① Like the first Chapter on Such Criminal
Ct.

MW01096798

INTERNATIONAL LAW AND WORLD ORDER

A PROBLEM-ORIENTED COURSEBOOK

Fourth Edition

By

Burns H. Weston

Bessie Dutton Murray Distinguished Professor of Law Emeritus
Senior Scholar, Center for Human Rights
The University of Iowa
and
Visiting Distinguished Professor of International Law and Policy
Vermont Law School

Richard A. Falk

Albert G. Milbank Professor of International Law and Practice Emeritus
Princeton University
and
Visiting Professor of Global and International Studies
University of California at Santa Barbara

Hilary Charlesworth

Professor of International Law
Australian National University

Andrew L. Strauss

Professor of Law
Widener University School of Law

AMERICAN CASEBOOK SERIES®

Mat #17741608

American Casebook Series and West Group are trademarks
registered in the U.S. Patent and Trademark Office.

COPYRIGHT © 1980, 1990 BURNS H. WESTON, RICHARD A. FALK, ANTHONY D'AMATO

© West, a Thomson business, 1997
© 2006 Thomson/West
  610 Opperman Drive
  P.O. Box 64526
  St. Paul, MN 55164–0526
  1–800–328–9352
Printed in the United States of America

ISBN–13: 978–0–314–25139–8
ISBN–10: 0–314–25139–1

 *TEXT IS PRINTED ON 10% POST CONSUMER RECYCLED PAPER*

For

Marta
Hilal
Charles
and
Renee

*

History says, Don't hope
on this side of the grave.
But then, once in a lifetime
the longed for tidal wave
of justice can rise up,
and hope and history rhyme.

—Seamus Heaney
from *Doubletake*,
The Cure at Troy (1991)

*

Preface

The fourth edition of this coursebook appears at a time of uncertainty and challenge in the global order. After the great hopes raised by the ending of the Cold War and the apparent democratization of much of the former Soviet Bloc and South Africa, significant issues have emerged (or reemerged) that suggest deep and unresolved tensions in global relations. These issues include devastating wars, gross violations of the most fundamental human rights as well as the continuing oppression of women and other marginalized groups, an increasing divide between rich and poor, rapid environmental degradation, and a significant decline in respect for, or adherence to, international law on the part of the major powers, especially the United States.

The aim of this coursebook is to introduce the field of international law to both law and liberal arts students to explore how the international legal system as presently constituted is able and unable to cope with these and related crises and trends. As in our earlier editions, we do so by posing four clusters of world order problems that require students to identify and frame legal issues in factual context and thereby determine the relevance of information given, to organize relevant law and policy and thereby test analytical skills, and to develop a critical understanding of the possibilities of international law and thereby engage the creative imagination. Engagement in problem-solving provides students with a concrete sense of the workings of international law. While we have attempted to provide materials that give an accurate account of the state of the law, our emphasis remains to encourage students to grapple with the normative, procedural, and institutional structures of the international legal system, to confront the range of policy choices available to decision-makers, and to relate immediate practical options to long-term policy goals.

As in the previous editions of this coursebook, this fourth edition is divided into three parts. The content of each part has changed—in many places significantly—from the earlier editions in response to global and theoretical developments and also to the comments and suggestions of colleagues.

Part I: The International Legal Process

Part I explores the nature of international law and the structure of its processes. It focuses on an actual "real world" problem, not the Nuremberg trial of the leading Nazi war criminals as in past editions, but the related current work of the new permanent International Criminal Court against the backdrop of the *ad hoc* International Criminal Tribunals for the Former Yugoslavia and Rwanda. This currency has added a certain tension to the preparation of this edition, as events have moved rapidly and may develop in ways that we cannot now foresee. However, we hope that the immediacy of the issues involved and their coverage in the media will better assist the student to understand the nature of international legal process, its sources of decision-making authority, and its force and effect—*i.e.*, the "basics" for *any* interna-

tional lawyer working with *any* international law problem, and thus essential
to the problem-solving that students will encounter in Part II.

Part II: Problems in International Law and World Order

As in the previous three editions, Part II comprises a series of hypothetical
problems involving fictional countries in "real world" decision-making settings, organized around themes that conveniently cluster the principal challenges to the present world order: "Problems in Conflict Prevention" (Chapter
4), "Problems in Sociopolitical Justice" (Chapter 5), "Problems in Economic
Well-Being" (Chapter 6), and "Problems in Environmental Protection" (Chapter 7). On occasion, colleagues have recommended that we use actual recent
problems rather than invented ones. However, we remain decided against
such an approach, for three reasons: first, because "real" problems risk unwanted associations and biases that potentially inhibit principled analysis; second, because such problems are vulnerable to rapid obsolescence; and third,
because the "solutions" to "real" problems are a matter of historical record
and thus potentially deprive students of the intellectual stimulation of re-
searching and arguing a case whose outcome is unknown or in doubt.

Also, reflecting our continuing concern to maximize instructional flexibility and substantive coverage, we again offer a total of twenty-four problems in
Part II: one *multi-issue or "maxi" problem* per chapter (Problems 4–1, 5–1,
6–1, and 7–1) and five more-or-less *single-issue or "mini" problems* per chapter (Problems 4–2 through 4–6, 5–2 through 5–6, 6–2 through 6–6, and 7–2
through 7–6). Additionally, consistent with our third edition, we have allowed
for the first two "mini" problems in each of the four chapters to be joined to
make one *multi-issue or "midi" problem* per chapter (*i.e.,* Problems 4–2 and
4–3, 5–2 and 5–3, 6–2 and 6–3, and 7–2 and 7–3). We have continued this
practice to maximize instructional flexibility and substantive coverage yet further.

On the other hand, Part II in this fourth edition is also noticeably different in that each of the problems in the four chapters comprising it has been
revised to some degree, often substantially. In many cases, indeed, the problems are entirely new—as in the case of problems 4–1, 5–1, and 6–1, for example, as well as many of those that follow each. As might be expected, revisions,
even wholesale innovations, were made necessary by the passage of time and
the need to remain up-to-date.

Part III: The Contributions of Law to a Peaceful, Just, Equitable, and Sustainable Global Future

In Part III, we shift to the ways in which international law and its practitioners (including scholars, government officials, and international bureaucrats) relate to the underlying structures of world order and to the dynamics
of change and struggle. It begins by exploring the idea that, in the last decade
of the 20th Century at least, since the collapse of the Berlin Wall in 1989, we
have been living in a "Grotian Moment"—a pivotal historical time in which
the structures of world order are changing, a time of opportunity as well as of
danger (Introduction). Then, after noting briefly the budding global civil society project that emerged in the immediate post-Cold War period of the 1990s
to achieve an equitable, sustainable, and democratically regulated form of

globalization, the countervailing impact of 11 September 2001 and especially the US belligerent response to it is explored, with special attention given to the debasement, largely at the hands of the United States, of the core prohibitions of the international use of force that, with due deliberation after World War II, were written into the United Nations Charter (Chapter 8: "Global Dreams and Geopolitical Nightmares"). Next, sensitive to the derailing of the normative energy of the 1990s in the aftermath of September 11, but with an eye to the future, we consider some of the principal components of the first genuine and sustained global justice movement in human history, taking into account resistances to it in the context of the American grand strategy that was fashioned in response to September 11, and thus acknowledging its as yet non-definitive character (Chapter 9: "The First Global Normative Revolution: Memories, Exaggerations, Hopes"). Finally, revealing our cautious optimism, we build on the efforts of peoples and governments to bring a global framework of law, ethics, and justice into being—described in Chapter 9 as a "global normative revolution"—by offering some sense of preferred direction for the future (Chapter 10: "Toward a Progressive Global Policy Agenda"). We conclude, as in our first three editions, with a final question that recalls the notion of individual responsibility that lies at the heart of the crimes trials that began our instructional journey: "Who, ultimately, is responsible for the future?"

*   *   *

Our coursebook is intended, as suggested above, for a one-semester course (although it certainly would work well—probably even better—in a year-long course). In a 60-hour course, the materials can be covered comfortably, albeit with little room to spare. In a 45-hour course, the materials can be adequately covered by making careful selections from amongst the problems in Part II. And in a 30-hour course, which we presume would be a seminar, it will be absolutely necessary to pick and choose. For our colleagues who must suffer the indignity of major time constraints and who would care to contact us, we will be happy to make suggestions for use of the materials. Our habit has been to follow a 45-hour course schedule, selecting one problem from each of the four chapters in Part II (usually Problems 4–1, 5–1, 6–1, and 7–1), leaving the remainder of the problems for supplemental lectures, special seminars, research papers, or "take-home" examinations. In our 3-hour courses, we ordinarily devote about four weeks (12 hours) to Part I, the next approximately eights weeks to Part II, and the remaining three to four weeks to Part III and a final wrap-up. Part II, we wish to stress, is adaptable to any teaching method. A lecture approach would deal straightforwardly with the problems and their legal and world order aspects. Another appropriate tack would be a discussion-lecture format, with the discussions devoted to the argumentation and resolution of the particular problems and the lectures to the legal and world order implications suggested by the problems. Further, a "Socratic" teaching method is possible, with the instructor eliciting arguments relative to the issues found in each of the problems.

We have used yet another approach, to wit, organizing "moot court" or equivalent simulation exercises for at least some of the problems presented, with the students variously divided among the key participants involved (*e.g,*

"petitioners," "respondents," and "judges") and the instructor playing a mediating role, guiding the argumentation and keeping it within assigned time limits. We have found that a "moot court" or other simulation approach to the
problems has had demonstrable educational value and that it has served to
make our classes lively. Like everyone else, students work hard when they
"get involved," and by actively "practicing" international law before their
peers they learn a great deal about it—often more than they immediately realize. Additionally, they develop heightened sensitivity to the variety of decision-making arenas in which international law "cases" typically are "decided,"
e.g, the UN Security Council (Problem 4–1); the UN Sub-Commission on the
Promotion and Protection of Human Rights, the Organization for Security
and Co-operation in Europe, the International Court of Justice, and the International Criminal Court (Problem 5–1); the NAFTA/ UNCITRAL Tribunal
and the US Senate Committee on Foreign Relations (Problem 6–1); and the
International Court of Justice (Problem 7–1)—also *ad hoc* tribunals (problems
4–4, 7–4, 7–5), specialized UN agencies (problems 5–5 and 7–6), WTO dispute
settlement panels (problems 6–4 and 6–5), and specialize treaty bodies (Problem 7–7). Regional tribunals, too, are invoked (Problem 5–2), as are also national decision-making institutions (problems 4–3, 4–5, 5–3, 5–4, 5–6, 6–2, 6–3,
6–6, and 7–2). And so forth. Regardless of the teaching method chosen, however, we strongly recommend that students be required to submit a written
outline of the legal issues present in each Part II problem assigned, preferably
as of the day on which the problem is first taken up in class. By this device,
discussions and arguments are carried out at a high level because at least
those assigned the task have an informed stake in the classroom proceedings.
Also, we strongly recommend deliberate attention to the Discussion
Notes/Questions that we have included throughout the coursebook. Intended
to expand the student's intellectual horizons, they contain instructive "hypotheticals," information collateral to the problems but nonetheless helpful in
"fleshing out" their larger contexts, and questions that challenge world order
thinking. Additionally, they contain bibliographies of specialized materials
helpful in the preparation of research papers. We realize, of course, that some
instructors will want to add certain materials of their own, and may even wish
to develop some "mini" problems of their own design. We welcome efforts of
this sort and hope you will share your ideas with us.

    Several additional pedagogical observations merit notice. *First,* to help fill
gaps in student background knowledge, we suggest that students consult as
needed R. Bledsoe & B. Boczek, *The International Law Dictionary* (1987) and
the *Encyclopaedia of Public International Law* (1992) published under the
auspices of the Max Planck Institute for Comparative Public Law and International Law (and totalling eleven volumes as of this writing). Each of these
publications constitute efficient sources of technical information. *Second,* we
urge students to study the Readings and Discussion Notes/Questions in the
order in which they are presented. Their order has been carefully planned,
such that "skipping around" will prove more confusing than efficient. *Third,*
we encourage instructors to use our Teacher's Manual. It has been prepared
particularly with an eye to the problem-oriented approach of Part II. *Finally,*
we urge that students acquire the independent supplement to this coursebook,
entitled Supplement of Basic Documents in International Law and World

Order. Most of the legal documents that are part of the readings in the coursebook are referenced to this supplement rather than being reprinted in the text.

We turn now to four editorial matters. *First,* since this coursebook is organized in problem-oriented rather than doctrine-oriented fashion, we have made a special effort to provide a comprehensive substantive index. The intent is to assist students and instructors in locating subject-matter which of necessity is scattered throughout the coursebook rather than being set out in one discrete unit. *Second,* original footnotes generally are omitted. However, when they are included they are denoted by numbers, with our own footnotes being indicated by letters. *Third,* we have tried to be as current as possible. Information cut-off dates range between 1 October 2005 and 1 March 2006 for the most part. *Fourth,* all URL links were last visited circa 1 March, 2005 when our manuscript went to press. We of course cannot guarantee their accessibility after that date.

Finally, three observations regarding language use. *First,* we have resorted to references such as "North," "South," "developing countries," "Third World," and the like. We recognize that these terms are inadequate reflections of the "real world," but we have found that they nevertheless are necessary for reasons of convenience. *Second,* we have left unamended the words of writers whose language implies that only men are international lawyers, judges, politicians, and other actors in the international legal process. It is important to appreciate that international law has developed in a lop-sided, gendered way and we hope that any sexist language in extracted materials will strike students as inappropriate and limited. *Finally,* even while recognizing that the term "world order" is susceptible to criticism for implying a rigid commitment to world government or a "brave new world" of Hitlerian or Stalinist autarchy, we use it here as purely an analytical/descriptive concept, referring to that aggregation of norms, procedures, and institutions that give shape and structure to international society at any given time. At least since the Peace of Westphalia, there always has been a world order. The transformation of the present world order of competing sovereign states to a new world order of universal peace and justice is the task that lies ahead.

We divided the work among ourselves, each of us contributing according to our respective backgrounds and interests, with Burns Weston again assuming stewardship for the coursebook overall. Each of us, however, accepts full responsibility for what is presented here. We would be surprised, of course, if there are no errors, and therefore would appreciate any corrections as well as other comments or suggestions that might improve our effort should it merit yet a fifth edition.

For this fourth edition, we are pleased to acknowledge with grateful appreciation all those who have assisted us in its preparation. Their names and our thanks may be found in the Acknowledgements. To anyone whose name we may have inadvertently omitted, we offer our apologies.

Not overlooked, however, is Professor Anthony D'Amato. Despite his departure as a co-author/co-editor after our second edition, his intellectual legacy is clearly present in this new edition, especially in Part I, and we are grateful to him for it.

Burns Weston, Richard Falk, and Hilary Charlesworth wish also to acknowledge their great good fortune to have been joined in this fourth edition by Professor Andrew Strauss. Professor Strauss provided not only substantial generalized knowledge and skills as an international law specialist, he ensured that highly technical issues of international trade and investment, among his specialty fields, would be accurately, clearly, and astutely represented.

We hope this fourth edition will be both controversial and useful. While we have tried to present a range of views in the materials contained here, our own commitments will be evident.

BURNS H. WESTON
IOWA CITY, IOWA AND SOUTH ROYALTON, VERMONT

RICHARD A. FALK
SANTA BARBARA, CALIFORNIA

HILARY CHARLESWORTH
CANBERRA, AUSTRALIA

ANDREW L. STRAUSS
WILMINGTON, DELAWARE

May 2006

Acknowledgements

We are greatly indebted to many generous people who contributed much to the realization of this fourth edition. We include all those persons we gratefully acknowledged in our first three editions, especially the many talented research assistants who, at The University of Iowa, the University of Adelaide, and Australian National University, came skillfully to our rescue: Yasir Aleemuddin, Jennifer Beard, Marci Cannon, Sarah Court, Julie Ann Fishel, Michelle Foster, Jeffrey Fuhrman, Julia Goings-Perot, Jyoti Larke, Ashish Mishra, Laura Olson, Shahyar Roushan, Noni Shannon, Jeremy Sosna, and Mark Teerink. Most if not all new editions, certainly this one, build on the ones preceding, including in this case the invaluable contributions of Professor Anthony D'Amato, which we acknowledge in the Preface and do so again.

We are especially indebted, however, to a number of student research assistants, past and present, who have contributed mightily to this fourth edition in particular. At Australian National University, assisting Hilary Charlesworth, they are Andrea Motbey, Alexandra Owens, Kim Pham, Xuelin Teo, Alexandra Strang, and Yanya Viskovich. At The University of Iowa College of Law, they are Jonathan Amarilio, Anne Burmeister, Christina Carmichael, Megan Dempsey, Jenna DiCocco, Jessica Downs, Demetrius Lambrinos, Victoria Kozyr, and Michael Okerlund, assisting primarily Burns Weston. At the Vermont Law School, assisting Burns Weston and Richard Falk, is Gavin Boyles. And at Widener University School of Law, assisting Andrew Strauss, are Santino Ceccotti, Andrew Dupre, Aron Gold, Gretchen Kwashnik, Nina Qureshi, and Maheen Siddiqui. Particularly to be praised for their huge kindness and skill in the last year, however, are Jonathan Amarilio, Gavin Boyles, Megan Dempsey, Alexandra Strang, and Yanya Viskovich. A very special great thanks goes also to Gretchen Kwashnik for her enormously adept help in securing the copyright permissions necessary for this coursebook to see the light of day. But everyone mentioned is to be abundantly thanked for their exceptionally adroit and gracious handling of various research, editorial, and clerical tasks, many of them onerous. Without these wonderful students, our work would have been rendered far more arduous, if not impossible.

For creative thinking and editorial assistance at different stages, we gratefully acknowledge as well the help of a number of our peers in Australia, the United Kingdom, and the United States. In Australia, we thank Mr. Phil Drury at Australian National University. In the United Kingdom, we thank Professor Robert McCorquodale at the University of Nottingham. And in the United States, in the order of their institutional affiliation, we thank: Professor Jonathan Van Dyke at the University of Hawaii School of Law (Manoa); Professor Francis A. Boyle at the University of Illinois School of Law (Champaign); professors Jonathan C. Carlson, Marcella David, and Mark D. Janis at The University of Iowa College of Law; professors Susan Franck and Matthew P. Schaefer at the University of Nebraska College of Law; Professor Roger S. Clark at Rutgers, The State University of New Jersey School of Law (Camden); Professor Joseph W. Dellapenna at Villanova University School of Law;

professors William T. Burke and the late Joan Fitzpatrick at the University of Washington School of Law; and Vice Dean Russell A. Hakes and professors Patrick J. Kelly, Juliet M. Moringiello, and Geoffrey H. Moulton, Jr., at the Widener University School of Law. Our thanks are extended also to Professor Lakshman D. Guruswamy, Sir Geoffrey W. R. Palmer, and Professor Jonathan C. Carlson for allowing us to borrow and revise several problems from Lakshman D. Guruswamy, Geoffrey W. R. Palmer, Burns H. Weston, and Jonathan C. Carlson (eds.), *International Environmental Law and World Order: A Problem- Oriented Coursebook* (2d ed. 1999), also published by West Group and soon forthcoming in a third edition.

For other expert advice and assistance, we thank additionally several colleagues in government at the Australian Department of Foreign Affairs and Trade the Office of Treaty Affairs and Office of Ocean Affairs at the US Department of State. Professor Strauss is especially grateful to Mr. Stefan Cassella at the US Department of Justice and to Mr. David Felsenthal, in private practice, for their generous expert assistance with Chapter 6. Of course, this coursebook would not have been possible without the help of the library staffs of our respective universities, but the eclectic and multidisciplinary nature of many of the readings that follow required a very special expertise and thus now require a very special word of gratitude. For this invaluable help, always generously and graciously offered, we tender our abundant thanks.

For dedication, skill, and unfailing good humor, we thank also our secretarial assistants who came to our rescue often in intense situations: Grace E. Tully at The University of Iowa College of Law; Laura Gillen at the Vermont Law School; and Debbe Patrick at Widener University School of Law. With their support, superb competence, and willingness always to go the extra mile, the lame did walk and were, indeed, inspired.

We are deeply grateful, too, to our academic institutions and other benefactors for their financial support of research assistants and other needs, never taken for granted, never unappreciated. Burns Weston wishes especially to acknowledge, with large gratitude, the supportive atmosphere provided by Dean Emeritus N. William Hines and Dean Carolyn C. Jones of The University of Iowa College of Law; also by Dean Geoffrey B. Shields, Vice Dean Stephanie J. Wilbanks, and former Vice Dean Bruce Duthu of the Vermont Law School. Richard Falk thanks the Global and International Studies Program of the University of California at Santa Barbara for the highly congenial and supportive working environment provided him. Hilary Charlesworth thanks the Australian Research Council and the John D. and Catherine T. MacArthur Foundation for their support of her research; also her colleagues in the Faculty of Law and the Regulatory Institutions Network in the Research School of Social Sciences at the Australian National University for their collegial assistance. And, in the same spirit, Andrew Strauss extends his sincere thanks to Dean Douglas E. Ray, Vice Dean Michael J. Goldberg, Vice Dean Russell A. Hakes, and his faculty colleagues at the Widener University School of Law for support and friendship invaluable to his scholarly undertakings.

For withstanding the long ordeal with unfailing kindness, humor, and warmth, Burns Weston, Richard Falk, and Andrew Strauss deeply thank their wives, respectively: Marta Cullberg Weston, Hilal Elver, and Renee Sherman Strauss. For his loving support and good humor, Hilary Charlesworth thanks her husband, Charles Guest. So indebted are we to these magnificently humane partners, indeed, we happily dedicate this fourth edition to them.

Finally, as the pages following will bear ample witness, we are indebted to many authors and publishers for permission to reprint materials used in this coursebook. We acknowledge with appreciation the permission granted to reprint copyrighted material by the following authors and publishers:

ABC-CLIO, for permission to reprint from R. Bledsoe & B. Boczek, The International Law Dictionary, 234-35 (1987).

American Bar Association, for permission to reprint from C. Brower, *Current Developments in the Law of Expropriation and Compensation: A Preliminary Survey of Awards of the Iran–United States Claims Tribunal*, 21 Int'l Law. 639, 643-52 (1987).

American University Journal of International Law and Policy, for permission to reprint from: Richard A. Falk, *Inhibiting Reliance on Biological Weaponry: The Role and Relevance of International Law*, 1 Am. U. J. Int'l L. & Pol'y 17, 23-27 (1986); Carol A. Petsonk, *The Role of the United Nations Environment Programme (UNEP) in the Development of International Environmental Law*, 5 Am. U. J. Int'l L. & Pol'y 351, 367-372 (1990).

Arizona Journal of International and Comparative Law, for permission to reprint from: S. James Anaya, *A Contemporary Definition of the International Norm of Self-Determination*, 3 Transnat'l L. & Contemp. Probs. 131, 143-62 (1993); H. Elizabeth Dallam, *The Growing Voice of Indigenous Peoples: Their Use of Storytelling and Rights Discourse to Transform Multilateral Development Bank Policies*, 8 Ariz. J. Int'l & Comp. L. 117, 142-48 (1991); Robert A Williams, Jr., *Comments on Energy and the Environment: Intersecting Global Issues*, 9 Ariz. J. Int'l & Comp. L. 199, 202-203 (1992).

Aspen Publishers, for permission to reprint from: Mark Janis, An Introduction to International Law 347-53 (4th ed. 2003).

Australian National University Centre for International and Public Law, for permission to reprint from Yash Ghai, *Human Rights and Governance: The Asia Debate*, 15 Austl. Y. B. Int'l L. 1, 5-6, 13, 16-18 (1994), first published in 1994 as Occasional Paper No. 1 of the Asia Foundation.

Australian Yearbook of International Law, for permission to reprint from: Christine Chinkin, *A Gendered Perspective to the International Use of Force*, 12 Austl. Y. B. Int'l L. 279, 291-93 (1988-89); J. Gardam, *A Feminist Analysis of Certain Aspects of International Humanitarian Law*, 12 Aust. Y. B. Int'l L. 265, 268, 277-78 (1992).

Blackwell Publishing, for permission to reprint from Sir Gerald Fitzmaurice, *The Foundations of the Authority of International Law and the Problem of Enforcement*, 19 Mod. L. Rev. 1, 8 (1956).

Boston University International Law Journal, for permission to reprint from Angela Thompson, *International Protection of Women's Rights: An*

Analysis of Open Door Counselling Ltd. and Dublin Well Woman Centre v. Ireland, 12 Boston U. Int'l L. J. 371, 399-401 (1994).

Brill Academic Publishers, for permission to reprint from: Derek Bowett, *The Use of Force for the Protection of Nationals Abroad*, The Current Legal Regulation of the Use of Force 39, 51 (A. Cassese ed., 1986); Ian Brownlie, *The United Nations Charter and the Use of Force, 1945-1985*, The Current Legal Regulation of the Use of Force 491, 501-02 (A. Cassese ed., 1986); Antonio Filippo Panzera, *Some Considerations on the Review of the 1977 Environmental Modification Techniques (ENMOD) Convention*, 6 Ital. Y. B. Int'l L. 96, 98-103 (1985); M. Sornarajah, The Pursuit of Nationalized Property 174-76 (1986); Tieya Wang, *The Third World and International Law*, The Structure and Process of International Law: Essays in Legal Philosophy Doctrine and Theory 955, 961-63, 970 (R. MacDonald & D. Johnston eds., 1983); Sylvia M. Williams, *A Historical Background on the Chlorofluorocarbon Ozone Depletion Theory and Its Legal Implications*, Transboundary Air Pollution 267, 274-77 (C. Flinterman et al. eds., 1986).

Brooklyn Journal of International Law, for permission to reprint from Shanker A. Singham, *Competition Policy and the Stimulation of Innovation: TRIPS and the Interface Between Competition and Patent Protection in the Pharmaceutical Industry*, 26 Brooklyn J. Int'l L. 363, 401-03 (2002).

Buttersworth, for permission to reprint from: D. W. Greig, International Law 47–48 (2d ed. 1976); Ivan Shearer, Starke's International Law, 471–514 (I. Shearer 11th ed. 1994).

Buttersworth Canada Limited, for permission to reprint from Sharon A. Williams & Armand L.C. de Mestral, An Introduction to International Law, Chiefly as Interpreted and Applied in Canada, 93–102 (2d ed. 1987).

California Law Review, for permission to reprint from Anthony A. D'Amato, Wesley L. Gould & Larry D. Woods, *War Crimes and Vietnam*, 57 Cal. L. Rev. 1055, 1062 (1969).

California Western School of Law, for permission to reprint from Louis Rene Beres, *Toward Prosecution of Iraqi Crimes under International Law: Jurisprudential Foundations and Jurisdictional Choices*, 22 Cal. W. Int'l L. J. 127 (1991); Carman Cassado, *Vessels on the High Seas: Using a Model Flag State Compliance Agreement to Control Marine Pollution*, 35 Cal. W. Intl'l L.J. 203, 205-07, 216-17, 222-23, 235 (2005).

Cambridge University Press, for permission to reprint from: Daniel P. O'Connell, 1 State Succession in Municipal Law and International Law, 3–7 vol. 1, Internal Relations (1967); Ann Orford, Reading Humanitarian Intervention: Human Rights and the Use of Force in International Law 6-37 (2003); Philippe J. Sands, *Chernobyl: Law and Communication—Transboundary Nuclear Air Pollution: The Legal Materials*, 40-42, 44-47, 51 (1988).

Cardozo Journal of International and Comparitive Law, for permission to reprint from Shashank Upadhye, *The International Watercourse: An Exploitable Resource for the Developing Nation Under International Law*, 8 Cardozo J. Int'l & Comp. L. 61, 61-83 (2000).

Carnegie Council on Ethics and International Affairs, for permission to reprint from Amartya Sen, *Thinking About Human Rights and Asian Values*, 4 Human Rights Dialogue 2, 2-3 (Carnegie Council on Ethics and International Affairs, March 1996). Copyright © 1996 by the Carnegie Council on Ethics and International Affairs.

Carnegie Endowment for International Peace, for permission to reprint from Morton H. Halperin, et. al., Self-Determination in the New World Order 56-60 (1992); Bilahari Kausikan, Asia's Different Standard, 92 Foreign Policy 24, 24-40 (1993). Copyright © 1993 by the Carnegie Endowment for International Peace.

Colorado Journal of International Environmental Law and Policy, for permission to reprint from: Charles Okidi, *"Preservation and Protection" Under the 1991 ILC Draft Articles on the Law of International Watercourses*, 3 Colo. J. Int'l Envtl. L. & Pol'y 143, 144-45 (1992).

Columbia Journal of Environmental Law, for permission to reprint from J. Wylie Donald, *Note, The Bamako Convention as a Solution to the Problem of Hazardous Waste Exports to Less Developed Countries*, 17 Colum. J. Envtl. L. 419, 422-24 (1992).

Columbia Journal of Transnational Law, for permission to reprint from: Charles Brower, *Investor-State Disputes Under NAFTA: The Empire Strikes Back*, 40 Colum. J. Transnat'l L. 43, 48 - 51 (2001); Mary Ellen O'Connell, *Regulating the Use of Force in the 21st Century: The Continuing Importance of State Autonomy*, 36 Colum. J. Transnat'l L. 473, 475-477, 479 (1997).

Columbia Law Review, for permission to reprint from Anne Marie Slaughter, *Law Among Liberal States: Liberal Internationalism and the Act of State Doctrine*, 92 Colum. L. Rev. 1907, 1983-1986 (1992).

Columbia University Press, for permission to reprint from: Louis Henkin, *How Nations Behave*, Law and Foreign Policy, 29-30 & 47 (2d ed. 1979). Copyright © 1979 by Columbia University Press.

Cornell International Law Journal, for permission to reprint from J. Patrick Kelly, *The Seduction of the Appellate Body: Shrimp/Sea Turtle I and II and the Proper Role of States in WTO Governance*, 38 Cornell Int'l L. J. 459, 460-66, 469 (2005).

Dickinson Journal of International Law, for permission to reprint from Philip Noonan, *Revolutions and Treaty Termination*, 2 Dickinson J. Int'l L. 301–29 (1984).

Duke University Press, for permission to reprint from Francis A. Boyle, World Politics and International Law 3 (1985).

Elsevier Science B.V., for permission to reprint from Jochen A. Frowein, *Recognition*, 4 Encyclopedia of Public International Law 34-40 (2000).

Encyclopaedia Britannica, for permission to reprint from: Burns H. Weston, *Human Rights,* Encyclopaedia Britannica (2005). Copyright © 2005 Encyclopaedia Britannica, Inc.

Environmental Law at Lewis and Clark Law School, for permission to reprint from C. Russell H. Shearer, *Comparative Analysis of the Basel and Bamako Conventions on Hazardous Waste*, 23 Envtl. L. 141, 146-47 (1993).

Environmental Law Reporter, for permission to reprint from: Jane A. Dwasi, *Regulation of Pesticides in Developing Countries*, 32 Envtl. L. Rep. 10045, 10055-60 (Jan 2002); David P. Fidler, *Challenges to Humanity's Health: The Contributions of International Environmental Law to National and Global Public Health*, 31 Envtl. L. Rep 10048, 10055 (Jan 2001).

European Journal of International Law, for permission to reprint from Christine Chinkin, *Rape and Sexual Abuse of Women in International Law*, 5 Eur. J. Int'l L. 326, 328-35 (1994).

Finnish Lawyers Publishing Company, for permission to reprint from Martti Koskenniemi, From Apology to Utopia: The Structure of International Legal Argument, 40-42, 44-48 (1989).

Foreign Affairs, for permission to reprint from: Jeffrey E. Garten, *Lessons for the next Financial Crisis*, Foreign Affairs, 78-81 (March/April 1999); Philip C. Jessup, *The Reality of International Law*, 18 For. Aff. 244-46 (1939-40).

Foundation Press, the Academic Division of West Publishing, for permission to reprint from David J. Bederman, International Law Frameworks 1-6 (2001).

FranÁois-Xavier Bagnoud Center for Health and Human Rights and the Presidents and Fellows of Harvard, for permission to reprint from Virginia A. Leary, *The Right To Health in International Human Rights Law*, 1 Health & Human Rights: An International Journal 24, 28-56 (1994).

George Braziller, Inc., for permission to reprint from Wolfgang Friedmann, The Future of the Oceans 1 (1971). Copyright © 1971 George Braziller, Inc.

George Washington International Law Review, for permission to reprint from Naomi A. Bass, *Implications of the TRIPS Agreement For Developing Countries: Pharmaceuticals Patent Laws In Brazil and South Africa in the 21st Century*, 34 Geo. Wash. Int'l L. Rev. 191, 191-97 (2002).

Georgetown International Environmental Law Review, for permission to reprint from: Paula Barrios, *The Rotterdam Convention on Hazardous Chemicals: A Meaningful Step Toward Environmental Protection?*, 16 Geo. Int'l Envtl. L. Rev. 679, 716-19, 725-27, 742 (2004); Will Martin, *Fisheries Conservation and Management of Straddling Stocks and Highly Migratory Stocks under the United Nations Convention on Law of the Sea*, 7 Geo. Int'l Envtl. L. Rev. 765. Copyright © 1995 Georgetown International Environmental Law Review.

Georgetown Journal of International Law, which is now named, Law and Policy in International Business, for permission to reprint from: Stefan Cassella, *Financial Aspects of the War on Terror, March 18, 2002: Forfeiture of Terrorist Assets Under the USA Patriot Act of 2001*, 34 Law & Pol'y Int'l Bus. 7 - 11, 13-14 (2002).

Georgetown Law Review © 2004, for permission to reprint from: Thomas M. Franck & Dennis M. Sughrue, *The International Role of Equity-as-Fairness*, 81 Geo. L. Rev. 563, 572, 580, 590–91 (1993).

Global Dialogue, for permission to reprint from Richard Falk, *Humanitarian Intervention: Elite and Critical Perspectives*, 7 Global Dialogue (Winter/Spring 2005) Nos. 1-2.

Greenpeace, for permission to reprint from William Arkin, Damian Durrant & Marianne Cherni, On Impact: Modern Warfare and the Environment: A Case Study of the Gulf War, Washington, Greenpeace (1991).

Florida Law Review, for permission to reprint from James Thuo Gathii, *Constructing Intellectual Property Rights and Competition Policy Consistently With Facilitating Access to Affordable Aids Drugs To Low-End Consumers*, 53 Fla. L. Rev. 727, 733-35 (2001).

Hague Academy of International Law, for permission to reprint from Louis Henkin, *International Law: Politics, Values and Functions*, 216 Recueil des Cours (Hague Acad. Int'l L.) 22 (1989-IV).

Harper Collins Publishers, for permission to reprint from: H. Bull, *The Grotian Conception of International Society*, in Diplomatic Investigations: Essays in Theory of International Relations 51-52, 64-73 (1966).

Harvard Human Rights Journal, for permission to reprint from: Deborah Anker, et. al., *Crisis and Cure: A Reply to Hathaway/Neve and Schuck*, 11 Harv. Hum. Rts. J. 295, 295-306, 308-310 (1998); James C. Hathaway & R. Alexander Neve, *Making International Refugee Law Relevant Again: A Proposal for Collectivized and Solution-Oriented Protection*, 10 Harv. Hum. Rts. J. 115, 115- 124, 126-129, 138-141, 143, 145, 155-156, 171-173, 211 (1997); David Kennedy, *The International Human Rights Movement: Part of the Problem?*, 15 Harv. Hum. Rts. J. 99, 101-102, 107-125 (2002).

Harvard International Law Journal, for permission to reprint from: Richard A. Falk & Burns H. Weston, *The Relevance of International Law to Palestinian Rights in the West Bank and Gaza: In Legal Defense of the Intifada*, 32 Harv. Int'l L.J. 129, 138-43 (1991); Makau Mutua, *Savages, Victims, and Saviors: The Metaphor of Human Rights*, 42 Harv. Int'l L.J. 201-208, 225-26, 243-245 (2001); Nigel Purvis, *Critical Legal Studies in Public International Law*, 32 Harv. Int'l L.J. 81 (1991).

Harvard Law Review, for permission to reprint from Roger Fisher, *Bringing Law to Bear on Governments*, 74 Harv. L. Rev. 1130, 1132-34 (1961).

Harvard University Press, for permission to reprint from Abram Chayes & Antonia Handler Chayes, *The New Sovereignty—Compliance with International Regulatory Agreements* 17, 22-26, 28 (1996); Albert E. Hindmarsh, Force in Peace: Force Short of War in International Relations 8-10, copyright © 1933 by the President and Fellows of Harvard College.

Holmes and Meier Publishers, Inc., for permission to reprint from Mohammed Bedjaoui, *Towards A New International Economic Order*, 49-50, 62-63 (1979).

Houston Journal of International Law, for permission to reprint from Kirsten Paris, *The Expansion of the Biological Weapons Convention: history and problems of a verification regime*, 24 Houst.J.Int'l.L, 510-12, 541-3 (2002).

Indian Journal of International Law, for permission to reprint from Makumi Mwagiru, *International Law, Politics, and the Re-invention of Humanitarian Intervention: The Lesson of Somalia*, 34 Indian J. Int'l L. 33, 33, 36-37, 41-44 (1994).

International and Comparative Law Review at Loyola of Los Angeles, for permission to reprint from: Christopher Joyner, International Extradition and Global Terrorism, 493, 496, 501, 538-39 (2003); Bruce Neuling, *The Shrimp-Turtle Case: Implications for Article XX of GATT and the Trade and Environment Debate*, 22 Loy. LA Int'l & Comp. L. Rev. 1, 18-28 (1999).

Iowa Law Review, for permission to reprint from: Robert L. Bard, *The Right to Food*, 70 Iowa L. Rev. 1279, 1287-90 (1985); Cheryl Christensen & Charles Hanrahan, *African Food Crises: Short-, Medium-, and Long-Term Responses*, 70 Iowa L. Rev. 1293, 1294 (1985); Catherine L. Piper, *Note, Reservations to Multinational Treaties: The Goal of Universality*, 71 Iowa L. Rev. 295, 298-300 (1985); Dinah L. Shelton, *The Duty to Assist Famine Victims*, 70 Iowa L. Rev. 1309, 1311, 1313-19 (1985).

Iowa State University Press, for permission to reprint from Richard A. Falk, Revitalizing International Law, 91-93 (1989).

Israel Law Review, for permission to reprint from Michla Pomerance, *Self-Determination Today: The Metamorphosis of an Ideal*, 19 Israel L. Rev. 310-15 (1984).

John Wiley & Sons, Ltd., for permission to reprint from: Richard A. Falk, *The Environmental Law of War: An Introduction*, Environmental Protection and the Law of War 78, 82-88 (G. Plant ed. 1992); Glen Plant, *Environmental Protection and the Law of War*, Environmental Protection and the Law of War 15- 18 (G. Plant ed. 1992); David Tolbert, *Defining the "Environment" Environmental Protection and the Law of War*, Environmental Protection and the Law of War 259-60 (G. Plant ed. 1992).

Journal of International Economic Law at the University of Pennsylvania, for permission to reprint from Andrew Strauss, *From GATTZILLA to the Green Giant: Winning the Environmental Battle for the Soul of the World Trade Organization*, 19 U. Pa. J. Int'l Econ. L. 769, 776-805 (1998).

Journal of Law and Commerce at the University of Pittsburgh School of Law, for permission to reprint from Marc Pallemaerts, *International Environmental Law in the Age of Sustainable Development: A Critical Assessment of the UNCED Process*, 15 J. L. & Com. 623, 630-34 (1996).

Juris Publishing, Inc., for permission to reprint from Robin Churchill & Alan V. Lowe, The Law of the Sea, 214-15 (1999).

Juris Publishing, Inc. and Manchester University Press, for permission to reprint from Hilary Charlesworth & Christine Chinkin, The Boundaries of International Law: A Feminist Analysis 96-123 (2000).

Kluwer Law International, for permission to reprint from: Charles B. Bourne, International Water Law: Selected Writings, 110-12 (P. Wouters ed., 1997); Bernard I. Logan, *An Assessment of the Environmental and Economic Implications of Toxic-Waste Disposal in Sub-Saharan Africa*, 25 J. World Trade 61, 65 (1991); Erik Jaap Molenaar, Coastal State Jurisdiction over Vessel-Source Pollution, Coastal State Jurisdiction over Vessel-Source Pollution 517-21 (1998); Ceasar P.R. Romano, The Peaceful Settlement of International Environmental Disputes 398 (2000).

Lynne Reinner Publishers, for permission to reprint from Gernot K^hler, *The Three Meanings of Global Apartheid: Empirical, Normative, Existential*, 20 Alternatives: Social Transformation and Humane Goverance 403, 403-04, 406-08 (1995). Copyright © 1996 by Lynne Reinner Publishers, Inc.

McGill Law Journal, for permission to reprint from Richard A. Falk, *Toward a Legal Regime for Nuclear Weapons*, 28 McGill L. J. 519, 535, 537 (1983).

McGeorge Law Review, for permission to reprint from Kojo Yelpaala, *Biotechnoloty and the Law: Owning the Secret of Life: Biotechnology and Property Rights Revisited*, 32 McGeorge L. Rev. 111, 202-04 (2000).

Michigan Journal of International Law, for permission to reprint from: Richard A. Falk, *The Complexities of Humanitarian Intervention: A New World Order Challenge*, 17 Mich. J. Int'l L. 491, 491-500, 511-13 (1996); Michael Scharf, *Clear and Present Danger: Enforcing the International Ban on Biological and Chemical Weapons Through Sanctions, Use of Force, and Criminalization*, 20 Mich. J. Int'l L. 484-5 (1999); Fernando R. Tesón, *Collective Humanitarian Intervention*, 17 Mich. J. Int'l L. 323, 325-38 (1996).

MIT Press Journals, for permission to reprint from: Jack Goldsmith & Stephen D. Krasner, *The Limits of Idealism*, Daedalus, 47-63 (Winter 2003); Carl Kaysen & George Rathjens, *The Case for a UN Force*, Daedalus, 91-103 (Winter 2003).

New Haven Press, for permission to reprint from: Myres S. McDougal & Florentino P. Feliciano, Law and Minimum World Public Order 732-33 (1961, 1994); Myres McDougal & Florentino P. Feliciano, Law and Minimum World Order–The Legal Regulation of International Coercion 231-40, 217-44 passim, 521-24 (1961); Myers S. McDougal & William Burke, The Public Order of the Oceans-A Contemporary International Law of the Sea, 1-2, 51-52 (1962).

New York University Law Review, for permission to reprint from Miriam E. Sapiro, *in an Era of Terrorism: The Need to Abolish the Political Offence Exception*, 61 N.Y.U. L. Rev. 654, 657, 689-93, 698-701 (1986).

Northwestern Journal of International Law and Business, for permission to reprint from Jason L. Godofsky, *Shedding Light on Article 1110 of the North American Free Trade Agreement (NAFTA) Concerning Expropriations, An Environmental Case Study*, 21 NW.J.Int'l L & Bus. 243, 281-284 (2000).

Northwestern University School of Law, for permission to reprint from: David A. Gantz, *Globalizing Sanctions Against Foreign Bribery: The Emergence of A New International Legal Consensus*, 18 Nw. J. Int'l L. & Bus. 457,

476-480 (1998); C. Todd Jones, *Compulsion Over Comity: The United States' Assault on Foreign Bank Secrecy*, 12 NW. J. Int'l L. & Bus. 454, 454-59, 461-464, 471-474, 484-488 (1992).

Ohio State Law Journal, for permission to reprint from Kevin Shook, *State Sponsors of Terroism Are Persons Too: The Flatow Mistake*, 61 Ohio St. L. J. 1301.

OMNI Publishing, for permission to reprint from Thor Heyerdahl, *How to Kill an Ocean*, Saturday Review, 29 Nov 75, at 12, 14-18.

Organization of American States, for permission to reprint from Edith Brown Weiss, *Environmental Disasters in International Law*, 1986 Ann. Jur. Interam. 141, 145-50 (1986).

Oxford University Press, for permission to reprint from: Alan E. Boyle, *Nuclear Energy and International Law: An Environmental Perspective*, 60 Brit. Y.B. Int'l L. 257, 261-65, 287-90, 292-97 (1989); James L. Brierly, The Outlook for International Law 5 (1944); Ian Brownlie, Principles of Public International Law 32–34 (4th ed. 1990); William Burke, The New International Law of Fisheries: UNCLOS 1982 and Beyond, 199-201, 205-08, 210-26, 228-29 (1994); Rachel Carson, The Sea Around Us, 218 (1951); Antonio Cassese, International Law in a Divided World 81-84, 280-82 (1986); James Crawford, The Creation of States in International Law, 405–06 (1979); H.L.A. Hart, Concept of Law 89-95, 209 & 212-215 (1970); Rosalyn Higgins, *Intervention and International Law*, Intervention in World Politics 29, 40-42 (H. Bull ed., 1984); Rosalyn Higgins, Problems and Process: International Law and How We Use It, 2-4, 19-22, 26-28 (1994); Robert McCorquodale, *Self-Determination: A Human Rights Approach*, 43 I.C.L.Q. 857, 875-83 (1994); Sally A. Meese, *When Jurisdictional Interests Collide: International, Domestic and State Efforts to Prevent Vessel-Source Oil Pollution*, 12 Ocean Dev. & Int'l L. 71, 75-81 (1982); Brian D. Smith, State Responsibility and the Marine Environment: The Rules of Decision, 193-203 (1988); Starke's International Law, 48-49, 63-64, 409–18 (I. Shearer 11th ed. 1994); Henry Steiner, *International Protection of Human Rights*, International Law 757 & 759-761 (Evans, M.D. ed. 2003); Nicholas J. Wheeler, Saving Strangers: Humanitarian Intervention in International Society XX, 293-95 (2000).

Palgrave Macmillan, for permission to reprint from Stephen John Stedman, *UN Intervention in Civil Wars: Imperatives of Choice and Strategy*, Beyond Traditional Peacekeeping 40, 40-41, 52-55, 58-60 (D. Daniel & B. Hayes eds., 1995).

Pearson, for permission to reprint from David H. Ott, Public International Law in the Modern World 13-16, 20–24, 192 (1987).

Polity Press, Ltd., for permission to reprint from Richard A. Falk, *The World Order Between Inter-State Law and the Law of Humanity: the Role of Civil Society Institutions*, Cosmopolitan Democracy: An Agenda for a New World Order 163 (D. Archibugi & D. Held eds., 1995).

Princeton University Press, for permission to reprint from Gidon Gottlieb, *The Nature of International Law: Toward A Second Concept of Law*, 4 The Future of the International Legal Order 331, 365-66 (C. Black & R. Falk eds. 1972).

Random House, for permission to reprint from Mary Ann Glendon, A World Made New: Eleanor Roosevelt and the Drafting of the Universal Declaration on Human Rights 221-223, 231-233 (2001).

Routledge, a member of the Taylor and Francis Group, for permission to reprint from Richard A. Falk, *The First Normative Global Revolution?: The Uncertain Political Future of Globalization*, Globalizations and Civilizations, 51- 76 (Medhi Mozaffari, ed. 2002).

Rutgers Law Journal, for permission to reprint from Maureen R. Berman & Roger S. Clark, *State Terrorism: Disappearances*, 13 Rutgers L. J. 531, 531-34, 547, 561-62 (1982).

San Diego International Law Journal, for permission to reprint from Christopher Greenwood, *International Law and the Pre-emptive Use of Force: Afghanistan, Al-Qaida, and Iraq*, 4 San Diego Int'l L.J. 7-16 (2003).

San Diego Law Review, for permission to reprint from: Christopher Greenwood, *International Law and the Pre-emptive Use of Force: Afghanistan, Al-Qaida, and Iraq*, 4 San Diego Int'l L.J. 7-16 (2003).

Saskatchewan Law Review, for permission to reprint from Noralee Gibson, *Comment, The Right to a Clean Environment*, 54 Saskatchewan L. Rev. 7, 14, 16- 17 (1990).

Simon & Schuster, for permission to reprint from Paul Bolster, *International Finance* in The Encyclopedia of Business 1019-20 (2d ed. 2000).

Springer, for permission to reprint from: Arie Bloed, *Two Decades of the CSCE Process: From Confrontation to Co-operation—An Introduction*, The Conference on Security and Co-operation in Europe: Analysis and Basic Documents, 1972-1993, at 1, 22-25 (A. Bloed ed., 1993); Professor Ndiva Kofele-Kale, *The Role of International Law in the Prevention and Punishment of Economic Crimes with Particular Reference to the Crime of Indigenous Spoilation* (International Economic Development Law, v.2), 11-14 International Law of Responsibility for Economic Crimes (1995); Myres S. McDougal, et. al., The Interpretation of Agreements and World Public Order 3–5 (1967); Fred L. Morrison & Wm. Carroll Muffett, *Hazardous Wastes*, International, Regional and National Environmental Law 409, 427-428 (F. Morrison & R. R¸diger eds., 2000); Oscar Schachter, International Law in Theory and Practice 38-39, 50–53, 55-56, 58 (1991); Peter-Tobias Stoll, *Hazardous Substances and Technologies*, International, Regional and National Environmental Law 437, 437-39 (F. Morrison & R. R¸diger eds., 2000).

Suffolk Transnational Law Review, for permission to reprint from Gabriel Eckstein, *Application of International Water Law to Transboundary Groundwater Resources, and the Slovak-Hungarian Dispute over Gabcikovo-Nagymaros*, 19 Suffolk Transnat'l L. Rev. 67, 79-81 (1995).

Sweet & Maxwell Limited, for permission to reprint from: B. Cheng, General Principles of Law-As Applied by International Courts and Tribunals 23-25 (1953); 1 D. O' Connell, International Law 455-60 (2d ed. 1970); J. Salter, *En-*

vironmental Legal Issues Arising From the Gulf Conflict, 10 Oil & Gas Law & Taxation Rev. 348 (1992), please note the name of this journal is now *International Energy Law and Taxation Review*.

Taylor and Francis Group, for permission to reprint from: Jozef Goldblat, *The Environmental Modification Convention of 1977: An Analysis* in Environmental Warfare: A Technical, Legal and Policy Appraisal, 53-57 (A. Westing 1984); Lawrence Juda, *Rio Plus Ten: The Evolution of International Marine Fisheries Governance,* 33 Ocean Dev. & Int'l L. J. 109, 116-23 (2002); Peter Malanczuk, Akehurst's Modern Introduction to International Law 36-37 (7th ed. 1997); R. Pohl, *Latin America's Influence and Role in the Third Conference on the Law of the Sea*, 7 Ocean Dev. & Int'l L. J. 65, 66-67 (1979); Brad Shingleton, *UNCLOS II and the Struggle for Law: The Elusive Customary Law of Seabed Mining*, 13 Ocean Dev. & Int'l L. J. 33, 37-55 (1983); Chen-Pan Wang, A Review of the Enforcement Regime for Vessel-Source Oil Pollution Control, 16 Ocean Dev. and Int'l L. J. 305, 312-330 (1986).

Temple International and Comparative Law Journal, for permission to reprint from: Thomas R. Phillips, *No Meeting of the Mines: An Analysis of the U.S. Policy regarding the International Ban on Anti-Personnel Landmines (The Ottawa Convention)*, 13 Temp. Int'l & Comp. L.J. 23, 35-46 (1999); Arcangelo Travaglini, *Reconciling Natural Law and Legal Positivism in the Deep Seabed Mining Provisions of the Convention on the Law of the Sea*, 15 Temp. Int'l & Comp. L.J. 313, 313-15 (2001).

Texas International Law Journal, for permission to reprint from: Timothy G. Ackermann, *Dis"ordre'ly Loopholes: TRIPS Patent Protection, GATT, and the ECJ*, 32 Tex. Int'l L.J. 489, 492-93, 496-99 (1997); John W. Kindt & Samuel P. Menefee, *The Vexing Problem of Ozone Depletion in International Law and Policy*, 24 Tex. Int'l L J. 261, 277-282 (1989); Eric Sievers, *Transboundary Jurisdiction and Watercourse Law: China, Kazakhstan, and The Irtysh*, 37 Tex. Int'l L. J. 1, 14-23 (2002).

Texas Law Review, for permission to reprint from William J. Davey, *Symposium: International Economic Conflict and Resolution: The World Trade Organization's Dispute Settlement System*, 42 S. Tex L. Rev. 1199-1203 (2001).

The Academy of Political Science, for permission to reprint from John Temple Swing, *The Law of the Sea*, The Proceedings of the Academy of Political Science vol.32, no.4 (1977) 128-141.

The American Law Institute, for permission to reprint excerpts of the Restatement (3D) Foreign Relations Law of the United States, copyright © 1987 by the American Law Institute. All rights reserved.

The American Society of International Law, for permission to reprint from: Antony Anghie & B.S. Chimni, *Third World Approaches to International Law and Individual Responsibility in Internal Conflicts* in The Methods of International Law 185, 185-95 (S. Ratner & A.-M. Slaughter, eds., 2004); M. Cherif Bassiouni, *Enforcing Human Rights through International Criminal Law and through an International Criminal Court*, Human Rights: An Agenda for the Next Century 347 (L. Henkin & J. Hargrove eds. 1994); Judith Bello, *The WTO Dispute Settlement Understanding: Less is More*, 90 Am. J. Int'l L.

416, 416-418 (1996); Derek Bowett, *Reprisals Involving Recourse to Armed Forces*, 66 Am. J. Int'l L. 1, 1-3, 10-11 (1972); Hilary Charlesworth, Panel on *Sources of International Law: Entrenching the Gender Bias*, Proceedings of the Second Joint Conference of the American Society of International Law and the Nederlandse Vereniging voor Internationaal Recht (at The Hague, 22–24 Jul 93) 418, 418–19 (1994) Recht(at The Hague, 22–24 July 1993) 421, 421–24 (1994); Hilary Charlesworth, *Feminist Methods in International Law*, 93 AJIL 379, 385-391, (1999); Hilary Charlesworth, et. al., *Feminist Approaches to International Law*, 85 Am. J. Int'l L. 613, 615, 621- 29 (1991); Christine Chinkin, *Panel on Sources of International Law: Entrenching the Gender Bias, Proceedings of the Second Joint Conference of the American Society of International Law and the Nederlandse Vereniging voor Internationaal Recht* (at The Hague, 22–24 Jul 93) 418, 418–19 (1994); Michael J. Dennis, *Current Development: The Fifty-Seventh Session of the UN Commission on Human Rights*, 96 Am. J. Int'l L. 181, 181-82, 190-91 (2002); Richard A. Falk, *The Beirut Raid and the International Law of Retaliation*, 63 Am. J. Int'l L. 415, 437-42 (1969); Richard Falk, *What Future for the UN Charter System of War Prevention?*, 97 Am. J. Int'l L.590, 590-98 (2003); Tom J. Farer, *Political and Economic Coercion in Contemporary International Law*, 79 Am. J. Int'l L. 405, 405–06 (1985); Joan Fitzpatrick, *Protection against Abuse of the Concept of Emergency*, Human Rights: An Agenda for the Next Century 203, 203-05 (L. Henkin & J. Hargrove eds. 1994); Thomas M. Franck, *Legitimacy in the International System*, 82 Am. J. Int'l L. 705, 705-07, 712-13 (1988); Thomas M. Franck, *What Happens Now? The United Nations after Iraq*, 97 Am. J. Int'l L. 607, 607-20 (2003); Judith Gardam, *Proportionality and Force in International Law*, 87 Am. J. Int'l L. 391, 404-05 (1993); Thomas Grant, *Iraq: How to reconcile conflicting obligations of occupation and reform*, American Society of International Law Insight (June 2003); Louis Henkin, *NATO's Kosovo Intervention: Kosovo and the Law of 'Humanitarian Intervention*, 93 Am. J. Int'l L. 824-828 (1999); Ruth Lapidoth, Equity in International Law, 81 Proceed. A.S.I.L. 138, 146–47 (1987); Richard Lillich, *The Constitution and International Human Rights*, 83 Am. J. Int'l L. 851, 856, 858-59 (1989); David A. Martin, *Large Scale Migrations of Asylum Seekers*, 76 Am. J. Int'l L. 598, n.15 (1982); Stephen McCaffrey & Sinjela Mpazi, *Current Development: The 1997 United Nations Convention on International Watercourses*, 92 Am. J. Int'l L. 97, 105-07 (1998); Myres McDougal, *The Effect of U.N. Resolutions on Emerging Legal Norms*, Proceed. A.S.I.L. 300 (1979); Diane F. Orentlicher, *Addressing Gross Human Rights Abuses: Punishment and Victim Compensation*, Human Rights: An Agenda for the Next Century 425, 425-26, 428-31, 448-53 (L. Henkin & J. Hargrove eds. 1994); Sir Geoffrey Palmer, *New Ways to Make International Environmental Law* 86 Am. J. Int'l L. 259, 269-70 (1992); S. N. Guha Roy, *Is the Law of Responsibility of States for Injuries to Aliens a Part of Universal Law?*, 55 Am. J. Int'l L. 863, 889 (1961); Romana Sadurska, *Threats of Force*, 82 Am. J. Int'l L. 239, 249-53, 260-66 (1988); Miriam Sapiro, *Changing the CSCE into the OSCE: Legal Aspects of a Political Transformation*, 89 Am. J. Int'l L. 631, 631-32, 636- 37 (1995); Thomas Schoenbaum, *Free International Trade and Protection of the Environment: Irreconcilable Conflict?*, 86 Am. J. Int'l L. 700, 700-704 (1992); John R. Stevenson & Bernard H. Oxman, *The Future of the United Nations Convention on the Law of the Sea*, 88 Am. J. Int'l L. 488, 488-99 (1994); Paul C. Szasz, *Remarks on the Gulf War: Environment as a Weapon*, 85 Proc. Am. J. Int'l L. 215, 219-20 (1991); Edith Weiss, *Environment and Trade as Partners in Sustainable Development: A Commentary*, 86 Am. J. Int'l L. 728, 728-735 (1992); Burns H. Weston, *The Charter of Economic Rights and Duties of States and the Deprivation of Foreign–Owned Wealth*, 75 Am. J. Int'l L. 437, 437–55 (1981); William H. Taft & Todd F. Buchwald, *Preemption, Iraq, & International Law*, Agora on Future Implications of the Iraq Conflict, 97 Am. J. Int'l L. 557, 557-63 (July, 2003).

The Free Press, a Division of Simon & Schuster, for permission to reprint from: Venkata Raman, Toward a General Theory of International Customary Law, Toward World Order and Human Dignity 365 (W. Reisman & B. Weston eds., copyright © 1976 by The Free Press); Burns H. Weston, *The Role of Law in Promoting Peace and Violence: A Matter of Definition, Social Values, and Individual Responsibility*, Toward World Order and Human Dignity 114, 116-17 (W. Reisman & B. Weston eds. and contribs., copyright © 1976 by The Free Press).

The Gale Group, for permission to reprint from: Burns H. Weston, *Executive Agreement,* 2 Encyclopedia of the American Constitution 666-68 (L. Levy, K. Karst & D. Mahoney eds. 1986); Burns H. Weston, *Treaty Power*, 4 Encyclopedia of the American Constitution 1910-11 (L. Levy, K. Karst & D. Mahoney eds. 1986).

The Georgetown Immigration Law Journal, for permission to reprint from Kristen Walker, *Defending the 1951 Convention Definition of Refugee*, 17 Geo. Immigr. L. J. 583, 608-609 (2003).

The Human Rights Brief, for permission to reprint from Azizah al-Hibri, *Who Defines Women's Rights? A Third World Woman's Response*, 2 Hum. Rts. Brief No. 1 (Washington College of Law, 29 Jul 96).

The Institute of International Public Law and International Relations, for permission to reprint from Rudolf Bernhardt, *Customary International Law New and Old Problems*, 19 Thesaurus Acroasium 199, 219–20 (1992).

The John Hopkins University Press, for permission to reprint from: R. Allen, M. Cherniak & G. Andreopoulos, *Refining War: Civil Wars and Humanitarian Controls*, 18 Hum. Rts. Q. 747, 777 (copyright © 1996 by the Johns Hopkins University Press); Philip Alston & Gerard Quinn, *The Nature and Scope of States Parties' Obligations under the ICESCR*, 9 Hum. Rts. Q. 156, 186-91 (copyright © 1987 by the Johns Hopkins University Press); Rachel Brett, *Human Rights and the OSCE*, 18 Hum. Rts. Q. 668, 678-82 (copyright © 1996 by the Johns Hopkins University Press); Audrey Macklin, Refugee Women and the Imperative of Categories, 17 Hum. Rts. Q. 213, 217-19, 225-29, 232, 237-38, 241-42, 247-48, 258-71 (copyright © 1995 by the Johns Hopkins University Press); Seymour J. Rubin, *Private Foreign Investment: Legal and Economic Realities*, 32-34, 40-43 (copyright © 1956 by the Johns Hopkins University Press).

The Nation, for permission to reprint from William Greider, *The Right and US Trade Law: Invalidating the 20th Century—Investor Protections in NAFTA Are One Manifestation of a Broad, Backdoor Effort to Restore the Pri-*

macy of Property Against Society's Broader Claims, The Nation 21 (15 Oct 2001).

The New York Times Syndicate, Paris, for permission to reprint from Philip Bowring, Look Who's Misbehaving, Int'l Herald Trib., 20 Aug 2003, at 6.

The Rector and Visitors of the University of Virginia, for permission to reprint from Richard B. Lillich, *The Valuation of Nationalized Property in International Law: Toward a Consensus or More 'Rich Chaos'?*, in 3 The Valuation of Nationalized Property in International Law, 183, 197–203 (R. Lillich ed. & contrib. 1975).

The Royal House of International Affairs, for permission to reprint from Sir Hersch Lauterpacht, *The Grotian Tradition in International Law*, 23 Brit. Y.B. Int'l L. 1, 18-53 (1946).

The South Dakota Law Review, for permission to reprint from Myres S. McDougal, *The Impact of International Law Upon National Law: A Policy-Oriented Perspective*, 4 S. Dak. L. Rev. 25, 35-36, 50-51 (1959).

The Stanford Law Review, for permission to reprint from: Edward T. Swaine, *Unsigning*, 55 Stan. L. Rev. 2061, 2066-2071 (2003); Phillip Trimble, *International Law, World Order and Critical Legal Studies*, 42 Stan. L. Rev. 811, 833-34 (1990).

The University of Chicago Journal of International Law, for permission to reprint from Alan O. Sykes, *Public Health and International Law: TRIPS, Pharmaceuticals, Developing Countries, and the Doha "Solution,"* 3 Chi. J. Int'l. L. 47-9, 55-8 (2002).

The University of Chicago Press, for permission to reprint from Thomas S. Kuhn, The Structure of Scientific Revolutions 111-13 (2d ed. 1970).

The University of Wisconsin Press, for permission to reprint from Richard B. Bilder, Managing the Risks of International Agreement 7-8, 10-11(1981).

The Washington Post Writers Group, for permission to reprint from Neely Tucker, Washington Post on April 6, 2003, F1.

The World Bank, for permission to reprint from Susan Rose-Ackerman, *Redesigning the State to Fight Corruption*, Viewpoint, Note No. 75 (The World Bank, April 1996); Susan Rose-Ackerman, *The Political Economy of Corruption–Causes and Consequences* Viewpoint, Note No. 74 (The World Bank, April 1996).

The Yale Law Journal Company and Fred B. Rothman & Company, for permission to reprint from Jordon Paust, *The Seizure and Recovery of the Mayaguez*, 85 Yale L.J. 774-81, 795-803 (1976).

The Yale Law Journal Company and William S. Hein Company, for permission to reprint from Harold Hongju Koh, *Why Do Nations Obey International Law?* 106 Yale L. J. 2599, 2599-59 (1998).

Thompson Publishing, on behalf of Taylor and Francis Books, for permission to reprint from: Bin Cheng, General Principles of Law–As Applied by International Courts and Tribunals 23-25 (1953); Peter Malanczuk, Akehurst's Modern Introduction to International Law 36-37 (7th ed. 1997).

Transaction Publishers, for permission to reprint from Joseph S. Nye, *Corruption and Political Development: A Cost–Benefit Analysis*, Political Corruption: A Handbook 973-75, 980-81 (A. Heidenheimer, M. Johnston, & V. LeVine eds., 1993).

Transnational Law & Contempory Problems at the University of Iowa School of Law, for permission to reprint from: Hurst Hannum, *Self-Determination, Yugoslavia, and Europe: Old Wine in New Bottles?*, 3 Transnat'l L. & Contemp. Probs. 57, 68-69 (1993); Brad Roberts, *Controlling Chemical Weapons*, 2 Transnat'l L. & Contemp. Probs. 435, 439-42, 451-52 (1992).

Transnational Publishers, Inc., for permission to reprint from: Alexandre C. Kiss and Dinah Shelton, International Environmental Law, 22-27, 225, 226, 228- 234 (2d ed. 2000); Nigel S. Rodley and David Weissbrodt, *United Nations Non- Treaty Procedures for Dealing with Human Rights Violations*, Guide to International Human Rights Practice 65-66, 75-88 (H. Hannum ed. 4th ed. 2004); Dinah Shelton, *The Promise of Regional Human Rights Systems*, The Future of International Human Rights 353-365, 396-398 (B. Weston & S. Marks eds., 1999); Burns H. Weston, International Claims: Their Settlement by Lump Sum Agreements, 208-42 (1975); Burns H. Weston, *The Universality of Human Rights in a Multicultured World: Toward Respectful Decision-Making*, reprinted from The Future of International Human Rights 65-66, 72-79 (B. Weston & S. Marks eds. & contribs., 1999).

Tulane Environmental Law Journal, for permission to reprint from Itzchak E. Kornfeld, *Groundwater and Hazardous Waste Landfills Do Not Mix*, 5 Tulane Envtl. L. J. 557, 568-69 (1992).

United Nations Publications, for permission to reprint from: Philip Alston, *International Law and the Right to Food,* Food as a Human Right 9, 37-38, 45-46, 162, 168-69 (A. Eide, W. Eide, S. Goohatilake, J. Gusson & Onawale eds. 1984); Heather Beach, et. al., Transboundary Freshwater Dispute Resolution: Theory, Practice, and Annotated References, 9-11 (2000); James P. Resor, Debt-for-Nature Swaps: A Decade of Experience and New Directions for the Future, 48 UNASYLVA No. 1 (FAO: Issuc 188, 1997).

University of Minnesota Press, for permission to reprint from Gerhard von Glahn, The Occupation Of Enemy Territory: A Commentary on the Law and Practice of Belligerent Occupation, 224-27 (1957).

University of Pennsylvania Journal of International Economic Law, for permission to reprint from Andrew Strauss, *From GATTZILLA to the Green Giant: Winning the Environmental Battle for the Soul of the World Trade Organization*, 19 U. Pa. J. Int'l Econ. L. 769, 776-805 (1998).

University of Pennsylvania Press, for permission to reprint from: Abullahi Ahmed An-Na`im, *Toward a Cross-Cultural Approach to Defining International Standards of Human Rights: The Meaning of Cruel, Inhuman or Degrading Treatment of Punishment*, Human Rights in Cross-Cultural Perspective 19, 20-21, 29, 33-38 (A. An-Na`im ed., 1992); Thomas Buergenthal, *The Helsinki Process: Birth of a Human Rights System*, Human Rights in the

World Community: Issues and Action 256, 257-59 (R. Claude & B. Weston eds. and contribs., 2d ed. 1992); *The Princton Principles on Universal Jurisdiction*, Universal Jurisdiction, 18-35 (Stephen Macedo, ed. 2004); Leo Kuper, *Theoretical Issues Relating to Genocide: Uses and Abuses*, Genocide 31, 33-40 (G. Andreopoulos ed., 1994); Sean D. Murphy, Humanitarian Intervention: The United Nations in an Evolving World Order 337-43 (1996).

University of Virginia Press, for permission to reprint from: Richard B. Lillich, *Economic Coercion and the International Legal Order*, in Economic Coercion and the New International Economic Order, 73, 79–82 (R. Lillich ed. & contrib. 1976).

Vanderbilt Journal of Transnational Law & International Legal Roundtable, for permission to reprint from Padideh Ala'i, *The Legacy of Geographical Morality and Colonialism: A Assessment of the Current Crusade Against Corruption*, 33 Vand. J. Transnat'l L. 877, 894-904 (2000); Burns H. Weston, R. Lukes & K. Hnatt, *Regional Human Rights Regimes: A Comparison and Appraisal*, 20 Vand. J. Transnat'l L. 585, 599 (1987).

Verso, for permission to reprint from: Daniele Archibugi, *Cosmopolitan Democracy*, Debating Cosmopolitics, 3-15 (Archibugi, ed. 2003); Richard A. Falk & Andrew Strauss, *The Deeper Challenges of Global Terrorism*, Debating Cosmopolitics, 203-231 (Archibugi, ed. 2003); Mario Pianta, *Democracy vs. Globalization: The Growth of Parallel Summits and Global Movements*, Debating Cosmopolitics, 232-256 (2003).

Virginia Law Review Association, for permission to reprint from Edwin A. Borchard, *The Relation Between International Law and Municipal Law*, 27 Va. L. Rev. 137, 140, 143-45 (1940).

Virginia Journal of International Law, for permission to reprint from: Derek W. Bowett, *Economic Coercion and Reprisals by States*, 13 Va. J. Int'l L. 1, 1–12 (1972); Jonathan I. Charney, *Entry into Force of the 1982 Convention*, 35 Va. J. Int'l L. 381, 392-400 (1995); Jonathan M. Clark, Jr., *Note: The Resolution of Act of State Disputes Involving Indefinitely Situated Property*, 25 Va. J. Int'l L. 901, 919, 926–32 (1985); J. Patrick Kelly, *The Twilight of Customary International Law*, 40 Va. J. Int'l L. 449, 452-53, 540-43 (2000); Deborah Perluss & Joan F. Hartman, *Temporary Refuge: Emergence of a Customary Norm*, 26 Va. J. Int'l L. 551, 554-621 (1986); Guy B. Roberts, *The New Rules for Waging War: The Case Against Ratification of Additional Protocol I*, 26 Va. J. Int'l L. 109, 146-47 (1985); Oscar Schachter, *State Succession: The Once and Future Law*, 33 Va. J. Int'l L. 253, 253–54, 256–60 (1993); Fernando R. Tesón, *Feminism and International Law: A Reply*, 33 Va. J. Int'l L. 647, 650-55, 665 (1993); Burns. H. Weston, *'Constructive Takings' Under International Law: A Modest Foray into the Problem of 'Creeping Expropriation'*, 16 Va. J. Int'l L 103, 113–26, 153-54 (1975).

Washington & Lee Law Review, for permission to reprint from: Hilary Charlesworth, *The Mid-Life Crisis of the Universal Declaration of Human Rights*, 55 Wash. & Lee L. Rev 781, 782-796 (1998); John Jackson, *World Trade Rules and Environmental Policies: Congruence or Conflict*, 49 Wash. & Lee L. Rev. 1227, 1230-31 (1992).

Washington University Journal of Law and Policy, for permission to reprint from Thomas M. Franck, *When, If Ever, May States Deploy Military Force Without Prior Security Council Authorization?*, 5 Wash. U. J.L. & Pol'y 51, 52-68 (2001).

West Group, for permission to reprint from John M. Johnson & George W. Ware, Pesticide Litigation Manual 11-3 to 11-4 (1995).

West Publishing Company, for permission to reprint from Anthony A. D'Amato, *Universality vs. Restructiveness of Custom*, International Law and World Order: A Problem–Oriented Casebook 76 (2d ed. 1990).

Widener Law Symposium Journal, for permission to reprint from Andrew Strauss, *The Case for Utilizing the World Trade Organization as a Forum for Global Environmental Regulation*, 3 Widener L. Symp J. 309, 323-24 (1998). Please note the name of this journal is now the *Widener Law Review*.

World Resources Institute, for permission to reprint from World Resources Institute, et al., Global Biodiversity Strategy: Guidelines for Action to Save, Study, and Use Earth's Biotic Wealth Sustainably and Equitably, 1-18, 27 (1992).

Wisconsin International Law Journal, for permission to reprint from, Peter Oppenheimer, *A Chemical Weapons Regime for the 1990s: Satisfying Seven Critical Criteria*, 11 Wis. Int'l L. J. 1, 5-14, 24-25, 40-46 (1992).

World Futures Studies Federation, for permission to reprint from Jimoh Omo-Fadaka, *The Misuse of Science and Technology*, Doc. No. 17, World Future Studies Conference on Science and Technology and the Future, Berlin, May 8-10, 1979.

W.W. Gaunt, for permission to reprint from Julius Stone, Legal Controls of Int'l Conflict 288-90, 555-56 (reprint ed. 1973).

W.W. Norton & Company, for permission to reprint from Elazar Barkan, *Amending Historical Injustices in International Morality*, from the introduction in The Guilt of Nations, xv-xli (Barkan ed. 2000).

Yale Journal of International Law, for permission to reprint from Edward Gordon, *Article 2(4) in Historical Context*, 10 Yale J. Int'l L. 271, 271-75 (1985).

Yale University Press, for permission to reprint from: Steve Charnovitz, *The Law of Environmental PPM's in the WTO: Debunking the Myth of Illegality*, 27 Yale J. Int'l L. 59, 64-65, 70-71, 75-76, 79-80, 83-86, 88-92 (2002); Lung-chu Chen, An Introduction to Contemporary International Law 359–65 (2nd ed. 2000).

IN ADDITION, the authors acknowledge with appreciation the permission granted to reprint previously and newly copyrighted material by the following authors and other individual copyright owners:

Daniele Archibugi, for permission to reprint from Daniele Archibugi, *Cosmopolitan Democracy*, Debating Cosmopolitics, 3-15 (Archibugi, ed. 2003).

Elizabeth DeSombre, for permission to reprint from Elizabeth R. DeSombre, *The Experience of the Montreal Protocol: Particularly Remarkable, and Remarkably Particular*, 19 U.C.L.A. J. Envtl. L. & Pol'y 49, 49-55, 57, 69-76 (2000-01), published by Journal of Environmental Law and Policy at the University of California at Los Angeles.

Mark A. Drumbl, for permission reprint from M. Drumbl, *Pluralizing International Criminal Justice*, 103 Mich. L. Rev. 1295, 1297, 1313-14 (2005), published by the Michigan Law Review.

Jean Bethke Elshtain, for permission to reprint from Jean Bethke Elshtain, *Just War and Humanitarian Intervention*, 17 Am. U. Int'l L. Rev. 1, 3-5, 9-17 (2001), published by American University International Law Review.

Richard A. Falk, for permission to reprint from Richard A. Falk & Andrew Strauss, *The Deeper Challenges of Global Terrorism*, Debating Cosmopolitics, 203-231 (Archibugi, ed. 2003).

David Frum, for permission to reprint from David Frum & Richard Perle, *U.N. Should Change - Or U.S. Should Quit; The World Body's Rules Prevent American from Answering Threat*, LA TIMES, Jan. 23, 2004, at B13, published by The Los Angeles Times.

Monica Hakimi, for permission to reprint from W. Reisman & Monica Hakimi, *Illusion and Reality in the Compensation of Victims of International Terrorism*, 54 Ala. L. Rev. 561 (2003), published by the Alabama Law Review.

John Jackson, for permission to reprint from John Jackson, *World Trade Rules and Environmental Policies: Congruence or Conflict*, 49 Wash. & Lee L. Rev. 1227, 1230-31 (1992), published by Washington & Lee Law Review.

Morton A. Kaplan, for permission to reprint from Morton A. Kaplan & Nicholas deB. Katzenbach, The Political Foundations of International Law 263 (1961).

Nicholas deB. Katzenbach, for permission to reprint from Morton A. Kaplan & Nicholas deB. Katzenbach, The Political Foundations of International Law 263 (1961).

Melissa Parker, for permission to reprint from Melissa Parker, *Rethinking Female Circumcision*, 65 Africa 506-23.

Richard Perle, for permission to reprint from David Frum & Richard Perle, *U.N. Should Change"–Or U.S. Should Quit; The World Body's Rules Prevent American from Answering Threat*, LA TIMES, Jan. 23, 2004, at B13, published by The Los Angeles Times.

Mario Pianta, for permission to reprint from Mario Pianta, *Democracy vs. Globalization: The Growth of Parallel Summits and Global Movements*, Debating Cosmopolitics, 232-256 (2003).*Cosmopolitan Democracy*, Debating Cosmopolitics, 3-15 (Archibugi, ed. 2003).

Andrew Strauss, for permission to reprint from: Andrew Strauss, *Could a Treaty Trump Supreme Court Jurisdictional Doctrine*, 61 Alb. L.Rev. 1237, published by the Albany Law Review; Richard A. Falk & Andrew Strauss, *The*

Deeper Challenges of Global Terrorism, Debating Cosmopolitics, 203-231 (Archibugi, ed. 2003).

W. Michael Reisman, for permission to reprint from W. Reisman & Monica Hakimi, *Illusion and Reality in the Compensation of Victims of International Terrorism*, 54 Ala. L. Rev. 561 (2003), published by the Alabama Law Review.

Finally, we acknowledge with appreciation the work of Sir Hersch Lauterpacht, International Law 68–74 (E. Lauterpacht ed., 1970), reprint permission for which proved unavailing despite our best efforts to locate or secure a response from the person or persons authorized to grant such permission.

B.H.W.
R.A.F.
H.C.
A.L.S.

Table of Abbreviations

The following abbreviations are used in the headnotes and footnotes to the instruments included in this documentary supplement:

A	United Nations General Assembly
Add.	Addendum
A.J.I.L.	*American Journal of International Law*
Alb.	Albania
A.M.R./S.C.M.	Document of the Session of the Special Consultative Meeting on Antarctic Mineral Resources
Ann.	Annual
App.	Appendix
ASEAN, A.S.E.A.N.	Association of South-East Asian Nations
A.T.S.	Australian Treaty Series
A.T.S.C.M.	Special Consultative Meeting of Antarctic Treaty Parties
AU, A.U.	African Union
Austl.	Australia
Belg.	Belgium
Bevans	Charles I. Bevans (ed.), U.S. Treaties and Other International Agreements of the US: I (1776- 1949), II (1918-30); III (1931-45); IV (1946- 49)
B.I.S.D.	GATT Basic Instruments and Selected Documents
B.F.S.P.	British and Foreign State Papers
B.Y.B.I.L	*British Yearbook of International Law*
Can.	Canada
Can. T.S.	Canadian Treaty Series
C/E, CoE	Council of Europe
C., Cd., Cmd., Cmnd.	U.K. Command Papers 1870-99, 1900-18, 1919-56, 1956- , respectively
CONF., Conf.	Conference
C.M.L.R.	Common Market Law Reports
C.S.C.E.	Conference on Security and Cooperation in Europe
C.T.S.	Clive Parry (ed.), Consolidated Treaty Series (1969-81)
Czech.	Czechoslovakia
Den.	Denmark
Doc.	Document
E, ECOSOC	United Nations Economic and Social Council
E.A.S.	U.S. Executive Agreement Series

E.C.E.	Economic Commission for Europe
E.E.C.	European Economic Community
EIF	Entry into force
E.J.I.L.	*European Journal of International Law*
E.T.S.	European Treaty Series
E.U.	European Union
E.Y.B.	European Yearbook (B. Landheer & A. Robertson eds.)
FAO, F.A.O.	United Nations Food and Agriculture Organisation
For. Rel.	U.S. Foreign Relations
Fr.	France
GA, G.A.	United Nations General Assembly
GAOR	United Nations General Assembly Official Records
Ger.	Germany
H.R.Q.	*Human Rights Quarterly*
Hudson	Manley O. Hudson (ed.), International Legislation (Washington, DC: Carnegie Endowment for International Peace, 1931- 1950) (9 vols.)
IAEA, I.A.E.A.	International Atomic Energy Agency
IAEA INFCIRC	International Atomic Energy Agency nformation Circular
IAEA Leg. Ser.	International Atomic Energy Agency Legal Series
I.C.C., ICC	International Chamber of Commerce; International Criminal Court
ICJ, I.C.J.	International Court of Justice
I.L.A.	International Law Association
I.L.C.	International Law Commission
I.L.M.	*International Legal Materials*
I.L.R.	International Law Reports
IMCO, I.M.C.O.	Inter-Governmental Maritime Consultative Organisation
IMO, I.M.O.	International Maritime Organisation
L.N.T.S.	League of Nations Treaty Series
Mtg.	Meeting
Neth.	Netherlands
N.Z.	New Zealand
N.Z.T.S.	New Zealand Treaty Series
No.	Number
OAS, O.A.S.	Organization of American States
O.A.S. Off. Rec.	Organization of American States Official Records
O.A.S.T.S.	Organization of American States Treaty Series
OAU, O.A.U.	Organisation of African Unity
OEA/Ser.	Organizacion Estados Americanos Series (Organisation of American States Series)

OECD, O.E.C.D.	Organisation for Economic Co-operation and Development
Off.	Official
OJ, O.J.	Official Journal of the French Republic
O.J.E.C.	Official Journal of the European Communities
P.A.U.L.T.S.	Pan American Union (Organization of American States) Law and Treaty Series
P.A.U.T.S	Pan American Union (Organization of American States) Treaty Series
PCIJ, P.C.I.J.	Permanent Court of International Justice
Proceed.	Proceedings
Pt., pt.	Part
Rep.	Report
RES, Res.	Resolution
Rev.	Revision, Revised
S	United Nations Security Council
S.A.T.S.	South African Treaty Series
SCOR	United Nations Security Council Official Records
Ser.	Series
Sess.	Session
Stat.	U.S. Statutes at Large
Supp.	Supplement
T.I.A.S.	U.S. Treaties and Other International Acts Series
T.S	Treaty Series
UK, U.K.	United Kingdom
U.K.T.S.	U.K. Treaty Series
UN, U.N.	United Nations
UNEP	United Nations Environment Programme
U.N.J.Y.B.	United Nations Juridical Yearbook
U.N.R.I.A.A.	United Nations Reports of International Arbitral Awards
U.N.T.S.	United Nations Treaty Series
US, U.S.	United States
USC, U.S.C.	United States Code
U.S.D.S.B.U.S.	Department of State Bulletin
U.S.T.	U.S. Treaties
Weston & Carlson	B. Weston & J. Carlson (eds.), International Law and World Order: Basic Documents, vols. 1-5 (1994-)
Y.B.I.L.C.	Yearbook of the International Law Commission
Y.B.U.N.	Yearbook of the United Nations

*

Summary of Contents

PART III. THE CONTRIBUTIONS OF LAW TO A PEACEFUL, JUST, EQUITABLE, AND SUSTAINABLE GLOBAL FUTURE

Table of Contents

lii

TABLE OF CONTENTS

Page

4. Readings—Continued

7. Protocol Additional (No. II) to the Geneva Conventions of August 12, 1949, and Relating to the Protection of Victims of Non-International Armed Conflicts 580

8. United Nations General Assembly Declaration for the Protection of War Victims 580

9. UN Security Council Resolution 827 on Establishing an International Tribunal for the Prosecution of Persons Responsible for Serious Violations of Humanitarian Law Committed in the Territory of the Former Yugoslavia 581

10. UN Security Council Resolution 955 Establishing the International Tribunal for Rwanda 581

11. Rome Statute of the International Criminal Court 581

12. Leo Kuper, *Theoretical Issues Relating to Genocide: Uses and Abuses* 581

13. Christine Chinkin, *Rape and Sexual Abuse of Women in International Law* 585

14. The Prosecutor v. Jean-Paul Akayesu 590

5. Discussion Notes/Questions 591

Problem 5-2. Women's Reproductive Rights in Hibernia 606

1. Facts 606
2. Questions Presented 607
3. Assignments 607
A. Reading Assignment 607
B. Recommended Writing Assignment 607
C. Recommended Oral Assignment 607
D. Recommended Reflective Assignment 607
4. Readings 608
1. Burns H. Weston, *Human Rights* 608
2. Dinah Shelton, *The Promise of Regional Human Rights Systems* 608
3. European Convention for the Protection of Human Rights and Fundamental Freedoms 614
4. Convention on the Elimination of All Forms of Discrimination Against Women 614
5. Convention on the Rights of the Child 614
6. Hilary Charlesworth, *The Mid-Life Crisis of the Universal Declaration of Human Rights* 614
7. Fernando R. Tesón, *Feminism and International Law: A Reply* 621
8. *Case of Open Door and Dublin Well Woman v. Ireland* 622
9. *Case of Schuler-Zgraggen v. Switzerland* 626
10. Programme of Action of the 1994 United Nations International Conference on Population and Development 627
11. Azizah al-Hibri, *Who Defines Women's Rights? A Third World Woman's Response* 627
5. Discussion Notes/Questions 629

PART III. THE CONTRIBUTIONS OF LAW TO A PEACEFUL, JUST, EQUITABLE, AND SUSTAINABLE GLOBAL FUTURE

Table of Arbitral and Judicial Decisions

The principal cases are in bold type. Cases cited or discussed in the text are roman type. References are to pages. Cases cited in principal cases and within other quoted materials are not included.

*

INTERNATIONAL LAW
AND
WORLD ORDER

A PROBLEM-ORIENTED
COURSEBOOK

Fourth Edition

*

Part I

THE INTERNATIONAL LEGAL PROCESS

INTRODUCTION

This coursebook introduces you to international law primarily through the study of problems of world order that we believe will be of vital concern for years to come—problems that arise out of conflicting claims of national, regional, and global security (including problems that spring from organizations and networks not officially connected to a particular state); problems that derive from alleged violations of internationally recognized human rights; problems that attend already widespread but widening poverty and maldevelopment; and problems that stem from humankind's disregard of the fragility of Earth's ecosystems.

The problems we have fashioned are hypothetical, to avoid associations and biases that potentially inhibit principled analysis, to resist too rapid obsolescence, and to facilitate thinking about the future. At the same time, they are true to life. We are concerned that you probe the complex webs of fact, law, and policy that typically confront international law decision-makers in the "real world." These problems will be found in Part II and reflect our belief that issue-spotting, problem-solving, and synthesis are more important in the legal learning experience than the mere assimilation of disembodied knowledge.

In this Part I, we focus on the analytical tools that are needed to work through the problems in Part II, with an eye to the wider fundamental setting of world order in which international law and lawyering has evolved over time, beginning with the emergence of the state system in the Seventeenth Century. Ever since that time, the guiding assumption has been that international law is primarily an instrument of, by, and for sovereign states—an assumption that has been a mixture of both ideology and fact, varying with the circumstances and interests of the strongest states.

Since the close of World War II in 1945, however, and especially since the end of the Cold War in 1989, two crucial developments have compelled policymakers, practitioners, scholars, and perhaps especially laypersons to question the adequacy, even as a matter of description, of conceiving of international law as "the Law of Nations," the law among and between states. The first is found in the realization of a cluster of complex integrative trends that are relocating economic and political power beyond the reach of even the most powerful states—as with the rise of global market forces, the threat of environmental degradation, the transnational flow of people, drugs, and popular culture, and so forth. The second has to do with the gradual but steady emergence of a global polity of individuals and groups harmed by state action or inaction, needing the protection of transnational human rights and environmental regimes, depending on citizens' initiatives at the grassroots and among nongovernmental organizations (NGOs) to exert pressures, and increasingly capable of ensuring constructive results through direct action, including the mobilization of modern information systems and communications technologies.

Therefore, sympathetic to the possibility that a *law of humanity* as the core of international legal process is superseding by gradual—though uneven—stages the *law of states*, we explore in this Part I the concept of international law, its so-called sources, and its means of implementation by adopting a critical perspective on the statist view of international law. And we do so against the backdrop of a real problem, involving the complexity of trying to impose criminal liability on individuals for inter-ethnic violence and other forms of severe abuse, prominent since the collapse of the Berlin Wall and the fall of the Soviet empire.

————

WE BEGIN WITH the newspaper and television images beamed worldwide, albeit unevenly, since the end of the Cold War from the former Yugoslavia—primarily Bosnia–Herzegovina (1992–95)—from Rwanda (1994–95), and from Sudan's Darfur province (since 2003):

• tens and hundreds of thousands of desperate men, women, and children fleeing their homes and across borders to escape what often is termed "ethnic cleansing"[a] and other premeditated abuse;

• huddled refugees and *déplacés* crammed into squalor, many of them further victimized by starvation and malnutrition, sometimes owing to deliberate policy;

• emaciated men, some old, clutching barbed wire prison fences, eyeballs sunken, ribs protruding, often the victims of torture and comparable atrocity;

• gaunt, terror-struck women haunted by systematic rapes and assaults, coerced pornography, and their forced witness to the sadistic murders of their children, families, and friends;

• bloodied and dismembered bodies, some the consequence of indiscriminate warfare, others of savage massacres, scattered on city streets and country hillsides, or heaped one upon the other in open charnel pits swarming with infectious flies; and more.

The saga of atrocity goes on and on, the enormity of it only partially revealed by the statistics. In *Bosnia–Herzegovina*, more than 200,000 killed and some 3 million driven from their homes from the outbreak of hostilities in 1992 to the Dayton Peace Accords in 1995, the vast majority of them Muslim. In *Rwanda*, between 800,000 and one million Tutsis and others (including moderate Hutus) exterminated during three months of fighting and up to two million forced into refugee camps since fighting began in 1994, three-fourths of the country's total population. In *Darfur*, more than 2 million people killed, wounded, displaced, or otherwise harmed by the civil war since its beginning in 2003. In towns and villages with unfamiliar names, nearly every building damaged or destroyed, little or no running water, little or no electricity, little

a. The term "ethnic cleansing" is problematic. Arguably it is a term of avoidance, a euphemism for "genocide," an international crime.

or no government infrastructure. Once more or less peaceful, the former Yugoslavia (Bosnia–Herzegovina especially), Rwanda, and Darfur are today's emblems of carnage and devastation,[b] the "killing-field metaphors"[c] of the end of the Twentieth Century.

Of course, the former Yugoslavia, Rwanda, and Darfur are not alone in this manner of horror. In whole or in part, any number of other post-Cold War nightmares would do—in alphabetical order: Abkhazia (1992–93), Burundi (1993–95), Central African Republic (since 2002), Chechnya (1994–96), Democratic Republic of the Congo (1996–2002), Haiti (1991–94), Kosovo (1996–99), Liberia (1989–2003), Sierra Leone (1998–99), Somalia (1992–95), and South Ossetia (1991–92). And they overlapped, or followed by only a few years, bloodbaths unleashed during the Cold War: Cambodia (Kampuchea) (1975–79), East Timor (1975–99), El Salvador (1980–92), Guatemala (1960–96), Guinea–Bissau (1980–84), Papua New Guinea (Bougainville) (1988–2003), and Uganda (1986–2005), to name a few.

We dwell here on the former Yugoslavia, Rwanda, and Darfur, however, because, directly or indirectly, they figure in potentially important ways in our decision-making venue of choice in this Part I—the International Criminal Court (ICC), established on 17 July 1998 when 120 states participating in the United Nations Diplomatic Conference of Plenipotentiaries on the Establishment of an International Criminal Court adopted the Rome Statute of the International Criminal Court **(Basic Document 1.16)**. The first ever *permanent* international criminal tribunal created "to promote the rule of law and to ensure that the gravest international crimes [genocide, crimes against humanity, and war crimes] do not go unpunished,"[d] the ICC, based in The Hague, The Netherlands, has had four cases referred to it at this writing— three by states parties to the Statute and one by the UN Security Council. Arguably the most prominent or pressing of these cases is the case of violations of international humanitarian law and human rights law in Darfur since 1 July 2002, referred to the ICC Prosecutor on 31 March 2005 by the UN Security Council[e] (after an initial, failed attempt by the United States to prevent ICC involvement with Darfur altogether[f]). Hence our focus on Darfur,

---

b. For accounts of the human tragedies in Bosnia–Herzegovina, Rwanda, and Darfur. see, respectively, *Tenth Periodic Report on the Situation of Human Rights in the Territory of the Former Yugoslavia*, UN Doc. A/50/69 & S/1995/79 of 26 Jan 95; UN ESCON, 51st Sess., 3400th mtg., UN Doc. S/RES/935 (1994); *Report of the Secretary–General on the Situation in Rwanda*, UN SCOR, 49th Sess., at 2, 11, UN Doc. S/1994/640 (1994); and *Monthly Report of the Secretary General on Darfur*, UN SCOR, 60th Sess., UN Doc. S/2005/523 (11 Aug 2005).

c. I. Cotler, *Foreword*, Nuremberg Forty Years Later: The Struggle Against Injustice in Our Time ix, xii (I. Cotler ed., 1995).

d. *Quoting* the ICC's website at <http://www.icc-cpi.GRt/home.html>.

e. *See* UN Security Council Resolution 1593 of 31 March 2005 (on the Situation in Darfur), S/RES/1593 (2005), Algeria, Brazil,

China, and the United States abstaining. The three other cases referred to the ICC by states parties to the Rome Statute as this text goes to press include a case referred by the Democratic Republic of Congo (for thousands of mass murders and summary executions within its territory in April 2004), by Uganda (for international crimes in Northern Uganda also in April 2004), and by the Central African Republic (for international crimes in its territory in January 2005).

f. Following a recommendation by a UN Commission of Inquiry stating that the ICC was the "single best mechanism" and the "only credible way" of ensuring justice for Darfur's victims, the United States, ignoring the Commission's recommendation (despite its having help to create the Commission), indicated that it opposed a Darfur referral to the Security Council because it did not want "to be party to legitimizing the ICC." For details, see the website of Human Rights Watch at

and notwithstanding that Sudan, though a signatory of the 1998 Rome Statute, was not a party to it at the time nor is it to this day. Anticipating claims of impunity in such instances, Article 13(b) of the Statute gives the ICC jurisdiction when "[a] situation in which one or more [grave international] crimes appears to have been committed is referred to the Prosecutor by the Security Council acting under Chapter VII of the Charter of the United Nations" as in this case.[g]

The 1998 Rome Statute, however, did not enter into force until 1 July 2002, so operationally the ICC is quite new. Moreover, a number of statutory and practical measures must be taken before it can become fully operational. As of this writing, indeed, none of the four cases so far referred to the Court, though formally under investigation, has been prosecuted or adjudicated. Accordingly, in this as yet untested jurisprudential setting, it is prudent to account for two *ad hoc* international criminal tribunals whose war crimes experience measurably shaped the creation of the ICC, each established early in the post-Cold War period by UN Security Council resolution and each still ongoing: the International Tribunal for the Prosecution of Persons Responsible for Serious Violations of International Humanitarian Law Committed in the Territory of the Former Yugoslavia since 1991 (the ICTY)[h] and the International Tribunal for the Prosecution of Persons Responsible for Genocide and Other Serious Violations of International Humanitarian Law Committed in the Territory of Rwanda between 1 January 1994 and 31 December 1994 (the ICTR).[i] Hence our focus also on the former Yugoslavia and Rwanda.

The facts that led the Security Council to act in the cases of the former Yugoslavia, Rwanda, and Darfur are complex and controversial. The essentials, however, are briefly summarized.

The Former Yugoslavia (principally Bosnia–Herzegovina)

The complexities of the crisis in the former Yugoslavia can be traced to the tortured history of the Balkans (much of it dominated by the Ottoman Empire from 1389 to 1878), the assassination of Austro–Hungarian Archduke Ferdinand on the streets of Sarajevo as the catalyst for World War I, the legacy of World War II, a post-Cold War leadership crisis following the death of Yugoslav dictator Marshall Tito, and a constitutional and economic structure (weakened by the withdrawal of IMF/World Bank funds when Yugoslavia was seen to be, after the end of the Cold War, no longer politically useful to the United States and Western Europe) that aggravated nationalist tensions. The immediate cause, however, lay in Serbian nationalism asserted within the

---

<http://hrw.org/english/docs/2005/02/15/sudan 10179.htm>.

g. Paragraph 2 of legally binding Security Council Resolution 1593, *supra* note **e**, provides that "the Government of Sudan and all other parties to the conflict in Darfur, shall cooperate fully with and provide any necessary assistance to the Court and the Prosecutor pursuant to this resolution and, while recognizing that States not party to the Rome Statute have no obligation under the Statute, urges all States and concerned regional and other international organizations to cooperate fully . . . ."

h. *See* UN Security Council Resolution 827 of 25 May 1993 (**Basic Document 2.44**). For an overview of the establishment of the Yugoslav tribunal, see J. O'Brien, *The International Tribunal for Violations of International Humanitarian Law in the Former Yugoslavia*, 87 A.J.I.L. 639 (1993).

i. *See* UN Security Council Resolution 955 of 8 November 1994 (**Basic Document 2.46**). For an overview of the establishment of the Rwanda tribunal, see P. Akhavam, *The International Criminal Tribunal for Rwanda: The Politics and Pragmatics of Punishment*, 90 A.J.I.L. 501 (1996).

established borders of Bosnia–Herzegovina and Croatia, undermining the constitutional arrangements guaranteeing the rights of non-Serbs.

The crisis began in 1990 when the then Yugoslav republics of Slovenia, Croatia, Macedonia, and Bosnia–Herzegovina, in that order, voted in free elections to install non-communist governments. Each showed strong secessionist sentiments. Not so, however, Serbia, which, then led by Serbian President Slobodan Milosevic, chose to retain its communist government and to press for a centralized Yugoslavia controlled by an all-Yugoslav communist party. Backed by the Yugoslav Federal Army, which was dominated by Serb officers, and capitalizing on genuine threats posed to Serbian minorities, the Milosevic government played the nationalist card and resisted all efforts by the four other republics to establish a loose Yugoslav federation.

The result was violence, first in the form of Serb-provoked skirmishes between Serbs and non-Serbs in Croatia and Bosnia–Herzegovina, next in the form of open warfare in Slovenia and Croatia, largely instigated by the Serb-dominated Yugoslav army, after those two republics declared their independence. Subsequent ceasefires in Slovenia and Croatia, brokered by the European Community[j] and the United Nations (UN), respectively, led to the successful withdrawal of the Yugoslav army in Slovenia, its replacement by a UN peacekeeping force in Croatia to maintain the ceasefire there, and, ultimately, the recognition of both Slovenia and Croatia as independent states by the European Community in January 1992—recognitions pressured by German foreign minister Hans Dietrich Genscher prematurely (and thus provocatively) according to many but accepted by Serbia in the case of Slovenia. An uneasy peace obtained in Croatia thereafter, due mainly to the efforts of the United Nations.

Meanwhile, tensions mounted in Bosnia–Herzegovina, where, in a population of 4.3 million, Muslim Slavs outnumbered Catholic Croats and Orthodox Serbs by 42% to 19% and 32%, respectively. When, in Summer 1991, it was revealed that Croatia and Serbia had secret talks about dividing Bosnia–Herzegovina between them, an uproar ensued, with Bosnia's Muslims declaring that a partition would lead to war and thereafter proposing and preparing for a referendum on independence. In late February 1992, the referendum succeeded and the Bosnian Croats and Muslims declared independence from Yugoslavia, after which the Bosnian Serbs, who had boycotted the referendum and refused to recognize the Muslim declaration in the interest of joining a "Greater Serbia," commenced hostilities in an effort to capture territory and dissuade the European Community and the United States from extending recognition. The effort failed. On 6 April 1992, the European Community recognized the independence of Bosnia–Herzegovina and, one day later, the United States followed suit (while simultaneously recognizing Croatia and Slovenia as well).

This recognition of Bosnia–Herzegovina served primarily to inflame the Serbs, however. Shortly thereafter, Bosnian Serb army troops and local militias, acting in the name of protecting the Serb minority in Bosnia, backed

j. The European Community was renamed the "European Union" upon the entry into force of the 1992 Treaty on European Union (also known as the "Maastricht Treaty") on 1 November 1993. For the original text of the treaty, see 31 I.L.M. 253 (1992). For its consolidated version, see 1997 O.J.(C430) 145, *reprinted in* 37 I.L.M. 56 (1998) and 1 Weston & Carlson I.B.13c.

by Serb leaders in Belgrade, and armed by the Serb-controlled Yugoslav army, proceeded to seize and shell predominantly Muslim villages and towns and to begin mortar attacks upon, and the attempted strangulation of, Bosnia's capital, Sarajevo. Meeting tenacious resistance, this pattern of hostility, which continued for 19 months, was relieved only by hesitant UN efforts at humanitarian aid, at establishing "safe havens" for Muslim civilians in six cities, and at the deployment of monitors on the Bosnian–Serbian border to verify Belgrade's promise not to further supply the Bosnian Serbs with weapons and munitions. Radovan Karadzic, head of the unrecognized Serb Republic of Bosnia, and General Ratko Mladic commander of the Army of the Serb Republic of Bosnia—comprised of some 50,000 well-armed soldiers from the Yugoslav army (predominantly Bosnian Serbs) bolstered by tens of thousands of reservists and irregulars—were unapologetic. Slobodan Milosevic, elected President of the "rump Yugoslavia" (Serbia and Montenegro) in December 1992, claimed to have no control over either of these Bosnian Serb leaders or their associates.

There is no doubt that atrocities were committed on all sides, Croat and Muslim as well as Serb. It also is clear, however, that the Bosnian Serbs, with help from the Milosevic government in Belgrade, were the main aggressor and the main perpetrators of a systematic campaign of "ethnic cleansing" pursuant to which primarily Bosnian Muslims were subjected to forced evacuations, pillage, compulsory detentions, torture, rape, disappearances, summary executions, selective murders, and massacres, including even heads on stakes. As part of this campaign as well, whole villages were burned to the ground; major and minor cities such as Bihac, Cerska, Goradze, Srebenica, Tuzla, and Zepa as well as Sarajevo were repeatedly besieged; hospitals were made the targets of periodic artillery shelling; UN convoys attempting to deliver humanitarian aid were at constant risk of being stopped and robbed; UN "safe havens" were defiantly attacked; and men, women, children, and even UN peacekeepers and Red Cross workers were taken hostage and used as human shields or killed. The carnage was substantial.

Rwanda

Rwanda, with a population comprised primarily of 85 percent Hutu (an agrarian Bantu people) and 14 percent Tutsi (a cattle-owning people with an Amharic warrior past), was a German colony placed under a Belgian-administered League of Nations mandate after World War I, an administration that was continued by Belgium following World War II under the UN trusteeship system. Prior to Rwanda's administration by European powers, the Tutsi dominated the Hutus in a complex system of governance that largely avoided conflict and bloodshed. With the advent of the Europeans, however, the traditional system eroded. While the Belgians, like the Germans before them, ruled largely through the Tutsi overlords, they did so in a manner that provoked conflict and exacerbated tensions between the two groups.

In 1961, the Belgian mandate was terminated and, in 1962, Rwanda became an independent republic. But not without violence between the Hutus and the Tutsis both before and after independence. As Rwanda moved toward independence under UN-sponsored elections that gave the country its first Hutu president in 1960, clashes between the two peoples, with the Tutsis attempting to topple the new Hutu government, resulted in the death of over

30,000 Tutsis and the creation of over 140,000 Rwandan refugees. In the years following independence, with the Hutus retaining political control, periodic clashes between the two groups became a standard feature of Rwandan life, with each side committing vengeful massacres resulting in thousands of deaths. In 1990, with economic conditions worsening, the Tutsi-led Rwandan Patriotic Front (R.P.F.), a rebel army formed in neighboring Uganda, launched an invasion to overthrow Rwanda's Hutu-led government, headed by President Juvenal Habyarimana, a Hutu and relative moderate in inter-ethnic relations who had seized power in a *coup d'état* in 1973 and ruled for 21 years thereafter. Habyarimana responded by arresting and imprisoning 8,000–10,000 people around the country, primarily Tutsis and other suspected opponents of his government. Civil war then broke out between the R.P.F. and Hutu government forces and lasted for three years, killing tens of thousands and displacing an estimated 100,000 from their homes. Early in 1992, political organizations affiliated with President Habyarimana formed two militias—the *Interahamwe* ("They Who Attack Together") and the *Impuzamyugambi* ("Those Who Have the Same Goal")—which, trained and supplied by the Rwandan army, were involved in the killing of more than 2,000 civilians, mostly Tutsis. In August 1993 in Arusha, Tanzania, after prolonged negotiations, Habyarimana agreed to a ceasefire, a programmed demobilization, the creation of an integrated army, a new transitional government with a prime minister acceptable to both sides, and multiparty elections with the full participation of the R.P.F.

The peace resulting from the Arusha Accords proved short-lived, however. On 6 April 1994, in unclear circumstances, President Habyarimana was killed in a plane crash outside Rwanda's capital, Kigali. Some believed that Tutsi rebels shot the plane down while others contended that the military forces of the Hutu government itself shot it down, disdainful of Habyarimana's reconciliation with the Tutsis at Arusha. In any event, militant Hutus then seized control of the government, killed Habyarimana's Prime Minister, and publicly charged that Habyarimana had been assassinated by Tutsi rebels using surface-to-air rockets. Almost instantly, Hutu gangs, paramilitary groups, and militias, using machetes, sharpened stakes, and other weapons, began indiscriminately to attack both Tutsis and moderate Hutus associated with the Habyarimana government. Evidence confirms that the slaughter that ensued was not chaotic, uncontrolled violence, but a planned and organized campaign of genocide. In most countries that suffer massive deprivations of human rights, the violations are perpetrated by the government and associated military and political groups while most of the rest of society is left to go about its business with relatively clean hands. In Rwanda, the atrocities were characterized by a deliberate attempt to force public participation on as broad a basis as possible, co-opting everyone into the carnage against the Tutsis and moderate Hutus. The militias were tightly organized throughout the country, inciting civilians to participate in the massacres, with many Hutus forced to choose between killing and being killed. If Tutsi deaths were not of sufficient number in a region, experienced killers were brought in from elsewhere to intensify the massacres.

On 18 July 1994, after the Tutsis managed to get the upper hand and with the Hutu-dominated government in flight, the R.P.F. declared victory and established a new government of national unity. After three months of fighting, between 500,000 and one million Tutsi were exterminated. Up to two million refugees, overwhelmingly Hutu and constituting 25–30 percent of Rwanda's pre-April population, are estimated to have fled to refugee camps in Zaire and Tanzania. Ugandan officials reported that as many as 10,000 bodies had floated down the Kagera River into Lake Victoria. In one incident, 500 Tutsis seeking refuge in a church compound were shot or hacked to death by Hutu soldiers over a two-day period. After a brief "humanitarian" intervention by French armed forces authorized by the UN Security Council and the installation of a new government, a tentative calm prevailed—threatened, however, by renewed warfare and genocide in Rwanda and neighboring Burundi.

Darfur

In Darfur, a poor western province of Sudan, "African" (dark-skinned) Fur, Masalit, and Zaghawa ethnic groups have long suffered abuse at the hands of both Sudan's "Arab" (lighter-skinned) leadership in Khartoum and militant "Arab" pastoralists driven to "African" farmlands by drought and desertification—to wit, nomadic "Arab" bandits and militiamen known as the "Janjaweed" (literally "men on horses with guns"). In February 2003, tensions escalated when two rebel movements from the ethnic groups—the Sudan Liberation Army/Movement (SLA/M) and the Justice and Equality Movement (JEM)—demanded an end to economic and political marginalization and requested government action to end the Janjaweed abuses. Instead, deliberately targeting civilians from the same ethnic groups as the rebels, government forces have aided and abetted Janjaweed massacres, summary executions of civilians (including women and children), burnings of towns and villages, and the forcible depopulation of wide swaths of land long inhabited by the Fur, Masalit and Zaghawa. Though Muslim like the ethnic groups they attack, the Janjaweed militias have destroyed mosques, killed Muslim religious leaders, and desecrated Qurans belonging to their enemies. And they continue to do so at this writing. Except for temporary lulls, the conflict proceeds essentially unabated.

The facts of this ongoing conflict are summarized in the 25 January 2005 Report of the International Commission of Inquiry on Darfur to the UN Secretary–General Pursuant to Security Council Resolution 1564 of 18 September 2004.[k] In its Executive Summary, the International Commission, chaired by Professor Antonio Cassese of Italy, wrote as follows:

> The Commission took as the starting point for its work two irrefutable facts regarding the situation in Darfur. Firstly, according to United Nations estimates there are 1.65 million internally displaced persons in Darfur, and more than 200,000 refugees from Darfur in neighbouring Chad. Secondly, there has been large-scale destruction of villages throughout the three states of Darfur. The Commission conducted independent investigations to establish additional facts and gathered extensive information on multiple incidents of violations affecting villages, towns and other locations across North, South and West Darfur. The conclusions of the Commission are based on the evaluation of the facts gathered or verified through its investigations.

k. *Available at* <http://www.un.org/News/dh/sudan/com_inq_darfur.pdf>.

Based on a thorough analysis of the information gathered in the course of its investigations, the Commission established that the Government of the Sudan and the Janjaweed are responsible for serious violations of international human rights and humanitarian law amounting to crimes under international law. In particular, the Commission found that Government forces and militias conducted indiscriminate attacks, including killing of civilians, torture, enforced disappearances, destruction of villages, rape and other forms of sexual violence, pillaging and forced displacement, throughout Darfur. These acts were conducted on a widespread and systematic basis, and therefore may amount to crimes against humanity. The extensive destruction and displacement have resulted in a loss of livelihood and means of survival for countless women, men and children. In addition to the large scale attacks, many people have been arrested and detained, and many have been held *incommunicado* for prolonged periods and tortured. The vast majority of the victims of all of these violations have been from the Fur, Zaghawa, Massalit, Jebel, Aranga and other so-called "African" tribes.

In their discussions with the Commission, Government of the Sudan officials stated that any attacks carried out by Government armed forces in Darfur were for counter-insurgency purposes and were conducted on the basis of military imperatives. However, it is clear from the Commission's findings that most attacks were deliberately and indiscriminately directed against civilians. Moreover even if rebels, or persons supporting rebels, were present in some of the villages—which the Commission considers likely in only a very small number of instances—the attackers did not take precautions to enable civilians to leave the villages or otherwise be shielded from attack. Even where rebels may have been present in villages, the impact of the attacks on civilians shows that the use of military force was manifestly disproportionate to any threat posed by the rebels.

The Commission is particularly alarmed that attacks on villages, killing of civilians, rape, pillaging and forced displacement have continued during the course of the Commission's mandate. . . . While the Commission did not find a systematic or a widespread pattern to these violations, it found credible evidence that rebel forces, namely members of the SLA and JEM, also are responsible for serious violations of international human rights and humanitarian law which may amount to war crimes. In particular, these violations include cases of murder of civilians and pillage.[1]

The Commission also concluded that the Sudanese government has not pursued a policy of genocide. A "crucial element" of genocide, it stated, "appears to be missing, at least as far as the central Government authorities are concerned"—that is, "a specific intent to annihilate, in whole or in part, a group distinguished on racial, ethnic, national or religious grounds." *Id*. The point is controversial, however.

––––––––

1. The UN estimated in early 2005 that some 180,000 people have died as a result of the conflict.

IT WAS WITH THESE HISTORIES IN MIND, then, that the Security Council, acting under Chapter VII of the United Nations Charter **(Basic Document 1.5)**, adopted resolutions 827 (1993) and 955 (1994) establishing *ad hoc* international criminal tribunals to bring international law formally to bear on heinous events in the former Yugoslavia and Rwanda, and Resolution 1593 (2005) referring the horrific case of Darfur to the newly established permanent International Criminal Court.[m] Its actions are explained by a number of factors, but key among them is the fact that the International Court of Justice ("the World Court")—one of the six principal organs of the United Nations[n]—does not possess criminal jurisdiction over individuals (or, indeed, criminal jurisdiction of any kind) and because egregious crimes must nevertheless not go unpunished. The Nuremberg principles of criminality and accountability had to be upheld, proponents of "final solutions" (*i.e.*, genocides) had to be deterred, the public had to be educated, and, above all, it has seemed the morally right thing to do. Additionally, commissions of inquiry such as have been used in the aftermath of significant human rights abuses in Argentina, El Salvador, South Africa and elsewhere ("truth commissions") have been judged unlikely to succeed given the scale of the atrocities and the intensity of the enmities involved.[o]

Of course, in establishing the *ad hoc* ICTY and ICTR and the permanent ICC, numerous and controversial questions of policy and practicality surfaced, not least of which have been how to staff and administer the tribunals cost-effectively; how to ensure efficiency and effectiveness in the task of investigation and inquiry; how to identify and obtain the custody of suspects; how to ensure the safety and security of defendants; how to guarantee reliable evidence and due process in the task of prosecution; how, when, and where to conduct the hearings and trials so that the victims of abuse will not feel irrelevant or marginalized; how and when, if at all, to compensate them; and so forth.

But even before questions of this sort could be answered—indeed, even before Security Council resolutions 827, 955, and 1593 could be passed—the Security Council had to confront, at least in theory, the far more fundamental question of whether *anything at all* should be done with the perpetrators of Yugoslavian, Rwandan, and Darfurian abuse—military and political, governmental official and civilian. It is well known that this question was answered in the affirmative after World War II in the form of two *ad hoc* international military tribunals established to bring to trial and punish where appropriate the major Axis leaders in Europe and the Far East for "crimes against peace" (*i.e.*, planning, initiating, or waging wars of aggression), "war crimes," and "crimes against humanity" committed during World War II—the first in

m. *See supra* notes **e** and **g**.

n. The other five organs are the General Assembly, the Security Council, the Economic and Social Council, the Trusteeship Council (essentially moribund as of this writing), and the Secretariat.

o. Paragraph 5 of UN Security Council Resolution 1593 *supra* note **e**, referring the case of Darfur to the ICC, however, does emphasize "the need to promote healing and rec-

onciliation and encourages ... the creation of institutions, involving all sectors of Sudanese society, such as truth and/or reconciliation commissions, in order to complement judicial processes and thereby reinforce the efforts to restore longlasting peace, with African Union and international support as necessary...." For pertinent discussion, see *infra* Discussion Note/Question 11 in Section A of Chapter 3, at 216–17.

Nuremberg, Germany, established by treaty;[p] the second in Tokyo, Japan, constituted by special proclamation.[q] And these historic precedents clearly paved the way for an affirmative answer from the Security Council relative to the international crimes alleged to have been committed in the former Yugoslavia, Rwanda, and, most recently, Darfur. The question in each of these cases really never has been whether to fight against impunity for crimes committed, but, rather, when, where, and how.

This fact raises the question, however, that surely did require an answer among the World War II Allied powers when they resolved to bring the Axis leaders to trial at Nuremberg and Tokyo after the war: whether or not to prosecute or summarily execute. And history, as it happens, did not serve them well as a sure-footed guide, providing too many inconsistent solutions. First, and farthest back in time, was the so-called "Carthaginian peace" whereby the entire defeated population—leaders and civilians alike—were executed by the winning side. Later, though the weapons of war had become more destructive, civilization modified the Carthaginian solution such that, up through the Middle Ages, the leaders of defeated powers often were executed while the enemy populations were spared (although frequently enemy populations were either looted of their property or, in some instances, enslaved). Later still, with the onset of the Renaissance and Reformation and the rise of nation-states, the practice of executing defeated enemy leaders became increasingly rare. And in 1918, after the biggest war in history—World War I—the leaders of the defeated powers signed the Peace Treaty in Versailles and returned to their homes essentially unscathed.[r]

Thus, while history provided a wide range of solutions prior to World War II, the trend up to it was nonetheless clear: enemy leaders and populations were to be left alone, free to go home and rebuild their war-torn nations pretty much as they saw fit. It can be said, of course, that this trend was ill-advised or misguided. History, after all, provided a spectrum of possible answers to the question of what to do with defeated enemy leaders, so surely such leaders need not have been allowed to get off entirely free. But was there not something to be learned from the increasingly humane (non-vindictive,

p. *See* the August 1945 Agreement by the Government of the United Kingdom of Great Britain and Northern Ireland, the Government of the United States of America, the Provisional Government of the French Republic, and the Government of the Union of Soviet Socialist Republics for the Prosecution and Punishment of the Major War Criminals of the European Axis Powers and Charter of the International Military Tribunal **(Basic Document 1.3)**.

q. *See* Special Proclamation Establishing an International Military Tribunal for the Far East and Charter of the International Military Tribunal for the Far East, issued 19 Jan 1946, *reprinted in* The Tokyo Judgment: The International Military Tribunal for the Far East (IMTFE), 29 Apr 46–12 Nov 48, at III–Annex Nos. A–4 and A–5 (Amsterdam: APA University Press, B. Röling & C. Ruter eds. 1977) and 2 Weston & Carlson II.E.2.

r. Observes M. C. Bassiouni, International Criminal Law: A Draft International Criminal Code (1980), at 9:

After World War I, the Treaty of Versailles in 1919 established the punishability of war criminals; ordered Germany to hand over to the Allies all Germans accused of war crimes to be tried by military tribunals; and allowed the Allies to establish national war crimes tribunals.... A special body was created to report on the persons to be prosecuted and the "Commission on the Responsibility of the Authors of the War and on Enforcement of Penalties" issued its report on 3 February 1920. In it, 896 names were submitted by the Allies to Germany of alleged war criminals, but for political reasons that list shrank to 45 and, of these, Germany tried only 12 before the Supreme Court of the Reich sitting in Leipzig, six of whom were acquitted. Article 228 was not applied because Germany refused to extradite its nationals.

non-punitive) nature of these solutions over time, from the fact that the "Carthaginian peace" did not furnish the model for all future wars?

———

THROUGHOUT THIS COURSEBOOK, questions such as these are asked, and when they are we hope you will pause briefly and venture an answer of your own before forging ahead. It is not essential or even important that you come up with the same answer that we, your authors/editors, might suggest because the principal point of asking the questions is to help you develop problem-solving skills. A primary goal of this book—no different than the goals of any other legal subject you might study—is to assist you in learning how to think like a lawyer, which means, in part, learning how to solve problems rationally and, we hope, humanely.

However, our aim is not only to help you acquire the techniques you need to identify and apply relevant international legal doctrines, principles, and rules; it is also to help you develop the ability critically to analyze and assess the existing law. As we shall see, many traditional doctrines, principles, and rules of the international legal order respond to the interests and concerns of the powerful states, many of them former colonial powers. Today, they are not infrequently called into question by nations from the developing world (which now make up two-thirds of the membership of the United Nations) on the grounds that they are inequitable and/or inappropriate. Increasingly, as well, women are challenging the objectivity of the international legal system, arguing that its male-dominated fora and agendas generate principles that privilege men's experiences and consequently do not take women's lives into account either seriously or at all. Other groups, such as minority indigenous peoples, also point to the inadequacy of a system built on the artificial construct of the nation-state. So, as you work through this coursebook, always consider the politics of international law: What values inform and what values are inculcated by particular doctrines, principles, and rules? Whose interests are being served? On what silences are the doctrines, principles, and rules built?

———

NOW, WITH THESE PEDAGOGICAL CONSIDERATIONS IN MIND, let us return to the question of the "Carthaginian peace," known to the Allied powers at the close of World War II. Why didn't that model "catch on" through the ages? Anthony D'Amato posed this key question in the second edition of this coursebook and responded to it as follows:

>   ... One answer is that, with the development of civilization through time, people had become less barbaric and perhaps more morally sensitive; over time, it increasingly became seen as cruel to slaughter defenseless persons who just happened to be on the losing side in a war. Thus, by the time of World War II, though the Allies insisted upon—and eventually got—"unconditional surrender" from Germany and Japan, there would have been no political support back home for any policy of mass murder of the defeated enemy populations. The possibility was too inhumane even to contemplate.

But "moral sensitivity" is only one "explanation," and you may be somewhat skeptical about it in any event (particularly in the light of the US atomic bombings of Hiroshima and Nagasaki at the very end of World War II). You may question whether it was a developing morality that changed what victorious powers did to vanquished enemies or whether it was the reverse; that is, you may wonder whether morality led practice or whether practice led morality?

A possible way of handling this latter question is to ask another: what other explanation can there be for the historical progression away from the "Carthaginian peace"? Think of a hardheaded, practical answer.

Here is one answer: a war (national or international) is always very costly to both sides; but omitting for the moment the cost to the losing side, how can the winning side minimize its own costs? Clearly the best way is to get the war over as soon as possible; the longer the war progresses, the higher the costs for the winning side. (When you consider costs, it does not matter that the losing side is incurring even greater costs as a war continues, because no matter what costs the losing side incurs those costs do not ameliorate the costs incurred by the winning side.)

So imagine a war in progress. W is clearly winning and L is clearly losing but is putting up fierce resistance. W wants to get L to surrender so as to put an end to the costs that L still is inflicting upon W through its resistance. But L will not surrender if L believes that, after the war, W will "eliminate" all of L's inhabitants. So W communicates "terms of peace" to L's leadership, offering to desist from any more killing if L surrenders. To be sure, the people of L may not trust W to keep its word, but if W has been a victorious power in other wars and has kept its word in the past, the people of L might "sue for peace." The terms of the peace might be harsh; all the people of L might become slaves to the conquering soldiers of W. But arguably even slavery seems preferable to death, so the people of L might accept enslavement as part of the peace treaty.[1]

Now let us leap forward a thousand years or so. We find that the fear of being enslaved keeps the losing side (L) fighting against the winning side (W). If W wants L to lay down its arms, W will have to offer better terms than enslavement. And so, gradually, W does offer better terms and keeps its promises. L may have to give up territories that it owns, [for it] certainly will have to pay huge sums of money to W in "reparation" for the war costs borne by W even though this would seem unfair if W had started the war. As a victorious power, W is able to extract huge financial reparations from L, and from L's point of view, paying much or most of its wealth to W is preferable to enslavement as well as preferable to continued fighting.

What would happen if W also demanded, as a condition of peace, the execution of L's leaders? Would L accept a peace treaty or would L go on

1. The peace treaty is one of the earliest examples of international law. It rapidly became the practice of states to adhere to the terms of peace treaties (do you see why?), and this consistent practice became a norm of customary international law. The norm says that all treaties—including treaties of peace—must be obeyed by the parties. The Latin expression for this norm is *pacta sunt servanda*.

fighting? Likely as not, L's leaders would urge the people of L to continue the war! But W might hope that the L populace would rise up against their leaders to obtain peace. If the people of L believed that their leaders led them into an unwanted war, then revolution might be possible. On the other hand, if W were the aggressor and the leaders of L did their best to defend friendly nation F, it is less likely that the people of L would overturn their leaders to sue for peace.

Around 1942—the precise date remains unclear—an idea was suggested by US President Franklin Delano Roosevelt to his World War II Allies: that they demand "unconditional surrender" of the Axis powers. This idea was resisted on the ground that it would prolong the war, giving the enemy nations no "bargaining power" for peace; it would give the Axis powers no incentive to surrender inasmuch as they would not know what draconian solution the Allies might impose upon them. Still, President Roosevelt prevailed. He prevailed in large part because the United States was contributing the decisive military power to the war effort. He also convinced the Allies that there was at least a chance that the people of Germany and Japan would rise up against their military dictators and thus topple the leadership that was causing the Allies all their problems. Perhaps President Roosevelt's most telling point, however, was that World War II should be a "war to end all wars," that we should not stop short of total victory lest the enemy leaders who led their nations into waging a war of aggression escape without punishment. In the President's view, punishing the enemy leaders was the only way to ensure that no new leadership would again emerge in Germany or Japan or elsewhere who might lead their countries into World War III. And, so, the Allies adopted the policy of "unconditional surrender" and proclaimed it publicly.

As is now known, the hope that the people of Germany and Japan would rise up and overthrow their military leaders proved completely unrealistic. The governments of both countries were so firmly in control that any indications of subversion or revolution were immediately suppressed. In 1944, for example, a group of disaffected German generals who were successful in planting and exploding a bomb in an attaché case under a table where Adolf Hitler was holding a meeting, but who were unsuccessful in killing or seriously injuring the Führer because the heavy table shielded him from the major force of the blast, were captured and executed. Moreover, the Axis governments provided their populations with false information about the progress of the war. Even in the final days of the war in 1945 the Japanese population believed that the Allies were on the verge of surrendering.[2]

Still, many rational observers of the Axis powers knew in 1943 that the tide of the war had turned in favor of the Allied powers and that defeat was but a matter of time.[3] It is quite apparent from what we now

2. False governmental information about the progress of war is a feature of all wars. The United States heavily censored war reports during World War II, and after the bombing of Pearl Harbor President Roosevelt, while reporting to the public on the heavy casualties and asking Congress for a declaration of war against Japan, deliberately minimized the extent of the damage.

3. It has been revealed that, remarkably, the military personnel in Japan who conceived of the devastating raid on Pearl Harbor argued

know that the German and Japanese leadership knew that their war effort was ultimately doomed, but fought on nevertheless because the idea of "unconditional surrender" meant that their own lives were at stake. They had no incentive to surrender because, they believed, surrender meant death for themselves. Roosevelt's "unconditional surrender" policy may have meant that World War II was prolonged and that many soldiers on both sides lost their lives or were wounded because of that policy.

Actually, no one knows how much longer World War II lasted because of the Allied insistence upon unconditional surrender. Historians are in disagreement on this issue. But it seems reasonable to assume that the war was protracted because the Allied powers offered no assurance to the enemy leaders that if they agreed to a peace treaty they themselves would be spared. Even if the war was protracted [for] only ... a few months, those months at the end witnessed the nuclear bombing of Hiroshima and Nagasaki. The enormous casualties inflicted by this use of the new nuclear weapon, and the cancer and leukemia induced in huge numbers of Japanese people who did not perish in the immediate fire-blast of the nuclear weapons, must be added to the "price" that was paid for attaining the unconditional surrender of the enemy, as must also the precedent set that has cast a shadow of dubious legal, moral, and political legitimacy over nuclear weaponry ever since.

In any event, toward the close of World War II, there was no doubt that when war would come finally to an end the enemy leaders responsible for it would be punished. The victorious Allies certainly were not going to exact a full-scale "Carthaginian peace" as a result of their victory. But neither were they going to repeat a World War I solution and send the enemy leaders home with scarcely a slap on the wrist while simultaneously nurturing a populist backlash through the imposition of humiliating conditions and insisting upon costly reparations, crippling the defeated country's recovery. Indeed, the Soviet Union wanted all the German Nazi leaders—even all the members of the German Nazi Party—to be summarily executed, as an administrative act without benefit of trial. Summary execution was favored, too, by the influential US Secretary of the Treasury, Henry Morgenthau Jr., although he confined it to a list of the highest Nazi officials. But the most important Allied leader—US President Harry S. Truman, a former judge—had made up his mind that there should be trials. And there were.

But consider: didn't Morgenthau have a point? He knew of the Nazi holocaust against the Jews, as many did not. He was aware of the mass deportations to the gas chambers of old men, women, and children. No more monstrous crime could be imagined. Surely, one might think, everyone responsible should have been executed. Moreover, the Nazis were responsible for launching aggressive wars that meant the death of hundreds of thousands of people and the destruction of homes, farms, and

that if the raid were successfully carried out Japan should sue for peace because a protracted war against the United States would ultimately end in certain defeat. Needless to say, once the raid was in fact successfully carried out, the Japanese leadership "forgot" the advice that accompanied the plan for the Pearl Harbor raid and, carried along by the momentum generated by their military success, considered it treason for anyone in the Government to talk about suing for peace with the United States.

cities. Weren't these wars nothing less than huge conspiracies to commit murder? Wasn't the war itself nothing less than mass murder? If capital punishment may be imposed upon a criminal for murdering another human being (as still is permitted in the United States, for example), why should not the Nazi leaders have been executed for carrying out murder on a vast scale?

There were, as one should expect, competing considerations. Hindsight helps to see at least some of them clearly.

First, the leading Nazis had surrendered and become Allied prisoners. Was it not unlawful to execute captured prisoners? It is true that they surrendered unconditionally, but once they surrendered and were at Allied mercy, should the Allies have had the right to execute them?

Also, some Nazi leaders would claim that they personally did not do the things the Allies indicted them for doing. Others would present evidence of having done everything possible to resist the Nazis while ostensibly going about everyday duties. And still others would claim cases of mistaken identity, that they were not the person who was in charge of a death camp but only resembled such a person. Did claimants such as these deserve summary execution without benefit of trial?

Additionally, the Nazi leaders would claim that they only followed the "superior orders" of Adolf Hitler, who personified the state. The Führer's orders were law, to be obeyed without question or hesitation, sometimes on penalty of death. If anyone was guilty, it was Hitler and not those who faithfully carried out his policies. They did what they did for the Third Reich, acting only as patriots or out of fear, but not for themselves as individuals. They bore no moral responsibility for the war.

Further, the lawyers for some of the Nazi leaders on trial would argue that the Allied leadership prosecuted the war in as criminal a fashion as anything that the German leaders did. Was it not criminal to engage in the saturation bombing of Dresden [and other German cities], where bombs were dropped on the homes of workers? Was it not a monstrous crime to firebomb Tokyo suburbs in 1945[4] and to incinerate Hiroshima and Nagasaki with atomic bombs? Why weren't the Allied leaders responsible for these acts to be prosecuted?[5] A variation of this

---

4. *Consider* 6 Foreign Rel. U.S. 471 (1945):

On the night of March 9, 1945, over 300 US B–29 superfortress bombers dropped over one thousand tons of incendiary bombs on an urban industrial area of Tokyo. Hundreds of thousands of homes were destroyed by the resulting firestorm. Over 72,000 people died and 130,000 were injured. On March 12, the raid was repeated in Nagoya in Tokyo's center, one of the densest population areas in the world (75,000 persons per square mile). Again, on March 14 and on March 17, General Curtis LeMay's incendiary bombers struck areas in Tokyo. According to a communiqué from the Japanese government handed to the Swiss Chargé, "the United States planes deliberately bombed such absolutely non-military objec-

tives as shrines, temples, schools, hospitals, and densely populated residential quarters and reduced them to ashes. They slaughtered an innumerable number of women, children, and aged people...."

Many of the homes destroyed by fire were contributing to the war effort by home-industry production. The avowed purpose of the American raids was to cripple the Japanese war effort.

5. As it happens, the only case brought for war crimes against the World War II Allies was one brought by some Japanese citizens for the use by the United States of atomic weapons at Hiroshima and Nagasaki. However, in the end, the case was rejected by the Supreme Court of Japan on jurisdictional grounds. *See* Shimoda v. The State, 355 Hanrel Jiho (Supreme Court

argument was called *"tu quoque"*—that the Allies should not have been able to prosecute the enemy for acts which the Allies committed themselves.

Finally, the Nazi leaders would claim that, even with a trial, the Allies were engaged in "victors' justice," that they were being tried and would be convicted and possibly even executed not because of any legally or morally deficient posture on their part but because they lost the war. What might have been the long-term—possibly even the short-term—political repercussions of this claim in the face of summary executions, in the absence of a trial? And, if the Allies had lost the war, wouldn't they have claimed loudly and bitterly about "victors' justice" had the Axis powers acted similarly?[6]

Surely, then, President Truman must have been right. A trial—not summary execution—was required, if only to determine individual guilt and responsibility.

WE NOW INVITE YOU to imagine yourself as a junior lawyer serving on the recently constituted prosecutorial staff of Luis Moreno–Ocampo of Argentina, the Prosecutor of the International Criminal Court at this writing. Your legal experience is primarily in national (or domestic or municipal) criminal law,[s] but you once took an introductory international law course, are analytically gifted, and have a knack for foreign languages.

It is early April 2005, you are in The Hague at the temporary quarters of the ICC on the capital city's outskirts, and Prosecutor Moreno–Ocampo, following up on UN Security Council Resolution 1593 of 31 March 2005,[t] has asked you and others on his growing staff to assist him with violations of international criminal law claimed to have been committed in Darfur since 1 July 2002. Specifically, he asks you to help him assess the "admissibility" of these claims in accordance with articles 17–19 of the Rome Statute of the International Criminal Court **(Basic Document 1.16)**, to help with his investigation of the claimed violations if found to be admissible, and then, if called for, to develop legal arguments for the indictment of individuals responsible for the violations alleged to have been committed. To these ends, searching for comprehensive guidance in as yet untested circumstances, he asks you to research, among other things, the trials of the Nazi and Japanese leaders captured at the end of World War II and prosecuted initially at Nuremberg and Tokyo; also the trials so far held under the aegis of the *ad hoc* ICTY and ICTR. These post-World War II, ICTY, and ICTR trials, he observes, are the only modern international precedents pertinent and available. Your assistance in all these ways, he adds, will prove useful also in the

of Japan, 7 December 1963). For additional detail, see R. Falk, *The Shimoda Case: A Legal Appraisal of the Atomic Attacks Upon Hiroshima and Nagasaki*, 59 A.J.I.L. 759 (1965).

6. Regarding this issue in the context of the Tokyo war crimes trial, see R. Minear, Victors' Justice: The Tokyo War Crimes Trial (1971). *See also* Judge Pal's dissent in the Tokyo trial, The Tokyo Judgment: The International Military Tribunal for the Far East (IMTFE), *supra* note p.

s. International lawyers use the terms "domestic law" and "municipal law" interchangeably with, and as synonyms for, "national law."

t. *See supra* notes **e** and **f**.

three cases referred to the ICC by the Democratic Republic of Congo (for thousands of mass murders and summary executions within its territory in April 2004), by Uganda (for international crimes in Northern Uganda also in April 2004),[u] and by the Central African Republic (for international crimes in its territory in January 2005).

You turn, therefore, to the bountiful international law library of the International Court of Justice (ICJ) at the nearby Peace Palace[v] and there discover, to your surprise, that the records of the Tokyo war crimes trials are skimpy relative to those of the International Military Tribunal established at Nuremberg. You learn that the reasons for this circumstance include the fact that it a took a long time for the Tokyo judgment to be published and that little of the Japanese literature on the trial has been available in translation.[w] Accordingly, briefly deferring your investigation of the ICTY and ICTR trials, you turn to the more abundant information available regarding Nuremberg, and quickly you learn that the lawyers for the Nazi leaders argued, *inter alia*, that their clients did nothing "illegal" because there was no applicable law to say that what they did was a crime. They argued that, though their clients were being prosecuted with all the trappings and appearance of a trial, the entire trial was a sham because the "law" was being applied *ex post facto*; the law was being invented by the Allies after the fact, after the events in question took place. A quick glance at the Rome Statute tells you, however, that this is not an issue for the ICC: Article 22 provides that "[a] person shall not be criminally responsible under this Statute unless the conduct in

u. "On 13 October 2005, Pre–Trial Chamber II unsealed the warrants of arrest for five senior leaders of the Lord's Resistance Army (LRA) for Crimes against Humanity and War Crimes committed in Uganda since July 2002. The Chamber concluded that 'there are reasonable grounds to believe' that Joseph Kony, Vincent Otti, Okot Odhiambo, Dominic Ongwen, and Raska Lukwiya 'ordered the commission of crimes within the jurisdiction of the Court.'" Press Release, International Criminal Court, "Warrant of Arrest unsealed against five LRA Commanders" (14 Oct 2005), *available at* <http://www.icc-cpi.int/press/pressreleases /114.html>.

v. The Peace Palace at The Hague is the site of the International Court of Justice (ICJ). It was a gift of philanthropist Andrew Carnegie to the League of Nations upon the founding of the ICJ's predecessor, the unfortunately-named Permanent Court of International Justice (PCIJ). The PCIJ and the ICJ are both jointly and separately referred to also as the "World Court."

w. C. Hosoya, N. Andō, Y. Ōnuma, & R. Minear further explain the lesser attention given to Tokyo relative to Nuremberg as follows:

... with the possible exception of former [Japanese] prime minister Tōjō Hideki, none of the defendants was as famous as Göring or Hess; ... the acts charged against the Japanese leaders were in no way comparable in sheer heinousness to those charged against the Nazi leaders, that few of the

Allied participants [in Tokyo] were people of great standing in their home countries; ... the trial dragged on so long; that by the time a judgment was reached the wartime alliance had already fallen apart; and ... the rest of the world was more interested in things European than things Asian.

Preface, The Tokyo War Crimes Trial: An International Symposium 7 ©. Hosoya, N. Andō, Y. Ōnuma & R. Minear eds. 1986). *See also* the *Introduction* to this book by the late Professor B.V.A. Röling, the Dutch judge on the Tokyo tribunal, who elaborates at 16 as follows:

The Nuremberg trial ... was the first trial in which leaders of a state ... stood trial, not only for crimes committed during the war, but also for launching the war itself. * * * Nuremberg also has more allure than the Tokyo trial.... Robert Jackson, the American chief prosecutor at Nuremberg, was a brilliant man who assumed his function convinced that this was one of those rare moments in history that might yield a fundamental change in thought and action, and who could express that deep conviction in words reminiscent of Churchill. * * * Compared with Jackson, Joseph B. Keenan [the chief prosecutor at Tokyo] was a mediocre man. The evidence suggests that he saw his job in Tokyo as a way to gain a seat in the US Senate....

See also M. C. Bassiouni, Crimes against Humanity in International Criminal Law xii (1992).

question constitutes, at the time it takes place, a crime within the jurisdiction of the Court" (the principle *nullum crimen sine lege*); Article 23 stipulates that "[a] person convicted by the Court may be punished only in accordance with this Statute" (*i.e.*, the principle *nulla poena sine lege*); and articles 5–8 and 21 spell out in great detail the crimes for which a person may be tried and convicted by the ICC and the legal authorities upon which the ICC may rely for this purpose.

Nevertheless, questions abound, and wanting to be helpful to Prosecutor Moreno–Ocampo you know that you must deepen your understanding of international law. You wonder whether there really was any "law" under which the Nazi leaders at Nuremberg (and the Japanese leaders at Tokyo) could be prosecuted. And you wonder, too, if the actions of the German (and Japanese) leaders were criminal as the Nuremberg (and Tokyo) trials said they were, what "law" made them criminal? Certainly the law of the Third Reich—which in fact authorized and even instructed the Nazi crimes—could not have been of any help in solving the problem at hand. Nor could the laws of the various World War II Allied countries given that disabling charges of bias would almost certainly have ensued and that, in any event, nations typically do not include in their criminal laws any crimes relating to warfare by the military forces of foreign countries or extend their laws into the territory of other countries.[x]

The answer is, of course, international law. But who makes international law and what makes it *law*? Where does it comes from? What does it embody? How is it enforced? You are of course aware that after World War II the victorious Allied Powers negotiated a "[Treaty] for the Prosecution and Punishment of the Major War Criminals of the European Axis Powers and Charter of the International Military Tribunal **(Basic Document 1.3)** established at Nuremberg. But you wonder how an agreement among certain but not all countries can create something we can think of as law. And, what about the connection between law and power? The Allied Powers could enforce their agreement on their defeated enemies because they won on the battlefield. Is international law therefore no more than an exercise in, or reflection of, naked power?

These questions provoke further questions. You know that the ICTY and the ICTR were established by the UN Security Council, but what is the source of the Security Council's authority to do such a thing? Upon what basis does it have the legal competence to establish international criminal tribunals, and what is the connection between that power and the ability for judgments of those tribunals to be enforced? And what about the ICC itself? You know that, like the Nuremberg Tribunal, it was established by a treaty (the Rome statute), but this time not by victorious powers as in the case of the Nuremberg Tribunal. Is the ICC, therefore, meaningfully different in a legal sense than the Nuremberg Tribunal and, for that matter, the ICTY and ICTR? Is its establishment indicative of an evolution in what we think of as

---

x. One prominent and time-honored exception is the law against counterfeiting currency. It is, for example, a crime under United States law to counterfeit US currency in any other nation. *See generally*, for example, §§ 402–433 Restatement (Third) of the Foreign Relations Law of the United States (1987) relative to the jurisdiction of the United States to prescribe, adjudicate, and enforce both territorially and extraterritorially.

international law? Without the force of a victorious army behind it, how does this new court enforce its judgements?

We, your authors/editors, have taken it upon ourselves to serve as your research assistants and thus to provide you with numerous materials and references relevant to these many and diverse questions. But, as elsewhere in this coursebook, we do not provide you with the thinking. That is for you to do with the materials and notes and other writings that we have assembled for you.

In particular, we make no claim that the materials we have found for you are always adequate. For example, there are many useful materials about the Tokyo wars crimes trials that, for reasons of space, we have not included. Decisions about adequacy are for you to make—just as when you are in a library doing research, selecting some articles and books and rejecting others. Indeed, you should treat the materials we have selected much as you would a library, pulling books off the shelves and looking through them to see if there is anything that you can use. Of course, our choice of materials is inevitably shaped by our own training and traditions; we are academics from the developed "North" and "West" and carry a variety of baggage that belongs to this heritage. You may well disagree with the positions taken by "the authorities"—the documents, the writers—we present, and you will need to evaluate carefully the weight you choose to give to each. However, we have included ideas, comments, and questions of our own to assist you in this task.

One final point. You will notice that the terminology of many of the authors whose work we use is sexist in that it refers only to men as potential actors in the international legal system and as beneficiaries of its doctrines, principles, and rules. This is the inevitable result of the long exclusion of women from the realm of international politics and law. It is a tangible symbol of one of the silences of international law to which we referred earlier and which underscores the importance of imagining how different the corpus of international law might be if women (as well as other historically marginalized people) from various ethnic and class backgrounds had contributed to its formation and participated equally and fully in its implementation.

Thus, with this caveat, we begin our exploration of international law and world order, a field of growing importance in an era of increasing globalization, uncertain in its ultimate destiny.

Chapter One

THE CONCEPT OF INTERNATIONAL LAW

In the Introduction immediately preceding, you were asked to imagine yourself working in early April 2005 as a junior prosecuting attorney at the International Criminal Court (ICC), established in The Hague pursuant to the Rome Statute of the International Criminal Court of 17 July 1998 **(Basic Document 1.16)** for the purpose of prosecuting persons alleged to be responsible for genocide, crimes against humanity, and war crimes in cases referred to the Court by states parties to the Statute or by the UN Security Council. You were asked also to imagine that then ICC Prosecutor, Luis Moreno–Ocampo of Argentina, following up on UN Security Council instructions, had asked you to assist him with violations of international criminal law claimed to have been committed in Darfur since 1 July 2002 (possibly also in the Democratic republic of Congo and Northern Uganda in April 2004 and in the Central African Republic in January 2005)—specifically, to help him assess the admissibility of the claims presented relative to Darfur, to help with his investigation of the claimed violations if found to be admissible, and then, if called for, to develop legal arguments for the indictment of individuals responsible for the violations alleged. However, as your professional experience has been more in domestic criminal law than in public international law, you have found it necessary to do some background study, beginning with the definition of international law, its history, and the structure of the international legal system. To this end you turn to a new international law treatise that recently you discovered in the law library of the Peace Palace in The Hague (*i.e.*, this Coursebook).[a]

A. DEFINITIONAL CONSIDERATIONS

You begin with the most basic lesson of all: clarifying the meaning of "international law" itself. The reason it is important to address this matter of definition is because of the relative absence in the international system of courts and legislatures and police forces in the commonly understood sense and therefore of the possibility of no international law at all but of something else that lawyers like to parade as international law. After all, how is it

---

a. You quickly note a remarkable feature of this new treatise: it contains materials from the future as well as the past. However, this magical quality, representing a literary license on your editors' part, makes you confident of the book's currency and reliability.

possible to have law without such manifestly legal institutions as courts, legislatures, and police forces as commonly understood? The question is no idle one. To the contrary, it is exceedingly important because definitions, like the words that make them up, are mental constructs—paradigms—that shape not only what we are willing to think about, but also how we go about looking at what we are willing to think about. You know, like Lewis Carroll's Humpty Dumpty, that words use us as much as we use words. Accordingly, you commence your reading.

————

The task of defining "law" itself, let alone "international law," is not easy. The point is clearly made in Sir Frederick Pollock, A First Book of Jurisprudence for Students of the Common Law (1929) 3–4 (6th ed. 1994):

> We find in all human sciences that those ideas which seem to be most simple are really the most difficult to grasp with certainty and express with accuracy. . . . It is not surprising, then, that the student approaching the science of law should find the formal definiteness of its ideas to vary inversely with their generality. No tolerably prepared candidate in an English or American law school will hesitate to define an estate in fee simple: on the other hand, the greater have been a lawyer's opportunities of knowledge, and the more time he has given to the study of legal principles, the greater will be his hesitation in face of the apparently simple question: What is Law?

No less difficult is the task of defining "international law"—or, more precisely, of reaching agreement on what we mean by "international law." Indeed, the very reality of international law is sometimes open to challenge, on the grounds that there can be no law governing sovereign states or that it is not "real law" because states obey it only when it is in their interest to do so. As Morton Kaplan and Nicholas Katzenbach put it in The Political Foundations of International Law 5 (1961): "A number of great legal philosophers . . . have . . . doubted the legal character of international law, and the charges and counter-charges which pervade the international community today seem to provide empirical support for their view. Clearly some definitions of law would exclude international law."

Consider, for example, the "analytical" or "legal positivist" school of jurisprudence, which holds that law is the command of a sovereign enforced by punitive sanction against persons subject to the sovereign's authority. John Austin, the influential Nineteenth Century founder of legal positivism, put it thus in The Province of Jurisprudence Determined (1832) 133, 201 (1954 ed.):

> . . . Laws properly so called are a species of commands. But, being a command, every law properly so called flows from a determinate source. . . . * * * [W]henever a command is expressed or intimated, one party signifies a wish that another shall do or forbear: and the latter is obnoxious to an evil which the former intends to inflict in case the wish be disregarded.

* * *

And hence it inevitably follows, that the law obtaining between nations is not positive law: for every positive law is set by a given sovereign to a person or persons in a state of subjection to its author. . . . [T]he law obtaining between nations is law (improperly so called) set by general opinion. The duties which it imposes are enforced by moral sanctions: by fear on the part of nations, or by fear on the part of sovereigns, of provoking general hostility, and incurring its probable evils, in case they shall violate maxims generally received and respected.

In sum, to the "analytical" or "legal positivist" way of thinking about law, the term "international law" is little more than a euphemism for international morality. International law is not "real law," not law "properly so called."

Consider, too, the views of the post-World War II American "realists" (sometimes called "Neo-realists" or "Skeptics"). In World Politics and International Law 3 (1985), law professor and political scientist Francis Boyle usefully summarizes their skepticism as follows:

From the moment of its creation as an intellectual discipline in the aftermath of the Second World War, international political science has maintained that international law and organizations are essentially irrelevant to a proper understanding of international politics and consequently are irrelevant to the progressive development of international political theory. * * * This denial of the relevance of international law and organizations to "high" international politics . . . is attributable to an extreme negative reaction to the so-called legalist-moralist or utopian approach to international affairs, said to have influenced the conduct of international relations by the United States and the other Western democracies during the period between the First and Second World Wars. . . . Its best exemplars [in the United States] were the writings of scholars such as Edward Hallett Carr and Hans Morgenthau, and the careers and publications of statesmen like Dean Acheson, George Kennan, and later Henry Kissinger.

In the realist view of international relations, international law and organizations totally lack any intrinsic significance within the utilitarian calculus of international political decision making. International law, morality, ethics, ideology and even knowledge itself are mere components in the power equation, devoid of non-instrumental significance or prescriptive worth, subject to compulsory service as tools of power when deemed necessary for the vital interests of state. There are no barriers to the acquisitive nature of the nation state beyond its own inherent limitations and those constraints imposed upon it by the international political milieu. Consequently, the analysis of international relations must concentrate exclusively upon the dynamics of power politics and the machinations of that metaphysical entity known as the "balance of power." Considerations of international law do not and should not intrude into such areas. Or, if they do intrude, it should be only for the instrumental purpose of serving as a source for the manufacture of ad hoc or ex post facto justifications for decisions taken on the basis of antinomian factors such as Machiavellian power politics and nation self-interest.

Thus, again, the term "international law" is perceived as little more than a euphemism for international morality, if that.

This "realist" response to the "legalist-moralist" or "utopian" approach to international affairs, it must be acknowledged, has not been without warrant. In a struggle that spanned three centuries, from the birth of the state system at the Peace of Westphalia in 1648 to the aftermath of World War II, classical legal theorists, particularly those espousing the polar doctrines of naturalism and positivism, battled one another to an intellectual impasse, each purporting but failing to answer convincingly the fundamental theoretical questions of international law—its origin, its status as law, its substantive content, its reformist and transformist possibilities—and thus each failing as well to respond adequately to controversies in the "real world." The natural law theorists (who maintained that international law binds sovereign states because law emanates from God or nature) ultimately were forced into retreat by the legal positivists (who, as noted, maintained that law emanates from sovereign will or consent); but the legal positivists also proved inadequate to the "real world" challenge. Whereas natural law theory was exposed as religiously arbitrary and unverifiable, legal positivism came up short for being unable to explain either the true normative beliefs of the day or actual behavior. The result: a discipline without convincing force and effect. As observed by Nigel Purvis in *Critical Legal Studies in Public International Law*, 32 Harv. Intl. L. J. 81, 82–83 (1991): "Theoretical discourse about international law repeatedly exposed the weaknesses of the two opposing positions without finding a way either to decide between them or to overcome the division.... The disharmony of the discipline made all theoretic enterprises seem impossible."

Nevertheless, there developed over the years a fairly standard usage of "international law" that has had great impact upon the practice as well as the theory of international law. The Permanent Court of International Justice put it this way in an oft-quoted statement in the Case of the S.S. "Lotus," 1927 P.C.I.J., ser. A, No. 10, at 18:

> International law governs relations between independent States. The rules of law binding upon States therefore emanate from their own free will as expressed in conventions or by usages generally accepted as expressing principles of law and established in order to regulate the relations between these coexisting independent communities or with a view to the achievement of common aims.

A similar formulation is found in James L. Brierly, The Law of Nations 1 (H. Waldock 6th ed. 1963), long considered a classic in the field: "The Law of Nations, or International Law, may be defined as the body of rules and principles of action which are binding upon civilized states in their relations with one another."

These traditional rule-oriented and statist definitions have been adopted more or less formally by most—perhaps even all—of the states of our present-day world, including such distinctive powers as the United States, the independent members of The Commonwealth, the states of the European Union, the republics of the former Soviet Union, and the People's Republic of China.[b]

b. For accounts of Chinese attitudes toward international law, see, *e.g.*, H. Chiu, *Chinese Attitudes Towards International Law in the Post–Mao Era, 1978–1987*, 21 Int'l Law. 1127 (1987); Rosemary Foot, Rights Beyond Borders: The Global Community and the Struggle over Human Rights in China (2000);Ann Kent, China, the United Nations,

With the passage of time, to be sure, new developments have added new elements. Thus, Section 101 of the 1986 revision of the American Law Institute's Restatement of Foreign Relations Law takes a small step toward recognizing the relevance of non-state actors to the international legal system:

> "International law," as used in this Restatement, consists of rules and principles of general application dealing with the conduct of states and of international organizations and with their relations inter se, as well as with some of their relations with persons, whether natural or juridical.

But by and large the factual and theoretical orientation has remained the same. Statist and rule-oriented definitions of international law continue to dominate.

Despite this formal adherence to the traditional view, however, international law scholarship and decision-making has come to conceive of international law increasingly from a contextually wider, more behaviorally responsive perspective. As the following four extracts make clear, this has been due, at least in part, to a growing sophistication about law and legal process generally.

LOUIS HENKIN, "INTERNATIONAL LAW: POLITICS, VALUES AND FUNCTIONS"
216 Recueil 22 (1989–IV)

First, law is politics. Students of law as well as students of politics are taught to distinguish law from politics. Law is normative, and failure to abide by legal obligations invites legal remedies and brings other legal responses; politics suggests freedom of choice, diplomacy, bargaining, accommodation. In fact, however, the distinction between law and politics is only a part-truth. In a larger, deeper sense, law is politics. Law is made by political actors (not by lawyers), through political procedures, for political ends. The law that emerges is the resultant of political forces; the influences of law on State behaviour are also determined by political forces.

Second ..., law is the normative expression of a political system. To appreciate the character of international law and its relation to the international political system, it is helpful to invoke (though with caution) domestic law as an analogue. Domestic (national) law ... is an expression of a domestic political system in a domestic (national) society. A domestic society consists of people, human beings, [and] artificial juristic persons (*e.g.*, companies, associations). Domestic law is a construct of norms, standards, principles, institutions and procedures that serve the purposes of society. Law serves, notably, to establish and maintain order and enhance the reliability of expectations; to protect persons, their property and other interests; to promote the welfare of individuals (or of some of them), and to further other societal values—justice, the good life, the good society.

Similarly ..., international law is the product of its particular "society," its political system. International law, too, is a construct of norms, standards,

and Human Rights (1999); S. Kim, *The Development of International Law in Post–Mao China: Change and Continuity*, 1 J. Chinese L. 117 (1987); T. Wang, *International Law in China: Historical and Contemporary Perspectives*, 221 Recueil des Cours (Hague Acad. Int'l L.) 195 (1990–II).

principles, institutions and procedures. The purposes of international law, like those of domestic law, are to establish and maintain order and hence reliable expectations, to protect "persons," their property and other interests, to further other values. But the constituency of the international society is different. The "persons" constituting international society are not [primarily] individual human beings but political entities, "States," and the society is [primarily] an inter-State system, a system [primarily] of States.

Myres S. McDougal, "The Impact of International Law Upon National Law: A Policy-Oriented Perspective"

4 S. Dak. L. Rev. 25, 35–36 (1959), *reprinted in* M. McDougal & Associates, Studies in World Public Order 157, 169–70 (1960)

... [T]he most appropriate [*i.e.*, usable] conception [of international law] requires emphasis not upon rules alone or operations alone, but upon rules and operations, and, further, not upon authority alone or control alone, but upon authority and control. Rules taken alone cannot be made to serve adequately to describe decisions or to account for decisions or to predict decisions or to appraise the consequences of decisions, much less to perform all these tasks at once. Focus upon operations only—when among the most important variables affecting decisions are the perspectives of participants, including their demands for values, their identifications, and their expectations about past and future events—is equally sterile. In comparable token, authority alone, when effective power is not at its disposal and expectations of decision in accordance with community prescription lack realism, is not law but sheer illusion. Effective control, on the other hand, when it asserts decision, in the sense of imposition or threat of severe deprivation, without regard for community expectations about how and what decision should be taken, is not law but naked power or unilateral coercion. The recommendation we make, from perspectives of human dignity and for efficiency of inquiry into varying patterns of authority and control, is, accordingly, that international law be regarded not as mere rules but as a whole process of authoritative decision in the world arena, a process in which authority and control are appropriately conjoined and which includes, along with an inherited body of flexible prescriptions explicitly related to community policies, both a structure of established decision-makers and a whole arsenal of methods and techniques by which policy is projected and implemented.

Rosalyn Higgins, Problems and Process: International Law and How We Use It

2–4 (1994)

There is a widely held perception of international law as "rules"—rules that are meant to be impartially applied but are frequently ignored. It is further suggested that these rules are ignored because of the absence of effective centralized sanctions—and, in turn, that all of this evidences that international law is not "real law" at all.

The view that international law is a body of rules that fails to restrain states falls short on several counts. In the first place, it assumes that law is indeed "rules." But the specialized social processes to which the word "law" refers include many things beside rules. Rules play a part in law, but not the only part. I remain committed to the analysis of international law as process rather than rules and to the view I expressed many years ago, when I said:

> When ... decisions are made by authorized persons or organs, in appropriate forums, within the framework of certain established practices and norms, then what occurs is legal decision-making. In other words, international law is [like all law] a continuing process of authoritative decisions. This view rejects the notion of law merely as the impartial application of rules. International law is the entire decision-making process, and not just the reference to the trend of past decisions which are termed "rules." There inevitably flows from this definition a concern, especially where the trend of past decision is not overwhelmingly clear, with policy alternatives for the future.[1]

Thus "rules" are just accumulated past decisions. And, if international law [were] just "rules," then international law would indeed be unable to contribute to, and cope with, a changing political world. To rely merely on accumulated past decisions (rules) when the context in which they are articulated has changed—and indeed when their content is often unclear—is to ensure that international law will not be able to contribute to today's problems and, further, that it will be disobeyed for that reason.

The rejection of the perception of law as [merely] "rules" entails a necessary consequence. It means that those who have to make decisions on the basis of international law—judges, but also legal advisers and others—are not really simply "finding the rule" and then applying it. That is because the determination of what is the relevant rule is part of the decision-makers' function; and because the accumulated trend of past decisions should never be applied oblivious of context. Although this reality has been regarded as anathema by many traditionalists, it was well understood by Sir Hersch Lauterpacht. He rejected the notion that the judicial function meant finding the appropriate "rule" in an impartial manner. The judge, he argued, does not "find rules" but he "makes choices"—and choices "not between claims which are fully justified and claims which have no foundation at all but between claims which have varying degrees of legal merit."[2]

The reasons why some insist that international law is "rules," and that all international lawyers have to do is to identify them and apply them, are not hard to find. They are an unconscious reflection of two beliefs, deeply held by many international lawyers. The first reason is that, if international law is regarded as more than rules, and the role of the authorized decision-maker as other than the automatic applier of such rules, international law becomes confused with other phenomena, such as power or social or humanitarian factors. The second reason is that it is felt by many that only by insisting on international law as rules to be impartially applied will it be possible to avoid the manifestation of international legal argument for political ends.

1. R. Higgins, *Policy Considerations and the International Judicial Process*, 17 I.C.L.Q. 58, 58–59 (1968).

2. H. Lauterpacht, The Development of International Law by the International Court 399 (1958).

I . . . deal with each of these reasons in turn, and [state] why I do not agree with them. To seek to contrast law with power (in which task the perception of law as "rules" plays an essential [role]) is fundamentally flawed. It assumes that law is concerned only with the concept of authority and not with power, or control. International law is indeed concerned with authority— and "authority" not just in the sense of binding decisions, but in the broader sense of jurisdictional competence, and more. Myres McDougal has explained:

> By authority is meant expectations of appropriateness in regard to the phases of effective decision processes. These expectations specifically relate to personnel appropriately endowed with decision-making power; the objectives they should pursue; the physical, temporal and institutional features of the situations in which lawful decisions are made; the values which may be used to sustain decision, and so forth . . . .[3]

So far, so good. But it is not the case, as is frequently supposed, that international law is concerned with authority alone, and that "power" stands somehow counterpoised to authority, and [has] nothing to do with law, and is indeed inimical to it. This view—which banishes power to the outer darkness (that is to say, to the province of international relations)—assumes that authority can exit in the total absence of supporting control, or power. But this is a fantasy. The authority which characterizes law exists not in a vacuum, but exactly where it intersects with power. Law, far from being authority battling against power, is the interlocking of authority with power. Authority cannot exist in the total absence of control. Of course, there will be particular circumstances when power overrides authority. On such occasions we will not have decision-making that we can term lawful. But that is not to say that law is about authority only, and not about power too; or that power is definitionally to be regarded as hostile to law. It is an integral element of it.

What then of the other argument—that a perception of international law as other than neutral rules inevitably leads to bias and partiality? A classical statement of this view was made by Judges Fitzmaurice and Spender in the South West Africa Cases in 1962, when they wrote:

> We are not unmindful of, nor are we insensible to, the various consider- ations of a non-judicial character, social, humanitarian, or other . . . but these are matters for the political rather than for the legal arena. They cannot be allowed to deflect us from our duty of reaching a conclusion strictly on the basis of what we believe to be the correct legal view.[4]

This formulation reflects certain assumptions: that "the correct legal view" is to be discerned by applying "rules"—the accumulated trend of past decisions, regardless of context or circumstance—and that "the correct legal view" has nothing to do with applying past decisions to current contexts by reference to objectives (values) that the law is designed to promote.

The classical view, so brilliantly articulated by Fitzmaurice but shared by very many others, is that international law can best perform its service to the community exactly by distancing itself from social policy. As the International Court of Justice put it in 1966: "Law exists, it is said, to serve a social need;

---

3. M. McDougal, H. Lasswell, & M. Reis- man, The World Constitutive Process of Au- thoritative Decision, 19 J. Legal Educ. 253, 256 (1966).

4. South West Africa Cases, 1962 ICJ 319, 466 (joint diss. op.).

but precisely for that reason it can do so only through and within the limits of its own discipline. Otherwise, it is not a legal service that would be rendered."[5] Of course, the International Court of Justice thought it self-evident as to where the law does draw "the limits of its own discipline." But what is self-evident to one is merely question-begging to another.

Reference to "the correct legal view" or "rules" can never avoid the element of choice (though it can seek to disguise it), nor can it provide guidance to the preferable decision. In making this choice one must inevitably have consideration for the humanitarian, moral, and social purposes of the law. As I have written elsewhere:

> Policy considerations, although they differ from "rules," are an integral part of that decision making process which we call international law; the assessment of so-called extralegal considerations is part of the legal process, just as is reference to the accumulation of past decisions and current norms. A refusal to acknowledge political and social factors cannot keep law "neutral," for even such a refusal is not without political and social consequence. There is no avoiding the essential relationship between law and politics.[6]

Because I believe there is no avoiding the essential relationship between law and policy, I also believe that it is desirable that the policy factors are dealt with systematically and openly. Dealing with them systematically means that all factors are properly considered and weighed, instead of the decision-maker unconsciously narrowing or selecting what he will take into account in order to reach a decision that he has instinctively predetermined is desirable. Dealing with policy factors openly means that the decision-maker himself is subjected to the discipline of facing them squarely (instead of achieving unconsciously desired policy objectives by making a particular choice, which is then given the label of "the correct legal rule"). It also means that the choices made are open to public scrutiny and discussion.

BURNS H. WESTON, "THE ROLE OF LAW IN PROMOTING PEACE AND VIOLENCE: A MATTER OF DEFINITION, SOCIAL VALUES, AND INDIVIDUAL RESPONSIBILITY"

in Toward World Order and Human Dignity 114, 116–17
(W. Reisman & B. Weston eds. and contribs., 1976)

The word "law" has . . . several diverse applications. Yet despite this fact we use the term with relative everyday ease. With little conspicuous difficulty, we use it to refer to matters essentially outside human intervention, as when we speak of "the law of gravity" or "the law of supply and demand"; and we use it to refer to matters which are, conversely, the product of human intervention, as when we speak of "the law of contracts," "criminal law," "the law of torts," "property law," and all the other breadwinners of the legal profession. Similarly, within the context of human intervention, we use it to refer to those social patterns which evolve essentially without benefit of

5. South West Africa Cases, 1966 ICJ 6, at ¶ 49.

6. R. Higgins, Integrations of Authority and Control: Trends in the Literature of International Law and Relations, in Towards World Order and Human Dignity 79, 85 (B. Weston & W. Reisman eds., 1976).

centralized decision-making mechanisms, as when we speak of "customary law" or "international law"; and we use it to refer to those social patterns which evolve from highly articulated command and enforcement structures, as when we speak of all those executive orders, legislative enactments, and judicial decisions we call "the law of Iowa" or "the law of the United States of America." The point is, of course, that none of these uses is incorrect. Fundamentally, each is proper. However applied, the concept "law" represents, in the end, a set of events whose common property is sanctioned regularity.

To most people, however, including many lawyers, this sanctioned regularity called "law," insofar as it pertains to social arrangements, is conceived largely as a body of rules affirmatively prescribed and enforced by the sovereign State, to the general exclusion of those regularities which, somehow mysteriously divorced from "the law," we are wont to call "customary morality." Except for the international lawyers and "jurisprudes" who take the challenge of defining "law" seriously, little attention is paid to those normative principles and practices which result from self-determinative interactions in the private sphere. Consider, thus, why Amy Vanderbilt's New Complete Book of Etiquette, manifestly descriptive of ordered social behavior in the absence of positive sovereign command, is not ordinarily considered relevant to law school study. Tenaciously wedded to the Legal Positivist tradition of nineteenth century English jurist John Austin and his followers, we cling to the belief that law is entirely or almost entirely a function of government—that it bespeaks only what governments say and do—and that it has little or no relation to what evolves in the absence of governmental intervention. So narrow a conception, I submit, is empirically unwarranted and socially detrimental, at least in the long run. It feeds the insidious notion that law is, or that it must be, as if some natural law of physics, only the expression of the will of the strongest.

But how, then, do we define "law" so as to avoid transforming the mere *characteristics* of the popular model into the *prerequisites* of a comprehensive theory about law; so as to avoid the allegation that law is not, or that it cannot be, the expression of the will of all or most of the people? The answer: to think upon law in functional rather than institutional terms, and from this perspective to acknowledge its invention, its application, and its appraisal both within and beyond the formal corridors of power. Law does not live by executives and legislators and judges alone. It lives also by individual human beings such as ourselves, pushing and pulling through reciprocal claim and mutual tolerance in our daily competition for power, wealth, respect, and other cherished values. To turn a phrase, law is legitimized politics—a Hydra-headed process of social decision, involving persons at all levels and from all walks of public and private life who, with authority derived both explicitly and implicitly from community consensus or expectation, and supported by formal and informal sanction, effect those codes or standards of everyday conduct by which we plan and go about our lives.

DISCUSSION NOTES/QUESTIONS

1. The traditional definition of international law emerged at a time when the principal actors on the world stage consisted of a small number of relatively

homogenous nation-states, mostly in Europe. Today, the international system has expanded greatly to include not only a large number of states of widely different ideological persuasion and levels of economic development from all regions of the globe, but also worldwide and regional international organizations, multinational business enterprises, transnational interest groups, and other non-state actors. When the UN was founded in 1945, it had fifty-one members, mainly European nations. Sixty-one years later, its membership stands at 191 states and functionally equivalent jurisdictions of which the majority are from the developing world. What implications does this have for the international legal system? To what extent is a definition of international law created for a simpler state-centric era still valid today? Should the new landscape provoke a different definitional response? Does the following excerpt from Thomas S. Kuhn, The Structure of Scientific Revolutions 111–13 (2d ed. 1970) suggest some answers?

Examining the record of past research from the vantage of contemporary historiography, the historian of science may be tempted to exclaim that when paradigms change, the world itself changes with them. Led by a new paradigm, scientists adopt new instruments and look in new places. Even more important, during revolutions scientists see new and different things when looking with familiar instruments in places they have looked before. It is as if the professional community had been suddenly transported to another planet where familiar objects are seen in a different light and are joined by unfamiliar ones as well. Of course, nothing of quite that sort does occur: there is no geographical transplantation; outside the laboratory everyday affairs usually continue as before. Nevertheless, paradigm changes do cause scientists to see the world of their research-engagement differently. * * * [Indeed,] [s]urveying the rich experimental literature from which ... examples [of perceptual transformation] are drawn makes one suspect that something like a paradigm is prerequisite to perception itself. What a man sees depends both upon what he looks at and also upon what his visual-conceptual experience has taught him to see. In the absence of such training there can only be, in William James's phrase, "a bloomin' buzzin' confusion."

2.   You will note that almost all the international lawyers mentioned or quoted thus far have been men. Is this significant for the definition of international law? *See* Doris Buss & Ambreena Manji, International Law: Modern Feminist Approaches (2005); Hilary Charlesworth & Christine Chinkin, The Boundaries of International Law: A Feminist Analysis (2000).

3.   Francis Boyle, *supra,* lists the late Hans Morgenthau as an "exemplar" of "political realism" which, like legal positivism as at least traditionally conceived, looks upon international law as little more than a euphemism for international morality. Yet in the same book from which the Boyle extract is drawn, Boyle reports that Morgenthau, toward the end of his life, repudiated political realism when he saw its consequences in the Vietnam War. May we conclude from Morgenthau's reversal that we cannot be "realistic" if we omit international law from our discussion of international politics? How can we explain many of the things states do if we do not invoke the idea of international law? More importantly, how can we explain the values states fight for if we disregard the legal principles that articulate those values? And is it not most important to consider what a "state" would be in the absence of international law? Isn't a "state" just a juridical entity? Does it not depend for its existence on a recognized legal concept—statehood; indeed, a legal concept that depends on what already-established states say and do and that thus is outside the state's control even though it is all-powerful vis-à-vis its own citizens?

Questions such as these, it must be allowed, clearly have influenced political scientists in recent years. As political scientist Anthony Clark Arend writes in Legal Rules and International Society 4–5 (1999):

Confronted with the difficulty of explaining cooperation among international actors under the logic of the realist paradigm, another approach to international relations has emerged in recent years—institutionalism. In contrast to the realists, institutionalists assert that international rules and institutions can indeed play a significant role in international relations and that a proper understanding of the international system requires an understanding of these rules and institutions.

On final analysis, however, does not Arend prove Boyle's primary point that international law remains still much in the grip of "political realism"? Why, for example, do Arend and his political science colleagues use the term "institutionalism" or the phrase "rules and institutions" to identify "another approach to international relations" rather than the more obvious and venerable term "international law"?

4. Professor Henkin, *supra*, asserts that "[l]aw is made by political actors (not by lawyers)," and that law serves, *inter alia*, "to protect persons, their property and other interests; to promote the welfare of individuals (or of some of them), and to further other societal values—justice, the good life, the good society." Are either of these statements altogether true? Are not many legislators also lawyers? Do not judges make law, and are not judges lawyers? And what about dictatorships and autocracies? Are their legal systems designed "to protect persons, their property and other interests; to promote the welfare of individuals (or of some of them), and to further other societal values—justice, the good life, the good society"? If not, then are their legal systems not legal systems or, alternatively, illegitimate legal systems? If so, who determines their non-legal status or illegitimacy? Is Henkin's view of law and legal process influenced by the more-or-less democratic climate of the United States, his national home?

In *International Law and International Relations Theory: A Dual Agenda*, 87 A.J.I.L. 205 (1993), Anne–Marie Slaughter Burley (now Anne–Marie Slaughter) argues for a more interdisciplinary approach from both international lawyers and international relations theorists. Her "dual agenda" refers to bringing international law together with two different strands in international relations: institutionalism and liberalism. "Institutionalism," she writes at 207, "means the study of the components of the international system. Liberal international relations theory focus[es] not on state-to-state interactions ... but on an analytically prior set of relationships among states and domestic and transnational civil society. The 'black box' of sovereignty becomes transparent, allowing examination of how and to what extent national governments represent individuals and groups operating in domestic and transnational society." If "liberal states" are presumed to act differently in international relations from dictatorships, what implications does this have for the international legal system?

5. Henkin, *supra*, asserts also that international law is an expression of international society. Given the well-known ethnic, ideological, socioeconomic, and political cleavages that have characterized world affairs from East to West and North to South, to what extent is it possible to speak of a present-day international society or world community? What do "society" and/or "community" mean? And to what extent can international law lay claim to universality? Is such a claim essential for international law to be called "law"? For domestic law to be called law?

6. In the foregoing extracts by professors McDougal and Higgins (newly elected President of the International Court of Justice), law generally and international law in particular are defined as a "process of authoritative and controlling decision." What is the meaning of "process"? Of "authoritative decision"? Of "controlling decision"? What do they mean by "authority"? By "control"? In *The Identification and Appraisal of Diverse Systems of Public Order*, 53 A.J.I.L. 1, 9 (1959), professors McDougal and Harold Lasswell write:

> ... *Authority* is the structure of expectation concerning who, with what qualifications and mode of selection, is competent to make which decisions by what criteria and what procedures. By *control* we refer to an effective voice in decision, whether authorized or not. The conjunction of common expectations concerning authority with a high degree of corroboration in actual operation is what we understand by law [emphasis added].

And in *Myres S. McDougal and Twentieth–Century Jurisprudence: A Comparative Essay,* in Toward World Order and Human Dignity: Essays in Honor of Myres S. McDougal 3, 14 (W. Reisman & B. Weston eds., 1976), Australian legal scholar William L. Morrison summarizes McDougal's conception of law as follows:

> Law is conceived as a social process of authoritative and controlling decision . . . . . [S]ocial process refers to interactions among participants in a context which maintain relatively stable, but not necessarily formally organized, patterns of value shaping and sharing. Decisions are taken to be commitments attended by threats of severe deprivation or extremely high indulgence. They are said to be *authoritative* when they are, in a stipulated degree, in accordance with community expectation about who is to make them, about the criteria in accordance with which they should be made, and about the situations in which, and the procedures by which, they are to be made. They are said to be *controlling* when the outcome sought is in fact realized to a significant degree. [Emphasis added.]

To what "stipulated degree" must decisions be in accord with "community expectation" about decision-making to qualify as legal decisions? Do you agree that, by implication, law does not exist when decisions are attended by threats of only mild rather than "severe" deprivation or merely high rather than "extremely high" indulgence? Or when the outcome sought is realized to only a modest rather than a "significant" degree? Why? Why not? Elsewhere McDougal writes (together with Harold D. Lasswell and W. Michael Reisman):

> By "law" or "authoritative decision" we refer to a process of decision characterized both by expectations of authority and by effective control. It may be observed, however, that no decision process, whatever the size of the community, is wholly effective. The aggregate degree of effectiveness of an authority system must be sufficient to sustain expectations of future decision largely in conformity with demanded authority. The precise degree of effectiveness or "control" required for "law"—whether in national or international arenas—cannot, thus, be stated absolutely; it is a function of context and will vary. An authoritative and controlling decision can be contrasted with decisions involving only effective power ("naked power") or mere barren authority ("pretended power"). We see "naked power" in action when a strong empire coerces a weak neighboring polity, and nothing happens. We identify "pretended power" when a superseded monarch vainly claims acceptance as the legitimate head of the body-politic from which [he/she] has been expelled.

Myres S. McDougal, Harold D. Lasswell, & W. Michael Reisman, *The World Constitutive Process of Authoritative Decision*, in International Law Essays 192, 193 (M. McDougal & W. M. Reisman eds., 1981).

7.   Burns Weston, *supra*, suggests that rules and patterns of social etiquette may be designated as "law." Is this appropriate? Consider the following quotation from Amy Vanderbilt's New Complete Book of Etiquette: The Guide to Gracious Living ix-xii (1971):

> The word "etiquette" . . . covers much more than "manners," the way in which we do things. [This guide] is considerably more than a treatise on a code of social behavior. . . . For we must all learn the socially acceptable ways of living with others in no matter what society we move. Even in primitive societies there are such rules, some of them as complex and inexplicable as many of our own. * * * I believe that knowledge of the rules of living in our society makes us more comfortable even though our particular circumstances may permit us to elide them somewhat. Some of the rudest and most objectionable people I have ever known have been technically the most "correct." Some of the warmest, most lovable, have had little more than an innate feeling of what is right toward others. But, at the same time, they have had the intelligence to inform themselves . . . on the rules of social intercourse as related to their own experiences. Only a great fool or a great genius is likely to flout all social grace with impunity, and neither one, doing so, makes the most comfortable companion.

If this quotation does not lead to the conclusion that rules and patterns of social etiquette are "law," is international law properly called "law"? If so (or if not), what do we mean by "law"? Does it require the participation, direct or indirect, of the state, as is implied by the standard curricula of most law faculties? If so, does that mean that it is not possible to have private legal systems? Does "law" include custom? If so, when is custom not law? In this connection, see *infra* Section B of Chapter 2.

8.   What are the principal indicia of "law" in national communities? In the world community? Do they differ? Is it valid to define "law" to include both domestic or municipal (*i.e.*, national) and international law? As for the international legal system, does the absence of a central executive agency with enforcement powers matter? The absence of a central legislative assembly? The absence of an international court with general, compulsory jurisdiction?

9.   In *International Law and the Controversy Concerning the Word "Law"*, 22 B.Y.B.I.L 146, 159–62 (1945), Glanville Williams contended that the jurisprudential debate over the reality of international law is merely a debate about words. Do you agree?

B.   INTERNATIONAL LAW IN HISTORICAL AND CONTEMPORARY PERSPECTIVE

As you prepare to assist ICC Prosecutor Moreno–Ocampo in the possible prosecution of persons responsible for atrocities and other abuses in Sudan's Darfur province (perhaps in relation to Congo, Uganda, and the Central African Republic as well), you now feel more refreshed about what international law purports to be. But you are hazy about its origins, about the factors that have shaped its growth and development, and about the extent to which, over the years, it has been successful or not in preventing and mitigating conflicts and disputes of one sort or another. So, you sensibly elect to read further.

1. HISTORICAL PERSPECTIVES

According to Arthur Nussbaum, A Concise History of the Law of Nations (1953 rev. ed.), "the law of nations"—or international law—can be traced to approximately 3100 B.C. when a treaty was concluded between two Mesopotamian city-states. And according to George A. Finch, The Sources of Modern International Law 313 (1937), the following historical factors "appear to have exerted an influence on growth and development of the principles of modern international law": (1) the spread of Roman law through Western Europe; (2) the revival of trade and commerce during the Middle Ages; (3) the formation of leagues of trading towns for the protection of their trade and their citizens engaged in trade; (4) the development of maritime law made necessary by the spread of international trade on the sea; (5) the growing custom on the part of States to send and receive permanent legations; (6) the establishment of permanent standing armies; (7) the Renaissance and the Reformation; (8) plans for maintaining international peace; (9) the discovery of America; and (10) the American Revolution. The next two selections make no attempt to report this entire history. They do, however, take stock of the principal events and perspectives that, both before and since the beginnings of the state system (around the Peace of Westphalia in 1648), have shaped the evolution and scope of contemporary international law theory and practice.

DAVID J. BEDERMAN, INTERNATIONAL LAW FRAMEWORKS
1–6 (2001)

Whether a rule of law for international relations can trace its origins to ancient times and classical antiquity is (fortunately enough) of little concern today. Suffice it to say, norms of international conduct have only developed when there is an authentic system of States and international actors in place. International law has never flourished in times of anarchy (think of the "Dark Ages" in Europe from 500–100 AD), nor, for that matter, in times of hegemony (consider the Roman Empire from 50 BC–300 AD). The ideal environment for the development of international law have been times of "multi-polar" international relations, where a number of States have competed and cooperated in a particular part of the world. Such conditions existed in various regions of Asia (China and the Indian sub-continent), as well as Africa, over the last three millennia.

But whether because of historical serendipity, or (more likely) Western ethnocentrism, the date that is commonly given as the birth of international law is one of peculiarly European significance. The year is 1648, the end of what has come to be known as the Thirty Years War (1618–48). This was a period of ferocious and bloody religious conflict in Europe, a war that resulted in the decimation of close to twenty percent of Europe's population. These events—culminating in the Peace of Westphalia, a comprehensive peace treaty signed by virtually all European nations—led to two significant observations about the development of international law.

The first, as already suggested, is that international law needs States in order to grow and develop. But more than that, it needs States with strong internal institutions and a profound self-awareness that we would today call nationalism. And it just so happens that the Thirty Years War saw the rise of modern nation-States like Great Britain, France, Spain, Portugal, Sweden, and Russia. The Thirty Years War also provided the ultimate intellectual and political justification for nation-States: States needed to be *sovereign* in order to confront the challenges that war and domestic upheaval brought.

So was born the notion of sovereignty in the writings of such political theorists as Jean Bodin, Thomas Hobbes, and (later) John Locke and Jean–Jacques Rousseau. Sovereignty became the linchpin of the notion that States are independent and autonomous, and accountable only to the whim of their rulers, or (in what was then the exceptional case) to the popular will of the people. States thus owed no allegiance to a higher authority—not to God, nor to a moral order or ideological ideal. States answered to nothing but themselves, and to the extent that a rule of law was possible between States, it was only because States had specifically consented to be bound by such rules.

There was a second phenomenon heralded by the 1648 Peace of Westphalia. It is that the defining moments for international law of the last three and a half centuries have come only after periods of intense global conflict. One can almost linearly chart the progress of new international organizations, new substantive rules of international conduct, and new procedures of dispute settlement between international actors by the dates that mark the end of cataclysmic wars: the 1763 Definitive Peace (concluding the Seven Years War or Great War for Empire), the 1815 Final Act at Vienna (ending the Wars of the French Revolution and Napoleon, 1791–1815), the 1919 Treaty of Versailles and Covenant of the League of Nations (completing the First World War, 1914–18), and the 1945 Charter of the United Nations (marking the end of World War Two, 1939–45). It thus appeared that international law was the step-child of war and destruction, offering a utopian hope of order and moral renewal.

So far, this historical narrative is pretty grim: international law has only prospered by extolling State power and sovereignty, and as an antidote to national conflict. Before one gets too discouraged by this doubtful pedigree of international law rules, it would be useful to chart other influences on norms of international conduct. One such consideration is that the notion of sovereignty—and its handmaiden of *positivism* (that States are subject to no moral authority above them)—has not always been ascendent, and is not so today. Indeed, international law was seen in the [European] Middle Ages as an outgrowth of universal values and norms, largely derived from Roman law (the *ius gentium* which applied to all peoples, and the *ius civile*, or civil law), religious institutions (the law of the Roman Catholic Church, or canon law), and common European customs involving such transnational issues as trade and control of conflict (the *ius commune*).

The earliest "classical" scholars (or publicists) of international law were writing before and during the Thirty Years War and were often reacting to the excesses of sovereignty and positivism. Writers such as Francisco de Vitoria (1486–1546), Alberico Gentili (1552–1608), Hugo de Groot ("Grotius") (1583–1645), and Samuel Pufendorf (1632–94) tended to emphasize the moral imperatives of law between nations and were part of a larger *natural law* tradition—a "common law" of State backed up by religious and philosophical principles of good faith and good will between men and nations. But by the late 1600's, publicists were starting to consider that the actual experience of State relations was the real basis of obligation in international affairs. This is the positivist tradition, reflected in the works of Richard Zouche (1590–1660), Cornelius van Bynkershoek (1673–1743), and Emmerich de Vattel (1714–69).

Of these great writers (who are still consulted on some points), Grotius and Vattel represented the best attempts at a naturalist and positivist synthesis of rules for international actors. Grotius has earned the title "father of international law," largely on the reputation of his volume *De jure belli ac pacis* ("On the Laws of War and Peace"), first published in 1625.[c] But Vattel probably had greater practical influence. His treatise, *Le droits des gens* ("The Law of Nations"), published in 1758, was widely read in European capitals and was admired both by the Founders of the United States (in 1776 and 1787) and the Jacobin leaders of France (in 1789).[d] Vattel's positivism was the favored instrument of international relations in the age of revolutions....

There was bound to be a collision between positivist and natural approaches to international law. It came in the early 1800's and was waged over the most compelling social issue of the day: the institution of slavery and the slave trade. The practical problem for international lawyers of that day was whether a small group of States (Great Britain and the United States) could unilaterally seek to suppress the international traffic in slaves. That question turned on whether the slave trade violated international law. For those who believed in natural law principles—that State conduct was subordinated to moral values—then the answer was easy: slavery was an abomination. But for the positivists, who embraced State sovereignty and the necessity of ascertaining State consent for new rules of international conduct, the issue was more difficult. And, ultimately, in a series of cases decided by English and US courts, the positivist view won and the decision was made that slavery and the slave trade could only be suppressed if States explicitly agreed that their nationals could not legally engage in it. Happily, this result was achieved by the late 1880's, although it came only after the bloody Civil War in the United States.

Positivism reigned supreme in international relations from 1848 to 1919. Gone were the days of nation-State building and the popular revolutions in Europe and the Americas. In their place was a period of colonialism and imperialism, in which explicitly (and exclusionary) European political and value systems were forcibly transmitted to Africa and Asia. Among these was a peculiarly European notion of a law of nations for "civilized" nations. Despite the fact that China, Japan and India each had their own historic conceptions of international rules of behavior, in the face of overweening European military and economic power their price of admission into the global order was acceptance of Western international law.

Ultimately, the European domination of international law collapsed in the charnel house of World War One. Four empires (the Austrian Hapsburg,

---

c. For a famous discussion of Grotius' contribution to international law, see H. Lauterpacht, *The Grotian Tradition in International Law*, 23 B.Y.B.I.L. 1 (1946) and reprinted in major part in the Introduction to Part III, *infra* at 1270–81.

d. In 1789, the English philosopher Jeremy Bentham renamed "the law of nations" as "international law." Today, the two terms are used interchangeably.

German Hohenzollern, Russian Romanov, and Ottoman Turkish) disintegrated into new ethnic States. Only the British Empire remained, and three new powers entered the international scene: Japan, the United States, and the communist Soviet Union. The 1919 Treaty of Versailles and the Covenant of the League of Nations (history's first attempt at an organization for global peace and security) was probably doomed to failure. What with the United States remaining outside the League, the Soviet Union disengaged, Britain and France morally and physically exhausted, the world was powerless to respond to the aggressions of new totalitarian powers (Germany, Italy and Japan).

But, to some degree, the League did break the pattern set in early centuries that substantive innovations made in international law came only after periods of warfare. The League set upon a relatively ambitious program for *codifying* international law, systematizing the rules of international conduct. A permanent international judicial tribunal [the PCIJ or "World Court"] was established. Conference diplomacy became more regular. International institutions began to operate in a more predictable fashion. And, just as important, the League became concerned with issues of significance to people, and not just governments: economic development, protection of the rights of minorities, and prevention of disease. But, ultimately, the League was unable to do the one task it had set for itself—keep the peace.

The cataclysm of the Second World War re-made the globe. First, it accelerated the process of decolonization. The British and French colonial empires collapsed by the early 1960's, and by the 1980's there remained no part of the world under unwilling colonial domination by Europeans. This meant that the international community—the family of nations—grew into a large, rowdy clan. Before 1945, the group of "civilized" nations had never numbered more than fifty. By 1960, it had increased to a hundred, and [in the year 2005] has topped out at about [193] States [and functionally equivalent jurisdictions]. The sheer increase in State entities (quite apart from other international actors) has changed the face of international law in fundamental and irreversible ways.

World War II and the Cold War rivalry that followed (particularly between the US and the Soviet Union) also set in motion a host of technological, social, environmental, and economic phenomena that we now identify as "globalism." Whether it is the integrated international economy and trade disciplines, nuclear power and proliferation, space exploration and computer applications, environmental pollution and habitat degradation, or intellectual properties and entertainment, we are gradually living in a shrinking, interdependent world. International law has been compelled to respond to the functional demands of the international community.[e]

Lastly, the end of World War Two brought a vision of world order that had only been incompletely realized by the League of Nations. Enshrined in the United Nations Charter, this dream created an organizational architecture for the international community. With the UN's political organs at its center, this system has reached out into every aspect and spectrum of human

---

e. Illustrative is the recent emergence of international environmental law. *See, e.g.,* L. Guruswamy, G. Palmer, B. Weston, & J. Carl- son, International Environmental Law and World Order: A Problem–Oriented Coursebook (2d ed. 1999).

cooperation. It has created progressively more complicated and supple legal and regulatory regimes for virtually all functional areas of international concern.

At the same time, this world order has managed to place State concerns (including sovereignty and maintaining international peace and security) side-by-side with the principle of protecting and extending the dignity of individual human beings. This vision is not exclusively one of State power and a positive grant of rights by nations to people. Instead, it is at least partly premised on a natural law notion of the inherent worth of human beings, and is manifested in the creation of rules by which a State must treat its own citizens. So the pendulum of natural and positive approaches to international legal obligation has swung back to a more neutral position in which the international community recognizes values separate and apart from State sovereignty.

RICHARD A. FALK, REVITALIZING INTERNATIONAL LAW
91–93 (1989)

Efforts in this century to deal with problems of international society have concentrated on four ... areas that exhibit both the capacities and the severe limits of international law and international institutions. The area of greatest success has been what I would call the management of complexity. There has been a surprisingly resilient capacity on the part of sovereign states ... to contrive mutually beneficial ways of dealing with the ... implications of interdependence.

The second area of effort, but one where until recently there has been less success despite strong efforts, has been the containment of conflict within tolerable limits. A major aspect of that containment has been the effort to build procedures and a consensus prohibiting aggressive uses of force. To abandon this search for agreed limits on conflict ... [would represent] a serious deterioration in the quality of international order.

The third area of considerable significance has been of relatively recent origin and is what I would call broadly the promotion of decency in the world; this has taken two principal forms. Perhaps the most important form is the notion that poverty and mass misery are matters not only of domestic concern, but also ... matters that affect the quality of international life as a whole including the possibilities of the space age, a psychological reality to our identity as a single species. Emerging alongside and underneath national and civilizational interests is a human interest that is not just sentimental; it is real. * * * [P]roblems involving the promotion of decency in relation to equity and development also have as their other side the whole question of human rights and the degree to which we tolerate torture, mass killing, extreme repression, and, to some extent, not only tolerate it but reinforce it by the kinds of foreign policies that are pursued.... [T]o the extent we do that, we deny our own dignity and esteem and are caught up in a process that is exceedingly destructive in its consequences....

The fourth general task and challenge has to do with the avoidance of catastrophe. It is here we encounter a colossal failure on the part of international law and the organized international community.... [W]eapons of mass destruction overwhelm the traditional law of war and yet how many law journal articles or serious treatment of these issues can one find?[f] The fundamental question, of course, is one of political will to achieve restraint. Such restraint is absent in the centers of power, thereby accenting the impotence of moral and legal reasoning. But this distance between the normative and the practical is something we need to acknowledge and interpret in an honest way; it is far better to take account of this distance than to pretend it does not exist.

2. CONTEMPORARY PERSPECTIVES

The historical evolution of international law and relations has stimulated considerable critical thinking in recent years. The next five extracts illustrate the most notable of the intellectual currents presently influencing international law's continuing development. The first is a voice from the "Third World," challenging many of international law's basic principles because of their early European derivation. The second elaborates on the themes of the first from the perspective of race and racism in global society. The third decries the pervasive patriarchy that dominates the organizational and normative structures of international law. The fourth reports on an intellectual enterprise that perceives international law as mainly an incoherent and self-validating ideological construct said to be incapable of responding to the fundamental questions of international life. And the fifth voices a cautiously optimistic world order view that international law is already in transition to a law of humanity through the agency of civil society.

ANTONY ANGHIE AND B.S. CHIMNI, "THIRD WORLD APPROACHES TO INTERNATIONAL LAW AND INDIVIDUAL RESPONSIBILITY IN INTERNAL CONFLICTS"

in The Methods of International Law 185, 185–95
(S. Ratner & A.-M. Slaughter, eds., 2004)

[*Eds.*—The authors introduce their essay with a description of "Third World Approaches to International Law" (TWAIL), distinguishing between "TWAIL I scholarship" ("produced by the first generation of post-colonial international lawyers") and "TWAIL II scholarship" (which "has broadly followed the TWAIL I tradition and elaborated upon it while, inevitably, departing from it in significant ways"). They do so with the caveat that "we are acutely aware of the fact that we cannot speak for the entire community of Third World international law scholars: we present only one version of this tradition, and other TWAIL scholars may very well disagree with the positions we outline here."]

* * *

f. For noteworthy exceptions, see R. Falk, E. Meyrowitz & J. Sanderson, *Nuclear Weapons and International Law*, 20 Indian J. Int'l L. 541 (1980); B. Weston, *Nuclear Weapons Versus International Law: A Contextual Reassessment*, 28 McGill L. J. 542 (1983); P. Weiss, B. Weston, S. Mendlovitz, & R. Falk, *Draft Memorial in Support of the Application by the World Health Organization for an Advisory Opinion by the International Court of Justice on the Legality of the Use of Nuclear Weapons* *under International Law, Including the WHO Constitution*, 4 T.L.C.P. 721 (1994); and B. Weston, *Nuclear Weapons and the World Court: Ambiguity's Consensus*, 7 T.L.C.P. 371 (1997). *See also* E. Meyrowitz, Prohibition of Nuclear Weapons: The Relevance of International Law (1990); N. Singh, Nuclear Weapons and International Law (1959); C. Weeramantry, Nuclear Weapons and Scientific Responsibility (1987); and *infra* Problem 4–5 ("Hindustan Threatens Nuclear Self–Defense"), in Chapter 4, at 437–61.

... At the risk of simplifying considerably, TWAIL I scholars[7] formulated a number of positions that had an important impact on all subsequent TWAIL scholarship.

First, TWAIL I indicted colonial international law for legitimizing the subjugation and oppression of Third World peoples. Nineteenth century international law, for instance, excluded non-European states from the realm of sovereignty, upheld the legality of unequal treaties between European powers and non-European powers, and ruled that it was completely legal to acquire sovereignty over non-European societies by conquest.

Second, TWAIL I emphasized that pre-colonial Third World states were not strangers to the idea of international law. Non–European societies had developed sophisticated rules relating, for example, to the law of treaties and the laws of war. TWAIL I, then, attempted to create a truly international law, both by pointing to the commonalities among ostensibly very different societies, and by identifying a rich body of doctrine and principle which was to be found in Third World legal systems and cultures, and which could be used for the benefit of the entire international community.

Third, TWAIL I adopted a non-rejectionist stance toward modern international law. TWAIL I believed that the contents of international law could be transformed to take into account the needs and aspirations of the peoples of the newly independent states. This was to be achieved principally through the United Nations system. TWAIL I scholarship was closely aligned with the diplomatic initiatives undertaken by newly independent Third World states, and it placed immense faith in the UN to bring about the changes necessary to usher in a just world order. In attempting to achieve these ends, the Third World states attempted, in effect, to formulate a new approach to sources doctrine by arguing that General Assembly resolutions passed by vast majorities had some binding legal effect. These TWAIL attempts to create a system of international law that was democratic and participatory were often defeated by positivist arguments regarding sources and consent.[8]

Fourth, TWAIL I laid great stress on the principles of sovereign equality of states and non-intervention, fundamentally important issues to societies that had just recovered their independence. Thus the Third World states initiated a number of resolutions in the United Nations which sought to advance these principles of sovereign equality and non-intervention.[9]

Fifth, it understood that political independence in itself was insufficient to achieve liberation, as the economic structures which linked the First and Third worlds, the North and South, continued to disadvantage the South and

---

7. These include pioneering scholars such as Georges Abi–Saab, F. Garcia–Amador, R. P. Anand, Mohammed Bedjaoui, and Taslim O. Elias. Needless to say, the complexity of the views of these individual scholars, whose own work has developed over time, cannot be done justice in our presentation here. Over the years, several Western scholars have been sympathetic to the Third World's position and made important contributions to this body of scholarship, and these include scholars such as C. H. Alexandrowicz, Richard Falk, Nico Schrijver, and P. J. I. M. de Waart. ...

8. The classic example of this type of positivist reasoning used to defeat Third World claims is found in *Texaco Overseas Petroleum et al. v. Libyan Arab Republic*, 17 ILM 1 (1978).

9. *See, e.g.*, [1965] Declaration on the Inadmissibility of Intervention in the Domestic Affairs of States and the Protection of Their Independence and Sovereignty [**Basic Document 2.20**]; [1970] Declaration on Principles of International Law Concerning Friendly Relations and Co-operation Among States in Accordance With the Charter of the United Nations [**Basic Document 1.11**].

needed to be reformed; thus it sought to inaugurate a New International Economic Order. The South sought in this way to make structural changes to an international economic system which was perceived to disadvantage developing countries, and, more specifically, it sought to regain control over its natural resources and to exercise effective control over foreign investors.[10]

[*Eds.*—The authors turn next to TWAIL II scholarship.]

In the last decade or so, what might be termed TWAIL II scholarship has attempted to reassess both the relationship between international law and the Third World, and the approaches outlined by TWAIL I [and thus] to further develop the analytical tools necessary to deal with Third World realities in a continuously shifting international setting.[11]

Critiquing the Post–Colonial State

First, TWAIL II has adopted a critical attitude toward many of the important tenets of TWAIL I. TWAIL I perceived the newly independent, post-colonial state as a unitary entity that transcended and stood above conflicts and tensions generated by class, race and gender within Third World societies. The task of intellectuals was viewed as supporting this state in its nation building tasks. Consequently, TWAIL I did not closely interrogate the idea of state sovereignty in order to align the language of international law with the destiny of Third World peoples as opposed to Third World states. This view of the transcendent post-colonial state prevented a focus on the violence of the state at home.

By contrast, while recognizing the fundamental importance of the doctrine of sovereignty for advancing Third World interests and for protecting and preserving Third World states against various forms of intervention, TWAIL II scholars have developed powerful critiques of the Third World nation-state, of the processes of its formation and its resort to violence and authoritarianism.[12] Corresponding with this is a concern to identify and give voice to the people within Third World states—women, peasants, workers, minorities—who had been generally excluded from consideration by TWAIL I scholarship. TWAIL scholars have examined, on one hand, how the great projects of "development" and nation building promoted by international law and institutions and embraced in some form by Third World leaders worked to the disadvantage of Third World peoples. On the other hand, they have examined whether and how international human rights norms may be used to protect Third World peoples against the state and other international actors.[13] By simultaneously examining the Third World state critically and recognizing the possibility of using international law to promote the interests of Third World peoples, these TWAIL II positions on international human rights law differ from either mainstream or critical Northern [including feminist] views

---

10. *See, e.g.,* Charter of Economic Rights and Duties of States **[Basic Document 4.9]**.

11. The work of several TWAIL II scholars has been influenced by the writings of post-colonial scholars. *See generally* Bart Moore–Gilbert, Postcolonial Theory: Contexts, Practices, Politics (1997); Laws of the Postcolonial (E. Darian–Smith & P. Fitzpatrick eds., 1999).

12. *See, e.g.,* M. Mutua, *Why Redraw the Map of Africa: A Moral and Legal Inquiry,* 16 Mich. J. Int'l L. 113 (1995); O. Okafor, Redefining Legitimate Statehood: International Law and State Fragmentation in Africa (2000).

13. *See, e.g.,* Legitimate Governance in Africa: International and Domestic Legal Perspectives (E. Quashigah & O. Okafor eds., 1999).

on human rights as well as from the views of the Third World states themselves. One of the major difficulties confronting TWAIL scholars arises precisely because it is sometimes through supporting the Third World state and sometimes by critiquing it, that the interests of Third World peoples may be advanced.

Theorizing the Fundamentals

In addition, TWAIL II has sought to further the analysis developed by TWAIL I of the structural factors promoting inequalities between First and Third World states. In this respect, TWAIL II has focused more explicitly on theoretical inquiry than TWAIL I, which adopted a relatively unproblematic view of international law and saw its task as using the established techniques of international law to address Third World concerns. As a consequence of the failure of a number of Third World initiatives, most prominently that of the New International Economic Order, TWAIL II scholars began to examine more closely the extent to which colonial relations had shaped the fundamentals of the discipline. Rather than seeing colonialism as external and incidental to international law, an aberration that could be quickly remedied once recognized, TWAIL II scholarship has focused on a more alarming proposition: that colonialism is central to the formation of international law.

This inquiry has been conducted through a study of particular doctrines of international law such as human rights, and through a critical examination of the history of international law. For TWAIL II scholars, the history of the relationship between international law and the non-European world was important not simply to demonstrate that the non-European world had developed a number of important principles which corresponded with well-recognized principles of international law but also to understand the extent to which the doctrines of international law had been created through the colonial encounter. It was principally through colonial expansion that international law achieved one of its defining characteristics: universality. Thus the doctrines used for the purpose of assimilating the non-European world into this "universal" system—the fundamental concept of sovereignty and even the concept of law itself—were inevitably shaped by the relationships of power and subordination inherent in the colonial relationship. It is thus hardly surprising that the Third World's attempts to use these same fundamental doctrines to advance its goals might encounter unique difficulties and challenges.

The Structure of Colonialism: The Civilizing Mission

We have said that international law has historically suppressed Third World peoples. How does this suppression take place, what are the techniques and technologies by which it is effected? This inquiry takes different forms depending on the area of international law involved. At a broader level, such inquiries use an analytic framework derived from the concept of the "civilizing mission." This concept justified the continuous intervention by the West in the affairs of Third World societies and provided the moral basis for the economic exploitation of the Third World that has been an essential part of colonialism.

The "civilizing mission" operates by characterizing non-European peoples as the "other"—the barbaric, the backward, the violent—who must be civilized, redeemed, developed, pacified. Race has played a crucially important role in constructing and defining the other.[14] This task of transforming the other requires the development of new doctrines, technologies and institutions. A number of issues arise from this reflex: how is this "other" constructed? How does this construction shape the legal framework which regulates the interaction between the West and the other? How does it determine what is legally permissible to each of the parties?

These ideas of the backward and the primitive, we argue, exercise a powerful and unstated influence on international law. More particularly, in the context of the ongoing problem of violence in the international system, it is significant that since the beginnings of international law, it is frequently the "other," the non-European tribes, infidels, barbarians, who are identified as the source of all violence, and who must therefore be suppressed by an even more intense violence. However, this violence, when administered by the colonial power, is legitimate because it is inflicted in self-defense, or because it is humanitarian in character and indeed seeks to save the non-European peoples from themselves.

What is remarkable is the way in which the project of the civilizing mission has endured over time, and how its essential structure is preserved in certain versions of contemporary initiatives, for example, of "development," democratization, human rights and "good governance," which posit a Third World that is lacking and deficient and in need of international intervention for its salvation. To understand the cunning of colonialism, the ways in which the civilizing mission reproduces itself in bewilderingly different forms, all of them presented as benevolent, TWAIL II scholars have focused more explicitly on the methodologies of international law and the ways in which those methodologies addressed Third World issues or else precluded consideration of those issues.[15]

TWAIL and the Politics of Knowledge

Given the importance of theoretical inquiry to our understanding and approach to international law, it is inevitable that TWAIL scholars have turned their attention to the question of how knowledge about international law is produced. How do we identify what counts as acceptable scholarship in the field of international law? Here a powerful international division of intellectual labor prevails: Northern scholars and Northern institutions set these important standards. Further, these scholars and institutions seem to assume that the most significant schools of thought originate in the North— or even more specifically, in the United States. In the words of [Stephen R. Ratner and Anne–Marie Slaughter], "although many of the methods have a distinctly American origin, the community of scholars for nearly all of them is

---

14. It is for this reason that TWAIL has much in common with a number of other important bodies of scholarship including Critical Race Theory and LatCrit theory. . . .

15. *See, e.g.,* B. S. Chimni, International Law and World Order: A Critique of Contemporary Approaches (1993) (critique, from a Third World perspective, of theories of international law proposed by Morgenthau, McDou-

gal–Lasswell, Richard Falk, and Grigory Tunkin); J. Gathii, *Neoliberalism, Colonialism and International Governance: Decentering the International Law of Government Legitimacy*, 98 Mich. L. Rev 1996 (2000); S. Grovogui, Sovereigns, Quasi–Sovereigns and Africans: Race and Self–Determination in International Law (1996).

now global."[16] We draw—unhappily wearisome—attention to this [fact] since it reflects a powerful reality that scholarship cannot be separated from the institutional resources—law schools, journals, publishers that enable its production.

TWAIL has thus found it difficult to assert itself in an institutional setting that, when it is not generally uncomprehending of TWAIL's history and its aims, seeks to incorporate TWAIL into a familiar geography of alliances and rivalries. Some Northern schools of thought that have generally neglected the subjects of race, colonialism and the Third World have recently developed an interest in TWAIL methodologies and concerns, which we welcome. However, to then see TWAIL as a product or subsidiary of these Northern schools would be to further the familiar pattern that all knowledge and theory—including TWAIL—originates in the North. This would disregard the enormous body of work that has been done by TWAIL scholars for more than five decades, work that has often not received proper recognition, and only a part of which we can present in these pages.

GERNOT KÖHLER, "THE THREE MEANINGS OF GLOBAL APARTHEID: EMPIRICAL, NORMATIVE, EXISTENTIAL"
20 Alternatives 403, 403–04, 406–08 (1995)

Political concepts can have alternative meanings, depending on the type of discourse in which they are employed. * * * As an empirical concept, global apartheid describes the structure of global society [and] is similar to several others, such as *industrialized-developing countries, First World–Third World, North-South, imperialism, center-periphery, world system, global stratification,* and others. * * * [It] has been defined as "a structure of world society [reflecting] extreme inequality in cultural, racial, political, economic, and legal terms, as ... South African apartheid."[17]

In this structure, "the affluent white minority possesses a disproportionately large share of world society's political, economic, and military power."[18] A similar description of the "system of global apartheid" is as follows: The "most economically developed and affluent countries are banding together to protect their privileged position in much the same way that South Afrikaners and others of European descent sought to maintain their dominance in South Africa."[19] One author speaks of a "diplomacy of apartheid on a global scale" that is "a dangerous exercise in the maintenance of inequality."[20]

* * *

Global Apartheid as a Negative Norm

The concept of global apartheid can be used [also] as a normative concept, in which case it implies a value judgment. The value judgment is: "That

16. S. Ratner & A.-M. Slaughter, Appraising the Methods of International Law: A Prospectus for Readers, 93. A.J.I.L. 291, 295 (1999).

17. G. Köhler, Global Apartheid, 4 Alternatives—A Journal of World Policy 263, 267 (1978).

18. *Id.*

19. A. Richmond, Global Apartheid: Refugees, Racism, and the New World Order 216 (1994).

20. J–C. Rufin, L'empire et les nouveaux barbares (1991), here quoted from the German translation: Das Reich und die Neuen Barbaren 247 (1991).

which we call global apartheid is as wrong, unjust, and objectionable as South African apartheid before Mandela." This statement requires further clarification, especially (1) to specify what is meant by global apartheid; (2) to explain in what sense it is wrong, unjust, and objectionable; and (3) to explain the basis on which this negative judgment is justified.

The target of the accusation implicit in the term global apartheid varies somewhat between writers, who may direct their negative judgment toward either (1) the entire world ("global society," "world order," "world structure"), or (2) one part of the world—namely, the North of the world or the dominant states of the North, or (3) certain policies by the North or certain states of the North, which may include international and domestic policies.

The content of the accusation implied in *global apartheid* is that the accused (that is, the world, the North, or a policy) exhibits global apartheid, practices global apartheid, or promotes global apartheid. Typically, the details of this accusation are as follows:

1. The *world order* is accused of

    - Exhibiting *"extreme inequality"* or "gross inequities." These inequities are between rich and poor countries and/or between the North and the South of the world and/or between the whites and nonwhites of the world, and/or between men and women.... These inequities are manifest in multiple dimensions: economic, social, health, power, violence, security from violence, and others.

    - Exhibiting *"domination"* by the North over the South of the world by military, economic, or other means, and *"subjugation"* and oppression of the South.

    - Exhibiting more *violence* and instability in the South than in the North.

    - Exhibiting economic *"exploitation"* of the South by the North.

    - Exhibiting *"structural racism"* between the white North and the nonwhite South.

2. The *North* of the world is accused of

    - Being affluent while oppressing the poor South; being affluent while exploiting the poor South; or being affluent while neglecting the poor South.

    - Controlling, dominating, or oppressing the South by various means and "recolonizing" the South.

    - Pursuing policies of racial segregation on a world scale, and thus of "institutionalized racial segregation."

    - Preventing poor nonwhites of the South from entering and working in rich white countries.

    - Being "overtly racist" and preaching the racial inferiority of non-whites.

    - Practicing domestic racism within the North.

3. Various *policies* of the North are similarly accused, including foreign and domestic policies, toxic waste disposal policies, and so on.

The Normative Basis of the Accusations

The above accusations against the existing world order and the North and its policies are based on several fundamental values and norms. It is claimed, explicitly or implicitly, that global apartheid violates the norms of

- *Justice and fairness.* The situation, structure, or behaviors are judged to be unjust and unfair.

- *Basic needs.* Irrespective of justice and fairness considerations, the basic needs for the necessities of life, including food, shelter, security, and dignity, are not met for vast numbers of people in the present world order.

- *Human rights.* The human rights of vast numbers of people are violated, including the rights to life, liberty, and employment.

- *Equality.* The norm of universal equality is grossly violated.

- *Democracy.* The domination and/or oppression of a majority by a minority violates principles of political democracy. In South Africa, Mandela and the ANC used the "one man, one vote" principle and slogan as their goal.

- *Racial nondiscrimination.* Global apartheid grossly violates the norm of racial nondiscrimination.

Furthermore, it is alleged that global apartheid replicates, on a world scale, the negative norm of apartheid.

This institutionalized practice of separate and unequal development of racial groups (segregation), combined with white minority rule over nonwhite majorities, has been condemned by the world community in the case of South Africa prior to Mandela, revealing a worldwide opinion, if not consensus, that a combination of gross inequality, minority rule, and racism is unacceptable to the modern mind.

HILARY CHARLESWORTH, CHRISTINE CHINKIN, AND SHELLEY WRIGHT, "FEMINIST APPROACHES TO INTERNATIONAL LAW"

85 A.J.I.L 613, 615, 621–29 (1991)

... A feminist account of international law suggests that we inhabit a world in which men of all nations have used the statist system to establish economic and nationalist priorities to serve male elites, while basic human, social and economic needs are not met. International institutions echo these same priorities. * * * [W]e argue that the international legal order is virtually impervious to the voices of women and propose two related explanations for this: the organizational and normative structures of international law.

The Organizational Structure of International Law

The structure of the international legal order reflects a male perspective and ensures its continued dominance. The primary subjects of international law are states and, increasingly, international organizations. In both states and international organizations the invisibility of women is striking. Power structures within governments are overwhelmingly masculine: women have significant positions of power in very few states, and in those where they do, their numbers are minuscule. Women are either unrepresented or under represented in the national and global decision-making processes.

States are patriarchal structures not only because they exclude women from elite positions and decision-making roles, but also because they are based on the concentration of power in, and control by, an elite and the domestic legitimation of a monopoly over the use of force to maintain that control. This foundation is reinforced by international legal principles of sovereign equality, political independence and territorial integrity and the legitimation of force to defend these attributes.

International organizations are functional extensions of states that allow them to act collectively to achieve their objectives. Not surprisingly, their structures replicate those of states, restricting women to insignificant and subordinate roles. Thus, in the United Nations itself, where the achievement of nearly universal membership is regarded as a major success of the international community, this universality does not apply to women.

* * *

Women are excluded from all major decision making by international institutions on global policies and guidelines, despite the often disparate impact of those decisions on women. Since 1985, there has been some improvement in the representation of women in the United Nations and its specialized agencies. It has been estimated, however, that "at the present rate of change it will take almost 4 decades (until 2021) to reach equality (*i.e.*: 50% of professional jobs held by women)."[21] This situation was recently described as "grotesque."[22]

The silence and invisibility of women also characterizes those bodies with special functions regarding the creation and progressive development of international law. Only [two women have] sat as a judge on the International Court of Justice[g] and no woman has ever been a member of the International Law Commission.[h] Critics have frequently pointed out that the distribution of judges on the Court does not reflect the makeup of the international community, a concern that peaked after the decision in the South West Africa cases in 1966.[23] Steps have since been taken to improve "the representation of the main forms of civilization and of the principal legal systems of the world" on the Court, but not in the direction of representing women, [over] half of the world's population. * * * [And despite] the common acceptance of human

21. Equal Time, July 1985, at 5.

22. B. Urquhart & E. Childers, A World in Need of Leadership: Tomorrow's United Nations 29 (1990)....

g. Currently, only one woman, Dame Rosalyn Higgins from the United Kingdom, serves as a judge on, and now President of, the International Court of Justice. Previously, in a case decided by the World Court in 1985, Mme. Suzanne Bastid of France sat as a judge *ad hoc*, as did also, more recently, Mme. Christine Van Den Wyngaert of Belgium in a case decided by the ICJ in 2002.

h. The International Law Commission (ILC) is a subsidiary body of the UN General Assembly established in 1947 and consisting of thirty-four members (originally fifteen, until 1956) chosen by the General Assembly for five-year terms, on the basis of their recognized expertise in international law, to initiate studies and make recommendations to encourage the progressive development of international law and its codification.

23. South West Africa (Eth. v. S. Afr.; Liber. v. S. Afr.) (Second Phase), 1966 ICJ 6.

rights in an area in which attention can be directed toward women, they are still vastly under represented on UN human rights bodies....

* * *

Why is it significant that all the major institutions of the international legal order are peopled by men? Long-term domination of all bodies wielding political power nationally and internationally means that issues traditionally of concern to men become seen as human concerns, while "women's concerns" are relegated to a special, limited category. * * * The orthodox face of international law and politics would change dramatically if their institutions were truly human in composition; their horizons would widen to include issues previously regarded as domestic—in the two senses of the word....

The Normative Structure of International Law

... International jurisprudence assumes that international law norms directed at individuals within states are universally applicable and neutral. It is not recognized, however, that such principles may impinge differently on men and women; consequently, women's experiences of the operation of these laws tend to be silenced or discounted.

The normative structure of international law has allowed issues of particular concern to women to be either ignored or undermined. For example, modern international law rests on and reproduces various dichotomies between the public and private spheres, and the "public" sphere is regarded as the province of international law. One such distinction is between public international law, the rules about conflicts between nation-states, and private international law, the rules about conflicts between national legal systems.[i] Another is the distinction between matters of international "public" concern and matters "private" to states that are considered within their domestic jurisdiction, in which the international community has no recognized legal interest. Yet another is the line drawn between law and other forms of "private" knowledge such as morality.

At a deeper level one finds a public/private dichotomy based on gender. One explanation feminist scholars offer for the dominance of men and the male voice in all areas of power and authority in the western liberal tradition is that a dichotomy is drawn between the public sphere and the private or domestic one. The public realm of the work place, the law, economics, politics and intellectual and cultural life, where power and authority are exercised, is regarded as the natural province of men; while the private world of the home, the hearth and children is seen as the appropriate domain of women. The public/private distinction has a normative, as well as a descriptive, dimension. Traditionally, the two spheres are accorded asymmetrical value: greater significance is attached to the public, male world than to the private, female one. The distinction drawn between the public and the private thus vindicates and makes natural the division of labor and allocation of rewards between the

---

i. Among common law countries such as Australia and the United States, the expression "conflicts of law" is typically substituted for the expression "private international law," the preferred expression among civil law countries such as France and Germany.

sexes. Its reproduction and acceptance in all areas of knowledge have conferred primacy on the male world and supported the dominance of men.

* * *

What force does the feminist critique of the public/private dichotomy in the foundation of domestic legal systems have for the international legal order? Traditionally, of course, international law was regarded as operating only in the most public of public spheres: the relations between nation-states. We argue, however, that the definition of certain principles of international law rests on and reproduces the public/private distinction. It thus privileges the male world view and supports male dominance in the international legal order.

[*Eds.*—The authors next illustrate their thesis by reference to the "generally accepted" international right to freedom from torture as defined in Article 1(1) of the 1984 United Nations Convention against Torture and Other Cruel, Inhuman or Degrading Treatment or Punishment **(Basic Document 3.26)**. They point out, *inter alia*, that the Convention's definition of torture, in addition to using the male pronoun which "immediately gives the definition a male, rather than a truly human, context," deliberately "relies on a distinction between public and private actions that obscures injuries ... typically sustained by women"; that it insists upon a primary and secondary intention to inflict suffering that necessarily excludes, for example, the victimization of women and children via "widespread and apparently random terror campaigns by both governments and guerilla groups in times of civil unrest or armed conflict"; and that it requires that "a public official or a person acting in official capacity ... be implicated in the pain and suffering" involved, thus relegating the prohibited conduct exclusively to the "public realm." The authors also point out that "States are not considered responsible if they have maintained a legal and social system in which violations or physical and mental integrity are endemic," noting that the International Law Commission, which drafted the 1984 convention, "did not widen the concept of imputability to incorporate such acts." They then conclude:]

The assumption that underlies all law, including international human rights law, is that the public/private distinction is real: human society, human lives can be separated into two distinct spheres. The division, however, is an ideological construct rationalizing the exclusion of women from the sources of power. It also makes it possible to maintain repressive systems of control over women without interference from human rights guarantees, which operate in the public sphere. By extending our vision beyond the public/private ideologies that rationalize limiting our analysis of power, human rights language as it currently exists can be used to describe serious forms of repression that go far beyond the juridically narrow view of international law....

EDITORS' NOTE

Starting in the early 1980s, a provocative attempt to rethink the basis of traditional legal theory began to make itself felt in the field of international law, challenging the view of law as rational, objective, and principled by deconstructing traditional legal argument and thereby exposing the contradictions and indeterminacies of legal doctrines, principles, and rules. An extension of the "post-modern" legal scholarship called "critical legal studies" (CLS) or "critical jurisprudence" (with its intellectual origins in Legal Realism, New Left anarchism, Sartrean existentialism, neo-progressive historiography, liberal sociology, radical social theory, and empirical social science), this "New Stream"[j] of internationally-oriented inquiry has had as its unifying theme, as noted in Nigel Purvis, *Critical Legal Studies in Public International Law*, 32 Harv. Int'l L. J. 81 (1991), large antipathy for what New Stream scholars David Kennedy (of the United States) and Martti Koskenniemi (of Finland) have called "conceptual pragmatism."[k] The term refers to the liberal international law scholarship that, in the wake of World War II, sought to transform the discipline by removing it from "the theoretical and doctrinal disharmony that had characterized much of its history."[l] Purvis summarizes, at 88–92:

> [Incorporating] insights from normative philosophy, critical theory, structuralism, anthropology, prepositional logic, literature, sociology, politics, and psychiatry * * *, New Stream scholarship [has] been directed against "the tragic voice of post-war public law liberalism"[m] * * * [and] has advanced on four principal fronts. Contemporary [critical] international law scholars have maintained (1) that the logic of liberalism in international law is internally incoherent; (2) that international legal discourse operates within a constrained structure; (3) that international legal analysis is indeterminate; and, (4) that whatever authority international law may have is self-validated.

While paralleling claims made by CLS scholars outside the international law field, these criticisms have been presented by New Stream scholars, Purvis notes, "as a unified theory of international legal analysis...." *Id.* at 92.

---

j. Professor David Kennedy coined this term in *A New Stream of International Legal Scholarship*, 7 Wis. Int'l L. J. 1, 6 (1988). For more recent "new stream" scholarship by Professor Kennedy, see his The Dark Sides of Virtue: Reassessing International Humanitarianism (2004).

k. D. Kennedy, *supra* note **j**, at 1–7; M. Koskenniemi, From Apology to Utopia: The Structure of International Legal Argument 131–91 (1989).

l. Purvis explains, at 84–86:

Conceptual pragmatists sought to use doctrinal analysis to mediate between positivism and naturalism. Recognizing the need for abstraction, they sought to turn abstraction into functionalism ..., producing a fantastic diversity of idiosyncratic theories about international law. Numerous schools of conceptual pragmatism developed. Most important among them were [the] "Rule-approach" [*i.e.*, the work of such theorists as Georg Schwarzenberger, James Brierly, and Lassa Oppenheim, "who emphasized abstracted doctrinal definitions and rules"], [the] "Policy-approach" [*i.e.*, the work of Harold Lasswell and Myres McDougal and their associates], Skepticism [*i.e.*, the "realists" whose

ranks included scholars and statesmen such as Hans Kelsen, Leo Gross, Louis Henkin, Hans Morgenthau, George Kennan, and Dean Acheson and who considered international law to be no more than what nations did in fact, preferring description and resisting abstraction], and idealism [*e.g.*, scholars and jurists such as Alejandro Alvarez and Mohammed Bedjaoui who "were prone to speculate about the existing normative character of international life"].... Each [of these schools] hoped to construct a view of international law that did not depend on the two rival theories about the fundamental nature of the international order. * * * [In the end, however,] all forms of modern conceptual pragmatism ... failed to escape the naturalism/positivism debate.... Within their pragmatic concepts the naturalism/positivism indeterminism reemerged in other dichotomies: idealism/realism, normativity/concreteness, rules/processes, law/policy, and utopias/apologies. Each of these dichotomies paralleled the irreconcilable sides of the classical debate....

m. *Id.* at 2.

Illustrative is the following passage from Martti Koskenniemi, From Apology to Utopia: The Structure of International Legal Argument 40–42, 44–48 (1989):

There are two ways of arguing about order and obligation in international affairs. One argument traces them down to justice, common interests, progress, nature of the world community or other similar ideas to which it is common that they are anterior, or superior, to State behaviour, will or interest. They are taken as a given normative code which precedes the State and effectively dictates how a State is allowed to behave, what it may will and what its legitimate interests can be. Another argument bases order and obligation on State behaviour, will or interest. It takes as given the existence of States and attempts to construct a normative order on the basis of the "factual" State behaviour, will and interest. Following Walter Ullmann, I shall call these the *"descending" and "ascending" patterns of justification.*[24]

The two patterns—or sets of arguments—are both exhaustive and mutually exclusive.... The former is premised on the assumption that a normative code *overrides* individual State behaviour, will or interest.... The latter is premised on the assumption that State behaviour, will and interest are determining of the law.... Either the normative code is superior to the State or the State is superior to the code. A middle position seems excluded.

It should not be difficult to recognize the normative/concrete opposition in these two argumentative patterns. The descending pattern privileges normativity over concreteness while the ascending pattern does the reverse.... The patterns oppose each other as they regard each other too subjectively. From the ascending perspective, the descending model falls into subjectivism as it cannot demonstrate the content of its aprioristic norms in a reliable manner (*i.e.*, it is vulnerable to the objection of utopianism). From the descending perspective, the ascending model seems subjective as it privileges State will or interest over objectively binding norms (*i.e.*, it is vulnerable to the charge of apologism).

Consequently, international legal discourse cannot fully accept either of the justificatory patterns. It works so as to make them seem compatible. The result, however, is an incoherent argument * * * as it incorporates *contradictory assumptions* about what it is to argue objectively about norms. This gives rise to conflicting legal arguments and the inability to prefer any of them.

* * *

Thus, *we cannot consistently prefer either set of arguments.* Adopting a descending pattern will seem political and subjective either because it assumes the existence of a natural morality or because it creates an arbitrary distinction between States. An ascending pattern will seem political and subjective because it cannot constrain at all. It simply accepts as law whatever the State will choose to regard as such at any

24. W. Ullmann, Law and Politics in the Middle Ages: An Introduction to the Sources of Medieval Political Ideas 30–31 (1975)....

moment. Both must be included in order to make law seem objective, that is, normative and concrete and, as such, something other than politics.

The standard strategy of reconciliation is recourse to tacit *consent*. That is, we assume that though the law can be justified only by subjective acceptance, no present acceptance is needed for its application. The norm is binding because the State had agreed by means of conduct, an anterior statement, during the *travaux préparatoires*, or the like. This seems to preserve the law's concreteness while maintaining its normative force. But this reconciliation is a failure.... [A]cceptance cannot be invoked against a State denying it without assuming either 1) that the law-applier "can know better" what the State has agreed to[,] or 2) that there is some non-acceptance-related criterion whereby we can judge whether acceptance is present or not. Both points involve assuming an objective theory of justice; the former under the guise of "objective interests," the latter by reference to a naturalistic theory of good faith, reasonableness, or the like. Both are vulnerable to the objection about utopianism.

Reconciliation is impossible. This results from the way both sets of arguments are based on the assumption that they overrule each other. Moreover, this is their only distinct sense. The point of making a descending argument is that it can override subjective acceptance. To make an ascending argument is to assume that subjective acceptance can overrule any alternative justification. The arguments are meaningful only in mutual exclusion....

The dynamic of international legal argument is provided by the contradiction between the ascending and descending patterns of argument and the inability to prefer either.... Consequently, doctrine is forced to maintain itself in *constant movement from emphasizing concreteness to emphasizing normativity and vice-versa* without being able to establish itself permanently in either position.

Different doctrinal and practical disputes turn out as transformations of this contradiction. Any doctrine, argument or position can be criticized [as] either utopian or apologist. The more it tries to escape from one, the deeper it sinks into the other. This will explain why familiar disputes keep recurring without there seeming to exist any way of disposing of them permanently. Law is contrasted to discretion, "positivism" to "naturalism," consent to justice, sovereignty to community, autonomy to organization[,] and so on.

The result is a curiously incoherent doctrine which is *ad hoc* and survives only because it is such. It retreats into general statements about the need to "combine" concreteness and normativity, realism and idealism which bear no consequence to its normative conclusions. It then advances in an *ad hoc* manner, emphasizing the contextuality of each solution—undermining its own emphasis on the general and impartial character of its system ..... The doctrine's own contradictions force it into an impoverished and unreflective pragmatism. On the one hand, the "idealist" illusion is preserved that law can and does play a role in the organization of social life among States. On the other, the "realist" criticisms have been accepted and the law is seen as distinctly secondary to power and politics....

The contradictions outlined in an abstract way give theoretical expression to the common feeling that international law is somehow "weak" or manipulable. One rule or argument seems to justify mutually opposing solutions. The same solutions are regularly justified by reference to contradictory arguments or rules. This feeling is ultimately explained by the contradictory nature of the liberal doctrine of politics.[25] ... The weakness of international legal argument appears as its incapability to provide a coherent, convincing justification for solving a normative problem. The choice of solution is dependent on an ultimately arbitrary choice to stop the criticisms at one point instead of another.

Koskenniemi then concludes, at 48: "In other words, my argument is that international law is singularly useless as a means for justifying or criticizing international behaviour. Because it is based on contradictory premises it remains both over- and under-legitimizing: it is over-legitimizing as it can ultimately be invoked to justify any behaviour (apologism); it is under-legitimizing because [it is] incapable of providing a convincing argument on the legitimacy of any practices (utopianism)."

Thus, voicing New Stream thinking, Koskenniemi's project is to show, as summarized by Hilary Charlesworth in *Subversive Trends in the Jurisprudence of International Law*, 1992 Proceed. A.S.I.L. 125, 126, that "the very notion of an objective legal order seems to conflict with the liberal rejection of all but subjective, individual values" and that, therefore, "[liberal] international legal argument cannot achieve the objective resolution of disputes, claimed as its principal virtue, with the aim of 'open[ing] up a possibility for alternative descriptive—and simultaneously normative—characteristics of the world in which states live.'"[26] But as Koskenniemi asks later, *supra*, at 497, "[d]oes this imply losing a commitment to the whole, to peace and world order?" He answers, at *id.*:

> No, but it does force one into seeing the commitment in a new light. It is not a commitment which seeks to realize given principles or ready-made social arrangements. It aims to construct the whole as a structure of open political conflict and constant institutional revision. The whole will be seen as a system which enables, as far as possible, particularized solutions, aimed at realizing authentic commitment. But it gives no intrinsic weight to solutions, once adopted, and it is ready to make constant adjustments once this seems called for. It positively *excludes imperialism and totalitarianism*. Beyond that, however, it makes no pretension to offer principles of the good life which would be valid in a global way.

In other words, "the lawyer [must] recognize that solving normative problems in a justifiable way requires ... wide knowledge of social causality and of political value and, above all, capacity to imagine alternative forms of social organization to cope with conflict." *Id.* at 498. Koskenniemi concludes: "As international lawyers ..., we [are] not relieved from the painful task of living and choosing in the midst of political conflict. Instead of impartial umpires or

---

25. ... Liberalism's internal contradictions have frequently been the subject of analysis. [T]he most useful ... [argue] that liberal political theory contains two separate strands: 1) the postulate of individual freedom and 2) a programme for collective decision. The strands are contradictory. Any political decision infringes individual freedom as liberalism cannot consistently define "freedom" otherwise than as absence of (collective) constraint....

26. *Id.* at xxiii....

spectators, we [are] cast as players in a game, members in somebody's team. It is not that we need to play the game better, or more self-consciously. We need to reimagine the game, reconstruct its rules, redistribute the prizes." *Id.* at 501.

RICHARD A. FALK, "THE WORLD ORDER BETWEEN INTER-STATE LAW AND THE LAW OF HUMANITY: THE ROLE OF CIVIL SOCIETY INSTITUTIONS"

in Cosmopolitan Democracy: An Agenda for a New World Order 163
(D. Archibugi & D. Held eds., 1995)

The [contemporary] notion of world order is situated between inter-state law and the law of humanity, although not necessarily at all in the middle. The inter-state is presumably the past, a time when clearly the inter-state dimension dominated our understanding of international law, but not the more distant past when states in the modern sense didn't exist....

The law of humanity is associated with the future, it is more a matter of potentiality than of history or experience. It is prefigured, and to some extent embodied, in the substance and theory of the international law of human rights. Its formal reality has been established through the primary agency of states, and qualifies as a domain of inter-state law. But the historical potency of the international law of human rights is predominantly a consequence of its implementation through the agency of civil society.

This agency of civil society needs to be understood in two senses. Firstly, in the transnational non-governmental sense, typified by Amnesty International and the various regional watch groups—that is, voluntary associations of citizens using information about abusive behaviour on the part of states, exerting influence to obtain compliance, and, failing this, to disclose information about abuses that challenges the legitimacy of the accused state. Here, the preoccupation is with the well-being of the individual human being, and, as such, satisfies one aspect of the law of humanity (in contrast, inter-state law is preoccupied with the interests of the state as promoted by its official representatives).

There is a second dimension of the agency of civil society in relation to the law of humanity: it is the activation of peoples to pursue their emancipation from oppressive structures of governance, social movements legitimated by their aspirations being embodied in inter-state law. The movements of emancipation in Eastern Europe (as, for instance, Solidarity in Poland and Charter 77 in Czechoslovakia) were sustained, in part, by the realization that their most fundamental grievances had already been validated by the state that was offering such blatant resistance. In this kind of setting, the law of humanity is buried in the forms of inter-state law, but must be exhumed, and made operative, by the militancy of civil society.

World order, then, is a composite reality, reflecting the persisting influence of states on its normative order, yet also exhibiting the effects of voluntary associations and social movements that are motivated by the law of humanity and situated in civil society. The global spread of political democracy, with its roots in constitutionalism, makes those persons within the territorial space controlled by the sovereign state increasingly aware of their political, moral and legal option to appeal to broader communities in the event of encroachment on their basic human rights.

The character of the law of humanity is not self-evident. It could mean law that is enacted by and for the peoples of the world, as distinct from the elites that act in law-making settings on behalf of states. Such a usage would correspond with "the rights of peoples," the innovation associated with the efforts of the radical Italian parliamentarian, Lelio Basso, leading to the establishment in the mid–1970s of the Permanent Peoples Tribunal with its site in Rome. Such an innovation is itself explicitly conceived to be a counter-institution intended to expose the abuses of states and the deficiencies of international institutions, and to provide civil society with its own autonomous voice. The formalization of this voice by way of legal instruments (for instance, The Algiers Declaration on the Rights of Peoples [1976] **[Basic Document 3.19]**) and acts (for instance, the various decisions of the Permanent Peoples Tribunal) constitutes the substance of the law of humanity so conceived. In this regard, then, states are not regarded as appropriate agents for the development of the law of humanity, and it depends on civil society to establish new forms of law-creation and law-application.

It is also necessary to distinguish the law of humanity from the phenomenon of globalization, although there are some connections that will be noted as well. Inter-state law presupposed the autonomy of the territorial state, although such a presupposition was always a legal fiction given the hierarchical reality of geopolitics. During most of the period of the ascendancy of the state, the largest part of humanity was excluded from its protective structures associated for convenience sake with the Peace of Westphalia (1648), being subordinated within the frame of one or another variety of imperial geopolitics. That is, the inter-state system was primarily a regional system centred in Europe, and only because the region projected its power globally did the illusion arise of a world system. Ironically, it is only in recent decades, with the collapse of colonialism, that inter-state law became an encompassing global reality. The irony arises because, at this historical point of climax for inter-state law as a framework of formal membership, the realities of interdependence and integration undermine the presupposition of autonomy, rendering partially obsolete the claims of inter-state law.

There is a certain confusion that follows from distinguishing the law of humanity as "the other" in relation to inter-state law. During the modern period the ideology of the state included the claim that such a system of distinct sovereignties upheld the well-being of humanity, that inter-state law was the best vehicle by which to achieve the objectives of the law of humanity. In this regard, inter-state law, with its positivist disposition, was seen as an improvement upon the naturalist approach that rested on a vague foundation of universalism that didn't correspond with the specific interests, cultural diversities and concrete values of separate peoples organized on the basis of distinct national identities. That is, the state reconciled the particular with the general in a satisfactory manner so long as territoriality approximated economic, social, political and cultural reality. Of course, here too, adequacy depended on fiction as illustrated by the terminology of nation-state, a juristic conception of nationality that often obscured the presence within state boundaries of several ethnic groups with separate, often antagonistic, psycho-political conceptions of national identity. The state-fracturing impact of the right of self-determination when extended to "peoples" (as in Article 1 of the human rights covenants **[Basic Documents 3.13 & 3.14]** and in the post–1989 practice relating to the former Yugoslavia and Soviet Union) has exploded once and for all the misleading pretension of designating states as "nation-states."

But, arguably, the erosion of territoriality has undermined the major premise of inter-state law and its derivative claim to operate as the guardian of human well-being. This erosion can be understood from different angles: matters of vulnerability—the state has lost the capacity to uphold security in light of nuclear weaponry and long-range delivery systems; matters of environmental protection—the state cannot safeguard its territory from the adverse effects of extra-territorial behaviour nor can it by its own efforts maintain the global commons (oceans, atmosphere); matters of economic viability—the state, even those that are well-endowed and large, can no longer provide an adequate framework for economic activity, and is gradually being superseded by an array of international regimes and by the regionalization and globalization of capital markets and corporate and banking organization. In these three types of erosion, the well-being of humanity requires law to be operative on a regional, or global, scale that corresponds to the scope of operations. It is here, however, that inter-state realities persist, and the law of humanity is mainly in the dreaming (or pure aspirational) phase. Inter-state law provides what control there is in relation to war/peace and environmental issues and, except for the European Community, with respect to transnational economic activity. Thus, the inability of inter-state law to rise to these challenges and the failure of the law of humanity to take effective shape is one way to express a critical view of world order; the deep structural quality of these criticisms also helps understand why even such a momentous historical occasion as the ending of the Cold War and the reuniting of Europe can have only a superficial relevance to an inquiry into prospects for the emergence of the law of humanity in an effective form.

DISCUSSION NOTES/QUESTIONS

1.   To understand the origins and development of international law is to understand world history. How, generally, would you describe the development of international law over the course of history? Would your answer differ were you to describe the development of any given municipal (*i.e.*, national) law system? How? Why?

2.   One might have expected that Grotius and other early writers would not have had very much previous international law to draw upon to make their arguments, since the nation-state was just beginning to emerge out of the medieval period. But a mere glance at the size of their tracts indicates that, in fact, they had an enormous body of doctrines, principles, and rules upon which to fashion their particular assertions. Where did all this previous authority come from?

3.   Through Bederman, *supra*, we can trace the emergence of the modern state system and the coordinate development of international law on the basis, at least initially, of "natural law" theorizing. He also indicates a resurgence of naturalist thinking in recent times, alluding to the experience of World War II, the Nuremberg and Tokyo trials, and, recently, the rapid development of international human rights law? But does not Bederman go even further to suggest a newly

emerging consensus on enduring values? Not so long ago it was fashionable to defer to anthropologists who, when investigating remote societies, claimed that all values were relative to time, place, and culture. But in a deep sense the Second World War and the development of weapons of global destruction may have changed our earlier attitudes. It is increasingly hard to maintain that any value is as good as another, that any morality is culturally determined and thus a matter only of social pressure, that any action by a government is all right as long as it has the support of its own people. What do you think?

4. Which of the forces shaping the organization and interrelation of human societies from early to modern times do you consider to have been most important in shaping the development of international law? And in answering this question, according to what criteria do you measure importance? Is it that the historical forces you identify have been more or less cataclysmic or threatening in character? What does your answer imply for how international law is likely to develop in the future? Do the extracts by Bederman, Bedjaoui, Charlesworth–Chinkin–Wright, Köhler, or Falk, *supra*, provide any clues?

5. Is there a Western bias in modern-day international law? A class bias? A racial bias? A gender bias? Do they persist? Is it a matter merely of perception or is it one of real substance? How might Bederman, Bedjaoui, Charlesworth–Chinkin–Wright, Köhler, and Falk, *supra*, answer these questions? What conclusions might we draw from Professor David Harris' observation, in Cases and Materials on International Law 16 (5th ed. 1998), that, for many generations, international law was "really no more than the Public Law of Europe"?

6. In Towards A New International Economic Order (1979), former World Court Judge Mohammed Bedjaoui contends, at 49, that "[t]raditional international law is derived from the laws of the capitalist economy and the liberal political system." This theme is echoed in R. P. Anand, International Law and the Developing Countries 24 (1987), referring to the 19th Century:

> With the increasing European need and demand for trade in an era of expanding economy, it came to be asserted "that there was a divine right to trade everywhere," and "that it was unnatural for governments to close their countries to the free flow of trade." It was asserted that,

> The inflow of the white race cannot be stopped where there is land to cultivate, ore to be mined, commerce to be developed, sport to enjoy, curiosity to be satisfied.

> If any people tried to keep the whites out, "international law has to treat such nations as uncivilized."

Do these words have any relevance for today's world within the framework of the World Trade Organization (WTO)? Is it possible that contemporary international trade law as promoted by today's large trading nations within the WTO framework may create injustices akin to those that were perpetrated during the 19th Century era of free trade? For pertinent discussion, see, *e.g.*, Frank J. Garcia, *Trade and Inequality: Economic Justice and the Developing World*, 21 Mich. J. Int'l L 975 (2000). *See also* Rhoda E. Howard–Hassmann, *The Second Great Transformation: Human Rights Leap–Frogging in the Era of Globalization Pursuing Global Justice*, 27 H.R.Q. 1 (2005).

7. The first Falk extract, *supra*, observes that international law and the organized international community have amounted to "a colossal failure" in the avoidance of catastrophe. Do you agree? Assuming Falk to be correct, do you

believe there are grounds for optimism that the practitioners of international law and policy can and will reverse this pattern? Why? Why not?

8.   In the continuation of his essay, Professor Köhler, *supra*, asks, at 408: "If the world had a court of justice where global apartheid was a punishable crime on a level with such crimes as waging [a] war of aggression or genocide, would the North be guilty or not guilty of such a crime?" How do you answer this question? What are your reasons?

9.   The Charlesworth–Chinkin–Wright extract, *supra*, asserts that the dichotomy drawn by international law (as well as national law) between public and private spheres of action prevent international legal processes from being gender neutral and consequently prejudice the position and role of women relative to men in international (and national) society. What do the authors mean? How does the public-private dichotomy to which they refer prejudice women? For more recent extensive explication, see Hilary Charlesworth & Christine Chinkin, The Boundaries of International Law: A Feminist Analysis (2000).

10.   Anghie–Chimni, Köhler, and Charlesworth–Chinkin–Wright, *supra*, all point to deep structural dislocations and malignancies in the international system. If it is true that law is an essentially conservative profession, how, if at all, might international law serve a reformist or transformist role in relation to these dislocations and malignancies?

11.   Purvis, in the Editors' Note, *supra*, observes, at 116, that "the most disappointing aspect of the New Stream literature has been its failure to commit to an affirmative image of international law's role in the world order"—in contrast to, for example, the "conceptual pragmatism" of the policy science approach of Harold Lasswell and Myres McDougal toward which New Stream scholars display some hostility. Rosalyn Higgins, a policy science scholar, now ICJ judge and President, writes as follows of critical jurisprudence in Problems and Process: International Law and How We Use It 8–9 (1994):

> [Critical legal studies] has more in common with policy science than either the policy scientists or the critical realists might wish to acknowledge. For both schools, the legal theory is applicable to law in general and not just to international law. . . . Both take as the starting-point that law is deeply rooted in social theory. Both locate legal process in social context and make the place of values quite explicit. Both reject law as rules and exceptions. But the critical-studies scholar will see law as contradictions or as essentially indeterminate at its core rather than as complementary or competing norms between which choices have to be made in particular circumstances. The critical-studies scholar believes that these contradictions are either historically contingent or inherent in the human experience. This view leads to the pessimistic conclusion that what international law can do is to point out the problems but not assist in the achievement of goals.

Do you agree with Judge Higgins' conclusion? Disagree? Why? What would Koskenniemi say? Note that his vision of world order "positively excludes imperialism and totalitarianism."

12.   The second Falk extract, *supra*, describes the present world order as somewhere between "inter-state law" and "the law of humanity," but moving in the direction of "the law of humanity." What does Falk mean?

13.   In their introduction to Rethinking Human Rights: Challenges for Theory and Action (1989), Indian scholars Smitu Kothari and Harsh Sethi write, at 9:

[W]hile recourse to law, or appealing to the state to enforce the law or legislate new ones, will and possibly must remain an important, maybe even the primary strategy to transform the human condition, equally important is to evolve and popularise a social praxis, rooted in the need of the most oppressed communities, that seeks to create shared norms of civilized existence. In any final instance, it is only this—shared vision of how we want to live as a collectivity—that can provide us the moral basis of evolving our own conduct.

Would Falk, on the basis of the second Falk extract, *supra*, agree with this statement, which, on final analysis, is skeptical of the law as a progressive social change agent? Do you? How might Anghie–Chimnii, Köhler, and Charlesworth–Chinkin–Wright respond? Do you agree with them? Why? Why not?

14. For insightful critique of "the most persuasive Western theories of international law"—"realist" (Morgenthau); "policy science" (McDougal–Lasswell); "world order" (Falk)—and of the Soviet approach to international law as well (Tunkin), see B. S. Chimni, International Law and World Order: A Critique of Contemporary Approaches (1993).

C. IS INTERNATIONAL LAW REALLY LAW?

In reviewing the definition of "international law" (*supra* Section A) as you prepare for the possible prosecution of violations of international criminal law in Sudan's Darfur province since 1 July 2002 (and perhaps also for crimes in Congo, Uganda, and the Central African Republic), you read some general observations supporting the proposition that international law deserves the title "law," a proposition that you found also to be assumed in the brief historical and contemporaneous views you just considered (*supra* Section B). But you are aware that much of the general public is skeptical about the "legal" status of international law, particularly in relation to such "gravest crimes" cases for which you are preparing. Are there really any means, many would ask, for legally impugning Sudanese officials and Janjaweed militiamen for their activities in Darfur? Is it not paradoxical to talk about law operating among "sovereign" states? Does not international law exist in name only, as merely a language for brokering international relations and politics? Suspecting that opposing counsel will be well versed in these kinds of questions and their theoretical responses, you again turn to your treatise.

—————

A modern-day example of skepticism about international law is to be found, as we saw in Section B, *supra*, in the "New Stream" scholarship of "Critical Legal Studies" (CLS) or "critical jurisprudence." As observed, New Stream scholars attack conclusory statements about law, which they perceive as commonly concealing the socioeconomic and political agendas of those with effective power. To the CLS theorist, objectivity does not exist except within the minds and prejudices of the naive. In *International Law, World Order and Critical Legal Studies*, 42 Stan. L. Rev. 811, 833–34 (1990), Philip Trimble summarizes an important aspect of the CLS argument in the context of international law:

A quick look at the rules of international law shows why governments love international law. Contrary to the ... view of law as a restraint on unruly governments, international law confirms much more authority and power than it denies. For example, the basic rule of international law is that a state generally has the exclusive authority to regulate conduct within its territory. International law thus confers authority to control entry and exit, to establish police control, to determine economic structure, to tax, to regulate, and to reinforce in many other ways the power and legitimacy of government. Public international law also grants governments sovereignty over air space and control over the continental shelf and economic resources 200 miles into the sea.

Of course, each rule conferring authority on a government denies it to all others. The United States government may be restrained in attempts to enforce its law in Canada, and Japanese fishermen may be barred from fishing near California's coast. Nevertheless, governments have little interest in extending their authority to that extent, at least when compared with their interest in controlling matters at home. For the most part governments do not want to invade other countries or apply their law or send their fishermen to other territories. To be sure, there are exceptions, and these exceptions can be of vital importance to the actors involved. In the aggregate, however, they are less important than the effect of the general rules.

Even the rules of public international law that expressly restrain government authority may at the same time give a government an excuse to impose its authority throughout its own society so that it can effectively discharge its obligations under international law. International human rights law, for example, promotes national judicial review, general criminal law procedures, and a host of objectives that can best be met by assertions of national government power, especially against village or other traditional structures. For example, a government's international responsibility for injuries to aliens gives that government a mandate to control local officials and practices.

Even when the rules do prevent a government from doing something that it otherwise wants to do, such as denying overflight rights to a hostile state's aircraft (contrary to a treaty obligation), it may decide to forego the short-term advantages derived from violating those rules because it has an overriding interest in maintaining the overall system. The rules comprising the system as a whole enable each government to achieve welfare goals for important parts of its population, and hence solidify its standing and legitimacy. Thus, the United States government may decide not to block transit of Cuban aircraft over United States territory because it derives support from the airline industry and the traveling public, both of which in turn benefit from transit over Cuba or from the system of which transit rights are an integral part. The rules of international law accordingly are very congenial to governments. They mostly justify or legitimate the practical exercise of state power.

For the CLS theorist, then, the claims of rational or objective rules only cloak the real forces behind all legal language and structure: politics.

As observed above, the New Stream of critical jurisprudence has as a predecessor in skepticism the philosophy about law known as legal positivism, a jurisprudence that has powerfully influenced legal thinking over the last two centuries and that strongly implies that law *within* states—the law familiar to people generally—is somehow *the* model for law against which international law must be measured *between* states. Thus John Austin, writing in the Nineteenth Century, examined law within states and found that it contained a "command" issuing from a determinate "sovereign" that was habitually obeyed by the citizenry. Then, looking at interactions between and among states, he found that there was no such habitually obeyed "command." Hence, he called international law "positive morality" and denied that it is "law, properly so called."[n]

Accordingly, many students of the law, especially those persuaded by the command theory of legal positivism, consider that the only "law" worth talking about is the "law" that is enforced. Citizen A sues Citizen B; A wins in court; B is very unhappy and refuses to pay the judgment; the sheriff seizes B's assets and pays them over to A. It is the last action—that of the sheriff or, in some cases, the military—that the positivists emphasize as giving the entire process the name "law."

When positivists look to international law, they have difficulty finding the international equivalent of a sheriff. Especially when a nation is the "defendant," they ask how any alleged "law" can be enforced against it. Nation A sues Nation B; A wins in an international court; B is very unhappy and refuses to pay the judgment. Then what? Suppose Nation A launches a war of retaliation against Nation B. Is such a war the equivalent of "enforcement action"? Theoretically one might so allege, but there is no guarantee that Nation A will win. Indeed, what if Nation B wins?

It is considerations such as these that have led many to conclude, akin to John Austin, that there is no such thing as international law because there is no third-party "command" that is routinely enforceable. As Gidon Gottlieb explains, "[d]ominant legal theories all relate to the legal order of vertical systems . . . in which, to borrow Professor Falk's phrase, there is a vertical or hierarchical relationship between unequal centers of power. This is in contrast to systems in which there is a horizontal or nonhierarchical order between equal centers of power."[o] Thus, leading modern-day legal positivist H. L. A. Hart has written, in The Concept of Law 209 (1961):

> [T]hough it is consistent with the usage of the last 150 years to use the expression "law" here, the absence of an international legislature, courts with compulsory jurisdiction, and centrally organized sanctions have inspired misgivings, at any rate in the breasts of legal theorists. The absence of these institutions means that the rules for states resemble the simple form of social structure, consisting only of primary rules of obligation, which, when we find it among societies of individuals, we are accustomed to contrast with a developed legal system. It is indeed arguable, as we shall show, that international law not only lacks the secondary rules of change and adjudication which provide for legislatures

n. *See, e.g.,* 2 J. Austin, Lectures on Jurisprudence 176–77 (R. Campbell ed., 1875): "[T]he greatest logical error of all that is committed by many continental jurists, who include in public law, not only the law of political conditions, of crimes, and of civil and criminal procedure, but also international law; which is not positive law at all, but a branch of positive morality."

o. G. Gottlieb, *The Nature of International Law: Toward a Second Concept of Law,* in The Future of the International Legal Order 331, 332 (C. Black & R. Falk eds., 1972).

and courts, but also a unifying rule of recognition specifying "sources" of law and providing general criteria for the identification of its rules. These differences are indeed striking and the question "Is international law really law?" can hardly be put aside.

Hart argues, in effect, that international law is not a system or process but a set of rules, and that, lacking any basic rules of recognition, it is not law.

But as we have seen not all students of international relations agree with the positivist view as traditionally conceived. Thus Roger Fisher has written, in a now classic essay based primarily on United States experience, *Bringing Law to Bear on Governments*, 74 Harv. L. Rev. 1130, 1132–34 (1961):

... I suggest that we lawyers, in uncritically accepting the command theory and applying it to international law have ourselves been guilty of woolly thinking. I suggest that in denying the status of international law because there is no apparent sovereign issuing the commands, we show a limited understanding of how [for example] a court system operates in its relations with a government. In blandly assuming that all law rests on superior force, we have ignored the cases in which the government loses a judgment and honors it.

Is organized force essential to such compliance? Clearly it is not. When a judgment is entered against the United States in the Court of Claims, no superior sovereign compels Congress to vote an appropriation. The judgment is paid because that is the law; but the law is not the articulate voice of a superior sovereign. When, in the *Youngstown* case, the Supreme Court ordered the Secretary of Commerce to return the steel mills which the President had ordered him to seize, the Court had no regiments at its command. But despite the fact that the Supreme Court sitting in Washington had no greater force at its command vis-à-vis the Government than does the International Court of Justice sitting at The Hague, the steel mills were returned.

The more closely one examines law within this country and within others, the less significant seems the element of force. Even such hard, positive laws as the criminal and tax laws depend ultimately on compliance with them by the Government, and the general pattern is one of compliance. To be sure, Congress, on perhaps a dozen occasions, has failed to honor a judgment of the Court of Claims. But the Government, which is never without funds or absent from the jurisdiction, has a far better record than the private judgment debtor. This record, even if less than perfect, demonstrates that a pattern of governmental compliance can be secured without a supragovernmental police force.

Moreover, even where the organized force of a superior sovereign is available it may be difficult to make a government comply. If a government is not persuaded to obey by other reasons, superior force alone may not be enough. In *Virginia v. West Virginia* the Supreme Court had before it the continuing failure of the West Virginia legislature to raise and appropriate the funds needed to pay Virginia that share of its public debt which West Virginia had undertaken upon becoming a separate state. Assuming that the United States Army was at the Court's disposal, what should the Army do to enforce the judgment? Should it seize the state capitol and sell it at auction? Should it raise funds at the point of a gun? If so, from whom? However effective force or the threat of force may be when applied to an individual, it is difficult to bring force to bear on a political enterprise which offers no obvious point of application. So long as a rule runs only to a political entity rather than to individuals, a superior power must face the problem of trying to apply force to an abstraction.

And to Professor Fisher's dissent may be added the curious fact that international law, despite few centralized or hierarchical command and enforcement structures, is widely obeyed on the whole. As Burns Weston observes in *Law and Alternative Security: Toward a Just World Peace*, in Alternative Security: Living Without Nuclear Deterrence 78, 80 (B. Weston ed., 1990):

> Every hour of every day ships ply the sea, planes pierce the clouds, and artificial satellites roam outer space. Every hour of every day communications are transmitted, goods and services traded, and people and things transported from one country to another. Every hour of every day, transactions are made, resources exploited, and institutions created across national and equivalent frontiers. And in all these respects, international law (by which I mean the many processes of authoritative and controlling transboundary decision at all levels of social organization that help to regulate such endeavors) is rather well observed on the whole; it is an important and relevant force in the ordering of human relationships worldwide. True, the international legal system is by no means adequate in its force and effect, and this is particularly true in the realm of war and peace.... But no legal system, not even the most advanced, can boast absolute effectiveness; and all legal systems, again including the most advanced, typically display a certain impotence when it comes to politically volatile or otherwise intractable issues of public policy.

See also Louis Henkin in How Nations Behave—Law and Foreign Policy 47 (2d ed. 1979): "It is probably the case that *almost all nations observe almost all principles of international law and almost all of their obligations almost all of the time.* Every day nations respect the borders of other nations, treat foreign diplomats and citizens and property as required by law, observe thousands of treaties with more than a hundred countries."

Actually, not even legal positivists such as H.L.A. Hart agree with the positivist view as originally or traditionally conceived. While not accepting international law as "law" in the same way or to the same degree they do domestic or municipal law, neither do they insist on "law" as solely a matter of orders (the command of the sovereign) backed by threats (sanctions). Thus Hart, for example, likens international law to the law of "primitive communities" which, he says, are lacking in so-called secondary *rules of recognition* (for conclusive identification of the authoritativeness of primary or substantive community norms), *rules of change* (for empowering individuals or groups to introduce or eliminate old primary or substantive norms), and *rules of adjudication* (for enabling individuals or groups to make authoritative determinations of the question whether a primary or substantive norm has been broken). However, he observes, they are *not* lacking in so-called primary *rules of obligation* ("that general attitude of the group towards its own standard modes of behaviour" that imposes "restrictions on the free use of violence, theft, and deception"). These latter "primary rules of obligation," he maintains, provided they are supported by majority consensus, may be understood to reflect at least a minimal legal system because, along with "secondary rules" of "recognition," "change," and "adjudication," they help to make up "the heart of a legal system." *See* H.L.A. Hart The Concept of Law 89–95, 212–15 (1961). Hart writes, at 212–13:

> To argue that international law is not binding because of its lack of organized sanctions is tacitly to accept the analysis of obligation contained in the theory that law is essentially a matter of orders backed by threats. This theory ... identifies "having an obligation" or "being bound" with "likely to suffer the sanction or punishment threatened for disobedience". Yet ..., this identification distorts the role played in all legal thought and discourse of the ideas of obligation and duty. Even in municipal law, where there are effective organized sanctions, we must distinguish ... the meaning of the external predictive statement "I (you) are likely to suffer for disobedience", from the internal normative statement "I (you) have an obligation to act thus" which assesses a particular person's situation from the point of view of rules accepted as guiding standards of behaviour. It is true that not all rules give rise to obligations or duties; and it is also true that the rules which do so generally call for some sacrifice of private interests, and are generally supported by serious demands for conformity and insistent criticism of deviations. Yet once we free ourselves from the predictive analysis and its parent conception of law as essentially an order backed by threats, there seems no good reason for limiting the normative idea of obligation to rules supported by organized sanctions.

Hart continues (and concludes), at 214–15:

> [T]here is general pressure for conformity to the [primary rules of international obligation]; claims and admissions are based on them and their breach is held to justify not only insistent demands for compensation, but reprisals and countermeasures. When the rules are disregarded, it is not on the footing that they are not binding; instead efforts are made to conceal the facts. It may of course be said that such rules are efficacious only so far as they concern issues over which states are unwilling to fight. This may be so, and may reflect adversely on the importance of the system and its value to humanity. Yet that even so much may be secured shows that no simple deduction can be made from the necessity of organized sanctions to municipal law, in its setting of physical and psychological facts, to the conclusion that without them international law, in its very different setting, imposes no obligations, is not "binding", and so not worthy the title of "law".

In short, says Hart, international law deserves to be called "law" even if its analogy to domestic or municipal law is more in its content than its form.

Thus it is possible to say that the positivist view of law and legal process as traditionally understood, though still influential in many respects, is no longer in ascendancy. It has given way to other, more complex theories about domestic and international law.

But if it is not necessarily the threat of force that induces governmental compliance with law in general, and international law in particular, on what basis is it possible to say that international law really is law and that it has force and effect most, if not all, of the time? As Thomas Franck has asked, in *Legitimacy in the International System*, 82 A.J.I.L. 705 (1988): "Why should rules, unsupported by an effective structure of coercion comparable to a national police force, nevertheless elicit so much compliance even against perceived self-interest, on the part of sovereign states?" This question has been asked even by a former judge of the International Court of Justice, Philip C. Jessup, in a now classic statement, *The Reality of International Law*, 18 Foreign Aff. 244 (1939–40), at 244–46:

Why do Foreign Ministers and Secretaries of State consult legal advisers about international law? * * * In most cases the layman is impressed by the reality of breaches of international law and is not sufficiently aware of the reality of reliance upon it. He does not pause to wonder why foreign offices bother to maintain legal staffs, which are an expense and sometimes a hindrance to the execution of policy. A distinguished student has remarked that in the seventeenth century "state papers are full of allusions and appeals not merely to reasons of policy but to principles of right, of justice and of equity—to the authority of public law and to those principles and rules by which the rights of the weak are protected against the invasion of superior force by the union of all who are interested in the common danger."

Why has this been true for three centuries? Why have the nations been willing . . . to subscribe to a budget . . . for the maintenance of the [World Court]? . . . Why have the governments of the United States and Mexico filled reams of paper with legal arguments concerning the property rights of American citizens in the latter country? Why does the Constitution of the United States, which, according to Chief Justice Marshall, cannot be presumed to contain any clause which "is intended to be without effect," give Congress the power "to define and punish . . . offenses against the law of nations"? Why has the United States Supreme Court, like the courts of most other countries, asserted that "international law is part of our law"? Why do people commonly emphasize the "lawlessness" of certain nations which have come to be known as "aggressors"?

There must be some reason for this habitual invocation of international law—an invocation which is even more frequent than the assertion of its nonexistence. Perhaps a subconscious human urge, a variety of wishful thinking, seeks to give reality to the ancient maxim: *ubi societas, ibi ius*. Perhaps "international law" is merely a slogan of diplomacy, like "manifest destiny," "the white man's burden," or "*Lebensraum*." Surely it is often a convenient weapon for a ministry of propaganda anxious to win the support of world opinion. Yet if international law has no reality, what is the use of convincing peoples in other lands that one's opponent is a violator of that law? Shall we chorus with the Pirate King: "A paradox, a paradox, a most ingenious paradox"? One would scarcely deny that international law is a comparatively weak sister of private law. Yet a great lawyer—John Bassett Moore—bears testimony as the result of wide experience and study that "international law is on the whole as well observed as municipal law."

How might Jessup have answered the questions he asks? How does one convincingly argue that international law really is law and that it has force and effect most if not all of the time? We here consider the principal arguments: obligation, rule-legitimacy, consensus, sanctions, self-interest, reciprocity, iterative management, and transnational legal process.

JAMES L. BRIERLY, THE OUTLOOK FOR INTERNATIONAL LAW
5 (1944)

The best evidence for the existence of international law is that every actual state recognizes that it does exist and that it is itself under obligation to observe it. States may often violate international law, just as individuals often violate municipal law; but no more than individuals do states defend their violations by claiming that they are above the law. It is only the philosopher in his study who sometimes makes that claim on their behalf. States may defend their conduct in all sorts of other ways, by denying that the rule they are alleged to have broken is a rule of law, by appealing to a supposed right of self-preservation superior to the ordinary law, and by other excuses more or less sincerely believed in as the case may be; but they do not use the explanation which would obviously be the natural one if there were any doubt that international law has a real existence and that they are bound by it.

SIR GERALD FITZMAURICE, "THE FOUNDATIONS OF THE AUTHORITY OF INTERNATIONAL LAW AND THE PROBLEM OF ENFORCEMENT"
19 Mod. L. Rev. 1, 8 (1956)

The real foundation of the authority of international law resides ... in the fact that the States making up ... international society recognize it as binding upon them, and, moreover, as a system that *ipso facto* binds them as members of that society, irrespective of their individual wills. * * * [I]t is not consent, as such, that creates the obligation, though it may be the occasion of it. It is a method of creating rules, but it is not, in the last resort, the element that makes the rules binding, when created. In short, consent could not in itself create obligations unless there were already in existence a rule of law according to which consent had just that effect.... Others have put it in the following way: "There is a customary rule of international law that the consent of the States to a rule makes that rule binding upon them." Be it so; but then, of course, the difficulty is merely removed a stage further back, and the inquirer will have to ask what is the juridical foundation for this customary rule itself, and what is it that makes that rule binding. To this question it is very difficult to give an answer. It can be said, with [Hans] Kelsen, that the reason why a customary rule is binding is that there is an antecedent and still more fundamental legal principle to the effect that "States have a duty to go on behaving as they have customarily behaved"— but then what is the source of that duty? Or can it be held, with [Sir Hersch] Lauterpacht, that the antecedent principle that confers binding force on customary rules is one according to which the general will of the community must prevail, and there is a duty to conform to that will as expressed in customary rules of law—but here again a duty is postulated that has itself ...

to be accounted for. The point is that, however the matter is put, finality can, in the nature of the case, never be attained. The discussion merely enters what is known to the mathematicians as an infinite regress—a series in which each proposition is explicable in terms of the previous one, and derives its validity from it; but this antecedent proposition itself requires to be accounted for by a similar process.

THOMAS M. FRANCK, "LEGITIMACY IN THE INTERNATIONAL SYSTEM"

82 A.J.I.L. 705, 705–07, 712–13 (1988)

... [The] observation [that nations obey international law most of the time may be made not only] to register optimism that the half-empty glass is also half full, but [also] to draw attention to a pregnant phenomenon: that most states observe systematic rules much of the time in their relations with other states. That they should do so is much more interesting than, say, the fact that most citizens usually obey their nation's laws, because the international system is organized in a voluntarist fashion, supported by so little coercive authority. This unenforced rule system can obligate states to profess, if not always to manifest, a significant level of day-to-day compliance even, at times, when that is not in their short-term self-interest. The element or paradox attracts our attention and challenges us to investigate it, perhaps in the hope of discovering a theory that can illuminate more generally the occurrence of voluntary normative compliance and even yield a prescription for enhancing aspects of world order.

* * *

[I submit] that, in a community organized around rules, compliance is secured—to whatever degree it is—at least in part by perception of a rule as legitimate by those to whom it is addressed.[p] Their perception of legitimacy will vary in degree from rule to rule and time to time. It becomes a crucial factor, however, in the capacity of any rule to secure compliance when, as in the international system, there are no other compliance-inducing mechanisms.

* * *

Four elements—the indicators of rule legitimacy in the community of states—[may be] identified and studied.... They are *determinacy*,[q] *symbolic validation*,[r] *coherence*[s] and *adherence* (to a normative hierarchy).[t] To the

---

p. Writes Franck, at 706: "Legitimacy is used here to mean that quality of a rule *which derives from a perception on the part of those to whom it is addressed that it has come into being in accordance with right process*. Right process includes the notion of valid sources but also encompasses literary, socio-anthropological and philosophical insights."

q. Defined by Franck as "the ability of the text to convey a clear message, to appear transparent in the sense that one can see through the language to the meaning." Franck, *supra*, at 713.

r. Writes Franck, *id.* at 725–26, "As determinacy is the linguistic or literary-structural

component of legitimacy, so *symbolic validation, ritual* and *pedigree* provide its cultural and anthropological dimension.... In this instance, however, what is to be communicated is not so much content as *authority*: the authority of a rule, the authority of the originator of a validating communication and, at times, the authority bestowed on the recipient of the communication. * * * These three concepts—symbolic validation, ritual and pedigree—are related, but not identical. The *symbolic validation* of a rule, or of a rule-making process or insti-

---

s-t.   See notes s-t on page 69.

extent rules exhibit these properties, they appear to exert a strong pull on states to comply with their commands. To the extent that these elements are not present, rules seem to be easier to avoid by a state tempted to pursue its short-term self-interest. This is not to say that the legitimacy of a rule can be deduced solely be counting how often it is obeyed or disobeyed. While its legitimacy may exert a powerful pull on state conduct, yet other pulls may be stronger in a particular circumstance. The chance to take a quick, decisive advantage may overcome the counterpull of even a highly legitimate rule. In such circumstances, legitimacy is indicated not by obedience, but by the discomfort disobedience induces in the violator. (Student demonstrations sometimes are a sensitive indicator of such discomfort.) The variable to watch is not compliance but the strength of the compliance pull, whether or not the rule achieves actual compliance in any one case.

* * *

The study of legitimacy ... focuses on the inherent capacity of a rule to exert pressure on states to comply. This focus on the properties of rules, of course, is not a self-sufficient account of the socialization process. How rules are made, interpreted and applied is part of a dynamic, expansive and complex set of social phenomena. That complexity can be approached, however, by beginning with the rules themselves. Those seemingly inert constructs are shaped by other, more dynamic forces and, like tree trunks and seashells, tell their own story about the winds and tides that become an experiential part of their shape and texture.

GIDON GOTTLIEB, "THE NATURE OF INTERNATIONAL LAW: TOWARD A SECOND CONCEPT OF LAW"

in 4 The Future of the International Legal
Order 331, 365–66 (C. Black & R. Falk eds., 1972)

It is correct to assert that a legal order exists when:

1. international actors (for example, states) accept sets of fairly specific rules, principles, and policies as binding—in the sense that they recognize

tution, occurs when a signal is used as a cue to elicit compliance with a command [*e.g.*, the singing of a national anthem to reinforce the citizen's relationship to the state]. * * * *Ritual* is a specialized form of symbolic validation marked by ceremonies, often—but not necessarily—mystical, that provide unenunciated reasons or cues for eliciting compliance with the commands of persons or institutions. * * * *Pedigree* is a different subset of cues that seek to enhance the compliance pull of rules or rule-making institutions by emphasizing their historical origins, their cultural or anthropological deep-rootedness."

s. "[C]oherence," asserts Franck, *id.* at 741, "encompasses the ... notion that a rule, standard or validating ritual gathers force if it is seen to be [uncapricious and] connected to a network of other rules by an underlying general principle."

t. States Franck, *id* at 752: "*Adherence* ... is used here to mean the vertical nexus between a single *primary rule of obligation* ("cross on the green; stop on the red") and a pyramid of secondary rules about how rules are made, interpreted and applied: rules, in other words, about rules. These may be labeled *secondary rules of process.* Primary rules of obligation that lack adherence to a system of secondary rules of process are mere ad hoc reciprocal arrangements.... A rule ... is more likely to obligate if it is made within the procedural and institutional framework of an organized community than if it is strictly an ad hoc agreement between parties in the state of nature. The same rule is still more likely to obligate if it is made within the hierarchically structured procedural and constitutional framework of a sophisticated community rather than in a primitive community lacking such secondary rules about rules."

they are not at liberty to disregard them—and as proper standards for assessing the legality of their own actions;

2.   international actors make demands, claims, complaints, and proposals to each other on the basis of such binding rules, principles, and policies and seek to settle their differences by reference to them;

3.   international actors attempt to secure compliance with such rules, principles, and policies and there is a measure of congruence between state action and accepted law;

4.   there are organizations established under such rules, principles, and policies and acting pursuant to them;

5.   there is a measure of consensus between international actors about the content of the rules, principles, and policies accepted as binding, and about criteria for identifying them;

6.   these rules, principles, and policies regulate significant aspects of the relationships between international actors and are designed to limit their unfettered discretion in decision-making;

7.   international actors are committed to accept the guidance of these binding rules, principles, and policies in good faith and to apply them evenhandedly in all situations.

Such a legal order involves then a process of authoritative decision-making leading to unavoidable principled choices between competing goals and policies. It requires a measure of congruence between state action and accepted law. This congruence is a central feature of the existence of any legal system. Accordingly, the earnestness with which major powers act upon international law considerations in good faith, and the intensity of their commitment to its principles and objectives, are good measures of the exis- tence of such a system. Deviant practices, invoking one set of standards for oneself and another for adversaries, stretching concepts to legitimize national policies of questionable legality, all these tend to undermine the existence of the international legal order. The health of a legal system is thus subject to fluctuations, declining at times of crisis and tension when legal scruples may be ignored to accommodate pressing political interests.

JAMES L. BRIERLY, "SANCTIONS"

17 Transact. Grot. Soc'y 68 (1932)

... [T]he habitual observance of International Law suggests, what every international lawyer knows to be the case, that there do exist sanctions behind the law. The real difference in this respect between municipal and International Law is not that the one is sanctioned and the other is not, but that in the one the sanctions are organized in a systematic procedure and that in the other they are left indeterminate. The true problem for consideration is therefore not whether we should try to create sanctions for International Law, but whether we should try to organize them in a system. In both kinds of law obedience is the rule and disobedience the exception, and in both the real inducing cause of the general obedience is the same....

LOUIS HENKIN, HOW NATIONS BEHAVE— LAW AND FOREIGN POLICY

29–30 (2d ed. 1979)

Every nation derives some benefits from international law and international agreements. Law keeps international society running, contributes to order and stability, provides for common enterprise and mutual intercourse. Because it limits the actions of other governments, law enhances each nation's independence and security; in other ways, too, by general law or particular agreement, one nation gets others to behave as it desires. General law establishes common standards where they seem desirable. Both general law and particular agreement avoid the need for negotiating anew in every new instance; both create justified expectation and warrant confidence as to how others will behave.

All these advantages of law and agreement have their price. Law limits freedom of action: nations are "bound" to do (or not to do) other than they might like when the time to act comes. Political arrangements legitimized by law are more difficult to undo or modify. Stability and order mean that a particular nation is not free to be disorderly or readily to promote external change. To promote its own independence and security and the inviolability of its territory, to control the behavior of other governments, a nation may have to accept corresponding limitations on its own behavior. For the confidence bred by law, one pays the price of not being free to frustrate the expectations of others.

MYRES S. McDOUGAL, "THE IMPACT OF INTERNATIONAL LAW UPON NATIONAL LAW: A POLICY-ORIENTED PERSPECTIVE"

4 S. Dak. L. Rev. 25, 50–51 (1959), *reprinted in* M. McDougal & Associates, Studies in World Public Order 157, 186–87 (1960)

It may perhaps require emphasis that, despite the absence from the world arena of a centralized executive organ, there are ample sanctions—if sanctions be defined as implementing techniques or available base values—at the disposal of the general community of states, assuming a willingness by states to employ sanctions, for securing that inclusive prescriptions are honored in actual conduct by a reasonable conformity. Exactly the same base values (power, wealth, respect, enlightenment, and so on) and exactly the same instruments of policy (diplomatic, ideological, economic, and military) may be used in support as an attack upon inclusive policy. The history of state interactions reveals a constant flow of examples in which all these base values and all these instruments of policy have been employed, in many differing combinations and in organized and unorganized modalities, for the enforcement of community prescription. The difficulty is that, on occasion, what has been missing is not efficient procedures but rather the appropriate predispositions of decision-makers, the general community consensus, necessary to sustain the application of sanctions. Decision-makers act ... like other men, to maximize their values as individuals and as members of all the groups and associations, including the state, with which they identify. The important decision-makers of the world arena have ... been able to clarify a long-term common interest in the enforcement of many inclusive prescriptions—such as with respect to the allocation of resources, the protection of diplomats, the making of agreements, the distribution of jurisdiction over particular events, and so on—and for sanctioning such prescriptions have established an elaborate network of expectations about reciprocal claim and mutual tolerance, promise of reciprocity and threat of retaliation, which in the main secures a high degree of effective application. For other prescriptions, such as the community prohibition of unauthorized violence, common interest has not yet been clarified in comparable degree, effective elites are not yet fully convinced that in destroying others they will destroy themselves, and expectations of enforcement are accordingly low. The task of enhancing the effectiveness of inclusive prescriptions in the world arena remains, in measure, a task of enlightenment.

ABRAM CHAYES AND ANTONIA HANDLER CHAYES, THE NEW SOVEREIGNTY—COMPLIANCE WITH INTERNATIONAL REGULATORY AGREEMENTS
17, 22–26, 28 (1995)

Compliance is not an on-off phenomenon. For a straightforward prohibitory norm like a highway speed limit, it is in principle a simple matter to determine whether any particular driver is in compliance. Yet there is a considerable zone within which behavior is accepted as adequately conforming. Most communities and law enforcement organizations in the United States, at least, seem to be perfectly comfortable with a situation in which the average speed on interstate highways is perhaps ten miles above the limit. The problem for the system is not how to induce all drivers to obey the speed limit, but how to contain deviance within acceptable levels. And so it is for international treaty obligations.

[*Eds.*—The authors, the first a former Legal Adviser to the US Department of State and the second a former Undersecretary of the US Air Force, next argue that "the principal source of noncompliance is not willful disobedience but the lack of capability or clarity or priority." They therefore conclude that compliance with international law at an acceptable level, at least within treaty regimes, is best cultivated not by "coercive enforcement," which "is as misguided as it is costly," but by a "management strategy" the elements of which "can be discerned in the characteristic activities of regulatory regimes, although they are not always employed with a full consciousness of their implications." They elaborate:]

At the simplest level, participating in the regime, attending meetings, responding to requests, and meeting deadline may lead to a realignment of domestic priorities and agendas, setting policies in motion that will operate to improve performance over time. But an array of more pointed activities can reinforce this general effect.

Ensuring Transparency

Transparency—the generation and dissemination of information about the requirements of the regime and the parties' performance under it—is an almost universal element of management strategy. Transparency influences strategic interaction among parties to the treaty in the direction of compliance....

* * *

Dispute Settlement

Where ambiguity or vagueness in treaty language creates compliance problems, the traditional prescription is dispute settlement machinery.... [M]ost treaty regimes turn to a variety of relatively informal mediative processes if the disputants are unable to resolve the issues among themselves.... On the whole, it has not seemed to matter whether the dispute settlement procedure is legally required or the decision is legally binding, so long as the outcome is treated as authoritative.

* * *

Capacity Building

Deficits of technical and financial resources have received increasing attention in the context of the difficulties of domestic enforcement of measures adopted in compliance with recent international environmental obligations. The current jargon is "capacity building," but technical assistance has been a major function of many treaty organizations for many years.

* * *

These disparate elements—transparency, dispute settlement, capacity building—all of which can be found in some regimes, can be considered to be parts of a management strategy. They merge into a broader process of "jawboning"—the effort to *persuade* the miscreant to change its ways—that is the characteristic method by which international regimes seek to induce compliance. It is remarkable that lawyers and international relations scholars, whose everyday stock-in-trade is persuasion—including persuasion of decision-makers—should pay so little attention and, by implication, attach so little significance to the role of argument, exposition, and persuasion in influencing state behavior. Our experience as well as our research indicates that, on the contrary, the fundamental instrument for maintaining compliance with treaties at an acceptable level is an iterative process of discourse among the parties, the treaty organization, and the wider public.

We propose that this process is usefully viewed as management, rather than enforcement. As in other managerial situations, the dominant atmosphere is one of actors engaged in a cooperative venture, in which performance that seems for some reason unsatisfactory represents a problem to be solved by mutual consultation and analysis, rather than an offense to be punished. States are under the practical necessity to give reasons and justifications for suspect conduct. These are viewed and critiqued not only in formal dispute settlement processes but also in a variety of other venues, public and private, formal and informal, where they are addressed and evaluated.... Often the upshot is agreement on a narrower and more concrete definition of the required performance, adapted to the circumstances of the case. At all stages, the putative offender is given every opportunity to conform. Persuasion and argument are the principal engines of this process, but if a party persistently fails to respond, the possibility of diffuse manifestations of disapproval or pressures from other actors in the regime is present in the background. * * * Inducing compliance through these interacting processes of justification, discourse, and persuasion is less dramatic than using coercive sanctions, but it is the way operational regimes in the real world go about it, for the most part.

HAROLD HONGJU KOH, "WHY DO NATIONS OBEY INTERNATIONAL LAW?"

106 Yale L. J. 2599, 2632–34, 2646, 2659 (1998)

The compliance literature has followed three distinct explanatory pathways.... The first, not surprisingly, is a rationalistic instrumentalist strand that views international rules as instruments whereby states seek to attain their interests in wealth, power, and the like [and use] increasingly sophisticated techniques of rational choice theory to argue that nation-states obey international law when it serves their short or long term self-interest to do so. Under this rationalistic account, pitched at the level of the international system, nations employ cooperative strategies to pursue a complex, multifaceted long-run national interest, in which compliance with negotiated legal norms serves as a winning long-term strategy in a reiterated "prisoner's dilemma" game.... [T]he more sophisticated instrumentalists are willing to disaggregate the state into its component parts, to introduce international institutions and transnational actors, to incorporate notions of long-term self-interest, and to consider the issue within the context of massively iterated multiparty games.

A second explanatory pathway follows a Kantian, liberal vein. The Kantian thread divides into two identifiable strands: one based on Franck's notion of rule-legitimacy, and another that makes more expansive claims for the causal role of national identity. "Liberal international relations" theorists ... have argued that the determinative factor for whether nations obey can be found, not at a systemic level, but at the level of domestic structure. Under this view, compliance depends significantly on whether or not the state can be characterized as "liberal" in identity, that is, having a form of representative government, guarantees of civil and political rights, and a judicial system dedicated to the rule of law. Flipping the now-familiar Kantian maxim that "democracies don't fight one another," these theorists posit that liberal democracies are more likely to "do law" with one another, while relations between liberal and illiberal states will more likely transpire in a zone of politics.

The third strand is a "constructivist" strand, based broadly on notions of both identity-formation and international society. Unlike interest theorists, who tend to treat state interests as given, "constructivists" have long argued that states and their interests are socially constructed by "commonly held philosophic principles, identities, norms of behavior, or shared terms of discourse"[27] [and thus] see norms as playing a critical role in the formation of national identities. * * * [T]he norms, values, and social structure of international society [help] to form the identity of actors who operate within it. Nations thus obey international rules not just because of sophisticated calcu-

27. M. Finnemore, National Interests in International Society 15 (1996).

lations about how compliance or noncompliance will affect their interests, but because a repeated habit of obedience remakes their interests so that they come to value rule compliance. In Andrew Hurrell's words, "[a] good deal of the compliance pull of international rules derives from the relationship between individual rules and the broader pattern of international relations: states follow specific rules, even when convenient, because they have a longer-term interest in the maintenance of law-impregnated international community."[28]

Each of these explanatory threads has significant persuasive power, and strongly complements the others. Yet ... none ... provides a sufficiently "thick" theory of the role of international law in promoting compliance with shared global norms. The short answer to the question, "Why do nations obey international law?" is not simply: "interest"; "identity"; "identity-formation"; and/or "international society." A complete answer must also account for the importance of *interaction* within the transnational legal process, *interpretation* of international norms, and domestic *internalization* of those norms as determinants of why nations obey. What is missing, in brief, is a modern version of the fourth historical strand of compliance theory—the strand based on *transnational legal process*.

* * *

... [S]uch a process can be viewed as having three phases. One or more transnational actors provokes an *interaction* (or series of interactions) with another, which forces an *interpretation* or enunciation of the global norm applicable to the situation. By so doing, the moving party seeks not simply to coerce the other party, but to *internalize* the new interpretation of the international norm into the other party's internal normative system. The aim is to "bind" that other party to obey the interpretation as part of its internal value set. Such a transnational legal process is normative, dynamic, and constitutive. The transaction generates a legal rule which will guide future transnational interactions between the parties; future transactions will further internalize those norms; and eventually, repeated participation in the process will help to reconstitute the interests and even the identities of the participants in the process.

* * *

"Why is it," Oran Young asked in 1992, "that an actor acquires and feels some sense of obligation to conform its behavior to the dictates or requirements of a regime or an institution? ... I think that there are differences in being obligated to do something because of a moral reason, a normative reason and a legal reason."[29] Although Young did not further specify, I would argue that these moral, normative, and legal reasons are in fact conjoined in the concept of obedience. A transnational actor's moral obligation to obey an international norm becomes an internally binding domestic legal obligation when that norm has been interpreted and internalized into its domestic legal system. Both Franck and the Chayeses, exemplars of the philosophical and

---

28. A. Hurrell, *International Society and the Study of Regimes: a Reflective Approach, in* Regime Theory and International Relations 49, 59 (V. Rittberger ed., 1993).

29. *International Law and International Relations Theory: Building Bridges,* 86 Am. Soc'y Int'l L. Proc. 172, 175 (1992) (remarks of Oran R. Young).

process traditions, respectively, recognize that transnational actors are more likely to comply with international law when they accept its legitimacy through some internal process.

It was precisely this "internal acceptance" that H.L.A. Hart found to be missing when he denied that international law satisfied the concept of law. Yet in Hart's own terms, a transnational legal process of interaction, interpretation, and internalization of global norms can provide both the "secondary rules" and the "rules of recognition" that Hart found missing from the international legal order.[u]

DISCUSSION NOTES/QUESTIONS

1. As noted above, even modern-day legal positivists concede the existence of international law. If the extracts from H.L.A. Hart, *supra*, are representative, however, they make this concession in only a limited sense; they ascribe to international law an elementary character analogous to the law found, ostensibly, in "primitive communities." According to Hart at least, international law manifests "primary rules of obligation," which are at "the heart a legal system," but not "secondary rules" of "recognition," "change," and "adjudication," which likewise are at "the heart of a legal system." Do you agree with Professor Hart's assessment of the primitiveness of international law? Is he correct in saying that the world community lacks rules of recognition, change, and adjudication? That so-called primitive communities lack such rules? Is it possible that Professor Hart may be exalting form over function?

2. "Up to a point," writes Thomas Franck, *supra*, at 68–69, "the Austinians are empirically right. The international system of states *is* fundamentally different from any national community of persons and of corporate entities." The implication of this statement is that international law and national law are fundamentally different. Do you agree? The international legal system, it is true, lacks the hierarchical decision-making institutions or structures present in national legal systems. But it nonetheless performs all of the same decision-making functions that national legal systems perform: intelligence-serving, recommending, invoking, prescribing, applying, appraising, and terminating. Is Franck's assertion thus vulnerable to criticism? Might it not be said that national and international law are fundamentally different institutionally but not functionally?

3. Professor Gottlieb refers to the existence of a "process of authoritative decision-making." What is a "process of authoritative decision"? What makes it authoritative? Do the Chayeses, Franck, Henkin, Koh, or McDougal, *supra*, shed any light on this question? What makes the decisions resulting from it authoritative? How do we know when a decision is "authoritative and controlling" and when it constitutes the exercise of merely "naked power"? How can we tell when a particular exercise of power is unauthoritative or lawless?

4. As we have seen, many scholars defend the existence of international law by pointing to its "binding" force, which in turn they validate by invoking notions of obligation, rule-legitimacy, consensus, sanctions, self-interest, reciprocity, iterative management, and transnational legal process, among others. In the end, is it not most accurate to say that none of these explanatory theories is invalid but that neither is any one of them fully explanatory, and that therefore only by accepting the entire intellectual landscape they cumulatively paint can we appreciate the full canvas of international law's existence and binding nature? Indeed, is

---

u. *See supra* text at 64–65.

it not possible that even this approach might be insufficient? Is it not possible that yet other theories might be added to the mix? If so, what might they be?

5. In everyday parlance, we speak of "the law of the jungle." Can there be a "law" of the jungle? Or is the jungle characterized by an absence of law? Is there "order" in the jungle? Is "law" synonymous with "order"? Is there international order? Is there international law? If so, is the law and/or order of the international system no more and no less than "the law of the jungle"?

6. Weston, *supra*, writes: "[N]o legal system, not even the most advanced, can boast absolute effectiveness; and all legal systems, again including the most advanced, typically display a certain impotence when it comes to politically volatile or otherwise intractable issues of public policy." Do you agree? Disagree? How might Brierly, the Chayeses, Gottlieb, Fitzmaurice, Franck, Henkin, Koh, and McDougal, *supra*, respond to this assertion. Does it threaten their theories about law compliance in the international system? What implications flow from an affirmative answer to this question? A negative answer?

7. Are the preconditions for effective law in the world community any different than the preconditions for effective law in national society? If so, how are they different? If not, how are they the same? Do Brierly, the Chayeses, Gottlieb, Fisher, Fitzmaurice, Franck, Henkin, Koh, or McDougal shed any light on these questions?

8. In general, from the standpoint of normative compliance, are national legal systems more effective or less effective than the international legal system? How? Why? Compare, in this connection, the following two comments:

> . . . I think it is very important to stress that it is true that 90 percent of the present system of international law is working [reasonably well]. Of course, we are worried about the remaining 10 percent in which we say the law is not working well enough just as we are worried domestically about teenage delinquency or about violations of human rights. Yes, we have the same problem internationally. We have the problem of proper international behaviour in the crucial area on which the peace of the world depends; and here, of course, I cannot say we have an adequate system. We are still far away from a system of world law which would really maintain peace and security, and of course this is what we are worried most about. Louis B. Sohn, *The Effectiveness of International Law, in* Essays on International Law 58, 63 (M. Nawaz ed., 1967).

> . . . [O]n empirical grounds, given the number of civil wars, wars of secession and *coups d'état* since—let us say—1945, a good case can be made out for saying that public international law is more efficacious than public law within States. At any rate, whether or not such a judgment is sustainable, those who would judge international law would do well, on grounds of logical consistency, to start out by taking a hard look at the performance of national legal systems. Ian Brownlie, *The Reality of International Law*, 52 B.Y.B.I.L. 1, 2–3 (1981).

With whom do you agree, Sohn or Brownlie? Both? Taking "effectiveness" to refer to the extent to which compliance with community norms is achieved, what conclusions do you reach when you act upon Professor Brownlie's suggestion?

9. Is there any legal system more effective than a national legal system in securing compliance with community-authorized norms? If so, which one(s) and why? If not, why not? Is there any legal system less effective than the internation-

al legal system? If so, which one(s) and why? If not, why not? Do your answers
depend at least in part on how you define "legal system"? On whether or not one
is considering "micro" and/or "private" legal systems (*e.g.,* church law, the law of
the playing field) as well as "macro" and/or "public" legal systems? All of the
above? None of the above? On "micro" legal systems, see W. Michael Reisman,
Law in Brief Encounters (1999).

10.   Is there any good reason not to consider international law as law?

CONCLUDING DISCUSSION NOTE/QUESTION

This chapter has dealt with international rules of great generality. We
have not yet considered the highly specific rules that were applied as war
crimes charges against the Nazi defendants at Nuremberg and that you might
seek to apply at the International Criminal Court. As we move from the broad
rule to the specific rule, are rules of international law likely to be harder or
easier to substantiate? To verify? To apply?

Chapter Two

INTERNATIONAL LEGAL PRESCRIPTION: THE "SOURCES" OF INTERNATIONAL LAW

Having recultivated your understanding of the concept of international law, you now turn to the matter of how international law is made—where we look to find the doctrines, principles, and rules that help to make up its content; and how we tell that a particular doctrine, principle, or rule actually has the force and effect of law. In your role as a junior lawyer assisting Prosecutor Luis Moreno–Ocampo of the International Criminal Court (ICC) in the investigation and possible prosecution of, *inter alia*, persons responsible for violations of international criminal law in Sudan's Darfur province since 1 July 2002, you know that no other aspect of your review of international law is likely to be more important, and few, if any, more difficult. You are aware, of course, that the ICC is an exception to the dearth of centralized legislative, judicial, and executive institutions in the international legal system and that Article 21 of the ICC's "constitution," the Rome Statute of the International Criminal Court **(Basic Document 1.16),** specifies the "sources" of law (the "applicable law") upon which the ICC Prosecutor and judges may rely when investigating and deciding cases brought to them Despite the relative absence of policy-and decision-making institutions at the regional and global levels in the present world order, Article 21 is proof that there are prescriptive (*i.e.,* law-making) processes by which expectations of authority and control become accepted as doctrines, principles, and rules of international law—that is, that there are "sources" of international law from which the norms (doctrines, principles, and rules) of international law may be extrapolated (including those applicable to the prosecution of war crimes and associated atrocities).

Your understanding of these so-called "sources" of international law is hazy, however, so you resume your study, knowing that this is the best way to respond, at least initially, to Prosecutor Moreno–Ocampo's request for legal assistance relative to Darfur. Thus, you reopen your treatise, turn to the chapter entitled "International Legal Prescription: The 'Sources' of International Law," and recommence your reading.

You begin by observing that the term "sources" is set off by quotation marks, as often it is in the legal literature, and you ask why. Another textbook addresses this question by another question, using the hydrographical analogy of a spring: "Is [the source of a spring] the place where water from the spring first appears on the surface of the ground," it asks, "or is it some subterranean area?"[a] You sense that the answer could be either or both of these alternatives, at least as applied to law or legal process. The water from the spring on the surface of the ground can be analogized to the statutes, administrative regulations, treaties, judicial decisions, customs, and other informational or material sources that communicate the doctrines, principles, and rules that are the corpus of the law in any given community. The water that is found in some subterranean area can be equated with the underlying community expectations that project the legal doctrines, principles, and rules and help to give them binding force and effect.

You reflect upon all of this, reminded of Professor M. H. Mendelson's warning on behalf of the International Law Association[b] in a working paper to the International Law Commission in 1988[c] that "in all discussions of theory metaphors should be treated with caution." Quickly, however, you note a widely accepted statement relied upon by the International Court of Justice (ICJ, or World Court) that indicates at least the "material sources" of international law, namely, Article 38 of the Statute of the International Court of Justice **(Basic Document 1.6)**:[d]

Article 38

1. The Court, whose function is to decide in accordance with international law such disputes as are submitted to it, shall apply:

(a) international conventions, whether general or particular, establishing rules expressly recognized by the contesting states;

(b) international custom, as evidence of a general practice accepted as law;

(c) the general principles of law recognized by civilized nations;

(d) subject to the provisions of Article 59,[e] judicial decisions and the teachings of the most highly qualified

a. The International Legal System—Cases and Materials 51 (W. Holder & G. Brennan eds., 1972).

b. The International Law Association was founded in Brussels in 1873. Its objectives, under its Constitution, include the "study, elucidation and advancement of international law, public and private, the study of comparative law, the making of proposals for the solution of conflicts of law and for the unification of law, and the furthering of international understanding and goodwill." The ILA has consultative status, as an international non-governmental organization, with a number of the United Nations specialised agencies. For details, see the ILA's web site at <http://www.ila-hq.org>.

c. See Appendix to First Report of the Rapporteur (1986): Formation of International Law and the Observational Standpoint, 63 Int'l L. Assoc., Report of the Conference 941, 954 (1988).

d. Hereinafter sometimes referred to as "the ICJ Statute." The ICJ is the principal judicial organ of the United Nations which, together with its unfortunately named predecessor, the Permanent Court of International Justice, is popularly known as "the World Court." The ICJ Statute is its "constitution."

e. Article 59 of the ICJ Statute provides: "The decision of the Court has no binding force except between the parties and in respect of that particular case."

publicists of the various nations, as subsidiary means for the determination of rules of law.

    2. This provision shall not prejudice the power of the Court to decide a case *ex aequo et bono*, **if the parties agree thereto.**

Technically speaking, you are aware, Article 38 is meant to apply to the ICJ. It is, after all, a provision of the legal instrument that governs the World Court. But you know, too, that Article 38 has come to have a life beyond the Court, helping to define the legal authority upon which decision-makers and theorists of all kinds decide cases, solve problems, and advocate policies throughout the international system. Additionally, its enumeration of "sources" or law-making processes is not complete. Drawn almost word-for-word from the statute that governed the Permanent Court of International Justice between World Wars I and II, its text does not account explicitly for the innovations in international law-making (prescription) that have emerged since that earlier time—for example, the resolutions and declarations of the United Nations and other international governmental institutions, many of which are of great importance to the laws of war, to human rights, and to other matters relevant to the prosecution of war crimes and associated atrocities. Nevertheless, Article 38 does address the historically venerable "sources" of international legal authority, and it is therefore fitting, you conclude, to revisit their meaning and significance.

    Before you do so, however, you wisely look at the Rome Statute **(Basic Document 1.16)** governing the ICC—a "convention" within the meaning of Article 38(1)(a) of the ICJ Statute—and in particular its Article 21.

Article 21

Applicable law

    1. The Court shall apply:

        (a) In the first place, this Statute, Elements of Crimes and its Rules of Procedure and Evidence;

        (b) In the second place, where appropriate, applicable treaties and the principles and rules of international law, including the established principles of the international law of armed conflict;

        (c) Failing that, general principles of law derived by the Court from national laws of legal systems of the world including, as appropriate, the national laws of States that would normally exercise jurisdiction over the crime, provided that those principles are not inconsistent with this Statute and with international law and internationally recognized norms and standards.

    2. The Court may apply principles and rules of law as interpreted in its previous decisions.

    3. The application and interpretation of law pursuant to this article must be consistent with internationally recognized human rights, and be without any adverse distinction founded on grounds such as gender as defined in article 7,

paragraph 3, age, race, colour, language, religion or belief, political or other opinion, national, ethnic or social origin, wealth, birth or other status.

You observe, of course, that, in contrast to Article 38(1)(b) of the ICJ Statute, Article 21 of the Rome Statute contains no general reference to "international custom." This is explained, you sense, first by the Rome Statute's seemingly implicit embrace of customary law in Paragraph 1(b), authorizing the ICC to apply "principles and rules of international law, including the established principles of the international law of armed conflict," and, second, by references to "custom" in its specialized provision defining "war crimes" (art. 8). Paragraphs 8(2)(b) and 8(2)(e) of the Rome Statute, you note, define "war crimes" to include, *inter alia*, "serious violations of the laws *and customs* applicable in international armed conflict, within the established framework of international law" and "serious violations of the laws *and customs* applicable in armed conflicts not of an international character, within the established framework of international law" (emphasis added). Unlike the Rome Statute's definitions of "genocide" (art. 6) and "crimes against humanity"(art. 7), which derive essentially from the 1948 Convention on the Prevention and Punishment of the Crime of Genocide **(Basic Document 3.2)** and the 1947 Final Judgment of the International Military Tribunal at Nuremberg **(Basic Document 7.4)**, the meaning of "war crimes," you are aware, necessarily entails centuries of state practice "accepted as law" prior to and following those post-World War II events. As noted hereinafter, international law prior to World War II relied mostly on doctrines, principles, and rules developed through the customary practice of states rather than treaties.[f]

Now, satisfied that your mandate from Prosecutor Moreno–Ocampo requires thorough understanding of international legal custom as well as treaties, general principles of law, and other "sources" relevant to the ICC's substantive jurisdiction, you resume your study.

A. TREATIES

The first "source" of international law listed in Article 38 of the ICJ Statute is "international conventions," another name for "treaties" and the preferred term in Article 1 of the Rome Statute where such instruments, including the Rome Statute itself, are also listed. Generally speaking, putting treaties first makes sense. Defined in Article 2(1)(a) of the 1969 Vienna Convention on the Law of Treaties **(Basic Document 1.10)** to mean "an international agreement concluded between states in written form and governed by international law," a treaty is the result ordinarily of extensive deliberation and negotiation and, as such, should be an especially strong "source" of law. But it is a strong source, too, because, more importantly, it contains the mutual promises of the states parties consenting to it, which of course is very powerful evidence that the terms agreed to should be "binding" on them. Indeed, the idea of mutual consent underlies one of the most basic principles of international law—the principle of *pacta sunt servanda*, to wit, that states are bound to keep the promises they make. In any event, the idea that treaties constitute a powerful "source" of international law was clearly

---

f. *See infra* text accompanying note **z**, at 106.

the legal perspective of the Allied Powers who, following World War II, prosecuted the German Nazi leaders at Nuremberg.[g] It was embedded in the governing instruments of the ICTY and ICTR.[h] And, obviously, it was fully understood by the drafters of the Rome Statute and, we may infer, the UN Security Council when it submitted the Darfur case to the ICC.[i] However, whereas the enumeration of "sources" in ICJ Statute Article 38 (and by implication the governing instruments of the ICTY and ICTR) may be misleading if the numerical sequence is seen as giving *absolute* priority to treaties over custom (or to custom over general principles, etc.),[j] treaties are most definitely accorded primary status in Rome Statute Article 21. Only ICC practice will tell just how strictly Article 21 is interpreted.[k]

Of course, as you contemplate the seeming disregard of treaties pertinent to the Darfur international crimes trials for which you are preparing—for example, the 1949 Geneva Convention (No. IV) Relative to the Protection of Civilian Persons in Time of War **(Basic Document 2.12)** or the 1966 International Covenant on Civil and Political Rights **(Basic Document 3.14)** to each of which Sudan is a party—you wonder whether this fact is fully appreciated by those who may be on trial by the ICC, and, if so, how they will be able to rationalize their behavior in light of the treaties. Taking no chances, you decide to explore the nature, meaning, and significance of treaties further, and, in particular, the extent to which they give international law shape and substance.

1.   THE IMPORTANCE OF TREATIES

PETER MALANCZUK, AKEHURST'S MODERN INTRODUCTION TO INTERNATIONAL LAW

36–37 (7th ed. 1997)

Treaties are of growing importance in international law.... Modern technology, communications and trade have made states more interdependent than ever before, and more willing to accept rules on a vast range of problems of common concern—extradition of criminals, safety regulations for ships and aircraft, economic aid, copyright, standardization of road signs, protection of foreign investment, environmental issues, and so on. The rules in question are usually laid down in treaties, with the result that international law has expanded beyond all recognition in the last [145] years (although it must be pointed out that most of the rules are too specialised to be dealt with in ordinary textbooks on international law). * * * Treaties are the major instrument of co-operation in international relations, and co-operation often in-

g. *See Indictment*, 1 International Military Tribunal, Trial of the Major War Criminals 29–40 (1947).

h. *See* the 1993 Statute of the International Tribunal [for the Prosecution of Persons Responsible for Serious Violations of International Humanitarian Law Committed in the Territory of the former Yugoslavia since 1991] **(Basic Document 2.43)** and 1994 UN Security Council Resolution 955 Establishing the International Tribunal for Rwanda **(Basic Document 2.46)**.

i. This is evident not only in Article 21(1)(b) of the Rome Statute **(Basic Document 1.16)** But, as well, in Article 21(1)(a) referencing the Statute (a treaty) itself.

j. For pertinent comment, see Discussion Note/Question 3 in "Concluding Notes/Questions" at the end of this chapter.

k. On the interpretation of treaties, see *infra* text, at 100–103.

volves a change in the relative positions of the states involved.... Treaties, therefore, are often an instrument of change—a point which is forgotten by those who regard international law as essentially a conservative force....

MYRES S. MCDOUGAL, HAROLD D. LASSWELL & JAMES C. MILLER, THE INTERPRETATION OF AGREEMENTS AND WORLD PUBLIC ORDER
3–5 (1967)

Even in a community which aspires only to minimum public order, in the sense of the prevention and repression of unauthorized violence, agreements are of central importance: agreements, explicit and implicit, are indispensable for establishing a stability in peoples' expectations which lessens predispositions for arbitrary resort to violence. In a community which projects, beyond minimum order, the goals of an optimum public order, in the sense of the greatest production and widest sharing of all human values, agreements assume an even greater significance. In such a community agreements serve both to secure that values are shaped and shared more by persuasion than coercion and to organize initiatives for the effective employment of resources in the maximum production and distribution of valued social outcomes.

The important role of agreements in the most comprehensive contemporary community of [humankind] relates, thus, to both minimum order and optimum order. It is by agreement most broadly conceived—that is, when agreement is conceived to include the whole flow of peoples' collaborative behavior—that the effective participants in earth-space power processes establish an overall "constitutive process"—identifying authoritative decision-makers, projecting fundamental community objectives, affording structure of authority, providing bases of power in authority and other values, legitimizing or condemning different strategies in persuasion and coercion, and allocating competence among effective participants over different authority functions and value interactions for the maintenance of a modest minimum order. It is by agreement, further, when agreement is no less broadly conceived, that the established decision-makers perform the important authority function of prescribing, of "legislating," general community policies about the detailed activities which comprise world social process in pursuit of all values. It is by agreement also, when the basic constitutive process of the general community is appropriately maintained, that the many different participants in the world social process—territorially organized communities, international governmental organizations, political parties, pressure groups, private associations, and individuals—express their creative initiatives and organize their base values to get on with the world's work in producing and distributing new values.

Given this important role of agreements in contemporary earth-space public order, the urgent need for appropriate general community procedures and principles to facilitate the making and application of agreements can scarcely require elaboration. The urgency of this need can, further, be expected to accelerate in proportion as the interdependencies of peoples accelerate in the [present] era, with both its threats of potentially comprehensive destruction and its promises of a productivity in all values hitherto beyond fantasy.

2. DEFINITION, NATURE, AND SIGNIFICANCE OF TREATIES

EDITORS' NOTE

As noted above, according to Article 2 of the 1969 Vienna Convention on the Law of Treaties **(Basic Document 1.10)** a treaty is "an international agreement concluded between states in written form and governed by international law." The form is of no consequence, and some writers say, contrary to the express language of Article 2, that it is not even necessary that a treaty be in writing. As stated in *Starke's* International Law 397 (I. Shearer 11th ed. 1994), "[a]n oral declaration in the nature of a promise made by the Minister of Foreign Affairs of one country to the Minister of Foreign Affairs of another and in a matter within his or her competence and authority may be as binding as a formal written treaty." To which may be added that, "even though the modern practice is for the original text of a treaty to be typed or printed, there is no reason why a treaty should not be contained in a telegram, telex, fax message or even email, or, rather, constituted by an exchange of such communications." Anthony Aust, Modern Treaty Law and Practice 16 (2000). In any event, a treaty need not be called a treaty to be one, as treaties go by different names (the Rome *Statute*, for example), indicating differences in procedure and/or formality. "Thus besides the term "treaty" itself, the following titles have been given: (1) *Convention.* (2) *Protocol.* (3) *Agreement.* (4) *Arrangement.* (5) *Procès-Verbal.* (6) *Statute.* (7) *Covenant.* (8) *Declaration.* (9) *Modus Vivendi.* (10) *Exchange of Notes (or of Letters).* (11) *Final Act.* (12) *General Act....* As to the term "treaty" itself, this tends to be given to formal agreements relative to peace, alliance, or the cession of territory, or some other fundamental matter." *Starke's, supra,* at 401.

DAVID H. OTT, PUBLIC INTERNATIONAL LAW IN THE MODERN WORLD
23–24 (1987)

Types of treaties. Treaties may be either *bilateral* (between only two parties) or *multilateral* (between more than two parties).

Nature of treaties. A treaty may serve in effect as an international contract between two states, or it may be what will be called here a "law-making" treaty, or it may very rarely have a legislative effect.

Contractual treaties. Some writers ... have suggested that treaties are strictly speaking sources of obligation rather than sources of law. That is, treaties of the kind intended do not establish a regime of legal principles and rules against which the conduct of the parties can be measured, but rather simply state the mutual obligations which the parties have undertaken to perform. Treaties which have this character may properly be called "contractual" by analogy to contracts in private law.

"Law-making" treaties. "Law-making" treaties are concerned with establishing general norms or overall legal regimes in accordance with which the parties to such a treaty agree to order their conduct and relations with each other.

Whereas the operative effect of a contractual agreement may come to an end when the parties have done (or failed to do) certain specified things, a law-making treaty may involve an open-ended commitment to a certain legal regime without regard to the parties' performance of reciprocal obligations. * * * The UN Charter **[Basic Document 1.5]**, as regards the members of the organization, ... functions as a constitutional and law-making treaty whereby, for example, the members have general obligations to the international community not to disrupt international peace and security as well as bilateral obligations to each other in that regard.

"Legislative" treaties. Although there is no reason in principle why states should not establish law-making treaties for themselves, there is an objection in principle to what we are calling here "legislative" treaties, *i.e.*, treaties concluded by some states which purport to determine law and obligations incumbent upon other states that are not parties.

Customary international law[l] and Article 34 of the Vienna Convention **[Basic Document 1.10]** adopt the position that in general a treaty does not create obligations or rights for a third state without its consent. The effect of this would be that there are no legislative treaties in the sense described, but occasionally suggestions are nevertheless made that certain treaties are in fact legislative.

Lord McNair, for example, argued that there could be "dispositive" treaties creating or affecting territorial rights and effectively imposing legal consequences on third parties, and "constitutive or semi-legislative" treaties establishing international legal regimes of one kind or another.

In 1920 a commission of jurists appointed by the League of Nations to consider the legal position regarding the Aaland Islands, lying at the mouth of the Gulf of Bothnia between Sweden and Finland, concluded that a treaty of 1856 created a special international status for the islands such that every interested state (whether party to the 1856 treaty or not) had the right to insist upon compliance with the treaty provisions.

In the *Reparation for Injuries Suffered in the Service of the United Nations Case* (1949),[m] the World Court held that the UN Charter created the UN as an entity possessing "objective international personality" such that Israel, though not a member of the UN at the relevant time, was obliged to acknowledge the UN's existence and pay it damages for the assassination of the UN's representative in Jerusalem by Jewish terrorists.

Professor Hans Kelsen has gone further and suggested that the Charter imposes general obligations on non-members by virtue of Article 2(6), which requires the UN to "ensure that states which are not members of the United Nations act in accordance with" the organisation's principles. Professor Kelsen himself calls this a "revolutionary" application of the Charter, and precisely for that reason it has been strongly contested by many writers.

HANS KELSEN, PRINCIPLES OF INTERNATIONAL LAW
456 (R. Tucker 2d rev. ed. 1966)

... By concluding a treaty the contracting states apply a norm of customary international law—the rule *pacta sunt servanda* (treaties must be,

---

l. *See infra* Section B of this chapter, at 106–39.

m. 1949 ICJ 174 (Advisory Opinion).

or ought to be, observed, that is, have binding force)—and at the same time create a norm of international law, the norm which presents itself as the treaty obligation of one or all of the contracting parties, and as the treaty right of the other or the others. Legal obligations and legal rights are always the function of a legal norm determining the behavior of an individual. The term "norm" designates the objective phenomenon whose subjective reflections are obligation and right. The statement that the treaty has "binding force" means nothing but that the treaty is or creates a norm establishing obligations and rights of the contracting parties. Thus the treaty has a law-applying and at the same time a law-creating character. It has a law-applying character because every conclusion of a treaty is the application of the rule of general international law *pacta sunt servanda*; it has a law-creating function because every treaty constitutes obligations and rights that, prior to the conclusion of the treaty, had not yet existed, obligations and rights which come into existence by the treaty.

Morton A. Kaplan and Nicholas deB. Katzenbach, The Political Foundations of International Law
239–40 (1961)

In the view of legal scholars, the "law of treaties" is largely derived from general principles of contract common to the various domestic legal systems. The consensual approach to international law promotes this analytical method. So, too, does the fact that most treaties are formally bilateral arrangements between two states, rather than general "legislation" for the international community. Many such arrangements are cast in the form, and perhaps even have the substance, of mutual advantage and reciprocal rights, thus promoting a "bargain" concept characteristic of a contractual prototype. But it is sobering to remember, too, that the parties to these "contracts" are political entities, represented by governments subject to the vicissitudes of politics, and that they double as international legislators. The contract analysis can be overdone, for there may be overriding considerations which demonstrate that it is no longer in the interest of the community as a whole to insist on literal compliance with a particular agreement, or situations where it is not possible politically for a government to honor its international commitments. It is certainly unrealistic now, and even yesterday, to think of the international community as little more than a series of bilateral arrangements among various participants. * * * [T]reaties are almost always something more than, or different from a contractual arrangement. And the legislative analogy helps us to see why this is true.

Richard B. Bilder, Managing the Risks of International Agreement
7–8, 10–11 (1981)

In the last analysis, of course, international agreements are only pieces of paper and nations can and on occasion do violate their agreements. But agreements are very special pieces of paper, which serve to reinforce the expectations of their parties by drawing upon deeply and widely held human norms, developed over millennia of social experience, supporting the sanctity of solemnly made promises. There is ample evidence that nations generally take their agreements very seriously, treat them as real commitments, and do not enter into them lightly. Indeed, if nations did not believe international agreements were useful and effective, they would not bother to enter into so many of them and would enter into them with less care and deliberation than they usually do. . . .

* * *

Nonetheless, to say that international agreements usually work does not mean that nations regard them as establishing completely rigid commitments or deal with treaty problems solely in legalistic terms. . . . [G]overnment officials probably look at questions of treaty obligation and breach more flexibly and in a broader context than traditional legal analysis assumes. For them, an agreement will often be not simply an instrument for creating legal rights and obligations but a multipurpose foreign policy tool, constituting one element in the more complex pattern of their nation's overall foreign policy. In this broader context, other foreign policy objectives will sometimes be more important than ensuring performance of the agreement. Indeed, decisions respecting international agreements will sometimes turn on solely domestic rather than foreign policy considerations; internal political pressures may dictate participation in agreements which otherwise make little sense, or prevent participation in agreements of great potential benefit. Moreover, government officials will recognize that agreements are made with varying degrees of commitment—that some are meant to be taken less seriously than others; that changing expectations and external or domestic circumstances can create pressures for one or more parties which must be pragmatically dealt with if the agreement is not to break; and that treaty disputes are more likely to signal real problems in the balance and fairness of the agreement than to result from attempts to "cheat." Consequently, they will tend to see the obligation to perform agreements in good faith in terms of these realities, to be interpreted and judged not only by the past balance of forces in which the treaty was formed but also by the present and future balance of forces in which it must be implemented. Finally, while legal rights and obligations will affect the perceived legitimacy of the different parties' positions in the event of a dispute, and thus their respective strategies in trying to resolve the dispute, law alone will not necessarily determine either the parties' responses or the eventual outcome. Government officials will be aware that a particular treaty dispute is only one incident in what must inevitably be a continuing relationship with the other nation; in an interdependent world, most countries will have little choice but, sooner or later, to do business with each other. As is often the case in business contract disputes, pressing one's treaty partner unduly, "taking him to court," or winning the dispute may be poor long-run policy, and accommodation and compromise through negotiation and express or tacit amendment will often appear much more sensible. The net result of these perceptions and tendencies towards accommodation is that in the real world, international agreements, far from creating once-and-for-all expectations and commitments, constantly change and evolve as the circumstances and the parties' expectations change.

HILARY CHARLESWORTH AND CHRISTINE CHINKIN, THE BOUNDARIES OF INTERNATIONAL LAW: A FEMINIST ANALYSIS

96–123 (2000)

Treaties have become increasingly important . . . as a means of securing states' commitment to legal obligations. The major advantages of treaties as a source of international law are perceived to be the certainty of a written text and the comparative ease of determining the parties. . . .

The process of treaty-making

Treaty-making is sometimes seen as analogous to the process of contract-making in national law. Common to both of these mechanisms is the idea of the autonomous person freely entering a binding agreement. The voluntarist understanding of international law underpins the law of treaties, emphasizing the importance of consent as a basis for obligation. . . . [T]his account of law is coded as "male" in contrast to alternatives that give priority to communitarian values.

Treaty negotiation

Treaty-making [involves] the doctrine of full powers whereby a state representative has authority to bind the state, and * * * [t]hroughout the process of treaty negotiation . . . [t]he subject matter for international regulation derives from the interests of states as articulated within domestic and international fora. The low level of women's participation in national government policy formulation and decision-making bodies, especially those relating to foreign and economic policies and national security, ensures that matters considered of international concern are defined by men. Women within negotiating teams may find it difficult to be taken seriously and to make their voices heard. . . .

Not only are women under-represented in government bodies that play leading roles in treaty-making, they also have little voice in the international law-making bodies. For example, there has never been a woman on the thirty-four member International Law Commission (ILC) which has the responsibility for the codification and progressive development of international law under the UN Charter.ⁿ . . . Similar law-making work has been undertaken by other bodies both within and outside the UN structure that have few active women members in positions of influence. The "invisible college" of scholars, described by Oscar Schachter as incorporating values and interests into the international legal process that do not necessarily reflect those of states,[1] has been traditionally dominated by men. Similarly the writers of the most frequently cited texts have also been men. There is an interactive process, as academics and non-governmental bodies draw upon the meticulous and detailed work of the ILC, and governments use these materials in preparing statements, briefs and policy positions, allowing what . . . Schachter has called

---

n. *See supra* note **h** in Chapter 1.

1. O. Schachter, *The Invisible College of International Lawyers*, 72 Nw. U. L. Rev. 217, 217 (1977).

a "*pénétration pacifique* of ideas from government to non-government."[2] The effect is an accumulation of material being consistently considered and evaluated from a single-gendered perspective.

NGOs and treaty-making

. . . NGOs have to some limited extent lessened the state monopoly in the treaty-drafting process . . . [and] women's NGOs have been strong in promoting humanitarian and social reform since before the time of the League of Nations. * * * [H]owever, the effect of NGOs on both treaty-making and the agreement of non-binding instruments remains limited in important ways. Throughout treaty negotiations the interests of all participants are mediated in the search for a mutually acceptable text. This leads to compromises and trading of texts and states may seek to neutralise NGO influence in these processes. Thus some international bodies remain impervious to NGO activity and access to international arenas remains susceptible to government exclusion. NGO registration practices at the global conferences have not been consistent, nor can NGOs participate directly in formal drafting sessions unless governments concur. . . .

Women's NGOs have been successful at recent UN conferences in inserting some reference to women's interests into final conference texts. However, men continue to dominate mainstream non-governmental bodies. This has led to a failure to recognise the relevance of power imbalances between women and men on social and economic issues. In this sense there must be caution about regarding the growing prominence of NGOs in international treaty-making as being inevitably of major benefit for women.

Reservations

The voluntarist account of international law underpins the right of a state to qualify its acceptance of treaty terms through reservations . . . [and] [s]tandard-setting human rights treaties have proved to be especially vulnerable to reservations. . . .

The Women's Convention **[Basic Document 3.21]** has been particularly susceptible to reservations and "interpretative declarations." As of December 1998 over fifty states had entered reservations to the Women's Convention. A number of these . . . raise fundamental questions about the purpose of the Convention and the seriousness with which the international community regards its objective of achieving equality for women. Article 28(2) . . . follows the Vienna Convention [on the Law of Treaties **(Basic Document 1.10)**] by prohibiting incompatible reservations . . . , [but] [t]here is no specific article to which reservations are prohibited, nor are there any non-derogable rights. The consequences of an incompatible reservation or of an objection to a reservation are not spelled out. Other states have made reservations to the effect that their domestic law prevails in specific instances. * * * The impression is created that the Convention is not as binding an international obligation as other treaties, and that these reservations need not be scrutinised against the yardstick of international standards of equality for women because of their religious and cultural sensitivity of the subject matter. In contrast there are few substantive reservations to the Convention on the

2. *Id.*

Elimination of All Forms of Racial Discrimination **[Basic Document 3.12]**
. . ., and none on the basis of religion or culture. . . . [R]eluctance to confront
Islamic, oil-producing states has undermined . . . support for the elimination
of gender [discrimination], as demonstrated by the adverse response within
the UN to proposals to tackle the reservations problem.

* * *

The international law relating to reservations reflects the problems of
constructing international communal norms in a system based on consent. In
the particular context of the equality of women, some states have used the
reservation mechanism effectively to hollow out the heart of their formal
obligations.

[*Eds.*—The authors turn next, under the heading "Treaty termination,"
to the question of "how states can be held to their obligations and what the
sanctions are for non-compliance." They first observe, approvingly, that
"withdrawal is not envisaged" under the Women's Convention (CEDAW), and
that "the drastic step of termination or suspension" on the grounds of
another party's material breach would be not only "counter-productive" but,
as well, contrary to Article 60(5) of the Vienna Convention exempting "provisions relating to the protection of the human person." They observe also,
again approvingly, that the Women's Convention grants jurisdiction to the
World Court relative to the interpretation and application of the Convention's
terms, including arguably "allegations of material breach," and, further, that
the 1999 Optional Protocol to the Convention **(Basic Document 3.52)**,
which entered into force in 2000, "allow[s] a new type of pressure for change"
by authorizing individuals to bring complaints about violations. However,
noting that the Women's Convention enforcement provision provides "only
for periodic state reporting" and that a potential for "restrictive interpretation" of the World Court's jurisdiction, supported by "the many reservations"
made relative to it, is real, the authors implicitly acknowledge the many
hurdles in the way of meaningful compliance. They then conclude:]

The law of treaties can be regarded with ambivalence by women. On the
one hand, . . . [treaties provide] greater certainty as to the extent of obligation
than customary international law. . . . [They] also can be incorporated into
national policies, guidelines and legislation. Women activists consequently
tend to regard the attainment of treaty support for their goals as a benchmark
of success. On the other hand, treaties as a source of law are limited by their
voluntaristic nature, based on a model of individual consent. The process of
giving consent has largely excluded women and the subject matter and
substantive content of most treaties reflect a limited perspective. In many
instances, international standards are not implemented into domestic law or
are simply not observed. The law of treaties reinforces voluntarism through
doctrines such as that relating to reservations and limited declarations. . . .

3. CONCLUSION AND ACCEPTANCE OF TREATIES

Starke's International Law
409–18 (I. Shearer 11th ed. 1994)

(2) Negotiation and adoption

Negotiations concerning a treaty are conducted either through discussions in the case of bilateral treaties or by a diplomatic Conference, the more

usual procedure when a multilateral treaty is to be adopted. In both cases the delegates remain in touch with their governments, they have with them preliminary instructions which are not communicated to the other parties, and at any stage they may consult their governments and, if necessary, obtain fresh instructions. As a matter of general practice, before appending their signature to the final text of the treaty, delegates do obtain fresh instructions to sign the instrument whether with or without reservations.

The procedure at diplomatic Conferences runs to a standard pattern. Apart from Steering Committees, Legal and Drafting Committees are appointed at an early stage to receive and review the draft provisions proposed by the various delegations. Usually, too, the Conference appoints a prominent delegate to act as rapporteur in order to assist the Conference in its deliberations. Besides the formal public sessions ..., many parleys are conducted in the "corridors," in hotel rooms, and at special dinners and functions. The results of these appear in due course in the decisions reached by the Conference.

Article 9, paragraph 2 of the Vienna Convention [on the Law of Treaties] **[Basic Document 1.10]** provides that the adoption of a treaty text at an international conference is to take place by the vote of two-thirds of the states present and voting, unless by the same majority these states decide to apply a different rule.

It should be mentioned that in respect of certain subjects at least, the procedure of adoption of multilateral instruments by diplomatic Conferences has been replaced by the method of their adoption by the organs of international institutions; for example, by—among others—the United Nations General Assembly, the World Health Assembly, and the Assembly of the International Civil Aviation Organization [ICAO]. The Conventions adopted by such Assembly are opened for signature or acceptance by member or non-member states.

* * *

(3) Authentication, signature and exchange of instruments

When the final draft of the treaty has been agreed upon, the instrument is ready for signature. The text may be made public for a certain period before signature.... The act of signature is usually a most formal matter, even in the case of bilateral treaties. As to multilateral conventions, signature is generally effected at a formal closing session (*séance de clôture*) in the course of which each delegate steps up to a table and signs on behalf of the head of state or government by whom they were appointed.°

Unless there is an agreement to dispense with signature, this is essential for a treaty, principally because it serves to authenticate the text. The rule, as stated in article 10 of the Vienna Convention, is that the text may be authenticated by such procedure as is laid down in the treaty itself, or as is agreed to by the negotiating states, or in the absence of such agreed procedure, by signature, signature ad referendum, initialing, or by incorporation in the Final Act of the conference. In practice, also, the text of an instrument may be authenticated by the resolution of an international organisation. If a treaty is signed, it is important that the signature should be made by each of

o. Sometimes not merely a delegate but a Head of State will sign a treaty.

the delegates at the same time and place, and in the presence of each other. Furthermore, the date of the treaty is usually taken to be the date on which it was signed.

* * *

It is a common practice to open a convention [or treaty] for signature by certain states until a certain date after the date of the formal session of signature. Generally, this period does not exceed nine months. The object is to obtain as many parties to the convention as possible, but inasmuch as new signatories can only be allowed with the consent of the original signatories, a special clause to this effect must be inserted in the convention. A current practice is to open a convention for signature to all members of the United Nations and the specialised agencies, to all parties to the Statute of the International Court of Justice **[Basic Document 1.6]**, and to any other state invited by the [UN] General Assembly. During the period mentioned, each state may sign at any time, but after the expiration of the period no further signatures are allowed and a non-signatory state desiring to become a party must accede or adhere to the convention but cannot ratify, inasmuch as it has not signed the instrument....

A further expedient has been, by the so-called *acceptance formula clause*, to open an instrument for an indefinite time for: (a) signature, without reservation as to acceptance; (b) signature subject to, and followed by later acceptance; and (c) acceptance simpliciter, leaving states free to become bound by any one of these three methods. The term "acceptance," used in this clause, has crept into recent treaty terminology to denote the act of becoming a party to a treaty by adherence of any kind, in accordance with a state's municipal constitutional law. The principal object of this clause was indeed to meet difficulties which might confront a potential state party under its municipal constitutional rules relative to treaty approval....

* * *

Effect of signature

The effect of signature of a treaty depends on whether or not the treaty is subject to ratification, acceptance, or approval.

If the treaty is subject to ratification, acceptance, or approval, signature means no more than that the delegates have agreed upon a text and are willing to accept it and refer it to their governments for such action as those governments may choose to take in regard to the acceptance or rejection of the treaty. It may also indicate an intention on the part of a government to make a fresh examination of the question dealt with by the treaty with a view to putting the treaty into force. In the absence of an express term to that effect, there is no binding obligation on a signatory state to submit the treaty to the national legislature for action or otherwise. On the other hand, it is laid down in [Article 18 of] the Vienna Convention that, where a treaty is subject to ratification, acceptance, or approval, signatory states are under an obligation of good faith to refrain from acts calculated to defeat the object of the treaty until they have made their intention clear of not becoming parties....

Where a treaty is subject to ratification, acceptance or approval, it is sometimes expressly stipulated in the treaty or in some related exchange of notes that, pending ratification, acceptance, or approval, the instrument is to operate on a provisional basis as from the date of signature. . . .

If the treaty is not subject to ratification, acceptance, or approval, or is silent on this point, the better opinion is that, in the absence of contrary provision, the instrument is binding as from signature. . . . Also many treaties relating to minor or technical matters, generally bearing the titles "Agreement," "Arrangement" or "Procès-Verbal," are simply signed but not ratified, and operate as from the date signature is appended. . . .

* * *

(4) Ratification

The next stage is that the delegates who signed the treaty or convention refer it back to their governments for approval, if such further act of confirmation be expressly or impliedly necessary.

In theory, ratification is the approval by the head of state or the government of the signature appended to the treaty by the duly appointed plenipotentiaries. In modern practice, however, it has come to possess more significance than a simple act of confirmation, being deemed to represent the formal declaration by a state of its consent to be bound by a treaty. So in article 2 of the Vienna Convention, ratification was defined to mean "the international act . . . whereby a state establishes on the international plane its consent to be bound by a treaty." Consistently with this, ratification is not held to have retroactive effect, so as to make the treaty obligatory from the date of signature.

* * *

Ratification and municipal constitutional law

The development of constitutional systems of government under which various organs other than the head of state are given a share in the treaty-making power has increased the importance of ratification. At the same time in each country the procedure followed in this regard differs. For instance, often states will insist on parliamentary approval or confirmation of a treaty although the treaty expressly provides that it operates as from signature, whereas other states follow the provisions of the treaty and regard it as binding them without further steps being taken.

* * *

Some treaties make signature subject to "acceptance" or "approval"; these terms may then denote a simplified form of ratification. In fact, in article 2 of the Vienna Convention, "acceptance" and "approval" have received the same definition as ratification, while the provisions of article 14 as to when ratification imports consent to be bound by a treaty apply mutatis mutandis to acceptance and approval.

Absence of duty to ratify

The power of refusing ratification is deemed to be inherent in state sovereignty, and accordingly at international law there is . . . [no] duty to ratify a treaty. Furthermore, there is no obligation other than one of ordinary courtesy to convey to other states concerned a statement of the reasons for refusing to ratify.

* * *

Obligation not to defeat the object and purpose of a treaty prior to its entry into force

The rule stated by article 18 of the Vienna Convention [not to defeat the object and purpose of a treaty following signature or expression of consent to be bound but prior to the treaty's entry into force] is regarded as one of customary international law.... The effect of this rule is not to make an unratified treaty, or one not yet in force, in all respects binding, for that would be to deprive those steps of meaning. Rather, a state is bound by good faith not to take up or persist in an action or posture fundamentally at variance with the treaty until it has definitively disavowed its intention to proceed to the ratification of the treaty that it has signed.

Exchange or deposit of ratifications

Unless the treaty itself otherwise provides, an instrument of ratification has no effect in finally establishing consent to be bound by the treaty until the exchange or deposit, as the case may be, of ratifications, or at least until some notice of ratification is given to the other state or states concerned, or to the depositary of the treaty, is so agreed [Vienna Convention, art. 16].... The same rule applies to an instrument of acceptance or approval.

In the case of bilateral treaties, ratifications are exchanged by the states parties concerned and each instrument is filed in the archives of the Treaty Department of each state's Foreign Office. Usually a Procès-Verbal is drawn up to record and certify the exchange.

[This] method of exchange is not appropriate for the ratification of multilateral treaties. Such a treaty usually provides for the deposit of all ratifications in a central headquarters such as the Foreign Office of the state where the treaty was signed....

(5) Accessions and adhesions

In practice, when a state has not signed a treaty it can only accede or adhere to it. According to present practice, a non-signatory state may accede or adhere even before the treaty enters into force. * * * No precise form is prescribed by international law for an instrument of accession, although generally it is in the same form as an instrument of ratification. A simple notification of intention to participate in a treaty may be sufficient.

* * *

(6) Entry into force

The entry into force of a treaty depends upon its provisions, or upon what the contracting states have otherwise agreed [Vienna Convention, art. 24(1)].... As already mentioned, many treaties become operative on the date of their signature, but where ratification, acceptance, or approval is necessary, the general rule of international law is that the treaty concerned comes into force only after the exchange or deposit of ratifications, acceptances, or approvals by all the states signatories. Multilateral treaties now usually make entry into force dependent on the deposit of a prescribed number of ratifications and like consents to be bound—usually from six to about thirty-five. Sometimes, however, a precise date for entry into force is fixed without regard to the number of ratifications received. Sometimes, also, the treaty is to come into operation only on the happening of a certain event. . . .

EDITORS' NOTE

When states signal their consent to be bound by a treaty, they sometimes also signal a wish to qualify that consent; they indicate that they accept the treaty in general but that, for constitutional or other reasons, they have reservations regarding certain of its provisions. The question then arises: what is the effect of a unilateral attempt to modify a treaty? In Public International Law in the Modern World 192 (1987), David H. Ott addresses the issue as follows:

> With a bilateral treaty an attempt to do this by a reservation would destroy the parties' original understanding of the agreement and would amount to a counter-offer and a reopening of negotiations. The other party would then accept or reject the reservation as, in effect, part of a new agreement. If the reservation were not acceptable, the treaty would fail.

> In the case of a multilateral treaty the situation is more complicated. If one state makes a reservation, some of the existing parties may accept it and consider that the reserving state is a party to the treaty, while other existing parties may reject the reservation and consider that the reserving state is not a party.

> The result would be that the applicability of the treaty's provisions would be in doubt and there would be disagreement about which states were parties and which were not. This could present a particular problem with regard to the treaty's coming into force. Most treaties require the adherence of a specified number of states before that can happen. If the adherence of some reserving states were in doubt, it might prove impossible to determine whether or when the treaty has entered into force, with serious consequences for the parties and the international community in general.

> The traditional response to this problem was to assume that a multilateral treaty was, in effect, a contract between all the existing parties on one side and the reserving state on the other. The choice for the reserving state would then be to accept without reservation what they had already agreed or alternatively to persuade them *all* to change their agreement in line with the reservation. This response was said to emphasize the *integrity of the convention*, that is, the integrated wholeness of the text, which was not to be undermined by reservations. In this view, unless all the existing parties to a multilateral treaty agreed to a reservation, the attempted adherence of the reserving state would be null and void.

> The problem usually came to a head at the time when the reserving state communicated its qualified adherence to the *depositary*, the state of organisation designated in the treaty as responsible for keeping records of the treaty and maintaining the official list of the parties to it. Should the depositary enter the reserving state's name on that list or not?

This question found its way to the World Court by way of a UN General Assembly request for an advisory opinion on whether reservations were permitted to avoid the compulsory jurisdiction of the Court under the 1948 Convention on the Prevention and Punishment of the Crime of Genocide (**Basic Document 3.2**). The Court, minimizing the contractual (as opposed to legislative) character of the

Genocide Convention, rejected the contention that the parties to the Convention could stipulate reservations to any provision they disliked. Otherwise, the Court concluded, state parties could act in "complete disregard of the object and purpose of the Convention." *Reservations to the Convention on the Prevention and Punishment of the Crime of Genocide,* 1951 ICJ 15, 24, 1951 WL 3 (Advisory Opinion). In this conclusion, the Court ruled consistently with Articles 2(d) and 19 through 21 of the 1969 Vienna Convention on the Law of Treaties **(Basic Document 1.10)** which indicate the generally accepted view that reservations are permissible except when (a) they are prohibited by the treaty, (b) they are not included among expressly authorized reservations, and (c) they are otherwise incompatible with the object and purpose of the treaty.

A "reservation," however, is not the only device used to signal a qualification to treaty consent. In addition, state parties resort to "understandings" and "declarations." For example, while Article 20 of the Rome Statute of the International Criminal Court **(Basic Document 1.16)** prohibits reservations to the Statute, states parties to it have made qualifying declarations in relation to it. In *Reservations to Multilateral Treaties: The Goal of Universality,* 71 Iowa L. Rev. 295, 298–300 (1985), Catherine L. Piper distinguishes these "treaty-qualifying" communications:

> The three major classifications of treaty-qualifying unilateral statements are reservations, understandings, and declarations. A reservation is a formal declaration that acts to limit or modify the effect of the treaty in application to the reserving state. A reservation is external to the text of the treaty and is an attempt to alter the negotiated package. Because reservations are made outside of the treaty negotiations, their amendment to the multilateral treaty may conflict with the original text of the treaty. The ultimate effect of the reservation will depend on the practice or rule of reservations applied and the existence or nonexistence of special provisions within the treaty governing inclusion and effect of reservations.

> The term "understanding" is used to designate a statement not intended to alter or limit the effect of the treaty, but rather to set forth a state's interpretation or explanation of a treaty provision. In practice, understandings are sometimes used to provide a memorandum of the nation's interpretation at the time of signing in case of future judicial or arbitral proceedings.

> A declaration is a unilateral statement of policy or opinion that, like an understanding, is not intended to alter or limit any provision of the treaty. It is considered to have the least effect on the original treaty text and is used primarily to articulate a signatory's purpose, position, or expectation, concerning the treaty in question.

> The use of the labels "reservation", "understanding," and "declaration" have created much confusion on both the international level and the domestic level. The problem arises because the label attached is not conclusive as to the substantive effect the statement has on the treaty. This is especially evident when dealing with understandings. A state may condition acceptance of a treaty on a specific interpretation, which may later be found contrary to the plain language of the treaty of intended meaning of other parties. As such, the understanding in effect alters or modifies the original treaty and amounts to a reservation. If a state were allowed to determine conclusively the treatment of a unilateral statement by attaching a label, the statement could alter the multilateral treaty and negate the application of reservation law. It is necessary, therefore, to distinguish qualifying statements by comparing the sub-

stance or contents of the statement with the original text of the treaty. If the qualifying statement in application alters the legal effect of the treaty, the statement should be considered a reservation and be governed by the applicable reservation law.

The Vienna Convention **[Basic Document 1.10]** has attempted to clarify the labeling confusion by formulating a broad definition of reservations that tends to focus on the substance of the statement rather than the label attached: " 'reservation' means a unilateral statement, however phrased or named, made by a State … whereby it purports to exclude or modify the legal effect of certain provisions of the treaty in their application to that State."

The Vienna Convention rule includes all unilateral statements, regardless of their labels, under the term "reservation" if the substantive content of the statement alters the effect of the treaty. The determination of whether a statement is a reservation is generally left to the other treaty signatories. The law of reservations, therefore, must be viewed as one governing all unilateral qualifying statements because the interpretative effect of any one statement may vary with the evaluating party.

For extended, more recent discussion of reservations, understandings, and declarations, see Anthony Aust, Modern Treaty Law and Practice ch 8 (2000).

4. AMENDMENT OF TREATIES

As time passes and circumstances change, reasons for altering agreements mount. In this respect, treaties are no less vulnerable than other agreements. Accordingly, many treaties contain provisions that establish a procedure for their amendment. In the case of bilateral treaties, typically either party may propose an amendment, but unanimity of agreement between both parties must be obtained for the proposed amendment to be adopted. In the case of multilateral treaties, typically any one or more of the parties may initiate the amendment procedure and usually only majority approval of the proposed amendment (commonly a two-thirds majority) is required for its adoption. In each case, however, usually the amendments are not enforceable until after they have been accepted or ratified by *all* the contracting parties. Articles 39 and 40 of the 1969 Vienna Convention on the Law of Treaties **(Basic Document 1.10)**, requiring amendments to be concluded and entered into force in the same way as treaties themselves, set out the generally accepted rules regarding these matters.

This traditional process of modifying treaties by negotiating and concluding new agreements has been found to be not quick enough to respond adequately to fast changing events—as in the discovery, for example, of a more rapidly depleting ozone layer than had been anticipated in the emission-curbing schedules of the 1987 Montreal Protocol on Substances that Deplete the Ozone Layer **(Basic Document 5.29)**. Though adding much-needed rigor to the 1985 Vienna Convention for the Protection of the Ozone Layer **(Basic Document 5.38)**, the Montreal Protocol has itself been modified, as of this writing, by the so-called London Agreements of June 1990, the Copenhagen Agreements of November 1992, the Vienna Agreements of December 1995, and the Montreal Agreements of September 1997 **(Basic Documents 5.33, 5.38, 5.45 & 5.47)**. In his famous treatise on The Law of Treaties, Lord McNair, noting the complexity of highly technical multilateral treaties, anticipated this problem when he observed that we are here addressing "one of the weakest spots in the now existing system of States." A. McNair, The Law of Treaties 534 (1961). "[I]t must be admitted," he continued, "that no national society which is not equipped with legislative and administrative machinery for effecting changes could hope to hold together for long. International society is clearly groping its way towards the creation of some escape from the present effect of the rule requiring consent of all the parties affected by a change...." *Id*. Earlier, in *International Legislation*, 19 Iowa L. Rev. 177 (1934), Lord McNair noted that some technical multilateral treaties contained provisions by which, within certain narrowly defined limits, the parties had agreed to permit treaty modifications by majority vote.

Today, echoing this history, an increasing number of treaties, especially environmental treaties, establish a bifurcated norm-modifying procedure: the fundamental obligations enunciated in the treaties are made subject to the traditional, rather difficult amendment process, while administrative and technical details are permitted to be altered informally and therefore quickly—that is, a general framework is set forth in the treaty proper which is supported by administrative and technical annexes that can be easily modified without amending the "framework treaty." Professor Kirgis has noted this "nontraditional" rule-altering technique in the context of the "constituent instruments" of the International Labour Organization (ILO), the Universal Postal Union (UPU), the World Health Organization (WHO), the International Civil Aviation Organization (ICAO), and the International Maritime Organization (IMO): "The constituent instruments of most specialized agencies contain amendment procedures that bind all members if some fraction—often two-thirds—of the total membership adopts and ratifies the amendment." Frederic L. Kirgis, Jr., *Specialized Law–Making Processes*, in 1 United Nations Legal Order 109, 121 (C. Joyner & O. Schachter eds., 1995). Noting that this norm-modifying "process of prolepsis" (*i.e.*, of providing an answer to an issue in anticipation of a circumstance that makes the answer applicable) has "clear applicability to global environmental problems," Sir Geoffrey Palmer observes—favorably—that "[t]he proleptic method of avoiding the rule of unanimous consent has already been employed in the environmental sphere in the Montreal Protocol on Substances that Deplete the Ozone Layer of 1987. Some little-noticed innovations," he adds, "were made that certainly go beyond the technical and change the rule of unanimous consent in dramatic ways." Sir Geoffrey Palmer, *New Ways to Make International Environmental Law*, 86 A.J.I.L. 259, 274 (1992). *See also* Anthony Aust, Modern Treaty Law and Practice ch. 15 (2000).

5. TERMINATION OF TREATIES

Most treaties have a limited life span; many are concluded for a limited duration only, and state parties always are free to suspend or terminate a treaty at any time by agreement. *See* Articles 54–55 and 57–59 of the 1969 Vienna Convention on the Law of Treaties **(Basic Document 1.10)**. A treaty may cease to operate, however, for reasons other than the agreement of the parties, *e.g.*, by denunciation or withdrawal[p] or by virtue of breach, impossibil-

---

p. In Military and Paramilitary Activities in and against Nicaragua (Nicar. v. U.S.) (Mer-   its),1984 ICJ 392, at 467, the International Court of Justice treated Article 56 as an accuity of performance, change of circumstances;[q] or the emergence of a new peremptory "higher law norm" of international law (*jus cogens*).[r] *See* Articles 56, 60–62, and 64 of the 1969 Vienna Convention.

6. INTERPRETATION OF TREATIES

How one interprets a legal text—a contract, a will, a judicial opinion, a statute, a constitution, etc.—is important, obviously, because legal benefits and burdens, often critical ones, always hang in the balance. The same is true for treaties, and over the years four principal approaches to treaty interpretation have emerged: *the ordinary meaning textual approach*, *the ordinary meaning contextual approach*, *the teleological or ultimate purpose approach*, and *the policy-oriented and configurative approach*. The first two of these approaches emphasize that the aim of treaty interpretation is to give effect to the original intentions of the parties. The last two, while not discounting the importance of party intent, give weight to other considerations in addition.

(a) The Ordinary Meaning Textual Approach

This approach, espoused (at least formerly) by the Institute of International Law (IIL),[s] avoids going beyond the treaty text and concentrates on analyzing the words in it according to their "plain and natural meaning." As IIL member Sir Eric Beckett once stated:

> . . . [T]he task of [a] Tribunal is that of interpreting a written document, a statute, a will, a contract in writing, or a treaty, and it has to proceed on the assumption that it finds the intention expressed in the words of the document which it has to interpret. There is a complete unreality in the references to the supposed intention of the legislature in the interpretation of the statute when in fact it is almost certain that the point which has arisen is one which the legislature never thought of at all. This is even more so in the case of the interpretation of treaties. As a matter of experience it often occurs that the difference between the parties to the treaties arises out of something which the parties never thought of when the treaty was concluded and that, therefore, they had absolutely no common intention with regard to it. In other cases the parties may all along have had divergent intentions with regard to the actual question which is in dispute . . ., possibly hoping that this point would not arise in practice, or possibly expecting that if it did the text which was agreed would produce the result which it desired. . . . [I]t is

rate statement of customary international law. For a brief extract from this case, see *infra* text at 117–21.

q. In the Fisheries Jurisdiction Case (Merits), 1974 ICJ 3, the International Court of Justice indicated that Article 62 is "in many respects" a codification of the customary international law doctrine of *rebus sic stantibus* ("things staying as they are"), an implicit provision in many treaties (a *clausula rebus sic stantibus*) that the treaty parties consider themselves bound only as long as the funda-

mental circumstances that prompted the treaty remained more or less constant.

r. For discussion of the doctrine of *jus cogens*, see *infra* Editors' Note, at 145–46.

s. The Institute of International Law (*Institut de Droit International*) is a transnational non-governmental organization founded in Belgium in 1873 for the purpose of developing and codifying international law. Its membership comprises persons chosen as a result of their contributions in the field of international law. It currently is headquartered in Geneva, Switzerland.

unrealistic to attempt to find a common intention of the parties when, in fact, they never had a common intention on the point that has arisen, but simply agreed on a text. . . .

Comments on the Report of M. H. Lauterpacht (of the Second Commission of the Institute of International Law) on the Interpretation of Treaties, 43–I Ann. Inst. D. Int'l 437–38 (1950):

(b) *The Ordinary Meaning Contextual Approach*

This approach, more liberal than the one preceding, is best represented by Article 31 and 32 of the 1969 Vienna Convention on the Law of Treaties **(Basic Document 1.10)**. Thus Article 31 provides that "[a] treaty shall be interpreted in good faith in accordance with the ordinary meaning to be given to the terms of the treaty in their context and in the light of its object and purpose" which, as stated by the International Law Commission in its commentary on its Draft Articles of the Law of Treaties,[t] "must be presumed to be the authentic expression of the intentions of the parties." Int'l L. Comm'n, Report on the Law of Treaties, UN GAOR, 19th Sess., Supp. No. 9, at 27, UN Doc. No. A/5809 (1964), *reprinted in* 61 A.J.I.L. 253 (1967). And to this end Article 31 goes on to authorize exploration of not only the treaty text, but, as well: (i) any agreement or other instrument made in connection with the treaty and accepted by the parties; (ii) subsequent agreements regarding the treaty's interpretation; (iii) post-signature practice establishing the under-standing of the parties relative to interpretation; and (iv) relevant rules of international law applicable in the relations between the parties. In addition, Article 32 authorizes recourse to "supplementary means of interpretation," including "the preparatory work" leading to signature (*i.e.,* the "*travaux préparatoires,*" or what in the domestic-law context we call the "legislative history") and "the circumstances of [the treaty's] conclusion." The International Law Commission's commentary on Article 31 states that the article comports with the approach of the International Court of Justice.

(c) *The Teleological or Ultimate Purpose Approach*

This approach, while not rejecting the elements stressed by the two preceding approaches, attaches special importance to giving effect to the ultimate aims or purposes of a treaty, particularly when constitutive treaties are involved. It is succinctly described in David H. Ott, Public International Law in the Modern World 195–96 (1987):

> It is true that in the *Interpretation of Peace Treaties Case* (1950)[u] the ICJ refused to allow the object and purpose of a treaty to override the clear language in it. The court held that it could not apply the rule of effectiveness (expressed in the maxim *ut res magis valeat quam pereat:* "that the thing may rather have effect than perish") whereby a tribunal may give effect to a treaty on the basis of implementing its purposes even though the treaty's language might make it inoperative in the case at hand.

---

t. The International Law Commission (regarding which see *supra* note **h** in Chapter 1) had the principal hand in drafting the Vienna Convention.

u. Interpretation of Peace Treaties with Bulgaria, Hungary and Romania (Advisory Opinion) (First Phase), 1950 ICJ 65.

However, the court has accepted the importance of giving effect to the purposes of treaties where their language is not definitive or where it is unclear. The ICJ has also relied on treaty purposes when interpreting and applying the UN Charter [**Basic Document 1.5**], most notably in the *Reparation Case*[v] (which derived the UN's international legal personality from the purposes set out in the Charter) and the *Certain Expenses Case*[w] (where the role of the General Assembly in organising peacekeeping forces was founded on the Charter's aims).

The distinction between the UN Charter and other treaties is that the Charter is a constitutional document in which the parties indicated, in Article 1, a special concern to achieve its purposes within the framework of a long-term and constantly developing legal regime. Judge Jessup in his dissent in the *South West Africa Cases* (1966)[x] emphasised the importance of the teleological approach in interpreting such a treaty.

(d) The Policy–Oriented and Configurative Approach

In contrast to the three foregoing approaches is the "policy-oriented and configurative approach" advocated in Myres S. McDougal, Harold A. Lasswell, and James C. Miller, The Interpretation of Agreements and World Public Order (1967). Building upon the other three approaches even while eschewing them, this controversial but critically acclaimed treatise holds that (i) it is the intentions of the parties—their "genuine shared expectations," which are not necessarily their original intentions—that should, together with overriding community policies, preeminently concern the interpretative enterprise; and (ii) that everything that throws light on those expectations (including, obviously, the text of the treaty) should be included in the interpreter's investigations. Thus, because "[t]he communications which constitute an international agreement ... are functions of a larger [than textual] context" (*id.* at 58), and as such "may be affected by any and all the variables in the process of agreement and its context" (*id.* at 11), the authors refuse to make the text the exclusive or even near-exclusive indicator of party expectation and community preference. Consequently, they urge the investigation of *all* relevant "pre-outcome" (*i.e.*, negotiation), "outcome" (*i.e.*, text), and "post-outcome" (*i.e.*, subsequent conduct) indices of such intention and preference. The Yale professors do not stop here, however. Proposing a host of "principles of content and procedure" designed to facilitate the fullest possible marshalling of all evidence relevant to party intention and community preference, *and refusing to accept any preordained hierarchy of factual inquiry* (because "[t]he significance of any particular factor may in different contexts vary greatly in relation to other factors"—*id.* at 116), they recommend a series of "goals of interpretation" (including the goal of according the highest possible deference, compatible with other constitutional policies, to the genuine shared expectations of the particular parties) for the purpose of guiding decision-makers through the labyrinths of interpretation and from which they deduce particu-

---

v. Reparation for Injuries Suffered in the Service of the United Nations (Advisory Opinion), 1949 ICJ 174.

w. Certain Expenses of the United Nations (Article 17, paragraph 2, of the Charter) (Advisory Opinion), 1962 ICJ 151.

x. South West Africa (Eth. v. S. Afr.) (Liber. v. S. Afr.) (Second Phase), 1966 ICJ 6.

lar policies to fit exact issues so as "to give effect to the goals of a public order of human dignity"[y] (*id.* at 40): "Our recommended goals of interpretation are based on the fundamental expectation that future events cannot fail to be affected in some degree by any decision outcome," they write. The authors continue:

> The decision-maker who engages in acts of interpretation is in search of the past and present; but the past and present are pursued as a way of accomplishing a future result. Obviously, decision of the particular case calls for action affecting the future relations of the parties, and particular consequences are expected to follow the decision. Results are not, however, restricted to the fate of the immediate parties, even when precautions are taken to circumscribe the significance of the decision as precedent. The chain of effect may prove to be visible for a very short time or it may be discerned for long periods and in many jurisdictions. In any event, effects are not to be eliminated by wishing or pretending that they will not occur.
>
> The goals of interpretation that we propose take into consideration the obligation of any decision-maker to act rationally in harmony with the fundamental objectives of the community whose authoritative spokesman he is. Decision outcomes have consequences that can and ought to be affected by deliberate efforts to further the realization of the basic pattern of value distribution and the fundamental institutions that are compatible with the preferred system of public order.

Id. at 39–40. For explanatory critiques of the McDougal–Lasswell–Miller study, see Richard A. Falk, *On Treaty Interpretation and the New Haven Approach: Achievements and Prospects*, 8 Va. J. Int'l L. 323 (1968); Gidon Gottlieb, *The Conceptual World of the Yale School of International Law*, 21 World Politics 108 (1968); and Burns H. Weston, *Book Review*, 117 U. Pa. L. Rev. 647 (1969).

For recent discussion on the interpretation of treaties by an experienced diplomat, including the interpretation of treaties in more than one language, see Anthony Aust, Modern Treaty Law and Practice ch. 13 (2000).

DISCUSSION NOTES/QUESTIONS

1. At the outset of this Section A discussion of treaties, we noted the definition of "treaty" in Article 2(1) of the 1969 Vienna Convention on the Law of Treaties **(Basic Document 1.10)** and the fact that this definition applies irrespective of a treaty's particular designation. We now know that the Rome Statute of the International Criminal Court is a treaty. But does an "Executive Agreement" amount to a "treaty"? The 1975 Final Act of the Conference on Security and Co-operation in Europe **(Basic Document 1.12)**?

2. Article 6 of the 1969 Vienna Convention **(Basic Document 1.10)** provides that "[e]very State possesses capacity to conclude treaties." What is a "state"? Is the United Nations a state? The International Labour Organization

---

y. A "public order of human dignity" is elsewhere defined by McDougal to mean a "public order in which values are shaped and shared more by persuasion than coercion, and which seeks to promote the greatest production and widest possible sharing, without discriminations irrelevant to merit, of all values among all human beings." M. McDougal & Associates, Studies in World Public Order 987 (1960).

(ILO)? The Vatican? Liechtenstein? Though not states as juridically conceived and constituted, each of these entities does in fact enter into treaties. What, then, does this say about Article 6? And what about Delaware, Iowa, New Jersey, and New South Wales, each of which are "states"? Can they enter into treaties? Can the District of Columbia or the Australian Capital Territory?

3.   Charlesworth and Chinkin, *supra*, contend that the process of treaty-making and reservations to treaty adoption are subject to gender bias in favor of men. Do you agree? If so, does it make any difference? What would be the effect of the absence of a gender bias in these respects?

4.   The negotiation, adoption, and ratification of treaties is often referred to by international lawyers as "the international legislative process." At the same time, some theorists look upon treaties as essentially "contractual" rather than "law-making" in character. Who is right? Does it matter? As observed *supra* in the Editors' Note, at 96–98, the International Court of Justice, in its *Advisory Opinion on Reservations to the Convention on Genocide*, 1951 ICJ 15, took notice of the two connotations and distinguished between them. States parties to so-called law-making conventions, it said, at 8, do not have any interests of their own; they merely have, one and all, a common interest, namely, the accomplishment of those high purposes which are the *raison d'etre* of the convention. Consequently, in a convention of this type one cannot speak of individual advantages or disadvantages to states, or of the maintenance of a perfect contractual balance between rights and duties. The high ideals which inspired the convention provide, by virtue of the common will of the parties, the foundation and measure of all its provisions.

Does the Court's comment answer the immediately foregoing questions?

5.   Many treaties cannot be truly successful if they are not ratified or acceded to by all or many states. A good example is the 1985 Vienna Convention on the Protection of the Ozone Layer **(Basic Document 5.23)** and its progeny, the focus of Problem 7–2 ("Hanguo Versus the Ozone Layer") in Chapter 7, *infra*. Without a system that can bind all or most nations, all efforts to protect the ozone layer would be, arguably, in vain. In this regard, what role, if any, is or might be played by the doctrine of obligations *erga omnes*, a Latin expression meaning "towards all" which, some argue, can have, like legislation, a regulatory connotation in service to common interests? If it has a role, would it be limited to international environmental law? What about the laws of war? Human rights law? The law appertaining to international trade or development?

6.   Is it possible for treaties, or at least some treaties, to be binding on non-ratifying states? Consider Article 11 of the 1969 Vienna Convention on the Law of Treaties **(Basic Document 1.10)**: "The consent of a State to be bound by a treaty may be expressed by signature, exchange of instruments constituting a treaty, ratification, acceptance, approval or accession, *or by any other means if so agreed*" (emphasis added). How does this square with Article 13(b) of the Rome Statute **(Basic Document 1.16)**, granting jurisdiction to the ICC in a situation when, irrespective of state non-adherence to the Statute (such as Sudan or the United States as of this writing), "one or more [crimes covered by the Statute] appears to have been committed is referred to the Prosecutor by the Security Council acting under Chapter VII of the Charter of the United Nations"? Observe that Article 11 does not prescribe an absolute means of consenting to a treaty. Indeed, it says, if anything, that the means are unimportant; that we have not to worry about some technical legal difference between "signature," "ratification," "acceptance," or "approval". Who, then, has to worry? When? What if a treaty

provides that it will enter into force when it is "signed"? Could the United States, with its constitutional requirements, ever "sign" such a treaty? Australia? Would a diplomat have the power to sign? How could he/she get the power?

7.   When does a treaty become "binding" (*i.e.*, enforceable)? Take, for example, the 1969 Vienna Convention on the Law of Treaties **(Basic Document 1.10)**, Article 84(1) of which provides that it "shall enter into force on the thirtieth day following the date of deposit of the thirty-fifth instrument of ratification or accession." As this text goes to press, 105 countries have become party to the Convention, 54 more than required by Article 84(1). But this represents just over only half the nations of the world. Are the many countries that are not party to the Convention legally bound by it (for example, the United States which, though a signatory, is a non-party)? If so, on what theory? Does it help to know that the Convention was carefully drafted? That most nations participated in its drafting? That it has been ratified by many countries in every region of the world? That many of its provisions are restatements of what, by 1969, was considered to be the customary international law of treaties? That it has been widely cited in both official and scholarly circles? What do these facts prove, if anything? That the Convention is enforceable generally, binding on parties and non-parties alike? If so, was the Convention necessary in the first place? If not, are the world's non-parties free to disregard its provisions with impunity?

8.   As noted in the readings, states often wish to make a reservation or some other qualifying statement when ratifying a treaty? Should treaties permit or disallow reservations and other qualifying expressions? Would not reservations often be contrary to the purpose of international agreements? On the one hand, there may be and often is a need to have many states join such treaties. On the other hand, reservations can render a whole treaty ineffective. What do you think?

9.   Article 56(1)(b) of the Vienna Convention on the Law of Treaties **(Basic Document 1.10)** provides that, in the absence of an explicit denunciation and/or withdrawal provision, a right to denounce or unilaterally withdraw from a treaty may be implied "by the nature of the treaty." What does this mean? That the presence of such a provision is to be presumed in "legislative" but not "contractual" treaties? That its absence in, say, a "*procès-verbal*" or an "exchange of notes (or letters)" is to be given less weight than its absence in a more formal treaty text? In any event, is the rule desirable? What margin does it leave for negligence or oversight in the drafting of treaties? Does it not risk rendering many treaties ineffective simply at the will of one party? If so, of what value is a treaty lacking an explicit denunciation and/or withdrawal provision?

10.   What constitutes a "material breach" of a treaty, justifying denunciation and/or withdrawal? What constitutes a "fundamental change of circumstances," justifying the same? Is a broad or narrow interpretation of "material breach" and "change of circumstances" to be preferred? Who should have the burden of proof?

11.   Why do treaty negotiations often take years? Why do states hesitate to conclude treaties? To what extent do domestic factors (*e.g.*, a full-employment economy) play a role? Should they play a role?

12.   Many environmental treaties provide for simplified amendment procedures when it comes to administrative and technical details. Would this approach be helpful in the field of, say, war and peace or human rights? Amendments still have to be negotiated and often will take a long time. Can you think of faster or more efficient amendment procedures? Better procedures, from the standpoint of responsiveness to particular needs? Not infrequently, a so-called technical change will constitute in reality a major modification of a treaty, but according to the

treaty provisions the state parties are not obliged to ask for the approval of their respective parliaments. Accordingly, national politicians often are skeptical about such procedures because they fear that the procedures facilitate circumvention of national approval prerogatives. What do you think?

13.   As we have seen, it is possible to identify at least four approaches to treaty interpretation. Which one do you prefer? Which makes the most sense (a) from a theoretical point of view, (b) from a practical (or operational) point of view, and (c) from both points of view? If you were in a position to render an authoritative interpretation of a written legal instrument other than a treaty (*e.g.*, a constitution, code, statute, resolution, administrative ruling, contract, etc.), which of the four approaches would you adopt, if any? Would it depend on the nature of the instrument? Whether you were situated in a domestic or international arena? Other considerations? Do any of the identified approaches serve as an unambiguous means for resolving disputes relative to provisions in treaties (and other legal instruments)? Is an unambiguous means for resolving textual disputes ever possible?

B.   CUSTOM

Next among the "sources" of international law listed in Article 38 of the Statute of the International Court of Justice **(Basic Document 1.6)** is "international custom, as evidence of a general practice accepted as law"— that is, customary international law, referenced also in Article 8 of the Rome Statute of the International Criminal Court **(Basic Document 1.16)**, as previously noted.[z] Prior to World War II, when the development of international law via treaties was less popular than it is today, international law consisted for the most part of doctrines, principles, and rules developed through the customary practice of states. Indeed, prior to World War II, custom often was viewed, if not as *the* principal "source" of international law, as at least equal to treaties in this regard.[aa] Without a doubt, this history was well known to the Allied Powers who sought to prosecute the German Nazi leaders at Nuremberg following World War II, again as evidenced by part of the general indictment drawn against them.[bb]

Likewise was the history of customary international law well known to the drafters of the Rome Statute, as noted above.[cc] Presumably in their application of articles 8 and 21 of the Statute, it will be invoked by the Prosecutor and judges at the ICC.

But what exactly is customary international law? What does it mean to talk about "a general practice accepted as law"? Is it binding on all states or only on some states? What constitutes evidence of it? Can treaties give rise to it? Does it include rules prohibiting "ethnic cleansing," mass rape, and other inhumane practices? If so, by what process do these rules arise? How do we know when a given state practice has matured into a rule of customary international law?

To these and related questions you now turn. They are important questions because, though international law is today shaped ever more by

---

z. *See supra* text at the beginning of Section A of this chapter, at 82.

aa. For related pertinent comment, see *supra* text accompanying note **f**, at 82.

bb. *Supra* note **g**, at 83.

cc. *See supra* text accompanying note **i**, at 83.

treaties, customary international law still plays an important role in contemporary international legal process. Most obviously, it helps to define legal rights and wrongs in areas of interaction not covered by treaties. In addition, however, it paves the way for the codification of doctrines, principles, and rules through treaties, domestic legislation, and other means of standard-setting (national as well as international); it facilitates the process of treaty interpretation by helping to fill *lacunae* in treaty law; it assists the definition of the rights and duties of states not party to treaty-based international organizations; and, as demonstrated in the case of Nicaragua against the United States before the International Court of Justice in the mid–1980s,[dd] it can give competence to an international tribunal to adjudicate in cases where, under conventional law, such competence is lacking. Not to be overlooked either, it often defies the second-level priority *textually assigned* to it by Article 38 of the Statute of the International Court of Justice (**Basic Document 1.6**), not infrequently demonstrating greater precision than treaties in reflecting community expectations about authority and control. The need to understand the meaning of customary international law—or, more precisely, the process by which customary international law norms are prescribed—is thus manifest.

EDITORS' NOTE

In his essay *Toward a General Theory of International Customary Law*, in Toward World Order and Human Dignity 365 (W. Reisman & B. Weston eds., 1976), Venkata Raman writes, at 365–66:

> Even within highly organized communities, where legislative and adjudicative functions are formally the prerogative of centralized institutions, it generally is recognized that legislation and adjudication do not exhaust the process by which "law" is prescribed. It is familiar knowledge that in applying [legal] prescriptions to any complex interaction there is a continuing interplay between the formulated and the unformulated components [of legal prescription]—evident whether a decisionmaker is concerned with interpreting a business contract or the constitution of the community itself—and generally is seen as a dependable guide for ascertaining what is truly regarded as "authoritative" at any given time. Even in societies structured to look to formal institutions for guidance, the lawmaking process cannot be described adequately without acknowledging the part played by customary practice. This is not just because of the reverence with which societies regard tradition in their social interaction. What is often treated functionally as [legal] prescription may not be readily traceable to any formal official source, just as a significant part of what is popularly termed "legislation" may have little or no relevance to community expectations of authority and control. Mistaking the structure for the function, many assume that is a technique of "primitive" societies and legislation a technique of "civilized" societies.

Thus Professor Raman concludes, perceptively, that "legal prescription" (or lawmaking) may be seen, in "primitive" *and* "advanced" societies alike, as "a comprehensive and continuing *process of communication* comprising primarily [1] an agreement process, [2] a process of formal enunciation through parliamentary organs, and [3] the customary process." *Id*. at 365. In the first two of these process categories, he observes, "legal prescription is communicated in some

---

dd. *Supra* note **p**, at 99. For a brief extract from this case, see *infra* text at 117–21.

stylized linguistic form" (*i.e.*, contracts, legislation, treaties, etc.); in the last or customary process, it is communicated "through uniformities of behavior." *Id*. Customary international law, in other words, "refers generally to the *unformulated* component of [legal] prescription [or law-making]." *Id*. (Emphasis added.)

But what criteria distinguish customs that generate rules of law from customs that generate merely rules of courtesy or convenience? Consider the following classic formulation by former World Court judge Manley O. Hudson from a working paper for the International Law Commission[ee] in 1950, UN Doc. A/CN.4/16, Mar. 3, 1950, at 5:

> ... [T]he emergence of a principle or rule of customary international law would seem to require presence of the following elements:
>
> (a) concordant practice by a number of States with reference to a type of situation falling within the domain of international relations;
>
> (b) continuation or repetition of the practice over a considerable period of time;
>
> (c) conception that the practice is required by, or consistent with prevailing international law; and
>
> (d) general acquiescence in the practice by other States.
>
> Of course the presence of each of these elements is to be established as a fact by a competent international authority.

Judge Hudson's formulation refers in essence to two criteria: (1) criteria that evince concern for state behavior, *i.e.*, what states do and how they do it (and by implication what states don't do and how they don't do it); and (2) criteria that evince concern for what states "think" about why they do and don't do—a psychological component that often is referred to as *"opinio juris,"* an abbreviation of the Latin phrase *opinio juris sive necessitatis* (a conviction that a particular behavior is or is not permitted or required by law). We have here a starting point for the readings that follow.

DAVID H. OTT, PUBLIC INTERNATIONAL LAW IN THE MODERN WORLD

13–16 (1987)

The process of forming customary law. The essence of the formation of customary international law is the gradually combining effect of the practice of a number of states with regard to a particular type of legal problem or situation.... The question then is: at what point ... [does] the rule come into existence?

To help in this determination international law has developed tests to be applied in evaluating instances of observed state action. One must examine the evidence for the nature, extent and significance of state practice and determine whether that practice establishes that the required elements are present and have in fact combined to generate a rule of law.

It is usual to distinguish customary law that is found in this way from mere *usage*, that is, a habitual state activity that is not required by interna-

---

ee. *See supra* note **h** in Chapter 1.

tional law but is observed as a matter of goodwill at the discretion of the particular state.[ff]

The problem of evaluating the evidence for state practice. In general, the examination of state activities is concerned with what states actually do when faced with a particular problem. The difficulty is that states may act out of some momentary interest which leads them away from what a more considered judgment might suggest international law requires. * * * In examining state actions, then, the international lawyer must be very careful not to attach undue weight to any particular act of state self-interest.

The evidence of state practice. With that caveat in mind, however, the lawyer may consider as evidence of state practice a wide variety of things, some of more value than others.

There are first the documents generated by states in their conduct of foreign relations. Diplomatic correspondence, policy statements, press releases, and opinions of official legal advisers may all come within this category.

Then one may find more general expressions of a state's views on international law in such things as official manuals on legal questions. Both the United States and the United Kingdom publish manuals on the law of war which may be taken as expressions of each state's views on the conduct of military activities.

The actual decisions of governments on questions with some international legal relevance are often good indications of state practice. Similarly, legislation and judicial decisions of the state's higher courts[gg] may reflect that state's practice on the international legal issues raised.

On the international level, the comments by a state on draft treaties produced by the UN International Law Commission, or the voting of that state in international bodies (particularly the UN General Assembly),[hh] may offer good indications of a state's practice—may indeed even in some sense be state practice.

More generally, the language used in the treaties a state signs may reflect its practice, as may also a pattern of treaties in which a state has fairly consistently agreed to a certain view of the relevant international law in agreements with its treaty partners.

It is within the framework of such evidences of state practice that the international lawyer must decide whether the elements of customary law are present.

The elements of custom. Once it has been determined what is the real practice of states with regard to some legal point, that practice must next be examined to see whether it reflects what are generally recognized to be the indispensable elements whose presence transforms practice into customary law. These elements are discussed below.... Element 1: *opinio juris*. This is the belief that a certain practice is obligatory as a matter of law. Thus Article

---

ff. "Although occasionally the terms are used interchangeably," writes Ian Brownlie in Principles of Public International Law 6 (6th ed. 2003), " 'custom' and 'usage' are terms of art and have different meanings. A usage is a general practice which does not reflect a legal obligation, and examples are ceremonial sa-

lutes at sea and, apart from a recent convention, the giving of customs exemption to the personal baggage of diplomatic agents."

gg. *See infra* Section D of this chapter, at 151.

hh. *See infra* Section F–1 of this chapter, at 162.

38(1)b of the ICJ Statute **[Basic Document 1.6]** speaks of a "general practice *accepted as law*". If a practice is not so accepted, but is regarded as simply a discretionary act performed out of a political or other non-legal motives, then it is an example of usage which may merely reflect international friendliness or diplomatic tact—what international law calls comity.

In the *Asylum Case* (1950)[ii] the World Court emphasised the importance of a practice being the expression of a right belonging to one party and a duty lying on the other party. Without that nexus of legal obligation, and the *opinio juris* which recognises it, there is no custom.

Unfortunately, although this requirement of *opinio juris* makes practical sense as a means of distinguishing from comity, it is illogical insofar as it requires new rules of customary law to be generated by a process which must assume a belief that those rules are *already* legally binding.

Nevertheless, the World Court has insisted on this, and the main question in several cases has been how to decide whether a practice is motivated by *opinio juris* or not. In the *Lotus Case* (P.C.I.J. 1927),[jj] the court indicated that one could not infer *opinio juris* from a particular practice unless the state involved was "conscious of having a duty" in that regard. This has been criticised as requiring the judges and others to determine the psychological viewpoint of a state as if it were a real person. Several respected writers have suggested that the better position is to infer *opinio juris* from practice which reasonably bears that inference unless there are clear indications from the state to the contrary. But in the *North Sea Continental Shelf Cases* (1969)[kk] the court reiterated the *Lotus* view although a slight shift occurred in *Nicaragua v. U.S.* (1984).[ll]

Element 2: duration. This has to do with the length of time a practice has been followed. Long duration may be helpful in establishing a custom, but the ICJ indicated in the North Sea Continental Self Cases that even a short duration might suffice when state practice has been extensive and virtually uniform. In other words, a short duration may be offset to some extent by a strong showing with regard to the remaining elements of custom....[mm]

Element 3: uniformity and consistency. Uniformity means that the practice of states should not vary greatly from state to state. Consistency

ii. Asylum (Colom./Peru), 1950 ICJ 266.

jj. (Fr. v. Turk.), 1927 P.C.I.J. (ser. A) No. 10, at 4.

kk. (F.R.G./Den.) (F.R.G./Neth.), 1969 ICJ 3. For a brief extract from this case, see *infra* text at 114–17.

ll. *Supra* note **p**, at 99. For a brief extract from this case, see *infra* text at 117–21.

mm. In *Customary International Law: New and Old Problems*, 19 Thesaurus Acroasium 199, 215 (1992), Rudolph Bernhardt asks: "Can 'customary law' come into existence without custom, as 'instant' customary law in the words of Bin Cheng [in *United Nations Resolutions on Outer Space: 'Instant' International Customary Law*, 5 Indian J. Int'l L. 28 (1965)]?" Bernhardt answers in the affirma-tive, but asserts that two conditions must first be met for customary international law to "come into existence spontaneously":

There must be quasi-unanimity in the community of States that a certain rule is necessary, and this unanimity must not be counterbalanced by adverse practices. If, for instance, the representatives of States in a universal organization or conference express the unanimous opinion that tests of nuclear weapons or the stationing of weapons of mass destruction in space and on celestial bodies should be totally excluded, why should this not create new law? Can the *opinio juris sive necessitatis* suffice in certain circumstances, if no adverse practices exist? I would answer this question affirmatively despite the undeniable dogmatic difficulties.

implies that there should not be contradictions or discrepancies in the practice of states between one relevant instance and another.

Element 4: generality. This relates to whether a practice is fairly widespread among a majority of states: a practice common in only one area of the world or observed by only a minority of states would not generate international customary law for all. However, all states may be bound by arising from generally followed practice without the need for universality.

It may be possible, nevertheless, for a state which objects to a particular general practice to avoid in certain circumstances being obligated as a matter of customary law. The *Anglo-Norwegian Fisheries Case* (1951)[nn] is generally understood to recognize the possibility of a state's being a *persistent objector* and thus not bound by a particular custom on account of having objected to the relevant practice right from the beginning of its transformation into a rule of customary international law. On the other hand, a *subsequent objector*, which remained silent while the custom was in the process of formation and spoke out only after it had become law, would not be able to escape being obligated unless other affected states acquiesced in the subsequent objector's attempt to avoid being bound.

These observations about the position of states that object to a rule of customary law are important for a corollary that is implicit in them, namely, that if a state makes neither a persistent objection nor a subsequent objection to a particular rule, then that state is bound by the rule, even without an explicit acceptance.

ANTHONY A. D'AMATO, THE CONCEPT OF CUSTOM IN INTERNATIONAL LAW

88–89 (1971)

What is an "act" of a state? In most cases, a state's action is easily recognized. A state ... engages in thousands of acts through its citizens and agents. On the other hand, a claim is not an act.... [A]lthough they may *articulate* a legal norm, [claims themselves] cannot constitute the material component of custom. For a state has not done anything when it makes a claim; until it takes enforcement action, the claim has little value as a prediction of what the state will actually do.

Harder to recognize as an "act" is a state's decision not to act in a situation where it could have acted. When the first Sputnik circled the globe, the non-actions of the states over whose territory the satellite passed were just as significant to the formation of custom as the action of the [former] Soviet Union in sending it up.

A more difficult question, insisted upon by many writers, relates to the number of acts (or restraints) necessary to satisfy the material element of custom formation. However, such an inquiry is misleading. There is no metaphysically precise (such as "seventeen repetitions") or vague (such as "in the Court's discretion") answer possible. States simply do not organize their behavior along absolute lines. There is no international "constitution" specifying when acts become law. Rather, states resort to international law in

---

nn. Fisheries (U.K. v. Nor.), 1951 ICJ 116.

claim-conflict situations. In such instances, counsel for either side will attempt to cite *as many acts as possible*. Thus we may say that persuasiveness in part depends upon the number of precedents. At the very least, the party asserting the existence of a custom must cite *one* instance of an act or restraint that followed the articulation of a rule. It was perhaps with this minimal requirement in mind that several writers have ... come out in favor of the proposition that only one act is necessary to constitute the material element of custom....

ROSALYN HIGGINS, PROBLEMS AND PROCESS: INTERNATIONAL LAW AND HOW WE USE IT
19–22 (1994)

One of the special circumstances of international law is that violations of law can lead to the formation of new law. Of course, this characteristic is more troublesome for those who regard law as rules, and less troublesome for those who regard law as process. But whether one believes that international law consists of rules ... derived from consent or natural law; or whether one believes international law is a process of decision-making, with appropriate reliance on past trends of decision-making in the light of current context ..., there still remains the question of how the "rules" or the "trends of decision" change through time. And, insofar as these rules or trends of decisions are based on custom, then there is the related question of what legal significance is to be given to practice that is inconsistent with the perceived rules or trends of decision.

Some rule-based international lawyers are apt to see rules as immutable. Repeated violations of these rules are to them a reflection of the reality that at the end of the day international law is dependent upon power[;] and, if there is a divergence between the two, it is power politics that will prevail. This ... is a view widely held by non-lawyers, and by students of international relations.... For those who regard international law as a process, however, the situation presents itself rather differently. That which we describe *as law* is the confluence of authority and control. Where there is substantial non-compliance, over a period of time, the norms concerned begin to lose their normative [*i.e.,* juridical] character. What has been lost is the community expectation that claimed requirements of behaviour reflect legal obligation.

But even for those who view international law as process, there are some difficult questions. What exactly causes a norm to lose its quality as law? Conceptually, this question is, of course, the same as that put regarding the formation of custom. To ask what is evidence of practice required for the loss of obligatory quality of a norm is the mirror of the evidence of practice required from the formation of the norm in the first place. As we have seen ..., practice and *opinio juris* are required.

If a customary rule loses its normative quality when it is widely ignored, over a significant period of time, does this not lead to a relativist view of the substantive content of international law, with disturbing implications? Let us take a spectrum of possibilities. In the *South West Africa Cases*,[oo] South Africa argued that there was not in reality any norm of [racial] non-discrimination,

oo. *Supra* note **x** (p. 102).

as—regardless of the way states voted on resolutions on the issue—the great majority of states routinely discriminated against persons of colour. This argument arose in the context of whether a norm of non-discrimination had ever developed and come into existence. A second example: all states agree that international law prohibits genocide (and that this total prohibition is today rooted in customary international law and not just in treaty obligations). So what if some states from time to time engage in genocide? Here we may safely answer that genocide, while it sometimes occurs …, is certainly not the majority practice. The customary law that prohibits genocide remains intact, notwithstanding appalling examples of non-compliance. Let us look at a third, more difficult example. No one doubts that there exists a norm prohibiting torture. No state denies the existence of such a norm; and, indeed, it is widely recognized as a customary rule of international law by national courts.[pp] But it is equally clear from, for example, the reports of Amnesty International, that *the great majority* of states systematically engage in torture. If one takes the view that non-compliance is relevant to the retention of normative quality, are we to conclude that there is not really any prohibition of torture under customary international law? The International Court of Justice touched on this issue in a rather general way in *Nicaragua v. United States*, when determining the law on intervention and permitted use of force. It said:

> If a State acts in a way prima facie incompatible with a recognized rule, but defends its conduct by appealing to exceptions or justifications contained within the rule itself, then whether or not the State's conduct is in fact justifiable on that basis, the significance of that attribute is to confirm rather than to weaken the rule.[qq]

For lawyers who do not approach matters from the perspective of the battle between "legal rules" and "power politics," this last type of example presents very real difficulties…. Essentially, the argument seems to be that, if [certain rules such as rules against aggression and on self-defence] are not treated as "rules of higher normativity" than ordinary rules, then they cannot be treated differently from ordinary rules so far as the evidence of practice is concerned; and, if they cannot be treated differently, then disaster will ensue. To assert an immutable core [of] norms which remain constant regardless of the attitudes of states is at once to insist upon one's own personal values (rather than internationally shared values) and to rely essentially on natural law in doing so. This is a perfectly possible position, but it is not one I take.

* * *

The answer, in my view, lies elsewhere. First, we must not lose sight of the fact that it is the practice of the vast majority of states that is critical, both in the formation of new norms and in their development and change and possible death. Thus, even if genocide and the killing of prisoners of war regrettably sometimes occur, if this is not the usual practice of most states, the status of the normative prohibitions is not changed. No special attribution of "high normative status" is needed. More difficult is the question of torture, because we are told, by reputable bodies in a position to know, that the

---

pp. *See, e.g.,* Filártiga v. Peña-Irala, 630 F.2d 878 (2d Cir. 1980).

qq. *Supra* note **p** (p. 99). For a brief extract from this case, see *infra* text at 117–21.

majority of states in the world do engage in this repugnant practice. It is at this point that a further factor comes into play.

New norms require both practice and *opinio juris* before they can be said to represent customary international law. And so it is with the gradual death of existing norms and their replacement by others. The reason that the prohibition on torture continues to be a requirement of customary international law, even though widely abused, is not because it has a higher normative status that allows us to ignore the abuse, but because *opinio juris* as to its normative status continues to exist. No state, not even a state that tortures, believes that the international law prohibition is undesirable and that it is not bound by the prohibition. A new norm cannot emerge without both practice and *opinio juris*; and an existing norm does not die without the great majority of states engaging in both contrary practice and withdrawing their *opinio juris*.

EDITORS' NOTE

Can a treaty give rise to customary law that is binding on all nations? At the turn of the Twentieth Century, a number of British scholars took the view that treaties prescribe only the contractual obligations of states, that they have no legal force and effect beyond them, and that their provisions could be declaratory or in derogation of customary law but that they could not alter it. But consider how the World Court has dealt with this question, as it did in the 1969 *North Sea Continental Shelf* cases and later in the 1986 case concerning *Military and Paramilitary Activities in and Against Nicaragua*.

NORTH SEA CONTINENTAL SHELF CASES (JUDGMENT) (FRG/DEN.) (FRG/NETH.)

1969 ICJ 3, 41–45, 1969 WL 1

[These cases involved three states (the Federal Republic of Germany, Denmark, and The Netherlands) bordering on the North Sea and asserting conflicting claims to its undersea land masses known as the "continental shelf." Denmark and The Netherlands claimed that the dispute should be decided according to the "principle of equidistance" per Article 6 of the 1958 Geneva Convention on the Continental Shelf **(Basic Document 5.4)**. The Court rejected the application of the Convention inasmuch as West Germany was not a party to it. It also rejected another claim advanced by Denmark and The Netherlands, to wit, that the equidistance principle in Article 6 of the same Convention had become part of the *corpus* of general international law and, in particular, customary international law. It addressed the question of whether a treaty give rise to customary law as follows:]

70.   ... [Denmark and The Netherlands contend] that even if there was at the date of the Geneva Convention [on the Continental Shelf] no rule of customary international law in favour of the equidistance principle, and no such rule was crystallized in Article 6 of the Convention, nevertheless such a rule has come into being since the Convention, partly because of its own impact, partly on the basis of subsequent State practice—and that this rule, being now a rule of customary international law binding on all States, including therefore the Federal Republic, should be declared applicable to the

delimitation of the boundaries between the Parties' respective continental shelf areas in the North Sea.

71.   In so far as this contention is based on the view that Article 6 of the Convention has had the influence, and has produced the effect, described, it clearly involves treating that Article as a norm-creating provision which has constituted the foundation of custom, or has generated a rule which, while only conventional or contractual in its origin, has since passed into the general *corpus* of international law, and is now accepted as such by the *opinio juris*, so as to have become binding even for countries which have never, and do not, become parties to the Convention. There is no doubt that this process is a perfectly possible one and does from time to time occur: it constitutes indeed one of the recognized methods by which new rules of customary international law may be formed. At the same time this result is not lightly to be regarded as having been attained.

72.   It would in the first place be necessary that the provision concerned should, at all events potentially, be of a fundamentally norm-creating character such as could be regarded as forming the basis of a general rule of law. Considered *in abstracto* the equidistance principle might be said to fulfil this requirement. Yet in the particular form in which it is embodied in Article 6 of the Geneva Convention, and having regard to the relationship of that Article to other provisions of the Convention, this must be open to some doubt. In the first place, Article 6 is so framed as to put second the obligation to make use of the equidistance method, causing it to come after a primary obligation to effect delimitation by agreement. Such a primary obligation constitutes an unusual preface to what is claimed to be a potential general rule of law.... Secondly the part played by the notion of special circumstances relative to the principle of equidistance as embodied in Article 6, and the very considerable, still unresolved controversies as to the exact meaning and scope of this notion, must raise further doubts as to the potentially norm-creating character of the rule. Finally, the faculty of making reservations to Article 6, while it might not of itself prevent the equidistance principle being eventually received as general law, does add considerably to the difficulty of regarding this result as having been brought about (or being potentially possible) on the basis of the Convention: for so long as this faculty continues to exist ..., it is the Convention itself which would, for the reasons already indicated, seem to deny to the provisions of Article 6 the same norm-creating character as, for instance, Articles 1 and 2 possess.

73.   With respect to the other elements usually regarded as necessary before a conventional rule can be considered to have become a general rule of international law, it might be that, even without the passage of any considerable period of time, a very widespread and representative participation in the convention might suffice of itself, provided it included that of States whose interests were specially affected. In the present case however, the Court notes that, even if allowance is made for the existence of a number of States to whom participation in the Geneva Convention is not open, or which, by reason for instance of being land-locked States, would have no interest in becoming parties to it, the number of ratifications and accessions so far secured is, though respectable, hardly sufficient. That non-ratification may sometimes be due to factors other than active disapproval of the convention

concerned can hardly constitute a basis on which positive acceptance of its principles can be implied. The reasons are speculative, but the facts remain.

74.   As regards the time element, the Court notes that it is over ten years since the Convention was signed, but that it is even now less than five since it came into force in June 1964.... Although the passage of only a short period of time is not necessarily, or of itself, a bar to the formation of a new rule of customary international law on the basis of what was originally a purely conventional rule, an indispensable requirement would be that within the period in question, short though it might be, State practice, including that of States whose interests are specially affected, should have been both extensive and virtually uniform in the sense of the provision invoked; and should moreover have occurred in such a way as to show a general recognition that a rule of law or legal obligation is involved.

75.   The Court must now consider whether State practice in the matter of continental shelf delimitation has, subsequent to the Geneva Convention, been of such a kind as to satisfy this requirement.... [S]ome fifteen cases have been cited in the course of the present proceedings, occurring mostly since the signature of the 1958 Geneva Convention, in which continental shelf boundaries have been delimited according to the equidistance principle—in the majority of the cases by agreement, in a few others unilaterally—or else the delimitation was foreshadowed but has not yet been carried out.... [However, there are] several grounds which deprive them of weight as precedents in the present context.

76.   To begin with, over half the States concerned, whether acting unilaterally or conjointly, were or shortly became parties to the Geneva Convention, and were therefore presumably ... acting actually or potentially in the application of the Convention. From their action no inference could legitimately be drawn as to the existence of a rule of customary international law in favour of the equidistance principle. As regards those States, on the other hand, which were not, and have not become parties to the Convention, the basis of their action can only be problematical and must remain entirely speculative. Clearly they were not applying the Convention. But from that no inference could justifiably be drawn that they believed themselves to be applying a mandatory rule of customary international law. There is not a shred of evidence that they did and ... there is no lack of other reasons for using the equidistance method, so that acting, or agreeing to act in a certain way, does not of itself demonstrate anything of a juridical nature.

77.   The essential point in this connection—and it seems necessary to stress it—is that even if these instances of action by non-parties to the Convention were much more numerous than they in fact are, they would not, even in the aggregate, suffice in themselves to constitute the *opinio juris;*— for, in order to achieve this result, two conditions must be fulfilled. Not only must the acts concerned amount to a settled practice, but they must also be such, or be carried out in such a way, as to be evidence of a belief that this practice is rendered obligatory by the existence of a rule of law requiring it. The need for such a belief, *i.e.,* the existence of a subjective element, is implicit in the very notion of the *opinio juris sive necessitatis.* The States concerned must therefore feel that they are conforming to what amounts to a legal obligation. The frequency, or even habitual character of the acts is not in

itself enough. There are many international acts, *e.g.*, in the field of ceremonial and protocol, which are performed almost invariably, but which are motivated only by considerations of courtesy, convenience or tradition, and not by any sense of legal duty.

78.   In this respect the Court follows the view adopted by the Permanent Court of International Justice in the *Lotus* case . . . (*P.C.I.J., Series A, No. 10,* 1927, at p.28).[rr] . . . [T]he position is simply that in certain cases—not a great number—the States concerned agreed to draw or did draw the boundaries concerned according to the principle of equidistance. There is no evidence that they so acted because they felt legally compelled to draw them in this way by reason of a rule of customary law obliging them to do so—especially considering that they might have been motivated by other obvious factors.

* * *

81.   The Court accordingly concludes that if the Geneva Convention was not in its origins or inception declaratory of a mandatory rule of customary international law enjoining the use of the equidistance principle for the delimitation of continental shelf areas between adjacent States, neither has its subsequent effect been constitutive of such a rule; and that State practice up-to-date has equally been insufficient for the purpose.

MILITARY AND PARAMILITARY ACTIVITIES IN AND AGAINST NICARAGUA (NICAR. V. US) (MERITS)

1986 ICJ 14, 1986 WL 522

[*Eds.*—In 1984 Nicaragua instituted proceedings against the United States in the World Court alleging military and paramilitary acts by the United States in Nicaragua in violation of international law. The United States contested the jurisdiction of the Court on several grounds, including a reservation it had made in accepting the Court's jurisdiction to the effect that its acceptance would not apply to disputes concerning the application of a treaty—in this case, the United Nations Charter **(Basic Document 1.5)** and the Charter of the Organization of American States **(Basic Document 1.7)**. Nicaragua responded by arguing that its claim was based on not only the Charter but also on rules of customary international law that were similar in content to the Charter and applicable to the facts in the case. The Court accepted the Nicaraguan argument for the reasons given in the ensuing extract from the Court's lengthy opinion.]

182.   The Court concludes that it should exercise the jurisdiction conferred upon it by the United States declaration of acceptance under Article 36, paragraph 2, of the Statute **[Basic Document 1.6]**, to determine the claims of Nicaragua based upon customary international law notwithstanding the exclusion from its jurisdiction of disputes "arising under" the United Nations and Organization of American States Charters.

183.   In view of this conclusion, the Court has next to consider what are the rules of customary international law applicable to the present dispute. For

---

rr. *See supra* text accompanying note **jj**, at
110.

this purpose, it has to direct its attention to the practice and *opinio juris* of States; as the Court recently observed,

> "It is of course axiomatic that the material of customary international law is to be looked for primarily in the actual practice and *opinio juris* of States, even though multilateral conventions may have an important role to play in recording and defining rules deriving from custom, or indeed in developing them." (*Continental Shelf (Libyan Arab Jamahiriya/Malta), ICJ Reports 1985, pp. 29–30, para. 27.*)

In this respect the Court must not lose sight of the Charter of the United Nations and that of the Organization of American States, notwithstanding the operation of the multilateral treaty reservation. Although the Court has no jurisdiction to determine whether the conduct of the United States constitutes a breach of those conventions, it can and must take them into account in ascertaining the content of the customary international law which the United States is also alleged to have infringed.

184. The Court notes that there is in fact evidence, to be examined below, of a considerable degree of agreement between the Parties as to the content of the customary international law relating to the non-use of force and non-intervention. This concurrence of their views does not however dispense the Court from having itself to ascertain what rules of customary international law are applicable. The mere fact that States declare their recognition of certain rules is not sufficient for the Court to consider these as being part of customary international law, and as applicable as such to those States. Bound as it is by Article 38 of its Statute to apply, *inter alia*, international custom "as evidence of a general practice accepted as law," the Court may not disregard the essential role played by general practice. Where two States agree to incorporate a particular rule in a treaty, their agreement suffices to make that rule a legal one, binding upon them; but in the field of customary international law, the shared view of the Parties as to the content of what they regard as the rule is not enough. The Court must satisfy itself that the existence of the rule in the *opinio juris* of States is confirmed by practice.

185. In the present dispute, the Court, while exercising its jurisdiction only in respect of the application of the customary rules of non-use of force and non-intervention, cannot disregard the fact that the Parties are bound by these rules as a matter of treaty law and of customary international law. Furthermore, in the present case, apart from the treaty commitments binding the Parties to the rules in question, there are various instances of their having expressed recognition of the validity thereof as customary international law in other ways. It is therefore in the light of this "subjective element"— the expression used by the Court in its 1969 Judgment in the *North Sea Continental Shelf* cases (*ICJ Reports 1969, p. 44*)—that the Court has to appraise the relevant practice.

186. It is not to be expected that in the practice of States the application of the rules in question should have been perfect, in the sense that States should have refrained, with complete consistency, from the use of force or from intervention in each other's internal affairs. The Court does not consider that, for a rule to be established as customary, the corresponding practice must be in absolutely rigorous conformity with the rule. In order to deduce

the existence of customary rules, the Court deems it sufficient that the conduct of States should, in general, be consistent with such rules, and that instances of State conduct inconsistent with a given rule should generally have been treated as breaches of that rule, not as indications of the recognition of a new rule. If a State acts in a way prima facie incompatible with a recognized rule, but defends its conduct by appealing to exceptions or justifications contained within the rule itself, then whether or not the State's conduct is in fact justifiable on that basis, the significance of that attitude is to confirm rather than to weaken the rule.

187. The Court must therefore determine, first, the substance of the customary rules relating to the use of force in international relations, applicable to the dispute submitted to it. The United States has argued that, on this crucial question of the lawfulness of the use of force in inter-State relations, the rules of general and customary international law, and those of the United Nations Charter, are in fact identical. In its view this identity is so complete that, as explained above . . ., it constitutes an argument to prevent the Court from applying this customary law, because it is indistinguishable from the multilateral treaty law which it may not apply. In its Counter–Memorial on jurisdiction and admissibility the United States asserts that "Article 2(4) of the Charter is customary and general international law." It quotes with approval an observation by the International Law Commission to the effect that

> "the great majority of international lawyers today unhesitatingly hold that Article 2, paragraph 4, together with other provisions of the Charter, authoritatively declares the modern customary law regarding the threat or use of force" (*ILC Yearbook*, 1966, Vol. II, p. 247).

The United States points out that Nicaragua has endorsed this view, since one of its counsel asserted that "indeed it is generally considered by publicists that Article 2, paragraph 4, of the United Nations Charter is in this respect an embodiment of existing general principles of international law." And the United States concludes:

> "In sum, the provisions of Article 2(4) with respect to the lawfulness of the use of force are 'modern customary law' (International Law Commission, *loc. cit.*) and the 'embodiment of general principles of international law' (counsel for Nicaragua, Hearing of 25 April 1984, morning, *loc. cit.*). There is no other 'customary and general international law' on which Nicaragua can rest its claims."

> "It is, in short, inconceivable that this Court could consider the lawfulness of an alleged use of armed force without referring to the principal source of the relevant international law—Article 2(4) of the United Nations Charter."

As for Nicaragua, the only noteworthy shade of difference in its view lies in Nicaragua's belief that:

> "in certain cases the rule of customary law will not necessarily be identical in content and mode of application to the conventional rule."

188. The Court thus finds that both Parties take the view that the principles as to the use of force incorporated in the United Nations Charter correspond, in essentials, to those found in customary international law. The

Parties thus both take the view that the fundamental principle in this area is expressed in the terms employed in Article 2, paragraph 4, of the United Nations Charter. They therefore accept a treaty-law obligation to refrain in their international relations from the threat or use of force against the territorial integrity or political independence of any State, or in any other manner inconsistent with the purposes of the United Nations. The Court has however to be satisfied that there exists in customary international law an *opinio juris* as to the binding character of such abstention. This *opinio juris* may, though with all due caution, be deduced from, *inter alia*, the attitude of the Parties and the attitude of States towards certain General Assembly resolutions, and particularly resolution 2625 (XXV) entitled "Declaration on Principles of International Law concerning Friendly Relations and Co-operation among States in accordance with the Charter of the United Nations" **[Basic Document 1.5]**. The effect of consent to the text of such resolutions cannot be understood as merely that of a "reiteration or elucidation" of the treaty commitment undertaken in the Charter. On the contrary, it may be understood as an acceptance of the validity of the rule or set of rules declared by the resolution by themselves. The principle of non-use of force, for example, may thus be regarded as a principle of customary international law, not as such conditioned by provisions relating to collective security, or to the facilities or armed contingents to be provided under Article 43 of the Charter. It would therefore seem apparent that the attitude referred to expresses an *opinio juris* respecting such rule (or set of rules), to be thenceforth treated separately from the provisions, especially those of an institutional kind, to which it is subject on the treaty-law plane of the Charter.

189. As regards the United States in particular, the weight of an expression of *opinio juris* can similarly be attached to its support of the resolution of the Sixth International Conference of American States condemning aggression (18 February 1928) and ratification of the Montevideo Convention on Rights and Duties of States (26 December 1933) **[Basic Document 1.2]**, Article 11 of which imposes the obligation not to recognize territorial acquisitions or special advantages which have been obtained by force. Also significant is United States acceptance of the principle of the prohibition of the use of force which is contained in the declaration on principles governing the mutual relations of States participating in the Conference on Security and Co-operation in Europe (Helsinki, 1 August 1975) **[Basic Document 1.12]**, whereby the participating States undertake to "refrain in their mutual relations, *as well as in their international relations in general*," (emphasis added) from the threat or use of force. Acceptance of a text in these terms confirms the existence of an *opinio juris* of the participating States prohibiting the use of force in international relations.

190. A further confirmation of the validity as customary international law of the principle of the prohibition of the use of force expressed in Article 2, paragraph 4, of the Charter of the United Nations may be found in the fact that it is frequently referred to in statements by State representatives as being not only a principle of customary international law but also a fundamental or cardinal principle of such law. The International Law Commission, in the course of its work on the codification of the law of treaties, expressed the view that "the law of the Charter concerning the prohibition of the use of force in itself constitutes a conspicuous example of a rule in international law

having the character of *jus cogens*"[ss] (paragraph (1) of the commentary of the Commission to Article 50 of its draft Articles on the Law of Treaties, *ILC Yearbook*, 1966–II, p. 247). Nicaragua in its Memorial on the Merits submitted in the present case states that the principle prohibiting the use of force embodied in Article 2, paragraph 4, of the Charter of the United Nations "has come to be recognized as *jus cogens*." The United States, in its Counter–Memorial on the questions of jurisdiction and admissibility, found it material to quote the views of scholars that this principle is a "universal norm," a "universal international law," a "universally recognized principle of international law," and a "principle of *jus cogens*."

ANTHONY A. D'AMATO, "UNIVERSALITY VS. RESTRICTIVENESS OF CUSTOM"

adapted from B. Weston, R. Falk & A. D'Amato, International Law and
World Order: A Problem–Oriented Coursebook 76 (2d ed. 1990)

If customary international law is "universal," then it is binding on *all* states. However, if it is not universal, then the question is left open as to whether, indeed, it is binding on any given state. Even a cursory look at the vast literature on the subject will show what the competing considerations are.

(a) Favoring the Universality of Custom: The "Objectivist" or "Sociological" View

Assume that it is, say, the Seventeenth Century and that Great Britain and The Netherlands are locked in a debate over the far-reaching question of the freedom of the high seas. "At that time," recount Anthony A. D'Amato & John L. Hargrove, *An Overview of the Problem, in* Who Protects the Ocean? 20–21 (J. Hargrove ed., 1975), "the Netherlands was the dominant maritime country, and its leading international lawyer, Hugo Grotius, spelled out the arguments in favor of freedom of navigation on all the oceans. John Selden for England countered in favor of a closed sea."[tt]

What really was at issue in this debate was the paying of tariffs to another nation for navigational use of the high seas off its coast. Grotius, representing an aspiring naval power, did not want Dutch ships to have to pay for a license to navigate and trade with a distant power; he feared the proliferation of fees from all countries along the route. Selden, on the other hand, believed that England stood to gain more than it would lose by the imposition of such fees in the waters around England, affecting not only trade with England but also trade through the Straits of Gibraltar.

But England was unable to enforce this collection of fees, and so the Dutch view of freedom of the high seas prevailed as between the two countries, and a customary practice respecting this view developed between them. Did this mean that the new custom between Great Britain and The Netherlands—freedom of navigation on the high seas—applied to all other countries? Does it today apply automatically between Australia and the United States?

---

ss. *i.e.,* a peremptory principle or norm from which, it is claimed, no derogation is permitted. For discussion of the doctrine of *jus cogens*, see *infra* the Editors' Note, at 145–46.

tt. Later, when England became the dominant naval power, England espoused freedom of the seas.

If the establishment of a legal custom between two or more states is automatically universalized, a proposition about which there is disagreement, the answer is of course "yes." But how does a principle of law become "automatically" universalized?

We need look no further than ordinary case law. Smith sues Jones and wins. A rule of law in *Smith v. Jones* is thus established and, through the force of precedent, deemed to apply to all future litigants similarly situated. In this way, the common law is certainly a rather undemocratic process. But it is quite normal and acceptable. If the same issue litigated in *Smith v. Jones* came up later in *Brown v. Green*, we would think it strange that the court in the latter case would refuse to follow the rule of *Smith v. Jones*. Such a refusal, we would say, would make the law unpredictable and uncertain. Thus, even though neither Brown nor Green were around when *Smith v. Jones* was decided, the rule of *Smith v. Jones* affects both Brown and Green in their dealings with one another.

If we take this "common law" analogy and apply it to customary international law, then the custom of freedom of navigation on the high seas—even if provable only between Great Britain and The Netherlands at a given point in time in the Seventeenth Century—becomes automatically extended to all nations wishing to navigate on the high seas. Historically, of course, it was the Grotian position that prevailed, and today it is even hard to find a copy of Selden's *Mare Clausum* in a law library.

(b) *Favoring the Restrictiveness of Custom: The "Participatory" or "Voluntarist" View*

Many writers have objected to this universalization thesis. For example, in past decades the former Soviet Union strenuously objected; and, today, many Third World countries say that the universalization of custom is "undemocratic" because it signals the extension to them of principles of law that had their origin in customs established primarily among the industrialized, liberal economy nations of the Western world over which they had little or no control. They do not want to be "told" what to do by customary practices in which they did not participate. Hence, various "voluntarist" theories have evolved, holding that rules of customary international law apply only to those nations that have participated in the custom.

* * *

Thus if under this "participatory" or "voluntarist" theory we want to apply the customary law of, say, transfrontier atmospheric pollution to a particular State, we would have to do historical research into the question of whether that state "participated" in the formation of the law of transfrontier atmospheric pollution or whether it rejected such norms. Surely we can expect the historical evidence to be mixed at best, and probably nonexistent in most instances.

More generally, when we look to "participation" (in some form or another) in the custom-formation process, we probably will find that, when actual cases come up, the nations party to them probably will *not* have participated in the relevant custom! For if they had, then the cases probably would not have come up; the practices between the states would have been in accordance with the custom. Cases only arise when we have divergent practices, and divergent practices usually indicate that both sides have not participated in the relevant custom-formation process.

So we see that any theory short of universality is likely to leave us with very little relevant international law to apply to disputes between states. Our view is that the "universality" principle of customary international law probably has prevailed, but this is only a guess. One should look to the leading cases on custom to obtain a more informed answer.

EDITORS' NOTE

In light of the immediately preceding discussion, consider the *Asylum Case* (Colom. v. Peru), 1950 ICJ 266, and the *Fisheries Case* (U.K. v. Nor.), 1951 ICJ 116. In the former, the ICJ stated, at 277–78, that "[e]ven if it could be supposed that ... a custom [of diplomatic asylum] existed between certain Latin American states only, it could not be invoked against Peru which, far from having by its attitude adhered to it, has on the contrary repudiated it...." Similarly, in the latter, after rejecting as a rule of customary international law claimed ten-mile baseline rule for bays,[uu] the Court stated, at 131, that, "[i]n any event, the ten-mile rule would appear to be inapplicable as against Norway, inasmuch as she has always opposed any attempt to apply it to the Norwegian coast." These pronouncements invoke what in the past has been a seldom claimed exception to the universality principle known as the persistent objector rule, to wit, that a customary rule, though it may come into being over the opposition of one state or a few states (assuming a sufficient degree of general acceptance), will not bind those who object persistently to it—which is to say that in international law there is no majority rule with respect to the formation of customary international law.

Though seldom relied upon in the past, this persistent objector rule is likely to be invoked increasingly in the future as new principles of customary international law merge from majority positions in intergovernmental conferences and in the organs of the United Nations and other international institutions. *See, e.g.,* Ted L. Stein, *The Approach of the Different Drummer: The Principle of the Persistent Objector in International Law*, 26 Harv. Int'l L. J. 457, 463–69 (1985). Accordingly, the rule has attracted ever more attention. *See, e.g.,* Jonathan I. Charney, *The Persistent Objector Rule and the Development of Customary International Law*, 56 B.Y.B.I.L. 1 (1985). It also has attracted controversy. *See, e.g.,* Olufemi A. Elias, *Some Remarks on the Persistent Objector Rule in Customary International Law*, 1991 Denning L. J. 37, who observes, *inter alia,* that "[a] striking feature of the discussions about the existence and vitality of the persistent objector rule is the lack of a common statement of the rule itself." *Id.* at 38. Rudolf Bernhardt comments upon the rule and its dilemmas in *Customary International Law: New and Old Problems*, 19 Thesaurus Acroasium 199, 219–20 (1992):

> Since, on the one hand, a strict majority rule is hardly compatible with the structure of [the international] community and the sovereignty of its member States, and, on the other hand, the emergence of new rules should not be made totally dependent on unanimity, a solution seems to be that all States which accept a new rule or at least acquiesce in regard to its application are bound, and only those which persistently reject the new rule are not bound.

uu. The "baseline" is the line from which the breadth of the territorial sea and other maritime zones of coastal states is measured.

This proposal would seem to satisfy the interests at stake, but it leaves a good number of very difficult questions open. Is one persistent objector enough to exclude its being bound by a new norm? The answer seems to be yes, but can it not be relevant how strong the objection is and which interests are at stake? And what is the legal position if a persistent objector rejects a norm which is widely considered to be a norm of *jus cogens*? This has been discussed for the [former] practice of apartheid [in South Africa], but other examples [can] also be found. If a State which is not a member of the United Nations would persistently deny the validity of the prohibition of the use of force at least in certain circumstances, would this mean that the objector is not bound? What is the situation in regard to the persistent rejection of the right of self-determination by one State or a small group of States, or the permanent violation of basic human rights?

There are no easy answers to these questions. Surely the constancy and intensity with which an objector dissents should bear some influence. But how much influence and under what circumstances? And surely, too, certain basic values or fundamental principles of the world community as expressed through customary international law should be binding upon a persistent objector even though these values or principles may have been rejected from the start. But which ones and who is to decide according to what criteria? As Bernhardt observes in conclusion, at 220, "[t]he formation and the content of customary law are not governed by strict logical rules; instead they follow the development of the international community." Again, thus, we are left to follow the leading cases and incidents on custom as they evolve.

TIEYA WANG, "THE THIRD WORLD AND INTERNATIONAL LAW"
in The Structure and Process of International Law: Essays in
Legal Philosophy Doctrine and Theory 955, 961–63, 970
(R. MacDonald & D. Johnston eds., 1983)

Although Third World countries are adamantly opposed to the imperialistic, colonialistic, oppressive and exploitative principles and rules of traditional [*i.e.*, customary] international law, they do not reject international law itself.... [T]he Third World objects only to parts of traditional international law; it has never and does not object to all of the rules of international law. * * * As Hazard puts it, "No one is asking that the books be burned and that we start afresh in rejection of the lessons history has given us as to the rules which minimize friction."[3] The Third World, however, will not suffer the continued existence of the principles and rules established to protect the interests of imperialism and colonialism.... [T]he Third World requires that international law be gradually re-written to reflect the revolutionary changes which have taken place since the Second World War. To this end, Third World nations have been eagerly participating in "legislative" activities. * * * Their collective importance to the formation and development of international law should not be underestimated.

EDITORS' NOTE

"Without denigrating the considerable utility of customary international law," writes Mark Janis in An Introduction to International Law 53 (4th ed. 2003), "it must be admitted that this form of international law is subject to a number of sometime crippling faults." He continues:

---

3.   J. Hazard, in 57 Proceed. A.S.I.L. 79.

... First and foremost is the fact that oftentimes state practice is so diverse that it may be difficult or even impossible to find enough consistency [or uniformity] of practice to warrant drawing a customary international legal rule from it.... If no treaty can be found to authoritatively regulate a matter, it is by no means certain that customary international law will provide a definite rule to fill the gap.

Second, even if one state, judge, or other observer decides that the available evidences establish a norm of customary international law, there is no assurance that another decisionmaker will reach the same conclusion. Customary international law is found by a more or less subjective weighing of the evidence and subjective scales tilt differently in different hands....

Third, the very process of making customary international law often stimulates conflict. When states have differing views of what international law ought to be and when they cannot agree to make common rules by treaty, then they may well act and react in international relations in a fashion consciously designed to make customary international law or, at least, to block another state's preferred version of the right rule from becoming customary international law or to establish an exception to the rule....

Id. at 53–55.

Professor Janis might usefully have recorded another deficiency of customary international law: its gender bias to the detriment of women and women's concerns. After noting customary law's quantitative and qualitative requirements (state practice and *opinio juris*), Professor Christine Chinkin has remarked insightfully as follows:

... The focus on official government action in the requirements of customary law makes the question [of customary law formation] one of simple exclusion. It leaves out the possibly many and varied practices of its citizens. There is an assumption of monolithic behaviour by the state, a single line of practice that can be viewed as state practice, without regard to the diversity of views and actions that may in fact exist. The low level of representation of women in high-ranking government positions has ... been noted. The effect in this context is that women's voices are not heard in the decision-making processes that lead to identifiable state practice.

However, there are other ways beyond simple lack of participation in which the determination of rules of customary law works to exclude the interests of women.... First, in some instances where the facts of state practice do not conform with assertions of customary law, there has been a tendency to disregard the reality in preference for the statements of governments that such acts are prohibited.... However, this approach does not allow a determination of a rule of customary law condemning violence against women that is likely to win widespread acceptance. [Second,] unlike other human rights abuses, violence against women is not even verbally condemned as illegal in many societies, but instead is regarded as acceptable on social, traditional or religious grounds.... It is impossible to assert that there is strong evidence of *opinio juris* to allow contrary state practice to be discounted. * * * The task for women has therefore been to struggle to have gender-specific violence placed on the international agenda and to take steps within the public arena whereby a rule of customary law may be generated.

Panel on Sources of International Law: Entrenching the Gender Bias, in Proceedings of the Second Joint Conference of the American Society of International Law and the Nederlandse Vereniging voor Internationaal Recht (at The Hague, 22–24 Jul 93) 418, 418–19 (1994).

J. Patrick Kelly, "The Twilight of Customary International Law"

40 Va. J. Int'l L. 449, 452–53, 537–38, 540–43 (2000)

In this article, I argue that CIL [customary international law] should be eliminated as a source of international legal norms and replaced by consensual processes. My goal is not to undermine international law, but to encourage the use of more democratic, deliberative processes in formulating this law. My argument has three components First, the substantive CIL norms of the literature lack the authority of customary law and therefore are not binding on states. CIL lacks authority as law because such norms are not, in fact, based on the implied consent or general acceptance of the international community that a norm is obligatory. Both implied consent and general acceptance are fictions used at different historical periods to justify the universalization of preferred norms. In a world of many cultures and values, general acceptance is neither ascertainable nor verifiable.

Second, CIL has evolved into a meaningless concept that furnishes neither a coherent nor objective means of determining the norms of international law, how and when they come into existence, and which nations are bound. As an undefined and indeterminant [sic] source, it is unable to perform its assigned function as a relatively objective source of international norms based on social fact.

Third, the CIL process lacks a procedural legitimacy. The process of norm formation, as actually practiced, violates the basic notion of democratic governance among states and is a particularly ineffective way to generate substantive norms that will command compliance. Few nations participate in the formation of norms said to be customary. The less powerful nations and voices are ignored. There is little consideration of alternatives and trade-offs in reconciling diverse values and interests. Consequently, CIL should be discarded as a source of law and replaced by consent-based processes that permit wide participation, the discussion of alternatives, and the commitment of nations to their norms.

The "custom-speak" used in international legal discourse is an indeterminate, normative discourse that varies from writer to writer and state to state. It is not customary law. Properly understood, customary law is empirical. It consists of those norms that a society, in fact, believes are legally required.[4] Customary law may be discerned by the inductive method. Norms may be inferred from repeated and consistent acts that are believed to be required by a community, but customary law is not state practice. It is the community-wide belief that a norm is legally required that provides customary law with authority and legitimacy. The asserted CIL norms of the literature, however,

---

4. The anthropology literature clarifies that customary law is a social fact subject to observation. *See* Social Anthropology and Law 7–11 (I. Hamnett ed., 1977). While some international law writers have recognized that the existence of custom is a question of fact, few engage in the necessary inquiry. *See, e.g.,* Lassa Oppenheim, International Law 17 (H. Lauterpacht ed., 8th ed. 1955).

are declared without either general, consistent practice or clear evidence that the vast majority of states have accepted the norm as a legal obligation.[5] In short, CIL norms are not customary.

* * *

Despite these defects, ... [t]here are strong arguments for the retention of CIL. The most powerful argument is based on necessity. Decentralized international society requires a source of universal norms to govern interactions among all nations when actual agreement is impossible or when many states are not party to treaties. There is a second, somewhat similar argument, that CIL is an essential source of progressive or other fundamental norms that could not easily be negotiated on a reciprocal basis as easily as trade norms.

These perceived advantages are not only illusory, but are more than offset by significant disadvantages. First, that CIL furnishes a means to develop universal norms when actual agreement is difficult or inconvenient, cannot justify norms when there is no genuine acceptance.... [M]any asserted CIL norms lack authority and legitimacy because acceptance has been presumed based on little evidence or even in the face of contrary evidence. * * * Moreover, CIL may no longer be necessary. If nations have, in fact, accepted legal norms and possess the necessary normative conviction, then the vast majority of states should have little difficulty signing a treaty. Modern communications and transportation have simplified the logistics of international meetings reducing treaty negotiations and international decisionmaking to a common occurrence. The customary norms, primarily structural, that do command near universal acceptance have, to a large extent, been memorialized in treaties.

* * *

The second argument that there is a need for a source of progressive or fundamental norms is, in actuality, an argument for the incorporation of preferred values into international law, without the inconvenience of democratic processes. The techniques of both Western traditionalists who would impose their essential norms, such as humanitarian intervention or full compensation for expropriation, and that of environmental and human rights activists armed with their own lists of preferred norms are remarkably similar. Each would create norms based on selected international materials, whether incidents, judicial and arbitral decisions, or non-binding international resolutions, without the agreement of nations or their actual acceptance of norms. Customary norms can be progressive or reactionary, universal exceptions to treaty norms depending upon who is spinning the tale. Customary law discourse is an exercise in the manipulation of legal materials, not of determining empirical law. If any possible norm can be justified, then no legitimate norms are possible through this sort of process.

* * *

5. The primary norms of the [American Law Institute's] Restatement [of the Foreign Relations Law of the United States] ... have not, in fact, been accepted by the overwhelming majority of states as legal norms, nor is there consistent, widespread practice to support an inference of customary law....

In addition to these specific concerns, there are several overarching systemic reasons why CIL should be eliminated as a source of international law in the modern era. First, the continued use and abuse of CIL has promoted cynicism and disenfranchisement of many nations and peoples. The nations excluded from this process are well aware of CIL's historic failure. CIL undermines the integrity of the international legal system which in turn encourages disrespect for the entire system of international law.

Second, the CIL process does not encourage compliance. With few effective means of enforcing norms, the international system relies on commitment and reciprocal self-interest for compliance. Nations that played no role in the formation of norms nor had their interests considered are unlikely to honor such norms.

Third, CIL creates inconsistency and exceptionalism. CIL theory is used by powerful nations to conjure up exceptions to fundamental norms such as the prohibition on the use of force in the Charter of the United Nations. Similarly, less powerful nations and advocacy scholars use non-binding resolutions to promote their own vision of a just order removed from actual agreement or effective action. Neither form of manipulation of legal material will contribute to a viable international order.

Fourth, there are a variety of other means of developing international norms that are more effective and more likely to promote a vital legal order. The ozone and trade regimes demonstrate that the world possesses a wealth of possible trade-offs, incentives, and other means of encouraging participation and compliance....

Finally, the fundamental question for international society is: Through what processes will international law be made? The CIL process cannot generate norms perceived as legitimate when there is conflict about these norms or their formulation. Domestic legislatures find it difficult to resolve normative conflicts even in relatively homogeneous societies. The CIL process encourages posturing and the hardening of positions, not the development of general law with majority support. In fact, this process, as it now stands, may engender bitterness and noncompliance....

[*Eds.*—Observing that "[i]ncreased globalization, the increasing convergence of information, values and perspectives, and the rising need for common principles to resolve international disputes portend a fertile period of international norm-creation and problem-solving," the author then concludes:]

If the function of CIL has been to create general law binding on all states, then there are other, more effective means of building a true international consensus. The world is moving to a new pre-federal stage in which global problems such as trade and the spillover effects of pollution, ethnic cleansing, and disease must be addressed in a systematic way. In an era of instantaneous communications and rapid global travel, there is no need for the use of the incomprehensible processes of CIL. The manipulation of ambiguous incidents and the universalizing of political events are no longer necessary and undermine the integrity of the international order. The fiction of general acceptance of common consent is a poor substitute for other modes of lawmaking. The US and many other nations will not accept norms that limit their sovereign prerogatives without specific agreement. Only a consensual process will permit nations with diverse values and interests to negotiate standards that reconcile differences and meet common needs.

State practices will continue to play a role in law formation. The customary practices of a few states, however, should not be seen as a source of law, but rather as the tentative steps in the ongoing process of the development and articulation of norms.... If the goal is a world legal order, then the attempts to universalize standards, without the participation and consent of states, impede progress rather than promote it. CIL, as a source of international law, should therefore be discarded.

ANTHEA ELIZABETH ROBERTS, TRADITIONAL AND MODERN APPROACHES TO CUSTOMARY INTERNATIONAL LAW: A RECONCILIATION
95 A.J.I.L. 757, 757–61, 788–91 (2001)

The demise of custom as a source of international law has been widely forecasted. This is because both the nature and the relative importance of custom's constituent elements are contentious. At the same time, custom has become an increasingly significant source of law in important areas such as human rights obligations. Codification conventions, academic commentary, and the case law of the International Court of Justice (the Court) have also contributed to a contemporary resurrection of custom. These developments have resulted in two apparently opposing approaches, which I term "traditional custom" and "modern custom." The renaissance of custom requires the articulation of a coherent theory that can accommodate its classic foundations and contemporary developments....

... Custom is generally considered to have two elements: state practice and *opinio juris*. State practice refers to general and consistent practice by states, while *opinio juris* means that the practice is followed out of a belief of legal obligation. This distinction is problematic because it is difficult to determine what states believe as opposed to what they say. Whether treaties and declarations constitute state practice or *opinio juris* is also controversial. For the sake of clarity, this article adopts Anthony D'Amato's distinction between action (state practice) and statements (*opinio juris*).[6] Thus, actions can form custom only if accompanied by an articulation of the legality of the action. *Opinio juris* concerns statements of belief rather than actual beliefs. Further, treaties and declarations represent *opinio juris* because they are statements about the legality of action, rather than examples of that action.... [T]raditional custom and modern custom are generally assumed to be alternatives because the former emphasizes state practice, whereas the latter emphasizes *opinio juris*.

What I have termed traditional custom results from general and consistent practice followed by states from a sense of legal obligation. It focuses primarily on state practice in the form of interstate interaction and acquiescence. *Opinio juris* is a secondary consideration invoked to distinguish be-

---

6. A. D'Amato, The Concept of Custom in International Law 89–90, 160 (1971). This distinction has been criticized by many commentators, who include certain statements as forms of state practice.... The distinction is also impliedly inconsistent with some case law of the Court. Fisheries Jurisdiction (U.K. v. Ice.), Merits, 1974 ICJ 3, 47, 56–58, 81–88, 118–20, 135, 161 (July 25); North Sea Continental Shelf, 1969 ICJ at 4, 32–33, 47, 53.

tween legal and nonlegal obligations. Traditional custom is evolutionary and is identified through an *inductive* process in which a general custom is derived from specific instances of state practice. This approach is evident in *S.S. Lotus*,[7] where the Permanent Court of International Justice inferred a general custom about objective territorial jurisdiction over ships on the high seas from previous instances of state action and acquiescence.

By contrast, modern custom is derived by a *deductive* process that begins with general statements of rules rather than particular instances of practice. This approach emphasizes *opinio juris* rather than state practice because it relies primarily on statements rather than actions. Modern custom can develop quickly because it is deduced from multilateral treaties and declarations by international fora such as the General Assembly, which can declare existing customs, crystallize emerging customs, and generate new customs. Whether these texts become custom depends on factors such as whether they are phrased in declaratory terms, supported by a widespread and representative body of states, and confirmed by state practice. A good example of the deductive approach is the Merits decision in *Military and Paramilitary Activities in and Against Nicaragua*.[8] The Court paid lip service to the traditional test for custom but derived customs of non-use of force and nonintervention from statements such as General Assembly resolutions. The Court did not make a serious inquiry into state practice, holding that it was sufficient for conduct to be generally consistent with statements of rules, provided that instances of inconsistent practice had been treated as breaches of the rule concerned rather than as generating a new rule.

The tests and justifications for traditional and modern custom appear to differ because the former develops slowly through state practice, while the latter can arise rapidly based on *opinio juris*. This difference has spurred considerable discussion over two related issues. First, the legitimacy of traditional and modern custom has been debated at length. David Fidler characterizes the various approaches to this issue as the dinosaur, dynamo, and dangerous perspectives.[9] The dinosaur approach focuses on traditional custom and argues that massive changes in the international system have rendered it an anachronism. For example, Jonathan Charney claims that the increasing number and diversity of states, as well as the emergence of global problems that are addressed in international fora, makes traditional custom an inappropriate means for developing law.[10] The dynamo perspective concentrates on modern custom and embraces it as a progressive source of law that can respond to moral issues and global challenges. For example, Theodor Meron, Richard Lillich, and Lori Bruun argue that modern custom based on declarations by international fora provides an important source of law for human

7. S.S. "Lotus," 1927 PCIJ (ser. A) No. 10, at 18, 29; *see also* Nottebohm (Liech. v. Guat.), Second Phase, 1955 ICJ 4, 22 (Apr. 6); S.S. Wimbledon, 1923 PCIJ (ser. A) No. 1, at 25 (Aug. 17).

8. Military and Paramilitary Activities in and Against Nicaragua (Nicar. v. U.S.), Merits, 1986 ICJ 14 (Jun 27) ...; *see also* Western Sahara, Advisory Opinion, 1975 ICJ 12, 30–37 (Oct 16); Legal Consequences for States of the Continued Presence of South Africa in Namibia (South West Africa) Notwithstanding Security Council Resolution 276 (1970), Advisory Opinion, 1971 ICJ 16, 31–32 (Jun 21)....

9. D. Fidler, *Challenging the Classical Concept of Custom*, 1996 Ger. Y.B.I.L. 198, 216–31.

10. J. Charney, *Universal International Law* 87 A.J.I.L. 529, 543 (1993).

rights obligations.[11] Finally, the dangerous perspective views modern custom as a departure from the traditional approach that has created an opportunity for legal and political abuse. Thus, Michael Reisman characterizes the increased dependence on custom as a "great leap backwards" designed to serve the interests of powerful states.[12] Similarly, Arthur Weisburd holds that modern custom often lacks the legitimacy of state consent because it is formed despite little, or conflicting, state practice.[13]

Second, the divergence between traditional and modern custom has been criticized as undermining the integrity of custom as a source of law. Patrick Kelly argues that custom is an indeterminate and malleable source of law, simply a "matter of taste."[14] According to D'Amato, the modern approach trashes the theoretical foundations of custom by inverting the traditional priority of state practice over *opinio juris*.[15] Sir Robert Jennings insists that "most of what we perversely persist in calling customary international law is not only *not* customary law: it does not even faintly resemble a customary law."[16] The phrases "modern," "new," "contemporary," and "instant" custom appear inherently contradictory and obscure the real basis for forming this law. Hilary Charlesworth contends that modern custom can be rationalized only by dispensing with the traditional rhetoric of custom.[17] Bruno Simma and Philip Alston argue that the modern approach has created an "identity crisis"[18] for custom and would be better understood as a general principle of international law. Likewise, Charney, Daniel Bodansky, and Hiram Chodosh conclude that modern custom is really a new species of universal declaratory law because it is based on authoritative statements about practice rather than observable regularities of behavior.[19]

Both the legitimacy and the integrity of traditional and modern custom have received considerable attention and polarized positions are evident. However, few commentators have transcended these debates by attempting to provide an overall theory of custom. Frederic Kirgis rationalizes the divergence in custom by analyzing the requirements of state practice and *opinio juris* on a sliding scale.[20] At one end, highly consistent state practice can

---

11. T. Meron, Human Rights and Humanitarian Norms as Customary Law (1989); L. Bruun, *Beyond the 1948 Convention—Emerging Principles of Genocide in Customary International Law,* 17 Md. J. Int'l L. & Trade 193, 216–17 (1993); R. Lillich, *The Growing Importance of Customary International Human Rights Law,* 25 Ga. J. Int'l & Comp. L. 1, 8 (1995/96).

12. W. M. Reisman, *The Cult of Custom in the Late 20th Century,* 17 Cal. W. Int'l L. J. 133, 135 (1987).

13. A. Weisburd, *Customary International Law: The Problem of Treaties,* 21 Vand. J. Transnat'l L. 1 (1988).

14. J.P. Kelly, *The Twilight of Customary International Law,* 40 Va. J. Int'l L. 449, 451 (2000) [excerpted *supra* at 126–29].

15. A. D'Amato, *Trashing Customary International Law,* 81 A.J.I.L. 101 (1987).

16. R. Jennings, *The Identification of International Law, in* International Law: Teaching

and Practice 3, 5 (B. Cheng ed., 1982); *see also* North Sea Continental Shelf (FRG/Den.; FRG/Neth.), 1969 ICJ 3, 224 (Feb. 20) (Srensen, J. *ad hoc,* dissenting) . . . .

17. H. Charlesworth, *Customary International Law and the* Nicaragua *Case,* 1984–87 Austl.Y.B.I.L. 1.

18. B. Simma & P. Alston, *The Sources of Human Rights Law: Custom, Jus Cogens, and General Principles,* 1988–89 Austl. Y.B.I.L. 82, 88, 96.

19. D. Bodansky, *Customary (and Not So Customary) International Environmental Law,* 3 Ind. Global Legal Stud. 105, 116–19 (1995); J. Charney, *supra* note 10, 543, 546–47; H. Chodosh, *Neither Treaty nor Custom: The Emergence of Declarative International Law,* 26 Tex. Int'l L. J. 87, 102 n.70 (1991).

20. F. Kirgis, Jr., *Custom on a Sliding Scale,* 81 A.J.I.L. 146 (1987); John Tasioulas, *In Defence of Relative Normativity: Communitarian Values and the* Nicaragua *Case,* 16 Oxford J. Legal Stud. 85 (1996).

establish a customary rule without requiring *opinio juris*. However, as the frequency and consistency of state practice decline, a stronger showing of *opinio juris* will be required. Kirgis argues that the exact trade-off between state practice and *opinio juris* will depend on the importance of the activity in question and the reasonableness of the rule involved. Simma and Alston claim that this approach reinterprets the concept of custom so as to produce the "right" answers.[21] However, John Tasioulas argues that the sliding scale can be rationalized on the basis of Ronald Dworkin's interpretive theory of law,[vv] which balances a description of what the law has been with normative considerations about what the law should be.[ww] This perspective shows why the Court may be less exacting in requiring state practice and *opinio juris* in cases that deal with important moral issues.

[*Eds.*—The remainder of this essay provides, in the author's words, "an enriched theoretical account of custom that incorporates both the traditional and the modern approaches rather than advocating one approach over the other" building on the work of Kirgis and Tasioulas. In the end, after rejecting the "custom on a sliding scale" approach "because it does not accurately describe the process of finding custom and would create customs that are apologies for power or utopian and unachievable [goals]," she presents "an alternative vision" of Ronald Dworkin's interpretive theory of law applied to custom, combining "a descriptive historical investigation about what the law has been (fit) with a normative moral inquiry about what it should be (substance)"—an alternative vision that "incorporates the justifications of descriptive accuracy and normative appeal and seeks to balance them in a Rawlsian reflective equilibrium." We conclude this reading with, next, her discussion of "the advantages of a reflective interpretive approach" to custom over the sliding-scale methodology.]

... [T]his article has sought to build an enriched theoretical account of custom that analyzes the competing justifications for traditional and modern custom and accommodates both approaches in a consistent interpretive theory. * * * This reconciliation provides a methodology for assessing asserted customs. After gathering evidence of state practice and *opinio juris*, one must apply the threshold criterion of fit to determine if there are any eligible interpretations that adequately explain the raw data of practice. Fit provides continuity and descriptive accuracy, so that state practice will assume primary importance at this stage. However, state practice is open to interpretation and should include intrastate action and inaction, not just interstate interaction and acquiescence.

Some articulation of legality is needed to differentiate between legal custom and social practice. If there is no eligible interpretation, then there is no custom. If there is one eligible interpretation, then the custom is clear. If there are multiple eligible interpretations, then one must weigh the dimensions of fit and substance to determine the best interpretation.

Strong statements of *opinio juris* become relevant at this third stage because they represent normative considerations about what the law should be. The best interpretation is the one that most *coherently* explains fit and

---

21. B. Simma & P. Alston, *supra* note 18, at 83.

vv. *See* R Dworkin, Law's Empire (1986).

ww. J. Tsioulas, *supra* note 20.

substance, which varies according to the facilitative or moral content of the custom involved. Primarily facilitative customs do not involve strong substantive considerations and thus will be determined principally by fit. Primarily moral customs give rise to strong procedural and substantive normative considerations, which must be balanced against deficiencies in fit. Custom is also a fluid source of law, which causes the point of equilibrium to vary over time in light of new state practice, *opinio juris*, and moral considerations. Consequently, the reflective interpretive approach results in a more sophisticated understanding of fit and substance and constitutes a more nuanced method for reconciling them than the sliding scale in various ways.

First, the reflective interpretive approach recognizes that the role of the dimension of fit is to provide descriptive accuracy. Questions of fit and descriptive accuracy are both backward looking because they focus on whether a custom is supported by past practice. Tasioulas claims that strong statements of *opinio juris* can form the basis of eligible interpretations at the dimension of fit. Similarly, Michael Akehurst has argued that state practice should include paper practice in the form of statements, declarations, and resolutions.[22] I have demonstrated that this approach is not feasible because statements often fuse *lex lata* [the law that exists] and *lex ferenda* [the law as it ought to be] and thus lack descriptive accuracy. However, one can still form eligible interpretations of traditional and modern custom by considering the open-textured nature of practice. State practice should also include consideration of intrastate action (not just interstate interaction), obligations being observed (not just obligations being breached), and reasons for a lack of protest over breaches (other than acquiescence in the legality of those breaches). These forms of practice reflect the changing subject matter of international law to include intrastate issues and are descriptively accurate because they focus on action and inaction.

Second, I have outlined a dimension of substance that embodies both substantive and procedural normativity. Kirgis refers to strong moral issues but does not provide a theory for determining them. Tasioulas deliberately limits his discussion of the substantive aims of international law to coexistence and cooperation. By contrast, my approach provides a more expansive understanding of the substantive aims of international law, which includes recognized moral aims (such as the protection of human rights) that do not necessarily affect coexistence and cooperation. Substantive aims are frequently criticized as being subjective value judgments that serve as a vehicle for normative chauvinism. For this reason, I have defined moral issues as commonly held subjective values about right and wrong that have been adopted by a representative majority of states in treaties and declarations. This approach has several advantages. Focusing on commonly held, or intersubjective, values avoids the need to consider whether moral values can be objectively determined and it explains why these values can change over time. It also denotes an agreed set of values rather than requiring interpreters to determine what they believe the substantive aims of international law should be. It builds the concept of procedural normativity into the dimension of substance because these values have been accepted by a majority of states, which helps prevent accusations of Western ideological bias. Finally, while

22. M. Akehurst, Custom as a Source of International Law, 1974–75 B.Y.B.I.L. 1, 53.

these statements may include *lex lata* and *lex ferenda*, the dimension of fit already provides a threshold test to determine if a custom is adequately supported by practice.

Third, I have suggested a more nuanced approach to balancing fit and substance than the crude sliding scale. Finding traditional custom on the strength of state practice and fit alone allows it to become an apology for state power. Similarly, deducing modern custom purely from *opinio juris* and substance can create utopian laws that cannot regulate reality. Thus, the sliding scale can allow one element completely to outweigh the other. While a reflective equilibrium will lean toward the stronger value, it avoids extremes of apology and utopia. The strength of fit and state practice in traditional customs must still be balanced against their substantive deficiencies, such as a lack of procedural normativity. Similarly, modern customs must be supported by state practice because they must pass the threshold of fit and deficiencies in their fit may still outweigh their moral content. A lower standard of practice may be tolerated for customs with a strong moral content because violations of ideal standards are expected. However, while occasional breaches may not nullify their legal character, massive, grave, and persistent violations will. The only exceptions are *jus cogens* norms,[xx] which by definition cannot be undermined by contrary practice unless that practice creates another rule of *jus cogens*.

Fourth, Kirgis and Tasioulas argue that the more morally distasteful an activity, the more readily the Court will substitute *opinio juris* for state practice and vice versa. However, I have explained that substantive considerations apply asymmetrically to traditional and modern customs because of their facilitative and moral content. This reasoning results in a better explanation of when, and on what basis, traditional and modern customs will be formed. It also means that, to the extent that the reflective equilibrium can still be criticized for apology and utopia, these criticisms are less compelling because they apply to facilitative and moral customs, respectively. Criticizing a facilitative custom for being an exercise of power is not problematic because it does not concern substantive moral issues. Instead, these customs are akin to domestic traffic rules. If developing states wish to challenge a traditional custom, they can enact declarations in international fora, as they did on whether there should be an international minimum standard of compensation for expropriation or a national treatment standard.[23] Similarly, modern customs that set up ideal standards about moral issues are expected to be somewhat utopian.[24] Meron argues that the international community is willing to accept gradual or partial compliance as fulfilling the requirements for forming moral customs.[25] Alasdair MacIntyre argues that the charge of utopianism is made by "the deliberately shortsighted who congratulate themselves upon the limits of their vision."[26] While hard law that is always enforced may be preferable to soft law, the choice in areas such as human

---

xx. For discussion of the doctrine of *jus cogens*, see *infra* the Editors' Note, at 145–46.

23. Supported by [1962] Resolution on Permanent Sovereignty over Natural Resources **[Basic Document 4.4]**.

24. Supported by Charter of Economic Rights and Duties of States **[Basic Document 4.9]**.

25. T. Meron, *supra* note 11, at 44.

26. A. MacIntryre, Three Rival Versions of Moral Inquiry: Encyclopædia, Genealogy, and Tradition 234 (1990); *see also* Tasioulas, *supra* note 20, at 127.

rights is often between soft law and no law. Giving these aspirations some legal force may be preferable to giving them no legal status, because they can be enforced in extreme situations such as apartheid in South Africa and their legal status may harden over time.

Finally, the reflective equilibrium can be used to explain the fluid nature of customary international law. The sliding scale assumes that state practice and *opinio juris* are fixed and irreconcilable quantities that must be traded off against each other to form eligible interpretations of custom. However, I have demonstrated that state practice is open textured and capable of being interpreted in various ways. For example, contrary state practice can be analyzed as a breach of an old rule or as the seed of a new rule. Finding the best interpretation of practice and principles requires one to determine the most coherent explanation of state practice and *opinio juris*, rather than simply giving preference to one and discounting the other. For this reason, conflicting state practice should never be discounted as irrelevant to interpretation, because it may contain the seed for a new custom. It also clarifies how customs change over time in light of new state practice, *opinio juris*, and moral considerations.

The reflective interpretive approach rearticulates the theoretical foundations of custom in a more principled and flexible fashion. Instead of debating the relative merits and legitimacy of traditional and modern custom, this interpretive theory seeks to justify and reconcile the two approaches and, in so doing, offers a coherent theory of custom that helps to defend its integrity as a source of international law.

DISCUSSION NOTES/QUESTIONS[yy]

1. In Global Order—Values and Power in International Politics (2d ed. 1990), political scientist Lynn H. Miller writes as follows, at 88:

[W]hat happens when, because of a malfunction of some kind, the traffic lights at a busy intersection suddenly fail? The symbol of government ceases to operate; yet we would not expect every semblance of social order there to break down as a result. The drivers of the cars approaching that intersection still have a mutual interest in their own safety. As a result, they almost certainly will begin to create an ordering, or quasi-governmental, system of their own, perhaps even without any verbal communication. We should expect such drivers at least to slow down when they see the traffic lights not functioning, and then proceed only when they deem it safe. Logically, each will defer to the driver who arrives at the intersection next before him, for if all drivers do that, none will be more than minimally inconvenienced, and a dependable stop-and-go system, clear to all, will be in place.

Does this passage help to explain how rules of customary international law come about? Can you relate it to the theoretical discussion of the elements of custom as explained in the foregoing readings? Does it help to clarify the "quantitative" element? The "qualitative" element?

2. What is the difference, if any, between "custom" and "usage" and "habit"?

---

yy. Discussion Notes/Questions 3, 4 and 6 derive from Anthony A. D'Amato's contributions to the first and second editions of this coursebook. Discussion Notes/Questions 7, 9 and 10 were for the most part written by him for those earlier editions.

3. As seen, one of the elements of customary international law is said to be state practice. But, specifically, what practice? Must it be some kind of action? Is a vote in the UN General Assembly (where resolutions are presumptively not binding) as opposed to the UN Security Council (where resolutions are presumptively binding) state practice? Do domestic executive, legislative, or judicial statements constitute state practice? If so, is it relevant by what internal organ state action is taken? Can acts of omission be a form of practice? If so, under what circumstances? Must the absence of action have been deliberate? Further:

    a. How general must state practice be to establish customary law? How many states are needed? Does one consider only the practice of affected states? Is the practice of some states more important than that of others? Can there be a customary rule if the United States or some other major power has a different state practice from the majority of states? Can there be regional customary international law? Bilateral customary international law?

    b. How much consistency is required to have state practice? How does one determine whether the state practice is consistent or not since the circumstances will be different in every case? How far back in time must we go to determine whether there is consistency? Or inconsistency? Is one inconsistency or are several minor inconsistencies sufficient to negate a customary rule?

    c. How much time must pass to create state practice? May a single act constitute State practice sufficient to establish customary law? Is it possible to have instant customary law? If so, is this desirable? Undesirable?

    d. How can there be "a general practice accepted as law," to quote Article 38(1)(b) of the Statute of the International Court of Justice **(Basic Document 1.6)**, in the case of an omission or absence of action?

4. Another key element of customary international law is captured in the expression *opinio juris or opinio juris sive necessitatis*. What does this mean?

    a. How does one determine the existence of this subjective element, *opinio juris*? Is it not determined by the consistency of state practice? Is it anything more than a tacit agreement among states? If not, then why is it necessary that there be this separate subjective element to establish customary international law? Does it not all add up to the fact that customary law consists only of one element? Or is something else involved? If so, what?

    b. Can we assume an *opinio juris* because a state practice is socially necessary or suited to international needs? Can there be a customary international rule if all states agree on the norm in theory but none act in accordance with it in practice?

    c. Whose *opinio juris* is relevant for the purpose of establishing customary international law? Can a state have an opinion, legal or otherwise? If we respond by saying that states, or governments, have opinions in the form of policies, who, then, speaks for the state or government? What if the government is not representative of the people?

5. Upon whom is customary international law binding? Are dissenting and non-participating states bound by customary rules? Is the burden upon the dissenting state to resist the binding effect of a customary international law rule? If so, when and how must a state express its opposition? Does only a persistent

objection deny the binding effect of the customary rule? If so, what qualifies as a persistent objection? Does a qualified persistent objection prevent the creation of the rule or is the rule not binding only on the particular state? Is customary law binding on states that were not in existence at its creation?

6.   It is said that treaties can create customary international law—for example, the 1907 Hague Convention (No. IV) Respecting the Laws and Customs of War on Land and its annexed Regulations **(Basic Document 2.2)**, upon which the Nuremberg tribunal heavily relied as a matter of customary law to convict most of the Nazi leaders of World War II who otherwise might have escaped the Convention's strictures because some of the war's belligerents were not party to it, thus failing a necessary precondition for the Convention's applicability as treaty law. Note also Article 8 of the Rome Statute of the International Criminal Court **(Basic Document1.16)** in this regard. But how does a treaty create customary law? And where do we draw the line between a treaty obligation and a customary rule? Can customary international law come into being via a treaty that has not been ratified or entered into force? Can resolutions and declarations of the General Assembly and other quasi-parliamentary institutions establish customary international law?

7.   If the 1907 Hague Convention (No. IV) Respecting the Laws and Customs of War on Land **(Basic Document 2.2)** could give rise to customary law binding on all nations, what is to be made of the fact that the Convention contains no provision dealing with the defense of "superior orders" (i.e., the plea that one is relieved of legal responsibility on the grounds that the crime committed was done pursuant to an order given by a government or a superior in a chain of command)? Pursuant to what authority or "source" of international law might such a defense be established or allowed? As of the time of the Nuremberg trials, is it possible that customary law could have evolved a defense of "superior orders"? Can you think of any customary law precedents?

    a.   In any event, does the failure of the 1907 Convention to provide for the defense of "superior orders" mean that no defendant in a war crimes trial can plead that he or she was following the orders of a superior under threat of severe penalty? Does not an affirmative answer to this question seem logical? After all, if the defense of "superior orders" were to be allowed, what would be the utility of the 1907 Convention and its annexed Regulations? Could not every officer then escape their application by "passing the buck" up the line to her or his superior officer? In the case of Nazi Germany specifically, could not everyone who was subordinate to the Führer then make a successful defense based on the principle of absolute loyalty to the Führer's will?

    b.   On the other hand, should a war crimes tribunal—say, the war crimes tribunals established in the cases of the former Yugoslavia and Rwanda or the International Criminal Court (ICC)—ever be deaf to such a plea? Is it not true that non-commissioned officers seldom were indicted and brought to trial in the hundreds of war crimes trials that were conducted after World War II, and that even among lower-ranking officers leniency was shown?

Consider these questions especially in relation to the *ad hoc* war crimes tribunals established to prosecute for atrocities committed in the former Yugoslavia and Rwanda and the ICC relative to Darfur.

8.   Can state practice negate a treaty commitment or obligation? What happens to a customary international law rule when the supporting state practice

changes? Is there law during the period of transition? What rules do we apply then, if any?

9. In an actual case, how does the international lawyer determine whether there exists a rule of customary law to be applied in that case? Can he or she look at judicial decisions and the teachings of qualified international law publicists to prove that a certain conduct constitutes a rule of customary international law? How do courts and arbitral tribunals do it? Do they engage in or refer to a detailed study of state practice? Is it not true that most of the time courts and arbitral tribunals simply announce that a particular customary law rule exists and that they rarely examine the actual state practice or consider whether it is accompanied by the subjective element of *opinio juris*?

To put these questions into immediately relevant context, is it possible to find in the practice of nations rules of customary international law that are of sufficient specificity as to define "war crimes" and "crimes against humanity" so that their violations may be legitimately prosecuted? Because of the precedent of Nuremberg, the answer to this question in the cases of the war crimes tribunals established relative to the former Yugoslavia and Rwanda must be in the affirmative. Likewise in relation to the ICC considering articles 7 and 8 of its Rome Statute **(Basic Document 1.16)**. But what of Nuremberg itself? By what process did these rules arise so as to be applicable there? How do we know when a given state practice has matured into a rule of customary international law? These are important questions. Knowing the process enables one to articulate the rule; and being able to articulate the rule obviously is significant in a context such as the Nuremberg trials where the defendants were charged and found guilty for having committed crimes violating customary rules of international law. How do you answer these questions in relation to the case of Darfur?

10. If war crimes are applicable to all fighting forces via customary international law, have we any choice but to look to the customary practices of all states to substantiate indictable offenses against the Axis leaders of World War II or the former leaders in Yugoslavia and Rwanda? Or the current leaders in Sudan? If so, what precedents would be appropriate? The "scorched earth" and "saturation bombing" policies of the World War II Allied Powers? The atomic bombings of Hiroshima and Nagasaki? The napalm bombing by the United States in Vietnam?

11. That customary international law is today marked by counter-positivist trend that exalts treaties (ratified or not), UN General Assembly resolutions, international commissions, and academic commentary is not to be denied. An important question is: why? In *The Cult of Custom in the Late 20th Century*, 17 Cal. W. Int'l L. J. 133, 135 (1987), W. Michael Reisman contends that it reflects "opposition to the *quantity* and the *style* of formal international legislation as it has developed in the last [several decades]. The setting of necessary [international] legislation is being shifted from the most inclusive and open international arenas, such as the General Assembly and universal conferences, to more limited alliances, regional and, within them, value sectoral conferences from which most of the new majority in the United Nations will be excluded. The "all states" trend of the last [half century], seeking to bring *everyone* into an inclusive conference arena, is being reversed in favor of a network of restrictive-access legislative arenas." Reisman is skeptical of the counter-positivist reaction. He writes: "Because this shift from the floors of the world legislatures to back rooms elsewhere is inconsistent with venerated international legal myth, it is more convenient, if less accurate, to describe it as the resurgence of custom." *Id.* Do you agree or disagree with Reisman? Why? Why not?

12. What is the value, if any, of customary international law today, particularly in relation to major world order problems? Does the process of customary law-making meet the needs of a Twenty-first Century global civilization? Can customary law change quickly enough to keep pace with scientific and technological breakthroughs? Is it adequately democratic to be representative of different legal expectations in a multicultured world?

C. GENERAL PRINCIPLES OF LAW

As a third "source" of international law, per Article 38(1)(c) of the Statute of the International Court of Justice **(Basic Document 1.6)**, what, you ask, are "general principles of law recognized by civilized nations"? How do they supplement treaties and customary international law? And what is meant by the expression "civilized nations"? One thing is clear: "general principles of law recognized by civilized nations" were relied upon by the World War II Allied Powers in their prosecution of the Nazi leaders following World War II.[zz] And they have been relied upon also by the drafters of the Rome Statute of the International Criminal Court (ICC). *See* Article 21(1)(c) and arguably also Article 21(1)(b) and (2) of the Rome Statute of the International Criminal Court (Basic Document **(Basic Document 1.16)**.

But what precisely is meant by the "general principles" phrase? As it happens, it depends at least in part on who you ask.

Thus Professor Mark Janis writes, in An Introduction to International Law 56 (3d ed. 1999), "some [scholars] liberally suggest that the availability of general principles as a source of international law permits international lawyers to apply natural law, while others restrictively contend that general principles of law may be international law only when drawn from customary international practice"—for example, legal positivists who insist upon state consent as a precondition to the establishment of any international law rule and who therefore are loathe to admit to international legal rules that are based on *nonconsensual* foundations such as natural law (hence their stress upon the qualitative element, or *opinio juris*, in the making of customary law). But "the most usual approach to general principles of law as a source of international law," Professor Janis continues, "relies upon techniques of comparative law. The basic notion is that a general principle of law is some proposition of law so fundamental that it will be found in virtually every legal system." *Id.* On the other hand, you wonder, is there really any reason why "general principles of law" cannot have all three meanings? After all, international tribunals had for many years relied upon all three meanings even before the phrase was inserted into the P.C.I.J.'s Statute in 1920.

As for the expression "civilized nations," did it, during World War II and the decade preceding, include Germany, the homeland not only of Bach, Beethoven, and Brahms (and Kant, Goethe, and Schiller) but also of Adolf Hitler, the killer of over six million Jews? In the horrible light of Hiroshima and Nagasaki—so far the only instances of innocent men, women, and children being incinerated and radiated by nuclear weapons—does it include the United States? For that matter, does it include the former Yugoslavia, Rwanda, Sudan? Also, may "general principles" be invoked to supplement or

---

zz. *Supra* note **g** (p. 83).

modify what treaty law and customary international law have to say on a given subject or may they be referred to only to fill gaps that treaty law and customary law fail to fill? Article 21(1)(c) of the Rome Statute suggests the latter, but this is not clear. It remains for ICC practice to give us the answer.

All of these and related issues compel you to resume your review of public international law. You turn to your treatise yet again.

HERSCH LAUTERPACHT, 1 INTERNATIONAL LAW
68–74 (E. Lauterpacht ed., 1970)

The fact that, on the face of it, there are no provisions of a treaty or of customary international law directly applicable to a given situation does not necessarily mean that there exists a gap in the law and that there is, therefore, no room for the application of international law.... [W]hen there might ... appear to exist a clear gap in the law as laid down by custom or treaty, international practice recognizes, and the very existence of the international community necessitates, a residuary source of law on which States are entitled to act and by reference to which international courts are bound to render decisions. That residuary source is, in the language of Article 38 of the Statute of the Court **[Basic Document 1.6]**, the body of "general principles of law recognized by civilized nations."

What is the meaning of that expression? These "general principles" are not, as such, principles of moral justice as distinguished from law; they are not rules of "equity" in the ethical sense; nor are they a speculative law conceived by way of deductive reasoning from legal and moral principles. They are, in the first instance, those principles of law, private and public, which contemplation of the legal experience of civilized nations leads one to regard as obvious maxims of jurisprudence of a general and fundamental character— such as the principle that no one can be judge in his own cause, that a breach of a legal duty entails the obligation of restitution, that a person cannot invoke his own wrong as a reason for release from a legal obligation, that the law will not countenance the abuse of a right, that legal obligations must be fulfilled and rights must be exercised in good faith, and the like. The International Court of Justice and its predecessor have occasionally acted on these and other general principles of law. So have international tribunals generally.

However, the recourse to and the utility of general principles of law are not confined to fundamental, or abstract, maxims of jurisprudence of a general character. "General principles of law" are, and have been, a legitimate source of judicial decision and State action in regard to specific rules and situations. * * * Whenever a question arises which is not governed by an existing rule of international law imposing an obligation upon a State or, in the absence of such a rule, acknowledging by implication its freedom from obligation, or in which the existing rule required elucidation or development, the rich repository of "general principles" may be legitimately resorted to by a tribunal, a Government, or the scholar grappling with a novel or difficult situation. Such instruction is available not automatically but only as the result of a search which may be exacting....

On occasions, the search for a general principle of law may fail to offer direct assistance for the reason that national systems of law differ with regard to the particular subject. Even in such cases the negative result may not be altogether without usefulness inasmuch as it may throw light on the intricacies of the problem involved. However, experience shows that in the vast majority of cases such differences are limited to questions of form and procedure and that behind national differences of technique and approach there asserts itself an essential uniformity of the law—a reminder that the increasingly frequent description of general principles of law as the modern law of nature is no mere form of words.

Finally, in the rapidly expanding field of relations between Governments which are substantially indistinguishable from that of ordinary commercial relations between private persons, circumstances call, on that account, for the application of general principles of law approximating to general principles of private law in the restricted sense. Thus, there has been a growing number of treaties between Governments providing for the sale or exchange of goods, the grant or opening of a credit, the loan of money or guarantee of a debt, the lease of property of an ordinary private law character, and the like.... [S]ome of these treaties ... may be governed by ... the rules of private law of one of the contracting parties. However, the circumstances of these transactions do not as a rule point to an intention of the parties to submit to the law of the other party. In view of this the relations in question ... are more properly governed by what has been described as the commercial law of nations, namely, general principles of private law applicable to the transaction in question.[aaa]

The same may apply to agreements, especially in the sphere of private law, between one [intergovernmental] organisation and another, between [intergovernmental] organisations and States, and, probably, between [intergovernmental] organisations and private individuals. The relations between public international organizations and their officials—an expanding field of international administrative law—[also] call for the application of "general principles of law" in that particular sphere.

BIN CHENG, GENERAL PRINCIPLES OF LAW—AS APPLIED BY INTERNATIONAL COURTS AND TRIBUNALS
23–25 (1953)

... [T]he line of demarcation between custom and general principles of law recognized by civilized nations is often not very clear, since international custom or customary international law, understood in a broad sense, may

---

aaa. *See, e.g.,* Award of Lord Asquith of Bishopstone in the Matter of an Arbitration "Between Petroleum Development (Trucial Coast) Ltd. and the Sheikh of Abu Dhabi," 1 I.C.L.Q. 247, 250 (1952):

What is the "Proper Law" applicable in construing this [oil concession] contract? This is a contract made in Abu Dhabi and wholly to be performed in that country. If any municipal system of law were applicable, it would prima facie be that of Abu Dhabi. But no such law can reasonably be said to exist. The Sheikh administers a purely discretionary justice with the assistance of the Koran; and it would be fanciful to suggest that in this very primitive region there is any settled body of legal principles applicable to the construction of modern commercial instruments. Nor can I see any basis on which the municipal law of England could apply. On the contrary, Clause 17 of the agreement, cited above, repels the notion that the municipal law of any country, as such, could be appropriate. The terms of that clause invite, indeed prescribe, the application of principles rooted in the good sense and common practice of the generality of civilised nations—a sort of "modern law of nature." I do not think that on this point there is any conflict between the parties.

include all that is unwritten in international law, *i.e.*, both custom and general principles of law. In Article 38 [of the ICJ Statute] **[Basic Document 1.6]**, however, custom is used in a strict sense, being confined to what is a general practice among States accepted by them as law....

In the definition of [general principles of law], there is also the element of recognition on the part of civilized peoples but the requirement of a general practice is absent. The object of recognition is, therefore, no longer the legal character of the rule implied in an international usage, but the existence of certain principles intrinsically legal in nature.... Principles are to be distinguished from rules.... This part of international law does not consist ... in specific rules formulated for practical purposes, but in general propositions underlying the various rules of law which express the essential qualities of juridical truth itself, in short of Law. Thus Lord Phillimore, who proposed the formula [of Article 38], explained that by general principles of law he meant "maxims of law."[27] But how is it possible to ascertain whether a given principle is a principle of law and not of another cognate social discipline, such as religion or morality? The recognition of its legal character by ... the municipal law of civilized peoples, where the conception of law is already highly developed, gives the necessary confirmation and evidence of the juridical character of the principle concerned. The qualification "recognized by civilized nations" was intended to safeguard against subjectivity and possible arbitrariness on the part of the judge. It should be noticed, however, that the word *nation* was originally used in the sense of "people" rather than "State." The qualifying epithet "civilized" was, therefore, necessary in order to exclude from consideration systems of law of primitive communities which were not yet civilized.... [28]

27. Lord Phillimore, Procès-verbaux 335.

28. The term "civilized nations" is no longer so restricted. Today the search for general principles, while still heavily influenced by the civil and common law traditions that have their origins in Europe, extends to all reaches of the globe. *See* H. Bokor–Szego, *General Principles of Law, in* International Law: Achievements and Prospects 213, 214–15 (M. Bedjaoui ed., 1991):

The origin of the expression "civilized nations" goes back to the colonial era, when the international community was mainly composed of European States. For a long time, this "traditional" international law meant, basically, European international law. This law was gradually expanded with the founding of the United States of America and subsequently the accession to independence of the Central American and South American States. Yet despite the expansion of international law, the gulf which existed at that time between the juridical status of States subject to international law and that of dependent territories persisted and indeed widened. The expression "civilized nations"

clearly reflected the wish to see international legal conflicts settled in terms of Anglo–Saxon [law] (common law) and the law of the European continental States based on Roman law, or according to legal systems derived from one or [the] other of these. After the First World War, and even more so after the Second, the composition of the international community changed radically with the accession to independence of a large number of States in Asia and Africa. The participation by the socialist States in international relations helped to bring pressure to bear on the "traditional" reference frames of international law. In 1973, some governments strongly criticized the expression "civilized nations" in their reply to the United Nations Secretary–General's questionnaire on a revision of the role of the International Court of Justice, considering it to be a relic of outdated colonialism, and proposing that it be defeated.* * * The prevailing view *is that today the expression "civilized nations" ... should be understood as meaning sovereign States irrespective of their political system and the degree of development of their economy.*

OSCAR SCHACHTER, INTERNATIONAL LAW IN THEORY AND PRACTICE

50–53 (1991)

... [The] category, general principles of municipal law, has given rise to a considerable body of writing and much controversy. Article 38(1)(c) of the Statute of the Court **[Basic Document 1.6]** does not expressly refer to principles of national law but rather [to] general principles "recognized by civilized nations." The travaux préparatoires reveal an interesting variety of views about this subparagraph during the drafting stage. Some of the participants had in mind equity and principles recognized "by the legal conscience of civilized nations." ... Elihu Root, the American member of the drafting committee, prepared the text finally adopted and it seemed clear that his amendment was intended to refer to principles "actually recognized and applied in national legal systems."[29] The fact that the subparagraph was distinct from those on treaty and custom indicated an intent to treat general principles as an independent source of law, and not as a subsidiary source. As an independent source, it did not appear to require any separate proof that such principles of national law had been "received" into international law.

However, a significant minority of jurists holds that national law principles, even if generally found in most legal systems, cannot *ipso facto* be international law. One view is that they must receive the *imprimatur* of State consent through custom or treaty in order to become international law. The strict positivist school adheres to that view. A somewhat modified version is adopted by others to the effect that rules of municipal law cannot be considered as recognized by civilized nations unless there is evidence of the concurrence of States on their status as international law. Such concurrence may occur through treaty, custom or other evidence of recognition. This would allow for some principles, such as *res judicata*, which are not customary law but are generally accepted in international law....

Several influential international legal scholars have considered municipal law an important means for developing international law and extending it into new areas of international concern.... The growth of transnational commercial and financial transactions has also been perceived as a fruitful area for the application of national law rules to create a "commercial law of nations," referred to as a "vast *terra incognita*."

Despite the eloquent arguments made for using national law principles as an independent source of international law, it cannot be said that either courts or the political organs of States have significantly drawn on municipal law principles as an autonomous and distinct ground for binding rules of conduct. It is true that the International Court and its predecessor the Permanent Court of International Justice have made reference on a number of occasions to "generally accepted practice" or "all systems of law" as a basis for its approval of a legal rule.... Those references to national law have most often been to highly general ideas of legal liability or precepts of judicial administration. In the former category, we find the much-quoted principles of the *Chorzów Factory* case[30] that "every violation of an engagement involves an

---

29. H. Waldock, *General Course on Public International Law*, 115 Recueil 237 (1965–II)....

30. Factory at Chorzów (Ger. v. Pol.) (Merits), 1928 P.C.I.J. (ser. A) No. 21, at 93, 17, 19.

obligation to make reparation" and that "a party cannot take advantage of his own wrong." These maxims and certain maxims of legal interpretation, as for example, *lex specialis derogat generalis*, and "no one may transfer more than he has," are also regarded as notions intrinsic to the idea of law and legal reasoning. As such they can be (and have been) accepted not as municipal law, but as general postulates of international law, even if not customary law in the specific sense of that concept.

The use of municipal law rules for international judicial and arbitral procedure has been more common and more specific than any other type of application. For example, the International Court has accepted *res judicata* as applicable to international litigation;[31] it has allowed recourse to indirect evidence (*i.e.,* inferences of fact and circumstantial evidence);[32] and it has approved the principle that legal remedies against a judgment are equally open to either party.[33] Arbitral tribunals have applied the principle of prescription (or laches) to international litigation relying on analogies from municipal law. Lauterpacht's *Private Law Sources and Analogies of International Law*, written in 1926, still remains a valuable repository of examples, as does Bin Cheng's later work on *General Principles as Applied by International Courts and Tribunals*.

But considerable caution is still required in inferring international law from municipal law, even where the principles of national law are found in many "representative" legal systems. The international cases show such use in a limited degree, nearly always as a supplement to fill in gaps left by the primary sources of treaty and custom.... The most important limitation on the use of municipal law principles arises from the requirement that the principle be appropriate for application on the international level. Thus, the universally accepted common crimes—murder, theft, assault, incest—that apply to individuals are not crimes under international law by virtue of their ubiquity. In the *Right of Passage Over Indian Territory* case (Port. v. India),[34] the Court rejected arguments that the municipal law of easements found in most legal systems were appropriate principles for determining rights of transit over State territory. Similarly, a contention that the law of trusts could be used to interpret the mandate of South Africa over South West Africa (Namibia) did not win approval as international law but it may possibly have had an indirect influence on the Court's reasoning in its advisory opinions. Lord McNair, in an individual opinion, in the 1950 Advisory Opinion on the *International Status of South West Africa*, expressed a balanced conclusion on the subject of analogies from private law that merits quotation here.

> International law has recruited and continues to recruit many of its rules and institutions from private systems of law.... The way in which international law borrows from the source is not by means of importing private law institutions "lock, stock and barrel," ready-made and fully equipped with a set of rules.... In my opinion the true view of the duty of international tribunals in this matter is to regard any features or

---

31. Effect of Awards Made by the United Nations Administrative Tribunal, 1956 ICJ 53 (Advisory Opinion).

32. Corfu Channel (U.K. v. Alb.) (Merits), 1949 ICJ 4. [*see also* **Basic Document 7.5**].

33. Judgments of the Administrative Tribunal of the ILO Upon Complaints Made Against UNESCO, 1956 ICJ 77, at 85–86. (Advisory Opinion).

34. Right of Passage Over Indian Territory (Port. v. India) (Merits), 1960 ICJ 6.

terminology which are reminiscent of the rules and institutions of private law as an indication of policy and principles rather than as directly importing these rules and institutions.[35]

I would subscribe to this general formulation and stress the requirement that the use of municipal law must be appropriate for international relations.

At the same time, I would suggest a somewhat more positive approach for the emergent international law concerned with the individual, business companies, environmental dangers and shared resources. Inasmuch as these areas have become the concern of international law, national law principles will often be suitable for international application. This does not mean importing municipal rules "lock, stock and barrel," but it suggests that domestic law rules applicable to such matters as individual rights, contractual remedies, liability for extra-hazardous activities, or restraints on use of common property, have now become pertinent for recruitment into international law. In these areas, we may look to representative legal systems not only for the highly abstract principles of the kind referred to earlier but to more specific rules that are sufficiently widespread as to be considered "recognized by civilized nations". . . .

EDITORS' NOTE

States and others frequently assert that certain principles of international law, whether nationally or internationally derived, are so fundamental as to be considered higher law (or *jus cogens*), *i.e.*, non-derogable or peremptory—for example, the basic principles of territorial sovereignty and *pacta sunt servanda*, found among the "general principles of law recognized by civilized nations" as well as in customary international law. But what, precisely, is this notion of higher law or *jus cogens*? Writes Malcolm Shaw, in International Law (4th ed. 1997), at 97: "The concept of *jus cogens* is based upon an acceptance of fundamental and superior values within the system and in some respects is akin to the notion of public order or public policy in domestic legal orders." To this may be added Professor Janis' observation that *"[j]us cogens* is a norm thought to be so fundamental that it invalidates rules drawn from treaty or custom. Usually, a *jus cogens* norm presupposes an international public order sufficiently potent to control states that might otherwise establish contrary rules on a consensual basis." Mark W. Janis, An Introduction to International Law 62–63 (4th ed. 2003). *See*, in this connection, Articles 53 and 64 of the Vienna Convention on the Law of Treaties **(Basic Document 1.10)** entitled, respectively, "Treaties Conflicting with a Peremptory Norm of General International Law (Jus Cogens)" and "Emergence of a New Peremptory Norm of General International Law (Jus Cogens)." Consider also the following excerpt from *Starke's* International Law 48–49 (I. Shearer 11th ed. 1994):

> . . . [M]ention should be made of the concept of *jus cogens* . . . which may . . . operate to invalidate a treaty or agreement between States to the extent of the inconsistency with any of such principles or norms. . . . There is undoubtedly some analogy between *jus cogens* and the principles of public policy which at common law render a contract void if it offends against these, such as the principle that parties cannot by agreement between themselves oust the ordinary courts from their jurisdiction. For example, in the international field, a treaty for the purpose of carrying out operations of piracy *jure*

---

35. International Status of South West-Africa, 1950 ICJ 128, at 148 (Advisory Opinion).

gentium would be void and would not be enforced by an international tribunal. Assuming that this analogy holds good, one must correspondingly bear in mind some of the metaphors used by harassed common law judges to describe the doctrine of public policy, such as "a very unruly horse," "treacherous ground," and "slippery ground." Critics of the concept of *jus cogens* in international law have also urged that it may be resorted to as a means of avoiding onerous treaty obligations, or even to justify interference in matters otherwise falling within the domestic jurisdiction of States.

One major difficulty is related to the identification of norms of *jus cogens*. First, should this function of identification be performed solely by multilateral law-making Conventions, or may a norm of *jus cogens* evolve through the same process as in the case of customary rules of international law? Article 64 of the Vienna Convention on the Law of Treaties provides that "if a new peremptory norm of general international law emerges, any existing treaty which is in conflict with that norm becomes void and terminates." The word "emerges" shows that it was contemplated that a norm of *jus cogens* could be one of customary international law. Second, there is a lack of consensus as to what, at the present time, are norms of *jus cogens*....

But see Roberto Ago, *The Law of Treaties in Light of the Vienna Convention*, 134 Recueil 297, 324 n.37 (1971–III) (editors' transl.), who views the *jus cogens* doctrine applicable to

the fundamental rules concern the safeguarding of peace and notably those which prohibit recourse to force or the threat of force; fundamental rules of a humanitarian nature (prohibitions of genocide, slavery, racial discrimination, protection of rights essential to the human person in times of peace and in times of war); rules which forbid infringement of the independence and the sovereign equality of States; rules which ensure to all members of the international community the enjoyment of certain common resources (high seas, outer space, etc.).

Arguably, *jus cogens* doctrines, principles, and rules forbidding infringement of the independence and sovereign equality of states can work against the goals of the tribunals established in The Hague to prosecute for war crimes and related atrocities committed in the former Yugoslavia and Rwanda. But others cited by Ago in 1971—rules prohibiting the threat or use of force and fundamental rules of a humanitarian nature—clearly do not.

REMARKS BY HILARY CHARLESWORTH, PANEL ON "SOURCES OF INTERNATIONAL LAW: ENTRENCHING THE GENDER BIAS"

in Proceedings of the Second Joint Conference of the American Society of International
Law and the Nederlandse Vereniging voor Internationaal
Recht (at The Hague, 22–24 July 1993) 421, 421–24 (1994)

The "general principles of law recognized by civilized nations" [including the *jus cogens* principle] are perhaps the most controversial source of international law. What I want to argue is that while general principles can be an essentially conservative force in entrenching the gender bias in international law, this source of law may also offer the possibility of transformation.... Professor Cherif Bassiouni has argued that, in the face of increasing global interdependence, customary and conventional law are not always adequate to respond to major contemporary issues, such as human rights, the environment, economic development and international criminality.[36] He contends that general principles may take up the slack, indeed that they may become "the most important and influential source of international law in this decade."[37]

What might be a feminist approach to this? * * * If one looks at the traditional way in which general principles are defined, it suggests they may well be a vehicle by which the androcentric assumptions of national legal systems are reproduced and reinforced in the international legal sphere. The subordination of women to men through both the structure and substance of law is one truly universal feature of national legal systems; implicitly, and sometime explicitly, a core legal concept. All national legal systems have been fashioned by men ... and reflect the interests of their designers.... A real danger of bringing general principles of domestic law into the international law system is that they will simply transpose the gender bias of national legal systems to the international plane. * * * [Additionally, a] core feature of many national legal systems is their concern to distinguish legal activity from politics and morality.... This leads to a very narrow form of dispute-resolution in which parties are viewed detached from their actual social context. Imbalances in social and economic power between individuals are regarded as irrelevant in legal terms.... Incorporation of general principles of this sort into the international sphere will not advance women's equality.

A second feminist criticism of Article 38(1)(c) is that it makes quite explicit the consensual assumptions of the international legal order; that the general principles can be translated to the international plane because all or some states have recognized them as such. Any feminist analysis of the international legal order must tackle this institutionalization of state perspectives in law-making. For a long time feminists accepted the state as a neutral institution which could be persuaded to accommodate women's interests, but this project has failed and has led to new understandings of the state.... [W]omen ... form the largest group whose interests remain unacknowledged in the state structure.

... The few general principles which are generally accepted as international law tend to be procedural or otherwise without immediate implications for gender. * * * One category of general principles, *jus cogens*, involves ... substantive commitments. [However, it] is not a properly universal one ...; [it] reflect[s] a male perspective of what is fundamental to international society that may not be shared by women or backed up by women's experience[s] of life ..., [with] [w]omen ... relegated to the periphery of communal values. My aim is not to challenge the powerful symbolic significance of *jus cogens*, but to argue that the symbolism is itself skewed and gendered. The content of *jus cogens* would be much richer if women's lives contributed to the designation of international fundamental values. The violations of human rights typically included in the catalogue of *jus cogens* norms are of undoubted seriousness: genocide, slavery, murder, systematic racial discrimination, etc. The silences of the list, however, indicate that women's experiences have not directly contributed to it. For example, although race discrimination consistently appears in *jus cogens* inventories, discrimination on the basis of

---

36. M. C. Bassiouni, *A Functional Approach to "General Principles of International Law,"* 77 Mich. J. Int'l L. 768 (1990).

37. *Id.* at 769.

sex does not. And yet, sex discrimination is an even more widespread injustice, affecting the lives of more than half the world's population.

How can a feminist analysis contribute to the development of general principles as a source of international law? One of the ways is to identify all the silences of the category and to ask, for example, why violence against women is not prohibited as a general principle of both national and international law? ... NGOs can have a particularly important role in this respect....

Another way that could improve general principles from a feminist perspective is to de-emphasize the state as their source. Accepting statehood and sovereignty as givens in the international legal order narrows our imaginative universe and the possibilities of reconstruction. Developing general principles of international law from the activities of international organizations is one way of reducing the androcentric influence of statehood. Another approach is a feminist reconstruction of the category of general principles. For example, notions of equity are often acknowledged as general principles and these could be developed to include the advancement of sexual equality. Feminist rethinking of *jus cogens* would give prominence to a range of human rights, including the right to sexual equality, to food, to reproductive freedom, to be free from fear of violence and oppression, and to peace. * * * [I]t should be possible for even traditional international legal theory to accommodate rights that are fundamental to the existence and dignity of [over] half the world's population.

DISCUSSION NOTES/QUESTIONS

1. The preceding extract by Hilary Charlesworth, citing Bassiouni, argues for the proposition that "general principles" provide a rich opportunity for developing new norms of conventional and customary international law and for developing a supplemental source to treaty law and customary international law. Consider, in this connection, the following quotation from Morton A. Kaplan & Nicholas deB. Katzenbach, The Political Foundations of International Law 263 (1961):

> As vague and discretionary as the injunction to use "general principles of law" may be, it is a limitation upon, rather than an extension of, the capacity of courts and other decision makers applying international law. We can see that this is true if we review the long and inconclusive debate about whether or not international arbitrators are free to decide *ex aequo et bono*—according to concepts of "justice and fairness."[bbb] Prevailing doctrine is that they are not free to do so unless specifically authorized by the parties, which rarely occurs. The phrasing suggests an absence of objective standards required by the judicial function. Although we suspect that it makes little difference to the decision arrived at, preference for "general principles of law" is a preference for principles that are as definite as possible. It reflects consensus that agreement would be impossible if nations had to agree on new rules or if judges were free to create new norms unrestrained by recorded common experience.

Does this quotation cause you to alter any conclusions you may have reached about "general principles" as a "source" of international law? Does it cause you

---

bbb. *See infra* Section E of this chapter, at 157.

to wonder about the capacity of international law, as circumscribed by Article 38 of the ICJ Statute **(Basic Document 1.6)**, to meet the unprecedented challenges to world order brought about by growing transnational economic and technological interdependence? How might Schachter, *supra*, react to this quotation?

2. Note that international tribunals often refer to general or well-recognized principles of international law when referring to rules of customary international law as opposed to "general principles of law recognized by civilized nations," *e.g.*, the principles of state sovereignty, territorial integrity, equality, non-intervention, self-defense, etc. So do international law publicists. Professor Schachter, *supra*, appears to consider them "general principles" within the meaning of Article 38(1)(c) of the ICJ Statute **(Basic Document 1.6)**. Do you agree with this conclusion? If so, what happens to the distinction between general principles of customary international law and "general principles of law recognized by civilized nations"?

3. "General principles of law recognized by civilized nations" is the third listed "source" of international law in Article 38 of the ICJ Statute **(Basic Document 1.6)** after treaties and custom and in Article 21 of the Rome Statute of the International Criminal Court **(Basic Document 1.16)** after treaties. Can you imagine a situation in which a general principle might take precedence over a treaty or a custom accepted as law, and thus challenge the hierarchy or sequence set forth in Article 38 and Article 21?

4. It is widely recognized among leading comparative law authorities that the major legal systems of the world include (a) the Romanist–Germanic–Civilist legal systems, (b) the Common Law legal systems, (c) the Marxist–Socialist legal systems, (d) the Islamic legal systems, and (e) the Asian legal systems. *See, e.g.*, R. David, Les Grands Systèmes de Droit Contemporaires 22–32 (5th ed. 1973). Is it reasonable to suppose that a "general principle of law recognized by civilized nations" cannot become part of international law unless it is recognized by all of these legal systems? A majority? One or two? When it comes to resolving international legal disputes, is it possible that some legal systems may be more helpful than others in supplying the necessary legal principles? If so, is it reasonable to suppose that a "general principle" can become part of international law *without* being recognized by all the major legal systems?

5. Notice that Article 38(1)(c) of the ICJ Statute **(Basic Document 1.6)** refers to "general principles of law *recognized* by civilized nations" (emphasis added). Does this mean that there must be some sort of consent to, or acknowledgment of, a general principle before it can become part of international law? If so, how is that consent or acknowledgment manifested? Is a tacit agreement sufficient? Must the general principle have matured into a rule of customary international law? Or is a general principle something that does not require "state practice" and therefore, to become part of international law, is not dependent on achieving customary law status?

6. Recall that, in theory, treaties are binding only on states that have consented to be bound by them and that customary international law is binding on a state only if it has not objected persistently. Is a "general principle of law recognized by civilized nations" binding on a state that has explicitly rejected—or refused to *recognize*—that principle? Does your answer depend on how you define "law" or on the school of jurisprudence that commands your intellectual loyalty?

7. Oscar Schachter, *supra*, argues that a municipal law principle must be not only "general" and "recognized" but also "appropriate" for international application to become part of international law. What conclusions may we draw from this

viewpoint relative to the expansion and strengthening of international law? How would an international lawyer transform a national norm into an international one? What would be required?

8. In the second edition of this coursebook, Anthony D'Amato posed the following questions and challenge:

> The defendants at Nuremberg were charged with, *inter alia*, crimes against humanity. Never having been invoked in state practice before World War II, and therefore never having been part of customary international law before the war, is one to conclude, as one might infer from the general indictment drawn up against the Nazi war leaders, that crimes against humanity implicate general principles of law recognized by civilized nations? If so, what general principles prior to Nuremberg? Prohibitions on state "murder," "extermination," and "enslavement"? Possibly. But persecutions on political, racial, and religious grounds? Recall that the former Soviet Union, one of the principal drafters of the general indictment against the Nuremberg defendants, committed vast purges under Stalin during the 1930s when millions of Soviet citizens were executed. And recall, too, that, during the same period, varying degrees of racial apartheid existed *de jure* as well as *de facto* in most of the United States, another principal drafter of the general indictment. In any event, what do you think the Nuremberg Tribunal held in respect of the crimes against humanity charges brought against the Nazi leaders? Attempt a reasoned position before reading on. As it happens, the Tribunal decided that "revolting and horrible as many of these crimes [against humanity] were," such crimes prior to 1939 were not "within the court's jurisdiction" (even though the charter that set up the Tribunal gave it jurisdiction over such crimes!). The judges *did* find that crimes against humanity *after* 1939 were in conjunction with other war crimes, and thus there was a "link" that made it possible for the Tribunal to assess guilt, in part, on the basis of crimes against humanity.

Do you agree with the Nuremberg Tribunal? For a study that concludes that the Tribunal's basis for assessing guilt was predicated mainly on the traditional war crimes category and not on crimes against humanity, see Anthony A. D'Amato, Wesley L. Gould & Larry D. Woods, *War Crimes & Vietnam*, 57 Cal. L. Rev. 1055, 1061–63 (1969), *reprinted in* 3 The Vietnam War and International Law 407 (R. Falk ed., 1972). Does this assessment apply as well to the ICC? Consider Article 7 of its Rome Statute **(Basic Document 1.16)**.

9. Roberto Ago contends, *supra*, that the prohibition of genocide is a prohibition having *jus cogens* status. One may add that it has had this status for quite some time. It surely is beyond doubt, for example, that the United States, which did not become a full party to the 1948 Convention on the Prevention and Punishment of the Crime of Genocide **(Basic Document 3.2)** until 25 November 1988, could not have entered into any treaty or other arrangement sometime before that date that would have had as its intent the killing or other infliction of serious mental or bodily harm of a national, ethnical, racial, or religious group as such (contrary to Articles I and II of the Convention). Might it, then, be fairly maintained that a government that deliberately kills or harms, say, an indigenous people as part of an effort to exploit the resources of a rainforest is violating not only a treaty prohibition but a "general principle of law" with *jus cogens* status as well?

D.   JUDICIAL DECISIONS AND THE TEACHINGS OF HIGHLY QUALIFIED PUBLICISTS

You now have renewed understanding that international legal authority may be derived from treaties, custom, and general principles of law—traditionally viewed as the primary means through which international law is made. However, you note from Article 38(1)(d) of the ICJ Statute **(Basic Document 1.6)** that there are yet other acknowledged "sources" of international law, to wit, "judicial decisions and the teachings of the most highly qualified publicists of the various nations, as subsidiary means for the determination of rules of law." But what judicial decisions? International ones only? National ones also? If so, which? Only the permanent? Also the *ad hoc*? The highest tribunals only? Adjudicative ones only? Other third-party decision-making processes? And who are "the most highly qualified publicists"? Is there a list of them somewhere? Is there some special standard to be applied? And why are they and "judicial decisions" designated as only "subsidiary means" for ascertaining rules of international law? Note, by the way, that, except, insofaras Article 21(b) of the Rome Statute of the International Criminal Court **(Basic Document 1.16)** authorizes the ICC "[to] apply principles and rules of law as interpreted in its previous decisions," judicial decisions are not explicitly recognized as a source of law upon which the ICC may rely in adjudicating cases brought to it. Nor are "the teachings of highly qualified publicists." But does this really matter? Is it even possible for the ICC to interpret and apply treaties, custom, or general principles of humanitarian law and human rights law accurately without consulting such "subsidiary means"? Is it reasonable or rational to conclude that the ICC should not consult, for example, the 1947 Final Judgment of the International Military Tribunal at Nuremberg **(Basic Document 7.4)** or the decisions of the *ad hoc* tribunals created to rule on war crimes in the former Yugoslavia and Rwanda? And how can the ICC fulfill its obligation under Article 21(3) of the Rome Statute to ensure "[t]he application and interpretation of law pursuant to this article ... consistent with internationally recognized human rights ..." without consulting the teachings of qualified publicists? Should the works of scholars who have spent lifetimes at understanding international humanitarian law and human rights law be disregarded or seconded?

1.   JUDICIAL DECISIONS

It is clear that, in general, judicial decisions in cases involving international law, domestic as well as international, can and will be cited for their persuasiveness by parties to an international legal dispute, the decisions of courts and other tribunals often being seen to affirm or announce a treaty-based rule or interpretation, a tenet of customary international law, or a general principle of law, international or domestic. Judicial decisions are seen as trustworthy evidence of what the law really is on a given subject; and this point is verified by most of the leading international adjudicative and arbitral decisions that have helped to lay the foundations of, and otherwise articulate, the substance of international law.

Each of these "judicial decisions" and others like them, however, are subject to the qualification, clearly stated in Article 38(1)(d) of the ICJ Statute, that they have no more than "subsidiary" value as reliable "sources" for international law doctrines, principles, and rules—a qualification that indicates, at least in theory, the reluctance of states, and perhaps most particularly states with a Civil Law tradition, to give to courts and other third-party decision-makers too much of a role in law-making. In addition, although a function of the same reluctance, there is Article 59 of the ICJ Statute which states that decisions of the World Court in contentious cases have no binding force except as between the parties and in respect of the case under consideration. The fact is, however, that the World Court itself and other tribunals as well have striven to follow their own and other previous rulings to ensure a measure of certainty and predictability in the development of international law, in a manner akin to the doctrine of precedent (*stare decisis*) well-known to the Common Law but theoretically foreign to the Civil Law upon which so much of international law has been erected. Article 21(2 of the Rome Statute of the International Criminal Court **(Basic Document 1.16)** (authorizing the ICC to "apply principles and rules of law as interpreted in its previous decisions") is illustrative. Indeed, in the course of interpreting and carefully distinguishing their prior judgments, the World Court and other tribunals sometimes actually *make* law and not merely *determine* it,[ccc] not least in their advisory opinions.[ddd]

But as is evident from the leading cases that have helped to lay the foundations of modern-day international law, "judicial decisions" as a "source" of international law need not be rendered solely by international adjudicative tribunals, such as the International Court of Justice. Frequently—perhaps the majority of times—the "judicial decisions" cited by parties to an international legal dispute will consist of arbitral awards (as opposed to *adjudicated* decisions *stricto sensu*) and, indeed, cases in *national* courts where issues of international law often are adjudicated (particularly in the absence of known pertinent precedent on the international plane). While technically not directly "binding," judges, arbitrators, and other third-party decision-makers—as a matter of training and habit—traditionally look to the disposition of other courts and tribunals in factually similar cases when attempting to reach decisions of their own. In this sense, strictly "binding precedent" is perhaps less important than the acknowledged fact that judges and analogous decision-makers typically attempt to adhere to prior third-party decisions whenever possible.

In any event, one thing is perfectly clear: the Final Judgment of the *ad hoc* International Military Tribunal at Nuremberg of 1 October 1946, in which the victorious Allied Powers of World War II ruled upon the trial of the defeated major Nazi German leaders of that war, has been widely accepted not only as an authoritative restatement of the then existing laws of war, but, as well, as an authoritative and even controlling source of new law for the prosecution of alleged war crimes, crimes against humanity, and related crimes. No better evidence can be given than the trials that took place at the time of, and right after, the Nuremberg trial. By some counts, there were over 3,000 trials of war criminals, most of which were conducted in the national

---

ccc. *See, e.g.,* Fisheries Case (U. K. v. Nor.), 1951 ICJ 116, 1951 WL 12; Nottebohm Case (Liech. v. Guat.), 1955 ICJ 4, 1955 WL 1.

ddd. *See, e.g.,* Reparation for Injuries Suffered in the Service of the United Nations,

1949 ICJ 174, 1949 WL 3 (Advisory Opinion); Reservations to the Convention on Genocide, 1951 ICJ 15, 1951 WL 3 (Advisory Opinion).

courts of the various Allied powers. In the Far East, the trials of Japanese leaders were conducted primarily under the auspices of the United States.[eee] In all of these trials, the national courts applied the international laws of war in ways that were similar to—and in many cases actually based upon—the Nuremberg Tribunal judgment. Also evidential are the "Principles of International Law Recognized in the Charter of the Nuremberg Tribunal and in the Judgment of the Tribunal," adopted by the UN International Law Commission on 2 August 1950 **(Basic Document 2.13)**, and such resolutions of the UN General Assembly as "Affirmation of the Principles of International Law Recognized by the Charter of the Nuremberg Tribunal," adopted 11 December 1946 **(Basic Document 2.6)**, and "Principles of International Co-operation in the Detection, Arrest, Extradition and Punishment of Persons Guilty of War Crimes and Crimes Against Humanity," adopted 3 December 1973 **(Basic Document 2.28)**. However vulnerable the Nuremberg judgment may be to charges of "victor's justice" and however otherwise imperfect, as the primary international precedent from modern times pertinent to the prosecution of alleged war crimes and related atrocities, it cannot be dismissed. Regrettably, the full text of the original judgment, which may be found in 1 International Military Tribunal, Trials of the Major War Criminals 171 (1947), is too lengthy to reproduce here, running 170 pages, plus 22 pages for the Soviet judge's dissenting opinion. However, an abridged version may be found in the documentary supplement to this coursebook **(Basic Document 7.4)**. As a lawyer on ICC Prosecutor Moreno–Ocampo's staff, you will want to read at least this version in full.

One further key point merits responsible attention, namely, the gendered way in which judicial and quasi-judicial bodies interpret and apply international (and national) law. The point was explicitly addressed relative to international judicial bodies at the Second Joint Conference of the American Society of International Law and the Nederlandse Vereniging voor Internationaal Recht in July 1993. Comparing the way the principles of equal treatment and non-discrimination as between men and women have been interpreted and applied by the European Court on Human Rights, the Court of Justice of the European Communities, and the UN Human Rights Commission, Dutch law professor Titia Loenen noted, in general, "a male bias [that] reflect[s] masculine norms and values under the guise of objectivity and neutrality," *i.e.*, "[a] legal focus ... on formal equality" that "start[s] from the presumption that men and women should always be treated the same [despite] the social and/or economic differences between men and women." *Remarks by Titia Loenen, Panel on "Sources of International Law: Entrenching the Gender Bias," in* Proceedings of the Second Joint Conference of the American Society of International Law and the Nederlandse Vereniging voor Internationaal Recht (at The Hague, 22–24 Jul 93) 424, 424–27 (1994). A "[s]tarting point for any court," Professor Loenen argued, "should be a contextual instead of an abstract approach to the concepts of equality and [non-discrimination]" that acknowledges "gender disadvantage." *Id*. at 428–29. For detailed treatment of judicial and quasi-judicial gender bias and pragmatic recommendations, see Hilary Charlesworth & Christine Chinkin, The Bound-

eee. For pertinent comment, see *supra* text following note **u** in the Introduction to this Part I, at 18.

aries of International Law: A Feminist Analysis 80–88 (2000). Note also that of the 18 judges currently elected to serve on the International Criminal Court, seven are women—four (from Brazil, Costa Rica, Ireland, and Mali) with established competence in criminal law and procedure (List A) and three (from Ghana, Latvia, and South Africa) with competence in relevant areas of international law such as international humanitarian law and human rights law (List B).

2. THE TEACHINGS OF PUBLICISTS

Under Article 38(1)(d) of the ICJ Statute **(Basic Document 1.6)**, the teachings of scholars (in French: *la doctrine*)—to which this coursebook gives obvious deference—are given a high, albeit "subsidiary," priority as an independent "source" of international law. Certainly this fact is gratifying to those who take up the study of international law as a life's work, the more so because it represents a significant break from the positivist doctrine of "sources" that became dominant in the Nineteenth Century and that continues to have substantial influence today, namely, an insistence upon empirically verifiable prescriptions that reveal themselves primarily, if not exclusively, in the "will" of states through treaties and customary practice accepted as law. But to what extent, precisely, do scholarly writings actually contribute to the formation of international law? Note that Article 21 of the Rome Statute of the International Criminal Court **(Basic Document 1.16)** contains no explicit reference to them. In any event, the following quotations from two celebrated domestic court decisions and from three "highly qualified publicists" are instructive. In reading them, bear in mind the fact, already several times noted, that the vast majority of international law publicists are men.

"THE PAQUETE HABANA, THE LOLA"
175 U.S. 677, 700 (1900)

International law is part of our law, and must be ascertained and administered by the courts of justice of appropriate jurisdiction, as often as questions of right depending upon it are duly presented for their determination. For this purpose, where there is no treaty, and no controlling executive or legislative act or judicial decision, resort must be had to the customs and usages of civilized nations; and as evidence of these, to the works of jurists and commentators, who by years of labor, research and experience, have made themselves peculiarly well acquainted with the subjects of which they treat. Such works are resorted to by judicial tribunals, not for the speculations of their authors concerning what the law ought to be, but for trustworthy evidence of what the law really is.

WEST RAND CENTRAL GOLD MINING CO. v. THE KING
[1905] 2 King's Bench 391, 402

... The views expressed by learned writers on international law have done in the past, and will do in the future, valuable service in helping to create the opinion by which the range of the consensus of civilized nations is enlarged. But in many instances their pronouncements must be regarded rather as the embodiments of their views as to what ought to be, from an ethical standpoint, the conduct of nations inter se, than the enunciation of a rule or practice so universally approved or assented to as to be fairly termed, even in the qualified sense in which that word can be understood in reference to the relations between independent political communities, "law."

D. W. GREIG, INTERNATIONAL LAW
47–48 (2d ed. 1976)

... [H]ow influential are juristic writings in the development of international law? Historically, before there existed any great wealth of state practice or judicial precedent, writers on international law held a pre-eminent position and it was impossible not to rely heavily on the writings of Suarez and Gentilis in the sixteenth century, of Grotius (volume II of whose *De Jure Belli ac Pacis* earned him the title of "Father of the Law of Nations"), Zouche and later Pufendorf in the seventeenth century, and the so-called "positivists," Bynkershoek, Moser and Van Martens, and the "Grotian" Vattel, of the eighteenth century. Even today, particularly where the law is uncertain, the advocate before an international tribunal, or the legal adviser to the foreign affairs department of a state, will make occasional reference to the works of these writers, the so-called "classics of international law," though more frequent citation is made to contemporary writings, particularly to Oppenheim's treatise,[fff] and to various monographs and articles on specialised fields of international law. [However,] [e]ven if it is possible to demonstrate the significance of international juristic writings to the advocate or legal adviser from the frequency with which use is made of such writings in written and oral pleadings submitted by states parties to cases before the International Court [of Justice], it is less apparent what impact these citations have either on the practice of states, or on actual decisions.

OSCAR SCHACHTER, INTERNATIONAL LAW IN THEORY AND PRACTICE
38–39 (1991)

... An examination of legal positions and argumentation of governments reveals that generally heavy reliance [has been] placed on principles and rules formulated in the [major] treatises [on international law]. In theory, most of the treatises written in the latter part of the nineteenth century and in the twentieth adhered to the doctrine of sources and the requirement of objective validation of claims on the basis of such sources. But the doctrinal adherence was significantly modified in the treatises themselves. Many of the treatises relied predominantly on quotations and paraphrases of statements by earlier writers of principles and rules. These were supported in many cases by references to State practice or judicial decision. But such references were frequently selected to confirm the norm that had been formulated by earlier writers or by the writer of the treatise. When we examine these treatises, we can readily see that pronouncements of impressive generality (and aphoristic form) were transmitted from treatise to treatise, quoted in judicial decisions and governmental statements.... [T]he selective tendency of the writers,

---

fff. *i.e.,* L. Oppenheim, International Law—A Treatise (H. Lauterpacht 8th ed. 1955 [vol. 1]; 7th ed. 1952 [vol. 2]).

especially their propensity to quote the generalities of other writers, meant that their statements of existing law were steps removed from the ideal of an inductive approach.

Furthermore, the scientific character of these scholarly works are [sic] . . . suspect because of the tendency in many of them to reflect positions and outlooks of their national States. . . . We are not really surprised by this though it is incompatible with the premise of scientific positivism. . . . These observations are not meant to suggest that deliberate bias of a national or political kind is characteristic of treatises and scientific articles. It is rather to point out that relatively few juristic studies, no matter how positivist in theory, fail to betray their national or ideological origins and indeed that more than a few clearly support partisan positions. That a degree of bias is inescapable is recognized by the common assumption that more credible judgments on controversial issues of international law were more likely if made by a broadly representative body than by persons (however expert) from a single country or a particular political outlook. . . .

If the question [before the International Court of Justice and other international bodies] concerns international law, it has become more usual to include citations of writers from a broad range of States, including the new States and those with different social systems. This reflects the expanded composition of the international community and a greater awareness that a heterogeneous society cannot have its law authoritatively determined by scholars from a small group of States. . . . But it does not follow that reliance on a plurality of writers brings one closer to the primary sources. Whether one or many, the jurists still engage in generalizing and abstraction that adds to the distance between their pronouncements of *lex lata* and the raw data of the sources.

DISCUSSION NOTES/QUESTIONS

1. Many respected publicists claim that a prohibition enunciated in Article 59 of the ICJ Statute **(Basic Document 1.6)**—forbidding the decisions of the World Court from having binding force except between the parties and in respect of the particular case adjudicated—applies to all cases decided by *all* international tribunals. *See, e.g.*, H. Lauterpacht, The Development of International Law by the International Court 20–22 (rev. ed. 1958). Is this viewpoint useful from the standpoint of the progressive development of international law? Does adherence to judicial or arbitral precedent via the doctrine of *stare decisis* help or hinder that development? Does Article 21(2) of the Rome Statute of the International Criminal Court **(Basic Document 1.16)**, providing that "[t]he Court may apply principles and rules of law as interpreted in its previous decisions" constitute a repudiation of this claim?

Many publicists also note approvingly the traditional view that *national* tribunals express the legal opinions only of the states in which they function. In part these viewpoints are the result of the Civil Law tradition which, in addition to an historical resistance to "judge-made" law in favor of legislation or codification, has greatly influenced the development of international law over the centuries. Historical explanations aside, if there are no unambiguous answers to a particular issue on the basis of international legal authority, does it make sense to disregard nationally-based judicial or arbitral decisions?

2.   The reputation of a court, whether national or international, depends in part on its ability to arrive at decisions free of political influence or pressure. Most observers give the ICJ high points in this regard. A well-known exception may be found in the United States' response to the case brought by Nicaragua against the United States for its support of military and paramilitary activities against Nicaragua in the early 1980s. *See Case Concerning Military and Paramilitary Activities in and Against Nicaragua* (Nicar. v. U.S.), 1986 ICJ 14, 1986 WL 522. The United States boycotted the Court and rescinded its acceptance of the compulsory jurisdiction of the Court in this instance because it believed the Court to be politically biased in the case brought by Nicaragua to seek vindication for its contention that it was being victimized by United States support of the *Contra* insurgents. *See* A. Sofaer, *The United States and the World Court*, US Dep't State Bureau Pub. Aff., Current Policy No. 769 (Dec. 1985). Professor Thomas Franck argued that the Nicaragua decision has to be interpreted objectively in light of the US role as a superpower entrusted "with responsibility for the defense of the free world." *See* T. Franck, Judging the World Court 23–71 (1986). How can international law provide a framework for restraint and cooperation in the face of such a mandate? Should a major power be willing to risk defeat in the World Court or any other international tribunal on such questions as a contested use of force? On other questions?

3.   Consider the final verdicts rendered by the International Military Tribunal relative to each of the leading Nazi Germans tried at Nuremberg—for Conspiracy to Wage Wars of Aggression (Count 1), for Crimes against Peace, *i.e.*, initiating or waging wars of aggression (Count 2), for War Crimes (Count 3), and for Crimes against Humanity (Count 4). They are conveniently summarized infra in Discussion Note/Question 1 of Section A of Chapter 3, *infra* at 213. On the basis of this record, is it fair to say, as many have done, that the Nuremberg trial was simply an exercise in "victor's justice"? If so, might the ICC be vulnerable to the same charge in the case of Darfur, it having been referred to the ICC by the UN Security Council without Sudan's participation?

E.   EQUITY

So far, in your preparation for the possible prosecution initially of persons responsible for violations of international criminal law in Sudan's Darfur province since 1 July 2002, you have reconsidered only those "sources" of international legal authority that are acknowledged in Article 38(1) of the ICJ Statute **(Basic Document 1.6)** and Article 21 of the Rome Statute of the International Criminal Court **(Basic Document 1.16)**. You now turn to Article 38(2), which states that Article 38 "shall not prejudice the power of the Court to decide a case *ex aequo et bono* [according to what is right and good], if the parties agree thereto." You note, however, that, with the possible exception of its Article 21(3), requiring the ICC to apply and interpret the law "consistent with internationally recognized human rights," the Rome Statute makes no such provision. Nevertheless, you sense that, to ensure just results, it is important to explore the meaning of this provision and the place of equity in international law generally.

DAVID H. OTT, PUBLIC INTERNATIONAL LAW IN THE MODERN WORLD

20–22 (1987)

Equity in international law: in the reservoir of principles or autonomous? In international law the position of equity is less restricted [than in national law], though there are theoretical problems regarding where it fits into the scheme of Article 38. When the *Diversion of Water from the Meuse Case* (1937) **[Basic Document 7.2]** was before the Permanent Court of International Justice, Judge Hudson, concurring, supported the view that equity was a part of international law and meant essentially "general principles of justice" derivable from the principles observable in national legal systems. Thus, equity would appear in this view to be a part of [the] reservoir of [general principles of law recognized by civilized nations].[ggg]

In more recent years, however, the ICJ has appeared to conceive of equity's being implicit in the rules of international law in a more general way than Judge Hudson did. In the *North Sea Continental Shelf Cases,*[hhh] the Court indicated that just and equitable decisions find their "objective justification in considerations lying not outside but within the rules."[iii] In the *Fisheries Jurisdiction (Merits) Case* (1974)[jjj] it saw the main problem as "not a matter of finding simply an equitable solution, but an equitable solution derived from the applicable law". In the *Continental Shelf (Tunisia v. Libya) Case* (1982)[kkk] the World Court continued the process of making equity an autonomous feature of international law. It said in part:

> Equity as a legal concept is a direct emanation of the idea of justice. The court whose task is by definition to administer justice is bound to apply it. In the course of the history of legal systems the term "equity" has been used to define various legal concepts. It was often contrasted with the rigid rules of positive law, the severity of which had to be mitigated in order to do justice. In general, this contrast has no parallel in the development of international law; the legal concept of equity is a general principle directly applicable as law. Moreover, when applying positive international law, a court may choose among several interpretations of the law the one which appears, in the light of the circumstances of the case, to be closest to the requirements of justice.... [The court] is bound to apply equitable principles as part of international law, and to balance up the various considerations which it regards as relevant in order to produce an equitable result. While it is clear that no rigid rules exist as to the exact weight to be attached to each element in the case, this is very far from being an exercise of discretion or conciliation; nor is it an operation of distributive justice.

ggg. A close reading of Judge Hudson's opinion permits the conclusion, however, that the applicability of equity does not depend on its introduction via general principles of law.

hhh. The decision is extracted in abridged form *supra* at 114–17.

iii. The case dealt with the delimitation of the shelf, it will be recalled, in a circumstance involving a concave coast. After the Court found that the relevant provisions of the 1958 Convention on the Continental Shelf **(Basic Document 5.4)** did not apply to the case, it found that in this matter customary international law required such delimitation to be established by reference to equitable principles.

jjj. Fisheries Jurisdiction (U.K. v. Ice.) (Merits), 1974 ICJ 3.

kkk. 1982 ICJ 18.

This view of equity implies a conception that has moved some distance from the reservoir of principles idea insofar as it sees equity arising from the nature of international law as a system seeking to achieve justice rather than from the specific principles of national legal systems.

Ex aequo et bono. Article 38(2) of the ICJ Statute [**Basic Document 1.6**] gives the court power to decide a case *ex aequo et bono, i.e.,* according to what is fair and appropriate, if the parties to the case agree. This is not the same as applying equity within the established system of law. *Ex aequo et bono* implies deciding according to what suits the facts of the case, regardless of the law. This is often said to be in effect a license for the court to legislate in the sense of creating new law for the parties, and is rarely resorted to because hardly ever authorised by the parties in cases before the court.

OSCAR SCHACHTER, INTERNATIONAL LAW IN THEORY AND PRACTICE
55–56, 58 (1991)

No concept of international law resists precise definition more than the notion of equity. It is often defined by listing approximate synonyms that seem equally elusive: fairness, justice, reasonableness, good faith. Apart from the imprecision of these terms, they are not adequate to convey the full use of equity in legal reasoning. Its almost protean character tempts one to speak of "equity in its infinite variety." But ... it is [nonetheless] convenient to distinguish the following five uses of equity and equitable principles:

(1) Equity as a basis for "individualized" justice tempering the rigours of strict law.

(2) Equity as consideration of fairness, reasonableness and good faith.

(3) Equity as a basis for certain specific principles of legal reasoning associated with fairness and reasonableness: to wit, estoppel, unjust enrichment, and abuse of rights.

(4) Equitable standards for the allocation and sharing of resources and benefits.

(5) Equity as a broad synonym for distributive justice used to justify demands for economic and social arrangements and redistribution of wealth.

* * *

Equitable principles of a ... specific substantive character have come to have an especially significant role in regard to shared resources and delimitation problems. It is interesting that these equitable principles of a "legislative" character have been developed in large measure by judicial or arbitral bodies, influenced by the work of nongovernmental international law bodies. One notable example has been the emergence of principles for the equitable sharing of rivers, lakes and ground waters that are a common resource of two or more States. The arbitral award of 1957 in the *Lac Lanoux* case between France and Spain [**Basic Document 7.7**] was a significant step in recognizing the claims of equitable sharing in limiting unilateral acts of riparian States. The Helsinki Rules on the Uses of the Waters of International Rivers adopted by the International Law Association in 1966 [**Basic Document 5.9**] and the resolution of the Institut de droit international on Pollution of Rivers and Lakes, adopted in 1979,[III] have advanced specific criteria for weighing the many factors that bear on the equities of sharing common resources.

RUTH LAPIDOTH, "EQUITY IN INTERNATIONAL LAW"
81 Proceed. A.S.I.L. 138, 146–47 (1987)

The advantages of the application of equity are obvious: in adjudication, it enhances the chances of bringing the law nearer to justice, which is one of the main objects of every legal system. It makes it possible to adapt the rule to individual cases and to prevent injustice resulting from the generality of law and from the impossibility of the legislature to predict in advance all possible situations that might arise. * * * In difficult negotiations, reference to an abstract although perhaps ambiguous equity or equitable principles may help the parties to reach an agreement that otherwise might be impossible.

The disadvantages should not be overlooked, however. . . . The subjectivity of the contents of equity is particularly dangerous in the international legal order due to the heterogeneity of the international community. Moreover, the notions that one may have of justice depend on his or her links to a certain ethical environment and to the municipal legal system in which he or she has grown up.

The great qualities of law are its generality, clarity, certainty and predictability. None of these virtues would exist in an individualized system of equity.

Moreover, if equity is part of international law, it is not only a source of inspiration for the judge and arbitrators, but also may be relied upon by the parties to justify their behavior. The possibility to invoke equity in a legal system with no compulsory jurisdiction may provide states with many loopholes and subterfuges that will help them to evade the application of the law.

* * *

Nevertheless, despite these shortcomings, equity is part of the law and has to be applied appropriately, in order to prevent grave injustice and to fill gaps. The need for equity in the administration of international law even has grown recently because more and more rules of law are of a rather general or abstract character, and because of the need to share and distribute the newly discovered natural and technological resources.

EDITORS' NOTE

The utility of equity as a means of sharing and distributing scarce resources, as noted in the foregoing extract by Ruth Lapidoth, is a focus of concern of the article *The International Role of Equity-as-Fairness*, 81 Geo. L. Rev. 563 (1993) by Thomas M. Franck & Dennis M. Sughrue. The authors write, at 572:

> Since World War I, equity-as-fairness has become relevant to one of the most vexing problems facing international courts: the allocation of scarce resources among states. This problem arises primarily from the failure of the earth's system of territorial boundaries to resolve satisfactorily the attribu-

III.   58 Ann. l'Institut Dr. Int'l 193 (1979).

tion of certain resources, such as the riches of the continental shelf. Equity brings important advantages to this task, affording judges a measure of discretion, within a flexible structure, commensurate with the uniqueness of each dispute and the rapid evolution of new resource recovery and management technology.

International lawyers are engaged in a debate as to the proper role of equity in this context. This debate shows that at least three approaches to equitable allocation have emerged. In the first model, which may be labeled "corrective equity," equity occupies the important, but fringe, role of tempering the gross unfairness that sometimes results from the application of strict law. In the second model, "broadly conceived equity," equity displaces law but is still rule-based, evolving into a set of principles for the accomplishment of an equitable allocation. In the third model, "common heritage equity," equity serves a dual creative function: determining the conditions for exploitation and ensuring the conservation of humankind's patrimony.

A relatively recent invocation of the "common heritage equity" model described by Franck and Sughrue is the theory of "intergenerational equity" advanced by Professor Edith Brown Weiss in Fairness to Future Generations: International Law, Common Patrimony, and Intergenerational Equity (1989).

DISCUSSION NOTES/QUESTIONS

1. What is the difference between law and equity? The relationship? Can equity serve to create law? Why has the World Court never explicitly stated that it applies equity or equitable principles? Might a reference to a specific equitable rule have raised too much criticism? What problems attend the application of equitable principles? Do they give third-party decision-makers too much discretion? Do they risk too much subjectivity in legal decision?

2. Ruth Lapidoth, *supra*, says that the "great qualities" of law include its clarity, certainty, and predictability. Do you agree? Professor Lapidoth also expresses concern that equity, which she says does not have these "virtues," would be relied upon, if as part of international law, to justify potentially unwanted subjectivities; one person's "justice" would be another's "injustice." Do you agree? How might such negative consequences be avoided?

3. Franck–Sughrue and Weiss give us examples of how equity can and might play a role in international environmental law. Is it implicit in their commentaries that conventional and customary rules are not flexible enough to meet the needs of the global environment? Or at least some of those needs? Can you think of other areas of international life that might benefit from the "common heritage equity" model or a version thereof? Would it or any other equity model have assisted at Nuremberg following World War II. Would it or any other equity model be useful in the tribunals established to prosecute war crimes and related atrocities in the former Yugoslavia and Rwanda? For example, "intergenerational equity" relative to the sustainability of ethnic/religious populations?

4. Is it possible to argue that all cases are decided according to "equity" in some sense of that word? If so, is the notion of "equity" a vacuous concept? Or does it have some substantive significance as a "source" of international law rules?

F. OTHER "SOURCES" OF INTERNATIONAL LAW

Up to this point in your preparations to assist ICC Prosecutor Moreno–Ocampo at The Hague, you have reconsidered only those "sources of international law" that are expressly chronicled in Article 38 of the Statute of the International Court of Justice **(Basic Document 1.6)** and Article 21 of the Rome Statute of the International Criminal Court **(Basic Document 1.16)**. But there are possible others—for immediately pertinent example, the Elements of Crimes, amendments thereto, and other work of the ICC's Assembly of States Parties (the ICC's management oversight and legislative body); additionally, the resolutions of international governmental organizations (IGOs) such as the United Nations and its allied agencies, expressions of consensus, declarations of intent, and so forth. However, the resolutions of the UN General Assembly and Security Council having been given the most serious scholarly attention in recent years, you consider them first and foremost.

At the same time, you approach these "other 'sources' " with caution. Although international law may be derived from them, from your formal studies you recall that what counts in the end, at least in the world order presently constituted, is the attitude of states toward these law-creating processes and their practices among one another. However much any potentially law-making process may stress that a given norm is a rule of international law, the acid test, especially in an essentially "horizontal" and voluntarist legal system such as the current international legal system, is whether nations accept that norm as one governing their international relations. The caveat applies, of course, to every "source" of international law without exception, including the ICC's Assembly of States and its Elements of Crimes and amendments thereto.

1. UNITED NATIONS AND OTHER INTERGOVERNMENTAL ORGANIZATIONAL RESOLUTIONS

Though nowhere mentioned in Article 38 of the ICJ Statute or Article 21 of the Rome Statute, declarations and resolutions of the United Nations, its allied agencies, and other intergovernmental organizations have been cited increasingly since 1945 as "evidence" for rules of international law, especially in the human rights and environmental realms. For this reason they merit our attention. It should be understood, however, that, while the readings that follow focus primarily on UN General Assembly declarations and resolutions, their essential teachings apply also to the declarations and resolutions of intergovernmental organizations (IGOs) generally. In addition to the UN and its specialized agencies, there exists a vast array of intergovernmental organizations, both global and regional, that contribute to the codification and development of international law. By interpreting their respective charters, by adopting and implementing declarations and resolutions, and by sponsoring treaties in their spheres of influence and competence, these diverse organizations contribute substantially to the creation and development of international law. In contrast to the United Nations and its allied agencies, however, all of which have global jurisdiction, these other IGOs tend to have less universal importance or significance. The same may be said, as a consequence, of their legal utterances.

DAVID H. OTT, PUBLIC INTERNATIONAL LAW IN THE MODERN WORLD
20–22 (1987)

... [Consider] the problem of the effect of [United Nations] General Assembly resolutions in the creation of new law. There are basically four possibilities:

- (*a*) that such resolutions have no legal effect;

- (*b*) that they are authoritative interpretations of the pre-existing law in the UN Charter;

- (*c*) that they help create customary law;

- (*d*) that they have an almost legislative effect.

Possibility (a): no legal effect. This argument depends on the statement in the UN Charter, Article 10 **[Basic Document 1.5]**, that the General Assembly may only "discuss" matters within the scope of the Charter and "make recommendations." By definition these are not orders and cannot have the binding effect necessary to create legal obligations and duties. It is sometimes also suggested that the act of voting for a mere recommendation cannot be state practice contributing to the growth of customary law since, it is said, the knowledge that the recommendation is not binding prevents the requisite *opinio juris*. Even if a state indicated that it felt obliged to vote for a certain recommendation, the obligation (and hence the rule of customary law) would exist independently and not in the resolution itself.

* * *

Possibility (b): authoritative interpretations. This view is less troubled by the limitations imposed by restriction of the Assembly to discussion and recommendation. International law recognises ... that the interpretation of a treaty may be affected by the subsequent practice of the parties to it. It is not too far from this to say that voting in the Assembly in favour of certain interpretations of the Charter ... amounts to practice that may clarify and develop the relevant Charter provisions.

This understanding is particularly apt when applied to resolutions that take the form of declarations of principle on legal questions, most notably the Universal Declaration of Human Rights of 1948 **[Basic Document 3.3]**. Thus, in the *Filártiga v. Peña-Irala* case[mmm] a United States federal court in 1980 said, on the question of whether torture was prohibited under international law, that "UN declarations are significant because they specify with great precision the obligations of member nations under the Charter."

A somewhat similar view of the role of General Assembly resolutions was put forward by Judge Jessup in his dissenting opinion in the *South West Africa Cases* (1966).[nnn] The judicial task of the court was, he said, to interpret constitutional documents like those in that case (and like the UN Charter) by applying contemporary international community standards for which statements in General Assembly resolutions provided proof.

mmm. *Supra* note **pp** (p. 113).   **nnn.** *Supra* note **x** (p. 102).

Possibility (c): creation of customary law. This could arguably happen in one of three ways:

(*a*) A state's vote in favour of a resolution might be state practice with *opinio juris* because the state regards the resolution as in itself legally binding. But this notion is open to the objection that under the UN Charter most General Assembly resolutions are only recommendatory and therefore cannot be binding.

(*b*) A state's vote for a resolution could be state practice with *opinio juris* because the vote is an acknowledgement by the state that the content of the resolution accords with the requirements of international law and cannot legitimately be rejected. From this possibility some writers have gone a step further to speak of a process of "parliamentary diplomacy" whereby the will of the international community can be quickly and accurately reflected in resolutions, with the accumulation of such authoritative pronouncements producing new international law. Judge Tanaka, dissenting in the *South West Africa Cases* (1966),[ooo] described the process as "the middle way between legislation by convention and the traditional process of custom making." The court in the *Filártiga* case ... implicitly endorsed this view with regard to resolutions on human rights. ...

(*c*) The resolution may enunciate principles or rules which later state practice (with *opinio juris*) adopts as customary law. This role for General Assembly resolutions is widely accepted, but one should remember that in this situation the subsequent practice, and not the resolution *per se*, is what is generating the new law.

Possibility (d): quasi-legislative effect. After the General Assembly in December 1963 adopted unanimously the "Declaration of Legal Principles Governing the Activities of States in the Exploration and Use of Outer Space,"[ppp] the United States representative said that a resolution of that kind, approved unanimously, "represented the law as generally accepted in the international community." This was understood to mean that one resolution of that kind could create law where none had existed previously, in effect could legislate new international law. The view was contested at the time and remains debatable.

The key to the American claim was the unanimity with which the resolution was adopted. If a resolution purporting to set out new "law" were adopted only by a majority, the situation would be different. In the *Texaco v Libya* arbitration of 1977,[qqq] the arbitrator held that such a resolution, if not simply reaffirming previously existing law (*lex lata*), would be merely *de lege ferenda*, that is, a suggestion of what the law ought to be rather than a statement of what it presently is. Although many international lawyers would accept this opinion in principle, considerable room for disagreement remains in trying to determine which resolutions it applies to.

ROSALYN HIGGINS, PROBLEMS AND PROCESS: INTERNATIONAL LAW AND HOW WE USE IT
26–28 (1994)

... Prominent among [the] activities [of international organizations] is the passing of resolutions that purport to be declaratory of contemporary

ooo. *Id.*
ppp. GA Res. 1962, UN GAOR, 18th Sess., Supp. No. 15, at 15, UN Doc. A/5515 (1963).
qqq. *Reprinted in* 17 I.L.M. 1 (1978).

international law. Can we reject their legal relevance *simply* on the ground that they are recommendatory, or incapable of directly binding the membership at large?"" What status is therefore to be accorded them?

There are a great range of opinions. Looking along a spectrum, we can perhaps see at one end those who are deeply skeptical, in the generalized fashion, about the relevance of General Assembly resolutions—such writers as Judge Sir Gerald Fitzmaurice, Judge Stephen Schwebel, and Sir Francis Vallat, Professors David Johnson and Gaetano Arangio–Ruiz. The Englishmen in this group all arrive at their position primarily by an emphasis in their writings, or judicial decisions, on the recommendatory nature of Assembly resolutions and their inability to bind.... Judge Schwebel and Professor Arangio–Ruiz arrive at their position through a different route. They fully accept that resolutions can contribute to the formation of customary international law, but express deep scepticism as to whether this really happens.

Professor Arangio–Ruiz says that General Assembly resolutions do not in fact contribute to the evolution of custom because states "don't mean it".... "That is to say, states often don't meaningfully support what a resolution says and they almost always do not mean that the resolution is law."[38] Judge Schwebel then adds a piercingly important point. Agreeing that states "don't mean it," he says: "This may be truer still of resolutions adopted by 'consensus.' "[39] Thus the size of the majority has nothing to do with the intentions of the states voting for it.

Somewhere towards the middle of the spectrum there are other international lawyers who downplay the significance of Assembly resolutions as non-binding, but accept that it would be wholly exceptional for any single resolution to have normative results. They argue ... [that] the decentralized method of international law-making can cause the metamorphosis of "General Assembly recommendations from non-binding resolutions to inchoate normative principles."[40] Certain resolutions may be a first step in the process of law creation; and looked at as a whole, they may in certain circumstances (depending on subject-matter, size and margin of majorities, *opinio juris*) be evidence of developing trends of customary law.

At what could be termed the radical end of the spectrum are those who invest Assembly resolutions with considerably greater legal significance. In this context can be mentioned Richard Falk, who has written of the "quasi-legislative" competence of the General Assembly,[41] and Jorge Castañeda, who

---

rrr. Earlier, Professor (now Judge) Higgins writes, at 24: "It is, of course, beyond all doubt that the drafters of the [UN] Charter **[Basic Document 1.5]** deliberately declined to give the General Assembly legislative authority. In other than budgetary matters, the resolutions of the General Assembly are recommendatory and not directly binding: see the wording of Articles 10, 11, 12, 13, and 14."

38. G. Arangio–Ruiz, *The Normative Role of the General Assembly of the United Nations and the Development of Principles of Friendly Relations*, 137 Recueil 419 (1972–III).

39. S. Schwebel, *The Effect of Resolutions of the UN General Assembly on Customary International Law*, 1979 Proceed. A.S.I.L. 301.

40. C. Joyner, *UN General Assembly Resolutions: Rethinking the Contemporary Dynamics of Norm–Creation*, 11 Calif. W. Int'l L. J. 445, 464 (1981).

41. R. Falk, *On the Quasi–Legislative Competence of the General Assembly*, 60 A.J.I.L. 782 (1966).

has argued that, through its repeated efforts to declare principles of international law, the General Assembly has secured powers beyond the recommendatory powers listed in the UN Charter **[Basic Document 1.5]**.[42]

Underlying these positions are many complicated and interesting issues, one or two of which may be mentioned briefly. When we look at resolutions as a first step in the formation of custom, or as part of the evidence of the existence of general practice, is it enough that we look at the resolutions alone?

Judge Schwebel has insisted that, because *opinio juris* remains a critical element, one must look to see if states "mean" what they voted for—and looking at their practice outside the United Nations is one way we can ascertain this. The [1977] arbitral award of Professor Dupuy in the Texaco Case[43] is interesting in this context, as well as in many others. It will be recalled that (unlike Judge Lagergren, when faced with similar issues in the *BP v. Libya Case*[44]) Dupuy closely examined the series of resolutions that are collectively regarded as the New International Economic Order resolutions, to see whether the traditional requirements for compensation had changed. He found that General Assembly Resolution 1803 **[Basic Document 4.4]** represented current international law, for it had passed with the support of the industrialized capital exporting states as well as the capital importing states; however, the same consensus was never really apparent in the voting on the Charter for Economic Rights and Duties **[Basic Document 4.9]** and the Declaration on the New International Economic Order **[Basic Document 4.8]**. In other words, Dupuy was engaged in trying to ascertain whether a resolution expressed a consensus on what was the existing customary rule. But one must take care not to use General Assembly resolutions as a short cut to ascertaining international practice in its entirety on a matter—practice in the larger world arena is still the relevant canvas, although UN resolutions are a part of the picture. Resolutions cannot be a *substitute* for ascertaining custom; this task will continue to require that other evidence of state practice be examined alongside those collective acts evidenced in General Assembly resolutions.

So far we have spoken of [General] Assembly resolutions. Yet we must not lose sight of Security Council resolutions in our examination of the process of creating norms in the international system. Professor Tunkin, in his 1956 study on the fundamental principles of contemporary international law,[45] indicated that decisions of the UN Security Council are not strictly speaking sources of international law. They have an *ad hoc* effect and may create binding obligations, but they are not sources of general applicability.... I think that this view is largely right—though sometimes the substance of the Security Council work, and the fact that it is legal work repeated year in and year out, makes it engage in the processes of customary [law] development as well as the mere imposing of obligation.

* * *

42. J. Castañeda, Legal Effects of United Nations Resolutions (1970).

43. Texaco Overseas Petroleum Co. v. Libyan Arab Republic, [1977] 53 I.L.R. 389 (1979) [*see also supra* text accompanying and following note **mmm**, at 163].

44. [1977] 53 I.L.R. 297 (1979).

45. G. Tunkin, Osnovy Sovremennogo Mezhdunarodnogo Prava (1956).

As with much of international law, there is no easy answer to the question: What is the role of resolutions of international organizations in the process of creating norms in the international system? To answer the question we need to look at the subject-matter of the resolutions in question, at whether they are binding or recommendatory, at the majorities supporting their adoption, at repeated practice in relation to them, at evidence of *opinio juris*. When we shake the kaleidoscope and the pattern falls in certain ways, they undoubtedly play a significant role in creating norms.

EDITORS' NOTE

Another response to the question of the legal nature of General Assembly resolutions is what van Hoof has called the "other source" or "new source" approach. Godefridus J.H. van Hoof, Rethinking the Sources of International Law 184 (1983). Rather than link General Assembly resolutions to one or more of the traditional "sources" set forth in Article 38 of the ICJ Statute **(Basic Document 1.6)**, this approach argues that those resolutions constitute a separate, independent "source" of international law. The late Nigerian jurist T. Olawale Elias, a former member and President of the World Court, may be the most conspicuous advocate of this view. He once wrote:

> Those states that vote for a particular resolution by the requisite majority are bound on the grounds of consent and of estoppel. Those that abstain are also bound on the ground of acquiescence and tacit consent, since an abstention is not a negative vote; while those that vote against the resolution should be regarded as bound by the democratic principle that the majority view should prevail when the vote has been free and fair and the requisite majority has been secured. . . .

Modern Sources of International Law, in Transnational Law in a Changing Society: Essays in Honor of Philip C. Jessup 34, 54 (W. Friedmann, L. Henkin & O. Lissitzyn eds., 1972).

A more cautious assessment, but still close enough to be identified with the "other source" or "new source" approach, may be seen in the writings of Louis B. Sohn, a long-time student of the United Nations. According to Professor Sohn, unanimously approved General Assembly declarations, such as the Declaration on Principles of International Law Concerning Friendly Relations and Cooperation among States **(Basic Document 1.11)**, may be seen as "leading to the creation of new international law applicable to all States" and as representing "a new method of creating customary international law." Louis B. Sohn, *The Development of the Charter of the United Nations: the Present State*, in The Present State of International Law and Other Essays 39, 52 (M. Bos ed., 1973). Van Hoof observes: "Despite his reference to customary international law, Sohn's treatment of the unanimous declarations leaves no doubt that he in fact drops the requirement of *usus* [*i.e.,* practice]" and that therefore one is faced here with "not just a new method of creating customary international law, but rather a new method of creating international law *tout court* [*i.e.,* altogether]." J. van Hoof, *supra*, at 185.

Finally, there is a school of thought, dubbed the "soft law" approach, that views General Assembly resolutions and other such prescriptive communications as not creating full-fledged rules of international law capable of fitting into the traditional "sources" categories but nonetheless fulfilling, in van Hoof's words, "at least some, if not a great number of the criteria required for rules to be considered rules of international law and [which therefore] cannot be put aside as non-law." J. van Hoof, *supra*, at 187–88. This "soft law," Pierre–Marie Dupuy avers, must be understood as "not merely a new term for an old (customary) process" but as "both a sign and product of the permanent state of multilateral cooperation and competition among the heterogeneous members of the contemporary world community," the existence of which "compels us to re-evaluate the general international law-making process and, in so doing, illuminates the difficulty of explaining this phenomenon by referring solely to the classical theory of formal sources of public international law." P.-M. Dupuy, *Soft Law and the International Law of the Environment*, 12 Mich. J. Int'l L. 420, 435 (1991). It is, he says, "a trouble maker because it is either not yet or not only law" and includes theoretically non-binding instruments "such as recommendations and resolutions of international organizations, declarations and 'final acts' published at the conclusion of international conferences and even draft proposals elaborated by groups of experts" create and delineate "goals to be achieved in the future rather than actual duties, programs rather than prescriptions, guidelines rather than strict obligations." *Id.* at 420 and 428. Illustrative, he observes, is the 1972 Stockholm Declaration on the Human Environment **(Basic Document 5.14)**. "Although, from a formal point of view, the Declaration is only a non-binding resolution," he writes, "many of its 'principles,' particularly Principle 21, have been relied upon by governments to justify their legal rights and duties . . ., [and] subsequent State practice has been, no doubt, influenced by such provisions." *Id.* at 422.

But why, one may ask, do governments generate and accept "soft" in contrast to "hard" law? Because, says Sir Geoffrey Palmer, former Prime Minister of New Zealand, "it is so politically convenient." G. Palmer, *New Ways to Make International Environmental Law*, 86 A.J.I.L. 259, 269 (1992). Hard law in the form of international custom, he writes, "takes time and often a lot of state practice before it hardens into a legally enforceable rule, [and] [t]reaties take a long time to negotiate and nations tend to shy away from the specificity they often involve." *Id*. Palmer elaborates at 269–70, noting the effect of "soft" law along the way:

> Resort to soft law leaves large amounts of discretion to states. The standards are often so vague that third-party adjudication would be impossible even if it were provided for. Often the standards themselves are discretionary. What is important about these instruments is not so much the form in which they appear but the manner in which the obligations, if any, created by them are expressed. Frequently, what is expressed is a series of political statements or values. The Stockholm Declaration is a good example.

* * *

> All politicians know the value of ambiguity. It can serve to secure agreement where agreement may otherwise not be achieved. International instruments are frequently drafted with studied ambiguity. Such an approach may have deceptive elements to it and may create wrong impressions, but it promotes feelings of international comity and cooperation that are very valuable. Since political leaders and countries must continue dealing with one another, it is better that those dealings be based on agreement than on disagreement—and soft law solutions produce agreement.

> More importantly, soft law solutions change the political thinking on an issue. They alter the circumstances in which an issue is considered; they cause opinion to coalesce. These changes can be a very important catalyst in securing an agreement with a harder edge later. Soft law solutions can thus

be useful steps on a longer journey. Soft law is where international law and international politics combine to build new norms. . . .

Political decision makers are influenced by soft law solutions. No political leader wants to endorse an empty declaration. They usually take a lot of care with the language since they have to defend it in the media and other public forums. The political impact of the statement is their prime concern, usually its impact on domestic political opinion. They want to have achieved something that is politically significant. Press statements are taken seriously by the politicians who make them. International instruments involving political leaders from other countries are taken even more seriously. Such soft law documents are often produced by lengthy negotiations simply because the statement is perceived to have political consequences of a serious sort. . . .

Considering that the system is somewhat short of means for establishing norms, it would be a great mistake to get too excited from an analytical point of view about the dangers of soft law. . . . [It] is a concept of both range and flexibility. It ranges from material that is not law at all, through a long spectrum to material so close to being hard law as to be indistinguishable from it. . . . It is a vital part of the continuous process of building norms.

Consider Palmer's experiential observations in the light of Professor Myres McDougal's reported scholarly remarks in a panel discussion on *The Effect of UN Resolutions on Emerging Legal Norms*, 1979 Proceed. A.S.I.L. 300, as summarized by the panel's chairman:

... Professor McDougal remarked that "sources of international law" presented not merely a theoretical problem, but in actuality, a very practical problem. The first question any operating lawyer would want to know was, "Who is going to decide my case?"; the second question which would naturally follow would be, "Who is making the law?" These were not just theoretical inquiries. Legal norms did not simply exist; they were manifested in a continuous process of evolution and hence emanate from several different sources.

For instance, in Article 38 of the Statute of International Court of Justice **[Basic Document 1.6]**, the traditional sources of international law were enumerated. . . . These were not homogeneous sources; they represented not only the most deliberate form of expression—formal agreement—but also the least deliberate form—the vast flow of expectations derived from uniformities in decision and behavior.

Regarding custom, it was supposed to arise when uniformities of behavior gave rise to expectations about authority and control in persons engaged over a long period of time in that behavior. Accordingly, the primary function of the longevity requirement was to clarify and substantiate what expectations were in fact held by members of the community.

In a real sense, then, the UN machinery entailed a facile means for finding out what the international community's expectations were concerning lawful and unlawful activities. In this regard, the concept of "binding obligation" became little more than meaningless noise if it omitted expectations of the community concerning authority (*i.e.*, who is competent to make decisions) and control (*i.e.*, what sanctions are in fact available to carry out decisions). As Hans Kelsen had noted, every norm possessed factual contingency, a policy content, and a sanctioning component. Hence, a norm must carry expectations of authority and control. In short, when looking for legal norms, we were actually searching for indices which express these expectations of authority and control.

Professor McDougal then posited that the notion of consensus was much too limited. The key to law was not consent, but expectation. It was not the intent of the communicator that held principal importance; rather, it was whether a certain policy expectation was shared by both the communicator and the communicatees. The key question was what did the community expect? For instance, at one time the laying of mines at sea had been considered wholly illegal. However, after parties had repeatedly engaged in this practice during two world wars, it had become accepted by the international community as being lawful. The intent of the communicator—be it a UN organ or any other party—was not of paramount consideration; rather, primacy should go to the expectations about authority and control which the communicator created for the larger community.

Consequently, it had to be realized that these expectations were being created all the time, in many different ways. There was in constant process an explicit, continuous flow of international agreements, as well as an outpouring of official decisions by courts and legislative bodies. Not to be overlooked either in this respect was the behavior of private parties engaged in multifaceted transnational activities. No one of these sources of law carried ultimate or exclusive importance; in each case, particular inferences might be drawn about expectations, but in the greatest likelihood, they would come from several diverse sources.

To be sure, the United Nations provided a forum for evaluating what the international community thought the law was. Yet, in order to decide whether UN statement reflected an accurate description of what peoples' expectations were concerning the law, one needed to know several facts: Who voted for that statement? Who voted against it? What was the relative and effective power of these voters? How compatible is the asserted policy with past expectations? What followed from the resolution? What were the expectations coming from other sources? And so on.

* * *

In reply to Professor McDougal's comments, Professor Garibaldi argued that it was incongruous to maintain that the binding nature of a General Assembly resolution depends on its acceptance by the major powers and, at the same time, that the major powers' opinions are irrelevant to the larger issue of whether some General Assembly resolutions are binding at all. The differences between his and Professor McDougal's views lay in the criterion of validity taken as reference. Community expectations constituted an *a priori* criterion; the speaker preferred an empirical criterion, more closely tied to the realities of international life.

Mr. Schwebel [recently retired Judge Schwebel of the ICJ] stated that if a major power or powers voted against a General Assembly resolution, that resolution could not *ipso facto* be considered declaratory of international law, or constitutive of what international law was.

Professor McDougal then responded that no nation state could effectively prevent the process of law creation. This related back to an ancient anthropological observation regarding what law was all about. Law served as a process of clarifying and implementing common interests of people, through explicit communications and by inferences from their behavior. This represented the most fundamental law in any society, namely, customary law. The argument was neither theoretical nor *a priori*; it was just an observation of historical fact. Furthermore, what was important in the legislative process was not the secret intent of the legislator, but rather the expectations which that legislation created for the community. Hence, the whole flow of behavior and inferences would guide expectations about content, authority, and control.[sss]

DISCUSSION NOTES/QUESTIONS

1. Is a resolution of the UN General Assembly a "source" of international law because it states a "general principle of law" that nations have accepted by virtue of their membership in the United Nations? Because it reflects customary international law? Is it an independent "source" in its own right?

2. Echoing the views of Professor Dupuy reported *supra* at 168, and agreeing with him that "international organizations and conferences ... contribute to the evolution and adoption of legal norms," Rudolf Bernhardt, in *Customary International Law New and Old Problems*, 19 Thesaurus Acroasium 199, 212–13 (1992), nevertheless cautions that "one should avoid the misleading notion of soft law and instead recognize that international practices and pronouncements of international organizations and conferences can contribute to the creation of *real customary law*" (emphasis added). States Bernhardt, at 212, "rules are either part of the law or legally not binding; they cannot be binding and non-binding at the same time." Do you agree with Bernhardt? Why? Why not?

3. Are resolutions of the UN General Assembly binding on the member states? Are some of them binding? What do UN Charter articles 10, 11, 12, 13, and 14 say? Are resolutions of the Security Council binding? What does Charter Article 25 say? What is the difference between "resolutions," "declarations," and "recommendations"?

4. Note that many legal scholars from northern industrialized countries deny the binding effect of UN General Assembly resolutions. Is this because developing countries are in the majority in that forum and that the industrialized world does not want to be bound by what they might call "the tyranny of the Third World majority"? Is it possible that the question of the legal effect of General Assembly resolutions is more political than legal?

5. Rosalyn Higgins, *supra*, states that "decisions of the UN Security Council ... may create binding obligations, but they are not sources of general applicability." Does this mean that Security Council resolutions do not "count as law"? If not, what does it mean?

6. In The Development of International Law through the Political Organs of the United Nations (1963), Professor [now Judge] Rosalyn Higgins observes that the law-creating role of political organs such as those of the United Nations "enables a quantitative problem of some magnitude." In this particular connection, she asks, at 6: "How many resolutions incorporating the same legal doctrine must be passed before that doctrine is deemed an international custom? How

sss. In a concluding remark, Mr. Schwebel stated that he believed Professor McDougal to be incorrect about the legal significance to be attributed to General Assembly actions. The widespread attitude of many States in the United Nations, especially those in the West, was, he said: "So what? It is only a recommen-datory resolution of the United Nations, so what does it matter? Why should we offend our friends in the Third World by voting against it?" In the light of this fact, he argued, to arrive at a conclusion that would hold these resolutions as binding or law creating would be at best questionable.

many states must vote in favour of those resolutions?—a simple majority?—a two-thirds majority? Must all the major powers be in favour of the implied legal prescription?" How would you answer these questions?

7. Suppose all the nations of the world were to agree to give full legislative power to the United Nations. Would that be desirable? What would be gained? Lost? What restrictions might there be, if any, on that legislative power? Who would define the restrictions? Who would interpret them? Would there have to be an international "Supreme Court"? If so, who would appoint the judges? Would the judges be capable of being impartial if a matter affected their own nations' vital interests? What other questions would be appropriate—indeed necessary—to ask? In this connection consider the following questions: is the world "ready" for centralized decision-making? Would centralized decision-making be more "rational" than what we have now? Assuming centralized decision-making would be more "rational," should each nation get a vote? Should "ministates" have the vote on a equal basis with, say, Australia, Brazil, China, India, Nigeria, Russia, or the United States?

8. What does McDougal, *supra*, mean when he says that the issue of the legal effect of UN resolutions and other prescriptive communications is one of community expectation, not consent? How does one substantiate community expectation? Is it easier or harder to substantiate than consent?

2. CONSENSUS AND GENERALLY ACCEPTED STANDARDS

As seen in the preceding discussion concerning the declarations and resolutions of international organizations, it often is loosely claimed that the consensus of states can be a "source" of international law. One should ask anyone making such a statement what is meant by "consensus." Is the claim merely a truism? If all the states in the world believe that proposition X is a rule of general customary law binding on all states, then who can say otherwise? Certainly not Professor McDougal, who argues that the key to law is not consent, but expectation. *See* the remarks of Myres McDougal, *supra*, in *The Effect of UN Resolutions on Emerging Legal Norms*, 1979 Proceed. A.S.I.L. 300. After all, no one other than "all the states" can define what international law is! Thus, to restate the truism: "international law consists of the international consensus about international law."

There is another key question: most practically, how can we establish what all the states believe? Many commentators have suggested that when the United Nations passes a resolution by unanimous vote, the content of that resolution *is* "international consensus" and hence becomes part of general customary law. What do you think of this position? Does the concept of "consensus" *add* anything to the discussion in the preceding section about the force and effect of UN resolutions?

The following summary paragraph from Ulrich Fastenrath, Lücken im Völkerrecht 291 (1991) provides a convenient overview that can help answer some of these questions. The insertion of the word "consensus" in brackets throughout is the result of an editorial judgment that the author, in translating from the German, mistakenly adopted the word "consent" instead of the word "consensus."

Among the controversial sources of international law is [consensus]. . . . According to the theory of [consensus] developed by *D'Amato* and *Cheng*

on the basis of psychological legal positivism,[ttt] a norm is a legal one if
states agree to see it as such. No express consent is necessary; acquiescence is sufficient. Ethiopia and Liberia pursued such a line of reasoning
in the *South West Africa* cases.[uuu] Presumably, according to this view,
consent could be withdrawn at any time. This result is avoided by *Onuf's*
theory of recognition.[vvv] Like the theory just mentioned, it is based on the
view that law is what states recognize as such. However, *Onuf* does not
construe common consent as a psychological fact but, in a more sociologi-
cal way, as a society's convention on the existence of a certain norm.
Once such a convention has been established it cannot simply be invalidated by changing one's mind. On the other hand, no formal cancellation
is necessary. Rather, according to the speech-act theory, a point must be
reached where the convention on the existence of the norm is not
generally accepted anymore. A much more stringent effect is attributed to
[consensus] by *Verdross, Simma,* and *van Hoof.* According to them, a
norm established by [consensus] is valid until it is abrogated or modified
by a new norm. Conversely, these authors are much more reluctant in
accepting the legal character of a rule established by [consensus]. However, they provide no evidence why such a norm can be nullified or modified
only by a new norm. It is well conceivable and, in international law, even
common practice that legal rules stemming from different sources are
changed or invalidated in different ways.

Closely related, if not identical, is the conception of "generally accepted
international standards," a phrase that has surfaced in recent years mainly in
relation to law of the sea and other environmental domains. *See, e.g.,*
Restatement (Third) of the Foreign Relations Law of the United States § 502,
Comment *c* of which states that "once a [marine safety] standard has been
generally accepted, a state is obligated in particular to apply it to all ships
flying its flag and to adopt any necessary laws or regulations." *See also,*
Comment *b* to § 601 which declares that a similar principle requires all states
to conform to international rules and standards derived from international
conventions or adopted by international organizations pursuant to such
conventions. Commenting, Professor Oxman writes, in *The Duty to Respect
Generally Accepted Standards,* 24 N.Y.U.J. Int'l L & Pol. 109, 143–44 (1991):

> The duty entails a legally binding obligation to observe generally
> accepted standards. This obligation, however, is created by general accep-
> tance of a standard in fact, rather than by the procedure by which the
> standard was articulated. Thus, it creates a useful bridge between so-
> called "soft law" and "hard law." This, indeed, was part of its original
> function. Where appropriate, standards (or guidelines) can be developed
> in a somewhat more relaxed procedural environment which is not specifi-
> cally designed to generate legally binding obligations as such; yet those
> same standards can become legally binding if they become generally
> accepted. * * * The effect ... is to impose a legal obligation on a state to
> respect a standard which it would not otherwise be legally bound to
> respect. The consensual requirements of international law for the imposi-

ttt. *See, e.g.,* A. D'Amato, *On Consensus,* 8 Can. Y.B.I.L. 104 (1970).
uuu. *Supra* note **x**.

vvv. *See, e.g.,* N. Onuf, *Do Rules Say What They Do? From Ordinary Language to Interna-tional Law,* 26 Harv. Int'l L. J. 385 (1985).

tion of legal obligations are not offended by this proposition; those requirements have previously been satisfied through acceptance of the general duty either by treaty or by customary international law. It is unnecessary to restrict the scope of the duty itself to conform to such requirements.

DISCUSSION NOTES/QUESTIONS

1. In *On Consensus*, 8 Can. Y.B.I.L. 104, 117 (1970), Anthony A. D'Amato took up the question of the weight to be given a dissenting vote by a major power in respect of a UN resolution:

> ... [W]e need not assume that the dissenting state be a powerful or major state or the leader of a bloc of states; such considerations of "weight" which often creep into the discussions of publicists confuse might with right in a manner which may these days be as anachronistic as gunboat diplomacy, let alone unjustifiable. The advent of the nuclear era has paradoxically created impotency in the highest places. Interbloc nuclear balance, the counter-productively excessive power of nuclear weapons, and the ability owing to modern mass communication of small nations to rally to the side of any one of them threatened by a larger power, make it necessary in any discussion of international law—which itself is designed to persuade the reader and not to force him to accept a position—to assume equality of states before the law and genuine reciprocity.

But could it not be argued that "major powers" should have a larger voice in determining the content of international law because (a) they usually have large populations, and "people count, not states"; (b) they command significant resources, including military resources that can be a force for world stability and order; (c) they are often more articulate about international law? How would a small power or a developing nation respond?

2. Is "consensus" as a possible "source" of international law anything more than the qualitative element of customary law (*opinio juris*) without the quantitative element of customary law (*usus*, or state practice)? Or is it both? And if it is both, how does it differ from customary law?

3. NON–CONVENTIONAL CONCERTED ACTS AND DECLARATIONS

It is common practice for governments to engage in collaborative acts that evince common understandings and outlooks but which are not viewed, at least not initially, as part of conventional or customary international law. Typically they are expressed in intergovernmental communications and *communiqués*. Sometimes, indeed, they are chronicled in more formal instruments, *e.g.*, the 1975 Final Act of the Conference on Security and Cooperation in Europe, the so-called Helsinki Accords **(Basic Document 1.12)**, and its multiple progeny. Deemed technically non-binding, they are nonetheless strictly observed.[www] The same is true of so-called memoranda of understanding (MOUs) or "gentlemen's agreements," characteristic of the practice

---

www. For details, see *infra* Problem 5–1 ("Ethnic Conflict and Its Consequences in Slavia, Candia, and Corcyra") in ch. 5, at 527–38.

For the texts of the many "Helsinki Process" instruments, see 1 Weston & Carlson §I.D.

of the International Monetary Fund.[xxx] Writes Anthony Aust, Modern Treaty Law and Practice (2000), at 17–18:

> [L]awyers practising in foreign or other ministries deliberately utilise instruments which employ carefully chosen terminology to indicate that, rather than create international legal rights and obligations, the intention of the participants is to record no more than mutual *understandings* as to how they will conduct themselves.... The existence of such instruments, and the extent to which they are significant for the conduct of business between states, is not well known outside government circles. In fact, a large number of such instruments, bilateral and multilateral [and most of which are never published], are concluded every year covering a wide range of subjects. * * * Such instruments have been variously described as "gentlemen's agreements," "non-binding agreements," "*de facto* agreements" and "non-legal agreements" ..., most commonly referred to by the initials "MOU."

Aust adds: "[C]alling an instrument a 'Memorandum of Understanding' does not, in itself, determine its status." *Id.* That is, an MOU (or gentleman's agreement) may or may not be legally binding depending on the circumstances or context. What matters is the expectations of the parties[yyy].

Similar observations attend presumptively non-legal intergovernmental declarations outside the framework of an international organization, used to settle disputes and chart the course for future relations—*e.g.*, the declarations at the Yalta, Potsdam, and Cairo conferences at the end of World War II relating to postwar territorial disposition and political organization. Professor Schachter, in International Law in Theory and Practice 129 (1991), describes these declaratory communications as official State acts from which "it is appropriate to draw inferences that the States concerned have recognized the principles, rules, status and rights acknowledged." He continues: "This does not mean that 'new law' or a new obligation is created. However, where the points of law are not entirely clear and are disputed the evidence of official positions drawn from these instruments can be significant." *Id.* Schachter then adds, at 130:

> ... States entering into a non-legal commitment generally view it as a political (or moral) obligation to carry it out in good faith. Other parties and other States concerned have reason to expect such compliance and to rely on it. What we must deduce from this, I submit, is that the political texts which express commitments and positions of one kind or another are governed by the general principle of good faith. Moreover, since good faith is an accepted general principle of international law, it is appropriate and even necessary to apply it in the legal sense.

DISCUSSION NOTES/QUESTIONS

1. According to James W. Garner, *The International Binding Force of Unilateral Oral Declarations,* 27 A.J.I.L. 493 (1933), unilateral declarations of states may give rise to international legal obligations by way of estoppel. However,

xxx. On the IMF, see *infra* Discussion Note/Question 5 in Problem 6–1 ("A Financial Crisis in Sundalau Spreads to Tolteca"), at 816–18.

yyy. For further treatment of MOUs, see A. Aust, Modern Treaty Law and Practice (2000), ch. 3.

the intention of a state making such a declaration must necessarily be a critical factor, as must also an element of publicity. But what constitutes a sufficient indication of intent and sufficient publicity for a unilateral declaration to be deemed binding? Indeed, given that states and governments do not have minds, how is it possible to determine the requisite intent in the first place? Does the customary law theory of *opinio juris* bear any relevance here? Consider in these connections that, in the *Nuclear Tests Cases* **(Basic Document 7.9)** wherein Australia and New Zealand challenged the atmospheric nuclear testing of France at its Muroroa atoll in the South Pacific, the World Court determined a unilateral declaration by France to halt further atmospheric testing to be a legally binding commitment sufficient to render the case moot. *See* 1973 ICJ 99, 135, 1973 WL 5.

2. If, as Schachter, *supra*, contends, voluntary governmental declarations are to be governed by the general principles of good faith (and its corollary estoppel), why is it necessary to posit a "source" of law distinct from "general principles of law recognized by civilized nations"? *See supra* Section E, at 157.

CONCLUDING DISCUSSION NOTES/QUESTIONS

1. The expression "sources of international law" is at best ambiguous. Worse, because it understates both the derivation and scope of law-creating processes, it is misconceived and therefore misleading. The case is persuasively made by professors McDougal, Lasswell, and Reisman who, in a germinal essay, observe that the law-creating processes which by tradition we call "sources" of law are best seen in terms of the seven component functions which comprise the various types of legal decision: intelligence, promotion, prescription, invocation, application, termination, and appraisal. *See* Myres S. McDougal, Harold D. Lasswell & W. Michael Reisman, *The World Constitutive Process of Authoritative Decision*, in 1 The Future of the International Legal Order 73 (R. Falk & C. Black eds., 1969).

Especially relevant is what these authors call the "prescriptive [or law-making] function." In *The Prescribing Function in World Constitutive Process: How International Law is Made*, 6 Yale Studies in World Public Order 249 (1980), McDougal and Reisman write, at 250: "The making of law is a decision function which may be conveniently described as prescription. By prescription, we refer to a process of communication which creates, in a target audience, a complex set of expectations comprising three distinctive components: expectations about a policy content; expectations about authority; and expectations about control." And "to speak meaningfully of law," they emphasize, "all three components must be copresent." *Id.* at 251. Equally important, Reisman adds, in *International Law-making: A Process of Communication*, 1981 Proceed. A.S.I.L. 101, 108, the three components "*must continue to be communicated* for the prescription, as such, to endure; if one or more of the components should cease to be communicated, the prescription undergoes a type of desuetude and is terminated."

2. Does there exist a hierarchy among the various "sources" of international law? Would you say that international law decision-makers are expected to treat the "sources" of international law embraced by Article 38 of the ICJ Statute **(Basic Document 1.6)**, or at least the first three major "sources" (treaties, custom, and general principles) noted therein, in hierarchical or sequential manner? Why? Why not? Do you conclude the same thing in respect of Article 21 of the Rome Statute of the International Criminal Court **(Basic Document 1.16)**? Why? Why not? Consider the following passage from W. Michael Reisman, Nullity

and Revision—The Review and Enforcement of International Judgments and Awards 555–57 (1971):

> In point of fact, the problem of [Article 38] priorities is artificial, since authoritative international policy does not present itself for application with a convenient label affixed, specifying its source. International prescription is an ongoing process. The purport of a convention cannot be grasped without consideration of prior and subsequent customary developments, their consonance with general principles, and the responses of quasi-authoritative doctrine. Initial focus on any one source will encounter a parallel necessity to be considered in the context of all other sources.

Do you agree with Reisman? What happens if a provision in a treaty clearly conflicts with a rule of customary international law? Is there a way to resolve the conflict according to the strategy he suggests? Suppose a treaty between states A and B clearly conflicts with customary law rights that A and B had in the absence of the treaty. Which prevails, the treaty or the custom? In considering your answer to this question, ask yourself why A and B signed the treaty when there were underlying customary rights in its absence. Would it matter which came first or last in time? In any case, does Reisman's argument regarding ICJ Statute Article 38 apply equally to Rome Statute Article 21?

3. Consider the following remarks by Liesbeth Lijnzaad of the Faculty of Law of the University of Limburg, in Maastricht, The Netherlands:

> Traditional international law is concerned with states.... What I find striking in the present international system is the lack of interest in the interests of people that states can get away with. That is related to the methods of creation of international law and the international legal system in which there is no central authority. In a domestic legal system there is a central authority which can steer if things go wrong. So if we try to change the indifference to the interests of people in the international legal system, that would have to include the methods of creation of law.

Panel on "Sources of International Law: Entrenching the Gender Bias" *in* Proceedings of the Second Joint Conference of the American Society of International Law and the Nederlandse Vereniging voor Internationaal Recht (at The Hague, 22–24 Jul 93) 432 (1994). Can you suggest how Professor Lijnzaad's concerns might be met? She suggests that feminist legal analysis might be helpful, commenting at 432–33:

> [F]eminist legal analysis is comparable to socialist legal theory of which the basic idea is that the law belonging to the superstructure is governed by production relationships in the base. There is a similarity between the way in which feminist legal analysis sees law as being created by what we all experience in everyday life. If you agree with this impression that might mean that we could look to socialist legal analysis and find ways of dealing with everyday problems.

Do you agree? *See generally* Hilary Charlesworth & Christine Chinkin, The Boundaries of International Law: A Feminist Analysis (2000).

In any event, on the basis of Professor Lijnzaad's comments and the chapter in general, would you say that the law-creating processes of the international law system are any different from the law-creating processes of municipal law systems? If so, what differences do you perceive? If not, why not? Consider Morton H. Kaplan & Nicholas deB. Katzenbach, The Political Foundations of International Law 235 (1961):

The techniques employed and the sources invoked are strikingly parallel in the domestic and international systems. The difference lies largely, as we have noted, in the difficulty of developing a system of legislation comparable to that developed by domestic governments, and of segregating, as a result, governmental functions structurally in the manner characteristic of domestic societies. The international process remains relatively undeveloped as a governmental system.

4. Finally, *á propos* the preceding question, in particular the preceding quotation, consider José Alvarez, *International Organizations as Law-makers* (2005), wherein Professor Alvarez addresses how the UN, the WTO, and other international organizations with "global reach" have been changing the mechanisms and reasoning behind the making, as well as the enforcement, of international law. How might the International Criminal Court fit into Alvarez's thesis?

Chapter Three

THE APPLICATION OF INTERNATIONAL LAW

A. THE APPLICATION OF INTERNATIONAL LAW AT THE INTERNATIONAL CRIMINAL COURT

It is September 2005, not yet six months since you began working as a junior lawyer on the prosecutorial staff of Luis Moreno–Ocampo, Prosecutor of the International Criminal Court (ICC) at The Hague. You and your colleagues have been very busy in this brief time, learning about the history of the ICC, its substantive jurisdiction, and the jurisprudence and procedures it is mandated to follow by its constitutive instrument, the Rome Statute of the International Criminal Court **(Basic Document 1.16)**. The Rome Statute, you have learned, was adopted on 17 July 1998 and entered into force on 1 July 2002, after being ratified by 60 states. As this coursebook went to press, 139 states had signed the Statute and 100 states (including the technically non-state polities of Andorra, Liechtenstein, Monaco, Nauru, and San Marino) had ratified it: 27 African states, 1 from North America, 8 from Asia (Central, Eastern and Southeastern), 1 from the Middle East, 14 from Eastern Europe, 20 from Latin America and the Caribbean, 6 from the South Pacific, and 22 from Western Europe—not yet a majority of the world's states, but an impressive number and array nonetheless.

You also have learned that the ICC mirrors to some extent the organization and structure of the *ad hoc* tribunals established by UN Security Council resolution to prosecute alleged international crimes committed in the former Yugoslavia and in Rwanda,[a] tribunals that have attracted no small amount of the world's attention since the early 1990s. And for good reason. While not without their own deficiencies (such as being limited by time and geography) and while they will be closed down as they complete their mandated work, both tribunals have demonstrated a seriousness of purpose and result sufficient to conclude that their jurisprudence will provide some guide to the work of the ICC.[b]

---

a. *See* UN Security Council Resolution 827 of 25 May 1993 on Establishing an International Tribunal for the Prosecution of Persons Responsible for Serious Violations of International Humanitarian Law Committed in the territory of the Former Yugoslavia **(Basic Document 2.44)** and UN Security Council Resolution 955 of 8 Nov 1994 Establishing the International Tribunal for Rwanda **(Basic Document 2.46)**.

b. To what extent will of course depend on how the ICC interprets Article 21 of its Rome Statute.

As this coursebook went to press, the International Tribunal for the Prosecution of Persons Responsible for Serious Violations of International Humanitarian Law Committed in the Territory of the Former Yugoslavia (the ICTY)[c] had called 3,500 witnesses, publicly indicted over 100 individuals (including former Yugoslav President Slobodan Milosevic, former Bosnian Serb leader Radovan Karadzic, and former Serbian General Ratko Mladic), held 56 indictees in custody (Mr. Milosevic among them), issued 40 sentencing judgments (27 on appeal and 13 on trial), and had 61 defendants in proceedings before it at the pre-trial, trial, appeal, and sentencing stages. A dramatic event was the "extradition" to the ICTY on 29 June 2001 of Slobodan Milosevic, to answer charges by the ICTY of war crimes and crimes against humanity committed in Kosovo during Serbia's conflict with ethnic Albanians in the 1990s.[d] This was the first time that a former head of state had ever been placed physically under the custody of an international criminal tribunal. The Kunarac, Kovac and Vukovic Case (the so-called "rape camp case") resulted in convictions for the first time by the ICTY (Judge Florence Ndepele Mwachande Mumba of Zambia presiding) of both rape and enslavement as a crime against humanity—the defendants, members of the Bosnian Serb armed forces, judged to be "lawless opportunists [who] should expect no mercy, no matter how low their position in the chain of command," having used rape "as an instrument of terror."[e]

From its inception, the ICTR has focused on the individuals alleged to have been the architects and perpetrators of the 1994 Rwanda genocide. Thus, with a current budget of almost US $256 million and after calling more than 1190 witnesses from twelve African, American, and European countries, the Tribunal has, as of this coursebook's presstime, 60 detainees, 51 cases in their pre-trial, trial, appeal, and sentencing stages, and custody of former political leaders such as former Prime Minister Jean Kambanda and ten Ministers of his 1994 Interim Government: the leadership of the Parliament and the dominant political party at the time (the National Republican Movement for Democracy and Development or MRND); high-ranking military commanders; senior government administrators such as the Governor (Prefects) of various regions; and lesser officials such as former Taba mayor Jean–Paul Akayesu. Most of these individuals were arrested in, and transferred from, cooperating neighboring countries such as Benin, Burkina Faso, Cameroon, Côte d'Ivoire, Kenya, Mali, Namibia, South Africa, Tanzania, Togo, and Zambia (also Belgium, Denmark, France, Switzerland, the United Kingdom, and the United States).[f] Kambanda's sentencing by a Trial Chamber of the ICTR was the first time in history that a former head of government had been sentenced for the crime of genocide by an international tribunal.

---

c. *See supra* note **a**; also note **h** in the Introduction to this Part I, at 4.

d. The term "extradition," widely used in the media to describe Mr. Milosevic's transfer from Belgrade to The Hague, is in fact a misnomer because Mr. Milosevic was not sent to another country at its request but to an international tribunal. "Deportation" would have been the correct term. For discussion of the law of extradition, see *infra* Problem 5–3

("Suspected Terrorists in Hibernia") in Chapter 5, at 643–59.

e. Prosecutor v. Dragolub Kunarac, Radomir Kovac, and Zoran Vukovic, Judgment of: 22 Feb 2001, Trial Chamber II, (IT–96–23) and (IT–96–23/1), available on the ICTY Web site at <http://www.un.org/icty/kunarac/trialc2/judgement/index.htm>.

f. *See supra* note **a**.

For all that these two *ad hoc* tribunals have done well, however, it has been regularly pointed out that they have dealt with the actions mainly of mid-or low-level personnel and that most of the leaders responsible for war crimes have somehow escaped being brought before a court. Indeed, despite considerable rhetoric to the contrary, the international community has done little to assist either tribunal in the fulfillment of its mandate. In Bosnia–Herzegovina, the NATO Implementation Force (IFOR), though with the capacity to make arrests, has refused to assist the ICTY in its search for indictees (including such conspicuous figures as Radovan Karadzic and Ratko Mladic, accused of genocide). In the case of the ICTR and of domestic procedures established relative to Rwanda, the processes of arrest, indictment, and prosecution have been severely hampered by insufficient funds and a Rwandan judiciary decimated by the 1994 genocide.

On the other hand, establishing the ICTY and ICTR reaffirmed and even advanced, at least in theory, the principles of criminality and individual accountability laid down at Nuremberg following World War II. Though they were not formally triggered by the massive and systematic Yugoslav and Rwandan humanitarian law and human rights violations as such, but, rather, by the determination that the violations constituted a "threat to international peace and security" under Chapter VII of the UN Charter **(Basic Document 1.5)**,[g] a failure to establish the two tribunals "would have eroded the values of Nuremberg and perpetuated worldwide the perception that even the most egregious crimes against humanity could go unpunished."[h]

The creation of the ICC—a completely new and permanent international organization, outside the framework of the United Nations, unlike the ICTY and ICTR and thus without exact precedent—has encountered more mixed reactions. The ICC can only hear cases which occur after 1 July 2002. Its geographic jurisdiction, however, is unlimited, which means that the Court has in theory jurisdiction over the actions of nationals of any country. Unlike the Nuremberg and *ad hoc* international tribunals, however, the ICC operates on the *principle of complementarity*, devised to preserve considerable state sovereignty.[i] "Complementarity" means that the ICC will have jurisdiction only when a national legal system is unable or unwilling to carry out a genuine investigation or prosecution of persons alleged to have committed international crimes. Thus the ICC is, in effect, a safety net for the failure of national legal systems, not the first port of call for the prosecution of international crimes.[j]

While some observers see the ICC as a vital step in creating a system of accountability for international crimes, others fear that it will be used for political advantage, especially against powerful countries such as the United States. This anxiety explains at least in part the hostility to the ICC in

---

g. Just as in the case of the ICC in relation to Darfur. *See* UN Security Council Resolution 1593 of 31 March 2005, *supra* note **e** in the Introduction to this Part I, at 3. *See also* text accompanying note **h** in the Introduction to this Part I, at 4.

h. T. Meron, *Answering for War Crimes: Lessons from the Balkans*, 76 Foreign Aff. 2 (Jan–Feb 1997), at 3.

i. *See* Article 17 of the Rome Statute **(Basic Document 1.16)**.

j. For discussion, see M. C. Bassiouni, The Statute of the International Criminal Court: a Documentary History (1998); Judging War Criminals: The Politics of International Justice (Y.Beigbeder ed., 1999); A. Cassese, International Criminal Law (2003).

particular by the US. The US joined six other nations in voting against the adoption of the ICC Statute in Rome in 1998.[k] In the last days of his administration, on 31 December 2000, US President Bill Clinton signed the ICC Statute, but this decision was revoked by President George W. Bush early in his first administration, on April 27 2002. Regrettably, impunity from the ICC has become a feature of US foreign policy. Indeed, the US Congress has enacted legislation whose purpose is to prevent the US government even from cooperating with the ICC. This law, termed "The Hague Invasion Act," allows the US military to rescue any member of American armed forces held by or on behalf of the ICC. In addition, the US has brought considerable pressure to bear on other countries to enter into bilateral agreements (which it argues are allowed under Rome Statute Article 98) to exempt US personnel from the jurisdiction of the ICC even if they are within the territory of a state party to the ICC Statute.[l] Many close allies of the US, including Australia and the United Kingdom, have become parties to the ICC's Rome Statute, and there is little international sympathy for the US refusal to participate in the work of the Court.[m]

How is the ICC likely to apply international law? Eighteen judges have been elected to the ICC and sit in The Hague awaiting the first cases. Meanwhile, the jurisprudence of the *ad hoc* tribunals provides some guide to what might be expected to evolve from ICC deliberations once they begin, including in the case of Darfur, to which you have been assigned by Prosecutor Moreno–Ocanpo, for alleged violations of international criminal law since July 2002. The opinion and judgment on the merits in the *Tadic case*, rendered by the ICTY's Trial Chamber on 7 May 1997, is of relevance to the question of application of international law. While it was appealed to the Tribunal's Appeals Chamber, this decision of the Trial Chamber, reached by a three-judge panel,[n] was the first of its kind since the Nuremberg and Tokyo trials after World War II. It is reproduced below in abridged form, following extracts from the thirty-four count amended indictment against Duško Tadić (and his colleague Goran Borovnica) of 14 December 1995.[o]

k. The other six countries were Algeria, China, Iraq, Israel, Libya, and Yemen.

l. *See* Leila Nadya Sadat, *Summer in Rome, Spring in The Hague, Winter in Washington? US Policy Towards the International Criminal Court*, 21 Wis. Int'l L. J. 557 (2003); Salvatore Zappalà, *The Reaction of the US to the Entry into Force of the ICC Statute: Comments on UN SC Resolution 1422 (2002) and Article 98 Agreements*, 1 J. Int'l Crim. Just. 114 (2003). *See also* SC Res. 1422, UN Doc. S/RES/1422 (12 Jul 2002), *available at* <http:// daccessdds.un.org/ doc/ UNDOC/GEN/ N02/ 477/ 61/ PDF/ N0247761.pdf?OpenElement> and SC Res. 1487, UN Doc S/RES/1487 (12 Jun 2003), *available at* <http://daccessdds.un.org/doc/UNDOC/ GEN/N03/394/51/ PDF/N0339451.pdf?OpenElement>, each requesting, "consistent with the provisions of Article 16 of the Rome Statute, that the ICC, if a case arises involving current or former officials or personnel from a contributing State not a Party to the Rome Statute over acts or omissions relating to a United Nations established or authorized operation, shall for a twelve-month period starting 1 July 2002 not commence or proceed with investigation or prosecution of any such case, unless the Security Council decides otherwise." For related comment, see *infra* Discussion Note/Question 19 in Problem 4–1 ("Intervention in Loango"), at 361–64.

m. It is rumored that, paradoxically, the ICC was able to organize itself more swiftly without US participation.

n. Members of the Trial Chamber panel were Judge Gabrielle Kirk McDonald, Presiding (United States), Judge Ninian Stephen (Australia), and Judge Lal Chand Vohrah (Malaysia).

o. The amended indictment is set out in full in Annex A to the Opinion and Judgment. *See also* the ICTY Web site at <http:// www.un.org/icty>.

The Prosecutor of the Tribunal
Against
Duško Tadić (a/k/a "Dule" or "Dušan")
and Goran Borovnica Indictment

Richard J. Goldstone, Prosecutor of the International Criminal Tribunal for the former Yugoslavia, pursuant to his authority under Article 18 of the Statute of the International Criminal Court for the former Yugoslavia ("The Statute of the Tribunal") **[Basic Document 2.43]** and Rule 50 of the Rules of Procedure and Evidence of the Tribunal,[1] charges:

1.   Beginning on about 23 May 1992, Serb forces, supported by artillery and heavy weapons, attacked Bosnian Muslim and Croat population centers in opstina Prijedor, Bosnia–Herzegovina. In the following days, most of the Muslims and Croats were forced from their homes and seized by the Serb forces. The Serb forces then unlawfully confined thousands of Muslims and Croats in the Omarska, Keraterm and Trnopolje camps. The accused, **Duško Tadić a/k/a "Dule" a/k/a "Dušan**," participated in the attack on, seizure, murder and maltreatment of Bosnian Muslims and Croats in collection and mistreatment, including killings, of Bosnian Muslims and Croats in opstina Prijedor both within the camps and outside the camps, between the period beginning about 23 May 1992 and ending about 31 December 1992. The accused, **Goran Borovnica,** participated with **Duško Tadić** in the killing of Bosnian Muslims in the Kozarac area, as set forth below:

Background

2.1.   About 23 May 1992, approximately three weeks after Serbs forcibly took control of governmental authority in opstina Prijedor, intensive shelling by Serb forces of Bosnian Muslim and Croat areas in opstina Prijedor caused Muslim and Croat residents to flee their homes. The majority of them were seized by Serb forces. As the Serb forces rounded up the Muslims and Croat residents, they forced the Muslims and Croats to march in columns bound for one or another of the prison camps that the Serbs had established in the opstina. The Serb forces pulled many of the Muslims and Croats from the columns and shot or beat them on the spot.

2.2.   On about 25 May 1992, shortly after the start of large scale military attacks on Muslim population centres, the Serb forces began taking prisoners to the Omarska, Keraterm and Trnopolje camps.

2.3.   During the next several weeks, the Serb forces continued to round up Muslim and Croats from Kozarac, Prijedor town, and other places in the opstina and interned them in the camps. Many of Prijedor's Muslim and Croat intellectuals, professional and political leaders were sent to Omarska. There were approximately 40 women in the camp, and all the other prisoners in the camp were men.

2.4.   Within the area of the Omarska mining complex that the Serb authorities used for the camp, the camp authorities generally confined the prisoners in three different buildings: the administration building, where interrogations

---

1.   IT/32/Rev 10.

took place and most of the women were confined; the garage or hangar building; the "white house," a small building where particularly severe beatings were administered; and on a cement courtyard area between the buildings known as the "pista." There was another small building, known as the "red house," where prisoners were sometimes taken but most often did not emerge alive.

2.5.   Living conditions at Omarska were brutal. Prisoners were crowded together with little or no facilities for personal hygiene. They were fed starvation rations once a day and given only three minutes to get into the canteen area, eat, and get out. The little water they received was ordinarily foul. Prisoners had no changes of clothing and no bedding. They received no medical care.

2.6.   Severe beatings were commonplace. The camp guards, and others who came to the camp and physically abused the prisoners, used all manner of weapons during these beatings, including wooden batons, metal rods and tools, lengths of thick industrial cable that had metal balls affixed to the end, rifle butts, and knives. Both female and male prisoners were beaten, tortured, raped, sexually assaulted, and humiliated. Many, whose identities are known and unknown, did not survive the camp. After the collection of thousands of Bosnian Muslims and Croats in late May, 1992, groups of Serbs, including the accused, continued to enter the villages in which Muslims and Croats remained, killing some villagers and driving others from their homes and into the camps.

2.7.   Keraterm camp was located at a former ceramics factory in Prijedor. Conditions for prisoners were similar to those in Omarska camp; physical and psychological abuse, including assaults and killings, were common. Trnopolje camp was established at the site of a former school in Trnopolje village. Men, women and children were detained in Trnopolje camp; the majority of those detained were then expelled from opstina Prijedor. In Trnopolje, female detainees were sexually abused, and detainees were murdered and otherwise physically and psychologically abused.

General Allegations

3.1.   At all times relevant to this indictment, a state of armed conflict and partial occupation existed in the territory of Bosnia–Herzegovina.

3.2.   All acts or omissions set forth as grave breaches recognised by Article 2 of the Statute of the Tribunal [**Basic Document 2.43**] occurred during that armed conflict and partial occupation.

3.3.   All of the prisoners at the Omarska, Keraterm and Trnopolje camps, and the Bosnian Muslims and Croats of opstina Prijedor referred to in this indictment were, at all relevant times, persons protected by the Geneva Conventions of 1949 [**Basic Documents 2.9 through 2.12**].

3.4.   The accused in this indictment were required to abide by the laws and customs governing the conduct of war, including the Geneva Conventions of 1949.

3.5.   Unless otherwise set forth below, all acts and omissions set forth in this indictment took place between about 23 May and about 31 December 1992.

3.6.   In each paragraph charging torture, the acts were committed by, or at the instigation of, or with the consent or acquiescence of, an official or person acting in an official capacity, and for one or more of the following purposes: to obtain information or a confession from the victim or a third person; to punish the victim for an act the victim or a third person committed or was suspected of having committed; to intimidate or coerce the victim or a third person; and/or for any reason based upon discrimination of any kind.

3.7.   In each paragraph charging crimes against humanity, a crime recognised by Article 5 of the Statute **[Basic Document 2.43]** of the Tribunal, the alleged acts or omissions were part of a widespread or large-scale or systematic attack directed against a civilian population, specifically the Muslim and Croat population of opstina Prijedor.

3.8.   The term "Serb" refers either to Bosnian citizens of Serbian descent or to individuals of Serbian descent whose citizenship in the former Yugoslavia is unknown.

3.9.   Paragraphs 3.1 through 3.8 are realleged and incorporated into each of the charges described below.

CHARGES:

PERSECUTION
(Count One)

4.   Between about 23 May 1992 and about 31 December 1992, **Duško Tadić** participated with Serb forces in the attack, destruction and plunder of Bosnian muslim and Croat residential areas, the seizure and imprisonment of thousands of Muslim and Croats under brutal conditions in camps located in Omarska, Keraterm and Trnopolje, and the deportation and/or expulsion of the majority of Muslim and Croat residents of opstina Prijedor by force or threat of force. During this time, Serb forces, including **Duško Tadić**, subjected Muslims and Croats inside and outside the camps to a campaign of terror which included killings, torture, sexual assaults, and other physical and psychological abuse.

4.1   Between the dates of 24 to 27 May 1992, Serb forces attacked the village of Kozarac and other villages and hamlets in the surrounding area. **Duško Tadić**, was actively involved in the attack. His participation included firing flares to illuminate the village at night for the artillery and tank guns as the village was being shelled, and physically assisting in the seizure, collection, segregation, and forced transfer to detention centres of the majority of the non-Serb population of the area during those first days. **Duško Tadić**, also took part in the killing and beating of a number of the seized persons, including: the killing and beating of an elderly man and woman near the cemetery in the area of "old" Kozarac, the acts described in paragraphs 11 and 12 below, the beatings of at least two former policemen from Kozarac at a road junction in the village of Kozarac, and the beating of a number of Muslim males who had been seized and detained at the Prijedor military barracks.

4.2   **Duško Tadić** was also seen on numerous occasions in the three main camps operating within the opstina Prijedor: Omarska, Keraterm and Trnopolje. During the period between 25 May 1992 and 8 August 1992, **Tadić,** physically took part or otherwise participated in the killing, torture, sexual assault, and beating of many detainees at Omarska camp, including those acts set forth in paragraphs 5 through 10 below and other instances of torture and beating prisoners in the "white house," the "administration building," the "pista" and the main garage area. During the same period, in Keraterm camp, **Duško Tadić**, physically took part or otherwise participated in the beating of detainees and looting of their personal property and valuables, including, on more than one occasion, the mass beating of a number of detainees from Kozarac being confined in "Room 2."

4.3   During the period 25 May 1992 and 31 December 1992, **Duško Tadić,** physically participated and otherwise assisted in the transfer to and unlawful confinement in Trnopolje camp of non-Serb persons from the Kozarac area. Additionally, during the period between September, 1992 and December, 1992, in Trnopolje camp or in the adjacent area, **Tadić,** physically took part or otherwise participated in the killing of more than 30 detainees, including groups of male detainees executed in a plum orchard adjacent to the camp. **Tadić,** also physically took part or otherwise participated in the torture of more than 12 female detainees, including several gang rapes, which occurred both in the camp and at a white house adjacent to the camp during the period between September, 1992 and December, 1992.

4.4   Between 25 May and 31 December 1992, **Tadić,** physically participated in the seizure and selection of individuals for detention in the camps and transported Muslims and Croats who had been seized, to the camps for detention. During the time he was engaged in this seizure, selection, and transfer of non-Serbs to various detention centres, **Duško Tadić,** was aware that the majority of those detainees who survived detention would be deported from the territory of Bosnia–Herzegovina.

4.5   Concurrent with the attack and seizure of the non-Serb population of Kozarac and the surrounding area, the Serb forces plundered and destroyed the homes, businesses, and other property of non-Serbs. The seizure, transfer and detention of the non-Serb population and the plundering and destruction of their property continued for a number of weeks. During the period 23 May and 31 August 1992, **Duško Tadić** was aware of the widespread nature of the plunder and destruction of personal and real property from non-Serbs and was physically involved and otherwise participated in that plunder and destruction, including the plunder of homes in Kozarac and the looting of valuables from non-Serbs as they were seized and upon their arrival at the camps and detention centres.

By his participation in these acts, **Duško Tadić,** committed:

> **Count 1:**
>
> a **CRIME AGAINST HUMANITY** recognised by Articles 5(h) (persecution on political, racial and/or religious grounds) and 7(1) of the Statute of the Tribunal **[Basic Document 2.43]**

FORCIBLE SEXUAL INTERCOURSE WITH "F"
(Counts 2–4)

5.   **"F"** was taken to Omarska camp as a prisoner in early June 1992. Sometime between early June and 3 August 1992, **"F"** was taken to the

Separacija building at the entrance to the Omarska camp and placed in a room where **Duško Tadić** subjected **"F"** to forcible sexual intercourse. By these acts, **Duško Tadić** committed:

Count 2:

a **GRAVE BREACH** recognised by Articles 2(b) (inhuman treatment) and 7(1) of the Statute of the Tribunal **[Basic Document 2.43]**; and

Count 3:

a **VIOLATION OF THE LAWS OR CUSTOMS OF WAR** recognised by Articles 3 and 7(1) of the Statute of the Tribunal and Article 3(1)(a) (cruel treatment) of the Geneva Conventions of 1949 **[Basic Documents 2.9 through 2.12]**; and

Count 4:

a **CRIME AGAINST HUMANITY** recognised by Articles 5(g) (rape) and 7(1) of the Statute of the Tribunal.

KILLING OF EMIR KARABASIC, JASMIN HRNIC, ENVER ALIC, FIKRET HARAMBASIC, BEATING EMIR BEGANOVIC AND INHUMANE ACTS AGAINST "G" AND "H" IN OMARSKA CAMP

(Counts 5–11)

6.   During the period 1 June and 31 July 1992, a group of Serbs, including from outside the camp, including **Duško Tadić**, severely beat numerous prisoners, including Emir KARABAIC, Jasmin HRNIC, Enver ALIC, Fikret HARAMBAIC and Emir BEGANOVIC, in the large garage building or hangar of omarska camp. The group forced two other prisoners, "G" and "H," to commit oral sexual acts on HARAMBAIC and forced "G" to sexually mutilate him. KARABASIC, HRNIC, ALIC and HARAMBIC died as a result of the assaults. By his participation in these acts, **Duško Tadić** committed:

Count 5:

a **GRAVE BREACH** recognised by Articles 2(a) (wilful killing) and 7(1) of the Statute of the Tribunal **[Basic Document 2.43]**; and

Count 6:

a **VIOLATION OF THE LAWS OR CUSTOMS OF WAR** recognised by Articles 3 and 7(1) of the Statute of the Tribunal and Article 3(1)(a) (murder) of the Geneva Conventions of 1949 **[Basic Documents 2.9 through 2.12]**; and

Count 7:

a **CRIME AGAINST HUMANITY** recognised by Articles 5(a) (murder) and 7(1) of the Statute of the Tribunal; and

Count 8:

a **GRAVE BREACH** recognised by Articles 2(b) (torture) and 7(1) of the Statute of the Tribunal; and

Count 9:

a **GRAVE BREACH** recognised by Articles 2(c) (wilfully causing great suffering or serious injury to body and health) and 7(1) of the Statute of the Tribunal; and

Count 10:

a **VIOLATION OF THE LAWS OR CUSTOMS OF WAR** recognised by Articles 3 and 7(1) of the Statute of the Tribunal and Article 3(1)(a) (cruel treatment) of the Geneva Conventions of 1949 **[Basic Documents 2.9 through 2.12]**; and

Count 11:

a **CRIME AGAINST HUMANITY** recognised by Articles 5(a) (inhumane acts) and 7(1) of the Statute of the Tribunal.

[*Eds.*—The indictment goes on to identify similar killings, beatings, and other abuses in which Duško Tadić, was alleged to have participated and for which he therefore was accused, in twenty-three additional counts, of "grave breaches" (counts 12, 15, 18, 21, 24, 27, 29, and 32), "violations of the laws or customs of war" (counts 13, 16, 19, 22, 25, 30, and 33), and "crimes against humanity" (counts 14, 17, 20, 23, 26, 28, 31, and 34) under articles 2, 3, 5 and 7 of the Statute of the Tribunal and Article 3(1)(a) of the Geneva conventions of 1949 **(Basic Documents 2.9 through 2.12).**]

EDITORS' NOTE

Following the filing of the above-quoted indictment with Trial Chamber II of the ICTY, the accused, Duško Tadić, responded by challenging the Tribunal's establishment, status, and jurisdiction, claiming that it was unlawfully constituted, that it lacked primacy over national courts, and that it was without subject-matter jurisdiction over the crimes alleged (on the theory that the scope of Tribunal's jurisdiction extends only to international conflicts and not to the conflict in Bosnia–Herzegovina which, Tadić claimed, was internal in character). Trial Chamber II ruled against Tadić on all three counts. Thereafter, he appealed to the International Criminal Tribunal's Appeals Chamber. The Appeals Chamber, Judge Antonio Cassese (Italy) presiding, also ruled against the accused, again on all three counts. The case then went to trial on the merits, Judge Gabriella Kirk McDonald (USA) presiding. On 7 May 1997, out of 31 counts, Duško Tadić was found guilty on 11 counts (persecution and beatings, *i.e.*, crimes against humanity and war crimes) and not guilty on 20 counts (9 murder counts because of insufficient evidence and 11 counts declared inapplicable). Judge McDonald dissented because she disagreed with her colleagues on whether the evidence supported the finding of an international war, thereby bringing to bear more stringent legal obligations on combatant officers. On 14 July 1997, Trail Chamber II sentenced Duško Tadić to 97 years in prison on 11 counts of crimes against humanity and war crimes, the sentences to run concurrently with the longest single term to be for 20 years.

Mr. Tadić subsequently appealed the judgment and sentence as did also the Prosecutor in a cross appeal relying upon Judge McDonald's dissent. On 15 July 1999, the Appeals Chamber, Judge Mohamed Shahabuddeen (Guyana) presiding, pronounced its judgment on the two appeals, denying defendant Tadić's appeal on all grounds and allowing the prosecution's cross-appeal by reversing Trial Chamber II and finding Duško Tadić guilty on counts 8, 9, 12, 15, 21, 29 and 32 of the indictment that charged him with "grave breaches" of the 1949 Geneva Conventions [**Basic Documents 2.9 through 2.12**] (Article 2 of the Statute of the Tribunal—*i.e.*, wilful killing, torture or inhuman treatment, and wilfully causing great suffering or serious injury to body or health). The Appeals Chamber also reversed the Trial Chamber II's judgment in respect of count 30, alleging a violation of the laws or customs of war (Article 3 of the Statute—*i.e.*, murder) and in respect of count 31, charging a crime against humanity (Article 5 of the Statute—*i.e.*, murder, mistreatment, and wilfully causing great suffering or serious injury to body or health). Thereafter, on 11 November 1999, Trial Chamber II, Judge McDonald again presiding, handed down nine separate sentences ranging from six to 25 years imprisonment, the sentences to be served concurrently, including each of the sentences imposed in the sentencing judgment of 14 July 1997.

Because it was the first judgment on the merits ever to be rendered by the ICTY, a situation potentially comparable to the circumstance of the International Criminal Court in the case against Darfur on which you are working alongside ICC Prosecutor Moreno–Ocampo, we excerpt next some of the key findings of fact and law set forth in the 1997 Trial Chamber II's Opinion and Judgment in relation to the charges brought against Duško Tadić in the above-quoted indictment, leaving it to you to review the 2000 judgment of the ICTY Appeal Chamber *available at* <http://www.un.org/icty/tadic/trialc2/judgement/tad-tsj70507JT2–e.pdf>. We excerpt also a portion of the Separate and Dissenting Opinion of Presiding Judge Gabriella Kirk McDonald (USA) mentioned above. We begin with a short selection from the majority opinion in which the trial panel gave its sense of the context.]

THE PROSECUTOR V. DUŠKO TADIĆ A/K/A "DULE"

In the Trial Chamber of the International Tribunal for the Prosecution of Persons
Responsible for Serious Violations of International Humanitarian Law
Committed in the Territory of Former Yugoslavia Since 1991
Case No. IT–94–1–T

OPINION AND JUDGMENT

7 May 1997

I. INTRODUCTION

A. The International Tribunal

1.   This Opinion and Judgment is rendered by Trial Chamber II of the International Tribunal for the Prosecution of Persons Responsible for Serious Violations of International Humanitarian Law Committed in the Territory of the Former Yugoslavia since 1991 ("International Tribunal") following the indictment and trial of Duško Tadić, a citizen of the former Yugoslavia, of Serb ethnic descent, and a resident of the Republic of Bosnia and Herzegovina at the time of the alleged crimes. It is the first determination of individual guilt or innocence in connection with serious violations of international humanitarian law by a truly international tribunal, the International Tribunal being the first such tribunal to be established by the United Nations. The international military tribunals at Nürnberg and Tokyo, its predecessors, were multinational in nature, representing only part of the world community.

2.   The International Tribunal was established by the Security Council of the United Nations in 1993, pursuant to resolution 808 of 22 February 1993 and resolution 827 of 25 May 1993 [**Basic Document 2.44**]. The Security

Council, having found that the widespread violations of international humanitarian law occurring within the territory of the former Yugoslavia, including the practice of "ethnic cleansing," constituted a threat to international peace and security, exercised its powers under Chapter VII of the Charter of the United Nations to establish the International Tribunal, determining that the creation of such a tribunal would contribute to the restoration and maintenance of peace. As such, the International Tribunal is a subsidiary organ of the Security Council and all Member States are required to cooperate fully with it and to comply with requests for assistance or with orders issued by it.

3.   The International Tribunal is governed by its Statute ("Statute"), adopted by the Security Council following a report by the Secretary–General of the United Nations presented on 3 May 1993 (*"Report of the Secretary–General"*) **[Basic Document 2.43]**. Its 11 Judges are drawn from States around the world. The proceedings are governed not only by the Statute but also by Rules of Procedure and Evidence ("Rules") adopted by the Judges in February 1994, as amended.[2] The International Tribunal is not subject to the national laws of any jurisdiction and has been granted both primacy and concurrent jurisdiction with the courts of States.

4.   The Statute grants competence to prosecute persons responsible for serious violations of international humanitarian law committed in the territory of the former Yugoslavia since 1991. Subject-matter jurisdiction is stated in Articles 2 to 5 of the Statute to consist of the power to prosecute persons responsible for grave breaches of the Geneva Conventions of 12 August 1949 **[Basic Documents 2.9 through 2.12]** (collectively the "Geneva Conventions") (Article 2), to prosecute persons violating the laws or customs of war (Article 3), to prosecute persons committing genocide, as a defined in the Statute (Article 4), and to prosecute persons responsible for crimes against humanity when committed in armed conflict (Article 5), which are beyond any doubt part of customary international law.

5.   Under the Statute the Prosecutor, an independent organ of the International Tribunal, is responsible for the investigation and prosecution of persons responsible for such offences. Upon determination that a prima facie case exists against a suspect, the Prosecutor may prepare an indictment, which is to contain a concise statement of the facts and the crime or crimes with which the accused is charged, and submit that indictment to a Judge of a Trial Chamber for review and confirmation.

B.   Procedural Background

6.   Duško Tadić was arrested in February 1994 in Germany, where he was then living, on suspicion of having committed offences at the Omarska camp in the former Yugoslavia in June 1992, including torture and aiding and abetting the commission of genocide, which constitute crimes under German law.

7.   Proceedings at the International Tribunal involving Duško Tadić, all of which have been held at the seat of the International Tribunal in The Hague, Netherlands, commenced on 12 October 1994 when the Prosecutor of the International Tribunal, at that time Richard J. Goldstone, filed an

2. *Id.*

application under Rule 9 of the Rules, seeking a formal request to the Federal Republic of Germany, pursuant to Rule 10, for deferral by the German courts to the competence of the International Tribunal. These provisions allow the International Tribunal to exercise its primacy jurisdiction in connection with proceedings already instituted in a State in cases where, *inter alia,* what is in issue is closely related to, or otherwise involves significant factual or legal questions which may have implications for investigations or prosecutions before the International Tribunal.

8. A public hearing on the deferral application was held on 8 November 1994, before Trial Chamber I, with Judge Adolphus Karibi–Whyte (Nigeria) presiding, sitting with Judge Elizabeth Odio Benito (Costa Rica) and Judge Claude Jorda (France). At that hearing, counsel for the Federal Republic of Germany and counsel for Duško Tadić appeared as *amici curiae.* The Federal Republic of Yugoslavia (Serbia and Montenegro) was also invited to appear as *amicus curiae* but declined to do so. Trial Chamber I found that both sets of investigations involved the same crimes and that, in addition, the International Tribunal would not be acting in the proper interests of justice if some of the alleged co-offenders of these serious violations of international humanitarian law were to be judged in national courts and others by the International Tribunal. Accordingly, a Formal Request for Deferral addressed to the Federal Republic of Germany was issued that day.

* * *

C.   The Indictment

36. The Indictment against Duško Tadić was issued by the Prosecutor of the International Tribunal in February 1995 and confirmed on 13 February 1995. It has been amended twice since then, in September and December 1995, and three of its counts were withdrawn at trial. . . .

37. The charges in the Indictment are divided by paragraphs, with paragraphs 1 to 3 setting out the background and general context of the allegations. The counts in paragraph 5 were withdrawn at trial. In all cases, the accused is charged with individual criminal responsibility pursuant to Article 7, paragraph 1, of the Statute.

* * *

II.   BACKGROUND AND PRELIMINARY FACTUAL FINDINGS

A.   The Context of the Conflict

53. In order to place in context the evidence relating to the counts of the Indictment, especially Count 1, persecution, it is necessary to say something in a preliminary way about the relevant historical, geographic, administrative and military setting about which evidence was received.

[*Eds.*—Through paragraph 179, the Trial Chamber panel next reviewed the relevant historical and geographic background, the disintegration of the Socialist Federal Republic of Yugoslavia (SFRY), events in Bosnia–Herzegovina, the concept of "Greater Serbia," the formation of Serb autonomous regions, the formation of "Crisis Staffs," the role of the Yugoslav People's Army (JNA), military action, and opstina Prijedor before and after its take-over by the Serb forces (including the treatment of non-Serbs there). It then turned to a consideration of the accused.]

C. The Accused

180.   The accused, Duško Tadić, was born on 1 October 1955 and grew up in Kozarac, living most of the time in the family home in the centre of the town. He came from a very prominent family of Serb ethnicity in Kozarac; his father was a decorated Second World War hero and well respected throughout the community. During the Second World War, his mother had been confined to the Jasenovac prison camp which was operated by Croats. Each of the accused's three elder brothers were well-known karate experts. The accused himself is an accomplished karate expert, having won numerous trophies. In 1979 the accused unofficially married Mira Tadić, who is from the neighboring hamlet of VidoviCi, with whom he has two daughters.... Although the couple has been officially divorced for several years, ostensibly because Mira Tadić could more easily find a job outside of the former Yugoslavia if she were single, they still consider themselves a married couple.

181.   Towards the end of 1990 or in the beginning of 1991 the accused opened a café in Kozarac, the Nipon café, attached to the family home on Marsla Tita Street in the center of town. At first it was a popular bar visited by Muslims and Serbs alike from Kozarac and the surrounding area. Ninety percent of the inhabitants of Kozarac were Muslims prior to the conflict and the accused testified that most of his friends were Muslim.

182.   Despite these friendships, the evidence demonstrates that the accused supported the Greater Serbia cause and all it involved, although he denies being a nationalist. He joined the SDS [Serb Democratic Party] in 1990, after he says he received a threatening letter from the "young Muslims of SDA [Muslim Party of Democratic Action] Kozarac." Testimony was received that some members of the community felt that the letter had, in fact, been written by the accused himself or his wife. Witness Q, who is a Muslim, testified that with his [Tadić's] growing nationalism more and more nationalistic Serbs began to frequent the accused's café and it began to be a gathering place for Serbs from outside the area. Sometimes as many as 30 Serbs dressed in the "Duke" or "Vojvode" coats, which were symbols of Serb nationalism, met there and sang Chetnik songs and used ethnic epithets, saying "we are going to kill all of the balijas, fuck the balijas's mother" and used the three-finger Serbian salute. This witness testified that many of the Serbs wore a "kokarda," a type of Serbian badge, and were armed, and stated that the accused appeared to be the leader of the group. As these incidents increased, Witness Q stopped frequenting the café.

183.   Witnesses testifying before the Trial Chamber noted the accused's acceptance of nationalistic ideas. For example, Sofia Tadić, the ex-wife of the accused's brother Mladen, testified that ... the accused stated that Slobodan Milosevic was the "only real man, the only real politician" among the political leaders and that the accused stated during his wife's pregnancy that if the child were a boy they would name it Slobodan after him.... She testified that the Serbs should go to Kosovo in order to repress the [Muslim] Albanians there. She also testified that the Tadić family became more active in the

Orthodox Christian church in Kozarac, and that the accused once commented, as Muslims were passing: "Look at the balijas going to their mosque."

* * *

185.   The accused himself acknowledges that several Serbs and Muslims began to boycott his café in the belief that he wanted to "disturb relations between ethnic groups" in a document he wrote on 8 August 1993 entitled "My Work Report in 1990–1993".... This work report, which described his activities during that period, indicates that copies of it were to be provided to [Serb party and governmental officials, among others]....

186.   The accused's involvement in nationalistic politics was also made apparent by other testimony. In November 1991 the SDS leadership requested that the accused and his wife organize in the Kozarac area [an] SDS plebiscite.... Witness P stated that the responsibility for conducting the plebiscite would have been given only to a person who was a loyal, reliable and committed member of the SDS political party, especially since the Kozarac area had greater significance as an area where Serbs did not constitute a majority.... [T]he fact that he was willing to take the risk involved in organizing the vote in a public place ... shows the dedication of the accused to the SDS and its platform.

* * *

191.   Between March and June 1991 the military attempted several times to enlist forcibly the accused for military service. He was arrested and threatened with arrest several times by the military police but the accused testified that he was released upon showing them a document which he says protected him from military service. On 9 or 10 June 1993 he was mobilized and posted to the war zone near Gradacac, from where he escaped the following day. Over the next two months, the accused went into hiding in an attempt to escape further mobilization. He was arrested several times during the ensuing months but always managed to escape.

192.   In his work report, the accused asserts that "after all I have done since 1990, only wishing to contribute to the creation of our common country even when it implied risking my life and my family safety, after all I have done as activist and a representative to the Prijedor Municipal Assembly. Tragedy befell us all and injustice which I am convinced will once come out." In August 1993 the accused resigned from his position of representative to the Prijedor Municipal Assembly and the Office of the Secretary to the Srpski Kozarac Local Commune. He traveled to Nürnberg, then to Munich, where he stayed with his brother Mladen who operated a club there. He was reunited with his wife who had been staying in Germany with Mladen's ex-wife ... and they moved into a room in part of Mladen's club, where they lived until 12 February 1994, when the accused was arrested by the German police. On 24 April 1995 the accused was transferred to the International Tribunal in The Hague.

[*Eds.*—The Trial Chamber panel next made its factual findings and then, on the basis of these, turned to consider the applicable law on the case. The next selections focus on the most important segments of applicable international law brought to bear by the court.]

VI. APPLICABLE LAW

A. General Requirements of Articles 2, 3 & 5 of the Statute

557.   Having considered the evidence offered at trial, it is now appropriate to discuss the law relating to the offences charged.

558.   The competence of this International Tribunal and hence of this Trial Chamber is determined by the terms of the Statute **[Basic Document 2.43]**. Article 1 of the Statute confers power to prosecute persons responsible for serious violations of international humanitarian law committed in the territory of the former Yugoslavia since 1991. The Statute then, in Articles 2, 3, 4 and 5, specifies the crimes under international law over which the International Tribunal has jurisdiction. In the present case, only Articles 2, 3 and 5 are relevant. It is not in dispute that the offences as alleged in the Indictment satisfy the requirements of time and place imposed by Article I and, as will be seen, each of the rules of customary international humanitarian law to which the Indictment directs the Trial Chamber is concerned with serious violations of that body of law.

559.   Each of the relevant Articles of the Statute, either by its terms or by virtue of the customary rules which it imports, proscribes certain acts when committed "within the context of" an "armed conflict." Article 2 of the Statute directs the Trial Chamber to the grave breaches regime of the Geneva Conventions which applies only to armed conflicts of an international character and to offences committed against persons or property regarded as "protected," in particular civilians in the hands of a party to a conflict of which they are not nationals. Article 3 of the Statute directs the Trial Chamber to those sources of customary international humanitarian law that comprise the "laws or customs of war." Article 3 is a general provision covering, subject to certain conditions, all violations of international humanitarian law which do not fall under Article 2 or are not covered by Articles 4 or 5. This includes violations of the rules contained in Article 3 common to the Geneva Conventions ("Common Article 3"), applicable to armed conflicts in general, with which the accused has been charged under Article 3 of the Statute. Article 5 of the Statute directs the Trial Chamber to crimes against humanity proscribed by customary international humanitarian law. By virtue of the Statute, those crimes must also occur in the context of an armed conflict, whether international or non-international in character. An armed conflict exists for the purposes of the application of Article 5 if it is found to exist for the purposes of either Article 2 or Article 3.

560.   Consequently, it is necessary to show, first, that an armed conflict existed at all relevant times in the territory of the Republic of Bosnia and Herzegovina and, secondly, that the acts of the accused were committed within the context of that armed conflict and for the application of Article 2, that the conflict was international in character and that the offences charged were committed against protected persons.

1. Existence of an Armed Conflict

561.   According to the Appeals Chamber Decision, the test for determining the existence of such a conflict is that

an armed conflict exists whenever there is a resort to armed force between States or protracted armed violence between governmental authorities and organized armed groups or between such groups within a State.

(a) Protracted armed violence between governmental forces and organized armed groups

562.　The test applied by the Appeals Chamber to the existence of an armed conflict for the purposes of the rules contained in Common Article 3 focuses on two aspects of a conflict; the intensity of the conflict and the organization of the parties to the conflict. In an armed conflict of an internal or mixed character, these closely related criteria are used solely for the purpose, as a minimum, of distinguishing an armed conflict from banditry, unorganized and short-lived insurrections, or terrorist activities, which are not subject to international humanitarian law. Factors relevant to this determination are addressed in the Commentary to Geneva Convention for the Amelioration of the Condition of the Wounded and Sick in Armed Forces in the Field, Convention I, (*"Commentary,* Geneva Convention I").

563.　The parties to the conflict in the area of opstina Prijedor and the main parties to the conflict in Bosnia and Herzegovina as a whole were the Government of the Republic of Bosnia and Herzegovina and the Bosnian Serb forces, the latter controlling territory under the banner of the *Republika Srpska* and, at least before 19 May 1992, supported by or under the command of the JNA. The Government of the Republic of Bosnia and Herzegovina was also in conflict with various Bosnian Croat forces supported by the Government of Croatia. The Republic of Bosnia and Herzegovina was admitted as a State member of the United Nations, following decisions adopted by the Security Council and the General Assembly, on 22 May 1992, two days before the shelling and take-over of Kozarac. It was the *de jure* State against which the Bosnian Serb forces were in revolt. Even before that date, the Republic of Bosnia and Herzegovina was an organized political entity, as one of the republics of the Socialist Federal Republic of Yugoslavia, having its own republican secretariat for defence and its own TO [Commander of the Territorial Defence].

564.　The territory controlled by the Bosnian Serb forces was known initially as the "Serbian Republic of Bosnia and Herzegovina" and renamed *Republika Srpska* on 10 January 1992. This entity did not come into being until the Assembly of the Serbian People of Bosnia and Herzegovina proclaimed the independence of that Republic on 9 January 1992. In its revolt against the *de jure* Government of the Republic of Bosnia and Herzegovina in Sarajevo, it possessed, at least from 19 May 1992, an organized military force, namely the VRS, comprising forces formerly part of the JNA and transferred to the *Republika Srpska* by the Federal Republic of Yugoslavia (Serbia and Montenegro). These forces were officially under various cease-fire agreements entered into in various parts of Bosnia and Herzegovina, no general cessation of hostilities had occurred there or elsewhere in the territory of the former Yugoslavia. The ongoing conflicts before, during and after the time of the attack on Kozarac on 24 May 1992 were taking place and continued to take place throughout the territory of Bosnia and Herzegovina between the Government of the Republic of Bosnia and Herzegovina, on the one hand, and, on the other hand, the Bosnian Serb forces, elements of the VJ operating from time to time in the territory of Bosnia and Herzegovina, and various paramilitary groups, all of which had occupied or were proceeding to occupy a significant portion of the territory of that State.

* * *

568.   Having regard then to the nature and scope of the conflict in the Republic of Bosnia and Herzegovina and the parties involved in that conflict, and irrespective of the relationship between the Federal Republic of Yugoslavia (Serbia and Montenegro) and the Bosnian Serb forces, the Trial Chamber finds that, at all relevant times, an armed conflict was taking place between the parties to the conflict in the Republic of Bosnia and Herzegovina of sufficient scope and intensity for the purposes of the application of the laws or customs of war embodied in Article 3 common to the four Geneva Conventions of 12 August 1949 **[Basic Documents 2.9 through 2.12]**, applicable as it is to armed conflicts in general, including armed conflicts not of an international character.

(b) Use of force between States

569.   Applying what the Appeals Chamber has said, it is clear from the evidence before the Trial Chamber that, from the beginning of 1992 until 19 May 1992, a state of international armed conflict existed in at least part of the territory of Bosnia and Herzegovina. This was an armed conflict between the forces of the Republic of Bosnia and Herzegovina on the one hand and those of the Federal Republic of Yugoslavia (Serbia and Montenegro), being the JNA (later the VJ), working with sundry paramilitary and Bosnian Serb forces, on the other. While the forces of the VJ continued to be involved in the armed conflict after that date, the character of the relationship between the VJ and the Bosnian Serb forces from that date, and hence the nature of the conflict in the areas with which this case is concerned, is discussed in the consideration of Article 2 of the Statute. It suffices for the moment to say that the level of intensity of the conflict, including the involvement of the JNA or the VJ in the conflict, was sufficient to meet the requirements for the existence of an international armed conflict for the purposes of the Statute.

570.   For evidence of this it is enough to refer generally to the evidence presented as to the bombardment of Sarajevo, the seat of government of the Republic of Bosnia and Herzegovina, in April 1992 by Serb forces, their attack on towns along Bosnia and Herzegovina's border with Serbia on the Drina River and their invasion of southeastern Herzegovina from Serbia and Montenegro. That the hostilities involved in this armed conflict extended into opstina Prijedor is also clear and is evidenced by the military occupation and armed seizure of power in the town of Prijedor itself on 30 April 1992 by JNA forces, aided by Bosnian Serb members of the police and administration and, following an unsuccessful revolt, their subsequent expulsion by force of arms of the majority of the non-Serb inhabitants from, and the bombardment and substantial destruction of, Stari Grad, the old, predominantly Muslim, section of Prijedor. These attacks were part of an armed conflict to which international humanitarian law applied up until the general cessation of hostilities.

571.   However, the extent of the application of international humanitarian law from one place to another in the Republic of Bosnia and Herzegovina depends upon the particular character of the conflict with which the Indictment is concerned. This depends in turn on the degree of involvement of the

VJ and the Government of the Federal Republic of Yugoslavia (Serbia and Montenegro) after the withdrawal of the JNA on 19 May 1992. That issue will be dealt with in Section VI.B of this Opinion and Judgment.

2. Nexus between the Acts of the Accused and the Armed Conflict

572. The existence of an armed conflict or occupation and the applicability of international humanitarian law to the territory is not sufficient to create international jurisdiction over each and every serious crime committed in the territory of the former Yugoslavia. For a crime to fall within the jurisdiction of the International Tribunal, a sufficient nexus must be established between the alleged offence and the armed conflict which gives rise to the applicability of international humanitarian law.

573. In relation to the applicability of international humanitarian law to the acts alleged in the Indictment, the Appeals Chamber has held that:

> Even if substantial clashes were not occurring in the Prijedor region at the time and place the crimes allegedly were committed—a factual issue on which the Appeals Chamber does not pronounce—international humanitarian law applies. It is sufficient that the alleged crimes were closely related to the hostilities occurring in other parts of the territories controlled by the parties to the conflict.

For an offense to be a violation of international humanitarian law, therefore, this Trial Chamber needs to be satisfied that each of the alleged acts was in fact closely related to the hostilities. It would be sufficient to prove that the crime was committed in the course of or as part of the hostilities in, or occupation of, an area controlled by one of the parties. It is not, however, necessary to show that armed conflict was occurring at the exact time and place of the proscribed acts alleged to have occurred, as the Appeals Chamber has indicated, nor is it necessary that the crime alleged takes place during combat, that it be part of a policy or of a practice officially endorsed or tolerated by one of the parties to the conflict, or that the act be in actual furtherance of a policy associated with the conduct of war or in the actual interest of a party to the conflict; the obligations of individuals under international humanitarian law are independent and apply without prejudice to any questions of the responsibility of States under international law. The only question, to be determined in the circumstances of each individual case, is whether the offences were closely related to the armed conflict as a whole.

574. In any event, acts of the accused related to the armed conflict in two distinct ways. First, there is the case of the acts of the accused in the take-over of Kozarac and the villages of Sivci and JaskiCi. Given the nature of the armed conflict as an ethnic war and the strategic aims of the *Republika Srpska* to create a purely Serbian State, the acts of the accused during the armed take-over and ethnic cleansing of Muslim and Croat areas of opstina Prijedor were directly connected with the armed conflict.

575. Secondly, there are the acts of the accused in the camps run by the authorities of the *Republika Srpska*. Those acts clearly occurred with the connivance or permission of the authorities running these camps and indicate that such acts were part of an accepted policy towards prisoners in the camps in opstina Prijedor. Indeed, such treatment effected the objective of the *Republika Srpska* to ethnically cleanse, by means of terror, killings or other-

wise, the areas of the Republic of Bosnia and Herzegovina controlled by Bosnian Serb forces. Accordingly, those acts too were directly connected with the armed conflict.

* * *

3. Legal Findings

607. The Trial Chamber is, by majority with the Presiding Judge dissenting, of the view that, on the evidence presented to it, after 19 May 1992 the armed forces of the *Republika Srpska* could not be considered as *de facto* organs or agents of the Government of the Federal Republic of Yugoslavia (Serbia and Montenegro), either in opstina Prijedor or more generally. For that reason, each of the victims of the acts ascribed to the accused in Section III of this Opinion and Judgment enjoy the protection of the prohibitions contained in Common Article 3, applicable as it is to all armed conflicts, rather than the protection of the more specific grave breaches regime applicable to civilians in the hands of a party to an armed conflict of which they are not nationals, which falls under Article 2 of the Statute. Such a conclusion is, of course, without prejudice to the position of those citizens of the Republic of Bosnia and Herzegovina who found themselves in the hands of forces of the JNA before 19 May 1992 or in the hands of forces of the VJ after that date, whether in the territory of the Republic of Bosnia and Herzegovina or elsewhere, or to those citizens of the Republic of Bosnia and Herzegovina in the hands of units of the VRS which, from time to time, may have fallen under the command and control of the VJ and of the Government of the Federal Republic of Yugoslavia (Serbia and Montenegro).

* * *

2. Conditions of Applicability of the Rules Contained in
Common Article 3

614. The rules contained in paragraph 1 of Common Article 3 proscribe a number of acts which: (i) are committed within the context of an armed conflict; (ii) have a close connection to the armed conflict; and (iii) are committed against persons taking no active part in hostilities. The first and second of these requirements have already been dealt with above. Consequently, the Trial Chamber turns to the third requirement.

615. The customary international humanitarian law regime governing conflicts not of an international character extends protection, from acts of murder, torture and other acts proscribed by Common Article 3, to:

> Persons taking no active part in the hostilities, including members of armed forces who have laid down their arms and those placed *hors de combat* by sickness, wounds, detention, or any other cause ... without any adverse distinction founded on race, colour, religion or faith, sex, birth or wealth, or any other similar criteria....

> This protection embraces, at the least, all of those protected persons covered by the grave breaches regime applicable to conflicts of an international character: civilians, prisoners of war, wounded and sick members of the armed forces in the field and wounded sick and shipwrecked members of the armed forces at sea. Whereas the concept of "protected person" under the

Geneva Conventions is defined positively, the class of persons protected by the operation of Common Article 3 is defined negatively. For that reason, the test the Trial Chamber has applied is to ask whether, at the time of the alleged offence, the alleged victim of the proscribed acts was directly taking part in hostilities, being those hostilities in the context of which the alleged offences are said to have been committed. If the answer to that question is negative, the victim will enjoy the protection of the proscriptions contained in Common Article 3.

616.   It is unnecessary to define exactly the line dividing those taking an active part in hostilities and those who are not so involved. It is sufficient to examine the relevant facts of each victim and to ascertain whether, in each individual's circumstances, that person was actively involved in hostilities at the relevant time. Violations of the rules contained in Common Article 3 are alleged to have been committed against persons who, on the evidence present-ed to this Trial Chamber, were captured or detained by Bosnian Serb forces, whether committed during the course of the armed take-over of the Kozarac area or while those persons were being rounded-up for transport to each of the camps in opstina Prijedor. Whatever their involvement in hostilities prior to that time, each of these classes of persons cannot be said to have been taking an active part in the hostilities. Even if they were members of the armed forces of the Government of the Republic of Bosnia and Herzegovina or otherwise engaging in hostile acts prior to capture, such persons would be considered "members of armed forces" who are "placed hors de combat by detention." Consequently, these persons enjoy the protection of those rules of customary international humanitarian law applicable to armed conflicts, as contained in Article 3 of the Statute.

3.   Legal Findings

617.   For the purposes of the application of the rules of customary international humanitarian law contained in Common Article 3, this Trial Chamber finds, in the present case, that: (i) an armed conflict existed at all relevant times in relation to the alleged offences; (ii) each of the victims of the acts charged was a person protected by those provisions being a person taking no active part in the hostilities; and (iii) the offences charged were committed within the context of that armed conflict. Accordingly, the requirements of Article 3 of the Statute are met.

D.   Article 5 of the Statute
1.   The Customary Status in International Humanitarian Law of the Prohibition Against Crimes Against Humanity

618.   The Appeals Chamber Decision discusses Articles 2 and 3 of the Statute at some length. In contrast, the discussion of Article 5 is confined to the requirement of a link to an armed conflict as provided in the Statute and thus now requires further discussion in considerable detail. The notion of crimes against humanity as an independent juridical concept, and the imputa-tion of individual criminal responsibility for their commission, was first recognized in Article 6(c) of the Nürnberg Charter **[Basic Document 1.3]** ("Nürnberg Charter"), which granted the International Military Tribunal for the Trial of the Major War Criminals ("Nürnberg Tribunal") jurisdiction over this crime. The term "crimes against humanity," although not previously codified, had been used in a nontechnical sense as far back as 1915 and in

subsequent statements concerning the First World War and was hinted at in the preamble to the 1907 Hague Convention in the so-called "Martens Clause." Thus when crimes against humanity were included in the Nürnberg Charter, although it was the first technical use of the term, it was not considered a novel concept. Nevertheless a new category of crime was created.

619.   The decision to include crimes against humanity in the Nürnberg Charter and thus grant the Nürnberg Tribunal jurisdiction over this crime resulted from the Allies' decision not to limit their retributive powers to those who committed war crimes in the traditional sense but to include those who committed other serious crimes that fall outside the ambit of traditional war crimes, such as crimes where the victim is stateless, has the same nationality as the perpetrator, or that of a state allied with that of the perpetrator. The origins of this decision can be found in assertions made by individual governments, the London International Assembly and the United Nations War Crimes Commission.

620.   Unlike the crime of aggression and war crimes, the Trial of the Major War Criminals before the International Military Tribunal ("Nürnberg Judgment") **[Basic Document 7.4]** does not delve into the legality of the inclusion of crimes against humanity in the Nürnberg Charter and the pre-existence of the prohibition, noting only that "from the beginning of the War in 1939 War Crimes were committed on a vast scale, which were also Crimes against Humanity." Thus the inclusion of crimes against humanity in the Nürnberg Charter was justified by their relation to war crimes, the gaps in the traditional definition of which it was designed to fill, the customary nature of which is described. Additionally, the Nürnberg Judgment noted that, in regard to the law to be applied, the Nürnberg Charter was decisive and binding on the Nürnberg Tribunal and that it "is the expression of international law existing at the time of its creation; and to that extent is itself a contribution to international law." On the basis of the Nürnberg Charter the prohibition against crimes against humanity, and the attribution of individual criminal responsibility for their commission, was also contained in the Charter of the International Military Tribunal for the Far East of 19 January 1946 ("Tokyo Charter") and in Law No. 10 of the Control Council for Germany ("Control Council Law No. 10"), which were utilised for additional prosecutions for atrocities committed during the Second World War.

621.   The prohibition of crimes against humanity was subsequently affirmed by the General Assembly in its resolution entitled Affirmation of the Principles of International Law recognized by the Charter of the Nürenberg [sic] Tribunal **[Basic Document 2.6]** and thereafter confirmed in the Principles of International Law Recognized in the Charter of the Nurenberg [sic] Tribunal and in the Judgement [sic] of the Tribunal (Nurenberg [sic] Principles) **[Basic Document 2.13]**, adopted by the International Law Commission in 1950 and submitted to the General Assembly, Principle VIc of which provides that a crime against humanity is punishable as a crime under international law. The attribution of individual criminal responsibility for the commission of crimes against humanity, as it was applied by the Nürnberg Tribunal, was also approved in Principle I of the Nurenberg [sic] Principles, which provides that "[a] person who commits an act which constitutes a crime under international law is responsible therefore and liable to punishment."

622.   The customary status of the Nürnberg Charter, and thus the attribution of individual criminal responsibility for the commission of crimes against humanity, was expressly noted by the Secretary–General. Additional codifications of international law have also confirmed the customary law status of the prohibition of crimes against humanity, as well as two of its most egregious manifestations: genocide and apartheid.

623.   Thus, since the Nürnberg Charter, the customary status of the prohibition against crimes against humanity and the attribution of individual criminal responsibility for their commission have not been seriously questioned. It would seem that this finding is implicit in the Appeals Chamber Decision which found that "[i]t is by now a settled rule of customary international law that crimes against humanity do not require a connection to international armed conflict." If customary international law is determinative of what type of conflict is required in order to constitute a crime against humanity, the prohibition against crimes against humanity is necessarily part of customary international law. As such, the commission of crimes against humanity violates customary international law, of which Article 5 of the Statute is, for the most part, reflective. As stated by the Appeals Chamber: "[T]here is no question ... that the definition of crimes against humanity adopted by the Security Council in Article 5 comports with the principle of *nullum crimen sine lege.*"

* * *

3.   Legal Findings

660.   As discussed, this Trial Chamber has found that an armed conflict existed in the territory of opstina Prijedor at the relevant time and that an aspect of this conflict was a policy to commit inhumane acts against the civilian population of the territory, in particular the non-Serb population, in the attempt to achieve the creation of a Greater Serbia. In furtherance of this policy these inhumane acts were committed against numerous victims and pursuant to a recognisable plan. As such the conditions of applicability for Article 5 are satisfied: the acts were directed against a civilian population on discriminatory grounds, they were committed on both a widespread basis and in a systematic fashion pursuant to a policy and they were committed in the context of, and related to, an armed conflict.

E.   Individual Criminal Responsibility Under Article 7, Paragraph 1

661.   The *Report of the Secretary–General* states that "all persons who participate in the planning, preparation or execution of serious violations of international humanitarian law in the former Yugoslavia contribute to the commission of the violation and are, therefore, individually responsible." Article 7 of the Statute, entitled individual criminal responsibility incorporates this concept by providing that "[a] person who planned, instigated, ordered, committed or otherwise aided and abetted in the planning, preparation or execution of a crime referred to in articles 2 to 5 of the present Statute, shall be individually responsible for the crime."

662.   Accordingly, the International Tribunal has jurisdiction to try a person who participates in crimes against humanity, grave breaches of the Geneva Conventions **[Basic Documents 2.9 through 2.12]**, violations of the

laws or customs of war or genocide in any one of several capacities. However, this provision, which the International Tribunal has not yet interpreted, does not specify the necessary degree of participation but first the objective basis for such individual responsibility as a matter of customary international law must be determined since the International Tribunal is only empowered to apply international humanitarian law that is "beyond any doubt customary law."

1.   The Customary Status of Article 7, Paragraph 1

663.   Certain types of conduct during armed conflict have been criminalised by the international community since at least the fifteenth century. In more modern times, the movement to abolish war that coalesced after the First World War resulted in the determination to reform the law of war and to make war conducted in contravention of international norms an international crime with a component of individual responsibility." After the First World War, the Preliminary Peace Conference of Paris created a Commission to investigate the responsibility for the war. On 29 March 1919 this Commission submitted its findings in a report that was unanimously adopted, although with reservations by the American and Japanese representatives. These findings included a provision addressing individual criminal responsibility for breaches of the laws and customs of war. The Commission recommended that all persons belonging to enemy countries, however high their position may have been, without distinction of rank, including chiefs of States, who have been guilty of offences against the laws and customs of war or the laws of humanity, are liable to criminal prosecution. This position was confirmed by several countries in the 1919 Paris Peace Treaty, which formally adopted the principle that any person could be tried and punished for violations of the laws of war by military courts of the adversary.

664.   The concept that an individual actor can be held personally responsible and punished for violations of international humanitarian law was first enunciated by the Nürnberg and Tokyo trials after the Second World War. Article 6 of the 1945 Nürnberg Charter **[Basic Document 1.3]** called for individual responsibility for crimes against peace, violations of the laws or customs of war, and crimes against humanity.

665.   Similarly, the Military Tribunals in occupied Germany enforced the Charter's principles under the terms of Article II, 2 of Control Council Law No. 10, which states:

> Any person without regard to nationality or the capacity in which he acted, is deemed to have committed a crime as defined in paragraph 1 of this Article, if he was (a) a principal or (b) was [sic] an accessory to the commission of any such crime or ordered or abetted the same or (c) took a consenting part there in or (d) was connected with plans or enterprises involving its commission or (e) was a member of any organisation or group connected with the commission of any such crime. . . .

Noting that the fact "[t]hat international law imposes duties and liabilities upon individuals as well as upon States has long been recognized," the court found punishment for individuals appropriate for violations of international law. Moreover, it is well recognized that

[t]he principle of individual responsibility and punishment for crimes under international law recognized at Nuremberg is the cornerstone of international criminal law. This principle is the enduring legacy of the Nuremberg Charter and Judgement [sic] which gives meaning to the prohibition of crimes under international law by ensuring that the individuals who commit such crimes incur responsibility and are liable to punishment.

666.   The concept of direct individual criminal responsibility and personal culpability for assisting, aiding and abetting, or participating in, in contrast to the direct commission of, a criminal endeavour or act also has a basis in customary international law. For example, Article 4(1) of the Convention Against Torture and Other Cruel, Inhuman or Degrading Treatment or Punishment **[Basic Document 3.26]** uses the phrase "complicity or participation in torture," and Article III of the International Convention on the Suppression and Punishment of the Crime of Apartheid[p] cites as criminally culpable those who "participate in, directly incite, or conspire in [, or] ... [d]irectly abet, encourage or cooperate in the commission of the crime. The prosecutions following the Second World War confirm this, revealing that participation in this way could entail culpability.

667.   For example, in the French war crimes trials after the Second World War, complicity was a basis for criminal culpability. *In the Trial of Wagner and Six Others,* the *Acte d'Accusation* and the judgment state the relevance of the French penal code to the charge and the sentence. Article 59 of the Code Pénal applicable at that time stated that "[t]he accomplices to a crime or a delict shall be visited with the same punishment as the authors therefor, excepting where the law makes other provisions" and Article 60, defined as an accomplice:

> Any person who, by gifts, promises, threats, abuse of power or authority, or guilty machinations or devices, has instigated a crime or delict or given orders for the perpetration of a crime or delict; any person who has supplied the arms, tools or any other means that have been used in the commission of the crime or offence, knowing that they would be so used; or who has wittingly aided or assisted the author or authors of the crime or offence in any acts preparatory to, of facilitating its perpetration, or in its execution.

With one exception, all the accused in that trial were charged with complicity as opposed to primary involvement.

668.   Likewise, in the *Trial of Martin Gottfried Weiss and 39 Others,* ("*Dachau* case"), the accused were charged with acting in "pursuance of a common design to commit acts hereinafter alleged as members of the staff of the Dachau Concentration Camp," and the allegation was that they did "wilfully, deliberately and wrongfully aid, abet and participate in the subjection of civilian nations. . . ." Finally, the Norwegian and the Netherlands war crimes laws explicitly made punishable complicity in war crimes and the British law also had such provisions.

p. Concluded at New York, 30 Nov 1973. Entered into force, 18 Jul 1976. 1015 U.N.T.S. 243, *reprinted in* 3 Weston & Carlson III.I.2.

669.   The foregoing establishes the basis in customary international law for both individual responsibility and of participation in the various ways provided by Article 7 of the Statute. The International Tribunal accordingly has the competence to exercise the authority granted to it by the Security Council to make findings in this case regarding the guilt of the accused, whether as a principal or an accessory or otherwise as a participant.

* * *

3.   Legal Findings

688.   The I.L.C. Draft Code **[Basic Document 2.16]** draws on these cases from the Nurnberg war crimes trials and other customary law, and concludes that an accused may be found culpable if it is proved that he "intentionally commits such a crime" or, *inter alia,* if he "knowingly aids, abets or otherwise assists, directly and substantially, in the commission of such a crime. . . ." The commentary to the I.L.C. Draft Code provides that the "accomplice must knowingly provide assistance to the perpetrator of the crime. Thus, an individual who provides some type of assistance to another individual without knowing that this assistance will facilitate the commission of a crime would not be held accountable." In addition, the commentary notes that

> the accomplice must provide the kind of assistance which contributes directly and substantially to the commission of the crime, for example by providing the means which enable the perpetrator to commit the crime. Thus, the form of participation of an accomplice must entail assistance which facilitates the commission of a crime in some significant way.

While there is no definition of "substantially," it is clear from the aforementioned cases that the substantial contribution requirement calls for a contribution that in fact has an effect on the commission of the crime. This is supported by the foregoing Nürnberg cases where, in virtually every situation, the criminal act most probably would not have occurred in the same way had not someone acted in the role that the accused in fact assumed. For example, if there had been no poison gas or gas chambers in the Zyllon B cases, mass exterminations would not have been carried out in the same manner. The same analysis applies to the cases where the men were prosecuted for providing lists of names to German authorities. Even in these cases, where the act in complicity was significantly removed from the ultimate illegal result, it was clear that the actions of the accused had a substantial and direct effect on the commission of the illegal act, and that they generally had knowledge of the likely effect of their actions.

689.   The Trial Chamber finds that aiding and abetting includes all acts of assistance by words or acts that lend encouragement or support, as long as the requisite intent is present. Under this theory, presence alone is not sufficient if it is an ignorant or unwilling presence. However, if the presence can be shown or inferred, by circumstantial or other evidence, to be knowing and to have a direct and substantial effect on the commission of the illegal act, then it is sufficient on which to base a finding of participation and assign the criminal culpability that accompanies it.

690. Moreover, when an accused is present and participates in the beating of one person and remains with the group when it moves on to beat another person, his presence would have an encouraging effect, even if he does not physically take part in this second beating, and he should be viewed as participating in this second beating as well. This is assuming that the accused has not actively withdrawn from the group or spoken out against the conduct of the group.

691. However, actual physical presence when the crime is committed is not necessary; just as with the defendants who only drove victims to the woods to be killed, an accused can be considered to have participated in the commission of a crime based on the precedent of the Nürnberg war crimes trials if he is found to be "concerned with the killing." However, the acts of the accused must be direct and substantial.

692. In sum, the accused will be found criminally culpable for any conduct where it is determined that he knowingly participated in the commission of an offence that violates international humanitarian law and his participation directly and substantially affected the commission of that offence through supporting the actual commission before, during, or after the incident. He will also be responsible for all that naturally results from the commission of the act in question.

* * *

VIII. JUDGMENT

FOR THE FOREGOING REASONS, having considered all of the evidence and the arguments, THE TRIAL CHAMBER finds as follows:

(1) By a majority, Judge McDonald dissenting,

Decides that the charges brought under Article 2 of the Statute of the International Tribunal **[Basic Document 2.43]** were, in the present case, inapplicable at the time in opstina Prijedor because it has not been proved that the victims were protected persons, which is an element of those offences, and therefore finds the accused, Duško Tadić, not guilty on counts 5, 8, 9, 12, 15, 18, 21, 24 and the alternative charge under count 27, counts 29 and 32;

(2) Unanimously finds on the remaining charges as follows:

Count 1: Guilty
Count 6: Not guilty
Count 7: Not guilty
Count 10: Guilty
Count 11: Guilty
Count 13: Guilty
Count 14: Guilty
Count 16: Guilty
Count 17: Guilty
Count 19: Not guilty
Count 20: Not guilty
Count 22: Guilty
Count 23: Guilty
Count 25: Not guilty
Count 26 and the alternative charge under count 28: Not guilty

Count 30:   Not guilty
Count 31:   Not guilty
Count 33:   Guilty in respect of Beido Balic, Sefik Balic, Ismet Jaskic and
             Salko Jaskic, Not Guilty as to Ilijas Elkasovic, Nijas Elkaso-
             vic, Meho Kenjar and Adam Jakupovic
Count 34:   Guilty in respect of Beido Balic, Sefik Balic, Ismet Jaskic and
             Salko Jaskic, Not Guilty as to Ilijas Elkasovic, Nijas Elkaso-
             vic, Meho Kenjar and Adam Jakupovic

* * *

SEPARATE AND DISSENTING OPINION OF JUDGE MCDONALD REGARDING
THE APPLICABILITY OF ARTICLE 2 OF THE STATUTE

1.   I completely agree with and share in the Opinion and Judgment with
the exception of the determination that Article 2 of the Statute is inapplicable
to the charges against the accused. I find that at all times relevant to the
Indictment, the armed conflict in opstina Prijedor was international in character and that the victims of the accused were persons protected by the
Geneva Convention Relative to the Protection of Civilian Persons in Time of
War ("Geneva Convention IV") [**Basic Document 2.12**]. Thus, I consider
that the Trial Chamber should apply the grave breaches regime to the
offences charged in the Indictment under Article 2 of the Statute [**Basic
Document 2.43**].

2.   The majority opinion correctly concludes that those alleged to have
been victims of the accused in this case were in the hands of a party to the
conflict or occupying power. However, for the reasons stated hereafter, I
disagree with the majority's finding that the Prosecution has failed to prove
that the victims were not nationals of the party or occupying power in whose
hands they were. The majority characterizes the issue before the Trial
Chamber as

> whether, after 19 May 1992, the Federal Republic of Yugoslavia (Serbia
> and Montenegro), by its withdrawal from the territory of the Republic of
> Bosnia and Herzegovina, and notwithstanding its continuing support for
> the VRS, had sufficiently distanced itself from the VRS that those forces
> could not be regarded as de facto organs or agents of the VJ and hence of
> the Federal Republic of Yugoslavia (Serbia and Montenegro).

3.   In considering this question, the majority defines the test as requiring
dependency on one side and "such a relationship of control on the other that,
on the facts of the instant case, the acts of the VRS, including its occupation
of opstina Prijedor, can be imputed to the Government of the Federal
Republic of Yugoslavia (Serbia and Montenegro)." The majority finds the
Judgment of the International Court of Justice ("ICJ") in the *Case Concerning Military and Paramilitary Activities in and Against Nicaragua,* Nicaragua
v United States (Merits) ("*Nicaragua*")[3] to be instructive and states that it is
applying "the essence of the test." The standard crafted by the majority,
however, departs from *Nicaragua,* and it provides that "it is neither necessary
nor sufficient merely to show that the VRS was dependent, even completely

---

3. *Supra* note **p** in Chapter 2 at 99. For a
brief extract from this case, see text at 117–21
in Chapter 2, *infra.*

dependent, on the VJ and the Federal Republic of Yugoslavia (Serbia and Montenegro) for the necessities of war. It must be shown that the VJ and the Federal Republic of Yugoslavia (Serbia and Montenegro) exercised the potential for control," which the majority construes to be "effective control." Although the majority acknowledges that *Nicaragua* established a "particularly high threshold test," the standard the majority has created is even more demanding. The exercise of this effective control is required after 19 May 1992, according to the majority, to establish that the VRS was an agent or organ of the Federal Republic of Yugoslavia (Serbia and Montenegro).

4.   I conclude in Section I of this Opinion that the evidence presented to the Trial Chamber supports a finding of effective control of the VRS by the Federal Republic of Yugoslavia (Serbia and Montenegro) in opstina Prijedor at all times relevant to the charges in the Indictment. However, as I discuss in Section II, the appropriate test of agency from *Nicaragua* is one of "dependency and control" and a showing of effective control is not required.

I.   The Federal Republic of Yugoslavia (Serbia and Montenegro) Effectively Controlled VRS

5.   The JNA's direct involvement in the armed conflict at various locations in Bosnia and Herzegovina including opstina Prijedor on behalf of the Federal Republic of Yugoslavia (Serbia and Montenegro) prior to 19 May 1992 rendered the conflict international at least in that opstina. International humanitarian law applicable to conflicts of an international character continues to apply until a general conclusion of peace is reached. The majority agrees that "from the beginning of 1992 until 19 May 1992, a state of international armed conflict existed in at least part of the territory of Bosnia and Herzegovina." After that date, the majority states that

> [w]hile the forces of the VJ continued to be involved in the armed conflict . . ., the character of the relationship between the VJ and the Bosnian Serb forces from that date, and hence the nature of the conflict in the areas with which this case is concerned, is discussed in the consideration of Article 2 of the Statute.

In the discussion referred to, the majority concludes that only if effective command and control of the VRS forces continued after 19 May through the times relevant to the charges in the Indictment in opstina Prijedor would the victims be protected persons. While the majority makes no clear finding regarding the character of the conflict after 19 May 1992, this statement implicitly establishes a requirement of effective command and control of the VRS in opstina Prijedor by the Federal Republic of Yugoslavia (Serbia and Montenegro) or VJ for a finding that the conflict was international. This standard is not required by the Appeals Chamber Decision, which holds that the conflict in Bosnia and Herzegovina was rendered international by the involvement of the JNA and that a conflict can become internationalized by external support. A review of the background of the division of the JNA and that a conflict can become internationalized by external support. A review of the background of the division of the JNA and the re-designation of the armed forces in Bosnia and Herzegovina in response to the 15 May 1992 Security Council resolution 752, demanding that the JNA cease all interference in Bosnia and Herzegovina, demonstrates that the victims of the offences charged in the Indictment are protected persons.

6.   The purported withdrawal of the JNA from Bosnia and Herzegovina took place on 19 May 1992, on which date the VRS was created. However, the withdrawal was not immediately successful as several Serbian Serbs remained in the military organisation of Bosnia and Herzegovina until at least early June 1992. Those remaining included many officers, commissioned and non-commissioned, who were not of Bosnian extraction, and the Federal Republic of Yugoslavia (Serbia and Montenegro) continued to pay all salaries and pensions of the VRS.

7.   The evidence proves that the creation of the VRS was a legal fiction. The only changes made after the 15 May 1992 Security Council resolution were the transfer of troops, the establishment of a Main Staff of the VRS, a change in the name of the military organisation and individual units, and a change in the insignia. There remained the same weapons, the same equipment, the same officers, the same commanders, largely the same troops, the same logistics centres, the same suppliers, the same infrastructure, the same source of payments, the same goals and mission, the same tactics, and the same operations. Importantly, the objective remained the same: to create an ethnically pure Serb State by uniting Serbs in Bosnia and Herzegovina and extending that State from the Federal Republic of Yugoslavia (Serbia and Montenegro) to the Croatian Krajina along the important logistics and supply line that went through opstina Prijedor, thereby necessitating the expulsion of the non-Serb population of the opstina.

8.   Although there is little evidence that the VRS was formally under the command of Belgrade after 19 May 1992, the VRS clearly continued to operate as an integrated and instrumental part of the Serbian war effort. This finding is supported by evidence that every VRS unit had been a unit in the JNA, the command and staffs remaining virtually the same after the re-designation. The VRS Main Staff, the members of which had all been generals in the JNA and many of whom were appointed to their positions by the JNA General Staff, maintained direct communications with the VJ General Staff via a communications link from Belgrade. Colonel Selak, commander of the logistics platoon that provided logistical support to units in the Banja Luka area (both before and after 19 May 1992), stated: "Some officers had been given direct [telephone] lines, Belgrade/Pale. There was a link there and it was used in everyday communication because there was a need for direct communication between the Chief of Staff of the Army of *Republika Srpska* with the Army of Yugoslavia." Moreover, the VRS continued to receive supplies from the same suppliers in the Federal Republic of Yugoslavia (Serbia and Montenegro) who had contracted with the JNA, although the requests after 19 May 1992 went through the Chief of Staff of the VRS who then sent them onto Belgrade. The ties between the military in Bosnia and Herzegovina and the SDS political party, which advocated a Greater Serbia, similarly remained unchanged after the redesignation.

* * *

15.   The continuity between the JNA and the VRS particularly as it relates to the military operations in the opstina Prijedor area, the presence of significant numbers of non-Bosnian former JNA officers in the VRS, the continued payment of salaries and pensions by Belgrade, the close proximity in time between the attack on Prijedor town and the attacks on Kozarac,

Jaskici and Sivci and the establishment of camps, and the relationship between the VRS and the VJ forces, taken together, establish that the change was in name only. Thus, if effective control is the degree of proof required to establish agency under Nicaragua, I conclude that this standard has been met. Therefore, the victims of the accused were in the hands of a party to which they were not nationals and Article 2 of the Statute is applicable to the offences in the Indictment.

II.   EFFECTIVE CONTROL: AN IMPROPER STANDARD
FOR AGENCY DETERMINATION IN THIS CASE

16.   Despite this conclusion, I find that the majority's requirement of effective control for making a determination of agency is founded on a misreading of the findings in *Nicaragua* and a misapplication of those findings to the facts of the case before the Trial Chamber. I would conclude that the effective control standard was never intended to describe the degree of proof necessary for a determination of agency founded on dependency and control as articulated in paragraph 109 of *Nicaragua*.[q] However, if *Nicaragua* did set the standards of proof required for agency as that of effective control, that finding should be limited to the facts of that case and is not applicable to the issues present to the Trial Chamber.

[*Eds.*—Judge McDonald goes on to observe, *inter alia,* that in *Nicaragua* the conflict was found to be internal as between the *contras* and the Nicaraguan government as distinct from "a conflict rendered international by the involvement of the Federal Republic of Yugoslavia (Serbia and Montenegro)" and that, in any event, the "primary issue in *Nicaragua* was whether the acts of the *contras* could be imputed so as to impose legal responsibility for monetary damages on the United States," not the applicability of the rule of international humanitarian law. She subsequently concludes:]

34.   In summary, the evidence supports a finding beyond reasonable doubt that the VRS acted as an agent of the Federal Republic of Yugoslavia (Serbia and Montenegro) in regard to the attack and occupation of opstina Prijedor during the times relevant to the charges in the Indictment and the victims are thus protected persons. The dependency of the VRS on and the exercise of control by the Federal Republic of Yugoslavia (Serbia and Montenegro) support this finding of agency under either the majority's standard of effective control or under the more general test of dependency and control. However, a close reading of *Nicaragua* leads me to conclude that the effective control standard supports a distinct and separate basis for the attribution of the conduct of non-agents to a State, and that it is not a necessary element for a finding of an agency relationship. For these reasons, I respectfully submit this Separate and Dissenting Opinion.

[*Eds.*—On 14 July 1997, Trail Chamber II sentenced Duško Tadić to 97 years in prison on 11 counts of crimes against humanity and war crimes, the sentences to run concurrently with the longest single term to be for 20 years. Mr. Tadić subsequently appealed the judgment and sentence as did also the

---

q.   In Paragraph 109 of *Nicaragua, supra* note **p** in Chapter 2, at 99, the ICJ framed the issue as being "whether or not the relationship of the *contras* to the United States Government was so much one of dependence on the one side and control on the other that it would be right to equate the *contras,* for legal purposes, with an organ of the United States Government, or acting on behalf of that Government."

Prosecutor in a cross appeal relying upon Judge McDonald's dissent. On 15 July 1999, the Appeals Chamber, Judge Mohamed Shahabuddeen (Guyana) presiding, pronounced its judgment on the two appeals, denying defendant Tadić's appeal on all grounds and allowing the prosecution's cross-appeal by reversing Trial Chamber II and finding Duško Tadić guilty on counts 8, 9, 12, 15, 21, 29 and 32 of the indictment that charged him with "grave breaches" of the 1949 Geneva Conventions **[Basic Document 2.9 through 2.12]** (Article 2 of the Statute of the Tribunal—*i.e.*, wilful killing, torture or inhuman treatment, and wilfully causing great suffering or serious injury to body or health). The Appeals Chamber also reversed the Trial Chamber II's judgment in respect of count 30, alleging a violation of the laws or customs of war (Article 3 of the Statute—*i.e.*, murder) and in respect of count 31, charging a crime against humanity (Article 5 of the Statute—*i.e.*, murder. treatment, and wilfully causing great suffering or serious injury to body or health). Thereafter, on 11 November 1999, Trial Chamber II, Judge McDonald again presiding, handed down nine separate sentences ranging from six to 25 years imprisonment, the sentences to be served concurrently, including each of the sentences imposed in the sentencing judgment of 14 July 1997].

————

As of this writing (1 May 2006), with no case yet decided by the ICC, it is of course impossible to know precisely how the Court will decide the case of Darfur or any of the other cases so far referred to it. But it is possible to speak of the successful application of international criminal law in a concrete case—the case of Duško Tadić at The Hague in the ICTY[r]—that may reflect how the ICC will reason and rule once it does proceed. As Professor Theodor Meron, who was involved in the prosecution of Duko Tadić and who now is President of the ICTY, has stated:

> [i]n the Tadić case alone, the tribunal ... advanced the state of the law governing international and internal armed conflicts, especially as it pertains to the conduct of hostilities and crimes against humanity. It ... also affirmed the customary, unwritten law that binds all states to international standards of behavior. Likewise, the appeals chamber's rulings on jurisdictional issues in the Tadić case [were] the first judicial affirmation of international criminality and individual responsibility for violations of international humanitarian law since Nuremberg. Both the statute and the indictments also confirmed the international criminalization of rape. The tribunal ... generated an unprecedented interest in humanitarian law and in punishing those who violate it. War crimes ... entered the mainstream of political debate and UN decision-making.[s]

Other scholars have been less optimistic about the value or success of international criminal law. Mark Drumbl, for example, has criticized what he terms the "comfortable metanarrative" of international criminal law, which represents mass violence as a transgression of universal norms.[t] He has pointed out that both the Nuremberg Tribunal and its companion institution,

---

r. *See supra* text, at 189–210.

s. T. Meron, *supra* note **h**, at 6.

t. M Drumbl, *Pluralizing International Criminal Justice*, 103 Mich. L. Rev. 1295, 1297 (2005).

the International Military Tribunal for the Far East (the Tokyo Tribunal) were deeply flawed. They were forms of "victors' justice" where prosecutions were highly selective and major atrocities by the Allied Powers were ignored. In the end, the Nuremberg Tribunal indicted only twenty-two defendants and, in the case of the Tokyo Tribunal, most of the people it convicted were released a few years later; indeed two of the most prominent convicted war criminals later became the Prime Minister and Foreign Minister of Japan.[u] Drumbl has argued that international criminal law has drawn too deeply on the models of criminality developed in national legal systems without paying attention to the need for new paradigms in the face of mass violence. One example of this is *Prosecutor v Krstić* (Case No. IT–98–33–A ICTY Appeals Chamber, 19 Apr 2004) which overturned the conviction of General Krstić, a leader of the Bosnia–Serb army when it massacred 7000 to 8000 Bosnian Muslim men and boys in Srebrenica in 1995. Krstić's initial conviction had been based on collective responsibility for genocide: he had done nothing to prevent the killings although he was aware that members of his army had a genocidal intent. The conviction had relied on the *Tadić* case's broad understanding of joint criminal enterprise. In the end, Krstić was convicted of the lesser offence of aiding and abetting genocide, which attracted a lower prison sentence. Drumbl writes:[v]

> Truly recognizing the riddle of collective action requires more than just an extension of the dominant discourse of ordinary criminal law, which embraces liberalism's understanding of the individual as the central unit of action and thereby deserving of blame when things go terribly wrong. This understanding echoes one of the most famous legacies of Nuremberg, namely the Tribunal's pronouncement that "[c]rimes against international law are committed by men, not by abstract entities, and only by punishing individuals who commit such crimes can the provisions of international law be enforced." This predicate carries through to modern institutions of international criminal justice, including the ICC, which only can try individuals. The complication, however, is that criminal law systems focused on individual responsibility may be ill-suited to promote accountability for collective wrongdoing. . . .
>
> * * *
>
> [I]nternational criminal law's reification of individual responsibility reflects a fear of collective responsibility, collective blame, and, especially, collective guilt. This fear ought to be reappraised dispassionately, by recognizing the specific nature of mass atrocity and differentiating it from ordinary criminal liability. Given the unique nature of the extraordinary criminality of mass atrocity, shouldn't this criminality be addressed through a unique and independent doctrinal and theoretical framework? . . . The absence of an independent theoretical framework obliges international criminal law to invoke the rationales of domestic criminal law. This invocation may be convenient, but it comes with a price: namely, such a system glosses over the fact that the perpetrator of mass atrocity is qualitatively different than the perpetrator of ordinary crime. Whereas

u. *Id.* at 1300, citing Jackson Nyamuya Maogoto, War Crimes and Realpolitik: International Justice from World War I to the 21st Century 103 (2004). *But see infra* Discussion Note/Question 1, at 213.

v. *Id.* at 1313–14.

ordinary criminals tend to deviate from mainstream society when they commit crimes, those individuals who perpetrate the extraordinary crimes that collectively lead to mass atrocity are not so deviant in the times and places in question. There is a deep contradiction in their behavior: although they transgress a *jus cogens* norm, this transgression often results from adhesion to a social norm that is much closer to home. This deep complicity cascade does not diminish the brutality or exculpate the aggressor, but it implicates, and in many ways problematizes, a variety of important issues. These include bystander innocence, reparations for victims, reconciliation, groupthink, reintegration of offenders, and the dual role of the international community as enabler of violence and as arbiter of right or wrong.

See also Allison Marston Stanner & Jenny S. Martinez, *Guilty Associations: Joint Criminal Enterprise, Command Responsibility, and the Development of International Criminal Law*, 93 Calif. L. Rev. 77 (2005).

Drumbl goes on to argue that international criminal tribunals may allow attention to be deflected from the deeper causes of the conflict. In the context of the Rwanda Tribunal, he writes:[w]

The deliberate choice by international criminal justice institutions to selectively blame a handful of individuals for mass violence also may serve selfish purposes. Pinning responsibility on a few erases not only the involvement of ordinary Rwandans, but also the involvement of the international community in the violence. The ICTR's judicial reductionism absolves the role of international agencies, transnational economic processes, the foreign policies of influential states, and colonial policies, each of which exacerbated ethnic conflict by creating an environment conducive to violence in Rwanda. It also glosses over decisions by foreign states to ignore the violence after it had begun,[4] and the international community's failure adequately to support peacekeeping or peace enforcement.[5]

It may be convenient to place blame for mass violence on selected savage individuals, instead of offering a fuller—and much more embarrassing—display of the multiple political, economic, historical, and colonial factors that facilitate violence. The trade-off for this convenience, though, is a narrower breadth of justice and a compromised preventative strategy. By virtue of its leaving the acts and omissions of international agents untouched, international criminal law fails to allocate blame according to degrees of responsibility. This, in turn, leads to a retributive shortfall, insofar as only a few people receive their just deserts while many powerful states and organizations avoid accountability.

Drumbl concludes that the law can be valuable in dealing with mass atrocities but that that "modesty about what the law can accomplish is an important virtue."[x] For further critiques see Ralph Zacklin, *The Failings of Ad Hoc Tribunals*, 2 J. Int'l Crim. Just. 541 (2004).

w. *Id.* at 1313–14.

4. S. Powers, "A Problem from Hell": America and the Age of Genocide (2002).

5. R. Dallaire, Shake Hands with the Devil 79 (2003).

x. M. Drumbl, *supra* note **t**, at 1302.

DISCUSSION NOTES/QUESTIONS

1. Mark Drumbl, *supra*, criticizes the post-World War II Nuremberg Tribunal (and its companion Tokyo Tribunal) for being deeply flawed, forms of "victors' justice" that meted out prosecutions and verdicts on a highly selective basis. Consider the final verdicts rendered by the International Military Tribunal relative to each of the leading Nazi Germans tried at Nuremberg—for Conspiracy to Wage Wars of Aggression (Count 1), for Crimes against Peace, *i.e.*, initiating or waging wars of aggression (Count 2), for War Crimes (Count 3), and for Crimes against Humanity (Count 4)—are conveniently summarized in the following table from Anthony A. D'Amato, Wesley L. Gould & Larry D. Woods, *War Crimes and Vietnam*, 57 Cal. L. Rev. 1055, 1062 (1969), *reprinted in* 3 The Vietnam and International Law 407, 414 (R. Falk ed., 1972):

Defendant	Counts				Sentence
	(1)	**(2)**	**(3)**	**(4)**	
Goering	1	1	1	1	D
Hess	1	1	0	0	C
von Ribbentrop	1	1	1	1	D
Keitel	1		1	1	D
Kaltenbrunner	0	1	1	1	D
Rosenberg	1	1	1	1	D
Frank	0		1	1	D
Frick	0	1	1	1	D
Streicher	0			1	D
Funk	0	1	1	1	C
Schacht	0	0			Acquitted
Doenitz	0	1		1	A
Raeder	1	1		1	C
vonSchirach	0			1	B
Sauckel	0	0	1	1	D
Jodl	1	1	1	1	D
von Papen	0	0			Acquitted
Seyss-Inquart	0	1	1	1	D
Speer	0	0	1	1	B
von Neurath	1	1	1	1	B
Fritzsche	0		0	0	Acquitted
Bormann	0	1	1		D(in absentia)
Total Indictments	22	16	18	18	
Total Convictions	8	12	16	16	

Key

0 = Indicted but not convicted	B = Fifteen to twenty years imprisonment
1 = Indicted and convicted	C = Life imprisonment
A = Ten years imprisonment	D = Death by hanging

On the basis of this record, is it fair to say that the Nuremberg trial was simply an exercise in "victor's justice"? Might the ICC be vulnerable to the same charge in the case of Darfur, it having been referred to the ICC by the UN Security Council without Sudan's participation? If you had been in charge and had had unlimited power at the time of Nuremberg, what differently would you have done? What differently would you do in the case of Darfur? Insofar as Nuremberg is concerned, consider what fifteen year-old Anne Frank had to say in her famous diary on 15 July 1944, about three months before her death in the concentration camp at Bergen–Belsen:

... [O]ur problems weigh down on us, problems for which we are probably much too young, but which thrust themselves upon us continually, until, after a long time, we think we've found a solution, but the solution doesn't seem able to resist the facts which reduce it to nothing again. That's the difficulty in these times: ideals, dreams, and cherished hopes rise within us, only to meet the horrible truth and be shattered.

It's really a wonder that I haven't dropped all my ideals, because they seem so absurd and impossible to carry out. Yet I keep them, because in spite of everything I still believe that people are really good at heart. I simply can't build up my hopes on a foundation consisting of confusion, misery, and death. I see the world gradually being turned into a wilderness, I hear the ever approaching thunder, which will destroy us too, I can feel the sufferings of millions and yet, if I look up into the heavens, I think that it will all come right, that this cruelty too will end, and that peace and tranquility will return again.

Anne Frank: The Diary of a Young Girl 237 (1952). How would Anne Frank have answered the questions posed?

2.   *Á propos* his criticism of the Nuremberg trials, Drumbl further states that "[i]n the end, the Nuremberg Tribunal indicted only twenty-two defendants...." Technically this is correct. But considering that many trials took place in German courts in the aftermath of the Nuremberg trials and convicting many of war crimes and associated atrocities while invoking its judgment, does this not leave a distorted impression? Should national tribunals be disregarded when conjuring the effectiveness of international law? For pertinent discussion, see *infra* Subsection B–2, at 2.34.

3.   Following Drumbl's critique of international criminal law, consider the situation of Duško Tadić—only a secondary figure in the Bosnian tragedy. Was it appropriate to prosecute and punish him and others like him while his superiors (Radovan Karadzic and Ratko Mladic) are allowed to remain free? If only a handful of perpetrators are caught and for whom there is evidence to support prosecution and conviction? Should the selectivity of prosecution be taken into account in determining punishment? Or should the gravity of the offenses be the controlling factor, with minimal attention to the wider context?

4.   If war crimes tribunals could be established in response to the genocide and other atrocities in the former Yugoslavia and Rwanda, why did not the same thing happen in response to genocide and other atrocities in Cambodia in the mid–1970s or in relation to the crimes of the Soviet government, especially in its early years? Why has the international law associated with individual accountability become of interest after so long? For discussion, see From Nuremberg to the Hague: The Future of International Criminal Justice (P. Sands ed., 2003). Over the last decade, the UN has been involved in negotiations to establish a special criminal tribunal to try some of the surviving participants in the Cambodian genocide, but no outcome has yet been determined. *See* Daniel K. Donovan, *Joint UN–Cambodia Efforts to Establish a Khmer Rouge Tribunal*, 44 Harv. Int'l L. J. 551 (2003).

5.   Professor Meron, *supra* note **h**, at 6, writes that "[t]he Rwanda tribunal ... belies complaints about the Eurocentric nature of international concern over Yugoslavia." In this connection, consider Payam Akhavan, *Justice and Reconcilia-*

*tion in the Great Lakes Region of Africa: The Contribution of the International Criminal Tribunal for Rwanda,*7 Duke J. Comp. & Int'l L. 325, 328 (1997):

> [The] significance [of the Rwanda Tribunal] has been overshadowed by the proceedings of the Yugoslav Tribunal. . . . One is tempted to ask a question with far-reaching consequences on the future of international justice: Was it simply Western cultural proximity with the Yugoslav victims which provoked the cries of indignation that resulted in the establishment of an International Tribunal? Had the Rwandan genocide occurred first, would we have resigned ourselves to the view of Africa as a continent where horror is commonplace, and where an International Tribunal would make no appreciable difference?

How would you answer these questions? Another African *ad hoc* tribunal is the Special Court for Sierra Leone, established in 2002 in the wake of a bitter civil war. It was created through an agreement between the United Nations and the Government of Sierra Leone to try those "who bear the greatest responsibility" for atrocities committed during the war. The judges are both international and from Sierra Leone (the President is an Australian–British lawyer, Geoffrey Robinson) and the first prosecutor was a US army lawyer, David Crane. *See* Nsongurua J. Udombana, *Globalization of Justice and the Special Court for Sierra Leone's War Crimes*, 17 Emory Int'l L. Rev. 55 (2003).

6. Compare the Hague (ICTY) and Arusha (ICTR) war crimes tribunals, the Special Court for Sierra Leone, and the ICC. What are the major similarities and differences? Which is better designed? Which is likely to be more effective? Why? According to what criteria? *Consult* Mark A. Drumbl, *Collective Violence and Individual Punishment*, 99 Nw. U. L. Rev. 539 (2005); Diane F. Orentlicher, *Judging Global Justice: Assessing the International Criminal* Court, 21 Wis. Int'l L. J. 495 (2003); Steven R. Ratner, *The International Criminal Court and the Limits of Global Judicialization*, 38 Tex. Int'l L. J. 445 (2003).

7. As this coursebook goes to press, former President of Iraq, Saddam Hussein, has been put on trial for crimes against humanity before the Supreme Iraqi Criminal Tribunal. The first case to be heard concerns the massacre and torture of 143 Shi'ite men in the village of Dujail in 1982. The choice of this case surprised some observers, given the well-documented wider scale atrocities of Saddam Hussein, such as the Anfal campaign against the Kurds. The Tribunal was established on 10 December 2003 by the adoption of a statute by the Iraqi Governing Council, just a few days before the capture of Saddam Hussein. Formally an Iraqi institution with Iraqi judges and prosecutors, though established and closely guided by the United States, it has jurisdiction over acts committed between 17 July 1968 and 1 May 2003 and a Statute with some features in common with the ICC Statute. Criticisms have been made of the Tribunal from a human rights perspective, however; some of its procedures do not accord with the standards established by the *ad hoc* UN tribunals nor those of the ICC—for example, the Iraqi Tribunal can issue the death penalty and there is mandatory execution within 30 days of a final judgment. Other issues raised have included whether Saddam Hussein can be accorded a fair trial. His defense counsel have argued that they have not had adequate notice of the material on which the charges are based nor sufficient time to prepare. Furthermore, its statute does not require that guilt be proved beyond a reasonable doubt and allows trials in absentia. It also does not protect either the right to counsel or the right to remain silent. Compare the Statute of the Iraqi Tribunal—*available at* http://www.cpa-iraq.org/human_rights/Statute.htm—with the ICC Statute and

identify their major points of similarity and difference. What are the competing advantages of international and domestic criminal tribunals in this context?

8.   The Rome Statute of the International Criminal Court **(Basic Document 1.16)** has been praised for the attention it pays to women. Article 36(8)(a) (iii) requires that there be "fair representation of female and male judges" and Article 36(8)(b) refers to "the need to include judges with legal expertise on specific issues, including, but not limited to, violence against women or children." The definition of the various crimes covered by the Rome Statute also gives some attention to women. Cherie Booth has argued that the role of women judges is vital and has described the important questioning of witnesses by Judge Navan-ethem Pillay, then President of the Rwanda Tribunal (and now a member of the International Criminal Court) in uncovering evidence of rape in the trial of Jean–Paul Akayesu. *See* Cherie Booth, *Prospects and Issues for the International Criminal Court: Lessons from Yugoslavia and Rwanda, in* From Nuremberg to the Hague: The Future of International Criminal Justice (Philippe Sands ed., 2003). *See also* excerpts from the *Akayesu* judgment in Reading 14 in Section 4–G of Problem 5–1 ("Ethnic Conflict and Its Consequences in Slavia, Candia, and Corcyra"), *infra* at 590. Additionally, see Christine Chinkin, *Feminist Reflections on International Criminal Law,* in International Criminal Law and the Current Development of Public International Law 125 (A. Zimmerman ed., 2003) for a skeptical look at the ICC and its possibilities for women. How important is it for women to serve on international criminal tribunals? While noting the involvement of women in the progressive development of international criminal law, Mark Drumbl has questioned Cherie Booth's enthusiasm for women judges by noting that it "may propound gender diversity while perpetuating the dominance of elite legal technocrats at the expense of the hard work required to integrate local communities and local women in the adjudicative process." Mark Drumbl, *Pluralizing International Criminal Justice*, 103 Mich. L. Rev. 1295, 1323 (2005).

9.   Traditionally, higher standards of legal accountability have obtained if warlike conflict can be characterized as "*inter*national" rather than "*intra*national"? How does one explain why this discrepancy in the treatment of identical behavior has insinuated itself into the substantive protection of civilian victims of belligerent abuse? How does one justify it?

10.   International criminal tribunals often are assigned what are considered the most serious of crimes committed during conflict, while national court systems may be left to manage other prosecutions. This has happened in Rwanda, for example. Does the experience of the Rwandan courts vindicate the national prosecution of war crimes and related crimes? As one may infer from the Introduction to this Part I, *supra* at 6–8, a major reason for concurrent jurisdiction of the Rwandan courts was the fact of 20,000 to 30,000 potential defendants or indictees. Realistically, could the ICTR have handled this number of cases? In the end, is it better to have an imperfect national war crimes prosecution process than no such process at all? What implications does the maltreatment of more than 80,000 potential war crimes defendants in Rwanda's jails have on the quest for the accountability of individuals for crimes of state? For discussion of these issues see Philippe Sands, *After Pinochet: The Role of National Courts, in* From Nuremberg to the Hague: The Future of International Criminal Justice (P. Sands ed., 2003).

11.   Truth and reconciliation commissions have become increasingly popular as a technique to deal with violence and injustice during armed conflict. They have been established in many South American countries as well as in East Timor, Sierra Leone, South Africa, and Sri Lanka, to name a few. Patricia Hayner

analyses many such commissions in Unspeakable Truths: Confronting State Terror and Atrocity (2001). South Africa's Truth and Reconciliation Commission is considered a notable success in securing from former police and other officials, in exchange for grants of amnesty, full confessions of human rights abuses and related crimes committed during the days of *apartheid*. The Commission was established as a way of putting to rest South Africa's brutal history of *apartheid*, serving as a kind of compromise that offers truth without the expense and other difficulties associated with legal prosecutions. *See* John Dugard, *Reconciliation and Justice: The South African Experience, in* The Future of International Human Rights 399 (B. Weston & S. Marks eds., 1999). Under what conditions is it possible to subordinate accountability to the quest for reconciliation and are such conditions present, for example, in the cases of the former Yugoslavia and Rwanda? To what extent do the politics of reconciliation depend upon effective procedures for imposing criminal accountability, at least on the main perpetrators of war crimes and crimes against humanity? In any event, do they not also depend, like adversarial prosecutions and adjudications, on authoritative legal guidelines to establish guilt and responsibility? It should be noted that Truth and Reconciliation Commissions have been strongly criticized by some human rights lawyers. For example, Diane Orentlicher has written: "Whatever salutary effects it can produce, [a truth commission] is no substitute for ... prosecutions. Indeed, to the extent that such an undertaking purports to replace criminal punishment ... it diminishes the authority of the legal process...." *Settling Accounts: The Duty to Prosecute Human Rights Violations of a Prior Regime*, 1000 Yale L. J. 257, 2546 n.32 (1991). What is your view on this issue? Some truth and reconciliation commissions operate in tandem with a system for criminal prosecution, for example in Peru, East Timor and Sierra Leone. And Paragraph 5 of UN Security Council Resolution 1593, *supra* note **e** in the Introduction to this Part I, at 3, referring the case of Darfur to the ICC, emphasizes their importance "to complement judicial processes." *See supra* text accompanying note **o** in the Introduction to this Part I, at 10. The relationship between these different institutions is often uneasy however. *See* Elizabeth M. Evenson, *Truth and Justice in Sierra Leone: Coordination between Commission and Court*, 104 Colum. L. Rev. 730 (2004).

12.   The doctrine of universal jurisdiction has been invoked to deal with the alleged perpetrators of mass atrocities. While Prosecution in national courts on this basis is rare, one conspicuous attempt involved General Augusto Pinochet, Chilean head of state from 1973–1990 who came to power through a violent coup against the elected government of Salvador Allende and then presided over a period of brutal repression. When Pinochet was visiting London for medical treatment in 1998, a Spanish judge hearing a criminal case relating to the deaths of Spanish citizens at the hands of Pinochet's regime made an extradition request to the United Kingdom. Unsurprisingly, the extradition order was contested by Pinochet and this resulted in a series of cases in the UK courts. One of Pinochet's arguments was that he could claim immunity for actions taken while he was head of state. This contention was rejected by the highest UK court, the Judicial Committee of the House of Lords. The House of Lords was, however, more reluctant to assert universal jurisdiction over atrocities attributed to Pinochet without a specific domestic legislative mandate. The final judgment of the House of Lords is reprinted in 38 I.L.M. 581 (1999). In the end, a claim that Pinochet was medically unfit to face trial was accepted by the UK government and Pinochet was allowed to return to Chile. For discussion of the Pinochet affair, see Christine Chinkin, *In re Pinochet*, 93 A.J.I.L. 703 (1999); Richard Falk, *Assessing the Pinochet Litigation: Whither Universal Jurisdiction?, in* Universal Jurisdiction:

National Courts and the Prosecution of Serious Crimes under International Law 97 (S. Macedo ed. 2004); Naomi Roht–Arriaza, *The Pinochet Effect: Transnational Justice in the Age of Human Rights* (2005). In May 2004, the Chilean government announced that General Pinochet would face trial for human rights abuses during his period as Chile's leader.

Belgium made a bold attempt to assert universal jurisdiction in a 1993 law, amended in 1999. *See* Act concerning the Punishment of Grave Breaches of International Humanitarian Law 10 Feb 1999, *reprinted in* 38 I.L.M. 918 (1999). The law allowed Belgian courts to hear charges of genocide, war crimes, and crimes against humanity against any person, whether or not they or the alleged crimes were within Belgium's territorial or nationality-based jurisdiction. Over forty cases were filed under the law, although only one case (concerning the 1994 Rwandan genocide) proceeded to judgment. The person bringing an action under the law did not require Belgian nationality or residence, and the law did not recognize any immunities based on the official status of the accused person. This aspect of the law was challenged before the International Court of Justice in a case against Belgium brought by the Democratic Republic of Congo. In 2002, the ICJ held that serving heads of state and government and ministers of foreign affairs had complete immunity from prosecution by a foreign jurisdiction for the term of their official position. *See Case Concerning the Arrest Warrant of 11 April 2000*, Judgment of 14 Feb. 2002, *reprinted in* 41 I.L.M. 536 (2002). The Belgian law was amended in 2003 to accord with the ICJ ruling. Note that Article 27 (2) of the Rome Statute of the International Criminal Court **(Basic Document 1.16)** states that immunities attaching to official positions under national or international law do not prevent the ICC from exercising jurisdiction over a person holding official status. The amended Belgian law nevertheless continued to cause tensions with other countries, particularly Israel and the United States. A case had been brought under it against Israeli Prime Minister Ariel Sharon under the Belgian law for his actions as a military commander in the 1982 massacre in the Sabraa and Shatila refugee camps in Lebanon; and in the wake of the invasion of Iraq in March 2003, a case was proposed against top US officials for war crimes. US Secretary of State, Colin Powell, threatened to move the headquarters of the North Atlantic Treaty Organization from Brussels unless Belgium changed the universal jurisdiction law, causing Belgium to agree to make further amendments to the law in 2003 to ensure that there was a clear link with Belgium in any case heard by a Belgian court. The new version of the law is based primarily on the nationality principle of jurisdiction, requiring that the accused person be a Belgian national or resident or that the victim be Belgian or have resided in Belgium for at least three years. In addition, a claim can only be made under the law if the accused is a national of a state that does not make genocide, war crimes and crimes against humanity criminal offences or that cannot guarantee a fair trial. The law is reprinted in 42 I.L.M. 749 (2003).

For discussion of universal jurisdiction as a response to international criminal acts generally, see Universal Jurisdiction: National Courts and the Prosecution of Serious Crimes under International Law (S. Macedo ed. 2004); The Law of War Crimes: National and International Approaches (Timothy McCormack & Gerry Simpson eds, 1996); Steven Ratner & Jason Abrams, Accountability for Human Rights Atrocities in International Law: Beyond the Nuremberg Legacy (1997). The Princeton Principles on Universal Jurisdiction were adopted in 2001 by a group of eminent jurists, scholars and legal experts to guide the exercise of universal jurisdiction. They are available at <http://www1.umn.edu/humanrts/instree/princeton.html>. The original Belgian universal jurisdiction law noted above has been described as a good reflection of the vision of the Princeton Principles in A. Hays Butler, *The Growing Support for Universal Jurisdiction in National Legislation*, *in* Universal Jurisdiction: National Courts and the Prosecution of Serious Crimes under International Law 67, 69 (S. Macedo ed. 2004). A debate between Henry Kissinger, former US Secretary of State, and Kenneth Roth, Executive Director of Human Rights Watch, summarizes the political tensions involved in exercises of universal jurisdiction: Henry Kissinger, *The Pitfalls of Universal Jurisdiction: Risking Judicial Tyranny*, 80 Foreign Aff. (2001); Kenneth Roth, *The Case for Universal Jurisdiction*, 80 Foreign Aff. (2001). Kissinger as well as other opponents of universal jurisdiction contend that it could subvert the goal of justice which its proponents seek to achieve. Dr. Kissinger's opposition may be self-serving, however, given that some journalists, most notably Christopher Hitchens, have argued that he should be put on trial for war crimes committed during the Vietnam War. *See* Christopher Hitchens, The Trial of Henry Kissinger (2002). Are there other methods for state officials to be held criminally accountable for their actions? *See generally* The Law and Enforcement of International Offenses: The Experience of International and National Courts (Gabrielle Kirk McDonald & Olivia Swaak–Goldman eds, 2000).

B. THE APPLICATION OF INTERNATIONAL LAW IN GENERAL

The application of international law doctrines, principles, and rules is indispensable to their counting as law. Unless they are applied to some degree, signaling an intention if not always a capacity to make them fully effective or controlling, they remain essentially aspirational or hortatory exercises—*moral* prescriptions, perhaps, but not *legal* ones. Such is one of the key lessons of the preceding section. In this section, we explore in further detail the many ways in which, in general, international law is applied, both on the international plane and the national plane.

1. THE APPLICATION OF INTERNATIONAL LAW ON THE INTERNATIONAL PLANE

Among the vast majority of international law decisions that are rendered on the international plane around the world every hour of every day, those that are discharged via the **adjudicative arena** of third-party decision-making with which we are so familiar in our national legal systems, are today in a distinct minority. In an essentially voluntarist legal system such as the international legal system (where there is primarily horizontal or nonhierarchical order among formally equal centers of legal authority, where few centralized command and enforcement structures have the capability to compel parties to comply with the rules consistently, and where autointerpretation prevails), legal prescriptions are relatively *infrequently* applied by third-party decision-makers such as courts and arbitral panels. Instead, they are applied, mainly, by national officials—functioning as claimant, judge, and police officer, often simultaneously[y]—in an ongoing transnational process of

---

y. The French jurist Georges Scelle used the term *dédoublement fonctionelle* to refer to the fact that a law officer (a lawyer for a government who also is an official of that government) typically has a double function: to make claims (as advocate) on behalf of her or his country, and to pass upon claims (as judge) made against her or his country by foreign countries or their citizens.

unilateral determination and reciprocal claim and response.[z] Of course, the application of international law does sometimes go forward, despite well-known limitations upon jurisdiction and access, through recourse to third-party decision-makers such as courts and arbitral tribunals, both permanent and temporary (as we have seen in the case of the ICTY, ICTR and ICC); and this happens with increasing frequency on the regional plane as well as the wider international and narrower national planes. Such permanently consti-tuted and highly specialized regional tribunals as the Court of Justice of the European Communities in Luxembourg, the Benelux Court of Justice in Brussels, the European Court of Human Rights in Strasbourg, and the Inter–American Court of Human Rights in San José (Costa Rica) are alone living testimony to this fact, not least because third-party adjudication is prized for its presumed impartiality and deliberateness. But the fact remains: the application of international law on the international plane goes forward most commonly not in arenas characterized by third-party decision-making (*e.g.,* arbitration and adjudication),[aa] but in arenas characterized by processes of unilateral determination and reciprocal response, to wit:

> the *diplomatic arena*, typically on a foreign office to foreign office basis, utilizing both persuasive (*e.g.,* fact-finding, negotiation, reporting) tech-niques[bb] and coercive (*e.g.,* economic, military) instruments of policy, in routine and exceptional circumstances alike;

> the *parliamentary-diplomatic arena*, through recourse to formal con-ferences, both official and unofficial;

> the *parliamentary arena*, in legislative and quasi-legislative assemblies on the global, regional, and national levels (as in such institutions as the United Nations Security Council or General Assembly, the General As-sembly of the Organization of American States, the European Parliament, and the Congress of the United States); and

> the *executive arena* via the secretariats of such international govern-mental organizations as the United Nations, the European Council, and NATO.

Never to be overlooked, of course, though it is highly susceptible to major abuse, is, in addition, resort to unilateral and collective *measures of self-help*, relying upon all the instruments of governmental policy—diplomatic, ideological, economic, and military.

Professor Lung-chu Chen writes of these matters in the following selec-tion.

z. For explication, see M. McDougal, H. Lasswell & W. Reisman, *The World Constitu-tive Process of Authoritative Decision, in* 1 The Future of the International Legal Order 73 (R. Falk & C. Black eds, 1969). *See also* L. Chen, An Introduction to Contemporary Internation-al Law ch. 24 (1989).

aa. To the extent that an ultimate settle-ment *is not* contingent on the consent of the disputing parties, good offices, mediation, and conciliation may be included among the tech-niques that are located within the adjudicative arena of third-party decision-making.

bb. To the extent that an ultimate settle-ment *is* contingent on the consent of the dis-puting parties, then good offices, mediation, and conciliation may be included among the persuasive techniques that are located within the diplomatic arena of unilateral determina-tion and reciprocal response.

LUNG-CHU CHEN, AN INTRODUCTION TO CONTEMPORARY INTERNATIONAL LAW

359–65 (2d ed. 2000)

RECOURSE TO DIRECT NEGOTIATIONS

The [usual] emphasis on "pacific" settlement of disputes through bilateral negotiations between "equal," "sovereign" states is understandable.... [The] overriding concern of international law is neither to punish states nor to embarrass them but to secure compliance with international legal norms. When compliance can be secured through peaceful, noncoercive procedures, it enhances the effectiveness of international law under the principle of economy with minimal insult or embarrassment to states.

In the contemporary world of decentralization, as sustained by shared perception of common interest and reciprocity, [transnational actors] are expected to act on their own to settle differences in a noncoercive manner with minimal involvement of inclusive authority. The most common procedure to settle differences and secure compliance is through diplomatic negotiations between contending states. Since most negotiations are conducted without drawing public attention, the achievement of ordinary diplomatic channels may always not be duly recognized. Numerous international agreements concerning the pacific settlement of disputes confine their application to disputes that cannot be solved by diplomacy. Recognizing the importance of diplomatic negotiations as a form of [international law] application, the Permanent Court of International Justice declared that "before a dispute can be made the subject of an action at law, its subject matter should have been clearly defined by means of diplomatic negotiations."[6]

Direct bilateral negotiations can be successful between contending parties. But such negotiations may often become deadlocked; hence the utility of such noncoercive devices as good offices, mediation, and conciliation. These devices inject into the application process a disinterested third party agreeable to both disputants, with varying degrees of authorized involvement, to facilitate peaceful settlement even for participants who have become too estranged to negotiate. The third party assists, not replaces, bilateral negotiations.[cc] The technical distinctions traditionally made regarding good offices, mediation, and conciliation reflect the degree of authorized involvement for the third party and do not affect the essence of bilateral negotiations. The ultimate settlement is contingent on the consent of the disputing parties.

These procedures have a long history in dispute settlement. Under the Hague Convention of 1899 for the Pacific Settlement of International Disputes,[dd] the signatory states, in consideration of the desirability of attempting

---

6. The Mavrommatis Palestine Concessions Case, 1924 P.C.I.J. (ser. A) No. 2, at 15.

cc. *But see* the Ruling in the *Rainbow Warrior* Affair Between France and New Zealand of 6 July 1986, 26 I.L.M. 1346 (1987) and 74 I.L.R. 256 (1987), which may be said to have resulted from the conciliatory efforts of the UN Secretary–General and which was deemed binding upon France and New Zealand by an international arbitral tribunal in an award of 30 April 1990 in respect of the two countries. For details, see L. Guruswamy, G. Palmer & B. Weston, International Environmental Law and

World Order: A Problem–Oriented Coursebook 146–69 (1994) (new third edition forthcoming in 2006).

dd. International Convention for the Pacific Settlement of International Disputes (Hague I), concluded 29 Jul 1899, entered into force 4 Sep 1900, 187 C.T.S. 410, 1 A.J.I.L. Supp. 107 (1907), superseded by the Convention for the Pacific Settlement of International Disputes (Hague I), concluded 18 Oct 1907, entered into force 26 Jan 10, 54 L.N.T.S. 435, 205 C.T.S. 233, 2 A.J.I.L. Supp. 43 (1908), *reprinted in* 1 Weston & Carlson I.H.1.

pacific settlement, pledged to make such efforts and acknowledged the right of third parties to offer assistance in arriving at peaceful solutions. With the establishment of the League of Nations, permanent agencies were created to perform functions of good offices, mediation, and conciliation. These procedures are incorporated in the Charter of the United Nations **[Basic Document 1.5]**. Commentators have sought to make technical distinctions among the procedures of good offices, mediation, and conciliation. But in practice these terms have been used with considerable flexibility. The tasks can be performed by a single third party but can also be done collectively. Their usefulness is limited in the sense that they cannot be successful, or even be initiated, without the cooperation of the disputants. But if such procedures do work toward composing differences and helping to secure compliance with international legal norms, so much the better.

THIRD–PARTY DECISION MAKING

Arbitration and judicial settlement . . . are typical modes of third-party decision making. The UN Charter explicitly includes both among the means of peaceful settlement of disputes. In arbitration and judicial settlement (through the International Court of Justice and other judicial tribunals), characterized by adverse proceedings with contending parties, the thrust of the emphasis differs from that prevailing in the previous phase of pacific settlement—with the third party playing the role the claimants want it to play [as often happens in the case of good offices, mediation, and conciliation].

During the nineteenth and the early part of the twentieth centuries, arbitration was frequently used to settle international disputes. In order to facilitate and encourage its use, nation-states entered into bilateral and multilateral agreements for arbitration. In spite of the establishment of the permanent Court of Arbitration in 1899,[ee] the procedure of arbitration is essentially ad hoc.

Widespread recognition of serious deficiencies in arbitral procedure led to the eventual establishment of the Permanent Court of International Justice, which was replaced by the International Court of Justice, one of the principal organs of the United Nations. [H]owever, because of a lack of compulsory jurisdiction—and in cases of acceptance of compulsory jurisdiction (by less than a third of the members of the UN), they are so highly qualified as to be more symbolic than substantial—the usefulness of judicial settlement by the court has not been maximized as contemplated. The US withdrawal, in October 1985, of its previous acceptance of compulsory jurisdiction in reaction to the court's assumption of jurisdiction in the case of *Nicaragua v. United States*[ff] was an especially severe blow,[7] although the United States (as most states) is bound by several treaties recognizing special acceptance of the

---

ee. The Permanent Court of Arbitration, established in 1900 under the 1899 Hague Convention for the Pacific Settlement of International Disputes (*seen supra* note **dd**), is not what its name implies. Apart from a permanent Bureau at The Hague, it consists simply of a standing panel of jurists from which States may select arbitrators to resolve their disputes together with machinery for facilitating the establishment of arbitral tribunals as needed.

ff. *Supra* note **p** in Chapter 2, at 99. For a brief extract from this case, see *supra* Ch. 2, at 117–21.

7. US Dep't State Letter and Statement Concerning Termination of Acceptance of ICJ Compulsory Jurisdiction, *reprinted in* 24 I.L.M. 1742 (1985).

court's competence to interpret and apply such treaties. Special acceptance seems to be the preferred mode at present.

The chamber procedure the ICJ used in the *Gulf of Maine* case (1984)[8] has somewhat encouraged more use of this economical and effective procedure.[gg] In this case Canada and the United States invoked Article 27 of the ICJ Statute [**Basic Document 1.6**], which provides for use of a Special Chamber by agreement of the parties. A five-person panel was selected by consent of the parties to decide the disputed fisheries jurisdiction in the Gulf of Maine. Both agreed to submit drafts of their proposed methods for drawing the baselines and settling the dispute, which would determine each state's territorial waters and continental shelf rights. But by virtue of Article 27 both parties also agreed to abide by the decision of the panel without reservation. The Special Chamber, after accepting proposals from each party, independently determined the new line. The compulsory third-party decision making mechanism of the Law of the Sea Convention has been another encouraging step toward the peaceful and lawful settlement of international disputes since it was implemented in 1994. Such dispute settlement processes are based on consent of the parties, and their involvement and participation in the decision process affords a greater chance of compliance.

Judicial adjudication has developed at the regional level—notably, the Court of European Communities, the European Court of Human Rights, and the Inter–American Court of Human Rights. The development of new forums to settle disputes peacefully increases the accessibility of various parties to effective arenas, thereby fostering greater compliance with community goals.

RECOURSE TO INTERNATIONAL GOVERNMENTAL ORGANIZATIONS (ESPECIALLY THE UNITED NATIONS)

When contending parties fail to settle disputes through either direct negotiations or third-party decision making, what can they do? Can they turn to international governmental organizations—most notably the United Nations—for help?

The United Nations is not designed to be a centralized agency for general law enforcement at the global level, though it is endowed with enormous responsibility to maintain international peace and security. The UN Charter encourages the settlement of disputes through noncoercive procedures outside the organization, expressing the policy of economy and effectiveness. The charter proclaims the basic principle of settling disputes by peaceful means in Articles 1(1) and 2(3). The charter's framers contemplated that most disputes should be settled by noncoercive methods and that settlement by organs of the United Nations should be resorted to only when other procedures fail. Article 33 thus obliges the member states to solve a dispute "by negotiation, enquiry, mediation, conciliation, arbitration, judicial settlement, resort to regional agencies or arrangements or other peaceful means of their own choice." In practice, member states tend to bring disputes before the Security Council without exhausting these peaceful means.

---

8. Case Concerning Delimitation of the Maritime Boundary in the Gulf of Maine Area (Can. v. U.S.), 1984 ICJ 246, 1984 WL 499.

gg. ICJ Communiqué 93/20, issued by the World Court on 19 July 1993, reported the formation of a "Chamber of the Court for Environmental Matters."

Although the United Nations is less than a general law enforcement agency, it is entrusted with the tremendous responsibility to maintain minimum world order. This has been especially the case in the past few years. As a whole, the charter is much more concerned with disputes that are likely to disrupt minimum order. Thus the application of Chapter VI of the charter is expressly limited to disputes "the continuance of which is likely to endanger the maintenance of international peace." Violations of international law embrace a range of situations; a violation may or may not constitute a breach of such magnitude. Unless requested otherwise by the contenders, the Security Council or the General Assembly is empowered to recommend either procedures of peaceful settlement or terms of settlement only if a preliminary investigation indicates that the "dispute or situation is likely to endanger the maintenance of international peace and security" (Article 34). The noncoercive procedures of settlement set forth in the charter have been carefully designed to permit a gradual approach to each dispute—the competence of the United Nations is contingent on the seriousness of the dispute and the degree of danger to minimum world order. The United Nations would normally step in only when a dispute is likely to disrupt minimum public order. Even then the United Nations is confined to recommending only procedures or terms of settlement.

In addition to the framework for peaceful settlement of disputes, the United Nations is authorized to take enforcement measures. The Security Council is empowered, under Article 39 of the charter, to determine the existence not only of "an act of aggression or breach of the peace" but also "a threat to the peace" and to take proper enforcement measures. Any violation falling short of threatening the peace will be outside the scope of the Security Council's competence. The concept of what constitutes such a threat has been increasingly broadened in the recent past, however, with the Security Council becoming a much more active decision making body since the end of the Cold War.

How effective has the United Nations been in performing its sanctioning functions? The veto power of the permanent members of the Security Council has made it extremely difficult, if not impossible, to enforce effectively the measures provided by Chapter VII of the charter, even against a clearly identified challenge to minimum world order. This has continued to be true after the Cold War, as witnessed by failure in Bosnia and difficulty in maintaining support from all the superpowers for sanctions against Iraq. In a bold peacetime experiment, the Security Council has undertaken multilateral efforts to destroy Iraq's warmaking capabilities through sanctions and on-site inspections. The Security Council has much at stake here. These sanctions, begun in 1990, could see the Security Council functioning in the way envisioned by the United Nations founders; their failure, however, could mean an erosion of council authority at a time when there is much hope invested in the new multilateralism in world security. The General Assembly's formal authority in peace-keeping ... has been greatly enlarged thanks to the Uniting for Peace Resolution and the Agenda for Peace, but it continues to be handicapped. The United Nations continues, despite some success in the Gulf War, to face limitations in performing the applying function to deal with a range of acts of lawlessness, especially in the very area that constitutes one of the organization's major goals.

RECOURSE TO UNILATERAL MEASURES OF SELF–HELP

The UN Charter represents the general efforts of the organized community of nations to substitute effective collective measures for unilateral measures of nation-state self-help, which are highly susceptible to abuse. Yet the existing structures of authority and procedure provided by the charter are not sufficiently comprehensive and effective to enable the United Nations to function as a centralized organ for securing compliance with international law across the board. When states that are victims of all sorts of lawless acts cannot, despite their genuine efforts, secure justice or peace through either noncoercive methods or international governmental organizations, will they be permitted to resort to unilateral coercive measures in response to prior unlawful acts?

In the past, resort to unilateral coercive measures was a recognized means of enforcement. Enforceability of international law depended in large measure on such patterns of unorganized and uninstitutionalized remedies. Measures thus taken by states were generally labeled self-help, reprisal, retaliation, or other measures short of war. Self-help would appear to be a generic term appropriate for the present purpose. Forcible self-help was regarded as permissible when it was reasonably necessary and taken in response to a prior unlawful act, including failure to carry out international obligations, when such act was imputable to the state against which the self-help measure was directed.

The UN Charter, with its general proscription of the threat or use of force as contained in Article 2(4), has generated a continuing controversy about the permissibility of self-help involving the use of armed force. . . . [W]e have reluctantly concluded that absent effective machinery for collective law enforcement under the present world conditions, self-help, even involving military force, remains permissible as a measure of last resort, subject to the rigorous requirements of necessity and proportionality. The necessity for self-help will occur only when all good faith efforts in exhausting all available noncoercive means in response to a prior act of lawlessness have proved futile. The requirement of proportionality must be appraised by reference to all factors relevant in a particular context, considering especially the nature of the precipitating act of lawlessness and the harm it has caused, and the modality (military or nonmilitary) of the responding measure and the deprivation it may cause.

Self-help measures that are nonmilitary in nature [*e.g.*, economic measures] can be permissible, provided the conditions of necessity and proportionality are met.

––––––––

TOUCHING UPON THEMES we addressed in Chapter 1, Professor Chen, *supra*, goes on to caution against "skeptics" [who] harbor the notion that international law is not law at all, because it lacks "enforceability" or has only "marginal enforceability." *Id.* at 384–85. "Such a view," he writes, "approaches the question of enforcement in terms of a centralized system of command and community coercion and fails to grasp the dynamics inherent in a decentralized legal system." *Id.* at 385. That is, it typically confuses "enforcement" and "sanctions" with resort to courts (adjudication) and exercise of the police power (military force) to the exclusion of, or without reference to, the real world impact of economic, diplomatic, and other more or less compromissory and nonconfrontational ways and means of managing disputes and achieving common goals.

These observations are validated among the many fields of human endeavor that have exploded across national boundaries in the last six decades— communications, economic development, education, the environment, health, human rights, labor, nuclear power, trade, transportation, and so forth. To handle the conflicts and realize the policies that inhere in these fields, new international legal norms, institutions, and procedures have had to be invented. Many of these, to ensure compliance with community norms and at the same time safeguard continuity among interdependent relationships, abjure adjudication after disputes have arisen in favor of regulatory regimes that prevent disputes before they take place. And nowhere is this approach more prominent, marking a distinctive shift in the way public international law gets enforced, than in almost countless new treaties and intergovernmental organizations that daily and significantly impact international trade and the protection and enhancement of the natural environment. Increasingly these new legal regimes, which typically reflect the growing perception that international well-being is less advanced by judicial decisions that remedy harm already inflicted (*ex post*) than by mutual and reciprocal regulatory policies and programs that prevent harm before it happens (*ex ante*), do not stop at establishing doctrines, principles, and rules of good citizenship. Increasingly they go further, promoting policies and obliging specified conduct that facilitate compliance with community norms more through *ex ante* treaty provisions and regulations than *ex post* judicial decisions and decrees, more through strategies of cooperation than those of competition. As one commentator has observed in this context, in "almost ... all cases where international law institutes administrative and judicial supervision side by side, the administrative method prevails and becomes the only one in operation to the almost entire exclusion of judicial supervision."[hh]

This development parallels similar developments in municipal law systems where public concern over social issues gives rise to regulatory regimes operating *ex ante*. Regulatory controls have been described by Robert Summers as the "administrative/regulatory method of legal control[ii]." According to Summers, this technique differs from the grievance-remedial approach primarily because it is designed to operate preventively before any grievance has arisen; officials adopt regulatory standards, communicate them to those subject to regulation, and take precautionary steps to ensure that those subject to regulation comply and thereby prevent untoward actions. Unlike the typical compensation claimant in the grievance-remedial mode or the typical prosecutor in the penal mode, the administrator need not wait until harm is done before taking action against a non-complying "regulatee."

The *ex ante* measures adopted in recent trade and environmental treaties typically include provisions requiring information and data collection, monitoring, reporting, reviews of performance, financial assistance, and arbitra-

hh. V. Kaasik, Le Contrôle en Droit International 145 (1933), *as quoted in* E. Landy, The Effectiveness of International Law 175 n.2 (1966).

ii. R. Summers, *The Technique Element in Law*, 59 Calif. L. Rev. 733 (1971).

tion. Such "techniques of inducement"[jj] or instruments in the "technology of international politics"[kk] help intergovernmental organizations push States toward better implementation of the treaties they have adopted. They are the bridge between "obligations of rule," such as the general principle that States shall not cause transboundary pollution, and the "obligations of result," such as those prescriptions that require a State to set up a specified system of monitoring.

The 1974 Paris Convention for the Prevention of Marine Pollution from Land–Based Sources[ll] is exemplary in this regard. Article 1(2) sets out the "obligations of rule" among the contracting State parties, requiring them to "adopt individually and jointly measures to combat land-based pollution...." Then, in Articles 4(2) and 4(3), the Convention establishes "obligations of result" by requiring the State parties to implement programs and measures that eliminate pollution caused by specified toxic substances. However, the elimination of marine pollution arising from land-based sources is an enormously complex enterprise. First the existing "baselines" and impacts of the pollutants have to be determined, a task that involves complicated scientific research and monitoring. Then it is necessary to ascertain and control each and every one of their possible sources (large plants and factories, small industries, domestic waste) and thereafter to identify and monitor on a continuous basis the pathways taken by them in their passage to the sea (rivers, canals, sewers, pipelines, the atmosphere). Finally, the steps taken in the jurisdiction of the contracting State parties to eliminate land-based pollution must be identified and the success or failure of the remedial measures instituted must be continuously monitored. Therefore, to better achieve its goals, the Paris Convention created a "Commission composed of representatives of each of the Contracting Parties" to perform a number of functions required by this difficult agenda. Per Article 16(d), the commission draws up programs and measures necessary for the implementation of the treaty obligations. Per Article 18(3), it conducts scientific research and monitoring. Per Articles 17 and 12(2), it oversees monitoring through reports that the contracting State parties are obliged to provide and scrutinizes the legislative and administrative measures taken by them to fulfill their obligations. And, per Articles 12(2) and 17, it is authorized to appoint, as needed, an independent committee of experts to review the extent to which obligations under the Convention have been satisfactorily implemented. In the light of these regulatory measures, demonstrating the kind of preventive role that can be played by intergovernmental organizations set up by environmental treaties, it can be seen how adjudicative supervision is relegated to a position of secondary importance.

In sum, to implement the policies and priorities defined by international law, one is well advised to cast a skeptical eye upon traditional approaches to implementation in favor of more sophisticated functional or programmatic techniques for making collective choices and taking positive action. *Ex ante* regulatory approaches brought about by multilateral agreement and implemented through collective measures may be seen to speak more for the

---

jj. V. Kaasik, *supra* note **hh.**

kk. P. Jessup & H. Taubenfeld, Controls for Outer Space 133 (1959).

ll. *Reprinted in* 13 I.L.M. 352 (1974) and 5 Weston & Carlson V.F.18.

common inclusive interest than the alternative *ex post* adversarial-adjudicative approach.

DISCUSSION NOTES/QUESTIONS

1.   Since the 1990s, the International Court of Justice has become considerably more active than in its first 45 years. *See, e.g.*, Keith Highet, *The Peace Palace Heats Up: The World Court in Business Again?*, 85 A.J.I.L. 646 (1991); Panel, *The Changing Role of the ICJ*, 85 A.S.I.L. Proceed. 31 (1991). Over the last 15 years, the Court has been called upon to resolve a number of diverse international disputes. As this coursebook goes to press, the Court has 14 cases on its docket. For an indication of the variety of cases decided by the World Court, especially in recent years, see Appendix II in the documentary supplement to this coursebook and the Court's own website at <http://www.icj-cij.org/>. For useful guides to the history and work of the Court, see Shabtai Rosenne, The Law and Practice of The International Court, 1920–2004 (2005). *See also* Thomas J. Bodie, Politics and the Emergence of an Activist International Court of Justice (1995); Robert Jennings, *The ICJ After Fifty Years*, 89 A.J.I.L. 493 (1995); Howard N. Meyer, The World Court in Action: Judging Among the Nations (2002); Fifty Years of the International Court of Justice (V. Lowe & M. Fitzmaurice eds., 1996).

Regardless of the Court's increased activity, however, and regardless of its substantive competence to hear virtually any dispute brought before it, its procedural competence rests, per Article 36(1) of its Statute **(Basic Document 1.6)**, on the willingness or consent of the contending parties, and for the most part, as noted in Discussion Note/Question 2, *infra*, states are reluctant to submit their legal disputes to the Court. As Oscar Schachter has written of international adjudication generally:

> Litigation is uncertain, time consuming, troublesome. Political officials do not want to lose control of a case that they might resolve by negotiation or political pressures. Diplomats naturally prefer diplomacy; political leaders value persuasion, manoeuvre and flexibility. They often prefer to "play it by ear," making their rules to fit the circumstances rather than submit to pre-existing rules. Political forums, such as the United Nations, are often more attractive, especially to those likely to get wide support for political reasons. We need only compare the large number of disputes brought to the United Nations with the few submitted to adjudication. One could go on with other reasons. States do not want to risk losing a case when the stakes are high or be troubled with litigation in minor matters. An international tribunal may not inspire confidence, especially when some judges are seen as "political" or hostile. There is apprehension that the law is too malleable or fragmentary to sustain "true" judicial decisions. In some situations, the legal issues are viewed as but one element in a complex political situation and consequently it is considered unwise or futile to deal with them separately. Finally we note the underlying perception of many governments that law essentially supports the *status quo* and that courts are [not] responsive to demands for justice or change.

Oscar Schachter, *International Law in Theory and Practice—General Course in Public International Law*, 178 Recueil 9, 208 (1982–V).

Should states be more willing to submit their international disputes to judicial settlement? Would increased resort to international adjudication help to develop and strengthen international law? Would it advance the cause of world peace? Social justice? Economic well-being? Ecological balance? Consider in these respects the following extract from Daniel G. Parton, *Increasing the Effectiveness of the International Court*, 18 Harv. Int'l. L. J. 559, 561 (1977), identifying three functions of the World Court specifically that can be said to characterize international adjudication generally:

> The effectiveness of the International Court, like that of any international institution, must be examined in terms of the purpose and functions of the Court. At the risk of over-simplification, three functions of the International Court might be distinguished. First, the Court functions as a vehicle for the peaceful settlement of international disputes. Second, in articulating international law and applying that law to disputes before it, the Court exerts a major influence on the progressive development of international law. Third, in carrying out its dispute settlement and law development roles, the Court must balance claims for legal change against claims for the enforcement of established rights under traditional international law.... [S]ubject to many intense differences of views as to their proper exercise, the three functions just stated would probably enjoy wide acceptance as a framework within which to define the Court's role and measure its effectiveness.

For elaboration on these and related themes, see Richard B. Bilder, *International Dispute Settlement and the Role of International Adjudication*, 1 Emory J. Int'l Dispute Resolution 131 (1987). *See also* Richard B. Bilder, *An Overview of International Dispute Settlement*, 1 Emory J. Int'l Dispute Resolution 1 (1986); John G. Merrills, International Dispute Settlement (3d ed. 1998); Onuma Yasuaki, *Is the International Court of Justice and Emperor without Clothes?*, 8 Int'l Leg. Theory 1 (2002).

2. All parties to the United Nations Charter **(Basic Document 1.5)**—*i.e.*, all UN members—are automatically parties to the Statute of the International Court of Justice **(Basic Document 1.6)**. It is not necessary, however, to be a UN member to accept the jurisdiction of the Court. For example, Nauru, when a non-member of the UN, became a party to the ICJ Statute so that it could bring a claim against Australia—*Certain Phosphate Lands in Nauru*, 1992 ICJ 240. As suggested in the preceding discussion note/question, however, being a party to the Statute does not signal acceptance of the Court's compulsory jurisdiction. Indeed, in many instances, states give their consent to ICJ adjudication, as in the present problem, only on a case-by-case basis, pursuant to a special agreement known as a *"compromis."* To signal their acceptance of the Court's compulsory jurisdiction, a strictly voluntary act, states must affirmatively declare, per Article 36(2) of the Court's Statute, that "they recognize [the Court's jurisdiction] as compulsory *ipso facto* and without special agreement, in relation to any other state accepting the same obligation." As this coursebook goes to press, only 68 states have accepted the Court's jurisdiction under Article 36(2)—including, among the leading common law jurisdictions, Australia, Canada, the United Kingdom, and New Zealand, although *not* the United States, which terminated its acceptance in October 1985 (*see* below). As authorized by Article 36(3) of the Court's Statute, some of these declarations of acceptance have been made "unconditionally"—for example, Costa Rica's declaration of acceptance—or virtually unconditionally, as in the case of the current Australian declaration of acceptance, with the reservation only that "this declaration does not apply to"

(a) any dispute in regard to which the parties thereto have agreed or shall agree to have recourse to some other method of peaceful settlement;

(b) any dispute concerning or relating to the delimitation of maritime zones, including the territorial sea, the exclusive economic zone, and the continental shelf, or arising out of, concerning, or relating to the exploitation of any disputed area of or adjacent to any such maritime zone pending its delimitation;

(c) any dispute in respect of which any other party to the dispute has accepted the compulsory jurisdiction of the Court only in relation to or for the purpose of the dispute; or where the acceptance of the Court's compulsory jurisdiction on behalf of any other party to the dispute was deposited less than 12 months prior to the filing of the application bringing the dispute before the Court.

However, as also authorized by Article 36(3), many declarations of acceptance are made "on condition of reciprocity on the part of several or certain states, or for a certain time," thus lending support to Professor Schachter's observations, *supra*, that general declarations of acceptance of the ICJ's jurisdiction can and do serve to limit that jurisdiction. Consider, thus, Canada's declaration of acceptance, which contains a clause similar to that found in Australia's declaration but also excludes from ICJ jurisdiction disputes with other members of the Commonwealth, "disputes with regard to questions which by international law fall exclusively within the jurisdiction of Canada," and disputes with respect to conservation and management measures taken by Canada with respect to fishing in the northwest Atlantic. For discussion of the issue of reservations to the ICJ Statute, see Stanimir A. Alexandrov, *Accepting the Compulsory Jurisdiction of the International Court of Justice with Reservations: An Overview of Practice with a Focus on Recent Trends and Cases*, 1 Leiden J. Int'l L. 89 (2001); John G. Merrills, *The Optional Clause Revisited*, 65 B.Y.B.I.L. 197 (1993).

The history of the declaration of acceptance made by the United States in 1946, since terminated (as hereinafter explained), is likewise illustrative of the more conditional sort reservation and reads in pertinent part as follows:

[T]he United States of America recognizes as compulsory *ipso facto* and without special agreement, in relation to any other state accepting the same obligation, the jurisdiction of the International Court of Justice in all legal disputes hereafter arising concerning:

  a. the interpretation of a treaty;

  b. any question of international law;

  c. the existence of any fact which, if established, would constitute a breach of an international obligation;

  d. the nature or extent of the reparation to be made for the breach of an international obligation;

Provided, that this declaration shall not apply to

  a. disputes the solution of which the parties shall entrust to other tribunals by virtue of agreements already in existence or which may be concluded in the future; or

  b. disputes with regard to matters which are essentially within the domestic jurisdiction of the United States of America as determined by the United States of America; or

  c. disputes arising under a multilateral treaty, unless (1) all parties to the treaty affected by the decision are also parties to the case before the Court, or (2) the United States of America specially agrees to jurisdiction....

Declaration by the President of the United States of America, 14 Aug 46, respecting recognition by the United States of America of the compulsory jurisdiction of the International Court of Justice, 61 Stat. 1218, T.I.A.S. No. 1598, 4 Bevans 140, 1 U.N.T.S. 9. Note especially the last eight words of reservation **b**: "as determined by the United States of America." Popularly known as the "Connally Amendment," after Senator Tom Connally of Texas (Chairman of the Senate Foreign Relations Committee when the Declaration was adopted), this language was for many years severely criticized by proponents of a stronger World Court, since, pursuant to the reciprocity doctrine embodied in Article 36(3) of the ICJ Statute, a state may use another state's reservation to defeat the jurisdiction of the Court. In addition, it was censured for its self-judging and self-serving character. In the words of former Vice–President Hubert Humphrey, the amendment "hampered the effectiveness of the Court [while rendering] little advantage and much embarrassment to this country." Hubert H. Humphrey, *The United States, the World Court and the Connally Amendment*, 11 Va. J .Int'l .L. 310, 311 (1971).

Proponents of a stronger World Court were to be yet further disappointed by the United States, however, following the Court's decision, on 26 November 1984, in *Military and Paramilitary Activities in and Against Nicaragua* (Nicar. v. U.S.) (Jurisdiction and Admissibility of the Application), 1984 ICJ 392, 1984 WL 501, *reprinted in* 24 I.L.M. 59 (1985), that it had jurisdiction to adjudicate claims alleging violations of international law by the United States in the aftermath of the Sandinista Revolution. In an earlier letter to the UN Secretary–General dated 5 April 1984, the United States had declared its "inherent right" to modify its August 1946 Declaration by excluding from the Court's jurisdiction "disputes with any Central American state or arising out of or related to events in Central America. . . ." Letter to UN Secretary–General Concerning Non–Applicability of Compulsory Jurisdiction of the International Court of Justice with Regard to Disputes with Central American States, *reprinted in* 23 I.L.M. 670 (1984). After the Court, in its November 26 judgment, denied that the United States had the right to thus modify its 1946 Declaration (ergo the Court's jurisdiction), the US Department of State issued a formal statement flatly denying the Court's jurisdiction and declaring a withdrawal by the United States from further proceedings in the case. Statement on the Withdrawal from the Proceedings Initiated by in the International Court of Justice (18 Jan 85), 85 Dep't State. Bull. 64 (Mar 85), *reprinted in* 24 I.L.M. 246 (1985). Thereafter, on 7 October 1985, ignoring the World Court's 26 November 1984 ruling, the United States terminated its 1946 Declaration and withdrew from the Court's compulsory jurisdiction altogether. *See* Letter to UN Secretary–General Concerning Termination of Acceptance of Compulsory Jurisdiction of the International Court of Justice (7 Oct 85), 86 Dep't State Bull. 67 (Jan 86). This withdrawal of the United States from the World Court's compulsory jurisdiction and the Court's 26 November 1984 jurisdictional ruling prompted a heated debate among international lawyers. *See, e.g.*, Herbert W. Briggs, *Nicaragua v. United States: Jurisdiction and Admissibility*, 79 A.J.I.L. 373 (1985); Anthony A. D'Amato, *Comment: Modifying US Acceptance of the Compulsory Jurisdiction of the World Court*, 79 A.J.I.L. 385 (1985); Monroe Leigh, *Comment: Military and Paramilitary Activities In and Against Nicaragua v. United States of America)*, 79 *id*. 442 (1985); John Norton Moore, *The Case: Political Questions Before the International Court of Justice*, 27 Va. J. Int'l L. 459 (1987); W. Michael Reisman, *Has the International Court Exceeded Its Jurisdiction?*, 80 A.J.I.L. 128 (1986). *See also* US Decision to Withdraw from the International Court of Justice: Hearing Before the Subcomm. on Human Rights and International Organizations of the House Comm. on Foreign Aff., 99th Cong., 1st Sess. (1985) (especially statements by Abraham D. Sofaer, Legal Adviser, Department of State; Professor Richard N. Gardner, Columbia University School of Law; and Professor Burns H. Weston, Independent Commission on Respect for International Law and University of Iowa College of Law). However, it should be noted that withdrawal from adherence to the compulsory jurisdiction of the Court does not signify withdrawal from the Court's jurisdiction in all cases and for all purposes; the United States is subject to the Court's jurisdiction under the compromissory provisions of over seventy treaties, under which disputes arising under the said treaties may be referred to the Court on the application of any party. *See,* in this connection, Fred L. Morrison, *Treaties as a Source of Jurisdiction, Especially in US Practice,* in The International Court of Justice at a Crossroads 58 (L. Damrosch ed., 1987). *See also* Michla Pomerance, The United States and the World Court as a "Supreme Court of the Nations": Dreams, Illusions, and Disillusion (1996). Indeed, the US submitted to the jurisdiction of the Court on the basis of a compromissory clause in a 1995 bilateral treaty with Iran in the *Oil Platforms Case* (Iran v. U.S.) 2003 ICJ 161.

Do you agree with the position taken by the United States government toward the compulsory jurisdiction of the ICJ ? How might it affect the work of the World Court in the future?

As this coursebook goes to press, there are no indications that the United States will soon reaccept the Court's compulsory jurisdiction except on a case-by-case basis and in respect of specific types of disputes. Imagine yourself as a lawyer in the Office of the Legal Adviser of the US Department of State. Would you, in this capacity, recommend such a selective step or would you argue against it? If you would not so recommend, why not? If you would so recommend, would you simultaneously recommend some qualifying language? For example, would you recommend that a United States declaration of acceptance of the general compulsory jurisdiction of the Court not extend to such disputes as were mentioned in the 1946 United States declaration, *supra*? To disputes in respect of which any party to the dispute has accepted the compulsory jurisdiction of the Court less than, say, a year prior to the filing of the application bringing the dispute before the Court? To disputes that relate to ongoing armed hostilities between the parties? Bear in mind that, first in the *Nuclear Tests Cases* [(Austl. v. Fr.) 1974 ICJ 253, 1974 WL 3 and (N.Z. v. Fr.) 1974 ICJ 457, 1974 WL 4] **(Basic Document 7.9)** and later in the Iranian *Hostage Case* [*Case Concerning United States Diplomatic and Consular Staff in Tehran* (United States v. Iran) 1979 ICJ 23, 1979 WL 119], as well as most recently in the case of *Nicaragua v. United States, supra*, respondent states have chosen to boycott the Court in the face of ongoing litigation, ergo to leave it in a position of rendering essentially *ex parte* decisions whose force and effect, in our decentralized international legal system, is thereby necessarily compromised. For this and related considerations, see The United States and the Compulsory Jurisdiction of the International Court of Justice (A. Arend ed., 1986); Anthony A. D'Amato, *Modifying US Acceptance of the Compulsory Jurisdiction of the World Court*, 79 A.J.I.L. 385 (1985); Louis B. Sohn, *Suggestions for the Limited Acceptance of Compulsory Jurisdiction of the International Court of Justice by the United States*, 18 Ga. J. Int'l & Comp. L. 1 (1988); The United States and the Compulsory Jurisdiction of the International Court of Justice (A. Arend ed., 1986); Shigeru Oda, *The Compulsory Jurisdiction of the International Court of Justice: A Myth—A Statistical Analysis of Contentious Cases*, 49 I.C.L.Q. 251 (2000).

For extensive discussion on how and in what ways to "revive" the World Court, see Richard A. Falk, Reviving the World Court (1986). *See also* Thomas M. Franck, Judging the World Court (Twentieth Century Fund Paper, 1986); The International Court of Justice at a Crossroads (L. Damrosch ed., 1987).

3.   An important aspect of the ICJ is its legal competence, under Article 65 of its Statute, to render Advisory Opinions. A request must be made by an international institution that is authorised to do so. Such bodies include the UN General Assembly. Interested states may make submissions to the Court. Requests for Advisory Opinions are often controversial, however, either because the question posed is highly contested (*e.g.*, Legality of the Threat or Use of Nuclear Weapons 1996 ICJ 225) or because the request is perceived as an indirect way of obtaining a ruling on what is properly a contentious case that cannot be litigated because the relevant parties have not accepted the jurisdiction of the ICJ (*e.g.*, Legal Consequences of the Construction of a Wall in the Occupied Palestinian Territory 2004 ICJ No. 131). For discussion, see Kenneth Keith, *The Advisory Jurisdiction of the International Court of Justice: Some Comparative Reflections* 17 Austl. Y.B.I.L. 39 (1996).

4.   As noted at the outset of this Subsection B–1, the International Court of Justice is not the only permanently constituted international tribunal. Except for the ICJ, however, all have limited subject-matter jurisdiction: the International Criminal Court, the Court of Justice of the European Communities, the Benelux Court of Justice, the European Court of Human Rights, the Inter–American Court of Human Rights, and an emerging African Court of Human Rights. Would the world benefit from an array of courts of general jurisdiction? How might this be accomplished? What would be the utility, given the "subsidiary" status accorded judicial decisions under Article 38 of the ICJ Statute **(Basic Document 1.6)**, widely accepted, at least in theory, to apply to all international tribunals?

5.   According to Chen, *supra*, the usefulness of non-adjudicative means of international dispute settlement such as mediation and conciliation is limited "[because] they cannot be successful ... without the cooperation of the disputants." Does this mean that decisions reached via these non-adjudicative modalities of international dispute settlement do not have the force and effect of law? What if the parties choose to treat these decisions as binding? What then?

6.   Professor Chen writes, *supra*, that he has "reluctantly concluded that absent effective machinery for collective law enforcement under the present world conditions, self-help, even involving military force, remains permissible as a measure of last resort, subject to the rigorous requirements of necessity and proportionality." Do you agree/disagree with this conclusion? What theory of world order lies behind this analysis? What problems does it raise? *See* Mary–Ellen O'Connell, *Controlling Countermeasures, in* International Responsibility Today: Essays in Memory of Oscar Schachter 49 (M. Ragazzi ed., 2005).

7.   A different form of adjudication may be found in various "peoples' tribunals" organized by civil society to respond to the limited formal mechanisms in international law. The first such tribunal was initiated by Bertrand Russell in 1967 to hear evidence on alleged United States aggression and war crimes in Vietnam. The French existentialist philosopher, Jean–Paul Sartre, was its chair. More recently peoples' tribunals have been formed to deal with issues such as environmental damage, corporate responsibility for crimes against humanity, Japanese treatment of Korean "comfort women" during World War II and the legality of the invasion of Iraq in 2003. For discussion of some of these tribunals and their public impact see Yves Beigbeder, Judging War Criminals: The Politics

of International Justice 137–140 (1999); Christine Chinkin, *Women's International Tribunal on Japanese Military Sexual Slavery*, 95 A.J.I.L. 335 (2001). What are the advantages and limitations of these developments? For pertinent related discussion focusing on the peoples' tribunal known as the World Tribunal on Iraq (WTI), see *infra* Chapter 10. *See also* the WTI's website at <http://www.worldtribunal.org/>.

2. THE APPLICATION OF INTERNATIONAL LAW ON THE NATIONAL PLANE

Contrary to popular impression, international law is not restricted to foreign offices, intergovernmental organizations, international tribunals such as the International Court of Justice or the International Criminal Court, and other decision-makers on the international plane. In fact, international law comes up often in national decision-making arenas; much of it depends for its effectiveness on enforcement through national (commonly called "domestic" or "municipal") legal systems. It is debatable whether international law serves as the ultimate legitimization of national law, as Hans Kelsen once argued.[mm] But it is beyond debate that it is invoked in varying degrees for the actual rules of decision in national courts and other national decision-making arenas. Writes Professor Bederman: "International environmental standards . . . are often actuated through domestic regulation. International human rights aspirations are practically enforced through municipal civil rights laws."[nn] In other words, when rendering decisions that extend the influence of international law, national decision-making institutions act, in effect, as agents of the international legal order. Witness, for example, the trials that took place in Germany in the aftermath of the Nuremberg trial or the trials that have taken place in the courts of Rwanda and Yugoslavia.

Therefore, before we delve into the problems in Part II of this coursebook, we here present material about the relation of international law to national arenas of decision, about the incorporation of international law as a rule of decision in domestic courts. In so doing, we focus primarily on the incorporation of international law as a rule of decision in *American* courts. We do this in part because this coursebook will likely be used mainly—though not exclusively—by American law students. It should be understood, however, that the issues raised in the United States relative to the interrelation of national and international law have their analogues in the legal systems of most other countries and therefore have broader relevance. It is thus not inappropriate to begin with citations to two leading English international law scholars.

Starke's International Law
63–64 (I. Shearer 11th ed. 1994)

Nothing is more essential to a proper grasp of the subject of international law than a clear understanding of its relation to State law. A thorough acquaintance with this topic is of the utmost practical importance. Particularly is it of value in clarifying the law of treaties—perhaps the most important

---

mm. *See generally* H. Kelsen, Principles of International law 551–88 (R. Tucker 2d rev. ed. 1966).

nn. D. Bederman, International Law Frameworks 149 (2001).

branch of international law, and one which impinges so frequently on the domain of State law. * * * The two principal theories are known as *monism* and *dualism*. According to monism, international law and State law are concomitant aspects of the one system—law in general; according to dualism, they represent two entirely distinct legal systems, international law having an *intrinsically* different character from that of State law. Because a large number of domestic legal systems are involved, the dualist theory is sometimes known as the "pluralistic" theory, but it is believed that the term "dualism" is more exact and less confusing.

Ian Brownlie, Principles of Public International Law
31–32 (6th ed. 2003)

The theoretical issue [of the relation of municipal and international law] is normally presented as a clash between dualism (or pluralism) and monism. Both these schools of thought assume that there is a common field in which the international and municipal legal orders can operate simultaneously in regard to the same subject-matter, and the problem then is, which is to be master? It is at once obvious that when the issue is taken up in this form a limit has already been set to the controversy and certain solutions ruled out. Dualist doctrine points to the essential difference of international law and municipal law, consisting primarily in the fact that the two systems regulate different subject-matter. International law is a law between sovereign states: municipal law applies within a state and regulates the relations of its citizens with each other and with the executive. On this view neither legal order has the power to create or alter rules of the other. When municipal law provides that international law applies in whole or in part within the jurisdiction, this is merely an exercise of the authority of municipal law, an adoption or transformation of the rules of international law. In case of a conflict between international law and municipal law the dualist would assume that a municipal court would apply municipal law.

Monism is represented by a number of jurists whose theories diverge in significant respects. In the United Kingdom Hersch Lauterpacht has been a forceful exponent of the doctrine. In his hands the theory has been no mere intellectual construction, and in his work monism takes the form of an assertion of the supremacy of international law even within the municipal sphere, coupled with well-developed views on the individual as a subject of international law. Such a doctrine is antipathetic to the legal corollaries of the existence of sovereign states, and reduces municipal law to the status of pensioner of international law. The state is disliked as an abstraction and distrusted as a vehicle for maintaining human rights: international law, like municipal law, is ultimately concerned with the conduct and welfare of individuals. International law is seen as the best available moderator of human affairs, and also as a logical condition of the *legal* existence of states and therefore of the municipal systems of law within the sphere of the legal competence of states.[oo]

---

oo. Brownlie subsequently adds, at 33: "There is also a monist-naturalist theory, which, superficially at least, resembles Kelsen's provision of a universal basic norm. According to this theory the international and municipal legal orders are subordinate to a third legal order, usually postulated in terms of natural law or 'general principles of law,' superior to both and capable of determining their respective spheres."

EDITORS' NOTE

The fact is, as international law scholar Edwin A. Borchard once wrote in *The Relation Between International Law and Municipal Law*, 27 Va. L. Rev. 137, 140 (1940), both the monist and dualist schools regarding the interrelation of national and international law are "partly right and partly wrong." Borchard continued:

> The error of each school appears to lie in the unwillingness to admit a principle of coordination between the two systems. They do have a relation and an easily established one. Although it is true that international law is addressed to States as entities, it exerts a command upon law-abiding States not to depart from its precepts, subject to international responsibility. The domestic instruments that the State employs to perform its international obligations are a matter of indifference to international law. It may employ statute or administrative official or judicial control. It may directly incorporate international law into the local system, or it may incorporate only treaties and not customary law. Its failure to enact the necessary implementing legislation or law may impose upon it international responsibility, as in the case of the *Alabama* claims. On the other hand, should its local legislation arrogate to itself privileges not permitted by international law, it will be bound either to make restitution or to pay damages through arbitration or diplomacy.

> In the United States the courts are by the Constitution bound to give effect to treaties which even an aggrieved individual may invoke. In England, the rule is different, for there treaties must be adopted or converted into legislation before they become invocable in the courts. But in both cases the treaty is binding on the nation and will be enforced, notwithstanding a conflicting municipal statute, by such instrumentalities as international law possesses. The American courts, like the English, are said to consider international law a part of the law of the land. And this is true, for international law will in principle be enforced directly in the municipal courts provided there is not statute *contra*. Where a reconciliation between international law and municipal law is possible, the courts will make it. Where there is a statute which conflicts with international law, instances of which will presently be noted, the courts must perforce give effect to the statute even as against the treaty, provided the treaty is earlier in time. But this merely indicates that the municipal economy or administration is so arranged that the enforcement of the international obligation is vested not in the courts but in a different department. This phenomenon has led to the inference that the municipal law enforceable in the courts prevails over a contrary rule of international law, which is enforceable by the Executive at the initiative of the aggrieved foreigner or his government. But this merely means that the courts have no local authority to give effect to international law *when it conflicts with municipal statute*, but that such function is vested in this country in the Secretary of State, who is the agent of the American people for the enforcement of international law. The rule that finally prevails on the American people is the rule of international law as evidenced in the taxes they may have to pay to make good the aberrations of the municipal statute.

Id. at 143–45.

Myres S. McDougal, arguably the preeminent international law theorist of the last half of the Twentieth Century, has given theoretical expression to Borchard's observations as follows:

From the perspective of our recommended conception of law, both international and national, as a process of authoritative decision, the problem of the impact of international law upon national law may now be given a much sharper focus. The problem is not, as the Austinians think, one of determining a relationship between mere rules of international morality and exclusive sovereign command; or, as the dualists think, of achieving some kind of logical explanation of how absolutely sovereign states can be subordinated to, or coordinated by, "binding" international rules; or, as the monists think, of demonstrating the common "validity" of a hierarchy of rules by syntactical derivations from the top of a rule pyramid downward or from the bottom upward. The problem is rather one of the reciprocal impact or interaction, in the world of operations as well as of words, of interpenetrating processes of international and national authority and control. The relevant hierarchies, if hierarchies are relevant, are not of rules but of entire social and power processes. The world power process as a whole may indeed perhaps be insightfully viewed as a complex hierarchy of power processes of varying degrees of comprehension (global, hemispheric, regional, national, local), with the more comprehensive affecting "inward" or "downward" the less comprehensive, and the latter in turn affecting "outward" or "upward" the former. The metaphor of "nesting" tables or cups might be apt if such tables and cups could be conceived as being in process of constant interaction and change. On the level of formal authority, there is in the power processes a thorough, continuing interpenetration of decision-makers, structures of interaction, and demanded policies, with the officials of international authority, for example, often acting in the arenas of national authority, and vice versa. On the level of effective power, of the factors which actually shape authoritative decision, it is a common-place that individuals, private associations, parties, and pressure groups being their base values to bear upon all levels of authority, and with little respect for state boundaries. The important questions are: how, and with what access to decision by interested participants, are inclusive policies, purporting to express a common interest, actually prescribed in the world arena for regulating the practices of states; what balance between the inclusive competence of the general community of states and the exclusive competence of particular states, in terms of control over interactions assigned to each, is in fact established by such prescription; in what degree, and by what practices, are inclusively prescribed policies effectively applied in action, in external and internal arenas, to regulate states both in their external strategies and in their internal policies; and, finally, how compatible are the aggregate effects achieved, by the impact of international upon national processes of authority, with shared values of human dignity?

Myres S. McDougal, *The Impact of International Law Upon National Law: A Policy-Oriented Perspective* 4 S. Dak. L. Rev. 25, 37–38 (1959), *reprinted in* Myres S. McDougal & Associates, Studies in World Public Order 157, 171–72 (1960).

Accurate though Borchard and McDougal are in describing the "real world" in which we live, the monist and dualist approaches to the interrelation of national and international law nevertheless find formal expression in the constitutive orders of many modern legal systems. Three examples follow.

A. *The monist approach to the relationship between national and international law*, prevalent in civil law countries that borrow heavily from the German legal experience, is illustrated by Articles 24–26 of the Basic Law for the Federal Republic of Germany (especially Article 25), as quoted in 6 Constitutions of the Countries of the World 50 (A. Blaustein & G. Flanz eds, 1985):

Art. 24

(1) The Federation may, by legislation, transfer sovereign powers to inter-governmental institutions.

(2) For the maintenance of peace, the Federation may enter a system of mutual collective security; in doing so it will consent to such limitations upon its rights of sovereignty as will bring about and secure a peaceful and lasting order in Europe and among the nations of the world.

(3) For the settlement of disputes between states, the Federation will accede to agreements concerning a general, comprehensive and obligatory system of international arbitration.

Art. 25

The general rules of public international law are an integral part of federal law. They shall take precedence over the laws and shall directly create rights and duties for the inhabitants of the federal territory.

Art. 26

(1) Acts tending and undertaken with the intent to disturb the peaceful relation between nations, especially to prepare for aggressive war, are unconstitutional. They shall be made a punishable offence.

(2) Weapons designed for warfare may not be manufactured, transported or issued except with the permission of the Federal Government. Details shall be regulated by a federal law.

B. *The dualist approach to the relationship between national and international law*, manifest in the United Kingdom and elsewhere in The Commonwealth where the Common Law prevails, is more or less illustrated by Australian law. We quote from Chapter 6 ("Treaties and Domestic Law") of Report by the Senate Legal and Constitutional References Committee of the Parliament of the Commonwealth of Australia, Trick or Treaty? Commonwealth Power to Make and Implement Treaties 86–95 (November 1995):

6.1   It has been generally accepted that treaties are not *directly* incorporated into Australian domestic law by the international act of ratification or accession by Australia. Treaties therefore do not run in domestic law unless implemented by legislation. This view has been shared by successive Governments of different political persuasions.

* * *

6.3   However, there have been important developments in recent years on the relationship between domestic law and international treaties. The submission of the Attorney–General's Department noted that treaties may have some *indirect* influence on Australian domestic law prior to their implementation through legislation.

6.4   In *Mabo v Queensland (No. 2)*, Justice Brennan stated:

The opening up of international remedies to individuals pursuant to Australia's accession to the Optional Protocol to the International Covenant on Civil and Political Rights brings to bear on the common law the powerful influence of the Covenant and the international standards it imports. The common law does not necessarily conform with international law, but international law is a legitimate and important influence on the development of the common law, especially when international law declares the existence of universal human rights.[9]

6.5   The Attorney–General's Department's submission to the Committee also discerned the following role for treaties from statements made by High Court Justices in the case of *Dietrich v The Queen*:

> Dietrich's case illustrates that treaties, particularly those dealing with human rights, can be used
>
> ● to resolve uncertainty or ambiguity in the common law;
>
> ● to support review of earlier decisions and then possibly their overruling; and
>
> ● to assist in the determination of community values and standards relevant to the development of the common law.[10]

6.6   The Hon. Elizabeth Evatt, former Chief Justice of the Family Court, made the following comments in relation to treaties, customary international law and the common law of Australia:

> Quite apart from conventions that Australia ratifies, some parts of that international law can, as a matter of common law, apply in Australia without any further action on the part of anyone. I think the recent High Court case of Teoh may have referred obliquely to this, but it could have said more about the fact that under common law, customary rules, and particularly principles of human rights, such as the principle against genocide and so on, are part of customary international law. Naturally as such, they can be overruled by legislation, as any part of the common law can. But we should not think of international law as being an entirely separate thing from the law of Australia. Some parts of it we would recognise.[11]

Teoh's case

6.7   A further *indirect* effect of treaties on Australian law was identified by the High Court in *Minister for Immigration and Ethnic Affairs v Teoh*.[12] The High Court held (by majority of 4:1) that ratification of an international convention by the Executive can create a legitimate expectation that the Executive will act in accordance with the convention:

> [R]atification of a convention is a positive statement by the Executive Government of this country to the world and to the Australian people that the Executive Government and its agencies will act in accordance with the Convention. That positive statement is an adequate formulation for a legitimate expectation, absent statutory or executive indications to the contrary, that administrative decision-makers will act in conformity with the Convention. . . .

* * *

6.9   *Teoh's* case does not alter the basic legal proposition that treaties are not *directly* incorporated into domestic law until they have been legislatively implemented:

9.   (1992) 175 C.L.R. 1, at 42.

10. Mr. H. Burmester, Submission No. 75, Vol. 4, p. 703.

11. *Hansard*, SLCRC, 16 May 1995, p. 379, per the Hon. E. Evatt.

12. (1995) 128 A.L.R. 353.

it is well established that the provisions of an international treaty to which Australia is a party do not form part of Australian law unless these provisions have been validly incorporated into our municipal law by statute. . . . This principle has its foundation in the proposition that in our constitutional system the making and ratification of treaties fall within the province of the Executive in the exercise of its prerogative power whereas the making and the alteration of the law fall within the province of parliament, not the Executive. . . . So, a treaty which has not been incorporated in our municipal law cannot operate as a direct source of individual rights and obligations under the law. In this case, it is common ground that the provisions of the convention have not been incorporated in this way.[13]

6.10   It has been argued by some, however, that the *indirect* effect of treaties on Australian law, as recognized by the High Court in *Teoh's* case, is so significant that it is undermining the rule of the Parliament as the only body which can *directly* implement treaties by way of legislation.

* * *

Government's response to Teoh's case

Press Release

6.13   On 10 May 1995, the Minister for Foreign Affairs, Senator Gareth Evans, and the Attorney–General, Michael Lavarch, published a joint press release on the *Teoh* case.

6.14   In their press release, the Ministers were critical of the potential consequence of the *Teoh* decision. They stated:

It may be only a small number of the approximately 920 treaties to which Australia is currently a party could provide a source for an expectation of the kind found by the High Court to arise in *Teoh*. But that can only be established as individual cases come to be litigated. In the meantime, the High Court decision gives little if any guidance on how decision-makers are to determine which of those treaty provisions will be relevant and to what decisions the provisions might be relevant, and because of the wide range and large number of decisions potentially affected by the decision, a great deal of uncertainty has been introduced into government activity. It is not in anybody's interests to allow such uncertainty to continue.[14]

6.15   The Ministers then stated that the fact that the Government enters into a treaty should not create an expectation that the Government and its officials will comply with Australia's treaty obligations. They announced:

We state on behalf of the Government, that entering into an international treaty is not reason for raising any expectation that government decision-makers will act in accordance with the treaty if the relevant provisions of that treaty have not been enacted into domestic Australian law. It is not legitimate, for the purpose of applying Australian law, to expect that the provisions of a treaty not incorporated by legislation should be applied by decision-makers. Any expectation that may arise

13. (1995) 128 A.L.R. 353 per Mason CJ and Denne J at 361–2. . . .

14. Joint Statement by the Minister for Foreign Affairs, Senator Gareth Evans, and the Attorney–General, Michael Lavarch, *International Treaties and the High Court Decision in Teoh*, 10 May 1995.

does not provide a ground for review of a decision. This is so, both for existing treaties and for future treaties that Australia may join.[pp]

6.16   The Ministers concluded, however, that this statement should not be taken as derogating from Australia's international obligations:

> We should emphasise that the Government remains fully committed to observing its treaty obligations. However, we believe it is appropriate to retain the long-standing, widely accepted and well-understood distinction between treaty action undertaken by the Executive which creates international rights and obligations and the implementation of treaty obligations in Australian law. The implementation of treaties by legislation is the way that the rights, benefits, and obligations set out in treaties to which Australia is a party are conferred or imposed on individuals in Australian law.[qq]

Administrative Decisions (Effect of International Instruments) Bill 1995

6.17   The Government reinforced its press release by introducing the *Administrative Decisions (Effect of International Instruments) Bill 1995* into the House of Representatives on 28 June 1995. The primary provision in the Bill is clause 5. It provides:

> The fact that Australia is bound by, or a party to, a particular international instrument, or that an enactment reproduces or refers to a particular international instrument, does not give rise to a legitimate expectation, on the part of any person, that:
>
> (a) an administrative decision will be made in conformity with the requirements of that instrument; or
>
> (b) if the decision were to be made contrary to any of those requirements, any person affected by the decision would be given notice and an adequate opportunity to present a case against the taking of such a course.

[*Eds.*—This legislation was never enacted. Similar legislation was introduced by the subsequent Coalition government in 1997, but at presstime for this coursebook, it had not been adopted.]

Criticism of the Government's response

6.18   The Committee received both evidence and submissions from a number of people, who were critical of the Government's response to the *Teoh* case, including two submissions from the President of the Human Rights and Equal Opportunity Commission. The Committee also received submissions supporting the Government's response.

* * *

Conclusion

6.26   Treaties are not directly incorporated into Australian law by the act of ratification or accession. Nevertheless, they can play an important role in a number of areas even when not incorporated into domestic law, particularly:

- in the development of the common law; and
- in influencing decision-makers at all levels of Government (particularly in relation to human rights treaties).

pp. *Id.*   **qq.** *Id.*

6.27   The *Teoh* decision and the reaction to it demonstrates the increasing impact that treaties have in Australia. This increasing impact of treaties is, in itself, reason for greater parliamentary involvement prior to the ratification of treaties. . . .

6.28   In particular, the reaction to the *Teoh* case has demonstrated a concern about the effect of treaties on Australian sovereignty.

[*Eds.*— The United Kingdom's approach to international law has been significantly altered in the area of human rights by the enactment of the Human Rights Act in 1998. This legislation effectively incorporates the European Convention on Human Rights into the law of the United Kingdom, although it allows Parliament to override the Convention.]

C.   A *mixed dualist-monist approach to the interrelation of national and international law* is illustrated by Article VI(2) of the United States Constitution, which reads as follows:

> This Constitution, and the Laws of the United States which shall be made in Pursuance thereof; and all Treaties made, or which shall be made, under the Authority of the United States, shall be the supreme Law of the Land; and the Judges in every State shall be bound thereby, any Thing in the Constitution or Laws of any State to the Contrary notwithstanding.

This mixed approach in the constitutive order of the United States, however, making treaties automatically part of "the supreme Law of the Land" but giving them no greater status than the Constitution or acts of Congress, tilts operationally in a dualist direction. The readings in subsections (a) and (b), immediately following, illustrate this point.

(a) The Impact of International Agreements Upon United States Law

BURNS H. WESTON, "TREATY POWER"

6 Encyclopedia of the American Constitution 2721–22
(L. Levy, K. Karst & D.Mahoney eds., 2d ed. 2000)

To enhance the pledged word of the United States in foreign relations, the Framers of the Constitution granted to the President, in cooperation with the Senate, the power to make and enter into treaties. They also provided that this power should vest exclusively in the federal government. The Framers neglected to define the term "treaty," however, leaving its meaning to subsequent clarification. Today, under ... United States law, the term "treaty" usually denotes only those international agreements that are concluded by the federal government and ratified by the President upon receiving the advice and consent of the Senate. All other international agreements— executive agreements, for example—are brought into force for the United States upon a constitutional basis other than senatorial advice and consent.

The process of treaty making involves negotiation, signature, ratification, exchange of instruments of ratification, publication, and proclamation; but, other than prescribing that two-thirds of the senators present must give their advice and consent to the ratification of a treaty, the Constitution is silent on the subject. In the early days of the Republic, it was thought that the Senate would participate with the President by giving its advice and consent at every negotiating juncture. Today, it is the accepted practice for the President to solicit the advice and consent of the Senate only after a treaty has been negotiated and signed, although in many—especially important—instances, Senate and even House committees play active roles in advance of the conclusion of a treaty, sometimes on their own initiative, sometimes at the behest of the executive branch.

Once the negotiation of a treaty is complete, the President decides whether to sign the treaty and, if so, whether to submit it to the Senate for advice and consent to ratification. If the Senate is perceived as hostile, the President may choose to let the treaty die rather than suffer defeat. If the Senate receives the treaty, it refers the treaty to the Committee on Foreign Relations, which may or may not report the treaty to the full Senate for its advice and consent. Committee inaction is the usual method for withholding consent to controversial treaties. Sometimes the executive branch will request that the committee withhold or suspend action. Few treaties are defeated by direct vote of the full Senate.

After the Senate gives its advice and consent to ratification, often subject to "reservations," "understandings," and "declarations" initiated by the Senate or the executive branch itself (to clarify, alter, or amend the treaty), the treaty is returned to the President for ratification. The President may choose to ratify the treaty or to return it to the Senate for further consideration. The President also may choose not to ratify the treaty at that time.

After a treaty is ratified, which is a national act, some international act—typically the exchange or deposit of instruments of ratification—usually is required to bring the treaty into force. Also upon ratification, the President issues a proclamation making the treaty officially public. There is disagreement over whether proclamation of a treaty is constitutionally required before the treaty takes effect domestically, but it is the norm to issue such a proclamation which, in any event, is useful in determining the date on which the treaty enters into force.

The Constitution does not limit the treaty power explicitly. Moreover, no treaty or treaty provision has ever been held unconstitutional. Nevertheless, it is generally agreed that such limitations exist. For example, the Supreme Court held, in *Reid v. Covert* (1957),[rr] that treaties may not contravene any constitutional prohibition, such as those of the Bill of Rights or in the Thirteenth, Fourteenth, and Fifteenth Amendments. Further, although *Missouri v. Holland* (1920)[ss] largely disposed of the argument that the subject matter of treaties is limited by the Tenth Amendment, it remains possible, as the Court hinted in *De Geofroy v. Riggs* (1890),[tt] that the treaty power may be limited by "restraints . . . arising from the nature . . . of the states."

Beyond these limitations, however, the treaty power is perceived as a broad power, extending to all matters of "international concern," a phrase that some claim limits the treaty power, but that the courts have used to illustrate the power's broad scope. Ordinarily it is difficult to show that a treaty matter is not of international concern even in the presence of domestic effects.

rr. 354 U.S. 1 (1957).   **tt.** 133 U.S. 258 (1890).
ss. 252 U.S. 416 (1920).

In addition to granting the power to make and enter into treaties, the Framers of the Constitution provided that resulting treaties, together with the duly enacted laws of the United States, should constitute part of the "supreme law of the land." Thus, as well as giving rise to international legal obligations, treaties have force as domestic law, to be applied as federal statutes and consequently to prevail at all times over inconsistent state laws (assuming no conflict with the Constitution).

Still, not all treaties are automatically binding on American courts. Aside from the general constitutionality requirement, two additional conditions must obtain for treaties to have domestic effect. First, a treaty must not conflict with a subsequent act of Congress. This is in keeping with the judiciary's interpretation of the supremacy clause, ranking treaties and acts of Congress equally and therefore ruling that the law later in time prevails. With the sole exception of *Cook v. United States* (1933),[uu] cases in this area have involved conflicts between an earlier treaty and a later statute, with the latter prevailing. The courts presume, however, that Congress does not intend to supersede treaties, and consequently the courts are disposed toward interpretations that will achieve compatibility between treaties and federal statutes on the same subject.[vv]

Second, for a treaty to bind courts it must be "self-executing" or, alternatively, "non-self-executing" but supported by enabling legislation. Such was the holding in *Foster v. Neilson* (1829).[ww] Judicial decisions vary widely in their application of this requirement, however. The distinction between "self-executing" and "non-self-executing" treaties is more easily stated than applied. A determination that a treaty fits one category or the other may be shown to depend on subjective, at times political, considerations.

Although the Constitution is silent on the question of who has the power to suspend or terminate treaties and under what circumstances, it is generally accepted that the President has such power, *without* the advice and consent of the Senate, based on the President's established constitutional authority to conduct the foreign affairs of the United States. A challenge to the President's authority in this connection has thus far arisen only in the one case of *Goldwater v. Carter* (1979),[xx] and that case was decided, on purely jurisdictional grounds, against the challenge. . . .

Burns H. Weston, "Executive Agreements"

2 Encyclopedia of the American Constitution 939–40
(L. Levy, K. Karst & D. Mahoney eds., 2d ed. 2000)

Executive agreements—that is, international agreements concluded between heads of state or their representatives, commonly without the necessity

---

uu. 288 U.S. 102 (1933).

vv. There are at least two exceptions to the "last in time" rule, one limiting and the other reinforcing the impact of international agreements within the United States. First, it has been held not to validate an *executive* agreement which, though last in time, was found to conflict with a substantive Federal statute. Seery v. United States, 127 F.Supp. 601 (Ct. Claims 1955). And second, pursuant to Article VI(2) of the Constitution **(Basic Document** 1.1)**, it has been shown not to operate in the case of state or local legislation, thereby giving effect to constitutionally valid treaties even when they pre-date the conflicting state or local laws, and even, indeed, when they are found to be "non-self-executing." Asakura v. City of Seattle, 265 U.S. 332 (1924).

ww. 27 U.S. 253 (1829).

xx. 481 F. Supp. 949 (D.D.C.1979).

of parliamentary approval—are nowhere explicitly authorized in the Constitution. The Constitution is silent about international agreement-making except as it vests in the President, in cooperation with the Senate, the power to make and enter into treaties. Nevertheless the principle has long been established that the capacity of the United States to negotiate and enter into international agreements is not exhausted by the treaty power. . . .

The expression "executive agreement," which is not widely used outside the United States but which has its equivalents abroad, is understood by the Department of State to refer, in general, to any international agreement brought into force relative to the United States without the advice and consent of the Senate that is constitutionally required for treaties. In particular, it is understood to refer to three kinds of agreements: those made pursuant to, or in accordance with, an existing treaty; those made subject to congressional approval or implementation ("congressional-executive agreements"); and those made under, and in accordance with, the President's constitutional powers ("sole executive agreements"). None of these executive agreements is subject to the formal treaty-making process specified in Article II, section 2, clause 2, of the Constitution.

A treaty-based executive agreement, provided that it is within the intent, scope, and subject matter of the parent treaty, has the same validity and effect as the treaty itself and is subject to the same constitutional limitations. Deriving from one of the elements of "the supreme law of the land," it takes precedence over all inconsistent state laws and follows the customary rule favoring the instrument later in time in case of inconsistency with a federal statute. A conspicuous example of a treaty-based executive agreement is the traditional *compromis* defining the terms of submission to adjudication or arbitration under a basic convention. Another is found in the hundreds of status of forces agreements and other agreements required to carry out the North Atlantic Treaty, the linchpin of United States policy in Europe since World War II.

A congressional-executive agreement is based on either a prior or a subsequent act of Congress authorizing the making of the agreement or providing general authority for the executive action needed internationally to implement the legislation in question. The scope or subject matter of the agreement is the same whether the congressional act comes before or after the negotiation of the agreement: the act of Congress often takes the form of an authorization to enter into or effectuate an agreement already negotiated. In principle, however, the agreement must reside within the joint powers of Congress or the President in order to have constitutional validity. An agreement outside the legal competence of Congress or the President, authorities generally agree, would be unconstitutional. On the other hand, as the American Law Institute has commented, "the source of authority to make a congressional-executive agreement may be broader even than the sum of the respective powers of Congress and the President," and "in international matters the President and Congress together have all the powers of the United States inherent in its sovereignty and nationhood and can therefore make any international agreement on any subject."[yy] In any event, partly out

yy. 1 Restatement (Third) of the Foreign   porters' note 7 (1987).
Relations Law of the United States § 303 re-

of a concern to check and balance the President in the conduct of foreign affairs, the vast majority of executive agreements entered into by the United States ... are of this type. Like its treaty-based counterpart, deriving from one of the elements of "the supreme law of the land," the congressional-executive agreement supersedes all inconsistent state law and follows the customary rule favoring the instrument later in time in case of inconsistency with a federal statute.

Sole executive agreements are international agreements entered into by the President without reference to a treaty or statutory authority, that is, exclusively on the basis of the President's constitutional powers as chief executive and commander-in-chief, responsible for United States foreign relations and military affairs. Department of State records indicate that only a small percentage of executive agreements are of this type and that the great majority have dealt with essentially routine diplomatic and military matters. Accordingly, with relatively minor exception ..., they have had little direct impact upon private interests and therefore have given rise to little domestic litigation. However, in part out of fear that the President might undertake by international agreement what would be unconstitutional by statute, as in fact occurred in *Missouri v. Holland* (1920),[zz] such agreements have not been free of controversy. Two issues in particular stand out.

First there is the question, not yet conclusively settled, of whether Congress may legislate to prohibit or otherwise limit sole executive agreements. Although comprehensive limitations on such agreements ... have so far failed to be adopted, Congress has nonetheless occasionally restricted presidential authority in ways that appear to preclude some executive agreements.... The validity of such restrictions upon presidential authority has been challenged by Presidents and has yet to be determined by the Supreme Court.

Second, while it is widely accepted that the President, under the "executive power" clause, has the authority to conclude sole executive agreements that are not inconsistent with legislation in areas where Congress has primary responsibility, there is a question as to whether the President alone may make an agreement inconsistent with an act of Congress or, alternatively, whether a sole executive agreement may supersede earlier inconsistent congressional legislation. The prevailing view, rooted in the belief that it would be unconscionable for an act of a single person—the President—to repeal an act of Congress, is that sole executive agreements are inoperative as law in the United States to the extent that they conflict with a prior act of Congress in an area of congressional competence. This is the position taken by a federal appeals court in *United States v. Guy W. Capps, Inc.* (4th Circuit, 1953)[aaa] and by the American Law Institute. The Supreme Court has not yet rendered a definitive decision in these respects, however.

The foregoing two issues aside, there is broad agreement about the scope and effect of sole executive agreements as a matter of constitutional law. Like the other two kinds of executive agreements, they are subject to the same

zz. *Supra* note **ss.**   **aaa.** 204 F.2d 655 (4th Cir.1953), *affirmed on other grounds*, 348 U.S. 296 (1955).

limitations applicable to treaties, they are not limited by the Tenth Amendment, and they supersede all inconsistent state law.[bbb]

(b) Customary International Law Before United States Courts

The following two cases outline in broad fashion the role of customary international law before American courts.

"THE PAQUETE HABANA, THE LOLA"

175 U.S. 677, 20 S. Ct. 290, 44 L. Ed. 320 (1900)

Mr. Justice GRAY delivered the opinion of the Court.

These are two appeals from decrees of the District Court of the United States for the Southern District of Florida, condemning two fishing vessels and their cargoes as prize of war.

Each vessel was a fishing smack, running in and out of Havana, and regularly engaged in fishing on the coast of Cuba; sailed under the Spanish flag; was owned by a Spanish subject of Cuban birth, living in the city of Havana; was commanded by a subject of Spain, also residing in Havana; and her master and crew had no interest in the vessel, but were entitled to shares, amounting in all to two thirds, of her catch, the other third belonging to her owner. Her cargo consisted of fresh fish, caught by her crew from the sea, put on board as they were caught, and kept and sold alive. Until stopped by the blockading squadron, she had no knowledge of the existence of the war, or of any blockade. She had no arms or ammunition on board, and made no attempt to run the blockade after she knew of its existence, nor any resistance at the time of the capture.

* * *

Both the fishing vessels were brought by their captors into Key West. A libel for the condemnation of each vessel and her cargo as prize of war was there filed on April 27, 1898; ... and on May 30, 1898, a final decree of condemnation and sale was entered, "the court not being satisfied that as a matter of law, without any ordinance, treaty or proclamation, fishing vessels of this class are exempt from seizure."

* * *

We are then brought to the consideration of the question whether, upon the facts appearing in these records, the fishing smacks were subject to capture by the armed vessels of the United States during the recent war with Spain.

By an ancient usage among civilized nations, beginning centuries ago, and gradually ripening into a rule of international law, coast fishing vessels, pursuing their vocation of catching and bringing in fresh fish, have been recognized as exempt, with their cargoes and crews, from capture as prize of war.

bbb. *See, e.g.,* United States v. Belmont, 301 U.S. 324 (1937); United States v. Pink, 315 U.S. 203 (1942).

This doctrine, however, has been earnestly contested at the bar; and no complete collection of the instances illustrating it is to be found, so far as we are aware, in a single published work, although many are referred to and discussed by the writers on international law.... It is therefore worth the while to trace the history of the rule, from the earliest accessible sources, through the increasing recognition of it, with occasional setbacks, to what we may now justly consider as its final establishment in our own country and generally throughout the civilized world.

[The Court then proceeds to review the history of the rule through a lengthy examination of State practice, beginning with the issuance of orders by Henry IV to his admirals in 1403 and 1406. It recites that France, Spain, Holland, England, Prussia, the United States, Japan, and other States had long followed the custom of exempting enemy fishing vessels from capture, even in the absence of treaties, although there sometimes had been exceptions to this custom. Referring to Lord Stowell's decision in *The Young Jacob and Johanna* (1798), 1 C. Rob 20, the Court went on:]

But some expressions in his opinion have been given so much weight by English writers, that it may be well to examine them particularly. The opinion begins by admitting the known custom in former wars not to capture such vessels—however, "but this was a rule of comity only, and not of legal decision." Assuming the phrase "legal decision" to have been there used, in the sense in which courts are accustomed to use it, as equivalent to "judicial decision," it is true that, so far as appears, there had been no such decision on the point in England. The word "comity" was apparently used by Lord Stowell as synonymous with courtesy or good will. But the period of a hundred years which has since elapsed is amply sufficient to have enabled what originally may have rested in custom or comity, courtesy or concession, to grow, by the general assent of civilized nations, into a settled rule of international law....

International law is part of our law, and must be ascertained and administered by the courts of justice of appropriate jurisdiction, as often as questions of right depending upon it are duly presented for their determination. For this purpose, where there is no treaty, and no controlling executive or legislative act or judicial decision, resort must be had to the customs and usages of civilized nations; and, as evidence of these, to the works of jurists and commentators, who by years of labor, research and experience, have made themselves peculiarly well acquainted with the subjects of which they treat. Such works are resorted to by judicial tribunals, not for the speculations of their authors concerning what the law ought to be, but for trustworthy evidence of what the law really is. *Hilton v. Guyot*, 159 U.S. 113, 163, 164, 214, 215.

Wheaton places among the principal sources of international law, "Text-writers of authority, showing what is the approved usage of nations, or the general opinion respecting their mutual conduct, with the definitions and modifications introduced by general consent."

As to these he forcibly observes: "Without wishing to exaggerate the importance of these writers, or to substitute, in any case, their authority for the principles of reason, it may be affirmed that they are generally impartial in their judgment. They are witnesses of the sentiments and usages of civilized nations, and the weight of their testimony increases every time that their authority is invoked by statesmen, and every year that passes without the rules laid down in their works being impugned by the avowal of contrary principles." Wheaton's International Law, (8th ed.) § 15.

Chancellor Kent says: "In the absence of higher and more authoritative sanctions, the ordinances of foreign States, the opinions of eminent statesmen, and the writings of distinguished jurists, are regarded as of great consideration on questions not settled by conventional law. In cases where the principal jurists agree, the presumption will be very great in favor of the solidity of their maxims; and no civilized nation, that does not arrogantly set all ordinary law and justice at defiance, will venture to disregard the uniform sense of the established writers on international law." 1 Kent Com. 18.

[The Court then reviews the opinions of French, Argentine, English, German, Swiss, Dutch, Austrian, Spanish, Portuguese, and Italian writers on international law, and thereafter continues.]

This review of the precedents and authorities on the subject appears to us abundantly to demonstrate that at the present day, by the general consent of the civilized nations of the world, and independently of any express treaty or other public act, it is an established rule of international law, founded on considerations of humanity to a poor and industrious order of men, and of the mutual convenience of belligerent States, that coast fishing vessels, with their implements and supplies, cargoes and crews, unarmed, and honestly pursuing their peaceful calling of catching and bringing in fresh fish, are exempt from capture as prize of war.

The exemption, of course, does not apply to coast fishermen or their vessels, if employed for a warlike purpose, or in such a way as to give aid or information to the enemy; nor when military or naval operations create a necessity to which all private interests must give way.

* * *

This rule of international law is one which prize courts, administering the law of nations, are bound to take judicial notice of, and to give effect to, in the absence of any treaty or other public act of their own government in relation to the matter.

* * *

Upon the facts proved in either case, it is the duty of this court, sitting as the highest prize court of the United States, and administering the law of nations, to declare and adjudge that the capture was unlawful, and without probable cause; and it is therefore, in each case,

Ordered, that the decree of the District Court be reversed, and the proceeds of the sale of the vessel, together with the proceeds of any sale of her cargo, be restored to the claimant, with damages and costs.

[Eds.—Mr. Chief Justice FULLER with whom concurred Mr. Justice HARLAN and Mr. Justice McKENNA, dissented on the ground that the practice of exempting enemy fishing vessels from capture had not become a customary rule of international law, but was only a rule of comity or courtesy and had not been authorized by the President.]

GARCIA-MIR, ET AL. V. MEESE, FERNANDEZ-ROQUE, ET AL. V. MEESE

788 F.2d 1446 (11th Cir.1986)

JOHNSON, Circuit Judge:

* * *

This is an appeal and cross-appeal from the final decision of the trial court ordering the government to prepare and implement a plan to provide individual parole revocation hearings for unadmitted aliens. The appellees-cross appellants ["appellees" or "aliens" or "Mariels"] are a certified class of Mariel Cuban refugees who were accorded a special immigration parole status by the Refugee Education Assistance Act of 1980. The district court has broken the class into two sub-classes. The "First Group" includes those who are guilty of crimes committed in Cuba before the boat-lift or who are mentally incompetent. They have never been paroled into this country. The "Second Group" consists of all other Mariels—those who, because there was no evidence of criminal or mental defect, were paroled under the provisions of the general alien parole statute, 8 U.S.C.A. 1182(d)(5) (1985) [*i.e.*, authorized to remain free in the United States pending resolution of their status], but whose parole was subsequently revoked. All are currently detained in the Atlanta Penitentiary.

* * *

B.   *International Law:*

The public law of nations was long ago incorporated into the common law of the United States. *The Paquete Habana*, 175 U.S. 677, 700 (1900); *The Nereide*, 13 U.S. (9 Cranch) 388, 423, 3 L. Ed. 769 (1815); *Restatement of the Law of Foreign Relations Law of the United States (Revised)* § 131 comment d (Tent. Draft No. 6, 1985) [hereinafter cited as "*Restatement* 6"]. To the extent possible, courts must construe American law so as to avoid violating principles of public international law. *Murray v. The Schooner Charming Betsy*, 6 U.S. (2 Cranch), 64, 102, 118 (1804); *Lauritzen v. Larsen*, 345 U.S. 571, 578 (1953). But public international law is controlling only "where there is no treaty and no controlling executive or legislative act or judicial decision. . . ." 175 U.S. at 700. Appellees argue that, because general principles of international law forbid prolonged arbitrary detention, we should hold that their current detention is unlawful.

We have previously determined that the general deportation statute, 8 U.S.C.A. 1227(a) (1985), does not restrict the power of the Attorney General to detain aliens indefinitely. *Fernandez–Roque II*, 734 F.2d at 580 n.6. But this does not resolve the question whether there has been an affirmative legislative grant of authority to detain. As to the First Group there is sufficiently express evidence of congressional intent as to interdict the application of international law. Pub. L. No. 96–533, Title VII, § 716. 94 Stat. 3162 (1980), *reprinted at* 8 U.S.C.A. § 1522 note.

The trial court found, correctly, that there has been no affirmative legislative grant to the Justice Department to detain the Second Group without hearings because 8 U.S.C.A. § 1227(c) does not expressly authorize indefinite detention.... Thus we must look for a controlling executive act. The trial court found that there was such a controlling act in the Attorney General's termination of the status review plan and in his decision to incarcerate indefinitely pending efforts to deport.... The appellees and the *amicus*[ccc] challenge this by arguing that a controlling executive act can only come from an act by or expressly sanctioned by the President himself, not one of his subordinates.... They rely for that proposition upon *The Paquete Habana* and upon the *Restatement of the Law of Foreign Relations Law of the United States (Revised)* § 131 comment c (Tent. Draft No. 1, 1980) [hereinafter cited as "Restatement 1"].

As to *The Paquete Habana*, that case involved the capture and sale as war prize of several fishing boats during the Spanish–American War. The Supreme Court found this contrary to the dictates of international law. The *amicus* characterizes the facts of the case such that the Secretary of the Navy authorized the capture and that the Supreme Court held that this did not constitute a controlling executive act because it was not ordered by the President himself. This is a mischaracterization. After the capture of the two vessels at issue, an admiral telegraphed the Secretary for permission to seize fishing ships, to which the Secretary responded that only those vessels " 'likely to aid enemy may be detained.' " 175 U.S. at 713, 20 S. Ct. at 304. Seizing fishing boats aiding the enemy would be in obvious accord with international law. But the facts of *The Paquete Habana* showed the boats in question to be innocent of aiding the Spanish. The Court held that the ships were seized in violation of international law because they were used solely for fishing. It was the *admiral* who acted in excess of the clearly delimited authority granted by the Secretary, who instructed him to act only consistent with international law. Thus *The Paquete Habana* does not support the proposition that the acts of cabinet officers cannot constitute controlling executive acts. At best it suggests that lower level officials cannot by their acts render international law inapplicable. That is not an issue in this case, where the challenge is to the acts of the Attorney General.

As to the *Restatement* 1, the provision upon which *amicus* relies has been removed in subsequent drafts. The most recent version of that provision notes that the President, "acting within his constitutional authority, may have the power under the Constitution to act in ways that constitute violations of international law by the United States." The Constitution provides for the creation of executive departments, *US Const.* art. 2, § 2, and the power of the President to delegate his authority to those departments to act on his behalf is unquestioned.... Likewise, in *Restatement* 6, § 135 Reporter's Note 3, the power of the President to disregard international law in service of domestic needs is reaffirmed. Thus we hold that the executive acts here evident constitute a sufficient basis for affirming the trial court's finding that international law does not control.

Even if we were to accept, *arguendo*, the appellees' interpretation of "controlling executive act," *The Paquete Habana* also provides that the reach of international law will be interdicted by a controlling judicial decision....

---

ccc. The Lawyers Committee for Human Rights filed a brief as *amicus curiae* in support   of the appellees.

DISCUSSION NOTES/QUESTIONS

1.   "Nothing is more essential to a proper grasp of the subject of international law," writes Starke, *supra*, "than a clear understanding of its relation to State law." Do you agree? Why? Why not?

2.   With which of the three theories set forth in the above readings describing the relationship between international and municipal law do you most agree? Monism? Dualism? McDougal's "nesting cup" or "nesting table" theory? Which best reflects the "real world" as you perceive it?

3.   The foregoing readings bear witness to the fact that nation-states variously commit themselves to the domestic application of international law. For example, note the bold, wholesale incorporation of international law by the Basic Law (or Constitution) of the German Federal Republic, *supra*, and compare this with the provisions of the United States Constitution, *supra*, together with the language of the US Supreme Court in *The Paquete Habana, supra.* In general, by what means, through what decision-making institutions, and to what degree do nation-states give "binding force and effect" to international law domestically? Is their commitment satisfactory in this respect? Unsatisfactory? Why?

4.   Sometimes even a *treaty* ratified by a State will not be given "binding force and effect" within that State itself. In the United States, for example, a court can refuse to give domestic effect to a treaty on the grounds that the treaty is found to be unconstitutional. In addition, there has developed in American courts at least a distinction between treaties that are "self-executing" versus those that are "non-self-executing," the latter being not automatically binding on the courts.

But when is a treaty "self-executing" or, alternatively, "non-self-executing"? According to Chief Justice Marshall, "when the terms of the [treaty] stipulation import a contract—when either of the parties [have] engaged to perform a particular act—the treaty addresses itself to the political, not the judicial department; and the legislature must execute the contract before it can become a rule for the Court." *Foster v. Neilson*, 27 U.S. (2 Pet.) 253, 314, 7 L. Ed. 415 (1829). Thus, a treaty that requires no legislation to make it operative within the national legal order is said to be "self-executing." Yet this seemingly clear-cut distinction turns out to be more easily stated than applied. For example, in *Sei Fujii v. California*, 217 P. 2d 481 (1950), the California District Court of Appeals, citing Articles 1, 55, and 56 of the United Nations Charter **(Basic Document 1.5)** and Articles 1, 2, and 7 of the Universal Declaration of Human Rights **(Basic Document 3.3),** invalidated certain California land laws discriminating against aliens. On appeal, however, although reaching the same results on constitutional grounds, the California Supreme Court found that the UN Charter provisions (and by implication, those of the Universal Declaration) were *not* "self-executing." *Sei Fujii v. California*, 38 Cal. 2d 718, 242 P. 2d 617 (1952). Stated Chief Justice Gibson, *id*. at 724, "they [the UN Charter provisions] are framed as a promise of future action by the member nations." Significantly, the US Supreme Court never has addressed the question of whether the UN Charter's human rights provisions are "self-executing" or not. What would you recommend to the Supreme Court if it ever should have the occasion to decide this question?

Consider, for example, Article 56 of the Charter of the United Nations requiring member states "to take joint and separate action in cooperation with the [United Nations] for the achievement of the purposes set forth in Article 55, among them "universal respect for, and observance of, human rights and fundamental freedoms for all without distinction as to race, sex, language, or religion." Is Article 56 self-executing? If a nation fails to implement Article 56, are not the "human rights and fundamental freedoms" invoked in Article 55 illusory for the people in that nation? For further thoughtful inquiry into the distinction between self-executing and non-self-executing treaties before United States courts, see John H. Jackson, *Status of Treaties in Domestic Legal Systems: A Policy Analysis*, 86 A.J.I.L. 310 (1992); Nicholas Quinn Rosenkranz, *Executing the Treaty Power*, 118 Harv. L. Rev. 1867 (2005).

Consider also the International Covenant on Civil and Political Rights **(Basic Document 3.14)** to which the United States is a party. Will it pass muster with the US Supreme Court? Consider Article 5 if and when it ever should get to the Court. Additionally, can you speculate as to what attitude the Court might take were it to have the "self-executing"/"non-self-executing" issue of the UN Charter's human rights provisions presented to it? What factors would have to be taken into account? Purely "legal" factors?

Not all states have to grapple with the issue of whether a treaty is self-executing or non-self-executing. As demonstrated by the above readings illustrating the dualist approach to the relationship between national and international law *(supra* at 234–42), the law in some states is that generally a treaty must be adopted through legislation before it can have full domestic effect. This rule, and a number of narrow exceptions to it are discussed in James Crawford & William R. Edeson, *International Law and Australian Law, in* International Law in Australia 71 (K. Ryan ed., 2d ed. 1994). *See also* Fluid States: International Law in National legal Systems (H. Charlesworth, M. Chiam, D. Hovell & G. Williams eds., 2005). For useful comparative coverage of this issue, see Martin Dixon & Robert McCorquodale, Cases and Materials on International Law 140–45 (2d ed. 1995).

5.   Generally, statutes later in time repeal earlier statutes that address the same subject-matter. What is the theory or rationale behind this "last-in-time" rule, and should it apply as between treaties and statutes? Is it ever appropriate for the President or the Senate, as the treaty-makers in the United States, to alter the will of Congress by concluding a self-executing treaty that provides for different rules?

6.   Suppose a treaty were to be signed by the US President on March 1, given advice and consent to ratification by the Senate (perhaps after national elections) on July 1 of the following year, but contravened by a clearly intended conflicting act of Congress on October 1 of the year of signature. What result? Would the treaty be binding on the American courts? Consider Articles 11–18 of the Vienna Convention on the Law of Treaties **(Basic Document 1.10)**.

7.   In the words of Mr. Justice Gray in *The Paquete Habana, supra,* "[i]nternational law is part of our [United States] law, and ... where there is no treaty, and no controlling executive or legislative act or judicial decision, resort must be had [by American courts] to the customs and usages of civilized nations...." Thus, just as international tribunals, *stricto sensu,* look to "international custom, as evidence of a general practice accepted as law" (per Article 38 of the Statute of the International Court of Justice **(Basic Document 1.6)**, so also do American courts look to custom as a "source" of law for resolving transnational disputes. But to what extent? What latitude is left to an American court after all treaties, controlling executive or legislative acts, and judicial decisions have been taken into account? How might the qualifying language "no treaty and no controlling

executive or legislative act or judicial decision,"as discussed in *Garcia–Mir, supra*, impact upon the application of a customary international law rule by US courts?

8. In their dissents in *The Paquete Habana, supra*, Justices Fuller, Harlan, and McKenna contended that the majority applied not a rule of customary international law but, rather, a rule of "comity" or "courtesy"? What is the difference between the two? In any event, on what did Mr. Justice Gray rely to substantiate the customary international law rule upon which, arguably, his majority opinion was premised? And where did he get the authority to do so? Finally, what was the holding in this case? What would the Court have held if there had been no reference to "the law of nations" in the presidential proclamation? What would the Court have held if Congress had provided in the declaration of war that all Spanish vessels were subject to arrest and capture?

9. Should a rule of customary international law be allowed to supersede a statute? This question is "answered" in Barry E. Carter & Phillip R. Trimble, International Law 280 (3rd ed. 1999) by a series of "hypotheticals":

> Consider these situations: (a) assume a statute provides for punishment of crimes within a three-mile zone of territorial sea, and a later development of customary law extends the territorial sea to 12 miles; (b) a statute requires felony trials within one year of arrest, and a later customary rule requires "prompt" trials; (c) a statute prohibits arms sales by foreign subsidiaries of US corporations, and a later rule of customary law forbids regulation of corporate activity outside the territory of the regulating state.

How would you answer these "hypotheticals"? Consider the heated debate over the use of customary international law in US courts: Alexander Aleinikoff, *International Law, Sovereignty, And American Constitutionalism: Reflections On The Customary International Law Debate*, 98 A.J.I.L. 91 (2004); Jordan J. Paust, *Customary International Law And Human Rights Treaties Are Law Of The United States*, 20 Mich. J. Int'l L. 301(1999); Garland A. Kelley, *Note—Does Customary International Law Supersede A Federal Statute?* 37 Colum. J. Transnat'l Law 507 (1999); Jack L. Goldsmith & Eric A. Posner, *A Theory of Customary International Law*, 66 U Chi. L. Rev.1113 (1999); ___ The Limits of International Law (2005).

10. What, in general, is the proper role of domestic courts in the application of international law? *Consider* Richard A. Falk, The Role of Domestic Courts in the International Legal Order xi-xii (1964):

> Two sets of considerations dominate my interpretation of the proper role for domestic courts to play. First, international law exists in a social system that possesses weak central institutions. As a result, international tribunals are not consistently or conveniently available to resolve most disputes involving questions of international law. Domestic courts can help to overcome this structural weakness in the international legal system. Also, since no international institution is endowed with legislative competence, it is difficult to change old rules in response to changes in the composition and character of international society. If international law is to develop into a universal basis of order, then it is necessary that divergent attitudes toward the content of law be treated with respect. The older states must put forth a special effort to broaden international law enough to make it compatible with the values of [the formerly colonized and other newer] states. It is of no value to insist upon the old rules developed when all of the active international actors accepted *laissez-faire* economics at home and imperialism abroad. Domestic courts in the older states can help adapt international law to the modern

world by developing principles that express tolerance for diverse social and economic systems.

Second, domestic courts must struggle to become their own masters in international law cases. The executive must not be allowed, and must certainly not be invited, to control the outcome of judicial proceedings by alleging precedence of foreign policy considerations. The courts are not good vehicles for the promotion of foreign policy; moreover, the independence of courts from national political control is essential if international legal order is to be upheld and developed. A legal tradition depends upon the autonomy of its method and the saliency of its governing principles. Only an independent judiciary can establish a tradition.

Do you agree with Falk? Is his approach realistic? Are domestic courts ever likely to achieve the independence from national policies and values that Falk advocates? If so, how? If not, should we conclude that domestic courts should not entertain international law cases at all? If so, is that realistic? Wise?

On the role of domestic courts in the application of international human rights law, see *infra* Problem 5–4 ("A Disappearance in Hispania") in Chapter 5, at 660.

11.   It is a truism that governments periodically violate rules of international law, and of course they are prohibited from doing so, at least in theory, by international law itself. But does domestic law prohibit them from doing so? Does the President of the United States have constitutional or statutory authority to violate rules of international law? If so, where in the US Constitution is this stated? And is it likely that the US Congress ever would authorize the President to do so explicitly? If not, why not? The answer is obvious, is it not? Even if sometimes governments do violate international law and even if the legality of their policies may be domestically challenged in parliamentary debate, no head of state or parliament is going to admit as much, much less explicitly authorize a violation of international law. Invariably they will rationalize their actions or interpret the law in ways that they believe will protect them against "rogue state" accusations.

12.   What responsibility do national courts bear for holding their own governments accountable for violations of international law? What responsibility should they bear? Are US federal courts, including of course the US Supreme Court, constitutionally empowered to rule against the United States when the United States is alleged to have violated international law? If not, should they be? If so, what likely effect would such rulings have? Would they be definitive within the United States? Outside the United States? What implications might your answers have for the expansion of international human rights law? International environmental law? This issue has been raised in the context of US treatment of prisoners taken in Afghanistan and Iraq since 2001. *See, e.g., Rasul et al. v. Bush et al.*, 542 U.S. 466, 124 S.Ct. 2686 (2004). *See also* Derek Jinks, *Is The President Bound by the Geneva Conventions?*, 90 Cornell L. Rev. 97 (2004).

*

Part II

PROBLEMS OF INTERNATIONAL LAW AND WORLD ORDER

INTRODUCTION

In the Index to his influential book *The Concept of Law*, published in 1961, English legal philosopher H.L.A. Hart allowed the following entry: "Certainty of Law, see Uncertainty." This ironic twist, intended or not, serves a useful purpose. Especially for those of us who have been nurtured in highly formalized legal traditions, it stands as a reminder that, no matter where operative, "the law" never is chiseled in granite.

This is not to say, of course, that there are no well-established legal norms. To the contrary, the majority of them, according to which we go about our everyday lives, are relatively uncontroversial and consequently helpful in channeling human conduct along fairly predictable lines most of the time. This condition of stability is especially evident, it is true, in the domestic-or municipal-law realm. However, as seen in Part I, it is observable also on the international plane where often it is assumed that everything can be argued either way, or alternatively, that few laws ever are acknowledged. For example, despite the disdain with which the Iranian Government of the Ayatollah Ruhollah Khomeini treated United States diplomatic personnel in the late 1970s, it is widely recognized and accepted that, as a matter of treaty and customary law, foreign governmental officials and offices are entitled to diplomatic immunity and host country protection. *See, e.g., Case Concerning United States Diplomatic and Consular Staff in Tehran* (U.S. v. Iran), 1980 ICJ 3. However morally defensible the particular non-conforming behavior and however difficult the job of enforcement against such behavior, there are many matters of international legal principle and practice about which few disagree.

It is important to bear this instruction in mind as we proceed through the "hypothetical" problems that comprise this second part of our coursebook; for, while all of them treat or assume a variety of principles and practices that are clear-cut and certain, much of the time they evoke answers that are ambiguous. The reason is simple: all address issues which are central to the unprecedented peril and change of our times, which therefore provide a great deal of controversy worldwide, and for which, consequently, universally acceptable solutions have yet to be found. Although neither topically nor doctrinally exhaustive, they are fashioned around those key questions that seem most demanding of investigation and solution as humankind moves into the Twenty-first Century:

- how to limit violence and prevent wars and other types of hostilities so that nations and peoples will be governed more by persuasion than by coercion;

- how to expand sociopolitical justice so that discrimination and oppression will be reduced and more people given more opportunity to say what should happen to their lives;

- how to raise levels of socioeconomic well-being so that degrading poverty and grinding misery will no longer be the fate of billions; and

- how to restore the global environment so that people can enjoy the benefits of Earth in good health and without fear of pollution and the squandering of finite resources.

It is the obligation of international law and lawyering, we believe, to confront these unsettled questions as expeditiously and conscientiously as possible. We seek to do so here, even if, in the process, it means paying less attention to those principles and practices in respect of which a good measure of certainty has been achieved.

The first problem in each of the next four chapters leaves to you, for pedagogical reasons, the task of identifying and organizing the legal issues involved. The next five problems in each chapter, some of which may be coupled together, identify and organize the principal issues for you. All the problems, however, addressing both "traditional" and "threshold" questions of international law, are meant to be consciously informed by the above world order questions. The existence and quality of life are increasingly threatened by forces over which humankind has so far evinced little or no control: war, nuclear proliferation, exploding populations, spreading famine, widening poverty, rampant pollution, and dwindling resources, to name a few. Some say there is nothing we can do to avert the ultimate catastrophe these forces imply. Others say civilization will survive no matter what. But whatever one's long-term viewpoint, the evidence is everywhere that these forces must be examined, discussed, and acted upon with urgency.

Chapter Four

PROBLEMS OF CONFLICT PREVENTION

THE VITAL PERSPECTIVE

The end of the Cold War appears to have produced a decline in aggregate world military expenditures and a reduction in the overall incidence of armed conflict, at least across national boundaries. In 1989, the final year of the Cold War, there were 36 major armed conflicts spread over all regions of the world; in 2003 there were 19 major armed conflicts being waged worldwide. Nevertheless, armed conflict remains a constant feature of the global order. The statistics are themselves proof of this, as is also rising military spending in politically volatile regions and consequent increased civil wars that today, more than wars between states, define post-Cold War armed conflicts (the wars in Darfur and the Congo, for example). Also, despite some progress in disarmament at the end of the Cold War, nuclear proliferation and the threat of nuclear war remain accepted aspects of international relations. In the early years of the Twenty-first Century, however, the nature of armed conflict is changing. Often the "new wars" of the new century are between asymmetrical parties—for example between technologically advanced armies and guerilla forces. There also is an increasing privatization of warfare in the sense that states are not necessarily the major players; groups such as transnational criminal or terrorist organizations may be involved. Moreover, the "new wars" are no longer confined to violence between military combatants, so that the vast majority of casualties are not the combatants themselves, but civilians—mostly older people, women, and children.[a] The most intractable current conflict is, perhaps, the "war against terrorism" launched in response to the 11 September 2001 attacks upon the United States. As of this writing, the campaign includes United States action in Afghanistan, Pakistan, and the Philippines against the Al Qaeda movement and the March 2003 attack by the "coalition of the willing" (principally the United States and the United Kingdom) against Iraq to remove the government of Saddam Hussein. The war against terrorism has reinvigorated the global military research and development industry. Often the laws of armed conflict are disregarded in this context, not least on the part of major powers such as the United Kingdom and the United States.

---

a. For a discussion of these features of the "new wars" see H. Münkler, *The Wars of the 21st Century*, 849 Int'l Rev. Red Cross 7 (2003). See also *The Human Security Report 2005* (2005) for statistics on the decline of armed conflicts.

Problem 4–1

Intervention in Loango

SECTION 1. FACTS

Loango, a former French colony, is a poor developing country in central Africa that became a member of the United Nations and the Organization of African Unity (now the African Union) when it became independent in 1969.[b] It is also a landlocked country that has always been heavily dependent economically on its large neighbor, Mayumba, a coastal state that provides access to sea transport for Loango's major export crop, ground nuts.

The major political parties in Loango are the "progressive" Loango Revolutionary Party (LRP) and the "conservative" National Democratic Party (NDP). The LRP is officially committed to national public ownership of major civil infrastructure in support of the government's development policies, while the NDP espouses free market economic principles that favor decentralized regional and tribal governance. Each party is associated with one of the two major ethnic groups in Loango: the LRP with the Bapounou and the NDP with the Lingala.

The LRP has been in power for much of Loango's post-independence period, although the NDP had a brief period of rule in the 1980s after being installed by a military coup. Military support for the NDP government dwindled after the NDP sought to restructure the army. The LRP has since used electoral laws to consolidate its position and NDP supporters regularly complain of harassment and intimidation. Recent elections produced a very close result, with neither party able to claim victory. The Loango Constitution requires that new elections be held in these circumstances, but before the elections could be held, armed conflict broke out between supporters of the two rival parties. Many members of the Loango army have left their barracks and joined in fighting for the political party they favor.

The conflict is both bitter and violent. The two warring groups are relatively evenly matched in terms of weapons and combatants. Each political party can claim support in different areas of the country, with the LRP's major base in the east and the NDP's in the west. Both sides have been recruiting children as young as nine to fight. There are reports of large scale massacre of civilians on the basis of suspicion about their political sympathies. Towns and villages have been destroyed and water supplies deliberately poisoned. Prisoners captured by one side are regularly tortured, brutalized, and killed by the other. Women and girls in particular have been targeted for rape and sexual assaults by both sides. Agricultural production has been greatly disrupted by the conflict, famine threatens the entire country, and infectious diseases, such as cholera and typhoid, are rife.

---

b. Thus Loango is a party to the United Nations Charter (**Basic Document 1.5**) and the Constitutive Act of the African Union (**Ba-** sic Document 1.17) which supersedes the Charter of the erstwhile Organization of African Unity (**Basic Document 1.9**).

The interior is now largely in the hands of the NDP, except for the traditional capital city of Ivoireville, the country's most populous, which, together with the several districts immediately surrounding it, is in the hands of the LRP. The NDP controls the interior principally from Iboundji, Loango's second largest city, where the NDP has established a government.

The LRP, claiming to represent Loango's legitimate government, maintains diplomatic relations with many members of the United Nations. An LRP appointee represents Loango at the United Nations. The LRP's particular supporters have included the Peoples' Republic of China, Cuba, and other members of the Non–Aligned Movement. Both China and Cuba have supplied fuel oil, foodstuffs, medical supplies and personnel to the LRP forces. Western newspaper reports suggest that the LRP also has received some small arms and munitions from these countries and that some LRP forces have been trained in China and Cuba.

The NDP also claims to represent the legitimate government of Loango. It has courted recognition by the United States in particular. Some of its leading officials have been educated in the United States, and the NDP has good links in the US Congress. The United States suspects the LRP of supporting terrorist organizations and is anxious to see the party removed from power. It has sent advisers to NDP-held areas to assist in the recruitment, outfitting, training, supply and direction of a 1500–person mercenary force to conduct raids against LRP targets. The United States has also made a grant of $1 billion for "humanitarian assistance in this time of peril." The International Committee of the Red Cross reports that the NDP has used most of these funds to purchase arms and recruit mercenaries in the United States and Europe.

The LRP has accused the United States of "criminal meddling in the internal affairs of a sovereign state." At the United Nations, members of the Non–Aligned Movement have introduced a General Assembly resolution to denounce the United States for its "activities in violation of international law."

Meanwhile, the Government of Mayumba has been observing the violence and chaos in Loango with increasing concern. Economic and social activity along the border with Loango has been severely disrupted, although no Mayumbans have been harmed physically. Mayumba is concerned about the impact that the destruction of a large part of Loango's ground nut crop will have on Mayumba's economy. In order to prevent any incursions into Mayumban territory, the Mayumban army made a series of raids on LRP camps in the border region and killed a number of LRP troops and, through error, some Loangoan civilians living in the area. The Foreign Minister of Mayumba has issued a statement warning that Mayumba will take further and stronger steps to prevent any possible attacks on Mayumbans and calling on the African Union to respond to what the Foreign Minister terms war crimes, genocide, and crimes against humanity. The Assembly of the African Union is divided on the issue and is unable to take any decision to intervene.

Belgium and Portugal have placed a draft resolution before the United Nations Security Council condemning the "unilateral military intervention" of the United States and of Mayumba. It calls for the prosecution of perpetrators of crimes against humanity. The United States, not wanting to be diplomatically isolated in relation to the conflict, also has placed a resolution before the Security Council, calling for "armed collective humanitarian intervention" for the purpose of imposing a ceasefire, preventing further atrocity and famine, and reconstituting order through supervised elections. The US resolution also expresses "deep concern" over "apparent violations" of the 1948 Convention on the Prevention and Punishment of the Crime of Genocide,[c] to which Loango is a party, and of the rules of armed conflict (known as international humanitarian law) as codified in the four 1949 Geneva conventions on the laws of war and the 1977 Protocols additional thereto.[d] The resolution exempts troops from the jurisdiction of the International Criminal Court if their state is not a party to its 1998 Rome Statute.[e] Both Loango and Mayumba are parties to the Rome Statute. The United States meanwhile invites Mayumba to join in a coalition force "of the willing" to "restore order" in Loango if the Security Council resolution it has sponsored is not successful.

SECTION 2.   PURPOSE OF THE PROBLEM

A primary purpose of this problem is to call attention to a significant aspect of the general world order problem of the prevention of armed conflict, namely, the legality of outside intervention in "internal" conflict and the role of the United Nations and regional organizations in reacting to such conflict. At what point, if any, can atrocities occurring within a state justify outside intervention? These questions have been much debated in the last few years, as the following extract from the report of the International Commission on Intervention and State Sovereignty, a group of experts convened by the Canadian government, explains.[f]

1.10   The issues and preoccupations of the 21st century present new and often fundamentally different types of challenges from those that faced the world in 1945, when the United Nations was founded. As new realities and challenges have emerged, so too have new expectations for action and new standards of conduct in national and international affairs. Since, for example, the terrorist attacks of 11 September 2001 on the World Trade Center and Pentagon, it has become evident that the war against terrorism the world must now fight—one with no contested frontiers and a largely invisible enemy—is one like no other war before it.

* * *

1.12   The current debate on intervention for human protection purposes is itself both a product and a reflection of how much has changed

c. See **Basic Document 3.2**.
d. See **Basic Documents 2.9, 2.10, 2.11, 2.12, 2.31**, and **2.32**.
e. See **Basic Document 1.16**.
f. See The Responsibility To Protect (2001).

since the UN was established. The current debate takes place in the context of a broadly expanded range of state, non-state, and institutional actors, and increasingly evident interaction and interdependence among them. It is a debate that reflects new sets of issues and new types of concerns. It is a debate that is being conducted within the framework of new standards of conduct for states and individuals, and in a context of greatly increased expectations for action. And it is a debate that takes place within an institutional framework that since the end of the Cold War has held out the prospect of effective joint international action to address issues of peace, security, human rights and sustainable development on a global scale.

* * *

1.22   All this presents the international community with acute dilemmas. If it stays disengaged, there is the risk of becoming complicit bystanders in massacre, ethnic cleansing, and even genocide. If the international community intervenes, it may or may not be able to mitigate such abuses. But even when it does, intervention sometimes means taking sides in intra-state conflicts. Once it does so, the international community may only be aiding in the further fragmentation of the state system. Interventions in the Balkans did manage to reduce the civilian death toll, but it has yet to produce a stable state order in the region. As both the Kosovo and Bosnian interventions show, even when the goal of international action is, as it should be, protecting ordinary human beings from gross and systematic abuse, it can be difficult to avoid doing rather more harm than good.

* * *

1.25   The current debate about intervention for human protection purposes also takes place in a historical, political and legal context of evolving international standards of conduct for states and individuals, including the development of new and stronger norms and mechanisms for the protection of human rights. Human rights have now become a mainstream part of international law, and respect for human rights a central subject and responsibility of international relations. Some key milestones in this progression have been the Universal Declaration of Human Rights [**Basic Document 3.3**]; the four Geneva Conventions and the two Additional Protocols on international humanitarian law in armed conflict [**Basic Documents 2.9, 2.10, 2.11 2.12, 2.31 & 2.32**]; the 1948 Convention on the Prevention and Punishment of the Crime of Genocide [**Basic Document 3.2**]; the two 1966 Covenants relating to civil, political, social, economic and cultural rights [**Basic Documents 3.13 & 3.14**]; and the adoption in 1998 of the statute for the establishment of an International Criminal Court [**Basic Document 1.16**]. Even though in some cases imperfectly implemented, these agreements and mechanisms have significantly changed expectations at all levels about what is and what is not acceptable conduct by states and other actors.

* * *

1.30   A critically important contextual dimension of the current debate on intervention for human protection purposes is the new opportunity and capacity for common action that has resulted from the end of the Cold War. For perhaps the first time since the UN was established, there is now a genuine prospect of the Security Council fulfilling the role envisioned for it in the UN Charter **[Basic Document 1.5]**. Despite some notable setbacks, the capacity for common action by the Security Council was shown during the 1990s to be real, with the authorization by the Council of nearly 40 peacekeeping or peace enforcement operations over the last decade.

1.31   Closely allied to this new awareness of world conditions and new visibility for human suffering has been the impact of globalization in intensifying economic interdependence between states. Globalization has led to closer ties at all levels and a pronounced trend towards multilateral cooperation. In the context of the debate surrounding the issue of intervention for human protection purposes, it is clear that the realities of globalization and growing interdependency have often been important factors in prompting states and others to become engaged positively both in promoting prevention, and also in calling for intervention in situations that seem to be spiraling out of control.

Another purpose of the problem is to explore the essentially horizontal character of the international legal system—in particular, the strengths and weaknesses of some of the unilateral and multilateral decision-making alternatives that help to make it up. This inquiry is important, clearly, whenever the exercise of military power is involved, a major feature of this problem; and it is, moreover, difficult when, as in this problem, military strategy based on the principle of sovereign territorial integrity and political independence (a fundamental postulate of the United Nations Charter) runs up against military strategy apparently based on respect for human rights and minimum world public order (other fundamental principles of the United Nations Charter). The present problem reflects the complex value choices that typically must be made whenever co-equal world order priorities such as war prevention and sociopolitical justice are involved. Traditionally, states have been allowed relatively broad unilateral competence to advance these sorts of interests as in their separate wisdoms they might choose. At the end of the Cold War, however, a trend emerged of increased multilateral involvement in preventing and mitigating armed conflict, although more recent events suggest a return to unilateralism, by the United States at least.

Finally, the problem is designed to stimulate analysis of a cluster of doctrines, principles, and rules with which international lawyers historically have been concerned. The Readings in Section 4, *infra*, are arranged according to these recognized legal themes. Related questions are considered in the Discussion Notes/Questions that follow.

SECTION 3. ASSIGNMENTS

A. READING ASSIGNMENT

Study the Readings presented in Section 4, *infra*, and the Discussion Notes/Questions that follow. Also, to the extent possible, consult the accompanying bibliographical references.

B. RECOMMENDED WRITING ASSIGNMENT

Prepare a comprehensive, logically sequenced, and *argumentative* brief in the form of an outline of the primary and subsidiary *legal* issues you see requiring resolution by the Security Council in this problem (approximately ten single-spaced, typewritten pages). Also, from the perspective of an international judge, indicate how each issue might be resolved and why. Retain a copy of your issue-outline (brief) for class discussion.

C. RECOMMENDED ORAL ASSIGNMENT

Assume you are the Permanent Representative to the United Nations from a country sympathetic to the United States and/or Mayumba or to those—including but not limited to the People's Republic of China and Cuba—supporting the LRP (as designated by your instructor); then, relying upon the Readings (and your issue-outline/brief, if prepared), present a 10–15 minute oral argument of your government's likely position on each of the key provisions embodied in the two proposed Security Council resolutions and the possibility of the United States and Mayumba intervening without Security Council authorization.

D. RECOMMENDED REFLECTIVE ASSIGNMENT

Consider (and recommend) alternative norms, procedures, and/or institutions that you believe might do better than existing world order arrangements to contend with situations of the kind posed by this problem. In so doing, but without insisting upon *immediate* political feasibility, identify the particular transition steps that would be needed to make your alternatives a reality.

SECTION 4. READINGS

The following readings are relevant to understanding this problem. They are divided according to those categories of recognized international legal inquiry and analysis that are principally implicated in the problem: "recognition of states and governments;" "civil war" (including "recognition of belligerent status" and "neutrality"); "unilateral intervention"; and "United Nations intervention." They are your law library for present purposes and should be treated as such, organized intelligibly for "shelving" and not necessarily according to the issues presented. Be sure to review Chapter 2 ("International Legal Prescription: The 'Sources' of International Law") in your consideration of them. It, too, should be treated as part of your law library (as, indeed, should this entire coursebook).

A. Recognition of States and Governments

1. Jochen A. Frowein, "Recognition," in 4 Encyclopedia of Public International Law 34–40 (2000).

3. Recognition of States

(a) Requirements

It is frequently stated that the recognition of States presupposes the existence of the criteria for statehood, *i.e.*, a fixed territory, a population and an effective government.[g] When the doctrine of recognition of States developed the emphasis was put on cases of forcible separation from the former mother-country. Here, the effectiveness of the separation was seen as the most important criterion. The development of the process of decolonization after 1945 has shown that recognition of States is a matter of normal routine where there is no dispute with a former mother-country. The many African, Asian and American States becoming independent on the basis of decisions taken by the former colonial powers were recognized immediately by the community of nations. This also happened where their borders were to a great extent in dispute or no effective government for the whole of the country existed (*e.g.*, the former Congo, 1960).

To establish what States consider to be the essential criteria for statehood it is more appropriate to consider under which circumstances they refuse recognition as a State. . . . There are two main reasons why States have withheld full recognition although, at least on the face of it, some entity resembling a State existed. The reason most frequently used is lack of independence in relation to some State which for political reasons wants to use the new State which it has helped come into existence. It is this reason which was advanced for the non-recognition of Manchukuo as a Japanese "puppet-State" or of Croatia as a German creation of that sort. The German Democratic Republic was for a long time not recognized as a sovereign State because it was not considered sufficiently independent *vis-à-vis* the Soviet Union and because no effective splitting-up of the German State was seen as permissible by intervention. . . . The South African homelands, although formally declared to be sovereign States by South Africa, have not been recognized as such by other States. The prevailing view would seem to be that they lack any real independence. . . .

A second reason, which was used to withhold recognition in the case of Rhodesia, was the fact that independence had been brought about by a white minority government in a former colonial territory. The clear lack of any part of self-determination by the whole people was seen as justifying non-recognition. Although democratic structures are not a prerequisite for recognition, this seems to establish that, in the case of States whose independence has not

---

g. A classical example is the oft-quoted Article 1 of the 1933 Convention on the Rights and Duties of States Adopted by the Seventh International Conference of American States (the "Montevideo Convention") (**Basic Document 1.2**): "The state as a person of international law should possess the following qualifications: (a) a permanent population; (b) defined territory; (c) a government; and (d) capacity to enter into relations with the other states." For a critique of the Montevideo formulation of statehood, see T. Grant, *Defining Statehood: The Montevideo Convention and its Discontents*, 37 Colum. J. Transnat'l L. 403 (1999).

been confirmed by a long history, some act at least tacitly confirmed by the attitude of the population may be required. It should be added here that non-recognition as a State does not mean, as was sometimes thought in early doctrine, that an entity falls outside the sphere of public international law.... Many rules of public international law are in fact applicable notwithstanding non-recognition as a State.

(b) Modes of recognition

Recognition may be express, especially after the granting of independence. In addition, it has long been accepted that there may be implied recognition. However, care should be used not to deduce recognition from acts which do not clearly show an intention to that effect. It would seem that there is only one unequivocal act from which full recognition can always be deduced: the establishment of full diplomatic relations. All other forms of contact do not necessarily lead to recognition as a State.

The distinction between *de jure* and *de facto* recognition has always been a source of difficulties. In most cases recognition will not be qualified by either of these terms. Where it is stated that recognition is *de facto*, this implies some hesitation on the part of the recognizing government either as to the coming into existence of the new State or its territorial situation. Probably the last clear example for *de facto* recognition of a State was the recognition of Israel in 1948 by Great Britain.... A further difficulty is added by the fact that the notion *de facto* may be used not to qualify the recognition, but to refer to the factual situation being recognized, as in the case of recognition of a *de facto* government or regime. The view that the *de facto* recognition may be revoked without a change of circumstances would not seem to be confirmed by State practice.

(c) Legal consequences

After recognition it is clear that all rules of public international law governing the relations between sovereign States are applicable *ipso jure*. Without recognition that may be a matter of dispute. Controversy has existed for a long time as to whether recognition has merely a declaratory or a constitutive effect.[h] Anzilotti and Kelsen, in particular, have advanced theoretical reasons why recognition must have a constitutive meaning in a system of law based on the understanding of States as to the legal consequences of a specific factual situation. Lauterpacht has argued that where dispute exists as to the existence of the criteria of statehood, recognition constitutively settles that dispute. He saw a duty for recognition where the criteria are met.

However, it is clear that recognition does not create the State. It only confirms that an entity has reached statehood. As soon as all or practically all States take the same view the matter is settled. Art. 12 of the OAS Charter **[Basic Document 1.7]** states: "The political existence of the State is

---

h. According to the *declaratory* theory, the act of recognition is merely an acknowledgment of pre-existing facts that meet the criteria of statehood as prescribed by international law. The primary function of the act of recognition, under this theory, is to acknowledge the *de facto* existence of the State and to indicate a willingness to accord it *de jure* status as a fully participating international person with all the rights and duties of a State under international law. According to the *constitutive* theory, the act of recognition creates or "constitutes" the new State, conferring international personality on the entity purporting to be a State. Conceptually, under this theory, one need but look to the presence or absence of acts of recognition to determine whether an entity is a State or not.

independent of recognition by other States. Even before being recognized, the State has the right to defend its integrity and independence." The two theories connected with recognition focus on different problems. In practice they do not help to explain recognition or to clarify the position of entities which are not recognized.

No obligation to establish full diplomatic relations or any specific links flow from recognition. This is a matter of discretion for the State concerned. Only those rules of international law which do not require a specific relationship apply automatically with recognition.

* * *

(e) The impact of the United Nations on recognition of States

It has been commented that recognition of a State, although very important in former times, has been substituted to a large extent by admission to the United Nations.... With the admission to the United Nations all the rules of the United Nations Charter apply to the new member. Although claims of non-recognition have been upheld even after the respective States became UN members (e.g., in the cases of the Arab States with respect to Israel and the Federal Republic of Germany with respect to the German Democratic Republic), it is clear that the quality as State of a UN member cannot be denied. Thus, while non-recognition will have a very specific political meaning, for example underlining the wish to have a change brought about in the future, that change can only be aimed at in full respect of Charter obligations, especially Art. 2(4).

It is of at least equal importance that the United Nations has become the forum to coordinate non-recognition. In several cases the ... Security Council, frequently on the basis of resolutions adopted by the ... General Assembly, has called upon States not to recognize specific entities as States. This was first done when Rhodesia declared its independence in 1965.... The same attitude was adopted after South Africa declared the independence of Transkei as a homeland.... When the Turkish Cypriot authorities proclaimed an independent State in northern Cyprus in 1983, the Security Council called upon all States not to recognize any Cypriot States other than the Republic of Cyprus.... In the last two cases the reason for the attitude of the United Nations which was not contested in the Security Council was similar: the lack of independence of the entities in question vis-à-vis South Africa or Turkey and some legal defects in their creation. In fact, the independence of the homelands was considered to be part of the apartheid policy, and independence of northern Cyprus as incompatible with the treaties of 1960. It is doubtful whether the resolutions of the Security Council in those cases are binding but they are clearly a justification for withholding recognition by all States.... In fact, in the cases in question non-recognition became the general attitude.... The examples show that the United Nations plays an important role in matters of recognition today.

4. Recognition of Governments

(a) Introductory remarks

Change of government in a given State is a matter within its domestic sphere and does not concern international law or the international community. This is true whether the procedure is in line with the constitutional rules applicable in the country or not. International law is not concerned with the constitutionality of any such change. This shows that there must be a special reason for the question of recognition of a new government to arise at all. The reason may be an uncertainty as to the effectiveness of the government after a period of revolutionary change, or the existence of two competing governments. . . .

(b) Requirements

A formal recognition of a new government is permissible only where there is some reason to clarify the situation after a revolutionary change. The first and generally accepted requirement for the recognition of a government is that this government be in control of the territory and the administration of the State. Where this control is unquestionable, no issue will arise. Therefore, this requirement has to be seen in the perspective of the need for the recognition of a government in doubtful circumstances. Effective control means control of at least the larger part of the territory with no real threat for the development of the state in the future. As for the recognition of States, effective control must not be brought about by foreign intervention. Indeed, foreign intervention in a change of government is a typical reason for non-recognition. Where there are still two competing governments, recognition of the revolutionary government as the government of the State is unlawful unless it has established its authority to such an extent that the outcome of the conflict is clear and the former government's authority is reduced to a negligible area. Typical examples of premature and unlawful recognition were the declarations by which Germany and Italy recognized the Franco Government as the government of Spain already at the beginning of the Spanish Civil War in 1936. Where a conflict exists for a longer time, limited recognition as a *de facto* regime may be extended to the revolutionary government.

Besides effectiveness, it is frequently stated by governments that two criteria may be taken into account for recognition: whether there is consent or at least acquiescence by the people, and whether the new government has indicated its willingness to comply with its obligations under international law. . . . While acquiescence may have some connection to the effective control and stability of the government, it may also refer to democratic legitimacy. It has clearly been used in the latter sense, for instance by taking into account whether elections have been announced by a revolutionary government. Insofar as these two criteria have nothing to do with the question of effectiveness of the new government, it is doubtful whether they can really be used to withhold recognition in the sense of not treating the new government as the government of the State. The correct view would seem to be that an effective government fully in control of the country must be accepted as the government of the State wherever contracts with that State exist. Since there is no obligation under general international law to establish or continue diplomatic relations, the criteria just discussed may be of importance concerning renewal or continuation of diplomatic relations. It is in this sense that one frequently uses the terminology "diplomatic recognition." However, one must conclude from State practice that States not infrequently justify their decision concerning the recognition of revolutionary governments with reasons going beyond the mere effectiveness of these governments.

(c) Modes

Although recognition may be express in the same way as for States, recognition of governments is more likely to be implied. The continuation of diplomatic relations is in fact the normal way to clarify the situation. It seems that more and more States avoid the label of recognition after revolutionary changes and prefer to take their decision in concrete dealings with the new government. The distinction between *de jure* and *de facto* recognition has apparently also become obsolete for the recognition of governments.

(d) Legal consequences

After recognition a government will be treated in all respects as fully entitled to represent the State concerned. In most instances diplomatic relations will be established or continued although no obligation is created in this respect. As a consequence of recognition, the right of the government concerned to represent its State in all international organizations in which the State is a member cannot subsequently be questioned. This does not mean that the acceptance by the other parties of a non-recognized government as representing its State in an international organization amounts to a full recognition. State practice clearly shows that not infrequently the position of non-recognition has been upheld although the government at issue was accepted as representing its State in the United Nations or other international organizations (*e.g.* China).

* * *

6. Evaluation

The importance of recognition in international law is a consequence of the imperfect nature of international law. Since disputes ... frequently [cannot] be settled by judicial procedures with binding results, the position which is taken by the other subjects of international law becomes crucial in case of doubt. Where the procedure of recognition is used *bona fide* by all members of the international community it will have no detrimental effects. However, where ideological and political motives influence the decision whether or not to recognize a State, a government or a territorial situation, abuse is quite possible. History and State practice clearly provide examples of such abuse.... Since international law is unable to eliminate such abuse it is of crucial importance that the legal position of non-recognized entities be clarified. Non-recognition must never mean that States are free to use force against an entity which they do not recognize as a State.

2. Arbitration Between Great Britain and Costa Rica (Tinoco Case), [1923] 1 U.N.R.I.A.A. 369 (1948); 18 A.J.I.L. 147 (1924).

[*Eds.*—After a successful *coup d'état* in January 1917, Frederico Tinoco governed Costa Rica under a new constitution for a little more than two years, until August 1919. The Tinoco regime was recognized by some governments but not by many of the leading powers of the day (*e.g.*, Great Britain and the United States). When the regime fell, the pre–1917 Costa Rican constitution was restored, and the new Costa Rican government nullified, *inter alia*, certain decisions of the Tinoco era, such as monetary transactions and the issuance of oil business licenses, which affected a bank and an oil company owned by British subjects. Great Britain, acting on behalf of the British companies, claimed that the new Costa Rican government was bound by the earlier decrees of the Tinoco government, and notwithstanding that the Tinoco government had not been recognized by Great Britain. Costa Rica denied the British allegation that the Tinoco regime constituted a *de facto* or *de jure* government, regarded Tinoco's decrees as void because they were violative of the old constitution of Costa Rica, and claimed an estoppel of the British claims based on Great Britain's failure to recognize the Tinoco government. The sole arbitrator, US Chief Justice William Howard Taft, discussed in his award and opinion the recognition issue as follows:]

First, what are the facts to be gathered from the documents and evidence submitted by the two parties as to the de facto character of the Tinoco government?

* * *

... Though Tinoco came in with popular approval, the result of his two years administration of the law was to rouse opposition to him. Conspiracies outside of the country were projected to organize a force to attack him. But this did not result in any substantial conflict or even a nominal provisional government on the soil until considerably more than two years after the inauguration of his government, and did not result in the establishment of any other real government until September of that year, he having renounced his Presidency in August preceding, on the score of his ill health, and withdrawn to Europe. The truth is that throughout the record as made by the case and counter case, there is no substantial evidence that Tinoco was not in actual and peaceable administration without resistance or conflict or contest by anyone until a few months before the time when he retired and resigned.

... It is not important, however, what were the causes that enabled Tinoco to carry on his government effectively and peaceably. The question is, must his government be considered a link in the continuity of the Government of Costa Rica? I must hold ... from the evidence that the Tinoco government was an actual sovereign government.

But it is urged that many leading Powers refused to recognize the Tinoco government, and that recognition by other nations is the chief and best evidence of the birth, existence and continuity of succession of a government. Undoubtedly recognition by other Powers is an important evidential factor in establishing proof of the existence of a government in the society of nations....

* * *

Probably because of the leadership of the United States in respect to a matter of this kind, her then Allies in [World War I], Great Britain, France and Italy, declined to recognize the Tinoco government. Costa Rica was, therefore, not permitted to sign the Treaty of Peace at Versailles, although the Tinoco government had declared war against Germany.

The merits of the policy of the United States in this non-recognition, it is not for the arbitrator to discuss, for the reason that in his consideration of this case, he is necessarily controlled by principles of international law, and however justified as a national policy non-recognition on such a ground may be, it certainly has not been acquiesced in by all the nations of the world, which is a condition precedent to considering it as a postulate of international law.

The non-recognition by other nations of a government claiming to be a national personality, is usually appropriate evidence that it has not attained the independence and control entitling it by international law to be classed as such. But when recognition *vel non* of a government is by such nations determined by inquiry, not into its *de facto* sovereignty and complete governmental control, but into its illegitimacy or irregularity of origin, their non-recognition loses something of evidential weight on the issue with which those applying the rules of international law are alone concerned. What is true of the non-recognition of the United States in its bearing upon the existence of a *de facto* government under Tinoco for thirty months is probably in a measure true of the non-recognition by her Allies in the European War. Such non-recognition for any reason, however, cannot outweigh the evidence disclosed by this record before me as to the *de facto* character of Tinoco's government, according to the standard set by international law.

Second, it is ably and earnestly argued on behalf of Costa Rica that the Tinoco government cannot be considered a *de facto* government, because it was not established and maintained in accord with the constitution of Costa Rica of 1871. To hold that a government which establishes itself and maintains a peaceful administration, with the acquiescence of the people for a substantial period of time, does not become a *de facto* government unless it conforms to a previous constitution would be to hold that within the rules of international law a revolution contrary to the fundamental law of the existing government cannot establish a new government. This cannot be, and is not, true.... The issue is not whether the new government assumes power or conducts its administration under constitutional limitations established by the people during the incumbency of the government it has overthrown. The question is, has it really established itself in such a way that all within its influence recognize its control, and that there is no opposing force assuming to be a government in its place? Is it discharging its functions as a government usually does, respected within its own jurisdiction?

[*Eds.*—Arbitrator Taft rejected the claim of estoppel on the grounds that Great Britain did not by non-recognition dispute the *de facto* existence of the Tinoco regime and because the successor government had not been led by Britain's non-recognition to alter its position.]

3.   **Editors' Note.** The "effective control" doctrine has been accepted as a guide to the recognition of governments. A different basis for recognition is that of legitimacy, sometimes known as the Tobar Doctrine (after the Foreign Minister of Ecuador who proposed the idea in 1907). This doctrine held that governments that came into power without benefit of elections or by extra-constitutional means should not be recognized. The doctrine, which was transmuted into the policy of political legitimacy of President Woodrow Wilson, was applied particularly by the United States in Central America to protect American interests in or near the Panama Canal. However, the Tobar Doctrine was never generally accepted, mainly for being out of step with revolutionary realities and attendant political considerations. It gave way to the Estrada Doctrine (named after the Mexican Secretary of Foreign Relations who articulated it in 1930), which held that a change of government is an

internal matter for each state, one in which other states have no right to intervene, and that foreign states should ignore revolutions and keep their diplomatic missions accredited to whoever may effectively occupy the government at any given moment. Chafing under the non-recognition of the dictatorial regime of General Victoriano Huerta and related consequences of the tumultuous years that followed the Mexican Revolution of 1910, Foreign Secretary Estrada stated, on September 27, 1930, that, to avoid the "insulting practice" of pronouncing judgment on the sovereign right of other states to maintain or replace their governments, the Government of Mexico would no longer extend or withhold grants of recognition but, instead, would confine itself "to the maintenance or withdrawal, as it may deem advisable, of its diplomatic agents, and to the continued acceptance, also when it may deem advisable, of such similar accredited diplomatic agents as the respective nations may have in Mexico." Press statement of 27 Sep 30, *translated in* 25 A.J.I.L. Supp. 203 (1931). In 1977, the US Department of State announced that "[i]n recent years, US practice has been to de-emphasize and avoid the use of recognition in cases of change of government and to concern ourselves with the question of whether we wish to have diplomatic relations with new governments." 77 Dep't State Bull. 462 (1977). It added that "establishment of relations does not involve approval or disapproval but merely demonstrates a willingness on our part to conduct our affairs with other governments directly." *Id.* at 463. Effective control is one important criterion for this decision.

In 1980, the United Kingdom adopted the same formal position with respect to recognition as the US. The Secretary of State for Foreign and Commonwealth Affairs announced that, after a comparison with the practice of partners and allies, it had been decided "that we shall no longer accord recognition to Governments. * * * We have ... concluded that there are practical advantages in following the policy of many other countries in not according recognition to Governments." Statement by the Secretary of State for Foreign and Commonwealth Affairs, 28 Apr. 80, Parl. Deb. H. L. (5th ser.) 1121–22. *See* Clive Symmons, *United Kingdom Abolition of the Doctrine of Recognition of Governments: A Rose By Another Name?*, 1981 Pub. L. 249. In 1988, the Australian government announced the abandonment of recognition of governments, partly as a response to a 1987 coup in Fiji in which the elected government had been replaced by a military government. *See* Hilary Charlesworth, *The New Australian Recognition Policy in Comparative Perspective*, 18 Melbourne U. L. Rev. 1 (1991). The question thus naturally arises: is recognition necessary? *See* L. Thomas Galloway, *Recognizing Foreign Governments—The Practice of the United States* (1978) which, in addition to discussing the Estrada Doctrine, urges the virtual termination of all recognition. For an argument that recognition of governments has both practical and theoretical value, see M. J. Peterson, *Recognition of Governments Should Not Be Abolished*, 77 A.J.I.L. 31 (1983).

At the UN level, there has been some change in practice relative to the recognition of governments. The UN Credentials Committee, which accredits governments to hold their countries' seats in the General Assembly, usually accredited the regime that could be said to be in effective control of the territory of a state, although it had notably failed to do so for many years in the case of the Peoples' Republic of China, whose government was not recognized by the UN until 1971. During the 1990s the Committee departed from its general practice. In the cases of Haiti, Sierra Leone, Cambodia, Liberia and Afghanistan, the Committee refused to accredit representatives of governments in effective control of the state and instead installed representatives of former regimes possessing few attributes of government. The decision in these cases rested on whether the government was seen to be democratic and whether it came to power by overthrowing a democratic government. Matthew Griffin, *Accrediting Democracies: Does the Credentials Committee of the United Nations Promote Democracy Through its Accreditation Process, and Should It?*, 32 N.Y.U. J. Int'l L. & Pol. 725 (2000). On UN practice with respect to the recognition of states and membership of the UN, see *infra* Discussion Note/Question 25.

The criteria for recognition of states have been developing some substantive features. Increasingly, international practice has been to impose conditions of democratic governance as a prerequisite for recognition of new states. For example, after the breakup of the Eastern European bloc in the early 1990s, the European Community, on 16 December 1991, adopted a Declaration on "Guidelines on the Recognition of New States in Eastern Europe and in the Soviet Union" **(Basic Document 1.15)**. In addition to proclaiming a readiness "to recognize ... those new states which ... have constituted themselves on a democratic basis, have accepted the appropriate international obligations and have committed themselves in good faith to a peaceful process and to negotiations," the Guidelines require, *inter alia*, "respect for "the rule of law, democracy and human rights," "guarantees for the rights of ethnic and national groups and minorities," "acceptance of all relevant commitments ... to disarmament ..., security and regional stability," and "commitment to settle by agreement ... all questions concerning state succession and regional disputes." Though the guidelines were substantially ignored in the case of the breakup of the former Yugoslavia, they thus go farther than the traditional law of recognition. *See generally,* Roland Rich, *Recognition of States: The Collapse of Yugoslavia and the Soviet Union*, 4 E.J.I.L. 36 (1993).

B.   CIVIL WAR

1.   Editors' Note. The rights and duties of nations in situations of internal conflict are governed in part by the level of crisis the conflict has achieved. According to traditional international law, three levels of crisis are relevant, each a point along a continuum of ascending intensity of challenge to the authority of the incumbent government: (a) rebellion, (b) insurgency, and (c) belligerency.

If the challenging faction seems capable of rapid suppression by normal internal security procedures, then the level of crisis is treated as a "rebellion," in which case external help to the "rebels" is said to constitute illegal intervention while foreign assistance to the incumbent government is said to be legal. Indeed, the incumbent government can insist that outside states accept the inconvenience of policies aimed at suppressing the rebellion (such as the closing of ports or interference with normal commerce) and that they not allow their own territory to be used as a base for organizing hostile activities against the incumbent government. When Nicaragua argued in the 1980s that US assistance to the Contras, a group opposed to the lawfully elected Sandinista government, constituted intervention in breach of international law, the International Court of Justice agreed. It stated:

> The principle of non-intervention involves the right of every sovereign State to conduct its affairs without outside interference.... If one State, with a view to the coercion of another State, arms, equips, finances and supports armed bands in that State whose purpose is to overthrow its government, that amounts to an intervention in its internal affairs, whatever the political objective of the State giving support.... It is clearly established that the United States intended, by its support of the *contras,* to coerce Nicaragua in respect of matters in which each State is permitted to decide freely.

Case concerning the Military and Paramilitary Activities in and against Nicaragua: Nicaragua v U.S.A., [1986] ICJ Rep. 14 [27 Jun], at ¶ ¶ 202, 239. For further discussion of aid as intervention see Oscar Schachter, *The Right of States to Use Armed Force,* 82 Mich. L. Rev. 1620, 1641–44 (1984).

Factually speaking, almost all that can be said about the crisis level called "insurgency" is that it is characterized by more sustained and substantial intrastate violence than is encountered in a "rebellion" and less sustained and substantial intrastate violence than is encountered in a "belligerency." Juridically speaking, it is a designation provided by international law to allow outside states to determine the nature of their own relations with the "insurgents" and thereby make possible a partial internationalization of the conflict without bringing the state of "belligerency" into being, which establishes a regime of rights and duties that exist independent of the will of a particular state. Characterizing an internal conflict situation as an "insurgency" permits outside states to participate in the internal conflict without finding themselves "at war"—for example, by allowing the use of the high seas for naval and air operations against the incumbent government (subject to the duty of the "insurgents" to conform to applicable rules of international law, including the laws of war)—even though such permissiveness represents a disregard of the incumbent government's normal claim to be the exclusive agent of the state for all matters within national jurisdiction. In general, the crisis level called "insurgency" is used to protect the economic and private interests of nationals and to acknowledge political facts arising from partial successes by the "insurgents" in an internal conflict situation without such acknowledgement amounting to a mode of illegal intervention in internal affairs.

Designating an internal conflict situation a "belligerency" places the conflict, legally speaking, on essentially the same footing as a war between independent sovereign states, giving rise to definite rights and obligations under international law. As with a truly interstate conflict, an outside state is given the formal option of joining with one of the "belligerents" against the other or of remaining strictly neutral, although, as one might expect, the sharpness of the choice is belied by history, which abounds with instances of partiality and participation that nevertheless are treated as consistent with neutral status. Also, the compatibility of this option with the United Nations system and its fundamental commitment to peaceful conflict resolution is open to serious question, even for non-Members.[i] In any event, if neutrality is

---

i. *See especially* articles 2(4) and 2(6) of the UN Charter **(Basic Document 1.5).**

undertaken, no assistance may be given even to the incumbent government, since this would constitute an illegal intervention and a violation of neutrality. That is, an intervention on behalf of either the incumbent or the challenger is considered, in theory at least, a calculated act of war against the other (making the intervening state likewise a "belligerent," deprived of the protection of the law of neutrality); and as a consequence traditional international law requires that certain factual conditions be met before outside states may accord recognition of belligerent status to factions challenging the incumbent government. Sir Hersch Lauterpacht summarizes these conditions in Recognition in International Law (1947), at 176:

> [F]irst, there must exist within the State an armed conflict of a general (as distinguished from a purely local) character; second, the insurgents must occupy and administer a substantial portion of national territory; third, they must conduct the hostilities in accordance with the rules of war and through organized armed forces acting under a responsible authority; fourthly, there must exist circumstances which make it necessary for outside States to define their attitude by means of recognition of belligerency.

If these conditions are not satisfied, then, in the eyes of traditional international law, it is premature to grant belligerent rights to either warring faction. Once these preconditions are met, however, then, arguably, it is intervention to refuse recognition of the internal conflict as "belligerency"; but as there is no objective way to meet the test of "belligerency," typically attention is given to the conduct of the incumbent that discloses a willingness to negotiate with the challenger on the basis of equality. Such a demonstration often forms part of an argument that there can arise a duty for outside states to treat a challenging faction as a "belligerent."

2. Antonio Cassese, International Law in a Divided World 81–84, 280–82 (1986).

States have traditionally been hostile to insurgents in their territory, on the obvious grounds that they do not like the status quo to be disrupted by people who seek to topple the "lawful government" and possibly to change the whole fabric of the State. Consequently they prefer to treat insurgency as a domestic occurrence and the rebels as common criminals; in their eyes, any "interference" from the international community is bound to bolster insurgents and make them even more dangerous. Traditional reluctance to grant civil upheaval the status of international armed conflict has become even more marked in recent times, for two reasons: first, the existence of tribal feuds or other forms of conflict in many Third World States, particularly in Africa, where the arbitrary borders decided upon by the colonial powers are likely to lead to secession, and second, the growing tendency of Great Powers to replace direct confrontation with war by proxy, through support for "loyal" or "friendly" political and military groups in small or middle-sized countries. Consequently, feeling more and more insecure, the overwhelming majority of States, and, above all, developing countries, show a growing tendency to withhold the granting of international legal standing to rebels and to treat them under the criminal laws of each country concerned.

The inimical attitude of States towards insurgents has manifested itself in three principal forms. First of all, the current regulation of insurgency is rather confused and rudimentary. International law does not specify when a group of rebels starts to possess international rights and duties. It only establishes certain loose minimum requirements (those indicated in the definition above) for being eligible to international subjectivity. It is for States (both the State against which civil strife breaks out and other parties) to decide—by granting or withholding recognition of insurgency or belligerency—whether these requirements have been fulfilled. In actual practice, the very existence of rebels as international legal persons largely depends on the attitude of other subjects. Theoretically, if all members of the international community were to decide that a certain insurrectional party is devoid of the requisite conditions, that party would not acquire any international status, however strong, effective, and protracted its authority over a portion of the territory belonging to a sovereign State. In practice, things are different, for two main reasons. First, in the international community there are several political and ideological alignments; any insurrectional party is likely to enlist the support of one or more States on account of political, religious, or ideological affinities, or because of military or strategic considerations. Consequently there will always be one or more States inclined to recognize certain rebels. Second, even other States may at a certain point find it useful to concede that a group of insurgents has become a legally independent subject: this may occur when the rebellious party exercises effective authority over a territory where foreigners live. Since it would be unrealistic for third States to claim respect for their nationals from the incumbent Government, they are forced to address their claim for protection of their citizens and their property to the rebels. They thus implicitly admit that rebels have a duty under international law to protect the lives and assets of foreigners.

Be that as it may, there is no gainsaying that in the case of rebels, recognition by existing States plays a more significant role than in the "birth" and legal personality of new States. The conspicuous reluctance of States to admit rebels to the "charmed circle" of the family of nations, the inherently provisional character of insurgency, the embryonic nature of most international rules concerning civil strife, are all factors determining the practical and legal importance of recognition.

There is a second way in which hostility to rebels comes to the fore. While third States are authorized to provide assistance of any kind, including the dispatch of armed forces, to the "lawful" government, they are duty-bound to refrain from supplying assistance (other than humanitarian) to rebels. Plainly, the current international regulation looks on insurgents with disfavour while granting the incumbent Government the right to enlist foreign help for wiping out rebels.

A third consequence of this hostility is the paucity of international rules applicable to the rebellious party. All in all, it can be argued that only very few general rules address themselves equally to rebels and to States (provided of course that the former prove they have control over the territory, and civil commotion reaches a certain degree of intensity and duration and that, in addition, at least a few States grant them recognition).

For example, the norms on treaty making: rebels are empowered to enter into agreements with those States which are willing to establish rapport with them. Similarly, the rules on the treatment of foreigners: rebels are to grant foreigners the treatment provided for under international law.... At the same time, rebels do not have a full correlative right to claim respect for their lives and property from all third States where their "nationals" (that is, people owing them allegiance) may find themselves. Such respect can be exacted only by way of reciprocity. If a "national" from an insurgent territory lives in a State unwilling to recognize rebels, that State's duty to protect that "national" only exists in relation to the "lawful" Government, of which the individual has citizenship. With regard to the rules on the immunity of foreign representatives: insurgents must treat as State organs all officials of third States in the territory under their control (they owe a special duty of protection, and must grant them immunity from jurisdiction for official acts, etc.). As to the persons acting for the rebellious party, they can claim international protection only in relation to those States which have granted them recognition. Other States are entitled to regard them simply as nationals of the country where civil strife is in progress.

A few rules on the enforcement of international law (unarmed reprisals and other peaceful sanctions) can also be applied. Insurgents can resort to all lawful sanctions both to enforce international agreements entered into with third States or the general international rules on foreigners and respect for officials, when applicable. Finally, there are rules concerning the conduct of hostilities with the "lawful" Government....

[But] [a]s ... pointed out above, the insurrectional party is provisional in character (insurgents are either quelled by the Government, and disappear; or they seize power, and install themselves in the place of the Government; or they secede and join another State, or become a new international subject). It follows that they cannot claim rights contingent upon the permanent character of international subjects. Thus, *inter alia*, insurgents do not possess any right of sovereignty proper over the territory they control (they cannot lawfully cede the territory or part of it to another international subject). They merely exercise *de facto* authority.

To conclude, insurgents are State-like subjects, for they exhibit all the major features of States. However, they are transient and, in addition, they have a limited international capacity in two respects: first, they have only a few international rights and duties; second, they are only "associated" to a limited number of existing States (those which by granting them recognition adopt the view that they fulfil all the conditions for international personality, and consequently engage in dealings with them).

* * *

General Features of the Legal Regulation of Civil Strife

At present, civil strife is viewed by international law from three different viewpoints: (1) the rights and obligations of third States with regard to the State where an internal armed conflict has broken out; (2) the conditions on which insurgents can claim international standing and the extent to which they consequently possess rights and obligations; (3) the extent to which international law regulates the fighting going on between the incumbent Government and the rebels.

[I here] turn to the third one. We should, however, remind ourselves . . . that the whole approach of international law to civil strife rests on an inherent clash of interests between the "lawful" Government on the one side (which is of course interested in regarding insurgents as mere bandits devoid of any international status) and rebels, on the other side (naturally eager to be internationally legitimized). Third States may, and actually do, side with either party, according to their own political or ideological leanings, and this, of course, further complicates the question.

All rules governing the struggle between the lawful Government and insurgents have one main feature in common: they do not grant rebels the status of lawful belligerents; in the eyes of both the Government against which they fight and of third States, rebels remain criminals infringing upon domestic penal law. Consequently, if captured, they do not enjoy the status of prisoner of war but can be tried and executed for the mere fact of having taken up arms against the central authorities. Insurgents can be upgraded to the status of lawful combatants only if the incumbent Government decides to grant them the so-called "recognition of belligerency". Obviously, this recognition has only been accorded in extreme situations. . . .

The obsolescence of the recognition of belligerency (mainly owing to the desire of the Governments involved in civil commotion to wipe out rebellion as soon as possible, as well as to the interest of the third States in either holding aloof or meddling *de facto* in the conflict without, however, going to the length of granting insurgents international legitimation) underlines the fact that rebels are in a greatly inferior position in relation to the central authorities against which they fight. One should not jump to the conclusion that if rebels come to possess international rights and duties, under certain circumstances . . . this achievement automatically entails the acquisition of the status of lawful combatants. . . . [O]n becoming international legal subjects they are enabled to enter into international agreements and to send or receive diplomatic missions, on the one hand, and are duty-bound to respect foreigners living in the areas under their control, on the other. The acquisition of international status also means the right to demand respect for certain international humanitarian rules on armed conflict and the obligation to abide by them. This does not mean, however, that these fighters legally cease to be criminals for the Government concerned—however abused this state of affairs may be.

Another important feature of the corpus of rules concerning internal armed conflict is that most of them aim at protecting non-combatants only, that is civilians who do not take part in hostilities and may directly or indirectly suffer from armed violence, the wounded and sick as well as those who, having taken part in the hostilities, are no longer willing, or in a position, to fight. Methods of combat are not regulated, except to the extent that they must aim at sparing civilians. In practice, there are almost no restraints on the armed engagements of Government authorities and rebels *inter se*. States have decided to leave fighting substantially unrestricted on the clear assumption that, being militarily stronger than insurgents, they may quell rebellion more easily by remaining untrammelled by law. This concept is proving increasingly fallacious, for, at present, rebels are assisted in various ways, especially militarily, by third States, and armed violence is therefore carried out with great intensity and cruelty on both sides.

Customary Law

... Owing to its ruinous effect and the magnitude of its armed hostilities, the Spanish Civil War (1936–9) acquired features comparable in several respects to an international war proper. This prompted the contending parties and several European States to affirm that certain general rules protecting civilians in interstate wars were applicable to this conflict as well, and to all similar examples of civil strife. Thus, a very interesting phenomenon took shape, which has become a major trend of the present century: the increasing extension to civil wars of the principles applicable to international armed conflicts. The rules on which general consent emerged were: the ban on deliberate bombing of civilians; the prohibition on attacking non-military objectives; the rule concerning the precautions which must be taken when attacking military objects; the rule authorizing reprisals against enemy civilians and consequently submitting them to the general conditions exacted for reprisals.

The four rules in point apply to any internal armed conflict, provided it has the characteristics of the Spanish Civil War. That is to say, the insurgents must exhibit the following features: an organized administration effectively controlling a portion of the territory of the State; and organized armed forces capable of abiding by international law. Internal armed conflicts having a lesser degree of intensity, for example, instances of minor rebellions, or uprisings which do not take on the proportions of a civil war proper, are not covered by the rules.

The formation of general norms on civilians was substantially borne out by the unanimous adoption by the General Assembly in 1968 of resolution no. 2444 (XXIII) **[Basic Document 2.23]**, and, again, in 1970, when resolution no. 2675 (XXV) **[Basic Document 2.24]** was passed. Interestingly, on a par with these UN resolutions, recent practice has reaffirmed the applicability to civil wars of at least some general rules on civilians. Such applicability was urged by the International Committee of the Red Cross on several occasions (for instance, in 1964 during the conflict in the Congo and during the 1966–9 Nigerian civil war), on none of which did it arouse any significant opposition.

Unfortunately these fairly satisfactory conditions of law are not matched by its observance in practice. It is dispiriting to notice that the Government and rebels of the same State—even though they pay lip-service to current legal standards, and in spite of the fact that, after all, the civilians suffering from the conflict are fellow-nationals—rarely protect non-combatants as requested by law.... A possible explanation is that, first, civilians often take sides in domestic strife and actually contribute, at various levels, to the struggle, and, second, that in many States (chiefly in Africa) the population is split into conflicting ethnic and cultural groups which consequently do not share the feeling of belonging to one and the same country.

[*Eds.*—Professor Cassese goes on to review some of the rules of international humanitarian law that are considered in Discussion Note/Question 19, *infra* at 361–64.]

3. Hilary Charlesworth, "Feminist Methods in International Law," 93 A.J.I.L. 379, 385–91 (1999).

How might a feminist international lawyer approach the specific question of individual accountability for human rights abuses in armed conflict? There is considerable empirical evidence that women are affected by armed conflict in ways that men are not.[1] The savagery of warfare seems closely linked to a wild form of male sexuality, a type of "toxic testosterone" in Michael Ignatieff's words,[2] and women and girls are the most obvious objects of this violence. Rape has been understood as one of the spoils of the victor, serving also to humiliate the vanquished. Globally, women form only 2 percent of regular army personnel, but as civilians they suffer disproportionately from armed conflict. For example, women and children constitute the majority of the victims in African conflict zones. In northern Uganda, young girls have been abducted to become the "wives" of commanders in the Lord's Resistance Army, which is fighting President Musuveni's government forces. In refugee camps, women tend to be responsible for the collection of food, fuel and water, requiring them to venture from the relative safety of the camps and thus to risk rape, torture and death from rebels, government soldiers and land mines. Women's lower social status also disadvantages them in the "relief" operations conducted during and after armed conflict. For example, in Somalia relief agencies often consult "household heads" when making decisions about the distribution of food and medicines, and these are usually regarded as the men. In Uganda, women survivors of decades of conflict claim that reproductive health has not been adequately attended to in relief work. Violence against women has been described more generally as "among the most serious and pervasive human rights abuses that the international community [now] confront[s]."[3] Nongovernmental organizations have chronicled, in particular, massive violence against women during armed conflict in Bosnia and Rwanda and the failure of their governments, international donors, humanitarian organizations, and reconstruction and development agencies to respond to women's needs in the "postwar" period.

Whether and how individuals should be held criminally accountable for human rights abuses in internal conflicts has increasingly exercised international lawyers. These questions have been prompted by the fact that the major overt manifestation of tension in the international community has shifted from wars between states to armed conflicts within states. What directions do feminist methodologies suggest for analyzing international law in this area? On one level, the acknowledgment of women's lives and the use of the vocabulary of gender in the statutes of the ad hoc Tribunals for the former Yugoslavia and for Rwanda and the International Criminal Court (ICC) might suggest that feminist activism has had a progressive effect on the law. On another level, it appears that even the "new" international criminal law remains primarily a system based on men's lives.

International law has traditionally drawn a distinction between the principles of individual conduct that apply in times of armed conflict (international humanitarian law, IHL) and those that operate in peacetime (human rights law). This dichotomy has led to many anomalies and inconsistencies.

---

1. *See, e.g.*, Special Rapporteur on Contemporary Forms of Slavery, Final Report on Systematic Rape, Sexual Slavery and Slavery-like Practices during Armed Conflict, UN Doc. E/CN.4/Sub.2/1998/13 (1998).

2. M. Ignatieff, The Warrior's Honor: Ethnic War and the Modern Conscience 127 (1998).

3. Human Rights Watch, World Report 1998, at 391 (1998).

From a feminist perspective, the distinction has allowed IHL, with its basis in codes of warriors' honor, to factor out issues that do not relate to the warrior caste. For example, the guardian of IHL, the International Committee of the Red Cross (ICRC), was able to consider the Taliban's exclusion of women from any workplace in Afghanistan as completely outside its mandate. Ignatieff has described the self-imposed constraints of the ICRC in this situation: "Its legitimacy depends on its working with warriors and warlords: if they insist that women be kept out of sight, it has no choice but to go along."[4] The honor of warriors has nothing to say about the oppression of women. Human rights law, while more expansive in its coverage than IHL ..., provided a more limited response to the harms that women generally face compared with those confronting men. International criminal law ... is an amalgam of IHL and human rights law. In many ways, it has combined the gendered blind spots of both traditions.

... What is the nature of international legal knowledge in this context? What knowledge is privileged and what knowledge is silenced and devalued?

Human Rights Abuses

The category of "human rights abuses" is a contested one from a feminist perspective. Analysis of the understanding of human rights in international law generally has shown that the definition of human rights is limited and androcentric.[5] The limitations of human rights law with respect to women are intensified in the context of IHL. Take, for example, the way that it deals with rape and sexual assault. Article 27 of the Fourth Geneva Convention [**Basic Document 2.12**] places states under an obligation to protect women in international armed conflict "against any attack on their honour, in particular against rape, enforced prostitution, or any form of indecent assault." The provision assumes that women should be protected from sexual crimes because they implicate a woman's honor, reinforcing the notion of women as men's property, rather than because they constitute violence. This proprietary image is underlined by the use of the language of protection rather than prohibition of the violence. Additional Protocol I [**Basic Document 2.31**] replaces the reference to a woman's honor with the notion that women should "be the object of special respect,"[6] implying that women's role in childbearing is the source of special status. Significantly, the provisions on rape are not specifically included in the category of grave breaches of international humanitarian law. In the context of noninternational armed conflict, common Article 3 of the Geneva Conventions does not specifically refer to sexual violence, generally prohibiting violence to life and the person, cruel treatment and torture, and humiliating and degrading treatment.

IHL, then, treats rape and sexual assault as an attack on (the warrior's) honor or on the sanctity of motherhood and not explicitly as of the same order as grave breaches such as compelling a prisoner of war to serve in enemy forces. The statutes of the two ad hoc Tribunals [**Basic Documents 2.43 & 2.46**] and the ICC [**Basic Document 1.16**], by contrast, provide much fuller responses to sexual violence, constructing it, depending on the circumstances,

4. Ignatieff, *supra* note 2, at 146.

5. *See generally*, *e.g.*, Human Rights of Women: National and International Perspectives (R. Cook ed., 1994).

6. Art. 76.

as potentially a crime of genocide, a crime against humanity and a war crime. This recognition was the result of considerable work and lobbying by women's organizations, but its limitations should be noted. In the statutes of the Yugoslav Tribunal and the ICC at least, all three categories of international crimes are concerned only with acts forming part of a widespread, systematic or large-scale attack. Thus, the "new" international criminal law engages sexual violence only when it is an aspect of the destruction of a community.

An example of this characteristic was the invitation to the prosecution by a trial chamber of the Yugoslav Tribunal, when reviewing indictments against Radovan Karadzic and Ratko Mladic, to consider broadening the characterization of the notion of genocide. It stated that "[t]he systematic rape of women ... is in some cases intended to transmit a new ethnic identity to the child. In other cases humiliation and terror serve to dismember the group."[7] This comment suggests that the primary problem with rape is either its effect on the ethnic identity of the child born as a result of the rape or the demoralizing effect on the group as a whole. This understanding of rape perpetuates a view of women as cultural objects or bodies on which and through which war can be waged. The decision in the 1998 Akayesu case by the Rwanda Tribunal that rape constituted an act of genocide if committed with the intention to destroy a particular group also rests on this limited image of women.[8]

The emphasis on the harm to the Tutsi people as a whole is, of course, required by the international definition of genocide, and the Akayesu decision on this point simply illustrates the inability of the law to properly name what is at stake: rape is wrong, not because it is a crime of violence against women and a manifestation of male dominance, but because it is an assault on a community defined only by its racial, religious, national or ethnic composition. In this account, the violation of a woman's body is secondary to the humiliation of the group. In this sense, international criminal law incorporates a problematic public/private distinction: it operates in the public realm of the collectivity, leaving the private sphere of the individual untouched. Because the notion of the community implicated here is one defined by the men within it, the distinction has gendered consequences.

Another public/private distinction incorporated (albeit unevenly) in international criminal law—via human rights law—is that between the acts of state and nonstate actors. Such a dichotomy has gendered aspects when mapped onto the reality of violence against women. Significantly, the ICC statute defines torture more broadly than the Convention against Torture **[Basic Document 3.26]**, omitting any reference to the involvement of public officials.[9] Steven Ratner has suggested, however, that some sort of distinction based on "official" involvement is useful as a criterion to sort out those actions against human dignity that should engender state and individual international criminal responsibility and those (such as common assault) that

---

7. Prosecutor v. Karadzic and Mladic, Review of the Indictment Pursuant to Rule 61 of the Rules of Procedure and Evidence, Nos. IT–95–5–R61 and IT–95–18–R61, ¶ ¶ 94–95 (11 Jul 1996), *reprinted in* 108 I.L.R. 85 (1998).

8. Prosecutor v. Akayesu, Judgment, No. 96–4–T (2 Sep 1998), *available at* <http://www.un.org/ictr>. [*Eds.*—For excerpts from the

Akayesu judgment, see Reading G–14 in Problem 5–1 ("Ethnic Conflict and Its Consequences in Slavia, Candia, and Corcyra"), at 590.

9. The Statute, however, appears to regard rape and sexual violence as distinct from torture. *See* Art. 7(1)(g).

should not.[10] The problem, from a feminist perspective, is not the drawing of public/private, or regulated/nonregulated, distinctions as such, but rather the reinforcement of gender inequality through the use of such distinctions. We need, then, to pay attention to the actual operation of boundary drawing in international law and whether it ends up affecting women's and men's lives differently. For example, the consequence of defining certain rapes as public in international law is to make private rapes seem somehow less serious. The distinction is made, not by reference to women's experiences, but by the implications for the male-dominated public sphere.[11]

A different type of silence that might be identified in the legal protection of the human rights of women in armed conflict is the almost exclusive focus on sexual violence. Insights generated by the "world traveling" method suggest that this emphasis obscures many other human rights issues in times of armed conflict, particularly the protection of economic, social and cultural rights of women. Conflict exacerbates the globally unequal position of women and men in many ways. We know, for example, of the distinctive burdens placed on women through food and medical shortages caused by conflict. When food is scarce, more women than men suffer from malnutrition, often because of cultural norms that require men and boys to eat before women and girls. Humanitarian relief for the victims of conflict regularly fails to reach women, as men are typically given responsibility for its distribution. Economic sanctions imposed before, during or after armed conflict have had particular impact on women and girls, who are disproportionately represented among the poor. Although the effect of these practices falls heavily on women, they are not understood by international law to be human rights abuses that would engage either state or individual responsibility.

Internal Conflict

What interests and voices are privileged or silenced in the distinction between international and noninternational conflicts ...? The Geneva Conventions, Additional Protocol II and the Statute of the International Criminal Court regulate noninternational conflicts in a more circumspect way than international conflicts. The explanation for this distinction is that states are reluctant to give international status to those challenging their authority by force, preferring to classify them as criminals subject to domestic jurisdiction. The category of noninternational conflicts regulated by IHL is a very limited one, excluding "situations of internal disturbances and tensions, such as riots, isolated and sporadic acts of violence or other acts of a similar nature."[12] The international/internal dichotomy has a gendered dimension because it underpins a detailed legal regime protecting combatants in international conflicts, almost invariably men, and a more general regime offering considerably weaker (and more contentious) protection to the civilian population, encom-

10. S. Ratner, *The Schizophrenias of International Criminal Law*, 33 Tex. Int'l L. J. 237 (1998).

11. *See* S. Chesterman, *Never Again ... And Again: Law, Order, and the Gender of War Crimes in Bosnia and Beyond*, 22 Yale J. Int'l L.299, 336 (1997).

12. ICC Statute **[Basic Document 1.16]**, Art. 8(2)(d). In the case of violations of human-

itarian law apart from common Article 3 to the Geneva Conventions, the statute adds that its provisions apply only to "armed conflicts that take place in the territory of a State when there is protracted armed conflict between governmental authorities and organized armed groups or between such groups." *Id.*, Art. 8(2)(f).

passing almost all women. From the perspective of those caught up in the conflict, the international/internal dichotomy makes little sense, as abuses of human rights do not change character according to this criterion.

On a broader level, the dichotomy between international and internal conflict distracts attention from the close relationship between international practices and internal conflict. For example, Anne Orford has drawn attention to the involvement of international institutions in the creation of "internal" tension.[13] In particular, she has shown how the activities of international economic institutions contributed to the terrible "internal" conflict in the former Yugoslavia and has concluded that "the failure to consider the possibility that the causes of the crisis might be related to the activities of international institutions or the influence of international law has meant that ... the causes of the conflict [were seen as] 'ethnic' or 'nationalist.' "[14] The distinction, then, is a construct that obscures both the human suffering created by, and the causes of, "internal" conflict.

The distinction between international and internal conflicts has to some extent been de-emphasized in international criminal law through the definition of the categories of genocide and crimes against humanity and through the inclusion of some human rights norms—for example, the prohibition on torture—that operate in times of war and peace. However, the categories of crimes against humanity and war crimes as defined in the ICC statute still assume the existence of some type of hostilities (a "widespread or systematic attack" on civilians in the case of crimes against humanity and the planned large-scale commission of crimes in the case of war crimes).

The notions of conflict and attacks are themselves contingent and controversial. When do they begin and end? For many women, violence is not reduced with the cessation of military hostilities, and ostensible times of peace may be full of conflict for women and produce serious human rights violations. For example, Cynthia Enloe has described the social structures surrounding many foreign military bases where women may be abducted and forced into prostitution or become prostitutes in order to survive.[15] Thus, in Honduras, women living on the fringes of United States bases have become caught up in a web of coercive and economic pressures to satisfy the military's expectation of the sexual services of local women. Women's experience of violence and sexual abuse at the hands of United Nations peacekeepers in Mozambique, Cambodia and Bosnia is another example of the unreality of the conflict/peace dichotomy: in this context the "peacekeepers" are the source of conflict and violence. Yet another example is the particularly harmful effects on women of economic sanctions imposed as a result of armed conflict. The negotiation of the Dayton Peace Accords shows how the achievement of "peace" may be at the expense of the recognition of, and compensation for, harm suffered by the most vulnerable groups.[16] The failure of the Dayton Accords to acknowledge the treatment of, or provide any assistance to, the

13. A. Orford, *Locating the International: Military and Monetary Interventions after the Cold War*, 38 Harv. Int'l L. J. 443 (1997).

14. *Id.* at 479–80.

15. C. Enloe, The Morning After: Sexual Politics at the End of the Cold War 118–20 (1993).

16. U. Dolgopol, *A Feminist Appraisal of the Dayton Peace Accords*, 19 Adelaide L. Rev. 59 (1997).

Bosnian women who were raped and sexually abused during the conflict has perpetuated their suffering.

Individual Accountability

The notion of "individual" accountability ... implies a contrast with (civil) state responsibility. Individual criminal accountability is regarded by most international lawyers as a higher, and more effective, deterrent to human rights abuses than state responsibility, because of the risk that the responsible state may choose not to impose any punishment on the actual perpetrator. In this sense, it might be argued that at the international level individual accountability for human rights abuses affecting women would be a valuable method to reduce these wrongs. In many countries, the international sphere is regarded as more hospitable to women's claims than national legal systems. What criterion, if any, should be used to distinguish those violations of human rights that generate individual accountability from those that do not? While we may not wish to allocate criminal responsibility for every breach of human rights, it is critical that the principle of accountability not effectively reinforce gendered differences. The criterion of official conduct, discussed above, may well have this effect.

Feminists have had mixed views on the appropriate reaction to crimes against women in national legal systems. Although they have often been skeptical of systems of criminal justice, many feminists have supported strict application of existing law and called for strong penalties in the case of violence against women. At the same time, they have pointed to the need to compensate and support victims of violence. Involvement in criminal legal processes, whether national or international, may bring about further trauma in the person who was the object of violence. Moreover, pursuing individual criminal accountability alone can distract us from investigating the causes of a problem. Focus on individual acts of violence against women may obscure the structural relations of power and domination that make them possible and the continuity between the ways women are treated in "peacetime" and in times of "conflict": rape in armed conflict is made possible by the prevalence of rape in times of peace. Such a focus will not necessarily provide an incentive to remedy human rights abuses that are the product of a systematic failure to create the conditions necessary to guarantee the security of women. International trials of individuals for human rights abuses during armed conflict serve a range of social functions, including retribution, deterrence and absolution through catharsis. The ideal of justice animating them is closely connected, as Simon Chesterman has shown, to a particular understanding of peace and order obtained through military means.[17] The trials allow a return to the "order" of the status quo, but this public order is dependent both on the acceptability of violence and on the domination of women in the private domain.

Schemes of accountability for human rights violations are not confined to criminal responsibility. For example, the "truth commissions" established in a number of states, including Uganda, Chile, El Salvador and South Africa, were designed to establish the facts about patterns of human rights violations, without necessarily leading to individual criminal prosecutions. The rationale of these investigatory mechanisms was that knowledge of the truth would

17. *See* Chesterman, *supra* note 11, at 311–17.

itself promote social healing and reconciliation.[18] The nonadversarial nature of these proceedings might appear to be consistent with some feminist scholars' reservations about criminal proceedings and support for alternative forms of dispute resolution. The experience of the commissions, however, is mixed. Their effectiveness in promoting reconciliation has been dependent on political support and broad terms of reference. Issues of gender have thus far not been seen as relevant to their mandates.

The notion of state responsibility has recently been developed in ways that encompass gendered harm. For example, in *Mejía Egocheaga v. Peru* the Inter-American Commission on Human Rights held Peru accountable for the rape of a woman, Raquel Mejía, by Peruvian security forces as an aspect of the campaign against civilians suspected of having connections with insurgents. The Commission observed that there were no effective remedies within Peru to pursue claims against the security forces. It stated:

> Current international law establishes that sexual assault committed by members of security forces, whether as a result of the deliberate practice promoted by the state or as a result of failure by the state to prevent the occurrence of this crime, constitutes a violation of the victim's human rights, especially the right to physical and mental integrity.[19]

The value of this principle is its recognition of international responsibility for an inadequate national structure to respond to crimes against women. When is a national legal system considered deficient in this context? International law appears able to recognize the Peruvian system as inadequate because it allowed no action against the security forces. It is less ready to respond to the significant structural problems in most legal systems, which may offer formal legal remedies for gendered harms but in practice fail to deliver justice to women.

4. Hague Convention (No. V) Respecting the Rights and Duties of Neutral Powers and Persons in Case of War on Land. Concluded, at The Hague, 18 Oct 1907. Entered into force, 26 Jan 1910. 205 C.T.S. 299 (French); 2 A.J.I.L.S. 117 (1908); *reprinted in* **2 Weston & Carlson II.B.2: Art. 4** (Basic Document 2.3).

5. Geneva Conventions (Nos. I–IV) for the Amelioration of the Condition of the Wounded and Sick in Armed Forces in the Field, for the Amelioration of the Condition of the Wounded, Sick and Shipwrecked Members of Armed Forces at Sea, (III) Relative to the Treatment of Prisoners of War, and (IV) Relative to the Protection of Civilian Persons in Time of War. Concluded, 12 Aug 1949. Entered into force, 21 Oct 1950. 75 U.N.T.S. 31, 85, 135, & 287, *reprinted in* **2 Weston & Carlson II.B.11–II.B.14: Art. 3** (Basic Documents 2.9, 2.10, 2.11 & 2.12).

6. Resolution on Respect for Human Rights in Armed Conflicts, 19 Dec 1968, GA Res. 2444, UN GAOR, 23rd Sess., Supp. No. 18, at 50, UN Doc. A/7128 (1969), *reprinted in* **2 Weston & Carlson II.B.16** (Basic Document 2.23).

---

18. *See* P. Hayner, *Fifteen Truth Commissions—1974 to 1994: A Comparative Study*, 16 H.R.Q. 597, 604 (1994).

19. Case 10.970, Report 5/96 (Mar. 1, 1996), *reprinted in* 1 Butterworths Hum. Rts. Cases 229 (1996).

7. **Resolution on the Basic Principles for the Protection of Civilian Populations in Armed Conflicts**, 9 Dec 1970, GA Res. 2675, UN GAOR, 25th Sess., Supp. No. 28, at 76, UN Doc. A/8028 (1970), *reprinted in* 2 Weston & Carlson II.B.16a (Basic Document 2.24).

8. **Protocol Additional (No II) to the Geneva Conventions of August 12, 1949, and Relating to the Protection of Victims of Non-International Armed Conflicts.** Concluded, 8 Jun 1977. Entered into force, 7 Dec 1978. 1977 U.N.J.Y.B. 135, *reprinted in* 16 I.L.M. 1442 (1977) and 2 Weston & Carlson II.B.21: Pmbl. & Arts. 1–18 (Basic Document 2.32).

9. **The Prosecutor v. Duško Tadić a/k/a "Dule" International Tribunal for the Prosecution of Persons Responsible for Serious Violations of International Humanitarian Law Committed in the Territory of Former Yugoslavia Since 1991**, Case No. IT–94–1–AR72, 2 Oct 95, *reprinted in* 35 I.L.M. 32 (1996): ¶ ¶ 79–145 (*see supra* Chapter 3, at 189–210).

10. **International Convention Against the Recruitment, Use, Financing and Training of Mercenaries.** Adopted by the UN General Assembly, 4 Dec 1989. Entered into force 20 Oct 2001. GA Res. 44/34 (Annex), UN GAOR, 44th Sess., Supp. No. 49, at 306, UN Doc. A/Res/44/49 (1990), *reprinted in* 29 I.L.M. 89 (1990) and 2 Weston & Carlson II.A.5: Arts. 1–8, 16–17 (Basic Document 2.39).

11. **Rome Statute of the International Criminal Court.** Concluded 17 Jul 1998. Entered into force 1 Jul 2002, UN Doc A/CONF.183/9 (1998), *reprinted in* 37 I.L.M. 999 (1998) and 1 Weston & Carlson I.H.13: Arts. 87, 89, 98, & 103 (Basic Document 1.16).

C. UNILATERAL INTERVENTION

1. **Charter of the United Nations.** Concluded, 26 Jun 1945. Entered into force, 24 Oct 1945. 1976 Y.B.U.N. 1043, *reprinted in* 1 Weston & Carlson I.A.1: Pmbl. & Arts. 1, 2(1), 2(3), 2(4), 2(7), 51 (Basic Document 1.5).

2. **Declaration on the Inadmissibility of Intervention in the Domestic Affairs of States and the Protection of their Independence and Sovereignty**, 21 Dec 1965, GA Res. 2131, UN GAOR, 20th Sess., Supp. No. 14, at 11, UN Doc. A/6014 (1966), *reprinted in* 5 I.L.M. 374 (1966) and 2 Weston & Carlson II.A.2 (Basic Document 2.20).

3. **Declaration on Principles of International Law Concerning Friendly Relations and Co-operation Among States in Accordance with the Charter of the United Nations**, 24 Oct 1970, GA Res. 2625, UN GAOR, 25th Sess., Supp. No. 28, at 121, UN Doc. A/8028 (1971), *reprinted in* 9 I.L.M. 1292 (1970) and 1 Weston & Carlson I.D.7 (Basic Document 1.11).

4. **Resolution on the Definition of Aggression**, 14 Dec 1974, GA Res. 3314, UN GAOR, 29th Sess., Supp. No. 31, at 142, UN Doc. A/9631 (1975), *reprinted in* 13 I.L.M. 710 (1974) and 2 Weston & Carlson II.A.4 (Basic Document 2.29).

5. Rosalyn Higgins, "Intervention and International Law," in Intervention in World Politics 29, 40–42 (H. Bull ed., 1984).[k]

... When one is dealing with military intervention in the context of Article 2(4) of the UN Charter [**Basic Document 1.5**], one is really simply dealing with the lawful and unlawful use of force. To call it "intervention" is simply a value-laden way of saying it is an impermissible use of force. Care should be taken about doing this in any lawyerish context, however. For example, the Declaration on the Definition of Aggression [**Basic Document 2.29**] makes it clear that "aggression" is not "intervention". "Aggression" involves the military use of force and the unlawful military use of force. "Intervention" ... is a term used to describe a spectrum of intrusions—some major, some minor, some lawful, some unlawful. One has to guard against using these phrases loosely and in an identical sense. "Intervention" in the military context has some reality to the international lawyer in the context of humanitarian intervention, and in the further context of participating at some level in civil wars, in internal wars. The traditional classical international law has it that once the insurgent party in a civil war has reached a certain standing, the status which affords it the right to be regarded by the international community as a belligerent (that is to say it has effective control over substantial parts of the territory and an organized fighting unit) requires third parties to be neutral in their relationships with each of the warring factions. The reality is vastly different. Indeed, there is evidence that the law is perceived differently today. The constitutional government will often itself ask for outside help. It will say that as the constitutional government it is indeed entitled to ask for help. The insurgents will themselves ask for help on the grounds that they are engaged in a battle for self-determination, or to overthrow an undemocratic government or a government that has been engaged in repression of human rights, or they will say they are entitled to recognition as the government perhaps of a ceded part of the territory. Looked at from the perspective of the outside states which have to respond to these requests to intervene, there are many arguments that can reasonably be adduced in favour of supporting the existing government. First of all, they will be able to argue that what is going on in the country concerned is at the moment mere insurgency, mere rebellion; it has not reached that level where neutrality is required. (But conversely, the responding state must bear in mind the growth of the contemporary doctrine of the right of self-determination. If a government is always entitled to ask for the assistance of an outside power it is hard to see the right of self-determination as a reality in the hands of a fighting secessionist or other rebellion movement.) Secondly, it is said that arms may continue to be sold to the lawful government provided that the belligerency has not been recognized. And sometimes it seems to be thought that it is perfectly appropriate for arms to be sold to recognized governments virtually regardless of the status of the rebels....

6. Editors' Note. Three exceptions historically invoked by states to justify intervention in situations of internal armed conflict outside the terms of Chapter VII of the UN Charter [**Basic Document 1.5**] are (a) intervention at the request or with the consent of the legitimate government, (b) intervention on the basis of a right conferred by treaty, and (c) "humanitarian"

---

k. The author has been a member (Judge) of the International Court of Justice since 12 July 1995 and was elected President in February 2006.

intervention to protect the human rights of those people caught up in the internal armed conflict. Each has been the subject of mounting concern in recent years.

(a) The case of intervention at the request or with the consent of the legitimate government is summarized by Ian Brownlie, *The United Nations Charter and the Use of Force, 1945–1985*, in The Current Legal Regulation of the Use of Force 491, 501–02 (A. Cassese ed., 1986):

> Intervention by request or consent was alleged in the case of Soviet interventions in Hungary in 1956 (two occasions), Czechoslovakia in 1968, and Afghanistan at the end of 1979. The United States used this justification in respect of Lebanon in 1958. France has intervened in a number of African States on the same basis. A complete list of similar instances would be of impressive length, and would include the Multinational Peacekeeping Force in Lebanon (1982–83).

> There can be little doubt but that this type of intervention is compatible with the Charter of the UN. The provisions of the Charter do not contain any provision related to the question and legality of such intervention flows from major principles of general international law: the principle of consent and the legal personality of the State producing the request for, or consent to, intervention. The legality of such intervention is confirmed by the subsequent practice of the Members of the UN either in giving consent or in acting in response to such request or consent. There is a certain qualification to be considered. In the case of intervention on the side of a government faced with a substantial rebellion, there is much to be said for the view that such intervention runs counter to the principle of self-determination of peoples which is also a significant part of the legal regime of the Charter. No doubt this position is open to question when the rebellion is supported from outside. However, provided the rebellion is in pursuit of the exercise of the right of self-determination, external assistance may be lawful and intervention on the side of the opposing forces may be unlawful: this would appear to be the effect of the Declaration of Principles of International Law concerning Friendly Relations of 1970 **[Basic Document 1.11]**. . . .

> The title of intervention by request or consent involves the request or consent of a lawful government and therein lies one of the major problems. In practice the request or consent emanates from an officer or organ of government at a time of constitutional crisis when the authority and status of the consenting agent is either questionable or, in some cases, the central issue in the crisis. The authority of the organ supposed to have given consent has been open to doubt (to say the least) in the cases of Hungary (1956), Lebanon (1958), Czechoslovakia (1968), Afghanistan (1979) and Grenada (1983). In cases of extreme confusion and civil strife there may be no lawfully constituted authority in being and in such case the standard of legality of a government set by public international law is simply that of effectiveness. This standard is by no means easy to apply to the claims of factions locked in an unresolved conflict. The dangers to peace in such cases are clear, since rival factions may purport to give licenses for foreign intervention. At least the international com-

munity has shown little patience with those pleas of consent which have a markedly weak basis in fact.

(b) The case of intervention grounded on a right conferred by treaty is likewise complicated by difficulties that arise when the legal status of the incumbent government is in doubt. Typically in cases of extreme civil strife—inescapably when the competing factions are locked in unresolved conflict—the question arises as to which of the competing factions is authorized to speak on behalf of the "legitimate" government or state with which the treaty originally was negotiated. Additionally, in such instances, the intervening state may face a conflict of obligations. On the one hand, the treaty may require assistance in the form of military advice, intelligence, arms, logistical support, and/or combat personnel; on the other hand, the internal conflict may have reached the point where the duty of non-intervention arises.

A problem is posed, too, when treaties purport to guarantee a right of intervention in the event a particular government or form of government is threatened by internal crisis. Historically, such arrangements have been criticized for being the product of unequal relationships in which the interests of one state may have been subordinated to the interests of another. They have also come under attack also for being contrary to post–1945 prohibitions on the use of force. *See, e.g.,* W. Michael Reisman, *Termination of the USSR's Treaty Right of Intervention in Iran*, 74 A.J.I.L. 144, 150–53 (1980). For a contrasting view, see Natalino Ronzitti, *Use of Force, Jus Cogens and State Consent*, in The Current Legal Regulation of the Use of Force 147, 159 (A. Cassese ed., 1986).

(c) "Humanitarian" reasons have been used to justify unilateral intervention in one state by another. They were the basis, for example, of the much debated NATO intervention in Kosovo in 1999. The status of unilateral humanitarian intervention in international law is controversial and is discussed in the readings that follow.

7. *Military and Paramilitary Activities In and Against Nicaragua* (Nicar. v. U.S.), 1986 ICJ 14 (27 Jun), 96–100.

202. The principle of non-intervention involves the right of every sovereign State to conduct its affairs without outside interference; though examples of trespass against this principle are not infrequent, the Court considers that it is part and parcel of customary international law. As the Court has observed: "Between independent States, respect for territorial sovereignty is an essential foundation of international relations"[1] . . ., and international law requires political integrity also to be respected. Expressions of an *opinio juris* regarding the existence of the principle of non-intervention in customary international law are numerous and not difficult to find. . . . The existence in the *opinio juris* of States of the principle of non-intervention is backed by established substantial practice. It has moreover been presented as a corollary of the principle of the sovereign equality of States. A particular instance of this is General Assembly resolution 2625 (XXV), the Declaration on the Principles of International Law concerning Friendly Relations and Co-operation among States **[Basic Document 1.11]**. In the *Corfu Channel* case[m]

---

l. Corfu Channel Case (U.K. v. Alb.), 1949   **m.** *Id.*
ICJ 4 (15 Dec) **(Basic Document 7.5).**

when a State claimed a right of intervention in order to secure evidence in the territory of another State for submission to an international tribunal ..., the Court observed that:

> the alleged right of intervention as the manifestation of a policy of force, such as has, in the past, given rise to most serious abuses and such as cannot, whatever be the present defects in international organization, find a place in international law. Intervention is perhaps still less admissible in the particular form it would take here; for, from the nature of things, it would be reserved for the most powerful States, and might easily lead to perverting the administration of international justice itself. (ICJ Reports 1949, p. 35.)

203. The principle has since been reflected in numerous declarations adopted by international organizations and conferences in which the United States and Nicaragua have participated, *e.g.*, General Assembly resolution 2131 (XX), the Declaration on the Inadmissibility of Intervention in the Domestic Affairs of States and the Protection of their Independence and Sovereignty **[Basic Document 2.20]** ..., [the essentials of which] are repeated in the Declaration approved by resolution 2625 (XXV)....

* * *

206. ... There have been in recent years a number of instances of foreign intervention for the benefit of forces opposed to the government of another State. The Court ... has to consider whether there might be indications of a practice illustrative of belief in a kind of general right for States to intervene, directly or indirectly, with or without armed force, in support of an internal opposition in another State, whose cause appeared particularly worthy by reason of the political and moral values with which it was identified. For such a general right to come into existence would involve a fundamental modification of the customary law principle of non-intervention.

207. ... In fact however the Court finds that States have not justified their conduct by reference to a new right of intervention or a new exception to the principle of its prohibition. The United States authorities have on some occasions clearly stated their grounds for intervening in the affairs of a foreign State for reasons connected with, for example, the domestic politics of that country, its ideology, the level of its armaments, or the direction of its foreign policy. But these were statements of international policy, and not an assertion of rules of existing international law.

* * *

209. The Court therefore finds that no ... general right of intervention, in support of an opposition within another State, exists in contemporary international law. The Court concludes that acts constituting a breach of the customary principle of non-intervention will also, if they directly or indirectly involve the use of force, constitute a breach of the principle of non-use of force in international relations.

8. Louis Henkin, "NATO's Kosovo Intervention: Kosovo and the Law of 'Humanitarian Intervention'," 93 A.J.I.L. 824, 824–28 (1999).

Was military intervention by NATO justified, lawful, under the UN Charter **[Basic Document 1.5]** and international law? Does Kosovo suggest the need for reaffirmation, or clarification, or modification, of the law as to humanitarian intervention? What should the law be, and can the law be construed or modified to be what it ought to be?

* * *

In my view, unilateral intervention, even for what the intervening state deems to be important humanitarian ends, is and should remain unlawful. But the principles of law, and the interpretations of the Charter, that prohibit unilateral humanitarian intervention do not reflect a conclusion that the "sovereignty" of the target state stands higher in the scale of values of contemporary international society than the human rights of its inhabitants to be protected from genocide and massive crimes against humanity. The law that prohibits unilateral humanitarian intervention rather reflects the judgment of the community that the justification for humanitarian intervention is often ambiguous, involving uncertainties of fact and motive, and difficult questions of degree and "balancing" of need and costs. The law against unilateral intervention may reflect, above all, the moral-political conclusion that no individual state can be trusted with authority to judge and determine wisely.

... The need for intervention may sometimes be compelling, and the safeguard against the dangers of unilateral intervention lies in developing bona fide, responsible, collective intervention.

Serious efforts to develop "some form of collective intervention" began soon after the end of the Cold War, when it ceased to be hopeless to pursue collective intervention by authority of the UN Security Council. In 1991 and 1992, the Security Council authorized military intervention for humanitarian purposes in Iraq and Somalia. In principle, those interventions were not justified as "humanitarian" (a term that does not appear in the UN Charter); the theory supporting such actions was that some internal wars, at least when accompanied by war crimes, and massive human rights violations and other crimes against humanity even if unrelated to war, may threaten international peace and security and therefore were within the jurisdiction and were the responsibility of the Security Council under Chapters VI and VII of the Charter. Of course, under Article 27(3) of the Charter, a Security Council resolution to authorize intervention, like other "nonprocedural" matters, was subject to veto by any permanent member. Thus, by the sum (or product) of law and politics, humanitarian intervention by any state was prohibited; humanitarian intervention was permissible if authorized by the Security Council, but a single permanent member could prevent such authorization.

Kosovo surely threatened international peace and security, as the Security Council had held in several prior resolutions. And, in 1998–1999, when negotiation and political-economic pressures appeared futile, for many Kosovo begged for intervention by any states that could do so, and by any means necessary. NATO heeded the call. It did not ask leave or authorization from the Security Council.

The reason why NATO did not seek explicit authorization from the Security Council is not difficult to fathom. Even after the Cold War, geography and politics rendered unanimity by the permanent members in support of military action (especially in the Balkans) highly unlikely. Evidently, NATO decided that not asking for authorization was preferable to having it frustrated by veto, which might have complicated diplomatic efforts to address the crisis, and would have rendered consequent military action politically more difficult.

* * *

The Charter prohibition on intervention, even for humanitarian ends, is addressed to individual states, but what the Charter prohibits to a single state does not become permissible to several states acting together. Intervention by several states is "unilateral," *i.e.*, "on their own authority," if not authorized by the Security Council. Was NATO intervention in Kosovo authorized? Was it a justifiable exception?

The argument for NATO might go something like this.

Human rights violations in Kosovo were horrendous; something had to be done. The Security Council was not in fact "available" to authorize intervention because of the veto. Faced with a grave threat to international peace and security within its region, and with rampant crimes reeking of genocide, NATO had to act.

NATO intervention was not "unilateral"; it was "collective," pursuant to a decision by a responsible body, including three of the five permanent members entrusted by the UN Charter with special responsibility to respond to threats to international peace and security. NATO did not pursue narrow parochial interests, either of the organization or of any of its members; it pursued recognized, clearly compelling humanitarian purposes. Intervention by NATO at Kosovo was a "collective" humanitarian intervention "in the common interest," carrying out the responsibility of the world community to address threats to international peace and security resulting from genocide and other crimes against humanity. The collective character of the organization provided safeguards against abuse by single powerful states pursuing egoistic national interests. And action by NATO could be monitored by the Security Council and ordered to be terminated. The NATO action in Kosovo had the support of the Security Council. Twelve (out of fifteen) members of the Council voted to reject the Russian resolution of March 26, thereby agreeing in effect that the NATO intervention had been called for and should continue. And on June 10, the Security Council, in Resolution 1244 approving the Kosovo settlement, effectively ratified the NATO action and gave it the Council's support.

In my view, the law is, and ought to be, that unilateral intervention by military force by a state or group of states is unlawful unless authorized by the Security Council. Some—governments and scholars—thought that NATO too needed, but had not had, such authorization, at least ab initio. But many—governments and scholars—thought that something had to be done to end the horrors of Kosovo, that NATO was the appropriate body to do it, and perhaps the only body that could do it, and that the law should not, did not, stand in the way.

* * *

Humanitarian intervention on the authority of the Security Council recognizes that the Charter prohibition on the use of force does not apply to the use of force "in the common interest"; it also recognizes that intervention authorized by the Security Council affords the strongest safeguard against abuse of humanitarian intervention that the contemporary political system provides. But, as Kosovo illustrated, the Council, as presently constituted and under prevailing procedures, remains seriously defective and may sometimes be unavailable for that awesome responsibility.

NATO did not seek the Council's mantle, presumably because of the fear of the veto. We are not about to see a major restructuring in the composition of the Security Council, and we are not likely soon to see an end to the veto generally. But might we pursue an exception to the veto, as regards humanitarian intervention, in practice if not in principle?

That may be what Kosovo in fact achieved, in some measure. For Kosovo, Council ratification after the fact in Resolution 1244[n]—formal ratification by an affirmative vote of the Council—effectively ratified what earlier might have constituted unilateral action questionable as a matter of law. Unless a decision to authorize intervention in advance can be liberated from the veto, the likely lesson of Kosovo is that states, or collectivities, confident that the Security Council will acquiesce in their decision to intervene, will shift the burden of the veto: instead of seeking authorization in advance by resolution subject to veto, states or collectivities will act, and challenge the Council to terminate the action. And a permanent member favoring the intervention could frustrate the adoption of such a resolution.

* * *

Kosovo demonstrates yet again a compelling need to address the deficiencies in the law and practice of the UN Charter. The sometimes-compelling need for humanitarian intervention (as at Kosovo), like the compelling need for responding to interstate aggression (as against Iraq over Kuwait), brings home again the need for responsible reaction to gross violations of the Charter, or to massive violations of human rights, by responsible forces acting in the common interest. We need Article 43 agreements for standby forces responsible to the Security Council, but neither action by the Security Council under Article 42, nor collective intervention as by NATO at Kosovo, can serve without some modification in the law and the practice of the veto. The NATO action in Kosovo, and the proceedings in the Security Council, may reflect a step toward a change in the law, part of the quest for developing "a form of collective intervention" beyond a veto-bound Security Council. That may be a desirable change, perhaps even an inevitable change. And it might be achieved without formal amendment of the Charter (which is virtually impossible to effect), by a "gentlemen's agreement" among the permanent members, or by wise self-restraint and acquiescence. That, some might suggest, is what the law ought to be, and proponents of a "living Charter" would support an interpretation of the law and an adaptation of UN procedures that rendered them what they ought to be. That might be the lesson of Kosovo.

n. SC Res. 1244 (On the situation in Kosovo), UN SCOR, 54th Sess., 4011th mtg, UN Doc. S/RES/1244 (10 Jun 1999).

9. Jean Bethke Elshtain, "Just War and Humanitarian Intervention," 17 Am. U. Int'l L. Rev. 1, 3–5, 9–17 (2001).

The just war tradition is a way of thinking that refuses to separate politics from ethics. Unlike the competing doctrine of state-centered strategic realism, just war argument insists one must not open up an unbridgeable gulf between "domestic" and "international" politics. The tradition of political realism and that of just war embrace contrasting presumptions about the human condition. The realpolitikers, whose great forefathers are Machiavelli and Hobbes, hold that men in general are ungrateful, dissembling, back-stabbing, and untrustworthy—Machiavelli here—or, in Hobbes' account, that humans are isolates driven into forward motion, bound to collide violently and that humanity in general is defined by the most horrible equality imaginable—the power each has to kill each other. It takes a lot of coercive force to hold such creatures in check, not in the interest of a positive vision of human possibility but simply to stop them marauding.

By contrast, just war thinkers begin with a commitment to a view of human beings as creatures who are always conflicted and torn and whose human relationships are characterized by love and kindness as well as selfishness and cruelty, human solidarity and human plurality. These are constant features of the human condition that are played out in a variety of plural ways in diverse cultures. Human motives and actions are always mixed: we both affirm and destroy solidaristic possibilities, often doing so simultaneously. For example, we affirm solidarity within the particular communities of which we are a part—for every human being is a member of a way of life that embodies itself institutionally as family, tribe, civil society, state. This plurality is a constant feature of human political and moral life. We may launch ourselves into wider or more universalistic possibilities from this particular site, seeking to affirm our common humanity through organizations, institutions, ways of being and thinking that draw us into wider streams of existence. Or we may not. And we may not in dreadful and destructive ways, for example, by denying the very humanity of those from different plural sites than our own. This denial of humanity is also a denial, or a refusal to recognize, that all cultures, without fail, define and refine moral codes and that these moral codes invariably set norms for the taking of human life; all have some notion of what counts as a violation of this norm. Standards of moral conduct pertain in all arenas in which human beings engage one another, from families to polities. The challenging question is what standards and to what ends, not whether moral norms are applicable to the arena of politics (as but one example) or not.

The tradition of *realpolitik*, by contrast, insists that the rules which govern domestic moral conduct—here the focus is a body politic internally—are inapplicable to the world of what used to be called "men and states." Just war as politics insists that while it would be utopian to presume that relations between states can be governed by the premises and care taking apposite in our dealings with family and friends, this does not mean a war of all against all must kick in once one leaves the hearth or the immediate neighborhood or even the borders of one's country. The strategic realist is governed by instrumental calculations and some concept of national interest; the just war thinker by a complex amalgam of normative commitments and pragmatic considerations that overlap in a number of important respects with those of strategic realism although the starting points vary. The just war thinker is not nearly so harsh in his or her evaluation of what is usually called liberal internationalism with its justifications of intervention in the name of sustaining, supporting, or building a universal culture of Kantian republics as is the *realpolitiker*. At the same time, he or she would voice considerable skepticism about any such project, not because she opposes making more robust an international regime of human rights and greater fairness and equity but, rather, because of her recognition of the intrinsic value of human cultural plurality. From the Augustinian side, nothing less than the sin of hubris is implicated in any attempt to weld humanity into a single monoculture: here the story of the Tower of Babel is instructive. The reason God intervened, scattered humanity, and set us to babbling was to remind humanity of the need for humility and limits. The Babel story is a cautionary tale concerning any and all attempts to forge a uniform humanity under a single scheme of things.

* * *

How well does the just war tradition bear up when it is specifically evoked as the grounding and framework for intervention? We have two examples of recent vintage that afford interesting and ambiguous case studies: the 1991 Persian Gulf War—not, to be sure, a humanitarian intervention per se although humanitarian grounds melded to traditional grounds of non-aggression against a sovereign state were evoked; and the 1999 intervention in Kosovo. The Persian Gulf War was prompted by the annexation of Kuwait, the brutalization of Kuwaitis, and the gutting of their country. These were clear violations of basic principles of international order that encode respect for the autonomy of states.

* * *

The American response to Iraqi aggression evoked just war imperatives from the beginning. Such considerations framed much of the debate about whether or not to intervene and what means to deploy once one had. The language of "just cause" was repeated endlessly as was "last resort": the argument here being that sanctions were tried and failed. Legitimate authority was articulated explicitly: a twenty-seven-nation coalition acting under the imprimatur of the United Nations and in the name of collective security. So far so good? Yes and no.

Just war principles are ambiguous and complex. Evaluations have to be made at each step along the way. Greater and lesser evils (injustices) must be taken into account. Thus, certain questions must be asked, including: What would be the cost of resisting Iraqi aggression? Would the post-war Gulf region be a more, or less, unjust and disordered region? Might not the human and environmental damage, and the assaults to the spirit each and every war trails in its wake, blight any peace? The ends may be justified—restitutive response to aggression—but the means may be unjust or unjustifiable, even if pains are taken to avoid direct targeting of civilians.

* * *

Just war thinking also requires sustained attention even after the shooting has stopped. Because the media focused nearly all its concerns on whether or not noncombatants were actual targets of coalition bombing strategy during the course of the conflict in the Gulf, the public's attention was deflected from the long-range effects of bombing, including life-threatening assaults to the infrastructure of Iraqi society—energy and water supplies, for example. These are matters that require explicit attention within a just war framework. The strategic realist can say, "Hit anything that makes them hurt and impairs their ability to fight." But the just war thinker must not move so hastily. He or she must sift out that which is vital to the opponent's war effort—including power and communication stations—from that which, while it may be drawn into support of military actions, is essential to sustain civilian life: here water and food supplies are foremost, even paradigmatic, as an example of what noncombatants require.

The First Geneva Protocol (1977) **[Basic Document 2.31]** codifies just war thinking on civilian and nonmilitary targeting in language that directs our attention not only to the buildup to war, or the war itself, but to its long-term consequences. Those consequences now include malnutrition and epidemics linked directly to inadequate food and water supplies and medicines.

* * *

The biggest problem from a just war perspective in the Kosovo war was the means deployed to halt and to punish ethnic cleansing. In the first instance, our means speeded up the process as the opening sorties in the bombing campaign gave Milosevic the excuse he needed to declare martial law and to move rapidly in order to complete what he had already begun, entrenching his forces in Kosovo before NATO might change its mind about introducing ground troops into the conflict—something the United States, rather astonishingly, announced it would not do from the get-go. We blundered into a strategy, not giving much consideration to the likely reaction to our bombs, namely, a deepening of the terror and expulsions. Hence, there was no preparation for the influx of desperate humanity to neighboring countries and regions, their plight made doubly desperate by lack of food, water, medicine, and shelter at their points of terrified egress. This doesn't seem a good way to run a humanitarian intervention whether in the name of justice or any other good.

The heart of the matter from a just war framework is this: We made no attempt to meet the strenuous demand of proportionality; rather, we violated the norm of discrimination in a strange up-ended kind of way, namely, by devising a new criterion: combatant immunity, as our combatants ranked higher as a consideration than did non-combatant immunity for Serbian—or Albanian Kosovar—civilians, for that matter. With our determination to keep NATO soldiers—read American combatants—for that was the overriding domestic political consideration that had nothing to do with just war or humanitarian issues—out of harm's way, we embraced combatant immunity for our combatants and indirectly for the Serb soldiers, too. Instead, we did a lot of damage from the air, reducing buildings to rubble, tearing up bridges, killing people in markets and television stations. It is harder by far to face determined combatants on the ground, to interpose one's combatants between the Kosovar Albanians and their predators. This wasn't given a second thought. We did not introduce Apache helicopters into the situation for fear of a loss of but one in combat. If combatant immunity is to become our new organizing principle, the United States will surely face in future situations in which we refuse or are unable not only to do what is right but to do what may be necessary, having set zero-casualties as a new norm for the way we do war.

10. Nicholas J. Wheeler, Saving Strangers: Humanitarian Intervention in International Society 293–95 (2000).

[H]ow many states have to validate a new norm before it can be said to have acquired the status of a new rule of customary international law? And what if some of the objectors to a new rule are among the most powerful states in the world? Michael Byers makes the important point that, where there is only one case of past practice in support of a new rule, states can easily nullify it by acting against it in future instances.[19] Consequently, given the record of state practice against a rule of unilateral humanitarian intervention, . . . it will require additional cases to the Kosovo one where practice and *opinio juris* support this rule before a judgement can be made as to how far there is a new custom of unilateral humanitarian intervention in the society of states.

In this context, it is important to realize that Kosovo is limited as a legal precedent for unilateral humanitarian intervention. It could plausibly be invoked by other states in a future context only where the Security Council has already adopted [UN Charter] Chapter VII resolutions identifying a government's human rights abuses as a threat to international peace and security, and where the threat or use of the veto prevented the Council authorizing the use of force. Restricting a legal right of unilateral humanitarian intervention to situations where the Council has already adopted Chapter VII resolutions reduces the dangers of states deciding for themselves when humanitarian intervention is permitted. As Vaughan Lowe put it in his Memorandum submitted to the Foreign Affairs Committee of the House of Commons, "the right to act [claimed by NATO over Kosovo] is not a unilateral right, under which each and every State may decide for itself that intervention is warranted. . . . The prior decision of the Security Council is asserted as a key element of the justification."[20] This restriction on the right of humanitarian intervention suits Western members of the Council, since they have the power of veto to ensure that no resolutions are adopted in cases where their interests might be affected. But this cuts both ways. If a legal right of unilateral humanitarian intervention is to be restricted in this manner, then NATO could well find itself deprived of this legal argument in future cases where it wants to act. Having watched NATO governments defend their military action in Kosovo by appealing to three resolutions adopted under Chapter VII, it is likely that Russia and China will be considerably more cautious about passing such resolutions in the future.

Given the volatile domestic situation in Russia, and the heightened sensitivity of Russia and China to actions that erode the sovereignty rule, it is highly unlikely that the permanent members of the Security Council will become a humanitarian 'coalition of the willing' in future cases of gross human rights abuses. It could be argued that whether there is a new legal custom supporting unilateral humanitarian intervention is beside the point,

---

19. M. Byers, Custom, Power and the Power of Rules: International Relations and Customary International Law 159 (1999).

20. V. Lowe, *International Legal Issues Arising in the Kosovo Crisis*, Memorandum

submitted to the Foreign Affairs Committee of the House of Commons 5 (Feb. 2000).

since, when acts of brutality offend against the conscience of humanity, those with the power to end this have a moral responsibility to act. If the words "We the Peoples," in the Preamble of the UN Charter **[Basic Document 1.5]**, have meaning, then the threat or use of a veto in the Security Council cannot be allowed to stand in the way of humanitarian intervention. This sentiment was echoed by Kofi Annan in his opening speech to the 1999 General Assembly, when he asked in relation to the Rwandan genocide: "If, in those dark days and hours leading up to the genocide, a coalition of States had been prepared to act in defence of the Tutsi population, but did not receive prompt Council authorization, should such a coalition have stood aside and allowed the horror to unfold?"[21]

This voice in the dialogue over the legitimacy of humanitarian intervention echoes the view of Franck and Rodley.[22] It may be recalled that they argued in the wake of the Bangladeshi case that, whilst humanitarian intervention breaks the law, this is morally justified in exceptional cases. The fundamental problem with this argument is that it plays into the hands of those states who maintain that humanitarian intervention is always a phenomenon of power, and that it issues a license for the powerful to impose their values on the weak. This objection was expressed by Russia in the General Assembly in September 1999 when it warned that "coercive measures . . . should not be allowed to turn into a repressive mechanism to influence States and peoples regarded by some as not being to their liking." The difficulty is that, if Western governments are perceived to be tearing up UN Charter principles when they want to intervene, other states might decide to treat these rules equally cavalierly in the future. Kofi Annan was well aware of this concern and cautioned those who welcomed NATO's action in Kosovo to remember that "actions without Security Council authorization threaten the very core of the international security system founded on the Charter of the United Nations."[23]

The challenge is to explore the possibilities of a solidarist third way that legitimates humanitarian intervention when the Security Council is prevented from authorizing the use of force, because of the threat or use of the veto, and that does not jeopardize existing restraints upon the use of force. Kofi Annan's response to the moral and legal dilemmas raised by the Kosovo crisis was to encourage the General Assembly to debate this question at its 54th session. In Kosovo, several governments argued that the defence of human rights by force was legitimate if authorized by the Security Council, but no government expressly advocated a right of unilateral humanitarian intervention, and many states strongly opposed this.

11.   Editors' Note. Writing on *The Use of Force for the Protection of Nationals Abroad*, in The Current Legal Regulation of the Use of Force 39, 51 (A. Cassese ed., 1986), Derek Bowett observes:

---

21. Press Release, Annual Report of the Secretary–General to the General Assembly, SG/SM/ 7136 GA/9596, 20 Sep 1999.

22. T. Franck & N. Rodley, *After Bangladesh: The Law of Humanitarian Intervention by Military Force*, 67 A.J.I.L. 275–305 (1973).

23. Kofi Annan, Report of the Secretary–General on the work of the Organization, General Assembly, Official Records, 54th Sess., Supp. No. 1, UN Doc. A/54/1, from ch. I, "Achieving Peace and Security," *available also at* <http://www.un.org/Docs/SG/Report99/toc.htm>.

There is an unfortunate tendency in some of the literature ... to confuse the right of protection of nationals with the quite separate, and more general right of humanitarian intervention. It is essential to keep the two distinct. For with humanitarian intervention the nationality of the persons to be rescued is essentially irrelevant and whatever the legal basis of such intervention might be, it is not self-defence. Moreover, with humanitarian intervention it is likely that the persons to be rescued are either nationals or permanent residents of the territorial State, the State in whose territory the intervention occurs. The degree of interference with the authority of that State is therefore greater than in the case of the protection of nationals who are aliens *vis-à-vis* the territorial State. The reason for insisting upon the separation of the right of protection from the right of humanitarian intervention is that ... the legality of the latter is far more controversial than the legality of the former. The danger exists, therefore, that by confusing the two, the controversies attaching to humanitarian intervention may affect and undermine the right of protection of nationals.

Professor Bowett argues that the protection of nationals abroad is permissible under Article 51 of the UN Charter **(Basic Document 1.5)** on the basis that the provision was intended to preserve the customary right of self-defense and that state practice under the Charter and policy considerations support this interpretation. Professor Bowett also concludes that the right extends to the protection of the property of nationals abroad. *See infra* Discussion Note/Question 5 at 348–49 for a brief discussion of the Israeli raid at Entebbe Airport in Uganda in 1976, justified as protection of nationals abroad.

D.   United Nations Intervention

1.   Charter of the United Nations. Concluded, 26 Jun 1945. Entered into force, 24 Oct 1945. 1976 Y.B.U.N. 1043, *reprinted in* **1 Weston & Carlson I.A.1: Pmbl. & Arts. 1, 2, 24–25, 33–56, 103** (Basic Document 1.5).

2.   Constitutive Act of the African Union. Concluded, 11 July 2000. Entered into force, 26 May 2001. OAU/CAB/LEG, *reprinted in* **1 Weston & Carlson I.B.1a: Arts. 2, 3, 4, 30** (Basic Document 1.17).

3.   Editors' Note. The United Nations Charter [**Basic Document 1.5**] gives the Security Council significant powers to maintain international peace and security. The Cold War split among the permanent members of the Security Council meant that the Council, during that period, never could exploit its collective security role. With the apparent end of the Cold War, however, the Security Council began to carve out a new role for itself in this area. The extracts in preceding Section C, while concerned primarily with unilateral intervention on humanitarian grounds, deal also with aspects of United Nations intervention on humanitarian grounds. The readings that follow further explore this realm, beginning with overviews of the UN's role in using military action to protect human rights, followed by a consideration of the peace-maintaining jurisdiction of the United Nations relative to that of regional organizations—such as the African Union, (formerly the Organization of African Unity (OAU))—associated with it, and concluding with a series of critiques of UN action.

4. Thomas M. Franck, "The UN and the Protection of Human Rights: When, If Ever, May States Deploy Military Force without Prior Security Council Authorization?," 5 Wash. U. J. L. & Pol'y 51, 52–68 (2001).

I. THE CHARTER LAW PERTAINING TO STATES' AUTONOMOUS USE OF FORCE

The noble plan for replacing state self-help with collective security failed because it was based on two wrong assumptions: first, that the Security Council could be expected to make speedy and objective decisions as to when collective measures were necessary; and second, that states would enter into the arrangements necessary to give the Council an effective policing capability.

The first of these assumptions simply was taken for granted on the strength of the wartime cooperation among allied powers. The drafters of the Charter **[Basic Document 1.5]**—those same allied powers—decided, in their planning for a new global system, not even to try to define what might constitute a "threat to, or breach of the peace" or act of aggression. Instead, they assumed that this could be left safely to future case-by-case interpretations by a willing and able Council.

The second assumption, that states would provide the new organization with a police force, was not so easily made. It was questioned by Secretary Hull in a 1943 memorandum to President Roosevelt raising the possibility that states, at first, might not be willing to pledge forces to UN command. He proposed that "in the absence of such agreement" the Council should be free to make such ad hoc arrangements "as [it] may deem appropriate."

By the time the Charter was finalized in San Francisco, these doubts had been swept aside, or repressed, as Articles 42 and 43 were adopted with relatively little debate. The drafting committee's Rapporteur merely observed that there was no contention about these "draft articles." It simply was assumed that states readily would enter into agreements with the Security Council to commit available specified forces for service when needed.

This may seem Panglossian in retrospect, but as a symptom of the then-prevalent "optimism," the US Congress enacted a law which authorizes the President:

> to negotiate a special agreement with the Security Council ... providing for the numbers and types of armed forces, their degree of readiness and general location, and the nature of facilities and assistance, including rights of passage, to be made available to the Security Council on its call for the purpose of maintaining international peace and security in accordance with article 43 of the Charter.[24]

It all seems so long ago!

No such negotiations, we know, ever took place: not by the United States or by any other nation as the Cold War cooled the impetus for globalist solutions.

---

24. An Act to Amend The United Nations Participation Act of 1945, Pub. L. No. 81–341, 63 Stat. 734 (1949), codified as amended at 22 USC § 287 *et seq* (2000).

What were the consequences for the UN of being built on these two wrong assumptions? Were the Charter a static instrument bound exclusively to the textually expressed intent of its drafters, the profound incapacitation of the Security Council and the absence of a stand-by police force might have put paid to the Charter's collective security system. Instead, the system has adapted, specifically by uncoupling Article 43 from Article 42 and by broadening the authority of states to act in self-defense under Article 51. These adaptations, brought about precedent-by-precedent, are worth noting.

II. COLLECTIVE FORCE WITHOUT ARTICLE FORTY-THREE

The Korean War was the first example of the Security Council resisting aggression by ad hoc collective measures, despite the absence of Article 43 forces. The North Koreans launched their attack in the night of June 24–25, 1950. Qualifying the situation as a threat to international peace, the Secretary–General immediately called on the Security Council to determine that the attack was a breach of the peace, demand a cessation of hostilities, and impose an embargo on all "assistance to the North Korean authorities." He proposed that the Council call "upon all Member States to render every assistance" in carrying out this plan of action. The Council adopted this proposal swiftly due to the fortuitous absence of its Soviet member. It determined that there had been a "breach of the peace" and thereby invoked Article 39, the prerequisite for collective measures under Chapter VII of the Charter. By June 25, 1950 with only Yugoslavia opposed, the Council passed a resolution asking "that the Members of the United Nations furnish such assistance to the Republic of Korea as may be necessary to repel the armed attack and to restore international peace and security in the area." On July 7, 1950 with the Soviets still absent and abstentions by Egypt, India, and Yugoslavia, the Council recommended that all members providing military assistance make such forces available to a unified military command headed by the United States. The Council authorized the command to use the UN flag and requested the United States to report "as appropriate" to the Security Council.

Since the Charter makes no provision for a UN military response other than with Article 43 forces, the Council was creatively adapting the text by authorizing action in its name by the United States and other national contingents in what became known as a "coalition of the willing."

Subsequently, authorization of such coalitions of the willing has become an established part of UN practice. In 1990, forty years after the Korean war, the Security Council—still lacking an Article 43–based military capability of its own—again authorized a massive coalition of the willing to undertake operation "Desert Storm" after Iraq's invasion of Kuwait. This began in August when, with all permanent members voting in favor and only Yemen abstaining, the Council found that Iraq's action constituted a breach of the peace. By November, it invoked Chapter VII and requested member states to "use all necessary means" to reverse Iraqi aggression. This resolution passed with only Cuba and Yemen opposed and with China abstaining.[25]

25. SC Res. 678, UN SCOR, 45th Sess., 2963rd mtg., at 27–28, UN Doc. S/RES/678 (1990) [*Eds.—See* **Basic Document 2.40**. For a critique of this resolution, see B. Weston, *Security Council Resolution 678 and Persian*

Somalia was the next instance of the Council exercising its adapted power to deploy military forces. On November 30, 1992 the Secretary–General informed the Council that "the situation in Somalia has deteriorated beyond the point at which it is susceptible to peace-keeping treatment." Accordingly, he reported, "I am more than ever convinced of the need for international military personnel to be deployed." He concluded that:

> the Security Council now has no alternative but to decide to adopt more forceful measures to secure the humanitarian operations.... It would therefore be necessary for the Security Council to make a determination under Article 39 of the Charter that a threat to the peace exists.... The Council would also have to determine that non-military measures as referred to in Chapter VII were not capable of giving effect to the Council's decision.[26]

Promptly, the Security Council, acting under Chapter VII, authorized the United States and any others willing to "use all necessary means" through an ad hoc Unified Task Force (UNITAF) to achieve the objectives specified in the Council resolution. This was adopted unanimously. On March 26, 1993 the Council, again acting under Chapter VII, authorized the replacement of the essentially American force of 37,000 with a multinational coalition of the willing without direct US participation to carry out an expanded peace and security mandate, the expanded United Nations in Somalia (UNOSOM II).

* * *

III.   THE VIABILITY OF ARTICLE FIFTY-ONE

The failure to realize the aims of Article 43 caused the Charter system to invent an alternative: the "coalition of the willing" authorized by the Council to use force collectively.

An additional important adaption of the Charter was dictated by changes in the way aggression came to be committed in the post-World War Two era. By the terms of Article 51, the Charter envisaged that states, individually or through treaty-based regional or mutual-defense systems, would defend themselves against an armed attack until such time as the UN, acting under Chapter VII of the Charter, could deploy Article 43 forces to combat the aggression. Not only were Article 43 forces not forthcoming, but neither were the sorts of conventional armed attacks visualized by Article 51. Thus the right of self-defense, just as it had became more important due to the system's failure to provide its promised collective security, also became more problematic as it was limited, textually, to responses to traditional armed attacks.

Three developments threatened to make this part of the Charter system unworkable. One was the virtual tactical replacement of military aggression with surrogate warfare, waged indirectly by subversion and covert foreign intervention in civil wars. This was not the kind of traditional "armed attack" against which the "inherent right of individual or collective self-defense" was designed to provide protection.

Gulf Decision–Making: Precarious Legitimacy, 85 A.J.I.L. 516 (1991)].

26. Letter from the Secretary–General, to the President of the Security Council (29 Nov 1992), 47th Sess., UN Doc. S/1992/24868.

The second development featured the transformation of weaponry to instruments of overwhelming and instant destruction. These brought into question the conditionality of Article 51, which limits states' exercise of the right of self-defense to the aftermath of an armed attack. Inevitably, first strike capabilities begat a doctrine of "anticipatory self-defense," for which the literal text of the Charter made no provision.

The third new development is the most difficult to assess. Undoubtedly, however, a new ethos had begun to develop that challenged traditional Westphalian notions of sovereignty. Article 2(7)'s promise that the UN will not intervene in matters "essentially within the domestic jurisdiction of any state" began to be tested against changing perceptions of sovereignty and new concepts of human rights. A doctrine of "humanitarian intervention" began to emerge in practice, for which the Charter provides no literal textual support.

These unanticipated circumstances have led the Charter system to confront new and controversial "interpretations" of the right of states to use armed force in the absence of Security Council authorization.

IV.   SELF-DEFENSE AGAINST ANTICIPATED AND INDIRECT AGGRESSION

Of particular difficulty in light of subsequent developments is the requirement in Article 51 that the "inherent right of self defense" can only be exercised "if an armed attack occurs against a member state." It was the United States that had insisted on inserting this phrase. Green Hackworth, the State Department's legal adviser, was alarmed that this language "greatly qualified the right of self-defense," but Governor Harold Stassen, deputy head of delegation at San Francisco, refused to yield, insisting "that this was intentional and sound. We did not want exercised the right of self-defense before an armed attack had occurred." When another member of the US delegation, Mr. Gates, "posed a question as to our freedom under this provision in case a fleet had started from abroad against an American republic, but had not yet attacked," Governor Stassen replied that "we could not under this provision attack the fleet but we could send a fleet of our own and be ready in case an attack came."

The exchange illustrates how little the contemporary advances in the technology of war had informed the thinking of the Charter's drafters, making it necessary for the Charter to respond in practice to these challenging transformations. In San Francisco, the founders deliberately closed the door to any claim of "anticipatory self-defense," but that posture was soon challenged by the exigencies of a new age of nuclear warheads and long-range rocketry.

It has been asserted that the emergence of "new age" weaponry makes it illogical to require states to sit still until an "armed attack" against them has occurred. Where the state is small and the potential attacker powerful or equipped with a "first strike capability," there is verisimilitude to the claim that Article 51 should be interpreted to allow anticipatory self-defense. This may even have been acknowledged tacitly by the UN when, after Israel's "preventive" attack on Egypt in 1956, it did not criticize this action but rather authorized the stationing of UN peacekeepers along a line that left Israel temporarily in occupation of much of the Sinai. Israel again made reference to anticipatory self-defense in 1967. And again, the UN "in its debates in the summer of 1967, apportioned no blame for the outbreak of fighting and specifically refused to condemn the exercise of self-defense by Israel." This time, Israel remained in occupation of most of the Sinai until a peace treaty with Egypt was negotiated.

Similar claims to use force in anticipatory self-defense were made by the United States in 1962 when it imposed a naval quarantine on Cuba to compel the removal of Soviet missiles said to pose an immediate threat to American security, and again in 1986 when US aircraft attacked bases in Libya allegedly used for terrorist attacks on its citizens abroad. Indeed, even the International Court has been ambiguous about the use of force in situations of supreme provocation. In its 1996 Advisory Opinion on the Legality of the Use of Nuclear Weapons in Armed Conflict, it was unable to decide definitively whether an otherwise unlawful act—recourse to nuclear weapons in anticipatory self-defense—would be lawful if the very existence of the state were threatened.

These instances pose an intractable dilemma. On the one hand, it is evident that any adaption of the Charter's absolute prohibitions on the unilateral or initiatory use of armed force would be nullified if each state were free to determine for itself whether a perceived danger of attack warrants anticipatory action. On the other hand, law that seeks to prohibit a state from protecting its very survival until the threat to it has eventuated is irrational and ineffectual.

This dilemma cannot be resolved in the abstract. Formulating an applicable principle may be easy, but the devil is in its application: how to make—credibly and impartially—the key determination that, in a particular instance, extreme necessity does or does not exist, so as to justify a military action? Who shall decide and on what facts?

Even traditional deference to US Secretary of State Daniel Webster's opinion in the arbitration arising out of the 1837 Caroline incident[27] does not go far to resolve the problem of its application to an infinite variety of factual situations in the absence of mandatory recourse to an impartial judge or jury. In seeking a resolution of this hiatus, it is less important to fine-tune the legal formula than to agree on institutions and procedures for getting the facts speedily and correctly, on which to base a sensible systemic response to the claim to have acted in "anticipatory self-defense."

Even more troublesome is the question whether force in self-defense may be used against indirect aggression by one state or its surrogates. Indirect aggression includes the fomenting of civil war by one state in another state, or supporting the export of insurgency, subversion, and terrorism. It includes

---

27. US Secretary of State Daniel Webster sent a note to British Foreign Secretary Fox in 1841 setting out the principles of self-defence in international law in order to settle a diplomatic dispute between the two countries over the Caroline (1837) and McLeod (1840) incidents. British troops in Canada had sent the steamer, Caroline, aflame over Niagara Falls, killing all on board because the Caroline was used by Canadian rebels against British rule.

Webster's statement that a state exercising the right of self-defense had to show "a necessity of self defence, instant, overwhelming, leaving no choice of means, and no moment for deliberation," and that it "did nothing unreasonable or excessive" has become part of international law. 21 B.F.S.P.1137, 30 B.F.S.P. 195. *See* R. Jennings, *The Caroline and McLeod Cases*, 32 A.J.I.L. 82 (1938); T. Kearley, *Raising the Caroline*, 17 Wis. Int'l L. J. 325 (1999).

acts perhaps analogous to, but not factually the same as, the conventional armed attack envisaged by the self-defense provision of the Charter.

With the beginning of the Cold War—inhibited by a nuclear balance of terror but otherwise unconstrained in zealotry—some states saw "surrogate warfare" as the best means to spread their influence and ideology. With the end of the Cold War, other states have felt freer to emulate this tactic.

Increasingly, states claiming to be the victim of indirect or surrogate aggression have sought recourse under the right of self-defense in Article 51. This sometimes has taken the form of an armed response against the state from which the indirect or surrogate attack is said to originate. In its controversial and deeply divided decision in Nicaragua v. U.S.A., the International Court of Justice appeared to uphold the right of a state subject to indirect aggression to receive military support in collective self-defense, but not its right to intervene militarily against the state from which the surrogate aggression was launched or supported.[28] The case also underscored the importance of basing any principled decision in any particular case on a credible assessment of the facts—something the UN system is not always well-equipped to provide.

Despite the court's Nicaragua ruling, the practice of intervening militarily in a country from which interventions emanate becomes increasingly tolerated practice. Turkey has occupied base areas in Iraq used by Turkish Kurds to fight for their independence. Russia has threatened to attack Afghanistani bases that support Chechen rebels. These events have passed with little or no comment at the UN, a sharp break with the vigorous condemnation that had earlier met Israeli occupation of PLO base areas in Lebanon.

Perhaps this growing tolerance is as it should be. Why should a state under attack from abroad by terrorists or insurgents supported by a foreign state grant those forces immunity in a so-called "safe haven"? When, after hundreds of persons were killed in the bombing of the United States embassies in Nairobi and Dar-es-Salaam, the United States launched retaliatory strikes against Osama bin-Laden's base in Afghanistan and a factory near Khartoum, there was scarcely any criticism and no recourse to the UN. On the other hand, while there may be support for the principle behind such actions, again the devil is in its contextual application. If admitted, how is the principle to be kept from becoming a license for every state taking the law into its own hands—no matter how flimsy its evidence of wrongdoing?

It is not merely new agreed upon principles that appear to be needed, but rather an effective, credible process for their implementation: a way to distinguish those instances where a state's recourse to force is factually and contextually justified and those where it is not. A white-knuckled insistence on the letter of the law embodied in Article 51 will lead to ever-greater disrespect for an obsolete principle. On the other hand, relaxation of Article 51's absolutism would be very dangerous to world peace unless new principles are not only agreed upon, but a process is instituted for these principles to be applied credibly. . . .

---

28. Military and Paramilitary Activities in and against Nicaragua (Nicar. v. U.S.), 1986 ICJ 14 (27 Jun), at ¶ ¶ 232, 249.

V. THE HUMANITARIAN INTERVENTION ISSUE

The UN system has not been oblivious to the fact that not all violations of Article 51—that is, resorts to armed force that were neither provoked by a direct armed attack nor authorized by the Security Council—are precisely the same. This is evidenced by the significant variation from case to case of the international system's reaction—the degree of approbation or disapprobation—when states have claimed to be acting in a reconfigured version of self-defense. In practice, the reactions of the system have varied across a broad spectrum. Benign silence greeted Tanzania's ouster of Idi Amin's brutal regime in Uganda, France's intervention against the mad Emperor Bokassa of the Central African "Empire," and America's air strike against the Sudan and Afghanistan after the destruction of US embassies in Dar-es-Salaam and Nairobi by the forces of Osama bin-Laden. The UN system appears tacitly to have accepted the need for allied intervention in northern Iraq in 1991–92 to save the Kurdish population, even though textually required authorization by the Security Council was not then forthcoming. Instead the UN, in effect, stepped in after the unauthorized allied military intervention had compelled Iraq to agree to the positioning of 500 UN guards to protect the local population's access to humanitarian efforts on their behalf. Mild formal reprimand greeted Israel's incursions into Uganda to rescue hijacked passengers at Entebbe and into Argentina to seize the war criminal, Eichmann. India's intervention in Bangladesh got off with a light reprimand.

On the other hand, there was fulsome condemnation of the Soviets' invasion of Hungary, and US occupation of Grenada. For years the UN steadfastly refused to recognize the results of the use of force by Vietnam in Cambodia, and still will not legitimate the military presence of Turkey in Cyprus. The UN system clearly refused to legitimate the use of force by Indonesia in East Timor or by Morocco in the Western Sahara.

Thus, it can be argued that the UN system, far from literally and mechanically applying Article 51 to each of these cases, has made a carefully nuanced analysis of each. Perhaps the system unselfconsciously has been reworking the Charter text to conform to a less rigid principle and is seeking to apply this adapted version of the applicable principle on a case-by-case basis, informed by the context and the facts as much as by an abstract normative concept.

Where would a more contextually sensitive adaption of Article 51 lead? That question arises most starkly in the context of humanitarian intervention.

Secretary–General Kofi Annan has captured the essence of this tension between an intolerably inflexible principle and the equally intolerable carte blanche that might result were the inflexible rule simply abandoned without any new checks and balances in place. The issue arises unavoidably out of NATO's action in Kosovo. Annan remarked on this profound dilemma:

> To those for whom the greatest threat to the future of the international order is the use of force in the absence of a Security Council mandate, one might ask, not in the context of Kosovo but in the context of Rwanda, if, in those dark days and hours leading up to the genocide, a coalition of states had been prepared to act in defence of the Tutsi

population, but did not receive prompt Council authorization, should such a coalition have stood aside and allowed the horror to unfold?

To those for whom the Kosovo action heralded a new era when States and groups of States can take military action outside the established mechanisms for enforcing international law, one might ask: Is there not a danger of such interventions undermining the imperfect, yet resilient, security system created after the Second World War, and of setting dangerous precedents for future interventions without a clear criterion to decide who might invoke these precedents and in what circumstances?

VI. IS THERE LIGHT AT THE END OF THIS DILEMMA?

One possible answer based on the actual practice of UN organs is that the UN system already tolerates, ultimately cooperates with, and may even commend military action by states when such action is taken to avert a demonstrable catastrophe. The kind of catastrophe is relatively easily answered in principle; the principle being derived from the actual responses of the UN system to such uses of unauthorized force.

The system has responded benevolently when anticipatory force has been used solely to prevent a demonstrably imminent and potentially overwhelming threat to a state's security. It has also responded benevolently when unauthorized force is used solely to contain or end a state's instigation of, or tolerance for, indirect aggression. Finally, the system has responded benevolently to the use of unauthorized force solely for the purpose of preventing a major humanitarian catastrophe.

"The system responded benevolently" means either specific consent or silent acquiescence. The Security Council or General Assembly have approved ex post facto the previously unauthorized use of force (as in the instance of ECOMOG's intervention in Liberia). The Council has defeated resoundingly a vote of censure of NATO's intervention in Kosovo. Both the Council and Assembly have avoided censure of the unauthorized use of force by Israel in its preemptive strike against Egypt in 1967, of the Turkish invasion of Cyprus in 1974, of Tanzania's invasion of Uganda in 1979, and of the US bombing of Osama bin-Laden's training camps in Afghanistan in 1998. These instances of benevolent response contrast eloquently with the systemic condemnation of uses of force that were not considered warranted by the facts and circumstances. Examples include the UN system's unrelenting opposition to the Israeli invasion of Lebanon, to Morocco's taking of the Western Sahara, and to Indonesia's seizure of East Timor.

It also may be argued that the system has responded benevolently to a use of force if the UN participates positively in its consequences: for example, by agreeing to provide the transitional regime for Kosovo, or by policing the Green Line created by Turkish intervention between ethnic Turks and Greeks in the Cyprus civil war. Was the admission of Bangladesh to the UN after Indian troops had won its independence not a form of absolution?

The UN organs have not always acted wisely, of course. It is difficult to defend as principled the General Assembly's ten-year-long rejection of the credentials of the Government of Cambodia. True, that government had been installed by invading forces from Vietnam; but it was surely an improvement, in humanitarian terms, over the Khmer Rouge. That Vietnam's use of force violated the Charter text is beyond question, but, in the absence of some collective remedy under UN auspices, can one really say that the world has an interest in defending Cambodian sovereignty even if it means the methodical murder of a large part of the Cambodian people? What kind of principle is that? Must the system always give preference to its rule against recourse to force over the emergent rules of humanitarian law and human rights?

* * *

VII. CONCLUSION

The Charter system has proven resilient in the face of changing fundamental circumstances to which it has learned to adapt. It is the practice of the principal organs—the Security Council, the General Assembly, and the Secretary–General, sometimes aided by the Court—that has helped it adapt.

Reading the practice of these organs, it is possible to conclude that the use of force by a state or regional or mutual-defense system is likely to be tolerated if there is credible evidence that such first-use was justified by the severe impact of another state's indirect aggression or by clear evidence of an impending, planned, and decisive attack by a state or by an egregious and potentially calamitous violation of humanitarian law by a government against its own population or a part of it.

Even if there appears to be a high level of agreement as to these emerging general principles, the more difficult challenge is to apply them, case-by-case, to the specifics of each crisis. There is no realistic alternative to the Council and Assembly as the global juries. True, the jurors are not all disinterested, unbiased citizens of the world community. But neither are they, or most of them, blind to credible evidence—evidence of states party to a crisis on their own behalf and evidence adduced by an augmented system of fact-finding reporting to the political organs through the Secretary–General. Most governments do respond to clear and unimpeachable evidence of the facts and of their sociopolitical context.

5. Stephen John Stedman, "UN Intervention in Civil Wars: Imperatives of Choice and Strategy," in Beyond Traditional Peacekeeping 40, 40–41, 52–55, 58–60 (D. Daniel & B. Hayes eds., 1995).

The United Nations has lost its direction concerning peacekeeping and intervention in civil wars. Its member states have asked the impossible from the organisation, and given it neither the resources, nor the clarity of purpose and strategy to achieve it. To get the United Nations back on track, the organisation and its member states must gain a realistic sense of the possibilities of making or enforcing peace in civil war; make choices about where and how the UN will intervene; and develop a capacity for thinking strategically about its interventions. In particular it must acknowledge the limitations imposed by civil war—what can realistically be accomplished by outside forces in violent internal conflict—and the limitations imposed by its own organisational makeup and procedures.

* * *

Prior to 1989 the United Nations had a coherent doctrine of peacekeeping. When there were agreements among warring parties who had command

and control over their people with weapons, the United Nations would interject troops in order to assist the parties in keeping the peace. Because the impetus for peace came from the parties themselves, UN troops could be lightly armed, have limited rules of engagement, and observe strict neutrality: peacekeepers are not supposed to have enemies, and their success rests on keeping it that way.

Starting in 1989 in Namibia, and subsequently in the Western Sahara, Angola, Cambodia and El Salvador, the UN was asked to incorporate elements of "peacebuilding" into its peacekeeping repertoire. These tasks included carrying out elections, registering and educating voters, supervising the demobilization and disarming of armies in civil war, monitoring elections, demining countrysides, and (in the case of El Salvador) carrying out land reform and investigation into human rights violations.

The first case of peacebuilding, Namibia, was a resounding success. The United Nations supervised the cease-fire and brief cantonment of guerilla forces, assisted voter-registration and education, and monitored the election that brought Namibia to independence. Like all successes, however, there has been a tendency of analysts to focus on the positive result and to ignore the myriad glitches during the success. The United Nations delayed establishing its presence for the cease-fire; never clarified its lines of authority *vis-à-vis* those of the South African provincial authorities; and did not create provisions if the loser in the election should have rejected the results. Success depended in part on good fortune; the process could easily have gone wrong.

The next four cases of civil conflict addressed by the UN (Western Sahara, Angola, Cambodia and El Salvador) placed greater demands on it and posed nasty dilemmas. Like Namibia, all these cases involved protracted wars where the parties had engaged in extended negotiations (with each other in the cases of Angola, Cambodia and El Salvador; with the United Nations in the case of the Western Sahara) and finally agreed to settle peacefully, when the UN agreed to step in. In all four cases recalcitrant parties tested the limits of UN authority; in all but one—El Salvador—signatories actually reneged on their commitments to peace.

* * *

TOWARDS A STRATEGY OF MAKING AND BUILDING PEACE

The United Nations should restrict its intervention in civil wars to peacemaking in "hot" civil wars and peacebuilding in civil wars where the parties agree to end their hostilities. This section addresses steps that the UN should adopt in the future in order to be effective at both tasks....

Getting An Agreement in Civil War

Effective mediation in civil war demands leverage and problem solving. Leverage is associated with the ability to create favourable alternatives at the negotiating table and lessen the desirability of alternatives away from the table for the antagonists. Leverage comes from five sources: coercion (the "stick"), remuneration (the "carrot"), identification ("charisma"), normative appeals, and knowledge (information). The effective use of leverage depends on appropriate strategy and tactics. Strategy requires that mediators combine a clear idea of their goal, an understanding of what is needed to attract and sustain support, and a feasible plan of administration and implementation.

The ability of a mediator to speak with one voice is usually crucial in bringing parties to agreement. Unilateral initiatives by individuals or states acting in competition with the mediator can prove disastrous to creating the conditions necessary for settlement. In active mediation where the mediator makes promises or threats, it is crucial that the parties in the conflict believe that the mediator is credible. When a mediator says one thing, only to be contradicted by another agent associated with the mediators, the parties to the conflict will be uncertain about the ability of a mediator to deliver on promises or threats. Moreover, disunity within the mediator's group can lead to the parties in conflict attempting to play off factions within the mediator's organisation to increase the likelihood of a settlement that favours them.

Any international organisation composed of member states who pursue their own policies must overcome the key problem of disunity. If the UN desires to actively mediate a settlement of civil war, then the following suggestions should be followed. While the suggestions are generic, I will refer to the Balkans example, where one not only has the problem of coordination between an international organisation and its member states, but also coordination among different international organisations.

> *(1) Define a structure for decision-making, with clearly delineated respon-*
> *sibilities and powers.*

As it stands now, decision-making by the West towards the Balkans has been *ad hoc*. Believing that they have the authority of the UN, mediators craft political solutions only to be overruled by United States foreign policy. UN soldiers in charge of humanitarian protection routinely find themselves out of the loop on decisions concerning military actions in their areas of engagement. US officials cry for war crimes prosecution against leaders who are invited to the United Nations to make peace. UN mediators struggle to continue peace talks, as a US special envoy travels to the region: to whom should the parties listen? Who has the credibility to deliver on promises and threats?

> *(2) Create a coherent strategy*

This demands an answer to the question discussed earlier: is the goal to make peace or enforce peace? Policies must be made subservient to one's choice. Before actions are taken, simple questions must be answered. Does providing humanitarian intervention serve the goal of forcing Serbia and Bosnian Serbs to stop their aggression? Or does it mean that UN forces are constrained from taking appropriate forceful action against them, for fear of putting humanitarian soldiers at risk? Does the threat of war crimes serve the goal of a negotiated settlement? Or does it force the antagonists to treat the war as a total one in fear that settlement will lead to their punishment? Does arming the Bosnian Muslims make it likely that a negotiated settlement will emerge or does it ensure a longer protracted war?

If getting the parties to reach a political settlement of their conflict is the goal, then other goals that may be good in and of themselves (such as provision of humanitarian assistance, protection of civilians, or investigation and prosecution of war crimes), must be subordinate to the larger goal of making peace.

> *(3) If the choice is to pursue a negotiated settlement, then a mediator must be informed by his or her superiors as to what terms are acceptable beforehand*

The Owen–Vance experience shows that not any Bosnian settlement will be acceptable to the international community. Objections have been raised by member states over the morality and practicability of various components of an agreement. Such objections should be worked out before settlement terms are developed.

> *(4) A negotiated settlement demands a workable solution*

The mediator, working under the constraints imposed by superiors, must create a settlement that will address the basic needs of the antagonists. If there is no possible solution that meets the needs of the warring parties and the constraints set by the international community, then the mediator must have the courage to say so and disengage. When superiors demand a just peace, and one is not possible because of the military power of one side, then the mediator should demand from his or her superiors a decision on whether to compromise one's morality to achieve peace, engage in peace-enforcement, or walk away from the conflict.

> *(5) Identify leverage and link it to the strategic goal*

Even when there exists a negotiated settlement that will meet all parties' needs, stronger parties may still prefer to hold out for a unilateral solution. The mediator must then use leverage to make such solutions impossible. If Serbia is the problem, then there are two sources of leverage: the threat of direct attack and the threat to arm Bosnia's Muslims. But threats must be credible, which makes unified command and control crucial. If a mediator threatens action and cannot deliver, then she/he is discredited. On the other hand, action *before* a threat robs one of leverage.

> *(6) Plan for failure*

Most civil wars do not end in a negotiated settlement, and those that do occur after long years of violence and international attention. Is the international community patient enough for the parties to fight themselves to exhaustion before being willing to settle? If not, what is the alternative? Is it better to quit the mediation effort so that the parties truly understand that negotiation is not an alternative? Or is it preferable to always keep the negotiation option available?

* * *

Negotiation versus War Crimes

The choices of making peace and implementing peace raise the issue of war crimes, a topic much discussed in the international community today. I have argued that if the interest of the United Nations is peacemaking in civil war and there is the belief that such a peace is attainable, then it should not threaten the participants with war crimes. I believe, however, that in those instances where a peace agreement has been reached and one party reneges, then the international community should investigate and if need be prosecute parties for war crimes.

The evaluation of sincerity ... is directly relevant to the question of war crimes in civil war. The international community must judge the hopes for peace in civil war based on an evaluation of the leaders' goals. Do they define the war as total? Would they be willing to share power if their legitimate security concerns can be met?

The judgment is a difficult one and mistakes are costly. If one misjudges a party as sincere in its desire for a settlement, there is a risk that party will strengthen itself and gain an advantage against a party that plays by the rules. On the other hand, a wrong evaluation that a party cannot be appeased can lead to an escalated, protracted conflict that could have been settled.

The investigation and possible prosecution of war crimes only make sense if the international community has judged the war to be total and that the offending party must be defeated. In an ongoing civil war, possible liability for war crimes is a powerful deterrent to negotiated settlement. It is very difficult to convince a party with a powerful military to put away its guns if that party believes that it will be punished afterwards for crimes committed in the course of the war. In a similar context, Samuel Huntington, writing on the democratic transitions in Latin America, contends that negotiated changes of government are easier if blanket amnesties are issued.[29] There is less of an incentive for recalcitrant forces to oppose negotiation, and there is a greater chance of reconciliation following such negotiation.

In the cases of Namibia and Zimbabwe, it was decided that peace would be based on no recrimination of individual actions during the civil war. It should be pointed out that in both of these wars there were terrible atrocities. A similar course of forgiveness was chosen for settlements in Angola, Mozambique and Cambodia. In the latter two cases, killing and atrocity were far greater than in the war in the Balkans.

Let me develop this line of argument with reference to the case of Yugoslavia. "Ethnic cleansing" by Serbians in Bosnia prompted the recent calls for international prosecution of those responsible. Without a United Nations mandate for a peace-enforcement operation against Serbia, and while UN mediators still attempted to hammer out a mediated solution, the UN decided to gather evidence of war crimes for possible prosecution. Assume for a moment that a negotiated peace is possible in Bosnia, a peace that is not dictated by Serbia. Would such a peace be more likely reached if some Serbians understand that a price of that peace will be their punishment for war crimes? Or does the establishment of such liability further convince Serbian leadership to make no concessions? Logic tells us that the second alternative is more likely.

A promise to hold parties responsible for war crimes makes sense only if the international community has judged a negotiated settlement with the present leadership as impossible. In such an instance the threat of war crimes may place a wedge within the warring party, and help leaders more willing to make peace overthrow recalcitrant leaders. But such a judgement must be accompanied by an effort to defeat the recalcitrant side. A determination of war crimes makes no sense when accompanied by attempts to reach a

---

29. S. Huntington, The Third Wave (1991).

negotiated settlement, but a lot of sense when accompanied by an effort to defeat the offending party.

6. Richard A. Falk, "Humanitarian Intervention: Imperatives and Problematics," reprinted with changes from Richard Falk, "Humanitarian Intervention: Elite and Critical Perspectives," 7 Global Dialogue (Winter/Spring 2005), Nos. 1–2, at 37–49.

Many developments account for the intensity of the recent debate concerning humanitarian intervention: the rise of humanitarian consciousness reinforced by an evolving sense of international accountability for political leaders; a post-Westphalian realization that ideas about territorial sovereignty need to be reconsidered in light of the various dimensions of globalization; suspicions that dominant states, especially the United States and its coalition partners, are using humanitarian pretexts to pursue otherwise unacceptable geopolitical goals and to evade legal prohibitions on the use of international force and the non-intervention norm; a series of high-profile instances (including Somalia, Bosnia, Rwanda, Kosovo, Darfur–Sudan) in which controversy arose about whether the international community was unacceptably doing too little or too much about a severe humanitarian emergency; and the post-hoc rationalization of the Iraq War as allegedly justified on humanitarian grounds, rescuing the Iraqi people from tyranny, despite the absence of any prior authorization by the UN Security Council and the opposition of world public opinion. Additionally, the contextualization of global security in relation to the American-led struggle against mega-terrorism tends to erode claims of sovereignty on the part of states seen as havens for anti-Western political extremism, but also gives rise to normative explanations of this erosion that appear to achieve humanitarian benefits (*e.g.* liberating women from an oppressive Taliban regime in Afghanistan).

There have been two sets of responses stimulated by this series of developments that pertain to the legal, ethical, and political status of humanitarian intervention: a statist response highlighted by reports of commissions composed of eminent persons and a civil society response highlighted by case-by-case advocacy and criticism of action and inaction by the international community, and various expressions of suspicion directed at self-serving accounts of motives on the part of intervening actors, with a particular concern associated with American claims to initiate wars in pursuit of its security without obtaining "a permission slip" from the United Nations.[30] It is not possible, especially in light of the Iraq War, to disentangle the US Government claim of right with respect to preemptive war from the diplomacy of the last decade or so associated with humanitarian intervention. The inhibitions on inter-governmental initiatives or on bodies constituted by "eminent persons," that is, persons prominently associated with governmental and inter-governmental careers, is such that these issues can only be addressed indirectly if at all.[31] This leaves the delicate task of disentangling

30. The phrase was first used by President Bush in the 2004 State of the Union Address to Congress: "America will never seek a permission slip to defend the security of our country." White House, 20 Jan 2004; *see also* "National Security Strategy of the United States of America," White House (Sep 2002), for an authoritative statement of the American claim to initiate a preemptive war whenever it perceives a security threat.

31. For discussion of the political constraints relevant to the operation of such international commissions, see Richard Falk, *Liberalism at the Global Level: Solidarity vs. Cooperation*, in The Globalization of Liberalism 75 (E. Hovden & E. Keene, eds., 2002).

geopolitics from humanitarianism to independent critical voices of opinion in global civil society.

What makes this subject-matter challenging from a normative perspective of law and ethics is that it is neither beneficial to give a green light to all interventionary diplomacy that proclaims humanitarian goals nor to absolutize the norm of non-intervention by posting a red light that prohibits humanitarian encroachments on sovereignty altogether. What seems appropriate is the yellow light of caution, recognizing the danger of either allowing intervention to proceed under the humanitarian banner or the corresponding danger of insisting on non-intervention despite the existence of a humanitarian emergency. Such a cautionary approach would seem to depend on an administering role for the United Nations, especially the Security Council. A precondition for a valid instance of humanitarian intervention is some explicit prior authorization by the UNSC. But suppose it is not forthcoming despite a severe, unfolding humanitarian catastrophe? Can the UN General Assembly or a regional organization play a residual authorizing role? A coalition of the willing? Or in an extreme case of unfolding genocide or massive crimes against humanity would there not be a tacit acquiescence regionally and globally that amounted to authorization, or at least acquiescence? This was the case when India entered East Pakistan (now Bangladesh) in 1971 to stop Pakistani atrocities, Vietnam entered Cambodia in 1978 to end the reign of terror by the Khmer Rouge, Tanzania entered Uganda in 1979 to depose the Idi Amin dictatorship. Each of these examples involved an intervention by a neighboring country, which seemed to act on the basis of strategic interests, but also appeared to be motivated by genuine humanitarian concerns. Such a setting, mingling self-interest with humanitarianism, arouses suspicions in various quarters about the true intentions of the intervention, but if a humanitarian catastrophe is truly unfolding, it also should strengthen confidence that such an intervention is at least more likely to be effective. In effect, realist incentives reinforce the humanitarian rationale for violating sovereign rights. To assess whether this rationale is but a pretext for intervention, consideration should also be given to factors such as whether the intervening state withdraws shortly after the humanitarian emergency has ended, does not insist on establishing strategic bases, a long-term military presence, and shows respect for the right of self-determination of the target country. . . .

The issue is complicated legally by the disposition in 1945 to reassure states joining the United Nations that the new Organization would not intervene in matters "essentially within domestic jurisdiction" (Article 2(7) of the UN Charter), a provision widely understood to encompass abuses of a citizenry by its own government and even instances of civil strife and insurgency. Obviously, if the United Nations was denied the right to intervene, then states and regional actors had no such legal authority to use non-defensive force for such a purpose. Article 51 of the Charter creates an exception to the prohibition on recourse to force, but only with respect to preserving the right of self-defense, and then appearing to limit this right to occasions where the state invoking self-defense has experienced a prior attack. In effect, humanitarian intervention appeared to be outlawed by the UN

Charter as initially drafted. But the Charter is a constitutional document that evolves as community values change and patterns of practice shape new understandings of the balance between the Westphalian autonomy of states and the global governance role of the international community. Integral to this shift in the direction of interventionary authority has been the unexpected rise of international human rights, and supportive notions and institutions of implementation, accountability, and even enforcement. The establishment in 2002 of the International Criminal Court is an institutional milestone in this process, although how far it will be able to realize its promise is uncertain, especially as it currently faces implacable opposition from the United States.

I.   COMMISSION REPORTS AND THE PERSPECTIVES OF EMINENT PERSONS

* * * [There was] a highly visible debate about whether the Kosovo War should be regarded as a positive precedent for humanitarian intervention.[32] On the one side, was concern about setting a precedent that allowed recourse to war outside the scope of the right of self-defense and in the absence of a mandate to intervene from the United Nations. On the other side, was the moral and political desirability of acting effectively in the face of a humanitarian emergency, confirmed by a welcoming population and the rapid return of most of the Albanian Kosovar refugees. Shortly after the war, an Independent International Commission on Kosovo was established by the Swedish government, acting in consultation with the Secretary–General of the United Nations, to address these issues, as well as to consider the future for Kosovo.

The basic effort of the Kosovo Commission, which issued its report in 2000, was to offer an approach to addressing the doctrinal tension identified above. The report suggested, first of all, that the Kosovo War was "legitimate, although illegal." In effect, this meant an acceptance of the argument that a humanitarian emergency existed, making it morally and politically justified, and hence legitimate, to intervene militarily to protect the vulnerable Kosovar population. At the same time the intervention was illegal because it involved a non-defensive use of international force that had not been authorized in advance by the United Nations.[33]

This circumstance of "legitimate, although illegal" was acknowledged as confusing and unfortunate, but it seemed highly unlikely in the near future that the UN would formally revise its conceptions on the legality of force so as to overcome this tension. And yet it also seemed important for the international community to act in the face of an unfolding humanitarian emergency as it had in Kosovo. One viewpoint that gained some attention at the time was to pronounce the law of the Charter to be essentially obsolete, and leave the decision to intervene, as in Kosovo, to coalitions of the willing.[34] Such an assessment, in effect, prematurely gives up on the Charter effort to prohibit non-defensive wars of choice, a viewpoint that would exempt the invasion and

---

32. I leave aside legal and moral criticisms of the war relating to the reliance on tactics of waging the war mainly by high altitude bombing, and the failure of occupying forces to avoid reverse ethnic cleansing and other abuses of the Serb minority, especially immediately following the cessation of hostilities.

33. *See* Independent Commission on Kosovo, Kosovo Report: Conflict, International Responses, Lessons Learned (2000).

34. Most fully argued by Michael J. Glennon, Limits of Law, Prerogatives of Power (2001). *See also* Glennon, *Why the Security Council Failed*, 82 Foreign Aff. No. 2., at 16 (2003).

subsequent occupation of Iraq from legal condemnation as a war of aggression. This "adjustment" unnecessarily concedes too much ground to geopolitical opportunism. An alternative adjustment would involve the suspension of the veto, either by formal arrangement or informal patterns of practice, in instances of humanitarian emergency of the Kosovo or Darfur variety. This adjustment would be beneficial, and would have enabled the Kosovo intervention to receive authorization from the Security Council, circumventing the expected vetoes of China and Russia. This adjustment is not politically acceptable at the present time as the tradeoff between sovereignty and humanitarianism is understood and interpreted differently by permanent members of the Security Council. It is not only differing degrees of attachment to sovereign rights, but the suspicion that humanitarian claims are often pretexts for the pursuit of grand strategy by hegemonic actors, including imperial ambitions. In effect, diminishing the relevance of the veto is also an unlikely adjustment under present world conditions. Slightly less unlikely, would be the evolution of a practice that allowed authorization to come from the General Assembly in those instances where a positive recommendation of humanitarian intervention was blocked solely because of negative votes by one or two permanent members with veto powers.

The Kosovo Commission, acknowledging these difficulties, seeks to endow the legitimate, but illegal approach with a principled framework that would test a claim of legitimacy.[35] The Kosovo Commission report sets forth eleven principles, divided into threshold principles and contextual principles that determine whether and to what extent the contention of legitimacy associated with the intervention is persuasive. There are three threshold principles, the first of which is that there are two sets of triggering circumstances: acute violations of human rights or of international humanitarian law; and state failure that exposes a population to mass suffering. The other two threshold principles insist that the intervention be undertaken for "the direct benefit of the victimized population" and that the method of intervention must be "reasonably calculated" to end the catastrophe as rapidly as possible and in a manner that protects civilians as a whole. There are eight further contextual principles: war must be last resort; efforts to gain UN authorization must be undertaken; efforts to resolve the conflict peacefully must be undertaken; some degree of multilateralism must guide the whole process; there should not exist a formal censure of the proposed intervention by either the Security Council or the International Court of Justice; the laws of war must be strictly upheld; the intervening states should obtain no territorial or economic rewards, and should show a readiness to withdraw as soon as normalcy is restored; sufficient resources should be made available at the post-conflict phases to facilitate economic, social, and political reconstruction.[36] Such a checklist of principles is meant to provide guidelines for policy and appraisal, and is obviously subject to wide variations of interpretation in specific circumstances. Whether such considerations help to identify occasions for legitimate intervention and to shape its implementation remains for the

---

35. See also the criteria for intervention set forth by the Danish Institute of International Affairs: serious violations of human rights or international humanitarian law; a failure by the UNSC to act; a multilateral basis for action undertaken; only necessary and proportionate force used; "disinterestedness" of the intervening states. Humanitarian Intervention: Legal and Political Aspects, Danish Institute of International Affairs 106–11 (1999)....

36. Kosovo Report, *supra* note 33, at 193–95.

future. Of course, as inaction in response to the unfolding and deepening humanitarian crisis in the Darfur region of Sudan illustrates, as Rwanda did in 1994, no matter how legitimate the case for humanitarian intervention, absent political will on the part of those actors with the capacity to intervene, there will not be forthcoming an effective international response. Paradoxically, it is one of the shadows cast upon claims of legitimacy, that is, the presence of strategic motives alongside the humanitarian considerations makes it more likely that *effective* action will be taken only in situations where the moral and political case for humanitarian intervention is reinforced by strategic incentives. In this sense, vulnerable peoples exposed to abuse and state failure in sub-Saharan Africa are not nearly as likely to be protected by an international initiative than those being victimized in regions that enjoy high geopolitical priorities.

A similar, but somewhat different tack was taken on interventionary diplomacy by the Canadian initiative that led to the establishment of the Commission on Intervention and State Sovereignty, which issued an influential report under the title of *The Responsibility to Protect*.[37] The report seeks to circumvent the controversy surrounding "humanitarian intervention" partly by adopting a different language, and shifting the locus of inquiry from the victimized population to the role of the international community in such circumstances. In this spirit, it abandons the terminology of "humanitarian intervention" as unnecessarily provocative because it so frontally poses issues of sovereign rights and of uses of force by the most powerful states. By substituting the language of responsibility and protection, it is hoped that hot button issues associated with interventionary diplomacy, evoking many bad memories of colonialism, can be circumvented or at least mitigated. "The Responsibility to Protect" frames the undertaking by reference to four basic objectives:

> to establish clearer rules, procedures and criteria for determining whether, when and how to intervene; to establish the legitimacy of military intervention when necessary and after all other approaches have failed; to ensure that military intervention, when it occurs, is carried out only for the purposes proposed, is effective, and is undertaken with proper concern to minimize human costs and institutional damage that will result; and to help eliminate, where possible, the causes of conflict while enhancing the prospects for durable and sustainable peace.[38]

As with the Kosovo Commission's eleven principles, these objectives of the Canadian Commission seem intended as guides to policy and assessment rather than to reinforce the red lines of international law that pertain to force and sovereignty. The engagement of national and international responsibility is inevitably related to political will, which is itself shaped by strategic interests, public opinion, media attention, and short-term memories of success and failures associated with prior interventionary undertakings. In the 1990s, the perceived failure of the American-led undertaking in Somalia contributed significantly to the refusal to support action by the United Nations in Rwanda despite the transparency of the genocidal dangers.[39] This refusal reflected both

37. Published by the International Development Research Centre, Ottawa, Canada, 2001.

38. *Id.* at 11.

39. For an excellent overview of these various cases arising in the 1900s that produced either action or inaction on the part of the international community, see N. Wheeler, Sav-

the sub-Saharan perceived absence of strategic interests by the dominant states and the realization that intervention could be costly in lives and resources. In contrast, Kosovo in 1999 generated an American sense of strategic stakes, combined with a shift of tactics to diminish the risk of casualties for the intervening side, the memories associated with impotence arising from the feeble role of the UN in Bosnia a few years earlier, and the impulse to show that a regional military alliance and innovations in weaponry and doctrine made NATO far more effective as an intervening actor than had been the United Nations.

The Commission on Intervention and State Sovereignty was also intent on suggesting that responsibility be substituted for rights when it comes to the understanding of sovereignty, rendering a state that fails to protect its citizenry "irresponsible," and no longer entitled to unqualified deference. Such a rhetorical move is explained as needed to incorporate the rise of human rights and to support the then emergent perspective on security that involved thinking less about the security of the state (national security) and more about the security of people (human security).[40] The report also urges that the main organs of the United Nations take steps to endorse this approach, and to act accordingly, seeking to shape the political climate of opinion by formalizing an inter-governmental and institutional level the consensus reached by the commission composed of eminent persons representative of the world as whole and mostly associated with prominent careers in the governments of their respective countries.

This report achieved considerable attention when issued, partly due to the energy of its co-Chair, Gareth Evans, former Foreign Minister of Australia, and partly because it made a successful effort to find a less threatening, yet sensible and clear, way to discuss humanitarian intervention. The approach has been adopted by the Report of the Secretary–General's High–Level Panel on Threats, Challenges and Change issued with considerable fanfare in November 2004.[o] Two elements can be highlighted, the explicit abridgement of the non-intervention norm: "The principle of non-intervention in internal affairs cannot be used to protect genocidal acts or atrocities, such as large-scale violations of international humanitarian law or large-scale ethnic cleansing, which can properly be considered a threat to international security and as such provoke action by the Security Council."[41] The report recommends against any effort to alter the Charter language to accommodate this approach, contending that it is not necessary and likely not politically feasible. It also moves directly to suggest that sovereignty is no longer operative as a shield for oppressive governments, suggesting that "[t]he successive humanitarian disasters in Somalia, Bosnia and Herzegovina, Rwanda, Kosovo and

ing Strangers: Humanitarian Intervention in International Society (2000). For an important sympathetic assessment of the UN response to the Rwanda crisis, see M. Barnett, Eyewitness to Genocide: The UN and Rwanda (2002).

40. The Responsibility to Protect, *supra* note 37, at 13; also Lloyd Axworthy, as Minister of External Affairs in Canada, made a special effort to introduce the idea of human security into the discourse of statecraft. Axworthy's important contributions to thinking about security are well expressed in his book

Navigating the World: Canada's Global Future (2003).

o. A More Secure World: Our Shared Responsibility, Report of the Secretary–General's High–Level Panel on Threats, Challenges and Change, UN Doc. A/59/565, published also in book form by the UN Department of Public Information in December 2004 and *available at* <http://www. un.org/secureworld>.

41. *Id.* at 65.

now Darfur, Sudan, have concentrated attention not on the immunities of sovereign Governments but their responsibilities, both to their own people and to the wider international community."[42] In this regard, 'responsibility' has a dual face, upward to impose duties of protection on the organized international community, and downward to confirm obligations of territorial governance on the sovereign state. Of course, given the nature of international society, as well as its normative framework, major states are essentially exempted from such obligations, being too large to be held accountable.

These developments await further incidents to determine whether their impact is mainly on the *style* of diplomatic language or affects, as well, *behavioral patterns of response*. What is excluded in these inquiries by credible individuals is the relevance, some would say the dominance, of geopolitics that seems crucial to the formation of political will, which in turn determines whether there is a strong prospect of an effective effort to insist on responsible behavior by governments and by the United Nations. The effects of the 9/11 attacks on the global policy agenda, the dithering response to Darfur, and the current leadership of the United States that appears hostile to 'humanitarian' nation-building (as contrasted with the enormous efforts undertaken by Washington in pursuance of strategic goals in Afghanistan and Iraq), combine to give an impression that humanitarian concerns and an ethos of human solidarity do not enjoy presently strong support from leading governments. Whether the epic natural disaster caused by the South Asian tsunami of December 2004 will give a more hopeful picture of the extent of humanitarian concerns remains to be seen. From a realist perspective, the appeal of responding to a natural disaster is that costs and risks can be fixed with relative certainty in advance, and no loss of life on the intervening side is likely. It is also worth noting that in the list of 'humanitarian disasters' in the UN High–Level report neither Afghanistan nor Iraq are mentioned, despite the American efforts, especially in Iraq, to justify its use of force after the fact by reference to the undoubted oppressive conditions existing in both countries.

* * *

III.   DOMAINS OF DOUBT AND BELIEF: CIVIL SOCIETY
PERSPECTIVES ON HUMANITARIAN INTERVENTION

Throughout the extensive literature on humanitarian intervention, almost all of it written by scholars living in the countries that do the intervening, either directly or through the agency of international institutions, there is encountered a self-serving, moralistic rhetoric and tone. Michael Walzer has long served as a leading exponent of geopolitically conservative moralistic advocacy, including with respect to humanitarian intervention. In this spirit he writes, "[w]henever the filthy work can be stopped, it should be stopped. And if not by us, the supposedly decent people of this world, then by whom?"[43]

---

42. *Id.*; see, at 66, endorsement of "the emerging norm that there is a collective international responsibility to protect" but seeming to confine its implementation to the Security Council, thereby indirectly invalidating the residual authority of such other actors as regional organizations or coalitions of the willing.

There is also presented a checklist of five criteria designed to provide a framework for principled action, and resembling the lists earlier discussed.

43. M. Walzer, Arguing About War 81, n.11 (2004).

Another stalwart moralist of the established order, Michael Ignatieff, who is even more explicitly supportive than Walzer of the moral claims of the leading political actors in the current makeup of world order, criticism should be mostly directed at the reluctance to intervene, rather than with the supposedly incidental harm done by intervention.[44] Such views by independent scholars provide invaluable aid and comfort to the United States and the former colonial states, casting them in the role of moral saviors of peoples trapped in barbaric circumstances. What such apologists for imperial prerogatives uniformly ignore is the historical record of cruel criminality on the part of these self-appointed, post-colonial guardians of world order. They also ignore the post-interventionary record of irresponsible withdrawal or the engagement with exploitative forms of reconstruction that ensure strategic control and economic benefits by way of lucrative investment contracts.

* * *

All of this contributes to sustaining a sort of "collective day-dream," as Edward Said describes the Orientalist process of visioning the other, which in the setting of humanitarian intervention allows the exploitative dominant side to sustain the illusion of moral distance between itself and evil out there at a distance. By so doing, the intervening state(s), or their constructed "international community" represents itself by contrasting images arising from being "sovereign, civilized, autonomous, powerful and humane."[45] Such critical thinking is definitely a needed corrective to patterns of naïve and uncritical liberal advocacy that has dominated mainstream discussions of humanitarian diplomacy, but does it go too far?

* * *

IV. CONCLUDING OBSERVATIONS

The subject-matter of humanitarian intervention has been foregrounded by the rise of human rights in a globalizing world. At the same time, the practice of rescuing populations raises a variety of *proximate* concerns associated with justification and effectiveness. It also raises more *fundamental* concerns associated with the causal onset of humanitarian emergencies and the impact of reconstructive efforts. There are two sets of responses that have been noted: the first consists of those who represent the established order, and seek to reconcile a sensitivity to the rights of independent states with actions designed to bring relief and rescue to peoples entrapped within oppressive or anarchic circumstances. These perspectives seek to make humanitarian intervention acceptable and operational, revising international law along the way, but without questioning underlying conditions or the motives of the intervenors. The second consists of critics of the established order that regard humanitarian intervention as a hypocritical exercise in post-colonial imperialism that not only fails to address basic issue generative of mass suffering, but may aggravate and intensify such suffering by diverting attention from real causes and available cures.

44. M. Ignatieff, *The Burden*, New York Times Magazine, 5 Jan 2003, 22–27, 50–54.

45. A. Orford, Reading Humanitarian Intervention: Human Rights and the Use of Force in International Law 204 (2003).

This whole setting of debate has been complicated by the 9/11 attacks on the United States, and the American response that has fused a new generation of real concerns about global security with a militarist push for global dominance by a Western power. In this latter setting, as seen in Iraq since the American invasion of 2003, the humanitarian intervention argument is invoked as a cover for aggressive warfare and a prolonged hostile occupation. At the same time, the massive humanitarian catastrophe festering in Darfur has evoked widespread global concern, but only minimalist protective action, again confirming that where strategic interests are weak, the needed political will for protective action will not be forthcoming no matter how grave and massive the unfolding tragedy and no matter how the intervention is sanitized by the language of protection. Rwanda *redux*.

The way forward is to proceed on complementary lines. Despite the difficulties and ambiguities of practice, it remains beneficial to counsel effective action in response to instances of ethnic cleansing, genocide, and crimes against humanity. It may be feasible to bring into being a volunteer, professional capability under the auspices of the United Nations that would be entrusted with the implementation of humanitarian diplomacy with reduced geopolitical interference....

**7.   Fernando R. Tesón, "Collective Humanitarian Intervention,"
17 Mich. J. Int'l L. 323, 325–38 (1996).**

I.   Soft, Hard, and Forcible Intervention

The customary meaning of prohibited intervention in international law denotes "dictatorial interference ... in the affairs of another State for the purpose of maintaining or altering the actual condition of things. Prohibited intervention in international law involves ... some kind of coercive action."[46] The International Court of Justice has confirmed this definition of prohibited intervention. According to the Court, acts of prohibited intervention must be coercive, and they must be aimed at thwarting choices by the target state that must remain free under international law.[47] Thus the *means* of the intervention must be coercive (although not necessarily *forcible*) and the *end* of the intervention must be to influence another state (by effect of the coercion exercised) on a matter falling under the state's domestic jurisdiction. Both requirements must be met for an action to be called "prohibited intervention" in this traditional sense.

Obviously, the word "intervene" in Article 2(7) [of the UN Charter **(Basic Document 1.5)**] cannot have this meaning. Rather, that article prohibits any United Nations organ from merely *discussing, examining, or issuing recommendations* on matters that fall within the state's domestic jurisdiction. The prohibition in Article 2(7) thus covers *non-coercive* action by the United Nations: the word "intervene" is used here in its ordinary, non-technical sense, not as a legal term of art. This is confirmed by the fact that Article 2(7) expressly *exempts* from the prohibition those cases where the organization is entitled to take coercive enforcement measures under Chapter VII of the UN Charter. Thus, in the context of United Nations law, we need to

---

46. L. Oppenheim, International Law 305 (H. Lauterpacht ed., 8th ed. 1955).

47. Military and Paramilitary Activities in and against Nicaragua (Nicar. v. U.S.), *supra*

note 28, at 107–08.... [*See also supra* Reading C–7 (p. 291)].

ask two questions. First, what is the present scope of domestic jurisdiction removed from the scrutiny of the United Nations under Article 2(7)? Second, can the United Nations validly adopt coercive measures, including force, to remedy a situation *other* than a breach of the peace or act of aggression?

As a preliminary matter, it is necessary to distinguish between three different meanings of "intervention," according to the degree of coercion utilized in the attempt to influence other states. The first is the sense in which the word is used in Article 2(7). In this sense, "intervention" means simply discussion, examination, and recommendatory action: this I will call *soft* intervention. The second meaning of the word "intervention" refers to the adoption of measures that (unlike soft intervention) are coercive but do not involve the use of force, such as economic and other kinds of sanctions: this I will refer to as *hard* intervention. And finally, the word "intervention" is often used to refer to acts involving the use of force (as in "humanitarian intervention"): this I call *forcible* intervention. The important issue regarding forcible intervention is that the use of force is subject to independent legal constraints. Therefore, a situation which could qualify for collective soft or hard intervention may nevertheless not be appropriate for collective forcible action.

The distinction between the different forms of intervention according to their degree of coercion leaves intact a common requirement: prohibited intervention has to be an action aimed at influencing a government on an issue where the target state has legal discretion. This is plain in the case of soft intervention, where the only issue is an issue of *ends*, not of means, since the means are perfectly permissible in principle. But the same is true in cases of hard and forcible intervention. If state A violates a fishing treaty with state B, and B adopts economic sanctions in retaliation, B's action will not be deemed "intervention." The matter did not fall within A's exclusive jurisdiction because A was not legally free to violate the treaty. Instead, the legality of B's retaliation will be determined by the law of countermeasures, in particular by the principle of proportionality. If, however, state A decides to nationalize certain natural resources, and B responds by declaring an economic embargo against A, this action amounts to prohibited hard intervention. B's action is coercive, although not forcible, and A has, in principle and absent an international commitment, exclusive jurisdiction over the question of nationalization of natural resources. In this example, B has no right to coerce A into reversing the nationalization.

The same analysis applies to forcible intervention. Applying the general requirements that define unlawful intervention, prohibited forcible intervention will occur when two conditions are met: first, the action by the intervenor can be described as indirect or direct use of force; and second, the "choices" that the intervenor attempts to influence should remain "free" for the target state—they must fall under its exclusive jurisdiction.[48] The same

48. I use the phrases "exclusive domestic jurisdiction" or "domestic" jurisdiction interchangeably, although technically those areas where the state is legally "free" may or may not concern "domestic" matters. For example, choices regarding foreign policy are not "domestic," but they may be legally discretionary and thus within the exclusive jurisdiction of the state.... Although the issue is a general one of the permissible limits of state influence, technically, only intervention in internal affairs gives rise to issues of domestic jurisdiction.

two requirements must be met. If a state violates a trade agreement with another state, and the latter retaliates with a limited forcible measure, this would violate the prohibition on the use of force, since treaty breaches of this kind do not justify the use of force. It would not violate the principle of non-intervention, however, because actions concerning a treaty are not within the legal discretion of the target state. The assessment of all three forms of intervention depends on the determination of whether a matter falls within the domestic jurisdiction of a state.

* * *

A. *Human Rights*

Human rights have long been subtracted from the exclusive domestic jurisdiction of states. This is notwithstanding the fact that they seem to constitute the paradigm of an "essentially" domestic matter since they define the relationship between government and subjects. Writers already had reached this conclusion in the early discussions of the concept of domestic jurisdiction in the UN Charter, citing not only the well-known provisions of the Charter, but also a number of human rights cases that had been addressed by the various organs of the United Nations.

The proposition that human rights are no longer a matter of exclusive domestic jurisdiction is indisputable, independently of the legal grounds for the obligation of states to respect human rights.[49] The General Assembly routinely adopts resolutions concerning human rights. Many are addressed to the membership in general, but some are addressed directly to particular states. Thus the General Assembly recently passed resolutions on the human rights situation in Bosnia–Herzegovina; El Salvador; Iraq; Myanmar (formerly Burma); Afghanistan; territories occupied by Israel; Haiti; and Iran. Admittedly, some of these cases, such as the "intifada" in the territories occupied by Israel or the situation in Afghanistan, do produce substantial international effects and can therefore be explained by reference to the traditional test. The General Assembly seldom offers this rationale, however. In the case of Myanmar, the General Assembly simply recalled that states have an obligation to promote and protect human rights in accordance with the applicable international human rights instruments. In the case of El Salvador, although a civil war of serious regional repercussions was taking place, the General Assembly could not overemphasize the importance of observing human rights, "full respect of which is essential to the attainment of a just and lasting peace." No references to international repercussions are cited in the case of Haiti either. In those cases of human rights violations that do threaten international peace and security, such as *apartheid* in South Africa, action by the United Nations is legally *overdetermined*: the "international effects" test *and* the human rights violations provide equally valid grounds for soft intervention.

49. *See generally* B. Weston, *Human Rights*, in Human Rights in the World Community 14 (R. Claude & B. Weston eds., 2d ed. 1992) [updated and revised in Encyclopædia Britannica (2005), available via Encyclopædia Britannica Online at <http//www.britannica.com/eb/article?tocId= 219350> and in Human Rights in the World Community 17 & 294 (R. Claude & B. Weston eds., 3d ed. 2006)].

That human rights violations warrant United Nations soft intervention has ceased to be a matter of controversy. Governments singled out by the General Assembly rarely claim nowadays that such action violates Article 2(7) of the UN Charter. Because the General Assembly treats the Charter and the Universal Declaration of Human Rights **[Basic Document 3.3]** as establishing definite obligations for members, violations of such obligations can trigger action by the appropriate United Nations body.

B. *Form of Government: Democracy*

Many writers and governments who accept the premise that the observance of human rights, in the sense of a government's *treatment* of its own citizens, is now an appropriate subject for international scrutiny, nonetheless draw the line at the question of the *legitimacy* of the government itself. They argue that *this* is a question of domestic jurisdiction, if there ever was one. In the absence of widespread human rights violations, so the argument goes, the international community should not be in the business of passing judgment on the legitimacy of the *origin* of a government. The question of internal political legitimacy is, in this view, a matter falling under the exclusive jurisdiction of the state and exempt from even soft intervention by international organizations or by the international community as a whole.

There are *a priori* reasons to doubt the conclusion that international law is or should not be concerned with democratic legitimacy. First and fundamental is the question of agency. If international law is largely created by nation-states, then the international community needs some criterion to determine when some official actually *represents* the state. Traditional international law has proposed the criterion of *effectiveness*. A government is the international representative of a people living in a territory if that government has effective political control over that people. Traditional international law is indifferent to how that political control has been acquired.

Such a view is indefensible. If the international system is going to be the result of what the "peoples of the United Nations" want it to be[50] then it makes sense to require that the government participating in the creation of international law be the real representative of the people who reside within the state's boundaries. A rule requiring democratic legitimacy in the form of free adult universal suffrage seems the best approximation to actual political consent and true representativeness.

Second, there are strong grounds for believing that democratic rule is a necessary condition for enjoying other human rights. While it is always possible to imagine a society where human rights are respected by an enlightened despot, this has never occurred in practice. This is why the right to political participation is included in the major human rights conventions. The right to participate in government is a very important human right in itself; it is also instrumental to the enjoyment of other rights. Its violation should therefore trigger appropriate international scrutiny.

The third reason for requiring democratic rule is the one indicated by Kant: democracies are more peaceful, and therefore a rule requiring democratic rule is consonant with the ideal of a lasting world peace, in a way that the rule of effectiveness, by countenancing tyranny, is not. This is because

50. *See* UN Charter **[Basic Document 1.5]**, pmbl.

tyrannies tend to be more aggressive *and* because the difference in regimes is a major cause of conflict. Democracies have built-in mechanisms which cause them to avoid war with one another altogether. The reason why democracies are sometimes belligerent is that they often perceive threats to their democratic institutions by illiberal regimes. These threats are sometimes real and sometimes imaginary, which is why democracies also get involved in unjustified wars. But these wars are always against illiberal regimes. Democracies *do not* make war against one another. If the aim of international law is to secure a lasting peace where the benefits of international cooperation can be reaped by all, then international law has to require democratic legitimacy.

But even if none of this was true, international law should require democratic rule simply because it is the right thing to do. I do not need a complicated philosophical defense of democracy: a simple comparison with the traditional rule of effectiveness will suffice. Traditional international law *authorizes* tyranny. It gives *carte-blanche* to anyone who wishes to bypass popular will and seize and maintain power by sheer political force. This is delicately described by pertinent international materials as a state's right to "choose" its political system. Such a state-centric view suffers from acute moral and conceptual poverty. Both ordinary common sense morality and the structure of international law, by presupposing agency and representation, require that governments should be recognized and accepted in the international community only if they genuinely represent their people.

These arguments suffice, I believe, to demonstrate why international law must recognize an individual and collective right to democratic rule. It has become abundantly clear, moreover, that the principle is supported by contemporary state practice. . . .

* * *

III.　Collective Humanitarian Intervention

A.　*General Principles*

In recent years, international lawyers have debated the legitimacy of using force to remedy serious human rights violations, a practice also known as humanitarian intervention. Some writers reject the legitimacy of humanitarian intervention altogether, whether it is collective or unilateral. For these authors, the intent of the intervenor is irrelevant, as are the *degree* of human rights violations and the attitude of the victims themselves—that is, whether the intervention is the product of a unilateral decision by the intervenor, or instead requested by the citizens of the target state. According to these authors, armed intervention for humanitarian purposes is flatly prohibited.

Undeniably, the anti-interventionist position has the support of traditional state-centric conceptions of international law and relations. It is also informed by the commendable moral purpose of reducing the permissible instances of war and containing armed conflict. This extreme position cannot be maintained today. The content and purpose of state sovereignty have undergone profound changes since 1945, and more dramatically since 1989. Human beings have claims against their own states and governments that the international community cannot merely ignore. While war ought to be the remedy of last resort to redress human rights violations, there are some, admittedly rare, serious cases of human rights deprivations where a strong case can and should be made for forcible intervention authorized by the international community or even by individual states. Whether these cases should be viewed as extreme instances of "moral catastrophe" and thus *outside* the law, or whether they are instead genuine exceptions to the legal prohibition is a jurisprudential preference to which little weight ought to be attached. I cannot see much consequence to the proposition that an act is illegal but morally permitted, or obligatory, as contrasted with the proposition that the act is legally permitted, or obligatory, in those rare instances. This is so because moral reasons are overriding. If anti-interventionists can agree on the kind of cases where the international community morally can or must intervene, their protests that the intervention is nevertheless illegal do not enjoy much credibility.

State practice since 1945 demonstrates that states have a right to intervene forcibly to put an end to serious human rights violations. Yet, here I wish to concentrate exclusively on *collective* humanitarian intervention. In more technical terms, the question is whether the Security Council may authorize [UN Charter] Article 42 measures to put an end to serious, or extreme, human rights violations. Some writers who are hostile to the legitimacy of unilateral action concede that the legal situation changes when the humanitarian intervention is authorized by the United Nations or an appropriate regional body. This support for multilateral action may be prompted by the feeling that if a coercive action is authorized by some kind of formal international *process*, such as voting by the Security Council, then it acquires a legality which it would lack if the decision to intervene were left to national governments acting unilaterally. Alternatively, they may think that collective humanitarian intervention is more apt to curb the danger of abuse posed by unilateral intervention. More technically, some may argue that the Security Council, unlike individual states, has absolute discretion in deciding when to authorize the use of force. According to this view, the Security Council *determines* the existence of a breach of the peace, threat to the peace, or act of aggression under Article 39 of the UN Charter. Therefore, if the Security Council authorizes enforcement measures in a case of serious human rights deprivations, it has determined that the situation qualifies under Article 39 as the kind of situation which *is* a breach of the peace.

Anti-interventionists disagree. They argue that under Article 39 the Security Council can only authorize collective forcible action in cases of threat to the peace, breach of the peace, and acts of aggression. Serious human rights violations, even genocide, do not constitute aggression or threat or breach of the (international) peace if contained within state borders. In addition, anti-interventionists deny absolute discretion to the Security Council in this regard. For them, the Security Council is subject to standards imposed by the UN Charter and cannot lawfully overstep those constraints. Unless a violation of human rights threatens international peace, the Security Council does not have the power to authorize forcible action. At most, these authors argue, the Security Council can criticize the dictatorial government and demand peremptorily that the violations cease. Such a demand will be legally binding under Article 25. The Security Council can even authorize *hard* intervention, such as economic or other sanctions, by members against the outlaw state. But these authors maintain that the Security Council may not authorize the use of force.

8. Makumi Mwagiru, "International Law, Politics, and the Reinvention of Humanitarian Intervention: The Lesson of Somalia," 34 Indian J. Int'l L. 33, 33, 36–37, 41–44 (1994).

This article ... investigates international responses to the Somalia conflict, and argues that on the evidence available, this response was characterised by the re-invention of the Cold War interventionist paradigm, rather than a creation of a new paradigm of intervention. It argues that notwithstanding this, responses to the Somalia conflict suggest that the old, Cold War interventionist paradigm displays significant anomalies, which international society will be called upon to examine critically as the parameters of the new world order emerge....

* * *

... [T]he three features of the UN Charter paradigm during the Cold War were the notion of non-use of force (or the pacific settlement of international disputes), collective security through measures approved by the Security Council, and the emphasis on the maintenance of international peace and security over the creation of a just international system. These were quintessentially Cold War preoccupations, and were designed to maintain the *status quo* that had been established by the realities of post second World War international political life.

Clearly, if there is to be a paradigm shift, the old paradigm must be shown to be unable to solve the pressing problems of the day. In the current international system, the pressing problems of the day have clearly changed: rather than the geopolitical problems of the Cold War, there are now new, and different problems. International society now has to deal with problems like those of conflicts based on emerging nationalisms, and the protection of human rights. It is also exercised with creating approaches to global problems such as those of poverty, and the protection of the environment. In addition, although this is not admitted in discourses about the new international world order, the place and role of small and weak states, devoid of the geopolitical underpinnings of the Cold War that made them important players, needs to be addressed in the substance of a new paradigm.

To date, however, although strains in the old paradigm are increasingly becoming evident in countries as diverse as Somalia, Bosnia and Haiti, there is little evidence that the international community has recognised anomalies in the old approaches, and hence their inability to resolve the pressing problems of the day. There has not yet been a paradigm shift in Kuhnian terms.[51] However, international society has witnessed a re-invention, and a reinterpretation of the old paradigm, in an attempt to meet the challenges of the new era. The new gloss on the old paradigm is that of multilateralism, which has in recent times been emphasised anew. This has in turn heralded a "return to the Charter" in the sense that provisions of the Charter [**Basic Document 1.5**] will in the future be more keenly resorted to, without the

---

51. *See* T. Kuhn, The Structure of Scientific Revolutions (1962) [*quoted in supra* Discussion Note/Question 1 in Chapter 1 (p. 31)].

fear of veto, which during the Cold War was the order of the day. Multilateralism, in the present climate, is buttressed by approaches such as preventive diplomacy, by which "leverage and persuasive power" will be used to lead conflicting parties to negotiations.[52]

In addition to this reinvention of the old paradigm, Cold War notions like those of intervention have also been boosted by new interpretations, with approaches to humanitarian intervention being elevated to a different status in the vocabulary of intervention. Apart from these, the structure of the old paradigm has been left intact: the Security Council, the International Court of Justice, and peace-keeping are still perceived to be central features of conflict management in international society. What is currently in place therefore, is not a new paradigm, but a reinvention of the old. At best, there is evidence that the old paradigm is developing significant anomalies, and that the process of its overthrow is in place, ready for eventual replacement....

* * *

Humanitarian Intervention and the Somalia Conflict

When President Bush sent American forces into Somalia in the winter of 1992, the rationale was that it was a humanitarian action, and that the American soldiers were going in to do "the work of God". Operation "Restore Hope" as it was dubbed, was also meant to be of short duration, aimed primarily at facilitating the safe passage of aid being provided by various relief agencies. However, although conceived of as a humanitarian mission, it soon took on the form of traditional intervention.

The ingredients of humanitarian intervention, as mentioned earlier, are that there must be an immediate threat to fundamental human rights, particularly a widespread threat to human life; the intervention must not be undertaken at the invitation of the legitimate government (to do so would destroy the whole edifice of the *humanitarian* element); and neither should the intervention be undertaken under the UN Charter.

On this basis, operation "Restore Hope" met two of the requirements of a humanitarian intervention: there was a widespread abuse of fundamental human rights in Somalia at the time, including the widespread loss of human life. Secondly, the operation was not undertaken pursuant of the invitation of a government, since indeed, there was no functional government in Somalia at that time. But the operation fails on the third and crucial test: it relied heavily for its effectuation on the United Nations, and particularly the Security Council. Security Council Resolution 794,[p] recognised the "unique character" and "complex and extraordinary nature" of the conflict in Somalia, which in its view constituted a threat to international peace and security. For these reasons, the Security Council invoked the provisions of Chapter VII of the Charter, and authorised the Secretary General and all member states "to use all necessary means to establish as soon as possible a secure environment for humanitarian relief operations in Somalia." This was the basis on

---

52. Military and Paramilitary Activities in and against Nicaragua (Nicar. v. U.S.), *supra* note 28, at 21.

p. United Nations Security Council Resolution 794 (Granting the Secretary–General Discretion in the Further Deployment of Personnel of the United Nations Operation in Somalia), 3 Dec 1992, UN SCOR, 47th Sess., 3145th mtg., at 63, UN Doc. S/RES/794 (1992), *reprinted in* 2 Weston & Carlson II. D.6.

which UNITAF (United Task Force), comprising almost thirty thousand US troops, went into Somalia. By thus resorting to the Security Council to legitimise its involvement, the United States lost a crucial basis on which it could have described the operation as humanitarian. As Arend and Beck have argued, the operation instead became one of collective use of force.[40]

The operation authorised by Resolution 794 was in any case not in itself a humanitarian operation, but one to *"establish as soon as possible a secure environment for humanitarian relief operations"* in Somalia. The question whether an intervention to facilitate humanitarian intervention is itself a humanitarian intervention can therefore only be answered in the negative. This point of view is further fortified by the differing perceptions of the United States Secretary General and President Bush as to the nature and import of the operation. While Bush contemplated a humanitarian intervention *strictu sensu,* Boutros–Ghali had in mind a wider perspective, that of peace enforcement. This in fact inexorably moved the operation even further from any notion of humanitarian intervention than before. The tragedy of Somalia was a humanitarian tragedy, but not one contemplated by Chapter VII of the Charter. Although the Security Council defined the Somali conflict as a threat to international peace and security, there are doubts as to whether the description properly applied to the Somalia situation especially after the end of the Cold War. During the Cold War, the Somalia conflict could have constituted a threat to international peace and security; post-Cold War, this was less true. The Security Council can therefore be criticised on this account in that it resorted to a Cold War paradigm to deal with a post Cold War problem, which called for a different paradigm. But the Charter in its unamended [form] provides no such paradigm yet, and the effect of this was the costly UNITAF/UNISOM exercise. The Security Council attempted to bell a cat which had barely been conceived.

The conclusions properly to be drawn from this are therefore that the conflict in Somalia represented a grave humanitarian problem, but not one which constituted a threat to international peace and security. By characterising the conflict as such the Security Council was in essence trying to justify the use of methodologies that were designed to cater for Cold War conflicts. The defining framework of international society had however changed, and the instruments designed in the old paradigm could not properly reflect this development. What is needed therefore, is a revision of the Charter to cater for humanitarian intervention, since the new pattern of the post-Cold War era will increasingly give rise to the need for such intervention. Such an amendment to the Charter (which will constitute devising a new paradigm rather than re-inventing the old), would in future obviate the need for the Security Council to authorise international humanitarian intervention on criteria which, given the new international order, are not objective.

Conclusions

The UN paradigm as stated in the Charter was state-centric, and saw states as the main players in international relations. In that paradigm, threats to international peace and security would only result from inter-state dis-

---

40. A. Arend & R. Beck, International Law and the Use of Force: Beyond the UN Charter Paradigm 113 (1993).

putes. Hence, Chapter VI of the Charter, on the pacific settlement of disputes, has in mind disputes between member states, which might endanger international peace and security. But the end of the Cold War has changed many of the underpinnings behind that formulation. In the post-Cold War world, as events in former Yugoslavia and former USSR, not to mention places like Somalia are revealing, the emerging pattern of conflict is not inter-state and ideological, but intra-state, ethnic and nationalist. Many of the conflicts are, indeed, internal conflicts, for which the Charter makes no adequate provision.

As the Somalia conflict showed, the mechanisms put in place to serve the old order are unsuitable for the realities of the new world. The old paradigm was based on the idea of collective enforcement of peace and security, and international action to resolve international conflict. That power-based paradigm is not equal to the challenges of the new type of conflicts, in which power, especially outside power, cannot address the causes of conflict, nor provide a framework for its resolution.

The new conflicts require resolution through negotiation. Intervention in these conflicts [encourages] the parties to them to sit down and negotiate a solution to their conflict. Multilateral institutions such as the United Nations, and indeed individual states, need to work out ways by which peaceful third party intervention in these conflicts can be effected. What needs to be strengthened, as Somalia has shown, are not the military capabilities of the United Nations, but its negotiating capabilities. Peaceful third party intervention in conflict contemplates a situation where the solution to conflict is also consensual, and worked out within a negotiating forum. In Somalia, solutions inherent in the old UN paradigm were re-invented and transposed on a situation where new realities cried for the overthrow of that paradigm, in favour of a new one. What was new in that approach was not the methodology adopted, but its justifications: it sought to impose old solutions on new problems by recourse to the notion of intervention, and to put a legalist veneer on that process by pleading its humanitarian character. It did not work and not surprisingly so. It however revealed that the old paradigm had developed significant anomalies. It is time for a new international conflict management paradigm. This is the lesson of Somalia.

9. Anne Orford, Reading Humanitarian Intervention: Human Rights and the Use of Force in International Law 6–37 (2003).

There are certainly some legal commentators who have continued to express concern about the apparent willingness of a largely unrestrained Security Council to expand its mandate to include authorising the use of force to remedy human rights abuses or "to make every State a democratic one." Many legal scholars, however, seem haunted by the fear that opposing military intervention in Bosnia, Haiti, Kosovo, or East Timor means opposing the only realistic possibility of international engagement to end the horrific human suffering witnessed in such conflicts. The need to halt the horrors of genocide or to address the effects of civil war and internal armed conflict on civilians has been accepted as sufficient justification for intervention, even if other motives may be involved.

Perhaps the most interesting place in the debate about the legality of humanitarian intervention is occupied by the new human rights warriors. In the popular scholarship of human rights lawyer Geoffrey Robertson, for example, humanitarian intervention demonstrates the possibility, too often deferred, of an international rule of law.[41] Robertson suggests that the world is entering a "third age of human rights," that of human rights enforcement. His vision of this age of enforcement is a potent blend of faith in the power of media images of suffering to mobilise public sentiment or the "indignant pity of the civilised world," and belief in the emergence of an international criminal justice system. According to Robertson, in the future the basis of human rights enforcement will be a combination of judicial remedies such as ad hoc tribunals, domestic prosecutions for crimes against humanity and an international criminal court. An important part of that system will be the willingness of states to use armed force to create this new world of enforceable human rights. Such force should ideally be authorised by the Security Council, according to the dictates of the UN Charter, but where Security Council approval is not politically feasible, international intervention should nonetheless go ahead, carried out by regional organisations or even a democratic "coalition of the willing." As he concludes, "there is as yet no court to stop a state which murders and extirpates its own people: for them, if the Security Council fails to reach superpower agreement, the only salvation can come through other states exercising the right of humanitarian intervention."[42]

This new support for humanitarian intervention is also evident in the work of NGOs such as Human Rights Watch. In its *World Report 2000*, Human Rights Watch treats the deployment of multinational troops in East Timor and the NATO bombing campaign in Kosovo as examples of a new willingness on behalf of the international community to deploy troops to stop crimes against humanity or to halt genocide or "massive slaughter."[43] Like Robertson, Human Rights Watch welcomes these developments as marking "a new era for the human rights movement", one in which human rights organisations can "count on governments to use their police powers to enforce human rights law." It sees the "growing willingness to transcend sovereignty in the face of crimes against humanity" as a positive development, one which promises that "victims of atrocities" will receive "effective assistance wherever they cry out for help." Any problems of selectivity or dangers that humanitarian intervention "might become a pretext for military adventures in pursuit of ulterior motives" can be met by ensuring that criteria are developed for when such intervention should occur, and by ensuring that no regions are "neglected" when it comes to the willingness to use force.

* * *

The conviction about the need for intervention expressed in post-Cold War legal and human rights literature mirrored the arguments made by European, US and Australian political leaders justifying international intervention during the 1990s. To give one example, British Prime Minister Tony Blair portrayed the NATO intervention in Kosovo as a "just war, based not on territorial ambitions, but on values." According to Blair, British foreign policy decisions in the post-Cold War era "are guided by a ... subtle blend of

41. Geoffrey Robertson, Crimes against Humanity: The Struggle for Global Justice (1999).

42. *Id.* at 420.

43. Human Rights Watch, World Report 2000, at 1 [*available at* <http://www.hrw.org/wr2k/>].

mutual self-interest and moral purpose in defending the values we cherish. . . . If we can establish and spread the values of liberty, the rule of law, human rights and an open society, then that is in our national interest."[44] The war in Kosovo was fought precisely to defend such values:

> This war was not fought for Albanians against Serbs. It was not fought for territory. Still less for NATO aggrandisement. It was fought for a fundamental principle necessary for humanity's progress: that every human being, regardless of race, religion or birth, has the inalienable right to live free from persecution.[45]

This was the broad climate within which the argument for humanitarian intervention in the case of East Timor was made. My immediate response to these calls for intervention was that here was a case where the willingness to kill people in the name of the international community might be ethical. I was moved by the sense that urgent action was the only way to prevent a genocide. This fear was evident in many calls for military intervention. A student asked to address one of my classes, and announced that "as we speak, people are being slaughtered in the streets of Dili. Timorese people in Australia are hysterical. Come and rally at Parliament House and demand intervention now." A newspaper head line on the same day read "Plea for peacekeepers as terror grips Timor."

The story the news article told was that violent pro-Jakarta militia were rampaging through Dili in response to the UN's announcement on 5 September [1999] that the overwhelming majority of East Timorese had voted for independence in the UN-sponsored referendum. More than one hundred people had already been killed or wounded, and many including injured children were seeking sanctuary at the UN headquarters. . . .

As I walked down to feed my son at the university childcare centre that afternoon, I was handed a leaflet advertising a rally. The leaflet stated that "the next few days will be critical in saving the lives of thousands of East Timorese" and urged that I "demand an international peacekeeping force." My desire for intervention was made more urgent by the repeated representation of the Timorese as defenceless, powerless, "hysterical" and unprotected, and by the focus on threats to babies, women and children. As one eyewitness cried on the radio, "The East Timorese are being slaughtered. There's no-one there to protect them." Hearing these reports left me feeling as unbearably and frustratingly powerless and helpless as the East Timorese. At the same time, if Australians and the international community were willing to use military force in response to this slaughter and devastation, we could be potential saviours of the East Timorese, agents of democracy and human rights able to overpower those bent on killing and destruction. It was up to us to offer protection to the people of East Timor.

Yet despite my growing sense that in this case intervention was necessary, I also had some doubts about my response. I had spent the last few years writing and thinking about how the desire for military intervention is produced. I had been interested in exploring the effects of the ways in which

---

44. Tony Blair, Doctrine of the International Community, Speech before the Economic Club of Chicago (22 Apr 1999), at <http://www.fco.gov.uk/news/speech text.asp?2316>.

45. *Id.*

internationalists spoke and wrote about collective security and international intervention in the post-Cold War era. Two features of the knowledge practices of international lawyers had interested me. First, I had been concerned to think about the claim that a right or duty of humanitarian intervention was somehow revolutionary, fulfilling the promise of a world based on respect for human rights rather than merely respect for state interests. My sense was that the way in which international law was narrated in fact served to confine any revolutionary potential inherent in human rights discourse, such that the right of intervention in the name of human rights became profoundly conservative in its meaning and effects. Any potentially revolutionary interpretations of humanitarian intervention as heralding a commitment to human rights over state interests had been constrained by the meanings that were made of international intervention in legal texts. I felt that in quite complicated ways, these legal intervention narratives served to preserve an unjust and exploitative status quo.

Second, the way in which humanitarian intervention was narrated had other less obviously "international" effects. For example, the way in which international law portrayed the need to intervene in order to protect and look after the people of "failed states," and the forms of dependence set up in post-conflict "peace-building" situations, seemed to rehearse colonial fantasies about the need for benevolent tutelage of uncivilised people who were as yet unable to govern themselves. The focus in international law's intervention narratives on the ways in which violence could be used by good and righteous men to achieve the best for those against whom that violence was directed seemed to me to reinforce many of the stories of masculinity against which feminists had been writing for decades. So, intervention narratives had a domestic or personal effect, despite their overtly international focus. These representations of international intervention help to shape the identities and world-view of all those who engage with them. Intervention stories work "by calling an audience into the story." Their appeal is premised upon learned assumptions about value based on old stereotypes of gender, race and class—assumptions that inform the way those who live inside such stories experience the world.

* * *

Experience had shown that armed intervention had not necessarily been humanitarian in effect. Those active in humanitarian organisations had argued that armed intervention, particularly aerial bombardment, often impeded humanitarian relief and was indiscriminate in its targets, generally proving counterproductive to the tasks of democratisation and peace-building. The disproportionate targeting of essential infrastructure and deaths of civilians through such air campaigns had itself been questioned as a breach of international humanitarian law. In addition, the introduction of large numbers of militarised men as peace-keepers had repeatedly led to increased exploitation, rape, prostitution and abuse of women and children.

The new enthusiasm for military intervention as a weapon of human rights enforcement also had systemic effects. The resort to ad hoc interventionist responses to human rights crises by major powers allowed them to avoid funding, supporting and strengthening the existing multilateral mechanisms for promoting and protecting human rights. The use of force as a response to security and humanitarian crises continued to mean that insufficient attention was paid to the extent to which the policies of international institutions themselves contribute to creating the conditions that lead to such crises. For example, the representation of the interventions in Bosnia and Kosovo as the actions of an international community interested in protecting human rights and humanitarian values served to obscure the extent to which the international community had itself contributed to the humanitarian crises that had emerged in those places. While ancient hatreds and ethnic tensions continue to be represented as the cause of the violence that erupted in the former Yugoslavia, critics have suggested that the crisis was equally a product of modern capitalist international relations.[46] In the former Yugoslavia as elsewhere, the project of economic restructuring and liberalisation which remains central to the new world order contributed to creating the conditions in which such hatreds were inflamed. For these and other reasons, I had argued that the desire to use violence and to take "action" by sending armed forces to create security had to be interrogated. As Edward Said has shown, the belief that "certain territories and people *require* and beseech domination" was at the heart of making colonialism palatable.[47] Given that it was so difficult for people to stand back from the culture that produced and legitimised imperialism, it seemed necessary to be cautious about any arguments that made the use of force appear benevolent to us today.

[The question] "What alternative can you offer at that moment when the choice is either intervention or genocide?" . . . is a compelling one. It raises a central theme underlying the debate about the legitimacy of humanitarian intervention—the idea that the choice facing the international community in security or humanitarian crises is one between action and inaction. In the case of East Timor, the story by which I was moved to advocate intervention was one in which slaughter, genocide and massive human rights abuses had to be met by action, specifically in the form of military intervention. Both those arguing for and those against the legitimacy of humanitarian intervention accept that the international community is faced with a choice as to whether or not to take action in states where conflicts arise. The argument made by those who support humanitarian intervention is based upon an assumption that post-Cold War crises are in part attributable to an absence of law, including international law, and a lack of sustained engagement by international organisations. Accordingly, a commitment to humanitarian ideals is seen to demand action from the international community, in the form of intervention. . . .

* * *

Even those who reject the legitimacy of collective humanitarian intervention appear haunted by the fear that failure to act under the auspices of the Security Council may represent a betrayal of our duty to be engaged in the world in the interests of humanity. Richard Falk's critical analysis of the precedent set by Security Council resolutions concerning Haiti provides a good illustration of that concern.[48] While Falk mounts a strong case against

46. P. Gowan, *The NATO Powers and the Balkan Tragedy*, 234 New Left Review 83 (1999).

47. E. Said, Culture and Imperialism 9 (1994).

48. R. Falk, *The Haiti Intervention: a Dangerous World Order Precedent for the United*

Security Council action in Haiti, he admits to a fear that advocating non-intervention may equal advocating inaction. "Having mounted this case against intervention, a haunting question must be posed: with all of its deficiencies, isn't it better to have confronted and deposed Cedras, to have provided relief to the Haitian people from the widespread daily brutality and to have given them an opportunity to compose a more democratic government that addresses the poverty of the people?"[49]

* * *

... [T]he assumption that the international community faces a choice between military intervention and inaction limits the capacity of international law to develop adequate responses to post-Cold War security and humanitarian crises.... The international community had already intervened on a large scale in [the former Yugoslavia, Rwanda, and East Timor] before the security crisis erupted, particularly through the activities of international economic institutions. Inactivity, in other words, is not the alternative to intervention. The international community is already profoundly engaged in shaping the structure of political, social, economic and cultural life in many states through the activities of, *inter alia,* international economic institutions. Indeed, intervention in the name of humanitarianism too readily provides an alibi for the continued involvement of those interested in exploiting and controlling the resources and people of target states. The "myopia" of international lawyers about the effects of the new interventionism means that, in general, international legal debate fails to address the ways in which the destructive consequences of coercive economic restructuring contributes to instability, leading to further violence and denials of human rights.

* * *

The question ... about the choices available when international law is confronted with genocide or mass human rights violations, like the discourse of humanitarian intervention more generally, adopts a particular temporal focus. International law is structured around a concern with serial security and humanitarian crises. The focus is always on the moment when military intervention is the only remaining credible foreign policy option. The question that is produced by law's focus on the moment of crisis is always "What would you suggest we do if we are in that situation again?" The assertion that this is the only moment which can be considered renders it impossible to analyse any other involvement of the international community or to think reflexively about law's role in producing the meaning of intervention. At the moment of crisis, the demands on law are so immediate and important that they replace everything else in the field of analysis—it is the duty of lawyers only ever to focus on specific crises and 'facts' rather than studying the narrating of legal texts or law as fiction....

* * *

Nations, 36 Harv. Int'l L. J. 341 (1995). *See also* Security Council Resolution 940, [UN SCOR, 49th Sess., 3413th mtg., UN Doc. S/INF/50 (1994)] adopted on 31 Jul 1994 (authorising member states to impose economic sanctions and use force to 'facilitate the departure from Haiti of the military leadership' and to return it to democratic rule under President Jean–Bertrand Aristide).

49. Falk, *supra* note 48, at 357.

Those international lawyers who support the new interventionism of the post-Cold War era have tended not to discuss the potential imperial character of multilateral intervention. Instead, they present an image of international institutions and international law as agents of democracy and human rights. That representation operates to reinforce the identity of international institutions and of major powers, particularly the USA, as in turn bearers of those progressive values. The UN and other post-World War II institutions have embodied the faith of many people in the ability of international institutions to protect ideals of universalism, humanitarianism, peace, security and human rights. Multilateralism has seemed to offer an escape from unrestrained self-interest and power politics. That faith, if anything, has grown stronger in the post-Soviet era, with commentators treating multilateral and regional institutions, particularly the UN and now NATO, as essentially benevolent and able to bring not only peace and security, but also human rights and democracy, to the world. Those who express concern about the potential for powerful states to abuse the emerging norm of humanitarian intervention tend to treat this as a problem for the future. For example, in his 1999 annual address to the General Assembly, Kofi Annan commented that the Kosovo action could set "dangerous precedents for *future* interventions without a clear criterion to decide who might invoke these precedents, and in what circumstances."[50] The faith in law's freedom from imperialist desire is clear in the general acceptance amongst legal commentators of the humanitarian motives behind intervention in the post-Cold War era.

* * *

[T]he Dayton Peace Agreement institutionalised the exclusion of the people of Bosnia and Herzegovina from vital economic and political decision-making. * * * Yet according to many legal accounts, the tension between law and empire was neatly, if belatedly, resolved in the case of East Timor. Portugal had held East Timor as one of its colonies from 1893. In 1960, the UN General Assembly placed East Timor on its list of non-self-governing territories, with Portugal as the administering power. Portugal initiated a decolonisation process in 1974, and sought to establish a provisional government and popular assembly to determine the future status of East Timor. The Indonesian invasion of East Timor in 1975 ended this move towards decolonisation. Nevertheless, despite Indonesia's purported integration of East Timor as an Indonesian province, the UN condemned Indonesia's aggression and continued to recognise Portugal as the administering authority over the territory. The more celebratory account of this period suggests that international law was able to oversee the chaotic and bloody end to the imperial overreach of Indonesia and the failed decolonisation attempt for which Portugal was responsible. In 1998, Indonesia proposed that East Timor be granted limited special autonomy within the Republic of Indonesia. The resulting talks involving Indonesia, Portugal and the UN Secretary–General saw the Secretary–General entrusted with the organisation and conduct of a popular consultation to ascertain whether the East Timorese people accepted Indonesia's special autonomy proposal. When the vote rejecting the autonomy

---

50. UN, Secretary–General Presents His Annual Report to General Assembly, UN Press   Release SG/SM/7136 GA/9596, 20 Sep 1999.

proposal in favour of independence resulted in a campaign of violence and destruction waged against the East Timorese, the international community responded by sending a multinational force to restore peace and security. International financial institutions were also able to help protect the people of East Timor against the violence sanctioned by Indonesia by exerting pressure on the Indonesian government during the post-ballot period. In the following months, the Indonesian armed forces, police and administrative officials withdrew from the territory and militia attacks were controlled.

According to this story, law champions the East Timorese and paves the way for the removal of imperialists, both old (Portugal) and new (Indonesia). Secretary–General Kofi Annan certainly saw these actions as signifying an important moment for the international community. For Annan, "the tragedy of East Timor, coming so soon after that of Kosovo, has focused attention once again on the need for timely intervention by the international community when death and suffering are being inflicted on large numbers of people."[51] He therefore welcomed the "developing international norm in favour of intervention to protect civilians from wholesale slaughter." ... Yet a consideration of the role of international organisations in East Timor in the period following intervention complicates this picture, particularly in the context of international law's imperial history. The UN and the World Bank have adopted a major 'trusteeship' role, taking over responsibility for administration in East Timor during the period of transition to independence. On 25 October 1999, the Security Council established the UN Transitional Administration in East Timor (UNTAET) as a peace-keeping operation "endowed with overall responsibility for the administration of East Timor and ... empowered to exercise all legislative and executive authority, including the administration of justice."[52] The UN granted itself a broad and ambitious mandate, including the provision of security and maintenance of law and order, the establishment of an effective administration, assisting in the development of civil and social services, supporting capacity-building for self-government and assisting in the establishment of conditions for sustainable development. The Secretary–General's Special Representative and Transitional Administrator, [the late] Sergio Vieira de Mello, was made "responsible for all aspects of the United Nations work in East Timor," with "the power to enact new laws and regulations and to amend, suspend or repeal existing ones."[53] The UN's view of its role in East Timor is well illustrated by Jean–Christian Cady, the Deputy Transitional Administrator of East Timor, who was to comment, "the United Nations found themselves in a situation without precedent in their history: to rebuild a country entirely."[54] The World Bank also plays a major role in the administration of East Timor. It administers the World Bank Administered Multilateral Trust Fund for East Timor, and works in consultation with the East Timorese and UNTAET representatives to facilitate economic development. The Bank has made clear that certain familiar Bank programmes and priorities are to be implemented in the management of East Timor. Its plans focus on ensuring that East Timor has a

---

51. K. Annan, *Two Concepts of Sovereignty*, The Economist, 18 Sep 1999, at 49, 50.

52. SC Res. 1272, UN SCOR, 54th Sess., 4057th mtg. ¶ 1, UN Doc. S/INF/55 (1999).

53. *Id.* ¶ 6.

54. J.-C. Cady, Building the New State of East Timor, lecture before the Centre for International and Public Law, Australian National University (18 May 2000).

small state and is quickly inserted into the global market economy, albeit as one of the poorest countries in the region.

The economic and political management being developed by these international organisations on behalf of East Timor sets the stage for the kind of limited sovereignty that Antony Anghie has analysed in his study of the operation of the mandate system under the League of Nations after World War I.[55] Under that system, territories belonging to defeated powers were placed under the control of mandate powers who were responsible for the administration of those territories and required to report back to the League concerning the measures taken to ensure the well-being and development of mandate peoples. The mandate system appeared to be premised on the international community's desire to move away from colonialism, and to represent a radical departure from international law's acceptance of colonialism towards an expression of condemnation of colonial exploitation and violence. In fact, Anghie argues that far from representing a move away from imperialism, the mandate system merely changed its legal form, instituting a new form of colonial power based not on political but on economic control. The neocolonial process would be overseen by an international institution, one which, like the World Bank in East Timor, saw its role as technical rather than political. Administration of a territory was to be undertaken by a disinterested body of international experts intent on ensuring the proper development and welfare of those subject to their trust. The policies of such institutions were seen as scientific and objective, rather than self-interested. The system as a whole, however, operated to integrate the mandate society into the international economy. Mandate territories were inserted into that economy in a subordinate role. As a result, while those territories appeared to be freed from political control, they remained subject to the control of the parties that exercised power within the international economy.

* * *

[T]he nature of post-conflict reconstruction in places such as Bosnia–Herzegovina and East Timor mirrors the way in which the international community supported colonialism in earlier periods. From its support for acquisition of territory belonging to uncivilised peoples through to the operation of the mandate system, the international community has systematically facilitated the enterprise of colonialism. Central to this support has been the limited meaning given to the concept of self-determination. Post-conflict reconstruction carried out under the auspices of international financial institutions is often concerned to create a secure environment in which foreign investment can produce profits for the shareholders of multinational and foreign corporations, free of the kinds of investment constraints that were the product of the efforts of decolonised states to create a new international economic order during the 1970s.

As a result, there appear to be limits on the capacity of those in whose name the exercise of reconstruction is conducted to participate fully in determining the conditions that will shape their lives. . . . [O]nly one "choice" is being made available to the new subjects of international law, such as the nation of East Timor. That choice is to be governed by economically rational

55. A. Anghie, *Time Present and Time Past: Globalization, International Financial In-* *stitutions, and the Third World*, 32 N.Y.U. J. Int'l L & Pol. 87, 243 (2000).

governments under the tutelage of the international economic institutions who follow the military as representatives of the international community. This illustrates a broader political problem facing the subjects of the international legal system. International law has always operated to constitute as its subjects those who resemble the idealised self-image of European sovereign peoples. The anxieties about who should count as international legal subjects generated by the nineteenth-century colonial enterprise were central to the ways questions about legal personality were posed and answered. The doctrinal attempt to define the "proper subjects of international law" was fuelled by the political imperative of European lawyers seeking to find a way to distinguish "sovereigns proper from other entities that also seemed to possess the attributes of sovereignty, such as pirates, non-European states, and nomads."[56] ... The ongoing struggle of indigenous peoples to be recognised as peoples entitled to self-determination and as subjects of international law is one of the contemporary manifestations of this history. The struggle of people in Bosnia, Haiti, Kuwait, East Timor and Kosovo to determine the nature of their conditions of existence and to be recognised as fully sovereign is another.

* * *

So, as I debated the promises of intervention with my friend, I argued that living under the administration of the UN and the World Bank promises little change—no real independence and new threats to life, health and security. I argued that the presence of the military as representatives of the "international community" provides an alibi for exploitation—we are able to portray our presence as offering salvation and protection. I argued that this is a revolution, that this has changed people's hearts and minds, that now people are ready to go on to the streets and protest for intervention, for the increased presence of US and Australian militaries in our region. Yet even as I argued, I thought about all the people protesting on the street, and I wanted to be part of that optimism. I wondered if I was missing something very fundamental here, if I was choosing not to believe in the good intentions of the international community in this case because I was lacking the necessary faith (in humanity? in law? in international organisations?). For my friend, the choice was clear. Living under UN and World Bank trusteeship is better than living under Indonesian governance. If she had the choice to live in Papua New Guinea under the World Bank, or West Papua under the Indonesian military, she argued, she would choose Papua New Guinea. People there eat better and are more secure. They are less likely to be subjected to rape and murder than those who are subject to the terror tactics of the Indonesian military or the pro-Indonesian militias.

I asked whether the choice between living under Indonesian soldiers or under international governance is after all a choice—"we," the "international community," were part of the conditions of the life of the East Timorese under Indonesian soldiers. Now we have changed the manner of our intervention, but does this mean we can treat "them" as somehow being about the East Timorese suffering purely under the governance of the Indonesian military? "Them" involved the US, British and Australian governments and militaries, arms manufacturers from Britain and the USA and the involve-

56. A. Anghie, *Finding the Peripheries: Sovereignty and Colonialism in Nineteenth-* Century International Law, 40 Harv. Int'l L. J. 1, 17 (1999).

ment of the World Bank and the IMF, whether through action or omission, in supporting the Indonesian government and military in its occupation of East Timor. So the choice between life in West Papua and Papua New Guinea seemed to me a false dichotomy, as they are both symptoms of global capitalism. Perhaps my friend was right though—it was extreme of me to argue that one symptom is no better than another. Yet how does it come down to these choices, to people arguing over whether it is better to be governed by the IMF and the World Bank or by the Indonesian military?

I worried about this conversation for days afterwards. Maybe on this one occasion it was better for there to be military intervention with the attendant international supervision, administration and governance that it legitimises. And yet didn't supporting this intervention support a dubious line of "human-itarian interventions" including the Gulf War and NATO's actions in bombing Kosovo? To support such a shift in policy towards the acceptability of humanitarian intervention surely increased the legitimacy of militarism in states such as the USA, the UK, France, Nigeria, Australia and Canada. It threatened to limit the role for no violent and principled means of addressing human rights abuses. It helped build the acceptance of the actions of the international community as unquestionably benevolent and charitable, a story that once played out as the civilising mission. Perhaps I am just wedded to this rejection of humanitarian intervention as an option because I am not able to see the particularity of the situation in East Timor. After all, justice is only possible in the particular case. If in the future this precedent is misused, that is something to be dealt with in the future. This case may indeed mean that the law has changed, and that may be a good thing. Certainly, that is what an increasing number of international lawyers have been advocating since the time of the Gulf War.

* * *

I think also of Rey Chow's argument, that the "Third World" is produced as spectacle, entertainment and monstrosity for those of us watching the media in the "First World." In her discussion of the meaning of the massacre in Tiananmen Square, Chow says:

> The "Third World," as the site of the "raw" material that is "monstrosi-ty," is produced for the surplus-value of spectacle, entertainment, and spiritual enrichment for the "First World." The intense productivity of the Western newsperson leads to the establishment of clear boundaries. Locked behind the bars of our television screens, we become repelled by what is happening "over there."[57]

Televised images of suffering people in the "Third World" function to explain the need for intervention, and in so doing act also as the forms of entertain-ment and spiritual enrichment to which Chow directs our attention. It is easy to forget that television news is part of a highly profitable entertainment industry, and that "entertaining" the audiences of that industry is at least one of the functions that the suffering Third World fulfils. In addition, we are shown nameless starving, weeping, mourning strangers as part of a narrative

57. R. Chow, *Violence in the Other Country: China as Crisis, Spectacle and Woman, in* Third World Women and the Politics of Femi- nism 81–100 (C. Mohanty, A. Russo & L. Tor- res eds., 1991).

in which we are spiritually enriched by the knowledge of our superiority and capacity to rescue and redeem these others. In the context of US reporting on the Tiananmen massacre, Chow points out that we should not take for granted the image of a US journalist "standing on the street in Beijing, speaking a language which is not Chinese, condemning the Chinese government."[58] She argues that we need to question the conditions that make such a fantastic spectacle appear normal. The "freedom" that makes it possible for such journalists to produce knowledge about the "non-West" is "not a basic existential condition to which all are entitled (though that is the claim that is made) but a network of demands, negotiations, and coercions that are themselves bound by historical determinants constructed on slaughter and bloodshed."[59]

* * *

The promise of humanitarian intervention

Humanitarian intervention draws its powerful appeal from the revolutionary discourse of human rights, which promises liberation from tyranny and a future built on something other than militarised and technocratic state interests. At its best, as Costas Douzinas comments, human rights expresses "concern for the unfinished person of the future for whom justice matters."[60] Many human rights activists see humanitarian intervention as unquestioningly a good thing precisely because it appears to enact a commitment to the emancipatory ideals of freedom from oppression, respect for human dignity and valuing of human life. For my friends, this is the meaning that was made of intervention by the people marching in the streets calling for UN action in East Timor.

Yet there has been little analysis of what happens to the revolutionary potential of human rights when those rights are invoked by lawyers and diplomats from powerful states in the name of the people of a territory they intend to invade, bomb or administer. Legal texts justifying interventions in the name of human rights protection offer a narrative in which the international community as heroic saviour rescues those passive victims who suffer at the hands of bullies and tyrants. According to this account of the current state of internationalism, the international community is motivated by the desire to promote and protect core values such as freedom, democracy and humanitarianism. It is international institutions, whether the Security Council or the IMF, the World Bank or NATO, who will operate to bring freedom and indeed salvation to the people of Africa, Asia, Eastern Europe and Latin America. Intervention by international institutions in the name of human rights and democracy provides a reason, or, as some have argued, an 'alibi,' for the presence of the international community in many parts of the world.

* * *

My discussions with friends who felt that intervention was necessary in the case of East Timor convinced me that there may be occasions where armed force is the only available option to deal with a security or humanitari-

---

58. *Id.* at 84.
59. *Id.* at 85.

60. C. Douzinas, The End of Human Rights 15 (2000).

an crisis, however that crisis has been reached. Their focus on solidarity, on standing with and beside the East Timorese, not as saviours but finally as comrades, helped me to see that there is more than one way to understand and narrate the meaning of intervention within a particular context. Yet my response to these conversations with my friends, and in particular my continued uneasiness about the implications of the official meanings made of humanitarian intervention, also reminded me that when we join our voices to the call for military intervention in a particular situation, we may find ourselves part of a different narrative. In this case, I remain concerned that the official narrative about intervention that was buttressed by the Security Council-authorised intervention in East Timor is a disturbing one. The challenge ... is to understand the effects of that dominant narrative, and to find ways to ensure that 'humanitarian intervention' has a more radical meaning than simply support for a particular kind of state-based, capitalist and militaristic world order. The discussions I have recounted helped me to realise that this is a far more complicated question than simply being for or against intervention. It involves thinking through the nature of the dominant intervention narrative, the imperial and patriarchal fantasies that haunt this narrative and the effects of particular interventions. It involves a focus on the way in which meanings are made about intervention, and the way those meanings shut out potentially revolutionary ways of understanding what is at stake.

Section 5.   Discussion Notes/Questions

1.   In working through the present as well as other problems in this coursebook, it is important to be alert to the factual and normative ambiguity of much of the legal language involved. Consider, for example, the key term "civil war." From the Readings it is clear that by "civil war" is meant a type of conflict, principally internal to a national community, that lies along a continuum ranging from relatively low-level, home-grown acts of violence—e.g., local terrorist activities—to full-scale hostilities involving even forces from foreign countries. The varying "foreign-ness" typically involved in "civil war" situations is of course widely accepted, as most of the recent literature bears testimony. But the appropriate world community response to such "foreign-ness" is not. Nor is the response to the different crisis levels involved. The rules applicable to war and peace have been made traditionally to hinge on such other factually and normatively ambiguous contrasts as "domestic" versus "international", and "rebellion" versus "insurgency" versus "belligerency." Indeed, the descriptive and legal value of the terms "war" and "peace" is open to question. The problems of some of these binary oppositions is discussed in the extract by Hilary Charlesworth, *supra* Reading B–3 (p. 281), at 385–91.

Consider also the term "intervention." As John Norton Moore has pointed out, the term has been used in at least four different senses: (1) "[a]s a synonym for transnational interaction or influence;" (2) "[a]s a statement that a particular transnational interaction violates community expectations about permissible international conduct;" (3) "[a]s a personal policy judgment that a particular transnational interaction is wrong;" and (4) "[i]n one or another specialized sense, as a definition of a problem for study." John Norton Moore, *Toward an Applied Theory for the Regulation of Intervention*, in Law and Civil War in the Modern World 9 (J.N. Moore ed., 1974). The extracts from Fernando Tesón (*supra* Reading

D–7, p. 323) and Anne Orford (*supra* Reading D–9, p. 332), also explore the diverse meanings of "intervention."

Thus, when a particular author uses the term "intervention," one must read carefully to determine what behavior is being talked about and whether that behavior is being described, predicted, or condemned. The point is that legal language purports often to perform three critically separate tasks simultaneously: the description of past decision, the prediction of future decision, and the declaration of policy preference. In so doing, to quote Professor Myres S. McDougal, it "refer[s] … with indiscriminate abandon to the facts to which decision-makers are responding, to the policies invoked before decision-makers, and to the particular responses of decision-makers which are sought to be predicted or justified." Myres S. McDougal, *Law as a Process of Decision: A Policy–Oriented Approach to Legal Study*, 1 Natural Law Forum 53, 59 (1956).

How can we deal with the politics of language and focus on the policy issues at stake in a particular situation? Compare the approaches proposed by Tesón (*supra* Reading D–7, p. 323) and Orford (*supra* Reading D–9, p. 332).

2. As we are advised by the readings in this problem, the end of the Cold War appeared to change significantly the politics of intervention in internal conflict; the bipolarity created by the rivalry between the formerly competing superpowers (the Soviet Union and the United States) gave way, at least for a while, to a revival of multilateralism involving reliance upon international institutions to respond to international disputes. United Nations activism in the 1990s in Somalia, the former Yugoslavia, and Rwanda are examples of this development. The revival of multilateralism, however, was accepted uncritically by international law scholars, as some of the preceding readings illustrate. One of the problems identified is that multilateralism may in some circumstances be a smokescreen for unilateral intervention: international institutions may be used by powerful nations such as the United States to "launder" otherwise questionable intervention. What other dangers of multilateralism are discussed in the readings? How serious do you consider them to be?

In the early years of the twenty-first century, multilateralism and international institutions have come under attack by the sole superpower, the United States, and some of its close allies, apparently because multilateral methods have made it difficult for the United States to achieve its foreign policy goals. For example, after the UN Security Council failed to authorize military action against Iraq, the Australian Foreign Minister, in June 2003, described multilateralism as "a synonym for an ineffective and unfocussed policy involving internationalism of the lowest common denominator." Minister for Foreign Affairs Alexander Downer, Security in an Unstable World, Speech at the National Press Club (26 Jun 2003) (transcript available at <http://www.foreignminister.gov.au/speeches/2003/030626_ unstable world.html>).

In thinking about international law relative to intervention in internal conflict situations, consider Antonio Cassese's perspective on the development of international law as he describes it in International Law in a Divided World 396–400 (1986). Professor Cassese identifies two competing models of international law. The first is the "Westphalian" model, based on a commitment to the sovereignty of states, where the only restrictions on sovereignty are entered into voluntarily. In this model, cooperation between states is minimal and force is an accepted method of dispute settlement. The second is the "Charter" model, which has a more idealistic and goal-oriented emphasis. While states are seen as the primary subjects of international law, the Charter model also gives prominence to international organizations, organized peoples, and individuals in creating international law. Cassese sees the two models coexisting in the international legal order, albeit often in tension with one another. Does Cassese's analysis shed any light on recent developments in the law relating to intervention?

3. Another theory once sometimes presented as justification for armed intervention into internal conflict situations is that the intervention is in support of a war of national liberation or self-determination—by which is meant, according to Natalino Ronzitti, *Wars of National Liberation—A Legal Definition*, 1 Ital. Y.B.I.L. 192 (1975), armed struggles by indigenous peoples against colonial rule, racist regimes, and governments which, even if not colonial or racist, are nonetheless unrepresentative or subordinating of certain clearly identifiable national constituencies. They are seen as being in furtherance of the principle of "self-determination of peoples," stated to be among the basic purposes and principles of the United Nations in Article 1(2) of the United Nations Charter **(Basic Document 1.5)**. *See* Christopher C. Mojekwu, *Self-Determination: The African Perspective*, in Self–Determination: National, Regional, and Global Dimensions 230 (Y. Alexander & R. Friedlander eds., 1980); S. Kwaw Nyameke Blay, *Changing African Perspectives on the Right of Self–Determination in the Wake of the Banjul Charter on Human and Peoples' Rights*, 29 J. African L. 147–59 (1985); M. Rafiqul Islam, *Use of Force in Self–Determination Claims*, 25 Ind. J. Int'l L. 424 (1985). Indeed several UN General Assembly resolutions actually have called upon member (and other) states to contribute material as well as moral assistance to national liberation movements. *See, e.g.*, GA Res. 2105, UN GAOR, 20th Sess., Supp. No. 14, at 16, UN Doc. A/6014 (1966). But is this desirable? Should wars of national liberation be treated differently from other internal conflicts?

In *Private Armies in a Global War System: Prologue to Decision*, 14 Va. J. Int'l L. 1, 5 (1973), Professor Michael Reisman contends that wars of national liberation should be subjected to the same evaluative criteria we apply to other internal conflicts. But he also implicitly endorses armed intervention on behalf of such wars whenever they are tested "in present and projected contexts" and found socially redeeming from the standpoint of augmented "human dignity"? In this connection, see W. Michael Reisman, *The Resistance in Afghanistan is Engaged in a War of National Liberation*, 81 A.J.I.L. 906 (1987). Do you agree? In this increasingly interdependent nuclear era, when even a small spark can ignite a major conflagration, should organized violence of any sort ever be encouraged or tolerated? Or are there times when we must risk rank-ordering the value of social justice above the value of peace? If so, when and under what conditions? What light does the Orford (*supra* Reading D–9, p. 332) shed on this question?

For further discussion, see Heather A. Wilson, International Law and the Use of Force by National Liberation Movements (1985); George Abi–Saab, *Wars of National Liberation and the Laws of War*, 3 Annals Int'l Stud. 93 (1972); Richard A. Falk, *Intervention and National Liberation*, in Intervention in World Politics 119 (H. Bull ed., 1984). The late Jonathan Charney identifies three conditions for international support for claims of self-determination outside a colonial context: a bona fide exhaustion of peaceful methods of resolving the dispute between the government and the minority group claiming an unjust denial of self-determination; evidence that the persons asserting the self-determination claim represent the will of the majority of the group; and a resort to force taken only as a means of last resort. Jonathan I. Charney, *Self-Determination: Chechnya, Kosovo, and East Timor*, 34 Vand. J. Transnat'l L. 455, 464 (2001). On this basis Charney argues that the Chechen claim to independence from Russia is less sustainable than that of the East Timorese.

4. What about unilateral humanitarian intervention, action taken outside the UN collective security system? Regardless of its formal legal standing, should it, like intervention on behalf of national liberation movements, be encouraged as an exception to the general prohibition of intervention? Professor Brownlie, for one, thinks not. He writes: "[A] rule allowing [unilateral] humanitarian intervention ... is a general license to vigilantes and opportunists to resort to hegemonical intervention." Ian Brownlie, *Thoughts on Kind–Hearted Gunmen*, in Humanitarian Intervention and the United Nations 147–48 (R. Lillich ed., 1973). Similarly, human rights scholar Louis Henkin has observed: "A humanitarian reason for military intervention is ... easy to fabricate.... Every case of intervention I can think of ... [has been] justified on some kind of humanitarian ground...." Louis Henkin, *Remarks on "Biafra, Bengal, and Beyond: International Responsibility and Genocidal Conflict,"* 1972 Proceed. A.S.I.L. 95, 96. *See also* Professor Henkin's comments in relation to the NATO intervention in Serbia in 1999 in Reading C–8, *supra*. The potential for self-serving abuse, it may be added, is something about which Americans in particular should be cautious. According to a leading American historian, intervening forcefully into other nations' affairs has been more the rule than the exception of United States foreign policy from 1776 to the present. *See* Walter LaFeber, The New Empire (1963); ___, Inevitable Revolutions–The United States in Central America (1993); Thomas G. Paterson, J. Garry Clifford & Kenneth J. Hagan, American Foreign Relations: A History (4th ed. 1995); Arthur M. Schlesinger, The Cycles of American History (1986). *See also* Noam Chomsky who, in *The New Military Humanism: Lessons from Kosovo* (1999), has authored the germinal text repudiating humanitarian claims by the United States. Still, in the absence of supranational institutions genuinely capable of averting gross violations of human rights, might we not risk too much by ruling out all unilateral use-of-force interventions? Fernando Tesón (*supra* Reading D–7, p. 323) would take this view. *See also* W. Michael Reisman, *Humanitarian Intervention to Protect the Ibos*, in Humanitarian Intervention and the United Nations 195 (R. Lillich ed., 1973); John Norton Moore, *Legal Standards for Intervention in Internal Conflicts*, 13 Ga. J. Int'l & Comp. L. 191 (1983). What are your views on this debate?

The distinction between unilateral intervention on humanitarian grounds and multilateral intervention (usually intervention under the auspices of an international organization) is often blurred. For example, in the case of Haiti in 1994, military intervention was the initiative of the United States which managed to secure a UN Security Council mandate for the operation and the endorsement of the Organization of American States. Richard Falk criticizes the Haiti intervention, but not without acknowledging the counter-arguments:

> Having mounted this case against intervention, a haunting question must be posed: with all of its deficiencies, isn't it better to have confronted and deposed Cedras, to have provided relief to the Haitian people from the widespread daily brutality and to have given them an opportunity to compose a more democratic government that addresses the poverty of the people? Even should the intervention lead over time to the reestablishment of the old dictatorial structures in Haiti, would the recent intervention not influence future leaders to refrain from terrorizing their citizens? And isn't it better that the United States government refrain from unilateralism, linking this intervention to prior approval and continued participation by the UN and the OAS? Furthermore, should not restoration of constitutionalism be the sole motivation for intervention, with the interventionary forces withdrawn once this objective is accomplished, so that the future of a country can be shaped

by the undisturbed interplay of indigenous forces, thereby upholding the Haitian people's right of self determination?

Richard A. Falk, *The Haitian Intervention: A Dangerous World Order Precedent for the United Nations*, 36 Harv. Int'l L. J. 341, 357 (1995). Compare Fernando Tesón's analysis of the Haitian intervention in *Collective Humanitarian Intervention*, 17 Mich. J. Int'l L. 883 (1995) (*see also supra* Reading D–7, p. 323). Tesón views the Haiti case as a genuine and worthy precedent for collective humanitarian intervention, primarily on human rights grounds.

The attack on Iraq in by a "coalition of the willing" in 2003, led by the United States without the approval of the UN Security Council, was justified in part as a humanitarian intervention. An argument that a threat by France (a permanent member of the Security Council) to exercise a veto over a resolution supporting the war constituted an unreasonable action and that the Security Council could thus be bypassed was made by British Prime Minister Tony Blair. A report adopted by the International Commission of Intervention and State Sovereignty—a group of eminent former politicians and scholars convened by the Canadian government (extracted *supra* at 262) provides a useful framework to consider the 2003 intervention in Iraq. The report recommends that the concept of "humanitarian intervention" is better characterised as "a responsibility to protect." The commission noted that this change in terminology "implies an evaluation of the issues from the point of view of those seeking or needing support, rather than those who may be considering intervention." The Responsibility to Protect: Report of the International Commission on Intervention and State Sovereignty ¶ 2.29 (Dec 2001).

The Commission's report attempts to find a balance between respect for state sovereignty and the need to respond to significant human rights violations. It identifies a responsibility to protect that may involve military intervention in international law but distills three guiding principles. First, there must be a just cause: "Military intervention for human protection purposes is an exceptional and extraordinary measure. To be warranted, there must be serious and irreparable harm occurring to human beings, or imminently likely to occur." The Commission identifies two types of harm as a large scale loss of life or a large scale ethnic cleansing. Second, the Commission states that the primary purpose of the intervention must be to avert human suffering; that intervention can be justified only when every other non-military option has been explored; that the scale, duration and intensity of the military intervention should be the minimum necessary to protect; and that there must be a reasonable chance of averting the suffering that has justified the intervention. The third principle identified by the Commission is that of "right authority." It argues that the UN Security Council is the most appropriate body in the first instance to authorise military intervention. If the Security Council were to reject a proposal for intervention, or fail to deal with it in a reasonable time, the Commission proposes that the UN General Assembly consider the matter under the 1950 Uniting for Peace Resolution which allows it to vote to support measures for the maintenance of international peace; or that action be taken by a regional organization.

How does the humanitarian intervention argument used by the "coalition of the willing" in the case of Iraq in 2003 measure against the criteria proposed by the International Commission on Intervention and State Sovereignty?

5. An example of truly unilateral intervention was the successful Israeli commando raid on the Entebbe Airport in Uganda in July 1976, freeing a number of Israeli and other nationals held hostage by a group of terrorists who had

hijacked an Air France plane in Athens (while en route from Israel to Paris) and who, according to some reports, were being given active assistance by the government of General Idi Amin. Three Israeli aircraft descended secretly and swiftly upon Entebbe to airlift the hostages to safety, and, in the course of the rescue mission, all the hijackers, 20 Ugandan soldiers, one Israeli commando, and three of the hostages were killed. Was the Entebbe raid a lawful act of humanitarian intervention? Was it an act of aggression? For discussion, see Natalino Ronzitti, Rescuing Nationals Abroad Through Military Coercion and Intervention on Grounds of Humanity (1985); Francis A. Boyle, *International Law in Time of Crisis: From the Entebbe Raid to the Hostages Convention*, 75 Nw. U. L. Rev. 769 (1980); Leslie C. Green, *Rescue at Entebbe—Legal Aspects*, 6 Israel Y. B. Hum. Rts. 312 (1976).

6. During the Cold War, both the United States and the Soviet Union argued for the right to police the alignment of states within a defensive perimeter, and also to support insurgents in particular states beyond the perimeter. In the case of the United States, support of insurgents was carried out under the guise of a pro-democracy orientation toward intervention. In fact, it was exclusively preoccupied with helping anti-left political forces regardless of their credentials as democrats and refused to challenge rightist modes of oppression, however severe. Michael Reisman discusses both the Reagan and Brezhnev doctrines in *Old Wine in New Bottles: The Reagan and Brezhnev Doctrines in Contemporary International Law and Practice*, 13 Yale J. Int'l L. 171 (1988). How do the Reagan and Brezhnev doctrines square with international law today? What is the international law relating to such intervention? Both the Reagan and Brezhnev doctrines may have outlasted their namesakes. For example, it might be argued that the United States intervention in Haiti was based on the notion that Haiti was within the United States' defensive perimeter and that the Russian intervention in Chechnya was premised on a parallel rationale. For a discussion of the background to the Haitian intervention, see Richard A. Falk, *The Haitian Intervention: A Dangerous World Order Precedent for the United Nations*, 36 Harv. Int'l L. J. 341 (1995). For a discussion of the background to the Russian intervention in Chechnya, see Nicolas M. L. Bovay, *The Russian Armed Intervention in Chechnya and its Human Rights Implications*, 54 Rev. Int'l Comm'n Jurists 29 (1995).

7. Is there a right to intervene militarily in another state to ensure that it becomes a democracy? Some international lawyers have asserted that this is a valid basis for intervention—for example, Fernando Tesón (*supra* Reading D–7, p. 323). The promotion of democracy in Iraq was one justification for the military intervention in 2003. For a debate on this issue see W. Michael Reisman, *Sovereignty and Human Rights in Contemporary International Law, in* Democratic Governance and International Law 239 (G. Fox & B. Roth eds., 2000); Michael Byers & Simon Chesterman, *"You, the People": Pro-democratic Intervention in International Law, id.* at 259. In July 2003, the editors of *The Nation* opened their pages to a twelve-person debate under the title "Humanitarian Intervention: A Forum." *See* 277 The Nation 11–20 (July 14, 2003). *See also* Oscar Schachter, *The Legality of Pro–Democratic Invasion*, 78 A.J.I.L. 645 (1984); F. Ruiz Ruiz, *Democratic Intervention: A Legal Analysis of its Lawfulness*, 41 Indian J. Int'l L. 377 (2001), Sean D. Murphy, *Assessing the Legality of Invading Iraq*, 92 Geo. L. J. 173 (2004).

8. In Reading C–7, (p. 291), we quote from the World Court's opinion in *Military and Paramilitary Activities In and Against Nicaragua* (Nicar. v. U.S.) (Merits), 1986 ICJ 14 (27 Jun). The case grew out of a policy of the administration of US President Ronald W. Reagan to oppose and, if possible, to replace the

Socialist Sandinista Government of Nicaragua which had overthrown the United States-backed Nicaraguan government of General Anastasio Somoza on 19 July 1979. Because the Reagan Administration regarded Nicaragua as a threat to the security of the region and because it had received a call for defense assistance from El Salvador, the United States gave support in the form of finance, military training, equipment, and other aid to a guerilla group known as the "Contras" formed by former members of General Somoza's National Guard and disaffected Sandinistas to overthrow the Sandinista Government. As a consequence of this aid and other operations of a military nature, such as the US mining of Nicaraguan harbors and the overflight by American aircraft of Nicaraguan territory for reconnaissance purposes, the Government of Nicaragua brought suit against the United States in the World Court. Initially, on 26 November 1984, the Court held by a majority of fifteen to one, against the objections of the United States, that it had jurisdiction over the claims raised by Nicaragua. *See Case Concerning Military and Paramilitary Activities in and Against Nicaragua* (Nicar. v. U.S.) (Jurisdiction), 1984 ICJ Reports 392 (26 Nov). Thereafter, on 18 January 1985, declaring the Court's assumption of jurisdiction erroneous on both fact and law, the United States withdrew from the Court and refused to appear in all subsequent hearings of the case on the merits. *See* 39 ICJ Yearbook 1984–1985, at 148; Dep't of State, *US Withdrawal from the Proceedings Initiated by Nicaragua in the International Court of Justice*, 18 Jan 85, 85 Dept. State Bull. 64 (March 1985), *reprinted in* 24 I.L.M. 246 (1985); Dep't of State, *Observations on the International Court of Justice's November 26, 1984 Judgment on Jurisdiction and Admissibility in the Case of Nicaragua v. United States of America, reprinted in* 24 I.L.M. 249 (1985). *See also* Robinson, *ICJ Hears US Argument Against Nicaraguan Claim*, in 85 Dep't State Bull. 24 (January 1985). Finally, in a judgment on the merits issued 27 June 1986, the World Court held, *inter alia*, that the military and paramilitary activities of the United States in and against Nicaragua, including support for the Contras, the mining of Nicaragua's harbors, and the practice of unauthorized overflights violated customary international law prohibitions on the use of force and intervention into the affairs of another state. Additionally it held that a US-declared economic embargo against Nicaragua had violated a 1956 Treaty of Friendship, Commerce and Navigation between the two countries. The Court rejected the claim that the activities of the United States were justified on grounds of collective self-defense because, it said, El Salvador (the assisted country) had not been the victim of an armed attack, a prerequisite of a valid claim of collective self-defense. It therefore called upon the United States to cease and desist from such activities and declared the United States to be liable for reparations to the Government of Nicaragua for the committed breaches of international law. As might be expected, this decision has provoked not a little comment. Anthony D'Amato, for example, noting that the decision "was not forged out of the heat of adversarial confrontation," finds the judges of the World Court to be "deciding the content of customary international law on a tabula rasa" in a manner that "reveals that [they] have little idea about what they are doing." Anthony A. D'Amato, *Trashing Customary International Law*, 81 A.J.I.L. 101, 101–02 (1987). Richard Falk, on the other hand, finds the judgment to be "a positive model of judicial style," succeeding in "conveying an overall impression of technical competence and fairness ..., [whose] quality of legal reasoning is admirable; the process by which [the Judgment] reaches its conclusions is developed with enviable clarity." Richard A. Falk, *The World Court's Achievement, id.*

at 106. Salman Rushdie describes the Nicaraguan reaction in his memoir, The Jaguar Smile: A Nicaraguan Journey 161–62 (1987):

> As I drove to the Managua airport ... Daniel Ortega was on the car radio, speaking at the UN Security Council.... He was asking for international law to be upheld, insisting upon Nicaragua's right to self-determination. Nicaragua against the United States, Daniel against Goliath. The International Court's judgment was a stone in his sling. The mouse roared.

For further debate, see Appraisals of the ICJ's Decision: Nicaragua v. United States (Merits), 81 *id*. 77–183 (1987). *See also* Eugene D. Rostow, *Nicaragua and the Law of Self–Defense Revisited*, 11 Yale J. Int'l L. 437 (1986); Paul S. Reichler & David Wippman, *United States Armed Intervention in Nicaragua: A Rejoinder, id.* at 462; Eugene D. Rostow, *Nicaragua: A Surreply to a Rejoinder, id.* at 474. For discussion of the Nicaraguan case by the Nicaraguan Ambassador to the United States, see Carlos Tünnermann Bernheim, *United States Armed Intervention in Nicaragua and Article 2(4) of the United Nations Charter*, 11 Yale J. Int'l L. 104 (1985). A jurisprudential overview may be found in John Tasioulas, *In Defence of Relative Normativity: Communitarian Values and the Nicaragua Case*, 16 Oxford J. Leg. Stud. 85 (1996).

9.   What are the prospects for the United Nations to end violence and gross deprivations of human rights in internal conflict situations via sanctions? Even when it is possible to muster the votes to impose sanctions or enforcement measures, there is no guarantee that the UN members will cooperate fully or at all as they are required to do under the UN Charter **[Basic Document 1.5]**. *See generally* Margaret P. Doxey, International Sanctions in Contemporary Perspective (1987); Robin Renwick, Economic Sanctions (1981); David Cortright & George A. Lopez, with Richard W. Conroy, Jaleh Dashti–Gibson & Julia Wagler, The Sanctions Decade: Assessing UN Strategies in the 1990s (2000).

Consider the example of *apartheid* South Africa. Although the UN General Assembly had passed numerous resolutions condemning its *apartheid* policies as posing "a real threat to the security and sovereignty" of African States opposing South Africa's institutionalized racism, the Security Council managed only to order a mandatory arms embargo against South Africa. *See* SC Res. 418, 32 UN SCOR Res. and Decs., at 5, UN Doc. S/INF/33 (1977). On 20 February 1987, a Draft Resolution mandating economic sanctions against South Africa could not be passed against the objections of the Federal Republic of Germany, the United Kingdom, and the United States and the abstentions of France and Japan. *See* Draft Resolution on Mandatory Sanctions against South Africa, UN Doc. S/18705 (adoption failed 20 Feb 87: UN SCOR (2738th Mtg.), UN Doc S/PV 2738 (1987)). For discussion and details, see Goler T. Butcher, *The Unique Nature of Sanctions Against South Africa, and Resulting Enforcement Issues*, 19 N.Y.U. J. Int'l L. & Pol. 821 (1987); Raymond Paretzky, Comment, *The United States Arms Embargo Against South Africa: An Analysis of the Laws, Regulations, and Loopholes*, 12 Yale J. Int'l L. 133 (1987). For related commentary, see Goler T. Butcher, *Legal Consequences for States of the Illegality of Apartheid*, 8 H.R.Q. 404 (1986); Henry J. Richardson, III, *The Obligation to Withdraw Recognition from Pretoria as the Government of South Africa*, 1 Temple Int'l & Comp. L. J. 153 (1987). Nevertheless, despite the problems associated with the imposition of sanctions, it is generally agreed that, in the case of South Africa, sanctions did play an important role in the eventual move to majoritarian democracy. Since the end of the Cold War, the Security Council has been much more prepared to impose sanctions in an attempt to curb ongoing violence within a state. Since 1990, the Security Council has agreed on a range of sanctions, from arms embargoes to comprehensive economic embargoes, in a variety of conflicts—*e.g.*, Liberia (1990), Iraq (1991, 1992), the former Yugoslavia (1992), Somalia (1992), and Haiti (1993–94). How can we explain this flurry of activity? It has been argued in Rodney G. Allen, Michael Cherniak & George J. Andreopoulos, *Refining War: Civil Wars and Humanitarian Controls*, 18 H.R.Q. 747, 777 (1996), that:

> Although no government would openly admit it, their preference for nonmilitary enforcement measures has precious little to do with a growing humanitarian awareness in the international community; rather, it is the low domestic political cost coupled with the minimal loss of failure (which is not the case with military failures) that render sanctions such a particularly attractive option. . . .

> Sanction-prone policy makers have a sympathetic constituency among certain antiwar circles who believe that economic sanctions, if judiciously enforced, are the most and perhaps the only appropriate response to international violence. Through the filter of commitment to nonmilitary forms of intervention, the ascendancy of finance ministers over armies represents a step in the humanization of international affairs. . . . Economic sanctions have proved to be problematic, however, not least because their proponents very often fail to make a convincing case regarding their strategic value. It seems that risk-averse policymakers and pacifistic humanitarians have formed a common discourse on the merits of sanctions based on their value as *symbolic* rather than as a *strategic* instrument of international concern.

Do you agree with this assessment of the value of sanctions? Is a focus on effectiveness an appropriate one? Should we also take into account a norm-enforcing rationale—*i.e.*, the need to reinforce the international community's commitment to particular norms, such as the protection of human rights? *See* Sean D. Murphy, Humanitarian Intervention: The United Nations in an Evolving World Order (1996); Lori F. Damrosch, *The Civilian Impact of Economic Sanctions*, in Enforcing Restraint: Collective Intervention in Internal Conflicts 118 (L. Damrosch ed., 1993). *See also* W. Michael Reisman, *Assessing the Lawfulness of Non–Military Enforcement: The Case of Economic Sanctions*, 89 Proceed. A.S.I.L. 350 (1995).

The effect of sanctions is also much debated. Anne Orford has pointed out that economic sanctions typically have harsher effect on women than on men: *The Politics of Collective Security*, 17 Mich. J. Int'l L. 373, 377 (1996). See also Sarah Zaidi, *War, Sanctions, and Humanitarian Assistance: The Case of Iraq 1990–1993*, 1 Med. & Global Survival 147 (1994). Does the difficulty of ensuring swift and effective UN action necessarily justify unilateral intervention? Should it?

10. Some of the above readings refer to the UN's intervention in Somalia in 1992–95. President Siad Barre's government was overthrown in January 1991 and the Somali state effectively collapsed in the ensuing civil war. By 1992, Somalis faced mass starvation. In response, there was limited UN intervention in early 1992, but this failed to maintain a ceasefire or to protect relief supplies. In December 1992, the Security Council adopted a resolution authorizing intervention by a US-led coalition, UNITAF, to establish a secure environment for relief operations (SC Res. 751). In 1993, a further resolution (SC Res. 814) created a new UN operation, UNOSOM II, to continue the work of UNITAF and to undertake rehabilitation and reconciliation of the warring factions. The UN's involvement in Somalia was bitterly resisted by the forces of the main Somali faction led by General Aideed and much of the UN's resources were taken up with

responding to this challenge. The last UNOSOM II forces left in March 1995, and the political situation has continued to deteriorate, although nutrition and health of the population has improved. In a statement on 6 April 1995, the President of the Security Council stated that the people of Somalia bear the ultimate responsibility for achieving national reconciliation and restoring peace to Somalia. S/PRST/1995/15 (6 Apr 95). For discussion, see Sean D. Murphy, Humanitarian Intervention: The United Nations in an Evolving World Order 217–43 (1996); Jeffrey Clark, *Debacle in Somalia: Failure of the Collective Response*, in Enforcing Restraint: Collective Intervention in Internal Conflicts 231 (L. Damrosch ed., 1993). For a useful documentary collection on the Somali intervention, see The United Nations and Somalia 1992–1996 (1996).

The UN's intervention in Somalia has been widely regarded as a failure, and was one of the reasons for the non-election of the then UN Secretary–General Boutros Boutros–Ghali to a second term in 1996. How can the UN best be used to support humanitarian objectives? In 1993, the then Australian Minister for Foreign Affairs and Trade, Senator Gareth Evans, drew the following lessons from the Somalia intervention:

A.   Interventions in situations of unresolved internal conflict under narrow short-term goals, i.e. the use of armed forces to establish secure conditions for delivery of relief supplies, are unlikely to be capable of early successful termination.

- UN forces should not be introduced unless it is agreed that they will remain as long as necessary for the establishment of conditions allowing for sustained relief, rehabilitation and reconstruction activities to continue on their withdrawal.

- Before deciding on coercive measures specifically to prevent loss of life and prevent human suffering, which should be a rare last resort, the Security Council should receive independent outside advice that the humanitarian situation is such that coercive measures are essential.

- The Rules of Engagement of UN forces introduced for humanitarian purposes should be carefully considered for each situation from the perspective of minimizing the impact of the use of force on the civilian population.

- . . . the importance of a clear mandate for enforcement operations.

Cooperating for Peace 154 (1993).

After considering these proposals and the extracts by Mwagiru (*supra* Reading D–8, p. 329) and Orford (*supra* Reading D–9, p. 332), what do you think are the most useful lessons to be drawn from the UN experience in Somalia?

11.   The intervention in East Timor 1999–2002, discussed in the Orford extract (*supra* Reading D–9, p. 332), brought rapidly to world attention this former "overseas province" of Portugal, half of an island at the eastern-most point of the Indonesian archipelago. After the Portuguese colonial administration withdrew in August 1975, there was great local dispute about the future of the territory. Some groups sought independence while others argued for union with Indonesia. On 28 November 1975, a proclamation of independence was issued by the Revolutionary Front for an Independent East Timor (Fretilin) which then was in control of most of East Timor. This was followed two days later by a proclamation of independence and integration with Indonesia issued by a coalition of smaller political parties. Thereafter, in December 1975, East Timor was invaded by Indonesia, which occupied by it for the following twenty-four years.

In 1976, Indonesia acted to integrate East Timor as its twenty-seventh province, but the integration remained controversial at the international level. It never was recognized by the United Nations, although condemnation of the occupation became progressively weaker over the years. A few countries, including Australia, formally recognized East Timor as Indonesian territory. East Timorese resistance movements, however, maintained a guerilla campaign against the Indonesian army throughout the occupation, leaving much of the civilian population to live in an atmosphere of repression and violence. The most prominent resistance organization was Fretilin and its military wing, Falantil. On 27 January 1999, President Habibie of Indonesia made the unexpected announcement that he would consider granting independence if the East Timorese people rejected a proposal of special autonomous status within the Republic of Indonesia. Indonesia, Portugal, and the UN then negotiated a set of agreements to ensure popular consultation on the issue. *See* Agreements on the Question of East Timor, 5 May 1999, at <http://www.un.org/peace/etimor99/agreement/ agreeFrame_ Eng01. html>. The agreements requested the UN, through a universal, direct, and secret ballot, to determine whether the East Timorese people would accept or reject a relationship of "special autonomy" with Indonesia. The UN Security Council created the UN Mission in East Timor (UNAMET) to organize the popular consultation. SC Res. 1246, UN SCOR, 54th Sess., 4013th mtg., UN Doc. S/INF/55 (1999). The referendum was held on 30 August 1999. The result was a vote of 78.5% against a "special autonomy" status within Indonesia and 21.5% in favor.

The announcement of the referendum outcome was met with great violence by opponents of independence. At least 600 people died and many more were attacked in the violence. Local and foreign UNAMET staff were killed. Most of the buildings and much of the infrastructure in Dili, the capital, were destroyed. Prior to the referendum, there were 880,000 people living in East Timor. Seven hundred fifty thousand people were displaced from their homes or became refugees in West Timor during the violence immediately after the independence vote.

The May 5 agreements had assigned responsibility for security in East Timor to Indonesia. A UN force, INTERFET, was eventually deployed in September after Indonesia was pressured to agree to prevent further violence. SC Res. 1264, UN SCOR, 54th Sess., 4045th mtg., UN Doc. S/INF/55 (1999). The UN Security Council decided to extend the peace-keeping role of the international community in East Timor to the formation and operation of a transitional government. SC Res 1272, UN SCOR, 54th Sess., 4057th mtg., UN Doc. S/INF/55 (1999). The Security Council created the United Nations Transitional Administration in East Timor (UNTAET), granting it "overall responsibility for the administration of East Timor" which involved "legislative and executive authority, including the administration of justice." UNTAET's mandate was, among other things, to "provide security and maintain law and order" throughout East Timor; to "support capacity for self-government"; and to "assist in the establishment of conditions for sustainable development." Timor Lorosa'e or East Timor finally became independent on 20 May 2002 and soon thereafter became the 191st member of the UN. *See* Ian Martin, Self–Determination in East Timor (2001); William Maley, *The UN and East Timor*, 12 Pacifica Rev. 63 (2000); Christine M. Chinkin, *East Timor: A Failure of Decolonisation*, 20 Austl. Y.B.I.L. 35 (1999).

12.   Various terms are used in the readings to describe the possibilities of United Nations interventionary action. What is the scope of, and difference between, the following terms: peacemaking, peacekeeping, peacebuilding, and peace enforcement? For discussion of these issues see Gareth J. Evans, Cooperating for Peace (1993) and Sally Morphet, *UN Peacekeeping and Election–Monitor-*

ing, in United Nations, Divided World 183 (A. Roberts & B. Kingsbury eds., 1993). In 2000, the Report of the Panel on United Nations Peace Operations (the Brahimi Report) was presented to the UN Secretary–General: UN GAOR, 55th Sess., Provisional Agenda Item 87, UN Doc. A/55/305–S/2000/809 (2000). The Report made a series of recommendations, including strengthening the mandates of UN peacekeepers to allow them to use force against aggressors.

13.   The readings by Falk, Tesón, Mwagiru, and Orford in Sections C and D, *supra*, adopt different approaches to collective humanitarian intervention. While Falk, Mwagiru, and Orford are skeptical about the legitimacy and moral objectives of collective humanitarian intervention, Tesón defends the right of the international community to intervene to uphold basic human rights. In his view, the profound changes to the content and purpose of state sovereignty since 1945, and more dramatically since 1989, have meant that human beings have claims against their own states and governments that the international community must not ignore. This view is challenged by Falk, Mwagiru, and Orford. Falk's skepticism is inspired primarily by the UN Charter's **(Basic Document 1.5)** renunciation of intervention in matters essentially within domestic jurisdiction, especially matters that do not pose a threat to international peace and security. Mwagiru, sharing a similar reformist attitude, points out that the state-centric paradigm of the UN Charter which saw threats to international peace and security as only arising from inter-state disputes is no longer applicable. He believes that, since the end of the Cold War, the emerging pattern of conflict is not inter-state and ideological, but intra-state, ethnic and nationalist and that these new conflicts require resolution through negotiation. For Mwagiru, effective intervention can be better achieved through the strengthening of the UN's negotiating capabilities rather than its military power. Orford takes a more radical approach, challenging us to understand the cultural processes and commitments behind the impulse to intervene. She cautions skepticism about the heroic tradition in intervention narratives in international law. What approaches do you find most useful and why?

14.   Assuming the requisite votes, according to what procedures does the United Nations make interventionary decisions (for humanitarian purposes or any other reason)? As it happens, owing to the changing composition and changing relative power of the member states, the way in which the United Nations proceeds in this connection has changed markedly from what was contemplated at the time of the drafting of the United Nations Charter **(Basic Document 1.5)** following World War II.

As the Franck extract points out (*supra* Reading D–4, p. 302), the original United Nations peacekeeping design, placing total responsibility for international peacekeeping in the Security Council (UN Charter, ch. VII), was premised on an assumption of continued cooperation among the major powers which emerged victorious from World War II. This design began to change quite early, however, when its underlying assumption was shattered by the onset of the Cold War. Due primarily to disagreements between the Soviet Union and the United States, agreements contemplated under UN Charter Article 43 for armed forces under the control of the Security Council never materialized, and the Security Council became increasingly unable to take decisive action. Stated UN Secretary–General Javier Pérez de Cuéllar in his annual report to the UN General Assembly in 1982, "the [Security] Council too often finds itself on the sidelines at a time when, according to the Charter, its possibilities should be used to a maximum." Work of the Organization: Report of the Secretary–General, 37 UN GAOR Supp. (No. 1) at 3, UN Doc. A/37/1 (1982). The veto power possessed by each of the five permanent powers, and as exercised especially by the Soviet Union in the early years, proved to be the major stumbling-block. *See, e.g.*, Richard A. Falk, *The Interplay of Westphalia and Charter Conceptions of International Order*, in 1 The Future of the International Legal Order 32–70 (R. Falk & C. Black eds., 1969); John G. Stoessinger, The United Nations and the Superpowers 3–19 (1965). *See also* Antonio Cassese, *Return to Westphalia? Considerations on the Gradual Erosion of the Charter System*, in The Current Legal Regulation of the Use of Force 505 (A. Cassese ed., 1986).

In any event, because of the former Soviet Union's initial extensive use of the veto during the Cold War era (later imitated by the United States), other organs of the United Nations, particularly the General Assembly (where once the United States usually could obtain a favorable majority) began to deal with matters originally entrusted exclusively to the Security Council. This trend reached its peak during the Korean Conflict (does it make any difference to say "Korean War" as most people do?) when the General Assembly, on 3 November 1950, passed the historic Uniting for Peace Resolution **(Basic Document 2.14)**, allowing itself to act upon threats to the peace when an exercise of the veto power prevented the Security Council from acting. Although the USSR was at first opposed to the Uniting for Peace Resolution, they subsequently relied upon it, at least when they saw it in their interest to do so, as when, in 1956, Security Council action in connection with the Suez Crisis was blocked by British and French vetoes. For details, see Inis L. Claude, Swords into Plowshares 271 (4th ed. 1984). It should be stressed, however, that the original American willingness to transfer peacekeeping functions from the Security Council to the General Assembly was based on the ability of the United States to command a General Assembly majority on most issues.

United States supremacy in the United Nations, while often substantial, is of course no longer a foregone conclusion, due mainly to the UN membership having expanded from its original 51 to present 191 Member States (as of 1 Mar 2006), the majority of them former colonies in Africa, Asia, and Latin America. It is, indeed, this decline in power relative to the UN's increased "Third World" membership that led to bitter attacks upon the UN's "tyranny of the majority" initially from Western scholars and subsequently from the United States and other Western governments, with controversial "neo-isolationist" policies to match. For an example of early scholarly criticism, see Agraham Yeselson & Anthony Gaglione, A Dangerous Place: The United Nations as a Weapon in World Politics (1974). For opinion contending that "a world without the United Nations would be a better world," see A World Without A UN (The Heritage Foundation, B. Pines ed., 1985). *See also The US Role in the United Nations: Hearing Before the Subcomm. on Human Rights and International Organizations of the House Comm. on Foreign Affairs*, 98th Cong., 1st Sess. (1983). In the 1990s and early 2000s, anti-UN rhetoric has been especially prevalent in the United States. *See* Michael J. Glennon, *Why the Security Council Failed*, 82 Foreign Aff. 82, No. 3, at 16 (2003). What are the advantages of UN membership for states? How can the United States and other Western countries adapt to the reality that they can no longer control the United Nations?

Whatever your answer to the foregoing questions, it would not be surprising, given the present situation in the United Nations, if the UN membership were to differ sharply on how to intervene in Loango, if at all. It seems a fair conclusion that there would be vigorous, possibly even disabling, debate not only over many of the substantive issues involved (including which, if either, faction to support), but, as well, over issues of military command and engagement. The present problem does not require debating and resolving these issues; but, because "rights" are for the most part meaningless without effective "remedies," they should be borne in mind throughout your analysis. As some of the readings argue, the question of whether individual states can properly claim a right to unilateral humanitarian intervention depends, at least in part, on whether there exist alternative multinational or supranational mechanisms capable of dealing effectively with major human suffering.

In this latter connection, note that, as of 17 July 2005, the United Nations had created 60 peacekeeping bodies, well over three-quarters of them since 1987. The character of peacekeeping has altered over time, becoming increasingly hybrid. A good example is UNTAC, the UN Transitional Authority in Cambodia, established by the Security Council in 1990. UNTAC's mandate had seven components: human rights, electoral, military, civil administration, police, repatriation, and rehabilitation. For a discussion of the development of UN peacekeeping see Sally Morphet, *UN Peacekeeping and Election–Monitoring*, in United Nations, Divided World 183 (A. Roberts & B. Kingsbury eds., 1993). *See also* Robert C. Johansen, *The Future of United Nations Peacekeeping and Enforcement: A Framework for Policymaking*, 2 Global Governance 299 (1996); Panel Discussion, *UN Peacekeeping: An Early Reckoning of the Second Generation*, in 89 Proceed. A.S.I.L. 275 (1995). The 2000 Brahimi Report (*see supra* Discussion Note/Question 12) addresses the perceived strategic and practical failures of UN peacekeeping. For discussion of the UN role in peacekeeping and nation-building in East Timor, see Jonathan Morrow & Rachel White, *The United Nations in Transitional East Timor: International Standards and the Reality of Governance*, 22 Austl. Y.B.I.L 1 (2002).

15.   One possibility that has been suggested to improve the capacity of the United Nations to respond to armed conflict is the creation of a standing UN army, or a standby UN army. *See, e.g.*, Robert C. Johansen, *Reforming the United Nations to Eliminate War*, in Preferred Futures for the United Nations (S. Mendolvitz & B. Weston eds., 1995); *Id.*, *The Future of United Nations Peacekeeping and Enforcement: A Framework for Policymaking*, 2 Global Governance 299 (1996). It is argued that this will reduce the *ad hoc* nature of UN peacekeeping efforts to date. Chapter VII of the UN Charter **(Basic Document 1.5)** provides for the creation of a Military Staff Committee which would be composed of the Chiefs of Staff of the five permanent members of the Security Council. The role of the MSC was to be responsible for the strategic direction of any armed forces placed at the disposal of the Security Council (Art. 47(3)). It was thought that the MSC would oversee the creation of some type of international force. The MSC's work was soon undermined by the Cold War, however, and the formation of a standing or standby force never was accomplished. For an account of the history of the idea, see Alex Morrison, *The Theoretical and Practical Feasibility of a United Nations Force*, 28 Cornell Int'l L. J. 661 (1995). After the Persian Gulf War, interest in the creation of some type of permanent UN force resurfaced. In his important paper, An Agenda for Peace (1992), then UN Secretary–General Boutros Boutros–Ghali supported the idea of establishing a peace enforcement force. The advantages of a permanent force include its greater responsiveness and efficiency. Critics of the idea point to the structural barriers within the UN (such as the lack of autonomous sources of income for the UN and the weakness of its logistical capabilities), and also the way that sovereignty and calculations of state interest complicate the UN's effectiveness. *See* Shibley Telhami, *Is a Standing United Nations Army Possible? Or Desirable?*, 28 Cornell Int'l L. J. 673 (1995). On the value of a regional collective approach see David D. Jividen, *It Takes a Region: A Proposal for an Alternative Regional Approach to UN Collective Force for*

Humanitarian Intervention, 10 USAFA J. Legal Stud. 109 (1999–2000). Consider the advantages and disadvantages of a standing or standby force and the practical implications of such a development. The UN Secretary–General's 2005 report, *In Larger Freedom: Towards Development, Security and Human Rights for All* (UN Doc. A/59/2005, 21 Mar 2005 at para 112) emphasized less the need for a UN standing army and more the need for the UN to work with regional organizations such as the European Union to improve the UN's peacekeeping capacities.

16. The issue of collective humanitarian intervention is further complicated when United Nations forces are involved—so far, in the absence of a standing UN army, on an *ad hoc* basis. According to the Secretary-General's Bulletin on the Observance by UN Forces of International Humanitarian Law (UN Doc. ST/SGB/1999/13) of 6 August 1999, UN forces are bound by international humanitarian law and are therefore liable for any damage caused by its breach. On the other hand, under the Convention on the Privileges and Immunities of the United Nations of 13 February 1946 (1 UNTS 16; 1949 ATS 3; 1950 UKTS 10, Cmd 7891, 146 BFSP 489; 21 UST 14318, TIAS 6900; *reprinted in* 1 Weston & Carlson I.D.2), the UN enjoys immunity from every form of legal process unless it has waived that immunity expressly. Should the UN be liable for violations of the laws of war, human rights abuse, or environmental damage caused by its forces? Why? Why not? Would immunity for UN forces strengthen or weaken UN enforcement mechanisms?

17. Not to be overlooked is the controversial issue of who will pay the costs of United Nations peacekeeping. Relatively early in the UN's history, the Soviet Union, France, and some other Member States refused to pay amounts assessed by the General Assembly to cover the cost of UN peacekeeping in the Middle East and the Congo. The refusal to pay was grounded on the general argument that the peacekeeping authorized by the General Assembly was illegal, and the specific issue was whether these assessments were "expenses of the [United Nations] Organization" within the meaning of Article 17(1) of the UN Charter (**Basic Document 1.5**). If so, it was argued, arrears in the payment of these expenses would be taken into account in determining, under Article 19, whether a delinquent member should lose its vote in the General Assembly because "the amount of its arrears equals or exceeds the amount of the contributions due from it for the preceding two full years." The General Assembly referred this question to the International Court of Justice, which later held that assessments for peacekeeping are "expenses of the Organization." *Case Concerning Certain Expenses of the United Nations,* 1962 ICJ 151 (20 Jul). Despite this advisory opinion, however, the Soviet Union refused to pay, and as a consequence the United States sought to force payment by threatening a loss of vote under Article 19. During the 1964 session of the General Assembly, a showdown was avoided only by conducting General Assembly business without roll-call votes. Finally, in August 1965, the United States, while expressly refusing to yield on the legal issue, ceased trying to enforce the Article 19 sanction, thereby allowing the General Assembly to continue business as usual. For details, see Stanley Hoffman, *A World Divided and a World Court Confused: The World Court's Opinion on UN Financing*, in International Law and Political Crisis 251 (L. Scheinman & D. Wilkinson eds., 1968); David Wilkinson, *The Article 17 Crisis: The Dispute Over Financing the United Nations, id.* at 211.

In October 1987, the USSR paid all its ordinary contributions to the UN for that year and started to pay all of its overdue bills from the previous years, including $197 million for peacekeeping expenses in the Middle East. *See* N.Y. Times, 16 Oct 1987, § I, at 1, col. 6. At the same time, with historic irony, the

United States, in arrears at over US $400 million, had become the UN's outstanding financial delinquent. Indeed, as a result of the so-called Kassebaum–Solomon Amendment to the Foreign Relations Authorization Act, Fiscal Years 1986 and 1987, § 143, Pub. L. No. 99–93, 99 Stat. 405, at 424, codified at 22 USC § 287e note (Supp. III 1985), which in turn was a consequence of heightened discontent with the United Nations during the years of the Reagan Administration especially, the US Congress legislated that "[n]o payment ... be made [by the United States] for an assessed contribution to the United Nations or its specialized agencies in excess of 20 percent of the total annual budget of the United Nations or its specialized agencies (respectively)," beginning in fiscal year 1987 and for every year thereafter, unless the United Nations and its specialized agencies shall have adopted "voting rights ... proportionate to the contribution of each member state to the budget of the United Nations and its specialized agencies." 22 USC § 287e (Supp. III, 1985). In late December 1996, the United States having succeeded at denying Secretary–General Boutros Boutros–Ghali a second term on the questionable grounds that he had not done enough to ensure UN budgetary and bureaucratic reform, the administration of US President Bill Clinton indicated a willingness to make good on its current billion or so dollars of unpaid UN dues via installment payments over several years. In light of the foregoing, what do you conclude to be "the law" as regards United Nations peacekeeping expenses? More precisely, is the World Court decision "law"? Is Article 19 "law"? Does withholding US contributions to the United Nations pursuant to the Kassebaum–Solomon Amendment constitute a violation of international law? Also, what lessons do you draw from the expenses crisis as regards the future of UN peacekeeping? The future of the UN itself? World order in general? Can you think of any other ways in which United Nations peacekeeping expenses might be met, and, if so, how feasible would be your proposed alternatives? Would they require any changes within the United Nations, or any innovations outside the United Nations? For a proposal that peacekeeping operations be funded by a tiny tax on the more than $900 billion of international currency exchanges that occur *each day*, see Martin Walker, *Global Taxation: Paying for Peace*, World Pol'y J. 7, 8 (Summer 1993). For a proposal that they be generated by a tax on airline tickets, see Gareth J. Evans, Cooperating for Peace (1993). In these various respects, consult Erskine B. Childers & Brian Urquhart, Renewing the United Nations System (1994); Grenville Clark & Louis B. Sohn, World Peace Through World Law—Two Alternative Plans (3rd ed. 1966); Preferred Futures for the United Nations (S. Mendlovitz & B. Weston eds., 1995); David Steele, The Reform of the United Nations (1987); The United Nations and the Maintenance of International Peace and Security (UNITAR ed., 1987); Chadwick Alger, *Thinking About the Future of the UN System*, 2 Global Governance 335 (1996); Richard A. Falk, *Explaining the UN's Unhappy 50th Anniversary: Toward Reclaiming the Next Half–Century, in* A United Nations for the Twenty–First Century 89 (D. Bourantonis & M. Evriviades eds., 1996); Samuel Kim, *The United Nations, Lawmaking, and World Order*, 10 Alternatives 643 (1985); Richard W. Nelson, *International Law and US Withholding of Payments to International Organizations*, 80 A.J.I.L. 973 (1986); Elisabeth Zoller, *The "Corporate Will" of the United Nations and the Rights of the Minority*, 81 A.J.I.L. 610 (1987).

18.   In the present problem, mercenaries were hired by the NDP to aid in its struggle against the LRP. Particularly in states that have weakened or under-resourced armed forces, mercenaries continue to play a significant role in some areas of armed conflict. For example, a group called "Executive Outcomes" (EO), led by white former South African security force officers, now offers its services as

mercenaries in Africa to what it considers "legitimate governments." For $60 million, according to the New York Times, EO led an operation to defeat some insurgents in Angola, and also was hired by the government of Sierra Leone to defeat a guerilla group there. Editorial, *Africa's New Dogs of War*, N.Y. Times, 2 Feb 1997, at § 4, p. 14, cols. 1–2. What is the problem with the use of mercenaries? One issue is their lack of accountability. If mercenaries violate the accepted rules of armed conflict as between states, who will be responsible? The 1997 New York Times editorial notes another issue: the form of payment of mercenaries. EO, for example, is linked to a company with mining interests. "If governments reimburse the group by granting it mining concessions ..., political leaders are effectively surrendering control of vital national resources. Regaining control when payment obligations have been met may not be easy." *Id.* The South African government, which at first tacitly approved the recruitment of mercenaries in its territory (apparently to remove persons likely to destabilize the first multiracial elections) has recently moved to curtail its operations. South Africa's move is consistent with international trends. While traditional international law did not impute responsibility to a a state for failing to prevent persons from enlisting in the armed forces of a foreign belligerent (*see* Henry C. Burmester, *The Recruitment and Use of Mercenaries in Armed Conflicts*, 72 A.J.I.L. 37 (1978)), the international community, by virtue of the 1989 International Convention Against the Recruitment, Use, Financing and Training of Mercenaries (*supra* Reading B–10, p. 288), has moved to change this position; and there are other signs of change as well. *First*, the UN General Assembly has adopted a series of resolutions condemning mercenary activity against national liberation movements and calling upon countries to legislate against such activity and also declared that the use of mercenaries and their recruitment, financing, and training violate the purposes and the principles of the UN Charter **(Basic Document 1.5)**. *See, e.g.*, GA Res. 2395, UN GAOR, 23rd Sess., Supp. No. 18, at 59, UN Doc. A/7218 (1968); GA Res. 47/84, UN GAOR, 47th Sess., Supp. No. 49, at 165, UN Doc. A/RES/47/84 (1993); GA Res. 49/150, UN GAOR, 49th Sess., Supp. No. 49, at 167, UN Doc. A/RES/ 49/150 (1995); GA Res. 50/138, UN GAOR, 50th Sess., Supp. No. 50, at 198, UN Doc. A/RES/50/138 (1996). *Second*, for the purpose of deterring persons from engaging in mercenarism, Article 47 of Protocol I to the 1949 Geneva Conventions on the Laws of War **(Basic Document 2.31)**, while providing fundamental guarantees of humane treatment, withholds from mercenaries the more favorable treatment afforded ordinary combatants and prisoners of war. *Third*, the Organization of African Unity (now the African Union) adopted in 1972 the Convention for the Elimination of Mercenaries in Africa, O.A.U. Doc. CM/433/Rev. L., Annex 1 (1972–1974), *reprinted in* Paul W. Mourning, *Leashing the Dogs of War: Outlawing the Recruitment and Use of Mercenaries*, 22 V.J.I.L. 589, at 613–15 (1982), making states parties thereto responsible for the prohibition and punishment of mercenarism in their respective jurisdictions. *Fourth*, the UN Commission on Human Rights appointed a Special Rapporteur on the question of the use of mercenaries and mercenary-related activities, and in 1995 the Secretary–General of the United Nations published a Note on "The Use of Mercenaries as a means of violating human rights and impeding the exercise of the right of Peoples to Self–Determination" (UN Doc. A/50/390/Add.1). Is this overall trend desirable? Why? Why not? For further discussion, see Edward Kwakwa, *The Current Status of Mercenaries in the Law of Armed Conflict*, 14 Hastings Int'l & Comp. L. Rev. 67 (1990); Marie–France Major, *Mercenaries and International Law*, 22 Ga. J. Int'l & Comp. L. 103 (1992); Gerry S. Thomas, *Mercenary Troops in Modern Africa* (1994).

19. The present problem involves much violence against civilians. The normative basis for individual rights and responsibilities in respect of wartime atrocities is contained, in large part, in a variety of formal instruments that go back as far as the Declaration of Paris Respecting Maritime Law of 16 April 1856 among Austria, England, France, Prussia, and Russia (115 C.T.S. 1.) and the International Convention with Respect to the Laws and Customs of War on Land (Hague II) of 29 July 1899 (187 C.T.S. 429). In the last century, the following major conventions have been adopted: (a) the Protocol of 1925 for the Prohibition of the Use in War of Asphyxiating, Poisonous or Other Gases, and of Bacteriological Methods of Warfare **(Basic Document 2.4)**; (b) the Geneva Conventions of 1929 stating the humane treatment of sick and wounded military personnel required during hostilities (118 L.N.T.S. 303), and treatment of prisoners of war (118 L.N.T.S. 343); (c) the Convention on the Prevention and Punishment of the Crime of Genocide **(Basic Document 3.2)**; (d) the Geneva Conventions of 1949: the Convention for the Amelioration of the Condition of the Wounded and Sick in Armed Forces of the Field **(Basic Document 2.9)**, the Convention for the Amelioration of the Condition of the Wounded, Sick and Shipwrecked Members of Armed Forces at Sea **(Basic Document 2.10)**, the Convention Relative to the Treatment of Prisoners of War **(Basic Document 2.11)**, and the Convention Relative to the Protection of Civilian Persons in Time of War **(Basic Document 2.12)**; (e) the Convention of 1972 on the Prohibition of the Development, Production and Stockpiling of Bacteriological (Biological) and Toxin Weapons and on Their Destruction **(Basic Document 2.25)**; (f) the Convention of 1976 on the Prohibition of Military or Any Other Hostile Use of Environmental Modification Techniques **(Basic Document 2.30)**; (g) Additional Protocols I & II to the Geneva Conventions of 1949 **(Basic Documents 2.31 & 2.32)**; and (h) the Rome Statute of the International Criminal Court **(Basic Document 1.16)**. *See generally* Antonio Cassese, International Law in a Divided World 81–84, 253–74 (1986); W. Michael Reisman, *Assessing Claims to Revise the Laws of War*, 97 A.J.I.L. 82 (2003).

While publicists have contended that the humanitarian rules of armed conflict always have applied to civil wars, it was not until the 1949 Geneva Conventions that this contention was expressly stipulated. Article 3 common to each of the four conventions adopted a "minimum" standard of humane treatment "[i]n the case of armed conflict not of an international character." Governments have proved reluctant to apply common Article 3, however, because they consider opposing civil war factions to be criminal by the State's internal law; and oppositional groups, though usually eager to enjoy the benefits of Article 3, often have shown themselves unwilling to be bound by the Geneva Conventions, particularly when resorting to terrorist tactics. *See generally* Thomas Fleiner–Gerster & Michael A. Meyer, *New Developments in Humanitarian Law: A Challenge to the Concept of Sovereignty*, 34 I.C.L.Q. 267 (1985). In addition, the protection granted by Article 3 is rudimentary at best. It does not guarantee prisoner of war treatment to captured insurgents; it does not obligate governments to utilize the medical and relief services of the Red Cross or a similar humanitarian agency; it does not prohibit the starvation of civilians through the erection of blockades; and so forth. *See* Michael Bothe, *Article 3 and Protocol II: Case Studies of Nigeria and El Salvador*, 31 Am. U. L. Rev. 899 (1982).

Hence the adoption in 1977 and the entry into force in 1978 of Protocol II Additional to the 1949 Geneva Conventions, *supra*. Entitled "Protocol Additional to the Geneva Conventions of 12 August 1949, and Relating to the Protection of Victims of Non–International Armed Conflicts," it contains extensive provisions for humane treatment of all persons who do not take a direct or active part in civil war hostilities. However, Article 1(1) provides that "[t]his Protocol ... develops and supplements Article 3 common to the Geneva Conventions ... *without modifying its existing conditions of application....*" (Emphasis added.) Additionally, Article 1(2) provides that it "shall not apply to situations of internal disturbances and tensions, such as riots, isolated and sporadic acts of violence and other acts of a similar nature...." In view of this language, does Protocol II remedy the deficiencies of common Article 3? Is it clear about the threshold of violence and unrest to which it applies?

Consider also Article 3 of Protocol II prohibiting intervention on the basis of the Protocol:

1. Nothing in this Protocol shall be invoked for the purpose of affecting the sovereignty of a State or the responsibility of the government, by all legitimate means, to maintain or re-establish law and order in the State or to defend the national unity and territorial integrity of the State.

2. Nothing in this Protocol shall be invoked as a justification for intervening, directly or indirectly, for any reason whatever, in the armed conflict or in the internal or external affairs of the High Contracting Party in the territory of which that conflict occurs.

Does this provision mean that unilateral intervention is impermissible in the face of even the most severe forms of inhumane treatment? Does it foreclose all possibility of humanitarian intervention by the United Nations? Suppose Loango had signed and ratified Protocol II. What then?

On the politics of the drafting Article 3 and Protocol II, see Laura Lopez, *Uncivil Wars: The Challenge of Applying International Humanitarian Law to Internal Armed Conflicts*, 69 N.Y.U. L. Rev. 916, 929–32 (1994). Lopez argues that important humanitarian principles were ignored in the drafting process because of the fear of many states that such principles would limit their sovereignty. On the role of customary international law in this area, see Theodor Meron, *The Continuing Role of Custom in the Formation of International Humanitarian Law*, 90 A.J.I.L. 238 (1996). For additional pertinent discussion, see Emmanuel G. Bello, African Customary Humanitarian Law (1980); Michael Bothe, Karl Josef Partsch, & Waldemar A. Solf, with the collaboration of Martin Eaton, New Rules for Victims of Armed Conflicts—Commentary on the Two 1977 Protocols Additional to the Geneva Conventions of 1949 (1982); Commentary on the Additional Protocols of 8 June 1977 to the Geneva Conventions of 12 August 1949 (Y. Sandoz, C. Swinarski, & B. Zimmerman eds., 1987); Judith G. Gardam, Non–Combatant Immunity As A Norm of International Humanitarian Law (1993); Géza Herczegh, Development of International Humanitarian Law (1984); Theodor Meron, Human Rights in Internal Strife: Their International Protection (1987); Jean Pictet, Development and Principles of International Humanitarian Law (1985).

The adequacy of the international regime governing internal armed conflict is discussed by Laura Lopez in the article cited at the outset of the preceding paragraph. She points out that, given the modern prevalence of civil rather than international armed conflict, the laws of war codified in the Geneva Conventions seem increasingly irrelevant. She writes, at 917:

Although civil wars present the same horrors as international ones, they are governed by only a few, largely ineffective provisions in the Geneva Conventions of 1949 and their Additional Protocols of 1977. These provisions offer little protection to combatants and civilians in conventional civil wars, resulting in an unfortunate disparity between the protections afforded during international and internal conflicts.

Concerns about state sovereignty consistently block any substantial progress in addressing the comparable horrors of civil wars. By its very nature, international humanitarian law conflicts with state sovereignty by placing the rights of individuals over the rights of states. A civil war heightens this inherent tension because the very identity of a state . . . is in jeopardy. Under desperate circumstances, a government may perceive that a threat to its own survival justifies ignoring humanitarian norms.

Lopez identifies four major inadequacies in the legal protections offered in a civil war: (1) combatants are not accorded prisoner-of-war status on capture and therefore may be prosecuted for treason; (2) civilians can be arbitrarily detained with no right to receive visits from relief agencies; (3) individual states are under no obligation to prosecute those who violate international humanitarian law with respect to civil wars; and (4) the Geneva Conventions regime does not address the treatment of United Nations peacekeepers in civil conflicts. One reform proposed by Lopez is that of drafting a human rights treaty to protect the rights of those affected by civil war. What are the advantages and disadvantages of such a proposal? For seven differing theoretical approaches to the question of accountability for human rights abuses in internal armed conflict see *Symposium on Method in International Law*, 93 A.J.I.L. (1999).

For a discussion of how the modern rules relating to the conduct of civil war would have applied to the American Civil War, see Rodney G. Allen, Martin Cherniak & George J. Andreopoulos, *Refining War: Civil Wars and Humanitarian Controls*, 18 H.R.Q. 747 (1996).

It has been argued by Judith Gardam that international humanitarian law generally is a gendered regime. Judith G. Gardam, *A Feminist Analysis of Certain Aspects of International Humanitarian Law*, 12 Austl. Y.B.I.L. 265 (1992). She writes, at 268 and 277–78:

From the perspective of women, the most important general principle of the law of armed conflict is that which requires parties to an armed conflict to distinguish at all times between civilians and combatants and between civilian and military objects and to direct their operations only against the latter. The development and implementation of the distinction has always had to be reconciled with the demands of military necessity. States and the military have traditionally supported initiatives aimed at the protection of combatants but have resisted inroads into freedom of military action designed to protect civilians. . . . The rationale for this . . . [is that] it is in the interests of all that soldiers are protected in order to carry on the fight and protect civilians from the consequences of military defeat. . . . But this analysis is based on a number of assumptions which as a feminist I would challenge. The question needs to be asked as to whose conflict it really is. It is not those who are told their sacrifice is necessary, without any involvement in the decision that led to the conflict or in the way it is conducted. The [fallacious] assumption is made by men that women's interests mirror their own. . . .

. . . [O]nce the fallacy that the goal of armed conflict is universal to men and women is exposed, all the arguments supporting military necessity as the primary consideration in the determination as to the rules governing such conflict lose their force. A recognition of the absence of women's voices in the decision making as to the use of force and . . . an acknowledgment of the price they pay in armed conflict would be a starting point towards a more equitable approach. . . .

How might feminist arguments be developed with respect to civil wars in particular? For further commentary, see Judith G. Gardam, *Women and International Humanitarian Law, in* Shelters from the Storm: Developments in International Humanitarian Law 205 (W. Maley ed., 1995); Deepika Udagama, *Women Victimized By War: A Call for Stronger Protection*, in *id.* at 219; Nurhalidi B. M. Khill, *Has International Humanitarian Law Failed Women?*, in *id.* at 229; Judith G. Gardam & Hilary Charlesworth, *Protection of Women in Armed Conflict*, 22 H.R.Q. 148 (2000). In 2000, the Security Council adopted Resolution 1325, the first ever to address specifically the impact of war on women **(Basic Document 2.57)**. Resolution 1325 calls on member states to ensure the increased representation of women at all levels of decision-making, particularly in UN peacekeeping operations. It also urges that special measures be taken to protect women and girls from gender-based violence. Two major reports on women and armed conflict and the implementation of Resolution 1325 are UNIFEM, Women, War and Peace: The Independent Experts' Assessment on the Impact of Armed Conflict on Women and Women's Role in Peace-building (2002) and the UN Secretary–General's Report on Women, Peace and Security UN Doc. S/2002/1154.

Another general critique of international humanitarian law is developed in Chris Af Jochnick & Roger Normand, *The Legitimation of Violence: A Critical History of the Laws of War*, 35 Harv. Int'l L. J. 49 (1994). Af Jochnick and Normand argue that, despite grand humanitarian rhetoric, powerful nations deliberately devised the laws of war to foster the primacy of military violence over humanitarian concerns. In other words, international humanitarian law has operated to legitimize, rather than limit, military violence against civilians. In a companion article, *The Legitimation of Violence: A Critical Analysis of the Gulf War*, 35 Harv. Int'l L. J. 387 (1994), the authors extend their analysis to the conduct of the Persian Gulf War and contend that it is a continuation of this historical pattern, rather than a positive example of post-Cold War cooperation, as many observers claim. Along the same lines, see also Burns H. Weston, *Security Council Resolution 678 and Persian Gulf Decision-Making: Precarious Legitimacy*, 85 A.J.I.L. 516 (1991). From the readings above, how persuasive do you find this argument?

For further discussion of the humanitarian rules of armed conflict, see Problem 4–3 ("Caucasia Occupies Parsa's NorthValley"), *infra* at 394, and Problem 4–5 ("Hindustan Threatens Nuclear Self–Defense"), *infra* at 437.

20. In the case of intervention in Loango, the Security Council resolution proposed by the United States provides immunity from the jurisdiction of the International Criminal Court for peacekeepers whose own state has not accepted the ICC's Rome Statute **(Basic Document 1.16)**. For a "real world" provision, see Security Council Resolution 1422 (first passed in July 2002 and renewed as Resolution 1487 in June 2003), UN SCOR, 57th Sess., 4572d mtg., UN Doc. S/RES/1422 (2002), at <http://daccessddsun.org/doc/UN-DOC/GEN/N02/477/61/PDF/N0247761.pdf?OpenElement> relative to intervention in the civil war in Liberia in August 2003. The United States has sought also to enter into bilateral treaties to prevent states parties to the Rome Statute from surrendering United States citizens to the Court. The United States has argued that such treaties are contemplated by article 98 of the Statute. What legal and policy issues are at stake here?

21. In her article cited in Discussion Note/Question 19, *supra*, Laura Lopez identifies the position of United Nations peacekeepers as one of the lacunae in international humanitarian law. She points out, at 944–45, that the Geneva Conventions **(Basic Documents 2.9, 2.10, 2.11 & 2.12)** and Protocols **(Basic Documents 2.31 & 2.32)** do not contain specific provisions for the protection of United Nations personnel. While in international conflicts the provisions of the Geneva Conventions covering combatants more generally may apply to peacekeepers, in civil wars only Article 3 and Protocol II would apply, with their very limited protection of combatants. Thus, states would not be obliged to punish those who attack United Nations personnel, nor would peacekeepers be assured of prisoner of war status if they were captured by one of the parties in a civil war.

One response to this gap in international law has been the 1994 Convention on the Safety of United Nations and Associated Personnel **(Basic Document 2.47)**. Lopez discusses the drafting of this treaty at 946–50. *See also* Kenneth J. Keith, *Protection of United Nations and Associated Personnel, in* Shelters from the Storm: Developments in International Humanitarian Law 87 (W. Maley ed., 1995); Ronald St. John McDonald, *The Convention on the Safety of United Nations and Associated Personnel, in id.* at 93; Stephen J. Lepper, *The Legal Status of Military Personnel in United Nations Peace Operations: One Delegate's Analysis,* 18 Hous. J. Int'l L. 359 (1996). A significant weakness of the Convention is that it does not apply to peacekeepers who are authorized to use force under Chapter VII of the United Nations Charter.

What of the violation of international humanitarian law by United Nations peacekeepers? In the 1990s, there have been a number of serious allegations of breaches of the laws of war by peacekeepers, including murder, torture, and rape of civilians and pillage of civilian property. *See* Judith G. Gardam, *Legal Restraints on Security Council Military Enforcement Action,* 17 Mich. J. Int'l L. 285, 289–93, 321–22 (1996); Anne Orford, *The Politics of Collective Security,* 17 *id.* 373 (1996); and Richard D. Glick, *Lip Service to the Laws of War: Humanitarian Law and United Nations Armed Forces,* 17 *id.* 53, 54 n.1 (1995). While the United Nations has acknowledged that its armed forces are bound by some form of customary international humanitarian law, it has argued that it is not bound by the full conventional humanitarian regime. Glick analyzes, and disagrees with, a number of arguments put by the United Nations to limit its obligations under international humanitarian law. These include: (1) the application of the law to the United Nations will undermine the effectiveness of the organization in promoting peace; (2) the UN cannot be considered a "party to an armed conflict" and its personnel cannot be "combatants" for the purposes of the Geneva Conventions regime; and (3) the humanitarian obligations of the states contributing troops satisfies the United Nations own obligations. *See supra* Richard D. Glick, at 70–105. Glick concludes, at 107:

> It is imperative that the United Nations accept its IHL [international humanitarian law] obligations fully. Existing problems with Organization funding, the recruitment of contingents from states, and political discomfort arising out of the assessment of responsibility for IHL violations can not, as a matter of law, justify the status quo. To the extent that this requires the United Nations to cease organizing peacekeeping or peace enforcement forces around troop contingents contributed by states, that must be done, even if it brings a halt to peacekeeping in the short term. The principle of humanity may not be subordinated to political or utilitarian goals.

In August 1999, the UN Secretary–General affirmed the applicability of many principles of humanitarian law to forces conducting operations under United Nations command and control. The Bulletin, Observance by United Nations Forces of International Humanitarian Law, (U. N. Doc. ST/SGB/1999/13) sets out a list of fundamental principles and rules of humanitarian law applicable to UN Forces, but it does not include all the principles of the Geneva Conventions regime. The obligation for UN forces to respect these fundamental principles and rules has also been included in the most recent agreements concluded between the United Nations and the countries in whose territory UN troops are deployed. *See also* Willy Lupin, *Towards the International Responsibility of the UN in Human Rights Violations During "Peace–Keeping" Operations: The Case of Somalia*, 52 Rev. Int'l Comm'n Jurists 47 (1994); Julianne Peck, *The UN and the Laws of War: How Can the World's Peacekeepers Be Held Accountable?*, 21 Syracuse J. Int'l L. & Com. 283 (1995).

22.   One consequence of the prevalence of civil or internal wars, as evidenced in this problem, is increasing danger for civilians. Statistical data on international conflicts is instructive. In the First World War, 20% of those killed were civilians. In World War II, the proportion was 50%. Today, 90% of those killed are civilians, and, among civilians, children are particularly vulnerable. A 1996 report commissioned by the United Nations, written by Graca Machel of Mozambique and entitled *The Impact of Armed Conflict on Children*, UN Doc. A/51/306 (1996), notes that, in the last ten years, two million children have been killed in wars. There are some 200,000 child soldiers in the world today, some as young as ten. Young girls are regularly forced into armies, sexually abused, raped, and sometimes granted to soldiers as "wives." Machel argues: "More and more of the world is being sucked into a desperate moral vacuum. This is a space devoid of the most basic human values; a space in which children are slaughtered, raped and maimed; a space in which children are exploited as soldiers.... There are few further depths to which humanity can sink." What practical measures can you think of to respond to this situation? Article 38 of the 1989 Convention on the Rights of the Child **(Basic Document 3.32)**, which provides some protection by requiring states parties "to ensure that persons who have not attained the age of fifteen years do not take part in hostilities," clearly is inadequate to deal with the problem. The Machel report calls for, among other things, the immediate demobilization of all child soldiers. In May 2000, the UN General Assembly adopted an Optional Protocol to the Convention on the Rights of the Child on the Involvement of Children in Armed Conflict **(Basic Document 3.53).** The Optional Protocol sets a higher minimum age (18 years) for the recruitment of volunteers into armed forces and imposes some governmental responsibility for the recruitment of children by nongovernmental armed groups. Will this help? What else might be done?

23.   This problem also tells us that mass starvation is one result of armed conflict. How does international law respond to such a phenomenon? Protocol I to the Geneva Conventions prohibits the use of starvation as a method of warfare. Review the provisions of Protocol II to determine whether they are relevant to this issue. For pertinent discussion, see Problem 5–5 ("Djourab Blocks Famine Relief in its North Province") in Chapter 5, *supra* at 688. *See also* Charles A. Allen, *Civilian Starvation and Relief During Armed Conflict: The Modern Humanitarian Law*, 19 Ga. J. Int'l & Comp. L. 1 (1989); René Provost, *Starvation As A Weapon: Legal Implications of the United Nations Food Blockade Against Iraq and Kuwait*, 30 Colum. J. Transnat'l L. 577 (1992); Jean E. Zeiler, Note, *The*

Applicability of the Genocide Convention to Government Imposed Famine in Eritrea, 19 Ga. J. Int'l & Comp. L. 589 (1989).

24. What are the appropriate forms of justice to deal with serious crimes once the immediate hostilities are over? The extract from Hilary Charlesworth, *supra* Reading B–3 (p. 280), discusses some of the options, and the other articles in the same Symposium on Method in International Law in 93 A.J.I.L. 302 (1999) debate the merits of various forms of "transitional justice." Are international or national war crimes trials the best course, or are methods that focus less on punishment and more on shaming, such as truth and reconciliation commissions, more productive? Many countries emerging from civil war have had to face these questions. For a discussion of the issues of transitional justice in the context of East Timor, see Carsten Stahn, *Current Development: Accommodating Individual Criminal Responsibility and National Reconciliation: The UN Truth Commission for East Timor*, 95 A.J.I.L. 952 (2001). *See also* John Dugard, *Reconciliation and Justice: The South African Experience, in* The Future of International Human Rights 399 (B. Weston & S. Marks eds., 1999). For a valuable overview see Patricia B. Hayner, Unspeakable Truths: Confronting State Terror and Atrocity (2001).

25. It has been argued that civil conflict might best be prevented through utilizing the international human rights system. In his note, *The Prevention of Civil War through the Use of the Human Rights System*, 27 N.Y.U. J. Int'l L. & Pol. 409 (1995), Virgil Wiebe describes a causal link between human rights violations and the outbreak or aggravation of civil wars. He emphasizes methods available for early warning and prevention of civil conflict. For a critical assessment of the role of the Security Council with respect to human rights, see Philip Alston, *The Security Council and Human Rights: Lessons to be Learned from the Iraq–Kuwait Crisis and its Aftermath*, 13 Austl. Y.B.I.L. 107 (1992).

26. One of the most basic of international law concepts—statehood—is introduced in the readings on "Recognition of States and Governments." Of course, despite the traditional theory that states are the only "subjects" of international law, the world social process embraces a diversity of participating entities other than states, some of them territorially based and some of them not, each with differing opportunity and capacity for affecting the processes of international law creation and application. For an influential collection of essays illustrating this point, see Robert O. Keohane & Joseph S. Nye, Transnational Relations and World Politics (1972). Nongovernmental organizations as diverse as transnational corporations, labor unions, religious bodies, and citizen's groups have become increasingly prominent in the international community. Then United Nations Secretary–General, Boutros Boutros–Ghali, emphasized the importance of what he termed "international civil society" in a number of speeches and reports. Do you agree with the implication that the days of the nation-state are numbered? In 1957, political scientist John Herz argued in a leading article that the nation-state, owing to modern military technology, was becoming less and less capable of fulfilling its primary function of providing security for its inhabitants and that therefore people would turn more and more to larger units of sociopolitical cohesion to ensure their protection. *See* John H. Herz, *The Rise and Demise of the Territorial State*, 9 World Politics 473 (1957). Was Herz correct in his diagnosis? In his prognosis? What is the available evidence? Most problems of the modern world—*e.g.*, nuclear proliferation, human rights deprivations, economic underdevelopment, environmental depletion and pollution—transcend the boundaries of the traditional nation-state. *See, e.g.*, Symposium, *Nationalism and Internationalism: Shifting World Spheres*, 33 Harv. Int'l L. J. 339 (1992); Louis Henkin, *The*

Mythology of Sovereignty, in Essays in Honour of Wang Tieya 351 (R. St. J. Macdonald ed., 1993); Karen Knop, Diversity and Self–Determination in International Law (2001); Ruth Lapidoth, *Sovereignty in Transition*, 45 J. Int'l Aff. 325 (1992); Neil MacCormick, *Beyond the Sovereign State*, 56 Modern L. Rev. 1 (1993); Oscar Schachter, *Sovereignty—Then and Now*, in Essays in Honour of Wang Tieya 671 (R. St. J. Macdonald ed., 1993); Christopher H. Schreuer, *The Waning of the Sovereign State: Towards a New Paradigm for International Law?*, 4 E.J.I.L. 447 (1993); Panel Discussion, *Theoretical Perspectives on the Transformation of Sovereignty*, in 88 Proceed. A.S.I.L. 1 (1994).

What are some of the key aspects of the theory and practice of statehood that traditionally have interested the international law profession (bearing in mind that this theory and practice is premised on a distinctly Euro–American conception of statehood[q])? A useful starting-point is the oft-quoted definition of the term "state" discussed in Reading A–1, *supra* at 266. It should be noted that, despite the language of Article 1, an entity may qualify as a "state" even if the precise extent of its population or territory is uncertain, even if it is temporarily without a government (as may happen in a "civil war," for example), and even if it does not manifest complete administration over its foreign relations. Also, it is clear that a state can continue to exist even if it undergoes territorial and governmental change, although such changes, if great enough, may cause its demise and the creation of a new state. This latter process, what international lawyers call "the process of state succession," is treated in some detail in Problem 6–1 ("A Financial Crisis in Sundalau Spreads to Tolteca"), *infra* at 796–806.

Feminist scholars have paid some attention to the notion of statehood in international law and relations and thereby offered a variety of feminist critiques of the state. For example, it has been argued that the analogy often drawn in the literature between states and individuals projects masculine assumptions about human nature onto the state. For a survey of feminist critiques, see Karen Knop, *Re Statements: Feminism and State Sovereignty in International Law*, 3 Transnat'l L. & Contemp. Probs. 293 (1993). But can we simply replace the autonomous individualized male model of the state with a female counterpart? For example, Mona Harrington has suggested that a feminist state would act to protect the weak within its borders. *See* Mona Harrington, *What Exactly is Wrong with the Liberal State as an Agent of Change?, in* Gendered States 65 (V.S. Peterson ed., 1992). Harrington also predicts that a feminized state may have implications for international law-making—for example, by making it more flexible. She envisages a feminist international law as involving "an ongoing formulation of rules responding to the particular shape of problems as they arise," devised democratically, rather than a more abstract, universal set of prescriptions created by sovereign states. Do you agree with this prediction? Why? Why not?

Another feminist strategy may be to undermine the centrality of the state in international law. Karen Knop draws attention to the value of international civil society—non-state groups and networks—as a site for the generation of international law: "[the] existence [of international civil society] at the edges of the system of states frees this mix of non-governmental organizations, unofficial groups of experts, and other initiatives from the calculus of self interest that often dictates the position of states, and enables it to be more responsive to women's aspirations and more creative in developing proposals for change. Karen Knop,

q. J. Crawford, The Creation of States in International Law (2d ed. 2006).

supra, at 316. As Knop acknowledges, however, civil society is not necessarily hospitable to women's interests; in many ways, international civil society tends to reflect the existing power imbalances in the nation-state system. It is critical, she argues, that women take an active role in international civil society and also in developing theoretical underpinnings for its role in the creation of international law. This can encompass a range of activities, from scholars at the margins challenging the basic assumptions of international law to the mainstream strategy of traditional lobbying. For a discussion of statehood in international law from a feminist perspective, see Hilary Charlesworth & Christine Chinkin, The Boundaries of International Law 124–70 (2000).

27. In 1947, the UN General Assembly asked the International Court of Justice for an advisory opinion on the question of the conditions of membership in the United Nations. The World Court responded in *Admission of a State to the United Nations*, 1948 ICJ 57 (28 May). Finding that Article 4(1) of the UN Charter **(Basic Document 1.5)** is "exhaustive" on the matter, the Court stated, *inter alia*, as follows:

> ... The requisite conditions are five in number: to be admitted to membership in the United Nations, an applicant must (1) be a State; (2) be peace-loving; (3) accept the obligations of the Charter; (4) be able to carry out these obligations; and (5) be willing to do so.

> All these conditions are subject to the judgment of the [United Nations] Organization. * * * [However,] these conditions constitute an exhaustive enumeration and are not merely stated by way of guidance or example. * * * [T]he spirit as well as the terms of [Article 4(1)] preclude the idea that considerations extraneous to these principles and obligations can prevent the admission of a State which complies with them.

In light of UN Charter Article 4(1) and this World Court ruling, does admission to membership in the United Nations constitute an implied recognition of statehood? If so, would it be binding? On UN members? On whether democratic governance is a requirement for statehood see Sean D. Murphy, *Democratic Legitimacy and the Recognition of States and Governments, in* Democracy and International Law 123 (G. Fox & B. Roth eds., 2000).

28. International law touches upon issues of recognition other than the recognition of states and governments. International governmental organizations (IGOs), too, are subjects of recognition. While their legal personality or competence is recognized by their member states by virtue of the latter's participation therein, non-member states recognize such personality or competence through the conclusion of treaties and other formal arrangements. However, in its advisory opinion in *Reparation for Injuries Suffered in the Service of the United Nations*, 1949 ICJ 174 (11 Apr), the International Court of Justice ruled that the United Nations is possessed of objective legal personality, competent to enter into treaties, engage in contracts, borrow money, etc., without requiring formal recognition by non-member states. While not a state, the Court found the UN to be a "subject" of international law with essentially the same rights and duties as a state.

Finally, recognition and non-recognition play an important role relative to territorial claims that are open to legal challenge. The Stimson Doctrine, for example, named after former US Secretary of State Henry L. Stimson, precipitated by the Japanese takeover of Manchuria in 1931–1932, endorsed by the League of Nations, and invoked in the cases of conquest and annexation of pre-World War II Albania, Austria, and Ethiopia as well as Manchuria, proclaimed a refusal to recognize "any situation, treaty or agreement which may be brought about contrary to the covenants and obligations of the [1928] Pact of Paris [**Basic Document 2.5**]." *Quoted in* 2 Whiteman 1145. For further material on the Stimson Doctrine, see 2 Whiteman 1111–62, 5 *id.* 874–84. Compare the tenth paragraph of Principle 1 of the 1970 Declaration on Principles of International Law Concerning Friendly Relations and Co–Operation Among States in Accordance with the Charter of the United Nations **(Basic Document 1.11)** which proclaims that "[n]o territorial acquisition resulting from the threat or use of force shall be recognized as legal." United Nations organs have from time to time called upon states not to recognize attempts at territorial change brought about by means of the threat or use of force or against UN decisions. UN General Assembly and Security Council resolutions declaring invalid Israel's "administrative unification" of the City of Jerusalem following the Arab–Israeli "Six Day" War in June 1967 is one example. *See, e.g.,* GA Res. 2253, UN GAOR, 22nd Sess., Supp. No. 1, at 4, UN Doc. A/6798 (1967); SC Res. 252, UN SCOR, 23rd Sess, 1426th Mtg., at 9, UN Doc. S/8590/Rev. 2 (1968); SC Res. 267, UN SCOR, 24th Sess., 1485th Mtg., at 3, UN Doc. S/9311 (1969); SC Res. 271, UN SCOR, 24th Sess, 1512th Mtg., at 5, UN Doc. S/9445 (1969); SC Res. 298, UN SCOR, 26th Sess., 1582nd Mtg., at 6, UN Doc. S/10337 (1971). Similarly, in its advisory opinion on the *Legal Consequences for States of the Continued Presence of South Africa in Namibia (South West Africa)*, 1971 ICJ 16 (21 Jun), the International Court of Justice ruled, at 54, "that member states of the United Nations were under an obligation not to recognize the legality of South Africa's presence in Namibia, or the validity of South Africa's acts on behalf of or concerning Namibia. . . ."

In the *Case Concerning East Timor* (Port. v Austl.) 1995 ICJ Rep. 90 (30 Jun), the International Court of Justice considered Portugal's argument that Australia had illegally entered into a treaty with Indonesia to set the maritime boundaries between Australia and East Timor (then under Indonesian rule). The Court stated, at ¶ ¶ 31–32: "[T]he argument of Portugal . . . rests on the premise that the UN resolutions . . . can be read as imposing an obligation on the States not to recognise any authority on the part of Indonesia over the Territory . . . . . The Court is not persuaded, however, that the resolutions went so far. . . . The Court finds that it cannot be inferred from the sole fact that the General Assembly and Security Council resolutions refer to Portugal as the administering Power of East Timor, that they intended to impose an obligation on third states to treat exclusively with Portugal as regards the continental shelf of East Timor." The Court concluded that UN resolutions acknowledging Portugal as the administering Power in East Timor, and East Timor as having the right to self-determination, were not, of themselves, unequivocal and unchallengeable legal bases on which to define recognition or otherwise of the status of East Timor by third parties.

While few of these appeals for the non-recognition of forcefully or illegally acquired territory have much direct effect upon the outlaw states involved, the question of non-recognition does become important in law suits in other countries when choice-of-law and similar issues arise. For example, in the United States, although a recognized foreign government generally is allowed to sue in domestic courts, this opportunity is not extended to unrecognized governments. *See, e.g., Russian Socialist Federal Soviet Republic v. Cibrario*, 235 N.Y. 255, 139 N.E. 259 (Ct.App.1923). *But see Upright v. Mercury Business Machines Co.*, 13 App. Div.2d 36, 213 N.Y.S.2d 417 (1961), wherein the Appellate Division of the New York Supreme Court, without deciding whether a corporation established by the German Democratic Republic could itself sue, allowed suit to be brought by an assignor of the corporation. For a contextually sensitive, policy-oriented treatment of recognition as an authoritative response to social change, see W. Michael Reisman & Eisuke Suzuki, *Recognition and Social Change in International Law: A Prologue for Decisionmaking*, in Toward World Order and Human Dignity 403 (W. M. Reisman & B. Weston eds. & contribs., 1976).

29. *Bibliographical Note*. For supplemental discussion concerning the principal themes addressed in this problem, consult the following additional specialized materials:

a. *Recognition of States and Governments*

(1) *Books/Monographs/Reports/Symposia*. J. Dugard, Recognition and the United Nations (Hersch Lauterpacht Memorial Lecture No. 3, 1987); H. Lauterpacht, Recognition in International Law (1947); M.J. Peterson, Recognition of Governments: Legal Doctrine and State Practice (1997).

(2) *Articles/Book Chapters*. E. Borchard, *Recognition and Non-recognition*, 36 A.J.I.L. 108 (1942).

b. *Civil War*

(1) *Books/Monographs/Reports/Symposia*. M. McDougal & F. Feliciano, Law and Minimum World Public Order (1961); L. Moir, The Law of Internal Armed Conflict (2001); The Vietnam War and International Law, vols. 1–4 (R. Falk ed., 1968–1976); L. Zegveld, The Accountability of Armed Opposition Groups in International Law (2002).

(2) *Articles/Book Chapters*. K. Annan, Peacekeeping in Situations of Civil War, 26 N.Y.U. J. Int'l L. & Pol. 623 (1994); J. Hasday, *Civil War as Paradigm: Reestablishing the Rule of Law at the End of the Cold War*, 5 Kan. J. Pub. L. & Pol'y 129 (1996); S. Marks, *The New Cambodian Constitution: From Civil War to a Fragile Democracy*, 26 Colum. Hum. Rts. L. Rev. 45 (1994); S. Tharoor, *The Changing Face of Peace-keeping and Peace-enforcement*, 19 Fordham Int'l L. J. 408 (1995); V. Wiebe, *The Prevention of Civil War Through the Use of the Human Rights System*, 27 N.Y.U. J. Int'l L. & Pol. 409. (1995).

c. *Intervention*

(1) *Books/Monographs/Reports/Symposia*. S. Chesterman, Just War or Just Peace? Humanitarian Intervention and International Law (2001); Council on Foreign Relations, Right v. Might—International Law and the Use of Force (1989); J. Harris, The Politics of Humanitarian Intervention (1995); S. Murphy, Humanitarian Intervention: United Nations in an Evolving World Order (1996); D. Sarooshi, Humanitarian Intervention and International Humanitarian Assistance: Law and Practice (1994); J. Stone, Aggression and World Order: A Critique of United Nations Theories of Aggression (1958); F. Tesón, Humanitarian Intervention: An Inquiry Into Law and Morality (2d ed., 1994); T. Weiss, The United Nations and Civil Wars (1995); I. Zartman, Collapsed States: The Disintegration and Restoration of Legitimate Authority (1995).

(2) *Articles/Book Chapters*. Y. Akashi, *The Use of Force in a United Nations Peace–Keeping Operation: Lessons Learnt From the Safe Areas Mandate*, 19 Fordham Int'l L. J. 312 (1995); D. Bills, *International Human Rights and Humanitarian Intervention: The Ramifications of Reform on the United Nation's Security Council*, 31 Tex. Int'l L. J. 107 (1996); A. Cassese, Ex Iniuria Ius Oritur: *Are We Moving Towards International Legitimation of Forcible Humanitarian Countermeasures in the World Community?*, 10 E.J.I.L. 23 (1999); B. S. Chimni,

Towards a Third World Approach to Non–Intervention: Through the Labyrinth of Western Doctrine, 20 Indian J. Int'l L. 243 (1980); D. Dallmeyer, *National Perspectives on International Intervention: From the Outside Looking In*, in Beyond Traditional Peacekeeping 20 (D. Daniel & B. Hayes eds., 1995); R. Gordon, *Humanitarian Intervention by the United Nations: Iraq, Somalia and Haiti*, 31 Tex. Int'l L. J. 43 (1996); R. Higgins, *The United Nations Role in Maintaining International Peace: The Lessons of the First Fifty Years*, 16 N.Y L. Sch. J. Int'l & Comp. L. 135 (1996); R. Kolb, *Note on Humanitarian Intervention*, 849 Int'l Rev. of Red Cross 119 (2003); M. Koskenniemi, *The Police in the Temple: Order, Justice and the United Nations*, 6 E.J.I.L. 325 (1995); S. Lee, *United Nations Peacekeeping: Developing and Prospects*, 28 Cornell Int'l L. J. 619 (1995); S. Murphy, *Assessing the Legality of Invading Iraq*, 92 Georgetown L. J. 173 (2004); B. Ove, *Peacekeeping to Peace Enforcement: Prospective Issues for the United Nations*, 20 Melb. U. L. Rev. 55 (1995); W. M. Reisman, *Humanitarian Intervention and Fledgling Democracies*, 18 Fordham Int'l L. J. 794 (1995); H. Richardson, *"Failed States," Self–Determination, and Preventive Diplomacy: Colonialist Nostalgia and Democratic Expectations*, 10 Temple Int'l & Comp. L. J. 1 (1996); D. Richmond, *Normativity in International Law: The Case of Unilateral Humanitarian Intervention*, 6 Yale H.R. & Dev. L. J. 45 (2003); F. Ruiz Ruiz, *Democratic Intervention: A Legal Analysis of its Lawfulness*, 41(3) Indian J. Int'l. L. 377 (2001); R. Wedgwood, *The Evolution of the United Nations Peacekeeping*, 28 Cornell Int'l L. J. 631 (1995).

Problem 4–2

War between Parsa and Caucasia

SECTION 1. FACTS

For many years, Parsa and Caucasia, two neighboring Central Asian countries—the first mostly Muslim, the second mostly Christian Orthodox—have lived in mutual enmity owing to deep-rooted religious differences and frequent border disputes. Following a systematic suppression of Islamic fundamentalists in Caucasia, tensions increased between the two countries and Parsa demanded the surrender of certain border areas "of high economic and strategic significance to our national security." Upon Caucasia's refusal to submit to this demand, minor but increasing armed border clashes flared up between the two countries. Subsequently, after Parsa realized that no diplomatic solution could be expected, it attacked Caucasia with the full strike power of its armed forces, arguing that Parsa had the right to take preemptive action in self-defense.

The United Nations Security Council, concerned to bring an end to the violence lest it spread throughout Central Asia and into the Middle East, has been convened to consider the crisis. Both Parsa and Caucasia are parties to the United Nations Charter. They are parties also to the Pact of Paris and the Pact of the League of Arab States. As Legal Adviser to your country's Ministry of Foreign Affairs, you have been asked to advise your Foreign Minister and Permanent Representative to the United Nations as to the international legality of Parsa's attack upon Caucasia.

SECTION 2. QUESTIONS PRESENTED

1. Has Parsa violated international law by attacking Caucasia?
2. In any event, are there any additional or alternative legal norms, procedures, and/or institutions to be recommended that might further help to prevent or discourage situations of the kind posed by this problem?

SECTION 3. ASSIGNMENTS

A. READING ASSIGNMENT

Study the Readings presented in Section 4, *infra*, and the Discussion Notes/Questions that follow. Also, time permitting, consult the accompanying bibliographical references.

B. RECOMMENDED WRITING ASSIGNMENT

Prepare a comprehensive, logically sequenced, and *argumentative* brief in the form of an outline of the primary and subsidiary *legal* issues you see requiring resolution for your country's Foreign Minister and Permanent Representative to the United Nations. Also, from the perspective of an independent judge, indicate which side ought to prevail on each issue and why. Retain a copy of your issue-outline/brief for class discussion.

C. Recommended Oral Assignment

Assume that your country has decided to lend its diplomatic support to Parsa or Caucasia (as designated by your instructor); then, relying upon the Readings (and your issue-outline if prepared), present a 10–15 minute oral argument of your government's likely positions before the United Nations Security Council.

D. Recommended Reflective Assignment

Consider (and recommend) alternative norms, institutions, and/or procedures that you believe might do better than existing world order arrangements to contend with situations of the kind posed by this problem. In so doing, but without insisting upon *immediate* feasibility, identify the particular transition steps that would be needed to make your alternatives a reality.

Section 4. Readings

The following readings are considered *prima facie* relevant to solving this problem. They are your law library for present purposes and should be treated as such, organized intelligibly for "shelving" and not necessarily according to the issues presented. Be sure to review Chapter 2 ("International Legal Prescription: The 'Sources' of International Law") in your consideration of them. It, too, should be treated as part of your law library (as, indeed, should this entire coursebook).

1. General Treaty Providing for the Renunciation of War as an Instrument of National Policy. Concluded, 27 Aug 1928. Entered into force, 24 Jul 1929. 94 L.N.T.S. 57 ("Pact of Paris" or "Kellogg–Briand Treaty"); *reprinted in* **2 Weston & Carlson II.A.1** (Basic Document 2.5).

2. Convention on Rights and Duties of States ("Montevideo Convention"). Concluded, 26 Dec 1933. Entered into force, 26 Dec 1934. 165 L.N.T.S. 19; *reprinted in* **1 Weston & Carlson I.D.1: Arts. 3, 4, 8, 10, 11** (Basic Document 1.2).

3. Charter of the United Nations. Concluded, 26 Jun 1945. Entered into force, 24 Oct 1945. 1976 Y.B.U.N. 1043; *reprinted in* **1 Weston & Carlson I.A.1: Pmbl. and Arts. 1(1) & (2), 2(3) & (4), 24(1), 33(1), 39, 43, 45, 51** (Basic Document 1.5).

4. Agreement by the Government of the United Kingdom of Great Britain and Northern Ireland, the Government of the United States of America, the Provisional Government of the French Republic, and the Government of the Union of Soviet Socialist Republics for the Prosecution and Punishment of the Major War Criminals of the European Axis and Charter of the International Military Tribu-

nal. Concluded at London, 8 August 1945. Entered into force, 8 August 1945. 82 U.N.T.S. 279; 1946 U.K.T.S. 27, Cmd. 6903, 145
B.F.S.P. 872, 59 Stat., 1544, E.A.S. 472; *reprinted in* 2 Weston & Carlson II.E.1: Art. 6 (Basic Document 1.3).

5.　**Declaration on the Inadmissibility of Intervention in the Domestic Affairs of States and the Protection of their Independence and Sovereignty, 21 Dec 1965, GA Res. 2131, 20 UN GAOR Supp. No. 14, at 11, UN Doc. A/6014 (1966);** *reprinted in* **5 I.L.M. 374 (1966) and 2 Weston & Carlson II.A.2** (Basic Document 2.20).

6.　**Declaration on Principles of International Law Concerning Friendly Relations and Co-operation Among States in Accordance with the Charter of the United Nations, 24 Oct 1970, GA Res. 2625, 25 UN GAOR Supp. No. 28, at 121, UN Doc. A/8028 (1971);** *reprinted in* **9 I.L.M. 1292 (1970) and 1 Weston & Carlson I.D.7** (Basic Document 1.11).

7.　**Resolution on the Definition of Aggression, 14 Dec 1974, GA Res. 3314, 29 UN GAOR Supp. No. 31, at 142, UN Doc. A/9631 (1975);** *reprinted in* **13 I.L.M. 710 (1974) and 2 Weston & Carlson II.A.4** (Basic Document 2.29).

8.　**Pact of the League of Arab States. Concluded, 22 Mar 1945. Entered into force, 10 May 1945. 70 U.N.T.S. 238;** *reprinted in* **1 Weston & Carlson I.B.16: Arts. 5, 6, 8** (Basic Documents 1.4).

9.　**Rome Statute of the International Criminal Court. Concluded 17 Jul 1998. Entered into force 1 Jul 2002, UN Doc A/CONF.183/9 (1998);** *reprinted in* **37 I.L.M. 999 (1998) and 1 Weston & Carlson & Carlson I.H.13: Art. 5** (Basic Document 1.16).

10.　**Edward Gordon, "Article 2(4) in Historical Context," 10 Yale. J. Int'l L. 271, 271–75 (1985).**

Until this century, the decision by states to employ armed force in their international relations enjoyed close to a full measure of legitimacy under international law. Force used in a way that clearly violated another state's established rights was treated as a subject of concern only between the state employing force and the target state.... [I]n general, states not directly affected were deemed not to have rights in jeopardy. If they interfered, it was as mediators or by offering their good offices; in either case upon sufferance.

The Convention for the Pacific Settlement of International Disputes, concluded at the first Hague Peace Conference in 1899,[a] critically weakened the theoretical foundations of this traditional perspective regarding the use of force.... [The principles of this Convention] established the international community's independent interest in the prevention or cessation of international armed conflict and deprived warfare of the legitimacy it derived from the presumed prerogatives of national sovereignty.

Despite the establishment of the international community's interest in narrowing this prerogative based on sovereignty, it must be remembered that

---

a.　29 Jul 1899, 32 Stat. 1779, T.S. 392, 1 Bevans 230.

World War I began with the denial by a major power that the Hague Convention, or any treaty, continued to be obligatory upon a party to it when that party no longer considered compliance to be in its national interest.... As a result, many of the rules of law that the world had thought were most firmly established were disregarded ... [and this fact] caused leaders to examine the premises upon which international society had been based. One of these leaders, Elihu Root, said at the time:

> [W]e may well ask ourselves whether that general acceptance which is necessary to the establishment of a rule of international law may be withdrawn by one or several nations and the rule be destroyed by that withdrawal so that the usage ceases and the whole subject to which it relates goes back to its original status as matter for new discussion as to what is just, convenient and reasonable.

* * *

Historical antecedents may offer some guidance as to the core meaning of Article 2(4) [of the UN Charter **(Basic Document 1.5)**]. After World War I, the adoption of the Covenant of the League of Nations[b] reestablished the international community's interest in a state's use of armed force in pursuit of its national interests. First, the Covenant declared in Article 10 that "any war or threat of war" was dangerous to the entire community. Except for the substitution of the more inclusive word "force" for "war," the language of Article 2(4) echoes this fundamental expression of community interest. Second, the Covenant ... institutionalized the power of public opinion as a sanction against the unlawful use of force by obligating members of the League in Article 11 "to respect and preserve as against external aggression the territorial integrity and existing political independence" of other members. The policies underlying the Covenant initiated the process and framed the words through which Article 2(4) came to be fashioned.

It is relevant to the interpretation of Article 2(4) that this process of reestablishing the international community's interest in a state's use of armed force did not come about overnight. The process gained momentum as a result of unanimous resolutions of the League Assembly between 1924 and 1927 condemning "wars of aggression" as international crimes; the declaration of the twenty-one American republics at the Pan American Conference in 1928 considering such wars an international crime "against the human species;" and the signing later that year of the Kellogg–Briand Pact **[Basic Document 2.5]** declaring "in the names of their [the signatory states'] respective peoples that they condemn recourse to war for the solution of international controversies, and renounce it as an instrument of national policy in their relations with one another." By 1934, with sixty-three states having participated in the Pact, it was said that the Pact had "abolished the conception of war as a legitimate means of exercising pressure on another state in the pursuit of national policy...."

The developmental process of Article 2(4) continued following the outbreak of World War II. In 1941, the leaders of Great Britain and the United States declared in the Atlantic Charter that "they believe that all nations of the world, for realistic as well as spiritual reasons must come to the abandon-

b. Adopted 28 Apr 1919, *reprinted in* 13 A.J.I.L. Supp. 128.

ment of the use of force." The following year, the State Department forwarded to President Roosevelt the first draft of its plan for what became the United Nations, articulating as its first purpose the prevention of "the use of force or threats of force in international relations except by authority of the international organization itself." Thus, even before the formal negotiations leading to the adoption of Article 2(4) in San Francisco in 1945, both the policy and the core of the language by which the community sought to deprive nations of the unlimited use of self-help were . . . well in place.

Article 2(4) is not merely the product of some momentary burst of enthusiasm; it is a deeply rooted rule of international law embodying a fundamental presumption that the use of force by states in pursuit of their national interests poses an unacceptable danger to the larger community.

11. Mary Ellen O'Connell, "Regulating the Use of Force in the 21st Century: The Continuing Importance of State Autonomy," 36 Colum. J. Transnat'l L. 473, 473, 475–77, 479 (1997).

The most important, and certainly the most ambitious, modification of international law in this century has been the outlawing of the use of force to settle international disputes. The definitive prohibition on the use of force came with the adoption of the United Nations Charter **[Basic Document 1.5]** and, in particular, Charter art. 2(4). Louis Henkin has written:

> Article 2(4) is the most important norm of international law, the distillation and embodiment of the primary value of the inter-State system, the defence of State independence and State autonomy. The Charter contemplated no exceptions. It prohibits the use of force for selfish State interests ("vital interests") as well as for benign purposes, human values. It declares peace as the supreme value, to secure not merely State autonomy, but fundamental order for all. It declares peace to be more compelling than inter-State justice, more compelling even than human rights or other human values.[1]

* * *

For the individual State, article 2(4) of the Charter prohibits the use of force except in self-defense against an actual armed attack, and even then only until the Security Council acts.[2] This rule provides ultimate protection for State autonomy—no State may be threatened by another State's decision to use force. Regardless of a State's violations of international law, it cannot be attacked by another State unless the violator State has attacked first. States have not opposed or attempted to reinterpret this basic principle since the Charter's adoption. For the most part, States have reinforced the principle. The International Court of Justice, in a case brought by Nicaragua against the United States in 1986,[3] authoritatively demonstrated the continuing vitality of article 2(4) in its original form. The Court confirmed that under international law States may only use force when responding to an actual armed attack. The Court stated that shipments of weapons from one State to rebels fighting the government of another State would not amount to an

---

1. Louis Henkin, International Law: Politics, Values and Functions 146 (1990).

2. . . . UN Charter, art. 51.

3. *See* Military and Paramilitary Activities in and against Nicaragua (Nicar. v. U.S.), 1986

ICJ 14 . . . [reprinted in part as Reading C–7 in Problem 4–1 ("Intervention in Loango"), *supra* at 291].

armed attack. This finding is consistent with the Definition of Aggression **[Basic Document 2.29]** which lists actions equivalent to an armed attack. According to article 3(g) of the Definition, an armed attack which triggers the right to use force includes: invasion of territory, bombardment of territory, blockade of ports, attack on air, sea, or land forces, and the sending ... of armed bands, groups, irregulars or mercenaries, which carry out acts of armed force against another State of such gravity as to amount to the acts listed above, or its substantial involvement therein."

While States have not challenged the core principle of article 2(4), some States have from time to time pressed for exceptions. For example, the drafters of the Definition of Aggression included a clear exception to the generally accepted meaning of 2(4). In article 7, the Definition says that the right of self-determination, particularly by peoples under "colonial and racist regimes or other forms of alien domination," is not intended to be limited by the Definition and neither is the "right of these peoples to struggle ... and to seek and receive support ...". This exception remains controversial. It certainly tended to undermine the autonomy of former colonial powers such as France and the United Kingdom. The United States, in particular, doubted its legality. Today, the chief sponsors of the exception argue that it is no longer relevant since the days of colonialism and apartheid are over. The States of the developing world, particularly in Africa, have spoken strongly in favor of the value of autonomy and have always considered the application of article 7 to be limited.[4]

* * *

... It would ... have been helpful if [the International Court of Justice in the *Nicaragua* case] had said something definitive about anticipatory self-defense. There seems to be no reason not to use the formula of the Caroline Doctrine, according to which a government may use force in anticipation of an armed attack if the "necessity of that self-defence, is instant, overwhelming, and leaving no choice of means, and no moment for deliberation."[5]

In summary, under the Charter as drafted and under the practice of the first fifty years after the adoption of the Charter, States could employ force under only one rule of international law: in self-defense. For part of this period, States might also have been permitted to use force to help realize the right of self-determination by peoples under colonial or racist domination. The legal right of States to challenge each others' autonomy for any reason by the use of force was eliminated with the adoption of the Charter.

12. Christopher Greenwood, "International Law and the Pre-emptive Use of Force: Afghanistan, Al–Qaida, and Iraq," 4 San Diego Int'l L. J. 7, 8–16 (2003).

The question whether international law permits the use of force not in response to existing violence but to avert future attacks has taken on added significance in the aftermath of the events of September 11, 2001 and with the debate about Iraqi weaponry. Referring both to the threat of terrorist

---

4. One sees the limitation quite clearly in, for example, The Charter of the Organization of African Unity **[Basic Document 1.9,** now the African Union per **Basic Document 1.17]**.

5. J. B. Moore, 2 A Digest of International Law 412 (1906). [The *Caroline Case* is discussed also in Reading D–4 in Problem 4–1 ("Intervention in Loango"), *supra* at 306].

attack and the dangers posed by "rogue States," the National Security Strategy document, issued by President Bush in September 2002, warns:

> The United States has long maintained the option of pre-emptive actions to counter a sufficient threat to our national security. The greater the threat, the greater is the risk of inaction—and the more compelling the case for taking anticipatory action to defend ourselves, even if uncertainty remains as to the time and place of the enemy's attack. To forestall or prevent such hostile acts by our adversaries, the United States will, if necessary, act preemptively.

> The United States will not use force in all cases to pre-empt emerging threats, nor should nations use pre-emption as a pretext for aggression. Yet in an age where the enemies of civilization openly and actively seek the world's most destructive technologies, the United States cannot remain idle while dangers gather....

> The purpose of our actions will always be to eliminate a specific threat to the United States or our allies and friends. The reason for our actions will be clear, the force measured, and the cause just.[6]

Nor have such sentiments been confined to the US administration. Members of the Australian government, for example, have called for a reconsideration of the UN Charter **[Basic Document 1.5]** provisions on self-defense to permit greater latitude for pre-emptive action.[7]

To some commentators, such statements are symptomatic of a disturbing willingness on the part of certain governments to disregard international law; others see them as indications of the need for a fundamental reconsideration of that law—possibly even including an amendment of the UN Charter—to meet a wholly new type of threat. Before embracing either school of thought, however, it is appropriate to examine whether, and if so under what circumstances, existing international law permits the use of force to prevent an attack that has not yet materialized....

At the outset ..., it is important to sound [some] notes of caution. First, there is no agreement regarding the use of terminology in this field. As a result, some commentators distinguish between "anticipatory" military action (which they generally use to describe military action against an imminent attack) and "pre-emptive" force (normally employed to describe the use of force against a threat that is more remote in time). Although this approach offers the appearance of precision, the appearance is deceptive because so many others use the two terms interchangeably. Statements about "pre-emptive" or "anticipatory" action need, therefore, to be treated with some caution.

* * *

6. President George W. Bush, The National Security Strategy of the United States of America, 15–16 (Sept. 17, 2002), at <http://www.whitehouse.gov/nsc/nss.pdf>.

7. *See, e.g.,* Senator Robert Hill, The John Bray Memorial Oration, 4, 6–8 (28 Nov 2002), *available at* <http://www.minister.de-fence.gov.au/2002/694281102.doc>; Doorstop Interview, 4–5 (28 Nov 28, 2002), at <http://www.minister.defence.gov.au/HillSpe echtpl.cfm? CurrentID=2120>; see also Interview by Neil Mitchell with Prime Minister John Howard, 5–6 (29 Nov 2002), *available at* <http://www.pm.gov.au/ news/interviews/2002 /interview2013.htm>.

[I]t is of course well-established that the use of force in international relations is lawful only if it satisfies two requirements. The recourse to force, and the degree of force employed, must be lawful under the legal regime codified in the UN Charter (the ius ad bellum). In addition, the conduct of hostilities must meet the requirements of international humanitarian law (the ius in bello).... [This] Article is ... confined to ius ad bellum questions.

II.   The Legal Framework of the Use of Force in International Relations

There is broad agreement on the main principles that make up the international law on the use of force. The starting point is the Preamble to the UN Charter, which affirms that the "Peoples of the United Nations" are "determined to save succeeding generations from the scourge of war, which twice in our lifetime has brought untold sorrow to mankind," and Article 1(1), which gives, as the first purpose of the United Nations:

> To maintain international peace and security, and to that end: to take effective collective measures for the prevention and removal of threats to the peace, and for the suppression of acts of aggression or other breaches of the peace, and to bring about by peaceful means, and in conformity with the principles of justice and international law, adjustment or settlement of international disputes or situations which might lead to a breach of the peace.

These provisions make clear the importance, in the legal order embodied in the Charter, of maintaining international peace but also the readiness to use force to combat aggression and to prevent threats to the peace from materializing into acts of aggression or breaches of the peace—the Charter is about keeping the peace, not about pacifism.

Article 2(4) then introduces into international law the most far-reaching limitation ever adopted on the use of force by States against one another:[c]

> All Members shall refrain in their international relations from the threat or use of force against the territorial integrity or political independence of any State, or in any other manner inconsistent with the Purposes of the United Nations.

This provision was an innovation in 1945[d] and is cast in terms of an obligation binding only upon Members of the United Nations, but it has long been recognized as stating a principle that has become part of customary international law and, indeed, a rule of ius cogens, binding all States.[8] Although it has sometimes been suggested that it states only a partial prohibition and that some instances of recourse to force between States fall wholly outside its scope,[9] this is very much a minority view and most States and commentators treat Article 2(4) as prohibiting all use of force by one State against another, or on the territory of another, unless that use of force is justified by one of the limited exceptions provided for in international law.

The Charter expressly provides for two such exceptions: military action in self-defense, the right to which is preserved by Article 51, and military action

---

c.   *But see* the 1928 Pact of Paris (**Basic Document 2.5**).

d.   *Id.*

8.   *Supra* note 3.

9.   *See, e.g.,* A. D'Amato, *Israel's Air Strike Upon the Iraqi Nuclear Reactor,* 77 A.J.I.L. 584 (1983).

taken or authorized by the UN Security Council under the collective security provisions of Chapter VII of the Charter. * * * [T]to what extent, if at all, does either the right of self-defense or the collective security powers of the Security Council permit military action to avert a threat that has not yet materialized in the form of actual violence? ...

A. Self–Defense

The right of self-defense is not created by the Charter—it is a customary law right of some antiquity and is said to be inherent in the concept of Statehood—but the conditions for its exercise are mostly to be found in the provisions of Article 51, which states that:

> Nothing in the present Charter shall impair the inherent right of individual or collective self-defense if an armed attack occurs against a Member of the United Nations, until the Security Council has taken measures necessary to maintain international peace and security. Measures taken by members in the exercise of this right of self-defense shall be immediately reported to the Security Council and shall not in any way affect the authority and responsibility of the Security Council under the present Charter to take at any time such action as it deems necessary to maintain or restore international peace and security.

The exercise of the right of self-defense is not subject to any requirement of prior authorization by the UN Security Council; it is an aspect of the sovereignty of the State (although subject to the limitations imposed by international law, as will be seen). Self-defense may be individual (in response to an armed attack upon the State exercising the right) or collective (where a State or group of States go to the assistance of a State that is the victim of an armed attack, even though they have not themselves been attacked and are not directly threatened).

It is noteworthy that Article 51 preserved the "inherent right" of self-defense, rather than creating a right, which otherwise would not have existed. Moreover, it was a comparatively late addition to the Charter, for most States initially assumed that "the right of self-defense was inherent in the proposals and did not need explicit mention in the Charter."[10] The customary law status of the right of self-defense and the close relationship between the customary principle and the provisions of Article 51 have been confirmed by the International Court and are not a matter of controversy.[11] That provision does not, however, state all of the requirements for a lawful resort to force in self-defense, for it is generally agreed that, to be lawful, the use of force must not exceed what is necessary and proportionate in self-defense.

1. Self–Defense Against Threatened Attacks

Although Article 51 refers to the right of self-defense "if an armed attack occurs," the United Kingdom and the United States have consistently maintained that the right of self-defense also applies when an armed attack has not yet taken place but is imminent. This view of self-defense can be traced back to the famous Caroline incident of 1837.[e] ... The Caroline test was applied by

10. United Kingdom Commentary on the United Nations Charter, Cmd. 6666, at 9.

e. *Supra* note 5.

11. Military and Paramilitary (Nicar. v. U.S.), *supra* note 3, at 102–03.

the International Military Tribunals at Nuremberg[12] and Tokyo.[13] This suggests that a right of anticipatory self-defense against imminent threats of armed attack was part of the customary law right preserved by Article 51 of the Charter.

Practice since 1945 (though not always unequivocal by any means) tends to support that conclusion and confirms that the right of self-defense in the Charter era continues to include a right to use force to avert imminent armed attack. The practice of the United Kingdom and the United States has already been mentioned. As Sir Derek Bowett has pointed out, even the Soviet Union, which was initially strongly opposed to any concept of anticipatory self-defense, itself relied on such a right at various times.[14] Two particularly revealing instances of State recognition of a right of anticipatory self-defense are the debates in the Security Council on the 1967 six-day war between Israel and the Arab States, as well as the 1981 Israeli attack on Iraq's nuclear reactor.

In the first case, although Israel's recourse to force against Egypt has sometimes (unconvincingly) been explained as a response to an actual attack or as the exercise of belligerent rights stemming from a war that had not formally been terminated, as Professor Franck has indicated, Israel's "words and actions clearly asserted a right of anticipatory self-defence against an imminent armed attack."[15] ... Moreover, the international reaction suggests that this claim struck a chord with other States. A Soviet draft resolution, which would have condemned Israel for an unlawful resort to force, achieved only four votes in the Security Council and was thus roundly defeated.[16] In the General Assembly, a similar resolution was also voted down.[17] The reaction of other States led Franck to conclude:

> [Israel's] attack on Egypt was in anticipation of an armed attack, not a reaction to it. Most States, on the basis of the evidence available to them, did however apparently conclude that such an armed attack was imminent, that Israel had reasonably surmised that it stood a better chance of survival if the attack were pre-empted, and that, therefore, in the circumstances, it had not acted unreasonably. This does not amount to an open-ended endorsement of a general right to anticipatory self-defence, but it does recognize that, in demonstrable circumstances of extreme necessity, anticipatory self-defence may be a legitimate exercise of a State's right to ensure its survival.[18]

Although international reaction to the 1981 Israeli attack on Iraq's nuclear reactor, on the other hand, was generally condemnatory of Israel,[19] in most

---

12. *See* 13 Ann. Dig. & Rep. Pub. Int'l L. Cases 203, 210; International Military Tribunal (Nuremberg), Judgment and Sentences, 41 A.J.I.L. 172, 205 (1947); Cmd. 6964, at 28–30.

13. *See* International Military Tribunal at Tokyo (1948), in 2 The Law of War: A Documentary History 1029, 1157–59 (L. Friedman ed., 1972).

14. D. Bowett, *The Use of Force for the Protection of Nationals Abroad*, in The Current Legal Regulation of the Use of Force 39, 40, n.26 (A. Cassese ed., 1986).

15. Thomas Franck, Recourse to Force 103 (2002); *but see* C. Gray, International Law and The Use of Force 112 (2000).

16. 1967 U.N.Y.B. 190.

17. A/L.521 was rejected on 4 Jul 1967 by 71 votes against to 22 in favor, with 27 abstentions. GA Draft Res. A/L.521, UN GAOR. 5th Emergency Spec. Sess., UN Doc. A/6717 (1967)....

18. Franck, *supra* note 15, at 105.

19. *See* SC Res. 487, UN SCOR, 36th Sess., 2288th mtg., UN Doc. S/RES/487 (1981)

cases that reaction was based on a conclusion that Israel had failed to demonstrate that there was an imminent threat from Iraq and had thus failed to satisfy the Caroline requirements for anticipatory self-defense, rather than on any rejection of anticipatory self-defense as such. Indeed, the emphasis on this failure to demonstrate the existence of an imminent threat tends, if anything, to confirm the existence of a right of self-defense in cases where such an imminent threat was shown to exist.

Academic opinion on this question is divided. Brownlie, Gray, and Henkin, among others, have argued that there is no right of self-defense until an armed attack has actually commenced.[g] Dinstein[20] also rejects anticipatory self-defense but accepts that there is a right of "interceptive self-defense," where a State has "committed itself to an armed attack in an ostensibly irrevocable way," an approach that differs but little from that in the Caroline case. On the other hand, in addition to Franck (whose work has already been cited), Waldock, Fitzmaurice, Bowett, Schwebel, and Jennings and Watts[h] have all argued that there is a right of anticipatory self-defense against an imminent armed attack.[21] The position is, perhaps, best summed up by Judge Higgins, who said:

> In a nuclear age, common sense cannot require one to interpret an ambiguous provision in a text in a way that requires a state passively to accept its fate before it can defend itself. And, even in the face of conventional warfare, this would also seem the only realistic interpretation of the contemporary right of self-defence. It is the potentially devastating consequences of prohibiting self-defence unless an armed attack has already occurred that leads one to prefer this interpretation—although it has to be said that, as a matter of simple construction of the words alone, another conclusion might be reached.[22]

In the present writer's opinion, this view accords better with State practice and with the realities of modern military conditions than with the more restrictive interpretation of Article 51, which would confine the right of self-defense to cases in which an armed attack had already occurred.

Nevertheless, that practice also shows that the right of anticipatory self-defense is confined to instances where the armed attack is imminent. Not only was this limitation a central feature of the Caroline correspondence, it was the basis on which the Nuremberg Tribunal, while affirming the Caroline test, rejected the defense plea that the German invasion of Norway had been an act of anticipatory self-defense. It was also the basis for rejection of the Israeli claim in the [Osirak] reactor case. In so far as talk of a doctrine of

---

(adopted unanimously, condemning the Israeli action).

g. The author cites, as follows: I. Brownlie, International Law and the Use of Force by States 112 (1963); Gray, *supra* note 15, at 112; L. Henkin, How Nations Behave 141–44 (1979).

20. Y. Dinstein, War, Aggression and Self–Defence 182 (3rd ed., 2001).

h. The author cites, as follows: H. Waldock, 81 Recueil (1952–II) 496–98; G. Fitzmaurice, 92 Recueil (1957–II) 171; D. Bowett, Self–Defence in International Law 187–92 (1958); S.

Schwebel, 136 Recueil (1972–II) 478–83; and 1 Oppenheim's International Law 421 (Sir Robert Jennings and Sir Arthur Watts eds., 9th ed. 1992).

21. Waldock, Schwebel, and Jennings are all past Presidents of the International Court of Justice; Fitzmaurice was a Judge of that Court.

22. Rosalyn Higgins, Problems and Process: International Law and How We Use It 242 (1994).

"pre-emption" is intended to refer to a broader right of self-defense to respond to threats that might materialize at some time in the future, such a doctrine has no basis in law.

In assessing what constitutes an imminent armed attack, however, it is necessary to take into account two factors that did not exist at the time of the Caroline incident. The first is the gravity of the threat. The threat posed by a nuclear weapon, or a biological or chemical weapon, if used against a city, is so horrific that it is in a different league from the threats posed (as in the Caroline) by cross-border raids conducted by men armed only with rifles. Where the threat is an attack by weapons of mass destruction, the risk imposed upon a State by waiting until that attack actually takes place compounded by the impossibility for that State to afford its population any effective protection once the attack has been launched, mean that such an attack can reasonably be treated as imminent in circumstances where an attack by conventional means would not be so regarded. The second consideration is the method of delivery of the threat. It is far more difficult to determine the time scale within which a threat of attack by terrorist means would materialize than it is with threats posed by, for example, regular armed forces. These would be material considerations in assessing whether, in any particular case, an attack should be treated as imminent.

Nevertheless, the requirement that the attack be imminent cannot be ignored or rendered meaningless. Even when taking into account the issues considered in the preceding paragraph, the right of self-defense will justify action only where there is sufficient evidence that the threat of attack exists. That will require evidence not only of the possession of weapons but also of an intention to use them.

[*Eds.*—The author considers the United States' use of force against Afghanistan in October 2001 and against Iraq in March 2003 and concludes that the use of force could be justified as actions in self-defence].

* * *

In his State of the Union address on 28 January 2003, President George W. Bush highlighted the importance of pre-empting attacks such as the one that occurred on September 11, 2001. In doing so, he made the following remark:

> Some have said that we must not act until the threat is imminent. Since when have terrorists and tyrants announced their intentions, politely putting us on notice before they strike. If this threat is permitted to fully and suddenly emerge, all actions, all words and all recriminations would come too late.[23]

This Article has sought to demonstrate that international law does not require that States wait until it is too late but nor does it give a broad general license for pre-emptive military action. The following conclusions seem warranted:

(1) All States have the right of self-defense against an armed attack, actual or imminent;

23. President's State of the Union Address (28 Jan 2003), *available at* <http://www.white house.gov/news/releases/2003/01/20030128–19.html>.

(2) There is, however, no right to take military action in self-defense against a threat that is not imminent;

(3) In determining whether an attack is imminent, the gravity of the threat and the means by which it would materialize in violence are relevant considerations and mean that the concept of imminence will vary from case to case;

(4) The Security Council can authorize States to use pre-emptive military force against a threat to the peace in circumstances where an attack is not yet imminent;

(5) The scope for pre-emptive action under the collective security regime is therefore more extensive than under the right of self-defense;

(6) Neither the right of self-defense nor the collective security regime is confined to threats emanating from States.

SECTION 5.   DISCUSSION NOTES/QUESTIONS

1.   As the 18th–19th century military strategist and writer Carl von Clausewitz once wrote (as quoted in Michael Howard, *Tempermamenta Belli: Can War Be Controlled?*, in Restraints On War: Studies in the Limitation of Armed Conflict 1 (M. Howard ed., 1979)):

> War is an act of force to compel our enemy to do our will. . . . Attached to force are certain self-imposed, imperceptible limitations hardly worth mentioning, known as international law and custom, but they scarcely weaken it. . . . To introduce the principle of moderation into the theory of war itself would always lead to logical absurdity.

On the basis of the foregoing readings and references, would you say that contemporary international law reflects this view? If so, how? If not, how not? Do you agree with von Clausewitz? Why? Why not?

2.   In an omitted portion of his historical analysis of Article 2(4), Edward Gordon (Reading 10, *supra*) writes, at 275:

> The rule embodied in Article 2(4) is not just a freestanding rule of customary law; it is also a formal treaty obligation. States may withdraw their consent to be bound by treaty obligations, but may not simply walk away from them. The existence of an operational code different from the formal commitment may be cause for withdrawing state consent, but it does not supplant the process for withdrawing consent called for by the treaty or by treaty law generally. Treaties, like free standing rules of customary law, are apt to be replaced if they are immoral, unfair, or not followed. However, an observer's inference that they are lagging behind actual practice is too subjective and fragile a criterion to replace the formal evidence of withdrawal of state consent as an indicator of the continuing force of treaty obligations.

Do you agree with this analysis? If so, how, juridically, and according to what criteria would you characterize, say, the act of jaywalking? Driving 72 mph on a freeway with a posted 65 mph speed limit? Are they legal? Illegal? According to a "formal code"? An "operational code"? Is there a difference? Factually? Juridically? Both?

3.   In *A Gendered Perspective to the International Use of Force*, 12 Austl. Y.B.I.L. 279 (1988–89), Christine Chinkin argues, at 291–93:

... [A]lthough contextual arguments for the non-applicability of Article 2(4) in the particular circumstances have been routinely presented in all instances of the international use of force, the commission of offences against women or their regular subordination within a patriarchal hierarchy have never been so used. The invisibility of women in any legal justifications for the use of force is striking. When assessing the impact of possible responses to aggression the concerns and needs of women are simply not raised by governments or even by other groups.

* * *

It seems that the Cold War analysis of incidents of the use of force that has dominated international law since the late 1940s will no longer be adequate. If there is to be rethinking on the appropriate norms governing both the collective and unilateral use of force with recognition that threats to other interests than State sovereignty may justify coercive response, ... the subordination of women within States or as a result of coercive action should no longer be ignored and regarded as irrelevant.

* * *

... [T]he objective of the prohibition of the use of force is the maintenance of international peace and security and the question to be asked about any claim as to the legitimacy of the use of force is whether it will undermine or preserve world order and community goals. Reisman has argued that mechanical application of Article 2(4) can lead to the continued denial of democracy for some peoples, but again this criticism is made without any reference to gender. Continued subordination of women cannot be conducive to the achievement of these goals.

Do you agree with Professor Chinkin's argument that the international law relating to the use of force should take the world-wide oppression of women into account as a threat to international peace and security? Why? Why not?

4. On 2 August 1990, Iraq invaded and quickly occupied its neighbor in the Persian Gulf, Kuwait. The UN Security Council immediately demanded Iraq's withdrawal from Kuwait. In the face of Iraq's continued occupation, on 29 November 1990, the Security Council authorized "member states cooperating with the government of Kuwait" to "use all necessary means to uphold and implement" earlier Security Council resolutions demanding Iraq's immediate and unconditional withdrawal. Security Council Resolution 678 (29 Nov 90) **(Basic Document 2.40)**. This was the first occasion since the Korean War that the United Nations had used its powers to respond to breaches of international peace to authorize the use of military force against a state. Thirty-eight UN members contributed troops to a coalition military force led by the United States that finally ejected the Iraqi army from Kuwait in February 1991. A formal ceasefire agreement terminated the military operations (Security Council Resolution 687 of 3 Apr 1991—**Basic Document 2.41**) and the UN Security Council administered and monitored the ceasefire until March 2003, when Iraq was invaded by the "Coalition of the Willing" led by the United States. As part of the 1991 ceasefire, Iraq agreed to eliminate its weapons of mass destruction and a reduction of its conventional weapons capacity. This commitment was monitored until March 2003 by the UN Special Commission on the disarmament of Iraq (UNSCOM) and its successor UNMOVIC.

On 13 April 1991, in a speech entitled *The Possibility of a New World Order* and delivered at Maxwell Air Force Base, US President George H. W. Bush claimed that the role of the UN in the Gulf War marked the beginning of a "new world order." He said:

> [The new world order] refers to new ways of working with other nations to deter aggression and to achieve stability, to achieve prosperity and, above all, to achieve peace. It springs from hopes for a world based on a shared commitment among nations large and small, to a set of principles that undergird our relations. Peaceful settlement of disputes, solidarity against aggression, reduced and controlled arsenals, and just treatment for all peoples.
>
> This order, this ability to work together, got its first real test in the Gulf War.... For the first time, the United Nations Security Council, free from the clash of Cold War ideologies, functioned as its designers intended, a force for conflict resolution in collective security.[24]

Was Security Council Resolution 678 within the powers of the Security Council under Chapter VII of the UN Charter **(Basic Document 1.5)**? Chapter VIII? Was subsequent action by the Coalition forces in accordance with Resolution 678? For a discussion of the legal basis of the UN actions in the Persian Gulf War, see Oscar Schachter, *United Nations Law in the Gulf Conflict*, 85 A.J.I.L. 452 (1991). For a critique of the process by which Resolution 678 was adopted, ergo its legitimacy, see Burns H. Weston, *Security Council Resolution 678 and Persian Gulf Decision Making: Precarious Legitimacy,* 85 A.J.I.L. 516 (1991).

In any event, did Resolution 678 provide authority for UN members to punish Iraq for violations of the ceasefire without further Security Coumcil authorization? On 23 February 1998, Iraq entered into a Memorandum of Understanding with the UN Secretary–General to cooperate fully with UNSCOM. It has been argued that the threat of devastating airstrikes against Iraq made by the United States and the United Kingdom unless Iraq signed the agreement constituted an illegal threat of force. *See, e.g.,* Nigel D. White & Robert Cryer, *Unilateral Enforcement of Resolution 687: A Threat too Far?*, 29 Cal. W. Int'l L. J. 243 (1999). In December 1998, the United States and the United Kingdom did in fact launch airstrikes against Iraq for non-compliance with inspection obligations. In March 2003, the same parties, forming a "Coalition of the Willing," mounted a full-scale invasion of Iraq on the same basis. For critiques of action against Iraq by individual members of the UN in the name of enforcement of Security Council resolutions see Jules Lobel & Michael Ratner, *Bypassing the Security Council: Ambiguous Authorizations to Use Force, Cease–Fires and the Iraqi Inspection Regime*, 93 A.J.I.L. 124 (1999); Sean D. Murphy, *Assessing the Legality of Invading Iraq*, 92 Geo. L. J. 173 (2004).

Many commentators have agreed with President George H. W. Bush that the Persian Gulf War marked a renaissance of the Security Council following the doldrums it suffered because of the Cold War. *See*, for example, the assessment of then Australian Minister of Foreign Affairs Gareth Evans in *Cooperating for Peace: The Global Agenda for the 1990s and Beyond* 147 (1993). The invasion of Iraq by a "Coalition of the Willing" in 2003, however, without explicit Security Council authorization, may suggest a retreat in Security Council influence. At the same time, it is striking that the United States soon found it needed the auspices of the Security Council to create a framework to rebuild Iraq after the invasion. *See* SC Res. 1483, UN SCOR, 67th Sess., 4761st mtg., UN Doc. S/RES/1483 (2003). *See also* Mats Berdahl, *The UN Security Council: Ineffective but Indispensable*, 45

---

24. 8 LVII Vital Speeches of the Day (15 Oct 1990).

Survival 2, 7–30 (2003). In *Cooperating for Peace*, Gareth Evans refers to the problems with the UN's "peace enforcement" actions in the 1990–91 Persian Gulf War that may help to explain the UN's continued relevance—importance—since the invasion of Iraq in 2003. For example, was the Persian Gulf action truly a United Nations action or one controlled in fact by the United States? Additionally, the international community seems to have been ill-prepared to respond to the aftermath of the "peace enforcement." Iraq sustained many internal crises after its defeat, including tremendous suffering imposed on its civilian population through destruction of the country's infrastructure and rebellions of Iraq's minorities, particularly the Kurds. For an argument that the "security" fostered by the Security Council in the Persian Gulf War was illusory and inadequate see Anne Orford, *The Politics of Collective Security*, 17 Mich. J. Int'l L. 373 (1996). *See also* Rafael A. Porrata–Doria, *The United Nations Response to Breaches of the Peace in the "New World Order": Lessons from the Korean and Gulf Wars*, 11 Wis. Int'l L. J. 259 (1992–93); Paul W. Kahn, *Lessons for International Law from the Gulf War*, 45 Stan. L. Rev. 425 (1993); and John B. Quigley, *The United States and the United Nations in the Persian Gulf War: New Order or Disorder?*, 25 Cornell Int'l L. J. 1 (1992).

5. Any legal prohibition in domestic or international law needs to be complied with to at least some extent to be considered valid or viable. When states do not obey the prohibition of Article 2(4) voluntarily, what might be the most efficient and realistic way to enforce it?

(a) The deployment of United Nations interpositional peacekeeping forces, such as the establishment of the United Nations Peace–Keeping Force in Cyprus (UNFICYP) established in 1964 and continuing to this day? *See, e.g.*, Elizabeth Abraham, *The Sins of The Savior: Holding the United Nations Accountable to International Human Rights Standards for Executive Order Detentions in Its Mission in Kosovo*, 52 Am. U. L. Rev. 1291 (2003); Saira Mohamed, *From Keeping Peace to Building Peace: A Proposal for A Revitalized United Nations Trusteeship Council*, 105 Colum. L. Rev. 809 (2005); No Exit Without Strategy: Security Council Decision–Making and the Closure or Transition of United Nations Peacekeeping: Report of the Secretary–General, UN Doc. S/2001/394 (2001).

(b) The payment of war damages and reparations, as was required of the World War I and World War II Axis powers? *See, e.g.*, Benjamin J. Cohen, Reparations in the Postwar Period: A Survey (1968); John Maynard Keynes, The Economic Consequences of the Peace (1920); Ignaz Seidl–Hohenveldern, *Reparations*, in 4 Encyclopedia of Public International Law 178 (1982) and *Reparations after World War II*, in *id.* at 180.

(c) The prosecution of civilian and military leaders who may be said to have committed war crimes, crimes against peace, or crimes against humanity, as at Nuremburg and in Tokyo following World War II? *See, e.g.*, The Tokyo War Crimes Trial—An International Symposium (C. Hosoya, N. Ando, Y. Onuma, & R. Minear eds., 1986); Robert H. Jackson, The Nürnberg Case (1947); Ann Tusa & John Tusa, The Nuremberg Trial (1984). *See also* Section A in Chapter 3, *supra*. Note that article 5 of the Statute of the International Criminal Court **(Basic Document 1.16)** gives the Court jurisdiction over acts of aggression once the parties to the Statute can agree on a definition of the term. Agreement on a definition is highly unlikely: Why?

Can you think of any other ways in which Article 2(4) and equivalent prohibitions on the use of force might be made more effective than currently they are?

6. The issue of war crimes was raised in the context of the 1990–91 Persian Gulf War and in the 2003 War on Iraq. For an argument that Iraq and its leader, Saddam Hussein, should be held accountable for the invasion of Kuwait in 1990, see Joseph E. Mayk, *Crimes Against Peace: An Analysis of the Nuremberg Prohibition on Planning and Waging Aggressive War and its Applicability to the Gulf War,* 24 Rutgers L. J. 253 (1992).

On the other hand, Professor John Quigley argues, in *The United States and the United Nations in the Persian Gulf War: New Order or Disorder?*, 25 Cornell Int'l L. J. 1 (1992), that several states and their officials are potentially liable for the unlawful use of force in the Persian Gulf War. He contends that Iraq's aggression against Kuwait leaves it and its officials open to liability. In addition, he argues that the states that attacked Iraq after its invasion of Kuwait, namely the United States and its allies, also used force unlawfully because they exceeded Resolution 678 (*supra* Discussion Note/Question 4) and because the resolution itself did not provide a lawful basis for action. Because, he asserts, the UN Charter **(Basic Document 1.5)** makes no distinction between unprovoked aggression and unlawful force used putatively but improperly in defense, the civilian and military leaders of the United States may have been guilty of planning and waging aggressive war against Iraq. Quigley also argues that the UN bears responsibility for authorizing force in violation of the Charter, and that all of its Member States may thus be liable.

As noted in Part I of this coursebook, the United Nations Security Council established *ad hoc* international criminal tribunals to deal with war crimes in the former Yugoslavia and Rwanda. The first such tribunals since those established in Nuremberg and Tokyo following World War II, their statutes give them jurisdiction over the prosecution of persons responsible for "serious violations of international humanitarian law," including the employment of poisonous weapons or other weapons calculated to cause unnecessary suffering; wanton destruction of cities, towns or villages, or devastation not justified by military necessity; attack or bombardment, by whatever means, of undefended towns, villages, dwellings or buildings; seizure of, destruction, or wilful damage done to institutions dedicated to religion, charity, education, the arts and sciences, historic monuments and works of art and science; and plunder of public or private property. The International Criminal Court (ICC) came into operation in July 2003, with jurisdiction over actions occurring after July 2002. Neither Iraq nor the United States have, at this writing (1 May 2006), accepted the jurisdiction of the ICC, although other members of the 2003 "Coalition of the Willing," such as Australia and the United Kingdom, have done so. Instead, Iraq and the United States have agreed that jurisdiction over war crimes alleged to have been committed by Saddam Hussein and his government should be handled by an Iraqi tribunal exclusively. Assuming *ad hoc* war crimes tribunals had been established following the 1990 and 2003 Gulf Wars, who might have been indicted and possibly found guilty? Assuming Iraq and the United States had accepted the jurisdiction of the ICC, who might have been indicted and possibly found guilty? In each case, why? Is a strictly Iraqi war crimes tribunal likely to be as impartial and just as an *ad hoc* international tribunal or the ICC? Why? Why not?

7. In the instant problem, can Parsa legitimately argue that its actions were justified under Article 51 of the UN Charter **(Basic Document 1.5)**? The scope of Article 51 has been hotly debated. *See, e.g.,* D. W. Greig, *Self-Defence and the Security Council: What Does Article 51 Require?*, 40 I.C.L.Q. 366 (1991); Louis René Beres, *After the Gulf War: Israel, Preemption and Anticipatory Self–Defence*, 13 Hous. J. Int'l L. 259 (1991); David R. Penna, *The Right to Self Defense in the*

Post–Cold War Era: The Role of the United Nations, 20 Denv. J. Int'l L. & Pol'y 41 (1991). The status of the doctrine of pre-emptive self-defence, articulated by President George W. Bush in 2002 (in an extract quoted in Greenwood, *supra* Reading 12), has been keenly debated. For an approach different to Greenwood, see Mary Ellen O'Connell, *The Myth of Preemptive Self–Defense* (A.S.I.L. Task Force on Terrorism, August 2002). See also the debate between former Legal Advisors to the United States State Department, Abraham D. Sofaer and Michael Bothe: Abraham D. Sofaer, *On the Necessity of Pre-emption*, 14 E.J.I.L. 209 (2003); Michael Bothe, *Terrorism and the Legality of Pre-emptive Force*, 14 E.J.I.L. 227 (2003). On self-defense generally, see Problem 4–5 ("Hindustan Threatens Nuclear Self–Defense"), *infra* at 437.

8.   In his dissenting opinion in the *Case Concerning Military and Paramilitary Activities In and Against Nicaragua* (Nicar. v. U.S.), 1986 ICJ 14 (Judgment of June 27), 212, Judge Oda objected to the justiciability of the case. One of his arguments, which also was an argument of the United States in the jurisdictional proceedings, was that Nicaragua's claims did not present a "legal dispute" in the sense of Article 36(2) of the Statute of the International Court of Justice **(Basic Document 1.6)**: "In my opinion," he wrote, at 236,

> judicial propriety dictates that the correct manner for dealing with the dispute would have been, and still may prove to be, a conciliation procedure through the political organs of the United Nations or a regional arrangement such as the Contadora Group, and not reference to the International Court of Justice, whose function, which is limited to the purely legal aspect of disputes, has theretofore not been exceeded.

Might Judge Oda reach the same conclusion were Caucasia to file suit against Parsa in the World Court? If so, or if Judge Oda was right in his dissent in the Nicaragua case, what are the prospects for the role of law in relation to the use of force in international affairs? Given the tremendous costs of the use of armed force in terms of human life and health, displacement of peoples, and environment degradation as well as financial costs, why is not greater attention paid to developing alternatives to the use of force? What are possible alternatives and what issues do they raise? *See, e.g.*, C. Milligan, *Alternatives to the Use of Force and the Role of the United Nations*, 20 Denv. J. Int'l L. & Pol'y 73 (1991).

9.   Parsa justified its attack upon Caucasia with claims to border areas "of high economic and strategic significance to our national security." Many wars are fought in defense of a claimant State's "national security." What is national security? Historically, how has it been defined? What factors have been traditionally taken into consideration? Have some been overlooked? If so, which ones? What factors would you include? Exclude? Consider in these regards the observation by Robin Luckham that

> security derives much of its ideological force from the myth that it is also the citizen who is secure.... This has much visceral appeal, especially as it readily connects to nationalism. Yet it is problematic whether State or ruling-class security actually has anything at all to do with the safety and well-being of ordinary citizens.

Robin Luckham, *Regional Security and Disarmament in Africa*, 9 Alternatives 203, 205 (1983). In terms of a rational cost-benefit analysis, who profits from the enlargement of Parsa's economic base and territory? Who pays the price?

Note also Anne Orford's discussion of the limiting assumptions of theories of security in *The Politics of Collective Security,* 17 Mich. J. Int'l L. 373 (1996). She argues, at 376:

> The power relations involved in producing knowledge about collective [and national] security operate to marginalize the security interests of many groups, including most women. The interests of men remain the unquestioned norm of collective [and national] security scholarship. My argument is not that such interests should be displaced or ignored altogether. Instead I ... [suggest] that the interests of elite men should be returned to their particularity. When those interests are seen as one set of interests which should be considered in thinking about security, rather than as a false universal, new visions about the necessary conditions for ... security might be possible.

For discussion of these and related security issues, see generally William E. Blatz, Human Security: Some Reflections (1967); Alan R. Collins, The Security Dilemma and the End of the Cold War (1997); Joseph P. Lorenz, Peace, Power, and the United Nations: a Security System for the Twenty-first Century (1999); Jorge Nef, Human Security and Mutual Vulnerability: the Global Political Economy of Development and Underdevelopment (2nd ed., 1999); A New Canadian International Security Policy? (D. Mutimer ed., 2001); Human Security and the New Diplomacy: Protecting People, Promoting Peace (R. McRae & D. Hubert eds., 2001); International Security in a Global Age: Securing the Twenty-first Century (C. Jones & C. Kennedy–Pipe eds., 2000); Margins of Insecurity: Minorities and International Security (S. C. Nolutshungu ed., 1996); New Millennium, New Perspectives The United Nations, Security, and Governance (R. Thakur & E. Newman eds., 2000); Power and the Purse: Economic Statecraft, Interdependence, and National Security (J. F. Blanchard, E. D. Mansfield, & N. M. Ripsman eds., 1999); Regional Approaches to Disarmament: Security and Stability (Jayantha Dhanapala ed., 1993); Security Issues in the Post–Cold War World (M. J. Davis ed., 1996); The United Nations and Human Security (Edward Newman & Oliver P. Richmond eds., 2001); Toward Nuclear Disarmament and Global Security: A Search for Alternatives (B. Weston ed., 1984); Worlds Apart: Human Security and Global Governance (M. Tehranian ed., 1999); M. C. Abad, Jr., *The Challenge of Balancing State Security with Human Security,* 4 Indonesian Q. 403 (2000); Lloyd N. Axworthy, *Canada and Human Security: The Need for Leadership,* 52 Int'l J. 183 (1997); ___, *Human Security and Global Governance: Putting People First,* 7 Global Governance 19 (2001); Leen Boer & Ad Koekkoek, *Development and Human Security,* 15 Third World Q. 519 (1994); Hans Van Ginkel & Edward Newman, *In Quest of "Human Security,"* 14 Japan Review of International Affairs 59 (2000); Samuel M. Makinda, *The United Nations and State Sovereignty: Mechanism for Managing International Security,* 33 Aust. J. Pol. Sc. 101 (1998); Dwight Newman, *A Human Security Council? Applying A "Human Security" Agenda to Security Council Reform,* 31 Ottawa L. Rev. 213 (2000).

10. *Bibliographical Note.* For supplemental discussion concerning the principal themes addressed in this problem, consult the following additional specialized materials:

(a) *Books/Monographs/Reports/Symposia.* S. Alexandrov, Self-defense Against the Use of Force in International Law (1996); D. Auerswald, Disarmed Democracies: Domestic Institutions and the Use of Force (2000); I. Brownlie, International Law and the Use of Force by States (1963); D. Byman & M. Waxman, Confronting Iraq: US Policy and the Use of Force Since the Gulf War (2000); T. Findlay, The

Use of Force in UN Peace Operations (2002); T. Franck, Recourse to Force: State Action Against Threats and Armed Attacks (2002); C. Gray, International Law and the Use of Force (2000); Democratic Accountability and the Use of Force in International Law (C. Ku & H. Jacobson eds., 2003); M. McDougal & F. Feliciano, Law and Minimum World Public Order–The Legal Regulation of International Coercion (1961); A. Orford, Reading Humanitarian Intervention: Human Rights and the Use of Force in International Law (2003); Peacemaking and Peacekeeping for the New Century (O. Otunnu & M. Doyle eds., 1998); The UN, Peace, and Force (M. Pugh ed., 1997); D. Sarooshi, The United Nations and the Development of Collective Security: the Delegation by the UN Security Council of its Chapter VII Powers (1999); J. Stone, Legal Controls of International Conflict (2nd ed. 1959); *Symposium on the Gulf War*, 10 Dick. J. Int'l L. (Spring 1992); *Symposium on the Non–Use of Force in International Law*, in 26 Coexistence–A Review of East–West and Development Issues No. 1 (W. Butler ed., 1989); M. Walzer, Just and Unjust Wars: A Moral Argument With Historical Illustrations (1977).

(b) *Specialized Articles/Book Chapters.* J. Bialke, *United Nations Peace Operations: Applicable Norms and the Application of the Law of Armed Conflict*, 50 A. F. L. Rev. 1 (2001); M. Bonafede, *Here, There, and Everywhere: Assessing the Proportionality Doctrine and US Uses of Force in Response to Terrorism After the September 11 Attacks*, 88 Cornell L. Rev. 155 (2002); D. Brown, *Use of Force Against Terrorism after September 11th: State Responsibility, Self–Defense and Other Responses*, 11 Cardozo J. Int'l & Comp. L. 1 (2003); S. Chesterman & N. Bhuta, *"Paved with Good Intentions . . ."—Humanitarian War, the New Interventionism and Legal Regulation of the Use of Force: Just War or Just Peace? Humanitarian Intervention and International Law*, 25 Melb. U. L. Rev. 843 (2001); B. Clemmons & G. Brown, *Rethinking International Self–Defense: The United Nations' Emerging Role*, 45 Naval L. Rev. 217 (1998); K. Cox, *Beyond Self–Defense: United Nations Peacekeeping Operations & The Use of Force*, 27 Denv. J. Int'l L. & Pol'y 239 (1999); A. De Saussure, *The Role of the Law of Armed Conflict During the Persian Gulf War: An Overview*, 37 Air Force L. Rev. 41 (1994); C. Edgar, *United States Use of Armed Force Under the United Nations . . . Who's in Charge?*, 10 J. L. & Pol. 299 (1994); T. Farer, *Law and War*, in 3 The Future of the International Legal Order–Conflict Management 15 (C. Black & R. Falk eds., 1971); T. Franck, *Terrorism and the Right of Self–Defense*, 95 A.J.I.L. 839 (2001); T. Graham, Jr, *Is International Law Relevant to Arms Control?: National Self–Defense, International Law, and Weapons of Mass Destruction*, 4 Chi. J. Int'l L. 1 (2003); S. Hoffmann, *International Law and the Control of Force*, in The Relevance of International Law 21 (K. Deutsch & S. Hoffmann eds., 1968); A. H-A Hsiao, *Is China's Policy to Use Force Against Taiwan a Violation of the Principle of Non–Use of Force Under International Law?* 32 New Eng. L. Rev. 715 (1998); J. Lobel, *Benign Hegemony? Kosovo and Article 2(4) of the UN Charter*, 1 Chi. J. Int'l L. 19 (2000); J. Lobel, *The Use of Force to Respond to Terrorist Attacks: The Bombing of Sudan and Afghanistan*, 24 Yale. J. Int'l L. 537 (1999); J. Lobel & M. Ratner, *Bypassing the Security Council: Ambiguous Authorizations to Use of Force, Cease–Fires and the Iraqi Inspection Regime*, 93 A.J.I.L. 124 (1999); K. Malone, *Preemptive Strikes and the Korean Nuclear Crisis: Legal and Political Limitations on the Use of Force*, 12 Pac. Rim L. & Pol'y 807 (2003); F. Martin, *Using International Human Rights Law for Establishing a Unified Use of Force Rule in the Law of Armed Conflict*, 64 Sask. L. Rev. 347 (2001); P. McLain, *Settling the Score with Saddam: Resolution 1441 and Parallel Justifications for the Use of Force Against Iraq*, 13 Duke J. Comp. & Int'l L. 233 (2003); T. Morth, *Considering Our Position: Viewing Information Warfare as a Use of Force Prohib-*

ited by Article 2(4) of the UN Charter, 30 Case W. Res. J. Int'l L. 567 (1998); R. Normand & C. Jochnick, *The Legitimation of Violence: A Critical Analysis of the Gulf War*, 35 Harv. Int'l L. J. 387 (1994); K. Nowrot & E. Schabacker, *The Use of Force to Restore Democracy: International Legal Implications of the ECOWAS Intervention in Sierra Leone*, 14 Am. U. Int'l L. Rev. 321 (1998); W. O'Brien, *Desert Storm: A Just War Analysis*, 66 St. John's L. Rev. 797 (1992); Panel Discussion, *The Prospective Role of the UN in Dealing with the International Use of Force in the Post–Cold War Period: an Analysis in Light of the Persian Gulf Crisis*, 22 Ga. J. Int'l & Comp. L. 9 (1992); A. Peterson, *Order Out of Chaos: Domestic Enforcement of the Law of Internal Armed Conflict*, 171 Mil. L. Rev. 1 (2002); D. Ridgway, *The Legal Legacy of the Gulf War: Claims Against Iraq*, 13 J. Int'l Arbitration 5 (1996); O. Schachter, *The Right of States to Use Armed Force*, 82 Mich. L. Rev. 1620 (1984); ___, *In Defense of International Rules on the Use of Force*, 53 U. Chi. L. Rev. 113 (1986); M. Schmitt, *Preemptive Strategies in International Law*, 24 Mich. J. Int'l L. 513 (2003); B. Simma, *NATO, the UN and the Use of Force: Legal Aspects*, 10 E.J.I.L. 1 (1999); D. Sloss, *Is International Law Relevant to Arms Control?: Forcible Arms Control: Preemptive Attacks on Nuclear Facilities*, 4 Chi. J. Int'l L. 39 (2003); A. Surchin, *Terror and the Law: The Unilateral Use of Force and the June '93 Bombing of Baghdad*, 5 Duke J. Comp. & Int'l L. 457 (1995); J. Terry, *Operation Desert Storm: Stark Contrasts in Compliance With the Rule of Law*, 41 Naval L. Rev. 83 (1993); G. Travalio, *Terrorism, International Law, and the Use of Military Force*, 18 Wis. Int'l L. J. 145 (2000); G. K. Walker, *Anticipatory Collective Self–Defense in the Charter Era: What the Treaties Have Said*, 31 Cornell Int'l L. J. 321 (1998).

Problem 4–3

Caucasia Occupies Parsa's North Valley

SECTION 1. FACTS

Assume the same facts as in Problem 4–2, *supra*.

Caucasia responded to Parsa's attack with devastating force and, by deft military strategy and maneuver, was able finally to push Parsa's forces across the Caucasia–Parsa border some 30 miles into Parsan territory. When the fighting ended, Caucasian troops were left occupying Parsa's fertile and resource-rich North Valley.

Several months thereafter, in an effort to deter further Parsan aggression, Caucasia transferred broad military and civilian authority to a newly constituted North Valley Administrative Council (NVAC), composed of high-ranking Caucasian officials, many of them Orthodox fundamentalists. The NVAC quickly acted to replace a number of Parsan laws—most notably those ensuring (a) freedom of movement, speech, and assembly, and (b) religious holidays and observances—with "more sacred" Caucasian rules and regulations. Also, following the forced transfer of some key landholdings, it arranged for a number of Caucasian mining companies to begin to exploit the newly occupied valley and helped several thousand Caucasian citizens, responding to Caucasian government inducements, to begin to establish "frontier settlements" there.

Parsan opposition to the Caucasian occupation of the North Valley in general, and to the NVAC's policies and practices in particular, has been widespread, with labor strikes, consumer boycotts, political rallies, and other forms of protest becoming commonplace. Until recently, this protest was non-violent for the most part. Once the Caucasian forces started making moves to disperse the large crowds, however, Parsan youth and young adults began to take matters into their own hands, barricading the streets and setting fire to cars and buildings. Also, extensive looting began to occur.

In response to these developments, the NVAC ordered a month-long curfew for the entire North Valley, the placing of Parsan demonstrators under house arrest on charges of incitement to riot, and the issuance of a special pass to all Parsan citizens seeking to enter or leave the occupied valley. Despite these measures, however, the Parsan opposition would not be subdued, and about two months ago, in several North Valley towns, in what appears to have been a coordinated act, seven Caucasian military police were killed by homemade bombs reliably reported to have been planted by a militant faction of the Popular Front for Parsan Resistance known as "Parsan Liberation." In turn, the Caucasian forces detained over 200 Parsan demonstrators for curfew violations in an isolated camp on the grounds that they are suspected terrorists. Caucasian troops instituted a house to house search for the perpetrators of the car bombings, a process that resulted in the arrest and internment of a prominent Parsan university professor and two associates (each members of Parsan Liberation) and the demolition of their respective homes. The three Parsans currently are being tried by a Caucasian military court for the bombing deaths of the seven Caucasian military police. They have been refused any form of legal assistance.

Both Parsa and Caucasia have asked the United States for economic and military assistance, the former "to terminate Caucasia's unlawful belligerent occupation and thereby to reverse the military conquest of the North Valley," the latter "to deter further unlawful aggression and ensure the continued necessity of Caucasia's lawful military administration." A joint hearing of the US Senate Foreign Relations Committee and the House Committee on Foreign Affairs has been convened to consider, among other things, the international legal rights and wrongs of the situation. Both countries are party to all the pertinent treaties on the law of war.

Section 2.   Questions Presented

1. Do Caucasia's belligerent occupation policies and practices violate international law, as Parsa charges, or are they lawful and justified on grounds of military necessity, as Caucasia claims?

2. In any event, are there any additional or alternative legal norms, procedures, and/or institutions to be recommended that might further help to prevent or discourage situations of the kind posed by this problem?

Section 3.   Assignments

A.   Reading Assignment

Study the Readings presented in Section 4, *infra*, and the Discussion Notes/Questions that follow. Also, time permitting, consult the accompanying bibliographical references.

B.   Recommended Writing Assignment

Prepare a comprehensive, logically sequenced, and *argumentative* brief in the form of an outline of the primary and subsidiary *legal* issues you see requiring resolution for the joint hearing of the US Senate Foreign Relations Committee and the House Committee on Foreign Affairs. Also, from the perspective of an independent judge, indicate which side ought to prevail on each issue and why. Retain a copy of your issue-outline/brief for class discussion.

C.   Recommended Oral Assignment

Assume that you represent a nongovernmental interest group or lobby sympathetic to the interests of Parsa or Caucasia (as designated by your instructor); then, relying upon the Readings (and your issue-outline if prepared), present a 10–15 minute oral argument of your interest group's likely positions before the joint hearing of the Senate Foreign Relations Committee and the House Committee on Foreign Affairs.

D. Recommended Reflective Assignment

Consider (and recommend) alternative norms, institutions, and/or procedures that you believe might do better than existing world order arrangements to contend with situations of the kind posed by this problem. In so doing, but without insisting upon *immediate* feasibility, identify the particular transition steps that would be needed to make your alternatives a reality.

Section 4. Readings

The following readings are considered *prima facie* relevant to solving this problem. They are your law library for present purposes and should be treated as such, organized intelligibly for "shelving" and not necessarily according to the issues presented. Be sure to review Chapter 2 ("International Legal Prescription: The 'Sources' of International Law") in your consideration of them. It, too, should be treated as part of your law library (as, indeed, should this entire coursebook).

1. Hague Convention (No. IV) Respecting the Laws and Customs of War on Land (with Annex of Regulations). Concluded, 18 Oct 1907. Entered into force, 26 Jan 1910. 205 C.T.S. 277 (French), 2 A.J.I.L. Supp. 90 (1908); *reprinted in* **2 Weston & Carlson II.B.1: Arts. 1–3 and Annex Arts. 22–28, 42–56** (Basic Document 2.2).

2. Geneva Convention (No. III) Relative to the Treatment of Prisoners of War. Concluded, 12 Aug 1949. Entered into force, 21 April 1951. 75 U.N.T.S. 115; *reprinted in* **2 Weston & Carlson II.B.13: Arts. 3–5, 17, 84–87, 99–108** (Basic Document 2.11)

3. Geneva Convention (No. IV) Relative to the Protection of Civilian Persons in Time of War. Concluded, 12 Aug 1949. Entered into force, 21 Oct 1950. 75 U.N.T.S. 287; *reprinted in* **2 & Carlson II.B.14: Arts. 1, 2, 4–6,12, 27–35, 47–78, 146–147** (Basic Document 2.12).

4. Protocol Additional (No. I) to the Geneva Conventions of August 12, 1949, and Relating to the Protection of Victims of International Armed Conflicts. Concluded, 8 Jun 1977. Entered into force, 7 Dec 1978. 1125 U.N.T.S. 3; *reprinted in* **16 I.L.M. 1391 (1977) and 2 Weston & Carlson II.B.20: Arts. 1, 4, 72–75** (Basic Document 2.31).

5. Editors' Note. The major rules relating to belligerent occupation were first codified in the 1907 Hague Convention (No IV) respecting the Laws and Customs of War on Land (*supra* Reading 1). They were further developed by the fourth 1949 Geneva Convention Relative to the Protection of Civil Persons in Time of War (*supra* Reading 3) and the first 1977 Protocol Additional thereto (*supra* Reading 4). The readings that follow explore and develop the relevant themes contained in them.

6. Gerhard von Glahn, The Occupation Of Enemy Territory: A Commentary on the Law and Practice of Belligerent Occupation 224–27 (1957).

Military Necessity

The modern rules governing belligerent occupation rest on two fundamental assumptions: war is still essentially a conflict between nations and not between private persons, and the rules of international law are binding on both occupant and legitimate sovereign of occupied territory.... [T]he first consideration of an occupant is the prosecution of the war to a successful conclusion. If this primary aim demands that certain measures be undertaken, the occupant might want to do so even if customary or conventional rules of law would have to be set aside for the time being. The preamble to the 1907 Hague Convention on the Laws of War **[Basic Document 2.2]** states that "military necessity has been taken into account in framing the regulations, and has not been left outside to control and limit their application"; however, several of the detailed provisions of the regulations contain a clause that while certain acts are forbidden, their commission may be undertaken in case of military necessity. If such a clause is *not* included in an article of the regulations, the prohibition contained in that article is *absolute*; but again, many of the most important articles do contain an "escape clause" relating to military necessity.

Max Huber, in his fundamental study of necessity in time of peace and war, developed four categories of necessity: (1) necessity of the State, that is, the necessity of safeguarding the vital interests, honor, and independence of the State; (2) necessity of war, that is, the necessity existing with reference to the attainment of the goal of the war, such as the siege of a city and the devastation of enemy territory (scorched earth policy); (3) military necessity, referring to the execution or securing of a single military operation, such as the use of certain means or methods of warfare, and seizure and destruction of property not specifically forbidden by mutual agreement; (4) real necessity *(eigentlicher Notstand)*, referring to the preservation of the life of a single person or several persons, such as the liberation or killing of prisoners because of a lack of food.

Practically all writers on the subject agreed in the past that there existed a necessity under certain conditions to do things and to use means which normally would be prohibited, even if they did not always go as far as the ancient maxim that "necessity knows no law". Regrettably enough, military manuals and law texts did not draw up any really clear-cut definition of necessity. Thus one otherwise excellent text stated that "military necessity sanctions measures by an occupant necessary to protect the safety of his forces and to facilitate the success of his operations." No formal qualification was given and a little later the authors amplified the foregoing by holding that "it [military necessity] would seem comprehensive enough to embrace the elimination of the source or cause of war although rooted in the enemy's traditional institutions." Such an unrestricted interpretation of the meaning of necessity could easily lead to serious breaches of international law and could serve as a virtually limitless reservoir of excuses for almost any and all acts of an occupant.

It has been said that "necessity" is used in three senses. First, there is the concept that all exercises of belligerent powers are justified only by military necessity in the sense of strategic advantage in winning the war. This interpretation would exclude all wanton destruction of life and property.

Second, there is the usual meaning of the term which recognizes that a special necessity to achieve an immediate military objective will justify exceptions from the rules of war, expressly justified by reference to military necessity. Third, there have been said to exist certain extreme types of necessity which would permit nonobservance of even the absolute rules of war. Conditions justifying reprisals, that is, retaliation for breaches of absolute rules of war by the enemy, are claimed to fall under this third type of necessity. The writer does not believe that absolute rules, or "positive prohibitions," can be set aside "lawfully" through a plan of "extreme necessity," as indicated below.

The widespread use of the concept of necessity as a defense by accused individuals in the various war crimes trials following the late [World War II] has started a re-examination of the problem on the part of courts, military personnel, and jurists. Little doubt can be found today for the view that military necessity cannot set aside the laws and customs of war and that a military commander cannot evade responsibility for his acts through a plea of necessity if there exists a *positive* prohibition, in customary or especially in conventional law, against a certain practice. In other words, the conventional law of war cannot recognize deviations from a rule through a claim of necessity unless that rule is qualified by an *explicit* reference to military necessity. That wording of Article 23(g) of the Hague Regulations **[Basic Document 2.2]** may be taken as a proof of this view—if necessity would or could override any or all provisions of the Regulations, necessity as a qualification would not have had to be spelled out in Article 23(g).

No general rule can be laid down as yet concerning the "escape clauses" in the Hague Regulations. Each particular instance in which a plea of military necessity is voiced in justification of the setting aside of a rule of law has to be judged on its own merits. The judgment of occupation authorities has to be measured against the known facts and, if at all possible, against any evidence that there existed an honest conviction to the effect that necessity proper existed. If a rule qualified by a reference to necessity has been set aside and it can be shown that an urgent need prompted the action in question, if the breach of the rule was accomplished, not by rash individual action, but under some form of supervised regulation or administration, then the plea of necessity would normally be upheld as valid. Yet, and this is the important point in view of the subject of this entire study, few if any of the measures likely to be undertaken by occupation authorities in enemy territory will reasonably contribute decisively to the end of the conflict, to the surrender of the enemy, or will be invested with supremely vital character; in other words, necessity proper will be almost impossible to prove, except in a few minor situations during the initial combat phases of the invasion of the enemy territory. It must be remembered that practically all measures of real importance undertaken by an occupant in hostile territory fall in a period of time when the military phase of active hostilities has passed from the occupied territory and when the occupant attempts to establish an orderly administration. Hence, there is an absence of nationally vital necessity and a lack of real necessity which would enable a successful employment of the defense in question.

THE DESTRUCTION OF PROPERTY

Article 23(g) of the Hague Regulations of 1907 supplies an excellent example of the compromise solution which has been produced by the recurring conflict between the humanitarian tendencies of international law and the stern realities of warfare: "It is especially forbidden ... to destroy or seize the enemy's property, unless such destruction or seizure be imperatively demanded by the necessities of war." Writers in other countries agree almost without exception but stress the important fact that the necessity has to be very urgent and vital if it is to justify any destruction of the property. If a real emergency forces an occupant to destroy public or private property, the injured party possesses no legal right to claim compensation either from the occupant or from its own legitimate sovereign (the same holds true in the case of destruction through direct military action during hostilities), although the latter quite commonly pays at least a part of the damage or loss after the end of the war as a gesture recognizing the suffering and losses of the affected party.

Any destruction, devastation, or seizure of private property beyond the obvious demands of a genuine military emergency places the occupant in the position of having violated the laws of war.... The writer believes that the offending belligerent would be subject to claims for such losses, that legal action could be undertaken against him [sic] and against the individuals responsible for the destruction even if a subsequent peace treaty were to provide for restitution or reparation. This opinion is based on the wording of Article 53 of the Fourth Geneva Convention of 1949 which reads:

> Any destruction by the Occupying Power of real or personal property belonging individually or collectively to private persons, or to the State, or to other public authorities, or to social or cooperative organizations, is prohibited, except where such destruction is rendered absolutely necessary by military operations.

7.   Richard A. Falk and Burns H. Weston, "The Relevance of International Law to Palestinian Rights in the West Bank and Gaza: In Legal Defense of the Intifada," 32 Harv. Int'l L. J. 129, 138–43 (1991).

Regarding the contention that Geneva IV [**Basic Document 2.12**] does not apply to Israel's presence in the West Bank and Gaza, the Israeli Government appears to have relied upon and adopted the argument of the "missing reversioner" advanced in 1968 by Professor Yehuda Z. Blum, then a lecturer in international law at the Hebrew University of Jerusalem, later Israel's Permanent Representative to the United Nations during the period of the government of Menachem Begin.[1] The crux of this argument is that the law of belligerent occupation in general, and Geneva IV in particular, presupposes that the belligerent occupant shall have displaced a "legitimate sovereign" (to whom the territory in question shall revert following the cessation of hostilities); that neither Jordan in the West Bank nor Egypt in Gaza were legitimate sovereigns (or "reversioners") in 1967 because of their acts of alleged unlawful aggression during Israel's "War of Independence" in 1948–49; and that the Government of Israel is therefore released from the constraints of the law of belligerent occupation in general and Geneva IV in particular. According to this argument, Israel's presence in the West Bank

---

1. See Y. Blum, *The Missing Reversioner:*   ria, 3 Isr. L. Rev. 279 (1968).
Reflections on the Status of Judea and Sama-

and Gaza is not an "occupation" that displaces a sovereign power, but an "administration" in the absence of a sovereign, unaccountable to Geneva IV and the law of belligerent occupation generally—although the argument is sometimes made, too, that Israel is present in the West Bank and Gaza as a result of a "defensive conquest" that confers legal title in the absence of a prior sovereign. Since 1977, when the Likud was first elected to power, Israel has insisted that the occupied territories fall within Israel's exclusive sovereign domain, that they form an integral part of "Greater Israel," constituting ancient Judea and Samaria, in respect of which the humanitarian laws of war are inapplicable.

Somewhat analogously, albeit less to escape the constraints of the humanitarian law of war than to ensure the legitimacy of Israeli settlements in the West Bank and Gaza, Professor Eugene V. Rostow, Professor Emeritus of the Yale Law School, now at the National Defense University in Washington, D.C., takes the view that the failure of the international community so far to achieve any final resolution of the underlying territorial status of the West Bank and Gaza results in a continuing lease on life for the Palestine Mandate which, authorizing Jews to settle throughout the mandate territory, includes the West Bank.[2] Relying upon analogies drawn from the Namibia advisory opinions of the International Court of Justice, including the Advisory Opinion on the International Status of South–West Africa,[3] Professor Rostow thus contends that the 1917 Balfour Declaration,[4] calling for a Jewish "national home" in Palestine and repeated in the 1922 League of Nations Mandate for Palestine,[5] is the law applicable in the occupied territories, not Geneva IV or the law of belligerent occupation generally.

Finally, there is Professor Allan Gerson's argument that the special, prolonged character of Israel's occupation [over thirty years as of the writing of this coursebook] renders Israel "a trustee-occupant" rather than "a belligerent-occupant" of the West Bank and Gaza.[6] Professor Gerson acknowledges that the Palestinian inhabitants possess a legal entitlement to some reasonable form of autonomy (to be shaped by an eventual settlement of the Israeli–Palestinian dispute); but the effect of his argument, which would terminate the status of belligerent occupation, is to give Israel greater discretion during the period of Israel's continuing occupation than is conferred by Geneva IV. Israel becomes the *de facto* sovereign power according to this line of thinking.

These and similar arguments, we submit, are strained and artificial, and have commanded little to no respect among "highly qualified publicists" or within the organized international community. Professor Blum's "missing reversioner" thesis, in addition to requiring a method of treaty interpretation that is unknown to international law (*i.e.*, a disregard of the expressed

---

2. *See* E. Rostow, *"Palestinian Self–Determination": Possible Futures for the Unallocated Territories of the Palestine Mandate*, 5 Yale Stud. World Pub. Order 147 (1979).

3. International Status of South–West Africa, 1950 ICJ 128 (Advisory Opinion of July 11).

4. For convenient text, see The Arab–Israeli Conflict—Readings and Documents 484–85 (J. N. Moore ed., 1977).

5. *See* 2 Report to the General Assembly of the United Nations Special Committee on Pal-

estine–Annexes, Appendix and Maps 18–22, UN Doc. A/364 Add. 1 (9 Sep 47). For convenient text, see Moore, *supra* note 4, at 891–901.

6. *See* A. Gerson, Israel, The West Bank and International Law 78–82 (1978); A. Gerson, *Trustee-Occupant: The Legal Status of Israel's Presence in the West Bank*, 14 Harv. Int'l L. J. 1 (1973).

purposes and cognate negotiating history of Geneva IV[7]), is premised on a wrong provision of Geneva IV[8] and, in any event, is unsupported by authority or practice. Professor Rostow's "continuing mandate" argument makes light of both the terminating acts of Great Britain as mandatory power and the unanimous authoritative decision of the United Nations mandate, which itself provides one of the firmest legal grounds for Israel's own legal status as a sovereign State. In addition, Professor Gerson's "trustee-occupant" theory rests essentially on the personal authority of Professor Gerson himself, having no support in the relevant legal literature or the appraisals of territorial status made by competent international institutions and being unpersuasive as a matter of policy. For all the ingenuity these lines of argument display, they are not juridically credible and have been influential neither with the wider community of international law specialists, including scholars more or less sympathetic to Israel, nor with diplomats. Not even the United States, Israel's principal ally and benefactor, gives credence to these arguments.

To be sure, the character of belligerent occupation always has been somewhat problematic, and it has been complicated in the present instance by the confused and overlapping claims to sovereign identity that have attached to the West Bank and Gaza both prior to and since the 1967 Six Day War. King Hussein's decision in July 1988 to respect "the wish of the P.L.O., the sole legitimate representative of the Palestinian people, to secede from us in an independent Palestinian state," and consequently to break Jordan's legal and administrative ties to the West Bank,[9] added a further layer of perplexity even as it simplified, for the moment, the number of political actors asserting sovereign rights in the territories.

Nevertheless, in its essence, the institution of belligerent occupation, however prolonged, represents an acknowledgment by governments (relatively recent, historically speaking) that territorial changes may not normally be effected by force of arms. It represents a step away from the notion that there is a right to territory acquired by conquest; it reinforces and complements the contemporary legal notion that war, regardless of circumstance, no longer provides a legal foundation for territorial claims. However instituted, belligerent occupation connotes only a temporary, provisional circumstance and an implicit duty to withdraw once hostilities have been brought to an end.

Thus, while a belligerent occupant clearly has certain rights—for example, to assert some practical claims against the indigenous population and to protect its own security interests, as acknowledged in Hague IV—the conventional and customary law of war requires the belligerent occupant to defer to the pre-belligerency political identity of the occupied territory and to act as if the territory's former status had not been superseded or even suspended for the duration of hostilities. This conception of belligerent occupation obliges

---

7. Professor Blum disregards the fact that Geneva IV is concerned with protecting an occupied people from the abuses of the occupying power at least as much as it is concerned with protecting the ousted sovereign's reversionary interest.

8. Professor Blum relied erroneously on the *second* paragraph of article 2, which addresses an occupation that "meets with no armed resistance," a circumstance quite unlike that

which greeted the commencement of Israel's occupation of the West Bank and Gaza, which began during the 1967 Six Day War. Professor Blum should have relied instead on the *first* paragraph of article 2, which addresses an occupation that begins in "cases of declared war or of any other armed conflict . . .".

9. N.Y. Times, 1 Aug 88, at A1, col. 6.

the occupant to sustain the pre-occupation character of all facets of civilian life, respecting the dignity and well-being of the occupied people as much as possible. Exceptions may be made only to the extent that they are *reasonably* required for the security of its occupation—and even then, doing so in a manner that places minimum burdens on the occupied population. The ultimate purpose of the law of belligerent occupation, it may be said, is to facilitate the prospects for an eventual peace agreement.

In sum, the forcible occupation of a territory beyond its existing boundaries is treated by the modern law of war, *including the customary law of war that applies in the current era*, as a temporary, provisional, reversible incident of ongoing hostilities. It is on the basis of this normative judgment that an overwhelming consensus of the world community, including on several occasions the United States government, endorses the view that Israel's maximum legal claim on the West Bank and in Gaza is based on its temporary supervisory control of these territories pursuant to the law of belligerent occupation, which entails a duty to comply with Hague IV and, more significantly, Geneva IV. It is not merely the Arab countries, the Islamic world, or even the Third World generally, but the entire United Nations—excepting Israel—that resists Israel's arguments to the contrary.

[*Eds.*—Professors Falk and Weston go on to consider the cogency of the defense of security concerns or military necessity. They conclude, at 150: "if it can be empirically substantiated, as indeed it can be, that Israel's unlawful policies and practices *vis-à-vis* the West Bank and Gaza are themselves the principal cause of the violence against which Israel retaliates on grounds of military necessity ..., then ... Israel is estopped from pleading a defense in respect of acts that have been provoked primarily by its own illegal policies and practices and for which it has ultimately itself to blame."]

8. Editors' Note. The occupation of Iraq after the March 2003 invasion by the United States and other members of the "Coalition of the Willing" raises important questions about the scope of the obligations imposed on occupying powers by the Geneva conventions regime. Given that one rationale for the invasion was the replacement of the government of Saddam Hussein, should the Geneva IV's conservative approach to changing the structures of governance in an occupied territory bind the coalition? The following reading addresses this issue.

9. Thomas Grant, "Iraq: How to Reconcile Conflicting Obligations of Occupation and Reform," A.S.I.L. Insight (June 2003).

When L. Paul Bremer III, the lead US administrator for the transition in Iraq, told a *Washington Post* reporter [in May 2003] "[o]ccupation is an ugly word, not one Americans feel comfortable with, but it's a fact,"[10] he stated the obvious: forces of the United States and its coalition allies stand in effective control of post-Saddam Iraq (or much of it). However, Mr. Bremer's statement raises a legal question without an obvious answer: how can restrictive language in the Fourth Geneva Convention and its implicit assumption that any occupation should be purely temporary and not for imposing a particular form of government be reconciled with obligations to rebuild and reform Iraq?

10. "Adjusting to Iraq," Sunday, 1 Jun 2003, p. B06

The 1949 Geneva Convention [No. IV] relative to the Protection of Civilian Persons in Time of War **[Basic Document 2.12]** provides that an Occupying Power (capitals provided in the Convention) may not "alter the status of public officials or judges in the occupied territories ... should they abstain from fulfilling their functions for reasons of conscience" (art. 54). It also requires the Occupying Power to leave the penal laws of the occupied country unchanged, subject to narrow exceptions (art. 64). The earlier Hague Regulations concerning the Law and Customs of War on Land **[Basic Document 2.2]** also restrict the occupant from changing local law. Both treaties are expressly invoked in paragraph 5 of Security Council resolution 1483 of May 22, 2003.[a]

But the resolution plainly conceives the coalition effecting on Iraqi politics, law, and institutions an overhaul, the scope of which will be nothing short of radical. In conjunction with the UN and an Iraqi interim administration, the coalition is called on to create "conditions in which the Iraqi people can freely determine their own political future" (resolution ¶ 4); "establish national and local institutions for representative governance;" and "encourag[e] international efforts to promote legal and judicial reform" (¶ 8). Scarcely any of the political, legal, or institutional infrastructure for this existed under the Ba'ath dictatorship, so it is not immediately clear how the coalition will both fulfill the task of reform identified in Res. 1483 and abide by the "no change" rule implied in the treaties.

One argument that might be made to avoid conflict is that the coalition powers do not constitute "occupying powers" for purposes of the Convention. This, however, would have to account for language in the preamble to Res. 1483. The preamble—though the preamble only—refers to the coalition powers in Iraq as "occupying powers," "recognizing the specific authorities, responsibilities, and obligations under applicable international law of these states as occupying powers." The British and American Permanent Representatives, in a letter delivered to the President of the Security Council on May 8, do not use the term "occupying power" at all.[11] It is far from clear that absence of the term is meant to characterize the coalition presence one way or the other. Substantive paragraphs 4 and 5 of Res. 1483 refer to obligations under international law—including, expressly, the Geneva Conventions and Hague Regulations which contain important provisions relevant to occupation—but any conclusion to be drawn from paragraphs 4 and 5 as to the status of the coalition Authority has to be drawn by inference; the paragraphs do not contain the term 'occupying power.' Inclusion of the term 'occupying power' in the substantive paragraphs of Res. 1483 would have clarified the situation. One may speculate whether its absence reflects a compromise at the drafting stage.

It may be wondered, too, whether the status "occupying power" is relevant, where no alternative locus of authority exists. The Hague Regula-

a. *See* SC Res. 1483, UN SCOR, 67th Sess., 4761st mtg., UN Doc. S/RES/1483 (2003).

11. Note citation by PBS to the May 8 letter as "the first time the United States has referred to its role in Iraq as an 'occupying power,'" at <http://www.pbs.org/newshour/updates/un_05–09–03.html>. The text of letter in fact does not contain the expression 'occupying power.' *See* S/2003/538. *Letter dated 8 May 2003 from the Permanent Representatives of the United Kingdom of Great Britain and Northern Ireland and the United States of America to the United Nations addressed to the President of the Security Council.*

tions and the Fourth Geneva Convention, in references to the "legitimate" authority and its on-going rights, might be seen to address situations where one military force continues in opposition against another—that is, situations where a force has lost effective control over territory but remains, to some degree, a viable entity, either continuing organized resistance from the unoccupied parts of its territory or establishing an exile presence with which to continue prosecuting, if only legally, a claim, broadly recognized, that its state holds *de jure* the rights of governance. The treaty obligations attach to the other force, which stands in occupation and must exercise certain incidents of local administration. The coalition in Iraq presents a case distinct from certain past cases of occupation, in the sense that, though the Iraqi state continues to hold all rights to its territory, there remains now no governmental organ that can exercise those rights—apart from the coalition itself. Yet the case of occupied Germany, much in the minds of the drafters of the Geneva Conventions in 1949, very much resembled that of Iraq, in the sense that, there too, no viable alternative locus of authority existed. The view will gain adherents that the coalition does constitute an Occupying Power and thus faces the restrictions inherent in that status. It is already the view prevalent amongst publicists,[12] and amongst governments and international organizations may become so as well.[13]

The "Coalition Provisional Authority" (as the May 8 letter titles it) or the "Authority" (as Res. 1483 titles it) therefore will be challenged to fulfill obligations incumbent upon and respect limits inhering in the status of an occupying power. A number of approaches present themselves. For one, the Authority may note that the restrictive language of the Fourth Geneva Convention is tempered by reservations permitting certain changes pursuant to good governance during occupation. For example, judges—whom the Convention permits to resign for reasons of conscience—may be replaced by the Occupying Power in the interests of maintaining the functions of the judiciary. The Occupying Power may take other legal and administrative measures to protect its own personnel, the Convention making allowance for such measures in light of the dangers an occupant well may face.

Yet the reservations to the restrictive language were tailored narrowly, and they were not intended in the nature of a license. Pictet noted in particular that the Occupying Power may not change the laws of the occupied territory "simply to bring them into accord with its own juridical conceptions."[14] This approaches the heart of the matter: Occupation was conceived as a temporary status, and effects it might have on a territory transitory. The specific provisions of the Fourth Convention restrict change by an Occupying Power, while leaving some margin for measures necessitated by circumstance. A purpose implied at root beneath the Fourth Convention, however, seems to

---

12. *See, e.g.,* J. Paust, *The US as Occupying Power Over Portions of Iraq and Relevant Responsibilities under International Law,* ASIL Insights (Apr. 2003).

13. The UN Secretary–General took the view on April 24, 2003. Reported in Jonathan Fowler, *US Bridles as UN's Kofi Annan Calls It "Occupying Power,"* Associated Press, 24 Apr 2003.

14. Jean S. Pictet, *Commentaire: IV La Convention de Genève relative à la protection*

des personnes civiles en temps de guerre (Comité International de la Croix–Rouge, 1956), p. 360. Exceptions to the requirement to leave local laws intact were also incorporated into the Hague Regulations of 1907, but, those, too, in the view of contemporary publicists, were to be applied narrowly. *See* T. Holland, *The Laws of War on Land* (Oxford: Clarendon Press, 1907), at 53.

have been to prevent an occupant from imposing its will through permanent constitutional change. In this, the reform mission expressed in Res. 1483 remains in tension with the treaty obligations of the Occupying Powers, even as they avail themselves of the reservations to the restrictive language of the Convention.

An alternative approach may be to bring Iraqi political organs rapidly into play as supervening instances over the Authority. Changes in governance in Iraq then might be characterized as the decisions of the interim administration—an organ defined in Res. 1483 as constituted by Iraqis and thus, perhaps, not under the limits facing an occupying power. But the Authority is itself bid in the reform process to act, suggesting that the responsibilities of the process are not meant to be discharged by the interim administration acting alone. Moreover, the interim administration itself seems to be conceived in the resolution as a creature of the Authority.

The better view may be that Res. 1483 has created a "carve out" from the Hague Regulations and Fourth Geneva Convention, leaving other provisions of the treaties in force, but suspending with respect to the Authority those provisions that otherwise would curb its license to change the laws, institutions, and personnel of the occupied state. This would reconcile the conflict noted above, without draining paragraph 5 of Res. 1483 of content.

It does not seem too remarkable a proposition, that a resolution of the Security Council could carve out such provisions. The Security Council has sweeping dispositive authority, as evidenced by its resolutions establishing a legal basis for such ambitious programs as the independence of East Timor or administration of Kosovo, not to mention power to create upon the member states obligations, which, owing to Article 103 of the Charter, enjoy primacy over treaty obligations, where the two conflict. If it has used the authority wisely, the Council will be seen to have carved from the treaties an exemption just broad enough to permit an Occupying Power to execute in Iraq the mission the Council itself has defined.

SECTION 5.   DISCUSSION NOTES/QUESTIONS

1. What constitutes "belligerent occupation?" Consider the following definition from Myres S. McDougal & Florentino P. Feliciano, Law and Minimum World Public Order 732–33 (1961, 1994):

> "Belligerent occupation" is used to refer to stages or specific contexts in which, following successful invasion, assault, and beginning stabilization, the destruction of organized resistance is effected within a larger or lesser area, the resulting enemy troops are expelled, and a considerable measure of effective control established. This degree of control signified by "belligerent occupation" is commonly accompanied by and manifested in the constituting of structures of governmental administration within the occupied territory. "Belligerent occupation" is, of course, "military" occupation in the sense that it is established and principally maintained by means of armed force. "Military occupation," however, in contradistinction to belligerent occupation, is appropriately taken to refer to occupation established and maintained at the termination stages of a process of coercion, that is, after the general close of hostilities and the final surrender of one belligerent to the other.... Success in establishing substantial control and firm possession distinguishes the stage

of belligerent occupation from that of invasion. It also serves to crystallize the expectations of the inhabitants of the region involved that, for the immediate foreseeable future, the belligerent occupant, in lieu of the ousted sovereign, will in fact assert and exercise authority over such region. . . .

Is Caucasia's occupation of Parsa's East Valley a "belligerent occupation" or a "military occupation"? What difference might it make, if any? For discussion in the context of Israel's relationship with Palestine, see John B. Quigley, *Loan Guarantees, Israeli Settlements and Middle East Peace*, 25 Vand. J. Transnat'l L. 547 (1992).

2. The laws of war and of belligerent occupation, as "codified" in the 1907 Hague Convention (No. IV) Respecting the Laws and Customs of War on Land **(Basic Document 2.2)**, the 1949 Geneva Convention (No. IV) Relative to the Protection of Civilian Persons in Time of War **(Basic Document 2.12)**, and the 1977 Geneva Protocol Additional (No. I) to the Geneva Conventions of 12 August 1949, and Relating to the Protection of Victims of International Armed Conflicts **(Basic Document 2.31)**, seek to achieve a balance between the customary principles of military necessity and humanity. As applied to the situation of belligerent occupancy, the belligerent occupant is conceded to have authority to promote and ensure the security of its occupation force and the civilian population of the occupied territory, but its actions taken to effectuate these ends are not unlimited. In general, the principles of military necessity and humanity limit the lawful exercise of coercion to that which is strictly necessary, relevant, and proportionate to the realization of legitimate military objectives and to respect the human rights of the occupied people. Precisely where the critical line is to be drawn, however, is not easily determined in many instances. Where should the presumption lie as between the duty of the inhabitants of a militarily occupied territory to obey the commands of the occupying authority and the duty of the occupying power to respect and provide for the humane treatment of the inhabitants of the occupied territory? Does the amorphous principle of military necessity give the occupying power a convenient pretext to disregard the well-being of an occupied people? Does the equally vague principle of humanity give to an occupied people an unlimited right to engage in civil disobedience?

An issue that emerged dramatically following the invasion of Iraq in 2003 was the duty of the occupying power to restore and ensure public order and safety per Article 6 of Geneva Convention No. IV. The National Museum of Iraq was looted shortly after the invasion, with Coalition troops doing little to prevent it. A further contentious issue is whether a Security Council resolution relating to the conduct of the occupation, such as Security Council Resolution 1483 discussed in Reading 9, *supra*, have the effect of superseding the Geneva Conventions regime?

For discussion of the bounds of military necessity and the principle of humanity, see Richard A. Falk & Burns H. Weston, *The Relevance of International Law to Palestinian Rights in the West Bank and Gaza: In Legal Defense of the Intifada*, 32 Harv. Int'l L. J. 129 (1991), at 144–50 (omitted from Reading 7, *supra*, wherein this article is extracted).

3. In *International Law and the Territories*, 32 Harv. J. Int'l L. 457 (1991), Professor Michael Curtis, a political scientist, contended that Geneva IV **(Basic Document 2.12)** does not apply in the case of Israel's military occupation of the West Bank and Gaza Strip, arguing, at 487, that the Convention is intended for short-term military occupation, not for what might be called the *sui generis* situation in the territories. He also contended, at 480–81, that 1977 Protocol Additional (No. I) to the Geneva Conventions **(Basic Document 2.31)** does not

apply to the West Bank and Gaza Strip either. In these contentions, he was in harmony with the Government of Israel which has further argued, in the case of Gaza, that, since the Gaza Strip had been under Egyptian administration when Israel occupied it in 1967, Israel had simply succeeded to the status of administrator and thus could not be considered a belligerent occupant. Based on your reading of Geneva IV and Protocol Additional No. I, do you agree with these arguments? Why? Why not? For pertinent discussion, see Ahmad H. Tabari, Note, *Humanitarian Law: Deportation of Palestinians from the West Bank and Gaza*, 29 Harv. Int'l L. J. 552 (1988).

Professor Curtis is of course at odds with the Falk–Weston article extracted in Reading 7, *supra*, and cited in foregoing Discussion Note/Question 2. Indeed, in his essay, he vigorously criticized the Falk–Weston article for being "political advocacy" rather than a proper, circumspect argument based on international law. Do you agree? Disagree? Professor Curtis, it merits notice, makes a number of points about the political context of the Israeli occupation. First, he writes, at 460, "the core of the Arab–Israeli conflict remains ... the implacable opposition by Arab states, except Egypt since 1979, to the Jewish presence in the Mandate area of Palestine and, since 1948, to the existence of the state of Israel." Second, he contends, at 461, "Israel is often unfairly held to a higher moral standard than that to which other countries are held." Additionally, he argues, at *id.*, "[t]hat the United Nations has focused its attention disproportionately on Israel, while generally ignoring other countries' blatant human rights violations, detracts from any legitimacy the resolutions may have as evidence of international law." Professor Curtis argues, at 463, that Arab belligerence against Israel, the then continuing Arab call for Israel's elimination, the emergence of Islamic extremism, and the nature of the Palestine Liberation Organization (specifically its support of Saddam Hussein during the 1990–91 Persian Gulf War) justify Israel's holding the occupied territories until peace is made. What weight should these factors be given in international law? How do they square with the international law of belligerent occupation? Is Professor Curtis himself engaging in "political advocacy"? For possible answers, see Professor Falk's and Professor Weston's response to Professor Curtis, in Richard A. Falk & Burns H. Weston, *The Israeli–Occupied Territories, International Law, and the Boundaries of Scholarly Discourse: A Reply to Michael Curtis*, 33 Harv. Int'l L. J. 191 (1992).

4.   Are arguments of self-determination relevant to Caucasia's occupation of Parsa's North Valley? How might they may be made? For readings on the right to self-determination, see *infra* Section 4–F in Problem 5–1 ("Ethnic Conflict and Its Consequences in Slavia, Candia, and Corcyra"), at 558.

5.   The prescriptions in the various modern conventions on the laws of war recognize that territorial changes normally may not be effected by force. This fact represents a profound change from past practice, which sanctioned territorial acquisition through conquest. A complementary principle is that belligerent occupation is to be only temporary with an implicit duty on the part of the occupying power to withdraw once hostilities have been terminated. Is this a desirable trend? Why? Why not?

6.   Common Article 2 of the Geneva Conventions **(Basic Documents 2.9, 2.10, 2.11, & 2.12)** declares that "the present Convention shall apply to all cases of declared war or any other armed conflict which may arise between two or more of the High Contracting Parties...." Are the terms of the Conventions binding only on States that are party to them? The issue of whether the Geneva Conventions are conventional or customary law has been widely discussed. *See,*

e.g. the decision of the International Court of Justice in *Military and Paramilitary Activities in and against Nicaragua (Nicaragua v. United States)*, 1986 ICJ 14 (Jun 27). *See also* Theodor Meron, *The Geneva Conventions as Customary Law*, 81 A.J.I.L. 348 (1987).

7.   The issue of control over natural resources, particularly water, has been a significant element in the Israeli–Palestinian conflict, as it is in the instant problem. In the case of the "Coalition of the Willing's" occupation of Iraq in 2003, control over Iraq's oil was contentious. Security Council Resolution 1483, discussed in Reading 9 *supra*, effectively gave control over disbursement of oil revenues to the Coalition rather than the UN, although it stipulated that the proceeds should be spent to benefit the people of Iraq. The Resolution also cancelled all existing legal rights to Iraq's oil, giving the Coalition the right to sell the oil to whoever it chose, on whatever terms. What are the international laws with respect to the use of natural resources in an occupied territory? *See* articles 53 and 55 of the 1907 Hague Regulations **(Basic Document 2.2)**, Article 55 of the 1949 Geneva Convention No. IV **(Basic Document 2.12)**, and Article 54 of 1977 Protocol Additional No. I **(Basic Document 2.31)**. For a discussion of the tensions provoked by Israel's use of the West Bank aquifer, see Jamal L. El–Hindi, Note, *The West Bank Aquifer and Conventions Regarding Laws of Belligerent Occupation*, 11 Mich. J. Int'l L. 1400 (1990).

8.   Another issue raised in this present problem is that of the replacement of Parsan laws on freedom of movement, speech, and assembly. What is the international law on the rights of a belligerent occupier in this respect? John Quigley discusses this question in *The Relation Between Human Rights Law and the Law of Belligerent Occupation: Does An Occupied Population Have A Right to Freedom of Assembly and Expression?*, 12 B.C. Int'l & Comp. L. Rev. 1 (1989).

9.   The Palestinian uprising ("intifada" or "intifadeh") begun in December 1987 helped to focus world attention on the almost four decades-old Israeli occupation of the West Bank and Gaza, found by many authoritative observers to be violative of the humanitarian rules of armed conflict specifically, and of the human rights of the occupied Palestinian people generally. Do these circumstances justify active, even armed, resistance by an occupied people in the face of a duty under the law of belligerent occupation to obey the rules and regulations of the occupier?

By the turn of the new century, proposals for new peace agreements made in the 1990s had failed and various vaguer alternatives took their place—for example, the United States—sponsored "Road Map." *See* SC Res 1515, UN SCOR, 58th Sess., 4862d mtg., UN Doc. S/RES/1515 (2003). Ongoing problems include the continued building of Israeli settlements in the West Bank and by the Israeli practice of closing off the Gaza Strip and West Bank at various times in retaliation to bomb attacks in Israel. For a discussion of the international legal implications of closure, see the Palestinian Centre for Human Rights, The Israeli Policy of Closure: Legal, Political and Humanitarian Evaluation (1996). The Palestinian Centre for Human Rights argues that Israel continues to be an Occupying Power, despite the limited autonomy granted under the interim agreements to the Palestine National Authority and the redeployment of the Israeli Army from most of the territories, citing articles 6, 7, 8 and 47 of 1949 Geneva Convention No. IV **(Basic Document 2.12)**. It contends that the closures violate Israel's obligations under the fourth Geneva Convention because they are reprisals for bomb attacks and effectively constitute collective punishment of the civilian population. The Centre also points to the blocking of imports of basic food and medical supplies and the continued building of Israeli settlements inside the territories as violations of the fourth Geneva Convention, citing articles 14–23, 33, 55–57, and 59–61. The Centre concludes, at xi:

> The extent of the social, political and economic damages sustained by the Palestinian people as a result of ... closure has been of such consequence that the peace process itself has been further undermined.... The closure is an all too tangible reminder for the Palestinian people that Israeli occupation and control over the lives of Palestinians in the Occupied Territories is still very much a reality, despite the re-deployment of Israeli forces out of major population centres and the existence of peace agreements and a peace process.

Israel's obligations under the Fourth Geneva Convention were considered also by the World Court in its advisory opinion on *The Legal Consequences of the Construction of a Wall in the Occupied Palestinian Territory*, 2004 ICJ 131 (Jul 9). The Court was asked by the UN General Assembly to rule on the legality of a barrier wall built by Israel to deter Palestinian attacks. Observing that the route of the wall chosen by Israel includes within its "Closed Area" (between the wall and the "Green Line") some 80% of the settlers living in the Occupied Palestinian Territory, recalling that previously the Security Council had ruled Israel's policy of establishing settlements in that Territory to be a "flagrant violation" of Geneva IV **(Basic Document 2.12)**, and noting that the route of the wall would prejudge the future frontier between Israel and Palestine, the Court found, 14 votes to one, Judge Buergenthal dissenting, that "the construction of the wall and its associated régime create[d] a 'fait accompli' on the ground that could well become permanent, in which case, and notwithstanding the formal characterization of the wall by Israel, it would be tantamount to *de facto* annexation" (¶ 121). The Court further concluded that the route chosen for the wall "gave expression *in loco* to the illegal measures taken by Israel" vis-à-vis the Israeli settlements and Jerusalem, also "entailed further alterations to the demographic composition of the Occupied Palestinian Territory," and thus "severely impedes the exercise by the Palestinian people of its right to self-determination, and is therefore a breach of Israel's obligation to respect that right" (¶ 122). The General Assembly's request to the Court for this advisory opinion was strongly opposed by a number of countries, including Australia and the US on the grounds that the question of the wall was a political rather than a legal issue. Do you agree with this "political question" claim? Why? Why not?

10. The Israeli Supreme Court has played an important role in the military occupation of the West Bank and Gaza Strip. Attempts have been made to use the Court to rule on aspects of the occupation. For example, the Court has considered the practice of demolishing the homes of Palestinians suspected or convicted of terrorism. In *The Demolition of Homes in the Israeli Occupied Territories*, 19 Yale J. Int'l L. 1 (1994), Dan Simon analyzed the attitude of the Court toward such demolitions, noting three distinct phases in the Court's rulings. Before 1979, the Court did not consider any demolitions; between 1979 and 1989, the Court approved the practice on the grounds that the local (military) law in force in the territories overrode international law; and since 1989 some judges have been much more critical of demolition orders, so as to lead to some curtailment of the practice. What scope should be given to local law in such contexts? *See* Article 43 of the 1907 Hague Regulations **(Basic Document 2.2)** and Article 64 of Geneva Convention No. IV **(Basic Document 2.12)**?

11. Caucasia's occupation of Parsa is based in part on the Israeli occupation of the West Bank and Gaza Strip. Another case of military occupation is that of

Indonesia's occupation of East Timor, one-half the island of Timor in the Timor Sea to the northwest of Australia from 1975 until 1999, although Indonesia consistently asserted that East Timor was a legitimate part of its territory. For an argument that Indonesia was a belligerent occupant of East Timor and thus bound by Geneva IV **(Basic Document 2.12)**, see Daniel Machover, *International Humanitarian Law and the Indonesian Occupation of East Timor*, in Catholic Institute for International Relations and International Platform of Jurists for East Timor: International Law and the Question of East Timor 205 (1995). *See also* Christine Chinkin, *East Timor: A Failure of Decolonisation* 20 Austl. Y.B.I.L. 35 (2000); Iain G. M. Scobbie & Catriona J. Drew, *Self-Determination Undetermined: The Case of East Timor*, 9 Leiden J. Int'l L. 185 (1996).

The US treatment of prisoners detained from the war in Afghanistan in 2001 and held at its naval base at Guantánamo Bay in Cuba also serves as backdrop for this Problem 4–3. Geneva III and IV **(Basic Documents 2.11 & 2.12)** grant a variety of procedural and substantive rights to prisoners of war and inhabitants of an occupied territory. A threshold issue is whether the Parsans held by Caucasia for their actions during the occupation can be termed "prisoners of war" as defined in Geneva III. Consider the definition of "prisoners of war" in Article 4 of Geneva III. What arguments can be made for and against this status? Note that Article 5 of Geneva III states that, where the status of a detainee is unclear, a special tribunal should be established to determine the matter and that, until the determination is made, the detainee should be considered a prisoner of war.

The United States initially refused to regard any of the detainees at its naval base at Guantánamo Bay as "prisoners of war," deeming all of them "unlawful combatants" who had no rights under Geneva III. Under international pressure, Washington modified this position somewhat to concede that those fighting for the Taliban, the then Afghan government against which war was waged, were covered by Geneva III; however, not as "prisoners of war" and excluding all al-Qaeda fighters not just from Geneva III but from the entire Geneva regime, including Geneva IV. Geneva IV provides broad protection for persons in the hands of an occupying power of which they are not nationals (art. 4). What are the requirements of Geneva III and IV for the constitution of courts to try prisoners of war or inhabitants of an occupied territory? For analysis of these issues, see, *e.g.*, Erin Choplak, *Dealing with the Detainees at Guantánamo Bay: Humanitarian and Human Rights Obligations under the Geneva Conventions*, 9 Hum. Rts. Br. 6 (Spring 2002). See also, generally, Lisa Hajjar, *Torture and the Future*, in Middle East Report Online (May 2004), *available at* <http://merip.org/mero/interventions/hajjar_interv.html>; Michael Ratner & Ellen Ray, *Guantánamo: What the World Should Know* (2004) and David Rose, *Guantánamo: America's War on Human Rights* (2004).

12. *Bibliographical Note.* For supplemental discussion concerning the principal themes addressed in this problem, consult the following additional specialized materials:

(a) *Books/Monographs/Reports/Symposia.* E. Benvenisti, The International Law of Occupation (1992); M. Bothe, K. Partsch, & W. Solf, with the collaboration of Martin Eaton, New Rules for Victims of Armed Conflicts—Commentary on the Two 1977 Protocols Additional to the Geneva Conventions of 1949 (1982); S. Flappan, The Birth of Israel—Myths and Realities (1987); G. Frankel, Beyond the Promised Land: Jews and Arabs on the Hard Road to a New Israel (1994); A. Gerson, Israel, The West Bank and International Law (1978); D. Grossman, The Yellow Wind (1988); The Laws of Armed Conflicts (D. Schindler & J. Toman eds.,

1988); W. Mallison & S. Mallison, The Palestine Problem In International Law And World Order (1986); W. O'Brien, Law and Morality in Israel's War with the PLO (1991); J. Quigley, Palestine and Israel: A Challenge to Justice (1990); R. Shehadeh, Occupier's Law: Israel And The West Bank (rev. ed. 1988); J. Stone, Israel And Palestine: Assault on The Law of Nations (1981); The Arab–Israeli Accords: Legal Perspectives (E. Cotran, C. Mallat & D. Scott eds., 1996).

(b) *Articles/Book Chapters*. Y. Blum, *The Missing Reversioner: Reflections on the Status of Judea and Samaria*, 3 Israel L. Rev. 279 (1968); M. Carroll, *The Israeli Demolition of Palestinian Houses in the Occupied Territories: An Analysis of Its Legality in International Law*, 11 Mich. J. Int'l L. 1195 (1990); A. Imseis, *On the Fourth Geneva Convention and the Occupied Palestinian Territory*, 44 Harv. Int'l L. J. 65 (2003); Y. Lootsteen, *The Concept of Belligerency in International Law,* 166 Mil. L. Rev. 109 (2000); M. Marcus, *Humanitarian Intervention without Borders: Belligerent Occupation or Colonization?*, 25 Hous. J. Int'l L 99 (2002); E. Rostow, *"Palestinian Self–Determination": Possible Futures for the Unallocated Territories of the Palestine Mandate*, 5 Yale Stud. World Pub. Order 147 (1979); A. Wing, *Legal Decision–Making During the Palestinian Intifada: Embryonic Self–Rule*, 18 Yale J. Int'l. L. 95 (1993).

Problem 4–4

Environmental Warfare in Khalifan

SECTION 1.   FACTS

A life-sustaining feature of Southwestern Asia is the Tiphrates River. Originating in the Anatolian Mountains, it flows southeasterly through Amirabia and Khalifan into the Arabian Gulf (*see infra* Figure 4–4.1). Amirabia is a modernizing oil-rich country under the military dictatorship of General Ali Tikrit. Its economy is based primarily on the export of oil and, to smaller extent, on agricultural products grown in the irrigated regions adjacent to the Tiphrates River. Khalifan, a two hundred years-old sheikdom, also exports oil and relies upon the rich soils of the Tiphrates River delta for substantial agricultural production.

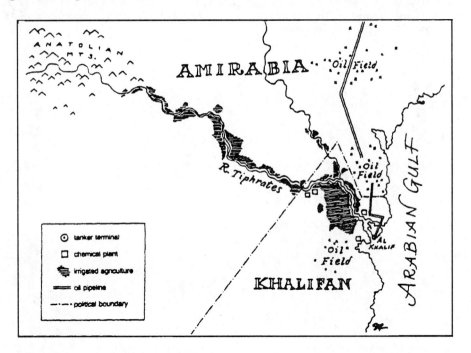

Figure 4-4.1

Both Amirabia and Khalifan have access to the Arabian Gulf and to the open seas beyond. Only Khalifan, however, has a port deep enough to accommodate the huge supertankers upon which Amirabia depends to export its oil, which it has done for more than three decades via a pipeline from its coastal storage facilities to Khalifan's deep water port. Thus, when Khalifan, never particularly friendly with Amirabia, three years ago proposed a substantial increase in its port taxes "to help upgrade Khalifan's petroleum and agricultural industries," Amirabia immediately protested, arguing that the proposed tax increase would severely burden Amirabia's economy. Despite Amirabia's protests, however, Khalifan increased its port taxes as proposed.

412

In addition, after repeated but unsuccessful appeals to Amirabia to renegotiate a treaty governing the Amirabian–Khalifani pipeline, and in apparent disregard of a treaty provision requiring "joint consultations" in respect of "any lessening of the [pipeline] flow," it shut down the pipeline.

Shortly thereafter, in a surprise move, General Tikrit ordered his army into Khalifan to repudiate, in his words, "this affront to Amirabia's national sovereignty and to international law." "The economic terrorists who have effectively taken our country hostage," he proclaimed, "must be taught a lesson." Within several days, Amirabia's military forced Khalifan's ruling family into exile, took control of the sheikdom's governmental apparatus, and proceeded to seize Khalifan's banks and businesses in the name of what General Tikrit called "economic equity."

The response of the organized international community was harsh. After many months of fruitless negotiations and unavailing economic sanctions, the United Nations Security Council, citing "unlawful aggression" on Amirabia's part, decided upon military sanctions to force Amirabia out of Khalifan. An international military coalition was assembled, air strikes began, and a land and sea invasion was launched. Shortly, General Tikrit ordered his army back across the Amirabian–Khalifani border.

In retreat, however, the Amirabian forces destroyed many of Khalifan's roads, railways, bridges, and anything else that might assist the advancing UN coalition. Several Amirabian and Khalifani oil wells and chemical plants situated near the Amirabian–Khalifani border alongside the Tiphrates River were destroyed, although it was unclear whether the destruction was caused by Amirabia or by the UN forces. The oil well fires, which darkened the surrounding skies for almost three weeks, were relatively quickly extinguished. The burning of the chemical plants, however, caused a large cloud of toxic smoke to billow into the atmosphere and an estimated two million gallons of agricultural chemicals to spill into the Tiphrates River. The cloud of smoke stretched for many miles across the Amirabian and Khalifani countryside, leaving sick and dying civilians urgently in need of evacuation and medical care.

In the chaos, it was several days before anyone noticed the extent of the Tiphrates River chemical spill. As the chemicals flowed downstream, they eliminated most forms of life in and near the river, especially in the delta area. Fish and other marine animals covered the river's surface in many places, aquatic vegetation slowly died, and riverside groves of citrus and other trees perished. Because it was not at first evident that chemicals had been released into the river, no immediate action was taken to prevent the pollution of a large percentage of Khalifan's irrigated fields, killing crops and rendering useless the land until the chemicals could be washed from the soil. Drinking water systems also were affected, and thousands of people suffered a variety of illnesses and death. Children were the hardest hit.

General Tikrit and his military commanders were subsequently captured by a squadron of British commandos and are being held in a British prison under UN auspices awaiting judgment by an *ad hoc* war crimes tribunal specially constituted by the UN Security Council. The Tribunal, Judge Yanya Viscovich presiding, has heard arguments from representatives of the UN military coalition on the violation of traditional humanitarian rules of armed conflict and now asks to hear arguments on alleged international environmental crimes. Specifically, the Tribunal seeks advice whether or not the "torching" of Khalifan's oil wells and the indiscriminate release of chemicals into the Tiphrates River constituted crimes under international law and, if so, what sanctions might be imposed upon General Tikrit and/or his government, if any. The Tribunal also requires advice on the legal liability of the UN coalition if evidence emerges that its actions were responsible for the environmental degradation. Khalifan and Amirabia are both parties to the 1976 Convention on the Prohibition of Military or any Other Hostile Use of Environmental Modification Techniques (ENMOD) and, while a party to the 1949 Geneva conventions on the laws of war, they have neither signed nor ratified the two 1977 protocols to the 1949 Geneva conventions or any other potentially relevant treaty, including the 1907 Hague Convention (No. IV) Respecting the Laws and Customs of War on Land.

SECTION 2.   QUESTIONS PRESENTED

1. Do Amirabia's and/or the UN military coalition's "torching" of Khalifan's oil wells and the release of chemicals into the Tiphrates River constitute violations of international law? If so, what sanctions, if any, may be imposed upon General Tikrit and/or members of the UN coalition?

2. In any event, are there any additional or alternative legal norms, procedures, and/or institutions to be recommended that might further help to prevent or discourage situations of the kind posed by this problem?

SECTION 3.   ASSIGNMENTS

A.   READING ASSIGNMENT

Study the Readings presented in Section 4, *infra*, and the Discussion Notes/Questions that follow. Also, time permitting, consult the accompanying bibliographical references.

B.   RECOMMENDED WRITING ASSIGNMENT

Prepare a comprehensive, logically sequenced, and *argumentative* brief in the form of an outline of the primary and subsidiary *legal* issues you see requiring resolution by the *ad hoc* war crimes tribunal. Also, from the perspective of an independent judge, indicate which side ought to prevail on each issue and why. Retain a copy of your issue-outline/brief for class discussion.

C. Recommended Oral Assignment

Assume you are legal counsel for Amirabia or Khalifan (as designated by your instructor); then, relying upon the Readings (and your issue-outline if prepared), present a 10–15 minute oral argument of your government's likely positions before the *ad hoc* war crimes tribunal.

D. Recommended Reflective Assignment

Consider (and recommend) alternative norms, institutions, and/or procedures that you believe might do better than existing world order arrangements to contend with situations of the kind posed by this problem. In so doing, but without insisting upon *immediate* feasibility, identify the particular transition steps that would be needed to make your alternatives a reality.

Section 4. Readings

The following readings are considered *prima facie* relevant to solving this problem. They are your law library for present purposes and should be treated as such, organized intelligibly for "shelving" and not necessarily according to the issues presented. Be sure to review Chapter 2 ("International Legal Prescription: The 'Sources' of International Law") in your consideration of them. It, too, should be treated as part of your law library (as, indeed, should this entire coursebook).

1. Hague Convention (No. IV) Respecting the Laws and Customs of War on Land (with annex of regulations). Concluded, 18 Oct 1907. Entered into force, 26 Jan 1910. 205 C.T.S. 277 (French); 2 A.J.I.L. Supp. 90 (1908); *reprinted in* **2 Weston & Carlson II.B.1: Pmbl., Art. 2, & Annexed Regs. 22, 23, 55** (Basic Document 2.2).

2. Geneva Convention (No. IV) Relative to the Protection of Civilian Persons in Time of War. Concluded, 12 Aug 1949. Entered into force, 21 Oct 1950. 75 U.N.T.S. 287; *reprinted in* **2 Weston & Carlson II.B.14: Arts. 2, 53, 147, 158** (Basic Document 2.12).

3. Stockholm Declaration of the United Nations Conference on the Human Environment. Adopted by the UN Conference on the Human Environment at Stockholm, 16 June 1972. *Report of the UN Conference on the Human Environment, Stockholm, 5–16 June 1972,* **UN Doc. A/CONF.48/14/Rev.1 at 3 (1973), UN Doc. A/CONF.48/14 at 2–65, and Corr. 1 (1972);** *reprinted in* **11 I.L.M. 1416 (1972) and 5 Weston & Carlson V.B.3: Princs. 2, 5–7, 21, 22, 26** (Basic Document 5.14).

4. Convention on the Prohibition of Military or Any Other Hostile Use of Environmental Modification Techniques (ENMOD). Adopted by the UN General Assembly, 10 Dec 1976. Entered into force, 5 Oct 1978. 1108 U.N.T.S. 151, 1976 U.N.J.Y.B. 1125, *reprinted in* **16 I.L.M. 88 (1977) and 2 Weston & Carlson II.B.19: Arts. I, II** (Basic Document 2.30).

5. Protocol Additional (No. I) to the Geneva Conventions of August 12, 1949, and Relating to the Protection of Victims of International Armed Conflict. Concluded, 8 Jun 1977. Entered into force, 7

Dec 1978. 1977 U.N.J.Y.B. 95; *reprinted in* 16 I.L.M. 1391 (1977) and 2 Weston & Carlson II.B.20: Arts. 35, 36, 51, 52, 54–58, 85 **(Basic Document 2.31).**

6. **World Charter for Nature. Adopted by the UN General Assembly, 28 Oct 1982. GA Res. 37/7 (Annex), UN GAOR, 37th Sess., Supp. No. 51, at 17, UN Doc. A/37/51; *reprinted in* 22 I.L.M. 455 (1983) and 5 Weston & Carlson V.B.11: Princs. 1, 5, 11, 12, 20, 24** (Basic Document 5.21).

7. **Rio Declaration on Environment and Development of the United Nations Conference on Environment and Development. Adopted by the UN Conference on Environment and Development (UNCED), 13 Jun 1992. UN Doc. A/CONF.151/26 (Vol. I) (1992); *reprinted in* 31 I.L.M. 874 (1992) and 5 Weston & Carlson V.B.16: Princs. 1, 2 & 24** (Basic Document 5.37).

8. **John Salter, "Environmental Legal Issues Arising from the Gulf Conflict," 10 Oil & Gas L. & Tax Rev. 348, 348–53 (1990).**

[*Eds.*—In late January 1991, Iraqi forces, in retreat from a military coalition authorized by the United Nations Security Council to reverse Iraq's August 1990 invasion of Kuwait, used the environment as a weapon of war by setting fire to hundreds of Kuwaiti oils wells and by spilling thousands of gallons of oil into the Persian Gulf. At the time, the author considered the ecological effects of these actions and the counteractions of the UN-authorized discussed military coalition.]

Air Pollution

The hundreds ... of well-head fires started by Iraqi soldiers before the Allied ground offensive was launched, and continued ... when later retreating, have caused the creation of columns of steam and thick dark clouds forming a vast pall of smoke as toxins poured into the air cutting out light during the day time. Estimated emission of smoke for the first 30 days is some 580,000 tonnes penetrating 0.6 miles into the atmosphere above burning wells and two miles above burning refineries.... Water, which provides pressure for exploitation of wells, is being sucked up through the oil and this may cause permanent damage to future commercial prospects of oil exploration....

Environmental Effects

Environmental effects could arise under at least four heads:

(1) From crude oil—from Iraqi/Kuwaiti oil terminals;

(2) From air pollution—from burning Iraqi/Kuwaiti installations;

(3) From windborne organisms—from Iraqi biological weapons plants;

(4) From radioactive contamination—from Iraqi nuclear installations.

The effects of marine oil pollution are reasonably well known.... However, the scale [here] is rather larger ..., [being, for example,] 13 times the size of the [March 1967] *Torrey Canyon* disaster.... The cost of the [*Torrey*

Canyon] clean-up exercise in [1967] was £100,000. The cost of the Gulf marine pollution clean-up in 1991 has been estimated at £500 million. . . .

The effects of . . . air strikes on stores of finished chemical weapons have not been so well studied. Professor Steven Rose of the Open University has stated that there could be a real danger of an epidemic spreading from the Gulf region. The Director of the United Nations Environmental Programme has said that the effects of any biological weapons used in the Gulf conflict could be felt as far away as Europe. Biological organisms such as anthrax live in the atmosphere for between 40 to 50 years and could be pushed by wind as far as Northern Europe. It would be difficult to contain the effects of any such attack. The effects of radioactive fall-out have been studied by the International Atomic Energy Agency who reported . . . that there was no evidence that attacks on the Iraqi nuclear installations had released any radioactive contamination. . . . [T]he Iraqi plants are small research reactors in which the field is immersed in a pool of water at least five metres deep. . . . Most are surrounded by large earth walls to protect them from the effects of bombing.

The effects of air pollution have also been extensively studied by the European Community. The environmental effects of the firing of well-heads and refineries relate not only to the Gulf States but also to Pakistan and possibly North India. These have so far been identified as covering:

(1) Acid or black toxic rain.

(2) Smog, being persistent air pollution and the reason for Gulf health officials warning people with respiratory problems to stay indoors, because of the increasing sulphur-dioxide levels.

(3) Farm produce and orchard failures (especially crops). Obstruction of sunlight could affect the double-cropping of rice. The first crop (assuming 120–day rice is planted) might not ripen in time for the second crop to be planted.

(4) Grazing herds affected by soot ingestion.

(5) Break up of desert pavement (a shield of pebbles laid down over thousands of years making it difficult for strong winds to dislodge sand) leading to erosion and violent dust and desert storms clogging up, for example, airport runways.

(6) Global warming and ozone effects which are thought probably not enough to cause measurable temperature change.

(7) Possible failure of Asian monsoons, although it is felt at present that the scale is not sufficiently large to affect monsoons.

Ecological Effects

The International Maritime Organisation[a] has . . . classified the Gulf area as a special area due to its sensitive ecology. Its shallow waters are significant in this connection. . . . In 1983 during the Iran–Iraq War the Iranian Nowruz field was allowed to leak some 30,000 tons of crude oil per day into the Gulf for a period of some nine months. . . . [I]n the short term [this will] have a

----

a. For details concerning the IMO, established in 1958 as the International Maritime Consultative Organization (IMCO), a specialized agency of the United Nations based in London, see *infra* Discussion Note/Question 10 in Problem 7–1 ("The Sea Around Antilla and Costa Grande"), at 1099.

considerably adverse effect on marine life.... Bahrain and other Gulf States are very dependent on fishing and, undoubtedly, such a large spill will affect this activity. Shrimp spawning-grounds are likely to be severely affected off Manifah. Fish nursery areas and fragile coral reefs would also be affected....

* * *

The effect of the firing of well-heads and refineries on ecology is ... quite serious, particularly having regard to water pollution by fall-out with its consequential threats to life itself.

9. Editors' Note. The harms inflicted upon the natural environment by the 1990–91 Persian Gulf War, as described above by John Salter, were the reason for a panel discussion on "The Gulf War: Environment as a Weapon" at the 85th Annual Meeting of the American Society of International Law in April 1991, 85 Proceed A.S.I.L. 215 (1991), wherein the following treaties and treaty provisions were observed to be of special relevance: the 1976 Convention on the Prohibition of Military or Any Other Hostile Use of Environmental Modification Techniques, the so-called ENMOD Convention **(Basic Document 2.30)**, and articles 35(3) and 55 of the 1977 Additional Protocol I to the 1949 Geneva Conventions Relating to the Protection of Victims of Armed Conflict **(Basic Documents 2.31)**. Also seen as relevant, despite "last minute and embarrassing US opposition," was the 1982 World Charter for Nature **(Basic Document 5.21)**, in particular paragraphs 5 and 20 thereof. Panelist Paul C. Szasz, former Deputy to the Legal Counsel and Director of General Legal Division of the Office of Legal Affairs at the United Nations commented: "I think it can safely be concluded that the principle expressed in all these instruments—that nature is no longer fair game in mankind's conflicts—is well on its way to becoming an accepted principle of international law." *Id.* at 217. Citing the above-noted instruments, Szasz might also have mentioned a number of other potentially relevant expressions of international legal expectation, including some of those noted immediately below (in their chronological order of appearance).

Other examples of environmental warfare include aspects of NATO's 1999 military campaign against the Former Republic of Yugoslavia (FRY). NATO's bombing raids targeted fuel storage facilities as well as oil refineries and petrochemical plants. The result was massive environmental damage. An unsuccessful request to the International Court of Justice by the FRY for the indication of provisional measures to stop the bombing relied in large part on environmental harm (Legality of the Use of Force (Yugo. v. U.S.), 1999 ICJ 916 (2 Jun) (Request for the Indication of Provisional Measures). Complaints were made also to the International Criminal Tribunal for the Former Yugoslavia (ICTY) about the damage to the environment. For a discussion of possible United States' liability for environmental damage caused by NATO see Nicholas G. Alexander, *Note: Airstrikes and Environmental Damage: Can the United States Be Held Liable for Operation Allied Force?*, 11 Colo. J. Int'l Envtl. L. & Pol'y 471 (2000). Alexander concludes that United States actions in Kosovo affecting the environment may have violated international law.

The invasion of Iraq by the "Coalition of the Willing," led by the United States, in March 2003 also involved environmental damage. The United Nations Environment Program (UNEP) noted the chronic environmental problems already existing in Iraq caused by the ravages of war, the low priority given to the environment by the government of Saddam Hussein, and the effects of UN sanctions. The Coalition forces used depleted uranium (DU) in ammunition used against Iraqi forces. This caused serious health risks through inhalation of DU dust and through contamination of the ground and possibly ground water. UNEP reported that oil-filled trenches in and around Baghdad were set alight by Iraqi forces in an attempt to impede Coalition weapons and prevent aerial and satellite surveillance. These fires generated large quantities of dense black smoke, containing a range of toxic substances that caused immediate air pollution and soil contamination threatening groundwater bodies and drinking water supplies. See UNEP Press Release, *UNEP outlines strategy for protecting people and the environment in post-war Iraq, Geneva,* 24 Apr 2003, *available at* <http://www.unep.org/Documents. multilingual/Default.asp?DocumentID=309&ArticleID=3965>.

10. Jozef Goldblat, "The Environmental Modification Convention of 1977: An Analysis," in Environmental Warfare: A Technical, Legal, and Policy Appraisal 53–57 (A. Westing ed., 1984).

The ENMOD Convention **[Basic Document 2.30]** deals with changes in the environment brought about by deliberate human manipulation of natural processes, as distinct from conventional acts of warfare which might result in adverse effects on the environment. Covered by the Convention are those changes which affect the dynamics, composition or structure of the Earth, including its biota, lithosphere, hydrosphere and atmosphere, or of outer space (article II). The employment of techniques producing such modifications as the means of destruction, damage or injury to another state party is prohibited. (This may be taken to 'mean that the use of environmental modification techniques to enhance the use of conventional weapons—for example, by dispersing fog covering airfields or other targets to be bombed—is not proscribed so long as the environmental modification technique itself produces no harm.) . . . . Nor is it allowed to assist, encourage or induce other nations to engage in these activities. . . .

* * *

The ban under the ENMOD Convention applies to the conduct of military operations during armed conflicts, as well as to hostile use (whether by military or non-military personnel) when no other weapon is being employed or when there is no overt conflict. It is applicable both to offence and defence, regardless of geographical boundaries. In the light of these explanations, which were given by the Soviet . . . and US . . . sponsors of the text, the term "hostile" alone would have sufficed as a purpose criterion upon which the Convention is based. But not all hostile uses causing harm to others are prohibited by the Convention; only those having "widespread, long-lasting or severe effects" are outlawed [in article I].[b] The meaning of these terms, according to the Understanding relating to article I, is as follows:

1. *widespread*: encompassing an area on the scale of several hundred square kilometres;[1]

b. Sometimes referred to as the "troika clause." *See, e.g.,* C. Wunsch, *The Environmental Modification Treaty,* 4 A.S.I.L.S Int'l L. J. 113, 115 (1980).

1. According to the interpretation provided by the USA, the entire area would have to experience destruction, damage or injury at approximately the same time to meet the

2. *long-lasting*: lasting for a period of months, or approximately a season; and

3. *severe*: involving serious or significant disruption or harm to human life, natural and economic resources or other assets.

It is noted in the Understanding that the above interpretation is intended exclusively for this Convention and should not prejudice the interpretation of the same or similar terms used in connection with any other international agreement. That proviso was found necessary ... to forestall an identical interpretation [of] the terms "widespread, long-term and severe" used in the 1977 Protocol I Additional to the Geneva Conventions of 1949, and Relating to the Protection of Victims of International Armed Conflicts **[Basic Document 2.31]** which was then under negotiation.... [T]o make this ban applicable, the presence of all three of the criteria—widespread, long term end severe—is required.... [In] the ENMOD Convention, [which] forbids the use (or manipulation) of the forces of the environment as "weapons" ..., the presence of only one of the three criteria—widespread, long-lasting, *or* severe—is enough for the environmental modification technique to be deemed outlawed.

Thus, the use of environmental modification techniques is prohibited if two requirements are met simultaneously: (*a*) that the use is hostile; and (*b*) that it causes destruction, damage or injury at, or in excess of, the threshold described above. Exempted from the prohibition are non-hostile uses of the modification techniques, even if they produce destructive effects exceeding the threshold. Equally permissible are hostile uses which produce destructive effects below the [troika] threshold. Assuming, therefore, that hostile intent has been proved (which may not be easy), it would still not be illegal, according to the Understanding, to devastate an area smaller than several hundred square kilometres ...; or to cause adverse effects lasting for a period of weeks instead of months, or less than a season; or to bring about disruption or harm to human life, natural and economic resources or other assets, which are not "severe", "serious" or "significant", whatever these subjective terms might mean to countries of different sizes, of different population densities or at different stages of economic development. For example, Trinidad and Tobago noted that the definitions of the terms "widespread, long-lasting or severe" do not address themselves to the situation of small entities, such as the islands of the Caribbean.... Moreover, the perpetrator's perception of the gravity of such acts may not coincide with that of the victim.

However, earthquakes, tsunamis (seismic sea waves), an upset in the ecological balance of a region, changes in weather patterns (clouds, precipitation, cyclones of various types, tornadic storms), changes in climate patterns, changes in ocean currents, changes in the state of the stratospheric ozone layer and changes in the state of the ionosphere appear to be definitely prohibited by the ENMOD Convention when produced by hostile use of environmental modification techniques. For it is understood that all these phenomena would result, or could reasonably be expected to result, in

"widespread" criterion.... This could result from a single operation or it could be the cumulative result of a series of operations conducted over a period of months or years. If, over the course of several years, a total area on the scale of several hundred square kilometres was affected, but the area actually suffering destruction, damage or injury at any one time was small, the "widespread" criterion would not be met.

widespread, long-lasting or severe destruction, damage or injury.... It has been recognized, in the Understanding relating to article II, that the use of techniques producing other phenomena could also be appropriately included, insofar as the criteria of hostility and destructiveness were met.... Nevertheless, only the most fanciful events are enumerated in the Understanding— those which ... would be felt only, or primarily, by the enemy....

As a consequence of the threshold approach, the techniques which can produce more limited effects (such as precipitation modification short of changing the "weather pattern") and which are, therefore, more likely to be used to influence the environment with hostile intent in a selected area, especially in tactical military operations, have escaped proscription. As noted earlier, the use of environmental modification techniques not as direct means of destruction, damage or injury, but to facilitate the effectiveness of other weapons in producing destruction, damage or injury, also does not appear to be covered. * * * Moreover, the imprecise and haphazard definition of the terms "widespread, long-lasting or severe" may generate controversies greater than a ban without any qualification. Thus, no convincing reason has been given as to why any hostile modification of the environment or any amount of damage caused by such modification should be tolerated at all. Even the right to use modification techniques on a state's own territory to forestall or stop foreign invasion (*e.g.*, by opening dams or producing massive landslides) might be legitimately challenged.

Evidently, certain powers preferred not to forswear altogether the possibility of using environmental methods of warfare and to keep future options open. This conclusion can also be drawn from the fact that the ENMOD Convention was conceived as a non-use agreement rather than as an arms-limitation measure. Hence, it does not prohibit the development of the prohibited techniques....

11. Richard A. Falk, "The Environmental Law of War: An Introduction," in Environmental Protection and the Law of War 78, 82–88 (G. Plant ed., 1992).

It should [now] be evident ... that ... existing law [relative to environmental protection during wartime] is ambiguous in extremely important respects.... At the same time, clarification of what exists is a necessary part of deciding upon and advocating what needs to be done [to strengthen] environmental protection in wartime by way of international law. * * * I am somewhat ... skeptical ... about the utility of treaty norms and somewhat ... affirmative in my attitude toward the role played by customary norms as part of the overall international picture.

* * *

Normative foundations: historic treaty prescriptions

Nineteenth and early twentieth-century attempts to develop the law of war rested upon broad normative mandates that continue to inform the efforts of international law. The St Petersburg Declaration of 1868 [**Basic Document 2.1**], despite proclaiming itself as a declaration, has come to be regarded as a binding agreement by the leading states of Europe to renounce the use of explosive or expanding bullets in wartime because of their cruel effects. It represented the first formal inter-governmental attempt to limit the tactics and methods of warfare, explicitly adopting the view that there are "technical limits at which the necessities of war ought to yield to the requirements of humanity" and that "the only legitimate object which states should endeavour to accomplish during war is to weaken the military force of the enemy". In the background to the St Petersburg Declaration is the central humanitarian objective of avoiding unnecessary suffering on the part of combatants and other war victims, and the importance of shaping choices about the development of and reliance upon weaponry in the light of such limiting considerations.

The St. Petersburg Declaration retains its relevance to the subject at hand for two reasons. First, it subordinates and restricts claims of "military necessity" by reference to a specific category of weaponry and through the coordinated action of the representatives of leading sovereign states; that is, from the outset of the modern law of war, absolute claims of "military necessity" have been rejected. At the same time, *ad hoc* considerations of military necessity have been allowed to prevail in the absence of specified prohibitions on weapons or targets (for example, nuclear weaponry); hence, the importance of having specific prohibitions in treaty form.

Second, the central notion that a mode of warfare must be relevant to a military purpose implies the "illegality" of all modes of behaviour that involve punitive or vindictive destruction, including, by implication, deliberate damage to resources, infrastructure and the environment.

The Hague Conferences of 1899 and 1907 produced a series of international agreements on various modes of warfare, including that upon land and sea.[c] These agreements, in many instances, continue to be the only codified formulation of restrictions on the generality of methods of warfare (often called the "Hague" law to distinguish it from the mainly humanitarian objectives of the "Geneva" law[d]). Article 22 of the [regulations annex to the] Hague Convention (IV) Respecting the Laws and Customs of War on Land (1907) **[Basic Document 2.2]** expresses a general normative sentiment that has often been invoked against military extremism: "The right of belligerents to adopt means of injuring the enemy is not unlimited." Such a general directive provides a legal foundation in certain settings for an authoritative condemnation of contested belligerent practices.

Of related, and reinforcing, significance is the "Martens Clause" that was included in the preamble to the Hague Convention (IV) of 1907, which is an insistence that states not adhering to the written laws of land warfare were nevertheless not liberated from legal restraint: "the inhabitants and belligerents remain under the protection and the rule of the principles of the law of nations, as they result from the usages established among civilized peoples, from the laws of humanity, and the dictates of the public conscience". Significantly, the Martens Clause is carried forward, although in more appropriate language, in Article I (2) of [Geneva] Protocol I **[Basic Document 2.31]**: "In cases not covered by this Protocol or by other international agreements, civilians and combatants remain under the protection and au-

---

c. Most of these agreements are reprinted in 1–2 Weston & Carlson.

d. To wit, the four conventions adopted in Geneva on 12 Aug 1949 **(Basic Documents 2.9, 2.10, 2.11 & 2.12)**.

thority of the principles of international law derived from established custom, from the principles of humanity and from the dictates of public conscience."

The Martens Clause is important, because it confirms the persistence of customary international law in relation to belligerent practices not covered by treaty norms, and extends the law of war to states that have failed to accede to recent developments in treaty law. The true relevance of this purported applicability of customary norms depends on the existence of a forum or tribunal that can offer authoritative interpretations of contested practices.

Normative foundations: the principles of customary international law of war

There is no single accepted text that formulates the principles of customary international law of war, but there is a fairly wide consensus on the identity and purpose of these principles. A summary follows of this consensus, organized around the four main principles ..., but with certain small changes in expression and content.

(a) *Principles of Discrimination.* To be lawful, weapons and tactics must clearly discriminate between military and non-military targets, and be confined in their application to military targets. Indiscriminate warfare is illegal *per se*, although indirect damage to civilians and civilian targets is not necessarily illegal.

(b) *Principle of Proportionality.* To be lawful, weapons and tactics must be proportional to their military objective. Disproportionate weaponry and tactics are excessive, and as such, illegal.

(c) *Principles of Necessity.* To be lawful, weapons and tactics involving the use of force must be reasonably necessary to the attainment of their military objective. No superfluous or excessive application of force is lawful, even if the damage done is confined to the environment, thereby sparing people and property.

(d) *Principles of Humanity.* To be lawful, no weapon or tactic can be validly employed if it causes unnecessary suffering to its victims, whether this is by way of prolonged or painful death or is in a form calculated to cause severe fright or terror. Accordingly, weapons and tactics that spread poison or disease or do genetic damage are generally illegal *per se*, as they inflict unacceptable forms of pain, damage, death and fear; all forms of deliberate ecological disruption would appear to fall within the sway of this overall prohibition.

In addition to these four cardinal principles, which are widely accepted in more or less the form I have expressed, two subsidiary principles seem to be well-grounded in authoritative custom and to have relevance to the array of special problems posed by deliberate and incidental environmental harm:

(e) *Principles of Neutrality.* To be lawful, no weapon or tactic can be relied upon if it seems likely that it will do harm to human beings, property, or the natural environment of neutral or non-participating countries. A country is neutral or non-participating if its government declares its neutrality and acts in a neutral manner, pursuing in relation to the armed conflict a policy that can be assessed to be impartial in view of its behaviour and situation.

(f) *Principle of Inter-generational Equity.* To be lawful, no weapon or tactic can be employed if it inflicts pain, risk of harm and damage, or if it can be reasonably apprehended to do so upon those unborn.

In my view these customary principles are of great importance in constructing the contours of existing international law pertaining to environmental harm arising out of warfare. Existing treaty law is, for various reasons, confined to the outer margins of these concerns and thus the only genuine basis for claiming violations of international law in relation to the sort of belligerent practices associated with recent war is based upon these customary principles.

* * *

At the same time ..., there are extreme limitations associated with the need to rely upon these customary principles. Their formulation is general and abstract and their application to concrete circumstances susceptible to extreme subjectivity and selectivity. Because of these features, the pedagogic and preventive functions of the law of war—that is, providing clear guidance to political leaders and military commanders, orienting public opinion and expert commentary—is not at all well-served. Indeed, the history of modern warfare shows the subordination, if not abandonment, of these customary principles in time of war, with postwar assessments of "illegality" confined generally to the practices of the losing side.

* * *

Normative foundations: declaratory principles relevant to environmental protection

The evolution of the law of war proceeded against a background of virtual environmental unconsciousness until some awareness was generated by critics of belligerent practices harmful to the environment during the latter stages of the Vietnam War.[2] In earlier wars, there were sporadic expressions of concern, and even legal condemnations, associated with punitive tactics toward a civilian population, such as the burning of croplands and forests and the poisoning of wells. Several Germans were convicted of the crime of "pillage" at the secondary Nuremberg trials for their wanton destruction of Polish forests. Projections of nuclear-war scenarios often rely on imagery of extreme environmental destruction to convey the full sense of the horror of such weapons. Yet, until the early 1970s, when a broader environmental concern took hold of the political imagination, no focused attention was directed toward protecting the environment from the ravages of war. Even at the 1972 Stockholm Conference on the Human Environment the topic was intentionally kept off the formal agenda because of the political sensitivity associated with implied criticism of US tactics in the Vietnam War, although it was addressed at a so-called "counter-conference," held simultaneously in Stockholm,[e] and received some media attention. Beginning in 1972, normative

2. *See* A. Westing, Ecological Consequences of the Second Indochina War (1976).

e. *See* "Self–Determination, National Liberation, War and Weaponry" in Declaration on the Third World and the Human Environment (Oi Committee Declaration, adopted by the participants in the Conference on Problems of the Third World and the Human Environment, paralleling the efforts of the United Nations Conference on the Human Environment attention began to be directed toward environmental protection as a distinct public concern.

Principles 21 and 26 of the Stockholm Declaration on the Human Environment **[Basic Document 5.14]** ... are often referred to as foundational. Principle 21 confirms that states can "exploit their own resources pursuant to their own environmental policies" but imposes "responsibility to ensure that activities within their jurisdiction or control do not cause damage to the environment of other states or of areas beyond the limits of national jurisdiction". This principle is not directly applicable to wartime, but it reinforces customary international law, particularly activities that cause transboundary pollution, climate change or release of radioactive, chemical and biological agents into the atmosphere. Principle 26, the very last provision in the Declaration, insists that "Man and his environment must be spared the effects of nuclear and other means of mass destruction"; states are implored "to reach prompt agreement on the elimination and complete destruction of such weapons". That is to say that war in general is not regarded as inherently destructive of the environment; only war fought with the weaponry of mass destruction is.

A decade later in 1982 the World Charter for Nature **[Basic Document 5.21]** was adopted in the form of a General Assembly Resolution ... widely endorsed by leading states, but opposed in isolation by the USA.... In the section dealing with General Principles, paragraph 5 deals directly with war: "Nature shall be secured against degradation caused by warfare or other hostile activities". Paragraph 11, although expressed in general terms, insists that: "Activities which might have an impact on nature shall be controlled, and the best available technologies that minimize significant risks to nature or other adverse effects shall be used." Sub-sections detail duties to avoid activities that cause "irreversible damage" and "significant risk to nature".

Several additional UN General Assembly resolutions deserve brief mention as building a normative climate: Resolutions 2849 (XXVI), 2994 (XXVII) and 3129 (XXVIII) affirmed and confirmed "the responsibility of the international community to take action to preserve and enhance the environment". On 14th December 1978 Resolution 3154 (XXVIII) deplored "environmental pollution by ionizing radiation from the testing of nuclear weapons". Passed on 9th December 1974, Resolution 3261 (XXIX) expressed the need "to adopt through the conclusion of an appropriate international convention, effective measures to prohibit action to influence the environment and climate for military and other hostile purposes, which are incompatible with the maintenance of international security, human well-being and health".

It should be stressed that these normative assertions are essentially aspirational, having as their most serious intention the encouragement of governments to take appropriate formal action. Such declaratory material, however, both shapes and reflects public opinion and is relevant to the activity of the NGO community. It builds support for strengthening international law through the adoption, if possible, of a comprehensive regulatory framework which is the outcome of a multilateral law-making process that

in Stockholm, 4–6 Jun 1972), *reprinted in* 5 Weston & Carlson V.B3 [*see also supra* Reading 3].

engages the active participation of leading governments and is subsequently widely signed and ratified. In this regard, this declaratory material is evidence of a legislative impulse, but little more than this if taken on its own.

12.   Editors' Note. It has long been accepted under traditional international law that self-defense is justified only when the necessity for action is "instant, overwhelming, and leaving no choice of means, and no moment for deliberation." Letter from Mr. Webster, Secretary of State to Lord Ashburton (6 Aug 1842), *reprinted in* 2 John Bassett Moore, A Digest of International Law 409, 412 (1906). Secretary Webster was addressing an incident of claimed anticipatory self-defense, the *Caroline* affair of 1837. Nevertheless, the quoted text reflects the customary law of self-defense generally both at the time of the *Caroline* incident and since that time. *See infra* Problem 4–1 ("Intervention in Loango"), at 260. Also, it gives content to the principle of military necessity, identified in the preceding extract by Richard Falk (Reading 11) as central to legal judgments about warfare, in general, and environmental warfare, in particular.

On the other hand, as stated in William M. Arkin, Damian Durrant & Marianne Cherni, On Impact: Modern Warfare and the Environment—A Case Study of the Gulf War (1991), at 115, "[i]t is in the interpretation of military action, and specifically the concept of "military necessity" (the anticipated value of one's own action), that there is significant international disagreement as to proper conduct during war." Indeed, according to the same authors, at 116 and 123:

> Military necessity has ... become the main justification for deviation from restrictions in customary law. * * * While a number of principles relate to protection of the environment during warfare, they are all subordinated to the principle of military necessity. Even in the Geneva Protocols **[Basic Documents 2.31 & 2.32]**, the new basic rule on protecting the natural environment (Article 35) is later subordinated to military necessity. Article 55 states that "*Care* shall be taken in warfare to protect the natural environment" (emphasis added), accepting that environmental protection is not absolute. Despite acknowledgement of the environmental effects of warfare, Richard Falk wrote in 1984, "to turn to international law for relief provides only the most scant basis for hope at present.... What is militarily attractive remains permissible, or at least not explicitly prohibited, whereas that which is of no evident relevance to war making is diligently proscribed."[f]

A similar, even if somewhat opposing, viewpoint is expressed in Guy B. Roberts, *The New Rules for Waging War: The Case Against Ratification of Additional Protocol I*, 26 Va. J. Int'l L. 109, 146–47 (1985):

> Article 35(3) [of Protocol I] introduces a new principle in the laws of war. It prohibits the use of "methods or means of warfare which are intended, or *may be expected*, to cause widespread, long term and severe damage to the environment." * * * By including the "may be expected" language of article 35(3), the drafters provided a legal ground for challenging the use of any weapon that may affect the environment. * * * [T]he "may be expected" language of articles 35(3) and 55 opens the door

f. Citing the article by Falk from which Reading 11, *supra,* is derived.

for war crimes prosecutions in every case where the environment suffers incidental damage as a result of military operations. The articles impose vague, unworkable, and impractical requirements on military commanders in an effort to prevent all collateral ecological damage, and should not be ratified.

13. Myres S. McDougal & Florentino P. Feliciano, Law and Minimum World Order: The Legal Regulation of International Coercion 521–24 (1961).

Throughout the sets of specific rules of warfare that authoritative decision-makers seek to prescribe and apply to specific problems ..., the familiar policies of military necessity and minimum destruction of values may be seen to recur continuously as basic themes.... Thus, it is commonly stated in the learned literature that three basic principles underlie the more detailed prescriptions of combatant law: the principle of military necessity, the principle of humanity, and the principle of chivalry. The principle of chivalry would seem little more than a somewhat romantic inheritance from the Medieval Ages when combat between mailed knights was surrounded by symbolic and ritualistic formalities. In an age increasingly marked by mechanized and automated warfare, the scope of application of chivalry as a principle distinct from humanity may very probably be expected to diminish in corresponding measure. The customary formulations of the remaining two principles in complementary terms and at highest level of abstraction appear, of course, at first glance, as largely tautologous: the principle of military necessity is said to be "subject to the principles of humanity [and chivalry]," while the principle of humanity is assumed to preclude only such kind or degree of violence as is "not actually necessary". Here, however, as in most of the other domains of the law of war, and of the law of nations generally, complementary general principles serve the important function of spotlighting broad categories of competing considerations that must be taken into account by decision-makers aspiring to rationality. What at highest level abstraction may appear to be tautologous opposites may, in contexts of specific application of policies, be indispensable preliminaries to, and anticipations of, inquiries for detailed factors of contexts and their appropriate relation to overriding community goals.

The principle of military necessity and the principle of humanity may be seen to express a genuine, inclusive interest of states and peoples. Each territorial community has a most direct and immediate interest in maintaining its security, that is, protecting the integrity of its fundamental bases of power and the continued functioning of its internal social processes from the obtrusion of unlawful violence. Each such community has consequently an interest in authority to exercise the force indispensable and appropriate for maintaining or re-establishing its security. Each territorial polity has at the same time an interest in reducing to minimal levels the destruction of values, both of itself and others, that attends such efforts. As we have earlier indicated, this interest has at least two interrelated, component elements. The first element is expressed in the demands, characteristic of a public order of human dignity, that the least possible coercion—not to mention violence—be applied to individual human beings, and that all authorized control over human beings be oriented toward strategies of persuasion with widest possible participation in decision, rather than toward strategies of coercion. The second equally pragmatic element is that of demand for economy in the outlay and expenditure of resources and other base values for safeguarding or restoring security. There is no ineluctable necessity for postulating the priority of one of these basic, complementary interests over the other. The point which does not bear emphasis is that the whole process of authoritative decision with respect to combat situations is a continuous effort to adjust and accommodate the specific requirements of both these interests in a series of concrete contexts. Historically, of course, the line of compromise has, more frequently than not, tended to be located closer to the polar terminus of military necessity than to that of humanity. Paradoxical as it may seem, the observation may not be inappropriate, however, that contemporary weapons whose destructiveness almost surpasses understanding may yet tend to push the line of compromise more toward the other terminus.

The content which has traditionally been written into the concept of military necessity is the policy of permitting the exercise of that violence necessary for the prompt realization of legitimate belligerent objectives. In terms of a theoretical image of the process of combat, one can of course conceive of the achievement of a clearly specified objective as requiring, under a given set of conditions, and at a given moment, the application of a particular (and no longer) period of time against a particular base of enemy power. In point of practical fact, however, no such perfection is achievable. The actual determinations of the lawfulness of particular exercises of violence, by military commanders on the spot as by war crimes tribunals reviewing the decisions of commanders, go forward in contexts of variables which, even when they can be identified, are hardly susceptible of precise quantification and measurement.

14. United Nations Security Council Resolution 687 (Concerning the Restoration of Peace and Security in Iraq and Kuwait). Adopted 3 Apr 1991. SC Res. 687, UN SCOR, 46th Sess., 2981st mtg., at 11, UN Doc. S/Res/687 (1991); *reprinted in* **30 I.L.M. 846 (1991) and 2 Weston & Carlson II.D.25: Paragraphs 1, 16, 18, 19, 33, 34** (Basic Document 2.41).

15. Hague Convention (No. IV) Respecting the Laws and Customs of War on Land (with annex of regulations). Concluded, 18 Oct 1907. Entered into force, 26 Jan 1910. 205 C.T.S. 277 (French); 2 A.J.I.L. Supp. 90 (1908); 36 Stat. 2277, T.S. No. 539; *reprinted in* **2 Weston & Carlson II.B.1: Arts. 2, 3 and Annexed Regulation 23(g)** (Basic Document 2.2).

16. Geneva Convention (No. IV) Relative to the Protection of Civilian Persons in Time of War. Concluded, 12 Aug 1949. Entered into force, 21 Oct 1950. 75 U.N.T.S. 287; 6 U.S.T. 3516, T.I.A.S. No. 3365; *reprinted in* **2 Weston & Carlson II.B.14: Art. 146** (Basic Document 2.12).

17. Experts Group on Environmental Law of the World Commission on Environment and Development, Legal Principles for Environmental Protection and Sustainable Development. Adopted by the WCED Experts Group on Environmental Law, 18–20 Jun 1986. UN Doc. WCED/86/23/Add.1 (1986); *reprinted in* **5 Weston & Carlson V.B.12: Princ. 21** (Basic Document 5.25).

18. Principles of International Law Recognized in the Charter of the Nuremberg Tribunal and in the Judgment of the Tribunal. Adopted by the UN International Law Commission, 2 Aug 1950. 2 Y.B.I.L.C. 374 (1950); *reprinted in* **2 Weston & Carlson II.E.4** (Basic Document 2.13).

SECTION 5.   DISCUSSION NOTES/QUESTIONS

1. We speak of damage to the environment as a result of intended and unintended acts of war. But what do we mean by "environmental damage"? Are mitigating solutions likely to depend on how we conceptualize it? Consider David Tolbert, *Defining the "Environment"*, in Environmental Protection and the Law of War (G. Plant, ed., 1992), at 259–60:

> [T]ension in defining environmental damage stems from an underlying conceptual problem which arises from what the "environment" is and how we define it. If the "environment" is defined in terms of human relationships to the resources of nature, then the "environment" becomes a term that simply describes a type of economic resource and environmental damage is simply a calculation of resultant economic and/or social loss arising out of injury to that economic resource. Although there is undoubted economic dimension to the environment ..., such a "human-centric" definition equates one consequence of environmental damage—damage to humans and their interests—as the sole or major determinant of environmental damage. [It is] submitted that for the "environment" to have any real meaning it must be defined in terms that do not principally rely on humans; * * * [And] one particularly good example in the area of armed conflict which takes a "nature-centric" approach [is] the Environmental Modification Convention of 1977 (ENMOD) **[Basic Document 2.30]** which seeks to prohibit "environmental modification techniques" of the "natural processes—the dynamics, composition or structure of the earth, including its biota, lithosphere, hydrosphere and atmosphere, or of outer space".... [T]his approach does not measure environmental degradation in terms of impact on human beings (although humans would clearly benefit from the enforcement of the treaty provisions), but in terms of the elements of the natural environment—water, air, space, seas and living matter, etc.

What are the consequences of taking a "human-centric" (*i.e.*, homocentric) view of the environment? A "nature-centric" view? Should warfare that is intentionally destructive of the environment be seen as a "crime against humanity"? Or should it be viewed as a "war crime"? What difference might it make? Is it reasonable to conclude that a "human-centric" view of the environment might limit compensation for environmental damage to human losses resulting from the destruction, whereas a "nature-centric" outlook would extend compensation for damage to wildlife and the natural environment as such?

2. However "nature-centric" the ENMOD Convention **(Basic Document 2.30)** may be, it is not perfect. In *Some Considerations on the Review of the 1977 Environmental Modification Techniques (ENMOD) Convention*, 6 Ital. Y.B.I.L. 96, 98–103 (1985), Antonio Filippo Panzera notes the following criticisms:

> a) according to the language of Art. 2 (which is supported also by the logical context and by the preparatory works), the Convention is concerned with environmental modifications produced by the deliberate use of special techniques intended for such purpose (which are prohibited) and not also (as

would have been desirable) with environmental modifications produced "indirectly" or by the use of conventional weapons or weapons of mass destruction;

b) the Convention only partially prohibits techniques that are able to modify the environment for military—or at least hostile—purposes because it prohibits only techniques "having widespread, longlasting or severe effects".... On the contrary, it appears to legitimize the use of techniques that are below this already high "threshold";

c) in ... real life it is not always easy to distinguish between peaceful aims ... and hostile aims ... in the use of environmental modification techniques;

d) the Convention prohibits the use of environmental modification techniques but not research and stockpiling activities and, in general, any kind of preparatory activity;

e) for the purpose of stimulating broader participation in the Convention, Art 1, n. 1 prohibits only the hostile use of techniques of environmental modification that may cause "damage or injury *to any other State Party*", and not to third States as well;

f) the control mechanism in Art. 5 appears weak. Indeed, the Consultative Committee of Experts' role is restricted to the mere verification of facts, whereas any possible decision is entrusted to the [UN] Security Council, with the drawback of the possible Permanent Members' resort to the veto;

g) sanctions are not provided in the hypothesis of an established breach of the Convention's obligations.

Do you agree that these criticisms render the ENMOD Convention essentially useless? What might you recommend to improve or strengthen it?

3. Articles 35 and 55 of 1977 Geneva Protocol I **(Basic Document 2.31)**, as we have seen, attempt to safeguard the natural environment against wartime activities. They provide important protections not previously found in the law. Significantly, however, such countries as France and the United States, key players in the 1990–91 Persian Gulf War, object to these provisions, refusing to consider them as binding principles of customary international law. As conveniently summarized in William Arkin, Damian Durrant & Marianne Cherni, On Impact: Modern Warfare and the Environment: A Case Study of the Gulf War 123–24 (1991), a Greenpeace study:

The US (and most western military powers') rejection is rooted in the concept of military necessity. The US government's position is that Article 35 is not part of customary law. The objection centers on the language of Article 35 of Protocol I, which prohibits acts that would have "widespread, long term and severe damage," while not defining these effects in the text. During the ... debate about the Protocols in 1987, Michael J. Matheson, Deputy Legal Adviser to the US State Department, reiterated that US objection:

We, however, consider that another principle in Article 35, which also appears later in the Protocol, namely, that the prohibition of methods or means of warfare intended or expected to cause widespread, long-term and severe damage to the environment, is too broad and ambiguous and is not part of customary law.

One opponent of the Protocols argued that Article 35 was objectionable, as it would open the door for war crimes prosecutions whenever the environment suffered serious environmental damage. However, an advocate of the

Protocols, its US negotiator, Ambassador George Aldrich, argued that "collateral damage from conventional warfare such as that which occurred in France in World War I was not intended to be covered. . . . [L]ong term should be understood in terms of decades."

The US also does not support . . . the new restrictions contained in the Protocols (Article 52) on attacking dangerous works and installations. The Joint Chiefs of Staff conducted a study of the military implications of Protocol I, concluding that it was "militarily unacceptable" because of new restrictions on objects of bombardment (as well as for other reasons). Abraham Sofaer, [former] State Department Legal Adviser, wrote that the new law "would protect objects that would be considered legitimate military objectives under customary international law." Sofaer argues that the Protocol would provide almost complete prohibition, and exempt such targets from the traditional considerations of proportionality:

> It is clear . . . that civilian losses are not to be balanced against the military value of the target. If severe losses would result, then the attack is forbidden, no matter how important the target. It also appears that Article 56 forbids any attack that raises the possibility of severe civilian losses. . . .

Is the US approach appropriate? Should the objections of a few nations be allowed to undermine the effectiveness of an otherwise widely endorsed agreement? How might such a world order situation be altered? What would you propose?

The United Kingdom ratified Protocol I in 1998. Its instrument of ratification contains an understanding that:

> both of these provisions [articles 35 (3) and 55] . . . cover the employment of methods and means of warfare and that the risk of environmental damage falling within the scope of these provisions arising from such methods and means of warfare is to be assessed objectively on the basis of the information available at the time.

See Ratification of the Additional Protocols by the United Kingdom of Great Britain and Northern Ireland 322 Int'l Rev. Red Cross 186 (1998), *available at* <http://www.icrc.org/web/eng/siteeng0.nsf/iwpList166/A06D567EA584477CC1256 B66005B94B8>.

4. The International Criminal Court has jurisdiction over actions taken in the 2003 Gulf War, but neither Iraq nor the United States has accepted the Statute of the International Criminal Court **(Basic Document 1.16)**. It should be noted however that various members of the 2003 "Coalition of the Willing" are parties to the Statute, including Australia and the United Kingdom. Under what circumstances could the International Criminal Court exercise jurisdiction over environmental damage caused in the 2003 invasion of Iraq?

5. It is widely appreciated that a nuclear war would have devastating effects upon the natural environment. It would risk the end of human civilization as we know it, in large part because of its probable climatic impacts (*e.g.*, "nuclear winter"). Thus in its July 1996 advisory opinion on the *Legality of the Threat or Use of Nuclear Weapons*, **(Basic Document 7.10)** the International Court of Justice states, at 15:

> The Court recognizes that the environment is under daily threat and that the use of nuclear weapons could constitute a catastrophe for the environment. The Court also recognizes that the environment is not an abstraction but represents the living space, the quality of life and the very health of

human beings, including generations unborn. The existence of the general obligation of States to ensure that activities within their jurisdiction and control respect the environment of other States or of areas beyond national control is now part of the corpus of international law relating to the environment.

Nevertheless, the Court concluded, at 16, that "existing international law relating to the protection and safeguarding of the environment does not specifically prohibit the use of nuclear weapons," only that "it indicates important environmental factors that are properly to be taken into account in the context of the implementation of the principles and rules of law applicable in armed conflict"— *e.g.*, the principles of necessity and proportionality. The Court reasoned: "the issue is not whether the treaties relating to the protection of the environment are or are not applicable during an armed conflict, but rather whether the obligations stemming from these treaties were intended to be obligations of total restraint during military conflict. * * * The Court does not consider that the treaties in question could have intended to deprive a State of the exercise of its right of self-defence under international law because of its obligations to protect the environment." *Id.*

The "treaties in question" to which the Court was referring included the 1976 ENMOD Convention **(Basic Document 2.30)** and the 1977 Additional Protocol I to the 1949 Geneva Conventions Relating to the Protection of Victims of Armed Conflict **(Basic Documents 2.31)**. Do you agree with the Court's argument? Disagree? Since when is a State's right of self-defense not limited by its environmental (and humanitarian) obligations? What might be a consequence of the Court's finding? Does it imply the need for some new treaty law? Does it make any difference? Is it possible to use nuclear weapons without violating the principles of necessity and proportionality? For a discussion of the opinion's relevance to environmental damage caused by warfare generally, see Deborah L. Houchins, *Extending The Application of the ICJ's July 8, 1996, Advisory Opinion to Environment–Altering Weapons in General: What Is the Role Of International Environmental Law in Warfare?*, 22 J. Land, Resources & Envtl. L. 463 (2002). For an overall assessment of the opinion, see Burns H. Weston, *Nuclear Weapons and the World Court: Ambiguity's Consensus,* 7 Transnat'l L. & Contemp. Probs. 371 (1997).

For additional discussion concerning the hazards of nuclear weapons, see *infra* Problem 4–5 ("Hindustan Threatens Nuclear Self–Defense"), at 437, and Problem 7–3 ("A Nuclear Accident in Hanguo") in Chapter 7, at 1135.

6. The history of environmental warfare can be traced back over two thousand years. As early as 401 B.C., the Greeks employed honey poisoned with gray anotoxins to render Pompey's troops incompetent during the Spartan Wars. Troops were led into valleys where poisoned honey was located and then attacked after eating the honey, when in a weakened condition. During the Fourteenth Century, the Tartars hurled plague victims over the walls of Kaffa to spread the disease. And during the French and Indian wars, smallpox was deliberately spread among American Indians via contaminated blankets. *See* Robert S. Root–Bernstein, *Biology: Infectious Terrorism* 44 (1991).

In modern times, given our systems of water supply and air ventilation in many large buildings, it has become even easier to imagine biological and environmental warfare. Experiments document the ease with which agents such as *Giardia lamblia,* a diarrheal micro-organism, can be spread through public water systems. In short, technology now makes the release of toxins and genetically altered substances into the civilian environment easy and untraceable, capable of affecting humans, animals, agriculture, and the wider environment sometimes in irreversible ways. Release of chemicals via large "spillage" as in the case of the Persian Gulf War (and Khalifan) are now threatening to damage the environment and affect civilian populations or many years to come. Release of flood waters has also become a real concern, as it is not difficult to destroy a dam or other hydroelectric facility with modern weapons. For useful summary and detail, see *id*.

How does ENMOD **(Basic Document 2.30)** address such environmental threats? How does Geneva Protocol I **(Basic Document 2.31)**. Would the spreading of a disease in the course of a war violate the text of either agreement? If so, how? If not, how would you amend these agreements so that they might address such threats directly and explicitly? Would it be better simply to draft an entire new convention?

7. In his introduction to Environmental Protection and the Law of War (G. Plant ed., 1992), Glen Plant identifies "four camps" representing a "spectrum of views" on the state of international environmental law relative to armed conflict. He summarizes, at 15–16:

> *Camp 1*, those who consider the existing law relevant to environmental protection in wartime to be an amalgamation of principles established in the customary international law of war and a number of codifying provisions to be found in the Regulations attached to the Hague Conventions of 1899 (II) and 1907 (IV) **[Basic Document 2.2]** and in the Geneva Conventions of 1949 **[Basic Documents 2.9, 2.10, 2.11 & 2.12]** and that this law reflects environmental concerns and is adequate to cover the worst environmental excesses of any foreseeable war; *Camp 2*, those who accept this but consider Protocol I to the 1949 Conventions **[Basic Document 2.31]** also to represent customary law, including among several relevant provisions two directly and expressly referring to environmental protection, Articles 33(5) and 55, and that this law, together with other relevant instruments such as the ENMOD **[Basic Document 2.30]** and the Inhuman Weapons Conventions (where they apply), is adequate to protect the environment in wartime, needing no further elaboration; *Camp 3*, those who consider the existing law of war, whatever it may be, to be inadequate or at least in need of restatement and who contemplate various means for improving the standards of, adherence to or implementation of that law, whether by using existing instruments and mechanisms or by developing new ones, such as a new Geneva-style Convention; this Camp generally inclines in favour of ensuring that developments in the international environmental law of peacetime are fully reflected in the law of war, but considers that the matter should be tackled essentially within the framework of the law of war; and *Camp 4*, which considers the distinction between wartime and peacetime acts in this context to be so vague, irrelevant or misleading that, if any new development is to take place, it should be concerned with environmental destruction in all scenarios, whether wartime or peacetime.

In which "camp" or "camps" do you fall? Why?

8. As by now must be clear, strengthening and enforcing the ENMOD Convention **(Basic Document 2.30)** and Geneva Protocol I **(Basic Document 2.31)** to help safeguard the natural environment against the ravages of war is a matter of high priority. Perhaps not so obvious is the possibility of assisting this process at the local level and not simply on the international plane. In August–

September 1990, for example, the Eighth United Nations Congress on the Prevention of Crime and the Treatment of Offenders, meeting in Havana, Cuba, adopted a resolution on "The Role of Criminal Law in the Protection of Nature and the Environment," in which the UN Congress called upon States to enact and enforce national criminal laws to protect nature and the environment. Does such a call add force to the argument that such serious violations of international environmental values as environmental warfare should constitute international crimes? Why? Why not?

9.   In *International Liability of States for Marine Pollution*, 21 Can. Y.B.I.L. 85, 88, Günther Handl writes that even if *prevention* of environmental harm is the best policy, state responsibility for such damage "would have to be emphasized as a key element." In other words, compensation for environmental damage often will be an important way to guarantee the international legal obligation not to do harm to "the environment of other States or of areas beyond the limits of national jurisdiction," per Principle 21 of the 1972 Stockholm Declaration of the United Nations Conference on the Human Environment **(Basic Document 5.14)**. However, as pointed out in Luan Low & David Hodgkinson, *Compensation for Wartime Environmental Damage: Challenges to International Law After the Gulf War*, 35 Va. J. Int'l L. 405 (1995), wartime environmental damage is typically not compensable under customary notions of *jus in bello*; and while compensable under Paragraph 16 of Security Council Resolution 687 **(Basic Document 2.41)** relative to the Persian Gulf War, that initiative, based on the *jus ad bellum*, may be said to have limited precedential value. Thus Low and Hodgkinson write, at 483: "The challenges for international law . . . are to provide obligations which directly protect the environment in wartime and to ensure that there is an adequate enforcement mechanism through the provision of liability and compensation. . . . Only when the legal system meets *both* challenges will international law offer full protection to the environment in wartime." What can you recommend that might fulfill this call to action?

10.   In response to criticisms of existing international law of war as regards protection of the environment, many have called for a fifth Geneva Convention to improve the status of the environment in the law of war. Professor Plant calls for a new convention rather than continued reliance on the 1949 Geneva Conventions and their supplementary protocols. In so doing, he lists "the common ground on the law of war," as follows:

1.   The law of war has been concerned with environmental protection since ancient times at least in the sense of prohibiting wanton destruction of forests, orchards, fruit trees and vines and forbidding the poisoning of wells, springs and rivers.

2.   Deliberate and wanton destruction of the environment in circumstances where no legitimate military objective is being served is contrary to international law.

3.   The principle of proportionality between means and methods employed in an attack and the military objective sought to be attained by it, the prohibition against military operations not directed against legitimate military targets, the prohibition against the destruction of enemy property not imperatively demanded by the necessities of war and other well established principles of customary international law have the indirect effect of protecting the environment in many wartime situations.

4.   The Martens Clause, formulated in its most modern version in Protocol I **[Basic Document 2.31]**, reads as follows:

> In cases not covered by this Protocol or by other international agreements, civilians and combatants remain under the protection and authority of the principles of international law derived from established custom, from the principles of humanity and from the dictates of public conscience.

> Thus the customary law of war, in reflecting the modern increase in concern for the environment as one of the dictates of public conscience in the sense understood in that Clause, now includes a requirement to avoid unjustifiable damage to the environment.

5. Violations of Article 23(g) of the Regulations attached to the Hague Convention of 1907 (IV) Respecting the Laws and Customs of War on Land **[Basic Document 2.2]**, or of Article 53 of the 1949 Geneva Convention (IV) Relative to the Protection of Civilian Persons in Time of War **[Basic Document 2.12]**, which prohibit destruction by an Occupying Power of enemy property not required by military necessity, give rise to civil liability. Wanton destruction is considered a grave breach, for which individual criminal responsibility can be attributed by virtue of Article 147 of the latter Convention.

6. States should ensure the wide dissemination and effective implementation of their existing obligations under the law of armed conflict as they may be relevant to the protection of the environment, as well as proper instruction of the military in their application. They should be adequately incorporated into military manuals and rules of engagement, in particular, through instructions to military commanders on the planning and preparation of military activities.

Glen Plant, *Introduction*, in Environmental Protection and the Law of War 17–18 (G. Plant ed., 1992). How, given this "common ground," might a better convention be conceived and drafted? Could it adequately address the problem of environmental protection in time of war? A draft of a fifth Geneva Convention on the Protection of the Environment in Times of Armed Conflict produced by a group of independent experts in 1991 provided that the principle of military necessity would not justify the destruction or damage of the environment. It also required states to undertake a type of environmental impact assessment before using a new weapons system. *See* Glen Plant, *Preface* in Environmental Protection and the Law of War x–xvii (Glen Plant ed., 1992). How effective would such a treaty be? What other provisions might it contain? Would it need to prescribe a new category of crime—crimes against nature or crimes against the environment—to supplement the existing "crimes against the peace," "war crimes," and "crimes against humanity" categories of international crime? See also Timothy Schofield, *Comment: The Environment as an Ideological Weapon: A Proposal to Criminalize Environmental Terrorism*, 26 B.C. Envtl. Aff. L. Rev. 619 (1999).

11. *Bibliographical Note.* For supplemental discussion concerning the principal themes addressed in this problem, consult the following additional specialized materials:

(a) *Books/Monographs/Reports/Symposia.* Environmental Warfare: A Technical, Legal and Policy Appraisal (A. Westing ed., 1984); Environmental Hazards of War (A. Westing ed., 1990); Explosive Remnants of War: Mitigating the Environmental Effects (A. Westing ed., 1985); F. Kalshoven, Constraints on the Waging of War (1987); Environmental Protection and the Law of War: A "Fifth Geneva" Convention on the Protection of the Environment in Time of Armed Conflict (G. Plant ed., 1992); A. Westing, Cultural Norms, War, and the Environment (1988).

(b) *Articles/Book Chapters*. H. Almond, Jr., *Weapons, War and the Environment*, 3 Georgetown Int'l Envtl. L. Rev. 117 (1990); A. Boyle, *State Responsibility for Breach of Obligations to Protect the Global Environment*, in Control Over Compliance with International Law 69 (W. Butler ed., 1991); J. Cohan, *Modes of Warfare and Evolving Standards of Environmental Protection Under the International Law of War*, 15 Fla. J. Int'l L. 481 (2003); A. Ehrlich, *Nuclear Winter: A Forecast of the Climatic and Biological Effects of Nuclear War*, 40 Bull. Atomic Scientists No. 40, at 15 (1984); P. Ehrlich *et al.*, *Long-term Biological Consequences of Nuclear War*, 222 Science 1293 (1983); R. Falk, *Environmental Warfare and Ecocide*, 4 Bull. Peace Proposals 1 (1973); ___ *Environmental Disruption by Military Means and International Law*, in Environmental Warfare: A Technical, Legal, and Policy Appraisal 33 (A. Westing ed., 1984); L. Green, *The Environment and the Law of Conventional Warfare*, 29 Can. Y.B.I.L. 222 (1991); L. Hourcle, *The Environmental Law of War*, 25 Vt. L. Rev. 653 (2001); A. Leibler, *Deliberate Wartime Environmental Damage: New Challenges for International Law*, 23 Cal. W. Int'l L. J. 67 (1992); L. Low & D. Hodgkinson, *Compensation for Wartime Environmental Damage: Challenges to International Law after the Gulf War*, 35 Va. J. Int'l L. 405 (1995); N. A. Robinson, *20th Annual Symposium: Lex & the Lorax: Enforcing Environmental Norms Under International Law: Enforcing Environmental Norms: Diplomatic and Judicial Approaches*, 26 Hastings Int'l & Comp. L. Rev. 387 (2003); J. Schafer, *The Relationship Between the International Law of Armed Conflict and Environmental Protection: The Need to Reevaluate What Types of Conduct Are Permissible During Hostilities*, 19 Cal. W. Int'l L. J. 287 (1989); M. Stuhltrager, *Combating Terrorism in the Environmental Trenches: Responding to Terrorism: Oil Pollution and Environmental Terrorism–An Overview of the Potential Legal Response in the United States*, 9 Wid. L. Symp. J. 401 (2003); R. Williamson, Jr., *Is International Law Relevant to Arms Control? Hard Law, Soft Law, and Non–Law in Multilateral Arms Control: Some Compliance Hypotheses*, 4 Chi. J. Int'l L. 59 (2003); F. Yuzon, *Deliberate Environmental Modification through the use of Chemical and Biological Weapons: "Greening" the International Laws of Armed Conflict to establish an Environmentally Protective Regime*, 11 Am. U. J. Int'l L. & Pol'y 793 (1996).

Problem 4–5

Hindustan Threatens Nuclear Self–Defense

SECTION 1.   FACTS

Hindustan and Islamistan are neighboring South Asian countries with a long history of mutual enmity, due in part to their religious differences. Soon after achieving political independence from their common colonial overlord in the wake of World War II, each claimed sovereignty over Karakorum, an economically and strategically important border territory whose population was, as it is now, 80% Muslim and thus a matter of great religious—and political—significance to Islamistan. However, because Hindustan had military superiority at the time of independence, it was able, via martial law, effectively to occupy and control Karakorum.

Until recently. Partly because Hindustani rule has continuously ignored the human rights of Karakorum's Muslim majority, partly because Islamistan has encouraged civil strife in the territory, and partly because each country has worked steadily over the years to build up its tactical and strategic armed forces, including the development and deployment of a limited number of nuclear weapons (which each country insists are necessary for self-defense), tensions finally reached a breaking point. Three months ago, Islamistan initiated conventional military action to wrest Karakorum from Hindustani control and since then has pursued Hindustani forces even into Hindustan itself. Hindustan, outraged by these actions and fearing a irreversible setback to its claim of sovereignty over Karakorum as well as an end to its military occupation, sternly warned Islamistan that any continuation of its "military aggression" would be met with a nuclear response in accordance with Hindustan's "inherent right of self-defense." It demanded that Islamistan totally withdraw its armed forces from both Hindustan and Karakorum within one week's time or suffer a nuclear missile attack against certain of its military installations within its territory.

Satellite data and intelligence sources from around the world confirm Hindustan's ability to carry out its nuclear threat. As Legal Adviser to your country's Ministry of Foreign Affairs, you have been asked to advise your country's Foreign Minister and its Permanent Representative to the United Nations as to the international legality of Hindustan's threat of nuclear self-defense. Both Hindustan and Islamistan are parties to the United Nations Charter and all other treaties pertinent except the 1968 Treaty on the Non–Proliferation of Nuclear Weapons (NPT) and the 1996 Comprehensive Test Ban Treaty (CTBT).

SECTION 2.   QUESTIONS PRESENTED

1. Has Hindustan violated international law by threatening the use of nuclear weapons as a measure of retaliatory self-defense against Islamistan?

2. In any event, are there any additional or alternative legal norms, procedures, and/or institutions to be recommended that might further help to prevent or discourage situations of the kind posed by this problem?

Section 3.   Assignments

A.   Reading Assignment

Study the Readings presented in Section 4, *infra*, and the Discussion Notes/Questions that follow. Also, time permitting, consult the accompanying bibliographical references.

B.   Recommended Writing Assignment

Prepare a comprehensive, logically sequenced, and *argumentative* brief in the form of an outline of the primary and subsidiary *legal* issues you see requiring resolution for your country's Foreign Minister and Permanent Representative to the United Nations. Also, from the perspective of an independent judge, indicate which side ought to prevail on each issue and why. Retain a copy of your issue-outline/brief for class discussion.

C.   Recommended Oral Assignment

Assume that, in your professional judgment, you have concluded that your country should lend its diplomatic support to Hindustan or Islamistan (as designated by your instructor); then, relying upon the Readings (and your issue-outline if prepared), present a 10–15 minute oral argument of your likely position before your country's national security advisors, among them your country's Foreign Minister and its Permanent Representative to the United Nations.

D.   Recommended Reflective Assignment

Consider (and recommend) alternative norms, institutions, and/or procedures that you believe might do better than existing world order arrangements to contend with situations of the kind posed by this problem. In so doing, but without insisting upon *immediate* feasibility, identify the particular transition steps that would be needed to make your alternatives a reality.

Section 4.   Readings

The following readings are *prima facie* relevant to solving this problem. They are your law library for present purposes and should be treated as such, organized intelligibly for "shelving" and not necessarily according to the issues presented. Be sure to review Chapter 2 ("International Legal Prescription: The 'Sources' of International Law") in your consideration of them. It, too, should be treated as part of your law library (as, indeed, should this entire coursebook).

1. **Hague Convention (No. IV) Respecting the Laws and Customs of War on Land (with annex of regulations). Concluded, 18 Oct 1907. Entered into force, 26 Jan 1910. 205 C.T.S. 277 (French); 2 A.J.I.L. Supp. 90 (1908);** *reprinted in* **2 Weston & Carlson II.B.1: Preamble, Art. 2, & Annexed Regs. 22, 23, 27** (Basic Document 2.2).

2. **Protocol for the Prohibition of the Use in War of Asphyxiating, Poisonous or Other Gases, and of Bacteriological Methods of Warfare. Concluded, 17 Jun 1925. Entered into force, 8 Feb 1928. 94 L.N.T.S. 65;** *reprinted in* **2 Weston & Carlson II.C.35** (Basic Document 2.4).

3. **General Treaty for Renunciation of War as an Instrument of National Policy ("Pact of Paris" or "Kellogg–Briand Pact"). Concluded, 27 Aug 1928. Entered into force, 24 Jul 1929. 94 L.N.T.S. 57;** *reprinted in* **2 Weston & Carlson II.A.1** (Basic Document 2.5).

4. **Charter of the United Nations. Concluded, 26 Jun 1945. Entered into force, 24 Oct 1945. 1976 Y.B.U.N. 1043;** *reprinted in* **1 Weston & Carlson I.A.1: Pmbl. and Arts. 1(1) & (2), 2(3) & (4), 24(1), 33(1), 39, 43, 45, 51** (Basic Document 1.5).

5. **Agreement of the Government of the United Kingdom of Great Britain and Northern Ireland, the Government of the United States of America, the Provisional Government of the French Republic, and the Government of the Union of Soviet Socialist Republics for the Prosecution and Punishment of the Major War Criminals of the European Axis and Charter of the International Military Tribunal. Concluded at London, 8 August 1945. Entered into force, 8 August 1945. 82 U.N.T.S. 279; 1946 U.K.T.S. 27, Cmd. 6903, 145 B.F.S.P. 872, 59 Stat., 1544, E.A.S. 472;** *reprinted in* **2 Weston & Carlson II.E.1: Charter Art. 6** (Basic Document 1.3).

6. **Affirmation of the Principles of International Law Recognized by the Charter of the Nuremberg Tribunal, 11 Dec 1946, GA Res. 95, 1st Sess., at 1144, UN Doc. A/236 (1946)** (Basic Document 2.6).

7. **Convention on the Prevention and Punishment of the Crime of Genocide. Concluded, 9 Dec 1948. Entered into force, 12 Jan 1951. 78 U.N.T.S. 277;** *reprinted in* **3 Weston & Carlson III.J.1** (Basic Document 3.2).

8. **Geneva Convention (No. IV) Relative to the Protection of Civilian Persons in Time of War. Concluded, 12 Aug 1949. Entered into force, 21 Oct 1950. 75 U.N.T.S. 287;** *reprinted in* **2 Weston & Carlson II.B.14: Arts. 2, 47–57, 64, 68, 147, 158** (Basic Document 2.12).

9. **Declaration on the Prohibition of the Use of Nuclear and Thermo–Nuclear Weapons, 24 Nov 1961, GA Res. 1653, UN GAOR, 16th Sess., Supp. No. 17, at 4, UN Doc. A/5100 (1961);** *reprinted in* **2 Weston & Carlson II.C.12a** (Basic Document 2.17).

10. **Declaration on the Inadmissibility of Intervention in the Domestic Affairs of States and the Protection of their Independence**

and Sovereignty, 21 Dec 1965, GA Res. 2131, 20 UN GAOR Supp. No. 14, at 11, UN Doc. A/6014 (1966); *reprinted in* 5 I.L.M. 374 (1966) and 2 Weston & Carlson II.A.2 (Basic Document 2.20).

11. **Treaty on the Non–Proliferation of Nuclear Weapons. Concluded, 1 Jul 1968. Entered into force, 5 Mar 1970. 729 U.N.T.S. 161;** *reprinted in* **2 Weston & Carlson II.C.17: Art. 6** (Basic Document 2.21).

12. **Resolution on Respect for Human Rights in Armed Conflicts, 19 Dec 1968, GA Res. 2444, UN GAOR, 23rd Sess., Supp. No. 18, at 50, UN Doc. A/7128 (1969);** *reprinted in* **2 Weston & Carlson II.B.16** (Basic Document 2.23).

13. **Declaration on Principles of International Law Concerning Friendly Relations and Co-operation Among States in Accordance with the Charter of the United Nations, 24 Oct 1970, GA Res. 2625, 25 UN GAOR Supp. No. 28, at 121, UN Doc. A/8028 (1971);** *reprinted in* **9 I.L.M. 1292 (1970) and 1 Weston & Carlson I.D.7** (Basic Document 1.11).

14. **Stockholm Declaration on the Human Environment of the United Nations Conference on the Human Environment. Adopted by the UN Conference on the Human Environment at Stockholm, 16 June 1972.** *Report of the UN Conference on the Human Environment, Stockholm, 5–16 Jun 1972,* **UN Doc. A/CONF.48/14/Rev.1 at 3 (1973), UN Doc. A/CONF.48/14 at 2–65, and Corr. 1 (1972);** *reprinted in* **11 I.L.M. 1416 (1972) and 5 Weston & Carlson V.B.3: Princs. 2, 5–7, 21, 22, 26** (Basic Document 5.14).

15. **Resolution on the Non-use of Force in International Relations and Permanent Prohibition of the Use of Nuclear Weapons, 29 Nov 1972, GA Res. 2936, UN GAOR, 27th Sess, Supp. No. 30, at 5, UN Doc. A/8730 (1972);** *reprinted in* **2 Weston & Carlson II.A.3** (Basic Document 2.27).

16. **Resolution on the Definition of Aggression, 14 Dec 1974, GA Res. 3314, 29 UN GAOR Supp. No. 31, at 142, UN Doc. A/9631 (1975);** *reprinted in* **13 I.L.M. 710 (1974) & 2 Weston & Carlson II.A.4** (Basic Document 2.29).

17. **Convention on the Prohibition of Military or Any Other Hostile Use of Environmental Modification Techniques (ENMOD). Adopted by the UN General Assembly, 10 Dec 1976. Entered into force, 5 Oct 1978. 1108 U.N.T.S. 151, 1976 U.N.J.Y.B. 1125;** *reprinted in* **16 I.L.M. 88 (1977) and 2 Weston & Carlson II.B.19: Arts. I, II** (Basic Document 2.30).

18. **Protocol Additional (No. I) to the Geneva Conventions of August 12, 1949, and Relating to the Protection of Victims of International Armed Conflict. Concluded, 8 Jun 1977. Entered into force, 7 Dec 1978. 1977 U.N.J.Y.B. 95;** *reprinted in* **16 I.L.M. 1391 (1977) and 2 Weston & Carlson II.B.20: Arts. 35, 36, 51, 52, 54–58, 85, 90, 91** (Basic Document 2.31).

19. **Fundamental Rules of International Humanitarian Law Applicable in Armed Conflicts.** *International Review of the Red Cross* **(Geneva: International Committee of the Red Cross, 1978): 248;** *reprinted in* **2 Weston & Carlson II.B.22** (Basic Document 2.33).

20. **World Charter for Nature. Adopted by the UN General Assembly, 28 Oct 1982. GA Res. 37/7 (Annex), UN GAOR, 37th Sess., Supp. No. 51, at 17, UN Doc. A/37/51;** *reprinted in* **22 I.L.M. 455 (1983) and 5 Weston & Carlson V.B.11: Princs. 1, 5, 11, 12, 20, 24** (Basic Document 5.21).

21. **Rio Declaration on Environment and Development of the United Nations Conference on Environment and Development. Adopted by the UN Conference on Environment and Development (UNCED), 13 Jun 1992. UN Doc. A/CONF.151/26 (Vol. I) (1992);** *reprinted in* **31 I.L.M. 874 (1992) and 5 Weston & Carlson V.B.16: Princs. 1, 2, 24** (Basic Document 5.37).

22. **Comprehensive Test Ban Treaty (CTBT). Adopted by the UN General Assembly, 10 Sep 1996. Not in force as of 1 Mar 2006. GA Res. 50/245, UN GAOR, 50th Sess., Supp. No. 49, at 14 (1996) (incorporating UN Doc. A/50/1027 of 26 Aug 1996);** *reprinted in* **2 Weston & Carlson II.C.33d** (Basic Document 2.50)

23. **Myres S. McDougal and Florentino P. Feliciano, Law and Minimum World Public Order—The Legal Regulation of International Coercion, 217–18, 231–40** *passim* **(1961).**

[T]he principal requirements which the "customary law" of self-defense makes prerequisite to the lawful assertion of [claims to self-defense] are commonly summarized in terms of necessity and proportionality.... [It] is the clear import of the classical peroration of Secretary of State Webster in the *Caroline* case—that there must be shown a "necessity of self-defense, instant, overwhelming, leaving no choice of means and no moment for deliberation."[1] ... There is, however, increasing recognition that the requirements of necessity and proportionality ... can ultimately be subjected only to that most comprehensive and fundamental test of all law, reasonableness in particular context.

* * *

Inquiry into the factors that are relevant to an appraisal of coercion claimed to be permissible self-defense parallel ... inquiry into factors that rationally bear upon judgments about impermissible initiating coercion [*i.e.,* the characteristics of the participants, the nature of the claimants' objectives, the modalities of response, the conditions under which alleged self-defense is exercised, and the effects of coercion claimed to be in self-defense].... The principal emphasis here, however, must be upon the need of relating particular factors to the requirements of necessity and proportionality.

* * *

The Exacting Standard of Customary Law

The structure of traditional prescription [relating to self-defense] has established a standard of justifying necessity commonly referred to in exacting terms. A high degree of necessity—a "great and immediate" necessity, "direct

---

1. Mr. Webster to Mr. Fox, 24 Apr 1841, in 29 Brit. & For. St. Papers 1129, 1138 (1840–1841). [The *Caroline Case* is discussed also in Reading D–4 in Problem 4–1 ("Intervention in Loango"), *supra,* at 306].

and immediate," "compelling and instant"—was prerequisite to a characterization of coercion as "legitimate self-defense." . . . It was of course the purpose of high requirements of necessity to contain and restrict the assertion of claims to apply preemptive violence, that is when the necessity pleaded consisted of alleged expectations of an attack which had yet actually to erupt.[a] In the *Caroline* case, it will be recalled, the British claim with which Secretary of State Webster was confronted was an assertion of anticipatory defense. There is a whole continuum of degrees of imminence or remoteness in future time, from the most imminent to the most remote, which, in the expectations of the claimant of self-defense, may characterize an expected attack. Decision-makers sought to limit lawful anticipatory defense by projecting a customary requirement that the expected attack exhibit so high a degree of imminence as to preclude effective resort by the intended victim to non-violent modalities of response.

* * *

Maintenance of Customary–Law Standard in the UN Charter

It is against the background of the high degree of necessity required in traditional prescription that Article 51 of the United Nations Charter [**Basic Document 1.5**] should be considered. . . . Some scholars have taken the view that Article 51 demands an even higher degree of necessity than customary law for the characterization of coercion as permissible defense, that it limits justifying necessity to an "armed attack" as distinguished both from an expected attack of whatever degree of imminence and from applications of nonmilitary types of intense coercion, and that it absolutely forbids any anticipatory self-defense. . . .

The major difficulties with this reading of what appears to be an inept piece of draftsmanship are twofold. In the first place, neither Article 51 nor any other word formula can have, apart from context, any single "clear and unambiguous" or "popular, natural and ordinary" meaning that predetermines decision in infinitely varying particular controversies. . . . It is of common record in the preparatory work on the Charter that Article 51 was not drafted for the purpose of deliberately narrowing the customary-law permission of self-defense against a current or imminent unlawful attack by raising the required degree of necessity. . . . Further, in the process of formulating the prohibition of unilateral coercion contained in Article 2(4), it was made quite clear at San Francisco that the traditional permission of self-defense was not intended to be abridged and attenuated but, on the contrary, to be reserved and maintained. . . .

* * *

The second major difficulty with a narrow reading of Article 51 is that it requires a serious underestimation of the potentialities both of the newer military weapons systems and of the contemporary techniques of nonmilitary coercion. If, in scholarly interpretation . . ., any operational reference is seriously intended to be made to realistically expected practice and decision,

---

a. The authors derive the three quoted phrases from, respectively: J. Westlake, International Law 300 (1904); T. Lawrence, The Principles of International Law 118 (2d ed. 1897); G. Schwarzenberger, *The Fundamental Principles of International Law*, 87 Recueil 195, 334 (1955).

an attempt to limit permissible defense to that against an actual "armed attack," when increases in the capacity of modern weapons systems for velocity and destruction are reported almost daily in the front pages of newspapers, reflects a surpassing optimism. In these circumstances, "to cut down," Professor Waldock suggests forcefully, "the customary right of self-defense beyond even the *Caroline* doctrine does not make sense...."[2] * * * [T]he whole tenor and effect of consistently requiring a "last irrevocable act" would seem to be to compel the target state to defer its reaction until it would no longer be possible to repel an attack and avoid damage to itself. In case of delivery by ballistic (as distinguished from guided) missiles, whose trajectory is traversed in a matter of minutes and against which effective repulsion measures have yet to be devised, it ... is in effect to reduce self-defense to the possible infliction, if enough defenders survive, of retaliatory damage upon the enemy.

24. *Legality of the Threat or Use of Nuclear Weapons* (Advisory Opinion), 1996 ICJ 226 (Basic Document 7.10).[b]

[*Eds.*—This Advisory Opinion was given at the request of the UN General Assembly pursuant to GA Res. 49/75K, UN GAOR, 49th Sess., 90th plen. mtg., Supp. No. 49, at 71, UN Doc. A/RES/49/75 (1994) asking the following question: "Is the threat or use of nuclear weapons in any circumstances permitted under international law?"[c]]

38. The [United Nations] Charter **[Basic Document 1.5]** contains several provisions relating to the threat and use of force. In Article 2, paragraph 4, the threat or use of force against the territorial integrity or political independence of another State or in any other manner inconsistent with the purposes of the United Nations is prohibited....

This prohibition of the use of force is to be considered in the light of other relevant provisions of the Charter. In Article 51, the Charter recognizes the inherent right of individual or collective self-defence if an armed attack occurs. A further lawful use of force is envisaged in Article 42, whereby the Security Council may take military enforcement measures in conformity with Chapter VII of the Charter.

39. These provisions do not refer to specific weapons. They apply to any use of force, regardless of the weapons employed. The Charter neither expressly prohibits, nor permits, the use of any specific weapon, including nuclear weapons. A weapon that is already unlawful *per se*, whether by treaty or custom, does not become lawful by reason of its being used for a legitimate purpose under the Charter.

---

2. H. Waldock, *The Regulation of the Use of Force by Individual States in International Law*, 81 Recueil 455, 498 (1952)....

b. *Also available at* <http://www.icj-cij.org/icjwww/idecisions/isummaries/iunanaummary 96 0708.htm>. For an extensive summary, see **Basic Document 7.10**. For detailed discussion of the Advisory Opinion, see B. Weston, *Nuclear Weapons and the World Court: Ambiguity's Consensus,* 7 Transnat'l L. & Contemp. Probs. 371 (1997).

c. A similar request for an advisory opinion was put to the World Court by the World Health Organization (WHO) as follows: "In view of the health and environmental effects, would the use of nuclear weapons by a State in war or other armed conflict be a breach of its obligations under international law including the WHO Constitution?" In an 11–3 decision, also on 8 Jul 1996, the Court ruled against the WHO, on the grounds that the WHO lacked the legal competence to request an advisory opinion on the question posed. *Legality of the Use of a State of Nuclear Weapons in Armed Conflict,* 1996 ICJ 66.

40. The entitlement to resort to self-defence under Article 51 is subject to certain constraints. Some of these constraints are inherent in the very concept of self defence. Other requirements are specified in Article 51.

41. The submission of the exercise of the right of self-defence to the conditions of necessity and proportionality is a rule of customary international law. As the Court stated in the case concerning *Military and Paramilitary Activities in and against Nicaragua (Nicaragua* v. *United States of America) (ICJ Reports 1986*, p. 94, ¶ 176): "there is a specific rule whereby self-defence would warrant only measures which are proportional to the armed attack and necessary to respond to it, a rule well established in customary international law." This dual condition applies equally to Article 51 of the Charter, whatever the means of force employed.

42. The proportionality principle may thus not in itself exclude the use of nuclear weapons in self-defence in all circumstances. But at the same time, a use of force that is proportionate under the law of self-defence, must, in order to be lawful, also meet the requirements of the law applicable in armed conflict which comprise in particular the principles and rules of humanitarian law.

43. Certain States have in their written and oral pleadings suggested that in the case of nuclear weapons, the condition of proportionality must be evaluated in the light of still further factors. They contend that the very nature of nuclear weapons, and the high probability of an escalation of nuclear exchanges, mean that there is an extremely strong risk of devastation. The risk factor is said to negate the possibility of the condition of proportionality being complied with. The Court does not find it necessary to embark upon the quantification of such risks; nor does it need to enquire into the question whether tactical nuclear weapons exist which are sufficiently precise to limit those risks: it suffices for the Court to note that the very nature of all nuclear weapons and the profound risks associated therewith are further considerations to be borne in mind by States believing they can exercise a nuclear response in self-defence in accordance with the requirements of proportionality.

44. Beyond the conditions of necessity and proportionality, Article 51 specifically requires that measures taken by States in the exercise of the right of self-defence shall be immediately reported to the Security Council; this article further provides that these measures shall not in any way affect the authority and responsibility of the Security Council under the Charter to take at any time such action as it deems necessary in order to maintain or restore international peace and security. These requirements of Article 51 apply whatever the means of force used in self defence.

* * *

46. Certain States asserted that the use of nuclear weapons in the conduct of reprisals would be lawful. The Court does not have to examine, in this context, the question of armed reprisals in time of peace, which are considered to be unlawful. Nor does it have to pronounce on the question of belligerent reprisals save to observe that in any case any right of recourse to such reprisals would, like self-defence, be governed *inter alia* by the principle of proportionality.

47.   In order to lessen or eliminate the risk of unlawful attack, States sometimes signal that they possess certain weapons to use in self-defence against any State violating their territorial integrity or political independence. Whether a signalled intention to use force if certain events occur is or is not a "threat" within Article 2, paragraph 4, of the Charter depends upon various factors. If the envisaged use of force is itself unlawful, the stated readiness to use it would be a threat prohibited under Article 2, paragraph 4. Thus it would be illegal for a State to threaten force to secure territory from another State, or to cause it to follow or not follow certain political or economic paths. The notions of "threat" and "use" of force under Article 2, paragraph 4, of the Charter stand together in the sense that if the use of force itself in a given case is illegal for whatever reason the threat to use such force will likewise be illegal. In short, if it is to be lawful, the declared readiness of a State to use force must be a use of force that is in conformity with the Charter. For the rest, no State whether or not it defended the policy of deterrence suggested to the Court that it would be lawful to threaten to use force if the use of force contemplated would be illegal.

48.   Some States put forward the argument that possession of nuclear weapons is itself an unlawful threat to use force. Possession of nuclear weapons may indeed justify an inference of preparedness to use them. In order to be effective, the policy of deterrence, by which those States possessing or under the umbrella of nuclear weapons seek to discourage military aggression by demonstrating that it will serve no purpose, necessitates that the intention to use nuclear weapons be credible. Whether this is a "threat" contrary to Article 2, paragraph 4, depends upon whether the particular use of force envisaged would be directed against the territorial integrity or political independence of a State, or against the Purposes of the United Nations or whether, in the event that it were intended as a means of defence, it would necessarily violate the principles of necessity and proportionality. In any of these circumstances the use of force, and the threat to use it, would be unlawful under the law of the Charter.

* * *

52.   The Court notes ... that international customary and treaty law does not contain any specific prescription authorizing the threat or use of nuclear weapons or any other weapon in general or in certain circumstances, in particular those of the exercise of legitimate self defence. Nor, however, is there any principle or rule of international law which would make the legality of the threat or use of nuclear weapons or of any other weapons dependent on a specific authorization. State practice shows that the illegality of the use of certain weapons as such does not result from an absence of authorization but, on the contrary, is formulated in terms of prohibition.

53.   The Court must therefore now examine whether there is any prohibition of recourse to nuclear weapons as such; it will first ascertain whether there is a conventional prescription to this effect.

[*Eds.*—The Court next discusses treaty law prohibiting "poisonous weapons"—Second Hague Declaration of 29 July 1899, *reprinted in* 1 A.J.I.L. 157 (Supp. 1907); Article 23(a) of the Regulations respecting the laws and customs of war on land annexed to the Hague Convention IV of 18 October 1907 **(Basic Document 2.2)**; the Geneva Protocol of 17 June 1925 **(Basic Docu-**

ment 2.4)—and concludes that this law does not specifically apply to nuclear weapons. The Court then continues:]

60.   Those States that believe that recourse to nuclear weapons is illegal stress that the conventions that include various rules providing for the limitation or elimination of nuclear weapons in certain areas (such as the Antarctic Treaty of 1959 **[Basic Document 5.7]** which prohibits the deployment of nuclear weapons in the Antarctic, or the Treaty of Tlatelolco of 1967 [634 U.N.T.S. 1970, *reprinted in* 2 Weston & Carlson II.C.16] which creates a nuclear-weapon-free zone in Latin America), or the conventions that apply certain measures of control and limitation to the existence of nuclear weapons (such as the 1963 Partial Test–Ban Treaty **[Basic Document 2.18]** or the Treaty on the Non–Proliferation of Nuclear Weapons **[Basic Document 2.21]**) all set limits to the use of nuclear weapons. In their view, these treaties bear witness, in their own way, to the emergence of a rule of complete legal prohibition of all uses of nuclear weapons.

61.   Those States who defend the position that recourse to nuclear weapons is legal in certain circumstances see a logical contradiction in reaching such a conclusion. According to them, those Treaties, such as the Treaty on the Non–Proliferation of Nuclear Weapons, as well as Security Council resolutions 255 (1968) and 984 (1995) which take note of the security assurances given by the nuclear-weapon States to the non-nuclear-weapon States in relation to any nuclear aggression against the latter, cannot be understood as prohibiting the use of nuclear weapons, and such a claim is contrary to the very text of those instruments. For those who support the legality in certain circumstances of recourse to nuclear weapons, there is no absolute prohibition against the use of such weapons. The very logic and construction of the Treaty on the Non–Proliferation of Nuclear Weapons, they assert, confirm this. This Treaty, whereby, they contend, the possession of nuclear weapons by the five nuclear-weapon States has been accepted, cannot be seen as a treaty banning their use by those States; to accept the fact that those States possess nuclear weapons is tantamount to recognizing that such weapons may be used in certain circumstances. Nor, they contend, could the security assurances given by the nuclear-weapon States in 1968, and more recently in connection with the Review and Extension Conference of the Parties to the Treaty on the Non–Proliferation of Nuclear Weapons in 1995, have been conceived without its being supposed that there were circumstances in which nuclear weapons could be used in a lawful manner. For those who defend the legality of the use, in certain circumstances, of nuclear weapons, the acceptance of those instruments by the different non-nuclear-weapon States confirms and reinforces the evident logic upon which those instruments are based.

62.   The Court notes that the treaties dealing exclusively with acquisition, manufacture, possession, deployment and testing of nuclear weapons, without specifically addressing their threat or use, certainly point to an increasing concern in the international community with these weapons; the Court concludes from this that these treaties could therefore be seen as foreshadowing a future general prohibition of the use of such weapons, but they do not constitute such a prohibition by themselves. . . .

* * *

85. Turning now to the applicability of the principles and rules of humanitarian law to a possible threat or use of nuclear weapons, the Court notes that doubts in this respect have sometimes been voiced on the ground that these principles and rules had evolved prior to the invention of nuclear weapons and that the Conferences of Geneva of 1949 and 1974–1977 which respectively adopted the four Geneva Conventions of 1949 **[Basic Documents 2.9, 2.10, 2.11 & 2.12]** and the two Additional Protocols **[Basic Document 2.31 & 2.32]** thereto did not deal with nuclear weapons specifically. Such views, however, are only held by a small minority. In the view of the vast majority of States as well as writers there can be no doubt as to the applicability of humanitarian law to nuclear weapons.

86. The Court shares that view. Indeed, nuclear weapons were invented after most of the principles and rules of humanitarian law applicable in armed conflict had already come into existence; the Conferences of 1949 and 1974–1977 left these weapons aside, and there is a qualitative as well as quantitative difference between nuclear weapons and all conventional arms. However, it cannot be concluded from this that the established principles and rules of humanitarian law applicable in armed conflict did not apply to nuclear weapons. Such a conclusion would be incompatible with the intrinsically humanitarian character of the legal principles in question which permeates the entire law of armed conflict and applies to all forms of warfare and to all kinds of weapons, those of the past, those of the present and those of the future . . .

* * *

95. [The Court cannot] make a determination on the validity of the view that the recourse to nuclear weapons would be illegal in any circumstance owing to their inherent and total incompatibility with the law applicable in armed conflict. Certainly, as the Court has already indicated, the principles and rules of law applicable in armed conflict at the heart of which is the overriding consideration of humanity make the conduct of armed hostilities subject to a number of strict requirements. Thus, methods and means of warfare, which would preclude any distinction between civilian and military targets, or which would result in unnecessary suffering to combatants, are prohibited. In view of the unique characteristics of nuclear weapons, to which the Court has referred above, the use of such weapons in fact seems scarcely reconcilable with respect for such requirements. Nevertheless, the Court considers that it does not have sufficient elements to enable it to conclude with certainty that the use of nuclear weapons would necessarily be at variance with the principles and rules of law applicable in armed conflict in any circumstance.

96. Furthermore, the Court cannot lose sight of the fundamental right of every State to survival, and thus its right to resort to self-defence, in accordance with Article 51 of the Charter, when its survival is at stake. Nor can it ignore the practice referred to as "policy of deterrence," to which an appreciable section of the international community adhered for many years. The Court also notes the reservations which certain nuclear-weapon States have appended to the undertakings they have given, notably under the Protocols to the Treaties of Tlatelolco and Rarotonga, and also under the

declarations made by them in connection with the extension of the Treaty on the Non–Proliferation of Nuclear Weapons, not to resort to such weapons.

97.   Accordingly, in view of the present state of international law viewed as a whole, as examined above by the Court, and of the elements of fact at its disposal, the Court is led to observe that it cannot reach a definitive conclusion as to the legality or illegality of the use of nuclear weapons by a State in an extreme circumstance of self-defence, in which its very survival would be at stake.

25.   Editors' Note. In the *Nuclear Weapons Case* the World Court ruled unanimously, first that "[a] threat or use of force by means of nuclear weapons that is contrary to Article 2(4) of the United Nations Charter and that fails to meet all the requirements of Article 51, is unlawful"; and, second that "[a] threat or use of nuclear weapons should also be compatible with the requirements of the international law applicable in armed conflict, particularly those of the principles and rules of international humanitarian law, as well as with specific obligations under treaties and other undertakings which expressly deal with nuclear weapons. It ruled by only seven votes to seven on the proposition that "the threat or use of nuclear weapons would generally be contrary to the rules of international law applicable in armed conflict, and in particular the principles and rules of humanitarian law...." It reached this particular result, on the other hand, because, "in view of the current state of international law, and of the elements of fact at its disposal," it could not conclude "definitively," one way or the other, "whether the threat or use of nuclear weapons would be lawful or unlawful in an extreme circumstance of self-defence, in which the very survival of a State would be at stake...." Moreover, three of the seven "dissenting" judges (Judges Shahabuddeen, Weeramantry, and Koroma) argued that the Court should have ruled that the threat or use of nuclear weapons would be unlawful under *all* circumstances, thus resulting in a *functional majority* of ten votes to seven in support of the proposition that "the threat or use of nuclear weapons would generally be contrary to the rules of international law applicable in armed conflict, and in particular the principles and rules of humanitarian law...." Each of these "dissenters" wrote separate opinions, the longest and perhaps most important of which is that of Judge Weeramantry of Sri Lanka. Particularly noteworthy for present purposes are his findings on the issue of nuclear self-defense:

> Self-defence raises probably the most serious problems in this case. The second sentence in paragraph 2(E) of the *dispositif* states that, in the current state of international law and of the elements of fact at its disposal, the Court cannot conclude definitively whether the threat or use of nuclear weapons would be lawful or unlawful in an extreme circumstance of self-defence, in which the very survival of a state would be at stake. I have voted against this clause as I am of the view that the threat or use of nuclear weapons would not be lawful in any circumstances whatsoever, as it offends the fundamental principles of the *ius in bello*. This conclusion is clear and follows inexorably from well-established principles of international law.

> If a nation is attacked, it is clearly entitled under the United Nations Charter to the right of self-defence. Once a nation thus enters into the domain of the *ius in bello*, the principles of humanitarian law apply to the

conduct of self-defence, just as they apply to the conduct of any other aspect of military operations. We must hence examine what principles of the *ius in bello* apply to the use of nuclear weapons in self-defence.

The first point to be noted is that the use of *force* in self-defence (which is an undoubted right) is one thing and the use of *nuclear weapons* in self-defence is another. The permission granted by international law for the first does not embrace the second, which is subject to other governing principles as well. * * * [P]rinciples of humanitarian law ... apply to the use of nuclear weapons in self-defence, just as they apply to their use in any aspect of war. Principles relating to unnecessary suffering, proportionality, discrimination, non-belligerent states, genocide, environmental damage and human rights would all be violated, no less in self-defence than in an open act of aggression. The *ius in bello* covers all use of force, whatever the reasons for resort to force. There can be no exceptions, without violating the essence of its principles.

The state subjected to the first attack could be expected to respond in kind. After the devastation caused by a first attack, especially if it be a nuclear attack, there will be a tendency to respond with any nuclear firepower that is available.

[Former US Secretary of Defense] Robert McNamara, in dealing with the response to initial strikes, states:

> "But under such circumstances, leaders on both sides would be under unimaginable pressure to avenge their losses and secure the interests being challenged. And each would fear that the opponent might launch a larger attack at any moment. Moreover, they would both be operating with only partial information because of the disruption to communications caused by the chaos on the battlefield (to say nothing of possible strikes against communication facilities). Under such conditions, it is highly likely that rather than surrender, each side would launch a larger attack, hoping that this step would bring the action to a halt by causing the opponent to capitulate."[3]

With such a response, the clock would accelerate towards global catastrophe, for a counter-response would be invited and, indeed, could be automatically triggered off.

It is necessary to reiterate here the undoubted right of the state that is attacked to use all the weaponry available to it for the purpose of repulsing the aggressor. Yet this principle holds only *so long as such weapons do not violate the fundamental rules of warfare embodied in those rules*. Within these constraints, and for the purpose of repulsing the enemy, the full military power of the state that is attacked can be unleashed upon the aggressor. While this is incontrovertible, one has yet to hear an argument in any forum, or a contention in any academic literature, that a nation attacked, for example, with chemical or biological weapons is entitled to use chemical or biological weapons in self-defence, or to annihilate the aggressor's population. It is strange that the most

---

3. R. McNamara, *The Military Role of Nuclear Weapons: Perceptions and Misperceptions,*   62 Foreign Aff. No. 1, at 71–72 (1983–84).

devastating of all the weapons of mass destruction can be conceived of as offering a singular exception to this most obvious conclusion following from the bedrock principles of humanitarian law.

[*Eds.*—Judge Weeramantry then catalogues various principles of humanitarian law which "could be violated by self-defence": unnecessary suffering, proportionality/ error, discrimination, damage to non-belligerent states, genocide, environmental damage, and human rights, discussed next.]

7. Human rights

* * *

The humanitarian principles discussed above have long passed the stage of being merely philosophical aspirations. They are the living law and represent the high water mark of legal achievement in the difficult task of imposing some restraints on the brutalities of unbridled war. They provide the ground rules for military action today and have been forged by the community of nations under the impact of the sufferings of untold millions in two global cataclysms and many smaller wars. As with all legal principles, they govern without distinction all nations great and small.

It seems difficult, with any due regard to the consistency that must underlie any credible legal system, to contemplate that all these hard-won principles should bend aside in their course and pass the nuclear weapon by leaving that unparalleled agency of destruction free to achieve on a magnified scale the very evils which these principles were designed to prevent.

* * *

Upon a review therefore, no exception can be made to the illegality of the use of nuclear weapons merely because the weapons are used in self-defence.

Collective self-defence, where another country has been attacked, raises the same issues as are discussed above.

Anticipatory self-defence—the pre-emptive strike before the enemy has actually attacked—cannot legally be effected by a nuclear strike, for a first strike with nuclear weapons would axiomatically be prohibited by the basic principles already referred to. In the context of non-nuclear weaponry, all the sophistication of modern technology and the precise targeting systems now developed would presumably be available for this purpose.

26. Romana Sadurska, "Threats of Force," 82 A.J.I.L. 239, 249–53, 260–66 (1988).

At first sight, it seems reasonable to say that when a threat is made in circumstances where resort to force would be unlawful, the threat itself is also unlawful. Ian Brownlie states: "If the promise is to resort to force in conditions in which no justification for the use of force exists, the threat itself is illegal." ...

In the international legal order, the view that the threat and use of force should be treated equally, at least as far as legal rhetoric goes, can be sustained if we accept the premise that the ultimate value protected by international law is the freedom of states from external pressure.... However, the preoccupation of international law with the political independence of states is not inspired by the concern of individualist liberalism with the freedom of political elites, but rather by the need for peace and order among nations....

The [United Nations] Charter **[Basic Document 1.5]** makes this premise explicit. The opening words of the Preamble express the determination of "the Peoples of the United Nations ... to save succeeding generations from the scourge of war," and Article 1(1) states as the first among the purposes of the Organization, "to maintain international peace and security." ... Respect for the political independence of states is not even included among these purposes. It is a principle that should be observed to further the purposes of the Organization, but it is not a purpose in itself.

The Charter prohibits the use of force in violation of the political independence and territorial integrity of a state *because* it may lead to international instability, breach of the peace and/or massive abuses of human rights. But if that is the rationale of Article 2(4), then there is no justification for the claim that the use of force and the threat of force should be treated equally. Typically, an effective threat of force can violate the political independence of a state, but even an effective threat will not have the same destructive consequences as the use of force. (As a matter of fact, in specific cases, an effective threat may be an economical guarantee against open violence.) Therefore, there is no reason to assume that the threat will *always* be unlawful if in the same circumstances the resort to force would be illicit. Consider, for instance, a nuclear strike in response to a conventional armed attack. Although prima facie it could well qualify as self-defense under Article 51 of the Charter, it is likely to fail the test of proportionality and ultimately be appraised as unlawful. Does it follow that the threat to use nuclear arms is also unlawful? Minimum nuclear deterrence, insofar as it discourages aggression against some targets, is perceived by many international actors as compatible with the purposes of the United Nations. In their view, the legal appraisal of the threat should be similar to the verdict on the use of force only if they produce comparable results.

It seems that as long as the threat of force does not jeopardize peace or lead to massive violations of human rights, international actors demonstrate varying degrees of approval or more or less reluctant tolerance for unilateral threats.... [But] [h]ow much unilaterally applied coercion the international community is prepared to tolerate is not clear. Practice does not seem sufficiently unambiguous to make unfailingly intelligible distinctions among genuine approval of acts of self-help, reluctant acquiescence in them and resigned recognition of a fait accompli. Commentators vary in their assessments of the present state of the law pertaining to armed coercion: from interpretations of Articles 2(4) and 51 as allowing strictly limited exceptions only, to suggestions of a "partial revival of a type of unilateral *jus ad bellum.*" . . .

* * *

The perception of threats as a prudent and economical sanction does not square comfortably with the standard picture of international law. [But] ...

some trends ... appear to form a pattern of shared expectations about the acceptability of this function of threats of force.

Considerations of Security. In the Cuban missile crisis ..., the quarantine [imposed on Cuba by the United States to interdict the entry into Cuba of Soviet offensive weapons and other military hardware] was specifically designed "to ensure that the Government of Cuba cannot continue to receive from the Sino–Soviet powers military material and related supplies which may threaten the peace and security of the Continent." By adopting a threatening posture, the United States communicated to the world its commitment to maintaining the status quo in the zone considered vital to its security.

International actors responded to this stance with varying degrees of support or tolerance. ... Since, in our volatile world, subjective perceptions of security dangers can lead to acts that jeopardize peace, states may be inclined to consider as licit those threats which help to restore an upset equilibrium in the international order. * * * Not every perception of threat, however, is taken as sufficient to justify a concern for security. The international community seems to examine the reasonableness of the perceptions of threat. ...

Vindication of a Denied Right. International actors seem to tolerate a threat of force for the vindication of a denied right, provided the right is well established in customary international law or in an agreement. Although this is not a sufficient condition of lawfulness, it remains its necessary and preliminary test. The decision of the International Court of Justice in the *Corfu Channel* case[d] [affirming a threat of force as a measure of enforcement of the right of innocent passage through an international waterway in peacetime] may be interpreted as confirming the point. ...

Prudence and Economy. The international community seems to approve, or at least tolerate, the actions of a threatener that proceeds with prudence, carefully balancing individual and community values, and strives to achieve the results in the most economical way, by rationally relating means to aims.

* * *

Consequences of the Threat. A threat may be carefully calculated and meet ... all the criteria of prudence and economy. It may aim at enforcing an illegally denied right without causing any prolonged violation of the territorial sovereignty, or fettering the political independence, of the target. It may be justified by the need for security. Yet it may fail to gain the approval of the international community. For ultimately, international law is less concerned with the intentions of the threatener than with the outcomes of the behavior. ...

In the final account, the threatener is judged by the consequences of the threatening action. The ultimate question is: have the benefits for the overall security and welfare of the community balanced the harm resulting from the conduct of the threatener? In a world full of tensions and sadly lacking in mutual trust, actions that further peace and stability deserve legal blessing.

SECTION 5. DISCUSSION NOTES/QUESTIONS

1. The doctrine of self-defense in international law is constrained by the requirement that the action be proportional in its context. What does the

---

d. 1949 ICJ 27.

requirement of proportionality entail? Judith Gardam discusses this issue in the context of the first Gulf War prompted by Iraq's invasion of Kuwait in *Proportionality and Force in International Law*, 87 A.J.I.L. 391, 404–05 (1993) as follows:

> A state cannot assess proportionality at the time it is deciding on the appropriate response to an armed attack and then dispense with it. In the Gulf conflict, for example, many of the decisions involving the application of proportionality would have been taken at the planning stage of the campaign. The decision to use massive aerial bombardment before the ground attack, the decision to attack targets in Iraq and the actual choice of these targets— all involved consideration of whether the actions were justified to achieve the legal result, the withdrawal of Iraq from Kuwait. The need to assess proportionality, however, would not have ended there. Each time targets were selected, for example, the relationship between the destruction of the target or targets and the scope of collective self-defense would have required assessment. In some cases, no doubt, the choice of targets raised questions as to whether the principle of proportionality in the law of armed conflict had been complied with. Even if under these rules the loss of civilian life was justified by the military advantage, the issue remained as to whether the destruction of the target was sufficiently related to the justifiable ends as to constitute a legitimate action in self-defense. In the Gulf conflict, the aerial bombardment of the infrastructure of Iraq had to be balanced against its contribution to the removal of Iraq from Kuwait. The decision to use this type of warfare was to a considerable extent dictated by the coalition forces' legitimate aim of minimizing their losses in the anticipated ground war. There is a limit, however, to the extent that such considerations can dictate the conduct of a campaign.

> Proportionality is a complex concept to apply to particular cases and there will inevitably be differences of opinion. It is difficult, therefore, to arrive at any firm conclusions about the proportionality in all its aspects of the coalition forces' response to the Iraqi invasion. It is not suggested that the actions of the coalition forces were so disproportionate as to convert a "just" resort to force into an "unjust" one. Such a result could have ensued if the overall response had been totally disproportionate in both *jus ad bellum* and *jus in bello* aspects, as measured against the legitimate ends. It is within the scope of legitimate self-defense for a state to undermine, as the coalition forces did, the military strength of an opposing state by aerial bombardment prior to the commencement of a ground offensive. In the Gulf conflict, achieving this aim necessarily encompassed attacks on targets within Iraq. It is, however, the massive destruction of the infrastructure of the state and the impact on the civilian population that are troubling. Certainly, these actions contributed to the early capitulation of Iraq, and the targets are within the definition of military targets under the customary rules. The legitimacy of such actions, however, is a question of degree, with civilian casualties a particularly relevant factor in assessing proportionality. It appears that more was done than was proportionate to expelling Iraq from Kuwait. As Walzer argues, these attacks indicate an illegitimate and unjust aim, the overthrow of the Iraqi regime, and thus lose their legitimacy as actions in self-defense.[8]

What arguments could Hindustan and Islamistan respectively make on the proportionality of the threat of nuclear action?

2.   In his "dissenting" opinion in *Legality of the Threat or Use of Nuclear Weapons* (*supra* Reading 25, p. 448), Judge Weeramantry differs from the majority

---

8. M. Walzer, Just and Unjust Wars xx (2d ed. 1991).

(*supra* Reading 24, p. 443) in his view of the legal requirments of the right to self-defense. Do you prefer the majority view or that of Judge Weeramantry? Why? For differing views on the relationship of the right to self-defense and nuclear weapons, compare, *e.g.*, Burns H. Weston, *Nuclear Weapons Versus International Law: A Contextual Reassessment*, 28 McGill L. J. 542 (1983) and Francis A. Boyle, *The Relevance of International Law to the Paradox of Nuclear Deterrence*, 80 Nw. U. L. Rev. 1407 (1986) with W. Michael Reisman, *Deterrence and International Law*, in Nuclear Weapons and Law 129 (A. Miller & M. Feinrider eds., 1984). For a useful overview of the debate, see Elliott L. Meyrowitz, *The Opinions of Legal Scholars on the Legal Status of Nuclear Weapons*, 24 Stan. J. Int'l L. 111 (1987). For other interesting discussions of the issues dealt with by the World Court include: B. S. Chimni, *Nuclear Weapons and International Law: Some Reflections*, in International Law in Transition 137 (R. S. Pathak & R. P. Dhokalia eds., 1992); William R. Hearn, The International Legal Regime Regulating Nuclear Deterrence and Warfare, 61 B.Y.B.I.L. 199 (1990); International Law, The International Court of Justice, and Nuclear Weapons (L. Boisson de Chazournes & P. Sands eds., 1999); Christopher C. Weeramantry, *The Law, Nuclear Weapons and the Real World*, 19 Denver J. Int'l L. & Pol'y 11 (1990); Nicholas C. Rostow, *The World Health Organization, The International Court of Justice, and Nuclear Weapons*, 20 Yale J. Int'l L. 151 (1995).

3.   In its advisory opinion entitled *Legality of the Threat or Use of Nuclear Weapons* (*supra* Reading 24, p. 443) and **Basic Document 7.10)**, the World Court concluded its assessment by holding that, per Article VI of the 1968 Treaty on the Non–Proliferation of Nuclear Weapons **(Basic Document 2.21)**, the nuclear-weapon-states are under a legal obligation "to negotiate in good faith a nuclear disarmament." The Court stated at ¶ 99: "The legal import of that obligation goes beyond that of a mere obligation of conduct; the obligation involved here is an obligation to achieve a precise result—nuclear disarmament in all its aspects—by adopting a particular course of conduct, namely, the pursuit of negotiations on the matter in good faith." The Court also held that the obligation extended even to non-parties to the NPT.

Do past efforts at nuclear arms *control* represent a fulfillment of this "good faith" legal obligation to achieve nuclear *disarmament*?

The United States and the Soviet Union agreed in 1961 in the McCloy–Zorin Agreement (UN Doc. A/4879, *reprinted in* 2 Weston & Carlson II.C.2) to work towards respectively an internationally acceptable program of general and complete disarmament that would lead to the eventual dissolution of national armed forces, the creation of a standing UN peacekeeping force, and the establishment of effective and reliable mechanisms for the peaceful settlement of international disputes. From the late 1960s, however, the Soviet Union and the United States negotiated the control and reduction of nuclear arms only intermittently, and then in a manner that may have made resort to nuclear weapons more acceptable than unacceptable as a policy option in a variety of confrontational contexts. Two distinct sets of negotiations were pursued.

For helpful discussion concerning the first of these sets of negotiations—the Strategic Arms Limitation Talks (SALT I), concentrating on the control rather than the reduction or elimination of nuclear weapons—see Robert C. Johansen, *SALT II: A Symptom of the Arms Race*, in Toward Nuclear Disarmament and Global Security: A Search for Alternatives (B. Weston ed., 1984); Notburga K. Calvo–Goller & Michael A. Calvo, The SALT Agreement: Content–Application–

Verification (1987); Committee on International Security and Arms Control, Nuclear Arms Control: Background and Issues (1985).

For helpful discussion concerning the second set of negotiations—the Strategic Arms Reduction Talks (START), begun in the early 1980s largely in reaction to the collapse of SALT II and aimed to reduce as well as control nuclear weapons and their delivery systems—see Patricia Hewitson, *Between Empire and Community: The United States and Multilateralism 2001–2003: A Mid-term Assessment: Arms Control, Nonproliferation and Reduction of Nuclear Weapons*, 21 Berkeley J. Int'l L. 405 (2003).

See generally also Antonio F. Perez, *Is International Law Relevant to Arms Control?*, 4 Chi. J. Int'l L. 19 (2003).

4. Another approach to the limitation and control of nuclear weapons has been the negotiation of nuclear test ban agreements, a subject of both bilateral and multilateral negotiation since the mid–1950s: (a) the 5 August 1963 Treaty Banning Nuclear Weapon Tests in the Atmosphere, in Outer Space and under Water ("Partial Test Ban Treaty" or "PTBT"), 480 U.N.T.S. 43, *reprinted in* 2 Weston & Carlson II.C.14, banning all nuclear tests except those conducted underground and ratified by over 113 countries as of April 2003; (b) the 3 July 1974 Treaty on the Limitation of Underground Nuclear Weapon Tests ("Threshold Test Ban Treaty"), 71 Dep't State Bull. 217 (1974), *reprinted in* 13 I.L.M. 906 (1974) and 2 Weston & Carlson II.C.24, banning underground tests above 150 kilotons;[e] and (c) the 28 May 1976 Treaty on Underground Nuclear Explosions for Peaceful Purposes, 74 Dep't State Bull. 801 (1978), *reprinted in* 15 I.L.M. 891 (1976) and 2 Weston & Carlson II.C.25, regulating nuclear explosions for peaceful purposes below the 150 kiloton threshhold; and, most recently but still not in force, (d) the 1996 Comprehensive Nuclear Test Ban Treaty (CTBT), GA Res. 50/245, UN GAOR, 50th Sess., Supp. No. 49, at 14 (1996) (incorporating UN Doc. A/50/1027 of 26 Aug 1996), *reprinted in* 2 Weston & Carlson II.C.33d **(Basic Document 2.50)** and listed as Reading 22, *supra*, at 441. The US Senate rejected the CTBT in 1999 under then President Bill Clinton [*see* Terry L. Deibel, *The Death of a Treaty*, Foreign Aff. 142 (Sept–Oct 2002)], and President George W. Bush, long opposed to the CTBT, thereafter refused to re-submit it to the Senate for advice and consent to ratification. The CTBT bans *all* nuclear explosions, underground and above ground, military or civilian, high yield or low yield, and thus replacing the PTBT. The CTBT provides for national implementation measures for each state party to implement its treaty obligations and sets up a verification regime consisting of an international monitoring system, consultation and clarification, on-site inspection and confidence-building measures. Work on the treaty had begun in the Conference on Disarmament (CD) in Geneva in 1994. India, however, which set off a nuclear explosion in 1974 and which is believed to have a clandestine nuclear weapons program, bitterly opposed the draft text of the CTBT, negotiated after two years work by the CD, and stated its intention not to sign a treaty in those terms; and Pakistan has said that it will boycott the CTBT if India does. India argued that, under the CTBT, the declared nuclear states (China, France, Russia, the U.K., and the US) have an unfair advantage over other states because they already possess stockpiles of weapons and that the CTBT regime simply would "freeze" this imbalance. Thus, India has insisted on a link being made between the CTBT and a general disarmament treaty, which

---

e. The atomic bomb dropped on Hiroshima on 6 Aug 1945 was a 12.5 kiloton (thousands of TNT equivalent weapon. The explosion killed 70,000 to 100,000 inhabitants and completely destroyed 13 square kilometres of the city.

would require the eradication of the stockpiles of the nuclear weapons states. India is considered a "threshold" (*i.e.*, undeclared) nuclear state, along with Pakistan and Israel, and Article XIV of the CTBT requires that all forty-four states that have nuclear research reactors or programs must ratify the treaty before it can come into effect. The text of the CTBT negotiated in the CD was adopted in a General Assembly resolution on 10 September 1996 in a move instigated by Australia to overcome India's veto of the draft treaty text in the CD. As formal consensus on the text was not achieved in the CD, direct endorsement by the General Assembly allowed the treaty to be opened for signature. The CTBT was adopted by a vote of 158 in favor, three against (India, Bhutan and Libya), and five abstentions (Cuba, Lebanon, Mauritius, Syria, and Tanzania). For relevant discussion, see George Perkovich, *India, Pakistan, and the United States: The Zero–Sum Game*, 13 World Pol'y J. 49 (Summer 1996). In July 1996, an independent commission comprised of international experts and established by the Australian government to propose practical steps towards a nuclear weapons-free world issued their report. The Canberra Commission on the Elimination of Nuclear Weapons called on the nuclear states to unequivocally commit themselves to eliminate all nuclear weapons, but proposed no timetable. For the complete text of the Commission's report, see its website at <http://www.dfat.gov.au/dfat/cc/cchome.html>. On 3 December 2004, in Resolution 59/102, the UN General Assembly called upon the CD to recommence negotiations to reach an agreement on an international convention prohibiting the use or threat of use of nuclear weapons under any circumstances. Do you believe that this is a realistic method to prevent nuclear warfare? What will be required for such a convention to be consummated?

Yet another approach to the limitation and control of nuclear weapons is found in the 1968 Treaty on the Non–Proliferation of Nuclear Weapons (NPT) **(Basic Document 2.21)**, the essential purpose of which is to prevent the spread of nuclear weapons. Following a month-long review conference in April 1995, it was determined by consensus to support the indefinite and unconditional extension of the NPT (which expired 25 Apr 1995) and on 11 May 1995, 178 nations agreed to extend the treaty permanently. The Conference also adopted three documents intended to strengthen the NPT's review process, establish a set of common principles and objectives for nuclear nonproliferation and disarmament, and promote measures to limit the proliferation of weapons of mass destruction in the Middle East. In July 2005, however, India announced that it would not sign the NPT because, according to Indian Defense Minister Pranab Mukeerjee, "it [is] discriminatory and flawed." *India Will Not Sign NPT: Pranab*, The Hindu, 20 Jul 2005, *available at* <http://www.hindu.com/thehindu/holnus/001200507202040.htm>. For further details, see C. Mierzwa, *The Indefinite Nuclear Non–Proliferation Treaty: Substantial Accomplishments or Ambitious Hopes?*, 4 J. Int'l L. & Prac. 555 (1995). *See also* William Epstein & Paul Szasz, *Extension of the Nuclear Non–Proliferation Treaty: A Means of Strengthening the Treaty*, 33 Va. J. Int'l L. 735 (1993); Antonio F. Perez, *Survival of Rights Under the Nuclear Non–Proliferation Treaty: Withdrawal and the Continuing Right of International Atomic Energy Agency Safeguards*, 34 Va. J. Int'l L. 749 (1994); Bryan Sutter, *The Nonproliferation Treaty and the New World Order*, 26 Vand. J. Trans'l L. 181 (1993); Richard L. Williamson, *Law and the H–Bomb: Strengthening the Nonproliferation Regime to Impede Advanced Proliferation,* 28 Cornell Int'l L.J. 71 (1995). International commitment to the NPT appears to be weakening, for example through the acceptance in the late 1990s of both India and Pakistan's nuclear capacities. These two countries and Israel have never ratified the NPT. In

January 2003, North Korea announced that it was withdrawing immediately from the NPT because of claimed US hostility towards it and threats to its security. North Korea's action raised questions of compliance with the three-month notice requirement of Article X of the NPT.

It is not only by international agreement, however, that the non-proliferation of nuclear weapons might be pursued. For example, on 7 June 1981, Israeli planes attacked and destroyed Iraq's nuclear research reactor at Osirak, claiming that the strike was a lawful act of self-defense designed to prevent Iraq from acquiring weapons-grade fissionable material that could be used against Israel. The UN Security Council condemned the attack. The lawfulness of this intervention might be questioned, but could not a "realist" regard Israel's behavior to constitute a vigorous commitment to a strict policy of non-proliferation of nuclear weapons. Would you? Why? Why not? For a discussion of the Osirak incident see Timothy L. H. McCormack, *Self-Defense in International Law: The Israeli Raid on the Iraqi Nuclear Reactor* (1996).

5.   Writing before the adoption of the 1963 Partial Test Ban Treaty (cited in Discussion Note/Question 4, *supra*), Myres S. McDougal and Norbert A. Schlei argued that atmospheric tests conducted by the United States in the area of the South Pacific high seas on the US-administered Bikini and Eniwetok atolls from 1946 to 1954 were reasonable and lawful activities in that their importance to the "free world" outweighed their interference with customary uses of the sea. *See* McDougal & Schlei, *The Hydrogen Bomb Tests in Perspective: Lawful Measures for Security*, 64 Yale L. J. 648 (1955). Would you have agreed? Disagreed? Why? *Compare* Emanuel Margolis, *The Hydrogen Bomb Experiments and International Law*, 64 Yale L. J. 629 (1955).

6.   In the *Nuclear Tests* cases between Australia and New Zealand on the one hand, and France on the other, 1973 ICJ 99 and 135, the World Court issued an "interim order of protection" calling upon France, neither a party to the proceeding nor to the 1963 Partial Test Ban Treaty **(Basic Document 2.18)**, to cease its atmospheric nuclear tests in French Polynesia on the grounds that the radioactive fallout from the tests was causing perhaps irreparable and illegal harm to Australian and New Zealand territory. Ignoring the interim order, France conducted further atmospheric tests, but shortly thereafter completed its testing program and indicated that it would conduct no further tests. Australia and New Zealand nevertheless pursued their claims before the ICJ; however, to no avail. The World Court, holding their cases to be mooted by the French decision to conduct no further tests, denied their requests for a declaratory judgment and, accordingly, dismissed their complaints. *Nuclear Tests* (Austl. v. Fr.) 1974 ICJ 253 and (N.Z. v. Fr.) 1974 ICJ 457. Was this a desirable result? Could it have been otherwise?

In any event, what action might have been taken to enforce the interim order? Note that Article 94 of the UN Charter **(Basic Document 1.5)** provides that any party to a case may have recourse to the Security Council if any other party "fails to perform the obligations incumbent upon it under a judgment rendered by the Court...." Do provisional measures of protection qualify as "a judgment" in this regard? If so, what might the results have been had Australia and New Zealand appealed to the Security Council? If not, what results might have been obtained had the Court, in its 1974 decisions, declared in favor of Australia and New Zealand instead of finding their cases moot? Does Article 27 of the UN Charter supply an answer to these last two questions? Observe, per Article 23, that France is a "permanent member" of the Security Council. Why might this fact be significant? What are its implications relative to the ICJ's mission of promoting a peaceful and just world order?

On 13 June 1995, the President of France, Jacques Chirac, announced that France would conduct a final series of 8 underground nuclear weapons tests in the South Pacific, breaking the moratorium on nuclear testing agreed to by France and other nuclear weapons states three years earlier. In August 1995, New Zealand decided to bring an action against France in the ICJ. However, France having withdrawn from the compulsory jurisdiction of the ICJ in January 1974, New Zealand's only option was to reopen the earlier nuclear test case of 1973/74. Following a two day hearing, the Court found that the 1974 judgment provided a *sui generis* procedure that enabled New Zealand to return to the Court and seek to have the case reopened. However, by a majority of 12 to 3, the Court found that the basis of the 1974 judgment was France's undertaking not to conduct any further atmospheric nuclear tests and that it was only in the event of a resumption of atmospheric tests that the Court could reconsider the issues. For further discussion, see Don MacKay, *New Zealand in the ICJ: French Nuclear Testing* and Alexander Gillespie, *The Third Attempt at the Hague*, in Proceedings of the Australian and New Zealand Society of International Law, Fourth Annual Meeting, Centre for International and Public Law, Australian National University, 17–19 May 1996.

7. If Hindustan used nuclear weapons in response to Islamistan's conventional attack, it would amount to a "first use" of nuclear weapons. In 1983, following the lead of the People's Republic of China in 1965, the Soviet Union pledged not to use nuclear weapons first:

> Guided by the desire to do all in its power to deliver the people from the threat of nuclear devastation and ultimately to exclude its very possibility from the life of mankind [sic], the Soviet Union solemnly declares: The Union of Soviet Socialist Republics assumes an obligation not to be the first to use nuclear weapons. This obligation shall become effective immediately from the rostrum of the UN General Assembly.

UN Doc. PUR/A/S–12, PV 12, 21–52, *reprinted in* Homer A. Jack, Disarm or Die 43 (1983). The United States, however, has so far resisted this course of action. Would a pledge not to be the first to use nuclear weapons (but to resort to them only in response to a nuclear attack) by all the nuclear weapons states increase or decrease the likelihood of nuclear war? Would such a pledge induce a build-up of conventional forces and make conventional warfare more likely? Why, in your opinion, did the Soviet Union pledge not to use nuclear weapons first? Is such a pledge legally binding? Consider the following statement by the International Court of Justice in the *Nuclear Tests* cases, in which Australia and New Zealand contended that French tests of nuclear weapons in the Pacific were illegal, in response to France's public announcement that it would abstain from such tests:

> Declarations of this kind may be, and often are, very specific. When it is the intention of the State making the declaration that it should become bound according to its terms, that intention confers on the declaration the character of a legal undertaking. . . . Any undertaking of this kind, *if given publicly, and with an intent to be bound*, even though not made within the context of international negotiations, is binding [emphasis added].

Nuclear Tests (Austrl. v. Fr.), 1974 ICJ 253, 267. Notwithstanding that the 1983 Soviet (now Russian) "no first use" declaration was given publicly and with an intention to be bound, can it be enforced? How?

8. Would Hindustan's use of nuclear weapons against Islamistan come within the jurisdiction of the International Criminal Court? Assume Hindustan is a party to the Rome Statute of the International Criminal Court **(Basic Document 1.16)** and consider whether ordering a nuclear strike might fall within the designated international crimes. In this respect, note the declarations attached to the ratifications of the Statute of New Zealand and France respectively, *available at* <http://untreaty.un.org/ENGLISH/bible/englishinternetbible/partI/chapterXVIII/treaty10.asp>. *See* Elaina I. Kalivretakis, *Are Nuclear Weapons above the Law? A Look at the International Criminal Court and the Prohibited Weapons Category* 628 (2001).

9. Richard Falk has outlined the contours of an interim legal regime that in his judgment responds to the three paramount policy goals of "(a) avoiding nuclear war, (b) minimizing crisis instability, and (c) reducing the arms race." Falk, *Toward a Legal Regime for Nuclear Weapons*, 28 McGill L. J. 519, 535 (1983). It would involve, he contends, at 537, the following considerations:

(a) public support for the idea that *any* actual use of nuclear weapons would violate the international law of war and would constitute a crime against humanity;

(b) public support for the rule that a first use of nuclear weapons, even in a defensive mode in response to or in reasonable anticipation of a prior non-nuclear armed attack, would violate international law and would constitute a crime against humanity;

(c) [the consequent conviction] that weapons systems (even at the research and development stage), war plans, strategic doctrines, and diplomatic threats that have first-strike characteristics are *per se* illegal, and that those political leaders, engineers, scientists, and defense workers knowingly associated with such "first-strike" roles are engaged in a continuing criminal enterprise;

(d) a definite consensus that second or retaliatory uses of nuclear weapons against cities and primarily civilian targets violate international law and constitute a crime against humanity;

(e) a clear obligation, recognized by all nuclear weapons states and by other states as well, to pursue arms control in the direction of minimizing the role of nuclear weapons in conflict behavior through negotiations in good faith; this obligation is a provision, Art. VI, of the widely ratified Non–Proliferation Treaty **[Basic Document 2.21]**, and is embodied in general terms as well in the Charter of the United Nations and in a variety of formal resolutions adopted over the years by the General Assembly; and

(f) a definite mandate directed toward citizens to take whatever steps are available to them to achieve a law-oriented foreign policy for their own country, including, as both conscience and good sense dictate, non-violent acts of civil disobedience, and efforts to persuade members of all branches of government to overcome the gap that separates the normative consensus of the public as to the illegality of the use of nuclear weapons from prevailing official policies.

How helpful are Professor Falk's recommendations? Do they afford feasible perspectives for governmental decision-makers in governments? If not, what kinds and degrees of global change might be necessary to make them feasible? To induce transition to a non-nuclear world, Falk argues, the "rules of prohibition [of nuclear weapons] need to be reinforced by making the prohibited activity as unnecessary as possible." *Id.* at 538. To this end, he advocates a clear separation of nuclear and conventional weapons, a no-first-use pledge, and comprehensive plans for non-nuclear defense capabilities. He stresses, however, that, over the long term, "assurances against the 'illegal' use of nuclear weapons will depend upon drastic global reform." *Id.* at 539. Do you agree? Disagree? Why? For discussion, incorporating but going beyond Falk's nuclear weapons ban proposals, see generally Alternative Security: Living Without Nuclear Deterrence (B. Weston ed., 1990). *See also* Burns H. Weston, *Law and Alternative Security: Toward A Just World Peace*, in Alternative Security, *supra*, at 43; ___, *Law and Alternative Security: Towards a Nuclear Weapons–Free World*, 75 Iowa L. Rev. 1077 (1990); ___,Toward Post–Cold War Global Security: A Legal Perspective 3–20 (Nuclear Age Peace Foundation, Waging Peace Series, Booklet 32, 1992).

10. *Bibliographical Note.* For supplemental discussion concerning the principal themes addressed in this problem, consult the following additional specialized materials:

(a) *Books/Monographs/Reports/Symposia.* Alternative Security: Living Without Nuclear Deterrence (B. Weston ed., 1990); Arms Control Toward the 21st Century (J. Larsen & G. Rattray eds., 1996); Department of Foreign Affairs and Trade, Report of the Canberra Commission on the Elimination of Nuclear Weapons (1996); Lawyers and the Nuclear Debate–Proceedings of the Canadian Conference on Nuclear Weapons and the Law (M. Cohen & M. Gouin eds., 1988); E. Meyrowitz, Prohibition of Nuclear Weapons: The Relevance of International Law (1990); H. Muller, D. Fischer & W. Kotter, Nuclear Nonproliferation and Global Order (1994); Nuclear Weapons After the Comprehensive Test Ban: Implications for Modernization and Proliferation (E. Arnett ed., 1996); Nuclear Weapons and Law (A. Miller & M. Feinrider eds., 1984); Nuclear Weapons and International Law (I. Pogany ed., 1987); B. Roling, The Impact of Nuclear Weapons on International Relations and International Law (1982); G. Schwarzenberger, The Legality of Nuclear Weapons (1958); N. Singh, Nuclear Weapons and International Law (1959); N. Singh & E. McWhinney, Nuclear Weapons and Contemporary International Law (1989); C. Weeramantry, Nuclear Weapons and Scientific Responsibility (1987); B. Weston, Toward Post–Cold War Global Security: A Legal Perspective (Nuclear Age Peace Foundation, 1992).

(b) *Articles/Book Chapters.* L. Beres, *On International Law and Nuclear Terrorism*, 24 Ga. J. Int'l & Comp. L. 1 (1994); D. Bolgiano, M. Leach, S. Smith, & J. Taylor, *Defining the Right of Self–Defense: Working Towards the Use of a Deadly Force Appendix to the Standing Rules of Engagement for the Department of Defense*, 31 U. Balt. L. Rev. 157 (2002); D. Brown, *Enforcing Arms Control Agreements by Military Force: Iraq and the 800–Pound Gorilla*, 26 Hastings Int'l & Comp. L. Rev. 159 (2003); R. Falk, E. Meyrowitz & J. Sanderson, *Nuclear Weapons and International Law*, 20 Indian J. Int'l L. 541 (1980); J. Fried, *International Law Prohibiting the First Use of Nuclear Weapons: Existing Prohibitions in International Law*, 12 Bull. Peace Proposals 21 (1981); T. Graham, Jr., *Is International Law Relevant To Arms Control?: National Self–Defense, International Law, and Weapons of Mass Destruction*, 4 Chi. J. Int'l L. 1 (2003); D. Karo, *Unfinished Business: Nuclear Weapons and the Post Cold War World*, 30 Tex. Int'l L. J. 411 (1995); K. Malone, *Preemptive Strikes and the Korean Nuclear Crisis: Legal and Political Limitations on the Use of Force*, 12 Pac. Rim L. & Pol'y 807 (2003); P. McLain, *Settling The Score With Saddam: Resolution 1441 and Parallel Justifications for the Use of Forces Against Iraq*, 13 Duke J. Comp. & Int'l L. 233 (2003); M. O'Connell, *American Exceptionalism and the International Law of Self–Defense*, 31 Denv. J. Int'l L. & Pol'y 43 (2002); M. Schmitt, *Preemptive Strategies in International Law*, 24 Mich. J. Int'l L. 513 (2003); D. Sloss, *Is International Law Relevant To Arms Control?: Forcible Arms Control: Preemptive Attacks on Nuclear Facilities*, 4 Chi. J. Int'l L. 39 (2003); H. Smith, *Is Honesty Still the Best Policy: Considering Legal Options for Missile Defense and the Antiballistic Missile Treaty*, 31 Ga. J. Int'l & Comp. L. 199 (2002); W. Taft & T. Buchwald, *Future Implications of the Iraq Conflict: Preemption, Iraq, and International Law*, 97 A.J.I.L. 557 (2003); L. Van Den Hole, *Anticipatory Self–Defence Under International Law*, 19 Am. U. Int'l L. Rev. 69 (2003); R. Williamson, *Law and the H–Bomb: Strengthening the Non–Proliferation Regime to Impede Advanced Proliferation*, 28 Cornell Int'l L. J. 71 (1995).

Problem 4–6

Chemical/Biological Weapons and Landmines
in Funan and Tongking

SECTION 1. FACTS

About a decade ago, Tongking invaded its western neighbor, Funan, deposed the existing government, and installed a puppet regime. Forces resisting the occupation took refuge in Sukhothai, a country to Funan's west, from where, ever since, they have supported guerilla operations aimed at overthrowing the Tongking-controlled regime in Funan.

Within the last few years, refugees managing to escape the fighting in Funan have reported unusual illnesses and deaths near locations where combat has taken place. Neutral observers from the International Committee of the Red Cross confirm the use by Tongking of chemical agents similar to mustard gas against the resistance forces, and report as well an outbreak of diseases inside Tongking and Funan that normally are associated with biological toxins. They also confirm that Tongking has placed landmines in strategic areas within Funan to deter resistance to its control.

Sukhothai, currently a member of the United Nations Security Council, has there formally accused Tongking of violating international law by its use of prohibited chemical agents and landmines against the resistance forces operating inside Funan and by its possession and use of biological agents in excess of what is needed for defensive research. Tongking is a party to both the 1925 Protocol for the Prohibition of the Use in War of Asphyxiating, Poisonous or Other Gases, and of Bacteriological Methods of Warfare and the 1972 Convention on the Prohibition of the Development, Production and Stockpiling of Bacteriological (Biological) and Toxic Weapons and On Their Destruction. Funan and Sukhothai are parties to this latter 1972 Convention and, as well, to the 1993 Convention on the Prohibition of the Development, Production, Stockpiling and Use of Chemical Weapons and on their Destruction, but not to the 1925 Geneva Gas Protocol. Tongking is not a party to the 1993 Chemical Weapons Convention. None are party to the 1997 Convention on the Prohibition of the Use, Stockpiling, Production and Transfer of Anti-Personnel Mines and on Their Destruction. A meeting of the Security Council has been called to consider Sukhothai's allegations.

SECTION 2. QUESTIONS PRESENTED

1. Has Tongking violated international law by its use of chemical weapons and landmines, and by its use and/or possession of biological toxins?

2. In any event, are there any additional or alternative legal norms, procedures, and/or institutions to be recommended that might further help to prevent or discourage situations of the kind posed by this problem?

SECTION 3. ASSIGNMENTS

A. READING ASSIGNMENT

Study the Readings presented in Section 4, *infra*, and the Discussion Notes/Questions that follow. Also, time permitting, consult the accompanying bibliographical references.

B. RECOMMENDED WRITING ASSIGNMENT

Prepare a comprehensive, logically sequenced, and *argumentative* brief in the form of an outline of the primary and subsidiary *legal* issues you see requiring resolution by the United Nations Security Council. Also, from the perspective of an independent objective judge, indicate which side ought to prevail on each issue and why. Retain a copy of your issue-outline/brief for class discussion.

C. RECOMMENDED ORAL ASSIGNMENT

Assume that your country has decided to lend is diplomatic support to Sukhothai or Tongking (as designated by your instructor); then, relying upon the Readings (and your issue-outline if prepared), present a 10–15 minute oral argument of your government's likely positions before the United Nations Security Council, convened to consider the crisis.

D. RECOMMENDED REFLECTIVE ASSIGNMENT

Consider (and recommend) alternative norms, institutions, and/or procedures that you believe might do better than existing world order arrangements to contend with situations of the kind posed by this problem. In so doing, but without insisting upon *immediate* feasibility, identify the particular transition steps that would be needed to make your alternatives a reality.

SECTION 4. READINGS

The following readings are considered *prima facie* relevant to solving this problem. They are your law library for present purposes and should be treated as such, organized intelligibly for "shelving" and not necessarily according to the issues presented. Be sure to review Chapter 2 ("International Legal Prescription: The 'Sources' of International Law") in your consideration of them. It, too, should be treated as part of your law library (as, indeed, should this entire coursebook).

1. Editors' Note. Chemical and biological weapons are not new. There are references to such weapons in early Greece and Rome. But it was not until the end of the nineteenth century, when developments in technology increased their destructiveness, that any international efforts were made to curb their use. The First Hague Peace Conference of 1899, initiated by Tzar Nicholas II, among other things adopted declarations limiting the use of weapons that diffused "asphyxiating or deleterious" gases. *See, e.g.,* Declaration (IV–2) Respecting the Prohibition of the Use of Projectiles Diffusing Asphyxiating Gases of 29 July 1899, 187 C.T.S. 459. The Hague Regulations of 1907 **(Basic Document 2.2)** set out the customary rules of warfare, including the provision that "[t]he right of belligerents to adopt means of injuring the enemy is not unlimited" (article 22) and prohibiting the use of "poison or poisoned weapons" (article 23(a)) and the employment of weapons "calculated to cause unnecessary suffering" (article 23 (e)).

These provisions were violated during World War I by both sides in that conflict through the use of poisonous gases, particularly chlorine and mustard gas, causing over a million casualties with 90,000 deaths. The Geneva Protocol of 1925 **(Basic Document 2.4)** was a direct response to these violations, restating the 1899 prohibition on the use of poisonous gases and extended it to bacteriological methods of warfare. It does not, however, prohibit the possession of chemical or biological weapons. Also, because its protections apply only with respect to states who are parties to it, and because it prohibits only the wartime use—not the peacetime use—of chemical or biological weapons, the Protocol's contribution to the development of customary international law is uncertain.

During World War II, apparently, these weapons were not used (although recent information suggests that Japan may have used biological weapons in China during the conflict). Both the Allies and the Axis powers held them in stockpiles, however, and, after World War II, the Cold War encouraged both the Soviet Union and the United States to expand these stockpiles. Increasingly, in addition, other nations have developed chemical and biological weapons, and allegedly chemical weapons have been used in a wide range of conflicts, including Afghanistan, Chechnya, Eritrea, Laos, Myanmar (Burma), Sri Lanka, Yemen, and the former Yugoslavia, although some of these allegations have not been substantiated. The best documented case is use by Iraq in its 1980–88 war against Iran, and against Kurdish groups in the north of Iraq. Few countries admit that they possess chemical weapons, but they are sometimes said to be a poor person's nuclear weapon because they can be cheaply and quickly produced without a sophisticated industrial base.

Fewer states have developed biological weapons, but concern with the threat posed by biological weapons stockpiles led, in 1972, to the adoption of the Biological and Toxin Weapons Convention **(Basic Document 2.25)**, which bans this type of weapon comprehensively. The Convention also requires state parties to continue negotiations to agree on an analogous prohibition of chemical weapons. As evidenced above, it took another twenty years for this to happen, in the form of the 1993 Chemical Weapons Convention **(Basic Document 2.42)**. While there had been some discussion in the 1960s of a treaty that would cover both biological and chemical weapons, it was decided that it would be easier to begin with biological weapons because they never had been used in war and because there was greater international abhorrence of them. As of 11 April 2006, 155 states were parties to the Convention on Biological Weapons and, as of 11 April 2006, 178 states were parties to the Chemical Weapons Convention. It may be noted, however, that, in the 1990s, Iraq had developed a sophisticated biological weapons program.

Further, observe that Article 35(2) of the 1977 Geneva Protocol I to the Geneva Conventions of 1949 **(Basic Document 2.31)** repeats the prohibition of the 1907 Hague Regulations against the employment of "weapons, projectiles and materials and methods of warfare of a nature to cause superfluous injury or unnecessary suffering"; also that Protocol III of the 1980 Convention on Prohibitions or Restrictions on the Use of Certain Conventional Weapons Which May be Deemed to be Excessively Injurious or to Have Indiscriminate Effects **(Basic Document 2.34)** imposes certain restrictions upon the use of "incendiary weapons," whose harm is produced by "a chemical reaction of a substance delivered on the target." As of 11 April 2006, 164 states were parties to Geneva Protocol I, and as of 11 April 2006, 100 were parties to the 1980 Convention.

For useful background information, see, *e.g.*, John R. Bolton, *War, International Law, And Sovereignty: Reevaluating The Rules Of The Game In A New Century: The Bush Administration's Forward Strategy For Nonproliferation*, 5 Chi. J. Int'l L. 395 (2005); Francis A. Boyle, *The Legal Distortions Behind the Reagan Administration's Chemical and Biological Weapons Buildup*, 30 St. Louis U. L. J. 1175 (1986); Randall Fosberg *et al.*, Nonproliferation Primer: Preventing The Spread Of Nuclear, Chemical And Biological Weapons (1995); L. P. Haines, *Controlling the Possession and Use of Biological and Chemical Weapons*, 99 Austl. Defence Force J. 43 (1993); Daniel H. Joyner, *The Proliferation Security Initiative: Nonproliferation, Counterproliferation, And International Law*, 30 Yale J. Int'l L. 507 (2005); and Peter H. Oppenheimer, *A Chemical Weapons Regime for the 1990s: Satisfying Seven Critical Criteria*, 11 Wis. Int'l L. J. 1 (1992).

By contrast, as we shall see below, the international law relating to the use of landmines is not as effective or developed as with chemical and biological weapons.

2. Declaration Renouncing the Use in Time of War of Explosive Projectiles Under 400 Grammes Weight. Adopted at St. Petersburg by the International Military Commission, 11 Dec 1868. 138 C.T.S. 297 (French), 1 A.J.I.L. Supp. 95 (1907); *reprinted in* **2 Weston & Carlson II.C.8** (Basic Document 2.1).

3. Hague Convention (No. IV) Respecting the Laws and Customs of War on Land (with annex of regulations). Concluded, 18 Oct 1907. Entered into force, 26 Jan 1910. 205 C.T.S. 277 (French), 2 A.J.I.L. Supp. 90 (1908); *reprinted in* **2 Weston & Carlson II.B.1: Arts. 1–3 and Annex Arts. 22, 23(a) & (e)** (Basic Document 2.2).

4. Protocol for the Prohibition of the Use in War of Asphyxiating, Poisonous or Other Gases, and of Bacteriological Methods of Warfare. Concluded, 17 Jun 1925. Entered into force, 8 Feb 1928. 94 L.N.T.S. 65; *reprinted in* **14 I.L.M. 49 (1975) and 2 Weston & Carlson II.C.35** (Basic Document 2.4).

5. Convention on the Prohibition of the Development, Production and Stockpiling of Bacteriological (Biological) and Toxin Weapons and on Their Destruction. Concluded, 10 Apr 1972. Entered into force, 26 Mar 1975. 1015 U.N.T.S. 163; *reprinted in* **11 I.L.M. 310 (1972) and 2 Weston & Carlson II.C.36: Pmbl. & Arts. 1–13** (Basic Document 2.25).

6. **Protocol Additional (No I) to the Geneva Conventions of August 12, 1949, and Relating to the Protection of Victims of International Armed Conflicts. Concluded, 8 Jun 1977. Entered into force, 7 Dec 1978. 1977 U.N.J.Y.B. 95;** *reprinted in* **16 I.L.M. 1391 (1977) and 2 Weston & Carlson II.B.20: Art. 35** (Basic Document 2.31).

7. **Convention on Prohibitions or Restrictions on the Use of Certain Conventional Weapons Which May be Deemed to be Excessively Injurious or to Have Indiscriminate Effects. Concluded, 10 Oct 1980. Entered into force, 2 Dec 1983. UN Doc. A/CONF.95/15 (1980) and UN Doc. A/CONF.95/15 Corr. 2;** *reprinted in* **19 I.L.M. 1524 (1980) and 2 Weston & Carlson II.C.10: Pmbl., Arts. 1, 2, & Protocol III** (Basic Document 2.34).

8. **World Charter for Nature, 28 Oct 1982, GA Res. 37/7 (Annex), UN GAOR, 37th Sess., Supp. No. 51, at 17, UN Doc. A/37/51;** *reprinted in* **22 I.L.M. 455 (1983) and 5 Weston & Carlson V.B.11: Princs. 1–5, 11, 20** (Basic Document 5.21).

9. **Convention on the Prohibition of the Development, Production, Stockpiling and Use of Chemical Weapons and on their Destruction. Concluded, 13 Jan 1993. Entered into force, 29 April 1997.** *Reprinted in* **31 I.L.M. 800 (1993) and 2 Weston & Carlson II.C.39: Pmbl. & Arts. I–VII, VIII(A), IX–XIV, XVI, XVII, XXI, XXII** (Basic Document 2.42).

10. **Julius Stone, Legal Controls of International Conflict 555–56 (1954).**

... Though in general the [1925 Geneva Gas] Protocol **[Basic Document 2.4]** is binding on each signatory as from ratification, a number of signatories, including Britain and France, made the reservations that it was binding only *vis-à-vis* States effectively bound by it, and so long as the enemy or his allies respect the prohibitions. This Protocol represented the state of the general treaty law on this matter through the Second World War.

At the outbreak of war Germany stated in reply to a British inquiry that she would on the basis of reciprocity observe the Protocol of 1925. While some belligerents found it necessary from time to time to issue dire warnings of retaliation which would follow violation of it, no clear violation occurred.

How far this observance was due to a special combination of circumstances rendering threat of reprisals unusually efficacious, how far it is to be attributed to the *opinio necessitatis* supporting an established rule of international law, is still debatable. The fact that Germany, while not using poison gas against combatants, put to death by poison gas millions of non-combatant men, women, and children in mass organised gas chambers, should at least restrain any tendency to be sanguine as to the latter possibility....

Since ... the Protocol of 1925 is subject to reciprocity, its compulsiveness *as law* seems difficult to distinguish from the *factual* compulsion arising from the mere threat of retaliation. And this view is confirmed by the fact that none of the military powers have relaxed their preparations for chemical warfare.

Whether such preparations are directed to the principle of reciprocity under the Geneva Protocol, or under the general rule of international law now

said to have emerged, or to retaliatory protection against a weapon still not
prohibited except to certain treaty-bound States in their mutual relations, it is
clear that international law does not prohibit either the *retaliatory* use of
poison gas against an enemy who has used it, or preparations for such
retaliation.

11. Brad Roberts, "Controlling Chemical Weapons," 2 Transnat'l L. & Contemp. Probs. 435, 439–42, 451–52 (1992).

[T]he proliferation of CW [chemical weapons] has come over the last
decade to pose sharper threats to international security than in prior years.
The reasons are numerous.

First, proliferation has occurred as part of a general accretion of military
capability among major states of the developing world, creating a Gordian
knot of armaments competition that has increased the risk of war in a variety
of regions as well as the likelihood that if war occurs it will be at a level of
destructiveness unprecedented in regional conflict outside Europe. CW have
proliferated conspicuously to regions where other weapons are being accumulated that offer adversaries more advanced and destructive military capabilities. This general trend has sharpened rather than dampened the political
sources of conflict in places like the Middle East, South Asia, and Northeast
Asia.

Second, CW have been mated to missile delivery systems with particularly
destabilizing implications. A state's ability to threaten attack with CW against
an opponent's population centers has encouraged leaders in the developing
world to think of CW as "the poor man's atom bomb." Whether such weapons
are reliable in this role is far from clear. But the fear that they might be
creates significant new forms of political leverage for threatening states and
new vulnerabilities for the threatened. One especially worrisome result of the
mating of chemical warheads to missiles is the compulsion this creates in time
of near war to strike first or risk annihilation. The need to strike preemptively seriously erodes crisis stability and makes war more likely. This accentuates the existing risks of miscalculation in time of crisis and war. The
destabilizing aspects of CW proliferation vary, of course, from region to
region. In South Asia and East Asia, the chemical dimension of major military
balances appears to be less significant than in the Middle East. Of course,
even there the necessity to strike at a potential opponent preemptively in time
of near war predates the perhaps growing sophistication of local CW arsenals.

Third, the prohibition against the use of CW is far weaker than the taboo
against other weapons, especially nuclear and biological. CW may be used
much more readily than other weapons deemed somehow out of bounds by the
international community. Iraq's use of CW with relative impunity in its war
against Iran showed that the moral norm embodied in the Geneva Protocol
was less strong than its advocates had hoped. The earlier debate about the
alleged use by Soviet or Soviet proxy forces in Afghanistan and Southeast Asia
of chemical and toxin weapons—the so-called Yellow Rain debate—also revealed the disinterest of many states in resolving allegations or redressing
instances of CW use.

Fourth, CW have proliferated to states whose use of force is inconsistent
with international standards. Iraq and North Korea stand out in this regard.
CW are in the arsenals of states known to sponsor terrorism. There is also

fear that the acquisition of CW by such states will precipitate their acquisition of biological weapons and an unraveling of the existing disarmament regime in that area.

Fifth, CW proliferation emerged as an important factor in regional conflicts and international diplomacy just at the time that the passing of the Cold War seemed to make conclusion of the [Chemical Weapons Convention (CWC)] negotiations imminent. The long-standing and sharp differences of view between East and West about the requirements of effective chemical disarmament were swept away by the "new thinking" of Mikhail Gorbachev and Eduard Shevardnadze, and by the late 1980s agreement between the United States and the Soviet Union about the essential elements of the chemical convention created a widespread optimism that the CWC would be rapidly concluded. Proliferation eroded this optimism. It stimulated a debate in the United States about the possible continuing need for CW by the US military for deterrence and retaliation purposes, although this seems to have concluded in a decision that the United States has preferable means to deal with the CW proliferation threat than retaliation in kind. It also sharpened the concern that states of the developing world might opt to keep their CW rather than join the convention.

There is a tendency among some observers to misunderstand the basic factors leading to CW proliferation. Most Westerners seem to attribute proliferation to one of two factors: greed within a business community willing to cut deals with unscrupulous leaders in the name of profits, or the desire of states to possess the equivalent of an atom bomb. Both views have some basis in fact. A few private firms of the developed countries have wittingly or unwittingly contributed to the build-up of CW production facilities in the developing world. (German firms have been singled out for international opprobrium but have not been the only ones engaged in this business.) Some leaders such as Saddam Hussein of Iraq or Muammar Qaddafi of Libya have evidently valued their CW arsenals as offering special strategic leverage. But these factors alone or in combination cannot account for the CW proliferation of recent years.

Rather, CW proliferation should be understood as the result of a lowering of barriers that previously had been significant. Some of these barriers were technical; but the globalization of industry has greatly eased access to the technology, expertise, and raw materials of CW. Other barriers were political, but the failure of the international community to respond forcefully to allegations of use by Iraq in the 1980s and to earlier charges of CW use by the USSR or its proxies undermined the expectation that a leader ordering the use of CW might expect to pay any significant international political costs. Perhaps the most important barriers were perceptual; but the view of CW as antiquated and unreliable was cast in doubt by Iraq's use of CW against Iran. Iraq's chemical arsenal suggested that CW might have a usefulness in conflicts between or within states of the developing world that they were not understood to have for the advanced militaries of the developed world.

Moreover, concurrent with the easing of the barriers to CW proliferation was the growing strength of a number of incentives to proliferation. These included the general accumulation of advanced military capabilities by states of the developing world, a perceived need within some states to substitute CW for nuclear ones beyond their reach and, in Iraq at least, a view that CW might be useful in carving out new areas of influence as the bipolar structure of regional conflicts passed along with the Cold War.

Because of the wholesale disavowal by states of the developing world of reports of indigenous CW programs, nothing is known about the strategic purposes for which those programs are intended. But it is possible to speculate about a number of different motives. Some states may desire a CW capability as a deterrent to the war-making intentions of another state, whether or not that state poses a specifically CW threat. Some states may desire a CW capability as an instrument of war-time self-defense, for use when deterrence has broken down and solely to preserve national independence or regime survival. Some states may desire CW for coercive purposes, as an instrument to bend others within reach of those weapons—whether domestically, within the region, or outside the region but reachable by missiles—to the political agenda of the threatening state. Still others may have little or no immediate strategic purpose and are engaged in CW programs for the purpose of better understanding the field or creating future options; this factor may account for the report noted above that only five or six states may possess CW arsenals of military significance. Of course, the purposes to which military instruments are put can change with time, and there is no guarantee that a weapon system acquired for purposes of deterrence for defense might not be turned to purposes of aggression at a future time.

It is important for a Western audience to note that not everyone agrees that CW proliferation is a problem. Among some states of the developing world, there is a conviction that CW are legitimate instruments of security until and if the international community agrees to a disarmament measure. They decry Western definitions of international security and stability and emphasize the ways in which CW and the threat of their use increase the security of individual countries. These states perceive a double standard in efforts by the developed world to constrain CW proliferation when leading members of the developed world possess such weapons of their own. Some have also criticized an effort to eliminate one class of weapons perceived to be of potential strategic significance for the developing world while not also eliminating the class of weapons of most strategic significance for the developed world—nuclear weapons. In the words of one analyst,

> The main hurdle to universalized acceptance of the chemical weapons ban treaty is likely to be the contradictory approaches adopted by the NATO allies in respect of different categories of weapons of mass destruction. While they urge adoption of a treaty to ban and eliminate chemical weapons they argue that they still need the more dangerous and feared weapon of mass destruction—the nuclear weapon—as weapons of last resort. This contradiction has become less justifiable after the end of the Cold War and the disappearance of a meaningful adversary for the Western industrialized nations. There is a view, however unjustified it may be, that chemical weapons are the weapons of last resort for the poorer and less industrialized nations.[1]

* * *

1. K. Subrahmanyam, Policy Proposals for Controlling Horizontal Proliferation of Dual

The past decade has brought the CW proliferation problem sharply into focus. Such weapons have proliferated in recent years and have emerged as significant military and political factors both regionally and globally. Non-proliferation policies have been tried and found wanting, as they lack the global political support necessary to make them effective. A comprehensive global ban on CW may enter into force in 1995, and although it will have considerable effectiveness as a non-proliferation measure it is hardly a panacea.

But policy analysts must also recognize that the CW proliferations subject cannot be considered in isolation from the broader political and military trends of the late twentieth century. Measures that isolate one technology without reference to this larger context are certain to fail, although the important differences between the nuclear, chemical, biological, and conventional armaments problems means that policy responses must be fine-tuned for each. This suggests that the fate of the CWC will depend not just on factors inherent to its specific provisions but also on the larger post-Cold War global agenda and the degree to which the international community makes progress on larger issues of war and peace in the years ahead. With the passing of the bipolar structure of world affairs wrought by the end of the Cold War, leaders in many nations are attempting to divine whether the future holds a new world order in which the cooperative will prosper or instead a new form of disorder and anarchy in which only the strong will survive. The CWC will set out a marker on the path to cooperation. It must be seen as one part of a broader strategy to redefine rights and responsibilities in the international system in a new era. It will not long survive if progress is not made on the other topics within the purview of this volume. But by reinforcing the importance of norms of collective responses to aggression, the CWC could be a leading feature of the movement toward a more stable era.

12. Michael P. Scharf, "Clear and Present Danger: Enforcing the International Ban on Biological and Chemical Weapons Through Sanctions, Use of Force, and Criminalization," 20 Mich. J. Int'l L. 477, 483–85 (1999).

"Given the inherent limitations of the [1925] Geneva Protocol [**Basic Document 2.4**], in 1968 the international community began negotiating a comprehensive chemical weapons convention that would ban not only the use, but also the production and stockpiling of chemical weapons, and that would additionally provide the means to verify compliance and to sanction violations."[2] The objective of the Chemical Weapons Convention (the Convention) [**Basic Document 2.42**] was to eliminate an entire class of weapons of mass destruction.

On April 29, 1997, the Convention entered into force. Over [150] states, including the United States, China, India, Iran and Russia, have ratified or acceded to the Convention [as of 11 April 2006]. The Convention prohibits the development, production, or other acquisition, retention, stockpiling, transfer,

Use Technology Without Undercutting the North–South Technological Transfer: A Personal Perspective from a Third World Country, 25–27 Oct 1991 (paper presented at the Seventh International AFES Press Conference, Gladbach, Germany).

2. Anne Q. Connaughton & Steven C. Goldman, *The Chemical Weapons Convention and Department of Commerce Responsibilities*, 760 PLI/Comm 533, 537–38 (1997).

and use of chemical weapons and chemical weapons production facilities. It also prohibits

State Parties from engaging in any military preparations to use chemical weapons and from assisting or inducing anyone to engage in an activity that is prohibited by the Convention. The Convention requires State Parties to eliminate all chemical weapons and chemical weapons production facilities under their jurisdiction or control within ten years of accession.

Most importantly, the Chemical Weapons Convention establishes a permanent Organization for the Prohibition of Chemical Weapons (the OPCW), whose role is to monitor implementation of the agreement through on-site inspections, including inspections of private, non-military chemical production facilities.[3] In addition, the Convention provides for challenge inspections of any facility or location, public or private, when a State Party suspects that the facility is not in compliance with the Convention. Because of its extensive verification procedures, the Convention is estimated to cost between $33 million and $500 million per year to operate.

While the verification provisions of the Chemical Weapons Convention have been heralded as "among the most intricate and intrusive ever designed for a disarmament regime,"[4] the Convention is not without its flaws. In particular, the Convention does not provide mandatory sanctions against violators. Nor does it apply to numerous "hold-out" states which continue to refuse to join[5] or non-State actors, such as terrorist or paramilitary groups. Moreover, it only "regulates chemical weapons and their precursors in terms of tons," even though technological developments have produced agents only a few grams of which are lethal. And it permits any State Party to withdraw from the regime in "the supreme interests of the country" on only ninety days notice.

The Convention's most significant weakness is the result of ill-conceived action by the US Congress. In enacting implementing legislation, Congress included three "poison-pill" provisions introduced by treaty opponents that could eviscerate the Chemical Weapons Convention's verification regime.[6] One provision authorizes the president to refuse a challenge inspection on "national security grounds," the second prevents the removal of samples from US territory for analysis, and the third sharply limits the number of US chemical plants subject to inspection. Other countries are likely to treat these as equivalent to reservations and assert them to frustrate verification.

13.   Richard A. Falk, "Inhibiting Reliance on Biological Weaponry: The Role and Relevance of International Law," 1 Am. U. J. Int'l L. & Pol'y 17, 23–27 (1986).

. . . Some of [the] weaknesses [of the 1925 Geneva Protocol **[Basic Document 2.4]** were eliminated with the signature and ratification of the 1972 Biological Weapons Convention ("Convention") **[Basic Document**

---

3. Under Article III of the Chemical Weapons Convention, parties must disclose to the OPCW the location of their production facilities and chemical weapons stockpiles.

4. P. Oppenheimer, *A Chemical Weapons Regime for the 1990s: Satisfying Seven Critical Criteria,* 11 Wis. Int'l L.J. 1 (1992) [*see also infra* Reading 13].

5. Most of the [M]iddle [E]astern countries did not sign and have not ratified or acceded to the Chemical Weapons Convention, citing Israel's refusal to sign the Nuclear Non-Proliferation Treaty.

6. *See* J. Tucker, Director of the Center for Nonproliferation Studies, The Current Status of the BCW Regimes, Paper Delivered at the Hoover Institution Conference on Biological and Chemical Weapons at Stanford University, November 16–18, 1998, at 7 (on file with the author).

2.25] which entered into force in 1975. The Preamble to the Convention places the prohibition in the wider context of "achieving effective progress toward *general* and *complete* disarmament, including the prohibition and elimination of *all* types of weapons of mass destruction." The Preamble also explicitly reaffirms the Geneva Protocol prohibition and augments its prohibitions on use, a feature reiterated in Article VIII. The Preamble also asserts that a legal regime prohibiting development, production, and stockpiling of biological weapons is "a first possible stem" toward the establishment of a comparable regime for chemical weapons. The linking of biological warfare and chemical warfare regimes is important because it acts to discourage acquisition of a deterrent capability, which would likely stimulate an arms race, as well as to achieve an unconditional and comprehensive regime of prohibition on these types of weapons. Finally, the Preamble asserts as the goal of the Convention the complete exclusion of the possibility of bacteriological (biological) agents and toxins being used as weapons and insists that "such use would be repugnant to the conscience of mankind." Here, particularly, the Convention invokes societal attitudes as a ground for the efforts of statesmen to achieve an effective legal regime. The Convention considers that the effectiveness of that regime involves prohibition of development and possession, as well as the threat of use and actual use. This extension of the prohibitions of the Protocol to stages prior to use is a practical recognition that inhibiting use in armed conflict requires a stable regime of non-possession. If states lack biological weapons capability, there is no need to induce respect for the norm prohibiting use; if they do have such capability, the prospect of inducing respect is fragile, at best, especially if considerations of military necessity appear to warrant use.

* * *

The signal achievement of this Convention should not be overlooked, nor should its contents be too easily deprecated. Both superpowers have legally committed themselves to forego possession as well as use. As a result, no retaliatory use, or even deterrent capability, is contemplated or permissible under the Convention and renunciation is unconditional. Furthermore, parties agreed to destroy stockpiles of biological weapons existing as of 1975 within nine months of the Convention's entry into force. Significantly, the parties to the Convention signed simultaneously in Washington, London, and Moscow. It enjoys the participation of the Soviet Union, the United States, the United Kingdom, and most other major states (with the exception of China and France). In this respect, the illegal status of biological weapons is more widely and significantly established than for any category of weaponry including chemical and nuclear. On its face then, the Convention seems to provide a comprehensive repudiation of development, production, and stockpiling of biological weaponry that does not depend upon deterrence for enforcement. What the Convention does permit is research associated with "defensive" or peaceful purposes.

Despite its numerous achievements, many recognize that the Convention, like the Protocol, suffers from many flaws and ambiguities. Particularly, critics assert that given the developments in biological capabilities and in the attitudes of states toward such weaponry, the Convention lacks sufficient restraints. First, "peaceful" applications can no longer be reliably distinguished from "military" applications. Similarly, "defensive" research, to protect populations by immunization and other methods, is also relevant for work toward a biological first-strike capability. Consequently, the Article I limitation to biological agents or toxins "that have no justification for prophylactic, protective or other peaceful purposes" is a gigantic loophole capable of being reconciled with almost any desired path of research. Similarly, the Article II obligation to destroy stockpiles exempts any biological agent or toxin that is diverted to peaceful purposes. This again allows states an alarming degree of discretion, which, when taken with ineffective verification procedures, means compliance almost entirely depends upon good faith and self-interest.

The veil of secrecy covering activities in this area arouses suspicions and makes it difficult to distinguish innocent from sinister activity on the part of foreign states and within our own [United States]. Malicious propaganda cannot easily be distinguished from disturbing revelation. Suspicions about violative behavior are, as a practical matter, impossible to verify by the procedures set forth in the Convention. Parties are not cooperative, tending to dismiss even reasonable suspicions as propaganda.

14. Kristen Paris, "The Expansion of the Biological Weapons Convention: History and Problems of a Verification Regime," 24 Houst. J. Int'l. L 509, 510–12, 541–43 (2002).

The threat of biological warfare is real. The September 11, 2001 attacks on New York and Washington, D.C. and the letters contaminated with anthrax that have killed five Americans and infected many others, show the willingness of terrorists to murder large numbers of people arbitrarily. Theoretically, however, there should be no threat of biological warfare, in light of the Biological Weapons Convention ("BWC") **[Basic Document 2.25]** ... which bans the development, production, and stockpiling of biological weapons for purposes other than preventive or peaceful reasons. The BWC also forbids developing, producing, stockpiling, acquiring, or retaining delivery systems, munitions, and other equipment used to launch biological weapons. The BWC, supported by both the United States and the former Soviet Union, is remarkable in the fact that it is the first international treaty to prohibit an entire class of weapons. As of April 2002, 162 nations have signed and 144 countries have ratified the BWC.[a]

However, the BWC is a weak agreement, and nations continue to develop, produce, stockpile, and use deadly biological agents for purposes other than preventive or peaceful reasons. Non-compliance with the BWC was made evident in 1992 when, then Russian President, Boris Yeltsin admitted that the former Soviet Union had possessed an offensive biological weapons program for twenty years. The world's confidence in the effectiveness of the BWC in banning biological weapons was further shaken in 1995 when Iraq was found to have a biological weapons program. More recently, North Korea, Syria, Iran, and Sudan, along with Iraq, were accused by the United States of violating the BWC.

One of the main reasons the BWC is such a weak agreement is because it does not have a verification regime. Only according to Article VI does any

---

a. As of 9 June 2005, 152 states were parties to the Convention.

party, "which finds that any other State Party is acting in breach of obligations deriving from the provisions of the Convention, [have the right to] lodge a complaint with the Security Council of the United Nations." When this occurs, "each State Party to this Convention [must] cooperate in carrying out any investigation which the Security Council may initiate...."

To strengthen the BWC, review conferences have been held in Geneva approximately every five years since the BWC went into effect. Overall, these conferences have reemphasized the basic prohibitions of the BWC and have attempted to resolve issues and problems that arise between the State Parties. Most importantly, the conferences have continually grappled with the absence of a verification regime.... [O]n December 7, 2001, the State Parties to the BWC adjourned the Fifth Review Conference in disarray and planned to meet again November 11–22, 2002 to continue the Fifth Review Conference.[b]

* * *

E. The Difficulties of a Verification Regime

Overall, it is difficult to create a verification regime. Verification "is not a mechanistic, cut and dried process that produces unambiguous evidence of noncompliance."[7] It is especially difficult to create a verification scheme for the BWC. First, verification is a daunting task in view of the number and variety of potential biological agents. A paper by a Brazilian official identified 148 bacteria, rickettsiae, fungi, and toxins that could be used as weapons.[8] This report included all naturally occurring agents, but did not include genetically engineered agents. A verification regime that provides assurance that biological agents are only used for permitted purposes is overwhelming.

Second, as Ambassador Ronald Lehman from the United States stated at the Third Review Conference, it is difficult to create a verification regime for the BWC because any nation with a developed pharmaceutical industry has the potential to make biological weapons,[9] because biological agents can be used for both legitimate and prohibited purposes. A verification regime would present difficulties in determining whether biological agents were being used for permitted purposes, such as vaccines, or whether they were being used for prohibited purposes, such as military weapons. In fact, the difference between

---

b. According to the author, the adjournment, done "to avoid failure," was brought about by an unexpected decision by the new US administration of President George W. Bush to terminate unilaterally an *ad hoc* working group that had been negotiating the verification Protocol. "The United States had numerous reasons for rejecting the draft Protocol," the author writes, at 535. "One of the main concerns of the Bush Administration," she states, "is that the measures proposed in the draft Protocol are intrusive on the US Government and private companies, putting their security and commercial proprietary information at risk." The author adds, at 540: "The United States proposal to terminate the Ad Hoc Group was not well received. European countries felt that the United States was acting unilaterally and not listening to concerns of allies."

7. L. Cole, The Eleventh Plague: The Politics of Biological and Chemical Warfare 179, 192 (1997) (quoting Michael Moodie, president of the Chemical and Biological Arms Control Institute).

8. *Id.* at 191–92 (citing Roque Monteleone Neto's paper, "Criteria for the Establishment of the First List of Agents," presented at Beyond VEREX, a forum sponsored by the Federation of American Scientists and the Special NGO Committee for Disarmament, Geneva, 21 Sep 1994).

9. Final Declaration of the Third Review Conference, BWC/CONF.III/23, *available at* <http:// projects.sipri.se/ cbw/docs/bw-btwc-review conf-3.html> (9–17 Sep 1991).

permitted use and prohibited use of biological agents may depend on the intent of the user, which is often impossible to verify.

In addition to the difficulties of creating a verification scheme, implementation will be troublesome. Because biological agents multiply, it is unnecessary to produce or store agents in large quantities. As a result, a biological warfare program does not necessarily imply large production sites or storage sites. This makes it very difficult for a verification regime to locate the small, prohibited facilities.

During the Third Review Conference, the first Bush Administration outlined many difficulties and concerns over the establishment of a verification regime. It claimed that biological weapons facilities cannot be located or monitored effectively because biological weapons do not leave distinctive "signatures." Compounding this problem is the inability of a verification regime "to detect clandestine facilities."

Perhaps the main source of concern regarding the verification of the BWC is the development of biotechnology. At the First Review Conference, biotechnology was not a concern.... However, by the Second Review Conference, concern about the potential use of biotechnology to change existing microorganisms into biological warfare weapons quickly developed.

Just within the past two decades, the business and science of biotechnology has grown rapidly. US firms developing new-generation drugs have increased from 45 in 1989 to 113 in 1996. Advances in microbiology, genetic engineering, and biotechnology have produced major benefits for the health of people and animals.

The growing biotechnology industry offers the potential of new and improved diagnostic techniques and medical countermeasures to an increasing range of naturally occurring diseases, however, problems developed with these advances. In order to counter diseases, the ways in which the diseases attack target populations must be understood. As scientists dissect how diseases spread and work, they gain an understanding of how these diseases could be used for military purposes. Therefore, those working in the biotechnology industry are constantly dealing with materials and concepts that could be used to devastate mankind.

The advances in biotechnology have simplified biological agent production and enhanced the agents' effects. For example, it might be possible to enhance a biological agent's resistance to degradation during its dissemination or even accelerate degradation after its use. A Russian state pharmaceutical agency called Biopreparat has already proven that viruses and toxins can be genetically altered to heighten their virulence, paving the way for development of pathogens capable of overcoming existing vaccines.

15. Convention on Prohibitions or Restrictions on the Use of Certain Conventional Weapons Which May be Deemed to be Excessively Injurious or to Have Indiscriminate Effects. Concluded, 10 Oct 1980. Entered into force, 2 Dec 1983. UN Doc. A/CONF.95/15 (1980); *reprinted in* **19 I.L.M. 1524 (1980) and 2 Weston & Carlson II.C.10: Pmbl., Arts. 1, 2, & Protocol II** (Basic Document 2.34).

16. Convention on the Prohibition of the Use, Stockpiling, Production and Transfer of Anti–Personnel Mines and on their Destruc-

tion. Concluded, 18 Sep 1997. Entered into force, 1 Mar 1999. 2056 U.N.T.S. 211; *reprinted in* 36 I.L.M. 1507 (1997) and 2 Weston & Carlson II.C.11b: Arts 1, 2, 7, 8, 9, & 10 (Basic Document 2.52).

17.   Thomas R. Phillips, "Note and Comment: No Meeting of the Mines: An Analysis of the US Policy regarding the International Ban on Anti–Personnel Landmines (The Ottawa Convention)," 13 Temp. Int'l & Comp. L. J. 23, 35–44 (1999).

On Wednesday, September 16, 1998, the nation-state of Burkina Faso became the fortieth nation to ratify the Convention on the Prohibition of the Use, Stockpiling, Production and Transfer of Anti–Personnel Mines and On Their Destruction [hereinafter "Ottawa Convention"] [**Basic Document 2.52**].[10] Thus the Ottawa Convention, which was ratified faster than any other major treaty in history, became binding as international law for the signatories after a brief waiting period of six months. The treaty took full effect on March 1, 1999.

Although the Ottawa Convention has broad international support from the 133 signatory nations, three of the five permanent members of the United Nations Security Council—China, Russia and the United States—did not sign the accord. The US position seems particularly ironic. When President Clinton addressed the United Nations General Assembly on September 26, 1994, he advocated the eventual elimination of anti-personnel landmines. Moreover, the US sponsored the UN resolution supporting the landmine ban treaty.

* * *

IV.   THE USE OF LANDMINES UNDER INTERNATIONAL LAW

Since the beginning of this century, there has been a restriction on the use of certain types of munitions, most notably poisonous gas and biological.[11] Later in the century the use of landmines was restricted in an international treaty, known as The Convention on Prohibitions or Restrictions on the Use of Certain Conventional Weapons Which May be Deemed to be Excessively Injurious or to Have Indiscriminate Effects [**Basic Document 2.34**]. However, those treaty restrictions were limited to declared international armed conflicts, while the current landmine crisis is largely the result of indiscriminate mining at the hands of factions engaged in internal fighting or undeclared wars. Therefore, the previous treaty restrictions are arguably ineffective in addressing this problem. Recent efforts have been made to expand the scope of existing protocols to fully protect noncombatants from indiscriminate mining. The following discussion outlines and analyzes those efforts.

A.   *International Law and Armed Conflict*

The evolution of international law condemns state military actions that violate basic humanitarian principles. Following the Battle of Solferino in

10. *See Land–Mine Pact Approved,* N.Y. Times, 17 Sep 1998; *see also* International Campaign to Ban Landmines [hereinafter ICBL], Press Release: *Landmine Treaty Ratified by Forty Countries in Record Time* (17 Sep 1998) (visited 14 Dec 1999), available also at <http://www.icbl.org/prelease/1998sept17.html>. [*Eds.*—As of 11 April 2006, 149 states were full parties to the Ottawa Convention while 5 were but signatories thereof (the United States among them)].

11. *See* Protocol for the Prohibition of the Use in War of Asphyxiating, Poisonous or Other Gases, and of Bacteriological Methods of Warfare, 17 Jun 1925 [**Basic Document 2.4**].

1859, the 1907 Hague Convention (IV) and the 1925 Geneva Protocol codified restrictions of military conduct [**Basic Documents 2.2 & 2.4**]. The overall goals of the codified norms were aimed to eliminate unnecessary suffering both to soldiers and noncombatants alike, and specifically to eliminate the use of poisonous gas and biological weapons. In 1949, the International Court of Justice (ICJ) addressed the unlawful use of mines in *United Kingdom v. Albania,* (**Basic Document 7.5)** which involved allegations of Albanian involvement of mining the North Corfu Strait. The case involved two ships from England's navy that unfortunately ran into freshly laid mines, which resulted in several deaths and injuries. The evidence pointed towards Albanian involvement. Since the United Kingdom and Albania were not at war in 1946, the International Court of Justice held that the Second Hague Convention of 1907 did not apply; however, it still found Albania liable under international law. The court's decision to hold Albania liable was founded on "elementary considerations of humanity, even more exacting in peace than in war."[12] Thus, the ICJ did not base the decision on any specific violation of an existing arms control or warfare treaty, but rather on basic humanitarian principles. As international law developed in this area, the use of landmines was specifically restricted under UN arms control protocols. These protocols are outlined below.

B.   *International Law and the Use of Landmines*

The United Nations adopted the Convention on Prohibitions or Restrictions on the Use of Certain Conventional Weapons Which May be Deemed to be Excessively Injurious or to Have Indiscriminate Effects [hereinafter CCW] [**Basic Document 2.34**] during a conference in Geneva. The final treaty was signed on October 10, 1980. The CCW was amended by the Protocol on Prohibitions or Restrictions on the Use of Mines, Booby–Traps and Other Devices [hereinafter Protocol II] that was annexed to the CCW. Under the original draft of Protocol II, the use of landmines was restricted to certain acceptable norms, but these restrictions only applied to conflicts between nation-states.

Considering the nature of recent conflicts (civil war, insurgencies and factional fighting) that have largely been responsible for the proliferation of landmines, the restrictions established under Protocol II were deemed largely ineffective. In 1993, France requested the UN to sponsor a conference to review the CCW. Thereafter, the 48th General Assembly agreed to sponsor a conference for governmental experts to review the CCW.

C.   *Amending Protocol II to Address the Anti–Personnel Landmine Crisis*

During the review conference held in Vienna, the US and others advocated several provisions to strengthen the ability of the original CCW to effectively address the landmine crisis. The provisions included the following: (1) applying the CCW to internal conflicts; (2) requiring all mines to be detectable (no pure plastic mines); (3) restricting the use of mines that do not self-destruct to areas that are marked, fenced and monitored until they are cleared; (4) prohibiting remotely delivered mines that are not self-destructing or self-deactivating; (5) prohibiting booby-traps; (6) restricting the transfer of

12.   *Id.* at 1949 I.C.J. 22.

landmines; (7) establishing a regime for verification and compliance; and (8) increasing cooperation in mine clearing, including transferring advanced technology for demining efforts. While there was general agreement on some basic provisions, however, there was no consensus on other technical provisions. The most difficult areas were the technical issues of detectability and the standards for self-destructing mines. Additional conferences were scheduled for January, April and May of 1996. The final version of Protocol II was adopted on May 3, 1996 and will go into effect on December 3, 1998 for those countries that are parties to the treaty. As of January 25, 1999, only thirty-one countries have ratified the amended Protocol II.[c] . . .

The focus of the amendments to Protocol II was to provide for greater protection against civilian casualties of landmines. Technological advancements and greater use restrictions were the means used to provide that protection. However, these provisions did not satisfy many of the participating parties and did not comport with the official position of the United Nations. These parties determined that regardless of the technological advancements, "smart" landmines are still incapable of differentiating between a soldier and a child, and as such, the threat of injury to noncombatants would remain unacceptably high. The call for a total ban on the use of landmines from NGOs, most notably, the Vietnam Veterans of America Foundation (VVAF) and the International Campaign to Ban Landmines (ICBL) gained support among UN members.

V. EVALUATING THE OTTAWA CONVENTION

The call for a total ban on landmines began with the efforts of several international NGOs. As the process moved forward, it was largely the efforts of these NGOs that served as the catalyst for achieving the international ban. That process began in November 1991, when the VVAF met with Medico International (MI) of Germany and agreed to launch a campaign to ban the use of landmines. In May 1993 the first NGO conference on landmines was held in London. At that conference forty different NGOs were represented and the VVAF was designated as the campaign coordinator. In May 1994, the second NGO conference on landmines was held in Geneva and was attended by seventy-five NGOs. Throughout 1995 and 1996, nation-wide campaigns were started in several countries advocating the total ban on landmines.

A. *"The Ottawa Process": A Call for a Total Ban on Landmines*

Following the Protocol II conference in May 1996 Canada decided to host an international strategy conference to address the landmine crisis. The conference was designated "Towards a Global Ban on Anti–Personnel Mines" and was held in Ottawa in October 1996. Attending the conference were representatives from fifty nations, the UN, the ICBL, and the International Committee of the Red Cross (ICRC). At the end of the conference participants agreed that a total ban on landmines was needed. Canada, again taking the lead on the issue, announced that it would sponsor a conference for the signing of a comprehensive treaty that would ban the use of anti-personnel landmines.

---

c. As of 11 April 2006, 86 states were parties to Protocol II, including the United States.

In November 1996, the US proposed [UN General Assembly Resolution 51/45S] which welcomed the initiatives developed at the Ottawa conference and called on all countries to "pursue vigorously an effective, legally binding international agreement to ban the use, stockpiling, production and transfer of anti-personnel landmines with a view to completing the negotiation as soon as possible."[13] Resolution 51/45S passed on a voice vote in the UN, with 156 members voting in favor, none opposing and ten abstaining.

The official second planning conference was held in Brussels on June 24–27, 1997. Representatives from 154 nations and several NGO's (including the ICRC and ICBL) attended the event. The conference concluded with 106 countries formally adopting the Convention on the Prohibition of the Use, Stockpiling, Production and Transfer of Anti–Personnel Mines and on their Destruction, commonly known as the "Ottawa Convention."[d] . . .

The Ottawa Process was proving successful. On October 10, 1997, Jody Williams, the ICBL leader, learned that she and her organization would share the 1997 Nobel Peace Prize for their efforts toward achieving a total ban on anti-personnel landmines. The fact that a private citizen and a non-governmental organization would receive recognition for achieving an international arms control treaty was remarkable. On December 10, 1997, less than a week after 122 nations officially signed the Ottawa Convention, Jody Williams traveled to Oslo once again, this time to personally receive her Nobel Peace Prize.[14]

There were two distinguishing features of the Ottawa Process. First, the ICBL (an NGO conglomerate with a membership of over 1,000 different NGOs) was a key player in developing the treaty framework. Secondly, in order to avoid Security Council veto power, the countries of Austria, Belgium, Canada, Mexico, Norway and South Africa began to draft the treaty apart from the normal UN framework. Their objective was to establish a set of norms acceptable to a core group of countries, and thereafter persuade the remainder of UN members to adopt the treaty provisions. The partnership between the NGOs and official representatives from several nation states seemed extremely effective—apparently the Nobel Committee agreed. However, the unusual framework in which the treaty was drafted also limited the ability of the US to influence the provisions of the accord.[15] When the US was unable to incorporate the provisions that it stated were required for future ratification, President Clinton announced that the US would be unable to become a party to the treaty.

B.   *The Ottawa Convention: What Does it Say?*

Article One of the Convention **[Basic Document 2.52]** directs that each State Party agrees never under any circumstances: "(a) To use anti-personnel

---

13. GA Res. 51/45S, 51st Sess., UN Doc. A/RES/51/45 (10 Jan 1997); *available also at* <http://www.unorg.ch/frames/disarm/resolut/51/45.htm>.

  d. *Supra* note 10.

14. *See* ICBL, *supra* note 10.

15. When the Senate Foreign Relations Committee was preparing to recommend approval of the Protocol II to the CCW, the

majority report indicated that the Ottawa Process empowered the NGOs to exclude the US and disregard the legitimate security requirements of the US. The committee found the treaty and the process flawed. . . .

  See The White House, Office of the Press Secretary, *Remarks by the President on Land Mines*, 17 Sep 1997, *available at* <http://www.defenselink.mil/speeches/1997/di1247.html> . . . .

mines; (b) To develop, produce, otherwise acquire, stockpile, retain or transfer to anyone, directly or indirectly, anti-personnel mines; (c) To assist, encourage or induce, in any way, anyone to engage in any activity prohibited to a State Party under this Convention." Thus, the treaty prohibits any use or retention of anti-personnel mines, with the limited exception for retaining a very limited amount of mines solely designated for demining training. The treaty defines an anti-personnel mine as a mine "designed to be exploded by the presence, proximity or contact of a person and that will incapacitate, injure or kill one or more persons" [art. 2]. Under ... Protocol II to the CCW, a very similar definition was used; however, it defined anti-personnel mines as a mine "primarily" designed to explode by the presence, proximity or contact of a person.[16] Thus, mines that have a dual purpose may be outside the scope of the CCW. By removing the word "primarily," the Ottawa Convention prohibits any mine that can act as a victim detonated anti-personnel mine, including "dual-purpose" mines. The treaty specifically excludes anti-vehicle mines, which are not prohibited under the treaty. Furthermore, any anti-vehicle mine that is equipped with an "anti-handling device" is not considered to be an anti-personnel mine and therefore is not prohibited under the treaty [art. 2]. The Ottawa Convention defines an anti-handling device as a "device intended to protect a mine and which is part of, linked to, attached to or placed under the mine and which activates when an attempt is made to tamper with or otherwise intentionally disturb the mine" [art. 2]. Any mine that is designed to explode by the presence, proximity or contact of a person is prohibited [art. 2]. These designs include the "smart" mines that self-destruct and self-deactivate [art. 2]. Thus, the Ottawa Convention prohibits the mixed systems (anti-personnel and anti-tank mines combined) currently used by the United States.[17] The parties to the treaty are required to accomplish the destruction of all prohibited mines as soon as possible, but in any event no later ten years after entry into force of the Convention for that State Party, which is six months after ratification [arts. 5, 17]. The treaty allows for a State Party to request an extension of up to an additional ten years, which must be approved by a majority vote of the other treaty parties [art. 5]. The Ottawa Convention provides for verification by allowing parties that are concerned about possible violations of the treaty to request the assistance of the United Nations [arts. 7, 8]. The Secretary–General can request the

16. *See* United Nations Protocol on Prohibitions or Restrictions on the Use of Mines, Booby–Traps and Other Devices (As Amended), 3 May 1996, *available at* <http://www.org.unorg.ch/frames/disarm/distreat/mines.htm> (hereinafter Protocol II). [*Eds.*—In an earlier footnote, the author writes: "Protocol II was annexed to the Convention of Prohibitions or Restrictions on the Use of Certain Conventional Weapons which may be Deemed to be Excessively Injurious or to have Indiscriminate Effects (commonly referred to as the 'CCW') **[Basic Document 2.34]**. In order to qualify as a self-destructing and self-deactivating landmine, the mine must self-destruct within 30 days after emplacement. The mines must have no more than a ten-percent failure rate for self-destruction. Additionally, the mines must have a backup feature, in case of the failure to

self-destruct, which deactivates the mine after no more than 120 days. These combined features must ensure that no more than one mine out of every 1,000 deployed remains active for more than 120 days. Types of landmines failing to meet these standards do not comply with the self-destructing and self-deactivating classifications and therefore, are prohibited from either being remotely deployed or deployed in areas without overt marking, fencing and monitoring. These standards are established in Protocol II to the CCW."

17. Indeed, this is the major point of contention between the US and the drafters of the treaty and the primary reason offered by President Clinton for why the US would not become a party to a treaty that the US first called for in the UN....

suspected violator to provide clarification on the issue of suspected use of prohibited landmines; the suspected party must respond within twenty-eight days to the Secretary–General [art. 8].[18] If the signatory countries determine that provisions of the Ottawa Convention are violated and that there are no circumstances beyond the control of the violating party which caused the violation, then all appropriate measures under international law will be considered [art. 8].

C.   The Ottawa Convention: Will it Work?

Critics of the Ottawa Convention simply state that it will actually accomplish very little. However, that criticism is under-developed and invites the equally under-developed response that a little is better than none— especially when the goal is to reduce the number of landmine victims. Notwithstanding the impact on the military capabilities of the US, there are legitimate issues regarding the efficacy of an international ban. Additionally, critics of the ban assert that verification will be difficult, if not impossible, and therefore, the ban will largely be ceremonial and ineffectual.

Paul A. S. Jefferson, who is involved in humanitarian demining operations, claims the movement toward an international ban on landmines is a failure.[19] In his opinion, the ban has not reduced the landmine casualty rate "by one leg" or restored "one acre" of land that was previously mined.[20] Jefferson, who himself was blinded and lost a leg in a mine blast in Kuwait, asserts that efforts to address the landmine crisis must be measured by the reduction in casualties and the ability to return previously mined land to the civilian population.[21] It is a compelling standard, since aside from the general estimates of landmines, the crisis is defined largely by the number of casualties that result from the proliferation of landmines. Indeed, the US Department of State now uses the landmine casualty rate and reclaimed land areas as the best assessment tools for the crisis.[22]

Furthermore, critics claim that the ICBL's ban campaign has diverted resources and attention away from more effective demining programs. They argue that because the ban campaigners have exaggerated the estimates of deployed landmines, the problem seems hopeless and the demining solution futile. Therefore, organizations such as the Open Society are willing to donate $3 million dollars to the ban campaign but unwilling to donate anything toward demining efforts. It may be impossible to empirically prove that dollars spent toward the ban campaign result in less demining resources.

---

18. . . . If the response is not submitted or is deemed insufficient, the originating party can request that the Secretary–General to convene a special meeting of the parties to the treaty to consider the matter. If one-third parties agree to a special meeting, the Secretary– General will convene such a meeting within fourteen days. If that meeting does not resolve the issue, than upon a majority vote among all parties present, a fact-finding mission, consisting of up to nine experts may be authorized to directly investigate the alleged treaty violation. The suspected party, who is able to present information at every forum, will receive at least seventy-two hours notice prior to the fact-finding mission deploying. Once deployed, the mission may remain inside the country for no more than fourteen days and may not stay more than seven days at any one site. The mission then submits a report to the Secretary–General and the remaining parties. *See id.*

19. *See generally* P. Jefferson, *A Political Minefield*, Wall St. J., 15 Oct 1997.

20. *See id.*

21. *See id.*

22. *See* Bureau of Political–Military Affairs, US Department of States, *Hidden Killers: The Global Landmine Crisis* 13–16 (1998) at Chapter III. . . .

However, if the assumption is made that both efforts are competing for the same limited resources, then it is arguable that demining efforts would be the wisest choice of investment. Demining has reduced dramatically the casualty rates in the countries most affected by this crisis. In Namibia alone, the casualty rate was reduced by ninety-percent because of effective demining.

As with any arms control agreement, monitoring is a vital element for the agreement's successful operation. Part of what makes other arms control treaties enforceable is the ability of intelligence systems to verify compliance or detect indicators of violations.... In verifying a treaty, intelligence indicators must reliably point toward either compliance or violations in order to be of any validity. It is difficult to imagine that a weapon as simple to manufacture and store as a landmine produces any unique signatures or indicators that may be effectively detected by intelligence systems. Detection would therefore have to come from labor intensive monitoring everywhere that landmines were suspected. Indeed, the common stick is the tool that is still widely used for detection and demining. This scheme of detection does not seem to adequately facilitate the enforcement of a global ban.

On balance, it appears that the Ottawa Convention is at best an unproven solution to the current crisis. However, that alone does not make it an unacceptable solution. But, if it diverts critical resources from demining, which has historically been successful, then the treaty may actually hurt and not help solve the problem. Most of the resistance toward adopting the ban is based on the alleged impact of reduced operational capabilities of US military forces....

[*Eds.*—The author proceeds to analyze US objections to the Ottawa Convention, the major objection being the need to use landmines in defending South Korea.]

SECTION 5. DISCUSSION NOTES/QUESTIONS

1. There is disagreement about the role of the 1925 Geneva Protocol **(Basic Document 2.4)** in preventing the use of chemical and biological weapons (CBW) in World War II. The few examples of World War II CBW use tend, however, to support the notion that the belligerents were deterred more by their mutual ability to use CBW than by concern to adhere to the Geneva Protocol. *See* Philip L. Reizenstein, Note, *Chemical and Biological Weapons—Recent Legal Developments May Prove to be a Turning Point in Arms Control,* 12 Brooklyn J. Int'l L. 95, 105 (1986):

> [During World War II], [t]he Italian army deployed an estimated 700 tons of chemical agents against the Ethiopian army, causing approximately 15,000 casualties. During the Japanese invasion of China, approximately 25–30 percent of all Japanese munitions were chemical in nature. Arguably, it was the prospect of Allied retaliation, not the respect of international law, which deterred Germany from ordering the use of chemical weapons. Indeed, most usages of chemical weapons ... in World War II [were] based on military commanders' evaluations that the target enemy had little defensive and no retaliatory capability.

If a state thought that it could gain a military advantage through use of CBW despite the possibility of retaliation, would the 1925 Protocol, the 1972 Biological Weapons Convention **(Basic Document 2.25)**, or the 1993 Chemical Weapons

Convention **(Basic Document 2.42)** prevent such action? How might prevention or deterrence be assured? Might your answer depend on the kind of deterrence that is practiced? Consider in this connection the following additional observations by the same author as above:

> Deterrence can take one of two forms, risk increase or gain decrease. Deterrence as practiced today is generally risk increase deterrence—a maintenance of the potential to inflict unacceptable harm upon whomever initiates a conflict. To achieve this goal, a continual and costly arms race is necessary.... [I]n the area of chemical warfare, the United States has followed in the general pattern of risk increase deterrence by engaging in a costly CBW arms race with the Soviet Union.... In the area of chemical warfare, gain decrease deterrence would involve the use of protective clothing which, when worn, would reduce the benefits that a state would obtain by using chemical weapons.

Id. at 124–25.

The existence of international customary law in addition to deterrence disincentives may act synergistically to prevent CBW use. As pointed out in Harry Almond, Jr., *US Chemical Weapons Policy,* 13 U. Tol. L. Rev. 1189, 1213 (1982), "[t]he perception of policy makers with respect to chemical weapons are affected by what they believe the weapons can do, their military utility, the possibility of use by adversaries, the improvement and modernization, and, of course, what they believe are the restraints on those weapons."

2. The facts of the present problem are based loosely on the "yellow rain" controversy in Southeast Asia during the 1970s and 1980s. Reports of possible chemical and biological weapons (CBW) use in Southeast Asia reached the West beginning in the mid–1970s. *See, e.g.,* Sterling Seagrave, Yellow Rain: A Journey through the Terror of Chemical Warfare (1981); US Department of State, Chemical Warfare in Southeast Asia and Afghanistan: Special Report No. 98, (March 1982). Hmong refugees in Thailand fleeing from Laos described a "yellow rain" and complained of dizziness, blisters, nausea, shock, coughing up of blood-stained tissue, vomiting of blood, and bloody diarrhea. Between 1978 and 1980 similar reports were heard from refugees fleeing Vietnamese intervention in Kampuchea. Many groups conducted ad hoc fact-finding missions. In 1981, the United States charged that the particular agent used in Southeast Asia was trichothecene and that it was used with the complicity of the Soviet Union. Several scientists have developed strong evidence, however, that these toxins are present in bee excrement, and that "yellow rain" is therefore a naturally occurring phenomena. *See* Julian Robinson, Jeanne Guillemin, & Matthew Meselson, *Yellow Rain: The Story Collapses,* 68 Foreign Pol'y 100 (1987). General scientific opinion tends to support this view.

What lessons may be drawn from this "yellow rain" controversy? That the 1925 Geneva Protocol **(Basic Document 2.4)**, the 1972 Biological Weapons Convention **(Basic Document 2.25)**, and the 1993 Chemical Weapons Convention **(Basic Document 2.42)** have been flagrantly violated and that their failure to provide for compliance verification or outside supervision is therefore fatal to their effectiveness? That a chemical or biological or chemical arms control regime cannot succeed without effective fact-finding? Consider Francis A. Boyle, *The Legal Distortions Behind the Reagan Administration's Chemical and Biological Warfare Buildup,* 30 St. Louis U. L. J. 1175, 1175 (1986):

> In my professional opinion, the Reagan administration did not make [its] charges in good faith. Instead, [the] charges represented part of an orchestrat-

ed attempt to convince the American people that the Soviet Union cannot be trusted to live up to the terms of already existing arms control agreements. These allegations were intended to diffuse public pressure upon the Reagan administration to conclude additional chemical, biological, and nuclear arms control agreements with the Soviet Union.

If Professor Boyle is right, what effect might the unsubstantiated charges of violation have had upon the CBW arms control regime established under the 1925 Protocol and the 1972 (biological) and 1993 (chemical) weapons conventions? Might unsubstantiated charges be used to mask a CBW build-up and therefore undercut the regime? Might a perceived need to justify such a build-up via unsubstantiated charges of violation by others evidence the vitality of the regime? On the politics of allegations of use of chemical weapons, see Thomas Stock, Maria Haug & Patricia Radler, *Chemical and Biological Weapon Developments and Arms Control*, 1996 SIPRI Y. B. 661, 662–63.

3. The issue of verification is crucial in arms control. How can we verify that a particular state is complying with its obligations under a particular treaty? Read the Convention on Biological and Toxin Weapons **(Basic Document 2.25)** to determine how compliance with it is to be verified. Note that it does not provide for on-site inspections. What are the pitfalls of reliance on "national technical means" for verification? Compare the verification procedures in the Chemical Weapons Convention **(Basic Document 2.42)**. Are they likely to be effective? A proposal has been made for a "verification protocol" to be drafted for the CBW Convention. This initiative was discussed at the Fourth Review Conference of the Convention held in late 1996. Recommendations for inclusion in such a protocol include: adherence to particular laboratory safety standards for infectious agents; annual declarations about facilities and activities that may raise compliance concerns; and provisions for "challenge inspections." *See* Marie I. Chevrier & Jessica E. Stern, *Chemical and Biological Weapons in the Third World*, 11 B. C. Third World L. J. 45, 79 (1991); Malcolm R. Dando, *Towards A Verification Protocol for the Biological Weapons Convention?*, 6 Pacific Research No. 4, at 11 (Nov 1993). What other provisions might be considered? Note the warning of Dando, at 13: "If the process of enhancing verification is delayed, rapid developments in biotechnology are almost certain to be the cause of increasing distrust in some conflict-prone regions of the world. The process of proliferation of biological weapons of mass destruction could then become unstoppable." How could verification work in the context of landmines?

4. It is interesting to note that the acceptance of the 1925 Geneva Protocol **(Basic Document 2.4)** and the Convention on Biological Weapons **(Basic Document 2.25)** by the United States was delayed because of concerns about whether chemicals used by the United States in Vietnam were covered by these treaties. Another concern was that the Geneva Protocol might prohibit the use of tear gas and other riot control agents in domestic police actions. *See* Marie I. Chevrier & Jessica E. Stern, *Chemical and Biological Weapons in the Third World*, 11 B.C. Third World L. J. 45, 53–4 (1991). What arguments might be made about the applicability of the 1925 Geneva Protocol to tear gas? *See* W. Hayes Parks, *Classification of Chemical–Biological Warfare*, 13 U. Tol. L. Rev. 1165 (1982).

5. The Chemical Weapons Convention **(Basic Document 2.42)** requires the dismantling of arsenals of obsolete but still lethal chemical weapons. How can this be achieved safely? What about potential conflicts with national environmental protection policies? These issues are considered by David A. Koplow in *How Do We*

Get Rid of These Things?: Dismantling Excess Weapons While Protecting the Environment, 89 Nw. U. L. Rev. 445 (1995). Koplow argues, at 448, that "environmentalism and arms control ... are now starting to intersect.... In the case of chemical weapons dismantling, these competing concerns can be accommodated— but only partially, temporarily, and uncomfortably."

6. In the instant problem, Tongking laid landmines in Funan. It has been estimated that there are 100 million landmines to be found in 64 countries and that over 10,000 people are killed by mines each year. Injuries are highest in Africa and Asia. In a section omitted from Reading 17, *supra,* author Thomas R. Phillips argues that a total ban on landmines presents risks to US forces. He proposes that US policy focus instead on an effective demining program, a prohibition on the indiscriminate use of landmines and ensuring the security of US military personnel through "smart" landmines. What are the consequences of the US remaining outside the Ottawa Convention?

7. *Bibliographical Note.* For supplemental discussion concerning the principal themes addressed in this problem, consult the following additional specialized materials:

(a) *Books/Monographs/Reports/Symposia.* Africa Watch, Landmines in Angola (1993); J. Austin & C. Bruch, The Environmental Consequences of War : Legal, Economic and Scientific Perspectives (2000); Biological Warfare and Disarmament: New Problems/New Perspectives (S. Wright ed., 2002); Preventing a Biological Arms Race (S. Wright ed., 1990); L. Cole, The Eleventh Plague: The Politics of Biological and Chemical Warfare (1996); Off. Int'l Security Operations, US Dep't State, Killers: The Global Problem with Uncleared Landmines (1993); Symposium on Anti–Personnel Mines: Montreux (1993); Symposium, *World Security and Weapons Proliferation,* 2 Transnation'l L. & Contemp. Probs. 331 (1992); The Arms Project and Physicians for Human Rights, Landmines: A Deadly Legacy (1993).

(b) *Articles/Book Chapters.* H. Blix, *Friedman Award Address: Developing International Law and Inducing Compliance,* 41 Colum. J. Transnat'l L. 1 (2002); J. Cohan, *Modes of Warfare and Evolving Standards of Environmental Protection under the International Law of War,* 15 Fla. J. Int'l L. 481 (2003); T. Graham, Jr., *Is International Law Relevant to Arms Control?: National Self–Defense, International Law, and Weapons of Mass Destruction,* 4 Chi. J. Int'l L. 1 (2003); D. Houchins, *Extending the Application of the ICJ's July 8, 1996, Advisory Opinion to Environment–Altering Weapons in General: What Is the Role of International Environmental Law in Warfare?,* 22 J. Land Resources & Envtl. L. 463 (2002); D. Kaye & S. Solomon, *Current Developments: The Second Review Conference of the 1980 Convention on Certain Conventional Weapons,* 96 A.J.I.L. 922 (2002); B. Kellman, *Responses to the September 11 Attacks: An International Criminal Law Approach to Bioterrorism,* 25 Harv. J. L. & Pub. Pol'y 721 (2002); P. Oppenheimer, *A Chemical Weapons Regime for the 1990s: Satisfying Seven Critical Criteria,* 11 Wis. Int'l L. J. 1 (1992); A. Perez, *Is International Law Relevant to Arms Control?: Delegalization of Arms Control—a Democracy Deficit in De Facto Treaties of Peace?,* 4 Chi. J. Int'l L. 19 (2003); M. Polkinghorne & J. Cockayne, *Dealing with the Risks and Responsibilities of Landmines and their Clearance,* 25 Fordham Int'l L. J. 1187 (2002); T. Stock, M. Haug & P. Radler, *Chemical and Biological Weapon Development and Arms Control,* 1996 SIPRI Y.B. 661; E. Tanzman & B. Kellman, *Legal Implementation of the Multilateral Chemical Weapons Convention: Integrating International Security with the Constitution,* 22 N.Y.U. J. Int'l L. & Pol. 475 (1990); J. Trahan, *Terrorism Conventions: Existing*

Gaps and Different Approaches, 8 New Eng. Int'l & Comp. L. Ann. 215 (2002); L. Wexler, *The International Deployment of Shame, Second–Best Responses, and Norm Entrepreneurship: The Campaign to Ban Landmines and the Landmine Ban Treaty*, 20 Ariz. J. Int'l & Comp. Law 561 (2003); R. Williamson, Jr., *Is International Law Relevant to Arms Control?: Hard Law, Soft Law, and Non–Law in Multilateral Arms Control: Some Compliance Hypotheses*, 4 Chi. J. Int'l L. 59 (2003); S. Wright, *Prospects for Biological Disarmament in the 1990s*, 2 Transnation'l L. & Contemp. Probs. 453 (1992).

Chapter Five

PROBLEMS OF SOCIO–POLITICAL JUSTICE

THE VITAL PERSPECTIVE

The values of freedom, equality, participation, and equity have powerful resonance in the international community and provide important yardsticks for the measurement of authority and legitimacy. But the concept of territorial sovereignty is regularly deployed to justify degrading social arrangements and repressive legal orders. Around the globe, we see governments kill, deport, incarcerate, rape, and torture. Non-state actors such as corporations and private military groups, too, are responsible for major human rights violations. Civil and political liberties, as well as social, economic, and cultural rights, are denied on a widespread basis, affecting particularly vulnerable groups—for example, indigenous peoples, women and children, and homosexuals. Prisoners of political and religious conscience fill many of the world's jails. Severe forms of racism and sexism persist everywhere. The present world order linchpin of territorial nationalism can itself operate as a form of discrimination and repression.

Problem 5–1

Ethnic Conflict and Its Consequences in Slavia, Candia, and Corcyra

SECTION 1.   FACTS

Slavia is a small republic in southeastern Europe comprised mainly of two populations with distinct linguistic and religious traditions. The Slavian majority is Orthodox Christian, comprises 75% of the population, and tends to live in the industrialized northern part of the country. The Illyrians are Muslim and live mainly in the poorer agricultural south. For almost 50 years after the formation of Slavia following World War II, the two groups lived in relative harmony. Slavian-dominated communist governments extended considerable autonomy to the Illyrians in respect of education, health, labor, police, and other matters of essentially local concern. Illyria was in fact a self-governing province of Slavia during this time.

Candia is an island republic some 1,000 kilometers to Slavia's south in the Mediterranean Sea. It has a prosperous economy, a low unemployment rate, a relatively homogenous ethnic population and a stable political culture. Ninety percent of Candia's population identify as Orthodox Christians.

Approximately half way between Slavia and Candia lies the smaller island state of Corcyra in the Ionian Sea, recently accepted as a member of the United Nations. Corcyra's environment is almost completely despoiled by phosphate mining conducted over the last century by Candian mining companies. Corcyra is deeply in debt and its economy is in tatters. It depends largely on economic support from Candia.

In 1989, coinciding with the collapse of communism and the emergence of ethnic rivalries elsewhere in Eastern Europe, a new Slavian government revoked Illyria's autonomy and officially supplanted Illyrian with Slavian governance relative to all matters local in Illyria. Almost ever since, a savage conflict has raged in Slavia between its two major ethnic groups—Slavians and Illyrians.

In the last few years, driven by its resurgent nationalism, Slavia's control of Illyria has taken a severe toll on Illyria and its majority Muslim population. In addition to revoking the self-governing status that Illyria enjoyed under communist rule, Slavia has pursued a host of policies hostile to the Illyrians. First it ignored ongoing demands of the League for a Democratic Illyria (LDI) for such reforms as one-person-one-vote in local elections, the removal of gerrymandered electoral districts, and the nondiscriminatory allocation of public services. Next, it proclaimed fast-growing separatist sentiments and activities among the Illyrians to constitute "a public emergency which threatens the life of the Slavian nation"; and, in response, it adopted and promulgated an Internal Security Act (ISA) outlawing the LDI and allowing for the indefinite detention of suspected "anti-Slavian terrorists" without charge or trial. Most recently, it has instituted a campaign of systematic discrimination, harassment, and repression against Illyria's Muslim majority, designed either to force it to submit to Slavian rule in all important respects or to quit the region and migrate elsewhere. Most observers agree that, by whatever means, the expulsion from Illyria of Illyria's Muslim majority is uppermost in the Slavian government's mind. "Slavia for the Slavians" is the Slavian government's most constant refrain.

Slavia has ordered the isolation and confinement of hundreds of Illyrians economists, political scientists, and other social theorists, replaced hundreds of Illyrian faculty with Slavian professors at The University of Illyria, dismissed thousands of Illyrian school teachers in favor of Slavian school teachers, and otherwise limited the intellectual and academic life of Illyria's majority population. Lodging at the university's dormitories has been denied to Illyrian students, and a sharp cut in the number of Illyrian students was recently authorized. Discriminatory policies now allow only 1,500 Illyrian youths to enroll for the first year of university study, and then to attend classes held only in Slavian; simultaneously, thousands of Slavian students from outside Illyria are being subsidized to pursue their university studies there.

Further, the Slavian government has initiated summary trials of Illyrian political activists, sentenced mass numbers of them to hard labor in prison for "misdemeanors with political elements," and killed several hundred unarmed Illyrian demonstrators protesting these trials and sentences. In these and other ways, Slavia has restricted freedom of speech and association in Illyria. Since the LDI's separatist activities began, Slavian internal security procedures have made it illegal for more than four Illyrians to gather anywhere (excepting families). "Anti-terrorist patrols" by paramilitary police regularly harass Illyrians on Illyrian streets and highways, demanding identification papers and breaking up any groups of four or more with threats of arrest. Police surveillance and body searches of Illyrians, however innocent their conduct, are now routine; and at night especially the Slavian police regularly enter Illyrian homes and businesses without warrants to investigate "anti-Slavian activities." Warrantless arrests often result from these encounters, as do also hostage-takings, forced evictions, and repeated accounts of physical abuse, even torture.

There are reliable reports of Slavian soldiers and civilian locals going on rampages and raping hundreds—some say thousands—of Illyrian women and girls, the apparent intent being not only generally to rape Illyrian females, but also, by virtue of the Muslim belief that one cannot be a Muslim if one is not born of a Muslim father, to reduce Illyria's Muslim population. When confronted by Amnesty International with these allegations,[a] the Slavian government denied the existence of large numbers of rapes as "absurd," but declared that such "indiscretions" would be strongly condemned if their occurrence could be proven. Rapes continue to such a degree, however, that Illyrian women and girls now venture out-of-doors only with male escorts.

Compounding the situation, Illyrian physicians and medical staff have been summarily dismissed from the Faculty of Medicine at The University of Illyria and other health facilities in Illyria; Illyrian medical workers have sustained much violence; and gynecology and obstetrics departments have been left without a single Illyrian physician or nurse. As a result, there are almost no medical personnel available to aid the many Illyrian women and girls who have been raped. Illyrian women and girls now usually deliver their babies without medical assistance and under poor sanitary conditions. The Illyrian infant mortality rate has soared.

---

a. Amnesty International (AI) is a London-based human rights organization and recipient of the 1977 Nobel Peace Price. *See infra* Discussion Note/Question 11, at 600.

Finally, the Slavian government has sought to erode the economic base of Illyria's Muslim majority. For "security" reasons, it has dismissed all of its Illyrian employees (including from the police forces in the area). Labor unions controlled by Illyrian workers have been repeatedly threatened and forced into clandestine operation when their offices have been raided and ransacked. Slavian businesses have been ordered to retain only those Illyrian workers who will sign "individual agreements" proclaiming their loyalty to the Slavian state and otherwise to dismiss Illyrian workers in favor of Slavian workers. And while Slavian businesses in Illyria are assisted by substantial grants-in-aid, Illyrians are now consistently denied the right to start businesses there and Illyrian marketplaces and street vendors are increasingly raided and stripped of their money and goods. The result has been to erode severely the purchasing power of Illyrians, many of whom have been forced into subsistence living.

All of which has fit Slavian governmental policy. The Slavian government, keenly interested in the rich soil of Illyria, has worked to force Illyrian farmers out of their homes and off their land, paying Slavians to settle in their stead and subsidizing Slavian housing whenever needed. The result: Illyrian farmers and others have been fleeing Illyria in droves, causing Illyria's ethnological structure to change dramatically. The French newspaper *Le Monde*, citing also the forced eviction of urban Illyrians from their homes, has called this "resettlement program" an "instance of 'ethnic cleansing.'"

Many Illyrians, despairing of their future in Slavia, have attempted to flee. Mainland neighbors of Slavia have been unwilling to accept the large numbers of Illyrian asylum seekers crossing into their countries. The unwillingness stems both from anxiety about the economic and social cost of resettlement of the Illyrians and from the inevitable antipathy this will cause in political relations with Slavia. Slavia's neighbors simply refuse entry to all Illyrians and forcibly return any Illyrians who cross the border illegally. The asylum seekers are then held under the ISA as anti-Slavian terrorists. These practices encourage Illyrians to devise other routes to new lives and increasing numbers to hire or purchase small boats in Slavian coastal ports and set sail for Candia. A lively trade in people-smuggling has thus developed along the coast as entrepreneurs exploit the Illyrian desire to leave Slavia, charging thousands of US dollars for each place in boats. The fleeing Illyrians claim refugee status as soon as they reach Candia.

The arrival of the Illyrian "boat people" (as they are termed in the Candian press) has caused intense alarm in Candia. The Muslim Illyrians are regarded as a threat to Candian social homogeneity and a drain on the Candian economy. The Candian Prime Minister described the Illyrians as a potential source of terrorist attacks because of their adherence to Islam. "Despite pressure from the United Nations to be politically correct," he told Candia's Parliament, "we would be foolish to deny that Islam was the religion of the September 11 terrorists and that many of its followers have applauded their wanton and cowardly acts." The Candian Parliament then acted quickly to declare all coastal land and sea below the high water mark as outside Candia's "immigration zone" and empowered the Candian Coast Guard to tow any boats in Candian waters back to the Slavian coast. Many Illyrians have been forcibly returned to Slavia in this way.

Because of criticism of these policies by Candian civil society, Candia entered into an agreement with Corcyra to house some of the Illyrian boat people. In return for significant financial assistance, Corcyra agreed to build temporary shelters for the Illyrians until their future can be determined. Reports from Corcyra are that the conditions of the temporary shelters are appalling, with inadequate sanitation. Corcyra refuses to grant entry visas to the media or human rights organizations to inspect the shelters.

Meanwhile Illyrians who have already arrived in Candia are being held in makeshift detention camps far from population centers. Candian law is amended to allow their detention until their claims to refugee status are determined. This process can take several years. The indefinite detention has caused severe trauma, especially among Illyrian children.

Assisted by Amnesty International, Illyrians inside Slavia have petitioned the United Nations Sub–Commission on the Promotion and Protection of Human Rights[b] about their treatment. Groups of detainees held in both Candia and Corcyra have appealed to the Organization for Security and Co-operation in Europe (OSCE) about the nature and conditions of their detention. And the United States and the United Kingdom have begun proceedings in the International Court of Justice, arguing that Slavia has violated the 1948 Convention on the Prevention and Punishment of Genocide. Meanwhile the Prosecutor of the International Criminal Court has begun investigations into the large-scale rape of Illyrian women and girls in Slavia.

Slavia and Candia as well as Corcyra are members of the United Nations. Also, all three are party to the 1951 Refugee Convention and its 1967 Protocol and are members of the Organization for Security and Co-operation in Europe. All countries are parties to the 1948 Convention on the Prevention and Punishment of Genocide and the International Covenants on Economic, Social and Cultural Rights and Civil and Political Rights, although not to the Optional Protocol to the latter.

SECTION 2.   PURPOSE OF PROBLEM

A primary purpose of this problem is to introduce, as a pivotal dimension of world order reform, the development of human rights prescription and enforcement in the years since the UN Charter of 1945 and the Universal Declaration of Human Rights of 1948. Before World War II and the founding of the United Nations, the bulk of international human rights law, except in relation to the protection of certain linguistic and religious minorities, centered upon the treatment to be accorded alien nationals living or traveling abroad (under the rubric of "the diplomatic protection of aliens)," and the

---

b.   *See infra* Discussion Note/Question 1, at 591.

humanitarian rules of armed conflict. In the post-Charter/Declaration era, however, international human rights law has undergone a dramatic shift, from almost total absorption with the protection of aliens to an ever-widening concern for the way governments treat persons within their jurisdiction, and in virtually every aspect of human endeavor. As Adolfo Perez Esquivel said when receiving the Nobel Peace Prize in 1980: "[t]he last few decades have seen a more extended and internationalized conscience in respect of human rights, such that we are confronted with and increasingly forced toward a deeper understanding of what the struggle for human rights means."[c]

A major reason for this development, partly catalyzed by the Nazi slaughter of six million Jews and the victimization of *apartheid*-controlled black South Africans, has been a growing recognition that major denials of sociopolitical and economic justice provoke violence, even war.[d] The continuing issue of Palestinian self-determination is today perhaps the most prominent case in point, but it is today recorded prominently elsewhere as well in the wake of the collapse of the former Soviet Union—in the Balkans, in Georgia, in Chechnya, and in East Timor, Sierra Leone, and Zimbabwe. Still, for all the gains that the growing recognition of these basic interdependencies has produced, progress has been slow and sketchy. The definition and implementation of international human rights, therefore, remains high among humanity's priorities. In the words of former US Supreme Court Justice and US Permanent Representative to the United Nations, Arthur J. Goldberg, several decades ago: "[the Universal Declaration] has received *universal* recognition, but it remains just that, a *declaration*. In these two words thus are reflected both the hope and the tragedy of human rights in our day. We agree all too often on principles, but practice and enforcement have not kept pace with pronouncements." Arthur J. Goldberg, *Our Concern for Human Rights*, 32 Congress Bi–Weekly, No. 13, p. 8, at 9 (Nov. 15, 1965).

Finally, a major purpose of the problem is to highlight the increasing institutionalization of international human rights law and policy, particularly at the regional level. To this end, it seeks to stimulate analysis of the following cluster of doctrines, principles, and rules of international law: international human rights law generally, the enforcement of international human rights generally, the enforcement of human rights through UN non-treaty-based procedures, the enforcement of human rights through the "Helsinki Process," international refugee law, self-determination and the rights of minorities, and international criminal law (including the issue of whether rape can constitute genocide). The Readings contained in Section 4, *infra*, are arranged, for convenience only, according to these recognized legal themes. Related normative questions are considered in the Discussion Notes/Questions that follow thereafter.

c. A. Perez Esquivel, *Afterword*, in The International Bill of Rights 105 (P. Williams ed., 1981).

d. As former US President John F. Kennedy once put it: "Is not peace, in the last analysis, basically a matter of human rights?" Remarks at the American University, 10 Jun 1963. Public Papers of the President: John F. Kennedy 1962 (1963).

SECTION 3.   ASSIGNMENTS

A.   READING ASSIGNMENT

Study the Readings presented in Section 4, *infra*, and the Discussion Notes/Questions that follow. Also, to the extent possible, consult the accompanying bibliographical references.

B.   RECOMMENDED WRITING ASSIGNMENT

Prepare a comprehensive, logically sequenced, and *argumentative* brief in the form of an outline of the primary and subsidiary *legal* issues you see requiring resolution by (1) the UN Sub–Commission on the Promotion and Protection of Human Rights; (2) the Organization for Security and Co-operation in Europe; and (3) the International Court of Justice (approximately ten single-spaced, typewritten pages). Also, from the perspective of an independent judge, indicate which side ought to prevail on each issue and why. Retain a copy of your issue-outline/brief for class discussion.

C.   RECOMMENDED ORAL ASSIGNMENT

Assume you are legal counsel for the Republic of Slavia or the Republic of Candia (as designated by your instructor); then, relying upon the Readings (and your issue-outline/brief, if prepared), present a 10–15 minute oral argument of your client's/government's likely positions before the Organization for Security and Co-operation in Europe, and the International Court of Justice.

D.   RECOMMENDED REFLECTIVE ASSIGNMENT

Consider (and recommend) alternative norms, procedures, and/or institutions that you believe might do better than existing world order arrangements to contend with situations of the kind posed by this problem. In so doing, but without insisting upon *immediate* political feasibility, identify the particular transition steps that would be needed to make your alternatives a reality.

SECTION 4.   READINGS

The following readings are *prima facie* relevant to solving this problem. They are divided according to those categories of recognized international legal inquiry and analysis that are principally implicated in the problem: "international human rights in general;" "enforcement of international human rights through the Organization for Security and Co-operation in Europe;" "international refugee law;" "the right to self-determination and minority rights;" and "war crimes, genocide, and crimes against humanity." They are your law library for present purposes and should be treated as such, organized intelligibly for "shelving" and not necessarily according to the issues presented. Be sure to review Chapter 2 ("International Legal Prescription: The 'Sources' of International Law") in your consideration of them. It, too, should be treated as part of your law library (as, indeed, should this entire coursebook).

A. International Human Rights in General

1. Burns H. Weston, "Human Rights," in *Encyclopædia Britannica* (2005), available from *Encyclopædia Britannica Online* at <http://www. britannica.com/eb/article?tocId=219350>.

Historical development

The expression "human rights" is relatively new, having come into everyday parlance only since World War II, the founding of the United Nations in 1945, and the adoption by the UN General Assembly of the Universal Declaration of Human Rights in 1948. It replaced the phrase "natural rights," which fell into disfavour in part because the concept of natural law (to which it was intimately linked) had become a matter of great controversy; and it replaced as well the later phrase "the rights of Man," which was not universally understood to include the rights of women.

* * *

Most students of human rights trace the origins of the concept to ancient Greece and Rome, where it was closely tied to the doctrines of the Stoics, who held that human conduct should be judged according to, and brought into harmony with, the law of nature. A classic example of this view is given in Sophocles' play *Antigone*, in which the title character, upon being reproached by King Creon for defying his command not to bury her slain brother, asserted that she acted in accordance with the immutable laws of the gods.

* * *

[It was primarily for the 17th and 18th centuries, however, to elaborate upon] natural law as meaning or implying natural rights.... The intellectual—and especially the scientific—achievements of the 17th century (including the materialism of Hobbes, the rationalism of Descartes and Leibniz, the pantheism of Spinoza, and the empiricism of Bacon and Locke) encouraged a belief in natural law and universal order; and during the 18th century, the so-called Age of Enlightenment, a growing confidence in human reason and in the perfectibility of human affairs led to the more comprehensive expression of this belief. Particularly important were the writings of John Locke, arguably the most important natural-law theorist of modern times, and the works of the 18th-century *philosophes* centred mainly in Paris, including Montesquieu, Voltaire, and Jean–Jacques Rousseau. Locke argued in detail, mainly in writings associated with the English Revolution of 1688 (the "Glorious Revolution"), that certain rights self-evidently pertain to individuals as human beings (because these rights existed in "the state of nature" before humankind entered civil society); that chief among them are the rights to life, liberty (freedom from arbitrary rule), and property; that, upon entering civil society, humankind surrendered to the state—pursuant to a "social contract"—only the right to enforce these natural rights and not the rights themselves; and that the state's failure to secure these rights gives rise to a right to responsible, popular revolution. The philosophers, building on Locke and others and embracing many and varied currents of thought with a common supreme faith in reason, vigorously attacked religious and scientific dogmatism, intolerance, censorship, and social and economic restraints. They sought to discover and act upon universally valid principles governing nature, humanity, and society, including the inalienable "rights of Man," which they treated as a fundamental ethical and social gospel.

Not surprisingly, this liberal intellectual ferment exerted a profound influence in the Western world of the late 18th and early 19th centuries. Together with the Revolution of 1688 in England and the resulting Bill of Rights, it provided the rationale for the wave of revolutionary agitation that swept the West, most notably in North America and France. Thomas Jefferson, who had studied Locke and Montesquieu, gave poetic eloquence to the plain prose of the 17th century in the Declaration of Independence, proclaimed by the 13 American colonies on July 4, 1776: "We hold these truths to be self-evident, that all men are created equal, that they are endowed by their Creator with certain unalienable Rights, that among these are Life, Liberty and the Pursuit of Happiness." Similarly, the Marquis de Lafayette, who won the close friendship of George Washington and who shared the hardships of the US War of Independence, imitated the pronouncements of the English and American revolutions in the Declaration of the Rights of Man and of the Citizen of August 26, 1789, proclaiming that "men are born and remain free and equal in rights" and that "the aim of every political association is the preservation of the natural and imprescriptible rights of man."

In sum, the idea of human rights, though known by another name, played a key role in late 18th- and early 19th-century struggles against political absolutism. It was, indeed, the failure of rulers to respect the principles of freedom and equality that was responsible for this development.

* * *

The idea of human rights as natural rights was not without its detractors, however. In the first place, because it was frequently associated with religious orthodoxy, the doctrine of natural rights became less attractive to philosophical and political liberals. Additionally, because they were conceived in essentially absolutist terms, natural rights were increasingly considered to conflict with one another. Most importantly, the doctrine of natural rights came under powerful philosophical and political attack from both the right and the left.

In England, for example, conservative political thinkers such as Edmund Burke and David Hume united with liberals such as Jeremy Bentham to condemn the doctrine, the former out of fear that public affirmation of natural rights would lead to social upheaval, the latter out of concern lest declarations and proclamations of natural rights substitute for effective legislation. In his *Reflections on the Revolution in France* (1790), Burke—a believer in natural law who nonetheless denied that the "rights of Man" could be derived from it—criticized the drafters of the Declaration of the Rights of Man and of the Citizen for proclaiming the "monstrous fiction" of human equality, which, he argued, serves but to inspire "false ideas and vain expectations in men destined to travel in the obscure walk of laborious life." Bentham, one of the founders of Utilitarianism, was no less scornful. "Rights," he wrote, "is the child of law; from real law come real rights; but from imaginary laws, from 'law of nature,' come imaginary rights.... Natural rights is simple nonsense; natural and imprescriptible rights (an American phrase) ... [is] rhetorical nonsense, nonsense upon stilts." Agreeing with

Bentham, Hume insisted that natural law and natural rights are unreal metaphysical phenomena.

This assault upon natural law and natural rights intensified and broadened during the 19th and early 20th centuries. John Stuart Mill, despite his vigorous defense of liberty, proclaimed that rights ultimately are founded on utility. The German jurist Friedrich Karl von Savigny, England's Sir Henry Maine, and other "historicalist" legal thinkers emphasized that rights are a function of cultural and environmental variables unique to particular communities. The English jurist John Austin argued that the only law is "the command of the sovereign" (a phrase of Hobbes'). And the logical positivists of the early 20th century insisted that the only truth is that which can be established by verifiable experience and that therefore ethical pronouncements are not cognitively significant. By World War I, there were scarcely any theorists who would defend the "rights of Man" along the lines of natural law. Indeed, under the influence of 19th-century German Idealism and parallel expressions of rising European nationalism, there were some—the Marxists, for example—who, though not rejecting individual rights altogether, maintained that rights, from whatever source derived, belong to communities or whole societies and nations preeminently.

* * *

Although the heyday of natural rights proved short, the idea of rights nonetheless endured. The abolition of slavery, the implementation of factory legislation, the rise of popular education and trade unionism, the universal suffrage movement—these and other examples of 19th-century reformist impulses afford ample evidence that the idea was not to be extinguished, even if its *a priori* derivation had become a matter of general skepticism. But it was not until the rise and fall of Nazi Germany that the idea of human rights truly came into its own. Many of the gruesome atrocities committed by the Nazi regime had been officially authorized by Nazi laws and decrees, and this fact convinced many that law and morality cannot be grounded in any purely Idealist or Utilitarian or other consequentialist doctrine. Certain actions, according to this view, are absolutely wrong, no matter what the circumstances; human beings are entitled to simple respect, at least.

Today, the vast majority of legal scholars and philosophers—particularly in the liberal West—agree that every human being has, at least in theory, some basic rights. Indeed, except for some essentially isolated late–19th century and early–20th century demonstrations of international humanitarian concern to be noted below, the last half of the 20th century may fairly be said to mark the birth of the international as well as the universal recognition of human rights [beginning with the 1945 Charter of the United Nations] **[Basic Document 1.5]** and the 1948 Universal Declaration of Human Rights **[Basic Document 3.3]**. . . .

Defining Human Rights

To say that there is widespread acceptance of the principle of human rights is not to say that there is complete agreement about the nature and scope of such rights—which is to say, their definition. Among the basic questions that have yet to receive conclusive answers are the following: whether human rights are to be viewed as divine, moral, or legal entitlements;

whether they are to be validated by intuition, culture, custom, social contract, principles of distributive justice, or as prerequisites for happiness; whether they are to be understood as irrevocable or partially revocable; and whether they are to be broad or limited in number and content.

The nature of human rights: Commonly accepted postulates

Despite this lack of consensus, a number of widely accepted (and interrelated) postulates can assist in the task of defining human rights. Five in particular stand out, though not even these are without controversy.

First, regardless of their ultimate origin or justification, human rights are understood to represent both individual and group demands for political power, wealth, enlightenment, and other cherished values or capabilities, the most fundamental of which is respect and its constituent elements of reciprocal tolerance and mutual forbearance in the pursuit of all other such values or capabilities. Consequently, human rights imply both claims against persons and institutions impeding the realization of these values or capabilities, and standards for judging the legitimacy of laws and traditions. At bottom, human rights qualify state sovereignty and power, sometimes expanding the latter even while circumscribing the former (as in the case of certain economic and social rights, for example—see below *Égalité*).

Second, human rights are commonly assumed to refer, in some vague sense, to "fundamental," as distinct from "nonessential," claims or "goods." In fact, some theorists go so far as to limit human rights to a single core right or two—for example, the right to life or the right to equal freedom of opportunity. The tendency is to emphasize "basic needs" and to rule out "mere wants."

Third, reflecting varying environmental circumstances, differing worldviews, and inescapable interdependencies within and between different value or capability systems, human rights refer to a wide continuum of claims, ranging from the most justiciable to the most aspirational. Human rights partake of both the legal and the moral orders, sometimes indistinguishably. They are expressive of both the "is" and the "ought" in human affairs.

Fourth, most assertions of human rights—though arguably not all—are qualified by the limitation that the rights of individuals or groups in particular instances are restricted as much as is necessary to secure the comparable rights of others and the aggregate common interest. Given this limitation, which connects rights to duties, human rights are sometimes designated prima facie rights, so that ordinarily it makes little or no sense to think or talk of them in absolutist terms.

Finally, if a right is determined to be a human right, it is understood to be quintessentially general or universal in character, in some sense equally possessed by all human beings everywhere, including in certain instances even the unborn. In stark contrast to the divine right of kings and other such conceptions of privilege, human rights extend in theory to every person on Earth, without discriminations irrelevant to merit or need, simply for being human.

In several critical respects, however, all these postulates raise more questions than they answer. Granted that human rights qualify state power, do they also qualify private power? If so, when and how? What does it mean to say that a right is fundamental, and according to what standards of importance or urgency is it so judged? What is the value of embracing nonjusticiable rights as part of the jurisprudence of human rights? Does it harbor more than rhetorical significance? If so, how? When and according to what criteria does the right of one person or group of people give way to the right of another? What happens when individual and group rights collide? How are universal human rights determined? Are they a function of culture or ideology, or are they determined according to some transnational consensus of merit or value? If the latter, is the consensus regional or global? How exactly would such a consensus be ascertained, and how would it be reconciled with the right of nations and peoples to self-determination? Is the existence of universal human rights incompatible with the notion of national sovereignty? Should supranational norms, institutions, and procedures have the power to nullify local, regional, and national laws on capital punishment, corporal punishment of children, "honor killing," veil wearing, female genital cutting, male circumcision, the claimed right to bear arms, and other practices? How would such a situation comport with Western conceptions of democracy and representative government?

In other words, though accurate, the five foregoing postulates are fraught with questions about the content and legitimate scope of human rights and about the priorities, if any, that exist among them. Like the issue of the origin and justification of human rights, all five are controversial.

The content of human rights: Three "generations" of rights

Like all normative traditions, the human rights tradition is a product of its time. Therefore, to understand better the debate over the content and legitimate scope of human rights and the priorities claimed among them, it is useful to note the dominant schools of thought and action that have informed the human rights tradition since the beginning of modern times.

Particularly helpful in this regard is the notion of three "generations" of human rights advanced by the French jurist Karel Vasak. Inspired by the three themes of the French Revolution, they are: the first generation of civil and political rights (*liberté*); the second generation of economic, social, and cultural rights (*égalité*); and the third generation of solidarity rights (*fraternité*).[e] Vasak's model is, of course, a simplified expression of an extremely complex historical record, and it is not intended to suggest a linear process in which each generation gives birth to the next and then dies away. Nor is it to imply that one generation is more important than another. The three generations are understood to be cumulative, overlapping, and, it is important to note, interdependent and interpenetrating.

Liberté: Civil and political rights

The first generation of civil and political rights derives primarily from the 17th- and 18th-century reformist theories noted above (*i.e.*, those associated with the English, American, and French revolutions). Infused with the political philosophy of liberal individualism and the related economic and social doctrine of laissez-faire, the first generation conceives of human rights more in negative terms ("freedoms from") than positive ones ("rights to"); it favours the abstention over the intervention of government in the quest for

e. Known also as communitarian rights and group rights.

human dignity. Belonging to this first generation, thus, are rights such as those set forth in Articles 2–21 of the Universal Declaration of Human Rights, including freedom from gender, racial, and equivalent forms of discrimination; the right to life, liberty, and security of the person; freedom from slavery or involuntary servitude; freedom from torture and from cruel, inhuman, or degrading treatment or punishment; freedom from arbitrary arrest, detention, or exile; the right to a fair and public trial; freedom from interference in privacy and correspondence; freedom of movement and residence; the right to asylum from persecution; freedom of thought, conscience, and religion; freedom of opinion and expression; freedom of peaceful assembly and association; and the right to participate in government, directly or through free elections. Also included are the right to own property and the right not to be deprived of it arbitrarily—rights that were fundamental to the interests fought for in the American and French revolutions and to the rise of capitalism.

Yet it would be wrong to assert that these and other first-generation rights correspond completely to the idea of "negative" as opposed to "positive" rights. The right to security of the person, to a fair and public trial, to asylum from persecution, and to free elections, for example, manifestly cannot be assured without some affirmative government action. What is constant in this first-generation conception is the notion of liberty, a shield that safeguards the individual—alone and in association with others—against the abuse of political authority. This is the core value. Featured in the constitution of almost every country in the world and dominating the majority of international declarations and covenants adopted since World War II, this essentially Western liberal conception of human rights is sometimes romanticized as a triumph of the individualism of Thomas Hobbes and John Locke over Hegelian statism.

Égalité: Economic, social, and cultural rights

The second generation of economic, social, and cultural rights originated primarily in the socialist tradition, which was foreshadowed among adherents of the Saint–Simonian movement of early 19th-century France and variously promoted by revolutionary struggles and welfare movements that have taken place since. In large part, it is a response to the abuses of capitalist development and its underlying and essentially uncritical conception of individual liberty, which tolerated, and even legitimized, the exploitation of working classes and colonial peoples. Historically, it is a counterpoint to the first generation of civil and political rights, conceiving of human rights more in positive terms ("rights to") than in negative ones ("freedoms from") and requiring more the intervention than the abstention of the state for the purpose of assuring the equitable production and distribution of the values or capabilities involved. Illustrative are some of the rights set forth in Articles 22–27 of the Universal Declaration of Human Rights, such as the right to social security; the right to work and to protection against unemployment; the right to rest and leisure, including periodic holidays with pay; the right to a standard of living adequate for the health and well-being of self and family; the right to education; and the right to the protection of one's scientific, literary, and artistic production.

But in the same way that all the rights embraced by the first generation of civil and political rights cannot properly be designated "negative rights," so all the rights embraced by the second generation of economic, social, and cultural rights cannot properly be labeled "positive rights." For example, the right to free choice of employment, the right to form and to join trade unions, and the right to participate freely in the cultural life of the community (Articles 23 and 27) do not inherently require affirmative state action to ensure their enjoyment. Nevertheless, most of the second-generation rights do necessitate state intervention because they subsume demands more for material than for intangible goods according to some criterion of distributive justice. Second-generation rights are, fundamentally, claims to social equality. However, partly because of the comparatively late arrival of socialist-communist and compatible "Third World" influence in international affairs, the internationalization of these rights has been relatively slow in coming, and with free-market capitalism in ascendancy under the banner of globalization at the turn of the 21st century, it is not likely that these rights will come of age any time soon. On the other hand, as the social inequities created by unregulated national and transnational capitalism become more and more evident over time and are not accounted for by explanations based on gender or race, it is probable that the demand for second-generation rights will grow and mature, and in some instances even lead to violence. This tendency is apparent already in the evolving European Union and in wider efforts to regulate intergovernmental financial institutions and transnational corporations to protect the public interest.

Fraternité: Solidarity rights

Finally, the third generation of solidarity rights, while drawing upon and reconceptualizing the demands associated with the first two generations of rights, is best understood as a product of both the rise and the decline of the nation-state in the last half of the 20th century. Foreshadowed in Article 28 of the Universal Declaration of Human Rights, which proclaims that "everyone is entitled to a social and international order in which the rights set forth in this declaration can be fully realized," this generation appears so far to embrace six claimed rights. Three of these rights reflect the emergence of Third World nationalism and its "revolution of rising expectations" (*i.e.*, its demand for a global redistribution of power, wealth, and other important values or capabilities): the right to political, economic, social, and cultural self-determination; the right to economic and social development; and the right to participate in and benefit from "the common heritage of mankind" (shared Earth and space resources, scientific, technical, and other information and progress, and cultural traditions, sites, and monuments). The other three third-generation rights—the right to peace, the right to a healthy and sustainable environment, and the right to humanitarian disaster relief—suggest the impotence or inefficiency of the nation-state in certain critical respects.

All six of these rights tend to be posed as collective rights, requiring the concerted efforts of all social forces, to a substantial degree on a planetary scale. However, each of them also manifests an individual dimension. For example, while it may be said to be the collective right of all countries and peoples (especially developing countries and non-self-governing peoples) to secure a "new international economic order" that would eliminate obstacles to their economic and social development, so also may it be said to be the individual right of every person to benefit from a developmental policy that is based on the satisfaction of material and nonmaterial human needs. It is important to note too that the majority of these solidarity rights are more aspirational than justiciable in character, and that their status as international human rights norms remains ambiguous.

Thus, at various stages of modern history, the content of human rights has been broadly defined not with any expectation that the rights associated with one generation would or should become outdated upon the ascendancy of another, but expansively or supplementally. The history of the content of human rights reflects evolving perceptions of which values or capabilities stand, at different times, most in need of responsible attention and, simultaneously, humankind's recurring demands for continuity and stability.

* * *

Human rights in the United Nations

The Charter of the United Nations (1945) begins by reaffirming a "faith in fundamental human rights, in the dignity and worth of the human person, in the equal rights of men and women and of nations large and small." It states that the purposes of the UN are, among other things: "to develop friendly relations among nations based on respect for the principle of equal rights and self-determination of peoples … [and] to achieve international co-operation … in promoting and encouraging respect for human rights and for fundamental freedoms for all without distinction as to race, sex, language, or religion." * * * In addition, in two key articles, all members "pledge themselves to take joint and separate action in co-operation with the Organization" for the achievement of these and related purposes….

* * *

Primary responsibility for the promotion and protection of human rights under the UN Charter rests in the General Assembly and, under its authority, in the Economic and Social Council (ECOSOC), the Commission on Human Rights, and the UN High Commissioner for Human Rights (UNHCHR). The UN Commission on Human Rights, an intergovernmental subsidiary body of ECOSOC that met for the first time in 1947, serves as the UN's central policy organ in the human rights field. The UNHCHR, a post created by the General Assembly in 1993, is the official principally responsible for implementing and coordinating UN human rights programs and projects, including overall supervision of the UN's Geneva-based Centre for Human Rights, a bureau of the UN Secretariat.

The UN Commission on Human Rights and its instruments

For the first 20 years of its existence (1947–66), the UN Commission on Human Rights concentrated … on setting human rights standards, believing itself unauthorized to deal with human rights complaints. Together with other UN bodies such as the ILO, … UNESCO, the UN Commission on the Status of Women, and the Commission on Crime Prevention and Criminal Justice, it … drafted standards and prepared a number of international human rights instruments. Among the most important [were] the Universal Declaration of Human Rights (1948) **[Basic Document 3.3]**, the International Covenant on Economic, Social and Cultural Rights (1966) **[Basic Docu-**

ment **3.13**], and the International Covenant on Civil and Political Rights (1966) **[Basic Document 3.14]** together with its Optional Protocols (1966; 1989) **[Basic Documents 3.15 & 3.33]**. Collectively known as the "International Bill of Human Rights," these three instruments serve as touchstones for interpreting the human rights provisions of the UN charter. Also central ... [were] the International Convention on the Elimination of All Forms of Racial Discrimination (1965) **[Basic Document 3.12]**, the Convention on the Elimination of All Forms of Discrimination against Women (1979) **[Basic Document 3.21]**, the Convention against Torture and Other Cruel, Inhuman or Degrading Treatment or Punishment (1984) **[Basic Document 3.26]**, and the Convention on the Rights of the Child (1989) **[Basic Document 3.32]**, each of which elaborates on provisions of the International Bill of Human Rights.

The commission continue[d] to perform this standard-setting role [for the next four decades. Beginning in 1967, however, when it was authorized to deal with violations of human rights, its work became highly investigatory, evaluative, and advisory in character. Each year it established working groups to consider and make recommendations concerning alleged "gross violations" of human rights referred to it by the commission's Sub-Commission on the Promotion and Protection of Human rights based on both "communications" from individuals and groups and investigations by the Sub-Commission. Also, on an ad hoc basis, it appointed Special Rapporteurs and other envoys to examine human rights situations—both country-oriented and thematic—and report back on the basis of trustworthy evidence.] These fact-finding and implementation mechanisms and procedures were the focus of the commission's attention during the 1970s and '80s. In the 1990s, it turned increasingly to economic, social, and cultural rights, including the right to development and the right to an adequate standard of living. Increased attention [was] paid also to the rights of minorities, indigenous peoples, women, and children. [In June 2006, the 53-member commission was replaced by a 47-member UN Human Rights Council (HRC), established by the UN General assembly with a larger mandate that includes all the best elements of the commission's investigatory, evaluative, and advisory functions. In a sudden reversal of policy regarded as unfortunate by many, the United States declined to seek election to it.]

The UN High Commissioner for Human Rights

Appointed by the Secretary-General in a regular rotation of geographic regions and approved by the General Assembly, the UNHCHR serves a fixed term of four years with the possibility of renewal for an additional four-year term.... Among other duties, the High Commissioner is charged by the General Assembly to promote and protect all civil, political, economic, social, and cultural rights; to provide advisory services and technical and financial assistance in the field of human rights to states that request them; to coordinate human rights promotion and protection activities throughout the UN system, including education and public-information programs; and otherwise to enhance international cooperation for the promotion and protection of human rights—all within the framework of the International Bill of Human Rights.

The Universal Declaration of Human Rights

The catalog of rights set out in the Universal Declaration of Human Rights, which was adopted without dissent by the General Assembly on December 10, 1948, is scarcely less than the sum of most of the important traditional political and civil rights of national constitutions and legal systems, including equality before the law; protection against arbitrary arrest; the right to a fair trial; freedom from *ex post facto* criminal laws; the right to own property; freedom of thought, conscience, and religion; freedom of opinion and expression; and freedom of peaceful assembly and association. Also enumerated are such economic, social, and cultural rights as the right to work, the right to form and join trade unions, the right to rest and leisure, the right to a standard of living adequate for health and well-being, and the right to education.

The Universal Declaration, it should be noted, is not a treaty. It was meant to proclaim "a common standard of achievement for all peoples and all nations" rather than enforceable legal obligations. Nevertheless, the Universal Declaration has acquired a status juridically more important than originally intended, and it has been widely used, even by national courts, as a means of judging compliance with human rights obligations under the UN Charter.

The International Covenant on Civil and Political Rights and its Optional Protocols

The civil and political rights guaranteed by the International Covenant on Civil and Political Rights, which was opened for signature on December 19, 1966, and entered into force on March 23, 1976, incorporate almost all those rights proclaimed in the Universal Declaration, including the right to nondiscrimination but excluding the right to own property and the right to asylum. The covenant also designates several rights that are not listed in the Universal Declaration, among them the right of all peoples to self-determination and the right of ethnic, religious, and linguistic minorities to enjoy their own culture, to profess and practice their own religion, and to use their own language. To the extent that the Universal Declaration and the covenant overlap, however, the latter is understood to explicate and to help interpret the former.

In addition, the covenant calls for the establishment of a Human Rights Committee, comprising persons serving in their individual expert capacities, to study reports submitted by the state parties on measures they have adopted to give effect to the rights recognized in the covenant. For state parties that have expressly recognized the competence of the committee in this regard, the committee also may respond to allegations by one state party that another state party is not fulfilling its obligations under the covenant.... State parties that become party to the covenant's first Optional Protocol further recognize the competence of the Human Rights Committee to consider and act upon communications from individuals claiming to be victims of covenant violations. Other treaty-based organs within the UN system that are empowered to consider grievances from individuals in quasi-judicial manner are the Committee on the Elimination of Racial Discrimination and the Committee on Torture, under the 1965 race discrimination and the 1984 torture conventions, respectively.

Also noteworthy is the covenant's Second Optional Protocol, which is aimed at abolishing the death penalty worldwide. Adopted in 1989 and entered into force in 1991, it has been favourably received in most of the countries of western Europe and many countries in the Americas, though not in the United States.

The International Covenant on Economic, Social and Cultural Rights

Just as the International Covenant on Civil and Political Rights elaborates upon most of the civil and political rights enumerated in the Universal

Declaration of Human Rights, so the International Covenant on Economic, Social and Cultural Rights elaborates upon most of the economic, social, and cultural rights set forth in the Universal Declaration: the right to work, the right to just and favourable conditions of work, trade union rights, the right to social security, rights relating to the protection of the family, the right to an adequate standard of living, the right to health, the right to education, and rights relating to culture and science. Unlike its companion agreement, the International Covenant on Civil and Political Rights, however, generally this covenant, sometimes called a "promotional convention," is not intended for immediate implementation, the state parties having agreed only "to take steps" toward "achieving progressively the full realization of the rights recognized in the . . . Covenant," and then subject to "the maximum of [their] available resources." One obligation, however, is subject to immediate application: the prohibition of discrimination in the enjoyment of the rights enumerated on grounds of race, colour, sex, language, religion, political or other opinion, national or social origin, property, and birth or other status. Also, the international supervisory measures that apply to the covenant oblige the state parties to report to the UN Economic and Social Council on the steps they have adopted and on the progress they have made in achieving the realization of the enumerated rights.

Other UN human rights conventions and declarations

Numerous other human rights treaties drafted under UN auspices address a broad range of concerns, including the prevention and punishment of the crime of genocide; the humane treatment of military and civilian personnel in time of war; the status of refugees; the protection of stateless persons; the abolition of slavery, forced labour, and discrimination in employment and occupation; the suppression and punishment of the crime of apartheid; the elimination of discrimination in education; the promotion of the political rights of women; the protection of minorities and indigenous peoples; and the promotion of equality of opportunity and treatment among migrant workers. In addition to overseeing human rights treaties, the UN also adopts declarations, in the form of resolutions, aimed at promoting human rights. Although technically not binding on member states in the sense of a treaty or a resolution of the Security Council, such declarations—particularly when they enunciate principles of great and solemn importance—may nevertheless create strong expectations about authority and control. Perhaps the best-known examples subsequent to the Universal Declaration are the Declaration on the Granting of Independence to Colonial Countries and Peoples (1960) and the Declaration on Principles of International Law concerning Friendly Relations and Co-operation among States in accordance with the Charter of the United Nations (1970), which affirms, among other things, "the duty of all states to refrain from organizing, instigating, assisting or participating in . . . terrorist acts."

Other declarations have addressed the rights of disabled persons; the elimination of all forms of intolerance and discrimination based on religion or belief; the right of peoples to peace; the right to development; the rights of persons belonging to national, ethnic, religious, and linguistic minorities; and the elimination of violence against women.

Human rights and the Helsinki process

After World War II, international concern for human rights was evident at the global level outside the UN as well as within it, most notably in the proceedings and aftermath of the Conference on Security and Co-operation in Europe (CSCE), convened in Helsinki, Finland, on July 3, 1973, and concluded there (after continuing deliberations in Geneva) on August 1, 1975. * * * From the earliest discussions, however, it was clear that the Helsinki Final Act was not intended as a legally binding instrument. The expression "determination to respect" and to "put into practice" were seen as moral commitments only, the Declaration of Principles was said not to prescribe international law, and nowhere did the participants provide for enforcement machinery. On the other hand, the Declaration of Principles, including its human rights principles, was always viewed as being at least consistent with international law, and in providing for periodic follow-up conferences, it made possible a unique negotiating process ("the Helsinki process") to review compliance with its terms, thus creating normative expectations concerning the conduct of the participating states. . . .

2.   Richard A. Falk, Human Rights Horizons: The Pursuit of Justice in a Globalizing World 24–35 (2000).

[*Eds.*—In this essay, the author describes "five contemporary dramas" in pursuit of "global justice."]

Peace versus Justice in the Setting of Democratization

One of the most persistent problems of this period is how to reconcile conflicting goals in the aftermath of severe criminality on the part of a past governing process. The regime responsible for crimes against humanity or genocidal behavior has passed from the scene but remains to varying degrees at large, often as part of a bargain by which its impunity was "purchased" in exchange for its voluntary relinquishment of power. From its modern origins in the Nuremberg and Tokyo trials of surviving German and Japanese leaders after the Second World War, international law has progressed to the point where such behavior is increasingly subject to indictment, prosecution, and punishment in various appropriate circumstances.

But the character of appropriate circumstances is far from self-evident. It often involves a delicate balancing of opposed considerations favoring either peace, in the sense of nonviolent coexistence between former leaders (the alleged perpetrators) and emergent leaders (the would-be constitutionalists), or justice, in the sense of imposing accountability for past conduct. The . . . anguish and controversy concerning the role and effects of the Truth and Reconciliation Commission in South Africa are a vivid example of the always risky search for peace. The optimistic view is that foregoing criminal prosecution while documenting, acknowledging, and denouncing the criminality of apartheid will avoid incensing the perpetrators of these crimes and yet provide satisfaction and relief to those South Africans who were victims or closely associated with victims. The less hopeful view is that the commission process will lead to a double failure. Namely, that the perpetrators and their friends will remain incensed by their public humiliation, and the victims and their associates will feel that far too little has been achieved to close the book on such acute and pervasive cruelty and abuse.

What gives the issue its unavoidable character as a matter of justice is the perceived character of past behavior as constituting unforgivable crimes. From the perspective of minimum international standards of law and morality, these crimes are perhaps best categorized as "crimes against humanity" and "genocide."[1] And yet, if the cost of prosecution is seen as jeopardizing the transition to democracy or the peace of the community, the decision to grant impunity or amnesty seems understandable, even beneficial.

A poignant example of this dilemma has been presented prominently by the Pinochet controversy. In the fall of 1998, while former Chilean dictator Augusto Pinochet was in Britain for medical treatment, a Spanish court requested his extradition to face charges relating to crimes of state involving Spaniards who were in Chile during Pinochet's rule. Several other European countries also issued such requests. The Chilean government requested the release of General Pinochet and his return to Chile, arguing that the former leader was entitled to diplomatic immunity with respect to the behavior in question and that he was the object of criminal prosecutions in Chile. After complex deliberations, the English House of Lords indicated by a 3–2 vote that the government of Britain should accede to the request for extradition so that Pinochet's alleged responsibility for crimes against humanity could be prosecuted in Spain. Unfortunately, that vote subsequently [was] set aside by the House of Lords for technical reasons, leaving the outcome uncertain once more. The House of Lords ... assembled a new panel of judges to hear a second presentation of the case.... In the end, the British courts upheld the contested finding that Pinochet is medically unfit to stand trial and should be returned to Chile.

Here, the complexity of justice assumes a very fundamental form. The essential dilemma is whether the final decision in Britain should be made by reference to international standards or whether deference should be accorded to the views of the Chilean government. It is the Chilean people who might well bear the burden of a regression to military rule or more probably to incidents of civil strife. At the same time, all of international society has an interest in the application of these international standards as part of a wider effort to establish an effective procedure to ensure the accountability of leaders for such criminality. In an important sense, grants of amnesty or impunity in such settings are always "Faustian bargains,"[2] in which Faust sells his soul to the devil in exchange for technological know-how. Yet even if the premise of unforgivable crime is accepted; given the suffering that a society has experienced, should not the decision of its democratically elected leaders prevail? But even if one posits this argument, the outcome may not be so evident. Perhaps the current leaders are making a pro forma show of seeking the return of Pinochet while making it clear through confidential diplomatic circles that their real preference is for him to face prosecution overseas. Should not the views of those who identify with the victims most directly be given great weight in reaching a decision? There is little doubt that

1. The standard definition of crimes against humanity is that given in Principle VI(c) of the Nuremberg Principles as formulated in 1950 by the International Law Commission **[Basic Document 2.13]**.... Genocide is defined in Article II of The Genocide Convention of 1948 ... **[Basic Document 3.2]**....

2. The reference here is to Johan Wolfgang Von Goethe, *Faust* (London: Heron Books, 1970), in which Faust sells his soul to the devil in exchange for technological know-how.

vocal anti-Pinochet Chileans would welcome his prosecution while pro-Pinochet Chileans would decry it.

At this stage of international history, it seems clear that these types of issues faced by many societies during the last decade need to be resolved on a contextual basis. The people that have endured the crimes, and their representatives, should have the first opportunity to resolve the dilemma of peace and justice. If the subject matter spills over the borders of a given country, as was the case with the Pinochet controversy, then the balance of considerations assumes a far more complex form. The dynamics of global justice would benefit from the expanded opportunities for prosecution and the denial of claims of immunity. But would the dynamics of peace be obstructed by undermining the reliability of impunity bargains struck in the past? Would dictators hesitate to relinquish the reins of power knowing that they may be vulnerable to future prosecutions if they should venture beyond the borders of their own country?

Such difficult questions suggest two conclusions: first, that the contextual attributes in each instance should be thoroughly explored, and second, that the process of appraisal and controversy should be carefully nurtured to clarify the issues at stake.

Economic Growth versus Social Equity

During recent decades, economic policy has been increasingly shaped by neoliberal criteria that emphasize the primacy of capital efficiency in the allocation of resources. Part of this emphasis involves privatization and liberalization, in which social and economic functions shift from the public to the private sector. The intranational result is the partial social disempowerment of the state. The international result is the decline of direct development assistance and the general conditionality of loans administered by the World Bank and International Monetary Fund. In effect, these institutions mount pressure to assure that a governmental recipient of funds does not use public resources for poverty alleviation and social distress, but rather to build a high-growth economy.

The ethical rationale buttressing such policies rests on variants of the invisible hand, by which the entire social spectrum automatically benefits, although not necessarily equally, from economic growth. In order to diminish the human suffering involved in achieving fiscal reform, there will need to be a greater willingness to take into balance social equity concerns against economistic goals

The empirical evidence suggests growing inequality across a range of dimensions * * *. These trends have ... been amply documented and summarized in the annual volumes of the UN Human Development Report. From this report emerge two important ideas that relate to the pursuit of global justice. First, the commitment to economic growth does improve the aggregate economic well-being of people in general, with overall reductions in various forms of impoverishment. Second, this process of growth also accentuates inequalities, making the rich richer and the poor poorer in every region of the world.

Such observations occur under conditions of limited ideological alternatives. A socialist ethos—or even an international welfare program—does not currently seem politically viable. At the same time, there are increasing acknowledgments of the problem, perhaps most comprehensively at the Copenhagen Social Summit in 1995, which called for more concerted action to provide jobs, address poverty, and overcome other types of social insecurity.

A further set of developments challenges the ideological primacy of neoliberalism, calling for various modifications in the direction of some social reempowerment of the state. The first includes the rethinking under way within the Bretton Woods institutions—a reaction to the inability of structural adjustment to arrest the deterioration of living standards for a substantial number of countries experiencing financial crisis since 1997. Of particular concern are their *efforts* to condition bailout relief on structural adjustments that produce political turmoil and massive impoverishment, as witnessed most alarmingly in Indonesia.

The second development concerns the mandate implied by a series of European elections that appeared to repudiate neoliberal political orientations in favor of more social-democratic outlooks, articulated in the context of economic globalization as "the Third Way" or as a call for the establishment of social Europe. The notion of social Europe as the Third Way seeks to reaffirm the social commitments to the poor or jobless without repudiating the move toward a dynamic model of European economic integration. In effect, social Europe implies that the advantages of this new phase of capitalism do not have to eclipse the human achievements of the welfare state, the labor movement, and social democracy....

The global justice aspects of this growth/equity dilemma relate both to the duties to alleviate distress, which are specified as economic and social rights of the disadvantaged, and to the moral obligation to adopt policies that diminish inequalities between countries, regions, races, genders, and civilizations. These concerns are often considered in relation to the question of distributive justice and its applicability to a world of sovereign states. These problems have recently highlighted the degree to which economic globalization, and its impact on national economic policy, have diminished the capacity and will of governments to be compassionate toward their own citizens. International institutions play an important role in gathering information about the degrees of deprivation and inequality, and about the adaptation of resource allocation in response to equity concerns. The rethinking apparently under way within the Bretton Woods institutions may well point toward a new balance between a purely economic view of growth and a more normative concern with overcoming human suffering and inequality.

Claims of Present Generations versus Claims of Future Generations

In this period of extraordinarily rapid technological change, and increasingly evident environmental decay and depletion of resources, ever greater attention has been devoted to the justice claims of future generations. International environmental treaty law has begun to acknowledge this obligation, and environmentalists have been urging a more rigorous application of "the precautionary principle" as one practical means of upholding the well-being of future generations. This principle urges that environmental risks be taken seriously as a guide to prudent behavior before conclusive scientific information is available to confirm the gravity of such risks.

This idea that global justice involves relations through time and space is gaining prominence. Global justice between spatial communities appears to be declining as a result of neoliberalism and globalization, as evidenced in the decline of foreign economic assistance in North–South relations. Global justice between temporal communities, however, actually seems to be increasing, as evidenced by various expressions of greater sensitivity to past injustices and future dangers.

The distinction between temporal and spatial communities is crucial. For centuries, the relations among territorially bounded sovereign entities called "states" ("spatial communities") preoccupied discussions of world order. More recently, this spatial focus has been attenuated by a rising concern about grievances from the past and worries about the life circumstances of future generations—that is, of "temporal communities."

There has also been an upsurge in efforts to rectify the injustices of the past, and in some instances, the rather distant past. Some of these efforts have involved substantive redress, although more often the results are largely symbolic. The recovery of Holocaust-era gold reserves from Swiss banks and of art treasures stolen by the Nazi regime constitutes instances of substantive redress. Instances of symbolic redress, on the other hand, include apologies by Japanese leaders for atrocities committed against China and Korea during its Imperial Era, by President Clinton to African societies for the cruelties of slavery, or by the Canadian government to indigenous peoples for their dispossession.

* * *

Many of the concerns about the future and unresolved past grievances call attention to the degree to which the pursuit of global justice involves the axis of time—an increasingly important focus for normative energies. International institutions can play a role in giving concrete meaning—in the form of specific prohibitions or through protective measures—to either claims of forbearance in view of future risks of harm or grievances derived from the past. With particular regard to contested views surrounding past events, institutions that embody commissions of experts or moral authority figures can play a constructive role in the search for acceptable solutions.

Tradition, Consensus, and Political Order versus the Rights of the Marginalized

A major preoccupation of recent decades has been to develop a framework of law for overcoming several forms of noneconomic inequality. This effort has focused on the protection of human rights and involves overcoming certain systemic forms of injustice. The pursuit of global justice, then, is a matter of diminishing the levels of injustice associated with the inequalities of race, gender, religious belief, civilizational orientation, and age.

International institutions have played a crucial role in this process, generating authoritative norms by way of lawmaking treaties, declarations, and reports on practice. One of the most impressive achievements of the United Nations in its first half-century has been to provide the peoples of the world with the normative architecture of a comprehensive human rights system. Such a development has assumed great practical relevance because of three complementary developments: first, the rise of human rights-oriented transnational nongovernmental organizations (NGOs), which have used their access to information about violations to promote compliance; second, the effectiveness of human rights as an instrument of struggle in the resistance movements in Eastern Europe during the 1980s and the anti-apartheid campaign in South Africa; and third, the increased prominence of human rights in the foreign policy of some major states.

* * *

This positive picture is not, unfortunately, the whole story. Geopolitical factors make the political reinforcement of human rights norms uneven, leading to perceptions of double standards and accusations of hypocrisy. Cultural practices may contradict human rights norms in ways that are exceedingly difficult to challenge effectively even if the territorial government acts in good faith. This is particularly true when long-entrenched religious beliefs oppose movements toward overcoming injustice, as in relation to the treatment of women.

* * *

The most pervasive forms of injustice are difficult to overcome because their existence is embedded in the deep structure of power and privilege. For example, male dominance of structures of authority and decision-making in all sectors of society is so pervasive that it is still treated as natural, despite important inroads made by feminism and the global human rights movement. Similarly, the modernist assumptions of society are so strongly held that efforts by indigenous peoples to retain their traditional ways of life are poorly understood and rarely appreciated beyond a small circle of sympathizers. In effect, established patterns—even if abusive—are very difficult to challenge effectively, especially by those at the margins of society, given their civilizational orientation and low social or economic status.

Some positive movement-based steps are being taken, however. Women and indigenous peoples have established their own networks and pressure groups that operate in institutional arenas throughout the world. The UN system has provided formal and informal arenas for both women and indigenous peoples to develop their own programs of action. Some concessions have been achieved by these transnational initiatives associated with an emergent global civil society. During the first half of the 1990s, such marginalized social forces made particularly good use of global conferences, under UN auspices, to put their grievances on the world policy agenda.[3] Indeed, these efforts were so successful that a statist backlash ensued, expressed in terms of budgetary concerns and the deriding of such global conferences as useless "spectacles." Cost cutting is often used by the established international order and its representatives as an excuse to mask the real concern over the threatening rise of transnational social forces. It has been widely noticed that the UN conferences provide such forces with increased political leverage and media access, thus eroding governmental control over policy outcomes with respect to such sensitive issues as abortion, the role of women, environmental

3. Among the more important of these conferences were the UN Conference on Environment and Development (1992), the UN Conference on Human Rights and Development (1993), the UN Conference on Population and Development (1994), and the UN Conference on Women and Development (1995).

regulation, and financial responsibility. As a result, these international institutional forums for political action are not nearly as likely to be available in the decade ahead, and this vehicle for the pursuit of global justice has been lost, at least temporarily.

* * *

Traditional Geopolitics versus the Legal Prohibition of International Aggression

A core goal associated with global justice has been minimizing the role of violence and warfare on all levels of political interaction, especially in the relations among states. There remains a fundamental disagreement about how such goals can be achieved given the structures and character of international society. The control of world politics remains firmly in the hands of realists—ideological descendants of Machiavelli—who believe that only countervailing power, combined with a credible will to use force if provoked, can maintain peace and stability in the world. Within this perspective, nuclear weaponry is considered an indispensable instrument of geopolitical management, dangerous only if these weapons fall into the wrong hands, but a generally constructive, stabilizing influence. On this basis, priority is accorded to antiproliferation efforts, and nuclear disarmament is perceived as politically unattractive and generally contributing to a less successfully managed world order.

The contrasting view has been that peace and justice in the world are best preserved by moving away from geopolitical management toward collective security, as embodied in the United Nations under the specific authority of the Security Council. The weakness of this challenge to realism is evident in the fact that the United Nations tends to incorporate the very ideas it opposes. The Security Council is itself a geopolitical instrument, giving each permanent member veto power, conducting its sensitive discussions in secret, and operating without any constraints that are not self-imposed. Consequently, the United Nations faithfully reflects prevailing patterns of geopolitics. It was largely gridlocked by the bipolar rivalry of the Cold War and, subsequently, has been responsive primarily to the United States as the manager of unipolar geopolitics.

The sharp ideological lines of debate are reductive, however, missing many valuable roles played by the United Nations. From time to time the United Nations does lend support to antiaggression norms and to closely related efforts to achieve other goals of global justice. The Security Council, partly in compensation for a failure of geopolitical will, established the war crimes tribunals in The Hague and in Arusha, Tanzania, to address the most severe wrongs associated with, respectively, the breakup of the former Yugoslavia and the genocidal outbreak in Rwanda. Furthermore, in mobilizing widespread support against Iraq's conquest of Kuwait in 1990, the United Nations managed to act effectively against Iraq's blatant aggression directed at another member of the organization.

An important secondary arena of controversy involves responses to intranational conflicts that are causing great human suffering. The issue has surfaced in the past decade in relation to whether the United Nations should serve as an agency for humanitarian intervention, and if so, whether it can do so successfully. Here, the relevance of geopolitics becomes evident. International institutions cannot act effectively unless their undertakings converge with the strategic interests, as well as the normative sentiments, of the geopolitical managers. Such were the painful lessons of Somalia, Bosnia, and Rwanda. There is also the legalist critique that relates global justice to adherence to international law. The original contract embedded in Article 2(7) of the UN Charter precludes intervention in domestic affairs of states. It can be maintained that such a constraint represents the limit of what can be expected from the United Nations given the persistence of geopolitical management of power and the consequent failure of the United Nations to command resources or independent peacekeeping capabilities.

So far as the nature of global justice is concerned in relation to uses of force, the core issues remain unresolved. An uneasy, suppressed tension exists between, on the one hand, legalist preferences for compliance with international law and for a gradual transfer of security functions to international institutions, and on the other, geopolitical preferences for configuring available power in such a manner as to discourage and punish antisocial behavior by irresponsible and evil political actors, pariah states, and terrorist movements.

TOWARD HUMANE GOVERNANCE

Global justice has so far been considered under the nonideal conditions of the established world order, which is evolving in the direction of some form of global governance. Whether this transition process, which appears to be superseding the Westphalian idea of territorial sovereignty, is leading humanity toward a beneficial form of global governance is unclear at present. Contradictory trends are evident.

It seems appropriate to end this [discussion] with a few indications of the positive prospects for reframing the pursuit of global justice. It needs to be emphasized that, at present, these prospects seem marginal to the main drift of change in the direction of a highly marketized, nonsustainable, and grossly unequal set of relations among the peoples of the world, with weak structures of legal authority and even weaker sentiments of human solidarity. Happily, however, our historical insight is often flawed, ignoring concealed forces. Such was the case with respect to the abrupt end of the Cold War and the Soviet collapse, as well as the peaceful dismantling of apartheid in South Africa. We do not understand political reality well enough to be pessimistic, or for that matter, optimistic.

What is positive can be identified in summary form: (1) The gradual realization that warfare among major, technologically advanced states is an obsolete form of conflict resolution, particularly given the increasingly nonterritorial bases of wealth and power; (2) the emergence of transnational networks of activists motivated by a commitment to human rights, the environment, humanitarian diplomacy, economic well-being, and civilizational dialogue; (3) the widespread adherence to democratic ideals as the moral foundation of humane governance in all arenas of authority and decision, including support for a vision of cosmopolitan democracy as the next stage of constitutionalism; (4) the beginnings of an ethos of criminal accountability that contains no exemptions for political leaders and is being implemented at the global level under the universal rubric of punishing anyone guilty of crimes against humanity and through the moves to establish a judicial institution of global character with such a mandate; and (5) the strong move toward integration at regional levels with accompanying shifts in allegiance away from the nation-state, moving outward in relation to species, civilization, and region, and inward toward local community identities.

Whether these positive elements can be fashioned in such a way as to lead toward humane governance, and the equally ambitious realization of global justice, remains uncertain. What is more evident is that such an outcome will be far more likely if it engages the peoples of the world and their associations in the struggle to achieve specific human rights. In essence, the future will be what we as individual citizens make it.

3. **Charter of the United Nations. Concluded, 26 Jun 1945. Entered into force, 24 Oct 1945. 1976 Y.B.U.N. 1043;** *reprinted in* **1 Weston & Carlson I.A.1: Pmbl. & Arts. 1, 13 & 55** (Basic Document 1.5).

4. **Universal Declaration of Human Rights, 10 Dec 1948, GA Res. 217A, UN GAOR, 3rd Sess., Pt. I, Resolutions, at 71, UN Doc. A/810 (1948);** *reprinted in* **3 Weston & Carlson III.A.1: Pmbl. & Arts. 30** (Basic Document 3.3).

5. **Convention against Discrimination in Education. Concluded, 14 Dec 1960. Entered into force, 22 May 1962. 429 U.N.T.S. 93;** *reprinted in* **3 Weston & Carlson III.P.1: Pmbl. & Arts. 1–5** (Basic Document 3.10).

6. **International Convention on the Elimination of All Forms of Racial Discrimination. Concluded, 7 Mar 1966. Entered into force, 4 Jan 1969. 660 U.N.T.S. 195;** *reprinted in* **3 Weston & Carlson III.I.1: Pmbl. & Arts. 1–7** (Basic Document 3.12).

7. **International Covenant on Economic, Social and Cultural Rights. Concluded, 16 Dec 1966. Entered into force, 3 Jan 1976. 993 U.N.T.S. 3;** *reprinted in* **3 Weston & Carlson III.A.2: Pmbl. & Arts. 1– 15** (Basic Document 3.13).

8. **International Covenant on Civil and Political Rights. Concluded, 16 Dec 1966. Entered into force, 23 Mar 1976. 999 U.N.T.S. 171;** *reprinted in* **3 Weston & Carlson III.A.3: Pmbl. & Arts. 1–27** (Basic Document 3.14).

9. **Convention on the Elimination of All Forms of Discrimination against Women. Concluded, 18 Dec 1979. Entered into force, 3 Sep 1981. 1249 U.N.T.S. 13;** *reprinted in* **3 Weston & Carlson III.C.13: Pmbl. & Arts. 1, 5, 12, 16** (Basic Document 3.21).

10. **United Nations General Assembly Declaration on the Elimination of All Forms of Intolerance and of Discrimination Based on Religion or Belief, 25 Nov 1981, GA Res. 36/55, UN GAOR, 36th Sess., Supp. No. 51, at 171, UN Doc. A/36/684 (1981);** *reprinted in* **21 I.L.M. 205 (1982) and 3 Weston & Carlson III.I.3: Arts. 1–4, 6** (Basic Document 3.23).

11. **Convention against Torture and Other Cruel, Inhuman or Degrading Treatment or Punishment. Concluded, 10 Dec 1984. En-**

tered into force, 26 Jun 1987. GA Res. 39/46 (Annex), UN GAOR, 39th Sess., Supp. No. 51, at 197, UN Doc. A/39/51 (1985); *reprinted in* 23 I.L.M. 1027 (1984) and 3 Weston & Carlson III.K.2: Pmbl. & Arts. 1–16 (Basic Document 3.26).

12.   **Convention on the Rights of the Child. Concluded, 20 Nov 1989. Entered into force, 2 Sep 1990. GA Res. 44/25 (Annex), UN GAOR, 44th Sess., Supp. No. 49, at 166, UN Doc. A/RES/44/49 (1990); *reprinted in* 30 I.L.M. 1448 (1989) and 3 Weston & Carlson III.D.3: Pmbl. & Arts. 1–41** (Basic Document 3.32).

13 **Vienna Declaration and Programme of Action, 25 Jun 1993, UN Doc. A/CONF.157/24 (Part I) (13 Oct 1993), at 20–46; *reprinted in* 32 I.L.M. 1661 (1993) and 3 Weston & Carlson III.U.2: Pmbl., § I (Arts. 1–8, 15, 19, 23, 27–30, 33, & 34), & § II (Arts. 19–27 & 36–62)** (Basic Document 3.40).

14.   **United Nations General Assembly Declaration on the Elimination of Violence against Women, 20 Dec 1993, GA Res. 48/104, UN GAOR, 48th Sess., Supp. No. 49, at 261, UN Doc. A/RES/48/104 (1994); *reprinted in* 33 I.L.M. 1049 (1994) and 3 Weston & Carlson III.C.14: Pmbl. & Arts. 1–6** (Basic Document 3.41).

B.   The Enforcement of International Human Rights in General

1.   Henry J. Steiner, "International Protection of Human Rights," in International Law 757, 759–61 (M. D. Evans ed., 2003).

Is it necessary or even useful to create intergovernmental human rights organizations (IGOs) to complement customary and treaty law? Are not matters like implementation and protection better left in the hands of governments and civil society in the different States, particularly since human rights issues are imbedded in national (and sub-national, local) governance, traditions and cultures? In such respects, human rights differ from situations presented by, say, international trade or environmental law where a State's violation of a treaty affects other treaty parties' interests more severely than it does its own population. In such typical kinds of treaty regimes based on reciprocity, the relevant issues about trade or environment are not as deeply imbedded in political structures, traditional practices, and cultural assumptions.

These doubts become the more plausible when we take into account that standard-setting by itself—the declarations and treaties that dominated the early decades of the human rights movement, and the related spread of this new discourse of international human rights—may advance the cause of human rights. The internalization and constitutionalization of treaty norms by many States has made those norms a key ingredient of the domestic legal system invoked by courts. The legislature, executive, and diverse groups in civil society absorb these norms into rich and ever more international legal and political debate.

As a consequence, human rights advocates and a politically mobilized population may now base their demands for political and social change on the new internal law responsive to treaty commitments as well as customary law.

The gap between that law and the government's actions becomes strikingly apparent to all. Even in the absence of intergovernmental organizations, at least rhetorical support for internal, advocates' arguments to narrow that gap may come from other States and NGOs. In such ways, the rhetoric of rights may serve to empower a population, spur demands for change, and increase the pressure on a State.

We can indeed imagine a world where all States are committed in good faith to observe human rights, and hence where international organizations would be unnecessary. But even in this ideal world, disputes will inevitably arise over questions of interpretation stemming from conflicts between rights, diverse political and cultural understandings about the meaning of a term or concept in the treaties, and the effect of changing circumstances such as the end of the Cold War on the human rights corpus. IGOs appear at least useful, perhaps essential, to deal with these varied perspectives and understandings. Their possibilities range from an organization charged with maintaining a forum for States to explore these issues, to a court whose opinions could have an advisory or recommendatory character or stand as legally binding judgments.

More to the point, the assumption above about the good-faith commitment of all States to a human rights regime defies our knowledge of the world and of the human rights movement's history. Reliance on States alone to observe such norms would be patently absurd. In recent decades, massive violations of basic physical security norms including genocide have captured the world's attention. Cambodia and Rwanda offer extreme examples. As most of these episodes demonstrate, we have no basis for relying on other States to apply economic or military force against such systemic violations, whether unilaterally or through coordinated action—let alone against delinquent States committing less dramatic violations of rights, perhaps related to a free press or due process.

If then the human rights treaties were left free floating rather than anchored in intergovernmental organizations endowed with some powers of protection, the movement would have achieved sonic but a very modest advance. IGOs are indispensable for a more effective movement. How should such organizations be constructed, what relationships should they bear to national systems, what powers and functions should they have vis-à-vis States? Moreover, what duties should States bear toward IGOs or their decisions?

Such issues were never systematically examined for IGOs as a group during the evolution of the universal human rights system. The UN Charter created or authorized the creation of the major organs and official posts that are now concerned with human rights issues: the Security Council and General Assembly, the UN Commission on Human Rights, its Sub–Commission on the Promotion and Protection of Human Rights, related working groups and rapporteurs, and more recently the Office of the High Commissioner of Human Rights. In addition, each of six human rights treaties is serviced by its own committee, the so-called treaty bodies or organs. These committees bear a close family resemblance, and as a whole differ markedly from the UN Commission on Human Rights. This range of universal organizations and organs developed at different times and in different contexts over a half century; indeed, many of them have played significant roles only over the last two decades. Moreover, each has experienced its independent and ongoing internal development with respect to its powers and functions, such that the original understandings about these now appear far more modest.

In the last decade, institutions and centres like the World Bank and the UN Development Program, as well as the International Criminal Tribunals and the new International Criminal Court, have become additional important actors in the field of human rights, further expanding the types of pressure against and forms of dialogue with delinquent States. Moreover, starting in the 1970s, non-governmental human rights organizations (NGOs) steadily gained power and influence. In addition to their independent activities of monitoring, reporting, and lobbying, they have interacted closely with and left a strong imprint on the entire network of IGOs.

The substantive provisions of the human rights treaties drew on several centuries of an evolving and expanding tradition of rights. But neither the architecture nor powers and functions of most of the intergovernmental institutions seemed obvious at the time of the drafting of their constitutive instruments. We can contrast a State in a period of transition from a repressive authoritarian regime to political democracy. Its planners for the structure of the new regime could adopt well understood principles for democratic government like the rule of law and the related separation of powers. But no common stock of principles was available to suggest the design of IGOs intended to protect human rights. In the universal system, close analogies to national legal-political institutions like a world court of human rights of broad jurisdiction lay beyond political possibility or even imagination.

The inevitably novel architecture and powers of these new institutions raised deep concerns among their planners—and potential members. After all, the IGO under negotiation might have power to implement a treaty through authoritative interpretation or even to apply telling pressure against a member State. Such powers would pose a far greater threat to a State's sovereign control over its own territory and population than would its bare agreement to observe norms. Indeed, many States saw even that bare agreement as a significant qualification of the sovereign control that was broadly thought to inhere in statehood. If IGOs gained in stature and increased their armoury of pressures against violator States, they could cut to the very bone of sovereignty.

Negotiations during the drafting of the treaties over powers and functions of IGOs were notoriously contentious. The inevitable compromises sometimes led to terse and vague provisions that left much for future decision. Neither basic principles nor a master plan, but rather contingent compromises over time responsive to the positions of the great powers and of regional or ideological blocs of countries, all as supplemented by a gradual increase in powers of international organizations through their internal development, explain our present institutional arrangements. However limited and inadequate those arrangements now appear, we should keep in mind how radical and politically implausible they would have seemed when the human rights movement got underway.

2. Joan Fitzpatrick, "Protection against Abuse of the Concept of 'Emergency'," in Human Rights: An Agenda for the Next Century 203, 203–05 (L. Henkin & J. Hargrove eds., 1994).

. . . Governments have frequently succumbed to the temptation to deflect criticism of their human rights violations by pleas of "emergency." Officials may even be tempted to manufacture crises in order to justify their denials of fundamental rights. The inherent danger and manipulability of states of emergency pose special conceptual and enforcement problems for the international community.

* * *

International law governing this highly charged area is evolving quickly, and contributing sources in this development are diverse. The doctrine of necessity is the most pertinent general norm of international law. The drafting history of the derogation clauses of three major human rights treaties also forms an important background,[4] along with minimal norms of humane treatment of detainees in humanitarian law.[5] Human rights implementation bodies have refined the treaty norms through review of state reports, decisions in interstate and individual cases, advisory opinions and special studies of the human rights situations in particular states. Ad hoc studies of the human rights situation in certain states undergoing emergencies have been undertaken by special rapporteurs and working groups of the United Nations Commission on Human Rights. Theme rapporteurs and working groups appointed by the same body have likewise confronted the problem of emergency-related violations. The Special Rapporteur on States of Emergency of the [UN] Sub–Commission on the Prevention of Discrimination and Protection of Minorities has made a special contribution to the development of norms and improvement in monitoring. Resolutions or bodies of principles on subjects related to states of emergency, such as those concerning treatment of detainees and disappearances must also be considered in assessing existing or developing norms. Finally, regional non-treaty bodies such as the Conference on Security and Cooperation in Europe (CSCE) have made distinct contributions to the evolution of norms and implementation mechanisms relating to emergencies.

The texts and the interpretations of the derogation clauses of the three key treaties establish several important principles. *First*, an emergency justifying suspension of guarantees must be actual or imminent; temporary; so grave as to threaten the existence of the nation; and so extensive as to affect the whole population. *Second*, the government must notify other state parties within a reasonable time and possibly officially proclaim the suspension of guarantees under the treaties.[6] *Third*, certain listed rights are nonderogable. However, nonderogable rights differ from treaty to treaty and additional nonlisted rights are increasingly recognized as essentially nonderogable.

---

4. International Covenant on Civil and Political Rights, *adopted* 19 Dec 1966 [**Basic Document 3.14**], art. 4; European Convention for the Protection of Human Rights and Fundamental Freedoms [**Basic Document 3.5**], art. 15; American Convention on Human Rights [**Basic Document 3.17**], art. 27.

5. *See, e.g.,* arts. 3, 32, 33, and 64–77 of the Geneva Convention Relative to the Protection of Civilian Persons in Time of War [**Basic Document 2.12**].

6. Only Article 4 of the [International Covenant on Civil and Political Rights] specifically requires official proclamation of the emergency. . . .

Fourth, the rule of proportionality establishes that guarantees may be suspended only to the degree and duration strictly required by the exigencies of the situation. *Fifth*, the principle of nondiscrimination requires that rights not be suspended solely on the basis of race, color, sex, language, religion, or social origin. *Sixth*, suspensions of rights that violate additional obligations of the derogating state, such as those imposed by humanitarian law, also violate the human rights treaties, which incorporate by reference the states parties' other international obligations.[f]

While these principles have become increasingly well-established in recent years, ambiguity remains with respect to certain issues. The treaty implementation bodies still encounter substantial obstacles in providing comprehensive interpretations of the derogation clauses and in applying them in a timely, accurate, and effective manner to curb abuses by derogating states. For states not parties to any of the key human rights treaties, other issues are central: which of these principles can be said to apply under customary law or by reference to other treaty obligations. . . .

3. **"The Siracusa Principles on the Limitation and Derogation Provisions in the International Covenant on Civil and Political Rights," 7 H.R.Q. 3, 4–12 (1985), *reprinted in* 3 Weston & Carlson III.T.8a: Principles 1–70 (Basic Document 3.25).**

4. **Diane F. Orentlicher, "Addressing Gross Human Rights Abuses: Punishment and Victim Compensation," in Human Rights: An Agenda for the Next Century 425, 425–26, 428–31, 448–53 (L. Henkin & J. Hargrove eds., 1994).**

International law has long recognized that human rights guarantees rest, above all, on a foundation of law—in particular, on the assurance of an effective legal response when violations occur. Notably, an act of law enforcement inaugurated the modern period of international protection of human rights. Through the prosecution of Nazi leaders for crimes against humanity at Nuremberg, the international community simultaneously asserted that all states are bound to respect fundamental rights, and that the vitality of these rights depends upon the assurance of their enforcement through legal process.

More recently, international law has continued to insist upon legal accountability for at least the most serious violations of human rights. Recently drafted human rights instruments explicitly recognize states' duty to punish violations of physical integrity, and authoritative interpretations of human rights treaties have repeatedly emphasized the role of punishment in securing fundamental rights. Human rights treaties also affirm the importance of civil redress for violations of protected rights, and in recent years international responses to gross violations have placed increasing emphasis on enforcement of states' duty to compensate victims.

The principle underlying these duties is straightforward: the only way to assure that rights are protected is to maintain effective legal safeguards against their breach. In particular, those who commit atrocious human rights crimes must be punished, and victims must be assured appropriate redress.

f. For amplification of these principles, see J. Fitzpatrick, Human Rights in Crisis: The International System for Protecting Rights During States of Emergency 36–38, 52–66 (1994).

But if international law has been emphatic in asserting states' duty to punish atrocious crimes, states' compliance with that duty has often been deficient, and international efforts to promote better compliance have been patently inadequate. States' compliance has been notably weak where it is most needed: in situations of massive violations. Not coincidentally, a general pattern of impunity has often been the context in which systematic abuses occur. At times, governments have enacted amnesties conferring legal impunity for grave violations of human rights; in other situations, de facto impunity has been the rule. Although international human rights bodies have recently begun to condemn amnesties for gross violations, little serious effort has been made to prevent states from using amnesties to consign atrocious crimes to legal oblivion. Too often, the international community has effectively condoned impunity.

* * *

1. Criminal Accountability

a. Current Law

Although few violations of human rights are international crimes, international criminal law played a crucial role in the development of human rights law. * * * Yet despite its origins, human rights law has, until recently, placed relatively little emphasis on criminal punishment. Although the Nuremberg precedent was in effect codified in the 1948 Convention for the Prevention and Punishment of the Crime of Genocide [**Basic Document 3.2**], that treaty has ... been invoked by states parties [only once] as the basis of international criminal enforcement.[g] On their face, the most comprehensive human rights instruments, such as the Universal Declaration of Human Rights [**Basic Document 3.3**] and the International Covenant on Civil and Political Rights (Covenant) [**Basic Document 3.14**], are silent about states' duty to punish those who commit serious abuses.

In recent years, however, the Covenant and its regional counterparts have been authoritatively interpreted to require that states parties bring to justice those who are responsible for certain violations. For example the Human Rights Committee [established pursuant to the Covenant], which monitors compliance with the Covenant, has repeatedly asserted that states parties must investigate torture, disappearances, and extra-legal executions and attempt to bring the wrongdoers to justice.

[*Eds.*—The author next describes how both the European Court of Human Rights and the Inter–American Court of Human Rights have interpreted their parent conventions—the 1950 European Convention for the Protection of Human Rights and Fundamental Freedoms (**Basic Document**

---

g. *See* Application of the Convention on the Prevention and Punishment of the Crime of Genocide (Bosnia and Herzegovina v. Yugo./Serbia and Montenegro) (Request for the Indication of Provisional Measures), 1993 ICJ 29 (16 Apr); Application of the Convention on the Prevention and Punishment of the Crime of Genocide (Bosnia and Herzegovina v. Yugo./Serbia and Montenegro) (Further Requests for the Indication of Provisional Measures), 1993 ICJ 325 (13 Sep); Application of the Convention on the Prevention and Punishment of the Crime of Genocide (Bosnia and Herzegovina v. Yugoslavia) (Preliminary Objections), 1996 ICJ 595 (11 Jul). In 1999, the Republic of Croatia began proceedings before the ICJ against Yugoslavia for the alleged 1995 genocide in the regions of Knin, Slavonia, and Dalmatia. For details on the history of these cases, see *infra* Discussion Note/Question 6, at 595.

3.5) and the 1969 American Convention on Human Rights **(Basic Document 3.17)**—to require the conscientious prosecution of, and criminal punishment for, at least serious violations of human rights, even while acknowledging that the State Parties to them enjoy a "margin of appreciation" (*i.e.*, a certain latitude) regarding the means they will use to secure the rights at issue. It is a duty, she notes, that persists despite a change in government and that has been explicitly recognized, at least in respect of grave violations of physical integrity, in more recent human rights instruments such as the 1984 Convention Against Torture and Other Cruel, Inhuman and Degrading Treatment or Punishment **(Basic Document 3.26)** and the 1992 Declaration on the Protection of All Persons From Enforced Disappearance **(Basic Document 3.38)**. Professor Orentlicher then continues:]

The frequent reiteration in international instruments of a duty to punish grave violations of physical integrity is evidence that the duty has become, or is emerging as, a rule of customary law. The *Restatement (Third) of the Foreign Relations Law of the United States* sheds light on the scope this duty. [It asserts in Section 702] that a state violates customary law "if, as a matter of state policy, it practices, encourages or condones" torture, murder, disappearances and several other human rights violations, and suggests that "[a] government may be presumed to have encouraged or condoned [these acts . . . if such acts, especially by its officials, have been repeated or notorious and no steps have been taken to prevent them or to punish the perpetrators.]" Echoing the logic of the *Restatement,* numerous reports prepared by Special Representatives, Special Rapporteurs, and Working Groups appointed by the United Nations Commission on Human Rights have condemned governments' consistent failure to punish widespread acts of torture, disappearance, and extra-legal executions and have suggested that the resulting impunity encourages further violations.

In sum, in recent years international law has placed growing emphasis on states' duty to assure freedom from serious violations of physical integrity through criminal sanctions. But if the principle itself has been firmly established, international efforts to enforce the law have been patently inadequate. . . .

* * *

2.   Civil Redress

a.   *Current Law*

An assurance of [civil] legal redress for violations of protected rights is commonplace in international human rights instruments. For example, Article 8 of the Universal Declaration of Human Rights **[Basic Document 3.3]** provides: "Everyone has the right to an effective remedy by the competent national tribunals for acts violating the fundamental rights granted him by the constitution or by law." Pursuant to Article 2(3) of the International Covenant on Civil and Political Rights, each state party undertakes

> (a) To ensure that any person whose rights or freedoms as herein recognized are violated shall have an effective remedy, notwithstanding that the violation has been committed by persons acting in an official capacity;

(b) To ensure that any person claiming such a remedy shall have his right thereto determined by competent judicial, administrative or legislative authorities, or by any other competent authority provided for by the legal system of the State, and to develop the possibilities of judicial remedy;

(c) To ensure that the competent authorities shall enforce such remedies when granted.

This duty is based on states parties' general duty under Article 2(1) to "ensure to all individuals within [their] territor[ies] and subject to [their] jurisdiction the rights recognized in the ... Covenant," and "to adopt such legislative or other measures as may be necessary to give effect to the rights recognized in the ... Covenant." The Covenant also establishes [in Article 9(5)] "an enforceable right to compensation" for those who have been "the victim of unlawful arrest or detention," and provides [in Article 14(6)] that someone who has suffered punishment as a result of a wrongful conviction generally "shall be compensated according to law." The right to an effective remedy for violations of human rights is also explicitly recognized in regional human rights treaties.

The scope and content of the right to redress is not entirely clear, however. For example, states parties' general duty to provide an effective remedy for violations of the Covenant does not necessarily require that they assure compensation for every type of violation. Indeed, the *travaux pré paratoires* make clear that the drafters sought to make Article 2 as broad as possible, so that remedies could be tailored to respond appropriately to specific violations. In some instances, injunctive relief might be sufficient; in others, judicially ordered compensation would be in order.

The Human Rights Committee has, however, consistently recognized a right to compensation for torture, disappearances, and extra-legal executions. Further, a UN expert, Theo van Boven, interprets the jurisprudence of the Committee to signify its view that states parties' general duty "to take effective measures to remedy violations" requires, in respect of serious violations of physical integrity, that states investigate the facts and bring the wrongdoers to justice.[9] In this view, states parties' duty to punish atrocious crimes constitutes part of their obligation to provide an effective remedy to the victims.

The Inter–American Court's judgment on compensation in the *Velásquez Rodriguez* [disappearance] case presents a broad view of the reparation owed to victims of serious violations under the American Convention. The Court interpreted the right to "[r]eparation of harm brought about by the violation of an international obligation" to consist of "full restitution, which includes the restoration of the prior situation, the reparation of the consequences of the violation, and indemnification for patrimonial and non-patrimonial damages, including emotional harm."[10] It also asserted that its earlier judgment

9. *Study concerning the right to restitution, compensation and rehabilitation for victims of gross violations of human rights and fundamental freedoms, Final report submitted by Mr. Theo van Boven, Special Rapporteur,* UN Doc. E/CN.4/Sub.2/1993/8, at 26, ¶ 56. . . .

10. Judgment of 21 Jul 1989, ¶ 26, Inter–Am. Ct. H.R. (ser. C), No. 7 (1989). . . . [For excerpts from this judgment, see *infra* Reading 17 in Problem 5–4 ("A Disappearance in Hispania"), at 677.]

on the merits, finding the Honduran government responsible for violations of the American Convention by virtue of the disappearance of certain individuals, "is in itself a type of reparation and moral satisfaction of significance and importance for the families of the victims." But the Court rejected the petitioners' request for punitive damages, concluding that the principle of punitive damages "is not applicable in international law at this time."

* * *

Outside the treaty context, various efforts have been made in recent years to identify and strengthen victims' right to an effective remedy for violations. For example, in 1985 the UN General Assembly adopted a Declaration of Basic Principles of Justice for Victims of Crime and Abuse of Power,[11] which elaborated general standards relating to compensation of victims of crime and of abuse of government power. Victims of the latter are defined as "persons who, individually or collectively, have suffered harm ... through acts or omissions that do not yet constitute violations of national criminal laws but of internationally recognized norms relating to human rights." The Declaration asserts that both types of victims should, where appropriate, receive restitution and/or compensation, including material, medical, psychological, and social assistance and support.

In 1989 the Sub–Commission on Prevention of Discrimination and Protection of Minorities (Sub–Commission)[h] of the UN Commission on Human Rights appointed one of its members, Theo van Boven, to study the right to restitution, compensation, and rehabilitation for victims of gross violations of human rights and fundamental freedoms. His final report, completed in July 1993, presents a comprehensive review of international law and practice in respect of reparation for victims of gross violations of human rights, and also describes several examples of national practice. The report recommends that the United Nations adopt a set of principles and guidelines "that give content to the right to reparation for victims of gross violations of human rights,"[12] and sets forth proposed principles and guidelines. * * * [S]ignificant are the Report's recognition that the right to reparation in international law includes a right to compensation for mental as well as physical harm, and its recommendation that states should "make adequate provision for groups of victims to bring collective claims and to obtain collective reparation" where appropriate.

C. The Enforcement of Human Rights through United Nations Non-Treaty Procedures

1. Nigel S. Rodley and David Weissbrodt, "United Nations Non-Treaty Procedures for Dealing with Human Rights Violations," in Guide to International Human Rights Practice 65–66 (H. Hannum ed., 4th ed. 2004).

The most important [non-treaty] procedures [to protect human rights at the global level] have been established within the UN Commission on Human

---

11. GA Res. 40/34, 29 Nov 1985.

h. Renamed the Sub–Commission on the Promotion and Protection of Human Rights in 2000.

12. *Supra* note 9, at 54, ¶ 136(4).

Rights [*Eds.*—replaced by the Human Rights Council in 2006] and its Sub–Commission on the Promotion and Protection of Human Rights (formerly the Sub–Commission on the Prevention of Discrimination and Protection of Minorities). The *Commission* ..., which meets annually in Geneva for six weeks beginning in March, consists of fifty-three members elected by the Economic and Social Council (ECOSOC). The Commission reports to ECOSOC which, in turn, reports to the General Assembly. Delegations make statements and vote on proposed resolutions and decisions in the same way as any other UN body, that is, on behalf of the governments they represent. Most other UN member states send observer delegations that can make statements but have no right to vote.

Governments may give their representatives broad discretion or strict instructions. The more sensitive the issue, the more likely that members will be obliged to seek instructions from their governments. Often, governments whose human rights practices are under challenge at the Commission will lobby the capitals of Commission members to avoid an adverse vote or action. It has therefore been difficult to condemn or challenge any but the most friendless of countries in the past.

The *Sub-Commission* ... also meets annually in Geneva, for three weeks beginning in late July or early August. Formally, the Sub–Commission reports to the following sessions of the Commission. It is composed of twenty-six individual experts nominated by their governments and elected by the Commission. In practice, some Sub–Commission members and their alternates are well-tuned to the policies of their governments and take positions that are consistent with those policies. It is not unusual for such members to have official positions or to serve in their governments delegation to the Commission. . . . On the whole, the Sub–Commission can be expected to act somewhat more on the merits than on the politics of human rights issues—a tendency which was reinforced by the Sub–Commission's adoption of voting by secret ballot on country-related matters since 1989. In 2000, however, the Commission forbade the Sub–Commission from adopting resolutions on country-related matters. The Sub–Commission still debates country situations and undertakes studies or adopts thematic resolutions on issues that impliedly relate to country situations.

A typical cycle of meetings thus starts with the Sub–Commission (July–August), continuing with the Commission (the following March–April), ECOSOC (July), and the General Assembly (September–December). Occasionally, the General Assembly may take up an issue raised during the immediately preceding Sub–Commission session.

2. Editors' Note. The right to petition the Sub–Commission is found in ECOSOC resolutions 1235 and 1503 of 6 June 1967 and 27 May 1970, respectively. *See* ECOSOC Resolution 1235 Concerning Questions of the Violation of Human Rights and Fundamental Freedoms, Including Policies of Racial Discrimination and Segregation and of Apartheid, in All Countries, with Particular Reference to Colonial and Other Dependent Countries and Territories, ESC Res. 1235, UN ESCOR, 42nd Sess., Supp. No. 1, at 17, UN Doc. E/4393 (1967), *reprinted in* 3 Weston & Carlson III.T.3, and ECOSOC Resolution 1503 Concerning the Procedure for Dealing with Communications Relating to Violations of Human Rights and Fundamental Freedoms, ESC Res. 1503, UN ESCOR, 48th Sess., Supp. No. 1A at 8, UN Doc. E/4832/Add. 1

(1970), *reprinted in* 3 Weston & Carlson III.T.6. The procedures made possible by these resolutions broke new ground in the protection of human rights via the UN system at the time of their creation, significantly changing the functions of the UN Commission of Human Rights which before 1967 had no power to take any action relative to complaints concerning human rights. While slow and unlikely to meet pressing needs, they continue today as the main procedures of the UN Commission on Human Rights and its Sub–Commission and thus merit attention.

ECOSOC Resolution 1235 authorizes the Commission on Human Rights and its Sub–Commission, in Paragraph 2, "to examine information relevant to gross violations of human rights and fundamental freedoms, as exemplified by the policy of *apartheid* as practiced in the Republic of South Africa and in the territory of South West Africa [now Namibia] . . . and to racial discrimination as practiced notably in Southern Rhodesia." . . . Precisely what it means to "examine information" and precisely what constitute "gross violations" are not explicitly clarified by Resolution 1235, but in Paragraph 3 it authorizes the Commission "[to] make a thorough study of situations which reveal a consistent pattern of violations of human rights, as exemplified by the policy of *apartheid* . . . and racial discrimination . . . and [to] report, with recommendations thereon, to the Economic and Social Council." In any event, the operational essence of "the 1235 procedure," as it has come to be called, is a public debate that can lead to the establishment of a mechanism for studying a country's human rights situation (in the form of, *e.g.*, a "working group," "observer delegation," "special rapporteur," "special representative," "special envoy," or "representative of the Secretary–General") and to the adoption of a resolution concerning the country situation examined or studied. In addition, the Sub–Commission can debate specific country situations and adopt resolutions expressing concern—but only concern—about them. The initiative for the 1235 procedure, it is important to recall, lies entirely in the hands of UN Member States (not private individuals or groups) and thus inevitably is influenced by political considerations.

ECOSOC Resolution 1503, a direct response to the Sub–Commission's reliance upon information derived from nongovernmental organizations (NGOs) under the 1235 procedure, gave the initiative for the first time to individuals and NGOs. Limited to cases that reveal "a *consistent pattern* of *gross* and *reliably attested* violations of human rights and fundamental freedoms" (emphasis added), it nevertheless was seen by many around the time of its adoption as "an enormously valuable precedent, a breach in the citadel of the mutual protection society, one that could be progressively enlarged." T. Farer, *The UN and Human Rights: At the End of the Beginning*, in United Nations, Divided World: The UN's Roles in International Relations 240, 279 (A. Roberts & B. Kingsbury eds., 2d ed. 1993). In practice, however, the 1503 procedure, though not without some notable successes, has fallen short of its promise. While it has sometimes served to facilitate gradually increased pressure on offending governments, often as a precursor to action under ECOSOC Resolution 1235, it is, in the words of F. Newman and D. Weissbrodt, International Human Rights: Law, Policy, and Process 122 (1990), "painfully slow, complex, secret, and vulnerable to political influence at many junctures." A non-anonymous "communication" (*i.e.*, petition) by an individual or NGO with "direct and reliable knowledge" of the situation (whether or not a victim of the alleged human rights abuse) is submitted to the Office of the UN High Commissioner for Human Rights in Geneva, describing the facts, stating its purpose, demonstrating the exhaustion of local remedies, and indicating the rights that have been violated. The Office, in turn, acknowledges receipt of the communication (while not otherwise communicating with its author), sends it to the government accused, summarizes it for a monthly confidential list, and forwards it to a "Communications Working Group" of the Sub–Commission on the Promotion and Protection of Human Rights, consisting of five members of the Sub–Commission from each of the UN's five major regions (Africa, Asia, Eastern Europe, Latin America, and "Western Europe and Others" which includes Australia, Canada, New Zealand, and, in practice, the United States). The Working Group meets privately for two weeks each summer immediately prior to the annual four-week meeting of the Sub–Commission to decide, by confidential majority vote, whether the communication should be considered by the full Sub–Commission. If so, the communication is placed on the Sub–Commission's agenda (except when it has been transmitted to the accused government less than twelve weeks before the Working Group's meeting and the government has not replied, in which case consideration of the communication is postponed until the next year). Then, in closed session, the full Sub–Commission decides whether the situation referred to it warrants forwarding to the next annual six-week session of the full Commission, approximately six months later. No public announcement is made as to which country is involved, but when, thereafter, in closed session, the Commission acts on the communication, if it does not decide simply to discontinue consideration of it, it is empowered to make a "thorough study" of it or an "investigation by an ad hoc committee"—although in practice it has relied upon a range of lesser techniques (such as, in ascending order of perceived importance, keeping the situation "under review," asking the concerned government for further information, requesting direct contacts by the Secretary–General, and appointing an independent expert/rapporteur). At the end of the Commission's closed discussions, the Chairperson announces publicly the name of the country involved and whether the communication has been considered or discontinued, but neither the nature of the claimed violations nor the action taken, if any. The Commission may also recommend that ECOSOC make the circumstances of the communication a matter of public record, although rarely has ECOSOC been called upon to do so. If it is thus called upon, however, then either it or the General Assembly may propound resolutions condemning the government in question.

In past years, the Commission on Human Rights has tended to encourage resort to the 1235 procedure over the 1503 procedure because it enables its members to place charges of gross violations of human rights on its agenda without having to wait for 1503 communications to be processed by the Sub–Commission and, unlike the 1503 procedure, to have them discussed in public. The confidentiality required by the 1503 procedure has been considered one of its most serious defects. Still, it reflects how much governments fear bad publicity and thereby demonstrates, indirectly, the power of world public opinion.

3. Nigel S. Rodley and David Weissbrodt, "United Nations Non–Treaty Procedures for Dealing with Human Rights Violations," in Guide to International Human Rights Practice 75–88 (H. Hannum ed., 4th ed. 2004).

One of the most positive developments in the UN's work in the past twenty-five years has been the development of thematic machinery to deal with violations of specific types of human rights. Unlike the [public (1235) and confidential (1503)] procedures that deal with general *situations*, the thematic mechanisms can deal with *individual cases* of human rights violations or threatened violations, particularly in countries in which a specific type of violation appears to be widespread.

The most important of these mechanisms which deal with threats to life or physical integrity were among the earliest to be created: the Working Group on Enforced or Involuntary Disappearances (created in 1980), the Special Rapporteur on Summary or Arbitrary Executions (1982), and the Special Rapporteur on Torture (1985). So many thematic mechanisms have been created subsequently that some concern at their proliferation, lack of resources to service them, and lack of time on the Commission agenda to consider the results of their work. Among the most significant to direct victims of violations are the rapporteurs or working groups on religious intolerance (1986), arbitrary detention (1991), the sale of children and child prostitution and pornography (1992), internally displaced persons (1993), racism and xenophobia (1993), freedom of opinion and expression (1993), the independence of the judiciary (1994), violence against women (1994), and human rights defenders (2000). Other rapporteurs deal with adequate housing, compensation for victims of human rights violations, education, extreme poverty, food, health, human trafficking, the impact of armed conflict on children, implementation of the 2001 Durban Declaration and Programme of Action [*available at* the Office of the UN High Commissioner for Human Rights (http://www.unhchr.ch/pdf/Durban/pdf)], indigenous peoples, migrants, racial discrimination faced by people of African descent, the right to development, structural adjustment policies, and mercenaries.

To date, these mechanisms have been genuinely impartial. In other words, their annual reports to the Commission indicate that cases and problems are taken up, regardless of the identity of the state whose behavior is called into question. This approach is a radical departure from the practice of some other UN bodies, including the Commission, where actions are partly (if not primarily) determined by political considerations.

4. Editors' Note. While varying in the character and scope of their operations, as well as in the degree to which they apply pressure against particular governments, the thematic mechanisms outlined in the foregoing reading have developed a variety of intelligence-retrieval techniques: requesting governments for information on specific cases; taking immediate action to reconcile or clarify a case; and making on-site visits to gain better knowledge and understanding of a series of cases. They report the substance of their findings annually to the Commission on Human Rights, generally tending to avoid concluding that any particular violation has been proven and thus serving more an informational than a judgmental function. Nevertheless, pursuing their inquiries fully and more or less impartially irrespective of the identity of the countries involved, elements of their reports serve a distinct "enforcement" function insofar as they facilitate firm world public opinion about the state of human rights in a given country.

D. The Enforcement of Human Rights through the Organization for Security and Co-operation in Europe: The "Helsinki Process"

1. Editors' Note. Apart from the various United Nations mechanisms for protecting human rights referred to in the readings above, there are a variety of regional human rights institutions. These are discussed in greater detail *infra* in Problem 5–2 ("Women's Reproductive Rights in Hibernia"). The facts of the present problem are set in Europe and implicate that region's human rights mechanisms. The principal European human rights institutions are those established by the European Convention on Human Rights and Fundamental Freedoms 1950 **(Basic Document 3.5)**, not relevant here as none of the states involved are parties to the treaty, and those created by the Organization for Security and Co-operation in Europe (OSCE), an outgrowth of what came to be known as the "Helsinki Process," born at the Conference on Security and Co-operation in Europe concluded at Helsinki on 1 August 1975.

The end-product of a concerted effort by the former Soviet Union and its allies to secure official recognition and acceptance of their post-World War II European frontiers (the Second World War having ended without the conclusion of an omnibus peace treaty), the Conference on Security and Co-operation in Europe met over two years. Thirty-five governments—including all the European states except Albania, plus Canada and the United States, the Holy See, Liechtenstein, Monaco, and San Marino—participated on a basis of formal equality. The West sought concessions primarily in relation to security requirements and human rights, largely in that order.

The Final Act of the Conference **(Basic Document 1.12)**, the importance of which is reflected in its having been signed by almost all of the principal governmental leaders of the day, was adopted on 1 August 1975 and comprised four key sections (or "baskets"), each the result of protracted diplomatic negotiation: (1) Questions Relating to Security in Europe; (2) Co-operation in the Fields of Economics, of Science and Technology, and of the Environment; (3) Co-operation in Humanitarian and Other fields; and (4) Follow-up to the Conference. Though not a treaty, it created expectations concerning the conduct of the "Participating States" (deliberately so-called) and provided for periodic review conferences to ensure that these expectations would be met. According to one informed observer, it was "a master-piece of diplomatic skill in the sense that a great number of problems between the Participating States were 'solved' by agreeing on compromissory clauses" and that it resulted in "a great number of agreements on which all parties are in clear accord." Arie Bloed, *Two Decades of the CSCE Process: From Confrontation to Co-operation–An Introduction*, in The Conference on Security and Co-operation in Europe: Analysis and Basic Documents, 1972–1993, at 1, 46 (A. Bloed ed., 1993). As stated in Thomas Buergenthal, *The Helsinki Process: Birth of a Human Rights System*, in Human Rights in the World Community:

Issues and Action 256, 256 (R. Claude & B. Weston eds. and contribs., 2d ed. 1992):[i]

> the [Helsinki Final Act] straddles the chasm that divided East from West in the 1970s, giving each side something it wanted. What is striking about the document is not that it is a compromise document; that was predictable. More significant is the fact that it proved possible in 1975 to draft an international instrument which laid the foundation for pan-European cooperation in areas as diverse as human rights and military security, and that this cooperative framework continues to play an ever greater role in shaping the Europe of the 1990s.

Indeed, as it turns out, the Helsinki Final Act, in its human rights component especially, proved to be an important force in the collapse of the Iron Curtain and the transformation of Eastern Europe. Professor Buergenthal writes: "The Solidarity movement in Poland, the Charter 77 in Czechoslovakia, the Helsinki Watch committees in the Soviet Union all trace their genesis to the [Helsinki Final Act]. This instrument and the publicity its adoption generated gave the Walesas, the Havels, the Sharanskys, and many others in the East political legitimacy. . . . By being reprinted in the government newspapers of all Iron Curtain countries, [it] gained an official imprimatur that greatly enhanced its value as a moral and political tool in the struggle for human rights." Buergenthal adds: "This phenomenon, not fully grasped at the time by the Communist leadership, is pregnant with the ironies of a propaganda that backfired. It also demonstrates the political impact of ideas whose time has come." *Id.*

Since the conclusion of the 1975 Final Act and in keeping with its Basket IV, long-running "Follow-up" and "Summit" meetings have been held. Serving the dual purpose of providing a forum to review compliance with the 1975 Final Act and establishing a mechanism for the normative, procedural, and institutional evolution of the CSCE, these meetings succeeded in establishing a unique negotiating process ("the Helsinki Process") that, over time, has permitted the reinterpretation and revision of the Final Act while simultaneously focusing responsible attention on the failure of certain states to live up to their human rights commitments.

Supplementing these "Follow-up" and "Summit" meetings—and the normative, institutional, and procedural outcomes they have produced—have been, especially in recent years, many specialized meetings and seminars on "military security issues," "the peaceful settlement of disputes," "economic and scientific co-operation and the environment," "the Mediterranean," and "the human dimension" (*i.e.*, human rights, the protection of national minorities, the rule of law, and democracy). "Spurred by the end of the Cold War and the re-emergence of ethnic tensions and territorial disputes," writes one informed observer, "the CSCE has been at the forefront of efforts to develop mechanisms that use collective political action to encourage peaceful resolution of disputes." Miriam Sapiro, *Dispute Resolution: General Methods and CSCE Mechanisms*, in ASIL Newsletter/ASIL Insight 1 (Sep–Oct 1994). One observer has noted, "[t]he Charter of Paris for a New Europe . . ., adopted in

---

i. Thomas Buergenthal is presently a judge of the International Court of Justice ("World Court") at The Hague.

1990, marked the beginning of institutionalization for the [CSCE] as well as the celebration of the historic changes taking place in Europe. In 1991, the [CSCE] started to become operational rather than serve simply as a forum for discussion, dialogue, verbal confrontation, and adoption of documents. Hence it needed more structure, and began to establish some skeleton institutions." Rachel Brett, *Human Rights and the OSCE*, 18 H.R.Q. 668, 670 (1996).

At the 1994 Budapest Summit Meeting and reflecting the substantial evolution of the Helsinki Process, the Conference on Security and Co-operation in Europe (CSCE) was renamed the "Organization on Security and Co-operation in Europe" (OSCE). Its principal organs and bureaus now include:

- the above-mentioned Parliamentary Assembly based in Copenhagen;

- the Ministerial Council (formerly the "CSCE Council of Ministers for Foreign Affairs"), which is the OSCE's central decision-making and governing body;

- the Senior Council (replacing the "Committee of Senior Officials");

- a general secretariat headquartered in Vienna and headed by a Secretary General who, as chief administrative officer, acts under the political guidance of a rotating Chairman-in-Office who is responsible for coordinating the fulfillment of the OSCE's objectives;

- a Permanent Council (formerly the "Permanent Committee") which remains the regular body for consultation and decision-making;

- an Office for Democratic Institutions and Human Rights (ODIHR) situated in Warsaw (formerly the "Office for Free Elections");

- Conflict Prevention Centre based in Vienna; and

- High Commissioner on National Minorities located in The Hague (HCNM).

In addition, an OSCE Court of Conciliation and Arbitration was established in Geneva, following the entry into force of—and in keeping with—the 1992 Convention on Conciliation and Arbitration within the CSCE.[j] The OSCE has also sponsored a number of international agreements: for example, the Treaty on Conventional Armed Forces in Europe (CFE) in 1990[k] and the Charter for European Security in 1999 adopted at the OSCE's Istanbul Summit.[l] The OSCE maintains a network of field missions in various conflict zones. In 2004, these included Georgia and Kosovo.

As this coursebook goes to press, 55 states are members of the OSCE, including all the republics of the former Soviet Union. As stated in Paragraph 3 of the 1994 Budapest Summit Declaration **(Basic Document 3.45)**, the OSCE is "the security structure embracing States from Vancouver to Vladivostok." On the whole, despite relatively low-level material support and

---

j. Concluded 15 Dec 1992. *Reprinted in* 32 I.L.M. 551 (1993) and 1 Weston & Carlson I.H.12. An outgrowth of CSCE meetings on the peaceful settlement of disputes, commencing in Valletta (Malta) in early 1991, its substantive jurisdiction extends to disputes concerning a state's territorial integrity, national defense, title to sovereignty over land territory, or competing claims with regard to jurisdiction over

other areas. It is not intended, at least at present, for the protection of human rights.

k. Concluded 19 Nov 1990. *Reprinted in* 30 I.L.M. 1 (1991) and 2 Weston & Carlson II. C.11.

l. Adopted 19 Nov 1999. *Reprinted in* 39 I.L.M. 255 (2000) and 1 Weston & Carlson I.D.24.

physically scattered institutions, its increased membership and infrastructural enhancement have been welcomed by most observers. The OSCE has a unique role in Europe partly because of its broad membership and partly because of its tradition of dialogue and negotiation. For up to date information on the OSCE see its website at <http://www.osce.org>.

   2.   Final Act of the Conference on Security and Co-operation in Europe ("Helsinki Accords"), 1 Aug 1975, *reprinted in* **14 I.L.M. 1292 (1975) & 1 Weston & Carlson I.D.9: Pmbl. & Princs. IV, VI, VII, VIII & X of Sec. 1(a) of "Questions Relating to Security in Europe" (Basket I); Pmbl. & §§ 1–4 of "Co-operation in Humanitarian and Other Fields" (Basket III)** (Basic Document 1.12).

   3.   Editors' Note. The first follow-up meeting to the 1975 Helsinki conference, in Belgrade during 1977–78, was divided along Cold War ideological lines and thus reached no meaningful agreement. Much the same can be said of the second follow-up meeting in Madrid from November 1980 to September 1983. While laying the foundation for the development of an informal practice of dealing with human rights violations, it produced no major breakthroughs. These were not to be had until the third follow-up meeting in Vienna between 1986 and 1989 and a series of meetings thereafter, in Copenhagen, Paris, and Moscow, among others.

   The Vienna follow-up conference, which was enabled by the policies of *perestroika* and *glasnost* of Soviet President Mikhail Gorbachev to avoid the usual ideological East–West debates, created a conceptual and institutional framework to advance the observance of human rights within the CSCE (now OSCE) process. It did so in two ways. First, it consolidated the human rights themes of Basket I with the human contact and related humanitarian topics of Basket III under a new heading entitled "the human dimension of the CSCE." Second, it established a process or institutional framework—the so-called Human Dimension Mechanism—for dealing with claims alleging the non-observance of human dimension commitments by Participating States. The Vienna Human Dimension Mechanism, as it has come to be called, was further refined by the June 1990 Concluding Document of the Copenhagen Meeting of the Participating States of the Conference on the Human Dimension of the Conference on Security and Co-operation in Europe **(Basic Document 3.34)**. It was reaffirmed and supported by the November 1990 Charter of Paris for a New Europe and Supplementary Document to Give Effect to Certain Provisions Contained in the Charter of Paris for a New Europe **(Basic Document 3.35)**, marking the beginning of the substantial institutionalization of the OSCE as well as celebrating the historic changes taking place in Europe at the time. And it was supplemented by the Moscow Human Dimension Mechanism as detailed in the October 1991 Document of the Moscow Meeting of the Conference on the Human Dimension of the Conference on Security and Co-operation in Europe **(Basic Document 3.37)**.

   In sum, the OSCE Human Dimension Mechanism formalizes, for all practical purposes, the informal negotiating process that had evolved over time within the CSCE and consists of two main elements: (a) the Vienna Mechanism, established in the Vienna Concluding Document of 1989; and (b) the Moscow Mechanism, which constitutes in part an elaboration of the Vienna Mechanism. A fundamental characteristic—some would say weakness—of each mechanism is that both represent predominantly an interstate process. Neither individuals nor NGOs have access to them except indirectly as providers of information or as pressure groups. They thus are to be sharply contrasted with individual complaint procedures available within the United Nations and Council of Europe human rights systems. Nevertheless, they together constitute, in the words of one close observer, "a sophisticated, permanent machinery for supervising the implementation of human dimension commitments." Arie Bloed, *Two Decades of the CSCE Process: From Confrontation to Co-operation–An Introduction*, in The Conference on Security and Co-operation in Europe: Analysis and Basic Documents, 1972–1993, at 40 (A. Bloed ed., 1993). For details concerning UN human rights procedures, see Discussion Notes/Questions 1 and 2, *infra* at 591.

4.   Concluding Document of the Madrid Meeting 1983 of Representatives of the Participating States of the Conference on Security and Co-operation in Europe, 9 Sep 1983, *reprinted in* 22 I.L.M. 1398 (1989) & 1 Weston & Carlson I.D.10: Princs. 1, 2, 4–6, 8–15 of "Questions Relating to Security in Europe" (Basket I) (Basic Document 3.24).

5.   Concluding Document of the Vienna Meeting 1986 of Representatives of the Participating States of the Conference on Security and Co-operation in Europe, 17 Jan 1989, *reprinted in* 28 I.L.M. 527 (1989) & 1 Weston & Carlson I.D.11: Pmbl. & Princs. 1–5, 8–24 of "Questions Relating to Security in Europe" (Basket I), "Co-operation in Humanitarian and Other Fields" (Basket III), & "Human Dimension in the CSCE" (Basic Document 3.30).

6.   Concluding Document of the Copenhagen Meeting of the Participating States of the Conference on the Human Dimension of the Conference on Security and Co-operation in Europe, 29 Jun 1990, *reprinted in* 29 I.L.M. 1305 (1990) & 1 Weston & Carlson III.B.20: Pmbl. & §§ I–IV (Basic Document 3.34).

7.   Charter of Paris for a New Europe and Supplementary Document to Give Effect to Certain Provisions Contained in the Charter of Paris for a New Europe (without annexes), 21 Nov 1990, *reprinted in* 30 I.L.M. 190 (1991) & 1 Weston & Carlson I.D.13: "A New Era of Democracy, Peace and Unity," "Guidelines for the Future," "New Structures and Institutions of the CSCE Process," and Supplementary Document to Give Effect to Certain Provisions Contained in the Charter of Paris for a New Europe I–V (Basic Document 3.35).

8.   Document to the Moscow Meeting of the Conference on Security and Co-operation in Europe, 3 Oct 1991, *reprinted in* 30 I.L.M. 1670 (1991) & 3 Weston & Carlson III.B.22: ¶¶ 1–16 (Basic Document 3.37).

9.   Editors' Note. From a human rights standpoint, the best known "baskets" of the 1975 Final Act of the Conference on Security and Co-operation in Europe **(Basic Document 1.12)** are Basket I (entitled "Questions Relating to Security in Europe") and Basket III, entitled "Cooperation in Humanitarian and Other Fields." The basic aims of Basket III were to facilitate greater freedom of movement between East and West, and thus has been rendered obsolete by the ending of the Cold War. Still highly relevant, however, is Basket I, containing, *inter alia*, a "Declaration of Principles

Guiding Relations between Participating States" (popularly known as "the ten Guiding Principles" or "Decalogue"). Especially relevant for human rights are Principle VI (non-intervention), Principle VII (respect for human rights), and Principle VIII (equal rights and self-determination), the subjects of the next reading.

10. Thomas Buergenthal, "The Helsinki Process: Birth of a Human Rights System," in Human Rights in the World Community: Issues and Action 256, 257–59 (R. Claude & B. Weston eds. and contribs., 2d ed. 1992).

Principle VI

Principle VI restates more or less the traditional ... international law rule prohibiting intervention by one state in the domestic affairs of another state. It constitutes an unequivocal rejection of the so-called Brezhnev doctrine, which was invoked by the USSR and its allies to legitimate their invasion of Czechoslovakia . . . . .

The obligation not to intervene in the internal affairs of a state has been invoked often by states to shield themselves against charges that they were violating the human rights of their nationals. In the CSCE context, Principle VI of the Helsinki Final Act [HFA] used to be invoked for many years by the Soviet Union and its allies whenever they were accused of violating their CSCE human rights commitments. It did not, however, prevent the airing of these charges. As in the UN, it was argued that a matter which is the subject of international agreements or commitments, for example, the commitments set out in Principle VII (respect for human rights), cannot be deemed to fall within a participating state's domestic jurisdiction because the inclusion of these commitments in the HFA has to that extent internationalized the subject they deal with. Principle VI must therefore be related to the human rights provisions of the HFA, which are spelled out in Principle VII.

Principle VII

The normative basis of the CSCE human rights system, as we know it today, rests on the commitments set forth in Principle VII. Entitled "Respect for human rights and fundamental freedoms, including freedom of thought, conscience, religion or belief," it contains elements that merely reaffirm preexisting human rights obligations. It also contains language that advances to a very significant extent the struggle to internationalize the protection of human rights. There is, first, the declaration by the participating states recognizing "the universal significance of human rights" and their acknowledgement that respect for these rights "is an essential factor for the peace, justice and well-being necessary to ensure the development of friendly relations" among states. By linking human rights to peace and friendly relations, the participating states transformed human rights from a marginal item on the pan-European political agenda into a subject of central importance to it. Henceforth it was politically legitimate to link the protection of human rights with arms control and the liberalization of trade relations. . . .

Another provision found in Principle VII ... is the declaration of the participating states confirming "the right of the individual to know and act upon his rights and duties in this field." This language needs to be read with the last chapter of the HFA wherein each participating state commits itself to publish the instrument and to "disseminate it and make it known as widely as possible." The publication of the Helsinki Final Act in the official government and party newspapers had a dramatic impact in a number of countries behind the Iron Curtain....

There is yet another provision found in Principle VII that deserves special attention. This clause deals with national minorities and has served, as we shall see, as the basis for an expanding body of CSCE norms that has evolved from non-discrimination and equal protection to the recognition of a special status for minority groups.

Principle VIII

Principle VIII of the HFA is titled "equal rights and self-determination of peoples." Although the UN Charter (Article 1[2]) **[Basic Document 1.5]** and the International Covenants on Human Rights (Article 1[1]) **[Basic Documents 3.13 & 3.14]** recognize the right to self-determination, Principle VIII clarifies the concept to a significant extent.... [It] leaves no doubt that the Helsinki Final Act recognizes the right of external and internal self-determination and that the right belongs to all peoples, whether they are subject to the jurisdiction of a state under colonial rule or fully independent.

It should be noted, however, that by dealing with the rights of individuals belonging to national minorities in Principle VII and with self-determination in Principle VIII, the HFA suggests that the concept of "peoples" differs from that of "minorities." Yet it must be recognized that the term "peoples" does not necessarily exclude national minorities from its reach, and may in fact embrace them in certain circumstances. The two terms are thus not mutually exclusive, enabling certain minorities to assert minority rights as well as the right of self-determination. However, it is very likely that the CSCE will focus more attention on minority rights and less on self-determination, although [this] is difficult to predict at this time....

11. Rachel Brett, "Human Rights and the OSCE," 18 H.R.Q. 668, 678–82 (1996).

A.   The Vienna Human Dimension Mechanism

... Subjected to only minor alterations since its creation, the Vienna Mechanism provides a structured means of raising and seeking to resolve disputes about violations of human dimension commitments through a four-stage intergovernmental process. Stage One provides for the exchange of information or responses to representations on questions relating to the human dimension. Stage Two concerns the holding of bilateral meetings, on request, to examine questions relating to the human dimension, including both situations and specific (individual) cases, with a view to resolving them. Stage Three enables states to bring situations and cases, including those raised in Stages One and Two, to the attention of other Participating States. And Stage Four extends the possibility of providing information to future OSCE meetings on issues raised and action taken under the other Stages, including details of specific cases.

This Mechanism fits into the traditional system of international dispute settlement rather than into the human rights implementation model. This is an important distinction. As Richard B. Bilder says:

The predominant, usual, and preferred method of resolving international disputes is negotiation.... [I]t is well established that, absent special agreement, a state is under no international legal obligation to submit a dispute with another state—or, *a fortiori,* an individual or nongovernmental organization—to judicial settlement by an international court or other third party.[13]

By contrast, human rights implementation procedures usually involve an independent third party, such as the European or American Human Rights Commissions or the various UN human rights treaty bodies. In an interstate dispute, the parties are in a position to reach an agreement that is more or less satisfactory to them both. However, in general, the implementation of human rights standards should not be a matter of negotiation because another state may accept an explanation or agreement concerning the violation of the human rights of an individual or group that would not be acceptable to the victim(s) or not in accordance with the commitments concerned....

Despite these limitations, the Vienna Mechanism was a breakthrough in terms of establishing an agreed upon procedure for raising human rights issues within the OSCE, particularly at a time (in January 1989) when no Eastern European country, except Hungary, had accepted the right of complaint under any international human rights procedure. The Vienna Mechanism was used more extensively than most interstate procedures....

However, since the changes in Eastern Europe, the Vienna Mechanism has scarcely been used.... This suggests that its earlier high level of usage was an aberration due to the particular circumstances of the time and to the strong incentive for states to make use of it, which overrode states' reluctance to indulge in behavior that the norms of international relations usually deem "unfriendly." ...

B.   The Moscow Human Dimension Mechanism

The Vienna Mechanism was supplemented in 1991 by the Moscow Human Dimension Mechanism ..., which left the earlier procedure intact but added to it the possibility of on-site investigation by independent experts. The Moscow Mechanism came into operation in May 1992. (The delay was due to the need to establish the list of experts.) The details are complex, but essentially one country can invite a mission of experts or be asked by another country that has used Stages One or Two of the Vienna Mechanism to invite a mission. If the requested country does not act, or the initiating one is not satisfied that the situation is resolved and can muster the support of five other countries, the mission (now called rapporteurs) can be sent without the consent of the country to be visited. If there is a particularly serious threat to the fulfilment of human dimension commitments, ten countries can initiate a rapporteur mission without the requirement of previous steps or the consent of the country to be visited. Finally, on the initiative of any Participating State, the Senior Council can decide to send a mission without any preconditions and without necessarily applying one of the specific procedures outlined above. In each case, the report of the mission goes to the country visited and,

13. R. Bilder, *Possibilities for Development of New International Judicial Mechanisms,* in Human Rights: An Agenda for the Next Century 317, 318–19 (L. Henkin & J. Hargrove eds., 1994).

where appropriate, to the initiating countries and then to all Participating States together with any observations. Finally, the report goes to the Permanent Council, which is charged with follow-up to all missions, and is then made public.

... [T]he Moscow Mechanism provides one of the rare exceptions to the OSCE's consensus rule. It also marked the first involvement of a nonstate element (the independent experts) in the OSCE implementation procedures, as well as the first fact-finding capacity. However, decision-making remains firmly in the hands of the governments, either individually or collectively in the form of the Permanent Council. (The Council's consideration of mission reports was originally permissive but the Rome Council Meeting in 1993 changed this to a mandatory requirement, thus abolishing one of the weaknesses of the system.)

12. Report of the CSCE Meeting of Experts on National Minorities, 19 Jul 1991, *reprinted in* **The Conference on Security and Co-operation in Europe: Analysis and Basic Documents, 1972–1993, at 593 (A. Bloed ed., 1993)** (Basic Document 3.36).

13. Arie Bloed, "Two Decades of the CSCE Process: From Confrontation to Co-operation–An Introduction," in The Conference on Security and Co-operation in Europe: Analysis and Basic Documents, 1972–1993, at 1, 22–25 (A. Bloed ed., 1993).

One of the most complicated aspects of the CSCE process is the legal characterization of CSCE commitments and of the CSCE's concluding documents. In legal doctrine the view generally adhered to is that the Final Act of Helsinki and the CSCE documents do not have the character of treaties. This was also explicitly stressed by the heads of state or government at the end of the Conference in 1975. Moreover, arguing that the Final Act would be a legally binding agreement on the basis of another source of international law would be futile. The intention of the parties, as expressed at the end of the Conference ..., clearly points ... to the fact that the Final Act has to be considered as a political, not as a legal document.

This observation should not be taken to imply, however, that the CSCE documents are not binding. The binding force of these documents is not seriously doubted. Van Dijk correctly states: "A commitment does not have to be legally binding in order to have binding force as the distinction between legal and non-legal binding force resides in the legal consequences attached to the binding force", not in the binding force as such.[14] Violation of politically, but not legally binding agreements is as inadmissible as violation of norms of international law. In this respect there is no difference between politically and legally binding rules.

Although the Final Act of Helsinki and the other Helsinki agreements are not legally binding, they contain numerous clauses which can be traced to international agreements to which a great number or all of the CSCE States are bound. The main example in this respect is the Charter of the United Nations **[Basic Document 1.5]**: the Helsinki agreements contain numerous

---

14. P. Van Dijk, The Final Act of Helsinki–
Basis for a Pan–European System?, 1980 Neth.
Y. B. Int'l L. 97, 110.

references to the purposes and principles of this Charter.... In addition, references are frequently made to more specific treaties, for instance the 1966 International Covenants on Human Rights **[Basic Documents 3.13 & 3.14]**.... Moreover, the Principles guiding the relations among the participating States contain several provisions which are binding upon States as fundamental principles of international law.

The fact that the Helsinki agreements are not legally binding agreements has not affected their political authority. The opposite is true. This becomes evident from the fact that the Helsinki agreements are very frequently invoked as an authoritative source of obligations in order to substantiate that the CSCE States are obliged to adopt certain behaviour or to refrain from certain actions. The great political authority of the Final Act of Helsinki also ensues from the fact that it [was] signed by the highest political representatives of the 35 CSCE States.

In fact, the Helsinki agreements are so often invoked by the CSCE States as an authoritative source of obligations ... that now and then the opinion is put forward that these agreements are in a process of developing into customary law. In other words, from this point of view the Helsinki agreements are international legal instruments *in statu nascendi* or *soft law*. Adherents of this view often refer to the way in which the Universal Declaration of Human Rights **[Basic Document 3.3]** is considered to have gradually acquired binding legal force. Moreover, they point to the fact the CSCE States often enact specific legislation in order to fulfil their obligations ensuing from adopted Helsinki agreements. Whatever view one adheres to, the fact should not be overlooked that, so far, the CSCE States have explicitly chosen a non-legally binding form for the CSCE documents. This intention is of tremendous importance in a discussion about the legal character of the Helsinki agreements. At the same time, we should not ignore the fact that these agreements may be important elements in a process of law-making.

It has to be observed that during the recent period the nature of certain CSCE documents has changed considerably. In the "new" CSCE, the emphasis in the decision-making process has shifted from the follow-up meetings and specialized conferences to the newly established and regularly meeting Council of Ministers and, in particular, to the CSO [Committee of Senior Officials, now the Senior Council]. This has resulted in the situation that other CSCE bodies, such as *ad hoc* meetings, are no longer entitled to adopt binding documents.[15] If they are entitled to produce documents at all, these documents have to be endorsed by the [Ministerial] Council or the [Senior Council] in order to obtain (politically) binding force. In addition, it has to be noted that recently a number of CSCE documents have been produced which explicitly state that they do "not purport to express any new commitments on the part of the participating States". It is, therefore, of great importance to take into account the specific clauses in each CSCE document and the

---

15. In the decision-making process in the "old" CSCE in the period prior to the Paris Summit in 1990, the emphasis was on the periodic follow-up meetings. These meetings determined the nature and mandate of any specialized meeting which had to be held between two follow-up meetings. Detailed rules about the precise competences of these special- ized meetings were lacking. In principle, the next follow-up meeting "welcomed" and/or "took note of" the results of the specialized meetings, but there was a common understanding that the commitments entered into at such specialized meetings were not dependent upon the final approval of the subsequent follow-up meeting....

corresponding decisions of the Council and/or CSO ... when judging the binding force of CSCE commitments.

Although the political character of CSCE commitments and documents is still largely unaffected, a certain trend towards a "legalization" of the CSCE process may be detected in the recent period. This is reflected in some far-reaching proposals to give the CSCE process a treaty basis or to "legalize" CSCE commitments. In 1990 and 1991 such proposals were put forward ... by [among others] the ... French President, François Mitterand, and the ... Czechoslovak President, Vacláv Hável. This would result in a transformation of the CSCE into a "traditional" international organization, based on a constituent treaty, and on the commencing of negotiations on the text of conventions which would contain CSCE commitments in legal terms. The proposals have so far been refuted. However, certain important developments in this respect have to be noticed. The fact that in the framework of the CSCE two treaties on disarmament and security issues have been negotiated—the Treaty on Conventional Armed Forces in Europe (CFE Treaty) in 1990[m] and the Open Skies Treaty in 1992[n]—is of little relevance in these respects, as the link between these negotiation processes and the CSCE was rather weak and clearly *sui generis*.... [I]mportant, however, is the fact the CSCE Council in Stockholm in December 1992 adopted the text of a Convention on Conciliation and Arbitration within the CSCE, and declared it open for signature by interested participating States.[o] In the spring of 1993 the Convention was signed by more than half of the CSCE States. This is the first CSCE convention in the proper sense of the word. This constitutes an important element, as for the first time in CSCE history a CSCE document has been adopted to which not all CSCE States are bound. This forms an important deviation to the (so far) fundamental principle of the "universalism" of CSCE commitments, which means that to date all CSCE commitments are fully applicable to all CSCE States.[16] This was also why a number of CSCE States refused to join the convention (such as the USA, the United Kingdom, Turkey and the Netherlands).

Another significant development is the fact that a CSCE group of experts has been established "to consider the relevance of an agreement granting an internationally recognized status to the CSCE Secretariat, the Conflict Prevention Center and the ODIHR [Office for Democratic Institutions and Human Rights]." This activity should lead to an agreement which would grant a certain legal capacity to the permanent administrative bodies of the CSCE which so far lack any formal legal status. A convention on the international legal status of the CSCE as a whole is not envisaged....

14. Budapest Summit Declaration and Decisions, 6 Dec 1994, *reprinted in* 34 I.L.M. 764 (1995) & 1 Weston & Carlson I.D.18: ¶ ¶ 1–22 ("Towards a Genuine Partnership in a New Era") and §§ I ("Strengthening the CSCE") and VIII ("Human Dimension") (Basic Document 3.45).

m. *Supra* note **k.**

n. S. Treaty Doc No 102–37, 102d Cong., 2d Sess (1992), *reprinted in* 2 Weston & Carlson II.D.17.

o. *Supra* note **j.**

16. The only exception [sic] to this principle are a number of confidence-and security-building measures (CSBMs) in the security area.

15.   Miriam Sapiro, "Changing the CSCE into the OSCE: Legal Aspects of a Political Transformation," 89 A.J.I.L. 631, 631–32, 636–37 (1995).

On January 1, 1995 [as a result of decisions taken at the CSCE's December 1994 Summit Meeting in Budapest, in December 1994], the Conference on Security and Co-operation in Europe (CSCE) became the Organization on Security and Co-operation in Europe (OSCE). Changing the name of the institution was the latest in a series of steps to transform the CSCE from a loosely structured conference of states into a more organized, effective political entity. It is natural to wonder whether the change in name signifies a change in legal status, since the term "organization" is typically ascribed to entities endowed with international juridical personality. In the case of the OSCE, however, the documents adopted by the leaders of the states participating in the CSCE Summit in Budapest on December 5–6, 1994, demonstrate that they did not intend to change the legal status of the entity or its institutions, much less to conclude an agreement to create an international legal personality. * * * The name was changed to reflect the determination "to give a new political impetus to the CSCE, thus enabling it to play a cardinal role in meeting the challenges of the twenty-first century."[17] * * * While there was little doubt before the Budapest Summit that the CSCE's existence was no longer a temporary phenomenon, the change in its name reflected both its evolution into a more established structure, and the expectation that it would play an even greater role in regional conflict prevention, crisis management and dispute settlement. From the legal perspective, novel arrangements were developed to address a specialized need for legal capacity and certain privileges and immunities without damaging the political flexibility or inclusive nature that are the hallmarks of the CSCE—now OSCE—process. . . .

E.   International Refugee Law

1.   Editors' Note. International refugee law is largely treaty-based. The central treaty obligations are contained in the 1951 Convention Relating to the Status of Refugees **(Basic Document 3.6)**, as extended by its 1967 Protocol Relating to the Status of Refugees **(Basic Document 3.16)** which consolidated earlier treaty obligations as well as codified customary norms. Most particularly, treaty parties must respect the obligation of *non-refoulement*, a French term used widely in refugee law and referring to a duty not to expel or return a refugee against her or his will to a territory where he or she fears persecution. The treaties establish basic minimum rules for the treatment of refugees and prohibit discrimination on the basis of race, religion, or country of origin. Article 1(A)(2) of the Convention confines refugee status to persons who are refugees "[a]s a result of events occurring before 1 January 1951," a phrase that is further restricted by the condition in Article 1(B)(1) that the events occurred in Europe or elsewhere. These limitations were removed in the 1967 Protocol. The Protocol is legally independent from the Convention and parties can accede to it without being a party to the Convention itself.

The protections set out in the treaties are available only to those who meet their definition of a refugee, one that reflects the era of the Convention

---

17. Budapest Summit Declaration [**Basic Document 3.45**], ¶ 3.

and does not respond to the problem of mass influx of refugees that character-izes the early 21st Century. To secure the protection of the Convention and Protocol refugees must meet the following four conditions: (1) they are outside their country of origin; (2) they are unable or unwilling to avail themselves of the protection of that country; (3) such inability or unwilling-ness is attributable to a well-founded fear of being persecuted; and (4) the persecution feared is based on reasons of race, religion, nationality, member-ship of a particular social group, or political opinion. However, neither the 1951 Convention nor its 1967 Protocol guarantees a refugee's or asylum seeker's right to be admitted to a country or her or his right to asylum. Indeed, these instruments are remarkable for the extent to which asylum—in the sense of admission and protection—is disregarded. The only generally applicable international instrument that acknowledges a right to seek and enjoy asylum from persecution is the Universal Declaration of Human Rights **(Basic Document 3.3)**, as set forth in its Article 14.

The Convention and Protocol are monitored by the Office of the United Nations High Commissioner for Refugees (UNHCR) established by the UN General Assembly in 1950, with operations commencing 1 January 1951. Parties to the refugee treaties undertake to cooperate with the UNHCR (*see* http://www.unhcr.ch). Based in Geneva and adopting the definition of "refu-gee" set out in the 1951 Convention, the UNHCR's mandate is to provide protection, emergency relief, and resettlement assistance to refugees, and to promote permanent and equitable solutions to refugee problems. To these ends, the UNHCR has developed five areas of action: (1) it provides an emergency response in times of major refugee influx; (2) it undertakes relief operations once an emergency stabilizes; (3) it supports local settlement efforts to help refugees become self-sufficient; (4) it assists with voluntary repatriation where possible and appropriate; and (5) it facilitates resettlement in third countries when refugees cannot return home. At present, over 17 million people worldwide fall within the mandate of the UNHCR. It also assists returnees (refugees who have returned home), internally displaced persons (people who have not crossed an international border but remain in their home countries), and, in special circumstances, victims of conflict. *See generally* United Nations High Commissioner for Refugees, The State of the World's Refugees: Fifty Years of Humanitarian Action (2000).

The UNHCR is funded almost entirely by voluntary contributions from states, with annual operations in 2003 approaching US$1 billion. It has offices in 120 countries and a staff of 5000 people representing over 100 different nationalities. As at this writing, the High Commissioner for Refugees is António Guterres, former Prime Minister of Portugal, who commenced in this position in 2005. He oversees all of the UNHCR operations and is a regular visitor to crisis areas, meeting with his staff, refugees, and local officials to gain firsthand knowledge of a given refugee situation and reports annually to the UN General Assembly through ECOSOC. The High Commissioner is advised by an Executive Committee (known as ExCom) consisting of 66 countries that meets regularly to review and approve the agency's programs and budgets and to advise on protection matters. ExCom also sets internation-al standards with respect to the treatment of refugees and provides a forum for exchanges among governments, UNHCR and its numerous partner agen-cies.

2. Convention Relating to the Status of Refugees. Concluded, 28 Jul 1951. Entered into force, 22 Apr 54. 189 U.N.T.S. 150, *reprinted in* **3 Weston & Carlson III.G.4: Arts. 1, 3, 32, 33, 38** (Basic Document 3.6).

3. Protocol Relating to the Status of Refugees. Concluded, 31 Jan 1967. Entered into force, 4 Oct 67. 606 U.N.T.S. 267, *reprinted in* **3 Weston & Carlson III.G.8: Arts. I, II, IV** (Basic Document 3.16).

4. James C. Hathaway and R. Alexander Neve, "Making International Refugee Law Relevant Again: A Proposal for Collectivized and Solution–Oriented Protection," 10 Harv. Hum. Rts. J. 115, 115–24, 126–29, 138–41, 143, 145, 155–56, 171–73, 211 (1997).

International refugee law is in crisis. Even as armed conflict and human rights abuse continue to force individuals and groups to flee their home countries, many governments are withdrawing from the legal duty to provide refugees with the protection they require. While governments proclaim a willingness to assist refugees as a matter of political discretion or humanitarian goodwill, they appear committed to a pattern of defensive strategies designed to avoid international legal responsibility toward involuntary migrants. Some see this shift away from a legal paradigm of refugee protection as a source for enhanced operational flexibility in the face of changed political circumstances. For refugees themselves, however, the increasingly marginal relevance of international refugee law has in practice signalled a shift to inferior or illusory protection. It has also imposed intolerable costs on many of the poorest countries, and has involved developed states in practices antithetical to their basic political values.

The argument that operational effectiveness will be enhanced by shifting away from reliance on legal principles reflects a serious misunderstanding of the function of international refugee law. The goal of refugee law, like that of public international law in general, is not enforceability in a strict sense. It is instead a mechanism by which governments agree to compromise their sovereign right to independent action in order to manage complexity, contain conflict, promote decency, or avoid catastrophe. International refugee law was established precisely because it was seen to afford states a politically and socially acceptable way to maximize border control in the face of inevitable involuntary migration. Refugee law has fallen out of favor because its mechanisms no longer achieve its fundamental purpose of balancing the rights of involuntary migrants and those of the states to which refugees flee.

Specifically, it is our view that the withdrawal of states from their legal responsibility to protect refugees stems primarily from two factors. First, governments increasingly believe that a concerted commitment to refugee protection is tantamount to an abdication of their migration control responsibilities. They see refugee protection as little more than an uncontrolled "back door" route to permanent immigration, in conflict with official efforts to tailor admissions on the basis of economic or other criteria. Second, neither the actual duty to admit refugees nor the real costs associated with their arrival are fairly apportioned among governments. There is a keen awareness that the states in which refugees arrive presently bear sole legal responsibility for what often amounts to indefinite protection.

In principle, refugee protection is not about immigration. It is intended to be a situation-specific human rights remedy: when the violence or other human rights abuse that induced refugee flight comes to an end, so does refugee status. Nor is this duty of limited duration logically assigned on the basis of accidents of geography or the relative ability of states to control their borders. Governments have regularly endorsed the importance of international solidarity and burden sharing, but collectivized efforts to date have been ad hoc and usually insufficient.

The challenge is to re-assert both the essence of refugee protection as a human rights remedy, and the logic of a shared commitment by governments to provide and fund that remedy. We can no longer insist on either the routine, permanent integration of all refugees, nor expect all governments, whatever their circumstances, simply to receive and provide quality protection to all refugees who arrive at their territory. The critical right of at-risk people to seek asylum will survive only if the mechanisms of international refugee protection can be reconceived to minimize conflict with the legitimate migration control objectives of states, and dependably and equitably to share responsibilities and burdens. In the analysis that follows, we argue for a shift to a solution-oriented temporary protection of refugees, conceived within a framework of common but differentiated responsibility among states.

* * *

I. The Need for Reform

Modern refugees increasingly encounter significant barriers erected to prevent them from reaching potential asylum states. Because particular states have legal obligations only toward refugees who are within the sphere of their formal or de facto jurisdiction, efforts to exclude refugees altogether are an effective means to avoid the duty to provide protection. Where the denial of entry is politically or logistically problematic, refugees who arrive in asylum states are often dealt with harshly and in violation of their human rights. Many states hope that refugees physically present will feel compelled to leave, or at least that would-be refugees will be diverted elsewhere. For those refugees able to enter and remain in an asylum state, the reality of protection is increasingly bleak. While fewer governments are prepared to link refugee status to a right of permanent residence, little thought is given to how to dovetail the modalities of temporary asylum with a serious commitment to solutions. The "warehousing" of refugees, long practiced by many states of the South, is therefore becoming a common feature of asylum in the North as well.

A. Refoulement

Even though international law presently requires no more than the provision of rights-regarding temporary protection, Northern states, in law or in practice, have historically afforded refugees permanent status. As the interest-convergence between refugees and developed countries has disappeared, Northern states have sought to avoid the arrival of refugees by adopting policies of external deterrence. Because developed states have the logistical capacity to prevent the arrival of many, and sometimes most, refugees, they have been able to implement *non-entrée* practices that prevent refugees from even reaching their frontiers. Since legal duties arise only once refugees successfully access a state's jurisdiction, *non-entrée* practices are a relatively invisible, and hence politically expedient, means to ensure that refugees are never in a position to assert their legal right to protection.

Specifically, most Northern states impose a visa requirement on the nationals of refugee-producing states, and penalize airlines and other transportation companies for bringing unauthorized refugees into their territories. By refusing to grant visas for the purpose of making a claim to asylum, Northern countries have been able to insulate themselves from many potential claimants of refugee status. The United Nations High Commissioner for Refugees (UNHCR) has expressed concern that visas are a serious obstacle to the admission to protection of refugees, and may in some instances put refugees at serious risk of *refoulement*[18] that is, of return to the country in which they assert they will be at risk of grave harm.

Multilateral burden-shifting arrangements and bilateral readmission treaties have also proved popular with Northern states. These arrangements deny entry to asylum-seekers who have not arrived by direct transportation, and authorize their summary removal to so-called "safe third countries" to pursue their claims. In Europe, refugees are thus removed from Northern and Western Europe to the transit states of Southern, Central, and Eastern Europe. The governments of Canada and the United States have similarly explored the possibility of an arrangement with Mexico that would authorize the return to that country of Central and South American asylum-seekers. These procedures are premised neither on substantive nor procedural harmonization of refugee determination at a level that ensures meaningful protection. Because the largely uncoordinated system of international refugee protection is incapable of delivering consistent results from state to state, burden-shifting arrangements can deprive persons who are genuine refugees of internationally guaranteed rights, including the right to protection against *refoulement*.

Even when refugees are able to navigate the course of visas, interdiction, and burden-shifting arrangements, they often remain at risk of *refoulement*. Developed states that wish to avoid receiving refugees adopt restrictive interpretations of the Convention refugee definition as a means of influencing refugees' choice of a destination state. The result is a downward spiral of protection toward the lowest common denominator, and a failure to recognize the claims of persons who are entitled to international protection. For example, the states of the European Union have recently adopted a common policy in which they refuse to recognize the refugee status of persons threatened by non-state actors unless the risk "is individual in nature and is encouraged or permitted by the authorities."[19] Only Sweden has formally opposed this reversal of the usual understanding that seriously at-risk persons are also refugees where the authorities are not complicitous in the harm, but nonetheless prove unable to offer effective protection.[20]

18. UNHCR, The State of the World's Refugees: In Search of Solutions 19 (1995), at 200–01.

19. Council of the European Union, Joint position defined by the Council on the basis of Article K.3 of the Treaty on European Union on the harmonized application of the definition of the term "refugee" in Article 1 of the Gene-

va Convention of 28 July 1951 relating to the status of refugees, 1996 O.J. (L 63).

20. *Id.* at Annex II. Denmark initially entered the same reservation as Sweden, but withdrew its objections. In contrast to the European Union position, the Office of the United Nations High Commissioner for Refugees affirms that "where serious discriminatory or

More dramatically, Northern states are beginning to adopt summary exclusion procedures and to interdict refugees at frontiers and in international waters. France, for example, detains asylum-seekers in artificially designated "international zones" of its airports, in which it has claimed to be free from the constraints of either domestic or international law. The interdiction at sea of Haitian refugees by the United States is another example. The US Coast Guard forced asylum-seekers onto its vessels, destroyed their boats, and returned them to Haiti where many suffered further human rights abuse. The US Supreme Court condoned this policy.[21] In addition, recent legislation adopted in the United States allows for the quick turnaround of refugees at border points. Refugees who rely on false documentation to avoid visa controls will now be subject to a summary removal process after no more than a rudimentary examination of their need for protection.[22] European governments have similarly approved expedited exclusion procedures for a wide-ranging category of asylum-seekers, including those whose claims are deemed (without a hearing on the merits) "inconsistent, contradictory or fundamentally improbable."[23] Because both the American and European procedures authorize the removal of asylum-seekers whose claims to refugee status have not been seriously considered, they raise the specter of *refoulement*.

It is also *refoulement* to require refugees to repatriate while a risk of persecution persists in their country of origin. In January 1996, Germany announced a two-stage plan for repatriation of Bosnian refugees, to begin on June 30, 1996, but then appropriately suspended the plan out of concern that conditions were still unsafe. Soon after the recent Bosnian elections, however, German authorities announced that repatriation efforts would proceed.[24] This time, the government ... minimized the significance of human rights concerns, turning a blind eye to widespread evidence of election fraud. Indeed, the fact that officials ... said they [would] not send refugees back to "areas now governed by hostile ethnic groups"[25] suggests that the situation in Bosnia [was] too unstable to warrant sending refugees back at all. The NATO-led peace force ... reported dozens of homes destroyed by fires or explosions, and observed that "using mines to blow up houses that refugees might fix up and move into is clearly designed to keep fear alive and intimidate refugees who

other offensive acts are committed by the local populace, they can be considered as persecution if they are knowingly tolerated by the authorities, or if the authorities refuse, *or prove unable*, to offer effective protection." UNHCR, Handbook on Procedures and Criteria for Determining Refugee Status 65 (1979) [hereinafter "UNHCR Handbook"] (emphasis added).

21. *See* Sale v. Haitian Centers Council, Inc., 509 U.S. 155 (1993)....

22. *See* Illegal Immigration Reform and Immigrant Responsibility Act of 1996, Pub. L. No. 104–208, 110 Stat. 3009 (1996).

23. Ministers of the Member States of the European Communities Responsible for Immigration, Resolution on manifestly unfounded applications for asylum (Nov. 30–Dec. 1, 1992), *reprinted in* European Consultation on Refugees and Exiles, Safe Countries, Myths and Realities, App. C (1995).

24. German authorities originally intended to begin repatriating Bosnians after March 31, 1996. At a January 26, 1996 meeting that date was delayed until June 30, 1996. US Committee for Refugees, World Refugee Survey 150 (1996). This deadline was again extended, but the intention to begin repatriations was reaffirmed, following a meeting of 16 German state interior ministers on September 19, 1996. A government spokesman indicated that "those who resist voluntary repatriation will face deportation." *Germany to Begin Returning Bosnians*, Refugee Rep., Sept. 30, 1996, at 13.

25. A. Cowell, *Germans Plan to Return Refugees to Bosnia*, N.Y. Times, Sept. 20, 1996, at A14; J. Borger, *Massive vote-rigging taints Bosnia election*, Manchester Guardian Wkly., Sept. 29, 1996, at 1.

might have wished to return to their homes."[26] There is even evidence of official hostility to the return of refugees, formal commitments notwithstanding. The forced return of refugees to such circumstances amounts to *refoulement.*

Southern states have historically demonstrated relatively scrupulous regard for the principle of *non-refoulement,* even under very difficult circumstances. A case in point was the admission to India of ten million refugees from Bangladesh (then East Pakistan) between March and December 1971. Most of the refugees were Bengali Hindus, many of whom had family or other connections in India. The massive numbers notwithstanding, "there was no question of turning any refugee back."[27] Increasingly, however, Southern states have taken decisive, and often unlawful, action to avert responsibility toward refugees. While usually lacking the resources and sophisticated border control systems to implement *non-entrée* policies, governments in the less developed world have engaged in several more direct forms of *refoulement.*

Most notoriously, Southern governments have sometimes forced refugees away from their territory by physical deterrence or the closure of borders. Between 1975 and 1980, for example, one million Indochinese refugees fled Vietnam, Cambodia, and Laos. Countries in the region were unwilling to admit them, even on a temporary basis. Concerned that there would be little effective international assistance, governments were convinced that temporary admission would lead to long-term responsibility for the refugees. These countries of first asylum only agreed to allow refugees to be admitted to temporary protection once they had received formal commitments from countries outside the region to accept the refugees for resettlement.

* * *

B. Denials of Refugee Rights

While Southern states have traditionally been less likely than Northern governments to block access to asylum altogether, refugee life in much of the less developed world is marked by insecurity and the inability to meet even basic needs. In part, this occurs because refugees are being protected in states in which citizens themselves suffer from a severe lack of economic resources.

* * *

Perhaps the most common denial of refugee rights in the South is the forced confinement of refugees. Mozambican refugees in South Africa were granted temporary resident status only in two South African homelands, and any Mozambican residing elsewhere in South Africa was considered an illegal alien subject to deportation. The majority of Vietnamese refugees in Thailand have been held in an isolated and overcrowded detention center in the northeast of the country, where there are concerns about inadequate water

26. *Dozens of Bosnian Homes Are Set Ablaze,* N.Y. Times, Oct. 26, 1996, at A7. . . .

27. B. Chimni, *The Legal Condition of Refugees in India,* 7 J. Refugee Stud. 378, 381 (1994). In emphasizing the temporary nature of the refuge India would provide, the government referred to the refugees as "evacuees," and housed them in short-term "transit relief camps." The refugees quickly returned home after the liberation of Bangladesh. The officially assisted repatriation movement of the refugees began on January 1, 1972 and was completed an extraordinary two and one-half months later. G. Coles, Temporary Refuge and the Large Scale Influx of Refugees 5 (submitted to UNHCR Expert Meeting, July 17, 1981).

and sanitation, an arbitrary code of justice, and physical abuse. Countries of first asylum routinely restrict Indochinese asylum-seekers to closed camps, which have been described as being "run in the same spirit and according to many of the same rules as the prisons[,] ... surrounded by tall fences and patrolled by guards."[28]

Relocation efforts have also been the source of rights violations, even when the efforts were undertaken to ensure greater safety for the refugees. In the early 1970s, the Sudanese government, with the cooperation of UNHCR, forcibly relocated Eritrean refugees from border camps to new, permanent settlements away from the frontier. The refugees, who were not consulted, resisted the move, primarily because they considered it incompatible with their desire to repatriate. In 1984, Mexico transferred Guatemalan refugees from self-settled camps near the border to interior locations in order to avoid attacks on the refugees by the Guatemalan military. To achieve this goal, Mexican authorities resorted to flagrant human rights violations, including burning settlements, cutting off food supplies, and forcibly evicting refugees.

In extreme cases, patterns of rights violation may be tantamount to *refoulement*.

Patterns of human rights violations against refugees have also been reported in Northern countries, particularly in states of the former Soviet bloc. In most cases, though, Northern governments have respected the human rights of refugees who manage to enter their territories, no doubt prompted by legal cultures receptive to holding states formally accountable to their treaty obligations. But when a significant number of Bosnian asylum-seekers successfully evaded European *non-entrée* policies, special legal regimes were devised coupling relaxed eligibility requirements with rights sometimes set below international legal standards. Under the guise of affording refugees from former Yugoslavia (legitimate) temporary protection, these schemes often suspended the usual procedures for processing refugee claims and required members of the designated groups to accept the lesser status and lesser rights provided for in the special legislation.

While European governments have the authority to enact supplementary protection regimes, they cannot rely on the existence of such programs to deny Convention rights to those entitled to Convention refugee status under international law. Yet, European countries have sometimes placed restrictions on the freedom of movement of temporarily protected refugees. In Germany, persons with a temporary residence authorization may not leave the lander or part of the lander that issued the authorization. In other countries, such as Norway, entitlement to social assistance and housing benefits may be expressly tied to residence in a certain municipality or reception center. More generally, temporary refugee protection is frequently coupled with policies that make it difficult for refugees to support themselves and their families.

* * *

28. Lawyers' Committee for Human Rights, Inhumane Detention: The Treatment of Vietnamese Boat People in Hong Kong 2 (1989). *See also* US Committee for Refugees, World Refugee Survey 81 (1993); US Committee for Refugees, World Refugee Survey 84 (1995).

1.   The Absence of a Meaningful Solution Orientation

Particularly in the North, resistance to honoring duties owed to refugees follows from a growing resistance on the part of governments to externally imposed changes to the composition of their societies. Because there is no longer a pervasive interest-convergence between refugees and asylum states, the legal right of refugees to trump immigration control rules means that persons not of a state's choosing will effectively be entitled to join its community. In states having a tradition of equating refugee status with the right to remain permanently in the asylum state, there is a fear that the arrival of refugees may, if sufficiently widespread, lead to social changes not desired by the host society. Even in those Northern states that have a long tradition of receiving immigrants, there is concern about the non-selective nature of the duty to admit refugees.

Concern about the impact of refugee arrivals on the make-up of an asylum state's community is not limited to Northern states. Vitit Muntarbhorn has argued that many states of East Asia, including Brunei, China, Japan, and Malaysia, are preoccupied with avoiding the arrival of refugees of distinct cultural or ethnic backgrounds.[29] As the bonds created by common opposition to colonialism and apartheid fade, some African governments are now affording truly dignified protection only to those refugees who are most similar to the citizens of the asylum state.

Where the community or its officials resist externally determined social transformation, efforts to control the arrival of refugees, harsh or otherwise, are the predictable result. One response is to condemn governments for their prejudice, or at least for pandering to the uninformed nativism of parts of their citizenry. Nativism, and even racism, have undoubtedly shaped the refugee policies of many governments. The growing influence of ethnic nationalism in many states, leading to a desire for segregation from "outsiders," clearly intensifies the problem. It is important to promote a breaking down of irrational fears of foreigners and, in particular, a credible understanding of the democratic limits to communal closure.

However, it is presently politically unwise to insist that states permanently enfranchise all refugees. Such a stance holds refugees hostage to a major project of social transformation. We need instead to accommodate the need of refugees to flee with the prevalence of often narrow understandings of community inspired by the rise of ethnic nationalism and the demise of the Cold War interest-convergence. This accommodation will clearly not amount to a complete recognition of the right of the present inhabitants of states to exclude all outsiders. Yet the terms upon which refugees enter a foreign state could be qualified to prevent refugees from becoming pawns in the internal struggles of asylum states over the meaning of community. In particular, a solid and dependable system of refugee protection need not have any enduring impact on the receiving state's communal self-definition. It could instead be oriented to ensuring that, at least in most cases, refugees ultimately repatriate to their own country when conditions permit.

This endorsement of temporary protection follows logically from the fact that refugees are exempted from the usual rules of immigration control solely

---

29. V. Muntarbhorn, The Status of Refugees in Asia 16–17, 68, 98, 116, 143 (1992).

on the basis of what amounts to a claim of necessity.[30] While they should be received with full respect for their human dignity and attention to the disabilities inflicted upon them by involuntary migration, there is no principled reason to insist that they be routinely admitted to permanent residence. We believe that it makes sense to define the duration of stay for refugees as a function of the risk that gives rise to the duty to admit them.

In referring to this approach as solution-oriented temporary protection, we do not mean to suggest that it should aspire to the generation of solutions. Refugee status ends only when the violence or other human rights abuse that induced flight is eradicated, matters clearly beyond the province of the refugee protection system itself. To the extent that the international community has begun to intervene against the phenomena that force refugees from their homes, the only true solution to the plight of refugees is at last being promoted. The refugee protection system, in contrast, is a palliative regime that protects desperate people until a fundamental change of circumstances allows them to go home safely.

Therefore, our reference to solution-oriented protection means that, while not a source of solutions, refugee protection should be implemented in a way that takes full advantage of opportunities for solutions. To counter the perception of refugee protection as an unwanted and externally imposed immigration system, repatriation must be made viable.... Repatriation will often be unsuccessful when family and collective social structures of refugees have not been preserved during the period of protection abroad, when refugees are denied opportunities to develop their skills and personalities in the asylum state, or when the place of origin sees the return of refugees as a threat or burden. In such circumstances, repatriation efforts may lead only to poverty, violence, and even further flight. On the other hand, temporary protection can be structured in a way that recognizes and protects core human rights, encourages self-reliance, and preserves the social, political, and cultural identity of the refugee community. If return is made practicable by an empowering system of repatriation aid and development assistance, the solution-oriented protection system we propose has the potential to renew asylum capacity regularly. As a reasonable and principled compromise between the needs of refugees and the migration control objectives of host governments, temporary protection will encourage states to live up to their international protection responsibilities, rather than avoid them.

This is because the repatriation of most, if not all, refugees sends a clear signal that the system is not just a "back door" route to permanent immigration. As it becomes understood that refugees are received on an extraordinary basis, and that their presence does not require any fundamental adjustment to the host community's self-definition, the implied threat presently associated with the arrival of refugees can be defused. The failure to promote repatriation, on the other hand, is inconsistent with the logic of refugee status as a situation-specific trump on immigration control rules. Because refugees are admitted on the basis of necessity, it cannot legitimately be asserted that

30. Walzer suggests that refugees have a special entitlement to be taken into a national community. This is because their claims "cannot be met by yielding territory or exporting wealth; they can be met only by taking people in ... [because their] need is for membership itself, a non-exportable good." M. Walzer, Spheres of Justice 48–49 (1983).

they should routinely be entitled to stay in the host state once the harm in their own country has been brought to an end.

2.   The Problem of Individuated State Responsibility

Even if the mechanisms of refugee protection are re-tooled to minimize conflict with migration control objectives, states may still seek to avoid their responsibilities because of the problem of individuated state responsibility. Under the present protection system, the government of the asylum state is solely responsible for delivering and funding the protection of all refugees who arrive at its jurisdiction. A shift to solution-oriented temporary protection would not alter that fact.

* * *

The answer we propose is to shift away from particularized duties and toward substantially greater collectivized protection efforts. The current system of unilateral, undifferentiated obligations is unfair and ultimately unsustainable. Building on previous examples of interstate cooperation in refugee protection and other fields, we therefore propose a new model of systematic and ongoing sharing within associations of states that we term "interest-convergence groups."

* * *

Under a regime of common responsibility, all members of the interest-convergence group agree in advance to contribute to protect refugees who arrive at the territory of any state member of the group. States will cooperate in a manner akin to participation in an insurance scheme. It must be stressed that we are not suggesting that states insure themselves against refugees, but rather that they minimize their particularized risks by joining with others to make protection feasible throughout the territories of all interest-convergence group member states. The notion of differentiated responsibility recognizes that it is unrealistic to expect all states to make an identical contribution both to receiving refugees and to financing the costs of the protection regime. We advocate allocational principles that take account of real differences in the relative abilities and circumstances of states and seek to maximize the overall commitment to protection by drawing on the comparative strengths of each member government. Each participating state would contribute by providing temporary protection, receiving refugees whose special needs make temporary protection inappropriate, resettling those refugees who cannot return home at the end of the period of temporary protection, funding the protection system, or through a combination of these roles.

* * *

II.   Can Reform Occur within the Prevailing Legal Framework?

For the reasons discussed in Part I, the moment is right to promote a new paradigm of refugee protection that is both human rights-based and pragmatic. Governments, however, exhibit little enthusiasm for engaging in the kind of major negotiations needed to establish a new international refugee convention. Moreover, members of official and nongovernmental communities alike have expressed concern that a decision to abandon the present Refugee Convention when most states appear focused on the promotion of narrowly defined self-interests may result in a serious diminution in the quality of protection formally guaranteed to refugees by international law. Sensitive to these concerns, we therefore [argue] that the kinds of reform we propose can be undertaken without amending the formal legal obligations owed to refugees.

* * *

III.   Reconceiving the Mechanisms of Refugee Protection

The present international legal framework will support a shift to the implementation of refugee law through a system of rights-regarding temporary protection. In a more fundamental sense, though, the Refugee Convention suffers from what Gervase Coles has accurately termed an "exile bias."[31] That is, while it links the duration of refugee status to the continuation of risk in the refugee's home state, it says nothing about how best to make repatriation a viable form of solution. This lapse reflects the Cold War-era pessimism that refugees would never return home. The prerogative of governments to withdraw protection when durable safety is restored in the country of origin is codified, but states are left largely to their own devices to decide how to *implement* termination of status. General human rights standards, such as the duty to avoid cruel, inhuman, or degrading treatment,[32] clearly set a minimalist standard for the way in which repatriation should be effected. There is, however, no international legal duty to proactively make repatriation viable. Similarly, the Refugee Convention says nothing about how states might cooperate to make refugee protection a fairly apportioned and sustainable endeavor.

We therefore propose activist measures that build on the guarantees of the Refugee Convention to facilitate a workable reform of the mechanisms of international refugee law. Five principles should govern this transition.

First, governments will only make a continuing commitment to refugee protection if a reform proposal is firmly solution-oriented. Temporary protection must be an empowering experience for refugees and their communities, delivered in a way that is dedicated to preparing refugees for a successful return when and if conditions allow.

Second, some needs-based exceptions to the norm of temporary protection must be recognized. In particular, temporary protection ought not continue when there is a risk of psychosocial damage to the refugee population. Equally important, the overall duration of temporary protection should be subject to principled limits. The system must therefore have the capacity to offer residual solutions to those refugees whose special needs make temporary protection an inappropriate response, or who are ultimately unable to return home at the end of a reasonable period of temporary protection.

Third, the protection system should anticipate and facilitate viable repatriation. Whether voluntary or mandated, return to the country of origin in

31. G. Coles, *Approaching the Refugee Problem Today, in* Refugees and International Relations 373, 390 (G. Loescher & L. Monahan eds., 1989).

32. International Covenant on Civil and Political Rights **[Basic Document 3.14]**, art.

7 . . .; Convention against Torture and Other Cruel, Inhuman or Degrading Treatment or Punishment **[Basic Document 3.26]**, arts. 1, 2. . . .

conditions of safety and dignity is an important means to continually regenerate asylum capacity. The feasibility of repatriation is enhanced when a clear commitment is made from the outset to support the family and communal structures of refugee communities, to keep links between the refugee and stayee communities alive, and ultimately to support return by a meaningful system of repatriation aid and development assistance.

Fourth, sub-global interstate associations, organized on the basis of trade, security, and other common interests, are an effective forum within which to collectivize this commitment to a more solution-oriented system of refugee protection. Because governments are already accustomed to practical collaboration in such associations, they are a sensible site in which to promote efforts to implement concrete mechanisms of collectivized protection.

Fifth, the obligations assumed by cooperating states should be defined on the basis of a theory of common but differentiated responsibility. This approach takes account of the very real differences in the manner in which different countries can best contribute to the successful implementation of a collectivized refugee protection regime. It is a practical means to preserve a continuing shared commitment to refugee protection without persisting in the unrealistic assumption that all countries are able and willing to make identical contributions to the implementation of refugee law.

Taken together, we believe that these five "building blocks" suggest a holistic structure that will enable states to protect their legitimate interests in migration control and fiscal and other resource accountability without withdrawing from the legal duty to meaningfully protect refugees.

* * *

The approach to refugee protection outlined in this Article is intended to encourage a transition away from traditional ways of thinking about refugee flows and solutions. Consideration should be given to implementing refugee law on the basis of a duty to equitably share the responsibilities and burdens of refugee protection. Collectivized and solution-oriented temporary protection presents the best option to replenish at least a substantial part of the world's asylum capacity. While some refugees, perhaps even a substantial minority, will still require residual or special needs resettlement, temporary protection will help to keep the number of such cases manageable, thereby more effectively reconciling the protection needs of refugees to the migration control objectives of governments.

No approach to refugee protection, standing on its own, can eradicate the need for persons to flee the risk of serious harm. Our model of protecting refugees neither aspires to be, nor in any sense contradicts, a program of timely, meaningful, and apolitical action to bring an end to the causes of refugee flight. Our goal, and the goal of refugee protection as conceived in international law, is instead to ensure the availability of solid and rights-regarding protection to refugees until and unless it is safe for them to return. Protection, if carefully designed and delivered, is the critical complement to root causes intervention. Even as states give increasing attention to efforts intended to end the need to flee, we must not fail to renovate the means by which we protect those who cannot wait for our efforts to succeed. Solution-oriented temporary protection, conceived within a framework of common but differentiated responsibility toward refugees, offers the best hope of keeping the institution of asylum alive.

5. Deborah Anker, Joan Fitzpatrick and Andrew Shacknove, "Crisis and Cure: A Reply to Hathaway/Neve and Schuck," 11 Harv. Hum. Rts. J. 295, 295–306, 308–10 (1998).

Two recent articles, one by James C. Hathaway and his co-author R. Alexander Neve and the other by Peter H. Schuck,[33] propose a radical reconfiguration of the international refugee regime. Neither intends to jettison the basic legal standards established by the 1951 Convention relating to the Status of Refugees nor to draft a new legal instrument defining forced migrants' rights to international protection. Indeed, each claims as a major objective the greater assurance of respect for the norm of non-refoulement articulated in Article 33 of the 1951 Convention. These two articles each perceive a crisis in protection and prescribe a similar cure—a dramatic departure from the existing individualized system for assessing and granting claims for refugee protection and its replacement by a collective framework emphasizing temporary protection in the region of origin rather than asylum.

Hathaway and Neve, summarizing a six year process of research and consultation organized at York University, propose creating "interest convergence groups" of states whose members would allocate responsibility for the physical and financial burdens of protecting refugees. They offer the analogy of an insurance scheme, arguing that states will recognize their need to plan for the equitable sharing of burdens arising from the massive influx of forced migrants. Their "solution-oriented" temporary protection envisions physical domicile primarily within the region of origin, standards of treatment consistent with fundamental human rights and devised to facilitate repatriation (for example, preservation of existing social structures within refugee communities), encouragement of contact with the internally displaced and communities staying behind in the country of origin, and close collaboration between agencies involved in development assistance and those working for the reintegration of refugees. Resettlement or asylum would be limited to the relatively small number of residual cases for whom safe and dignified return to the country of origin is impossible.

Schuck's approach in many ways is similar, though he devotes less attention than Hathaway and Neve to durable solutions, concentrating instead on describing a new system for allocating the burdens of protecting and financially supporting migrants during their displacement. Schuck's innovation is the creation of a market in refugee quotas within groups of states, which would come together voluntarily out of a perception of the same type of "interest convergence" that Hathaway and Neve imagine. Quotas could be met by transferring financial resources primarily from developed states to developing states located in the region of origin, which in turn would provide physical protection to refugees.

* * *

33. J. Hathaway & R. Neve, *Making International Refugee Law Relevant Again: A Proposal for Collectivized and Solution–Oriented* *Protection*, 10 Harv. Hum. Rts. J. 115 (1997); P. Schuck, *Refugee Burden–Sharing: A Modest Proposal*, 22 Yale J. Int'l L. 243 (1997).

Four questions should be addressed respecting these proposals:

(1) Do the authors correctly characterize the current situation of refugee protection as a definable "crisis"?

(2) Are their proposed alternatives feasible and politically viable, and would their implementation promote protection?

(3) Are their proposed alternatives legally and morally sound?

(4) If these proposals are not advisable, what other steps are needed to insure that the protection needs of refugees are met?

I. IDENTIFYING THE "CRISIS"

Professor Hathaway is a leading analyst of refugee law, and we have long admired his original and incisive writings.

We do not, and believe no one can, seriously dispute that refugee protection is under assault in first-asylum states in the South and, most critically, in the developed states of the North. The clever dodges and flat breaches of the non-refoulement norm documented by these authors are both wearily familiar and intensely disturbing. Our criticism of these articles' description of the current situation has three aspects. First, we do not agree that a single, discrete crisis exists, amenable to one over-arching solution. Second, as Hathaway and Neve agree, the visible failure of many Northern states to implement their obligations under international refugee law in good faith is a major precipitating cause for the current situation. Yet, these articles tend to capitulate to the underlying loss of the North's political will to comply with refugee law. Third, we do not accept that individualized status determination procedures contribute to current protection failures, as Hathaway and Neve argue.

We believe that we face not a single crisis, but a series of weaknesses in the existing protection regime, some of which predate the end of the Cold War. The context in which refugee crises of various origins unfold is too complex and unpredictable for one over-arching structural cure. In our conclusion, we sketch a variety of ameliorative measures that we believe have potential to enhance refugee protection while posing fewer risks than these sweeping proposals. The responsibility of Northern states for many of the worst aspects of the current situation needs to be especially emphasized. The mass refoulements, border closures and pushbacks of seaborne asylum-seekers that have occurred in the developing world in recent years were strongly influenced by the example of Northern states successfully shirking their responsibilities to refugees. It is primarily the influential states of the North that have pressured the United Nations High Commissioner for Refugees (UNHCR) to redefine its mission as one of humanitarian assistance rather than legal protection. Northern failures stem from a lack of political will to comply in good faith with international legal obligations. The conclusion of Hathaway/Neve and Schuck that the current system of refugee protection cannot be salvaged is premised in part on their acceptance, certainly reluctant, that anti-immigrant forces will continue to drive refugee policy in key Northern states. While we do not suggest in any way that either Hathaway/Neve or Schuck share an anti-rights orientation, their proposals do not sufficiently challenge the continued dominance of those values in shaping refugee policy. We continue to hope that humane values will again prevail in

Northern states, and we believe that large segments of Northern publics are deeply sympathetic to forced migrants.

Hathaway and Neve explicitly identify "individuated state responsibility" under the 1951 Convention regime as a contributing cause of recent failures in protection. We accept their point that the current decentralized design (typical of multilateral international legal obligations) contributes to several factors that may aggravate the pattern of evasion. * * * However, we fear that in their effort to achieve the greater good for the greater number, Hathaway and Neve overemphasize the drawbacks of the current individuated system of protection and do not acknowledge its continued strengths. We believe there are many valid reasons why refugees seek protection in developed states, and it is important to underscore that those states have assumed binding legal obligations to protect refugees without regard to their nationality. The existing "individuated" system still saves lives and extends asylum to significant numbers of persons (as well as generating alternative protections); moral and legal constraints still prevent Northern democracies from renouncing the 1951 Convention and 1967 Protocol.

We find these proposals in an important respect overly state-focused. They exaggerate the dominance of states, assume that states are the sole actors in the system, that their motives largely will be self-interested, and that this reality explains many of the current failures of refugee protection. We question these assumptions in two respects: (1) international and nongovernmental organizations are increasingly important actors on the international scene, demonstrably so in the refugee realm; and (2) if states retain the high degree of sovereignty suggested by these articles, the solutions the authors propose simply cannot succeed.

Thus, while we acknowledge the accuracy of Hathaway/Neve's and Schuck's factual description of recent failures of protection, we dispute their causal analysis and their optimism that their proposals would resolve a definable crisis.

II. FEASIBILITY AND POLITICAL VIABILITY

Our pessimism concerning the viability of these proposals can be summarized as follows: (1) there is little empirical data to support a thesis that regionally based solutions constructed within existing "subregional" or newly constructed interest convergence groups will provide more protection for refugees than the existing system under which obligations are universal but protection is provided by individual states; (2) once refugees are contained in the South, the interests of the North will not be sufficiently implicated to produce the large cash transfer payments which these proposals anticipate and which are crucial to their success in enhancing refugee protection; (3) the savings, if any, from diminished refugee status determination procedures are highly unlikely to be diverted in whole or substantial part to support refugee communities in the regions of origin; (4) states will not agree to a binding prior commitment to grant first asylum to future refugee flows, and agreements among interest convergence groups will not guarantee that physical protection for refugees will actually be extended; and (5) increased population containment in the South may adversely affect stability and peace.

* * *

These articles' analogy to an insurance scheme raises the issue of resources and the need for wealthier states to participate in the interest
convergence groups. If states perceive that they are not very vulnerable over
the long term, that they can self-insure against occasional crises, or that they
will be assisted in any case without an advance commitment, then the capital
necessary to construct the system of burdensharing will not materialize.
Democratic states are especially poor at long-term financial planning and
their commitments may not be enduring. If the proposals succeed in confining
refugees within the poorer states of the South, the commitment of Northern
democratic states is likely to erode over time as refugee crises become more
remote. The costs of financing the system will compete against pressing and
more palpable demands for important domestic programs, such as health care
and education. In the United States context, for example, the division of
power between the executive and legislative branches, and the frequent
hostility of leaders of the latter branch to foreign assistance and recently even
to domestic social programs, will imperil commitments to support interest
convergence groups, except in unusual circumstances where partisan political
objectives are implicated.

* * *

One of the most serious flaws in a reformulation of refugee law [that]
emphasize[s] temporary protection is the fact that many refugee crises are
enduring. It is the exception rather than the rule that the causes of flight can
be resolved within the approximately five-year period that defines the outer
bounds of a temporary protection system meeting basic standards of humane
treatment. The flight of refugees from East Pakistan (Bangladesh) to India is
the rare exception to the rule of enduring refugee flows, such as those from
Chile, Afghanistan, Vietnam, El Salvador, Haiti, Eritrea, Sudan, Angola, and
so forth.

While Hathaway and Neve clearly are concerned with preserving and
enhancing the rights of refugees, we fear that respect for the human rights
and welfare standards in the 1951 Convention will be eroded rather than
strengthened under a system so focused on temporary protection in the poorer
states of the South. We also believe that there will be many more residual
populations requiring resettlement than Hathaway and Neve predict. Yet,
relief from the burden of providing enduring physical protection to refugees is
the primary inducement both proposals offer to the richer states of the North
to construct these ambitious new systems of protection.

While we agree that repatriation in safety and dignity can often be the
optimal solution to a refugee crisis, we fear that placing it at the center of the
protection system, as Hathaway and Neve have done, increases the risk that
refugees will be improperly refouled. We do agree that greater efforts should
be made to enhance the skills of refugees during their exile so as to facilitate
possibilities for successful repatriation and we accept that greater coordination between development and refugee assistance agencies could be productive. But we do not believe the costs of such enhancements should include the
dismantling, with limited exceptions, of the asylum systems of the North.

* * *

III.　Legal and Moral Soundness

A.　*Legal Concerns*

Both proposals emphasize temporary protection, primarily in lesser developed regions; a greater degree of control over the movement of refugees; and collective rather than individualized protection. The primary legal issue posed by these proposals is an enhanced risk of refoulement, as groups of refugees will be prematurely repatriated under conditions in which their safety and dignity cannot be insured. There is also a risk that, by emphasizing the temporary nature of physical asylum and conferring it through voluntary coalitions of states, the economic and social rights of refugees under the Convention and Protocol will be de-emphasized.

It is true that the Refugee Convention and Protocol under Article 31 provide some scope for returning refugees who do not arrive directly from countries of origin but transit "safe third countries," so such returns would not in principle offend the norm of refoulement. However, states designated as "safe third countries," for example the developing world and eastern Europe, have been empirically shown to be unsafe. By encouraging developed states to treat physical protection for refugees as an object for bargaining, these proposals may jeopardize the safety of asylum-seekers. We appreciate that Hathaway and Neve explicitly reject the view expressed by some Northern governments, that extension of temporary protection to asylum-seekers removes them from the realm of legal obligation. Yet it is precisely because such notions have received great currency in recent years that we fear that implementation of the Hathaway/Neve or Schuck proposals will lead to serious breaches of international norms. Actions resulting in foreseeable refoulement of refugees do violate international law. We fear that eliminating asylum adjudication systems in Northern states will accelerate rather than diminish the trend toward such violations.

B.　*Moral Concerns*

We also contest the arguments of Hathaway/Neve and Schuck that their proposals are morally preferable because of the failures of the current regime. Both articles frankly concede that their proposals, if implemented, would confine an even greater percentage (than the estimated current eighty percent) of refugees in the South, in minimal accommodations. Asylum-seekers arriving in the North would presumably be removed involuntarily to temporary protection sites within their regions of origin; many fewer would be granted asylum and permitted to build new lives in the societies of the North. The authors assume that the funds currently expended by Northern states on nonentree and asylum adjudication processes would be diverted, at least partly, to support refugee communities in their regions of origin. Hathaway/Neve anticipate that greater numbers of refugees consequently would have an opportunity to repatriate in conditions of safety and dignity, as more concerted international action would be taken to link repatriation to protection and development.

* * *

Under the present system for refugee protection, concrete obligations run directly from the asylum state to the refugee. At least in developed democracies, asylum claimants have access to legal procedures and defined rights to protection. While Northern states do sometimes breach their legal obligations to refugees, their actions are subject to challenge in their own independent courts and also, under some circumstances, before international tribunals.[34] The poorer states in the South provide refugee protection because many have accepted treaty obligations to do so, have a tradition of humanitarianism and generosity or wish to avoid the condemnation of the international community.

Under the Hathaway/Neve and Schuck proposals, asylum-seekers would largely be removed from the realm of law and consigned to the realm of political bargaining. While, under these proposals, refugees are intended to be the indirect beneficiaries of developed states' promises of financial support to lesser developed states providing physical protection, the strength and enforceability of those promises is questionable. Under their own models, the Hathaway/Neve and Schuck proposals will result in a diminished level of refugee protection unless all parts of the bargain are respected. If Northern states fail to honor their financial pledges, the predictable result is the repudiation of the reciprocal commitments by poorer states to provide refuge, triggering unsafe refoulement or resulting in poor conditions for asylum-seekers transferred to temporary protection zones. We fear that if Northern states fail to keep their financial promises, such breaches will be concealed from the public gaze and insulated from processes of legal redress. Proposing a program of "plausible deniability" for violators of international refugee law strikes us as, at best, a morally ambiguous undertaking.

Both proposals are frankly utilitarian. On this aspect, moral views will vary, depending on the philosophical orientation of the observer. We do not doubt the good intentions of the authors nor their hopes that greater numbers of forced migrants will derive enhanced protection from the most dire risks of displacement should these proposals be implemented. Still, we are concerned that, despite serious efforts to respond to early critics, neither proposal has avoided the "commodification" of refugees. By analogizing these proposals to an insurance scheme, the authors associate refugee flows with other forms of insurable risk, such as natural disaster. While we recognize the burdens mass influx can impose on asylum states, we find this characterization of forced human migration to be morally troubling. Schuck's proposal to create a market in refugee quotas pushes commodification even further, as he cordially seeks to justify on the grounds that his proposal is no more dehumanizing or arbitrary than the existing regime and potentially more efficient.[35]

The fundamental premise of the Refugee Convention, although drafted in the context of mass displacement after World War II, was a right to personal protection and the chance to rebuild a life of human dignity. The Hathaway/Neve and Schuck proposals shift to a group-based concept of protection. While an excessive focus upon an individualized concept of refugee status can be harmful, suppression of the individuality of forced migrants also has moral costs.

34. *See, e.g., Ahmed v. Austria* (European Court of Human Rights, 17 Dec 1996) *at* <http://www.dhcour.coe.fr/eng/AHMED.html> (holding deportation of Somali refugee, on basis of criminal conviction, invalid because his return to Somalia might expose him to torture, in violation of Article 3 of the European Convention for the Protection of Human Rights and Fundamental Freedoms).

35. *See* P. Schuck, *supra* note 33.

We do not believe that claims to protection by future groups of refugees should be subject to denial based on extension of protection to earlier groups, or, conversely, that earlier groups can be acceptably exposed to danger or designedly harsh conditions in order to provide relief to later victims. Although governments assert limits on their "absorptive capacity" for immigrants, including refugees, no quantifiable and morally valid indicators of such capacity exist. Assessments of the political aspects of absorptive capacity may give undue weight to the vociferous objections of small but organized political groups that do not reflect the general tolerance of the majority of citizens.

* * *

It is a tactical error, for those committed to enhanced refugee protection, to accept fatalistically recent, clear breaches of international legal obligations. We believe that the legal framework for refugee protection can be made to meet the needs of today's forced migrants, if the political will to respect these norms can be reinvigorated.

These studies are out of step, in important respects, with the development of international human rights law after World War II, which emphasizes individual rights under the rule of law. The proposals are also out of sync with modern trends in de-emphasizing the universal dimension of responsibility for refugee protection. They stress the role of states, whereas the international human rights regime recognizes and promotes the increased role of civil society and non-state actors in the legal and policy realms. We do not believe that Northern states should be allowed to strike a "Faustian bargain" under which they would jettison their systems for individually assessing refugee claims and eliminate asylum in order to substitute financial assistance to Southern states providing temporary protection. We do not believe that such an approach will actually cure the current defects of the system, nor that it will provide acceptable levels of protection to future forced migrants.

C. *Alternatives*

... Our aim is to build upon the current framework of international legal obligation, to preserve existing systems for determining refugee status and to reinforce the norm of non-refoulement. We concede that our proposals will not provide a simple and conclusive solution to today's refugee crises. We acknowledge that we take a more idealistic approach to the current state of affairs. Yet, we believe that they pose fewer risks to forced migrants; that they are more likely to pressure states, especially in the North, to comply with their international legal obligations to refugees; and that they give greater recognition to the dignity and individuality of refugees.

1.   The international community must recognize that the flight of refugees is a chronic problem which will persist and recur. Gross human rights violations and conflict will continue to impel population displacement until these root causes are adequately addressed in a manner that protects the fundamental rights of victims.

2.   Different refugee emergencies will call for different solutions and will implicate varying constellations of states and interests. While "interest convergence groups" of states may coalesce in the interests of solving a particular refugee emergency, such a voluntary framework is unlikely to emerge in all

situations or to serve as an adequate substitute for the existing system of obligation based on multilateral conventions and customary international law.

3. States must continually be pressed by academics, non-governmental organizations and other concerned parties to honor their commitments to the Refugee Convention and Protocol and to human rights instruments.

4. The refugee regime must coordinate more closely with human rights institutions to ameliorate the human rights violations that precipitate many refugee flows.

5. The independence, professionalism and institutional capacity of the UNHCR, UN and regional organs and national institutions must be enhanced so that sophisticated approaches can be taken to complex emergencies.

6. The UNHCR must be placed on a more secure and independent financial basis. The agency must renew its commitment to its legal protection mandate and alter its orientation toward accommodating the demands of powerful states.

7. Parties concerned with the situation of refugees should make greater use of established human rights techniques. Inter-governmental organizations and non-governmental organizations should send more frequent monitoring missions to assess the condition of refugees and the prospects for their safe return, and mobilize shame through the international media to expose gross breaches of the rights of refugees.

8. While group-based status determination procedures can advance refugee protection in cases of true emergency, when individual hearings are infeasible, such substitutes should not undercut the availability of access to asylum adjudication procedures.

F. THE RIGHT TO SELF-DETERMINATION AND MINORITY RIGHTS

1. **Editors' Note.** The right to self-determination and minority rights are addressed expressly in many of the instruments cited in preceding Sections A and D. *See especially, but not exclusively,* Principles IV, VII, and VIII of Sec. 1(a) of the 1975 Final Act of the Conference on Security and Co-operation in Europe (*supra* Reading D–2); Principles 4, 5, and 19 of the 1989 Concluding Document of the Vienna Meeting 1986 of Representatives of the Participating States of the Conference on Security and Co-operation in Europe (*supra* Reading D–5); Articles 5–8, 23, 24, 26, 30–37, and 40 of the 1990 Concluding Document of the Copenhagen Meeting of the Participating States of the Conference on the Human Dimension of the Conference on Security and Co-operation in Europe (*supra* Reading D–6); Articles 1, 55, 73, and 76(b) of the Charter of the United Nations (*supra* Reading A–3); Articles 1 and 27 of the 1948 Universal Declaration of Human Rights (*supra* Reading A–4); Articles 1 and 15 of the 1966 International Covenant on Economic, Social and Cultural Rights (*supra* Reading A–7); Articles 1 and 27 of the 1966 International Covenant on Civil and Political Rights (*supra* Reading A–8); and § I (Arts. 1, 2, 15, 17, & 19) and § II (Arts. 19–27) of the 1993 Vienna Declaration and Programme of Action (*supra* Reading A–13).

2. Human Rights Committee, General Comment 23, Article 27 (Fifth Session, 1994), Compilation of General Comments and General Recommendations Adopted by Human Rights Treaty Bodies, UN Doc. HR/GEN/1/Rev.1, at 38 (1994).

1.   Article 27 of the Covenant provides that, in those States in which ethnic, religious or linguistic minorities exist, persons belonging to these minorities shall not be denied the right, in community with the other members of their group, to enjoy their own culture, to profess and practise their own religion, or to use their own language. The Committee observes that this article establishes and recognizes a right which is conferred on individuals belonging to minority groups and which is distinct from, and additional to, all the other rights which, as individuals in common with everyone else, they are already entitled to enjoy under the Covenant.

2.   In some communications submitted to the Committee under the Optional Protocol, the right protected under article 27 has been confused with the right of peoples to self-determination proclaimed in article 1 of the Covenant. Further, in reports submitted by States parties under article 40 of the Covenant, the obligations placed upon States parties under article 27 have sometimes been confused with their duty under article 2.1 to ensure the enjoyment of the rights guaranteed under the Covenant without discrimination and also with equality before the law and equal protection of the law under article 26.

3.1.   The Covenant draws a distinction between the right to self-determination and the rights protected under article 27. The former is expressed to be a right belonging to peoples and is dealt with in a separate part (Part I) of the Covenant. Self-determination is not a right cognizable under the Optional Protocol. Article 27, on the other hand, relates to rights conferred on individuals as such and is included, like the articles relating to other personal rights conferred on individuals, in Part III of the Covenant and is cognizable under the Optional Protocol.

3.2.   The enjoyment of the rights to which article 27 relates does not prejudice the sovereignty and territorial integrity of a State party. At the same time, one or other aspect of the rights of individuals protected under that article—for example, to enjoy a particular culture—may consist in a way of life which is closely associated with territory and use of its resources. This may particularly be true of members of indigenous communities constituting a minority.

4.   The Covenant also distinguishes the rights protected under article 27 from the guarantees under articles 2.1 and 26. The entitlement, under article 2.1, to enjoy the rights under the Covenant without discrimination applies to all individuals within the territory or under the jurisdiction of the State whether or not those persons belong to a minority. In addition, there is a distinct right provided under article 26 for equality before the law, equal protection of the law, and non-discrimination in respect of rights granted and obligations imposed by the States. It governs the exercise of all rights, whether protected under the Covenant or not, which the State party confers by law on individuals within its territory or under its jurisdiction, irrespective of whether they belong to the minorities specified in article 27 or not. Some States parties who claim that they do not discriminate on grounds of ethnici-

ty, language or religion, wrongly contend, on that basis alone, that they have no minorities.

5.1.   The terms used in article 27 indicate that the persons designed to be protected are those who belong to a group and who share in common a culture, a religion and/or a language. Those terms also indicate that the individuals designed to be protected need not be citizens of the State party. In this regard, the obligations deriving from article 2.1 are also relevant, since a State party is required under that article to ensure that the rights protected under the Covenant are available to all individuals within its territory and subject to its jurisdiction, except rights which are expressly made to apply to citizens, for example, political rights under article 25. A State party may not, therefore, restrict the rights under article 27 to its citizens alone.

5.2.   Article 27 confers rights on persons belonging to minorities which "exist" in a State party. Given the nature and scope of the rights envisaged under that article, it is not relevant to determine the degree of permanence that the term "exist" connotes. Those rights simply are that individuals belonging to those minorities should not be denied the right, in community with members of their group, to enjoy their own culture, to practise their religion and speak their language. Just as they need not be nationals or citizens, they need not be permanent residents. Thus, migrant workers or even visitors in a State party constituting such minorities are entitled not to be denied the exercise of those rights. As any other individual in the territory of the State party, they would, also for this purpose, have the general rights, for example, to freedom of association, of assembly, and of expression. The existence of an ethnic, religious or linguistic minority in a given State party does not depend upon a decision by that State party but requires to be established by objective criteria.

5.3.   The right of individuals belonging to a linguistic minority to use their language among themselves, in private or in public, is distinct from other language rights protected under the Covenant. In particular, it should be distinguished from the general right to freedom of expression protected under article 19. The latter right is available to all persons, irrespective of whether they belong to minorities or not. Further, the right protected under article 27 should be distinguished from the particular right which article 14.3 (f) of the Covenant confers on accused persons to interpretation where they cannot understand or speak the language used in the courts. Article 14.3 (f) does not, in any other circumstances, confer on accused persons the right to use or speak the language of their choice in court proceedings.

6.1.   Although article 27 is expressed in negative terms, that article, nevertheless, does recognize the existence of a "right" and requires that it shall not be denied. Consequently, a State party is under an obligation to ensure that the existence and the exercise of this right are protected against their denial or violation. Positive measures of protection are, therefore, required not only against the acts of the State party itself, whether through its legislative, judicial or administrative authorities, but also against the acts of other persons within the State party.

6.2.   Although the rights protected under article 27 are individual rights, they depend in turn on the ability of the minority group to maintain its culture, language or religion. Accordingly, positive measures by States may also be necessary to protect the identity of a minority and the rights of its members to enjoy and develop their culture and language and to practise their religion, in community with the other members of the group. In this connection, it has to be observed that such positive measures must respect the provisions of articles 2.1 and 26 of the Covenant both as regards the treatment between different minorities and the treatment between the persons belonging to them and the remaining part of the population. However, as long as those measures are aimed at correcting conditions which prevent or impair the enjoyment of the rights guaranteed under article 27, they may constitute a legitimate differentiation under the Covenant, provided that they are based on reasonable and objective criteria.

7.   With regard to the exercise of the cultural rights protected under article 27, the Committee observes that culture manifests itself in many forms, including a particular way of life associated with the use of land resources, especially in the case of indigenous peoples. That right may include such traditional activities as fishing or hunting and the right to live in reserves protected by law. The enjoyment of those rights may require positive legal measures of protection and measures to ensure the effective participation of members of minority communities in decisions which affect them.

8.   The Committee observes that none of the rights protected under article 27 of the Covenant may be legitimately exercised in a manner or to an extent inconsistent with the other provisions of the Covenant.

9.   The Committee concludes that article 27 relates to rights whose protection imposes specific obligations on States parties. The protection of these rights is directed towards ensuring the survival and continued development of the cultural, religious and social identity of the minorities concerned, thus enriching the fabric of society as a whole. Accordingly, the Committee observes that these rights must be protected as such and should not be confused with other personal rights conferred on one and all under the Covenant. States parties, therefore, have an obligation to ensure that the exercise of these rights is fully protected and they should indicate in their reports the measures they have adopted to this end.

3.   United Nations General Assembly Declaration on the Granting of Independence to Colonial Countries and Peoples, 14 Dec 1960, GA Res. 1514, UN GAOR, 15th Sess, Supp. No. 16, at 66, UN Doc. A/4684 (1961), *reprinted in* **3 Weston & Carlson III.Q.2** (Basic Document 3.9).

4.   United Nations General Assembly Declaration on Principles of International Law Concerning Friendly Relations and Co-operation Among States in Accordance With the Charter of the United Nations, 24 Oct 1970, GA Res. 2625, UN GAOR, 25th Sess., Supp. No. 28, at 121, UN Doc. A/8028 (1971), *reprinted in* **9 I.L.M. 1292 (1970) & 1 Weston & Carlson I.D.7** (Basic Document 1.11).

5.   United Nations General Assembly Declaration of the Rights of Persons Belonging to National or Ethnic, Religious and Linguistic Minorities, 18 Dec 1992, GA Res. 47/135 (Annex), UN GAOR, 47th Sess., Supp. No. 49, at 210, UN Doc. A/RES/47/135 (1993), *reprinted in* **(3 Weston & Carlson III.I.5)** (Basic Document 3.39).

6. Council of Europe Framework Convention for the Protection of National Minorities. Concluded 1 Feb 95. Entered into force, 2 Jan 1998, E.T.S No. 157, *reprinted in* **3 Weston & Carlson III.I.7** (Basic Document 3.46).

7. Editors' Note. The political origins of the principle of self-determination can be traced to the American Declaration of Independence of 1776. During the nineteenth and early twentieth centuries it was interpreted by nationalist movements to mean that each nation had a right to form an independent state and, further, that only nationally homogenous states were legitimate. It further evolved at the close of World War I when US President Woodrow Wilson championed it in his so-called Fourteen Points, which served as the basis of the peace negotiations with the Central Powers. However, though reflected in a number of plebiscites held by the Allies in certain disputed areas and though a basic component of a series of treaties concluded by the League of Nations for the protection of linguistic and religious minorities (largely in the Balkans), its impact between World War I and World War II was minimal. For example, in the mandate system established by Article 22 of the Covenant of the League of Nations (pursuant to which the colonies and territories of defeated Germany and Turkey were placed under the tutelage of a victorious ally), it was actualized substantially with the interests of the occupying powers in mind.

Following World War II, however, the modern principle of self-determination began to come into its own. Presaged in the Atlantic Charter of 14 August 1941 (in which US President Roosevelt and British Prime Minister Winston Churchill declared, *inter alia*, "the right of all peoples to choose the form of government under which they will live" and their wish to see "sovereign rights and self-determination restored to those who have been forcibly deprived of them"), it took shape and was incorporated into Articles 1, 55, 73, and 76(b) of the United Nations Charter **(Basic Document 1.5)**. However, as Professor Daniel Thürer observes in *Self-Determination*, 8 Encycl. Pub. Int'l L. 470, 471 (1985), "it should not be assumed that the concept of self-determination [had] become a legally binding principle of conventional international law by the mere fact of its incorporation into the UN Charter." Thürer explains: "Although the provisions concerning non-self-governing and trust territories entail binding international obligations, the general principles of 'self-determination' and of 'equal rights' of peoples, which in the formula used by the Charter appear to be two component elements of the same concept, seem to be too vague and also too complex to entail specific rights and obligations." *Id.* at 471–72.

Accordingly, it took further initiatives to cause the principle of self-determination to acquire a genuinely legal status, among them the 1960 Declaration on the Granting of Independence to Colonial Countries and Peoples **(Basic Document 3.9),** adopted by the General Assembly without dissenting vote; the 1966 International Covenant on Economic, Social and Cultural Rights and the 1966 International Covenant on Civil and Political Rights **(Basic Documents 3.13 & 3.14)**, each proclaiming the human right of self-determination in their identically worded Article 1; and the 1970 Declaration on Principles of International Law Concerning Friendly Relations and Cooperation among States in accordance with the Charter of the United

Nations **(Basic Document 1.11)**, adopted by the General Assembly by consensus.

It is, in any event, a given today that the principle of self-determination is part of modern international law. At issue is the extent to which it operates as a legal right under international law, and how. It should be noted, however, that, apart from the law of decolonization as specified in the UN Charter, it does not seem to include, in Thürer's words, "a general right of groups to secede from the States of which they form a part. . . . State practice in general and particularly with regard to cases such as Tibet, Katanga, Biafra and Bangladesh do not lend support to the thesis." *Id.* at 474. Thürer adds: "On the contrary, it seems to be sound to agree with a whole body of General Assembly resolutions which assume that the fundamental principles underlying the present international order such as sovereignty, territorial integrity and political independence preclude the existence of such a right." *Id.*

8.   Michla Pomerance, "Self–Determination Today: The Metamorphosis of an Ideal," 19 Israel L. Rev. 310–15 (1984).

I.   Introduction

"Self-determination," the famous catchword of World War I, has become one of the most potent political slogans of our time. In its name battles continue to be waged, and no continent—and scarcely any country—is immune from its grip. . . . Within the UN, self-determination is viewed by the majority as a kind of "supernorm," a principle which has been lifted from the realm of politics and morality to the very pinnacle of legal rules. According to this perspective, even the linchpin of the UN Charter **[Basic Document 1.5]**, the principle prohibiting the threat or use of force in international relations (Art. 2, ¶ 4), may be overridden in the name of the more sacred "right of self-determination."

It is perhaps not surprising that discussions of self-determination in the media and the UN have been characterized by confusion, misunderstandings and oversimplification. But woolly thinking on the subject is also common in academic circles, where one might expect more rigorous analysis to prevail. At root, the misunderstandings derive from a common basic premise: that to invoke the right * * * is to give the solution to a problem. This premise, however, is fallacious. As Arnold Toynbee wrote in 1925, "self-determination is merely the statement of a problem and not the solution of it."[36]

* * *

II.   Self-Determination as a Problem

A.   Defining the "Self"

First and foremost, there is need to define the bearer of the right. Who is the "self" to whom self-determination attaches? Is it Biafra or Nigeria? Northern Ireland, Ireland, or the United Kingdom together with Northern Ireland? The present population of Taiwan (consisting mainly of Nationalist Chinese), the indigenous islanders, or Communist China? Gibraltar or Spain? . . . The Kurds, or, respectively, Iraq, Iran, the Soviet Union, and Turkey?

36.   A. Toynbee, *Self-Determination*, 484
The Quarterly Rev. 319 (1925).

Very early in the history of self-determination, the question of definition worried US Secretary of State Robert Lansing, who accompanied Wilson to Versailles in 1919. He expressed his doubts in his diary in these terms:

> When the President talks of "self-determination," what unit has he in mind? Does he mean a race, a territorial area, or a community? Without a definite unit which is practical, application of this principle is dangerous to peace and stability. . . . [37]

In fact, the problem of definition goes beyond the question which troubled Lansing—whether to adopt a territorial or an ethnographic criterion. It is far more complex. Selection of either criterion necessitates further decisions with respect to delimitation, exclusion and inclusion. What are the boundaries of the area? Who are its inhabitants? Who are the members of the "race" or the "community"? The territorial and ethnic criteria are *not* neatly separable; they are rather inextricably interwoven, and are bound up with yet a third factor, the factor of time. It is necessary to determine which population belongs to which area, an exercise which is particularly delicate where significant population movements, of recent or more ancient origin have occurred. Such movements complicate the ethnographic map and raise thorny questions regarding the identification and rights of "indigenous" and "settler" populations. The issue of the "critical date" or "critical period" inescapably enters the calculus. The definition of "self" is clearly not only space-bound and group-bound; it is also time-bound. In Lansing's own time the population in Alsace–Lorraine in 1919, following fifty years of German rule and colonization, was not considered a "self" whose wishes needed to be consulted. The historic rights of an earlier community were preferred over the desires of the existing inhabitants.

* * *

B. A Non–Universalizable Principle

Self-determination claims generally do not clash with non-self-determination or anti-self-determination claims but with some countervailing self-determination claims. This is probably the most basic dilemma in the matter of self-determination: recognition of the rights of one "self" almost always entails the denial of the rights of a competing "self." The problem may be formulated in three alternative ways:

a) The demand for secession or *separate self-determination* by one "self" clashes with the claim to territorial integrity or political independence put forward by the unit of which the first "self" is felt to be a part.

b) "Self-determination" by the smaller unit conflicts with the "self-determination" to which the larger unit claims to be entitled.

c) There is an opposition between two claims to territorial integrity that of the larger as against that of the smaller unit.

There may also be competing claims by different ethnic groups. . . .

Inherently, self-determination, in the sense of full independence and sovereignty, cannot be given to all peoples, unless the "self" is reduced to the individual "self" of the term's metaphysical origin. For the very act of

---

37. R. Lansing, *Self-Determination*, Saturday Evening Post, 9 Apr 21, p. 7.

fulfilling one claimant's right of self-determination will generally constitute the denial of the claim of another contender to the right.

C. Conflict With Other Principles of International Law and International Relations

Claims to self-determination often clash with other, at least equally hallowed, principles of international law and international relations. Apart from the principle, already mentioned, of territorial integrity, there are further principles—such as sovereign equality and the maintenance of international peace and security—which may conflict with the attempt to realize self-determination in specific instances. . . .

* * *

D. A One–Time Exercise or a Continuing Process?

What happens when new demands for secession arise? Is a limit to be set to the process of self-determination, or should the process be seen as continuing and open-ended? Did the South of the United States have the right to secede from the North, even as the thirteen colonies severed themselves from England? Could Biafra separate itself from Nigeria, Eritrea from Ethiopia? Are minorities within states—for example, Croats and Albanians in Yugoslavia and the diverse ethnic groups in Lebanon—to be granted separate self-determination? Since the right of self-determination, in the form of full independence, cannot, in practice or in theory, be granted to all claimants, may some other solutions—federal scheme, autonomy, minority rights, guarantees of non-discrimination—be viewed as alternative forms of self-determination? Can the right of option be seen as a way of permitting individuals to "vote with their feet," indicating thereby whether they feel a subjective need to align their political with their ethnic allegiance? Could it be said, then, that the only way to grant self-determination as a universal and continuing right to all people, is by recognizing self-determination as a continuum of rights, rather than as a one-time, all-or-nothing, exercise?

E. "External" Self–Determination, "Internal" Self–Determination and Democracy

In Wilsonian thought, "self-determination," the right of a people to determine its own fate, was clearly a composite concept involving, chiefly, the following three ideas: a) the right of a people to be free from alien rule and to choose the sovereignty under which it will live (an idea often referred to as "external" self-determination); b) the right of a people to select its own form of government ("internal" self-determination); and c) continuous consent of the governed in the form of representative democratic government.

How are these three components of self-determination to be linked? In the Wilsonian view, which remains the Western view today, self-determination is intimately bound with representative government. Unless there is continuous consent of the governed, the rule of the prevailing government will always be experienced as "alien." On the other hand, in the presence of true democracy, the question of who possesses sovereignty ("external" self-determination) is not really so important. (The second part of the proposition is, of course, more debatable, since it ignores the problem of permanent minorities, such as the Turks in Cyprus and the Catholics in Northern Ireland. Apart from democratic regimes, special minority arrangements may be warranted.) . . . .

9. S. James Anaya, "A Contemporary Definition of the International Norm of Self–Determination," 3 Transnat'l L. & Contemp. Probs. 131, 143–62 (1993).

. . . Given the prominence of decolonization in the international practice of self-determination, there has been a tendency to define self-determination by reference to the specific prescriptions developed in that context, which for most of the subject territories meant procedures resulting in independent statehood. * * * If, however, self-determination fundamentally entails a standard of governmental legitimacy that benefits all segments of humanity, a different interpretation of decolonization ensues: Decolonization procedures did not themselves embody the *substance* of the norm of self-determination; rather they were measures to *remedy* a sui generis deviation from the norm that existed in the prior condition of binding colonialism. Self-determination precepts define a standard in the governing institutional order, a standard with which colonialism was at odds and with which other institutions of government also may conflict.

The substantive content of the international norm of self-determination, therefore, inheres in the precepts by which the international community held colonialism illegitimate and which apply universally to human beings in regard to their governing institutions. The *substance* of the norm—the precepts that define a standard of governmental legitimacy—must be distinguished from the *remedial* prescriptions that may follow a violation of the norm, such as those developed to undo colonization.

A. Substantive Aspects

The substance of the international norm of self-determination by which the international community held colonialism illegitimate, and which applies more generally in regards to the political order, comprises two elements. First, in what I will call its *constitutive* aspect, self-determination enjoins the episodic procedures by which the governing institutional order comes about. Secondly, in what I will call its *ongoing* aspect, self-determination applies continuously to enjoin the form, content, and functioning of the governing order itself.

1. Constitutive Self–Determination

In self-determination's constitutive aspect, core values of freedom and equality translate into a requirement that individuals and groups be accorded meaningful participation, commensurate with their interests, in procedures leading to the creation of or change in the institutions of government under which they live. Constitutive self-determination does not itself dictate the outcome of such procedures; but where they occur it imposes requirements of participation such that the end result in the political order can be said to reflect the collective will of the people, or peoples, concerned. This aspect of self-determination corresponds with the provision common to the International Human Rights Covenants **[Basic Documents 3.13 & 3.14]** and other instruments which state that peoples "freely determine their political status" by virtue of the right of self-determination. It is not possible to identify with precision the bounds of international consensus concerning the required levels and means of individual or group participation in all contexts of institutional birth or change. Certain minimum standards, however, are evident. * * * Today, procedures toward the creation or territorial extension of governmental authority are regulated by self-determination precepts requiring [at least] minimum levels of participation on the part of all affected, as evident in the context of European integration. The steps of institution building within the umbrella of the European Community have been taken through processes of consultation involving government representatives who are presumed to be acting not simply on behalf of their state governments, but more fundamentally on behalf of the *people* of the countries they represent. . . .

Self-determination precepts also are apparent in constitutive procedures of disintegration. . . . As recent events tell . . ., political movements may well result in the breakup of states, and it is increasingly apparent that in such instances the international community expects the outcome to be minimally grounded in democratic procedures that can be said to reflect the aspirations of the people concerned. International recognition of states emerging from the dissolution of the former Soviet Union, Yugoslavia, and Czechoslovakia followed referenda or other expressions of popular support by the constituents of the nascent independent states. . . . The ensuing conflicts in the former Yugoslavia attest to the volatility of political dissolution and the need for the international community to moderate disintegrative procedures more aggressively and carefully, particularly those procedures which involve discrete groups with antagonistic interests.

* * *

2. *Ongoing Self–Determination*

Apart from its constitutive aspect, which applies at discrete episodes of institutional birth or change, self-determination applies continuously in what I have designated its *ongoing* aspect. Ongoing self-determination requires a governing institutional order under which individuals and groups are able to make meaningful choices in matters touching upon all spheres of life on a continuous basis. In the words of the self-determination provision common to the International Human Rights Covenants and other instruments, peoples are to "freely pursue their economic, social and cultural development." In this respect as well, the international community's condemnation of colonialism represents a minimum standard.

* * *

Two significant developments in dominant conceptions about the requirements of governmental legitimacy have emerged since the height of the decolonization movement, developments which have expanded the common denominator of global opinion that defines the normative content of self-determination particularly in its ongoing aspect. One is the dramatic decline of Marxism, accompanied by a worldwide movement toward an ever greater embrace of nonauthoritarian democratic institutions. Especially since the demise of the Soviet Union, this democratic movement is reflected in developments worldwide and has been promoted through the United Nations and other international institutions. Accordingly, there is a budding scholarly literature articulating emerging rights of "political participation" and "democratic governance" under international law.[38] Closely linked with modern precepts of democracy is the idea that, consistent with the values promoted by patterns of political integration, decisions should be made at the most local level possible. Thus, for example, an important part of the Russian Federation's reform movement is the devolution of authority to its constituent parts. And while Europe moves toward greater integration, the principle of "subsidiarity" has taken hold to guard against unnecessary centralization of power that might come at the expense of local units of governance....

A second major development is the ever greater embrace of notions of cultural pluralism [in contrast to the earlier ideal model] of the culturally homogenous independent nation-state. * * * Over the last several years the international community increasingly has come to value and promote the integrity of diverse cultures, including non-European cultures. This tendency is manifested *not* in a growing sentiment in favor of independent statehood for each of the world's cultural or ethnic groups, but rather in a discernible trend in the world's multiple systems of governance toward the accommodation of diverse cultural identities ..., promoted by the international community through its emboldened system of minority rights protections [as evidenced, for example, by the UN General Assembly's adoption in 1992 of its Declaration on the Rights of Persons Belonging to National or Ethnic, Religious, and Linguistic Minorities **[Basic Document 3.39]** and the burgeoning body of international norms to protect the integrity and survival of indigenous communities.[p]

Many have viewed the minority and indigenous rights regimes as existing apart from the concept of self-determination. This view, however, does not fully appreciate the relationship between cultural integrity precepts, which are central to the minority and indigenous rights regimes, and notions of freedom and equality implicit in the concept of self-determination. If the cultures of diverse groups are not valued, neither are their distinctive ways of life or interactive patterns which extend well into the social and political realms. Under such a perceptual gloss, freedom and equality may be considered satisfied by simple inclusion of the groups' individual members as participants in political systems based on traditional Western liberal conceptions of democracy (or, until recently, Marxist proletarianism). But once diverse cultural groupings are acknowledged and valued, their associational patterns and community aspirations become factors that must be reflected in the governing institutional order if self-determination notions are to prevail.

Accordingly, the contemporary global trend is toward securing for cultural groups and their members contextually appropriate accommodations in the governing order. A number of groups, particularly indigenous peoples, are pursuing spheres of autonomy over a range of policy and administrative matters, while at the same time enhancing their effective participation in all decisions affecting them left to the larger institutions of government. Although there is no one formula of structural accommodation in this global

38. *See, e.g.,* M. Halperin, et al., Self–Determination in the New World Order 420–24 (1992); G. Fox, *The Right to Political Participation in International Law,* 17 Yale J. Int'l L 539 (1992); T. Franck, *The Emerging Right to Democratic Governance,* 86 A.J.I.L. 46 (1992).

p. *See infra* Problem 7–6 ("A Rainforest and the Guahibo Are Threatened in Amazonia and Caribia") in Chapter 7, at 1226. *See also* S. J. Anaya, Indigenous Peoples in International Law, ch. 6 (1996).

trend—and indeed the very fact of the diversity of cultures and their surrounding circumstances belies a singular formula—the underlying and increasingly widespread premise is that of promoting the free development of
diverse cultures.

The norm of self-determination, therefore, promotes an ongoing condition
of freedom and equality among and within peoples in relation to the institutions of government under which they live, a condition today substantially
defined by precepts of democracy and cultural pluralism. * * * In its *constitutive* aspect, the norm entitles individuals and groups to meaningful participation in episodic procedures leading to the creation of or change in the
governing institutional order. In its *ongoing* aspect, self-determination requires that the governing institutional order itself be one in which individuals
and groups live and develop freely on a continuous basis.

B. Self–Determination Remedies

Where substantive elements of the norm of self-determination are violated, a remedy should be forthcoming. The prescriptions promoted through the
international system to undo colonization, while not themselves equal to the
norm of self-determination, were contextually specific *remedial* prescriptions
arising from colonialism's deviation from the generally applicable norm....

Significantly, the remedy for this infraction of self-determination did not
entail a reversion to the status quo prior to the historical patterns of
colonization but rather to the creation of an altogether new institutional
order viewed as appropriate to "implementing" self-determination.... In
most instances, independent statehood was the presumed or express preference.

To the extent the international community is generally concerned with
the promotion of self-determination precepts, and as it expands its common
understanding about those precepts, it may identify other contextual deviations from self-determination and promote appropriate remedies. With appropriate attentiveness to the particular character of deviant conditions or
events, and with an understanding of the interconnected character of virtually
all forms of modern human association, these remedies need not entail the
formation of new states. Secession, however, may be an appropriate remedy in
limited contexts (as opposed to a generally available "right") where substantive self-determination for a particular group cannot otherwise be ensured.
* * * [S]ince the atrocities and suffering of the two world wars, international
law does not much uphold sovereignty principles when they would serve as an
accomplice to the subjugation of human rights or act as a shield against
international concern that coalesces to promote human rights. The proliferation of a floor of human rights norms that are deemed applicable to all states
as to their own citizens and the decolonization remedy itself both demonstrate
the yielding of sovereignty principles to human rights imperatives in modern
international law. Ideally, then, sovereignty principles and human rights
precepts, including the norm of self-determination, work in tandem to promote a stable and peaceful world. Where there is a trampling of self-
determination, however, the presumption in favor of non-intervention, territorial integrity, or political unity of existing states may be offset to the extent
required by an appropriate self-determination remedy.

10. Committee on the Elimination of Racial Discrimination, General Comment 21, UN Doc. A/51/18, Annex VIII A, p. 125–26; HRI/GEN/1/Rev.3, at 113 (1996).

* * *

6. The Committee notes that ethnic or religious groups or minorities frequently refer to the right to self-determination as a basis for an alleged right to secession. In this connection the Committee wishes to express the following views.

7. The right to self-determination of peoples is a fundamental principle of international law. It is enshrined in article 1 of the Charter of the United Nations [**Basic Document 1.5**], in article 1 of the International Covenant on Economic, Social and Cultural Rights [**Basic Document 3.13**] and article 1 of the International Covenant on Civil and Political Rights [**Basic Document 3.14**], as well as in other international human rights instruments. The International Covenant on Civil and Political Rights provides for the rights of peoples to self-determination besides the right of ethnic, religious or linguistic minorities to enjoy their own culture, to profess and practise their own religion or to use their own language.

8. The Committee emphasizes that in accordance with the Declaration on Principles of International Law concerning Friendly Relations and Cooperation among States in accordance with the Charter of the United Nations, approved by the United Nations General Assembly in its resolution 2625 (XXV) of 24 October 1970 [**Basic Document 1.11**], it is the duty of States to promote the right to self-determination of peoples. But the implementation of the principle of self-determination requires every State to promote, through joint and separate action, universal respect for and observance of human rights and fundamental freedoms in accordance with the Charter of the United Nations. In this context the Committee draws the attention of Governments to the Declaration on the Rights of Persons Belonging to National or Ethnic, Religious and Linguistic Minorities, adopted by the General Assembly in its resolution 47/135 of 18 December 1992 [**Basic Document 3.39**].

9. In respect of the self-determination of peoples two aspects have to be distinguished. The right to self-determination of peoples has an internal aspect, that is to say, the rights of all peoples to pursue freely their economic, social and cultural development without outside interference. In that respect there exists a link with the right of every citizen to take part in the conduct of public affairs at any level, as referred to in article 5 (c) of the International Convention on the Elimination of All Forms of Racial Discrimination [**Basic Document 3.12**]. In consequence, Governments are to represent the whole population without distinction as to race, colour, descent or national or ethnic origin. The external aspect of self-determination implies that all peoples have the right to determine freely their political status and their place in the international community based upon the principle of equal rights and exemplified by the liberation of peoples from colonialism and by the prohibition to subject peoples to alien subjugation, domination and exploitation.

10. In order to respect fully the rights of all peoples within a State, Governments are again called upon to adhere to and implement fully the international human rights instruments and in particular the International

Convention on the Elimination of All Forms of Racial Discrimination. Concern for the protection of individual rights without discrimination on racial, ethnic, tribal, religious or other grounds must guide the policies of Governments. In accordance with article 2 of the International Convention on the Elimination of All Forms of Racial Discrimination and other relevant international documents, Governments should be sensitive towards the rights of persons belonging to ethnic groups, particularly their right to lead lives of dignity, to preserve their culture, to share equitably in the fruits of national growth and to play their part in the Government of the country of which they are citizens. Also, Governments should consider, within their respective constitutional frameworks, vesting persons belonging to ethnic or linguistic groups comprised of their citizens, where appropriate, with the right to engage in activities which are particularly relevant to the preservation of the identity of such persons or groups.

11. The Committee emphasizes that, in accordance with the Declaration on Friendly Relations, none of the Committee's actions shall be construed as authorizing or encouraging any action which would dismember or impair, totally or in part, the territorial integrity or political unity of sovereign and independent States conducting themselves in compliance with the principle of equal rights and self-determination of peoples and possessing a Government representing the whole people belonging to the territory, without distinction as to race, creed or colour. In the view of the Committee, international law has not recognized a general right of peoples unilaterally to declare secession from a State. In this respect, the Committee follows the views expressed in An Agenda for Peace (paras. 17 and following), namely, that a fragmentation of States may be detrimental to the protection of human rights, as well as to the preservation of peace and security. This does not, however, exclude the possibility of arrangements reached by free agreements of all parties concerned.

11. Robert McCorquodale, "Self–Determination: A Human Rights Approach," 43 I.C.L.Q. 857, 875–83 (1994).

A. *Self–Determination Has Limitations on its Exercise*

It has already been demonstrated that the international community now applies the right of self-determination to any situation, internal and external, where peoples are subject to oppression by subjugation, domination and exploitation. * * * However, the right of self-determination is not an absolute right without any limitations. Its purpose is not directly to protect the personal or physical integrity of individuals or groups as is the purpose of the absolute rights and, unlike the absolute rights, the exercise of this right can involve major structural and institutional changes to a State and must affect, often significantly, most groups and individuals in that State and beyond that State. Therefore, the nature of the right does require some limitations to be implied on its exercise. These limitations on the right of self-determination, designed to protect the rights of everyone (not just those seeking self-determination) and the general interests of the international community, can be appropriately dealt with by a human rights approach....

B. *Self–Determination Has Limitations to Protect Other Rights*

Despite the lack of express limitations on the right of self-determination in common Article 1 of the ICCPR [International Covenant on Civil and

Political Rights **(Basic Document 3.14)**] and ICESCR [International Covenant on Economic, Social and Cultural Rights **(Basic Document 3.13)**], common Article 5(1) of those Covenants provides that "nothing in the present Covenant may be interpreted as implying for any State, group or person any right to engage in any activity or perform any act aimed at the destruction of any of the rights and freedoms recognized herein". This provision—which is also found in the European Convention **[Basic Document 3.5]** and the American Convention **[Basic Document 3.17]**—implies a limitation on the right of self-determination to the extent that any exercise of the right cannot result in the destruction (or impairment) of any of the other rights protected. . . .

The particular concern of the international community in regard to this limitation has been to protect the rights of other groups affected by the exercise of the right of self-determination. . . . This is seen both where [a] new State has come into existence by independence, such as Namibia, or by secession, as with the former Yugoslavia and the former Soviet States. . . .

In resolving these competing rights the human rights approach, by using the international human rights law framework, aims to protect all rights and not the right of self-determination in isolation. Rights can then be balanced and a solution can be found which protects both rights as far as possible in the particular circumstances. Thus, instead of secession being the only option, peoples would be able to exercise their right of self-determination by such methods as the creation of a federation; guarantees of political power to defend or promote group interests; the giving of special assurances (as with minority rights); providing for a specific recognised status to a group; or by "consociational democracy."[39] This framework allows flexibility in resolutions of conflicts and even allows flexibility in sovereignty and so would allow the possibility that nationality be given to citizens of another State, for example by giving Serbian nationality to a Serbian citizen of the State of Bosnia–Herzegovina. . . .

Above all, if there were enforceable national and international guarantees of human rights so that the rights of every person and group in each State were protected and judicially enforced then there would probably be fewer claims of violation of the right of self-determination. The consequence should then be that each government did represent "the whole people belonging to the territory without distinction as to race, creed or colour," or any other form of discrimination, and so the right of self-determination would not be infringed. . . .

C. Self–Determination Has Limitations to Protect the General Interests of Society

Common Article 1(3) of the ICCPR and ICESCR implies a limitation on the right of self-determination as it provides that States have an obligation to respect the right "in conformity with the provisions of the Charter of the United Nations" **[Basic Document 1.5]**. The relevant obligations of States

39. This has four elements: a "grand coalition" of political leaders representative of the different groups in society; the presence of a mutual veto for the protection of minority interests; proportionality in political representation and appointments; and a high degree of autonomy for each group in running its internal affairs. A. Lijphart, Democracy in Plural Societies (1977).

under the provisions of the UN Charter were clarified by the Declaration on Principles of International Law [**Basic Document 1.11**] which set out seven principles of international law. As well as equal rights and self-determination of peoples, these principles were: prohibition on the use of force; prohibition on intervention in the domestic jurisdiction of a State; duty to settle disputes by peaceful means; duty to co-operate with other States; sovereign equality of States; and States should fulfil obligations in good faith. The Declaration expressly states that "in their interpretation and application the above principles are interrelated and each principle should be construed in the context of the other principles." In other words, there is a requirement to take into account these other principles when construing the right of self-determination. These other principles as a whole reassert the general purposes of the United Nations and principally its purpose to maintain international peace and security. So there is the general interest of international society in maintaining international peace and security, which creates a limitation on the right of self-determination. This general interest is often expressed in two ways: territorial integrity of States and the maintenance of colonial boundaries (*uti possidetis juris*).

1.   *Territorial integrity*

A part of the general limitation on the right of self-determination is the specific limitation of territorial integrity. The Declaration on Principles of International Law provides that the right of self-determination shall not "be construed as authorizing or encouraging any action which would dismember or impair, totally or in part, the territorial integrity or political unity of sovereign and independent States." This limitation is an extension of the desire in most societies to create a social and legal system which is relatively stable. In the international community, dominated as it is by States, the stability desired primarily concerns territorial boundaries. This limitation was . . . evident in the initial response by the European Community to the break-up of Yugoslavia.

However, the territorial integrity limitation cannot be asserted in all situations. The Declaration on Principles of International Law provides that only "States conducting themselves in compliance with the principle of equal rights and self-determination of peoples . . . and thus possessed of a government representing the whole people belonging to the territory without distinction as to race, creed or colour" can rely on this limitation. So a government of a State which does not represent the whole population on its territory without discrimination . . . cannot succeed in limiting the right of self-determination on the basis that it would infringe that State's territorial integrity. After the recognition by the international community of the disintegration . . . of the Soviet Union and Yugoslavia, it could now be the case that any government which is oppressive to peoples within its territory may no longer be able to rely on the general interest of territorial integrity as a limitation on the right of self-determination. * * * It appears that only a government of a State which allows all its peoples to decide freely their political status and economic, social and cultural development has an interest of territorial integrity which can possibly limit the exercise of a right of self-determination. . . .

2. *Uti possidetis juris*

Where the exercise of the right of self-determination is to become independent from a colonial power or to secede from an independent State, the limitation of the principle of *uti possidetis* may apply. The aim of this principle is to achieve stability of territorial boundaries by preserving the colonial boundaries of a State. It is a limitation based on the maintenance of international peace and security as was made clear by a Chamber of the International Court of Justice when it said that:[40]

> the maintenance of the territorial status quo in Africa is often seen as the wisest course, to preserve what has been achieved by peoples who have struggled for their independence, and to avoid a disruption which would deprive the continent of the gains achieved by much sacrifice ... [and] induced African States ... to take account of [*uti possidetis*] in the interpretation of the principle of self-determination of peoples.

This principle arose in the South American context but has begun to be applied to territorial disputes wherever occurring, including in Europe. In a world where boundary disputes are a constant source of instability and tension, this principle of *uti possidetis* seems to have been adopted by some international tribunals as a broad limitation on the exercise of the right of self-determination.

Yet State practice is inconclusive.... In addition, the inequities of the colonial boundaries cannot be ignored as these boundaries were the result of dispositions by colonial powers, often in complete disregard for natural geographical or ethnic boundaries.... Indeed, the International Court of Justice Chamber in the *Land, Island and Maritime Dispute* case cautioned that "*uti possidetis juris* is essentially a retrospective principle, investing as international boundaries administrative limits intended originally for quite other purposes."[41]

Despite the uncertainties in the universal application of the principle of *uti possidetis*, it is a principle which does need to be considered as a limitation on the right of self-determination. However, it is relevant only in those very few situations when the claimed exercise of the right is for secession and that secession has an effect on a colonial [or other pre-existing] boundary.

3. *Other aspects of international peace and security interests*

While there are general prohibitions on the use of force and intervention as part of the general interest of international society in peace and security, there has been an acceptance of the need to ease those prohibitions in order to protect those whose right of self-determination is being infringed. It is clear that those deprived of the right of self-determination can seek forcible international support to uphold their right of self-determination and no State can use force against such groups. It may even be the case that groups seeking to exercise their right could use armed force if that was the only means to resist forcible action against them. The increase in actions by the international community which could be classed as humanitarian intervention ... indicates the reduced importance given by the international community to the

---

40. Case Concerning the Frontier Dispute (Burkina Faso and Mali), 1986 ICJ 554 (22 Dec), 567.

41. (El Sal. v. Hond.) (Merits), 1992 ICJ 351 (11 Sep), 388.

territorial integrity of a State when human rights, including the right of self-determination, are grossly and systematically violated.[q]

Thus a special status has developed for the right of self-determination in which the usual general limitations of the international society might not be applied. This status is consistent with the first clear international declaration upholding the right of self-determination—the Declaration on Independence for Colonial Countries and Peoples 1960 **[Basic Document 3.9]**—as that Declaration provides that "the subjection of peoples to alien subjugation, domination and exploitation constitutes a denial of fundamental human rights, is contrary to the Charter of the United Nations and is an impediment to the promotion of world peace and co-operation". . . .

[Nevertheless,] [t]here are limitations on the right of self-determination to protect the general interests of international society, and of the society within the State as a whole, to maintain peace and security. The two specific limitations on the right in this area are to protect the territorial integrity of a State and to uphold colonial boundaries by use of the principle of *uti possidetis* . . . .

12. Editors' Note. International law has never prohibited secession from, or dissolution of, a state when the secession or dissolution has resulted from consensual processes. The world community's almost immediate recognition of Singapore's claim to statehood when it left Malaysia by agreement in 1965 and the consensual (arguably inevitable) dissolution and division of the Soviet Union and Czechoslovakia into independent republics in 1992 and 1993, respectively, are cases in point. But neither has international law ever stood for a *right* to secession or dissolution. Though in the process of fundamental change, the international legal system remains, essentially, a state-centric system and therefore not predisposed to encouraging the dismemberment or dissolution of states. When, however, in 1991, the world community—principally its European members—came face to face with the disintegration of the former Yugoslavia and thereafter proceeded, with not a little alacrity, to accede to dissolutionist demands, this historic posture became confused. Following armed clashes between federal Yugoslav forces, on the one hand, and the forces of Croatia and Slovenia, on the other, the European Community (now European Union), with the support of the United States, adopted its 16 December 1991 Declaration on the "Guidelines on the Recognition of New States in Eastern Europe and in the Soviet Union" **(Basic Document 1.15)**. In excess of what traditionally has been demanded of new states, the EC Declaration tied recognition to the rule of law, democracy, and respect for human rights; guarantees for the right of ethnic and national groups and minorities (in keeping with CSCE/OSCE undertakings); disarmament and nuclear nonproliferation; and commitment to diplomatic or arbitral settlement of state succession and regional disputes. Notably missing was any reference to a right of secession or even to the right of "peoples" to self-determination. Nevertheless, led by the European Community, the world community made haste to recognize the dissolutionist/secessionist claims involved, and seemingly on the basis of little more than the desire of a particular territorially-based leadership to secede.

q. For extensive treatment of the doctrine of humanitarian intervention, see *supra* Problem 4–1 ("Intervention in Loango") in Chapter 4, at 301.

This outcome further muddled the distinction between the right to self-determination and the rights of minorities, respectively proclaimed, as previously observed, in articles 1 and 27 of the 1966 International Covenant on Civil and Political Rights **(Basic Document 3.14)**, a distinction that is not easy to apply in the first place. In International Law, Rights and Politics: Developments in Eastern Europe and the CIS 74–75 (1994), Rein A. Müllerson observes that "contemporary international practice tends to ... the conclusion that[,] in the post-colonial era[,] peoples, for the purposes of self-determination under international law, can be defined as populations of independent states, while minorities constitute a part of peoples, having distinctive ethnic, religious or linguistic characteristics." He is, however, skeptical. He writes, at 74:

> [O]ne may say that while there is more or less a clear distinction between the rights of peoples and the rights of minorities, it is impossible to make such a distinction between peoples and minorities themselves. The UNESCO meeting of experts on the further study of the rights of peoples (Paris, 1990) ... identified the following criteria as being commonly taken into account in deciding that a group of individuals is a "people": common historical tradition, racial or ethnic identity, cultural homogeneity, linguistic unity, religious or ideological affinity, territorial connection and common economic life.
>
> But the more I think of this problem, the more I become convinced that it is impossible to find an international law criterion or criteria which would help us to divide ethnicities into peoples, minorities, tribes, nations, etc. Why do, for example, the Russians constitute a people, while the Tartars should be dealt with as a minority? Or why is the population of Bosnia–Herzegovina more of a people than are the ethnic Serbs who live in Bosnia–Herzegovina? The criteria proposed above are applicable to hundreds of ethnicities which do not form their own individual nation-states, and many apply also to populations which belong to different states.

In any event, the confused response of the European Community and the United States to the breakup of the former Yugoslavia has come under severe scholarly criticism. Writes Professor Hurst Hannum, in *Self-Determination, Yugoslavia, and Europe: Old Wine in New Bottles?*, 3 Transnat'l L. & Contemp. Probs. 57, 68–69 (1993):

> The fundamental problem with the European (and, ultimately, United Nations') approach to the Yugoslav conflict is that it adopted a one-time-only approach to secessionist demands based on no discernable criteria—except the desire of some territorially based population to secede. The principle that borders should not be altered except by mutual agreement has been elevated to a hypocritical immutability that is contradicted by the very act of recognizing secessionist states. The traditional international practice of non-intervention in civil wars has been replaced by a selective rule which prohibits some central governments (for example, Belgrade) from suppressing secession by force, accepts the use of force by others (for example, Colombo and New Delhi), and has yet to make up its mind about even more compelling cases (for example, Kurds and Tibetans).

New minorities are trapped in new ethnically based states not because of any international legal principle which such minorities can comprehend, but by the historical accident of finding themselves within administrative borders drawn decades ago for domestic purposes by an undemocratic government. As at Versailles in 1919, the ethnic factor is ignored on one side of a border, yet is cited as the primary justification for self-determination on the other side. Indeed, violence was much greater in Croatia and Bosnia–Herzegovina than in Slovenia precisely because Slovenia is a much more ethnically homogeneous state.

* * *

The attempt to link recognition of new states to the protection of human rights and specific guarantees for minorities is laudable, but the ad hoc, one-sided, and ultimately failed approach adopted by the EC with respect to Yugoslavia is insufficient to deal with the many ethnic conflicts and claims for self-determination with which the world is now faced.

Hannum concludes: "Until we move from the nineteenth-century, ethnic-state approach to self-determination, we will be condemned to more Yugoslavias." *Id.* at 69.

13.　Morton H. Halperin & David L. Scheffer (with Patricia L. Small), Self–Determination in the New World Order 56–60 (1992).

After World War II, the protection of minorities receded as both a political concern and a legal right. There is no mention of minority rights in the UN Charter (1945) **[Basic Document 1.5]** or the Universal Declaration of Human Rights (1948) **[Basic Document 3.3]**. The notable exception immediately after the war was the Genocide Convention (1948) **[Basic Document 3.2]**, which indirectly refers to minority groups in its formulation of a right of existence for human groups....

In large part because of the influence of the United States ..., the protection of *individual* human rights became the dominant human rights concern. The protection of the individual encouraged the view that the way to manage minority groups was to assimilate them within an existing state, rather than cater to their group identities or cultivate any possible interest in self-determination. With a few exceptions, minority rights were essentially buried as an international legal concern.

Minority rights reappeared in Article 27 of the 1966 International Covenant on Civil and Political Rights **[Basic Document 3.14]**.... The rights (culture, religion, language) protected, however, for many years were viewed as limited in scope and lacking sufficient definition. Further, the beneficiary is the individual member of the minority group and not the group as a whole. This interpretation prevails as the dominant view.

In the aftermath of the Cold War, minority rights in a collective sense have found their expression again in several important documents.... [One such is the 1992 Declaration on the Rights of Persons Belonging to National or Ethnic, Religious, and Linguistic Minorities **(Basic Document 3.39)**]. It is not a manifesto for self-determination; in its preamble it affirms protection of minority rights as a contribution "to the political and social stability of States in which [the minority lives]." ...

The Conference on Security and Cooperation in Europe (CSCE) has taken a renewed interest in minority rights. . . . The Copenhagen Document **[Basic Document 3.34]** includes an entire section on the rights of national minorities and strongly affirms linguistic freedom for minorities as well as the right of national minorities to establish and maintain their own educational institutions. It notes the efforts by states to establish "appropriate local or autonomous administrations" for minority groups. Though weakly stated, the provision . . . suggests that democracy and individual human rights guarantees alone may not adequately protect minorities—that it may be necessary to devolve to a minority group as a whole certain political functions and powers . . . in order to protect not only minority rights but also the territorial integrity of the state. * * * The [1990] Charter of Paris for a New Europe **[Basic Document 3.35]** . . . echoes the Copenhagen Document's concern for minority rights. . . .

The Report of the Geneva CSCE Meeting of Experts on National Minorities, adopted July 19, 1991, goes further in fusing protection of minority rights with democratic systems and the rule of law:

> Human rights and fundamental freedoms are the basis for the protection and promotion of rights of persons belonging to national minorities. . . . Questions relating to national minorities can only be satisfactorily resolved in a democratic political framework based on the rule of law, with a functioning independent judiciary. This framework guarantees full respect for human rights and fundamental freedoms, equal rights and status for all citizens, including persons belonging to national minorities, the free expression of all their legitimate interests and aspirations, political pluralism, social tolerance and the implementation of legal rules that place effective restraints on the abuse of government power.

> Issues concerning national minorities, as well as compliance with international obligations and commitments concerning the rights of persons belonging to them, are matters of legitimate international concern and consequently do not constitute exclusively an internal affair of the respective State.[42]

The Report describes positive results in democratic systems as including "local and autonomous administration, as well as autonomy on a territorial basis, including the existence of consultative, legislative and executive bodies chosen through free and periodic elections," and other forms of decentralized government for national minorities.[43]

[*Eds.*—The authors next discuss, in its draft form, the Council of Europe's Framework Convention for the Protection of National Minorities **(Basic Document 3.46)**, since opened for signature (on 1 February 1995) and entered into force 2 January 1998. Characterizing the Convention as "[a] more extreme endorsement of minorities rights," they correctly observe that the Convention essentially requires "blanket protection of minorities." They also take note of Article 5(2) which they describe as "[o]ne of the most controversial provisions" because it stipulates that the state parties "shall

42. CSCE, Report of the CSCE Meeting of Experts on National Minorities, 1–19 July 1991, *reprinted in* 30 I.L.M. 1692 (1991).

43. *Id.* at 1698.

refrain from policies or practices aimed at assimilation of persons belonging to national minorities against their will and shall protect these persons from any action aimed at such assimilation." The authors comment: "This would appear to be an anti-integration stance even when the government's efforts to promote integration are non-coercive." The authors then summarize, by way of conclusion:]

The traditional rights of minorities—religion, language, and culture—are embodied in international law, particularly when expressed in terms of the individual belonging to a minority. Beyond that, despite the advances of the documents just described, governments remain reluctant to obligate themselves to protect group rights that they fear may lead to secessionist pressures. Governments are even less willing to grant minority groups the political freedom to wage a campaign for secession that would ultimately lead to the disaggregation of the country. The real mistake occurs when a government is so fearful of self-determination—even when it is not aimed at secession—that it denies minority groups the protection of their traditional rights. Such negativist actions can easily trigger minority discontent and upheaval, and create the surge toward self-determination that the government so fears.

The reassertion of the protection of minority rights, particularly by the CSCE and the Council of Europe, points the way toward international regional involvement in a self-determination dispute where a minority's rights are being violated. The goal of that involvement must initially be to press a government to see that its self-interest lies in accommodating the interests of a minority group, rather than triggering more extreme self-determination claims—even secessionist demands—by alienating it. Only if such efforts fail is it necessary to consider whether the protection of minority rights justifies support for the creation of a new state.

G. WAR CRIMES, GENOCIDE, AND CRIMES AGAINST HUMANITY

1. Hague Convention (No. IV) Respecting the Laws and Customs of War on Land (with annexed regulations). Concluded, 18 Oct 1907. Entered into force, 26 Jan 1910. C.T.S. 277 (French), 2 A.J.I.L. Supp. 90 (1908); *reprinted in* **2 Weston & Carlson II.B.1: Arts. 21, 42–56 of annexed regulations** (Basic Document 2.2).

2. Convention on the Prevention and Punishment of the Crime of Genocide. Concluded, 9 Dec 1948. Entered into force, 12 Jan 1951. 78 U.N.T.S. 277; *reprinted in* **3 Weston & Carlson III.J.1** (Basic Document 3.2).

3. Geneva Convention (No. IV) Relative to the Protection of Civilian Persons in Time of War (with Annex II). Concluded, 12 Aug 1949. Entered into force, 21 Oct 1950. 75 U.N.T.S. 287; *reprinted in* **2 Weston & Carlson II.B.14: Arts. 47–78** (Basic Document 2.12).

4. Principles of International Law Recognized in the Charter of the Nuremberg Tribunal and in the Judgment of the Tribunal, 2 Aug 1950, 2 Y.B.I.L.C. 374 (1950); *reprinted in* **2 Weston & Carlson II.E.4: Principles VI and VII** (Basic Document 2.13).

5. **Editors' Note.** Important in helping to define the modern-day laws of armed conflict have been the judgments of the war crimes tribunals established following World War II, in particular the 1 October 1946 Final Judgment of the International Military Tribunal at Nuremberg, organized pursuant to the London Agreement and Charter of 8 August 1945 **(Basic Document 1.3)**. An abridged version of the Tribunal's lengthy opinion and judgment is reproduced in the documentary supplement to this coursebook **(Basic Document 7.4)**. The UN General Assembly, by unanimous vote, affirmed the principles of international law recognized in the Charter and Judgment in GA Res 95, 1st Sess., Supp. for 23 Oct.–15 Dec. 1946, at 188, UN Doc.A/236 (1946). They were further reaffirmed—and explained—in a resolution adopted by the International Law Commission on 2 August 1950 and in a Draft Code of Crimes Against the Peace and Security of Mankind that the General Assembly asked the International Law Commission to prepare in 1950. The culmination of this work was the 1998 Rome Statute of the International Criminal Court **(Basic Document 1.16)** which came into force on 1 July 2003. For documentation and analysis of this effort at its earlier stages, see Benjamin Ferencz, An International Criminal Court: A Step Toward World Peace (1980). *See* Draft Statute for an International Criminal Tribunal (with commentaries), as reported by the Working Group on a Draft Statute for an International Criminal Court of the International Law Commission at its Forty-sixth Session, UN GAOR, 49th Sess., Supp. No. 10, at 320, UN Doc. A/49/10 (1994). For informative commentary, see M. Cherif Bassiouni, Draft Statute–International Criminal Tribunal (1992); James Crawford, *The ILC's Draft Statute for an International Criminal Court*, 88 A.J.I.L. 140 (1994); _____, *The ILC Adopts a Statute for an International Criminal Court*, 89 A.J.I.L. 404 (1995); Commentary on the Rome Statute of the International Criminal Court (Otto Triffterer ed., 1999); Steven Ratner & Jason S. Abrams, Accountability for Human Rights Atrocities in International Law: Beyond the Nuremberg Legacy (1997). Until the creation of the International Criminal Court, a permanent institution, only *ad hoc* and temporary courts existed *e.g.*, the still functioning International Tribunal for the Prosecution of Persons Responsible for Serious Violations of International Humanitarian Law in the Territory of the Former Yugoslavia and its companion International Tribunal for Rwanda, each considered in some detail in Chapter 3, *supra*.

6. **Protocol Additional (No. I) to the Geneva Conventions of August 12, 1949, and Relating to the Protection of Victims of Non-International Armed Conflicts. Concluded, 8 Jun 1977. Entered into force, 7 Dec 1978. 1977 U.N.J.Y.B. 95** *reprinted in* **16 I.L.M. 1391 (1977) & 2 Weston & Carlson II.B.20: Section III** (Basic Document 2.31).

7. **Protocol Additional (No. II) to the Geneva Conventions of August 12, 1949, and Relating to the Protection of Victims of Non-International Armed Conflicts. Concluded, 8 Jun 1977. Entered into force, 7 Dec 1978. 1977 U.N.J.Y.B. 135,** *reprinted in* **16 I.L.M. 1442 (1977) & 2 Weston & Carlson II.B.21: Parts II and IV** (Basic Document 2.32).

8. **United Nations General Assembly Declaration for the Protection of War Victims, 1 Sep 1993, UN Doc. A/48/742 (Annex), 33 I.L.M.**

297 (1994), *reprinted in* **2 Weston & Carlson II.B.23** (Basic Document 2.45).

    9.   UN Security Council Resolution 827 on Establishing an International Tribunal for the Prosecution of Persons Responsible for Serious Violations of Humanitarian Law Committed in the Territory of the Former Yugoslavia, 25 May 1993, SC Res. 827, UN SCOR, 48th Sess., 3217th mtg., at 29, UN Doc. S/RES/827 (1992), *reprinted in* **32 I.L.M. 1203 (1993) & 2 Weston II.E.12** (Basic Document 2.44).

    10.   UN Security Council Resolution 955 Establishing the International Tribunal for Rwanda, 8 Nov 1994, SC Res. 955, UN SCOR, 49th Sess., 3453rd mtg., at 15, UN Doc. S/RES/955 (1994), *reprinted in* **33 I.L.M. 1598 (1994) & 2 Weston & Carlson II.E.12: Arts. 2–4** (Basic Document 2.46).

    11.   Rome Statute of the International Criminal Court. Concluded 17 July 1998. Entered into force 1 July 2002, UN Doc A/CONF. 183/9 *reprinted in* **37 I.L.M. 999 (1998) & 2 Weston & Carlson I.H.13** (Basic Document 1.16).

    12.   Leo Kuper, "Theoretical Issues Relating to Genocide: Uses and Abuses," in Genocide 31, 33–40 (G. Andreopoulos ed., 1994).

Under Article I of the [United Nations Convention on the Prevention and Punishment of the Crime of Genocide **[Basic Document 3.2]**, the contracting parties confirm that genocide, whether committed in time of peace or in time of war, is a crime under international law. This cannot be interpreted as equating genocides in time of peace with those committed during war. It is only at a very general level of abstraction that genocide is a uniform phenomenon. Its manifestations and processes and contexts are quite varied and need to be distinguished. I draw a basic distinction between "domestic" genocides and genocides committed in the course of inter-national war.

The domestic genocides are those which arise on the basis of internal divisions within a single society. They are a phenomenon of the plural society, with its marked divisions between racial, ethnic, and/or religious groups. Plural society theory deals with the relations between these groups, and the conditions promoting peaceful cohabitation, integration, or violent polarization leading to genocide. It has no application to the genocides of international war, committed in armed conflict between separate states.

Genocide in international war is by no means an exclusive category. It may also be a war crime, as [in the case of] the Sabra and Shatila massacres. These were committed [in 1982] against the inhabitants of two Palestinian camps in Beirut by Christian Phalangists during Israel's military occupation of the area, and, accordingly, responsibility attaches to Israel as an occupying army. . . .

So too, the incendiary pattern bombing of Hamburg, Dresden, and Tokyo, and the atomic bombings of Hiroshima and Nagasaki may constitute both genocides and war crimes. The distinctive feature of pattern bombing is that the entire population of a city becomes the target of annihilatory assault. . . .

[*Eds.*—The author next discusses the World War II Nazi bombings of Coventry, London, and Rotterdam. While acknowledging them as war crimes, he dismisses them as acts of genocide on the grounds that they did not constitute "pattern bombings." He then continues:]

The pattern bombings were a significant step in the movement toward total war, attaining their apotheosis in the atomic bombings. Destruction was not limited to war-related targets, and noncombatants became the innocent victims of indiscriminate annihilation in contravention of the humanitarian laws governing international war.

Are these humanitarian laws now being abrogated by current practice and by technological advances for the deployment against distant targets of high-powered missiles conveying nuclear, incendiary, chemical, and biological bombs of devastating lethal power, all weapons of indiscriminate effect and of mass murder? Has technological invention rendered international warfare inevitably genocidal? Meanwhile, the United Nations' record, in either times of war or of peace, hardly encourages confidence in its ability or its commitment to restrain genocide.

United Nations—Uses and Abuses

With the adoption of the United Nations Genocide Convention, the concept of genocide gained currency as a most horrendous crime. It was, therefore, to be expected that the charge of genocide would become a weapon in the defense against discrimination and injustice and oppression. Experiencing the indifference of the outside world to their suffering, disadvantaged groups sought to gain a sympathetic hearing by dramatic denunciation.

Hence birth control clinics, for example, were interpreted as instruments of genocide. This presumably relied on Article II(d) of the Convention, which specified as one of the acts constituting genocide the imposition of measures "intended to prevent births within [a] group," but ignored the overall context for commission of the crime, namely the intent to destroy the victim group in whole or in part. More generally, violations of human rights, or a pattern of violations, were denounced as genocide.

The resultant abuse of the concept proved counterproductive in the United Nations, which turned a deaf ear to these extravagant charges. In fact, in some situations, the avoidance of extreme charges and rhetoric might contribute to a favorable response. Thus, the representatives of the Bahais, threatened with the violent eradication of their religion in Iran and subjected to systematic discrimination reminiscent of the persecution of Jews by the Nazis in the 1930s, were advised to avoid the charge of genocide, a strategy they successfully followed.

The resistance of the United Nations to charges of genocide is not simply a reaction to the trivializing abuse of the concept. A significant factor is that genocide is usually, though not exclusively, a crime committed by governments or with governments' condonation or complicity. And, as Franck and Rodley comment, the United Nations is a professional association of governments which cannot be counted upon to act in any way likely to undermine the authority of—and, by implication, all of—the member regimes.[44]

---

44. T. Franck & N. Rodley, *The Law, United Nations and Bangladesh*, 2 Isr. Y. B. Hum. Rts. 165 (1972).

This supportive stance is reflected in the primacy accorded by the UN to norms protective of the status quo, such as its emphasis on sovereignty, on territorial integrity, and on nonintervention in the internal affairs of member states. It is also reflected in the UN's failure to respond to valid charges of genocide and to emergency situations of mass murder.

Examples of the UN's reluctance to respond abound, though there has been a continuing incidence of genocide since the adoption of the Genocide Convention. Offending regimes might be protected during years of annihilatory violence by regional and ideological alliances, as in the case of Uganda under Amin in the 1970s. Or the Cold War, with veto-empowered superpowers divided in their support for the contending parties, might [have] frustrate[d] the efforts of the Secretary–General to convene the Security Council and ensure United Nations intervention, as in the case of Bangladesh. Some regimes, such as the Khmer Rouge in Democratic Kampuchea, were so intransigent, and so contemptuous of outside involvement, that war and invasion were the only effective measures against genocide.

In contrast to the protective stance toward member states, and the failure to take action against genocide or even to invoke the assistance of the International Court of Justice, certain vilified states, and notably Israel, are vulnerable to charges of genocide. This availability of a scapegoat state in the UN restores to members with a record for murderous violence against their subjects a self-righteous sense of moral purpose as principled members of "the community of nations." * * * [While] the numbers killed in the Sabra–Shatila massacres range from about four hundred to eight hundred ... , a carefully planned UN campaign found Israel guilty of genocide, without reference to the role of the Phalangists in perpetrating the massacres on their own initiative. The procedures were unique in the annals of the United Nations * * * [and need] to be set against the failure of the Security Council to meet on Bangladesh, in a case where millions of lives were imperiled.

The ... condemnation of Israel as guilty of the crime of genocide is in strong contrast to the careful phrasing of [the] decision on South African apartheid at the same session. International concern over South Africa's gross violations of the rights of subject races [went] back to the very inception of the United Nations, a reminder that the infrastructure of racial oppression [had been] already firmly established prior to the Nationalist Party's apartheid regime. From the time of the first meeting of the General Assembly in 1946, the monitoring of South Africa's performance on human rights [became] a major UN industry, with a vast proliferation of reports.

Inevitably the issue of genocide would be raised, given the close resemblance of the key apartheid statutes to the Nuremberg laws, the brutality of the systematic deprivation of human rights, and the implementation of a policy designed to ensure the perpetuity of a hierarchy of racial domination, with each race encouraged (forced) "to develop in its own way." And in 1967, the Commission on Human Rights had appointed the Ad Hoc Working Group of Experts, who extended their mandate to investigate torture and ill-treatment into a sort of preparatory examination of the South African government on charges of genocide.

After taking the testimony of witnesses who had been victims of persecution, the group concluded that the intention of the government to destroy a racial group in whole or in part was not established in law. This showed surprising integrity, given the pariah status of South Africa.

Two later reports dealt with the relationship between apartheid and genocide and with crimes against humanity, and the group finally recommended that the Genocide Convention be amended to make punishable inhuman practices resulting from apartheid. This was not accepted. Instead the United Nations introduced a new [1973] Convention on the Suppression and Punishment of the Crime of Apartheid.[r] ... Whereas the governments of member states are by no means immune to the temptations of genocide, apartheid [was] a uniquely South African phenomenon.

* * *

International Human Rights: Theory and Practice

Self-determination might conceivably have assisted in the prevention of genocide, but the doctrine has been appreciably modified in the United Nations and rejected in practice by member states. And the doctrine of humanitarian intervention, also relevant for the prevention of genocide, is in considerable disrepute.[s]

* * *

[Moreover,] [t]here is an inherent contradiction in the cardinal principles of international law as described in the General Assembly's *Declaration Concerning Friendly Relations and Co-operation Among States* [**Basic Document 1.11**]. The preamble declares that "the subjection of peoples to alien subjugation, domination and exploitation constitutes a major obstacle to the promotion of international peace and security." It then reaffirms the principle of equal rights and self-determination as being of "paramount importance for the promotion of friendly relations among States, based on respect for the principle of sovereign equality." But at the same time, the preamble emphasizes the contradictory principle "that any attempt aimed at the partial or total disruption of the national unity and territorial integrity of a State or country or at its political independence is incompatible with the purposes and principles of the Charter."

The contradiction arises from the fact that many of the member states are in fact plural societies, composed of a variety of ethnic or national groups. This is appreciably a heritage of colonization with its often arbitrary grouping of peoples in a single administrative entity. As a result, claims for self-determination by former subject peoples in the form of secession from the now independent state, or claims for greater autonomy, or indeed for freedom from discrimination, conflict with concern for national unity, territorial integrity, or political independence.

Movements for independence, for secession, are most likely to evoke an extreme response from the state to the threat of a diminution in territory and power. Notable examples are the West Pakistan genocidal assault on East Pakistan (Bangladesh) [in 1971 when an estimated one million Bengalis were

---

r. Concluded, 30 Nov 1973. 1015 U.N.T.S. 243, *reprinted in* 13 I.L.M. 50 (1974) and 3 Weston & Carlson III.I.2.

s. For extensive treatment of the doctrine of humanitarian intervention, see *supra* Prob-

lem 4–1 ("Intervention in Loango") in Chapter 4, at 301.

killed and ten million more took refuge in India], and the Nigerian federal government assault on the Ibos [in the late 1960s during the Biafran civil war], with its deliberate use of starvation as a weapon in the final stages of the ... war.

In the debate on Bangladesh, the Pakistan representative warned delegates that the pluralistic structure of many of their societies rendered them equally vulnerable to fragmentation.

> Today you may rejoice over what is happening to us. But if you think that today you are going to dismember Pakistan and the germs of dismemberment are not going to spread to your country, you are sadly mistaken. And where is this Pandora's box going to be closed? Is it going to be closed in Yugoslavia? Why not Czechoslovakia? ... And Brittany, the Basque country, Morocco, Algeria, all the countries in Africa? Can it not happen in any single country in Africa and Asia. If there is Bangladesh in Africa, there must be Bangladesh everywhere.... Let us open the floodgates, because if sovereign States are going to be mutated in this fashion, let the deluge come.[45]

His warning had a prophetic quality, as we witnessed the dismemberment of the Soviet Empire, and the resultant lethal [and often genocidal] conflicts, not only in the movements for independence, but also between the plural sections in different societies.

13. Christine Chinkin, "Rape and Sexual Abuse of Women in International Law," 5 E.J.I.L. 326, 328–35 (1994).

Rape in war is not merely a matter of chance, of women victims being in the wrong place at the wrong time. Nor is it a question of sex. It is rather a question of power and control which is "structured by male soldiers" notions of their masculine privilege, by the strength of the military's lines of command and by class and ethnic inequalities among women. Radhika Coomaraswamy has identified a number of reasons for sexual violence against women, two of which are especially applicable to rape in armed conflict: violence against women may be directed towards the social group of which she is a member because "to rape a woman is to humiliate her community."[46] Complex, combined emotions of hatred, superiority, vengeance for real or imagined past wrongs and national pride are engendered and deliberately manipulated in armed conflict. They are given expression through rape of the other side's women. For the men of the community rape encapsulates the totality of their defeat; they have failed to protect "their" women. Second, studies have indicated the connection between militarization of the nation State and violence against women. Other connections have been drawn between "normal" peacetime attitudes towards women and rape in armed conflict; one that has been controversial in the context of the former Yugoslavia is the direct causal link that has been made by Catharine MacKinnon between pornography in that country and the mass rapes of Muslim women.[47] The connection between pornographic projections of women and the use as war propaganda of

---

45. S/PV 1611, 21.

46. R. Coomaraswamy, *Of Kali Born: Violence and he Law in Sri Lanka*, in Freedom from Violence: Women's Strategies from Around the World 49 (M. Schuler ed. 1992).

47. C. MacKinnon, *Turning Rape into Pornography*, Ms Magazine, Jul/Aug 1992....

these and other media images can be readily accepted; but to identify these as the sole, or even major cause of the abuse of women throughout that area is simplistic and misleading.

Licence to rape has been included as a term of employment for mercenary soldiers. In determining why such a condition is repugnant, Walzer discounts the utilitarian argument that it acts as a spur to military courage. Instead he goes to the heart of the matter:

> Rape is a crime, in war as in peace, because it violates the rights of the woman who is attacked. To offer her as bait to a mercenary soldier is to treat her as if she were not a person at all but a mere object, a prize, a trophy of war. It is the recognition of her personality that shapes our judgment.[48]

Rape has also been directed as an instrument of war. In the former Yugoslavia rape has been "massive, organized and systematic." It was perceived by the Special Rapporteur appointed by the United Nations Commission on Human Rights not only as an instrument of war but as a method of ethnic cleansing "intended to humiliate, shame, degrade and terrify the entire ethnic group."[49]

* * *

The consequences of rape continue beyond the actual attack or attacks, often lasting for the rest of the women's lives. As well as the degradation, pain and terror caused at the time, the fear engendered remains long after. This fear is also experienced by other women who were not themselves attacked but are aware that they might have been, or might be in the future. Rape centred within a community undermines the well-being and secure existence of the community. For survivors, rape carries the risk of sexually-transmitted diseases, including of course AIDS. It also can result in pregnancy. Women have to face the prospect of bearing the child of the invader (of their State, their community and their bodies), or of seeking an abortion at a time of intense social dislocation and when scarce medical supplies are directed as a priority to military personnel. This same factor reduces availability of treatment of sexually-transmitted diseases. Abortion is restricted under the teachings of a number of religions, or women have been forcibly detained to prevent abortion. Other women have been so badly internally injured that they will never be able to bear the children they would have chosen to have; infertility and loss of virginity make women unmarriageable in some societies. Still others have been unable to bear their shame and have committed suicide. Where the effects of conflict have caused shortages of food and shelter, and priority health care is directed towards the military, child bearing can impose an impossibly high additional material, as well as psychological, burden upon their mothers. This can be further exacerbated by the child-being seen by family or compatriots as "proof" of the woman's collaboration with the enemy, or of her immoral behaviour. Women fear they have become unacceptable to their families and communities, a fear which may be enhanced where the rape was committed publicly in the presence of members of these

48. M. Walzer, Just and Unjust Wars: A Moral Argument with Historical Illustrations ch. 8 (2d ed. 1992).

49. T. Mazowiecki, Special Rapporteur of the Commission on Human Rights, Report Pursuant to Commission Resolution 1992/S–I/1 of 14 Aug 92, E/CN.4/1993/50 (10 Feb 93).

communities. Public rape terrorizes and traumatizes the civilian population. There is also only just beginning to be some understanding of the psychological damage caused by the trauma of violent sexual abuse.

[*Eds.*—The author next turns to the ways in which international law responds to rape and other abuses of women during wartime.]

A number of substantive international legal regimes are currently applicable. States are liable for harm done to individuals which constitutes violation of the laws and customs of war by troops under their authority and command, for violations of internationally guaranteed human rights, including genocide and torture, and for wrongdoing to aliens under the normal principles of State responsibility. These different legal regimes allow for analysis of rape through different lenses: violations of the laws of war, violence against women as a violation of women's human rights, and protection of ethnic groups against genocide. In addition to State responsibility there is individual criminal responsibility for the commission of war crimes and crimes against humanity. The plea of superior orders is not available as a defence to such actions.

Meron has demonstrated that rape has long been prohibited by the laws of war and has been incorporated into various modern Codes of Military Conduct.[50] The currently applicable laws of war are contained within the 1949 Geneva Conventions [**Basic Documents 2.9, 2.10, 2.11 & 2.12**], the 1977 supplementary Protocols [**Basic Documents 2.31 & 2.32**], and in the body of law arising from the judgment of the Nuremberg Tribunal[x] and the Military Tribunal for the Far East. Unfortunately, in these documents the position with respect to rape is ambiguous. Rape was not included in the listed war crimes in Article 6 of the Nuremberg Charter [**Basic Document 1.3**], although the list was specifically stated not to be exhaustive.

The Fourth Geneva Convention [**Basic Document 2.12**] provides protection for civilians in international armed conflict and specifically provides that women should be protected against rape. This provision is almost exactly reiterated in Protocol I. It is [notable] that these provisions do not impose a blanket prohibition against sexual abuse, but rather oblige States to offer women protection against attacks on their honour and to accord them special respect. Article 4 of the Fourth Geneva Convention applies to those "who at a given moment and in any manner whatsoever find themselves, in case of a conflict or occupation, in the hands of a Party to the conflict or Occupying Power of which they are not nationals." Article 76 of Protocol I enhances this protection by extending its scope to all women in the power of a Party to the conflict including a Party's own nationals. In non-international armed conflict, Article 3 to the Geneva Conventions provides a minimum standard of behaviour that applies both to government and non-government forces. Prohibited actions include violence to life and the person, cruel treatment and torture, and humiliating and degrading treatment. It is easy to interpret these Articles so as to include rape, but it is nevertheless unfortunate that it is not spelled out as an explicit prohibition. For this reason the affirmation by the

---

50. T. Meron, *Shakespeare's Henry the Fifth and the Law of War*, 86 A.J.I.L. 1 (1992); ____, *Rape as a Crime under International Humanitarian Law*, 87 A.J.I.L. 424 (1993).

x. *See supra* Ch. 3, § A, at 179–219.

World Conference on Human Rights in Vienna in 1993 that "violations of the human rights of women in situations of armed conflict [with no distinction drawn between international and non-international armed conflict] are violations of the humanitarian principles of international human rights and humanitarian law" is to be welcomed. The Declaration and Programme of Action **[Basic Document 3.40]** continues that violations, including systematic rape and sexual slavery "require a particularly effective response."

The same is true of the enforcement provisions. States are under an obligation to make grave breaches of the Geneva Conventions and Protocols subject to the jurisdiction of their own courts and punishable by severe penalties. Rape is not however explicitly listed as a grave breach of the Convention, although acts wilfully committed and causing great suffering or causing injury to body or health do constitute grave breaches. Protocol I includes among its list of grave breaches "degrading practices involving outrages upon personal dignity based upon racial discrimination" but makes no reference to gender discrimination.

War crimes, that is violations of the laws or customs of war, are not the only possible legal regime for the prosecution of rape committed during international armed conflict. There is also the concept of a crime against humanity and, it has been argued in the context of the former Yugoslavia, genocide. A crime against humanity was defined in the Nuremberg Charter as:

> murder, extermination, enslavement, deportation, and other inhumane acts committed against any civilian population before or during the war, or persecutions on political, racial, or religious grounds in execution of or in connection with any crime within the jurisdiction of the Tribunal whether or not in violation of the domestic law of the country where perpetrated.

A number of points require special mention. First, although crimes against humanity were established as a separate category from war crimes, the crimes in question were inevitably associated with the occurrence of the Second World War. This association between armed conflict and crimes against humanity has been continued in the case of the former Yugoslavia. Second, despite the enormous incidence of rape of civilian populations during the Second World War, prosecutions of crimes against humanity were limited to persecutions on racial, political or religious grounds, in accordance with the wording of Article 6. These words import a requirement of discriminatory behaviour into the concept of crimes against humanity, which is equally well provided by the gender discrimination inherent in violent crimes against women. Thirdly, for actions to come within the category of crimes against humanity they had to be committed against a civilian population, not against individual civilians. Fourthly, in contrast to war crimes, it has been necessary to establish systematic government planning for crimes against humanity. Crimes against humanity are not easily established in light of these restrictive requirements. Nevertheless, when the four occupying powers in Germany adopted Control Council Law No. 10 they departed from the Nuremberg precedent and incorporated rape as a crime against humanity.

Genocide is defined in Article II of the Genocide Convention. There must be an intention to destroy, in whole or in part, a national, ethnic, racial or religious group through the commission of such acts as killing or causing serious bodily or mental harm to members of the group; deliberately inflicting on the group conditions of life calculated to bring about its physical destruction in whole or in part; imposing measures to prevent births within the group; or forcibly transferring children of the group to another group. At first sight rape does not appear to fall within this definition, but it has been forcefully argued that where it has been carried out on a massive and systematic basis for the purposes of producing babies of the ethnic class of the rapists, of destroying the family life of the victims and of cleansing the surrounding area of all other ethnic groups rape becomes genocidal. This categorization has been further supported by allegations that impregnated women were forcibly detained until it was too late to abort.

Despite this impressive body of formal prohibition, the incidence of rape in armed conflict has been widely ignored, underplayed or tolerated. Rape is too frequently regarded as an unfortunate but inevitable side-effect of conflict, or as an anticipated bonus for soldiers on all sides. Rape did not figure prominently at Nuremberg, "not because the Germans were not guilty of rape, but because the allied forces, especially the Russians and the Moroccan forces under French control, were also guilty of many rapes."[51] Rape was also largely invisible in the trials of the Japanese war criminals.

This silence by international law enforcement agencies denotes a double irony for women. Feminist writers have argued that the distinction drawn in international law between public acts of the State and private actions has been an important factor in its failure to address denial of human rights to women. Violence against women for example has not been readily viewed as torture, or as being imputable to the State, because of its widespread commission by private actors within the private arena of the home. Yet rape in international armed conflict, which is largely committed by military agents of the State under public authority, has also been ignored.

* * *

However, in the context of the former Yugoslavia there has been widespread pressure to ensure that this long silence is broken. The substantive law on rape in armed conflict has now become entangled with the question of arenas for its application. Condemnation of violations and calls for compliance have been made within international political fora, notably the Security Council, the Human Rights Commission, the Commission on the Status of Women, and the Committee on the Elimination of Discrimination Against Women. Proceedings have been [brought] against Yugoslavia (Serbia–Montenegro) in the International Court of Justice by Bosnia–Herzegovina. Yugoslavia (Serbia–Montenegro) has counter-claimed in similar terms. Since under Article 34 of the Statute of the Court **[Basic Document 1.6]** only States can be parties before it, [such] litigation [can] deal [only] with the question of the responsibility of the State under the relevant treaties and customary international law. The options for the prosecution of individuals alleged to have committed such crimes are the domestic courts of any State, or an international war crimes tribunal on the precedent of Nuremberg.

51. J. Laber, *Bosnia: Questions About Rape*, 40 N.Y. Rev. Bks. 3 (25 Mar 93).

14.   The Prosecutor v. Jean–Paul Akayesu, Case No. ICTR–96–4–T (Decision of 2 September 1998), ¶ ¶ 730–34.

[*Eds.*—Jean-Paul Akayesu, a former *bourgmestre* (mayor) of Taba commune, Prefecture Gitarama, in Rwanda, was charged on indictment before the International Criminal Tribunal for Rwanda for crimes against humanity, breaches of international law, and genocide allegedly perpetrated by him while he was in office. This extract deals with Mr. Akayesu's incitement of, and failure to prevent, sexual violence against Tutsi women and girls.]

730.   . . . [T]he Chamber has already established that genocide was committed against the Tutsi group in Rwanda in 1994, throughout the period covering the events alleged in the Indictment. Owing to the very high number of atrocities committed against the Tutsi, their widespread nature not only in the commune of Taba, but also throughout Rwanda, and to the fact that the victims were systematically and deliberately selected because they belonged to the Tutsi group, with persons belonging to other groups being excluded, the Chamber is also able to infer, beyond reasonable doubt, the genocidal intent of the accused in the commission of the above-mentioned crimes.

731.   With regard, particularly, to the acts described in . . . the Indictment, that is, rape and sexual violence, the Chamber wishes to underscore the fact that in its opinion, they constitute genocide in the same way as any other act as long as they were committed with the specific intent to destroy, in whole or in part, a particular group, targeted as such. Indeed, rape and sexual violence certainly constitute infliction of serious bodily and mental harm on the victims and are even, according to the Chamber, one of the worst ways of inflicting harm on the victim as he or she suffers both bodily and mental harm. In light of all the evidence before it, the Chamber is satisfied that the acts of rape and sexual violence . . ., were committed solely against Tutsi women, many of whom were subjected to the worst public humiliation, mutilated, and raped several times, often in public, in the Bureau Communal premises or in other public places, and often by more than one assailant. These rapes resulted in physical and psychological destruction of Tutsi women, their families and their communities. Sexual violence was an integral part of the process of destruction, specifically targeting Tutsi women and specifically contributing to their destruction and to the destruction of the Tutsi group as a whole.

732.   The rape of Tutsi women was systematic and was perpetrated against all Tutsi women and solely against them. A Tutsi woman, married to a Hutu, testified before the Chamber that she was not raped because her ethnic background was unknown. As part of the propaganda campaign geared to mobilizing the Hutu against the Tutsi, the Tutsi women were presented as sexual objects. Indeed, the Chamber was told, for an example, that before being raped and killed, Alexia, who was the wife of the Professor, Ntereye, and her two nieces, were forced by the Interahamwe to undress and ordered to run and do exercises "in order to display the thighs of Tutsi women". The Interahamwe who raped Alexia said, as he threw her on the ground and got on top of her, "let us now see what the vagina of a Tutsi woman takes like." As stated above, Akayesu himself, speaking to the Interahamwe who were committing the rapes, said to them: "don't ever ask again what a Tutsi woman tastes like." This sexualized representation of ethnic identity graphi-

cally illustrates that Tutsi women were subjected to sexual violence because they were Tutsi. Sexual violence was a step in the process of destruction of the Tutsi group—destruction of the spirit, of the will to live, and of life itself.

733.   On the basis of the substantial testimonies brought before it, the Chamber finds that in most cases, the rapes of Tutsi women in Taba were accompanied with the intent to kill those women. Many rapes were perpetrated near mass graves where the women were taken to be killed. A victim testified that Tutsi women caught could be taken away by peasants and men with the promise that they would be collected later to be executed. Following an act of gang rape, a witness heard Akayesu say "tomorrow they will be killed" and they were actually killed. In this respect, it appears clearly to the Chamber that the acts of rape and sexual violence, as other acts of serious bodily and mental harm committed against the Tutsi, reflected the determination to make Tutsi women suffer and to mutilate them even before killing them, the intent being to destroy the Tutsi group while inflicting acute suffering on its members in the process.

734.   In light of the foregoing, the Chamber finds firstly that the acts described *supra* are indeed acts as enumerated in Article 2 (2) of the Statute, which constitute the factual elements of the crime of genocide, namely the killings of Tutsi or the serious bodily and mental harm inflicted on the Tutsi. The Chamber is further satisfied beyond reasonable doubt that these various acts were committed by Akayesu with the specific intent to destroy the Tutsi group, as such. Consequently ..., the Chamber finds Akayesu individually criminally responsible for genocide.

Section 5.   Discussion Notes/Questions

1.   In the present problem, it is stated that a group of Illyrians in Slavia petitioned the UN Sub–Commission on the Promotion and Protection of Human Rights (which until 2000 was known as the Sub–Commission on Prevention of Discrimination and Protection of Minorities). How do you evaluate its 1235 and 1503 procedures? Which would be the most useful for the Illyrians? What criteria would you use? What reforms would you recommend? For further discussion of the 1235 and 1503 procedures, see Philip Alston, *The Commission on Human Rights*, in The United Nations and Human Rights 139 (P. Alston ed., 1992); Richard B. Lillich & Hurst Hannum, International Human Rights: Problems of Law, Policy, and Practice 340–407 (3rd ed. 1995); Frank C. Newman & David S. Weissbrodt, International Human Rights: Law, Policy, and Process 101–43 (1990); Nigel Rodley, *United Nations Non–Treaty Procedures for Dealing with Human Rights Violations*, in Guide to International Human Rights Practice 65 (H. Hannum ed., 4th ed. 2004); Henry J. Steiner & Philip Alston, International Human Rights in Context: Law, Politics, Morals 611–647 (2d ed. 2000); Howard Tolley, The UN Commission on Human Rights 55–82 (1987); Ton J. M. Zuijdwijk, Petitioning the United Nations: A Study in Human Rights 39–116 (1982).

2.   Like the 1235 and 1503 procedures of the UN Commission on Human Rights and its Sub–Commisson, the thematic mechanisms procedure discussed in Reading C–3, *supra*, are based on the authority of the United Nations Charter, not the authority of any specialized treaty. Of what value might this procedure be in the present case, if any? For further reading on the thematic mechanisms and their techniques, see Nigel Rodley, *United Nations Human Rights Treaty Bodies and Special Procedures of the Commission on Human Rights–Complementarity or*

Competition? 25 H.R.Q. 882 (2003). *See also* the references cited in preceding Discussion Note/Question 1, *supra.*[52]

3.   The UN Human Rights Committee established under Article 28 of the 1966 International Covenant on Civil and Political Rights **(Basic Document 3.14)** (hereinafter "the HRC" to avoid confusion with the UN Charter-based Commission on Human Rights) is not available to the Illyrians as a means to press their human rights grievances against Slavia because Slavia is not a party to the Covenant's first Optional Protocol **(Basic Document 3.15)** pursuant to which Slavia would be otherwise subject to direct challenge. Article 1 of the Optional Protocol provides that "[a] State Party to the Covenant that becomes a party to the present Protocol recognizes the competence of the [Human Rights] Committee to receive and consider communications [*i.e.*, complaints or petitions] from individuals subject to its jurisdiction who claim to be victims of a violation by that State Party of any of the rights set forth in the Covenant." It also provides that "[n]o communication shall be received by the Committee if it concerns a State Party to the Covenant which is not a party to the present Protocol." Actually, even if the HRC were available to the Illyrians, their ability to press their grievances against Slavia would be somewhat constricted. According to the HRC's jurisprudence, only individual Illyrians personally affected by a violation of the Covenant, not Illyrians seeking to challenge Slavian law in the abstract by way of, for example, an *actio popularis* or a request for a declaratory judgment, can petition the HRC. Additionally, neither the right to self-determination (because it is a right conferred on peoples) nor the right to property (because it is not protected by the Covenant) can be the subject of a complaint before the HRC. Nevertheless, as part of the complex of human rights grievance procedures within the UN system, it merits study.

The HRC is so far one of four treaty-based organs within the UN system competent to receive and consider, in quasi-judicial manner, grievances from individuals claiming to be victims of human rights violations. The other three are the Committee on the Elimination of Racial Discrimination (CERD) established under Article 8 of the 1966 International Convention on the Elimination of All Forms of Racial Discrimination **(Basic Document 3.12)**, the Committee on Torture established under Article 17 of the 1984 Convention against Torture and Other Forms of Cruel, Inhuman or Degrading Treatment **(Basic Document 3.26)** and the Committee on the Elimination of Discrimination against Women under its 1999 Optional Protocol **(Basic Document 3.52)**. Since they operate along similar confidential lines (all proceedings involving the consideration of individual communications are held in private) and since the HRC has the most experience to date, we focus here on the HRC. As of 10 May 2006, the ICCPR Optional Protocol had 105 parties.

The HRC is composed, per Articles 28 and 29 of the Covenant, of eighteen "persons of high moral character and recognized competence in the field of human rights" who are elected from and by the State Parties to the Covenant but who "serve in their individual [expert] capacity" (in contrast, for example, to the UN Commission on Human Rights). Normally meeting for three weeks three times each year (twice in Geneva and once in New York), with its working groups meeting for one week prior to the commencement of each session, its main function, under the Covenant proper, is to review reports that the State Parties are required by Article 40(1) of the Covenant to submit "on the measures they have adopted which give effect to the rights recognized ... [in the Covenant] and on the progress made in the enjoyment of these rights." Proceedings discussing these reports are public (though generally poorly attended by the public). Under

---

52. As this book was going to press, the United Nations agreed to replace the Commission on Human Rights with a Human Rights Council. Membership of the Council will be elected by a majority of the General Assembly in order to ensure accountability to the broader UN membership. See UN Doc. A/60/L.48, A/RES/6/251 23 Feb. 2006.

the Optional Protocol, the main function of the HRC is to receive and consider individual communications alleging violations of human rights obligations under the Covenant. These proceedings are always in private. To date, the HCR never has been called upon to receive and consider a communication by one State Party to the Covenant against another State Party though this option is available under Article 41 of the Covenant.

For a communication to be admissible, it need not allege that the violation complained of involves "a consistent pattern of gross violations of human rights" as in the case of the Charter-based 1235 and 1503 procedures considered in Discussion Note/Question 1, *supra*. However, per Optional Protocol Article 5, the complainant may not complain about a matter identical to one being examined under another procedure of international investigation or settlement and must first exhaust domestic remedies (unless unduly prolonged or manifestly futile). Only the entire HRC can declare a case inadmissible, although it considers the advice of the rapporteur and working group that shall have made an earlier review of the communication's admissibility.

If the communication is deemed admissible, the HRC, per Article 4 of the Optional Protocol, brings it to the attention of the accused state, which then is given up to six months "[to] submit to the Committee written explanations or statements clarifying the matter and the remedy, if any, that may have been taken," with the petitioner usually receiving six weeks to reply to the accused state's submissions. The written communications of the petitioner and the State Party are then reviewed by the HRC, its findings are communicated to the parties, and a summary of these findings is reproduced in the HRC's annual report to the UN General Assembly. No provision exists for oral hearings or on-site investigations of complaints, and, unlike other international procedures, the HRC may not arrange a friendly settlement between the parties.

The HRC's decision, which is required by a majority vote of its members present, is not legally binding and, until recently, no sanctions were available for noncompliance with the Covenant. In 1990, however, the HRC adopted several compliance measures. Pursuant to them, first, the HRC may request the violating state to inform it of any action it has taken in relation to the case, within a period of 180 days. Second, as of 1991, the HRC, in its annual report, may indicate which states have complied with its decisions and which have not. Third, State Parties must now, in their required periodic reports, include information concerning steps they have taken to remedy violations. Finally, a "Special Rapporteur for the Follow–Up of Views," appointed by the HRC, now acts as a liaison between the violating government and the claimant victim. This last measure is analysed by Sian Lewis–Anthony in *Treaty-based Procedures for Making Human Rights Complaints with the UN System*, in Guide to International Human Rights Practice 43, 51–52 (H. Hannum ed., 4th ed. 2004). She notes that lack of funding has restricted the Special Rapporteur's efficacy.

For further reading on the HRC and other treaty-based human rights organs, see Christof H. Heyns & Frans Viljoen, *The Impact of the United Nations Human Rights Treaties on the Domestic Level,* 23 H.R.Q. 483 (2001); Sarah Joseph, Jenny Schultz & Melissa Castan, The International Covenant on Civil and Political Rights (2nd ed. 2004); Torkel Opsahl, *The Human Rights Committee*, in The United Nations and Human Rights 369 (P. Alston ed., 1992); Henry J. Steiner & Philip Alston, International Human Rights in Context: Law, Politics, Morals 738–

778 (2nd ed. 2000); Sian Lewis–Anthony, *supra*; The Future of the UN Human Rights Treaty Monitoring System (P. Alston & J. Crawford eds., 2000); David Weissbrodt, Joan Fitzpatrick & Frank Newman, International Human Rights: Law, Policy, and Process (2001); Kirsten A. Young, The Law and Process of the UN Human Rights Committee (2002). *See also* Anne F. Bayefsky, The UN Human Rights Treaty System: Universality at the Crossroads (2001), *available at* <http://www.yorku.ca/hrights>.

4. In the enforcement of human rights, ultimately the United Nations has authority, via Security Council actions under Chapter VII of the UN Charter **(Basic Document 1.5)**, to resort to coercive action in the form of economic and military measures of "humanitarian intervention." To date, this has required a finding, under Article 39, of "a threat to the peace, a breach of the peace, or an act of aggression." Increasingly, as demonstrated in the case of the UN's 1992–94 humanitarian intervention into Somalia, this language has become the subject of liberal interpretation. For details, see Sean D. Murphy, Humanitarian Intervention, the United Nations, and an Evolving World Order (1996). For extensive treatment of the issue, see Problem 4–1 ("Intervention in Loango") in Chapter 4, *supra*.

5. What enforcement mechanisms are contemplated in the 1951 Refugee Convention **(Basic Document 3.6)** and its 1967 Protocol **(Basic Document 3.16)**? As noted in the readings, these instruments are supervised by the Office of the UN High Commissioner for Refugees. They rely on parties implementing the terms of the treaties into domestic law. Faced with a global refugee population of over 17 million, increasingly states are moving to restrict the protection offered by international refugee law in the name of preservation of sovereignty.

Recent Australian law and practice provides a good case study of the tendency to redefine international legal standards. Australia, the world's largest island, has declared outlying islands and areas on which asylum seekers traveling by boat are likely to land to be outside its immigration zone. This is an attempt to preclude the operation of the Refugee Convention and its Protocol. Australia has set up a system of mandatory detention of all asylum seekers arriving by boat. The conditions of detention have been criticized by the UN Human Rights Committee in its views on a communication made under the Optional Protocol to the Covenant on Civil and Political Rights by a Cambodian asylum seeker held in a remote detention centre in Western Australia. The applicant (or author as complainants are termed) was detained for four years while his application for refugee status was being considered. He argued that he had been detained arbitrarily within the meaning of Article 9 (1) of the Covenant and the Committee agreed with him saying that "the notion of 'arbitrariness' must not be equated with 'against the law' but be interpreted more broadly to include such elements as inappropriateness and injustice." *See* A v. Australia, Case No. 560/93, at ¶ 9.2. The Australian government simply rejected the Committee's views as an unacceptable interpretation of Article 14 of the Covenant. *See* 19 Austl. Y.B.I.L. 208 (1998). For an account of recent Australian refugee law and politics see *Symposium on Refugees* 23 U. New So.Wales L. J. (2000); Frank Brennan, S.J., Tampering with Asylum: A Universal Humanitarian Problem (2003).

Whatever their rights under the Refugee Convention and Protocol, asylum seekers are able to claim the protection also of international human rights law. Relevant obligations include the right not to be subject to torture or cruel and inhuman or degrading treatment or punishment (contained, for example, in

Article 7 of the Covenant on Civil and Political Rights), the right to be free from arbitrary detention (contained, for example, in Article 9 of the Covenant on Civil and Political Rights) and the right not to be expelled, returned or extradited to a country where the person is likely to be subject to torture (Article 3 of the 1984 Convention against Torture **(Basic Document 3.26)**). Parallel rights exist under the various regional systems of human rights. See Ralph Allenweldt, *Protection against Expulsion under Article 3 of the European Convention on Human Rights*, 4 E.J. I.L. 360 (1993).

The materials extracted in Section E, *supra*, are evidence of lively debate among international refugee lawyers about future directions in this area of law. What do you think of the proposals made by Hathaway and Neve (Reading E–4, *supra*) to reconfigure the law to respond better to the reality of considerable state reluctance to accept refugees? How persuasive is the response by Anker, Fitzpatrick and Shaknove (Reading E–5, *supra*)?

In 2002, the UN High Commissioner for Refugees announced an initiative to improve refugee protection worldwide called "Convention Plus." Although the 1951 Convention and its 1967 Protocol remain the corner stone of international refugee protection, the "Convention Plus" program is designed to create further special agreements to deal with issues such as resettlement and the responsibilities of states in the event of secondary movements (when refugees and asylum-seekers move from the initial country of refuge to another country).

A further issue is the capacity of treaties drafted with very different circumstances in mind to respond to the mass movement of asylum seekers, often in search of better economic opportunities. Should poverty be a valid ground to seek asylum in a different country? For discussion of this issue see Kristen Walker, *Defending the 1951 Convention Definition of Refugees*, 17 Geo. Immigr. L. J. 583 (2003) and readings in Problem 5–3 ("Suspected Terrorists in Hibernia"), *infra*.

6. Implicated in the present problem is the crime of genocide, defined in Article II of the 1948 Convention on the Prevention and Punishment of the Crime of Genocide **(Basic Document 3.2)** to mean

> the following acts committed with intent to destroy, in whole or in part, a national, ethnical, racial or religious group, as such:
>
> (a) Killing members of the group;
>
> (b) Causing serious bodily or mental harm to members of the group;
>
> (c) Deliberately inflicting on the group conditions of life calculated to bring about its physical destruction in whole or in part;
>
> (d) Imposing measures intended to prevent births within the group;
>
> (e) Forcibly transferring children of the group to another group.

Was genocide committed in Bosnia–Herzegovina during 1992–95? No legally explicit answer to this question has yet been given. However, according to the former General Agent of the Republic of Bosnia and Herzegovina in the Republic's suit before the International Court of Justice to cause Yugoslavia/Serbia and Montenegro to cease and desist from violating the United Nations Genocide Convention, "Bosnia has ... won what is tantamount to two pre-judgments on the merits of the case in the World Court's Order of 8 April 1993 and the Court's Order of 13 September 1993, as conceded by the late Judge Tarasov in his Declaration attached to the former Order, and in his Dissenting Opinion attached to the latter Order." Francis E. Boyle, *Disposition of the Case Concerning Application of the Convention on the Prevention and Punishment of the Crime of*

Genocide, in The Bosnian People Charge Genocide: Proceedings at the International Court of Justice Concerning Bosnia v. Serbia on the Prevention and Punishment of the Crime of Genocide xx (F. Boyle ed., 1996). The basis for the jurisdiction of the ICJ is Article IX of the Genocide Convention **(Basic Document 3.2)** to which both Bosnia and the former Yugoslavia were parties. That Article provides that disputes between contracting parties relating to the interpretation, application or fulfilment of the Convention shall be submitted to the International Court of Justice. While not deciding on the merits that "genocide" was in fact committed by Serbia in Bosnia–Herzegovina during 1992–95, the Court did observe in its 8 April 1993 Order, quoting UN, General Assembly Resolution 96 (I) of 11 December 1946, that "the crime of genocide 'shocks the conscience of mankind, results in great losses to humanity . . . and is contrary to moral law and to the spirit and aims of the United Nations' " [1993 ICJ 4, ¶ 49 (16 Apr)], and then, later, in its 13 September 1993 Order, reiterated this observation and further observed that "since the Order of 8 April 1993 was made, and despite that Order, and despite many resolutions of the Security Council of the United Nations, great suffering and loss of life has been sustained by the population of Bosnia–Herzegovina in circumstances which shock the conscience of mankind and flagrantly conflict with moral law and the spirit and aims of the United Nations" [1993 ICJ 325, ¶¶ 51–52 (13 Sep)]. On 11 July 1966, the World Court ruled in favor of the Republic of Bosnia–Herzegovina on the issues of the Court's jurisdiction and the admissibility of the Republic's case. Case Concerning the Application of the Convention on the Prevention and Punishment of the Crime of Genocide (Bosnia and Herzegovina v. Yugo./Serbia and Montenegro) (Preliminary Objections), 1996 ICJ (II) 595 (11 Jul). The ICJ case has been bogged down in procedural questions, particularly the issue whether the "rump" state of Yugoslavia had succeeded to the former Yugoslavia's acceptance of the Genocide Convention. Following the judgment on preliminary objections, Yugoslavia filed counter-claims (submitted on 22 July 1997 in its Counter–Memorial), requesting the ICJ to adjudge that "Bosnia and Herzegovina is responsible for the acts of genocide committed against the Serbs in Bosnia and Herzegovina" and that it "has the obligation to punish the persons held responsible" for these acts. It also asked the Court to rule that "Bosnia and Herzegovina is bound to take necessary measures so that the said acts would not be repeated" and "to eliminate all consequences of the violation" of the Genocide Convention. On 28 July 1997, Bosnia and Herzegovina challenged the Yugoslavian counter-claims. By an Order of December 17 1997, the ICJ held by 13 votes to 1 that Yugoslavia's counter-claims were "admissible as such" and that they "form part of the current proceedings" in the case. Following the fall of the Milosevic government in Yugoslavia, that country withdrew its counter-claims on 10 September 2001. Yugoslavia however requested the Court to revise its 1996 preliminary objections judgment because it argued that the Federal Republic of Yugoslavia's admission to the UN in 2000 proved that it had not succeeded to Yugoslavia's ratification of the Genocide Convention. On 3 February 2003 the ICJ delivered its Judgment on the admissibility of the Application filed by Yugoslavia for the revision of the Judgment of 11 July 1996 in the case of Bosnia and Herzegovina v Yugoslavia. The Court, by ten votes to three, found that "the Application submitted by the Federal Republic of Yugoslavia for revision . . . is inadmissible."

Meanwhile, on 2 July 1999 the Republic of Croatia instituted proceedings before the ICJ against the Federal Republic of Yugoslavia (FRY) for violations of the 1948 Genocide Convention alleged to have been committed between 1991 and 1995. As in Bosnia's action, Croatia based ICJ jurisdiction on Article IX of the

Convention. In its Application, Croatia contended that "by directly controlling the activity of its armed forces, intelligence agents, and various paramilitary detachments, on the territory of ... Croatia, in the Knin region, eastern and western Slavonia, and Dalmatia, [Yugoslavia] is liable [for] the 'ethnic cleansing' of Croatian citizens from these areas ... as well as extensive property destruction— and is required to provide reparation for the resulting damage". Croatia went on to state that "in addition, by directing, encouraging, and urging Croatian citizens of Serb ethnicity in the Knin region to evacuate the area in 1995, as ... Croatia reasserted its legitimate governmental authority ... [Yugoslavia] engaged in conduct amounting to a second round of 'ethnic cleansing.'" According to Croatia, "the aggression waged by [Yugoslavia]" resulted in 20,000 dead, 55,000 injured and over 3,000 individuals still unaccounted for. Of this number, 1,700 were killed and more than 4,000 injured in Vukovar alone. Furthermore, 10 per cent of the country's housing capacity is alleged to have been destroyed, with 590 towns and villages having suffered damage (including 35 razed to the ground), while 1,821 cultural monuments, 323 historical sites and 450 Croatian catholic churches were also destroyed or damaged. Croatia further claims that some 3 million explosive devices of various kinds were planted in Croatia, mostly anti-personnel and anti-tank devices, currently rendering some 300,000 hectares of arable land unusable, and that around 25 per cent of its total economic capacity, including major facilities such as the Adriatic pipeline, was damaged or destroyed. Accordingly, Croatia requested the Court to adjudge and declare that Yugoslavia "breached its legal obligations" to Croatia under the Genocide Convention and that it "has an obligation to pay to ... Croatia, in its own right and as parens patriae for its citizens, reparations for damages to persons and property, as well as to the Croatian economy and environment caused by the foregoing violations of international law in a sum to be determined by the Court". After delays in filing Memorials by both parties, on 11 September 2002, Yugoslavia filed preliminary objections to the jurisdiction of the Court and to admissibility. Pursuant to Article 79 of the Rules of Court, the proceedings on the merits were then suspended.

There is little international jurisprudence on what constitutes an act of genocide, although there are some interesting national court decisions such as those of Israeli courts in *A.G. Israel v. Eichmann* (1968) 36 I.L.R. 18 (D.C.) and 277 (S.Ct.) and the Australian Federal Court in *Nulyarimma v. Thompson* [1999] F.C.A. 1192. The International Criminal Tribunal for the Former Yugoslavia has considered the issue raised in *Akayesu* before the International Tribunal for Rwanda (Reading G–14, *supra*) of whether sexual violence can constitute genocide. In *Prosecutor v. Furundzija* Case No. IT–95–17/1–T, 10 December 1998, the Tribunal agreed that rape could be genocide, although it was not required to decide this issue. For further discussion see Sherrie Lynne Russell–Brown, *Rape as an Act of Genocide,* 21 Berkeley J. Int'l L. 350 (2003); Michelle J. Jarvis, *An Emerging Gender Perspective on International Crimes*, in International Criminal Law Developments in the Case Law of the ICTY 157 (G. Boas & W. Schabas eds., 2003); Kristen Boon, *Rape and Forced Pregnancy under the ICC Statute: Human Dignity, Autonomy, and Consent*, 32 Colum. Hum. Rts. L. Rev. 625 (2001).

Are you satisfied with the definition given to genocide in the 1948 Convention? Is it sufficiently inclusive? Frank Chalk, in *Redefining Genocide*, in Genocide 47 (G. Andreopoulos ed., 1994), comments, at 48, that the definition "was the direct result of a political compromise designed to preserve the remainder of the Genocide Convention. It answered the practical needs of governments as well as the strictures of international lawyers." What is Chalk saying? Does his comment imply that the 1948 Convention's definition may be too narrow, that there may be alternative more expansive definitions that would be more suitable to contemporary global life? For guidance, consult Thomas W. Simon, *Defining Genocide,* 15 Wis. In'l L. J. 243 (1996); Pieter N. Drost, *The Crime of State* 125 (1959); *Encyclopedia of Genocide* (I. Charny ed., 1999); Steven R. Ratner & Jason S. Abrams, Accountability for Human Rights Atrocities in International Law: Beyond the Nuremburg Legacy (1997).

7.   In the present problem, two permanent members of the Security Council, the United States and the United Kingdom, resort to the International Court of Justice (ICJ) at The Hague for the purpose of holding Slavia accountable for claimed violations of the 1948 Convention on the Prevention and Punishment of the Crime of Genocide **(Basic Document 3.2)**. Popularly known, together with its inaccurately named predecessor (the Permanent Court of International Justice), as the "World Court," the ICJ is one of the six principal organs of the United Nations, along with the Economic and Social Council, the General Assembly, the Security Council, the Trusteeship Council, and the Secretariat. For details concerning the Court and its procedural competence, see Discussion Note/Questions 1–3 in Section B–1 of Chapter 3, *supra* at 228–33. For details concerning the Court's treatment so far of allegations of genocide, see Discussion Note/Question 6, *supra*. The possibility of the United States taking judicial action with respect to genocide may seem unlikely in view of its tradition of inaction over the last century. In "A Problem from Hell:" America and the Age of Genocide (2002), Samantha Power chronicles the US indifference to genocide occurring in Armenia, in Europe during World War II, in Cambodia, Rwanda and Bosnia. She argues that the failure to take any action was typically a political choice and not the product of ignorance.

8.   The principal human rights enforcement regime invoked in the present problem is the Organization of Security and Co-operation in Europe (OSCE). The choice seems fitting, even if not ideal. Consider, thus, the following appraisal by Professor Forsythe:

> Whereas over time the [OSCE] finally found an important niche for it-self in "first-era issues" involving liberalism versus communism, the task in the 1990s is for [the OSCE] to define its place in "second-era issues" involving transitions to democracy in a context of economic difficulty and communal friction. The almost complete acceptance—in principle at least—of liberal political philosophy within the [OSCE], symbolized by the Concluding Document of the Copenhagen Meeting on the Human Dimension in 1990 **[Basic Document 3.34]**, does not mean that there is less need for multilateral help in solving complex and thorny problems. For example, before 1989 much [OSCE] time was spent trying to obtain acceptance of a human right to leave a country; after 1989 a major problem lay in getting people to stay in their country and not become an unwanted economic migrant in the West....

> It may turn out to be the case that the [OSCE] will prove itself moderately influential for the protection of human rights in the near future in one of three types of situations. Where there is already, or will soon be, a situation of relatively stable democracy (relative to the rest of East–Central Europe), the [OSCE] will probably be mostly irrelevant. The Council of Europe [based in Strasbourg] is likely to be the primary multilateral institution for protecting rights.... Where there are systematic and massive violations of human rights involving considerable violence, like that arising out of ethnic/national passions and manifesting genocide, the [OSCE] is, on the

evidence thus far, also likely to be mostly irrelevant—although there may be one or two exceptions.

The [OSCE] "never got into the game in Yugoslavia" regarding hostility between Serbs and Croats. It was also mostly irrelevant in the hostility between Serbs and Bosnians, Armenians and Azeris, ethnic Russians and Moldavians. It did vote to suspend Serbia for its aggression against Bosnia. And it might be the locus of a call for military force to terminate or reduce human rights violations, perhaps linked to NATO.

This record would leave the [OSCE], at least as now constituted, with perhaps some influence in the intermediate situation between relatively stable democracy on the one hand, and extensive communal violence on the other. That is the situation in which a government has accepted, with some degree of good faith, the [OSCE] norms on human rights, but has not yet been able to make much progress on securing them. Such governments might be susceptible to the international embarrassment involved in [OSCE] pressures, especially if bilateral and other multilateral transactions, as on foreign assistance of various sorts, were tied to living up to [OSCE] human rights provisions.

David P. Forsythe, Human Rights in the New Europe 178–79 (1994).

Hathaway and Neve (Reading E–4, *supra*) refer to the OSCE process for conflict resolution as "a useful model for structured collaboration with a relatively informal association of states." They point to its ability "to get a disparate group of states to come quickly to the negotiating table." However, in the context of refugee crises, they express concern that the quorum requirement for convening a meeting of senior OSCE officials "is unduly onerous." They add, at p. 200: "A government faced with a refugee influx that it believes threatens key interests might be tempted to resort to *refoulement* or other violation of refugee rights if it cannot immediately secure a high level of agreement to meet in order to share-out responsibilities and burdens. As well, the OSCE requirement that all decisions be arrived at by consensus may prove an obstacle to the ability of the process to generate clear and workable decisions...."

9. Also implicated in the present problem, indeed a central theme, is the human right to self-determination. In its early incarnation, as we have seen, it was the battle-cry of the post-World War II movement of Third World peoples that led to the dismantling of colonial empires. Today, as in the instant problem, it is at the heart of nationalistic demands for independent statehood both following the breakup of the Soviet empire and in other contexts such as East Timor. Another and perhaps yet more dominant way in which it is invoked, as evidenced in the extract by Professor Anaya in Reading F–9, *supra*, is in the context of indigenous peoples rights, often in relation to the natural environment from which such peoples derive their sustenance. Although the first victims of "ethnic cleansing" and genocidal behavior if not genocide itself, typically indigenous peoples have been ignored in the mainstream literature. For consideration of this aspect of the human right to self-determination, see Problem 7–6 ("A Rainforest and the Guahibo Are Threatened in Amazonia and Caribia") in Chapter 7, *infra* at 1241–58.

10. Considering the vast numbers of people worldwide who are denied even the most basic of needs and decencies, how can we—lawyers and non-lawyers alike—use the term "human rights" and believe ourselves to be talking about reality? To illustrate, how is it that some of us can say that freedom of thought and expression is a "fundamental human right" while knowing that freedom of thought and expression is not widely practiced in the world today? Or, alternative-

ly, how is it that others of us can say that the right to work is a "fundamental human right"—as it is declared to be, for example, in Article 1 of the European Social Charter **(Basic Document 3.11)**—while knowing that this so-called right is at best marginally guaranteed in the most powerful capitalist states of the present global system? Saying something is so does not necessarily make it so; and, as Mr. Justice Holmes is reputed to have said—overstated, we submit—"a right without a remedy is no right at all."

In other words, what do we mean by the expression "human rights"? Do we mean, simply, the sum of social priorities that are variously set forth in the numerous declarations and conventions which have been promulgated under the auspices of the United Nations and its allied agencies—most conspicuously, perhaps, the Universal Declaration of Human Rights? Or do we mean something else? Is it possible that your answer could be influenced by how you define "law" or "international law"? By whether you were trained in the Liberal or Socialist tradition? By your personal values? This issue of definition, it must be emphasized, is not a trivial matter. As one astute observer has warned, "what we think human rights really are will inevitably influence not only our judgment as to which types of claims to recognize as human rights, but also our expectations and programs for implementation and compliance with these standards." Richard B. Bilder, *Rethinking International Human Rights: Some Basic Questions*, 1969 Wis. L. Rev. 171, 174.

For further related discussion, consult: Myres S. McDougal, Harold D. Lasswell & Lung-chu Chen, Human Rights and World Public Order—The Basic Policies of an International Law of Human Dignity (1980); Alan John Mitchell, Human Rights and Human Diversity (1986); Henry J. Steiner & Philip Alston, International Human Rights in Context: Law, Politics, Morals (2d ed. 2000); Christian Tomuschat, Human Rights: Between Idealism and Realism (2003); Elizabeth K. Spahn, *Waiting for Credentials: Feminist Theories of Enforcement of International Human Rights*, 44 Am. U. L. Rev. 1053 (1995); Barbara Stark, *International Human Rights Law, Feminist Jurisprudence, and Nietzche's "Eternal Return": Turning the Wheel*, 19 Harv. Women's L. J. 169 (1996); David Weissbrodt, Joan Fitzpatrick & Frank Newman, International Human Rights: Law, Policy, and Process (2001).

11. Whatever we may mean by "human rights" or "human rights law," it is undeniable that much work is now being done to promote and protect human rights by a growing number of independent-minded nongovernmental organizations (NGOs) in the international human rights field—for example, Amnesty International (mentioned in the fact statement of the instant problem). Six other NGOs especially to be noted are Human Rights Watch, the International Commission of Jurists, the International Human Rights Law Group, the International League for Human Rights, the Lawyers Committee for Human Rights, and Physicians for Human Rights. For details on these and other groups, see, *e.g.*, Roger S. Clark, *The International League for Human Rights and Southwest Africa, 1945–1957: The Human Rights NGO as Catalyst in the International Legal Process*, 2 H.R.Q. 101 (1981); Richard Pierre Claude, *What Do Human Rights NGOs Do?*, in Human Rights in the World Community 424 (R. Claude & B. Weston eds., 3d ed., 2006); Holly Cullen & Karen Morrow, *International Civil Society in International Law: The Growth of NGO Participation*, 1 Non–State Actors & Int'l L. 7 (2001); David S. Weissbrodt, *The Contribution of International Nongovernmental Organizations to the Protection of Human Rights*, in 2 Human Rights in International Law 403 (T. Meron ed., 1984); ____, *Fact-finding by International Nongovernmental Human Rights Organizations*, 22 Va. J. Int'l L. 1

(1981); ___, *The Role of International Non–Governmental Organizations in the Implementation of Human Rights*, 12 T.IL.J. 293 (1977); Laurie S. Wiseberg, *Nongovenmental Organizations in the Struggle against Child Labor*, in Child Labor and Human Rights 343 (B. Weston ed., 2005).

12.   David Kennedy has offered a strong critique of the international human rights system in *The International Human Rights Movement: Part of the Problem?*, 15 Harv. Hum. Rts. J. 99 (2002). He lists a series of "pragmatic worries and polemical charges" about the modern human rights movement. These include the concern that human rights have come to occupy the field of emancipatory possibility, edging out other critiques of the social order (such as economic ones), and that human rights talk promises more than it can ever deliver; the claim that human rights discourse views both the problems and solutions to injustice too narrowly; the sense that human rights are too closely tied to a particular, western, Enlightenment model; and the suggestion that the international human rights movement reinforces bad international governance. How do you assess Kennedy's arguments? Do you agree with them? Why or why not? What reforms of the international human rights movement do they suggest? For a reaction to Kennedy's article, see Hilary Charlesworth, *Author! Author! A Response to David Kennedy*, 15 Harv. Hum. Rts. J. 127 (2002). For a different style of philosophical and theoretical critique of human rights to that of David Kennedy, see Costas Douzinas, The End of Rights (1999).

13.   Judging from the foregoing readings about the Final Act of the Conference on Security and Co-operation in Europe **(Basic Document 1.12)** and its progeny, it is not just the term "human rights" that appears problematic, but also the term "law." Arie Bloed (Reading D–13, *supra*) points out that neither the Final Act nor any of it associated instruments constitute a treaty and that therefore they are not legally binding upon the OSCE Participating States. Why, then, do the OSCE Participating States act as if they are binding or, more precisely, as if the pledges contained in them are binding? Is it possible that the Final Act and its progeny may count as law even though the Participating States say that they do not have legal force and effect? Reconsider Bloed:

> The binding force of these documents is not seriously doubted. Van Dijk correctly states: "A commitment does not have to be legally binding in order to have binding force as the distinction between legal and non-legal binding force resides in the legal consequences attached to the binding force," not in the binding force as such. Violation of politically, but not legally binding agreements is as inadmissible as violation of norms of international law. In this respect there is no difference between politically and legally binding rules.

What is Bloed saying? Does he make sense? Is the Final Act law or isn't it? Is Bloed (and, by implication, Van Dijk) trying to have it both ways? What is law? In *Human Rights and the OSCE*, 18 H.R.Q. 668, 676 (1996), Rachel Brett writes of the OSCE "political commitments" as follows:

> The distinction between political and legal force is . . . significant even if the degree of binding force is deemed to be the same. There is no way in which political commitments can have legal effect internationally or domestically. In particular, they cannot be invoked in domestic courts, do not have direct effect, and are less likely to be incorporated into domestic law—not only because of their nonlegal character per se but also because, not being negotiated as legal documents, the degree of precision of the latter is frequently lacking.

Does this help? Is Brett convincing? Is international law any less law for not being enforceable domestically?

20. *Bibliographical Note.* For supplemental discussion concerning the principal themes addressed in this problem, consult the following additional specialized materials:

a. International Human Rights in General

(1) *Books/Monographs/Reports/Symposia.* C. Douzinas, The End of Rights (1999); Guide to International Human Rights Practice (H. Hannum ed., 4th ed. 2004); Human Rights: An Agenda for the Next Century (L. Henkin & J. Hargrove eds., 1994); Human Rights in the World Community (R. Claude & B. Weston eds., 1989); M. Ignatieff, Human Rights as Politics and Idolatry (2001); Human Rights in the National and International Law (A. Robertson ed., 1968); Human Rights of Women: National and International Perspectives (R. Cook ed., 1994); 1–2 International Dimensions of Human Rights (K. Vasak ed., 1982); International Human Rights Law (M. Addo ed., 2001); R. Lillich & H. Hannum, International Human Rights: Problems of Law, Policy, and Practice (3rd ed. 1995); M. McDougal, H. Lasswell & L. Chen, Human Rights and World Public Order—The Basic Policies of an International Law of Human Dignity (1980); R. Provost, International Human Rights and Humanitarian Law (2002); H. Steiner & P. Alston, International Human Rights in Context: Law, Politics, Morals (2d. ed. 2000).

(2) *Articles/Book Chapters.* A. Bayefsky, *Making the Human Rights Treaties Work*, in Human Rights: An Agenda for the Next Century 229 (L. Henkin & J. Hargrove eds., 1994); J. Bond, *International Intersectionality: A Theoretical and Pragmatic Exploration of Women's International Human Rights Violations*, 52 Emory L.J. 71 (2003); J. Burgers, *The Road to San Francisco: The Revival of the Human Rights Idea in the Twentieth Century*, 14 H.R.Q. 447 (1992); D. Cassel, *International Human Rights Law in Practice: Does International Human Rights Law Make a Difference?* 2 Chi. J. Int'l L. 121 (2001); M. Koskenniemi, *The Effect of Rights on Political Culture*, in The EU and Human Rights (P. Alston ed., 1999).

b. The Organization on Security and Co-operation in Europe

(1) *Books/Monographs/Reports/Symposia.* M. Arnheim, The Handbook of Human Rights Law: An Accessible Approach to the Issues and Principles (2004); Fundamental Rights in Europe: the European Convention on Human Rights and its member states, 1950–2000 (R. Blackburn & J. Polakiewicz eds., 2001); F. Mastny, The Helsinki Process and the Reintegration of Europe 1986–1991: Analysis and Documentation (1992); J. Matlary, Intervention for Human Rights in Europe (2002); The Challenges of Change: The Helsinki Summit of the CSCE and Its Aftermath (A. Bloed ed., 1994).

(2) *Articles/Book Chapters.* K. Boyle, *Europe: The Council of Europe, the OSCE, and the European Union*, in Guide to International Human Rights Practice 143 (H. Hannum ed., 4th ed. 2004); R. Brett, *Human Rights and the OSCE*, 18 H.R.Q. 668 (1996); D. Shelton, *The Boundaries of Human Rights Jurisdiction in Europe*, 13 Duke J. Comp. & Int'l L. 95 (2003).

c. International Refugee Law

(1) *Books/Monographs/Reports/Symposia.* G. Goodwin–Gill, The Refugee in International Law (2d ed. 1996); 1–2 A. Grahl–Madsen, The Emergent International Law Relating to Refugees: Past, Present, Future (1982); J. Hathaway, The Rights of Refugees under International Law (2005); M. Ignatieff, Blood and

Belonging: Journeys into the New Nationalism (1993); Reconceiving International Refugee Law (J. Hathaway ed., 1997); The Refugees Convention, 1951: The Travaux Préparatoires Analyzed (P. Weis ed., 1994); D. Weissbrodt & L. Danielson, Immigration Law and Procedure in a Nutshell (5th ed. 2005).

(2) *Articles/Book Chapters.* B. Alexander, *Detention of Asylum–Seekers in the United States*, 7. Hum. Rts. Br. 20 (2000); Anonymous, *The UNHCR Note on International Protection You Won't See*, 9 Int'l J. Refugee L. 267 (1997); G. Coles, *Approaching the Refugee Problem Today, in* Refugees and International Relations 373 (G. Loescher & L. Monahan eds., 1989); B. Donkoh, *A Half–Century of International Refugee Protection: Who's Responsible, What's Ahead?* 18 Berkeley J. Int'l L. 260 (2000); E. Feller, *International Refugee Protection 50 Years On: The Protection Challenges of the Past, Present and Future*, 83(843) IRRC 581 (2001); J. Fitzpatrick, *Revitalizing the 1951 Refugee Convention*, 9 Harv. Hum. Rts. J. 229 (1996); B. Frelick, *Haitian Boat Interdiction and Return: First Asylum and First Principles of Refugee Protection*, 26 Cornell Int'l L. J. 675 (1993); G. Goodwin–Gill, *The Haitian Refoulement Case: A Comment*, 6 Int'l J. Refugee L. 103 (1994); A. Hans & A. Suhrke, *Responsibility Sharing, in* Reconceiving International Refugee Law (J. C. Hathaway ed., 1997); A. Helton, *Toward Harmonized Asylum Procedures in North America: The Proposed United States–Canada Memorandum of Understanding for Cooperation in the Examination of Refugee Status Claims from Nationals of Third Countries*, 26 Cornell Int'l L. J. 737 (1993); _____, *The United States Government Program of Intercepting and Forcibly Returning Haitian Boat People to Haiti: Policy Implications and Prospects*, 10 N.Y.L.S.J. Hum. Rts. 325 (1993); _____, *United States Immigration Policy: The Conflict Between Human Rights and Perceptions of National Identity and Self–Interest, in* Legitimate and Illegitimate Discrimination: New Issues in Migration 235 (Howard Adelman ed., 1995); _____, *Refugee Rights and Realities: Evolving International Concepts and Regimes*, 95. A.J.I.L. 478 (2001); L. Henkin, *That "S" Word: Sovereignty, And Globalization, And Human Rights, Et Cetera*, 68 Fordham L. Rev. 1 (1999); S. Jaquemet, *The Cross–Fertilization of International Humanitarian Law and International Refugee Law*, 83 (843) IRRC 651 (September 2001); S.S. Juss, *Sovereignty, Culture, And Community: Refugee Policy and Human Rights in Europe*, 3 ULCA J. Int'l L. & Foreign Aff. 463 (1998 /1999); H. Leary, *The Nature of Global Commitments and Obligations: Limits on State Sovereignty in the Area of Asylum*, 5. Ind. J. Global Leg. Stud. 297 (1997); T. Magner, *Does a Failed State Country of Origin Result in a Failure of International Protection? A Review of Policies Toward Asylum–Seekers in Leading Asylum Nations*, 15 Geo. Immigr. L.J. 703 (2001); S. Martin & A. Schoenholtz, *Asylum in Practice: Successes, Failures, and the Challenges Ahead*, 14 Geo. Immigr. L. J. 589 (2000); M. Parrish, *Redefining the Refugee: The Universal Declaration of Human Rights as a Basis for Refugee Protection*, 22 Cardozo L. Rev. 223, (2000); P. Schuck, *Refugee Burden–Sharing: A Modest Proposal*, 22 Yale J. Int'l L. 243 (1997).

d.   *Self–Determination and Minority Rights*

(1) *Books/Monographs/Reports/Symposia.* S. Anaya, Indigenous Peoples in International Law (2d ed. 2004); G. Gottlieb, Nation Against State: A New Approach to Ethnic Conflicts and the Decline of Sovereignty (1993); T. Gurr, Minorities At Risk: A Global View of Ethno-political Conflicts (1993); M. Halperin et al., Self–Determination in the New World Order (1992); H. Hannum, Autonomy, Sovereignty, and Self–Determination: The Accommodation of Conflicting Rights (rev. ed. 1996); K. Knop, Diversity and Self–Determination in International Law (2002); Self–Determination in International Law (R. McCorquodale ed.,

2000); The Rights of Nations: Nations and Nationalism in a Changing World (D. Clarke & C. Jones eds., 1999); J. Valadez, Deliberative Democracy: Political Legitimacy, and Self–Determination in Multicultural Societies (2001).

(2) *Articles/Book Chapters*. R. Araujo, *Sovereignty, Human Rights, and Self–Determination: The Meaning of International Law*, 24 F.I.L.J. 1477 (2001); T. Farer. *The Ethics of Intervention in Self–Determination Struggles*, 25 H.R.Q. 382 (2003); T. Franck, *The Emerging Right to Democratic Governance*, 86 A.J.I.L. 46 (1992); G. Gilbert, *The Burgeoning Minority Rights Jurisprudence of the European Court of Human Rights*, 24 H.R.Q. 736 (2002); R. Murray & S. Wheatley, *Groups and the African Charter on Human and Peoples' Rights*, 25 H.R.Q. 213 (2003); R. Miller, *Self-Determination in International Law and the Demise of Democracy?* 41 Colum. J. Transnat'l L. 601 (2003); J. Oloka–Onyango, *Heretical Reflections on the Right to Self–Determination: Prospects and Problems for a Democratic Global Future in the New Millennium*, 15 Am. U. Int'l L. Rev. 151 (1999); H. Richardson, *"Failed States," Self–Determination, and Preventive Diplomacy: Colonialist Nostalgia and Democratic Expectations*, 10 Temple Int'l & Comp. L. J. 1 (1996).

e. War Crimes, Genocide, and Crimes Against Humanity

(1) *Books/Monographs/Reports/Symposia*. K. Askin, War Crimes Against Women: Prosecution in International War Crimes Tribunals (1997); M. Bassiouni, Crimes Against Humanity in International Criminal Law (1992); M. Bassiouni & M. McCormick, Sexual Violence: An Invisible Weapon of War in the Former Yugoslavia (Int'l Hum. Rts. L. Inst. Occasional Paper No. 1, 1996); International Criminal Law Developments in the Case Law of the ICTY 157 (Gideon Boas & William Schabas eds., 2003); Genocide: Uses and Abuses (G. Andreopoulos ed., 1994); *Encyclopedia of Genocide* (I. Charny ed., 1999); I. Horowitz, Taking Lives: Genocide and State Power (4th ed. 1996); L. Kuper, Genocide: Its Political Use in the Twentieth Century (1981); R. Kerr, The International Criminal Tribunal for the Former Yugoslavia (2004); 1–2 War Crimes, Genocide and Crimes Against Humanity: An Insider's Guide to the International Criminal Tribunal for the Former Yugoslavia (V. Morris & M. Scharf eds., 1995); S. Ratner & J. Abrams, Accountability for Human Rights Atrocities in International Law: Beyond the Nuremburg Legacy (1997); G. Robertson & K. Roth, Crimes Against Humanity: The Struggle for Global Justice (2003); M. Walzer, Just and Unjust Wars: A Moral Argument with Historical Illustrations (2d ed. 1992); P. Williams & M. Scharf, Peace with Justice? War Crimes and Accountability in the Former Yugoslavia (2002).

(2) *Articles/Book Chapters*. P. Akhavan, *Punishing War Crimes in the Former Yugoslavia: A Critical Juncture for the New World Order*, 15 H.R.Q. 262 (1993); R. Coomaraswamy, *Of Kali Born: Violence and the Law in Sri Lanka*, in Freedom from Violence: Women's Strategies from Around the World (M. Schuler ed., 1992); J. Fitzpatrick, *The Use of International Human Rights Norms to Combat Violence against Women*, in Human Rights of Women: National and International Perspectives 532 (R. Cook ed., 1994); J. Gardam, *Gender and Non–Combatant Immunity*, 3 Transnat'l L. & Contemp. Probs. 345 (1993); T. Meron, *Shakespeare's Henry the Fifth and the Law of War*, 86 A.J.I.L. 1 (1992); ———, *Rape as a Crime under International Humanitarian Law*, 87 A.J.I.L. 424 (1993); M. Mills, *War Crimes in the 21st Century*, 3 Hofstra L. & Pol'y Symp. 47 (1999); C. Niarchos, *Women, War, and Rape: Challenges Facing the International Tribunal for the Former Yugoslavia*, 17 H.R.Q. 650 (1995); B. Van Schaack, *The Definition of Crimes Against Humanity: Resolving the Incoherence*, 37 Colum. J. Transnat'l L. 787 (1999); M.

Scharf, *Swapping Amnesty for Peace: Was There A Duty to Prosecute International Crimes in Haiti?*, 31 T.I.L.J. 1 (1996); D. Scheffer, *International Judicial Intervention*, 102 Foreign Pol'y 34 (Spring 1996); J. van der Vyver, *Prosecution and Punishment of the Crime of Genocide*, 23 F.I.L.J. 286 (1999); A. de Waal & R. Omaar, *The Genocide in Rwanda and the International Response*, 94 Current History 156 (1995).

Problem 5-2

Women's Reproductive Rights in Hibernia

SECTION 1. FACTS

Hibernia is a small republic in Europe with a strong Catholic tradition. Indeed, Catholicism is declared the official state religion in Hibernia's constitution.

One aspect of this national religious commitment is a constitutional provision that protects the right to life and that explicitly extends this right to the unborn. A recent decision of Hibernia's highest court considered the scope of this provision and held that the right to life of the unborn could be superseded only if the mother's life were in "imminent danger." In addition, Hibernian law makes it a crime to procure or perform an abortion. Provision of information about abortion services also is illegal, punishable by fines and prison sentences of six months to three years.

Kerry Kildare, a citizen of Hibernia, is employed as an engineer at Hibernia State Motors, an automobile manufacturing company. One day, while performing a routine assembly line procedure, a faulty machine collapsed and crushed her left hand. She was declared unfit for work, and, under Hibernian industrial legislation, given indefinite leave and a disability pension equal to her annual salary until her hand recovered adequately.

About two and a half months ago, or two years after her accident, Ms. Kildare became pregnant, for the first time, and soon thereafter was advised by the Hibernian Disability Pension Board that her pension would be canceled upon the birth of her child. After protesting this advisory, she received the Board's formal determination. It provided, among other things, as follows:

> A woman's entitlement to a disability pension ceases upon the birth of her first child. This is in accord with the long-held policy of the Disability Pension Board that women should discontinue working when they give birth to a child in order to promote traditional family values.

The Board's decision threw Ms. Kildare into deep despair. As her partner is unemployed, she is completely financially dependent on her pension for her economic well-being.

Thus, Ms. Kildare decided to investigate the possibility of an abortion. Hearing of a local women's health clinic, she promptly made an appointment to see a counselor there. The women's health clinic, she was informed, would provide information and non-directive counseling on abortion. Also, if requested, it would arrange appointments for Hibernian women to have legal abortions in neighboring countries.

On the day of Ms. Kildare's appointment, the women's health clinic was raided by the local Hibernian police who, in addition to confiscating the clinic's books, pamphlets, and videos, promptly arrested both Ms. Kildare and the counselor interviewing her, Meath Galway. Kerry Kildare was arrested for attempting to procure an abortion and Meath Galway for providing abortion information. Two weeks ago, in a local Hibernian magistrate's court, both women were found guilty of the charges brought against them, and each were sentenced to six months' imprisonment and heavy fines.

Angered by what has happened to them, Ms. Kildare and Ms. Galway, through their lawyers, submitted individual petitions to the European Court of Human Rights in Strasbourg, France, under Article 34 of the 1950 European Convention on Human Rights and Fundamental Freedoms **(Basic Document 3.5)**. Hibernia is a party to that treaty.

SECTION 2. QUESTIONS PRESENTED

1. Has Hibernia violated Kerry Kildare's and Meath Galway's human rights? If so, what rights?

2. In any event, are there any additional or alternative legal norms, procedures, and/or institutions to be recommended that might further help to prevent or discourage situations of the kind posed by this problem?

SECTION 3. ASSIGNMENTS

A. READING ASSIGNMENT

Study the Readings presented in Section 4, *infra*, and the Discussion Notes/Questions that follow. Also, time permitting, consult the accompanying bibliographical references.

B. RECOMMENDED WRITING ASSIGNMENT

Prepare a comprehensive, logically sequenced, and *argumentative* brief in the form of an outline of the primary and subsidiary *legal* issues you see requiring resolution by the European Court of Human Rights. Also, from the perspective of an independent judge, indicate which side ought to prevail on each issue and why. Retain a copy of your issue-outline/brief for class discussion.

C. RECOMMENDED ORAL ASSIGNMENT

Assume you are legal counsel for Kerry Kildare and Meath Galway, on the one hand, or Hibernia, on the other (as designated by your instructor); then, relying upon the Readings (and your issue-outline if prepared), present a 15–10 minute oral argument of your clients'/government's likely positions before the European Court of Human Rights.

D. RECOMMENDED REFLECTIVE ASSIGNMENT

Consider (and recommend) alternative norms, institutions, and/or procedures that you believe might do better than existing world order arrangements to contend with situations of the kind posed by this problem. In so doing, but without insisting upon *immediate* feasibility, identify the particular transition steps that would be needed to make your alternatives a reality.

SECTION 4.   READINGS

The following readings are considered *prima facie* relevant to solving this problem. They are your law library for present purposes and should be treated as such, organized intelligibly for "shelving" and not necessarily according to the issues presented. Be sure to review Chapter 2 ("International Legal Prescription: The 'Sources' of International Law") in your consideration of them. It, too, should be treated as part of your law library (as, indeed, should this entire coursebook).

1.   Burns H. Weston, "Human Rights," in *Encyclopædia Britannica* **(2005), available from** *Encyclopædia Britannica Online* **at <http:// www. britannica.com/eb/article?tocId=219350>** (*see supra* Reading A–1 in Problem 5–1, at 494).

2.   Dinah Shelton, "The Promise of Regional Human Rights Systems," in The Future of International Human Rights 353–65, 396–97 (B. Weston & S. Marks eds., 1999).

The promise of regional systems can be understood initially by considering why regional systems exist. First, regional systems are a product of the global concern for human rights that emerged at the end of the Second World War. Given the widespread movement for human rights that followed, it should not be surprising that regional organizations created or reformed after the war should have added human rights to their agendas. All of them drew inspiration from the human rights provisions of the United Nations Charter **[Basic Document 1.5]** and the Universal Declaration of Human Rights **[Basic Document 3.3]**.

Second, historical and political factors encouraged each region to focus on human rights issues. The Americas had a tradition of regional approaches to international issues, including human rights that grew out of regional solidarity developed during the movements for independence. Pan American Conferences had taken action on several human rights matters well before the creation of the United Nations, and this history led the Organization of American States to refer to human rights in its Charter **[Basic Document 1.7]** and to adopt the American Declaration on the Rights and Duties of Man **[Basic Document 3.1]** some months before the United Nations completed the Universal Declaration of Human Rights.

Europe had been the theater of the greatest atrocities of the Second World War and felt compelled to press for international human rights guarantees as part of European reconstruction. Faith in western European traditions of democracy, the rule of law, and individual rights inspired the belief that a regional system could be successful in avoiding future conflict and stemming post-war revolutionary impulses supported by the Soviet Union.

Somewhat later, in Africa, claims to self-determination became a recognized part of the human rights agenda as African states emerged from colonization and continued struggles for national cohesion. Resistance to human rights abuses in South Africa also contributed to regional efforts for all of Africa.

A third impulse to regionalism came from frustration at the long-stalled efforts of the United Nations to produce a human rights treaty that would complete the international bill of rights. Indeed, it took nearly two decades to finalize and adopt the two United Nations covenants. During the process, it became clear that the compliance mechanisms at the global level would not be strong and that any judicial procedures to enforce human rights would have to be on the regional level. As a result, beginning with Europe, regional systems focused on the creation of procedures of redress, establishing control machinery to supervise the implementation and enforcement of the guaranteed rights. The functioning European and Inter–American courts are among the great contributors to the protection of human rights by regional systems. A June 10, 1998 protocol to the African Charter, which will create a court in the African system, promises to add to the regional protections [**Basic Document 3.50**].[a]

Thus, regional systems have elements of uniformity and diversity in their origins. All of them began as the global human rights system was developing and each was inspired by the agreed universal norms. At the same time, each region had its own issues and concerns. As the systems have evolved, the universal framework within which they began, together with their own interactions, have had surprisingly strong influence, leading to converging norms and procedures in an overarching interdependent and dynamic system. In many respects they are thinking globally and acting regionally. Each uses the jurisprudence of the other systems and amends and strengthens its procedures with reference to the experience of the others. In general, their mutual influence is highly progressive, both in normative development and institutional reform.

III.   Regional Human Rights Systems

As noted, regional human rights systems exist in Europe, the Americas, and Africa. The Arab League has assisted a nascent system in the Middle East, having adopted the Arab Charter for Human Rights in 1994 [**Basic Document 3.44**]. Continuing efforts are underway to create a regional system or systems within the Asia–Pacific region. All of the systems have experienced important recent changes in membership and enacted new normative instruments and procedural reforms.

A.   The European System

The European system, the first to be fully operational, began with the creation of the Council of Europe by ten Western European states in 1949. It has since expanded to include Central and Eastern European countries, bringing the total membership to [46 as this coursebook goes to press]. Article 3 of the Council's Statute provides that every member state must accept the principles of the rule of law and of the enjoyment by all persons within its jurisdiction of human rights and fundamental freedoms; membership in the Council is conditioned *de facto* upon adherence to the European Convention on Human Rights and Fundamental Freedoms (ECHR) [**Basic Document 3.5**] and its eleven protocols.

---

a. The Protocol entered into force 25 January 2004.

As the first of its kind, the ECHR began with a short list of civil and political rights, to which additional guarantees have been added over time. The European system was the first to create an international court for the protection of human rights and to create a procedure for individual denunciations of human rights violations. But the jurisprudence of the European Court of Human Rights has been relatively conservative compared to that of other systems, reflecting an early concern for maintaining state support in light of the innovations of the European system and the then-optional nature of the Court's jurisdiction. The role of the victim was initially very limited and admissibility requirements were stringent. As the system has matured, however, the institutional structures and normative guarantees have been considerably strengthened. Although most of the changes result from efforts to improve the effectiveness of the system and add to its guarantees, some of the evolution reflects a responsiveness to the activities of other regional organizations both within and outside Europe, while still other changes have resulted from the impact of expanding membership in the Council of Europe.

The evolution of the European system is in fact characterized by the adoption of numerous treaties and protocols. Through its Parliamentary Assembly, the Council has drafted a series of human rights instruments. The most significant of these are the 1950 ECHR and its eleven protocols, the 1961 European Social Charter (ESC) **[Basic Document 3.11]** with its protocols, the 1987 European Convention for the Prevention of Torture and its protocols, the European Charter for Regional or Minority Languages, the 1995 Framework Convention for the Protection of National Minorities, and the 1997 Convention on Human Rights and Biomedicine, with its protocol banning human cloning. Together these instruments form a network of mutually reinforcing human rights protections in Europe.

B.   The Inter–American System

The Inter–American system began with the transformation of the Pan American Union into the Organization of American States (OAS), the Charter of which proclaims the "fundamental rights of the individual" as one of the Organization's basic principles. The 1948 American Declaration on the Rights and Duties of Man gives definition to the Charter's general commitment to human rights. Over a decade later, in 1959, the OAS created a seven member Inter–American Commission of Human Rights with a mandate to further respect for human rights among the OAS member states. In 1965, the Commission's competence was expanded to accept communications, request information from governments, and make recommendations to bring about the more effective observance of human rights. In 1969, the American Convention of Human Rights **[Basic Document 3.17]** which entered into force in 1978, conferred additional competence on the Commission to oversee compliance with the Convention.

The Commission's jurisdiction extends to all thirty-five OAS member states. The twenty-five states that have ratified the Convention are bound by its provisions, while other member states are held to the standards of the American Declaration. Communications may be filed against any state; the optional clause applies only to interstate cases. Standing for non-state actors to file communications is broad.

The Commission may also prepare country reports and conduct on-site visits to examine the human rights situations in individual countries and make recommendations to the government in question. Country reports have been prepared on the Commission's own initiative and at the request of the country concerned. The Commission may also appoint special rapporteurs to prepare studies on hemisphere-wide problems.

The American Convention also created the Inter–American Court of Human Rights. The Court has jurisdiction over contentious cases submitted against states that accept its jurisdiction and it may issue advisory opinions.

Like the European system, the Inter–American system has expanded its protections over time through the adoption of additional human rights prescriptions. The major instruments are: the 1985 Inter–American Convention to Prevent and Punish Torture; the 1988 Additional Protocol to the American Convention on Human Rights in the Area of Economic, Social and Cultural Rights; the 1990 Second Additional Protocol to the American Convention on Human Rights to Abolish the Death Penalty; the 1994 Inter–American Convention on the Prevention, Punishment, and Eradication of Violence against Women; the 1994 Inter–American Convention on Forced Disappearance of Persons; and the 1998 Declaration of the Rights of Indigenous Peoples.

C.   The African System

The regional promotion and protection of human rights in Africa is established by the African Charter on Human and Peoples' Rights (African Charter) **[Basic Document 3.22]**, designed to function within the framework of the Organization of African Unity (OAU).[b] The OAU Assembly of Heads of State and Government adopted the African Charter on June 27, 1981, and as of January 1, 1998 it had been ratified by fifty-two of the fifty-three OAU member states.

The African Charter differs from other regional human rights treaties in its inclusion of ''peoples' rights.'' It also includes economic, social, and cultural rights to a greater extent than either the European or the American conventions. Like its European and American counterparts, however, it establishes a human rights commission, the African Commission on Human and Peoples' Rights, comprising eleven independent members elected for a renewable period of six years. The Charter confers four functions on the Commission: the promotion of human and peoples' rights; the protection of those rights; interpretation of the Charter; and the performance of other tasks that may be entrusted to it by the OAU Assembly of Heads of State and Government. In addition, the Commission may undertake studies, perform training and teaching functions, convene conferences, initiate publication programs, disseminate information, and collaborate with national and local institutions concerned with human and peoples' rights. Unlike the other regional systems, the African system envisages not only interstate and individual communications procedures, but a special procedure for the handling of gross and systematic violations of human rights.

b. Now known as the African Union (AU) pursuant to the Constitutive Act of the African Union of 11 Jul 2000, OAU/CAB/LEG, *reprinted in* 1 Weston & Carlson I.B.1a.

D.   The Nascent Middle East System

On September 15, 1994, building on earlier texts adopted by regional nongovernmental and inter-governmental organizations, the League of Arab States, which did not mention human rights in its founding charter, approved an Arab Charter on Human Rights. The Charter requires acceptance by seven states before it will enter into force; until then there are no Middle Eastern regional institutions or procedures for monitoring human rights. The Charter foresees the election by its states parties of a seven-member independent Committee of Experts to serve for three years, subject to the possibility of a single re-election. Article 41 foresees periodic reporting by the states parties and implies that the Committee may request a report by submitting inquiries to a state party, with the Committee studying the reports and distributing its own report to the Human Rights Committee of the Arab League. No other functions of human rights promotion or protection are specified in the Charter.

The emerging Middle East system is marked probably more than other regional systems by the great division among its states in their willingness to accept and give effect to international human rights law. These divisions have slowed progress in achieving a true human rights system.

E.   Asia

No human rights system exists in Asia, despite efforts by nongovernmental organizations and the United Nations to create one. In 1993, over one hundred Asia–Pacific nongovernmental organizations adopted an Asia–Pacific Declaration of Human Rights supporting the universality of human rights and the creation of a regional system, but governments have been slow to respond. At a 1996 UN-sponsored workshop on the issue, the thirty participating governments concluded that "it was premature, at the current stage, to discuss specific arrangements relating to the setting up of a formal human rights mechanism in the Asian and Pacific region." The participating governments agreed, however, to explore "the options available and the process necessary for establishing a regional mechanism."

There are many hurdles to creating an Asian–Pacific regional system. First, there is far greater diversity of language, culture, legal systems, religious traditions, and history in the Asia–Pacific region than in other regions of the world. Second, the geographic limits of the region are as unclear as they are vast. These two factors suggest that the region may be better served by "sub-regional" mechanisms that could be more easily and quickly developed on the basis of the closer ties and geographic proximity of states in smaller areas. A third factor hindering the development of an Asian regional system is that, in general, governments in the region have been unwilling to ratify human rights instruments, a reluctance that makes it unlikely that an effective regional system can garner widespread support in the near future.

Finally, recent economic crises in Asia have put additional pressures on governments trying to survive in the wake of growing unrest; the crises create risks of repression in the short term. "Asian values," observes Thai human rights scholar Vitit Muntarbhorn, may become even more "a tool of some authoritarian regimes to suppress individual rights, especially freedom of expression and association which are at the heart of democratic aspirations." On the other hand, the regional economic and political crises have led many to question the concept of "Asian values" as a means to progress. Political movements and nongovernmental organizations have renewed efforts to ensure greater respect for human rights in the region. If the crisis continues and the economic justification often given for limiting civil and political rights disappears, the opportunity to create a regional system may improve quickly and dramatically, as it did in Central and Eastern Europe.

* * *

VIII.   Conclusions

The evolution in regional norms and procedures does not address the fundamental question of whether regional systems actually have had a positive impact on respect for human rights, but there can be little doubt in this regard. While compliance is not as good as it should be and while much remains to be done, there is considerable evidence that states have responded to judgments of the regional tribunals, changing their laws and practices as a result. In Europe it is relatively easy to demonstrate the effect of the Convention and Court judgments: Austria, for example, has modified its Code of Criminal Procedure; Belgium has amended its Penal Code, its laws on vagrancy, and its Civil Code; France has strengthened the protection for privacy of telephone communications; Germany has modified its Code of Criminal Procedure regarding pretrial detention, given legal recognition to transsexuals, and taken action to expedite criminal and civil proceedings; The Netherlands has modified its Code of Military Justice and the law on detention of mental patients; Ireland created a system of legal aid; Sweden introduced rules on expropriation and legislation on building permits; Switzerland amended its Military Penal Code and completely reviewed its judicial organization and criminal procedure applicable to the army; France has strengthened the protection for privacy of telephone conversations. According to Buergenthal,

> the decisions of the European Court are routinely complied with by European governments. As a matter of fact, the system has been so effective in the last decade that the Court has become, for all practical purposes, Western Europe's constitutional court. Its case law and practice resembles that of the United States Supreme Court.

The impact of the European human rights system is relatively easy to demonstrate because of the follow-up procedure which requires states to report to the Committee of Ministers on their compliance with decisions of the European Court. In a similar fashion, the Inter–American Court maintains open files on cases until the defendant state carries out the judgment. It has closed a number of cases following compliance. The impact of the decisions of the Inter–American Commission is harder to measure, but in the field of criminal justice there have been significant changes in laws and practices throughout the hemisphere—for example, in regard to amnesty for human rights violators. According to a former member of the Inter–American Commission,

> [i]n many ways the Inter–American system has not been as efficient as the European regional system, though its mandate is notably broader. The challenges the Inter–American system has faced are, however, severe and make its accomplishments all the more impressive. The fact that

government leaders, diplomats, commission and court members, and many non-governmental organizations in the Americas have been able, often in an ongoing adversarial collaboration, to fashion and implement a useful human rights instrument may be of particular importance to those interested in establishing regional human rights systems.

Even without undertaking a detailed empirical analysis of the impact of the regional human rights systems, it is clear that they contribute to the functioning and improvement of the global human rights system....

3. European Convention for the Protection of Human Rights and Fundamental Freedoms. Concluded, 4 Nov 1950. Entered into force, 3 Sep 1953. 213 U.N.T.S. 221; *reprinted in* **3 Weston & Carlson III.B.2: Arts. 2, 8, 10, 14, 17, 60** (Basic Document 3.5).

4. Convention on the Elimination of All Forms of Discrimination against Women. Concluded, 18 Dec 1979. Entered into force, 3 Sep 1981. 1249 U.N.T.S. 13; *reprinted in* **3 Weston & Carlson III.C.13: Arts. 5, 10, 16, 12, 11(2)** (Basic Document 3.21).

5. Convention on the Rights of the Child. Concluded, 20 Nov 1989. Entered into force, 2 Sep 1990. GA Res. 44/25 (Annex), UN GAOR, 44th Sess., Supp. No. 49, at 166, UN Doc. A/RES/44/49 (1990); *reprinted in* **30 I.L.M. 1448 (1989) and 3 Weston & Carlson III.D.3: Preamble** (Basic Document 3.32).

6. Hilary Charlesworth, "The Mid–Life Crisis of the Universal Declaration of Human Rights," 55 Wash. & Lee L. Rev 781, 782–795 (1998).

What relevance is the Universal Declaration [**Basic Document 3.3**]— and the body of human rights law it has generated—to women's lives around the world? My argument is that the Universal Declaration can be likened to a certain type of fifty-year-old man. It was born in an era when the rights of men to control and dominate the public spheres of the economy, politics, law, and culture were unquestioned. It may have been shaken a little by the increasing claims of women to participate in life beyond the private sphere, but it nonetheless has settled into a rather self-satisfied middle age in which society accommodates women by changing slogans or vocabulary. The Universal Declaration needs a mid-life crisis of identity to force it to reexamine its existence in a radical way and to launch it into an energetic middle age that is not set in traditional male patterns. This is, of course, an unpredictable journey that may antagonize those who have relied on the Universal Declaration as a stable symbol of international values....

II.   Text of the Universal Declaration

Eleanor Roosevelt chaired the Commission on Human Rights's (CHR) drafting committee that was responsible for the Universal Declaration. All of the other committee members were men. The language of the Universal Declaration reflects this uneven representation of the sexes. The new Commission on the Status of Women (CSW), however, kept a watching brief on the creation of the instrument. John Humphrey's account of the drafting of the Universal Declaration notes that the CSW successfully objected to Rene Cassin's draft of article 1 that stated: "All men are brothers. Being endowed

[with] reason, members of one family, they are free and possess equal dignity and rights." The final version of article 1 refers to human "beings" as born free and equal in dignity and rights, but article 1 nevertheless retains a reference to "the spirit of brotherhood." Throughout the Universal Declaration, "man" is used as a general category (although the terms "human beings" and "person" are also used) and the male pronoun is used consistently. We now know that such word use is significant in reinforcing hierarchies based on gender, even if the drafters intended the language to be generic. The origins of the use of the masculine as generic were to give prominence and deference to men. It is still often unclear whether a writer's intention in using masculine terms is to signify a generic category. As Helen Bequaert Holmes writes regarding the use of "generic" masculine terms, "[a] man is sure that he is included; a woman is uncertain."[1]

The Universal Declaration does, however, implicitly or explicitly acknowledge women in a number of articles. Article 2 promises entitlement to the rights set out in the Universal Declaration "without distinction of any kind," including sex. A more general guarantee of nondiscrimination in article 7 does not refer to any categories of discrimination. Article 16 sets forth the right for "[m]en and women of full age" to marry and to have a family. The right to an adequate standard of living in article 25 refers specifically to the need for security in the event of widowhood. It also states that "[m]otherhood and childhood are entitled to special care and assistance."

The Universal Declaration's acknowledgment of women's lives clearly is quite limited. Women enter the picture only insofar as they are connected to men. The Universal Declaration depicts women as wives and mothers and, in the latter capacity, as particularly vulnerable individuals. The constant references to the family in the Universal Declaration reinforce the restricted image of women. In fact, the Universal Declaration presents the family as "the natural and fundamental group unit of society" and as a unit that is "entitled to protection by society and the State." The language of the Universal Declaration suggests that a family comprises only a heterosexual married couple and their offspring. Indeed, the Universal Declaration assumes that the primary purpose of marriage is to have children. In a marriage, a woman will be economically dependent on her husband such that, if she is widowed, she will have a special claim to social security. One could interpret the Universal Declaration as indicating that the right to leave a marriage is very limited, although the Universal Declaration does provide equal rights to men and women on dissolution of marriage. The Universal Declaration's emphasis on the family as the foundation of society also may suggest that human rights are not applicable within the family context. The sacrosanct image of the family in the Universal Declaration discourages proper scrutiny of whether the rights to life, liberty, freedom from slavery, and security of the person are realized within particular family contexts.

Fifty years after its drafting, we can see that the Universal Declaration has limits. For example, the Universal Declaration contains no reference to self-determination nor to the rights of minorities. Can we now single out its

1. H. Holmes, *A Feminist Analysis of the Universal Declaration of Human Rights*, in Beyond Domination: New Perspectives on women and Philosophy 250, 259 (C. Gould ed. 1983).

provisions and silences with respect to women? One might argue that this would be an unfair use of current standards to assess a fifty-year-old document. However, international concern with the position of women in particular contexts was well-established at the time of the drafting of the Universal Declaration. For example, prior to the Universal Declaration, there were conventions on trafficking in women and on women in the work place. This suggests that human rights relevant to women's lives were seen as a discrete and separate category to the "general" human rights guarantees that were designed with men in mind. Moreover, the Universal Declaration's image of women is reflected in all of the subsequent "general" international human rights treaties. These documents similarly rely on a generalized male experience and attend to a very limited notion of women's lives. Women's submission to male authority appears as a "natural" consequence of their reproductive role.[2] In other words, as Spike Peterson writes, "a woman's capacity for biological reproduction becomes essentialized as her nature; the 'givenness' of this capacity is then extended to the entire process of social reproduction, thereby consigning women to a restricted 'family' domain."[3]

* * *

III. Feminist Critiques of the UN Human Rights System

Although treaties devoted to particular rights of women were adopted by the UN system in the 1950s, recognition that the UN human rights system did not adequately respond to women's situations did not begin until after the 1975 Mexico World Conference on the International Women's Year that launched the UN Decade for Women (1976–85). The adoption of the Convention on the Elimination of All Forms of Discrimination Against Women in 1979 **[Basic Document 3.21]** elaborated on the norm of nondiscrimination on the basis of sex. It took another decade for women to begin interrogating the generally applicable human rights instruments and to show that, in fact, they gave particular prominence and protection to men's lives.

There is now significant literature critiquing the international system for the protection of human rights from a feminist perspective. Following are the main themes of this work:

1. Feminist activists and scholars point out that there exists an absence of women in the processes of defining and implementing human rights standards. For example, none of the human rights treaty-monitoring bodies (apart from the Committee on the Elimination of Discrimination Against Women) have an equal number of women and men members. Many see this non-participation by women as a human rights issue in itself. Many scholars also conclude that the lack of participation by women is connected to the lopsided concerns of the traditional human rights canon.

2. The monitoring and enforcement of the specialized women's treaties is weaker than that of their "general" counterparts. For example, the Convention on the Elimination of All Forms of Discrimination Against Women is monitored only through a reporting system. The International Convention on the Elimination of All Forms of Racial Discrimination **[Basic Document**

2. *See* V. S. Peterson, *Whose Rights? A Critique of the "Givens,"* 15 Alternatives 303, 314–15 (1990).

3. *Id.*

3.12], the International Covenant on Civil and Political Rights **[Basic Document 3.14]**, and the Convention Against Torture and Other Cruel, Inhuman or Degrading Treatment or Punishment **[Basic Document 3.26]**, on the other hand, offer reporting as well as individual and state complaint mechanisms. Moreover, the institutions designed to promote and monitor the observance of women's human rights have less resources than the comparable institutions of "general" human rights.

3.   The traditional human rights canon does not cover issues that have a particular significance for women. For example, the issues of illiteracy, development, and sexual violence are dealt with in "soft" law instruments but are not addressed in legally binding norms. Moreover, international law focuses on states as the primary violators of human rights. More significant are the activities of nonstate actors, such as international monetary institutions, which have the power to impose social and economic conditions that can adversely affect women's lives through their loans.

4.   The ideas of equality and nondiscrimination that animate the Convention on the Elimination of All Forms of Discrimination Against Women, the flagship of women's human rights, are very limited in the sense that they promise equality on male-defined terms only. The terms of the Convention require that women be treated in the same way as a similarly situated man. The Convention does not recognize the effects of structural discrimination against women.

5.   Feminists have argued that the focus on activities that occur in the public sphere introduces a significant bias against women into human rights law. For example, the accepted international definition of "torture" requires the involvement of a "public official." Also, the guarantee of a right to work applies to the paid, public workforce only. Although many women do suffer from this public type of human rights violation, the violations of rights that take place in the "private" sphere are much more significant in women's lives globally.

6.   More generally, the model of human nature that underlies the human rights tradition is gendered and cannot claim to have an "objective" core. The Western, liberal, and individualistic underpinnings of human rights law all contribute to its male bias. Feminists from the South have particularly criticized the Western framework of human rights law and indeed of much feminist criticism.

7.   Even when women can be shown to have suffered violations of human rights in the traditional, male-defined sense, these violations are given much less attention and publicity than is accorded to violations of men's rights. For example, the reports by the special rapporteurs of the Commission on Human Rights have typically ignored human rights violations against women. The methods of investigating and documenting human rights abuses can often obscure or even conceal abuses against women. As a result, the UN's "fact finding" in Rwanda in 1994 did not detect systematic sexual violence against women until nine months after the attack and genocide, when women began to give birth in unprecedented numbers.[4]

---

4.   A. Gallagher, *Ending the Marginalization: Strategies for Incorporating Women into* the *United Nations Human Rights System*, 19 H.R.Q. 283, 292 n.31 (1997).

8. Society justifies many violations of women's rights on the grounds that the violations are an aspect of particular religious or cultural practices. States, religious communities, and individuals invoke the rights to religious freedom or cultural integrity as "trumping" women's rights. The pattern of reservations to the Convention on the Elimination of All Forms of Discrimination Against Women provides a good example of this phenomenon.

IV. UN Responses

How has the UN system responded to the wave of feminist critiques of its protection of human rights? On one level, the response has been surprisingly rapid and impressive. For example, at the United Nations World Conference on Human Rights in 1993, the international community formally recognized that the human rights system did not adequately respond to women's lives. The community committed itself to the furtherance of the belief that the human rights of women were "an inalienable, integral and indivisible part of universal human rights." It also accepted that gender-specific violations of human rights were part of the human rights agenda. Another significant development was the adoption by the UN General Assembly of the Declaration on the Elimination of Violence Against Women in December 1993 **[Basic Document 3.41]**. The Declaration contains a broad definition of the notion of gender-based violence. It acknowledges gender-based violence as an international issue and more specifically, as an issue of sex discrimination. The Beijing Declaration and Platform for Action, adopted at the Fourth World Conference on Women in September 1995 **[Basic Document 3.47]**, identifies the human rights of women as a critical area of concern.

While these developments have generally been hailed by feminist scholars and activists, they are worth a closer look. How far do they respond to the criticisms of the international human rights system outlined above? It is striking that the assertion that "[w]omen's rights are human rights," while contained in the Beijing Declaration, is not reiterated in the more action-oriented Platform for Action because of an apparent anxiety of states about recognizing "new" human rights.[5] Thus, the Platform distinguishes between human rights of women (meaning the application of the traditional human rights canon to women), which are universal and women's rights (meaning rights that are of especial relevance to women only), which are not universal. Moreover, the model of women's existence presupposed by the Beijing Platform is quite restricted. Although the Platform for Action gives a nod in the direction of the diversity of women's experiences, it nevertheless presents women in a very limited and encumbered way. The major role for women remains that which is described in the Universal Declaration—wife and mother. As Dianne Otto points out in her analysis of the Beijing negotiations, the only acknowledged development in the role of women is that women are expected to participate in decision-making structures and to play a part in the free market economy. Attempts to raise the diversity of women's identities, most particularly with respect to sexual orientation, were unsuccessful at Beijing.

5. D. Otto, *A Post–Beijing Reflection on the Limitations and Potential of Human Rights Discourse for Women*, in Women's Human Rights Reference Guide (K. Askin & D. Koenig eds., 1998).

The new international concern with women's rights also is limited in the way it understands the notion of equality. Although there have been significant moves to recognize some gendered harms, particularly violence against women, the major remedy for the global subordination of women has been to increase women's roles in decision-making. This simply allows women access to a world that is already constituted by men. Dianne Otto argues that "[i]n the absence of a recognition that the decision-making structures must themselves change, it is not clear what difference women's equal participation could make. Ultimately, it may merely equally implicate women in the perpetuation of the masculinist liberal forms of minimalist representative democracy and capitalist economics."[6] The new international discourse on women's rights also gives prominence to civil and political rights of women at the expense of economic and social rights. Health and reproductive rights are much more likely to be controversial in international fora than civil rights. Although the feminization of poverty clearly is acknowledged in the Beijing Platform, it was not placed squarely in a rights context. It has been noted that the Platform "assumes ... that capitalism has the ability to deliver economic equality to the poor women of the world and ... that the obligation of states to guarantee certain economic and social rights is made redundant by the more 'efficient' processes of free market forces."[7] The practices of international monetary institutions such as the World Bank and International Monetary Fund also have serious implications for economic and social rights. The narrow notion of development that animates these institutions elevates private sector interests over public funding for food, health, education, and social security.

In the last few years, the various levels of the UN human rights machinery have shown an interest in women's rights. In March 1994, the CHR appointed Radhika Coomaraswamy as Special Rapporteur on Violence Against Women. Coomaraswamy is the first Special Rapporteur with a gender-specific mandate. Some of the human rights treaty monitoring bodies have announced changes to their procedures in order to better respond to women's concerns. In 1995, for example, the Centre for Human Rights in collaboration with the United Nations Development Fund for Women organized a meeting of experts to create guidelines for "mainstreaming" gender perspectives into the human rights system. Also, the CSW currently is considering a draft Optional Protocol to the Women's Convention that would allow individual and group complaints of noncompliance with the Convention.[c]

Thus, the international community seems to have accepted the rhetoric of women's rights. What effect has this had in practice? ...

* * *

The [Human Rights] Committee has given a mixed reception to complaints under the Optional Protocol [to the ICCPR] involving gender issues. The Committee has found that cases of direct discrimination on the basis of sex—for example, a Mauritian law that gave greater status to foreign wives of Mauritian men than to foreign husbands of Mauritian women—breach the article 26 guarantee of nondiscrimination. However, in other cases of direct

---

6. *Id.*

7. *Id.*

c. For further consideration of the Optional Protocol, now in force, *see infra* Discussion Note/Question 14, at 641.

discrimination on the basis of sex, the Committee has permitted a considerable margin of appreciation to states. For example, in *Vos v. The Netherlands*, the Committee found that a Dutch law that allowed disabled men to retain a disability allowance on the death of their wives but that did not allow disabled women to retain disability on the death of their husbands was not a violation of article 26. The Committee also has had much more difficulty with cases that involve laws or practices that are facially gender neutral but that, in effect, discriminate against women. Overall, gender mainstreaming has had a mixed fate. It has been relatively easy to obtain a revision of reporting guidelines but much more difficult to obtain practical follow-through on these revisions, such as through the systematic questioning of states.

V.   Future Development of Women's Rights in International Law

The sheaf of resolutions that the various UN bodies adopted in commemoration of the fiftieth anniversary of the Universal Declaration acknowledge in various ways that there are significant problems with the international protection of rights. These resolutions outline the major concerns with the Universal Declaration's protection of rights as nondissemination and nonimplementation of the pertinent Universal Declaration provisions. In other words, the problems are external to the Universal Declaration and to the UN human rights system itself. The UN bodies see the Universal Declaration as having a continuing and universal relevance. To these UN bodies, then, the cure for the mid-life crisis is better coordination, better promotion, better evaluation, better information, and better implementation. I argue, in contrast, that for women, the Universal Declaration and its progeny themselves may be the problem.

The UN human rights system and the Universal Declaration have grown into middle age. Like many fifty-year-old men today, the Universal Declaration is rather smug in its attitude towards women. The UN's reactions to criticism of the Universal Declaration include simply ignoring the issue and hoping that, in time, it will go away. Another argument sometimes made is that taking the specificity of women's lives into account will undermine the objectivity and universality of the system. Yet another reaction is that of the double message—the public use of "politically correct" language acknowledging the problem and the announcement of special programs to alleviate it, but failure to tailor the programs to the specific problem or to give enough weight or resources to the programs to ensure their success. The human rights system appears to have learned that the art of politically correct rhetoric is an effective tool in silencing potential critics. It finds it very hard, however, to institute significant change. The human rights system's responses to the criticisms of feminist activists and scholars have been very mixed. Generally, the human rights system has only recognized claims of women that involve rights violations akin to those that men might sustain. Recognition of rights violations in the "private" sphere are still the exception. For example, the negotiations on the text of the Declaration on the Elimination of Violence Against Women, in which some states resisted the definition of violence against women as a human rights issue on the grounds that this would water down the concept of human rights, indicate the problems of enlarging the androcentric focus of human rights law. The overarching slogan of the UN human rights system with respect to women seems to be just "add women and stir." A mid-life crisis is necessary for the system to change course in a more radical way to ensure that there is substantive change.

7. Fernando R. Tesón, "Feminism and International Law: A Reply," 33 Va. J. Int'l L. 647, 650–55, 665 (1993).

Feminists criticize the international lawmaking process for depriving women of the access and opportunity to take part in lawmaking in two important ways. First, feminists argue that women are *under-represented* in international relations, that is, in high positions in international organizations, in diplomatic services, and as heads of state and government. Second, they contend that because of this underrepresentation, the *creation* of international law is reserved almost exclusively to men. Women are thus effectively prevented from participating in the processes of international lawmaking.

Central to the claim of exclusion is the fact that women are underrepresented in international relations. There is no doubt that there are relatively few women heads of state, diplomats, or international organizations officials. Is this state of things, however, an injustice? And how can the statistical underrepresentation (whether or not it is an injustice) be redressed? ...

* * *

Radical feminists ... seem to believe that there is a global injustice even where, as a result of democratic elections held in independent, rights-respecting states, it is mostly men who are elected to government, or if in such states mostly men traditionally seek admission to the diplomatic service. An example is the discussion by Charlesworth and her associates of the Women's Convention [**Basic Document 3.21**]. They strongly criticize the Convention for assuming that men and women should be treated alike, which is the liberal outlook. The Charlesworth view is that sexism is "a pervasive, structural problem."[4] Further, it is male dominance which lies at the root of the structural problem and which must be addressed as a means to reach the structural issues. But what are the authors' suggestions? If we descend from the abstract slogan that liberal equality is just the men's measure of things, how do they suggest rewriting each of the rights recognized by the Convention to meet their concerns? Take article 7, for example, which directs states to eliminate all discrimination against women in the political and public life of the country. Would a radical feminist rewriting of this article require states to *appoint* women, regardless of popular vote? Would it impose a 50% gender quota for elected positions, or force women who do not want to run for office to do so? These are not just rhetorical questions: given the radical feminists' rejection of rights discourse and formal political equality, it is difficult to imagine what a radical list of international women's rights would look like.

* * *

In addition to criticizing the processes of international lawmaking, many feminists argue that the *content* of international law privileges men to the detriment of women. The claim that the content of international law favors the interests of men may incorporate either or both of the following argu-

4. H. Charlesworth, C. Chinkin & S. Wright, *Feminist Approaches to International Law*, 85 A.J.I.L. 613, 631–32 (1991).

ments: first, international law rules in general are "gendered" to privilege men; and second, international rules such as sovereign equality and nonintervention protect states, and states are instrumental in disadvantaging or oppressing women. The latter claim, in turn, may intend either or both of the following: first, international law is too tolerant of violations of women's rights *by governments*; and second, international law is too tolerant of violations of the rights of women *by private individuals* within states, such as physical abuse by men in the home.

* * *

In response to [this] point, I find little plausibility in the claim of some feminists that the specific content of international law rules systematically privileges men. Positive international law is a vast and heterogeneous system consisting of principles, rules, and standards of varying degrees of generality, many of a technical nature. Rules such as the principle of territoriality in criminal jurisdiction, or the rule that third states should in principle have access to the surplus of the entire allowable catch of fish in a coastal state's exclusive economic zone are not "thoroughly gendered" but, on the contrary, gender-neutral. It cannot be seriously maintained that such norms operate overtly or covertly to the detriment of women. The same can be said of the great bulk of international legal rules. * * *

... Some feminists argue that because current international law derives from European, male, liberal legalism, its very form and structure are inherently patriarchal and oppressive. In response to this contention, I first argue that the foundations of the "inherent oppressiveness" thesis are faulty, that nothing in the philosophic "nature" of a state makes it oppressive or non-oppressive, and that the radical feminists' nominalism only serves to obscure differences between states that defenders of women's interests ought to care about.

8.   Case of Open Door and Dublin Well Woman v. Ireland, 246 Eur. Ct. Hum. Rts. (ser. A) 8 (29 Oct 92).

[*Eds.*—In 1991, the Court of Justice of the European Communities in Luxembourg held that Europe's open trade borders require the free flow of information about medical services, including abortion services. *See Society for the Protection of Unborn Children Ireland Ltd. v. Grogan*, 3 C.M.L.R. 849 (E.C.J. 1991). The applicants in the instant case of Open Door Counselling Ltd. and Dublin Well Women Centre Ltd. were Irish corporations providing "non-directive" counseling for women on a range of reproductive issues, including contraception and abortion. Two women counselors joined the action, as did also Mrs. X and Ms. Geraghty, each a woman of childbearing age. All complained of an injunction imposed by Irish courts on Open Door and Dublin Well Women restraining them from providing information to pregnant women relative to abortion facilities outside Ireland. Previously, Dublin Well Women had issued a pamphlet stating, *inter alia*, that the implication of the wording of a 1983 referendum amending the Irish Constitution meant that a court injunction could be obtained to prevent the "non-directive" counseling offered by Well Women and that it also would be possible "for an individual to seek a court injunction to prevent a woman travelling abroad if they believe she intends to have an abortion."

In 1985, the Society for the Protection of the Unborn Children Ltd. (SPUC) sought a declaration that the activities of the applicant corporations in counseling pregnant women to travel abroad to obtain an abortion were unlawful activities, having regard to Article 40.3.3 of the Irish Constitution, which provides as follows: "The State acknowledges the right to life of the unborn, and, with due regard to the equal right to life of the mother, guarantees in its laws to respect, and, as far as practicable, by its laws to defend and vindicate that right." The case was converted into a relator action brought by the Attorney–General by order of the High Court. Justice Hamilton, President of the High Court, found that the activities of the corporations were unlawful under Article 40.3.3 and granted the injunction requested, causing Open Door and Dublin Well Women to appeal to the Irish Supreme Court. They did so unsuccessfully, however. After determining that the issue and question of fact to be determined in the case was whether the applicants were assisting in the destruction of the lives of the unborn, the Supreme Court, in a unanimous decision delivered by Chief Justice Finlay, found that the applicants were assisting in the destruction of life and consequently upheld the injunction granted by the High Court.

Thereafter, in late 1988, Open Door, Dublin Well Women, Mrs. X, and Ms. Geraghty lodged a complaint with the European Commission on Human Rights (an institution which is now defunct following the entry into force in 1998 of Protocol 11 to the 1950 European Convention for the Protection of Human Rights and Fundamental Freedoms **(Basic Document 3.5)**). The complaint stated that the injunction constituted an unjustified interference with their right to respect for private life in breach of Article 8 of the European Convention. Open Door also claimed discrimination contrary to Article 14, first in conjunction with Article 8 (alleging that the injunction discriminated against women since men were not denied the information "critical to their reproductive and health choices") and second in conjunction with Article 10 (claiming discrimination on the grounds of political or other opinion since those who seek counsel against abortion are permitted to express their views without restriction). Dublin Well Women also complained of discrimination contrary to Article 14 in conjunction with Article 8 as well as in conjunction with Article 10 (protecting the right to freedom of information) on the basis that Dublin Well Women was an "economic operator" that should be permitted to distribute and receive such information in the interests of free trade in services. In its report of 7 March 1991, the Commission expressed the opinion that there had been a violation of Article 10 relative to all the complainants and that it was not necessary to examine further the complaints of Mrs. X and Ms. Geraghty under Article 8. It also found, unanimously, that here had been no violation of Article 8 against Open Door.

On appeal, the European Court of Human Rights ruled as follows with respect to the alleged violation of Article 10:]

53.   The applicants alleged that the Supreme Court injunction, restraining them from assisting pregnant women to travel abroad to obtain abortions, infringed the rights of the corporate applicants and the two counsellors to impart information, as well as the rights of Mrs. X and Ms. Geraghty to receive information. They confined their complaint to that part of the injunction which concerned the provision of information to pregnant women as

opposed to the making of travel arrangements or referral to clinics. . . . They invoked Article 10. . . .

54. In their submissions to the Court the Government contested these claims and also contended that Article 10 should be interpreted against the background of Articles 2, 17 and 60 of the Convention. . . .

* * *

67. . . . The Government also emphasised that, in granting the injunction, the Supreme Court was merely sustaining the logic of Article 40.3.3 of the Constitution. The determination by the Irish courts that the provision of information by the relevant applicants assisted in the destruction of unborn life was not open to review by the Convention institutions.

68. The Court cannot agree that the State's discretion in the field of protection of morals is unfettered and unreviewable. . . .

It acknowledges that the national authorities enjoy a wide margin of appreciation in matters of morals, particularly in an area such as the present which touches on matters of belief concerning the nature of human life. As the Court has observed before, it is not possible to find in the legal and social orders of the Contracting States a uniform European conception of morals, and the State authorities are, in principle, in a better position than the international judge to give an opinion on the exact content of the requirements of morals as well as, on the "necessity" of a "restriction" or "penalty" intended to meet them.

However this power of appreciation is not unlimited. It is for the Court, in this field also, to supervise whether a restriction is compatible with the Convention.

69. As regards the application of the "proportionality" test, the logical consequence of the Government's argument is that measures taken by the national authorities to protect the right to life of the unborn or to uphold the constitutional guarantee on the subject would be automatically justified under the Convention where infringement of a right of a lesser stature was alleged. It is, in principle, open to the national authorities to take such action as they consider necessary to respect the rule of law or to give effect to constitutional rights. However, they must do so in a manner which is compatible with their obligations under the Convention and subject to review by the Convention institutions. To accept the Government's pleading on this point would amount to an abdication of the Court's responsibility under Article 19 "to ensure the observance of the engagements undertaken by the High Contracting Parties. . . ."

70. Accordingly, the Court must examine the question of "necessity" in the light of the principles developed in its case-law. . . . It must determine whether there existed a pressing social need for the measures in question and, in particular, whether the restriction complained of was "proportionate to the legitimate aim pursued". . . .

71. In this context, it is appropriate to recall that freedom of expression is also applicable to "information" or "ideas" that offend, shock or disturb the State or any sector of the population. Such are the demands of that

pluralism, tolerance and broadmindedness without which there is no "democratic society." . . .

72. While the relevant restriction, as observed by the Government, is limited to the provision of information, it is recalled that it is not a criminal offence under Irish law for a pregnant woman to travel abroad in order to have an abortion. Furthermore, the injunction limited the freedom to receive and impart information with respect to services which are lawful in other Convention countries and may be crucial to a woman's health and well-being. Limitations on information concerning activities which, notwithstanding their moral implications, have been and continue to be tolerated by national authorities, call for careful scrutiny by the Convention institutions as to their conformity with the tenets of a democratic society.

73. The Court is first struck by the absolute nature of the Supreme Court injunction which imposed a "perpetual" restraint on the provision of information to pregnant women concerning abortion facilities abroad, regardless of age or state of health or their reasons for seeking counselling on the termination of pregnancy . . .

74. On that ground alone the restriction appears over broad and disproportionate. Moreover, this assessment is confirmed by other factors.

75. In the first place, it is to be noted that the corporate applicants were engaged in the counselling of pregnant women in the course of which counsellors neither advocated nor encouraged abortion, but confined themselves to an explanation of the available options. . . . The decision as to whether or not to act on the information so provided was that of the woman concerned. There can be little doubt that following such counselling there were women who decided against a termination of pregnancy. Accordingly, the link between the provision of information and the destruction of unborn life is not as definite as contended. Such counselling had in fact been tolerated by the State authorities even after the passing of the Eighth Amendment in 1983 until the Supreme Court's judgment in the present case. Furthermore, the information that was provided by the relevant applicants concerning abortion facilities abroad was not made available to the public at large.

76. It has not been seriously contested by the Government that information concerning abortion facilities abroad can be obtained from other sources in Ireland such as magazines and telephone directories . . . or by persons with contacts in Great Britain. Accordingly, information that the injunction sought to restrict was already available elsewhere although in a manner which was not supervised by qualified personnel and thus less protective of women's health. Furthermore, the injunction appears to have been largely ineffective in protecting the right to life of the unborn since it did not prevent large numbers of Irish women from continuing to obtain abortions in Great Britain. . . .

77. In addition, the available evidence, which has not been disputed by the Government, suggests that the injunction has created a risk to the health of those women who are now seeking abortions at a later stage in their pregnancy, due to lack of proper counselling, and who are not availing of customary medical supervision after the abortion has taken place. . . . Moreover, the injunction may have had more adverse effects on women who were not sufficiently resourceful or had not the necessary level of education to have

access to alternative sources of information.... These are certainly legitimate factors to take into consideration in assessing the proportionality of the restriction.

* * *

78. The Government, invoking Articles 17 and 60 of the Convention, have submitted that Article 10 should not be interpreted in such a manner as to limit, destroy or derogate from the right to life of the unborn which enjoys special protection under Irish law.

79. Without calling into question under the Convention the regime of protection of unborn life that exists under Irish law, the Court recalls that the injunction did not prevent Irish women from having abortions abroad and that the information it sought to restrain was available from other sources.... Accordingly, it is not the interpretation of Article 10 but the position in Ireland as regards the implementation of the law that makes possible the continuance of the current level of abortions obtained by Irish women abroad.

* * *

80. ... The Court concludes that the restraint imposed on the applicants from receiving or imparting information is disproportionate to the aims pursued. Accordingly there has been a breach of Article 10.

[*Eds.*—Having regard to its finding that there had been a violation of Article 10 of the European Convention for the Protection of Human Rights and Fundamental Freedoms, the Court considered it unnecessary to examine the complaints raised with respect to articles 8 and 14.]

9. Case of Schuler–Zgraggen v. Switzerland, 263 Eur. Ct. Hum. Rts. (ser. A) 9 (24 Jun 93).

[*Eds.*—Mrs. Schuler–Zgraggen, a Swiss national, received a full state invalidity pension as a result of an incapacitating illness. After bearing a child and submitting to medical examination by the invalidity insurance authorities, however, her pension was terminated, on the grounds that she was 60–70 percent able to look after her home and child. Mrs. Schuler–Zgraggen appealed the decision to the Canton of Uri Appeals Board for Old Age, Survivors' and Invalidity Insurance and requested access to her file and the right to make copies of important documents. The request was initially refused, but later granted on a further administrative law appeal to the Swiss Federal Insurance Court. However, without an oral hearing, the Federal Insurance Court ruled that, because Mrs. Schuler–Zgraggen was a woman with a child, it had to be assumed that even without her disability she would not have gone to work and that, because her income was above the hardship level, she was not entitled to a pension. Whereupon Mrs. Schuler–Zgraggen petitioned the European Commission of Human Rights, claiming that she had been denied the right to a fair trial within the meaning of Article 6(1) of the 1950 European Convention for the Protection of Human Rights and Fundamental Freedoms **(Basic Document 3.5)** (in that she had insufficient access to her medical records and was provided no oral hearing by the Federal Insurance Court) and been made to suffer discrimination within the meaning of Article 14 (on the grounds of gender) taken together with Article 6(1). Following is an extract from the judgment of the European Court of Human Rights to which the Commission's decision was appealed, relating to the alleged violation of Article 14 taken together with Article 6(1), to wit, Mrs. Schuler–Zgraggen's claim of gender discrimination in the exercise of her right to a fair trial:]

64.   According to the applicant, the Federal Insurance Court based its judgment on an "assumption based on experience of everyday life," namely that many married women give up their jobs when their first child is born and resume it only later. It inferred from this that Mrs. Schuler–Zgraggen would have given up work even if she had not had health problems. The applicant considered that if she had been a man, the Federal Insurance Court would never have made such an assumption, which was contradicted by numerous scientific studies.

65.   The Government argued that Article 6(1) and thus, indirectly, Article 14 were not applicable, as the complaint was concerned with the taking of evidence, a sphere which essentially came within the State authorities' competence.

66.   The Court reiterates that the admissibility of evidence is governed primarily by the rules of domestic law, and that it is normally for the national courts to assess the evidence before them. The Court's task under the Convention is to ascertain whether the proceedings, considered as a whole, including the way in which the evidence was submitted, were fair.

67.   In this instance, the Federal Insurance Court adopted in its entirety the Appeals Board's assumption that women gave up work when they gave birth to a child. It did not attempt to probe the validity of that assumption itself by weighing arguments to the contrary.

As worded in the Federal Court's judgment, the assumption cannot be regarded—as asserted by the Government—as an incidental remark, clumsily drafted but of negligible effect. On the contrary, it constitutes the sole basis for the reasoning, thus being decisive, and introduces a difference of treatment based on the ground of sex only.

The advancement of the equality of the sexes is today a major goal in the member-States of the Council of Europe and very weighty reasons would have to be put forward before such a difference of treatment could be regarded as compatible with the Convention. The Court discerns no such reason in the instant case. It therefore concludes that for want of any reasonable and objective justification, there has been a breach of Article 14 taken together with Article 6(1).

10.   Programme of Action of the 1994 United Nations International Conference on Population and Development. Adopted 13 Sep 1994. UN Doc. A/CONF.177/20; *reprinted in* 35 I.L.M. 401 (1996) and 5 Weston & Carlson V.I.20: chs. I, II, IV, VII (Basic Document 5.41).

11.   Azizah al-Hibri, "Who Defines Women's Rights? A Third World Woman's Response," 2 Hum. Rts. Brief No. 1 (Washington College of Law, 29 Jul 96).

The 1993 World Conference on Human Rights in Vienna revealed the wide gulf that separates "Third World" women from "First World" women. Arriving at the conference to discuss their human rights issues, Third World women were surprised to see that this task had been performed on their behalf by First World women, who used their organizational skills to take control of the conference and determine its agenda. * * * [They] were frustrated by attempts on the part of First World women to speak for all participants. They were also frustrated with the First World women's selection of Third World spokeswomen representing a First World point of view. The [1994] International Conference on Population and Development (ICPD) in Cairo unfortunately replicated these earlier patterns. For this reason, as well as others, some Third World women carried placards during their last days of the ICPD criticizing it for not being responsive to their concerns.

The impact of American feminism on Third World women has been positive. Unfortunately, however, the positive effects have been diminished by some vocal First World women activists who appear to dominate international fora. The problem lies with the approach these activists take. They refuse to treat Third World women as equals, even as they claim to fight for their human rights. In a real sense, the approach reeks of the attitude of early colonialist women, in places such as Algeria, who appropriated and silenced the colonized woman's voice. In her new book, The Eloquence of Silence (Routledge 1994), Marina Lazreg, an Algerian-born feminist, provides an insightful analysis of this problem. She uses the issue of the veil as an example:

> The veil made colonial women uncomfortable, as did every task that Algerian women performed, from rearing children to cooking and taking care of their homes. The veil, for the colonial woman, was the perfect alibi for rejecting the Algerian woman's culture and denigrating her. But it was also a constant reminder of her powerlessness in erasing the existence of a different way of being a woman. She often overcame her handicap by turning it into an advantage. She is superior to these veiled women....

In Copenhagen, at the 1981 UN Mid–Decade for Women Conference, Third World women were told that their highest priorities related to the veil and clitoridectomy (female genital mutilation). In Cairo, they were told that their highest priorities related to contraception and abortion. In both cases, Third World women begged to differ. They repeatedly announced that their highest priorities were peace and development. They noted that they could not very well worry about other matters when their children were dying from thirst, hunger or war. Sometimes, First World women shook their heads and indicated that they understood. But nothing has changed. First World women still do not listen; they still do not hear.

Many Third World women went to Cairo with a sense of hope. Finally, a conference was prepared to address their issues. After all, it was clearly billed as a "development" conference. But, again, their hopes were left unrealized. The conference instead centered around reducing the number of Third World babies in order to preserve the earth's resources, despite (or is it "because of") the fact that the First World consumes much of these resources.

What First World women succeeded in doing at Cairo, however, in fact damaged Third World women. They forced the issue of abortion on everyone, from a First World perspective. Many Third World governments allied to the United States acquiesced in the demands of the conference, thus making women's issues appear to their citizens (including women) as suspect, and the proposals as "foreign" and offensive. Other Third World countries were forced to evaluate their public policies on the matter from the First World's perspective. Because of the apparent racism motivating some of these First World reproductive concerns, the outcome in some cases has been disastrous to women.

In the case of abortion rights specifically, in certain Muslim countries the result was to produce a highly conservative official juristic analysis of the issue. This presents a retrenchment, since, for hundreds of years, Muslim jurists have had quite a liberal analysis of abortion, and, unlike the situation that used to exist in the United States, safe abortions were widely available in many Muslim countries.

The reason for this retrenchment derives to a great extent from the perception that the First World reproductive rights movements are part of a concentrated racist Western onslaught on Third World population. Had Muslim women been afforded the space to speak in their own voices, the results may have been remarkably different.

SECTION 5.   DISCUSSION NOTES/QUESTIONS

1.   In Reading 2, *supra*, we noted the existence and purpose of the Council of Europe, which drafted and implemented, among many other important treaties, the 1950 European Convention for the Protection of Human Rights and Fundamental Freedoms **(Basic Document 3.5)** and the 1961 European Social Charter **(Basic Document 3.11)**. Established by agreement ("statute") in 1949 (*see* Statute of Council of Europe, Europ). T.S. No. 1, 87 U.N.T.S. 103, *reprinted in* 1 Weston & Carlson I.B.4), the Council is composed of 46 European states or principalities as of 28 July 2005; its original ten member states (Belgium, Denmark, France, Ireland, Italy, Luxembourg, the Netherlands, Norway, Sweden, and the United Kingdom) plus 36 additional members (Albania, Andorra, Armenia, Austria, Ajerbaijan, Bosnia and Herzegovina, Bulgaria, Croatia, Cyprus, Czech Republic, Estonia, Finland, Georgia, Germany, Greece, Hungary, Iceland, Latvia, Liechtenstein, Lithuania, Macedonia, Malta, Moldova, Monaco, Poland, Portugal, Romania, Russia, San Marino, Serbia and Montenegro, Slovakia, Slovenia, Spain, Switzerland, Turkey, and Ukraine. Canada, Israel and Mexico) enjoy Parliamentary Assembly observer status.

The Council consists of three principal organs: a Parliamentary Assembly, comprised of delegates from the national parliaments of the Member States [and Principalities] (who, however, speak in individual capacity); a Committee of Ministers, made up of the foreign ministers of each of the Member States [and Principalities]; and a Secretariat, headquartered in Strasbourg, France. According to Article 1 of its Statute, the purpose of the Council is "to achieve a greater unity between its Members for the purpose of safeguarding and realizing the ideals and principles which are their common heritage and facilitating their economic and social progress." Despite its lofty ideals, however, the Council is best characterized as a discussion forum. Originally inspired by British Prime Minister Winston Churchill's 1946 call and plan for a "United States of Europe," it never has emerged, in the words of two authorities, "beyond the nuclear stage of a federal organization." Dominik Lasok & J.W. Bridge, An Introduction to the Law and Institutions of the European Communities 9 (4th ed. 1987). Still, the Council has done important work, proposing and formulating agreements and other modes of cooperation in the fields of social security, social and medical assistance, public health, agriculture, transport, trade and tariffs, dispute settlement, cultural exchange, and, as we have seen, extradition, terrorism, and, above all, human rights.

One central instrument in the Council of Europe's human rights mandate is the European Social Charter of 1961 **(Basic Document 3.11)**. Burns H. Weston, Robin Ann Lukes, and Kelly M. Hnatt describe the Social Charter in "Regional Human Rights Regimes: A Comparison and Appraisal," 20 Vand. J. Transnat'l L. 585, 599 (1987) thus:

> Under the Charter, in force and effect relative to the Member States [and two Principalities] of the Council of Europe, the States Parties undertake to consider the economic, social, and cultural rights enumerated therein "as a declaration of aims which [they] will pursue by all appropriate means" and to submit biennial progress reports to the Council's Secretary–General concerning those substantive provisions "as they have accepted." A Committee of Experts, consisting of not more than seven members nominated by the States Parties and appointed by the Council's Committee of Ministers "from a list of independent experts of the highest integrity and or recognized competence in international social questions," examines the reports the Secretary–General has received. A subcommittee of the Governmental Social Committee then considers both the reports of the States Parties and the conclusions of the Committee of Experts, and the Secretary–General submits the conclusions of the Committee of Experts to the Council's [Parliamentary] Assembly. Ultimately, however, similar to its enforcement powers under the European Convention relative to civil and political rights, the Committee of Ministers is responsible for the promotion and protection of the economic, social and cultural rights that the Charter enumerates. Article 29 of the Charter provides that "the Committee of Ministers may, on the basis of the report of the Sub-committee, and after consultation with the [Parliamentary] Assembly, make to each Contracting Party any necessary recommendations."

In 1995 the Council of Europe adopted an Amending Protocol (E.T.S. No. 158) providing for a system of collective complaints. The Protocol came into force in 1998. It allows complaints of violations of the Social Charter to be made to the European Committee on Social Rights by certain organizations including NGOs who have consultative status with the Council of Europe. If the complaint is declared admissible by the Committee, a written procedure is set in motion, although the Committee can call a public hearing. Compliance with the Committee's decision on the merits of a particular complaint is monitored by the Council of Ministers, which may recommend that the state involved take specific measures. As of this writing, 31 complaints had been made under the Protocol. For details, see <http://www.coe.int/T/E/Human_Rights/Esc>. If Hibernia were a party to the Protocol, could a complaint be made about its criminalization of abortion and provision of related information?

In 1999, the Council of Europe established the Office of the European Commissioner for Human Rights. A Spanish law professor, Alvaro Gil–Robles, was the first and, at this writing, is the current Commissioner. See <http://www.coe.int/T/E/Commissioner_H.R/ Communication_ Unit>. The Commissioner's mandate covers the promotion of the education in and awareness of human rights, the encouragement for the establishment of national human rights structures where they do not exist and facilitate their activities where they do exist, the identification of short-comings in the law and practice with regards to human rights and, lastly, the promotion of their effective respect and full enjoyment in all the member states of the Council of Europe. For further details concerning the Council of Europe, in relation to human rights especially, see Informational Ministerial Conference, 40 Years of Human Rights protection by the Council of Europe: Achievements, Prospects, and Pan–European Vocation (1994); Human Rights: A Continuing Challenge of the Council of Europe (1995); Perspectives of an All–European System of Human Rights protection: The Role of the Council of Europe, the Conference on Security and Co-operation in Europe, and the European Communities (Z. Kedzia, A. Korula & M. Nowak eds., 1991); The Challenge of a Greater Europe: The Council of Europe and Democratic Security (1996). *See also*, Council of Europe and the Protection of Human Rights passim Council of Europe, The Council of Europe and the Protection of Human Rights passim (2004), *available at* <http://www.coe.int/T/E/Human_ rights/ prothr_eng.pdf>. For a description of the Court's procedural requirements for bringing a claim under the Convention, *see* Kevin Boyle, *Council of Europe, OSCE, and European Union*, in Guide to International Human Rights Practice 143, 143–70 (Hurst Hannum ed., 4th ed. 2004).

For a discussion of regionalism in general, see A. LeRoy Bennett, International Organizations: Principles and Issues (7th ed. 2001), especially Chapter 10 entitled "Varieties of Regionalism."

A parallel postwar development in Western European integration now known as the "European Union" (*see* Treaty on European Union, 7 Feb 1992, 31 I.L.M. 253 (1992), *reprinted in* 1 Weston & Carlson I.B.13a) has important functions with respect to human rights. *See generally* The EU and Human Rights (Philip Alston ed., 1999). European Union law deals with economic and political issues but it also has jurisdiction over a range of human rights issues through the Maastricht Treaty's commitment to the protection of the fundamental human rights of citizens in member states. In *Society for the Unborn Child v Grogan* (discussed above in the Editors' note preceding Reading 8, *supra*) the Irish High Court requested the European Court of Justice, based in Luxembourg, to rule on whether the Irish prohibition on the carrying out of an abortion or the provision of information about abortions was consistent with European Community law. A result of the decision by the ECJ that the Irish law was inconsistent with the law of the European Community was the insertion of Protocol No. 17 in the 1992 Maastricht Treaty. That instrument states:

> Nothing in the Treaty on European Union [or other constitutive treaties of the European Communities] shall affect the application in Ireland of Article 40.3.3. of the Constitution of Ireland [the 1983 amendment which guarantees the right to life of the unborn "with due regard to the equal right to life of the mother."]

Protocol No. 17 thus serves to protect Ireland from any EU pressure towards increasing women's reproductive rights. The response to the *Grogan* case is discussed in *Member State Sovereignty and Women's Reproductive Rights: The European Union's Response*, 22 B.C. Int'l & Comp. L. Rev 195 (1999) by Peta–Gaye Miller. She argues that the EU must take firmer steps in the protection of human rights of women and be less deferential to national sensitivities on moral issues. At least one step in this direction is the Treaty of Amsterdam of 1997, which came into force on 1 May 1999. That treaty inserts a new Article 6 into the Maastricht Treaty reaffirming that the EU is founded on the principles of liberty, democracy, respect for human rights and fundamental freedoms and the rule of law. Member states that violate these principles in a "serious and persistent way" may have certain of their rights under the Maastricht Treaty suspended. The

Amsterdam Treaty also requires that the European Court of Justice apply human rights standards, as set out *inter alia* in the European Convention on Human Rights, to the acts of European Community institutions. In 2000, the EU adopted the EU Charter of Fundamental Rights. The aim of the Charter is to give prominence to human rights by codifying material from the European Convention on Human Rights, common constitutional traditions and international instruments. For a discussion of the Charter see Rose M. D'Sa, *The EU Charter on Fundamental Rights: A Contribution to Regional Human Rights Norms?* 20 Austl.Y.B.I.L. 55 (1999).

Besides the Council of Europe and the European Union, Europe also offers the mechanism of the OSCE to protect human rights. The role of the OSCE is discussed extensively in Problem 5–1, *supra*.

2.   As noted in Reading 2, *supra*, Europe is not unique in having a regional system designed to protect human rights. The Protocol establishing an African Court of Human Rights came into force on 25 January 2004 after it received fifteen ratifications (Algeria, Burkina–Faso, Burundi, Comoros, Cote d'Ivoire, Gambia, Lesotho, Libya, Mali, Mauritius, Rwanda, Senegal, South Africa, Togo and Uganda). For discussion of the African human rights system see The African Charter on Human and Peoples' Rights: The System in Practice (M. Evans & R. Murray eds., 2002); Rachel Murray & Steven Wheatley, *Groups and the African Charter of Human and Peoples' Rights*, 25 H.R.Q. 213 (2003). In light of the differences between the various human rights regimes, as described by Dinah Shelton, *supra* Reading 2, which do you believe is the most effective? Why? For insights comparing the European and Inter–American systems, see Jochen A. Frowein, *The European and the American Conventions on Human Rights—A Comparison*, 1 Hum. Rts. L. J. 44 (1980); A. Glenn Mower, Jr., Regional Human Rights: A Comparative Study of the West European and Inter–American Systems (1991). For comparisons of the African and other regional systems see Rachel Murray, *Serious or Massive Violations under the African Charter on Human and Peoples' Rights: A Comparison with the Inter–American and European Mechanisms*, 17 Neth. Q. Hum. Rts. 109 (1999); _____, *A Comparison between the African and European Courts of Human Rights*, 2 African Hum. Rts. L. J. (2002). *See also*, W. Michael Reisman, *Practical Matters for Consideration in the Establishment of a Regional Human Rights Mechanism: Lessons from the Inter–American Experience*, 1995 St. Louis–Warsaw Transatlantic L. J. 89. A useful website for information on international human rights courts generally is that of the Project on International Courts and Tribunals at <http://www.pict-pcti.org/index. html>.

As yet, no states have ratified the Arab Charter. For a critical account of the Arab system, see Abdullahi Ahmed An–Naim, *Human Rights in the Arab World: A Regional Perspective*, 23 H.R.Q. 701 (2001). On the difficulties of developing an Asian system of rights protection *see, e.g.,* Abdul Hasnat Monjurul Kabir, *Establishing National Human Rights Commissions in South Asia: A Critical Analysis of the Processes and the Prospects*, 2 Asia–Pac. J. Hum. Rts. & L. 1 (2001); Pamela A. Jefferies, *Human Rights, Foreign Policy, and Religious Belief: An Asia/Pacific Perspective*, 2000 B.Y.U.L. Rev. 885 (2000) (speculating briefly on the Malaysian human rights commission); Vitit Muntarbhorn, *Asia, Human Rights and the New Millenium: Time For a Regional Human Rights Charter?*, 8 Transnat'l L. & Contemp. Probs. 407 (1998). For an overview of the Southeast Asian region and a close examination of commissions in Indonesia and the Philippines, *see*, Li-ann Thio, *Implementing Human Rights in ASEAN Countries: "Promises to Keep and Miles to Go Before I Sleep"*, 2 Yale Hum. Rts. & Dev. L. J. 1 (1999). It is worth noting that a group of Asian NGOs adopted an Asian Human Rights Charter in 1998 to mark the fiftieth anniversary of the Universal Declaration of Human Rights. The text may be found at <http://www.ahrchk.net/charter/main-file.php/eng_charter>.

3. Enforcing the 1950 European Convention for the Protection of Human Rights and Fundamental Freedoms **(Basic Document 3.5)** and its associated protocols has been no easy task, especially given the vastly expanding workload involved. The general acceptance of the right to individual petition under former Article 25 of the Convention and the active approach to human rights protection by both the European Commission and the Court led to a great increase in cases. In 1996 the European Commission registered 4,758 new cases. It also gave rulings on 3,469 applications, of which 614 were declared admissible and 2,776 were declared inadmissible or struck off. The Commission drew up reports in 552 cases, giving its opinion before passing them to the Court or the Committee of Ministers. The biggest rises in new cases were in Turkey by 162% (214 in 1995; 562 in 1996); in Poland by 106% (222 to 458); in Germany by 50% (223 to 334); in Italy by 32% (554 to 729); in France by 27% (471 to 600). In 1997 the number of judgments given by the European Court was up by forty-five percent from the previous year. Extended sessions helped to break the log-jam, but there still was a forty percent rise in cases pending, and cases took on average four and a half years to complete their path through Commission and Court.

Because of the increasing workload, a significant streamlining of the European human rights regime occurred in 1998 pursuant to Protocol No. 11 to the European Convention. Its effect was to merge the European Commission of Human Rights and the European Court of Human Rights to eliminate the Commission and reconstitute the Court in a more efficient mode and on a permanent full time basis. *See* E.T.S. No. 146, *reprinted in* 33 I.L.M. 943 (1994) and 3 Weston & Carlson III.B.16a.

The Protocol replaced articles 19–58 of the Convention, which dealt with the institutional arrangements, as well as protocols 2 and 9, which dealt with advisory opinions and access to the Court, respectively. Protocol 11 provided that the number of judges on the Court will be equal the number of states parties to the European Convention and that they will be elected for six-year, potentially renewable terms. Per Article 34, the formerly optional procedure of individual complaint under Article 25 was made mandatory so that the Court now receives applications from "any person, nongovernmental organization, or group of individuals claiming to be the victim of a violation by one of the High Contracting Parties of the rights set forth in the Convention or the protocols thereto." Cases are now normally decided by a "chamber" of seven judges, while appeal to the "Grand Chamber" of seventeen judges is exceptional. The Court places itself at the disposal of the parties concerned with a view to securing a friendly settlement, the negotiation of which is expressly confidential. In all cases, a High Contracting Party whose national is an applicant has the right to submit written comments and to take part in the hearings. In addition, per Article 36(2), the President of the Court, in the interests of the proper administration of justice, may invite any High Contracting Party which is not a party to the proceedings, or any person concerned who is not an applicant, to submit written comments and to take part in a hearing before a chamber or the Grand Chamber. Protocol 11 also reduced the role of the Committee of Ministers in the European human rights system.

Despite (or perhaps because of) the reforms introduced by Protocol 11, the case load of the European Court has continued to grow at a daunting pace. The

President of the Court, Luzius Wildhaber, stated in 2003 that the Court expected 38,000 applications to be lodged in 2004 and 46,000 or more in 2005. He noted with concern the ever increasing backlog of cases raising substantial human rights issues. For a discussion of the problems faced by the Court and proposals for introducing a filtering mechanism for cases, *see* Leo Zwaak & Therese Cachia, *The European Court of Human Rights: A Success Story?*, 11 Human Rights Brief 32 (Issue 3 Spring 2004).

For a detailed account and evaluation of the changes in Protocol 11, see Henry G. Shermers, *The Eleventh Protocol to the European Convention on Human Rights*, 19 Eur. Hum. Rts. L. Rev. 367 (1994); Rudolph Bernhardt, *Reform of the control machinery under the European Convention on Human Rights*, 89 A.J.I.L. 145 (1995); John G. Merrills & Arthur H. Robertson, Human Rights in Europe (4th ed. 2001). For up-to-date information on the European human rights system in general, see generally the *European Human Rights Law Review*, first published in 1995 and the *European Journal of International Law*.

4. In an article on the *Open Door* case (*supra* Reading 8), Angela Thompson criticizes the apparent deference given by the European Court of Human Rights to domestic legal policy on issues of reproduction, arguing that the "margin of appreciation" doctrine disparately harms women. *See* Angela Thompson, *International Protection of Women's Rights: An Analysis of Open Door Counselling Ltd. and Dublin Well Woman Centre v. Ireland*, 12 Boston U. Int'l L. J. 371 (1994). She writes, at 399–401:

> The criteria for determining the scope of the margin of appreciation in each case seems to vary in part according to the provision of the Convention being interpreted, and in part according to the characterization of the State's justification for the restriction. In *Dudgeon*, the Court examined whether the Convention could tolerate a law that criminalized the inherently private act of homosexual sodomy. By minimizing the morality argument, the Court found a violation of the right of privacy. By contrast, the *Open Door Counselling* Court examined whether the Convention could tolerate a restriction on reproductive decision-making when done for the protection of unborn life and morality. By emphasizing the morality argument, the Court justified a wide margin of appreciation. The opinion of the Court seems to be that domestic institutions are in a far better position to properly regulate the protection of morals, "particularly in an area such as the present which touches on matters of belief concerning the nature of human life."

* * *

> ... As the [European] Convention's supranational supervisor ... , the [European] Court has a responsibility to ensure that the signatory States adhere to their obligations under the Convention. The Court's handling of the issues presented in the *Open Door Counselling* litigation raise grave concerns over the protection of women's rights under the Convention. By declining to comment on the fundamental nature of the underlying right involved in that case, a broader implication may be drawn that the individual rights unique to women are not afforded equal treatment by the Convention organs. The Court, in fact, was not squarely faced with the issue of whether a woman's right to make reproductive choices is protected by the Convention. Its application of a wide margin of appreciation, however, indicates a willingness to shield domestic regulation of reproductive choice from challenges based on Article 8 privacy, and Article 14 equal protection guarantees.

One reading of the case might suggest that the issues involved were simply too narrow to permit the Court to comment on a general right to unencumbered reproductive decisionmaking under the Convention. Upon closer examination, however, the decision seems far more offensive. The Court's application of the margin of appreciation and the extent to which it differs from its application in the *Dudgeon* case more aptly suggests that the Court is likely to defer to the domestic institutions of High Contracting Parties on matters involving a women's right to control reproductive choices. In this way, *Open Door Counselling* represents a missed opportunity; here, the Court had a chance to definitively transform the rhetoric of universal human rights into a reality by acknowledging the fundamental nature of the issue at stake. Ironically, that the issue is peculiar to women is itself a justification for the Court to apply the margin of appreciation more narrowly.

Do you agree with this analysis? Why? Why not?

5. In the same year as the *Open Door* case (*supra* Reading 8), and as in that case, the Irish appellate courts, in *Attorney-General v. X and Others*, 1992 I.R. 1 (Ir. H. Ct.), 1992 I.L.R.M. 401 (Ir. S.Ct.), used a variety of tactics to avoid pronouncing directly on whether the 1950 European Convention for the Protection of Human Rights and Fundamental Freedoms **(Basic Document 3.5)** protects a woman's right to abortion. In that case, a 14 year-old Irish girl (the first defendant) was allegedly raped and became pregnant. The girl and her parents (the second and third defendants) decided that she should travel to England to have an abortion. However, the Attorney General made an *ex parte* application to the Irish High Court for an interim injunction to prevent the defendants from leaving the country for a period of nine months or arranging an abortion. The defendants contested the order, arguing, *inter alia*, that they had the right to travel to obtain a service lawfully available in another state and that X's life was at risk.

In the High Court, Justice Costello upheld the injunction on the basis of Article 40.3.3 of the Irish Constitution which, provides that "[t]he State acknowledges the right to life of the unborn, and, with due regard to the equal right to life of the mother, guarantees in its laws to respect, and, as far as practicable, by its laws to defend and vindicate that right." He found that the risk to X's life posed by the injunction was "much less and of a different order of magnitude than the certainty that the life of the unborn would be terminated if the order was not made." Further, with respect to articles 59 and 60 of the 1957 Treaty Establishing the European Economic Community, 298 U.N.T.S. 11, *reprinted in* 1 Weston & Carlson I.B.7, which protect the freedom to receive a service without subjugation to restrictions, he held that, although an abortion is a service, the freedom to receive a service was subject to a state's right to derogate on the grounds of public policy. The protection of an unborn baby, he determined, was such a permitted derogation. After considering the jurisprudence of the European Court of Human Rights, he found that, when considering the application of the European Convention's guaranteed rights, a "margin of appreciation" was allowed for national authorities in relation to laws dealing with moral issues. Article 40.3.3 of the Irish constitution reflected deeply held convictions on a moral issue, he found, and therefore was a valid derogation.

Following the High Court's decision, the defendants appealed to the Irish Supreme Court, which upheld the appeal by a majority of 4 to 1. Chief Justice Finlay found that the proper test to be applied in interpreting Article 40.3.3 was whether, as a matter of probability, there was a real and substantial risk to the life of the mother that could be avoided only by the termination of her pregnancy. In this case, he found that there was a real and substantial risk to the life of the mother by self-destruction which could only be avoided by termination of her pregnancy. Justice McCarthy concurred and emphasized that it was not a question of balancing the life of the unborn against the life of the mother, because if it were the life of the unborn would virtually always have to be preserved. Rather the true construction of Article 40.3.3 was that, paying due regard to the equal right to life of the mother, when there was a real and substantial risk attached to her survival, then it may not be practicable to vindicate the life of the unborn.

What were the views of the Irish courts on whether Article 2 of the European Convention protects the right to life of the unborn? *See* Katherine Freeman, *The Unborn Child and the European Convention on Human Rights: To Whom Does "Everyone's Right to Life" Belong?*, 8 Emory Int'l L. Rev. 615 (1994).

6. In *Webster v. Reproductive Health Services*, 492 U.S. 490 (1989), Justice Harry Blackmun stated, at 557–58, that "[t]he result [of making abortion illegal], as we know from experience, . . . would be that every year hundreds of thousands of women, in desperation, would defy the law, and place their health and safety in the unclean and unsympathetic hands of back-alley abortionists, or they would attempt to perform abortions on themselves, with disastrous results." Is this argument relevant in international law? If so, how?

7. In *Planned Parenthood v. Casey*, 505 U.S. 833 (1992), the United States Supreme Court stated as follows, at 950–51:

Men and women of good conscience can disagree, and we suppose some always shall disagree, about the profound moral and spiritual implications of terminating a pregnancy, even in its earliest stage. Some of us as individuals find abortion offensive to our most basic principles of morality, but that cannot control our decision. Our obligation is to define the liberty of all, not to mandate one moral code. The underlying constitutional issue is whether the State can resolve these philosophical questions in such a definitive way that a woman lacks all choice in the matter, except perhaps in those rare circumstances in which pregnancy is itself a danger to her own life or health, or is the result of rape or incest. . . . * * * At the heart of liberty is the right to define one's own concept of existence, of meaning, of the universe and of the mystery of human life. Beliefs about these matters could not define the attributes of parenthood were they formed under compulsion of the State.

If abortion is a moral decision, as the US Supreme Court says, should the law become involved at all? Is this what pro-choice activists are advocating?

8. Women's rights often appear to conflict with "cultural" or "religious" values, as illustrated by events surrounding the Indian Supreme Court's decision in *Md. Ahmed Khan v. Shah Bano Begum*, 3 S.C.R. 844 (1985). While not finding a conflict between India's Criminal Code (to which all Indians are subject) and Muslim personal law relative to a Muslim woman's right to maintenance from her former husband, the Indian Supreme Court stated categorically that in a case of conflict between the Code and the personal law of any religious group, the former would prevail. The decision caused such controversy within Indian society that the Indian government, in 1986, enacted The Muslim Women (Protection of Rights on Divorce) Act, reversing the Supreme Court's ruling. *See* Anika Rahman, *Religious Rights Versus Women's Rights in India: A Test Case for International Human Rights Law*, 28 Colum. J. Transnat'l. L. 473 (1990); Hilary Charlesworth & Christine Chinkin, The Boundaries of International Law 116–17, 224–25 (2000). How should women's rights be balanced with competing religious or cultural

values? A good discussion of this question is found in Arati Rao, *The politics of gender and culture in international human rights discourse*, in Women's Rights Human Rights 167 (J. Peters & A. Wolper eds., 1995).

9. Can abortion be separated as an issue of national culture? Given that Catholicism is the state religion in Hibernia, could an argument be made that Hibernian cultural values should trump any international human rights regime? For treatment of the question of cultural relativism versus universal human rights, see *infra* Problem 5–6 ("Cultural Difference in Malacca"), at 712.

10. In *Human Rights and Reproductive Self–Determination*, 44 Am. U. L. Rev. 975 (1995), Professor Rebecca Cook has proposed the recognition of a right to reproductive self-determination that divides into four broad categories of rights: reproductive security and sexuality, reproductive health, reproductive equality, and reproductive decision-making. Each, she writes, draws upon a number of well-established rights. For example, rights relating to reproductive security and sexuality include the right to life and survival, to liberty and security of the person, to freedom from torture and ill-treatment, to marry and found a family, and to the enjoyment of private and family life. Thus, she argues, while noting that 500,000 women die each year for pregnancy-related reasons, the right to life and survival is a precondition of all other human rights. This right, she contends, should be developed to serve each woman whose life is liable to end through avoidable or postponable pregnancy. Is Cook's notion of a right to reproductive self-determination persuasive? How could it be invoked in the instant problem? *See also* Rebecca Cook & Bernard Dickens, *Abortion Law Reform*, 25 H.R.Q. 1 (2003).

Article 10(h) of the 1979 Convention on the Elimination of All Forms of Discrimination Against Women **(Basic Document 3.21)** obligates states to take "all appropriate measures" to eliminate those forms of discrimination against women that result from lack of education and reproductive health services. Should women have the liberty to choose their own beliefs, sexuality, and participation in reproduction? What competing rights are there? Should access to information concerning contraception and/or abortion be freely available to women? In the present problem, imagine Kerry Kildare as not disabled and choosing to carry the fetus until birth. Would she still have the same opportunities and access to the employment market after the birth of her child?

11. Closely related to the issue of women's rights, in particular the right of a woman to determine for herself her own biological functions, is the global issue of overpopulation, impliedly raised in the present problem in the context of a relatively industrialized Western society. As stated in Paragraph 1.4 of the Preamble to the 13 September 1994 Programme of Action of the 1994 United Nations International Conference on Population and Development, UN Doc. A/CONF.171/13 (28 Oct 94), *reprinted in* 5 Weston & Carlson V.I.20:

> During the remaining six years of this critical decade, the world's nations by their actions and inactions will choose from among a range of alternative demographic futures. The low, medium and high variants range from a low of 7.1 billion people to the medium variant of 7.5 billion and a high of 7.8 billion. The difference of 720 million people in the short span of 20 years exceeds the current population of the African continent. Further into the future, the projections diverge even more significantly. By the year 2050, the United Nations projections range from 7.9 billion to the medium variant of 9.8 billion and a high of 11.9 billion....

In light of these projections and a present world population of about 5 billion people, consider the following:

(a) Is "the population problem" primarily a matter of too many people? Too many poor people? Too many rich people using up too many resources? A mixture of all of these?

(b) Is the present or future world population reconcilable with long-run ecological and political stability? Is it primarily a matter of sufficiency of resources, of environment quality, or of political milieu? A mixture of all of these?

(c) How does population increase bear upon the prospects for development? It often is argued, especially by Third World thinkers, that the essence of the problem of meeting "basic needs" is more one of equitable distribution than of expanded production. At the same time, even if the short-term challenge is distributional, each additional person is a proportionate burden on resources, and rapid increases in population do complicate the task of providing jobs and of improving the social services (*e.g.*, schools, hospitals, public recreational facilities) in countries where deficiencies already exist. Indeed, it is argued that population growth imperils the prospect of democratic governance in poor countries. The economic surplus is not sufficient to sustain both profit margins for the rich and social dividends for the poor. As a consequence, savings and investment are required to make the economic system work, and this leads to holding the wage and social services demands of the poor in check. There is thus an apparent correlation between demographic pressure and recourse to authoritarian patterns of rule.

(d) What should be the role of the state in relation to "the population problem"? Should it have the authority to restrict family size by fiat? By influencing calculations via tax and inheritance policies? By some other devices?

(e) How does (should) population policy correlate with the values of peace, sociopolitical justice, economic well-being, and ecological balance? Is the answer different in the industrial countries of the North than in the developing countries of the South? If not, should it be?

* * *

(g) Would you favor an international legal regime that tied foreign aid and developmental capital from international financial institutions to some evidence of a national population policy committed to lowering the birth rate to acceptable levels? Some liberals in the North have advocated such "world order bargains." Do you? What are the arguments pro and con?

(h) Azizah al-Hibri (*supra* Reading 11) argues that the population debate has been hijacked by the First World to focus on the need for birth control in the developing world rather than on the need to reduce First World consumption. She is very critical of First World feminist reproductive movements for this reason. Do you agree with al-Hibri? Why? Why not? *See generally* Paula Abrams, *Reservations About Women: Population Policy and Reproductive Rights*, 39 C.I.L.J. 1 (1996). For another Third World critique of feminist discourse in international law see Joe Oloka–Onyango & Sylvia Tamale, *"The Personal Is Political," or Why Women's Rights Are Indeed Human Rights: An African Perspective on International Feminism*, 17 H.R.Q. 691 (1995).

(i) What can international law and lawyers do to play a useful role in relation to global population policy? Is the subject-matter suitable for the articulation of standards comparable to those formulated in such human rights documents as the

Universal Declaration of Human Rights **(Basic Document 3.3)** or the European Social Charter **(Basic Document 3.11)**? What specific legal recommendations can you propose?

For preliminary assistance, see William G. Hollingsworth, Ending the Explosion: Population Policies and Ethics for a Humane Future (1996).

See also Maria Sophia Aguirre & Anne Wolfgram, *United Nations Policy and the Family: Redefining the Ties that Bind a Study of History, Forces, and Trends*, 16 B.Y.U. J. Pub. L. 113 (2002). *See also* Tara A. Gellman, *The Blurred Line Between Aiding Progress and Sanctioning Abuse: United States Appropriations, the UNFPA and Family Planning in the P.R.C.*, 17 N.Y.L. Sch. J. Hum. Rts. 1063 (2001); Amy Hampton, *Population Control in China: Sacrificing Human Rights for the Greater Good?*, 11 Tulsa J. Comp. & Int'l L. 321 (2003); Carol A. Kates, *Reproductive Liberty and Overpopulation*, 13(1) Envtl. Values 51 (2004); George D. Moffett, Critical Masses: The Global Population Challenge (1994); Anup Shah, Ecology and the Crisis of Overpopulation: Future Prospects for Global Sustainability (1998); "Coercive Population Control in China: New Evidence of Forced Abortion and Forced Sterilization." Hearing before the Committee on International Relations, House of Representatives, 107th Congress, 1st Sess., 17 Oct 2001, *available at* <http://www.house. gov/international_relations/107/75761.pdf>; Katarina Tomasevski, Human Rights in Population Policies (Swedish International Development Agency, 1994). For earlier pioneering analyses, see Barry Commoner, *Rapid Population Growth and Environmental Stress*, 21 Int'l J. Health Services 199 (1991); Paul R. Ehrlich & Anne H. Ehrlich, Population, Resources, Environment: Issues in Human Ecology (2d ed. 1972); _____, The Population Explosion (1980); Garrett J. Hardin, *Living On A Lifeboat*, 24 Bioscience 561 (1974); and Gordon R. Taylor, The Biological Time Bomb (1968).

12.   In Reading 6, *supra*, Hilary Charlesworth argues that the international law of human rights is effectively a law protecting the rights of men rather than the rights of women. *See also* Hilary Charlesworth, Christine Chinkin, & Shelley Wright, *Feminist Approaches to International Law*, 85 A.J.I.L 613 (1991); Hilary Charlesworth & Christine Chinkin, The Boundaries of International Law (2000), chapter 7. *See also supra* Section B–2 in Chapter 1, at 40. What are your views of this argument in the context of the present problem? If the claim is correct, what can be done in response. In a portion of the article not excerpted above, Charlesworth writes (at 795–96, footnotes omitted):

> There has been much debate among feminists about whether human rights discourse is a useful strategy. Many have argued, for example, that civil and political rights are manipulable, individualistic, and unlikely to respond to the more general structural disadvantages that women face. In my view, however, the significance of human rights discourse outweighs its disadvantages. Human rights provide an alternative language and framework to the existing welfare and protection approach to the global situation of women as victims or dependents. Human rights allow women to claim specific entitlements from a specified obligation-holder. Moreover, there are international, regional, and national systems in place that can be invoked to protect human rights. Human rights discourse is the dominant progressive moral philosophy operating at the global level. It is important for women to engage in such discourse and contest its parameters.

What might the Universal Declaration's mid-life crisis produce? One outcome could be attention to the gendered model of human nature embedded in the human rights system. Just as some men at fifty suddenly regret the limitations of traditional male roles, the human rights system should develop rights responding to the life experiences of women, rather than forcing women to articulate their concerns in terms of rights based on male lives. Radhika Coomaraswamy, the UN Special Rapporteur on Violence Against Women, proposes the creation of a "fourth generation" of women's rights. This "fourth generation" of rights includes "new" rights such as the right to sexual autonomy as well as a reinterpretation of the earlier generations of rights in order to respond to women's concerns.

The use of an equality paradigm in women's human rights law needs to be reassessed. While it can offer some progress for women, it also can rationalize the deeper inequities in social structures around the world. As Nicola Lacey writes, the idea of equality as sameness cuts little ice when men and women are simply running different races. Dianne Otto proposes that women reclaim the language of equity from states that have used it to signal a lesser standard than equality to achieve substantive redistributive outcomes. She also emphasizes the need to respond to the diversity of women's experiences in a meaningful way. One way to do this is to focus on economic and social rights that would draw attention to "the operation of systems of privilege among women" and the inequitable structures of global capital.

13. The treatment of women has been the subject of over twenty international legal instruments since 1945. In addition to the 1979 Convention on the Elimination of All Forms of Discrimination Against Women **(Basic Document 3.21)**, see, *e.g.*, International Agreement for the Suppression of the White Slave Traffic (as amended by Protocol of 4 May 49), 18 May 1904, 92 U.N.T.S. 19, *reprinted in* 3 Weston & Carlson III.C.1; International Convention for the Suppression of the White Slave Traffic (as amended by Protocol of 4 May 49 and with final protocol), 4 May 10, 98 U.N.T.S. 101, *reprinted in* 3 Weston & Carlson III.C.2; International Convention for the Suppression of Traffic in Women and Children (as amended by Protocol of 12 Nov 47), 30 Sep 21, 53 U.N.T.S. 39, *reprinted in* 3 Weston & Carlson III.C.3; International Convention for the Suppression of Traffic in Women of Full Age (as amended by Protocol of 12 Nov 47), 11 Oct 33, 53 U.N.T.S. 49, *reprinted in* 3 Weston & Carlson III.C.4; Inter–American Convention on the Granting of Political Rights to Women, 2 May 48, OASTS No. 3, *reprinted in* 3 Weston & Carlson III.C.5; Inter–American Convention on the Granting of Civil Rights to Women, 2 May 48, OASTS No. 23, *reprinted in* 3 Weston & Carlson III.C.6; ILO Convention (No. 90) on Night Work of Young Persons (Industry), 10 Jul 48, 91 U.N.T.S. 3 (1951); ILO Convention (No. 95) on Protection of Wages, 1 Jul 49, 138 U.N.T.S. 225 (1952); Convention for the Suppression of the Traffic in Persons and of the Exploitation of the Prostitution of Others, 2 Dec 49, 96 U.N.T.S. 271, *reprinted in* 3 Weston & Carlson III.C.7; ILO Convention (No. 100) Concerning Equal Remuneration for Men and Women Workers for Work of Equal Value, 29 Jun 51, 165 U.N.T.S. 303; ILO Convention (No. 103) on Maternity Protection (Revised 1952), 28 Jun 52, 214 U.N.T.S. 321, *reprinted in* 3 Weston & Carlson III.C.8; Convention on the Political Rights of Women, 31 Mar 53, 193 U.N.T.S. 135, *reprinted in* 3 Weston & Carlson III.C.9; Convention on the Nationality of Married Women, 20 Feb 57, 309 U.N.T.S., *reprinted in* 3 Weston & Carlson III.C.10; ILO Convention (No. 111) Concerning Discrimination in Respect of Employment and Occupation, 25 Jun 58, 362 U.N.T.S. 31; and Convention on the Consent to Marriage, Minimum Age for Marriage and Registration of Marriages, 10 Dec 62, 512 U.N.T.S. 231, *reprinted in* 3 Weston & Carlson III.C.11. In 2003, the Organisation of African States adopted a Protocol to the African Charter on Human and Peoples' Rights on the Rights of

Women in Africa. The provisions of the Protocol are justiciable before the African Court of Human Rights. *See also* Natalie Kaufman Hevener, *An Analysis of Gender Based Treaty Law: Contemporary Developments in Historical Perspective*, 8 H.R.Q. 70 (1986). Are any of the above-cited ILO conventions relevant to Kerry Kildare's and Meath Galway's legal action? Will they be effective?

14. An Optional Protocol to the 1979 Convention on the Elimination of All Forms of Discrimination Against Women was adopted by the United Nations on 10 December 1999 **(Basic Document 3.52)**. It entered into force on 22 December 2000 after being ratified by ten states. As at 10 June 2005, the Optional Protocol has been accepted by 71 states. The Optional Protocol allows women within the jurisdiction of states parties to make a complaint about breaches of the Convention (termed a "communication") directly to the Committee on the Elimination of Discrimination Against Women, the treaty's monitoring body. Assume Hibernia is a party to the Optional Protocol. How could it be used by Kerry Kildare and Meath Galway? What arguments could be made by these two women and Hibernia respectively before the Committee? In 1999 the Committee on the Elimination of Discrimination against Women adopted General Recommendation 24 on Women and Health (UN Doc. A/54/38/Rev. 1, 3–7.) General Recommendation 24 elaborated the right of women to health care as requiring *inter alia* the removal of barriers to access to health care for women including "laws that criminalize medical procedures only needed by women and that punish women that undergo these procedures."

15. *Bibliographical Note.* For supplemental discussion concerning the principal themes addressed in this problem, consult the following additional specialized materials:

(a) *Books/Monographs/Reports/Symposia.* H. Charlesworth & C. Chinkin, The Boundaries of International Law (2000); R. Coomaraswamy, Reinventing International Law: Women's Rights as Human Rights (1997); M. Eriksson, Reproductive Freedom in the Context of International Human Rights and Humanitarian Law (2000); R. Graycar & J. Morgan, The Hidden Gender of Law (2d ed. 2002); Human Rights of Women: National and International Perspectives (R. Cook ed., 1994); C. Meyer, Wandering Uterus: Politics and the Reproductive Rights of Women (1997); Negotiating Reproductive Rights: Women's Perspectives Across Countries and Cultures (R. Petchesky & K. Judd eds., 1998); C. Packer, The Right to Reproductive Choice: A Study in International Law (1996); R. Petchesky, Abortion and Women's Choice: The State, Sexuality and Reproductive Freedom (1984); Pilipina Legal Resources Center, Gender, Muslim Laws and Reproductive Rights (2001); Reproductive Rights in Practice: A Feminist Report on Quality of Care (A. Hardon & E. Hayes eds., 1997); R. Rosen, Reproductive Health, Reproductive Rights: Reformers and the Politics of Maternal Welfare, 1917–1940 (2003); A. Sanger, Beyond Choice: Reproductive Freedom in the 21st Century (2004); 1–3 Women's Human Rights: A Reference Guide (K. Askin & D. Koenig eds., 1998); Women's Rights, Human Rights: International Feminist Perspectives (J. Peters & A. Wolper eds., 1995).

(b) *Articles/Book Chapters.* P. Abrams, *Population Politics: Reproductive Rights and U. S. Asylum Policy*, 14 Geo. Immigr. L.J. 881 (2000); P. Abrams, *Reservations About Women: Population Policy and Reproductive Rights*, 39 C.I.L.J. 1 (1996); P. Abrams, *Symposium on Population Law: Population Control and Sustainability: It's the Same Old Song but with a Different Meaning*, 27 Envt'l. L. 1111 (1997); D. Babor, *Population Growth and Reproductive Rights in International Human Rights Law*, 14 Conn. J. Int'l L. 83 (1999); C. Bateup, *Can reproductive rights be 'human' rights? Some thoughts on the inclusion of women's rights in mainstream human rights discourse,* 6 Austl. J. Hum. Rts. 33 (2000); F. Beckwith, *Cloning and Reproductive Liberty,* 3 Nev. L.J. 61 (2002); M. Brookes, *Reproductive Rights in Afghanistan: Considerations of Abortion Regulation in Light of the Afghan Reconstruction Process,* 18 Conn. J. Int'l L. 595 (2003); C. Bustelo, *Reproductive Health and CEDAW,* 44 Am. Univ. L. Rev. 1145 (1995); T. Cho, *The Double Moral: Compliance of International Legal Obligations of Reproductive Rights vs. Allegiance to the Catholic Church,* 5 Sw. J. of L. & Trade Am. 421 (1998); D. Cole, *Going to England: Irish Abortion Law and the European Community,* 17 Hastings Int'l & Comp. L. Rev. 113 (1993); B. Crane & S. Isaacs, *Symposium: The United Nations Family: Challenges of Law and Development: The Cairo Programme of Action: A New Framework for International Cooperation on Population and Development Issues,* 36 Harv. Int'l L. J. 295 (1995); A. Dubler, A. Rahman, K. Rodgers, & J. Spinak, *Women's Rights: Reframing the Issues for the Future,* 12 Colum. J. Gender & L. 333 (2003); I. Feitshans, *Is There a Human Right to Reproductive Health?* 8 Tex. J. Women & L. 93 (1998); R. Fleishman, *The Battle Against Reproductive Right: The Impact of the Catholic Church on Abortion Law in both International and Domestic Arenas,* 14 Emory Int'l . Rev. 277 (2000); A. Haroz, *South Africa's 1996 Choice on Termination of Pregnancy Act: Expanding Choice and International Human Rights to Black South African Women,* 30 Van. J. Transnat'l L. 863 (1997); *Women's Rights as Human Rights–Rules, Realities and the Role of Culture: A Formula for Reform,* 21 Brooklyn J. Int'l L. 605 (1996); R. Howard–Hassmann, *Dueling Fates: Should the International Legal Regime Accept a Collective or Individual Paradigm to Protect Women's Rights?* 24 Mich. J. Int'l L. 227 (2002); K. Johns, *Reproductive Rights of Women: Construction and Reality in International and United States Law,* 5 Cardozo Women's L. J. 1 (1998); M. Lee, *Defining the Agenda: A New Struggle for African–American Women in the Fight for Reproductive Self–Determination,* 6 Wash. & Lee Race and Ethnic Ancestry L. J. 87 (2000); C. Obermeyer, *A Cross–Cultural Perspective on Reproductive Rights,* 17 H.R.Q. 366 (1995); A. Orford, *Contesting Globalization: A Feminist Perspective on the Future of Human Rights,* 8 Transnat'l L. & Contemp. Probs. (1998); A. Orford, *Locating the International: Military and Monetary Interventions after the Cold War,* 38 Harv. Int'l. L. J. 443 (1997); D. Otto, *Holding Up Half the Sky, But for Whose Benefit?: A Critical Analysis of the Fourth World Conference on Women,* 6 Aust. Feminist L. J. 7 (1996); V. Peterson, *Whose Rights? A Critique of the "Givens" in Human Rights Discourse,* 15 Alternatives 303; M. Plata, *Reproductive Rights as Human Rights: The Colombian Case,* in Human Rights of Women: National and International Perspectives 515 (R. Cook ed., 1994); A. Rao, *Home-Word Bound: Women's Place in the Family of International Human Rights,* 2 Global Governance 241 (1996); H. Soana, *The Protection of Reproductive Rights under International Law: The Bush Administration's Policy Shift and China's Family Planning Practices,* 13 Pac. Rim L. & Pol'y 229 (2004); B. Stark, *International Human Rights Law, Feminist Jurisprudence, and Nietzche's "Eternal Return": Turning the Wheel,* 19 Harv. Women's L. J. 169 (1996); M. Sunder, *Piercing the Veil,* 112 Yale L. J. 1399 (2003); Symposium, *Women's Rights Are Human Rights: Selected Articles Dedicated to Women in the International Human Rights Area,* 21 Brooklyn J. Int'l L. No. 3 (1996).

Problem 5–3

Suspected Terrorists in Hibernia

Section 1. Facts

Assume the same facts as in Problem 5–2, *supra*.

Another aspect of Hibernia's national religious commitment is a resolve, especially among church groups and others in the private sector, to assist the poor and otherwise less privileged. Thus Hibernia has become known as a place of refuge for persons seeking escape from autocratic and discriminatory rule. This fact has not gone unnoticed among Muslims in southeastern Europe and the Middle East where war and other violence have prevailed in recent years. Nor has it gone unnoticed among their compatriots seeking asylum in neighboring Albion, a parliamentary democracy recently attacked via suicide and remote control bombings apparently by Islamic persons claiming association with the terrorist organization known as al-Qaeda.

Amatullah Aziz and Najwa Hussein are two young Arab women of Shi'ite Muslim faith recently arrived in Hibernia from Albion where, despite help from refugee assistance organizations, they had been unable to secure legal refuge from the strife prevailing in their Middle East homeland. It seemed to matter not at all that they had been sexually assaulted by Christian and Sunni–Muslim militants in their native land, in part because their fathers were politically active and outspoken against the Christian and Sunni–Muslim majorities there. Furthermore, rising anti-Islamic sentiment in Albion, nurtured by Albion's new anti-terrorist Internal Security Act (ISA), which profiles and targets persons of Islamic origin and belief, made it seem unlikely that refugee status would be granted them in Albion. Among other things, the ISA outlaws "public Muslim gatherings" of more than three people without governmental permission and allows for the indefinite detention of "suspected anti-Albion terrorists" without charge or trial. Stated Albion's Home Secretary recently: "Preachers of hate and purveyors of terrorism have no place in our country. They are a threat to our freedom."

Angry at this state of affairs, Amatullah Aziz and Najwa Hussein joined with fellow Muslims to denounce publicly the discrimination and consequent victimization that, collectively as well as individually, they felt being inflicted upon them by the Albion authorities and members of Albion society. At a pro-Muslim rally on a public square—a rally for which no permit had been sought or granted—Amatullah Aziz was heard to say: "Allah condemns Albion for its inhumane fascistic ways." To which Najwa Hussein was heard to have added: "Allah will have his revenge against Albion's democratic pretense."

Soon the two women were jeered and threatened whenever they left their boarding house. Many of their Muslim women friends and relatives were likewise jeered and threatened. One was gang-raped by a group of Albion men. A popular neighborhood mosque was set afire. After a while, Amatullah Aziz and Najwa Hussein feared leaving their boarding house and remained there as virtual prisoners, visiting with Muslim friends in their small room only at night under cover of darkness.

With the help of some of these friends, the two women managed to escape across the border to Hibernia where, by prearrangement with a Hibernian human rights lawyer, they immediately applied for political asylum, hoping later to qualify for Hibernian citizenship. Immediately thereafter, however, they were taken into custody by the Hibernian officials. The day before their arrival in Hibernia, it turns out, another series of both suicide and remote controlled bombs destroyed numerous components of Albion's public transportation system—trains, subways, and buses—killing hundreds and wounding thousands. It also turns out that cell phone photographs appear to have placed Amatullah Aziz and Najwa Hussein, arm in arm, in the general vicinity of one of the bombings.

Albion is now demanding the extradition of Amatullah Aziz and Najwa Hussein from Hibernia to Albion—for incitement to revolt, murder, conspiracy to commit murder, criminal assault, and "other terrorist activities"— pursuant to the Council of Europe's 1957 Convention on Extradition (as amended by its two additional protocols) and its 1977 Convention on the Suppression of Terrorism, two agreements to which both Albion and Hibernia are parties. Also referencing these two conventions, the lawyer representing the two women in Hibernia is resisting extradition through application to Hibernia's Minister of Justice, who, under Hibernian law and consistent with the 1957 extradition convention, is empowered, after a hearing, to grant or refuse extradition. In mid–2004, both Albion and Hibernia, members of the European Union (EU), enacted legislation—called the "European Arrest Warrant Act" (EAWA) in Hibernia—to implement the EU Council Framework Decision of 13 June 2002 on the European Arrest Warrant and the Surrender Procedures between Member States which, as of 1 January 2004, replaced the "corresponding provisions" of both the 1957 extradition convention, as amended, and the 1977 anti-terrorism convention. In mid–2005, however, Hibernia's Supreme Court, Chief Judge Gavin Boyles presiding, declared Hibernia's 2004 EAWA unconstitutional for failing to protect adequately the rights of Hibernian citizens and of persons seeking asylum and/or citizenship in Hibernia. As a consequence, Hibernia has not yet effectively implemented the 2002 EU Council Framework Decision, and in this setting, as confirmed by German as well as Hibernian case law, Article 31 of the Framework Decision instructs that the 1957 Convention on Extradition and 1977 Convention on the Suppression of Terrorism apply.[a]

Section 2.   Questions Presented

1. Is Hibernia obligated under international law to extradite Amatullah Aziz and Najwa Hussein to Albion?

2. In any event, are there any additional or alternative legal norms, procedures, and/or institutions to be recommended that might further help to prevent or discourage situations of the kind posed by this problem?

a. For pertinent discussion, see *infra* Discussion Note/Question 1, at 652.

SECTION 3.   ASSIGNMENTS

A.   READING ASSIGNMENT

Study the Readings presented in Section 4, *infra*, and the Discussion Notes/Questions that follow. Also, time permitting, consult the accompanying bibliographical references.

B.   RECOMMENDED WRITING ASSIGNMENT

Prepare a comprehensive, logically sequenced, and *argumentative* brief in the form of an outline of the primary and subsidiary *legal* issues you see requiring resolution by the Hibernian Minister of Justice. Also, from the perspective of an independent judge, indicate which side ought to prevail on each issue and why. Retain a copy of your issue-outline/brief for class discussion.

C.   RECOMMENDED ORAL ASSIGNMENT

Assume you are legal counsel for Amatullah Aziz and Najwa Hussein, on the one hand, or Albion, on the other (as designated by your instructor); then, relying upon the Readings (and your issue-outline if prepared), present a 15–10 minute oral argument of your client's/government's likely positions before the Hibernian Minister of Justice.

D.   RECOMMENDED REFLECTIVE ASSIGNMENT

Consider (and recommend) alternative norms, institutions, and/or procedures that you believe might do better than existing world order arrangements to contend with situations of the kind posed by this problem. In so doing, but without insisting upon *immediate* feasibility, identify the particular transition steps that would be needed to make your alternatives a reality.

SECTION 4.   READINGS

The following readings are considered *prima facie* relevant to solving this problem. They are your law library for present purposes and should be treated as such, organized intelligibly for "shelving" and not necessarily according to the issues presented. Be sure to review Chapter 2 ("International Legal Prescription: The 'Sources' of International Law") in your consideration of them. It, too, should be treated as part of your law library (as, indeed, should this entire coursebook).

1.   Marjorie M. Whiteman, 6 Digest of International Law 727–28 (1968).

Extradition is the process by which persons charged with or convicted of a crime against the law of a State and found in a foreign State are returned by the latter to the former for trial or punishment. It applies [a] to those who are merely charged with an offense but have not been brought to trial; [b] to those who have been tried and convicted and have subsequently escaped from custody; and [c] to those who have been convicted *in absentia*. It does not apply to persons merely suspected of having committed an offense but against whom no charge has been laid or to a person whose presence is desired as a witness or for obtaining or enforcing a civil judgment.

Extradition is a national act. Requesting and granting extradition from or to a foreign State is, apart from any treaty to the contrary, a prerogative of the national government of a State.... It is ... distinguishable from deportation or expulsion whereby an alien is removed from the territory of a State for reasons of concern to that State.

Although in the absence of a treaty a State is ... under no legal obligation to do so, most States may, under their law, extradite fugitives from justice to a foreign State without an extradition agreement with that State. Nevertheless, most States have entered into extradition agreements with foreign States. Under United States law the United States may grant extradition only pursuant to a treaty.

Extradition treaties normally provide that the two contracting States agree reciprocally to surrender persons found in their territories who are accused of crimes committed within the jurisdiction of the other contracting State. The crimes covered by the treaty may be all those acts which are offenses under the laws of both States and punishable by a certain minimum term of imprisonment or, as in the case of the treaties of the United States and of Great Britain, only those offenses enumerated in the treaty itself.

Extradition treaties and the extradition laws of some States require that to obtain the extradition of a fugitive from justice, the State making the request must produce sufficient evidence to show probable cause to believe the fugitive committed the offense for which ... extradition is requested and that the act charged is a crime in both States. Treaties and laws usually except extradition in certain circumstances such as when the offense is political in character[b] or has become barred by prescription and, frequently, when the accused is a national of the requested State. Generally, a condition of surrender [commonly known as "the doctrine of specialty"] is that the accused will not be tried or punished for any offense previously committed other than that for which ... extradition is granted. Under the laws of most States the extradition request when received is subject first to judicial examination prior to its consideration by the executive branch of the government. Depending on the law of the State concerned the judicial branch may or may not have the power to render a binding decision against the extradition of the fugitive. But in all cases, the ultimate decision to grant extradition rests with the executive.

2. European Convention on Extradition. Concluded, 13 Dec 1957. Entered into force, 18 Apr 1960. 359 U.N.T.S. 274, E.T.S. No. 24; *reprinted in* 3 Weston & Carlson III.M.2: Arts. 1–3, 12, 14, 18, 22, 25 (Basic Document 6.1).

3. Additional Protocol to the European Convention on Extradition. Concluded, 13 Dec 1957. Entered into force, 20 Aug 1979. E.T.S.

---

b. *But see infra* Discussion Notes/Questions 2–4, at 653–56.

No. 86, *reprinted in* 3 Weston & Carlson III.M.2: Additional Protocol (15 Oct 1975), Art. 1 (Basic Document 6.1).

4. **European Convention on Extradition. Concluded, 13 Dec 1957. Entered into force, 5 Jun 1983. E.T.S. No. 98;** *reprinted in* 3 **Weston & Carlson III.M.2: Second Additional Protocol (17 Mar 1978), Arts. 1, 3, 5** (Basic Document 6.1).

5. **Model Treaty on Extradition. GA Res. 45/116, UN Doc. A/RES/ 45/116 (14 Dec 1990): Art. 3** (Basic Document 6.4).

6. **Convention Relating to Extradition between Member States of the European Union. Concluded, 27 Sep 1996. Entered into force, 27 Sep 1996. O.J. (C313) 12–23: Art. 5** (Basic Document 6.5).

7. **European Convention on the Suppression of Terrorism. Concluded, 27 Jan 1977. Entered into force, 4 Aug 1978. 1137 U.N.T.S. 93, E.T.S. No. 90: Arts 1–5, 7** (Basic Document 3.20).

8. **EU Council Framework Decision on the European Arrest Warrant and the Surrender Procedures between Member States. Council Decision 2002/584/JHA (13 Jun 2002), 2002 O.J. (L 190), 1–20: Prmbl. & Arts. 1–8, 31, & 34** (Basic Document 6.8).

9. **Miriam E. Sapiro,** *In an Era of Terrorism: The Need to Abolish the Political Offence Exception*, **61 N.Y.U. L. Rev. 654, 657, 689–93, 698–701 (1986).**

This Note challenges the widespread assumption that the POE [political offense exception] doctrine should be an essential component of the United States's extradition practice. It argues that there are serious problems with the theoretical purposes and justifications of the POE, as well as flaws in its practical application. Because it is nearly impossible to distinguish between a political offense and a nonpolitical crime on a theoretical or a practical level, protection of the person sought against unfair treatment by the requesting state emerges as the only rational and attainable objective of the POE. This goal can be readily achieved by alternative means, and therefore it is possible to eliminate the POE as a barrier to extradition without diminishing the rights of the requested person.

* * *

PROPOSED SOLUTION

In attempting to solve the problems caused by the POE, many have tried to adapt it to terrorism, but few have questioned its functional necessity. Recent judicial decisions and reform efforts indicate that the line between a protected political act and an extraditable terrorist act is difficult—if not impossible—to draw, ... The inability to resolve the complex issue results, in part, from a myopic focus on how to classify particular offenses. The one rational purpose of the POE—to protect the offender from unfair treatment by the requesting state—is frequently overlooked. In light of the present abuses of the doctrine, it is imperative to consider whether the POE is indeed an indispensible element of the extradition process, or whether its sole justifiable function can be better fulfilled by other means.

A. Alternative Means of Protection

The concern of . . . commentators has focused primarily on the problem of defining and determining the legitimacy of the political act, and not on the impartiality of the prospective trial or punishment. This focus is misguided because the justifications advanced for protecting the act are not persuasive, and it is difficult to differentiate between political and nonpolitical offenses. Instead, another purpose of the POE—the protection of the requested person from unfair treatment by the requesting state—should be emphasized. The offender's legal interest in the extradition process consists of, and should be limited to, the right not to be returned to a state that may unfairly prosecute or punish him. The person sought deserves a fair trial on the merits of the charge and just punishment regardless of the act and its connection to a political objective. Although the political nature of an offense may in some cases decrease the likelihood of due process, the POE irrebuttable presumption of unfairness is unwarranted. When the emphasis is properly shifted from the nature of the act to the fairness of the requesting state's treatment of the person sought, the reasons for the traditional POE are eliminated because better means of protecting this interest exist. Principally, these means consist of the double criminality principle, the specialty doctrine, and the discrimination clause. Together, these mechanisms can operate to ensure that all requested persons, and not just those accused of politically motivated offenses, will not be subject to unfair treatment upon extradition.

1. Double Criminality Principle

The established principle of double criminality operates to prohibit extradition on any charge that would not constitute a serious crime under the laws of both the requesting state and the requested state, although identical terminology is not necessary. For example, a request from Chile to the United States for extradition of a person convicted of demonstrating against the government would be denied because the act is not an offense under American law. In addition, extradition may be denied under the double criminality principle if the requesting state relies upon a theory of jurisdiction not recognized by the requested state.

2. Doctrine of Specialty

The doctrine of specialty, which is explicitly incorporated in most extradition agreements, provides both the requested state and the person sought with certain rights in the post-extradition process. The purpose of the doctrine is to prevent punishment of a person who might not have been extradited if the plans of the extraditing state had been fully disclosed. It achieves this by ensuring that the extradited offender is not prosecuted or punished for an offense committed prior to the extradition that is not contained in the grant of extradition. As additional precautions against the possibility of unjust treatment by the requesting state, the doctrine prohibits the imposition of a punishment that is more severe than that which was provided for when the extradition request was made, and it requires the requesting state to give an acquitted person a reasonable opportunity to leave the state.

* * *

Perhaps most importantly, the doctrine of specialty enables the requested state to make the grant of extradition contingent upon agreement regarding procedural or substantive aspects of the trial or punishment. For example, in the case of Eain v. Wilkes (Eain III),[1] the Secretary of State agreed to extradite Eain to Israel after receiving assurances that he would receive a public trial in a civilian court, normal rules of criminal procedure would apply, Eain would have counsel of his choice, the prosecution would have to prove guilt beyond a reasonable doubt, if convicted Eain would have a right of appeal, and under no circumstances would he receive the death penalty.[2] Similarly, in the extradition of Marcos Perez Jimenez, a former President of Venezuela, the court considered carefully which of the murder and embezzlement charges warranted extradition, and concluded that there was only sufficient evidence to sustain extradition for certain of the charged crimes.[3] The Secretary of State therefore granted the extradition request on the conditions that Jimenez be tried only for these crimes, and that a representative of the United States be allowed to observe the trial.[4]

3. Discrimination Clause

Incorporating a discrimination clause in each extradition treaty, or achieving the same result through legislation, is the most effective way to ensure that an extradited person will be fairly prosecuted and punished. Under the clause, if the person sought demonstrates that there exists a likelihood of unfair treatment or persecution, he cannot be extradited to the requesting state. The discrimination clause, which has been included in a number of recent treaties, precludes extradition if he person sought is by reason of his race, religion, nationality, or political opinions, likely to be denied a fair trial or punished, detained or restricted in his personal liberty for such reasons. The best formulation would also include a provision prohibiting extradition if the person sought as established by a preponderance of the evidence that such person . . . would, as a result of extradition, be subjected to fundamental unfairness.

* * *

B. Abolition of the POE

Given the safeguards provided by the double criminality principle, the doctrine of specialty, and the discrimination clause, there is no justification for retaining the POE, and there are compelling reasons to eliminate it from extradition practice. First, as examined earlier in this Note, in both theory and practice the POE does not effectively serve its intended purposes. The doctrine was developed to secure freedom of political expression by armed force if necessary, but the POE's overly broad protection of this liberty also permits terrorists to commit serious, violent crimes with impunity. Paradoxically, no such right extends to those caught within the borders of the state where the act occurred. The POE is also meant to maintain neutrality among states, but it is a dubious means of achieving this goal because the automatic denial of extradition can easily be perceived as aiding a requesting state's

---

1. 641 F.2d 504 (7th Cir.), cert. denied, 454 U.S. 894 (1981).

2. Memorandum of decision by William Clark, Deputy Secretary of State, in the Case of Abu Eain, reprinted in GA Res. 36/171, UN Doc. A/36/51, Annex II app. (1982) (note verbale, 4 Jan 1982).

3. *See Jimenez v. Aristeguieta*, 311 F.2d 547, 558–60 (5th Cir. 1962), cert. denied, 373 U.S. 914 (1963).

4. *See* 6 M. Whiteman, Digest of International Law 727, 737–38, 1051–52 (1968).

adversaries and thus harm relations between the two states. A broad interpretation of the POE may also hinder the ability of the United States successfully to request the extradition of accused persons from foreign states.[5] More generally, a denial of extradition under the POE may be construed, both at home and abroad, as condonement of the offense. Thus, continued unrestricted use of the POE could encourage dangerous offenders to flee to the United States. The only objective of the POE that is both rational and attainable is the protection of the person sought against unfair treatment. In this regard, individual adjudication of each extradition request makes far more sense than the irrebuttable presumption of unjust treatment inherent in the POE doctrine. Second, courts have been unable to use the traditional political incidence test or an adaptation of it to distinguish persuasively the political offender from the terrorist; indeed, such a distinction may be illusory. For its part, Congress has failed to give the judiciary effective guidance, which could have mitigated the inconsistent and unpredictable application of the doctrine. Further attempts by either the courts or Congress to alter the POE will only prolong the charade of using a doctrine that is based on a fictional and impractical distinction between political and ordinary offenders. Furthermore, the POE is already subject to a number of exemptions created by treaty and judicial interpretation, including the attentat clause and the exclusion of anarchy.[6] Instead of attempting to carve out yet more exemptions from the exception, thus making the doctrine even more internally inconsistent, the POE should be abolished.

Finally, it is important to remember that the POE doctrine is not a binding rule of international law. Rather, it is an exception created principally

---

5. France's refusal of two extradition requests by the United States illustrate how a broad interpretation of the POE may operate against American interests. In one instance, a French court deemed an airline hijacking to be a political offense on the strength of the hijackers' vague references to Black Panther leaders and Hanoi, despite their pecuniary demand for $500,000. See E. McDowell, Digest of United States Practice in International Law 1975, 168–75 (1976). In another case, hijackers demanded and received $1 million, and were then flown from the United States to Algeria. Following their arrest in Paris, a French court accepted their claims that the hijacking was committed in order to escape racial segregation in the United States and therefore denied extradition on the basis of the POE. See E. McDowell, Digest of United States Practice in International Law 1976, 124–25 (1977).

6. *E.g., In re Meunier*, [1894] 2 Q.B. 415, 419 (POE is inapplicable to anarchists because "there must be two or more parties in the State, each seeking to impose the Government of their own choice on the 'other' "); accord *Eain v. Wilkes (Eain III)*, 641 F.2d 504, 521–22 (7th Cir.), cert. denied, 454 U.S. 894 (1981); *see also supra* note 92. *Id.* at 166 (Hawkins, J.) (quoting J. Stephen, 2 A History of the Criminal Law of England 71 (1883)). Justice Denman wrote that it must at least be shewn that the act is done in furtherance of, done with the

intention of assistance, as a sort of overt act in the course of acting in a political matter, a political rising, or a dispute between two parties in the State as to which is to have the government in its hands.... Id. at 156. This interpretation of the POE was narrowed slightly four years later by *In re Meunier*, [1894] 2 Q.B. 415. France charged Meunier with causing explosions at a cafe and barracks and requested England to extradite him. The accused claimed that, as an anarchist, he was entitled to immunity from extradition under the POE. Id. at 415–16. The court disagreed and held that in order to constitute an offense of a political character, there must be two or more parties in the State, each seeking to impose the Government of their own choice on the other, and that, if the offence is committed by one side or the other in pursuance of that object, it is a political offence, otherwise it is not. Id. at 419. Because there was no conflict between two or more parties in the state—"the party of anarchy, is the enemy of all Governments' " and its "efforts are directed primarily against the general body of 'citizens' "—the court concluded that the POE was inapplicable. Id. For a detailed description of British extradition practice, see United Kingdom Criminal Justice Department, A Review of the Law and Practice of Extradition in the United Kingdom: Report of an Interdepartmental Working Party (1982) (on file at New York University Law Review).

by treaty and thus included at the discretion of the parties. Just as there is no international legal obligation to extradite absent a treaty between two states, there is also no duty to prevent the extradition of a political offender.

Elimination of the POE does not mean that persons who previously invoked the POE to avoid extradition will automatically be sent to the requesting state. Three safeguards can protect the person sought if the POE is abolished. First, the double criminality principle operates to ensure that the courts will not certify a case to the Secretary of State unless the offense is a serious crime in both the requesting state and the United States. This principle is already included in extradition treaties and used by the courts. Second, the doctrine of specialty, which is also a part of present extradition practice, prohibits the requesting state from trying the accused on charges not specified in the extradition request. It further protects the person sought by permitting the executive to grant extradition upon the fulfillment of certain conditions. Finally, although the executive has always been expected to deny extradition if it appears that the requested person will receive an unfair trial or be persecuted, incorporation of the discrimination clause in all treaties, or codification by Congress in an amended extradition statute, will require the Secretary of State to deny extradition in such cases. Furthermore, the clause will explicitly articulate the reasons that would mandate the denial of extradition.

10.   Christopher C. Joyner, *International Extradition and Global Terrorism: Bringing International Criminals to Justice*, 25 Loy. L.A. Int'l & Comp. L. Rev. 493, 496, 501, 538–9 (2003).

An act of terrorism is generally a political act. Terrorism is meant to inflict dramatic and deadly injury on civilians and to create an atmosphere of fear, generally for a political or ideological (whether secular or religious) purpose. Acts of terrorism are more than mere criminal actions. Terrorist acts entail a systematic tactic used to attain political or strategic ends. They involve calculated political strategies of fear, coercion, and warfare. More recently, terrorist activities have arguably become convenient instruments of certain states' foreign policies against other states. The concept of terrorism defies precise definition. Because of its highly subjective and politicized nature, an exact, universally-agreed upon definition of terrorism remains elusive. In a sense, the difficulties associated with defining terrorism recall Justice Stewart's reflection on the nuances of defining obscenity—we know it when we see it—but there is no generally established definition. Consequently acts of terrorism are easier to identify than to define in precise legal terms acceptable to most governments.

* * *

Perhaps most problematic for extradition cases involving acts of terrorism is the political offense exception. Many modern extradition treaties specifically exempt political offenses from extradition, since liberal and democratic governments developed a strong antipathy toward the idea of surrendering dissidents into the hands of a despotic government. There are, however, no recognized criteria as to what constitutes a "political" offense, nor is there a rule of international law prohibiting the extradition of political offenders. As a result, the decision whether to extradite rests on subjective criteria, as determined by the holding government. Accordingly, the bilateral extradition system can provide only partial remedies for bringing international terrorists to justice. The consequence is that, while governments might agree that terrorist acts rise to being criminal offenses against the international community, strict multilateral enforcement through extradition in prosecuting such acts may still be lacking.

Since 1970, the threat of various international terrorist activities prompted the ad hoc negotiation of a series of special multilateral agreements dealing with criminal activities, nearly all of which contain specific extradition provisions. These instruments contribute much to expanding the opportunities for governments to extradite accused offenders to other states, even in the absence of specific bilateral treaties. Preeminent among the concerns for which multilateral agreements have been negotiated are the international criminal offenses associated with terrorist acts.

[*Eds.*—The author then proceeds to describe the 12 UN treaties dealing with terrorism adopted between 1963 and 1999. Extradition plays a central role in enforcing these treaties. These instruments deal with terrorism in specific contexts, such as aircraft hijacking, kidnapping, hostage-taking and terrorist bombings.]

The UN counter-terrorism instruments address the question of extraditable offenses and proffer mandatory requirements for extradition with few grounds for refusal to do so. Considered collectively, they provide a wider basis for extradition arrangements by eliminating the list-of-specific-offenses approach in favor of a more generalized, indeed, universal jurisdictional approach for extraditing terrorist offenders. Further, where no bilateral treaty exists between states, extradition traditionally could be premised upon the customary international law principles of reciprocity and comity. The constellation of UN agreements gives formal structure and direction for using the extradition process over a broad multilateral jurisdictional scope. In addition, these instruments aim to coordinate and enhance mutual assistance among parties with the goal of combating serious transnational terrorist crimes.

The most recent of these instruments seeks to impose limits on the mandatory political offense exception by excluding terrorist acts that are recognized in multilateral conventions as being especially grave criminal offenses. Indeed, the political offense exception is specifically declared not to be a bar to extradition for crimes of terrorist violence. Yet, it is important to realize that a government's decision to extradite is still subjective because extradition can be denied if government officials believe the prosecution of an accused offender might be motivated by that person's race, religion, nationality, ethnic origin, or political opinion. The problem with such a prophylactic stipulation seems plainly obvious. Persons might commit terrorist acts in violent reaction to a government's policies that affect their racial, religious, ethnic, or national minority group in that state. This situation therefore might qualify for a denial of extradition from another government, even though the person sought was not attempting to change the political system of the requesting state.

SECTION 5.   DISCUSSION NOTES/QUESTIONS

1. In this problem, the Supreme Court of Hibernia is reported to have declared unconstitutional Hibernian legislation (the EAWA) intended to im-

plement the EU Council Framework Decision of 13 June 2002 on the European Arrest Warrant and the Surrender Procedures between Member States **(Basic Document 6.8)**. This ruling portends national and international legal issues of major and potentially controversial import. By conscious design, however, we have not presented facts sufficient to resolve these issues here. Our present interest is to explore the law of extradition generally, as more or less represented by the 1957 European Convention on Extradition **(Basic Document 6.1)**, not the law of extradition as more particularistically defined by the EU Council Framework Decision of 13 June 2002. Nevertheless, insight into the arguable correctness or incorrectness of such a ruling is provided by the majority and dissenting opinions in a German constitutional law decision that inspired our fact pattern, to wit, the 18 July 2005 judgment of the Second Senate of the German Federal Constitutional Court which, for reasons similar to those of the Hibernian Supreme Court, declared a violation of German constitutional law German legislation equivalent to the Hibernian EAWA. *See* BVerfG, 58 Neue Juristische Wochenschrift 2289 (2005). For extensive focused discussion of this case, see Simone Mölders, *European Arrest Warrant Act is Void—The Decision of the German Federal Constitutional Court of 18 July 2005*, 7 German L. J. 45–57 (2005).

Also note that EU Council Framework Decision of 13 June 2002 is part of what is known as the "Third Pillar" of European Union law and policy. The "First Pillar," made up of the three European Communities—the European Community (EC), the European Coal and Steel Community (ECSC), and the European Atomic Energy Community (EURATOM)—embodies EU jurisdiction in its most developed and binding form. The "Second Pillar," built upon common "foreign and security policy," is based principally upon step by step cooperation between the Member States, each concerned to safeguard their own national sovereignty in this realm. The "Third Pillar," concerning "Police and Justicial Cooperation in Criminal Justice Matters" and of which the 2002 EU Council Framework Decision is one expression, is founded on cooperation between national police and judicial authorities relative to crime (especially terrorism, human trafficking, illicit drug and arms trafficking, corruption, and fraud), racism, and xenophobia. As with the "Second Pillar," cooperation in this area takes place outside the decision-making processes of the EC on the basis of Member State collaboration. Framework decisions in particular, though similar to EC directives are not valid or directly applicable in the Member States. Nor can they be challenged before the European Court of Justice. Nevertheless, if only to understand the direction that EU extradition law is now taking, we urge review of at least the Preamble and Articles 1–8 of the EU Council Framework Decision of 13 June 2002. It is for this reason also that we have included it as Reading 8, *supra*.

2.   This problem raises the definition of an offence that is "political" in character. The references to such offences in multilateral and bilateral extradition treaties rarely offer an exhaustive definition of this term. One such attempt is in the Australian Extradition Act 1988 (Cth) which in section 5 defines a political offence as one "of a political character, (whether because of the circumstances in which it is committed or otherwise and whether or not there are competing political parties in the country)." The legislation excludes from the definition a range of crimes such as genocide, hostage taking, torture, hijacking, murder and kidnapping. It is widely accepted that the

exception is intended to cover crimes such as insulting a head of state and offences based on political protest; but can it cover the serious crimes with which Amatullah Aziz and Najwa Hussein are charged? In Schtraks v Government of Israel [1964] AC 556 at 591, the United Kingdom House of Lords said "the idea that lies behind the phrase 'offence of a political character' is that the fugitive is at odds with the State that applies for his extradition on some issue connected with the political control or government of the country." Can this interpretation be made of Aziz and Hussein's conduct? Why? Why not? Other unsatisfactorily vague attempts to define a "political offence" include the approach by the Ninth Circuit Court of Appeals in McMullen v. INS, 788 F 2d 591, 596 (9th Cir. 1985) to the effect that the nature and degree of such an offence must be in proportion to its political ends.

3.   Article 1 of Protocol (No. 1) to the 1957 European Convention on Extradition provides that, for the purposes of Article 3 of the Convention (**Basic Document 6.1**), political offenses shall not be considered to include:

   (a) the crimes against humanity specified in the Convention on the Prevention and Punishment of the Crime of Genocide **[Basic Document 3.2]** . . . ;

   (b) the violations specified in Article 50 of the 1949 Geneva Convention for the Amelioration of the Condition of the Wounded and Sick in Armed Forces in the Field **[Basic Document 2.9]**, Article 51 of the 1949 Geneva Convention for the Amelioration of the Condition of Wounded, Sick and Shipwrecked Members of Armed Forces at Sea **[Basic Document 2.10]**, Article 130 of the 1949 Geneva Convention Relative to the Treatment of Prisoners of War **[Basic Document 2.11]** and Article 147 of the 1949 Geneva Convention relative to the Protection of Civilian Persons in Time of War **[Basic Document 2.12]**;

   (c) any comparable violations of the laws of war having effect at the time when this Protocol enters into force and of customs of war existing at that time, which are not already provided for in the above-mentioned provisions of the Geneva Conventions.

How might these provisions assist the case of Amatullah Aziz and Najwa Hussein against extradition, if at all?

In *Cabal v. United Mexican States* [No 3] (2000) 186 ALR 188, a Mexican national, Cabal, resisted extradition from Australia to Mexico among other grounds on the basis that the extradition was sought for offences based on his political opinions. Justice French of the Federal Court of Australia stated that the onus of proof on the person resisting extradition on this ground was a heavy one. He said "It is no light matter for [a Court] to conclude that there are substantial grounds for believing that the requesting country is acting in bad faith, especially given the necessary assumption that the offences have been committed." Id. at 268. How might Aziz and Hussein argue to discharge this burden of proof? For a discussion of the Cabal case see Gavan Griffith & Claire Harris, *Recent Developments in the Law of Extradition*, 6 Melbourne J. Int'l L. 33, 44–45 (2005).

4.   A critical issue in this problem is whether the offences with which Amatullah Aziz and Najwa Hussein are charged can be termed "terrorist" offences. Do the crimes alleged against them fall under the crimes set out in

the 1977 European Convention on the Suppression of Terrorism **(Basic Document 3.20)**? Consider the impact of Article 5 of the 1996 Convention Relating to Extradition between Member States of the European Union **(Basic Document 6.5)** on the arguments Aziz and Hussein might make. *See also* the 1986 Supplementary Treaty to the Treaty on Extradition of 8 June 1972 between the United States and the United Kingdom, 29 U.S.T. 229, T.I.A.S. No. 8468, *reprinted in* 24 I.L.M. 1105 (1985) and 3 Weston & Carlson III.M.5. The Supplemental Treaty was a direct reaction to four court cases in the United States in which the United Kingdom was denied the extradition of members of the Irish Republican Army (IRA) on the grounds that the crimes committed by the IRA members were political offenses. Article 1 of the Supplementary Treaty excludes from the political offense exception (as between the United Kingdom and the United States) the following crimes and offenses:

(a) an offense for which both Contracting Parties have the obligation pursuant to a multilateral international agreement to extradite the person sought or to submit his case to their competent authorities for decision as to prosecution;

(b) murder, voluntary manslaughter, and assault causing grievous bodily harm;

(c) kidnapping, abduction, or serious unlawful detention, including taking a hostage;

(d) an offense involving the use of a bomb, grenade, rocket, firearm, letter or parcel bomb, or any incendiary device if this use endangers any person;

(e) an attempt to commit any of the foregoing offenses or participation as an accomplice of a person who commits or attempts to commit such an offense.

For a discussion of the IRA cases, see Christie A. Leary, *The Political Offence Exception, The Irish Republican army, and the Supplementary Treaty–The Inadequacy of Anglo–American Extradition Policy*, 5 J. Int'l Legal Studies 293 (1999). These demonstrations of exceptions to the political offense exception are part of what appears to be an emerging consensus in extradition law and policy. Do you agree that the political offense exception should be narrowed? If not, why not? If so, to what extent? Would you exclude all of the following from the exception, as recommended by Professor Cherif Bassiouni in *The Penal Characteristics of Conventional International Criminal Law*, 15 Case W. Res. J. Int'l L. 27, 28 (1983): "aggression, war crimes, unlawful use of weapons, crimes against humanity, genocide, apartheid, slavery and slave-related practices, torture, unlawful medical experimentation, piracy, hijacking, kidnapping of diplomats, taking of civilian hostages, unlawful use of the mails, drug offenses, falsification and counterfeiting, theft of archeological and national treasures, bribery of public officials, interference with submarine cables, and international traffic in obscene publications"? What are the world order consequences of narrow and broad readings of the political offense exception? Consider, in this connection, the caution of Christopher Pyle, *The Political Offense Exception*, in Legal Responses to International Terrorism: US Procedural Aspects 181, 201–02 (M. C. Bassiouni ed., 1988), that "it must be remembered that the primary function of the political crimes defense is not to provide an opportunity to express our abhorrence of terrorism (by either side), or to achieve neutrality toward foreign conflicts, but to avoid judicial complicity in victor's justice." Pyle adds, at 202: "In some instances, courts will not be able, in good conscience, to send an alleged terrorist back for punishment because the people who seek his extradition are terrorists too."

This caution notwithstanding, students of international terrorism increasingly agree that acts of terrorism such as hijacking, the kidnapping of diplomats, the taking of civilian hostages, and the unlawful use of the mails should be denied the legal protection of the political offense defense altogether. Indeed, some contend that *all* acts of terrorism should be thus denied.

Yet what of the adage that one person's terrorist is another person's freedom fighter? Does the exclusion of all acts of terrorism from the political offense exception evince adequate sensitivity to the oppressive and repressive conditions that many believe are at the root of the problem? Were the "terrorist acts" of the South–West Africa People's Organization (SWAPO) in what today is Namibia or of South African groups battling apartheid on the one hand, and those of Al–Qaeda on the other, each of the same cloth? Many of the paramilitary operations that have been labelled "terrorist" have their roots in the struggle for national and cultural self-determination, a struggle that in turn has its roots in discrimination, racism, poverty, and other such offenses to human dignity. The Abkhaz and South Ossetians in Georgia, the Basques in France and Spain, the Catholics in Northern Ireland, the Chechnyians in Russia, the Kurds in Iraq and Turkey, the Sikhs in India, the Tamils in Sri Lanka, and of course the more than 2 million displaced Palestinians throughout the Middle East—all share the common perception that their political, cultural, and/or religious rights have been or are being denied, even ignored, and that their options for peaceful political change have been exhausted. Not until their human rights are taken seriously, it is submitted, not until there are credible options through which the aggrieved and the oppressed can pursue their moral and political claims peacefully, will the problem of terrorism go away.

Thus it seems necessary to ask: is not the suggestion to withhold the political offense exception from *all* acts of terrorism to risk too much? Should not the motivation of the act be taken into account as well as the nature of the act itself? In other words, should not a less blunt analytical instrument be fashioned? Miriam Sapiro in *supra* Reading 9 argues for the abolition of the political offence exception entirely. Are you convinced by her arguments? Why? Why Not? How would her arguments assist the case of either Amatullah Aziz and Najwa Hussein or of Albion?

5. Attempting to narrow the political offense exception in extradition theory and practice, first through a series of meetings during the late 1920's and early 1930's under the auspices of the International Conference for the Unification of Penal Law, and subsequently through diplomatic initiatives (usually bilateral) of one sort or another, is but one way in which criminologists and governments have sought to curb transnational terrorism. As Christopher Joyner (*supra* Reading 10) explains in a section of his article not extracted here, there has been a continuing resort to the international treaty-making process via the International Civil Aviation Organization (ICAO), the Organization of American States (OAS), and the United Nations in direct

response to a rash of hijackings and kidnappings that came to figure promi-
nently in daily headlines beginning in the 1960s. Hence, for example: the 1963
Convention on Offenses and Certain Other Acts Committed on Board Aircraft
("the Tokyo Convention"), 704 U.N.T.S. 219, *reprinted in* 3 Weston &
Carlson III.L.1; the 1970 Convention for the Suppression of Unlawful Seizure
of Aircraft ("the Hague Convention"), 860 U.N.T.S. 105, *reprinted in* 3
Weston & Carlson III.L.2; the 1971 Convention for the Suppression of
Unlawful Attacks Against the Safety of Civil Aviation ("the Montreal Conven-
tion"), 1971 U.N.J.Y.B. 143, *reprinted in* 3 Weston & Carlson III.L.3; the 1973
Convention on the Prevention and Punishment of Crimes against Internation-
ally Protected Persons, Including Diplomatic Agents, 1035 U.N.T.S. 167,
reprinted in 3 Weston & Carlson III.L.4; and the 1979 International Conven-
tion against the Taking of Hostages, 1316 U.N.T.S. 205, *reprinted in* 3 Weston
& Carlson III.L.6, in addition to the 1976 European Convention on the
Suppression of Terrorism **(Basic Document 3.20)**.

These limited successes aside, however, the diplomatic road to thwarting
terrorism has not been easy. In fact, except for the 1976 European Convention, all diplomatic efforts to prevent terrorism or to punish terrorist acts on a
more-or-less general or comprehensive basis have proven unsuccessful. For
example, the 1937 Convention for the Prevention and Punishment of Terrorism, prepared under the auspices of the League of Nations [*see* League of
Nations, Monthly Supp., Vol. 17, No. 11, Annex p. 284 (Nov. 1937)], ultimately was ratified only by India. The 1954 Draft Code of Offenses Against the
Peace and Security of Mankind **(Basic Document 2.16)**, prepared and
revised by the International Law Commission for the UN General Assembly,
never has come to a conclusive vote. And a US-sponsored Draft Convention
for the Prevention and Punishment of Certain Acts of International Terrorism [*see* 127 UN GAOR, Supp. No. 10, at 91, UN Doc. A/2710/Rev. 1 (1972)],
though relatively modest in scope and though promoted in the wake of the
Black September massacre of Israeli athletes at the 1972 Munich Olympics,
never has managed to win widespread endorsement. At the time of writing,
the most current legal initiative against terrorist activities is a UN comprehensive draft treaty, first proposed by India in 1996. The UN General
Assembly is sponsoring the drafting of the treaty through its Sixth (Legal)
Committee. Not surprisingly, the three most controversial areas during the
drafting process have been the definition of terrorism; the relationship of the
comprehensive treaty to the existing more specialized treaties referred to
above; and the distinction between terrorist activities and the right of peoples
to self-determination. The major enforcement mechanism in the draft Anti–
Terrorism Convention is extradition. For discussion of the Convention see,
Jackson N. Maogoto, *Countering Terrorism: From Wigged Judges To Helmet-
ed Soldiers—Legal Perspectives On America's Counter–Terrorism Responses*, 6
San Diego Int'l L.J. 243 (2005); and Peter J. Van Krieken, Terrorism and the
International Legal Order (2002).

6. Expressly implicated in the instant problem are the 1957 European
Convention on Extradition **(Basic Document 6.1)** and its 1976 European
Convention on the Suppression of Terrorism **(Basic Document 3.20)**, each
products of the Council of Europe. For details concerning the Council of
Europe see *supra* Problem 5–2 ("Women's Reproductive Rights in Hibernia"),
at 609. How do the provisions of the European Convention on Human Rights

and Fundamental Freedoms **(Basic Document 3.5)** interact with measures taken to suppress terrorism? Does the Convention provide legal arguments for any of the parties in this case? Could, for example, the validity of Albion's ISA be challenged as a breach of international human rights standards? How could this be done? For discussion of these issues see Edward J. Flynn, *Counter Terrorism and Human Rights: The View from the United Nations*, European Human Rights Law Review 29(1) (2005); C.A. Gearty, *Terrorism and Human Rights*, European Human Rights Law Review 1 (Issue 1, 2005); Emanuel Gross, *Legal Aspects of Tackling Terrorism: The Balance Between the Right of a Democracy to Defend Itself and the Protection of Human Rights*, 6 UCLA J. Int'l L. & Foreign Aff. 89 (2001); John Hedigan, *The European Convention on Human Rights and Counter–Terrorism*, 28 Fordham Int'l L.J. 392 (2005); Barry Kellman, *Catastrophic Terrorism—Thinking Fearfully, Acting Legally* 20 Michigan J. Int'l L. 537 (1999).

7. Suppose that Hibernia refused to extradite Amatullah Aziz and Najwa Hussein to Albion and, instead, made it possible for them to seek asylum in Hibernia. Assuming that Hibernia is a party to the 1951 Convention Relating to the Status of Refugees and its 1967 Protocol (discussed in Problem 5–1, *supra*), what evidentiary and normative hurdles would Aziz and Hussein have to overcome to gain refugee status in Hibernia? A number of public and private initiatives have undertaken to draft guidelines and recommendations relative to the treatment of female asylum claimants. Among the best known of these, is the UN High Commissioner for Refugees, Guidelines on the Protection of Refugee Women, UN Doc. ES/SCP/67 (1991). Canada (1993), the United States (1995) and Australia (1996) have all adopted specific guidelines for the treatment of women's claims to refugee status. A useful comparative analysis of these national guidelines of offered by Audrey Macklin in *Cross-Border Shopping for Ideas: A Critical Review of United States, Canadian, and Australian Approaches to Gender–Based Asylum Claims*, 13 Geo. Immigr. L. J. 25 (1998). The Office of the UNHCR has also published Sexual and Gender–Based Violence against Refugees, Returnees and Internally Displaced Persons: Guidelines for Prevention and Response (May 2003). Relevant to the adjudication of refugee status in cases of sexual violence is UNHCR's Gender–Related Persecution: 2000 Complementary Guidelines on Procedures and Criteria for Determining Refugee Status (2000). Another effort is found in the *Guidelines for Women's Asylum Claims* issued in 1994 by the Women Refugees Project of the Harvard Law School's Immigration and Refugee Clinic in cooperation with Cambridge and Somerville Legal Services. Endorsed by thirty-six nongovernmental organizations, these guidelines analyze the individual components in the definition of "refugee" incorporated in the US Immigration and Naturalization Act, 8 § 1101(a)(42) (1982), incorporating the definition set forth in the 1951 United Nations Convention Relating to the Status of Refugees **(Basic Document 3.6)**. The Guidelines are discussed in Nancy Kelly, "Guidelines for Women's Asylum Claims," 6 Int'l J. Refugee L. 517 (1994). For discussion of relevant US jurisprudence, see Daniel McLaughlin, *Recognizing Gender–Based Persecution as a Grounds for Asylum*, 13 Wis. Int'l L. J. 217 (1994); Mattie L. Stevens, *Recognizing Gender–Specific Persecution: A Proposal to Add Gender as a Sixth Refugee Category*, 3 Cornell J. L. & Pub. Pol'y 179 (1993); Melanie Randall, *Refugee Law and State Accountability for Violence Against Women: A Comparative Analysis of Legal*

Approaches to Recognizing Asylum Claims Based on Gender Persecution, 25 Harv. Women's L.J. 281 (2002).

8. *Bibliographical Note.* For supplemental discussion concerning the principal themes addressed in this problem, consult the following additional specialized materials.

(a) *Books/Monographs/Reports/Symposia.* M. Forde, The Law of Extradition in the United Kingdom (1995); A. Jones Q.C., Jones on Extradition (1995); C.H. Pyle, Extradition, Politics, and Human Rights (2001); I. Shearer, Extradition in International Law (1971); C. Van de Wijngaert, The Political Offence Exception to Extradition: The Delicate Problem of Balancing the Rights of the Individual and the International Public Order (1980).

(b) *Articles/Book Chapters.* M. C. Bassiouni, *Reforming International Extradition: Lessons of the Past for a Radical New Approach*, 25 Loy. L.A. Int'l & Comp. L. Rev. 389 (2003); J. Dugard & C. Van Den Wyngaert, *Reconciling Extradition with Human Rights*, 92 Am. J. Int'l L. 187 (1998); V. Epps, *The Development Of The Conceptual Framework Supporting International Extradition*, 25 Loy. L.A. Int'l & Comp. L. Rev. 369 (2003); S. Gosser, *In Re Requested Extradition of Artt, Brennan, and Kirby: Counterterrorism and the Court*, 6 Tul. J. Int'l & Comp. L. 633 (1998); M. Halberstam, *The Evolution Of The United Nations Position On Terrorism: From Exempting National Liberation Movements To Criminalizing Terrorism Wherever And By Whomever Committed*, 41 Colum. J. Transnat'l L. 573 (2003); E. Lagos & T. Rudy, *Preventing, Punishing, and Eliminating Terrorism in the Western Hemisphere: A Post–9/11 Inter–American Treaty*, 26 Fordham Int'l L.J. 1619 (2003); M. Lewis, *The Political Offense Exception: Reconciling the Tension Between Human Rights and International Public Order*, 63 Geo. Wash. L. Rev. 585 (1995); M. Lippman, *The New Terrorism And International Law*, 10 Tulsa J. Comp. & Int'l L. 297 (2003); Renuka E. Rao, *Protecting Fugitives' Rights While Ensuring The Prosecution And Punishment Of Criminals: An Examination of the New EU Extradition Treaty*, 21 B.C. Int'l & Comp. L. Rev. 229 (1998); G. Vermeulen & T. Vander Beken, *New Conventions on Extradition in the European Union: Analysis and Evaluation*, 15 Dick. J. Int'l L. 265 (1997); J. Yoo, *Transferring Terrorists*, 79 Notre Dame L. Rev. 1183 (2004).

Problem 5–4

A Disappearance in Hispania

SECTION 1.   FACTS

Hispania, a Central American republic with a long history of military dictatorships, is currently led by a democratically elected government that about five years ago, with the backing of Hispania's military, assumed near-dictatorial powers. Soon after the elections, for example, it dissolved Hispania's National Congress and suspended its Supreme Court. Faced with a weak economy, a surge in drug trafficking, and threats from a guerilla insurgency seeking broad-based land reform, there was, according to Hispania's President Julia Césaron, "no alternative." Democratic institutions would be fully restored, she said, "when public order and economic stability are firmly re-established." In the name of a "program of national unity," she ordered economic and security measures to stimulate business confidence at home and abroad.

Never popular among Hispania's poor, the Césaron government's national unity policies soon came increasingly under fire when outspoken critics of the government, known to have been taken into custody by the police or the military without warrant, began mysteriously to disappear, never to be heard from again. Even less outspoken Hispanians began to vanish without a trace, particularly members of the Committee for the Defense of Human Rights in Hispania (CDHRH) who, apparently at no small risk, undertook to document the disappearances with an eye to petitioning the Inter–American Commission on Human Rights under the 1969 American Convention on Human Rights, to which Hispania is a party. Conservative estimates place the number of "disappeared," or "*desaparecidos*," at more than 3,000 persons, although efforts to elicit information as to the precise whereabouts and fate of the *desaparecidos* have proved futile for the most part. Hispanian authorities deny ever having detained anyone. The disappearances, they say, are "part of a planned conspiracy among the shameless guerilla insurgents to make the government look bad."

Approximately two years ago, however, on the basis of eyewitness reports and other credible information successfully gathered by the CDHRH and other human rights groups, the wife and adult children of one Francisco Morazán, a "disappeared" past president of the CDHRH, were able to bring suit in the United States District Court for the Southern District of Iowa against a regional commander of the Hispanian National Security Forces, Colonel Rafael Carrera, then in the United States for extended medical treatment and to attend to some agricultural and other real estate investments. According to the plaintiffs' complaint and supporting evidence, Colonel Carrera was responsible for the torture and disappearance—unacknowledged detention and presumed extrajudicial execution—of their husband and father by virtue of Morazán having been subjected to harsh interrogation and caused to vanish while in the custody of personnel under Colonel Carrera's command. The plaintiffs, Hispanian citizens who had been granted political asylum in the United States and who had learned of the colonel's medical sojourn via the television news, predicated federal jurisdiction on 28 USC § 1350 (the "Alien Tort Claims Act" or ATCA)[a] and requested the court to attach assets of the colonel based in California, Iowa, and Delaware and to pay them compensation for the "torture," "cruel, inhuman or degrading treatment," and "wrongful disappearance" of Morazán. In their legal brief, they noted that, in addition to Hispania's adherence to the 1969 American Convention on Human Rights, both Hispania and the United States are parties to the Charter of the United Nations, the Charter of the Organization of American States, and the 1966 International Covenant on Civil and Political Rights, although not to any other treaty potentially relevant to their case.

The District Court, on Defendant's motion, dismissed the action for want of subject-matter jurisdiction and on the grounds that "the law of nations does not provide for the torts of 'cruel, inhuman, or degrading treatment' and 'wrongful disappearance.' " The Court of Appeals for the Eighth Circuit reversed on all three counts.

SECTION 2. QUESTIONS PRESENTED

1. May the United States Supreme Court find in favor of the plaintiffs or must it reverse the Court of Appeals for lack of subject-matter jurisdiction and on the grounds that the law of nations does not provide for torts of "disappearance" and "cruel, unusual, or inhumane treatment or punishment"?

2. In any event, are there any additional or alternative legal norms, procedures, and/or institutions to be recommended that might further help to prevent or discourage situations of the kind posed by this problem?

SECTION 3. ASSIGNMENTS

A. READING ASSIGNMENT

Study the Readings presented in Section 4, *infra*, and the Discussion Notes/Questions that follow. Also, time permitting, consult the accompanying bibliographical references.

B. RECOMMENDED WRITING ASSIGNMENT

Prepare a comprehensive, logically sequenced, and *argumentative* brief in the form of an outline of the primary and subsidiary *legal* issues you see requiring resolution by the US Supreme Court. Also, from the perspective of an independent judge, indicate which side ought to prevail on each issue and why. Retain a copy of your issue-outline/brief for class discussion.

---

a. *See infra* Reading 13, beginning especially with the third paragraph therein.

C. RECOMMENDED ORAL ASSIGNMENT

Assume you are legal counsel for the wife and adult children of Francisco Morazán, on the one hand, or Colonel Carrera, on the other (as designated by your instructor); then, relying upon the Readings (and your issue-outline if prepared), present a 10–15 minute oral argument of your client's likely positions before the US Supreme Court.

D. RECOMMENDED REFLECTIVE ASSIGNMENT

Consider (and recommend) alternative norms, institutions, and/or procedures that you believe might do better than existing world order arrangements to contend with situations of the kind posed by this problem. In so doing, but without insisting upon *immediate* feasibility, identify the particular transition steps that would be needed to make your alternatives a reality.

SECTION 4. READINGS

The following readings are considered *prima facie* relevant to solving this problem. They are your law library for present purposes and should be treated as such, organized intelligibly for "shelving" and not necessarily according to the issues presented. Be sure to review Chapter 2 ("International Legal Prescription: The 'Sources' of International Law") in your consideration of them. It, too, should be treated as part of your law library (as, indeed, should this entire coursebook).

1.   Burns H. Weston, "Human Rights," in *Encyclopædia Britannica* (2005), available from *Encyclopædia Britannica Online* at <http:// www. britannica.com/eb/article?tocId=219350> (*see supra* Reading A–1 in Problem 5–1, at 494).

2.   United Nations Charter. Concluded, 26 Jun 1945. Entered into force, 24 Oct 1945. 1976 Y.B.U.N. 1043; *reprinted in* 1 Weston & Carlson I.A.1: Pmbl., Arts. 2(7), 55, 56 (Basic Document 1.5).

3.   American Declaration of the Rights and Duties of Man, O.A.S. Res. XXX, adopted by the Ninth International Conference of American States, Bogota, 30 Mar 48–2 May 1948, O.A.S. Off. Rec. OEA/ Ser.L./V/I.4 Rev. (965); *reprinted in* 3 Weston & Carlson III.B.23: Arts. I, XVII, XVIII, XXV, XXVI, XXXIII (Basic Document 3.1).

4.   Universal Declaration of Human Rights, 10 Dec 1948, GA Res. 217A (III), UN Doc. A./810, at 71 (1948); *reprinted in* 3 Weston & Carlson III.A.1: Arts. 2, 3, 5–11, 13, 28, 30 (Basic Document 3.3).

5.   International Covenant on Civil and Political Rights. Concluded, 16 Dec 1966. Entered into force, 23 Mar 1976. 999 U.N.T.S. 171; *reprinted in* 6 I.L.M. 368 (1967) and 3 Weston & Carlson III.A.3: Arts. 2, 6, 7, 9, 10, 12, 14–17, 26 (Basic Document 3.14).

6.   American Convention on Human Rights. Concluded, 22 Nov 1969. Entered into force, 18 Jul 1978. 1144 U.N.T.S. 123, O.A.S.T.S. No. 36; *reprinted in* 9 I.L.M. 99 (1970) and 3 Weston & Carlson III.B.24: Arts. 1, 2–5, 7, 8, 22, 24, 25, 27, 29, 30 (Basic Document 3.17).

7.   Convention Against Torture and Other Cruel, Inhuman or Degrading Treatment or Punishment. Concluded, 10 Dec 1984. Entered into force, 26 Jun 1987. GA Res. 39/46 (Annex), UN GAOR, 39th Sess., Supp. No. 51, at 197, UN Doc. A/39/51 (1985); *reprinted in* **23 I.L.M. 1027 (1984) and 3 Weston & Carlson III.K.2: Arts. 1, 2, 13, 14, 16** (Basic Document 3.26).

8.   Inter-American Convention to Prevent and Punish Torture. Concluded, 9 Dec 1985. Entered into force, 28 Feb 1987. O.A.S.T.S. No. 67; *reprinted in* **25 I.L.M. 519 (1986) and 3 Weston & Carlson III.K.3: Arts. 1-9** (Basic Document 3.27).

9.   Restatement (Third) of the Foreign Relations Law of the United States § 702 ("Customary International Law of Human Rights") (1987).

A state violates international law if, as a matter of state policy, it practices, encourages, or condones:

(a) genocide,

(b) slavery or slave trade,

(c) the murder or causing the disappearance of individuals,

(d) torture or other cruel, inhuman, or degrading treatment or punishment,

(e) prolonged arbitrary detention,

(f) systematic racial discrimination, or

(g) a consistent pattern of gross violations of internationally recognized human rights.

10.   Declaration on the Protection of All Persons from Enforced Disappearance, 18 Dec 1992, GA Res. 47/133, UN GAOR, 47th Sess., Supp. No. 49, at 207, UN Doc. A/RES/47/133 (1993); *reprinted in* **3 Weston & Carlson III.K.5** (Basic Document 3.38).

11.   Inter-American Convention on the Forced Disappearance of Persons. Concluded, 9 Jun 1994. Entered into force, 28 Mar 1996. 33 I.L.M. 1429 (1994) (Basic Document 3.42).

12.   Maureen R. Berman & Roger S. Clark, "State Terrorism: Disappearances," 13 Rutgers L. J. 531, 531-34, 547, 561-62 (1982).

The term disappearance, a translation of the Spanish *desaparecido*, was first used to describe a government practice employed in the mid-1960's in Guatemala when so-called "death squads" abducted and assassinated anti-government forces. Developments in Chile following the military coup in September 1973 focused worldwide attention on the phenomenon.... The pattern ... was to be repeated following the military coup in Argentina in March 1976 where responsible estimates of the number of disappearance victims are put between 10,000 and 15,000.

Although the practice of massive disappearance is widely associated with the nations in the Southern Cone of Latin America, the technique has been employed by a substantial number of governments in regions around the world. Apart from Argentina, Chile, and Uruguay, large-scale disappearances have been reported in Afghanistan, Cambodia ..., Ethiopia, Equatorial Guinea, the Philippines, and Uganda. The practice has proved to be all too easily exportable.

* * *

In countries where large-scale disappearances have been reported, there are remarkable similarities in the pattern of treatment of the victims. Five characteristics should be noted:

1. The individuals who are kidnapped or abducted are subjected to unacknowledged detention, torture, and, typically, death.

2. The abductors are well-organized and well-armed; they are government agents, members of the military and police forces, and people dressed in civilian attire who often identify themselves as security forces.

3. The "disappearances" are a conscious and deliberate policy on the part of the government in an attempt to eliminate what it perceives as threatening, destabilizing opposition forces. The abductions are often carried out with the direct participation of government agents, military personnel, or those responsible for enforcing the law within the country. In some cases, the governments have actually conferred upon security personnel the unbridled power to arrest, interrogate, imprison, and kill citizens.

4. There is no way in which targets can be identified. The disappeared come from all sectors of society—some are terrorists, suspected terrorists, or more often individuals suspected of involvement in subversive activities. Some are union leaders or political activists or individuals simply opposed to the existing regime. Some are abducted incidentally—because they happen to be in the wrong place at the wrong time. Family groups have been abducted and disappeared together.

5. Information and evidence relating to the disappeared is extremely difficult to obtain, and as a result, family members often suffer severe psychological stress. Out of fear for their own safety or of further endangering the victim, family members and friends often are afraid to speak out publicly.

The denial of accountability is the factor which makes disappearance unique among human rights violations and so dangerous for the victims. * * * [When] the authorities refuse to acknowledge the detention of a disappearance victim—even if the family can produce credible evidence that an individual was taken into custody—no assistance can be provided by the international humanitarian agencies or intergovernmental bodies who visit prisons to determine the welfare of detainees. The victims of the crime of disappearance simply vanish and thus disappearance becomes an expedient measure to avoid application of legal standards guaranteeing individual rights.

* * *

. . . How are we to describe, in terms of international law, the "wrong" of disappearance? * * * An important function of a legal system is to provide a conceptual framework for the analysis of a societal phenomenon. A characterization in legal terms shapes the ways in which criticisms and claims may be made against states and individuals, and points to possible procedural ways of dealing with the matter.

[*Eds.*—The authors next examine three ways in which international lawyers look at disappearances—as a crime against humanity after the Charter of the Nuremberg Tribunal **(Basic Document 1.3)**, as a breach of human rights instruments, and as an international crime committed by the state concerned—and stress the importance of viewing disappearances as an example of the category of most egregious human rights violations, international crimes.]

There is some promise . . . of . . . development of international standards and procedures for responding to disappearances. But it would be foolish to expect that these developments will be rapid. Consideration must therefore be given to . . . the utilization of domestic legal procedures in states other than those in which the disappearances occur. * * * [G]iven the decentralized nature of the international legal order, it is desirable to encourage domestic courts (and the legislatures that typically regulate their sphere of authority) to exercise jurisdiction to enforce fundamental policies of international law. There are some basic standards here which are capable of being objectively determined. Encouraging diverse states to adjudicate such cases need not lead to hopeless confusion and conflict. We believe that this is particularly true where the exercise of civil jurisdiction is concerned.

13.   Editors' Note. United States courts have not been especially hospitable to human rights lawyers over the years.[b] One reason is that the United States, though pledged via Articles 55 and 56 of the UN Charter **(Basic Document 1.5)** to take action in cooperation with the United Nations for the achievement of universal respect for, and observance of, human rights, is not party to many important human rights conventions—for pertinent example, the 1969 American Convention on Human Rights **(Basic Document 3.17)**.[c] Consequently not part of the "supreme Law of the Land," these conventions are incapable of being directly invoked in domestic litigation. Another reason is that United States courts, even when in a position to apply treaties to which the United States is a party, have been reluctant to do so. In *Sei Fujii v. State of California*, 38 Cal.2d 718, 242 P.2d 617 (1952), for example, a leading case holding invalid under the Fourteenth Amendment a state statute forbidding aliens not eligible for citizenship to "acquire, possess, enjoy, use, cultivate, occupy, and transfer" real property in California, the California Supreme Court rejected a lower state court's view that the UN Charter's human rights provisions had become part of the "supreme Law of the Land" and, hence, domestically applicable. The UN Charter, it declared, is not a "self-executing" treaty and therefore, absent an act of the US Congress, does not automatically supersede domestic legislation that may be at odds with it.

A US court would be likely (although arguably not constitutionally obliged) to reach the same conclusion in respect of the domestic application of the 1966 International Covenant on Civil and Political Rights **(Basic Document 3.14)**, the 1966 International Convention on the Elimination of All Forms of Racial Discrimination **(Basic Document 3.12)**, or the 1984 Con-

---

b. See R. Lillich, *The Constitution and International Human Rights*, 83 A.J.I.L. 851 (1989).

c. For further related discussion, see *infra* Discussion/Note Question 5, at 682.

vention Against Torture and Other Cruel, Inhuman or Degrading Treatment or Punishment **(Basic Document 3.26)**—all treaties to which the United States has become a party (in 1992, 1994, and 1994, respectively), but in each case subject to a declaration that the treaty in question or its principal substantive provisions "are not self-executing." Such a result would be likely, indeed, even in the absence of such a declaration of non-justiciability. Some American international law scholarship, including that of the prestigious American Law Institute, has argued in favor of a general presumption that treaties are self-executing. *See, e.g.*, Jordan J. Paust, *Self-Executing Treaties*, 82 A.J.I.L. 760 (1988); Restatement (Third) of the Foreign Relations Law of the United States § 111(3) & (4), comment *h*, at 46–47 and Reporter's Note 5 at 53–56 (1987). However, as pointed out by Thomas Buergenthal, in *Self-Executing and Non–Self–Executing Treaties in National and International Law*, 235 Recueil 303, 382 (1992–IV), "the presumption in the United States in favour of holding treaties to be self-executing ... may well be true" but "only as far as bilateral treaties are concerned." Buergenthal continues, at *id.*:

> In recent years, a contrary presumption appears to be emerging with regard to multilateral treaties. This may be so because these treaties tend to be invoked more frequently in cases that challenge executive or legislative policies of the United States Government, thus raising issues the courts consider political in character. By holding these treaties to be non-self-executing, American courts resort to this label as a stand-in for the "political question" doctrine, which has traditionally enabled them to avoid deciding issues they consider to be the proper province of the political branches of Government.

In 1979, on the other hand, a little known provision of the United States Judiciary Act of 1789, ch. 20, § 9(b), 1 Stat. 73, 77—better known as the Alien Tort Claims Act (ATCA), codified as 28 USC § 1350, and providing that "[t]he district courts [of the United States] shall have original jurisdiction of any civil action by an alien for a tort only, committed in violation of the law of nations or a treaty of the United States"—came to play an important role in US domestic human rights litigation, being successfully invoked on behalf of Dr. Joel Filártiga, a Paraguayan physician and opponent of former Paraguayan *caudillo* Alfredo Stroessner. Dr. Filártiga, together with his daughter, had fled to New York City and subsequently brought a wrongful death action there against a former Paraguayan police official alleged to have been responsible for the death by torture of his 17–year old son, Joelito. The plaintiffs contended that the conduct resulting in the wrongful death constituted official torture and that such conduct violated the "law of nations" referred to in ATCA, *i.e.*, customary international law. The District Court dismissed the complaint on jurisdictional grounds, Judge Nickerson believing himself to be bound by higher court rulings to construe narrowly "the law of nations" as employed in the Statute as excluding that law which governs a state's treatment of its own citizens. On appeal, however, in *Filártiga v. Peña-Irala*, 630 F.2d 876 (2d Cir. 1980), the United States Second Circuit Court of Appeals reversed the District Court, ruled that the ATCA provides federal jurisdiction, and held that official torture is prohibited by "the law of nations," a prohibition that "is clear and unambiguous and admits of no distinction between treatment of aliens and citizens." *Id.* at 884. In reaching the conclusion that official torture is prohibited by customary international law, the court referred as evidence to, *inter alia*, the 1948 Universal Declaration of Human Rights **(Basic Document 3.3)**, various regional human rights instruments, and the 1975 Declaration on the Protection of All Persons from Being Subjected to Torture, GA Res. 3452, 30 UN GAOR Supp No. 31, at 91, UN Doc. A/10034 (1975).

The *Filártiga* decision, a victory for human rights activists, had the support of the departments of Justice and State in the administration of US President Jimmy Carter. It was not well received, however, by the subsequent Reagan Administration and other persons sympathetic to the "original intent" argument that the drafters of the ATCA could not possibly have contemplated or expected that the Statute would or should have been used by foreign nationals to redress human rights violations committed by other foreign nationals outside the United States. For example, Judge Robert Bork, in the next case after *Filártiga* to consider foreign-based human rights violations in the context of the ATCA, *Tel–Oren, et al. v. Libyan Arab Republic, et al.*, 726 F.2d 774 (D.C. Cir. 1984), *cert. denied*, 470 U.S. 1003 (1985), essentially embraced this "original intent" argument. Contending that Congress in 1789 probably had in mind only three classes of cases (violation of safe conducts, infringement of ambassadorial rights, and piracy), that torture surely did not fall under any of them, and that, in any event, neither the Founding Fathers nor Congress had intended for the courts to become entangled in foreign affairs questions. In *Tel–Oren*, via three separate concurring opinions and in sharp contrast to *Filártiga*, the court dismissed a complaint brought under the ATCA by the survivors and representatives of 121 bus passengers—primarily Israelis—captured, held hostage, tortured, and murdered in Israel on the main highway between Haifa and Tel Aviv by thirteen armed members of the Palestine Liberation Organization (PLO) who secretly had entered Israel by boat from Lebanon under instructions to seize and hold Israeli citizens in ransom for the release of PLO members incarcerated in Israel.

It is not, however, only Judge Bork's narrow reading of the ATCA that makes *Tel–Oren* a problematic precedent from the standpoint of human rights advocacy. Judge Harry Edwards, who agreed with *Filártiga* that the ATCA provides federal jurisdiction but who did not agree that *Filártiga* should be extended to torture by non-state actors, refused to honor the plaintiff-appellants' claims because "the law of nations ... [does not outlaw] politically motivated terrorism, no matter how repugnant it might be to our own legal system." *Id.* at 796. Judge Roger Robb, although not addressing the jurisdictional issues raised by the ATCA, recommended dismissal on the grounds that the action was non-justiciable primarily for "political question" reasons. And Judge Bork, in further defense of his decision to dismiss, maintained that neither the human rights treaties pleaded as binding on the United States nor violations of "the law of nations" (*i.e.*, customary international law) provided the "explicit grant of a cause of action" that, he argued, is required for the judiciary to become involved with the executive and legislative branches in the conduct of foreign relations, thus leaving the plaintiff-appellants without a cause of action even if federal jurisdiction under the ATCA could be established. The treaties in question were not self-executing, according to Judge Bork, hence were incapable of granting plaintiff-appellants a cause of action to seek damages for violation of their provisions; and customary international law, he contended, does not itself provide a cause of action in United States courts, only those customary rules which themselves *explicitly* authorize individuals to sue to enforce them. In addition, Judge Bork insisted, the "[a]djudication of [plaintiff-appellants'] claims would require the analysis of international legal principles that are anything but clearly defined and that are the subject of controversy touching 'sharply on national nerves.'" *Id.* at 805, citing *Banco Nacional de Cuba v. Sabbatino*, 376 U.S. 398, 428 (1964).[d]

The Bork approach in *Tel–Oren* has had however limited influence. In 1994, specifically endorsing *Filártiga*, the US Ninth Circuit Court of Appeals joined the Second Circuit in concluding that "the Alien Tort Act ... creates a cause of action for violations of specific, universal and obligatory international human rights standards which 'confer fundamental rights upon all people vis-à-vis their own governments.' ..." *Hilao v. Marcos*, 25 F.3d 1467, 1475–1476 (9th Cir. 1994). The fact that *Tel-Oren* resulted in three separate opinions, reflecting no consensus other than a decision to dismiss, may have undercut its impact. So also, perhaps, the passage of the Torture Victim Protection Act of 1987, H.R. 1417, 100th Cong., 1st Sess. (1987), by Congress over the opposition of the Reagan and Bush administrations to provide alien victims of torture with a private right of action in United States courts.

In any event, there have been many invocations of the ATCA in the two decades since *Filártiga*, and numerous important advances have been made. In *Filártiga*, the actual perpetrator was sued and found liable; in subsequent cases the range of defendants was expanded to include those who have ordered or authorized the violations or those persons with command responsibility who knew, or should have known, and failed to stop violations. *See, e.g., Forti v. Suarez–Mason*, Readings 14 and 15, *infra*; *Paul v. Avril*, 901 F.Supp. 330 (S.D. Fla., 1 Jul 1994); *Todd v. Panjaitan*, Civ. No. 92–12255–PBS (D. Mass., 26 Oct 1994); *Xuncax v. Gramajo*, 886 F.Supp. 162 (D. Mass., 12 Apr 1995). In addition, groups as well as individual defendants involved in human rights violations have been sued, as have also non-state actors responsible for human rights violations. *See, e.g., Kadic v. Karadzic*, 70 F.3d 232 (2d Cir. 1995). For elaboration, see PBS, Justice and the Generals, <http://www.pbs.org/wnet/justice/law_backgroundtorture.html>. What is more, though not all ATCA suits have proved successful—*e.g., Flores v. Southern Peru Copper Corp.*, 343 F.3d 140 (2d Cir. 2003), involving allegations of international environmental rights violations but dismissed for failure to submit evidence sufficient to establish that intranational pollution violates customary international law—the cases have involved international legal issues as varied as; child labor violations (*Deutsch v. Turner Corp.*, 324 F.3d 692 (9th Cir. 2003) (cert. denied, 540 U.S. 820 (2003)); imprisonment and torture (*Carmichael v. United Technologies Corp.*, 835 F.2d 109 (5th Cir. 1988)); mass rape and sexual assault (*Kadic v. Karadzic*, 70 F 3d 232 (2d Cir. 1995)); and racial discrimination (*Tachiona v. Mugabe*, 234 F.Supp.2d 401 (S.D.N.Y. 2002)).

d. For a lively exchange on *Tel–Oren*, in particular Judge Bork's reasoning, see A. D'Amato, *Judge Bork's Concept of the Law of Nations is Seriously Mistaken*, 79 A.J.I.L. 92 (1985); A. Rubin, *Professor D'Amato's Concept of American Jurisdiction is Seriously Mistaken*, *id.* at 105; A. D'Amato, *Professor Rubin's Reply Does Not Live Up to its Title*, *id.* at 112.

On 29 June 2004, the US Supreme Court decided a major case on the operation of the ATCA, Sosa v. Alvarez–Machain, 542 U.S. 692 (2004). At issue was whether a Mexican national, abducted and transported to the United States to face prosecution for alleged torture and murder and thereafter acquitted, could succeed in an action brought under the ATCA and the Federal Tort Claims Act (FTCA) against US Drug Enforcement Agency (DEA) agents, former Mexican policeman, and Mexican civilians, on the grounds of his abduction having violated his civil rights. The courts below had agreed with Alvarez–Machain, although the Ninth Circuit was divided 6–5. The Supreme Court, in an opinion by Justice Souter, reversed, holding that:

1. whatever liability the United States allegedly had for [Dr. Alvarez–Machain's] arrest by Mexican nationals, allegedly at [the] instigation of the DEA, so that he could be transported across the border and lawfully arrested by federal officers, rested on events that occurred in Mexico, so as to fall within the "foreign country" exception to waiver of [the] government's immunity under the FTCA;

2. the "foreign country" exception to waiver of [a] government's immunity bars all claims against the government based on any injury suffered in the foreign country, regardless of where the tortious act or omission giving rise to that injury occurred; and

3. a single illegal detention of less than one day of [Dr. Alvarez–Machain], custody of whom was then transferred to lawful authorities in the United States for prompt arraignment, violated no norm of customary international law so well defined as to support creation of cause of action that district court could hear under the [ATCA]. . . .

The Supreme Court's holding makes clear that not all claims brought under the ATCA will be successful. It may make difficult, for example, claims brought by victims of military torture and other abuse in Afghanistan and Iraq. Nevertheless, *Alvarez–Machain* did preserve the right of individuals to bring suits in US courts alleging tortious violations of international law.

For discussion of the *Alvarez–Machain* cases, see Brad R. Roth, *Sosa v. Alvarez–Machain; United States v. Alvarez–Machain*, 98 A.S.I.L. 798 (2004). The recent vast literature about *Filártiga* and its progeny includes Rachel Bart, *Using the American Courts to Prosecute International Crimes Against Women: Jane Doe v. Radovan Karadzic and S. Kadic v. Radovan Karadzic*, 3 Cardozo Women's L.J. 467 (1996); Curtis A. Bradley, *The Alien Tort Statute and Article III*, 42 Va. J. Int'l L. 587 (2002); Kathryn L. Boyd, *The Inconvenience of Victims: Abolishing Forum Non Conveniens in US Human Rights Litigation*, 39 Va. J. Int'l L. 41 (1998); John F. Carella, *Of Foreign Plaintiffs and Proper Fora: Forum Non Conveniens and ATCA Class Actions*, U. Chi. Legal F. 717 (2003); William S. Dodge, *The Constitutionality of the Alien Tort Statute: Some Observations on Text and Context*, 42 Va. J. Int'l L. 687 (2002); Amy E. Eckert, *Kadic v. Karadzic: Whose International Law?* 25 Denv. J. Int'l L. & Pol'y 173 (1996); Ryan Goodman & Derek P. Jinks, *Human Rights on the Eve of the Next Century: UN Human Rights Standards & US Law: Filartiga's Firm Footing: International Human Rights and Federal Common Law*, 66 Fordham L. Rev. 463 (1997); Jed Greer, *Plaintiff Pseudonymity and the Alien Tort Claims Act: Questions and Challenges*, 32 Colum. Hum. Rts. L. Rev. 517 (2001); Natalie I. Johnson, *Justice for "Comfort Women": Will the*

Alien Tort Claims Act Bring Them the Remedies They Seek? 20 Penn St. Int'l
L. Rev. 253 (2001); Samuel A. Khalil, *The Alien Tort Claims Act and Section
1983: The Improper Use of Domestic Laws to "Create" and "Define" Interna-
tional Liability for Multinational Corporations*, 31 Hofstra L. Rev. 207 (2002);
Donald J. Kochan, *Constitutional Structure as a Limitation on the Scope of the
"Law of Nations" in the Alien Tort Claims Act*, 31 Cornell Int'l L. J. 153
(1998); David P. Kunstle, *Kadic v. Karadzic: Do Private Individuals have
Enforceable Rights and Obligations under the Alien Tort Claims Act?* 6 Duke
J. Comp. & Int'l L. 319 (1996); Lisa Lambert, *At the Crossroads of Environ-
mental and Human Rights Standards: Aguinda v. Texaco, Inc. Using the
Alien Tort Claims Act to Hold Multinational Corporate Violators of Interna-
tional Laws Accountable in US Courts*, 10 J. Transnat'l L. & Pol'y 109 (2000);
Justin Lu, *Jurisdiction over Non–State Activity under the Alien Tort Claims
Act*, 35 C.J.T.L. 531 (1997); Marissa Anne Pagnattaro, *Enforcing Internation-
al Labor Standards: The Potential of the Alien Tort Claims Act*, 37 Vand. J.
Transnat'l L. 203 (2004); Michael Ratner, *Civil Remedies for Gross Human
Rights Violations*, in Human Rights in the World Community: Issues and
Action 390 (R. Claude & B. Weston eds., 2006); Francisco Rivera, *A Response
to the Corporate Campaign Against the Alien Tort Claims Act*, 14 Ind. Int'l &
Comp. L. Rev. 251 (2003); Marc Rosen, *The Alien Tort Claims Act and the
Foreign Sovereign Immunities Act: A Policy Solution*, 6 Cardozo J. Int'l &
Comp. L. 461 (1998); Courtney Shaw, *Uncertain Justice: Liability of Multina-
tionals under the Alien Tort Claims Act*, 54 Stanford L. R. 1359 (2001); Aric
K. Short, *Is the Alien Tort Statute Sacrosanct? Retaining Forum Non Conve-
niens in Human Rights Litigation*, 33 N.Y.U. J. Int'l L. & Pol. 1001 (2001);
Ralph G. Steinhardt & Anthony A. D'Amato, The Alien Tort Claims Act: An
Analytical Anthology (1999); Ralph G. Steinhardt, *International Humanitari-
an Law in the Courts of the United States: Yamashita, Filartiga, and 911*, 36
George Wash. Int'l L. R. 1 (2004); Pamela J. Stephens, *Beyond Torture:
Enforcing International Human Rights in Federal Courts*, 51 Syracuse L. Rev.
941 (2001); ———, *Translating Filartiga: A Comparative and International
Law Analysis of Domestic Remedies For International Human Rights Viola-
tions*, 27 Yale J. Int'l.L. 1 (2002).

**14. Forti v. Suarez–Mason, 672 F.Supp. 1531, 1538–1543 (N.D.
Cal. 1987).**

[*Eds.*—This case, decided on 6 October 1987, was brought under 28 USC
§ 1350 (the ATCA or Alien Tort Statute) against a former Argentine general
(Carlos Guillermo Suarez–Mason) by two Argentine citizens (Alfredo Forti
and Debora Benchoam) residing in the United States. It arose out of events in
Argentina in the mid-to late–1970s when a military junta seized the government of President Isabelita Peron and waged a "dirty war" against suspected
subversives. In the period 1976–1979, tens of thousands of persons were
detained by the military without charge, and it is estimated that more than
12,000 were "disappeared." The plaintiffs sued on their own behalf and on
behalf of family members, seeking damages from defendant Suarez–Mason
and alleging eleven causes of action: torture; prolonged arbitrary detention
without trial; cruel, inhuman and degrading treatment; false imprisonment;
assault and battery (including rape); intentional infliction of emotional distress; and conversion. Additionally, Forti claimed damages for the "disappearance" of his mother and Benchoam asserted claims for "murder and summary

execution," wrongful death, and a survival action relative to her 17–year old brother. The plaintiffs contended that the acts complained of were committed by military and police officials under defendant's authority and control and pursuant to a "policy, pattern and practice" of the First Army Corps under defendant's command. In response to the allegations, the defendant moved to dismiss the entire complaint, arguing, *inter alia*, that the Court lacked subject matter jurisdiction under 28 USC § 1350 to adjudicate tort claims arising out of "politically motivated acts of violence in other countries" and, alternatively, that not all of the torts alleged constitute violations of the law of nations. Pertinent portions of District Judge D. Lowell Jensen's opinion follow.]

... For the reasons set out below, the Court rejects defendant's construction of § 1350 and finds that plaintiffs allege sufficient facts to establish subject matter jurisdiction.... However, the Court agrees with defendant that not all of the alleged claims constitute "international torts" cognizable under 28 USC § 1350. Accordingly, the Court dismisses with prejudice the claims for "causing disappearance" and "cruel, inhuman, or degrading treatment." Further, the Court orders plaintiffs to amend the Complaint to state more definitely the facts constituting their claim for official torture.

A. THE ALIEN TORT STATUTE

The Alien Tort Statute provides that federal district courts shall have "original jurisdiction of any civil action by an alien for a tort only, committed in violation of the law of nations or a treaty of the United States." 28 USC § 1350 (1982).... As the cases and commentaries recognize, the history of the Alien Tort Statute is obscure. *See, e.g., IIT v. Vencap, Ltd.*, 519 F.2d 1001, 1015 (2d Cir. 1975) (§ 1350 a "kind of legal Lohengrin"). Nonetheless, the proper interpretation of the statute has been discussed at some length in the principal decisions upon which the parties rely: the unanimous decision in *Filártiga v. Peña–Irala*, 630 F.2d 876 (2d Cir. 1980) and the three concurring opinions in *Tel–Oren v. Libyan Arab Republic*, 726 F.2d 774 (D.C.Cir. 1984), *cert. denied*, 470 U.S. 1003, 105 S.Ct. 1354, 84 L.Ed.2d 377 (1985).

Defendant urges the Court to adopt the reasoning of Judges Bork and Robb in *Tel–Oren, supra*, where the court affirmed the dismissal of a § 1350 tort action ... based on a terrorist attack in Israel.... While the three judges concurred in the result, they were unable to agree on the rationale. Judge Bork found that § 1350 constitutes no more than a grant of jurisdiction; that plaintiffs seeking to invoke it must establish a private right of action under either a treaty or the law of nations; and that in the latter category the statute can support jurisdiction at most over only three international crimes recognized in 1789.... Judge Robb, on the other hand, found that the dispute involved international political violence and so was "nonjusticiable" within the meaning of the political question doctrine....

The Court is persuaded, however, that the interpretation of § 1350 forwarded by the Second Circuit in *Filártiga, supra*, and largely adopted by Judge Edwards in *Tel–Oren*, is better reasoned and more consistent with principles of international law. There appears to be a growing consensus that § 1350 provides a cause of action for certain "international common law torts." ... It is unnecessary that plaintiffs establish the existence of an independent, express right of action, since the law of nations clearly does not create or define civil actions, and to require such an explicit grant under international law would effectively nullify that portion of the statute which confers jurisdiction over tort suits involving the law of nations.... Rather, a plaintiff seeking to predicate jurisdiction on the Alien Tort Statute need only plead a "tort ... in violation of the law of nations."

* * *

The Court thus interprets 28 USC § 1350 to provide not merely jurisdiction but a cause of action, with the federal cause of action arising by recognition of certain "international torts" through the vehicle of § 1350. These international torts, violations of current customary international law, are characterized by universal consensus in the international community as to their binding status and their content. That is, they are universal, definable, and obligatory international norms. The Court now examines the allegations of the Complaint to determine whether plaintiffs have stated cognizable international torts for purposes of jurisdiction under § 1350.

B. Analysis Under 28 USC § 1350

In determining whether plaintiffs have stated cognizable claims under Section 1350, the Court has recourse to "the works of jurists, writing professedly on public law; ... the general usage and practice of nations; [and] judicial decisions recognizing and enforcing that law." ... For purposes of defendant's motion to dismiss, the Court must accept as true all of plaintiffs' allegations, construing them in the light most favorable to plaintiffs.... The Court may grant dismissal only if it is clear that plaintiffs can prove no set of facts which would entitle them to relief....

[Eds.—The Court proceeds to find that official torture, prolonged arbitrary detention, and summary execution constitute "cognizable" violations of "the law of nations" under § 1350. However, because the plaintiffs alleged torture in "conclusionary" and "general" terms and because of "the seriousness of this claim," the Court ordered the plaintiffs to amend their complaint "to state specific acts on which they base their claim of official torture." The Court then continues:]

4. Causing Disappearances

In Count Three plaintiff Forti alleges a claim for "causing the disappearance" of his mother, in that defendant "arbitrarily and without justification, cause or privilege, abducted Nelida Azucena Sosa de Forti, held her in secret captivity and caused her 'disappearance' to this day." ...

Sadly, the practice of "disappearing" individuals—*i.e.*, abduction, secret detention, and torture, followed generally by either secret execution or release—during Argentina's "dirty war" is now well documented in the official report of the Argentine National Commission on the Disappeared, *Nunca Mas*. Nor are such practices necessarily restricted to Argentina. With mounting publicity over the years, such conduct has begun to draw censure as a violation of the basic right to life. Plaintiff cites a 1978 United Nations resolution and a 1980 congressional resolution to this effect.... The Court notes, too, that the proposed Restatement of the Law of Foreign Relations lists "the murder or causing the disappearance of individuals," where practiced, encouraged, or condoned by the state, as a violation of international law. *Restatement (Revised) of the Foreign Relations Law of the United States*, § 702 (Tenth Draft No. 6, 1985). However, plaintiffs do not cite the Court to any case finding that causing the disappearance of an individual constitutes a violation of the law of nations.

Before this Court may adjudicate a tort claim under § 1350, it must be satisfied that the legal standard it is to apply is one with universal acceptance and definition.... Unfortunately, the Court cannot say, on the basis of the evidence submitted, that there yet exists the requisite degree of international consensus which demonstrates a customary international norm. Even if there were greater evidence of universality, there remain definitional problems. It is not clear precisely what conduct falls within the proposed norm, or how this proscription would differ from that of summary execution. The other torts condemned by the international community and discussed above—official torture, prolonged arbitrary detention, and summary execution—involve two types of conduct by the official actor: (1) taking the individual into custody; and (2) committing a wrongful, tortious act in excess of his [sic] authority over that person. In the case of "causing disappearance," only the first of these two actions can be proven—the taking into custody. However, the sole act of taking an individual into custody does not suffice to prove conduct which the international community proscribes. The Court recognizes the very real problems of proof presented by the disappearance of an individual following such custody. Yet there is no apparent international consensus as to the additional elements needed to make out a claim for causing the disappearance of an individual. For instance, plaintiffs have not shown that customary international law creates a presumption of causing disappearance upon a showing of prolonged absence after initial custody.

* * *

Accordingly, the Court must dismiss Count Four for failure to state a claim upon which relief may be granted.

5. *Cruel, Inhuman and Degrading Treatment*

* * *

The claim suffers the same defects as Count Four. Plaintiffs do not cite, and the Court is not aware of, such evidence of universal consensus regarding the right to be free from "cruel, inhuman and degrading treatment as exists, for example, with respect to official torture." Further, any such right poses problems of definability.... [I]t is unclear what behavior falls within the proscription—beyond such obvious torts as are already encompassed by the proscriptions of torture, summary execution and prolonged arbitrary detention. Lacking the requisite elements of universality and definability, this proposed tort cannot qualify as a violation of the law of nations....

15.   **Forti v. Suarez–Mason, 694 F.Supp. 707 (N.D. Cal. 1988).**

On October, 6, 1987 this Court [held, *inter alia*,] that "on the basis of the evidence submitted" plaintiff Forti had failed to establish "the requisite degree of international consensus which demonstrates a customary international norm" in regard to his claim for causing the disappearance of his mother. The Court also dismissed both plaintiffs' claims for "cruel, inhuman or degrading treatment," holding that plaintiffs had failed to bring forth sufficient evidence of international consensus, and moreover that the tort "lacks readily ascertainable parameters." . . .

Plaintiffs subsequently filed this Motion, supported by numerous international legal authorities, as well as affidavits from eight renowned international law scholars.[1] The Court has reviewed these materials and concludes that plaintiffs have met their burden of showing an international consensus as to the status and content of the international tort of "causing disappearance." . . . The Court also concludes that plaintiffs have again failed to establish that there is any international consensus as to what conduct falls within the category of "cruel, inhuman or degrading treatment." Absent such consensus as to the content of this alleged tort, it is not cognizable under the Alien Tort Statute [28 USC § 1350]. . . .

. . . The plaintiff's burden in stating a claim is to establish the existence of a "universal, definable, and obligatory international norm." To meet this burden plaintiffs need not establish unanimity among nations. Rather, they must show a general recognition among states that a specific practice is prohibited. It is with this standard in mind that the Court examines the evidence presented by plaintiffs.

* * *

The legal scholars whose declarations have been submitted in connection with this Motion are in agreement that there is universal consensus as to the two essential elements of a claim for "disappearance." In Professor Franck's words:

> The international community has also reached a consensus on the definition of a "disappearance." It has two essential elements: (a) abduction by a state official or by persons acting under state approval or authority; and (b) refusal by the state to acknowledge the abduction and detention. . . .

Plaintiffs cite numerous international legal authorities which support the assertion that "disappearance" is a universally recognized wrong under the law of nations. For example, United Nations General Assembly Resolution 33/173[e] recognizes "disappearance" as violative of many of the rights recognized in the Universal Declaration of Human Rights **[Basic Document 3.3]**. . . . These rights include: (1) the right to life; (2) the right to liberty and security of the person; (3) the right to freedom from torture; (4) the right to freedom from arbitrary arrest and detention; and (5) the right to a fair and public trial. *Id.*, articles 3, 5, 9, 10, 11. *See also* International Covenant on Political and Civil Rights [sic] **[Basic Document 3.14]** . . . , articles 6, 7, 9, 10, 14, 15, 17.

Other documents support this characterization of "disappearance" as violative of universally recognized human rights. The United States Congress

---

1. These include Richard Anderson Falk of Princeton University, Thomas Franck of New York University, Louis Henkin of Columbia University, Richard B. Lillich of the University of Virginia, Phillipe Sands of Cambridge University and Boston College Law School, Henry J. Steiner of Harvard Law School, David Weissbrodt of the University of Minnesota Law School, and Burns H. Weston of the University of Iowa College of Law.

e. Favorably cited in the preamble to the Declaration on the Protection of All Persons from Enforced Disappearance, GA Res. 47/133, UN GAOR, 46th Sess., Supp. No. 49, at 207, UN Doc. A/RES/47/133 (1993), *reprinted in* 3 Weston & Carlson III.K.5 **(Basic Document 3.38)**, listed as Reading 10, *supra*.

has denounced "prolonged detention without charges and trial" along with other "flagrant denial[s] of the right to life, liberty, or the security of person." 22 USC § 2304(d)(1). The recently published Restatement (Third) of the Foreign Relations Law of the United States § 702 includes "disappearance" as a violation of international law of human rights. The Organization of American States has also denounced "disappearance" as "an affront to the conscience of the hemisphere and . . . a crime against humanity." Organization of American States, Inter–American Commission on Human Rights, General Assembly Resolution 666 (November 18, 1983).

Of equal importance, plaintiffs' submissions support their assertion that there is a universally recognized legal definition of what constitutes the tort of "causing disappearance." The Court's earlier order expressed concern that "the sole act of taking an individual into custody does not suffice to prove conduct which the international community proscribes." . . . Plaintiffs' submissions on the Motion, however, establish recognition of a second essential element—official refusal to acknowledge that the individual has been taken into custody. For example, the United Nations General Assembly has expressed concern at the

> difficulties in obtaining reliable information from competent authorities as to the circumstances of such persons, including reports or organizations to acknowledge that they hold such persons in custody or otherwise to account for them.

UN General Assembly Resolution 33/173 (December 20, 1978).

Likewise, the Organization of American States has recognized the importance of this element, commenting on the

> numerous cases wherein the government systematically denies the detention of individuals, despite the convincing evidence that the claimants provide to verify their allegations that such persons have been detained by police or military authorities and, in some cases, that those person are, or have been, confined in specified detention centers.

Organization of American States, Inter–American Commission on Human Rights, 1977 Annual Report, at 26. . . .

In the Court's view, the submitted materials are sufficient to establish the existence of a universal and obligatory international proscription of the tort of "causing disappearance." . . . Therefore, the Motion to Reconsider is GRANTED in part and plaintiff Forti's claim is reinstated.

* * *

In its October 1987 Order the Court found that plaintiffs had stated claims . . . for "official torture" . . ., but had failed to state claims for "cruel, inhuman or degrading treatment or punishment." . . . The Second Amended Complaint does not state precisely what alleged actions constitute the proposed tort. Rather, it merely incorporates *all* the factual allegations and alleges that these acts constitute "torture or other cruel, inhuman or degrading treatment or punishment." * * * Specifically, the plaintiffs argue that [torture and cruel, inhuman or degrading treatment or punishment] are properly viewed on a continuum . . . [differing] "essentially in the degree of ill treatment suffered." . . .

Plaintiffs emphasize that virtually all international legal authorities which prohibit torture also prohibit cruel, inhuman or degrading treatment. * * * While these and other materials establish a recognized proscription of "cruel, inhuman or degrading treatment," they offer no guidance as to what constitutes such treatment.... The scholars whose declarations have been submitted likewise decline to offer any definition of the proposed tort. In fact, one of the declarations appears to concede the lack of a universally recognized definition. *See Lillich Declaration* ... ("only the contours of the prohibition, not its existence as a norm of customary international law, are the subject of legitimate debate.").

* * *

Plaintiffs cite *The Greek Case*, 12 Y. B. Eur. Conv. on Human Rights 186 (1969), for a definition of "degrading treatment" as that which "grossly humiliates [the victim] before others or drives him to act against his will or conscience." ... But this definitional gloss is of no help. From our necessarily global perspective, conduct, particularly verbal conduct, which is humiliating in one cultural context is of no moment in another. An international tort which appears and disappears as one travels around the world is clearly lacking in that level of common understanding necessary to create universal consensus. Likewise, the term "against his will or conscience" is too abstract to be of help. For example, a pacifist who is conscripted to serve in his country's military has arguably been forced to act "against his will or conscience." Would he thus have a claim for degrading treatment?

... Plaintiffs' submissions fail to establish that there is anything even remotely approaching universal consensus as to what constitutes "cruel, inhuman or degrading treatment." ... Therefore, the Motion to Reconsider the Dismissal of the Claim is DENIED.

16. Editors' Note. It will be noted that both of the foregoing *Forti v. Suarez–Mason* opinions cite § 702(c) of the Restatement (Third) of the Foreign Relations Law of the United States as adopted by the American Law Institute in May 1986, published in 1987, and quoted in Reading 9, *supra*. It also will be noted, however, that this particular reliance upon § 702 (entitled "Customary International Law of Human Rights") is not self-evidently warranted. Neither in the "Comment" to § 702 nor in its accompanying "Reporters' Notes" is any explicit authority or explanation given to support the assertion that "the murder or causing the disappearance of individuals" constitutes a violation of customary international human rights law. And the same may be said of the 1994 *Final Report on the Status of the Universal Declaration of Human Rights in National and International Law* of the Committee on the Enforcement of Human Rights Law of the International Law Association. While praising "[t]he American Law Institute's *Restatement* ... [as] one of the most explicit and authoritative opinions as to the content of the customary international law of human rights, at least as of 1987," it merely observes, without further comment, that "[t]he prohibition against murder and causing 'disappearances' is included in the *Restatement's* list...." I.L.A. Report of the Sixty–Sixth Conference 525, 544–45 (Buenos Aires, 1994).

17. Velásquez Rodriguez Case, Inter–Am. Ct. H.R. (ser. C, no. 4) (1988).

[*Eds.*—This case, submitted by the Inter–American Commission on Human Rights (IACHR) to the Inter–American Court of Human Rights was decided on 29 July, 1988. According to Sonia Picado, a former judge of the Inter–American Court of Human Rights, it is the Court's "most important precedent to date": *The Evolution of Democracy and Human Rights in Latin America: A Ten Year Perspective*, 11 Human Rights Brief 28 (Spring 2004). The case arose out of an individual petition against the Republic of Honduras submitted to the IACHR on October 7, 1981. The IACHR invoked Articles 50 and 51 of the American Convention on Human Rights **(Basic Document 3.17)** (hereinafter "the Convention" or "the American Convention") and asked the Court to decide whether Honduras had violated Articles 4 (Right to Life), 5 (Right to Humane Treatment), and 7 (Right to Personal Liberty) of the Convention. The case involved Angel Manfredo Velásquez Rodriguez, a student at the National Autonomous University of Honduras. He was alleged to have been "violently detained without a warrant" by members of the National Office of Investigations (DNI) and G–2 of the Armed Forces of Honduras, subsequently accused of political crimes and subjected to "harsh interrogation and cruel torture," and thereafter moved to a military post where interrogation continued. He was never heard from again. The police and security forces denied that Manfredo Velásquez was ever detained. "Today, nearly seven years later," the Court concluded on the basis of the facts it found to have been proven, "he [Manfredo Velásquez] remains disappeared, which creates a reasonable presumption that he has died." The disappearance of Manfredo Velásquez took place, the Court went on to note, during the period 1981–84 when 100 to 150 persons disappeared in Honduras, usually persons Honduran officials considered dangerous to state security. The Court then turned to the legal issues presented:]

150. The phenomenon of disappearances is a complex form of human rights violation that must be understood and confronted in an integral fashion.

* * *

153. International practice and doctrine have often categorized disappearances as a crime against humanity, although there is no treaty in force which is applicable to the States Parties to the [American] Convention and which uses this terminology (Inter–American Yearbook on Human Rights, 1985, pp. 368, 686 and 1102). The General Assembly of the OAS has resolved that it "is an affront to the conscience of the hemisphere and constitutes a crime against humanity" ... and that "this practice is cruel and inhuman, mocks the rule of law, and undermines those norms which guarantee protection against arbitrary detention and the right to personal security and safety"....

* * *

155. The forced disappearance of human beings is a multiple and continuous violation of many rights under the Convention that the States Parties are obligated to respect and guarantee. The kidnapping of a person is an arbitrary deprivation of liberty, an infringement of a detainee's right to be taken without delay before a judge and to invoke the appropriate procedures

to review the legality of the arrest, all in violation of Article 7 of the Convention which recognizes the right to personal liberty. . . .

156.   Moreover, prolonged isolation and deprivation of communication are in themselves cruel and inhuman treatment, harmful to the psychological and moral integrity of the person and a violation of the right of any detainee to respect for his [sic] inherent dignity as a human being. Such treatment, therefore, violates Article 5 of the Convention, which recognizes the right to the integrity of the person. . . . In addition, investigations into the practice of disappearances and the testimony of victims who have regained their liberty show that those who are disappeared are often subjected to merciless treatment, including all types of indignities, torture and other cruel, inhuman and degrading treatment, also in violation of the right to physical integrity recognized in Article 5 of the Convention.

157.   The practice of disappearances often involves secret execution without trial, followed by concealment of the body to eliminate any material evidence of the crime and to ensure the impunity of those responsible. This is a flagrant violation of the right to life, recognized in Article 4 of the Convention. . . .

158.   The practice of disappearances, in addition to directly violating many provisions of the Convention, such as those noted above, constitutes a radical breach of the treaty in that it shows a crass abandonment of the values which emanate from the concept of human dignity and of the most basic principles of the inter-American system and the Convention. The existence of this practice, moreover, evinces a disregard of the duty to organize the State in such a manner as to guarantee the rights recognized in the Convention. . . .

[*Eds.*—The Court next considers whether the rights guaranteed to Manfredo Velásquez by Articles 4, 5, and 7 of the Convention were violated and, if so, whether the acts of violation can be imputed to the State of Honduras and thereby establish its international responsibility. The Court resolves both of these questions in the affirmative, stating:]

178.   In the instant case, the evidence shows a complete inability of the procedures of the State of Honduras, which were theoretically adequate, to ensure the investigation of the disappearance of Manfredo Velásquez and the fulfillment of its duties to pay compensation and punish those responsible, as set out in Article 1(1) of the Convention.

* * *

182.   The Court is convinced, and has so found, that the disappearance of Manfredo Velásquez was carried out by agents who acted under cover of public authority. However, even had that fact not been proven, the failure of the State apparatus to act, which is clearly proven, is a failure on the part of Honduras to fulfil the duties it assumed under Article 1(1) of the Convention, obligating it to guarantee Manfredo Velásquez the free and full exercise of his human rights.

* * *

185.   From the above, the Court concludes that the facts found in this proceeding show that the State of Honduras is responsible for the involuntary

disappearance of Angel Manfredo Velásquez Rodriguez. Thus, Honduras has violated Articles 7, 5 and 4 of the Convention.

186.   As a result of the disappearance, Manfredo Velásquez was the victim of an arbitrary detention, which deprived him of his physical liberty without legal cause and without a determination of the lawfulness of his detention by a judge or competent tribunal. Those acts directly violate the right to personal liberty recognized by Article 7 of the Convention ... [and are a] violation imputable to Honduras of the duties to respect and ensure that right under Article 1(1).

187.   The disappearance of Manfredo Velásquez violates the right to personal integrity recognized by Article 5 of the Convention.... The guarantee of physical integrity and the right of detainees to treatment respectful of their human dignity require State Parties to take reasonable steps to prevent situations which are truly harmful to the rights protected.

188.   The above reasoning is applicable to the right to life recognized by Article 4 of the Convention.... The context in which the disappearance occurred and the lack of knowledge seven years later as to the victim's fate create a reasonable presumption that he was killed. Even if there is a minimal margin of doubt in this respect, it must be presumed that his fate was decided by authorities who systematically executed detainees without trial and concealed their bodies in order to avoid punishment....

[*Eds.*—The Court ruled against Honduras on each count and, citing Article 63(1) of the American Convention, ordered it "to pay fair compensation to the next-of-kin of the victim."[f]]

SECTION 5.   DISCUSSION NOTES/QUESTIONS

1.   The scope of violence and "disappearances" in Latin America in the 1960s and 1970s, described in Reading 12, *supra*, has only recently begun to be documented in a systematic manner. For accounts, see, *e.g.*, Julia Boyle, *The International Obligation to Prosecute Human Rights Violators: Spain's Jurisdiction over Argentine Dirty War Participants*, 22 Hastings Int'l & Comp. L. Rev. 187 (1998); Roseann Latore, *Coming Out of the Dark: Achieving Justice for Victims of Human Rights Violations by South American Military Regimes*, 25 B.C. Int'l & Comp. L. Rev. 419 (2002); Sonia Picado, *The Evolution of Democracy and Human Rights in Latin America: A Ten Year Perspective*, 11 Human Rights Brief 28 (Spring 2004).

2.   In the present problem, might defendant Carrera have raised the non-justiciability plea of sovereign immunity, on the grounds of being an agent of the state of Hispania? Should not forum states, to avoid stirring up international tensions, simply decline to hear tort suits involving other sovereign states, including tort suits against their agents? Compare, in this connection, *Frolova v. USSR*, 761 F.2d 370 (7th Cir. 1985) (granting immunity) with *Von Dardel v. USSR*, 623 F.Supp. 246 (D.D.C. 1985) (denying immunity), judgment vacated and complaint dismissed, 736 F.Supp. 1 (D.D.C. 1990) (granting immunity). In *Argentine Republic v. Amerada Hess Shipping Corporation, et al.*, 488 U.S. 428 (1989), a suit by two Liberian corporations against the Republic of Argentina for damages resulting from an Argentine military attack upon a Liberian tanker during

---

f. For a similar subsequent ruling by the Inter-American Court of Human Rights, see the *Godinez Cruz Case*, Inter-Am. Ct. H.R. (ser. C, no. 5) (1989).

Argentina's 1982 Falkland Islands war with Great Britain, the US Supreme Court held that the US Foreign Sovereign Immunities Act (FSIA) of 1976 (**Basic Document 6.2**) protected Argentina from suit in a United States court notwithstanding that the suit had been brought under ATCA, 28 USC § 1350, because § 1605(a) of the FSIA limits the "tort exception" to sovereign immunity to cases where the tortious acts occur *within* the United States. *See, e.g., Letelier v. Republic of Chile*, 488 F.Supp. 665 (D.D.C. 1980), involving a suit for damages against the Republic of Chile for its part in the deaths of former Chilean ambassador to the United States and Chilean Foreign Minister Orlando Letelier and one Ronni Moffit resulting from the bombing of Ambassador Letelier's car in the District of Columbia on 21 September 1976.

Note: The enforcement of the *Letelier* judgment became a diplomatic matter and therefore was referred to an arbitral commission of the Organization of American States (OAS), which ordered Chile to pay $2.6 million in damages to the plaintiff-heirs of Ambassador Letelier and Mr. Moffit. The former head of Chile's military secret police, Manuel Contreras, and his deputy, Pedro Espinoza, who were found guilty by the Chilean Supreme Court of having plotted Letelier's and Moffit's deaths, were sentenced to seven and six years in jail, respectively—part of Chile's painful struggle to mete out justice to its former oppressors under the military rule of General Augusto Pinochet. Contreras and Espinoza began serving their prison terms, after unsuccessful appeals, on 21 October 1995.

3. Why should foreigners be free to bring suits in the domestic courts of one country for tortious actions committed in their own country or another? In Kenneth Jost, *Don't Say "No" to Human Rights*, Nat'l L. J., 16 January 1989, at 13, col. 1, two reasons are proffered insofar as the United States is concerned (each "beyond the traditional impulse of Anglo–American common law to provide a remedy to the innocent victims of wrongful conduct"): "One reason, suggested by Northwestern University Prof., Anthony D'Amato, is to serve notice to the world that the United States is committed to deal fairly and impartially—in the courts—with cases having foreign policy implications, and not make 'political bargaining chips' out of them. A second reason is to promote the evolution of international law in ways that advance both our ideals and our self-interest in world affairs." Do you agree? What about the possibility of the judiciary embarrassing the executive branch in "cases having foreign policy implications"? What about the possibility that courts in one society or culture will insist upon outcomes incompatible with the values of other societies or cultures? What in fact is the proper role of domestic courts in the struggle for internationally guaranteed human rights? For commentary on international human rights in US domestic courts, see Richard A. Falk, The Role of Domestic Courts in the International Legal Order (1964); Kenneth C. Randall, Federal Courts and the International Human Rights Paradigm (1990); Beth Stephens & Michael Ratner, International Human Rights Litigation in US Courts (1996); Penny J. White, *Legal, Political, and Ethical Hurdles to Applying International Human Rights Law in the State Courts of the United States (and Arguments for Scaling Them)*, 71 U. Cinn. L. Rev. 937 (2003). *See also* Curtis A. Bradley, *The Costs of International Human Rights Litigation*, 2 Chi. J. Int'l L. 457 (2001); Cynthia R. L. Fairweather, *Obstacles to Enforcing International Human Rights Law in Domestic Courts*, 4 U.C. Davis J. Int'l L. & Pol'y 119 (1998); Mark P. Gibney, *Human Rights Litigation in US Courts: A Hypocritical Approach*, 3 Buff. Jour. Int'l L. 261 (1996–97); Richard B. Lillich, *The Role of Domestic Courts in Promoting International Human Rights Norms*, 24 N.Y.L.S.L. Rev. 153 (1978); ___, *Invoking International Human Rights Law in Domestic Courts*, 54 U. Cinn. L. Rev. 367 (1985); _____,

The Constitution and International Human Rights, 83 A.J.I.L. 851 (1989); Beth Stephens, *Taking Pride in International Human Rights Litigation*, 2 Chi. J. Int'l L. 485 (2001). *See also* the references cited at the end of Reading 13, *supra,* and Discussion Note/Question 5, *infra.*

4.   As noted in Reading 13, *supra,* the United States is not party to many of the major international human rights treaties, and United States courts tend to construe any international human rights treaty in the most narrow terms, thus requiring what the late Professor Lillich called a "pessimistic assessment of the role of international human rights treaties in the American legal system." Richard B. Lillich, *The Constitution and International Human Rights*, 83 A.J.I.L. 851, 856 (1989). But, in light of *Filártiga,* what about the domestic application of *customary* international human rights law? After indicating a "somewhat more optimistic outlook about the potential effect of customary international human rights law" (in contrast to treaty-based international human rights law), Lillich comments in *id.* at 858–59 as follows:

> A core list of human rights that arguably have achieved customary international law status, including the prohibition against torture, may be found in section 702 of the *Restatement (Third) of the Foreign Relations law of the United States*. Of the additional rights listed, US Courts during this decade [of the 1980s] have held that prolonged arbitrary detention and "causing the disappearance" of individuals are prohibited by customary international law.... Arguments that other human rights now are part of customary international law can be expected to be made with increasing frequency.

Lillich adds: "These arguments, of course, can be raised in other contexts than the Alien Tort Act, since customary international human rights law, being part of US law, has potentially wider application." *Id.* He then continues:

> An example of the relevance (and current limits) of such arguments can be found in *Garcia–Mir v. Meese,*[2] a ... case involving excludable Cuban aliens, where the US District Court for the Northern District of Georgia observed that "[e]ven the government admits that [the] customary international law of human rights contains at least a general principle prohibiting prolonged arbitrary detention." The Government, however, then proceeded to argue that, under the caveats the Supreme Court attached to its oft-quoted holding in *The Paquete Habana,*[3] there existed both legislation and a "controlling executive act" that provided a rule of decision, making resort to customary international law inappropriate. * * * The district court accepted the contention that a controlling executive act effectively preempts customary international law.... On appeal, the US Court of Appeals for the Eleventh Circuit, after advancing the extraordinary view that the President possesses the power "to disregard international law in service to domestic needs," concluded that the Attorney General's "executive acts here evident constitute a sufficient basis for affirming the trial court's finding that international law does not control." The decision, which has been rightly criticized for misreading The Paquete Habana, puts a severe restraint upon the use of customary

2.   788 F.2d 1446 (11th Cir.), *cert. denied,* 479 U.S. 889 (1986).

3.   [175 U.S. 677 (1900).] Immediately after its holding [that customary international law is "part of our law"] ..., the Court added the following important caveats: "For this purpose [the application of international law by US courts], where there is no treaty, *and no controlling executive or legislative act or judicial decision,* resort must be had to the customs and usages of civilized nations...." 175 U.S. at 700 (emphasis added).

international human rights law by US courts, at least in those (rare, one hopes) cases where the executive branch is willing to take, identify and rely upon acts that are contrary to it.

For discussion of the adherence by national governments and legal systems to international law, see *supra* Chapter 3.

5. Given the reluctance of United States courts to entertain claims based directly on human rights treaties or customary international human rights law, the indirect use of conventional and customary international human rights law to infuse the substance of US constitutional and statutory law standards could be a promising alternative for the extension of international human rights protection on the domestic plane. Some US courts have cited the UN Charter **(Basic Document 1.5)**, the Universal Declaration of Human Rights **(Basic Document 3.3)**, and other international human rights instruments to define the scope and content of rights guaranteed by US law. This judicial strategy has been controversial. When some members of the US Supreme Court have referred to international law standards in cases involving the death penalty—Thompson v. Oklahoma, 487 U.S. 815 (1998)—and the criminalization of homosexuality—*Lawrence v. Texas*, 539 U.S. 558 (2003)—the response in some quarters has been negative. In *Thompson* Supreme Court Justice Antonin Scalia criticized references in Justice Stevens' judgment for the Court to the provisions of International Covenant on Civil and Political Rights **(Basic Document 3.14)** and the American Convention on Human Rights **(Basic Document 3.17)** that prohibit the execution of children under the age of 18 at the time an offence is committed by stating that "civilized standards of decency in other countries are totally inappropriate as a means of establishing the fundamental beliefs of *this* Nation." Justice Scalia similarly dismissed the invocation of decisions of the European Court of Human Rights in *Lawrence* by Justice Kennedy writing for the Court about a right to sexual preference as "meaningless" and "dangerous." He presented international legal principles as "foreign moods, fads [and] fashions" that should be resisted in interpretation of the US Constitution. It is to be noted, however, that other Supreme Court justices take a less hostile approach to international law. In *Roper v. Simmons*, 543 U.S. 551 (2005), for example, holding unconstitutional (*i.e.*, in violation of the Eighth and Fourteenth amendments) the execution of persons under age 18 who have committed capital crimes, the Court, citing state practice state practice relative to the execution of juvenile offenders in addition to international human rights treaties, declared it mete and proper to acknowledge "the overwhelming weight of international opinion against the juvenile death penalty." The world community, wrote Justice Kennedy for the Court, provides "respected and significant confirmation of our own conclusions. . . . It does not lessen our fidelity to the Constitution," he explained, to recognize "the express affirmation of certain fundamental rights by other nations and peoples," and affirmation that "underscores the centrality of those same rights within our own heritage of freedom." It is not unreasonable to suggest that *Roper* with its precedents may have hastened the acceptance of customary international human rights law in American jurisprudence. For example Justice Ruth Ginsberg referred to the International Convention on the Elimination of All Forms of Racial Discrimination of 1966 **(Basic Document 3.12)** and the International Convention on the Elimination of All Forms of Discrimination against Women of 1979 **(Basic Document 3.21)** in discussing racial preferences in University admissions in *Grutter v. Bollinger*, 539 U.S. 306 (2003).

The process of "indirect incorporation" need not be restricted to the courts or even altogether indirect. For example, in September 1986, before the United

States became a party to the 1966 International Convention on the Elimination of All Forms of Racial Discrimination **(Basic Document 3.12)** and at a time when its ratification by the United States seemed bleak, the City of Burlington, Iowa, at the suggestion of Professor Francis A. Boyle of the University of Illinois College of Law, adopted an ordinance specifically adding the Convention's substantive provisions to the city's governing human rights law, a procedure that was utilized later in two other Iowa cities as well—in Iowa City, for example, where also the substantive provisions of the 1979 International Convention on the Elimination of All Forms of Discrimination against Women **(Basic Document 3.21)** were incorporated into local law. Editorialized the principal Burlington newspaper at the time, in *City [of Burlington] Shows Local Issues Have Global Roots*, Burlington Hawkeye, 21 September 1986: "The idea of turning international conventions into local ordinances proposes an end run around the recalcitrant [US] Senate. Widespread adoption by localities will constitute a national endorsement which the Senate will be under pressure to recognize." The Burlington Hawkeye also quoted Professor Burns Weston, who helped to inspire the initiative, as saying that "[t]his will force judges in local jurisdictions to pay attention to international justice.... [It is] a case of thinking globally and acting locally." Given the US propensity to declare all human rights treaties non-self-executing, would communities throughout the United States be well advised to consider this approach to the extension of international human rights law even when the United States shall have ratified an international human rights treaty?

6. In Australia, as in the United Kingdom, but in contrast to the United States, there is a strict theoretical separation between the power to enter into human rights and other treaties and the power to implement them. Grounded in the bicameral Westminster system of government, whereby the executive branch is made up of members of the majority party in the legislative branch (*i.e.*, the House of Representatives in Australia and the House of Commons in the United Kingdom), treaties are concluded by the executive branch alone and do not operate internally until they are incorporated into domestic law by parliamentary enactment. *See Walker v. Baird*, 1892 A.C. 491. Nevertheless, in Australia, as in the United Kingdom, international human rights law has been promoted domestically with somewhat greater alacrity than in the United States—and notwithstanding that, unlike the United States, Australia, as the United Kingdom, has no constitutional guarantees of rights; human rights protection depends on a rather sporadic coverage of particular rights in the common law and in certain statutory provisions such as those prohibiting particular forms of discrimination. In Australia, though in different ways than in the United Kingdom, international human rights law has played a significant role in developing national human rights protection.

The federal division of powers under the Australian Constitution gives the federal government no specific competence relative to human rights, and thus for many years it was assumed that human rights were the province of the separate states. The states were slow to act in this regard, however. Thus, in 1982, in *Koowarta v. Bjelke–Petersen*, 56 Austl. L.J.R. 625 (1982), a suit by an Australian Aborigine invoking legislation designed to implement the 1966 International Convention on the Elimination of All Forms of Racial Discrimination **(Basic Document 3.12)** against the State of Queensland, the Australian High Court, in a vote of four to three, decided that, under § 51(29) of the Australian Constitution (known as the "external affairs" power), the federal government could legislate to implement international human rights law. Queensland's main defense was that the federal legislation was not valid because the subject of racial discrimination was not constitutionally assigned to the federal government and therefore fell within the reserved powers of the states. For further details, see Andrew Byrnes & Hilary Charlesworth, *Federalism and the International Legal Order: Recent Developments in Australia*, 79 A.J.I.L. 622, 626–33 (1985).

Since *Koowarta*, the Australian federal government has enacted legislation implementing a number of important human rights treaties, *e.g.*, the 1966 Convention on the Elimination of All Forms of Racial Discrimination (CERD) **(Basic Document 3.12)**, the 1979 Convention on the Elimination of All Forms of Discrimination against Women (CEDAW) **(Basic Document 3.21)**, and the 1984 Convention Against Torture and Other Cruel, Inhuman or Degrading Treatment or Punishment (CAT) **(Basic Document 3.26)**. In addition, while failing to legislate to implement the rights set out in the 1966 International Covenant on Economic, Social and Cultural Rights (ICESR) **(Basic Document 3.13)** and many of those in the companion International Covenant on Civil and Political Rights (ICCPR) **(Basic Document 3.14)**, it has established a statutory body known as the Human Rights and Equal Opportunity Commission (HREOC), empowered, even if only occasionally respected, to advise the federal government as to any of its activities that might violate the rights set out in the ICCPR. Further, since 1991, Australia, has accepted the individual "communication" procedure set out under the 1966 first Optional Protocol to the ICCPR **(Basic Document 3.15)** pursuant to which human rights claims against Australia may be brought to the Human Rights Committee (HRC) established under the ICCPR.[g] It has accepted as well the right of individual petition under the CERD and the CAT, and also the right of state-to-state complaint under the ICCPR, the CERD and the CAT. The first Australian case to reach the merits phase of the ICCPR Optional Protocol procedure was the case of a gay activist, living in Tasmania, who argued that the State of Tasmania's criminalization of homosexuality violated his right to privacy and to equality under Articles 17 and 26, respectively, of the ICCPR. The HRC found that Article 17 had been violated and called upon Australia to take steps to override Tasmania's law. *Toonen v. Australia*, Communication No. 488/1992, HRC, View of Committee, 31 March 1994, 1 Int'l Hum. Rts. Rep. 97 (No. 3 1994). In 1994, the Australian Parliament enacted the Human Rights (Sexual Privacy) Act 1994 (Austl. C. Acts) in response to *Toonen*. A change of federal government in 1996 led however to a different approach to international human rights law. This has been manifest, for example, in the Australian government's rejection of views adopted by the UN human rights treaty bodies in relation to Australia. *See* Hilary Charlesworth, Madelaine Chiam, Devika Hovell & George Williams, *Deep Anxieties: Australia and the International Legal Order*, 25 *Sydney Law Review* 243 (2003).

As for the United Kingdom, the 1950 European Convention for the Protection of Human Rights and Fundamental Freedoms **(Basic Document 3.5)** has played an increasingly significant role. First, many cases were brought against the UK under former Article 25 (now Article 34) of the Convention, authorizing individual "petitions" to the European Court on Human Rights (in much the same manner that the first Optional Protocol to the ICCPR authorizes individual "communications" to the HRC)—for example, in regard to harsh contempt laws that effectively muzzled the freedom of journalistic expression, declared to be in violation of the right to freedom of speech under the European Convention. Between 1975 and 1998, the European Court of Human Rights ruled against the United Kingdom in over sixty cases. Second, British courts developed certain doctrines relative to

g. For brief explication, see *supra* Discussion Note/Question 3 in Problem 5–1 ("Ethnic Conflict and its Consequences in Slavia, Candia, and Corcyra"), at 592.

statutory interpretation and the review of administrative actions in an effort to bring the UK more in line with the Convention than otherwise it was. For example, in *Derbyshire County Council v. Times Newspapers Ltd.*, [1992] Q.B. 770, the Court of Appeal relied on Article 10 of the European Convention (protecting freedom of expression) to interpret an uncertain common law principle relating to defamation actions. The Court held that, where the law is uncertain, a court should ensure that it not involve a breach of treaty obligation. *See generally* Andrew Drzemczewski, European Human Rights Conventions in Domestic Law: A Comparative Study (1996). In 1998, the United Kingdom Parliament enacted the Human Rights Act, the effect of which is to give the European Convention formal status in UK domestic law. The Human Rights Act protects the rights set out in the European Convention and some of its protocols through a series of mechanisms. The Act requires that all legislation is to be interpreted, as far as possible, to be consistent with the Convention rights. If a court cannot interpret a particular law in this way, it may issue a Declaration of Incompatibility with respect to the legislation. The Declaration is, in effect, a notice to Parliament of a law that is inconsistent with human rights guarantees. The Declaration does not, however, invalidate the law. The Human Rights Act requires all public authorities to act consistently with the Convention rights, unless there is legislation to the contrary. It has been said that the UK Human Rights Act is based on a "dialogue" approach to human rights, in that it does not give the courts the final say with respect to their enforcement. The idea is that the courts, the legislature, and the executive are partners in the protection of human rights. *See* Julie Debeljak, *Rights Protection without Judicial Supremacy*, 16 Melb. U. L. Rev. 285 (2002); Francesca Klug, Values for a Godless Age: The Story of the United Kingdom's New Bill of Rights (2000).

Since 1982, Canadians have been able to rely on the Charter of Rights and Freedoms enshrined in the Canadian Constitution. The Charter was modelled on the 1966 ICCPR to some extent, and provides significant guarantees of rights, subject to the explicit limitation, in Section 1, that they may be "subject ... to such reasonable limits prescribed by law as can be demonstrably justified in a free and democratic society." Canada has also accepted the right of individual communication (or petition) under the first Optional Protocol to the ICCPR, and a number of important cases have been brought against Canada before the UN Human Rights Committee. *See generally* Promoting Human Rights through Bills of Rights: Comparative Perspectives (P. Alston ed., 1999); Litigating Rights: Perspectives from Domestic and International Law (G. Huscroft & P. Rishworth eds., 2002).

7. The present problem considers the exercise of civil jurisdiction in domestic courts to redress human rights infractions. What about *criminal* jurisdiction? The principal bases upon which international law recognizes the competence of states to punish crimes are that the criminal act must have taken place or had substantial effect in the state exercising jurisdiction (territorial principle) or that the persons committing the crime are nationals of said state even though they may have been acting elsewhere (nationality principle). What are the chances of a state whose officials have committed, say, torture or a disappearance or any of the discrete wrongs that constitute "cruel, inhuman or degrading treatment or punishment" ever bringing the guilty to trial absent a change of regime? The Restatement (Third) of the Foreign Relations Law of the United States § 404 (1987) asserts that

[a] state has jurisdiction to define and prescribe punishment for certain offenses recognized by the community of nations as of universal concern, such

as piracy, slave trade, attacks on or hijacking of aircraft, genocide, war crimes, and perhaps certain acts of terrorism, even where none of the bases of jurisdiction [such as territoriality or nationality] is present.

On the basis of the cases reported in this problem, is it possible to conclude that, say, an act of official torture, a disappearance, or cruel, inhuman or degrading treatment or punishment constitutes an offense of "universal concern"? Chapter 3 discusses the prosecution of cases in national courts on the basis of universal jurisdiction and should be consulted on this issues.

8.   Since the mid–1980s, increasing attention has been paid to alternative methods of accountability for grave human rights violations—for example, the creation of "truth commissions," a mechanism allowing public testimony by victims and perpetrators of abuse to create an historical record. Truth commissions are often attractive to governments after a lengthy period of domestic violence and upheaval, and there are many different models. Some have offered amnesty from criminal prosecution for those who appear before them and acknowledge their past behavior, leading to the possibility of impunity for crimes. *See* Diane Orentlicher, *Settling Accounts: The Duty to Prosecute Human Rights Violations of a Past Regime*, 100 Yale L. J. 25 (1991); Naomi Roht–Arriaza & Lauren Gibson, *The Developing Jurisprudence on Amnesty*, 20 H.R.Q. 849 (1998). Others have retained the possibility of prosecution for serious crimes, as in the case of the South African Truth and Reconciliation Commission, for example, established at the end of the apartheid era. For discussion of the South African Commission see John Dugard, *Reconciliation and Justice: The South African Experience*, 8 Transnat'l L. & Contemp. Probs. 286 (1998), *reprinted in* The Future of International Human Rights 399 (B. Weston & S. Marks eds., 1999); Jeremy Sarkin, *The Trials and Tribulations of South Africa's Truth and Reconciliation Commission*, 12 S. Afr. J. Hum. Rts. 617 (1996); Patricia B. Hayner offers a useful comparative study of truth commissions in Unspeakable Truths: Confronting State Terror and Atrocity (2001). In the context of the present problem, how valuable would a truth commission in Hispania be (assuming the resumption of its democratic institutions)? What would be the advantages and disadvantages of a truth commission? *See* Julia K. Boyle, *The International Obligation to Prosecute Human Rights Violators: Spain's Jurisdiction over Argentine Dirty War Participants,* 22 Hastings Int'l & Comp. L. Rev. 187 (1998); Evelyn Bradley, *In Search for Justice: A Truth and Reconciliation Commission for Rwanda*, 7 J. Int'l L. & Prac. 140 (1998); Richard J. Goldstone, *Past Human Rights Violations: Truth Commissions and Amnesties or Prosecutions*, 51 N. Ireland Legal Q. 164 (2000); Roseann M. Latore, *Coming Out of the Dark: Achieving Justice for Victims of Human Rights Violations by South American Military Regimes*, 25 B.C. Int'l & Comp. L. Rev. 419 (2002); Leila Nadya Sadat, *Universal Jurisdiction, National Amnesties, and Truth Commissions: Reconciling the Irreconcilable*, in Universal Jurisdiction: National Courts and the Prosecution of Serious Crimes under International Law 193 (S. Macedo ed., 2004).

9.   In the present problem, Francisco Morazán has disappeared because of his work with the Committee for the Defense of Human Rights in Hispania. The situation of human rights defenders is particularly vulnerable in repressive societies. In 1999, the UN General Assembly adopted a Declaration on the Right and Responsibility of Individuals, Groups and Organs of Society to Promote and Protect Universally Recognized Human Rights and Fundamental Freedoms, UN Doc. A/Res/53/144, 8 Mar 1999, *reprinted in* 3 Weston & Carlson III.T.20. The Declaration affirms the right to promote the protection of human rights at the national and international levels. The UN Commission on Human Rights in 2000

appointed a Special Representative of the UN Secretary–General on Human Rights Defenders. Ms Hina Jilani of Pakistan is the current Special Representative.

10. *Bibliographical Note.* For supplemental discussion concerning the principal themes addressed in this problem, consult the following additional specialized materials:

(a) *Books/Monographs/Reports/Symposia.* Amnesty International, "Disappearances" and Political Killings–Human Rights of the 1990s: A Manual for Action (1994); J. Brohmer, State Immunity and the Violation of Human Rights (1997); A. Clark, Diplomacy of Conscience: Amnesty International and Changing Human Rights Norms (2001); Human Rights, Labor Rights, and International Trade (L. Compa & S. Diamond eds., 1996); A. Drzemczewski, European Human Rights Conventions in Domestic Law: A Comparative Study (1996); P. Flood, The Effectiveness of UN Human Rights Institutions (1998); Nunca Mas: The Report of the Argentine National Commission on the Disappeared (1986); Torture as Tort: Comparative Perspectives on the Development of Transnational Human Rights Litigation (C. Scott ed., 2001); B. Stephens & M. Ratner, International Human Rights Litigation in US Courts (1996); J. Timmerman, Prisoner Without a Name, Cell Without a Number (1981); United Nations Office at Geneva, Enforced or Involuntary Disappearances (1997). J. Rogers, International Law and United States Law (1999).

(b) *Articles/Book Chapters.* G. Christenson, *Customary International Human Rights Law in Domestic Court Decisions*, 25 Ga. J. Int'l & Comp. L. 225 (1995–96); W. Dodge, *The Historical Origins of the Alien Tort Statute: A Response to the "Originalists,"* 19 Hastings Int'l & Comp. L. Rev. 221 (1996); M. Pettyjohn, *"Bring me your Tired, your Poor, your Egregious Torts Yearning to See Green:" The Alien Tort Statute*, 10 Tulsa J. Comp. & Int'l L. 513 (2003); S. Pritchard, *The Jurisprudence of Human Rights: Some Thoughts and Developments in Practice*, 2 Austl. J. Hum. Rts. 3 (1995).

Problem 5–5

Djourab Blocks Famine Relief in its North Province

SECTION 1. FACTS

Djourab, a poor African country, is suffering from widespread famine and malnutrition due to a severe lack of rainfall and climate change, with children among the most severely affected. It recently requested food aid from the World Food Programme ("Programme") of the United Nations Food and Agriculture Organization (FAO), based in Rome, Italy. Pursuant to Article 21 of the Programme's regulations on "Types and Fields of Activity," as approved by the United Nations Economic and Social Council (ECOSOC) and the FAO Council, the Director–General of the FAO approved the request. She instructed the Programme's Executive Director to conclude an agreement to provide Djourab with emergency food relief.[a] The Agreement between the Programme and Djourab reads in part as follows:

> The Government of Djourab shall ensure that the commodities supplied by the FAO/World Food Programme shall be handled, transported, stored, and distributed with adequate care and efficiency and that the commodities and the proceeds from their sale, when authorized, shall be utilized in the manner agreed upon between the parties to this agreement. In the event they are not so utilized, the Programme may require the return to it of the commodities or the sales proceeds or both, as the case may be.

On the basis of the aforementioned Agreement, Djourab received shipments of emergency food aid from the FAO/World Food Programme. In addition, it received 125,000 metric tons of grain from Australia as a gesture of humanitarian concern.

However, though eager to distribute some of the Programme's food aid and Australia's grain to most regions, Djourab refuses to distribute any of the Programme's food aid or Australia's grain to its rebellious North Province. Djourab's North Province is the source of much anti-government agitation and resistance.

---

a. The World Food Programme, established in 1961 for the purpose of effectively utilizing available surplus foodstuffs in emergency situations of hunger and malnutrition and operating under the auspices of the FAO, is supported by annual pledges of grain from at least seventy countries. Article 21 of the World Food Programme Types and Fields of Activity provides: "Upon approval of an emergency operation by the Director General of FAO, an agreement, which may be in the form of an exchange of letters, shall be concluded forthwith between the Executive Director and the recipient government."

The FAO claims that Djourab's refusal to distribute the Programme's food aid to its North Province violates Djourab's obligations under international law and accordingly seeks to enforce its rights under its agreement with Djourab. Australia, acting in keeping with Article 22 of the 1966 International Covenant on Economic, Social and Cultural Rights and making the same claim with respect to its grain shipments, seeks a resolution of the Economic and Social Council condemning Djourab in this regard and recommending that other appropriate United Nations organs and agencies, including the Security Council, instruct Djourab to comply with its international legal obligations.

Djourab is a member of the United Nations, a signatory of the 1948 Universal Declaration of Human Rights, and a party to the 1966 International Covenant on Civil and Political Rights, the 1966 International Covenant on Economic, Social and Cultural Rights, and the 1989 Convention on the Rights of the Child.

SECTION 2. QUESTIONS PRESENTED

1. May Djourab's refusal to distribute to its North Province the FAO/World Food Programme's emergency relief and Australia's gift of grain be successfully challenged under international law by, respectively, the FAO and Australia?

2. In any event, are there any additional or alternative legal norms, procedures, and/or institutions to be recommended that might further help to prevent or discourage situations of the kind posed by this problem?

SECTION 3. ASSIGNMENTS

A. READING ASSIGNMENT

Study the Readings presented in Section 4, *infra*, and the Discussion Notes/Questions that follow. Also, time permitting, consult the accompanying bibliographical references.

B. RECOMMENDED WRITING ASSIGNMENT

Prepare a comprehensive, logically sequenced, and *argumentative* brief in the form of an outline of the primary and subsidiary *legal* issues you see requiring resolution by the FAO and the Economic and Social Council. Also, from the perspective of an independent judge, indicate which side ought to prevail on each issue and why. Retain a copy of your issue-outline/brief for class discussion.

C. RECOMMENDED ORAL ASSIGNMENT

Assume you are legal counsel for the FAO and Australia, on the one hand, or Djourab, on the other (as designated by your instructor); then, relying upon the Readings (and your issue-outline if prepared), present a 10–15 minute oral argument of your government's likely positions before the FAO and ECOSOC.

D. RECOMMENDED REFLECTIVE ASSIGNMENT

Consider (and recommend) alternative norms, institutions, and/or procedures that you believe might do better than existing world order arrangements to contend with situations of the kind posed by this problem. In so doing, but without insisting upon *immediate* feasibility, identify the particular transition steps that would be needed to make your alternatives a reality.

SECTION 4. READINGS

The following readings are considered *prima facie* relevant to solving this problem. They are your law library for present purposes and should be treated as such, organized intelligibly for "shelving" and not necessarily according to the issues presented. Be sure to review Chapter 2 ("International Legal Prescription: The 'Sources' of International Law") in your consideration of them. It, too, should be treated as part of your law library (as, indeed, should this entire coursebook).

1. **Burns H. Weston, "Human Rights," in *Encyclopædia Britannica* (2005), available from *Encyclopædia Britannica Online* at <http://www. britannica.com/eb/article?tocId=219350>** (*see supra* Reading A–1 in Problem 5–1, at 494).

2. **United Nations Charter. Concluded, 26 Jun 1945. Entered into force, 24 Oct 1945. 1976 Y.B.U.N. 1043; *reprinted in* 1 Weston & Carlson I.A.1: Arts. 55 & 56** (Basic Document 1.5).

3. **Universal Declaration of Human Rights, 10 Dec 1948, GA Res. 217A, UN GAOR, 3rd Sess., Pt. I, Resolutions, at 71, UN Doc. A/810 (1948); *reprinted in* 3 Weston & Carlson III.A.1: Arts. 3, 22, 25(1), 28, 29(1)** (Basic Document 3.3).

4. **International Covenant on Economic, Social and Cultural Rights. Concluded, 16 Dec 1966. Entered into force, 3 Jan 1976. 993 U.N.T.S. 3; *reprinted in* 3 Weston & Carlson III.A.2: Arts. 11(1) & (2)** (Basic Document 3.13).

5. **International Covenant on Civil and Political Rights. Concluded, 16 Dec 1966. Entered into force, 23 Mar 1976. 999 U.N.T.S. 171; *reprinted in* 3 Weston & Carlson III.A.3: Arts. 1 & 6** (Basic Document 3.14).

6. **Universal Declaration on the Eradication of Hunger and Malnutrition, Adopted by the UN World Food Conference, 16 Nov 1974. Report of the World Food Conference, Rome, UN Doc E/CONF. 65/20 (1974). *reprinted in* 3 Weston III.N.1** (Basic Document 3.18).

7. **Protocol Additional (No. II) to the Geneva Conventions of 12 August 1949, and Relating to the Protection of Victims of Non–International Armed Conflicts. Concluded, 8 Jun 1977. Entered into force, 7 Dec 1978. 1977 U.N.J.Y.B. 135; *reprinted in* 16 I.L.M. 1442 (1977) and 2 Weston & Carlson II.B.21: Arts. 4, 5, 7, 13, 14, 18** (Basic Document 2.32).

8. **Food Aid Convention. Concluded, 13 Apr 1999. Entered into force, 1 Jul 1999. 2073 U.N.T.S. 135; *reprinted in* 3 Weston & Carlson III.N.2: Arts I–IV, VII–XI, XIII–XIV, XX** (Basic Document 3.51).

9.   **Convention on the Rights of the Child. Concluded, 20 Nov 1989. Entered into force, 2 Sep 1990. GA Res. 44/25 (Annex), UN GAOR, 44th Sess., Supp. No. 49, at 166, UN Doc. A/RES/44/49 (1990); *reprinted in* 30 I.L.M. 1448 (1989) and 3 Weston & Carlson III.D.3: Arts. 1–6, 19, 24, 27, 37, 38** (Basic Document 3.32).

10.   **Additional Protocol to the American Convention on Human Rights in the Area of Economic, Social and Cultural Rights. Concluded, 17 Nov 1988. Entered into force, 16 Nov 1999. O.A.S.T.S. No. 69; *reprinted in* 28 I.L.M. 156 (1989) and 3 Weston & Carlson III.B.25: Art. 12** (Basic Document 3.29).

11.   **Vienna Declaration and Programme of Action, 25 Jun 1993, UN Doc. A/CONF.157/24 (Part I) (13 Oct 1993), at 20–46; *reprinted in* 32 I.L.M. 1661 (1993) and 3 Weston & Carlson III.U.2: § I, Art. 31** (Basic Document 3.40).

12.   **Rome Declaration on World Food Security and World Food Summit Plan of Action, 13 Nov 1996, FAO/SAD, W3613/E, 1998; *reprinted in* 3 Weston & Carlson III.N.1a: Commitments 1, 2, 5** (Basic Document 3.48).

13.   **UN General Assembly Resolution on the Right to Food, 15 Feb 2002, GA Res. 56/155, UN Doc. A/RES/56/155; *reprinted in* 3 Weston & Carlson III.N.3a** (Basic Document 3.54).

14.   **Declaration of World Food Security: *five years later*, 11–13 Jun 2002, at <http://www.fao.org/worldfoodsummit/english/index. html>; *reprinted in* 3 Weston & Carlson III.N.4: ¶ ¶ 3, 6, 7, 18** (Basic Document 3.55).

15.   **Philip Alston, "International Law and the Human Right to Food," in The Right To Food 9, 13–14, 38–39, 42–43 (P. Alston & K. Tomasevski eds., 1984).**

The right to adequate food is already an integral part of the existing structure of contemporary international law, whether we approach it from the perspective of those principles dealing with food or of those relating to human rights. It is important to note, however, that in practice the convergence between these two sets of principles is extremely limited.

In the area of international law dealing with food, the proposition that the continuation of widespread hunger in the world is unacceptable and the notion that individuals have a right not to die from hunger and not to suffer (either physically or mentally) from malnutrition (*i.e.*, that they have a right to food), have long been accepted by the international community. Whether in the context of global statements of policy such as the [1974] Universal Declaration on the Eradication of Hunger and Malnutrition **[Basic Document 3.18]** or the strategy for the Third United Nations Development Decade or in specific instruments such as the Food Aid Convention **[Basic Document 3.51]**[b] or through institutional arrangements such as those relating to

b.   At the time of writing, the author was referring to the Food Aid Convention of 6 Mar 1980, 32 U.S.T. 5753, T.I.A.S. No. 10015, which since has been superseded and replaced by the Food Aid Convention of 13 Apr 1999 **(Basic Document 3.51)**, cited as Reading 8, *supra*, which in turn is designated, per Art. XXVI, as one of the "constituent instruments of the International Grains Agreement, 1995," 1882 U.N.T.S. 195.

FAO [Food and Agriculture Organization], IFAD [International Fund for Agricultural Development], or the WFC [World Food Council], all states have unambiguously committed themselves to these principles. As in all areas of law, the fact that their actions are not always consistent with the obligations thereby assumed does not in itself contradict the validity of the basic principles. Rather it points to the need to devise more effective means by which to increase the account-ability of states to ensure the consistency of their rhetoric with their actions in this domain.

* * *

In the area of international law dealing with human rights the right to food is equally firmly entrenched as a basic norm. Whether on the basis of treaty obligations, of customary international law principles, or of established practice, all states in the international community have recognized the existence of the right to adequate food. Indeed, in many respects, the human rights regime provides the essential ethical framework within which the policy governing specific issue areas in international law should evolve. . . .

[*Eds.*—The author goes on to discuss the existing international human rights instruments formally recognizing the right to food. He includes in his discussion: Articles 55 and 56 of the United Nations Charter **(Basic Document 1.5)**; Articles 3, 22, 28, and 29 of the Universal Declaration of Human Rights **(Basic Document 3.3)**; Articles 1 and 6 of the International Covenant on Civil and Political Rights **(Basic Document 3.14)**; Article 26 of the 1949 Geneva Convention (III) Relative to the Treatment of Prisoners of War **(Basic Document 2.11)**; Article 55 of the 1949 Geneva Convention (IV) Relative to the Protection of Civilian Persons in Time of War **(Basic Document 2.12)**; Articles 14 and 18(2) of the 1977 Protocol Additional II to the 1949 Geneva Conventions **(Basic Document 2.32)**; Paragraph 20(1) of the Standard Minimum Rules for the Treatment of Prisoners **(Basic Document 3.7)**; Article 11 of the European Social Charter **(Basic Document 3.11)**; and Article 11 of the International Covenant on Economic, Social and Cultural Rights **(Basic Document 3.13)**, discussed in detail in the next two ensuing readings. The author continues with a discussion of Covenant Article 11, as follows:]

Clearly the obligation does not require that a State should expend resources . . . it does not have or that it is bound to spend all its resources on satisfying these rights. Nevertheless it does comport [with] some freely accepted limitations on the State Party's freedom to allocate its resources, and also accords a degree of priority, over and above other goals, to promotion of the rights specifically proclaimed in the Covenant. This does not necessarily mean that an authoritative statement can be made as to a State Party's duties in a particular situation. For example, if a State's total resources are sufficient to ensure full domestic realization of the right to food, is it entitled under the terms of the Covenant to opt instead to devote its resources to other objectives such as building nuclear power facilities or luxury hotels, or reinforcing its military strength at the expense of causing hunger? Or can a government say: yes, there are people starving who could be fed but the country's need for foreign exchange earnings compels us to export food crops? Obviously there are no easy answers in practice to such questions although there may be situations which cannot under any reasonable interpretation be justified, when judged against the obligations assumed under the Covenant. In this respect, the government is accountable to its people for the manner in which it allocates its resources and for the consequences of such allocations in terms of food availability. Moreover, these allocations may justifiably be taken into account by other States and by the international community in assessing what is required in the circumstances to satisfy their obligation to provide assistance to the State concerned to ensure realization of the right to food.

The obligation of States Parties under article 2 and 11 is not, however, only a question of appropriate budgetary allocations. Although the Covenant does not contain any provision which is equivalent to article 2 of the International Covenant on Civil and Political Rights **[Basic Document 3.14]** which specifically requires States to take "necessary" legislative and other measures, it is reasonable to assume on the basis of the *travaux préparatoires* and of the practice of States in their reports under the Covenant that the "steps" required to be taken include the adoption of some type of legislative, executive and/or administrative measures oriented specifically towards the realization of the right in question. The validity of such an emphasis on the role of law is also confirmed by the provisions of: article 2(2) whereby States Parties "undertake to guarantee" the exercise of the relevant rights without discrimination on certain grounds; article 3 by which States Parties "undertake to ensure the equal right of men and women to the enjoyment" of the relevant rights; and article 4 whereby limitations on the enjoyment of rights are restricted to those "determined by law." In addition, article 11(1) commits States Parties to "take appropriate steps to ensure the realization of this right."

* * *

A duty of a different type ... is the duty of governments to seek international assistance in situations where widespread starvation would otherwise occur. The relevance of this duty was most dramatically illustrated in Ethiopia in early 1973 when the government of Emperor Haile Selassie sought to avoid adverse publicity by refusing to acknowledge the existence of a serious famine. As a result hundreds of thousands of people are estimated to have died. In analyzing how such a tragedy could have been permitted to happen [Stephen J.] Green has written:

> Perhaps the most serious crime that a government can commit, short of a campaign of genocide against its own people, is consciously to ignore the existence of a major disaster, or knowingly to deny the needed relief.... And yet, for this most serious of crimes, there is no international remedy, nor even any means of calling attention to it.[1]

Although [Green] was writing before the entry into force of the Covenant, his analysis would probably be the same today. However, at least in theory, the Covenant does provide a mechanism by which attention could be called to such a serious violation of a State Party's duties under the Covenant.

16. Committee on Economic, Social and Cultural Rights, General Comment 12: *The Right to Adequate Food (Art.11),* **UN Doc. E/C.12/1999/5 (20th session, 1999).**

1. S. Green, *Afterword, in* The Politics of Starvation 87 (J. Shepherd ed. 1975).

1.   The human right to adequate food is recognized in several instruments under international law. The International Covenant on Economic, Social and Cultural Rights deals more comprehensively than any other instrument with this right.... The human right to adequate food is of crucial importance for the enjoyment of all rights. It applies to everyone; thus the reference in Article 11.1 to "himself and his family" does not imply any limitation upon the applicability of this right to individuals or to female-headed households.

* * *

4.   The Committee affirms that the right to adequate food is indivisibly linked to the inherent dignity of the human person and is indispensable for the fulfilment of other human rights enshrined in the International Bill of Human Rights. It is also inseparable from social justice, requiring the adoption of appropriate economic, environmental and social policies, at both the national and international levels, oriented to the eradication of poverty and the fulfilment of all human rights for all.

5.   Despite the fact that the international community has frequently reaffirmed the importance of full respect for the right to adequate food, a disturbing gap still exists between the standards set in article 11 of the Covenant and the situation prevailing in many parts of the world. More than 840 million people throughout the world, most of them in developing countries, are chronically hungry; millions of people are suffering from famine as the result of natural disasters, the increasing incidence of civil strife and wars in some regions and the use of food as a political weapon. The Committee observes that while the problems of hunger and malnutrition are often particularly acute in developing countries, malnutrition, under-nutrition and other problems which relate to the right to adequate food and the right to freedom from hunger, also exist in some of the most economically developed countries. Fundamentally, the roots of the problem of hunger and malnutrition are not lack of food but lack of *access to* available food, *inter alia* because of poverty, by large segments of the world's population.

6.   The right to adequate food is realized when every man, woman and child, alone or in community with others, has physical and economic access at all times to adequate food or means for its procurement. The *right to adequate food* shall therefore not be interpreted in a narrow or restrictive sense which equates it with a minimum package of calories, proteins and other specific nutrients. The *right to adequate food* will have to be realized progressively. However, States have a core obligation to take the necessary action to mitigate and alleviate hunger as provided for in paragraph 2 of article 11, even in times of natural or other disasters.

Adequacy and sustainability of food availability and access

7.   The concept of *adequacy* is particularly significant in relation to the right to food since it serves to underline a number of factors which must be taken into account in determining whether particular foods or diets that are accessible can be considered the most appropriate under given circumstances for the purposes of article 11 of the Covenant. The notion of *sustainability* is intrinsically linked to the notion of adequate food or food *security*, implying food being accessible for both present and future generations. The precise

meaning of "adequacy" is to a large extent determined by prevailing social, economic, cultural, climatic, ecological and other conditions, while "sustainability" incorporates the notion of long-term availability and accessibility.

8. The Committee considers that the core content of the right to adequate food implies:

The availability of food in a quantity and quality sufficient to satisfy the dietary needs of individuals, free from adverse substances, and acceptable within a given culture;

The accessibility of such food in ways that are sustainable and that do not interfere with the enjoyment of other human rights.

9. *Dietary needs* implies that the diet as a whole contains a mix of nutrients for physical and mental growth, development and maintenance, and physical activity that are in compliance with human physiological needs at all stages throughout the life cycle and according to gender and occupation. Measures may therefore need to be taken to maintain, adapt or strengthen dietary diversity and appropriate consumption and feeding patterns, including breast-feeding, while ensuring that changes in availability and access to food supply as a minimum do not negatively affect dietary composition and intake.

10. *Free from adverse substances* sets requirements for food safety and for a range of protective measures by both public and private means to prevent contamination of foodstuffs through adulteration and/or through bad environmental hygiene or inappropriate handling at different stages throughout the food chain; care must also be taken to identify and avoid or destroy naturally occurring toxins.

11. *Cultural or consumer acceptability* implies the need also to take into account, as far as possible, perceived non nutrient-based values attached to food and food consumption and informed consumer concerns regarding the nature of accessible food supplies.

12. *Availability* refers to the possibilities either for feeding oneself directly from productive land or other natural resources, or for well functioning distribution, processing and market systems that can move food from the site of production to where it is needed in accordance with demand.

13. *Accessibility* encompasses both economic and physical accessibility:

Economic accessibility implies that personal or household financial costs associated with the acquisition of food for an adequate diet should be at a level such that the attainment and satisfaction of other basic needs are not threatened or compromised.... Socially vulnerable groups such as landless persons and other particularly impoverished segments of the population may need attention through special programmes.

Physical accessibility implies that adequate food must be accessible to everyone, including physically vulnerable individuals, such as infants and young children, elderly people, the physically disabled, the terminally ill and persons with persistent medical problems, including the mentally ill. Victims of natural disasters, people living in disaster-prone areas and other specially disadvantaged groups may need special attention and sometimes priority consideration with respect to accessibility of food. A particular vulnerability is that of many indigenous population groups whose access to their ancestral lands may be threatened.

14. The nature of the legal obligations of States parties are set out in article 2 of the Covenant. . . . The principal obligation is to take steps to achieve *progressively* the full realization of the right to adequate food. This imposes an obligation to move as expeditiously as possible towards that goal. Every State is obliged to ensure for everyone under its jurisdiction access to the minimum essential food which is sufficient, nutritionally adequate and safe, to ensure their freedom from hunger.

15. The right to adequate food, like any other human right, imposes three types or levels of obligations on States parties: the obligations to *respect*, to *protect* and to *fulfil*. In turn, the obligation to *fulfil* incorporates both an obligation to *facilitate* and an obligation to *provide*. The obligation to *respect* existing access to adequate food requires States parties not to take any measures that result in preventing such access. The obligation to *protect* requires measures by the State to ensure that enterprises or individuals do not deprive individuals of their access to adequate food. The obligation to *fulfil (facilitate)* means the State must pro-actively engage in activities intend-ed to strengthen people's access to and utilization of resources and means to ensure their livelihood, including food security. Finally, whenever an individu-al or group is unable, for reasons beyond their control, to enjoy the right to adequate food by the means at their disposal, States have the obligation to *fulfil (provide)* that right directly. This obligation also applies for persons who are victims of natural or other disasters.

16. Some measures at these different levels of obligations of States parties are of a more immediate nature, while other measures are more of a long-term character, to achieve progressively the full realization of the right to food.

17. Violations of the Covenant occur when a State fails to ensure the satisfaction of, at the very least, the minimum essential level required to be free from hunger. In determining which actions or omissions amount to a violation of the right to food, it is important to distinguish the inability from the unwillingness of a State party to comply. Should a State party argue that resource constraints make it impossible to provide access to food for those who are unable by themselves to secure such access, the State has to demonstrate that every effort has been made to use all the resources at its disposal in an effort to satisfy, as a matter of priority, those minimum obligations. This follows from Article 2.1 of the Covenant, which obliges a State party to take the necessary steps to the maximum of its available resources. . . . A State claiming that it is unable to carry out its obligation for reasons beyond its control therefore has the burden of proving that this is the case and that it has unsuccessfully sought to obtain international support to ensure the availability and accessibility of the necessary food.

18. Furthermore, any discrimination in access to food, as well as to means and entitlements for its procurement, on the grounds of race, colour, sex, language, age, religion, political or other opinion, national or social origin, property, birth or other status with the purpose or effect of nullifying or impairing the equal enjoyment or exercise of economic, social and cultural rights constitutes a violation of the Covenant.

19.   Violations of the right to food can occur through the direct action of States or other entities insufficiently regulated by States. These include: the formal repeal or suspension of legislation necessary for the continued enjoyment of the right to food; denial of access to food to particular individuals or groups, whether the discrimination is based on legislation or is pro-active; the prevention of access to humanitarian food aid in internal conflicts or other emergency situations; adoption of legislation or policies which are manifestly incompatible with pre-existing legal obligations relating to the right to food; and failure to regulate activities of individuals or groups so as to prevent them from violating the right to food of others, or the failure of a State to take into account its international legal obligations regarding the right to food when entering into agreements with other States or with international organizations.

20.   While only States are parties to the Covenant and are thus ultimately accountable for compliance with it, all members of society—individuals, families, local communities, non-governmental organizations, civil society organizations, as well as the private business sector—have responsibilities in the realization of the right to adequate food. The State should provide an environment that facilitates implementation of these responsibilities. The private business sector—national and transnational—should pursue its activities within the framework of a code of conduct conducive to respect of the right to adequate food, agreed upon jointly with the Government and civil society.

21.   The most appropriate ways and means of implementing the right to adequate food will inevitably vary significantly from one State party to another. Every State will have a margin of discretion in choosing its own approaches, but the Covenant clearly requires that each State party take whatever steps are necessary to ensure that everyone is free from hunger and as soon as possible can enjoy the right to adequate food. This will require the adoption of a national strategy to ensure food and nutrition security for all, based on human rights principles that define the objectives, and the formulation of policies and corresponding benchmarks. It should also identify the resources available to meet the objectives and the most cost-effective way of using them.

* * *

36.   In the spirit of article 56 of the Charter of the United Nations, the specific provisions contained in articles 11, 2.1, and 23 of the Covenant and the Rome Declaration of the World Food Summit, States parties should recognize the essential role of international cooperation and comply with their commitment to take joint and separate action to achieve the full realization of the right to adequate food. . . .

37.   States parties should refrain at all times from food embargoes or similar measures which endanger conditions for food production and access to food in other countries. Food should never be used as an instrument of political and economic pressure. In this regard, the Committee recalls its position, stated in its General Comment No. 8, on the relationship between economic sanctions and respect for economic, social and cultural rights.

17.   Dinah L. Shelton, "The Duty to Assist Famine Victims," 70 Iowa L. Rev. 1309, 1311, 1313–19 (1985).

. . . That food aid is available is undeniable: "If total world food supplies were divided equally—all food grown divided in equal portions—there would be plenty for everyone, with some to spare."[1] Nonetheless, food security is established on a precarious basis. While food reserves exist in wealthier developed countries, governmental policies may prevent those reserves from being tapped. Elsewhere, food reserves may be available only at prices too high to meet the needs of the poor. Often, reserves are established as part of domestic agricultural policies, without regard to the needs of famine areas. In times of scarcity, reserves come under the control of private exporters or of exporting countries, in which governments have at best only a secondary interest in ensuring that the hungry poor receive adequate food.

The question then arises whether there is an international right to food and whether that right imposes an obligation on states that have food surpluses to assist those states facing famine, by directly assisting them in the short-term and contributing to a global reserve system in the long-term. In answering these questions, recourse [may] be made not only to positive international law expressed in treaties and declarations, but also to general principles of law reflected in common provisions of national legislation throughout the world.

* * *

The exact dimensions of each state's duties, either domestically or internationally, have not been developed. In formulating proposals, one source of international legal obligations is "the general principles of law recognized by civilized nations." Although this language has been uniformly interpreted by neither the International Court [of Justice] nor commentators, it may allow application of laws and principles common to many countries.[2]

If application of principles of municipal law is an acceptable means of enforcing broad legal obligations such as those flowing from the right to food, then the question arises whether a duty to rescue constitutes a "general principle of law" within the terms of article 38 of the [Statute of the] International Court. If such a duty constitutes a general principle of law within article 38, the next question is whether the duty may be extended to economic circumstances such as starvation, or whether the duty must be limited to immediate, noneconomic perils such as assault or traffic accidents.

Continental legal systems, following the tradition of Roman law, generally require assistance to those in peril and provide criminal and civil penalties for violators. Such statutes exist in Belgium, China, France, Germany, Italy, Denmark, Hungary, [the former] Czechoslovakia, the Netherlands, Norway, Poland, Portugal, Romania, Switzerland, the [the former] USSR, and Turkey. The obligation applies to strangers and is not fault based. The French statute is typical: anyone who abstains from rendering assistance to a person in peril when he could do so without risk to himself or to third parties may be

---

1. National Committee for World Food Day Hunger Primer 5 (1984). . . .

2. *E.g.,* Temple of Preah Vihear (Cambodia v. Thailand), 1962 ICJ 6, 26, 31–32 [15 Jun];

The Diversion of Water from the Meuse (Netherlands v. Belgium) **[Basic Document 7.2]**; Factory at Chorzow, 1928 P.C.I.J., ser. A, No. 17, at 32 [13 Sep]. . . .

punished by up to five years in prison and a fine of 20,000 French francs. The duty applies if the peril is constant and necessitates immediate intervention, regardless of its cause or nature.

Common-law jurisdictions have shown more hostility toward imposing a duty to rescue on strangers. In American law the traditional view, expressed in the *Restatement of Torts*, provides that "[t]he fact that the actor realizes or should realize that action on his part is necessary for another's aid or protection does not of itself impose upon him a duty to take such action." American courts originally adopted a strict no-duty rule, describing the rescuer as "a mere volunteer" or "officious intermeddler" and sometimes imposed damages for actions undertaken. . . .

* * *

American courts have carved out three exceptions to the no duty rule, when: (1) the rescuer created the peril, either innocently or negligently; (2) the rescuer has undertaken to assist, creating reliance on further aid; or (3) the relationship between the individuals involved leads to an expectation of assistance. These relationships often are found on the basis of economic circumstances or positions of trust and are particularly easy to impose where the duty-holder derives an advantage from the relationship.

* * *

Generally, courts have not applied the duty to assist, either statutorily or through common law, to situations of economic peril. The language in statutes and cases, however, does not appear to preclude such application. Thus, it may not be unreasonable to extend the duty to assist to the case of starving individuals, depending on how one distinguishes that case from cases in which the duty has been applied. Are the objections overcome if the duty is imposed on states in international context rather than on individuals within a community?

International instruments provide a right to food and require states to establish a legal order, both nationally and internationally, in which the right may be exercised. This framework could support the enforcement of a duty to assist famine victims. Yet, it is sometimes asserted that economic rights are positive in nature and, therefore, either are not true rights or are less important than negative civil and political rights. . . .

The concepts of positive and negative rights—action and inaction—are considerably intertwined. Civil rights, generally considered to be negative, may impose extensive positive obligations. For example, the right to a fair trial requires appointing judges and administrators, building courtrooms, and acquiring juries. Conversely, a positive right, such as the right to food, may in some instances be implemented passively by simply not interfering with a population's ability to produce or otherwise acquire food. Thus, the right does not absolutely determine the nature of the duty.

* * *

The purpose of a basic right is to provide a shield, some minimal protection against helplessness, for those unable to protect themselves. It is a social guarantee to fulfill a basic need and acts as a restraint on economic and political power. . . . Rights are basic when the enjoyment of all other rights depends on their fulfillment. The right to food, as part of the right to life and personal security, is such a basic right. . . .

* * *

The argument that it is impossible to determine the scope of the obligation loses force in the economic arena if the obligation is societal (and international) rather than individual. A system of world food reserves based on annual yield would allocate the duty equitably among those actually in a position to assist. The duty then clearly would shift from year to year as production and climates change. Of course, whether based on potential production or actual production, allocation decisions would be difficult. Such a system, however, would support the internationally recognized right to food and implement the correlative duty to assist, by applying principles already recognized in legal systems throughout the world.

Even the restrictive common-law rule of causation, reliance, and special relationship could support a duty to assist famine victims. When developed countries' trade and aid policies have contributed to agricultural policies that have exacerbated the effects of natural disasters and contributed to famine contributions, those countries should recognize a duty to assist the victims of the peril they helped to create. Countries that have made food aid pledges have induced reliance that would support a duty even under common law. Additionally, former colonial countries may owe a particular duty based on their relationship to their former colonies. In sum, the three recognized exceptions to the common-law, no-duty rule can be found in the case of famine and would therefore support implementation of a duty to assist famine victims. Furthermore, common-law countries have increasingly recognized a general duty to rescue, perhaps because the early common-law approach, which denied a duty to assist as well as any recovery to an injured rescuer (who even might be held liable for any damage caused), "could hardly have encouraged altruism."[4]

Finally, the question of allocating risk must be addressed. . . . More specifically, the question arises whether individuals should be forced to assume the risk of starvation when food surplus countries have contributed to famine through their trade and other economic policies. By having recognized the right to food, the international community no longer asks individuals to bear the risk of starvation. Implementing a duty to assist would contribute to the fulfillment of this right by alleviating famine conditions. Because the duty to assist those in peril is recognized in most non-common-law countries and has increasingly been given effect in common-law jurisdictions, this doctrine justifies requiring famine relief as part of an international implementation of the right to food.

18. Robert L. Bard, "The Right to Food," 70 Iowa L. Rev. 1279, 1287–90 (1985).

Although the dominant American scholars of international law flatly reject the concept of international law as strictly limited to those rule systems that command explicit and continuing consent of the relevant objects of a rule, they do not dispute that this is one method of establishing binding and effective international law. But no advocate of the right to food claims that

---

4. A. Linden, *Rescuers and Good Samaritans*, 34 Mod. L. Rev. 241, 241 (1971).

such a right has been established by either of the two "conservative" methods of international lawmaking—development of a near-unanimous consensus or the adherence of the requisite number of countries to binding international convention.

The most authoritative international pronouncement in this regard is article 11 of the International Covenant on Economic, Social and Cultural Rights **[Basic Document 3.13]**. Section 1 of article 11 of this Covenant provides that "[t]he States Parties to the present Covenant recognize the right of everyone to an adequate standard of living for himself and his family, including adequate food, clothing and housing, and to the continuous improvement of living conditions." According to section 1 of article 2, these objectives are to be achieved by each state taking "steps, individually and through international assistance and co-operation, especially economic and technical, to the maximum of its available resources, with a view to achieving progressively the full realization of the rights recognized in the present Covenant by all appropriate means, including particularly the adoption of legislative measures."

The key phrase is "to the maximum of its available resources." How is the quality of resources for international and economic development purposes to be determined, and by whom? The availability language was inserted to prevent the Covenant from achieving legal status. As long as a country is taking any actions that arguably promote the economic well-being of other countries, it is meeting its obligations under this Covenant. Perhaps such a covenant could be deemed an example of "soft law"—establishing objectives but mandating no particular course of action.

The peculiar nature of the Covenant on Economic Rights is highlighted by comparing it with the International Covenant on Civil and Political Rights **[Basic Document 3.14]**. . . . The sharp contrast between economic rights on the one hand, and political and civil rights on the other hand, is quite clear. Political and civil rights concern the kinds of restraints on government that are commonplace in any society recognizing individual rights. The right to food belongs to a second category of international obligations—obligations that consist of pledges to take actions to more equitably share the world's resources.

The United States has signed both covenants, but has ratified [only the International Covenant on Civil and Political Rights]. Therefore, the establishment of a right to food faces two formidable obstacles: it attempts to establish an international system of economic redistribution rather than imposing limits on governmental assertions of power against individuals, and it lacks the consent of one of the essential contributors to any effort to guarantee a universal minimum standard of living. But even if the United States were to ratify the Covenant on Economic, Social and Cultural Rights, the obligations regarding food under article 11 fall short of a legally cognizable right to food. In any case, no right to food has been accepted explicitly by a sufficient number of nations as a binding rule to be established as a rule by the customary process of international law. Therefore, unless rules of international law can be imposed on nations without their consent, no such rule exists. Moreover, one of the strongest reasons for limiting international law to consensually developed rules is that, absent any universally recognized rule-making and rule-implementing authorities, a plausible case can be made for a wide array of rules of international law based on morality, convenience, or necessity. Such a rulemaking system simply does not provide the reliability of response by appropriate power-wielders necessary to produce those expectations of official behavior that are essential to legal arrangements.

Not only does no right to food exist, but it is unlikely that one can be established. That is, both poor and wealthy nations are unlikely to subject themselves to law-based claims of either their own citizens or foreign governments pertaining to access to food. The reluctance of wealthy nations to accept any *formal* economic or welfare obligations toward the poor not only is well established by conduct, but is inherent in the existing international political order. Poor countries have long been trying to persuade or coerce the rich to make formal commitments to share the rich nations' advantages, most recently in the campaign for the New International Economic Order. Western nations have resisted such efforts, and they will likely continue to resist. As previously noted, asserting a duty on the rich to guarantee adequate food for the poor is a welfare concept, and few nations have achieved a guaranteed, minimally accepted life for their people. Extending it to foreigners is grossly utopian. This does not mean that individual nations will not recognize obligations to less fortunate nations, only that they will refuse to accept this as a legally imposed obligation. Nation-states will insist on a right to retain absolute discretion in determining the level of their contribution to world welfare requirements.

Economically developed countries would not be alone in their resistance to the establishment of a right to food. Third World countries might be happy to impose legal requirements on other nations toward themselves, but they will strongly resist any legal norms that obligate them to their own citizens. The current situation in Africa demonstrates why nations will resist recognizing a right to food. The press contains numerous allegations that the governments of particular famine-stricken nations are to some degree responsible for the terrible plight of their citizens. Some nations have been accused of spending excessive amounts for arms, others of using famine relief for political purposes. Accusations of inefficiency and graft in distributing food aid are common. In some cases, countries have been accused of deliberately concealing the existence of famine to avoid political embarrassment. In defense, the accused countries claim that they are doing their best under the most difficult circumstances.

Poor nations that attempt to meet unlimited needs with scant resources would resist any attempt to establish legal standards to be applied to their responses to their citizens' needs. But legal duties must be expressed in terms of rules. Otherwise they cannot serve to guide conduct and are not subject to adjudicatory processes. No such rules can be formulated regarding a right to food. Most important, nations would hesitate to render themselves liable to such determinations, because their only gain would be the possibility of imposing similar requirements on other countries. But the risks of being the object of such claims would exceed the benefits of acquiring the power to subject other nations to similar restrictions.

SECTION 5.   DISCUSSION NOTES/QUESTIONS

1.   Famine has afflicted African countries on many occasions: in Biafra in the late 1960s, in Ethiopia and Sudan in the mid–1970s to early–1980s, in Mozambique and Angola in the mid-to late–1980s, Somalia, on the eastern edge of the horn of Africa, in 1991–92, Darfur in Sudan in 2004. What have been the causes of the Sub–Saharan food crises? According to Cheryl Christensen and Charles Hanrahan, *African Food Crises: Short-, Medium-, and Long–Term Responses*, 70 Iowa L. Rev. 1293, 1294 (1985), discussing the Sub–Saharan food crisis of the 1970s and 1980s, droughts and agricultural malpractices are among them:

> The [Sub–Saharan] food crisis illustrate[d] the region's vulnerability to erratic rainfall patterns. For the most part African agriculture is highly dependent on rainfall; irrigation is not widely practiced. Successive drought years not only reduce[d] crop production but also deplete[d] food stocks with little possibility of replenishment. Drought can be particularly hard on nomadic peoples heavily dependent on cereals, which creates both higher import requirements and delivery problems.

* * *

> ... [F]ood problems in Sub–Saharan Africa also result from a number of long-run problems in African agriculture. Sub–Saharan Africa is the only region in the world where food production per capita ... declin[ed] over the ... decades [1965–85].... If the total amount of food available [had been] distributed equally, there would not [have been] enough to provide everyone with an adequate diet.

But as Christensen and Hanrahan further point out, at *id.*, Sub–Saharan famines have been due also to political and social unrest, including civil war:

> The African food situation [was] also complicated by civil war.... [A]rmed conflict in Chad, Ethiopia, and Mozambique, three of the most seriously drought-affected countries in the region, additionally burden[ed] these already vulnerable countries. Unsettled political conditions ... triggered refugee movements that complicate[d] logistics and [made] the delivery of emergency food aid more difficult and costly. Political conflict in one country often causes food problems to spill over into other countries, as in the case of refugees from Ethiopia's northern provinces who ... crossed the border into Sudan to seek relief from both food shortages and political strife.

The International Crisis Group, an NGO, has documented the political uses of famine in many of its reports on Africa. *See, e.g.,* Sudan: Now or Never in Darfur (23 May 2004), *available at* <http://www.crisisweb.org>.

2.   Who is entitled to claim the right to food? Individuals? Groups? Whole populations? The state? Does it matter? Consider the following extract from Philip Alston, former first chair of the UN Committee on Economic, Social and Cultural Rights, in *International Law and the Right to Food*, in Food as a Human Right 162, 168–69 (A. Eide, W. Eide, S. Goohatilake, J. Gusson & Onawale eds., 1984):

> The principal holders of the right to food under the terms of article 11 [of the International Covenant on Economic, Social and Cultural Rights **(Basic Document 3.13)**] are individuals. The right of individuals is formulated in terms of "the right of everyone." Whereas subparagraph 2 uses only this phrase, the terminology used in sub-paragraph 1 is "the right of everyone ... for himself [sic] and his [sic] family." The question which then arises is to

what exactly is the individual entitled? In practical terms, the answer will depend on the circumstances of the individual and of his or her geographical location at a given time. From the present perspective the most important point is to recognize the need to develop, at the national level, a set of relevant legal norms which reflects and seeks to satisfy the state's international legal obligation to promote realization of the right of everyone to adequate food.

Another level at which one can identify a holder of the right to food is that of the state. Whether this is a collective right attaching directly to peoples or to states or whether it is rather an aggregation of the human rights of individuals which is articulated through the medium of the state is an important theoretical question, but it is of limited practical relevance in the present context.

Article 11 does not specifically identify states as holders of the right to food. Nevertheless by imposing duties upon states to act, "through international co-operation," the article implicitly vests rights in certain states as a corollary of the duty of all states to act. Moreover, in practical terms, the obligation of states parties "to ensure an equitable distribution of world food supplies in relation to need" can only be operationalized on an inter-state basis. The shield (or the sword) of state sovereignty severely restricts the possibility of implementing such an obligation at any other level.

Assuming Professor Alston is correct in his analysis, can it be legitimately concluded that every individual or every state has an equal claim to assert the right to food as against, respectively, all other individuals or states? If not, which individuals might have a greater claim? Which states? What criteria would be determinative? Also, if all individuals or states do not have an equal claim, what does it means to speak of international human rights as being in some way "universal"? For helpful guidance, see George Kent, Freedom from Want: The Human Right to Adequate Food (2005); _____, *Food Is A Human Right*, in Human Rights in the World Community: Issues and Action (R. Claude & B. Weston eds., 3rd ed. 2006).

3. Can the right to food be considered part of customary international law? Robert Bard, Reading 18, *supra*, argues that the right does not have this status. However, as noted by the ICJ in the *Nicaragua Case* (excerpted in Chapter 2 (p. 117), resolutions of international organizations can be evidence of both state practice and *opinio juris*. Consider the jurisprudential impact of UN Security Council resolutions dealing with the right to food, such as Resolution 1472 (2003) on the UN's "oil for food" program in Iraq, as well as General Assembly resolutions, such as that contained in Reading 13 *supra*. For helpful guidance, see George Kent, *Food Is A Human Right*, in Human Rights in the World Community: Issues and Action (R. Claude & B. Weston eds., 3rd ed. 2006). *See also* Anthony P. Kearns, *The Right to Food Exists Via Customary International Law* 22 Suffolk Transnat'l L. Rev. 223 (1998). A useful timeline on the development of the right to food has been prepared by the F.A.O. at <http://www.fao.org/Legal/rtf/time-e.htm>.

4. Assuming there is a right to food, who are the duty-holders of the norm—that is, who is bound to make good on it? States in respect of their domestic populations? States in respect of foreign populations? Individuals? Corporations? The international community via multilateral organizations? Anyone? There is much debate among international lawyers about the nature of the duty imposed by economic, social and cultural rights. In theory, says Philip Alston (*supra*

Reading 15), the 1966 Covenant on Economic, Social and Cultural Rights (ICESCR) does provide a mechanism—a periodic reporting system, monitored by the Committee on Economic, Social and Cultural Rights (CESCR), established by ECOSOC resolution rather than by the ICESCR itself)—through which attention could be called to so serious a violation of a state party's duties under the Covenant. These arrangements notwithstanding, however, the CESCR is not, at this writing, empowered to receive and adjudicate complaints of violations of the Covenant. "The absence of a direct complaints procedure," the CESCR has noted, "places significant constraints on the ability of the Committee to develop jurisprudence or case-law and, of course, greatly limits the chances of victims of abuses of the ICESCR obtaining international redress" (Office of the High Commissioner for Human Rights, Fact Sheet No.16 [Rev.1] § 8). Accordingly, write Burns H. Weston and Mark B. Teerink, *Abolishing Child Labor: A Multifaceted Human Rights Solution*, in Child Labor and Human Rights: Making Children Matter (2005), at 235,

> the CESCR has promoted for adoption an optional individual complaints protocol similar to the one provided for in the first Optional Protocol to the [Interneational Covenant on Cvivil and Political Rights (ICCPR)]. Thus far unsuccessfully, however, and as a consequence the CESCR has signaled that, "[p]ending the addition of an optional protocol, beneficiaries of the rights contained in the Covenant may still have recourse to the general procedures of the Committee, and may utilize what has been called an 'unofficial petition procedure' based on the modalities of the Committee." Also, the Committee has drawn up a "Plan of Action to Strengthen the Implementation of the International Covenant on Economic, Social and Cultural Rights" with emphasis on "substantive, analytical, expert, and general support (a) to facilitate the Committee's work with States parties in relation to the reporting process; (b) for the preparation of various substantive background papers to enable the Committee to contribute effectively to the various activities which it is increasingly being called upon to perform; [and] (c) to enable the Committee to work constructively with States parties and United Nations agencies and others in following up on its recommendations designed to enhance the realization of economic, social and cultural rights" [footnotes omitted].

The proposed optional protocol to which Weston and Teerink refer is available on the website of the Office of the High Commissioner for Human Rights (OHCHR) at <http://daccessdds.un.org/doc/UN-DOC/GEN/G04/120/29/PDF/G0412029.pdf? OpenElement>. For helpful discussion, see, *e.g.* Manfred Nowak, *The Need for an Optional Protocol to the International Covenant on Economic, Social and Cultural Rights*, 55 ICJ Rev. 153 (1995). In 2002, the UN Commission on Human Rights established an open-ended working group to consider the matter. *See* CHR Res. 2002/24 (22 Apr 2002) at ¶ 9(f). The vote was in the Commission was 44 in favor, one vote against (United States) and four abstentions (Australia, India, Japan and Pakistan). Proposals for an Optional Protocol are criticized in Michael J. Dennis & David P. Stewart, *Justiciability of Economic, Social and Cultural Rights: Should There Be An International Complaints Mechanism to Adjudicate the Rights to Food, Water, Health and Housing?*, 98 A.J.I.L. 462 (2004).

5. Assuming the right to adequate food has duty-holders, but in the absence of strong implementation measures under the International Covenant on Economic, Social and Cultural Rights (ICESCR), how does one enforce ICESCR norms against the states parties to the ICESCR? For helpful discussion bearing upon the related right to development, see Philip Alston & Gerard Quinn, *The Nature and*

Scope of States Parties' Obligations under the ICESCR, 9 H.R.Q. 156, 186–91 (1987). Consider also the following quotation by Algerian jurist Mohammed Bedjaoui, Judge and former President of the International Court of Justice, who advocates that all the world's food stocks that are essential to life, *i.e.*, principally grain stocks, be declared part of "the common heritage of mankind." He writes that it is necessary to do this "so as to guarantee every people the vital minimum of a bowl of rice or loaf of bread in order to eradicate the hunger which kills fifty million human beings a year. We are not suggesting this out of moral idealism but out of concern to avoid a dangerous impasse in international relations." Mohammed Bedjaoui, *The Right to Development*, in International Law: Achievements and Prospects 1177, 1196 (M. Bedjaoui ed., 1991). He continues, at 1196–97:

> Why, as the twentieth century, with its astounding technical and scientific progress and its present keen awareness of the interdependence of peoples, draws to a close, should not its thinking be equal to the ideas of the sixteenth century when lawyers such as the Spaniard Vitoria affirmed that the Christian Holy Scriptures intended "the goods of the earth" for "the whole of the human race", for "common use" and for "a universal purpose"? * * * Why ... should not the twentieth century also be equal to the spirituality of the seventh century when the Koran announced to all humankind that "all wealth, all things, belong to God" and thus to all members of the human community and that consequently the "Zakat", the act of charity, should be seen rather as a compulsory institutionalized act, a manifestation of human solidarity, making it every man's duty to give away one tenth of his wealth each year? * * * Is the twentieth century incapable of matching the principles of solidarity stated by the lawyer Emeric de Vattel in 1758 when he affirmed that each nation must contribute, by every means in its power, to the happiness and perfection of the others?

Bedjaoui then asks, at 1197, how the world's essential food stocks as part of the common heritage of mankind might come into being, and observes: "It is a matter for politicians, economists, lawyers and financiers to think about." What is your answer? Would you agree that a first step might be, as Bedjaoui goes on to suggest, an "international Fund for Food Stocks" funded by value-added taxes levied in each country of products manufactured from the raw materials of the developing world and/or by a one percent tax on all military budgets? Is such a suggestion realistic? What would be necessary to make it happen?

For suggestions on realizing the right to food, see George Kent, Freedom from Want: The Human Right to Adequate Food (2005); Asbjørn Eide, Arne Oshuag & Wench Barth Eide, *Food Security and the Right to Food in International Law and Development*, 1 Transnat'l L. & Contemp. Probs. 415, 448–67 (1991); Asbjorn Eide, *Strategies for the Realization of the Right to Food*, in Human Rights in the Twenty-first Century: A Global Challenge 459 (K. Mahoney & P. Mahoney eds., 1993). Norwegian expert Asbjørn Eide prepared a major update of an earlier study on the right to adequate food and freedom from hunger for the Sub–Commission on Prevention of Discrimination and Protection of Minorities (now the Sub–Commission on the Promotion and Protection of Human Rights) in 1999. *See* UN Doc. E/CN.4/Sub. 2/1999/12 (12 June 1999). For wide-ranging, and often provocative, discussion, see *Report of the International Committee on the Right to Food*, in International Law Association, Report of the Sixty-fourth Conference Held at Warsaw (1988).

In 1996, 185 states gathered at the World Food Summit, held in Rome, reaffirmed the right to food and committed to halve the number of people suffering from hunger by 2015 in the Rome Declaration **(Basic Document 3.48)**. In 2002, a follow-up "five years later" summit revealed that very little action had been taken on the 1996 commitments. At the 2002 meeting, while a proposal for a code of conduct on the right to food was rejected, governments undertook to devise voluntary guidelines for the implementation of the right to food. What might such guidelines contain? *See* UN High Commissioner for Human Rights, The Right to Food: Achievements and Challenges, World Food Summit: Five Years Later (2002).

6. In 2000, the UN Commission on Human Rights, appointed a Special Rapporteur on the Right to Food (C.H.R. Res. 2000/10). The inaugural Special Rapporteur is Jean Ziegler and his mandate is to receive information and highlight violations of the right to food, cooperate with the UN and civil society to realize the right to food, and identify emerging issues with respect to the right. The Special Rapporteur reports annually to both the Commission and to the UN General Assembly. Ziegler has made a series of country missions to assess the right to food and his reports are available at <http://www.righttofood.org>. In his statement to the 2002 meeting on the World Food Summit: Five Years Later, the Special Rapporteur stated:

> I am convinced that there are profound internal contradictions in the United Nations system. On the one hand, the UN agencies emphasise social justice and human rights. In Vienna, at the 1993 World Conference on Human Rights, member States proclaimed the importance of economic, social and cultural rights, including the right to food. UN agencies, including FAO, UNDP, UNICEF and the WFP and many others do excellent work in promoting development. On the other hand, the Bretton Woods Institutions, along with the Government of the United States of America and the World Trade Organisation oppose the right to food, prefering the Washington Consensus, which emphasises liberalisation, deregulation, privatisation, and the compression of State domestic budgets. A model which in many cases produces greater inequalities. As all the United Nations organisations, including the Bretton Woods institutions, have the obligation to report to the Economic and Social Council of the United Nations, I recommend that these contradictions be addressed by States that are Parties to both the human rights treaties and the financial institutions.

How might the contradictions identified by the Special Rapporteur be addressed? Responded to?

7. Food crises are likely to result in malnutrition and consequent widespread diseases. Consider extending the right to food to a more encompassing argument—the right to health care. A useful starting point is the Committee on Economic, Social and Cultural Rights, General Comment 14: *The Right to the Highest Attainable Standard of Health (Art. 12)*, E/C.12/2000/4 (22nd session, 2000). One writer suggests that health care includes, *inter alia*, public health, nutrition and medical treatment and "any benefits under it must be provided in a non-discriminatory fashion with concomitant universality of the right." Steven D. Jamar, *The International Human Right to Health*, 22 S. U. L. Rev. 1, 2 (1994). Explore this notion in light of the Djourab food crisis. Assuming there is a right to food, how might the arguments differ if that right is extended to embrace the right to health? Even if there were no international right to food and freedom from malnutrition, what arguments could be made in support of an international right to health that would include a right to food? How would such a right be recognized and enforced? Compare these issues with the perennial US health care

debate. What is "adequate" care? What about funding? What would be the role of health care providers? Of international and nongovernmental organizations? For further discussion, see Michle Jacquart, *Economic, Social and Cultural Rights*, in International Law: Achievements and Prospects 1083, 1087–90 (M. Bedjaoui ed., 1991); Audrey R. Chapman, *Conceptualizing the Right to Health: A Violations Approach*, 65 Tenn. L. Rev. 389 (1998); Eleanor D. Kinney, *The International Human Right to Health: What does this Mean for our Nation and World?* 34 Ind. L. Rev. 1457 (2001); Sheetal B. Shah, *Illuminating the Possible in the Developing World: Guaranteeing the Human Right to Health in India*, 32 Vand. J. Transnat'l L. 435 (1999).

8.   Hunger and malnutrition, as has been observed in these materials, is largely a result of "man-made" factors. Among these factors is the feminization of poverty or the marginalization of women, who otherwise could provide important and powerful tools to combat hunger and malnutrition. "The availability of food," writes Margaret Snyder in *Gender and the Food Regime: Some Transnational and Human Issues*, 1 Transnat'l L. & Contemp. Probs. 469, 504 (1991), "is increasingly dependent upon women's productivity and purchasing power, which in turn rests on their access to resources—technologies, land, and incomes. Until planners recognize and act on these facts, the global food regime cannot be equitable or efficient." For further discussion, see Christine M. Chinkin & Shelley Wright, *The Hunger Trap: Women, Food and Self–Determination*, 14 Mich. J. Int'l L. 262 (1993); Barbara Stark, *The "Other" Half of the International Bill of Rights as a Postmodern Feminist Text*, in Reconceiving Reality: Women and International Law 19 (D. Dallmeyer ed., 1993); Shelley Wright, *Economic Rights and Social Justice: A Feminist Analysis of Some International Human Rights Conventions*, 12 Aust'l YB Int;' L. 241 (1992). The 2002 UN General Assembly Resolution on the Right to Food **(Basic Document 3.54)** calls for the Commission on Human Rights' Special Rapporteur on the Right to Food to "mainstream a gender perspective in the activities relating to his mandate." What could "gender mainstreaming" mean in practical terms in this context? For an analysis of the problems associated with gender mainstreaming in the F.A.O., *see* Elizabeth Harrison, *Fish, Feminists and the FAO: Translating "Gender" Through Different Institutions in the Development Process*, in Getting Institutions Right for Women in Development 61 (A. Goetz ed., 1997).

9.   Is it justified to use food as a sanction, to punish behavior that violates the policies—particularly the clear policies—of the donor country? If so, when? In the past, the use of such a sanction has been for the most part ineffective. Would your answer be any different if it could be shown that the use of food as a sanction would positively influence oppressive regimes to move toward more democratic governance? Suppose, for example, that in the present problem Australia were to withhold food aid to Djourab on the grounds that the government of Djourab constituted a repressive, authoritarian regime inimical to the interests of Australia and the Djouraban people. According to articles I and VII–IX of the 1999 Food Aid Convention **(Basic Document 3.51)**, donor state Parties are not legally obligated to provide food aid, suggesting that Australia could lawfully refuse aid to Djourab if it so chose. But what about Article 11 of the 1966 International Covenant on Economic, Social and Cultural Rights **(Basic Document 3.13)** which requires the states parties to take "appropriate steps" to ensure the realization of the right to "adequate food"? Would not Article 11 prohibit Australia from using food as a weapon against Djourab? Is it clear? Consider the following extract from Philip Alston, *International Law and the Human Right to Food (supra,* in Reading 15), at 45–46:

The proliferating use in recent years of both unilaterally and multilaterally imposed restrictions on the sale or transfer of food to countries such as Iran, Poland, the [former] USSR and Afghanistan raises the question of the compatibility of such sanctions with existing international instruments. Morally, the use of food sanctions has long been frowned upon. Legally, the position is less clear, except with respect to the provisions of the Geneva Convention[s] **[Basic Documents 2.9, 2.10, 2.11, & 2.12]** which are applicable in times of war and with respect to economic warfare in general. In regard to the latter Whiteman has argued that economic warfare undertaken "with the purpose of upsetting . . . the world's food supply" is either an emerging or already existing peremptory norm of international law (*jus cogens*). However, the position with respect to limited sanctions against a particular government is more complex. In 1981 the General Assembly adopted the Declaration of the Inadmissibility of Intervention and Interference in the Internal Affairs of States **[Basic Document 2.36]** which "solemnly declares" *inter alia*: "the duty of a State not to use its external economic assistance programme or adopt any multilateral or unilateral economic reprisal or blockade and to prevent the use of transnational and multinational corporations under its jurisdiction and control as instruments of political pressure or coercion against another State. . . ."

But since that controversial Declaration, the soundness of which is highly questionable in terms of international law, was adopted with 6 recorded abstentions and 22 "no" votes (mainly OECD member States) it is far from being determinative of the issue. However in another resolution, adopted later in the same session by consensus, the Assembly reaffirmed "that food is a universal human right . . . and, in that context, stresses its belief in the general principle that food should not be used as an instrument of political pressure."[5] By contrast, although the 1947 General Agreement on Tariffs and Trade is generally designed to outlaw discriminatory trade measures, Article XXI nevertheless preserves the right of a contracting party to take "any action which it considers necessary for the protection of its essential security interests . . . taken in time of war or other emergency in international relations."

The position under the [International] Covenant [on Economic, Social and Cultural Rights **(Basic Document 2.13)**] is similar although slightly more restrictive. The duties under article 11, which include the duty to cooperate internationally to promote realization of the right to food, may be derogated from only in accordance with article 4. That article is however not formulated in such a way as to provide an indication of the legitimacy or otherwise of sanctions unless the sanctioning state could claim that its actions are for the purpose of promoting the general welfare in a democratic state (*e.g.* upholding national security?). In reality, international law as reflected in the Covenant and elsewhere is unlikely to be the deciding factor in a situation involving sanctions. Nevertheless the duty to co-operate and the specific provisions of article 11, both support the view that there is a general duty not to use food as an international sanction and never to do so in cases where starvation and death are inevitable consequences.

5.　GA Res 36/185, UN GAOR, 36th Sess., Supp. No. 51, at 118, UN Doc. A/36/51 (1981), ¶ 10.

In light of the authorities he cites, is Professor Alston justified in concluding that "there is a general duty not to use food as an international sanction and never to do so in cases where starvation and death are inevitable consequences"? Why? Why not?

10.   What if the Djourab government had denied the North Province access to a usable water supply? Would its international legal obligations be the same? What if the Djourab government did not actively withhold water, but refused to provide relief during a drought? Do state populations possess a right of access to water? Domestic populations only? The Committee on Economic, Social and Cultural Rights has adopted a General Comment on the Right to Water which elaborates its elements: General Comment 15, *The Right to Water (Arts. 11 and 12)*, E/C.12/2002/11 (29th session, 2002). *See also* Mélanne Andromecca Civic, *A Comparative Analysis of the Israeli and Arab Water Law Traditions and Insights for Modern Water Sharing Agreements*, 26 Denv. J. Int'l L. & Pol'y 437 (1998); Stephen C. McCaffrey, *A Human Right to Water: Domestic and International Implications*, 5 Geo. Int'l Envt'l L. Rev. 1, 19 (1992).

11.   *Bibliographical Note.* For supplemental discussion concerning the principal themes addressed in this problem, consult the following additional specialized materials:

(a) *Books/Monographs/Report/Symposia.* K. Arambulo, Strengthening the Supervision of the International Covenant on Economic, Social and Cultural Rights: Theoretical and Procedural Aspects (1999); I. Brownlie, The Human Right to Food (London, Commonwealth Secretariat, 1987); C. Christensen, The Right to Food: How To Guarantee (1978); M. Craven, The International Covenant on Economic, Social and Cultural Rights (1995); Economic, Social and Cultural Rights: A Textbook (A. Eide, Krause & A. Rosas eds., 2d ed. 2001); P. Farmer, Pathologies of Power: Health, Human Rights, and the New War on the Poor (2003); First World Hunger: Food Security and Welfare Politics (G. Riches ed., 1997); UN Food and Agriculture Organization, The Right to Food: In Theory and Practice (1998); Food Policy: The Responsibility of the United States in the Life and Death Choices (P. Brown & H. Shue eds., 1977); J. Drèze & A. Sen, Hunger and Public Action (1989); Food as a Human Right (A. Eide, W. Eide, S. Goonatilake, J. Gussow & Onawale eds., 1984); G. Kent, Freedom from Want: The Human Right to Adequate Food (2005); F. Lappe & J. Collins, Food First—Beyond the Myth of Scarcity (1979); I. Palmer, Women, Food Chains and Agrarian Reform (1981); A. Sen, Poverty and Famines: An Essay on Entitlement and Deprivation (1981); A. Sen, Development as Freedom (1999); The Global Political Economy of Food (R. Hopkins & D. Puchala eds., 1978); B. Toebes, The Right to Health as a Human Right in International Law (1999); *Report of the International Committee on the Right to Food, in* International Law Association, Report of the Sixty-fourth Conference Held at Warsaw (1988); The Right to Food (P. Alston & K. Tomasevski eds., 1984); H. Shue, Basic Rights (1980); Symposium, *World Food Day Food and Law Conference: The Legal Faces of the Hunger Problem*, 30 Howard L. J. 225 (1987); Symposium, *International Law and World Hunger*, 70 Iowa L. Rev. 1183 (1985); Symposium, *Human Rights and Development, in* Third World Legal Stud. (1984); Symposium, *The Global Food Regime in the 1990s: Efficiency, Stability, and Equity*, 1 Transnat'l L. & Contemp. Probs. i (1991); N. Twose, Behind the Weather–Why the Poor Suffer Most: Drought and the Sahel (1984); _____ Fighting the Famine (1985); J. Warnock, The Politics of Hunger: The Global Food System (1987); UN High Commissioner for Human Rights, The Right to Food: Achievements and Challenges, World Food Summit: Five Years Later (2002).

(b) *Articles/Book Chapters.* P. Alston & K. Tomasevski, The Right to Food: Guide through Applicable International Law, 84 A.J.I.L. 309 (1990); R. Bonner, Famine, The New Yorker 85 (13 Mar 89); D. Buckingham, A Recipe for Change: Towards an Integrated Approach to Food Under International Law, 6 Pace Int'l L. Rev. 285 (1994); C. Chinkin & S. Wright, The Hunger Trap: Women, Food and Self–Determination, 14 Mich. J. Int'l L. 262 (1993); K. Cox, Should Amnesty International Expand its Mandate to Cover Economic, Social and Cultural Rights? 16 Ariz. J. Int'l & Comp. Law 261 (1999); A. Eide, Strategies for the Realization of the Right to Food, in Human Rights in the Twenty-first Century: A Global Challenge 459 (K. Mahoney & P. Mahoney eds., 1993); G. Kent, *Food Is A Human Right*, in Human Rights in the World Community: Issues and Action (R. Claude & B. Weston eds., 3rd ed. 2006); D. MacDonald, International Responsibility to Implement the Right to Food, in Human Rights in the Twenty-first Century: A Global Challenge 473 (K. Mahoney & P. Mahoney eds., 1993); M. Ritchie & K. Dawkins, WTO Food and Agricultural Rules: Sustainable Agriculture and the Human Right to Food, 9 Minn. J. Global Trade 9 (2000); R. Roberston, The Right to Food in International Law, in Human Rights in the Twenty-first Century: A Global Challenge 451 (K. Mahoney & P. Mahoney eds., 1993); K. Roth, Defending Economic, Social and Cultural Rights: Practical Issues Faced by an International Human Rights Organization, 26 H.R.Q. 63 (2004); R. Schechter, Intentional Starvation as Torture: Exploring the Gray Area Between Ill–Treatment and Torture, 18 Am. U. Int'l L. Rev. 1233 (2003); M. Snyder, Gender and the Food Regime: Some Transnational and Human Issues, 1 Transnat'l L. & Contemp. Probs. 469 (1991).

Problem 5–6

Cultural Difference in Malacca

Section 1.   Facts

The Republic of Malacca, a newly industrialized country and member of the United Nations, is situated in southeast Asia. Its government is dominated by a single political organization, the Malaccan Action Party (MAP), which is vociferously pro-capitalist, politically pragmatic, and authoritarian. It controls Malacca's unicameral parliament.

Since assuming power in the early 1960s, the MAP government has established a highly-developed social security system for the Malaccan people, with the government providing benefits for retirement, work-related disability, widowhood, and low-cost medical care. Also, it has ensured mandatory but free primary and secondary education plus higher education at no cost to any student who qualifies academically. A healthy and highly educated citizenry, capable of competing effectively in world markets, is a very high priority. As a result, Malacca has managed to achieve health and educational levels which compare favorably to the most highly-developed nations. Life expectancy ranges into the 70s, and infectious disease, once a common killer, is now of negligible significance. Generally, the Malaccan standard of living has risen to heights unimaginable a generation ago, and is the envy of many of Malacca's southeast Asian neighbors.

The MAP government maintains, and the vast majority of Malaccans agree, that this extraordinary progress, nicknamed the "Malaccan Miracle," was achievable only through the establishment and enforcement of strict rules of public conduct and personal discipline. These rules, codified in the nation's criminal law, prohibit conduct ranging from defacing public property to spitting in public. Littering on public property is an offense punishable by a fine of up to the equivalent of US $1,000 and 30 days in jail. Additionally, great respect for civil authorities is not only expected but required by Malaccan law, and criticism of governmental authorities is officially discouraged.

In October of last year, Christina Cairns, a professor of journalism at Queen's University in New Britain, a Commonwealth state in the South Pacific, traveled to the Malaccan capital of Malacao to attend a regional forum on the role of the media in international trade. During the first days of the conference, Malaccan police presence was conspicuous: agents attended each meeting, photographed participants, regularly demanded identification from the conferees, turned away Malaccan citizens, and, according to several journalists, followed the conferees from the conference to their hotels and around town. On the third day, several of the journalists (including Professor Cairns), upset by what they called "police harassment," staged a protest in the city's central park. Professor Cairns stood on a park bench and loudly criticized the Malaccan government for its treatment of the foreign journalists and condemned its recent adoption of a prohibition on media reports critical of the Malaccan Ministry of Justice—the government's chief law enforcement agency. Meanwhile, a research associate of Professor Cairns from Queen's University, David Dunedin, walked about the park placing stickers with slogans saying "Demand Freedom" and "Speak Out" on park benches and light posts. A dozen or so Malaccans, loyal to the government, stood around the journalists, jeering them and trying to shout down Professor Cairns.

Suddenly uniformed police officers charged the group and, with night-sticks, knocked Professor Cairns to the ground. At the same time, David Dunedin was confronted by two other police officers and arrested on the spot. Both Professor Cairns and Mr. Dunedin were then handcuffed, shoved into a police wagon, and brought to jail. Professor Cairns was charged with incitement to criminal conduct, malicious defamation of governmental officials, and disruption of the peace, offenses carrying penalties of up to 15 years in prison at hard labor. Mr. Dunedin was charged with littering and defacement of public property. He faces a potential six months in prison and "caning"—a punishment whereby the offender is bound to a post in the main city square, stripped to the waist, and flogged with a water-soaked bamboo rod. This punishment can result in lacerations to the back and arms, potentially to leave permanent scars. Both Professor Cairns and Mr. Dunedin were ordered held indefinitely with no legal counsel or outside contact until a hearing could be held, procedures expressly allowed under Malaccan criminal law.

Meanwhile, colleagues of Professor Cairns and Mr. Dunedin at the conference, angered by what had happened, went to New Britain's embassy in Malacao and related the story to New Britain officials. The New Britain government has since lodged a formal complaint with the Malaccan government, alleging that the treatment of prisoners prior to trial and especially the threatened caning violate international human rights standards requiring due process and prohibiting cruel, inhuman, and degrading treatment; also that the Malaccan government's treatment of the journalists violated other rights protected by international law, including freedom of expression, peaceful assembly, association and movement. Particularly, New Britain cites the United Nations Charter, the 1948 Universal Declaration of Human Rights and the 1966 International Covenant on Civil and Political Rights, arguing that these norms are now part of customary international law as well. Both Malacca and New Britain are signatories of the Universal Declaration, but only New Britain has ratified the 1966 Covenant.

Recognizing the urgency of the situation and knowing that any action via the usual channels of the United Nations or other human rights mechanisms would not take place quickly enough to spare Mr. Dunedin from his threatened caning, New Britain is considering action through the International Bank for Reconstruction and Development (the "World Bank"). The Bank is currently weighing the possibility of a loan to Malacca, directed at assisting the development of Malacca's industrial infrastructure. New Britain law requires that its representatives to the Bank use all means at their disposal to prevent the Bank from lending money to governments found to be involved in "gross violations of fundamental human rights." New Britain has therefore been contacting other governmental representatives to the Bank, seeking their support in opposing the Malaccan loan. Among those who have responded favorably to the New Britain position is the United States, which controls 17% of the Bank's votes as of this writing.

Meanwhile, a committee of New Britain's parliament with jurisdiction over matters of foreign policy, the Joint Committee on Foreign Affairs, Defence and Trade, is now considering a resolution to establish official parliamentary opposition to the World Bank loan to Malacca—a move that would not only require the New Britain representative to the Bank to oppose the loan, but would likely cause the United States and other governments friendly to New Britain to follow suit. The Malaccan government has responded to New Britain's charges by arguing that its strict laws and severe penalties are founded in a strong tradition of respect for, and obedience to, government and the law, a tradition deeply rooted in Malaccan social mores. It maintains that strict discipline and public order are required to ensure the continued well-being and development of Malaccan society, and public opinion polls taken there show broad public support for this position. Malacca therefore argues that international norms must give way to local norms in societies like Malacca, where they are based on long-standing tradition and culture and are necessary to maintain order and general well-being.

The Joint Committee on Foreign Affairs, Defence and Trade has invited representatives from both the New Britain Foreign Office and the Embassy of Malacca in New Britain to present their respective positions on whether there exists a "cultural relativism" exception to international human rights obligations, deferring to a later meeting the issue of whether the Malaccan government's actions in fact constitute "gross violations of fundamental human rights" in this case.

Section 2.   Questions Presented

1. Is Malacca's treatment of Professor Cairns and Mr. Dunedin a violation of international human rights law from which there can be no derogation on grounds of cultural difference?

2. In any event, are there any additional or alternative legal norms, procedures, and/or institutions to be recommended that might further help to prevent or discourage situations of the kind posed by this problem?

Section 3.   Assignments

A.   Reading Assignment

Study the Readings presented in Section 4, *infra*, and the Discussion Notes/Questions that follow. Also, time permitting, consult the accompanying bibliographical references.

B.   Recommended Writing Assignment

Prepare a comprehensive, logically sequenced, and *argumentative* brief in the form of an outline of the primary and subsidiary *legal* issues you see requiring resolution by New Britain's Joint Committee on Foreign Affairs, Defence and Trade. Also, from the perspective of an independent judge, indicate which side ought to prevail on each issue and why. Retain a copy of your issue-outline/brief for class discussion.

C. RECOMMENDED ORAL ASSIGNMENT

Assume you are legal counsel for New Britain or Malacca (as designated by your instructor); then, relying upon the Readings (and your issue-outline if prepared), present a 10–15 minute oral argument of your government's likely positions before New Britain's Joint Committee on Foreign Affairs, Defence and Trade.

D. RECOMMENDED REFLECTIVE ASSIGNMENT

Consider (and recommend) alternative norms, institutions, and/or procedures that you believe might do better than existing world order arrangements to contend with situations of the kind posed by this problem. In so doing, but without insisting upon *immediate* feasibility, identify the particular transition steps that would be needed to make your alternatives a reality.

SECTION 4. READINGS

The following readings are considered *prima facie* relevant to solving this problem. They are your law library for present purposes and should be treated as such, organized intelligibly for "shelving" and not necessarily according to the issues presented. Be sure to review Chapter 2 ("International Legal Prescription: The 'Sources' of International Law") in your consideration of them. It, too, should be treated as part of your law library (as, indeed, should this entire coursebook).

1. Burns H. Weston, "Human Rights," in *Encyclopædia Britannica* (2005), available from *Encyclopædia Britannica Online* at <http://www. britannica.com/eb/article?tocId=219350> (*see supra* Reading A–1 in Problem 5–1, at 494).

2. Charter of the United Nations. Concluded, 26 Jun 1945. Entered into force, 24 Oct 1945. 1976 Y.B.U.N. 1043; *reprinted in* 1 Weston & Carlson I.A.1: Pmbl. & Arts. 1 & 55 (Basic Document 1.5).

3. Universal Declaration of Human Rights, 10 Dec 1948, GA Res. 217A, UN GAOR, 3rd Sess., Pt. I, Resolutions, at 71, UN Doc. A/810 (1948); *reprinted in* 3 Weston & Carlson III.A.1: Pmbl. & Arts. 1, 3, 5, 9, 13, 18, 19, 20 (Basic Document 3.3).

4. International Covenant on Civil and Political Rights. Concluded, 16 Dec 1966. Entered into force, 23 Mar 1976. 999 U.N.T.S. 171; *reprinted in* 3 Weston & Carlson III.A.3: Pmbl. & Arts. 1, 7, 9, 10, 12, 18, 19, 21, 22, 27 (Basic Document 3.14).

5. Declaration of Principles of International Law Concerning Friendly Relations and Co-operation among States in accordance with the Charter of the United Nations, 24 Oct 1970, GA Res. 2625 (Annex), UN GAOR, 25th Sess., Supp. No. 28, at 122, UN Doc. A/8028

(1971); *reprinted in* 9 I.L.M. 1292 (1970) and 1 Weston & Carlson I.D.7 (Basic Document 1.11).

6.   Editors' Note. In June 1993, twenty-five years after the first United Nations International Conference on Human Rights in Teheran, Iran, in May 1968,[a] a second UN World Conference on Human Rights convened in Vienna, Austria. Preceding the conference were four preparatory meetings in four different regions of the world, including Asia. The culminating expression of the Asian preparatory meeting, held in Bangkok, Thailand, in March–April 1993, was the "Final Declaration of the Regional Meeting for Asia of the World Conference on Human Rights" of 2 April 1993, also known as "The Bangkok Declaration," *reprinted in* 14 H.R.L.J. 370 (1993). After reaffirming their "commitment to principles contained in the Charter of the United Nations **(Basic Document 1.5)** and the Universal Declaration of Human Rights **(Basic Document 3.3)**," the ministers and representatives of the over forty participating Asian states stressed "the urgent need to ... ensure a positive, balanced and non-confrontational approach to addressing and realizing all aspects of human rights" (¶ 3); emphasized "the principles of respect for national sovereignty and territorial integrity as well as non-interference in the internal affairs of States, and the non-use of human rights as an instrument of political pressure" (¶ 5); and recognized "that while human rights are universal in nature, they must be considered in the context of a dynamic and evolving process of international norm-setting, bearing in mind the significance of national and regional particularities and various historical, cultural and religious backgrounds...." (para 8). Although the Bangkok Declaration does not use the term "Asian values" it was regarded by both its defenders and critics as expressing a particular Asian perspective on human rights. For a perceptive analysis of the Declaration, see Karen Engle, *Culture and Human Rights: The Asian Values Debate in Context*, 32 N.Y.U. J. Int'l L. & Pol. 291 (2000). The culminating expression of the later Vienna conference was the Vienna Declaration and Programme of Action **(Basic Document 3.40)**. After observing that they had "taken into account the Declarations adopted by the ... regional [preparatory] meetings," the governmental conferees, responding to the Bangkok challenge, declared that "[a]ll human rights are universal, indivisible and interdependent and interrelated. The international community must treat human rights globally in a fair and equal manner, on the same footing, and with the same emphasis. While the significance of national and regional particularities and various historical, cultural and religious backgrounds must be borne in mind, it is the duty of States, regardless of their political, economic and cultural systems, to promote and protect all human rights and fundamental freedoms" (§ 1, ¶ 5). A close reading of the Declaration, however, reveals that the universalists at the conference nonetheless made important concessions.

Thus the debate between "cultural relativism" and "universalism," a feature of the drafting of the Universal Declaration of Human Rights, remains alive. "Cultural relativism," a term borrowed from anthropology and moral philosophy, may be defined generally, in the context of arguments about the

---

a. For the consensus reached at the Te-heran conference, see Final Act of the United Nations International Conference on Human Rights at Teheran (a/k/a "the Proclamation of Teheran"), adopted 13 May 68, *reprinted in* Human Rights: A Compilation of International Instruments 43 (1988) and 3 Weston & Carlson III. U.1.

role of internationally prescribed human rights in the contemporary world, as the position according to which local legal, political, religious, and other customs and traditions fundamentally determine the existence and scope of at least civil and political rights in a given society. Human rights standards, "relativists" contend, are locally defined and interpreted, differing from culture to culture, in keeping with the values of cultural pluralism, and thus are not to be judged against transboundary legal or moral standards without running afoul of the right of all peoples to self-determination. "Universalists," on the other hand, insist that internationally prescribed human rights are quintessentially general or universal in character, in some sense equally possessed by all human beings everywhere, irrespective of race, color, sex, language, religion, political or other opinion, national or social origin, property, birth, or other status.

7. Mary Ann Glendon, A World Made New: Eleanor Roosevelt and the Drafting of the Universal Declaration on Human Rights 221–23, 231–33 (2001).

In 1998, a few days before the fiftieth anniversary of the Universal Declaration of Human Rights **[Basic Document 3.3]**, Chinese activist Xu Wenli, who had spent twelve years in prison for his part in the 1978 "democracy wall" movement, was jailed for trying to register a new political party. The Beijing government issued its standard response to the charge that such treatment of dissidents violates human rights: Rights are relative to local conditions and many so-called human rights are merely parochial Western notions inapplicable to Chinese circumstances.

Protesting her father's arrest in a *Boston Globe* article, Xu Wenli's daughter scornfully dismissed the idea of blanket cultural exemptions from universal rights. One of the most influential framers of the Universal Declaration, she pointed out, was P. C. Chang—who "believed that rights are for everyone, not just westerners." And his credo lives on: "When the Chinese people have spoken—P. C. Chang in 1948, Wei Jinsheng, Xu Wenli and other members of the democracy wall movement in 1978, Tiananmen worker and student demonstrators in 1989, and Xu Wenli again this year—they have claimed their right to all of the universally acknowledged human liberties, not to a list impoverished by some supposed peculiarity of culture."

The problem of what universality might mean in a multicultural world haunted the United Nations human rights project from the beginning. In June 1947, when word of a proposed human rights declaration reached the American Anthropological Association, that group's executive board sent a letter to the Human Rights Commission warning that the document could not be "a statement of rights conceived only in terms of the values prevalent in the countries of Western Europe and America." The challenge would be "to formulate a statement of human rights that will do more than just phrase respect for the individual as an individual. It must also take into full account the individual as member of the social group of which he is part, whose sanctioned modes of life shape his behavior, and with whose fate his own is thus inextricably bound." Earlier that year some of the world's best-known philosophers had been asked to ponder the question, "How is an agreement conceivable among men who come from the four corners of the earth and who belong not only to different cultures and civilizations, but to different spiritual families and antagonistic schools of thought?"

No one has yet improved on the answer of the UNESCO philosophers: Where basic human values are concerned, cultural diversity has been exaggerated. The group found, after consulting with Confucian, Hindu, Muslim, and European thinkers, that a core of fundamental principles was widely shared in countries that had not yet adopted rights instruments and in cultures that had not embraced the language of rights. Their survey persuaded them that basic human rights rest on "common convictions," even though those convictions "are stated in terms of different philosophic principles and on the background of divergent political and economic systems." The philosophers concluded that even people who seem to be far apart in theory can agree that certain things are so terrible in practice that no one will publicly approve them and that certain things are so good in practice that no one will publicly oppose them.

The Human Rights Commission heeded the anthropologists' advice, and its experience seemed, on the whole, to bear out the philosophers' conclusion. In 1948, when Saudi Arabia made the isolated claim that freedom to marry and to change one's religion were Western ideas ill suited for universal application, no other country objected on cultural or religious grounds to those or any other parts of the Declaration. Nor did any country use those grounds to oppose the idea of a universal standard of human rights. The most philosophical of the framers, Charles Malik, believed that, over time, the Declaration's principles would "either bring to light an implicit agreement already operative, perhaps dimly and unconsciously, in the systems and ways of life of the various states, or consciously and creatively advance further and higher the area of agreement."

Though the UNESCO philosophers were confident that such an implicit agreement existed, they left the task of proving it for another day. What needed to be investigated was precisely how, and to what extent, various cultural, philosophical, and religious traditions have affirmed the universality of certain basic values.

* * *

The Declaration's framers did not imagine in 1948 that they had discovered the whole truth about human beings and human rights. They never claimed that the document they had produced under difficult circumstances represented the last word. Indeed, one speaker after another on December 9, 1948, had acknowledged that the Declaration was not perfect. The dominant metaphor was that of an important milestone on a long and difficult journey. They were content to have advanced the quest and confident that experiences gained in implementing the Declaration's principles would lead to deeper understanding in the future.

* * *

If the door is left open to different ways of balancing and enforcing the Declaration's principles, friends of human rights must wonder nervously whether this will not play into the hands of international actors, who, like China's rulers, maintain that cultural and economic disparities among nations require all human rights to be understood as relative. Does pluralism not give comfort to leaders who have argued that temporary suspension of civil liberties is necessary in order to build democratic systems in the wake of repressive regimes? Or to liberal democratic governments that, while paying lip service to universality, often turn a blind eye when their allies or trading partners commit the same abuses that they condemn in an enemy or rival?

The Declaration's vulnerability to political manipulation is heightened by the popularity of philosophies that deny the existence of any moral truths. * * * The framers were not oblivious of such dangers. All they could do was to state the truths they believed to be self-evident and suggest the outer bounds of legitimate pluralism in the document itself. The structure they fashioned is flexible enough to allow for differences in emphasis and means of implementation, but not so malleable as to permit any basic human right to be completely eclipsed or unnecessarily subordinated for the sake of other rights.

At [a] 1998 Harvard symposium [on human rights], a Chinese dissident, Xiao Quiang, departed from his prepared remarks in order to respond to the charge that the Declaration was an arrogant attempt to impose "Judeo–Christian" values on non-Western peoples. Xiao said he had often heard that argument in China—and Burma, and North Korea, and Indonesia. He agreed that human rights was a Western idea insofar as its origin was concerned. Communism, he noted, was a Western idea, too. But had Professor Mutua considered what a luxury it was to be able to voice his critical opinions on that subject freely? he asked. Turning to Matua, he said, "If you were to voice dissent from the prevailing view in China, you would end up in jail, and there you would soon be asking for your rights, without worrying about whether they were 'American' or 'Chinese.' "[b]

There is little doubt about how the principal framers of the Universal Declaration would have responded to the charge of "Western-ness." What was crucial for them—indeed, what made universal human rights possible—was the *similarity* among all human beings. Their starting point was the simple fact of the common humanity shared by every man, woman, and child on earth, a fact that, for them, put linguistic, racial, religious, and other differences into their proper perspective. A strong emphasis on racial and cultural difference was, after all, one of the worst evils of colonialism and Nazism.

Cassin, Chang, Humphrey, Malik, and Roosevelt would have agreed with the eloquent statement made by a representative of Human Rights Watch/Asia shortly before the 1993 Vienna Human Rights Conference. Speaking in Jakarta to an audience that included many skeptics, Daniel S. Lev said:

> Values, traditions, customs, and habits naturally vary, as do languages and religions, but do they differ on the fundamental questions with which we are concerned? Whatever else may separate them, human beings belong to a single biological species, the simplest and most fundamental commonality before which the significance of human differences quickly fades.... The argument of cultural specificity cannot over-ride the reality that we all share the most basic attributes in common. We are all capable, in exactly the same ways, of feeling pain, hunger, and a hundred kinds of deprivation. Consequently, people nowhere routinely

b. *See infra* Reading 10, for some of Professor Makau Matua's views.

concede that those with enough power to do so ought to be able at will to kill, torture, imprison, and generally abuse others. There may be no choice in the matter, given realities, of power, but submission is different from moral approval.

The great religious traditions ... take for granted the principle of common humanity. Islam, Buddhism, Catholicism, Protestantism, Judaism, Hinduism, Taoism, and most of their variants share a recognition of the human condition. Their explanations of it and their solutions for it may differ, but not their concern. The idea of universal human rights shares the recognition of one common humanity, and provides a minimum solution to deal with its miseries.

8. Bilahari Kausikan, "Asia's Different Standard," 92 Foreign Pol'y 24, 24–40 (1993).[c]

East and Southeast Asia must respond to a new phenomenon: Human rights have become a legitimate issue in interstate relations. How a country treats its citizens is no longer a matter for its own exclusive determination. Others can and do legitimately claim a concern. There is an emerging global culture of human rights, and a body of international law on human rights has gradually developed, codified in the United Nations Charter [**Basic Document 1.5**], the Universal Declaration of Human Rights [**Basic Document 3.3**], and other international instruments....

In response, East and Southeast Asia are reexamining their own human rights standards. Of the noncommunist states in the region, only Japan, South Korea, and the Philippines are parties to both the International Covenant on Civil and Political Rights and the International Covenant on Economic, Social and Cultural Rights. Seoul and Manila have also accepted the Optional Protocol to the International Covenant on Civil and Political Rights. Tokyo has partially adopted the Western approach to human rights. [And] there is a more general acceptance of many international human rights norms, even among states that have not acceded to the two covenants or are accused by the West of human rights abuses. * * * The human rights situation in the region, whether measured by the standard of civil and political rights or by social, cultural, and economic rights, has improved greatly over the last 20 years....

... But it is too simplistic to dismiss what has been achieved as mere gestures intended to appease Western critics. Such inclinations may well be an element in the overall calculation of interests. And Western pressure undeniably plays a role. But in themselves, self-interest and pressure are insufficient and condescendingly ethnocentric Western explanations. They do less than justice to the states concerned, most of which have their own traditions in which the rulers have a duty to govern in a way consonant with the human dignity of their subjects, even if there is no clear concept of "rights" as has evolved in the West. China today, for all its imperfections, is a vast improvement over the China of the Cultural Revolution. So too has the situation in Taiwan, South Korea, and the Association of Southeast Asian

c. At the time of his essay, the author was the Director of the East Asian and Pacific Bureau of the Ministry of Foreign Affairs of Singapore.

Nations (ASEAN) improved. Western critics who deny the improvements lose credibility.

* * *

The diversity of cultural traditions, political structures, and levels of development will make it difficult, if not impossible, to define a single distinctive and coherent human rights regime that can encompass the vast region from Japan to Burma, with its Confucianist, Buddhist, Islamic, and Hindu traditions. Nonetheless, the movement toward such a goal is likely to continue. What is clear is that there is a general discontent throughout the region with a purely Western interpretation of human rights. * * * [Moreover,] efforts to promote human rights in Asia must also reckon with the altered distribution of power in the post-Cold War world. Power, especially economic power, has been diffused. For the last two decades, most of East and Southeast Asia has experienced strong economic growth and will probably keep growing faster than other regions well into the next century. Not just Japan, but increasingly also the newly industrialized economies (NIEs), near NIEs like Thailand and Malaysia, and sub-regions such as southern China are considerable forces in the global economy. The economic success of East and Southeast Asia is the central strategic fact of the 1990s. . . .

* * *

East and Southeast Asia are now significant actors in the world economy. * * * [They] are now capable of exerting considerable influence on the international politics of human rights, and their interests, values, and cultures cannot be disregarded. Most of the region's countries can no longer be pushed or coerced. Unlike Eastern Europe, Russia, or many states of the former Soviet Union, Asians do not wish to be considered good Westerners, even if they are friendly to the West. At least two countries, Japan and China, have the power to make a major impact on the international system.

For the first time since the Universal Declaration was adopted in 1948, countries not thoroughly steeped in the Judeo–Christian and natural law traditions are in the first rank. That unprecedented situation will define the new international politics of human rights. It will also multiply the occasions for conflict. In the process, will the human rights dialogue between the West and East and Southeast Asia become a dialogue of the deaf, with each side proclaiming its superior virtue without advancing the common interests of humanity? Or can it be a genuine and fruitful dialogue, expanding and deepening consensus? . . . The myth of the universality of all human rights is harmful if it masks the real gap that exists between Asian and Western perceptions of human rights. The gap will not be bridged if it is denied.

The June 1993 Vienna UN conference on human rights did not even attempt to do so. The West went to Vienna accusing Asia of trying to undermine the ideal of universality, and determined to blame Asia if the conference failed. Inevitably, Asia resisted. The result after weeks of wrangling was a predictable diplomatic compromise ambiguous enough so all could live with it, but that settled very few things. There was no real dialogue between Asia and the West, no genuine attempt to address the issues or forge a meeting of the minds. If anything, the Vienna conference may only have hardened attitudes on both sides and increased the deep skepticism with which many Asian countries regard Western posturing on human rights.

* * *

For many in the West, the end of the Cold War was not just the defeat or collapse of communist regimes, but the supreme triumph and vindication of Western systems and values. It has become the lens through which they view developments in other regions. There has been a tendency since 1989 to draw parallels between developments in the Third World and those in Eastern Europe and the former USSR, measuring all states by the advance of what the West regards as "democracy." That is a value-laden term, itself susceptible to multiple interpretations, but usually understood by Western human rights activists and the media as the establishment of political institutions and practices akin to those existing in the United States and Europe. * * * [T]he Western approach is ideological, not empirical. The West needs its myths; missionary zeal to whip the heathen along the path of righteousness and remake the world in its own image is deeply ingrained in Western (especially American) political culture. It is entirely understandable that Western human rights advocates choose to interpret reality in the way they believe helps their cause most.

* * *

The hard core of rights that are truly universal is smaller than many in the West are wont to pretend. Forty-five years after the Universal Declaration was adopted, many of its 30 articles are still subject to debate over interpretation and application—not just between Asia and the West, but within the West itself. Not every one of the 50 states of the United States would apply the provisions of the Universal Declaration in the same way. It is not only pretentious but wrong to insist that everything has been settled once and forever. The Universal Declaration is not a tablet Moses brought down from the mountain. It was drafted by mortals. All international norms must evolve through continuing debate among different points of view if consensus is to be maintained.

Most East and Southeast Asian governments are uneasy with the propensity of many American and some European human rights activists to place more emphasis on civil and political rights than on economic, social, and cultural rights. They would probably not be convinced, for instance, by a September 1992 report issued by Human Rights Watch entitled *Indivisible Human Rights: The Relationship of Political and Civil Rights to Survival, Subsistence and Poverty*. They would find the report's argument that "political and civil rights, especially those related to democratic accountability," are basic to survival and "not luxuries to be enjoyed only after a certain level of economic development has been reached" to be grossly overstated. Such an argument does not accord with their own historical experience. That experience sees order and stability as preconditions for economic growth, and growth as the necessary foundation of any political order that claims to advance human dignity.

The Asian record of economic success is a powerful claim that cannot be easily dismissed. Both the West and Asia can agree that values and institutions are important determinants of development. But what institutions and which values? The individualistic ethos of the West or the communitarian traditions of Asia? The consensus-seeking approach of East and Southeast Asia or the adversarial institutions of the West? . . .

Poverty, insecurity, and instability breed human rights abuses, while wealth creates the stability of Western societies and allows the operation of political institutions that in less-favorable circumstances could lead to disaster. Only America's wealth, for example, allows it to operate a political system that elevates conflict to the status of principle and makes a virtue of a tendency toward paralysis in all but exceptional circumstances. Wealth makes political institutions almost irrelevant to the well-being and happiness of the majority in many Western societies. Many Americans do not even bother to vote and the popular estimation of American politicians is low. Those are among the luxuries that wealth buys. But the costs are already becoming evident.

* * *

At any rate, many East and Southeast Asians tend to look askance at the starkly individualistic ethos of the West in which authority tends to be seen as oppressive and rights are an individual's "trump" over the state. Most people of the region prefer a situation in which distinctions between the individual, society, and state are less clear-cut, or at least less adversarial. It will be far more difficult to deepen and expand the international consensus on human rights if East and Southeast Asian countries believe that the Western promotion of human rights is aimed at what they regard as the foundation of their economic success. In fact, many Asians perceive the values and practices insisted upon by Western human rights purists as exacerbating the thorny problems faced by the West.

* * *

One explanation of the contradictions in Asian attitudes is that popular pressures against East and Southeast Asian governments may not be so much for "human rights" or "democracy" but for good government: effective, efficient, and honest administrations able to provide security and basic needs with good opportunities for an improved standard of living. To be sure, good government, human rights, and democracy are overlapping concepts. Good government requires the protection of human dignity and accountability through periodic fair and free elections. But they are not always the same thing; it cannot be blithely assumed . . . that more democracy and human rights will inevitably lead to good government. . . . The apparent contradictions mirror a complex reality: Good government may well require, among other things, detention without trial to deal with military rebels or religious and other extremists; curbs on press freedoms to avoid fanning racial tensions or exacerbating social divisions; and draconian laws to break the power of entrenched interests in order to, for instance, establish land reforms.

Future Western approaches on human rights will have to be formulated with greater nuance and precision. It makes a great deal of difference if the West insists on humane standards of behavior by vigorously protesting genocide, murder, torture, or slavery. Here there is a clear consensus on a core of international law that does not admit of derogation on any grounds. The West has a legitimate right and moral duty to promote those core human rights, even if it is tempered by limited influence. But if the West objects to, say, capital punishment, detention without trial, or curbs on press freedoms, it should recognize that it does so in a context where the international law is less definitive and more open to interpretation and where there is room for further elaboration through debate. The West will have to accept that no universal consensus may be possible and that states can legitimately agree to disagree without being guilty of sinister designs or bad faith. Trying to impose pet Western definitions of "freedom" and "democracy" is an incitement to destructive conflict, best foregone in the interest of promoting real human rights.

9. Yash Ghai, "Human Rights and Governance: The Asia Debate," 15 Austl. Y. B. I. L. 1, 5–6, 13, 16–18 (1994).

. . . It is easy to believe that there is a distinct Asian approach to human rights because some government leaders speak as if they represent the whole continent when they make their pronouncements on human rights. This view is reinforced because they claim that their views are based on perspectives which emerge from the Asian culture or religion or Asian realities. The gist of their position is that human rights as propounded in the West are founded on individualism and therefore have no relevance to Asia which is based on the primacy of the community. It is also sometimes argued that economic under-development renders most of the political and civil rights (emphasised in the West) irrelevant in Asia. Indeed, it is sometimes alleged that such rights are dangerous in view of fragmented nationalism and fragile Statehood.

It would be surprising if there were indeed one Asian perspective, since neither Asian culture nor Asian realities are homogenous throughout the continent. All the world's major religions are represented in Asia, and are in one place or another State religions (or enjoy a comparable status: Christianity in the Philippines, Islam in Malaysia, Hinduism in Nepal and Buddhism in Sri Lanka and Thailand). To this list we may add political ideologies like socialism, democracy or feudalism which animate peoples and governments of the region. Even apart from religious differences, there are other factors which have produced a rich diversity of cultures. A culture, moreover, is not static and many accounts given of Asian culture are probably true of an age long ago. Nor are the economic circumstances of all the Asian countries similar. Japan, Singapore and Hong Kong are among the world's most prosperous countries, while there is grinding poverty in Bangladesh, India and the Philippines. The economic and political systems in Asia likewise show a remarkable diversity, ranging from semi-feudal kingdoms in Kuwait and Saudi Arabia, through military dictatorships in Burma and formerly Cambodia, effectively one party regimes in Singapore and Indonesia, communist regimes in China and Vietnam, ambiguous democracies in Malaysia and Sri Lanka, to well established democracies like India. There are similarly differences in their economic systems, ranging from tribal subsistence economies in parts of Indonesia through highly developed market economies of Singapore, Hong Kong and Taiwan and the mixed economy model of India to the planned economies of China and Vietnam. Perceptions of human rights are undoubtedly reflective of these conditions, and suggest that they would vary from country to country.

* * *

Perceptions of human rights are reflective [also] of social and class positions in society. What conveys an apparent picture of a uniform Asian perspective on human rights is that it is the perspective of a particular group, that of the ruling elites, which gets international attention. What unites these elites is their notion of governance and the expediency of their rule. For the most part, the political systems they represent are not open or democratic, and their publicly expressed views on human rights are an emanation of these systems, of the need to justify authoritarianism and occasional repression. It is their views which are given wide publicity domestically and internationally.

* * *

[However,] [t]here are other Asian voices as well. There are, admittedly somewhat muted or censored, the voices of the oppressed and the marginalised. There are the passionate voices of indigenous peoples whose cultures are destroyed by governments which claim to be the custodians of Asian cultures.... There is the voice, rising in density, of the middle classes, with a stake in affluence whose new found prosperity and economic enterprise shows to them the virtues of legal protection of property and the rule of law. There are the strident voices of ethnic minorities who seek collective autonomies which challenge governments' claims of political monopoly and State sovereignty. An important and articulate group are intellectuals who are alienated from the State ..., [who] engage in international debates [and who] form networks with their counterparts in other parts of the world.... They have a commitment to human rights and democracy [though they] are less ready to accept Western conceptions in totality, and attempt to relate questions of human rights to specific national conditions.

* * *

... [Nevertheless,] some Asian governments claim that their societies place a higher value on the community than in the West, that individuals find fulfilment in their participation in communal life and community tasks, and that this factor constitutes a primary distinction in the approach to human rights.... This argument is advanced as an instance of the general proposition that rights are culture specific.

The "communitarian" argument is Janus-faced. It is used against the claim of universal human rights to distinguish the allegedly Western, individual-oriented approaches to rights from the community centred values of the East. Yet it is also used to deny the claims and assertions of communities in the name of "national unity and stability". It suffers from at least two further weaknesses. First, it overstates the "individualism" of Western society and traditions of thought. Even within Western liberalism, there are strands of analysis which assert claims of community (for example, Rousseau); and most Western human rights instruments allow limitations on and derogations from human rights in the public interest, or for reasons of State.... Furthermore, liberalism does not exhaust Western political thought or practice. There is social democracy, which emphasises collective and economic rights, and Marxism, which elevates the community to a high moral order, is also reflective of an important school of Western thought. There is much celebration in Western political thought of "civil society."

Secondly, Asian governments ... fall into the easy but wrong assumption that they or the State are the "community".... Nothing can be more destructive of the community than this conflation. The community and State are different institutions and to some extent in a contrary juxtaposition. The community ... depends on popular norms developed through forms of consensus and enforced through mediation and persuasion. The State is an imposition on society, and unless humanised and democratised (as it has not been in most of Asia), it relies on edicts, the military, coercion and sanctions. It is the tension between them which has elsewhere underpinned human rights. In the name of the community, most Asian governments have stifled social and political initiatives of private groups.... Governments have destroyed many communities in the name of development or State stability....

Another attack on the community comes from the economic, market oriented policies of the governments. Although Asian capitalism appears to rely on the family and clan associations, there is little doubt that it weakens the community and its cohesion. The organising matrix of the market is not the same as that of the community. Nor are its values or methods particularly "communitarian". The moving frontier of the market, seeking new resources, has been particularly disruptive of communities which have managed to preserve intact a great deal of their culture and organisation during the colonial and post-colonial periods. The emphasis on the market, and with it individual rights of property are also at odds with communal organisation and enjoyment of property....

A final point is the contradiction between claims of a consensus and harmonious society, and the extensive arming of the state apparatus. The pervasive use of draconian legislation like administrative detention, disestablishment of societies, press censorship, and sedition, belies claims to respect alternative views, promote a dialogue, and seek consensus. The contemporary State intolerance of opposition is inconsistent with traditional communal values and processes....

10. Makau Matua, "Savages, Victims, and Saviors: The Metaphor of Human Rights," 42 Harv. Int'l L. J. 201, 201–08, 243–45 (2001).

The human rights movement is marked by a damning metaphor. The grand narrative of human rights contains a subtext that depicts an epochal contest pitting savages, on the one hand, against victims and saviors, on the other. The savages-victims-saviors (SVS) construction is a three-dimensional compound metaphor in which each dimension is a metaphor in itself. The main authors of the human rights discourse, including the United Nations, Western states, international non-governmental organizations (INGOs), and senior Western academics, constructed this three-dimensional prism. This rendering of the human rights corpus and its discourse is unidirectional and predictable, a black-and-white construction that pits good against evil.

* * *

The first dimension of the prism depicts a savage and evokes images of barbarism. The abominations of the savage are presented as so cruel and unimaginable as to represent their state as a negation of humanity. The human rights story presents the state as the classic savage, an ogre forever bent on the consumption of humans. Although savagery in human rights discourse connotes much more than the state, the state is depicted as the operational instrument of savagery. States become savage when they choke off and oust civil society. The "good" state controls its demonic proclivities by cleansing itself with, and internalizing, human rights. The "evil" state, on the other hand, expresses itself through an illiberal, anti-democratic, or other authoritarian culture. The redemption or salvation of the state is solely dependent on its submission to human rights norms. The state is the guarantor of human rights; it is also the target and *raison d'être* of human rights law.

But the reality is far more complex. While the metaphor may suggest otherwise, it is not the state per se that is barbaric but the cultural foundation of the state. The state only becomes a vampire when "bad" culture overcomes or disallows the development of "good" culture. The real savage, though, is not the state but a cultural deviation from human rights. That savagery inheres in the theory and practice of the one-party state, military junta, controlled or closed state, theocracy, or even cultural practices such as the one popularly known in the West as female genital mutilation (FGM), not in the state per se. The state itself is a neutral, passive instrumentality—a receptacle or an empty vessel—that conveys savagery by implementing the project of the savage culture.

The second dimension of the prism depicts the face and the fact of a victim as well as the essence and the idea of victimhood. A human being whose "dignity and worth" have been violated by the savage is the victim. The victim figure is a powerless, helpless innocent whose naturalist attributes have been negated by the primitive and offensive actions of the state or the cultural foundation of the state. The entire human rights structure is both anticatastrophic and reconstructive. It is anti-catastrophic because it is designed to prevent more calamities through the creation of more victims. It is reconstructive because it seeks to re-engineer the state and the society to reduce the number of victims, as it defines them, and prevent conditions that give rise to victims. The classic human rights document—the human rights report—embodies these two mutually reinforcing strategies. An INGO human rights report is usually a catalogue of horrible catastrophes visited on individuals. As a rule, each report also carries a diagnostic epilogue and recommended therapies and remedies.

The third dimension of the prism is the savior or the redeemer, the good angel who protects, vindicates, civilizes, restrains, and safeguards. The savior is the victim's bulwark against tyranny. The simple, yet complex promise of the savior is freedom: freedom from the tyrannies of the state, tradition, and culture. But it is also the freedom to create a better society based on particular values. In the human rights story, the savior is the human rights corpus itself, with the United Nations, Western governments, INGOs, and Western charities as the actual rescuers, redeemers of a benighted world. In reality, however, these institutions are merely fronts. The savior is ultimately a set of culturally based norms and practices that inhere in liberal thought and philosophy.

The human rights corpus, though well-meaning, is fundamentally Eurocentric, and suffers from several basic and interdependent flaws captured in the SVS metaphor. First, the corpus falls within the historical continuum of the Eurocentric colonial project, in which actors are cast into superior and subordinate positions. Precisely because of this cultural and historical context, the human rights movement's basic claim of universality is undermined. Instead, a historical understanding of the struggle for human dignity should locate the impetus of a universal conception of human rights in those societies *subjected* to European tyranny and imperialism. Unfortunately, this is not part of the official human rights narrative. Some of the most important events preceding the post–1945, United Nations-led human rights movement include the anti-slavery campaigns in both Africa and the United States, the anti-colonial struggles in Africa, Asia, and Latin America, and the struggles for women's suffrage and equal rights throughout the world. But the pioneering work of many non-Western activists and other human rights heroes are not acknowledged by the contemporary human rights movement. These historically important struggles, together with the norms anchored in non-Western cultures and societies, have either been overlooked or rejected in the construction of the current understanding of human rights.

Second, the SVS metaphor and narrative rejects the cross-contamination of cultures and instead promotes a Eurocentric ideal. The metaphor is premised on the transformation by Western cultures of non-Western cultures into a Eurocentric prototype and not the fashioning of a multicultural mosaic. The SVS metaphor results in an "othering" process that imagines the creation of inferior clones, in effect dumb copies of the original. For example, Western political democracy is in effect an organic element of human rights. "Savage" cultures and peoples are seen as lying outside the human rights orbit, and by implication, outside the regime of political democracy. It is this distance from human rights that allows certain cultures to create victims. Political democracy is then viewed as a panacea. Other textual examples anchored in the treatment of cultural phenomena, such as "traditional" practices that appear to negate the equal protection for women, also illustrate the gulf between human rights and non-liberal, non-European cultures.

Third, the language and rhetoric of the human rights corpus present significant theoretical problems. The arrogant and biased rhetoric of the human rights movement prevents the movement from gaining cross-cultural legitimacy. This curse of the SVS rhetoric has no bearing on the substance of the normative judgment being rendered. A particular leader, for example, could be labeled a war criminal, but such a label may carry no validity locally because of the curse of the SVS rhetoric. In other words, the SVS rhetoric may undermine the universalist warrant that it claims and thus engender resistance to the apprehension and punishment of real violators.

The subtext of human rights is a grand narrative hidden in the seemingly neutral and universal language of the corpus. For example, the UN Charter describes its mandate to "reaffirm faith in fundamental human rights, in the dignity and worth of the human person, in the equal rights of men and women and of nations large and small." This is certainly a noble ideal. But what exactly does that terminology mean here? This phraseology conceals more than it reveals. What, for example, are fundamental human rights, and how are they determined? Do such rights have cultural, religious, ethical, moral, political, or other biases? What exactly is meant by the "dignity and worth" of the human person? Is there an essentialized human being that the corpus imagines? Is the individual found in the streets of Nairobi, the slums of Boston, the deserts of Iraq, or the rainforests of Brazil? In addition to the Herculean task of defining the prototypical human being, the UN Charter puts forward another pretense—that all nations "large and small" enjoy some equality. Even as it ratified power imbalances between the Third World and the dominant American and European powers, the United Nations gave the latter the primary power to define and determine "world peace" and "stability." These fictions of neutrality and universality, like so much else in a lopsided world, undergird the human rights corpus and belie its true identity and purposes. This international rhetoric of goodwill reveals, just beneath the surface, intentions and reality that stand in great tension and contradiction with it. . . .

If the human rights movement is driven by a totalitarian or totalizing impulse, that is, the mission to require that all human societies transform themselves to fit a particular blueprint, then there is an acute shortage of deep reflection and a troubling abundance of zealotry in the human rights community. This vision of the "good society" must be vigorously questioned and contested.

Fourth, the issue of power is largely ignored in the human rights corpus. There is an urgent need for a human rights movement that is multicultural, inclusive, and deeply political. Thus, while it is essential that a new human rights movement overcome Eurocentrism, it is equally important that it also address deeply lopsided power relations among and within cultures, national economies, states, genders, religions, races and ethnic groups, and other societal cleavages. Such a movement cannot treat Eurocentrism as the starting point and other cultures as peripheral. The point of departure for the movement must be a basic assumption about the moral equivalency of all cultures. . . .

The fifth flaw concerns the role of race in the development of the human rights narrative. The SVS metaphor of human rights carries racial connotations in which the international hierarchy of race and color is reintrenched and revitalized. The metaphor is in fact necessary for the continuation of the global racial hierarchy. In the human rights narrative, savages and victims are generally non-white and non-Western, while the saviors are white. This old truism has found new life in the metaphor of human rights. But there is also a sense in which human rights can be seen as a project for the redemption of the redeemers, in which whites who are privileged globally as a people—who have historically visited untold suffering and savage atrocities against non-whites—redeem themselves by "defending" and "civilizing" "lower," "unfortunate," and "inferior" peoples. The metaphor is thus laced with the pathology of self-redemption.

As currently constituted and deployed, the human rights movement will ultimately fail because it is perceived as an alien ideology in non-Western societies. The movement does not deeply resonate in the cultural fabrics of non-Western states, except among hypocritical elites steeped in Western ideas. In order ultimately to prevail, the human rights movement must be moored in the cultures of all peoples.

The project of reconsidering rights, with claims to their supremacy, is not new. The culture of rights in the present milieu stretches back at least to the rise of the modern state in Europe. It is that state's monopoly of violence and the instruments of coercion that gave rise to the culture of rights to counterbalance the abusive state. Robert Cover refers to this construction as the myth of the jurisprudence of rights that allows society to both legitimize and control the state.[1] Human rights, however, renew the meaning and scope of rights in a radical way. Human rights bestow naturalness, transhistoricity [sic], and universality to rights.

* * *

The promise that human rights holds out to the Third World is that problems of cruel conditions of life, state instability, and other social crises can be contained, if not substantially eliminated, through the rule of law, grants of individual rights, and a state based on constitutionalism. Through the metaphor of human rights and its grand narrative, the Third World is asked to follow a particular script of history. That script places hope for the future of the international community in liberal nationalism and democratic internal self-determination. The impression given is that a unitary international community is possible within this template if only the Third World followed suit by climbing up the civilizational ladder. However, I argue that this historical model, as now diffused through the human rights movement, cannot respond to the needs of the Third World absent some radical rethinking and restructuring of the international order.

The human rights movement must abandon the SVS metaphor if there is going to be real hope in a genuine international discourse on rights. The relentless efforts to universalize an essentially European corpus of human rights through Western crusades cannot succeed. Nor will demonizing those who resist these efforts achieve a truly international approach. The critiques of the corpus from Africans, Asians, Muslims, Hindus, and a host of critical thinkers from around the world are the one avenue through which human rights can be redeemed and truly universalized. This multiculturalization of the corpus could be attempted in a number of areas: balancing between individual and group rights, giving more substance to social and economic rights, relating rights to duties, and addressing the relationship between the corpus and economic systems. This Article does not develop those substantive critiques, but it is important that these issues be raised. Further work must done on these questions to chart out how such a vision affects or distorts non-European societies.

Ultimately, a new theory of internationalism and human rights, one that responds to diverse cultures, must confront the inequities of the international order. In this respect, human rights must break from the historical continuum—expressed in the metaphor and the grand narrative of human rights—that keeps intact the hierarchical relationships between European and non-European populations. . . .

* * *

Using political democracy as one medium through which the human rights culture is conveyed, one is able to capture the imperial project at work. First, the choice of a political ideology that is necessary for human rights is an

---

1. *See* Robert M. Cover, *Obligation: A Jewish Jurisprudence of the Social Order*, 5 J. L. & Religion 65, 69 (1987).

exclusionary act. Thus, cultures that fall outside that ideological box immediately wear the label of the savage. To be redeemed from their culture and history, which may be thousands of years old, a people must then deny themselves or continue to churn out victims. The savior in this case becomes the norms of democratic governments, however those are transmitted or imposed on the offending cultures. Institutions and other media—both those that purport to have a universalist warrant and those that are the obvious instruments of a particular nation's foreign policy and its interests—are critical to the realization of the grand script and metaphor of human rights explored [here]. However, the imposition of the current dogma of human rights on non-European societies contradicts conceptions of human dignity and rejects the contributions of other cultures in efforts to create a universal corpus of human rights. Proponents of human rights should first accept the limitations of working within the metaphor. Then they must reject it and seek a truly universal platform.

11. Abullahi Ahmed An–Na'im,"Toward a Cross–Cultural Approach to Defining International Standards of Human Rights: The Meaning of Cruel, Inhuman or Degrading Treatment of Punishment," in Human Rights in Cross–Cultural Perspective 19, 20–21, 29, 33–38 (A. An–Na'im ed., 1992).

The general thesis of my approach is that, since people are more likely to observe normative propositions if they believe them to be sanctioned by their own cultural traditions, observance of human rights standards can be improved through the enhancement of the cultural legitimacy of those standards. * * * [It] accepts the existing international standards while seeking to enhance their cultural legitimacy within the major traditions of the world through internal dialogue and struggle to establish enlightened perceptions and interpretations of cultural values and norms. Having achieved an adequate level of legitimacy *within* each tradition, through this internal stage, human rights scholars and advocates should work for *cross-cultural* legitimacy, so that peoples of diverse cultural traditions can agree on the meaning, scope, and methods of implementing these rights. * * * This approach is based on the belief that, despite their apparent peculiarities and diversity, human being and societies share certain fundamental interests, concerns, qualities, traits, and values that can be identified and articulated as the framework for a common "culture" of universal human rights. . . .

[*Eds.*—To illustrate his argument, the author turns to consider the right not to be subjected to cruel, inhuman, or degrading treatment or punishment in the context of Islamic criminal law, in particular the criminal offense of *sariqa*, or theft, which is punishable by the amputation of the right hand. He begins by observing that "Islamic law, commonly know as Shari'a, is based on the Qur'an, which Muslims believe to be the literal and final word of God, and on Sunna, or traditions of the Prophet Muhammad." He then continues:]

. . . The question being raised is: Are Muslims likely to accept the repudiation of punishments [such as amputation of the right hand] *as a matter of lslamic law* on the ground that they are cruel, inhuman, or degrading? This question should not be confused with the very important but distinct issue of whether [such] punishments have been or are being applied legitimately and in accordance with all the general and specific requirements of Islamic law.

Islamic law requires the state to fulfill its obligation to secure social and economic justice and to ensure decent standards of living for all its citizens before it can enforce these punishments. The law also provides for very narrow definitions of these offenses, makes an extensive range of defenses against the charge available to the accused person, and requires strict standards of proof. Moreover, Islamic law demands total fairness and equality in law enforcement. In my view, the prerequisite conditions for the enforcement of these punishments are extremely difficult to satisfy in practice and are certainly unlikely to materialize in any Muslim country in the foreseeable future. Nevertheless, the question remains, can [such] punishments be abolished as a matter of Islamic law [on the grounds that they are cruel, inhuman, or degrading]?

* * *

The basic question here is one of interpretation and application of a universally accepted human right. . . . Muslims would accept the human right not to be subjected to cruel inhuman, or degrading treatment or punishment. Their Islamic culture may indicate to them a different interpretation of this human right, however.

From a secular or humanist point of view, inflicting such a severe permanent punishment for any offense, especially for theft, is obviously cruel and inhuman, and probably also degrading. This may well be the private intuitive reaction of many educated modernized Muslims. However, to the vast majority of Muslims, the matter is settled by the categorical will of God as expressed in the Qur'an and, as such, is not open to question by human beings. Even the educated modernized Muslim, who may be privately repelled by this punishment, cannot risk the consequences of openly questioning the will of God. In addition to the danger of losing his or her faith and the probability of severe social chastisement, a Muslim who disputes the binding authority of the Qur'an is liable to the death penalty for apostasy (heresy) under Shari'a.

Thus, in all Muslim societies, the possibility of human judgment regarding the appropriateness or cruelty of a punishment decreed by God is simply out of the question. Furthermore, this belief is supported by what Muslims accept as rational arguments. From the religious point of view, human life does not end at death, but extends beyond that to the next life. In fact, religious sources strongly emphasize that the next life is the true and ultimate reality, to which this life is merely a prelude. In the next eternal life, every human being will stand judgment and suffer the consequences of his or her actions in this life. A religiously sanctioned punishment, however, will absolve an offender from punishment in the next life because God does not punish twice for the same offense. Accordingly, a thief who suffers the religiously sanctioned punishment of amputation of the right hand in this life will not be liable to the much harsher punishment in the next life. To people who hold this belief, however severe the Qur'anic punishment may appear to be, it is in fact extremely lenient and merciful in comparison to what the offender will suffer in the next life should the religious punishment not be enforced in this life.

* * *

Neither internal Islamic reinterpretation nor cross-cultural dialogue is likely to lead to the total abolition of this punishment as a matter of Islamic law. Much can be done, however, to restrict its implementation in practice. For example, there is room for developing stronger general social and economic prerequisites and stricter procedural requirements for the enforcement of the punishment. Islamic religious texts emphasize extreme caution in inflicting any criminal punishment. The Prophet said that if there is any doubt (*shubha*), the Qur'anic punishments should not be imposed. He also said that it is better to err on the side of refraining from imposing the punishment than to err on the side of imposing it in a doubtful case. Although these directives have already been incorporated into definitions of the offenses and the applicable rules of evidence and procedure, it is still possible to develop a broader concept of *shubha* to include, for example, psychological disorders as a defense against criminal responsibility. For instance, kleptomania may be taken as *shubha* barring punishment for theft. Economic need may also be a defense against a charge of theft.

Cross-cultural dialogue may also be helpful in this regard. In the Jewish tradition, for instance, jurists have sought to restrict the practical application of equally harsh punishment by stipulating strict procedural and other requirements. This theoretical Jewish jurisprudence may be useful to Muslim jurists and leaders seeking to restrict the practical application of Qur'anic punishments.... In fact, the jurisprudence of each tradition has borrowed heavily from the other in the past and may do so in the future once the present conflict is resolved.

I believe that in the final analysis, the interpretation and practical application of the protection against cruel, inhuman, or degrading treatment or punishment in the context of a particular society should be determined by the moral standards of that society. I also believe that there are many legitimate ways of influencing and informing the moral standards of a society. To dictate to a society is both unacceptable as a matter of principle and unlikely to succeed in practice. Cross-cultural dialogue and mutual influence, however, is acceptable in principle and continuously occurring in practice. To harness the power of cultural legitimacy in support of human rights, we need to develop techniques for internal cultural discourse and cross-cultural dialogue, and to work toward establishing general conditions conducive to constructive discourse and dialogue.

* * *

... The fundamental objective of the modern human rights movement is to protect citizens from the brutality and excesses of their own governments. On the other hand, it is extremely important to be sensitive to the dangers of cultural imperialism, whether it is a product of colonialism a tool of international economic exploitation and political subjugation, or simply a product of extreme ethnocentricity. Since we would not accept others' imposing their moral standards on us, we should not impose our own moral standards on them. In any case, external imposition is normally counterproductive and unlikely to succeed in changing the practice in question.... Greater consensus on international standards for the protection of the individual against cruel, inhuman, or degrading treatment or punishment [and other human rights deprivations] can be achieved through internal cultural discourse and cross-cultural dialogue.

It is unrealistic to expect this approach to achieve total agreement on the interpretation and application of standards, whether of treatment or punishment or any other human right.... If one reflects on the interpretation she or he would like to make the norm, it will probably be the one set by the person's culture.... [A] North American may think that a short term of imprisonment is the appropriate punishment for theft, and wish that to be the universal punishment for this offense. A Muslim, on the other hand, may feel that the amputation of the hand is appropriate under certain conditions and after satisfying strict safeguards.... I am not suggesting that we should make the Islamic or any other particular punishment the universal norm. I merely wish to point out that agreeing on a universal standard may not be as simple as we may think or wish it to be.

12. Burns H. Weston, "The Universality of Human Rights in a Multicultured World: Toward Respectful Decision–Making," *reprinted from* The Future of International Human Rights 65–66, 72–79 (B. Weston & S. Marks eds. & contribs., 1999).

Values are preferred events, "goods" we cherish; and ... the value of respect, conceived as the reciprocal honoring of freedom of choice about participation in value processes,[2] is "the core value of human rights."[3] In a world of diverse cultural traditions that is simultaneously distinguished by the widespread universalist claim that "human rights extend in theory to every person on earth without discriminations irrelevant to merit,"[4] the question thus unavoidably arises: when, in international human rights decision-making, are cultural differences to be respected and when are they not?[d]

* * *

2. M. McDougal, H. Lasswell & L. Chen, Human Rights and World Public Order: The Basic Policies of an International Law of Human Dignity 7 (1980).

3. *Id.* at 451. The authors impose an individualistic perspective on the meaning of this "core value." They write: "[R]espect is defined as an interrelation *among individual human beings* in which they reciprocally recognize and honor each other's freedom of choice about participation in the value processes of the world community or any of its component parts." *Id.* (emphasis added).

4. B. Weston, *Human Rights, supra* Reading A–1 in Problem 5–1, at 494. Reconsidering this phrase, I am today inclined to add "capability" to "merit" (and possibly also "basic need" insofar as it is not a function of "capability") as potentially a permissible basis for discrimination in otherwise equal arenas of claim and decision.

d. Weston next cites, at 67, many "physical practices" that provoke this question: abortion,

cannibalism, corporal disfigurement (foot binding, genital cutting, scarring, tatooing), corporal punishment (amputation; caning, flogging, lashing, spanking, and whipping; honor killing; execution by electric chair, firing squad, hanging, lethal injection, stoning), euthanasia, genocide, "ethnic cleansing," imprisonment (life, solitary, hard labor), infanticide, torture. He cites also many "behavioral practices": banishment (including "ethnic cleansing" and social ostracization), discrimination/segregation, divorce/separation (especially unilateral), dress codes (body covering, veil wearing), marriage (arranged, bride price/dower, forced, homosexual, polygamy/polygyny), slavery/forced labor, civil/political deprivations (assembly, association, expression, opinion, speech, etc.), economic/social deprivations (education, employment, etc.). He is at pains to point out that "[s]uch illustrations of the possible non-universality of alleged universal human rights are ... in no way restricted to 'Third World' settings. The long-standing resistance of the capitalist coun-

A survey of the literature reveals that the vast majority of commentators, most of them intellectually indebted or sympathetic to Western thought and tradition, come down on the side of universalism. Cultural relativism, if not criticized for preventing transnational moral judgments altogether, is repeatedly denounced as a "new excuse for an old strategy,"[5] used "to justify limitations on speech, subjugation of women, female genital mutilation, amputation of limbs and other cruel punishment, arbitrary use of power, and other violations of international human rights conventions."[6] . . .

Are these choices and conclusions unequivocally favoring universalism over relativism legitimate? In a critical sense, I think not, though not because they are the result of simplistic *a priori* reasoning or even that they are wrong. * * * My concern is that, without an analytically neutral approach to deciding when cultural differences are to be respected and when they are not, the pro-universalist choices and conclusions undermine the credibility and defensibility of their own particularistic objectives and thus make the idea of international human rights law as a basis for rendering moral judgments very difficult, perhaps even unworkable on occasion. One-sided assertions of legitimacy and priority, by definition discounting the centrality of the value of respect in human rights, invite countervailing charges of cultural imperialism (defending against real or imagined claims of cultural superiority—"colonizing") and cultural ethnocentrism (defending against real or imagined claims of cultural bias—"Westernizing"), and thus defeat the core goals they seek to achieve. True, cultural relativists also . . . express themselves in ways that subvert their own credo—as when, for example, non-Western and sometimes even Western proponents of cultural pluralism evince absolutist outrage at the supposed moral decay of the West. But this is only to prove my point. Any human rights orientation that is not genuinely in support of the widest possible embrace of the value of respect in the prescription and application of human rights norms in a multicultured world is likely to provoke substantial and widespread skepticism if not unreserved hostility.

It is of course tempting to argue that international human rights law settles the issue. . . . In human rights convention after human rights convention, after all, states have committed themselves to the universality of human rights, [and as required by] the rudimentary—indeed foundational—international law principle *pacta sunt servanda*, they are duty bound to uphold that universality. * * * This argument, however, falls woefully short of the cross-cultural challenge, and there are at least four reasons why.

First, not all states, certainly not all "relativist states," have ratified even some of the core international human rights instruments, thus thwarting the *pacta sunt servanda* argument *ab initio* in many if not most instances of relativist-universalist contestation. * * * Second . . ., much of international

tries, particularly the United States, to economic and social rights, and of the communist countries, past and present, to civil and political rights, attest to this fact. So too do the abortion and nuclear weapons policies in the industrialized world, challenging the 'right to life' set forth in UDHR Article 3 just as do the practices of infanticide and female sacrifice (*e.g.*, Sati) in 'pre-modern' societies." *Id.* at 68–69.

5. *See* A. Bayefsky, *Cultural Sovereignty, Relativism, and International Human Rights: New Excuses for Old Strategies*, 9 Ratio Juris 42 (1996).

6. J. Shestack, *The Philosophical Foundations of Human Rights*, 20 H.R.Q. 201, 231 (1998).

human rights law, particularly as it relates to such "first generation" rights as are reflected in the ICCPR [International Covenant on Civil and Political Rights] **[Basic Document 3.14]**, may be said to be Western inspired, thus fueling the conflict rather than resolving it. * * * Third, all human rights instruments are filled with ambiguity and indeterminacy, sometimes deliberately to ensure signature and ratification, [and] [t]hus require interpretation to inform the *content* of universalism even when the *concept* of it has been accepted. * * * Finally, when their plenipotentiaries are not signing human rights treaties and voting for human rights resolutions "as mere gestures for temporary public relations purposes,"[7] states, including states that profess the universality of human rights, typically hedge their bets by resort to reservations, statements of understanding, and declarations so as to ensure that certain practices deemed central to their legal or other cultural traditions will not be rendered unlawful or otherwise anachronistic. . . .

. . . There is, thus, no escaping that claims of cultural relativism demand and deserve thoughtful responses. * * * But how, one may ask, is this to be done . . . in the particular case? [How do we reach the conclusion that a particular claim of universalism] should trump a competing claim of cultural relativism or *vice versa*?

The remainder of this essay explores this question, detailing a *methodology of respect* according to which competing relativist-universalist claims can be assessed objectively and thereby escape, hopefully, charges of cultural imperialism and ethnocentrism. . . .

[*Eds.*—The author begins by delineating, at 77–80, the observational standpoint he says is needed "to render human rights judgments about particular cultural practices in transnational settings in an objectively respectful manner." Borrowing from the late John Rawls who, in A Theory of Justice 11 (1971), reasoned that "[t]he true principles of justice" are those that "free and rational persons concerned to further their own interests would accept in an *initial position* of equality as defining the fundamental terms of their association," he argues, at 77–78, that an observational standpoint capable of such objectivity is that "of thinking men and women who, each in their private capacity (*i.e.*, not as state representatives) in some original social setting, but without knowledge of the details of their own physical and social identity (creed, gender, race, etc.), freely choose a public order that is fair to all in its distribution of benefits (rights) and burdens (duties) because, rationally contemplating their own self-interests, they choose a public order that will not cause anyone, including of course themselves, to be disadvantaged in the real world; they choose principles of governance that are good for all, not simply for some or a few"—*i.e.*, "principles that identify more with the human species as a whole than with the primacy of any of its individual or group." From this observational standpoint, Weston asserts, it is possible to articulate "a set of public order value preferences that transcend parochial interest and selfish motive, a map of basic values or blueprint of fundamental laws that can win the assent of persons everywhere, and thereby facilitate

7. S. Marks & B. Weston, *International Human Rights at Fifty: A Foreward*, 8 Transnat'l L. & Contemp. Probs. 112, 119 (1998).

respectful decision when it comes to legal and moral judgments about particular cultural practices across national boundaries."

Weston then asks, at 80–81, what would be, from this perspective, the "map of basic values or blueprint of fundamental laws" that "our initial position decision-makers [would] choose to guide their transnational judgments about particular cultural practices?" Rejecting the notion that his preferred observational standpoint is subject to criticism for being "too Western inspired, too individualistically oriented,"[e] he demurs from Rawls' proposition that decision-makers in the "initial position" would intuitively choose two "principles of justice"—liberty and equality. While not discounting the importance of these ordering principles, he argues that "cultural practices for which relativist claims have been or might be made commonly reach beyond the values of liberty and equality that Rawls stresses." Concluding that "neither liberty nor equality are sufficient to serve adequately as the exclusive determinants of relativist-universalist contests," he urges instead "[all] the basic values of human dignity or of a free society"—that is, citing Myres S. McDougal, Harold D. Lasswell, and Lung-chi Chen, Human Rights and World Public Order: The Basic Policies of An International Law of Human Dignity 90 (1980), "those [values] which have been bequeathed to us by all the great democratic movements of humankind and which are being more insistently expressed in the rising common demands and expectations of peoples everywhere."

Even this alternative, however, is seen by Weston to betray "a distinct Western bias that appears ... to prejudge the outcome of ... relativist-universalist controversies." Accordingly, he advocates a compromise, drawing from both Rawls and McDougal–Lasswell–Chen, at 81–82 as follows:]

... [T]he map of basic values or decision-making principles that should guide transnational judgments about particular cultural practices should be ... both more expansive or inclusive than that proposed by Rawls and ... less vulnerable than the McDougal–Lasswell–Chen formulation to accusations of Western/universalist bias, ergo one ... that embraces the following self-interested *desiderata*:

- the widest possible shaping and sharing of *all* the values of human dignity, including but not limited to (political) liberty and (socioeconomic) equality,

- without discrimination of any kind save that of merit and basic need (*e.g.,* physical/mental handicap, rank poverty) in many though not necessarily all instances,

e. Rational people acting individually behind a "veil of ignorance," Weston reasons, at 79, "can foresee the possibility that they [may] belong to social groups that espouse spiritual/dialectic and collectivist/communitarian as well as Western/individualistic values, and that therefore they may belong to a public order that embraces all of these community values."

- consistent with the truism that in a world of finite possibility, 'most assertions of human rights are qualified by the limitation that the rights of any particular individual or group in any particular instance are restricted as much as is necessary to secure the comparable rights of others and the aggregate common interest.'[8]

It need here be added only that, in choosing this policy guide to respectful relativist-universalist decision, our "initial position" decision-makers might substitute Martha Nussbaum's (and Amartya Sen's) language of "capabilities"[9] for the more commonly used language of "rights"—[i.e., thinking upon] all the values of human dignity ... not in terms of *abstract goals* but, rather, in terms of the concrete and more readily *measurable needs* that all people must have satisfied to fulfill at least the minimal requirements of human dignity (however defined).

[*Eds.*—On the basis of the above-recommended observational standpoint and guiding principles, the author next details his proposed "methodology of respect," *i.e.*, "the intellectual tasks of relativist-universalist decision."]

Having ... postulated the world public order goals that optimally should define and govern [relativist-universalist] appraisal, emphasizing the widest possible shaping and sharing of *all* the values (or capabilities) of human dignity, it is tempting to argue that local practices that are indisputably destructive of the values (or capabilities) of human dignity must be altogether rejected and that such rejection should not be confused with disrespect for cultural differences or the principles of nonintervention and self-determination that afford them protection. I have in mind such policies and practices as genocide, ethnic cleansing, imposed starvation, physical and mental torture, [systematic rape], arbitrary arrest, detention, and execution, slavery, forced labor, and racial *apartheid*. If they are not entirely without cultural basis in the first place, these policies and practices are now so widely condemned that they no longer can be justified by any local custom or rationale.

Or so it might be initially argued.... [However, to ensure] fully respectful decision when cross-cultural legal and moral judgments are being rendred ..., [i]t is, I believe, [essential first to embrace] *all* the intellectual tasks that seem required to resolve, from an "initial position" policy-oriented perspective, a particular relativist-universalist controversy: (1) the clarification of community policies relevant to the specific cultural practice at issue, (2) the description of past trends in decision relevant to that practice, (3) the analysis of factors affecting these trends, (4) the projection of future trends in decision relevant to the specific cultural practice in question, and (5) the invention and evaluation of policy alternatives to that practice. An analytical flow chart of these relevant intellectual tasks looks as follows:

8. Weston, *supra* note 4.

9. *See, e.g,* M. Nussbaum, *Capabilities, Human Rights, and the Universal Declaration*, in

The Future of International Human Rights 25 (B. Weston & S. Marks eds & contribs., 1999).

Clarification of Community Policies

↕

Description of Past Trends in Decision

↕

Analysis of Factors Affecting Decision

↕

Projection of Future Trends in Decision

↕

Invention and Evaluation of Policy Alternatives

Although ... presented in logically sequenced order here, they must be applied configuratively (as the two-way arrows suggest) ..., each task informing and being informed by the others, to achieve as comprehensive a contextual analysis as possible. The goal is to test each dimension of policy-oriented inquiry for its ability to contribute to rational but respectful choice in decision, and to obtain guidance in the development of international community policy relative to the practices in question. Of course ..., a preliminary issue is the threshold question of whether or not the practice in question is a *cultural* practice as distinct from one that might be, say, *idiosyncratic* to the particular governing elite involved. If the latter, then the relativist-universalist issue is by definition not implicated, and a decision about the practice may be taken according to potentially different policy criteria. If, however, the practice in question can be properly denominated a cultural one, then it is incumbent upon us, from the standpoint of our "initial position" decision-makers, to pursue the policy-oriented inquiry outlined.

[*Eds.*—The author then proceeds to detail at length, at 84–98, each of the five intellectual tasks he advocates. We summarize in the following five key points.]

1. While the values of liberty and equality advocated by Rawls are essential to respectful cross-cultural decision, Weston argues, "[they] do not of themselves provide a reliable exit from the relativist-universalist conundrum" because, in addition to being often competitive, they do not sufficiently pinpoint the community policies that are at stake relative to the two principal "social functions" on which the vast majority of cross-cultural normative judgments are centered: punishment (its severity) and societal differentiation (its justification). Also, he contends, "[e]xalting liberty and equality to the disregard of other principles or values [has] diverted responsible attention from the centrality of respect in human rights decision-making and thus thwarted clear-headed thinking about the relativist-universalist choice." As a "guide to respectful decision," he therefore recommends "the map of basic values or fundamental principles of decision-making that our hypothetical 'initial position' decision-makers would choose behind a 'veil of ignorance' to ensure the greatest possible equal distribution of rights and duties within the public order of which they are a part." Only by relating these broad goals to specific instances of relativist-universalist controversy—be it hand amputation in the former Afghanistan or outright execution in the United States—is it possible to ensure respectful decision about the competing values of cultural

pluralism and universalist principle. Weston continues: "[T]he task of relating these goals to specific cultural practices is no easy one. Nor is it made easier by the fact that behind the relativist-universalist debate lurks a desire, evident on *both* sides of the debate, less to ensure cultural pluralism than to further the interests of the private and public governing elites who currently are engaged in a grand global struggle for economic and political influence (to the shameful disregard of the interests of the 'Other' who typically are the victims of globalization's highly uneven—unjust—distribution of economic benefits and burdens and whose pain always must be central to human rights discourse and action). The relativist-universalist debate is not merely a conflict between differing cultural and universal norms. It is, often, a high-level confrontation between competing conservative and liberal versions of capitalism, none of which is *a priori* superior to the other, especially when expressed in cultural terms. Neither the relativist nor the universalist, therefor, may dismiss the other's claims without a reasoned response. The policies that underwrite their claims must be understood for what they are and properly measured for their compatibility with the wider public order goals that our neutral 'initial position' decision-makers would have chosen to ensure respectful decision when rendering cross-cultural moral judgments."

2. "A key task in . . . cross-cultural judgment," Weston argues, "is to describe the past trends in cross-cultural decision that are relevant to the particular practice that is in question." An understanding of past cross-cultural decision, he contends, "can reveal the extent to which the world community . . . has actively denounced/supported, passively opposed/tolerated, or otherwise disapproved/condoned the particular practice across space, time, institution, and crisis, and [thus] reveal as well the extent to which one should or should not take seriously the immediate objection to it."

3. Weston argues that it is next important "to analyze the factors that have influenced . . . decisional trends" in [relativist-universalist controversy] and thus also the case at hand. It is important, he says, "because such analysis helps us to understand not only how and why relevant precedents were reached but also what factors are likely to serve as useful indicators for present and future decisions, particularly as they may prove useful in guiding the evaluation and recommendation of policy alternatives." To demonstrate his point, he entertains "impressionistic forays" into these conditioning factors, organized around the principal elements of social process—"who (participants), with what views or outlooks (perspectives), in what spatial, temporal, and other circumstances (situations), with what capabilities (bases of power), by what methods or techniques (strategies), produces what results (outcomes and effects), is influenced by what more-or-less exogenous factors (general conditions)"—and subject to the caveat that "it is seldom the investigation of one conditioning factor alone but, rather, the in-depth exploration of all of them that provides the comprehensive knowledge that is needed to reach a respectful decision, our objective."[f]

4. For "at least two reasons," Weston argues, "[t]he projection of probable future developments relative to given cultural practices—in the sense of the broad trend, not the particular instance—is an important variable

---

f. For illustration of the kind of policy-oriented inquiry Weston advocates for respect- ful cross-cultural decision-making, see *infra* Discussion Note/Question 5, at 743.

... in cross-cultural decision-making...." He writes: "First it can help us see whether continuation of the given practice will reveal movement toward or away from the postulated public order goals of our 'initial position' decision-makers. If so, then the practice [merits] at least *prima facie* deference; if not, then the opposite. Second, to minimize the [diminution] of cultural pluralism where continuation of the given practice will reveal movement away from the postulated goals of our 'initial position' decision-makers, it can help to simulate creativity in the invention and evaluation of alternatives to the manner in which the given cultural practice is currently being exercised so as ... to preserve the essence of the practice [while simultaneously making it] comport with our postulated public order goals."

5. The final intellectual task of respectful decision-making in relativist-universalist controversies relates, according to Weston, to "the deliberate search for, and assessment of, alternatives either to the given cultural practice itself or to the manner in which it is exercised in cases where it [or its manner of exercise] may be found ... at odds with the postulated public order goals of our 'initial position' decision-makers." It is, he says, "the last task towards which all the preceding intellectual tasks accumulate and therefore the one to be pursued after all of its predecessors have been credibly exhausted." The point, he contends, "is not to declare a 'winner,' but, rather, to enhance the possibility of ensuring the world's rich diversity (cultural pluralism) while at the same time serving the values of *human* dignity as defined by the postulated public order goals of our 'initial position' decision-makers." To the extent feasible, he asserts, "respectful decision-making in cross-cultural context should seek integrative solutions characterized by maximum gains and minimum losses for all sides of the relativist-universalist debate; it should seek diversity in unity."

To the foregoing and critical to respectful cross-cultural decision must be added, the author further argues, "an honest assessment of the very decision process pursuant to which that judgment is being rendered." He writes: "As any sophisticated law student knows, who decides what,why, when, where, and how often has as much and sometimes more to do with the resolution of legal controversies as the facts and pertinent doctrines, principles, and rules themselves." The author then concludes:

"[O]ne thing is certain: if one is to take seriously the proposition that respect is 'the core value of all human rights,' there is no escaping that cross-cultural decision-making about relativist-universalist controversies cannot be a simpleminded affair. Necessarily, it must reflect the complexity of life itself, implicating a whole series of interrelated activities and events that are indispensable to effective inquiry and therefore to rational and respectful choice in decision. And to this end, I therefore join other human rights theorists and activists in advocating the importance of dialogue across cultures and societies. But not only ethical or moral dialogue. Also needed is that kind of cross-cultural dialogue that can yield substantial detailed consensus on the many factual and policy-oriented questions that absolutely need to be asked—hopefully systematically in keeping with the *methodology of respect* that I have urged here—so as to guarantee that the core value of respect will be present in all relativist-universalist decision-making...."

SECTION 5. DISCUSSION NOTES/QUESTIONS

1. States have regularly invoked claims of "national sovereignty" or "domestic jurisdiction" to stay the international community's community's efforts to promote and especially protect human rights. Examples of such claims are those of South Africa during the *apartheid* era, and the United States with respect to criticism of the use of the death penalty. Are claims of "cultural difference" simply a variant of the same argument? If not, how do they differ?

2. Is cultural pluralism a desirable value? If so, in what way or ways might the doctrine of cultural relativism be of help in relation to it? If not, why is the preservation of cultural differences not a good thing?

3. As seen from the readings, *supra*, cultural relativism tends to favor duty-based over rights-based social orders. Does this necessarily mean or require a less strong commitment to human rights, as some of the readings suggest? If so, how does one explain the 1948 American Declaration of the Rights and Duties of Man **(Basic Document 3.1)**, which contains ten articles devoted to the duties that individuals and groups of individuals owe to civil society, or the 1981 African (Banjul) Charter on Human and Peoples' Rights **(Basic Document 3.22)**, which contains three such articles? In any event, is a duty-based social order or a rights-based social order more likely to ensure a public order of human dignity? Does your answer to this question depend on how you define "human dignity"? How might a relativist define the concept? A universalist? To mark the fiftieth anniversary of the Universal Declaration of Human Rights of 1948 **(Basic Document 3.3)** a group of eminent former politicians and scholars organized by an NGO, the InterAction Council, issued a Universal Declaration of Human Responsibilities, *available at* <http://www.interactioncouncil.org>. The Council hoped that the Declaration would be adopted by the UN General Assembly, but it did not attract enough support from states. After reading the Declaration, why do you think it failed to garner state backing?

4. "Women's issues," observes Burns Weston (*supra* Reading 1, at 84), "lie at the heart of many relativist-universalist controversies, both directly and indirectly, particularly at the intersection between masculine hegemony and women's sexual and reproductive identities." This may be seen in the extensive reservations made to the Convention on the Elimination of All Forms of Discrimination Against Women of 1979 **(Basic Document 3.21)**, many made in the name of preservation of cultural and religious identities. *See* Hilary Charlesworth and Christine Chinkin, *The Boundaries of International Law* 102–13 (2000). Feminist scholars have emphasized the value of an investigation into the gender of the "cultures" that relativism privileges. Arati Rao, who writes in *The Politics of Gender and Culture in International Human Rights Discourse, in* Women's Rights Human Rights 167, 169 (J. Peters & A. Wolper eds., 1995) that "[n]o social group has suffered greater violation of its rights in the name of culture than women," has proposed a series of questions to assess claims of culture, particularly those used to counter claims of women's human rights: whose culture is being invoked? What is the status of the interpreter? In whose name is the argument being advanced? Who are the primary beneficiaries of the claim? *See id.* at 174. A passionate debate has occurred over international approaches to the practices of clitoridectomy and infibulation, also termed genital surgeries or genital mutilation. Some states have been resistant to international criticism of these practices on the basis that they are matters of domestic jurisdiction. Women within states where these practices occur may support the goal of their eradication but de-

nounce the punitive approach of Western feminists. Isabelle Gunning has argued, for example, that education and dialogue are the best responses: *Arrogant Perception, World Traveling and Multicultural Feminism: The Case of Female Genital Surgeries*, 23 Colum. Hum. Rts. L. Rev. 189 (1992). *See also* Leslie Obiora, *Bridges and Barricades: Rethinking Polemics and Intransigence in the Campaign against Female Circumcision*, 47 Case W. Res. L. Rev. 275 (1997). In a similar vein Makau Matua (*supra* Reading 10) writes at 225–26

> Perhaps in no other area than in the advocacy over FGM [female genital mutilation] is the image of culture as the savage more poignant. The word "mutilation" itself implies the willful, sadistic infliction of pain on a hapless victim, and stigmatizes the practitioners and their cultures as barbaric savages. Descriptions of the practice are so searing and revolting that they evoke images of a barbarism that defies civilization. Although the practice has dissipated over the last several decades, it is still carried out in parts of Africa and the Middle East. Given Western stereotypes of barbaric natives in the "dark" continent, Western advocacy over FGM has evoked images of machete-wielding natives only too eager to inflict pain on women in their societies.

Matua concludes, at 244–45:

> Stepping back from the SVS [savages-victims-saviors] rhetoric creates a new basis for calculating human dignity and identifies ways and societal structures through which such dignity could be protected or enhanced. Such an approach would not assume, *ab initio*, that a particular cultural practice was offensive to human rights. It would respect cultural pluralism as a basis for finding common universality on some issues. With regard to FGM, for instance, such an approach would first excavate the social meaning and purposes of the practice, as well as its effects, and then investigate the conflicting positions over the practice in that society. Rather than demonizing and finger-pointing, under the tutelage of outsiders and their local supporters, the contending positions would be carefully examined and compared to find ways of either modifying or discarding the practice without making its practitioners feel shameful of their culture and of themselves. The zealotry of the SVS approach leaves no room for a deliberative intra-cultural dialogue and introspection.

For a thoughtful perspective on human rights law from a "Third World" perspective see Ratna Kapur, *The Tragedy of Victimization Rhetoric: Resurrecting the "Native" Subject in International/Post–Colonial Feminist Legal Politics*,15 Harv. Hum. Rts. J. 1 (2002).

5. Weston's "methodology of respect" (*supra* Reading 12) is an attempt to formulate an "analytically neutral approach for deciding when cultural differences are to be respected and when they are not." Why is neutrality important? Is it possible? Consider Weston's "impressionistic foray" into the first of the "conditioning factors" that influence cross-cultural decision: *participants*. He writes, at 88–89:

> In all cultural practices, individual human beings are the ultimate actors, either because they are themselves the *masters* of the practice or its *servants*, or because they are affiliated with a group that is either way directly involved.[10] If only just to comprehend the practice, therefore, it is important

---

10. There are no perfect words of common usage to identify the key participants in cultur- al practices. Therefore, for lack of more suitable alternatives and for purely descriptive

to ask ... such descriptively-oriented questions as: Who are the key participants in the practice (*e.g.*, individuals, families, clans, ecclesiastical organizations, private associations, pressure groups, political parties, governments, international institutions)? Who is responsible for the practice, who are its principal masters? Who is the object of it, who are its primary servants? What biological characteristics (race, sex, age, sexual orientation), culture (ethnicity, nationality), class (wealth, power), interest (group membership), or personality (authoritarian, submissive) may be attributed to each? And so forth. But participatory questions such as these, helping us to understand the identity and roles of the different participants involved, can also greatly assist the issue of whether or not to honor a cultural practice, particularly where the resolution of that issue turns on the legal and moral rationales given for social differentiation. Indeed, together with other considerations, they may, in such instances, prove decisive in the given case. Consider, for example, the practice of racial *apartheid* in pre–1990 South Africa. In addition to its violating [the] general "initial position" public order postulate of nondiscrimination in the shaping and sharing of all values, the fact that it privileged minority whites of European origin over majority blacks of indigenous origin obviously had much to do with the world's having outlawed it. Might similar conclusions be reached *vis-à-vis* the Hindu and Muslim traditions in Central and South Asia and in the Middle East of segregating women (*Harem, Purdah*)? Of veil wearing (*Chador, Hijab, Niqab*) and total body covering (per the *Shari'a* doctrine of *Urf*)? Of the erstwhile Chinese practice of female foot binding were it still exercised today? In light of [the] nondiscrimination postulate, surely the participatory (patriarchal) dynamics of such practices (privileging men over women) are important, sometimes perhaps even decisive, to the issue of whether they should or should not be honored in cross-cultural judgment. For example, if the practice can be shown to involve a broad cross-section of society participating in decision-making about it, including its servants as well as its masters, we might tentatively conclude that the practice has some at least *prima facie* legitimacy. If, on the other hand, it can be found that only privileged persons make the relevant decisions about it (*e.g.*, men, people from elite castes/races, etc.), we would apply, in light of the postulated public order goal values of our "initial position" decision-makers, a higher level of scrutiny to the cultural practice. Likewise, if only one group benefits—particularly if the benefit is at the expense of another group or if only one group "loses"—the practice, according to the same criteria, should be called into question.

Does this sort of questioning lend credence to the possibility of analytic neutrality in cross-cultural decision-making? If so, how? If not, why not?

6. *Bibliographical Note.* For supplemental discussion concerning the principal themes addressed in this problem, consult the following additional specialized materials:

(a) *Books/Monographs/Report/Symposia.* P. Baehr, Human Rights: Universality in Practice (1999); The East Asian Challenge for Human Rights (J.Bauer & D. Bell eds., 1999); _____, Universal Human Rights in Theory and Practice (2d ed. 2003); Michael Freeman, Human Rights (2002); Human Rights and Societies in

purposes (*i.e.*, free of bias or preference), I adopt the term "master" to refer to those persons who define, execute, administer, and otherwise govern cultural practices, and the term "servant" to refer to those persons who follow or who are expected to follow such practices. It must be understood, however, that neither the masters nor servants of cultural practices are restricted to their most distinctive participatory characteristics. On many occasions, the same participant or participants will perform both roles simultaneously.

Transition: Causes, Consequences, Responses (S. Horowitz & A. Schnabel eds., 2004); Human Rights in Cross–Cultural Perspective (A. An–Na'im ed., 1992); S. Huntington, The Clash of Civilizations: The Debate (1993); ___, The Clash of Civilizations and the Remaking of World Order (1996); M. McDougal, H. Lasswell, & L. Chen, Human Rights and World Public Order (1980); A. Renteln, International Human Rights: Universalism Versus Relativism (1990).

(b) *Articles/Book Chapters*. G. Binder, *Cultural Relativism and Cultural Imperialism in Human Rights Law*, 5 Buff. Hum. Rts. L. Rev. 211 (1999); R. Bahdi, *Truth and Method in the Domestic Application of International Law*, 15 Can. J. L. & Juris. 255 (2002); J. Chan, *The Task for Asians: To Discover Their Own Political Morality for Human Rights*, 4 Hum. Rts. Dialogue 5 (Carnegie Council on Ethics and International Affairs, Mar. 1996); M. Davis, *Constitutionalism and Political Culture: The Debate over Human Rights and Asian Values*, 11 Harv. Hum. Rts. J. 109 (1998); J. Donnelly, *Cultural Relativism and Universal Rights*, 6 H.R.Q. 400 (1984); _____, *Human Rights and Human Dignity: An Analytical Critique of Non–Western Conceptions of Human Rights*, 76 Am. Pol. Sci. Rev. 303 (1982); M. Goodhart, *Origins and Universality in the Human Rights Debates: Cultural Essentialism and the Challenge of Globalization*, 25 H.R.Q. 935 (2003); Y. Ghai, *Universal Rights and Cultural Pluralism: Universalism and Relativism: Human Rights as a Framework for Negotiating Interethnic Claims*, 21 Cardozo L. Rev. 1095 (2000); R. Howard, *Dignity, Community, and Human Rights*, in Human Rights in Cross–Cultural Perspective 81 (A. An–Na'im ed., 1992); S. Huntington, *The West and the World*, 75 For. Aff. 28 (Nov/Dec 1996); D. Otto, *Rethinking the "Universality" of Human Rights Law*, 29 Colum. Hum. Rts. L. Rev. 1 (1997); O. Schachter, *Human Dignity as a Normative Concept*, 77 A.J.I.L. 848 (1983); R. Sloane, *Outrelativizing Relativism: A Liberal Defense of the Universality of Human Rights*, 32 Vand. J. Transnat'l L. 527 (2001); K. Sorrell, *Cultural Pluralism and International Rights*, 10 Tulsa J. Comp. & Int'l L. 369 (2003); K. Tan, *What Asians Think about the West's Response to the Human Rights Debate*, 4 Hum. Rts. Dialogue 3 (Carnegie Council on Ethics and International Affairs, March 1996); S. Tay, *Human Rights, Culture, and the Singapore Example*, 41 McGill L. J. 743 (1996).

Chapter Six

PROBLEMS OF ECONOMIC WELL–BEING

THE VITAL PERSPECTIVE

The globalization of trade, capital, and technology that began in earnest during the last decade of the 20th century, commonly called "economic globalization," is one of the most defining phenomena of our time, and it is having a profound impact on world order. Presenting new regulatory challenges, it has brought into play global economic institutions that, though evolving, appear at once menacingly powerful and unable either to fulfill their missions successfully or to ensure the values of social justice and economic and environmental sustainability—the International Monetary Fund (IMF) and the World Trade Organization (WTO), for example. At the same time, more people suffer from hunger, malnutrition, and disease today than at the end of World War II. Well over half the world's population receives a per capita income of less than two dollars a day, under life conditions that are monstrously grim and worsening. With population increases absorbing over half the economic gains made since 1960, with concentrations of power and wealth nesting higher and higher on the social pyramids, with domestic and foreign policies resistant to defining where business profit ends and social responsibility begins, and with mere fractions of huge GNPs being consigned away from colossal military budgets to the alleviation of human want, the gap between the "haves" and "have-nots" widens, both nationally and internationally. The social deficit of the approximately three billion who comprise the poorest 60% of the world's population is larger than ever before, with women faring far worse than men in all the indicators. There are more children without schools to attend, more adult illiterates, more people in ill health and lacking in adequate medical services, more unemployed, more unable to satisfy the most basic of human needs. In other words, as it responds to economic globalization, the international system is taking on more and more the role of national governments without any assurance that it is up to the task. A fundamental world order challenge, therefore, is the creation of an international system that responds to economic globalization and its attendant problems not only holistically but, as well, with deference to transparency, accountability, and social justice.

Problem 6–1

A Financial Crisis in Sundalau Spreads to Tolteca

SECTION 1. FACTS

Sundalau is a Southeast Asian country that, beginning in the 1980s, came to enjoy extremely rapid—often double-digit—economic growth rates annually. This success, however, disguised serious underlying problems with Sundalau's financial system. Corruption, including at the highest levels, was rampant. Many of the most sizable industries were in the hands of politically connected elites and, though poorly run, many were propped up by friendly bankers who extended credit long after it was clear that loans could not be repaid. Compounding the problem, a lack of transparency and shoddy accounting practices obscured the full extent to which these practices had damaged the banking system.

A combination of other factors added to the precariousness of the country's financial situation. Over the last decade, Sundalaun enterprises borrowed significantly, mostly in US dollars, from foreign banks. Sundalau's extremely inflated property market, especially in its capital city, Bandabang, was highly leveraged. As a result of the country's economic boom, consumers had begun to purchase large quantities of imported goods, causing a chronic and growing current account deficit. Finally, following the elimination of capital controls, a great deal of speculative "hot" money was invested in the country's stock market.

Approximately one year ago, investigative articles in the international financial press began to expose the nature of the bad commercial debt, current account, and other problems in Sundalau, making the international investment community extremely nervous. Sundalau maintained a pegged exchange rate of forty Sundalaun rupiahs to the US dollar. Particularly in light of the current account problem, investors began to fear that Sundalau might not be able to maintain that value and thus began selling their Sundalaun securities to cash out of the rupiah. Whereupon, in an attempt to stave off financial panic, the Sundalaun Minister of Finance, Grace Namominda, appeared with the country's Prime Minister and, putting on a brave face, declared that the country's central bank would vigorously defend the rupiah, asserting that there was "absolutely no foreseeable scenario under which the Rupiah would be devalued."

Two days later, the *World Financial Daily* ran a front page exposé alleging that Sundalau's foreign exchange reserves (which had been thought to be large) were almost depleted, and a full-scale panic ensued. Believing a devaluation of the rupiah to be inevitable, investors *en masse* began to sell their Sundalaun securities and cash out of the rupiah. At the same time, as pressure on the rupiah began to build, Sundalau's central bank attempted to maintain its defense of the rupiah by seeking and receiving an emergency loan from the International Monetary Fund (IMF). Ms. Namominda appeared again, this time with the President of the IMF, and reiterated that the rupiah would not be devalued. She followed by raising short-term interest rates to 60%.

Nevertheless, the stampede out of the rupiah continued, making the eventual devaluation of the currency a self-fulfilling prophecy; and as foreign exchange reserves became almost completely exhausted, Ms. Namominda conceded defeat with an announcement that the rupiah would be left to "float at its natural level." In the next week, the rupiah—before finally stabilizing—lost almost 65% of its value.

A major economic recession—more accurately a depression—ensued as thousands of enterprises all over the country could not maintain the liquidity necessary to stay in business. Foreign loans, which were denominated in dollars and other foreign currencies, could no longer be repaid, and foreign banks declared many of the country's businesses to be in default. Even access to domestic credit became nearly impossible, as the government's efforts to keep the rupiah from further collapse required it to maintain the previously introduced high, short-term interest rates. Businesses, as a result, no longer had the liquidity necessary to meet domestic expenses, let alone pay for the now hugely expensive US dollar and other foreign currency denominated imports, including essentials such as petroleum. As businesses closed, overnight almost one-half of the country's workers found themselves unemployed. The resulting lack of consumer demand further exacerbated the country's depression.

Observing in horror the unfolding of events in Sundalau, investors worried that a similar fate would befall other neighboring Asian countries with more or less similar economic profiles.[a] As panicky investors sold national securities to cash out of local currencies, the Sundalaun disaster began to repeat itself in varying degrees throughout Southeast Asia. The contagion then began to spread to Latin America and the territories of the former Soviet Union. A full-scale global crisis was at hand.

Strongly affected was the Latin American country of Tolteca, a founding member of both the Organization of American States (OAS) and the IMF.[b] The Sundalaun crisis came at a crucial time in Tolteca's political development. After a long period of military rule and moderate economic progress, the country had returned to democracy in the early 1980s. To deter the possibility of a future authoritarian leader coming to power, the country's new democratic constitution included a provision limiting the President to one five-year term.

Presidential transitions took place smoothly and without incident until 2000 when Humberto Gonzalez was elected President on a left-leaning populist platform. However, Gonzalez, a former general who had led an unsuccessful *coup de état* only a few months after the country was returned to

---

a. Several foreign investors, however, took advantage of the opportunity to buy Sundalaun companies very inexpensively either from banks or directly from their owners.

b. When Tolteca joined the IMF, its government notified the organization that the country intended to avail itself of transitional arrangements under Article XIV, Section 2 of the IMF Articles of Agreement to grandfather

in the previously enacted National Currency Control Law. This law allowed for the Toltecan government to limit the amount of Toltecan pesos that could be exchanged for foreign currency for purposes of foreign travel by Toltecan nationals. While the Toltecan government had only utilized this power on a few occasions over the years, the law remained in effect.

democratic rule, betrayed his populist campaign promises almost immediately after becoming President and adopted the neoliberal economic policies that were much in vogue at the time. He dramatically cut back social welfare spending, privatized most of the country's state-owned businesses, opened the door wide to foreign investment, and began negotiating to join the North American Free Trade Agreement (NAFTA). The Tolteca citizenry generally accepted President Gonzalez's justification (based on the economic thinking then dominant) that the social pain associated with these changes would lead to strong economic growth and ultimately benefit the working class and poor. This prognosis did not come to pass, however. Only the economic elite profited from the President's neoliberal policies. When, in early 2004, President Gonzalez's term was entering its final year, the poor and working class found themselves, if anything, worse off than when President Gonzalez had won office.

Concerned to ensure a favorable historical legacy but consistent with his undemocratic past, President Gonzalez therefore determined to continue in office despite the constitutional provision barring re-election. In pursuit of this goal, he initiated a legal action before the Toltecan Supreme Court asserting that the Constitution's provision barring re-election conflicted with a more fundamental provision guaranteeing political freedom, and, midst allegations of intimidation and impropriety,[c] the Court ruled in his favor. Though President Gonzalez won the election that followed in 2005, the results were tainted by significant evidence of organized voter fraud on the part of the President's supporters. Election monitors from the OAS reported that the election was a "sham" and that it was "not free and fair even in the most minimal sense."

Following the election, President Gonzalez took the constitutionally dubious position that Tolteca could accede to NAFTA solely on his presidential authority without the consent and ratification of the Toltecan parliament. The Supreme Court again backed President Gonzalez and, after the decision, Tolteca joined NAFTA.

Despite President Gonzalez's increasingly authoritarian drift, an alliance of political parties and civil society organizations known as the Coalition for a Return to Democracy (CRD) emerged as a major challenge to him; and, as the country began to experience the effects of the global financial crisis begun in Sundalau, many of his allies, particularly among the wealthy, began to defect to the CRD. Mass protests soon followed, and President Gonzalez found himself forced to call early elections in accordance with the Toltecan constitution. Whereupon the CRD unified behind a single candidate, José Castillo, who had served as Vice President in the second administration elected after Tolteca's return to democracy in the early 1980s. Despite attempts by President Gonzalez to rig the election, Señor Castillo won and was sworn in as president.

Immediately upon assuming the presidency, and against the backdrop of an ever worsening economic crisis that had begun in Sundalau, President Castillo made several statements ensuring foreign investors in Tolteca that

---

c. For example, the three Supreme Court justices that were most likely to rule against President Gonzalez were forced to resign because of unsubstantiated allegations made by the President of financial corruption.

"their interests would be respected." Unlike the Sundalaun Finance Minister Namominda, Castillo refused to raise interest rates, the traditional IMF orthodoxy in response to such a crisis. Instead, without seeking the approval or review of the IMF, he pushed through parliament an amendment of Tolteca's National Currency Control Law (NCCL) directing the Toltecan government to impose currency controls. The controls specifically required that dividend, interest, or other income derived from portfolio investment in the Toltecan stock, bond, or money markets, as well as proceeds from the liquidation of portfolio investment in those markets, could not be converted into foreign exchange for one year, and then only after an "exit" tax equivalent to 10% of the monies being exchanged was paid to the government. The amendment did not affect foreign direct investment or trade in goods and services. Nor did it affect domestically owned and operated enterprises[d] that required access to foreign exchange to pay principal or interest on bank loans denominated in foreign currencies.

Initially, after the imposition of the capital controls, the Toltecan peso continued its decline, losing another 30% of its value. In the months that followed, however, the peso began to strengthen, recovering one-half of what it had lost after the imposition of the currency controls. Tolteca has been in consultation with the IMF since the imposition of its currency controls, but the IMF has not as of yet taken any position on the controls.

In the United States, responding to pressure from American investors, Charles Chauvin, a United States Senator, introduced legislation that would impose US trade sanctions against Tolteca "in defense against Tolteca's illegal expropriation" of US investor assets. Additionally, his proposed legislation directed the United States to vote against the extension of future IMF loans to Tolteca. Hearings before the Senate Committee on Foreign Relations are scheduled to address the question of whether Senator Chauvin's bill, if adopted and implemented as national policy, would constitute a violation of international law.

The American investors, not content to limit their strategy to one of economic pressure on Tolteca, have initiated a legal case against the country.[e] The case is before a panel convened under the rules of the UN Commission on International Trade Law (UNCITRAL) pursuant to Chapter 11 of NAFTA, to be resolved in accordance with the procedural provisions of Section B of Chapter 11, and to be decided in conformity with the relevant substantive provisions of NAFTA, the Articles of Agreement of the IMF, and/or customary international law. The investors have requested (a) that, Tolteca be ordered, pursuant to NAFTA Article 1135, to allow them immediately to exchange for foreign currency Toltecan pesos derived from the income from, or sale of, portfolio investment in Tolteca; and (b) that Tolteca be further required to pay as damages the difference between the value of the peso on the date of judgment and its value on the date that (i) the currency controls went into effect, and in the event that later portfolio income was accrued, on the date of such accrual (including reasonable interest) or (ii) the value of the peso on the date of the exchange of currencies and the date that the currency controls

---

d. Defined in relevant part as "Toltecan incorporated enterprises over 50% of whose voting securities are owned by Toltecan citizens."

e. The investor cases have been consolidated in accordance with NAFTA Article 1126.

went into effect, and in the event that later portfolio income was accrued, on the date of such accrual (including reasonable interest), which ever is the lesser amount. The investors have further requested that Tolteca be ordered to pay as additional damages the amount of any loss in the value of investor portfolios, independent of changes in exchange rates, from the date on which the currency controls took effect and the date of judgment, or the date of sale of portfolio investments, which ever is the lesser amount. Responding to the law suit, Tolteca declared that as a matter of good faith it recognizes the jurisdiction of the Chapter 11 tribunals for purposes of resolving the investor disputes. Notwithstanding this declaration, however, Tolteca has taken the position that it is not bound by NAFTA, or alternatively, that if it is bound by NAFTA, it is in full compliance with its provisions and should be allowed to maintain its currency controls and should not be required to pay damages. Tolteca is a party to the 1969 Vienna Convention on the Law of Treaties, but not to the 1978 Vienna Convention on Succession of States in Respect of Treaties.

SECTION 2.   PURPOSE OF PROBLEM

A major purpose of this problem is to explore the ways in which changes in global finance are intricately connected to the evolving world order and the development of international law in relation to it. This is a topic that seldom receives attention in traditional international law or political science classes. The politically transformative effects of global finance are obscure to lay people and for the most part are completely ignored in the popular discourse. To provide the foundation for this exploration, this problem aims to furnish a quick course in the underlying economic causes of the crisis that besets Sundalau and Tolteca.[f]

At the same time, the problem critically examines the workings of the international organization whose mandate is to oversee the international financial system, *i.e.*, the International Monetary Fund (IMF). As economic globalization has evolved, the international financial system has been afflicted by a series of financial crises that have devastated whole economies, thrown millions out of work, and, each in their own way, left an imprint on the global system. No sooner had the developing world sovereign debt crisis of the 1980s begun to fade into memory than Mexico was hit with a major financial calamity in 1994, followed quickly, in 1997, by an Asian financial crisis that was far worse than its Mexican counterpart three years earlier. This was followed by the Argentine financial crisis of 2002; and now, as this coursebook goes to press, the persistent and growing current account deficit and federal budget deficit of the United States have left observers wondering whether the next crisis may be a US dollar crisis. A key purpose of this problem is to explore the effects of these crises and ask how the global system might be placed on a more stable foundation or be otherwise reformed so that the world's most vulnerable citizens from its most vulnerable reaches will not continuously have to bear the brunt of such instability.

Another purpose of this problem is to introduce the important topic of foreign investment within the context of the North American Free Trade

f. *See* in particular *infra* Discussion Note/Question 1, at 815, which is designed to be a relatively simple tutorial in the economics behind the problem.

Agreement (NAFTA), encouraging familiarity not only with a treaty regime that is highly important in its own right but, as well, familiarity with its extremely liberal investment provisions, an excellent setting for examining the controversial issue of how freely private capital should be allowed to move across national borders. Relatedly, the problem introduces the classic international law question of the extent to which governments should be allowed to interfere with the property interests of private foreign investors.

Also embedded in this problem are two world order issues of especially great significance in recent times. One concerns the doctrine of state and governmental succession, very much in play since the dissolution of the former Soviet Union and the subsequent emergence of many new states. The other concerns the extent to which governments should be at liberty to use their economic power transnationally (*i.e.*, extraterritorially) to achieve their national objectives, a question that has recurred frequently since the beginning of the 21st Century as evidenced by the fact that the United States now imposes some form of economic sanctions on more than seventy countries worldwide.

Finally, this problem is designed to stimulate analysis of a cluster of doctrines, principles, and rules with which international lawyers historically have been concerned. The Readings contained in Section 4, *infra*, are arranged according to these recognized legal themes. Related normative questions are considered in the Discussion Notes/Questions that follow.

Section 3.   Assignments

A.   Reading Assignment

Study the Readings presented in Section 4, *infra*, and the Discussion Notes/Questions that follow. Also, to the extent possible, consult the accompanying bibliographical references.

B.   Recommended Writing Assignment

Prepare a comprehensive, logically sequenced, and *argumentative* brief in the form of an outline of the primary and subsidiary *legal* issues you see requiring resolution by (1) the NAFTA Chapter 11 UNCITRAL Tribunal, and (2) the US Senate Committee on Foreign Relations (approximately ten single spaced, typewritten pages). Also, from the perspective of an independent judge, indicate which side ought to prevail on each issue and why. Retain a copy of your issue outline-brief for class discussion.

C.   Recommended Oral Assignments

Assume that you are legal counsel for the American investors or Tolteca (as designated by your instructor) appointed to argue before the NAFTA/UNCITRAL Tribunal; then, relying upon the Readings (and your issue outline-brief, if prepared), present a 10–15 minute oral argument of your client's position before the Tribunal. In addition or alternatively (as determined by your instructor), assume that you are an expert international law witness before the US Senate Committee on Foreign Relations called to testify in favor of Senator Chauvin's bill on behalf of the nationalistically oriented

Homeland Institute or against it on behalf of the universally inclined Transnational Foundation (as designated by your instructor); then, relying upon the Readings (and your issue outline-brief, if prepared), present a 10–15 minute oral argument reflecting the viewpoint you represent.

D. Recommended Reflective Assignment

Consider (and recommend) alternative norms, procedures, and/or institutions that you believe might do better than existing world order arrangements to contend with situations of the kind posed by this problem. In so doing, but without insisting upon *immediate* feasibility, identify the particular transition steps that would be needed to make your alternative a reality.

Section 4. Readings

The following readings are considered *prima facie* relevant to solving this problem. They are divided according to those categories of accepted international legal analysis that are principally implicated in the problem: "the international financial system," "Chapter 11 and other relevant provisions of the North American Free Trade Agreement," "treatment of alien property under customary international law," "the rules of the International Monetary Fund," "legal personality and binding obligation under international law," and "economic retorsion and reprisals." They are your law library for present purposes and should be treated as such, organized intelligibly for "shelving" and not necessarily according to the issues presented. Be sure to review Chapter 2 ("International Legal Prescription: The 'Sources' of International Law") in your consideration of them. It, too, should be treated as part of your law library (as, indeed, should this entire coursebook).

A. The International Financial System

1. Paul Bolster, "International Finance," The Encyclopedia of Business 1019–20 (2d ed. 2000).

International Finance is the examination of institutions, practices, and analysis of cash flows that move from one country to another. There are several prominent distinctions between international finance and its purely domestic counterpart, but the most important one is exchange rate risk. Exchange rate risk refers to the uncertainty injected into any international financial decision that results from changes in the price of one country's currency per unit of another country's currency. Examples of other distinctions include the environment for direct foreign investment, new risks resulting from changes in the political environment, and differential taxation of assets and income.

The level of international trade is a relevant indicator of economic growth worldwide. Foreign exchange markets facilitate this trade by providing a resource where currencies from all nations can be bought and sold. While there is a heavy volume of foreign exchange between some countries, such as the United States and Canada, other countries with little international trade may have only intermittent need for such transactions. Current exchange rates of one country's currency versus another are determined by supply and demand for these currencies. . . .

In addition to international trade, there is a second motivation for international financial activity [and that motivation is investment]. * * * The short-term motive for foreign exchange (trade) and the long-term motive [investment] are related. For example, for most of the 1980s Japan maintained a sizeable balance of trade surplus with the United States. This is because Japan exports more to the United States than they import from the United States, resulting in a flow of funds from the United States to Japan. This was also a period, however, when Japan provided considerable capital investments in automobile plants and other US securities. These investment funds from Japan far outweighed the flow of investment funds moving from the United States to Japan. While some motivation for Japan's large investment in US assets is strategic, the overall result is an inflow of investment funds from Japan that offsets the outflow created by the trade imbalance.

By the late 1990s the Japanese economy was in a deep recession. This made the trade imbalance even more extreme as demand for US exports declined precipitously. The lack of appealing domestic investment alternatives in Japan, however, encouraged Japanese investors to pursue international options. Again, the flow of investment funds tends to offset the trade imbalance. While the two motives for foreign exchanges do not always offset, they typically do for major trading partners over longer periods.

The Nature of Exchange Rates and Exchange Rate Risk

Consider two developed countries, A and B. If A and B are trading partners and make investments in each other's country, then there must also be a well-developed market for exchange of the two currencies. From A's perspective, demand for B's currency will depend on the cost of B's products when compared with domestic substitutes. It will also depend on investment opportunities in B compared with those available domestically in A. Likewise, the supply of B's currency depends on the same issues when examined from B's perspective.

Ignoring everything else, A will demand more of B's currency if it can buy it more cheaply. For example, if the exchange rate moves from 2 B per 1 A to 3 B per 1 A, imports from B become cheaper since it costs A's residents fewer units of their own currency to buy them. Conversely, if the exchange rate moves to 1.5 B per 1 A, the cost of imports has risen and demand for B's currency will fall. The supply of B's currency will change for the same reasons, but the change will be in the opposite direction. If B's citizens can trade the same number of their own currency units for fewer units of A's currency, they will offer less currency for exchange. At some exchange rate, the supply of B's currency will exactly satisfy the demand and an equilibrium, or market-clearing rate, will be established.

The market-clearing exchange rate does not stay in one place. This is because of a variety of events including: (1) changes in the relative inflation rates of the two countries, (2) changes in the relative rates of return on investments in the two countries, and (3) government intervention. Examples of government intervention include quotas on imports or restrictions on foreign exchange. As a brief example of how the market-clearing exchange rate can move, suppose that the current equilibrium exchange rate is 2 B per 1 A. Next, consider new information that indicates investors can achieve a higher rate of return on investments in B while returns on investments available domestically in A remain the same. As investors in A realize this, they have greater interest in making investments in B. This increases the demand for B's currency and means that investors in A are now willing to pay more for a unit of B's currency. B's investors however, now see that investment prospects in A have deteriorated in relative terms. They are less interested in making these investments and will supply fewer units of B's currency in exchange for A's currency. The dual influences of A's investors becoming more eager to buy B's currency and the increased reluctance of B's investors to offer their currency indicates that the market clearing exchange rate must be different than the prior rate of 2 B per 1 A. In this example, to reach equilibrium, the rate should move to a point where 1 unit of A's currency can be exchanged for less then 2 units of B's currency. This movement can be interpreted as a weakening of A's currency and strengthening of B's currency.

Specific movements in the market-clearing exchange rate can be modeled by several economic equalities called parity conditions. Three specific parity conditions are commonly used to model exchange rate equilibrium. Purchasing power parity indicates that currencies experiencing high inflation are likely to weaken while those experiencing low inflation are likely to strengthen. The international Fisher effect[g] indicates that currencies with high interest rates will tend to strengthen while currencies with low level of interest will weaken. A third parity condition, interest rate parity, indicates that exchange rates must move to a level where investors in either country cannot make a riskless profit by borrowing or lending a foreign currency.

Examples of Exchange Rate Risk

Since forecasts of future inflation rates, interest rates, and government actions are uncertain, exchange rates are also uncertain. This means that an investment that will pay its return in units of a foreign currency has an uncertain return in the home currency. For example, suppose an investor in A bought a security [denominated in] B for 100 B. This one-year investment has a guaranteed return of 10 B, or 10 percent. If the exchange rate remains at a constant 2 B per 1 A over the life of the investment, the investor must initially commit 50 A to exchange for 100 B to make the investment. After one year, the 110 B returned (including the 10 B in interest) is exchanged for 55 A. The profit of 5 A on an investment of 50 A represents a 10 percent return to the investor from A. If, however, the exchange rate moved to 1.8 B per 1 A during the year, the investor would now receive the same 110 B from the investment, but when converted to the home currency, 61.1 A is received. This represents a profit of 11.1 A on an investment of 50 A, or 22.2 percent. Note that the return is amplified because B's currency strengthened during the holding period. Likewise, if the exchange rates moved to 2.2 B per 1 A, the return of 110 B translates to 50 A and a rate of return of 0 percent.

As another example, suppose an importer in country A purchases a quantity of goods from an exporter in country B and agrees to pay 1,000 B in 90 days. The importer is now obligated to make a foreign exchange transac-

---

g. The Fisher effect states that the interest rate differential between two countries should be an unbiased predictor of the future change in the spot rate.

tion and must purchase the units of B's currency at the exchange rate that prevails in 90 days. Since the rate is likely to be different from the current rate, the importer is exposed to exchange rate risk. * * *

2. Editors' Note. The preceding reading from the *Encyclopedia of Business* explains the market factors that cause exchange rates to fluctuate. As the present problem makes clear, fluctuations in exchange rates can lead to financial crises and other problems. For this reason, following the end of World War II, John Maynard Keynes, Harry Dexter White, and other architects of the post-World War II global economic order established the International Monetary Fund (IMF) to oversee what were called "fixed" exchange rates. The intention was that exchange rates among currencies would not fluctuate except in rare cases and then as a result of conscious policy determinations.

Given that the market forces that cause currencies to appreciate or depreciate (described in Reading 1, *supra*) could not be eliminated, specific tools had to be used to influence or even counter these market forces. Thus, pursuant to Article IV(1) of the Articles of Agreement of the International Monetary Fund **(Basic Document 4.2)**, countries "undertake to collaborate with the Fund and other members to assure orderly exchange arrangements and to promote a stable system of exchange rates"—meaning, as further specified in the Articles of Agreement, that countries would not pursue either a monetary policy (expanding the money supply) or fiscal policy (deficit spending) that would cause excessive inflation destabilizing to exchange rates. If, however, as a result of inflationary government policies or for other reasons identified in preceding Reading 1, downward market pressures on a country's currency build, three policy tools are available to maintain that country's exchange rate. The intention was to utilize each as needed.

First, as suggested in Reading 1, a country can impose what are called currency controls—that is, by fiat, governments can limit the amount of foreign currency that can be exchanged for domestic currency. Typically, governments imposing currency controls allow holders of domestic currency to exchange that currency for foreign currency only for certain specified purposes and only in limited amounts. This artificially restricts the demand for foreign currency and thereby drives up the value of the domestic currency. Generally speaking, the IMF Articles of Agreement allowed for currency controls on capital transactions (investments) but not for current transactions (trade).

Second, a county's exchange rate can be maintained through the manipulation of interest rates. By restricting the domestic money supply (assuming a relatively stable demand for money), governments can, in accordance with the normal laws of supply and demand, cause the price (*i.e.*, the interest rate on that money) to rise. As the preceding reading explains, relatively higher returns will discourage local currency holders from buying foreign currency to invest overseas and will encourage foreign currency holders to buy local currency to invest locally. This causes the demand for the local currency to rise and, hence, stems the downward pressure on it.

Finally, governments can maintain fixed exchange rates by intervening in the foreign exchange markets. The central banks of governments typically hold reserve supplies of gold and foreign exchange. When necessary to maintain the value of their currency, these reserves are available to buy up their own currency which, if done, creates an artificial demand for their currency and thus helps to maintain its price. If governments run out of foreign exchange, they can borrow more foreign exchange from the IMF, which will extend initial loans as a matter of course. However, the more that countries become indebted to the IMF, the more it places conditions on their borrowings. Typically conditions are designed, in theory at least, to force countries to redress the underlying economic policies that cause their currencies to decline in value.

Despite the availability of these tools, they often fail to work, and during the period of fixed exchange rates following World War II there were many currency devaluations. The United States was the lynchpin of the fixed exchange rate system, but after many years of large current account deficits it became clear that the US dollar itself was vastly overvalued. In 1971, US President Richard Nixon declared that the dollar would no longer be redeemable for gold at $35 per ounce, effectively ending the fixed exchange rate regime. The above-described policy tools, however, continue to be used to influence the price of currencies relative to each other. Even today, some countries attempt individually to maintain a fixed exchange rate with another country's currency (called "pegging"), often (like Sundalau) to the US Dollar. The IMF continues to loan money to countries to help maintain some amount of stability between currencies, and particularly becomes involved in the types of situations described in the present problem.

3. Jeffrey Garten, "Lessons for the Next Financial Crisis," 78 Foreign Aff. 76, 78–83 (Mar–Apr 1999).

Wall Street and Washington do seem able to agree on the following few key areas:

The financial system is not stable. Even a quick glance at the 1990s—the Latin American debt crisis, the European monetary upheaval of 1992, the Mexican bailout of 1994, and now the current debacle—shows that the evolution of a global market has been tortuous. In developing nations in particular, the last two decades reveal increasingly volatile markets and increasingly massive economic damage. While every crisis is embedded in a different set of circumstances—bad macroeconomic policies in 1980s Latin America, excessive private sector debt in 1990s Asia—there are many common elements too, such as unwarranted euphoria on the part of lenders and investors and a rush to the exits when the bubble bursts. There is also solid agreement among Washington and Wall Street leaders that no matter what measures are now put in place, more crises inevitably lie ahead.

The implications of what started in Thailand were badly underestimated. Major mistakes were made in reacting to the Asian crisis. For one thing, nearly all parties failed to correctly appraise the risk of contagion. At the annual meetings of the International Monetary Fund and World Bank in November 1997 in Hong Kong, shortly after the Thai economy started to implode, the consensus was that Indonesia was "safe." Even after Asian problems began to spread, most forecasters did not understand the impact on economic conditions. The IMF alone lowered its forecasts for global and emerging market growth twice in the last three months of 1998. In fact, as late as last summer, concern in the United States and Europe remained muted, and it took the combination of a Russian default and the near collapse of the Long Term Capital Management hedge fund to focus serious international attention on the growing problems. The changing rhetoric of President Clinton says it all. In November 1997 he called the Asian crisis a mere "glitch." In October 1998 he called it the most serious financial crisis in 50 years.

Lenders and investors deluded themselves. They stampeded into emerging markets when interest rates were low in the West and potential returns were higher in Asia and Latin America. In the mid–1990s, when new terminology transformed "developing countries" into "emerging markets," lenders and investors got sucked into thinking that the regulatory oversight in these countries was far more sophisticated than it was. They fooled themselves into believing that emerging markets were ready to fully participate in the turbulent world economy.

The nature of contagion was not well understood. In the past, a problem in one country—especially a small one like Thailand—would usually spread mostly to its principal trading partners and to countries in the region. But what happened in 1997 was more complicated. Inflated expectations about virtually all emerging markets had been building for several years in financial institutions around the world. When lenders and investors saw these hopes dashed in one country, they were quick to downgrade all other nations in the same category. In other words, contagion was as much in the mind of lenders and investors as in the markets themselves. Moreover, bankers and officials underestimated both the downward pressure on global commodity markets from the collapse in demand in Southeast Asia and the impact this would have on the many other emerging markets that are major raw-material exporters. And governments and markets alike failed to understand that in a crisis, market risk, credit risk, and political risk would all blend together. They were also taken aback by how quickly liquidity would dry up in a situation in which so much lending and investing was short-term and comprised of securities rather than conventional banking transactions.

The initial diagnosis missed the mark. The first analyses of the crisis in Southeast Asia failed to take enough account of the private-sector roots of the crisis—not government finances as much as overindebtedness of local corporations and poor debt and currency management on the part of local banks. The early assessments of the situation in Japan were also overly optimistic; some Western officials mistakenly thought that Japan would rescue Thailand the same way the United States helped Mexico in 1995.

All risk management systems failed. The risk assessment and risk management of foreign lenders and investors in emerging markets—both in private institutions and in governments—failed to foresee the buildup of unsustainable financial leverage. The IMF monitoring system did just as poorly. Everyone agrees that all these mechanisms need strengthening, and no one denies being totally surprised by the way that markets seized up and closed down in August and September of 1998—even in the United States, where the economy was so strong.

New financial players changed the rules of the game. Global finance is no longer a cozy club of finance ministers, central bankers, and big commercial banks. The Asian crisis revealed a much wider group of players. The evolution is clear: in the first two decades after World War II, foreign aid and other "official" capital was the main source of funds flowing to developing countries. In the 1970s and 1980s, commercial banks became the primary source. In the 1990s, a much larger cast took the stage: insurance companies, pension funds, hedge funds, and mutual funds. Future financial crises will increasingly involve securities markets, with their multiplicity of instruments, markets, trading strategies, and global linkages. All this will make crisis management infinitely more complicated because there is no one mindset at play, no one set of regulators, and no way to negotiate anything with so many diverse parties. Moreover, many participants who have not one iota of genuine interest in a country or the "global system" will flee at the first sign that the good times are over.

Local politics are crucial. In retrospect, Wall Street and Washington now realize the overwhelming role that domestic politics played in frustrating crisis management. The Thai bailout unfolded amid a constitutional crisis, the South Korean rescue during a leadership transition, the Indonesian package amid widespread rioting that eventually led to the downfall of a dictator, and the Russian plan while the government was crumbling. It is now better understood that a successful stabilization and restructuring package cannot be forced down a country's throat. One of the enduring images of a mistaken approach is likely to be the photo carried in major newspapers of the IMF's managing director, Michel Camdessus, arms defiantly crossed over his chest, standing over former Indonesian President Suharto as the latter reluctantly signed an IMF agreement that was soon to collapse.

Transparency, information disclosure, and adequate financial regulation were sorely lacking. There is no controversy in principle about the need to strengthen the financial systems of individual countries via more accurate and timely financial reporting, tighter financial regulations, and better corporate governance of private-sector banks and companies. The fact is that emerging market countries often have not disclosed their true reserves or their total liabilities in a regular and up-to-date way. Their lax banking supervision and corporate oversight fell far short of what was necessary for an open global economy.

The IMF, mistakes notwithstanding, was and remains crucial to economic stabilization and recovery. Despite all the controversy surrounding the IMF's policies and the withering criticism of several highly respected economists, the overwhelming weight of opinion on Wall Street and in Washington favors strengthening the fund. Not everyone agrees on the exact nature of its role, but all believe that some global institution needs to be in the center of the storm and that it is wiser to use the IMF as the starting point than to craft something altogether new.

In sum, while many serious mistakes were made, there is broad agreement on the need to strengthen the global financial system so that it is as strong as some of the better-run national financial systems. And there is no doubt, either, that this is among the most difficult public policy challenges of our times.

THE BATTLEGROUND

In some cases key officials diagnose the financial crisis differently; in others, they disagree on the details of implementing the next steps. Among the main questions being argued over are the following:

Were the IMF stabilization packages poorly constructed? The fund's many defenders say that it did the best it could with the information available at the time, particularly given the fact that countries came to it late in the game and agreed to its programs only well after the crisis became advanced. For its part, the IMF itself conceded in January that it had been too sanguine about the prospect of a serious economic downturn and that its assessments of the markets' response had been flawed. But there is still serious criticism, too, and it goes like this: The IMF was too focused on defending fixed exchange rates. In so doing, it let speculation build up, which eventually forced the rates to collapse anyway but also did more damage to the country in question than would have happened had devaluation occurred at the outset. The IMF failed to see that the Asian crisis was primarily about excessive leverage in the private sector. In forcing tighter fiscal and monetary policy, the fund precipitated widespread bankruptcies where there were not effective bankruptcy laws and killed the growth that would have been essential for private-sector restructuring and recovery. Some critics further argue that the fund should have been far less intrusive, focusing on stability first and phasing in large-scale restructuring of the economies later; others accuse the IMF of failing to take societal needs into account, thereby sowing the seeds for political problems for years to come.

Is it a mistake to push financial liberalization in emerging markets so fast? For several years the conventional wisdom in Washington was that emerging markets should quickly dismantle financial controls on all kinds of capital inflows. This free market doctrine was mirrored by similar calls to lift restrictions on trade and to hold democratic elections. Everyone now realizes that emerging markets were walloped by the quick exit of short-term capital, but there is no consensus on whether capital controls on short-term inflows should be encouraged in the future. Some key officials still hold that full financial liberalization is the least bad alternative and that the imperative now is to move ahead simultaneously with financial liberalization and the shoring up of domestic financial systems. But many others believe this approach is now discredited, that adequate domestic regulation in emerging markets will take many years at best, and that some controls on incoming short-term capital are essential.

What are the relative roles of the public and private sectors? Officials argue intensely about the issue of "moral hazard"—the awkward term used to signify the danger that lenders can be reckless because they feel assured that the government will bail them out. A key dispute revolves around the question of who should construct rescue packages—the IMF and governments alone, or these public entities along with private lenders and investors? (Here, private participation could mean some combination of maintaining credit lines, providing new money, and negotiating debt-restructuring agreements.) Some Washington politicians need to show the voting public that private lenders and investors are suffering some losses from the debacle and that government funds are not just being used to bail out Wall Street. But beyond that, many see that the problems in emerging markets were in large part caused by overlending and overinvesting by the private sector, which therefore has some responsibility for cleaning up the mess it created.

4. Philip Bowring, "Look Who's Misbehaving," Int'l Herald Trib., 20 Aug 2003, at 6.

* * *

Why is Brazil in trouble? The marketplace attributes it to the threat of a left-wing electoral victory. Wall Street and Latin democracy are uncomfortable with each other. But who has really been the driving force in the fall of the real and a vicious cycle of rising interest rates and government deficits? Answer: the financial institutions which purport to be interested in stability but have been repeating their earlier behavior in Asia—lend thoughtlessly when times look good, then pull it out at the first sign of trouble.

According to Bloomberg, Citigroup alone reduced its exposure to Brazil by $2.1 billion to $9.3 billion in the first quarter of this year. J.P. Morgan cut its exposure by around 20 percent. Assume that 10 other big banks do likewise and you have an international crisis based not on assessment of actual or likely policies in Brazil but on the herd instincts of Wall Streeters.

Citigroup has two men on its payroll who not long ago were at the epicenter of financial power—a former US Treasury secretary, Robert Rubin, and a former IMF deputy managing director, Stanley Fischer. Fischer was the IMF's key player during the Asian crisis. After that crisis, experts were supposed to lead the creation of improved international financial architecture. Now they seem to be participants, indirectly, in the violent flows that call out for regulation.

Like other major banks, Citigroup has made big profits from providing channels for capital flight from Latin America, as earlier from Asia, to tax-free locations offshore. Insistence, backed by the IMF, on the right to free flow of short-term capital remains at the root of global instability. * * *

B.   Chapter 11 and other relevant provisions of
the North American Free Trade Agreement

1.   North American Free Trade Agreement (NAFTA), Concluded, 8–17 Dec 1992. Entered into force, 1 Jan 1994. *Reprinted in* **32 I.L.M. 289 & 605 (1993) and Weston & Carlson IV.C.7: Arts. 1102–05, 1109–39, 1410, 2104, 2205** (Basic Document 4.13).

2.   Charles N. Brower, "Investor–State Disputes Under NAFTA: The Empire Strikes Back," 40 Colum. J. Transnat'l L. 43, 48–51 (2001).

In ratifying NAFTA **[Basic Document 4.13]**, Canada, Mexico and the United States resolved to "ensure a predictable commercial framework for business planning and investment,"[1] "increase substantially investment opportunities in their territories,"[2] and "create effective procedures for . . . the resolution of disputes."[3] Chapter 11 implements these objectives by identifying the standards for treatment of investors and establishing procedures for arbitration of investor-state disputes.

---

1. NAFTA, 32 I.L.M. 289 & 605 (1993)   **3.** *Id*. art. 102(1)(e), at 297.
[Basic Document 4.13], at 297.

2. *Id*. art. 102(1)(c), at 297.

For example, Section A of Chapter 11 permits expropriation and measures tantamount to expropriation only for a public purpose, on a nondiscriminatory basis, in accordance with due process of law and the minimum standard of treatment under Chapter 11, and upon prompt payment of fair market value (plus interest) in freely-transferable funds.[4] In addition, Section A prohibits certain performance requirements, including requirements to export a given level or percentage of goods or services, or to achieve a given level or percentage of domestic content.[5] Furthermore, Section A requires NAFTA Parties to treat each others' investors in accordance with the relative standards of national treatment and most-favored-nation (MFN) treatment.[6] Finally, Section A establishes a minimum standard of treatment, which mandates treatment in accordance with international law, including fair and equitable treatment.[7]

Section B of Chapter 11 secures these obligations by "establishing a mechanism for the settlement of investment disputes that assures both equal treatment among investors of the Parties ... and due process before an impartial tribunal."[8] To this end, the NAFTA Parties have consented to investor-state arbitration in accordance with the procedures set forth in Section B.[9] Their consent represents a standing offer, which investors may accept by submitting disputes to arbitration under the Convention on the Settlement of Investment Disputes between States and Nationals of Other States (the "ICSID Convention")[10] (if the investor's home state and the disputing NAFTA Party are both states parties to that convention),[11] the Additional Facility Rules of ICSID (if either the investor's home state or the disputing NAFTA Party is a state party to the ICSID Convention), or the United Nations Commission on International Trade Law ("UNCITRAL") Arbitration Rules.[12] Article 1122(2) recognizes that, when taken together, the treaty-based consent of NAFTA Parties and the submission of claims by investors satisfy the requirements for written arbitration agreements under the ICSID Convention, the New York Convention,[13] and the Inter–American Convention.[14]

4. *Id,* art. 1110(1)-(6), at 641–42.

5. *See id.* art. 1106(1)(a)-(b), 1106(3)(b), at 640.

6. *See id.* arts. 1102, 1103, at 639.

7. *See id.* art. 1105(1), at 639. Because Article 1105(1) creates a "minimum standard" for all treatment of investments, its express incorporation by reference into Article 1110 seems unnecessary. The overlap between many substantive provisions of Chapter 11 seems to reflect a belt-and-suspenders approach to investor protection.

8. *Id.* art. 1115, at 642.

9. *See id.* art. 1122(1), at 644.

10. The Convention on the Settlement of Investment Disputes between States and Nationals of other States, 18 Mar 1965, 17 U.S.T. 1270, 575 U.N.T.S. 159 [*reprinted in* 4 Weston & Carlson IV.G.2]. *See* NAFTA, *supra* note 1, art. 1139, at 647. Presently, the United States is a state party to the ICSID Convention, but Canada and Mexico are not. *See* Ethyl Corp. v.

Canada, Decision Regarding the Place of Arbitration (Nov. 28, 1997), *reprinted in* 38 I.L.M. 702, 703 n.5 (1999).

11. *See* NAFTA, *supra* note 1, art. 1120(1), at 643.

12. The United Nations Commission on International Trade Law (UNCITRAL) Arbitration Rules, GA Res. 31/98, UN Commission on International Trade Law, 31st Sess., Supp. No. 17, at Ch. V, Sec. C, UN Doc. A/31/17 (1976) [*reprinted in* 4 Weston & Carlson IV.G.3]. *See* NAFTA, *supra* note 1, art. 1120(1), at 643.

13. The "New York Convention" means the Convention on the Recognition and Enforcement of Foreign Awards, 10 Jun 1958, 21 U.S.T. 2517, 330 U.N.T.S. 38 [*reprinted in* 1 Weston & Carlson I.H.6]. *See* NAFTA, *supra* note 1, art. 1139, at 647.

14. The "Inter–American Convention" means the Inter–American Convention on Commercial Arbitration, 30 Jan 1975, 104 Stat. 448 (1990), OAS Treaty Series no. 42, *reprinted*

Following submission of a claim, the arbitration rules selected by the investor govern the proceedings except to the extent modified by Section B of Chapter 11.[15] Section B modifies the arbitration rules by creating a limited right of audience for non-disputing NAFTA Parties, identifying the proper law for Chapter 11 disputes, and imposing strict limits on the form of interim and final relief that Chapter 11 tribunals may award. Thus, Articles 1127 and 1129 entitle non-disputing NAFTA Parties to receive copies of all pleadings, evidence and written arguments.[16] Article 1128 also grants non-disputing NAFTA Parties the right to make submissions to Chapter 11 tribunals regarding the interpretation of NAFTA.[17] Article 1131(1) requires tribunals to render decisions in accordance with NAFTA and other "applicable rules of international law."[18] Tribunals must also apply interpretations of NAFTA made by the Free Trade Commission (i.e., the three NAFTA Parties acting in concert through cabinet-level representatives).[19] Although tribunals may order interim relief to preserve their own jurisdiction and the rights of the parties, they cannot order attachments or enjoin the application of the measures alleged to constitute a breach of Section A.[20] In their final awards, tribunals may only grant compensatory damages plus interest, restitution of property (subject to the NAFTA Party's right to pay monetary damages in lieu of restitution), and the costs of arbitration.[21]

3. North American Free Trade Agreement, United Nations Commission on International Trade Law Tribunal Decision: *Pope & Talbot, Inc. v. Government of Canada*, Interim Award (NAFTA Arb. 2000).

[*Eds.*—Under a treaty between the United States and Canada (the Softwood Lumber Agreement) Canada was required to allocate quotas for the export of lumber from certain Canadian Provinces to the United States. Pope & Talbot, Inc., a US corporation operating in Canada, challenged Canada's implementation of the treaty, alleging that Canada denied it the percentage of the quota to which it was entitled and did not provide adequate review in violation of NAFTA articles 1102, 1105, 1106, and 1110. The NAFTA Tribunal rejected Pope & Talbot's claim under 1102 and 1106, but found that Canada had breached 1105. The Tribunal's analysis and conclusions in regard to Article 1110 are excerpted below.]

96. [T]he Tribunal concludes that the Investment's access to the US market is a property interest subject to protection under Article 1110 and that the scope of that article does cover nondiscriminatory regulation that might be said to fall within an exercise of a state's so-called police powers. However, the Tribunal does not believe that those regulatory measures constitute an interference with the Investment's business activities substantial enough to be characterized as an expropriation under international law. Finally, the Tribunal does not believe that the phrase "measures tantamount to nationalization or expropriation" in Article 1110 broadens the ordinary concept of expropriation under international law to require compensation for measures

in 14 I.L.M. 336 (1975). *See* NAFTA, *supra* note 1, art. 1139, at 647.

15. *See* NAFTA, *supra* note 1, art. 1120(2), at 643.

16. *See id*. arts. 1127, 1129, at 645.

17. *See id*. art. 1128, at 645.

18. *Id*. art. 1131(1), at 645.

19. *See id*. art. 1131(2), at 645.

20. *See id*. art. 1134, at 646 …

21. *See* [*id*], art. 1135(1), at 646. Chapter 11 tribunals cannot order NAFTA Parties to pay punitive damages. *Id*. art. 1135(3), at 646.

affecting property interests without regard to the magnitude or severity of that effect.

97.   As noted, Article 1110 sets requirements that must be met by Parties expropriating "an investment of an investor of another Party." The Investor is acknowledged to be an "investor of another Party," but Canada claims that the ability to sell lumber to the US market is not an investment within the meaning of NAFTA. Article 1139(g) defines investment to include among other things, "property, tangible or intangible, acquired in the expectation or used for the purpose of economic benefit or other business purpose."

98.   While Canada suggests that the ability to sell softwood lumber from British Columbia to the US is an abstraction, it is, in fact, a very important part of the "business" of the Investment. Interference with that business would necessarily have an adverse effect on the property that the Investor had acquired in Canada which, of course, constitutes the Investment. While Canada's focus on the "access to the US market" may reflect only the Investor's own terminology, that terminology should not mask the fact that the true interests at stake are the Investment's asset base, the value of which is largely dependent on its export business. The Tribunal concludes that the Investor properly asserts that Canada has taken measures affecting its "investment," as that term is defined in Article 1139 and used in Article 1110.

99.   Canada appears to claim that, because the measures under consideration are cast in the form of regulations, they constitute an exercise of "police powers," which if nondiscriminatory, are supposedly beyond the reach of the NAFTA rules regarding expropriations. While the exercise of police powers must be analyzed with special care, the Tribunal believes that Canada's formulation goes too far. Regulations can indeed be exercised in a way that would constitute creeping expropriation:

> Subsection (1) [relating to responsibility for injury from improper takings] applies not only to avowed expropriations in which the government formally takes title to property, but also to other actions of the government that have the effect of "taking" the property in whole or in large part, outright or in stages ("creeping expropriation"). A state is responsible as for an expropriation of property under Subsection (1) when it subjects alien property to taxation, *regulation*, or other action that is confiscatory, or that prevents, unreasonably interferes with, or unduly delays, effective enjoyment of an alien's property or its removal from the state's territory.[22]

Indeed much creeping expropriation could be conducted by regulation, and a blanket exception for regulatory measures would create a gaping loophole in international protections against expropriations.[23] For these rea-

---

22.   Third Restatement of the Foreign Relations Law of the US § 712, comment (g) (emphasis added) **[Basic Document 6.3]**.

23.   This is not to say that every regulatory restraint can be likened to expropriation. The *Restatement* **[Basic Document 6.3]** recognizes that the distinction between taking and regulation is not always clear but may rest on the degree of interference with the property interest. *See Restatement* § 712 comment (g) and note 6. Canada's suggestion that regulations can run afoul of international legal requirements only if discriminatory is inconsistent with the *Restatement:* "[A] state is responsible for expropriation of alien property without just compensation even if property of nationals is treated similarly." *Id.* comment (i).

sons, the Tribunal rejects the argument of Canada that the Export Control Regime, as a regulatory measure is beyond the coverage of Article 1110.

100. The next question is whether the Export Control Regime has caused an expropriation of the Investor's investment, creeping or otherwise. Using the ordinary meaning of those terms under international law, the answer must be negative. First of all, there is no allegation that the Investment has been nationalized[24] or that the Regime is confiscatory.[25] The Investor's (and the Investment's) Operations Controller testified at the hearing that the Investor remains in control of the Investment, it directs the day-to-day operations of the Investment, and no officers or employees of the Investment have been detained by virtue of the Regime. Canada does not supervise the work of the officers or employees of the Investment, does not take any of the proceeds of company sales (apart from taxation), does not interfere with management or shareholders' activities, does not prevent the Investment from paying dividends to its shareholders, does not interfere with the appointment of directors or management and does not take any other actions ousting the Investor from full ownership and control of the Investment.

101. The sole "taking that the Investor has identified is interference with the Investment's ability to carry on its business or exporting softwood lumber to the US." While this interference has, according to the Investor, resulted in reduced profits for the Investment, it continues to export substantial quantities of softwood lumber to the US and to earn substantial profits on those sales.

102. Even accepting (for the purpose of this analysis) the allegations of the Investor concerning diminished profits, the Tribunal concludes that the degree of interference with the Investment's operations due to the Export Control Regime does not rise to an expropriation (creeping or otherwise) within the meaning of Article 1110. While it may sometimes be uncertain whether a particular interference with business activities amounts to an expropriation, the test is whether that interference is sufficiently restrictive to support a conclusion that the property has been "taken" from the owner. Thus, the *Harvard Draft* defines the standard as requiring interference that would "justify an inference that the owner * * * will not be able to use, enjoy or dispose of the property . . ."[26] The *Restatement* in addressing the question whether regulation may be considered expropriation, speaks of "action that is confiscatory, or that prevents, unreasonably interferes with, or unduly delays, effective enjoyment of an alien's property."[27] Indeed, at the hearing the Investor's Counsel conceded, correctly, that under international law, expropriation requires a "substantial deprivation." The Export Control Regime has not restricted the Investment in ways that meet these standards.

---

24. *See* Article 1110 (1).

25. *See* Restatement **[Basic Document 6.3]** § 712 comment (g).

26. Draft Convention on the International Responsibility of States for Injuries to Aliens, Art 10(3).

27. Restatement **[Basic Document 6.3]** § 712 comment (g). The *Restatement* also suggests that one test is "the degree to which the government action deprives the investor of effective control over the enterprise," and another is whether the government has made it "impossible for the firm to operate at a profit."

. . .

103. As noted, the Investor expressly agreed that "the Export Control Regime is a measure not covered by customary international law definitions or interpretations of the term expropriation." It contends that NAFTA goes beyond those customary definitions and interpretations to adopt broader requirements that include under the purview of Article 1110 "measures of general application which have the effect of substantially interfering with the investments of investors of NAFTA Parties." The Investor discerns this additional [requirement] because of the use of the phrase "measures tantamount to * * * expropriation" in Article 1110.

104. The Tribunal is unable to accept the Investor's reading of Article 1110. "Tantamount" means nothing more than equivalent.[28] Something that is equivalent to something else cannot logically encompass more. No authority cited by the Investor supports a contrary conclusion. References to the decision of the Iran–US Claims Tribunal ignore the fact that that tribunal's mandate expressly extends beyond expropriation to include "other measures affecting property rights."[29] And, to the extent the Investor is correct in urging that the comments of Dolzer and Stevens suggest that measures "tantamount" to expropriation can encompass restraints less severe than expropriation itself (creeping or otherwise), those comments would not be well founded under a reasonable interpretation of the treaties that the authors analyze.[30]

105. Based upon the foregoing, the Tribunal rejects the Investor's claim under Article 1110.

4. North American Free Trade Agreement, International Centre for the Settlement of Investor Disputes Tribunal Decision: *Metalclad Corp. v. Mexico* (NAFTA Arb. 2000).

[*Eds.*—In 1990, the Mexican federal government granted a Mexican company, Coterin, permits to operate a hazardous waste facility in the state of San Luis Potosi (SLP). In 1993, Metalclad, a US corporation, purchased Coterin. Metalclad's plan was to up-grade the site and build a modern waste treatment facility. Though SLP never granted Metalclad a permit, the company went ahead with construction based on the federal government's assurance that local permits would be granted. Metalclad, was ultimately barred from opening the site, however, because of a last minute ecological decree passed by the municipality. The NAFTA tribunal reported its decision in August of 2000, as follows:]

28. Indeed ... the French text uses the word "equivalent" and the Spanish text "equivalente."

29. *Declaration of the Government of the Democratic and Popular Republic of Algeria Concerning the Settlement of Claims by the Government of the United States of America and the Government of the Islamic Republic of Iran,* 19 Jan 1981.

30. The authors suggest that treaty provisions that define "measures * * * tantamount to expropriation" to include "impairment * * * of economic value" represents the broadest scope of indirect expropriation. *Bilateral Investment Treaties,* (The Netherlands: Kluwer Law International), p. 102. But it has long been accepted that measures should be subject to the requirements of international law if they impair the economic value of an investment to a degree that is equivalent to expropriation. "[A] state may seek to achieve the same result [as outright expropriation] by taxation and regulatory measures designed to make continued operation of the project uneconomical." *Restatement* **[Basic Document 6.3]** § 712, note 7. Thus, the authors' analysis does not change the basic concept at work in the treaties, NAFTA included: measures are covered only if they achieve the same results as expropriation.

NAFTA Article 1105: Fair and Equitable Treatment

74. NAFTA Article 1105(1) provides that "each Party shall accord to investments of investors of another Party treatment in accordance with international law, including fair and equitable treatment and full protection and security." For the reasons set out below, the Tribunal finds that Metalclad's investment was not accorded fair and equitable treatment in accordance with international law, and that Mexico has violated NAFTA Article 1105(1).

* * *

85. Metalclad was led to believe and did believe, that the federal and state permits allowed for the construction and operation of the landfill.

* * *

87. Relying on the representations of the federal government Metalclad started constructing the landfill, and did this openly and continuously and with the full knowledge of the federal, state and municipal governments.

* * *

99. Mexico failed to ensure a transparent and predictable framework for Metalclad's business planning and investment. The totality of these circumstances demonstrates a lack of orderly process and timely disposition in relation to an investor of a Party acting in the expectation that it would be treated fairly and justly in accordance with NAFTA.

100. Moreover, the acts of the State and the Municipality—and therefore the acts of Mexico—fail to comply with or adhere to the requirements of NAFTA, Article 1105(1) that each Party accord to investments of investors of another Party treatment in accordance with international law, including fair and equitable treatment. This is so particularly in light of the governing principle that internal law (such as the Municipality's stated permit requirements) does not justify failure to perform a treaty.[h]

101. The Tribunal, therefore, holds that Metalclad was not treated fairly or equitably under the NAFTA and succeeds on its claim under Article 1105.

NAFTA Article 1110: Expropriation

102. NAFTA Article 1110 provides that "no party shall directly or indirectly ... expropriate an investment ... or take a measure tantamount to ... expropriation ... except (a)" for a public purpose; (b) on a non-discriminatory basis; c) in accordance with due process of law and Article 1105(1); and (d) on payment of compensation ... "A Measure" is defined in Article 201(1) as including "any law, regulation, procedure, requirement or practice."

103. Thus expropriation under NAFTA includes not only open, deliberate and acknowledged takings of property, such as outright seizure or formal or obligatory transfers of title in favour of the host State, but also covert or incidental interference with the use of property which has the effect of depriving the owner, in whole or in significant part, of the use or reasonably-to-be-expected economic benefit of property even if not necessarily to the obvious benefit of the host State.

---

h. See Vienna Convention on the Law of Treaties **(Basic Document 1.10)**, arts 26, 27.

104. By permitting or tolerating the conduct of Guadalcazar in relation to Metalclad which the Tribunal already held amounts to unfair and inequitable treatment breaching Article 1105 and by thus participating or acquiescing in the denial to Metalclad of the right to operate the landfill, notwithstanding the fact that the project was fully approved and endorsed by the federal government, Mexico must be held to have taken a measure tantamount to expropriation in violation of NAFTA Article 1110 (1).

* * *

107. These measures taken together with the representations of the Mexican federal government, on which Metalclad relied, and the absence of a timely, orderly or substantive basis for the denial of the Municipality of the local construction permit, amount to an indirect expropriation.

108. The present case resembles in a number of pertinent respects that of *Biloune, et al. v. Ghana Investment Centre, et al.* 95 ILR 183, 207–10 (7993) (Judge Schwebel, President; Wallace and Leigh, Arbitrators). In that case, a private investor was renovating and expanding a resort restaurant in Ghana. As with Metalclad, the investor, basing itself on the representation of a government affiliated entity, began construction before applying for a building permit. As with Metalclad, a stop work order was issued after a substantial amount of work has been completed. The order was based on the absence of a building permit. An application was submitted, but although it was not expressly denied a permit was never issued. The Tribunal found that an indirect expropriation had taken place because the totality of the circumstances had the effect of causing the irreparable cessation of work on the project. The Tribunal paid particular regard to the investor's justified reliance on the government's representations regarding the permit, the fact that government authorities knew of the construction for more than one year before issuing the stop work order, the fact that permits had not been required for other projects and the fact that no procedure was in place for dealing with building permit applications. Although the decision in *Biloune* does not bind this Tribunal, it is a persuasive authority and the Tribunal is in agreement with its analysis and its conclusion.

* * *

112. In conclusion, the Tribunal holds that Mexico has indirectly expropriated Metalclad's investment without providing compensation to Metalclad for the expropriation. Mexico has violated Article 1110 of NAFTA.

* * *

[*Eds.*—Following the decision Mexico challenged the Metalclad Tribunal's award in Vancouver, British Columbia, the situs of the arbitration. Purporting to address whether the Tribunal had exceeded its jurisdiction (one of the only allowable bases for review) the judge, in fact, conducted a *de novo* review and rejected the Tribunal's Article 1105 analysis. Accepting, however, the Tribunal's conclusions under Article 1110, the judge did not overturn the award of damages itself. Because the parties then settled, the decision was not reviewed by the appellate court.]

5. NAFTA Free Trade Commission, Notes of Interpretation of Certain Chapter 11 Provisions (31 Jul 2001).

[*Eds.*—Partially in response to the *Metalclad* decision, pursuant to NAF-TA Article 1131(2)[i] the NAFTA trade ministers, sitting as the NAFTA Free Trade Commission, issued the following interpretation of Article 1105(1).]

1. Article 1105(1) prescribes the customary international law minimum standard of treatment of aliens as the minimum standard of treatment to be afforded to investments of investors of another Party.

2. The concepts of "fair and equitable treatment" and "full protection and security" do not require treatment in addition to or beyond that which is required by the customary international law minimum standard of treatment of aliens.

3. A determination that there has been a breach of another provision of the NAFTA, or of a separate international agreement, does not establish that there has been a breach of Article 1105(1).

6. North American Free Trade Agreement, United Nations Commission on International Trade Law Tribunal Decision: *Pope & Talbot, Inc. v. Government of Canada*, Award in Respect of Damages (NAFTA Arb. 2002).

[*Eds.*—Subsequent to the *Pope & Talbot* tribunal's interim award (*supra* Reading B–3, p. 763), the NAFTA Free Trade Commission issued its interpretation of Article 1105 of July 31, 2001 (*supra* Reading B–5) prompting the tribunal to revisit below its discussion of 1105 in light of the Commission's interpretation. Pope & Talbot had initially alleged that Canada had breached its obligations under Article 1105 because it did not grant the company a fair hearing respecting its lumber quota, fully inform it of the governmental decision-making process, provide adequate reasons for the quota, or provide any review procedure.]

52. Viewing the Interpretation as binding on the Tribunal does not necessitate a finding that it overturns the Tribunal's previous Award under Article 1105. That Award could remain either because the Tribunal's interpretation of Article 1105 is compatible with the Commission's, or, if it is not, because the application of the Interpretation to the facts found by the Tribunal leads to the same conclusion that there was a breach by Canada of its obligations under Article 1105. If upon either basis the answer is in the affirmative, the Tribunal may proceed to award damages. If, however, the conclusion is that, upon those facts, the application of the Interpretation leads to a finding of no breach of Article 1105, the Tribunal may not proceed to award damages.

53. The Interpretation concluded that Article 1105 prescribes the customary international law minimum standard of treatment of aliens as the minimum standard of treatment to be afforded to investments of investors of other Parties. The Interpretation does not require that the concepts of "fair and equitable treatment" and "full protection and security"[31] be ignored, but rather that they be considered included as part of the minimum standard of

---

i. NAFTA Article 1131(2) reads: "An interpretation by the Commission of a provision of this Agreement shall be binding on a Tribunal established under this Section."

31. As it did in its Award of April 10, 2001, the Tribunal will henceforth use "fairness elements" to refer to both the "fair and equitable treatment" and "full protection and security" requirements of Article 1105.

treatment that it prescribes. Parenthetically, any other construction of the Interpretation whereby the fairness elements were treated as having no effect, would be to suggest that the Commission required the word "including" in Article 1105(1) to be read as "excluding." Such an approach has only to be stated to be rejected.

54. Therefore, the Interpretation requires each Party to accord to investments of investors of the other Parties the fairness elements as subsumed in, rather than additive to, customary international law.

55. Was the decision made by the Tribunal based on an interpretation different from that made by the Commission? At one level this might appear to be so since the Tribunal expressly referred to the fairness elements as being additions to the requirements of the international law minimum and interpreted Article 1105 to require that covered investors and investments receive the benefits of the fairness elements under ordinary standards applied in the NAFTA countries without any threshold limitation.

56. However, that conclusion alone does not mean that the Tribunal's award was incompatible with the Interpretation. Whether the two are consistent in this case depends on whether the concept behind the fairness elements under customary international law is different from those elements under ordinary standards applied in NAFTA countries.

57. Based upon its submissions in these proceedings[32] and confirmed internationally in its proposals in the [Free Trade Area of the Americas Agreement] negotiations,[33] Canada considers that the principles of customary international law were frozen in amber at the time of the *Neer*[j] decision.[34] It was on this basis that it urged the Tribunal to award damages only if its conduct was found to be an "egregious" act or failure to meet internationally required standards.[35]

58. The Tribunal rejects this static conception of customary international law for the following reasons:

59. First, as admitted by one of the NAFTA Parties,[36] and even by counsel for Canada,[37] there has been evolution in customary international law concepts since the 1920's. It is a facet of international law that customary international law evolves through state practice. International agreements

32. Canada's view was "The conduct of government toward the investment must amount to gross misconduct, manifest injustice or, in the classic words of the *Neer* claim, an outrage, bad faith or the wilful neglect of duty." Counter Memorial Phase 2 § 309

33. [T]he language offered by Canada used the precise language of *Neer* to explain what it meant by the customary international law minimum standard of treatment.

j. Neer v. United Mexican States, 4 U.N.R.I.A.A. 60 (1926).

34. To recall, the passage from *Neer* relied upon by Canada states: "[T]he treatment of an alien, in order to constitute an international delinquency, should amount to an outrage, to bad faith, to wilful neglect of duty, or to an insufficiency of governmental action so far short of international standards that every rea-

sonable and impartial man would readily recognize its insufficiency." 1927 A.J.I.L. 555, 556.

35. Canada used this term to "encapsulate" what it believed were the standards of customary international law. See Nov. 2000 Trl, Vol. 2, at 58:8–20.

36. See Post Hearing Submission Damages Phase for Mexico at paragraph § 8: "Mexico also agrees that the standard is relative and that conduct which may not have violated international law (sic) the 1920's might very well be seen to offend internationally accepted principles today."

37. See Nov. 2001 Tr. at 830:8–11. "We also said that that standard, obviously, develops over time, but that does not take away from the fact that the threshold is high."

constitute practice of states and contribute to the grounds of customary international law.[38]

60. Secondly, since the 1920's the range of actions subject to international concern has broadened beyond the international delinquencies considered in *Neer* to include the concept of fair and equitable treatment. This development was focused in the work of the OECD on its Draft Convention on the Protection of Foreign Property,[39] which recognized that that concept was already customary in bilateral agreements then in effect. That draft did not rest upon an effort to discern the ingredients of international law but upon an independent consideration of how host countries should treat foreign owned property. However, the comments to the draft made two observations that are pertinent here: fair and equitable treatment requires treatment at least as good as that accorded by a state to its own nationals and that concept was embodied in "customary" international law.[40]

61. Thirdly, the standard of fair and equitable treatment was central to BITs [bilateral investment treaties] negotiated since the work of the OECD. Many of those agreements, as the Tribunal has previously observed, require state conduct to be evaluated under the fairness elements apart from the standards of customary international law. And even those that do not provide that those elements are owed independently of the requirements of customary international law do add the fair and equitable treatment protections to those rights formerly protected by customary international law. That is, the BITs are not limited to protection against "international delinquencies."[41]

62. Canada's views on the appropriate standard of customary international law for today were perhaps shaped by its erroneous belief that only some 70 bilateral investment treaties have been negotiated;[42] however, the true number, now acknowledged by Canada[43] is in excess of 1800.[44] Therefore, applying the ordinary rules for determining the content of custom in international law,[45] one must conclude that the practice of states is now represented by those treaties.[46]

63. The International Court of Justice has moved away from the *Neer* formulation:

> Arbitrariness is not so much something opposed to a rule of law, as something opposed to the rule of law. * * * It is a wilful disregard of due

38. I. Brownlie: Principles of Public International Law 12 (5th ed. 1998).

39. OECD Publication 23081 (Nov. 1967).

40. *Id.* ...

41. As Professor Sir Robert Jennings cogently observed in an Opinion furnished by him in another NAFTA case (*Methanex v. United States*) and provided to this Tribunal by the United States, the *Neer* case relied upon for that standard was not one concerned with fair and equitable treatment but with whether the state concerned had committed an "international delinquency."

42. Nov. 2001 Tr. at 730–32.

43. *See* Canada's Post Hearing Submission Arising Out of Article 1128, etc. (Damages Phase) at paragraph 14.

44. A. Parra, *Applicable Substantive Law in ICSID Arbitrations Initiated Under Investment Treaties,* ICSID News, Vol 17, No. 2.

45. As stated by counsel for Canada, "Customary international law is based on the practice of states or diplomatic correspondence." Nov. 2001 Tr. at 731:2–4.

46. Of course, as noted in the Tribunal's April 10, 2001 Award under Article 1105, every NAFTA investor is entitled, by virtue of Article 1103, to the treatment accorded nationals of other states under BITs containing the fairness elements unlimited by customary international law.... The Interpretation did not purport to change that fact, nor could it.

process of law, an act which shocks, or at least surprises a sense of judicial propriety.[47]

64.   That formulation leaves out any requirement that *every* reasonable and impartial person be dissatisfied and perhaps permits a bit less injury to the psyche of the observer, who need no longer be outraged, but only surprised by what the government has done. And, of course, replacing the neutral "governmental action" with the concept of "due process" perforce makes the formulation more dynamic and responsive to evolving and more rigorous standards for evaluating what governments do to people and companies.

65.   Based upon the foregoing, the Tribunal rejects Canada's contention on the present content of customary international law concerning the protection of foreign property. Those standards have evolved since 1926, and, were the issue necessary to the Tribunal's decision here, it would propose a formulation more in keeping with the present practice of states. However, because the Tribunal concludes that, *even applying Canada's proposed standard,* damages would be owing to the Investor as a result of the Verification Review Episode, that reformulation is unnecessary here.

66.   The Tribunal having thus concluded that the Investor is entitled to damages by reason of the breach by Canada of Article 1105, it is unnecessary to consider issues relating to Articles 1102 or 1103 which had been raised following upon the Interpretation. The Tribunal accordingly does not do so.

7.   William Greider, "The Right and US Trade Law: Invalidating the 20th Century—Investor Protections in NAFTA Are One Manifestation of a Broad, Backdoor Effort to Restore the Primacy of Property Against Society's Broader Claims," The Nation 21 (15 Oct 2001).

I.   Beyond the Law

The case of *Methanex v. United States* originated in California in the mid–1990s, when people began to notice a foul taste in their drinking water, a smell like turpentine. Santa Monica had to shut down half its supply wells and purchase clean water from elsewhere. The contamination turned up in thirty public water systems, Lake Tahoe and Shasta Lake, plus 3,500 groundwater sites. The source was quickly identified as methyl tertiary butyl ether (MTBE), a methanol-based gasoline additive that creates cleaner-burning fuel, thus reducing air pollution. But even small amounts of MTBE leaking from storage tanks, pipeline breaks or car accidents made water unfit to drink—and extremely difficult to clean up. A study team from the University of California, Davis, added that in lab tests on rats and mice, MTBE was also carcinogenic, raising the possibility of human risk.

The state government acted promptly. In 1997 the legislature authorized a ban on MTBE if further investigations confirmed the health risks. In March 1999, after more research and lengthy public hearings, Governor Gray Davis issued an executive order to begin the phaseout. Other states were acting too. The oxygenating additive is used in one-fourth of the US gasoline supply, especially in pollution-prone big cities, so New York, New Jersey and other places were also discovering MTBE's unintended consequences for clean

47. *Case Concerning Elettronica Sicula S.P.A. (ELSI),* 1989 ICJ 15, at 76.

water. Up to this point, the story sounded like an alarming but fairly conventional environmental problem.

Then, four months after Governor Davis's order, a Canadian company from Vancouver, British Columbia, filed a daring lawsuit against the US government, demanding $970 million in compensation for the damage California was inflicting on its future profits. Methanex Corporation, which manufactures methanol, principal ingredient of MTBE, claimed that banning the additive in the largest US market violates the foreign-investment guarantees embodied in Chapter 11 of the North American Free Trade Agreement. Under Chapter 11, foreign investors from Canada, Mexico and the United States can sue a national government if their company's property assets, including the intangible property of expected profits, are damaged by laws or regulations of virtually any kind. Who knew?

The company did not take its case to US federal court. Instead, it hired a leading Washington law firm, Jones, Day, Reavis & Pogue, to argue the billion-dollar claim before a private three-judge arbitration tribunal, an "offshore" legal venue created by NAFTA. Each side—the plaintiff company and defendant government—gets to choose one of the three arbitrators who will hear the case, then they jointly select the third, who presides. The proceedings are in secret—no public notice whatever—unless both sides agree to disclose the case. Sacramento had difficulty finding out what was happening, though it was California's environmental law that was under attack.

Methanex and the other controversial corporate claims pending before NAFTA tribunals are like a slow-ticking time bomb in the politics of globalization. As nervous members of Congress inquire into what they unwittingly created back in 1993, environmentalists and other critics explain the implications: Multinational investors can randomly second-guess the legitimacy of environmental laws or any other public-welfare or economic regulation, including agency decisions, even jury verdicts. The open-ended test for winning damages is whether the regulation illegitimately injured a company's investments and can be construed as "tantamount to expropriation," though no assets were physically taken (as is the case when a government seizes an oil field or nationalizes banks).

NAFTA's arbitrators cannot overturn domestic laws, but their huge damage awards may be nearly as crippling—chilling governments from acting once they realize they will be "paying to regulate," as William Waren, a fellow at Georgetown law school, puts it. On its face, this strange new legal system's ability to check democratically elected governments confirms a principal accusation of those much-disparaged protesters against corporate-dominated globalization. Elite power politics, they contend, is imposing rules on the global economy that effectively shut out competing voices and values, that slyly undermine the sovereign capacity of a nation to defend its own citizens' broader interests. Indeed, the US multinational community dreams of establishing Chapter 11's provisions as the worldwide standard, to be applied next in the proposed Free Trade Area of the Americas.

The most disturbing aspect of Chapter 11, however, is not its private arbitration system but its expansive new definition of property rights—far beyond the established terms in US jurisprudence and with a potential to override established rights in domestic law. NAFTA's new investor protections actually mimic a radical revision of constitutional law that the American right has been aggressively pushing for years—redefining public regulation as a government "taking" of private property that requires compensation to the owners, just as when government takes private land for a highway or park it has to pay its fair value. Because any new regulation is bound to have some economic impact on private assets, this doctrine is a formula to shrink the reach of modern government and cripple the regulatory state—undermining long-established protections for social welfare and economic justice, environmental values and individual rights. Right-wing advocates frankly state that objective—restoring the primacy of property against society's broader claims.

* * *

How could all this have transpired so unobtrusively? And how did the right wing's novel concept of "regulatory takings" find its way into an international trade agreement? The story, in passing, is another devastating commentary on the decay of representative democracy. These now-controversial legal innovations were ostensibly adopted in broad daylight, yet the public never had a clue. Nor did the media, watchful policy experts or members of Congress. Yet the stakes are as fundamental to public life as the Constitution itself. The transmission of big ideas among elite interests is always a more supple and elusive process than backroom conspiracy—not exactly secret, yet withheld from general understanding. To fully appreciate the momentous risks for law and justice, one starts by stepping back in history to see what exactly the right-wingers are trying to overthrow. The answer, in their own words, is the twentieth century.

II. Rolling Back the New Deal

Political conflict over property rights has of course been central to American life since the first colonies, starting most obviously with human slavery and the brutal confiscation of Indian lands. But the property issue never really went away; it only became less visible. The conservative mind sees private ownership of property (correctly, in my view) as an essential element undergirding individual freedom. Yet conservatives typically have trouble accepting that property also regularly comes into collision with society's other values: claims for the common good, the rights of individual citizens who own little or nothing. The tension of deciding which comes first—property or people—has always generated the deepest conflicts, including the Civil War.

The last great confrontation over property rights occurred at the dawn of the twentieth century, when modern corporations emerged with national scope and scale and awesome new influence over society. A broad tide of reformers, led by labor, arose in opposition, demanding new social and economic laws to protect people and social values, but the federal judiciary blocked their way. The Supreme Court relentlessly defended business and the old order—the "classical legal doctrine" of limited government and laissez-faire economics. It spoke most defiantly in the *Lochner* decision of 1905, in which the Justices threw out an early New York State labor-reform law that required a ten-hour day and safer conditions for bakery workers. The law, they ruled, unconstitutionally deprived bakery owners of their property rights. Over the next three decades, the logic of *Lochner* was applied to invalidate more than 200 state and federal statutes—the progressive income tax, minimum-wage laws, health and safety codes, workers' right to organize independent unions and other public measures that have since become common features of US governance.

The *Lochner* era did not actually end until deep into the New Deal. When a liberal majority was finally achieved at the Supreme Court in 1937, it promptly upheld the National Labor Relations Act and declared that social and economic regulatory laws are constitutional after all. Government, the court affirmed, has constitutional obligations to protect society's general health and welfare, and its so-called police powers justify intrusions into the private sphere—these public necessities come before property rights. This decision opened the floodgates for expanding government and elaborating new regulatory powers in myriad ways.

In our era, conservatives think they have finally found a way to close the gates. This past March in Chicago, the Federalist Society organized a lawyers' forum with a provocative title—"Rolling Back the New Deal"—and its star attraction was Richard Epstein, law professor at the University of Chicago and intellectual lion of the right. Epstein's theory of "regulatory takings" galvanized the movement fifteen years ago when his book Takings: Private Property and the Power of Eminent Domain first appeared, describing an ingenious new constitutional interpretation designed to rein in modern government.

Regulations, he argued, should be properly understood as "takings" under the Fifth Amendment (" . . . nor shall private property be taken for public purpose without just compensation"), so government must pay those businesses or individuals whose property value is in some way diminished by public actions.

* * *

While his conservative brethren on the Supreme Court have so far declined to accept his radical redefinition of the Constitution, multinational business has already succeeded in planting his premise in NAFTA and promoting it for other trade agreements. The claims are being heard, some companies have already won huge awards for regulatory injury to investments. The professor's contribution didn't even get a footnote. "I am aware that what I have said has been very influential in the NAFTA debate and that, strangely enough, much of what I say seems to have more resonance in the international context than it did in the domestic context," Epstein said. "Nobody from any of those [business] organizations even thought to ask me to give an opinion, let alone hire me as a consultant. I think they should have asked me."

III. Think Locally, Act Globally

How did the professor's ideas migrate from one realm to the other? * * * The problem [the American multinational community] foresaw, as US capital invested heavily abroad, was not the old-style expropriation of outright seizure, but a more subtle process in which foreign governments, by enacting progressively stiffer regulatory measures, could effectively take control of assets and profits. Economist Edward Graham, NAFTA expert at the Institute for International Economics (IIE), a think tank supported by international business and finance, thought the fears were legitimate. "There had been problems in Latin America, though not so much Mexico, I think, and some other developing countries, particularly in Southeast Asia, with what came to be known as creeping expropriation. Measures were taken by governments that were regulatory in nature but clearly expropriatory in intent. For example, taxes. You just keep pumping the taxes, you claim the company had used various tax-avoidance mechanisms in the past. So the government would present them with a big bill for back taxes and say, Look, if you don't pay up on this, we are taking 25 percent of equity for the government."

* * *

When NAFTA negotiations began in 1990, the multinationals' lawyers already had the investor protection scheme in hand, the arbitration feature borrowed from prior bilateral agreements. Then they expanded it vigorously during the negotiations. . . . The ostensible purpose and the explanation given to Congress [of the investor-state provisions]—was that US investors needed an insurance policy in Mexico, whose courts were notoriously corrupt. . . . [A]dvocates claim that Chapter 11's "enormously broad" definition of property rights is in accord with US law—though any diligent law student could demonstrate that the claim is fallacious.

C. Treatment of Alien Property Under Customary International Law

1. Seymour J. Rubin, Private Foreign Investment 32–34, 40–43 (1956).

As every lawyer knows, there is a wealth of literature in the United States on the subject of what constitutes a "taking"—or, if the more general international-law word is preferred, an "expropriation."[48] The Fifth Amendment to the Constitution of the United States prohibits the taking of private property except on the payment of "just compensation." What constitutes a taking, under this provision, has been litigated time and again in the courts of the United States.

Even in the situation in which there obviously has been a dispossession of the owner for the benefit of the government, whether there has been a taking is not always clear. . . . [C]oncepts of the public interest and its superiority to private rights may result in this act of the state being considered not to be a taking. In United States law, a taking generally involves exercise of the power of eminent domain, whereas a non-taking involves exercise of the police power.

Thus, if there is a "valid exercise of the police power" it is generally held that there has not been a taking within the Constitutional sense. The

---

48. Some writers use the word "expropriation" only where compensation has been paid. "Confiscation" is then used for those situations in which no compensation or perhaps inadequate or ineffective or dilatory compensation is offered. "Nationalization" is often applied to the situation of a general "expropriation," distinguishing the taking of an entire industry from the taking of one house or plant. These words are, however, often used without these connotations, and I have made no particular effort to employ them here as exact terms. A "taking" is involved whether the general term is confiscation, expropriation, or nationalization.

difficulty here is that the phrase, exercise of the police power, more often describes a result than it defines a process of reasoning by which the result is reached. To the disinterested observer, the conclusion that there has been a valid exercise of the police power may well seem more indicative of the conclusion that compensation need not be paid than of the fact that no taking has occurred.

* * *

We may here find it useful to pose a hypothetical case.... Let us suppose a company engaged in the production of iron ore in the prosperous little country of Ruritania. The company is owned by foreign capitalists for the most part, though there is some local capital participation. The supervisory personnel of the company are nationals of countries other than Ruritania, chiefly for the reason that ore in commercial quantities and quality was only recently discovered in Ruritania, and there are few local experts. The company exports most of its ore to consumers abroad, makes reasonable earnings, reinvests a substantial part of its income in capital improvements, new exploration, and modern equipment, and remits good dividends to its shareholders, local and foreign.

Into this picture there now enter, first of all, exchange controls. Ruritania finds that, despite the earnings of the ore company and its other export industries, it is experiencing a serious shortage of foreign exchange. The Ruritanian standard of living, under the impetus of a wartime and postwar export boom, has been rising. Ruritanians have been buying refrigerators, automobiles, and nylons, and the country now finds itself lacking sufficient dollars and pounds sterling to purchase these as well as its essential imports of wheat, cotton, and machinery. So exchange controls, a device of which the world has seen much since World War I, are brought into play; and the foreign shareholders of the ore company find that they are not able to get dollar or sterling remittances of their earnings.

The Ruritanian government, however, still finds the economic going heavy. Merely cutting down on remittances of earnings and on nonessential imports is not enough to remedy its balance of payments deficit. Nor does it feel that fundamental problems can be solved merely by such negative measures. What the country needs, say its sages, is a more diversified economy. Particularly, it needs to build up manufacturing facilities at home. For this purpose, the government drafts an ambitious five-year plan for expansion of domestic manufacturing, as part of which they propose to produce steel rather than export ore. A smelter and steel mill is constructed.

Such an enterprise, of course, means increased consumption of ore at home. Thus, regulations are enacted prohibiting the export of ore except under special license—which is now rarely granted. These regulations cause considerable conflict between the ore company, which points out that it is no longer allowed to earn foreign currencies which it needs in order to purchase equipment and supplies, and the government, which views with increasing distaste the representations made to it by the foreign manager of the company. This is especially true since these representations frankly state the view that the entire five-year plan is overambitious and not likely to achieve its objectives. The next governmental move is to pass a new labor law that requires all supervisory personnel to be local nationals and sets up a labor-management committee to which major issues of company policy must be referred. In rapid order there then follow, "in the interests of the national economy," regulations with respect to allocation of ore mined within the country, regulations with respect to ceiling prices, and regulations calling for governmental supervision of all companies which exploit the natural resources of Ruritania—which are declared in a special preamble to the latter law to be part of the inalienable national patrimony. By this time, the foreign share-holders are thoroughly unhappy. They feel that their rights have been infringed, and they therefore call upon their own government for assistance.

When the foreign government makes representations, however, the gov-ernment of Ruritania quotes from [a] United Nations resolution ... : "The right of peoples freely to use and exploit their natural wealth and resources is inherent in their sovereignty." The government of Ruritania further points out that it has not expropriated the property of the foreign owners; far from that, it has encouraged the mining operations of the ore company by enact-ment of laws which will penalize the ore company or any other company which is engaged in exploitation of natural resources for not producing to capacity. Moreover, Ruritania states that it has declared a condition of national economic emergency; and it suggests that in time of such emergency (and perhaps even when the emergency has passed) other countries have enacted or continued exchange controls, allocation measures, price controls, and labor laws. Such legislation therefore cannot be considered other than legitimate internal laws.

If this seems an overdrawn picture, it is because countries adhering to a democratic and fundamentally capitalist organization have not imposed such a series of controls on industry. But a stage very similar to the one described was in fact reached in [post-World War II Eastern Europe] before [it was] decided ... to cease this process of inch-by-inch amputation and make an outright seizure of foreign investment properties. And one or more of the measures described can be found in almost every country of the ... world.

The problem of creeping expropriation, of nibbling the foreign property owner to death, is therefore one which must be faced. It will not be solved by being ignored. The rule of international law requires compensation when property of foreign nationals has been taken; but what constitutes a taking? Where in this modern world of regulation in which we live is the line to be drawn between regulation power and expropriation? At what point does the conceded power of the state to organize its own economy in that way which seems to it most appropriate and useful so impinge on property rights as to require that the foreign possessor of those rights be compensated?

2. Burns H. Weston, " 'Constructive Takings' Under Internation-al Law: A Modest Foray into the Problem of 'Creeping Expropria-tion,' " 16 Va. J. Int'l L. 103, 113–26, 153–54 (1975).

Even when we lawyers try to solve the "taking"-"regulation" problem by carefully avoiding the ambiguities and imprecisions of our introverted termi-nology, we remain, by and large, in a definitional morass. The reason seems clear. Nurtured by a tradition of distorting dogmatisms, we train upon a particular configuration of facts, conclude that it can rationalize the "taking"-"regulation" dilemma posed (because it squares with some autochthonous "property rights" conception), and elevate it to a "rule of decision" that is supposed to distinguish between "the power of eminent domain" and the "police power" for all cases at all times. Invariably, because we proceed in this uniaxial (and rather ethnocentric) fashion, we author definitional distinctions that are empirically and ethnically unsatisfying.

Consider, thus, some of the more common distinctions (or tests) that traditionally have been used, bearing in mind that, like most definitions, they are neither true or false, but, rather, of potentially limited utility....

[*Eds.*—The author next critiques the "common distinctions (or tests)" mentioned, namely, that it is a "taking" in the compensable sense

1.   when the "regulating" agency acts more as "enterpriser" than as "mediator" in the competition for economic values;

2.   when the governmental "regulation" results from "capricious," "discriminatory," or otherwise "improper" motives and/or does not advance some "recognized social purpose";

3.   when an allegedly provisional governmental "regulation," valid for advancing some "recognized social purpose" (usually in the face of an "emergency"), works a "permanent" rather than a "temporary" loss;

4.   when "the thing affected" by the governmental "regulation" is not of itself socially undesirable;

5.   when the governmental "regulation," even though it does not effect a formal transfer of title, works a "physical invasion" over the "property" in question; and

6.   when the "property" subjected to governmental "regulation" is thereby damaged to a "substantial" or "excessive" degree.

None of these tests, Weston concludes, even though admittedly relevant to the "taking"-"regulation" dilemma, are or can be conclusive discriminants in all cases at all times. He writes: "The 'taking'-'regulation' problem, being Hydra-headed and therefore given to many different issues of fact and policy, simply cannot be defined, let alone resolved, by 'rules of decision' which look only to one or two of its diverse aspects.... However attractive and relevant they may be, the harsh reality is that, at least separately, they yield conceptually ambiguous, and so operationally paradoxical, results." Accordingly, Weston contends, the "true test" resides ultimately in social policy and, in particular, those social policies that condition compensatory decisions. "When all is said and done," he observes, the " 'taking'-'regulation' problem is a compensatory problem and therefore incapable of rational solution except by reference to, or guidance from, the overriding social policies which compensatory decisions are meant to serve." He continues:]

Thus, to resolve the "taking"-"regulation" dilemma in the international realm—to decide when compensation should or should not be paid for the "regulatory" deprivation of foreign wealth—one should look to see whether, *in total context*, the "regulations" under challenge do or do not advance a world public order which holds out at least the prospect of universal security and abundance, the *desideratum* of compensatory decision generally. If so, ... the deprivative intervention [should be] held liability-free. If not, then the reverse is true, and compensation should be paid. It is understood that the traditional definitional tests do point to factors that are pertinent to this sort of analysis, and they must therefore be taken into account. But because they reside in ethnocentric (Western) "acquired rights" conceptions, and because they lead to ambiguous, occasionally irrelevant, and endless theoretical spirals, they do not by themselves assure that the above-stated or any other policy which bespeaks the holistic adjustment of competing legitimate interests ever will be realized. . . . The only true test of the international "taking"-"regulation" (compensation) problem would seem to be, in short, the test of a policy which favors a peaceful, productive, and equitable global economy perceived in terms of the common *inclusive* interests of the world community, perceived in terms of aggregate well-being. To quote Professor Michelman . . ., "[w]e might restate the balancing test by asking whether a distribution could be arrived at, under the regime to be established by the proposed measure, whereby everyone will be at least as well off as he was before, while at least some people will be better off."[49]

* * *

Of course, it is not enough to speak only in general terms about the policy test which is here recommended to guide the "taking"-"regulation" decision. To avoid the charge of excessive abstraction (and therefore inutility), it is necessary to relate it more precisely to the concrete cases; and this injunction, in turn, requires yet greater explicitness about the underlying policies which "taking"-"regulation" decisions should serve. . . .

In more familiar parlance, then, although in rough symmetry to the postulate of a peaceful, productive, and equitable global economy, these basic policies would appear to include (1) the reduction of the use of force, (2) the promotion of worldwide economic development, and (3) the preservation of at least minimum human rights.[k] [T]hey are not conceived as separately determinative, rank-ordered expressions of preferred policy. To the contrary, they are seen as interdependent (even to some degree redundant) and adjustable formulations which, when taken as a whole, represent the overarching goal—central to the Law of State Responsibility—of achieving a genuinely cooperative balance between (a) the exclusive interests that all States share in exercising effective control over persons and property within their jurisdictions, and (b) the exclusive interest that all States also share in gaining secure access to the world's economic resources wherever situated. . . .

[*Eds.*—The author next explores these "basic policies" as guides for resolving the "taking"-"regulation" issue and thereafter applies them to specific deprivation strategy contexts. His discussions of the general claim "that certain uses of the economic instrument of policy do (do not) serve as the functional equivalents of deprivations that give rise to international responsibility" is particularly pertinent. We conclude here with only his introductory statement, at 153–54:]

Economic exercises of public power, regardless if they actually serve in particular instances as the functional equivalents of deprivations for which compensation traditionally has been expected, can be conveniently, although not rigidly, grouped according to the techniques governments commonly use

---

49. F. Michelman, *Property, Utility, and Fairness: Comments on the Ethical Foundations of "Just Compensation" Law*, 80 Harv. L. Rev. 1165, 1195 (1967).

k. In light of ecological developments since his article was written, the author now recommends also the encouragement of a sustainable global environment.

to affect not title to, but (a) participation in, (b) use of, and c) benefit or yield from wealth processes and values. Compared to diplomatic, ideological, and military exercises of public power, they provoke ... by far the greatest number of "constructive taking"/"creeping expropriation" claims. Falling into the first ("participation in") subcategory have been, for example, so-called State administration measures, the creation of public and private monopolies, the granting of exclusive concessions, and the non-renewal of previously authorized licenses and charters. Falling into the second ("use of") subcategory have been, *inter alia*, restrictions upon the entry of capital and labor, ("participation in") wage and price controls, distribution and sales prohibitions, the "freezing" or "blocking" of assets, land-use zoning, and the imposition of "servitudes." And falling into the third ("benefit or yield from") subcategory have been such other familiar measures as taxation (in diverse forms) and monetary revaluation. As might be expected, "constructive takings" have been most often determined when these kinds of "regulations" have operated, singly or in combination, so as to span or embrace all three of the above subcategories.

3.   Charles N. Brower, "Current Developments in the Law of Expropriation and Compensation: A Preliminary Survey of Awards of the Iran–United States Claims Tribunal," 21 Int'l Law. 639, 643–52 (1987).[1]

The Tribunal has had no difficulty in recognizing the expropriatory effect of Iranian public laws expressly nationalizing industries or particular entities. * * * Most cases brought before the Tribunal, however, involve the gray area of expropriation in which no formal taking is announced by the host government, but the alien argues that the property has been seized de facto. In deciding these cases the Tribunal has consistently ruled that interference by the Government with the alien's enjoyment of the incidents of ownership—such as the use or control of the property, or the income and economic benefits derived therefrom—constitutes a compensable taking. The Tribunal's decisions vary slightly in their discussion of the degree of interference necessary to a finding of expropriation, but the most common benchmark appears to be reasonableness. In one of its earliest cases the Tribunal suggested in dictum that an unreasonable interference is sufficient to find expropriation.[m] ... Other awards describe the standard as requiring an "interfere[nce] ... to such an extent that these [property] rights are rendered so useless that they must be deemed to have been expropriated"[n] or state that a taking occurs whenever an owner is "deprived of fundamental rights of ownership" and "the deprivation is not merely ephemeral."[o] While these last

1. On 19 January 1981, the governments of the United States of America and the Islamic Republic of Iran established the Iran–United States Claims Tribunal to resolve, *inter alia*, disputes then outstanding between United States nationals and the Government of Iran arising out of "expropriations or other measures affecting property rights." The author, a US national, was a member of the Tribunal at the time of this writing.

m. Harza Eng'g Co. v. Iran, Award No. 19-98–2 (30 Dec 1982), 1 Iran-U.S. C.T.R. 499, 504 (1981–82).

n. Starrett Hous. Corp. v. Iran, Award No. ITL 32-24–1 at 51 (19 Dec 1983), 4 Iran–U.S. C.T.R. 122, 154 (1983); Foremost Tehran, Inc. v. Iran, Award No. 220-$^{37}\!/_{231}$-1 at 22, 28 (11 Apr 1986).

o. Tippetts v. TAMS–AFFA Consulting Eng'rs of Iran, Award No. 141-7–2 at 10, 11 (29 June 1948), 6 Iran-U.S. C.T.R. 219, 225 (1984); Phelps Dodge Corp. v. Iran, Award No. 217-99–2 at 14 (19 Mar 1986), *reprinted in* 25 I.L.M. 619, 626 (1986).

two groups of cases could be interpreted as somewhat divergent—the one requiring that the arguably more difficult standard of uselessness be proved, the other that of a non-ephemeral loss of fundamental rights—both tend to rely on the others for general support. Similarly, in still other cases, the Tribunal examines whether the effective use of the property has been lost.[p] The decisions of the Tribunal, therefore, have not focused on semantics, but rather on the reality of the impact of the alleged expropriation. Consequently, the standard both explicitly and implicitly adopted by the Tribunal requires an unreasonable interference with property rights caused by actions attributable to the Government.

4. Jason L. Godofsky, "Shedding Light on Article 1110 of the North American Free Trade Agreement (NAFTA) Concerning Expropriations: An Environmental Case Study," 21 N.W. J. Int'l L. Bus. 243, 281–284 (2000).

If abused, currency-related measures, including inflation, deflation, transfer and/or exchange restrictions and monetary policies can have an expropriatory effect on foreign property holders. However, like with taxation, tribunals have accorded extreme deference to these types of policies. Once again, except in obvious situations, and likely only where it is applied in a discriminatory manner, aliens are faced with a difficult task where trying to establish a State delinquency on the basis of a currency regulation.

According to general principles of international law, every State has the sovereign right to establish and regulate its currency.[q] In most circumstances a State may determine without the scrutiny of the community of nations whether, for example, to counter inflation, support its currency or place limitations on exchange and foreign transfers.[r] While currency regulation is a municipal and internal matter, like with taxation, it enters into the realm of international law when an alien enters into commercial relations with a foreign State.[s] This may occur, for example, where an alien places money in a foreign bank, retains foreign currency or in any other manner which places an alien in the position of a creditor to a foreign State. Furthermore, an alien is not required to actually reside in the debtor State for that State to owe it an obligation pursuant to international law.

Most expropriatory measures involving currency policies have occurred in the so-called lesser-income countries.[t] Generally speaking, currency-related

p. *See* Gianoplus v. Iran, Award No. 237–314–1 at 7 (20 Jun 1986)....

q. *See* Case Concerning the Payment of Various Serbian Loans Issued in France (France v. Kingdom of the Serbs, Croats and Slovenes), 1929 PCIJ (ser. A) Nos. 20/21.

r. *See* F.A. Mann, The Legal Aspect of Money (1992). Dr. Mann provides that: "Money, like tariffs or taxation or the admission of aliens, is one of these matters which prima facie must be considered as falling essentially within the domestic jurisdiction of States ... Customary international law does not normally fetter the municipal legislator's discretion in these matters or characterize his measures as an international wrong for which he could be held responsible, just as it leaves him the free-

dom to decide whether he wishes to introduce a particular type of tax and whether he levies tax at a particular rate." *Id* at 461.

s. Case of Certain Norwegian Loans (France v. Norway), 1957 ICJ 9, 37 (separate opinion of Judge Lauterpacht).

t. For example, in a peculiar twist, Rosenn chronicled how the extreme inflationary period between the early–1950s to the mid–1960s in Brazil and Argentina allowed both States to expropriate compensation awards gained through earlier expropriation proceedings. By the time the Governments paid their compensation, particularly because the rate of inflation exceeded interest rates given on such awards, the actual money a property owner received for its taken property was nominal.

claims arise out of situations where a country is attempting to reorder and take control of its economy.[u] Except for certain comments made in dissent, which are discussed below, the case law has overwhelmingly sided with respondent host States where an expropriation claim is made on the basis of a currency policy.

The first hurdle to meet in establishing an expropriation claim arising from a currency measure is in demonstrating a loss of property. It is difficult to conceptualize this form of taking. The problem lies in that there is often not an accompanying direct loss. The losses are notional, and may only apply for a temporary period. Furthermore, currency legislation is often applied in a very broad and general fashion. While the creditor of a host state may very well receive the face value of his or her investment as at the date of maturity, in actuality, the real value of his or her payment will have severely declined.

Alternatively, a State may adopt a currency conversion regulation which provides that aliens may not redeem their investments, or, if they can redeem them, that the amount be reduced by a specified rate. For example, in *Eisner*,[v] a US national alleged that her property was "taken" when, following the liberation of Germany after the Second World War, the American Military Commander in Berlin ordered that German Reichmarks be converted into a "new" currency. Because the conversion rates were not applied equally (*e.g.*, residents of Germany received a better rate than did aliens), the plaintiff asserted that such actions were expropriatory. In finding against the plaintiff, the United States Court of Claims noted that when dealing with currency conversion it is very difficult to even know whether there has been a loss of real value.[w] Similarly, in *French*, despite the fact that the claimant was not permitted to redeem his certificates worth US$150,000 outside of Cuba, the New York Court of Appeals found that the fact that "it is still his or his assignee's to enforce or attempt to enforce . . ." demonstrates that it has not been taken.[x] Hence, when raising an expropriation claim on the basis of fiscal

---

Rosenn noted that the monetary policies of both countries "operated confiscatorily, and thus have severely strained the confidence of property owners and investors in the promises of both governments to protect private investment." K. Rosenn, *Expropriation, Inflation and Development,* 1972 Wis. L. Rev. 845, 847 (1972).

u. At the same time, it must not be lost that a State can manipulate its monetary policy in such a way as to extract a supreme advantage over its creditors. For example, it can support a program of devaluation in order to erase its debt. However, for an alien, the difficulty is in substantiating his or her claim. Even if a purely effects-based test were applied, an alien would still be faced with a difficult challenge in establishing both a loss of property and that his or her loss was attributable to its host State. *See* Edwin Borchard, State Insolvency and Foreign Bondholders—General Principles vol. 1 136 (1951), who noted that currency regulations can be used in an expropriatory manner. On the other hand, Wortley notes that "when devaluation is a genuine defensive measure to counterbalance a

disastrous fall in prices, it is not abusive." B.A. Wortley, Expropriation in Public International Law 48 (1959).

v. Eisner v. United States, 1954 I.L.R. 476 (U.S. Ct. of Claims, 1954).

w. A similar finding was reached in the *Adam's* Case where, though the facts were slightly different, the Commissioners did not even consider the Claimant's case be a valid one. Adam's Case (Great Britain v. United States), in 3 History and Digest, Moore Arbitrations 3066, 3067 (1898).

x. French v. Banco Nacional de Cuba, 66 I.L.R. 6, 16 (N.Y. 1968). Essentially, the Court adopted a direct physical invasion test whereby, as long as a property owner retains title, even if it means that a property owner merely has the right to "burn" his or her property (*i.e.*, left valueless), then no action may be raised. In light of the very nature of an indirect expropriation, this type of reasoning is not likely to be followed. Instead, the following minority opinion of Keating J. is more reflective of the present state of international law:

There is sufficient authority in international law for the proposition that a taking of prop-

policies or currency measures, a claimant faces an initial formidable barrier in having to substantiate a loss.

Assuming that a loss can be established, as described above, the next hurdle is to demonstrate that such loss is attributable to the debtor-State. In *French*, Fuld C.J. asserted that:

> This is not an era, surely, in which there is anything novel or internationally reprehensible about even the most stringent regulation of national currencies and the flow of foreign exchange. Such practices have been followed, as the exigencies of international economics have required—and despite resulting losses to individuals—by capitalist countries and communist countries alike, by the United States and its allies as well as by those with whom our country has had profound differences. They are practices which are not even of recent origin but which have been recognized as a normal measure of government for hundreds of years, if not, indeed, as long as currency has been used as the medium of international exchange.[y]

As well, in the *Furst* Claim, the United States Foreign Claims Commission held that a State cannot be held liable for fluctuations in its currency when attempting to bring order "in time of financial stress."[z]

Thus, similar to taxation and other fiscal measures, international tribunals are not likely to consider currency measures as amounting to an expropriation.

5. Editors' Note. Assuming there has been a "taking" (or wealth deprivation), what of its legality? Once upon a time publicists sought to argue that any "taking" was wrongful *per se*, under a doctrine of "acquired" or "vested" rights. The beginnings of this doctrine can be traced to a distinction between two classes of private rights in the legal theory of medieval Europe. Vested rights rested in part on rules of natural law and were not at the disposition of the state. The second class of private rights was derived only from statutory prescription (or "positive law") and was subjected to modification or elimination by the state. *See, e.g.*, Gillian M. White, Nationalisation of Foreign Property 33 (1961); Georges S.F.C. Kaeckenbeeck, *The Protection of Vested Rights in International Law*, 17 B.Y.B.I.L. 1, 2–3 (1936). The special

erty can occur without first depriving the owner of legal title if the foreigner is effectively deprived of all benefit of the property ... Moreover, simply because Decision No. 346 was initially necessitated by Cuba's need to protect its foreign exchange, it does not follow that it remains valid under international law permanently. *Id*. at 42.

Although stated in relation to the US's Fifth Amendment, similar reasoning to the above was adopted by the US Court of Appeals, Second Circuit, in Sardino v. Federal Reserve Bank of New York, where eventually finding for the US Government on the basis of the police powers exception, the Court rejected the Respondent Government's contention that no taking had occurred. 361 F.2d 106, 110 (2d Cir. 1966). The plaintiff was denied the transfer of its money out of the US, because "it has mere-ly placed a temporary barrier to its transfer outside the United States ... [the plaintiff may] ... use the account to pay customs duties, taxes or fees owing to the United States, a state, or any instrumentality of either." *Id*. The Court, in response to the above argument, noted that "we find it hard to say there is no deprivation when a man is prevented both from obtaining his property and from realizing any benefit from it for a period of indefinite duration which may outrun his life." *Id*. at 111. However, these cases effectively demonstrate the hesitancy which tribunals have had with finding the existence of an expropriation out of a currency measure.

y. French, 66 I.L.R. at 19.

z. Furst Claim, 42 I.L.R. 153, 154 (U.S. Foreign Claims Comm'n, 1960).

protection of vested rights against retroactive legislation later served as a model for conflict of laws rules which claimed that a right acquired under the legal system of one country must be recognized and respected in another country. *See, e.g.*, Isi Foighel, Nationalization and Compensation 124 (1963).

Some publicists have borrowed these ideas from domestic law and placed them within the framework of international law, claiming that states are forbidden to destroy a foreigner's rights acquired or vested under pre-existing legislation. *See, e.g.*, references in Samy S. Friedman, Expropriation in International Law 122 n.44 (1953). However, the notion of absolute protection for acquired or vested rights under international law has been doubtful, at best, for a long time. The diverse replies of states to a questionnaire of the Preparatory Committee of the League of Nations assigned to codify rules on state responsibility, for example, demonstrated the complete absence of any rule on the absolute recognition of acquired or vested rights. *See id.* at 123 n.50. Today, the doctrine of acquired or vested rights is almost never invoked as a basis for establishing the *per se* illegality of foreign "takings." As Ingrid Detter De Lupis has put it:

> [I] suggest that the theory of acquired [or vested rights] was never justified, at any time, in public international law. It has, at times, been borrowed, like a *cliché*, from the field of conflict of laws.... But even in this field the theory of acquired rights is not without opponents. The theory appears to have little justification in public international law.... [T]he theory has little or nothing to add to the general rules on state succession or to the general rules on expropriation in international law.

Ingrid D. De Lupis, Finance and Protection of Investments in Developing Countries 113 (2d ed. 1987).

The contemporary and more realistic view of the doctrine of acquired or vested rights is to recognize that the power of eminent domain—of "expropriation"—is a prerogative of the sovereign state and that the doctrine thus "merely indemnifies ... titleholders from complete and arbitrary destruction of their interests," serving, consequently, as a basis for compensation and restitution claims. Daniel P. O'Connell, 1 State Succession in Municipal Law and International Law 266 (1967).[m] Today, there is universal agreement that a "taking" of foreign property is not unlawful *per se* and that a state's power of eminent domain includes the right to "expropriate" and "nationalize" foreign as well as domestic property. All that is required today, to be entirely free of allegations of illegality under international law, is that a "taking" satisfy a few more-or-less accepted conditions, and most jurists now speak of only four: (1) that there be no denial of procedural justice; (2) that there be no discrimination; (3) that the "taking" be for a public purpose; and (4) that there be fair compensation, except if the "taking" is a "confiscation" as an element of a penal action under criminal law. It should be noted, however, that some of the conditions listed above have been greatly criticized, by the

m. *See also, e.g.*, I. De Lupis, Finance and Protection of Investments in Developing Countries 105–13 (2d ed. 1987); C. Lipson, Standing Guard: Protecting Foreign Capital in the Nineteenth and Twentieth Centuries (1985); B. Wortley, Expropriation in Public International Law 125–28 (1959); K. Sik, *The Concept of Acquired Rights in International Law*, 24 Neth. Int'l L. Rev. 120 (1977); J. Stevenson, *International Protection of Acquired Rights*, 54 Proceed. AS.I.L. 102 (1960).

developing States especially, and thus have undergone reinterpretation and modification.

6. Restatement (Third) of The Foreign Relations Law of the United States §§ 711–712, Comment (1987) (Basic Document 6.3).

7. Ingrid Detter De Lupis, Finance and Protection of Investments in Developing Countries 68–71 (2d ed. 1987).

There is a rule that there must be no discrimination, a rule which implies that no distinction must be made between nationals and aliens: the expropriation law must be "general" in its scope and not directed only against foreigners.

This rule has been invoked in several cases to substantiate a claim that a nationalization was "wrongful" [*i.e.* a violation of international law].[n] But, naturally, a state cannot refrain from nationalizing just because such a measure would affect only certain foreign-owned property. . . .

* * *

However, it appears unlikely that a nationalization would be contrary to international law if there is a patent public purpose even if the expropriating measures are exclusively directed against aliens. I would submit that it is the public purpose of nationalization which is of paramount importance and such valid purpose appears to outweigh the necessity of non-discrimination.[o] The rule that there must be no discrimination and that nationalization laws must have a "general" scope to be valid under international law is obviously borrowed from national law. . . .

But in the international community, considering the pattern of foreign investment in other countries, it seems that, more often than not, natural resources are exploited by foreign enterprises in developing countries. Any nationalizing measures of such enterprises are then likely to be "discriminatory" in so far as only foreigners hold concessions to exploit natural resources.

In sectors of the economy outside natural resources, where it is more common for both nationals and aliens to carry on the business the rule of non-discrimination may be of importance. But, I submit, particularly in the field of natural resources, the rule of non-discrimination is merely subsidiary to the rule demanding a valid public purpose and, being subsidiary, it is a rule which can be dispensed with, provided there is an overriding public purpose.

n. The author cites, *inter alia*, the pleadings in Anglo–Iranian Oil Co. (U.K. v. Iran), 1952 ICJ Pleadings 96–98, and the opinions in Phosphates in Morocco (Italy v. Fr.), 1938 PCIJ (ser. A/B), No. 74, at 10; Oscar Chinn, 1934 PCIJ (ser. A/B/), No. 63, at 65; and the Deutsche Amerikanische Petroleum Gesellschaft Oil Tankers Case, [1926] U.N.R.I.A.A. 777 (1949).

o. Writes M. Sornarajah, *infra* Reading C–8, at 185:

There are alternative ways of rationalizing the principle of non-discrimination with the validity of nationalization measures aimed at a dominant, alien group. Non-discrimination is not an absolute principle either in municipal law or in international law. The idea of reverse discrimination to favour historically disadvantaged groups has been accepted in domestic systems. It has been suggested that such a principle may be accepted in international law as well. If this principle does exist, it can be argued that a nationalization measure directed at a dominant alien group, particularly one holding dominance from colonial times, is a measure justifiable as reverse discrimination in that it restores the other groups into the economic life of the State by ending the dominance of the alien group.

8. M. Sornarajah, The Pursuit of Nationalized Property 174–76 (1986).

There is some authority in traditional international law for the requirement that an act of nationalization should be for a public purpose. But such authority is weak.... In the *Walter Fletcher Smith Case*,[64] the arbitrator made a reference to the absence of public utility of the taking of property but the dictum in the award is open to the interpretation that the arbitrator was referring to an internal requirement of Cuban law and not to a principle of international law. Dicta in other awards supporting the public utility principle seem to be similarly equivocal and there are contrary dicta in other awards. Writers are also divided on whether the requirement of a public purpose is a limitation on the right to nationalize.

The public purpose limitation may have had some significance in the period when the distinction between expropriations and nationalizations had an importance in the law, for the motive behind the taking was the basis of the distinction.... State regulation of private property, over four decades later, is so commonplace that the inquiry into the motives behind the taking of foreign property, especially by a foreign court or tribunal, would be a task that would not only involve an affront to the sovereignty of the nationalizing state but would lead to charges of prejudice against a tribunal which makes the decision. The better proposition seems to be that even if there is a requirement of public policy, the determination made by the state that its acts of nationalization had a public purpose should be regarded as conclusive.

To some extent, the public purpose requirement may be an affirmation of the requirement of non-discrimination. For, if the taking was indeed for a public purpose, it would not have been aimed at any particular ethnic group.[p] But, if this is a reason for maintaining the requirement of public purpose, it is unnecessary. That objective could be achieved by the recognition of nondiscrimination as a requirement of a valid act of nationalization. In any event ..., new developments asserting the right to nationalization and permanent sovereignty over natural resources must be taken as having eroded the basis of this limitation. Resolution 1803 (XVII) on permanent sovereignty over natural resources **[Basic Document 4.4]** which received the support of both developed and developing countries requires that nationalizations should be for purposes of "public utility, security and national interest." The linking of national security interests with public utility indicates that the state alone can be the arbiter of these requirements.

9. Charter of Economic Rights and Duties of States, 12 Dec 1974, GA Res. 3281, UN GAOR, 29th Sess., Supp. No. 31, at 50, UNDoc.A/9631 (1975); *reprinted in* 15 I.L.M. 251 (1975) and 5 Weston & Carlson IV.F.5: Arts. 1–3, 7 (Basic Document 4.9).

10. Richard B. Lillich and Burns H. Weston, 1 International Claims: Their Settlement by Lump Sum Agreements 208–42 (1975).

When a State deprives foreigners of their property or otherwise injures them in a fashion giving rise to international responsibility, "orthodox com-

---

64. 24 A.J.I.L. 384 (1930).

p. *Cf.* I. De Lupis, *supra* Reading C–7, at 71: "[R]ecent events have shown that if the effects of a nationalization are 'retaliatory' or aimed at 'harming' interests of other nationals, one may be entitled to question whether there was, in fact, any valid public purpose."

pensation preferences," generally traced back to Secretary of State Hull's attempt to spell out the doctrine of just compensation during correspondence between the United States and Mexico in 1938, require the payment of "prompt, adequate and effective" compensation. The precise meaning of these adjectives, however, never has been made altogether clear, although a yeoman effort to give them juridical content may be found in the American Law Institute's Restatement [Second] of the Foreign Relations Law of the United States. Without accepting or rejecting this traditional formulation of customary international law, which has achieved widespread if far from universal recognition, the analysis [of post-World War II lump sum settlement agreements ("Settlement Agreements")] . . . which follows is organized around the above trio of supposed "requirements."[q]

A. Promptness

The Restatement [Second] specifie[d] that compensation must be paid "with reasonable promptness," a phrase defined to mean "payment as soon as is reasonable under the circumstances. . . ."[r] The Reporters add[ed] in their notes that "[p]ayment in marketable bonds promptly delivered satisfies the requirement," while payment in nonmarketable bonds does not "unless the maturity date of the bonds is within a reasonable time under the circumstances."[s] While they do not mention lump sum settlements in this connection, reasoning by analogy one may conclude that the Reporters would require any deferred compensation thereunder, *i.e.*, any compensation by installments, to be paid within a few years at the most. Otherwise, absent the payment of interest, the nominal amount of compensation specified in the Settlement Agreement presumably would be diluted to the point of inadequacy. This linkage between the terms of payment and the amount of compensation needs be kept in mind throughout. . . .

[*Eds.*—The authors next examine the extent to which lump sum settlement agreements have satisfied "the promptness requirement," and conclude that "the time between claim accrual and eventual redress . . . is substantially longer than conventional wisdom has assumed."]

The above examination of the Settlement Agreements, moreover, also justifies concluding that most States now accept the principle of payment by installment. . . . [However,] certainly the *sine qua non* of its acceptance should be . . . the payment of at least nominal interest. The use of installments, after

---

q. A lump sum settlement agreement is an agreement between a state that is home to nationals whose property has been expropriated and the state that has expropriated the property. Such agreements provide for the expropriating state to make an aggregate payment to the home state in place of individual payments to the nationals whose property was expropriated. The home state may then establish a national claims commission to determine how the compensation paid pursuant to the Agreement should be allocated between the various nationals who had their property expropriated.

r. Section 712(c) of the Restatement (Third) of the Foreign Relations Law of the

United States (hereinafter "Restatement Third")[**Basic Document 6.3**] specifies "within a reasonable time."

s. In their notes to § 712 of Restatement Third [**Basic Document 6.3**], the Reporters observe that ("[t]he First Hickenlooper Amendment [22 USC § 2370(e)(1)] requires the expropriating state to take appropriate steps to fix compensation within a reasonable time (six months)" and that "payment is generally regarded as having been timely if compensation is tendered at the time of the taking or if compensation plus interest from that time is paid at a later date." *See also infra* note **w**.

all, represents only a compromise in the *method*, not necessarily the *amount*, of compensation. . . .

B. Adequacy

Concerning the adequacy of compensation, the Restatement [Second] takes the position that *"[u]nder ordinary conditions* . . . the amount must be equivalent to the full value of the property taken, together with interest to the date of payment. . . ."[t] [I]t also contains an enlightened provision suspending the full value requirement when "special circumstances make such requirement unreasonable."[u] . . .

[It is a] widely held belief that most if not all of the Settlement Agreements have afforded claimants substantially less than "adequate," much less "full," compensation. Garcia–Amador, for instance, concluded from his survey of postwar settlements that "lump-sum agreements, far from envisaging 'just' or 'adequate' compensation, provide for 'partial' indemnification, the amount of which varies appreciably depending on the case and the circumstances," while Professor [formerly World Court Judge] Aréchaga observed that "[t]hese agreements do not provide in all cases for full or even adequate compensation and often they only represent a percentage of the existing claims."[65] . . .

Several factors, however, require consideration, although relatively little revision, of this point of view . . ., [including the fact that] under many of the Settlement Agreements the respondent State, in addition to its promise to pay compensation, also agrees to waive various claims against the claimant State which the latter may or may not pass on to its own nationals. Although hard if not impossible to quantify, these waivers obviously add to the totality of compensation paid.

This last factor, heretofore largely ignored by all commentators, including the present writers, surely deserves extended consideration in any contextual analysis of the compensation question. To base estimates of percentage returns solely upon lump sums paid, overlooking other *quid pro quos* from respondent States, may understate considerably the amount of compensation which claimant States actually have been able to obtain. . . .

[*Eds.*—The authors then consider the following four categories of *respondent* state *quid pro quos*: the waiver of taxes and similar changes owed by eligible claimants; the waiver of claims held by the respondent state; and the granting of other *quid pro quos* from respondent state such as the express assignment of a group of claims to the claimant state for collection. They point out, *inter alia*, that these *quid pro quos* have their counterparts in the waiver of claims or analogous *quid pro quos* conferred by claimant states, a fact that sometimes "may undercut the adequacy of compensation received."

---

t. Comment *d* to § 712 of Restatement Third **[Basic Document 6.3]** takes the same position, observing that "full value" usually means "fair market value," taking into account "going concern value" and "other generally recognized principles of valuation" where appropriate.

u. Comment *d* to § 712 of Restatement Third **[Basic Document 6.3]** allows "some deviation" in "exceptional circumstances,"

which is said not to obtain "if . . . the property taken had been used in a business enterprise that was specifically authorized or encouraged by the state."

65. E. Jimenez de Aréchaga, *The Duty to Compensate for the Nationalization of Foreign Property*, [1963] 2 Y.B. Int'l L. Comm'n 237, 239, UN Doc. A/CN.4/152 (1963).

The authors then consider the following three categories of *claimant* state *quid pro quos*: the waiver of additional claims held by the claimant state; and the granting of other *quid pro quos* by the claimant state such as a long-term trade agreement with compensation being paid from earnings derived from the export of goods to the claimant state. The authors conclude:]

The above examination of various *quid pro quos* flowing from respondent to claimant States, and vice versa, demonstrates beyond doubt that the adequacy of compensation received under lump sum settlements cannot be judged simply by comparing the compensation actually paid with the amount of the awards subsequently rendered by a national claims commission....

Nevertheless, assuming *arguendo* the universality of the valuation standards employed by claimant States, it is apparent that "partial" compensation has become, if indeed it already was not, the general norm. Since these valuation standards are not universally accepted as the touchstone for determining the amount of compensation due and, hence, the adequacy of the amount actually paid, however, what claimant States regard as "partial," respondent States may view as "adequate," "just," or even "full." Indeed, absent well-recognized international valuation standards any consensus about the adequacy of compensation under lump sum settlements is well-nigh impossible....

* * *

C. *Effectiveness*

"Although damages may be adequate in amount and promptly paid," explain the Reporters of the Harvard Convention,[v] "they cannot be effective if they are paid in a currency which cannot be utilized by the injured alien." Put succinctly, albeit too simply, by White, "[t]he question of effectiveness turns on the currency in which compensation should be paid."[66] Three possibilities exist: (1) payment in the currency of the claimant State; (2) payment in the currency of the respondent State; and (3) payment in the currency of a third State. While acknowledging that international law precedents on this point are scanty, the Restatement [Second] adopts the view that compensation, "[i]f not in the currency of the state in which the alien was a national at the time of taking," at least "must be convertible into such currency and withdrawable, either before or after conversion, to the territory of the state of the alien's nationality...."[w] Here, to a much greater degree than in the case of promptness or adequacy, the Settlement Agreements support the Restatement's position.

11. Editors' Note. In their 1975 treatise on lump sum agreements from which preceding Reading 10, *supra*, is excerpted, Richard Lillich and Burns Weston concluded that reliance on lump sum agreements as a source of

---

v. Harvard Draft Convention (No. 12) on the International Responsibility of States for Injuries to Aliens (L. Sohn & R. Baxter, Reps., 15 Apr 61).

66. G. White, Nationalisation of Foreign Property 16 (1961).

w. The comments upon Restatement Third [**Basic Document 6.3**] take essentially the same position, adding that "payment in bonds may satisfy the requirement of just compensation if they bear interest at an economically reasonable rate and if there is a market for them...." *See also supra* notes **r** & **s**.

international law, to be treated in the same manner as any other international prescription, is entirely warranted. They wrote, at 43:

> Continued adherence to a theory that would deny the validity of these conclusions by relegating the whole phenomenon of lump sum agreement-making to an inferior status within the pantheon of international [legal] prescription is . . . to deny a growing edge of international law. Worse, it is to misconceive the nature of law and legal process.

However, in Burns H. Weston, Richard B. Lillich and David J. Bederman, International Claims: Their Settlement by Lump Sum Agreements, 1975–1995, at 7–20 (1999), a sequel to the 1975 Lillich–Weston treatise a quarter century later, the authors write that "certain events have occurred that oblige us to acknowledge that, as an empirical matter, lump sum agreements have yet to be accorded the full jurisprudential significance that we believe should attach to them." Among these events, they list *Banco Nacional de Cuba v. Chase Manhattan Bank*,[x] wherein the the US Court of Appeals for the Second Circuit rejected the argument, advanced by Cuba's counsel, that lump sum agreements had contributed to the development of a partial compensation rule. They cite also *In the Matter of an Arbitration Between the Government of the State of Kuwait and the American Independent Oil Co. (AMINOIL)*,[y] to acknowledge that "[i]nternational arbitral tribunals . . . have weighed the jurisprudential importance of lump sum agreements and reached somewhat the same conclusion as the Second Circuit." Finally, they cite scholars unsupportive of their view (Sornarajah, Clagett).[z]

They do not relinquish their argument, however, citing two leading scholars supportive of their view (Dolzer, Pechota):[aa]

> Both Dolzer and Pechota thus endorse our view that lump sum agreements are important sources of the Law of International Claims in general, and, more specifically, that such settlements, together with investment treaties, arbitral awards and other relevant expressions of community expectation, support "the proposition that the principle of compensation as an international regulatory norm is yet alive even if under attack."

Weston, Lillich, and Bederman then continue:

> It bears repeating that our jurisprudential point is *not* that lump sum agreements by themselves state *the* rule of international law relative to compensation and other issues but that, despite all their deficiencies, they should be treated equally with other expressions of international lawmaking in helping to determine what the international law rules relative to compensation and other issues really are. . . .

* * *

x. 658 F.2d 875 (2d Cir.1981). . . .

y. 21 I.L.M. 976, 1035–37 (1982).

z. B. Clagett, *Just Compensation in International Law: The Issues Before the Iran–United States Claims Tribunal*, in 4 The Valuation of Nationalized Property in International Law 31, 78 (R. Lillich ed. & contrib. 1987); M. Sornarajah, The Pursuit of Nationalized Property 215 (1986).

aa. *See* R. Dolzer, *New Foundations of the Law of Expropriation of Alien Property*, 75 A.J.I.L. 553, 559–60 (1981); V. Pechota, *The 1981 US–Czechoslovak Claims Settlement Agreement: An Epilogue to Postwar Nationalization and Expropriation Disputes*, 76 A.J.I.L. 639 (1982).

As for the compensation controversy, it presently focuses (just as it did when we first addressed the question ...), not upon the *principle* but upon the *amount* of compensation. This question, in turn, raises the important issue of precisely what constitutes "just" compensation, as well as the technical questions concerning the valuation standards to be used in determining it. And here ... the lump sum settlement-national claims commission device has made a real contribution towards a new consensus on compensation. For example, although considerable additional data gathering will be required before any definitive conclusion can be reached, it now appears that the less lump sum settlements involve wartime or immediate postwar deprivations, the more compensation they provide. A preliminary assessment of the additional sixty-nine lump sum agreements now extant suggests that such settlements continue to have a useful impact upon the compensation question, although one not always appreciated by courts and commentators.

The authors then conclude:

One final point needs making, and it is one that cannot be overstressed. All the dissents from, or reservations to, the norm-creating impact of lump sum agreements that have been made by courts and commentators ... pertain *exclusively* to matters of compensation (and, to a lesser extent, valuation). With respect to the other norms, standards or rules found in them—for instance, the continuous nationality requirement, the eligibility of direct or indirect stockholder claims, the rules of attribution, and whether certain claims (such as "creeping expropriation" claims), are compensable—lump sum agreements never have been the object of criticism. Indeed, as to these norms, they are widely and frequently relied upon as relevant sources of international law, even by the Iran–United States Claims Tribunal. Moreover, whatever the response of courts and commentators to lump sum agreements, the response of governments has been to continue to use them extensively as precedent for further such settlements.... However much some international lawyers may wish the contrary, lump sum agreements, unlike the Cheshire cat, stubbornly refuse to fade away....

D. THE RULES OF THE INTERNATIONAL MONETARY FUND

1. Articles of Agreement of the International Monetary Fund, Concluded, 22 July 1944. Entered into force 27 Dec. 1945. T.I.A.S. No. 1501, 2 U.N.T.S. 39; *reprinted in* 15 I.L.M. 546 (1976) and 5 Weston & Carlson IV.A.3: Intro. & Arts. IV, VI, VII, VIII, XIV, XXX (Basic Document 4.2).

2. James Evans, "Current and Capital Transactions: How the Fund Defines Them" 3 Fin. and Dev., 30, 31, 33–35 (Sep. 1968).

Code of Conduct

Article I of the Fund Agreement lists the purposes for which the Fund was created. Item (iv) of Article I indicates where the distinction between payments for current and capital transactions is relevant to the code of conduct. It states that the Fund is established and shall operate "to assist in the establishment of a multilateral system of payments in respect to current transactions between members and in the elimination of foreign exchange restrictions which hamper the growth of world trade." This purpose is carried out in the code of conduct by the obligation members undertake pursuant to the provisions of Article VIII, Section 2(a). Section 2 is entitled "Avoidance of restrictions on current payments" and paragraph (a) states that (subject to certain provisions) "no member shall, without the approval of the Fund, impose restrictions on the making of payments and transfers for current international transactions." It should be observed that the terms of this provision cover only exchange restrictions and are not intended to prevent a member from regulating either the receipt of payments or the underlying transactions which give rise to the making of a payment.

Thus a member may require, for example, that exporters sell only for specified currencies and that they surrender all export proceeds. The member may also prohibit or limit the importation of particular commodities or services, or may require that an exporter or importer insure all his risks of loss with a local insurance company.

The complimentary provision, found in Article VI, Section 3, entitled "Controls of capital transfers," states: "Members may exercise such controls as are necessary to regulate international capital movements, but no member may exercise these controls in a manner which will restrict payments for current transactions or which will unduly delay transfers of funds in settlement of commitments, except as provided in Article VII, Section 3(b), and in Article XIV, Section 2." It could be argued that in a strict legal sense Article VI, Section 3, is not a necessary provision in the Agreement since it imposes no new undertaking on members but only recognizes that members do not undertake any obligation not to impose restrictions on the making of payments for capital transactions. It does show, however, the importance attached to the principle that current payments should be free from restrictions, and it disposes any argument that a member might have made that a restriction on a current payment that incidentally arises from its capital controls can be imposed under the provisions of the Fund Agreement.

Of the two other provisions referred to in each of these Sections, Article VII, Section 3(b) need not concern us at present since it applies only in circumstances that the Fund has so far not found to have arisen.

The other provision, Article XIV, Section 2, is, however, of the greatest importance. It permits a member, if it so desires, and without obtaining Fund approval, to maintain for balance of payments reasons those restrictions on payments and transfers for current transactions which it imposes when it joins the Fund and to adapt them to changing circumstances. The member is required, however, to remove these measures as its balance of payments situation improves and finally, when its balance of payments position permits, to forgo all reliance on this provision and accept the obligations of Article VIII. The majority of Fund members still avail themselves of these "transitional arrangements" set forth in Article XIV, Section 2. Even though a member is availing itself of these "transitional arrangements," it may not introduce new restrictions on payments for current international transactions without Fund approval under Article VIII. Further, the road from Article XIV to Article VII is one way. Once restrictions have been removed, they may not be reintroduced, except under Article VIII with Fund approval.

* * *

Fund Definition

In Article [XXX.] Explanation of Terms, the definition of what is to be considered a "payment for a current transaction" for the purposes of the Fund agreement is contained in paragraph [d] which reads as follows:

"Payments for current transactions means payments which are not for the purpose of transferring capital, and includes, without limitation:

(1) All payments due in connection with foreign trade, other current business, including services, and normal short-term banking and credit facilities;

(2) Payments due as interest on loans and as net income from other investments;

(3) Payments of moderate amount for amortization of loans or for depreciation of direct investments;

(4) Moderate remittances for family living expenses.

The Fund may, after consultation with the members concerned, determine whether certain specific transactions are to be considered current transactions or capital transactions."

The three elements of this provision are the general test, the list of items, and the express grant of authority to the Fund to determine whether the particular transactions are capital or current.

* * *

Some of the particular items in the list of current transactions in Article [XXX(d)] have raised problems of interpretations. The treatment that must be accorded income from investment, or depreciation or amortization of an investment, has raised the question in practice that may indicate why the drafters of the Fund Agreement specifically included interest and net income as payments for current transactions. Since a member country is free to regulate capital movements and may attach conditions to the inflow of capital, it has sometimes been assumed that it may, as a capital control measure, also require the investor to forgo the repatriation of income, amortization, or depreciation as a condition of permitting the capital inflow. This is not so as the terms of Article VI, Section 3 make clear. Such a requirement would clearly be a restriction on the making of payments for current transactions and accordingly prohibited under the Fund Agreement, and it can hardly be argued that there is in fact no restriction merely because the person against whom the restriction is imposed is compelled to agree to accept such a restriction.

With respect to payments for amortization, depreciation, or family remittances, the question which recurs is what is meant by a "moderate amount" or a "moderate remittance." No precise figure can be said to be "moderate" for any of these payments in every situation. However, amortization payments which, for example, equal one twentieth of the amount of a 20–year loan would certainly appear to qualify everywhere. In determining whether a payment on account of depreciation is "moderate," local experience as to the useful lifespan of any item of plant or equipment would have to be the first consideration. The provision does not reject any appropriate method of computing depreciation.

With regard to remittances for family living expenses, what is "moderate" can only be judged in the light of the particular circumstances, such as the size of the family and the expenses which are to be met.

The terms "interest," "income," "amortization," and "depreciation" denote concepts that are generally accepted and require little further explanation. This is not so with the words "normal short-term banking and credit facilities" used in the first item in the list in Article [XXX(d)]. Three basic questions are raised: What is the nature of these "banking and credit facilities"? What is "normal"? And what is "short-term"? The kind of banking and credit facilities intended is indicated by several factors. One of the items on the original list at Bretton Woods referred to "payments due on maturing obligations for the above where the obligations were incurred within one year." Further evidence is found by contrasting the words in the definition with the words of Article VI, Section 1(b)(i) which refers to "capital transactions ... required for the expansion of exports or in the ordinary course of trade, banking, or other business." In addition, the term is part of item (1) of Article [XXX(d)] which deals with "foreign trade, other current business, including services" and "normal short-term banking and credit facilities" together. Each of these indicates that the "facilities" (and the use of the word "facilities" itself strengthens the conclusion), are those banking and credit facilities which are necessary to keep trade moving and to sustain current business operations. This is in contrast to those capital transactions referred to in Article VI, Section 1(b)(i) which are needed to promote or expand operations above present level by direct investment and transfers of working capital and which therefore can be regarded as being more than the "facilities" needed for current operations.

The "normal" facility is the customary practice in the particular trade or business for which the facility is being made available. The custom and practice as it changes from time to time may mean that the term "short-term banking and credit facilities" may have a different content from time to time as well as from place to place.

In this context, the shortness of "short-term" must also be judged against what is usual in that part of the trade or business under consideration. As with the term "moderate," there do not appear to be hard and fast rules, and practice may change. One definition of a "short-dated bill" is a "bill of exchange drawn for a short term, not exceeding three months, after date." The original draft at Bretton Woods seemed to place a one-year limit on obligations incurred for current purposes. Since it is custom and practice that set the limit, it seems that a period of more than one year would probably not be generally considered "short term" and in many instances even shorter periods could be the outside limit.

3. *Weston Banking Corp. v. Turkiye Guaranti Bankasi, A.S.,* 57 N.Y.2d 315, 442 N.E.2d 1195 (1982).

[*Eds.*—In analyzing whether it should enforce a debt owed by Turkiye Guaranti Bankasi, a Turkish Bank, to Weston Banking Corp., a Panamanian Bank, the court had to determine whether Turkish exchange controls arguably justifying non-payment by Turkiye Guaranti Bankasi were consistent with the IMF Articles of Agreement. In coming to the conclusion that they were, the dissent argued as follows:]

* * *

Plaintiff suggests that the regulation is not maintained consistently with the Agreement because the purpose of the agreement is to promote exchange stability, because Article VIII (Section 2, Subd, [a]) provides that "no member shall, without approval of the Fund, impose restrictions on the making of payments and transfers for current international transactions," and because paragraph (a) of Section 1 of Article V requires members to avoid manipulating exchange rates in order to prevent effective balance of payment adjustments or to gain an unfair competitive advantage over other members. The argument overlooks the provisions of Section 2 of Article XIV which permits "restrictions on payments and transfers for current international transactions" during the "post-war transitional period" even though not approved by the Fund, and the powers of the Fund under Section 4 of that Article to make representations that such controls be withdrawn, and under Section 2 of Article XV to compel withdrawal of a member whose regulations offend against the Agreements provisions. Plaintiff presents nothing to suggest that Turkey has violated Article IV, to indicate that the Turkish regulation first imposed in 1930 and amended postwar many times is not a permitted transitional period restriction, or indeed that if [that is not so] the restriction has not been approved by the fund.

E. Legal Personality and Binding Obligation Under International Law

1. Vienna Convention on the Law of Treaties, Concluded, 23 May 1969. Entered into force, 27 Jan. 1988, 1155 U.N.T.S. 331; *reprinted in* 8 I.L.M. 679 (1969) and 5 Weston & Carlson *i.e.*1: Arts 46, 54, 62 (Basic Document 1.10).

2. Restatement (Third) of The Foreign Relations Law of the United States § 311 (1987) (Basic Document 6.3).

3. International Law Commission Report [on draft Article 62 of the Vienna Convention on the Law of Treaties] 2 Y B. I.L.C. 169, 256–258 (1966).

[*Eds.*—The International Law Commission provided the commentary excerpted in part below to its draft of Article 62 (Fundamental Change in Circumstances) of the Vienna Convention on the Law of Treaties **(Basic Document 1.10)**.]

(1) ... [J]ust as many systems of municipal law recognize that, quite apart from any actual *impossibility* of performance, contracts may become inapplicable through a fundamental change of circumstances [or *rebus sic stantibus*], so also treaties may become inapplicable for the same reason. Most jurists, however, at the same time enter a strong *caveat* as to the need to

confine the scope of the doctrine within narrow limits and to regulate strictly the conditions under which it may be invoked; for the risks to the security of treaties which this doctrine presents in the absence of any general system of compulsory jurisdiction are obvious. The circumstances of international life are always changing and it is easy to allege that the changes render the treaty inapplicable.

* * *

(6) The Commission concluded that the principle, if its application were carefully delimited and regulated, should find a place in the modern law of treaties. A treaty may remain in force for a long time and its stipulations come to place an undue burden on one of the parties as a result of a fundamental change of circumstances. Then, if the other party were obdurate in opposing any change, the fact that international law recognized no legal means of terminating or modifying the treaty otherwise than through a further agreement between the same parties might impose a serious strain on the relations between the States concerned; and the dissatisfied State might ultimately be driven to take action outside the law. The number of cases calling for the application of the rule is likely to be comparatively small. . . . [T]he majority of modern treaties are expressed to be of short duration, or are entered into for recurrent terms of years with a right to denounce the treaty at the end of each term, or are expressly or implicitly terminable upon notice. In all these cases either the treaty expires automatically or each party, having the power to terminate the treaty, has the power also to apply pressure upon the other party to revise its provisions. Nevertheless, there may remain a residue of cases in which, failing any agreement, one party may be left powerless under the treaty to obtain any legal relief from outmoded and burdensome provisions. It is in these cases that the *rebus sic stantibus* doctrine could serve a purpose as a lever to induce a spirit of compromise in the other party. Moreover, despite the strong reservations often expressed with regard to it, the evidence of the acceptance of the doctrine in international law is so considerable that it seems to indicate a recognition of a need for this safety-valve in the law of treaties.

4. Oscar Schachter, "State Succession: The Once and Future Law," 33 Va. J. Int'l L. 253, 253–54, 256–58 (1993).

[State] "succession" [is] a somewhat imprecise term that deals with the transmission or extinction of rights and obligations of a state that no longer exists or has lost part of its territory. [It] is one of the oldest subjects of international law. Even Aristotle speculated in his *Politics* on the problem of continuity when "the state is no longer the same."[67] . . . Underlying the legal discourse we can discern the human dramas: the break-up of age-old empires and the emergence of new identities, new voices, new frontiers separating peoples or uniting them, deeply affecting their personal lives. These events are not only the stuff of history; they foreshadow the future. We can be quite sure, as we look around us today, that some states will split, others will be absorbed, frontiers will be moved, and new generations will question old alliances and commitments. The problem that concerned Aristotle in the

67. Aristotle, The Politics, bk. III, ch. 3 (Stephen Everson ed. 1988).

fourth century B.C., of the stability of legal obligation when political identities change, will persist on both the international as well as the domestic level.

... The prevailing legal view in the nineteenth and much of the twentieth century accepted two basic principles relating to succession. One was the critical difference between succession of states and changes in government. The principle of succession was relevant only where the state was replaced by another in the responsibility for the international relations of a territory. The legal problem of succession did not arise when governments ... changed, no matter how profound or revolutionary a change. This principle, traced by scholars to Grotius, has been generally accepted by scholars, courts and foreign ministries. It was challenged ... by the Soviet regime in its early effort to repudiate obligations of the Czarist government, an effort that did not succeed in changing doctrine or practice. It is evident that in sharply differentiating between "sovereignty" and "government," the law weighs heavily on the side of continuity of obligations when major political changes occur within sovereign states.

This basic differentiation between changes in government and changes in sovereignty is rarely questioned but, as pointed out by Daniel O'Connell (an eminent authority), the distinction "in some instances wears thin to the point of disappearance" and may be "quite arbitrary."[68] In his words, "[t]o permit the solution of complex political and economic problems to depend on this arbitrary cataloguing is to divorce the law from the actualities of international life."[69]

5. Daniel P. O'Connell, 1 State Succession in Municipal Law and International Law 3–7 (1967).

As Hall, in a much quoted passage, expressed it, personality has been regarded as the key to the problem of State succession. The consequences of change of sovereignty may vary according to the extent to which such personality is affected.... [70]

At the present time the boundary between change of sovereignty and change of government often wears thin to the point of disappearance, and the question has now arisen whether or not there is any utility in maintaining a rigid distinction between the legal consequences of the one and the other situation. * * * [T]he solution of the problem raised by political change cannot be left to the hazard of characterizing the event as a succession of States or a succession of governments. There is evident at the present time a developing pressure in the direction of assimilating these two categories of events, and as the nineteenth-century theory of the State, with its concomitant metaphysics of political personality, loses its cogency, legal theory will tend more and more to return to its eighteenth-century position.

* * *

6. Sharon A. Williams and Armand L.C. de Mestral, An Introduction to International Law, Chiefly as Interpreted and Applied in Canada 93–102 (2d ed. 1987).

Once a state has come into existence, it continues to exist until extinguished by absorption into another state or by dissolution. Changes in the

---

68. 1 D. O'Connell, State Succession in Municipal and International Law vi (1967).

69. *Id.*

70. W. Hall, International Law 114 (8th ed., A. Higgins rev., 1926).

government, or in the types of government, for example from a monarchy to a republic, by legal or by unconstitutional or violent means, do not affect the continuity or the identity of the state in terms of its international legal personality. All rights and title to property remain vested in the state regardless of such changes....

By this same principle of continuity, a state is bound by any acts and engagements of governments that have become extinct.[71] ... A government represents the state, succeeds to any debts of the government it follows and passes any obligations it incurs to the next regime. * * * The questions of international law which arise in [the context of succession] are to what extent the existing rights and obligations of the predecessor state are extinguished and to what extent the successor state takes up those rights and obligations.

* * *

I. TREATIES

... Treaties can relate to a wide variety of matters, from exclusively political agreements to multilateral conventions and conveyances of territory between states.

The traditional method of viewing treaties in relation to state succession has been to determine firstly whether the treaty concerned is a "personal" treaty or a "real" treaty. "Personal" treaties ... were based on the premise that the parties would continue to exist unchanged. This was an essential element of their contract. "Personal" treaties were primarily political—alliances, pacts of mutual defence, settlements of disputes, economic—such as commercial arrangements, administrative—relating, for example, to postal and telegraphic communications, and judicial—concerning matters such as extradition.... The new state was said to start off with a limited *tabula rasa* (a clean slate) and succeeded to no such personal—political obligations.

"Real" or dispositive treaties, on the other hand, were said to comprise boundary treaties and other rights of transit, over territory. These treaties, as they depended less on the particular personality of the states in question, were held generally to survive a change in sovereignty thus posing an exception to the complete *tabula rasa* doctrine.

* * *

Since 1945, some states have departed from this traditional approach and consequently the law is now far from certain. The most extreme view that has been put forward by many newly independent developing countries is that the doctrine of equality of states requires that upon independence a state should have the right and the absolute freedom either to accept or reject any treaty obligations which have been incurred on its behalf by the former metropolitan colonial power....

In effect, the uncertainty as to state succession revolves around the newly independent states. They have adopted varying procedures. The interim

---

71. The Tinoco Concessions Case, [1923] 1 U.N.R.I.A.A. 369 (1948).

report which was presented to the Helsinki Conference of the International Law Association in 1966 distinguished four trends in post-war practice. . . .

First, the successor state accepts all pre-existing treaty obligations. Nigeria adopted this procedure. Secondly, the successor state provisionally accepts all treaties during a trial period and at the end of that time makes a declaration as to which treaties it accepts definitively and which it declines to follow. Malawi adopted this procedure. Thirdly, the successor state avoids making any declarations or statements as to whether or not it accepts certain treaties, and instead leaves the matter to be determined by customary international law. Zambia followed this procedure. Fourthly, the successor state makes a general declaration of its policy in the matter of succession to treaties.

The International Law Commission has also considered the issue of state succession with respect to treaty and other matters. It presented its study in the form of draft articles ... [and the] draft was used as the basis for the Vienna Convention on Succession of States in Respect of Treaties that was adopted by the United Nations Conference on August 22, 1978.[72] This Convention purports to codify customary international law. Article 11 provides that state succession does not affect boundaries established by treaties or obligations and rights established by treaty and relating to a boundary regime. Article 12(1) and 12(2)c likewise provide that succession shall not affect obligations relating to the use of territory or restrictions upon use established by treaty for the benefit of any foreign state or group of states or of all states and attaching to that territory. . . . Article 16 provides that a newly independent state is not bound either to maintain in force, or to become a party to, any treaty by reason of the fact that it was in force in respect of the territory to which the succession of states relates. Under Article 17(1) a newly independent state may, by notification of succession, establish itself as a party to a multilateral treaty which at the date of the succession was in force in the predecessor state. . . . As regards bilateral treaties, there can only be succession where both parties are in agreement.

* * *

II. PUBLIC PROPERTY

A successor state, when it acquires the entire territory of the predecessor state, takes over all the public or state property, movable or immovable, wherever that property is situated. . . .

III. PUBLIC DEBTS

How far does a new state have to succeed to the debts of the predecessor state? * * * It has been suggested that if the debt has been incurred in order to improve the territory of the state, the successor state has benefitted from the loan when taking over the territory and should be responsible for the debt. In other words, the successor has to take up the burdens and not only

72. UN Doc. A/CONF.80/31, 22 Aug 1978, *as corrected by* A/CONF.80/31/Corr. 2, 27 Oct. 1978, *reprinted in* 17 I.L.M. 1488 (1978) [and 5   Weston & Carlson I.F.1]. . . . [The Convention entered into force on 6 Nov 1996.]

the benefits of succession. Where[,] however, the debt was incurred for some purpose hostile to the successor state, the latter will not be bound to repay it.

* * *

The 1983 Vienna Convention on Succession of States in Respect of State Property, Archives and Debts[73] provides for succession to financial obligations chargeable to a state.... Article 38(1), in laying down the rules of newly independent states, provides that no state debt shall be transferred unless there is an agreement with the predecessor state. However, under Article 38(2) no such agreement "shall infringe upon the permanent sovereignty of every people over its wealth and natural resources, nor shall the implementation endanger the fundamental economic equilibria of the newly independent state."

IV.   PRIVATE RIGHTS

Vested or acquired rights should be respected by the successor state. * * * The question is, does state succession transmit all private rights? ... Nothing prevents the successor state from changing the domestic system and laws and in this way extinguishing existing rights. Nevertheless, a successor state has a duty under international law to observe the minimum international standard for the treatment of aliens. For instance, if the successor state wishes to nationalize or expropriate property belonging to foreigners, then even if it has changed its municipal law to allow itself to do so, it must still comply with the international rules so far as public purpose and fair and adequate compensation are concerned.

... [M]any newly independent states have criticized these principles of international law as being biased in favour of Western interests. As regards investments, some maintain that those made in a state after its independence should be respected. However, different considerations apply to those made before independence when the dependent state was not in a position to protect its interests.... On the other side, it has been argued that the international rules providing for compensation where expropriation takes place, are designed to prevent unjust enrichment. On this basis, compensation should be paid but can be reduced where a foreigner has profited himself at the expense of the former dependent state.

Thus, many of the problems encountered in the area of vested or acquired rights and state succession arise from the protection given to foreigners by international law. * * * The principles that have emerged from the case law affirm the continuation of acquired rights....

It must be stressed that these cases do not mean that a successor state [may not] alter such rights.... The doctrine of acquired rights merely emphasizes that there is a presumption that [such] rights will continue regardless of changes in sovereignty.

73. UN Doc. A/CONF.117/14, Apr. 7, 1983, *reprinted in* 22 I.L.M. 306 (1983) [and 5 Wes- ton & Carlson I.F.2].... [The Convention had not entered into force as of 1 Mar 2006.]

7. James Crawford, The Creation of States in International Law 405–06 (1979).

It has long been established that, in the case of an "internal revolution, merely altering the municipal constitution and form of government, the State remains the same; it neither loses any of its rights, nor is discharged from any of its obligations."[74] Despite the question-begging nature of this and other formulations, the rule that revolution *prima facie* does not affect the continuity of the State in which it occurs has been consistently applied to the innumerable revolutions, *coups d'état* and the like in the nineteenth and twentieth centuries. After some hesitation, it was for example established that the R.F.S.F.R. (later the Soviet Union) was a continuation of Imperial Russia. A *fortiori*, continuity is not affected by alterations in a municipal constitution according to its own amendment provisions; or by a change in the name of the State; or by non-recognition of the revolutionary government of a State. Although it is sometimes argued that "socialist revolutions," which result in a changed class-structure of the State, bring about a fundamental discontinuity in relations, it is not at all clear whether this claim is directed to the notion of legal continuity of the State, or is a claim to a more liberal regime of succession. Neither the Soviet Union nor the People's Republic of China have asserted such discontinuity; while problems of succession of governments in the two cases have tended to be worked out on an *ad hoc* basis.

8. Philip Noonan, "Revolutions and Treaty Termination," 2 Dickinson J. Int'l L. 301, 301–29 (1984).

It is a widely accepted principle of international law that ordinary changes in government do not affect treaty obligations. During the course of the twentieth century, however, certain states and some writers have asserted that revolutionary changes in government do affect treaty obligations. * * * Typically, these authors believe that certain characteristics of a revolution set it apart from other governmental changes; that such characteristics may warrant an approach more sophisticated than the bald application of a general rule of treaty continuation. Thus, Starke writes that, "[t]here may be such fundamental revolutionary changes with the advent of the new Government, politically, economically or socially, that it is impossible in fact to hold the Government to certain serious or burdensome obligations."[75]

[*Eds.*—The author next notes the inconsistent treatment accorded by international legal doctrine to revolutions and unconstitutional secessions, the former being theoretically without effect upon existing treaties, the latter being theoretically free to disregard them. He then continues:]

... The extent to which it is observed in practice is perhaps the most powerful reason for questioning the correctness of the rule that insists upon virtually total treaty continuation. Revolutionary states in fact refuse to be bound by treaties that they regard as against the best interests of the state. In other words, the rule "is a paradigm of the over-ambitious norm."

* * *

It can be seen that with respect to three important revolutions in this century, the post-revolutionary government has claimed the right to be free of

74. H. Wheaton, Elements of International Law (8th ed., 1866) I, § 22, *citing* H. Grotius. De Jure Belli ac Pacis II, Ch. 9 § 8 (1646) (trans. F. Kelsey, 1925); S. von Pufendorf, De Iure Naturae et Gentium Libri Octo, Ch. 12, §§ 1–3 (1672) (trans. C. & W. Oldfather, 1934).

75. J. Starke, An Introduction to International Law 334 (7th ed. 1972).

at least some of its predecessor's treaty obligations. The People's Republic of China has based this squarely on the principle of *rebus sic stantibus*, the revolution being the *rebus*. The Soviet argument is less obvious, but seems to represent a similar plea that the changed circumstances associated with the revolution have rendered certain treaties invalid. While Iranian theory is as yet unclear, the importance of changes in circumstances may be relevant there too.

* * *

Some writers have searched for such a paramount rationale. They have proceeded from the basis that this area of international law, as with many others, ought to be oriented primarily toward a peaceful banning of the ever-competing forces for stability and change. O'Connell states, "The problem is to give expression in normative form to a reconciliation of two competitive pressures, that of stability in the international and internal orders, and that of adjustment of legal relationships to the social and economic effects of change."[76]

* * *

What then are the particular factors to be considered when a government changes? * * * Writing about the status of treaties during a revolution, Graham identifies five factors:

(1) conditions at the time of making the agreement,

(2) the nature of the agreement,

(3) the type of revolution; its purpose, duration and factual effect,

(4) the nature and extent of the changed conditions associated with the revolution,

(5) the factual effect of these changed conditions on the agreement.[77]

* * *

When assessing the extent of change in a state, it is necessary to remember that a revolution is not an instantaneous event. Even when the old government has been decisively defeated, the character of the changes promoted by the new government may depend upon which of the various factions, perhaps united in warfare but rivals in victory, gains full power. Hasty decisions, based upon insufficient information, may well yield inadequate results.

9. Oscar Schachter, "State Succession: The Once and Future Law," 33 Va. J. Int'l L. 253, 256–60 (1993).

In the 1960's, state succession was placed high on the agenda of international lawyers ... as a result of the wave of decolonization and the efforts of the UN International Law Commission to codify the law of succession in relation to treaties and, separately, to debts, state property and state archives. In the 1960's and 1970's, this gave rise to considerable controversy centered

---

76. 1 D. O'Connell, State Succession in Municipal and International Law 34–35 (1967).

77. A. Graham, Note, *The Effects of Domestic Hostilities on Public and Private International Agreements: A Tentative Approach*, 3 W. Ontario L. Rev. 128 (1964).

mainly on the applicability of the clean slate principle to the newly independent states resulting from decolonization. Many members of the International Law Commission and the majority of states concluded that new states should not be bound by agreements made by former colonial rulers. Self-determination was often cited in support of this principle. It was included in the convention on treaty succession proposed by the International Law Commission and adopted by a majority of states at the Vienna Plenipotentiary Conference in 1978.[78] That Vienna Convention did not, however, apply the clean slate principle to new states that arose from separation rather than decolonization. Unlike colonies, those new states presumably had a voice in making and accepting the treaty. As Professor Vagts observes,[79] this differentiation was rejected by the Restatement (Third) of the Foreign Relations Law of the United States ("Restatement") **[Basic Document 6.3]**, which favored giving all newly independent states freedom to start afresh. The Vienna Convention went a step beyond the clean slate rule by giving the ex-colonial state a right to become a party to a multilateral agreement to which its predecessor state had adhered unless the new state's adherence would radically change the conditions for the operation of the treaty or if the consent of all treaty parties is expressly or impliedly required. Thus, ex-colonial states not only had a right to escape the obligations of the predecessor state in this respect; they also could choose to become a party to a multilateral treaty in many cases irrespective of the consent of other parties.... [T]he State Department Legal Adviser expressed the opinion in 1980 that the rules of the Vienna Convention were "generally regarded as declarative of existing customary law by the United States."[80]

Now that decolonization has come to an end, questions still remain whether states that have separated (*i.e.*, seceded) will be able to claim the right to pick and choose (as the Restatement would allow) or whether they would be bound by the principle of the Vienna Convention (but as a customary law rule) that a separated state which was not a colony is presumed to succeed to the treaty obligations and rights of the predecessor state unless this result would be incompatible with the object of the treaty. The experience thus far with respect to the cases of the former Soviet Union and the former Yugoslavia supports a general presumption of continuity. That presumption would not, however, apply to membership in the United Nations or other general international organizations that provide for the election of new members. Nor would the separated states continue to have the rights of the predecessor where this would be contrary to the object of a treaty. A good example of the latter point ... relates to the important Nuclear Non–Proliferation Treaty ("NPT") of 1968, a general multilateral treaty open to all states **[Basic Document 2.21]**. Under that treaty, the USSR was designated as a nuclear power. After the dissolution, Russia was recognized as the successor in this respect to the former USSR. However, to recognize some or all of the other republics as successors to the USSR with the right to have

---

78. Vienna Convention on Succession of States in Respect of Treaties, art. 16, 17 I.L.M. 1488 (1978) [hereinafter Treaty Succession Convention] [*reprinted in* 5 Weston & Carlson I.F.1]. The treaty was opened for signature on 23 Aug 1978, [and went into effect on 6 Nov 1996].

79. *See* D. Vagts, *State Succession: The Codifier's View*, 33 Va. J. Int'l L. 275 (1993).

80. 1980 Digest of United States Practice in International Law 1041 n.43 (quoting memorandum of Roberts Owen, US State Department Legal Adviser).

nuclear weapons would undoubtedly be incompatible with the main objective of the NPT, which was to limit nuclear weapons to the five states that were nuclear powers prior to January 1, 1967. Obviously, a presumption of continuity that would give nuclear rights to the new states could not be acceptable.

* * *

Although state succession has been a subject of great controversy in the last fifty years ..., it seems probable that a general presumption of continuity of the obligations of a predecessor state will be accepted for new states that have come into being by secession or by dissolution of existing states. This is in accord with the position of the United States.... Most other countries may be expected to follow. Thus it is unlikely that the Restatement's rule of a clean slate for all new states will prevail in practice or theory.... We might recall, as James Crawford has pointed out, that "[t]he process of evolution towards a general regime of treaty continuity ... was, remarkably, completed at the Second Session of the Vienna Conference."[81]

A presumption of continuity does not mean a categorical black letter rule of succession. It is important to recognize that the particular circumstances may call for non-succession. This would apply to all successions whether of treaty, debt or delictual liability....

As a matter of policy, the case for presuming continuity makes sense today when the state system is increasingly fluid. Nation-states no longer appear immortal. Many seem likely to split or to be absorbed by others. Autonomous regions are likely to increase, central governments may even disappear for a time (as in Somalia or Cambodia), and mergers and integration will probably occur.

In this predictably pluralist world of kaleidoscopic change, stability in expectations will matter; it becomes more important than would be the case in a more settled period. The responses to the fragmentation of the Eastern European regimes revealed the concerns over the disruption of treaty relations. At the same time, the diversity and the particularities call for avoiding rigidities and for taking account of context in specific cases. Contextual solutions may be facilitated by relying on treaty rules, such as *rebus sic stantibus* or on equitable principles applicable to state debts or liability.

An especially strong case for continuity can be made in respect of multilateral treaties of a so-called "universal" character that are open to all states. Such treaties include the codification conventions like those on the law of treaties and on diplomatic and consular relations. In addition, there is good reason to include in this category other law-making treaties that have been widely accepted, even though they fall in the category of "development" of new law rather than codification of preexisting law. Müllerson supports this view, mentioning especially the UN human rights treaties which, while not codificatory, have been adhered to by the majority of states.[82] He notes that Croatia and Slovenia declared themselves to be successor states to the former Yugoslavia in regard to human rights treaties which had been in force for Yugoslavia. While Müllerson is cautious in asserting a legal rule in this

81. J. Crawford, *The Contribution of Professor D.P. O'Connell to the Discipline of International Law*, 1980 B.Y.B.I.L. 1, 40.

82. *See* R. Mullerson, *New Developments in the Former USSR and Yugoslavia*, 33 Va. J. Int'l L. 299 (1993).

connection, I am inclined to predict that most such treaties of a general "legislative" character will be treated ... as automatically binding on new states on the basis of adherence by their respective predecessor states. Support for this conclusion can even be found in earlier writings of European jurists. The increase in such universal conventions expressing norms adopted at international assemblies by near-unanimity on the part of states from all regions of the world is indicative of a trend that should support succession by new states as a matter of course.

Müllerson also brings a helpful reminder that many treaties create acquired rights on the part of individuals. In this connection he refers to the decision of the Permanent Court of International Justice in the case of the German settlers which declared that acquired rights of individuals do not cease on a change of sovereignty.[83] Müllerson's suggestion that individual human rights should also be treated like acquired property rights entitled to respect in successor states is likely to be a much-cited legal contention on behalf of individuals in new states.

Still another reason to expect that a presumption of continuity will be widely accepted by new states is that it is helpful to the administration of treaties and other international legal relations of new states. International lawyers in the United States probably do not realize how difficult it is for new states to cope with the hundreds, even thousands, of treaties to which their predecessor states were parties. Lacking adequate documentation, severely limited in legally trained personnel and administrative resources, they cannot examine most treaties afresh and pick or choose among them. If these states are not considered presumptive successors to the treaties, they may not become parties because of their own administrative and technical deficiencies.... For this reason, among others, it makes good sense for states to accept prima facie continuity as a basic premise, leaving room for adjustment or exceptions when they appear necessary or desirable in a particular case.

In sum, my speculation about the future law of state succession rests on what appear to be the political trends relating to changes and turbulence in the nation-state system. It also gives weight to the practical aspects of administering the complicated effects of transfers of sovereignty and the need to avoid rigidity and doctrinaire solutions.

This approach ... is far removed from the learned discourse of the renowned international legal authorities who discussed state succession largely in terms of philosophical theories of the state and justice. Enticing as these works may be to students of legal and political philosophy, they offer little guidance to the solution of actual problems. Our hope for a more orderly and equitable adjustment to political change lies in practical wisdom rather than in abstract theory.

F. Economic Retorsion and Reprisal

1. Charter of the United Nations, 26 Jun 1945, 1976 Y.B.U.N. 1043, 59 Stat. 1031, T.S. No.993; *reprinted in* 5 Weston & Carlson 1.A.1: Arts. 1(1) & (2), 2(3) & (4), 33 (Basic Document 1.5).

---

83. Advisory Opinion No. 6, 1923 PCIJ (ser. B) No 6, at 36.

2. Charter of the Organization of American States 30 Apr 1948, 2 U.S.T.2394, T.I.A.S. No. 2361; *reprinted in* 5 Weston & Carlson I.B.14: Arts. 3, 12, 16–20 (Basic Document 1.7).

3. Declaration on the Inadmissibility of Intervention in the Domestic Affairs of States and the Protection of Their Independence and Sovereignty, 21 Dec 1965, GA Res. 2131 (XX), 20 UN GAOR, Supp. (No. 14) 11, UN Doc. A/6014 (1966); *reprinted in* 5 I.L.M. 374 (1966) and 5 Weston & Carlson II.A.2 (Basic Document 2.20).

4. Declaration on Principles of International Law Concerning Friendly Relations and Co-operation among States in Accordance with the Charter of the United Nations, 24 Oct 1970, GA Res. 2625 (XXV), 25 UN GAOR, Supp. (No.28) 121, UN Doc. A/8028 (1971); *reprinted in* 9 I.L.M. 1292 (1970) and 5 Weston & Carlson I.D.7 (Basic Document 1.11).

5. Charter of Economic Rights and Duties of States, 12 Dec 1974, GA Res. 3281 (XXIX), 29 UN GAOR, Supp. (No. 31) 50, UN Doc. A/9631 (1975); *reprinted in* 14 I.L.M. 251 (1975) and 5 Weston & Carlson IV.F.5: Art. 6, 32 (Basic Document 4.9).

6. Resolution on the Definition of Aggression, 14 Dec 1974, GA Res. 3314 (XXIX), 29 UN GAOR, Supp. (No. 31) 142, UN Doc. A/9631 (1975); *reprinted in* 13 I.L.M. 710 (1974) and 5 Weston & Carlson II.A.4 (Basic Document 2.29).

7. *Starke's* International Law 471–14 (I. Shearer 11th ed. 1994).

When States cannot agree to solve their disputes amicably a solution may have to be found and imposed by unilateral means. The principal forcible and non-forcible modes of settlement are:

a. War and non-war armed action.

b. Retorsion.

c. Reprisals and countermeasures.

d. Pacific blockade.

e. Intervention.

* * *

(b) Retorsion

Retorsion is the technical term for retaliation by a state against discourteous or inequitable acts of another state, such retaliation taking the form of unfriendly legitimate acts within the competence of the state whose dignity has been affronted; for example, severance of diplomatic relations, revocation of diplomatic privileges, or withdrawal of fiscal or tariff concessions.

So greatly has the practice as to retorsion varied that it is impossible to define precisely the conditions under which it is justified. At all events it need not be a retaliation in kind.

The legitimate use of retorsion by Member States of the United Nations has probably been affected by the United Nations Charter [**Basic Document 1.5**]. For example, under paragraph 3 of article 2, Member States are to settle their disputes by peaceful means in such a way as not to "endanger" international peace and security, and justice. It is possible that an otherwise legitimate act of retorsion may in certain circumstances be such as to endanger international peace and security, and justice, in which event it would seemingly be illegal under the Charter.

(c) Reprisals

Reprisals (now more often referred to in situations not involving the use of armed force as countermeasures) are methods adopted by states for securing redress from another state by taking retaliatory measures. Formerly, the term was restricted to the seizure of property or persons, but in its modern acceptation connotes coercive measures adopted by one state against another for the purpose of settling some dispute brought about by the latter's illegal or unjustified conduct. The distinction between reprisals and retorsion is that reprisals consist of acts which would generally otherwise be illegal whereas retorsion consists of retaliatory conduct to which no legal objection can be taken. Reprisals and countermeasures may assume various forms, for example, a boycott of the goods of a particular state, an embargo, a naval demonstration, or bombardment. Few topics of international practice are more controversial. . . .

It is now generally established by international practice that a reprisal or countermeasure is only justified, if at all, where the state against which it is directed has been guilty of conduct in the nature of an international delinquency. Moreover, a reprisal would not be justified if the delinquent state had not been previously requested to give satisfaction for the wrong done, or if the measures of reprisals were "excessive" proportionately in relation to the injury suffered[84] . . . .

Some authorities hold that reprisals are only justified if their purpose is to bring about a satisfactory settlement of a dispute. Hence the principle referred to above that reprisals should not be resorted to unless and until negotiations for the purpose of securing redress from the delinquent state fail.

* * *

As in the case of retorsion, the use of reprisals by member states of the United Nations has been affected by the Charter. Not only is there paragraph 3 of article 2 mentioned above in connection with retorsion, but there is also the provision in paragraph 4 of the same article that Member States are to refrain from the threat or use of force against the territorial integrity or political independence of any state, or in any other manner inconsistent with the Purposes of the United Nations. Also, the Declaration on Principles of International Law Concerning Friendly Relations and Co-operation Among States in Accordance with the United Nations Charter **[Basic Document 1.5]** . . . expressly declares: "States have a duty to refrain from acts of reprisal involving the use of force." . . . Moreover under article 33 the states parties to a dispute, the continuance of which is likely to endanger peace and security are "first of all" to seek a solution by negotiation, and other peaceful means. . . .

---

84. *See* the Naulilaa Case, 8 Trib. Arb. Mixtes 409, 422–25 (1928) [*reprinted in* [1928] 2 U.N.R.I.A.A. 1012 (1949)] and the Air Ser- vices Agreement Case (Fr. v. U.S.) (1978), [1946] U.N.R.I.A.A. 416. . . .

8. Report by the Secretary–General on the Question of Defining Aggression, 3 Oct 1952, 7 UN GAOR, Annex (Agenda Item 54) 17, 74 UN Doc. A/2211 (1953).

2.   *Economic Aggression*

(a) Emergence of the concept of economic aggression

441.   The concept of economic aggression is new. Economic aggression was covered in the draft definition submitted to the Sixth Committee by Bolivia on 11 January 1952, which states:

> "Also to be considered as an act of aggression shall be ... unilateral action to deprive a State of the economic resources derived from the fair practice of international trade, or to endanger its basic economy, thus jeopardizing the security of that State or rendering it incapable of acting in its own defense and co-operating in the collective defense of peace."

* * *

445.   It will be noted that article 16 [now Article 19] of the Charter of the Organization of American States signed at Bogotá on 30 April 1948 **[Basic Document 1.7]** states that:

> "No State may use or encourage the use of coercive measures of an economic or political character in order to force the sovereign will of another State and obtain from it advantages of any kind."

(b) Criticism of the concept of economic aggression

446.   The concept of economic aggression appears particularly liable to extend the concept of aggression almost indefinitely. The acts in question not only do not involve the use of force, but are usually carried out by a State by virtue of its sovereignty or discretionary power. Where there are no commitments a State is free to fix its custom tariffs and to limit or prohibit exports and imports. If it concludes a commercial treaty with another State, superior political, economic and financial strength may of course give it an advantage over the weaker party; but that applies to every treaty, and it is difficult to see how such inequalities, which arise from differences in situation, can be evened out short of changing the entire structure of international society and transferring powers inherent in States to international organs.

9. Derek W. Bowett, "Economic Coercion and Reprisals by States," 13 Va. J. Int'l L. 1, 1–12 (1972).

There is a general agreement with the proposition that reprisals involving recourse to armed force and undertaken by States on their own initiative are illegal. * * * It is significant that no similar forthright statement is made about economic reprisals....

I.   *The Possibility of Characterizing Economic Measures as Illegal*

If we have no specific statement about reprisals we at least now have the possibility of characterizing certain kinds of economic coercion by States as illegal on the following grounds:

(1) economic coercion in violation of specific treaty commitments such as those found in treaties of trade and commerce; treaties on transit

rights, air services and fisheries, multilateral treaties on telecommunications, trade (GATT, for example), monetary policy, and treaties establishing Free Trade Areas or Economic Unions;

(2) economic coercion in violation of general principles of international law such as freedom of the seas, principles of State responsibility for acts economically harmful to aliens, and possibly principles such as those regulating the utilization of international rivers; and

(3) economic coercion in violation of the principle of nonintervention.

As we have shown, the recent formulations of this latter principle within the United Nations embrace economic coercion. It may be expected that, in the future, States will invoke this principle rather than rely on vague allegations of "economic aggression"....[bb]

Despite the above formulation, the principle remains all too vague. First, the measures must be coercive to be illegal. Yet any measures by State A (the establishment of rival industries, for example) may be regarded as coercion by State B in the sense that State B may be forced to take them into account in planning its own economy. In short, economic "pressure" can assume many forms.

Second, the measures must have the aim of obtaining from another State "the subordination of the exercise of its sovereign rights and to secure from it advantages of any kind." Much depends upon what a State assumes its sovereign rights to be. There have been cases where States have assumed the "right" to expropriate in breach of treaties or concession agreements as if this were a part of "sovereignty." As to advantages, a great many economic relationships are established on the basis of reciprocal advantage and it would be ludicrous to characterize a State's economic action as illegal simply because it sought some advantage from another State....

* * *

Much of the State economic activity is harmful to other States for the very obvious reason that State economies are competitive and that promoting one's own economy may well be injurious to others. This suggests that it will be necessary to characterize unlawful economic measures by their intent rather than their effect. In other words, measures not illegal per se may become illegal only upon proof of an improper motive or purpose. This idea is found in the English common law. For example, the tort of conspiracy evolved to cover the situation in which two or more persons conspire to commit acts which are lawful per se but are motivated predominantly by the desire to injure the economic interests of the plaintiff rather than to protect the interests of the defendants. Such an emphasis upon predominant purpose would probably provide a more effective criterion for defining illegal economic coercion than the notions of "subordination of sovereign rights" or "securing advantages" used in the General Assembly Declaration. However, the test of

bb. Writes Daniel P. O'Connell, International Law 300–01 (2d ed. 1970): "[A]ttempts to formulate "economic aggression" have been tiresomely unsuccessful. The most that we can expect is particular rules related to particular occasions. Economic blockade has always been illegal except as an exercise of belligerent rights in wartime; formal interference with trade and shipping, and denial of access by land and water are covered by the rules relating to the sea, rivers, canals and enclaves. More recently economic and financial behavior has been regulated by GATT and other international institutions."

predominant purpose is not necessarily incompatible with these vague criteria. Hopefully, it can be used to give them substance.

It must finally be emphasized that the inherent vagueness of the non-intervention principle does not affect the characterization of measures as illegal where the illegality derives from a breach of specific treaty commitments or established general principles of international law.

II.   The Consequences of Characterizing Economic Activity as Illegal

Measures characterized as prima facie illegal by reference to any one of the three headings listed above may nevertheless be justified on three possible grounds.

A.   Economic Sanctions Authorized by a Competent Organ of the International Community

The power of the Security Council to authorize economic sanctions is beyond dispute. It is expressly recognized by Article 41 of the UN Charter. . . .

The competence of the General Assembly in this area is arguable. . . . However, some States would argue that the Assembly clearly can authorize, if not order, economic sanctions. . . .

Equally arguable is the question of the competence of a regional organization to authorize coercive economic measures. . . . [I]t may be argued that sanctions, whether military or economic, can be taken only by the Security Council or by a regional organization pursuant to Security Council authorization.

* * *

B.   Economic Measures of Self–Defense

Just as a legitimate claim of self-defense may justify unilateral measures involving force which would otherwise be illegal under Article 2(4) of the Charter, a State may justify unilateral economic measures which might otherwise be illegal if it can show that these measures are taken in self-defense. Of course, the essentials of self-defense must be proved. The State would have to show that it was reacting to a delict by another State, posing an immediate danger to its security or independence in a situation affording no alternative means of protection and, lastly, that the reaction was proportionate to the harm threatened.

* * *

C.   Economic Measures of Reprisal

Economic measures openly admitted to be retaliatory are rare for the rather obvious reason that States will usually justify their measures as lawful per se or justifiable self-defense. * * * As we have seen, there has been no agreement within the United Nations that economic reprisals are illegal under the Charter. Indeed, given the rather low level of compliance accorded by States to the prohibition of armed reprisals, it would seem excessively optimistic to argue that economic reprisals are illegal per se.

* * *

The limiting or controlling of State economic reprisals must be accomplished in terms of the accepted traditional preconditions for reprisals. These require:

1. A prior international delinquency against the claimant State. (This would exclude reprisals against economic measures not in themselves unlawful.)

2. Redress by other means must be either exhausted or unavailable.

3. The economic measures taken must be limited to the necessities of the case and proportionate to the wrong done.

One difference between forceful and economic reprisals is that, while States have a virtual monopoly over armed forces, they have no monopoly over the capacity to inflict economic harm. The question then arises whether a State should bear the responsibility for the use of force by non-State entities such as companies incorporated in its territory and controlled by its nationals. To permit reprisals against the State for the actions of such private entities goes far beyond established international law. Such practice exists in relation to military expeditions, but not, it is believed, in relation to economic activities.

The involvement of non-State entities also occurs when they are regarded as the victims of reprisals.... The principle is not an attractive one, for it smacks of the victimization of innocent parties. However, realistically, States taking reprisals have always regarded nationals of the delinquent State as permissible objects of reprisals and in many situations they are the only available objects. It seems unrealistic to attempt to develop a prohibition of reprisals against non-State entities for State delicts.

A principal difference between economic and forceful reprisals stems from the second base condition, the exhaustion or unavailability of other means of redress. Whereas, with forceful reprisals, justification rests essentially on the inability of the Security Council to provide the necessary protection of rights and deterrence of further wrong-doing, thus leaving the injured State to its own measures of self-help, in the economic field there are likely to be specific obligations of pacific settlement as well as defined, effective procedures therefor....

* * *

III. *Conclusion*

Given the prohibition against armed coercion, the future is likely to bring increasing reliance on economic reprisals. Doubtless, more concrete norms governing the limits of permissible economic coercion will emerge in the same way as the norm or norms on military coercion. The main hope for a policy of restraint on economic reprisals is, however, likely to lie in the more general development of mandatory dispute procedures and institutionalized sanctions. In the economic field States may be more sympathetic to such a development than in that of military concern.

10.   Tom J. Farer, "Political and Economic Coercion in Contemporary International Law," 79 A.J.I.L. 405, 405–06 (1985).

The issues implied by the term "political and economic aggression" cannot be considered adequately outside the context of the broad questions: In their ongoing relations, what means may states employ to influence each other's policies? And to what ends? Means may for analytical purposes be divided into those of a cooperative and those of a coercive character. The former are proposals of all kinds of joint and mutually beneficial action, the mutual benefits being a function of cooperative behavior. The latter, however disguised, are threats.

* * *

The nub of the matter is that the word "coercion" has no normative significance; there is nothing illegal about coercion. Coercion is normal in all human relationships, including those between lovers. It's part of life. So is cooperation. Indeed, every human relationship is some mixture of coercion and cooperation. So to say that a particular relationship is coercive is to say nothing at all about its legitimacy.

The failure to draw explicit and detailed instructions and the related preference for abstract, consensus statements in international forums have succeeded only in obscuring the real legal and moral choices. Nor has analysis of the limits of legitimate coercion been helped by a tendency to speak about coercion in static terms, that is, to attempt to look at or to legislate about discrete events. One singles out a particular event and says, "Ah, this is aggression" of one kind or another, ignoring the fact that every event is embedded in an ongoing process of relations between states that goes on forever, particularly in the era of the United Nations when no state is allowed to disappear involuntarily.

11.   Statement by David H. Small, Assistant Legal Adviser for Near Eastern and South Asian Affairs, Department of State, 12 Nov 1976, Digest of United States Practice in International Law 576, 577–78 (E. McDowell ed., 1976).

The Charter of the United Nations **[Basic Document 1.5]** ... says nothing at all about restrictions on the use of economic measures of coercion by individual States or groups of States. Conceivably, economic measures could give rise to a dispute, "the continuance of which is likely to endanger the maintenance of international peace and security" within the meaning of Article 33 of the Charter, but even that is nowhere made clear. Economic pressure may be unfriendly and even unfair, but economic coercion, *per se*, cannot generally be said to be prohibited by the U.N. Charter.

In 1970, the Twenty-fifth General Assembly attempted to elaborate the law of the U.N. Charter by adopting a resolution approving the "Declaration on Principles of International Law Concerning Friendly Relations and Cooperation Among States" **[Basic Document 1.11]**. . . . [T]here are two provisions relevant to economic coercion. A preambular provision recalls "the duty of States to refrain in their international relations from military, political, economic or any other form of coercion aimed against the political independence or territorial integrity of any State." This seems to acknowledge the existence of a duty not to use economic coercion for the purpose of destroying or dismembering a State. This is scarcely a radical rule. While the passage could imply more, its possible further implications are not widely agreed. The second reference to economic coercion in the Declaration is more important. In elaborating on the duty not to intervene in matters within the domestic jurisdiction of a State, it says:

> No State may use or encourage the use of economic, political or any other type of measures to coerce another State in order to obtain from it the subordination of the exercise of its sovereign rights and to secure from it advantages of any kind.

This latter provision is far from clear, but it seems to mean that two types of economic coercion are prohibited: that which attempts to coerce a State not to exercise its legal rights and that which attempts to extort advantages. The origin of this provision is to be found in Article 15 [now Article 19] of the Charter of the Organization of American States **[Basic Document 1.7]**. . . . [I]t seems fair to say that the broad acceptability of this formulation results from its ambiguity. Under it . . . the United States can defend suspension of economic assistance pursuant to the . . . Hickenlooper amendment [22 USC 2370(e)(2)] on the grounds that the other State has no legal right to expropriate property without paying just compensation—and, on the contrary, that the other State has a duty to pay such compensation. . . .

In view of the extensive use of economic coercion by one State against another throughout the twentieth century, and in view of these rather modest legal efforts to restrict it, existing international law can probably best be described as narrowing only slightly the permissive legal regime of the past. The direction of development of the law is toward greater restriction on the use of economic coercion, but it has been a slow movement with, thus far, limited effects.

12.   Richard B. Lillich, "Economic Coercion and the International Legal Order," in Economic Coercion and the New International Economic Order 73, 79–82 (R. Lillich ed. & contrib. 1976).

If . . . there are now some restraints, however nebulous, upon a state's unilateral resort to economic coercion, what are they and how can they be enforced? Before exploring these questions it is perhaps worth emphasizing that, . . . [notwithstanding] the [1973] Arab oil embargo, Arab states certainly have no monopoly on the use or abuse of economic coercion. In response to Dr. Kissinger's characterization of the embargo as "blackmail," George Ball, former Under Secretary of State in the Kennedy and Johnson Administrations, noted in the New York Times that it "has the sour sound of sanctimony in the chancelleries of other nations. We Americans, after all, have been leading practitioners of economic sanctions to advance our own political—and even moral—policies, and if those sanctions have rarely, if ever, achieved the intended result, that has not deterred us."

More detailed criticism has come from [Richard] Gardner who, warning against "an unduly self-righteous attitude on these matters," points out that the United States itself has been one of the worst offenders in using trade controls in ways which have adversely affected other countries. . . .

Thus, in recommending normative guidelines and procedural sanctions in this area of international law, as in all areas of law generally, the "mirror image" principle must be kept in mind: namely, that the claims one projects against others inevitably will be reflected in similar claims against oneself.

* * * [B]ut one can sketch out an approach based upon the general principle that serious and sustained economic coercion should be accepted as a form of permissible self-help only when it is also compatible with the overall interests of the world community, as manifested in the principles of the UN Charter or in decisions taken or documents promulgated thereunder. This approach, like the determination of many other issues in international law, rests more upon subjective than objective standards.... Lawyers, of course, are quite familiar with this approach in the context of domestic law....

SECTION 5.   DISCUSSION NOTES/QUESTIONS

1.   The international financial system is one of the primary edifices of the present world order. It has been argued with some justification that the dynamism of the international financial system is the driving force behind economic, political, and even social globalization. It is a mistake, however, to begin an exploration of this system and its relationship to international law without first establishing a primary understanding of the fundamental economic relationships upon which it is based. As a learning exercise, first read the straight-forward explanation from the *The Encyclopedia of Business* (*supra* Reading A–1, p. 753) and the Editors' Note that follows (*supra* Reading A–2, p. 756); then, using this material, answer the following questions derived from the facts of the present problem as detailed in Section 1, *supra* (once you understand the primary relationships you will find that most of the questions are variations on the same theme):

a.   Explain why it is that investors become "extremely nervous" upon learning of Sundalau's bad commercial debt and current account problems? What do they fear might happen? Would it matter whether or not the bad commercial debt was owed in local currency (the rupiah) or in US dollars?

b.   What is Sundalau's Minister of Finance hoping to accomplish by her "brave face" appearance with her Prime Minister and, in particular, by her declaration that Sundalau's central bank would vigorously defend the rupiah and that "there was absolutely no foreseeable scenario under which the rupiah would be devalued"?

c.   Why does the *World Financial Daily* exposé alleging that Sundalau's foreign exchange reserves were almost depleted cause a financial panic? Why would investors begin selling Sundalaun securities if they considered a devaluation of the rupiah to be inevitable? What effect would such investor behavior have on the rupiah?

d.   What does Sundalau's central bank presumably do to defend the rupiah? Explain how the "emergency loans" from the IMF contributes to this effort. What is Ms. Namominda hoping to accomplish by raising the short term interest rate to 60%?

e.   Explain what it means in economic terms that the rupiah is left to float. Explain why the high interest rates and devaluation of the rupiah cause a major economic recession or, more accurately, a depression. Explain what accounts for the contagion effect that causes the disaster to spread throughout Asia and beyond.

Continue this exercise on your own, re-reading line by line the extract from *Foreign Affairs* by Jeffrey Garten (*supra* Reading A–3, p. 757) and asking yourself, as above, what the fundamental economic relationships are behind the events that he describes having transpired in the international economy.

2.   Capital controls were only discontinued by most developed countries in the early 1980s after having been in place since the end of the second world war. In the relatively recent past Malaysia is best known for implementing controls during the Asia financial crisis. The Malaysian controls on the outflow of capital were in some respects similar to those imposed by Tolteca in the present problem and included a tax on investment capital that was withdrawn from the country in under one year. The intended purpose of the Malaysian controls was to help strengthen the Malaysian currency while allowing the government to lower interest rates. Generally considered to have been successful, Malaysia's controls resulted in an initial sell-off of stocks after which the Malaysian stock market recovered and the country's currency gradually strengthened. The IMF was initially critical of Malaysia and refused to render economic assistance to it. In a later study, however, the organization suggests that Malaysian style capital controls may be beneficial. In 1999 Malaysia's controls were replaced by a graduated exit tax on capital outflows such that the longer capital was in the country the less taxes that were owed.

Also, well known are the capital controls imposed by Chile. In the early 1990's Chile found itself in the opposite situation from Malaysia with an overall capital account surplus equal to 10% of GDP and highly volatile short term capital flows accounting for much of the surplus. Feeling vulnerable to a reversal in capital flows as had happened in that country before, Chile introduced capital controls in 1991. Chile modified the controls twice during the decade, and suspended them in 1998.

3.   Reading D–2, *supra,* at 792 explains in some detail the difference between current and capital transactions and the legal implications of this difference under the IMF Articles of Agreement **(Basic Document 4.2)**. Why do you suppose that currency controls on one type of transaction are with certain exceptions allowed while they are generally not allowed on the other? Of what relevance might it be that the IMF has a considerable overlap in membership with the World Trade Organization[cc] whose primary purpose is to subject national restrictions on international trade to its discipline? What are the implications of the IMF rules distinguishing current transactions from capital transactions for the Toltecan controls?

4.   In the present problem to what extent is the investors' claim for relief premised on the assumption that they suffered a monetary loss as a result of the currency controls? How much did the investors' lose due to the currency controls? Is it possible to know? Upon what assumptions is your answer based? Do your conclusions depend upon the success of the currency controls? Could it be argued, for example, that the investors might in fact gain financially as a result of the controls? How should your answers to these questions be factored into the NAFTA Chapter 11 UNCITRAL tribunal's determination of appropriate relief? How have courts dealt with this problem in the past (*see supra* Reading C–4, at 782)?

5.   The IMF, almost since its inception, has been a lightning rod for criticism. Doubtless part of the reason is the unique role that it plays in world affairs. As the present problem and its readings indicate, the organization is frequently the final source of liquidity for countries facing exchange rate meltdowns. In exchange for such liquidity, the Fund often requires governments to reduce expenditures— sometimes dictating national budgets, including social spending priorities—that in its view are necessary for a return to financial health (why might that be?).

cc.   *See infra* Problem 6–4 ("The UFC and the EU Dispute the GATT and Global Warm- ing") and Problem 6–5 ("AIDS Meets TRIPS in Gondowana"), at 886 and 926, respectively.

Though arguably such actions are necessary at times, they have not always been able to avert recurrent developing world financial panics and, in the face of borderless global capital markets, the devastation of whole economies (as in Indonesia and Kenya, for example). Thus, the Fund is seldom popular with constituents, and governments have historically found in the IMF a convenient scapegoat for politically unpopular policies.[dd] However, there also has been a good deal of serious independent criticism of the organization.

One strand of criticism has focused on the institutional structure of the organization. Voting within the IMF is based on the size of a country's financial subscription to the organization. Thus, the larger a country's economic resources, the more potential voting power it has. This raises obvious problems from the point of view of democracy, especially relative to developing countries. In fact, because of super-majority provisions in the IMF's Articles of Agreement, the United States, with the largest single vote, can independently veto certain measures.

A related criticism focuses on the IMF's lack of transparency. Meetings take place in secret, and those who participate in the organization's decision-making, narrowly drawn from finance ministries and central banks, tend to be responsive to a small constituency of banking and financial elites. These elites often have a direct interest in rescue packages that can allow for their outstanding loans to countries in crisis to be repaid. Members of civil society organizations, on the other hand, have had a difficult time gaining access to the organization. Compounding this concern about the organization's democratic deficit is the fact that the scope of the organization's lending conditions, particularly in recent years, has more and more encroached on the domain of what was once considered national autonomy. In the Brazilian financial crisis of 2002, for example, facing the likely election of a left-wing populist president, the IMF offered a rescue package to be doled out mostly after the election of the new president, an action that significantly hampered his ability to engage in the economic reforms upon which he had campaigned. In recent years, the Fund has intruded in the public policy domain even to the extent of demanding privatization of national economic sectors.

Yet another strand of criticism has focused on the substance of the economic prescriptions imposed by the Fund. Politics, at times, colors the Fund's decision-making, as it did perhaps most notably in 1996 when Russian President Yeltsin's re-election was put in peril from Communist Party challenger Gennadi Zyuganov. US President Bill Clinton, and his partners in the G7, resolving to support Yeltsin, directed an extension of US$10.2 billion of the IMF's resources despite clear indications that its normal lending criteria would not be met. But even when politics has not been a clear factor, the Fund's economic prescriptions have been controversial. As noted above, the IMF has been partial in the past to shoring up countries' currencies by requiring governments to balance their budgets. As in the facts of the present problem, this induces economic recession, potentially causing tremendous hardship to the domestic population. Liberal economists in particular have been critical of this approach. *See* Joseph Stiglitz, Globalization and Its Discontents (2002). Some conservative economists, on the other hand, have been

---

dd. Similar misgivings attend The World Trade Organization (WTO), which is beginning to have a significant impact upon the lives of ordinary citizens. Workers often lose their jobs as a result of trade decisions made at the WTO. Consumers must increasingly contend with markets in which state-proscribed protections (such as the European ban on hormone-fed beef) can be overridden by WTO regulations. Patients who need medicines pay prices influenced by WTO-enforced patent rules that allow pharmaceutical companies to monopolize drug pricing. *See infra* Problem 6–5 ("AIDS Meets TRIPS in Gondowana").

critical of the IMF's very mission of providing liquidity to rescue failing economies. Their complaint is that this encourages "moral hazard," the willingness of private investors to make risky investments that they would avoid but for the knowledge that if things turn bad they will be rescued by the IMF. *See* Meltzer Commission Report, International Financial Institutions Advisory Commission: Hearing before the Senate Committee on Foreign Relations, 106th Cong. (2000).

6. The present problem exposes the issue of "indirect" or "creeping" expropriation. The salient question of when a regulatory act becomes a confiscatory or expropriatory act is the primary concern of "the international law of expropriation" at the present historical time. This is a change from the relatively recent past. In the years following political decolonization, during the 1960s and 1970s, the wounds of colonialism were still fresh, and an ideology that denied the legitimacy of the local property rights of the nationals of former colonial or "neo-colonial" powers easily gained popular support. Taking advantage of the maneuvering room provided by the Cold War's bipolar world order, certain developing countries directly seized foreign concerns. Though even the more radical developing countries usually paid symbolic compensation, as the readings suggest, these countries typically maintained that international law generally allowed for the deprivation of foreign wealth without compensation being required. Some of the more well-known takings of the period were Castro's 1960 nationalization of American sugar holdings in Cuba and Allende's nationalization of American copper interests in Chile in 1971. The decline in direct takings in the years since has likely been due more to determinations by developing countries that such actions are not in their economic interest than to considerations of international law. Based on your reading of the present problem, particularly in light of the dynamics exposed in Discussion Note/Question 1, *supra*, why might developing countries have come to the determination that direct takings are not in their economic interest? Might the ending of Cold War rivalries have had anything to do with it? Anything else?

7. As the readings in this problem make clear, there is today, as a result of Articles 1102–05 regarding standards of treatment for investors and Article 1110 regarding expropriation of the North American Free Trade Agreement (NAFTA) **(Basic Document 4.13)**, renewed interest in "indirect" or "creeping" expropriation. *See, e.g.,* Vicki Been & Joel C. Beauvais, *The Global Fifth Amendment? NAFTA's Investment Protections and the Misguided Quest for an International "Regulatory Takings" Doctrine,* 8 NYU L. Rev. 30 (2003); David Schneiderman, *NAFTA's Takings Rule: American Constitutionalism Comes to Canada,* 46 U. Toronto L. J. 499 (1996).

In this connection, several other NAFTA provisions specifically applying to transfers of financial assets are noteworthy. Article 1109 proscribes limitations on financial transfers related to foreign investment. Article 1410 lays out certain exceptions related to financial services. Finally, Article 2104 applies specifically to parties experiencing balance of payments problems. Unlike Articles 1102–05 and Article 1110, these other provisions have not yet been judicially tested and therefore their meaning is still open to interpretation.

Article 1109(1) mandates that "[e]ach Party shall permit all transfers relating to an investment of an investor of another Party in the territory of the Party to be made freely and without delay." Paragraph (4) of Article 1109, however, provides an exception: "Notwithstanding paragraphs 1 and 2, a Party may prevent a transfer through the equitable, nondiscriminatory and good faith application of its law relating to ... issuing, trading or dealing in securities...." Given the lack of an official legislative history (*travaux préparatoires*), most commentators have assumed that this and other accompanying exceptions are designed to allow the prevention of specific transfers to preserve assets necessary to enforce criminal laws or satisfy civil judgments.[ee] *See* Robert K. Paterson, *A New Pandora's Box? Private Remedies for Foreign Investors Under the North American Free Trade Agreement,* 8 Williamette J. Int'l L. & Dispute Res. 77, 102 (2000). Query, however, whether it could be alternatively interpreted to mean that certain classes of transfers can be generally prohibited so long as the directive providing for their prohibition meets the specified requirements of equitability, non-discrimination, and good faith. Does the specific way in which the provision was drafted lend credence to one interpretation over the other? Can you infer what the underlying policy rationale for this exception most likely was? Does this help? Article 1410(4) provides as follows:

> Notwithstanding Article 1109(1),(2) and (3), as incorporated into this Chapter, and without limiting the applicability of Article 1109(4), as incorporated into this Chapter, a Party may prevent or limit transfers by a financial institution or cross-border financial services provider to, or for the benefit of, an affiliate of or person related to such institution or provider, through the equitable, non-discriminatory and good faith application of measures relating to maintenance of the safety, soundness, integrity or financial responsibility of financial institutions or cross-border financial service providers. This paragraph does not prejudice any other provision of this Agreement that permits a Party to restrict transfers.

What effect does Article 1410(4) have on your analysis?

The extent to which NAFTA proscribes a Party's ability to limit financial transfers is made more complicated by the balance of payments exception of Article 2104. The Article provides that nothing in the Agreement "shall be construed to prevent a party from adopting or maintaining measures that restrict transfers where the party experiences serious balance of payments difficulties...." This provision, is qualified, however, by several restrictions that should be reviewed carefully. Most significantly, the Article incorporates by reference the requirements of Articles VI and VIII of the Articles of Agreement of the International Monetary Fund **(Basic Document 4.2)**. What is it exactly that these Articles require? Given what you have learned about which of the NAFTA countries is most influential in the IMF review process, who gains the ability to review whose policies under NAFTA Article 2104?

8. Many people have assumed in the past that if the nation-state were to give way to a more centralized global system of government it would happen either as a result of a Napoleonic-like conquest or a conscious effort to create a comprehensive treaty founding a new global order, a sort of super United Nations.[ff] In fact, much of the decline in state sovereignty that currently is occurring in favor of transnational governance is the result of piecemeal solutions

---

ee. The provision as a whole reads: "Notwithstanding paragraphs 1 and 2, a Party may prevent a transfer through the equitable, non-discriminatory and good faith application of its laws relating to: (a) bankruptcy, insolvency or the protection of the rights of creditors; (b) issuing, trading or dealing in securities; (c) criminal or penal offenses; (d) reports of transfers of currency or other monetary instru-ments; or (e) ensuring the satisfaction of judgments in adjudicatory proceedings."

ff. For one of the more influential proposals of the latter sort popularized in the middle part of the last century, see Grenville Clark & Louis B. Sohn, World Peace Through World Law (1966).

to practical legal problems that arise from the need to maintain transnational economic relationships. Drawing on a model originally found in some bilateral investment treaties (BITs), the dispute resolution provisions of NAFTA Chapter 11 (Part B) **(Basic Document 4.13)** allow for foreign investors to bring legal actions directly against states before international tribunals. What is the practical legal problem that Chapter 11 is designed to resolve? Why not allow investors to follow the conventional path of suing for alleged wrongs in domestic courts or of providing mechanisms for the investor's home country to bring a legal action in an international forum on behalf of the investor? In what way do the above referenced provisions of Chapter 11 compromise the traditional paradigm of state sovereignty?

Other provisions of NAFTA, in particular Chapter 19, also erode the traditional sovereignty paradigm. Chapter 19 was adapted from the predecessor agreement to NAFTA, the US–Canada Free Trade Agreement. One of the main purposes of that Agreement was to eliminate tariffs on trade between the two countries. In the negotiations over the Agreement, however, the parties could not agree on whether to allow for the continued maintenance of anti-dumping and countervailing duties. If a foreign government gives its industry a subsidy or if a foreign industry engages in dumping—what in antitrust terms is called predatory pricing (selling at below market cost to drive competitors out of business)—the traditional rules of the GATT allowed for countries to impose countervailing or offsetting duties on the theory that such duties will level the competitive playing field. Canada argued that these duties are contrary to the tariff-eliminating spirit of the Agreement. The US countered that if Canadian companies were dumping products, or if Canada was subsidizing its companies, it was fair that the United States should be able to impose off-setting duties. The Canadian rejoinder: perhaps in principle, but these rules are applied in a biased way by the United States International Trade Commission and appellate courts to favor US companies. The negotiators argued back and forth on this point until they resurrected a solution proposed by Congressman Samuel Gibbons of Florida that would accommodate both countries' concerns in what was to become Chapter 19. His suggestion was that each country could keep its anti-dumping and countervailing duty laws, but that national administrative determinations of whether such duties were legally justified would be reviewed by a NAFTA tribunal. No appeals would be allowed within either countries' domestic system, except to challenge the basic constitutionality of the provision. With the implementation of Chapter 19, then, for the first time, an international tribunal instead of a US domestic court was charged with applying and being the final determiner of US domestic law. Query: in what way is Chapter 19 inconsistent with the paradigm of sovereignty. Is its approach likely to be extended to other areas? If so, what would this portend for the future of sovereignty, if anything? For further discussion of the negotiating history that led to Chapter 19, see Raymond Vernon, Debora Spar & Glenn Tobin, Iron Triangles and Revolving Doors: Cases in US Foreign Economic Policymaking 21–54 (1991).

9. Long before the birth of NAFTA and its Chapter 11 investor dispute provisions, the paradigm of sovereignty began to be challenged by institutional innovations designed to legally protect foreign investment. As noted above, bilateral investment treaties pioneered the idea of providing investors with an international forum to bring claims against states. An even more fundamental challenge to sovereignty came in the form of concession agreements, more recently called economic development agreements. These agreements, first occurring in the early post colonial days, and almost always in the extractive resource sector, provided

that governments cede often vast territorial expanses to foreign mining concerns. In the traditional agreements, companies would exercise something approaching sovereign-like control over the entire area within the concession. They would build infrastructure such as roads and schools and even would provide for basic public services. As under the bilateral investment treaties (BITs) referenced above, conflict between the investor and the state, typically would cause resort to international arbitration. Unlike those treaties, however, the legal relationship requiring arbitration is lodged in an agreement not between two states but between a state and a private investor, and as a result the status of such agreements in international law is unclear. Some have argued that corporations as private entities have no standing under international law and that their agreements with states should be considered as nothing more than domestic contracts subject to superseding legislation by the host country. Others have argued that the unique nature of these agreements, their international arbitration provisions, and choice of law provisions often specifying international law are all evidence of their international character. *See, e.g.,* Leo T. Kissam & Edmond K. Leach, *Sovereign Expropriation of Property and Abrogation of Concession Contracts,* 28 Fordham L. Rev., 177, 194–214 (1959). In the present problem, assume that in the place of Chapter 11 the investors had their own private contractual agreement with Tolteca containing provisions identical to those found in Chapter 11. In what way would the investors' claims be weakened? Can you think of any way in which this might help their claims?

10. William Greider's article from *The Nation* (*supra* Reading B–7, p. 772) reflects the critical view of NAFTA Chapter 11 **(Basic Document 4.13)** held by much of the anti-globalization/global justice movement. What is the basis of his criticism? To what extent is Grieder's critique based on the diminution of sovereignty engendered by Chapter 11? By its affront to democracy and transparency? To what extent is it based on his perception that it gives precedence to property rights over public health and safety? Greider argues that US business interests have found in Chapter 11 a backdoor way around Supreme Court precedent on the "Takings Clause" of the United States Constitution. Given, however, that Chapter 11 as applied within the United States can be used only by foreign companies, what do US corporate interests gain, if anything? Given the ability of companies to reincorporate overseas, could "US" businesses, practically speaking, come to benefit within the United States from Chapter 11? Does Greider help make the interpretative case for those sympathetic to Professor Epstein's position? Is it clear from the language of Article 1110 that it should be read as more deferential to property interests than the takings clause of the US Constitution? Given your knowledge of how political factors influence legal developments, as well as the ministerial note excerpted in *supra* Reading B–5, at 769, what would be your prediction for how Article 1110 of Chapter 11 is likely to be interpreted in the future? In making your prediction, it may be useful to know that, to date, no Chapter 11 tribunal has found the US liable for monetary damages and that a final decision in the *Methanex* case itself finally came down in 2005 absolving the US of liability. Academic commentators writing in law journals have on the whole been considerably more sympathetic to Chapter 11 than has William Greider and other popular critics of globalization. *See, for example*, Charles H. Brower II, *Investor-State Disputes Under NAFTA: The Empire Strikes Back,* 40 Colum. J. Transnat'l L. 43 (2001); Barton Legum, *Emerging Fora for International Litigation (Part 1): The Innovation of Investor–State Arbitration Under NAFTA,* 43 Harv. Int'l L. J. 531 (2002).

11.   The political situation in Tolteca under the Gonzalez regime suggests the problem of what Fareed Zakaria has called "illiberal democracies." According to Zakaria, many countries have leaders who are elected but who rule nevertheless in authoritarian ways. Zakaria estimates that at least half of the world's 118 "democratizing" countries could be considered illiberal. *See* Fareed Zakaria, The Future of Freedom: Illiberal Democracy at Home and Abroad, (2003). What role do elections play in such societies? Are they useful? How realistic do you find the Toltecan election scenario, depicting an authoritarian leader being unseated despite his attempt to manipulate the electoral process? *See* Bryan Johnson, The Four Days of Courage: The Untold Story of the People Who Brought Marcos Down (1987) and Lucy Komisar, Corazon Aquino: The Story of a Revolution (1987) (describing the 1986 elections in the Philippines); also Roger Cohen, *Who Really Brought Down Milosevic?,* The New York Times Magazine, 26 Nov 2000, at 43 (describing the 2000 election in Serbia), *An Orange Victory; Ukraine's Presidential Election,* The Economist, 1 Jan 2005, at 7 (describing the 2004 election in the Ukraine). Are illiberal democracies meaningfully different form purely authoritarian political systems that operate without even the pretense of elections?

12.   In the present problem, Senator Chauvin introduces legislation intended to make Tolteca a target of economic retaliation by the United States, much as Cuba was the target of US economic retaliation when, following Fidel Castro's successful revolution in 1959, the United States sharply reduced a preferential Cuban sugar import quota upon which, at the time, the Cuban economy significantly depended. As should be clear from the Readings in Section 4(F), *supra* at 806, the matter of economic coercion rarely gets the attention of effective decision-makers, at least not in the industrialized world which tends, naturally, to be more on the giving-than the receiving-end of economic and other forms of state power. In *Banco Nacional de Cuba v. Sabbatino*, 307 F.2d 845 (2d Cir.1962), however, the only known case in the United States ever to consider the problem of economic coercion directly, the Court of Appeals for the Second Circuit, assessing the lawfulness of the Cuban nationalization of some American-owned sugar plantations in Cuba, did flirt briefly with the issue, deciding that

> whether she was wise or unwise, fair or unfair, in what she did, the United States did not breach a rule of international law in deciding, for whatever reason she deemed sufficient, the sources from which she would buy her sugar. We cannot find any established principle of international jurisprudence that requires a nation to continue buying commodities from an unfriendly source.

The court was unpersuaded by Banco Nacional's argument that Cuba's nationalization measure was justified because "the United States was the first offender against international law by an attempt to coerce Cuba through the reduction of American purchases of Cuban sugar." From a human rights point of view, the Circuit Court may well have been right. However, as pointed out in Frank G. Dawson & Burns H. Weston, *Banco Nacional de Cuba v. Sabbatino: New Wine in Old Bottles*, 31 U. Chi. L. Rev. 63 (1963), rather than deny flatly the relevance of *any* inquiry into the legality of the sugar quota reduction the Court of Appeals would have been well-advised to contemplate the meaning and effect of the United States action before rendering judgment. The authors write, at 94:

> Whether United States policy "was wise or unwise, fair or unfair," it might be considered by some as a recrudescence of that economic intervention repudiated by the United States at the Seventh Pan–American Conference in Montevideo in 1933 and in the Buenos Aires Protocol of Non–Intervention of

1936. Indeed the United States' action might legitimately be deemed a violation of her existing treaty obligations. Article 15 [now Article 18] of the Charter of the OAS **[Basic Document 1.7]**, to which the United States and Cuba were both signatories in 1960, provides:

> No State or group of States has the right to intervene, directly or indirectly, for any reason whatever, in the internal or external affairs of any State. The foregoing principle prohibits not only armed force but also any other form of interference or attempted threat against the personality of the State or against its political, economic and cultural elements.

While experts may differ on whether the United States violated the OAS Charter, it is clear from this language that Banco Nacional's defense merited at least minimum evaluation. Given the first of the criteria formulated in the *Naulilaa Case* [that the State against which a reprisal is taken must first be in breach of international law], Cuba's seizure of ... American sugar enterprises may have been justified.

A similar conclusion has been reached by M. Sornarajah, The Pursuit of Nationalized Property, at 180 (1986): "[T]here seems to have been sufficient functional bases on which the Cuban measures [*i.e.* nationalizations] could have been regarded as lawful economic reprisals. There was evidence of US efforts to destabilize the Castro regime culminating in the later Bay of Pigs incident." To similar critical effect, see Cornelius F. Murphy, Jr., *Limitations Upon the Power of a State to Determine the Amount of Compensation Payable to an Alien Upon Nationalization*, in 3 The Valuation of Nationalized Property in International Law 49, 62 (R. Lillich ed. & Contrib. 1975): "An impartial tribunal, taking [these] circumstance[s] into consideration, [might] have reached a different conclusion." Do you agree? Disagree?

13. *Bibliographical Note.* For supplemental discussion concerning the principal themes addressed in this problem, consult the following additional specialized materials:

a. International Finance and The IMF

(1) *Books/Monographs/Reports/Symposia*: Asian Financial Crisis and the Architecture of Global Finance (J. Ravenhill & G. Noble eds., 2000); G. Bird, IMF and the Future: Issues and Options Facing the International Monetary Fund (2002); P. Blustein, Chastening: Inside the Crisis that Rocked the Global Financial System & Humbled the IMF (2001); P. Bond, Against Global Apartheid: South Africa Meets the World Bank, IMF and International Finance (2004); R. Bryant, Crisis Prevention and Prosperity Management for the World Economy: Pragmatic Choices for the International Financial Governance, Part 1 (2005); D. Coyle, Governing the World Economy (Themes for the 21st Century) (2000); B. Eichengreen & C. Bergsten, Toward a New International Financial Architecture: A Practical Post–Asia Agenda (1999); Financial Crises, Contagion, and the Lender of Last Resort (C. Goodhart & G. Illing ed., 2002); Governing Global Finance: New Challenges, G7 and IMF Contributions (Global Finance Series) (M. Fratianni, P. Savona, J. Kirton & D. Yu eds., 2002); R. Harper, Inside the IMF (1998); IMF–Supported Programs in Indonesia, Korea and Thailand: A Preliminary Assessment (Occasional Paper (International Monetary Fund), No. 178.) (T. Lane ed., 1999); H. Kaufman & P. Volcker, On Money and Markets: A Wall Street Memoir (2000); D. Kirk, Korean Crisis: Unraveling of the Miracle in the IMF Era (2001); M. Mussa, Argentina and the Fund: From Triumph to Tragedy (2002); R. Peet, Unholy Trinity: The IMF, World Bank and WTO (2003); E. Riesenhuber, The

International Monetary Fund Under Constraint: Legitimacy of Its Crisis Management (Legal Aspects of International Organization, 39) (2001); J. Stiglitz, Globalization and Its Discontents (3d ed. 2002); R. Stone, Lending Credibility: The International Monetary Fund and the Post Communist Transition (2002); J. Stotsky, Revenue Implications of Trade Liberalization (Occasional Paper (International Monetary Fund), No. 180.) (1999); The International Monetary Fund (L. McQuillan & P. Montgomery ed., 1999); J. Vreeland, The IMF and Economic Development (2003).

(2) *Articles/BookChapters.* R. Bejesky, *Exchange Rate Stability: Domestic and International Institutions Enhancing Credibility of Government Intervention Policy*, 8 MSU–DCL J. Int'l L. 673 (1999); Guy Brucculeri, *A Need to Refocus the Mandate of the International Monetary Fund and the World Bank*, 17 Windsor Rev. Legal & Social Issues 53 (2004); R. Buckley, *A Tale of Two Crises: The Search for the Enduring Reform of the International Financial System*, 6 UCLA J. Int'l L. & Foreign Aff. 1 (2001); T. Canova, *Banking and Financial Reform at the Crossroads of the Neoliberal Contagion*, 14 Am. U. Int'l L. Rev. 1571 (1999); T. Canova, *Financial Liberalization, International Monetary Dis/Order, and the Neoliberal State*, 15 Am. U. Int'l L. Rev. 1279 (2000); E. Carrasco & K. Berg, *Transnational Law and Contemporary Problems Spring, 1999 Symposium, The E–Book on International Financial Finance and Development*, 9 Transnat'l L. & Contemp. Probs. I (1999); W. Coats, *The Asian Meltdown of 1997: The Role of the Financial Sector and Bank Exit Policies*, 23–SPG Fletcher F. World Aff. 77 (1999); B. Eichengreen, *Bailing in the Private Sector: Burden Sharing in International cs. Financial Crisis Management*, 23–SPG Fletcher F. World Aff. 57 (1999); F. Gianviti, *2001 Symposium—International Monetary and Financial Law in the New Millennium: Dedication Conference of Sir Joseph Gold Library Collection Evolving Role and Challenges for the International Monetary Fund*, 35 Int'l Law. 1371 (2001); J. Head, *Lessons from the Asian Financial Crisis: The Role of the IMF and the United States*, 7–SPG Kan. J.L. & Pub. Pol'y 70 (1998); R. Hockett, *From Macro to Micro to "Mission–Creep": Defending the IMF's Emerging Concern with the Infrastructural Prerequisites to Global Financial Stability*, 41 Colum. J. Transnat'l L. 153 (2002); H. Kim, *Living with the IMF: A New Approach to Corporate Governance and Regulation of Financial Institutions in Korea*, 17 Berkeley J. Int'l L. 61 (1999); J. Levinson, *The International Financial System: A Flawed Architecture*, 23–SPG Fletcher F. World Aff. 1 (1999); J. Norton, *2001 Symposium—International Monetary and Financial Law in the New Millennium: Dedication Conference of Sir Joseph Gold Library Collection International Financial Institutions and the Movement Toward Greater Accountability and Transparency: The Case of Legal Reform Programs and the Problem of Evaluation*, 35 Int'l Law. 1443 (2001); J. Norton, *1999 Symposium: Law–Based Nature of the New International Financial Infrastructure A "New International Financial Architecture?"-Reflections on the Possible Law–Based Dimension*, 33 Int'l Law. 891 (1999); J. Sanders, *THE World Bank and the IMF: Fostering the Growth in Global Markett*, 9–WTR Currents: Int'l Trade L.J. 37 (2000); I. Shihata, *2001 Symposium—International Monetary and Financial Law in the New Millennium: Dedication Conference of Sir Joseph Gold Library Collection The World Bank and the IMF Relationship–Quo Vadis?*, 35 Int'l Law. 1349 (2001); R. Weber, *Challenges for the New Financial Architecture*, 31 HKLJ 241 (2001).

b. NAFTA General Structure and Dispute Resolution and Investor Protection Provisions

(1) *Books/Monographs/Reports/Symposia.* R. Folsom & W. Folsom, Understanding NAFTA and Its International Business Implications (1998); R. Folsom, J.

Spanogle & M. Gordon, Handbook of NAFTA Dispute Settlement (1998); R. Folsom, Folsom's NAFTA in a Nutshell (1999); G. Horlick, WTO & NAFTA Rules and Dispute Resolution (2003); S. R. Jablonski, NAFTA Chapter 11 dispute resolution and Mexico: a healthy mix of international law, economics and politics (2004); F. Mayer, Interpreting NAFTA (1998); J. McKinney, Created from NAF-TA: The Structure, Function & Significance of the Treaty's Related Institutions (2000); Trading Punches: Trade Remedy Law and Disputes Under NAFTA (B. Leycegui, W. Robson, & S. Stein eds., 1995); L. Trakman, Dispute Settlement Under the NAFTA: Manual and Source Book (1998); S. Weintraub, Nafta's Impact On North America: The First Decade (CSIS Significant Issues Series) (2004)

(2) *Articles/BookChapters*. F. Abbott, *The Political Economy of NAFTA Chapter Eleven: Equality Before the Law and the Boundaries of North American Integration*, 23 Hastings Int'l & Comp. L. Rev. 303, 308 (2000); A. Afilalo, *Towards a Common Law of International Investment: How NAFTA Chapter 11 Panels Should Solve Their Legitimacy Crisis*, 17 Geo. Int'l Envtl. L. Rev. 51 (2004); A. Afilalo, *Meaning, Ambiguity and Legitimacy: Judicial (Re-)Construction of NAFTA Chapter 11*, 25 Nw. J. Int'l l. & Bus. 279 (2005); K. Banks, *NAFTA's Article 1110–Can Regulation Be Expropriation?, 5 NAFTA: L. & Bus. Rev. Am. 499 (1999);* C. Brower & L. Steven, *Who then Should Judge?: Developing the International Rule of Law under NAFTA Chapter 11,* 2 Chi. J. Int'l L. 193 (2001); W. Dodge, *National Courts and International Arbitration: Exhaustion of Remedies and Res Judicata under Chapter Eleven of NAFTA,* 23 Hastings Int'l & Comp. L. Rev. 357 (2000); F. Fracassi, *Confidentiality and NAFTA Chapter 11 Arbitrations,* 2 Chi. J. Int'l L. 213 (2001); D. Gantz, *Reconciling Environmental Protection and Investor Rights Under Chapter 11 of NAFTA,* 31 Envtl. L. Rep. 10646 (June 2001); M. Gordon, *Forms of Dispute Resolution in the North American Free Trade Agreement,* 13 Fla. J. Int'l L. 16 (2000); B. Hodges, *Where the Grass Is Always Greener: Foreign Investor Actions against Environmental Regulations under NAFTA's Chapter 11, S.D. Myers, Inc. V. Canada,* 14 Geo. Int'l Envtl. L. Rev. 367 (2001); *Investment Disputes and NAFTA Chapter 11,* 95 Am. Soc'y Int'l L. Proc. 196 (2001); M. Jiménez, *Considerations of NAFTA Chapter 11,* 2 Chi. J. Int'l L. 243, 244 (2001); B. Legum, *The Innovation of Investor–State Arbitration Under NAFTA,* 43 Harv. Int'l L.J. 531 (2002); H. Mann, *Private Rights, Public Problems: A Guide to NAFTA's Chapter on Investor Rights (2001), available at* <http://www.iisd.org/trade/private_rights.htm>; L. Díaz & N. Oretskin, *Medication Furthers the Principles of Transparency and Cooperation to Solve Disputes in the NAFTA Free Trade Area,* 30 Denv. J. Int'l L. & Pol'y 73 (2001); C. Pearce & J. Coe, *Arbitration under NAFTA Chapter Eleven: Some Pragmatic Reflections upon the First Case Filed against Mexico,* 23 Hastings Int'l & Comp. L. Rev. 311 (2000); J. Pencier, *Investment, Environment and Dispute Settlement: Arbitration under NAFTA Chapter Eleven,* 23 Hastings Int'l & Comp. L. Rev. 409 (2000); D. Posin, *The Multi–Faceted Investment Arbitration Rules of NAFTA,* 13 World Arb. & Mediation Rep. 13 (2002); D. Price, *Some Observations on Chapter Eleven of NAFTA,* 23 Hastings Int'l & Comp. L. Rev. 421 (2001); D. Price, *Chapter 11— Private Party vs. Government, Investor–State Dispute Settlement: Frankenstein or Safety Valve?,* 26 Can.-US L.J. 107, 113 (2000); D. St. Louis, *The Anatomy of a Chapter Eleven Arbitration: Affidavits, Affiant, and Burdens of Proof,* 23 Hastings Int'l & Comp. L. Rev. 345, 352 (2000); C. Tollefson, *Games Without Frontiers: Investor Claims and Citizen Submissions under the NAFTA Regime,* 27 Yale J. Int'l L. 141 (2002); C. Tollefson, *Metalclad v. United Mexican States Revisited: Judicial Oversight of NAFTA's Chapter Eleven Investor–State Claim Process,* 11 Minn. J. Global Trade 183 (2002); D. Wallace, *State Responsibility for Denial of*

Substantive and Procedural Justice under NAFTA Chapter Eleven, 23 Hastings Int'l & Comp. L. Rev. 393 (2000); T. Weiler, *NAFTA Investment Law in 2001: As the Legal Order Starts to Settle, The Bureaucrats Strike back*, 36 Int'l Law 345 (2002); T. Weiler, *A First Look at the Interim Merits Award in S.D. Myers, Inc. v. Canada: It Is Possible to Balance Legitimate Environmental Concerns with Investment Protection*, 24 Hastings Int'l & Comp. L. Rev. 173 (2001); G. Word, *NAFTA Standards Regulation: The US Perspective*, 9 US–Mex. L.J. 1 (2001).

c. Treatment of Alien Property Under Customary International Law

(1) *Books/Monographs/Reports/Symposia.* A. Akinsanya, Expropriation of Multinational Property in the Third World: Finance Trade and Investment (1980); R. Allison & J. Coe, Protecting against the Expropriation Risk in Investing Abroad (1999); Attacking Foreign Assets (D. Campbell ed., 1992); J. Coates, New Law of Expropriation (1995); I. Foighel, Nationalization: A Study in the Protection of Alien Property in International Law (1982); S. Friedman, Expropriation in International Law (1981); The Valuation of Nationalized Property in International Law, Vol. 4 (R. Lillich ed., 1987); A. Mouri, International Law of Expropriation As Reflected in the Work of the Iran–U. S. Claims Tribunal (1994); G. Neuman, Strangers to the Constitution: Immigrants, Borders, and Fundamental Law (1996); M. Sornarajah, The Pursuit of Nationalized Property (1986); E. Todd, The law of expropriation and compensation in Canada (2d ed. 1992); J. Truitt, Expropriation of Private Foreign Investment (1974); B. Weston, R. Lillich & D. Bederman, Their Settlement by Lump Sum Agreements. 1975–1995 (1999); B. Wortley, Expropriation in public international law (M. Wilkins ed., 1977).

(2) *Articles/Book Chapters.* M. Brunetti, *The Iran–United States Claims Tribunal, NAFTA Chapter 11, and the Doctrine of Indirect Expropriation*, 2 Chi. J. Int'l L. 203 (2001); G. Chifor, *Caveat Emptor: Developing International Disciplines for Deterring Third Party Investment in Unlawfully Expropriated Property*, 33 Law & Pol'y Int'l Bus. 179 (2002); S. Djajic, *The Right to Property and Thevasilescu v. Romania case*, 27 Syracuse J. Int'l L. & Com. 363 (2000); A. Maniruzzaman, *Expropriation of Alien Property and Principle of Non-discrimination in International Law of Foreign Investment: An Overview*, 8 J. Transnat'l L. & Pol'y 57 (1998); J. Nolan, *A Comparative Analysis of the Laotian Law on Foreign Investment, the World Bank Guidelines on the Treatment of Foreign Direct Investment, and Normative Rules of International Law on Foreign Direct Investment*, 15 Ariz. J. Int'l & Comp. L. 659 (1998); E. Williamson, *US—EU Understanding on Helms–Burton: A Missed Opportunity to Fix International Law on Property Rights*, 48 Cath. U. L. Rev. 293 (1999); E. Young, *Sorting out the Debate over Customary International Law*, 42 Va. J. Int'l L. 365 (2002).

d. Legal Personality and Binding Obligation Under International Law

(1) *Books/Monographs/Reports/Symposia.* 2002 Canadian Council on International Law 31st Annual Conference, The Measure Of International Law: Effectiveness, Fairness And Validity (2004); K. Buhler, State Succession and Membership in International Organizations: Legal Theories Versus Political Pragmatism (Legal Aspects of International Organization) (2001); Dissolution, Continuation and Succession in Eastern Europe (B. Stern ed., 1998); P. Eisemann & M. Koskenniemi, State Succession: Codification Tested Against the Facts/La Succession D'Etats: La Codification a L'Epreuve des Faits (Recueil, vol 20., 2000); P. Groarke, Dividing the State: Legitimacy, Secession and the Doctrine of Oppression (Applied Legal Philosophy) (2004); E. McWhinney, The United Nations and a New World Order for a New Millenium: Self–Determination, State Succession, and

Humanitarian Intervention (2000); National Self–Determination and Secession (M. Moore ed., 1998); D. Shelton, Commitment and Compliance: The Role of Non–Binding Norms in the International Legal System (2000); D. State Practice Regarding State Succession and Issues of Recognition: The Pilot Project of the Council of Europe Pratique Des Etats Concernant LA Succession D'Etats Et Les Questions De Reconnaissance: Le Projet pilote (J. Klabbers, M. Koskenniemi, O. Ribbelink & A. Zimmermann eds., 1999); Succession of States (Developments in International Law, V. 33) (M. Mrak ed., 1999).

(2) *Articles/Book Chapters*. J. Blackman, *State Successions and Statelessness: The Emerging Right to An Effective Nationality Under International Law*, 19 Mich. J. Int'l L. 1141 (1998); W. Dodge, *Succeeding in Seceding?: Internationalizing the Quebec Secession Reference under NAFTA*, 34 Tex. Int'l L.J. 287 (1999); F. Francioni, *Diversity or Cacophony?: New Sources of Norms in International Law Symposium: Article: Beyond State Sovereignty: The Protection of Cultural Heritage as a Shared Interest of Humanity*, 25 Mich. J. Int'l L. 1209 (2004); E. Huang, *The Evolution of the Concept of Self-determination and the Right of the People Taiwan to Self-determination*, 14 N.Y. Int'l L. Rev. 167 (2001); B. R. Roth, *The Enduring Significance of State Sovereignty*, 56 Fla. L. Rev. 1017 (2004); B. Schwartz & S. Waywood, *A Model Declaration on the Right of Secession*, 11 N.Y. Int'l L. Rev. 1 (1998); J. Shen, *Sovereignty, Statehood, Self-determination, and the Issue of Taiwan*, 15 Am. U. Int'l L. Rev. 1101 (2000); C. Stahn, *The Agreement on Succession issues of the Former Socialist Federal Republic of Yugoslavia*, 96 Am. J. Int'l L. 379 (2002); P. Williams & J. Harris, *State Succession to Debts and Assets: The Modern Law and Policy*, 42 Harv. Int'l L.J. 355 (2001).

e.   Economic Retorsions and Reprisals

(1) *Books/Monographs/Reports/Symposia*. H. Alikhani, Sᴀɴᴄᴛɪᴏɴɪɴɢ Iʀᴀɴ: Anatomy of a Failed Policy (2000); H. Askari, J. Forrer, H. Teegen, & J. Yang, Economic Sanctions: Examining Their Philosophy and Efficacy (2003); H. Askari, J. Forrer, H. Teegen, & J. Yang, Case Studies of US Economic Sanctions: The Chinese, Cuban, and Iranian Experience (2003); J. Blanchard, Power and the Purse: Economic Statecraft, Interdependence, and National Security (Case Series on Security Studies) (2000); J. Collins & G. Bowdoin, Beyond Unilateral Economic Sanctions: Better Alternatives for US Foreign Policy (CSIS Report) (1999); D. Cortright, Sanctions and the Search for Security: Challenges to UN Action (2002); A. Dobson, United States Economic Statecraft for Survival, 1933–1991: Of Sanctions and Strategic Embargoes (Routledge Advances in International Relations and Politics) (2002); D. Drezner, The Sanctions Paradox: Economic Statecraft and International Relations (Cambridge Studies in International Relations, 65) (1999); A. C. Drury, Economic Sanctions and Presidential Decisions: Models of Political Rationality (Advances in Foreign Policy Analysis) (2005); Economic Casualties: How US Foreign Policy Undermines Trade, Growth, and Liberty (1999); Economic Sanctions and American Diplomacy (R. Haass ed., 1998); G. Feiler, From Boycott to Economic Cooperation: The Political Economy of the Arab Boycott of Israel (1998); G. C. Hufbauer, Economic Sanctions Reconsidered (2005); How Sanctions Work: Lessons from South Africa (International Political Economy) (N. Crawford & A. Klotz eds., 1999); D. Johnston & S. Weintraub, Altering US Sanctions Policy: Final Report of the CSIS Project on Unilateral Economic Sanctions (Center for Strategic and International Studies Report) (1999); D. Kaplowitz, Anatomy of a Failed Embargo: US Sanctions Against Cuba (1998); R. Naylor & J. Blum, Economic Warfare: Sanctions, Embargo Busting, and Their Human Cost (2001); E. Preeg, Feeling Good or Doing Good With Sanctions: Unilateral Economic Sanctions and the US National Interest (Significant Issues Series, Vol 21 No 3) (1999); K. Rodman, Sanctions Beyond Borders (2001); M. Malloy, United States

Economic Sanctions: Theory and Practice (2001); D. Rowe, Manipulating the Market: Understanding Economic Sanctions, Institutional Change, and the Political Unity of White Rhodesia (2001); J. Roy, Cuba, the United States, and the Helms–Burton Doctrine: International Reactions (Contemporary Cuba Series) (2000); G. Simons, Imposing Economic Sanctions: Legal Remedy or Genocidal Tool? (1999); Smart Sanctions: Targeting Economic Statecraft (D. Cortright, G. Lopez & J. Stephanides eds., 2002); Sanctions As Economic Statecraft: Theory and Practice (International Political Economy) (S. Chan & A. Drury eds., 2000); Honey and Vinegar: Incentives, Sanctions, and Foreign Policy (R. Haass & M. O'Sullivan eds., 2000); The Sanctions Decade: Assessing UN Strategies in the 1990s (D. Cortright & G. Lopez eds., 2000); G. Shambaugh, States, Firms, and Power: Successful Sanctions in United States Foreign Policy (Suny Series in Global Politics) (1999); Z. Selden, Economic Sanctions as Instruments of American Foreign Policy (1999); S. Zhang, Economic Cold War: America's Embargo Against China and the Sino–Soviet Alliance 1949–1963 (Cold War International History Project Series) (2001).

(2) *Articles/Book Chapters.* M. Boersma, *Analysis of the Application of Economic Coercion to Correct Breaches of International Obligations: The Use of Force by the United States to Correct Cuba's Breaches of Its International Obligations,* 10 Msu–Dcl J. Int'l L. 281 (2001); S. Cleveland, *Norm Internationalization and US Economic Sanctions,* 26 Yale J. Int'l L. 1 (2001); L. Delmonte, *Symposium International Sanctions against Iraq: Where are we after Ten Years?: Economic Sanctions, Iraq, and US Foreign Policy,* 11 Transnat'l L. & Contemp. Probs. 345 (2001); M. Ehrmann, *Procedures of Compliance Control in International Environmental Treaties,* 13 Colo. J. Int'l Envtl. L. & Pol'y 377 (2002); K. Elliott, *The Sanctions Glass: Half Full or Completely Empty?,* 23 Int'l Security 50 (1998); R. Pape, *Why Economic Sanctions Still Do Not Work,* 23 Int'l Security 66 (1998); S. Gibson, *International Economic Sanctions: The Importance Of Government Structures,* 13 Emory Int'l L. Rev. 161 (1999); J. Gordon, *A Peaceful, Silent, Deadly Remedy: The Ethics of Economic Sanctions,* 13 Ethics & Int'l Aff. 123 (1999); C. Grave, *Extraterritoriality and its limits: The Iran and Libya Sanctions Act of 1996,* 21 Hastings Int'l & Comp. L. Rev. 715 (1998); A. Howlett, *Colloquium: Deborah L. Rhodes Access to Justice: Note: Getting "Smart": Crafting Economic Sanctions that Respect All Human Rights,* 73 Fordham L. Rev. 1199 (2004); G. Hufbauer & B. Oegg, *Economic Sanctions: A Primer for Journalists,* 87 The Quill 21 (1999); R. Parker, *The Use and Abuse of Trade Leverage to Protect the Global Commons: What We Can Learn from the Tuna–Dolphin Conflict,* 12 Geo. Int'l. Envtl. L. Rev. 1 (1999); P. Kozal, *Is The Continued Use of Sanctions As Implemented Against Iraq a Violation of International Human Rights?,* 28 Denv. J. Int'l L. & Pol'y 383 (2000); C. LaRae–Perez, *Economic Sanctions as A Use of Force: Re-evaluating the Legality of Sanctions From An Effects-based Perspective,* 20 B.U. Int'l L.J. 161 (2002); D. Losman, *Economic Sanctions: An Emerging Business Menace,* 33 Business Econ. 37 (1998); R. Normand & C. Wilcke, *Symposium Human Rights, Sanctions, and Terrorist Threats: The United Nations Sanctions against Iraq,* 11 Transnat'l L. & Contemp. Probs. 299 (2001); L. Nouraee, *Reassessing US Policy toward Iran: Stimulating Reform through Economic Means,* 25 Suffolk Transnat'l L. Rev. 535 (2002); R. Parker, *The Problem With Scorecards: How (and How Not) to Measure the Cost–Effectiveness of Economic Sanctions,* 21 Mich. J. Int'l L. 235, 250 (2000); A. Reinisch, *Note and Comment, Developing Human Rights and Humanitarian Law Accountability of the Security Council for the Imposition of Economic Sanctions,* 95 A.J.I.L. 851 (2001); D. Santeusanio, *Extraterritoriality and Secondary Boycotts: A Critical and Legal Analysis of United States Foreign Policy,* 21 Suffolk Transnat'l L. Rev. 367 (1998); C. Wall, *Human Rights and Economic Sanctions: The New Imperialism,* 22 Fordham Int'l L.J. 577 (1998).

Problem 6–2

The "War on Terrorism" and Foreign Bank Accounts in United States Courts

Section 1. Facts

The Kingdom of Tarragonia, located on Europe's Mediterranean coast, shares its northeastern border with the Republic of Narbonna. Ninety percent of Tarragonia's population is ethnic Tarragonian. Ten percent, however, located principally in Tarragonia's northeastern provinces adjacent to Narbonna, are ethnic Narbonnans. They have long desired to secede from Tarragonia and unite with their ethnic community in Narbonna.

In November of 1998 a previously unknown organization calling itself the Narbonnan Liberation Alliance (NLA) launched a series of bombings in various Tarragonian cities. Since that time, the NLA has continued to grow and to launch terrorist attacks against Tarragonian civilian targets inside Tarragonia. Despite continued efforts, however, Tarragonia has been unable to eradicate the NLA or seriously to curb its terrorist activities. Tarragonian intelligence has learned that the NLA receives considerable financial support from individuals within Narbonna as well as from the Government of Narbonna itself. Despite repeated diplomatic protests, and even some military threats, however, Tarragonia has been unable to make Narbonna stop the flow of money from Narbonna to the NLA.

The United States enjoys a close diplomatic relationship with Tarragonia, and after the terrorist attacks in New York City and Washington, DC on 11 September 2001 it began to speak out strongly against the NLA and Narbonnan irredentism. In early 2005, as part of its "war on terrorism," the United States committed a small number of troops to help the Tarragonian government root out NLA cells, to which the NLA responded by issuing a statement proclaiming that "the United States has chosen to enter our war on the opposing side. From now on, all Americans are lawful military targets in our struggle." Soon after the statement was issued, the NLA claimed credit for a terrorist bombing at a major Tarragonian Mediterranean resort. The target was the Hotel Nueva York, an American-owned hotel whose guests were known to be primarily American. Four-hundred people were killed in the attack, 350 of them American citizens.

The reaction in the United States was one of great anger as well as anguish. Vowing to "rout the NLA by all means necessary" the US government took action on several fronts. It added significantly to the number of American troops already operating in Tarragonia. It demanded that Narbonna crack down on money flows to the NLA. Finally, acting under § 806 of the USA Patriot Act, codified at 18 USC § 981(a)(1)(G)—which allows forfeiture to the United States of "all assets, foreign or domestic, of any individual ... engaged in planning or perpetrating any act of domestic or international terrorism ... against the United States, citizens or residents of the United States, or their property, and all assets, foreign or domestic, affording any person a source of influence over any such entity or organization"—it seized the assets of several individuals it believed to be contributing to the NLA, among them Jaime Rodolfo, Narbonna's wealthiest national and an outspoken supporter of the NLA. Based on an intercepted communication that "El Gordito de Playa Linda" (a pseudonym by which Rodolfo was known) was involved in financing the bombing of the hotel Nueva York, the US Attorney General secured a warrant from the US District Court for the District of Columbia to seize the contents (US $50 million) of three of Rodolfo's known accounts with the Mediterranean International Bank (MIB), a bank chartered in Narbonna.

As a non-American bank that allows customers to hold US dollar denominated accounts, the MIB does not have direct access to the US dollar settlements system; rather, it maintains a correspondent account with Metro-Bank, a US chartered bank. Incapable of directly seizing Rodolfo's accounts with the MIB, the US government, pursuant to its authority under § 319 of the Patriot Act, codified at 18 USC § 981(k), required Metrobank to transfer the US $50 million from MIB's correspondent account to an account of the US Treasury. As per the design of the USA Patriot Act, the MIB was then forced either to assume the loss of the fifty million dollars itself or to pass it on by debiting Rodolfo's account with it for that amount.[a]

The bank debited Rodolfo's account completing the initial asset seizure. The US government then, moving to the next stage of the process, filed a complaint for forfeiture with the US District Court for the District of Columbia to dispossess Rodolfo permanently of his fifty million dollars. Under the USA Patriot Act, Rodolfo could defeat the forfeiture if he could prove by a preponderance of the evidence that, as he maintained, he was not involved in financing the bombing of the Hotel Nueva York.[b] In its attempt to discover evidence demonstrating the existence of the alleged contribution, the United States Attorney General pursuant to § 319 of the USA Patriot Act, codified at 31 USC § 5318(k)(3), issued a subpoena to MIB requiring MIB to divulge "any and all information in its possession relating to the accounts of Jaime Rodolfo." Upon receiving the subpoena in accordance with § 911 of the Narbonnan Penal Code,[c] MIB sent a certified letter to Jaime Rodolfo at his

a. For a description of the correspondent banking system helpful to understanding the process described in this paragraph, see *infra* Reading 6 (p. 843).

b. *See* 18 USC § 981(a)(1)(G) **(Basic Document 6.7)**.

c. Section 911 of the Narbonnan Penal Code provides in relevant part as follows:

A. Non–Disclosure Requirement

It shall be a felony punishable by a fine and/or imprisonment for anyone with knowl-edge of nonpublic information relating to a bank account maintained in a Narbonnan Chartered Bank to disclose to any person or agency, public or private, domestic or foreign, any information relating to such account without the permission of the holder of such account.

B. Exception to Non–Disclosure Requirement

The Narbonnan Ministry of Finance may grant an exception in a particular case to the Non–Disclosure Requirement in Paragraph

residence in Narbonna seeking his permission to release the sought after information to the United States Attorney General. Rodolfo responded promptly that he agreed to the release of "all information related to his accounts," whereupon MIB forwarded Rodolfo's account information to the US Department of Justice. In reviewing Rodolfo's banking statements the Justice Department found that in early 2004 Rodolfo had written a check for US $25,000 in favor of AG Mediterranean Regent, Inc. Justice Department investigation of the check's clearing history revealed that the check had been deposited in a AG Mediterranean Regent dollar account with the Narbonna International Bank (NIB), a Narbonnan chartered bank that maintains a correspondent account with AmericaBank, a US chartered bank.[d] AG Mediterranean Regent, further investigation revealed, was a shell corporation whose true owner was legally obscure.[e] Suspecting, but unable to substantiate, that the NLA was the indirect owner of AG Mediterranean Regent, the US Attorney General issued a subpoena to NIB demanding information related to the identity of the beneficial owner of AG Mediterranean Regent. Citing Narbonnan Penal Code § 911, NIB refused to comply with the subpoena, whereupon the US Justice Department initiated remedial action against it pursuant to the USA Patriot Act.[f] With no US–Narbonna mutual legal assistance treaty at its disposal, and unable to make progress with NIB, the Justice Department issued a subpoena *duces tecum* to Rodolfo for the information that would reveal the identity of AG Mediterranean Regent's beneficial owner. Rodolfo averred in a sworn statement that, upon receiving the subpoena at his home in Narbonna, he tried unsuccessfully several times to contact AG Mediterranean Regent with the intention of securing permission to disclose account information. Rodolfo petitioned the Ministry of Finance for a determination that the information requested by the US government did not fall within § 911 on the basis that "the identity of AG Mediterranean Regent's beneficial owner is not specifically related to a bank account." In the event that the Ministry could not make such a determination, Roldolfo asked for permission nonetheless to divulge the requested information under § 911(B) of the Narbonnan Penal Code. Denying Rodolfo's petition, the Ministry wrote in relevant part: "As the US government's purpose in requesting the beneficial owner of AG Mediterranean Regent is directly related to a banking transaction, the Ministry finds such information to be information relating to [a Narbonnan chartered bank] account under § 911 A." Further-

A upon a determination that the compelling national interest of Narbonna in allowing a disclosure would outweigh the privacy interest of an account holder.

d. NIB is headquartered in Narbonna and has branches in 25 countries. It has no branch or other physical presence in the United States, but it does have a virtual "Internet Branch" which allows anyone with access to the Internet anywhere in the world to open "full service" online checking and savings accounts. Close to 2,000 of the bank's 5 million customers bank online from the United States.

e. The ability not only of terrorists, but also of drug dealers, tax evaders, and other criminals to obscure their identities through the use of corporate vehicles is a significant global concern. Because, commonly, only the name of a corporation's original "incorporator" (often a lawyer or other professional former of corporations) appears on the officially filed founding corporate documents, the identities of the actual owner-shareholders can be difficult to ascertain. The Organization of Economic Cooperation and Development studied the dimensions of this problem in depth in 2001. For its conclusions see OECD Report, *Behind the Corporate Veil: Using Corporate Entities for Illicit Purposes* (2001) *available at* <http://www1.oecd.org/publications/e-book/2101131e.pdf>.

f. Pursuant to § 319(b) of the USA Patriot Act, codified at 31 USC § 5318(k)(3)(c) (**Basic Document 6.7)** the Attorney General ordered AmericaBank to terminate its correspondent relationship with NIB.

more, the Ministry finds that in this case Narbonna has no compelling interest in favor of disclosure. In fact, Narbonna's national interest militates against cooperating with US judicial process as US seizure and forfeiture of Narbonnan bank accounts, including under the USA Patriot Act, are a violation of the right of Narbonna to exercise sovereign control over its own national banking system. In addition, such seizures and forfeitures extraterritorially violate the individual rights guaranteed under the Narbonnan Constitution to property and to be considered "innocent until proven guilty."

Narbonnan law allows for judicial appeals of such rulings stating that they should be overturned if the Ministry of Finance "clearly erred in its balancing of national and privacy interests." Rodolfo chose not to exercise this right of appeal, arguing to the US District Court that such an appeal would be futile because "in each of the five cases where such Ministry of Finance rulings have been appealed, they have been upheld." The United States moved for the Court to render a verdict upholding the forfeiture by default (under Rule 37 of the Federal Rules of Civil Procedure[g]) on the grounds of Rodolfo's noncompliance with the subpoena. Rodolfo countered that because his compliance with the subpoena is legally prohibited by the laws of Narbonna, such noncompliance should be excused.

SECTION 2.   QUESTIONS PRESENTED

1. Should the US District Court for the District of Columbia rule favorably on the US government's motion to render a verdict against Jaime Rodolfo based on his lack of compliance with the subpoena?

2. In any event, are there any additional or alternative legal norms, procedures, and/or institutions to be recommended that might further help to prevent or discourage situations of the kind posed by this problem?

SECTION 3.   ASSIGNMENTS

A.   READING ASSIGNMENT

Study the Readings presented in Section 4, *infra*, and the Discussion Notes/Questions that follow. Also, time permitting, consult the accompanying bibliographical references.

B.   RECOMMENDED WRITING ASSIGNMENT

Prepare a comprehensive, logically sequenced, and *argumentative* brief in the form of an outline of the primary and subsidiary *legal* issues you see requiring resolution by the Federal District Court for the District of Columbia. Also, from the perspective of an independent judge, indicate which side

g. Rule 37B(2) of the Federal Rules of Civil Procedure provides in part:

If a party ... fails to obey an order to provide ... discovery ... the court in which the action is pending may make such order in regard to the failures as are just, and among others the following: ...

c) An order striking out pleadings or parts thereof, or staying further proceedings until the order is obeyed, or dismissing the action or proceeding or any part thereof, or rendering a judgment by default against the disobedient party.

ought to prevail on each issue and why. Retain a copy of your issue-outline/brief for class discussion.

C.   Recommended Oral Assignment

Assume you are legal counsel for Jaime Rodolfo or that you are an Assistant US Attorney for the US Attorney's Office for the District of Columbia (as designated by your instructor); then, relying upon the Readings (and your issue-outline if prepared), present a 10–15 minute oral argument of your client's likely positions before the Federal District Court for the District of Columbia.

D.   Recommended Reflective Assignment

Consider (and recommend) alternative norms, institutions, and/or procedures that you believe might do better than existing world order arrangements to contend with situations of the kind posed by this problem. In so doing, but without insisting upon *immediate* feasibility, identify the particular transition steps that would be needed to make your alternatives a reality.

Section 4.   Readings

The following readings are considered *prima facie* relevant to solving this problem. They are your law library for present purposes and should be treated as such, organized intelligibly for "shelving" and not necessarily according to the issues presented. Be sure to review Chapter 2 ("International Legal Prescription: The 'Sources' of International Law") in your consideration of them. It, too, should be treated as part of your law library (as, indeed, should this entire coursebook).

1.   Uniting and Strengthening America by Providing Appropriate Tools Required to Intercept and Obstruct Terrorism Act of 2001[h] § 806 and § 319, 19 USC § 981(a)(1)(G), § 981(k) and 31 USC § 5318(k) (2005) (Basic Document 6.7).

2.   Stefan D. Cassella, "Financial Aspects of the War on Terror, March 18, 2002: Forfeiture of Terrorist Assets Under the USA Patriot Act of 2001," 34 Law & Pol'y Int'l Bus. 7–11, 13–14 (2002).

The USA PATRIOT Act contains a number of provisions that may be used by federal law enforcement authorities to seize and forfeit the assets of terrorist organizations, assets that are derived from terrorist acts, and assets that are intended to be used to commit terrorist acts in the future. Some of the new provisions are specifically intended to be used in, and are limited to, the terrorism context. Others apply more generally, but will undoubtedly be used in terrorism cases.

I.   *18 USC § 981(A)(1)(G)*

Title 18, section 981 of the United States Code is the general-purpose civil forfeiture statute applicable to most federal crimes. Among other things, it authorizes the forfeiture of property involved in money laundering cases,

---

h.   Known also as the USA Patriot Act.

property derived from or used to commit certain foreign crimes, and the proceeds of any offense designated as a "specified unlawful activity."

Section 806 of the Patriot Act added a new provision to § 981 that is an obvious response to September 11. Section 981(a)(1)(G) **[Basic Document 6.7]** authorizes forfeiture of all assets of anyone engaged in terrorism, any property affording any person a "source of influence" over a terrorist organization, and any property derived from or used to commit a terrorist act.

This language is extraordinarily broad. Unlike the money laundering statute, which authorizes the forfeiture only of property "involved" in the money laundering offense, or the drug statute, which authorizes forfeiture only of property derived from or used to commit the drug offense, § 981(a)(1)(G) does not require any nexus between the property and any terrorism offense. To the contrary, once the Government establishes that a person, entity, or organization is engaged in terrorism against the United States, its citizens or residents, or their property, the Government can seize and ultimately mandate forfeiture of *all assets*, foreign or domestic, of the terrorist entity, whether those assets are connected to terrorism or not.

The only parallel in federal law is the Racketeer Influenced and Corrupt Organizations (RICO) statute, which permits the forfeiture of all interests a person has in a RICO enterprise, or any property affording that person a source of influence over the enterprise, whether or not the forfeited property was tainted in any way by the racketeering activity. In fact, the "source of influence" language that appears in the RICO statute is repeated in § 981(a)(1)(G). Enactment of § 981(a)(1)(G) was necessary because the law previously had no forfeiture provisions tailored to terrorism.

A. Civil Versus Criminal Forfeiture

Section 981(a)(1)(G) appears in the general purpose civil forfeiture statute, but it is really both a civil and criminal forfeiture provision. This is because federal law now provides that any civil forfeiture may also be classified as a criminal forfeiture. Thus, if the United States apprehends and prosecutes a terrorist, the Government can seek forfeiture of all of his assets in the criminal case under the new statute, provided that the act giving rise to the forfeiture occurred after October 21, 2001, when the new law took effect. Nonetheless, the true utility of § 981(a)(1)(G) is likely to be in the civil forfeiture context, because in civil forfeiture cases, the Government can proceed against the assets even if it does not apprehend the defendant because he is dead or because he remains a fugitive from justice.

B. Procedure for Civil Forfeiture

In most respects, a forfeiture under § 981(a)(1)(G) will work just like any other civil forfeiture action under federal law. The Government can seize property based on probable cause. Generally, the seizure must be pursuant to a warrant, but warrantless seizures are authorized under certain circumstances. The seizure of the property is, however, only the beginning of the process. Seized property may be under Government control, but it still belongs to the property owner. To convert a seizure into a forfeiture—that is, to take title to the property permanently away from the property owner and transfer it to the Government—the Government must commence a formal forfeiture action.

The provisions of the Civil Asset Forfeiture Act of 2001 (CAFRA) set forth the procedure for converting a seizure into a forfeiture. In short, the Government has sixty days from the date of the seizure to send notice of the forfeiture action to all interested parties. If no one files a claim challenging the forfeiture within thirty days, the Government can declare the property forfeited by default. If someone does challenge the forfeiture, however, the Government has ninety days to return the property or to commence either a civil or criminal forfeiture action in federal court.

All of that is standard civil forfeiture law. It would work the same way in a terrorism case as in any other case. In other words, if the United States seizes a terrorist's assets under § 981(a)(1)(G), the Government could be in federal court, trying the case to a jury, in less than six months. The only concession Congress has made to the unique nature of terrorism cases concerns the procedure at trial. Under section 316 of the Patriot Act, if the case goes to trial under § 981(a)(1)(G), and the property involves the assets of "suspected international terrorists," the normal burden of proof is reversed: once the Government makes its initial showing of probable cause, the claimant has the burden of proving, by a preponderance of the evidence, that his property is *not* subject to confiscation. In almost all other forfeiture cases, of course, the Government has the burden of proving the forfeitability of the property. Moreover, in the forfeiture trial, hearsay is admissible if the evidence is reliable and compliance with the normal Rules of Evidence might "jeopardize the national security interests of the United States."

These two exceptions aside, the forfeiture of terrorist assets under § 981(a)(1)(G) would proceed along a very short timetable, would likely involve a full-blown jury trial if contested, and could result in the payment of attorneys fees to the claimant if the Government fails to prevail.

C. *Relationship to IEEPA*

For a variety of reasons, there have been few instances since September 11 in which the Government has sought to seize or forfeit terrorist assets under the new statute. The fact is that the Treasury Department has separate authority to freeze and confiscate terrorist assets under the International Emergency Economic Powers Act (IEEPA), which is specifically exempted from CAFRA and from virtually all of the other evidentiary and due process requirements of federal forfeiture law. Therefore, since September 11, 2001, virtually all of the press reports concerning the freezing of terrorist-related bank accounts have been IEEPA cases, not cases brought by the Justice Department under § 981(a)(1)(G).

Under IEEPA, the Office of Foreign Asset Control (OFAC) of the Treasury Department can freeze (*i.e.*, seize) suspected terrorist assets indefinitely based on a presidential order. Furthermore, if Treasury ultimately decides to convert its blocking order into a forfeiture (or "confiscation," which is the same thing), it would not be bound by any of the CAFRA procedures, except for the right of the property owner to contest the forfeiture by filing a claim in federal court.

On the other hand, Treasury could decide to refer a case to the Department of Justice for formal forfeiture of the property under § 981(a)(1)(G).

The Justice Department stands ready to pursue any such cases that are referred.

* * *

IV.   18 USC § 981(K)

Finally, there is one other new tool relating to asset forfeiture in the Patriot Act that is worth mentioning. Historically, it has been very difficult for the United States to recover forfeitable property that has been deposited into a foreign bank. The federal courts have jurisdiction to enter forfeiture orders against funds in foreign banks if the act giving rise to the forfeiture occurred here, but the forfeiture still requires the cooperation of the foreign government. Sometimes that cooperation is forthcoming, and sometimes it is not.

Congress addressed this in the Patriot Act by enacting a new provision at 18 USC § 981(k) **[Basic Document 6.7]**. Under that statute, if the Government can show that forfeitable property was deposited into an account at a foreign bank, the Government can now recover the property by filing a civil forfeiture action against the equivalent amount of money that is found in any correspondent account of the foreign bank that is located in the United States. It is not necessary to trace the money in the correspondent account to the foreign deposit. Furthermore, the foreign bank does not have standing to object to the forfeiture action. Only the customer who deposited the forfeitable funds into the foreign bank has standing to contest the forfeiture.

For example, if the United States learns that the assets of an international terrorist are on deposit in a bank on a Pacific island, and that bank has a correspondent account at a bank in New York, the Government may effectively seize the terrorist's assets by bringing a civil forfeiture action under § 981(k) against the equivalent sum in the correspondent account of the foreign bank in New York.

The theory is that when the US forfeiture action results in the forfeiture of a given sum of money from the correspondent account of the foreign bank, the bank will then debit the customer's account abroad, leaving the bank in a wash situation and depriving the foreign customer of the funds that have been forfeited to the United States. Before § 981(k) was enacted this would have been impractical because the foreign bank would have had the right to object to the forfeiture of funds in its correspondent account, claiming that the money belongs to it, not its customer, and raising the innocent owner defense. Because this will be controversial, however, forfeitures under § 981(k) require approval from Justice Department headquarters.

3.   C. Todd Jones, "Compulsion Over Comity: The United States' Assault on Foreign Bank Secrecy, 12 Nw. J. Int'l L. & Bus. 454, 454– 59, 461–64, 471–74, 484–88 (1992).

"Upon fundamental principles of international comity, our courts dedicated to the enforcement of our laws should not take such action as may cause a violation of the laws of a friendly neighbor or, at least, an unnecessary circumvention of its procedures."[1] Circuit Judge Leonard Moore's statement in 1960 in one of the first US bank secrecy cases evidences a respect for

---

1. Ings v. Ferguson, 282 F.2d 149, 152 (2d Cir. 1960).

foreign nations and tribunals no longer present. Because of their physical proximities and tory secrecy laws, many nations have become bank secrecy havens, providing financial services and anonymity to people and business enterprises, both legitimate and illegitimate. In response, US courts have systematically circumvented almost any challenge to the authority of our prosecutors and judicial procedures presented by nations that respect and uphold financial privacy. . . .

* * *

I. HISTORICAL BANK SECRECY

While banking, money changing, and finance are as old as civilization, the practice of bank secrecy developed in recent centuries. Modern bank secrecy evolved after World War I when hyperinflation and exchange controls forced prudent individuals to hold assets outside of their home nations. Other nations attempted to control their economies with restrictive monetary practices which enhanced the appeal of other more stable and friendly economic environments. The first major international conflict challenging the new bank secrecy order occurred during this post-war economic upheaval. In 1933, the Nazis published regulations requiring all German nationals to declare assets held outside of Germany. The penalty for noncompliance was the death sentence. The execution of three Germans one year later prompted the Swiss government to codify what until then had been only an unofficial secrecy practice among Swiss bankers. The new law provided for strong criminal penalties for violations.

The first international counter-attack against the Swiss law, however, came not from Germany but from the United States. When the Germans invaded Poland, the Swiss kept their bank assets in US financial institutions. After the fall of France, the Swiss, fearing an invasion, physically moved their national gold supply to New York. In mid–1941, US government officials became convinced that Nazis were hiding their wealth in Swiss deposit accounts. Based on the personal jurisdiction over the Swiss branches located in the United States, the government attempted to obtain account holder names from the branches, only to discover that the holdings were in the names of the banks and not the clients. In response, the US government blocked the expatriation of all Swiss assets and gold reserves. This plenary use of personal jurisdiction over both persons and property would later be repeated to obtain the secret bank information the United States desired.

After World War II, the reasons for bank secrecy expanded. Currency and other government economic controls remained after the war while the expansion of socialism and, concomitantly, heavy income taxes drove money to secrecy havens. Criminal tax statutes, a new prosecutorial weapon, increased investors' desires for secret locales to hide assets from government investigation. The growth of international crime also facilitated the growth of banking centers that protected bank customers' identities and assets. Many small nations, given this currency flight and their own lack of hard currency, catered to such customers with favorable bank secrecy laws.

The United States has taken a completely opposite view of the practice, viewing foreign bank secrecy as a mechanism to facilitate and promote illegal activity. As reported from the House Committee on Banking and Currency twenty-two years ago:

> Secret foreign bank accounts and secret foreign financial institutions have permitted a proliferation of "white collar" crimes; have served as the financial underpinning of organized criminal operation in the United States; have been utilized by Americans to evade income taxes, conceal assets illegally and purchase gold; have allowed Americans and others to avoid the law and regulations governing securities and exchanges; have served as essential ingredients in frauds including schemes to defraud the United States; have served as the ultimate depository of black market proceeds from Vietnam; have served as a source of questionable financing for stock acquisitions, mergers and takeovers; have covered conspiracy to steal from the US defense and foreign aid funds; and have served as the cleansing agent for 'hot' or illegally obtained monies.... The debilitating effects of the use of these secret institutions on Americans and the American economy are vast. It has been estimated that hundreds of millions in tax revenues have been lost.[2]

While the report might have overstated the cause of such activities, it reflects many of the illegal uses of bank secrecy as well as the federal government's attitude toward enforcing its laws. Since that time, the government's passion for enforcing the laws most likely to implicate bank secrecy (*i.e.,* tax, economic regulation, and narcotics laws) and blocking statutes has not diminished.

An institutionally separate but effectually similar legal device has arisen since World War II. Blocking laws were designed to prevent persons and enterprises from complying with orders of foreign tribunals and governments. These laws originated in Canada and have spread throughout the world as a means of protecting domestic interests from foreign legal interference. Nations generally enacted such laws in reaction to countries such as the United States whose aggressive litigation rules were considered by blocking law jurisdictions to be an infringement upon their sovereignty. The first Canadian law was created in 1947 due to a US grand jury investigation of the Canadian paper industry. The Netherlands enacted a law in reaction to US investigations of the petroleum industry. The broadest international response came when the United States conducted investigations of the international shipping industry and the world uranium cartel. The nations in the later cases viewed US antitrust laws and discovery procedures as a means of protecting US industry against foreign competition as well as enabling US competitors to gain competitive advantages through litigation.

[*Eds.*—The author goes on to consider issues of "financial privacy," including "blocking laws." He writes:]

Blocking laws "prohibit the disclosure, copying, inspection or removal of documents located in the host country in compliance with orders of foreign authorities,"[3] and are designed to take advantage of the foreign government compulsion defense. There are two categories of blocking laws. The first

---

2. H. Rep. No. 975, 91st Cong., 2d Sess. 12 (1970).

3. Staff of Senate Comm. On Governmental Affairs, Crime and Secrecy, 98th Cong., 1st Sess, The Use of Offshore Banks and Companies 13 (Comm. Print 1983).

prohibits production of documents or testimony before a foreign tribunal. Some of these statutes provide general protection of business and commercial documents while others are directed at protecting specific industries; general business practice statutes prevent the disclosure of all business records, including bank records. . . .

A second class of blocking statutes prohibits substantive compliance with foreign government orders. Substantive statutes prevent parties from complying with the orders of foreign government officials.

Blocking laws usually provide an even stronger defense against foreign government action. While bank secrecy laws protect a range of banking relationships, blocking laws are designed either to protect certain industries or repel particular discovery techniques. Consequently, nations are more likely to selectively waive bank secrecy laws in a particular case than blocking laws.

* * *

IV. THE LIMITS OF INTERNATIONAL COOPERATION

Because of the conflict between domestic and foreign policies and procedures, nations attempt to cooperate when possible to meet the needs of each. Their efforts include treaties, informal agreements, and multilateral cooperation to improve upon the traditional non-treaty mechanisms for obtaining evidence abroad.

A. Non–Treaty Mechanisms for Obtaining Evidence Abroad

Letters rogatory are the oldest bilateral procedure for obtaining information in a foreign jurisdiction. "Letters rogatory are the medium ... whereby one country, speaking through one of its courts, requests another country, acting through its own courts and by methods of court procedure peculiar thereto and entirely within the latter's control, to assist the administration of justice in the former country. . . ."[4] Based on international comity, nations ordinarily grant such requests absent unusual circumstances. Letters rogatory can be used for both private and government actions.

Although letters rogatory can produce information, several drawbacks limit their value. First, few specific procedures exist with respect to letters rogatory. While some nations require a formal request through diplomatic channels, others do not. Even when the letter can be directly sent from the domestic court to the foreign court, the procedure still takes time. To discover the correct procedures requires litigants to expend not only extensive time but also money, a second drawback to the procedure. Third, the letter itself must be simple enough to be understood but sufficiently complete to convince a foreign judge to act. This requires careful drafting to avoid confusion with US legal terms and peculiar names for offenses. Fourth, the foreign procedure may prevent the domestic party from obtaining sufficient information. Because the letters rogatory process is limited by the laws and procedures of the jurisdiction, foreign judges might not assist US courts; this is especially so with fiscal offenses (*i.e.,* currency, securities, or tax offenses).

---

4. The Signe, 37 F.Supp. 819, 820 (E.D. La 1941).

Finally, other nations have a general antipathy for US litigation procedures and practice. Many countries find it unreasonable to compel individuals to expend extensive time, effort, and money to produce records for an adverse party on a fishing expedition. Similarly, foreign jurisdictions often do not recognize United States grand jury and administrative procedures as valid bases for letters rogatory because they do not meet their "judicial proceeding" requirement for answering a letter rogatory. Parties have no certainty that the procedure will be successful in procuring information, particularly when attempting to overcome bank secrecy laws. For these reasons, letters rogatory are often used as a last resort when evidence cannot otherwise be compelled, especially in the case of bank records protected by foreign law.

Employed only in civil matters, the Hague Evidence Convention has, for some nations, supplanted the use of letters rogatory. Civil law nations interpret the Hague Convention as not applying to criminal, government fiscal, or administrative matters, "as well as other cases in which the government is the plaintiff."[5] The Convention itself also effectively excludes injunctions and restraining orders. This leaves letters rogatory or procedures established under treaties as the only available alternative.

B.   Bilateral Agreements

1.   Mutual Legal Assistance Treaties

Faced with the problems of transboundary litigation and crime, among others, the United States started negotiating bilateral treaties designed to effectuate a better system of obtaining evidence and piercing bank secrecy. The mutual legal assistance treaty (MLAT) between the United States and Switzerland (Swiss Treaty) was the first of these treaties. It created an obligation between the nations "to afford each other ... mutual assistance" in investigations and the return of property obtained through crimes. Although every bilateral MLAT negotiated by the United States has been tailored to the specific needs of the contracting parties, they tend to have some common elements. The treaties generally exclude political, military, and in some cases, tax offenses. Employing a "dual criminality" prerequisite, these treaties require that the offense either be a crime in both nations or a crime listed in the treaty. Nations limit the use of information to the purpose in the assistance request in order to prevent circumvention of the dual criminality requirement. The treaties also establish general guidelines for the evidence request process.

[*Eds.*—The author turns to issues of "judicial compulsion," including "Comity and the Restatements." He writes:]

Because treaties, informal agreements, and international organizations provide only patchwork links through the broad range of financial relationships, US courts developed their own tests to solve conflicts stemming from secrecy laws. To assist the courts, the American Law Institute (ALI) published the Restatement Second. The Restatement Second proposed a model balancing test to remedy jurisdictional conflicts. Section 40 stated that where two courts have prescriptive jurisdiction and each could apply rules requiring

---

5. E. Prescott & D. Alley, *Effective Evidence-Taking Under the Hague Convention*, 22 Int'l Law 947 (1988).

inconsistent conduct, international law requires each tribunal to consider, [specific enumerated factors] in moderating its enforcement jurisdiction. . . .

* * *

Many of the circuits adopted the section 40 test while others did not. Of the panels that used the formula, actual application was so diverse that today's precedents do not represent a uniform test. . . .

In 1988, ALI published the Restatement (Third) of the Foreign Policy Law of the United States (Restatement Third) **[Basic Document 6.3]**. In part because the Restatement Second was not precisely tailored to conflicts between discovery procedures and foreign laws barring document production, the Restatement Third created a more detailed analytical structure for courts to use. According to the Restatement Third, US courts have "jurisdiction to prescribe law with respect to (a) conduct that, wholly or in substantial part, takes place within its territory [and] (b) the status of persons, or interests in things, present within its territory."[6] Civil discovery, grand jury subpoenas, and agency demands represent legitimate exercises of such jurisdiction. In the interest of comity, however, courts should limit the exercise of that jurisdiction by the standard of reasonableness. Restatement Third section 403(2) [lists several factors] that courts should [use to] determine reasonableness. . . .

If a US court determines that jurisdiction exists, that court should consider, in deciding whether to order production of information and in framing a production order, [other] factors [identified] in Restatement Third section 442(1)(c). . . .

If a court determines that issuing an order is appropriate and a foreign law or court order prohibits disclosure of the information, a US judge may enforce that order and, under section 442(2): a) require a person to make a good faith attempt to secure permission from a foreign authority to obtain requested information; b) impose sanctions of contempt, dismissal, or default for failure to make a good faith effort or deliberately concealing or removing information; or c) make adverse findings of fact for failure to obtain the requested information, regardless of any good faith attempt to procure it.

The Restatement Third essentially divides judicial analysis in bank secrecy and blocking law situations into three separate and structured steps. First, a court should determine whether it should exercise jurisdiction based on the section 403(2) "reasonableness test." If the court decides it has jurisdiction, it should then consider other factors in the section 442(1)(c) "order test" in deciding whether to issue an order and how to phrase an order if its issuance were appropriate. Finally, if a party fails to comply with an order, a judge should analyze the section 442(2) "enforcement test" to ascertain what, if any, penalty should be assessed against the non-complying party.

The Restatement Third three-step analysis represents restatements, extensions, or additions to the Restatement Second balancing test. The reasonableness test requires a court to evaluate three former Restatement Second factors before issuing a production order. Factors (c), (d), and (e) in the Restatement Second balancing test—the extent to which the conduct would

---

6. Restatement (Third) of Foreign Relations Law of the United States § 402(1)(a)-(b).

occur outside the US, the nationality of the persons, and the expected compliance—must be considered during the initial comity analysis under the reasonableness test. However, the Restatement Third replaces the "expected compliance" factor with the lesser standard of "likelihood of conflict." The vital national interests of the states, formerly considered by courts as the Restatement Second balancing test factor (a), must now be considered in the reasonableness test, section 403(2)(g), and at the order issuance stage under part five of the order test.

The hardship test of Restatement Second section 40(b) has only been partially integrated into the Restatement Third tests. The hardship imposed upon the party producing the records can be considered by the court under the reasonableness test, but only as the "justified expectations" of the party, which is a lower standard than actual hardship. Hardship must again be judged in the "enforcement test" but can clearly be ignored at a court's discretion.

4. Editors' Note. The Restatement (Third) of the Foreign Relations Law of the United States **(Basic Document 6.3)** reports on two distinct bodies of law in its articulation of the law regarding jurisdictional conflicts between states, referred to in Reading 3, *supra*. In the case of §§ 402, 403, and 441 the Restatement attempts to codify the rules of international law, and in the case of § 442, it attempts to codify the domestic American legal rules. This distinction has significant implications for applicability in American courts. Each country decides when international law will be applied by its own courts and when it will be given precedence over domestic law. Some countries ascribe to what is called a monist approach that generally speaking gives precedence to international law rules when in conflict with domestic law. The United States, on the other hand, ascribes to what is called dualism described by Andrew Strauss in *A Global Paradigm Shattered: The Jurisdictional Nihilism of the Supreme Court's Abduction Decision in Alvarez–Machain,* 67 Temp. L. Rev. 1209, 1243–45 (1994) as follows:

> The dualist model of [the] relationship [between international law and domestic law], which the American judiciary has adopted, posits that domestic and international legal systems are completely separate and distinct. As distinct systems, they each have their own sources of law and their own separate law-applying institutions. Emanating from the international system, international law is mostly created by nation-states through procedures which manifest their consent to be legally bound either explicitly through treaties or implicitly through customary practice. Domestic law, on the other hand, emanates from an individual nation-state's domestic system. Legislatures, administrative agencies, and tribunals, for example, serve as law-making bodies in the American domestic system. International legal disputes are largely resolved through international dispute resolution mechanisms such as diplomacy, international arbitration, or the International Court of Justice. Domestic legal disputes are resolved within the legal bodies of the particular nation-states, most notably domestic courts.

> The seamless nature of law, however, often necessitates that domestic courts interpret and apply international law despite this theoretically strict separation between the domestic and international legal systems. In

the United States, for example, this is accomplished consistently with the dualist model by incorporating international law into federal law. This convoluted approach permits the United States to break international law by employing the "later-in-time rule." Since the most recent enactments of federal law take precedence, the courts are required to recognize the most recent federal law as authoritative even if such federal law is preceded by an international legal obligation.

The precedence of domestic over international law in the United States is codified at § 115 (1)(a) of the Restatement (Third) **(Basic Document 6.3)** which provides that:

> An act of Congress supercedes an earlier rule of international law or a provision of an international agreement as law of the United States if the purpose of the act to supercede the earlier rule or provision is clear or if the act and the earlier rule or provision cannot be fairly reconciled.

Thus, for example, whatever international law as codified at §§ 402, 403, or 441 of the Restatement may hold § 319(b) of the USA Patriot Act codified at 31 USC § 5318(k)(3) **(Basic Document 6.7)** prescribes a superceding later in time pronouncement:

> The Secretary of the Treasury or the Attorney General may issue summons or subpoena to any foreign bank that maintains a correspondent account in the United States and request records related to such correspondent account, including records maintained outside the United States relating to the deposits of funds into the foreign bank.

Of potential relevance to the present problem, it should be noted, § 319(b) does not authorize the issuance of summons or subpoenas to foreign or nonresident individuals.

5. Restatement (Third) of the Foreign Relations Law of the United States: § 111 (International Law and Agreements as Law of the United States), § 115 (Inconsistency Between International Law or Agreements and Domestic Law: Law of the United States), § 402 (Bases of Jurisdiction to Prescribe), § 403 (Limitations on Jurisdiction to Prescribe), § 404 (Universal Jurisdiction to Define and Punish Certain Offenses), § 441 (Foreign State Compulsion) & § 442 (Requests for Disclosure: Law of the United States (1987) (Basic Document 6.3).

6. Editors' Note. The Restatement (Third) **(Basic Document 6.3)** approach to jurisdiction (*supra* Reading 5) and referred to in Readings 3 and 4, *supra*, gives precedence to territoriality and to a lesser extent nationality as legitimate basis for states to exercise jurisdiction. That states should be able to exercise legal control over what takes place in their territory or over what their nationals do outside of state boundaries equates well with our traditional understanding of state power. To draw a parental analogy, the territorial basis for jurisdiction could be thought of intuitively as the international law equivalent of "my home is my castle and making the rules for what takes place inside it are mine to make." Likewise, the nationality basis for jurisdiction could be thought of as the international law equivalent of, "I don't care what the neighbor parents say you can do in their home. As long as you are my children, I'll set the rules for your behavior wherever you might be."

Though these doctrines fit well with traditional understandings of state control over a defined national territory and over the "national family," they are becoming harder to apply in the increasingly symbolic information economy. The problem of jurisdiction over bank accounts or the Internet as presented in this Problem 6–2 demonstrates well this evolving complexity.

To understand the application of jurisdictional theory to international banking in this problem, it is necessary to know something of the nature of bank accounts and especially correspondent bank accounts. Many people believe that banks physically keep what customers deposit in a safe. This is, for the most part, untrue. The vast majority of what we commonly think of as money is nothing more than notations on bank balance sheets. Part of the function that banks play is to be *notation keepers* in a vast *notation keeping* system. If Ms. Smith has $1 million in an account with MetroBank, it means that she has 1 million units of purchasing power that will be accepted by others in exchange for goods and services. When she pays a seller for those goods or services she directs (usually by check or wire transfer) that some of her units are debited from her account and credited to the seller's account. (Only a small proportion of transactions in dollar terms take place by withdrawing cash—*i.e.* converting the units to paper money—and then physically paying with the cash.)

In the course of a day, there are millions of such transactions debiting one bank account and crediting another. Because, for example, every day tens of thousands of Citibank account holders write checks to Bank of America account holders and vice versa, at the end of each day, all of the dollars owed from Citibank customers to Bank of America customers and from Bank of America customers to Citibank customers are netted out through a complex system overseen by the Federal Reserve. All US banks are part of this giant dollar *settlements* system, and the banks that on balance net additions in money will be able to lend more money while those that have a decrease will have to cut back on their loans.

Only US banks or US branches of foreign banks have access to the federal reserve supervised dollar settlement system. This means that foreign banks that want to allow customers to maintain dollar denominated accounts must enter into what is called a correspondent banking relationship with a US bank. To do this the foreign (called "respondent") bank establishes the functional equivalent of a checking account with the US bank. When the respondent bank's customers write a dollar denominated check, the respondent bank directs the US bank to pay out of the respondent Bank's funds. Under what amounts to a two tiered system, the respondent bank then debits on its own books what could be thought of as the sub-account of the individual check writing customer.

The traditional territorial and national approaches to jurisdiction described above assume not an intangible like a bank account or information but a person or physical commodity that exists in a particular place at a particular time. This jurisdictional paradigm is being put under increasing stress by a global economy that is more and more oriented around symbols and information. For further discussion *see infra* Discussion Note/Question 1.

7. *United States v. The First National Bank of Chicago,* 699 F.2d. 341, 343–47 (7th Cir. 1983).

* * *

On September 24, 1979, Internal Revenue Service Officer Earl Tripplett issued a summons to the First National Bank of Chicago ("First Chicago") requiring production of bank statements of Christ and Helen Panos for the month of June 1978 and the balance of funds in their account at the Athens, Greece, branch of First Chicago on June 19, 1978. (The Panoses now reside in Greece.)

* * *

First Chicago ... filed a motion to vacate the enforcement order, arguing that disclosure would expose its employees to penal sanctions under Greek law. The motion was supported by a memorandum and copies of two unsworn letters from ... First Chicago's Greek counsel ... interpreting the Greek Bank Secrecy Act (the "Act"). In relevant part, the letters stated that information concerning customer deposits could not lawfully be supplied to American authorities, that the penalty for violation was at least six months in prison, and that such sanction could not be suspended or converted into fines.[i] After receiving the Government's answering memorandum, accompanied by a Library of Congress translation of the Act, the court, without opinion, denied the motion to vacate on September 15, 1980.

* * *

First Chicago does not argue that the Government failed to make out a *prima facie* case for enforcement. And indeed there is no suggestion that the summons did not relate to a proper purpose, albeit levy and collection rather than determination of tax liability, that the material sought was irrelevant or already within the Commissioner's possession, or that necessary administrative steps remained to be taken.... Rather, First Chicago urges that [as a result of conflicting Greek law] cause has been established for denying enforcement, notwithstanding the Government's *prima facie* showing.

* * *

The fact that foreign law may subject a person to criminal sanctions in the foreign country if he produces certain information does not automatically

---

i. Elsewhere in the opinion the court reprints the following Library of Congress translation of the Act, submitted by the Government to the district court:

Article 1: Deposits in Greek banks are regarded as secret.

Article 2:

1. Governors, members of the board, [members of] other collective bodies, or employees of a bank who, in the course of their duties acquire knowledge of deposits, convey any information in any manner are punished with a minimum of 6 months' imprisonment. The consent or approval of the depositor who has the right to secrecy does not change the punishable nature of the act.

2. Upon conviction for the offense mentioned in the above paragraph, the court cannot order suspension of the penalty nor can it change a conviction to a fine.

3. The persons mentioned in paragraph 1, called upon as witnesses at a civil or criminal trial, cannot be questioned on the secret deposits, even though the depositor consents.

Article 3: As an exception, information is allowed on secret bank deposits only by virtue of a specially justified decision of a domestic court, to the extent that the information is regarded as absolutely necessary for searching and punishing offenses which are regarded as felonies committed in Greece.

bar a domestic court from compelling production. . . . Rather what is required is a sensitive balancing of the competing interests at stake. A number of circuits have utilized a test derived from the Restatement (Second) Foreign Relations Law of the United States (1965). . . . Section 40 of the Restatement ["Limitations on Exercise of Enforcement Jurisdiction"] provides:

> Where two states have jurisdiction to prescribe and enforce rules of law and the rules they may prescribe require inconsistent conduct upon the part of a person, each state is required by international law to consider, in good faith, moderating the exercise of its enforcement jurisdiction, in light of such factors as
>
> (a) vital national interests of each of the states,
>
> (b) the extent and the nature of the hardship that inconsistent enforcement actions would impose upon the person,
>
> (c) the extent to which the required conduct is to take place in the territory of the other state,
>
> (d) the nationality of the person, and
>
> (e) the extent to which enforcement by action of either state can reasonably be expected to achieve compliance with the rule prescribed by that state.

Applying the test just set forth, we conclude that it was an abuse of discretion to enter an unqualified order compelling production, particularly where there is no indication of the rationale of the decision.

It seems clear that the critical act of initially conveying the information would take place in Greece (factor (c)), and highly probable that persons of Greek nationality would make the initial disclosure (factor (d)). Factor (b), extent and nature of hardship, bears great weight. Those acting in Greece would be exposed to criminal liability, not merely a fine, but imprisonment. Comment c to § 40 of the Restatement observes:

> In determining whether to refrain from exercising jurisdiction, a state must give special weight to the nature of the penalty that may be imposed by the other state. A state will be less likely to refrain from exercising its jurisdiction when the consequence of obedience to its order will be a civil liability abroad. Similarly, a state will be less likely to exercise jurisdiction, where there is a possibility that obedience to its command may put an alien in jeopardy under the criminal laws of his own country, than it will if one of its own nationals may be subjected to foreign liability under similar circumstances.

We think it significant in weighing the hardship factor that the Bank employees who would be exposed to penalty and First Chicago, which would be ordering its Greek employees to act unlawfully, are involved only as neutral sources of information and not as taxpayers or adverse parties in litigation.

Although the interest of the United States in collecting taxes is of importance to the financial integrity of the nation, the interest of Greece, served by its bank secrecy law is also important, and so conceded by Government counsel (factor (a)). In connection with this factor it seems significant that the amount of tax liability of the Panoses has already been determined, the information is sought as a step toward levy and collection, the amount of the asset is comparatively small, and there are legal restrictions on the conversion and export of Greek funds.

We note further that Restatement (Second) of the Foreign Relations Law of the United States is being revised, and the substance of § 40, with some modification, is being reflected in § 403 of Tentative Draft No. 2 and §§ 419 and 420 of Tentative Draft No. 3, Foreign Relations Law of the United States (Revised).[j]

Section 419(1) provides that "A person may not ordinarily be required by authority of the United States ... to do an act outside the United States prohibited by the law of the state where the act is to be done." Section 420 deals specifically with court ordered production of information located outside the United States. Section 420(2) provides that "If disclosure of information located outside the United States is prohibited by a law or regulation of the state in which the information or prospective witness is located ... the person to whom the order is directed may be required by the court to make a good faith effort to secure permission from the foreign authorities to make the information available."

In the case before us, we note that Article 3 of the Greek Act provides what seems to be a closely limited exception. The question whether this exception would be liberally construed in a case like the present does not appear to have been explored, and it seems to us that a reasonable, good faith effort to explore it might fairly be imposed on First Chicago. The furnishing of information by the Greek branch to the home office may possibly not be considered an offense, and a reasonable, good faith effort to determine that question of law might fairly be imposed on First Chicago. If the information came into the possession of First Chicago employees in the United States without violation of law in Greece, the result of the balancing test might well be different.

First Chicago tells us that the United States and Greece have a treaty, Convention Between The United States of America And The Kingdom Of Greece For The Avoidance Of Double Taxation And The Prevention Of Fiscal Evasion With Respect To Taxes On Income, entered into on February 10, 1950 and ratified in 1953, and that the IRS maintains a regional representative in Europe to coordinate efforts to collect delinquent taxes through diplomatic means. We are not aware of the Government's position as to the relevancy of either of these facts to the problem with which we are confronted.

On remand, the district court is directed to conduct further inquiry consistent with this opinion and to consider whether to issue an order requiring First Chicago to make a good faith effort to receive permission from the Greek authorities to produce the information specified in the summons.

We are aware that the Eleventh Circuit has reached a different result in a case involving a bank which was apparently a neutral source of information, as here. *In re Grand Jury Proceedings, 691 F.2d 1384 (11th Cir. 1982).* In that

---

j. The final provisions are found in §§ 403, 441, and 442 and contain slightly modified   language **(Basic Document 6.3)**.

case, however, the court of appeals had the benefit of findings by the district court, including a finding that the bank had not made a good faith effort to comply with the subpoena. The information was sought by a grand jury conducting a tax and narcotics investigation, so that the interest of the United States in the grand jury process of investigation and enforcement of its criminal laws was involved as well as its interest in determination and collection of taxes. There was evidence, though contested, that all banking transactions for the foreign branch could be handled by the United States branch. The foreign law (Bahamian) was different from the Greek law involved here in that disclosure with the consent of the customer would not be a criminal offense, and the power of a Bahamian court to permit disclosure did not appear to be as strictly limited. We consider the decision distinguishable.

The order appealed from is REVERSED, and the cause REMANDED for further proceedings.

8. *United States v. The Bank of Nova Scotia*, 691 F.2d 1384, 1385–91 (11th Cir. 1982).

The Bank of Nova Scotia appeals from an order of the United States District Court for the Southern District of Florida holding the Bank of Nova Scotia in civil contempt for failing to comply with an order of the court enforcing a grand jury subpoena duces tecum. The Bank of Nova Scotia (the Bank) presents three arguments against enforcing the subpoena. The Bank first contends that there were insufficient grounds to enforce the subpoena. The Bank also contends that enforcing the subpoena would violate due process. Finally, the Bank argues that the subpoena should not be enforced as a matter of comity between nations. We find the Bank's contentions to be without merit, and therefore we affirm the district court.

I. FACTS

The Bank of Nova Scotia is a Canadian chartered bank with branches and agencies in forty-five countries, including the United States and the Bahamas. A federal grand jury conducting a tax and narcotics investigation issued a subpoena duces tecum to the Bank calling for the production of certain records maintained at the Bank's main branch or any of its branch offices in Nassau, Bahamas and Antigua, Lesser Antilles, relating to the bank accounts of a customer of the Bank. The subpoena was served on the Bank's Miami, Florida agency on September 23, 1981. The Bank declined to produce the documents asserting that compliance with the subpoena without the customer's consent or an order of the Bahamian courts would violate Bahamian bank secrecy laws.[7]

---

7. Banks and Trust Companies Regulations Act of 1965, 1965 Bah. Acts No. 64, as amended by the Banks and Trust Companies Regulation (Amendment) Act, 1980, 1980 Bah. Acts No. 3, and Section 19 of the Banks Act, III Bah.Rev. Laws, c. 96 (1965), as amended by the Banks Amendment Act 1980, 1980 Bah. Acts No. Both Section 10 and Section 19 are identical. Section 10 of the Bank and Trust Companies Regulation Act as amended provides:

Preservation of secrecy

10.–(1) No person who has acquired information in his capacity as—

(a) director, officer, employee or agent of any licensee or former licensee;

(b) counsel and attorney, consultant or auditor of the Central Bank of The Bahamas, established under section 3 of the Central Bank of The Bahamas Act 1974, or as an employee or agent of such counsel and attorney, consultant or auditor;

A hearing was held on the government's motion to compel the Bank to comply with the subpoena on January 13, 1982. At the hearing conflicting evidence was presented as to the degree of control the Miami agency held over documents held by the Nassau branch. The government presented evidence that all banking transactions for accounts in the Bahamian branch could be handled by the Miami agency. The Bank presented evidence that the Miami agency is a one-way conduit for customer communication with the Nassau branch. The Bank also presented an affidavit showing that compliance with the subpoena could expose the Bank to prosecution under the Bahamian bank secrecy law. The affidavit also showed that the government could obtain an order of judicial assistance from the Supreme Court of the Bahamas allowing disclosure if the subject of the grand jury investigation is a crime under Bahamian law and not solely criminal under United States tax laws. The government did not make a showing that the documents sought are relevant and necessary to the grand jury's investigation.

After the district court entered an order compelling the Bank to comply with the subpoena, the Bank's Miami agent appeared before the grand jury and formally declined to produce the documents called for by the subpoena. The district court held the Bank in civil contempt and the Bank brings this appeal.

II. RELEVANCE OF THE DOCUMENTS

The Bank urges this court to follow the Third Circuit's holdings in *In re Grand Jury Proceedings, 486 F.2d 85* (Schofield I), (3rd Cir.1973), and *In re Grand Jury Proceedings, 507 F.2d 963* (Schofield II), (3rd Cir. 1975), *cert.*

(c) counsel and attorney, consultant, auditor, accountant, receiver or liquidator of any licensee or former licensee or as an employee or agent of such counsel and attorney, consultant, auditor, accountant, receiver or liquidator;

(d) auditor of any customer of any licensee or former licensee or as an employee or agent of such auditor;

(e) the Inspector under the provisions of this Act,

shall, without the express or implied consent of the customer concerned, disclose to any person any such information relating to the identity, assets, liabilities, transactions, accounts of a customer of a licensee or relating to any application by any person under the provisions of this Act, as the case may be, except—

(i) for the purpose of the performance of his duties or the exercise of his functions under this Act, if any; or

(ii) for the purpose of the performance of his duties within the scope of his employment; or

(iii) when a licensee is lawfully required to make disclosure by any court of competent jurisdiction within The Bahamas, or under the provisions of any law of The Bahamas.

–(2) Nothing contained in this section shall—

(a) prejudice or derogate from the rights and duties subsisting at common law between a licensee and its customer; or

(b) prevent a licensee from providing upon a legitimate business request in the normal course of business a general credit rating with respect to a customer.

–(3) Every person who contravenes the provisions of subsection (1) of this section shall be guilty of an offense against this Act and shall be liable on summary conviction to a fine not exceeding fifteen thousand dollars or to a term of imprisonment not exceeding two years or to both such fine and imprisonment.

The government argues the Bank would not be successfully prosecuted by Bahamian authorities if it complied with the subpoena. In this regard it argues that because Section 10(2)(a) expressly preserves the common law relationship between bank and customers, the Bank is authorized to disclose the requested information. . . . Although the determination of foreign law is reviewable on appeal, *F.R.Civ.P. 44.1*, we shall assume for purposes of this appeal that the Bank will be subject to criminal sanctions in the Bahamas.

denied, 421 U.S. 1015, 95 S. Ct. 2424, 44 L. Ed. 2d 685 (1975), and require the government to show that the documents sought are relevant to an investigation properly within the grand jury's jurisdiction and not sought primarily for another purpose. . . .

* * *

The guidelines established by the Third Circuit in *Schofield* are not mandated by the Constitution; the Third Circuit imposed the requirements under that court's inherent supervisory power. *Schofield, 486 F.2d at 89; McLean, 565 F.2d at 320.* We decline to impose any undue restrictions upon the grand jury investigative process pursuant to this court's supervisory power. . . .

* * *

While it is true courts should not impinge upon the political prerogatives of the government in the sensitive area of foreign relations . . . accepting the Bank's position would be a greater interference with foreign relations than the procedures employed here. In essence, the Bank would require the government to chose between impeding the grand jury's investigation and petitioning the Supreme Court of the Bahamas for an order of disclosure.

This court is cognizant that international friction has been provoked by enforcement of subpoenas such as the one in question. See, Restatement (Revised) of Foreign Relations Law of the United States § 420, Reporter's Note 1. . . . But as recognized in *United States v. First National City Bank, 379 U.S. 378, 384–385, 85 S. Ct. 528, 531–532, 13 L. Ed. 2d 365 (1965),* the various federal courts remain open to the legislative and executive branches of our government if matters such as this prove to have international repercussions. See, *e.g.,* Convention on Double Taxation of Income, September 27, 1951. United States–Switzerland, *2 U.S.T. 1751,* T.I.A.S. No. 2316 (Swiss–US Tax Treaty providing for exchange of information for, inter alia, the prevention of fraud.)

III.   DUE PROCESS

The Bank contends that compliance with the subpoena would require it to violate the Bahamian bank secrecy law and therefore enforcing the subpoena and imposing contempt sanctions for noncompliance violates due process under *Société Internationale Pour Participations Industrielles v. Rogers, 357 U.S. 197, 78 S. Ct. 1087, 2 L. Ed. 2d 1255 (1958).* The Bank argues that once it has shown Bahamian law bars production of the documents and that it is a disinterested custodian of the documents due process prohibits enforcement of the subpoena. We disagree.

The Bank attempts to fashion a due process defense to the contempt proceedings because of its lack of purposeful involvement or responsibility in the subject matter before the court. In essence, the Bank asserts it is fundamentally unfair to require a "mere stakeholder" to incur criminal liability in the Bahamas. The Bank's position does not withstand analysis.

In *Société Internationale* a Swiss holding company brought an action to recover assets seized under the Trading with the Enemy Act. The district court had ordered production of certain banking records of a Swiss bank pursuant to the government's discovery request. The holding company failed to comply with the court's order, after good faith efforts were made to comply, on the grounds that compliance would violate Swiss penal laws. The district court then dismissed the suit with prejudice due to noncompliance with the production order. In reversing the district court, the Supreme Court did not erect an absolute bar to sanctions being imposed for noncompliance with summons or subpoenas whenever compliance is prohibited by foreign law. *Société Internationale, 357 U.S. at 205–06, 78 S. Ct. at 1092–93....* *Société Internationale* held only that the sanction of outright dismissal of that plaintiff's complaint could not be imposed where that plaintiff had acted in good faith, was unable to comply because of foreign law, and was entitled to a hearing on the merits in order for the Trading with the Enemy Act to withstand constitutional challenge. *Société Internationale, 352 U.S. at 211–12, 78 S. Ct. at 1095–96. ...* The Court left the district court free to impose other sanctions. *Société Internationale, 357 U.S. at 213, 78 S. Ct. at 1096. Société Internationale* does not stand for the proposition that a lawfully issued grand jury subpoena may be resisted on constitutional grounds where compliance would violate foreign criminal law....

The Bank has failed to bring itself within the holding of *Société Internationale*. The district court found the Bank had not made a good faith effort to comply with the subpoena in its order of June 11, 1982.... The Bahamian government has not acted to prevent the Bank from complying with the subpoena. Finally, the Bank is not being denied a constitutionally required forum to recover confiscated assets.[8]

IV. COMITY

The Bank's final contention is that comity between nations precludes enforcement of the subpoena. The Bank argues that the district court improperly analyzed this case under the balancing test of the Restatement (Second) of Foreign Relations Law of the United States § 40 (1965) adopted in *In re Grand Jury Proceedings. United States v. Field, 532 F.2d 404 (5th Cir.1976), cert. denied, 429 U.S. 940, 97 S. Ct. 354, 50 L. Ed. 2d 309 (1976).* The district court concluded that because compliance with the subpoena may cause the Bank to violate Bahamian penal laws, it was appropriate to follow the balancing test adopted in *Field*. Because we conclude this case is controlled by *Field*, we affirm the court below.

In *Field* contempt penalties were upheld against a nonresident alien who, having been subpoenaed to testify before a grand jury while present in the United States, refused to answer questions before the grand jury, despite the witness' assertion that the very act of testifying would subject him to criminal penalties in his country of residence. *Id. at 405.* The grand jury was investigating the use of foreign banks in evading tax enforcement. Field was an officer of a bank located in the Grand Cayman Islands, British West Indies, and was subpoenaed to testify about matters concerning his bank and its clients. *Id. at 405–06.* After balancing the competing interests of the United States and the Cayman Islands under the Restatement approach, the court

---

8. It is difficult to fashion due process protections recognizing the differential argued by the Bank, *i.e.*, stakeholder vs. participant. If fairness is the key, as is asserted here, then it seems hardly offensive to "traditional notions of fair play and substantial justice," *Milliken v.* *Meyer, 311 U.S. 457, 463, 61 S. Ct. 339, 343, 85 L. Ed. 278 (1940),* to exempt entities who do business in the United States and thereby voluntarily bring themselves within the jurisdiction of our courts and legislatures from the burdens of United States law.

affirmed the district court's imposition of contempt sanctions against Field. *Id.* at 407–09.

The situation before us is similar to that in *Field* in all material respects. The Bank has been subpoenaed while subject to the jurisdiction of our courts and has been required to disclose information before a grand jury even though the very fact of disclosure may subject the Bank to criminal sanctions by a foreign sovereign.

The Bank attempts to distinguish *Field* from the case before us on four grounds. The Bank first asserts that the Bank itself is not under investigation by the grand jury, unlike the situation in *Field.* . . . A careful reading of *Field* reveals that the fact that Castle Bank and Trust Company was under investigation did not affect the court's analysis. That court was concerned with the proliferation of foreign secret bank accounts utilized by Americans to evade income taxes and conceal crimes. *In re Grand Jury Proceedings. United States v. Field, 523 F.2d at 407–08.* The instant subpoena calls for the production of certain records relating to bank accounts of a United States citizen pursuant to a tax and narcotics investigation.

Second, the Bank argues this case is distinguishable from *Field* because documentary evidence is requested here rather than testimonial evidence as in *Field*. The distinction, while real, is immaterial. The case before us concerns the relations among nations; whether the subpoena will be enforced is a matter of international comity. *Id. at 407.* Comity is "a nation's expression of understanding which demonstrates due regard both to international duty and convenience and to the rights of persons protected by its own laws." *Somportex Limited v. Philadelphia Chewing Gum Corp., 453 F.2d 435 (3rd Cir.1971), cert. denied, 405 U.S. 1017, 92 S. Ct. 1294, 31 L. Ed. 2d 479 (1972).* Whether the requested information is testimonial or documentary, the effect on the competing state interests will be the same. The deference accorded the Bahamian interest is not to be diminished by the form of the requested information.

Third, the bank argues this case is distinguishable from *Field* because the instant subpoena calls for information located in the Bahamas instead of the United States. This argument is without merit for two reasons. First, the disclosure to the grand jury will occur in this country. . . . Second, the affront to the Bahamas occurs no matter where the information is originally located; the interest of the Bahamas in preserving the secrecy of these records is impinged by the fact of disclosure itself.

Finally, the Bank contends the government "could avoid rather than provoke disrespect for the sovereignty of a friendly nation" by pursuing the alternative of applying for an order of judicial assistance permitting disclosure from the Supreme Court of the Bahamas. . . . Restatement (Revised) of Foreign Relations Law of the United States § 420 (Tent. Draft No. 3, 1982). Applying for judicial assistance, however, is not a substantially equivalent means for obtaining production because of the cost in time and money and the uncertain likelihood of success in obtaining the order. According to the affidavit from a member of the Honorable Society of Lincoln's Inn, England, and of the Bahamas Bar, the Supreme Court of the Bahamas does not have power to order disclosure if the subject of the investigation is criminal only under the tax laws of the United States. Therefore, it is not clear to any degree of certainty that the Bahamian court would order disclosure of all the requested documents.[9]

The judicial assistance procedure does not afford due deference to the United States' interests. In essence, the Bank asks the court to require our government to ask the courts of the Bahamas to be allowed to do something lawful under United States law. We conclude such a procedure to be contrary to the interests of our nation and outweigh the interests of the Bahamas.

In *Field* the vital role of a grand jury's investigative function to our system of jurisprudence and the crucial importance of the collection of revenue to the "financial integrity of the republic" outweighed the Cayman Islands' interest in protecting the right of privacy incorporated into its bank secrecy laws. *In re Grand Jury Proceedings. United States v. Field, 532 F.2d at 407–08.* The United States' interest in the case before us has not been diminished since *Field* was decided. The Bank asserts the Bahamas' interest in the right of privacy; this interest is similarly outweighed. A Bahamian court would be able to order production of these documents. Banks and Trust Companies Regulation Act, 1965 Bah. Acts No. 64, § 10(I)(iii), as amended 1980 Bah. Acts No. 3. In addition, numerous officials, employees, attorneys, and agents of the Bank of Nova Scotia or the Central Bank of the Bahamas may disclose information regarding the account in the performance of their various functions under the Bank Act. *Id.* § 10(1)(a-e). It is incongruous to suggest that a United States court afford greater protection to the customer's right of privacy than would a Bahamian court simply because this is a foreign tribunal. *In re Grand Jury Proceedings. United States v. Field, 535 F.2d at 408.* A statute that is "hardly a blanket guarantee of privacy" does not present a Bahamian interest sufficient to outweigh the United States' interest in collecting revenues and insuring an unimpeded and efficacious grand jury process. . . .

V. CONCLUSION

Absent direction from the Legislative and Executive branches of our federal government, we are not willing to emasculate the grand jury process whenever a foreign nation attempts to block our criminal justice process. It is unfortunate the Bank of Nova Scotia suffers from differing legal commands of separate sovereigns, but as we stated in *Field*:

> In a world where commercial transactions are international in scope, conflicts are inevitable. Courts and legislatures should take every reasonable precaution to avoid placing individuals in the situation [the Bank] finds itself. Yet, this court simply cannot acquiesce in the proposition that United States criminal investigations must be thwarted whenever there is conflict with the interest of other states.

In re Grand Jury Proceedings. United States v. Field, 535 F.2d at 410.

For the reasons stated above, the judgment entered by the district court is AFFIRMED.

---

9. The Bank conceded at oral argument that if the grand jury is conducting a tax investigation the documents could not be ob- tained through the judicial assistance proce- dure.

9. **United Nations Security Council Resolution 1373, 28 Sep 2001, S/RES/1373, UN SCOR, 56th Sess., 4385 mtg., UN Doc. S/RES/ 1573 (2001),** *reprinted in* **40 I.L.M. 1278 (2001) and 2 Weston & Carlson II.F.36** (Basic Document 2.58).

SECTION 5. DISCUSSION NOTES/QUESTIONS

1. Reading 6, *supra*, explains that international jurisdiction as conceptualized by the Restatement (Third) **(Basic Document 6.3)** gives precedence to territoriality and, to lesser extent, nationality as legitimate basis for states to exercise jurisdiction. It goes on to describe the intangible nature of bank accounts generally and correspondent accounts specifically. This understanding raises several fundamental jurisdictional questions: what does it mean to say that an account is "located" in Narbonna? Since there is no physical commodity actually located in Narbonna, or in the United States for that matter, is the concept of territoriality obsolete as applied to this problem? Is it possible to say that anything relevant is taking place in either county's territory? Since legally speaking banks and depositors have a debtor-creditor relationship (the deposit being a loan to the bank), many courts have held that a bank account is located where the debt exists, and that the debt exists in the state that has the power to enforce it. Is this helpful? Despite the lack of a physical commodity, is it possible to characterize the United States or Narbonna as having legitimate interests in regulating matters relevant to "Narbonnan" accounts? Likewise, of what relevance is the national basis of jurisdiction? Should it make a difference that a bank is chartered or incorporated in a particular jurisdiction? Does this have any necessary connection to the location of a bank's customers (account holders or borrowers), owners (shareholders), or workers? Many small countries in the Caribbean and elsewhere have instituted bank secrecy and other laws to attract offshore banking business. In addition to helping finance political violence, accounts with such banks are often utilized by tax cheats, money launderers and other criminals. Often times the banks booking accounts through these countries will have no actual physical presence in them. What effect does this have on your analysis?

In a world where state power is based on the concept of sovereign control over territory, the ethereal nature of banking and more generally (and perhaps to the point in the present problem) of information in the information economy has significant world order implications. Query, in a world of overlapping national interests, including in the control of terrorism, how might the global system evolve to regulate such economic transactions? For further discussion, see Joseph H. Sommer, *Where is a Bank Account*, 57 Md. L. Rev. 1 (1998) and the collection of articles in The International Lawyer's *Symposium on Jurisdiction and the Internet,* beginning at 32 Int'l Law. 959 (1998). For an excellent and very comprehensive overview, see Paul S. Berman, *The Globalization of Jurisdiction,* 151 U. Pa. L. Rev. 311 (2002).

2. The instant problem poses the question of how domestic courts should deal with conflicting jurisdictional assertions by states. One answer to the question is the interest balancing approach primarily relied upon by courts in the absence of a congressional directive mandating discovery when dealing with foreign bank secrecy and blocking statutes. Another answer would be to apply the act of state doctrine, one of the most often discussed, complex and controversial international legal canons. The classic American statement of the doctrine comes from the 1897 case of *Underhill v. Hernandez* 168 U.S. 250 at 252:

> Every sovereign state is bound to respect the independence of every other sovereign state, and the courts of one country will not sit in judgment on the

acts of the government of another, done within its own territory. Redress of grievances by reason of such acts must be obtained through the means open to be availed of by sovereign powers as between themselves.

In the United States two primary rationales have been offered for the continued application of this doctrine. The first is that it protects the sovereignty of each state within a coequal international system to exercise political control over its own territory. The second—and more accepted today, but somewhat less obvious—is that it upholds the prerogative of the executive within the American system to conduct foreign relations without judicial interference. When American courts negatively adjudge what foreign governments do in their own territories, so the argument goes, they necessarily interfere with the President's ability to negotiate executive level solutions to problems with those governments. Presumably the application of the act of state doctrine to facts such as those in the present problem would lead to more predictable results than would interest balancing. How so? Why do you think courts have avoided using the act of state doctrine to resolve cases involving foreign bank secrecy and blocking statutes? Does the ethereal nature of money and information identified in Reading 6 and Discussion Note/Question 1, *supra,* also pose a challenge to the application of the act of state doctrine? Why? Why not? For pertinent discussion, *see* Carsten–Thomas Ebenroth & Louise Ellen Teitz, Banking on the Act of State: International Lending and the Act of State Doctrine (1985). For an early work that provides a political as well as theoretical understanding of the act of state doctrine, *see* Richard Falk, The Role of Domestic Courts in the International Legal Order (1964).

3. In the immediate aftermath of 11 September 2001, the US Congress passed, and President George W. Bush signed into law, The Uniting and Strengthening America by Providing Appropriate Tools Required to Intercept and Obstruct Terrorism, also known as the USA Patriot Act. Many provisions of the Patriot Act have been quite controversial, especially those affecting civil liberties. Among the most discussed provisions are those that deal with the ability of law enforcement to conduct secret searches and phone and Internet surveillance as well as those that expand the instances in which the FBI can utilize counter intelligence provisions to conduct investigations. Largely having escaped notice, however, are provisions dealing with civil forfeiture of alleged terrorist assets and thus applicable to the present problem. As Stefan D. Cassella points out in Reading 2, *supra,* USC § 981(a)(1)(G) provides that all of the property of anyone coming within the provision is subject to forfeiture without regard to any connection between the property and terrorist activities. That said, however, perhaps the USA Patriot Act provisions are only a relatively insignificant side show inasmuch as confiscations under the more used International Emergency Economic Powers Act, 50 USC § 1702 (2005), are subject to even less civil liberties protections. What do you think?

4. *Bibliographical Note.* For supplemental discussion concerning the principal themes addressed in this problem, consult the following additional specialized materials:

(a) *Books/Monographs/Reports/Symposia.* A. Block & C. Weaver, All Is Clouded by Desire: Global Banking, Money Laundering, and International Organized Crime (International and Comparative Criminology) (2004); D. Campbell & S. Woodley, E–Commerce: Law and Jurisdiction (2002); J. Pachkowski, CCH guide to anti-money laundering and bank secrecy: Compliance and the USA Patriot Act (2002); W. M. Reisman, Jurisdiction in International Law (Libraries of Essays in

International Law.) (1999); P. Sarbanes, Financial War on Terrorism And the Administration's Implementation of Title III of the USA Patriot Act: Hearing Before the Committee on Banking, Housing, And Urban Affairs, US Senate (2002); United States Senate, Crime and Secrecy: The Use of Offshore Banks and Companies (2002); J. Vervaele, European Cooperation Between Tax, Customs and Judicial Authorities (2001); G. Walker, International Banking Regulation Law, Policy and Practice (International Banking, Finance and Economic Law, Volume 19) (2001).

(b) *Articles/BookChapters.* A. Aguilar–Zinser, *2003 Stefan A. Riesenfeld Symposium: International Money Laundering: From Latin America to Asia, Who Pays?,* 22 Berkeley J. Int'l L. 8 (2004); R. August, *International Cyber–Jurisdiction: A Comparative Analysis,* 39 Am. Bus. L.J. 531 (2002); K. Fisher, *In Rem Alternatives to Extradition for Money Laundering,* 25 Loy. L.A. Int'l & Comp. L. Rev. 409 (2003); J. Goldsmith, *Against Cyberanarchy,* 65 U. Chi. L. Rev 1199 (1998); E. Gouvin, *Bringing Out the Big Guns: The USA Patriot Act, Money Laundering, and the War on Terrorism,* 55 Baylor L. Rev. 955 (2003); A. Hardister, *Can we Buy Peace on Earth?: The Price of Freezing Terrorist Assets in a Post–September 11 World,* 28 N.C.J. Int'l L. & Com. Reg. 605 (2003); C. Linn, *International Asset Forfeiture and the Constitution: The Limits of Forfeiture Jurisdiction over Foreign Assets Under 28 USC 1355(b)(2),* 31 Am. J. Crim. L. 251 (2004); W. Perkel, *Money Laundering and Terrorism: Informal Value Transfer Systems,* 41 Am. Crim. L. Rev. 183 (2004); D.G. Post, *"Against Cyberanarchy,"* 17 Berkeley Tech. L. J. 1365 (2002); K. Raustiala, *The Evolution of Territoriality: International Relations & American Law* in Territoriality and Conflict in the Era of Globalization (M. Kahler & B. Walter eds., (2006); E. Sanders, Jr. & G. Sanders, *The Effect of the USA Patriot Act on the Money Laundering and Currency Transaction Laws,* 4 Rich. J. Global L. & Bus. 47 (2004); S. Turner, *US Anti–Money Laundering Regulations: An Economic Approach to Cyberlaundering,* 54 Case W. Res. L. Rev. 1389 (2004); C. Wallace, *Extraterritorial Discovery: Ongoing Challenges for Antitrust Litigation in An Environment of Global Investment,* 5 JIEL 353 (2002); M. Waters, *Mediating Norms and Identity: The Role of Transnational Judicial Dialogue in Creating and Enforcing International Law,* 93 Geo. L.J. 487 (2005).

Problem 6–3

Suing Narbonna as a State Sponsor of Terrorism in United States Courts

SECTION 1. FACTS

Assume the same facts as in Problem 6–2, *supra*.

Diplomatic relations between Narbonna and the United States had not been good for many years, but as a result of the bombing of the Hotel Nueva York the relationship went from bad to worse. The US Secretary of State designated Narbonna a state sponsor of terrorism pursuant to Section 6(j) of the Export Administration Act of 1979 and Section 620A of the Foreign Assistance Act of 1961 as specified in 28 USC § 1605(a)(7). The United States instituted an economic embargo against Narbonna and cut off all diplomatic relations. As a result, almost all connections between the two countries were severed. Even Narbonna's embassy in Washington, DC was closed, and the building is standing empty.

As the bilateral relationship between the United States and Narbonna deteriorated, private lawyers from Holmes and Hughes, LLP, a successful New York personal injury law firm, approached bereaved family members of many of the US citizens killed in the Hotel Nueva York bombing. Holmes and Hughes solicited them to become plaintiffs in a lawsuit against Narbonna for its alleged support of the NLA.

After securing the agreement of the families, Holmes and Hughes petitioned Narbonna to agree to submit the claims against it to arbitration. When Narbonna refused, Holmes and Hughes brought suit in US District Court for the Southern District of New York. Narbonna's response to the law suit was to move for dismissal based on the forum's lack of personal jurisdiction over it. Narbonna argued that it did not have the requisite contacts with the forum to be subject to its jurisdiction. Decision on the jurisdictional question is now pending.

SECTION 2. QUESTIONS PRESENTED

1. Does the applicable law of personal jurisdiction allow for the US District Court for the Southern District of New York to assert jurisdiction over Narbonna?

2. In any event, are there any additional or alternative legal norms, procedures, and/or institutions to be recommended that might further help to prevent or discourage situations of the kind posed by this problem?

SECTION 3.   ASSIGNMENTS

A.   READING ASSIGNMENT

Study the Readings presented in Section 4, *infra*, and the Discussion Notes/Questions that follow. Also, time permitting, consult the accompanying bibliographical references.

B.   RECOMMENDED WRITING ASSIGNMENT

Prepare a comprehensive, logically sequenced, and *argumentative* brief in the form of an outline of the primary and subsidiary *legal* issues you see requiring resolution by the Federal District Court for the Southern District of New York. Also, from the perspective of an independent judge, indicate which side ought to prevail on each issue and why. Retain a copy of your issue-outline/brief for class discussion.

C.   RECOMMENDED ORAL ASSIGNMENT

Assume you are newly a partner at Holmes and Hughes and legal counsel for the families of the American victims of the Hotel Nueva York attack or the Government of Narbonna (as designated by your instructor); then, relying upon the Readings (and your issue-outline if prepared), present a 10–15 minute oral argument of your client's likely positions before the Federal District Court for the Southern District of New York.

D.   RECOMMENDED REFLECTIVE ASSIGNMENT

Consider (and recommend) alternative norms, institutions, and/or procedures that you believe might do better than existing world order arrangements to contend with situations of the kind posed by this problem. In so doing, but without insisting upon *immediate* feasibility, identify the particular transition steps that would be needed to make your alternatives a reality.

SECTION 4.   READINGS

The following readings are considered *prima facie* relevant to solving this problem. They are your law library for present purposes and should be treated as such, organized intelligibly for "shelving" and not necessarily according to the issues presented. Be sure to review Chapter 2 ("International Legal Prescription: The 'Sources' of International Law") in your consideration of them. It, too, should be treated as part of your law library (as, indeed, should this entire coursebook).

1. Mark W. Janis, An Introduction to International Law 347–53 (4th ed. 2003).

The doctrine of foreign sovereign immunity shields foreign sovereigns from the jurisdictional reach of municipal courts on the theory that to implead the foreign sovereign could upset the friendly relations of the states involved. It has been reported that questions relating to jurisdictional immunities figure more before national courts than do any other questions of international law.

In the United States, the doctrine of foreign sovereign immunity was first authoritatively rendered by Chief Justice John Marshall in 1812 in *The Schooner Exchange v. McFaddon*.[1] A French warship, the *Balaou*, was forced by bad weather to enter the port of Philadelphia where it was libeled by US citizens who alleged that the ship was in reality *The Schooner Exchange*, a merchant vessel wrongfully seized and confiscated on the high seas by the French government. Marshall held that though "[t]he jurisdiction of the nation within its own territory is necessarily exclusive and absolute,"[2] such theoretically absolute territorial jurisdiction had to be limited in practice with respect to foreign sovereigns:

> One sovereign being in no respect amenable to another, and being bound by obligations of the highest character not to degrade the dignity of his nation, by placing himself or its sovereign rights within the jurisdiction of another, can be supposed to enter a foreign territory only under an express license, or in the confidence that the immunities belonging to his independent sovereign station, though not expressly stipulated, are reserved by implication, and will be extended to him.[3]

As for foreign sovereigns, so for their warships: It was "a principle of public law, that national ships of war, entering the port of a friendly power open for their reception, are to be considered as exempted by the consent of that power from its jurisdiction."[4]

Affording a foreign sovereign immunity does not deny plaintiffs all redress; it only forecloses their national courts. Claimants may always turn to the foreign sovereign's judicial system or avail themselves of diplomatic channels. Indeed, diplomacy in the *Exchange* case finally led to a measure of compensation.

The Foreign Sovereign Immunities Act of 1976 (FSIA) codifies what had been in the United States an area of common law. The FSIA provides that "[s]ubject to existing international agreements to which the United States is a party at the time of enactment of this Act a foreign state shall be immune from the jurisdiction of the courts of the United States and of the States except as provided [in the Act]."[5] A "foreign state" is defined to include "an agency or instrumentality of a foreign state," which in turn is defined as including separate legal entities that are either "an organ of a foreign state or political subdivision thereof, or a majority of whose shares or other ownership interest is owned by a foreign state or political subdivision thereof" and "which is neither a citizen of a State of the United States ... nor created under the laws of any third country."[6]

Before the passage of the FSIA, the granting of immunity was often decided on the basis of a formal suggestion made by the Department of State. One of the principal objects of the FSIA was to relieve the State Department of the burden and possible diplomatic repercussions of determining whether immunity should be afforded. The FSIA now provides that claims of foreign states to immunity are to be decided by the courts. The FSIA, however, does

---

1. 11 U.S. (7 Cranch) 116 (1812).

2. *Id.* at 136.

3. *Id.* at 137.

4. *Id.* at 145–46.

5. Pub. L. No. 94–583, 90 Stat. 2891, as amended, Pub. L. No. 100–669 (1988), 28 USC § 1604 [hereinafter "FSIA"].

6. *Id.,* § 1603(a), (b).

not preclude the State Department from filing with a court its suggestions about the granting of sovereign immunity. . . .

The most important exception to the rule of foreign sovereign immunity exposes a foreign sovereign to suit when the foreign government engages in commercial rather than public activities. The commercial activities exception is based on the notion that, though a state's acts may sometimes be those of a sovereign, *acta imperii,* they are at other times those of a merchant, *acta gestionis.* As states in the nineteenth and twentieth centuries increasingly engaged in business pursuits, it seemed unfair to shield such commercial activities from litigation in the national courts of foreign countries.

The commercial activities exception, also known as the restrictive theory of foreign sovereign immunity, was relatively late in arriving in the United States. For many years, the US rule was the principle of absolute sovereign immunity. Jurisdiction over the commercial activities of foreign states, such as merchant shipping, was regularly rejected by the US courts. The restrictive theory was adopted in the United States in 1952 when in the Tate letter the Acting Legal Adviser to the State Department communicated his opinion to the Justice Department that because many countries had adopted or were contemplating adopting the restrictive theory and because "the widespread and increasing practice on the part of governments of engaging in commercial activities makes necessary a practice which will enable persons doing business with them to have their rights determined in the courts," the United States should no longer afford absolute immunity to foreign states.[7] Although perhaps not bound in law to follow such advice from the Executive Branch, US courts did in fact change course and begin to hear and decide cases brought against foreign sovereigns for their commercial activities.

Like the doctrine of foreign sovereign immunity in general, the restrictive theory has moved from its common law foundations into US statute. Section 1605 of the FSIA establishes a foreign state's commercial activities as one of a number of exceptions to Section 1604's presumptive grant of immunity to foreign states and to their political subdivisions, agencies, and instrumentalities:

> A foreign state shall not be immune from the jurisdiction of courts of the United States or of the States in any case. . . in which the action is based upon a commercial activity carried on in the United States by the foreign state; or upon an act performed in the United States in connection with a commercial activity of the foreign state elsewhere; or upon an act outside the territory of the United States in connection with a commercial activity of the foreign state elsewhere and that act causes a direct effect in the United States.[8]

The FSIA provides only slight guidance as to what is or is not commercial activity:

> A "commercial activity" means either a regular course of commercial conduct or a particular commercial transaction or act. The commercial character of an activity shall be determined by reference to the nature of

---

7. Letter of Acting Legal Adviser, Jack B. Tate, to Department of Justice, 19 May 1952, 26 Dep't State Bull. 984, 1985 (1952).

8. FSIA, *supra* note 5, § 1605(a)(2).

the course of conduct or particular transaction or act, rather than by reference to its purpose.[9]

Thus, what constitutes commercial activity in any particular case is more a question of judicial precedent and discretion than it is one of statutory direction.

The FSIA codifies several other exceptions to foreign state immunity of which the most important, next to the commercial activities exception, is the exception relating to waivers, that is, permitting suit in any case "in which the foreign state has waived its immunity either explicitly or by implication, notwithstanding any withdrawal of the waiver which the foreign state may purport to effect except in accordance with the terms of the waiver."[10]

* * *

In the United States, besides the exceptions to a state's sovereign immunity for commercial activities and for its waivers, the FSIA provides an exception for cases involving property "taken in violation of international law," or for property acquired by succession or gift or for property that is immovable and located in the United States.[11] The Act also excepts personal injury claims such as those likely to occur in automobile accidents. There is no immunity in admiralty suits where a "maritime lien is based upon a commercial activity of the foreign state."[12] A new exception was added by the Antiterrorism and Effective Death Penalty Act of 1996 to cover cases "in which money damages are sought against a foreign state for personal injury or death that was caused by an act of torture, extrajudicial killing, aircraft sabotage, hostage taking or the provision of material support or resources" for such acts.[13]

2. W. Michael Reisman and Monica Hakimi, "Illusion and Reality in the Compensation of Victims of International Terrorism," 54 Ala. L. Rev. 561, 563–68 (2003).

In 1976, Congress enacted the Foreign Sovereign Immunities Act (FSIA). The FSIA was a complex legal instrument that subjected foreign states to the jurisdiction of US courts in a variety of commercial matters, as interpreted and understood by the United States. Moreover, it gave courts, rather than the executive, the power to determine whether, in a particular instance, the foreign state was immune. The FSIA thus effectively restored the playing field that existed before the development of command economies, again enabling judicial relief for international commercial disputes regardless of whether one party to the dispute was a government entity.

The FSIA was expected to be, and in fact was, a major event in international commercial law. However, the impact that the FSIA had on the protection of human rights by national courts was not anticipated. Until the FSIA's enactment in 1976, the human rights bar had, rather unsuccessfully, sought to enforce and implement human rights before inter-governmental bodies, because those bodies were, in effect, "the only game in town." With passage of the FSIA, American human rights lawyers shifted their efforts for

---

9. *Id.,* § 1603(d).

10. *Id.,* § 1605(a)(1).

11. *Id.,* § 1605(a)(3), (4).

12. *Id.,* § 1605(b).

13. *Id.,* § 1605(a)(7).

enforcement of human rights from various international fora to the national judiciary. By combining the new FSIA with the Alien Tort Claims Act (ATCA), an obscure instrument dating from the earliest days of the Republic, human rights lawyers discovered a venue for suits in US courts against foreign governments that allegedly had violated the human rights of their own nationals.[a] This national, "judicialist" initiative received early encouragement from the Second Circuit in the case of *Filártiga v. Peña-Irala.* In *Filartiga,* the father and sister of a Paraguayan national who had been tortured and killed in Paraguay sued the victim's torturer, a Paraguayan state official. After finding that torture violated the law of nations, the Second Circuit held that the ATCA allowed for the exercise of federal court jurisdiction. The D.C. Circuit, in *Tel-Oren v. Libyan Arab Republic*, dampened somewhat the Second Circuit's encouragement by applying a more restrictive interpretation to the phrase "law of nations" in the ATCA. In other US jurisdictions, however, the felicitous conjunction of the FSIA and the ATCA provided opportunities for human rights suits against foreign governments, brought first by the human rights bar and, later, by the plaintiff's bar. To be sure, these judgments could not be enforced, because any damage awards that might be secured could find no readily accessible assets of the defendant. Nevertheless, from the perspective of the human rights advocate, the fact that the national judiciary affirmed the violation and obliged a remedy reinforced international human rights law. That reinforcement was no minor achievement.

However, the Supreme Court to some extent reversed that progress in *Argentine Republic v. Amerada Hess Shipping Corp.* by restricting the jurisdictional scope of the FSIA for potential human rights cases. The plaintiffs in *Amerada Hess* were Liberian corporations that sued the Argentine Republic for bombing their cargo ship on the high seas during the Falklands War. The plaintiffs claimed that their dispute with Argentina was entirely commercial and, therefore, that it fit within the exceptions to the FSIA. The Supreme Court disagreed. The Court concluded that, because no specific exception to the FSIA applied to the type of dispute at issue, the Argentine Republic was immune from suit in US courts. The Court thus interpreted the FSIA as the sole basis for jurisdiction over a foreign sovereign and instructed lower courts to construe the FSIA restrictively in this regard. Foreign sovereign immunity again became the default position, and the FSIA, a long-arm statute for only the specifically enumerated applications set forth therein.

The United States is a vibrant democracy in which dissatisfactions with an existing legal situation quickly generate demands for legal adjustments, which then are effected in proportion to the political influence that the dissatisfied groups are able to mobilize. In this instance, individuals who sought to expand the restrictive exceptions of the FSIA but found themselves blocked in the courts turned to the legislature to alter the FSIA's legal framework, which, in turn, would enable a subsequent judicial remedy. In the environment of political lobbying in Washington, a second convergence of events led to unexpected consequences for the protection of human rights, in particular, and for the development of international law, more generally. In 1995, Timothy McVeigh and others bombed the federal building in Oklahoma

a. For pertinent detailed discussion, see *supra* Problem 5–4 ("A Disappearance in Hispa-   nia"), at 660, especially Reading 13 and the Discussion Notes/Questions.

City, causing enormous loss of life. When those responsible were apprehended, the families of the victims intensely demanded justice. To many of the families, justice in that context meant the execution of the perpetrators. When the families learned that those responsible might use the courts to defer the death penalty for decades, if not to avoid it entirely, the families descended on Washington to secure legislative change and to increase the likelihood that capital punishment could be meted out against McVeigh and his accomplices. In Washington, the Oklahoma families encountered another group of families, those of the victims of the bombing of Pan Am Flight 103 over Lockerbie, Scotland. Neither group, on its own, could likely achieve its desired enactment. However, the groups realized that if they joined forces, each might achieve its objectives. And they did. Working together, the two groups secured passage of the chillingly titled Antiterrorism and Effective Death Penalty Act of 1996 (AEDPA).

The convergence of AEDPA's "effective death penalty" component with its "anti-terrorism" component is somewhat ironic. The "effective death penalty" component narrowed the opportunities available to defendants for challenging their state convictions in federal courts. Human rights activists often criticize this component of AEDPA, contending that Congress essentially closed the safety valve by which federal courts rescue state prisoners from unconstitutional state convictions. At the same time, however, the human rights movement appreciated the potential of the "anti-terrorism" component, which amended the FSIA to allow US nationals to sue foreign states for violations of human rights that can be deemed "terrorist activities." Under the 1996 amendment to the FSIA, a foreign state no longer is immune from jurisdiction in any case

> [i]n which money damages are sought against a foreign state for personal injury or death that was caused by an act of torture, extrajudicial killing, aircraft sabotage, hostage taking, or the provision of material support or resources ... for such act if such act or provision of material support is engaged in by an official, employee, or agent of such foreign state while acting within the scope of his or her office, employment, or agency.[14]

For the amendment to apply, either the victim or the survivor bringing the claim must be a US national. In addition, the US Secretary of State must have designated the foreign state a state sponsor of terrorism, either at the time the event occurred or after that time but as a result of the particular event that gave rise to the suit. Finally, the American plaintiff must allow the defendant foreign state a reasonable opportunity to arbitrate the claim. Of course, everyone recognized that the probability of the foreign state agreeing to arbitrate a claim arising out of the state's terrorist activities was remote and, thus, that the claims would likely proceed before United States courts.

The 1996 amendment to the FSIA was accompanied a few months later by another act, the Civil Liability for Acts of State Sponsored Terrorism Act (the "Civil Liability Act"), passed as part of the 1997 Omnibus Consolidated Appropriations Act. The Civil Liability Act, sometimes referred to as the "Flatow Amendment," in memory of an American college student, Alisa Flatow, who was killed in a suicide attack in Israel, provides, in relevant part, as follows:

---

14. 28 USC § 1605(a)(7) (2000).

> An official, employee, or agent of a foreign state designated as a state sponsor of terrorism ... while acting within the scope of his or her office, employment, or agency shall be liable to a United States national ... for personal injury or death caused by acts of that official, employee, or agent for which the courts of the United States may maintain jurisdiction under [28 USC 1605(a)(7)].[15]

The 1996 amendment to the FSIA and the Civil Liability Act together broadened the scope for judicial action and of potential liability for acts of terrorism. First, AEDPA's new exception to the FSIA created an innovative threshold of causality: A foreign state now could be subjected to US jurisdiction even if it only indirectly caused the act of terrorism at issue, *i.e.*, through the provision of material support or resources. Second, the new exception adopted the principles of agency: A foreign state could be subjected to US jurisdiction on the basis of the act of terrorism of an agent or employee, acting within his or her scope of authority. Third, with the Civil Liability Act, plaintiffs no longer needed to incorporate the provisions of ATCA for a cause of action against individual agents or employees of a terrorist state. And finally, the Civil Liability Act specifically allowed recovery for pain and suffering, economic damages, solatium, and punitive damages.

By allowing recovery for pain and suffering, economic damages, solatium, and punitive damages, the Civil Liability Act introduced an element that had theretofore not been part of the emerging legislative ensemble or, arguably, of international law. US plaintiffs now could receive awards of damages—and, potentially, very high awards—for certain human rights abuses.

3. International Law Commission, Draft Articles on Jurisdictional Immunities of States and Their Property, UN GAOR, 46th Sess., Supp. No. 10, UN Doc. A/46/10 (1991).

PART I

INTRODUCTION

Article 1

Scope of the present articles

The present articles apply to the immunity of a State and its property from the jurisdiction of the courts of another State.

* * *

PART II

GENERAL PRINCIPLES

Article 5

State immunity

A State enjoys immunity, in respect of itself and its property, from the jurisdiction of the courts of another State subject to the provisions of the present articles.

* * *

---

15. 28 USC § 1605 note.

Article 7

Express consent to exercise jurisdiction

1.   A State cannot invoke immunity from jurisdiction in a proceeding before a court of another State with regard to a matter or case if it has expressly consented to the exercise of jurisdiction by the court with regard to the matter or case:

(a) by international agreement;

(b) in a written contract; or

(c) in a declaration before the court or by a written communication in a specific proceeding.

2.   Agreement by a State for the application of the law of another State shall not be interpreted as consent to the exercise of jurisdiction by the courts of that other State.

Article 8

[*Eds.*—This Article, which deals with effect of participation in a proceeding before a court, includes a provision that a State shall not be considered to have consented to the exercise of jurisdiction if it intervenes in a proceeding for the sole purpose of invoking immunity.]

* * *

PART III

PROCEEDINGS IN WHICH IMMUNITY CANNOT BE INVOKED

Article 10

Commercial Transactions

1.   If a State engages in a commercial transaction with a foreign natural or juridical person and, by virtue of the applicable rules of private international law, differences relating to the commercial transaction fall within the jurisdiction of a court of another State, the State cannot invoke immunity from that jurisdiction in a proceeding arising out of that commercial transaction.

2.   Paragraph 1 does not apply:

(a) in the case of a commercial transaction between States; or

(b) if the parties to the commercial transaction have expressly agreed otherwise.

3.   The immunity from jurisdiction enjoyed by a State shall not be affected with regard to a proceeding which relates to a commercial transaction engaged in by a State enterprise or other entity established by the State which has an independent legal personality and is capable of:

(a) suing or being sued; and

(b) acquiring, owning or possessing and disposing of property, including property which the State has authorized it to operate or manage.

* * *

Article 12
Personal injuries and damage to property

Unless otherwise agreed between the States concerned, a State cannot invoke immunity from jurisdiction before a court of another State which is otherwise competent in a proceeding which relates to pecuniary compensation for death or injury to the person, or damage to or loss of tangible property, caused by an act or omission which is alleged to be attributable to the State, if the act or omission occurred in whole or in part in the territory of that other State and if the author of the act or omission was present in that territory at the time of the act or omission.

4. Foreign Sovereign Immunities Act of 1976, 28 USCA §§ 1602–1611 (Supp. 1989) (Basic Document 6.2).

5. Andrew L. Strauss, "Symposium: Could a Treaty Trump Supreme Court Jurisdictional Doctrine? Where America Ends and the International Order Begins: Interpreting the Jurisdictional Reach of the US Constitution in Light of a Proposed Hague Convention on Jurisdiction and Satisfaction of Judgments," 61 Alb. L. Rev. 1237, 1245–63 (1998).

Despite all of the attention given to personal jurisdiction in civil cases by the United States Supreme Court, the Court has never articulated a discrete approach to international jurisdiction. Rather, in cases with foreign plaintiffs or defendants ..., the Court has approached international jurisdiction as an ad hoc appendage to its doctrine of domestic jurisdiction. Specifically, the Court, as well as the legal community in general, has assumed that the US Constitution prescribes America's international jurisdictional reach as if it were prescribing domestic jurisdiction among states within the United States. Thus, with minor variation, the Court applies the constitutionally-derived minimum contacts test to international cases.

* * *

II.   Interpreting the Constitution
A.   The Sovereignty Paradigm and the US Constitution

Finding the answer to the question of whether the Constitution is meant to prescribe international jurisdiction lies in understanding the intellectual universe in which the architects of the Constitution were operating. In this universe, the distribution of all global political power, including the extent to which the authority of nation-states yields to the authority of the international system, is derived from the paradigm of state sovereignty. Under the classic formulation of the sovereignty paradigm, the state is the ultimate and supreme political entity within its jurisdictional sphere. As such, all private, non-state actors coming within a state's jurisdictional sphere, as well as the state's own internal organs of administration, are subject to the absolute exercise of that state's domestic authority. What is left to the international order under this paradigm is to govern relations between these sovereign political entities.

Because state sovereignty despite certain qualifications continues to be the basic organizing principle of the international system, most of us continue to accept implicitly its basic allocation of responsibility between the domestic and international orders. Highway speed limits are decided domestically. Laws regulating the rules of international armed conflict are the province of the international order. While rarely stated explicitly, the allocation of responsibility is implicit throughout the entire Constitution. The document's first three Articles establish the basic framework for internal self-governance. They do not attempt to establish a regulatory structure for the world at large. Article I establishes a legislative branch with powers vested in "a Congress of the United States" to "provide for the common Defence and general Welfare of the United States." Article II establishes the executive powers of the United States, the office of President to be held only by a natural born citizen of the United States. Article III establishes the "judicial Power of the United States," which "extends to all Cases, in Law and Equity, arising under this Constitution, the Laws of the United States, and Treaties made ... under their Authority." As a framework for internal governance, the document functions to allocate power among the fifty states of the Union and between those fifty states and the federal government, not among the nation-states of the global community. For example, the Full Faith and Credit Clause of Article IV requires that "full Faith and Credit shall be given in each State to the public Acts, Records, and judicial Proceedings of every other State." Thus, the Constitution establishes the deference in certain matters that the fifty states within the Union owe to each other. Nowhere does the Constitution purport to establish similar reciprocal obligations upon the nation-states of the world. Defining such reciprocal obligations between the nation-states of the world, it is well-established, is the province of international law. Likewise, it is clear, from the context of Article III's identification of the limited subject matter jurisdiction of the Supreme Court and other federal courts to be established, that Article III provides an alternative to the courts of the fifty states within the United States, and is not intended to allocate authority between courts within the United States and those within foreign countries.

The implied general distinction between an inner-realm under the domain of the Constitution and an outer-realm under the domain of the international order surfaces in Article II, Section 2, which establishes the treaty-making power of the Executive and the Senate. By providing a process for internal ratification of the external obligations undertaken by the United States, the Constitution manifests the Framers' understanding that the document is meant to establish a structural framework for American self-regulation, and that the country is only one of many participants in a separate international law making system whose domain is relations among nation-states. . . .

All of this analysis merely makes explicit what is implied in undertaking to draft a constitution for the United States: that the Framers incorporated into the Constitution their understanding of where America ends and the international order begins.

B. The Constitutionally Accepted Sovereignty Paradigm and Personal Jurisdiction

How does this constitutionally reflected allocation of responsibility apply to personal jurisdiction? An elemental understanding of personal jurisdiction unencumbered by the highly particularized US Supreme Court jurisprudence on the subject reveals that personal jurisdiction, like all jurisdiction, is about the allocation of administrative authority between subunits of an organizational system. The concept is so basic that without it, anything but small-scale social organization would be impossible. There simply would be no way to determine which administrative subunits of an organization have the responsibility for exercising authority in which areas. Chaos would ensue.

Consistent with the basic concept of jurisdiction, subunits cannot self-define their own jurisdiction. Our own federal system makes this obvious. If Louisiana was charged with deciding its own jurisdiction, there would be no jurisdictional constraints on Louisiana. In a hypothetical federal system of jurisdictional self-prescription, Louisiana and every other state could exercise regulatory authority in whatever area they pleased, and the fundamental organizational purpose of jurisdiction would be defeated.

If self-prescription is inconsistent with the premise underlying jurisdiction, then the allocation of jurisdictional responsibilities between the nation-states of the world must be left to the international order. Under the constitutionally-reflected sovereignty paradigm, international jurisdiction cannot be a matter for domestic regulation, but rather, as a question necessarily involving relations between nation-states, it is a classic subject for prescription by the international order. The Constitution, therefore, must intend itself to prescribe the jurisdictional responsibilities of the fifty states within the United States and the federal government and leave the allocation of jurisdiction among the nation-states of the world to the international order.

As I will now demonstrate, that the Constitution is not meant to extend into the realm of prescribing international jurisdiction was taken for granted during the era of territorial jurisdiction.

III. Applying the Constitutionally–Accepted Sovereignty Paradigm to International Cases

A. *Easy Application: The Era of Territorial Jurisdiction*

During the era of territorial jurisdiction (predating the founding of the United States and ending definitively in 1945), the courts, and the legal community in general, assumed that the US Constitution's role was not to prescribe personal jurisdiction in international cases. Rather, in assuming that the limits of nation-state jurisdiction came from the international order, courts during this period took for granted that our Constitution was not intended to upset the allocation of responsibility between the domestic and international orders implied by the sovereignty paradigm.

The hallmark of the territorial era was an understanding that nation-states possessed absolute sovereignty over their territories and conversely were excluded from exercising sovereign powers in the territories of other nation-states. It followed that a nation-state only had personal jurisdiction over a defendant who was inside of its own territory. A state asserted this jurisdiction by physically seizing or arresting the defendant. Eventually the system evolved to allow symbolic seizure of the defendant through service of process. That in this simple jurisdictional world the Constitution was not intended to claim authority to prescribe whether the United States could assert personal jurisdiction over someone who was in another country was taken as obvious by the legal community, which assumed implicitly the sovereignty paradigm's division of domestic from international responsibility.

So straightforward was the territorial formula and so clear was its international function of allocating power among nation-states that no one would have assumed that it was a creation of our own Constitution. In fact, quite the opposite was the case. Courts explicitly reported their understanding that the international order governed jurisdiction between nation-states in their attempts to derive an analogous system of jurisdiction for the parallel community of states within the United States.

Pennoyer v. Neff, the 1877 case which, in many people's minds, exemplifies the territorial era, provides the most famous such reference. In that case, the Court needed an authoritative basis to justify its use of the territorial approach to allocating judicial powers among the "sovereign" states of the American federation. The Court found such a basis in the "well-established principles of public [international] law respecting the jurisdiction of an independent [nation-]State over persons and property."[16]

Many other nineteenth-century cases also stand as evidence of the implied presumption that the international order prescribes the jurisdiction of nation-states. For example, in the 1828 case of *Picquet v. Swan*, the former Federal Circuit Court for the District of Massachusetts proclaimed:

> the courts of a state, however general may be their jurisdiction, are necessarily confined to the territorial limits of the state. Their process cannot be executed beyond those limits; and any attempt to act upon persons or things beyond them, would be deemed an usurpation of foreign sovereignty, not justified or acknowledged by the law of nations.[17]

Likewise in 1848, the Supreme Court of Georgia, in holding that Georgia could not assert personal jurisdiction over a resident of South Carolina, reported its understanding that "the rule is firmly fixed, that no sovereignty can extend its process beyond its territorial limits, to subject either persons or property to its judicial decisions. This is the rule, by the laws of nations—by the Common Law, and [it] is recognized by the American Courts."[18] Additionally, in 1850 in *D'Arcy v. Ketchum*, the Supreme Court itself, anticipating its decision in *Pennoyer*, made reference to the international order's prescription of international jurisdiction. Holding that an American state could refuse to give effect to a sister American state's judgment on the basis of a claim of lack of jurisdiction, the Court proclaimed that, "we deem it to be free from controversy that these adjudications are in conformity to the well-established rules of international law, regulating governments foreign to each other."[19] Many other cases of the era evidenced a similar understanding.

With the rise of contacts jurisdiction, however, this simple territorial model of jurisdiction would lose its viability, and with it would go the clarity of understanding that made the application of international law to international cases appear so natural.

16. 95 U.S. 714, 722 (1877).

17. 19 F. Cas. 609, 611 (C.C.D. Mass. 1828) (No. 11,134).

18. Dearing v. Bank of Charleston, 5 Ga. 497, 515 (1848).

19. 52 U.S. (11 How.) 165, 174 (1850).

I will now turn to explaining how courts and commentators came to misunderstand the nature of jurisdiction during the contacts era, and how this misunderstanding led to the assumption that domestic jurisdictional principles should be applied in international cases.

B.   The Conundrum of Contacts Analysis

1.   The Conversion to Contacts

In 1945, the landmark case of *International Shoe Co. v. Washington* brought the era of territorial jurisdiction to an end. In that case, which presented a question regarding the jurisdiction of a state within the United States, the Supreme Court explicitly endorsed what came to be identified as the minimum contacts test. The Court proclaimed that:

> Due process requires only that in order to subject a defendant to a judgment in personam, if he be not present within the territory of the forum, he have certain minimum contacts with it such that the mainte-nance of the suit does not offend "traditional notions of fair play and substantial justice."[20]

Commentators generally agree that economic developments forced the Supreme Court to make the transition from territoriality to contacts jurisdic-tion. Most significant was the increasing number of corporate defendants which made reliance on the defendant's presence within the forum as the sine qua non for the exercise of state power no longer possible. As the facts in *International Shoe* itself made clear, while the corporation is metaphorically deemed to be a person, it is in reality a legal "fiction" composed of a multitude of many different persons all performing different functions. The entity, therefore, has no physical presence, much less one in a particular jurisdiction. Should the entity be deemed "to be" where it was formally incorporated, where its board of directors sat, where its owners (the share-holders) were, where its workers were, or where its customers were? Without a satisfactory answer to these questions, the courts were forced to change the basis for jurisdiction. For many years before *International Shoe*, lower courts had been moving away from a territorial approach toward a more expansive view of jurisdiction. In *International Shoe*, literal presence within the forum was replaced by the notion that under the Due Process Clause of the US Constitution, certain contacts with the forum justified jurisdiction.

2.   The Illusion that Contacts Jurisdiction Is Not About the Allocation of Regulatory Authority

Today, as evidenced by the question before this Symposium, courts and commentators operating within the new contacts framework no longer as-sume that the international order should prescribe international jurisdiction. Rather, to the contrary, they assume that the Constitution prescribes the contacts that are necessary for assertions of jurisdiction. This is equally true whether the assertion of jurisdiction is by one of the fifty states who collectively operate as constituent units of the American federation or wheth-er it is by the United States as a whole operating as a part of the international order.

---

20.   326 U.S. 310, 316 (1945) (quoting Mil-liken v. Meyer, 311 U.S. 457, 463 (1940)).

Where does this assumption come from? There are two common underlying illusions about contacts jurisdiction. These illusions give rise to this assumption that international jurisdiction is no longer about the international question of the allocation of authority between the constituent subunits of the international system. First, the fact that contacts jurisdiction allows for nation-states to have overlapping jurisdictional realms obscures the fact that jurisdiction continues to be about the allocation of authority. Under the territorial scheme, because jurisdiction was mutually exclusive—assigned only to the one forum where the defendant was present—quite obviously a finite reserve of regulatory power was being allocated among states. But under contacts jurisdiction, defendants potentially have requisite contacts with multiple forums, each of which possess the simultaneous power to exercise jurisdiction in a given case. The existence of non-exclusive, overlapping jurisdiction creates the impression that administrative power does not need to be allocated among nation-states. Jurisdiction, one might come to assume, must be about something other than the international allocation of administrative authority. Nevertheless, it is essential to remember that jurisdiction remains about what jurisdiction always has been fundamentally about: the allocation of sovereign authority. Even overlapping and non-exclusive jurisdictional realms serve to distribute administrative authority.

At an even more fundamental level, contacts doctrine, as formulated by the US Supreme Court, denies that the Court, in authorizing states within the United States to exercise authority outside their traditional territorial confines, was engineering a transformation of state jurisdictional powers. Rather, under the Supreme Court's formulation, state jurisdictional powers do not change. Instead, the state's ability to assert jurisdiction extraterritorially is premised upon the agreement of out-of-state defendants to acquiesce to state powers. Because contacts jurisdiction under this formulation is not about empowering the state to exercise new jurisdictional powers, contacts doctrine applied internationally brings with it no new power to, in fact, be allocated by the international order.

The Supreme Court adopted this formulation because it did not appear to believe that it could alter the basic territorial powers of the state. The reasons for this probably lie in history and in psychology. The state, and especially the popular conception of it as a territorially-defined sovereign entity, has not been just a political convention of the modern world. Since the emergence of the nation-state after the Thirty Years War in 1648, humankind has been so psychologically wedded to the idea of the territorially sovereign state as to have turned it into a kind of religious icon. The absolutist formulation of the state as an immutably defined territorial entity is reflected in Chief Justice John Marshall's famous 1812 declaration in *Schooner Exchange v. M'Faddon:*

> The jurisdiction of the nation within its own territory is necessarily exclusive and absolute. It is susceptible of no limitation not imposed by itself. Any restriction upon it, deriving validity from an external source, would imply a diminution of its sovereignty to the extent of the restriction, and an investment of that sovereignty to the same extent in that power which could impose such restriction.[21]

---

21.   11 U.S. (7 Cranch) 116 (1812).

With the arrival of the contacts era, the Justices of the Supreme Court, operating as the high priests of this secular religious tradition, seem to have simply assumed that it was beyond their power to alter the fundamental territorial character of the fifty "sovereign" united states. Instead of simply expanding the powers of these states to allow for contacts jurisdiction, they evidently felt it necessary to invent a formulation which only allowed the states to assert jurisdiction if "there be some act by which the defendant purposefully avails itself of the privilege of conducting activities within the forum State, thus invoking the benefits and protections of its laws."[22] Thus, the state could remain exclusively territorial and yet exercise jurisdiction over defendants who had in some way independently acquiesced to its power. The Supreme Court, in endorsing this new jurisdiction, was, despite the pretense of maintaining territoriality, altering fundamentally the nature of state power. In reality, the state's powers were being expanded to cover situations where the defendant had extraterritorial contacts with the state, and it did not matter whether the defendant actually accepted this power. Tracking a development that had been taking place for a long period of time in prescriptive jurisdiction, the state was losing its exclusively territorial dimension. No longer did state jurisdiction (either for states within the United States or for the nation-states of the world) begin and end with the state's territorial boundaries. Contacts jurisdiction meant a redefinition of the powers of both the states within the United States and of the nation-states of the world, and, as we have seen under the constitutionally reflected sovereignty paradigm, it is the domain of the international order to oversee the allocation of such new powers among nation-states.

Contacts jurisdiction's nonexclusive, overlapping jurisdictional realms and the Supreme Court's denial that such jurisdiction involved expanding state powers caused jurisdiction in the contacts era to appear to lose its raison d'être—the allocation of regulatory authority. Jurisdiction was not, however, to be left by courts and commentators as an empty procedural vessel without an underlying rationale. And so into the conceptual void (courtesy of the perceived need to look to the acquiescence of defendants to rationalize extraterritorial jurisdiction) came a new jurisdictional mission—protecting the rights of defendants. The Court in *Insurance Corp. of Ireland v. Compagnie des Bauxites de Guinee* articulated it most strongly. That personal jurisdiction can be waived by the defendant, declared the Court, "portrays it for what it is—a legal right protecting the individual."[23] More accurately stated, the convenience of litigating in a particular forum for defendants was the primary (though not only) criterion used to allocate authority for forum courts to hear civil disputes in the contacts era. With the jurisdictional purpose hidden from view, however, all that remained visible in the jurisdictional exercise was the criterion that was used for allocating judicial power. It was, therefore, easy for the primary criterion for allocating such power to become confused with the underlying purpose of jurisdiction. Following this substitution, this new "purpose" of jurisdiction came itself to reinforce the perception that jurisdiction is unrelated to the international order's domain of relations between nations. The focus on defendants, private actors who are subject to domestic

22. Hanson v. Denckla, 357 U.S. 235, 253   **23.** 456 U.S. 694, 704 (1982).
(1958).

regulation under the paradigm, adds to the appearance that jurisdiction should fall within the realm of domestic law.

But by confusing criteria for allocating jurisdiction with the subject matter of jurisdiction, courts and commentators have confused the fundamental question of when states can assert authority over private actors with their ability to assert such authority once they have jurisdiction. The former, involving the distribution of the authority among the states to regulate private actors, is a matter—as we have seen—for the international order, while the latter, involving the use of that authority once granted to regulate private actors, is properly the domain of the domestic order.

6. Restatement (Third) of the Foreign Relations Law of the United States § 421 (Jurisdiction to Adjudicate) (1987) (Basic Document 6.3).

7. *Michael H. Price and Roger K. Frey v. Socialist People's Libyan Arab Jamahiriya*, 294 F.3d 82, 86–87, 95–99 (D.C. Ct. of App. 2002).

I. BACKGROUND

The facts and procedural history of this case are relatively straightforward. Plaintiffs Michael Price and Roger Frey, Americans who had been living in Libya in the employ of a Libyan company, were arrested in March of 1980 after taking pictures of various places in and around Tripoli. Libyan government officials apparently believed that these photographs constituted anti-revolutionary propaganda, because they would portray unfavorable images of life in Libya.

Price and Frey allege that, following their arrest, they were denied bail and kept in a "political prison" for 105 days pending the outcome of their trial. In their complaint, plaintiffs assert that they endured deplorable conditions while incarcerated.... The complaint also asserts that the plaintiffs were "kicked, clubbed and beaten" by prison guards, and "interrogated and subjected to physical, mental and verbal abuse." ... The complaint contends that this incarceration was "for the purpose of demonstrating Defendant's support of the government of Iran which held hostages in the US Embassy in Tehran, Iran." ...

Ultimately, plaintiffs were tried and acquitted of the crimes with which they had been charged....

On May 7, 1997, Price and Frey commenced a civil action against Libya in federal court. Their complaint asserted claims for hostage taking and torture and sought $20 million in damages for each man. Following receipt of process, Libya filed a motion to dismiss, arguing [in part] that ... the court's exercise of personal jurisdiction was unconstitutional.... The District Court rejection of [this argument].... allow[s] the court to assert.... personal jurisdiction over the defendant. Libya now pursues an interlocutory appeal.

II. DISCUSSION

Libya asserts that the Due Process Clause does not permit an American court to take jurisdiction over a foreign sovereign based on conduct that has no connection to the United States save for the nationality of the plaintiff.

A. Plaintiffs' Cause of Action

Before we address the issues arising under the.... Due Process Clause, we first want to make it clear that our decision today does not address or decide whether the plaintiffs have stated a *cause of action* against Libya. The parties appear to assume that a substantive claim against Libya arises under the FSIA, but this is far from clear. The FSIA is undoubtedly a jurisdictional statute which, in specified cases, eliminates foreign sovereign immunity and opens the door to subject matter jurisdiction in the federal courts. There is a question, however, whether the FSIA creates a federal cause of action for torture and hostage taking *against foreign states. See Roeder v. Islamic Republic of Iran, 195 F.Supp.2d 140, 171–73 (D.D.C. 2002).*

The "Flatow Amendment" to the FSIA confers a right of action for torture and hostage taking against an "official, employee, or agent of a foreign state," ... but the amendment does not list "foreign states" among the parties against whom such an action may be brought.

* * *

G. Personal Jurisdiction

The ... question that we face is whether the Due Process Clause is offended by the District Court's assertion of personal jurisdiction over Libya. [Even] [i]f ... personal jurisdiction [is] established under the FSIA ... it is well-settled that "a statute cannot grant personal jurisdiction where the Constitution forbids it." *Gilson v. Republic of Ireland, 221 U.S.App.D.C. 73, 682 F.2d 1022, 1028 (D.C. Cir. 1982).*

The Due Process Clause requires that if the defendant "be not present within the territory of the forum, he have certain minimum contacts with it such that the maintenance of the suit does not offend 'traditional notions of fair play and substantial justice.' " *Int'l Shoe, 326 U.S. at 316* (quoting *Milliken v. Meyer, 311 U.S. 457, 463, 85 L. Ed. 278, 61 S. Ct. 339 (1940)).* In the absence of such contacts, the liberty interest protected by the Due Process Clause shields the defendant from the burden of litigating in that forum. ... Libya argues that foreign states, no less than private individuals and corporations, are protected by these constitutional strictures.

In the present case, it is undisputed that Libya has no connection with the District of Columbia or with the United States, except for the alleged fact that it tortured two American citizens in Libya. This would be insufficient to satisfy the usual "minimum contacts" requirement.... Therefore, Libya argues, the Fifth Amendment precludes the exercise of personal jurisdiction in this case.

Implicit in Libya's argument is the claim that a foreign state is a "person" within the meaning of the Due Process Clause.... In previous cases, we have proceeded *as if* this proposition were true, but we have never so held....

Moreover, both the Supreme Court and this court have expressly indicated that the constitutional issue remains an open one.... Now, however, this assumption has been challenged. And, with the issue directly before us, we hold that foreign states are not "persons" protected by the Fifth Amendment.

Our conclusion is based on a number of considerations. First, as the Supreme Court noted in *Will v. Michigan Department of State Police*, there is an "often-expressed understanding that 'in common usage, the term "person" does not include the sovereign, and statutes employing the word are ordinarily construed to exclude it.' " *491 U.S. 58, 64, 105 L. Ed. 2d 45, 109 S. Ct. 2304 (1989)* (quoting *Wilson v. Omaha Indian Tribe, 442 U.S. 653, 667, 61 L. Ed. 2d 153, 99 S. Ct. 2529 (1979)*.... In this case, however, what is at issue is the meaning of the Due Process Clause, not a statutory provision. And, on this score, it is highly significant that in *South Carolina v. Katzenbach, 383 U.S. 301, 323–24, 15 L. Ed. 2d 769, 86 S. Ct. 803 (1966),* the Court was unequivocal in holding that "the word 'person' in the context of the Due Process Clause of the Fifth Amendment cannot, by any reasonable mode of interpretation, be expanded to encompass the States of the Union." Therefore, absent some compelling reason to treat foreign sovereigns more favorably than "States of the Union," it would make no sense to view foreign states as "persons" under the Due Process Clause.

Indeed, we think it would be highly incongruous to afford greater Fifth Amendment rights to foreign nations, who are entirely alien to our constitutional system, than are afforded to the states, who help make up the very fabric of that system. The States are integral and active participants in the Constitution's infrastructure, and they both derive important benefits and must abide by significant limitations as a consequence of their participation. *Compare* US CONST. art. IV § 4 ("The United States shall guarantee to every State in this Union a Republican form of Government, and shall protect each of them against Invasion;"), *with id.* at art. VI, cl. 2 ("This Constitution ... shall be the supreme Law of the Land; and the Judges in every State shall be bound thereby, any Thing in the Constitution or Law of the State to the Contrary notwithstanding."), *and id.* at art. 1 § 10 (listing specific acts prohibited to the States). However, a "foreign State lies outside the structure of the Union." *Principality of Monaco v. Mississippi, 292 U.S. 313, 330, 78 L. Ed. 1282, 54 S. Ct. 745 (1934).* Given this fundamental dichotomy between the constitutional status of foreign states and States within the United States, we cannot perceive why the former should be permitted to avail themselves of the fundamental safeguards of the Due Process Clause if the latter may not.

It is especially significant that the Constitution does not limit foreign states, as it does the States of the Union, in the power they can exert against the United States or its government. Indeed, the federal government cannot invoke the Constitution, save possibly to declare war, to prevent a foreign nation from taking action adverse to the interest of the United States or to compel it to take action favorable to the United States. It would therefore be quite strange to interpret the Due Process Clause as conferring upon Libya rights and protections *against* the power of federal government.

In addition to text and structure, history and tradition support our conclusion. Never has the Supreme Court suggested that foreign nations enjoy rights derived from the Constitution, or that they can use such rights to shield themselves from adverse actions taken by the United States. This is not surprising. Relations between nations in the international community are seldom governed by the domestic law of one state or the other.... And legal disputes between the United States and foreign governments are not mediated through the Constitution....

Rather, the federal judiciary has relied on principles of comity and international law to protect foreign governments in the American legal system. This approach recognizes the reality that foreign nations are external to the constitutional compact, and it preserves the flexibility and discretion of the political branches in conducting this country's relations with other nations. . . .

An example of this approach is seen with respect to the right of access to the courts, that is, the "right to sue and defend in the courts," *Chambers v. Baltimore & Ohio R.R., 207 U.S. 142 (1907)*. Private individuals have "a constitutional right of access to the courts." Foreign states also have been afforded the right to use the courts of the United States to prosecute civil claims "upon the same basis as a domestic corporation or individual might do." *Pfizer, 434 U.S. at 318–19* . . . . But the right of access enjoyed by foreign nations derives from "principles of comity," and it is "neither a matter of absolute obligation, on the one hand, nor of mere courtesy and good will, upon the other." *Banco Nacional de Cuba v. Sabbatino, 376 U.S. 398, 408–09, 11 L. Ed. 2d 804, 84 S. Ct. 923 (1964)* (quoting *Hilton v. Guyot, 159 U.S. 113, 164– 65, 40 L. Ed. 95, 16 S. Ct. 139 (1895))*. This privilege is not to be denied lightly, because to do so "would manifest a want of comity and friendly feeling." *The Sapphire, 78 U.S. (11 Wall.) 164, 167, 20 L. Ed. 127 (1870)*. Nonetheless, foreign nations do not have a *constitutional* right of access to the courts of the United States. Indeed, only nations recognized by and at peace with the United States may avail themselves of our courts, and "it is within the exclusive power of the Executive Branch to determine which nations are entitled to sue." *Pfizer, 434 U.S. at 319–20* . . . .

While we recognize that the present case implicates not the right of affirmative access to the courts, but rather its reverse—the right not to be haled into court—this does not change the analysis under the Due Process Clause. The personal jurisdiction requirement is not a structural limitation on the power of courts. Rather, "the personal jurisdiction requirement recognizes and protects an individual liberty interest. It represents a restriction on judicial power not as a matter of sovereignty, but as a matter of individual liberty." *Ins. Corp. of Ire. v. Compagnie des Bauxites de Guinee, 456 U.S. 694, 702, 72 L. Ed. 2d 492, 102 S. Ct. 2099 (1982)*. This makes sense, because "the requirement that a court have personal jurisdiction flows not from Art. III, but from the Due Process Clause." *Id*. And the "core of the concept" of due process is "to secure the individual from the arbitrary exercise of the powers of government, unrestrained by the established principles of private right and distributive justice." *County of Sacramento v. Lewis, 523 U.S. 833, 845–46, 140 L. Ed. 2d 1043, 118 S. Ct. 1708 (1998)*. It is thus quite clear that the constitutional law of personal jurisdiction secures interests quite different from those at stake when a sovereign nation such as Libya seeks to defend itself against the prerogatives of a rival government. It therefore follows that foreign states stand on a fundamentally different footing than do private litigants who are compelled to defend themselves in American courts.

Unlike private entities, foreign nations are the juridical equals of the government that seeks to assert jurisdiction over them. . . . If they believe that they have suffered harm by virtue of being haled into court in the United States, foreign states have available to them a panoply of mechanisms in the international arena through which to seek vindication or redress. . . . These mechanisms, not the Constitution, set the terms by which sovereigns relate to one another. We would break with the norms of international law and the structure of domestic law were we to extend a constitutional rule meant to protect individual liberty so as to frustrate the United States government's clear statutory command that Libya be subject to the jurisdiction of the federal courts in the circumstances of this case. The constitutional limits that have been placed on the exercise of personal jurisdiction do not limit the prerogative of our nation to authorize legal action against another sovereign. Conferring on Libya the due process trump that it seeks against the authority of the United States is thus not only textually and structurally unsound, but it would distort the very notion of "liberty" that underlies the Due Process Clause.

8. Kevin Todd Shook, "Note: State Sponsors of Terrorism Are Persons Too: The Flatow Mistake," 61 Ohio St. L. J. 1301, 1313–1319 (2000).

[*Eds.*—In *Flatow v. Islamic Republic of Iran*, 999 F.Supp. 1 (D.D.C. 1998) the Plaintiff brought suit under 28 USC § 1605(a)(7) in the United States District Court for the District of Columbia against the Islamic Republic of Iran. The Plaintiff alleged that Iran's support for Palestine Islamic Jihad, the party that claimed responsibility for the suicide attack that killed his daughter in the Gaza Strip, amounted to that country having committed a wilful and deliberate act of extrajudicial killing within the meaning of 28 USC § 1605(a)(7). In determining whether it had jurisdiction over Iran, the District Court, like the D.C. Court of Appeals in *Price*, found that foreign states are not "persons" for purposes of the Fifth Amendment and are, therefore, not entitled to the Due Process protection of minimum contacts. This author contends below that the *Flatow* court erred in holding that a foreign state is not a person entitled to due process protection.]

A. *Textual Considerations: The Fifth Amendment Meaning of "Person"*

The Fifth Amendment provides that "[n]o person shall be ... deprived of life, liberty, or property, without due process of law." At first blush, it would seem that the text of the Constitution lends support to the *Flatow* holding that a foreign state is not a person. After all, in common usage a "person" is a "human being; a man, woman, or child," and a "state" represents "a politically unified people occupying a definite territory." Thus, it would seem that a foreign state is not really a person, but a collection of persons. However, the term "person" has a much broader meaning in legal usage—both Congress and the Supreme Court have supplied definitions of "person" that include many things beyond the scope of "human being."

1. *Corporations and Governmental Bodies Are Persons*

First of all, the Supreme Court has found that a corporation is a "person" for purposes of the Fourteenth Amendment. Beginning in 1886, the Supreme Court has found that "defendant corporations are persons within the intent ... of the Fourteenth Amendment" which forbids a state from denying "any person ... equal protection of the laws."[24] Similarly, the Court has extended double jeopardy protections of the Fifth Amendment to corporate persons.

24. Santa Clara County v. S. Pac. R.R., 118 U.S. 394, 396 (1886).

Furthermore, the Supreme Court has found that governmental bodies such as states are "persons" for purposes of various federal statutes. In *Chattanooga Foundry & Pipe Works v. Atlanta*,[25] the Supreme Court held that a municipality is a "person" within the meaning of the general definitions section of the Sherman Act. Similarly, the Supreme Court has found that local governments, municipal corporations, and school boards are "persons" subject to liability under the Civil Rights Act, which imposes civil liability on every "person" who deprives another of his federally protected rights. Lastly, in *Georgia v. Evans*,[26] the Court held that the words "any person" in section 7 of the Sherman Act included states of the union. Although the Supreme Court looked beyond the text and also considered the intent and history behind these statutory provisions, these cases clearly demonstrate that the legal meaning of "person" has come to include many entities not included in common usage.

2. *Distinguishing* Katzenbach*: States Are Not Persons*

The Supreme Court's holding in *South Carolina v. Katzenbach*[27] presents the greatest hurdle to the contention that a foreign state is a person for purposes of the Fifth Amendment. In that case, the Court found that "States of the Union" are not "persons" entitled to due process protection. In *Republic of Argentina v. Weltover, Inc.*,[28] the Supreme Court assumed without deciding that a foreign state is a "person" for purposes of the Fifth Amendment, but cited *Katzenbach* in a footnote. The *Flatow* court argued that the *Katzenbach* footnote was an "invitation" to revisit the issue, arguing that "[i]f the States of the Union have no due process rights, then a foreign mission . . . surely can have none."

However, the *Katzenbach* decision is clearly distinguishable from the question presented in *Flatow*. First of all, in *Katzenbach*, South Carolina sought to invoke Due Process as a plaintiff seeking to invalidate an act of Congress. The issue in *Flatow* was whether Iran could invoke Due Process as an unwilling defendant. Second, South Carolina did not invoke Due Process by arguing that the claim had no nexus or connection with the United States. Instead, they argued that an Act of Congress aimed at eliminating racial discrimination in voting violated the State's Due Process right to have the question adjudicated in court.

Not only were the facts and issues different in *Katzenbach*, but the Court also rendered its decision with logic that is inapplicable to foreign states. For example, the *Katzenbach* court stated that to its knowledge, no court had ever found the meaning of person under the Fifth Amendment to include states of the union. This is certainly not true in the case of foreign states. The overwhelming and almost unanimous body of case law in lower courts has established that foreign states are persons for purposes of the Fifth Amendment. Also, *Katzenbach* reasoned that a state could not have standing to invoke constitutional rights, as the parent of its citizens, against the federal government because the federal government is the ultimate parens patriae of every American citizen. This, of course, is not true for all foreign states. Unlike the states of the United States, every foreign country is the ultimate

25. 203 U.S. 390 (1906).   **27.** 383 U.S. 301 (1966).
26. 316 U.S. 159, 162 (1942).   **28.** 504 U.S. 607, 619 (1992).

parent of its own citizens and should be permitted to invoke constitutional rights on their behalf.

3. *The Fifth Amendment "Person" Includes Foreign Entities*

Significantly, the Supreme Court has already found that due process rights are not necessarily domestic. The "person" referred to in the Due Process Clause includes foreign corporations and individuals that are not American citizens. In *Western and Southern Life Insurance Co. v. State Board of Equalization of California*,[29] the Supreme Court held that the "Equal Protection Clause imposes limits upon a [s]tate's power to condition the right of a foreign corporation to do business within its borders." Furthermore, in *United States v. Pink*,[30] the Supreme Court explicitly found that aliens, as well as citizens, are entitled to the due process protections of the Fifth Amendment. A logical extension of this holding is that foreign states, like foreign corporations, are persons entitled to due process protection.

Thus, the Supreme Court should find that a foreign state is a "person" for purposes of the Fifth Amendment. The Court has already found that various governmental bodies, both foreign and domestic, can fall within the legal meaning of person. The *Katzenbach* holding, that states of the union are not persons, is clearly distinguishable and inapplicable to the question regarding foreign states. For these reasons, Congress has never doubted the applicability of the Fifth Amendment to foreign states.

[B.] *Legislative Assumptions: Foreign States Have Due Process Rights*

The legislative history of both the FSIA and the earliest versions of the 1996 Amendment clearly indicate that Congress intended the Fifth Amendment Due Process Clause to apply to foreign states. Committee reports of both acts indicate that it was the purpose of Congress to craft legislation that asserted jurisdiction only over those foreign states that had minimum contacts with the United States.

The House Committee Report for the FSIA provides clear guidance on this issue, stating that section 1330(b) of the FSIA "provides, in effect, a federal long-arm statute over foreign states" patterned after the District of Columbia long-arm statute. The Report states under no uncertain terms that "[t]he requirements of minimum jurisdictional contacts and adequate notice are embodied in [1330(b)]." Clearly, the drafters of the FSIA believed the Fifth Amendment applied to foreign states, and the due process minimum contacts test placed additional limitations on a federal court's power to assert jurisdiction in international litigation.

The 1996 Amendment to the FSIA was part of a much larger terrorism package passed in the wake of the Oklahoma City Bombing. This may explain why the legislative history regarding Fifth Amendment limitations of the 1996 Amendment is virtually nonexistent. Nevertheless, the House Reports of two earlier versions[31] of the 1996 Amendment make it very clear that the amendment would assert personal jurisdiction, "subject to the Due Process Clause's requirement of 'minimum contacts.' "

---

29.   451 U.S. 648 (1981).

30.   315 U.S. 203, 226–28 (1942).

31.   H.R. Rep. No. 102–900, at 1–2 (1992); H.R. Rep. No. 103–702, at 1–2 (1994).

Thus, the drafters of both the FSIA and the earliest versions of the 1996 Amendment believed that the legislation embraced the principles of minimum contacts. Without a doubt, Congress never intended for the FSIA to permit courts to assert jurisdiction over foreign states that do not have minimum contacts with the United States.

[C.]   *The Case Law Extending Due Process Rights to Foreign States*

"If there is any reason to doubt that foreign sovereigns are protected by the Due Process Clause, it does not arise from the case law under the FSIA."[32] To date, the Supreme Court has only "assum[ed], without deciding that a foreign state is a person for purposes of the due process clause."[33] Nevertheless, the lower federal courts have almost unanimously found that a foreign state is entitled to Due Process protections requiring they have minimum contacts.

The principal case discussing personal jurisdiction over a foreign state is *Texas Trading & Milling Corp. v. Federal Republic of Nigeria*, decided just five years after the FSIA was enacted into law. In that case, the Republic of Nigeria, "developing at breakneck speed . . ., contracted to buy huge quantities of Portland cement," but later repudiated those contracts when its docks became so clogged with ships that all exports and imports ground to a halt.[34] The American cement companies sued for breach of contract and the Republic of Nigeria argued that the court lacked personal jurisdiction. The Second Circuit found that the FSIA "cannot create personal jurisdiction where the Constitution forbids it. Accordingly, each finding of personal jurisdiction under the FSIA requires, in addition, a due process scrutiny of the court's power to exercise its authority over a particular defendant."[35]

The *Texas Trading* decision has become the standard authority for the proposition that a foreign state is a person for purposes of the Fifth Amendment. As a result, courts confronted with FSIA cases have routinely cited the *Texas Trading* mantra and applied the traditional minimum contacts test. The *Texas Trading* view has become so ingrained in jurisprudence that it is cited as authoritative in the *Restatement of Foreign Relations Law*. Clearly, the lower courts have left their mark with consistent opinions of learned judges.

SECTION 5.   DISCUSSION NOTES/QUESTIONS

1.   As is discussed in the *Price & Frey* decision (Reading 7, *supra*), the amendment to the FSIA contained in the Antiterrorism and Effective Death Penalty Act of 1996 eliminates sovereign immunity only for specified state sponsors of terrorism. It does not provide for an affirmative cause of action against them. Congress provided an affirmative cause of action several months later in the so-called Flatow Amendment, but the specific language of the amendment referred to suits against individuals ("an official, employee, or agent of a foreign state designated as a state sponsor of terrorism"), not designated terrorist states themselves. The *Flatow* court, however, interpreted the Flatow Amendment to provide a cause of action against designated terrorist states:

32. Joseph W. Glannon & Jeffrey Atik, *Politics and Personal Jurisdiction: Suing State Sponsors of Terrorism Under the 1996 Amendments to the Foreign Sovereign Immunities Act*, 87 Geo. L.J. 675, 682 (1999).

33. Republic of Argentina v. Weltover, Inc., 504 U.S. 607, 619 (1992).

34. 647 F.2d at 300 (2d Cir. 1981).

35. *Id.* at 308.

The Flatow Amendment is apparently an independent pronouncement of law, yet it has been published as a note to 28 USC § 1605, and requires several references to 28 USC § 1605(a)(7) *et seq.* to reach even a preliminary interpretation. As it also effects a substantial change to 28 USC § 1605(a)(7), it appears to be an implied amendment.... The brief explanation of the Flatow Amendment's purpose in the House Conference Report explicitly states that it was intended to increase the measure of damages available in suits under 28 USC § 1605(a)(7). ... Both the Flatow Amendment and 28 USC § 1605(a)(7) address the same subject matter, and were enacted during the same session of Congress, only five months apart. Interpretation *in pari materia* is therefore the most appropriate approach to the construction of both provisions.... The amendment should be considered to relate back to the enactment of 28 USC § 1605(a)(7) as if they had been enacted as one provision.... and the two provisions should be construed together and in reference to one another. *Flatow v. Islamic Republic of Iran*, 999 F.Supp. 1, 21–24 (D.D.C. 1998).

Is the Court's logic persuasive? The DC Court of Appeals thought not. In 2004, in *Cicippio-Puleo v. Islamic Republic of Iran*, 353 F.3d 1024 (D.C. Cir. 2004), after years of hedging on this issue, the Court held definitively that Congress had created no private right of action against a foreign state. Because the District of Columbia has been the primary venue for cases alleging foreign state sponsorship of terrorism, this case is likely to be an impediment to the bringing of such cases in the future. *Cicippio-Puleo* did, however, leave open the possibility that plaintiffs could "state a cause of action under some other source of law, including state law." *Id* at 1036. Do you agree? Why? Why not?

2. The availability of a legally cognizable cause of action and the lack of absolute procedural obstacles (such as foreign sovereign immunity), is only the first step to achieving ultimate success in a civil lawsuit in the United States. Plaintiffs must, of course, win on the merits, and then if financial recompense is called for, the money judgment must be collected. If the defendant's financial assets do not exist within the jurisdiction of the presiding forum, a foreign court where the assets exist must be petitioned to "satisfy the judgment." If that court agrees to so satisfy the judgment, it will order the attachment of the local assets.

Not surprisingly the courts in the countries designated by the US Secretary of State as state sponsors of terrorism have been unwilling to order the attachment of their own state's assets. This has meant that the assets potentially available to satisfy a judgment against a foreign state for supporting terrorism have been those located in the United States. Such assets have broken down into two categories: First, diplomatic and consular properties, and second, state assets frozen by the United States government subsequent to previous breakdown in diplomatic relations.

Attempts by plaintiffs to attach either category of assets have met with considerable resistance by both the Clinton and Bush administrations. The executive branch has been concerned about the questionable international legality of using these assets to satisfy judicial judgments. This has been especially true of consular and diplomatic property. International legal issues aside, both administrations have also been conscious that there are many other competing demands for these assets, including the existence of other parties with potential claims. In addition, the United States has a longstanding practice of using frozen assets as leverage in negotiations to resume normal diplomatic relations. In this regard, both administrations have been concerned that in exchange for important concessions (perhaps involving support for terrorism), the United States might need to concede that frozen funds be returned to their state owners. If this were to happen the American tax payer would have to make up for any funds that had been drawn down to pay legal judgments. *See* Hearing of the Senate Foreign Relations Committee, 17 July 2003, testimony of William H. Taft IV, Legal Advisor, US Department of State.

As a result of the Executive Branch's obstructionism in allowing the attachment of assets in the United States, plaintiffs have sought specific legislative relief from a more ostensibly sympathetic US Congress. First, in the Justice for Victims of Terrorism Act, Congress provided that specific judgments for certain amounts should be paid. To avoid international legal problems the US treasury chose to pay judgments to Iran from another account with the hope of collecting from that country at a later date. Subsequently as part of an appropriations act in 2001 Congress attempted to designate that payments be made in one specific case originating from the Iranian hostage crisis of 1979. Because the Act had language arguably prohibiting such payment as inconsistent with the Algiers Accords (ending the hostage crisis) between the United States and Iran, it ultimately did not result in the outstanding judgment in that case being satisfied. Finally, Congress included a fairly general provision the Terrorism Risk Insurance Act of 2002 providing for payments to plaintiffs in terrorism related law suits. *But see Acree v. Snow*, 276 F.Supp.2d 31, 32 (D.D.C. 2003), aff'd, 78 Fed.Appx. 133 (D.C. Cir. 2003) (holding that as regards Iraq specifically the Executive's authority pursuant to the Emergency Wartime Supplemental Appropriations Act takes precedence over the Terrorism Risk Insurance Act).

3. As mentioned in Discussion Note/Question 1, *supra*, under 28 USC § 1605 (a) (7)(A) only claims against states designated by the Secretary of State as "state sponsors of terrorism" are actionable. As this coursebook goes to press, the following states have been so designated: Cuba, Iran, Libya, North Korea, Sudan and Syria. What was Congress' rationale for allowing only specific states to be subject to terrorism law suits? What potential problems might arise if Congress had allowed all states to be sued in US Courts for supporting terrorism? Does discriminating between states in this way politicize the judicial system? Those who believe that the anti-terrorism amendments to the Foreign Sovereign Immunities Act have interjected politics into the legal system point to the very large size of judgments that have been awarded under the amendments. For example, in *Alejandre v. Cuba,* 996 F.Supp. 1239 (S.D.Fla. 1997), the default judgment was $187 million. Default judgments against Iran have been $225 million [*Flatow v. Islamic Republic of Iran*, 999 F.Supp. 1, 34 (D.D.C. 1998)], $65 million [*Cicippio v. Islamic Republic of Iran*, 18 F.Supp.2d 62, 70 (D.D.C. 1998)], $342 million [*Anderson v. Islamic Republic of Iran*, 90 F.Supp.2d 107, 112–114 (D.D.C. 2000)], and $327 million [*Eisenfeld v. Islamic Republic of Iran*, 172 F.Supp.2d 1, 2 (D.D.C. 2000)]. If, in fact, the anti-terrorism amendments do represent something other than blind justice, is that necessarily a problem?

4. As is implicit in the language quoted from *The Schooner Exchange* in Reading 1, *supra,* part of the rationale for the doctrine of foreign sovereign immunity is that states as coequal entities inherently lack the authority to stand in judgment of one another. On a practical level one concern is that politics rather than law would dominate an interstate dispute resolution system where states come to mutually entertain suits against each other regarding matters of interstate conflict. Also, with no supreme arbiter to make definitive determinations such disputes could not be finally resolved. Is the rationale for the doctrine of foreign sovereign immunity that states lack the inherent authority to stand in

judgment of one another specifically relevant to whether or not foreign states should be allowed to be sued in national courts for supporting terrorism? To what extent do the above identified practical concerns militate against allowing suits against foreign states as supporters of terrorism in national courts? Perhaps, the willingness of the United States to entertain terrorism lawsuits against foreign states is itself strong evidence against the reality of the normative assumption that states are in fact coequal. To what extent might it be relevant that the United States' political, economic and military power put it in a class of its own? If you believe that the United States should uniquely entertain such suits is your rationale based on power, morality or a combination of the two? Does the following extract from the *Washington Post* (6 Apr 2003, p. F1) affect your thinking?

It turns out that Hossein Alikhani has a judgment to collect, too. He is owed $115 million for an ugly kidnapping episode. The guilty party? The United States. It happened in 1992, in the Bahamas. Alikhani got busted in a bungled sting operation by US customs agents. They knew he was a business-man looking for spare oil-field parts for Libya, a country under sanctions for supporting terrorism. So they set him up—posing as swank operators taking him on a luxury fishing trip—lured him onto a private jet, then popped out the handcuffs. He was hustled to a series of hotel rooms in Florida for interrogation, cuffed to the bed at night, then thrown in jail. Then it all blew up. The Bahamian government was furious, saying that the United States had "kidnapped" someone on its soil. Congress demanded answers.

Alikhani copped a plea to a token charge and walked out of jail after three months. And there the case might have died, had it not been for a flood of lawsuits by American victims of terrorism against Iran and a handful of other nations. They infuriated Alikhani.

He likes Americans—he runs the Center for World Dialogue, a Cyprus-based organization that gets American and Iranian citizens to talk face to face—but thinks his Yankee friends tend to look at the world with blinders on. These allow Americans to see their own pain but not the suffering their lumbering nation sometimes causes, he says.

So he flew home to Tehran last year, filed a suit against the United States for "kidnapping" him and, bam, won the first lawsuit by an Iranian against the United States for supporting terrorism. "Kidnapping, false impris-onment, using force, battering, abusing and ultimately inflicting physical and psychological injuries," wrote Chief Justice Mansour Pour Nouri of the Third Branch of the Tehran Public Court, describing the conduct of US investiga-tors. "The acts of United States officials ... ran counter to Articles 5, 6, 8, 11 and 12 of the Universal Declaration of Human Rights [**Basic Document 3.3**] and the provisions of the International Covenant on Civil and Political Rights"[**Basic Document 3.14**].

Alikhani says his case "opens the floodgates" for suits against the United States. "Iran supports terrorism, yes, but so does the US," he says. "The US supported a coup in Iran in 1953, so the survivors or descendants of those victims can sue. Is there any doubt Saddam is a terrorist? Doesn't President Bush say so daily? Saddam used chemical weapons against us in the Iran–Iraq war. The US supported him. So the US has supported a terrorist, and the Iranian victims of those attacks can now sue. We're talking about billions and billions of dollars in damages."

The point, Alikhani is saying, is that the spate of antiterrorism lawsuits in the United States is not a blow against faceless killers but an exercise in bad diplomacy. He espouses a litigious detente: You sue us, we sue you. You seize our assets, we seize yours.

5.   Might terrorism based civil cases be better resolved by an international court of some sort. To what extent do the rules of the new International Criminal Court allow for individuals responsible for terrorism to be tried before it? *See supra* Chapter 3.

6.   Andrew Strauss (*supra* Reading 5) argues that the American constitutional framers assumed that the international law of jurisdiction should apply to domestic cases involving foreign defendants or plaintiffs. Is Professor Strauss' case made stronger or weaker when the foreign defendant happens, as in the present problem, to be a state? If the international law of jurisdiction should be applied to cases involving domestic jurisdiction over foreign states, then what is the international law that should be applied? Is it the legal rules identified in the Restatement (*supra* Reading 6) or does/should international law have a different test for sovereign states? What role, if any, should the specifically international rules codified by the International Law Commission regarding sovereign immunity play (*supra* Reading 3)? Finally, Professor Strauss bases his argument on what the constitutional framers intended. Can you think of a logical/theoretical argument that the intention of the framers of the Constitution should be irrelevant to whether or not the international law of jurisdiction applies to international cases? In considering your answer to this question think about whether there are or should be any limits to the ability of countries to define the extent of their own international jurisdiction?

7.   In the *Price* case (*supra* Reading 7), the US Court of Appeals for the District of Columbia premised its analysis on the assumption that Libya did not have minimum contacts with the United States. Is this necessarily true? How could the *Price* court have side-stepped the difficult constitutional question of whether states have due process rights and still reached the same result? Could it be argued that states always have minimum contacts with each other? Consider part of the Court's opinion in *Flatow v. Islamic Republic of Iran,* 999 F.Supp. 1 (D.D.C. 1998):

> Even in the absence of diplomatic relations, state actors, as a matter of necessity, have substantial sovereign contact with each other. They inherently interact as state actors in the international community and as members of the United Nations.... This Court concludes that even if a foreign state is accorded the status of a "person" for the purposes of Constitutional Due Process analysis, a foreign state that sponsors terrorist activities which causes [sic] the death or personal injury of a United States national will invariably have sufficient contacts with the United States to satisfy Due Process. *Id* at 59.

8.   In the present case, plaintiffs filed suit in the Southern District of New York, rather than in Washington D.C., where Narbonna's embassy property was located, or another jurisdiction. When the personal jurisdiction of a federal court is at issue, these courts have interpreted the general language of Rule 4 of the Federal Rules of Civil Procedure to direct them to apply the long-arm provision of the federal legislation being substantively applied, if such a provision exists. Such provisions have generally been interpreted to provide that contacts with the United States as a whole (national contacts) rather than with any particular US state, is sufficient to establish the personal jurisdiction of the federal forum. The

non-state specific language of the Foreign Sovereign Immunities Act implies that, to the extent contacts are needed, national contacts are sufficient. *See* Graham C.Lilly, *Jurisdiction Over Domestic and Alien Defendants*, 69 Va. L. Rev. 85, 130 (1983), stating at 130 that the FSIA **(Basic Document 6.2)**, "makes it reasonably clear that national—not state—contacts are decisive." In federal question cases where there is no applicable long-arm statute Rule 4(K)(2) of the Federal Rules of Civil Procedure specifically prescribes that if the foreign defendant does not have sufficient contacts with any individual state, but does have the requisite national contacts under the Due Process Clause of the Fifth Amendment, any federal court can assert personal jurisdiction. Although the Supreme Court has yet to rule on the constitutionality of national contacts, the lower federal courts have generally upheld the approach. *See SEC v. Carrillo,* 115 F.3d 1540, 1543 (11th Cir. 1997) (upholding the constitutionality of the national contacts approach and citing six other circuits as in accord).

9. *Bibliographical Note.* For supplemental discussion concerning the principal themes addressed in this problem, consult the following additional specialized materials:

(a) *Books/Monographs/Report/Symposia.* A. Dikinson, R. Lindsay, & J. P. Loonam, State Immunity: Selected Materials and Commentary (2004); H. Fox, The Law of State Immunity (Foundations of Public International Law) (2003); A. Gerson & J. Adler, The Price of Terror. One Bomb. One Plane. 270 Lives. The History–Making Struggle for Justice After Pan Am 103 (2000); P. Jan Slot, M. Bulterman, Globalisation and Jurisdiction (2004); M. S. O'Sullivan, Shrewd Sanctions: Statecraft and State Sponsors of Terrorism (2003); S. Ratner & J. Abrams, Accountability for Human Rights Atrocities in International Law: Beyond the Nuremberg Legacy (2nd ed. 2001).

(b) *Articles/Book Chapters.* J. Dellapenna, *Civil Remedies for International Terrorism,* 12 DePaul Bus. L. J. 169; R. M. Deutsch, *Suing State–Sponsors of Terrorism Under the Foreign Sovereign Immunities Act: Giving Life to the Jurisdictional Grant After Cicippio–Pule,* 38 Int'l Law. 891 (2004); J. Glannon & J Atik, *Politics and Personal Jurisdiction: Suing State Sponsors of Terrorism Under the 1996 Amendments to the Foreign Sovereign Immunities Act,* 87 Geo.L. J. 675 (1999); W. Heiser, *Civil Litigation as a Means of Compensating Victims of International Terrorism,* 3 San Diego Int'l L. J. 1 (2002); W. Hoye, *Fighting Fire With ... Mire? Civil Remedies and the New War on State–Sponsored Terrorism,* 12 Duke J. Comp. & Int'l L. 105 (2002); F. McKay, *US Unilateralism and International Crimes: The International Criminal Court and Terrorism,* 36 Cornell Int'l L. J. 455(2004); D. Mostaghel, *Wrong Place, Wrong Time, Unfair Treatment? Aid to Victims of Terrorist Attacks,* 40 Brandeis L. J. 83 (2001); J. Murphy, *Civil Liability for the Commission of International Crimes as an Alternative to Criminal Prosecution,* 12 Harv. Hum. Rts. J. 1 (1999); E. Re, *The Universal Declaration of Human Rights: Effective Remedies and the Domestic Courts,* 33 Cal. W. Int'l L. J. 137 (2003); K. Sealing, *"State Sponsors of Terrorism" is a Question, Not an Answer: The Terrorism Amendment to the FSIA Makes Less Sense Now Than It Did Before 9/11,* 38 Tex. Int'l L.J. 119 (2003); H. Sommer, *Providing Compensation for Harm Caused by Terrorism: Lessons Learned in the Israeli Experience,* 36 Ind. L. Rev. 335 (2003).

Problem 6–4

The UFC and the EU Dispute the
GATT and Global Warming

Section 1.   Facts

The United Federation of Columbia (UFC) is an advanced industrial country in North America with a population of 150 million people. Responsible for over 25% of aggregate greenhouse gas emission, the UFC is one of the world's major contributors of greenhouse gases, both on an absolute and per capita basis. Greenhouse gases are a major cause of global warming which, in turn, could cause catastrophic changes to the earth's ecological system.

In 1992 at the Rio Conference on Trade and the Environment, most of the countries of the world adopted the United Nations Framework Convention on Climate Change (UNFCCC) pursuant to which advanced industrialized countries committed themselves to greenhouse gas emission reduction targets, the UFC among them. The UFC was one of the original signatories of the Convention and was early to ratify it as well. The UNFCCC, however, set no binding limits on greenhouse gases, so that, five years later, under the auspices of the regime established by the Convention, and after long and difficult negotiations, the states parties to the Convention concluded a protocol to it commonly known as the "Kyoto Protocol."[a] Under the Kyoto Protocol, the industrialized states parties to it bound themselves to adopt greenhouse gas emission reduction targets that they determined to be legally binding.

Toward the end of the Kyoto Protocol negotiations, federal elections in the UFC resulted in the conservative government of Prime Minister Benjamin Compton taking office. During his campaign for office, candidate Compton had argued that global warming was "far more hype than threat," and that "compliance with the Kyoto Protocol would be too expensive for the UFC." Once in office, the Compton government refused to sign or ratify the Kyoto Protocol. On 16 February 2005, however, following its ratification by the Russian Federation and despite the UFC refusal, the Kyoto Protocol entered into force and became binding on its then 128 states parties.

Not long after, under internal pressure from domestic producers, the European Union ("EU") resolved to take retaliatory trade action against the UFC for its failure to join the Kyoto Protocol. At this time, without consulting with the UFC, the EU Council, acting on a recommendation of the European Commission, decided to approve a recently proposed EU Kyoto Enforcement

---

a.   *See* Basic Document 5.48.

886

Regime ("KER"),[b] providing for the imposition of trade sanctions against countries that either do not become parties to the Kyoto Protocol or who become parties to it but do not comply with their obligations under it ("Non–Conforming Countries"). Under the KER, EU member countries are to ban imports from Non–Conforming Countries that have been manufactured in ways that contribute "disproportionately" to global warming. Whenever the average emissions of greenhouse gases for a particular industry in a Non–Conforming Country exceeds industry-wide the industry-wide average for the same industry within the EU by more than 10%, the importation of goods produced by that industry into European Union countries will be disallowed.

The European Commission, moving quickly to implement the KER, established a schedule of UFC goods that it pronounced subject to an immediate import ban. The UFC, alleging the KER to be in violation of the GATT,[c] responded by threatening trade retaliation against the EU and requesting the World Trade Organization ("WTO") to constitute a trade panel to decide the matter.[d] All parties consented and a panel was commissioned.[e]

SECTION 2.   QUESTIONS PRESENTED

1. Did the European Union's actions placing a ban on certain UFC imports constitute a violation of international law?

2. In any event, are there any additional or alternative legal norms, procedures, and/or institutions to be recommended that might further help to prevent or discourage situations of the kind posed by this problem?

---

b. The Kyoto Enforcement Regime is fictional.

c. The GATT referred to here is the General Agreement on Tariffs and Trade 1994 (**Basic Document 4.14**) in combination with the General Agreement on Tariffs and Trade of 30 Oct 1947 (**Basic Document 4.3**). One of several instruments incorporated by reference in, and annexed to, the 1994 Agreement Establishing the WTO, *infra* note **c**, GATT 1994, in turn, incorporates GATT 1947, including all changes made to GATT 1947 prior to the entry into force of the 1994 WTO agreement and six "understandings" on the interpretation of various GATT provisions that were agreed to at the Uruguay Round of trade negotiations. Fundamentally, GATT 1994 is GATT 1947 renamed. If GATT 1947 had remained in force, countries could have declined to sign on to the WTO agreement yet benefitted from its provisions by invoking their most-favored-nation (MFN) rights under GATT 1947. The solution was to replace GATT 1947 with GATT 1994, make GATT 1994 part of the WTO agreement, and then have all countries who join the WTO agreement withdraw from GATT 1947. Thus,

no country wishing to continue receiving the benefits of GATT law could do so without joining the WTO and having GATT 1994 applied to it. However, the amended GATT fails to address explicitly the issue of "unrelated" extrajurisdictional trade sanctions, such as those imposed by the EU in this problem, leaving resolution of that matter unsettled. The readings that follow therefore encompass the emerging law on this issue, the GATT's reform notwithstanding.

d. The WTO panels are provided for by the 1994 Understanding on Rules and Procedures Governing the Settlement of Disputes (**Basic Document 4.16**). The Understanding is one of several instruments incorporated by reference in, and annexed to, the 1994 Agreement Establishing the World Trade Organization, *reprinted in* 33 I.L.M. 1144 (1994) and 5 Weston & Carlson IV.C.2a.

e. For the procedural details, see the Understanding on Rules and Procedures Governing the Settlement of Disputes, (**Basic Document 4.16**), *supra* note **c**, especially Articles 2(1), 3, 6, 11, 16(4), 17(1) & (14), and 21(1) thereof.

Section 3. Assignments

A. Reading Assignment

Study the Readings presented in Section 4, *infra*, and the Discussion Notes/Questions that follow. Also, time permitting, consult the accompanying bibliographical references.

B. Recommended Writing Assignment

Prepare a comprehensive, logically sequenced, and *argumentative* brief in the form of an outline of the primary and subsidiary *legal* issues you see requiring resolution by the WTO panel. Also, from the perspective of an independent judge, indicate which side ought to prevail on each issue and why. Retain a copy of your issue-outline/brief for class discussion.

C. Recommended Oral Assignment

Assume you are legal counsel for the UFC or the European Union (as designated by your instructor); then, relying upon the Readings (and your issue-outline if prepared), present a 10–15 minute oral argument of your government's likely positions before the WTO panel.

D. Recommended Reflective Assignment

Consider (and recommend) alternative norms, institutions, and/or procedures that you believe might do better than existing world order arrangements to contend with situations of the kind posed by this problem. In so doing, but without insisting upon *immediate* feasibility, identify the particular transition steps that would be needed to make your alternatives a reality.

Section 4. Readings

The following readings are considered *prima facie* relevant to solving this problem. They are your law library for present purposes and should be treated as such, organized intelligibly for "shelving" and not necessarily according to the issues presented. Be sure to review Chapter 2 ("International Legal Prescription: The 'Sources' of International Law") in your consideration of them. It, too, should be treated as part of your law library (as, indeed, should this entire coursebook).

1. Third Assessment Report of the Intergovernmental Panel on Climate Change, Report of Working Group 1, Summary for Policymakers 2–7 (Robert T. Watson ed., 2001).[f]

The Third Assessment Report of Working Group I of the Intergovernmental Panel on Climate Change (IPCC) builds upon past assessments and incorporates new results from the past five years of research on climate change. Many hundreds of scientists from many countries participated in its preparation and review.

This Summary for Policymakers (SPM), which was approved by IPCC member governments in Shanghai in January 2001 describes the current

---

f. Graphs and tables omitted.

state of understanding of the climate system and provides estimates of its projected future evolution and their uncertainties. . . .

* * *

The global average surface temperature (the average of near surface air temperature over land, and sea surface temperature) has increased since 1861. Over the 20th century the increase has been 0.6 ± 0.2°C. . . . The record shows a great deal of variability; for example, most of the warming occurred during the 20th century, during two periods, 1910 to 1945 and 1976 to 2000.

Globally, it is very likely that the 1990s was the warmest decade and 1998 the warmest year in the instrumental record, since 1861.

New analyses of proxy data for the Northern Hemisphere indicate that the increase in temperature in the 20th century is likely to have been the largest of any century during the past 1,000 years. It is also likely that, in the Northern Hemisphere, the 1990s was the warmest decade and 1998 the warmest year. Because less data are available, less is known about annual averages prior to 1,000 years before present and for conditions prevailing in most of the Southern Hemisphere prior to 1861.

On average, between 1950 and 1993, night-time daily minimum air temperatures over land increased by about 0.2°C per decade. This is about twice the rate of increase in daytime daily maximum air temperatures (0.1°C per decade). This has lengthened the freeze-free season in many mid- and high latitude regions. The increase in sea surface temperature over this period is about half that of the mean land surface air temperature. . . .

* * *

Since the start of the satellite record in 1979, both satellite and weather balloon measurements show that the global average temperature of the lowest 8 kilometres of the atmosphere has changed by +0.05 ± 0.10°C per decade, but the global average surface temperature has increased significantly by +0.15 ± 0.05°C per decade. The difference in the warming rates is statistically significant. This difference occurs primarily over the tropical and subtropical regions. . . .

* * *

Satellite data show that there are very likely to have been decreases of about 10% in the extent of snow cover since the late 1960s, and ground-based observations show that there is very likely to have been a reduction of about two weeks in the annual duration of lake and river ice cover in the mid- and high latitudes of the Northern Hemisphere, over the 20th century.

There has been a widespread retreat of mountain glaciers in non-polar regions during the 20th century.

Northern Hemisphere spring and summer sea-ice extent has decreased by about 10 to 15% since the 1950s. It is likely that there has been about a 40% decline in Arctic sea-ice thickness during late summer to early autumn in recent decades and a considerably slower decline in winter sea-ice thickness.

Tide gauge data show that global average sea level rose between 0.1 and 0.2 metres during the 20th century.

Global ocean heat content has increased since the late 1950s, the period for which adequate observations of sub-surface ocean temperatures have been available.

It is very likely that precipitation has increased by 0.5 to 1% per decade in the 20th century over most mid- and high latitudes of the Northern Hemisphere continents, and it is likely that rainfall has increased by 0.2 to 0.3% per decade over the tropical (10°N to 10°S) land areas. Increases in the tropics are not evident over the past few decades. It is also likely that rainfall has decreased over much of the Northern Hemisphere sub-tropical (10°N to 30°N) land areas during the 20th century by about 0.3% per decade. In contrast to the Northern Hemisphere, no comparable systematic changes have been detected in broad latitudinal averages over the Southern Hemisphere. There are insufficient data to establish trends in precipitation over the oceans.

In the mid- and high latitudes of the Northern Hemisphere over the latter half of the 20th century, it is likely that there has been a 2 to 4% increase in the frequency of heavy precipitation events. Increases in heavy precipitation events can arise from a number of causes, *e.g.*, changes in atmospheric moisture, thunderstorm activity and large-scale storm activity.

It is likely that there has been a 2% increase in cloud cover over mid-to-high latitude land areas during the 20th century. In most areas the trends relate well to the observed decrease in daily temperature range.

* * *

A few areas of the globe have not warmed in recent decades, mainly over some parts of the Southern Hemisphere oceans and parts of Antarctica.

No significant trends of Antarctic sea-ice extent are apparent since 1978, the period of reliable satellite measurements.

Changes globally in tropical and extra-tropical storm intensity and frequency are dominated by inter-decadal to multi-decadal variations, with no significant trends evident over the 20th century. Conflicting analyses make it difficult to draw definitive conclusions about changes in storm activity, especially in the extra-tropics.

No systematic changes in the frequency of tornadoes, thunder days, or hail events are evident in the limited areas analysed.

Changes in climate occur as a result of both internal variability within the climate system and external factors (both natural and anthropogenic)....

The atmospheric concentration of carbon dioxide (CO_2) has increased by 31% since 1750. The present CO_2 concentration has not been exceeded during the past 420,000 years and likely not during the past 20 million years. The current rate of increase is unprecedented during at least the past 20,000 years.

About three-quarters of the anthropogenic emissions of CO_2 to the atmosphere during the past 20 years is due to fossil fuel burning. The rest is predominantly due to land-use change, especially deforestation.

2.   General Agreement on Tariffs and Trade (GATT 1947). Concluded, 30 Oct 1947. Entered into force (provisionally), 1 Jan 1948. 55 U.N.T.S. 187; *reprinted in* **5 Weston & Carlson IV.C.1: Arts. I, III, IX, XI, XX, and Ad Art. III** (Basic Document 4.3).

3.   General Agreement on Tariffs and Trade 1994 (GATT 1994). Concluded, 15 Apr 1994. Entered into force, 1 Jan 1995. *Reprinted in* **33 I.L.M. 1154 (1994) and 5 Weston & Carlson IV.C.2b: Art. 1** (Basic Document 4.14).

4.   John H. Jackson, "World Trade Rules and Environmental Policies: Congruence or Conflict?," 49 Wash. & Lee L. Rev. 1227, 1230–31 (1992).

The most significant and widespread rule system for international trade is the GATT system * * *. The basic policy underlying the GATT (and the broader "Bretton Woods System" established in 1944–1948) is well known. The objective is to liberalize trade that crosses national boundaries, and to pursue the benefits described in economic theory as "comparative advantage" [which] relates partly to the theories of economies of scale. When nations specialize, they become more efficient in producing a product (and possibly also a service). If they can trade their products or services for the different products or services that other countries specialize in producing, then all parties involved will be better off because countries will not waste resources producing products that other countries can produce more efficiently. The international rules are designed to restrain governmental interference with this type of trade.

5.   William J. Davey, "Symposium: International Economic Conflict and Resolution: The World Trade Organization's Dispute Settlement System," 42 S. Tex L. Rev. 1199, 1199–1203 (2001).

In the WTO, [an effective system of dispute resolution] is provided by the Dispute Settlement Understanding **[Basic Document 4.16].** As stated in the DSU, the dispute settlement system of the WTO is a central element in providing security and predictability to the multilateral trading system. In reality, in the commercial world, such security and predictability are viewed as fundamental prerequisites to conducting business internationally.

The DSU is effectively an interpretation and elaboration of GATT Article XXIII. This Article was the basis for dispute settlement in GATT, the predecessor organization of the WTO. The GATT dispute settlement system was relatively successful, as instruments of state-to-state dispute settlement go. It was active; there were far more disputes that went through it than the International Court of Justice during the same period, and it was reasonably effective in resolving disputes. Typically, eighty to ninety percent of complainants that were legitimate had their complaint totally or partially resolved in the system. . . .

* * *

In describing the WTO process, I will try to indicate how it solves these problems of delay, blocking of results, and resort to unilateral measures. As to unilateralism, part of the DSU contains a commitment that the members of the WTO will use only the WTO dispute settlement system to resolve their WTO disputes. Thus, taking unilateral action with respect to a WTO dispute without having gone through the WTO system would be a violation of WTO rules.

Now I will examine the four phases of WTO dispute settlement: consultation, the panel process, the appellate process, and surveillance of implementation of the results. First, as to consultations under the WTO procedures, a Member may ask for consultation with another WTO Member if the complaining Member believes that the other Member has violated a WTO agreement or otherwise nullified or impaired benefits that should have accrued to the complaining Member. Note that private parties have no access to the system. It is a system of state-to-state dispute settlement. The goal of the consultation stage is to enable the disputing parties to better understand the background of the dispute, to understand the legal claims that each side is making, and, hopefully, to resolve the matter without the need to resort to panel proceedings. In fact, the DSU states that the aim of the dispute settlement mechanism is to secure a positive solution to a dispute. A mutually acceptable solution to the parties of the dispute, which is consistent with the WTO agreements, is clearly preferred. The manner in which the consultations are conducted is up to the parties. Despite the fact that the consultations are somewhat undefined, statistics indicate that roughly one-half of the matters that are brought to consultation are either resolved, settled at that stage, or abandoned. So roughly one-half of the cases are weeded out of the system through the consultation requirement.

The second stage in the dispute settlement system is the panel process. If consultations fail to resolve the dispute within sixty days, the complaining party can request what is called the Dispute Settlement Body to establish a panel to consider the dispute. The DSB is composed of all WTO members. It is the WTO body that is in charge of the operation of the dispute settlement system. Under the rules of the DSU, if requested, the DSB must establish a panel to consider the dispute at the second meeting at which the request is made, unless there is a consensus to the contrary. Thus, unless the member requesting the panel consents to the delay of the establishment of the panel, the panel will be established within about ninety days of the initial request for consultations.

* * *

The function of the panel is to make an objective assessment of the matter before it, which includes an analysis of the facts and the legal issues.... After it completes the fact-finding and hearing phase, the panel issues what is called an interim report. This interim report is its proposed result. The parties are allowed to comment on that result, and they may ask the panel to grant them one more hearing. The panels virtually never change the ultimate result between the interim report and the final report they issue, although occasionally there are some significant changes in the language used in the report.

* * *

After the panel report has been circulated to the WTO membership, it is referred to the DSB for formal adoption. This is to take place within sixty days of the issuance of the report unless there is a consensus not to adopt the report or there is an appeal. Now the so-called negative consensus rule, which was the same with respect to panel establishment, is a fundamental change from the GATT system, where a positive consensus was needed to adopt the report. The negative consensus rule—that is, the report will be adopted unless there is a consensus to the contrary—effectively means that as long as somebody wants the report adopted, and presumably the winner will, the report will be adopted. So the problem of blockage has been solved. But, as I mentioned, there is an alternative to having the report adopted, and that is an appeal.

Now we turn to the third stage of the process, the appellate process. An appeal can be made to the Appellate Body.... The job of the Appellate Body is limited to reviewing issues of law and legal interpretation developed by the panel. The Appellate Body, though, has taken a broad view of its power to review panel decisions and has typically reviewed them rather thoroughly. It has the express power to reverse, modify, or affirm panel decisions. There is no possibility of remand, and, as a result, the Appellate Body will address issues it thinks will resolve the case if it significantly modifies the panel opinion.[g] . . .

6. Andrew Strauss, "From GATTZILLA to the Green Giant: Winning the Environmental Battle for the Soul of the World Trade Organization," 19 U. Pa. J. Int'l Econ. L. 769, 776–805 (1998).

2. THE FRAMEWORK: THE GATT, THE WTO, AND THE POROUS BOUNDARIES SEPARATING TRADE AND ENVIRONMENTAL REGULATION

2.1. The History and Function of the GATT and the WTO

The sixty-four year time-line leading to the establishment of the WTO began with Congressional passage of the Smoot–Hawley Tariff Act in 1930.[1] Smoot–Hawley dramatically increased United States tariffs on foreign goods, triggering retaliatory tariff increases by other countries. In the eyes of American and British post-war planners, these increases caused a contraction in international trade, greatly exacerbating the depression of the 1930s. They saw the resulting economic turmoil, particularly in Germany, as a major contributing cause of the Second World War. In their attempts to learn the lessons of history, the post-war planners ultimately succeeded in establishing a global trade regime. This regime, the GATT, was designed to discourage governments from pursuing policies which placed imports from foreign countries at a disadvantage relative either to domestically produced goods or goods produced in other foreign countries.

The primary rules promoting this objective were the following: (1) Article I, the "Most Favored Nation" provision which required that countries not discriminate in trading between foreign nations; (2) Article III, the "National Treatment" provision, which required that countries not discriminate against foreign importers in establishing or applying domestic regulations; and (3) Article XI which prohibited (subject to exceptions) the use of quantitative restrictions, such as quotas, on the import of foreign goods.

The post-war planners only intended that the GATT provide substantive trade rules. They did not intend for it to endure as an international organization. An institutional structure was to be created in a separate treaty

g. The weight of scholarly opinion holds that neither decisions by panels nor the Appellate Body create binding precedent that must be followed in future cases.

1. Pub. L. No. 71–361, 46 Stat. 590 (1930).

establishing what was to be called the International Trade Organization ("ITO"). As a result of opposition within the United States Congress, however, this agreement never came into being and the GATT was left to assume, by default, the administrative burdens created by the growth of international trade. Rising to this challenge, the GATT took on the responsibilities of an international organization. Acting in this capacity, over the years, it sponsored a series of multilateral negotiations which succeeded in virtually eliminating tariffs on manufactured goods. Under the GATT, international trade has increased dramatically during the last half century.

By 1986 most of the countries in the world had signed the GATT and had become members of the Organization. That year, in Punta del Este, Uruguay, these members initiated the most ambitious round of trade negotiations ever undertaken. In 1994, after eight years of discussion, the Uruguay Round finally came to an end with the establishment of the WTO, a de jure international trade organization. Today, the WTO administers the trading rules established by the GATT, as well as several other trade related agreements, that resulted from the Uruguay Round. These include agreements related to trade in services and the protection of intellectual property.

2.2.   *Emergence and Scope of International Environmental Law*

The early 1970s saw the emergence of, or what appeared to be at the time, the distinct area of international environmental law. The seminal event was the 1972 Stockholm Conference on the Human Environment. In addition to catalyzing the international environmental movement, the Stockholm Conference succeeded in articulating a statement of fundamental international environmental principles known as the Stockholm Declaration, and in serving as the impetus for the United Nations Environment Programme ("UNEP"). In the ensuing years, multilateral environmental agreements ("MEAs") were promulgated in a wide variety of areas, including the protection of plant and animal species, the climate, and waste disposal.

2.3.   *The Overlap Between Trade and Environmental Regulation*

As I will explain shortly, powerful state and commercial interests are committed to the ideological proposition that the regime that regulates international trade should not concern itself with the environment. Such ideology notwithstanding, the regulatory spheres governed by international trade law and international environmental law have increasingly come to converge. The first reason for this convergence has been the increasing use of trade restrictive measures in MEAs. For example, the Convention on the International Trade in Endangered Species requires signatories to prohibit importation of certain species that are threatened with extinction. This presents a potential conflict between GATT rules (guaranteeing free trade) and environmental rules (promoting species survival).

The second reason for this convergence has been the tendency of some countries to resort to unilateral trade restrictions in order to remedy what they perceive to be extrajurisdictional environmental infractions. The best known examples of this have been American attempts to restrict the import of foreign tuna that are caught outside of US territorial waters in ways that kill large numbers of dolphins, and of shrimp caught outside of US waters in ways that kill a large number of endangered sea turtles. Such unilateral attempts to promote global environmental norms come into conflict with GATT-based provisions designed to ensure that foreign "products" are allowed access to domestic markets.

This creation of both international and domestic environmental law that impacts international trade is based on an increasing understanding of the profound link that exists between global trade and the global environment. The extent to which this link justifies giving the WTO a role in environmental regulation is the topic to which we will now turn.

3. THE RELATIONSHIP BETWEEN THE WORLD TRADE ORGANIZATION AND THE ENVIRONMENT

3.1. *The Case for Environmental Sovereignty*

In order to understand the environmentalist criticism of the WTO, some knowledge of the WTO's historic position on the link between trade and the environment is necessary. Many of the industry and developing country supporters of free trade argue that the WTO should respect and even protect what I will call the "environmental sovereignty" of its members. They claim that in fulfilling its mandate to promote free trade, the Organization should not interfere or allow interference with what they consider to be the entirely domestic concern of deciding the appropriate level of local environmental protection. Poorer countries they claim, for example, might well wish to tolerate higher levels of environmental degradation in exchange for certain economic benefits and should be left free to do so. This is an application of the still dominant view of state sovereignty, which asserts that states should be left free to regulate all matters of human activity within their territories.

The GATT's articles ... work to protect the thus described "environmental sovereignty" of its members.... Nothing in the WTO Agreement provides for the imposition of substantive environmental standards on countries, and the Organization does not presently attempt to do this.

Two provisions circumscribing the permissible scope of domestic regulation are particularly important. Article III establishes what is called "the National Treatment" standard. Generally, this allows countries to require that foreign products conform to domestic regulations as long as such regulations treat foreign products no less favorably than like domestically produced goods. The other important provision, Article XX, allows for GATT inconsistent measures (specifically, for the purposes of this Article, to protect human, animal, or plant life or health, or to conserve exhaustible natural resources) as long as such measures do not arbitrarily or unjustifiably discriminate between countries where the same conditions prevail, or restrict international trade.

[Those committed to environmental sovereignty] have interpreted these two articles to mean that states can require environmental health and safety standards for foreign manufactured imports, but may not use trade measures in an attempt to impose their own standards on the off-shore production processes used to fabricate such products. Thus, for example, (subject to what has become a major exception[2]) [this view would hold that] the United States

---

2. This exception is found in the SPS Agreement [*i.e.*, Agreement on the Application of Sanitary and Phytosanitary Measures, in WTO Agreement, 15 Apr 1994, Marrakesh Agreement Establishing the World Trade Or- ganization, Annex 1A, *in* World Trade Organization, The Legal Texts: The Results of the Uruguay Round of Multilateral Trade Negotiations 59 (1999)]. The agreement sets limits on states' ability to restrict imports that are not

may impose any limits on automobile emissions that it desires, as long as it does not establish more burdensome standards for imported cars than for domestic cars. It may not, however, restrict the import of cars from foreign nations based upon the amount of effluents that car factories inside those countries are releasing into the air.

3.2. *Responding to the Case for Environmental Sovereignty*

Environmentalists are justifiably critical of this approach. The WTO's limited mission does not, in fact, leave each state free to choose its own level of ecological welfare. This is so for several reasons. We are increasingly coming to understand that the whole of the earth's biosphere is ecologically interconnected and that seemingly isolated damage to local environments has complex and deleterious effects throughout the planetary system, though these effects may be difficult to observe. Sometimes, so-called domestic pollution can have quite obvious effects beyond national borders. Those emissions from automobile assembly plants in foreign nations contribute to global warming and may be a cause of air pollution and/or acid rain in neighboring countries. The danger to the earth's ozone layer is caused by chlorofluorocarbons ("CFCs") regardless of the country in which they are produced or used. Deforestation, especially the destruction of tropical rain forests, has obvious effects on the global climate, as well as on the planet's biological diversity. Intensifying these global environmental problems, one of the main purposes of WTO-supported free trade is to promote economic growth. Such growth will result in increased industrial activity, and without enhanced pollution controls, this will result in more degradation to the global environment.

There is another important reason that the WTO's promotion of free trade does not leave each state free to choose its own level of ecological welfare. By establishing the preconditions for free trade, the Organization facilitates the unleashing of an environmentally destructive global regulatory and economic dynamic that is beyond the power of individual states to curtail.

This is true because free trade furthers a so-called regulatory "race to the bottom," whereby independent national regulatory regimes are all forced to lower their environmental standards. In the contemporary world of relatively free trade, promoted by the WTO, and open capital markets, free-flowing capital gravitates towards global export operations in those places where the cost of meeting regulatory burdens are the lowest and profits are the highest. In what has become a global regulatory market place, states are forced to

in compliance with domestic environmental standards, thereby undermining the claim that the WTO supports environmental sovereignty. Under the SPS Agreement, WTO member states have the right to take sanitary and phytosanitary measures that are "necessary" for the protection of human and animal health. *See* SPS Agreement art. 2:2. One of the requirements that must be fulfilled is that the measure must be based on "scientific principles" and "sufficient scientific evidence." *Id.* Recently, a WTO dispute resolution panel found a European Union regulation banning (for health reasons) the domestic selling of beef that is hormone fed not to be based on scienti- fic evidence. The WTO found the European Union in violation of its treaty obligations despite the fact that the regulation banning hormones was applied to domestic and foreign beef alike. *See* Report of the 1997 Panel on the EC, Measures Concerning Meat and Meat Products (Hormones), WT/0S26/R/USA (18 Aug 1997). For further discussion of the SPS agreement and its effect on the environment, see John J. Barcelo, *Product Standards to Protect the Local Environment—the GATT and the Uruguay Round Sanitary and Phytosanitary Agreement*, 27 Cornell Int'l L.J. 755, 769 (1994).

relax domestic environmental regulations while attempting to out-bid each other to attract jobs and tax revenues. A systematic reduction of global environmental standards is the result.

A second related concern is competitiveness. Within a globalized system of free trade, companies that operate in countries with stricter environmental regulations will tend to be burdened by higher production costs and will, therefore, have difficulty selling their goods at prices which are competitive with firms which do not have to bear these costs. Therefore, even controlling for free mobility of capital and disregarding the dynamic of the race to the bottom, such firms will tend to be either driven out of business or forced to devote their production resources to industries that are less environmentally problematic.

Some free trade apologists for the status quo justify this as a beneficial environmental application of David Ricardo's famous rationale for international trade, the law of comparative advantage. According to Ricardo's theory, if trade barriers between nations are removed, each nation will come to produce what it can produce most advantageously, and the greatest sum total of world production will occur. Under the classic theory, a country gains a comparative advantage in producing certain goods if it has access to factors of production which allow such goods to be produced at a relatively lower cost than in other countries. For example, a country may have a comparative advantage in growing roses if soil and rainfall are conducive to rose production.

The argument that lax environmental standards should be considered a way of gaining a comparative advantage rests on the assumption that a preference for degrading the local environment should be seen as a low cost factor of economic production. This is a false assumption. The appearance of comparative advantage is created because neither the producer who sells the product, nor the consumer who buys it has to pay for the environmental costs of the pollution. These costs are instead borne by those third parties whose quality of life the pollution adversely effects. Because the cost of pollution is not borne internally by the participants in the market transaction, economists refer to it as an "externality." Once environmental degradation is correctly understood to be an externalized cost of production, it becomes clear that when that cost is correctly attributed to the market cost of the products, the advantage disappears.

[Former Harvard University president] Lawrence Summers made the economic argument for encouraging environmental degradation in developing countries when he was the Chief Economist at the World Bank. In an internal memorandum that ultimately became public (generating considerable controversy), Summers argued that the World Bank should be encouraging migration of "dirty" industries to developing countries. Part of his rationale rested on the contention that "the demand for a clean environment for aesthetic and health reasons is likely to have very high income-elasticity." In other words, the demand for a clean environment, like the demand for many other goods, is likely to increase as people have more money. In a poor society, people would be less likely to choose to utilize scarce resources to clean up the environment. This assumes that pollution is not a true externality, but rather that the local population has collectively chosen to bear this cost because of a perceived group benefit.

If there is such a benefit to the local population, however, it is not clear what it is. While there may be some effect on local employment or wages, determining whether this would be the case, how many people it would effect, and the extent to which this would be adequate compensation for the environmental degradation is quite complex and speculative. What is obvious is that only in the most fictitious sense are local populations in developing countries making a collective market decision to choose domestic pollution in exchange for perceived economic rewards. Rather, a sovereign preference for such environmental degradation is a function of the observable fact that in most developing countries, such third party locals are not as politically influential as producers.

In trade terms, forcing local populations in developing countries to bear pollution costs is the equivalent of a general tax on the local population that is being used to subsidize producers. It is well accepted that subsidies that can give a competitive advantage to certain products are not sovereign matters immune from discipline by the WTO. Therefore, understood correctly as a subsidy, under basic GATT principles, environmental degradation is not exclusively a matter of domestic concern.

Even if local populations in developing countries could be understood to be choosing domestic pollution in exchange for perceived economic rewards, the sovereignty rationale for allowing states to gain an environmental "comparative advantage" still does not hold. If the prior argument that the effects of environmental degradation transcend national borders is correct, a choice to create an environmental comparative advantage cannot be seen as an exclusively sovereign matter.

4. The Danger of the Unilateral Alternative to Global Environmental Regulation

Given the WTO's failure to address environmental concerns, why should environmentalists work within its framework? Part of the answer lies in understanding the unsatisfactory nature of the isolationist approach, manifested by Ralph Nader's suggestion that the United States consider withdrawing from the WTO, and unilaterally enforce environmental standards by closing its markets to goods that are produced in environmentally unacceptable ways. Even if the United States were to stop short of withdrawal from the WTO, such unilateralism would not be the answer.

Most importantly, such a unilateral approach would very likely be completely ineffective at stemming the long-term tide towards global environmental degradation. Regulatory standards which are unilaterally imposed by the United States are simply not going to be considered legitimate, and countries' willingness to comply voluntarily with international norms is highly dependent upon their legitimacy. It is possible, of course, that under the threat of unilateral United States sanctions, some countries sometimes may be bullied into implementing stricter environmental regulations. However, the United States is obviously not capable of single-handedly coercing the world into adopting the comprehensive environmental standards necessary to secure a world in environmental harmony. In fact, the international ill will that would result from such a heavy handed American effort would make it very difficult to create the type of positive negotiating atmosphere conducive to successfully concluding MEAs.

It is true that, if the United States resorts to such an approach, many countries would probably act unilaterally as well. This "help," however, would hardly improve the chances of successfully meeting global environmental challenges. The success of a global regime based on each country's establishment of its own idiosyncratic scheme of excluding foreign goods would be impaired by its incoherence. Given the myriad of haphazard and conflicting requirements for exporting goods that global industries would face, any overall benefit to the environment would be far from ensured. This ineffectiveness would be compounded by the political reality that without the discipline of international oversight, many country regimes would be prone to lose touch with their environmental raison d'etat. Given the inherent complexity of differentiating between legitimate environmental measures and disguised trade barriers, such national regimes would be very susceptible to cooptation by their own domestic protectionist interest.

Logistical realities related to the complexity of enforcement would further undermine such an approach. Given that national environmental regulators are already over-burdened, imagine the cost and difficulty (especially, but not only, for poor countries) of attempting to unilaterally assess environmental problems in countries all over the world. Countries would be assessing pollution controls in places where technologies and appropriate environmental solutions may differ from their own, and where the local authorities would have little incentive to be cooperative with what they would likely deem intrusive foreign regulators.

A unilateral approach would not only fail to protect environmental interests, but it could also spell disaster for the international trade order. The reality or perception that trade restrictions on targeted countries were being used for protectionist ends, coupled with a general aversion to foreign attempts to export environmental standards, would very likely lead target countries to impose their own retaliatory trade restrictions. More fundamentally, significant implosion of the international trading system would become almost inevitable as disagreements over approaches to local environmental regulations have caused countries to mutually restrict the import of each others products. A consideration of the arguments for and against free trade is outside the scope of this Article. Suffice it to say, however, that as we learned in the 1930s, such an implosion of the international trading system could cause widespread and serious economic hardship for many people, even heightening the possibility for war.

5.   Accomplishing Global Environmental Regulation With the Help of the WTO

5.1.   *WTO's Limitations as a Forum of Environmental Regulation*

Clearly, when the implications are examined, unilateralism is not the answer. Global environmental regulation requires a multilateral regime. Many environmentalists accept this, but nevertheless argue that the WTO should not be that regime. They do not believe that the Organization can make the transition from promoting "environmental sovereignty" into a force for global environmentalism. They contend that it is inherently biased in favor of business and against environmental interests. In support of this contention they point to its fundamental mandate and mind set of advancing free trade. They point to its traditional function as a forum where governments represented by trade ministries bargain for trade concessions on behalf of various industrial constituents. Finally, they point to its secretive and exclusionary processes under which environmentalists have a hard time gaining a seat at the table. While these arguments raise real problems, they overlook the fact that the GATT historically, and to a lesser extent the WTO today, do not have an agenda distinct from that of their member states. Until very recently, the WTO had a small secretariat that rarely took action which could be construed as independent of direct control by its member states.

While national trade ministries, with an arguable bias in favor of trade over environmental protection, are the lead agencies working with the WTO, this arrangement is not written in stone. In fact, to the extent environmental matters begin to come before the WTO, states are likely to increasingly rely on environmental ministries in dealing with the WTO. This means that, ultimately, the ability to overcome existing institutional bias and to make the environmental voice heard is contingent upon the overall strength of the global environmental movement and not upon the ephemeral architecture of the trade regime.

In addition to concerns about institutionalized bias, some environmentalists argue (oddly enough, together with the anti-environmentalists) that the WTO lacks the expertise necessary to create and monitor environmental agreements because it was not founded as an environmental organization. Just as there is no inherent reason why the Organization's anti-environmental bias cannot be overcome, so too is there no inherent reason why such expertise cannot be acquired. The World Bank was certainly not established as an environmental organization and yet, born out of a realization of the connection between development, lending, and the environment, the World Bank established an environmental department and now requires environmental impact statements on loans. Similar institutional changes have also occurred at the major regional development banks.

To be clear, I wish to emphasize that I am not proposing a specific, definitive environmental mandate for the WTO. While institutional change is possible, there may be many reasons, including the extent to which critical expertise could be best found outside the WTO, that the WTO should not take the lead in global environmental regulation. There are clearly many ways the Organization could play a role in the negotiation and enforcement of global environmental agreements. My purpose here is to point to the advantages that the WTO offers generally, not to rigidly advance any particular institutional structure as necessary for implementing these advantages.

7. Steve Charnovitz, "The Law of Environmental PPM's in the WTO: Debunking the Myth of Illegality," 27 Yale J. Int'l L. 59, 64–65, 70–71, 75–76, 79–80, 83–86, 88–92 (2002).

The term "processes and production methods" [PPMs] originated in the GATT agreement of 1979 on Technical Barriers to Trade and referred to product standards focused on the production method rather than product characteristics. For example, a law prohibiting the landing of fish caught using a driftnet is a PPM. By contrast, a law prohibiting the sale of fish smaller than a prescribed size is not a PPM. . . .

* * *

Non-product-related PPMs are a response to humankind's shared habitation on the planet. The driftnet fishing example is just one of a wide array of concerns that consumers may have about the side effects of production. Various terms are used to describe this concern, such as the "environmental profile" of a product or its "ecological footprint." Citizens and consumers have these concerns because the public in one country can be affected by the production methods used in another.

While it is easy to criticize PPMs as a manifestation of eco-imperialism, that characterization is too simplistic. PPMs are a symptom of the dysfunctions in international environmental governance. Among the biggest problems are poor stewardship of the global commons, lack of liability for transboundary environmental harms, and free riding in treaties. PPMs are an inevitable response to the disagreements between countries at different stages of development. Addressing these root causes would not only obviate many PPMs, but could also improve prospects for economic growth and environmental protection.

PPMs have always been a feature of environmental law. For example, in 1906, the US Congress passed a law banning the landing of sponges taken by means of a diving apparatus from the waters of the Gulf of Mexico. The diving techniques at issue were destructive of the sponge bed, as compared to the use of simple hooks. Another example comes from 1925, when a treaty between Mexico and the United States set up an International Fisheries Commission to conserve marine life in the Pacific Ocean. The treaty committed the parties to refuse the landing of any fish taken in violation of the Commission's regulations. This treaty is noteworthy in demonstrating the early acceptance by Mexico of the application of PPMs to imported fish. Another early example of a trade PPM occurred in the 1931 treaty between Denmark and Sweden to protect migratory birds. This treaty forbade the use of nets for catching seabirds and prohibited the sale or transport of such birds when caught in nets.

Even when a treaty is in place, a government may use unilateral trade measures to seek to enhance the treaty's effectiveness. For instance, in 1950 the United States enacted a law prohibiting the import of whale products taken in violation of the Whaling Convention. The Whaling Convention itself did not provide for the use of trade measures as a means of enforcement.

Because many important international environmental treaties have been developed during the past three decades, there is sometimes a tendency to assume that any significant transborder environmental problem will lead to a treaty that averts the need for unilateral PPMs. Throughout the 1990s this belief was a common theme in the criticism of PPMs, which assumed that countries like the United States were choosing national action over equally available multilateral action. But the reality is that effective, broad-membership treaties are difficult to achieve. Furthermore, treatymaking negotiations sometimes succeed because leading countries have manifested a willingness to act alone if necessary. . . .

* * *

If a WTO Member government believes that a PPM in another WTO Member country violates trade rules, the complaining government may raise the issue in WTO dispute settlement. A three-person panel will be appointed, which will review briefs, hold oral hearings, and issue a decision in about six months. This panel's decision may be appealed by either a plaintiff government or the defendant government to the WTO Appellate Body, which assigns three of its jurists to hear the appeal and issues a final ruling in about sixty days. The Appellate Body may uphold, modify, or reverse the legal findings and conclusions of the panel. The reports of the panel and the Appellate Body are then automatically adopted by the WTO Dispute Settlement Body, which consists of delegates of all of the WTO Member countries. At that point, defendant governments are under a treaty obligation to comply promptly. Of course, the drafters of the WTO recognized the possibility that a government might not comply and that the WTO (or a winning plaintiff) has no way to compel compliance by seeking court orders within the defendant government's national legal system. In an effort to induce compliance, the WTO rules provide for trade retaliation by a winning plaintiff government against a non-complying defendant government. The experience so far demonstrates a good record of compliance.

* * *

The structure of GATT obligations is as follows: A PPM could violate GATT Article I (most-favored-nation), or GATT Article III (national treatment), or GATT Article XI (elimination of quantitative restrictions). If so, it would be reviewed under the General Exceptions in Article XX when there is an applicable exception. GATT Article I requires parties to treat a product of another party no less favorably than the like product of any other party. GATT Article III requires treating imported products from a party no less favorably than like domestic products. GATT Article XI prohibits import and export bans and quotas (subject to certain exceptions not relevant here). GATT Article XX provides for General Exceptions to the entire Agreement.

* * *

B.   GATT Article I—Most Favored Nation (MFN) Rule

GATT Article I:1 (General Most–Favored–Nation Treatment) provides that with respect to customs duties, taxes, regulations, and import rules, any advantage or favor granted by a Party to any product shall be accorded immediately and unconditionally to the "like" product of all other Parties. This provision means that a WTO Member government cannot discriminate by treating the product of one WTO Member country better than the like product of another member country. The decision as to whether two products are "like" will often determine the outcome of a case because Article I does not prohibit differential treatment of unlike products.

* * *

The WTO has considered two GATT Article I disputes involving PPMs, both concerning automobiles. In the Indonesia Automobile case, Japan, the European Communities, and the United States complained that Indonesia applied higher customs duties and sales taxes to imported products when the exporting manufacturer did not utilize a sufficient amount of Indonesian parts or labor. In the Canada Automotive case, Japan and the European Communities complained that Canada provided an import duty exemption for an eligible corporation conditioned on its having a manufacturing presence and sufficient value-added in Canada. In both cases, the panels found a violation of GATT Article I. In neither case did the defendant invoke an Article XX exception.

In the Indonesia Automobile decision, the panel held that according to GATT Article I, an advantage "cannot be made conditional on any criteria that is not related to the imported product itself." Elaborating on this point, the panel stated that "in the GATT/WTO, the right of Members cannot be made dependent upon, conditional on or even affected by, any private contractual obligations in place." The panel concluded that Indonesia was levying a PPM tax and tariff based on producer characteristics and domestic content, and deemed that to be an Article I violation.

In the Canada Automotive decision, the panel held that GATT Article I was being violated, but adopted a more nuanced interpretation of the Article I discipline. Specifically, the panel said, "We therefore do not believe that . . . Article I:1 must be interpreted to mean that making an advantage conditional on criteria not related to the imported product itself is per se inconsistent with Article I:1, irrespective of whether and how such criteria relate to the origin of the imported products." In other words, the panel suggested that truly origin-neutral criteria might be permissible under Article I. The panel was careful to distinguish the holdings in the . . . Indonesia Automobile [case], which it viewed as relating to origin-based discrimination. In the instant case, the panel concluded that the criteria were not origin-neutral, and so Article I was being violated. On appeal, the Appellate Body upheld the panel's finding of the Article I:1 violation but did not address the panel's interpretive point.

The Article I case law reviewed above can be summarized as follows: A government policy standard violates MFN because it is origin-contingent. A producer characteristics standard was held to be a violation in the Indonesia and Canada automobile cases, but the latter panel suggested that PPMs are not per se violations of MFN. As this discussion shows, the law of PPMs under Article I is somewhat unsettled. It is also worth noting that no how-produced standard has been reviewed under Article I.

C.   GATT Article III—National Treatment Rule

GATT Article III (National Treatment) contains disciplines on domestic taxation and regulation. Under Article III:2, imported products shall not be subject to taxes of any kind in excess of those applied to like domestic products. Under Article III:4, imported products shall be accorded treatment no less favorable than that accorded to like products of national origin.

The drafters of Article III recognized that governments sometimes utilize processing regulations, and Article III does not prohibit that practice. Article III:1 provides that internal taxes and regulations affecting the internal sale, transportation, distribution or use of products, "and internal quantitative regulations requiring the mixture, processing or use of products in specified amounts or proportions, should not be applied to imported or domestic products so as to afford protection to domestic production." In stating that such regulations should not afford protection to domestic production, Article III:1 implies that mixture or processing regulations that do not afford protection to domestic production are not prohibited. . . .

* * *

Suppose that a government had a regulation prohibiting the sale of a wood product unless at least eighty percent of its weight came from sustainably harvested timber of any national origin. That how-produced PPM would specify a minimum proportion for processing. Written this way, such a measure would not seem to be a per se violation of Article III.

Nevertheless, as shown below, adjudicatory panels considering Article III have objected to PPMs in the few cases where such measures were reviewed. During the GATT era (1947–94), there were four cases, all against the United States. Since the advent of the WTO, two cases have arisen, but other decisions may bear on how Article III would be applied to PPMs.

The earliest GATT case, decided in 1991, is known as the Tuna–Dolphin I Report. At that time, the United States imposed a "primary" import ban on tuna from countries that did not have a regulatory regime to protect dolphins comparable to the US regime. Mexico, one of the embargoed countries, complained that this law violated Article III. The US import ban was a government policy standard aimed at foreign laws. Indeed, the law also contained a fishery-practice standard by requiring Mexico to keep its overall dolphin killing rate no more than 25 percent higher than the United States' annual rate. The panel ruled that Article III "covers only those measures that are applied to the product as such." Therefore, the US measure regarding dolphins did not fit within the confines of Article III because this PPM "could not possibly affect tuna as a product." The panel went on to say that if the US measure were covered by Article III, such a measure would constitute a violation because the United States treatment of Mexico cannot be predicated on whether or not the incidental taking of dolphins by Mexican vessels corresponds to that of US-flag vessels. When the matter was debated before the Council in 1992, the European Commission called for the adoption of the Tuna–Dolphin report as "a necessary first step in clarifying the relationship between environmental policies and GATT provisions." Nevertheless, this judgment was not adopted by the GATT Council and today carries no legal weight in the WTO.

* * *

The second Tuna–Dolphin decision came in 1994 and it too was not adopted. The plaintiffs were the European Communities and the Netherlands acting for the Netherlands Antilles. This panel's Article III holding was similar to that of the first Tuna–Dolphin panel. The second panel contended that Article III did not apply to laws "related to policies or practices that could not affect the product as such."

The last pre-WTO decision was US Automobile Taxes, and it too was not adopted. The European Communities lodged several complaints, one of which was that the US Corporate Average Fuel Economy (CAFÉ) regulation violated

Article III:4 because it was based on a fleet averaging method that treated domestic and foreign-made autos separately. The panel issued a broad ruling that "Article III:4 does not permit treatment of an imported product less favourable than that accorded to a like domestic product, based on factors not directly relating to the product as such." Thus, fleet averaging violated Article III because this method was "based on the ownership or control relationship of the car manufacturer" and therefore "did not relate to cars as products." This was a producer characteristics PPM. The panel found that this Article III violation did not qualify for GATT's environmental exception, and it therefore held that the CAFÉ law violated the GATT.

The first WTO panel decision—the US Gasoline case—involved a producer characteristics PPM regulation for gasoline composition. Venezuela and Brazil complained that the US regulation, which required reduction from a pollution baseline, was discriminatory because it assigned foreign producers a standard baseline while giving domestic refiners an individual baseline. The regulation was not based on the chemical composition of a particular shipment of gasoline, but rather on the entire output of a domestic refinery or entire output of a foreign refinery that was to be exported to the United States. The complaining governments argued that because foreign gasoline was generally higher-polluting, the assignment of a standard baseline required some of those producers to undertake greater reductions in polluting ingredients than if they had been given an individual baseline.

The US regulation was undoubtedly a violation of the national treatment rule. Yet in so holding, the US Gasoline panel went farther, issuing a broad decision that built on the US Alcoholic Beverages and Automobile Taxes decisions. Noting that the US regulation had been defended on the ground that data from foreign producers was unverifiable, the panel held that Article III:4 "does not allow less favorable treatment dependent on the characteristics of the producer and the nature of the data held by it." More generally, the panel suggested that the identification of like products in Article III:4 needs to be done "on the objective basis of their likeness as products" and not according to "extraneous factors" like those in the US Gasoline dispute. This Article III:4 holding was not appealed and was the backbone of the WTO decision that the US measure violated the GATT.

The second WTO case was Indonesia Automobile. The panel found an Article III:2 violation because the tax measures were based on nationality and origin, and "other factors not related to the product itself." This was similar to the panel's ruling on Article I.

The third case, Japan Alcoholic Beverages, did not consider a PPM, but in rejecting the so-called "aim-and-effect" test, its holding makes it more likely that PPMs will be found to violate GATT Article III. Aim-and-effect was a treaty interpretation developed in GATT caselaw and commentary during the 1990s, which sought to define product likeness more narrowly so as to prevent Article III from unnecessarily infringing on national regulatory autonomy. As the US Alcoholic Beverages panel explained in 1992, "once products are designated as like products, a regulatory product differentiation, *e.g.*, for standardization or environmental purposes, becomes inconsistent with Article III even if the regulation is not 'applied ... so as [to] afford protection to domestic production.'" In other words, if two products I and D are deemed "like" products, then taxing or regulating them differently, even when based on an objective environmental distinction, could be found to violate Article III if I is taxed more or treated less favorably than D. To avoid such a holding, the proponents of the "aim-and-effect" test sought to have panels consider whether the disputed tax or regulation had a protective aim or effect, and, if it did not, then products I and D, treated differently based on the tax or regulation, could perhaps avoid characterization as like products.

The first time this test was invoked in a WTO proceeding, in the Japan Alcoholic Beverages dispute, the panel rejected such a test in an Article III:2 case. The Appellate Body upheld the panel and, in a later decision, the European Communities (EC) Bananas case, the Appellate Body stated its rejection of "aim-and-effect" explicitly with respect to GATT Article III:1.

Although it was not propounded as a way to defend PPMs, the aim-and-effect test could have provided a doctrinal basis for distinguishing two otherwise like products that differ only in conformity to the PPM. Without the aim-and-effect test, a PPM-compliant domestic product may be easily deemed a "like" product to a PPM-non-compliant imported product. If so, an Article III violation will occur when government action denies the imported product an equal opportunity to compete in the domestic market.

* * *

In summary, the textual ambiguities in Article III have been resolved unfavorably to PPMs. A producer characteristics standard was held to be a violation of Article III in the US Alcoholic Beverages, US Gasoline, and Indonesia Automobile decisions. No how-produced standard has been tested, but WTO jurisprudence points to the likelihood that such a standard would be deemed a national treatment violation.

* * *

D. GATT Article XX—General Exceptions

GATT Article XX lists ten exceptions to GATT disciplines. These exceptions are "subject to the requirement that such measures are not applied in a manner which would constitute a means of arbitrary or unjustifiable discrimination between countries where the same conditions prevail, or a disguised restriction on international trade." This requirement is now known as the "chapeau" of Article XX. Two of the exceptions would be available for environmental measures—paragraph (b) for measures "necessary to protect human, animal or plant life or health," and paragraph (g) for measures "relating to the conservation of exhaustible natural resources if such measures are made effective in conjunction with restrictions on domestic production or consumption." Article XX will be central to an analysis of PPMs because, as discussed above, many PPMs will violate Articles I, III, or XI.

8. Bruce Neuling, "The Shrimp–Turtle Case: Implications for Article XX of GATT and the Trade and Environment Debate," 22 Loy. LA Int'l & Comp. L. Rev. 1, 17–28 (1999).

In the 1990s, the putative environmental provisions of Article XX were at the heart of several WTO/GATT cases. The results disappointed environmentalists, further fostering their suspicion that "trade bureaucrats" were incapable of taking a broad view of the relationship between environmental protection and the world trading system. The issues raised in these cases not only framed the jurisprudence in Shrimp–Turtle, but also contributed to the polarized political atmosphere in which trade and the environment are continuously debated.

A. Thai Cigarettes

Although not an environmental case, the 1990 Panel Report on Thailand—Restrictions on Importation of and Internal Taxes on Cigarettes (Thai Cigarettes) has important environmental implications. The Report interpreted the phrase "necessary to protect human ... life or health" in Article XX(b). The case dealt with an import ban on cigarettes imposed by the Thai Government. The United States challenged the ban as a violation of Article XI. In response, Thailand invoked Article XX(b), arguing that the ban was necessary to protect the public from harmful ingredients in imported cigarettes and to reduce the consumption of cigarettes in Thailand. The Panel rejected the Thai Government's argument on the ground that "the import restrictions imposed by Thailand could be considered to be 'necessary' in terms of Article XX(b) only if there were no alternative measure consistent with the General Agreement, or less inconsistent with it, which Thailand could reasonably be expected to employ to achieve its health policy objectives."

The Panel reasoned that alternative methods consistent with GATT, such as advertising restrictions and mandatory labeling, were available to Thailand to achieve its public health objectives. Therefore, the import ban was not "necessary" within the terms of Article XX.

Many environmentalists have argued that this result set an almost "impossibly high hurdle" for environmental measures under Article XX(b). They argued that a less trade-intrusive policy "is almost always conceivable and therefore in some sense 'available.' " ...

* * *

B. Tuna–Dolphin I

The 1991 Dispute Panel Report in United States—Restrictions on Imports of Tuna from Mexico (Tuna Dolphin I) served as a landmark event in the trade and environment debate. Probably more than any other event prior to the implementation of the North American Free Trade Agreement (NAFTA), the Panel Report mobilized environmental NGOs to oppose GATT....

Tuna–Dolphin I stemmed from violations of provisions of the 1972 US Marine Mammal Protection Act (MMPA). The MMPA requires fishermen operating in US waters to use certain techniques to reduce the incidental killing of marine mammals such as dolphins. The MMPA also requires that the US Government ban imports of commercial fish caught with fishing technology that result in the incidental killing of marine mammals in excess of US standards....

Mexico argued that its right to sell tuna in the United States had been violated and requested a GATT Dispute Panel to adjudicate the matter. The Panel ruled in Mexico's favor. It rejected the United States' argument that the MMPA was consistent with GATT Article III because it did not treat imported products less favorably than similar products of national origin.

Even though US and foreign fishermen were both required to reduce the incidental killing of dolphins, the Panel found that GATT Article III was not applicable to the case because it only covers regulations affecting products and does not apply to PPMs. Having decided that Article III did not apply, the Panel stated:

> The MMPA regulates the domestic harvesting of yellowfin tuna to reduce the incidental taking of dolphin, but these regulations could not be regarded as being applied to tuna products as such because they would not directly regulate the sale of tuna and could not possibly affect tuna as a product. Therefore, ... the import prohibition on certain yellowfin tuna and certain yellowfin tuna products of Mexico ... did not constitute internal regulations covered by ... Article III.

In other words, the United States was obligated to treat tuna produced by Mexico no less favorably than tuna produced by the United States, regardless of how the tuna was harvested. The Mexican and US tuna were "like" products and required equal treatment, even though they were caught under different circumstances. Under Article III, different production methods do not differentiate products and render them "unlike." The Panel next considered the United States' arguments that the ban was justifiable under Article XX(b) and Article XX(g). It rejected the Article XX(b) argument on the basis that the ban was not necessary to protect animal life. It stated "the United States had not demonstrated ... that it had exhausted all options reasonably available to it to pursue its dolphin protection objectives through measures consistent with the General Agreement, in particular through the negotiation of international cooperative arrangements...."

The Panel also rejected the argument that Article XX(g) protected the ban. Construing the language in Article XX(g) that conservation measures be taken "in conjunction with restrictions on domestic production or consumption," the Panel concluded that Article XX(g) applied only to measures aimed at rendering domestic restrictions effective and not to measures taken jointly with, or otherwise related to, domestic restrictions. It then reasoned:

> A country can effectively control the production or consumption of an exhaustible natural resource only to the extent that the production or consumption is under its jurisdiction. This suggests that Article XX(g) was intended to permit contracting parties to take trade measures primarily aimed at rendering effective restrictions on production or consumption within their jurisdiction.

Because the import ban would not help conserve dolphins found within US jurisdiction, it was not justifiable under Article XX(g). The clear implication was that Article XX(g) is limited to measures taken to conserve only domestic natural resources.

Finally, the Panel rejected the notion that a GATT party could use trade measures to press foreign governments to modify their policies. It thus dismissed the idea that a GATT party could condition access to its market on its trading partners' adoption of certain environmental practices. According to the Panel:

> [A] contracting party may not restrict imports of a product merely because it originates in a country with environmental policies different

from its own.... If the CONTRACTING PARTIES were to permit import restrictions in response to differences in environmental policies ... they would need to impose limits on the range of policy differences justifying such responses and to develop criteria so as to prevent abuse. If the CONTRACTING PARTIES were to decide to permit trade measures of this type in particular circumstances it would therefore be preferable for them to do so not by interpreting Article XX, but by amending or supplementing the provisions of the General Agreement or waiving obligations thereunder.

The Report was not adopted by the GATT Council. Nor did Mexico push for its adoption, partly because of the ongoing NAFTA negotiations. Environmental groups bitterly denounced the Report. It was perceived as a clear warning that trade considerations would invariably trump the environmental protection in GATT.

C.　Tuna–Dolphin II

The European community brought its own case, Tuna–Dolphin II, against the MMPA, focusing on the law's "secondary embargo." This provision barred tuna imports to the United States from countries engaging in tuna trade with an embargoed country such as Mexico. Several European countries imported tuna from Mexico. The European Community argued that the secondary embargo was not covered by Article III, violated Article XI, and could not be justified under Article XX.

In June 1994, the Panel ruled that the secondary embargo violated GATT. Unlike the Panel in Tuna–Dolphin I, the Tuna–Dolphin II Panel concluded that Articles XX(b) and XX(g) could be applied extraterritorially, because "it could not ... be said that the General Agreement proscribed in an absolute manner measures that related to things or actions outside the territorial jurisdiction of the party taking the measure." The Panel, however, found measures that force other countries to effectively change their policies with respect to persons or things within their own jurisdictions were not covered by Articles XX(b) and (g) in that:

> If ... Article XX was interpreted to permit contracting parties to take trade measures so as to force other contracting parties to change their policies within their jurisdiction, including their conservation policies, the balance of rights and obligations among contracting parties, in particular the right of access to markets, would be seriously impaired. Under such an interpretation the General Agreement could no longer serve as multilateral framework for trade among contracting parties.

It was clear the embargo was designed to force policy changes in third countries, such as Mexico, because the secondary embargo prohibited imports of tuna regardless of whether the tuna was harvested in a manner harming dolphins, or whether tuna fishing practices in the exporting country as a whole harmed dolphins. Therefore, the secondary embargo was not justifiable under Article XX. The Report was not, however, adopted by the GATT Council.

D.　Reformulated Gas

United States–Standards for Reformulated and Conventional Gasoline (Reformulated Gas) was the first environmental case decided after the establishment of the WTO. It involved a provision of the Clean Air Act that required oil refiners to reduce a variety of smog-causing contaminants in their gasoline from a baseline determined by the composition of the gasoline in 1990. In 1993, the Environmental Protection Administration (EPA) issued regulations permitting most domestic refiners to establish their baseline using their own actual data from 1990. Most foreign refiners were required to use the US industry's average level of contaminants in 1990 as their baseline. The rule for importers stemmed from the EPA's conclusion that requirements applied to US refiners could not be applied to foreign refiners without raising substantial concerns regarding the availability of foreign data and enforcement methods.

Venezuela and Brazil challenged the regulation arguing that it discriminated against foreign gasoline. In 1996, a WTO Dispute Panel found that the regulation violated Article III. The Panel concluded that the inability of foreign refiners to use individual baselines meant that imported gasoline was treated less favorably than domestic gasoline (a "like" product). The Panel also rejected the argument that the regulation was "necessary" within the meaning of Article XX(b).

The Panel then considered whether the discrimination was justified under Article XX(g). It rejected the argument of Venezuela and Brazil that clean air is not a "natural resource." It concluded, however, that in the absence of a "direct connection" between the less favorable treatment of foreign gasoline and the air quality goals of the United States, the regulation was not "primarily aimed" at the conservation of a natural resource. The regulation therefore failed the "relating to" condition of Article XX(g).

On appeal, the US Government contended that the regulation met the requirements of Article XX(g), and the Appellate Body agreed. It rejected the finding that the regulation was not "primarily aimed at," and thus not "related to," the conservation of clean air. According to the Appellate Body, the Panel seemed to equate "related to" with "necessary," which was incorrect under the "fundamental" rule of treaty interpretation. The Appellate Body also found the regulation was "made effective in conjunction with" domestic conservation measures. This result was reached because restrictions on domestic production had been "established jointly" with restrictions on foreign gasoline. Under these circumstances the regulation satisfied Article XX(g).

For a measure to be upheld under Article XX, however, it must do more than simply satisfy one of the particular exceptions that are listed in paragraphs (b) and (g). It must also satisfy the general conditions found in the chapeau.

* * *

The chapeau ... requires that a measure taken pursuant to one of the specific paragraphs does not constitute "arbitrary or unjustifiable discrimination," or a "disguised restriction on international trade." Although the Appellate Body wrestled with these phrases, it did not provide a clear definition. Perhaps the clearest and most comprehensive analysis it offered was:

"Arbitrary discrimination," "unjustifiable discrimination" and "disguised restriction" on international trade may ... be read side-by-side; they impart meaning to one another. It is clear to us that "disguised restriction" includes disguised discrimination....

It is questionable whether this explanation added much clarity to the language already in the chapeau. It served, however, as the basis for finding the EPA regulation defective. The Appellate Body cited two distinct shortcomings in the regulation. First, the EPA had not adequately explored means of mitigating the verification and enforcement problems associated with individual baselines for foreign refiners. In particular, "the United States had not pursued the possibility of entering into cooperative arrangements with the governments of Venezuela and Brazil ..." in order to gather and verify information on gasoline refiners, and thus permit the use of individual company baselines in those countries. In this regard, the Appellate Body noted that foreign company data is routinely used in anti-dumping investigations. It also noted that the United States had entered into numerous agreements with other countries to share information in antitrust, tax, securities, and other cases. The regulation's second shortcoming was that the EPA had considered the costs of various regulatory options available to domestic refiners, but not to foreign refiners. Because of these defects, the Appellate Body concluded that the gasoline regulation constituted "unjustifiable discrimination" and was in reality a "disguised restriction on international trade." As a result, the regulation failed to satisfy Article XX.

* * *

The litigation of the 1990s did much to shape and provide content to the environmental provisions of Article XX. The emerging legal picture, however, was not particularly hospitable to the goal of environmental protection.

A restrictive interpretation of the "life or health" exception in paragraph (b) was adopted. The notion that PPMs could distinguish between products for the purposes of Article III was rejected. Additionally, serious restrictions were placed on the extraterritorial application of environmental measures. Discriminatory measures designed to simplify environmental enforcement might be unjustified if alternative diplomatic solutions are not first explored.

As a result, many environmentalists in the United States, Europe, and elsewhere worried that adequate protection of the environment was not possible within the existing framework of the WTO. Environmentalists were often drawn into trade politics where they tended to side with critics of globalization in order to achieve their goal of environmental protection. Shrimp–Turtle took place within this polarized atmosphere and was watched with great interest by environmentalists everywhere.

9. World Trade Organization: Dispute Settlement Appellate Body Report on United States—Import Prohibition of Certain Shrimp and Shrimp Products, No. WT/DS58/AB/R 12 October 1998.

[*Eds.*—To protect sea turtles, an endangered species, the United States required American shrimp trawlers to use nets equipped with "turtle excluder devices" (TEDs), which allowed turtles to escape the net. Pursuant to Section 609 of Public Law 101–162 this requirement was extended to foreign states wishing to export shrimp to the United States. Shrimp imports were prohibited from countries that were not certified as having a marine turtle conservation program "comparable" to that of the United States and as having a "comparable" rate of incidental taking of turtles during shrimp trawling. In 1996, India, Malaysia, Pakistan, and Thailand all challenged this ban before the WTO dispute resolution system. The Panel convened to hear the dispute found that the United States had violated its obligation not to impose quantitative restrictions on imports under Article XI of the GATT and that this violation was not justified by an Article XX exception. In its appeal to the Appellate Body, the US did not challenge the Panel's determination that Section 609 violated Article XI but only its determination that an Article XX exception did not apply. The United States did not argue legality under Article III apparently conceding that the trade restriction was an import ban and not the sort of internal regulation that is governed by Article III.]

127. We begin with the threshold question of whether Section 609 is a measure concerned with the conservation of "exhaustible natural resources" within the meaning of Article XX(g)…. In the proceedings before the Panel … the parties to the dispute argued this issue vigorously and extensively. India, Pakistan and Thailand contended that a "reasonable interpretation" of the term "exhaustible" is that the term refers to "finite resources such as minerals, rather than biological or renewable resources." … For its part, Malaysia added that sea turtles, being living creatures, could only be considered under Article XX(b), since Article XX(g) was meant for "nonliving exhaustible natural resources"….

128. We are not convinced by these arguments. Textually, Article XX(g) is *not* limited to the conservation of "mineral" or "non-living" natural resources…. One lesson that modern biological sciences teach us is that living species, though in principle, capable of reproduction and, in that sense, "renewable", are in certain circumstances indeed susceptible of depletion, exhaustion and extinction, frequently because of human activities….

129. The words of Article XX(g), "exhaustible natural resources", were actually crafted more than 50 years ago. They must be read by a treaty interpreter in the light of contemporary concerns of the community of nations about the protection and conservation of the environment. While Article XX was not modified in the Uruguay Round, the preamble attached to the *WTO Agreement* shows that the signatories to that Agreement were, in 1994, fully aware of the importance and legitimacy of environmental protection as a goal of national and international policy. The preamble of the *WTO Agreement*— which informs not only the GATT 1994, but also the other covered agreements—explicitly acknowledges "the objective of sustainable development":

> The *Parties* to this Agreement,
>
> *Recognizing* that their relations in the field of trade and economic endeavour should be conducted *with a view to raising standards of living, ensuring full employment and a large and steadily growing volume of real income and effective demand*, and *expanding the production of and trade in goods and services*, while allowing for the optimal use of the world's resources in accordance with the *objective of sustainable development, seeking both to protect and preserve the environment and to enhance the means for doing so* in a manner consistent with their respective needs

and concerns at different levels of economic development . . . [emphases added].

130. From the perspective embodied in the preamble of the *WTO Agreement*, we note that the generic term "natural resources" in Article XX(g) is not "static" in its content or reference but is rather "by definition, evolutionary". It is, therefore, pertinent to note that modern international conventions and declarations make frequent references to natural resources as embracing both living and non-living resources. . . .

* * *

133. Finally, we observe that sea turtles are highly migratory animals, passing in and out of waters subject to the rights of jurisdiction of various coastal states and the high seas. In the Panel Report, the Panel said:

> . . . Information brought to the attention of the Panel, including documented statements from the experts, tends to *confirm the fact that sea turtles, in certain circumstances of their lives, migrate through the waters of several countries and the high sea* . . . [emphasis added].

The sea turtle species here at stake, *i.e.*, covered by Section 609, are all known to occur in waters over which the United States exercises jurisdiction. Of course, it is not claimed that *all* populations of these species migrate to, or traverse, at one time or another, waters subject to United States jurisdiction. Neither the appellant nor any of the appellees claims any rights of exclusive ownership over the sea turtles, at least not while they are swimming freely in their natural habitat—the oceans. We do not pass upon the question of whether there is an implied jurisdictional limitation in Article XX(g), and if so, the nature or extent of that limitation. We note only that in the specific circumstances of the case before us, there is a sufficient nexus between the migratory and endangered marine populations involved and the United States for purposes of Article XX(g).

134. For all the foregoing reasons, we find that the sea turtles here involved constitute "exhaustible natural resources" for purposes of Article XX(g) of the GATT 1994. . . .

[*Eds.*— The Appellate Body next determines that, as required by Article XX(g), Section 609 "*relat[es] to the conservation* of exhaustible natural resources" and is "made effective in conjunction with restrictions on domestic production or consumption."]

    C. *The Introductory Clauses of Article XX: Characterizing Section 609 under the Chapeau's Standards*

146. As noted earlier, the United States invokes Article XX(b) only if and to the extent that we hold that Section 609 falls outside the scope of Article XX(g). Having found that Section 609 does come within the terms of Article XX(g), it is not, therefore, necessary to analyze the measure in terms of Article XX(b).

147. Although provisionally justified under Article XX(g), Section 609, if it is ultimately to be justified as an exception under Article XX, must also satisfy the requirements of the introductory clauses—the "chapeau"—of Article XX, that is,

Article XX

General Exceptions

Subject to the requirement that such measures are *not applied in a manner which would constitute a means of arbitrary or unjustifiable discrimination between countries where the same conditions prevail*, or a *disguised restriction on international trade*, nothing in this Agreement shall be construed to prevent the adoption or enforcement by any Member of measures . . . [emphasis added].

We turn, hence, to the task of appraising Section 609, and specifically the manner in which it is applied under the chapeau of Article XX; that is, to the second part of the two-tier analysis required under Article XX.

* * *

150. . . . The precise language of the chapeau requires that a measure not be applied in a manner which would constitute a means of "arbitrary or unjustifiable discrimination between countries where the same conditions prevail" or a "disguised restriction on international trade." There are three standards contained in the chapeau: first, arbitrary discrimination between countries where the same conditions prevail; second, unjustifiable discrimination between countries where the same conditions prevail; and third, a disguised restriction on international trade. In order for a measure to be applied in a manner which would constitute "arbitrary or unjustifiable discrimination between countries where the same conditions prevail," three elements must exist. First, the application of the measure must result in *discrimination*. As we stated in *United States–Gasoline*, the nature and quality of this discrimination is different from the discrimination in the treatment of products which was already found to be inconsistent with one of the substantive obligations of the GATT 1994, such as Articles I, III or XI. Second, the discrimination must be *arbitrary* or *unjustifiable* in character. We will examine this element of *arbitrariness* or *unjustifiability* in detail below. Third, this discrimination must occur *between countries where the same conditions prevail*. In *United States–Gasoline*, we accepted the assumption of the participants in that appeal that such discrimination could occur not only between different exporting Members, but also between exporting Members and the importing Member concerned. Thus, the standards embodied in the language of the chapeau are not only different from the requirements of Article XX(g); they are also different from the standard used in determining that Section 609 is violative of the substantive rules of Article XI:1 of the GATT 1994.

151. In *United States–Gasoline*, we stated that "the purpose and object of the introductory clauses of Article XX is generally the prevention of 'abuse of the exceptions of [Article XX]'." We went on to say that:

. . . The chapeau is animated by the principle that while the exceptions of Article XX may be invoked as a matter of legal right, they should not be so applied as to frustrate or defeat the legal obligations of the holder of the right under the substantive rules of the *General Agreement*. If those exceptions are not to be abused or misused, in other words, the measures falling within the particular exceptions must be applied reasonably, with due regard both to the legal duties of the party claiming the exception and the legal rights of the other parties concerned.

152.   At the end of the Uruguay Round, negotiators fashioned an appropriate preamble for the new WTO Agreement * * *. Those negotiators evidently believed, however, that the objective of "full use of the resources of the world" set forth in the preamble of the GATT 1947 was no longer appropriate to the world trading system of the 1990's. As a result, they decided to qualify the original objectives of the GATT 1947 with the following words:

> ... while allowing for the optimal use of the world's resources in accordance with the objective of sustainable development, seeking both to protect and preserve the environment and to enhance the means for doing so in a manner consistent with their respective needs and concerns at different levels of economic development, ...

153.   We note once more that this language demonstrates a recognition by WTO negotiators that optimal use of the world's resources should be made in accordance with the objective of sustainable development. As this preambular language reflects the intentions of negotiators of the *WTO Agreement*, we believe it must add colour, texture and shading to our interpretation of the agreements annexed to the *WTO Agreement*, in this case, the GATT 1994. . . .

154.   We also note that since this preambular language was negotiated, certain other developments have occurred which help to elucidate the objectives of WTO Members with respect to the relationship between trade and the environment. The most significant, in our view, was the Decision of Ministers at Marrakesh to establish a permanent Committee on Trade and Environment (the "CTE"). In their Decision on Trade and Environment, Ministers expressed their intentions, in part, as follows:

> ... *Considering* that there should not be, nor need be, any policy contradiction between upholding and safeguarding an open, non-discriminatory and equitable multilateral trading system on the one hand, and acting for the protection of the environment, and the promotion of sustainable development on the other, ...

In this Decision, Ministers took "note" of the Rio Declaration on Environment and Development, Agenda 21, and "its follow-up in the GATT, as reflected in the statement of the Council of Representatives to the CONTRACTING PARTIES at their 48th Session in 1992. . . ."

* * *

159.   The task of interpreting and applying the chapeau is, hence, essentially the delicate one of locating and marking out a line of equilibrium between the right of a Member to invoke an exception under Article XX and the rights of the other Members under varying substantive provisions (*e.g.*, Article XI) of the GATT 1994, so that neither of the competing rights will cancel out the other and thereby distort and nullify or impair the balance of rights and obligations constructed by the Members themselves in that Agreement. The location of the line of equilibrium, as expressed in the chapeau, is not fixed and unchanging; the line moves as the kind and the shape of the measures at stake vary and as the facts making up specific cases differ.

160.   With these general considerations in mind, we address now the issue of whether the *application* of the United States measure, although the measure itself falls within the terms of Article XX(g), nevertheless constitutes "a means of arbitrary or unjustifiable discrimination between countries where the same conditions prevail" or "a disguised restriction on international trade." . . .

* * *

2. *"Unjustifiable Discrimination"*

161.   We scrutinize first whether Section 609 has been applied in a manner constituting "unjustifiable discrimination between countries where the same conditions prevail." Perhaps the most conspicuous flaw in this measure's application relates to its intended and actual coercive effect on the specific policy decisions made by foreign governments, Members of the WTO. Section 609, in its application, is, in effect, an economic embargo which requires *all other exporting Members*, if they wish to exercise their GATT rights, to adopt *essentially the same* policy (together with an approved enforcement program) as that applied to, and enforced on, United States domestic shrimp trawlers.

* * *

163.   The actual *application* of the measure . . . *requires* other WTO Members to adopt a regulatory program that is not merely *comparable*, but rather *essentially the same*, as that applied to the United States shrimp trawl vessels. Thus, [the United States establishes] a rigid and unbending standard by which United States officials determine whether or not countries will be certified, thus granting or refusing other countries the right to export shrimp to the United States. Other specific policies and measures that an exporting country may have adopted for the protection and conservation of sea turtles are not taken into account, in practice, by the administrators making the comparability determination.

164.   . . . [I]t is not acceptable, in international trade relations, for one WTO Member to use an economic embargo to *require* other Members to adopt essentially the same comprehensive regulatory program, to achieve a certain policy goal, as that in force within that Member's territory, *without* taking into consideration different conditions which may occur in the territories of those other Members.

165.   Furthermore, when this dispute was before the Panel and before us, the United States did not permit imports of shrimp harvested by commercial shrimp trawl vessels using TEDs comparable in effectiveness to those required in the United States if those shrimp originated in waters of countries not certified under Section 609. In other words, *shrimp caught using methods identical to those employed in the United States* have been excluded from the United States market solely because they have been caught in waters of *countries that have not been certified by the United States*. . . . We believe that discrimination results not only when countries in which the same conditions prevail are differently treated, but also when the application of the measure at issue does not allow for any inquiry into the appropriateness of the regulatory program for the conditions prevailing in those exporting countries.

166.   Another aspect of the application of Section 609 that bears heavily in any appraisal of justifiable or unjustifiable discrimination is the failure of the United States to engage the appellees, as well as other Members exporting shrimp to the United States, in serious, across-the-board negotiations with the objective of concluding bilateral or multilateral agreements for the protection and conservation of sea turtles, before enforcing the import prohibition against the shrimp exports of those other Members. The relevant factual finding of the Panel reads:

> ... However, *we have no evidence that the United States actually undertook negotiations on an agreement on sea turtle conservation techniques which would have included the complainants before the imposition of the import ban as a result of the CIT [Court of International Trade] judgement*.... As we consider that the measures sought by the United States were of the type that would normally require international cooperation, we do not find it necessary to examine whether parties entered into negotiations in good faith and whether the United States, absent any result, would have been entitled to adopt unilateral measures [emphasis added].

* * *

169.   ... [T]he United States did negotiate and conclude one regional international agreement for the protection and conservation of sea turtles: The Inter–American Convention.

* * *

171.   The Inter–American Convention thus provides convincing demonstration that an alternative course of action was reasonably open to the United States for securing the legitimate policy goal of its measure, a course of action other than the unilateral and non-consensual procedures of the import prohibition under Section 609. It is relevant to observe that an import prohibition is, ordinarily, the heaviest "weapon" in a Member's armoury of trade measures. The record does not, however, show that serious efforts were made by the United States to negotiate similar agreements with any other country or group of countries before (and, as far as the record shows, after) Section 609 was enforced on a world-wide basis on 1 May 1996....

172.   Clearly, the United States negotiated seriously with some, but not with other Members (including the appellees), that export shrimp to the United States. The effect is plainly discriminatory and, in our view, unjustifiable.

* * *

3.   *"Arbitrary Discrimination"*

177.   We next consider whether Section 609 has been applied in a manner constituting "arbitrary discrimination between countries where the same conditions prevail." We have already observed that Section 609, in its application, imposes a single, rigid and unbending requirement that countries applying for certification under Section 609(b)(2)(A) and (B) adopt a comprehensive regulatory program that is essentially the same as the United States' program, without inquiring into the appropriateness of that program for the conditions prevailing in the exporting countries. Furthermore, there is little

or no flexibility in how officials make the determination for certification pursuant to these provisions. In our view, this rigidity and inflexibility also constitute "arbitrary discrimination" within the meaning of the chapeau.

* * *

184. We find, accordingly, that ... [t]he measure ... is not entitled to the justifying protection of Article XX of the GATT 1994. Having made this finding, it is not necessary for us to examine also whether the United States measure is applied in a manner that constitutes a "disguised restriction on international trade" under the chapeau of Article XX.

185. In reaching these conclusions, we wish to underscore what we have *not* decided in this appeal. We have *not* decided that the protection and preservation of the environment is of no significance to the Members of the WTO. Clearly, it is. We have *not* decided that the sovereign nations that are Members of the WTO cannot adopt effective measures to protect endangered species, such as sea turtles. Clearly, they can and should. And we have *not* decided that sovereign states should not act together bilaterally, plurilaterally or multilaterally, either within the WTO or in other international fora, to protect endangered species or to otherwise protect the environment. Clearly, they should and do.

186. What we *have* decided in this appeal is simply this: although the measure of the United States in dispute in this appeal serves an environmental objective that is recognized as legitimate under paragraph (g) of Article XX of the GATT 1994, this measure has been applied by the United States in a manner which constitutes arbitrary and unjustifiable discrimination between Members of the WTO, contrary to the requirements of the chapeau of Article XX. For all of the specific reasons outlined in this Report, this measure does not qualify for the exemption Article XX of the GATT 1994 affords to measures which serve certain recognized, legitimate environmental purposes but which, at the same time, are not applied in a manner that constitutes a means of arbitrary or unjustifiable discrimination between countries where the same conditions prevail or a disguised restriction on international trade. As we emphasized in *United States–Gasoline*, WTO Members are free to adopt their own policies aimed at protecting the environment as long as, in so doing, they fulfill their obligations and respect the rights of other Members under the *WTO Agreement*.

* * *

10. World Trade Organization: Dispute Settlement Appellate Body Report on United States–Import Prohibition of Certain Shrimp and Shrimp Products, No. WT/DS58/AB/RW (22 Oct 2001).

[*Eds.*—Following the Appellate Body's decision against the United States in the Shrimp Turtle case (*i.e.*, "Shrimp Turtle 1," *supra* Reading 9), the United States revised its guidelines for the implementation of Section 609 and began efforts to enter into a new sea turtle conservation agreement with countries such as Malaysia. In October 2000, based in part on the United States' failure to conclude an agreement with it, Malaysia asserted that the United States was not in compliance with the Shrimp Turtle 1 Appellate Body Report and requested that a compliance panel be convened pursuant to Article 21.5 of the Dispute Settlement Understanding. The panel convened at the request of Malaysia concluded that the United States was at that time in compliance with its obligations under the GATT. In determining that the United States was engaged in ongoing serious good faith efforts to reach a multilateral agreement the panel pointed to the following:

— A document communicated on 14 October 1998 by the United States Department of State to a number of countries of the Indian Ocean and the South–East Asia region. This document contained possible elements of a regional convention on sea turtles in this region.

— The contribution of the United States to a symposium held in Sabah on 15–17 July 1999. The Sabah Symposium led to the adoption of a Declaration calling for the negotiation and implementation of a regional agreement throughout the Indian Ocean and South–East Asia region.

— The Perth Conference in October 1999, where participating governments, including the United States, committed themselves to developing an international agreement on sea turtles for the Indian Ocean and South–East Asia region.

— The contribution of the United States to the Kuantan round of negotiations, 11–14 July 2000. This first round of negotiations towards the conclusion of a regional agreement resulted in the adoption of the Memorandum of Understanding on the Conservation and Management of Marine Turtles and their Habitats of the Indian Ocean and South–East Asia (the "South–East Asian MOU"). The Final Act of the Kuantan meeting provided that before the South–East Asian MOU can be finalized, a Conservation and Management Plan must be negotiated and annexed to the South–East Asian MOU. At the time of the Panel proceedings, the Conservation and Management Plan was still being drafted.

Malaysia appealed the Panel's determination to the Appellate Body ("Shrimp Turtle 2").]

122.   We concluded in *United States–Shrimp* that, to avoid "arbitrary or unjustifiable discrimination," the United States had to provide all exporting countries "similar opportunities to negotiate" an international agreement. Given the specific mandate contained in Section 609, and given the decided preference for multilateral approaches voiced by WTO Members and others in the international community in various international agreements for the protection and conservation of endangered sea turtles that were cited in our previous Report, the United States, in our view, would be expected to make good faith efforts to reach international agreements that are comparable from one forum of negotiation to the other. The negotiations need not be identical. Indeed, no two negotiations can ever be identical, or lead to identical results. Yet the negotiations must be *comparable* in the sense that comparable efforts are made, comparable resources are invested, and comparable energies are devoted to securing an international agreement. So long as such comparable efforts are made, it is more likely that "arbitrary or unjustifiable discrimination" will be avoided between countries where an importing Member concludes an agreement with one group of countries, but fails to do so with another group of countries.

123.   Under the chapeau of Article XX, an importing Member may not treat its trading partners in a manner that would constitute "arbitrary or unjustifiable discrimination." With respect to this measure, the United States could conceivably respect this obligation, and the conclusion of an international agreement might nevertheless not be possible despite the serious, good faith efforts of the United States. Requiring that a multilateral agreement be *concluded* by the United States in order to avoid "arbitrary or unjustifiable discrimination" in applying its measure would mean that any country party to the negotiations with the United States, whether a WTO Member or not, would have, in effect, a veto over whether the United States could fulfill its WTO obligations. Such a requirement would not be reasonable. For a variety of reasons, it may be possible to conclude an agreement with one group of countries but not another. The conclusion of a multilateral agreement requires the cooperation and commitment of many countries. In our view, the United States cannot be held to have engaged in "arbitrary or unjustifiable discrimination" under Article XX solely because one international negotiation resulted in an agreement while another did not.

124.   As we stated in *United States–Shrimp*, "the protection and conservation of highly migratory species of sea turtles . . . demands concerted and cooperative efforts on the part of the many countries whose waters are traversed in the course of recurrent sea turtle migrations". Further, the "need for, and the appropriateness of, such efforts have been recognized in the WTO itself as well as in a significant number of other international instruments and declarations." For example, Principle 12 of the Rio Declaration on Environment and Development states, in part, that "[e]nvironmental measures addressing transboundary or global environmental problems should, as far as possible, be based on international consensus." Clearly, and "as far as possible," a multilateral approach is strongly preferred. Yet it is one thing to *prefer* a multilateral approach in the application of a measure that is provisionally justified under one of the subparagraphs of Article XX of the GATT 1994; it is another to require the *conclusion* of a multilateral agreement as a condition of avoiding "arbitrary or unjustifiable discrimination" under the chapeau of Article XX. We see, in this case, no such requirement.

* * *

134.   In sum, Malaysia is incorrect in its contention that avoiding "arbitrary and unjustifiable discrimination" under the chapeau of Article XX requires the *conclusion* of an international agreement on the protection and conservation of sea turtles. Therefore, we uphold the Panels finding that, in view of the serious, good faith efforts made by the United States to negotiate an international agreement, "Section 609 is now applied in a manner that no longer constitutes a means of unjustifiable or arbitrary discrimination, as identified by the Appellate Body in its Report."

11. J. Patrick Kelly, "The Seduction of the Appellate Body: Shrimp/Sea Turtle I and II and the Proper Role of States in WTO Governance," 38 Cornell Int'l L. J. 459, 460–66, 469 (2005).

The recent *Shrimp/Turtle* decisions (*Shrimp/Turtle* I and *Shrimp/Turtle* II) of the Appellate Body ("AB") effectively reversed longstanding, although unadopted, decisions of the GATT/WTO dispute resolution system that had been supported by a majority of States. These remarkable examples of judicial activism constitute a transfer of the power to make fundamental policy decisions from WTO Member states to the Appellate Body. *Shrimp/Turtle I* interpreted the Article XX(g) exception for the "conservation of exhaustible natural resources" to include living, renewable resources, thereby permitting a Member state to unilaterally exclude imports if other Member states fail to adopt that Member's preferred conservation policy, as long as its trade measure meets the general standards in the Article XX chapeau.

* * *

The *Shrimp/Turtle I* opinion occurred after an outcry from international environmental NGOs, angry demonstrations in the streets, and the development of an extensive literature within the environmental and trade communities arguing that the WTO adjudicative bodies were acting contrary to accepted international environmental policy. The AB's opinion may have solved a public relations problem with the environmental community, but it will create an even greater one with developing countries and with advanced industrial societies in which access to foreign markets is restricted.

Environmentalists' concerns about the plight of endangered species, the emission of greenhouse gases, and the destruction of biodiversity are well-founded. However, the question of how such policy decisions are to be made and which institutions should engage in the balancing of the many factors and perspectives relating to these issues is a question of the appropriate form of global governance.

There are, in general, two competing paradigms of how international law and policy should be made. The State Consent paradigm asserts that legitimate international norms that limit the sovereign prerogatives of states require the express consent of the affected states, which are then accountable to their domestic polities. As embodied in the WTO system this model requires that changes in rights or obligations be negotiated and concluded by a formal agreement or other authorized process. The second paradigm, which I am characterizing as the Naturalist paradigm, implicitly or explicitly draws on the much older tradition of natural law or assumed global values as a source of international norms. It postulates that universal norms, or norms perceived to be generally accepted by the observer, bind states even without their express consent. Advocates of this approach use non-binding resolutions at international forums, selected domestic court decisions from the United States and Europe, and general language from treaties to generate binding legal norms when there is, in fact, no agreement that these norms constitute binding legal obligations, and explicit state consent would be difficult or impossible to obtain.

Advocates of the Naturalist paradigm rely on judicial activism and the cosmopolitan conscience to inject new norms into what appear to be consensual regimes. There is a vast and growing body of work supporting judicial activist interpretations of UN resolutions, general nonbinding declarations, and domestic judicial decisions to create legal norms. . . .

* * *

The WTO Agreement and the Dispute Settlement Understanding ("DSU") **[Basic Document 4.16]**, however, contain a detailed structure of governance based on state consent and a textualist interpretation methodology. The AB's infusion of what are essentially the value preferences of particular interest groups and some scholars into the trade regime through the technique of "evolutionary" interpretation in *Shrimp/Turtle I* is a dangerous trend for global governance. The Naturalist approach to law formation is, first, less democratic than nation-state representation under a consensual regime and, second, a process of lawmaking that most states have not accepted. Judicial innovations like those in *Shrimp/Turtle I* and *II* will inevitably create conflicts about the legitimacy of AB policymaking and undermine support for the trade regime in many domestic societies.

* * *

In *Shrimp/Turtle I* the AB determined that US measures prohibiting the import of shrimp captured in a manner causing the incidental killing of sea turtles did relate to the "conservation of exhaustible natural resources" and were therefore provisionally exempt. In reaching this conclusion the Appellate Body utilized what it termed an "evolutionary" approach to the problem of the interpretation of agreements in a treaty regime. Rather than use the textual approach of the Vienna Convention on the Law of Treaties **[Basic Document 1.10]** or attempt to determine what Member states intended in negotiating the GATT agreement, the AB announced that Article XX(g) must be interpreted "in the light of the contemporary concerns of the community of nations about the protection and conservation of the environment."

First, the particular "evolutionary" approach the AB used in this case is directly contrary to the clearly articulated structure of governance in the WTO agreements. The DSU, in allocating responsibility to the dispute settlement bodies, establishes a consent-based legal system allocating only a limited law-applying role for the Appellate Body. Article 3.2 specifies that the purpose of the dispute settlement system is "to preserve the rights and obligations of Members under the covered agreements" and that rulings "cannot add to or diminish the rights and obligations provided in the covered agreements." This limited mandate is reinforced by the clear language of Article 19.2 that "the panel and Appellate Body cannot add to or diminish the rights and obligations provided in the covered agreements."

* * *

Rather Member states, consistent with a consent approach, selected a method of interpretation in the DSU that preserves state sovereignty by requiring Member participation in policy determinations. This selection inherently rejects a more teleological approach to interpretation, such as that of the jurisprudence of the European Court of Justice and the United States Supreme Court, both of which adjudicate in the context of relatively homogeneous domestic societies. For good or ill, the Vienna Convention on [the Law of] Treaties ..., codifying the customary rules of interpretation, articulates an essentially textualist method of interpretation. The International Law Commission, in proposing the draft articles of the Vienna Convention, described the general rule of interpretation now codified in Article 31 as follows: "A treaty shall be interpreted in good faith in accordance with the ordinary meaning to be given to the terms of the treaty in their context and in the light of its object and purpose."

SECTION 5.   DISCUSSION NOTES/QUESTIONS

1. In this problem, the EU chose to ban imports from "Non–Conforming Countries" that were manufactured in ways that contribute "disproportionately" to global warming. An alternative way for the EU to have proceeded with remedial trade action against the UFC would have been to impose "countervailing duties" on such imports pursuant to Articles VI and XVI of the GATT **(Basic Document 4.3)** and the Agreement on Subsidies and Countervailing Measures. In *The Legal Option: Suing the United States in International Forums for Global Warming Emissions,* 33 Envtl. L. Rep. 10185 (2003) at 10188–89, Andrew Strauss has described such an approach:

> [P]articipants in the Kyoto process [could continue] to proceed without the United States, [while] introducing a provision into the regime which would allow participating countries to impose countervailing duties on products made in ways that contribute disproportionately to global warming from certain or all nonparticipating countries. The WTO, pursuant to the General Agreement on Tariffs and Trade (GATT), currently allows countries to impose countervailing duties to offset the competitive trade advantage that foreign companies gain when they receive subsidies from their governments. The identification of a subsidy is very complex. Clearly, a cash hand-out to industry by a government qualifies, but what about equivalent tax breaks, special government services, etc.? Some environmentalists have argued that lax environmental standards externalize the costs of production and should be considered de facto subsidies. It could be argued that emission of [greenhouse gases] is far more insidious than most subsidies. Rather than the countries own tax payers bearing the cost of advantaging favored industries, the cost is placed in this instance on the citizens (human and nonhuman) of the entire planet. In addition, there is jurisprudence by WTO panels and the Appellate Body indicating that multilateral attempts to remedy environmental problems through trade restrictions would be given a deference under the WTO regime that unilateral trade actions would not be given. The prospect of countries taking potentially embarrassing, expensive and arguably legal remedial trade action against the United States could help encourage it to engage in serious negotiations over global warming.

Assume that instead of a ban, the KER established a mechanism whereby countervailing duties were imposed in accordance with a complex formula to offset directly the amount saved by manufacturers in Non–Conforming Countries by not having borne the costs of complying with the Kyoto Protocol **(Basic Document 5.48)**. After considering Professor Strauss's discussion above and examining GATT articles VI and VXI **(Basic Document 4.3)**, what advantages and/or disadvantages would such an approach have offered the EU over the ban approach adopted in the present problem? Taking into account the GATT/WTO case law you have read in Section 4 above, would the legal argument in support of a countervailing duty approach be stronger or weaker than the argument in favor of a ban? For further discussion of environmental externalities and subsidies *see* Naomi Roht–Arriaza, *Shifting the Point of Regulations: The International Organization for Standardization and Global Lawmaking on Trade and the Environment,* 22 Ecology L.Q. 479, 521 (1995); Thomas J. Schoenbaum, *International Trade and Protection of the Environment: The Continuing Search for Reconciliation,* 91

A.J.I.L. 268, 188–89 (1997). For a similar discussion regarding border tax adjustments allowed under GATT Article III, *see* John A. Barett, *The Global Environment and Free Trade: A Vexing Problem and a Taxing Solution*, 76 Ind. L.J. 829 (2001).

2. Suppose the following additional variation on the instant problem: UFC's parliament, responding to public outcries against the utilization of child labor in developing countries, adopts legislation banning the importation of products manufactured in whole or in part by children under the age of fifteen, requiring every manufactured import to display a label or tag stipulating that it was not made by child labor in whole or in part, and calling upon the UFC to seek the worldwide implementation of the 1989 Convention on the Rights of the Child **(Basic Document 3.32)**? Would this scenario fit among the exceptions of Article XX? How would the UFC legislation comport with the national treatment obligations and other provisions of the GATT? To the extent that it is inconsistent with these provisions might it, nevertheless, be allowed under an exception to Article XX? If so which one(s)? For pertinent discussion, see Frank J. Garcia & Soohyun Jun, *Trade-Based Strategies for Combating Child Labor*, in Child Labor and Human Rights: Making Children Matter 401 (B. Weston ed. & contrib., 2005).

3. *Bibliographical Note.* For supplemental discussion concerning the principal themes addressed in this problem, consult the following additional specialized materials:

(a) *Books/Monographs/Report/Symposia.* C. Barfield, Free Trade, Sovereignty, Democracy: The Future of the World Trade Organization (2001); D. Brack, M. Grubb, & C. Windram, International Trade and Climate Change Policies (Trade and Environment Series) (2000); B. Guha–Khasnobis, The WTO, Developing Countries, and the Doha Development Agenda: Prospects and Challenges for Trade–Led Growth (Studies in Development Economics and Policy) (2004); J. Jackson, The Jurisprudence of GATT and WTO: Insights on Treaty Law and Economic Relations (2000); P. Mavroidis, The Role of the Judge: Lessons for the WTO (Studies in International Economics) (2000); M. Moore, A World Without Walls: Freedom, Development, Free Trade and Global Governance (2003); M.S. Taylor & B. Copeland, Trade and the Environment: Theory and Evidence (2003); G. Sampson & J. Pronk, Trade, Environment, and the WTO: The Post–Seattle Agenda (Policy Essay, No. 27) (2000); X. Yi–Chong, P. Weller, E. Elgar, & Y. Xu, The Governance Of World Trade: International Civil Servants and the GATT / WTO (2004).

(b) *Articles/Book Chapters.* J. Alvarez, *How Not to Link: Institutional Conundrums of an Expanded Trade Regime,* 7 Wid. L. Symp. J. 1 (2001); S. Charnovitz, *Symposium: The Boundaries of the WTO: Triangulating the World Trade Organization,* 96 A.J.I.L. 28 (2002); D. Esty, *Toward Optimal Environmental Governance,* 74 N.Y.U. L. Rev. 1495 (1999); J. Dunoff, *The Death of the Trade Regime*, 10 EUR. J. INT'L L. 733 (1999); S. Gaines, *Process and Production Methods: How to Produce Sound Policy for Environmental PPM–Based Trade Measures,* 27 Colum. J. Envtl. L. 383 (2002); R. Howse, *The Appellate Body Rulings in the Shrimp/Turtle Case: A New Legal Baseline for the Trade and Environment Debate,* 27 Colum. J. Envtl. L. 383 (2002); J. H. Jackson, *International Law Status of WTO Dispute Settlement Reports: Obligation to Comply or Option to "Buy Out"?,* 98 A.J.I.L. 109 (2004); K. Kennedy, *Trade and the Environment: Implications for Global Governance: Why Multilateralism Matters in Resolving Trade–Environment Disputes,* 7 Wid. L. Symp. J. 31 (2001); J. McGinnis & M. Movsesian, *Commentary: The World Trade Constitution*, 114 Harv. L. Rev. 511 (2000); J. Pauwelyn, *The Role of Public*

International Law in the WTO: How Far Can We Go?, 95 A.J.I.L. 535 (2001); T. Reif and J. Eckert, *Courage You Can't Understand: How to Achieve the Right Balance Between Shaping and Policing Commerce in Disputes Before the World Trade Organization,* 42 Colum. J. Transnat'l L. 657 (2004); G. Shaffer, *The World Trade Organization Under Challenge: Democracy and the Law and Politics of the WTO's Treatment of Trade and Environment,* 25 Harv. Envtl. L. Rev. 1 (2001); M. Schaefer, *Sovereignty, Influence, Realpolitik, and the World Trade Organization,* 25 Hastings Int'l & Comp. L. Rev. 341 (2002); J. Vallely, *Developments: Tension between the Cartagena Protocol and the WTO: The Significance of Recent WTO Developments in an Ongoing Debate,* 5 Chi. J. Int'l L. 369 (2004).

Problem 6–5

AIDS Meets TRIPS in Gondowana

SECTION 1. FACTS

Gondowana is a medium size developing country in southern Africa, possessed of a middle class and a modest technological base. Owing to its colonial history, however, a hugely disproportionate share of its middle class is made up of a European-descended minority. The vast majority of Gondowana's population is black and extremely poor, many suffering from HIV/AIDS. The World Health Organization (WHO) recently estimated that 20% of Gondowana's population is HIV positive, giving the country one of the highest incidences of HIV/AIDS anywhere in the world.

Poor prevention planning has been a major contributing factor to Gondowana's HIV/AIDS epidemic. But so also has been the unaffordability of existing HIV/AIDS drugs, all of which were developed by foreign pharmaceutical companies. With the annual cost of an HIV/AIDS antiviral regime at close to US $1,200 per person, these drugs are significantly out of the reach of the vast majority of poor Gondowanans who, on average, live on the equivalent of one dollar (US) per day. Notwithstanding, Gondowana is not a party to any international instrument that explicitly or implicitly proclaims and seeks to safeguard the human right to health.

A few years ago, however, in an effort to strengthen its economy, in major part to deal with its critical public health problem, Gondowana joined the World Trade Organization (WTO), established by treaty at the close of the Uruguay Round of the GATT trade negotiations in April 1994.[a] As one of the requirements of membership in the WTO, it was required to accede to the constituent 1994 General Agreement On Trade–Related Aspects of Intellectual Property Rights ("TRIPS"),[b] although as a "developing country member" of TRIPS, it had under TRIPS Article 65 until 2000 to bring its laws into compliance with that agreement. In 1999, Gondowana's parliament enacted an updated patent law, modeled on United States law, which significantly strengthened the protection of patents.

Following implementation of Gondowana's updated patent law and pursuant to its terms, drug companies from all over the world immediately refiled their Gondowanan patents to protect their right exclusively to control the production and distribution of their drugs in Gondowana, including HIV/AIDS and other drugs to treat sexually transmitted diseases such as herpes. Because

---

a. Agreement Establishing the World Trade Organization (WTO), *reprinted in* 33 I.L.M. 1125, 1144 (1994) and 4 Weston & Carlson IV.C.2a.

b. The TRIPS Agreement **(Basic Document 4.15)** is one of several instruments incorporated by reference in, and annexed to, the 1994 Agreement Establishing the World Trade Organization, *supra* note **a.**

of the limited number of people living in Gondowana who could afford HIV/AIDS drugs, however, the pharmaceutical companies' profits on these drugs proved to be extremely modest.

Nevertheless, after intensive but largely unsuccessful efforts by Gondowana's government to persuade the foreign manufacturers of the HIV/AIDS drugs to significantly lower their prices, the Gondowanan Prime Minister issued a statement that his government would introduce legislation into parliament to make AIDS drugs more affordable. Once the government's bill was submitted to Parliament, in response to domestic lobbying pressure, the bill's coverage was expanded also to include drugs that treat the sexually transmitted forms of the herpes virus.[c] Proponents of expanding the bill's coverage pointed to credible clinical studies suggesting that herpes sores or lesions in the genital area make people more prone to AIDS infection. Declaring a "state of national emergency" the Gondowanan parliament passed legislation known as the Medicines and Related Substances Access (MARSA) Act.

The MARSA Act distinguishes between "Category I Drugs" and "Category II Drugs." Category I Drugs are defined to include "prophylactic drugs to prevent the onset of disease symptoms in people who are carriers of the HIV virus or the herpes simplex virus 2." The MARSA Act specifies that for the treatment of people who are HIV positive these include "protease inhibitors and other prophylactic drugs which prevent the onset of AIDS among persons carrying the HIV virus." The MARSA Act specifies that for the treatment of people who are carriers of the herpes virus 2 these include antiviral drugs which can be administered as a suppressive therapy to reduce the frequency and severity of herpes symptoms.

Category II Drugs are defined to include "therapeutic drugs designed to treat opportunistic infections which occur in individuals with AIDS." As of the date of the Act, all Category I and Category II drugs available in Gondowana were developed and manufactured by foreign pharmaceutical companies, which also maintained all Gondowanan patent rights on them.

The MARSA Act provides that Category I drugs will be subject to compulsory licensing by a governmental Office of Patent License Control (OPLC) within Gondowana's Ministry of Health charged with awarding local enterprises licenses to utilize Category I Gondowanan drug patents. Section 3 of the Act provides that the OPLC shall "determine the fair price that the licensee shall pay to the licensor," and that, in determining such price, "overriding importance" shall be given to "the affordability of Category I

---

c. Twenty percent of Gondowana's adult population is infected with the genital herpes simplex virus 2. This is similar to the percentage of infection found in the United States. While genital herpes is not life threatening, symptoms and severity can very greatly from person to person. Some people experience severe recurrent outbreaks with very painful burning and sores in the genital area, as well as flu-like symptoms. Other people seldom experience outbreaks, and when they do, they have milder symptoms such as itching and redness. An annual supply of herpes drugs (which have all been developed by foreign pharmaceutical companies) in Gondowana costs US$1,000; but, as is the case with HIV/AIDS drugs, few Gondowanans can afford them and drug company profits are consequently quite modest. Neither the Gondowanan government nor anyone else in Gondowana has made an effort to negotiate licenses from the foreign holders of herpes drug patents.

drugs for Gondowanan citizens in need of such drugs." Section 6 of the Act provides that "an interested party" may appeal the price determination made by the OPLC to the Minister of Health, and that "all appeals are final and not subject to judicial review."

The MARSA Act further provides, under its Section 10, that Category II drugs will no longer be subject to patent protection. Pursuant to Section 12 "Category II drugs will be manufactured under the direction of the Ministry of Health and distributed to Gondowanan citizens free of charge, all expenses to be born by the Ministry of Health."

A third category of drugs, vaccines that can prevent the contraction of HIV, are not covered by the MARSA Act. In a very unusual achievement for local enterprises, Gondowanan companies have developed—and own—patents on two of the most promising of such vaccines, each currently in clinical trials. The patents on three less promising vaccines, also in clinical trials, are owned by foreign pharmaceutical manufacturers.

The major American pharmaceutical manufacturers have reacted with great alarm to the passage of the MARSA Act, claiming that it violates international law, including the specific requirements of the relevant provisions of TRIPS, and therefore are demanding that Gondowana rescind it. Accordingly, they have requested that the United States Trade Representative, Megan Dempsey, on behalf of the United States, also a member of the WTO, invoke the WTO dispute resolution procedures to determine whether the provisions relating to both Category I and Category II drugs are consistent with the requirements of TRIPS. She has acceded to this request and a dispute settlement panel has been constituted pursuant to the 1994 WTO Understanding on Rules and Procedures Governing the Settlement of Disputes.

Section 2.   Questions Presented

1. Does Gondowana's Medicines and Related Substances Access (MARSA) Act constitute a violation of international law, including the specific requirements of the relevant provisions of TRIPS; and, if so, to what extent, if at all, is Gondowana legally required to rescind this law?

2. In any event, are there any additional or alternative legal norms, procedures, and/or institutions to be recommended that might further help to prevent or discourage situations of the kind posed by this problem?

Section 3.   Assignments

A.   Reading Assignment

Study the Readings presented in Section 4, *infra*, and the Discussion Notes/Questions that follow. Also, time permitting, consult the accompanying bibliographical references.

B. Recommended Writing Assignment

Prepare a comprehensive, logically sequenced, and *argumentative* brief in the form of an outline of the primary and subsidiary *legal* issues you see requiring resolution by the WTO dispute settlement panel. Also, from the perspective of an independent judge, indicate which side ought to prevail on each issue and why. Retain a copy of your issue-outline/brief for class discussion.

C. Recommended Oral Assignment

Assume that you are legal counsel for Gondowana or the United States (as designated by your instructor); then, relying upon the Readings (and your issue-outline if prepared), present a 10–15 minute oral argument of your government's likely positions before the WTO dispute settlement panel.

D. Recommended Reflective Assignment

Consider (and recommend) alternative norms, institutions, and/or procedures that you believe might do better than existing world order arrangements to contend with situations of the kind posed by this problem. In so doing, but without insisting upon *immediate* feasibility, identify the particular transition steps that would be needed to make your alternatives a reality.

Section 4. Readings

The following readings are considered *prima facie* relevant to solving this problem. They are your law library for present purposes and should be treated as such, organized intelligibly for "shelving" and not necessarily according to the issues presented. Be sure to review Chapter 2 ("International Legal Prescription: The 'Sources' of International Law") in your consideration of them. It, too, should be treated as part of your law library (as, indeed, should this entire coursebook).

1. General Agreement on Trade–Related Aspects of Intellectual Property Rights, Including Trade in Counterfeit Goods. Concluded at Marrakesh, 15 Apr 1994. Entered into force, 1 Jan 1995. *Reprinted in* **33 I.L.M. 1197 (1994) and 4 Weston & Carlson IV.C.2d: Pmbl. & Arts. 1–4, 7–8, 27–34, 40–50, 63–69, 71(1)** (Basic Document 4.15).

2. James Thuo Gathii, "Constructing Intellectual Property Rights and Competition Policy Consistently with Facilitating Access to Affordable AIDS Drugs to Low–End Consumers," 53 Fla. L. Rev. 727, 733–35 (2001).

The leading cause of death in Sub–Saharan Africa today is AIDS. In southern African countries, the infection rate is as high as 20% of the population. In 1999, for example, Botswana had an infection rate of 35.80%, Swaziland 25.25%, Zimbabwe 25.06%, Lesotho 23.57%, and South Africa 19.94%. By 1999, at least fifteen million Africans had died of AIDS and another twenty-five million in sub-Saharan Africa were living with the disease. Four million sub-Saharan Africans were newly infected in 1999.

AIDS, contrary to the view that it is a death warrant, is a treatable disease. In the United States, for example, drug treatment has quadrupled the median survival time for Americans diagnosed with AIDS from one to four years. This stunning achievement is the result of a combination of initiatives that has galvanized public attention in treating AIDS for about twenty years. Intense public pressure on the government and the pharmaceutical industry by AIDS activists, including the efforts of non-governmental organizations working with AIDS patients, has led to greater availability and accessibility of AIDS drugs, health services and support services for AIDS patients.

Among these initiatives is the availability of a complex combination of drugs known as a cocktail. A cocktail includes protease inhibitors and reverse transcriptase inhibitors. These drugs interrupt the cycle of HIV infection, allow an infected person's immune system to rebuild itself, and allow the person to live much longer than the person would without treatment. In the United States, a strict cocktail regimen costs on average between $10,000 and $15,000 per year. These regimens have reduced mortality rates by a phenomenal 75% in the United States. AZT (Zidovudine) has been shown to reduce mother-to-child transmission by up to 70% when administered to the mother during pregnancy or to the child immediately after birth. By contrast, in sub-Saharan Africa and for low-end consumers in general, AIDS has become history's worst pandemic in part because the cocktails that have been used successfully in the United States are too expensive. In addition, the provision of health services has been undermined substantially by reallocation of funds to other sectors of the economy. It seems, therefore, that unless measures are taken to provide affordable drugs to the millions with AIDS in Africa, they may be "already . . . beyond hope."

In Brazil, the government has produced at least five generic AIDS drugs that have been available to its citizens for free since 1997. Brazil's policy of universal access to AIDS drugs has led to dramatic reductions in the rate of AIDS deaths and the incidence of opportunistic infections. While the death rate between 1996 and 1999 fell by about half, the rate of incidence of opportunistic infections fell by 60–80%. The Brazilian government invested over US $339 million in 1999 and over US $462 million in 2000 into the project. In January 2001, the United States requested that the WTO establish a panel to determine the legality of Brazil's compulsory licensing laws.

As the experience of the United States and Brazil demonstrates, AIDS is a treatable disease, and levels of infection can drop dramatically with increased availability of drugs: the same should be so in Sub–Saharan Africa. While the AIDS problem in Africa is part of a bigger picture of a health sector in crisis, that is no reason not to take action to facilitate access to affordable AIDS drugs in sub-Saharan Africa. There can be no gainsaying that low income levels in sub-Saharan Africa make costs of over $10,000 per year prohibitive. Yet, the pharmaceutical industry has quietly argued that selling AIDS drugs at discounts in sub-Saharan Africa portends doom with respect to the ability to finance further research and development. In effect, it argues that the AIDS crisis in Africa is intractable because providing AIDS drugs, which still enjoy patent protection in Western markets, conflicts with its commercial objectives. The handouts that pharmaceutical companies have announced are laudable, but the existence of such handouts does not address the question of affordability in the long term. In addition, it is possible that these ad hoc responses and the infrequency with which AIDS drugs are consumed in Africa may contribute to the creation of drug-resistant strains of the virus.

However, addressing the needs of low-end consumers is not a problem specific to sub-Saharan Africa. Low-end consumers, or consumers with little or no income, who have HIV, are found in all countries of the world. Thus, while most of these consumers are in sub-Saharan Africa, the problem is an international one, not merely a regional one. . . .

3.   Naomi A. Bass, Note, "Implications of the TRIPS Agreement For Developing Countries: Pharmaceuticals Patent Laws In Brazil and South Africa in the 21st Century," 34 Geo. Wash. Int'l L. Rev. 191, 191–97 (2002).

A.   The History of International Patent Laws

Prior to the TRIPs Agreement [**Basic Document 4.15**], several multilateral treaties provided basic protection of intellectual property. In 1883 the Paris Convention for the Protection of Industrial Property (subsequently modified in 1967)[1] endeavored to safeguard a variety of industrial property, including the rights of patent holders. The Paris Convention did not, however, impose obligations on a member country to protect the rights of foreigners if the member country did not grant protection to its own nationals. As a result, member countries could easily circumvent the requirements of the Paris Convention by universally withholding protection of intellectual property. This fundamental limitation of the Paris Convention, whereby "member nations [were] free to treat foreign interests poorly as long as domestic interests [were] treated just as poorly"[2] undermined efforts to provide comprehensive intellectual property protection.

Originally adopted in 1887 and most recently modified in 1971, the Berne Convention for the Protection of Literary and Artistic Works[3] established protection for the rights of copyright owners' technical and creative material. Similar to the Paris Convention, the Berne Convention was criticized for its limitations, including the failure to devise provisions for empowering intellectual property holders to enforce their rights and resolve disputes.

These conventions ultimately led to the Stockholm Convention of 1967, which established the World Intellectual Property Organization (WIPO).[4] WIPO symbolized international efforts to implement global intellectual property protection. WIPO's primary objective is to foster "cooperation among the [member] nations in cooperation with various international organizations . . . [and to] insure administrative cooperation among the various intellectual property unions."[5]

WIPO received criticism for its tendency to give priority to the objectives of developing countries, failing to establish sufficient protection and enforcement of intellectual property. Perceived by many representatives of the international community as "out of touch with modern times and the chang-

1. 828 U.N.T.S. 305 ... [*reprinted in* 4 Weston & Carlson IV.E.1].

2. R. Pechman, Note, *Seeking Multilateral Protection for Intellectual Property: The United States "TRIPs" over Special 301*, 7 Minn. J. Global Trade 179, 181–82 (1998).

3. 828 U.N.T.S. 221 ... [*reprinted in* 4 Weston & Carlson IV.E.2].

4. 828 U.N.T.S. 3.

5. F. Romano, International Conventions and Treaties, 536 PLI/Pat 545, 554 (1998).

ing norms of an innovative community,"[6] WIPO failed to create an effective regime for the protection of intellectual property. The inability of WIPO to adequately accomplish its primary objectives ultimately motivated the creation of the WTO and the implementation of the TRIPs Agreement.

B.   The Modern Approach: The Agreement on Trade–
Related Intellectual Property Rights

The TRIPs Agreement was one achievement of the Uruguay Round of the GATT, concluded in Morocco on April 15, 1994. The TRIPs Agreement became effective on January 1, 1995 and is one of the most far-reaching multilateral agreements on intellectual property. Expanding upon existing obligations under WIPO, the Paris Convention, and the Berne Convention, the TRIPs Agreement encompasses the protection of copyrights, trademarks, geographical indications, industrial designs, patents, layout-designs of integrated circuits, and undisclosed information including trade secrets and test dates. All members of the WTO must comply with the 73 articles comprising the TRIPs Agreement, which stipulates minimum standards for the protection of intellectual property and the enforcement of patent laws. Despite the comprehensive, unprecedented requirements, however, the TRIPs Agreement permits some flexibility in the manner in which member countries choose to execute their intellectual property laws domestically.

Part I of the TRIPs Agreement sets forth the general provisions and basic principles of the Agreement. Articles 2.1 and 9.1 of the TRIPs Agreement directly reference the Paris and Berne Conventions, instructing member countries to adhere to existing obligations set forth in these preceding treaties. Article 3 of the TRIPs Agreement requires uniform, national treatment standards, obligating each WTO member country to provide comparable intellectual property protection for the products and processes of its nationals, in addition to the nationals of all other member countries. The TRIPs Agreement also contains an expansive most-favored-nation requirement in Article 4, specifying that each WTO member country must grant to nationals of other member countries any "advantage, favor, privilege, or immunity" given to nationals of any other country with regard to the protection of intellectual property.

Finally, Article 8 grants WTO members the authority ["in formulating or amending their laws and regulations"] to "adopt measures necessary to protect public health and nutrition, and to promote the public interest in sectors of vital importance to their socioeconomic and technological development, provided that such measures are consistent with the provisions of the TRIPs Agreement." The TRIPs Agreement's failure to explicitly define acceptable procedures for accomplishing the objectives of ensuring public health and welfare creates a vague allocation of power that is vulnerable to multiple, conflicting interpretations. The resulting disagreement emerging from WTO members' disparate interpretations of TRIPs will not receive swift reconciliation.

Part II of the TRIPs Agreement governs the standards concerning the availability, scope and use of intellectual property rights. Included within Part II is Article 27, defining the scope of patentable subject matter. Specifically,

---

6. *Id* at 559.

Article 27 requires each member country to make patents available in all fields of technology—including pharmaceuticals—provided that the inventions are "new, involve an inventive step, and are capable of industrial application." This description is consistent with the definition of patentable subject matter under US patent laws. Article 27 further mandates equitable treatment of all patent rights, irrespective of the place of invention, field of technology, or whether the products are imported or locally manufactured. Despite this seemingly rigid definition of patentable subject matter, Article 27 permits select governments the opportunity to exclude a pharmaceutical product from patentability when essential to protect the public health or environment.

In addition to Article 27, Article 30 sets forth a second exception to the TRIPs Agreement, stipulating that WTO member countries may "provide limited exceptions to the exclusive rights conferred by a patent, provided that such exceptions do not unreasonably conflict with a normal exploitation of the patent and do not unreasonably prejudice the legitimate interests of the patent owner, taking account of the legitimate interests of third parties." This provision suggests the need for a balancing test to compare the needs of patent-holding, multinational pharmaceutical manufacturers with the concerns of consumers and domestic drug manufacturers in developing countries. Particularly in times of economic hardship and domestic public health crises, efforts to provide essential medicine to the poor should outweigh profit-maximizing agendas set by large, multinational pharmaceutical corporations. Article 30 does not condone alleviating a patent system entirely. It is, however, appropriate under Article 30 to reduce the term of a patent from twenty years as a means of promoting faster access to innovative medicine to poor people in developing countries, but limiting such reduction to the extent that the patent holder will not suffer from inequitable treatment.

4. Editors' Note. The ability to engage the WTO system of dispute resolution to resolve intellectual property disputes—such as, for example, when the United States invoked the system in respect of pharmaceuticals in Brazil (see, *e.g., supra* Reading 2)—is one of the major benefits that developed countries derived from the bringing of the global intellectual property regime into the WTO. Resort to this system to ensure compliance with TRIPS **(Basic Document 4.15)** permits enhanced mechanisms for both adjudication and enforcement. Andrew Strauss, in somewhat different context, describes this WTO dispute resolution process succinctly as follows:

> The WTO's adjudicative mechanisms are established in several key provisions of the "Dispute Settlement Understanding" that arose out of the Uruguay Round Agreements. The Dispute Settlement Understanding specifies that parties to a dispute must first attempt to resolve their differences through consultations with each other. If unsuccessful, and if both parties agree, they can request good offices conciliation or mediation from the Director General of the World Trade Organization. If a settlement continues to be illusive, the complainant can request a three member panel to adjudicate the dispute. The losing party may appeal issues of law to a permanent appellate body. Once the adjudication process has run its course, a final decision identifying whether or not an infraction has occurred becomes binding when adopted by the membership of the WTO. This is now automatic unless all members agree that it

should not be adopted (a most unlikely possibility). After a decision, the losing party is required to comply with the decision or, in the alternative, offer compensation.

Once the WTO authoritatively identifies an infraction [the WTO dispute resolution system also provides advantages for enforcement]. In the first place, because the continuing integrity of the international trading order depends upon the willingness of countries to abide by WTO determinations, voluntary compliance is likely to be much higher than if another body was used to adjudicate ... disputes. Even under the older and much weaker GATT system, the vast majority of panel decisions were honored. To the extent that a commitment to the multilateral trading system alone, is not sufficient to ensure compliance, the WTO employs a uniquely powerful system of sanctions which could be used to enforce international environmental standards. The Dispute Settlement Understanding provides that if a party is judged not to be in compliance with WTO rules, and does not remedy the situation or pay compensation to the winning party, the winning party can seek permission from the WTO to withdraw trade concessions previously given to the loser. These can be very costly, and can be strategically targeted against specific politically powerful national industries of the recalcitrant parties. Thus, in addition to facing international pressures to comply with [pertinent] treaty obligations, the system is designed so that targeted industries place additional internal pressures on their governments to comply. Because such sanctions are legalized, and therefore deemed legitimate, the loser is unlikely to retaliate in kind, thus averting the potential for a trade war.

Andrew Strauss, *The Case for Utilizing the World Trade Organization as a Forum for Global Environmental Regulation*, 3 Widener L. Symp. J. 309, 323–24 (1998).

5. World Trade Organization: Dispute Settlement Panel Report on Canada—Patent Protection of Pharmaceutical Products, WT/DS114/R (17 Mar 2000).

[*Eds.*—From 1923 to 1992, Canada maintained a system of compulsory licensing to ensure cheap domestic production of food and medicine products. In 1992, Canada passed the Patent Act Amendment Act, 1992 (Bill C–91). The act eliminated the compulsory license system to conform to the NAFTA and TRIPS agreements **(Basic Documents 4.13 & 4.15)**, both then in the late stages of negotiation. Stiff parliamentary opposition had argued that enforcement of this TRIPS regime would cause drug prices to skyrocket and cripple the public health service. In compromise, the new act contained two "exceptions" to the exclusive patent rights of TRIPS Article 28. The "regulatory review exception"[d] allowed competitors to produce generic versions of patented drugs during the life of the patents, for the purpose of gaining regulatory approval. This eliminated the 3 to 6 year delay between the time a drug patent expired and the time it took generic versions to get approved and on market. The "stockpiling exception"[e] permitted competitors to manufacture

---

d. *Patent Act, Section 55.2(1)*: "It is not an infringement of a patent for any person to make, construct, use or sell the patented invention solely for uses reasonably related to the development and submission of informa-

tion required under any law ... that regulates the manufacture, construction, use or sale of any product."

e. *Patent Act, Section 55.2(2)*: "It is not an infringement of a patent for any person who

generic versions of a drug during the life of its patent, so that large quantities would be available for purchase the moment the patent expired. Canada contended that both were "limited exceptions" justified by TRIPS Article 30.

In 1998, after engaging in unsuccessful consultations with Canada pursuant to Article 4 of the Understanding on Rules and Procedures Governing the Settlement of Disputes (DSU) and Article 64 of TRIPS, the European Community (EC) (now known as the European Union or EU) requested that the Dispute Settlement Body (DSB) establish a panel to examine the matter.

Before the panel, the EC argued that the "exceptions" to Canada's Patent Act violated TRIPS Articles 28 and 27.1. Canada conceded that the Act violated Article 28.1(a) by allowing competitors to make use of and import a patented product without the patent holder's permission, but argued that Article 30 permitted such "limited exceptions." The EC countered that Canada's exceptions were not "limited" and that even if the Act was a valid Article 30 exception to Article 28, it still singled out pharmaceuticals in violation of the anti-discrimination clause of Article 27.1. Canada claimed that Article 27.1 did not apply to Article 30 exceptions or, alternatively, that if Article 27.1 did apply, the Act did not discriminate within the meaning of Article 27. Excerpts from the panels decision follow.]

Article 30

(7.20) Article 30 establishes three criteria: . . . (1) the exception must be "limited"; (2) the exception must not "unreasonably conflict with normal exploitation of the patent"; (3) the exception must not "unreasonably prejudice the legitimate interests of the patent owner, taking account of the legitimate interests of third parties." The three conditions are cumulative, each being a separate . . . requirement.

* * *

(7.27) [Canada argued that] an exception is "limited" as long as the exclusive right to sell to the ultimate consumer during the term of the patent is preserved. . . .

(7.28) The EC interpreted . . . "limited" to connote a narrow exception, . . . described by words such as "narrow, small, minor, insignificant or restricted." . . . [It] contended that the stockpiling exception is not "limited" because it takes away three of the five Article 28.1 rights—the rights to exclude "making," "using" and "importing."

* * *

(7.30) The Panel agreed with the EC that . . . the narrower definition is . . . appropriate when the word "limited" is used as part of the phrase "limited exception". The word "exception" by itself connotes a limited derogation. . . . When a treaty uses the term "limited exception," . . . "limited" must be given a meaning separate from the limitation implicit in the word

makes, constructs, uses or sells a patented invention [per 55.2(1)] . . . to make, construct or use the invention, during the . . . [patent], for the manufacture and storage of articles intended for sale after the date . . . the patent expires."

"exception." ... The term "limited exception" must therefore ... [make] only a small diminution of the rights in question.

* * *

(7.35) In practical terms [addressing Canada's argument], it must be recognized that enforcement of the right to exclude "making" and "using" during the patent term will necessarily give all patent owners, for all products, a short period of extended market exclusivity after the patent expires. The repeated enactment of such exclusionary rights with knowledge of their universal market effects ... [is] an affirmation of the purpose to produce those market effects.... [Thus the stockpiling exception] does not satisfy the first condition of Article 30 ... [and] therefore ... is inconsistent with Canada's obligations under Article 28.1.

* * *

(7.45) In the Panel's view, however, Canada's regulatory review exception is a "limited exception." ... As long as the exception is confined to conduct needed to comply with the requirements of the regulatory approval process, the extent of the acts ... permitted ... will be small and narrowly bounded. Even though regulatory approval processes may require substantial amounts of test production ... the patent owner's rights ... are not impaired ... as long as they are solely for regulatory purposes and no commercial use is made of resulting ... products.

[*Eds.*—The Panel found that the "regulatory review exception" met the remaining prongs of Article 30. It ruled that approval delays were an unintended consequence of the crossover of regulatory and patent legal regimes and therefore were not protected "normal exploitation." The Panel also found that patent owners do not, as a matter of law, have a "legitimate interest" in the post patent monopoly period caused by regulatory delay. Since there was clear disagreement on the question at the time TRIPS was signed, the Panel found that further political debate and negotiation, rather than an adjudicatory decision, should determine whether the interest was legitimate. Finally, the Panel found that the general public has a legitimate third party interest in drug patents. Since the stockpiling exception failed the "limited" prong, the Panel did not examine it further.]

Article 27

(7.91) The Panel was unable to agree with Canada's contention that Article 27.1 did not apply to exceptions granted under Article 30.... Article 30 exceptions are explicitly described as "exceptions to the exclusive rights conferred by a patent" and contain no indication that any exemption from non-discrimination rules is intended. The Panel concluded, therefore, that the anti-discrimination rule of Article 27.1 does apply to exceptions of the kind authorized by Article 30.

* * *

(7.93) We turn, accordingly, to the question of whether [the regulatory review exception] discriminates as to fields of technology....

* * *

(7.95) The European Communities acknowledged that the words of the regulatory review exception ... do not limit its application to pharmaceutical products....

(7.96) The EC pointed out, however, that pharmaceuticals were the only products mentioned in ... [the] legislative debates [leading to] enactment. It also asserted that [the regulatory review exception] was "in effect applied only to pharmaceuticals products." These assertions led to two distinct allegations of discrimination. The first claim of discrimination was the claim that the legislative history's concentration on pharmaceuticals actually governs the legal scope of the measure, so that, as a matter of law, [the regulatory review exception] applied only to pharmaceuticals [*i.e. de jure* discrimination]. The second claim of discrimination was the claim that, whatever the *de jure* scope, ... the actual effects of [the regulatory review exception] are limited to pharmaceutical producers, and these differential effects amount to a case of de facto discrimination.

* * *

(7.99) ... [T]he Panel concluded that the European Communities had not presented sufficient evidence to [overcome] Canada's formal declaration that the exception ... was not limited to pharmaceutical products....

* * *

(7.104) The Panel did not find [the] evidence from the debates ... to be persuasive evidence of a discriminatory purpose.... [P]reoccupation with the effects of a statute in one area does not necessarily mean that the provisions applicable to other areas are a sham, or of no actual or potential importance. Individual problems are frequently the driving force behind legislative actions of broader scope.... So long as the broader application is not a sham, the legislation cannot be considered discriminatory.... In sum, the Panel found that the evidence in record before it did not raise a plausible claim of discrimination under Article 27.1 of the TRIPS Agreement.

* * *

(8.1) In light of the findings above, the Panel has concluded as follows: (1) [The regulatory review exception] ... is not inconsistent with Canada's obligations under Article 27.1 and Article 28.1 of the TRIPS Agreement. (2) [The stockpiling exception] ... is not consistent with the requirements of Article 28.1 of the TRIPS Agreement.

6. Shanker A. Singham, "Competition Policy and the Stimulation of Innovation: TRIPS and the Interface Between Competition and Patent Protection in the Pharmaceutical Industry," 26 Brooklyn J. Int'l L. 363, 401–03 (2002).

The TRIPS Agreement **[Basic Document 4.15]** allows for compulsory licensing under Articles 27(1), 31 and 65(4), but limits these circumstances to cases of antitrust violation, national emergency, and public noncommercial use. The damaging effect of compulsory licenses was recognized by the WTO, and hence, where WTO Members insist on maintaining such provisions, the WTO rules strictly regulate what can be used as a basis for compulsory licensing. Indeed, laws can be TRIPS compliant with no provision for compulsory licensing at all. TRIPS Article 31 states that, "Where the law of a Member allows for [compulsory licensing] ... the following provisions shall be respected." In other words, even if Members have compulsory licensing provisions, they must respect certain basic provisions.

Article 31 of TRIPS lists, conjunctively, the criteria which must be met before a compulsory licensing regime is deemed to be TRIPS compliant.... Although much has been made of the fact that Article 31 of TRIPS is ambiguous, this should not cloud those aspects of the article which are clear and unambiguous. Compulsory licensing is subject to very strict conditions, which must all apply (except in cases of anti-competitive conduct by the patentee). The references to a reason behind the need for the license grant, and the fact that the license only will be granted while that reason prevails, is strongly suggestive that the compulsory licensing regime should be used as a remedy for some form of market failure only, and, therefore, should not be universally applicable. The foregoing addresses what constitutes anti-competitive behavior, and what might further constitute patent misuse. However, many countries' submissions to the WTO trade and competition group help to further clarify this issue....

7. Kojo Yelpaala, "Biotechnology and the Law: Owning the Secret of Life: Biotechnology and Property Rights Revisited," 32 McGeorge L. Rev. 111, 202–04 (2000).

Article 27 (2) of TRIPs [**Basic Document 4.15**] permits member states to exclude an invention from patentability if doing so is "necessary to protect *ordre public* or morality." Article 27(2) states as follows:

> Members may exclude from patentability inventions, the prevention within their territory of the commercial exploitation of which is necessary to protect ordre public or morality, including to protect human, animal or plant life or health or to avoid serious prejudice to the environment, provided that such exclusion is not made merely because the exploitation is prohibited by their law.

The acceptance of the public policy or morality exception under TRIPs by its member states signifies the endorsement of that principle by a large number of states albeit in a limited form. Since TRIPs is only enabling, any perceived limitations suggested by the use of the term commercial exploitation as opposed to publication and exploitation might be handled, in good faith, by signatory states through their domestic legislation. It is important to note, however, that Article 27(2) opens the door for the development of the public policy concept internationally.

[*Eds.*—The author next addresses relevant public policy in the United States.]

Unlike the United Kingdom or the European Union, the United States patent statute does not contain an explicit public policy exception. However, the public policy exception is not foreign to US patent law. In the 1817 case of *Lowell v. Lewis*,[7] Justice Story was called upon to decide whether a patent was

7. 15 F.Cas. 1018 (C.C. Mass. 1817) (No. 8,568).

invalid under the Patent Act of 1793 for not being a "useful invention." In view of the fact that the statute contained no explicit public policy exception, the issue was raised in terms of the usefulness of the invention. Relying on the "utility" concept, Justice Story held that a patent would be invalid if it was "frivolous or injurious to the well-being, good policy, or sound morals of society." In spite of the generality and seeming timelessness of the language used by Justice Story, it is doubtful whether a public policy exception extracted from a statute lacking specific statutory mandate over 150 years ago should control issues of patentability today. Certainly the moral compass of Eighteenth century United States has experienced significant shifts between the 1793 Patent Statute and the current 1952 Patent Act. Within that time period, the atom was split giving impetus to the development of the atomic bomb; the theory of relativity was discovered; the technology for transportation went from horse and buggy to jet airlines; and penicillin was discovered, just to mention a few. The moral and ethical issues raised by these monumental scientific and technological advances were certainly different from those that existed in the early days of the Republic. The moral and ethical issues have, since 1952, been further complicated by the discovery of DNA and the resulting explosion in the advances in biotechnological research. How then could Justice Story's formulation be controlling today without some adjustment? The need for an explicit public policy exception is further demonstrated of the decision by the US Supreme Court in *Diamond v. Chakrabarty*[8] that genetically engineered bacteria and micro-organisms are patentable and the proliferation of biotechnological patents that followed.

In 1998, the US PTO [Patent and Trademark Office] sought to address the issue of the public policy exception in a press release. Allegedly, the PTO received a patent application for a technique that combines human and animal embryo to produce a single animal-human embryo or "chimera." Apparently, the patent was filed by a cellular biologist to instigate a public debate over the appropriateness of patenting genetically engineered biological life forms and genetic components. Confronted with the general public outcry against genetic engineering and the publicity generated by the animal-human embryo patent application, the PTO felt obliged to respond. It issued a press release in which it suggested that a patent might be denied on public policy grounds under the *Lowell v. Lewis* decision. To achieve its objectives, the PTO indicated that it would review patent applications with an eye toward seeking compliance with the strict patentability requirements contained in the patent statute, including the requirement that inventions have "utility." ...

8.   Timothy G. Ackermann, Comment, "Dis'ordre'ly Loopholes: TRIPS Patent Protection, GATT, and the ECJ," 32 Tex. Int'l L. J. 489, 492–93, 496–99 (1997).

... TRIPS **[Basic Document 4.15]** expressly grants Member States the right to exclude inventions from patentability under certain conditions. * * * Under [TRIPS Article 27(2)], a state may exclude an invention from patent protection if prevention of "commercial exploitation" of that invention in their territory is "necessary" in order to "protect ordre public or morality."

8.   447 U.S. 303 (1980).

There is, however, a limitation: the term "necessary" does not encompass an exclusion based solely on a domestic law prohibition. Further, GATT jurisprudence does provide guidance as to the interpretation of "necessary."[f] The TRIPS article also explicitly includes examples of several concerns that are justifiable grounds for exclusion under the "ordre public and morality" clause: "protection of human, animal or plant life or health or ... [avoidance of] serious prejudice to the environment." An exclusion of an invention from patent protection complies with the terms of TRIPS if it falls within these limitations.

* * *

[However,] TRIPS provides definition of the dual reasons for derogation—ordre public and morality—by providing [also] a nonexhaustive list of acceptable justifications: protection of "human, animal or plant life or health [and avoidance of] serious prejudice to the environment." This nonexhaustive list should be viewed as broadening the already potentially broad scope of the grounds for derogation. The concerns enumerated in the list might have been found to be already within the intended scope of the grounds for derogation. Their explicit inclusion, however, provides approved grounds to states looking for a means to exclude a technology from patent protection. Some countries already claim that their refusal to grant patent protection for certain areas of technology or inventions are based on reasons similar to those described in TRIPS.

* * *

As a result of the inherent lack of specificity of the terms used in TRIPS and the broadening effect of the nonexhaustive list, the potential exists for Member States to base their patentability determinations on economic interests of the state, rather than on the legal requirements presented by TRIPS. Several reasons exist for fearing that this potential might be realized. First, the economic interests that would drive such behavior are present, probably have been for a long time, and will continue to be so. Second, states have made decisions concerning intellectual property in the past that were based on economic needs or interests. In order to fully understand the potential for such actions, one must start at the foundation of these decisions—the LDCs' [Less Developed Countries'] conception of intellectual property.

* * *

Many of the LDCs view the purposes and uses of intellectual property in a fundamentally different manner than the developed countries. Several broad theories held by LDCs regarding intellectual property may be identified. One view is that certain kinds of idea-based property are, or should be, pure public goods. One result of this conception of intellectual property is the belief that knowledge, and its products, should be used for the "benefit of all mankind." A related view is reflected in the bureaucratic ethos of the LDCs, which is based on that of the scientific community. This ethos is based on complete disclosure of knowledge. Bureaucracies, as a consequence, have a philosoph-

f. For further discussion of the meaning of "necessary" under the GATT, see *supra* Reading 8 in Problem 6–4 ("The UFC and the EU Dispute the GATT and Global Warming"), at 906, dealing with the interpretation of GATT Article XXB. For citation to and brief explanation of the GATT itself, see note **c** in Problem 6–4, *supra*, at 887.

ical basis for hostility toward a system which treats knowledge as a private right or property.

Finally, LDCs may view intellectual property as a tool for accomplishing public policy goals, rather than as a property right, or as a means to encourage innovation. As an example, increased technology transfer may be considered a public policy goal. Some states view such transfer as a key to industrial (and, thus, economic) growth and believe that granting increased intellectual property rights would work against that goal. It is especially in the technology transfer area that one often finds a close interconnection to the economic interests of the state in question.

This connection between intellectual property and economics has significant implications. Some argue that any attempt to completely separate intellectual property and economics—in the real world, at least—will be unsuccessful. If this is so, then one must consider the economic interests of the LDCs when evaluating the effects of TRIPS. These interests undoubtedly exist, and they have caused states to alter their intellectual property systems in the past.

9. Declaration on the TRIPS Agreement and Public Health. Adopted by the Fourth WTO Ministerial Conference in Doha, Qatar, 14 Nov 2001. WT/MIN(01)/DEC/2 (20 Nov 2001), *reprinted from* **the WTO website at <http://www.wto.org/english/thewto_e/min-ist_e/min01_e/mindecl_trips_e. htm>.**[g]

1. We recognize the gravity of the public health problems afflicting many developing and least-developed countries, especially those resulting from HIV/AIDS, tuberculosis, malaria and other epidemics.

2. We stress the need for the WTO Agreement on Trade–Related Aspects of Intellectual Property Rights (TRIPS Agreement) **[Basic Document 4.15]** to be part of the wider national and international action to address these problems.

3. We recognize that intellectual property protection is important for the development of new medicines. We also recognize the concerns about its effects on prices.

4. We agree that the TRIPS Agreement does not and should not prevent members from taking measures to protect public health. Accordingly, while reiterating our commitment to the TRIPS Agreement, we affirm that the Agreement can and should be interpreted and implemented in a manner supportive of WTO members' right to protect public health and, in particular, to promote access to medicines for all.

g. Unlike WTO panels or the Appellate Body whose decisions are generally not thought to create binding precedent, the membership of the WTO represented either by countries' trade ministers as The Ministerial Conference or by lesser officials as the General Council shall have, according to Article IX (2) of the Marrakesh Agreement Establishing the World Trade Organization, exclusive authority to adopt interpretations of TRIPS and the other Multilateral Trade Agreements. The Article requires that the decision to adopt an interpretation must be approved by a 3/4 majority of the Members. It also specifies that such interpretative authority "not be used in a manner that would undermine" the WTO's amendment provisions. In exceptional circumstances and subject to specific conditions, Article IX (3) allows the Ministerial Conference to decide to waive an obligation imposed on a Member also by a 3/4 vote of the Members.

In this connection, we reaffirm the right of WTO members to use, to the full, the provisions in the TRIPS Agreement, which provide flexibility for this purpose.

5.   Accordingly and in the light of paragraph 4 above, while maintaining our commitments in the TRIPS Agreement, we recognize that these flexibilities include:

a.   In applying the customary rules of interpretation of public international law, each provision of the TRIPS Agreement shall be read in the light of the object and purpose of the Agreement as expressed, in particular, in its objectives and principles.

b.   Each member has the right to grant compulsory licences and the freedom to determine the grounds upon which such licences are granted.

c.   Each member has the right to determine what constitutes a national emergency or other circumstances of extreme urgency, it being understood that public health crises, including those relating to HIV/AIDS, tuberculosis, malaria and other epidemics, can represent a national emergency or other circumstances of extreme urgency.

d.   The effect of the provisions in the TRIPS Agreement that are relevant to the exhaustion of intellectual property rights is to leave each member free to establish its own regime for such exhaustion without challenge, subject to the MFN [Most Favored Nation] and national treatment provisions of Articles 3 and 4.

6.   We recognize that WTO members with insufficient or no manufacturing capacities in the pharmaceutical sector could face difficulties in making effective use of compulsory licensing under the TRIPS Agreement. We instruct the Council for TRIPS to find an expeditious solution to this problem and to report to the General Council before the end of 2002.

7.   We reaffirm the commitment of developed-country members to provide incentives to their enterprises and institutions to promote and encourage technology transfer to least-developed country members.... We also agree that the least-developed country members will not be obliged, with respect to pharmaceutical products, to implement or apply Sections 5 and 7 of Part II of the TRIPS Agreement or to enforce rights provided for under these Sections until 1 January 2016, without prejudice to the right of least-developed country members to seek other extensions of the transition periods as provided for in Article 66.1 of the TRIPS Agreement. We instruct the Council for TRIPS to take the necessary action to give effect to this pursuant to Article 66.1 of the TRIPS Agreement.

10. Alan O. Sykes, "Public Health and International Law: TRIPS, Pharmaceuticals, Developing Countries, and the Doha Solution," 3 Chi. J. Int'l. L. 47–9, 55–8 (2002).

Pharmaceutical prices in the developing world have been much in the news lately.... Much of the problem [of high pricing] is attributed to the prices charged by pharmaceutical companies for their patented medications.... Developing nations where patents are in place seek to reduce those prices with measures that the pharmaceutical manufacturers say would infringe their intellectual property rights. Some of these initiatives have already brought forth legal challenges. South Africa was the target of litigation initiated by a number of pharmaceutical manufacturers over South Africa's Medicines and Related Substances Control Act of 1997. The US government also initiated an action against Brazil within the World Trade Organization ("WTO") over the compulsory licensing provisions in Brazil's Industrial Property Law.[9]

Developing nations subsequently united in an effort to relax (or at least "clarify") the scope of intellectual property protection required for pharmaceuticals under ... TRIPS [**Basic Document 4.15**].... Certain developed nations, most prominently the United States and Switzerland, responded with a campaign to protect their interpretation of TRIPS against any developments that might undermine it. The eventual result was a ministerial interpretation of the TRIPS agreement in the form of a "Declaration on the TRIPS Agreement and Public Health," one of the few concrete legal developments during the recent WTO ministerial meetings in Doha, Qatar. The Declaration gave the developing nations many of the legal "clarifications" that they were seeking, although a number of issues remain unresolved.

The precise impact of the Doha Declaration on the policies of developing nations remains to be seen, but it seems likely that the Declaration will embolden them to enact measures that will reduce the returns to pharmaceutical patent holders, at least with respect to drugs that are used to treat certain diseases. Such measures will likely include the award of compulsory licenses for the production of patented medications (with minimal royalties payable to the patent holder), and the allowance of "parallel imports" of medications from nations where prices are lower. This essay will take a preliminary look at the merits of such policies from an economic perspective, and draw on this analysis to suggest some directions for the resolution of legal issues that remain on the table after Doha.

The ultimate wisdom of measures that relax intellectual property protection for pharmaceuticals in developing countries turns on complex matters, including empirical issues about which one can only hazard an educated guess. It is conceivable that patent rights in the developing world have negligible impact on research incentives. They may simply raise prices on patented drugs, transferring rents to foreign pharmaceutical patent holders, and creating deadweight losses by pricing consumers out of the market who are willing to pay the marginal cost of medicines but not the monopoly markup charged by the patent holder.

But there is another possibility, one which in my view better accords with what we know about the importance of patents to pharmaceutical research, and with the extraordinary value to consumers of medicines that successfully treat serious conditions. Developing nations have long had little intellectual property protection for pharmaceuticals, and we have concurrently witnessed an apparent dearth of research into diseases such as malaria and drug-resistant tuberculosis that are of particular importance to these nations. The lack of patent protection may have resulted, at least in part, from an acute collective action problem—developing nations reap the full benefits from lower prices when they do not create pharmaceutical patents, yet the costs in terms of diminished research incentives are largely externalized to the rest of

9. The United States subsequently dropped this action.

the developing world. The WTO TRIPS agreement held out some promise of overcoming part of this problem. Yet, just as the obligations of developing nations under TRIPS are beginning to take hold, the Doha Declaration casts great doubt on the future credibility of patent rights for pharmaceuticals in developing nations. The result may be quite unfortunate for research incentives, especially those relating to particular diseases.

* * *

I begin with some questions that a Socratic teacher might ask. Imagine a developing nation with a severe housing crisis, a famine, or an extraordinary natural disaster. It believes itself to have a desperate need for funds as a result, and asserts that it cannot obtain the needed funds through general taxation or available aid programs. Would we then think it appropriate for the nation in question to expropriate the property of foreign corporations (say, their mineral rights and manufacturing facilities), and to auction it off to raise needed funds? Or would we think it appropriate for the nation simply to repudiate its external public debt, leaving foreign lending institutions as the parties implicitly "expropriated?" If not, how would we distinguish measures that "expropriate" the rents otherwise due to pharmaceutical patent holders in the face of public health crises?

The most obvious response is that a property right cannot be "expropriated" unless it exists in the first instance. If the TRIPS Agreement affords developing countries the right to respond to public health emergencies through compulsory licensing and the right to allow parallel imports on a non-discriminatory basis, the argument would run, these policies are readily distinguishable from my hypothetical on the grounds that they do no violence to the legitimate entitlement of the right holder.

Even if TRIPS affords developing countries enough flexibility to distinguish their plans for compulsory licensing and parallel importation from my hypothetical case of expropriation as a legal matter, however, it remains to inquire whether policies that eliminate the rents of pharmaceutical patent holders in response to public health "emergencies" are wise. To those issues we now turn.

A. The Monopoly/Innovation Tradeoff and Its General Implications

Patent rights allow inventors and their licensees to prevent potential competitors from selling products covered by the patent during its duration (now twenty years). If a product has no close substitutes and there are significant numbers of consumers willing to pay more than the cost of production to acquire the product, the patent holder will then enjoy a period of significant "monopoly power" during the life of the patent, defined as an ability to elevate price above cost.

Ordinarily, public policy is hostile to monopoly. In economic parlance, it is a source of "deadweight losses." Monopolists charge more for goods and services than the cost of producing them, thereby pricing consumers willing to pay cost but not the full monopoly price out of the market. Monopolists' loss of "consumer surplus" represents the standard deadweight loss triangle in price theoretic discussions of the evils of monopoly. In addition, monopolists may invest resources in obtaining monopoly, thereby dissipating monopoly profits ex ante and causing further deadweight losses. With patents in particular, monopoly rents may be dissipated by excessive investment in the race to develop a new invention—a so-called patent race.

Depending on the degree of monopoly power enjoyed by a patent holder, therefore, the existence of a patent may cause significant deadweight losses. The justification for tolerating them, of course, is that they provide a desirable return to inventors. Invention is costly, runs the argument, and if inventions can be copied and sold by competitors of the inventor immediately, their prices will be driven down to the marginal cost of producing them exclusive of the cost of innovation. As a result, inventors will be unable to recoup research and development costs. Knowing that fact ex ante, potential inventors will be unwilling to incur such costs and technical progress will be stifled. Patent rights overcome this problem by affording the patent holder a period of monopoly rents that allows the recoupment of research and development costs. The magnitude of the rents to inventors under a patent system is reasonably correlated with the value of an invention—monopoly rents will be greater the lesser the extent to which close substitutes for the patented good exist, and the greater the degree to which consumers value it in excess of its cost.

11. Universal Declaration of Human Rights, 10 Dec 1948, GA Res. 217 A (III), UN Doc. A/810, at 71 (1948); *reprinted in* **3 Weston & Carlson III.A.1: Arts. 17, 27** (Basic Document 3.3).

12. International Covenant on Economic, Social and Cultural Rights, 19 Dec 1966, GA Res. 2200 (XXI), 21 UN GAOR, Supp. (No. 16) 49, UN Doc. A/6316 (1967); *reprinted in* **6 I.L.M. 360 (1967) and 3 Weston & Carlson III.A.2: Arts. 1, 4, 15, 25** (Basic Document 3.13).

13. Charter of Economic Rights and Duties of States, 12 Dec 1974, GA Res. 3281, UN GAOR, 29th Sess., Supp. No. 31, at 50, UNDoc.A/9631 (1975); *reprinted in* **15 I.L.M. 251 (1975) and 4 Weston & Carlson IV.F.5: Arts. 1–3, 6–9, 13, 14, 18, 19, 24** (Basic Document 4.9).

14. Michael J. Dennis, "Current Development: The Fifty–Seventh Session of the UN Commission on Human Rights," 96 A.J.I.L. 181, 181–82, 190–91 (2002).

The fifty-seventh session of the United Nations Commission on Human Rights took place in Geneva from March 19 to April 27, 2001, under the chairmanship of Ambassador Leandro Despouy of Argentina. More than thirty-six hundred individuals were in attendance, representing 53 member states, 93 observer states, 250 nongovernmental organizations, 37 national human rights institutions, and 31 specialized agencies. The Commission adopted eighty-two resolutions and nineteen decisions, two-thirds of them by consensus. The debate was more confrontational than in prior years because the Commission faced numerous politically divisive texts and amendments, many sponsored by Cuba. Some participants and observers attributed this development to the election to the Commission of Algeria, the Democratic Republic of the Congo, Libya, Malaysia, Syria, and Viet Nam....

Like similar reports on earlier sessions, the following account highlights new directions in the development of human rights law.

* * *

[A] new Brazilian resolution [2001/33] on "Access to Medications in the Context of Pandemics Such as HIV/AIDS," [was] adopted by a vote of 52–0–1. The Brazilian text sparked substantial controversy among Commission members, however, because it called into question the impact of the Trade–Related Aspects of Intellectual Property Rights (TRIPS) regime of the World Trade Organization (WTO) **[Basic Document 4.15]**. The resolution mandates that states, in implementing the right to the highest attainable standard of health [found in several major human rights documents], "adopt legislation or other measures, in accordance with applicable international law" to "safeguard access" to such medications "from any limitations by third parties.". . . .

The United States maintained that by questioning "the validity of internationally agreed protections of intellectual property rights," the text was "simply put, bad public health policy" that could "have the unintended consequence of discouraging investment in the important research desperately needed to find the cures of the future." It further declared that it did not accept the implication contained in the text that the "presumed" right to the highest attainable standard of health creates "legally enforceable entitlements" or requires "the establishment of judicial or administrative remedies at the national or international levels." The EU [European Union], while joining consensus on the text, expressed its understanding that "no provisions in this resolution can be interpreted as undermining or limiting existing international agreements, including in the field of intellectual property."

Notwithstanding the position taken by the Brazilian text, international trade law does not appear to be in conflict with international human rights law. Article 27(2) of the Universal Declaration **[Basic Document 3.3]** provides that "everyone has the right to the protection of the moral and material interests resulting from any scientific, literary or artistic production of which he is author." The article recognizes implicitly that intellectual property laws play a role in the protection of human rights—in particular, health-related rights—since they encourage investment in research and development. Nevertheless, the TRIPS agreement also expressly recognizes that trade protections are not absolute. TRIPS Article 31 provides that generic production of medications may be permitted "without authorization of the right holder" in the case of "a national emergency or other circumstances of extreme urgency." Subsequently, in reliance on this provision, Brazil declared HIV/AIDS a "national emergency" and authorized generic domestic production of all HIV/AIDS medications.

15. The Fifty–Fourth World Health Assembly of the World Health Organization, WHO Medicines Strategy, WHA54.11, Agenda item 13.8 (21 May 2001).[h]

The Fifty-fourth World Health Assembly,

Recalling resolutions, nominally WHA39.27, WHA41.16, WHA43.20, WHA45.27, WHA47.12, WHA47.16, WHA47.17, WHA49.14 and WHA52.19;

h. The World Health Assembly (WHA) is the supreme decision-making body for the World Health Organization (WHO). It meets in Geneva once a year, and is attended by delegations from all WHO member states, 192 as of this writing. Its main function is to determine the policies of the Organization. It can adopt international conventions on health which are binding only upon acceding countries; and, as a very unusual power for an international organ- ization, it can promulgate, in certain very limited areas, binding "international health regulations" subject to the ability of member states to opt out of the regulations. Finally, under Article 23 of the WHO Constitution (14 UNTS 185), it can make recommendations to member states, "with respect to any matter within the competence of the [WHO]." This Resolution WHA 54.11 is an example of a recommendation of the World Health Assembly.

Having considered the report on the revised drug strategy, and bearing in mind the previous report on the subject, that highlight challenges related to international trade agreements, access to essential drugs, drug quality and rational use of medicines, together with the urgent need to improve access to drugs for treating priority health problems such as malaria, childhood illnesses, HIV/AIDS and tuberculosis, among others;

Acknowledging the four main objectives of WHO's medicines strategy, namely, to frame and implement policy, to ensure access; to ensure quality, safety and efficacy, and to promote rational use of medicines;

Taking into account that the aforementioned health problems are particularly acute among poor and vulnerable populations, entrapping them in poverty, and substantially inhibiting the growth of national and international economies to the detriment of all humanity;

Recalling that the Constitution of the World Health Organization provides that the enjoyment of the highest attainable standard of health is one of the fundamental rights of every human being without distinction of race, religion, political belief, economic or social condition, and considering that progressive realization of that right should involve access, on a non-discriminatory basis, to health facilities, prevention, care, treatment and support in the context of access to medicines;

Bearing in mind the WHO global framework for expanding access to essential drugs, and its four components: the rational selection and use of medicines, reliable health and supply systems, sustainable financing, and affordable prices;

Taking into account that access to medicines is particularly price sensitive, since most people in developing countries have to pay personally for health care, and that the commitment of governments, organizations of the United Nations system, the private sector, and the civil society is necessary in order to achieve universal access;

Taking into account the urgency of implementing the WHO medicines strategy in order fully to realize the enormous health benefits that essential drugs can offer to the one-third of the human population now lacking them;

Taking into account the need to increase the current levels of international technical and economic assistance channeled to implementation of the WHO medicines strategy; Recognizing the importance of national drug policies established in accordance with WHO guidelines;

Commending the strong leadership that WHO has shown in re-emphasizing the essential drugs concept, and the contribution of nongovernmental organizations working in public health to attaining such objectives as the framing of national drug policies and related aspects;

Noting that the impact of international trade agreements on access to, or local manufacturing of, essential drugs and on the development of new drugs needs to be further evaluated;

Recognizing that well-functioning and equitable health systems, including reliable supply systems, are key elements in any framework for expanding access to essential drugs;

Noting resolution 2001/33 on access to medication in the context of pandemics such as HIV/AIDS adopted by the United Nations Commission on Human Rights at its 57th session;

1.   URGES Member States:

(1) to reaffirm their commitment to ensuring public health interests and to make every effort to promote equitable access to medicines, and to undertake the necessary action within their national health policies, including for priority diseases and pandemics, as an important element for progressively achieving the highest attainable standard of health;

(2) to take effective measures in accordance with international law and international agreements acceded to in order to ensure improved access to medicines;

(3) to cooperate with respect to resolution 2001/33 of the United Nations Commission on Human Rights;

(4) to pursue measures directed to expanding access of their populations to essential drugs, including the implementation of resolution WHA52.19[10] taking into account the cost-effectiveness of rational drug use as well as affordability;

(5) in order to increase access to medicines, and in accordance with the health needs of people, especially those who can least afford the costs, and recognizing the efforts of Member States to expand access to drugs and promote domestic industry, cooperate constructively in strengthening pharmaceutical policies and practices, including those applicable to generic drugs, and intellectual property regimes in order further to promote innovation and the development of domestic industries, consistent with applicable international law;

(6) to provide financial support and technical cooperation to enable Member States in need to expand access of their populations to essential drugs....

16.   Virginia A. Leary, "The Right To Health in International Human Rights Law," 1 Health & Human Rights: An International Journal 24, 28–56 (1994).

On first hearing it, the phrase "right to health" strikes many as strange. It is not a common expression in national legal systems and it is not a term familiar to many in the field of medicine and public health. Notwithstanding, there are a number of references to the right to health (and health care) in philosophical literature, and it is becoming a familiar term in the context of international human rights. Superficially, the "right to health" seems to presume that government or international organizations or individuals must

---

10. Identifying principles and goals for the WHO's work in the Pharmaceutical sector.

guarantee a person's good health. This interpretation is obviously absurd and the phrase is not given such an interpretation in the context of human rights law.... [T]he term "right to health" is currently used in the context of human rights as shorthand, referring to the more detailed language contained in international treaties and to fundamental human rights principles. The precise terminology "right to health," without further explanation, is not used in most provisions of treaties relating to health.

* * *

In a paper submitted to the workshop entitled "The Right to Health," Professor Theo C. Van Boven, then Director of the United Nations Division of Human Rights and subsequently Professor of International Law at Limburg University, Netherlands uses the term "right to health" to refer to provisions in the founding documents of international human rights law. Cited were provisions in the Universal Declaration of Human Rights and the Economic Covenant and a number of other declarations. Van Boven wrote, "Three aspects of the right to health have been enshrined in the international instruments on human rights: the declaration of the right to health as a basic human right; the prescription of standards aimed at meeting the health needs of specific groups of persons; and the prescription of ways and means for implementing the right to health."[11]

The use of shorthand expressions to express more complete concepts is common in human rights, civil rights, and fundamental rights. Reference may be made in fundamental rights literature to the "right to property"; the acquired meaning is not that everyone has the right to demand some property, but that no one may be arbitrarily deprived of his or her property. The term's meaning has developed through long usage and application in legal systems. This is in keeping with the evolution of the scope of concepts like "due process," "natural justice," "equal protection," and of rights to freedom of expression or freedom of association. At first these terms were not self-evident, but through judicial, legislative and scholarly use in many countries they have acquired a generally recognized meaning.

Use of rights language in connection with health has led to controversy in the United States, despite its acceptance internationally. Furthermore, whereas the concept of a right to health *care* is more specific and more readily understood than the right to health, the use of this more specific phrase has also been criticized. For example, a recent publication entitled *The Right to Health Care,* edited by two American authors, contains a number of chapters by philosophers and economists, some favoring the concept of a right to health *care* and some opposing it as rhetorical, lacking in specificity and diversionary from the real problems of medical care.[12] In that publication, some contributors reject a right to health care on ideological grounds as authorizing "the coercive redistribution of individuals' resources."[13] Those writing in favor of the terminology perceive the use of rights language as emphasizing aspects of equity and fairness in the provision of medical care. Only one contribution in

11. *The Right to Health as a Human Right,* Workshop, The Hague Academy of International Law and the United Nations University 54, at 54–55 (R.-J. Dupuy ed., 1979).

12. Thomas J. Bole and William A. Bondeson, Rights to Health Care (1991).

13. Thomas J. Bole, *The Rhetoric of Rights and Justice in Health Care, id.,* at 7.

the volume makes even passing reference to international declarations or treaties relating to the right to health and health care.

* * *

A number of international treaties and declarations use the language of rights in referring to health issues. Only those paragraphs of articles using rights language are cited in this section. A number of these same articles contain additional paragraphs listing measures to be taken by states parties to ensure the enjoyment of the rights. . . .

Although the 1948 Universal Declaration of Human Rights [**Basic Document 3.3**] is not a treaty, most of its provisions are now considered by legal scholars as constituting customary international law. Article 25 of the Declaration reads:

> Everyone has the right to a standard of living adequate for the health and well-being of himself and his family, including food, clothing, housing and medical care and the right to security in the event of . . . sickness, disability. . . .

The language of the WHO Constitution has inspired the provisions of several treaties:

WHO Constitution (Preamble)[i]

> The enjoyment of the highest attainable standard of health is one of the fundamental rights of every human being without distinction of race, religion, political belief, economic or social conditions.

International Covenant on Economic, Social and Cultural Rights [**Basic Document 3.13**]

> Article 12(*l*): The States Parties to the present Covenant recognize the right of everyone to the enjoyment of the highest attainable standard of physical and mental health.

Convention on the Rights of the Child [**Basic Document 3.32**]

> Article 24(1): States Parties recognize the right of the child to the enjoyment of the highest attainable standard of health.

African Charter on Human and Peoples' Rights [**Basic Document 3.22**]

> Article 16: Every individual shall have the right to enjoy the best attainable state of physical and mental health.

The important WHO and UNICEF Declaration of AlmaAta adopted at the International Conference on Primary Health Care in 1978, also used similar language:

> The Conference strongly reaffirms that health, which is a state of complete physical, mental and social wellbeing, and not merely the absence of disease or infirmity, is a fundamental human right and that the attainment of the highest possible level of health is a most important world-wide social goal whose realization requires the action of many other social and economic sectors in addition to the health sector.[j]

---

i.   14 U.N.T.S. 185.

j.   To similar effect and self-consciously building upon the Declaration of Alma Ata, see

It should be noted that the use of the language "highest attainable standard" in these documents presupposes a reasonable, not an absolute, standard. Also, the language of the WHO Constitution emphasizes an essential element implicit in the shorter phrase "right to health" by referring to non-discrimination on the grounds of race, religion, political belief, economic, or social conditions. Emphasis on non-discrimination in relation to health is reiterated in the following discrimination conventions.

Convention on the Elimination of All Forms of Racial Discrimination **[Basic Document 3.12]**

Article 5(e)(iv) provides that States Parties undertake to prohibit and eliminate racial discrimination in the enjoyment of "the right to public health, medical care, social security and social services."

Convention on the Elimination of All Forms of Discrimination Against Women **[Basic Document 3.21]**

Article 11(1)(f) provides that States Parties shall take all appropriate measures to eliminate discrimination against women in the enjoyment of "the right to protection of health and to safety in working conditions, including the safeguarding of the function of reproduction."

Article 12 of the same convention provides that all appropriate measures should be taken by States Parties to eliminate discrimination against women "in the field of health care in order to ensure on a basis of equality of men and women, access to health care services, including those related to family planning."

The *Additional Protocol to the American Convention on Human Rights in the Area of Economic, Social and Cultural Rights (Protocol of San Salvador)* **[Basic Document 3.29]** uses the precise language "right to health." Article 10, entitled "Right to Health," reads: "(1) Everyone shall have the right to health, understood to mean the enjoyment of the highest level of physical, mental and social well-being. (2) In order to ensure the exercise of the right to health, the States Parties agree to recognize health as a public good...."

The *American Declaration of the Rights and Duties of Man* **[Basic Document 3.1]** contains the following similar language:

> Article XI: Every person has the right to the preservation of his health through sanitary and social measures relating to food, clothing, housing and medical care, to the extent permitted by public and community resources.

As stated earlier, these provisions employ a wide variety of language: some use the terminology "right to protection of health" or "right to preservation of health"; others intersperse additional language between the terminology of "right" and "health." Naturally, when a particular treaty or declaration is considered for application in a concrete case, the specific language of the provision involved should be referred to, rather than the more general concept of a right to health.

* * *

Iowa City Appeal on Advancing the Human Right to Health, adopted 22 April 2001 by The Global Assembly on Advancing the Human Right to Health convened at The University of Iowa, Iowa City, Iowa, 20–22 Apr 2001, *reprinted in* 3 Weston & Carlson III.V.5.

What do human rights have to do with health issues? What does rights discourse add to consideration of complex technical, economic, and practical issues involved in health care and status? . . .[k]

* * *

Rights as Trumps

The use of rights language vis à vis social goals confers a special status on those goals. As Ronald Dworkin puts it, categorizing something as a right means that the right "trumps" many other claims or goods.[l] A special importance, status, priority, is implied in categorizing something as a right. Therefore, the use of rights language in connection with health issues emphasizes the importance of health care and health status. To speak of a right to health does not mean that that right should always take priority over all other goods, claims, or other rights; but it does emphasize that health issues are of special importance given the impact of health on the life and survival of individuals.

* * *

Dignity as the Foundation of Human Rights

. . . The concept of rights grows out of a perception of the inherent dignity of every human being. Thus, use of rights language in connection with health emphasizes that the dignity of each person must be central in all aspects of health. . . . The focus must be on the dignity of the individual rather than the good of the collectivity. The utilitarian principle is rejected by a rights approach. The greater good of the greater number may not override individual dignity. For example, although medical experimentation may result in good for the general populace, it must not violate the dignity of the individuals subjected to it. The dignity of all must be respected in particular, the dignity of society's most vulnerable elements: the poor, racial and ethnic minorities, disabled persons, the mentally handicapped.

The Equality or Non–Discrimination Principle

Equality or non-discrimination is a fundamental principle of human rights law, and prohibition of discrimination is a leitmotif running through all of international human rights law. Article 2 of the Universal Declaration of Human Rights provides, "Everyone is entitled to all the rights and freedoms set forth in this Declaration, without distinction of any kind such as race, colour, sex, language, religion, political or other opinion, national or social origin." The major international covenants on human rights contain similar non-discrimination clauses. Specific international treaties have been adopted prohibiting discrimination on the basis of sex or race. The rights approach, with its emphasis on non-discrimination (including on the grounds of limited economic resources) implies rejection of a solely market-based approach to the social good of health care and health status. Cost-containment and cost-benefit analyses in the health care allocation remain important but need not be determinative in matters of social goals relating to health.

k. For similar questioning and response in a related field likewise affected by HIV/AIDS, see B. Weston & M. Teerink, *Rethinking Child Labor: A Multidimensional Human Rights Problem*, in Child Labor and Human Rights 3 (B. Weston ed. & contrib., 2005).

l. R. Dworkin, Taking Rights Seriously (1977).

As the WHO Declaration of Alma–Ata on Primary Health Care states:

> The existing gross inequality in the health status of the people particularly between developed and developing countries as well as within countries is politically, socially and economically unacceptable and is, therefore, of common concern to all countries. . . .

SECTION 5.   DISCUSSION NOTES/QUESTIONS

1. As James Thuo Gathii explains in Reading 1, *supra*, lack of access to AIDS drugs is one of the major factors behind the continuation of an immense human tragedy. The primary socio-economic question the instant problem presents is, therefore, the extent to which private property should be protected and at what social cost, one of the most enduring questions of public order from local to global. Even with the demise of communist and even many socialist economic systems, the 21st century reality that millions of human beings without resources continue to die from diseases with known treatments most starkly demonstrates why this discussion is not likely to end soon. As the reading by Alan O. Sykes reflects, the theoretical debate about what is sometimes referred to as distributive justice has centered around philosophical ideas having to do with ethics and justice as much as economic notions stressing the link between deference for private property and economic productivity. Religious ideals have also greatly influenced the debate. For the beginning of the Western thinking on distributive justice, see Aristotle, The Nicomachean Ethics, 109 (D. Ross transl., 1983). For a contemporary exploration of the problem that has become one of the most influential philosophical works of the modern era see John Rawls, A Theory of Justice (1971). For a contrary and extremely influential view in its own right, see Milton Friedman & Rose Friedman, Free to Choose (1979). Finally, for concrete application to the problem of global health, see Paul Hunt, *The UN Special Rapporteur on the Right to Health: Key Objectives, Themes, and Interventions*, 7 Health and Human Rights 1 (2003), reprinted in abridged form in Human Rights in the World Community: Issues and Action 201 (R. Claude & B. Weston eds. & contribs., 3rd ed., 2006).

2. The present problem demonstrates the way in which international law is a seamless web. The extent to which international law, as a comprehensive legal order (as distinguished from, *e.g.*, TRIPS standing alone), requires states to give deference to patent holders cannot be determined without analyzing international human rights law as well as TRIPS **(Basic Document 4.15)** and the relationship between the two. Because the international adjudicatory system is balkanized, the extent to which specialized tribunals, such as the WTO Dispute Settlement Body, should examine all areas of law necessary to making a holistic decision on the legal merits of a case is the subject of current discussion. Article 3.2 of the WTO's Dispute Settlement Understanding identifies the purpose of dispute settlement as clarifying the provisions of the WTO Agreements "in accordance with customary rules of interpretation of public international law." This impliedly refers to the Vienna Convention, particularly Articles 31 and 32, and, of possible relevance to this problem, Articles 53 and 64 **(Basic Document 1.10)**. For an argument that the WTO tribunal should take an expansive view of its ability to consider sources of international law beyond the treaties governed by the WTO, see David Palmeter & Petros Malvroides, *The WTO Legal System: Sources of Law*, 92 A.J.I.L. 398 (1998). For a contrary view, see J. Patrick Kelly, *Judicial Activism at the World Trade Organization: Developing Principles of Self–Restraint*, 22 NW J. Int'l L. & Bus. 353 (2002).

3.   Developed countries (particularly the United States), the United Nations, the WTO, the WHO, developing countries, NGOs, and drug companies all have been involved in ongoing, often acrimonious negotiations over the extent to which intellectual property rights of patent holders of HIV/AIDS drugs should be respected. The Doha Ministerial Declaration on the TRIPS Agreement and Public Health (*supra* Reading 9) constituted a victory for the developing countries and activist NGOs dedicated to the treatment of AIDS patients. However, despite doing much to relax intellectual property limitations on the ability of poor countries to produce generic pharmaceutical products for their home markets, the Doha Declaration left unresolved the question of whether such generics could be exported to other poor countries. This question is important since only a few of the world's developing nations have substantial drug manufacturing capacity, and Paragraph F of Article 31 of TRIPS mandates that compulsory licenses be "predominantly for the supply of the domestic market" of the country conferring a compulsory license.

Paragraph 6 of The Doha Declaration instructed the Council for TRIPS to "find an expeditious solution to this problem" by the end of 2002. In the acrimonious Council negotiations that ensued the US took the position that compulsory licensing for export be permitted only for HIV/AIDS, malaria, tuberculosis, and other severe infectious illnesses while developing countries pushed for a much broader waiver. The Paragraph 6 deadline passed without a resolution of the issue. Finally in the face of mounting criticism over its lack of concern for the poor, in September of 2003 the United States largely acquiesced to the demands of the developing world. The resulting decision by the General Council ("Implementation of paragraph 6 of the Doha Declaration on the TRIPS Agreement and public health") waived the TRIPS restrictions on the rights of individual member states to decide which health problems merit compulsory licenses for export.

The United States has, however, subsequently attempted to circumvent the Doha Declaration understanding by insisting that legal impediments to the manufacture of generic antiviral drugs be included in the free trade agreements it has negotiated with developing countries including the August 5, 2004 United States–Central American–Dominican Republic Free Trade Agreement (CAFTA), available on the website of the US Department of Agriculture Foreign Agriculture Service at <http://www.fas.usda.gov/itp/CAFTA/cafta.html>. This and other political barriers to the implementation of the Doha Declaration created by the United States and certain other pharmaceutical exporting countries have thus far significantly limited the impact of the Doha Declaration. For further helpful discussion of the pertinent events, see Brook K. Baker, *Arthritic Flexibilities for Accessing Medicines: Analysis of WTO Action Regarding Paragraph 6 of the Doha Declaration on the TRIPS Agreement and Public Health,* 14 Ind. Int'l & Comp. L. Rev. 613 (2004).

4.   Another important aspect of the emerging international intellectual property regime in relation to developing countries concerns intellectual property rights in products from plant genetic resources. Imagine a developing country that is rich in plant resources, some of which are reputed to have medicinal value (*e.g.,* the Pacific Yew, the bark from which is used to produce cancer-fighting drugs). Suppose that a multinational pharmaceutical company from a developed country sends scientists to the developing country to gather samples of plant material ("bioprospecting," as it is sometimes called). The scientists return to their labs and there undertake analytical techniques to isolate the active chemical substance that appears to provide the therapeutic benefit. The isolate itself or products derived from the isolate may well be eligible for patent protection. Is there a role

for international law in controlling commercial exploitation of such resources? The issue is multifaceted, touching on international environmental law (inasmuch as it concerns efforts to preserve biodiversity), international human rights law (inasmuch as it concerns the protection of the ethnobiological knowledge of indigenous peoples), and, of course, international intellectual property law. For pertinent scholarly commentary, see Edgar J. Asebey & Jill D. Kempenaar, *Biodiversity Prospecting: Fulfilling the Mandate of the Biodiversity Convention*, 28 Van. J. Transnat'l L. 703 (1995); Mark Hannig, *An Examination of the Possibility to Secure Intellectual Property Rights for Plant Genetic resources Developed by Indigenous Peoples of the NAFTA States: Domestic Legislation Under the International Convention for the Protection of New Plant Varieties*, 13 Ariz. J. Int'l & Comp. L. 175 (1996).

5. Finally, this problem raises a variety of world order issues relevant to the structure of the international system. Consider the following questions raised by Andrew Strauss:

> [Thinking about] international AIDS as a case study in the challenges of globalization . . . raises a host of questions. . . . How do you create an effective strategy for dealing with the spread of a truly transnational pandemic? . . . What should be done at the level of the state and what should be done internationally? What is the role for international human rights? How intrusive should the international community be in countries where governments seem to be following wrong headed or even wholly irrational policies? Do we at this point have the basic institutional infrastructure to accomplish an effective global strategy? Questions of distributive justice abound as well. Clearly, the disease knows no boundaries, but why is it that the poor, and the dispossessed, and the marginalized, are its greatest victims? What are the obligations of specific industrial sectors such as drug companies or of wealthy citizens in general to help? What do ongoing debates about intellectual property rights and economic theory have to contribute to this discussion?

Andrew Strauss, *Introductory Remarks: AIDS and Globalization—The Question Presented*, 35 J. Marshall L. Rev. 398, 398–99 (2002).

6. *Bibliographical Note*. For supplemental discussion concerning the principal themes addressed in this problem, consult the following additional specialized materials:

(a) *Books/Monographs/Reports/Symposia*. D. Adesky, Moving Mountains: The Race to Treat Global AIDS (2004); F. K. Beier & G. Schricker, eds, From GATT to TRIPS: The Agreement on Trade–Related Aspects of Intellectual Property Rights (1994); C. Correa, Intellectual Property Rights, The WTO and Developing Countries: The TRIPS Agreement and Policy Options (2000); A. Kotin & R. Marlink, Global AIDS Crisis: A Reference Handbook (Contemporary World Issues) (2004); R. Rikowski, Globalisation, Information And Libraries: The Implications of the World Trade Organisation's GATS and TRIPS Agreements (2005); P. Roffe, Resource Book on TRIPS and Development (2005); M. Ryan, Knowledge Diplomacy: Global Competition and the Politics of Intellectual Property (1998); Symposium, *The Global Aids Crisis; Human Rights, International Pharmaceutical Markets and Intellectual Property*, 117 Conn J. Int'l L 311 (2002).

(b) *Articles/Book Chapters*. W.J. Davey, *The World Trade Organization Dispute Settlement System*, 42 S. Tex L. Rev. 1199 (2001); A. X. Fellmeth, *Secrecy, Monopoly, and Access to Pharmaceuticals in International Trade Law: Protection of Marketing Approval Data Under the TRIPs Agreement*, 45 Harv. Int'l L.J. 443 (2004); L. R. Hellfner, *Regime Shifting: The TRIPs Agreement and New Dynamics of International Intellectual Property Lawmaking*, 29 Yale J. Int'l L. 1 (2004); J. Martin, *TRIPS Agreement: Towards a Better Protection for Geographical Indications?*, 30 Brooklyn J. Int'l L. 117 (2004); J. H. Reichman, *The TRIPS Agreement Comes of Age: Conflict or Cooperation With the Developing Countries?* 32 Case W. Res. J. Int'l L. 441 (2000); J. Rein, *International Governance Through Trade Agreements: Patent Protection for Essential Medicines* 21 J. Int'l L. Bus. 379 (2001); A. Subramanian, *Medicines, Patents, and TRIPS: Has the Intellectual Property Pact Opened a Pandora's Box for the Pharmaceuticals Industry?*, 41 Fin & Dev 22 (2004).

Problem 6–6

Corruption in Maurya

SECTION 1. FACTS

Maurya (mah-oo´-rya) is a medium-sized country in South Asia, bordering the northern reaches of the Bay of Bengal. Until a few years ago, aided by fertile agricultural land, other abundant resources, and an emergent industrial sector, Maurya boasted one of the fastest growing economies in the region. However, a three-year recession, a sharp increase in population growth, and consequent mounting socioeconomic problems have led to a declining standard of living and resultant severe pressures on its economy.

Paralleling Maurya's socioeconomic problems is a growing discontent with the government of Prime Minister Chandra Gupta, now nine years old. Much of the dissatisfaction is traceable to a public perception that, wealthy and otherwise privileged, many of Prime Minister Gupta's cabinet, perhaps even Prime Minister Gupta himself, are corrupt. This image is shared by many people doing business in Maurya, as reflected in a recently released Internet Corruption Index sponsored by Transparency International[a] and ranking Maurya among the ten most corrupt countries in the world. Anecdotes of corruption on a grand scale are commonplace.

Before independence in 1971, Maurya had been a colony of the Western European state of Anglia, and to this day many Anglian companies continue to engage in substantial business in Maurya. Two years ago, Anglia signed the 1997 Organization of Economic Cooperation and Development (OECD)[b] Convention on Combating Bribery of Foreign Public Officials in International Business Transactions ("the Convention"). However, as a result of opposition by several members of Parliament close to Anglian multinational interests, ratification of the Convention is now bogged down in the Anglian Parliament. The opponents of the Convention argue that it will put Anglian companies at

---

a. Transparency International (TI) is a nongovernmental organization devoted to fighting corruption. Based in Berlin, Germany, it issues an annual index on corruption, developed from polls of business people regarding their perceptions of corruption in countries in which they do business. For TI's website, see <http://www.transparency.org>. *See also* the TI Corruption Perceptions Index in *infra* Discussion Note/Question 6, at 985–86.

b. The OECD is an intergovernmental organization established in 1961 to promote economic growth and freer trade and to expand and improve Western aid to developing countries. Replacing the Organization for European

Economic Cooperation (OEEC) established in 1948 to further common action among Marshall Plan recipients so as to assist their recovery from World War II, its 30 Member States include as of this writing: Australia, Austria, Belgium, Canada, the Czech Republic, Denmark, Finland, France, Germany, Greece, Hungary, Iceland, Ireland, Italy, Japan, Luxembourg, Mexico, the Netherlands, New Zealand, Norway, Poland, Portugal, Slovak Republic, South Korea, Spain, Sweden, Switzerland, Turkey, the United Kingdom and the United States. For more details, see the OECD's website at <http://www.oecd.org/home/0, 2605,-en_2649_ 201185_1_1_1_1_1,00.html>.

an economic disadvantage relative to foreign competitors. Under international pressure from the United States, the OECD, and anti-corruption NGOs both inside and outside of Anglia, the Minister of Justice nevertheless promulgated Decree 12–15 which states:

> Pursuant to Article 16 of the Anglian Constitution[c] and Section 40 of the Securities and Company Law,[d] it shall be unlawful and punishable in accordance with the requirements of the Anglian Penal Code for any Anglian concern or agent of such Anglian concern to offer anything of value to any foreign official for the purpose of influencing an official decision related to the awarding of business contracts.

After receiving an anonymous tip, *The Herald*, the major Anglian daily newspaper, began an investigation of Anglian business practices in Maurya. Its investigation focused primarily on LuxAuto, a large Anglian manufacturer and exporter of luxury cars and sports-utility vehicles. In a series of stories, it alleged that LuxAuto paid over US$500,000 to Mauryan customs officials, including a US$300,000 payment to Maurya's Minister of Finance and Development; also, that it had spent nearly US$1.5 million on the construction of a modern highway from Maurya's capital and principal port city of Buddhagong on its eastern border to the town of Hindipur on Maurya's western border, President Gupta's birthplace and home and also LuxAuto's point of entry into South Asia. *The Herald* quoted a high-level LuxAuto whistle blower as acknowledging that these expenditures were negotiated with top Mauryan officials in return for LuxAuto being able to bring its vehicles into the country and through Maurya duty-free, in clear violation of Mauryan law.

Following the furor over the revelations in the *The Herald* article, the Anglian Ministry of Justice began an investigation of its own. This investigation eventually led to the filing of charges pursuant to Decree 12–15. A subsequent trial resulted in the conviction of LuxAuto and three of its senior executives. LuxAuto and its executives have appealed their conviction arguing that international law does not prohibit the payment of foreign bribes and that, for this reason, in the absence of enacted legislation prohibiting such bribes, the Justice Ministry exceeded its juridical authority. The case is now pending decision on final appeal.

Section 2. Questions Presented

1. Does international law provide the Anglian Ministry of Justice with a legal basis for prosecuting LuxAuto and its officials for engaging in foreign bribery?

2. In any event, are there any additional or alternative legal norms, procedures, and/or institutions to be recommended that might

---

c. Article 16 of the Anglian Constitution provides: "Where there is no treaty and no controlling executive or parliamentary act or judicial decision, the general rules of public international law are an integral part of the law of Anglia and shall create rights and duties for its inhabitants.

d. Section 40 of the Securities and Company Law gives the Minister of Justice the "authority to define elements of economic offenses recognized under Anglian law."

further help to prevent or discourage situations of the kind posed
by this problem?

SECTION 3.   ASSIGNMENTS

A.   READING ASSIGNMENT

Study the Readings presented in Section 4, *infra*, and the Discussion
Notes/Questions that follow. Also, time permitting, consult the accompanying
bibliographical references.

B.   RECOMMENDED WRITING ASSIGNMENT

Prepare a comprehensive, logically sequenced, and *argumentative* brief in
the form of an outline of the primary and subsidiary *legal* issues you see
requiring resolution by Anglia's Court of Tax Appeals. Also, from the perspective of an independent judge, indicate which side ought to prevail on each
issue and why. Retain a copy of your issue-outline/brief for class discussion.

C.   RECOMMENDED ORAL ASSIGNMENT

Assume you are legal counsel for the Government of Anglia or LuxAuto
(as designated by your instructor); then, relying upon the Readings (and your
issue-outline if prepared), present a 10–15 minute oral argument of your
party's likely positions before Anglia's Court of Tax Appeals.

D.   RECOMMENDED REFLECTIVE ASSIGNMENT

Consider (and recommend) alternative norms, institutions, and/or procedures that you believe might do better than existing world order arrangements to contend with situations of the kind posed by this problem. In so
doing, but without insisting upon *immediate* feasibility, identify the particular
transition steps that would be needed to make your alternatives a reality.

SECTION 4.   READINGS

The following readings are considered *prima facie* relevant to solving this
problem. They are your law library for present purposes and should be treated
as such, organized intelligibly for "shelving" and not necessarily according to
the issues presented. Be sure to review Chapter 2 ("International Legal
Prescription: The 'Sources' of International Law") in your consideration of
them. It, too, should be treated as part of your law library (as, indeed, should
this entire coursebook).

1.   Editors' Note.[e] At its core, "corruption" is the abuse of public trust
for private gain. Though as old as history itself and endemic in many cultures,
it is an appalling problem throughout the world—and growing. According to
some studies, corruption is increasing in frequency and cost. Perhaps, now, as
much as 10–15 percent of an international contract or other project cost may

---

e. The authors are indebted to Professor
Steven J. Burton of The University of Iowa

College of Law for his collaborative drafting of
this note.

be allocated for questionable payments. Corrupt international entities, such as black marketeers in arms and nuclear materials, organized crime, and drug cartels, are globalizing and regularizing corrupt practices. Also, the unfortunate consequences of corruption are broad and deep.

Arms and Nuclear Materials Trade. Corrupt practices aggravate the possibilities for violent conflict. The International Atomic Energy Agency recorded 130 cases of nuclear smuggling between 1993 and 1996. The German Federal Intelligence Service estimates there were nearly 300 nuclear smuggling cases in 1994–1995 alone. This intelligence takes on new urgency in the wake of the 11 September 2001 and 7 July 2005 terrorist attacks in New York–Washington and London, respectively. Bribery, extortion, and the embezzlement of government property are at the heart of attempts to transfer nuclear arms and materials on the black market. Brokers and black marketeers evade arms control and nonproliferation laws, undermine the policies they implement, and weaken the prospects for international peace and security.

Democratization and Decentralization. There are official and unofficial means of conducting politics and business: the official means seek to foster democratic politics in a decentralized economy; the unofficial means undermine such efforts. More advanced market economies—even established democracies—are surely not immune.

International Trade, Foreign Investment, and Development Aid. International trade and foreign investment foster economic well-being, but depend on stable political and economic environments to be successful. Corruption destabilizes these environments by making governmental interventions in markets less predictable and business more costly. Public (and private) efforts to aid development, by building social and physical infrastructures, are made more expensive and less reliable by corrupt practices. Bribes channel state contracts to worthy contractors, and embezzlements deprive contractors of project materials, leaving countries with shoddy roads, dams, and communications systems. Funds, goods, and services for schools, hospitals, humanitarian relief, and other public purposes are similarly diverted.

Humane Market Regulation. Corrupt practices are used to circumvent labor and safety laws, anti-pollution and other environmental controls, and other regulatory measures governments use to moderate the harshness of unfettered markets. Bribes are used to induce government actions that enable a business or group of businesses to exclude competitors or place them at a disadvantage, permitting monopoly pricing and other market distortions. At worst, corruption induces sales of public assets to private holders, concentrating economic and political power in the hands of a few unscrupulous actors.

Rule of Law. The corruption manifest in Russia and the the other former Soviet Republics dramatizes its inherent incompatibility with a government of integrity under the Rule of Law. To repeat, at its core, corruption is the abuse of public trust for private gain. Legitimate governments employ public power for the public good. The Rule of Law confines the use of public power to its authorized purposes, as embodied in the law. Corruption, therefore, delegitimizes government and sabotages the Rule of Law. Over time, it undermines public confidence to the point of facilitating support for demagogues, desperate devolutions, and other developments that undermine human rights, in particular, and social and political stability, in general.

In sum, corruption tends to impede the adoption and implementation of almost any kind of public policy. However, because it plays differing roles in different cultures, it cannot be contained or managed without a rich understanding of its functions in context.

2. Susan Rose–Ackerman, "The Political Economy of Corruption—Causes and Consequences," Viewpoint, Note No. 74 (The World Bank, April 1996).

Corruption occurs at the interface of the public and private sectors. Sometimes officials simply steal state assets. But the more interesting and complex cases occur when a private individual or organization bribes a state official with power over the distribution of public benefits or costs.

What determines the level of corruption? The question is a vexing one, especially since no comprehensive empirical research exists on the incidence of corruption or its impact on resource use and the distribution of income. Many officials remain honest in the face of considerable temptation, and others accept payoffs that seem small relative to the benefits under their control. Others, however, amass fortunes. The level of malfeasance depends not only on the volume of potential benefits, but also on the riskiness of corrupt deals and on the participants' moral scruples and bargaining power. The overall impact of corruption, however, depends not just on the size of payoffs, but also on their distortionary effects on the economy. But even when the impact is significant, the efficient level of bribery will not be zero. Bribery is costly to control, and reforms must consider the costs as well as the benefits of fighting it.

* * *

Economic opportunities for corruption

Bribes are paid for two reasons—to obtain government benefits and to avoid costs.

Paying for benefits

Governments buy and sell goods and services and distribute subsidies. More recently, many governments have sold state firms and provided infrastructure service concessions to private operators. All these activities can create corrupt incentives. When the government is a buyer or a contractor, for example, there are several reasons why a corrupt firm may pay off officials. A corrupt firm may pay to be included in the list of qualified bidders, to have officials structure the bidding specifications so that it is the only qualified supplier, or to be selected as the winning contractor. And once selected, it may pay for the opportunity to charge inflated prices or to skimp on quality.

Similarly, when governments sell goods or services at below-market prices, firms will often pay off officials for access to state supplies. In China, for example, where many raw materials are sold both at state subsidized prices and on the free market, payoffs reportedly are common. When the state controls the supply of credit and the rate of interest, bribes may be paid for access. Businesspeople in Eastern Europe and Russia report that payoffs are often necessary to obtain credit. And, when the state maintains multiple exchange rates at artificially low levels, firms often pay bribes to get scarce foreign exchange.

Corruption can also occur when spending on subsidies and benefits is too low to satisfy all who qualify, or when officials must use discretion in allocating services. People may pay to be judged qualified for a public benefit or to be selected to receive a scarce benefit. In the United States, for example, corruption has periodically surfaced in public housing programs....

Although privatizing state-owned enterprises reduces opportunities for corruption, the privatization process itself can create corrupt incentives. A firm may pay to be included in the list of qualified bidders or to restrict their number. It may pay to obtain a low assessment of the public property to be leased or sold off, or to be favored in the selection process....

In all these types of government programs officials are likely to amass valuable information. Private individuals and firms may be willing to pay for information such as bidding specifications, the actual condition of soon-to-be-privatized firms, and the location of future capital projects.

Paying to avoid costs

Governments also impose regulations, levy taxes, and enforce criminal laws. As they carry out these functions, officials can delay and harass those they deal with, and they can impose costs selectively in a way that affects firms' competitive position. Under public regulatory programs, firms may pay for a favorable interpretation of the rules or a discretionary judgment in their favor. The incentives to do so are especially high when the regulatory requirements are unclear, giving much discretion to officials, or when regulatory agencies are new and unproven.

To reduce their tax payments, businesses and individuals may collude with tax collectors, dividing the savings with them.... Customs officials are particularly likely to engage in corruption since they control access to the outside world, something that firms value highly....

Firms and individuals everywhere will pay to avoid the costs of delay. For example, if the government or a parastatal does not pay its bills on time, contractors may pay to get speedy settlement. In many countries, informal payoffs are required to obtain even ordinary services such as a telephone, a passport, or a driver's license....

Businesses selling outlawed goods and services are especially prone to extortion. Law enforcement authorities can demand payments to overlook criminal law violations or limit penalties. If the evidence of criminal behavior is clear, such firms are unable to credibly threaten to report corrupt authorities. Of course, illegal businesspeople are hardly innocent victims. They may purposely corrupt the police, seeking not only immunity from prosecution, but also monopoly power in the illegal market....

The size and incidence of bribes

The level of corruption is a function of the honesty and integrity of both public officials and private individuals. With these factors held constant, the size and incidence of bribe payments are determined by the overall *level* of benefits available, the *riskiness* of corrupt deals, and the relative *bargaining power* of briber and bribee. The level of benefits is determined by the nature of government programs, but corrupt public officials themselves often influence the supply of benefits up for negotiation. For example, they may be able to extract some of a contractor's profits by delaying payments or inventing ex post regulatory hurdles. They can threaten to enforce criminal and regulatory laws more vigorously than is the norm. They can also propose "white elephant" projects, or structure privatization projects or natural resource concessions to include high monopoly profits.

If the likelihood of detection and punishment is high, bribes may not be worthwhile. As the riskiness of corruption rises, the division of gains from corruption will depend in part on the briber['s] and bribee['s] relative tolerance for risk. It may also depend on whether the probability of detection and punishment is a function of the size of bribes. One possible result of stepped-up enforcement is a lower incidence of corruption, but an increase in the size of bribes paid.

Generally, the division of gains between the payer and the recipient of the bribe depends on their relative bargaining power. One aspect of this is their relative vulnerability to prosecution. For example, if firms are punished less severely than public officials, their threat to reveal a corrupt arrangement is more credible, and they ought to be able to garner a larger share of the monopoly gains of bribery. In such cases the size of the bribes is a poor guide to their distortionary effect.

The relative position of a potential briber also depends on whether there are other ways of obtaining the desired benefit. The potential briber might be able to obtain the same benefit by relocating to another jurisdiction or country, by following legal processes at some additional cost, or by using threats and intimidation rather than payoffs. Or it might be able to obtain a comparable benefit by applying to another official in the same government. This is a real possibility when many officials can provide a benefit, such as a license, a passport, or help in smuggling goods. Similarly, in a democratic legislature, where a majority would have to be bribed, no one legislator has much bargaining power. Individual payoffs will be low, but the overall incidence of corruption may be high. In general it seems that when firms have other options, they can more easily avoid making high payoffs and may be able to avoid corruption entirely.

The costs of corruption

How often do officials, private firms, and individuals take advantage of corrupt opportunities, and how much money is paid in bribes? Not surprisingly, there is little solid evidence on the incidence and magnitude of corruption. Surveys of businesspeople indicate that the problem varies widely across countries. And within countries, some public agencies—for example, customs and tax collection—are more of a problem than others. Surveys also suggest that where corruption is endemic, it imposes a disproportionately high burden on the smallest firms. But, importantly, the most severe costs often are not the bribes themselves, but the underlying distortions they reveal.

Inefficiency and unfairness

When payoffs are commonplace, government contracts, privatized firms, and concessions may not be allocated to the most efficient bidders. One might argue that the most efficient firm would be willing to pay the highest bribe, but this would not be the case if this firm happens to be scrupulous. Corruption favors those with no scruples and those with connections over those that are the most efficient. It produces inefficiency because the need to pay bribes is an entry barrier, and firms that make payoffs may expect not only to win the contract or the privatization auction, but also to obtain inefficient subsidies, monopoly benefits, and regulatory laxness in the future.

Corruption introduces other kinds inefficiencies into government contracting. Projects may be too large and too numerous if bribe revenues increase with the dollar volume of procurement. They may also be too technically complex, since corrupt payments are easier to hide in one-of-a-kind projects. Quality may suffer if contractors make payoffs to be allowed to cut corners. In privatizations there is a more subtle reason why the most corrupt firm will not necessarily be the most efficient. A corrupt bidder with inside access may persuade officials to badly manage a parastatal in order to lower its value. The insider then emerges as the high bidder. Such behavior is difficult to detect since, ex post, the privatization will appear to be a smashing success.

Officials may raise firms' costs by introducing delays and unnecessary requirements as a way of inducing payoffs. This can happen in contracting and auctioning, for example, or in the administration of regulatory and tax laws. Furthermore, the process of paying bribes is itself costly. For example, a firm might need to establish a web of offshore bank accounts to hide its illegal gains.

Corruption in contracting and privatizations also has distributive consequences. The gains of bribery accrue to winning bidders and public officials rather than to the state and ordinary citizens. To make up for high contract prices and the disappointing revenue generated by privatizations, the state must raise taxes or cut spending. Third parties may suffer in other ways too. Consumers may end up with low-quality products if bribes are paid to induce regulatory officials to overlook dangerous conditions or permit firms to reduce quality. Enforcement of workplace safety rules and environmental regulations can be compromised by payoffs.

Undermining political legitimacy

Systemic corruption undermines the legitimacy of governments, especially in democracies, where it can even lead to coups by undemocratic leaders. By contrast, nondemocratic governments can use corruption to maintain power by spreading its benefits. If most wealthy and powerful individuals are part of a web of corrupt payoffs and favors, the threat of exposure can help current rulers to maintain power. Thus, corruption need not be destabilizing, but it always runs against norms of open and fair dealing.

Conclusions

Although no definitive evidence exists, there are good reasons to suspect that even in high growth countries, corruption is both unfair and inefficient.

Corrupt countries can still grow ... as long as corruption has not gone so far as to undermine economic fundamentals totally.... But recent econometric research suggests a negative association between growth and high levels of corruption. Case study material from around the world indicates that illegal payoffs can increase the cost and lower the quality of public works projects by as much as 30 percent to 50 percent.

Despite the costs of widespread corruption, they are a symptom of disease, not the disease itself. Eliminating corruption makes no sense if the result is a rigid, unresponsive, autocratic government. Instead, anticorruption strategies should seek to improve the efficiency and fairness of government and ... the efficiency of the private sector....

3. Padideh Ala'i, "The Legacy of Geographical Morality and Colonialism: An Assessment of the Current Crusade against Corruption," 33 Vand. J. Transnat'l L. 877, 894–904 (2000).

II. The Moralist and Revisionist Approaches to Corruption and the Continued Acceptance of the Rule of Geographical Morality

A. The Moralist Approach

Prior to the 1960s all discussion of corruption and bribery was based on a moralist perspective. Corruption was viewed first as a moral failing and also, at times, as a violation of the dictates of positive law, such as penal legislation against bribery. It has specifically been argued that the concept of bribery is fundamentally informed by religion, which created in the first instance the idea of a "transcendental Judge" immune from ordinary reciprocities....

* * *

In sum, the moralist approach lent itself to an a priori condemnation of all non-Western and non-Christian societies and cultures as morally inferior without any attempt to understand the culture or religious traditions of the East. This condemnation in turn was used by [colonists] to justify despotic acts as being necessitated by the lower moral standards of non-Western and non-Christian societies.

The morality-based approach to, and discourse on, corruption and bribery was rejected by social scientists in the 1960s. These social scientists argued that the moralist approach that dominated the discourse on corruption and bribery at the time was unacceptable because it lacked a working definition of corruption and relied on an a priori condemnation based on moral principles....

* * *

B. The Revisionist Approach

The revisionist school of thought on corruption and bribery developed during the decolonization period of the 1960s and 1970s. This approach is exemplified by the works of Samuel Huntington, J.S. Nye, A.J. Heidenheimer, and Nathaniel H. Leff. The revisionists challenged the ipso facto condemnation of corruption as something evil men did. Contrary to the traditional moralist approach, revisionism emphasized the "unavoidable character of corruption at certain stages of development and the contributions of the practice to processes of modernization and development.''[1] The revisionists' definition of corruption has been summarized as follows: ''a 'revisionist' approach ... defined corruption in terms of divergence from a specific norm of accepted behavior, explained its existence by reference to social mores and deficiencies in economic and political systems, and enumerated conditions in which it might elicit approval rather than condemnation.''[2] The most striking feature of the revisionist definition is that it is intended to be amoral. The revisionists used concepts from economics, sociology, anthropology, and other social sciences to make two arguments: (1) the definitions of corruption and bribery varied with societal values and inherited cultural and religious traditions, and (2) an increase in the incidence of corruption and bribery was a necessary and inevitable part of the modernization process. Despite an overall unity of concepts which coalesce the revisionist thought, their discourse on corruption in the developing world has been divided into three different approaches: (1) the functional-integrationist approach of sociology and anthropology, (2) the economic-market approach, and (3) the institutionalist approach, proposed by Samuel Huntington.

1.   Functional–Integrationist Revisionists

The works of Merton, Bayley, Abueva, and Scott exemplify the functional-integrationist approach to political corruption that drew largely upon the US experience with political machines in US cities. The functional-integrationists believed that corruption may contribute positively to development when it allows the integration of various groups who otherwise would not be able to participate in the political process. They saw corruption not only as giving the rich access to top-level decision making, but also as giving ordinary citizens access to lower levels of government bureaucracy. According to this school, corruption at the ''lower levels'' of bureaucracy may have ''an important humanizing element,'' enabling ordinary people to overcome their impotence in dealing with a ''huge, impersonal governmental apparatus.''[3] It is interesting to note that the functional-integrationists believed that it may be better ''that people in developing nations misuse modern agencies to their own ends than that they reject the new because they cannot work the handles.''[4]

* * *

... They also recognized that in some societies, cultural practices that we may consider ''corrupt,'' may be closer to their traditional way of doing things. Therefore, by integrating traditional ways of interacting with governmental officials, *e.g.*, gift-giving, we may allow these new institutions to survive and gain acceptance.

2.   Economic–Market Revisionists

The works of Leff, Nye, Bayley, and Scott exemplify the economic-market revisionist school. The economic-market revisionists argued that corruption may introduce efficiency into a system where there is none. The underlying

1. G. Ben–Dor, *Corruption, Institutionalization, and Political Development: The Revisionist Thesis Revisited*, 62 Comp. Pol. Stud. 63, 65 (1974).

2. G. Caiden & N. Caiden, *Administrative Corruption*, 37 Pub. Admin. Rev. 301 (1977).

3. Ben–Dor, *supra* note 1, at 72.

4. D. Bayley, *The Effects of Corruption in a Developing Nation*, 19 W. Pol. Q. 719, 729 (1966).

problem they saw was that, where government policies are imperfect, government bureaucracy and regulation become overly burdensome, inefficient, and replete with red tape. In addition, specific acts of corruption, such as bribery, can allow entrepreneurs to enter the market who otherwise would be excluded.

In his often-quoted article, Corruption and Political Development: A Cost–Benefit Analysis [*infra* Reading 4], J. S. Nye not only attacked the moralist analysis of corruption, but went on to outline the possible benefits and costs of corruption and bribery.

3. Institutional Revisionists

Sharing with the other revisionists a distaste for the moralist a priori condemnation of corruption, the institutionalists attributed corruption to the absence of effective political institutionalization. Huntington argued that modernization and development create new sources of wealth and power that are outside the traditional norms of a developing society and that are regulated by more modern norms not yet accepted by that society's majority. Modernization entails increased corruption because modernization or development "involves the expansion of the output side of the political system, and the multiplication of governmental activities multiplies the opportunities for corruption."[5] The institutionalists argued that corruption can play a useful role when it contributes to political development by "preventing the alienation of certain groups from society and the political system, . . . particularly if it contributes to the building of new and stronger institutions."[6] Echoing the functional-integrationists, the institutionalist approach maintained that "like machine politics or clientalistic politics in general, corruption provides immediate, specific, and concrete benefits to groups which might otherwise be thoroughly alienated from society."[7] The institutionalists believed that corruption in certain developing countries may be positive because it is an acceptable alternative to violence in times of change when it facilitates elite integration and humanizes government for non-elites; that is, one who corrupts a system is more likely to identify with it than one who attacks a system. In addition, according to Huntington, institutionalization will ultimately reduce opportunities for corruption by strengthening political parties, *i.e.*, corruption will indirectly undermine itself.

4. The Revisionist Approach and the Principle of Geographical Morality

In the words of one commentator, the revisionist view amounted to the following:

Poor countries for cultural and historical reasons have a propensity toward corruption, seen as a violation of Western norms. To this propensity may be added a breakdown in the allocative mechanisms of society, or economic, political, and administrative reasons, so that corruption steps in to fulfill the missing functions. Corruption is thus legitimized in terms of its prevalence, and of its functionality: indeed, given the inappropriateness of Western norms and inadequacy of Western institutions, corrup-

5. Ben–Dor, *supra* note 1, at 74.
6. *Id.* at 75.

7. S. Huntington, Political Order in Changing Societies 64 (1968).

tion does not really exist at all—it is simply a different way of doing business.[8]

The removal of the moral aspect of corruption meant that Westerners could act corruptly without any moral misgivings. The revisionist discourse on political corruption provided the intellectual and moral justification for multinational corporations—the new colonial masters—to apply a different, lower standard of conduct to their actions in the South than they would apply to their actions in the North. This analysis is supported by the comment of Singapore's Minister of Foreign Affairs and Labour in 1968 on the revisionist discourse on corruption in Asia:

> I think it is monstrous for these well-intentioned and largely misguided scholars to suggest corruption as a practical and efficient instrument for rapid development in Asia and Africa. Once upon a time, Westerners tried to subjugate Asia ... by selling opium. The current defense of Kleptocracy is a new kind of opium by some Western intellectuals, devised to perpetuate Asian backwardness and degradation. I think the only people ... pleased with the contribution of these scholars are the Asian Kleptocrats.[9]

In other words, the revisionist discourse on corruption ironically perpetuated the rule of geographical morality, while denying the relevance of morality.

III. The Post–Cold War Crusade Against Transnational Bribery and Corruption and the Rule of Geographical Morality

A. Globalization and the End of the Cold War

The end of the Cold War and the subsequent process of globalization gave rise to the current anti-corruption movement and the rejection of the revisionist hypothesis that corruption is necessary and sometimes good for development. The defeat of Communism contributed to the rejection of the revisionist discourse on corruption because it was no longer necessary to defend corruption as a weapon to combat socialism and its "systematic bias" against "the market mechanism." The anti-corruption movement gained strength when Europe felt the effects of the explosion of corruption closer to home in the transitional economies of Eastern Europe and the former Soviet Union. Globalization also increased the opportunities for, and incidence of, corruption as more and more businesses "went international." This trend led both multinational corporations and peoples from the South to join the anti-corruption movement for the first time.

B. The Current Anti–Corruption Discourse

The current anti-corruption discourse has had three distinctive characteristics. The first characteristic is its rejection of "geographical morality," including a rejection and minimization of the importance of cultural differences as to what constitutes "corrupt practices," such as bribery. The second characteristic is its reliance on economic arguments: corruption has been opposed primarily on economic, not moral, grounds. The final characteristic, related to the second, is a heavy reliance on social science methodology and empirical data to prove the detrimental economic consequences of corruption

8. Caiden & Caiden, *supra* note 2, at 304. **9.** R. Klitgaard, Controlling Corruption 29 (1988) (citing the statements of Minister S. Rajaratnam in 1968).

in the South. The first of these characteristics is a reaction against the revisionist discourse on political corruption. The second and third are inherited from the revisionist approach in that they attempted to surgically remove any discussion of morality from the analysis of corruption in the South and relied instead on economic and empirical data. This modern, amoral, economically-based approach to corruption, however, categorically rejects the revisionist approach to corruption.

4. Joseph S. Nye, "Corruption and Political Development: A Cost–Benefit Analysis," in Political Corruption: A Handbook 973–75, 980–81 (A. Heidenheimer, M. Johnston, & V. LeVine eds., 1993).

... [We] have established that under some circumstances corruption can have beneficial effects on [certain] development problems.... It remains to offer hypotheses about the *probabilities* of benefits outweighing costs. In general terms, such probabilities will vary with at least three conditions: (1) a tolerant culture and dominant groups; (2) a degree of security on the part of the members of the elite being corrupted; (3) the existence of societal and institutional checks and restraints on corrupt behavior.

1. Attitudes toward corruption vary greatly [from country to country]. In certain West African countries, observers have reported little widespread sense of indignation about corruption.... [T]he Indonesian attitude to corruption (which began on a large scale only in 1954) is that it is sinful.... [However,] variations of attitude within a country can be as important (or more so) than differences between countries. Very often, traditional sectors of the populace are likely to be more tolerant of corruption than some of the modern sectors (students, army, civil service). Thus the hypothesis must take into account not only the tolerant nature of the culture, but also the relative power of groups representing more and less tolerant subcultures in a country....

2. Another condition which increases the probability that the benefits of corruption will outweigh the costs is a degree of security (and perception thereof) by the members of the elites indulging in corrupt practices. Too great insecurity means that any capital formed by corruption will tend to be exported rather than invested at home....

3. It is probable that for the benefits of corruption to outweigh the costs depends on its being limited in various ways, much as the beneficial effects of inflation for economic growth tends to depend on limits. These limits depend upon the existence of societal or institutional restraints on corruption. These can be external to the leaders, *e.g.*, the existence of an independent press, and honest elections; or internalized conceptions of public interest by a ruling group....

Given the characteristics of less developed countries, one can see that the general probability of the presence of one or more of these conditions (and thus of benefits outweighing costs) is not high. But to conclude merely that the moralists are more right than wrong ... is insufficient because the whole issue remains unsatisfactory if left in these general terms. Though corruption may not prove beneficial for resolution of development problems in general, it may prove to be the only means to solution of a particular problem. If a country has some overriding problem, some "obstacle to development"—for instance, if capital can be formed by no other means, or ethnic hatred threatens all legal activities aimed at its alleviation—then it is possible that corruption is beneficial for development despite the high costs and risks involved. While there are dangers in identifying "obstacles to development," and while the corruption that is beneficial to the solution of one problem may be detrimental to another, we need to get away from general statements which are difficult to test and which provide us with no means of ordering the vast number of variables involved. We are more likely to advance this argument if we distinguish the roles of different types of corruption in relation to different types of development problems.

[*Eds.*—Professor Nye next develops a "matrix" of probabilities, based on the conditions outlined above (favorable conditions being a tolerant culture or dominance of tolerant groups, security of the corrupted elite, and social and institutional limits on corruption; and unfavorable conditions being the opposites of those factors) and three types of development problems (economic development, national integration, and governmental capacity). He then hypothesizes the relative likelihood that the costs of corruption will outweigh the benefits in each of those particular problems. He acknowledges that his conclusions are based on *a priori* judgments, begging clarification or refutation by hard data. He then concludes:]

The scoring of the matrix suggests that we can refine the general statements about corruption and political development to read "it is probable that the costs of corruption in less developed countries will exceed its benefits except for top level corruption involving modern inducements and marginal deviations and except for situations where corruption provides the only solution to an important obstacle to development." . . . [C]orruption can provide the solution to several of the more limited problems of development. Whether this is beneficial to development as a whole depends on how important the problems are and what alternatives exist. It is also interesting to note that while the three conditions we have identified seem to be necessary for corruption to be beneficial in general terms, they are not necessary for it to be beneficial in the solution of a number of particular problems.

* * *

. . . [T]here is probably much more data on corruption and development gleaned during field work on other topics than we realize. What we need to advance the study of the problem is to refute and replace *specific* a priori hypotheses with propositions based on such data rather than with the generalities of the moralists. Corruption in developing countries is too important a phenomenon to be left to moralists.

5. Editors' Note. The move toward the internationalization of anti-corruption norms has been a slow one. Beginning in 1972 the Paris-based International Chamber of Commerce, a nongovernmental organization of thousands of companies and business associations in more than 140 countries, sought to discourage corrupt practices in its "Guidelines for International Investments," I.C.C. Pub. No. 272 (1973). It revised its standards in 1977 in its "Commission Recommendations on Ethical Practices to Combat Extortion and Bribery in Business Transactions," I.C.C. Pub. No. 315 (1977), and again in 1996 in its "Recommendations to Combat Extortion and Bribery in International Business Transactions." I.C.C. Pub. No. 412 (1996), and finally in 2005 in its "Rules of Conduct and Recommendations Combating Extortion and Bribery" **(Basic Document 4.24)**, available also at <http://www.iccwbo.org>. In 1976, the OECD similarly sought to discourage corruption as part its "Guidelines for Multinational Enterprises" **(Basic Document 4.10)**. In 1994 the OECD exclusively addressed the problem of corruption in its Recommendation on Bribery in International Business Transactions **(Basic Document 4.17)**, and in 1997 it issued strengthened Revised Recommendations **(Basic Document 4.20)**. The most significant early development in the effort to counter international corruption occurred in 1977, when the United States Congress passed the Foreign Corrupt Practices Act (FCPA), Pub. L. No. 95–213, 91 Stat. 1494 (codified as amended at 15 USC § 78dd–1 et seq. (1988 & Supp. V 1993) **(Basic Document 4.22)**. The FCPA forbids United States business enterprises and individuals from offering money, gifts, promises, or anything of value, to any foreign official who assists in obtaining or retaining business in a corrupt fashion.[f] For many years the FCPA stood as a lone effort by a major investor country to extraterritorially police its own nationals. In fact, until recently many countries even allowed domestic concerns to deduct the costs of foreign bribes on their domestic income tax returns.

In the years that followed the passage of the FCPA, global efforts to combat corruption through the introduction of soft law continued. For example, in 1988, the United Nations Economic and Social Council addressed corruption in its "Draft Code of Conduct on Transnational Corporations" **(Basic Document 4.11)**. In the 1990's the World Bank began to implement enhanced procedures for guarding against corruption in its lending practices, and the IMF as part of its focus on "good governance" made the control of corruption by borrowing governments part of its own lending criteria.

The major legal breakthrough towards the internationalization of anti-corruption norms occurred in 1997 with the OECD adoption of the Convention on Combating Bribery of Foreign Public Officials in International Business Transactions **(Basic Document 4.21)**. The Convention which entered into force in 1999 obligates all parties to adopt their own version of legislation similar to the FCPA. The core of the Convention is Article 1 which requires that each Party criminalize the payment of extraterritorial bribes "in order to obtain or retain business or other improper advantage." The Foreign Corrupt Practices Act was amended in fairly minor ways to bring it into conformance with the Convention. Presently there are thirty-five Parties to the Convention. These include Argentina, Australia, Austria, Belgium, Brazil, Bulgaria, Canada, Chile, the Czech Republic, Denmark, Finland, France, Germany, Greece, Hungary, Iceland, Ireland, Japan, Luxembourg, Mexico, Netherlands, New Zealand, Norway, Poland, Portugal, Slovakia, Slovenia, South Korea, Spain, Sweden, Switzerland, Turkey, the United Kingdom, and the United States.

f. Significantly, an exception exists for payments made for routine government actions, defined as obtaining permits or government documents to authorize one to do business, processing paper work, obtaining visas, and the like. Payments for police protection, mail pick-up, inspections related to goods in transit across country, obtaining phone service or utilities, and loading and unloading cargo are likewise exempted and are distinguished from larger governmental decisions to award contracts. Affirmative defenses are available, *e.g.*, if the action was legal in the host country, if it was a bona fide business expenditure, or if it involved the execution or performance of a contract.

Another major development in the internationalization of anti-corruption norms on a regional level is the Inter–American Convention Against Corruption which was adopted by the Organization of American States in 1996 and went into force in 1997 **(Basic Document 4.18)**. Presently there are 32 American states that are parties to the Convention. While the OAS Convention is similar to the OECD Convention, it differs in that in addition to requiring the criminalization of the giving of foreign bribes, it requires as well that states take action against domestic corruption. It is also broader in its coverage than the OECD Convention in that it includes in its ambit payment for routine governmental actions.

While the OECD and OAS conventions hold great promise, unfortunately, thus far there has been a failure of compliance. For example, while US enforcement of the FCPA has historically been less than vigorous, other countries have yet to impose the first fine or prison sentence for extraterritorial bribery under their domestic laws promulgated pursuant to the OECD Convention.

Finally, of significant potential importance, the United Nations Convention Against Corruption was adopted by the United Nations General Assembly in 2003 and went into force in late 2005 **(Basic Document 4.23)**. While not intended to deal narrowly with the problem of extraterritorial corruption, the United Nations Convention broadly requires the criminalization of corrupt practices and contains provisions that require countries to cooperate with each other in fighting corruption.

6.   Convention on Combating Bribery of Foreign Public Officials in International Business Transactions, Concluded, 21 Nov 1997. Entered into force, Feb 1999. *Reprinted in* **37 I.L.M. 1 (1998) and 5 Weston & Carlson IV.D.19** (Basic Document 4.21).

7.   Stuart Eizenstat, Under Secretary of State for Economic, Business and Agricultural Affairs, Prepared Testimony Regarding the OECD Anti Bribery Convention before the US Senate, Committee on Foreign Relations, Washington, DC (9 Jun 1998).

Mr. Chairman and Members of the Committee: Ten years ago this summer, the United States Congress passed the Omnibus Trade Act which, in part, amended our Foreign Corrupt Practices Act. The amendments were a reaffirmation of the strong support of the Congress for effective anti-bribery legislation. As part of this action, the Congress called on the executive branch to negotiate—with our major trading partners in the Organization for Economic Cooperation and Development—an international agreement prohibiting bribery of foreign public officials in international business transactions. Such action has been a goal of successive US administrations since passage of the 1977 US Foreign Corrupt Practices Act. As then-President Carter's chief domestic advisor, I was involved in development and passage of the FCPA, and can attest to the high priority attached to getting a commitment from the world's largest industrial countries that they adopt strict anti-bribery laws of their own. The goal was to internationalize the principles in the FCPA so that other countries would rise to our high standards and so that US businesses would not be at a competitive disadvantage doing business abroad. The US Government, with the support of the business community and members of Congress, both Republicans and Democrats, has been working steadily for years to convince our trading partners to criminalize the bribery of foreign public officials. I am very pleased to inform you today that we have met this goal. And we have done so in a manner which will provide for freer and fairer international competition, will strengthen the rule of law in international business and will provide for a more level playing field for US businesses overseas. On December 17 of last year, on behalf of the United States, Secretary of State Madeleine Albright signed the OECD Convention on Combating Bribery of Foreign Public Officials in International Business Transactions. We were right to enact the Foreign Corrupt Practices Act over 20 years ago. And we have been right to press hard for our trade competitors to enact similar prohibitions. We have succeeded with the OECD Convention.... This is a major achievement for the rule of law....

* * *

Let me briefly highlight for you what this Convention does:

The Convention obligates the Parties to criminalize bribery of foreign public officials, including officials in all branches of government, whether appointed or elected. This prohibition includes payments to officials of public agencies, public enterprises, and public international organizations. This, therefore, would cover government-controlled parastatals, such as airlines, utilities, state telecommunications companies, which are increasingly important in public procurement. Only those operating on a purely commercial basis would be exempt.

The Parties must apply "effective, proportionate and dissuasive criminal penalties" to those who bribe foreign public officials. If a country's legal system lacks the concept of criminal corporate liability, it must provide for equivalent non-criminal sanctions, including monetary penalties.

The Convention requires that parties be able to seize or confiscate both the bribe and the bribe proceeds—the net profits that result from the illegal transaction—or to impose equivalent fines so as to provide a powerful disincentive to bribery. Under our law, substantial fines have had significant impact on corporate compliance.

The Convention has strong provisions to prohibit accounting omissions and falsification, and to provide for mutual legal assistance and extradition. These mutual legal assistance provisions, in particular, will greatly enhance cooperation with foreign governments in cases of alleged bribery, improving both our own enforcement of the FCPA and foreign governments' enforcement of anti-bribery laws. The Convention will cover business-related bribes to foreign public officials made through political parties, party officials, and candidates, as well as those bribes that corrupt foreign public officials direct to them....

* * *

IMPLEMENTING LEGISLATION

Since the Convention follows our FCPA closely, we have submitted to Congress only those amendments designed to bring our law into full compliance with its obligations and to implement the Convention. We have tailored our proposed amendments so that our law will have a scope similar to that we expect our major trading partners to achieve as they enact their own laws. We have been careful not to put US firms at a disadvantage. First, the FCPA currently criminalizes payments made to influence any decision of a foreign official or to induce that official to do or omit to do any act, in order to obtain or retain business. An amendment will clarify that the scope of the FCPA includes payments made to secure "any improper advantage," the language used in the OECD Convention, in order to obtain or retain business. Second, the OECD Convention requires parties to cover prohibited acts by "any person." The current FCPA covers only issuers with securities registered with the Securities and Exchange Commission and "domestic concerns." An amendment will expand the scope of the FPCA to cover acts prohibited by the Convention of persons other than issuers or domestic concerns (*i.e.*, all foreign natural and legal persons), committed while in the territory of the United States, regardless of whether the mails or a means or instrumentality of interstate commerce are used, in furtherance of the prohibited acts. Third, the OECD Convention calls on parties with jurisdiction to prosecute their nationals for offenses committed abroad to assert nationality jurisdiction over the bribery of foreign public officials, consistent with national legal and constitutional principles. Accordingly, an amendment will provide for jurisdiction over the acts of US businesses and nationals, in furtherance of unlawful payments, that take place wholly outside the United States. Fourth, the OECD Convention includes officials of international agencies within the definition of foreign public official. Accordingly, an amendment will expand the FCPA definition of foreign official to include officials of public international organizations. Finally, under the current FCPA, non-US citizen employees and agents of issuers and domestic concerns are subject only to civil, rather than criminal, penalties. A proposed amendment to the penalty sections relating to issuers and domestic concerns will ensure that penalties for non-US citizen employees and agents of issuers and domestic concerns accord with those of US citizen employees and agents.[g]

8. International Chamber of Commerce Rules of Conduct and Recommendations Combating Extortion and Bribery. Report of the Commission on Anti-Corruption. International Chamber of Commerce Document Number 517 (2005) (Basic Document 4.24).

9. Inter–American Convention Against Corruption. Concluded, 29 Mar 1996. Entered into force, 6 Mar 1997. OAS Off. Rec. OEA/Ser. K/XXXIV.1 CICOR/Doc. 14/96, Rev. 2 (1996); *reprinted in* 35 I.L.M. 724 (1996) and 5 Weston & Carlson IV.D.14: Pmbl. & Arts. I–IX, XI, XIII–XV, XVII (Basic Document 4.18).

10. David A. Gantz, "Globalizing Sanctions Against Foreign Bribery: The Emergence of A New International Legal Consensus," 18 Nw. J. Int'l L. & Bus. 457, 476–80 (1998).

V.   The Inter–American Convention Against Corruption

The first, historic, binding international agreement dealing with foreign corruption is the Inter–American Convention Against Corruption. Twenty-two

---

g.   All of the proposed amendments referred to were enacted into law. *See* Basic Document 4.22.

OAS [Organization of American States] member nations, including the United States, signed the Inter–American Convention within a few months of its completion on March 29, 1996. The Inter–American Convention entered into force on March 6, 1997, after the deposit of the second instrument of ratification. . . .

* * *

A. A Latin American Initiative Against Corruption

Given the United States' long-term interest in international agreements that would require nations to criminalize foreign corruption, it is perhaps surprising that the Inter–American Convention was not a US initiative at the outset. Rather, it was a group of Latin American governments, led by Venezuela, that first proposed the concept at the Meeting of Western Hemisphere Presidents in Miami in December 1994. The United States gave its strong support to the proposal and encouraged the OAS, at a conference in Caracas in March 1996, to adopt the Inter–American Convention, which applies to both the "supply" and the "demand" aspects of the problem by requiring criminalization of both domestic and foreign corruption.

In retrospect, it seems evident that the Inter–American Convention is, most of all, a manifestation of the spread of popularly-elected government in Latin America, which in turn has led to much less patience with, and in some instances a rejection of, corruption, at least in public. This is reflected in the fact that the Convention is not grounded principally on trade or economic development concerns, but on morality and the need to preserve and protect democratic institutions:

> Representative democracy, an essential condition for stability, peace and development of the region, requires, by its nature, the combating of every form of corruption in the performance of public functions . . . fighting corruption strengthens democratic institutions and prevents distortions in the economy, improprieties in public administration and damage to a society's moral fiber. . . .[10]

* * *

B. Scope and Major Features of the Inter–American Convention

When the Inter–American Convention was concluded in March 1996, it went much further than any other actual or proposed international agreement in seeking not only to make bribery of foreign officials a crime in the country of the exporting firm or individuals, but also in encouraging local governments to deal more effectively with the problem of domestic corruption. The latter aim appears particularly important given that only two major capital goods exporting countries, the United States and Canada, are members of the OAS, although foreign investment by firms headquartered in other western hemisphere states, particularly Argentina, Brazil, Mexico, and Venezuela, is increasing.

The Inter–American Convention requires the Parties to establish as criminal offenses, under their domestic laws: the solicitation or acceptance of

---

10. Inter–American Convention Against Corruption, pmbl [*supra* Reading 9, and **Basic Document 4.18**].

illicit payments; the offering of illicit payments; acts or omissions by government officials for the purpose of obtaining a bribe; fraudulent use of property derived from such activities; and participation as a principal, accomplice, accessory after the fact, etc., in a conspiracy to commit the enumerated acts. The Parties also "agree to consider the applicability of measures within their own institutional systems" to "create, maintain and strengthen" standards of conduct for their own government officials, define acts of corruption, and provide for methods to enforce the standards of conduct.[11] Among other preventive measures is a requirement that the Parties "consider the applicability of measures to create, maintain and strengthen ... laws that deny favorable tax treatment for any individual or corporation for expenditures made in violation of the anticorruption laws of the States Parties."[12]

The Inter–American Convention also provides for the establishment of the criminal offense of "illicit enrichment," under which an inexplicable significant increase in the assets of a government official is to be considered an act of corruption under the Convention in jurisdictions where this is constitutionally permissible.[13] In civil law jurisdictions, if an official is discovered with great wealth that is otherwise inexplicable, there may be a presumption of criminal guilt. While such an approach would be questionable in the United States, the concept is important to many Latin American jurisdictions where investigatory institutions are not always capable of complex investigations. Moreover, even in the United States, a form of unjust enrichment is addressed in the "net worth" method of proof used in prosecuting certain US tax evasion actions.

Most significantly in light of the need to control foreign ("transnational") bribery, the Inter–American Convention also requires each state party, "subject to its Constitution and the fundamental principles of its legal system," to prohibit and punish the offering or granting, directly or indirectly, by its nationals, persons having their habitual residence in its territory, and businesses domiciled there, to a government official of another State, of any article of monetary value, or other benefit, such as a gift, favor, promise or advantage, in connection with any economic or commercial transaction in exchange for any act or omission in the performance of that official's public functions.[14]

This provision is clearly intended to require and facilitate extraterritorial application of the Parties' laws to foreign bribery because "the Convention is applicable provided that the alleged act of corruption has been committed or has effects in a State Party."[15] Also, the offenses covered by the Convention must be treated as extraditable offenses under any existing extradition treaties that are in force between or among the Parties.[16] The Parties are obligated to provide mutual assistance and technical cooperation to each other in investigating and prosecuting offenses under the Inter–American Convention, including the furnishing of technical cooperation.[17] In a departure from the FCPA, there is no explicit exception for facilitating or "grease" payments. However, it can be argued that facilitating payments are not designed to elicit

11. *Id.*, arts. III, VI.
12. *Id.*, art. IV(7).
13. *Id.*, art. IX.
14. *Id.*, art. VIII.
15. *Id.*, art. IV.
16. *Id.*, art. XIII(2).
17. *Id.*, art. XIV.

an improper "act or omission" by a government official, but rather to encourage that official to perform a ministerial duty that is a part of his or her normal responsibilities, and therefore are not covered offenses. The Inter–American Convention thus follows a multi-pronged approach that seeks to control both the supply of and demand for bribery. The Parties accept binding international legal obligations: to criminalize domestic bribery within their own jurisdictions; to strengthen domestic prevention and detection methodology; to punish foreign bribery by their own officials; and to improve methods of cooperation among the nations that are parties to the convention. As one senior US official has suggested, corruption is like adultery: ninety percent of it is a matter of opportunity. If you eliminate the opportunities, you eliminate the crime. Even if the Inter–American Convention only assists in reducing the opportunities for foreign bribery, it would have achieved a significant benefit.

11. Susan Rose–Ackerman, "Redesigning the State to Fight Corruption," Viewpoint, Note No. 75 (The World Bank, April 1996).

... [W]ith norms of honesty constant, corruption depends on three factors: the overall level of public benefits available, the riskiness of corrupt deals, and the relative bargaining power of briber and bribee. Anticorruption strategies must operate in parallel, by reducing the benefits under the control of officials, increasing the costs of bribery, and limiting the bargaining power of officials. This Note proposes reforms to achieve these objectives, beginning with measures to increase the riskiness of corruption.

Risks and costs of bribery

Government policy can reduce corruption by increasing the benefits of being honest, increasing the probability of detection and punishment, and increasing the penalties levied on those caught. Such measures will usually require substantive law reform to tighten internal controls, strengthen external monitoring, and introduce more transparency.

Civil service reform

Reforming the civil service is an obvious first step. Often the pay structure needs adjustment. If officials are paid much less than those with similar training elsewhere in the economy, people willing to accept bribes will be disproportionately attracted to the public sector. Officials with discretionary control of large benefits may need to be paid much more than the going rate for people with similar skills, to increase their willingness to resist the high bribes they may be offered. But adequate civil service pay is only a necessary condition, not a sufficient one. Paradoxically, an official whose pay is boosted may demand higher bribes—to offset the risk of losing what is now a very desirable job. Thus, the incidence of bribery falls as fewer officials are willing to accept payoffs, but the size of the bribes paid increases.

Civil service reform must therefore include features tied to the marginal benefits of accepting payoffs. There are two parts to such a strategy. The first is to set civil service wages above the going private sector wage, or to grant public employees generous benefits such as pensions, that they will receive only if they retire in good order. But, again, such reforms may not be sufficient, since they are not tied to the benefits of individual corrupt deals. Once an official steps over the line and begins to take bribes, these policies will encourage him to take ever-higher and more frequent payoffs. If he faces a high probability of losing his job anyway, why not take as much as possible? Thus, a second step is also necessary. Penalties should be tied to the marginal benefits of the payoffs received. The probability of detection and punishment and the level of punishment, given conviction, should increase with the level of speculation.

Furthermore, to be effective, antibribery laws must apply both to those who pay and to those who receive bribes. Convicted public officials should pay a penalty equal to a multiple of bribes received, and penalties for convicted bribers should be tied to their gains (their excess profits, for example), not to the amount paid. One effective deterrent is debarment procedures that prohibit corrupt firms from contracting with the government for a period of years.

Law enforcement and administrative penalties focus on locating corruption after it has occurred. They can deter civil servants from accepting or extorting payments if they create the perception that corruption carries high risks. The goal is to use a combination of carrots (desirable pay and benefits) and sticks (legal and administrative penalties) to deter payoffs.

External bodies and whistleblower statutes

Outside institutions can complement internal controls. An independent and honest judiciary, from lower-level clerks to judges, is essential for effective legal sanctions. As alternatives or supplements, other independent review and investigative systems have been proposed, such as an anticorruption commission, an ombudsman, or other independent administrative tribunals. Such external review bodies (Hong Kong's Independent Commission against Corruption, for example) can be valuable, but they carry the risk of arbitrariness if they report only to the country's ruler.

Uncovering evidence of corruption is notoriously difficult because both sides to the transaction have an interest in keeping it secret. In fact, reporting the speculations of others can be dangerous. If corruption is systemic, a "whistleblower" risks being disciplined by corrupt superiors and attacked by coworkers, and may even end up being accused of corruption himself. Governments should consider promulgating whistleblower statutes that protect and reward those in the public and private sector who report malfeasance. The United States, for example, has a statute that rewards those who report irregularities in government contracts.

When corruption is systemic, solutions that appear reasonable in other contexts can have perverse effects. For example, some recommend rotating officials so that they are unable to develop the close, trusting relations in which payoffs may be more likely. But if the entire government agency is corrupt, superiors can use their ability to reassign staff to punish those who refuse to play along. . . .

Increased transparency

Those concerned with fighting corruption should support a free press, few constraints on the creation and operation of watchdog and good-government groups and freedom of information laws. They should oppose restrictive libel laws, especially those that give special protection to public officials. Elected politicians ought not be immune from charges of corruption.

Within the public sector certain structures and systems can make government actions more transparent. Corruption is deterred because it is more difficult to hide. For example, strong financial management systems are essential that audit government accounts and make financial information about the government public. Open and fair procurement regulations are also necessary. Similarly, corruption among politicians can be deterred through campaign finance reform and conflict of interest rules. But restrictions on legal donations must not be so restrictive that they push candidates off the books. Legal controls must be combined with effective methods of financing campaigns from public money or private contributions.

Integrated approach

It is hard to evaluate the relative merits of these options in the abstract, because their costs and benefits depend on the context. But most cannot stand alone. For example, increases in civil service pay and benefits are pointless if credible monitoring systems are not in place to detect wrongdoing. Policies to increase the risks and costs of corruption are usually part of reform strategies designed to reduce the potential benefits. For example, when Mexico reformed its customs service, it not only simplified the underlying regulations, but also improved civil service pay and improved auditing and control.

Reducing discretionary benefits

The most promising anticorruption reforms are those that reduce the discretionary benefits under the control of public officials. This must be done without simply shifting the benefits to private sector elites, where they will show up as monopoly profits.

Less intervention

The first and most obvious way to reduce payoff opportunities is simply to eliminate those programs riddled with corruption—though this is not an option for programs with strong public policy rationales. If the state has no authority to restrict exports or license businesses, there is no opportunity for bribes. If a subsidy program is eliminated, the associated bribes will also disappear. If price controls are lifted, market prices will express scarcity values, not bribes. If a parastatal that is the locus of corrupt payoffs is moved into the private sector, those payoffs will end.

Of course, many regulatory and spending programs have strong justifications and ought to be reformed, not eliminated.

Competition and market forces

In general, any reform that increases the competitiveness of the economy helps reduce corrupt incentives. Policies that lower the controls on foreign trade, remove entry barriers for private industry, and privatize state firms in a way that assures competition, all contribute to the fight against corruption. But deregulation and privatization must be carried out with care. Deregulating in one area may increase corruption elsewhere. For example, a successful effort to reduce corruption in the transport of agricultural products in one

African country increased corruption and legal tariffs in neighboring countries on the same transport route. The privatization process can itself be corrupted, as can new regulatory institutions. Rather than bribing the parastatal to obtain contracts and favorable treatment, bidders bribe officials in the privatization authority. This is not to say that privatization and deregulation are not, on balance, desirable in most cases, but only to caution reformers to be aware of the incentives for malfeasance along the way.

Economists have long recommended reforming regulatory laws in such areas as environmental protection by introducing market-based schemes and charging user fees for scarce government services. In addition to improving efficiency, these reforms reduce corrupt incentives. The sale of water and grazing rights, pollution rights, and import and export licenses can limit corruption by replacing bribes with legal payments.

Administrative reforms can also be important in lowering corrupt incentives. One such reform is the introduction of competition within government to reduce the bargaining power of officials. When bribes are paid for benefits such as licenses and permits, overlapping, competitive bureaucratic jurisdictions can reduce corruption. Since clients can apply to any of a number of officials and go to a second one if the first turns them down, no one official has much monopoly power, and, therefore, no one can extract a very large payoff. For qualified clients, bribes will be no larger than the cost of reapplication. Unqualified clients will still pay bribes, but even they will not pay much so long as they too can try another official. This model can be extended to law enforcement, giving police officers who control illegal businesses overlapping enforcement areas. Gamblers and drug dealers will not pay much to an individual policeman if a second one may come along later and also demand a payoff. The system may work better if the law enforcement officers belong to different police forces—local, state, or federal, for example—making collusion among officers less likely.

Clear rules, simple processes

When corruption is difficult to observe, administrative reforms can be designed to make its effects more easily observed. For example, the state might use private market prices as benchmarks to judge public contracts. Clear rules of proper behavior could be established so violations can be spotted even if the bribery itself is not. Procurement decisions could favor standard off-the-shelf items to provide a benchmark and to lower the cost of submitting a bid.

Corruption in the collection of taxes cannot, of course, be solved by failing to collect revenue. In such cases, one solution is to clarify and streamline the necessary laws. The reform of the Mexican customs service, for example, reduced the steps in the customs process from twelve to four, and streamlined the remaining service to reduce delays. Rules should be transparent and publicly justified. A government could move toward simple nondiscretionary tax, spending, and regulatory laws as a way of limiting corrupt opportunities. But the value of such reforms depends on the costs of limiting the flexibility of public officials. Some risk of corruption often needs to be tolerated in exchange for the benefits of a case-by-case approach in administering programs. But even in these cases, transparency and publicity can reduce corrupt incentives.

Many corrupt situations have both winners and losers. The state could introduce ways for the potential losers to protest or to organize ahead of time, or make it hard for corrupt officials to organize themselves or bribe payers. Sometimes bribe payers view themselves as losers who would be better off in an honest world and are potential allies in an anticorruption effort. But when bribery makes both the payer and the recipient better off than they would be in a no-bribery world, control incentives must rest with outsiders (for example, disappointed bidders, taxpayers, consumers). The existence of losers with a large stake in the outcome, such as disappointed bidders, can facilitate efforts to limit corruption.

Conclusions

Some argue that bribes help firms and individuals circumvent government requirements—reducing delays and avoiding burdensome regulations and taxes. Payoffs seem to be nothing more than the grease needed to move the gears of complex machinery. But corruption cannot be limited to situations where the rules are inefficient. Incentives to make and ask for payoffs exist whenever a government official has economic power over a private firm or individual. It does not matter whether the power is justified or unjustified. Once a pattern of successful payoffs is institutionalized, corrupt officials have an incentive to demand larger bribes and seek new ways to extract payments. Therefore, even when illegal payoffs appear to facilitate commerce, governments and private citizens should not respond with tolerance. Instead, they must move vigorously to stem a "culture" of illegality. Illegal markets are always inefficient relative to a well-functioning legal market. Those with scruples will not participate, price information will be poor because of the illegality of the trades, and time and energy must be expended to keep the deal secret and to enforce its terms. In some cases, paying bribes may be more efficient than complying with existing rules, but corruption is always a second-best response to government failures.

Corruption can never be entirely eliminated. Under many realistic conditions, it is simply too expensive to reduce corruption to zero. And a single-minded focus on preventing corruption can impinge on personal freedoms and human rights. Such a focus could produce a government that is rigid and unresponsive. The aim, therefore, should be not complete rectitude, but a fundamental increase in the honesty—and thus the efficiency, fairness, and political legitimacy—of government.

12.   Edward T. Swaine, "Unsigning," 55 Stan. L. Rev. 2061, 2066–2071 (2003).

The history of the law of treaties, greatly simplified, supports a shift in gravity from signature to ratification. Signature was generally regarded as sufficient between monarchs or, for that matter, between their duly authorized representatives. Even in the early twentieth century, dictators sometimes personally negotiated, signed, and through those acts made binding treaties along much the same lines. But separate ratification procedures also have an ancient pedigree in international relations, have come to be required by numerous national constitutions, and are now the default procedure for international agreements.

The relationship among negotiating authority, signature, and ratification raises a host of technical issues, but at least one of potential consequence: If ratification is required before a state can become a party, what significance remains for prior acts, particularly signature? To be sure, signature has some recognizable, if often overlooked, consequences. Collectively, signature tends to fix the treaty's substantive terms—at least in the absence of reservations. It also establishes the terms by which a treaty is to come into force, such as by setting a time limit for ratification or stipulating the minimum number of signatories.

Commentators puzzled, however, over the significance of individual signatures for state consent, a problem made more acute by widespread and prolonged delays in ratification. Some conceded that the signature lacked any legal effect, but most shrunk from such a nihilistic view. At the opposite end of the spectrum, some claimed that signature created an obligation to ratify. But this would basically divest ratification of significance, and in the process slight the functional arguments for it. Because adding discrete stages to the consent process may improve the likelihood of cooperation, rendering ratification redundant may harm the objectives of treatymaking. Moreover, to the extent that domestic ratification processes broaden participation—as in the United States, where ratification increases public scrutiny, requires legislative participation, and presents the executive branch with a second opportunity to evaluate the treaty—requiring ratification on the international plane may improve the credibility of treaty commitments.

* * *

By the time the Harvard Research in International Law project was compiling a code of treaty law, it felt comfortable stating conclusively that there was no duty whatsoever to ratify a signed treaty. Special Rapporteurs to the International Law Commission's subsequent efforts at codification, which formed the basis for what became the Vienna Convention [**Basic Document 1.10**], urged inclusion of a binding legal duty "to submit the instrument to the proper constitutional authorities for examination with the view to ratification," but admitted that such a duty went beyond what existing law provided, and that, together with the obligation's vague character, ultimately doomed it.

A third, intermediate possibility was that ratification, though necessary to make an obligation binding, had an effect retroactive to the time of signature. Whatever the potential merits of that rule, it too was regarded as inconsistent with the migration from ratification of the signature to ratification as a separable mechanism for indicating consent. By the time of the Harvard Research project in 1935, retroactive ratification was considered "obsolete," a judgment reiterated in the International Law Commission's proceedings.

A fourth possibility, that endorsed by the Harvard project, the International Law Commission, and ultimately by those negotiating the Vienna Convention, was to redeem the signature by imposing a distinct duty on signatories. A handful of cases decided following World War I indicated that signatories—including, at least arguably, mere signatories—assumed some kind of duty not to disrupt the treaty's operation. In that spirit, article 18 of the Vienna Convention provides that:

A State is obliged to refrain from acts which would defeat the object and purpose of a treaty when:

(a) It has signed the treaty or has exchanged instruments constituting the treaty subject to ratification, acceptance or approval, until it shall have made its intention clear not to become a party to the treaty; or

(b) It has expressed its consent to be bound by the treaty, pending the entry into force of the treaty and provided that such entry into force is not unduly delayed.

[A]rticle 18's terms, and its influence, are unclear. But its dominance as a legal tactic for coping with the diminished checks on treaty signatures is beyond dispute. The Vienna Convention made no attempt to revive signature as the legally definitive juncture for state consent, and there has been little attempt to do so outside the Convention. Similarly, the Convention bypassed the opportunity to endorse the civil law principle of culpa in contrahendo, according to which liability may be imposed for bad faith conduct during negotiations. Even if the failure to adopt such alternatives is of little assistance in interpreting article 18, the choice to adopt exclusively the interim obligation approach—which has been followed by commentators and non-parties as well—makes it relatively easy to assess the default rules for treaty formation.

SECTION 5.   DISCUSSION NOTES/QUESTIONS

1.   The present problem has jurisdictional undertones. As the commentary and discussion in problems 6–2 and 6–3 indicate, the primary basis of jurisdiction is territorial. Under the principle of territorial jurisdiction states have the international legal authority to regulate what takes place within their own territory. Underpinning this jurisdictional basis is the simple presupposition that when in Rome one should do as the Romans do. The Foreign Corrupt Practices Act (FCPA) and similar laws promulgated in other countries pursuant to the OECD and OAS conventions attempt to prescribe the conduct mostly of one's own nationals that takes place primarily in foreign countries. The jurisdictional foundation for such extraterritorial regulation of a country's own citizens is called the nationality basis of jurisdiction. The nationality basis of jurisdiction is fairly well accepted under international law, although it is somewhat more controversial than the territoriality principle. As applied to foreign bribery, are there good reasons for large investor countries to attempt to regulate corruption in foreign countries, at least to the extent of involvement by their own nationals? Should it matter if corruption in Rome is commonplace, even a part of Roman economic culture? What effect does such an extension of the nationality basis of jurisdiction have for the paradigm of state sovereignty? Does such an extension of the nationality basis of jurisdiction have imperial overtones?

In addition to the "horizontal" jurisdictional question of how authority should be allocated among the different states, there is the "vertical" jurisdictional question of how authority should be allocated between states and the international system. The OAS and OECD treaties require the institution of extraterritorial anti-corruption legislation. Is the regulation of corruption an appropriate area of authority for the international system? Why not leave it to each state to individually decide whether it wishes to regulate in this area? Should it matter that the regulation as discussed above is extraterritorial in nature?

2.   As Reading 5, *supra*, suggests, the OECD Convention **(Basic Document 4.21)** supplanted earlier recommendations concerning foreign bribery. Is the Convention necessarily a step forward in combating foreign bribery? How does the lack of state compliance with the Convention to date mentioned in the last paragraph of Reading 5 influence your answer? In developing your response to this question, consider the following by Peter Eigen:

> [I]n 1994 the OECD issued a recommendation for its 29 member countries to end the practice of tax-deductibility for bribes paid abroad and to criminalize foreign bribery. Transparency International supported this OECD process from the beginning as it promised to be both effective and to yield results soon. In fact, what the OECD aimed at was direct action by all member countries at the respective national levels. Although such a "soft law" approach has been practiced highly successfully–not least by the OECD itself, with its recommendations against money laundering–several member countries felt uneasy having to rely on the good will of other countries. It was France and Germany that called most prominently for a legally binding international convention against foreign corruption, arguing that only a convention would give their exporters the certainty that they would not have to compete against corrupt competitors from other OECD countries that had not yet enacted the OECD recommendations.

Peter Eigen, *The OECD Convention on Combating Bribery of Foreign Public Officials in International Business Transactions*, 45–Aug Fed. Law 22 (1998).

3.   A commonly accepted definition of corruption is "private gain at public expense." *See* Carl J. Friedrich, *Corruption Concepts in Historical Perspective*, in Political Corruption: A Handbook 15, 15 (A. Heidenheimer, M. Johnston, & V. LeVine eds., 1993). This definition suggests that corruption is always a negative. After reviewing the material presented by professors Ala'i and Nye (*supra* Readings 3 and 4), do you conclude that corruption may play a positive role in economic and political development—if not generally, then at least in certain circumstances? Does a tolerance of corruption in developing countries by those representing the developed world suggest a self-serving neo-colonial outlook?

4.   The instant problem deals primarily with what is called "grand corruption," that is, corruption on a large-scale involving large sums of money or objects of great value. The most prevalent form of corruption, however, is what is known as "petty corruption," *e.g.*, "grease money," "speed money," or "dashes"—small-scale bribes or favors in return for favorable treatment by (usually) low-level governmental officers. Such corruption is a common, daily experience for many people in many parts of the world, part of everyday transactions to obtain mail, travel through government checkpoints, secure licenses, or avoid arrest for some minor or even non-existent infraction. Note the difference in this regard between the FCPA and the OECD Convention **(Basic Document 4.21)** on the one hand and the OAS Convention **(Basic Document 4.18)** on the other. Is it appropriate and/or desirable to seek the eradication of petty corruption when it is endemic to a particular culture or cultural traditions? Why? Why not?

5.   What about the truly grand corruption problem of national leaders, not atypically from the Third World, who betray the public trust by sacking their national treasuries to live a life of luxury (commonly abroad in Europe or North America) while their people, usually already impoverished, scratch out the most meagre of existences midst the most degrading of circumstances? The names of

Suharto (Indonesia), Nicolae Ceausescu (Romania), Umaru Dikkos (Nigeria), Jean–Claude Duvalier (Haiti), Ferdinand Marcos (Philippines), and Mobutu Sese Seko (Congo) come to mind, among others. In International Law of Responsibility for Economic Crimes (1995), Professor Ndiva Kofele–Kale has written of this problem, what he calls "indigenous spoliation," insightfully and creatively, as follows, at 11–14:

> Such terms as "embezzlement" or "misappropriation" or "corruption" or "graft" or "fraudulent enrichment" have been, and continue to be used to describe the widespread practice of office holders confusing the public fisc with their private accounts, but these concepts do not adequately convey the full force of the relatively new phenomenon of indigenous spoliation. If anything, they signify only the raw act of depredation but not its effect which is the destruction of the social, economic and moral foundation of the victim nation. What has been taking place in the last two decades or so is a coordinated plan whose effect, if not objective, is the destruction of the essential foundations of the economic life of a society. It is the systematic looting and stashing in foreign banks of the financial resources of a State; the arbitrary and systematic deprivation of the economic rights of the citizens of a nation by its leaders, elected and appointed, in military regimes as well as civilian governments in Africa, Asia, Latin America and Eastern Europe, on a scale so vast and never before seen in history. This activity deserves a new name, for, as Raphael Lemkin argued some four decades ago when he introduced the word "genocide" into the lexicon of political discourse, a new crime deserves a new name.

The new term "patrimonicide" is Professor Kofele–Kale's preferred name. Invoking international human rights law and such venerable doctrines of domestic law as the doctrine of fiduciary relations and the public trust doctrine, he makes a case for indigenous spoliation or patrimonicide as an *independent* breach of individual and group rights under both conventional and customary international law, and then argues the issue of responsibility and accountability for this economic crime under international law. Does Professor Kofele–Kale's approach suggest an effective alternative to problems of corruption such as are hypothesized in the Maurya scenario? Putting aside the question of whether international law *does* provide recourse against indigenous spoliation, *should* such conduct by national leaders be subject to international legal process? If so, can the law be enforced against them?

6.   What causes corruption? Where does it flourish? Professor Rose–Ackerman (*supra* Reading 2) argues that, while corruption depends on "the overall *level* of benefits available, the *riskiness* of corrupt deals, and the relative *bargaining power* of briber and bribee," discretion in the hands of government officials and control by bureaucrats of valuable assets (e.g., licenses, access to government contracts) invites corruption. She therefore concludes that reducing the control and bargaining power of bureaucrats over such benefits, though possibly increasing the size of bribes paid, can enhance both public and private sector efficiency, ergo economic growth. Thus, some argue, greater democracy and transparency in government is the best defense against corruption. Others stress economic factors, particularly the sufficiency of bureaucrats' salaries and benefits, or the overall economic conditions of the country in question. Transparency International (TI), mentioned in footnote **a**, *supra*, publishes an annual "Corruption Perceptions

Index" drawn from ten different sources reflecting business persons' perceptions of corruption in individual countries and ranking them based on these perceptions. The following is drawn from 158 rankings issued for 2005 (with 0 = "totally corrupt" and 10 = "zero corruption"): Iceland, 9.7 (**#1**); Singapore 9.4; Sweden, 9.2; Switzerland, 9.1; Australia, 8.8 (**#9**); United Kingdom, 8.6; Canada, 8.4; Hong Kong 8.3, Germany, 8.2; United States, 7.6 (**#17**); France, 7.5; Chile/Japan 7.3; Estonia, 6.4; Israel, 6.3; United Arab Emirates, 6.2; Botswana/Taiwan, 5.9; Malaysia, 5.1; South Korea, 5.0; South Africa, 4.5; Czech Republic, 4.3; Thailand, 3.8; Brazil, 3.7; Mexico, 3.5; Egypt/Saudi Arabia, 3.4; China, 3.2; India, 2.9; Argentina, 2.8; Russia, 2.4; Venezuela, 2.3; Indonesia, 2.2; Nigeria, 1.9; Haiti/Myanmar, 1.8; Bangladesh/Chad, 1.7 (**#158**). TI also publishes a "Bribe Payers Index" identifying perceptions of the relative propensity of companies from leading exporting countries to pay bribes. For details, see TI's web site at <http://www.transparency.org>.

7. Suppose that, in the instant problem, LuxAuto were to have sued the Government of Maurya for the millions it paid in bribes as a cost of doing business in Maurya? In such an event, it doubtless would face immediately the defense of sovereign immunity, explored in some detail in readings 1 through 4 of Problem 6–3 ("Suing Narbonna as a State Sponsor of Terrorism in United States Courts"), *supra,* at 857. Using United States law as our source of legal authority, what counterclaims might LuxAuto raise? Would the claim of official corruption standing alone or, alternatively, as part of a "commercial activity" exception suffice to overcome this defense?

In *W. S. Kirkpatrick & Co., Inc. v. Environmental Tectonics Corporation, International,* 493 U.S. 400 (1990), an antitrust suit under US law, the US Supreme Court held that the *act of state doctrine* did not bar adjudication where a company was alleged to have obtained a military procurement contract from the Government of Nigeria through bribery of Nigerian officials. However, in that case, the legality of the Nigerian contract, ergo Nigerian official behavior, was not in issue, but, rather, the conduct of the bribing company; and thus, according to the Court, "there was no occasion to apply the rule of decision that the act of state doctrine requires." Stated the Court: "Act of state issues only arise when a court must decide—that is, when the outcome of the case turns upon—the effect of official action by a foreign sovereign. When that question is not in the case, neither is the act of state doctrine." 493 U.S. at 406. Hence, even if the sovereign immunity doctrine can be analogized to the act of state doctrine, *Kirkpatrick* would not afford LuxAuto a defense to Maurya's sovereign immunity defense.

But does *Kirkpatrick* provide support for the argument that bribery is a "commercial activity"? Note that the Supreme Court has said that

> "when a foreign government acts, not as regulator of a market, but in the manner of a private player within it, the foreign sovereign's actions are 'commercial' within the meaning of the Foreign Sovereign Immunities Act (**Basic Document 6.2**). Moreover, because the Act provides that the commercial character of an act is to be determined by reference to its 'nature' rather than its 'purpose' ..., the question is not whether the foreign government is acting with a profit motive or instead with the aim of fulfilling uniquely sovereign objectives. Rather, the issue is whether the particular actions that the foreign state performs ... are the type of actions by which a private party engages in 'trade and traffic or commerce'...."

Republic of Argentina and Banco Central De La Republica Argentina v. Weltover, Inc., et al., 504 U.S. 607 (1992).

8. As Reading 5, *supra,* indicates, until recently it had been official policy for many investor nations actually to allow for the tax deductibility of bribes paid to foreign government officials. In 1996 and 1997, the OECD adopted recommenda-

tions calling on member countries to deny such deductibility. The OECD Convention **(Basic Document 4.21)** arguably incorporates by reference these recommendations. All OECD countries have now reported that they no longer allow for the tax deductibility of foreign bribes though the level of their actual compliance is not yet clear.

9.   In concluding Reading 11, *supra*, Professor Rose–Ackerman enumerates ways to combat corruption. Essentially international solutions are not among them, however. Why might this be? The lack of such solutions? Problems of achieving transnational consensus, cooperation, and/or enforcement? Insufficient space? Oversight?

10.   *Bibliographical Note*. For supplemental discussion concerning the principal themes addressed in this problem, consult the following additional specialized materials:

(a) *Books/Monographs/Report/Symposia*. Anti–Corruption Measures in South Eastern Europe: Civil Society's Involvement, Organization for Economic Cooperation and Development (2002); M. Bull, Corruption in Contemporary Politics (2003); G. Caiden, Where Corruption Lives (2001); Corruption, Integrity and Law Enforcement, Nethe Global Forum on Fighting and Safeguarding Integrity (2002); Corruption and Good Governance, United Nations Development Programme (2000); O. Echezonam, Espionage and Corruption in African Nations (2003); D. Fleischer, Corruption in Brazil: Defense, Measuring and Reducing (2002); M. Johnston, Cross Border Corruption: Points of Vulnerability and Challenges for Reform (2001); M. Johnston, Syndromes of Corruption: Wealth, Power, and Democracy (2005); J. Kidd, Corruption and Governance in Asia (2003); W. Miller, A Culture of Corruption: Coping With Government in Post Communist Europe (2001); W. Ofosu–Amaah, Combating Corruption: A Comparative Review of Selected Legal Aspects of State Practice and Major International Initiatives (1999); J. Quah, Curbing Corruption in Asian Countries: A Comparative Analysis (2003); C.P. Srivastava, India's Enemy Within (2001); B. I. Spector, Fighting Corruption In Developing Countries: Strategies And Analysis (2005); R. Stapenhurst, Curbing Corruption: Toward a Model for Building National Integrity (Edi Development Studies) (1999); Taking Action Against Corruption in the Asian and Pacific Rim, Asian Development Bank (2003); Transparency International, Global Corruption Report (2003); Transparency International, Source Book, Confronting Corruption: The Elements of a National Integrity System (2000); J. Tulchin, Combating Corruption in Latin America (2000); R. Williams, Corruption in the Developed World (2000); R. Williams, Corruption in the Developing World (2000).

(b) *Specialized Articles/Book Chapters*. A. DeAses, *Developing Countries: Increasing Transparency and Other Methods of Eliminating Corruption in the Public Procurement Process*, 34 Pub. Cont. L. J. 553 (2005); B. Harnes, *Holding Public Officials Accountable in the International Realm: A New Multi–Layered Strategy to Combat Corruption*, 33 Cornell Int'l. L. J. 159 (2000); C. R. Kumar, *Human Rights Approaches of Corruption Control Mechanisms—Enhancing the Hong Kong Experience of Corruption Prevention Strategies*, 5 San Diego Int'l L.J. 323 (2004); P. Nichols, G. Siedel, & M. Kasdin, *Corruption as a Pan–Cultural Phenomenon: An Empirical Study in Countries at Opposite Ends of the Former Soviet Empire*, 39 Tex. Int'l L. J. 215 (2004); P. Nichols, *Symposium, Fighting International Corruption and Bribery in the 21st Century*, 33 Cornell Int'l. L. J. 627 (2000); O. Oko, *Subverting the Scourge of Corruption in Nigeria: A Reform Prospectus*, 34 N.Y.U. J. Int'l L. & Pol. 397 (2002); A. Posada, *Combating Corruption Under International Law*, 10 Duke J. Comp. & Intl. L. 345 (2000); S. Salbu, *Information Technology in the War Against International Bribery and Corruption: The Next Frontier of Institutional Reform*, 38 Harv. J. on Legis. 6 (2001).

Chapter Seven

PROBLEMS OF ENVIRONMENTAL PROTECTION

THE VITAL PERSPECTIVE

Since the first Earth Day in 1970, our environment has been noisily rediscovered. Genuine efforts at population control, resource conservation, and pollution abatement have been made. But the world's population continues to grow alarmingly, and the squandering of nonrenewable resources, the wanton killing of precious species, and the contamination of delicate ecosystems persist with only marginal relief. To date, albeit with growing exception, there is mostly modest evidence that humankind is seriously prepared, psychologically and politically, to assume the courageous planetary stewardship that is needed to avoid major disasters. Governments remain committed to economic expansion as the *sine qua non* of social progress and well-being. Pollution is widely perceived as *the* central theme of environmental concern, except when there is talk or movement in the direction of competitive resource grabs. Too few evince wholesale regard for "the closing circle" and the consequent need to see our world as a total living organism, with appropriate coherent policies to match.

Problem 7–1

The Sea around Antilla and Costa Grande

Section 1. Facts

Antilla, a mid-sized island democracy on the northeast margin of the Caribbean Sea [*see* Figure 7–1.1], is an independent member of The Commonwealth.[a] Known as "The Pearl of the Caribbean," it is a developing country economically dependent on tourism and anchovy, shrimp, and yellowfin tuna fisheries. Costa Grande, a large and modestly industrialized country, ruled by a democratically elected but somewhat autocratic government and situated on the Caribbean coast of South America about 600 nautical miles southwest of Antilla [*see* Figure 7–1.1], earns the bulk of its foreign exchange from oil and other minerals and, to lesser extent, from cacao, cattle, and fish products, including yellowfin tuna (Thunnus albacares).

---

a. Sometimes loosely but incorrectly referred to as "the British Commonwealth of Nations."

Both countries are members of the United Nations (UN) and the Organization of American States (OAS), and each is a party or signatory to the following international instruments: the 1947 Inter–American Treaty of Reciprocal Assistance ("Rio Pact"); the 1948 American Treaty on Pacific Settlement ("Pact of Bogota"); the 1958 Convention on the Territorial Sea and the Contiguous Zone; the 1958 Convention on the Continental Shelf; the 1958 Convention on the High Seas; the 1958 Convention on Fishing and Conservation of the Living Resources of the High Seas; the 1969 Vienna Convention on the Law of Treaties; the 1970 Declaration of the Latin American States on the Law of the Sea; and the 1973 International Convention for the Prevention of Pollution from Ships together with its 1978 Protocol Concerning Reports of Incidents Involving Harmful Substances ("MARPOL 73/78"). In addition, Antilla, though not Costa Grande, is a signatory to the 1970 Declaration of Montevideo on the Law of the Sea. At the same time, Costa Grande, though not Antilla, is a party to the 1999 International Convention on Arrest of Ships.

In 1975, in keeping with the 1970 Declaration of Montevideo and prompted by a marked rise in unrestrained yellowfin tuna fishing by foreign commercial fleets between 100 and 300 nautical miles off its coast, the Government of Antilla enacted the "Fishery Conservation and Management Law" (FCML), one provision of which declared a "fishery jurisdiction" of up to 250 nautical miles, coextensive with the breadth of Antilla's continental shelf at its widest point.[b] The law was intended mainly to guard against excessive fishing of the living resources of the sea adjacent to Antilla's coast, yellowfin tuna in particular. Yellowfin tuna is a highly migratory fish that accounts for 75 percent of Antilla's annual commercial fishing catch, and all efforts by Antilla since 1975 to achieve intergovernmental cooperation for the conservation and management of this vital fish stock have failed. Ever optimistic, however, the Antillan government last year signed the 1995 Agreement for the Implementation of the Provisions of the United Nations Convention on the Law of the Sea of 10 December 1982, Relating to the Conservation and Management of Straddling Fish Stocks and Highly Migratory Fish Stocks. Its parliament is currently considering the agreement's ratification. Costa Grande, on the other hand, has so far taken no action.

b. "Fishing," according to the Fishery Conservation and Management Law, means:

"(A) the catching, taking, or harvesting of fish;

"(B) the attempted catching, taking, or harvesting of fish;

"(C) any other activity which can reasonably be expected to result in the catching, taking, or harvesting of fish; or

"(D) any operations at sea in support of, or in preparation for, any activity described in subparagraphs (A) through (C)."

[*Note*: The foregoing definition is based on § 2(10) of the US Fishery Conservation and Management Act of 1976, 16 USC § 1802 (1982).]

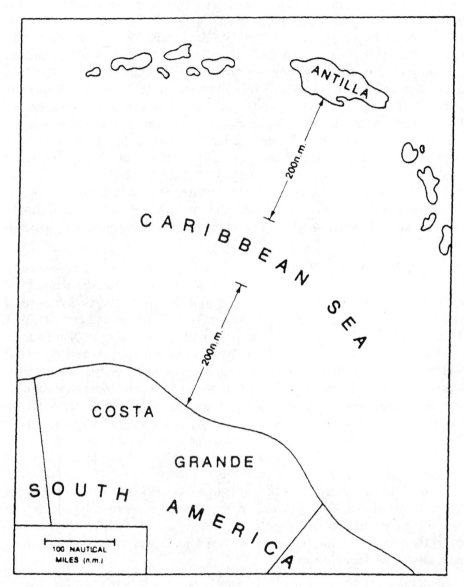

Figure 7-1.1

As implied by its endorsement of the 1995 agreement, Antilla's interest in equitably regulating its surrounding sea areas does not stop here. Several years ago, it deposited its instrument of ratification of the 1982 United Nations Convention on the Law of the Sea (1982 CLOS) upon which the 1995 agreement is premised; and, pursuant to Article 3, Article 33, and Part V of the 1982 CLOS, simultaneously proclaimed, respectively, a territorial sea of 12 nautical miles, a contiguous zone of an additional 12 nautical miles, and an exclusive economic zone (EEZ) of 200 nautical miles. At the same time, it enacted legislation defining its previously proclaimed "fishery jurisdiction" to include, at its most distant point, a "special zone of fishery protection" of 50 nautical miles. Further, it issued the following qualifying declaration as adopted by its parliament in accordance with its Constitution:

> WHEREAS continuation of unregulated fishing of yellowfin tuna on the high seas adjacent to Antilla's exclusive economic zone could precipitate a collapse of Antilla's yellowfin tuna stocks within its exclusive economic zone, threatening Antilla's largest renewable food resource;
>
> WHEREAS the Government of Antilla has sought without success to achieve international cooperation appropriate to the conservation and management of yellowfin tuna which migrate between Antilla's exclusive economic zone and the high seas adjacent thereto;
>
> NOW, THEREFORE, the Government of Antilla, without seeking to impose any unlawful restrictions on the internationally recognized rights and freedoms of vessel transit, declares that, to ensure the conservation and promote the optimum utilization of yellowfin tuna adjacent to its coast, nothing in the Convention shall be understood to nullify or impair Antilla's fishery jurisdiction over yellowfin tuna, including its special zone of fishery protection, or otherwise to deprive Antilla of its right to enact legislation, including moratoriums on all tuna fishing, to protect and manage this highly migratory species pursuant to such jurisdiction.

Finally, in early 2002, Antilla signed and ratified the 1993 FAO Agreement to Promote Compliance with International Conservation and Management Measures by Fishing Vessels on the High Seas. At the same time, it signed the 1994 Agreement Relating to the Implementation of Part XI of the United Nations Convention on the Law of the Sea of 10 December 1982. It has yet to ratify this 1994 agreement, however.

For its part, Costa Grande has become a party neither to the 1982 CLOS nor to the 1993 FAO Agreement to Promote Compliance with International Conservation and Management Measures by Fishing Vessels on the High Seas. Nor has it become a party to the 1994 Agreement Relating to the Implementation of Part XI of the United Nations Convention on the Law of the Sea of 10 December 1982. Nevertheless, apparently encouraged by the UN General Assembly's adoption of this 1994 implementation agreement, it last year proclaimed, like Antilla, a 12 nautical mile territorial sea, a 12 nautical mile contiguous zone, and a 200 nautical mile EEZ.

Historically, relations between Antilla and Costa Grande have been amicable. In the last few years, however, relations between the two countries have become strained. Three maritime encounters between them bear witness to this fact.

The first encounter involved a marine scientific research mission dispatched by Costa Grande to study the migratory habits of the yellowfin tuna for the purpose of enhancing Costa Grande's annual catch of this commercially important fish. About one year ago, approximately 240 nautical miles off Antilla's coast, the patrol ship *Vigilant* (of Antilla's flag) intercepted, by visual and auditory signal, the vessel *Observador* (of Costa Grande's flag), a 50–meter diesel-powered trawler replete with equipment to conduct marine scientific research, including visible fishing gear. Believing itself to be in international waters, however, and therefore uncertain about the *Vigilant's* intentions, the *Observador* refused to heave to and, instead, headed further out to sea. Whereupon the *Vigilant* dropped a red interception marker, gave chase, and, at a point approximately 255 nautical miles out to sea, fired a warning shot, arrested the *Observador* and its master, roughed up two of its crew in the process, and brought the ship into Antilla's principal port where it was declared seized and its crew officially detained. Later, Antilla released the *Observador's* master and crew. However, it has refused to release the *Observador*, stating that it will not do so until Costa Grande recognizes Antilla's claim to a 250–mile fishery jurisdiction and Antilla's constituent right to insist upon its consent to all marine scientific research therein.

The second encounter, about six months ago, involved a deep seabed mining ship, the *Minero*, a former US Navy minesweeper owned by a consortium of Belgian, Japanese, and Costa Grandean interests and flying Costa Grande's flag. Constituting a tangible outcome of an early decision on the part of Costa Grande's government to facilitate corporate ventures likely to expand Costa Grande's mineral extraction and production capabilities, the *Minero* was outfitted with sophisticated equipment for sighting and retrieving ocean floor mineral deposits. It was not, however, immune from mishap. While passing through Antilla's territorial sea, en route to Costa Grande from a deep seabed mining operation in international waters, the *Minero* suffered a minor explosion which resulted in a fire that necessitated putting into port in Antilla. Consistent with its international obligations, Antilla provided medical assistance to the injured and helped to replenish the *Minero's* food and water supplies. At the same time, however, it confiscated the ship's cargo, discovered to be manganese nodules recovered from the ocean floor. "Except as provided in the 1982 Convention on the Law of the Sea," the Antillan Government contended, "neither Costa Grande nor the consortium has the right to resources belonging to the 'common heritage of Mankind.' This unilateral taking of such resources constitutes international piracy." Antilla, it is well known, has openly opposed the unilateral exploitation of the deep seabed and consistently denounced such exploitation as contrary to international law and sound public policy.

The third encounter was the culmination of a series of both accidental and intentional oil tanker discharges that lately have threatened Antilla's economy. For the last five years, ever since Costa Grande began to use sea lanes near Antilla to transport oil to North America and Western Europe, Antilla has been the victim of several minor oil spills and of frequent seepage, tank washing, and deballasting by numerous oil tankers of foreign origin, including tankers flying Costa Grande's flag. This has resulted over time in the contamination and consequent shutdown of a number of Antilla's resort beaches and the threat of injury to large quantities of anchovy, shrimp, and other commercially important fishery stock. Numerous protests by Antilla, however, made in conformity with Antilla's maritime pollution control laws (which, in turn, conform to standards established by the International Maritime Organization[c]), have proved unavailing. Thus, one month ago, when seepage and deballasting by the Costa Grande oil tanker *Oro Negro* (well in excess of that permitted under the 1973 International Convention for the Prevention of Pollution from Ships) threatened a further setback to Antilla's tourism trade and further potential harm to Antilla's fishing industry, the Government of Antilla took matters into its own hands. After obtaining an authorizing court order, it dispatched the gunboat *Defender* to arrest and detain the *Oro Negro*, then 18 nautical miles off Antilla's coast. However, claiming that the *Defender* was violating its internationally guaranteed right to freedom of navigation on the high seas, the *Oro Negro* refused to comply and resumed its voyage. Whereupon the *Defender* fired upon and disabled the *Oro Negro*, causing the *Oro Negro* to radio for help. In less than two hours, but not until after Antillan tugboats had towed the *Oro Negro* to within Antilla's territorial sea, a Costa Grande destroyer and two Costa Grande fighter planes appeared and threatened to sink the *Defender* and the tugboats. No seriously damaging shots were fired, however. The Costa Grande destroyer and fighter planes succeeded in escorting the *Oro Negro* out to the high seas beyond 200 nautical miles from Antilla's coast.

At this point, fearing further tensions, yet hopeful of achieving a peaceful settlement of their disputes, Antilla and Costa Grande agreed to submit their claims to the International Court of Justice (ICJ) in The Hague, including a claim by Antilla for damages resulting from the pollution of its coast by oil.[d] Antilla and Costa Grande have stipulated that the facts as given are true, and the case is now pending before the Court.

c. The International Maritime Organization (IMO), formerly known as the International Maritime Consultative Organization (IMCO), is a specialized agency of the United Nations based in London. It was established in 1958 for the purpose of promoting cooperation and encouraging high standards of safety and navigation in the maritime field. For details, see *infra* Reading D–1, at 1051, and *infra* Discussion Note/Question 10, at 1099.

d. Even if Costa Grande were, like Antilla, a party to the 1982 CLOS, resort to the ICJ would be an option. Article 287 of 1982 CLOS allows for the settlement of disputes arising under the Convention via the International Tribunal for the Law of the Sea (ITLOS), the ICJ, and two arbitral tribunals constituted in accordance with Articles VII and VIII. For pertinent discussion, see *infra* Discussion Note/Question 14, at 1101; also Discussion Note/Question 16, at 1102.

SECTION 2. PURPOSE OF PROBLEM

A primary purpose of this problem is to call attention to a complex and important area of world order concern, the world's seas and, more particularly, the Law of the Sea. The world's seas are of course important to all of humanity and influence all life. As legendary oceanographer Rachel L. Carson wrote in *The Sea Around Us* 216 (1951):

> [T]he sea lies all about us. The commerce of all lands must cross it. The very winds that move over the lands have been cradled on its broad expanse and seek ever to return to it. The continents themselves dissolve and pass to the sea, in grain after grain of eroded land. So the rains that rose from it return again in rivers. In its mysterious past it encompasses all the dim origins of life and receives in the end, after, it may be, many transmutations, the dead husks of that same life. For all at last return to the sea—to Oceanus, the ocean river, like the ever-flowing stream of time, the beginning and the end.

And thus, not surprisingly, the Law of the Sea is complex and increasingly important. It is complex because it involves many competing and potentially conflicting state interests (coastal v. non-coastal, land-locked v. shelf-locked, maritime v. non-maritime, developed v. underdeveloped, etc.) and many competing and potentially conflicting uses (commercial and military navigation, coastal and deep-sea fishing, hard and soft mineral mining, scientific and strategic exploration, etc.). And it is increasingly important because, since the Truman Proclamation of September 28, 1945, 59 Stat. 884, which declared United States jurisdiction over the natural resources of the subsoil and the seabed of the continental shelf, it has been ever more challenged by technological advances and jurisdictional claims that threaten the ecologically wise and politically just management of those ocean bounties upon which a world urgently in need of alternative sources of energy, food, and wealth is manifestly dependent. Anticipating the Third United Nations Conference on the Law of the Sea (UNCLOS III), Wolfgang Friedmann put it this way in The Future of the Oceans 1 (1971):

> Among the many challenges that face mankind in the remaining decades of the twentieth century two stand out as of crucial importance for the very survival of civilization. One is the ecological problem of man's ability to cope with an environment of his own creation, which now threatens to overwhelm him. The other is the political problem of choosing between a competitive race of nations for power and wealth—a race that can only lead to the ultimate confrontation of a few superpowers—and ordered co-operation, in which countries can combine their purposes, their ingenuity, and their resources in an international order that envisages mankind as a whole.

> The ecological and political challenges are closely connected. And of all the many areas in which a fateful choice must be made, there is none

more important or urgent, both qualitatively and quantitatively, than the future status of the oceans.

Toward the close of his book, after reviewing positive as well as negative developments in ocean use and management, Professor Friedmann warned—ominously—that "[t]he tragedy of mankind may prove to be the inability to adapt its modes of behavior to the products of its intellect. Twentieth-century man threatens to be a new kind of dinosaur, an animal suffering from a brain ill-adjusted to its environment." *Id.* at 120.

Another purpose of the problem is to facilitate at least preliminary understanding of the concept of jurisdiction, one of the most basic of legal concepts. Derived from the Latin *jurisdictio* and meaning, literally, "the declaring of the law," it refers, essentially, to those processes by which organized communities both assert and allocate competence among and between themselves to exercise control over people, resources, institutions, and events within their scope of operation. In the world arena, these assertions and allocations of competence, at least insofar as they are made by interacting national communities, rest primarily on the principles of territoriality and nationality. In addition, however, states seek to prescribe and apply policy by virtue of events occurring near their claimed territories (jurisdiction based on contiguity), by virtue of events allegedly affecting their national interests (jurisdiction based on impact), and, at times, by virtue of events perceived as inimical to common world interests (jurisdiction based on universal concern).[e] Of course, states may choose against asserting jurisdictional competence where considerations of reciprocity and retaliation press hard—as, for example, on the high seas, in Antarctica, or in outer space. Moreover, even where jurisdictional competence is properly claimed, states will, for a variety of legal and policy reasons, forgo the prescription and application of their laws. It is, therefore, essential to think about jurisdiction in the real world of acts and events in which we live. The nature of the jurisdictional claimants involved, the objectives they seek to maximize, the spatial and other concrete situations in which they purport to operate, the means and strategies they utilize to achieve their goals, the short- and long-term consequences of their words and deeds—these and other variables determine whether, in any particular case, an assertion or forswearing of jurisdictional competence is or is not permissible and/or desirable. The term "jurisdiction," because it often is used to refer indiscriminately to what has been, what will be, and what ought to be decided in given cases, is normatively ambiguous, so it serves no rational purpose—least of all the cause of justice—to assume that it is somehow etched in stone, performing all three functions simultaneously and in a manner that disregards the vicissitudes of everyday life.

Finally, the problem is designed to stimulate analysis of a cluster of doctrines, principles, and rules with which international lawyers historically have been concerned. The Readings contained in Section 4, *infra*, are ar-

---

e. An act of piracy on the high seas, long recognized as entitled to the protection of no nation and susceptible of punishment by any nation capable of capture, is illustrative of an event that can justify claims to "universal ju- risdiction." For relevant additional discussion concerning universal and other claims to juris- diction, see *supra* Discussion Note/Question 12 in Chapter 3, at 217.

ranged according to these recognized legal themes. Related normative questions are considered in the Discussion Notes/Questions that follow.

Section 3.   Assignments

A.   Reading Assignment

Study the Readings presented in Section 4, *infra*, and the Discussion Notes/Questions that follow. Also, to the extent possible, consult the accompanying bibliographical references.

B.   Recommended Writing Assignment

Prepare a comprehensive, logically sequenced, and *argumentative* brief in the form of an outline of the primary and subsidiary *legal* issues you see requiring resolution by the International Court of Justice in this problem (approximately ten single-spaced, typewritten pages). Also, from the perspective of an independent judge, indicate which side ought to prevail on each issue and why. Retain a copy of your issue-outline (brief) for class discussion.

C.   Recommended Oral Assignment

Assume you are an official of Antilla or Costa Grande (as designated by your instructor) appointed to argue before the International Court of Justice; then, relying upon the Readings (and your issue outline-brief, if prepared), present a 10–15 minute oral argument of your government's likely positions before the Court.

D.   Recommended Reflective Assignment

Consider (and recommend) alternative norms, procedures, and/or institutions that you believe might do better than existing world order arrangements to contend with situations of the kind posed by this problem. In so doing, but without insisting upon *immediate* political feasibility, identify the particular transition steps that would be needed to make your alternatives a reality.

Section 4.   Readings

The following readings are considered prima facie relevant to solving this problem. They are divided according to those categories of accepted international legal analysis that are principally implicated in the problem: "the law of the sea in general," "jurisdiction over ocean resources: highly migratory species," "jurisdiction over ocean resources: deep seabed mining," "marine pollution," and "military retorsion and reprisals." They are your law library for present purposes and should be treated as such, organized intelligibly for "shelving" and not necessarily according to the issues presented. Be sure to review Chapter 2 ("International Legal Prescription: The 'Sources' of International Law") in your consideration of them. It, too, should be treated as part of your law library (as, indeed, should this entire coursebook).

A. THE LAW OF THE SEA IN GENERAL

1. Myres S. McDougal and William T. Burke, The Public Order of the Oceans—A Contemporary International Law of the Sea 1–2, 51–52 (1962).

The historic function of the law of the sea has long been recognized as that of protecting and balancing the common interests, inclusive and exclusive, of all peoples in the use and enjoyment of the oceans, while rejecting all egocentric assertions of special interests in contravention of general community interest.[f] Historically, the record is familiar: the oceans of the world, or great segments thereof, were at one time claimed for the exclusive use of a limited number of states, but concern for the more general interest of the whole community of states ultimately succeeded in freeing the larger expanses of the sea for relatively unhampered use by all. The knowledge is equally familiar, however, that coastal states never surrendered their claim to exclusive and comprehensive authority over certain adjacent areas of the sea and that, even after a consensus developed that states were not to exercise a continuing and comprehensive authority beyond a relatively narrow belt of such waters, it was quickly discovered that the occasional exercise of some exclusive authority beyond this belt had necessarily to be honored if the common interests of all states in the security of the social processes upon their land masses were to be given adequate protection. Through several centuries of interaction, of particular claims and of general community acceptance or rejection in response to such claims, a body of principles and a process of decision were thus developed which restrained the assertion of special interests and achieved an economic balancing of demands for protection of both exclusive and inclusive interests, effectively internationalizing in the common interest a great resource covering two-thirds of the earth's surface.

* * *

The common interest of all states and their peoples in both exclusive and inclusive uses of the oceans of the world and in an economic accommodation of all uses is not, from the perspective of an observer who identifies with the whole of [humankind], difficult to demonstrate. If the several centuries of experience of territorially organized communities is to be trusted, it is reasonably clear that all states which border upon the oceans have a common interest in those traditional exclusive assertions of control in nearby areas which permit a state both to protect its territorial base and organized social life from too easy invasion or attack from the sea and to take advantage of any unique proximity it may have to the riches of the sea bed and marine life. It is no less clear that each state, whether coastal or not, has an interest in the fullest possible access, either for itself or for others on its behalf, to all the inclusive uses of the ocean, such as navigation, fishing, cable-laying, and so on, for the richest possible production of values. From this mutual interest of all states in all types of uses, it follows that each state has an interest in accommodation of such uses, when they conflict, which will yield both an

---

f. The most important exclusive claims to the use of oceans are made by coastal states, but states on occasion assert exclusive claims over waters far removed from their shores.

adequate protection to exclusive claims and yet the greatest possible access to inclusive uses. The net total of inclusive uses available for sharing among all states is directly dependent, further, upon the restriction of exclusive claims to the minimum reasonably necessary to the protection of common interest. If all states asserted and were protected in extravagant, disproportionate, exclusive claims, there would be little, if any, net total of inclusive use for common enjoyment. The ancient fable of a group of monkeys on one end of a seesaw is relevant: a single monkey may be able to race to the other end and pluck grapes from vines on an overhanging tree, but if all the monkeys suddenly race, no monkey gets any grapes.... For states tightly locked in a global arena in an irrevocable interdependence with respect to all values, and highly dependent upon specialization among themselves for the production of many values, the conclusion would seem inescapable: the common interest is in an accommodation of exclusive and inclusive claims which will produce the largest total output of community values at the least cost.

2.   1 Daniel P. O'Connell, International Law 455–60 (2d ed. 1970).

The Roman lawyers characterized the sea as *res communis*, by which they meant that it was beyond appropriation. They were thinking, of course, in terms of appropriation by private persons, and the problem of appropriation by the State could not have occurred within the context of the Roman Empire. None the less their characterization was to influence the outcome of the passionate debate in the seventeenth century on the freedom of the sea which began in earnest when James I of England, who had inherited a developed doctrine of the rights of the King of Scotland in the sea, issued in 1609 a proclamation excluding Dutch fishermen from operating off the shores of England. By coincidence the same year saw the publication of Grotius' treatise *Mare Liberum* which was a counterblast, not to James' pretensions, but to those of the Portuguese.[g] Just as today, fisheries in the seventeenth century were vital national interests, and the collision of these interests between Holland and England prompted a reply to Grotius on the part of several English lawyers. Actually Grotius had written on the freedom of navigation, but Welwood, a Scottish lawyer in 1613 attacked him on the ground that *mare liberum* would leave England's fisheries to the mercy of every comer. Grotius was stimulated to a retort, later embodied in *De jure belli ac pacis*. In turn the challenge was taken up by ... Boroughs[h] and Selden.[i]

At this point, then, the question of fishery became inextricably entangled with the question of the extent of national territory.... Out of the controversy evolved the two conceptions, each the corollary of the other, of the freedom of the seas and the territorial sea.

... The eighteenth century ... is the period when the new conception of the territorial sea was in process of crystallization. In 1704 Bynkershoek, discarding Grotius' distinction between *imperium* and *dominium*, proposed

---

g. At the time, Hugo Grotius was legal counsel for the Dutch East India Company which, by the freedom-of-the-seas doctrine propounded in Grotius' treatise, sought to break the hegemony of Spain and Portugal which were bent upon establishing dominion over the seas and lands divided between them along a line close to that assigned to them by Pope Pius VI.

h. The Sovereignty of the British Seas (1633) (*reprinted in* 1920).

i. Mare Clausum (1635).

that sovereignty should be exercised as far as authority extends by force of arms. Vattel to some extent put the question back in the melting pot by advancing an argument anticipating those in favor of the continental shelf of today, but most of his contemporaries settled for Bynkershoek's principle, which came to be known as the cannon-shot rule. . . .

The same criterion was adopted when neutrality questions became prominent in the American War of Independence, and . . . the proposal that war could not be waged within three miles of a neutral coast . . ., the ultimate range of artillery at that time. Whether the three-mile rule was ever regarded as a mere fixing of the limits of the cannon shot is disputable. In fact all through the eighteenth century, for one purpose or another, varying distances were adopted in the exercise of maritime jurisdiction. . . .

Sometime during the French Revolutionary period disparate jurisdictions such as fishing, police, revenue and neutrality, each claiming the privilege of the cannon-shot rule, came to be fused in British and American practice under the comprehensive notion of the territorial sea. . . . Actually, the United States, except for neutrality purposes, at that time favored a three-league territorial sea, and it seems to have been British pressure that consolidated the three-mile rule and brought fishery jurisdiction within it.

[*Eds.*—The author next traces the history of the three-mile "cannon shot rule" during the Nineteenth Century, noting that "the three-mile rule for fishery remained one of controversy" even while "the era of the great arbitrations," from the 1880s until World War I, "settled the freedom of the sea" outside territorial waters. He then continues, noting first a failure of agreement at the League of Nations Codification Conference at The Hague in 1930.]

Between . . . 1930 and 1958 great changes in the practice of States concerning the maritime domain had occurred. In the first place the continental shelf doctrine had emerged and had to be rationalized in terms of the freedom of the seas. Secondly, there was a strong pressure in favor of a much wider area of territorial sea. Thirdly, the decision of the International Court of Justice in the Anglo–Norwegian Fisheries case **[Basic Document 7.6]** had added new considerations to the law. Fourthly, a large number of new States had emerged which were uncommitted to any traditional doctrine and had varying economic interests in the exploitation of the sea and in the conservation of its resources. . . .

It was fishery that was critical. In short, the emphasis in this century has shifted from the sea as a highway to the sea as a reservoir of economic resources.

The International Law Commission's report was debated during the 1957 session of the General Assembly of the United Nations and in the Sixth Committee. Drafts of proposals were distributed to governments and their comments taken into account in the several revisions. The *Geneva Conference* of 1958 was intended in part to explore the possibility of finding agreement on the existing law, and in part to formulate certain proposals to be embodied in draft conventions. A two-third voting rule was adopted. The result, where agreement was reached, was in part declaratory of the law and in part legislative.[j] . . .

3. UN Office of Legal Affairs (OLA), Division of Oceans and the Law of the Sea (DOALOS), The United Nations Convention on the Law of the Sea: A Historical Perspective (originally prepared for the International Year of the Oceans, 1998), *available at* <http://www.un.org/Depts/los/convention_agreements/convention_ historical_ perspective.htm>.

A Historical Perspective

The oceans had long been subject to the freedom-of-the-seas doctrine—a principle put forth in the seventeenth century essentially limiting national rights and jurisdiction over the oceans to a narrow belt of sea surrounding a nation's coastline. The remainder of the seas was proclaimed to be free to all and belonging to none. While this situation prevailed into the twentieth century, by mid-century there was an impetus to extend national claims over offshore resources. There was growing concern over the toll taken on coastal fish stocks by long-distance fishing fleets and over the threat of pollution and wastes from transport ships and oil tankers carrying noxious cargoes that plied sea routes across the globe. The hazard of pollution was ever present, threatening coastal resorts and all forms of ocean life. The navies of the maritime powers were competing to maintain a presence across the globe on the surface waters and even under the sea.

A tangle of claims, spreading pollution, competing demands for lucrative fish stocks in coastal waters and adjacent seas, growing tension between coastal nations' rights to these resources and those of distant-water fishermen, the prospects of a rich harvest of resources on the sea floor, the increased presence of maritime powers and the pressures of long-distance navigation and a seemingly outdated, if not inherently conflicting, freedom-of-the-seas doctrine—all these were threatening to transform the oceans into another arena for conflict and instability.

In 1945, President Harry S. Truman, responding in part to pressure from domestic oil interests, unilaterally extended United States jurisdiction over all natural resources on that nation's continental shelf—oil, gas, minerals, etc. This was the first major challenge to the freedom-of-the-seas doctrine. Other nations soon followed suit.

In October 1946, Argentina claimed its shelf and the epicontinental sea above it. Chile and Peru in 1947, and Ecuador in 1950, asserted sovereign rights over a 200–mile zone, hoping thereby to limit the access of distant-water fishing fleets and to control the depletion of fish stocks in their adjacent seas.

Soon after the Second World War, Egypt, Ethiopia, Saudi Arabia, Libya, Venezuela and some Eastern European countries laid claim to a 12–mile territorial sea, thus clearly departing from the traditional three-mile limit.

---

j. The result of the 1958 Geneva Law of the Sea Conference was the Convention on the High Seas **(Basic Document 5.3)**, the Convention on the Continental Shelf **(Basic Document 5.4)**, the Convention on the Territorial Sea and Contiguous Zone **(Basic Document 5.5)**, and the Convention on Fishing and Conservation of Living Resources of the High Seas **(Basic Document 5.6)**.

Later, the archipelagic nation of Indonesia asserted the right to dominion over the water that separated its 13,000 islands. The Philippines did likewise. In 1970, Canada asserted the right to regulate navigation in an area extending for 100 miles from its shores in order to protect Arctic water against pollution.

From oil to tin, diamonds to gravel, metals to fish, the resources of the sea are enormous. The reality of their exploitation grows day by day as technology opens new ways to tap those resources.

In the late 1960s, oil exploration was moving further and further from land, deeper and deeper into the bedrock of continental margins. From a modest beginning in 1947 in the Gulf of Mexico, offshore oil production, still less than a million tons in 1954, had grown to close to 400 million tons. Oil drilling equipment was already going as far as 4,000 metres below the ocean surface.

The oceans were being exploited as never before. Activities unknown barely two decades earlier were in full swing around the world. Tin had been mined in the shallow waters off Thailand and Indonesia. South Africa was about to tap the Namibian coast for diamonds. Potato-shaped nodules, found almost a century earlier and lying on the seabed some five kilometres below, were attracting increased interest because of their metal content.

And then there was fishing. Large fishing vessels were roaming the oceans far from their native shores, capable of staying away from port for months at a time. Fish stocks began to show signs of depletion as fleet after fleet swept distant coastlines. Nations were flooding the richest fishing waters with their fishing fleets virtually unrestrained: coastal States setting limits and fishing States contesting them. The so-called "Cod War" between Iceland and the United Kingdom had brought about the spectacle of British Navy ships dispatched to rescue a fishing vessel seized by Iceland for violating its fishing rules.

Offshore oil was the centre of attraction in the North Sea. Britain, Denmark and Germany were in conflict as to how to carve up the continental shelf, with its rich oil resources.

It was late 1967 and the tranquillity of the sea was slowly being disrupted by technological breakthroughs, accelerating and multiplying uses, and a super-Power rivalry that stood poised to enter man's last preserve—the seabed.

It was a time that held both dangers and promises, risks and hopes. The dangers were numerous: nuclear submarines charting deep waters never before explored; designs for antiballistic missile systems to be placed on the seabed; supertankers ferrying oil from the Middle East to European and other ports, passing through congested straits and leaving behind a trail of oil spills; and rising tensions between nations over conflicting claims to ocean space and resources.

The oceans were generating a multitude of claims, counterclaims and sovereignty disputes.

The hope was for a more stable order, promoting greater use and better management of ocean resources and generating harmony and goodwill among

States that would no longer have to eye each other suspiciously over conflicting claims.

Third United Nations Conference on the Law of the Sea

On 1 November 1967, Malta's Ambassador to the United Nations, Arvid Pardo, asked the nations of the world to look around them and open their eyes to a looming conflict that could devastate the oceans, the lifeline of man's very survival. In a speech to the United Nations General Assembly, he spoke of the super-Power rivalry that was spreading to the oceans, of the pollution that was poisoning the seas, of the conflicting legal claims and their implications for a stable order and of the rich potential that lay on the seabed.

Pardo ended with a call for "an effective international regime over the seabed and the ocean floor beyond a clearly defined national jurisdiction." "It is the only alternative by which we can hope to avoid the escalating tension that will be inevitable if the present situation is allowed to continue," he said.

Pardo's urging came at a time when many recognized the need for updating the freedom-of-the-seas doctrine to take into account the technological changes that had altered man's relationship to the oceans. It set in motion a process that spanned 15 years and saw the creation of the United Nations Seabed Committee, the signing of a treaty banning nuclear weapons on the seabed, the adoption of the declaration by the General Assembly that all resources of the seabed beyond the limits of national jurisdiction are the common heritage of mankind and the convening of the Stockholm Conference on the Human Environment. What started as an exercise to regulate the seabed turned into a global diplomatic effort to regulate and write rules for all ocean areas, all uses of the seas and all of its resources. These were some of the factors that led to the convening of the Third United Nations Conference on the Law of the Sea, to write a comprehensive treaty for the oceans.

The Conference was convened in New York in 1973. It ended nine years later with the adoption in 1982 of a constitution for the seas—the United Nations Convention on the Law of the Sea **[Basic Document 5.22]**. During those nine years, shuttling back and forth between New York and Geneva, representatives of more than 160 sovereign States sat down and discussed the issues, bargained and traded national rights and obligations in the course of the marathon negotiations that produced the Convention.

The Convention

Navigational rights, territorial sea limits, economic jurisdiction, legal status of resources on the seabed beyond the limits of national jurisdiction, passage of ships through narrow straits, conservation and management of living marine resources, protection of the marine environment, a marine research regime and, a more unique feature, a binding procedure for settlement of disputes between States—these are among the important features of the treaty. In short, the Convention is an unprecedented attempt by the international community to regulate all aspects of the resources of the sea and uses of the ocean, and thus bring a stable order to mankind's very source of life.

"Possibly the most significant legal instrument of this century" is how the United Nations Secretary–General described the treaty after its signing. The Convention was adopted as a "Package deal," to be accepted as a whole in all its parts without reservation on any aspect. The signature of the Convention by Governments carries the undertaking not to take any action that might defeat its objects and purposes. Ratification of, or accession to, the Convention expresses the consent of a State to be bound by its provisions. The Convention came into force on 16 November 1994, one year after Guyana became the 60th State to adhere to it.

Across the globe, Governments have taken steps to bring their extended areas of adjacent ocean within their jurisdiction. They are taking steps to exercise their rights over neighbouring seas, to assess the resources of their waters and on the floor of the continental shelf. The practice of States has in nearly all respects been carried out in a manner consistent with the Convention, particularly after its entry into force [on 16 November 1994] and its rapid acceptance by the international community as the basis for all actions dealing with the oceans and the law of the sea.

The definition of the territorial sea has brought relief from conflicting claims. Navigation through the territorial sea and narrow straits is now based on legal principles. Coastal States are already reaping the benefits of provisions giving them extensive economic rights over a 200–mile wide zone along their shores. The right of landlocked countries of access to and from the sea is now stipulated unequivocally. The right to conduct marine scientific research is now based on accepted principles and cannot be unreasonably denied. Already established and functioning are the International Seabed Authority, which organize and control activities in the deep seabed beyond national jurisdiction with a view to administering its resources; as well as the International Tribunal for the Law of the Sea, which has competence to settle ocean related disputes arising from the application or interpretation of the Convention.

Wider understanding of the Convention will bring yet wider application. Stability promises order and harmonious development. However, Part XI, which deals with mining of minerals lying on the deep ocean floor outside of nationally regulated ocean areas, in what is commonly known as the international seabed area, had raised many concerns especially from industrialized States. The Secretary–General, in an attempt to achieve universal participation in the Convention, initiated a series of informal consultations among States in order to resolve those areas of concern. The consultations successfully achieved, in July 1998, an Agreement Related to the Implementation of Part XI of the Convention. The Agreement, which is part of the Convention, is now deemed to have paved the way for all States to become parties to the Convention.

Setting Limits

The dispute over who controls the oceans probably dates back to the days when the Egyptians first plied the Mediterranean in papyrus rafts. Over the years and centuries, countries large and small, possessing vast ocean-going fleets or small fishing flotillas, husbanding rich fishing grounds close to shore or eyeing distant harvests, have all vied for the right to call long stretches of oceans and seas their own.

Conflicting claims, even extravagant ones, over the oceans were not new. In 1494, two years after Christopher Columbus' first expedition to America, Pope Alexander VI met with representatives of two of the great maritime

Powers of the day—Spain and Portugal—and neatly divided the Atlantic Ocean between them. A Papal Bull gave Spain everything west of the line the Pope drew down the Atlantic and Portugal everything east of it. On that basis, the Pacific and the Gulf of Mexico were acknowledged as Spain's, while Portugal was given the South Atlantic and the Indian Ocean.

Before the Convention on the Law of the Sea could address the exploitation of the riches underneath the high seas, navigation rights, economic jurisdiction, or any other pressing matter, it had to face one major and primary issue—the setting of limits. Everything else would depend on clearly defining the line separating national and international waters. Though the right of a coastal State to complete control over a belt of water along its shoreline—the territorial sea—had long been recognized in international law, up until the Third United Nations Conference on the Law of the Sea, States could not see eye to eye on how narrow or wide this belt should be.

At the start of the Conference, the States that maintained the traditional claims to a three-mile territorial sea had numbered a mere 25. Sixty-six countries had by then claimed a 12–mile territorial sea limit. Fifteen others claimed between 4 and 10 miles, and one remaining major group of eight States claimed 200 nautical miles.

Traditionally, smaller States and those not possessing large, ocean-going navies or merchant fleets favoured a wide territorial sea in order to protect their coastal waters from infringements by those States that did. Naval and maritime Powers, on the other hand, sought to limit the territorial sea as much as possible, in order to protect their fleets' freedom of movement.

As the work of the Conference progressed, the move towards a 12–mile territorial sea gained wider and eventually universal acceptance. Within this limit, States are in principle free to enforce any law, regulate any use and exploit any resource.

The Convention retains for naval and merchant ships the right of "innocent passage" through the territorial seas of a coastal State. This means, for example, that a Japanese ship, picking up oil from a Gulf State, would not have to make a 3,000–mile detour in order to avoid the territorial sea of Indonesia, provided passage is not detrimental to Indonesia and does not threaten its security or violate its laws.

In addition to their right to enforce any law within their territorial seas, coastal States are also empowered to implement certain rights in an area beyond the territorial sea, extending for 24 nautical miles from their shores, for the purpose of preventing certain violations and enforcing police powers. This area, known as the "contiguous zone," may be used by a coast guard or its naval equivalent to pursue and, if necessary, arrest and detain suspected drug smugglers, illegal immigrants and customs or tax evaders violating the laws of the coastal State within its territory or the territorial sea.

PROFILE OF OFFSHORE ZONES[k]

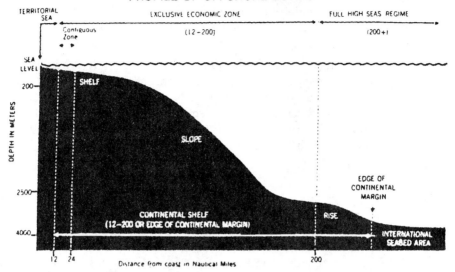

Figure 7-1.2

The Convention also contains a new feature in international law, which is the regime for archipelagic States (States such as the Philippines and Indonesia, which are made up of a group of closely spaced islands). For those States, the territorial sea is a 12–mile zone extending from a line drawn joining the outermost points of the outermost islands of the group that are in close proximity to each other. The waters between the islands are declared archipelagic waters, where ships of all States enjoy the right of innocent passage. In those waters, States may establish sea lanes and air routes where all ships and aircraft enjoy the right of expeditious and unobstructed passage.

Navigation

Perhaps no other issue was considered as vital or presented the negotiators of the Convention on the Law of the Sea with as much difficulty as that of navigational rights.

Countries have generally claimed some part of the seas beyond their shores as part of their territory, as a zone of protection to be patrolled against smugglers, warships and other intruders. At its origin, the basis of the claim of coastal States to a belt of the sea was the principle of protection; during the seventeenth and eighteenth centuries another principle gradually evolved: that the extent of this belt should be measured by the power of the littoral sovereign to control the area.

In the eighteenth century, the so-called "cannon-shot" rule gained wide acceptance in Europe. Coastal States were to exercise dominion over their territorial seas as far as projectiles could be fired from a cannon based on the shore. According to some scholars, in the eighteenth century the range of land-based cannons was approximately one marine league, or three nautical miles. It is believed that on the basis of this formula developed the traditional three-mile territorial sea limit.

k. Editors' addition.

By the late 1960s, a trend to a 12–mile territorial sea had gradually emerged throughout the world, with a great majority of nations claiming sovereignty out to that seaward limit. However, the major maritime and naval Powers clung to a three-mile limit on territorial seas, primarily because a 12–mile limit would effectively close off and place under national sovereignty more than 100 straits used for international navigation.

A 12–mile territorial sea would place under national jurisdiction of riparian States strategic passages such as the Strait of Gibraltar (8 miles wide and the only open access to the Mediterranean), the Strait of Malacca (20 miles wide and the main sea route between the Pacific and Indian Oceans), the Strait of Hormuz (21 miles wide and the only passage to the oil-producing areas of the Gulf) and Bab el Mandeb (14 miles wide, connecting the Indian Ocean with the Red Sea).

At the Third United Nations Conference on the Law of the Sea, the issue of passage through straits placed the major naval Powers on one side and coastal States controlling narrow straits on the other. The United States and the Soviet Union insisted on free passage through straits, in effect giving straits the same legal status as the international waters of the high seas. The coastal States, concerned that passage of foreign warships so close to their shores might pose a threat to their national security and possibly involve them in conflicts among outside Powers, rejected this demand.

Instead, coastal States insisted on the designation of straits as territorial seas and were willing to grant to foreign warships only the right of "innocent passage," a term that was generally recognized to mean passage "not prejudicial to the peace, good order or security of the coastal State." The major naval Powers rejected this concept, since, under international law, a submarine exercising its right of innocent passage, for example, would have to surface and show its flag—an unacceptable security risk in the eyes of naval Powers. Also, innocent passage does not guarantee the aircraft of foreign States the right of overflight over waters where only such passage is guaranteed.

In fact, the issue of passage through straits was one of the early driving forces behind the Third United Nations Conference on the Law of the Sea, when, in early 1967, the United States and the Soviet Union proposed to other Member countries of the United Nations that an international conference be held to deal specifically with the entangled issues of straits, overflight, the width of the territorial sea and fisheries.

The compromise that emerged in the Convention is a new concept that combines the legally accepted provisions of innocent passage through territorial waters and freedom of navigation on the high seas. The new concept, "transit passage," required concessions from both sides.

The regime of transit passage retains the international status of the straits and gives the naval Powers the right to unimpeded navigation and overflight that they had insisted on. Ships and vessels in transit passage, however, must observe international regulations on navigational safety, civilian air-traffic control and prohibition of vessel-source pollution and the conditions that ships and aircraft proceed without delay and without stopping except in distress situations and that they refrain from any threat or use of force against the coastal State. In all matters other than such transient navigation, straits are to be considered part of the territorial sea of the coastal State.

Exclusive Economic Zone

The exclusive economic zone (EEZ) is one of the most revolutionary features of the Convention, and one which already has had a profound impact on the management and conservation of the resources of the oceans. Simply put, it recognizes the right of coastal States to jurisdiction over the resources of some 38 million square nautical miles of ocean space. To the coastal State falls the right to exploit, develop, manage and conserve all resources—fish or oil, gas or gravel, nodules or sulphur—to be found in the waters, on the ocean floor and in the subsoil of an area extending 200 miles from its shore.

The EEZs are a generous endowment indeed. About 87 per cent of all known and estimated hydrocarbon reserves under the sea fall under some national jurisdiction as a result. So too will almost all known and potential offshore mineral resources, excluding the mineral resources (mainly manganese nodules and metallic crusts) of the deep ocean floor beyond national limits. And whatever the value of the nodules, it is the other non-living resources, such as hydrocarbons, that represent the presently attainable and readily exploitable wealth.

The most lucrative fishing grounds too are predominantly the coastal waters. This is because the richest phytoplankton pastures lie within 200 miles of the continental masses. Phytoplankton, the basic food of fish, is brought up from the deep by currents and ocean streams at their strongest near land, and by the upwelling of cold waters where there are strong offshore winds.

The desire of coastal States to control the fish harvest in adjacent waters was a major driving force behind the creation of the EEZs. Fishing, the prototypical cottage industry before the Second World War, had grown tremendously by the 1950s and 1960s. Fifteen million tons in 1938, the world fish catch stood at 86 million tons in 1989. No longer the domain of a lone fisherman plying the sea in a wooden dhow, fishing, to be competitive in world markets, now requires armadas of factory-fishing vessels, able to stay months at sea far from their native shores, and carrying sophisticated equipment for tracking their prey.

The special interest of coastal States in the conservation and management of fisheries in adjacent waters was first recognized in the 1958 Convention on Fishing and Conservation of the Living Resources of the High Seas. That Convention allowed coastal States to take "unilateral measures" of conservation on what was then the high seas adjacent to their territorial waters. It required that if six months of prior negotiations with foreign fishing nations had failed to find a formula for sharing, the coastal State could impose terms. But still the rules were disorderly, procedures undefined, and rights and obligations a web of confusion. On the whole, these rules were never implemented.

The claim for 200–mile offshore sovereignty made by Peru, Chile and Ecuador in the late 1940s and early 1950s was sparked by their desire to protect from foreign fishermen the rich waters of the Humboldt Current (more or less coinciding with the 200–mile offshore belt). This limit was incorporated in the Santiago Declaration of 1952 and reaffirmed by other Latin American States joining the three in the Montevideo and Lima Declarations of 1970. The idea of sovereignty over coastal-area resources continued to gain ground.

As long-utilized fishing grounds began to show signs of depletion, as long-distance ships came to fish waters local fishermen claimed by tradition, as competition increased, so too did conflict. Between 1974 and 1979 alone there were some 20 disputes over cod, anchovies or tuna and other species between, for example, the United Kingdom and Iceland, Morocco and Spain, and the United States and Peru.

And then there was the offshore oil.

The Third United Nations Conference on the Law of the Sea was launched shortly after the October 1973 Arab–Israeli war. The subsequent oil embargo and skyrocketing of prices only helped to heighten concern over control of offshore oil reserves. Already, significant amounts of oil were coming from offshore facilities: 376 million of the 483 million tons produced in the Middle East in 1973; 431 million barrels a day in Nigeria, 141 million barrels in Malaysia, 246 million barrels in Indonesia. And all of this with barely 2 per cent of the continental shelf explored. Clearly, there was hope all around for a fortunate discovery and a potential to be protected.

Today, the benefits brought by the EEZs are more clearly evident. Already 86 coastal States have economic jurisdiction up to the 200–mile limit. As a result, almost 99 per cent of the world's fisheries now fall under some nation's jurisdiction. Also, a large percentage of world oil and gas production is offshore. Many other marine resources also fall within coastal-State control. This provides a long-needed opportunity for rational, well-managed exploitation under an assured authority.

Figures on known offshore oil reserves now range from 240 to 300 billion tons. Production from these reserves amounted to a little more than 25 per cent of total world production in 1996. Experts estimate that of the 150 countries with offshore jurisdiction, over 100, many of them developing countries, have medium to excellent prospects of finding and developing new oil and natural gas fields.

It is evident that it is archipelagic States and large nations endowed with long coastlines that naturally acquire the greatest areas under the EEZ regime. Among the major beneficiaries of the EEZ regime are the United States, France, Indonesia, New Zealand, Australia and the Russian Federation.

But with exclusive rights come responsibilities and obligations. For example, the Convention encourages optimum use of fish stocks without risking depletion through overfishing. Each coastal State is to determine the total allowable catch for each fish species within its economic zone and is also to estimate its harvest capacity and what it can and cannot itself catch. Coastal States are obliged to give access to others, particularly neighbouring States and land-locked countries, to the surplus of the allowable catch. Such access must be done in accordance with the conservation measures established in the laws and regulations of the coastal State.

Coastal States have certain other obligations, including the adoption of measures to prevent and limit pollution and to facilitate marine scientific research in their EEZs.

Continental Shelf

In ancient times, navigation and fishing were the primary uses of the seas. As man progressed, pulled by technology in some instances and pushing that technology at other times in order to satisfy his needs, a rich bounty of other resources and uses were found underneath the waves on and under the ocean floor—minerals, natural gas, oil, sand and gravel, diamonds and gold. What should be the extent of a coastal State's jurisdiction over these resources? Where and how should the lines demarcating their continental shelves be drawn? How should these resources be exploited? These were among the important questions facing lawyers, scientists and diplomats as they assembled in New York in 1973 for the Third Conference.

Given the real and potential continental shelf riches, there naturally was a scramble by nations to assert shelf rights. Two difficulties quickly arose. States with a naturally wide shelf had a basis for their claims, but the geologically disadvantaged might have almost no shelf at all. The latter were not ready to accept geological discrimination. Also, there was no agreed method on how to define the shelf's outer limits, and there was a danger of the claims to continental shelves being overextended—so much so as to eventually divide up the entire ocean floor among such shelves.

Although many States had started claiming wide continental-shelf jurisdiction since the Truman Proclamation of 1945, these States did not use the term "continental shelf" in the same sense. In fact, the expression became no more than a convenient formula covering a diversity of titles or claims to the seabed and subsoil adjacent to the territorial seas of States. In the mid–1950s the International Law Commission made a number of attempts to define the "continental shelf" and coastal State jurisdiction over its resources.

In 1958, the first United Nations Conference on the Law of the Sea accepted a definition adopted by the International Law Commission, which defined the continental shelf to include "the seabed and subsoil of the submarine areas adjacent to the coast but outside the area of the territorial sea, to a depth of 200 metres, or, beyond that limit, to where the depth of the superjacent waters admits of the exploitation of the natural resources of the said areas".

Already, as the Third United Nations Conference on the Law of the Sea got under way, there was a strong consensus in favour of extending coastal-State control over ocean resources out to 200 miles from shore so that the outer limit coincides with that of the EEZ. But the Conference had to tackle the demand by States with a geographical shelf extending beyond 200 miles for wider economic jurisdiction.

The Convention resolves conflicting claims, interpretations and measuring techniques by setting the 200–mile EEZ limit as the boundary of the continental shelf for seabed and subsoil exploitation, satisfying the geologically disadvantaged. It satisfied those nations with a broader shelf—about 30 States, including Argentina, Australia, Canada, India, Madagascar, Mexico, Sri Lanka and France with respect to its overseas possessions—by giving them the possibility of establishing a boundary going out to 350 miles from their shores or further, depending on certain geological criteria.

Thus, the continental shelf of a coastal State comprises the seabed and its subsoil that extend beyond the limits of its territorial sea throughout the natural prolongation of its land territory to the outer edge of the continental margin, or to a distance of 200 miles from the baselines from which the territorial sea is measured, where the outer edge of the continental margin does not extend up to that distance.

In cases where the continental margin extends further than 200 miles, nations may claim jurisdiction up to 350 miles from the baseline or 100 miles from the 2,500 metre depth, depending on certain criteria such as the thickness of sedimentary deposits. These rights would not affect the legal status of the waters or that of the airspace above the continental shelf.

To counterbalance the continental shelf extensions, coastal States must also contribute to a system of sharing the revenue derived from the exploitation of mineral resources beyond 200 miles. These payments or contributions—from which developing countries that are net importers of the mineral in question are exempt—are to be equitably distributed among States parties to the Convention through the International Seabed Authority.

To control the claims extending beyond 200 miles, the Commission on the Limits of the Continental Shelf was established to consider the data submitted by the coastal States and make recommendations

Deep Seabed Mining

Deep seabed mining is an enormous challenge that has been compared to standing atop a New York City skyscraper on a windy day, trying to suck up marbles off the street below with a vacuum cleaner attached to a long hose.

Mining will take place at a depth of more than fifteen thousand feet of open ocean, thousands of miles from land. Mining ships are expected to remain on station five years at a time, working without a stop, and to transfer the seabed minerals they bring up to auxiliary vessels.

At the centre of the controversy were potato-sized manganese nodules found on the deep ocean floor and containing a number of important metals and minerals.

On 13 March 1874, somewhere between Hawaii and Tahiti, the crew of the British research vessel HMS *Challenger,* on the first great oceanographic expedition of modern times, hauled in from a depth of 15,600 feet a trawl containing the first known deposits of manganese nodules. Analysis of the samples in 1891 showed the Pacific Ocean nodules to contain important metals, particularly nickel, copper and cobalt. Subsequent sampling demonstrated that nodules were abundant throughout the deep regions of the Pacific.

In the 1950s, the potential of these deposits as sources of nickel, copper and cobalt ore was finally appreciated. Between 1958 and 1968, numerous companies began serious prospecting of the nodule fields to estimate their economic potential. By 1974, 100 years after the first samples were taken, it was well established that a broad belt of sea floor between Mexico and Hawaii and a few degrees north of the equator (the so-called Clarion Clipperton zone) was literally paved with nodules over an area of more than 1.35 million square miles.

In 1970 the United Nations General Assembly declared the resources of the seabed beyond the limits of national jurisdiction to be "the common heritage of mankind." For 12 years from then, up to 1982 when the Convention on the Law of the Sea was adopted, nothing tested so sorely the ability of diplomats from various corners of the world to reach common ground than the goal of conserving that common heritage and profiting from it at the same time.

The Exploitation Regime

Having established that the resources of the seabed beyond the limits of national jurisdiction are the common heritage of mankind, the framers of the treaty faced the question of who should mine the minerals and under what rules. The developed countries took the view that the resources should be commercially exploited by mining companies in consortia and that an international authority should grant licenses to those companies. The developing countries objected to this view on the grounds that the resource was unique and belonged to the whole of mankind, and that the most appropriate way to benefit from it was for the international community to establish a public enterprise to mine the international seabed area.

Thus, the gamut of proposals ran from a "weak" international authority, noting claims and collecting fees, to a "strong" one with exclusive rights to mine the common heritage area, involving States or private groups only as it saw fit. The solution found was to make possible both the public and private enterprises on one hand and the collective mining on the other—the so-called "parallel system."

This complex system, though simplified to a great degree by the Agreement on Part XI, is administered by the International Seabed Authority, headquartered in Jamaica. The Authority is divided into three principal organs, an Assembly, made up of all members of the Authority with power to set general policy, a council, with powers to make executive decisions, made up of 36 members elected from among the members of the Authority, and a secretariat headed by a secretary-general.

Technological Prospects

Unfortunately, the road to the market is long, hard and expensive. The nodules lie two to three miles—about 5 kilometres—down, in pitch-black water where pressures exceed 7,000 pounds per square inch and temperatures are near freezing. Many of the ocean floors are filled with treacherous hills and valleys. Appropriate deep-sea mining technology must be developed to accommodate this environment.

* * *

Extracting metals from the nodules is another task altogether. All agree that this phase will be the most expensive, even if only at the initial investment stage. Technologically, however, processing does not pose as much of a challenge as the recovery of manganese nodules. That is because it is thought that the two processing techniques applied to land-derived ores—heat and chemical separation of the metals—will apply just as well to the seabed resources.

Because of their porous nature, recovered nodules retain a great deal of water. Heat processing would therefore require a great amount of energy in order to dry the nodules prior to extracting the metals. It is for that reason that some believe that chemical techniques will prove to be the most efficient and least costly.

Moreover, processing would involve such waste that special barren sites would have to be found to carry out operations. Yet, others believe that the economic viability of seabed mining would be greatly enhanced if a method is devised to process the nodules at sea, saving enormous energy costs involved in the transfer of nodules to land-based processing plants.

The Question of Universal Participation in the Convention

Prospects for seabed mining depend to a large degree on the market conditions for the metals to be produced from seabed nodules. While one of the driving forces behind the Convention on the Law of the Sea was the prevailing belief in the 1970s that commercial seabed mining was imminent, today the prospects for the inherently expensive process of mining the seabed have greatly receded with changing economic and other conditions since the early 1980s. Indeed, some experts predict that commercial mining operations are not likely to begin until well after the year 2000.

A number of important political and economic changes have taken place in the 10 years that have elapsed since the adoption of the Convention, some directly affecting the deep seabed mining provisions of the Convention, others affecting international relations in general. In the meantime, the prevailing economic prognosis on which the seabed mining regime was built has not been realized.

The Convention on the Law of the Sea holds out the promise of an orderly and equitable regime or system to govern all uses of the sea. But it is a club that one must join in order to fully share in the benefits. The Convention—like other treaties—creates rights only for those who become parties to it and thereby accept its obligations, except for the provisions which apply to all States because they either merely confirm existing customary law or are becoming customary law.

However, as its preamble states, the Convention starts from the premise that the problems of ocean space are closely interrelated and need to be considered as a whole. The desire for a comprehensive Convention arose from the recognition that traditional sea law was disintegrating and that the international community could not be expected to behave in a consistent manner without dialogue, negotiations and agreement.

In this context, it must be underscored that the Convention was adopted as a "package deal", with one aim above all, namely universal participation in the Convention. No State can claim that it has achieved quite all it wanted. Yet every State benefits from the provisions of the Convention and from the certainty that it has established in international law in relation to the law of the sea. It has defined rights while underscoring the obligations that must be performed in order to benefit from those rights. Any trend towards exercising those rights without complying with the corresponding obligations, or towards exercising rights inconsistent with the Convention, must be viewed as damaging to the universal regime that the Convention establishes.

The adoption of the Agreement on Part XI has eliminated this threat. With nearly all States now adhering, even on a provisional basis pending ratification or accession, to the Convention, the threat to the Convention has been eliminated. The Agreement has particularly removed those obstacles which had prevented the industrialized countries from adhering to the Convention. Those same countries have either ratified the Convention or submitted it for their internal legislative procedures. Even more important, is their active participation in the institutions created by the Convention and their strong support for the regime contained in it.

Pioneer Investors

The Preparatory Commission for the International Seabed Authority and for the International Tribunal for the Law of the Sea was established, prior to the [16 November 1994] entry into force of the Convention, to prepare for the setting up of both institutions. The Preparatory Commission proceeded with the implementation of an interim regime adopted by the Third United Nations Conference on the Law of the Sea, designed to protect those States or entities that have already made a large investment in seabed mining. This so-called Pioneer Investor Protection regime allows a State, or consortia of mining companies to be sponsored by a State, to be registered as a Pioneer Investor. Registration reserves for the Pioneer Investor a specific mine site in which the registered Investor is allowed to explore for, but not exploit, manganese nodules. Registered Investors are also obligated to explore a mine site reserved for the Enterprise and undertake other obligations, including the provision of training to individuals to be designated by the Preparatory Commission.

* * *

Protection of the Marine Environment

Thor Heyerdahl, sailing the Atlantic in his papyrus raft, Ra, found globs of oil, tar and plastics stretching from the coast of Africa to South America. Parts of the Baltic, Mediterranean and Black Sea are already so polluted that marine life is severely threatened. And waste dumped in the Pacific and Atlantic Oceans has washed up on the shores of Antarctica.

In the United States, long stretches of beaches are often closed because of medical and other waste washing up on shore. And every time an oil tanker is involved in an accident, the world's pulse quickens a bit in fear of a major catastrophe. In fact, every time a tanker cleans its tanks at sea, every time a factory channels toxic residues to coastal waters or a city conveniently releases raw sewage into the sea, every time a service station changes the oil of an automobile and pours the waste oil into the sewers, the oceans become a little more polluted. Eventually, scientists fear, the oceans' regenerative capacity will be overwhelmed by the amount of pollution it is subjected to by man. Signs of such catastrophe are clearly observed in many seas—particularly along the heavily populated coasts and enclosed or semi-enclosed seas.

There are six main sources of ocean pollution addressed in the Convention: land-based and coastal activities; continental-shelf drilling; potential seabed mining; ocean dumping; vessel-source pollution; and pollution from or through the atmosphere.

The Convention lays down, first of all, the fundamental obligation of all States to protect and preserve the marine environment. It further urges all States to cooperate on a global and regional basis in formulating rules and standards and otherwise take measures for the same purpose.

Coastal States are empowered to enforce their national standards and anti-pollution measures within their territorial sea. Every coastal State is granted jurisdiction for the protection and preservation of the marine environment of its EEZ. Such jurisdiction allows coastal States to control, prevent and reduce marine pollution from dumping, land-based sources or seabed activities subject to national jurisdiction, or from or through the atmosphere. With regard to marine pollution from foreign vessels, coastal States can exercise jurisdiction only for the enforcement of laws and regulations adopted in accordance with the Convention or for "generally accepted international rules and standards." Such rules and standards, many of which are already in place, are adopted through the competent international organization, namely the International Maritime Organization (IMO).

On the other hand, it is the duty of the "flag State," the State where a ship is registered and whose flag it flies, to enforce the rules adopted for the control of marine pollution from vessels, irrespective of where a violation occurs. This serves as a safeguard for the enforcement of international rules, particularly in waters beyond the national jurisdiction of the coastal State, *i.e.*, on the high seas.

Furthermore, the Convention gives enforcement powers to the "port State," or the State where a ship is destined. In doing so it has incorporated a method developed in other Conventions for the enforcement of treaty obligations dealing with shipping standards, marine safety and pollution prevention. The port State can enforce any type of international rule or national regulations adopted in accordance with the Convention or applicable international rules as a condition for the entry of foreign vessels into their ports or internal waters or for a call at their offshore terminals. This has already become a significant factor in the strengthening of international standards.

Finally, as far as the international seabed area is concerned, the International Seabed Authority, through its Council, is given broad discretionary powers to assess the potential environmental impact of a given deep seabed mining operation, recommend changes, formulate rules and regulations, establish a monitoring programme and recommend issuance of emergency orders by the Council to prevent serious environmental damage. States are to be held liable for any damage caused by either their own enterprise or contractors under their jurisdiction.

With the passage of time, United Nations involvement with the law of the sea has expanded as awareness increases that not only ocean problems but global problems as a whole are interrelated. Already, the 1992 United Nations Conference on Environment and Development (UNCED) held in Rio de Janeiro, Brazil in 1992, placed a great deal of emphasis on the protection and preservation of the oceans' environment in harmony with the rational use and development of their living resources, thus establishing the concept of "sustainable development" embodied in Agenda 21, the programme of action adopted at the Conference.

The necessity to combat the degradation and depletion of fish stocks, both in the zones under national jurisdiction and in the high seas and its causes, such as overfishing and excess fishing capacity, by-catch and discards, has been one of the recurrent topics in the process of implementation of the programme of action adopted in Rio de Janeiro.

In this respect, among the most important outputs of the Conference was the convening of an intergovernmental conference under United Nations auspices with a view to resolving the old conflict between coastal States and distant-water fishing States over straddling and highly migratory fish stocks in the areas adjacent to the 200 nautical-mile exclusive economic zones. This Conference adopted the 1995 Agreement on Straddling Fish Stocks and Highly Migratory Fish Stocks, which introduces a number of innovative measures, particularly in the area of environmental and resource protection obliging States to adopt a precautionary approach to fisheries exploitation and giving expanded powers to port States to enforce proper management of fisheries resources.

Marine Scientific Research

With the extension of the territorial sea to 12 miles and the establishment of the new 200–mile EEZ, the area open to unrestricted scientific research was circumscribed. The Convention thus had to balance the concerns of major research States, mostly developed countries, which saw any coastal-state limitation on research as a restriction of a traditional freedom that would not only adversely affect the advancement of science but also deny its potential benefits to all nations in fields such as weather forecasting and the study of effects of ocean currents and the natural forces at work on the ocean floor.

On the other side, many developing countries had become extremely wary of the possibility of scientific expeditions being used as a cover for intelligence gathering or economic gain, particularly in relatively uncharted areas, scientific research was yielding knowledge of potential economic significance.

The developing countries demanded "prior consent" of a coastal State to all scientific research on the continental shelf and within the EEZ. The developed countries offered to give coastal States "prior notification" of research projects to be carried out on the continental shelf and within the EEZ, and to share any data pertinent to offshore resources.

The final provisions of the Convention represent a concession on the part of developed States. Coastal State jurisdiction within its territorial sea remains absolute. Within the EEZ and in cases involving research on the continental shelf, the coastal State must give its prior consent. However, such consent for research for peaceful purposes is to be granted "in normal circumstances" and "shall not be delayed or denied unreasonably," except under certain specific circumstances identified in the Convention. In case the consent of the coastal State is requested and such State does not reply within six months of the date of the request, the coastal State is deemed to have implicitly given its consent. These last provisions were intended to circumvent the long bureaucratic delays and frequent burdensome differences in coastal State regulations.

Settlement of Disputes

Provisions for the settlement of disputes arising out of an international treaty are often contained in a separate optional protocol. Parties to the treaty could choose to be bound by those provisions or not by accepting or not accepting the Protocol. The Convention on the Law of the Sea is unique in that the mechanism for the settlement of disputes is incorporated into the document, making it obligatory for parties to the Convention to go through the settlement procedure in case of a dispute with another party.

During the drafting of the Convention, some countries were opposed in principle to binding settlement to be decided by third party judges or arbitrators, insisting that issues could best be resolved by direct negotiations between States without requiring them to bring in outsiders. Others, pointing to a history of failed negotiations and long-standing disputes often leading to a use of force, argued that the only sure chance for peaceful settlement lay in the willingness of States to bind themselves in advance to accept the decisions of judicial bodies.

What emerged from the negotiations was a combination of the two approaches, regarded by many as a landmark in international law.

If direct talks between the parties fail, the Convention gives them a choice among four procedures—some new, some old: submission of the dispute to the International Tribunal for the Law of the Sea, adjudication by the International Court of Justice, submission to binding international arbitration procedures, or submission to special arbitration tribunals with expertise in specific types of disputes. All of these procedures involve binding third-party settlement, in which an agent other than the parties directly involved hands down a decision that the parties are committed in advance to respect.

The only exception to these provisions is made for sensitive cases involving national sovereignty. In such circumstances, the parties are obliged to submit their dispute to a conciliation commission, but they will not be bound by any decision or finding of the commission. The moral pressure resulting was argued as being persuasive and adequate to ensure compliance with the findings. The Convention also contains so-called "optional exceptions," which can be specified at the time a country signs, ratifies or accedes to the Convention or at any later time. A State may declare that it chooses not to be bound by one or more of the mandatory procedures if they involve existing maritime boundary disputes, military activities or issues under discussion in the United Nations Security Council.

Disputes over seabed activities will be arbitrated by an 11–member Seabed Disputes Chamber, within the International Tribunal for the Law of the Sea. The Chamber has compulsory jurisdiction over all such conflicts, whether involving States, the International Seabed Authority or companies or individuals having seabed mining contracts.

The United Nations and the Law of the Sea

Throughout the years, beginning with the work of the Seabed Committee in 1968 and later during the nine-year duration of the Third United Nations Conference on the Law of the Sea, the United Nations has been actively engaged in encouraging and guiding the development and eventual adoption of the Law of the Sea Convention. Today, it continues to be engaged in this process, by monitoring developments as they relate to the Convention and providing assistance to States, when called for, in either the ratification or the implementation process.

The goal of the Organization is to help States to better understand and implement the Convention in order to utilize their marine resources in an environment relatively free of conflict and conducive to development, safeguarding the rule of law in the oceans. * * * The United Nations also gives assistance to the two newly created institutions—the International Seabed Authority and the International Tribunal for the Law of the Sea.

The Future

The entry into force of the Convention [on 16 November 1994], together with extended jurisdiction, new fields of activity and increased uses of the oceans, will continue to confront all States with important challenges. These challenges will include how to apply the new provisions in accordance with the letter and spirit of the Convention, how to harmonize national legislation with it and how to fulfil the obligations incumbent upon States under the Convention.

Another major challenge will be to provide the necessary assistance, particularly to developing States, in order to allow them to benefit from the rights they have acquired under the new regime. For example, a great many of the States that have established their EEZs are not at present in a position to exercise all their rights and perform duties under the Convention. The delimitation of EEZ, the surveying of its area, its monitoring, the utilization of its resources and, generally speaking, its management and development are long-term endeavours beyond the present and possibly near-term capabilities of most developing countries.

The United Nations will continue to play a major role in the monitoring of, collection of information on and reporting on State practice in the implementation of the new legal regime. It will also have a significant role to play in reporting on activities of States and relevant international organizations in marine affairs and on major trends and developments. This information will be of great assistance to States in the acceptance and ratification of the Convention, as well as its early entry into force and implementation.

* * *

The United Nations will continue to strengthen the cooperation that has developed over the last two decades among the organizations in the United Nations system involved in marine affairs. Such close cooperation would be of great benefit to States, since it would avoid duplication and overlapping of activities. It would also help to coordinate multidisciplinary activities related to the management of marine affairs.

With the passage of time, United Nations involvement with the law of the sea is expected to expand as awareness increases that not only ocean problems but also global problems as a whole are interrelated.

4. Editors' Note. As noted in preceding Reading 3, the 1982 CLOS **(Basic Document 5.22)** entered into force among the states party to it on 16 November 1994. But not without some difficulties along the way. While finding most of the provisions of the 1982 CLOS compatible with their interests and the interests of all other nations, Belgium, Italy, Luxembourg, the United Kingdom, the United States, and West Germany (now Germany) refused to sign and become party to the Convention when it was opened for signature on 10 December 1982, principally because of disagreement with its deep seabed mining provisions which, they contended, favored the interests of the developing world at the expense of those of the industrialized world. Since that time, all of these countries, with the exception of the United States, have become parties to the Convention. Largely responsible was the successful conclusion and provisional entry into force of the 1994 Agreement Relating to the Implementation of Part XI of the United Nations Convention on the Law of the Sea of 10 December 1982 ("Seabed Mining Agreement") **(Basic Document 5.40)** which, after several years of quiet negotiation under the auspices of the Secretary–General of the United Nations, substantially accommodates the seabed mining objections previously raised. Indeed, it appears that this 1994 Seabed Mining Agreement, which entered fully into force on 28 July 1996 (again without US ratification), actually hastened broad participation in the 1982 CLOS. In toto, as of this writing (1 May 2006), 149 states have become parties to the 1982 CLOS, 78 more than were required for it to enter into force. However, several major maritime powers, including the United States, are not yet among them, and thus it is prudent still to be cautious about the Convention's ultimate fate. On the other hand, from its very beginning, the 1982 CLOS has been respected and even invoked by those very governments—including perhaps most importantly the United States—that registered dissatisfaction with its deep seabed mining provisions. On 7 October 1994, US President Bill Clinton transmitted to the US Senate the 1982 CLOS and the 1994 Seabed Mining Agreement for advice and consent to ratification; and while this initiative did not succeed, it is noteworthy that, on 17 December 2004, President George W. Bush, responding to a report of the US Commission on Ocean Policy recommending US accession to the two instruments, urged "Congress to provide its advice and consent to this treaty as early as possible in the 109th Congress." On 25 February 2004, the Senate Foreign Relations Committee, by a unanimous vote of 15–0, approved the 1982 CLOS and thus it looked as though the treaty would be quickly approved by the full Senate. Since then, however, a small faction of conservatives in the Senate have sought to block a vote and thus prevent its ratification, citing concerns that the treaty would undermine US sovereignty. Nevertheless, it is not without reason that the UN Convention on the Law of the Sea, in many respects a "framework-convention," is frequently referred to as a "Constitution for the Oceans." One ignores these realities at one's analytical—and possibly political—peril.

B.   JURISDICTION OVER OCEAN RESOURCES: HIGHLY MIGRATORY SPECIES

1.   Convention on the High Seas. Concluded, 29 Apr 1958. Entered into force, 30 Sep 1962. 450 U.N.T.S. 82; *reprinted in* **5 Weston & Carlson V.F.3: Arts. 1, 2, 9, 14–23** (Basic Document 5.3).

2.   Convention on the Continental Shelf. Concluded, 29 Apr 1958. Entered into force, 30 Sep 1962. 499 U.N.T.S. 311; *reprinted in* **5 Weston & Carlson V.F.4: Arts. 1, 2, 5** (Basic Document 5.4).

3. Convention on Fishing and Conservation of the Living Resources of the High Seas. Concluded, 29 Apr 1958. Entered into force, 30 Sep 1962. 559 U.N.T.S. 285; *reprinted in* **5 Weston & Carlson V.F.5: Arts. 1–3, 6–8** (Basic Document 5.6).

4. Declaration of Montevideo on Law of the Sea. Adopted as Doc No. 39 of the Montevideo Conference on the Law of the Sea, 8 May 1970. *Reprinted in* **9 I.L.M. 1081 (1970).**[1]

The states represented at the Montevideo meeting on the law of the sea:

Recognizing that ties of geographic, economic and social nature bind the sea, the land and man [sic] who inhabits it, from which there arises a legitimate priority in favor of littoral peoples to benefit from the natural resources offered to them by their maritime environment; recognizing further, that rules relevant to delimitation of national sovereignty and jurisdiction over the sea, the seabed and the subsoil thereof, and that measures concerning exploitation of resources, must always be mindful of the geographic realities of coastal States and of the special economic and social requirements of the less developed States;

* * *

Do declare, as Basic Principles of the Law of the Sea:

1. The right of littoral States to exercise control over the natural resources of the sea adjacent to their coasts and of the seabed and the soil and subsoil thereof in order to achieve the maximum development of their economy and to raise the living standards of their peoples;

2. The right to delimit their maritime sovereignty and jurisdiction in conformity with their own geographic and geological characteristics and consonant with factors that condition the existence of marine resources and the need for national exploitation;

3. The right to explore, conserve and exploit the living resources of the sea adjacent to their territories, and to control fishing and aquatic game hunting operations;

4. The right to explore, conserve and exploit the natural resources of their respective continental shelf out to where the depth of the superjacent waters admits of exploitation of said resources;

5. The right to explore, conserve and exploit the natural resources of the seabed and of the subsoil of the ocean floor out to where the littoral State claims jurisdiction over the sea;

6. The right to enact regulatory measures to achieve the aforecited goals applicable within the zones of their maritime sovereignty and jurisdiction, without prejudice to freedom of navigation and to the passage of vessels and overflight by aircraft of any flag.

Inspired by the results of this Meeting, the signatory States express in addition their goal to coordinate their future actions to assure effective defense of the principles enunciated in the present Declaration.

1. This Declaration was signed by Argentina, Brazil, Chile, Ecuador, El Salvador, Panama, Peru, Nicaragua, and Uruguay.

This Declaration shall be known as the "Declaration of Montevideo on Law of the Sea."

5. Declaration of the Latin American States on the Law of the Sea, 14 Aug 1970, UN Doc. A/AC.138/28, *reprinted in* 10 I.L.M. 207 (1971).

The Latin American Meeting on Aspects of the Law of the Sea, ...

* * *

Declares as common principles of the Law of the Sea:

1. The inherent right of the coastal State to explore, conserve and exploit the natural resources of the sea adjacent to its coasts and the soil and subsoil thereof, likewise of the Continental Shelf and its subsoil, in order to promote the maximum development of its economy and to raise the level of living of its people;

2. The right of the coastal State to establish the limits of its maritime sovereignty or jurisdiction in accordance with reasonable criteria, having regard to its geographical, geological and biological characteristics, and the need to make rational use of its resources;

3. The right of the coastal State to take regulatory measures for the aforementioned purposes, applicable in the areas of its maritime sovereignty or jurisdiction, without prejudice to freedom of navigation and flight in transit of ships and aircraft, without distinction as to flag;

4. The right of the coastal State to prevent contamination of the waters and other dangerous and harmful effects that may result from the use, exploration or exploitation of the area adjacent to its coasts;

5. The right of the coastal State to authorize, supervise and participate in all scientific research activities which may be carried out in the maritime zones subject to its sovereignty or jurisdiction, and to be informed of the findings and the results of such research.

This Declaration shall be known as the "Declaration of the Latin American States on the Law of the Sea."

6. Summary of *Fisheries Jurisdiction Case* (U.K. v. Ice.), 1974 ICJ 3 (Judgment of 25 Jul 1974) (Basic Document 7.8).

7. United Nations Convention on the Law of the Sea. Concluded, 10 Dec 1982. Entered into force, 16 Nov 1994. 1833 U.N.T.S. 3; *reprinted in* 21 I.L.M. 1261 (1982) and 5 Weston & Carlson V.F.22: Arts. 55–59, 61–64, 73, 76–78, 86–91, 94, 96–98, 100–03, 105–07, 111, 116–19, 238–40, 242–46, 252, 255, 257, 300 (Basic Document 5.22).

8. Will Martin, "Fisheries Conservation and Management of Straddling Stocks and Highly Migratory Stocks under the United Nations Convention on the Law of the Sea," 7 Geo. Int'l Envtl. L. Rev 765, 765–66 (1995).[m]

The management and conservation of living marine resources is extremely complex and involves many biological, economic, and political factors.

---

m. At the time of writing, the author was Deputy Assistant Secretary of Commerce for International Affairs at the US National Oceanic and Atmospheric Administration.

Needless to say, biology and conservation do not always mix well with economic and political factors. Human nature compels many fishermen to resist the catch reductions necessary for conservation of the resource because those reductions translate directly and immediately into reduced income. This reality, in turn, translates into political reluctance to impose such conservation measures.

These economic and political realities have produced a woeful condition in today's world fisheries. A global crisis has developed and is growing. Most commercial fish stocks have been overfished. Many are seriously overexploited and depleted. Some face the possibility of commercial extinction or even biological extinction. Four principal factors have caused this crisis: world population growth; widespread degradation of habitat; enormous growth in fishing technology and the size of fishing fleets; and failure of the regulators to say "no" to overfishing.

What was once proclaimed to be the limitless abundance of the oceans is now generally recognized as a shrinking resource whose management is unsustainable in most parts of the world.... In addressing the problems, both domestically and internationally, we must tailor our actions to be consistent with the provisions of the [1982 United Nations Convention on the Law of the Sea], since it is now regarded as customary international fisheries law. Many fish stocks generally fit within the 200–mile band within which one state can claim and manage an exclusive economic zone (EEZ). Part V of the Convention provides guidance for the management of these resources. However, there are some situations in which the fish stocks do not fit so neatly within an EEZ. These "international" situations are addressed by special provisions in the Convention. Two important problem areas are "straddling stocks" and highly migratory stocks. Straddling stocks overlap the EEZ of a coastal state and the high seas area which adjoins and is beyond the EEZ. An example is the cod stocks occurring in both the Canadian EEZ on the Atlantic and the high seas area beyond the Canadian EEZ. Fishing on the portion of a straddling stock which is within the EEZ of a coastal state is regulated by the coastal state and thus subject to the provisions of Part V of the Convention regarding management of living marine resources within the EEZ. Fishing on the portion of a straddling stock which is on the high seas area, adjacent to and beyond the coastal state's EEZ, is subject to Part VII of the Convention. While some regard the freedom of all countries to fish on the high seas as a license for unrestrained exploitation, Articles 116–119 of Part VII actually impose a duty of conservation upon the fishermen in high seas areas.

In the case of straddling stock, Article 63(2) of Part V of the Convention additionally provides that, "the coastal state and the states fishing for such stocks in the adjacent area shall seek, either directly or through appropriate subregional or regional organizations, to agree upon the measures necessary for the conservation of these stocks in the adjacent area."

I believe most experts would agree that the provisions of Article 63(2), taken in conjunction with other Convention provisions, such as Article 116, imply a degree of primacy to the coastal states in the management and conservation of straddling stocks. This tip of the balance toward coastal state interests is beneficial, since the coastal states are probably more "invested" in the long-term health of the straddling stock resource than a distant-water fishing nation and, thus, are more motivated to preserve that resource.

* * *

Annex I to the Convention lists the highly migratory species of the oceans. Article 64 requires that coastal states and other states fishing for the species in the region "co-operate directly or through appropriate international organizations with a view to ensuring conservation and promoting the objective of optimum utilization of such species throughout the region, both within and beyond the exclusive economic zone." (Note that this Article, unlike Article 63(2) on straddling stocks, requires that the cooperative agreements apply both within EEZs and on the high seas, implying that the coastal states have less primacy in the case of highly migratory fish than in the case of straddling stocks.)

Article 64 further requires that, if no international organization exists to manage highly migratory species in the region, the coastal states and other states harvesting the species in the region shall co-operate to establish one. An example of an international organization which manages highly migratory species is the International Commission for the Conservation of Atlantic Tunas, or ICCAT.... ICCAT is a [41–nation] commission[n] which manages tuna, swordfish, sailfish, and marlin throughout the Atlantic.

Problems have arisen in ICCAT in the past because some key fishing nations ... have not joined the organization. Their failure to cooperate in the conservation of the species tends to undermine ICCAT. Another problem has been the failure of countries to adopt serious conservation measures throughout the migratory range of the fish. Without concerted action by the parties, the stocks managed by ICCAT have declined, in some cases perilously.... [T]he problems of ICCAT highlight the need for strong international cooperation in the case of highly migratory species.

9. William T. Burke, The New International Law of Fisheries: UNCLOS 1982 and Beyond 199–201, 205–08, 210–26, 228–29 (1994).

... [T]he 1982 Convention on the Law of the Sea **[Basic Document 5.22]** ... has a special provision for a category of marine animals called highly migratory species (HMS). Prior to this negotiation, this categorization of species was unknown. Separate treaty provision was made for them for two principal reasons: (1) a number of states, most prominently the United States and Japan, had a particular interest in tuna fishing because their nationals are among the most important participants in the fishery and (2) effective management is affected by the fact that some species of tuna move considerable distances in the ocean, sometimes entering or crossing through several zones of national jurisdiction as well as vast expanses of the high seas.

* * *

FACTUAL BACKGROUND

The HMS category is political, not biological.... [B]ecause the political interest was confined to tuna, the number of [HMS] species identified in the annex to the [1982 CLOS] is limited.

n. Forty-one plus the European Community as of 1 May 2006.

At least a dozen species of tuna are harvested commercially; the most important species are skipjack and yellowfin, which constitute the preponderance of the world catch. Tuna are widely distributed around the globe and are pursued in every ocean. * * * [However,] [w]ith the extension of national jurisdiction to 200 miles, the association of tuna with open ocean has lost a good deal of its significance. Tuna are frequently harvested within 200 nautical miles of a coastal state, which means that it is caught within national jurisdiction. In particular ocean regions, the proportion of annual harvests within and beyond national zones varies over time. . . .

In recent years the tuna industry has been in considerable ferment in response to changes in national jurisdiction, fluctuations in fuel prices, and the impacts of national legislation affecting fishing practices. A large number of nations have tuna fishing vessels, but the most important tuna fishing nations have been Japan, Mexico, Indonesia, the Philippines, Taiwan, South Korea, the United States, Spain, France, and Venezuela. . . .

* * *

POLICY: THE INTERESTS AT STAKE

In general terms, the goals of tuna management should be to maintain a stock at desirable levels, to facilitate its exploitation for optimum social and economic benefits, and to avoid undesirable effects on other parts of the ecosystem.

A main biological objective of management should be to avoid a level of exploitation that would either bring a species of stock to commercial extinction, or threaten to do so. . . . Another main management goal is securing the maximum benefits at the least cost. . . .

* * *

[However,] [a]chieving optimum utilization [defined as providing for production efficiency and maximizing the net benefits from the fishery] is especially difficult for migratory species that move through several jurisdictions. In the tuna fisheries, the conflicting interests are those between coastal states, which wish to decide the level and distribution of benefits from taking tuna in the EEZ and fishing states which seek to support their flag vessels in the fishery in the use of strategies on the high seas that are not consistent with coastal interests. This problem is not peculiar to tuna fishing, but generally occurs where there are straddling stocks. A notable instance is that of the cod fishery in the Northeast Atlantic where the high seas states have very different interests.

Thus the mobility of tuna complicates the conflicting interests between coastal and distant water fishing states. Although this is not invariably true, these fish are usually vulnerable to harvest in both the EEZ and the high seas, and a single coastal state or several coastal states cannot necessarily exercise sufficient control over their harvest to manage them properly. A coastal state with a 200–mile EEZ can lawfully control the use of fish within its jurisdiction, and can capture the benefits of such use. But because the harvesting also may occur outside coastal control, it cannot fully control the level of obtainable benefits. . . .

In most instances, however, it is probably desirable to allow the coastal state to determine the level of fishing *within* its zone and to decide upon the distribution of benefits.º For coastal states, especially some of the smaller ones, the tuna resource is valuable and can yield significant economic benefit through arrangements with foreign tuna harvesters and processors. In tropical areas, most coastal states are developing states whose economies and sources of revenue require expansion. In many instances, these developing states are also island states which commonly have no other significant resources from which to gain income, employment, or food. Allowing these states to benefit from tuna resources within their national jurisdiction is justifiable. However, because of lack of local capital it is reasonable that foreign fishing enterprises must also be permitted to share in the benefits.

Most tuna species are underexploited and it is doubtful whether they or other HMS need to have catches restricted except in limited situations. Expert observers have recently declared that the major market species of yellowfin tuna and skipjack tuna are substantially underexploited on a global basis. * * * [However,] [i]t is still necessary to continue research into [their] life history, their behaviour, and the environmental conditions affecting them. There are still significant management problems relating to levels of abundance, the influence of the marine environment on both abundance and distribution, and, not least, relations with other species. . . .

TREND IN DECISIONS

A. Tradition fishing regime for highly migratory species

Before the general expansion of fishery jurisdiction which began in the mid–1970s, tuna fishing had been the centre of one of the principal controversies regarding the lawfulness of large extensions of national jurisdiction to include fisheries. . . . For a quarter-century, the claims to 200–mile zones of Peru, Ecuador, and Chile were a major focus of attention. . . .

The 1958 United Nations Conference on the Law of the Sea did not reach agreement . . . on the limit of fisheries jurisdiction. But during the negotiations, no one supported the argument advanced by some Latin American states that each state was exclusively competent to determine its own jurisdictional limits in the ocean. . . . During this period of widespread unilateral claims to extended jurisdiction, the general belief prevailed that tuna fishing was an exercise of the freedom of fishing.

* * *

*B. The 1982 Convention and coastal state rights
to conserve and manage fisheries in the EEZ*

1.   Scope and content of sovereign rights

Under [the 1982] CLOS the coastal state's sovereign rights are for the purpose of exploring and exploiting, conserving and managing the natural resources of the EEZ, including all living resources except those subject to the regime of the continental shelf. . . . HMS are subject to coastal authority in the EEZ exactly as are all other species except that coastal states are, in addition, obliged by Article 64 to co-operate with states fishing in the region

---

o.   Emphasis added.

... "both within and beyond the exclusive economic zone." Because of their mobility, HMS may be available simultaneously within and beyond the zone, or they may be available mainly outside at one time and inside at another. Amounts taken within may affect catches beyond and vice versa....

The rights and duties of states fishing in the region must also be considered. According to Article 64 such states are obliged to co-operate with coastal states regarding fishing for HMS within the zone and in the region beyond. At the same time, Article 116 provides that "All States have the right for their nationals to engage in fishing on the high seas subject to (a) their treaty obligations; (b) the rights and duties as well as the interests of coastal States provided for, *inter alia*, in article 63, paragraph 2, and articles 64 to 67; and (c) the provisions of this section." The combined effect of Articles 64 and 116 appears to be that high seas fishing states are not free to adopt conservation and allocation measures applicable only to their own high seas fishing without having sought to co-operate with coastal states in the region whose rights and interests are superior ... since [such unilateralism] could prejudice ultimate conservation and allocation measures, both inside and outside the zone. Article 116 appears to introduce a drastic change in high seas fishing rights by providing a priority for coastal states rights and interests affecting high seas fishing states. How far this interpretation of articles 64 and 116 can be carried is not clear. One view is that a high seas fishing state may not fish, or impose management measures, in a manner inconsistent with coastal state management measures.

* * *

C. Conditions and limitations on coastal state rights regarding HMS

Tuna, and other species defined as highly migratory in annex I of the [1982 CLOS], are fully subject to articles 56, 61, and 62, as well as article 64.... [T]he purport of article 64 is to subject tuna to the same general authority as other species but to add other considerations....

* * *

1. The Requirements of Article 64

Article 64 requires coastal and fishing states to co-operate regarding "conservation" and "optimum utilization" of the specified HMS both within the EEZ and on the high seas.... Since articles 61 and 62 provide for coastal authority to make these choices, article 64 can be taken to require co-operation regarding the decisions addressed by these articles.

Some significant questions about article 64 include the meaning of co-operation and the scope of its subject-matter; when the duty to co-operate is discharged; the consequences of failure or termination of co-operation; the manner and forms of co-operation; and co-operation with respect to fishing in high seas enclaves....

(i) The duty of co-operation and its subject-matter

The combined CLOS provisions directly relating to HMS in the EEZ establish that ..., while the coastal state has final decision-making authority in the exercise of its sovereign rights over HMS, just as it does for other species, it cannot lawfully exercise that authority and employ its discretion until it has discharged its duty to co-operate with other coastal states and with distant-water fishing nations (DWFN) to "ensure conservation and promote optimum utilization." According to article 64, co-operative measures are to deal with stocks and fishing within and beyond 200 miles. In some instances, this may involve a relatively large number of states ... and an enormous geographic area....

* * *

Because of the nature of HMS, which move in and out of any single national jurisdiction, co-operation in this context should aim at a coherent, unified management regime applicable to the stock within and beyond the EEZ. It seems unlikely that "co-operation" could be achieved if any state takes unilateral decisions or actions that are not preceded by communications designed to lead or to establish *agreed* measures to be implemented by coastal states within an EEZ and by fishing states beyond....

However, it seems reasonably obvious that states might not agree and that dissatisfied states may question the process leading to this outcome.

(ii) Failure to co-operate and its consequences

Co-operative activities may be continued for an indefinite period, irrespective of the need for a particular decision involving a specific fishery, but eventually the coastal state with sovereign rights to conserve and to manage within its 200–mile zone must take some action. The question of whether that state, or any other state involved, has discharged its duty to co-operate appears to depend on the ingredients of the choices to be made and the functions required to make decisions. At some point, the state needs to make concrete choices in selecting an allowable catch, promulgating conservation measures, determining the appropriate yield, and so forth....

If co-operation fails to result in the needed conservation and allocation measures, despite good faith efforts, then even though the parties continue to interact co-operatively on some other issues or some later time period, it should be permissible for coastal states to take action to initiate the needed measures, at least in the EEZ, and, probably, beyond....

This interpretation of article 64 allows coastal states in a region to join in making decisions regarding a stock of common interest that is available for harvest in each of their zones....

A most significant issue is what are the respective rights and duties of coastal and fishing states when the failure to agree on measures for stocks within an EEZ means there are no agreed measures for the same stocks outside the EEZ. Coastal states are authorized, as noted, to make independent decisions regarding all fishing for stocks within the EEZ, but what happens when those same stocks are available outside? This is a critical question because it is generally believed that proper conservation and management measures must include the total area within which stocks are harvested. Tuna cannot be managed successfully if management measures are applicable only within 200 nautical miles, but the stocks are fished in significant degree beyond this limit. The problem is to resolve this dilemma under the treaty.

Article 64 deals with HMS both within the EEZ and beyond, joining articles 56, 61, and 62 for application within the EEZ and articles 87 and 116–19 for application beyond the EEZ. Articles 64, 87, and 116–19 provide a treaty basis for resolving the dilemma where coastal and fishing states fail to agree on needed conservation and allocation measures after efforts at co-operation are no longer timely. This set of provisions appears to alter substantially the traditional law regarding freedom to fish on the high seas.

Article 87 provides that freedom of the high seas comprises, *inter alia*, "freedom of fishing, subject to the conditions laid down in section 2." Article 116 in section 2 declares that "All States have the right for their nationals to engage in fishing on the high seas subject to: (a) their treaty obligations; (b) the rights and duties as well as the interests of coastal States provided for, *inter alia*, in Article 63, paragraph 2, and Articles 64 and 67; (c) the provisions of this section." This established that the right to fish for HMS beyond 200 miles is subject to article 64, among others.

Article 64, in turn, recognizes that the coastal state has sovereign rights over HMS within 200 miles, these being the same HMS that are available on the high seas. Article 116, therefore, provides that high seas fishing for HMS is subject to the sovereign rights of the coastal states over the same stock when the latter is within the EEZ. The question is how to interpret the effect of these provisions upon the freedom of fishing for HMS on the high seas?

This question is relatively unimportant if fishing states must, as a practical matter, fish within coastal state zones as well as on the high seas. If the DWFN must have access to the EEZ of ... coastal states in a region ... , then the coastal states can apply terms and conditions regarding high seas fishing to that access. So long as these terms and conditions are consistent with the [1982 CLOS], there would be no legal basis for complaint under the treaty.

An important question remaining, then, concerns the possibility that DWFN might seek to operate only within a high seas area, beyond any EEZ, and to do so independently of coastal state control. What, if any, obligation does the fishing state have regarding the coastal state in light of the article 116 provision that the right to fish there is subject to coastal rights, duties, and interests?

Absent agreement between coastal states and DWFN, articles 64 and 116–19 might be interpreted in a number of very different ways, with different consequences for conservation measures affecting high seas fishing for stocks found both on the high seas and within the EEZ.

One interpretation is that failure to agree is not necessarily the same as the end of co-operation and that, so long as the parties continue to co-operate, neither the coastal state nor the fishing state can independently promulgate conservation measures applicable on the high seas. This interpretation should be rejected because it deprives articles 64 and 116 of any meaning at all and simply blocks action....

Another possible effect of this interpretation is to encourage the coastal state to terminate co-operation on some plausible pretext, because continuation of any form of co-operation might be considered to disable that state from needed measures of conservation.

Another interpretation is that, when good faith negotiations for a season fail to produce agreed measures, the coastal states concerned are authorized ... to establish an allowable catch for the entire region, including the high seas ..., based on the precondition that the negotiations were genuine and pursued in good faith....

* * *

The difficulty with this interpretation, and any other implying the exercise of enforcement jurisdiction, is that the treaty contains no provision at all for any such authority on the high seas beyond the zone. While the coastal state could prescribe for activity beyond the EEZ, its only enforcement power would be within the EEZ, not beyond.

Another interpretation is that in the absence of agreement on measures applicable within the EEZ and beyond, the coastal states are entitled to establish an allowable catch for each EEZ in the region, as well as determinations of each state's harvesting capacity, so long as they take account of all fishing in the region....

This interpretation might be supported specifically by reference to article 117, which provides that "all States have the duty to take, or to co-operate with other States in taking, such measures for their nationals as may be necessary for the conservation of the living resources of the high seas." Since coastal states are entitled to establish an allowable catch for tuna within the EEZ and the fishing state's right is subject to that, it follows that the fishing state is required to conserve tuna on the high seas in light of the collective allowable catch of all coastal states in the region. In this context, conservation means observing the allowable catch established by coastal states.

The major problem with this interpretation is that it is probably impractical or even impossible to forecast where tuna or any other HMS will be caught. It seems unfair to foreclose any fishing in the high seas area on the basis of predictions by coastal states that the allowable catch can be taken within the EEZ. This appears to be an entirely theoretical calculation—where the fish are available for harvesting may vary from week to week, or even more frequently.

As noted, a difficulty with any interpretation of article 116 is that the coastal state has no enforcement authority beyond 200 miles. None the less, the treaty contains provisions that may assist both coastal and distant water states in this area. Either the coastal or the distant water state is competent under the treaty to invoke compulsory dispute settlement procedures concerning fishing in the high seas....

* * *

The above interpretations of the treaty seek to address a difficult but likely situation, namely one in which the states concerned cannot agree on concerted action even though the lawful alternative of independent action by the coastal state would deprive each side of benefits. Unregulated high seas fishing appears to be inconsistent with a coastal state's rights to set the allowable catch in its own zone and to ensure that stocks are not endangered by exploitation. On the other hand, coastal state measures, adopted without the agreement of fishing states, also cannot accomplish these objectives if high seas fishing remains unregulated. There must be some way out of this dilemma consistent with the treaty.

While it may not be clear how articles 64 and 116 should be interpreted to provide for conservation when the parties disagree, it is clear that unregulated foreign fishing [on the high seas] infringes on coastal rights as formulated in the treaty. Although the treaty gives coastal states wide discretion regarding fisheries in the EEZ and, as interpreted here, gives some degree of authority over high seas fishing, it also emphasizes that these states are obliged to act reasonably in decisions that include high seas fishing. . . . Coastal states have wide leeway in managing fisheries occurring wholly within 200 miles, but the treaty does not provide for similar unreviewable discretion when management measures are directed at high seas fishing rights. Although these rights are subject to coastal rights and interests, the coastal rights must be exercised reasonably. . . .

(iii) Manner of co-operation: direct interaction and international organizations

Article 64 clearly calls for international co-operation for conservation and utilization, but it presents important questions about the manner and form of co-operation, including the following: (a) whether it permits a choice between direct co-operation and use of an international organization (IO) or whether an IO must be employed even if direct co-operation is preferred, and (b) what characteristics or elements of an IO are required by article 64. * * * The major pattern of the several decades since World War II has been to employ simultaneously direct co-operation between states *and* international organizations. . . .

* * *

In any event, these seeming inconsistencies are resolved by the total absence of any details regarding an appropriate IO. Without the requirements being spelled out, the obligation to establish an IO means whatever the parties are able to agree upon and this is not an effective obligation.

* * *

2. Measures to Ensure Against Overexploitation

The coastal state, "taking into account the best scientific evidence available to it," has the obligation to adopt "proper conservation and management measures" to ensure that living resources in its zone are not endangered by overexploitation. For species found wholly within the coastal state's zone this obligation can be discharged with no unusual difficulty. . . .

The situation is very different for HMS because they can be, and typically are, exploited outside the coastal state's zone and sometimes outside any state's zone. Accordingly the relevant scientific evidence pertains to the target HMS throughout its range. The "best scientific evidence" includes data that might come from sources outside the coastal state. Whether or not that data is "available" to the coastal state is a question of fact. Article 61(2) declares that the coastal state "shall cooperate" with competent international organizations to avoid overexploitation which endangers maintenance of the living resources of its zone.

The effect of these provisions is to require a management process that may be different for HMS than for other species. To adopt "proper" measures, the coastal state must seek out information concerning fishing activities and fishing stocks located outside its own jurisdiction, at least for some period of time. . . .

10. Editors' Note. Notwithstanding the special deference that Article 63 of the 1982 CLOS **(Basic Document 5.22)** appears to give to coastal state fishery interests and management, state practice records several instances where coastal state efforts to protect against overfishing have led the coastal state to assert jurisdiction over the activities of foreign vessels on the high seas beyond, first, the territorial sea and contiguous zone and, more recently, beyond the 200–mile EEZ.

An early example of fishery stock management along these lines is found in the "epicontinental sea doctrine," reportedly first propounded by the Argentine jurist José-Léon Suárez as early as 1918 and employed by the Government of Argentina in Decree No. 14,708 Concerning National Sovereignty over the Epicontinental Sea and the Argentine Continental Shelf, adopted 11 October 1946. According to this decree, Argentina claimed jurisdiction over fish stock superjacent to, and coextensive with, its continental shelf, the outer edge of which was in some places as far as 400 miles distant from Argentina's coast. *See* Winston C. Extavour, The Exclusive Economic Zone: A Study of the Evolution and Progressive Development of the International Law of the Sea 74–76 (1979).

Another, more recent example is seen in the response of the United States Senate in 1988 to an area of the Bering Sea called the "Doughnut Hole," a large high seas area of productive mixed stock fishery resources— mainly pollock—resulting from parts of the Bering Sea being surrounded by the 200 nautical mile EEZs of the United States and the former USSR. Concerned about "a massive increase" in fishing in the Doughnut Hole and worried that vessels of foreign nations were using it "as a staging ground for raids into the US EEZ for the purpose of illegally fishing US stocks," the Senate, on 21 March 1988, adopted Senate Resolution 396, 100th Cong., 2d Sess., 134 Cong. Rec. S2621 (daily ed. Mar. 21, 1988). In that Resolution, the "sense of the Senate" was that a moratorium on all fishing within the Doughnut Hole should be observed until "such time as the United States and the Soviet Union have entered into an agreement with a majority of other interested nations for the conservation and management of fishery resources in the Doughnut."

Expressing the "sense of the Senate" and therefore in theory not constituting a binding resolution, the 1988 Senate resolution nevertheless corresponds well with the reasoning behind the "species approach" to fishery stock management suggested in 1972 in the Seabed Committee by the United States and Canada. Stated the Canadian delegation:

> In the view of the delegation of Canada the functional approach provides the soundest basis for a rational system of management of the living resources of the sea. On this basis it would be recognized that different management régimes may be required for different species groups [including large pelagic fish such as tunas and most of the marine mammals]. * * * As regards the *limits* of the area under the management authority of the coastal state, these could be biological or geographical in nature. If biological, the functional authority of the coastal state could be exercised in accordance with the known distribution and zoogeographical

limits of the stocks being managed, excepting the territorial or jurisdictional waters of another state. It may be, however, that some form of geographic delimitation of authority, related to the relevant biological limits, will be considered desirable or necessary for practical administrative purposes.

Report of the Committee on the Peaceful Uses of the Sea–Bed and the Ocean Floor Beyond the Limits of National Jurisdiction, GAOR, 27th Sess., Supp. (No. 21) 164 & 168, UN Doc. A/8721 (972).

Also to be noted is the idea of the *Mar Presencial* (Presencial Sea) suggested by some Chilean officials in the early 1990s. *See* Francisco Orrego Vicuña, *Toward an Effective Management of High Seas Fisheries and the Settlement of the Pending Issues of the Law of the Sea*, 24 Ocean Dev. & Int'l L. 81 (1993). The Presencial Sea, according to Dr. Orrego, involves three concepts: (1) "the participation in and surveillance of the activities undertaken by other states in the high seas areas of particular interest for the coastal state"; (2) encouragement of the "coastal state to undertake economic activities in the high seas in order to promote national economic development and to ensure that other activities there are conducted in such a way as to avoid direct or indirect harmful effects upon this development"; and (3) "a broad view of national security, understood not in a strict military sense but in terms of protection of the national interest ... with particular reference to the Exclusive Economic Zone and the territorial sea." *Id.* at 88.

More recently, in 1994, out of concern for the depletion of cod stocks off eastern Canada in the North Atlantic and seemingly reflecting the "functional approach" cited by the US Senate in relation to the Doughnut Hole, the Canadian government unilaterally extended its coastal state fisheries management authority to cover the area where the straddling cod are located.[p] The legislation authorized the Canadian authorities to seize, arrest, prosecute, and penalize foreign vessels that fish on the high seas adjacent to Canada's EEZ in a manner that diminished the effectiveness of the conservation management rules of the North Atlantic Fisheries Organization (NAFO), the international fisheries management organization for the North Atlantic region.

The United States, it should be noted, firmly opposed Canada's unilateral assertion of extra-EEZ authority, contending that devices such as its "zone of protection" were inconsistent with the 1982 CLOS and threatened to undermine it. *See, e.g.*, Will Martin, *Fisheries Conservation and Management of Straddling Stocks and Highly Migratory Stocks under the United Nations Convention on the Law of the Sea*, 7 Geo. Int'l Envtl. L. Rev. 765, 767 (1995). Consistent with this stance, it successfully negotiated, with the Russian Federation and thereafter China, Japan, Poland, and South Korea, the 1994 Convention on the Conservation and Management of Pollock Resources of the Central Bering Sea (commonly known as the "Doughnut Hole Convention"), concluded 16 December 1994, entered into force 8 December 1995, S. Treaty Doc. No. 27, 103d Cong., 2d Sess. (1994), *reprinted in* 34 I.L.M. 67 (1995). The Convention, calling for individual national quotas or allowable high seas harvest levels (AHL) to be decided by the states parties for allocation among themselves based on biomass considerations, protects the straddling stock resources from overfishing in the area by recognizing a special role for the two

p. *See* An Act to Amend the Coastal Fisheries Protection Act, I S.C. ch. 14 (12 May 1994).

coastal states (Russia and the United States) should consensus on AHL prove impossible and by providing for real-time vessel-position reporting by satellite, boarding and inspection by state party officials, and advance notification of the trans-shipment of fish taken from the Doughnut Hole area.

The 1994 Doughnut Hole Convention, it turns out, was among the first of a growing number of ecologically oriented fisheries agreements to emerge regionally in recent years, the result of pressures associated with fish stock overexploitation and a consequent perceived need to manage fish stocks according to principles of ecosystem sustainability. All but one of these agreements, including the Doughnut Hole Convention, are in force at this writing, and thus merit notice because the environmental trend they signify is likely to influence fisheries decision-making for years to come. On 15 May 1999, Iceland, Norway, and the Russian Federation successfully concluded the Agreement Concerning Certain Aspects of Cooperation in the Area of Fisheries relative to the Barents Sea (the "Barents Sea Loophole Agreement"), the principal purpose of which is a mutual exchange of quotas between the three states parties, combined with ceilings on the total catch that may be taken of particular species.[q] On 14 August 2000, Chile, Colombia, Ecuador, and Peru concluded the Framework Agreement for the Conservation of Living Marine Resources on the High Seas of the South Pacific (the "Galapagos Agreement"), with special reference to straddling and highly migratory fish populations in the high seas zones of the Southeast Pacific.[r] On 5 September 2000, eleven nations with fisheries interests in the Southeast Pacific Ocean (including the United States) concluded the Convention on the Conservation and Management of Highly Migratory Fish Stocks in the Western and Central Pacific Ocean,[s] creating a new international commission to manage highly migratory fish stocks in that region, the consequence of a growing tension between coastal state and distant-water fishing state interests. Most recently, on 20 April 2001, Angola, Iceland, Namibia, Norway, South Africa, South Korea, the United Kingdom (on behalf of St. Helena and its dependencies), the United States, and the European Community signed the Convention on the Conservation and Management of Fishery Resources in the South–East Atlantic Ocean, establishing the South–East Atlantic Fisheries Organization (SEAFO)[t] for the purpose of ensuring the long-term conservation and sustainable use of the fishery resources in the Convention area.

Once in force, these new treaty regimes will join a host of regional fisheries organizations and arrangements, such as the International Commission for the Conservation of Atlantic Tunas (ICCAT), that are either newly emerging or undergoing significant change in purpose and governance. Unfortunately, as noted by Lawrence Juda in *Rio Plus Ten: The Evolution of International Marine Fisheries Governance*, 33 Ocean Dev. & Int'l L. J. 109,

---

q. For the text of this agreement (including two protocols of the same date, see <http://www.oceanlaw.net/texts/barents.htm>. The agreement entered into force 15 Jul 1999.

r. For the text of this agreement, not yet in force, see <http://www.oceanlaw.net /texts/galapagos.htm>. Despite applying to the high seas, it is not currently open to signature by non-coastal states.

s. The text of this agreement, which entered into force 19 Jun 2004, is found in *Report of the Seventh and Final Session of the Multilateral High Level Conference on the Conservation and Management of Highly Migratory Fish Stocks in the Western and Central Pacific* (Aug–Sep 2000).

t. For the text of this agreement, which entered into force 30 Apr 2003, see <http:// www.oceanlaw.net/texts/seafo.htm>.

124–25 (2002), the effectiveness of these organizations and arrangements has been frustrated by insufficient data, inadequate resources to compel compliance among member states that fail to meet their consensual obligations (made even more difficult by the threat of "opt out" clauses that allow the unilateral rejection of fishery body management efforts), and, generally, a reactive rather than proactive approach to fish stocks management.

Paralleling these regional fisheries developments has been the work of the Food and Agriculture Organization (FAO), a United Nations "specialized agency" founded in 1945 and based in Rome. Among its diverse activities, the FAO promotes the sustainable development of responsible fisheries to improve worldwide food security. In 1991, mindful that the world's fisheries could not sustain the exploitation of them that had resulted from the widespread introduction of EEZs in the mid–1970s, the FAO Committee on Fisheries (COFI) requested the development of new concepts to better manage them. Responding to COFI and to an International Conference on Responsible Fishing held in Cancún, Mexico in 1992, the FAO subsequently prepared a Code of Conduct for Responsible Fisheries which, on 31 October 1995, was adopted by the FAO Conference. A non-binding instrument, the Code provides a detailed framework for national and international efforts to ensure the conservation, management, and sustainable development of all fisheries in harmony with the environment. For background information on its adoption, see D. Doulman, *The Code of Conduct for Responsible Fisheries: The Requirement for Structural Change and Adjustment in the Fisheries Sector* (November 1998) <http://www.fao.org/fi/ agreem/codecond/codnov98.asp>.

The ecologically oriented Code of Conduct notwithstanding, however, 90 percent of the world's marine fisheries, many of which involve straddling and highly migratory fish species, are located within EEZs of states that lack the experience and/or the financial and physical resources necessary to assure the Code's effective implementation. Accordingly, in 1993, the FAO also parented the 1993 Agreement to Promote Compliance with International Conservation and Management Measures by Fishing Vessels on the High Seas **(Basic Document 5.39)**. As of this writing, this agreement had not yet entered into force.

Also to be noted, not least because it has helped to shape the regional fishery organizations and regimes noted above, is the 1995 United Nations Agreement for the Implementation of the Provisions of the United Nations Convention on the Law of the Sea of 10 December 1982, Relating to the Conservation and Management of Straddling Fish Stocks and Highly Migratory Fish Stocks **(Basic Document 5.43)**. Sometimes called the United Nations Fish Stocks Agreement (UNFSA), it was adopted as a supplement to the 1982 United Nations Convention on the Law of the Sea **(Basic Document 5.22)** and may be seen as a response to the call for effective monitoring and enforcement of high seas fishing in Chapter 17 of Agenda 21 of the germinal United Nations Conference on the Environment and Development (UNCED), held in Rio de Janeiro in June 1992.

11.   Code of Conduct for Responsible Fisheries. Adopted by the FAO Conference, 31 Oct 1995, *available at* **<ftp://ftp.fao.org/docrep/ fao/005/v9878e/V9878E00.pdf>: Arts. 1, 2, 6, 7, 8, & 10** (Basic Document 5.44).

12. FAO Agreement to Promote Compliance with International Conservation and Management Measures by Fishing Vessels on the High Seas. Adopted by the the Twenty-seventh Session of the FAO Conference, 24 Nov 1993. Entered into force, 24 Apr 2003. *Reprinted in* **33 I.L.M. 968 (1994): Arts. III(1)(a), III(8), & VIII(2)** (Basic Document 5.39).

13. Agreement for the Implementation of the Provisions of the United Nations Convention on the Law of the Sea of 10 December 1982, Relating to the Conservation and Management of Straddling Fish Stocks and Highly Migratory Fish Stocks. Concluded, 4 Aug 1995. Entered into force, 11 Dec 2001. UN Doc. A/CONF.151/26 (12 Aug 1992); *reprinted in* **34 I.L.M. 1542 (1995) and 5 Weston & Carlson V.H.24: Pts. I–III, V–VII, X, XI, XIII (Art. 48), & Annexes I & II** (Basic Document 5.43).

14. Lawrence Juda, "Rio Plus Ten: The Evolution of International Marine Fisheries Governance," 33 Ocean Dev. & Int'l L. J. 109, 116–23 (2002).

A number of new legal instruments that affect the international governance of marine fisheries have been adopted since the 1992 United Nations Conference on the Human Environment, and others already in existence have been modified to bring them into line with recommendations made at the Rio meeting. In considering these developments there is a need to distinguish in international law between what is termed "hard law" and "soft law." Hard law refers to legally binding agreements that are typically embodied in international treaties and that require party states to behave in accord with their stipulations. They are the product of negotiations among states and, together with customary rules, are the basis of an increasingly complex system of binding international law.

Soft law is typically used to refer to nonbinding multilateral declarations or intergovernmental conferences, such as the [1992] United Nations Conference on Environment and Development, or recommendations or resolutions of intergovernmental bodies such as the United Nations General Assembly. While not binding, and thus unlike treaties in this important respect, soft law instruments are also the product of careful negotiations and may have substantial significance as a reflection of emerging international consensus and general statements of principles that may later be developed and incorporated into future treaties or emerge as norms of customary law over time. Indeed, the process of developing the hard law of treaties increasingly appears to be preceded by evolution of soft law instruments. Further, soft law becomes part of the broader context in which existing (hard law) treaties are interpreted and implemented over time. Such realities explain why states exert efforts to influence the nature and wording of nonbinding soft law instruments.

Soft Law Developments

FAO Code of Conduct for Responsible Fisheries. The FAO Code of Conduct [Basic Document 5.44], is a nonbinding instrument that, in sweeping fashion, addresses a variety of aspects of fishing, integrating these aspects so as to encourage sustainability of living resources and the ecological conditions that support them. * * * Laying out a broad array of principles and standards for the conservation, management, and development of all fisheries, the provisions of the code are believed to be applicable globally.

* * *

While from an international law perspective the code is a voluntary instrument without binding effect. It must be viewed as embodying a broad international consensus and a framework for future treatment of ongoing fisheries problems worldwide. Discussions leading to the adoption of the Code of Conduct have no doubt contributed to the development of the FAO Compliance Agreement **[Basic Document 5.39]** and the United Nations Fish Stocks Agreement (UNFSA) **[Basic Document 5.43]**; and the code has influenced the work of existing regional fisheries bodies and helped shape the treaties of newly emerging fisheries. . . . It is also influencing actions at the national level. Continuing and broad-based support for the principles of the code and the use of an ecosystem approach to fisheries is seen in the 1999 Rome Declaration on the Implementation of the Code of Conduct for Responsible Fisheries adopted unanimously by ministers from some 126 states and the European Union.[u]

* * *

Hard Law Developments: Treaties

FAO Compliance Agreement. This agreement **[Basic Document 5.39]** responds directly to the recommendation made in Agenda 21 for action to ensure effective monitoring and enforcement of high seas fishing activities. In brief, the 1993 Compliance Agreement specifies the responsibilities of a state for ships that fish on the high seas and fly the state's flag. It requires flag state authorization for such fishing and obligates a state to ensure that fishing by vessels under its flag does not undermine international conservation and management efforts. Flag states are to make available to [the] FAO stipulated information on each of its fishing vessels authorized to fish on the high seas, a development that may be helpful in enforcing international fishery management measures. Perhaps most important of all, a state is not to allow the use of its flag unless it can effectively exercise its Compliance Agreement responsibilities. These requirements constitute a response to problems associated with the reflagging of fishing vessels under the flag of a state that is either unwilling or unable to enforce fisheries regulations.

To supplement the sometimes insufficient enforcement capabilities (or willingness) of flag states, the Compliance Agreement provides a limited opening for port state action against a foreign flag fishing vessel voluntarily entering its port if that port state "has reasonable grounds for believing that the fishing vessel has been used for an activity that undermines the effectiveness of international conservation and management measures. . . ."[v] The action that may be taken by the port state is limited, however, to notifying the flag state, and arrangements "may" be made between the port state and the flag state for port state investigation.

u. The full text of this declaration is found online at <http://www.fao.org/fi/agreem/declar/dece.asp>.

v. Compliance Agreement, Art. V(2).

United Nations Fish Stocks Agreement (UNFSA). As in the case of the FAO Compliance Convention, the UNFSA **[Basic Document 5.43]** may be seen as fulfilling recommendations of Agenda 21. Adopted in 1995, the UNFSA supplements the 1982 UN Convention on the Law of the Sea **[Basic Document 5.22]** and details state obligations with respect to marine fisheries. While great emphasis was placed on the need for the agreement to be fully consistent with the Law of the Sea Convention of 1982, the fact remains that in addressing the void left by the 1982 convention, the agreement represents an effort in both the codification and progressive development of international law. To the end of achieving the objective of sustainable use of straddling and highly migratory fish stocks, an ecosystem-based approach to management is employed, making reference to principles such as:

- unity of stocks and the need for management of stocks over their entire migratory range [Arts. 5 & 7];

- the necessity for compatibility of EEZ and high seas fisheries regimes [Art. 7];

- concern with the catch of nontargeted species and the interdependence of stocks [Arts. 5(b)-(e) & 6(3)(c)];

- the need for a precautionary approach to fisheries management [Arts. 5(c) & 6]; and

- transparency in the decision making and activities of regional fisheries management organizations and arrangements [Art. 12].

Significantly, the UNFSA provides means with which to give effect to this new conceptualization of fisheries management, underscoring the role and responsibility of regional fisheries bodies to ensure protection of stocks in areas beyond the jurisdiction of coastal states. [*Eds.*—The author goes on to describe the liability and enforcement mechanism of the UNFSA, which involves member states, the flag state, and port states, and therefore undermines the historically exclusive jurisdiction of a flag state over vessels on the high seas that fly that state's flag.]

But perhaps even more astonishing is the acceptance by party states of the obligation that if ships of their flag are to fish in high seas areas in which there are regional organizations or arrangements for conservation and management, then the state is to join the organization or participate in the arrangement as a price of access to the fishery resources that are governed by that organization or arrangement. This provision, if made effective, would address the problem of the "free rider" who benefits from the efforts of others at no cost to himself. Significantly, in an effort to ensure transparency, the increasing significance of nongovernmental organizations is recognized with assurance that they will be allowed to take part in meetings of regional fishery management bodies.... Finally, the agreement provides that the dispute settlement provisions contained in the Law of the Sea Convention **(Basic Document 5.22)** will apply to disputes among parties to the agreement, even should they not be party to the convention.

Depending on how the agreement's provisions are executed, entry into force and implementation may have substantial effects on the sustainability of fisheries if those states most actively participating in high seas fisheries become party to the agreement.... [T]he UNFSA entered into force on

December 11, 2001. Of considerable concern is the fact that key high seas fishing states have not ratified or acceded to the agreement. It is estimated that some 90% of high seas catch is taken by nationals of six states or entities: Japan, Spain, Poland, the Republic of Korea, the Russian Federation, and Taiwan, province of China.... Concerned with the reality that many commercially significant straddling and highly migratory fish stocks remain subject to insufficiently regulated fishing efforts, the United Nations General Assembly has called repeatedly on states and other entities ... to ratify or accede to it....

15. Editors' Note. As noted in preceding Reading 13, commercially significant straddling and highly migratory fish stocks are not regulated very well, the 1995 United Nations Fish Stocks Agreement **(Basic Document 5.43)** notwithstanding. The world community, still clinging to notions of national sovereignty that have been outstripped by economic, environmental, and other challenging forces, has yet to devise adequate law enforcement mechanisms even for the global commons. Such policing capabilities as do exist to safeguard commercially significant straddling and highly migratory fish stocks as well as other maritime matters remain principally the province of individual sea-going states, unequal in wealth and power. Nevertheless, sometimes these states, even some of the less powerful, do assert themselves, not infrequently to the farthest reaches of their coastal jurisdictions; and when this happens the international law doctrine of hot pursuit sometimes comes into play.

The doctrine of hot pursuit, a limitation on the principle of the freedom of the high seas, has long been recognized under customary international law, allowing the warships or military aircraft of a coastal state to pursue foreign ships that violate that state's laws within its internal waters or territorial sea and to arrest them, if necessary, on the high seas. *See, e.g.*, the *"I'm Alone"Case* (Can. v. U.S.), [1935] 3 UNRIAA 1609 (1949). This principle is recognized in both Article 23 of the 1958 Convention on the High Seas (1958 CHS) **(Basic Document 5.3)** and Article 111 of the 1982 Convention on the Law of the Sea (1982 CLOS) **(Basic Document 5.22)**. Pursuit must be begun, these provisions stipulate, while a foreign ship "or one of its boats" (*i.e.*, a boat of a "mother ship") is within the territorial sea of the coastal state or its contiguous zone in the case of customs, fiscal, immigration or sanitary laws); it must begin by the giving, within range of the ship, of a visual or auditory signal to stop and when the foreign ship has failed to yield (the signaling ship or aircraft not needing to be within the territorial sea or contiguous zone at the time); and it must be continuous (*i.e.*, not interrupted). Article 111 (1) of the 1982 CLOS has extended the right to include hot pursuit from archipelagic waters, and Article 111(2) has done the same in respect of hot pursuit from the EEZ and the waters above the continental shelf in cases where there has been a violation of laws the coastal state is entitled to make in respect of the EEZ or continental shelf. In other words, under the 1982 CLOS at least, a coastal state is authorized to pursue a foreign vessel from its archipelagic waters and EEZ as well as its territorial sea and contiguous zone if it reasonably suspects that a foreign ship has violated a bona fide law within one of these zones. Additionally, the pursuing coastal state ship may use any necessary and reasonable means to arrest the foreign ship and escort it back to port, but must then promptly release it pending an inquiry by the coastal state's competent authorities. However, the right of hot pursuit ceases as soon as the foreign ship enters its own territorial sea or that of a third state, for to continue would violate the sovereignty of the flag or other state. At the same time, write Robin R. Churchill and Alan V. Lowe in The Law of the Sea 215 (3d ed. 1999), "[t]here is no reason why the right of pursuit should cease when the vessel pursued enters the EEZ of its own or a third State.'"[w]

A prominent US federal district court case, *United States v. F/V Taiyo Maru, No. 28*, 395 F. Supp. 413 (D. Me. 1975), marks the development of the hot pursuit doctrine in the context of 1958 CHS and the 1958 Geneva Convention on the Territorial Sea and Contiguous Zone (1958 CTSCZ) **(Basic Document 5.5)**. In this case, a US Coast Guard ship, on 5 September 1974, sighted a commercial Japanese fishing vessel, the *Taiyo Maru* 28, within waters claimed by the United States to be part of its contiguous fisheries zone, in violation of the Bartlett Act 16 USCA § 1801 et seq., and the Contiguous Fisheries Zone Act, 16 USC § 1091 et seq. The Coast Guard signaled the *Taiyo Maru* 28 and, after giving immediate and continuous hot pursuit, seized the vessel on the high seas. Defendant's sole contention was that the United States "had no right to conduct hot pursuit from the contiguous zone and to effect seizure of the *Taiyo Maru* 28 because the vessel was seized on the high seas in violation of Article 23 of the [1958 CHS]" which, when read together with Article 24 of the 1958 CTSCZ, evidenced that the United States had undertaken a "specific obligation" not to institute hot pursuit of foreign ships from its contiguous fisheries zone for violation of its fisheries laws. Article 24, defendant asserted, enumerated only four purposes for which a coastal state may initiate hot pursuit, none of which applied to the facts of this case. The district court disagreed and denied defendant's motion to dismiss for lack of jurisdiction. It reasoned:

> ... It is true that Article 23 permits hot pursuit from a contiguous zone, created for one of the four purposes enumerated in Article 24 of the Convention on the Territorial Sea and the Contiguous Zone, only if there has been a violation of the rights for the protection of which the zone was established. But Article 23 does not in terms deny a coastal State the right to commence hot pursuit from a contiguous zone established for a purpose other than one of the purposes listed in Article 24. Nor does Article 24 in terms prohibit the establishment of a contiguous zone for a purpose other than one of those specified in the Article. The language of Article 24, relating to the purposes for which a contiguous zone may be established, is permissive, rather than restrictive. It provides that a coastal State "may" establish a contiguous zone for the purposes of enforcing its customs, fiscal, immigration or sanitary regulations.... [T]he Conventions in the case at bar contain no specific undertaking by the United States not to conduct hot pursuit from a contiguous fisheries zone extending 12 miles from its coast....
>
> The history of the 1958 Conventions confirms the conclusion that the United States did not specifically undertake to limit its authority to exercise exclusive fisheries jurisdiction within 12 miles of its coast, to

w. [However,] some States, such as Brazil (in the context of the 1988 UN Convention against Illicit Traffic in Narcotic Drugs ...), have taken the view that arrests of ships within the EEZ need the consent of the coastal State. Brazil's statement was the subject of an objection by EC member States.

establish a contiguous zone for such a purpose, or to conduct hot pursuit from such a zone. * * * [T]he United States could not have intended to accept any limitation ... since the Geneva Conference could not agree as to whether a contiguous zone would be established for the purpose of enforcing domestic fisheries law.

It is apparent that Congress was well aware of its obligations under the 1958 Conventions when the 1966 Contiguous Fisheries Zone Act was enacted, and that Congress perceived no conflict between the Act and the treaty provisions. . . .

More recently, in 1999, in the *The M/V "Saiga" (No. 2) Case* between St. Vincent and the Grenadines and Guinea, the International Tribunal for the Law of the Sea (ITLOS) dealt with many of the same issues raised in *Taiyo Maru* and further clarified the outer boundaries of the right of hot pursuit, this time in the context of the 1982 Convention on the Law of the Sea (1982 CLOS) **(Basic Document 5.22)** to which both St. Vincent/Grenadines and Guinea were party.

16.   Summary of the M/V "Saiga" (No. 2) Case (St. Vincent and the Grenadines v. Guinea), 1999 ITLOS Case No. 2 (1 July 1999), *available at* <http://www.itlos.org/start2_en.html> (Basic Document 7.12).

17.   Editors' Note. A question remains: when one of the disputing states is not a party to the 1982 Convention on the Law of the Seas (1982 CLOS) **(Basic Document 5.22)**, does there exist a right of arrest and hot pursuit onto the high seas for offences committed in the exclusive economic zone (EEZ)? In other words, does there now exist a customary international law right of arrest and hot pursuit relative to the EEZ? In The Law of the Sea 215 (3d ed. 1999), Robin R. Churchill and Alan V. Lowe suggest that there is. They write:

There is . . . , in customary international law, a right to arrest foreign ships which use their boats to commit offences within the territorial sea (and, perhaps, now the EEZ) while themselves remaining on the high seas. This is the doctrine of constructive presence, implicitly recognised in the provisions of the High Seas and Law of the Sea Conventions relating to hot pursuit. . . . The doctrine of constructive presence may operate together with the right of hot pursuit so as to give coastal States some flexibility in the manner in which they enforce their laws.

Others argue that the right exists also by virtue of the large majority of states that have ratified or acceded to the 1982 CLOS, 149 as of this writing (1 May 2006). They point to, *inter alia*, the decisions of the World Court in the 1969 *North Sea Continental Shelf Cases* (F.R.G./Den.) (F.R.G./Neth.), 1969 ICJ 3, and the 1986 case concerning *Military and Paramilitary Activities in and Against Nicaragua* (Nicar. v. U.S.) (Merits),1984 ICJ 392, each reprinted in pertinent part in Section B of Chapter 2, *supra* at 114–21.

18.   International Convention on Arrest of Ships. Concluded at the UN/IMO Diplomatic Conference on Arrest of Ships, 12 Mar 1999. Not yet in force. UN Doc. A/CONF.188.6 (19 Mar 1999): Arts. 1–4 & 8 (5.50).

C. JURISDICTION OVER RESOURCES: DEEP SEABED MINERALS

1. Arcangelo Travaglini, Note, "Reconciling Natural Law and Legal Positivism in the Deep Seabed Mining Provisions of the Convention on the Law of the Sea," 15 Temp. Int'l & Comp. L. J. 313, 313–15 (2001).

The discovery of rich deposits of nickel and manganese at the bottom of the oceans, and the development of technologies capable of harvesting such valuable ores in the near future, inaugurated an international legal debate, beginning in the 1960s, over the rights of the individual states to mine the world's untapped mineral wealth. Specifically, one block, represented by most developing nations, maintains that the natural resources of the deep oceans are the common heritage of mankind, and their exploitation as a consequence, should take place under a communal regime. Conversely, another faction, headed by the United States, and including the most developed nations, argues that the high economic value of the seabed minerals, and their strategic value to the First–World states, requires free access by the technologically and financially richer countries as a matter of economic interest. The conflict between those in favor of a communal regime, and those in favor of unfettered access, reflects a classic contradiction of international law: on one hand, numerous underdeveloped states attempt to redress the world's inequalities through a regime of shared participation in the mining of the seabed; on the other, a limited number of powerful nations view the equal parceling of the seafloor's natural resources as a scheme at odds with national sovereign interests. In essence, this contradiction mirrors an old antagonism between natural law and legal positivism, through which the former proclaims the primacy of universal supranational rights, while the latter declares that discrete nation states are the sole entities with an implicit right to reject or accept legal norms in the name of sovereign interests. * * * Thus ... , the economic question of who should harvest the mineral wealth of the sea, and in what percentage, if any, has added another point of contention in the North-South conflict. Indeed, in 1982, the incarnation of such a chasm occurred when President Reagan refused to sign the Third United Nations Convention on the Law of the Sea **[Basic Document 5.22]**, arguing that the United States would first attempt to redress the objectionable elements in the agreement that threatened the economic interests of the individual states. In addition, President Reagan asserted the seabed's mining rights of the technologically advanced states, and declared that the communal regime under [the 1982 CLOS] discriminated unfairly against the "free enterprise" culture....

2. Declaration of Principles Governing the Sea–Bed and Ocean Floor, and the Subsoil Thereof, Beyond the Limits of National Jurisdiction, 17 Dec 1970, GA Res. 2749 (XXV), 25 UN GAOR, Supp. (No. 28) 24, UN Doc. A/8028 (1971); *reprinted in* **10 I.L.M. 220 (1971) and 5 Weston & Carlson V.F.10** (Basic Document 5.12).

3. Question of the Reservation Exclusively for Peaceful Purposes of the Sea–Bed and the Ocean Floor, and Subsoil Thereof, Underlying the High Seas Beyond the Limits of Present National Jurisdiction, and the Use of Their Resources in the Interests of Mankind, 15 Dec 1969, GA Res. 2574D (XXIV), 24 UN GAOR, Supp.

(No. 30) 11, UN Doc. A/7630 (1970); *reprinted in* 9 I.L.M. 422 (1970) and 5 Weston & Carlson V.F.9 (Basic Document 5.11).[x]

4.   Brad Shingleton, "UNCLOS III and the Struggle for Law: The Elusive Customary Law of Seabed Mining," 13 Ocean Dev. & Int'l L. J. 33, 37–55 (1983).

II.   Is There a Customary Law Regime of the Seabed?

Obviously, the existence or absence of a customary legal regime of the seabed must necessarily affect any attempt to create a legal regime for the seabed by convention. If there is a preexisting customary regime, a conventional regime will displace it so far as the parties to the convention are concerned; conversely, if a convention is not concluded, the customary regime remains in force subject to the usual powers of protest....

A.   The Customary Regime Before 1958

The legal regime of the seabed has been historically tied to that of the high seas ... , [and from] Roman times the high seas have been seen as *res communis*, belonging to all, for use by all.... Only in recent years has the seabed begun to assume a separate legal identity ... , viewed as *res nullius*, thus not owned by anyone, but capable of being acquired through certain acts. The emerging distinction between the seabed and the sea surface was generally based on the dissimilar uses of the respective areas: different uses suggested different controlling principles.... It is important to note that, in contrast to the historical seas uses, the seabed, lacking navigational and fishing uses, did not appear to require a distinct regime. This historical fact contradicts any inference that the high seas regime never applied to the seabed. If a separate seabed regime was not considered necessary, there is no reason, per se, to assume that it was, or was not, part of the general high seas regime.

... But with the discovery of desirable and recoverable seabed resources [the seabed's] legal status came into question. Two alternative regimes were proposed as the controlling customary regimes of the seabed. Under the first regime, the seabed was seen as *res nullius*, open to sovereign acquisition by virtue of: a) its resemblance to unclaimed land territory, or alternatively, b) because of the presence of harvestable resources on its surface. According to the second theory, the seabed was *res communis*, and, in the absence of separate identities, the sea and seabed constitute a legal unity....

Proponents of the *res nullius* approach to the seabed have appealed to two supports: a) the analogy of *terra nullius*, and b) historical cases of international recognition of claims to sedentary resources on the seabed. The analogy approach asserts that the seabed is more akin to *terra nullius* than to the high seas and that therefore it can be, and has been, appropriated by a combination of claims and peaceful, continuous, and sufficient exercise of sovereignty. The requisite imposition of seabed sovereignty, according to this view, has traditionally arisen upon the exploitation of sedentary resources, such as oyster beds and sponge fisheries. The problem with the analogy is, simply put, that the nature of land acquisition by appropriation is different in kind from that for the seabed. As Professor Burton has pointed out, the *terra nullius* doctrine was always linked to the internationally recognized obligation of protection of territory and its inhabitants, which could not conceivably

x. This resolution is popularly known as "the Moratorium Resolution."

apply to seabed appropriations.[1] Appropriation of the seabed under some adaption of the *terra nullius* appropriation test would be a misapplication of the doctrine, for it would allow geographically unbound claims over vast areas without any correlative obligations. . . .

The argument based on appropriation of the seabed through sedentary resource exploitation is also defective. Professor Biggs has noted that historically recognized claims to seabed areas on the basis of resource exploitation have only occurred a) where historical usage of the resources was present, and b) where the area claimed was geographically contiguous to the claiming state.[2] * * * Since manganese nodules have never been historically exploited, the seabed itself could not be appropriated in that way. Moreover, this version of the appropriation argument has been rendered nugatory by the 1958 Convention on the Continental Shelf **[Basic Document 5.4]**, which recognized coastal state sovereignty over its adjacent continental shelf on the geographical basis of natural prolongation of the mainland, not use or occupation.

Though some seabed claims appear to have been recognized under customary law on the basis of historic resource exploitation combined with physical contiguity, some scholars reason that the very nature of these claims, with their appeals to history and geographical circumstances, inevitably implies a general norm holding the seabed to be *res communis*. . . . This interpretation of the true legal status of historic resource rights appears quite sound; but whether the seabed itself has therefore customarily been considered *res communis* is somewhat less certain. An underlying problem with the concept of *res communis* is its imprecise content and limited scope. . . . [It] does have some generally undisputed prohibitive content, namely, that "common things" are not subject to unilateral appropriation, and that use of these "things" requires the consent of all. This much follows logically from the seabed *not* being *res nullius*. But the unglossed doctrine of *res communis* does not specify what uses are permissible, in what manner, and by whom. In light of the fact that seabed exploitation was not technologically conceivable until this century, the shortcomings of the doctrine did not historically give rise to legal problems. Yet inasmuch as it was acknowledged as having communal, universalistic associations without substantive, normative content, it stands as a precursor of the "common heritage of mankind" notion proposed by Ambassador Pardo [from Malta] in 1967. Indeed, Professor Burton has argued against the *res communis* doctrine for this reason. It is for him more of a political tool than an international norm, and its requirement of common consent for use served as unfortunate precedent for the [1969] UN Moratorium Resolution **[Basic Document 5.11]** . . . and for the developing world's claim for the moratorium's effect.

However . . . , the theory that the seabed is *res communis* does undoubtedly have some positive precedential weight. The development of the continental shelf doctrine after the Truman Proclamation carried with it the assumption that the deep seabed is a common area, and that claims over it must be justified on some basis. The true substance of the doctrine must be

---

1. *See* S. Burton, *Freedom of the Seas: International Law Applicable to Deep Seabed Mining Claims*, 29 Stan. L. R. 1135, 1165 (1977).

2. G. Biggs, *Deepsea's Adventures: Grotius Revisited*, 9 Int'l Law. 271 (1975).

found in the prohibitions it contains against exclusive exploitation rights and unilateral appropriation. In short, *res communis* seems to be, for reasons of logic, consistency, and history, the most likely customary seabed regime.

B.   *The Customary Status of Seabed Resources*

The fundamental question of the customary status of seabed resources, and especially of mineral nodules, is whether they share the same legal status as the underlying seabed. The generally acknowledged answer to this question is that they probably do not, for following [Hugo] Grotius's arguments on unclaimed ocean resources, they are capable of appropriation by capture.... What can be won through capture becomes property of the captor, and applied to mineral nodules, this inevitably implies that they are subject to a legal regime of *res nullius* separate from the seabed regime of *res communis*. This theory appears to have been historically recognized in a number of precedents involving ocean resources. The earliest precedent occurred in 1872 with the taking of some mineral nodules from the seabed by a British ship, the *H.M.S. Challenger*. However, * * * though it may not have been inherently limited by the *res communis* regime of the sea, the right of capture has always been subject to other freedom of the seas principles. The existence of other uses of the high seas and its resources implied that acts of capture could not inhibit the rights of others to use the oceans freely. For this reason exclusive exploitation claims, even if only prospective, would then be always subject to the overriding *mare liberum* regime. Appropriation of ocean resources, like any other use of the high seas, required a concomitant and reasonable regard for others' rights, and in this way a balance was achieved between resource exploitation and other uses of the oceans.... The only limitation on exploitation was functional, *i.e.*, it could not interfere with the *exercise* of other rights.

... [T]wo further reasons suggest that the general high seas regime can furnish legal support for nodule exploitation. First, no ocean resource has ever been specifically immune from capture, and therefore no derogation of the general right of capture in the case of nodules has been acknowledged. Second, the presence of nodules has been known since 1873. No state has suggested until recently that nodules should be distinguished from other resources of the water column or seabed. Consequently, the lack of technological ability to harvest the nodules does not in itself imply that nodules were not theoretically, or legally, subject to the traditional right of capture in customary law. * * * In the absence of customary, or conventional, rules circumscribing its sovereignty, a state has full sovereign rights within an existing legal regime. If restrictions on sovereignty exist, they must be explicitly assented to. This principle was unequivocally affirmed by the Permanent Court of International Justice in the case of *S.S. Lotus*, where it said " ... restrictions upon the independence of States cannot be presumed."[3]

. . .

* * *

III.   CONVENTIONAL AND OTHER APPROACHES TO THE SEABED: THE 1958 GENEVA CONVENTIONS AND THE UN RESOLUTIONS

A.   *The 1958 Geneva Conventions*

The first UN Conference on the Law of the Sea ... produced four Conventions (High Seas, Continental Shelf, Territorial Shelf, Territorial Sea

---

3. The S.S. Lotus (Fr. v. Turk.), 1927 PCIJ (ser. A) No. 10, at 18.

and Contiguous Zone, and Fisheries) **[Basic Documents 5.3, 5.4, 5.5 & 5.6]**. No explicit seabed regime was proposed or negotiated ..., [but the seabed's] status was present in the thoughts of the International Law Commission (ILC) during their preparations for the Geneva Conference.... In referring to its draft of Article 2 of the High Seas Convention, [the ILC] said in 1955:

> The list of freedoms of the high seas contained in this article is not restrictive; the Commission has merely specified four of the main freedoms. It is aware that there are other freedoms, such as freedom to explore or exploit the subsoil of the high seas....

Again in 1956, the ILC noted this omission:

> The Commission has not made specific mention of the freedom to explore or to exploit the subsoil of the high seas. It considered that apart from the case of the exploitation or exploration of the soil or subsoil of a continental shelf ... such exploitation has not yet assumed sufficient practical importance to justify special regulation.

This attitude, supported by the final results of the Conference, implies that deep seabed exploitation was seen as associated with high seas freedoms....

The presence [in Article 2 of the High Seas Convention] of the term *inter alia* indicates that the enumerated uses are exemplary and not exhaustive. This interpretation is also supported by the reference in the second clause to other exercisable freedoms, provided that these unenumerated freedoms are recognized by general principles of international law. Given the customary existence of seabed resource exploitation, as well as the *Lotus* doctrine of plenary state sovereignty, seabed exploitation was neither prohibited nor singled out for special treatment, and therefore, arguably, was recognized....

Article 2 of the same convention does require that freedoms be exercised with reasonable regard for other states' interests. For example, the freedom of laying submarine cables is affirmed in Article 2(3). If that activity can be done with requisite care, presumably seabed exploitation could as well since it involves a similar degree of seabed intrusion. Indeed, the only mention of seabed exploitation anywhere in the Conventions suggests this interpretation:

> Every State shall draw up regulations to prevent pollution of the seas by the discharge of oil from ships or resulting from the exploitation and exploration of the seabed and its subsoil. (Convention on High Seas, Art. 24).

This reference reinforces the interpretation that seabed exploitation was seen, to some degree, as an activity which could be, and was, accommodated within the joint scope of the Conventions and customary international law. It is worth reiterating, though, that the seabed's status was not squarely confronted....

B. *The UN Resolutions*

The next major events in the evolution of a seabed regime were the Pardo speech of 1967 [calling for the seabed and its resources beyond the limits of national jurisdiction to be considered part of "the common heritage of mankind"]^y and the UN Resolutions on the seabed of 1968–1970 [*i.e.*, GA Res. 2574D (XXIV) of December 15, 1969 **(Basic Document 5.11)]** and the Declaration of Principles of December 17, 1970 **[Basic Document 5.12]** declaring, *inter alia*, the seabed and ocean floor to be part of "the common heritage of mankind"]. . . .

* * *

Regarding the legal quality of the resolutions, supporters of a binding interpretation have raised essentially a two-stage argument. First, they argue that, since the 1958 Geneva Conventions did not recognize seabed exploitation as a high seas freedom, no customary legal regime regarding that activity exists. This assumption, discussed above, effectively reverses the *Lotus* principle in presuming limitation on state sovereignty absent affirmation of a right by a legal norm. Nevertheless, upon this assumption, the UN resolutions are therefore the initial positive enactments in a legal vacuum.

How did they attain the status of legal enactments? This is the second stage of the argument, and it takes two directions. The resolutions are interpreted, on the one hand, as basically legislative enactments of international law. However, . . . the General Assembly was specifically denied power to enact rules of international law at the UN San Francisco Conference in 1945.

The other direction of the argument is that the resolutions constitute newly emerging customary law. According to this, they attained this status through consensual approval by the Assembly and its constituent committees, thus manifesting a balanced and universal character. This process has been validated, for developing countries, by the mutually supportive trends from consent to consensus as a measurement of international approval, and the rise of the quasi-legislative influence of the General Assembly, such that "Expressing, as a resolution does, the *opinio juris communis* of states, the vital element of custom, a unanimously adopted resolution creates, according to some jurists, 'instant' customary international law." * * * [However,] during the votes on the resolutions and subsequently, the United States . . . consistently denied any legal effect to the resolutions. In voting for the Declaration of Principles, the United States and many other states, including the USSR, stated that they understood it to be a set of political recommendations, a general basis for future negotiation. The Principles were not, it was emphatically stated," . . . an interim deep seabed mining regime." This interpretation was shared by some developing countries as well. The commendatory character and broad terminology of the Declaration seem to support this view. * * * [Furthermore,] [t]he *opinio juris* requirement of customary law cannot reasonably be said to exist in the face of consistent exercise of the recognized right of protest by several states. Assertions by the Group of 77 [G–77]^z of the

y. *See supra* Reading A–3, at 1000.

z. The Group of 77 (G–77) is a UN General Assembly intergovernmental caucus that originated in 1963 with the presentation of the Joint Declaration of the Developing Countries [UN GAOR, 18th Sess., Supp. No. 15, at 24, UN Doc. A.5515 (1964)] to the Eighteenth Session of the UN General Assembly. The Declaration, which in fact was signed by 75 developing countries in anticipation of the 1964 Conference on Trade and Development, asserted the interest of developing nations in redressing international economic imbalances between their countries and the more advanced States. Although the G–77 (so named from the fact that 77 countries were included in it as an unofficial regional political unit at the 1964 Conference) has changed its size and

Declaration's legality seem to be based exclusively on the unanimous vote it received. These votes, subsequent events have made clear, were cast with diverse and contending motives and understandings, and to overlook this is to deny the consensual nature of customary law and to eliminate effectively a state's right of protest.

The fundamental opposition among states on the legal status of the resolutions can be seen even more clearly in the interpretive problems the "common heritage" concept has generated. * * * The developing countries' basic construction of the common heritage concept contrasts it with the *res communis* doctrine. Ambassador de Soto has stated: " ... the difference between common heritage and *res communis* is not that common heritage implies everyone owns the area or has equal access to it, but rather that it must be jointly administered and jointly managed.[aa] It is more like *res communis communitatus usus*, where mankind is considered to be a title bearer to an area."[bb] Further, the chairman of the Group of 77 has proclaimed: "It [the common heritage] had to imply the idea of a common administration and therefore, not only the freedom of access and utilization but also the regulation of that exploitation and of equitable sharing of the benefits between the members of the international community." This position is distinctive for its contention that common heritage is a *complex* principle, composed of several associated elements such as:

- inalienable title to the area and its resources,
- implied trustee duties over it for the benefit of present and future humanity,
- internationally exercised exploitation and administration rights, through international machinery,
- equitable distribution of the benefits of the area.

* * *

The United States and the major developed states have taken the view that the common heritage principle is imprecise and in need of negotiated

complexion over the years, it continues to press the economic needs and interests of the developing Third World and, through its Panel of Experts, to prepare draft codes and recommend action for those UN organs and agencies that deal with economic development and related human rights issues.

aa. *Accord* G. Van Hoof, *Legal Status of the Concept of the Common Heritage of Mankind*, 7 Grotiana 49 (1986), at 55:

... [T]he *res communis* theory ... [i]n the case of the seabed ... means that only a handful [of] rather highly industrialized States could benefit ... because they are the only ones to command the technology to engage in deep seabed mining.

It is at this point that the concept of the Common Heritage of Mankind departs from ... the *res communis* theory. The concept of the Common Heritage ... purports to ensure that the benefits flowing from the use

of areas beyond the limits of national jurisdiction and the exploitation of their resources are equitably shared by all States. It is in particular this element of equitable sharing of benefits which makes the Common Heritage concept representative of the new international law of co-operation as opposed to the traditional international law of co-existence.

Van Hoof further observes that the "common heritage" concept implies the creation of "some type of international machinery" to regulate and supervise the areas concerned and the exploitation of their resources. *Id.* at 56. He also notes that "areas beyond the limits of national jurisdiction may be used for peaceful purposes only." *Id.*

bb. A. De Soto, *The Developing Countries and Deep Seabed Mining*, in International Law of the Sea and the Future of Deep Seabed Mining 47 (C. Joyner ed. 1975).

definition.... It has been viewed ... as a limited, fundamental principle, the exact consequences of which, in terms of rights and duties, require explicit agreement. Its immediate effect for these states is to affirm the right of countries to exploit seabed mineral resources, subject to corresponding duties not to interfere with other ocean uses and to share the revenue derived. Unilateral seabed mining legislation ... passed in both the United States and ... Germany [also now in France, Great Britain, Japan, and the nations formerly comprising the Soviet Union, among other countries] incorporates the common heritage concept but within the context of a system of private, licensed exploitation with revenue-sharing obligations[cc] This again shows the amenability of the concept to a plurality of meanings and applications.

5. United Nations Convention on the Law of the Sea. Concluded, 10 Dec 1982. Entered into force, 16 Nov 1994. 1833 U.N.T.S. 3; *reprinted in* **21 I.L.M. 1261 (1982) and 5 & Carlson V.F.22: Arts. 133–43, 150–53** (Basic Document 5.22).

6. Agreement Relating to the Implementation of Part XI of the United Nations Convention on the Law of the Sea of 10 December 1982. Concluded, 28 Jul 1994. Entered into force, 16 Nov 1994 (provisionally) and 28 Jul 1996 (definitively). GA Res 48/263 (Annex), UN GAOR, 48th Sess., Supp. No. 49, at 7, UN Doc. A/RES/48/263 (1994); *reprinted in* **33 I.L.M. 1309 (1994) and 5 Weston & Carlson V.F.30a: Arts. 1, 2 & 7 and Annex (Basic Document 5.40).**

7. Editors' Note. In 1982, as earlier observed,[dd] US President Ronald Reagan declared that the United States would not sign the 1982 CLOS (**Basic Document 5.22**) because of objections to Part XI of the Convention, the then proposed regime for deep seabed mining. Joining the United States in this refusal were Belgium, Italy, Luxembourg, the United Kingdom, and West Germany. Also effectively joining the United States were most of the other industrialized states which, though they signed the Convention, withheld their ratification of it pending some resolution of the deep seabed mining controversy.

In July 1990, when the ending of the Cold War created the conditions needed to re-visit Part XI, UN Secretary–General Javier Perez de Cuellar initiated informal consultations to address the objections of the industrialized states. His successor, Secretary–General Boutros Boutros–Ghali, continued this initiative and saw the consultations to successful conclusion. Aided by an awakened consciousness that the 1982 CLOS would receive sufficient ratifications to enter into force before the end of 1994, he was assisted also by a change of government in Washington. "In particular, the Clinton Administration attempted to resurrect [the 1982 CLOS] by hinting that the advantages for the United States—namely, the preservation of unhindered navigational rights, and the freedom to conduct military activities on the seafloor—outweighed the single disadvantage of relinquishing all unilateral claims to the oceanic mineral wealth. The common ownership claims that had impeded adhesion to [the 1982 CLOS] by the United States in 1982, became irrelevant once the emerging countries began to embrace the principles of democratic

cc. *See, e.g.*, the Deep Seabed Hard Minerals Resources Act, Pub. L. No. 96–283, 94 Stat. 553, passed by the U.S. Congress in 1980. For further details, see Discussion/Note Question 7, at 1095.

dd. *See supra* Reading C–1 (p. 1040).

capitalism." Arcangelo Travaglini, Note, *Reconciling Natural Law and Legal Positivism in the Deep Seabed Mining Provisions of the Convention on the Law of the Sea*, 15 Temp. Int'l & Comp. L. J. 313, 328 (2001). The end result: an amended Part XI in the form of the 1994 Agreement Relating to the Implementation of Part XI of the United Nations Convention on the Law of the Sea of 10 December 1982 **(Basic Document 5.40)**, adopted by the UN General Assembly on 28 July 1994, pursuant to GA Res. 48/263, by a vote of 121–0–7 which, though designed to represent all the differing state interests, nevertheless "substantially accommodates the objections of the United States and other industrial states to the deep seabed mining provisions of the Law of the Sea Convention." Bernard H. Oxman, *The 1994 Agreement and the Convention*, 88 A.J.I.L. 687, 695 (1994). "The Agreement embraces market-oriented policies and eliminates provisions identified as posing significant problems of principle and precedent, such as those dealing with production limitations, mandatory transfer of technology, and the review conference. It increases the influence of the United States and other industrial states in the Sea–Bed Authority, and reflects their longstanding preference for emphasizing interests, not merely numbers, in the structure and voting arrangements of international organizations." *Id.*

The Agreement, according to its Article 2, is to be interpreted and applied together with Part XI of the 1982 CLOS as a single instrument. In the event of inconsistency between the two, the Agreement is to prevail. Opened for signature on the day of its adoption by the General Assembly, it entered into force *provisionally* on 16 November 1994 and *definitively* on 28 July 1996. As of this writing (1 May 2006), 122 states had become party to the Agreement and 79 additional had signed it, most of them provisionally in accordance with Article 7 of the Agreement, the United States included.

8.   Jonathan I. Charney, "Entry into Force of the 1982 Convention on the Law of the Sea," 35 Va. J. Int'l L. 381, 392–400 (1995).

With the conclusion of the [1994 Agreement Relating to the Implementation of Part XI of the United Nations Convention on the Law of the Sea of 10 December 1982 **(Basic Document 5.40)**], the international community . . . put to rest the essentially hypothetical dispute over deep seabed mining and the regime that would oversee this potential activity. The revised regime limits full implementation of the deep seabed regime to the time when the activity is really justified—when deep seabed mining is about to become economically viable under free market principles. . . .

The new Agreement also improves the decision-making processes of the ISA [International Seabed Authority]. The key provisions of the Agreement assign the Legal and Technical Commission (Commission), a professionally staffed organ, responsibility to receive applications from developers to recommend approval by the ISA Council solely on the basis of technical issues. Approval by the ISA Council is deemed to be granted if, after sixty days from submission by the Commission, the Council has not voted to disapprove the Commission's recommendations.

Disapproval must be based upon the affirmative vote of two-thirds of the Council members, and in no chamber may a majority be opposed. The Council is composed of four chambers of special interest groups, each of which is composed by the states that are qualified to serve in those chambers They are:

(1) states that have invested in deep seabed mining; (2) states that are consumers of the categories of minerals to be derived from the deep seabed; (3) states that are land-based producers of minerals expected to be derived from the deep seabed; and (4) states representing developing countries selected on the basis of special interests and geographical distribution. In addition, the United States is assured a seat on the Council while it applies to the deep seabed regime provisionally and afterwards if it becomes a party to the LOS Convention **[Basic Document 5.22]** and the Agreement. Other states that are not developing countries may be elected to the Council also in order to assure equitable geographical distribution, but these states would not be included in any of the four chambers. Other important, substantive issues require the same voting majority. The composition of the ISA Council and its voting structure were designed to make certain that decisions to disapprove development after objectively defined financial, technical and environmental requirements are met will be based on an international consensus of diverse states. . . .

If deep seabed mining does become an economic reality, it will be a market-based system under the revised deep seabed regime. The system will provide for the phase-in of regulations necessary for deep seabed mineral resource development. The regime balances the multiple and diverse interests at stake, including those of industry, the environment, consumer states, land-based producer states, developed states and developing states. . . . Thus, the Agreement provides for necessary regulations to efficiently conduct activities in the area, taking into account the wide variety of interests that may be present when deep seabed mining becomes economically viable, if ever. . . .

* * *

The new Agreement touches on some interesting international law issues. First, the Agreement raises the question of whether states can become bound to changes to a treaty that they have ratified, even though the treaty makes no provision for the instant modification procedure. The UNGA Resolution [pursuant to which the UN General Assembly adopted the Agreement] purports to make all subsequent ratifications and accessions of the LOS Convention subject to changes contained in the new Agreement. The Agreement provides for states that previously ratified the LOS Convention and signed the Agreement to be bound by the Agreement if they fail to give notice to the contrary within twelve months of its entry into force. Unless a state indicates a contrary intention, the Agreement may apply provisionally pursuant to a state's signature of the Agreement, its vote in favor of the UNGA Resolution, its accession to the Agreement or its written notification to the depository of the Agreement.

Some may argue that states cannot be bound to modifications of the LOS Convention by these means, even though individual states have notice of the breadth of the consent to be implied and the right to opt out of the new Agreement. I would disagree. International law permits states to be bound to international obligations by a variety of methods. The traditional doctrine of customary international law allows uniform state practice and *opinio juris* to lead to new obligations under international law without the consent of any particular state, so long as the international community in general supports the new law. Non-acting states are deemed to have acquiesced to the new law and are bound by it regardless of their real intentions, if not expressed. In the instant case, actual notice to states of the new agreement, participation through signature or voting and express procedures for opting out are more powerful indications of consent than those required for the creation of general customary international law. Furthermore, customary international law permits implied consent even to treaty reservations. That rule is also more liberal than the approach taken for the new Agreement; in the case of reservations, states can be bound by their actual consent, but also by their implied consent or acquiescence after the passage of twelve months from deposit of the reservation. Finally, some argue that actual consent of states lies at the foundation of international legal obligations.... [T]his proposition itself is open to serious question.

A second issue presented is whether, by accepting the LOS Convention and the new Agreement, states will surrender an existing freedom to mine the deep seabed unilaterally. This view is simply incorrect. The law for the deep seabed has never been settled; this ambiguity was especially present following the UNGA resolutions that formed the basis for the LOS Conference negotiations that produced the LOS Convention. Even the domestic legislation of the United States on deep seabed mining accepts the deep seabed as the "common heritage of mankind." The fact that this domestic legislation is interim— pending an international regime for deep seabed mining—acknowledges the ambiguous state of the law, if not the rights and interests of the international community. The domestic laws of other states on deep seabed mining are similar in this regard. All of the potential deep seabed mining states are committed to become parties to the LOS Convention with the revised deep seabed regime of the Agreement. Furthermore, in addition to the lack of economic viability of deep seabed mining at present, it is inconceivable that the necessary financial markets would support unilateral deep seabed mining if it is contrary to development under the LOS Convention. Deep seabed mining is simply too vulnerable to proceed even unilaterally under controversial circumstances.

Another legal question that may arise from the new Agreement is whether a state that signed or ratified the LOS Convention prior to the conclusion of the Agreement would violate its obligation not to defeat the "object and purposes" of the LOS Convention by participating in the Agreement. This obligation is found in the Vienna Convention on the Law of Treaties **[Basic Document 1.10]** and is considered to be general international law. Although the Agreement does change the deep seabed mining regime of the LOS Convention by a method not provided in the Convention, I believe that these changes do not violate the above obligation. First, it is not clear how one identifies the "object and purpose" of international agreements. States do have a general obligation not to defeat the ultimate entry into force of an international agreement and the execution of its purposes, but the obligation does not extend to the specific articles if they are not fundamental. Prior to the conclusion of the new Agreement, the LOS Convention was about to enter into force, but all the states able to lead the effort to conduct deep seabed mining refused to participate. Part XI seemed doomed to fail, and to take with it the entire LOS Convention as a near universal international agreement. The new Agreement makes it possible for an international deep seabed regime and the entire LOS Convention to enter into force with widespread participation, especially by those states that are the potential sponsors of deep seabed mining. Furthermore, the changes made by the Agreement to Part XI are technical and do not go to the likely object and purpose of the Convention as a whole, much less to that of Part XI. The object and purpose of the LOS Convention, if it may be divined, is to provide a comprehensive legal regime for the oceans accepted by widespread participation. The new Agreement facilitates this objective. The object and purpose of Part XI was to put in place an international regime for deep seabed mining and perhaps to give substance to the rather empty phrase "common heritage of mankind." The Agreement seeks to accomplish this goal and to attract widespread participation in order to make this regime truly effective if deep seabed mining becomes an economic reality. Thus, signatories to the LOS Convention are unquestionably promoting, not undermining, the object and purposes of the Convention by adhering to the Agreement.

9. Regulations on Prospecting and Exploration for Polymetallic Nodules in the Area, ISBA Doc. 6/A/18 (2000), adopted by the Council of the International Seabed Authority, 13 Jul 2000; *reprinted in* **5 Weston & Carlson V.F.30d:**[ee] **Preamble and Regs. 1, 2, & 31(1) & (2)** (Basic Document 5.53).

10. Rio Declaration on Environment and Development. Adopted by the UN Conference on Environment and Development (UNCED) at Rio de Janeiro, 13 Jun 1992, UN Doc. A/CONF.151/26 (vol. I) (1992); *reprinted in* **31 I.L.M. 874 (1992) and 5 Weston & Carlson V.B.16: Principle 15** (Basic Document 5.37).

D. MARINE POLLUTION

1. Editors' Note. "Sea pollution by oil," write David M. Dzidzornu and B. Martin Tsamenyi in *Enhancing International Control of Vessel–Source Oil Pollution Under the Law of the Sea Convention, 1982: A Reassessment*, 10 U. Tasmania L. Rev. 269, 269 (1991), "is a major phenomenon capable of making our seas virtually biological deserts." This is so, the authors observe, because "the ability of the oceans to tolerate continued pollution is not interminably elastic. The real danger is that whilst there may seem to be an ebb and flow to their ability to neutralise pollutants, persistent fouling by oil and other substances disposes the oceans to reach a point of sudden biological collapse." *Id*. The oil flow into the marine environment resulting from the Kharg Island oil spill in the Persian Gulf in 1982, for example, nearly continuous ever since, has caused an entire fishing industry to be destroyed, complete populations of some fish species to become extinct, and desalination plants to become inoperative. It is not yet known if or when the Persian Gulf waters will return to normal.

According to oceanographic research from the Space Shuttle, the amount of petroleum products ending up in the ocean is estimated at 25 percent of

ee. It bears noting that these Regulations are limited to the prospecting and exploration of polymetallic nodules. They do not apply to the full commercial mining of nodules, nor to the exploration or exploitation of deep-sea "vent chimneys" ("smokestacks" that are formed atop bio-organically and mineral-rich seafloor geysers from dissolved metals that precipitate out when the super-hot vent water meets the surrounding deep ocean water that typically is but a few degrees above freezing).

world oil production (about six million tons per year), with the greatest volume being carried there by rivers, triple the quantity coming from all tankers and other ships. *See* the NASA website at <http://disc.gsfc.nasa.gov/oceancolor/shuttle_oceanography_web/oss_122.shtml>. Industrial enterprises, including oil refineries and oil storage installations, regularly discharge oil and other petroleum products into the ocean via rivers as well as into the oceans directly. Gasoline stations alone dump petroleum products into the marine environment in an amount that twice exceeds that resulting from ship disasters. *Id.*

Nevertheless, vessel-source oil pollution is an important and ubiquitous contributor to marine pollution.... According to A.S. Monin and V. P. Krasitskiy, Ocean Surface Phenomena (1985), oceanic pollution is commonly caused when seagoing tankers, which carry 60 percent of all oil extracted, flush their tanks with sea water and when, though in smaller amount, passenger ships and freighters drain water ballast from their fuel tanks.

Of course, the ultimate effects that oil and other petroleum-based products have on the marine environment depend on a number of variables, including the quantity and type of oil discharged, the nature of the marine environment into which it is introduced, and its reaction to the pollution. Still, the risks associated with oil pollution are greatest in and near coastal zones where most maritime activity takes place. Writes Sally A. Meese, *When Jurisdictional Interests Collide: International, Domestic, and State Efforts to Prevent Vessel–Source Oil Pollution*, 12 Ocean Dev. & Int'l L. 79–80 (1982):

> ... [A] more rapid evaporation and breakdown of toxic compounds occur with higher temperatures. A spill in the Arctic or sub-Arctic would persist much longer than one in a tropical region. Spills become more dangerous as they progress from the open ocean through near-shore, and into the enclosed estuaries and rivers. In the open ocean, the increased turbulence by waves and the vastness of space allow a large proportion of the oil to degrade or disperse before any harm can be done. The open sea is relatively immune to inputs of oil, especially in diffuse concentrations (as allowed presently by ballasting and tank cleaning operations). Closer, to the coast, esthetics also begin to play a role, and spills may curtail tourism in some areas.... Beaches and rocky coastlines can be smothered under a layer of persistent oils. Waterways, estuaries, and rivers are even more susceptible to damage because they are enclosed, and because they have a high productivity. They are often the site for intense fishing of invertebrates for human consumption.

Thus, oil that is discharged into the marine environment tends not only to do damage to kelp, fisheries, marine mammals, and birds directly, it also disrupts the food chain by poisoning the algae, plankton, and other intertidal organisms upon which these creatures—and ultimately human beings—depend. The repercussions are felt throughout the entire ecosystem. Moreover, "scientists have theorized that organisms which are not killed immediately may absorb oil and introduce the toxins into the food chain at other stages and produce long-term sub-lethal genetic effects." Meese, *supra*, at 78.

Until recently, however, legal rules governing vessel-source pollution have favored the freedom of the seas without impediment or interference. As observed by Dzidzornu and Tsamenyi, *supra* at 272, "[s]ince Hugo Grotius' concept of *mare liberum* won the day in the debate over the juridical nature of the sea, the only restraint on national conduct in the maritime realm has been the concept of *abuse of rights* which seeks to ensure that States use the seas reasonably in due consideration of the interests and rights of other users. Thus, when ... the Geneva Conference 1958 sought to codify the Law of the Sea, jurisdiction over pollution control by States was barely recognized."

Illustrative is the 1958 Convention on the High Seas **(Basic Document 5.3)**. It guarantees freedom of navigation to every state party and the right of each to bestow its nationality to ships properly registered under its laws. It gives each state party exclusive jurisdiction over the construction, design, equipment and manning (so-called CDEM standards) of its flag vessels. It leaves to each sole discretion to ensure that these standards "conform to generally accepted international standards"[ff] and that they are observed by its flag vessels. And it leaves also to each the obligation not to prevent oil pollution *per se* but to "*draw up regulations* to prevent pollution of the seas by the discharge of oil from ships or pipelines" (emphasis added). As a corollary, only the flag state is given authority to institute legal and disciplinary procedures against its vessels in the event of a collision or other incident.

It is in part because of this essentially unbridled freedom-of-the-seas orientation, along with an incipient awareness of the world's growing economic and ecological interdependence, that the Intergovernmental Maritime Consultative Organization, now known as the International Maritime Organization (IMO), was born. As summarized in Article 1(a) of its constitutive convention (298 UNTS 48), concluded on 6 March 1948 and entered into force on 17 March 1958, the organization's purposes are "to provide machinery for cooperation among Governments in the field of governmental regulation and practices relating to technical matters of all kinds affecting shipping engaged in international trade; to encourage and facilitate the general adoption of the highest practicable standards in matters concerning maritime safety, efficiency of navigation *and prevention and control of marine pollution from ships*" (emphasis added). Established six weeks prior to the conclusion of the 1958 Convention on the High Seas and its companion Convention on the Continental Shelf **(Basic Document 5.4)**, Convention on the Territorial Sea and Contiguous Zone **(Basic Document 5.5)**, and Convention on Fishing and Conservation of the Living Resources of the High Seas **(Basic Document 5.6)**, it was to the IMO that the international community—ergo these 1958 law of the sea conventions—deferred to develop the applicable rules and jurisdictions for the prevention of vessel-source oil pollution. Though it was not until 1975 that the IMO Convention was amended to give it the authority to lay down anti-pollution measures, the technical rules (CDEM standards) it has laid down in its conventions, beginning in 1954, have been aimed at preventing, minimizing and, to the extent possible, eliminating marine pollution from vessel oil.

The IMO's first task was to adopt a new version of the International Convention for the Safety of Life at Sea (SOLAS) (1184 UNTS 2, 1185 UNTS 2), the most important of all treaties dealing with maritime safety. Yet, while safety at sea remains the IMO's most important responsibility, vessel-source oil pollution soon began to capture much of the IMO's attention. The growth

---

ff. Also known as "GAIRAS" (generally accepted international rules and standards).

in the size of oil tankers and the amount of oil being transported by sea was of particular concern, and the *Torrey Canyon* supertanker disaster of March 1967, in which 120,000 tons (or 31,000,000 gallons) of oil were spilled between the Scilly Isles and Land's End, England, demonstrated the scope of the problem. The spilled oil spread across the sea between England and France, killing most of the marine life it touched along the entire southern coast of England and the Normandy shores of France. It was not long thereafter, in 1969, that the IMO's Convention relating to Intervention on the High Seas in Case of Oil Pollution Casualties **(Basic Document 5.10)** was concluded.

During the next few years, the IMO introduced a series of measures designed to prevent tanker accidents and to minimize their consequences. It also tackled the environmental threat caused by routine operations such as the cleaning of oil cargo tanks and the disposal of engine room wastes—in tonnage terms a bigger menace than accidental pollution. Among the first of these measures was the IMO's 1954 Convention for Prevention of Pollution of the Sea by Oil (OILPOL 54) **(Basic Document 5.1)**, several times amended. But the most important, and superseding the 1954 Convention, was the IMO's 1973 International Convention for the Prevention of Pollution from Ships **(Basic Document 5.16)** as modified by its 1978 Protocol **(Basic Document 5.18)**. Jointly known as "MARPOL 73/78," these instruments cover not only accidental and operational oil pollution but also pollution by chemicals, goods in packaged form, sewage, garbage, and air pollution.

At about the same time, the IMO was given the additional task of establishing a system for providing compensation to those who suffer financially from pollution. Two treaties were adopted, in 1969, and 1971, which enabled victims of oil pollution to obtain compensation more easily and quickly than previously. Both treaties were amended in 1992, and again in 2000, to increase the limits of compensation payable to victims of pollution.

But it was the period 1973–82, during which the Third UN Conference on the Law of the Sea was deliberating the 1982 CLOS **(Basic Document 5.22)**, that, in the words of the Senior Deputy Director of the IMO's Legal Affairs and External Relations Division, was "the most prolific in the history of the IMO. The most important IMO treaties . . . were [then] adopted while, at the same time, the Third Conference was finally developing a comprehensive convention which would provide an appropriate jurisdictional framework for the enforcement of IMO treaties." Agustín Blanco–Bazán, *IMO Interface with the Law of the Sea Convention*, <http://www.imo.org/InfoResource/main-frame.asp?topic_id=406&doc_id=1077>.

2. Convention on the High Seas. Concluded, 29 Apr 1958. Entered into force, 30 Sep 1962. 450 U.N.T.S. 82; *reprinted in* **5 Weston & Carlson V.F.3: Arts. 1, 6, 9–11, 10, 24, 217** (Basic Document 5.3).

3. Convention on the Territorial Sea and the Contiguous Zone. Concluded, 29 Apr 1958. Entered into force, 30 Sep 1962. 516 U.N.T.S. 205; *reprinted in* **5 Weston & Carlson V.F.5: Arts. 1, 3, 5, 10, 14–17, 19, 24** (Basic Document 5.5).

4. Convention on Fishing and Conservation of the Living Resources of the High Seas. Concluded, 29 Apr 1958. Entered into force, 30 Sep 1962. 559 U.N.T.S. 285; *reprinted in* **5 Weston & Carlson V.F.6: Arts. 1, 2, 6, 7, 9** (Basic Document 5.6).

5. **Convention on the Prevention of Marine Pollution by Dumping Wastes and Other Matter. Concluded, 29 Dec 1972. Entered into force, 30 August 1975. 1046 U.N.T.S. 120;** *reprinted in* **11 I.L.M. 1294 (1972) and 5 Weston & Carlson V.F.14: Art. 1–4, 7, 12, Annexes I & II** (Basic Document 5.15).

6. **International Convention for the Prevention of Pollution from Ships (with annex) (MARPOL 73). Concluded, 2 Nov 1973. Entered into force, 2 Oct 1983. I.M.C.O. Doc. MP/CONF/WP.35 (1973);** *reprinted in* **12 I.L.M. 1319 (1973) and 5 Weston & Carlson V.F.15: Pmbl. (¶¶ 1, 2, 4) & Arts. 1–4, 6–12, & Annex Regs. 1, 2, 9, 11** (Basic Document 5.16).

7. **Protocol of 1978 Relating to the 1973 International Convention for the Prevention of Pollution from Ships (with annex) (MARPOL 78). Concluded 17 Feb 1978. Entered into force, 2 Oct 1983. I.M.C.O. Doc. TSPP/CONF/11 (1978);** *reprinted in* **17 I.L.M. 546 (1978) and 5 Weston & Carlson V.F.20: Arts. 1–3 & Annex Regs. 1, 2, 9, 11** (Basic Document 5.18).

8. **Chen–Pang Wang, "A Review of the Enforcement Regime for Vessel–Source Oil Pollution Control," 16 Ocean Dev. & Int'l L. 305, 315–20 (1986).**

[*Eds.*—The international law concerning vessel-source oil pollution control, the author observes, "has been complicated by jurisdictional issues, technology immaturity, and the passive attitude of the maritime states." Nevertheless, he says, "we have developed a relatively recognizable international law regime for vessel-source oil pollution control," referring in particular to "the MARPOL Convention" (*i.e.*, MARPOL 73/78) **(Basic Documents 5.16 & 5.18)** which superseded the amended 1954 International Convention for the Prevention of Pollution of the Sea by Oil **(Basic Document 5.1)**, also known as "the 1954 OILPOL Convention," as well as earlier oil-pollution control conventions (or "OILPOLs") developed by the IMO. He cautions, however, that " 'supersede' does not necessarily mean 'terminate' "—which is to say "that contracting states of the OILPOLs who do not sign and ratify the MARPOL Convention would still be bound by the standards in the OILPOLs to regulate culprit vessels." He then proceeds to consider the vessel-source pollution control scheme (a "mutual enforcement scheme") constituted in the MARPOL Convention (MARPOL 73/78).]

Flag State Jurisdiction to be Enforced Under the 1973 MARPOL Convention with 1978 Protocol

The MARPOL Convention still relies on the states to enforce the rules and standards, just like the 1954 OILPOL Convention, as amended in 1962 and 1969.

A. Discharge Standard Violations

The enforcement of OILPOL [conventions] relies on the conscience of the crews to write down all their violations into the Oil Record Book. The flag state can then use this self-incrimination to apprehend the ship. The MARPOL continues the flag state scheme and the Oil Record Book requirement, but gives some "improvement" in requiring ships to install automatic monitoring devices in order to have an "objective" oil discharge record. But the problem is that reliable monitoring devices have not yet been successfully developed. This has created an unenforceable requirement similar to the OILPOL's 100 ppm discharge-limitation standard which has been perceived as unenforceable beyond the port water due to technological limitations.

Although ... reliable monitoring devices have not become technologically feasible, the validity of the Oil Record Book can be checked.... [I]t is now possible to detect the creditability of the Oil Record Book by physically inspecting the tankers.... However, the tasks of combining the use of the Oil Record Book with physical inspection to detect violations ... was largely left to the flag states. Port-state authority has been limited by the MARPOL which does not give the port authority jurisdiction to inspect the Oil Record Book of a foreign ship on the port's own initiative. The inspection of the Oil Record Book can be allowed only after the port authority has received a request concerning an alleged violation that could be backed by "sufficient evidence".... The MARPOL Convention has made no attempt to increase the port authority's incentive. * * * [Moreover, if] a ship captain expects his ship to be examined in the next port of call, he would presumably be careful not to conduct an illegal discharge....

* * *

B. Construction, Design, Equipment, and Manning (CDEM) Standards Violations

The MARPOL Convention has also strengthened the flag states' obligation to control tankers' CDEM standards by requiring the flag states to issue certificates to guarantee flag ships' conditions. The port authority's competence to question the validity of the certificate has been limited, and the port state has to carry the burden of proving that there are "clear grounds" to justify inspection of the ship. Obviously the certificate approach is based on the assumption that states seek to avoid losing face by being accused of issuing false certificates. Since the flag states are bound to issue certificates, the only alternative left for them is to inspect the ships carefully before any certificates have been issued.

* * *

Coastal State Competence to Enforce

In the MARPOL negotiations the jurisdictional issues aroused "the most discordant debate of the month-long gathering." The central issue was "the concern over the content of the coastal jurisdiction which was compounded by another basic disagreement as to the proper geographical extent of coastal jurisdiction." Although the delegates to the MARPOL negotiation had sensed the traditional division of legal authority between a narrow territorial sea and the high seas as "dangerously anachronistic," the final decision was to leave this issue and the jurisdictional issue to the [1982] UN Convention to determine. In the text of the MARPOL Convention, this attitude is evidenced by the words of Article 9(3): "The term 'jurisdiction' ... shall be construed in the light of international law in force at the time of application or interpretation of this Convention."

The attempt to establish a port state jurisdiction regime in MARPOL in addition to the coastal state regime was defeated. The port competence to question foreign vessels' CDEM or discharge violation in either the national zones or the port of that state or anywhere else was treated as part of coastal power. The reasons for the defeat are:

(a) The [IMO]'s traditional conservative attitude to keep the Convention from "wandering too close to the boundaries set for it by the prevailing laws of the sea." I believe it includes the flag state/coastal state dichotomy which was still prevailing in 1973.

(b) The power of the concern about foreign interference with shipping and the fear of uncontrollable costs caused by discretionary detention in foreign ports.

(c) All delegates were unwilling to concede any bargaining chips on an issue which might later be offered as part of a package deal at the UNCLOS III negotiation. . . .

* * *

Assessment of the MARPOL Convention

According to what we have discussed, we could say that the significance of the MARPOL Convention is not in allocating the enforcement jurisdiction, but in serving as a "technical convention" to consolidate the CDEM and the discharge standards of the OILPOL Conventions. In terms of the discharge standards, MARPOL has incorporated some easier-to-enforce approaches of OILPOL. The "prohibited zone approach" prohibited any discharge from various tonnages of tankers and other types of vessels within a certain distance from the nearest land. The "clear ballast approach" allows the coastal state to apprehend a vessel whenever visible traces of oil are observed on or below the surface of the water in the immediate vicinity of a ship or its wake, by taking any other possible sources of the traces into consideration. But MARPOL has also contained some standards which are more difficult, if not impossible, to enforce, especially for less affluent developing coastal states. One example is that a tanker should not discharge more than 60 liters of oil per nautical mile.

* * *

The MARPOL Convention has put heavy pressure upon the flag states to assume a supervisory role over their flag ships' CDEM standards, by requiring them to conduct annual mandatory inspections. But there is no requirement for flag states to inspect their vessels for discharge violations.

The coastal states have the potential power to inspect foreign vessels in their ports. But for vessels which are in the waters out of the port-water, the MARPOL Convention only gave an ambiguous description about the competence of the coastal states in Article 4(2). Therefore, the coastal states' competence to inspect ships in out-of-port waters has not been confirmed by the MARPOL Convention.

* * *

My last comment about the MARPOL Convention is how it has contributed to protect vessels from wanton port apprehensions. Under Article 10(2) of the 1954 OILPOL Convention, as amended in 1962, the coastal state has the right to determine whether it will inform the flag state that one of its ships has violated an applicable law. Article 6(2–3) and Article 8(3) of the MARPOL Convention have changed the right of the coastal state into an obligation of the port state to report the violation to the flag state (the administration). It is hoped that this arrangement will give the vessels more sense of security. If the ship is unduly detained or delayed, it is entitled to compensation for any loss or damage suffered.

9. **Editors' Note**. As noted above, the most important of the IMO oil-pollution control treaties, MARPOL 73 and 78 **(Basic Documents 5.16 & 5.18)**, were initiated by the IMO at the same time as UNCLOS III was deliberating the 1982 CLOS **(Basic Document 5.22)**,[gg] a milestone in the annals of international law that is best understood in at least three ways: "first, as a source of balance between the ever-competing interests of coastal and maritime nations; second, as a means of preserving vital national interests ...; and third, as a basis for persuading others to ... 'roll back' excessive claims." William L. Schachte, Jr., *The Value of the 1982 UN Convention on the Law of the Sea: Preserving Our Freedoms and Protecting the Environment*, 23 Ocean Dev. & Int'l L. 55, 59 (1992). Schachte continues: "The impact of the Convention lies in the fact that it is a comprehensive restatement of customary international law of the sea. The Convention's value, therefore, is its unprecedented scope of codification and its role in shaping the behavior of nations. This is ... no less important when dealing with environmental issues than with any other problem associated with ocean law and policy." *Id*. Thus, when assessing the juridical role of MARPOL 73/78 and other IMO oil-pollution control treaties in the context of the present problem, it is useful to bear in mind the words of the Senior Deputy Director of the IMO's Legal Affairs and External Relations Division:

> The interaction between treaty making activities at the Third Conference and those at IMO is reflected not only in continuous consultations to avoid overlapping but also in temporary clauses included in IMO treaties indicating that these treaties should not be interpreted as prejudicing the codification and development of the law of the sea being undertaken by UNCLOS III. Another proviso establishes the basis for the avoidance of jurisdictional conflicts between the law of the sea and IMO rules and standards. It stipulates that nothing in these treaties shall prejudice present or future claims and legal views of any State concerning the law of the sea and the nature and extent of coastal and flag state jurisdiction.

Agustín Blanco–Bazán, *IMO Interface with the Law of the Sea Convention*, <http://www.imo.org/InfoResource/mainframe.asp?topic_id=406&doc_id=1077>.

10. **United Nations Convention on the Law of the Sea. Concluded, 10 Dec 1982. Entered into force, 16 Nov 1994. 1833 U.N.T.S 3; *reprinted in* 21 I.L.M. 1261 (1982) and 5 Weston & Carlson V.F.22: Arts. 1–5, 8, 17–22, 24, 25, 27–28, 33, 87–88, 94, 96–98, 121, 192, 194–95, 197–99, 210–11, 216–21, 233** (Basic Document 5.22).

11. **Chen–Pang Wang, "A Review of the Enforcement Regime for Vessel–Source Oil Pollution Control," 16 Ocean Dev. & Int'l L. 305, 321–30 (1986).**

[Eds.—Noting that the activities of the [IMO] and the UN Law of the Sea Conference have overlapped "in the areas of standards setting and enforce-

---

gg. *See supra* Reading D–1 (p. 1051).

ment jurisdiction, but not on technical shipping regulations," the author argues that "to have a complete picture about what international conventions have done in the realm of vessel-source oil pollution control, we should look not only at the [IMO] Conventions but also at the [1982] Convention" **(Basic Document 5.22)**. These two instruments, he observes, "supplement each other."]

Coastal State Enforcement Jurisdiction

At issue is the violation by foreign vessels of the applicable rules and standards of the territorial sea and the international CDEM rules and standards and conforming national CDEM laws and regulations.

The relevant provisions are Article 220.2, Article 21.2, Article 24.1(a), and the Section 7 safeguard provisions of Part XII [of the 1982 UN Convention on the Law of the Sea **(Basic Document 5.22)**]. However, these provisions have certain ambiguities, and the interpretation of the regime could be manipulated by the flag state to emasculate the coastal state's competence to enforce under certain conditions.

According to Article 220.2, the existence of "clear grounds" and "where the evidence so warrants" are the premises for allowing the coastal states to exercise enforcement measures. The crucial point is to determine "clear grounds" for allowing the coastal states to enforce CDEM standards ... [and] the probability is the coastal state will only have prima facie evidence or questionably "clear grounds" to justify police action. Perhaps the only way to have *adequate* evidence constituting "clear grounds" for CDEM violations is through physical inspection, which can be made only if clear grounds have already been established. One need not, or should not, take the extreme argument that only evidence gathered by physical inspection can be deemed "clear grounds." Such extremes could defeat the legislative purpose of Article 220.2. However, the possibility of interpreting the "clear grounds" provision narrowly could offer the foreign vessels the means to resist the coastal states' attempt to inspect CDEM violations, and thereby reduce, if not defeat, the enthusiasm of the bureaucrats of the coastal state to question the ships' CDEM violations.

Even if one could bypass the labyrinth of the "clear grounds" argument, the innocent passage regime would constitute [a] second line of defense for ships against the coastal states. The coastal states have ... the burden of proving that their policing operations ... [do not violate] the international law of innocent passage. Of course, how heavy the burden is depends on how one defines the term "innocent passage".... Nevertheless, the burden [offers] more ammunition for ships resisting the coastal state's enforcement measures.

* * *

Yet another issue deals with violated international discharge rules and standards and national laws and regulations conforming to the international discharge rules and standards. The relevant provisions are Article 220.2, Article 221.4, Article 24.1(a), and Section 7 Safeguard Provisions of Part XII. Here, the basic requirement of "clear grounds" and "where the evidence so warrants" for a coastal state to conduct physical inspection is a lesser controversy because the oil discharge is easier to detect beyond the hull of the vessels than are the CDEM violations.

The major issue here is how the coastal state can exercise its inspection in opposition to the ship's innocent passage right. Can the ship be stopped for the inspection? The answer to the question depends on the understanding of the innocent passage regime. . . . In traditional international law, the coastal state could adopt appropriate enforcement measures against a vessel exercising the right of innocent passage as long as the measures were considered not to have "hampered" innocent passage. The term "hamper" is a matter of degree, which could be interpreted as having exceeded the restraints of customary international law such as the principles of proportionality and reasonableness. Perhaps detaining a ship might be considered "excessive" and therefore an infringement of the ship's right of innocent passage, but a few minutes' or a few hours' delay might not be excessive so long as there were "clear grounds" to justify the delay. The practice of requiring a ship to stop has not been prohibited per se.

If the coastal state intends to apprehend a passing vessel, however, that state must have a lawful reason for doing so. In terms of oil discharge, pursuant to Article 19.2(h) of the UN Convention, the criterion is that the discharge has been both "willful and serious." However, without stopping the ship for interrogation and inspection, how can the coastal state obtain the evidence of "willful" violation, necessary to negate the right of innocent passage? . . .

For the violation of national discharge laws and standards the relevant provisions are Article 220.2, Article 211.4, Article 19.2(h), Article 24.1(a), and Section 7 Safeguard provisions of Part XII. The coastal state is entitled to establish national laws and regulations exceeding the degree set by international rules and standards in its territorial sea. However, the national prescription should not "hamper" the right of innocent passage. According to the innocent passage criteria stated in Article 19.2(h) of the UN Convention, the state must be able to prove that the discharge is both willful and serious if the coastal state wants to negate the innocent passage right of the ship. . . . After comparing the difference between the UN Convention and earlier conventions, it seems clear that the UN Convention has sought to lessen coastal state authority to regulate passage in its territorial sea.

When foreign vessels violate applicable law in the Exclusive Economic Zone, or violate international CDEM standards and national laws conforming to the international standards, the relevant provisions are Article 220.3, and Section 7 Safeguard provisions of Part XII. The "clear grounds" argument still has its application here even though it is difficult to establish CDEM violations. What has further complicated the difficulty here is that the coastal state can only "require the vessel to give information," regarding the ship's identity, port of registry, last and next port of call, and other relevant information required to establish whether a violation has occurred.

The coastal states' enforcement practice in territorial sea also rely on the documents as a matter of principle. According to Article 226 of the UN Convention the coastal state could "physically inspect" the documents in the territorial sea, and if the state felt that documentary inspection is not sufficient, further physical inspection could be undertaken. However, if the ship is in the EEZ, the coastal state could only "inquire information." The question is how would that information be secured? Could the coastal state "physically inspect" the documents in order to have the information, or could the coastal state get what it wants only by radio or visual signals? . . .

Traditional international law has made it clear that freedom of navigation in the high seas is not an absolute right. . . . In balancing the free navigation rights against coastal states' preservation interests, customary international law leads us to the principle[s] of reasonableness, proportionality, and necessity. Provided that the intended coastal state enforcement action could be justified as a necessary matter and the enforcement measures as reasonable and proportionate, the coastal states' competence to apprehend ships in the EEZ has not been prohibited by customary international law. Enforcement measures that involve "physical inspection," however, may give the benefit of the doubt to the vessel. Comparing Article 220.2 and Article 220.3 of the UN Convention, we find the term "physical inspection" deliberately omitted from the latter Article. The participants in the UNCLOS III negotiation understood that the coastal states should have lesser competence in their EEZ than in their territorial seas to apprehend foreign ships. . . .

* * *

In sum, innocent passage serves as the minimum standard for navigation rights for vessels in coastal states' national zones. As far as a CDEM violation in the special area is concerned, coastal state enforcement action should be under the restrictions which that state would face in enforcement against CDEM violations in her own territorial sea. . . .

* * *

For violations of international discharge rules and standards, the relevant provisions are Article 220.3, Article 220.5, Article 220.6, Article 226.1, and Section 7 Safeguard provisions of Part XII. If a foreign vessel has only slightly violated international discharge standards, the coastal state could only resort to Article 220.3 to inspect the certificates, records, or other documents that the ship is required to carry. If the discharge is . . . "substantial" and has caused or is threatening to cause significant pollution . . . , the coastal state could conduct further inspection under Article 226.1. Slight discharge and substantial discharge have not been defined by either the UN Convention or the [IMO] Convention. The dividing line is left to the discretion of the coastal state.

If the oil discharge has caused or is threatening to cause major damage to the coastal area or related interests of the coastal state, or to any resources of its territorial sea or EEZ, according to Article 220.6, the coastal state can detain the ship. The dividing line between "major damage" to the interests of the coastal state and "substantial discharge" in Article 226.1 is ambiguous and so is the dividing line between substantial discharge that is "threatening to cause major damage." The ambiguities are significant because they have blurred the enforcement jurisdiction of the coastal state. These ambiguities provide the coastal state with the opportunity to adopt rigid application in actual practice, and thereby through subjective discretion allow it to wield its enforcement powers in an arbitrary manner. These ambiguities might be clarified with the developments in practice and through third-party dispute settlement procedures.

For the violation of national discharge laws and regulations the relevant provisions are Article 211.5, Article 211.6, Article 220.8, and Section 7 Safeguard provisions of Part XII. The coastal state can only prescribe laws and regulations conforming to the international regulations and standards unless the coastal state has been allowed to establish an Article 211.6 special area in its EEZ [to regulate the right of free navigation]. However, the power to establish a special area might not be as significant as it appears.... In the high seas area the flag states and the port states enforce discharge rules and standards. The coastal state has only the competence to take measures to avoid pollution arising from maritime casualties. The relevant provisions are Article 221 and Section 7 Safeguard provisions.

Article 220.1 of the UN Convention allows the coastal state to apprehend a ship in its ports for a discharge or a CDEM violation in the territorial sea or in the EEZ of that state. Article 219 allows the coastal state to prevent a ship in its ports from sailing provided that ship's CDEM standards are defined as international standards. However, the term "condition for the entry of foreign vessels" used in Article 211.3 and Article 25.2 could be interpreted as including the consent of the foreign ship to follow the coastal state's national CDEM standards. Thereby the coastal state could enforce its national CDEM standards upon any ship in its ports.

The real understanding of the current coastal state competence in its own ports, however, cannot be gleaned solely from the provisions of the UN Convention. The relevant MARPOL provisions should also be taken into consideration.

* * *

Flag State Enforcement Jurisdiction

The UN Convention inherited the 1973 MARPOL flag state enforcement regime, such as the obligation of issuing certificates in order to assure the state's flag ships' good conditions; the obligation of conducting periodical inspections to verify the credibility of the certificates issued; and the obligation of investigating and prosecuting its flag ships which have violated applicable pollution control laws. The obligation to inform has also been embodied in the sequence of [IMO] Conventions, but was largely ignored by most nations. How nations will respect this provision is a question left for the future.

[Eds.—The author concludes by noting that upon the entry into force of the 1982 CLOS "the international law for vessel-source oil pollution control [became] a combined reading of the MARPOL Convention and all related IMO Conventions negotiated and accepted, and the UN Convention itself." Generally speaking, he states, "the [IMO] conventions ... constructed [among the states party to them] a relatively comprehensive legal framework with regard to [vessel-source oil pollution] by allocating national competence to apprehend ships and by delineating the extent of national jurisdictions." However, he says, there is no guarantee that everything said above will be implemented.... The regime, he observes, "still [has] certain problems, such as the overrigid non-innocent-passage definitions; and inconsistencies, such as the provisions relevant to enforcement of international CDEM standards."]

12.   Erik Jaap Molenaar, Coastal State Jurisdiction over Vessel–Source Pollution 517–21(1998).

[*Eds.*—Compared to the customary law of the sea as reflected largely in the 1958 Convention on the Territorial Sea and Contiguous Zone **(Basic Document 5.5)** and the 1958 Convention on the High Seas **(Basic Document 5.3)**, the author writes, the 1982 CLOS regime of jurisdiction over vessel-source pollution is "considerably more elaborated ..., differentiated with respect to not only the increased number of maritime zones, but also with respect to different types of standards, *viz.* discharge (emissions), CDEM, and navigation standards...." Yet, however comprehensive the 1982 CLOS regime for jurisdiction over vessel-source pollution was meant to be, he argues, it is possible to identify "several situations in which no particular regime seems explicitly applicable," *i.e.*, ambiguities that supplement the problems and inconsistencies noted at the conclusion of immediately preceding Reading 11. The author continues:]

... Suggestions for dealing with these ambiguous situations are aimed at ensuring consistency with the regime as a whole, and its object and purpose. Identified ambiguities led to the following suggestions:

- coastal States have prescriptive and in-port enforcement jurisdiction over discharge violations occurring beyond a coastal State's maritime zones that have an adverse impact on that coastal State. This exercise of jurisdiction can be based on the effects or impact principle, and is justified by the intention behind Article 218;

- coastal State jurisdiction in straits normally subject to the regime of transit passage is governed by Article 234 where such straits fall within ice-covered areas;

- coastal State jurisdiction in areas where a (non-suspendable) regime of innocent passage applies is identical to that of the territorial sea. This regime is governed not only by Section 3 of Part II, but also by Part XII. These areas include: archipelagic waters beyond ASLs [archipelagic sea lanes], internal waters created pursuant to Article 7 (as referred to in Articles 8(2) and 35(a)), and straits used for international navigation where a regime of non-suspendable innocent passage applies under Article 45. References to the territorial sea in Part XII should for the purpose of jurisdiction over vessel-source pollution be read to include these areas;

- the regime of enforcement jurisdiction within areas subject to the regime of transit passage is identical to that in areas subject to the regime of ASLs passage;

- coastal State enforcement jurisdiction over ships navigating in the EEZ that have committed violations in a coastal State's internal waters or territorial sea, should be identical to the enforcement regime over violations in the EEZ governed by Article 220(3, 5 and 6);

- strait and archipelagic State enforcement powers under Article 233 should also be permitted for violations meant in Article 42(1)(a and b) committed within areas subject to transit or ASLs passage where at the time of enforcement the ship is navigating beyond these areas, *viz.* in archipelagic waters, the territorial sea or the EEZ. This should also be allowed in a similar situation where the *locus* of violation and ship is reversed.

In addition to these ambiguities, there are several instances where the jurisdictional regime seems illogical. One example is that of enforcement jurisdiction over violations committed in the EEZ. Enforcement powers do not vary on account of the location of the ship at the time of enforcement. Rather, these powers are identical for ships navigating in the territorial sea or the EEZ, even though more extensive powers would be expected in the territorial sea. Rather than an omission this seems to be the LOSC's express purpose, and should therefore not be ignored. A distinction would probably even further complicate the existing enforcement regime and, as state practice reveals no real interest in enforcement at sea ..., this issue is largely devoid of importance.

Another example of an illogical or unreasonable distribution of jurisdiction concerns areas where the transit and ASLs passage regimes apply. The very limited coastal State enforcement powers under Article 233 seem not unreasonable in light of the fear for overzealous or non-justified use with their consequential impact on international shipping. The same cannot be said of prescriptive jurisdiction, which is first of all limited to internationally agreed standards, *viz.* all types of navigational measures and discharge standards in Annexes I and II of MARPOL 73/78 **[Basic Documents 5.16 & 5.18]**. Secondly, jurisdiction over discharge standards for other substances, and over all CDEM standards, even those that are generally accepted, is altogether excluded. Presumably, this perhaps unnecessarily strict regime was thought to be justified for the reason that even a modest measure of jurisdiction has the risk of being extensively interpreted or abused.... [S]tate practice ... suggests that this distribution of jurisdiction is not in all aspects closely observed.

* * *

[Nevertheless, in] the light of the concept of jurisdiction in international law, the LOSC regime for coastal State jurisdiction over vessel-source pollution reflects the fundamental point of departure that jurisdiction is only upheld or granted where the coastal State has a legitimate interest, and this interest is balanced with the interests of others, *viz.* the flag State. In one special case, coastal States are granted jurisdiction in the broader meaning of encompassing port State jurisdiction, to safeguard the interests of the international community. The LOSC explicitly provides for this "universal" port State jurisdiction in Article 218.

Although as a general rule a legitimate interest of the coastal State is presumed to exist within areas in which it exercises sovereignty, the LOSC shows that even within the territorial sea the regime of innocent passage restricts coastal State jurisdiction. This is adequately captured in the obligation in Article 24 that coastal States should not unreasonably hamper innocent passage.[hh] From the prescriptive side Article 21(2) indicates CDEM standards are unreasonable if they are not "generally accepted" and not

---

hh. *See also* 1982 LOSC (or CLOS), Article 211(4).

established at the international level. As regards enforcement, even though Article 220(2) does not require the occurrence of certain damage before enforcement action can be undertaken, this provision and Article 27 nevertheless require a coastal State to have "clear grounds" and due regard to the interests of navigation. Coastal State jurisdiction is even more restricted in areas subject to the regimes of transit and ASLs [archipelagic sea lanes] passage, even though these areas generally fall under that State's sovereignty. This is due to the key importance of these "choke points" to international shipping.

Within the EEZ, coastal State jurisdiction is based on the quasi-territorial principle. In comparison with the territorial sea, coastal States have a less prominent interest to exercise jurisdiction when balanced against the interests of the flag State. This is reflected in the LOSC by the absence of unilateral prescription and the fact that enforcement is limited to requests for information unless considerable damage has arisen or threatens to arise. This limited measure of coastal State jurisdiction does not affect the conclusion that freedom of navigation comparable to that on the high seas does not exist in the EEZ. The exceptionally fragile marine environment in ice-covered areas shifts the jurisdictional balance in favor of the coastal State. In fragile marine areas which are not covered by ice, this shift is, by way of IMO approval, only possible with the consent of flag States.

13. Brian D. Smith, State Responsibility and the Marine Environment: The Rules of Decision 193–203 (1988).

[*Eds.*—With one exception, the prescriptive and enforcement powers exercised by a coastal state over its territorial sea is coextensive with the powers it exercises over its land mass and internal waters. The one exception concerns the right of foreign vessels to "innocent passage." The author traces the evolution of this right, observing that "[i]t was not until the middle of the nineteenth century that the concept of a *right* of "innocent passage" in the territorial sea was articulated. Prior to that period, there was some recognition in the literature that non-threatening passage ought to be tolerated by the coastal state. Nevertheless, the [then] contemporary absolutist definition of sovereign prerogative dictated that passage in territorial waters remain subject to coastal state discretion." Thereafter, he discusses three events in the period intervening between the 1930 Hague Conference and the 1958 United Nations Conference on the Law of the Sea, among them the *Corfu Channel Case* **(Basic Document 7.5)**. He continues:]

Following this decision, there could be little question that a right of innocent passage had risen to the dignity of a rule of international law. Yet, the decision only directly affirmed the existence of a right with respect to passage in international straits—zones of crucial navigational significance. Moreover, the analysis engaged [in] by the Court raised a subsidiary set of questions as to the criteria of "innocence." Certain commentators ascribed the Court's inquiry into the manner of the vessels' passage to the conclusion that manner is the determinant of innocence. Others voiced the broader perspective that the Court only defined otherwise patently threatening warship passage as innocent due to the unique facts with respect to motivation; but for the evidence that the British intent was only to test the right, the manner of the passage would not have been deemed innocent. The *Corfu*

Channel decision, then, illuminated, without solution, certain of the basic uncertainties in the definition and interpretation of the right of innocent passage.

[*Eds.*—The author then discusses the right of innocent passage under the 1958 Geneva Convention on the Territorial Sea and Contiguous Zone **(Basic Document 5.5)** and the 1982 CLOS **(Basic Document 5.22)**.]

b.   The 1958 Geneva Convention

The first multilateral forum for the resolution of such uncertainties [as were raised in *Corfu Channel*] was the 1958 Geneva conference; having confirmed a regime of sovereignty, the conferees were compelled to define the qualifications to that regime. Article 14 of the [Territorial Sea] Convention sets forth the basic rule that "ships of all States, whether coastal or not, shall enjoy the right of innocent passage through the territorial sea." "Passage" is then defined as "navigation through the territorial sea for the purpose either of traversing that sea without entering internal waters, or of proceeding to internal waters, or of making for the high seas from internal waters." Passage is to be conferred the privileges of "innocence" "so long as it is not prejudicial to the peace, good order or security of the coastal State."

Notably, the language of the 1930 draft requiring a "use" of the sea with the "purpose" of committing a "prejudicial act" was not incorporated in the definition of innocence.... Presumably ..., the rationale of the deletion of "purpose" was to codify the propriety of the inquiry into *both* manner and purpose of passage suggested, under its most persuasive interpretation, by the *Corfu Channel* decision. Furthermore, by deletion of the references to "use" and "prejudicial act," the Geneva text had the apparent intent to expand the bounds of the analysis of innocence even beyond consideration of actual conduct and its purpose engaged by the ICJ. Activity was no longer a requisite component of the definition of "prejudice" to the coastal state. Hence, the broad language of the Convention generally has been interpreted as establishing the relevance of, and the legitimacy of an inquiry into, additional passive characteristics such as species of cargo and destination.

Article 15 supports the preceding general grant of a right of innocent passage with the statement that "[t]he coastal State must not hamper innocent passage." As with the parallel 930 provisions, this prohibition was not intended to suggest the absence of coastal state regulatory authority. To the contrary, Article 16 clearly acknowledges the state's authority to take any action to prevent non-innocent passage. Moreover, Article 17 recognizes the coastal state's right to regulate the passage of even innocent vessels with the admonition that "vessels exercising the right of innocent passage shall comply with the laws and regulations of the coastal State enacted in conformity with these Articles and other rules of international law."

One of the principal drafting objectives of these provisions was to disassociate the idea of non-innocence of passage from that of infringements of local laws. In other words, the intent of the participants, not expressed in the text, was to establish an objective definition of innocence. In the words of Fitzmaurice:

> If a vessel infringes such a [local] law or regulation, she may indeed be liable to a fine or other penalty. But her passage does not, merely on that

account, cease to be innocent, or become liable to be prevented or denied entirely.... To render a passage non-innocent, there must be something more than a mere infringement of a local law or regulation. There must really be something ... that could be considered as tainting the passage even if there happened not to be any specific domestic law or regulation under which it was logically illegal.[4]

A violation of law, therefore, justifies prohibition of passage only to the extent that the coastal state law or regulation which has been transgressed reflects the objective definition. McDougal and Burke have succinctly summarized the object and effect of the disassociation:

> For violation of coastal prescriptions ... relating to interests broadly formulated as "peace, good order, or security," the coastal State would be competent to prohibit passage as non-innocent. For failure to comply with other coastal laws, however, passing vessels could not be excluded from the territorial sea but they could be subject to other forms of coastal authority.[5]

The basic issues unresolved by the Convention's approach relate precisely to the character of authority retained by the coastal state with respect to matters which do not rise to the level of implicating innocence itself. With respect to environmental matters, it is quite clear, from the comments prepared in conjunction with the Convention itself and the predecessor 1930 text, that coastal state authority to prescribe and enforce regulations designed to protect the environment against vessels in innocent passage was indeed contemplated by the Geneva participants. Yet, that competence, together with all other coastal state authority, is expressly subject to the rule that innocent passage shall not be "hampered." The interpretative problem, of course, is that any exercise of coastal state legal authority may, to some degree, hamper passage. The very existence of a prescription which requires compliance of all actors within the territorial sea may have a chilling effect on the exercise of the right of innocent passage. This is true even in the absence of any enforcement action ... which physically interferes with innocent passage itself. The penalty for a violation of a coastal regulation may be enforced at another opportunity by methods or actions other than direct physical interference with the navigation of an offending vessel. Hence, the simple presence of rules subject to such subsequent enforcement would constitute an impediment to the exercise of innocent passage by any vessel that might anticipate a violation; the threat of incurring liability may effectively impede the exercise of navigational rights.

The utility of the restriction against hampering passage may be found, however, in its logical implication: a test of proportionality or reasonableness. It is submitted that the object of the "hampering" language must be to strike an appropriate balance among (a) the significance of the interest which the coastal state seeks to protect or advance, (b) the threat to such interest in the absence of prescriptive authority and (c) the character and magnitude of the attendant interference with the exercise of innocent passage. Expressed in its most abstract form, the rule of decision that will lead to such a balance must

4. G. Fitzmaurice, *Some Results of the Geneva Conference on the Law of the Sea*, 8 I.C.L.Q. 72, 94–95 (1979).

5. M. McDougal & W. Burke, The Public Order of the Oceans 254 (1972).

be one of "reasonableness." Coastal state prescriptions designed to protect minor interests which materially impair navigational rights . . . ought not to be tolerated. Such regulations would not survive scrutiny under a test of reasonableness. As unreasonable prescriptions, they must be deemed to "hamper" the exercise of innocent passage. On the other hand, the same degree of hindrance to foreign vessels might well be defined as reasonable in connection with the application of a prescription designed to safeguard a seriously threatened interest of greater significance. Notwithstanding their practical effect, such prescriptions should not be viewed as impermissibly "hampering" to passage.

* * *

The reconciliation of the coastal state's right to regulate vessels in innocent passage and the imperative not to hamper such passage is even more difficult in the context of enforcement authority. Even a minor enforcement action, such as detention for inspection, taken against a vessel in innocent passage, directly interferes with the course of its navigation. Indeed, McDougal and Burke, in a critique following the 1958 Convention, persuasively argue that denial of entry to the territorial sea represents a far less intrusive or hampering exercise of enforcement authority than do other acts such as arrest, seizure, or judicial sale.[6] They submit, therefore, that the 1958 provisions which preclude only prohibitions of innocent passage fail to impose limits on enforcement actions of even greater detriment to the enjoyment of navigational rights.

The latter conclusion, however, fails to recognize the applicability of the provision forbidding acts which hamper innocent passage to the exercise of coastal state enforcement authority. The subsumed test of reasonableness would dictate that the degree of interference attendant to any enforcement act must be proportionate to the interests of the coastal state, including the importance of the interest protected, the nature of the prescription violated, the risk of harm in the absence of enforcement, etc. It may indeed be appropriate to immunize a vessel from direct interference with passage caused by the enforcement of a rule forbidding the introduction of pollution, when the violation consists of the discard of a small bin of garbage. On the other hand, a discharge of oil, although perhaps not rising to the level of "serious" pollution, may merit a limited enforcement response such as inspection and brief detention. The prohibition against "hampering" thus provides a flexible rule of decision for determining the reasonableness, *i.e.* legality, of any exercise of enforcement authority.

Abuse of enforcement, however, represents such a threat to innocent passage that the 1958 [Territorial Sea] Convention text set forth a series of guidelines as to when a coastal state may take any action to enforce a prescription against a vessel in passage. Article 19 first provides that a state "should not" conduct an arrest or investigation on board such a vessel for the commission of a crime during passage unless: (*a*) "the consequences of the crime extend to the coastal State"; (*b*) "the crime is of a kind to disturb the peace of the country or the good order of the territorial sea"; (*c*) requested to do so by the captain or the flag state's consul; or (*d*) "it is necessary for the

---

6. *Id.* at 260–61.

suppression of illicit traffic in narcotic drugs." Article 20 then states that a passing vessel "should not" be stopped or diverted in innocent passage for the exercise of civil jurisdiction over a person on board and "may not" be so interfered with for the exercise of civil jurisdiction over the vessel itself for liabilities not related to the current passage. Finally, coastal states are precluded from enforcing extraterritorial prescriptions against vessels in innocent passage not on their way to internal waters; no arrest may be made for crimes committed prior to entry into the territorial sea. It is noteworthy that only the text regarding arrest for prior or extraterritorial crimes and civil jurisdiction is unequivocally mandatory. Although the conclusion is not without its critics, most commentators have concluded that the "should not" language in the balance of Articles 19 and 20 was "intended to reflect the fact that the rule enunciated represents standard international practice rather than strict international law."[7]

c. The LOS III Regime

1. Definition of "Innocence"

In basic structure, the regime of innocent passage defined in the 1982 LOS Convention closely parallels that described in the provisions of the 1958 [Territorial Sea] Convention. Article 17 commences with a statement of the affirmative right of innocent passage through the territorial sea. Article 18 recites, with certain expansion, the definition of "passage" articulated in 1958. Article 19(1) continues with the familiar language as to the meaning of "innocence": "Passage is innocent so long as it is not prejudicial to the peace, good order or security of the coastal State." The Convention then seeks to reduce the level of abstraction of this definition. Article 19(2) provides:

> Passage of a foreign ship shall be considered to be prejudicial to the peace, good order or security of the coastal State if in the territorial sea it engages in any of the following activities: ... *(h)* any act of wilful and serious pollution contrary to the Convention; ... *(l)* any other activity not having a direct bearing on passage.

... [T]his elaboration represents a deviation from custom and the 1958 text. * * * Article 19 would deny to the coastal state the legal authority to prohibit passage or exercise plenary authority with respect to vessels discharging pollution unless that discharge is "wilful." There would seem little question that the 1958 Convention contemplated coastal competence to prevent passage to polluting vessels as non-innocent. Indeed, it is difficult to comprehend an argument that the preservation of aesthetic and recreational amenities, resource productivity, related general economic welfare, and the physical well-being of the population does not constitute a core interest embraced in the language "peace, good order or security." The Convention's introduction of a standard of intent is, therefore, perplexing. The polluter's state of mind would not seem relevant to the issue of the magnitude and character of the threat to the coastal state.... In short, the *mens rea* component of the Convention's definition of innocence is consistent with neither the underlying logic nor the current state of the customary regime.

* * *

---

7. G. Fitzmaurice, *supra* note 4 (p. 1067).

The harm with which a vessel with inherently hazardous cargo or inadequate CDEM threatens the coastal state may occur, on the other hand, absent any intentional activity or even any human agency whatsoever. Accidents do happen. The prejudice to coastal state interests occurs, therefore, merely with presence. Hence the only opportunity the coastal state has to prevent the threat or the actual harm is to deny the right to such presence.

* * *

2. Prescriptive Authority

The LOS Convention treats the issue of the prescriptive authority of the coastal state over vessels in innocent passage in substantially the same fashion as the 1958 text. Article 21(1) recites the authority of the coastal state to prescribe laws and regulations in connection with the exercise of innocent passage with respect to a substantial list of matters, including "the preservation of the environment of the coastal State and the prevention, reduction and control of pollution thereof." The provision of the text relating exclusively to the protection of the marine environment underscores this prescriptive right: "Coastal States may, in the exercise of their sovereignty within their territorial sea, adopt laws and regulations for the prevention, reduction and control of marine pollution from foreign vessels, including vessels exercising the right of innocent passage." Finally, the Convention states explicitly the correlative: "[f]oreign ships exercising the right of innocent passage through the territorial sea shall comply with all such laws and regulations."

As in the 1958 text, the basic qualification to this grant of coastal state prescriptive authority is the prohibition against "hampering" innocent passage. With one exception, no provision either elaborates on the definition of hampering or suggests any limitation to environmental prescriptions. That exception is a requirement that coastal state laws applicable to vessels in innocent passage "shall not apply to the design, construction, manning or equipment of foreign ships unless they are giving effect to generally accepted international rules or standards [Art. 21(2)]."

14. Editors' Note. In the years since the entry into force of the 1982 CLOS **(Basic Document 5.22)**, despite the freedom extended to coastal states to prevent, reduce, and control marine pollution from foreign vessels even when exercising the right of innocent passage, relatively few have enacted detailed legislation relevant to vessel-source pollution. Writes Erik Jaap Molenaar, Coastal State Jurisdiction over Vessel–Source Pollution 521 (1998): "Many [coastal states] merely claim jurisdiction within their maritime zones in general terms, thereby in principle covering jurisdiction over vessel-source pollution." A general conclusion which can be drawn, he ventures, is that "there seems to be more consistency with the [1982 CLOS] in the exercise of coastal State *prescriptive* jurisdiction in comparison with *enforcement* jurisdiction [emphasis added]. Legislation on enforcement seems to reveal more deviations and also less uniformity...." Molenaar explains: "The relatively large measure of consistency in prescriptive jurisdiction, even by States not bound by the [1982 CLOS] or relevant regulatory conventions, could in part be explained by pragmatic reasons. Even though coastal States might be dissatisfied with existing international rules, prescribing standards with a high level of stringency could have significant competitive and political implications. Moreover, the prescription of certain standards, in particular

CDEM standards, requires technical expertise which many coastal States simply do not have." Molenaar notes further, at 525:

> More than one explanation ... seems possible. Some coastal States could simply not be very interested in jurisdiction over vessel-source pollution. Environmental jurisdiction was certainly not one of the main issues at UNCLOS III. Some coastal States could also regard the detailed provisions as unworkable and develop their own, more pragmatic approaches. This raises the question whether it was appropriate to adopt such detailed legal regimes at the global level if States apparently do not feel the urge to implement them. Of course, detailed provisions can often provide more guidance should conflicts arise. In some situations, however, less complex solutions could have been opted for as well.

However, Molenaar adds, at 530, "[w]ith the geographical and substantive increase of port and coastal State jurisdiction under the [1982 CLOS] and, perhaps even more importantly, the wider use of port State jurisdiction through the establishment of regional agreements on port State control ... in most regions of the world, [traditional] flag State primacy is certainly undermined, although not necessarily at a fundamental level."

Confirming Molenaar's judgment, is the saga of the single-hulled oil tanker *Prestige*, which, on 19 November 2002, carrying 77,000 metric tons of crude oil, split in half 133 miles west of the Spanish coast, with devastating consequences. The saga, evidencing greater coastal state assertions of jurisdiction over navigation in the EEZ and appearing to be leading to a change in the balance between navigational freedoms and coastal state environmental protection, is briefly recounted and assessed in Reading 15, next.]

15.   Carmen Cassado, "Vessels on the High Seas: Using a Model Flag State Compliance Agreement to Control Marine Pollution," 35 Cal. W. Int'l L. J. 203, 205–07, 216–17, 222–23, 235 (2005).

A.   The *Prestige* Incident

The *Aframax Prestige Tanker* began her journey in Latvia, destined for Singapore, and stopped in St. Petersburg, Russia where she loaded up with 77,000 metric tons of crude oil. Her journey ended tragically on November 19, 2002, when she broke in half on the high seas and sank off the Spanish Costa de la Muerte, or Coast of the Dead. . . .

The *Prestige Tanker* was owned by a Greek company, Mare Shipping, and operated by Swiss-based Crown Resources. She was registered in Liberia as a way of limiting taxes and liabilities. She flew the flag of the Bahamas. Her captain, Apostolos Mangouras, is Greek and her crew, Filipino.

As she approached the Spanish Costa de la Muerte ..., the *Prestige* encountered a windstorm with twenty-foot waves that punctured a hole in her starboard side tank. Her captain called for help, whereby rescue helicopters from Spain evacuated the crew. The Prestige began to leak crude oil and drifted within four miles of the Spanish Coast.

Due to the severity of the accident, the Spanish Government ordered Serafin Diaz, a veteran Captain, dispatched to the scene in order to steer the *Prestige* out to sea and away from Spain to avoid environmental devastation to the Spanish coasts. . . . After several days of sailing and being towed, the

Prestige snapped in two, spewing crude oil, and sank 130 miles off the Spanish coast. Captain Mangouras was arrested and charged with negligence.

The accident produced black tides of oil that swept the northern coast of Spain, and parts of France, killing millions of fish, birds and other species. The tide contaminated 350 miles of coastline with almost twice the oil from the Exxon Valdez spill in Alaska.... The cleanup took approximately 6 months and cost an estimated $2 billion. It will take decades for the Galician marine ecosystem to recover.

* * *

B. International Measures Being Implemented

The European Union has since taken measures to prevent laden vessels, and especially tankers, from traversing EU waters. The leaders, Spain, France and Portugal, initiated this movement by collectively banning single hull tankers from their 200–mile exclusive economic zones prior to legislation being in place. The ban was enforced in December 2002, when a Greek tanker carrying 81,000 tons of fuel oil heading for Spain through the Strait of Gibraltar was ordered to keep 200 miles away from the coasts of France and Spain. Also, three Maltese-flagged vessels have been escorted out of the French, Spanish and Portuguese exclusive economic zones. However, according to the International Chamber of Shipping (ICS), the actions taken by these countries are clearly in violation of Articles 56, 211 and 220 of UNC-LOS. The Convention offers the right of freedom of navigation to ships traveling through Coastal States' exclusive economic zones.

* * *

C. Flag State Compliance Agreement

The FAO Flag State Compliance Agreement **[Basic Document 5.39]** was approved by the Food and Agriculture Organization Conference at its Twenty–Seventh Session on November 24, 1993 [entered into force April 23, 2003]. The purpose of the Agreement is to develop management measures for the conservation of living resources on the high seas. It is "designed to strengthen enforcement of high seas conservation obligations arising under UNCLOS by elaborating on flag state duties...."

Amongst the more important areas the Agreement touches on are the following: the responsibility of Flag States to consider the past history of vessels and the vessels' past relationships with other Flag States; national enforcement mechanisms against non-compliant vessels including possible sanctions; the marking of vessels for identification purposes; international cooperation among Flag States; the duty of parties to the Agreement to persuade non-Members to accept the Agreement; assistance to developing countries provided by developed member states and the FAO; the oversight of the system by the FAO who plays a critical administrative role; and the establishment of a much needed information bank, or global registry.

* * *

V. Conclusion

The evolution of international laws of the seas has created a legal system of mare liberum. This system is increasingly less compatible with globalization, which is demanding domination of the seas for commerce, causing serious global problems such as marine pollution. Despite numerous international efforts to address these emerging problems, including the implementation of many international and regional agreements, and the creation of international organizations dedicated to addressing the issues, we continue to experience large-scale problems like the sinking of the *Prestige* oil tanker.

It is crucial that our competing interests on the high seas—the importance of the shipping industry to the world economy, the protection of the marine environment, and state autonomy—be reconciled with one another. The sinking of the *Prestige* is just one more reminder that the need for effective oversight, accountability and regulation of the shipping industry has never been greater.

A model FAO Compliance Agreement that applies to the shipping industry in its entirety would be a significant step towards controlling Flag States and vessels, making our oceans more secure....

16.   Editors' Note. In 1969, the IMO saw the adoption of the Convention on Civil Liability for Oil Pollution Damage, 973 U.N.T.S. 3, *reprinted in* 5 Weston & Carlson V.J.5, the first of several civil liability (or compensation) conventions carried out under its auspices over the last several decades to safeguard against the consequences of pollution from oil and other substances. This convention, which entered into force in 1981, adopted uniform international rules and procedures for determining questions of liability for oil pollution damage and for providing compensation where "pollution damage" occurs or where costs are incurred when attempting to prevent or minimize such damage. In 1971, the correlative Convention on the Establishment of an International Fund for Compensation for Oil Pollution Damage ("Fund Convention") **(Basic Document 5.13)**, which entered into force in 1978, authorized extra compensation to cover pollution damage beyond the limit of compensation available under the 1969 convention. In 1996, the International Convention on Liability and Compensation for Damage in Connection with the Carriage of Hazardous and Noxious Substances by Sea, IMO Doc. LEG/CONF.10/8/2, *reprinted in* 35 I.L.M. 1415 (1996), was adopted to ensure, as its title indicates, liability and compensation for damage resulting from the carriage by sea of hazardous and noxious substances, mainly chemicals but including oil. And, most recently, in March 2001, the International Convention on Civil Liability for Bunker Oil Pollution Damage (2001) (text available from the IMO) was adopted to ensure that prompt, adequate, and effective compensation is available to persons who suffer damage caused by spills of oil, when carried as fuel in ships' bunkers. A 1984 protocol to the 1969 convention, IMO Doc. LEG/CONF.6/66, 973 U.N.T.S. 1969, makes compensation available to states parties for pollution damage caused within the EEZ. A similar 1984 protocol to the 1971 convention, IMO Doc. LEG/CONF.6/67 (superseded but not contradicted by a 1992 protocol, IMO Doc. LEG/CONF.9/16) does the same thing for that convention. The 1996 "HNS Convention" and 2001 "Bunker Convention" also extend to the EEZ. However, neither of these latter two conventions has entered into force as of this writing.

Each of the aforementioned liability and compensation conventions oblige flag states to ensure that their vessels carry insurance or otherwise provide for compensation to safeguard against pollution harm to coastal states and others. Accordingly, they demonstrate the principle of state responsibility for transnational environmental harm. Derived initially from the traditional norms of state responsibility for the treatment of aliens and their property, this principle is rooted in the long-accepted proposition that states, the so-called subjects of international law, are responsible for such violations of law as are attributable to them and that, consequently, they are legally obligated to aggrieved other states and even private parties to make reparations whenever such attributable violations occur. Over the years, it has come to embrace as well, although more controversially, notions of liability for transnational environmental harms that arise out of acts *not* prohibited by international law—akin to what, in domestic law systems, we call "strict" or "absolute" liability.

The 1996 "HNS Convention" is testimony to this fact. Today, with major environmental harms occurring and threatening across national boundaries daily, the need to define and refine this jurisprudence, its scope, and conditions, is an imperative of the first magnitude. For the foundations of the modern-day customary international law of global environmental protection, see the following leading arbitral and judicial decisions excerpted or summarized in the documentary supplement to this coursebook: the *Case Relating to the Territorial Jurisdiction of the International Commission of the River Oder* **(Basic Document 7.1)**, the *Diversion of Water from the Meuse Case* **(Basic Document 7.2)**, the *Trail Smelter Arbitration* **(Basic Document 7.3)**, the *Corfu Channel Case* **(Basic Document 7.5)**, the *Lake Lanoux Arbitration* **(Basic Document 7.7)**, the *Nuclear Tests Cases* **(Basic Document 7.9)**, and the *Case Concerning the Gabcikovo–Nagymaros Project* **(Basic Document 7.11)**. The 1972 Stockholm Declaration on the Human Environment **(Basic Document 5.14)**, the 1974 Charter of Economic Rights and Duties of States **(Basic Document 4.9)**, the 1982 World Charter for Nature **(Basic Document 5.21)**, and the 1992 Rio Declaration on Environment and Development **(Basic Document 5.37)** are four instruments that explicitly extend the principle of state responsibility to transnational environmental harm to a Twenty-first Century marked by greater and greater environmental interconnectedness. For usefully abridged treatment, see Lakshman D. Guruswamy, Sir Geoffrey W. R. Palmer, Burns H. Weston, and Jonathan C. Carlson, International Environmental Law and World Order: A Problem–Oriented Coursebook ch. 5 ("International Environmental Wrongs") (2nd ed. 1999).

17.   International Convention on the Establishment of an International Fund for Compensation for Oil Pollution Damages. Concluded, 18 Dec 1971. Entered into force, 16 Oct 1978. 1110 U.N.T.S. 57; *reprinted in* **5 Weston & Carlson V.F.12: Arts. 2–4** (Basic Document 5.13).

18.   Stockholm Declaration of the United Nations Conference on the Human Environment, adopted by the UN Conference on the Human Environment at Stockholm, 16 Jun 1972, Report of the UN Conference on the Human Environment, 5–16 June 1972, UN Doc. A/CONF.48/14/Rev.1 at 3 (1973), UN Doc. A/CONF.48/14 at 2–65, and Corr. 1 (1972); *reprinted in* **11 I.L.M. 1416 (1972) and 5 Weston & Carlson V.B.3: Pmbl. & Princs. 2, 6, 7, 21** (Basic Document 5.14).

19. Charter of Economic Rights and Duties of States, 12 Dec 1974, GA Res. 3281, 29th Sess., Supp. No. 31, at 50, UN Doc. A/9631 (1975); *reprinted in* **14 I.L.M. 251 (1975) and 4 Weston & Carlson IV.F.5: Art. 30** (Basic Document 4.9).

20. World Charter for Nature, 28 Oct 1982, GA Res. 37/7, UN GAOR, 37th Sess., Supp. No. 51, at 17, UN Doc. A/37/51; *reprinted in* **22 I.L.M. 455 (1983) and 5 Weston & Carlson V.B.11: Princs. 1–4, 11, 12, 22, 24** (Basic Document 5.21).

21. Rio Declaration on Environment and Development, 13 Jun 1992, UNCED Doc. A/CONF.151/5/Rev. 1; *reprinted in* **31 I.L.M. 874 (1992) and 5 Weston & Carlson V.B.16: Princs. 1, 2, 7, 14, 15** (Basic Document 5.37).

22. Alexandre C. Kiss and Dinah Shelton, International Environmental Law 225, 226, 228–234 (2d ed. 2000).

Despite efforts to prevent pollution and protect the environment, human activities and accidents give rise to environmental damage. In order to deter harmful acts and remedy damage as fully as possible, legal consequences attach to those acts that cause injury. International agreements and domestic law may refer liability issues to national fora for determination between the actor and the injured parties or may provide for both inter-state and private actions. The increasingly accepted solution is to transfer the question from the interstate level to the inter-personal level, that is, from public to private international law where the polluter and victim are brought directly before the competent domestic authorities. A transnational element is present in all these cases, creating potential jurisdictional problems. It is not surprising, therefore, that states have sought to overcome the difficulties by prior agreement, concluding treaties or adopting other international texts to resolve at least some of the problems.

Civil liability refers to the liability of any legal or natural person under rules of national law adopted pursuant to international treaty obligations which establish harmonized minimum national standards. Several treaties establish rules on civil liability for environmental or related damage. These regimes usually have developed regarding specific activities, such as nuclear installations and oil transport. Recent regional treaties in Europe apply more generally to industrial operations. Civil liability agreements generally define the activities or substances covered and the harm, channel liability, establish a standard of care and exceptions, set limitations on the amount of liability, and provide for enforcement of judgments. In addition, most include a provision for mandatory insurance or other financial guarantees.

. . . Some national laws permit consumers or even those with no direct injury to sue. While the international law of strict liability is less developed than is national law, the concept applies in most of the treaties concerned with hazardous activities and substances. In this type of case, and in those of international responsibility, fundamental problems exist in establishing causation, identifying the polluter, and proving damage. To these difficulties are added four issues particular to the field of private international law: jurisdiction, choice of law, assessing damages, and execution of judgments.

Providing a remedy of compensation for environmental harm requires consideration of the amount of damage that has occurred. The concept of harm to the environment is often viewed as a property concept, where economic value is placed on the lost or damaged object. This may include market value, loss of income, and damage to moral, aesthetic, and scientific interest. The economic approach poses problems for protection of species of wild fauna and flora that are not exploited and thus have no market value, as well as for ecosystems or landscapes the economic value of which cannot be assessed. Evaluating the economic value of the intangible aspects of the environment, such as biological diversity and balanced ecosystems, is difficult. The situation is similar for areas that are under common ownership, and even more for those areas that are for common use but not capable of ownership, such as the high seas and outer space. Measurement or evaluation of harm for the purpose of damage awards also involves important questions of the threshold or *de minimis* level of harm, proximity of harm, especially for long-term, long-distance, multiple-authored actions and, finally, the possible irreversibility of the harm caused. The last issue is something that is thus far largely ignored in law.

One of the most difficult issues in environmental litigation is the scope of damage. The key question is whether damage extends beyond persons and properties to include damage to the environment itself. Increasingly, relevant civil liability conventions are addressing damage to the environment but generally limit recovery to the costs of reasonable measures of reinstatement and the costs of preventive measures. The UNECE Task Force on Responsibility and Liability regarding Transboundary Water Pollution has proposed a definition of damage that includes "detrimental changes in ecosystems." For this there may be awarded the equivalent costs of reasonable measures of reinstatement actually undertaken and further damages exceeding those provided for under the first measure, *i.e.*, there may be substitute damages where reinstatement is impossible because of the irremediable nature of the harm.[8]

The *Amoco Cadiz* case illustrates the current problems in the civil liability regime, especially in regard to the assessment of damages. The Amoco Cadiz tanker ran aground on March 16, 1978, due to damage to its navigational equipment. The accident occurred two miles from the small port of Portsall on the coast of Brittany. During the following three weeks, nearly all the 219,617 tons of oil, escaped into the sea, creating an oil slick eighteen miles wide and eight miles long. Part of the oil evaporated and another part broke down by natural means, but the rest filtered to the seabed or reached the coastline, creating ecological disaster.

Normally, the pollution victims would have been able to bring an action in French court for damages under the Brussels Liability Convention, discussed infra, which France had ratified. However, their damages substantially exceeded the limits of seventy-seven million francs which would have been due under the original Liability Convention formula. According to estimates prepared at the time, the cleanup alone cost some 450 million francs, the

8. See A. Rest, *New Tendencies in Environmental Responsibility/Liability Law: The Work of the UNECE Task Force on Responsibility* and Liability regarding Transboundary Water Pollution, 21 E.P.L. 137 (1991).

damage caused to fish and shellfish was estimated to equal 140 million, and the losses caused by the reduction in tourism were placed at more than 400 million. In these circumstances, the victims sought to take the case to the United States courts because the United States is not a party to the Liability Convention and therefore is not bound by its limits. The complaint sought $2.2 billion in damages for environmental harm suffered due to the negligence of the companies in the construction, maintenance, and operations of the Amoco Cadiz.

Four years later, the court examined in detail the question of damages, awarding the plaintiffs $85.2 million. The court's 435–page opinion[9] addressed the claims made by France, the harmed cities and towns, individuals, farmers, fishermen, and environmental protection groups[10] discussing several categories of damages:

—Cleanup operations made by public employees. The court accepted the claim for costs of the cleanup to the extent that public employees, including elected officials and the military, took time from their regular duties or put in overtime to assist. Travel costs incurred in the cleanup were also reimbursed. The time of volunteers was not compensated because their efforts were donated, but the proven costs of transportation, food and lodging could be claimed.

—Gifts made by local communities in money or goods to volunteers or military officials were found to be inappropriate for inclusion in the damage claim, being in the nature of recognition of and gratitude for the services rendered.

—Costs of material and equipment purchased for the cleanup. The Court allowed recovery, less the residual value of purchased items, provided the acquisition was reasonable and the equipment was, in fact, used during the cleanup and that a residual value could be proven. . . .

—Costs of using public buildings. The damage suffered by buildings during the cleanup operations was compensated and reimbursement was awarded for the extra coast arising from use of the buildings during the cleanup, such as increased water, power, and telephone usage.

—Coastline and harbor restoration. The expenses for these purposes were included.

—Lost enjoyment. The court applied French law and rejected this claim, which it viewed as a claim for damage to the quality of life and public services.

—Loss of reputation and public image of the towns. . . . The Court rejected the claim, finding that it was more precisely covered and measurable in individual claims brought by hotels, restaurants, campgrounds and other businesses.

—Individual claims. The Court accepted some of the numerous individual claims, applying as a general rule the loss of income for one year. . . .

---

9. In re Oil Spill by Amoco Cadiz off the Coast of France on 16 Mar 1978, No. MDL376 (N.D. Ill. 1988), 1988 U.S. Dist. LEXIS 16832.

10. The various claimants initially demanded $2.2 billion in damages. *See* Business Insur-ance, 30 April 1984, at 1. *Final Cost of Amoco Cadiz*, 14 Mar. Pollution Bull.12 (1983).

—Ecological harm.... The Court did not award damages for injury to the biomass, the totality of life in the sea and on the bottom in the affected zone, deeming the matter complex, attenuated, speculative and based on a chain of assumptions....

* * *

Given the myriad uncertainties and risks of litigation, a plaintiff could become involved in a legal steeplechase where one hurdle after another must be overcome in order to receive compensation for environmental harm. States have agreed on special procedures in an effort to reduce the hurdles in two fields where the effects of environmental harm may be the most serious: the transportation of hazardous substances by sea and the production and use of nuclear energy.

Marine oil pollution, in particular compensation for environmental injury caused by it, is regulated by an entire system based on the 1969 International Convention on Civil Liability for Oil Pollution, 973 U.N.T.S. 3, *reprinted in* 5 Weston and Carlson V.J.5, as modified in 1971, 1976, 1984, and 1992. To this must be added the 1971 Convention on the Establishment of an International Fund for Compensation for Oil Pollution Damage **[Basic Document 5.13]**, also modified by protocols.

The 1992 Liability Protocol makes clear that this includes environmental harm. It states that compensation for impairment of the environment other than loss of profit from such impairment shall be limited to costs of reasonable measures of reinstatement actually undertaken or to be undertaken.[11] The owner may limit liability except in case of actual fault and must maintain insurance or other financial security to cover its liability.

E.   MILITARY RETORSIONS AND REPRISALS

1.   Charter of the United Nations. Concluded, 26 Jun 1945. Entered into force, 24 Oct 1945. 1976 Y.B.U.N. 1043, 59 Stat. 1031, T.S. No. 993, 3 Bevans 1153; *reprinted in* **1 Weston & Carlson I.A.1; Pmbl. & Arts. 1, 2, 33, 51** (Basic Document 1.5).

2.   Charter of the Organization of American States (as amended). Concluded, 30 Apr 1948. Entered into force, 13 Dec 1951. 2 U.S.T. 2394, T.I.A.S. No. 2361, 119 U.N.T.S. 3, amended by Protocol of Amendment, 27 Feb 1967, 21 U.S.T. 607, T.I.A.S. No. 6847, 721 U.N.T.S. 324; *reprinted in* **6 I.L.M. 310 (1967) and 1 Weston & Carlson I.B.14: Arts. 1–3, 9–12, 14, 18–21, 23–25** (Basic Document 1.7).

3.   Inter–American Treaty of Reciprocal Assistance ("Rio Pact"). Concluded, 2 Sep 1947. Entered into force, 3 Dec 1948. 62 Stat. 1681,

---

11. Article 8(2) of the Antarctic Mineral Resource Activities Convention also provides for strict liability for damages "in the event that there has been no restoration to the status quo ante." The Council of Europe rules on compensation for damage caused to the environment include among the definitions given in Rule 2: "(9) Measures of reinstatement means any appropriate and reasonable measures aiming to reinstate or restore damaged or destroyed natural resources or where appropriate or reasonable to introduce the equivalent of these resources into the environment." In all cases, restoring the environment to its *status quo ante* is the preferred remedy and this is especially true where it is difficult to assess the harm and the corresponding compensation. Only when restoration is not possible would it then be necessary to measure the damages.

T.I.A.S. No. 1838, 21 U.N.T.S. 77; *reprinted in* 2 Weston & Carlson II.D.18: Arts. 1, 2 (Basic Document 2.7).

4. American Treaty on Pacific Settlement ("Pact of Bogota"). Concluded, 30 Apr 1948. Entered into force, 6 May 1949. 30 U.N.T.S. 55; *reprinted in* **1 Weston & Carlson I.H.3: Arts. 1, 2, 8** (Basic Document 2.8).

5. Declaration on Principles of International Law Concerning Friendly Relations and Co–Operation Among States in accordance with the Charter of the United Nations. Adopted, 24 Oct 1970. GA Res. 2625 (XXV), 25 UN GAOR, Supp. (No. 28) 121, UN Doc. A/8028 (1971); *reprinted in* **9 I.L.M. 1292 (1970) and 1 Weston & Carlson I.D.7** (Basic Document 1.11).

6. United Nations Convention on the Law of the Sea. Concluded, 10 Dec 1982. Entered into force, 16 Nov 1994. 1833 U.N.T.S. 3; *reprinted in* **21 I.L.M. 1261 (1982) and 5 Weston & Carlson V.F.22**: Arts. 279, 280 (Basic Document 5.22).

7. International Convention on Arrest of Ships. Concluded at the at the UN/IMO Diplomatic Conference on Arrest of Ships, 12 Mar 1999. Not yet in force. UN Doc A/CONF.188.6 (19 Mar 1999): Arts. 1–4 & 8 (Basic Document 5.50).

8. Albert E. Hindmarsh, Force in Peace—Force Short of War in International Relations 8–10 (1933).[ii]

There are several reasons for studying the problems raised by the state use of force in time of peace. It is desirable to know how deeply founded in customary law is a practice which has long been justified on the ground that it is a necessary ultimate sanction of international law. Its abuses and its inherent contradictions are apparent when it is recognized as an arbitrary self-help method which is founded on physical force but is defended as a means of supporting law. The history of the development of international law, especially during the nineteenth century, indicates that a large part of our substantive law today represents mere crystallization of state practices. However much we may decry the acts of states and statesmen, we find that international law in general tends to follow the facts of international life. From an idealistic point of view, law should more often accord with abstract principles of justice, usually anticipatory of practice and present law. This is but another way of asserting, without approving a process which often renders international law out of harmony with actual conditions in a rapidly changing world, that we may safely forecast developments in international law and international relations only after a study of the actual practices of states. In a system of law which is based very largely on custom and usage, past practices are evidence of what states will continue to demand as rights. . . . The exercise of rights derived from customary law and not clearly renounced cannot be condemned on legal grounds, however great the moral offense may be. No state has thus far renounced the right to use armed force under all circumstances. Practically all states have renounced, in a limited set of circumstances, the right to have recourse to war, but that is not enough to render all use of force illegal.

ii. Note that this excerpt was published in 1933. Is it outdated? Should it be?

The established legality of state self-help methods short of war ... and the absence of international machinery competent to adjust all international differences by purely amicable methods, justify continued study of the practice of state self-help short of war. There is one more significant reason for examining the history of the practice. States have constantly refused to abjure the right to use coercive measures in their own behalf prior to appeal to impartial judgment. It has seemed futile to hold out moral guarantee as a substitute for national armaments until the international community is sufficiently organized to provide adequate material guarantees of their rights under international law. The enforcement of national rights and interests rests today very largely on the possession of physical force by plaintiff states. Such a condition is likely to continue until the international community becomes willing to assume responsibility for rendering its rules of conduct effective. The question is, which method is in the real interests of world order—unrestrained and unregulated state self-help, or provision for sanctions to be exercised by the organized community of states after impartial judgment?

9. Julius Stone, Legal Controls of International Conflict 288–90 (reprint ed. 1973).

... It can ... be argued that ... it would be a disservice to international peace, and to international law, to prohibit resort to ... degrees of force [short of war]. For such prohibition may tend to drive States to seek to vindicate their claims by war, in circumstances when they might otherwise well have been content with measures less disturbing to international order. It is necessary, however, regrettable, to see such problems in their historico-political context....

[Stone next describes "the main coercive methods short of war" to which States have been given over the years, including "severance of diplomatic relations," "embargo," "boycott," and "pacific blockade." He then discusses "retorsion" and "reprisals:"[jj]]

B. Retorsion

Retorsion consists of an unfriendly act or acts whereby one State answers *objectionable* (though not necessarily illegal) conduct of another State in a retaliatory manner. There appears to be general agreement that the retorsion itself must be a legitimate act within the competence of the retorting State, that is to say, not contrary to public international law or to any treaty binding the State. Such, for example, would be the revocation of non-treaty tariff concessions, or the withdrawal of any privileges granted on a basis of reciprocity to the citizens of the other State.... There is, however, some disagreement among authors as to whether it is a retorsion to retaliate against objectionable conduct of the offending State which is contrary to public international law, and not merely of the nature of an unfriendly act or acts. There is some weight of opinion to the effect that this constitutes rather a reprisal. It seems clear from the practice that the retorsion need not take the form of a retaliation in kind.

---

jj. For additional discussion on retorsion and reprisals, see the readings in Section F of Problem 6–1 ("A Financial Crisis in Sundalau Spreads to Tolteca"), *supra* at 806–15.

Although legitimate in itself, an act of retorsion may constitute a danger to justice within the meaning of paragraph 3 of Article 2 of the United Nations Charter [**Basic Document 1.5**].... If this be so, it might (though very vaguely) be prohibited by the Charter.

C. Reprisals

Reprisals in the modern sense denote any kind of forcible or coercive measures whereby one State seeks to exercise a deterrent effect or to obtain redress or satisfaction, directly or indirectly, for the consequences of the *illegal* acts of another State, which has refused to make amends for such conduct. This definition has been carefully framed in order to embrace the multifarious acts which, according to doctrine, are usually referred to as "reprisals." These acts may consist of the bombardment or occupation of territory of the alleged offending State (for example, the Italian bombardment and occupation of Corfu in 1923 in order to secure redress from the Greek Government for the murder of the Italian General Tellini); the seizure of ships of such State (as, for example, by the Netherlands of Venezuelan public vessels in 1908); the freezing of the assets of its citizens, and the taking generally of any kind of property belonging to it.

The nature of non-belligerent reprisals was discussed by the German–Portuguese Arbitral Tribunal in the *Naulilaa Case* (1929),[12] which arose out of certain measures taken by Germany against Portuguese territory in retaliation for the killing of three German officers in Portuguese territory by the members of a Portuguese frontier post, at a time in the First World War when Portugal was still neutral. The Tribunal enunciated three conditions for the legitimate applicability of reprisals: (i) That in the first instance the State against which reprisals are taken, must have been guilty of a breach of public international law; (ii) That prior to the recourse to reprisals an adequate attempt had been made to obtain from such State redress for the consequences of its illegal conduct, without success; (iii) That the reprisals should not be "excessive." As the Tribunal pointed out, the test of "excessiveness" is somewhat different from the test whether or not the reprisals are out of proportion to the alleged illegal conduct of the offending State.

* * *

The line between reprisals and retorsion is not clearly defined, and in a particular case is often difficult to mark. Presumably, however, reprisals must consist of measures which are contrary to international law or in breach of a treaty binding the State which institutes them, whereas, as already pointed out above, a retorsion is an act which is legitimate and not in breach of international law, although it may be regarded as of an unfriendly character. The acts, moreover, against which retorsion or retaliation are respectively resorted to usually show a similar difference. A further distinction may be that the primary purpose of reprisals is as a rule to secure redress, while a retorsion is most generally of a retaliatory nature; but this is scarcely a proposition of law.

* * *

12. (Port. v. Ger.), [1928] 2 U.N.R.I.A.A. 1012 (1949).

The scope for the application of reprisals has now been limited by the provisions of the United Nations Charter ..., and in view of these provisions the distinction between a retorsion and reprisals seems scarcely worth maintaining.

10. Derek Bowett, "Reprisals Involving Recourse to Armed Force," 66 A.J.I.L. 1, 1–3, 10–11 (1972).

Few propositions about international law have enjoyed more support than the proposition that, under the Charter of the United Nations **[Basic Document 1.5]**, the use of force by way of reprisals is illegal. Although, indeed, the words "reprisals" and "retaliation" are not to be found in the Charter, this proposition was generally regarded by writers and by the Security Council as the logical and necessary consequence of the prohibition of force in Article 2(4), the injunction to settle disputes peacefully in Article 2(3) and the limiting of permissible force by states to self-defense. The UN Declaration on Principles of International Law concerning Friendly Relations and Co-operation among States, adopted by the General Assembly Resolution 2625 (XXV) on October 24, 1970 **[Basic Document 1.11]**, contains the following categorical statement: "States have a duty to refrain from acts of reprisal involving the use of force."

* * *

It cannot be doubted that a total outlawry of armed reprisals, such as the drafters of the Charter intended, presupposed a degree of community cohesiveness and, with it, a capacity for collective action to suppress any resort to unlawful force which has simply not been achieved. Not surprisingly, as states have grown increasingly disillusioned about the capacity of the Security Council to afford them protection against what they would regard as illegal and highly injurious conduct directed at them, they have resorted to self-help in the form of reprisals and have acquired the confidence that, in so doing, they will not incur anything more than a formal censure from the Security Council. The law on reprisals is, because of its divorce from actual practice, rapidly degenerating to a stage where its normative character is in question.

[*Eds.*—The author, seeking to clarify the "normative character" of the law of reprisals, subsequently turns to the distinction between reprisals and self-defense (as guaranteed by UN Charter Article 51).]

Reprisals and self-defense are forms of the same generic remedy, self-help. They have, in common, the preconditions that:

(1) The target state must be guilty of a prior international delinquency against the claimant state.

(2) An attempt by the claimant state to obtain redress or protection by other means must be known to have been made, and failed, or to be inappropriate or impossible in the circumstances.

(3) The claimant's use of force must be limited to the necessities of the case and proportionate to the wrong done by the target state.

The difference between the two forms of self-help lies essentially in their aim or purpose. Self-defense is permissible for the purpose of protecting the security of the state and the essential rights—in particular the rights of territorial integrity and political independence—upon which that security depends. In contrast, reprisals are punitive in character: they seek to impose reparation for the harm done, or to compel a satisfactory settlement of the dispute created by the initial illegal act, or to compel the delinquent state to abide by the law in the future. But, coming after the event and when the harm has already been inflicted, reprisals cannot be characterized as a means of protection. This distinction would fit neatly into the general theory that punishment is a matter for society as a whole, whereas self-defense must still be permitted to the individual member, as an interim measure of protection and subject to a subsequent evaluation of the correctness of the individual's judgment as to the necessity for self-defense by the organized community of states.

This seemingly simple distinction abounds with difficulties. Not only is the motive or purpose of a state notoriously difficult to elucidate but, even more important, the dividing line between protection and retribution becomes more and more obscure as one moves away from the particular incident and examines the whole context in which the two or more acts of violence have occurred. Indeed, within the whole context of a continuing state of antagonism between states, with recurring acts of violence, an act of reprisal may be regarded as being at the same time both a form of punishment and the best form of protection for the future, since it may act as a deterrent against future acts of violence by the other party. . . .

11. Jordan J. Paust, "The Seizure and Recovery of the Mayaguez," 85 Yale L. J. 774, 774–81, 795–803 (1976).

I. Factual Background

A. The Seizure of the Mayaguez

The merchant ship *Mayaguez* was seized some six-and-one-half miles off the Pouli Wai Islands, in an area claimed by Cambodia to be within its territorial waters, at 3:18 a.m. (Washington, D.C. time) on May 12, 1975. * * * For at least 10 days prior to [its] seizure . . . , the Cambodians had fired on or captured 25 ships and fishing boats in the same area [later claiming that some of these had engaged in espionage activities]. * * * Amidst this rash of seizures . . . and warnings, the *Mayaguez* proceeded calmly toward the Gulf of Thailand. On May 12 the vessel was spotted heading toward claimed Cambodian waters. The Cambodians described the incident thus:

> [The *Mayaguez*] continued to intrude deeper into our waters. . . . Seeing that this ship intentionally violated our waters, our patrol then stopped in order to examine and question it and report back to our higher authorities. * * * [W]e have no intention of detaining it permanently. . . . We only wanted to know the reason for its coming and to warn it against violating our waters again. This is why our coast guard seized this ship. * * * [W]e will release this ship, but we will not allow the US imperialists to violate our territorial waters, conduct espionage in our territorial waters or force us to release their ships whenever they want, by applying threats.

These stated objectives of the Cambodian seizure were confirmed by the captain of the *Mayaguez*, Charles Miller. . . . Meanwhile, President Ford was aware of the following message from the ship, received in Indonesia: "Have been fired upon and boarded by Cambodian armed forces. Ship being towed to unknown Cambodian port."

* * *

At noon on May 12, President Ford had a 45–minute meeting with the National Security Council to discuss the seizure of the *Mayaguez*. Later that afternoon Press Secretary Nessen issued the following statement:

> We have been informed that a Cambodian naval vessel has seized an American merchant ship on the high seas and forced it to the port of Kompong Som. The President . . . has instructed the State Department to demand the immediate release of the ship. Failure to do so would have the most serious consequences.

At the same time Nessen also admitted that the United States . . . was aware that Cambodia had claimed a 12–mile territorial sea limit since 1969, when Prince Sihanouk was first in power. . . .

B. *Diplomatic Efforts (May 12 and May 14) and the First Attack (May 13)*

  1. *May 12*

Diplomatic effort to gain release of the *Mayaguez* began with Press Secretary Nessen's announcement of President Ford's demand for the "immediate release of the ship" and his warning that "most serious consequences" could follow if the demand went unheeded. Later that day (May 12), Ambassador Huang Chen, head of the Chinese liaison office in Washington, went to the office of Deputy Secretary of State Robert Ingersoll, at Ingersoll's request. There he was given a diplomatic note conveying a 24–hour ultimatum from the United States for communication to the Cambodians. . . . No further diplomatic messages are known to have been transmitted to Cambodia before the use of force by the United States to stop the transport of the crew of the *Mayaguez* to the Cambodian mainland.

  2. *May 13—the First Attack*

During the first evening (local time) . . ., [f]earing that it would be difficult to get the crew back once they reached the Cambodian mainland, the United States launched an air attack on the Cambodian naval vessels escorting the crew of the *Mayaguez* to the mainland. The Pentagon news release was cryptic:

> After giving warning, US aircraft began efforts to block this movement [of the fishing boat carrying the crew of the *Mayaguez*]. Three Cambodian patrol craft were destroyed, about four others were damaged and immobilized. One boat succeeded in reaching Kompong Som.

* * *

  3. *May 14—14 Hours After the First Attack*

. . . Some 14 hours after the raid, on May 14, the United States turned for the first time to the existing United Nations machinery for handling international disputes. Two days after the seizure of the *Mayaguez*, Ambassador John Scali handed a letter to United Nations Secretary General Waldheim which asked him to obtain the release of the crew and ship. The Secretary General responded by offering his good offices and appealed to the United States and

Cambodia to "refrain from further acts of force in order to facilitate the process of peaceful settlement." The letter delivered by Ambassador Scali claimed that the Cambodian seizure was illegal and posed a threat to international peace. It also "reserved" the right to take "such measures as may be necessary to protect the lives of American citizens and property, including appropriate measures of self-defense under Article 51 of the United Nations Charter **[Basic Document 1.5]**."

* * *

Three hours after this contact with the Secretary General, the fourth National Security Council meeting on the *Mayaguez* incident began. As the meeting started, "all were convinced" that the diplomatic effort was "getting nowhere." In addition, as the Secretary of State would later admit to reporters, the Ford Administration already had resolved not to engage in "humiliating" negotiations.

C. The Second Attack (May 14)

At 4:45 p.m. President Ford decided to send in the Marines. At 5:45 the order left the Pentagon. The President met with certain congressional leaders at 6:40. Independently of these events, the crew of the *Mayaguez* left the mainland to return to the ship (7:00 p.m. Washington time; 6:00 a.m. Cambodian time) and the Cambodians began to broadcast on local radio that the crew and ship were being released (7:07). At 7:20 the Marine assault force landed on Tang Island under heavy fire. Meanwhile, American planes bombed Ream airport on the Cambodian mainland near Sihanoukville and an unused oil refinery, also on the mainland.

This second attack, then, began just as the crew was to be released....

* * *

III. The Peaceful Settlement of Disputes

... Whether or not Cambodia's seizure of the *Mayaguez* was lawful ..., another issue must be analyzed: the lawfulness of the response of the United States.

A. Legal Norms

1. The United Nations Charter

When confronted with what it considered to be an illegal seizure of a United States merchant vessel, the Ford Administration was bound to respond in accordance with the basic commands of the United Nations Charter. [See Charter, arts. 2(3) and 33(1).]

No state may threaten ... or use force for the settlement of a dispute. The 1970 United Nations Declaration on Principles of International Law Concerning Friendly Relations and Co-operation **[Basic Document 1.11]** adds [equivalent language]....

2. Prior Cases

Traditionally, states challenging the legality of the seizure and search of merchant vessels either in coastal waters or on the high seas have presented their challenges through peaceful settlement processes. In *Church v. Hub-*

bard,[13] claim and counterclaim were raised before a national court. The case of the *Virginius* was settled by diplomatic process[14] the case of the *I'm Alone* by international arbitration[15] and the *Corfu Channel* case by the International Court.[16]

The United States has been a party to many peaceful settlements of such disputes. Indeed, the United States has actively sought peaceful solutions to disputes involving conflicting claims for access to ocean resources and conflicting claims concerning state security interests and freedom of the seas. Through the last five administrations, the United States has never used armed force to obtain the release of any of the numerous captured crews from fishing vessels seized off the coasts of the Latin American states.

* * *

B. The United States Response to the Seizure of the Mayaguez

When President Ford presented the Cambodian regime with a 24–hour ultimatum and a demand for the immediate release of the *Mayaguez* and crew, he left no room for negotiation for a release of the crew and detention of the ship, for a reasonable questioning of the crew, or for a search of the ship. Nor did the ultimatum allow adequate time to communicate with a new regime, with which the United States did not have normal diplomatic relations. Such an ultimatum was not in reasonable conformity with articles 2(3) and 33(1) of the United Nations Charter; nor was it consistent with previous United States practice....

The American ultimatum was not simply inconsistent with accepted standards of international law; it was, in reality, a hollow gesture without substance. Some seven hours before the ultimatum was returned unanswered, American planes had fired warning shots across the bow of the *Mayaguez*, then in Cambodian territorial waters off Tang Island, and President Ford had ordered "the United States armed forces to isolate the island and interdict any movement between the ship or the island and the mainland, and to prevent movement of the ship itself...." These actions, in addition to the terms of the ultimatum itself, were hardly conducive to the peaceful settlement of a dispute about the propriety of the detention of the *Mayaguez*.

* * *

C. The Use of Force

Article 2(4) of the United Nations Charter prohibits "the threat or use of force against the territorial integrity or political independence of any state, or in any other manner inconsistent with the Purposes of the United Nations." In contrast, Article 51 recognizes the inherent right of states to engage in necessary and proportionate measures of self-defense. Many writers recognize a right of self-help for sanctioning violations of international law when other remedies are ineffective, the action is otherwise necessary and proportionate, and intended targets are not otherwise immune.

13. 6 U.S. (2 Cranch) 187 (1804).

14. See 2 J.B. Moore, Digest of International Law 895 (1906).

15. (Can. v. U.S.), [1935] 3 U.N.R.I.A.A 1609 (1949).

16. (U.K. v. Alb.) 1949 ICJ 4.

In this case, the Ford Administration ... argued that armed force was necessary "to protect the lives of American citizens and property, including appropriate measures of self-defense under Article 51 of the United Nations Charter." If legal advisors had been contacted, however, it would have been known that the United States could not use force to protect the property of United States citizens. The only possible argument—that armed force was necessary to protect American lives and was a proportionate response to a claimed Cambodian violation of international law—does not appear to be any more plausible. There was never any showing that the lives of the crew were in danger, nor were there any reasonable grounds for believing that they were....

* * *

If armed intervention was not necessary to save the lives of the *Mayaguez* crew, it was also not a proportionate response to the Cambodian detention of the crew. A disproportionate response can be just as illegal as an unnecessary response. As Professors McDougal and Feliciano have written:

> Coercion that is grossly in excess of what, in a particular context, may be reasonably required for conservation of values against a particular attack, or that is obviously irrelevant or unrelated to this purpose, itself constitutes an unlawful initiation of coercive or violent change.

* * *

The bombing of the Cambodian mainland and the landing of Marines on a Cambodian island were completely disproportionate responses to a dispute concerning the seizure of a merchant vessel and the detention of her crew. The most telling symbol of the degree to which the United States overreacted was the dropping of a 15,000–ton bomb—the largest conventional bomb in the United States arsenal—on a small Cambodian island.

The United States has an obligation to seek the peaceful settlement of disputes, including prompt and fair use of the United Nations machinery. The only two exceptions recognized by international law are, first, the necessary and proportionate use of self-help, when the United Nations machinery is inoperative, and, second, self-defense, as defined in Article 51 of the United Nations Charter, when there is an actual or imminent attack. In this case, the response of the United States to the seizure of the *Mayaguez* crew was not only unnecessary to protect the lives of the *Mayaguez* crew; it actually endangered them. In addition, the American response was wholly disproportionate to the Cambodian action—an action that was, moreover, lawful ..., including appropriate measures of self-defense under Article 51 of the United Nations Charter **[Basic Document 1.5]**."

12.   Richard A. Falk, "The Beirut Raid and the International Law of Retaliation," 63 A.J.I.L. 415, 437–42 (1969).

... [I]t is important to sustain some framework of constraint in circumstances of conflict.... There is, in particular, a need to establish indicators of reasonableness that can be applied to appraise specific flash-points in a setting of continuous conflict. These indicators can influence, above all else, national decision-making processes to adopt a course of conduct that tends to appear reasonable from an objective or third-party point of view. The structuring of expectations, those of the adversary and of the community, are normally the principal purpose of retaliatory uses of force. . . . In such a context of conflict, world public opinion can become influential should it crystallize in favor of one party in a dispute; this influence can affect what the parties regard as a reasonable basis of settlement, and hence, the shape and prospects for a negotiated settlement. . . .

The principal point is that a retaliatory use of force that is perceived as excessive tends to engender a variety of bad consequences, including some that may be detrimental to the user. The further point is that rules of international law, as traditionally conceived, are too rigidly formulated to give appropriate insight into the factors that shape a decisional process of government and thus do not, in a realistic way, help officials or observers identify when a use of force is "excessive." The excessiveness of a particular use of force depends upon a combination of objective and subjective (value and ideological outlooks) factors, including the effort at justification made by the claimant state. A more useful conception of international law than the specification of categorical rules would be the enumeration of objective factors likely to shape authoritative judgment and expert commentary. Such an enumeration would be useful for legal advisers to the adversary governments and to those passing judgment on contested behavior. * * * [Here], some effort is made to suggest a suitable framework for claims to use force in retaliation. . . .

(1) That the burden of persuasion is upon the government that initiates an official use of force across international boundaries;

(2) That the governmental user of force will demonstrate its defensive character convincingly by connecting the use of force to the protection of territorial integrity, national security, or political independence;

(3) That a genuine and substantial link exists between the prior commission of provocative acts and the resultant claim to be acting in retaliation;

(4) That a diligent effort be made to obtain satisfaction by persuasion and pacific means over a reasonable period of time, including recourse to international organizations;

(5) That the use of force is proportional to the provocation and calculated to avoid its repetition in the future, and that every precaution be taken to avoid excessive damage and unnecessary loss of life, especially with respect to innocent citizens;

(6) That the retaliatory force is directed primarily against military and paramilitary targets and against military personnel;

(7) That the user of force make a prompt and serious explanation of its conduct before the relevant organ(s) of community review and seek vindication there from its course of action;

(8) That the use of force amounts to a clear message of communication to the target government so that the contours of what constituted the unacceptable provocation are clearly conveyed;

(9) That the user of force cannot achieve its retaliatory purposes by acting within its own territorial domain and thus cannot avoid interference with the sovereign prerogatives of a foreign state;

(10) That the user of force seek a pacific settlement to the underlying dispute on terms that appear to be just and sensitive to the interests of its adversary;

(11) That the pattern of conduct of which the retaliatory use of force is an instance exhibits deference to considerations (1)-(10), and that a disposition to accord respect to the will of the international community be evident. . . .

* * *

The role of legal analysis is to facilitate the process of shaping and judging action: specifically, to promote constructive effects to the action and to the community. The assumption underlying such an approach is that the primary role of international law is to help governments plan how to act, rather than to permit some third-party judge to determine whether contested action is legal or not. In fact the function of the third-party judge can be performed properly only by attempting to assess *in what respects* and *to what extent* the governmental actor "violated" community norms of a prescriptive nature. Given the present character of international legal order, the essence of law consists of an interactive process of communication among governments and between governments and international institutions as to the character of acceptable behavior. The more this communication is premised upon a consensus as to relevant considerations and the more it reflects the dominance of objective over subjective factors, the more plausible it becomes to say that international law is playing a significant role.

SECTION 5. DISCUSSION NOTES/QUESTIONS

1. The oceans cover approximately three-fourths of the surface of our planet. Accordingly, for the "average person," it is not always easy to see how endangered the oceans really are. Such expressions as "the bottomless sea" and "the boundless ocean" still are a part of our everyday vocabulary. But consider the following dissent and warning, as long ago as the mid–1970s, by Norwegian explorer and ethnologist Thor Heyerdahl, *How to Kill an Ocean*, Saturday Review, 29 Nov 75, at 12, 14–18:

> It is time to ask: is the ocean vulnerable? And if so, can man survive on a planet with a dead ocean? Both questions can be answered, and they are worthy of our attention.

> First, the degree of vulnerability of any body of water would of course depend on two factors: the volume of the water and the nature of the pollutants. We know the volume of the ocean, its surface measure, and its average depth. We know that it covers 71 percent of the surface of the planet, and we are impressed, with good reason, when all these measurements are given in almost astronomical figures. If we resort to a more visual image, however, the dimensions lose their magic. The average depth of all oceans is only 1,700 meters. The Empire State Building is 448 meters high. The average depth of the North Sea, however, is not 1,700 meters, but only 80 meters. . . . In this shallow water, until only recently, all the industrial nations of Western Europe have conducted year-round routine dumping of hundreds of thousands of tons of their most toxic industrial refuse. All the world's sewers and most of its waste are dumped into waters as shallow as, or shallower than, the North Sea . . .

* * *

After we abandon the outworn image of infinite space in the ocean, we are still left with many wrong or useless notions about biological life and vulnerability. Marine life is concentrated in about 4 percent of the ocean's total body of water, whereas roughly 96 percent is just about as poor in life as is a desert ashore. We all know, and should bear in mind, that sunlight is needed to permit photosynthesis for the marine plankton on which all fishes and whales directly or indirectly base their subsistence. In the sunny tropics the upper layer of light used in photosynthesis extends down to a maximum depth of 80 to 100 meters. In the northern latitudes, even on a bright summer's day, this zone reaches no more than 15 to 20 meters below the surface. Because much of the most toxic pollutants are buoyant and stay on the surface (notably all the pesticides and other poisons based on chlorinated hydrocarbons), this concentration of both life and venom in the same restricted body of water is most unfortunate.

What is worse is the fact that life is not evenly distributed throughout this thin surface layer. Ninety percent of all marine species are concentrated above the continental shelves next to land. The water above these littoral shelves represents an area of only 8 percent of the total ocean surface, which itself represents only 4 percent of the total body of water, and means that much less than half a percent of the ocean space represents the home of 90 percent of all marine life. This concentration of marine life in shallow waters next to the coasts happens to coincide with the area of concentrated dumping and the outlet of all sewers and polluted river mouths, not to mention silt from chemically treated farmland. The bulk of some 20,000 known species of fish, some 30,000 species of mollusks, and nearly all the main crustaceans live in the most exposed waters around the littoral areas. As we know, the reason is that this is the most fertile breeding ground for marine plankton....

When we speak of farmable land in any country, we do not include deserts or sterile rock in our calculations. Why then shall we deceive ourselves by the total size of the ocean when we know that not even 1 percent of its water volume is fertile for the fisherman?

Much has been written for or against the activities of some nations that have dumped vast quantities of nuclear waste and obsolete war gases in the sea and excused their actions on the grounds that it was all sealed in special containers. In such shallow waters as the Irish Sea, the English Channel, and the North Sea there are already enough examples of similar "foolproof" containers moving about with bottom currents until they are totally displaced and even crack open with the result that millions of fish are killed or mutilated. In the Baltic Sea, which is shallower than many lakes and which—except for the thin surface layer—has already been killed by pollution, 7,000 tons of arsenic were dumped in cement containers some 40 years ago. These containers [are now leaking]. Their combined contents are three times more than is needed to kill the entire population of the earth today.

Fortunately, in certain regions modern laws have impeded the danger of dumpings; yet a major threat to marine life remains—the less spectacular but more effective ocean pollution through continuous discharge from sewers and seepage....

* * *

The world was upset when the *Torrey Canyon* unintentionally spilled 100,000 tons of oil into the English Channel ...; yet this is only a small fraction of the international discharge of crude oil sludge through less spectacular, routine tank cleaning. Every year more than the *Torrey Canyon's* spill of a 100,000 tons of oil is intentionally pumped into the Mediterranean alone, and a survey of the sea south of Italy yielded 500 liters of solidified oil for every square kilometer of surface . . .

* * *

The problem of oil pollution is in itself a complex one. Various types of crude oil are toxic in different degrees. But they all have one property in common: they attract other chemicals and absorb them like blotting paper, notably the various kinds of pesticides. DDT and other chlorinated hydrocarbons do not dissolve in water, nor do they sink: just as they are absorbed by plankton and other surface organisms, so are they drawn into oil slicks and oil clots, where in some cases they have been rediscovered in stronger concentrations than when originally mixed with dissolvents in the spraying bottles. Oil clots, used as floating support for barnacles, marine worms, and pelagic crabs, [are common events] and these riders are attractive bait for filter-feeding fish and whales, which cannot avoid getting gills and baleens cluttered up by the tarlike oil. Even sharks with their rows of teeth plastered with black oil clots are now reported from the Caribbean Sea. Yet the oil spills and dumping of waste from ships represent a very modest contribution compared with the urban and industrial refuse released from land.

No breathing species could live on this planet until the surface layer of the ocean was filled with phytoplankton, as our planet in the beginning was only surrounded by sterile gases. These minute planet species manufactured so much oxygen that it rose above the surface to help form the atmosphere we have today. All life on earth depended upon this marine plankton for its evolution and continued subsistence. Today, more than ever before, mankind depends on the welfare of this marine plankton for its future survival as a species. With the population explosion we need to harvest even more protein from the sea. Without plankton there will be no fish. With our rapid expansion of urban and industrial areas and the continuous disappearance of jungle and forest, we shall be ever more dependent on the plankton for the very air we breathe. Neither man nor any other terrestrial beast could have bred had plankton not preceded them. Take away this indispensable life in the shallow surface areas of the sea, and the life ashore will be unfit for coming generations. A dead ocean means a dead planet.

In light of what you have come to know about "the living sea," do you believe that existing norms, institutions, and procedures are adequate to the challenge described by Heyerdahl? Are contemporary trends in ocean use and management encouraging? Discouraging?

2.   Jurisdiction (literally, legal say-so) is a key variable in ocean use and management, perhaps *the* key variable. And it is not without controversy. Not even the breadth of the territorial sea is entirely settled. As of 26 August 2005, according to the Division for Ocean Affairs and the Law of the Sea of the United Nations Office of Legal Affairs, three states claimed a three (3) nautical mile territorial sea, three claimed six (6) nautical miles, 134 claimed twelve (12) nautical miles, and seven claimed 200 nautical miles, and one state (Philippines) claimed a territorial sea, defined by coordinates of points, that extends beyond twelve (12) nautical miles.

For further details concerning territorial sea claims and other maritime claims, see the website of the Division for Ocean Affairs and the Law of the Sea of the United Nations Office of Legal Affairs at <http://www.un.org/Depts/los/LEG-ISLATIONANDTREATIES/PDFFILES/claims_2005.pdf>. The following table, current to 26 August 2005, summarizes the information contained therein, reflecting claims regarding the breadth of given zones (in nautical miles) as contained in national legislation—"regardless," according to the Division of Ocean Affairs, "of whether the legislation contains an additional specific reference to the need for delimitation of maritime boundaries with adjacent or opposite states." However, again quoting the Division, "where the national legislation establishes the limits of a given zone only by, or to a median (equidistant) line in the absence of a maritime boundary agreement, the symbol DLM is used."

TERRITORIAL SEA CLAIMS

Breadth (nautical miles)	Number of States
3	3
6	3
12	134 [17]
Rectangular/Polygonal	1

CONTIGUOUS CLAIMS

Breadth (nautical miles)	Number of States
14	1
15	1
18	4
24	68 [18]

FISHERY CLAIMS

Breadth (nautical miles)	Number of States
25	1
32 or 52	1
62	1
200	6
200 or 12	1
Defined by coordinates of points	3

EXCLUSIVE ECONOMIC ZONE

Breadth (nautical miles)	Number of States
200	104 [19]
Defined by coordinates of points	1
No legislation available [20]	1
DLM	10

17. Does not include North Korea's military boundary.

18. Does not include North Korea's military boundary.

19. Including Australia and the United States.

20. *See* ICJ Judgment of 10 Oct 2002 in the Case Concerning the Land and Maritime Boundary between Cameroon and Nigeria, *available at* <http://www.icj-cij.org/cjwww/idocket/icn/icnframe htm>.

3. In addition to the issue of the distance to which a coastal state may measure its territorial sea, international law has had to deal with the question of the baseline from which the territorial sea is to be measured. The leading case on this question is the *Fisheries Case* (U.K. v. Nor.), 1951 ICJ 116 **(Basic Document 7.6)**, in which the World Court was called to judge the validity of Norway's practice of measuring its territorial sea from a line connecting the approximately 12,000 islands, rocks, and reefs ("skjaegaard") off the Norwegian coast. Although agreeing that the baseline used should not depart from the general direction of the coast, the Court rejected Britain's argument that the outer limit of the territorial sea must never be more than four miles (then the width of Norway's territorial sea) from some point on the coast. Following the Court's lead, international lawyers developed a detailed set of rules governing the drawing of baselines which now are codified in Articles 3–9 of the 1958 Convention on the Territorial Sea and the Contiguous Zone **(Basic Document 5.5)**. This codification was essentially incorporated in Articles 3–16 of the 1982 CLOS **(Basic Document 5.22)**, although the provisions of the 1982 Convention are more inclusive as they naturally take into account developments since the adoption of the 1958 Conventions. On various aspects of the *Anglo-Norwegian Fisheries Case*, see 4 Marjorie M. Whiteman, Digest of International Law 137–94 (1965); Gerald. Fitzmaurice, *The Law and Procedure of the International Court of Justice*, 1951–1954, [1954] B.Y.B.I.L. 371; D.H.N. Johnson, *Anglo-Norwegian Fisheries Case*, 1 I.C.L.Q. 145 (1952); C. Humphrey. M. Waldock, *The Anglo–Norwegian Fisheries Case*, [1951] B.Y.B.I.L. 114. *See also* the following World Court decisions implicating maritime boundaries generally: *Delimitation of the Maritime Boundary in the Gulf of Maine Area* (Can. v. U.S.), 1984 ICJ 246; *Land, Island and Maritime Frontier Dispute* (El Sal./Hond.:Nicaragua Intervening), 1992 ICJ 351; *Land and Maritime Boundary Between Cameroon and Nigeria* (Cameroon v. Nig.), 1994 ICJ 105; *Maritime Delimitation in Area between Greenland and Jan Mayen* (Den. v. Nor.), 1993 ICJ 38; *Maritime Delimitation and Territorial Questions between Qatar and Bahrain* (Qatar v. Bahr.) (Jurisdiction and Admissibility), 1994 ICJ 112 and 1995 ICJ 6.

4. Are foreign warships barred from claiming the right of innocent passage by definition? The former Soviet Union and other communist countries tended to answer this question in the affirmative, asserting that such ships may exercise rights in a coastal state's maritime jurisdiction only with the coastal state's authorization or prior notification. Western countries tended toward the opposite view. Which view is legally correct? Note that Article 23 of the 1958 Convention on the Territorial Sea and Contiguous Zone **(Basic Document 5.5)** authorizes the coastal state to require a warship "to leave the territorial sea" if the latter "does not comply with the regulations of the coastal state concerning passage through the territorial sea and disregards any request for compliance which is made to it.... " Note also that Article 30 of the 1982 CLOS **(Basic Document 5.22)** simply inserts the word "immediately" before the word "comply." Note still further that Article 14(1) of the Territorial Sea Convention provides that, "ships of all States ... shall enjoy the right of innocent passage through the territorial sea" and that Article 14(6) requires submarines (which usually are warships) passing through a coastal State's territorial sea "to navigate on the surface and to show their flag." Are these provisions persuasive relative to the right of warships to innocent passage? Should they be? Under customary international law, according to Philip C. Jessup, The Law of Territorial Waters and Maritime Jurisdiction 120 (1927), "the sound rule seems to be that [warships] should not enjoy an

absolute legal right to pass through a state's territorial waters any more than an army may cross the land territory." For a variety of views, see 4 M. Whiteman, Digest of International Law 404–17 (1965).

5.   The concept of the exclusive economic zone (EEZ) was a consequence, in part, of the growing tendency of coastal states to exploit the living and nonliving resources of their continental shelves following World War II—as in the seminal case, for example, of President Truman's 1945 proclamation asserting the exclusive rights of the United States to the living and nonliving resources of its continental shelf following the discovery of offshore oil and gas in the Gulf of Mexico. *See* Presidential Proclamation 2667, 28 Sep 45, 10 Fed. Reg. 12303 (1945). Not surprisingly, disputes over the delimitation of the continental shelf proliferated. *See, e.g.*, the *North Sea Continental Shelf Cases* (F.R.G. v. Den.; F.R.G. v. Neth.), 1969 ICJ 3; the *Aegean Sea Continental Shelf Case*, 1976 ICJ 3; the *Continental Shelf Case* (Tunis. v. Libya), 1982 ICJ 18; the *Gulf of Maine Case* (Can. v. U.S.), 1984 ICJ 246; the *Continental Shelf Case* (Libya v. Malta), 1985 ICJ 13; and *Application for Revision and Interpretation of the Judgment of 24 February 1982 in the Case Concerning the Continental Shelf* (Tunis. v. Libya), 1985 ICJ 192. The *North Sea Continental Shelf Cases* are criticized in Wolfgang Friedmann, *The North Sea Continental Shelf Cases*, 64 A.J.I.L. 229 (1970). The two more recent cases are the subject of comment in Mark B. Feldman, *Tunisia-Libya Continental Shelf Case: Geographic Justice or Judicial Compromise?*, 77 A.J.I.L. 219 (1985) and Jan Schneider, *The Gulf of Maine Case*, 79 A.J.I.L. 539 (1985). *See generally* Jonathan I. Charney, *Ocean Boundaries Between Nations: A Theory for Progress*, 78 A.J.I.L. 582 (1984).

For the most part, however, by virtue of Article 76(1) of the 1982 CLOS **(Basic Document 5.22)**, consensus as to the basic definition and delimitation of the continental shelf has been achieved, to wit:

> the seabed and subsoil of the submarine areas that extend beyond its territorial sea throughout the natural prolongation of its land territory to the outer edge of the continental margin, or to a distance of 200 nautical miles from the baselines from which the breadth of the territorial sea is measured where the outer edge of the continental margin does not extend up to that distance.

Sections 4–7 of Article 76 provide that, wherever it extends beyond 200 nautical miles, the outer edge of the continental margin shall not exceed 350 nautical miles from the baseline or 100 nautical miles from the 2,500 meter isobath. Compare Article 1 of the 1958 Convention on the Continental Shelf **(Basic Document 5.4)**, defining "continental shelf" as "the seabed and subsoil of the submarine areas adjacent to the coast but outside the area of the territorial sea, to a depth of 200 metres or, beyond that limit, to where the depth of the superjacent waters admits of the exploitation of the natural resources of the said areas.... " The expansion of the definition of the continental shelf in the 1982 CLOS in contrast to the 1958 Convention relates to the widespread acceptance of a 200–mile exclusive economic zone.

Despite this general consensus, however, the diversity of geographic and other elements suggests that precise definition and delimitation of the continental shelf in individual cases especially will be the subject of continuing controversy for years to come. At this writing, for example, China, Japan, and South Korea continue many years of tensions over estimated oil reserves of 10 to 100 billion barrels located in the South China Sea where each of these states claim 200–mile EEZ jurisdictions even though they are less than 400 miles apart. The South

China Sea, through which more than half of the world's supertanker traffic passes, extends from Singapore and the Strait of Malacca in the southwest to the Strait of Taiwan between Taiwan and China in the northeast, and includes more than 200 small islands, rocks, and reefs, the majority of them located in the Paracel and Spratly Island chains, few of which are fit for human habitation. They are, however, important nonetheless because ownership claims to them are used to bolster claims to the surrounding sea and its vast oil and gas resources. Other contestants include Indonesia, Malaysia, the Philippines, Thailand, and Vietnam. Most of these claims are historical, but they are based also upon internationally accepted principles extending territorial claims to a country's continental shelf, as well as on the 1982 CLOS. For further details, see the website of the Energy Information Adminstration of the US Department of Energy at <http://www.eia.doe.gov/emeu/cabs/schina.html>.

6. States sometimes go to great lengths to ensure broad maritime jurisdiction, particularly now that EEZ claims have become so important. Japan's efforts to build up Okinotorishima island is a novel case in point. Located 6,800 kilometers (kms) south of Tokyo, the island boasts only a few rocks standing some 70 centimeters above the water's surface at high tide. If the erosion that already has caused the island to disappear in part should claim these remaining rocks, Japan would lose its claim under the 1982 CLOS (**Basic Document 5.22**) to nearly 400,000 sq. kms of its EEZ, abounding with tuna and bonita and cobalt-rich mineral deposits. Thus, in 1987, to preserve the island, the Japanese government built a retaining wall around the remaining rocks, taking care not to pave them over with cement so as to conform to the provisions of the 1982 CLOS governing exclusive economic zones. *See*, in particular, Articles 55–75 and 121 of the Convention. For details concerning the Japanese effort, see David Swinbanks, *Rock Holds Key to Mineral Riches*, 333 Nature 4 (1988); ___, *Saving Japanese Rocks Out at Sea*, *id.* at 487. See also the website of the Keihin Working Office of the Kanto Regional Development Bureau of the Japanese Ministry of Land, Infrastructure and Transport at <http://www.keihin.ktr.mlit.go.jp/english/ okino-tori>.

7. In 1980, the US Congress passed the Deep Seabed Hard Minerals Resources Act, Pub. L. No. 96–283, 94 Stat. 553, with the US explicitly adopting the position that, in the absence of a supervening treaty and as an aspect of the principle of the freedom of the seas, states have a right to mine the ocean floor. Congress' declared purpose was to provide "assured and nondiscriminatory access" plus "security of tenure" to US corporations seeking to exploit deep seabed resources, including the assurance that any licenses resulting from the Act's passage would remain valid insofar as they would not be inconsistent with any subsequent supervening treaty. Still, Congress recognized the character of deep seabed resources as "the common heritage of mankind" and provided for the establishment of an international revenue-sharing fund. Also, it declared the Act to be transitional pending the results of UNCLOS III.

Still, the legality of this legislation was challenged by the Group of 77 (G–77) in 1979. *See* Letter dated 23 April 1979 from the Group of Legal Experts on the Question of Unilateral Legislation to the Chairman of the Group of 77, UN Doc. A/CONF. 62/77. Essentially, G–77 took the position that the UN General Assembly's Declaration of Principles Governing the Sea–Bed and Ocean Floor, and the Subsoil Thereof, Beyond the Limits of National Jurisdiction (**Basic Document 5.12**)—declaring, *inter alia*, that the named area and its resources "are the common heritage of mankind"—created legal as well as moral obligations and that, though not yet adopted and opened for signature, the 1982 CLOS (**Basic**

Document 5.22), with its Article 136 on the "common heritage of mankind" and 159 signatures, represented *jus cogens*. Nevertheless, on 3 August 1984, two years after the General Assembly's adoption of the 1982 CLOS and not least to overcome a perceived unattractiveness in unilateral seabed mining legislation from a diplomatic point of view, the United States, together with Belgium, France, West Germany, Italy, Japan, the Netherlands, and the United Kingdom entered into a Provisional Understanding Regarding Deep Seabed Mining, *reprinted in* 23 I.L.M. 1354 (1984), the primary purpose of which was to prevent and/or resolve overlapping deep seabed mine site claims among the major industrial powers and to permit multinational consortia to engage in deep seabed mining at least until a supervening treaty enters into force. The eight signatories to the Provisional Understanding state, in the final paragraph, that "this agreement is without prejudice to, nor does it affect, the positions of the parties, or any obligations assumed by any of the parties, in respect of the United Nations Convention on the Law of the Sea."

The G–77 immediately challenged the legitimacy of the Provisional Understanding, however, stating that it went "beyond the resolution of conflicts arising from overlapping claims by including provisions regarding exploration and exploitation of the seabed resources outside of the LOS Convention" and that it is therefore "wholly illegal." *Statement by the Chairman of the Group of 77 Delivered on 13 August 1984*, United Nations Convention on the Law of the Sea: Preparatory Commission for the International Seabed Authority and for the International Tribunal for the Law of the Sea, UN Doc. LOS/PCN/48 (16 Aug 84). Or as one developing world observer critically commented, "[t]he Provisional Understanding, albeit an impermanent agreement, represents a commitment to an alternative regime for the industrialized mining states outside the UNCLOS III framework.... The main benefit, from the point of view of these states ... lies in avoiding their financial or technological obligations to the [International Seabed] Authority and Enterprise [provided for in Part XI of the 1982 UN Convention on the Law of the Sea]. Also of importance (particularly to the Reagan administration) were ideological advantages: the rejection of the application of collectivist principles to the oceans, and the preservation of sovereignty against a perceived Third World-dominated United Nations system." Bharat Dube, *The Deep Seabed and North–South Politics: Cooperation or Confrontation?*, 25 Indian J. Int'l L. 245, 259 (1985).

8. Two critically important shareable resource areas that have encountered problems similar to those arising from the increased use and exploitation of the oceans are the continent of Antarctica and the area known as "outer space." Page limitations preclude extensive discussion of these two realms, but they merit at least brief mention.

(a) The denomination of the deep seabed as "the common heritage of mankind" has been the result, to large degree, of efforts especially on the part of the developing countries to establish a principle of global sharing in respect of the world's shareable resources. This principle is currently being sought to be applied in relation also to the continent of Antarctica. Thus, even though the subject of a multilateral treaty that was created to ensure that this southernmost region of our planet "shall not become the scene or object of international discord" [Antarctic Treaty **(Basic Document 5.7)**], Antarctica remains the focus of jurisdictional debate and the object of competing claims to resource access and economic activity. Thus, a series of consultative meetings among the parties to the 1959 Antarctic Treaty has led to the adoption of several additional treaties dealing with issues critical to the protection of Antarctica. *See, e.g.,* Convention for the

Conservation of Antarctic Seals, 11 Feb 72, 29 U.S.T. 441, T.I.A.S. No. 8826, *reprinted in* 11 I.L.M. 251 (1972) & 5 Weston & Carlson V.D.3; Convention on the Conservation of Antarctic Marine Living Resources (CCAMLR), 20 May 80, T.I.A.S. No. 10240, *reprinted in* 19 I.L.M. 841 (1980) & 5 Weston & Carlson V.D.4; Convention on the Regulation of Antarctic Mineral Resource Activities, 2 Jun 1988, Document AMR/SCM/88/78 of the Antarctic Treaty Special Consultative Meeting on Mineral Resources, *reprinted in* 27 I.L.M. 859 (1988) & 5 Weston & Carlson V.D.5. However, borrowing from the experience of UNCLOS III in negotiating principles and strategies relative to global sharing, it is possible that an equitable Antarctic regime might be established. For a mere sampling of the vast literature on this and related themes, see Ian Anderson, *Oil and Geological Chaos Found off Antarctica*, 106 New Scientist 9 (1985); Antarctic Challenge: Proceedings of an Interdisciplinary Symposium, 22–24 Jun 83 (R. Wolfrum ed., 1984); Antarctic Challenge II: Proceedings of an Interdisciplinary Symposium, 17–21 Sep 85 (R. Wolfrum ed., 1986); Antarctic Ecology (R. Laws ed., 1984); Antarctic Politics and Marine Resources: Critical Choices for the 1980s (L. Alexander & L. Carter eds., 1985); Antarctic Resources Policy (F. Orrego Vicuña ed., 1983); F. M. Auburn, Antarctic Law and Politics (1982); F. M. Auburn, Antarctic Law and Politics (1982); Peter J. Beck, The International Politics of Antarctica 1986); William N. Bonner & D.W.H. Walton, Key Environments: Antarctica (1985); Lorraine M. Elliott, Continuity and Change in Cooperative International Regimes: The Politics of the Recent Environment Debate in Antarctica (1991); Vladimir Golitsyn, Antarctica: The International Law Regime (1983); Governing the Antarctic: The Effectiveness and legitimacy of the Antarctic Treaty System (O. Stokke & D. Vidas eds., 1997); Christopher C. Joyner, Antarctica and the Law of the Sea (1992); Christopher C. Joyner & Ethel R. Theis, Eagle Over the Ice: The United States in Antarctica (1997); John May, The Greenpeace Book of Antarctica: A New View of the Seventh Continent (1989); Jeffrey D. Myhre, The Antarctic Treaty System: Politics, Law, and Diplomacy (1986); Deborah Shapley, The Seventh Continent (1985); John Stewart, Antarctica: An Encyclopedia (1990); Keith Suter, Antarctica: Private Property or Public Heritage? (1991); The Antarctic Legal Regime (C. Joyner & S. Chopra eds., 1988); The Antarctic Treaty Regime: Law, Environment and Resources (G. Triggs ed., 1987); The Antarctic Treaty System in World Politics (A. Jorgensen–Dahl & W. Ostreng eds., 1991); The Future of Antarctica: Exploitation versus Preservation (G. Cook ed., 1990); The New Nationalism and the Use of Common Spaces (J. Charney ed., 1982); US Polar Research Board, Antarctic Treaty System: An Assessment (1986).

(b) As for "outer space," perhaps the most conspicuous area of concern, which has resulted from the largely unregulated scientific and technological revolution of the last half-century especially, is the damage that has been done and threatens to be done to the earth's ozone layer, from radioactive and other atmospheric pollution. For preliminary discussion, see Problems 7–2 ("Hanguo Versus the Ozone Layer") and 7–3 ("A Nuclear Accident in Hanguo"), *supra* at 1105 and 1135. Of course, the subject of outer space use and management, like that of ocean use and management, covers a range of issues that extend beyond the matter of environmental protection. Topics receiving widespread attention include limitations on outer space exploitation and research, militarism, and allocation of jurisdiction and responsibility. International efforts to address these and related issues are evidenced in such instruments as the 1963 Resolution Regarding Weapons of Mass Destruction in Outer Space **(Basic Document 2.19)**; the Declaration of Legal Principles Governing the Activities of States in the Exploration and Use of Outer Space, 13 Dec 63, GA Res. 1962 (XVIII), 18 UN

GAOR, Supp. (No. 15) 15, UN Doc. A/5515 (1964), *reprinted in* 3 I.L.M. 157 (1964); the 1967 Treaty on Principles Governing the Activities of States in the Exploration and Use of Outer Space, Including the Moon and Other Celestial Bodies, 27 Jan 67 & 10 Oct 67, 610 U.N.T.S. 205, *reprinted in* 5 Weston V.E.21. For general reference, see Myres S. McDougal, Harold D. Lasswell, & Ivan A. Vlasic, Law and Public Order in Space (1963); Glenn H. Reynolds, *International Space Law: Into the Twenty-first Century*, 25 Vand. J. Transnat'l L. 225 (1992).

9.   Since the adoption of the 1995 Agreement for the Implementation of the Provisions of the United Nations Convention on the Law of the Sea of 10 December 1982 Relating to the Conservation and Management of Straddling Fish Stocks and Highly Migratory Fish Stocks **(Basic Document 5.43)**, regional fishing organizations (RFOs) have assumed an increasingly important role in the conservation and management of the ocean's fisheries by means of facilitating regional cooperation. Although critics have pointed out that lack of political will, funding, and scientific research has prevented RFOs from taking the proactive role necessary to halt the depletion of threatened fish populations, most agree that they provide the only realistic mechanism for cooperation. Consider the following comment on the 1995 Straddling Stock Agreement by Rebecca Bratspies, *Finessing King Neptune: Fisheries Management and the Limits of International Law*, 25 Harv. Envt'l L. Rev. 213, 238–40 (2001):

> Historically, RFOs were not supranational organizations and had no independent power. They were only as strong (or, more accurately, as weak) as their member states chose to make them. RFOs typically suffered from three structural weaknesses: no ability to adopt or enforce management measures, no way to bind non-parties fishing in the management area, and an easy opt-out provision for members that refused to be bound by specific RFO measures.

> In contrast, the Straddling Stock Agreement bars any non-complying state from access to fisheries, including the high seas portions of these fisheries. Under the Agreement, states that do not cooperate in the regulation of high seas fisheries are not allowed to fish. In particular, Article 8(4) of the Agreement provides:

>> Only those States which are members of such an organization or participants in such an arrangement, or which agree to apply the conservation and management measures established by such organization or arrangement, shall have access to the fishery resources to which those measures apply.

> Article 17(1) provides:

>> A State which is not a member of a subregional or regional fisheries management organization or is not a participant in a subregional or regional fisheries management arrangement, and which does not otherwise agree to apply the conservation and management measures established by such organization or arrangement, is not discharged from the obligation to cooperate, in accordance with the Convention and this Agreement, in the conservation and management of the relevant straddling fish stocks and highly migratory fish stocks.

When read together, Articles 8 and 17 of the Agreement purport to impose conservation obligations on all vessels—even those whose flag state is party to neither the Straddling Stock Agreement nor the RFO under which the conservation obligations arise. Any vessels that refuse to comply with obligations its flag state has not assumed (and may even be presumed to have rejected) on their behalf will be excluded from the fisheries. Moreover, inspectors are authorized to use force on the high seas against vessels flying the flags of other states. Such a regime is a remarkable revision of *mare liberum.* Indeed, at the close of the negotiations, Ambassador Sitya N. Nandan of Fiji, who acted as chair of the Conference, proclaimed that "the freedom to fish on the high seas no longer exists as it did under the old law of the sea."

In light of the apparent reliance upon RFOs to do the heavy lifting in the conservation and management of ocean fisheries, do you believe that such organizations are adequate to the task? Why? Why not?

10. Centrally positioned in the struggle against abusive ocean practices, especially as regards marine pollution, is the International Maritime Organization (IMO), a specialized agency of the United Nations established in 1958 (as the International Maritime Consultative Organization, or IMCO) and since then an important force in the development of international pollution control law. As noted in the readings, the IMO has sponsored such conventions as: the 1969 International Convention Relating to Intervention on the High Seas in Cases of Oil Pollution Casualties **(Basic Document 5.10)**, the 1969 Convention on Civil Liability for Oil Pollution Damage (973 U.N.T.S. 3, *reprinted in* 5 Weston & Carlson V.J.5), the 1971 Convention for the Establishment of an International Fund for Compensation for Oil Pollution Damage **(Basic Document 5.13)**, the 1972 Convention on the Prevention of Marine Pollution by Dumping Wastes and Other Matter **(Basic Document 5.15)**, and the 1973 International Convention for the Prevention of Pollution from Ships (MARPOL 73) (Basic Document 5.16) as modified by its 1978 Protocol (MARPOL 78) **(Basic Document 5.18)** which together are known as "the MARPOL Convention" or "MARPOL 73/78. More recently, the IMO sponsored the 1990 International Convention on Oil Pollution Preparedness, Response and Co-operation, 1891 U.N.T.S. 51, *reprinted in* 5 Weston & Carlson V.F.28; the 1996 International Convention on Liability and Compensation for Damage in Connection with the Carriage of Hazardous and Noxious Substances by Sea, IMO Doc LEG/CONF.10/8/2; and four instruments available only from the IMO at this writing: the 2000 Protocol on Preparedness, Response and Co-operation to Pollution Incidents by Hazardous and Noxious Substances; the 2001 International Convention on the Control of Harmful Anti-fouling Systems on Ships; the 2001 International Convention on Civil Liability for Bunker Oil Pollution Damage; and the 2004 International Convention for the Control and Management of Ships' Ballast Water and Sediments. As of this writing (1 Mar 2006), however, all but the first of these last six instruments have yet to enter into force.

The IMO's function, which has expanded over the years to meet the increasingly complex needs of maritime activity, is essentially to facilitate intergovernmental cooperation and exchange of information on technical matters affecting shipping and to ensure high standards of maritime safety and efficient navigation. With a staff of about 300 people, making it one of the smallest of all UN agencies, the IMO, headquartered in London, operates through an Assembly (the policy-making organ of the agency), a Council and Secretariat (which perform the administrative and normal operational functions of the agency), and the Maritime Safety and Marine Environment Protection Committees (which serve the needs of their respective specialized interests). As of 1 Mar 2006, it had a membership of 166 states (plus Hong Kong and Macao as associate members). Also, as of 30 Nov. 2005, it had concluded "agreements of cooperation" with 36 inter-governmental organizations (IGOs and, as of 14 Oct 2005, granted "consultative status" to 63 nongovernmental organizations (NGOs). Thus, a central force in international pollution control and maritime rule and standard setting, the IMO is likely to play an increasingly important role in the future development of the Law of the Sea. In this connection, see Articles 197–212 of the 1982 CLOS **(Basic Document 5.22)**.

On the IMO's work on pollution, see Cleopatra E. Henry, The Carriage of Dangerous Goods by Sea: The Role of the International Maritime Organization in International Legislation (1985); Ronald B. Mitchell, Intentional Oil Pollution at Sea: Environmental Policy and Treaty Compliance (1994); David W. Abecassis, *IMO and Liability for Oil Pollution from Ships: A Retrospective*, 1983 Lloyd's Mar. & Comm. L. Q. 45; Alan E. Boyle, *Marine Pollution Under the Law of the Sea Convention*, 79 A.J.I.L. 347 (1985); Mario Valenzuela, *IMO: Public International Law and Regulation*, in The Law of the Sea and Ocean Industry: New Opportunities and Restraints 141 (D. Johnston & N. Letalik eds., 1984). For more detailed discussion of the IMO in general, see 1–2 Samir Mankabady, The International Maritime Organization (2d rev. ed. 1986). *See also* the IMO's website, *supra* at <http://www.imo.org>.

11.   As suggested in the readings on marine pollution, *supra* at 1051—78, one reason it has been difficult to secure coastal state jurisdiction over polluting vessels located in the adjacent ocean beyond the territorial sea is because of a substantial fear, on the part of the major maritime powers especially, that anti-pollution controls in this context could serve as a pretext for unwarranted coastal state interference with freedom of navigation. Accordingly, the custom has been to leave the competence to apply authority relative to marine pollution beyond the territorial sea primarily to the state of registry (or flag state). A noteworthy innovation that has emerged from UNCLOS III in this connection, however, is, as noted in the readings, the notion of enforcement by the port state. According to Article 218 of the 1982 CLOS **(Basic Document 5.22),** any state in which a polluting vessel voluntarily makes port may investigate and, subject to some qualification, cause legal proceedings to be brought against such vessel even though the violation of applicable anti-pollution rules and standards may occur wholly outside the port state's usual jurisdiction. Certainly this innovation advances the world order goal of environmental protection relative to marine pollution. But is it sufficient? Note that Article 218 of the 1982 CLOS leaves a coastal state threatened or damaged by a discharge violation essentially in the position of having to find a port state willing to undertake investigations or cause proceedings to be brought. Apart from whether or not such actions would be warranted by evidence, what factors might get in the way? Might they be substantial enough to justify a campaign against the fear of coastal state interference with freedom of navigation? If so, is it realistic to expect that such a campaign would be successful? Might a negative answer suggest the need for some additional normative or structural solutions? What might such solutions be?

12.   Suppose, in the instant problem, that the *Oro Negro* had been situated not 18 but 10 miles off Antilla's coast. Is it clear that Antilla's territorial sea jurisdiction would strengthen its legal control over the *Oro Negro* for oil seepage and/or deballasting, routine events that might be considered innocent for purposes of the law of innocent passage? What about a fully loaded oil tanker? Irrespective of routine seepage, tank washing, or deballasting, would such a vessel pose a pollution hazard serious enough to make innocent passage in fact impossible? Should it? If so, what might some of the practical consequences be? Expensive rerouting? Consequent high energy costs? Other?

13. An historical note. As can be inferred from the readings and the foregoing discussion notes/questions, Latin America's influence upon and contribution to the Law of the Sea has been particularly notable. In fact, it is fair to say that the Latin American countries have been on the vanguard of the endeavor to revise the Law of the Sea, playing a major integrative role among the nations of the "Third World" in general. Why is this so? *See* Bibliography on Latin America and the Development of the Law of the Sea (A. Szekely ed., 1984).

14. If both Antilla and Costa Grande had been parties to the 1982 CLOS **(Basic Document 5.22)**, they would have had the option to seek a binding judgment from not only the International Court of Justice (ICJ) in The Hague, Netherlands, but, as well, the International Tribunal for the Law of the Sea (ITLOS) in Hamburg, Germany, part of a detailed system for the settlement of disputes relating to all aspects of the Law of the Sea dealt within the 1982 CLOS. This system, which came into force upon the entry into force of the 1982 CLOS on 16 November 1994, is set out in Part XV (Articles 279–298) of the Convention and Articles 186–191 regarding disputes arising under the International Sea–Bed Authority as amended by the 1994 Seabed Mining Agreement **(Basic Document 5.40)**. Among these Articles are provisions relating to the obligation to settle disputes by peaceful means (Article 279), applicable law (Article 293), and the binding nature of decisions rendered in settling disputes (Article 296). Also stipulated is a choice of procedure (Article 287), including: (a) the ITLOS, in accordance with 1982 CLOS Annex VI; (b) the ICJ; (c) an arbitral tribunal constituted in accordance with 1982 CLOS Annex VII; and (d) a special arbitral tribunal constituted in accordance with 1982 CLOS Annex VIII for one or more of the categories of disputes specified therein. "The convention is the first global treaty of its kind to require, without a right of reservation, that an unresolved dispute between states parties concerning its interpretation or application be submitted at the request of either party to the dispute to arbitration or adjudication for a decision binding on the other party." Bernard Oxman, *The New Law of the Sea*, 69 A.B.A.J. 157, 162 (Feb 1983).

The Statute of the ITLOS is set out in Annex VI of the 1982 CLOS, and it reflects both the Tribunal's global perspective and its expertise on maritime issues. Article 2 calls for the election by the states parties of 21 judges "enjoying the highest reputation for fairness and integrity and of recognized competence in the field of the law of the sea," and Article 3 provides that at least three of the Tribunal's judges shall be "from each geographical group established by the General Assembly of the United Nations." Indicative of the Tribunal's expertise is the creation of specialized chambers, including the Seabed Disputes Chamber, the Chamber of Summary Procedure, the Chamber of Fisheries Disputes, and the Chamber for Marine Environment Disputes (arts. 14–16).

For details concerning the 1982 CLOS disputes settlement scheme see, Shigeru Oda, *Some Reflections on the Dispute Settlement Clauses in the United Nations Convention on the Law of the Sea*, in Essays in International Law in Honour of Judge Manfred Lachs 645 (J. Makarczyk ed., 1984); Elliot. Richardson, *Dispute Settlement Under the Convention on the Law of the Sea: A Flexible and Comprehensive Extension of the Rule of Law to Ocean Space*, in Contemporary Issues in International Law: Essays in Honor of Louis B. Sohn 149 (T. Buergenthal ed., 1984); Louis B. Sohn, *Dispute Settlement*, in The United States Without the Law of the Sea Treaty: Opportunities and Costs 126 (L. Juda ed., 1983); ___, The System for Settlement of Disputes under the 1982 United Nations Convention on the Law of the Sea: A Drafting History and Commentary (1987); Jorge R. Coquia, *Settlement of Disputes in the UN Convention on the Law of the Sea*, 25

Indian J. Int'l L. 171 (1985); John K. Gamble, *The 1982 UN Convention on the Law of the Sea: Binding Dispute Settlement?*, 9 B.U. Int'l L. J. 39 (1991); Mark W. Janis, *The Law of the Sea Tribunal and the ICJ: Some Notions About Utility*, 16 Marine Pol'y 102 (1992).

15.   Three of the 13 cases that have come before the ITLOS as of this writing (1 Mar 2006)—*The M/V "SAIGA" (No. 2) Case* (Saint Vincent and the Grenadines v. Guinea), the *Southern Bluefin Tuna Cases, Provisional Measures* (New Zealand v. Japan; Australia v. Japan), and *The MOX Plant Case, Provisional Measures* (Ireland v. United Kingdom)—bear relevance to the instant problem. *Saiga* is of such relevance that we have incorporated it as Reading 16, *supra*, and **Basic Document 7.12**. *Bluefin* and *Mox Plant* **(Basic Documents 7.13 and 7.14)** also merit notice. Do you believe that the outcome of *Southern Bluefin* is what the drafters of the 1982 CLOS intended? If not, is it a function of faulty interpretation? Poor drafting? A too narrow conception of the norms, institutions, and/or procedures needed to cope with the environmental problem posed? Consider in this latter connection the words of Steven Broad, Executive Director of TRAFFIC, the wildlife trade monitoring programme of the World Wide Fund for Nature (WWF) and the World Conservation Union (IUCN), who, in August 1999, remarked on the *Southern Bluefin Tuna* dispute as follows:

> The appearance of this issue in an international court is a very poor omen for the future of Southern Bluefin Tuna stocks and for the success of wider international efforts to manage sustainable fisheries around the world.... All countries involved in the dispute, including non-members of [Commission for the Conservation of Bluefin Tuna (*see* <http://www.ccsbt.org/docs/about.html>) who continue to fish outside any quota agreement, need to face the fact that a precautionary management approach backed up by an effective trade certification scheme is essential to ensure a future for this fishery.

Quoted on TRAFFIC's website at <http://www.traffic.org/news/press-releases/tunafishingdispute.html>.

As for *Mox Plant*, note that the Tribunal did not follow the precedent of *Southern Bluefin* wherein it prescribed provisional measures meant to preserve the existing the situation. Why? Is it possible that, as Christoph Schwarte *Environmental Concerns in the Adjudication of the International Tribunal for the Law of the Sea*, 16 Geo. Int'l Envtl. L. Rev. 421 (2004), it actually raised the bar by requiring that the fear of damage to the marine environment must be accompanied by an element of irreversibility or irreparability, thus adopting the jurisprudence of the ICJ in *Case Concerning the Gabcikovo–Nagymaros Project* (Hung. v. Slov.), 1997 ICJ 92 (Sep 25)? If so, do you agree with the decision. Was the Tribunal's decision unequivocal? Note that it did not draw a bright line that might be used in future cases to distinguish serious and irreparable harm from that which could have resulted in this case. What are the reasons for its not doing so? The consequences?

For commentary on *Southern Bluefin* and *Mox Plant*, see Barbara Kwiatkowska, *International Decision: The Southern Bluefin Tuna Case*, 95 A.J.I.L. 162 (2001); Christoph Schwarte *Environmental Concerns in the Adjudication of the International Tribunal for the Law of the Sea*, 16 Geo. Int'l Envtl. L. Rev. 421 (2004); Ted L. McDorman, *International Decision: Access to Information Under Article 9 of the Ospar Convention*, 98 A J.I.L. 330 (2004).

16.   Finally, it is useful to make explicit a fact that is implicit in the materials preceding, namely, that the World Court—first as the Permanent Court of International Justice and subsequently as the International Court of Justice— has played an important ongoing role in the development of the law of the sea.

Since 1920, the World Court has decided the following law of the sea cases: *Delimitation of the Territorial Waters between the Island of Castellorizo and the Coasts of Anatolia*, 1933 PCIJ No. 51 at 4; *The Corfu Channel* (U.K. v. Alb.), 1949 ICJ 237 **(Basic Document 7.5)**; *Fisheries* (U.K. v. Nor.), 1951 ICJ 116 **(Basic Document 7.6)**; *Constitution of the Maritime Safety Committee of the Inter-Governmental Maritime Consultative Organization*, 1960 ICJ 150; *Fisheries Jurisdiction* (U.K. v. Ice.), 1974 ICJ 3 **(Basic Document 7.8)**; *Fisheries Jurisdiction* (F.R.G. v. Ice.), 1974 ICJ 175; *Delimitation of the Maritime Boundary in the Gulf of Maine Area* (Can. v. U.S.), 1984 ICJ 246; *Land, Island and Maritime Frontier Dispute* (El Sal./Hond.:Nicaragua Intervening), 1992 ICJ 351; *Land and Maritime Boundary Between Cameroon and Nigeria* (Cameroon v. Nig.), 1994 ICJ 105, 1996 ICJ 13 (Provisional Measures), 1998 ICJ 275 (Preliminary Objections); *Maritime Delimitation in Area between Greenland and Jan Mayen* (Den. v. Nor.), 1993 ICJ 38; *Maritime Delimitation and Territorial Questions between Qatar and Bahrain* (Qatar v. Bahr.) (Jurisdiction and Admissibility), 1994 ICJ 112 and 1995 ICJ 6; *Oil Platforms* (Iran v. U.S.) (Preliminary Objections), 1996 ICJ 803; *Fisheries Jurisdiction* (Sp. v. Can.), 1998 ICJ 432; and the numerous continental shelf cases cited in Discussion Note/Question 7, *supra*. Pending as of this writing are *Maritime Delimitation between Nicaragua and Honduras in the Caribbean Sea* (Nic. v. Hond.) (General List No. 120) and *Maritime Delimitation between Nicaragua and Colombia in the Caribbean Sea* (Nic. v. Colom.) (General List No. ___).

Considering the complexities of the law of the sea, however, and therefore the large potential for disagreement, only seventeen law of the sea cases in 75 years is scarcely overwhelming. On the other hand, neither is it difficult to understand. Regardless of the Court's substantive competence to hear virtually any dispute brought to it, per Article 36(2) of its Statute **(Basic Document 1.6)**, its procedural competence rests, per Article 36(1), on the willingness or consent of the contending parties, and for the most part States are reluctant to submit their legal disputes to the Court. For illustration, see Discussion Note/Question 7 in Problem 5–1 ("Ethnic Conflict and Its Consequences in Slavia, Candia, and Corcyra"), *supra* at 598.

20. *Bibliographical Note*. For supplemental discussion concerning the principal themes addressed in this problem, consult the following additional specialized materials:

a. The Law of the Sea in General

(1) *Books/Monographs/Reports/Symposia*. Handbook on the New Law of the Sea (R. Depuy & D. Vignes eds., 1991); P. Birnie & A. Boyle, International Law and the Environment (1992); R. Friedheim, Negotiating the New Ocean regime (1993); L. Kimball, D. Johnston, P. Saunders & P. Payayo, The Law of the Sea: Priorities and Responsibilities in Implementing the Convention (1995); M. McDougal & W. Burke, The Public Order of the Oceans (1962); New Directions in the Law of the Sea: Global Developments (R. Lee & M. Hayashi eds., 1996); Pacem in Maribus (E. Borgese ed., 1972); J. Schneider, World Public Order and the Environment: Towards an International Ecolgical Law and Organization (1979).

(2) *Articles/Book Chapters*. J. Charney, *The Delimitation of Ocean Boundaries*, 18 Ocean Dev. & Int'l L. 497 (1987); T. Koh, *Negotiating a New World Order for the Sea*, in Third World Attitudes Toward International Law 715 (F. Snyder & S. Sathirathai eds., 1987); A. Pardo, *The Convention on the Law of the Sea: A Preliminary Appraisal*, in Third World Attitudes Toward International Law 737 (F. Snyder & S. Sathirathai eds., 1987); J. Stevenson & B. Oxman, *The Third United Nations Conference on the Law of the Sea: The 1974 Caracas Session*, 69 A.J.I.L. 1 (1975); ___, *The Third United Nations Conference on the*

Law of the Sea: The 1975 Geneva Session, 69 A.J.I.L. 763 (1975); ___, *The Future of the United Nations Convention on the Law of the Sea*, 88 A.J.I.L. 488 (1994); J. Van Dyke, *International Governance and Stewardship of the High Seas and Its Resources*, in Freedom for the Seas in the 21st Century (Jon M. Van Dyke et al. ed., 1993).

b. Jurisdiction Over Ocean Resources

(1) *Books/Monographs/Reports/Symposia.* F. Ahnish, The International law of Maritime Boundaries and the Practice of States in the Mediterranean Sea (1993); M. Ball, Lying Down Together: Law, Metaphor, and Theology (1985); E. Brown, Sea-bed Energy and Minerals: The International Legal Regime (1992); W. Burke, The New International Law of Fisheries: UNCLOS 1982 and Beyond (1994); D. Johnston, The International Law of Fisheries (1965); E. Luard, The Control of the Seabed: A New International Issue (1974); D. Pharand, The Continental Shelf and the Exclusive Economic Zone: Delimitation and Legal Regime (1993); L. Sohn, The Seabed Beyond National Jurisdiction and the Law of the Sea (1975).

(2) *Articles/Book Chapters.* M. Bleicher, *Equitable Delimitation of Continental Shelf*, 73 A.J.I.L. 60 (1979); B. Oxman, *The High Seas and the International Seabed Area*, 10 Mich. J. Int'l L. 526 (1989); B. Oxman, *The High Seas and the International Seabed Area*, 10 Mich. J. Int'l L. 526 (1989); J. Van Dyke & S. Hefter, *Tuna Management in the Pacific: An Analysis of the South Pacific Forum Fisheries Agency*, 3 U. Haw. L. Rev. 1 (1981).

c. Marine Pollution

(1) *Books/Monographs/Reports/Symposia.* E. Borgese & D. Krieger, The Tides of Change: Peace, Pollution, and Potential of the Oceans (1975); Freedom for the Seas in the Twenty-first Century: Ocean Governance and Environmental Harmony (J. Van Dyke, D. Zaelke & G. Hewison eds., 1993); M. Gavounelli, Pollution from Offshore Installations (1995).

(2) *Articles/Book Chapters.* A. Bernhardt, *A Schematic Analysis of Vessel–Source Pollution: Prescriptive and Enforcement Regimes in the Law of the Sea Conference*, 20 V.J.I.L. 265 (1980); P. Dempsey, *Compliance and Enforcement in International Law—Oil Pollution of the Marine Environment by Ocean Vessels*, 6 Nw. J. Int'l L. & Bus. 459 (1984); R. Mitchell, Compliance with International Treaties: Lessons from Intentional Oil Pollution, 37 Env't 10 (1995); P. Sands, *The Environment, Community and International Law*, 30 Harv. Int'l L. J. 393 (1989); M. Stephenson, *Vessel-Source Pollution Under the Law of the Sea Convention—An Analysis of the Prescriptive Standards*, 17 U. Queensland L. J. 117 (1992); J. Van Dyke, Applying the Precautionary Principle to Ocean Shipments of Radioactive Materials, 24 Ocean Dev. & Int'l L. 399 (1996).

d. Military Retorsion and Reprisals

(1) *Books/Monographs/Reports/Symposia.* D. Bowett, Self–Defense in International Law (1958); I. Brownlie, International Law and the Use of Force by States (1963); E. Colbert, Retaliation in International Law (1948); F. Kalshoven, Belligerent Reprisals (1971).

(2) *Articles/Book Chapters.* H. Almond, *Reprisals: The Global Community Is Not Yet Ready to Abandon Them*, 74 A.S.I.L. Proc. 196 (1980); D. Bowett, *Economic Coercion and Reprisal of States*, 13 V.J.I.L. 1 (1972); L. Damrosch, *Retaliation or Arbitration or Both*, 74 A.J.I.L. 785 (1980); J. McCredie, *The April 14, 1986 Bombing of Libya: Act of Self–Defense or Reprisal?*, 19 Case West. Res. J. Int'l L. 215 (1987); R. Tucker, *Reprisals and Self–Defense: The Customary Law*, 66 A.J.I.L. 586 (1972).

Problem 7–2

Hanguo Versus the Ozone Layer

Section 1.   Facts

Hanguo,[a] a member state of the United Nations, is a technologically developing country on the East Asian continent. In the last three decades, it has sought vigorously to modernize its economy and to raise the living standards of its people. To these ends, it has encouraged direct foreign investment, in part by promising the avoidance of burdensome labor laws and environmental regulations.

In keeping with these promises, Hanguo has taken a deliberately recalcitrant stance toward international instruments that are designed to protect the earth's ozone layer—for example, the 1985 Vienna Convention for the Protection of the Ozone Layer. On the basis of numerous scientific findings, the ozone layer (a thin protective layer of gas that shields Earth from the harmful consequences of ultraviolet radiation (*e.g.*, skin cancer epidemics in humans and unforeseen genetic damage to Earth's flora and fauna) has been seen to be, by developed nations especially, in grave danger of serious depletion. Hanguo, however, though a party to the 1985 Vienna Convention as of the late 1980s, has refused to sign and ratify the 1987 Montreal Protocol thereto or any of the Vienna Convention's other progeny. Instead, it insists upon, *inter alia*, its right to sovereign control over its own resources and the urgent need of its people to lift themselves out of longstanding poverty and social chaos brought about by centuries of abusive exploitation, domestic and foreign. While it attended all the international ozone layer negotiations called by the United Nations Environment Programme (UNEP),[b] it always passionately declared that it would not sign or ratify any of the instruments coming out of the post-Vienna negotiations. It was free to do as it pleased, it contended, because, it claimed, no international legal rules require it to change its behavior. Moreover, it asserted, the developed nations were "hypocrites"; having used ozone-depleting technology for their own gain, they now attempt to decree that no-one else may do the same.

Among the ozone-depleting technologies much used by the developed nations have been artificial chemicals known as chlorofluorocarbons (CFCs) and halons. CFCs were used as propellants in aerosol sprays, as coolants in refrigerators and air conditioners, for the blowing of various foam products (*e.g.* styrofoam), and as a cleaning agent for various electrical processes and appliances, including computers. Halons were used to extinguish fires. During the 1970s and 1980s, scientists found these chemicals to be the cause of ozone

---

a. Pronounced "Hängwua."

b. UNEP is headquartered in Nairobi, Kenya.

layer depletion, so it was to the control of their emission that all the diplomatic instruments were directed. However, it took some time for a scientific consensus to emerge, and as a consequence a number of dissenters always could be found. Hanguo paid the scientific skeptics handsomely to continue their research, and it vigorously trumpeted their findings at all the international meetings. As the evidence became clearer, however, the controls on emission became stricter.

The Hanguoan government's legal advisors were familiar with the nuances of the international instruments that aimed to control CFC emissions, having been active participants in the negotiations leading to them. Accordingly, they were able to structure governmental policies that made possible the creation of a significant CFC manufacturing industry in Hanguo. Some of the CFCs produced were used to meet Hanguo's growing domestic demand for refrigerators, air conditioners, and like products. Others were exported to other developing countries. The remainder were used in industrial processes in Hanguo, with the resultant products being exported. The proportions were roughly one-third for each use. The exported products, though requiring CFCs for their manufacture, did not appear on the list of products produced with controlled substances compiled under Article 4 of the 1987 Montreal Protocol. In most instances, in part because these products were free from ozone-depleting substances at the time of their export, it was not possible to tell whether they had been manufactured with ozone-depleting substances or not.

As more and more international corporations located manufacturing plants in Hanguo to take advantage of the situation created there, Hanguo developed a quite substantial industrial base to its economy. And as other countries sharply reduced their manufacture of ozone-depleting goods and substances in conformity with the international instruments on ozone depletion, Hanguo's production of like goods and substances rose dramatically. Indeed, by the turn of the 21st Century, Hanguo was producing an estimated 15% of the total annual world production of ozone-depleting goods and substances.

But Hanguo's policy was becoming increasingly difficult to maintain. Many developing countries had acceded to the instruments on ozone depletion when funding became available to help them comply, which meant that they could no longer trade with Hanguo in CFC products without violating their treaty commitments. In addition, the provisions of the international instruments relating to trade in ozone-depleting goods and substances were tightened up in London in 1990 and again in Copenhagen in 1992. At this writing, 189 nations had ratified the 1987 Montreal Protocol, which is a very high number of states to become party to any international agreement. International pressure was mounting.

The Australian and United States governments, concerned about the deleterious effect that Hanguo's ozone policy could have on their territories and peoples, decided to try and put a stop to Hanguo's ozone policy, which they considered to be an evasion of an international legal consensus achieved after much diplomatic effort and at considerable economic cost to the world. Breach of this legal consensus, they claimed, endangers the future of life on

Earth. While conceding that Hanguo is a technologically developing country entitled to the deferences provided by Article 5 of the 1987 Montreal Protocol, they requested that Hanguo abide by the emission levels that had been established in the 1985 Vienna Convention and its progeny, and limit and reduce its manufacture of ozone-depleting goods and substances. Hanguo, however, adamantly refused to alter its policy and, citing the US and Australian resistance to the 1997 Kyoto Protocol to the United Nations Framework Convention on Climate Change,[c] asserted strongly, in the words of its prime minister, that it is entitled under international law to pursue its existing policies "uninterrupted and without external interference." To date, it has not changed its position significantly and continues to manufacture ozone-depleting goods and substances.

You are a lawyer in the Office of the Legal Adviser of the United States Department of State working closely with your counterpart in the Australian Department of Foreign Affairs and Trade. You have been asked for authoritative *legal* advice to be submitted by way of confidential memorandum to the Prime Minister of Australia and the President of the United States (without regard to any specialized trade rules that might apply).

SECTION 2.   QUESTIONS PRESENTED

1. Is Hanguo violating international law? If so, what rights/remedies do Australia and the United States have against Hanguo? If not, what lawful political (or practical) steps might Australia and/or the United States take to bring about a change in Hanguo's policy?

2. In any event, are there any additional or alternative legal norms, procedures, and/or institutions to be recommended that might further help to prevent or discourage situations of the kind posed by this problem?

SECTION 3.   ASSIGNMENTS

A.   READING ASSIGNMENT

Study the Readings presented in Section 4, *infra*, and the Discussion Notes/Questions that follow. Also, to the extent possible, consult the accompanying bibliographical references.

B.   RECOMMENDED WRITING ASSIGNMENT

Prepare a comprehensive, logically sequenced, and *argumentative* brief in the form of an outline of the primary and subsidiary *legal* issues you see requiring resolution for the Prime Minister of Australia and the President of the United States. Also, from the perspective of an independent observer, indicate which side ought to prevail on each issue and why. Retain a copy of your issue-outline (brief) for class discussion.

c. FCCC/CP/1997/7/Add.1, *reprinted in* 37 ILM 32 (1998) and 5 Weston & Carlson V.E.20d. For further discussion of the Kyoto Protocol, see *supra* Problem 6–4 ("The UFC and the EU Dispute the GATT and Global Warming"), at 886.

C. Recommended Oral Assignment

Assume that you have been asked by the Legal Adviser, who is responsible for the legal memorandum to be submitted to the Prime Minister of Australia and the President of the United States, to pose as legal counsel for Hanguo, on the one hand, or Australia and the United States, on the other (as designated by your instructor); then, relying upon the Readings (and your issue-outline if prepared), present a 10–15 minute oral argument of your government's likely positions before the Legal Adviser.

D. Recommended Reflective Assignment

Consider (and recommend) alternative norms, institutions, and/or procedures that you believe might do better than existing world order arrangements to contend with situations of the kind posed by this problem. In so doing, but without insisting upon *immediate* feasibility, identify the particular transition steps that would be needed to make your alternatives a reality.

Section 4. Readings

The following readings are considered *prima facie* relevant to solving this problem. They are your law library for present purposes and should be treated as such, organized intelligibly for "shelving" and not necessarily according to the issues presented. Be sure to review Chapter 2 ("International Legal Prescription: The 'Sources' of International Law") in your consideration of them. It, too, should be treated as part of your law library (as, indeed, should this entire coursebook).

1. Editors' Note. In the late 1970s, in response to scientific findings, including the ground-breaking research of scientists Sherwood Rowland and Mario Molina of the University of California (as reported in Sharon Begley, *A Gaping Hole in the Sky*, Newsweek, 11 Jul 1988, at 21), several countries, the United States among them, banned CFC aerosols. However, as Carol Petsonk writes, in *The Role of the United Nations Environment Programme (UNEP) in the Development of International Environmental Law*, 5 Am. U. J. Int'l L. & Pol'y 351, 367–68 (1990), "[g]lobal CFC consumption continued to climb ... as the chemicals were put to other uses. In 1980 the Governing Council [GC] directed UNEP to under-take measures to protect the ozone layer from modifications due to human activities, and in 1981 the GC called for a convention." Thus, Petsonk continues, "[t]he Montevideo Programme [of UNEP] gave high priority to the development of a convention on ozone layer protection. Building on its Barcelona Convention model,[1] UNEP sought to obtain simultaneous adoption of a framework convention and a protocol controlling CFCs. There was no scientific consensus, however, on the extent of CFC-catalyzed ozone layer depletion. Several CFC-producing countries, most notably Japan, questioned the need for a CFC protocol. By 1985 UNEP had achieved consensus on only the framework convention **[Basic Document 5.23]**."

---

1. *See* Barcelona Convention for the Protection of the Mediterranean Sea Against Pollution, concluded 16 Feb 1976, entered into force, 12 Feb 1978, 15 ILM 290 (1976) (adopting convention and protocols together).

2. John W. Kindt and Samuel P. Menefee, "The Vexing Problem of Ozone Depletion in International Law and Policy," 24 Tex. Int'l L. Rev. 261, 277–282 (1989).

For environmentalists, 1985 began in a promising manner, with forty-one countries in attendance at the UNEP-sponsored Vienna Conference of Plenipotentiaries on Protection of the Ozone Layer. Of the participant countries, eighteen ended the conference on March 22nd by signing the Vienna Convention for the Protection of the Ozone Layer **[Basic Document 5.23]**. Interestingly, in the United States the Convention had the support of both the CFC industry and environmentalists, because of its potential contribution to the development of better scientific data. The Ozone Convention's stated purpose was "to promote exchanges of information, research, and data on monitoring to protect human health and the environment against activities that have an adverse effect on the ozone layer."[2] As the US Department of State noted, "[t]he Convention . . . [was] an important step in protecting the environment and preserving public health from the potential effects of ozone depletion."[3] Furthermore, the State Department had decided that "[d]ue to the nature of the ozone layer, a multilateral undertaking such as the Convention [was] the only way to promote the global coordination and harmonization necessary for protection of stratospheric ozone."[4]

* * *

. . . Revised five times, the document embodied not only the view of the attendees, but also the written comments solicited from non-attending states. Despite last-minute efforts, the Ozone Convention did not adopt a protocol for future CFC control measures. * * * [Nevertheless], the . . . Convention was a success because it provided an umbrella treaty on the ozone problem, along with annexes on "Research and Systematic Observation" and "Information Exchange." Specific accomplishments included:

a. defining the general obligations of parties to protect human health and the environment from adverse effects "resulting or likely to result" from activities "which modify or are likely to modify" the ozone layer;

b. calling for research and systematic observations, as well as cooperation in science, technology, law, and data transmission;

c. establishing a "Conference of the Parties" and a Secretariat to implement the Convention and its protocols; and

d. providing for the negotiated settlement of disputes concerning interpretation or application of the Convention.

Soon after this success, while the Bonn Economic Summit was in session, the United States strongly urged an international ban on CFC use in aerosols. The Summit resulted in an agreement, based on the December 1984 recom-

2. P. Sand, *Protecting the Ozone Layer: The Vienna Convention is Adopted*, 18 Environment 19 (Jun 85).

3. *Id.*

4. Letter from John C. Whitehead, US Dep't of State, to President Ronald W. Reagan, submitting the Vienna Convention for the Protection of the Ozone Layer, 22 Aug 1985, *reprinted in* President's Ozone Message Treaty Doc. No. 9, 99th Cong., 1st Sess. 12 (1985).

mendations of EEC environment ministers, to devise internationally accepted standards to measure environmental changes.

With the Ozone Convention and the Summit agreement, environmentalists began to think that the process for reaching a solution to the problem was well underway, but in May of 1985 there was an alarming report[5] of an "ozone hole" over Antarctica.[6] * * * [And] [a]s this information became public, "[e]verything about ... [the hole] seemed ominous.... One scientist, who's not known for hyperbole, compared the hole to 'the canary in the mine.'"[7]

The ozone hole placed the entire ozone problem back on the world's diplomatic agenda. Unfortunately, scientists were unsure of the hole's cause. While many scientists [looked for a chemical culprit (usually chlorine) and blamed CFCs, others [dubbed "dynamicists"] "thought the effect to be a natural fluctuation, one possibly connected with the solar cycle."[8] * * * [Throughout 1986 and much of 1987, and despite numerous reports and publications, it] was still far from clear ... whether the ozone hole was an isolated problem or was symptomatic of a global [ecological] decline.

3. Vienna Convention for the Protection of the Ozone Layer. Concluded at Vienna, 22 Mar 1985. Entered into force, 22 Sep 1988. 1513 U.N.T.S. 293; *reprinted in* 26 I.L.M. 1529 (1987) and 5 Weston & Carlson V.E.5 (Basic Document 5.23).

4. Carol A. Petsonk, "The Role of the United Nations Environment Programme (UNEP) in the Development of International Environmental Law," 5 Am. U. J. Int'l L. & Pol'y 351, 367–372 (1990).

... Almost immediately after the [Vienna Convention **(Basic Document 5.23)**] was adopted, UNEP resumed intensive negotiations on [a] protocol. Irish reports of a hole in the ozone layer over Antarctica spurred the momentum. Scientific evidence also began to implicate substances other than CFCs. In mid–1987 the Governing Council recommended that the protocol negotiations consider the full range of ozone-depleting substances. Barely three months later, a UNEP-convened diplomatic conference adopted the Montreal Protocol **[Basic Document 5.29]**.

* * *

UNEP's strategy in ozone layer protection was to go for a convention directly without getting bogged down in soft law preliminaries. This strategy was aided by the emergence, over the six years of negotiations, of a set of governmental negotiators—scientists and legal/political experts from developing and developed countries—who understood the importance of the issue and were committed to reaching consensus.

UNEP took care to involve not only environmental NGOs, but also industry groups. UNEP recognized that without industry support, CFC production controls would be meaningless. Fortunately for UNEP's efforts, CFC

5. *See* National Aeronautics and Space Admn., Present State of Knowledge of the Upper Atmosphere: An Assessment Report at 15, 106–07 (1986).

6. *See* US Nat'l Science Foundation, Press Release No. 86–89, Nat'l Ozone Expedition Statement 1 (20 Oct 1986)....

7. G. Taubes & A. Chen, *Made in the Shade? No Way*, 8 Discover 62, at 63 (Aug 1987)....

8. R. Hallgreen, *Earth Sciences: Meteorology*, 1987 Britannica Book of the Year 175, 176.

production is concentrated among relatively few countries and companies. The major producers and some of the major consumers are large, publicly held firms and are thus increasingly sensitive to public pressure of the environmental kind.

The constituency that presented the greatest challenge to UNEP's drive for consensus was comprised of Asian and Pacific countries. Many of these had recently joined the ranks of CFC-producing countries and were seeking greater shares of the global market. . . .

* * *

Potentially, the Vienna Convention and Montreal Protocol constitute a highly effective regime for reducing—and possibly, in the future, eliminating—emissions of ozone layer-depleting chemicals. Unlike most other environmental agreements, the Montreal Protocol also contains economic incentives to encourage participation and compliance. It further provides for assessment of its efficacy and for readjustment.

The Vienna Convention is the central international mechanism for harmonizing national and international policies and strategies on ozone layer research. The Montreal Protocol is the central international control instrument.

It freezes CFC consumption as of January 1, 1990, requires 50% reductions in CFC production and consumption by mid–1998, and mandates a 1992 freeze on the consumption of halons. The parties have agreed to establish a working group to develop recommendations concerning the determination and consequences of noncompliance.

The Montreal Protocol uses three kinds of provisions as economic incentives to encourage participation in and compliance with the Protocol's control regime: (1) entry into force requirements, (2) controls on trade with nonparties, and (3) research and technology transfer benefits. While the Protocol could have used other types of economic incentives, each of these kinds of provisions aims to make continued production of ozone-destroying CFCs less profitable, while boosting the market for safer substitutes.

Article 16 of the Montreal Protocol provides that eleven countries representing two-thirds of global consumption of controlled substances must ratify the Protocol before it may enter into force.[d] Thus, the Protocol creates a cartel of consumers who control the consumption market, and who have agreed to reduce their consumption. Since most of the major consuming countries are also major producers, the consumption cartel also operates as a production cartel which has effectively agreed to scale back production. Furthermore, as a result of the consumption cutback, this production cartel will face a shrinking market, with correspondingly lower prices and profits, discouraging continued production.

Article 4 of the Montreal Protocol gradually prohibits trade in controlled substances with nonparties. Consequently, nonparty producing states will also face declining demand, with similar effects on prices, profits and production.

As a further result of Article 4's ban on trade with nonparties, nonparty consuming states will face a diminishing legal supply of controlled substances.

d. The Protocol entered into force on 1 January 1989.

This could give rise to black markets, were it not for the fact that the Vienna Convention specifically encourages research on the development of substitutes. The Montreal Protocol's consumption controls should accelerate these processes. Nonparty consumer states should therefore find increased availability of safe substitutes, which they can obtain legally from states party to the Protocol. The prices for these substitutes should become competitive as producers in party states shift to producing substitutes instead of producing controlled substances.

The Protocol promotes technology transfer to parties who are developing countries, thereby offering economic incentives for developing countries to join and comply. The benefits of technology transfer should improve the ability of newly industrialized producing countries to penetrate the growing substitutes market. In addition, countries that are located in tropical climates, where demand for coolants is presumably high, should be interested in developing local production of substitutes in order to reduce dependence on expensive imports. The rewards of obtaining technology to develop local production, coupled with the difficulties of obtaining products from other nonparties, should encourage developing countries to join the Protocol.

The Montreal Protocol specifically provides for readjustment of its controls. The parties can undertake such readjustment on the basis of new information about the state of the ozone.[e] * * * The parties to the Protocol [can] also re-evaluate the control measures based on the degree of compliance achieved. Compliance [can] be measured in terms of reductions in CFC emissions over time, compared against 1986 consumption. In the short term, the relatively concentrated nature of the CFC industry, its susceptibility to the current climate of pro-environment political pressures, and the sense of personal commitment that many negotiators developed over the past ten years, increase the likelihood that compliance will continue with measurable results. Over time, however, if the Montreal Protocol increases competition in the substitutes industry, production may shift to smaller companies less susceptible to these compliance pressures. Hopefully, the Protocol's economic incentives, as well as increased global awareness of the ozone layer problem will continue to foster compliance with these much-needed control measures.

5. Montreal Protocol on Substances that Deplete the Ozone Layer. Concluded, 16 Sep 1987. Entered into force, 1 Jan 1989. 1522 U.N.T.S. 3; *reprinted in* **26 I.L.M. 1541 (1987)** *and in consolidated form with Basic Documents 5.33, 5.42, 5.45, 5.47, and 5.52 in* **5 Weston & Carlson V.E.9** (Basic Document 5.29).

6. Helsinki Declaration on the Protection of the Ozone Layer. Adopted, 2 May 1989. *Reprinted in* **28 I.L.M. 1335 (1989) and 5 Weston & Carlson V.E.14** (Basic Document 5.31).

7. London Amendment to the Montreal Protocol on Substances that Deplete the Ozone Layer. Adopted by the Parties, 29 Jun 1990. Entered into force, 10 Aug 1992. 1598 U.N.T.S. 469; *reprinted in* **30 I.L.M. 537 (1991)** *and consolidated with Basic Document 5.29 in* **5 Weston & Carlson V.E.9** (Basic Document 5.33)

e. The Protocol has been formally amended and adjusted five times as of this writing. *See infra* readings 7–11.

8. Copenhagen Amendment to the Montreal Protocol on Substances that Deplete the Ozone Layer. Adopted by the Parties, 25 Nov 1992. Entered into force, 14 Jun 1994. 1785 U.N.T.S. 517; *reprinted in* **32 I.L.M. 874 (1993)** *and consolidated with Basic Document 5.29 in* **5 Weston & Carlson V.E.9** (Basic Document 5.38).

9. Vienna Adjustments to the Montreal Protocol on Substances that Deplete the Ozone Layer. Adopted by the Parties, 7 Dec 1995. Entered into force, 5 Aug 1996. 1931 U.N.T.S. 423; *consolidated with Basic Document 5.29 in* **5 Weston & Carlson V.E.20b** (Basic Document 5.45).

10. Montreal Amendment to the Montreal Protocol of September 16, 1987 on Substances that Deplete the Ozone Layer. Adopted by the Parties, 17 Sep 1997. Entered into force, 10 Nov 1999. UN Doc. UNEP/OzL.Pro.9/12; *reprinted in* **1996 WL 806145 (Treaty)** *and consolidated with Basic Document 5.29 in* **5 Weston & Carlson V.E.9** (Basic Document 5.47).

11. Beijing Amendment to the Montreal Protocol on Substances that Deplete the Ozone Layer. Adopted by the Parties, 3 Dec 1999. Entered into force, 25 Feb 2002. UN Doc. UNEP/OzL.Pro.11/10; *reprinted in* **5 Weston & Carlson V.E.20h** (Basic Document 5.51).

12. Elizabeth R. DeSombre, "The Experience of the Montreal Protocol: Particularly Remarkable, and Remarkably Particular," 19 UCLA J. Envtl. L. & Pol'y 49, 49–55, 57, 69–76 (2000–01).

By most accounts, the treaty process for addressing ozone depletion is an unqualified success. It has achieved near universal participation, with 170 states party to the Montreal Protocol **[Basic Document 5.29]**[f] and a substantial fraction of those party to the London, Copenhagen, and Montreal Amendments to the Protocol **[Basic Documents 5.33, 5.38 & 5.47]**. It has fundamentally changed the way certain industries conduct their business, already creating in some countries a complete phaseout of certain classes of chemicals.

The process itself is particularly impressive. Negotiations began under conditions of uncertainty, over both the existence and extent of environmental harm and the costliness of taking action to mitigate it. The Vienna Convention **[Basic Document 5.23]**, the Montreal Protocol, and subsequent amendments have created the ability to adapt to changes in scientific understanding of the problem and its potential solutions. The environment is responding as well. Although it is too soon to expect to see improvement in the ozone layer, measurements indicate that it is deteriorating at a decreasing rate, and concentrations of some ozone depleting substances in the atmosphere are starting to decline.

* * *

The process of responding to ozone depletion has not been entirely simple. It has faced a number of unforeseen problems, some of them more serious than they appear; some less so. As a representative of the environmental group Friends of the Earth pointed out, "[n]one of our models predicting

f. One hundred eighty-nine (189) states parties as of this writing (1 Mar 2006).

when CFC releases will peak and when the ozone hole will close up take into account smuggling and large countries that don't comply."[9] These difficulties, primarily relating to the thriving black market in ozone depleting substances and the uncertainty over developing country phaseout of these substances, are both in some ways side effects of precisely the things that made the Montreal Protocol successful. The black market arises in part out of the non-treaty ways states have chosen to implement the agreement. While not part of the agreement, these mechanisms of implementation were important in setting up the industrial incentives to create and use non-ozone depleting substances. It is thus a side effect, and probably not a fatal one. The possibility that large developing countries may ultimately refuse to phase out their use of ozone depleting substances is an open question at this point but a greater potential danger. It is a more direct effect of the way the treaty enticed developing countries to join, and it too may not have had any reasonable alternatives. These potential difficulties should not, for now, overshadow the dramatic improvements the treaty has initiated.

* * *

One of the notable features of the Montreal Protocol process is the extent to which it is designed to allow for adjustments when scientific understanding or political willingness to address the issue changes. This flexibility was particularly important for a treaty that was negotiated when there was no clear evidence of human-induced destruction of the ozone layer and certainly no measurable effect or environmental damage as a result of such depletion. The major factors allowing for change in regulations include the type of treaty used to regulate, an additional adjustments process included in the treaty, and the existence and autonomy of bodies within the treaty organization that have the ability to study or suggest changes in various policies.

* * *

The use of a Convention/Protocol treaty structure allowed negotiation to begin when there was uncertainty about the extent of the environmental problem, and a disinclination to take action under those conditions. While this regulatory format did not begin with the Vienna Convention and the Montreal Protocol, the experience with the ozone depletion issue popularized this approach, which is now seen as commonplace in international environmental regulation.

The Vienna Convention for the Protection of the Ozone Layer creates a framework in which states agree to take "appropriate" (but unspecified) measures to protect the ozone layer, cooperate in scientific research, and exchange information. It indicates that the Conference of the Parties to the treaty "may adopt protocols" in order to create substantive obligations. The 1985 Convention was followed by the negotiation in 1987 of the Montreal Protocol on Substances that Deplete the Ozone Layer, which required specific abatement measures for ozone depleting substances. As laid out in the Vienna Convention, amendments to the Protocol can be made with a 2/3 majority vote and are then subject to ratification by the Parties. Only those that ratify the Amendments are bound by them, although states that ratify the Protocol are bound by any Amendments in force at the time of ratification. Amendments

9. W. Gibbs, *The Treaty that Worked—Al-* most, *273 Sci. Am. 20 (Sep 1995).*

were agreed to in London in 1990, Copenhagen in 1992, and Montreal in 1997.[g]

The Convention/Protocol process resulted in a more robust agreement, at an earlier point, than would have occurred if negotiations had only begun once serious abatement measures could have been agreed upon. The Montreal Protocol added specific abatement measures and the amendments added new regulated substances and new regulatory processes. The London amendments added regulations for carbon tetrachloride, methyl chloroform, and fully halogenated CFCs, as well as introducing the funding mechanism to provide assistance to developing countries. The Copenhagen Amendments added HCFCs, hydrobromide fluorocarbons, and methyl bromide to the list of controlled substances, and made the funding mechanism permanent. The Montreal Amendments adjusted the timetable for phaseout of some substances and modified trade restrictions, including the creation of a licensing system to attempt to decrease the black market in ozone depleting substances. An agreement that would have addressed all these issues could certainly not have been negotiated in 1985 or even 1987, and arguably is only because of the incremental action that further regulations were made possible within an existing framework.

* * *

... [T]he Montreal Protocol adjustment system ... circumvents both of the standard approaches to the making of international environmental law. It neither empowers a commission to make rules that states are allowed to opt out of, nor requires that all changes be ratified by all parties before they take effect. Unusual among treaties that follow the Convention/Protocol approach, the Montreal Protocol also allows for adjustments within the agreement. Adjustments require the consent of 2/3 of the Parties, representing a majority of both developed and developing countries (the latter part an addition of the London Amendments). They become binding on all Parties six months after they are formally notified about them, even those states that did not vote in favor of them.

Adjustments have taken place at meetings of the parties and other negotiations and have addressed such issues as faster phaseout of certain chemicals. Many of the most dramatic changes in the phaseout schedule for various ozone depleting substances have come through adjustments rather than Amendments. For example, the original Montreal Protocol called for a 55 freeze at 1986 levels for the main halons by 1993 for non-Article 5 countries. That was first adjusted in 1990 to a freeze in 1992 and a complete phaseout by 2000. In 1992 it was adjusted to consumption by 1994 at 25% of 1989 levels and a complete phaseout by 1996. Similarly, the initial Montreal Protocol requirement that developed countries cut their use of the major CFCs to 50% of 1986 levels by 1999 was ultimately adjusted to a complete phaseout by 1996. Similar adjustments were made for developing country parties.

The adjustments process ... has made substantive and dramatic changes in abatement obligations possible more quickly than would have taken place otherwise. It allows for changes when new information on environmental damage or technological options suggest that faster phaseout is necessary or

g.   Also in Beijing in 1999.

possible. * * * [T]he role that the secretariats, committees, and subsidiary bodies to the Conference of the Parties play in working behind the scenes has added flexibility to the static language of the Treaty in ways that make implementation of the agreement more successful. The combination of the overall Convention/Protocol process and the adjustments process, allow for adaptations to policies without the need to renegotiate and ratify the entire agreement for every change taken. These elements of flexibility have been essential in allowing the Montreal Protocol process to adapt to changing environmental conditions, scientific and technical understanding, and political realities.

[*Eds.*—The author, of the Wellesley College Environmental Studies and Political Science faculties, next recounts the "central role" that industry has played in the Montreal Protocol process, spurred by Protocol process incentives, governmental regulations, and global market forces to contribute to "the successful mitigation of ozone depletion" by developing and using substitute technologies to replace ozone-depleting substances (ODS). She also details the emergence of an "unforeseen but perhaps not unforeseeable" ODS black market caused by, *inter alia*, differential phaseout dates between developed and developing countries, difficulties faced by countries with economies in transition (*e.g.*, Russia), the ease of smuggling itself, and, most importantly, consumer demand—"the ultimate creator of supply"—provoked by legal prohibitions, high excise taxes that make the legal purchase of ODS too expensive, and "the high cost of retrofitting some CFC-based equipment to use other non-ozone depleting substances" (*e.g.*, in automobile air conditioning). Concluding that, while "less than ideal" and to be ameliorated "to the extent possible," this black market "does not pose a long-term threat to the health of the Montreal Protocol system," the author then turns to consider what she perceives to be the more problematic issue of developing country participation in the ozone layer protection process.]

The participation of developing countries [has been] essential to the success of the Montreal Protocol process. Although at the time the Protocol was signed the per capita consumption of ODS by these countries was miniscule and production in most countries negligible, both these figures were likely to grow significantly. Chlorofluorocarbons had been essential in the process of industrialization for the countries of the North, and others at early stages of development were likely to use these cheap, safe chemicals in their process of industrialization as well. It was estimated at the time that India and China alone would account for one-third of the world's consumption of CFCs by 2008.

Moreover, the problem had clearly been created by Northern industries, and the concern about the environmental problem was most prevalent in the industrialized world. Absent sufficient incentives to join the agreement, developing countries showed every sign of remaining outside the regulatory system. By the time of the London negotiations in 1989 the only major CFC-using developing countries that had joined the agreement were Mexico, Nigeria, and Venezuela. Any successful effort to protect the ozone layer had to gain the participation of all the major developing countries.

The most innovative and essential element in bringing these states into the agreement was the elaboration of a financial transfer mechanism. The

Multilateral Fund, as the mechanism was ultimately named, was the element that allowed for universal participation in the agreement, and facilitated the process of moving away from ozone depleting substances in developing countries. It is a generally well-designed instrument for bringing developing states into the Montreal Protocol and helping their implementation of the agreement. However, two concerns arise from the functioning of the mechanisms to encourage developing country participation in the process. One is the precedent that the Multilateral Fund has set. The other is the uncertainty at this point over whether the major developing countries will actually stop using ozone-depleting substances. Although there are some encouraging signs there are also indicators of concern. Without success at this goal, the protection of the ozone layer will ultimately fail.

a.   Bringing Developing Countries In

The initial efforts to bring developing countries into the agreement revolved around a grace-period (initially 10 years, though it has been renegotiated for a variety of different ODS) during which developing countries would not have to meet the obligations of the Protocol. This measure allowed member states operating under Article 5 (developing countries whose annual per capita consumption of ODS was less than 0.3 kg) to continue and even increase their use of these substances. The Protocol acknowledged that these countries had special needs for financial and technical assistance to meet their obligations, but without specifying the way in which these needs would be met, the lag-time was insufficient to convince most developing countries to join.

The second effort was a trade incentive: states that are party to the agreement can only trade in controlled substances with those that are in the agreement. For states that did not produce ozone-depleting substances but hoped to use them, joining the agreement was the obvious way to guarantee their access to these chemicals. The scenario would only work, however, if the developing countries capable of producing ozone-depleting substances were brought into the agreement as well. Otherwise a separate trading bloc could emerge outside of the agreement that could undermine, rather than encourage, participation. Mexico was the only developing country producer of ODS that initially signed the Protocol. The reluctance of other producer states such as China and India to join the Montreal Protocol initially indicated that the trade sanctions would be insufficient to bring developing countries into the agreement. These states, potentially unaffected by the sanctions, would have to be convinced to join.

Although the Montreal Protocol acknowledged the special needs of developing countries for funding and access to technology, the actual funding mechanism was specified under the London Amendments to the Protocol and the details worked out in difficult negotiations. These created the mechanism that came to be known as the Multilateral Fund [for the Implementation of the Montreal Protocol].[h]

The organization of the Multilateral Fund is innovative and well designed to mitigate the North/South conflict that inspired it. The rotating member-

---

h. The World Bank, one of the world's largest sources of development assistance, is the implementing agency of the Multilateral Fund. For more on the World Bank, see *infra* note **a** in Problem 7–3 ("A Nuclear Accident in Hanguo") at 1135.

ship on the Executive Committee that oversees fund decisionmaking involves equal numbers of Article 5 and non-Article 5 countries. Decisions are taken by consensus where possible; if votes must be taken they require a two-thirds majority vote that represents a majority among both developed and developing countries. Although votes remain unlikely, the double majority voting structure helped to convince both sets of parties that decisions could not be taken solely under the influence of the other group.... [T]he Fund is served by a Secretariat that operates independently.

The specification of the Fund had the intended effect. China joined the Protocol immediately, followed by India and Brazil in 1992 and eventually by almost all developing countries. Importantly, the operation of the Fund has gone a long way toward helping some developing countries avoid ozone depleting substances or change over their use of ODS to ozone-safe chemicals or processes. By early 1999 developed countries had contributed more than $847 million to the fund, and the Executive Committee had approved nearly 3,000 projects, expected to result in the phaseout of the consumption of more than 119,000 OPD tonnes and the consumption of 42,000 ODP tonnes.[i] Approximately one-third that amount has already been phased out.

The Multilateral Fund process has not been free of difficulties, but the independence of the Secretariat, the Executive Committee, and the ability of the system as a whole to adjust to changes has been invaluable in addressing these problems. * * * The Executive Committee and the Multilateral Fund Secretariat have been instrumental in preventing some of the most egregious potential problems of developing country phaseout. At the recommendation of the Secretariat and the Executive Committee, a number of Multilateral Fund policies have been changed. For example states must now show that their overall consumption of a controlled substance goes down if they are to receive funding to close down or retrofit a production facility. The Executive Committee also took the somewhat radical move of deciding that plants built after August 1995 would be ineligible for funding to retrofit or close them, and that no Article 5 countries would be allowed to build new plants after December of that year. To the extent that the problems discussed below can be avoided, it will be because of the independence of these decision-making bodies and their willingness to make difficult or unpopular decisions.

b. The Precedent

One of the stumbling blocks to the initial creation of the Multilateral Fund was the fear of the precedent it would create. Initial US opposition to a fund was based on this fear, and explicit efforts were made to indicate that it should not be taken as an indication that funding would be forthcoming to address other environmental issues.

The precedent has nevertheless been set, and strengthened, as all major global environmental agreements negotiated since Montreal have included provisions for aid to cover the incremental costs to developing countries of meeting their obligations under the agreements. Moreover, these new agreements have taken the funding precedent one step further, indicating (as in

i. According to more recent World Bank statistics, the World Bank has phased out 104,911 tons of Ozone Depleting Potential (ODP) through 777 approved projects resulting in approval funds of over US$434 million. *See* <http://lnweb18.worldbank.org/ESSD/envext.nsf/49ByDocName/MontrealProtocol>.

the Convention on Biological Diversity) that developing country requirements to uphold their obligations are contingent on "the effective implementation by developed country Parties of their commitments under this Convention related to financial resources and transfer of technology."[10] This type of clause is a clear response to possible funding shortfalls or delays in the Montreal Protocol case.

It is certainly possible to argue that such assistance to developing countries in cases of environmental problems caused primarily in the course of industrialization is fair, and that the precedent is therefore a valuable one. On the other hand, such a precedent may be seen to contribute to moral hazard. Developing countries may forego action they would otherwise take because they can persuade others to fund it. The funding undertaken in the Montreal Protocol, the result of a difficult negotiating process to agree upon, is modest compared with what will be required to address other environmental issues such as climate change. The precedent set that all developing country costs of environmental agreements will be borne by the developed world may make negotiation of obligations more difficult, and their implementation far more costly.

c. Developing Country Phaseout Concerns

... The extent to which [Article 5] developing countries will actually meet the phaseout requirements for CFCs and then other ozone depleting substances is an open question, and one that will ultimately determine the overall success of the Montreal Protocol process. There are some encouraging signs. Some developing countries, such as Mexico and Venezuela, indicated an early interest in phasing out on the developed country schedule, and have been able to do so to some extent. Others are making efforts to meet accelerated schedules as well.

There are also some concerns. In particular, the Montreal Protocol explicitly allows for the increase in consumption of ODS by Article 5 countries until control measures take effect, provided they do not exceed .3 kg per capita ODS consumption. Some developing countries, particularly the major producers of ozone depleting substances, have therefore increased their ODS consumption throughout the period leading to the CFC freeze. They have had every incentive (and legal right) to do so: many ozone depleting substances, particularly CFCs, are cheap, safe, and easy to produce. Moreover, with the implicit guarantee that the costs of their phaseout would ultimately be covered by the multilateral fund, they gained little advantage from refraining from increased production. These countries gain the benefit of using these chemicals and are assured of increased funding and technical assistance later for switching their already-increased technical capabilities over to newer production processes and chemicals. An increased consumption level during the 1990s also increased the level at which consumption would be frozen.

The way the Fund was initially structured, developing countries did not even need to forego funding during the period when their production was increasing. The issue that eventually convinced the Executive Committee to restrict funding for phasing out production at some plants when new produc-

---

10. United Nations Convention on Biological Diversity, art. 20, ¶ 4 [1760 U.N.T.S. 79, reprinted in *5 Weston & Carlson V.H.22*].

tion was increasing occurred in 1996. China applied for funding to retrofit one halon plant while simultaneously building others to increase its halon output, something allowed by the letter of the law, but certainly contrary to the spirit. This type of funding was ultimately disallowed. So while this was an issue that the regulatory process eventually addressed successfully, it indicated the willingness of major ODS-producing developing countries to work the system to their advantage, in a way that contributed to the environmental problem and increased mitigation activities required later.

The production capabilities of the major developing country ODS producers has grown dramatically. China now accounts for 90 percent of global production of halons, and the emissions of these substances are rising annually by three percent, despite the phaseout in developed countries. As the developed world has almost completely ceased the use of a number of ozone depleting substances and the developing world increased its production and consumption of these substances, developing countries increase their bargaining position to demand greater compensation or assistance with phaseout. There are signs already of this phenomenon. Developing countries preparing for the 1999 Meeting of the Parties to the Montreal Protocol agitated for greater funding when the Multilateral Fund was being replenished. Malaysia indicated that it would have to delay its planned phase-out of CFCs until more funding was made available. Whether Article 5 countries will be able, or willing, to meet their phaseout obligations is therefore still unclear. An encouraging study by the Multilateral Fund Secretariat was generally optimistic about the "ability of Article 5 countries to comply with the [CFC] freeze."[11] But the increased production capacity, and the increased political bargaining power that confers, leaves open the question of whether, and at what price, developing countries will cease their use of ozone depleting substances.

[*Eds.*—In conclusion, Professor DeSombre restates her belief that the Montreal Protocol "has been remarkable in its ability to bring almost all the world's states into an agreement that fundamentally changes the way industrial activity takes place." She also reiterates her view that "[t]he most identifiable problem with the system as it stands, the black market in ozone depleting substances, is not as bad as most fear." She then cautions, in closing:]

The potential problem to which not enough academic attention is currently directed is the possibility that developing countries, with increased political power and increasing consumption and production of ozone depleting substances, may either refuse to take action to protect the ozone layer or may demand increasingly costly compensation for doing so. Even if this type of assistance can be considered ethically necessary, it may make protection of the ozone layer less likely or more costly, and may make developed states even more hesitant to take action to prevent or mitigate other global environmental problems. . . .

---

11. Report of the Tenth Meeting of the Parties to the Montreal Protocol on Substances that Deplete the Ozone Layer, UN Environmental Program, UNEP/OzL.Pro.10/9, ¶ 83 (3 Dec 1998).

13.   Sylvia M. Williams, "A Historical Background on the Chloro-fluorocarbon Ozone Depletion Theory and Its Legal Implications," in Transboundary Air Pollution 267, 274–77 (C. Flinterman et al. eds., 1986).

Contrary to other branches of international law ... where, in the initial stages at least, the conclusion of regional arrangements appears to be the most sensible step, the protection of the ozone layer from the use of CFCs ... calls for global regulation from the outset. * * * [T]he issue is global in scope and involves the whole international community because one country's overhead zone is not protected by that country's unilateral restrictions on the use of CFCs. Hence, a set of rules of a regional scope would not provide an effective solution.

A number of principles of international law are applicable, *ab initio*, to the problem in question. First and foremost, mention should be made of the principle of international responsibility of states which has kept appearing over the years in the decisions of international courts and tribunals and has been the subject of lengthy debates at [the] doctrinal level.

The well-known principle underlying the *Trail Smelter* arbitration [**Basic Document 7.3**] and later, the *Corfu Channel* judgment [**Basic Document 7.5**], that no state has the right to allow its territory to be used for acts contrary to the rights of other states is, without doubt, applicable to the ozone depletion problem except that conditions are somewhat different. Whereas in the *Trail Smelter* and *Corfu Channel* cases the responsibility of the state causing the damage arises *vis-à-vis* another specific country and, therefore, indemnities are more easily determined, in the present instance, the damage affecting the ozone layer—perhaps irreversible and, certainly, retarded—would be reaching the whole international community. The state would, therefore, be responsible *erga omnes* for environmental damage. It necessarily follows that the assessment of the damage and the obligation to restore to the *status quo ante* become far more complex. However so, there exists today a rule of general international law prohibiting states to allow the use of their territory in a way that affects the rights of other states. This rule—which clearly covers the possibility of ozone depletion by the use of CFCs—is binding upon all states and its breach entails the international responsibility of the state causing the injury.

Of no small importance in the discussion of the legal aspects of ozone depletion is, next to the principle of state responsibility, the role played by the principles relating to abuse of rights and good neighborliness with, of course, the limitations [posed by] the global nature of the ozone protection issue. We should be equally aware, however, of the difficulty of drawing a clear line between an abuse as distinct from a harsh but justified use of a right under international law. It is sometimes extremely difficult to determine when a legitimate right is overstepped. Similarly, one ought to bear in mind that, in this assumption, the concept of good neighborliness would include all nations of the world irrespective of their geographic proximity.

The United Nations Stockholm Declaration on the Human Environment of 1972 [**Basic Document 5.14**] has, conversely, provided a number of principles concerning damage to the environment in general and not only damage from one state to another. Principle 6 is of special significance: it calls for the halting of the release of toxic substances in quantities to exceed the capacity of the environment to render them harmless. Principle 21 recognizes the rights of states to exploit their resources under international law provided they ensure that these activities do not cause damage to the environment of other states or to areas beyond national jurisdiction. Principle 22 stresses the need for progressive development of international law in connection with liability and compensation for the victims of pollution or other environmental damage. The [1985 Vienna] Convention for the Protection of the Ozone Layer **[Basic Document 5.23]**—where the recurring note is the need for scientific and technological co-operation—has embodied some of these principles in its context, such as principle 21 to which express reference is made in the preamble. . . .

14. **Stockholm Declaration of the United Nations Conference on the Human Environment adopted by the UN Conference on the Human Environment at Stockholm, 16 Jun 1972, Report of the UN Conference on the Human Environment, UN Doc. A/CONF. 48/14/ Rev. 1 at 3 (1973), UN Doc. A/CONF. 48/14 at 2–65, and Corr. 1 (1972); *reprinted in* 5 Weston & Carlson V.B.3: Pmbl. & Princs. 1–3, 6, 11–13, 21–24** (Basic Document 5.14).

15. **Charter of Economic Rights and Duties of States. Adopted, 12 Dec 1974. GA Res. 3281, 29th Sess., Supp. No. 31, at 50, UN Doc. A/9631 (1975); *reprinted in* 4 Weston & Carlson IV.F.5: Art. 30** (Basic Document 4.9).

16. **World Charter for Nature. Adopted, 28 Oct 1982. GA Res. 37/7, UN GAOR, 37th Sess., Supp. No. 51, at 17, UN Doc. A/37/51; *reprinted in* 5 Weston & Carlson V.B.11: Princs. 1–4, 6–9, 11, 12, 14, 16, 19, 20, 24** (Basic Document 5.21).

17. **Experts Group on Environmental Law of the World Commission on Environment and Development, Legal Principles for Environmental Protection and Sustainable Development. Adopted, 18–20 Jun 1986. UN Doc. WCED/86/23/Add.1 (1986); *reprinted in* 5 Weston & Carlson V.B.12: Arts. 1 & 21** (Basic Document 5.25).

18. **Rio Declaration on Environment and Development. Adopted, 13 Jun 1992. UNCED Doc. A/CONF.151/5/Rev. 1; *reprinted in* 5 Weston & Carlson V.B.16: Princs. 2, 7, 14, 15** (Basic Document 5.37).

19. **Editors' Note.** The five immediately preceding instruments, perhaps most importantly the 1972 Stockholm Declaration on the Human Environment **(Basic Document 5.14)** and the 1992 Rio Declaration on Environment and Development **(Basic Document 5.37)**, contain the principle of state responsibility for transnational environmental harm. Derived initially from the traditional norms of state responsibility for the treatment of aliens and their property, this principle is rooted in the long-accepted proposition that states, the so-called subjects of international law, are responsible for such violations of law as are attributable to them and that, consequently, they are legally obligated to aggrieved other states and even private parties to make reparations whenever such attributable violations occur. Over the years, it has come to embrace as well, although more controversially, notions of liability for transnational environmental harms that arise out of acts *not* prohibited by international law—akin to what, in domestic law systems, we call "strict" or "absolute" liability. Today, with major environmental harms occurring and threatening across national boundaries daily, the need to define

and refine this jurisprudence, its scope, and conditions, is an imperative of the first magnitude. For the foundations of the modern-day customary international law of global environmental protection, see the following leading arbitral and judicial decisions excerpted or summarized in the documentary supplement to this coursebook: the *Case Relating to the Territorial Jurisdiction of the International Commission of the River Oder* (**Basic Document 7.1**); the *Diversion of Water from the Meuse Case* (**Basic Document 7.2**); the *Trail Smelter Arbitration* (**Basic Document 7.3**); the *Corfu Channel Case* (**Basic Document 7.5**); the *Lake Lanoux Arbitration* (**Basic Document 7.7**); the *Nuclear Tests Cases* (**Basic Document 7.9**) and the *Case Concerning the Gabcikovo–Nagymaros Project* (**Basic Document 7.11**). The 1972 Stockholm Declaration on the Human Environment (**Basic Document 5.14**), the 1974 Charter of Economic Rights and Duties of States Environment (**Basic Document 4.9**), the 1982 World Charter for Nature Environment (**Basic Document 5.21**), and the 1992 Rio Declaration on Environment and Development (**Basic Document 5.37**) are four instruments that explicitly extend the principle of state responsibility to transnational environmental harm to a Twenty-first Century marked by greater and greater environmental interconnectedness. For usefully abridged treatment, see Lakshman D. Guruswamy, Sir Geoffrey W. R. Palmer, Burns H. Weston, and Jonathan C. Carlson, International Environmental Law and World Order: A Problem–Oriented Coursebook ch. 5 ("International Environmental Wrongs") (2nd ed. 1999).

20. Noralee Gibson, Comment, "The Right to a Clean Environment," 54 Saskatchewan L. Rev. 7, 14, 16–17 (1990).

Human rights are but one type of right, namely those rights one holds by virtue of being a person. Not all rights held by human beings are human rights. Contractual and constitutional rights are held by human beings and are not necessarily human rights. They are rights of persons without being "human rights." The right to a clean environment is an important right, but it does not amount to a "human" right.

* * *

It is submitted that a right to a clean environment is an essential condition for the fulfillment of all human rights. It may be considered a precondition for the enjoyment of human rights. This is called the "indispensability" theory. The satisfaction of collective rights, such as the right to a clean environment, is a prerequisite for the materialization of individual human rights. A clean and healthy environment is essential to the enjoyment of basic human rights—even the right to life itself. We are confronted by the need for humans and all other species to survive. The international community must aim at saving all members of the ecosystem. Part of that aim will be the protection of the most basic human right, the need to survive. To talk of protecting other human needs is academic unless that need is met.

In conjunction with the broader international goal of saving the ecosystem, one can formulate an international right to a clean environment. This right would be extended to all members of the ecosystem including humans. It is a right based on need. This right would be viewed as the most basic need of all living organisms. It is even more fundamentally important than individual human rights; it is concerned with the collective survival of all human beings. It is this most important objective to which the right to a clean environment should be linked and not to individual human rights. Granting of rights to the environment as a whole is a recognition of its value, not to us as consumers of environmental amenities, but as an integral part of life itself. This is consistent with the philosophy of deep ecologists.[j]

Also, if the right to a clean environment can be viewed as a survival *need*, it is truly a "universal" right since the cultural aspect of legitimization is not a factor. The *need* for survival is universal due to every organism's inherent need and desire to survive. This need is not linked to notions of culture, therefore, cross-cultural analysis is not required to determine the legitimacy of such a right.

What is required to realize this international right to a clean environment? To speak of a universal right is to speak of a universal duty. As part of the universe, all humans have a right to a clean environment, but to say they have this right is to also impose on all humans the duty of respecting the environment. Discharging this duty and realizing this right will require international acceptance of a right to benefit individuals, peoples, animals and plant life in a holistic and interconnected manner. It can be realized only through the concerted efforts of all actors: the individual, the state, public and private bodies and the international community. In defining this right, one would have to consider the responsibilities it imposes on nongovernmental groups and individuals in addition to the responsibilities of the state. Finally, a specific definition of this right would have to be conceived. "The right to a clean environment" is much too vague. Concrete rights, duties and responsibilities have to be defined in order to begin the process of implementing and enforcing such a right.

The right to a clean environment has not formally been recognized as an international human right. Nor should we recognize it as such without following a procedure that would ensure adequate debate and definition of the right. Moreover, in the course of the debate, we must keep in mind what makes a "human right" unique. If this is done, the conclusion may well be that the right to a clean environment is more properly seen as a universal right and not a "human right." This conceptualization is based on a more

---

j. According to A. Naess, *The Deep Ecological Movement: Some Philosophical Aspects*, 8 Phil. Inquiry 10, 14 (1986), the following set of eight principles are basic to "deep ecology":

(1) The well-being and flourishing of human and non-human Life on Earth have value in themselves (synonyms: intrinsic value, inherent value). These values are independent of the usefulness of the non-human world for human purposes.

(2) Richness and diversity of life forms contribute to the realization of these values and are also values in themselves.

(3) Humans have no right to reduce this richness and diversity except to satisfy vital needs.

(4) The flourishing human life and cultures is compatible with a substantial decrease of the human population. The flourishing of non-human life requires such a decrease.

(5) Present human interference with the non-human world is excessive, and the situation is rapidly worsening.

(6) Policies must therefore by changed. These policies affect basic economic, technological, and ideological structures. These policies affect basic economic, technological, and ideological structures. The resulting state of affairs will be deeply different from the present.

(7) The ideological change is mainly that of appreciating life quality (dwelling in situations of inherent value) rather than adhering to an increasingly higher standard of living. There will be a profound awareness of the difference between big and great.

(8) Those who subscribe to the foregoing points have an obligation directly or indirectly to try to implement the necessary changes.

realistic view of our ecosystem and would be more congenial to, and less disruptive of, existing human rights.

   21.   Editors' Note. As observed in Chapter 2 ("International Legal Prescription: The 'Sources' of International Law"), *supra*, some norms of international law are more important than others. Not all are of equal legal force. Some are so basic that nations are not free to enter into treaties not to follow them. There exists, in short, a hierarchy of norms.

   To be sure, there is disagreement among publicists about which principles fall within the category of fundamental norms. But there is general agreement that such a category exits, and it goes by the name of *jus cogens*, the doctrine of peremptory norms, expressed as follows in Article 53 of the Vienna Convention on the Law of Treaties **(Basic Document 1.10):**

> A treaty is void if, at the time of its conclusion, it conflicts with a peremptory norm of general international law. For the purposes of the present Convention, a peremptory norm of general international law is a norm accepted and recognized by the international community of States as a whole as a norm from which no derogation is permitted and which can be modified only by a subsequent norm of general international law having the same character.

According to *Starke's* International Law 49 (I. Shearer 11th ed., 1994), analogizing to domestic law, "[t]here is undoubtedly some analogy between jus cogens and the principles of public policy which at common law render a contract void if it offends against these, such as the principle that parties cannot by agreement between them oust the ordinary courts from their jurisdiction." And in Principles of Public International Law 513 (4th ed. 1990), Ian Brownlie identifies the international norms that are considered to be *jus cogens* norms: the prohibition on the aggressive use of force, the principle of nondiscrimination on grounds of race, and rules against the slave trade, piracy, and genocide.

   Permanent sovereignty over natural resources may also be included, although it is both uncertain and contentious as to how far the doctrine of *jus cogens* extends. Article 64 of the same Vienna Convention provides that "[i]f a new peremptory norm of general international law emerges, any existing treaty which is in conflict with that norm becomes void and terminates." Thus, there exists within that text both flexibility and scope for dynamic development of principles to meet changing circumstances. While the idea appears to have been developed in the context of treaty law, particularly addressing the problem of states seeking to avoid general rules through bilateral treaty, it is not logically restricted to that. Indeed, in the rapidly developing area of international environmental law, it is possible that the doctrine of *jus cogens* may be capable of wider development. There conceivably may be some norms of good environmental behavior so basic and fundamental to the future of the planet that nations cannot do as they please about following them.

   In *Barcelona Traction, Light and Power Company, Limited* (Belg. v. Spain) (Second Phase), 1970 ICJ 3, the International Court of Justice spoke of obligations owed towards the international community *as a whole* (obligations *erga omnes*), stating that "[s]uch obligations derive ... in contemporary international law, from the outlawing of acts of aggression, and of genocide, as also from the principles and rules concerning the basic rights of the human person, including protection from slavery and racial discrimination." *Id.* at 32. Similarly, in International Law—A Textbook 76–77, published in the USSR in 1986, Professor Grigorii I. Tunkin, a highly respected Russian international lawyer, took the following expansive view of *jus cogens*:

> The basic cause for the emergence of peremptory norms is the growing internationalization of various aspects of social life, especially economic life, and the increasing role of global international problems. This serves to increase the number of issues whose uncontrolled regulation on a local multilateral or bilateral basis may harm the interests of other States. Similarly, the increasing role and influence of the forces of socialism and of progress in the world and the correspondingly greater role of moral principles of international relations also encourage the development of peremptory principles and norms.

And in An Introduction to International Law 62 (2003), Professor Mark Janis writes that "*[j]us cogens* is a norm thought to be so fundamental that it even invalidates rules drawn from treaty or custom. Usually a *jus cogens* norm presupposes an international public order sufficiently potent to control states that might otherwise establish contrary rules on a consensual basis."

As yet, regrettably, there is no authoritative exposition or application of the *jus cogens* doctrine to the problems of the global environment. But the scope for development is obvious in situations where the state of scientific knowledge advances rapidly and the cumbersome machinery of multilateral negotiation, agreement, and subsequent ratification lags behind.

SECTION 5. DISCUSSION NOTES/QUESTIONS

1. The "ozone layer" refers to a thin sheet of O_3 molecules (ozone) that are found in the stratosphere and that, until recently, completely covered the earth, shielding it from harmful dosages of ultra violet radiation (UVR) from the sun. Ozone, however, is highly reactive; it can be destroyed by a number of complex chemical reactions involving chlorine, bromine, nitrogen, and other elements (*see* Figure 7–2.1).

After the atmospheric nuclear tests carried out by the Soviet Union and United States in the late 1950s and early 1960s—prior to the 1963 Partial Test Ban Treaty **(Basic Document 2.18)**[k]—it was discovered that nitrogen oxides and

---

k. For discussion concerning the Partial Test Ban Treaty and related arms control initiatives, see Discussion Notes/Questions 3 and 4 in Problem 4–5 ("Hindustan Threatens Nuclear Self–Defense"), *supra* at 437.

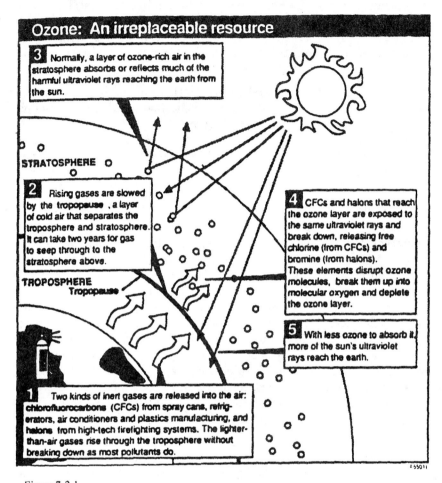

Figure 7-2.1

ozone-attacking chlorine derived from the tests had created a hole in the ozone layer. At present, however, the major threat to the ozone layer comes not from atmospheric nuclear testing (the last known such test having been conducted by China in 1980) but from the extensive production and use of chlorofluorocarbons (CFCs) by industrialized and industrializing nations—in the form of refrigerator and air conditioner coolants, aerosol spray can propellants, and products used to make styrofoam, among other things. While numerous topospheric trace gases have been identified as affecting the ozone layer—methane (CH_4), nitrous oxide (N_2O), other nitrogen oxides (NO_x), source gases for stratospheric sulfate aerosols (OCS, CS_2), carbon monoxide (CO), carbon dioxide (CO_2)—it is predominantly a class of manmade compounds, namely "halocarbons," that include chlorofluorocarbons, or "CFCs," that damage the ozone layer.

And such damage, in turn, threatens life on earth. As stated by the US National Academy of Sciences on its website at <http://www.beyonddiscovery.org/content/view.page.asp?I=92>: "With less ozone in the atmosphere, more ultraviolet radiation reaches Earth. Scientists estimated that increased exposure would lead to a higher incidence of skin cancer, cataracts, and damage to the immune system and to slowed plant growth. Because some CFCs persist in the atmosphere for more than 100 years, these effects would last throughout the twenty-first century."

The first CFCs were produced in 1928. Their impact on the ozone layer, however, did not come to public attention until the publication of M. Molina & F. Rowland, *Chlorofluorocarbons: Chlorine Atom–Catalyzed Destruction of Ozone*, 249 Nature 810 (1974). Writing for UNEP in 1997, Dr. Molina, joint winner of the 1995 Nobel Prize for Chemistry for his work on ozone depletion, expressed optimism about the CFC problem at <http://www.ourplanet.com/imgversn/85/molina.html>:

> The CFC problem is largely under control, thanks to the Montreal Protocol on Substances that Deplete the Ozone Layer **[Basic Document 5.29]**—an unprecedented international agreement negotiated under the auspices of UNEP. * * * Atmospheric scientists estimate that if the global production of CFCs had continued unrestricted, globally averaged ozone depletion would have been close to 10 per cent by the year 2000, instead of the 4 per cent measured today, and the damage would have been much more dramatic in subsequent decades, particularly at high latitudes. We are indeed fortunate that much of the basic scientific research in stratospheric chemistry was in place when the ozone hole was discovered in 1985, thus allowing the policy makers to take decisive action to protect the ozone layer. Ozone depletion is expected to reverse and recover measurably towards the beginning of the next century. And, of course, society still enjoys the benefits of refrigeration, air conditioning, plastic foams, aerosol cans, etc.—but now with new, CFC-free technologies.

> My own experience with the CFC-ozone depletion phenomenon prompts me to believe that we can meet the challenge presented by global environmental issues in the 21st century. My optimism stems from observations of major changes in people's attitudes about environmental problems when considering that the health of the entire planet is at stake. . . .

Dr. Molina would be among the first to admit, of course, that threats to the ozone persist. A 2005 study by the British Institute of Physics makes the point abundantly clear.

> "It will be decades before the ozone layer is restored to levels that existed before the 1970s, as the ozone destroying compounds can be extremely long-lived. The ozone 'holes' over the polar regions are currently as deep and persistent as ever observed, leading to elevated levels of damaging ultraviolet radiation at the Earth's surface and a rise in the incidence of skin and eye disease. Levels of some ozone-depleting substances in the stratosphere are stabilising, in response to concerted action and legislation for the control of damaging emissions. However, the abundance of other damaging compounds, including those derived from chlorofluorocarbon replacement compounds, continues to rise."

The Rise of Ozone Research, British Institute of Physics <http://policy.iop.org/Policy/Ozone% 20Report.pdf>.

Bromine levels in particular are continuing to rise. Under the Montreal Protocol, developed country use of methyl bromide (an inexpensive pesticide which becomes Bromine in the atmosphere) was to be completely phased out by 1 January 2005. A so-called "critical use exemption," however, allowed countries to temporarily continue to use a banned substances until an alternative can be found. Despite the availability of more expensive alternatives, the United States under pressure from its farm industry, is continuing to exploit this exemption. At the time this casebook went to press the United States was using approximately 10 million kilograms of the pesticide, more than the rest of the developed world combined.

Also to be noted is the now rapid development of CFC and halon substitutes, *e.g.*, hydrochlorofluorocarbons (HCFCs), low ozone-depleting substances that replace most existing uses of CFCs. The problem is that some replacements for the ozone-depleting CFCs and halons could themselves become a threat. If used in large quantities over a long period, they too could prevent the ozone layer from returning to its natural state. Many are potent greenhouse gases.

It is thus not without good reason that, in his 1997 UNEP statement, *supra*, Dr. Molina added the following note of caution: "We must change our view of the world and adopt new ways of thinking. The quality of life of future generations will be based to a large extent on our ability to deal intelligently with these global problems."

Assuming Dr. Molina to be correct, how must we "change our view of the world" and what "new ways of thinking" must we adopt? Dr. Molina further observes that "[o]ne of the key steps in any rational approach to addressing global environmental issues is to promote internationalism—a widespread understanding that all our human problems are interconnected." *Id.* What does this mean exactly? In what way or ways does it translate into concrete policy? For Australia? For the United States? For other countries? For global governance?

2. The ozone layer as a global commons is a classic case of what Garrett Hardin, in his germinal article, called the "Tragedy of the Commons." *See* G. Hardin, *The Tragedy of the Commons*, 162 Science 1243 (1968). The ozone layer is a "pasture open to all," and is therefore likely to be "overgrazed," without international accord. Hardin suggests the privatization of the commons as a solution. This is not a feasible approach for the ozone layer. Reversing the current destruction of our global commons requires a rethinking of the traditional concepts of state sovereignty, national security, and international law. Hardin recognized nearly thirty years ago that "[t]he law, always behind the times, requires elaborate stitching and fitting to adapt it to this newly perceived aspect of the commons." *Id.* at 1245. Relative to ozone layer depletion, what do your recommend?

3. The World Commission on Environment and Development, also known as the "Brundtland Commission" (after Prime Minister Gro Brundtland of Norway), proposed the principle of sustainable development. *See* The World Commission on Environmental Development, Our Common Future (1987). In view of the ozone

depletion problem, has humanity reached the point where if development is to be sustainable it must be rationed? How might this be done? What role can international law play, if any, in dealing with these questions?

4. In Annex I of World Commission on Environmental Development, *Our Common Future* (1987) is set forth a "Summary of Proposed Legal Principles for Environmental Protection and Sustainable Development Adopted by the WCED Experts Group on Environmental Law" **(Basic Document 5.25)**. Principle 1 ("Fundamental Human Right") states that "[a]ll human beings have the fundamental right to an environment adequate for their health and well-being." This principle is also found in the 1989 Declaration of the Hague (UN Doc. A/44/340, E/1989/120, *reprinted in* 28 I.L.M. 1308 (1989) and 5 Weston & Carlson V.E. 13), which begins by recognizing that "the right to live is the right from which all other rights stem. Guaranteeing this right is the paramount duty of those in charge of all states throughout the world." Do these communications represent a new or emerging principle of customary law in the environmental field? Are the 1972 Stockholm Declaration on the Human Environment **(Basic Document 5.14)**, the 1985 Vienna Convention for the Protection of the Ozone Layer **(Basic Document 5.23)**, the 1987 Montreal Protocol **(Basic Document 5.29)**, and other treaties of a global nature regulating the global commons like the marine pollution treaties, evidence of such an emerging principle? What might this mean for the present problem? What would Noralee Gibson (*supra* Reading 20) say?

5. As observed, ozone depletion is closely linked to issues of industrial development and the international economy. Developing countries argue that industrialized countries caused the problem in their drive to development and that they cannot and should not be expected now to forego the opportunity to pursue an equal path of development. If developing countries are to avoid the potentially disastrous course followed by industrialized countries in the past, they argue, then they need to be able to adopt modern technologies early in the process of development, to "leapfrog" directly from a state of underdevelopment to efficient, environmentally benign technologies. And, they contend, because the developed nations cause the problem the developing nations should not have to pay for it. The developed nations, they assert, should take responsibility for the extra costs involved, with new CFC-free technology given, not sold, to developing countries, and a fund set up to help cover their increased costs. Do you agree? If so, how should this technology transfer be financed? If not, why not?

6. Noted *supra* in Reading 12, in the extract from Elizabeth R. DeSombre, *The Experience of the Montreal Protocol: Particularly Remarkable, and Remarkably Particular*, 19 UCLA J. Envtl. L. & Pol'y 49 (2000–2001), is the emergence in recent years of a not inconsiderable illegal trade in CFCs and other ozone-depleting substances. As stated in the 15 October 2001 UNEP press release cited in Discussion Note/Question 1, *supra*: "Millions of CFC-dependent refrigerators, automobile air conditioners and other equipment are still in service around the world. Criminals clearly have a strong incentive to smuggle CFCs and other banned substances across borders."

And as the UNEP press release further reports, the problem is spreading: "Since developing countries are now subject to phase-out schedules [under the Montreal Protocol], they too are increasingly exposed to illegal trade." *Id*. In other words, as Professor DeSombre observes, at 68, "the very factors that gave rise to the black market are among those that have made the Montreal Protocol as successful as it has been." She continues:

Many who write about the black market refer to the "loophole" that allows for continued Article 5 consumption of ODS while others are required to end their consumption of particular substances, thus creating the supply side of the black market. As discussed below, the Montreal Protocol would not have been politically possible without this type of differentially timed obligations, so it is not realistic to imagine removing that element of the treaty in order to combat the black market. On the demand side, the other main contributor to the black market is the excise tax that makes legal CFCs at least ten times more expensive than illegal ones. The excise tax within the US and Europe, however, also helped make the phaseout of these substances politically possible, and certainly made it happen more quickly. The increased cost of CFCs relative to substitute chemicals or processes gave industries the incentive to make the switch from ozone depleting substances much faster than they would have absent such a measure. The advantage to the ozone layer from this faster phaseout is likely to dwarf the damage caused by black market CFCs. A Montreal Protocol without these elements, while perhaps less likely to lead to a black market, would at the same time be less likely to have rescued the ozone layer as effectively as the current Treaty has.

How, then, is the black market problem to be solved? Is it enough for governments to pursue, as increasingly the states parties to the Montreal Protocol are doing, better monitoring of imports and exports, improved customs cooperation and control, more training of enforcement officers, and enhanced informational networking? If not, what more needs to be done?

7. Ozone protection measures impact also on the emerging "right to development," claimed by all nations. The UN Declaration on the Right to Development **(Basic Document 3.28)**, adopted in December 1986, emphasizes the well-being of the human person. Can the "right to development" be reconciled with the principle of sustainable development proposed by the World Commission on Environment and Development? What are the limits to this claimed right to development? Should developing countries be expected to follow a different development path from the one taken by developed countries? Why? Why not? *See, e.g.*, Jennifer M. Drogula, *Developed & Developing Countries: Sharing the Burden of Protecting the Atmosphere*, 4 Georgetown Int'l Envtl L. Rev. 257 (1992).

8. Article 2(9)(c) of the Montreal Protocol **(Basic Document 5.29)** provides that the parties must make every effort to reach agreement by consensus on the assessment and review of the control measures. If there is no consensus, decisions "shall, as a last resort, be adopted by two-third majority vote of the Parties present and voting representing at least fifty per cent of the total consumption of the controlled substances of the parties." The 1990 London amendments to the Montreal Protocol substituted for the final sixteen words the words: "a majority of the parties operating under paragraph 1 of Article 5 present and voting and majority of the parties not so operating present and voting." What does this mean for the rule of unanimous consent? Why was it necessary? Are there other environmental issues where a similar approach would be justified?

Nations, unhappy with the adjustments made under the foregoing rule, still have a way out. Any party can withdraw from the Protocol at any time after four years of assuming the obligations of reducing the consumption of controlled substances. The withdrawal takes effect one year after giving notice. Should nations be able to withdraw? If they withdraw, will they be caught by similar restrictions in customary law? When might state practice under a treaty become customary law?

9. Related to the problem of ozone depletion is the problem of climate change or global warming, also known as the greenhouse effect. A dissipating ozone layer results in an increase in the amount of carbon dioxide (CO_2) in the earth's atmosphere, and this, in turn, increases temperatures worldwide, thereby contributing to global warming. The world's leading scientists project that, during our children's lifetimes, global warming will raise the average temperature of the planet by 2.7 to 11 degrees Fahrenheit, a statistical projection that may be compared to the fact that, at present, Earth is only 5 to 9 degrees warmer today than it was 10,000 years ago, during the last ice age. In other words, human-made global warming is occurring much faster than at any time in the past 10,000 years. For convenient extensive treatment, see Third Assessment Report of the Intergovernmental Panel on Climate Change, Report of Working Group 1, Summary for Policymakers 2–7 (Robert T. Watson ed., 2001), extracted as Reading 1 in Problem 6–4 ("The UFC and the EU Dispute the GATT and Global Warming), *supra* at 888.

Throughout history, major shifts in Earth's temperature, which occurred at a rate of a few degrees over thousands of years, were accompanied by radical ecological changes, including the extinction of species. Some consequences of global warming could be severe climatic changes and other large-scale environmental alterations. According to many reliable assessments, it is within a matter of decades—not millennia—that humankind will have to adapt rising sea levels resulting from melting icecaps and consequent changes in weather patterns that may cause increased flooding, storms, and agricultural losses that could have serious consequences upon human health and national economies. Plants and animals that cannot adapt to new conditions will become extinct.

It is against this backdrop that was adopted, on 9 May 1992, the United Nations Framework Convention on Climate Change, 1771 U.N.T.S. 107, *reprinted in* 5 Weston & Carlson V.E.19, and that, on 10 December 1997, following the Convention's entry into force, its Conference of the Parties concluded the Kyoto Protocol to the United Nations Framework Convention on Climate Change, FCCC/CP/1997/7/Add.1, *reprinted in* 5 Weston & Carlson V.E.20d. The Convention entered into force on 21 March 1994 and, as of Mar 2006, boasts 188 states parties and the European Union. The Protocol entered into force on 16 February 2005 and at this writing (28 Feb 2006) has 161 state parties and the European Community. While both Australia and the United States are parties to the Convention, each has signed but not ratified the Kyoto Protocol. Indeed, the United States, under the authority President George W. Bush, claiming the Kyoto Protocol to be "fundamentally flawed," has notified the international community of its intention *not* to ratify the Protocol. *See* Public Affairs Section, United States Embassy, Vienna, Austria Fact Sheet: United States Policy on the Kyoto Protocol, at <http://www.usembassy.at/en/download/pdf/kyoto.pdf>.

Because of considerable scientific uncertainties, global warming is a much more complex problem than is ozone depletion today. What lessons might be drawn from the problem of ozone depletion that could help with global warming? *See, e.g.,* Alan S. Miller, *Incentives for CFC Substitutes: Lessons for Other Greenhouse Gases, in* Coping with Climate Change: Proceedings of the Second North American Conference on Preparing for Climate Change 547 (J. Topping ed., Washington DC: Climate Institute, 1989). In *The Evolution of Policy Responses to Stratospheric Ozone Depletion,* 29 N.R.J. 793 (1989), Peter M. Morrisette, argues that the approach to ozone can best be understood as a two-stage process. The first stage involved ozone depletion as a domestic issue in the United States and several other countries in the 1970s. The second stage was its transformation to an international issue in the 1980s. Morrisette maintains that factors critical to building international consensus on the need for strong measures controlling the production and use of CFCs were: the evolving scientific understanding of the problem, increasing public concern based on the threat of skin cancer, the perception of potential global catastrophe associated with the discovery of the Antarctic ozone hole (the "dread" factor), and the availability of acceptable substitutes. Thus, ozone depletion may be seen as a test case for the ability of the international community to deal with other global environmental problems such as global warming. What does Morrisette's analysis mean for other environmental issues such as the loss of biodiversity in the form, say, of deforestation?

10. Preparatory work has been undertaken to develop a comprehensive "Law of the Atmosphere," modeled on the Law of the Sea. But there has been criticism of the Law of the Atmosphere as too ambitious and slowing agreement on climate change. Critics point out that the Law of the Sea conference was not a total success. It took nine years to negotiate and many governments, including those of the United States and the United Kingdom, could not accept the results. On the basis of this record, what would you say are the prospects of a comprehensive Law of the Atmosphere?

11. *Bibliographical Note.* For supplemental discussion concerning the principal themes addressed in this problem, consult the following additional specialized materials:

(a) *Books/Monographs/Reports/Symposia.* S. Anderson, Protecting the Ozone Layer: The United Nations History, (2005); S. Barrett, The Environment and Statecraft: The Strategy of Environmental Treaty–Making (2003); K. Daigaku & K. Junshu, Economic Globalization and Compliance With International Environmental Agreements (2003); E. DeSombre, Domestic Sources of International Environmental Policy: Industry, Environmentalists, and US Power (2000); A. Kiss & D. Shelton, International Environmental Law (2d ed. 2000); V. Nanda, International Environmental Law and Policy (1995) E. Parson, Protecting the Ozone Layer: Science and Strategy (2003); C. Reus–Smit, The Politics of International Law (2004); E. Shea, Environmental Law and Compliance Methods (2002); E. Weiss & H. Jacobson, Engaging Countries: Strengthening Compliance with International Environmental Accords (1998).

(b) *Articles/Book Chapters.* J. Dernbach, *Sustainable Development as a Framework for National Governance,* 49 Case W. Res. L. Rev. 3 (1998); C. Dove, *Can Voluntary Compliance Protect the Environment?: The North American Agreement on Environmental Cooperation,* 50 Kan. L. Rev. 867 (2002); O. Greene, *The System for Implementation Review in the Ozone Regime, in* The Implementation and Effectiveness of International Environmental Commitments 89 (D. Victor, K. Raustiala, & E. Skolnikoff eds., 1998); S. Kass and J. McCarroll, *Standing Alone on Climate Change,* 227 N.Y.L.J. 3 (4 Jan 2002); J. Knox, *The International Legal Framework for Addressing Climate Change,* 12 Penn St. Envtl. L. Rev. 135 (2004); E. Mossos, *The Montreal Protocol and the Difficulty with International Change, 10 Alb. L. Envtl. Outlook 1 (2005);* S. Montzka, J. Butler, J. Elkins, T. Thompson, A. Clarke, & L. Locke, *Present and Future Trends in the Atmospheric Burden on Ozone-Depleting Halogens,* 398 Nature 690 (22 Apr 1999); M. A. Sullivan, *Kyoto Wasn't Last Gasp; Even Without the Protocol, Greenhouse Gas Regulation is Coming Here,* Legal Times, 10 Jun 2002, at 30; P. Taylor, *Heads in the Sand as the Tide Rises: Environmental Ethics and Climate Change,* 19 UCLA J. L. & Envtl. Pol'y 247 (Summer 2001); L. Thoms, *A Comparative Analysis of International Regimes on Ozone and Climate Change with Implications for Regime*

Design, 41 Colum. J. Transnat'l L. 795 (2003); D. Victor *Enforcing International Law: Implications for An Effective Global Warming Regime,* 10 Duke Envtl. L. & Pol'y F. 147 (1999); M. Weisslitz, *Rethinking the Equitable Principle of Common but Differentiated Responsibility: Differential Versus Absolute Norms of Compliance and Contribution in the Global Climate Change Context,* 13 Colo. J. Int'l Envtl. L. & Pol'y 473 (2002); O. Yoshida, *Soft Enforcement of Treaties: The Montreal Protocol's Noncompliance Procedure and the Functions of Internal International Institutions,* 10 Colo. J. Int'l Envtl. L. & Pol'y 95 (Winter 1999).

Problem 7–3

A Nuclear Accident in Hanguo

Section 1. Facts

Assume the same facts as in Problem 7–2, *supra*.

In addition to inducing private foreign capital to help with its economic development, Hanguo chose to modernize through nuclear energy. Its native coal, oil, and other fossil fuel resources, though of high grade, were judged to be of insufficient quantity to meet Hanguo's energy needs, and its hydroelectric, solar, and wind power alternatives were found to be either too limited or too costly to be of much help. Thus, in 1995, it resolved to complete a large nuclear power station in its Yangshao province, begun in the early 1980s with the financial and technological assistance of the (former) Soviet Union but left half-completed following that country's disintegration in the early 1990s.

To this end, in 1996, Hanguo sought and received a loan from the World Bank.[a] At the same time, it won from Gallia, a technologically advanced West European country, a commitment to provide financial capital, engineers, and equipment so that the Yangshao power station could be completed expeditiously and with regard to high safety standards. After lengthy negotiations, Gallia and Hanguo entered into an agreement pursuant to which Gallia agreed to provide Hanguo with the necessary technology and information. For its part, Hanguo, a non-nuclear-weapon state, promised to use this materiel and expertise for peaceful purposes exclusively, and to accept the imposition of safeguards by the Vienna-based International Atomic Energy Agency (IAEA)[b] in accordance with a verification agreement also concluded between Hanguo and IAEA under Article III of the 1968 Treaty on the Non–Proliferation of Nuclear Weapons (NPT) to which both Gallia and Hanguo were and remain party.

---

a. The World Bank, or International Bank for Reconstruction and Development (IBRD), is a specialized agency of the United Nations, established at the Bretton Woods Conference in 1944. The bank grants loans only to member states and for the purpose of financing specific developmental projects. To ensure repayment, member governments must guarantee loans made to private concerns within their territories. Early in its existence, the World Bank extended loans mainly to European countries seeking to rebuild after World War II. Since the late 1960s, however, most loans have been granted to economically developing countries in Africa, Asia, and Latin America. Since the 1980s, the Bank has particularly focused on projects intended to benefit directly the poorest people in the economically developing world by helping them to raise their productivity and gain access to such basic needs as safe water and waste-disposal facilities, nutrition, health care, family-planning assistance, education, housing, and the like. For details, see the World Bank's website at <http://web.worldbank.org>. *See also* the website for the World Bank Group at <http://www.worldbank.org>.

b. The IAEA, a member of the United Nations System of Organizations, serves as the world's central intergovernmental forum for scientific and technical co-operation in the nuclear field, and as the international inspectorate for the application of nuclear safeguards and verification measures covering civilian nuclear programmes. For details, see the IAEA website, at <http://www.iaea.org>.

But it did not take long for problems to emerge. Because of deteriorating economic and political conditions brought about by numerous instances of grand corruption at the highest levels, many of them involving sweetheart deals with foreign investors, Hanguo's leadership became discredited, and the military took over the government. Soon thereafter, with much fanfare about "the need to protect the Motherland against external forces of greed," it was decided that investment in some nuclear weaponry would be a good way for Hanguo to overcome its economic and political troubles; and thus did Hanguo's new military government begin to take steps to use for military purposes the technology being installed in the Yangshao power plant. These initiatives soon came to the attention of the IAEA, however, which quickly publicized the facts and condemned Hanguo's actions. Additionally, relying on the provisions of its Statute, the IAEA ordered Gallia to withdraw its technological assistance and expert personnel from Hanguo. Whereupon, pointing to the aid and verification agreements concluded earlier (an objective reading of which confirms that Gallia's technology and know-how were to be used exclusively for peaceful purposes), Gallia immediately complied. Hanguo's new military government, Gallia asserted, was in "gross violation" of international law and policy.

Following Gallia's withdrawal of support, Hanguo cast around for other assistance. However, due to the IAEA condemnation, no other nation was prepared to give any help. Thus the Government of Hanguo decided to continue the construction of the Yangshao power station with the expertise available within Hanguo. The knowledge and methods used by Hanguo to complete the project were clearly below the safety standards approved by reputable nuclear experts in technologically advanced countries, but it nevertheless completed the Yangshao plant in 1998.

Recently, during a scheduled safety check at the plant, when engineers were testing the plant's cooling systems, disaster struck: an explosion occurred in the inner core of the main Yangshao reactor, an ensuing fire nearly destroyed the structure, and a steady stream of smoke, gas, and radiation was released into the atmosphere. These emissions were made worse in their effects by the absence of a containment building, a usual feature of nuclear plants. This design feature had been omitted to save money when Hanguo took over sole responsibility for the project.

When the explosion occurred, the Hanguoan government, fearing widespread radioactive contamination, quickly moved to evacuate all inhabitants from the area and to destroy all local milk supplies and fresh produce. For three days, however, in the resulting confusion and embarrassment, Hanguoan officials failed to notify anyone outside the country about the disaster. While technicians in Cascadia, an industrialized country in North America about 9,000 kilometers northeast of Yangshao, began, because of the northern hemispheric jet stream, to pick up significant traces of radioactive atmospheric debris just two and a half days after the accident, it was not until the fourth day, when people fleeing the plant area began to seek entry into adjacent countries, that the Hanguoan government was forced to announce the disaster publicly and to request emergency help.

Upon learning officially of the accident, the Cascadian government mobilized its health care and military services to check its population and livestock for contamination. Additionally, it issued large quantities of iodide tablets to its people to combat possible health effects and ordered the destruction of all unsheltered agricultural produce and fresh milk supplies. Further, it destroyed large numbers of animals and crops over a wide area and paid compensation to the farmers who owned them. Finally, expensive measures were instituted to monitor the health of its population, so far as their exposure to radiation was concerned.

Other countries took similar measures and, together with Cascadia, expressed great alarm at the situation. So busy were these countries with their own emergency activities, indeed, that they were unable to come to the aid of the Hanguoan government with the degree of help necessary to extinguish the fire and address the radioactive contamination quickly and efficiently. Cascadia especially, which had begun to experience unusually high levels of atmospheric radioactivity relative to other nearby countries, was unable to provide help. Thus, the Yangshao plant continued to burn for several days more, exacerbating the damage. It was not until scientists and technicians from the Vienna-based International Atomic Energy Agency (IAEA) arrived nearly a week after the accident that the fire was put out and a true assessment of the damage made.

In the months immediately following, all of Hanguo's Southeast Asian neighbors and others affected, including Australia and New Zealand, protested strongly to the Hanguoan government, complaining that it should have taken greater precautions to ensure the Yangshao plant's safety, such as constructing a containment building common to most reactors. Further, they threatened court action for compensatory damages to recover the cost of preventive and decontamination measures taken in response to the accident. At the end of half a year, however, only Cascadia took this course of action, demanding compensation in the amount of US$1 billion. Outraged, Hanguo countered that the costs incurred were the fault of Cascadia for failing to come immediately to Hanguo's rescue. In any event, it asserted that Cascadia had overreacted to the accident and stated that it was "under no legal obligation" to meet Cascadia's demands.

Talks between Cascadia and Hanguo eventually broke down. After several months, however, Hanguo proposed to bring the dispute before the International Court of Justice at The Hague. Cascadia agreed, and the case is now pending. Both countries are members of the United Nations and the IAEA. Also, in addition to the NPT, both are party to the 1963 Vienna Convention on Civil Liability for Nuclear Damage. However, neither has signed either the 1997 Protocol to Amend the Vienna Convention on Civil Liability for Nuclear Damage or the 1997 Convention on Supplementary Compensation for Nuclear Damage.[c] Additionally, while Cascadia is a party to the 1986 IAEA Convention

---

c. Each of these 1997 protocols was concluded 12 Sep 1997. The 1997 Protocol to Amend the Vienna Convention on Civil Liability for Nuclear Damage entered into force on 4

Oct. 2003. However, the 1997 Convention on Supplementary Compensation for Nuclear Damage was not in force as of this writing (1 Mar 2006). Available from the International

on Early Notification of a Nuclear Accident and the 1986 IAEA Convention on Assistance in the Case of a Nuclear Accident or Radiological Emergency, Hanguo is not, having signed but not yet ratified the two 1986 conventions.

SECTION 2.   QUESTIONS PRESENTED

1. Is Hanguo liable to Cascadia for damages caused by the Yangshao disaster? If so, on what grounds or in what way?

2. In any event, are there any additional or alternative legal norms, procedures, and/or institutions to be recommended that might further help to prevent or discourage situations of the kind posed by this problem?

SECTION 3.   ASSIGNMENTS

A.   READING ASSIGNMENT

Study the Readings presented in Section 4, *infra*, and the Discussion Notes/Questions that follow. Also, to the extent possible, consult the accompanying bibliographical references.

B.   RECOMMENDED WRITING ASSIGNMENT

Prepare a comprehensive, logically sequenced, and *argumentative* brief in the form of an outline of the primary and subsidiary *legal* issues you see requiring resolution by the International Court of Justice. Also, from the perspective of an independent observer, indicate which side ought to prevail on each issue and why. Retain a copy of your issue-outline (brief) for class discussion.

C.   RECOMMENDED ORAL ASSIGNMENT

Assume that you are legal counsel for Hanguo or Cascadia (as designated by your instructor); then, relying upon the Readings (and your issue-outline if prepared), present a 10–15 minute oral argument of your government's likely positions before the World Court.

D.   RECOMMENDED REFLECTIVE ASSIGNMENT

Consider (and recommend) alternative norms, institutions, and/or procedures that you believe might do better than existing world order arrangements to contend with situations of the kind posed by this problem. In so doing, but without insisting upon *immediate* feasibility, identify the particular transition steps that would be needed to make your alternatives a reality.

SECTION 4.   READINGS

The following readings are considered *prima facie* relevant to solving this problem. They are your law library for present purposes and should be treated

Atomic Energy Agency, they also are reprinted
in 36 I.L.M. 1454 (1997) and 5 Weston &
Carlson V.J.13 and V.J.14.

as such, organized intelligibly for "shelving" and not necessarily according to the issues presented. Be sure to review Chapter 2 ("International Legal Prescription: The 'Sources' of International Law") in your consideration of them. It, too, should be treated as part of your law library (as, indeed, should this entire coursebook).

1. Editors' Note. On 26 April 1986, a chemical explosion occurred in one of the four reactors of the state-run Chernobyl nuclear power plant near Kiev in the former Soviet Union. Over the following days, a fire in the damaged reactor caused the release of radioactive elements into the atmosphere. The radiation fallout caused considerable concern and damage in many European countries. Scandinavia also experienced increased radiation levels. Reactions by nations to radiation levels varied. Some nations took preventive actions, such as banning the pasturing of cows and forbidding children in some regions to drink milk. A number of countries intervened in the import and sale of food. Some iodine 131 was detected in rainwater samples in the United States and the State of Oregon advised people not to drink rainwater.

The effects in the then Federal Republic of Germany were described at the time in *Legislative and Regulatory Activities, Federal Republic of Germany*, 38 Nuclear L. Bull. 7, 21 (Dec 1986) as follows:

> The widespread radioactive contamination of the air, water and soil entailed direct damage to spring vegetables; milk-producing cattle had to be kept from grazing; the consumption of milk and other foodstuffs had to be supervised; import restrictions became necessary; the fixing of state intervention levels led to a change in consumers' eating and buying habits; travel agencies and transport undertakings specializing in Eastern European business lost their clientele; and finally, seasonal workers in agriculture lost their jobs.

In 1987, there were reports that the clean-up in the Chernobyl area involved the decontamination of 60,000 buildings and 500 villages, and the building of a special subterranean concrete wall to prevent groundwater from penetrating into nearby rivers. This concrete wall surrounded the nuclear power station to a depth of 15 meters. Radioactive topsoil from several square miles had been carted away. A "quite small" increase in cancer deaths in the future was predicted. And those evacuated from the area had been rehoused elsewhere. It now is clear, however, that the extent of the damage is much greater than was known or predicted at that time and that there is a greater need for effective international control in this realm than previously was realized.

Three major international governmental organizations operate in the nuclear field: the International Atomic Energy Agency (IAEA), established under the aegis of the United Nations;[d] the Nuclear Energy Agency (NEA) of the Organization of Economic Cooperation and Development (OECD);[e] and

---

d. *See supra* note **b.**

e. The Organisation for Economic Co-operation and Development (OECD) is an intergovernmental organization of industrialized countries (including Australia and the United States) based in Paris. The mission of its NEA is, in the words of its website (http://

www.nea.fr/html/pub/newsletter/edito17–1.pdf), "[t]o assist its Member countries in maintaining and further developing, through international co-operation, the scientific, technological and legal bases required for the safe, environmentally friendly and economical use of nuclear energy for peaceful purposes....." To the European Atomic Energy Community (EAEC/EURATOM).[f] The IAEA is both a regulator and a promoter of nuclear energy worldwide. The NEA represents the industrialized market economy countries with the most advanced nuclear programs. EURATOM represents certain European countries only.

Critics argue that the IAEA's dual role as both a regulator and a promoter of nuclear energy results in conflicts that reduce the Agency's effectiveness. The Agency has been particularly criticized for its impotence in the first few days following the Chernobyl explosion. The Soviet Union was a member of the IAEA, yet for three days after the accident the USSR remained silent, a fact that caused additional damage to its own people and to its European neighbors that could have been avoided had Moscow disclosed the mishap without delay. It was only later, after radioactivity spread throughout much of Europe and beyond, that the Soviet authorities, in a report to a "Post Accident Review Meeting" called by the IAEA in Vienna during 25–29 August 1986, described in detail the causes and circumstances of the accident, its evolution, the emergency actions taken by the Soviet authorities, and their efforts at site decontamination and rehabilitation. *See* IAEA, Summary Report on the Post Accident Review Meeting on the Chernobyl Accident (1986). While the IAEA moved quickly to negotiate a notification convention and assistance convention—respectively, the 1986 Convention on Early Notification of a Nuclear Accident **(Basic Document 5.26)** and the 1986 Convention on Assistance in the Case of a Nuclear Accident or Radiological Emergency **(Basic Document 5.27)**—these instruments have shortcomings (discussed in the later readings). There is a serious question as to whether an organization like the IAEA can even hope to resolve the issues involved in preventing and dealing with the consequences of transboundary nuclear pollution.[g]

While the IAEA has responsibility for establishing health and safety standards to protect health and minimize danger to life and property, there are no mandatory international safety standards applicable to all nuclear installations. A large number of member states oppose binding standards. Opponents maintain that mandatory standards would decrease worldwide nuclear safety because they would reflect the lowest common denominator of safety. Some also argue that such standards would not be sensitive to local conditions and that the objectives of nuclear safety are better served if each

---

achieve this end, the "NEA will aim at fulfilling three major objectives, namely: to provide Member countries and other parts of the OECD with nuclear policy analyses based on its technical work; to offer a forum for information and experience among Member countries and for promoting international co-operation; to create a centre of nuclear competence which helps Member countries pool and maintain their technical expertise and support their nuclear policies."

f. The EAEC or EURATOM came into being as the third treaty organization (along with European Economic Community and the European Coal and Steel Community) of what now is called the European Union. EURATOM member states are pledged to coordinate their nuclear research and development programs and to permit the free movement of nuclear

materials, equipment, investment capital, and specialists within the community. Vested with wide powers, including the power to conclude contracts, obtain raw materials, and establish standards to protect workers and the general population against the dangers of radiation, it is administered by the European Commission, which in turn is advised by the Scientific and Technical Committee and the Economic and Social Committee of the European Union.

g. This expression of skepticism notwithstanding, the IAEA continues to struggle for worldwide nuclear safety. For conspicuous evidence, see the Convention on Nuclear Safety **(Basic Document 5.42)**, included as Reading 8, *infra*, and adopted by the IAEA in 1994. The Convention had been ratified by 57 states as of 3 Feb 2006.

state assumes responsibility for nuclear safety. It needs to be considered whether these objections are convincing when weighed against the need for states to be globally accountable for their nuclear safety practices. In this connection, see Günter Handl, *Transboundary Nuclear Accidents: the Post–Chernobyl Multilateral Legislative Agenda,* 15 Ecology L. Q. 202, 223 (1988).

Another major problem for the IAEA is monitoring compliance with safety standards. On-site inspections are essential. However, as the case of Iraq makes clear, this is likely to meet resistance from states inasmuch as an erosion of their territorial sovereignty is involved, particularly where there is nuclear power in military installations. The IAEA currently undertakes voluntary nuclear and radiological safety assessment services, and, as the number of countries using these services grows, political pressure is likely to increase on holdout states to allow such services. States may find that there is political advantage in allowing such services, both domestically and in their relations with neighboring states.

The exchange of information on nuclear safety incidents is another important need. The IAEA has set up an incident reporting system, but there are problems with it. One difficulty is that not all countries with nuclear power plants participate. There also is debate over whether there should be a principle that nuclear-supplier states have a responsibility to provide recipient states with up-to-date safety information throughout the operational life of the nuclear technology supplied.

Mandatory technical safety standards for plant design and operation, safety audits and independent inspections, and information exchange obviously will enhance nuclear safety. But a major contributing factor to the Chernobyl catastrophe was human error and poor judgment. No amount of legal regulation can eliminate such factors. Thus, it is important to consider how the international community might minimize the risk. What about a principle of individual responsibility applicable to nuclear energy operators and administrators, similar to the kind established at Nuremberg after World War II? Or for exporters of nuclear technology? *See, e.g.,* Anthony D'Amato & Kirsten Engel, *State Responsibility for the Exportation of Nuclear Power Technology,* 74 Va. L. Rev. 1011 (1988). Who would apply and enforce such a principle? What about the abolition of nuclear power altogether? Is this desirable? Possible? *See, e.g.,* Richard Falk, *Nuclear Policy and World Order: Why Denuclearization,* 3 Alternatives–A Journal of World Policy 321 (1978).

2. Alan E. Boyle, "Nuclear Energy and International Law: An Environmental Perspective," 60 B.Y.B.I.L. 257, 261–65 (1989).

(a) *IAEA and the Regulation of Nuclear Power*

The International Atomic Energy Agency was the product of compromise following failure to agree on United States' proposals for international management of all nuclear power by an international body. [In the beginning,] its main tasks were to encourage and facilitate the development and dissemination of nuclear power, and to ensure through non-proliferation safeguards that it was used for peaceful purposes only. Setting standards for health and safety in collaboration with other international agencies was very much an incidental or secondary responsibility.

The Chernobyl accident has called for significant alteration of the Agency's priorities.... Among the recommendations of a review group were that the Agency should promote better exchanges of information among States on safety and accident experience, develop additional safety guidelines and enhance its capacity to perform safety evaluations and inspections on request. The Convention on Assistance in cases of Nuclear Emergency **[Basic Document 5.27]** also gives it the new task of co-ordinating assistance and responding to requests for help.

Thus, despite the very different objectives it had in 1956, the Agency now attaches high importance to its nuclear safety role.... [I]t has acquired a new environmental perspective as perhaps the one positive result of Chernobyl.

(b) *Powers over Health and Safety*

The [IAEA] Statute **[Basic Document 5.2]** requires the IAEA to establish "standards" for protecting health and minimizing danger to life and property. In addition, its health and safety document[1] sets out a policy on the inclusion of safety standards in agreements with States. This refers to "standards, regulations, rules or codes of practice established to protect man and the environment against ionising radiation and to minimise danger to life and property." "Standards" may thus take a number of different forms, depending on their function, but all serve the same broad purpose of seeking to prevent harm to the environment and adverse effects on other States. * * * The important point is ... that the Agency has competence over a wide range of safety and health issues relating to all aspects of the use of nuclear energy: what it lacks is the ability to give these standards obligatory force.

(c) *The Legal Effect of IAEA Health and Safety Standards*

Nothing in the Statute confers any binding force on IAEA standards, or requires member States to comply with them. While, under the Statute, the same is true of non-proliferation safeguards, in practice the IAEA enjoys much stronger powers in that field as a result of the 1968 Non–Proliferation Treaty **[Basic Document 2.21]** and regional agreements.

The effect of the NPT treaty is to make obligatory the acceptance of nonproliferation safeguards through bilateral agreements with the Agency, and to allow periodic compulsory Agency inspection for the purpose of verification. Compliance with the overall scheme of non-proliferation safeguards is monitored by the UN General Assembly and Security Council.

No comparable attempt has been made to require universal adherence to health and safety standards. Safeguards agreements and safeguards inspections relate only to non-proliferation; they give the IAEA no power over health and safety. Only where the Agency supplies materials, facilities or services to States does the Statute give it the power to ensure, through project agreements, that acceptable health, safety and design standards are adopted. In such cases, but only in such cases, it also has the right to examine the design of equipment and facilities to ensure compatibility with its standards, and the right to send inspectors to verify compliance. If these are not met, further assistance may be terminated and membership of the Agency withdrawn. Considerable latitude is normally allowed, however, provided national

---

1. Revised safety standards and measures
(1976), INFCIRC/18/Rev.1.

practices meet the minimum criterion of offering an "adequate" means of controlling hazards and ensuring effective compliance.

These powers over safety relate only to materials or facilities supplied by or through the IAEA; States cannot be required to place their other facilities or materials under its standards merely because they seek its assistance, although they may do so voluntarily. Where assistance is supplied under bilateral agreement without IAEA involvement, even these limited powers are lost, and the practice in such cases has been to provide only for safety consultations with the supplier State.

* * *

(d) *Assessing the Role of IAEA Standards*

Despite their non-binding character, IAEA health and safety standards are a significant contribution to controlling the risks of nuclear energy. Governments are consulted during the formulation stage and in some cases drafting is carried out in co-operation with specialist bodies, such as the International Committee on Radiological Protection. The Agency's standards thus reflect a large measure of expert and technical consensus, and it is for this reason, and not because of their legal status, that they have been influential and do serve as important guidelines for most States in regulating their nuclear facilities.

At their thirtieth conference in 1986, prompted by the Chernobyl disaster, IAEA member States considered the question of obligatory international minimum safety standards for reactors, but reached no agreement.... Instead the conference affirmed the responsibility of each State engaged in nuclear energy activities for ensuring nuclear and radiation safety, security and environmental compatibility, and the central role of the Agency in encouraging and facilitating co-operation on safety and radiological protection. But it is clear that the opportunity which might have existed in the early stages of nuclear power for stronger international safety regulations has been missed, and that it may now be too late to move significantly in that direction.

(e) *The IEAE as an International Inspectorate*

The IAEA has very limited power to act as an international nuclear safety inspectorate. Compulsory inspections are possible only where an assistance agreement is in force, and in practice this power is rarely used. The Agency can, if requested, provide safety advice and a review of safety practices at nuclear power stations.... [I]f unsafe practices are found, the Agency can only recommend, not enforce, changes.

3. Philippe J. Sands, "Chernobyl: Law and Communication–Transboundary Nuclear Air Pollution—The Legal Materials," 40–42, 44–47, 51 (1988).

The failure of the [former] USSR to provide immediate information [following the Chernobyl accident] led to prompt action. Under the auspices of the IAEA the Notification Convention **[Basic Document 5.26]** was drawn up and opened for signature within six months of the Chernobyl accident.

The Convention incorporates many of the recommendations set out in the Information Guidelines and applies in the event of any "accident involving facilities or activities of a State Party or of persons or legal entities under its jurisdiction or control." In the event of such an accident States Parties are required to notify, directly or through the IAEA, those States which are or may be physically affected with details of the accident, its nature, time of occurrence and exact location. They are also to promptly provide the States, directly or through the IAEA, and the IAEA with such available information as relevant to minimize the radiological consequences in those States. This includes the cause and foreseeable development of the accident, the general characteristics of the radioactive release (including its nature, form, quantity, composition and effective weight), current and future meteorological and hydrological conditions, planned or taken protective measures, and the predicted behavior over time of the release. Such information is to be supplemented at "appropriate intervals" by the provision of relevant information including the foreseeable or actual termination of the emergency situation. States should also respond "promptly" to a request for further information or consultations sought by an affected State.

According to one writer the substantive provisions of the Notification Convention, imposing a clear obligation on States to provide immediate, regular and detailed information relating to the actual or potential transborder release of radioactive material, merely reflect pre-existing customary international law and in some parts are less stringent.[2] The significance of the Convention is that it is the first multilateral agreement to provide a detailed framework for the application of clearly identified rules requiring the provision of information in emergency situations, involving a role for the national authorities of States Parties and the IAEA, as well as a binding dispute settlement mechanism.

It is not, however, exhaustive, nor immune from a number of important criticisms. First, the Convention applies only to non-military nuclear accidents.[3] Second, certain of the recommendations contained in the Information Guidelines were not included.... Third, the reference in Article 1(l) to an accident that "could be of radiological safety significance for another State" leaves it to the discretion of the State in whose territory or under whose jurisdiction or control the accident has occurred to determine what is or is not of radiological safety significance and what are the chances that another State would be affected. Given the dangers of radioactivity it would have been preferable that all radioactive releases be notified to the IAEA. Failing that, there should be an agreed level which would trigger the obligation to provide information. Fourth, a number of States have entered reservations restricting the application of the Convention. Most relate to the non-applicability of the dispute settlement provision, but some relate to the substantive provisions. Thus, the Government of the People's Republic of China stated that the Convention did not apply to cases caused by "gross negligence."

Finally, the Convention does not establish any obligation on States giving or receiving information to make [the information] available to members of the public. The 1985 IAEA Guidelines noted that:

2. *See* G. Silagi, *Volkerrechtliche Verpflichtungen des Genehmigungsstaates bei Stor- und Unfallen, in* Friedliche Kernenergienutzung und Staatsgrenzen in Mitteleuropa (N. Pelzer ed., 1987).

3. The five [declared] nuclear weapons States have declared that they will voluntarily apply the convention to all nuclear accidents, irrespective of origin.

Dissemination of information to the public is an important responsibility of the appropriate authorities in each State. Particular arrangements ensuring the necessary co-ordination across international borders should be established.[4]

Desirable as it may be, there is no obligation under international law for a State to provide assistance in the event of a major disaster, nuclear or otherwise. States may, of course, offer assistance on humanitarian grounds.... The provision of such assistance nevertheless raises certain legal questions. The most important relate to the direction and control of the assistance: the reimbursement of any costs incurred; the attribution of liability in the event of damage being suffered by the assisting State in the course of assistance: and the liability of the assisting State for damage it might cause during the course of assistance, including any privileges and immunities attaching to the assisting State. These questions require clear answers if the provision of assistance is to be encouraged.

* * *

The IAEA has recognized for some time that "the speed of initial response to a nuclear accident or radiological emergency could be crucial in minimizing the extent of the physical damage and the subsequent release of radioactive material."[5] In 1977 the IAEA concluded an agreement with the UNDRO (United Nations Disaster Relief Agency) for close coordination of their activities in providing assistance in connection with nuclear accidents; and in 1984 it drew up the Guidelines for Mutual Emergency Assistance Arrangements in Connection with a Nuclear Accident or Radiological Emergency (Assistance Guidelines). These are designed for use as the basis for the negotiation of bilateral or regional arrangements to encourage the provision of assistance and contain very similar provisions to the Nordic Assistance Agreement, including the establishment of channels for communication and, if appropriate, the designation of working languages.

The Chernobyl accident gave fresh impetus for the further development of a legal framework for assistance. Within six months a new multilateral instrument had been drawn up and opened for signature. The 1986 Assistance Convention **[Basic Document 5.27]**, which is closely modeled on the Assistance Guidelines, seeks to facilitate prompt assistance in the event of a nuclear accident or radiological emergency:

> to minimize its consequences and to protect life, property and the environment from the effects of radioactive releases.[6]

The Convention applies whether or not the accident occurred within the requesting State's territory or jurisdiction and it extends to the provision of assistance in relation to medical treatment or the temporary relocation of displaced persons.

4. International Atomic Energy Agency, Guidelines on Reportable Events, Integrated Planning and Information Exchange in Transboundary Release of Radioactive Materials (Information Guidelines) (1985), ¶ 4.5.1.

5. *Id.* Technical Annex, ¶ 4.

6. ... art. 1(1).

Requesting States are required to specify the scope and type of assistance they require and, where practicable, to provide any necessary information. A State receiving such a request is under an obligation to:

promptly decide and notify the requesting State Party ... whether it is in a position to render the assistance requested, and the scope and terms of the assistance that might be rendered.[7]

States Parties are under an obligation

within the limits of their capabilities [to] identify and notify the [IAEA] of experts, equipment and materials which could be made available ... as well as the terms, especially financial, under which such assistance could be provided.[8]

The IAEA is to make available appropriate resources allocated for emergency purposes, to transmit information relating to resources and, if asked by the requesting State, to coordinate available assistance at the national level.

The Convention contains provisions for the establishment of the direction and control of assistance, the competent national authorities and points of contact and the reimbursement of costs. It also requires the assisting State to maintain the confidentiality of certain information, and establishes rules on privileges and immunities and claims and compensation relating to persons or property injured or damaged in the course of providing the assistance requested. It also sets out a binding dispute settlement provision.

The Convention is a significant contribution to international cooperation in the event of a nuclear accident. Significantly, it establishes an important role for the IAEA, as a channel for the provision of information and assistance to the States Parties or Member States. However, the Convention can be criticized on a number of grounds. It clearly emphasizes the protection of the assisting State. As the Argentinean representative at the Special Session noted, under Article 10(2) the State receiving assistance is to be held responsible for all damage suffered by the assisting State, but the assisting State apparently assumes no responsibility for any damage which it might cause. Furthermore Article 7, on the reimbursement of costs, has the result that a State which has caused a nuclear accident and which agrees to provide assistance to another affected State has the right to require reimbursement of assistance costs. This seems most unsatisfactory, and led the representative from Luxembourg to conclude that the fundamental question of responsibility had not been properly resolved. Moreover, a number of States have entered reservations and declarations restricting the application of the provisions relating to dispute settlement, privileges and immunities, and claims and compensation.

4.   Statute of the International Atomic Energy Agency (IAEA). Concluded, 26 Oct 1956. Entered into force, 29 Jul 1957. 276 U.N.T.S. 3, 8 U.S.T 1093, T.I.A.S. No. 3837; *reprinted in* **5 Weston & Carlson V.A.3: Arts. II, III, XII** (Basic Document 5.2).

5.   Vienna Convention on Civil Liability for Nuclear Damage. Concluded, 21 May 1963. Entered into force, 12 Nov 1977. 1063

7.   ... art. 2(3).
8.   ... art. 2(4).

U.N.T.S. 265; *reprinted in* 5 Weston & Carlson V.J.3: Arts. I, II, IV–VI, XI (Basic Document 5.8).

6.   IAEA Convention on Early Notification of a Nuclear Accident. Concluded, 26 Sep 1986. Entered into force, 27 Oct 1986. IAEA INFCIRC 335; *reprinted in* **5 Weston & Carlson V.I.2: Arts. 2, 5, 8** (Basic Document 5.26).

7.   IAEA Convention on Assistance in the Case of a Nuclear Accident or Radiological Emergency. Concluded, 26 Sep 1986. Entered into force, 26 Feb 1987. IAEA INFCIRC 336; *reprinted in* **5 Weston & Carlson V.I.3: Arts. 2, 3** (Basic Document 5.27).

8.   IAEA Convention on Nuclear Safety. Concluded, 20 Sep 1994. Entered into force, 24 Oct 1996. 1963 U.N.T.S. 293; *reprinted in* **5 Weston & Carlson V.I.6a** (Basic Document 5.42).

9.   Treaty on the Non–Proliferation of Nuclear Weapons. Concluded, 1 Jul 1968. Entered into force, 5 Mar 1970. 729 U.N.T.S. 161; *reprinted in* **2 Weston & Carlson II.C.17: Art. III** (Basic Document 2.21).

10.   Stockholm Declaration of the United Nations Conference on the Human Environment adopted by the UN Conference on the Human Environment at Stockholm, 16 Jun 72, Report of the UN Conference on the Human Environment, UN Doc. A/CONF.48/14/Rev.1 at 3 (1973), UN Doc. A/CONF.48/14 at 2–65, and Corr. 1 (1972); *reprinted in* **5 Weston & Carlson V.B.3: Pmbl. & Princs. 1–4, 6, 8, 9, 11, 12, 18, 21, 22, 24** (Basic Document 5.14).

11.   Charter of Economic Rights and Duties of States. Adopted, 12 Dec 1974. GA Res. 3281, 29th Sess., Supp. No. 31, at 50, UN Doc. A/9631 (1975); *reprinted in* **4 Weston & Carlson IV.F.5: Art. 30** (Basic Document 4.9).

12.   World Charter for Nature. Adopted, 28 Oct 1982. GA Res. 37/7, UN GAOR, 37th Sess., Supp. No. 51, at 17, UN Doc. A/37/51; *reprinted in* **5 Weston & Carlson V.B.11: Princs. 1–5, 11, 12, 20, 21, 24** (Basic Document 5.21).

13.   Rio Declaration on Environment and Development. Adopted, 13 Jun 1992. UNCED Doc. A/CONF.151/5/Rev. 1; *reprinted in* **5 Weston & Carlson V.B.16: Princs. 1, 2, 3, 7, 18, 19** (Basic Document 5.37).

14.   Editors' Note. *See* Reading 19 (Editors' Note) in Section D–4 of Problem 7–2 ("Hanguo Versus the Ozone Layer"), *supra* at 1122.

15.   Edith Brown Weiss, "Environmental Disasters in International Law," 1986 Ann. Jur. Interam. 141, 145–50 (1986).

The duty to minimize damage and to provide emergency assistance [in the event of environmental disaster] applies both to the State in which the accident occurs and to those States that are in a position to help alleviate the damage. Many bilateral and multilateral agreements contain these obligations. Certain obligations of States in responding to major environmental disasters exist as customary international law.

A State in which a major environmental disaster occurs has the duty to minimize the damage to the human environment. At a minimum this requires that a State promptly notify countries that may be affected, provide available information about the course of the accident, and inform affected States of measures it is taking to reduce the damage. States must also take necessary and practicable steps to prevent or reduce injury to other States from the accident. They must do so for both natural and man-induced disasters, although the State may bear no responsibility for injury caused by the natural disaster. Those States potentially affected by an environmental disaster have an obligation to cooperate in minimizing the damage. The failure to do so on their own territory may be a defense available to the State in which the accident occurred, if claims for reparation are made against it . . . .

The duty to minimize damage from environmental disasters derives from the principle of State responsibility. Principle 21 of the Stockholm Declaration on the Human Environment **[Basic Document 5.14]** . . . reflects customary international law. Support for it is contained in the resolution of earlier disputes, such as the Trail Smelter Arbitration **[Basic Document 7.3]**, and in the multitude of international agreements which implement it. The US Restatement on Foreign Relations Law confirms this obligation of States to "reduce and control" injury to the environment of other States and areas beyond national jurisdiction.[9]

There are four aspects to the duty to minimize damage: the duty to notify promptly; the duty to provide information to potentially affected States; the duty to develop contingency plans; and the duty to cooperate in minimizing damage, as by providing emergency assistance.

1. *The Obligation to Notify*

As early as 1949, the International Court of Justice in the Corfu Channel case **[Basic Document 7.5]** affirmed the obligation of a State to warn other countries exposed to dangers in its territory which could cause serious injury or death. The Court cited a State's duty not to permit knowingly the use of its territory in such a way as to violate the rights of others and "elementary considerations of humanity" as bases for this duty. The same considerations underlie the extension of the duty to notify the other States of major environmental disasters which may affect them.

The duty to notify appears in many treaties concerned with environmental disasters and in Sec. 602 of the Restatement of Foreign Relations Law on the Law of the Environment **[Basic Document 6.3]**, Article 9 of the Montreal Rules of the International Law Association [ILA] **[Basic Document 5.20]**, and Article 19 of the Legal Principles proposed in the report of the World Commission on Environment and Development **[Basic Document 5.25]**.

Treaties concerned with international waterways, marine pollution, nuclear accidents, forest fires, and other environmental catastrophes embody this duty. The provisions normally call for immediate notification when the State becomes aware that an emergency exists which could affect other countries or territories . . . . The duty to notify promptly and in good faith is firmly established in international law.

---

9. 2 Restatement (Third) of the Foreign Relations law of the United States, § 601 **[Basic Document 6.3]**.

2. *The Obligation to Provide Information*

There is also an obligation in international law to provide timely and relevant information to the potentially affected States. This has several aspects. The first is the need to provide relevant information about the accident to enable States to take their own measures to minimize the damage; the second is to inform States of measures that the host State is taking to prevent or reduce damage. Both aspects of this obligation appear in the Montreal Rules of the ILA and in the Legal Principles proposed by the World Commission on Environment and Development. Many of the international agreements which provide for notification specifically refer to one or both aspects. The 1986 IAEA Convention [on Early Notification of a Nuclear Accident] **[Basic Document 5.26]** provides in Article 5 a detailed list of information to be provided, if available, which includes information relevant to forecasting the scope and effects of the accident and the off-site protective measures planned. It is important for States in which an environmental disaster occurs to provide both kinds of information to enable potentially affected State[s] to take appropriate preventive or mitigating measures. If notice is to be effective, it must include relevant and appropriate information.

3. *The Obligation to Develop Contingency Plans.*

There is arguably a duty in customary international law to develop contingency plans for responding to marine pollution disasters in nearby areas, which may soon extend to other kinds of disasters. * * * Certainly the development of contingency plans is essential for effective responses to environmental disasters and should be part of customary international law applicable to major environmental disasters, particularly those that may be ultrahazardous. It is, however, doubtful that international law as yet requires States in the absence of an international agreement to develop such national contingency plans for disasters other than marine pollution.

4. *The Obligation to Cooperate in Minimizing Damage*

As part of the duty to minimize damage from environmental disasters, there is an emerging duty in international law which requires States to cooperate with each other in combating environmental disasters and preventing damage. This duty is reflected in the increasingly large number of bilateral and multilateral agreements which provide for emergency assistance and for mutual cooperation with mitigating damage. The details of this obligation are, however, by no means clear. For example, do all States have a duty to provide emergency assistance if requested? Must they be potentially affected by the disaster or is it sufficient that they have the capability to render assistance? What kinds of assistance must be provided? Who is responsible for paying the cost of the emergency assistance? The existing agreements address these issues in different ways.

16. Alan E. Boyle, "Nuclear Energy and International Law: An Environmental Perspective," 60 B.Y.B.I.L. 257, 287–90, 292–97 (1989).

(b) *Fault and Strict or Absolute Responsibility*

The point has ... been made that the obligation to control sources of harm represented by Principle 21 of the Stockholm Declaration **[Basic Document 5.14]** is capable of interpretation either as an obligation of due diligence or as one of absolute prevention of harm. The latter possibility may support strict or absolute responsibility for the fact of harm in international law, but the nature of such a principle must be considered.

The question cannot be reduced to a simple choice between "fault" and some stricter standard of responsibility, since "fault," as Corfu Channel **[Basic Document 7.5]** illustrates, can be used both subjectively, requiring intention or negligence on the part of the State or its agents, and objectively, meaning simply the breach of an international obligation. Used in the former, subjective, sense, "fault" is, as Handl observes, almost never the basis of responsibility in environmental disputes.[10] Jimenez de Aréchaga aptly explains the essential point:

> The decisive consideration is that unless the rule of international law which has been violated specifically envisages malice or culpable negligence, the rules of international law do not contain a general floating requirement of malice or culpable negligence as a condition of responsibility.[11]

Used in the objective sense, "fault" is simply tautologous, unless the particular obligation itself incorporates subjective elements.

This merely indicates that it is more productive to leave aside doctrinal arguments about the role and character of fault, and to concentrate instead on the essential point, that responsibility for a failure to prevent environmental harm will normally entail no more than the objective breach of an international obligation, however defined. Thus in choosing between diligent or absolute standards of responsibility, it is once more the definition of the primary obligation represented by Principle 21 of the Stockholm Declaration which is important, not the presence or absence of "subjective" fault. Simply to show that *dolus* or *culpa* is not required is not enough to demonstrate that States are strictly or absolutely responsible for nuclear damage.

* * *

(d) The Case Law

This is certainly inconclusive. The final award of the tribunal in *Trail Smelter* **[Basic Document 7.3]** required payment of further compensation if harm occurred notwithstanding Canada's compliance with the regime of control laid down, and has thus been variously read as supporting either strict or absolute responsibility. These concepts are often used interchangeably, as they will be [here] for the sake of convenience, but the point should be made at once that they differ significantly in the degree to which exculpation is permitted by international law. Strict responsibility places the burden of proof on the respondent but permits exculpation; absolute liability does not permit exculpation. Not all writers observe this basic distinction, but it indicates the difficulty of drawing firm conclusions from the *Trail Smelter* case. Since Canada's responsibility for damage was of course accepted by the parties at the outset, the award was not concerned with establishing a standard of

10. G. Handl, *International Liability for Pollution of International Watercourses: Balancing Interests*, 13 Can. Y. B. Int'l L. 156, 164 (1975)....

11. E. Jiménez de Aréchaga, *International Responsibility*, in Manual of Public International Law 531, at 539 (M. Sørensen ed. 1968).

responsibility in international law, but only with deciding what compensation was due and what the terms of future operation of the smelter should be. In any event, as Dupuy points out, whatever the case decides, it must be read in the light of subsequent State practice, which in his view favours due diligence.[12]

The decision in the *Corfu Channel* case **[Basic Document 7.5]** has suffered widely varied interpretations but in reality tells us only that States must make diligent efforts to warn other States of known hazards. It permits no definitive conclusions about the role of due diligence in cases of environmental injury, but it is difficult to reconcile the Court's efforts to establish what preventive steps the Albanian authorities could have taken with the view that States are strictly or absolutely responsible for injury. Most of the debate about the role of fault in this case has centred on the choice between subjective and objective definitions of fault referred to earlier, not on the question whether the obligations of States are absolute or qualified by diligent conduct.

For different reasons, the *Nuclear Tests* cases **[Basic Document 7.9]** are also unhelpful. Decided by the [International Court of Justice] in 1974, they deal with a series of deliberate test explosions, not with operational pollution or nuclear accidents. The claimants did not seek reparation for proven damage, but only a judgment that there should be no further testing, no deposit of nuclear fallout in breach of their territorial sovereignty and no more interference with high seas freedoms. The Court made no findings on any of these issues but dismissed the case on the ground that it no longer had any object, France having pledged unilaterally to discontinue further atmospheric tests. Only Judge de Castro made reference to the argument that nuclear testing may involve the breach of a State's obligation not to use its territory for acts contrary to the rights of other States.

Although Principle 21 of the Stockholm Declaration **[Basic Document 5.14]** now incorporates this obligation, it too is an inconclusive guide to the nature of responsibility for environmental damage, and must be interpreted within the framework of customary rules on which it is based. Reviewing the proceedings of the Preparatory Committee for the Stockholm Conference, Handl concludes that they provide little or no support in favour of any specific theory of liability, let alone a form of liability that is dependent on a link of causation in fact as the only prerequisite.[13]

(e) *Treaty Practice*

Only exceptionally does treaty practice adopt a form of responsibility for damage placed directly on States without more. Most treaty obligations are expressed in terms of diligent control of sources of harm ..., which requires States to take "all measures necessary" to protect other States against damage.... [I]t is only for non-fulfillment of this and other obligations under [conventional and customary] international law that the State is to be responsible....

---

12. P.-M. Dupuy, *International Liability for Transfrontier Pollution*, in Trends in Environmental Policy and Law 363, 369, 373 (M. Bothe ed. 1980).

13. G. Handl, *supra* note 10 (p. 1150).

The tendency to avoid direct implication of the State in responsibility for damage is complemented in many cases by emphasizing the liability in national law of the relevant operator or company which caused it. Significantly, this practice is adopted in treaties dealing with liability for nuclear damage. These do not preclude the possibility of State responsibility for harmful nuclear activities, but their scheme involves States only as guarantors of the operator's strict liability, or in providing additional compensation funds. Moreover, the burden of this residual responsibility is either spread equitably across a group of nuclear States, as under the Brussels Supplementary Convention,[h] or left in part to lie where it falls, by limiting liability. In neither case does the polluting State bear responsibility for the whole loss. The extent of its exposure is further limited by the narrow definition given to nuclear damage.

These factors make the nuclear liability conventions weak precedents for any particular theory or standard of State responsibility and are inconsistent with the view that States are absolutely or strictly responsible in international law for damage emanating from their territory. As with national laws employing standards of strict or absolute liability contingent on compulsory insurance and limitation of exposure, it is difficult to treat complex schemes of loss distribution as indicating a standard of responsibility for States themselves in the less highly developed circumstances of international law.

(f) *State Claims*

State claims, or settlements involving damage caused by nuclear activities, provide little support for any one standard of responsibility and demonstrate the lack of international consensus on this point, [and] [r]esponses to the Chernobyl disaster provide the most telling evidence of State practice so far. * * * Despite ... provable loss, no claims have been made against the [former] Soviet Union by any affected State, although the possibility was considered by some governments. Uncertainty over the basis for such a claim, reluctance to establish a precedent with possible future implications for States which themselves operate nuclear power plants, and the absence of any appropriate [binding] treaty ... are the main reasons for this inaction. It is also unclear whether damage to the environment or the costs of precautionary measures taken by governments can be included. The [former] Soviet Union ... made no voluntary offer of compensation and ... questioned the necessity for precautionary measures taken by its neighbours.

The failure to demand, or to offer, compensation in this case shows the difficulty of reconciling doctrinal support for any standard of strict or absolute responsibility with the evidence of State practice, limited as it is. It points to the conclusion that responsibility for a failure of due diligence, that is, for causing avoidable loss only, provides a more convincing interpretation of the actual practice of States and the present state of customary law in cases of environmental damage.

h. Convention Supplementary to the 1960 Convention on Third Party Liability in the Field of Nuclear Energy (as amended), 31 Jan 1963, *reprinted in* 2 I.L.M. 685 (1963) & 5 Weston & Carlson V.J.2.

(g) *Developing Trends*

The arguments for using a standard more demanding than due diligence to shift the burden of unavoidable loss back to the polluter remain strong, particularly where the source is an ultra-hazardous activity, such as a nuclear power plant. In the absence of reciprocal acceptance of risk, making the victim suffer is not an attractive policy. Nor in cases of nuclear accidents is due diligence an easy standard to administer. As we have seen, it is not possible to identify clearly accepted international standards defining the content of this duty in the case of nuclear activities. A heavy burden of proof will be placed on the State which has to establish a failure of due diligence; in the case of complex processes, such as the operation of nuclear reactors, this will be especially difficult unless liberal inferences of fact are allowed or the burden of proof is placed on the polluter.

The desirability of international agreement on appropriate principles of responsibility for inter-State claims [was] acknowledged by the [former] Soviet Union following Chernobyl. The ILC's proposed articles on "International Liability"[i] have since attracted some attention in the IAEA as a possible model. These provide reparation for injury on a strict liability basis that aims at restoring an equitable balance of interests between the parties. The articles now apply both to ultra-hazardous activities and to those with a higher probability of more minor but still appreciable injury. However, the introduction of equitable balancing would inevitably tend to dilute the force of present customary obligations of responsibility for harm prevention, such as they are.

Another possibility is to rely on a reformed system of civil liability conventions, hoping that these will attract more support from States. But even this would not render recourse to State responsibility unnecessary in all cases, and for various reasons considered below, the two systems are better seen as complementary, not alternative.

At present, however, it is difficult to conclude that State responsibility itself affords a sufficiently principled basis for the settlement of international claims arising out of nuclear damage. Without further agreement on the conditions and extent of its application, and on how the burden of reparation should be allocated, State responsibility is unlikely to supply answers which are either clear or predictable.

17. Draft Articles on Prevention of Transboundary Harm from Hazardous Activities. Adopted by the International Law Commission. Adopted, 11 May 2001. Report of the International Law Commission on the Work of its Fifty-third Session, UN GAOR, 56th Sess., Supp. No. 10, at 370–76, UN Doc. A/56/10 and Corr.1 (2001); *reprinted in* **5 Weston & Carlson V.J.17** (Basic Document 5.54).

18. Articles on Responsibility of States for Internationally Wrongful Acts. Adolpted by the International Law Commission. Adopted, 2 Aug 2001. Report of the International Law Commission on the Work of its Fifty-third Session, UN GAOR, 56th Sess., Supp. No. 10, at 43–58, UN Doc. A/56/10 and Corr. 1 (2001); commended to the attention of governments by the UN General Assembly, UNGAOR,

---

i. See note **g**, *supra*.

56th Sess., Supp. No. 49, at 499, UN Doc. A/RES/56/83 (12 Dec 2001);
reprinted in **1 Weston & Carlson I.G.4** (Basic Document 1.18).

    19. Editors' Note. Another way to deal with transboundary environ-
mental damage, *i.e.,* not invoking the juridical regime of responsibility of
states under international law, is to proceed via domestic civil liability actions
on the part of the individual victims of such damage. This approach requires
removing or reducing the jurisdictional hurdles that commonly hinder foreign
plaintiffs. It also requires shifting the burden of liability from the state to the
private entrepreneurs who operate the industry or activity involved. An
important advantage, however, is that it frees injured parties from having to
rely upon their governments to pursue interstate diplomatic claims on their
behalfs, rarely if ever an obligation under domestic law and reportedly never
done even in the extreme case of Chernobyl. Observes Günter Handl in
*Transboundary Nuclear Accidents: The Post–Chernobyl Multilateral Legisla-
tive Agenda*, 15 Ecology L. Q. 203, 222 (1988):

> What is striking about the "legal fallout" from Chernobyl . . . is that . . .
> reparation of the transboundary costs [turned out to be] an unlikely
> prospect despite the accident's massive impact on the environment and
> the economies of neighboring countries. None of the affected governments
> formally . . . lodged an international legal claim for damages. . . . Indeed,
> some West European countries . . . intimated that they believe[d] there
> [was] no international legal basis for securing damages from the [former]
> Soviet government. Immediately after the accident, the [former] Soviet
> Union itself disclaimed any international obligation to make reparation
> for damages abroad, even though it indicated a willingness to cooperate in
> clarifying the international liability issue *pro futuro.*[j]

Thus, making it possible for individual victims of environmental damage to
take matters into their own hands has an obvious appeal.

    The international framework for civil liability for nuclear damage is
conveniently summarized by the IAEA on its website at <http://www.iaea.org/
Publications/Documents/Conventions/liability.html>. The IAEA summarizes:

> At a Diplomatic Conference at IAEA Headquarters in Vienna, 8–12
> September 1997, delegates from over 80 States adopted a Protocol to
> Amend the 1963 Vienna Convention on Civil Liability for Nuclear Dam-
> age and also adopted a Convention on Supplementary Compensation for
> Nuclear Damage. The Protocol sets the possible limit of the operator's
> liability at not less than 300 million Special Drawing Rights (SDRs)
> (roughly equivalent to 400 million US dollars). The Convention on
> Supplementary Compensation defines additional amounts to be provided
> through contributions by States Parties on the basis of installed nuclear
> capacity and UN rate of assessment. The Convention is an instrument to

---

    j. Professor Handl cautions, however, that,
Moscow's "deplorable" failure to provide compensation aside, "it would be a mistake to
ignore certain idiosyncratic features of the incident and to attribute this failure exclusively, or
even primarily, to a lack of international
norms bearing on the liability issue. Political
expediency and the existence of a rather obvious causation problem, for example, probably

dissuaded affected governments from pursuing
the issue of reparation through diplomatic
channels. In the case of at least one affected
Western European country, moreover, the [for-
mer] Soviet Union agreed to a trade deal immediately after the accident that [had] the
clear marks of a compensatory payment."
Handl, *supra* note 10, at 223–24.

which all States may adhere regardless of whether they are parties to any existing nuclear liability conventions or have nuclear installations on their territories. The Protocol contains *inter alia* a better definition of nuclear damage (now also addressing the concept of environmental damage and preventive measures), extends the geographical scope of the Vienna Convention, and extends the period during which claims may be brought for loss of life and personal injury. It also provides for jurisdiction of coastal states over actions incurring nuclear damage during transport. Taken together, the two instruments should substantially enhance the global framework for compensation well beyond that foreseen by existing Conventions. Before the action in September 1997, the international liability regime was embodied primarily in two instruments, *i.e.* the Vienna Convention on Civil Liability for Nuclear Damage of 1963 **[Basic Document 5.8]** and the Paris Convention on Third Party Liability in the Field of Nuclear Energy of 1960,[k] linked by the Joint Protocol adopted in 1988.[l] The Paris Convention was later built up by the 1963 Brussels Supplementary Convention.[m] These Conventions are based on the civil law concept and share the following main principles:

a. Liability is channeled exclusively to the operators of the nuclear installations;

b. Liability of the operator is absolute, *i.e.*, the operator is held liable irrespective of fault;

c. Liability is limited in amount. Under the Vienna Convention, it may be limited to not less than US$5 million (value in gold on 29 April 1963), but an upper ceiling is not fixed. The Paris Convention sets a maximum liability of 15 million SDR provided that the installation State may provide for a greater or lesser amount but not below 5 million SDRs taking into account the availability of insurance coverage. The Brussels Supplementary Convention established additional funding beyond the amount available under the Paris Convention up to a total of 300 million SDRs, consisting of contributions by the installation State and contracting parties;

d. Liability is limited in time. Compensation rights are extinguished under both Conventions if an action is not brought within ten years from the date of the nuclear incident. Longer periods are permissible if, under the law of the installation State, the liability of the operator is covered by financial security. National law may establish a shorter time limit, but not less than two years (the Paris Convention) or three years (the Vienna Convention) from the date the claimant knew or ought to have known of the damage and the operator liable;

e. The operator must maintain insurance of other financial security for an amount corresponding to his liability; if such security is insufficient, the installation State is obliged to make up the difference up to the limit of the operator's liability;

---

k. 956 U.N.T.S. 251, *reprinted in* 5 Weston & Carlson V.J.1.

l. 1672 U.N.T.S. 293, *reprinted in* 5 Weston & Carlson V.J.8.

m. 1041 U.N.T.S. 350, *reprinted in* 5 Weston & Carlson V.J.2.

f. Jurisdiction over actions lies exclusively with the courts of the Contracting Party in whose territory the nuclear incident occurred;

g. Non-discrimination of victims on the grounds of nationality, domicile or residence.

Following the Chernobyl accident, the IAEA initiated work on all aspects of nuclear liability with a view to improving the basic Conventions and establishing a comprehensive liability regime. In 1988, as a result of joint efforts by the IAEA and OECD/NEA, the Joint Protocol Relating to the Application of the Vienna Convention and the Paris Convention was adopted. The Joint Protocol established a link between the Conventions combining them into one expanded liability regime. Parties to the Joint Protocol are treated as though they were Parties to both Conventions and a choice of law rule is provided to determine which of the two Conventions should apply to the exclusion of the other in respect of the same incident.

A regional model for civil liability is the 1993 Council of Europe Convention on Civil Liability for Damages Resulting from the Exercise of Activities Dangerous for the Environment, E.T.S. 150, *reprinted* in 32 I.L.M. 1228 (1993), establishing general standards for indemnification of those injured by hazardous activities and products. Kiss and Shelton explain in International Environmental Law 294–95 (3d ed. 2004), as follows:

> [The Convention] establishes general standards for indemnification of those injured by hazardous activities and products. [It] broadly imposes responsibility on all persons and companies and the state and all agencies exercising control over dangerous activities, irrespective of the place of the harm. However if the damage occurs in a non-contracting state, the convention permits reservations to be filed demanding reciprocity of remedies.

> The Convention applies to dangerous activities and substances including living modified organisms. The quality of dangerousness is largely based upon assessment of the risk of harm to man, the environment or property. Nuclear damage is excluded if the incident is regulated by the Paris Convention on Civil Liability of 1960[n] or by the Vienna Convention of 1963 **[Basic document 5.8]** with its amendments, or by national legislation at least as favorable to the plaintiffs as the Convention. Work place accidents covered by social security and automobile accidents in places inaccessible to the public as well as assimilated to other activities within the installation also are excluded.

> In addition to compensation for death, bodily harm, and injury to property other than that found on the sight or within the installation where the dangerous activity has taken place, recovery can be had for environmental harm, limited to the costs of reasonable measures taken to restore or rehabilitate the environment to its prior state. Recovery is also possible for the costs of mitigating measures and any losses or damage costs by such measures after an incident or event. The maximum amount on liability may be fixed by local law, which should also insist upon adequate insurance coverage taking into account the risks associated with the activity. . . .

n. *Supra* note **k** (p. 1155).

All this said, however, it is sobering to note that, though requiring only three ratifications to enter into force, this convention has yet to do so ten years after its adoption. Indeed, of the 45 eligible participants in the Council of Europe, only eight have signed the treaty and none have ratified it since 21 June 1993 when it was opened for signature. One is thus led to wonder if Professor Sands, deploring the "unwillingness of states to act as guardians of the environment," was not prescient when, in 1989, he thought it "doubtful whether traditional international law will succeed in establishing either an effective substantive regime or effective procedures for protecting the environment." Philippe J. Sands, *The Environment, Community and International Law*, 30 Harv. Int'l L. J. 393, 396 (1989).

20. Alexandre C. Kiss & Dinah Shelton, International Environmental Law 74–82 (3d ed. 2004).

. . . [S]ome international jurists have posited the existence in international law of "treaty-laws," distinguished from "treaty-contracts." The distinction may have meaning in the sense that "treaty-laws" are concluded in the common interest of humanity, while "treaty-contracts" are based on the principle of reciprocity.

* * *

Common interests shared by the international community may be protected as obligations *erga omnes*.° In *Barcelona Traction Light and Power Company, Limited*,[17] the International Court of Justice recognized the distinction between reciprocal and regulatory norms [and] included in the category of obligations *erga omnes* the international laws prohibiting aggression, genocide, slavery, and racial discrimination. More recently, the International Court of Justice has cited with approval the view of the International Law Commission that safeguarding the earth's ecological balance has come to be considered an essential interest of all states, to protect the international community as a whole.[18] This factor, plus the absence of reciprocity [*i.e.*, the absence of a perfect contractual balance between rights and duties among formally obligated parties in a highly interdependent community], characterizes much of international environmental law. Thus, many of the codified norms and customary standards in the environmental field may be viewed as obligations *erga omnes*.

Rules of international environmental law, adopted in the common interest of humanity, generally do not bring immediate advantages to contracting states when their objective is to protect species of wild plant and animal life, the oceans, the air, the soil, and the countryside. Even treaties concluded among a small number of states generally lack reciprocity. For example, states upstream on a river are not in the same situation as those downstream. The

---

o. The doctrine of obligations *erga omnes*, a Latin expression meaning "towards all," can have, as Kiss and Shelton contend here, a regulatory connotation, like legislation, in service to common interests. For pertinent commentary, see Discussion Note/Question 5 in Section A of Chapter 2, *supra* at 104.

17. Barcelona Traction, Light and Power Company, Limited (New Application: 1962) (Belg. v. Spain, Second Phase) 1970 ICJ 312.

18. Case Concerning the Gabcikovo–Nagymaros Project (Hungary/Slovakia), 1997 ICJ ¶ 53, citing the Interna-tional Law Commission, Commentary to Article 33 of the Draft Articles on the International Responsibility of States. *See Yearbook of the I.L.C,* 1980, Vol. II, Part 2, at 39, ¶ 14.

general direction of winds and ocean currents can substantially affect legal obligations, cut against the equality of the parties, and diminish the importance of reciprocity.

International environmental obligations also differ from most international law in calling upon the state to regulate the behavior of non-state actors that are the source of most harm to the environment. The obligations must be implemented in national law to control the non-state actors within the state's territory and jurisdiction. In contrast, treaties to establish diplomatic relations, or to lower trade barriers, generally impact the state and its agents only. Human rights law also primarily applies to the conduct of state authorities.

* * *

International conventions seeking to proclaim and establish the common interest of humanity, distinguished by the restricted role of reciprocity in their provisions, pose particular problems of enforcement. In an international society without institutional strength, bilateral reciprocity has provided an essential guarantee of respect for obligations undertaken, due to the implicit threat of sanctions imposed in the event obligations are breached. With an agreement that contains reciprocal rights and duties, a state violating the treaty rights of another state risks losing benefits under the same agreement. Such results are inconceivable in a conventional system aimed at the common interest: violation of human rights by one state cannot be sanctioned by another state engaging in similar violations. It is the same for international environmental law: norms against pollution of the sea or the air cannot be enforced by reciprocal pollution. Enforcement must be by other means, especially by international control mechanisms that supervise the implementation of international environmental law by states.

Section 5.   Discussion Notes/Questions

1.   What should be the standard of care for any obligation to avoid harmful increase in levels of transboundary radioactivity? The possibilities are fault (intention or negligence), strict liability (basically a *prima facie* liability with various defenses or qualifications), and absolute liability (for which there is no exculpation). *See* L. Goldie, *Liability for Damage and the Progressive Development of International Law,* 14 I.C.L.Q. 1189, 1202–20 (1965) for a discussion of the distinction between strict and absolute liability in the context of environmental damage. The dangers of nuclear activity mean that the standard of care should be a high one. The national law of many countries has a standard of strict liability for ultra-hazardous activities. Some treaties regulating nuclear activities and other ultra-hazardous activities establish a principle of absolute liability. However, the use of the word "absolute" is misleading, as many of these treaties provide exceptions to the rule, *e.g.* Article 3 of the 1960 Paris Convention on Third Party Liability in the Field of Nuclear Energy (as amended), 956 U.N.T.S. 251, *reprinted in* 5 Weston & Carlson V.J.1, and Article IV(1) of the 1962 Brussels Convention on the Liability of Operators of Nuclear Ships, IAEA Leg. Ser. No. 4, at 34 (25 May 1962). By contrast the 1972 Convention on International Liability for Damage Caused by Space Objects, 1961 U.N.T.S. 187, *reprinted in* 5 Weston & Carlson V.J.4, provides for objective responsibility for space objects falling on the ground irrespective of fault and has no ceiling or limit on possible compensation.

In 1981, the USSR paid $3 million compensation in final settlement for damage incurred in locating and cleaning-up after the disintegration of a nuclear-powered satellite, Cosmos 954, on Canadian territory in 1978. In its statement of claim, Canada relied on Article 2 of the 1972 Convention on International Liability for Damage Caused by Space Objects, *supra*, and maintained that the principle of absolute liability applies to fields of activity having in common a high degree of risk in international law. Is absolute liability a principle in customary law for abnormally dangerous activities? Should it be?

What standard of care would be most likely to achieve the objective of preventing nuclear accidents? There is an argument that strict or absolute liability might make it impossible for operators to obtain financial security (insurance) coverage. Should this be a consideration when dealing with questions concerning global environmental security?

2.   What type of reparation would be best for pollution from a nuclear power plant? Indemnity in the form of monetary compensation? Restoration (if possible)? Satisfaction? Which is the most likely to achieve the objective of prevention? Should there be different criteria for determining reparations for activities with a higher-than-normal likelihood of causing substantial injuries within the territory of another state? Is the "polluter pays" principle appropriate for nuclear pollution given its widespread, long-lasting, and serious effects on the environment? Are there other possible ways of handling the question of reparations?

Taking the compensation route raises the issue of how to quantify the value of damage caused in monetary terms. Some losses cannot be quantified. For example, what value would be placed on the destruction of the traditional Lapp way of life, alleged to be a casualty of the effect of radioactivity from Chernobyl on lichen which reindeer eat. States are unlikely to agree on any monetary value, given that it reflects a different set of cultural assumptions. One possible measure of damages would be the cost of making the environment whole. This approach finds support in traditional international law, which provides that "reparation must, as far as possible, wipe out all the consequences of the illegal act and establish the situation which would in all probability have existed if the act had not been committed." Chorzow Factory Case (Ger. v. Pol.), 1928 PCIJ (ser. A) No. 17, at 47.

3.   The consequences of a nuclear accident are difficult to establish. There are major problems in proving damage and loss over the long term. Could Cascadia succeed with a claim based on an alleged infliction of a moral injury? Is material damage required? Would the psychological impact of radioactive fallout on the state's people suffice as a basis for a claim? Günter Handl, *Territorial Sovereignty and the Problem of Transnational Pollution*, 69 A.J.I.L. 50 (1975) concludes that moral injury is not enough. International law requires proof of material damage, but this could include psychological impact.

The *Nuclear Tests Cases* **(Basic Document 7.9)** raised these issues; but the International Court of Justice did not deal with them because France undertook to stop nuclear testing. Australia and New Zealand argued that radioactive fallout from the French tests on their territory and its dispersion within their airspace without their consent violated their territorial sovereignty. They claimed also that it impaired their independent right to determine what acts should take place within their territories and, in particular, whether each state and its people shall be exposed to radiation from artificial sources. If the International Court of Justice had considered these issues, how do you think it might have decided?

Why? For pertinent comment, see Discussion Note/Question 6 in Problem 4–5 ("Hindustan Threatens Nuclear Self–Defense"), *supra* at 437.

4. What if Gallia supplied the up-to-date technological equipment and then the accident happened? What if there were a Calvo-type clause in the contract which stated that Hanguo exempted Gallia from any responsibility? Would Gallia be liable to the injured populations under the law of state responsibility? Is there a human rights argument? For a discussion of these questions, see Anthony A. D'Amato & Kirsten Engel, *State Responsibility for the Exportation of Nuclear Power Technology*, 74 Va. L. Rev. 1011 (1988).

5. Where to with the law now? There are two views on the best approach to handle the law on international liability for nuclear damage. The first considers the 1960 Paris Convention (956 U.N.T.S. 251, *reprinted in* 5 Weston & Carlson V.J.1) and the 1963 Vienna Convention **(Basic Document 5.8)** and its 1997 Protocol [36 I.L.M. 1454 (1997), *reprinted in* 5 Weston & Carlson V.J.13, with wider acceptance, as the way to proceed (*N.B.*: neither Australia nor the United States is a party to any of these instruments at this writing). This approach would harmonize, and perhaps simultaneously apply, the two Conventions. The second view believes that there is a need for a new instrument on state liability for nuclear damage. The conventions deal with liability primarily under civil law. They address the liability of individuals or juridical persons for damage resulting in loss of life or damage to the property of individuals. They do not deal with damage to the environment or with claims between states. Such a multilateral instrument would take full account of the work of the International Law Commission on international liability.

6. At the time of Chernobyl, there were no international standards on what constitutes harmful levels of radioactivity. This caused problems. The former USSR claimed that states took unjustified action in placing restrictions on trade in agricultural products. There were allegations that some states took action for reasons other than the threat of nuclear contamination, such as for trade advantage. The USSR suggested that a new instrument could deal with material, moral, and political damage caused by unwarranted action taken under the pretext of protecting against the consequences of nuclear accidents (the spreading of untrue information, introduction of unjustified restrictive measures, etc). What would such an instrument look like? How would it work?

7. What should Hanguo have done prior to the development of the nuclear facility? What is a state's responsibility under international law for transboundary environmental risks and potential harm? Does international law recognize the principle of international liability for risk? Is the source state under a legal obligation to take certain procedural steps—*e.g.*, providing prior information, offering or accepting a request for consultation, and undertaking a transboundary impact assessment—designed to minimize the risk? Does such a duty raise practical problems of implementation and enforcement? How might these problems be overcome? *See, e.g.,* Roda Mushkat, *The Daya Bay Nuclear Plant Project in the Light of International Law,* 7 U.C.L.A. Pac. Basin L. J. 87 (1990).

8. Should neighboring states have a legal right of veto or co-decision relative to the construction of a nuclear facility? Should the people and local authorities affected in neighboring states have the same procedural rights as those enjoyed during a public inquiry by general public and local authorities in the constructing state? Should the constructing state be obliged to include the observations made by the affected people and local authorities of the neighboring state in its decision-making? Should the mere risk of a major accident be regarded as damage to the

other state? What about the possible psychological effects of a nuclear power plant on the inhabitants of a region, or any effect on aesthetics and tourism? *See. e.g.,* Koen Lenaerts, *Border Installations, in* Nuclear Energy Law After Chernobyl (P. Cameron *et al.* eds., 1988). How can states decide what constitutes neighboring territories when distance does not always equate to danger of transboundary pollution?

9.   After Chernobyl, some countries abandoned plans for developing new nuclear power plants. Others looked at phasing out nuclear power. This would mean the use of alternative sources of power (sun, wind, water, biomass, etc.), which also could have undesirable environmental consequences. In Europe, for example, greater use of coal-fired and oil-fired power plants has the potential to increase emissions of sulfur and nitrogen oxides, both contributors to acid rain. There is also the potential effect on global warming. Nuclear power generation involves the release of negligible quantities of carbon dioxide, acidifying gases, and other air pollutants associated with fuel combustion. However, nuclear power has health, safety, and security risks. And there are problems regarding the safe disposal of nuclear waste and the de-commissioning of nuclear plants. What implications do these questions have for the treatment of nuclear technology in international law?

10.   A relatively recent crisis in transboundary nuclear pollution is found in the radioactive waste that has resulted from reactors of decommissioned nuclear submarines belonging to Russia's Northern Fleet and situated on the Kola Peninsula adjacent to the Barents and White seas. It is a crisis that is not widely appreciated by the general public, but one that could affect the whole of Europe if not brought quickly under strict control.

Following the breakup of the Soviet Union in late 1991, newly sovereign Russia, in furtherance of arms control agreements reached between its predecessor Soviet Union, the United States and others in the late 1980s, undertook to reduce drastically its nuclear and conventional arms pursuant to a set of negotiations begun between the United States and the USSR in 1982, known as the "Strategic Arms Reduction Talks" (START). For summary description, see Discussion Note/Question 3 in Problem 4–5 ("Hindustan Threatens Nuclear Self–Defense") in Chapter 4, *supra* at 437. Many of the weapons covered by the arms reduction agreements resulting from START were on Russian submarines that generally are powered by two nuclear reactors (in contrast to one reactor which typically characterizes the nuclear submarines of France, the United Kingdom, and the United States). Most of these Russian submarines are based in Russian ports on the Kola Peninsula near Murmansk in the West and in and around Vladivostok in the East. Many of these decommissioned submarines have yet to have their reactors removed. In such cases they have simply been cut open to remove the warheads and then patched back together and stored in the harbors. As a result, each of these submarines, while inoperative for lack of missiles, still contains the two nuclear reactors that once powered them.

All of which has created a huge stockpile of submarine nuclear reactors equal to about 60 percent of the nuclear power reactors presently generating civilian electric power worldwide, most of them on the Kola Peninsula, only one hour's drive from northern Norway and Finland. Indeed, combined with Russia's Atom-flot fleet of nuclear-powered ice breakers in Kola Bay, the Kola nuclear power plant near Polyarny Zori, and the nuclear submarine shipbuilders in Severodvinsk, Russia's Northern Fleet of active and decommissioned submarines help to make the Kola Peninsula–White Sea region home to the largest concentration of nuclear reactors anywhere in the world. Partly because most of these reactors are themselves mismanaged and partly because the waste generated by them is stored or disposed of under unsafe conditions, they present a large danger to human health and to the natural environment both on land and at sea, exacerbated by accidents on land that release radioactive material into the Arctic environment and by the intentional discharge of radioactive pollutants on the land that later migrate into the neighboring Arctic seas. Also contributing to the toxicity of the region are more than 700,000 tons of sulphur dioxide that are each year released into the Kola Peninsula by Russian factories in Severonickel and Pechenganickel, where aluminum and nickel minerals are extracted practically unfiltered, endangering thousands of square miles of taiga, tundra, and mixed forests.

In sum, the Arctic environment is grievously threatened by nuclear pollution emanating from the Russian Federation, emanations that poison not just that immediate region but, as well, the entire Arctic environment, including the northern reaches of countries such as Finland and Norway. The total amount of radioactivity in the Murmansk area alone is thought to be in the hundreds of millions of curies. It is a threat that the world can disregard or downplay only at its peril.

For summary detail, see Lakshman D. Guruswamy, Sir Geoffrey W.R. Palmer, Burns H. Weston & Jonathan C. Carlson, International Environmental Law and World Order: A Problem–Oriented Coursebook 2–10 (2d ed., 1999). For extensive up-to-date detail, see Nils Boehmer, Aleksandr Nikitin, Igor Kudrik, Thomas Nilsen, Michael H. McGovern, & Andrey Zolotkov, The Arctic Challenge (Bellona Report No. 3, 2001), containing an extensive chapter on the Russian Northern Fleet and available at the website of the Bellona Foundation, at <http://www.bellona.org>. The Bellona Foundation is a nongovernmental, nonprofit organization formed in 1986 and based in Oslo, Norway.

How would you propose to solve the problems of radioactive environmental contamination and the ensuing adverse health effects, both actual and potential, to the people living in the Arctic areas and beyond as a result of this northwest Russian nuclear crisis? Two further broad questions should spring immediately to mind. First, to what extent can the Russians be held responsible and liable for their past actions? Second, how might the impending environmental catastrophe be avoided? Numerous off-shoots of these basic questions emerge. Is the Russian government responsible for hazards to human health and the natural environmental created in fulfillment of its arms control agreements? If Russia can be held internationally accountable for these hazards, on the basis of what legal doctrines, principles, or rules may this be so? Under international law, may, say, Finland, Norway, or even the Arctic Council of which they are members demand that Russia specifically perform remedial measures designed to eliminate or reduce the health and environmental hazards it is posing? If so, what measures and according to what procedures? In addition, or in the alternative, may Finland, Norway, or the Arctic Council, under international law, demand reparations from Russia for damage done? May private Finnish, Norwegian, or other foreign victims do so via civil liability proceedings? If so, what damages may be assessed? Personal damages? Property damages? Punitive damages for arguable violations of international environmental law? Prospective damage? Other damages? If any of these, in what amount and according to what valuation criteria? Criteria established by Finnish or Norwegian law? Russian law? International law? Does the international law of state responsibility help? Are civil liability proceedings a likely route to success? Is the law even relevant? For preliminary discussion of some of these issues, see

Justin Mellor, *Radioactive Waste and Russia's Northern Fleet: Sinking the Principles of International Environmental Law*, 51 Denver J. Int'l L. & Pol'y 51 (1999).

11. Not to be overlooked either is the nexus between nuclear power and the spread of nuclear weapons. Despite many pressures and blandishments, it has been argued, nuclear weapons proliferation is not likely to be halted until there is a total renunciation of nuclear power for whatever purpose, on the part of the nuclear weapons states especially, and its substitution with other less centralized, less costly, and pollution-free sources of energy such as sun, wind, water, and biomass. *See* Richard A. Falk, *Nuclear Policy and World Order: Why Denuclearization*, 3 Alternatives–A Journal of World Policy 321 (1978). Is it feasible to eliminate commercial nuclear power from the world scene? For powerful, seminal advocacy in the affirmative, see Amory Lovins, *Energy Strategy: The Road Not Taken?*, 55 Foreign Aff. 65 (1976). *See also* Amory Lovins, Soft Energy Paths: Toward a Durable Peace (1977).

12. *Bibliographical Note.* For supplemental discussion concerning the principal themes addressed in this problem, consult the following additional specialized materials:

(a) *Books/Monographs/Reports/Symposia.* R. Avenhaus, Containing the Atom: International Negotiations on Nuclear Security and Safety (2002); X. Hanqin, Transboundary Damage in International Law (2003); IAEA, Topical Issues In Nuclear Safety: Proceedings of An International Conference on Topical Issues (2002); NEA, Indemnification of Damage in the Event of a Nuclear Accident (2003); M. Wilde, Civil Liability for Environmental Damage: A Comparative Analysis of Law and Policy in Europe and the United States (2002); L. Zanardi et al, Nuclear Nonproliferation And Safety: Challenges Facing The International Atomic Energy Agency (2002).

(b) *Articles/Book Chapters.* K. McMillan, *Strengthening the International Legal Framework for Nuclear Energy*, 13 Geo. Int'l Envtl. L. Rev. 983 (2001); V. Nee & B. Sewall, *Can Kazakhstan Profit from Radioactive Waste? Domestic and International Legal Perspectives on a Proposal to Import Radioactive Waste*, 15 Geo. Int'l Envtl. L. Rev. 429 (2003); B. Richardson, *Mandating Environmental Liability Insurance*, 12 Duke Env L & Pol'y F 293 (2002); D. J. Steding, *Russian Floating Nuclear Reactors: Lacuane in Current International Environmental and Maritime Law and the Need for Proactive International Cooperation in the Development of Sustainable Energy Sources*, 13 Pac. Rim L. & Pol'y 711 (2004).

Problem 7–4

The Sindhu River in Punjamir and Rajatan

SECTION 1. FACTS

Originating in the Karakush Mountains in the central Himalayas and flowing southwesterly some 2000 miles to the Indian Ocean, the Sindhu River is a life sustaining source of water for the two bordering South Asian nations of Punjamir and Rajatan, each members of the United Nations. Beginning about twenty years ago, however, extended drought conditions caused the Sindhu to shrink to half its normal size, leading to forced water rationing in both countries, crop failures, food shortages, and related misfortunes that brought not inconsiderable grief to their respective populations.

Punjamir sought to rectify this problem by constructing, with foreign capital, a large dam on that part of the Sindhu that runs through its territory, to the north and upstream from Rajatan. According to Punjamir, the dam would make possible the recovery of arable land lost through desertification. Also, it would permit the development of irrigated "green belts" and the generation of rural hydroelectric power, vital to elevating the standard of living of its farming communities. The building of the dam, however, together with a diversion of water for irrigation greater than originally had been planned, led to rapidly increased desertification in Rajatan to the south and downstream from Punjamir, and a consequent severe decline in a certain river fish upon which, historically, Rajatani diets have depended. Additionally, it caused a decline in the quality of the river water flowing to Rajatan because of increased pesticide use and run-off in Punjamir's newly created "green belts."

Rajatan now demands that the flow of the Sindhu River be restored to its normal level and that Punjamir take steps to remedy the pesticide problem. It is a party to the 1966 International Covenant on Economic, Social, and Cultural Rights, the 1992 Convention on Biological Diversity, and the 1997 United Nations Convention on the Law of the Non-navigational Uses of International Watercourses, but to no other relevant environmental or human rights treaty. Punjamir, which also is a party to 1966 International Covenant on Economic, Social, and Cultural Rights but to neither of the aforementioned environmental conventions nor to any other relevant environmental or human rights treaty, has responded that the current river flow is critical to the success of its "green belt" irrigation program and has dismissed the suggestion that the use of pesticides damages the health of Rajatani citizens. In the face of threats of military action on Rajatan's part, a mixed arbitral panel of international law experts, including one each from Punjamir and Rajatan, has been convened to resolve the legal issues between the two countries.

SECTION 2.   QUESTIONS PRESENTED

1.   Has Punjamir violated international law by diminishing the quantity and quality of the flow of the Sindhu River to Rajatan?

2.   In any event, are there any additional or alternative legal norms, procedures, and/or institutions to be recommended that might further help to prevent or discourage situations of the kind posed by this problem?

SECTION 3.   ASSIGNMENTS

A.   READING ASSIGNMENT

Study the Readings presented in Section 4, *infra*, and the Discussion Notes/Questions that follow. Also, time permitting, consult the accompanying bibliographical references.

B.   RECOMMENDED WRITING ASSIGNMENT

Prepare a comprehensive, logically sequenced, and *argumentative* brief in the form of an outline of the primary and subsidiary *legal* issues you see requiring resolution by the ad hoc arbitral tribunal. Also, from the perspective of an independent judge, indicate which side ought to prevail on each issue and why. Retain a copy of your issue-outline (brief) for class discussion.

C.   RECOMMENDED ORAL ASSIGNMENT

Assume you are legal counsel for Punjamir or Rajatan (as designated by your instructor); then, relying upon the Readings (and your issue-outline if prepared), present a 10–15 minute oral argument of your government's likely positions before the ad hoc arbitral tribunal.

D.   RECOMMENDED REFLECTIVE ASSIGNMENT

Consider (and recommend) alternative norms, institutions, and/or procedures that you believe might do better than existing world order arrangements to contend with situations of the kind posed by this problem. In so doing, but without insisting upon *immediate* feasibility, identify the particular transition steps that would be needed to make your alternatives a reality.

SECTION 4.   READINGS

The following readings are considered *prima facie* relevant to solving this problem. They are your law library for present purposes and should be treated as such, organized intelligibly for "shelving" and not necessarily according to the issues presented. Be sure to review Chapter 2 ("International Legal Prescription: The 'Sources' of International Law") in your consideration of them. It, too, should be treated as part of your law library (as, indeed, should this entire coursebook).

1. International Water Law: Selected Writings of Professor Charles B. Bourne 110–12 (P. Wouters ed., 1997).

Before 1900, little attention was paid to the legal aspects of the utilization of waters for purposes other than navigation. And, even in the case of navigation, no customary international law had been developed by that time.... It is, therefore, hardly an exaggeration to say that international lawyers started the twentieth century with a clean slate insofar as water resources were concerned.

The reason for this is that there were few urgent problems in the utilization of international waters to engage the attention of lawyers before 1900. Modern technology soon changed that. The capacity to build huge dams to store water for generating hydroelectric power or to divert water from its natural channel to distant places, even outside the drainage basin, coinciding with heavy new demands for more food to feed a growing world population and for more energy to sustain a rapidly expanding industrial society, made water a coveted commodity. Consequently, before long, rules were needed to help resolve the conflicting interests of states sharing international drainage basins.

Four theories have been advocated as the proper basis for these rules. First is the well-known "Harmon Doctrine." When the Mexican government had complained for a number of years that Mexican farms were being ruined because the waters of the Rio Grande were being diverted for irrigation in the United States, the United States government in 1895 asked Attorney–General Harmon for his opinion on the legality of the American diversions. His reply was that "rules, principles and precedents of international law impose no liability or obligation upon the United States" and that the recognition of the Mexican claim would be "entirely inconsistent with the sovereignty of the United States over its national domain."[1] In short, the doctrine is a brutal assertion of the unfettered right of a territorial sovereign to do as it pleases.[a]

Second is the riparian rights doctrine [also known as "the doctrine of absolute territorial integrity"]. Under it a state with territory in an international drainage basin would have the right to have water continue to flow into its territory from that of another state "undiminished in quantity and unimpaired in quality"; its effect would be that upstream states could not utilize the waters of the basin without the consent of downstream states. The doctrine is supposedly based on the common law riparian rights rules but the common law, especially as it has developed in the eastern United States, allows upper riparians to make a reasonable use of water flowing through their lands and does not give lower riparians a veto over that use. The

---

1. *Treaty of Guadalupe Hidalgo—International Law*, 21 Op. Att'y Gen. 274, 282–83 (1895).

a. This statement appears somewhat exaggerated. As pointed out in J. Lipper, *Equitable Utilization, in* The Law of International Drainage Basins 15, 22 (A. Garretson, R. Hayton & C. Olmstead eds., 1967), Attorney–General Harmon's statement implied that the United States was free to continue at will because there was no established international conventional or customary law rule prohibiting the US conduct. Nevertheless, in support of his claim, Harmon cited as authority US Chief Justice John Marshall's opinion in an early US Supreme Court case involving quite another matter, namely, jurisdiction over a foreign ves-

sel within United States territory. In that case, *Schooner Exchange v. McFaddon*, 11 U.S. (7 Cranch) 116 (1812), Justice Marshall said that "the jurisdiction of the nation within its own territory is necessarily exclusive and absolute." However, the Harmon Doctrine "was eventually rejected by the United States (itself a downstream riparian of several rivers originating in Canada)"—*see, e.g.*, Agreement With Mexico, 21 May 1906, 34 Stat. 2953, T.S. No.455, 9 Bevans 924—and "never [has been] implemented in any water treaty, nor invoked as a source for judgment in any international water legal ruling...." H. Beach *et al.*, Transboundary Freshwater Dispute Resolution: Theory, Practice, and Annotated References 11 (2000).

doctrine has been invoked by states.[b] Pakistan did so in its dispute with India over the waters of the Indus River in response to India's invocation of the Harmon Doctrine. And, in the controversy between Canada and the United States about the development of the Columbia River, overtones of this doctrine could be heard in the American arguments.

A third theory is the doctrine of "prior appropriation." It simply asserts the proposition, "first in time, first in right": that is to say, the person who first establishes a utilization of water thereby acquires a good title to it. In an arid country where the demand for water exceeds supply, this doctrine, protecting the investment of the prior user, was found to be more acceptable than the territorial sovereignty doctrine (might is right) and the riparian rights doctrine (the last person downstream gets all the water). It was first developed in the arid regions of the western United States. When applied in international relations, it tends to favour downstream states which, in the ordinary course of events, always seem to develop economically ahead of states upstream. It is therefore popular with downstream states. Upstream states, however, are not impressed with its justice; even though their need of the water may arise later than that of downstream states, they feel entitled to share some of the benefits to be derived from the utilization of waters that pass through their territories; they reject the notion that all of the prizes in the utilization of water resources should go to a state that gets the quickest start.

A fourth doctrine is therefore brought forward, namely, that of "equitable utilization" or, as it is sometimes called, limited territorial sovereignty.[c] It is the doctrine that has gained the overwhelming support of the international community. In particular, it . . . [has] the blessing of the Institute of International Law[d] and of the International Law Association;[e] it is found at the heart of the Institute's 1961 Salzburg Resolution[2] and of the International Law Association's and of the International Law Association's 1966 Helsinki Rules **(Basic Document 5.9)** [which, in 2004, were superseded but reaffirmed by the ILA's more detailed Berlin Rules on Water Resources **(Basic Document 5.56)**].

2. Editors' Note. The principle of equitable utilization is newly rearticulated in the International Law Association's Berlin Rules on Water Resources **(Basic Document 5.56)** promulgated in 2004. *See infra* Readings 3 and 4. Article 12 demands that each State shall "manage the waters of an international drainage basin in an equitable and reasonable manner having

---

b. *Cf.* G. Eckstein, *Application of International Water Law to Transboundary Groundwater Resources, and the Slovak–Hungarian Dispute over Gabcikovo–Nagymaros*, 19 Suffolk Transnat'l L. Rev. 67, 74–75 (1995): "This principle, like the principle of absolute territorial sovereignty, has received little support amongst legal publicists and in state practice. Indeed, no contemporary authority espouses the postulate as a modern principle of international law. It is regarded as inequitable in its allocation of water resources, as well as in its biased preference for downstream states, particularly because it does not require lower riparian states to compensate upstream states for preserving the waters."

c. The doctrine is grounded on the principle of *sic utere tuo ut alienum non laedas* ("one must so use one's own as not to do injury to another"), employed, *e.g.*, in the 1941 *Trail Smelter Arbitration* between the United States and Canada **(Basic Document 7.3)**.

d. On the Institute of International Law (IIL), *see supra* note **s** in Chapter 2.

e. On the International Law Association (ILA), *see supra* note **b** in Chapter 2.

2. Resolution on the Utilization of Non-maritime International Waters (except for Navigation) . . . , 49 Annuaire de l'Institut Droit International 381 (1961–II).

due regard for the obligation not to cause significant harm to other States," and Article 13 defines "equitable and reasonable" as something to be determined through "consideration of all relevant factors in each particular case," referencing a list of such factors. In other words, decision-makers are instructed to determine the reasonableness of any use by applying a kind of cost-benefit balancing test.

Like their predecessor Helsinki Rules and other developments in international water law, the Berlin Rules are based in part on a number of judicial and arbitral decisions that, over the years, have greatly influenced the evolution of international environmental law generally, among them the *Case Relating to the Territorial Jurisdiction of the International Commission of the River Oder* (Czech., Den., Fr., Ger., Swed., U.K./Pol.), 1929 PCIJ (ser. A) No. 23, at 5; the *Diversion of Water from the Meuse Case* (Neth. v. Belg.), 1937 PCIJ (ser. A/B) No. 7, at 4; the *Trail Smelter Arbitration* (U.S. v. Can.), [1941] 3 U.N.R.I.A.A. 1938 (1949); the *Corfu Channel Case* (U.K. v. Alb.), 1949 ICJ 4; and the *Lake Lanoux Arbitration* (Spain v. Fr.), 12 U.N.R.I.A.A. 281 (1964). Summaries of each of these decisions are included in the documentary supplement to this coursebook as **Basic Documents 7.1** (*Oder*), **7.2** (*Meuse*), **7.3** (*Trail Smelter*), **7.5** (*Corfu Channel*), and **7.7** (*Lake Lanoux*). Together with the *Corfu Channel Case*, the *Trail Smelter Arbitration* (by analogy) and the *Lake Lanoux Arbitration* (by way of dictum) have become the most celebrated examples, each of them explicitly expressing the view that there is an international obligation not to cause transboundary environmental injuries. Charles Okidi summarizes:

> The emphasis [in the *Trail Smelter Arbitration*] is on the responsibility of the Dominion to reduce or otherwise control pollution, even though Trail Smelter was a private firm. This is the point which brings the jurisprudence of the *Trail Smelter* case close to that of the *Corfu Channel* case. In the latter case the International Court of Justice (ICJ) found Albania responsible for the placement of the mines at Corfu Channel even though there was no proof that Albania, the State, had actually performed the wrongful act. Responsibility was based on the fact of sovereignty. In a separate concurring opinion, Judge Alvarez put forth the point forcefully that "[e]very State is considered as having known, or as having a duty to have known, of prejudicial acts committed in parts of its territory where local authorities are installed; that this is not a presumption, nor is it a hypothesis, it is the consequence of sovereignty." Then he added in the same lines that "[e]very State is bound to take preventive measures to forestall the execution in its territory of criminal or prejudicial acts to the detriment of other States or of their nationals."

> Clearly, then, the *Corfu Channel* case and the *Trail Smelter* decision seem to articulate rather forcefully the rule of state responsibility to prevent environmental pollution which may injure the interest of other States.

> [The] *Lac Lanoux* arbitration was between France and Spain. * * * France proposed to construct a dam on the River Carol to raise the capacity of Lac Lanoux and create a head for hydroelectric power generation.... Spain objected plainly to the very fact of the construction of the dam and control of the flow because it introduced human discretion into

the regime of international drainage systems, possibly jeopardizing Spanish interest in irrigation.

> The Tribunal rejected [this] argument ... , specifically because no
> harm to Spanish interests was actually established. * * * [But] [i]t is this
> reference to possible change in quality or composition of the water which
> makes the Lac Lanoux decision significant as evidence of international
> obligation not to cause harm to an international watercourse. It also
> offers support to the provisions of the [1991] ILC draft articles on
> preservation and protection of the quality of such watercourses [supersed-
> ed in 1997 by the UN Convention on the Law of the Non-navigational
> Uses of International Watercourses **(Basic Document 5.46)**].

Charles O. Okidi, *"Preservation and Protection" Under the 1991 ILC Draft
Articles on the Law of International Watercourses*, 3 Colo. J. Int'l Envtl. L. &
Pol'y 143, 144–45 (1992).

**3.   Berlin Rules on Water Resources (Revision of the Helsinki
Rules and other International Law Association Rules on Water Resources), ILA Report of the Berlin Conference, 21 Aug 2004, 71 I.L.A.
337; *reprinted in* 5 Weston & Carlson V.F.39: Arts. 1–28** (Basic Document 5.56).

4.   Editors' Note. The foregoing 2004 Berlin Rules **(Basic Document
5.56)** update and supersede the 1966 Helsinki Rules on the Uses of the
Waters of International Rivers **(Basic Document 5.9)**, ILA Report of the
Fifty–Second Conference, Helsinki, 20 Aug 1966, *reprinted in* 5 Weston &
Carlson V.F.32. The following official comments on articles 12, 13, 14 and 27
of the Berlin Rules are *prima facie* relevant to the present problem:

Commentary to Article 12

Today the principle of equitable utilization is universally accepted as
basic to the management of the waters of an international drainage basin.
The principle was first formulated in the original *Helsinki Rules,* art IV. The
principle was reformulated in [the 1997] *UN Convention* [on the Law of the
Non-navigational Uses of International Watercourses **(Basic Document
5.46)**[f]], art. 5(1). The language in this Article is based on the *UN Convention's*
language, without limiting it to watercourses. This formulation reflects the
approach of the original *Helsinki Rules* and is consistent with the emphasis
on conjunctive management in Article 5. The language introduces another
change from the *UN Convention* in order to resolve the most debated issue in
the drafting of the *UN Convention:* the relationship of the principle of
equitable utilization to the obligation not to harm another basin State (Article
16). The phrasing adopted here emphasizes that the right to an equitable and
reasonable share of the waters of an international drainage basin carries with
it certain duties in the use of those waters. The change of phrase from the
original *Helsinki Rules* is not a turning away from the right to share in the
benefits of the transboundary resource. Rather, it recognizes that with the
right to share come from obligations that can only be fulfilled by acting in an
equitable and reasonable manner, having due regard to the obligation not to
cause significant harm to another basin State. The interrelation of these

---

f.   *See infra* Reading 6 (p. 1173).

obligations must be worked out in each case individually, in particular through the balancing process expressed in Articles 13 and 14.

Paragraph 2 tracks the language of the second sentence of the *UN Convention,* art. 5(1), with vocabulary changes to reflect usage in these Rules. As with the corresponding sentence in the *UN Convention,* paragraph 2 sets forth the principle that the right to an equitable utilization does not trump the obligations to assure the optimal and, most centrally, sustainable use of the waters, and the obligation to assure adequate protection to the waters (Article 7). The last point refers back to the obligation to minimize environmental harm (Article 8).

Commentary to Article 13

This Article originated in the original *Helsinki Rules,* art. V, but has been revised by adopting the provisions of the *UN Convention,* art. 6. Empirical surveys have found that these lists describe the actual variables that influence actual allocations under particular transboundary water treaties. There are a few changes in paragraph 2 reflecting the emphases of these Rules.... Consistent with the emphasis of these Rules on sustainability and on the minimization of environmental harm, this draft adds those factors to the end of the list in paragraph 2 although they do not appear either in the original *Helsinki Rules* or in the *UN Convention.* The *UN Convention* includes one variable that was not recognized explicitly in the original *Helsinki Rules*: the need for water for future uses in the basin States. The need to consider foreseeable future uses was implicit in the original Helsinki Rules.

Commentary to Article 14

Generally, categories or kinds of use have no inherent preference over each other in international water law, with one important exception. Legal institutions have long recognized a preference in municipal law for domestic uses of water, or as the *UN Convention* describes it, "vital human needs." Comparable preferences are found in particular treaties. This Article makes explicit what was implicit in the original *Helsinki Rules,* art. V. This Article tracks the language of the *UN Convention,* art. 10. The preference in this Article is stronger, but the concept vital human needs is defined more clearly in Article 2(20) than in the *UN Convention.* It does not extend to water needed to support general economic activity even though some have argued that such activity is included in "vital human needs." Unquestionably, the provision of jobs as well as the other benefits from enhanced economic activity are important concerns, but those concerns need to be balanced under Articles 12 and 13 against the like needs in other basin States and against the obligations of ecological integrity and sustainable development.

* * *

Commentary to Article 27

The original *Helsinki Rules* addressed three articles to pollution, arts. IX–XI, focusing only on the risk that activities in one basin State would cause injury in other basin States. With the growing interest in protecting the environment, the International Law Association subsequently approved the *Marine Pollution Rules* (1972), the *Belgrade Rules on the Relationship of*

International Water Resources with Other Natural Resources and Environmental Elements (1980), the *Montreal Rules on Pollution* (1982), and the *Supplemental Rules on Pollution* (1996). These several rules began as recommendations that States strengthen their steps to prevent or correct the pollution of internationally shared waters, and gradually strengthened the strictures into obligations. This progression matched the evolving practice of States, including multilateral and bilateral agreements, which was also moving in the direction of definite obligations regarding pollution. A similar rule was included in the *UN Convention* art. 21. Today, the obligation to control pollution in order to produce the least net environmental harm is part of the customary international law of the environment. As the *Rio Declaration* **[Basic Document 5.37]** and other instruments make clear, this obligation applies to the management of the waters within a States jurisdiction and control as much as it applies to any other resource.

The *UN Convention,* art. 21, is limited to cross-border situations, but spells out in more detail the obligation of States to act against pollution. This Article sets forth the obligation in more general terms as an expression of the general obligation to minimize environmental harm as provided in Article 8. The obligation draws upon international environmental law to go beyond the earlier efforts of the *Helsinki Rules* and its supplements and the *UN Convention.* This Article not only dispenses with the limited view of preventing injury only to other basin States, but also transcends concerns limited solely to the pollution of water. It commands basin States to handle, treat, and dispose of wastes, pollutants, and hazardous materials with the best environmental practices or best available techniques as appropriate in order to minimize environmental harm.

"Best environmental practices" refers to practices to prevent or reduce the effects of nonpoint sources of pollution, while "best available techniques" refers to techniques applied to prevent or reduce the effects of point sources of pollution. These are evolving concepts that cannot be precisely codified without preventing their further evolution. As indicated in Article 1(2), nothing in these Rules or in customary international law generally displaces the specific obligations spelled out in various treaties, including the growing body of treaties that define more precisely how wastes, pollutants, and hazardous materials are to be treated. These treaties define current standards of best environmental practices and best available techniques.

The goal of minimizing environmental harm recognizes that occasionally some degree of environmental harm must be accepted, but that overall environmental harm must be minimized if resource use is to be sustainable. The principle of integrated management further requires that the determination of how to proceed regarding wastes, pollutants, and hazardous materials should not be limited to consideration of only one medium or resource. These obligations apply to the transportation of wastes, pollutants, and hazardous materials as well as to their use or disposal.

This and other Articles do not mention the "polluter pays" principle, summarized in the *Rio Declaration,* pr. 16. This principle is built upon in *Agenda 21,* ch. 20, and has been widely embraced in European environmental law. The *International Convention on Oil Pollution Preparedness, Response, and Co–Operation,* in its preamble, even describes "polluter pays" as a "general principle of international law. Despite such assertions, however, the polluter pays principle has not been widely adopted in international agreements outside of Europe. Most of the instruments referred to in this commentary describe the polluter pays principle as a goal ("insofar as possible") rather than as a binding norm. One cannot conclude that the polluter pays principle is in fact part of customary international law. The increasingly frequent recourse by States to economic incentives to prevent, eliminate, reduce, or control pollution is neither required nor precluded by this Article, but it serves to introduce at least some aspects of the polluter pays principle into water management.

5. Heather L. Beach, Jesse Hammer, J. Joseph Hewitt, Edy Kaufman, Anja Kurki, Joe A. Oppenheimer, and Aaron T. Wolf, Transboundary Freshwater Dispute Resolution: Theory, Practice, and Annotated References 9–11 (2000).

. . . Since [World War I], organs of international law have tried to provide a framework for increasingly intensive water use, focusing on general guidelines that could be applied to the world's watersheds. These general principles of customary law, codified and progressively developed by advisory bodies and private organizations, are terms [of] "soft law," and are not intended to be legally binding, but can provide evidence of customary law and may help crystallize that law. While it is tempting to look to these principles for clear and binding rules, it is more accurate to think of them in terms of guidelines for the process of conflict resolution.

* * *

. . . On 8 December 1970, the [UN] General Assembly directed its own legal advisory body, the International Law Commission (ILC) to study the "Codification of the Law on Water Courses for Purposes other than Navigation." * * * It is testimony to the difficulty of merging legal and hydrologic intricacies that the ILC, despite an additional call for codification at the UN Water Conference at Mar de Plata in 1977, . . . only completed its task [in the mid–1990s]. For example, it took until 1984 for the term "international watercourse" to be satisfactorily defined. Problems both political and hydrological slowed the definition: in a 1974 questionnaire submitted to [UN] Member States, about half the respondents (only 20 per cent responded after eight years) supported the concept of a drainage basin (*e.g.* Argentina, Finland, and the Netherlands), while half were strongly negative (*e.g.*, Austria, Brazil, and Spain) or ambivalent; "watercourse basin" connoted a basin, which threatened sovereignty issues; and borderline cases, such as glaciers and confined aquifers, both now excluded, had to be determined. In 1994, more than two decades after receiving its charge, the ILC adopted a set of 32 draft articles which, with revisions, were adopted by the UN General Assembly on 21 May 1997 as the "Convention on the Law of the Non–Navigational Uses of International Watercourses" **[Basic Document 5.46]**.

The convention articles include language very similar to the Helsinki Rules,[g] requiring riparian states along an international watercourse in general to communicate and cooperate. Included are provisions for exchange of data

g. *See supra* Reading 4 for details on the relationship between the 1966 Helsinki Rules   and the 2004 Berlin Rules **(Basic Documents 5.9 and 5.56)**.

and information, notification of possible adverse effects, protection of ecosystems, and emergency situations. Allocations are dealt with through equally vague but positive language. Balanced with an obligation not to cause significant harm is "reasonable and equitable use" within each watercourse state, "with a view to attaining optimal utilization thereof and benefits therefrom. Based on seven factors, reasonable and equitable is defined similarly to Helsinki. The text of the convention does not mention a hierarchy of these factors, although Article 10 says both that, "in the absence of agreement or custom to the contrary, no use . . . enjoys inherent priority over other uses," and that, "in the event of a conflict between uses . . . [it shall be resolved] with special regard begin given to the requirements of vital human needs."

When attempting to apply this reasonable but vague language to specific water conflicts, problems arise. For example, riparian position and consequent legal rights shift with changing borders, many of which are still not recognized by the world community. Furthermore, international law only concerns itself with the rights and responsibilities of nations. Some political entities who might claim water rights, therefore, would not be represented, such as the Palestinians along the Jordan River or the Kurds along the Euphrates river.

6.   Convention on the Law of the Non-navigational Uses of International Watercourses. Concluded, 21 May 1997. Not yet in force. UN Doc. A/51/869; *reprinted in* 36 I.L.M. 700 (1997) and 5 Weston & Carlson V.F.37: Arts. 1–36 (Basic Document 5.46).[h]

7.   Stephen C. McCaffrey and Mpazi Sinjela, "Current Development: The 1997 United Nations Convention on International Watercourses," 92 A.J.I.L. 97, 105–07 (1998).

When the resolution containing the [1997 U.N Convention on the Law of the Non-navigational Uses of International Watercourses **(Basic Document 5.46)**] came before the General Assembly for adoption on May 21, 1997, Turkey requested a recorded vote. The vote was 103 in favor and 3 against (Burundi, China and Turkey), with 27 abstentions. In the context of a convention on international watercourses, 103 affirmative votes seem to constitute a strong endorsement: quite a few countries would not be interested in the subject matter for the reasons already indicated. While General Assembly votes are notoriously opaque, this one appears to hold out hope that the [NUIW] Convention may actually enter into force. The significant number of abstentions does not bode particularly well, but the fact that only three states could bring themselves to vote against the resolution suggests a sense among the overwhelming majority of delegations that the rules embodied in the Convention are generally acceptable and, on the whole, reflect a reasonable balance between the interests of upstream and downstream states. The negative votes of China and Turkey are probably attributable to their positions as upstream states in ongoing controversies rather than to a dispassionate assessment of the law. The vote of Burundi came as something of a surprise since it did not participate at the working-group level and since the hydro-geography of the states in the upper Nile basin, including Burundi, will prevent their activities from affecting Egypt or Sudan. Burundi's position may owe more to political considerations than to hydro-geographic reality.

h. The Convention is often cited as the "NUIW Convention."

Even if the Convention never enters into force, it is likely to prove of significant value for several reasons, some of which have already been alluded to. First, it was based on, and hews closely to, a draft prepared by the International Law Commission, the United Nations body responsible for the "progressive development of international law and its codification." As is its practice, the ILC did not indicate which of the provisions codify, and which progressively develop, the law. But it seems clear that the most important elements of the Convention—equitable utilization, "no harm," prior notification—are, in large measure, codifications of existing norms. That the working group did not fundamentally alter the ILC's approach betokens general satisfaction with the Commission's efforts at codification and progressive development in this field. The report of the working group to the General Assembly notes: "Throughout the elaboration of the draft Convention, reference had been made to the commentaries to the draft articles prepared by the International Law Commission to clarify the contents of the articles."[3] Even the provisions of the Convention that do not reflect current law are likely to give rise to expectations of behavior on the part of riparian states that may, over time, ripen into international obligations.

Second, the Convention will have value even if it does not enter into force because it was negotiated in a forum that permitted virtually any interested state to participate. It is the only convention of a universal character on international watercourses. It was adopted by a weighty majority of countries, with only three negative votes, indicating broad agreement in the international community on the general principles governing the non-navigational uses of international watercourses. These considerations also mean that if it does enter into force, the Convention will have significant bearing on controversies between states, one or more of which is not a party to it. In addition, the Convention may be helpful in interpreting other general or specific watercourse agreements that are binding on the parties to a controversy, whether or not the Convention is itself binding on those parties.

Third, even before the Convention's adoption, the ILC's draft articles on which it was based had influenced the drafting of specific agreements. These include the 1995 Protocol on Shared Watercourse Systems in the Southern African Development Community Region,[4] the 1991 Protocol on Common Water Resources concluded between Argentina and Chile,[5] and the 1995 Agreement on the Cooperation for the Sustainable Development of the Mekong River Basin.[6] It is likely that, with the adoption of the Convention, states negotiating future agreements will resort to its provisions as a starting point.

Thus, in the words of Ambassador Tello of Mexico, introducing the draft resolution containing the Convention, "[t]his instrument undoubtedly marks an important step in the progressive development and codification of international law...."[7] It does not go as far as it might have gone in some areas,[8]

---

3. Report of the Sixth Committee, ... 36 I.L.M. at 720 (1997).

4. Signed at Maseru, Lesotho, 16 May 1995 (copy on file with the authors).

5. Integracion LatinoAmericana, Revista Mensuel del Intal 116 (Sep–Oct 1997).

6. 5 Apr 1995, 34 I.L.M. 864 (1995).

7. Verbatim record, 99th plenary meeting, UN Doc. A/51/PV.99, at 2 (1997).

8. For example, a significant group of delegations believed its provisions concerning pollution and the ecosystems of international

and goes farther than some states would have liked in others.[9] The sponsors of the resolution containing the Convention declared that they were "convinced" that it "will contribute to the equitable and reasonable use of transboundary water resources and their ecosystems, as well as to their preservation, to the benefit of current and future generations," and that it "will contribute to enhancing cooperation and communication among riparian States of international watercourses."[10] In its resolution first calling for negotiation of a convention, the General Assembly had declared its conviction "that successful codification and progressive development of the rules of international law governing the non-navigational uses of international watercourses would assist in promoting and implementing the purposes and principles set forth in Articles 1 and 2 of the [UN] Charter."[11] Now that the work has been completed, it seems fair to conclude that the Convention will indeed assist in promoting and implementing those purposes and principles.

8. Editors' Note. A regional transboundary water law development paralleling in time but not altogether in substance the UN Convention on the Law of the Non-navigational Uses of International Waterways or NUIW Convention **(Basic Document 5.46)** is the 1992 Convention on the Protection and Use of Transboundary Watercourses and International Lakes (TWIL Convention),[i] open for signature and participation only to member states of the UN Economic Commission for Europe (UNECE) plus states having consultative status with the UNECE (altogether the countries of Europe, Canada, the United States, and the nations of the former Soviet Union). Together with its 1999 Protocol on Water and Health,[j] it is more attentive to environmental concerns than the NUIW Convention, which devotes more attention to development and thus challenges some of the NIUW's central-most provisions. "This difference," as observed by Eric W. Sievers in *Transboundary Jurisdiction and Watercourse Law: China, Kazakhstan, and The Irtysh*, 37 Tex. Int'l L. J. 1, 24 (2002), "highlights a North/South tension between environmental and developmental goals." Thus, in contrast to the 1997 NUIW Convention, the 1992 TWIL Convention and its 1999 Protocol, which aim to achieve, per Article 2(2)(b) of the TWIL Convention, "ecologically sound and rational water management, conservation of water resources and environmental protection," give expression to what one commentator has called a "community of interests theory [that] goes a step beyond the principle of reasonable and equitable utilization in that it advances the goal of the most optimal use and development of a transboundary water resource system." Gabriel Eckstein, *Application of International Water Law to Transboundary Groundwater Resources, and the Slovak–Hungarian Dispute over Gabcikovo–Nagymaros*, 19 Suffolk Transnat'l L. Rev. 67, 79 (1995). Eckstein continues, at 79–81:

watercourses could have been strengthened....

9. For example, the provisions of part III ["Planned Measurers"] drew fire from some delegations.... However, they were strongly supported by others. That they survived the negotiation process bespeaks their overall balance.

10. Verbatim record, *supra* note 7, at 2.

11. GA Res. 49/52, ¶ 3, UN GAOR, 49th Sess., Supp. No. 49, Vol. 1, at 2, UN Doc.A/49/49 (1994)....

i. Concluded 17 Mar 1992. Entered into force, 6 Oct 1996. UN Doc. ENVWA/R.53, UN Doc. E/ECE/1267, *reprinted in* 31 I.L.M. 1312 (2000) and 5 Weston & Carlson V.F.36.

j. Concluded 27 Jun 1999, entered into force 4 Aug 2005. UN Doc. E/MP.WAT/AC.1/1999/1, *reprinted in* 5 Weston & Carlson V.F.38.

Fundamentally, this theory seeks to achieve economic efficiency and the greatest beneficial use possible, though often at the cost of equitable distribution and benefit among the states sharing the resource. Furthermore, founded on the principles of "natural law," it ignores all national boundaries and regards the entire hydrologically connected water system as a single economic and geographic unit.

Of significance is the case of the International Commission of the River Oder **[Basic Document 7.1]**. In deferring to principles of "international fluvial law," the tribunal remarked that when considering transboundary water systems—here, an international river—and the desire to advance the principles of justice and utility, [the] community of interest in a navigable river becomes the basis of a common legal right, the essential features of which are the perfect equality of all riparian States in the use of the whole course of the river and the exclusion of any preferential privilege of any one riparian State in relation to the others.

Eckstein concludes: "While the community of interests theory may be regarded as the most efficient and advantageous for the international management of shared transboundary natural resources, its acceptance within the international community is sparse." *Id.* at 80–81.

Arguably confirming this conclusion are two relatively recent transboundary river agreements in South Asia (the locus of the instant problem): the 12 Feb 1996 Treaty between India and Nepal Concerning the Integrated Development of the Mahakali River, *reprinted in* 36 I.L.M. 531 (1997), and the 12 Dec 1996 Treaty between India and Bangladesh on Sharing of the Ganges Waters at Farakka, *reprinted in* 36 I.L.M. 519 (1997). Each of these agreements is intended to bring about an end to long-standing differences between India and its two neighbors, Nepal and Bangladesh, in respect of water flow entitlements following the construction by India of "barrages" (dams, irrigation channels, or other artificial formations built in a watercourse to increase its depth or divert its flow) on the Ganges and Mahakali rivers. Even while differing in their scope of application, the extent of their reliance upon general shared watercourse principles, and on dispute settlement arrangements, each establishes water discharge regimes of long duration (75 and 30 years, respectively) and, as such, contribute to increased stability among the countries involved. As one international environmental law expert has noted, however, each of the treaties "[focuses] on the utilization of waters rather than their conservation" and takes "only limited account, if any, of recent developments in the international law of watercourses or current efforts to promote sustainable development." Philippe Sands, *Introductory Note*, 36 I.L.M. 519 (1997).

These two South Asian treaties are of course only two of the more than 2,000 bilateral and multilateral treaties regulating navigation, hydroelectric power, irrigation, agriculture, drinking, and recreation among close to 300 transboundary watercourses around the world today, including such well known rivers as the Congo, Niger, Nile, and Zambezi in Africa; the Ganges, Indus, and Mekong in Asia; the Columbia, St. Lawrence, Niagara, and Rio Grande in North America; the Amazon in South America; and the Danube, Oder, Rhine, and Volga in Europe. Nevertheless, despite the recent emergence of a number of treaties that seek to regulate a handful of watercourses on a comprehensive "community of interests" or "basin management" basis, they probably do reflect a majority riparian state view that resists the cession or sharing of sovereign power, even in the name of "reasonable and equitable use," except within the framework of an exclusively or specially defined bilateral arrangement. The declaration affixed by France upon its approval of the 1992 TWIL Convention illustrates the point clearly:

> The Government of the French Republic, in approving the Convention on the Protection and Use of Transboundary Watercourses and International Lakes, declares that reference to the concept of reasonable and equitable use of transboundary waters does not constitute recognition of a principle of customary law, but illustrates a principle of cooperation between Parties to the Convention; the scope of such cooperation is specified in agreements, . . . such agreements being concluded on the basis of equality and reciprocity. . . .

A *New York Times* article published on the eve of the 1992 United Nations World Summit on Sustainable Development put it this way: "Despite efforts by the United Nations and others, the world has yet to come up with an accepted formula on how shared waters should be divided. That situation applies to nearly 300 rivers, including the Nile, the Danube, the Colorado, and the Rio Grande, all subject to major disputes." Douglas Jehl, *In Race to Tap the Euphrates, The Upper Hand is Upstream*, N.Y. Times, 25 Aug 2002, at 1, 6.

It is fair to ask, in other words, "whether state practice has given rise to a substantial number of norms of transboundary water law" and "to what degree the last decade's two framework multilateral watercourse treaties [*i.e.*, the 1992 TWIL and 1997 NUIW conventions] codify existing law or contribute to the progressive development of international law." Sievers, *supra*, at 14. In search of an answer to this question, it is useful to consider, next, the *Case Concerning the Gabcíkovo-Nagymaros Project*, decided by the World Court on 25 Sep 1997.

9. Summary of Case Concerning the Gabcikovo–Nagymaros Project (Hung. v. Slovk.), 1997 ICJ 7 (Basic Document 7.11).

10. Eric W. Sievers, "Transboundary Jurisdiction and Watercourse Law: China, Kazakhstan, and The Irtysh," 37 Tex. Int'l L. J. 1, 14–23 (2002).

[*Eds.*—In this article, the author discusses the international legal implications of a "simmering dispute" between Kazakhstan and China relative to the latter's diversion of the Black Irtysh River which, "arising in a sparse border region of Mongolia and China, . . . flows 700 kilometers before crossing Kazakhstan's border to empty into Lake Zaisan, one of the thirty largest lakes in the world. On the other side of Lake Zaisan, the river, now the Irtysh proper, forms Kazakhstan's industrial heartland, crosses into Russia, joins the Ob River, and finally empties into the Arctic Ocean. . . . The world's fifth largest river, the Irtysh, flows north; does not contain within its drainage basin, which is the size of India, the capital of any state; and is the only river to flow through three of the planet's ten largest states." The author argues that China's diversion project, which threatens water levels both in the Irtysh–Ob Basin and the millions of people and dozens of ecosystems that line the Irtysh's 5,000–plus kilometer length, is "a 'totalitarian, gigomaniac monument which is against nature'[12]" and "violates customary international law both in its conception and in China's dealings with co-riparians." He also argues that "ironically, the emerging international law of watercourses may, in time, support China because of structural weaknesses in this law," including a failure of international law, "Pollyannaish scholars and international agencies notwithstanding," to "direct or substantially inform decision-making in many contemporary situations." Along the way, challenged by the task of "redeeming a role for the application of international law in non-European watercourse disputes," he usefully opines the current state of transboundary watercourse law.]

... Today, the state of transboundary watercourse law lies somewhere along a continuum between unrestrained state discretion, a customary rule against any inequitable utilization that infringes on co-riparian interests, and, at the outer fringes, an *erga omnes* prohibition, based on the concept of common heritage, against degradation of riparian ecosystems.

* * *

A. Customary Law

* * *

Evidence of customary law, while ultimately founded in the actions and *opinio juris* of states, can be gleaned from a variety of sources, including historically important and representative treaties, arbitration and court judgments, and recent framework watercourse treaties, such as the 1997 United Nations Convention on the Law of the Non-navigational Uses of International Watercourses (the NUIW Convention) **[Basic Document 5.46]**. While all the Irtysh riparians actively negotiated the NUIW Convention, none has ratified the Convention, although Kazakhstan did vote for its adoption. China was one of only three states to vote against the NUIW Convention. Accordingly, the NUIW Convention is of, at best, questionable applicability to the Irtysh diversion dispute as a treaty. However, as a codification of customary law, it directly applies to the Irtysh controversy. Even though the NUIW Convention is not in force, those of its provisions that merely codify existing customary law already bind all states.

Although transboundary watercourse law is an esoteric branch of international public law, with the Gabcikovo–Nagymaros case **[Basic Document 7.11]**, it had its day in court. While the International Court of Justice (ICJ) stopped short of making any sweeping rulings on the content of international customary watercourse law, it accorded notable deference to the NUIW Convention as a document that codifies customary law. As a result, the Gabcikovo–Nagymaros case and the NUIW Convention together allow for a fuller explication of watercourse custom than would have been possible five years ago.

1. Limited Territorial Sovereignty, Equitable Use, and Sustainable Development

Clarification of transboundary watercourse law depends in large part on state agreement about what foundational policy should inform this law. There

---

12. Czechsolovak President Vaclav Havel thus described the Gabcikovo–Nagymaros Dam Project in the early 1990s....

exist four general candidates: absolute territorial sovereignty, absolute territorial integrity, limited territorial sovereignty, and community of interests. Scholars generally agree that the first two approaches (which, in the first case, burden upstream states with no duties to downstream states and, in the second case, give downstream states an effective veto over proposed upstream uses) do not embody customary law and do not have a place in emerging treaties.

In contrast, limited territorial sovereignty and community of interests enjoy support from scholarly circles and in practice, with the more conservative limited territorial sovereignty informing the greater mass of current customs, but with community of interests quickly gaining ground. Indeed, for navigation issues, discussed below, community of interests long ago displaced limited territorial sovereignty.

Limited territorial sovereignty, broadly understood, places some restrictions on state discretion, primarily based on the principle of *sic utere tuo ut alienum non laedes*. In turn, community of interests requires that decision-making be undertaken collectively and in consideration of the best use of the entire basin. To distinguish between these two approaches, while limited territorial sovereignty does not burden states with any substantive obligation to maximize the efficiency of allocation of watercourse resources, community of interests takes efficiency as a starting point.

To the extent that limited territorial sovereignty is gradually giving way to community of interests, the current name for the shifting middle ground between the two is equitable utilization, also known as equitable and reasonable use. Article 5 of the NUIW Convention [which calls for equitable and reasonable use] * * * codifies existing customary law; equitable utilization is a requirement under customary law. As a result, at present, watercourse law possesses a framework principle, but this principle is founded not in a single clear policy, but rather in a policy that is cobbled together out of two often consonant, but ultimately dissimilar, policies. The two most recent ICJ cases to visit watercourse issues in detail provide support for the view that equitable utilization, despite its ambivalent ontogeny, is now custom.[13]

Because a principle of customary law is nonetheless abstract, for customary law to be substantive at an operational level there must also be rules. At the present stage of the evolution of transboundary watercourse law, in addition to the principle of equitable utilization, five customary norms appear solidly established. These include a requirement of notice prior to any diversion, a requirement of consultation prior to any diversion that will result in a substantive (*i.e.*, material) decrease in the quality or quantity of waterflow to a lower riparian, automatic succession for treaties that regulate boundary waters and/or navigation, a presumption of illegality for any diversion that interrupts navigation, and a presumption of illegality for any diversion that will result in an environmental (*i.e.*, a species extinction) or human tragedy (*i.e.*, a loss of subsistence water supply).

13. "[A riparian has a] basic right to an equitable and reasonable sharing of the resources of an international watercourse." *Gabcikovo–Nagymaros Project (Hung. v. Slovk.)* **[Basic Document 7.11]**; *see also* Kasikili/Se- dudu Island (Bots. v. Namib.), 39 I.L.M. 310, 380 (2000) (separate opinion of Judge Kooijmans stating that Article 5 is customary law and contending that state practice supports this view).

2. The Notice Rule

The notice rule, simply stated, holds that an upper riparian must provide formal notice to lower riparians prior to effecting any substantial project on a transboundary watercourse. Under community of interests, lower riparians would ostensibly incur a similar obligation. While a co-riparian could react to such notice by claiming that a proposed project infringed on its interests, nothing more than notice is required if the quantity and quality of water, as well as freedom of navigation, are not adversely affected in other riparians' territories.

The accepted authority on this notice rule is the 1957 Lake Lanoux Arbitration between France and Spain **[Basic Document 7.7]**. In the tribunal's influential holding, France was required to give notice and nothing more to Spain about French plans to divert, but then restitute in full, a supply of water from the Carol River.

3. The Consultation Rule

Had France anticipated reducing the actual flow of water transversing into Spain, it would have been required to engage in prior consultations with Spain. The consultation rule holds that prior consultations must be held or at least offered prior to the initiation of any project that may have a substantive impact on the freedom of navigation and/or a co-riparian's ability to enjoy its current quality and quantity of water.

Support for the long existence of this rule is founded in more than the Lake Lanoux Arbitration. In deciding a case concerning unilateral diversion of water from the Meuse **[Basic Document 7.2]**, the Permanent Court of International Justice in 1937 held that as long as either party did not adversely affect the current, flow, or volume of water available to the other party, there was no breach of law. More recently, in the Gabcikovo–Nagymaros case **[Basic Document 7.11]**, the ICJ suggested that, for diversion projects in which the affected state played no role in contributing to or developing the project, serious prospective threats of species extirpation, ecological degradation, and disruption of navigation may alone constitute violations, if there have been no meaningful consultations.

4. The Succession Rule

Under Articles 11 and 12 of the Vienna Convention on Succession of States in Respect of Treaties **[Basic Document 1.13]**, "succession of States does not affect ... obligations [or] ... rights established by a treaty ... relating to the use of any territory ... and considered as attaching to that territory" [Article 12] or "relating to the regime of a boundary" [Article 11].

The ICJ's promotion of these articles as mere codification of a customary law of "automatic succession" is frequent and unequivocal. If a treaty that concerns water rights or navigation on transboundary watercourses is in force at the time of succession, it qualifies as an Article 12 treaty. Naturally, if such a treaty applied to a contiguous border river like the Horgos, a tributary of the Ili, on the China–Kazakhstan border, it would simultaneously qualify as an Article 11 treaty.

I would go so far as to posit that, of the five rules mentioned, the rule of succession is the strongest ... [although] that does not at all mean that it is the rule most understood or least often violated in practice....

* * *

5.   The Community of Navigation Rule

Accounting for and understanding the Community of Navigation Rule requires understanding the genesis of watercourse law. The rule holds that any action of a riparian state that limits a co-riparian's enjoyment of its freedom of navigation is presumed to be unlawful. This rule is not a positive rule, such as the tradition whereby watercourse treaties establish freedom of navigation on a watercourse, but a negative rule, prohibiting any substantive worsening of conditions for navigation.

The historical roots of the rule rest in conditions that do not today vivify the hottest controversies about transboundary rivers. These roots are that, formerly, navigation was the most important use of such watercourses and that, formerly, non-riparians were often the major users of such rivers. Addressing the latter point, Britain's domination of Nile River navigation and British and French dominance of Danube navigation in the nineteenth and twentieth centuries are not relevant to modern customary law because of last century's *jus cogens* rejection of colonialism. This rejection lays the basis for the current content of the rule that limits rights of freedom of navigation to riparians [subject, however, to the prohibition of any substantive worsening of the conditions of navigation which continues to trump other watercourse uses absent the consent of all the relevant co-riparians]. * * * The fact that recent treaties, like the NUIW Convention, stress that their lawmaking efforts are only for the "non-navigational uses" of transboundary watercourses illustrates the special and established weight of navigational rights....

* * *

6.   The Human and Environmental Disaster Rules

The obligation to refrain from causing an imminent and substantial environmental or human disaster is founded in the progressive development of environmental and human rights law in recent decades.[14] To begin with the environmental case, since all the Irtysh riparians are parties to the [1992] Convention on Biological Diversity (CBD) [**Basic Document 5.36**], they are clearly subject to the environmental obligation described above.

The obligations imposed by the CBD are stated strongly, and Article 22 provides that the provisions of the CBD shall not affect the rights and obligations of contracting parties, deriving from any existing international agreement "except where the exercise of those rights and obligations would

---

14. In the Gabcikovo–Nagymaros case [**Basic Document 7.11**], the Court established that a "state of ecological necessity" could only exist if a threat was both substantial and imminent.... By analogy, since states of necessity are "a ground recognized by customary international law for precluding the wrongfulness of an act not in conformity with an inter- national obligation," this may overstate the requirements for "disasters," but certainly does not understate them. However, that the standard is quite clearly not one of optimality or utility illustrates that this rule is firmly within the limited territorial sovereignty paradigm.

cause a serious damage or threat to biological diversity." The obligations imposed by the CBD are, thus, compelling and should not be ignored in any determination defining inter-state rights and obligations, if such determination entails a risk of damage to ecosystems, which it was the object of the CBD to prevent.[15]

Accordingly, to the extent that other environmental conventions create or codify similar requirements regarding certain types of species (*i.e.*, migratory species), ecosystems (*i.e.*, wetlands), or pollutants, the environmental obligation can be expanded within a watercourse basin even in the absence of a specific treaty, or amendments to a treaty, regulating that transboundary watercourse.

Similarly, a riparian cannot subject a neighboring riparian's population to substantial and imminent danger through unilateral use of a watercourse. Such danger could arise through denying a population its ability to meet its "vital human needs" (*i.e.*, subsistence irrigation or drinking water), which are accorded paramount importance under Article 10 of the NUIW Convention,[16] or through some other action (*i.e.*, causing flooding). General norms of humanitarian law and the human right to water underlie this norm.

7.   General International Environmental Law

Taking equitable utilization and the five rules listed above as the core of modern transboundary watercourse law, some other norms begin deductively to reveal themselves. While the scope of such norms is probably wider than discussed here, in an effort to avoid being Pollyannaish, these norms only include a few other articles of the NUIW Convention, sustainable development, and environmental impact assessment.

The concept of equitable utilization, especially as currently envisioned by the scholars and judges cited here, as a merging of environmental and economic concerns is intrinsically close to the principle of sustainable development. Indeed, the Gabcikovo–Nagymaros court comes very close to stating explicitly that sustainable development is a customary norm.[17]

---

15. Kasikili/Sedudu Island (Bots. v. Namib.) [1999 ICJ 1045, 39 I.L.M. 310 (2000), at 400 (separate opinion of Judge Weeramantry).

16. In stressing the paramount importance of "vital human needs," the NUIW Convention may in fact be restating customary law. Gleick makes this argument by pointing out that the 1977 Mar del Plata Statement [resulting from the 1977 United Nations Water Conference in Mar del Plata, Argentina, the first such international gathering on fresh water] recognized the right of people "to have access to drinking water in quantities and of a quality equal to their basic needs," and then arguing that successive similar statements reinforce this right. P. Gleick, *The Human Right to Water*, 1 Water Pol'y 487, 493, 493–94 (1999), available at <http://www.pacinst.org/gleickrw.pdf>. Gleick is correct that "vital human needs" reflect custom, but incorrect in implying that Article 10 of the NUIW Convention codifies customary law. The NUIW Convention's elevation of basic/vital human needs to an importance above

all other concerns is not supported by precedent. In the additional sources Gleick cites (namely the 1992 Agenda 21, UN Conference on Environment and Development, UN GAOR, UN Doc. A/CONF.151/26/Rev. 1 (1993), and the 1997 UN Comprehensive Assessment of the Freshwater Resources of the World, UN Commission on Sustainable Development, 5th Sess., UN Doc. E/CN.17/1997/9 (1997)), protection of ecosystems is listed as an equivalent priority. Thus, Article 10 of the NUIW Convention, being the only modern source of which the author is aware in which human needs explicitly trump environmental needs, is really an innovation and not a reflection of a customary rule.

17. The judgment merely implies sustainable development ... (citing unnamed "new norms and prescriptions of international environmental law"). However, Judge Weeramantry fills in this gap with a very sweeping endorsement of sustainable development as a

Articles 4, 6, 7, 8, and 12 of the NUIW Convention codify existing customary law. Article 4 disallows the exclusion of any riparian state from negotiations for and party status to any agreement that applies to or affects the entirety of a watercourse. This rule logically flows from the interaction of the principle of equitable utilization and the consultation rule.

Article 6 lists seven types of factors relevant to an analysis of equitable utilization; since this list derives from and reflects the experiences of state negotiations involving transboundary watercourses, it constitutes a general statement of customary law. Because a "reasonable" standard explicitly attaches to Article 5, Article 6 is an indispensable corollary to Article 5. Essentially, Article 6 clarifies that dismissal of attention to any of these seven fairly self-evident factors would be prima facie unreasonable.

Article 7 merely restates and explicates the established customary principle of *sic utere tuo ut alienum non laedes*. Article 8 simply states that in pursuing equitable utilization, states should cooperate, a restatement of the customary requirement for peaceful resolution of disputes. Finally, Article 12 restates the notification rule, but for measures that would produce a "significant adverse effect." While on the one hand, this would seem to contradict the notification rule as described above, the article continues on to state that notification must be accompanied by "available technical data and information," which essentially means that the article is a combination of the consultation requirement and the general customary rule that negotiations be meaningful.

In addition to these rules, there now exists a customary obligation to conduct an environmental impact assessment (EIA). Especially in "the transboundary context, the duty to conduct an EIA is probably now a requirement of customary law."[18] To the extent that this is true, lower riparians must be accorded the opportunity to consult with project planners, comment on the assessment, and provide technical and other information relevant to the assessment, and especially relating to consequences of the planned project, that may not be in the possession of the planning state.

11.   Stockholm Declaration of the United Nations Conference on the Human Environment, adopted by the UN Conference on the Human Environment at Stockholm, 16 Jun 1972, Report of the UN Conference on the Human Environment, UN Doc. A/CONF.48/14/ Rev.1 at 3 (1973), UN Doc. A/CONF.48/14 at 2–65, and Corr. 1 (1972); *reprinted in* 11 I.L.M. 1416 (1972) and 5 Weston & Carlson V.B.3: Princs. 6, 11, 13, 14, 18, 21, 22 (Basic Document 5.14).

12.   Charter of Economic Rights and Duties of States. Adopted, 12 Dec 1974. GA Res. 3281 (XXIX), 29 UN GAOR, Supp. (No. 31) 50, UNDoc. A/9631 (1975); *reprinted in* 14 I.L.M. 251 (1975) and 4 Weston & Carlson IV.F.5: Articles 2, 3, & 30 (Basic Document 4.9).

13.   Draft Principles of Conduct in the Field of the Environment for the Guidance of States in the Conservation and Harmonious Utilization of Natural Resources Shared by Two or More States.

fundamental principle that "command[s] recognition in international law" ... (separate opinion of Judge Weeramantry).

18.   D. Hunter et al., International Environmental Law and Policy 367 (1998).

Adopted, 19 May 1978. UNEP Doc. GC.6/17, at 9; *reprinted in* 17 I.L.M. 1097 (1978) and 5 Weston & Carlson V.B.8: Princs. 1, 3–7, 9, 13, 15 (Basic Document 5.17).

14. **World Charter for Nature. Adopted, 28 Oct 1982. GA Res 37/7, UN GAOR Supp. (No. 51) 21, UN Doc. A/37/L.4 and Add. 1 (1982);** *reprinted in* **5 Weston & Carlson V.B.11: Principles 1–4, 7–9, 11, 13, 19, 21, 22, 24** (Basic Document 5.21).

15. **Experts Group on Environmental Law of the World Commission on Environment and Development, Legal Principles for Environmental Protection and Sustainable Development. Adopted, 4 Aug 1987. UN Doc. WCED/86/23/Add.1 (1986);** *reprinted in* **5 Weston & Carlson V.B.12: Arts. 1 & 21** (Basic Document 5.25).

16. **Rio Declaration on Environment and Development. Adopted, 13 Jun 1992. UNCED Doc. A/CONF.151/5/Rev. 1;** *reprinted in* **5 Weston & Carlson V.B.16: Principles 2, 7, 14, 15** (Basic Document 5.37).

17. **Editors' Note.** Five of the six immediately preceding instruments contain the principle of economic self-determination of states, particularly as it applies to the development of natural wealth and resources. *See* Principle 21 of the 1972 Stockholm Declaration of the United Nations Conference on the Human Environment **(Basic Document 5.14)**; Article 2 of the 1978 Charter of Economic Rights and Duties of States **(Basic Document 4.9)**; Principle 3(1) of the 1978 Draft Principles of Conduct in the Field of the Environment for the Guidance of States in the Conservation and Harmonious Utilization of Natural Resources Shared by Two or More States **(Basic Document 5.17)**; Principle 22 of the 1982 World Charter for Nature **(Basic Document 5.21)**; and Principle 3 of the 1992 Rio Declaration on Environment and Development **(Basic Document 5.37)**. So also do the instruments cited in the next three readings.

18. **International Covenant on Economic, Social and Cultural Rights. Concluded, 16 Dec 1966. Entered into force, 3 Jan 1976. 993 U.N.T.S. 3;** *reprinted in* **3 Weston & Carlson III.A.2: Article 1** (Basic Document 3.13).

19. **Resolution on Permanent Sovereignty over Natural Resources. Adopted, 14 Dec 1962. GA Res. 1803, UN GAOR, 17th Sess., Supp. No. 17, at 15, UN Doc. A/5217;** *reprinted in* **2 I.L.M. 223 (1963) and 4 Weston & Carlson IV.F.1.** (Basic Document 4.4).[k]

20. **Declaration on the Right to Development. Adopted , 4 Dec 1986. GA Res. 41/128 (Annex), UN GAOR, 41st Sess., Supp. No. 53, at 186, UN Doc. A/41/53 (1987);** *reprinted in* **3 Weston & Carlson III.R.2** (Basic Document 3.28).

21. **The Hague Report, Sustainable Development: From Concept to Action 6–7, 10–12, 14–15 (March 1992).**[l]

The call for sustainable development is not simply a call for environmental protection. Instead, sustainable development implies a new concept of

---

k. Reaffirmed in Resolution on Permanent Sovereignty over Natural Resources, GA Res. 3171, UN GAOR, 28th Sess., Supp. No. 30, at 52, UN Doc. A/9030; *reprinted in* 13 I.L.M. 238 (1974) and 4 Weston & Carlson IV.F.2.

l. Summarizing the main conclusions of the Hague Symposium, held November 25–27, 1991, co-sponsored by the Dutch Ministry of Development Cooperation, the UNDP and

economic growth—one that provides fairness and opportunity for all the world's people, not just the privileged few, without further destroying the world's finite natural resources and carrying capacity.

Sustainable development is a process in which economic, fiscal, trade, energy, agricultural, industrial and all other polices are so designed as to bring about development that is economically, socially, ecologically sustainable. This means that current consumption cannot be financed for long by incurring economic debts that others must repay. This also means that sufficient investment must be made in the education and health of today's population so as not to create a social debt for future generations. And natural resources must be used in ways that do not create ecological debts by overexploiting the carrying and productive capacity of the earth. All postponed debts mortgage sustainability—whether economic debts or social debts or ecological debts.

* * *

At the global level, sustainable models of development require no less than a new global ethics, a clear understanding that the world cannot be made safe for anyone without the willing cooperation of everyone. Concern for common survival must also lead to policies for a more equitable world order, based on fundamental global reforms. Such a world order cannot be based on a passive continuation of the existing international economic system which denies over $500 billion of economic opportunities each year to poor nations because of their restricted or unequal access to global markets of trade, labour and capital; which leads to a reverse net resource transfer of over $50 billion a year from poor to rich nations; in which richer nations reluctantly spare only 0.35% of their GNP in official development assistance for the 1.2 billion absolute poor in the developing world while earmarking 15–20% of the GNP in their budgets for social safety nets for their own 100 million people below the official poverty line; where income disparities between the top 20% and the bottom 20% of the world's people have doubled over the last three decades and stand now at a staggering level of 150:1.[m] Out of such an unequal world of the poor and the rich, the concept of one world and one planet simply cannot emerge without some basic reforms. Nor can shared responsibility be created for the health of the global commons without some measure of shared global prosperity. Global sustainability without global justice will always remain an elusive goal.

* * *

For developing countries, the choice is not to sustain poverty but to overcome ... poverty through growth. Continuation of the present state of poverty, after all, will be one of the greatest threats to the sustainability of the physical planet, not just to the sustainability of human life. Poor people and poor countries depend on the soil for food, the rivers for water, and the forests for fuel. Even though they need these resources desperately, the poor

UNCED, and "attended by about forty leading thinkers from all over the world."

m. The statistics cited are of course dated; but it would not be incorrect to assume that they are today higher than they were in 1992.

have little choice—without assets or income—but to overuse and to destroy their natural environment, simply to survive. In so doing, they threaten their own health and the lives of their children. In developing countries, it is not the quality of life that is at risk—it is life itself. Economic growth is vital to give more options to these poor societies. But their models of development must become less energy-intensive and more environmentally sound than has been the historic experience.

For industrial countries also, stoppage of growth or even a serious slow down is not much of an option for the protection of [the] global environment. For one thing, slower growth in the developed countries will imperil growth rates in the poor nations, dependent as they are on the markets of the rich nations. For another, continued growth in the industrial nations is necessary to generate both the new environmentally-safe technologies and the extra margin of resources for transfer to poor nations. The current growth models of the industrial nations must change drastically. The current emphasis on quantitative growth should certainly be replaced by more concern with qualitative growth. But this should not be confused with zero growth, which is largely a sterile and disruptive dialogue.

* * *

The new models of sustainable development must * * * place people at the very centre of their concern. Environmental protection is vital. But it is not an end in itself. Like economic growth, it is merely a means. The primary objective of our efforts must be to protect human life and human options. Every environmental measure must be tested against that yardstick: to what extent it adds to the human welfare of the majority of the world's population. In other words, we must opt for sustainable *human* development. And we must begin to recognize that the most endangered species in many places on our planet are the people.

* * *

If we are to build a bridge of understanding between the North and the South, we must readily concede that environmental priorities can greatly differ at different stages of development. Developed countries are preoccupied at present with global warming, depletion of ozone layers and disposal of chemical wastes. Developing countries are concerned with much more basic issues of human survival: water and land. Polluted water is a threat to life: 1.3 billion people in the developing countries still do not have access to safe drinking water. Erosion of land is a threat to livelihood: an estimated 135 million people lived in 1984 in areas affected by desertification (up from 57 million in 1977). Thus, at the lower end of the income scale, poverty is as great an enemy of the environment as misspent affluence by rich societies.

It is unfortunate that "loud" environmental emergencies (*e.g.* global warming) have been receiving [more] of the media attention at present than the "silent" environmental emergencies which affect the lives of many more people in the world. The loud emergencies have yet to affect many people; the silent emergencies are already wasting many lives. For instance, 750 million children suffer from acute diarrheal diseases annually, of which 4 million die; 500 million people suffer from trachoma, 200 million from schistosomiasis, and 800 million from hookworm. Just the provision of safe drinking water and sanitation and some education in hygiene can alleviate these environmental problems and relieve much human suffering. Surely, these issues have as great a claim on [responsible] attention ... as the much louder environmental emergencies.

It must also be recognized that environmental standards for various projects and programmes may be vastly different in developing and developed countries. Poor nations will naturally discount the future at a higher rate than the rich nations, confronted as they are with the struggle for daily survival within limited resource options. Also, they may not yet have used up even a fraction of their ecospace compared to the industrial nations. They cannot—and need not—adopt the environmental standards of Pittsburgh or Lancashire at their present stage of development. They may have to make their choices from a whole range of environmentally-safe technologies. Search for *similar* environmental standards for all nations is based on a profound misconception and can only lead to unnecessary conflicts.

22.   Shashank Upadhye, "The International Watercourse: An Exploitable Resource for the Developing Nation Under International Law," 8 Cardozo J. Int'l & Comp. L. 61, 61–83 (2000).

International law does not forbid a developing country from exploiting an international watercourse, despite lofty commentary otherwise. Although it has been suggested that international law imposes a mandatory duty of reasonable and equitable use of a watercourse, this is not so. A developing nation must be allowed to exploit an international watercourse to the utmost within the prescribed rules of international law. Grounded in the right of self-determination,[19] a developing nation has the undisputed right of permanent sovereignty over its natural resources, including international watercourses and,[20] as such, a right of exploitation. Respect for international environmental law is of little concern to a developing nation since the lesser developed nations will not abide by current ambiguous international law adverse to their own developmental and sovereignty policies. Taming a watercourse is a catalyst for evolutionary societal progression and it behooves a developing nation to act consistently with development, not necessarily with respect for the international environment. The only constraint is that the development of the watercourse cannot significantly damage other nations. Since under-development is the linchpin for developing nations, the development of watercourses supersedes environmental concerns.[21] Today, the most effective regulation of the use of an international watercourse will only occur through the creation of a joint commission between the nations affected or by an

19. UN Charter art. 55(a) [**Basic Document 1.5)**]; *see also* Rio Declaration on Environment and Development, Principle 2 [**Basic Document 5.37**]; Declaration of the United Nations Conference on the Human Environment ..., Principle 21 [**Basic Document 5.14**].... *See also* Art. 1(1), International Covenant on Economic, Social and Cultural Rights [**Basic Document 3.13**]....

20. Art. 1(1), Declaration on the Right to Development [**Basic Document 3.28**] ... ;

see also Art. 28, Universal Declaration of Human Rights [**Basic Document 3.3**]....

21. Rio Declaration on Environment and Development ... , Principle 3 [**Basic Document 5.37**] ... ; Article 30, Charter of Economic Rights and Duties of States [**Basic Document 4.9**] ... ; Art. 20(4), Convention of Biological Diversity [**Basic Document 5.36**] ... ; *see also* Art. 4(7), Framework Convention on Climate Change [**Basic Document 5.35**]....

affirmative declaration that watercourse use is squarely within the scope of established international law.[22]

[*Eds.*—Next, after introducing how international law applies to international watercourses and briefly discussing the theories of sovereignty and territoriality concerning natural resource exploitation, the author examines "the sparse international environmental case law" and argues that "international law is lacking and fails to justify the imposition of non-binding, non-customary international law on the developing nation." He then continues:]

Against this inchoate backdrop, the development of international environmental law must be examined to see if it reflects any precedential or binding norms. Many United Nations documents espouse the international law that a State has permanent sovereignty over natural resources (PSONR) within its borders.[23] The Resolutions, Covenants, and Declarations of the UN General Assembly may be a source of international law, even though these documents do not compartmentalize neatly into one of the categories of Article 38 of the ICJ The general definition of PSONR is the inalienable right of each nation to fully exercise authority over its natural wealth and the correlative right to dispose of its resources fully and freely. Under PSONR, a State is precluded from divesting itself of its sovereign rights over natural resources but may, by agreement, accept a partial limitation in particular areas for a specified period of time.[24]

The principle of PSONR enjoys, at a minimum, the status of customary international law since it stems from the right of development. * * * [It] may possess an even stronger right. It is undisputed that the right of development is the right of people to freely use and exploit their own natural resources and that this is in accord with the principles of the UN Charter **[Basic Document 1.5]**. Furthermore, since the right of development enjoys the status of *jus cogens* (a peremptory norm) it follows that since the PSONR right sprouts from that right of development, it too enjoys the status of *jus cogens*. Once the right of general exploitation of a resource is found, the developing nation can exploit the watercourse since a watercourse qualifies as a resource.

Commensurate with the above discussion, one can examine the several alternative sovereignty theories in watercourse exploitation. They are as follows:

1. *Absolute Territorial Sovereignty.*[n] * * * At first glance, it appears that PSONR is exactly this principle. However, this is not the case.... Permanent sovereignty ... lends a certain measure of absolute sovereignty but yields eventually to established customary international law or new peremptory norms. Liability, therefore, attaches to a nation asserting PSONR if the

---

22. Another alternative, albeit not an attractive one, would be to encourage the interested nations to petition the International Court of Justice for intervention. The ICJ could then create an *ad hoc* special panel to resolve the dispute. Articles 92–96, Statute of International Court of Justice **[Basic Document 1.6]**....

23. Resolution on the Permanent Sovereignty Over Natural Resources, GA Res. 1803 **[Basic Document 4.4]** ...; *reaffirmed in* Res-

olution on Permanent Sovereignty Over Natural Resources ..., GA Res. 3171 **[Basic Document 4.6]** ...; *see also* World Charter for Nature ... , Principle 22 **[Basic Document 5.21]** ...; Rio Declaration on Environment and Development ..., Principle 2 **[Basic Document 5.37]**....

24. *See* Texaco v. Libya Arbitration, 53 I.L.R. 389, 481–82 (1979).

n. *See supra* Reading 1, at p. 1165.

nation breaches its treaty obligations, or if the ICJ renders an unfavorable decision against it, predicated on established law. Therefore, PSONR, deeply rooted in *jus cogens*, customary, or conventional international law, creates a rebuttable and reviewable presumption that nations can exploit their resources to the fullest extent possible. Any conflict concerning the degree of PSONR exercised can only be determined on a case by case basis.

2. *Absolute Territorial Integrity.*[o] ... This theory ... cannot create customary international law because watercourse development of any type will alter water flow to some extent and absolute territoriality strictly prohibits any changes to water flow. Therefore, absolute territoriality would effectively prohibit all watercourse development by placing a burden on the upper riparian without placing an equivalent duty on the lower riparian State. Neither developing nor developed nations would tolerate such a law....

3. *Limited Territorial Sovereignty and Integrity*. This is an amalgamation of the above two theories. Though it rejects both of the absolute principles it is not yet the community or reasonable principle discussed below.... [T]he nation still retains rights of territoriality and sovereignty albeit to a slightly diminished extent. One such example is the principle of prior appropriation.[p] ... The self-evident problem with this theory is that it rewards the first user to the detriment of the later user. If the first user is a developed country and the later user is a less developed country, then the less developed country cannot use the watercourse to further develop. The theory also fails to consider whether the first user conducted a thorough plan for water allocation or pollution control. This is different from the reasonable and equitable use principle discussed below, which mandates that certain factors be considered, because there are no obligatory factors used in the consideration.

4. *Community Resource*[q].... [T]his theory will never become customary international law nor a principle of international law recognized by civilized nations despite its supporters as it relies completely on mutual cooperation, a misplaced sense of altruism and, most importantly, wholly disregards sovereignty and territoriality. In fact, this approach is diametrically opposed to well-established customary and conventional law, such as PSONR, self-determination, and sovereign equality. Further, the theory encompasses the entire watershed basin, rather than just the watercourse. As such, it seeks to regulate more territory than permitted.[25]

5. *Reasonable and Equitable Use*.[r] By and large the most popular theory ..., [t]his theory is the emerging trend and perhaps might, but has not yet become unequivocal customary international law.[26]

---

o. Also known as "the riparian rights doctrine." *See supra* Reading 1, at 1165.

p. *Id.*

q. *Id.*

25. The Convention on the Law of the Non–Navigational Uses Of International Watercourses of 1997 [**Basic Document 5.46**] restricts itself to watercourses only....

r. *See supra* Reading 1 at (p. 1165).

26. The Permanent Court of International Justice (PCIJ) recognized the community of interests theory in 1929.... *See Territorial Jurisdiction of the International Commission of the River Oder* [**Basic Document 7.1**]. However, in the *Gabcikovo-Nagymaros Dam* case [**Basic Document 7.11**], the ICJ stated that the reasonable and equitable use theory has gained momentum in international law. The ICJ stated that "Czechoslovakia, by unilaterally assuming control of a shared resource, and thereby depriving Hungary of its right to an equitable and reasonable share of the natural resources of the Danube, with the continuing

If the reasonable and equitable use theory is not customary international law then it certainly has not achieved the status of *jus cogens*, thereby supplanting the PSONR right. The right of PSONR and the reasonable and equitable use theories, however, are not mutually inconsistent. A nation can exercise full dominion over the watercourse yet consider its own use reasonable and equitable. After all, what is perfectly reasonable to one may be wholly unreasonable to another. Equitable utilization is an equality of rights, not an equality of shares in the water at issue.

[*Eds.*—The author next considers the meaning of "reasonable and equitable use" as articulated in the International Law Association's (ILA) 1966 Helsinki Rules **(Basic Document 5.9)**, and continued in its superseding 2004 Berlin Rules **(Basic Document 5.56)** promulgated after the publication of his article on the 1997 International Law Commission (ILC) Convention on the Law of the Non–Navigational Uses of International Watercourses of 1997 **(Basic Document 5.46)**. In passing, he asserts that the former "are not legally binding unless adopted in conventions" because the ILA, which propounded them, is "an unofficial organization." He also asserts that the 1997 ILC Convention, as he refers to it, rejects the Helsinki Rules concept (continued in the Berlin Rules) of "drainage basin" regulation in favor of the geophysically narrower concept of "watercourse" regulation; also that it raised the threshold of prohibited harm from altered watercourse flows from "appreciable" to "significant," *i.e.*, more than "mere inconvenience or *de minimus* damage." He then continues:]

Neither the Helsinki Rules nor the I.L.C. Convention provide adequate evidence of the existence of binding rules of international law since the rules themselves expressly respect the will of the parties. This focus on subjectivity invites varying interpretations about the status of obligations, the binding or non-binding nature of the law, and, in addition, the circumstances dictate what is unreasonable, harmful, and inequitable.[27] The Helsinki Rules have not reached the level of customary international law, nor do they purport to. Moreover, there is insufficient evidence to show widespread State practice, and no evidence indicating States feel bound to follow the Rules. The Rules and the I.L.C. Convention, however, are a source of international law insofar as they are the teachings of highly publicized legal scholars and, therefore, under Article 38 of the ICJ Statute, they indicate some international law. Further, a negotiated but unratified treaty may be a potential source of international law.

What is considered reasonable and equitable must be analyzed in light of the nation developing the watercourse. The reasonableness depends on the natural features of the watercourse whereas the equity depends on the circumstances surrounding the use of the watercourse. These factors are best considered by the developing nation itself.[28] Since each watercourse has its

effects of the diversion of these waters on the ecology of the riparian area ... failed to respect the proportionality which is required by international law."

27. Appreciable harm is harm that has some detrimental impact of some consequence upon the industry, the public health, property, agriculture, and the environment of another

State. *See* Report of the I.L.C. to the General Assembly on the Work of its Fortieth Session, UN GAOR, 43rd Sess., Supp. No. 10, at 85, UN Doc. A/43/10 (1988).

28. Domestic use of a river is a high priority since the community depends on it for survival. An expanding community increases its needs for water and thus its uses become even

own unique characteristics, it is unrealistic to proffer a coterie of rules that attempt to encompass the needs of all involved.

[*Eds.*—The author next considers whether, according to his understanding of the international law of treaty interpretation,[s] the 1997 ILC Convention "purports to represent customary law." He begins by observing that, "despite a predilection to state in the preamble of the Convention the I.L.C.'s views of the existing customary law at the time, the plain language of the Convention's preamble does not purport to codify existing customary law." Next, eschewing resort to the 1997 ILC Convention's "legislative history" or *travaux préparatoires* to answer the question, he argues that "resort to the *travaux préparatoires* is misplaced"; "the use of *travaux préparatoires*," he asserts, "requires that the *travaux préparatoires* represent customary international law and that the customary law is clear." In this instance, he contends, it is not. Therefore, because it is "the closest the ICJ came to interpreting the I.L.C. Watercourse Convention," he turns to the *Case Concerning the Gabcikovo–Nagymaros Project* (**Basic Document 7.11**). In this case, he acknowledges, "the ICJ used the terms 'reasonable' and 'equitable' in interpreting the 1977 Treaty between Hungary and the then Czechoslovakian Republics." But, he argues, "the ICJ did not pronounce this theory in declaring some customary international law, rather the Court interpreted the provisions of the Treaty. In essence, when faced with the opportunity to unravel the imbroglio, the Court failed to do so." The author explains: "what is clear is that the ICJ did not declare the reasonable and equitable use theory to be customary international law, for it stated that the requirement of international law was proportionality. Therefore, the ICJ determined that proportionality was the key and did not refer to the I.L.C. Watercourse Convention as mandating the reasonable and equitable use theory." The author then continues:]

In addition, other arguments exist to vitiate the factors stated in the I.L.C. Convention and the Helsinki Rules. In the situation where the two States at different levels of development share the watercourse, scrutiny must be given to the interests of the lesser developed State. Although one factor of the equitable use theory may entail an integrated utilization approach, this approach may not be applicable where the States vary on the development levels. In developing countries, a watercourse may have multiple uses, such as irrigation, hydroelectricity, and sustenance, and thus requires more deference to its uses before another State labels those uses as illegal under international law. The multiple benefits may also spill over into the neighboring riparian States and thus the developing country's use becomes more acceptable as it furthers the goals of sustainable development.

Another argument involves the geography of the developing nation. If the nation is land-locked, then its only source of utilizable water is the international watercourse. To this end, unitary use of the watercourse becomes highly favorable to the developing nation and international law supports its use.

---

more higher in priority. In arid or semi-arid areas, water consumption becomes of paramount importance as no other viable means of sustenance may exist....

s. On the law of treaty interpretation, see *supra* Section A(6) of Chapter 2, at 99–103.

The importance and problems of pronouncing a statement of international law becomes evident in relation to the I.L.A. Helsinki Rules and the I.L.C. Watercourse Convention. First, when these documents were in the draft stage, the opinions of the legal scholars working on the drafts could have represented persuasive opinions for the ICJ to consider under Article 38(1)(d) [of its Statute **[Basic Document 1.6)]**. While giving fidelity to the work of the scholars, the ICJ may be investigating the law as it should be (*lex ferenda*) as opposed to what the law is (*lex lata*).

Second, the mere creation of a treaty does not, *ipso facto*, demonstrate any customary international law as there may be many countries that choose not to adopt the treaty, thus indicating anti-*opinio juris*. Therefore, an attempt to codify customary international law is severely undermined by the lack of States' adopting those laws.

Third, as States sign on to a treaty, litigants will likely argue that after some numerical threshold is reached, the treaty provisions squarely represent *opinio juris*. However, the issue of whether the numerical threshold is empirically acceptable and adequately represents the international community arises. Further, the nature of State conduct must be examined to determine if it parallels the treaty provisions; if it does not, the widespread, consistent treaty practice that is necessary to establish customary international law will be undermined. In essence, the mere presence of a treaty that is not yet in force clouds the issue of whether the treaty's provisions truly represent an attempted codification of customary international law as presented by legal scholars, or whether the provisions represent scholarly views that are predicated on inconsistent State practice. Even Sir Robert Jennings, former Excellency of the ICJ, commented that most of what is called customary international law is not only not customary, but does not even faintly resemble a customary law.[29] This is clear, for instance, in the Gabcikovo–Nagymaros Dam case, where the treaty between Hungary and the then Czechoslovakian Republic did not *ipso facto* displace any existing customary international law relating to watercourse use. The same applies to the I.L.C. Watercourse Convention since its codification does not purport to represent customary international law.

One final consideration in the I.L.C. Watercourse Convention concerns the standard applied to the equitable use. The central question becomes: is equity measured against whether the State's use is equitable in relation to the underlying activity, or [is it] measured in relation to the rights of the other riparian States? The Convention fails to answer this question, except that the terms of the Convention may require further explication by the international community.

In sum, the I.L.C. Watercourse Convention ... and its provisions do not clearly evidence a representation of customary international law. In a case squarely addressing the Convention, the ICJ did not declare the Convention's provisions to be binding principles of law and resorted to the 1977 Treaty for resolution. Since there is no express statement by high authorities that customary international environmental law exists, and express teachings

29. R. Jennings, *The Identification of International Law, in International Law: Teaching*   *and Practice* 3, 5 (Bin Cheng ed. 1982).

indicate customary international environmental law does not exist, it likely does not. Only time will tell whether States will sign on to the treaty and then engage in conduct consistent with the proposed treaty provisions.

[*Eds.*—The author next discusses several environmental law cases, including the *Trail Smelter Arbitration* (**Basic Document 7.3**) and *Lake Lanoux Arbitration* (**Basic Document 7.7**), as well as the *Gabcikovo-Nagymaros Case* (**Basic Document 7.11**). He concludes this discussion as follows:]

In summary, the above indicates that several theories of sovereignty over natural resources exist and international law is presently equivocal as to the status of international watercourse utilization. Even assuming that international law pronounces a reasonable and equitable rule for use of the watercourse regime, this theory is flexible and can provide for many differing views. The I.L.C. Watercourse Convention binds only its signatories and has no hold over non-signatories. It, therefore, becomes perfectly reasonable for nations to exploit their resources since no clear customary international law exists to the contrary. To this end, a developing nation will exploit its resources if it can, and will seek out international participation to do so. The most accessible source of international participation is through multinational funding organizations, and the impetus to reach out to these sources is great.

[*Eds.*—Finally, after addressing, first, the "Economics of Development and the Role of the World Bank" (wherein the author argues that watercourse development, especially hydroelectric generation, is in the best interest of a developing state "because it attracts vast sums of foreign development capital and generates vast sums of money from the export of goods and services created therefrom") and, second, "International Environmental Impact Surveys and the Problem of Standards" (wherein the author argues that watercourse utilization and disputes arising therefrom are best left to the nations involved because "mutual cooperation through joint commissions is more effective in watercourse management than through equivocal pronouncements of sweeping international law"), the author concludes:]

. . . Cognizant that the reasonable and equitable use law is unclear and that the ICJ did not pronounce it as a binding law, one of the only practicable solutions to international watercourse development and management is the creation of the joint commission via bilateral (or multilateral) treaty. The States directly concerned with an environmental problem should be the States to deal with the issue. After all, given the lack of clarity on any issue involving watercourse use, each State must have the ability to craft joint documents individually tailored to the circumstances at hand. . . .

* * *

Regionalization recognizes problems in the environmental sphere that transcend the States in scope, but do not rise to the level of global cooperation and do not affect the global commons. In fact, there is an increasing recognition that while an environmental problem is global in nature, its solution need not be. Especially in the context of developing nations and the hostility to the imposition of developed nation's will, deferential consideration must be given to the developing State in the management of its watercourse. Even former Secretary–General U. Thant stated, with respect to a developing

State's control over its own resources by the creation of regional joint commissions, that

> [t]he developing countries are intimately concerned with these problems, which are crucial both to their own future and to the future of the environment. Their voices must be heard, and listened to.... Their confidence and their cooperation, as representing the largest part of the world's population, are vital. Otherwise we shall once again increase the gap between advanced and developing nations which is already one of the major sources of tension in the world.[30]

As evidence that joint commissions do work despite the lack of rules in the international realm, there are several examples of joint commissions over international watercourses. These include the Rhine River Commission, the Danube River Commission, and the International Joint Commission [between Canada and the United States].

* * *

Commissions finding success in developing States include the Committee for the Lower Mekong River, which promotes, coordinates, supervises, and plans water development projects on the Mekong.

The Permanent Indus Commission, established between India and Pakistan in 1960, has jurisdiction over disputes concerning the Indus River and coordinates the parties' water development policies. A noteworthy feature is that the World Bank is a party to the treaty which monitors how the loans are distributed. Similarly, in India, the Joint Ganges Commission was created between India and Bangladesh. This Commission also regulates the use of water and mandates a duty of prior consultation before undertaking any development.

* * *

... In sum, the joint commission is the most practicable means for solving international watercourse disputes. * * * General principles of international law cannot cope with the reality that each watercourse system has its own physical peculiarities and it is governed by nations with their own peculiar sensitivities regarding development. As developed nations push harder for environmental respect in the wake of their own destructive policies, they try to create binding obligations of customary international law. However, developing nations resist this trend by falling back on current entrenched principles of sovereignty over natural resources. As binding international law is not present, the most sensible approach to international watercourse management is to expand and improve intergovernmental relations by creating joint commissions. Thus the use, administration, and protection of the international watercourse can be maximized by allowing the regional nations to govern the watercourse.

SECTION 5.　DISCUSSION NOTES/QUESTIONS

1. The multifactoral tests of Article 13 of the 2004 Berlin Rules **(Basic Document 5.56)** and Article 6 of the 1997 UN Convention on the Law of Non–

---

30. U. Thant, Human Environment and World Order, Address to University of Texas at Austin, 14 May 1970, in UN Press Release SG/SM/1259 (1970).

Navigational Uses of International Watercourses **(Basic Document 5.46)** differ. How? Regardless, are they adequate to the task of resolving disputes relative to the sharing of the waters of international rivers?

2.   Currently there is no international law duty requiring co-basin states to seek the optimum rational development of common water resources on a basin-wide scale. It has been inferred from the decision in the 1957 *Lake Lanoux Arbitration* **(Basic Document 7.7)**, for example, that there is no duty to attempt types of water utilization that would lead to an optimal use of the waters considering all the interests involved. Also, as has been pointed out in the foregoing readings (Reading 8 especially), the UN Convention on the Non-navigational Uses of International Waterways **(Basic Document 5.46)** imposes not a duty of optimal use but only a duty to develop the resources of an international river basin as efficiently as co-basin state financial resources will allow. Further, that Convention is textually restricted to water "courses" and therefore does not expressly address river "basins" at all. Nevertheless, a principle of optimal use, requiring co-basin states to cooperate in making the most economically efficient use of transboundary rivers and their basins appears today to be emerging in part due to the pressure of increased demand for water by ever growing populations. Evidence of this development is found in Articles 10 and 11 of the Berlin Rules which provides that, "Basin States have the right to participate in the management of waters of an international drainage in an equitable, reasonable and sustainable manner," and that "Basin States shall cooperate in good faith in the management of waters of an international drainage basin for the mutual benefit of the participating states." Perhaps more importantly, however, is the experiential evidence; in recognition of their common interests co-basin states now seem increasingly inclined to develop transboundary watercourse resources on a multistate basis through joint planning and development agreements governing international drainage basins. *See, e.g.,* the 1996 Treaty between India and Nepal Concerning the Integrated Development of the Mahakali River, *reprinted in* 36 I.L.M. 531 (1997), and the 1996 Treaty between India and Bangladesh on Sharing of the Ganges Waters at Farakka, *reprinted in* 36 I.L.M. 519 (1997). *See also* the 1978 Draft Treaty for Amazonian Cooperation **(Basic Document 5.19)**. An especially noteworthy case in point is the Treaty between the United States and Canada Relating to the Cooperative Development of Resources of the Columbia River Basin, 17 Jan 1961, 15 U.S.T. 1555, T.I.A.S. No. 5638, which authorized the United States to construct a hydroelectric dam on Canadian territory for energy production and flood control purposes on condition of recompense to Canada in the form of both hydroelectric power and dollars. It is an excellent example of how one co-basin state (a lower riparian) with the resources to make optimal use of a river's potential was allowed by another co-basin state (an upper riparian) to exploit the latter's river jurisdiction to the benefit of both states to a degree greater than either could have obtained independently. For pertinent discussion, see, *e.g.,* Patricia Jones, *Operationalizing Equitable and Reasonable Utilization: Practice on the Columbia River*, International Speciality Conference on Globalization and Water Resources Management: the Changing Value of Water, University of Dundee, 6–8 Aug 2001, available at <http://www.awra.org/proceedings/dundee01/Documents/Jones.pdf>. Should international law impose a duty of optimal use on co-basin states?

3.   Transboundary river pollution has been addressed elsewhere besides Article 27 of the Berlin Rules on Water Resources **(Basic Document 5.57)**. For example, in 1974 the Council of the Organization for Economic Co-operation and Development (OECD) adopted a Recommendation on Principles Concerning

Transfrontier Pollution, OECD Doc. C(74) 224 of 21 Nov 1974, *reprinted in* 14 I.L.M. 242 (1975); in 1982 the International Law Association (ILA) adopted Rules on International Law Applicable to Transfrontier Pollution, **(Basic Document 5.20)**; and in 1999 the UN Economic Commission for Europe adopted the Protocol on Water and Health to the 1992 Convention on the Protection and Use of Transboundary Watercourses and International Lakes, *supra* note j. The central concern is to ensure that water is sufficient, healthful, and free of pollutants, including agriculturally based pollutants. Also working to establish guidelines for the use and preservation of internationally shared natural resources has been the United Nations Environment Programme (UNEP) which, in May 1978, issued Draft Principles of Conduct in the Field of the Environment for the Guidance of States in the Conservation and Harmonious Utilization of Natural Resources Shared by Two or More States **(Basic Document 5.17)**. While the Draft Principles never have been formally adopted by the UN General Assembly, in December 1979 the General Assembly did "[request] all States to use the principles as guidelines and recommendations in the formulation of bilateral and multilateral conventions regarding natural resources shared by two or more States, on the basis of the principle of good faith and in the spirit of good neighbourliness and in such a way as to enhance and not adversely affect development and the interests of countries, in particular the developing countries." Resolution on Co-operation in the Field of the Environment Concerning Natural Resources Shared by Two or More States, GA Res. 34/186, Supp. (No. 46) 128, UN Doc. A/34/46 (1978). An example of the utilization of the Draft Principles can be found in the 1978 Treaty for Amazonian Cooperation **(Basic Document 5.19)**. The Treaty, which entered into force 12 Aug 1980, serves as another example of the emerging pattern of co-basin states attempting to make provision for the sharing of the economic potential of international watercourses while providing for conservation and rational utilization of the natural resources of the region.

4.   When manipulating river systems for flood-control, irrigation, hydroelectric, and other praiseworthy purposes, governmental authorities and private contractors do not always take adequately into account the potential consequences of their environmental intervention—as, for example, in the instant case of Punjamir whose dam resulted in a "major decline in a certain river fish upon which Rajatani diets historically have depended." In this connection, consider the following remarks of Dr. Jimoh Omo–Fadaka, *The Misuse of Science and Technology*, Doc. No. 17, World Future Studies Conference on Science and Technology and the Future, Berlin, 8–10 May 1979. While somewhat dated, they are nonetheless insightfully instructive:

> What happens when we dam the flow of a great river and create an immense body of water where there was none before? Not enough thought was given to this question in the 1950's and 1960's as dozens of big dams went up from Pakistan to Ghana, Egypt to Brazil. Everybody thought big dams meant instant progress, and that there was nothing like a big dam for a fast economic take off. Few people were worried about aftershocks in the ecosystem.

> In the past few years, however, big dam owners the world over have begun to compare notes and discover that when a dam backs up waters behind it, everything changes: the water's chemistry; kinds and numbers of indigenous flora and fauna; the way of life for all the people who lived on the land before the lake came; the fertility and salinity of the soil downstream; the pressure on the earth's crusts and the tendency, therefore, to earthquakes

and landslides. Moreover, while the promised progress is usually less than expected, these changes produce problems that are real and proliferating.

It has been found that Egypt's Aswan High Dam project has eliminated vital nutrients that used to maintain the sardine supply; has shrunk lakes, reducing the available fish protein; has concentrated insecticides, herbicides and molluscides which produce massive fish kill. In addition, the Nile Delta which is constantly eroded by the wash of the river, is no longer protected by the sediment which used to be carried down the river before the dam was built. The dam's electricity-generating capacity is enormous—10,000 million kilowatt-hours yearly. But power installed is not necessarily power consumed. According to the latest reports of the Egyptian Ministry of Energy, Egypt is short of electricity. Many Egyptians have yet to benefit from the abundant energy that Aswan was supposed to produce.

Lake Nasser, which covers the Sudanese town of Wadi Halfa, was designed to store some 35.2 billion gallons and reach capacity by 1970. Now, it is only half full and may never be full. Evaporation alone takes 3.3 billion gallons of water a year from the lake, 50 per cent more than the engineers' original estimate. Moreover, Lake Nasser's entire 300 mile western bank is porous Nubian sandstone, which can absorb still more quantities of water. Altogether the Lake is losing about one-third of the water flowing into it—6.6. billion gallons yearly.

True, Egyptians are no longer threatened by the Nile's yearly floods. But they are no longer getting the flood's priceless gift: the annual 100 million tons of silt that made the Nile Delta so fertile. This precious substance is dropping to the bottom of Lake Nasser. All six million of Egypt's cultivated acres will soon be needing much more fertilizer—to make up for what used to come from the Nile's once inexhaustible silt. Already the yearly cost of the necessary extra fertilizer comes to upwards of US $100 million.

Egypt loses 18,000 tons of sardines a year because the now diminished silt was part of the aquatic food chain at the Nile's mouth. What is more, the heavy use of water in irrigation projects and generally poor drainage have caused a rise in underground water levels and a consequent accumulation of soil salts. Egypt has been forced to start installing expensive underground drains on a million waterlogged acres on the delta—the most ambitious drainage project in the world, costing more than US $180 million.

Wherever superdams have gone up in Africa and Asia, the reservoir lakes and irrigation canals have brought an explosion of water borne diseases. This happens partly because people accustomed to relieving themselves in the bush do so in the water instead. But, also, the surfaces of lakes and canals offer superb breeding conditions for malarial mosquitoes. Similarly, conditions favour the kinds of mosquito that bear yellow fever, dengue fever, elephantiasis—the Guinea worm that grows three feet long in the human body and causes painful ulcers—and that scourge of so many Third World countries, the bilharzia-carrying snail.

Thus, the decision of a state to build a dam, "super" or otherwise, obviously can have vast ramifications for itself and its neighbors.

Perhaps the best known contemporary major dam project is the largest hydroelectric project in the world on the third largest river in the world, the Three Gorges Dam project on China's Yangtze River, begun in 1994 and scheduled to be completed in 2009 at an *official* estimated cost of US$29 billion. If and when it is completed, it will span nearly a mile across, tower 575 feet above the Yangtze, contain an upstream reservoir stretching more than 350 miles (farther than New York City to Montreal), and force the displacement of close to 1.9 million people. Because the Yangtze, though rising in the Tibetan highlands before coursing 3,450 miles to the East China Sea at Shanghai, is not otherwise a transboundary river, its social and environmental costs will be primarily internal to China. Those costs, however, will be unprecedentedly huge and thus the project is worthy of attention for this reason alone. Chinese officials claim the dam will control the unpredictable river which frequently floods and kills thousands of people. Others, including transnational environmental groups specialized to the protection of transboundary rivers and watersheds, oppose its construction and seek to mitigate as much as possible its likely effects, including the displacement of an estimated 1.9 million people as a result of a reservoir that will stretch over 350 miles upstream and thus disrupt what has for centuries been China's ventral highway. For helpful detail, see, *e.g.*, the web site for the US-based International Rivers Network, at <http://www.irn.org/programs/threeg>.

Is there any role for international law to play in the initial decision of whether or not to build a super dam? If the river involved is a transboundary watercourse? A watercourse that is entirely or essentially internal to a given territorial state? Or is international law, as to the really "big" questions, called upon too late to do much good? Would it be possible in such situations to require an assessment procedure that includes impact analyses before at least major environmental initiatives are undertaken?

5. Over the years, as highlighted in Reading 22, *supra*, developing countries such as Punjamir have been concerned that the growing interest of the economically developed nations in international environmental protection will, because of the cost of such protection, impact negatively upon their economic development. Indeed, believing that most of the world's environmental problems are caused by the industrialized countries, many have viewed the imposition of international environmental controls upon them as a form of neocolonialism. What kind and degree of environmental responsibility should be imposed upon developing countries in their pursuit of economic development? Upon international, national, and private lending institutions that help to finance development projects? Upon public and private contractors that carry the projects out? Should persons responsible for the planning, financing, and implementation of development projects be held individually responsible for failing to safeguard against environmental harms that foreseeably could result from the development projects they plan, finance, and carry out? If so, to what extent? If not, why not?

6. *Bibliographical Note.* For supplemental discussion concerning the principal themes addressed in this problem, consult the following additional specialized materials:

(a) *Books/Monographs/Reports/Symposia.* H. Beach et al, Transboundary Freshwater Dispute Resolution: Theory, Practice, and Annotated References, (2000); S. Bogdanovic, International Law of Water Resources–Contribution of the International Law Association (1954–2000) (International and National Water Law and Policy Series, Volume 4) (2001); H. Elver, Peaceful Uses of International Rivers: The Euphrates and Tigris Rivers Dispute (Innovation in International Law) (2002); M. Frank, Managing International Rivers: Problems, Politics and Institutions (2001); M. Haddadin, Diplomacy on the Jordan: International Conflict and Negotiated Resolution (Natural Resource Management and Policy) (2002); S. McCaffrey, The Law of International Watercourses: Non–Navigational Uses

(2003); S. Salman & L. Boisson De Chazournes, International Watercourses: Enhancing Cooperation and Managing Conflict: Proceedings of a World Bank Seminar (World Bank Technical Paper) (1998); S. Salman & K. Uprety, Conflict and Cooperation on South Asia's International Rivers: A Legal Perspective (Law, Justice, and Development) (2003); J. B. Skjaerseth, North Sea Cooperation: Linking International and Domestic Pollution Control (2000); S. Suvedi, International Watercourses Law for the 21st Century: The Case of the River Ganges Basin, (2005); The International Bureau of the Permanent Court of Arbitration, Resolution of International Water Disputes (Permanent Court of Arbitration/Peace Palace Papers) (2003); A. Utton and L. Teclaff, Transboundary Resources Law 5 (Westview Special Studies Ed., 1987).

(b) *Articles/Book Chapters.* E. Benvenisti, *Sharing Transboundary Resources: International Law and Optimal Resource Use*, 17 Emory Int'l L. Rev. 1091 (2003); G. Eckstein & Y. Eckstein, *A Hydrogeological Approach to Transboundary Ground Water Resources and International Law*, 19 Am. U. Int'l L. Rev. 201 (2003); A. Parrish, *Trail Smelter Deja Vu: Extraterritoriality, International Environmental Law, and the Search* for *Solutions to Canadian*-US *Transboundary Water Pollution Disputes,* 85 B.U.L. Rev. 363 (2005); E. Sievers, *Transboundary Jurisdiction and Watercourse Law: China, Kazakhstan, and the Irtysh*, 37 Tex. Int'l L.J. 1 (2002).

Problem 7–5

Toxic Pollution in Yoribo and Bamileko

Section 1. Facts

In 1980, PanAfrica AgChem (PAAC) was incorporated under the laws of
Yoribo, a developing country in sub-Saharan West Africa on the Gulf of
Guinea. Its goal was to promote sub-Saharan agricultural products and
productivity. A later secondary goal was to profit from a growing regional as
well as worldwide concern to reduce or eliminate the use of pesticides, other
agriculturally-based chemicals, and miscellaneous wastes deemed hazardous
to human health or the environment[a] by providing both neighboring and
distant sub-Saharan countries a convenient and inexpensive means of disposing them. Thus, in 1983, on the advice of Nippon Chemicals Corporation, a
Japanese multinational company with which it had a consultation agreement,
PAAC began construction of an agricultural chemical production plant and, in
1993, an adjacent chemical and hazardous waste disposal facility—each at
Khasa, a small city near Yoribo's Mimbu River boundary with Bamileko, a
neighboring agricultural producer to Yoribo's southeast. In 1985, the new
plant began to produce insecticides, herbicides, and rodenticides for both
domestic use and export. Ten years later, in 1995, the disposal facility began
to collect and store for ultimate disposal both organochlorines and agriculturally-based wastes deemed hazardous to human health and the environment.
In each case, the pesticides involved included DDT and other organochlorines:
aldrin, chlordane, dieldrin, endrin, and heptachlor.[b]

Soon after PAAC's chemical plant began production, international pressures on the Yoribon government to ensure the safe treatment of the
hazardous chemicals and wastes that would result from it quickly mounted.
By 1990, they reached a boiling point. The evidence was that Yoribo had
taken only minimal legislative steps to classify and ban or regulate such
chemicals and wastes to prevent pollution. Accordingly, the Yoribon government, by this time advised of PAAC's disposal facility plans, called upon
PAAC to incorporate into its plans the construction of underground treatment
and disposal units (TDUs) for the reprocessing and disposal of the hazardous
chemicals and waste and, in addition, the implementation of a treatment and
disposal strategy (TDS) for the same that Yoribon officials would monitor.
PAAC complied by acquiring both the TDUs and a TDS from TechnoChemi-

---

a. As exemplified by the Basel Convention
on the Control of Transboundary Movements
of Hazardous Waste and Their Disposal of 22
Mar 1989 (**Basic Document 5.30**) and the
Bamako Convention on the Ban of Import into
Africa and the Control of Transboundary
Movements of Hazardous Wastes within Africa
of 30 Jan 1991 (**Basic Document 5.34**).

b. Organochlorines are insecticides that
contain carbon (hence "organo"), chlorine, and
hydrogen. They are sometimes referred to by
other names: chlorinated hydrocarbons, chlorinated organics, chlorinated insecticides, and
chlorinated synthetics.

cals, which, in turn, had obtained them from one of its US subsidiaries, a consequence of which was that the TDUs and the TDS were designed to meet the chemical and chemical waste disposal standards of the United States. The design and operation standards for the TDUs were aimed at preventing pollution and groundwater contamination. The TDS dealt with, among other things, various kinds of pre-treatment to prevent the formation of leachate.[c] Specifications for liners and leachate collection systems were intended to minimize the migration of any leachate into the adjacent subsurface soil and groundwater, and a three-stage program to detect, evaluate, and correct groundwater contamination was an integral part of these standards. Each TDU was estimated to cost $US 5 million to construct and a half million US dollars annually to maintain.

In 1995, after a comprehensive resource allocation study, PAAC embarked upon a plan to construct ten TDUs phased in at the rate of one each year so as to avoid maintaining empty units. Lacking sufficient capital to undertake this program in its entirety, it sought a subsidy from the Yoribon government. As the country's economy was enjoying a petroleum boom at the time, the Yoribon government, acting pursuant to its national investment program, agreed to subsidize for a "reasonable period" two-thirds of the cost of building the TDUs. During the first five years of the ten-year plan, the TDUs were built and operated on schedule.

The pesticides produced at PAAC's Khasa plant sold well throughout sub-Saharan Africa. Neighboring Bamileko, which had undertaken a major national effort to gain food self-sufficiency, became one of PAAC's principal customers, purchasing agricultural chemicals from PAAC in bulk in order to get lower prices and then selling them to farmers at subsidized rates. DDT and other organochlorines were shipped by road from Khasa to a Bamilekon government distribution point about 100 miles within Bamileko. There, the chemicals, which had been shipped in large metal drums that carried warnings and instructions in English and in pictograms, were re-packaged in available cans, bottles, and other receptacles by largely illiterate day laborers who simply glued paper labels on the containers that said in English—not in native Bamilekon—"agriculture chemicals." They then dispatched the receptacles to small-scale farmers in various parts of the country, particularly in and around the maize, millet, peanut, and sorghum fields that border the Mimbu on Bamileko's side of the river. Bamileko did not request, and PAAC did not provide, suitable packaging for small-scale farmers.

Once launched, PAAC's disposal facility at Khasa began to make a profit also. Shipments of organochlorines and agriculturally-based chemical wastes from around Yoribo and several nearby countries grew steadily, many of them derived originally from PAAC's chemical production plant and all of them supplementing chemicals and wastes turned over to the facility from the plant. Bamileko, however, was slow to respond to the opportunity presented by the disposal facility. Still committed to achieving food self-sufficiency, it continued for almost a decade to press the importation and use of DDT and

---

c. A product or solution, usually containing contaminates, formed by the leaching of soil.

other pesticides to enhance agricultural productivity rather than encourage
the shipment of these chemicals for disposal at PAAC's Khasa facility in
Yoribo. There is no evidence that, until late–2004 when it ceased to treat its
agricultural fields with DDT and other organochlorines, it had taken any
significant steps to classify and ban or regulate chemical pesticides.

In 2000, oil prices began a decline that caused the Yoribon economy to
stall and retreat, with individual incomes cut in half in just three years. This
sharp decline prompted a successful coup attempt by Army officers who, in a
firestorm effort to cut national spending, withdrew Yoribo's TDU subsidy and
dramatically reduced public sector employment, including that of officials
charged with monitoring PAAC's activities. Concurrently, neighboring countries faced similar economic difficulties, which led to a slump in demand for
agricultural chemicals from PAAC's chemical plant and in the shipment of
chemicals and chemical waste to its disposal facility.

Ultimately these factors led to PAAC's fall from profitability and accountability, so much so that PAAC found itself unable to build and maintain the
remaining five TDUs. Therefore, as part of its own austerity program, it
canceled its consultation agreement with TechnoChemicals. The new Yoribon
government, however, was only partially sympathetic to PAAC's financial
predicament. While understanding PAAC's need to scale back its production
of agricultural chemicals and particularly the dangerously hazardous ones,
but alert to international environmental pressures, it prevailed upon PAAC to
agree to maintain full operation of its Khasa disposal facility without the
additional TDUs.

Predictably, in the absence of the additional TDUs, there quickly developed an accumulation of hazardous chemicals and chemical wastes in and
around the Khasa facility, and for this reason PAAC began immediately to
look for less expensive ways to store the accumulating toxic chemicals and
their wastes. After an extensive search, in which the Yoribon government
chose not to participate, PAAC located a site several miles away from the
Khasa facility.

The new site was at Mt. Mandara, a 3,000–feet high ridge located in a
northeastern stretch of unpopulated land adjacent to the Mimbu River that
separates Yoribo and Bamileko. Without consulting the Yoribon government
but with its knowledge, PAAC hired local laborers to tunnel 150 feet through
the ridge and into a large "dead" cavern.[d] Thereafter, for the next three
years, until late–2003 when the cavern's storage capacity was reached and
with only occasional government oversight during that time, work crews from
the surrounding region deposited directly onto the floor of the cavern large
55–gallon metal drums of chemicals and chemical waste that had been
accumulating at the Khasa facility. The drums carried warnings written with
chalk in the Yoribon language that quickly became blurred and illegible. Many
of the drums were stacked on top of one another with little knowledge of, or
regard for, the chemical compatibility of their contents. The crews closed the
site with earth, rock, and cement over the opening they had made. PAAC
maintained general records of the types of chemicals and chemical waste
byproducts being stored at the Mandara site, but a precise inventory of the

d. A "dead" cavern is one through which calcitic growths such as stalactites and stalag-
water is no longer flowing and contributing to mites.

number of drums and the exact contents of each was neither kept nor supplied to the Yoribon government. No provision was made for follow-up analysis of the waste dumped at the site or for groundwater monitoring by either PAAC or Yoribo.

In 2004, a wetter than usual rainy season in Yoribo and its surrounding region caused considerable erosion around Mt. Mandara. The rains soaked the land surrounding the Mandara cavern and water migrated into the cavern and the drums. The intrusion of water resulted in rust, rot, and general disintegration that, in turn, led to the escape of various toxic and hazardous substances into the soil. Eventually, the toxins leached through the soil at Mt. Mandara and into the Mimbu River. At the same time, the heavy rains led to unprecedented runoffs from the maize, millet, peanut, and sorghum fields that Bamileko had continued to treat with DDT and other organochlorines on its side of the Mimbu River. Upon entering the water, the toxic compounds rapidly worked their way through the food chain, accumulating in the livers and fatty tissues of carp, trout, and various tilapia. Some of the toxins bonded with other organic matter and were carried downstream. Some of it settled on the riverbed as sediment.

Downriver, in Douaundé, Bamileko's largest metropolitan area, the impact of these toxins gradually became apparent. Thousands of Bamilekon citizens who consumed riverbed feeding fish, such as carp and tilapia, complained of joint pain, extreme muscular weakness, anxiety, vomiting, mild jerking, dizziness, and convulsions. Textile factories that traded with Europe and the United States had to cut production by 40 percent due to worker illnesses, losing new contracts as a result. Local hospitals reported a significant increase in the number of babies born with birth defects.

Alarmed by these events, Bamilekon authorities set up a Commission of Inquiry consisting of biology, chemistry, zoology, and medical experts from Douaundé University who were teamed with public health care officials from the local office of the World Health Organization (WHO). During its three-month inquiry the Commission sampled fish, mollusks, plankton, and other life from the Mimbu, and found much higher traces of organochlorines, including DDT, heptachlor, and chlordane, than might be expected even for a country like Bamileko that used these chemicals in its own agricultural programs. After sampling drinking water drawn from wells fed by the river, the Commission found levels of pesticides 1,500 times in excess of Bamilekon and WHO standards. It also discovered that toxic concentrations in river water increased steadily as samples were drawn further upriver, but then abruptly dropped to lower—though not normal—levels immediately after passing Yoribo's Mt. Mandara. In early 2005, the Commission reported accordingly to the Bamilekon government.

Later in 2005, after considering the Commission's report, the Government of Bamileko accused the Government of Yoribo of violating international law by secretly dumping hazardous chemicals and chemical waste that damaged the environment and people of Bamileko. Bamileko argued that Yoribo had violated the 1989 Basel Convention on the Control of Transboundary Movements of Hazardous Waste and Their Disposal, the 1991 Bamako Convention on the Ban of Import into Africa and the Control of Transboundary Movements of Hazardous Wastes within Africa, and, as well, the 1997 United

Nations Convention on the Law of the Non-navigational Uses of International Watercourses, and the 1998 Rotterdam Convention on the Prior Informed Consent Procedure for Certain Hazardous Chemicals and Pesticides in International Trade. Bamileko had become a party to each of these for treaty instruments in mid–2004 when, as indicated, it ceased to treat its agricultural fields with DDT and other organochlorines. Yoribo had become a party to the first two of them several years earlier but has yet to sign and ratify the third and fourth. Beyond these breaches of conventional international law, Bamileko asserted that Yoribo had violated customary international law as reflected in the general principle of good neighborliness and the 1985 Cairo Guidelines and Principles of Environmentally Sound Management of Hazardous Waste.[e] In addition, in mid–2006, Bamileko accused Yoribo of violating the 2001 Stockholm Convention on Persistent Organic Pollutants to which Bamileko, but not yet Yoribo, had become a party. The Stockholm Convention, Bamileko argued, was reflective of newly emerged customary international law.

Yoribo refuted these allegations, asserting, *inter alia*, that the cheap disposal of hazardous chemicals and their wastes in the best practicable manner within its own borders constitutes both an equitable and reasonable use of its territory and compliance with relevant conventional and customary international law. Assuming, though not admitting to, some leaching at Mt. Mandara, Yoribo stated first that the use of Mt. Mandara was both equitable and reasonable, and amounted to good management. Additionally, it argued that Bamileko was primarily responsible for the chemical levels in the Mimbu River and the harm the chemicals might have caused. Yoribo claimed that its own studies revealed high toxicity levels upstream from Mt. Mandara in an area of intensive Bamileko agriculture, caused by runoff. Furthermore, Yoribo asserted that Bamileko had negligently used higher than recommended doses of the agricultural chemicals it imported from Yoribo, in clear violation of instructions and warnings on the drums PAAC had supplied.

Angry that the Yoribon reply amounted to a complete repudiation of its claim, Bamileko froze Yoribon assets totaling $US 80 million, including an airplane, real estate, and securities. Bamileko claims that this was the only way to recoup even a part of the costs of the Commission, the skyrocketing medical expenses incurred in treating Bamilekon citizens affected by toxic chemicals, and the enormous losses suffered by its textile industry. It also asserts that the frozen Yoribon assets are insufficient to meet these damages, and therefore it has demanded pecuniary compensation from Yoribo. Neither Bamileko nor Yoribo has yet signed the 1999 Basel Protocol on Liability and Compensation for Damage Resulting from Transboundary Movements of Hazardous Wastes and Their Disposal.

Protesting the illegality of Bamileko's actions, yet troubled that the international publicity given to these incidents might damage its delicate negotiations with various OECD nations for substantial development assistance, the new Government of Yoribo proposed that the two countries submit

---

e. The two governments have issued statements affirming their acceptance of the 1987 Cairo Guidelines and Principles for the Environmentally Sound Management of Hazardous Wastes [**Basic Document 5.28**]. They have done so also in respect of the 1989 London Guidelines for the Exchange of Information on Chemicals in International Trade [**Basic Document 5.32**] and the 1985 FAO Code of Conduct on the Distribution and Use of Pesticides [**Basic Document 5.24**].

their dispute to an *ad hoc* tribunal established under Article 20(2) of the Bamako Convention which had been signed and ratified by both countries. Bamileko has agreed to submit to the jurisdiction of such an *ad hoc* tribunal, and both parties agree that the tribunal should resolve their dispute according to international law.

SECTION 2.   QUESTIONS PRESENTED

1. Has Yoribo or Bamileko violated international law; and, if so, to what damages is either entitled, if any?

2. In any event, are there any additional or alternative legal norms, procedures, and/or institutions to be recommended that might further help to prevent or discourage situations of the kind posed by this problem?

SECTION 3.   ASSIGNMENTS

A.   READING ASSIGNMENT

Study the Readings presented in Section 4, *infra*, and the Discussion Notes/Questions that follow. Also, to the extent possible, consult the accompanying bibliographical references.

B.   RECOMMENDED WRITING ASSIGNMENT

Prepare a comprehensive, logically sequenced, and *argumentative* brief in the form of an outline of the primary and subsidiary *legal* issues you see requiring resolution by the Yoribo–Bamileko *ad hoc* tribunal. Also, from the perspective of an independent judge, indicate which side ought to prevail on each issue and why. Retain a copy of your issue-outline (brief) for class discussion.

C.   RECOMMENDED ORAL ASSIGNMENT

Assume you are legal counsel for Yoribo or Bamileko (as designated by your instructor); then, relying upon the Readings (and your issue-outline if prepared), present a 10–15 minute oral argument of your government's likely positions before the *ad hoc* tribunal.

D.   RECOMMENDED REFLECTIVE ASSIGNMENT

Consider (and recommend) alternative norms, institutions, and/or procedures that you believe might do better than existing world order arrangements to contend with situations of the kind posed by this problem. In so doing, but without insisting upon *immediate* feasibility, identify the particular transition steps that would be needed to make your alternatives a reality.

SECTION 4.   READINGS

The following readings are considered *prima facie* relevant to solving this problem. They are your law library for present purposes and should be treated as such, organized intelligibly for "shelving" and not necessarily according to the issues presented. Be sure to review Chapter 2 ("International Legal Prescription: The 'Sources' of International Law") in your consideration of them. It, too, should be treated as part of your law library (as, indeed, should this entire coursebook).

1. Peter–Tobias Stoll, "Hazardous Substances and Technologies," *in* International, Regional and National Environmental Law 437, 437–39 (F. Morrison & R. Rüdiger eds., 2000).

Recalling the major accidents in Seveso, Bhopal, and Basel, it is evident that chemicals, and the technologies designed for their production and use, may have a catastrophic impact on human life and the environment. While such emergencies dramatize the dangers of widespread chemical production, however, they are not the only cause for concern. Scientists, politicians and the general public are increasingly recognizing that even the controlled use of such substances can ... lead to serious environmental and health effects. Chemicals once considered safe and beneficial, such as PCBs,[f] DDT, and other pesticides, have been shown to accumulate in the environment and in the bodies of living things, with dangerous consequences. Many such substances were in widespread—even global—use for decades before these toxic effects were discovered.

In the last twenty-five years, many countries have taken steps to control the production, distribution and use of hazardous substances and technologies. It is only recently, however, that the international community has begun to confront the international aspects of the problem. To a limited degree, international concern with hazardous substances is based on their direct physical transborder effects, which may cause harm to another state's territory or an international common. * * * However, there is a more specific international concern about hazardous substances and technologies, or rather, two closely related concerns. First, these substances and technologies often require specific handling and control measures, which—due to inadequate information or differing legal, administrative and technological environments—may not be applied properly during their transport and ultimate use. Second, hazardous substances and technologies may involve risks so severe as to outweigh any positive usefulness they might have. In such cases, a national or international authority may have restricted their use.

The dangers associated with hazardous substances and technologies are particularly acute when they have moved as goods in international commerce. The dangers are magnified because, once placed in the stream of trade, hazardous substances continue to circulate not only as primary products but also as ingredients in other products, and ultimately as waste. The resulting dispersion of hazardous substances across geographic regions and economic sectors has been termed the "cycle of poison."[1]

* * *

... [I]t bears mention that the problem of hazardous substance control has a development aspect. Most industrialized countries have established national systems for monitoring and controlling hazardous substances and

---

f. Polychlorinated biphenyls.

1. V. Nanda & B. Bailey, *Nature and Scope of the Problem, in* Transferring Hazardous Technologies and Substances: The International Legal Challenge 3, 42 (G. Handl & R. Lutz eds., 1989).

technologies. Many developing countries, by contrast, lack the legislation necessary for such control, the administrative machinery necessary for enforcing that legislation, or both. Businesses based in industrialized countries have often exploited this gap by exporting hazardous substances and technologies that are banned on domestic markets to developing countries where there are fewer restrictions. In some cases, these businesses transferred production facilities to developing countries in order to circumvent domestic bans. Developed countries did little to prevent such activities until it became apparent that the banned substances—for example, on fruits and vegetables imported from developing countries—and into developed country environments in the form of polluted air, rivers, and rain.

    2. Editors' Note. In the immediately preceding reading, Peter–Tobias Stoll observes that chemicals once considered safe and beneficial (*e.g.*, PCBs, DDT) have later been proven dangerous to human health and the environment but that, through international trade, they have dispersed globally, especially in the developing world. It thus behooves one to consider the nature of the chemicals involved.

Consider first the well-known pesticide DDT, banned in much of the industrialized world, but still widely used in the Global South. Write John M. Johnson & George W. Ware, Pesticide Litigation Manual (1995), at 11–3 to 11–4:

> Let us consider a few salient points concerning DDT in order to understand some of the well-documented evils attributed to it. The first point is DDT's chemical stability. DDT and TDE are *persistent*, that is, their chemical stability gives the products long lives in soil and aquatic environments and in animal and plant tissues. They are not readily broken down by microorganisms, enzymes, heat, or ultraviolet light. . . .
>
> Second, we note that DDT's solubility in water is only about six parts per billion parts (ppb) of water. DDT has been reported in the chemical literature to be probably the most water-insoluble compound ever synthesized. However, it is quite soluble in fatty tissue, and, as a consequence of its resistance to metabolism, it is readily stored in fatty tissue of any animal ingesting DDT alone or DDT dissolved in the food it eats, even when it is part of another animal.
>
> Since DDT is not readily metabolized and thus not excreted, and it is freely stored in body fat, it accumulates in every animal that preys on other animals. It also accumulates in animals that eat plant tissue bearing traces of DDT. For example, a dairy cow excretes (or secretes) a large share of the ingested DDT in its milk fat. Humans drink milk and eat the fatted calf, and thereby ingest DDT. The same story was repeated in food chains ending in the osprey, falcon, golden eagle, seagull, pelican, and so on.
>
> The principle of these food chain oddities is this: Any chemical that possesses the characteristics of stability and fat solubility will follow the same biological magnification (biomagnification) as DDT. The polychlorinated biphenyls (PCBs), a group of chemicals that have no insecticidal properties, are stable and fat soluble and have climbed the food chain just as DDT has. Other insecticides incriminated to some extent in biomagnification, belonging to the organochlorine group, are TDE, DDE (a major

metabolite of DDT), dieldrin, aldrin, several isomers of HCH, endrin, heptachlor, and mirex.

Additionally, consider James R. Allen, Walter A. Hargrave, M. T. Stephen Hsia & Francis S. D. Lin, *Comparative Toxicology of Chlorinated Compounds on Mammalian Species*, in Differential Toxicities of Insecticides and Halogenated Aromatics 469 (F. Matsumura ed., 1984), at 474–75:

2.1. TOXICITY [OF DDT] TO HUMANS

Severe cases of accidental poisoning of humans with massive amounts of DDT have been reported. The main symptoms are extreme muscular weakness, joint pain, extreme nervous tension, anxiety, confusion, inability to concentrate and depression. Other than the incidents of acute poisoning, it appears that DDT is generally not very toxic to man. . . .

* * *

3.1. TOXICITY [OF CYCLODIENE INSECTICIDES] TO HUMANS

The chlorinated cyclodienes can be classified as neurotoxins, and many of the signs and symptoms of poisoning resemble those produced by DDT. Unlike DDT, however, these compounds tend to produce convulsions before other less serious signs of illness have appeared. Persons who have been exposed to cyclodiene insecticides report headaches, nausea, vomiting, dizziness and mild chronic jerking. On the other hand, patients occasionally have convulsions with no previous symptoms. There have been a number of fatalities resulting from acute poisoning by the cyclodiene insecticides.

Finally, consider Fumio Matsumura, Toxicology of Insecticides 496 (2d ed. 1985):

In man, the signs of dieldrin poisoning . . . include headache, nausea, vomiting, dizziness, and general malaise. In severe cases, convulsions are the only symptom observed. A coma may or may not follow a convulsion. Hyperexcitation and irritability are common. However, all these symptoms do not always appear in human poisoning. In some spray operators with repeated exposure, a condition similar to epilepsy has resulted. Laboratory tests have shown the presence of dieldrin in the tissues and urine after poisoning, but this finding is not proof of poisoning, for dieldrin has been found in the blood and urine of spraymen who showed no symptoms. Workers who had convulsions and other signs of poisoning tended to show a high concentration of dieldrin in the blood. . . .

In sum, though it is stating what is now widely accepted as obvious, pesticides and other toxic substances, even in small quantities, are harmful and in many cases life-threatening to all living things, human beings included. While most persistent pesticides are no longer used extensively in the industrial North, why then are they still used (and misused) widely in the developing South?

A principal explanation for the continued use of DDT and other organochlorines in the developing world is the large-scale need to boost agricultural productivity to feed hungry populations. But powerful economic and political influences, aided and abetted by the dubious production and export practices noted by Stoll in the immediately preceding reading are also explanatory. David P. Fidler writes:

> ... Economically, the "export" of pollution or dangerous products is a convenient way for a country and its companies to shift costs onto other governments and peoples. Experts see economic externalities in transboundary pollution, which means that the countries and companies producing the pollution do not internalize all the costs such pollution creates. The policy objective, therefore, becomes getting the polluter to internalize more or all of the cost of pollution. Or, more succinctly, make the polluter pay. The "polluter pays" principle means higher production costs in the country where the pollution originates, which portends higher prices for consumers in that country. This economic dynamic makes it easy to see why transboundary pollution is economically attractive to countries and their companies. . . .

> Politically, a number of issues are pertinent. First, the transboundary polluters are often (but not always) powerful developed states and, therefore, can frustrate international efforts to deal with this international environmental problem. Second, there is the "silent conspiracy" among states engaging in and affected by transboundary pollution. A state may be adversely affected by another state's transboundary pollution, but unwilling to challenge that state because it is also "exporting" its pollution across borders. No state wants to throw what Brownlie called the "normative boomerang" that might return against the thrower.[2] Third, in some situations, tensions between developed and developing countries complicate international cooperation, such as [has] happened with the transboundary trade in hazardous substances.

Challenges to Humanity's Health: The Contributions of International Environmental Law to National and Global Public Health, 31 Envtl. L. Rep. 10048, 10055 (Jan 2001).

Another conspicuous explanation is, simply put, that many if not most developing countries, due to extremely limited governmental funds, lack the official controls, resources, and information that are needed to protect human health and the environment from the adverse effects of pesticides and other toxic substances. In the absence of such costly infrastructure, they have been unable to implement systems to generate and analyze the information needed to assess the relative dangers of a particular pesticide or chemical[3]. It is, indeed, for this reason that, in 1985, the United Nations Food and Agriculture Organization (FAO) adopted its International Code of Conduct on the Distribution and Use of Pesticides **(Basic Document 5.24)** and that, in 1989, the

2. *See* I. Brownlie, *State Responsibility and International Pollution: A Practical Perspective*, in International Law and Pollution 120, 123 (D.B. McGraw ed., 1991).

3. Experience with the 1985 FAO International Code of Conduct on the Distribution and Use of Pesticides **(Basic Document 5.24)** is a case in point. In response to a questionnaire distributed by the FAO in 1988 pursuant to Code Article 12 (which requires governments to "monitor the observance of the Code and report on progress made to the Director–Gen-

eral of [the] FAO"), many countries indicated that they were not observing the Code. *See* Charlotte Uram, *International Regulation of the Sale and Use of Pesticides*, 10 Nw. J. Int'l L. & Bus. 460, 470 (1990). The author writes, at 471, that of the 73 percent responding to the questionnaire (*i.e.*, 115 countries), "84 developing countries stated that they did not have adequate governmental resources to control pesticides and comply fully with the Code [with] Africa [having] the greatest number of countries with difficulty observing the Code."

Governing Council of the United Nations Environment Programme (UNEP) adopted its London Guidelines for the Exchange of Information on Chemicals in International Trade **(Basic Document 5.32)**. Each in their own way, emphasizing what today is called "the principle of prior informed consent" or "PIC," constituted important steps in the development of international environmental "right-to-know" law, now enshrined, with an assist from Principle 10 of the 1991 Rio Declaration on Environment and Development **(Basic Document 5.37)**, in the 1998 Rotterdam Convention on the Prior Informed Consent Procedure for Certain Hazardous Chemicals and Pesticides in International Trade **(Basic Document 5.49)**, also known as the "PIC" Convention.

3. **FAO International Code of Conduct on the Distribution and Use of Pesticides (as amended in 1989). Adopted, 28 Nov 1985. 23 FAO Conf. Res. 10/85;** *reprinted in* **5 Weston & Carlson V.H.17: Arts. 1–3, 5–10** (Basic Document 5.24).

4. **Editors' Note.** Originally promulgated in 1985, the Food and Agricultural Organization's International Code of Conduct on the Distribution and Use of Pesticides **(Basic Document 5.24)** is intended to establish standards of conduct applicable to both governments and industry governing the management of pesticides. With a small budget dedicated to implementation of the Guidelines, the FAO proactively convenes an "expert group" which meets on an ad hoc basis to review and encourage implementation of various aspects of the Code.[4] In 1989, in addition, a voluntary prior informed consent procedure was added to the Code, giving importing countries the opportunity to be notified of, and to refuse the importation of, chemicals banned or severely restricted in other countries. In 1998 the FAO began the process of revising the Code. This was seen as a necessary response to the changing nature of global pesticide usage. Also, the Rotterdam Convention, **(Basic Document 5.49)]** adopted in 1998 (*see infra* Readings 7 and 8) had included a mechanism to implement prior informed consent rendering the FAO Code's overlapping provisions anachronistic. In November 2002, the Hundred and Twenty-third session of the FAO Council approved the revised version of the Code. Despite the removal of its regime to implement the prior informed consent rules, the Code continues to provide guidelines to reduce the environmental and health risks of pesticides through proscribing standards for management, testing, labeling, advertising, distribution and information exchange.

5. **UNEP Governing Council Decision on London Guidelines for the Exchange of Information on Chemicals in International Trade. Adopted by the Environment Programme Governing Council, 25 May 1989. UN Doc. UNEP/PIC.WG2/4, at 9 (1989);** *reprinted in* **5 Weston & Carlson V.I.24: Guidelines 1–3, 13** (Basic Document 5.32).

6. **Jane A. Dwasi, Regulation of Pesticides in Developing Countries, 32 Envtl. L. Rep. 10045, 10056–57 (Jan 2002).**

. . . The London Guidelines [for the Exchange of Information on Chemicals in International Trade **(Basic Document 5.32)**, adopted by the Govern-

---

4. Email message from Barbara Dinham, Director, Pesticide Action Network UK (14 Jul 2005) (on file with the editors). For further information, see the Pesticide Action Network UK website at <http://www.pan-uk.org>.

ing Council of the UN Environment Programme (UNEP) in 1989,] are addressed to governments and are intended to assist countries in the process of increasing chemical safety through the exchange of information and through a PIC procedure for pesticides in international trade.[5] Information exchange basically involves submission of information by states regarding any actions taken by their governments to ban or restrict pesticides to the International Register of Potentially Toxic Chemicals, which is managed under the London Guidelines. Along with this information, participating countries are required to indicate whether or not they wish to receive any imports of the chemicals they have banned or severely restricted. If imports of the chemicals are allowed on specified conditions, this must be stated [pt. II, ¶ 7.2(a)]. This information would then be transmitted by UNEP to other countries that have adopted the London Guidelines, along with an alert list of chemicals that 10 or more countries have banned or severely restricted and a technical guidance document comprising UNEP's recommendations regarding those chemicals. It was hoped that this would give countries information and a basis on which to make their own assessment of risks associated with the banned or severely restricted chemicals and to transmit information regarding the status of other countries with regard to these chemicals to their industry. They would also be able to make timely and informed decisions on the chemicals, taking their local circumstances into consideration [pt. II, ¶ 6]. One notable aspect of the information exchange system under the London Guidelines is that it allows countries to participate in information exchange without similarly participating in the London Guidelines' PIC procedure [pt. II, ¶ 7.1(a)].

The PIC procedure established by the London Guidelines was founded on the principle that an export of a chemical that is banned or severely restricted because of human health or environmental concerns should not proceed without formal agreement of the importing country where such agreement exists, or contrary to the decision of a relevant authority in the importing country. The London Guidelines required that exporting countries send information to importing countries that an export will occur, or is occurring. Further, the London Guidelines recommended that this information be sent to importers when the first export following control action occurs [pt. II, ¶ 8]. If an importing country fails to declare its decision of a particular chemical, the status quo regarding its importation continues.

Although the London Guidelines would have had a bearing on some of the problems associated with exports of banned pesticides to developing countries, they fail to effectively address these problems for a variety of reasons. First, the London Guidelines were purely guidelines that countries have the option to adopt or to participate in the procedures they recommended. Voluntary participation of countries would not, and has not, ensured any protection of the kind necessary for health and the environment resulting from exports of banned, never-registered, severely restricted, and obsolete pesticides. Moreover, the London Guidelines were only intended to operate at the internation-

---

5. According to the Director of the Pesticide Action Network UK, *supra* note **4**, UNEP does not have a process for regular review or implementation paralleling the FAO's in relation to its 1985 Code of Conduct, thus causing the London Guidelines to "stand alone as guid- ance." For a proactive implementation process to be instituted, she reports, "it would need to be requested at a Governing Council meeting of UNEP, which takes place every second year."

al trade level and were never intended to address situations of risk in specific countries. In addition, introductions to the London Guidelines explicitly acknowledge that the London Guidelines were not prepared specifically to address the situation of developing countries. Further, a country has to be participating in the London Guidelines to receive important information such as those regarding intended exports of banned pesticides. . . . It was these weaknesses that created the need to come up with a binding international instrument to regulate international trade in chemicals, which the Rotterdam Convention [on the Prior Informed Consent Procedure for Certain Hazardous Chemicals and Pesticides in International Trade **(Basic Document 5.49)**] attempts to accomplish.

7. Convention on the Prior Informed Consent Procedure for Certain Hazardous Chemicals and Pesticides in International Trade. Concluded, 10 Sep 1998. Entered into force, 24 Feb 2004. UN Doc. UNEP/FAO/PIC/ CONF/2; *reprinted in* **38 I.L.M. 1 (1999) and 5 Weston & Carlson V.G.5: Arts. 1–3, 6–15** (Basic Document 5.49).

8. Paula Barrios, "The Rotterdam Convention on Hazardous Chemicals: A Meaningful Step Toward Environmental Protection?", 16 Geo. Int'l Envtl. L. Rev. 679, 716–19, 725–27, 742 (2004).

Not long after the [voluntary] PIC [Prior Informed Consent] procedure was introduced into the [1985 FAO] Code of Conduct **[Basic Document 5.24]** and the [1989] London Guidelines **[Basic Document 5.32]**, developing countries, some European states (notably Belgium and the Netherlands), the EC and public interest groups started to claim that a binding PIC procedure would be more effective * * * The formal decision to negotiate a convention was made by the FAO Council at its 107th meeting in 1994 * * * [I]n March 1998, ninety-five governments finalized the text of the Rotterdam Convention on the Prior Informed Consent Procedure for Certain Hazardous Chemicals and Pesticides in International Trade.

* * *

3.   The Rotterdam Convention

i.   *Information Exchange, Export Notification and PIC Procedure*

Like the London Guidelines and the Code of conduct, the Rotterdam Convention covers three types of procedures: (1) information exchange; (2) export notification of domestically banned or severely restricted chemicals not subject to PIC; and (3) prior informed consent for [certain specified] chemicals [which are listed in an addendum identified as] Annex III.

Information exchange requires each party to notify the Secretariat in writing on each ban or severe restriction on a chemical it adopts. The chemical could potentially be included in Annex III and thus be subject to the PIC procedure, providing some requirements—moderately stricter than those of the voluntary system—are met. Export notification, in turn, requires a party that plans to export a banned or severely restricted chemical for use within its territory to inform the importing party of such export before the first shipment and annually thereafter. This obligation ceases if the chemical is listed in Annex III, since it is then covered by the PIC procedure. As in the voluntary system, the exporting party must also provide an updated export notification if it has adopted a final regulatory action that has resulted in a major change of the ban or severe restriction of the chemical being exported.

... Once a decision has been made to include a chemical in Annex III, [the PIC procedure requires that] a decision guidance document (DGD) with all the relevant information must be sent by the Secretariat to all parties so that they can decide whether to import the chemical in the future. No later than nine months after the date of dispatch of the DGD, Parties must inform the Secretariat whether or not they will receive future imports of the chemical. A decision could consist of consent, no consent or consent to import under certain conditions, or contain an interim response. In all cases, the decision must be "trade neutral." This means that if a party decides to refuse an import or consents to an import under certain conditions, the same restrictions must apply to imports of that chemical from any source and to domestic production. Exporting parties must take appropriate legislative or administrative measures to ensure that exporters within their jurisdiction comply with the decisions of importing parties in relation to PIC decisions. According to Article 11(2), exporting parties must also ensure that, in the absence of a response by an importing party, no export takes place....

Article 11(2) seems to establish the rule that no export should take place unless expressly agreed upon by the importing country, and a narrow exemption that an export without such consent can occur under three exceptional circumstances. In practice, however, Article 11(2), referred to as the "status quo" clause, guarantees that trade in hazardous chemicals will continue unless the importing country impedes it through effective participation in the PIC procedure. This is because the three exceptional circumstances contemplated by the rule are very broad, placing the burden of preventing an export on the importing country. To prevent an export, the importing country must give a negative response on the import of the substance through the PIC system. This requirement presumes that the importing country has, among other things, the technical capacity, sufficient qualified staff, and adequate laboratories to establish a basis for its negative response. In order to give that response, the country must be able to analyze the data received to study the possible effects of the substance under its own environmental conditions, and to consider viable and affordable alternatives. Perhaps more importantly, the country must make sure that its response, whether provisional or final, is consistent with the rules of international trade. Thus, in order to ensure that its decision will not be challenged in international trade tribunals because it contradicts, for instance, the principle of nondiscrimination, the importing country must disclose whether it is currently importing the chemical, the history of imports from different sources, and whether there is local production of the chemical. Since many countries lack the capacity to fulfill these requirements, they might prefer to give an interim response which allows the import of the chemical, or to register no decision at all, as evidenced by the high occurrences of failures to respond.

* * *

4. Will a Binding PIC Make a Difference?

Even by its own standards, one can say that the Rotterdam Convention fails to respond to its objective. This is not because the treaty is limited to PIC, which is in itself unfortunate, as the treaty could have dealt with needed provisions on chemical management, but because it does not address any of the elements upon which a successful PIC depends, namely: (1) capacity building of developing countries to effectively implement the procedure; (2) provisions to facilitate the promotion of alternatives so that countries can actually reject an import; and (3) trade with non-Parties to ensure participation of all relevant countries. All these factors point to the conclusion that the transformation of the voluntary PIC procedure into a binding system will be of little consequence. This is because an instrument that makes a procedure binding without providing the means for all parties to implement it; alternatives to importing countries so that they actually refuse imports; and measures to promote participation of all relevant countries, is virtually meaningless.

9.   Editors' Note. What are hazardous wastes and how and in what ways do such wastes, pesticides, and other toxic substances give rise to long-term and potentially widespread environmental risks? Responding to the first part of this question, Fred L. Morrison & Wm. Carroll Muffett write as follows in *Hazardous Wastes*, in International, Regional and National Environmental Law 409 (F. Morrison & R. Rüdiger eds., 2000):

> The term "hazardous waste" evokes images of inadequately stored, toxin-filled drums leaking into the earth, polluting the water supply, and endangering the lives and genetic constitution of thousands of people. There have been well-publicized instances of such harm. But the concept of "hazardous waste" is much broader. Applying the precautionary principle includes a wide array of items that "might be" hazardous, or are so only when the aggregate of human activity is considered. Thus, all medical waste is hazardous waste by definition. Even simple bandages fall within its scope, because some might carry infection. All batteries are also hazardous because, in the aggregate, the acid and metal they contain pose a threat to human health and the environment.

Responding to the second, more complex part of the question, Itzchak E. Kornfeld, in *Groundwater and Hazardous Waste Landfills Do Not Mix*, 5 Tulane Envtl. L. J. 557 (1992), observes, at 568–69, that a partial answer is found in the physical environment in which they are placed:

> The "[l]and disposal of liquids and highly mobile or persistent hazardous wastes can present significant long-term risks to ground and surface water because, eventually, the wastes or their constituents will leak or leach from the disposal unit."[6] Additionally, in any situation where a landfill is involved, a major concern of both the surrounding community and the regulating agencies is whether the nature of the geological environment underlying the site is composed of unconsolidated or consolidated soils, bedrock, sandstone, or shales. This concern is founded on the type of geological environment underlying the landfill, as the site's geology dictates the physical and chemical variables involved.
>
> Two major physical variables are the porosity and permeability of the rocks underlying the facility. Porosity refers to the percentage of voids verses the solid part of a rock. . . . Primary porosity is formed at the time

---

6. W. Rosbe & R. Gulley, *The Hazardous and Solid Waste Amendments of 1984: A Dramatic Overhaul of the Way America Manages Its Hazardous Waste*, 14 Envtl. L. Rep. (Envtl. L. Inst.) 10,458, 10,460 (Dec 1984).

of deposition or formation of the rock. Where the particles are of uniform size, the porosity will be greater than where the particles are of varying sizes. Secondary porosity is formed after the deposition or formation of the rock. This type of porosity is usually an enhancer of primary porosity and manifests itself as fractures, caverns, or caves. Permeability, on the other hand, refers to the ability of a rock to transmit fluids.

A further environmental response to the second part of the question is provided in Bernard I. Logan, *An Assessment of the Environmental and Economic Implications of Toxic–Waste Disposal in Sub–Saharan Africa*, 25 J. World Trade 61, 65 (1991):

> It is well known that the dangers of landfilling, reported to be the prevalent practice in legal dumping in Africa, are most serious in areas of heavy rainfall, because of the potential for contaminating ground and surface water systems. Given this concern, it is doubtful whether any region in sub-Saharan Africa is suitable for landfilling, or represents what has been referred to as a Best Practicable Environmental Option or BPEO.[7] ...
>
> The relationship between the human and environmental dimensions of toxic-waste dumping as they relate to precipitation, geology, drainage patterns and population distribution, are further complicated by two additional factors in sub-Saharan Africa: (i) the status of water-resource management, namely that much of the population of the region derives its water from untreated natural sources; (ii) the heavy reliance of African societies on natural products, which increases their vulnerability to even slight toxicity-induced disequilibria in the food chain....

Of course, not to be overlooked is the human element. Observes J. Wylie Donald, Note, *The Bamako Convention as a Solution to the Problem of Hazardous Waste Exports to Less Developed Countries*, 17 Colum. J. Envtl. L. 419 (1992), at 422–24:

> Improper storage, treatment, or disposal of hazardous wastes can lead to serious human health effects. These effects can be particularly severe in LDCs [Less Developed Countries] that are incapable of dealing with hazardous wastes in an environmentally sound manner. Dumpsites can be hazardous to the public through fire or explosion. Solvents leaking from dumps can contaminate groundwater supplies. Disease and infection can spread from hospital waste, fecal material, and rotting garbage. Many hazardous materials are carcinogens.... Workers, as well as people scavenging at dumpsites, can expose themselves and their families to these poisons. People living next to the dump site or whose water supply is contaminated by the waste are likely to be injured. Crops planted on these poisoned lands are likely to fail. * * * [Also,] [t]he improper disposal of hazardous wastes can ... cause substantial changes in the local environment. Careless disposal of persistent chemicals can contaminate the food chain, threatening both sensitive species and human health. Leachates and sewage sludges can cause massive fish kills or oxygen depletion in marine environments....

7. British Institute of Water and Environmental Management, *Evidence to the Environment Committee of the House of Commons on* *Their Inquiry into Toxic Wastes*, 2 J. Inst. of Water and Envtl. Mgmt. 350 (1988).

And in all these and related respects, poverty—or perhaps more precisely, the culture of poverty—must be accounted for, especially in the Global South. Writes C. Russell H. Shearer, *Comparative Analysis of the Basel and Bamako Conventions on Hazardous Waste*, 23 Envtl. L. 141 (1993), 146–47:

> The developing nations have several problems in managing waste. First, the forces of nature conspire to thwart environmentally sound management. For example, in the tropics' heavy rains, wastes leach into the soil under landfills, causing the contamination of water supplies. Second, landfills are usually located near the residences of the poorest people. In fact, the poorest neighborhoods may be located in waste disposal sites. . . . Third, developing nations often do not have competent administrative agencies or administrators to regulate waste disposal. Finally, developing nations are attractive disposal sites because of their need for capital, even though they lack environmentally sound disposal sites and adequate land-use planning strategies.

> The developing nations face additional problems which are not solely their province. Improper waste disposal poses a grave danger even for wastes which are relatively harmless or easy to manage. During the 1950s and 1960s, residents of Minamata and Niigata, Japan, suffered neurological diseases resulting from the consumption of fish which had been contaminated by the discharge of mercury into the ocean. Of those poisoned by the mercury, 400 died. Ground wells throughout the world have been contaminated by leaks from waste storage facilities. Improper disposal of waste has resulted in mass evacuations and relocations, most notably at Love Canal in the United States and Lekkerkerk in the Netherlands. Transboundary waste movements have also resulted in nomadic waste barges that are not welcome in their state of origin, destination, or any other state.

The ultimate legal question is, of course, who should be held responsible for pesticides and other toxic substances becoming long-term and widespread environmental risks, and on what grounds. The question is not a little troublesome when it comes to states that do not, as in the instant controversy between Yoribo and Bamileo, share coextensively in the conventional environmental law that has grown exponentially in the last quarter century.

10. Stockholm Declaration of the United Nations Conference on the Human Environment, adopted by the UN Conference on the Human Environment at Stockholm, 16 Jun 1972. Report of the UN Conference on the Human Environment, UN Doc. A/CONF.48/14/ Rev.1 at 3 (1973), UN Doc. A/CONF.48/14 at 2–65, and Corr. 1 (1972); *reprinted in* 11 I.L.M. 1416 (1972) and 5 Weston & Carlson V.B.3: Pmbl. & Princs. 2, 6, 7, 21 (Basic Document 5.14).

11. Charter of Economic Rights and Duties of States. Adopted, 12 Dec 1974. GA Res. 3281, 29th Sess., Supp. No. 31, at 50, UN Doc. A/9631 (1975); *reprinted in* 14 I.L.M. 251 (1975) and 4 Weston & Carlson IV.F.5: Art. 30 (Basic Document 4.9).

12. World Charter for Nature. Adopted, 28 Oct 1982. GA Res. 37/7, UN GAOR, 37th Sess., Supp. No. 51, at 17, UN Doc. A/37/51; *reprinted in* 22 I.L.M. 455 (1983) and 5 Weston & Carlson V.B.11: Princs. 1–5, 11, 12, 20, 21, 24 (Basic Document 5.21).

13.   Experts Group on Environmental Law of the World Commission on Environment and Development, Legal Principles for Environmental Protection and Sustainable Development. Adopted, 18–20 Jun 1986. UN Doc. WCED/86/23/Add.1 (1986); *reprinted in* **5 Weston & Carlson V.B.12: Arts. 1 & 21** (Basic Document 5.25).

14.   Rio Declaration on Environment and Development. Adopted, 13 Jun 1992, UNCED Doc. A/CONF.151/5/Rev. 1; *reprinted in* **31 I.L.M. 874 (1992) and 5 Weston & Carlson V.B.16: Princs. 1, 2–5, 7, 14, 15, 18, 19** (Basic Document 5.37).

15.   Editors' Note. *See supra* Reading 19 (Editors' Note) in Problem 7–2 ("Hanguo Versus the Ozone Layer"), at 1122. *See supra also* Readings 1 (Bourne) and 2 (Editors' Note) in Problem 7–4 ("The Sindhu River in Punjamir and Rajatan"), at 1165 and 1167.

16.   Berlin Rules on Water Resources (Revision of the Helsinki Rules and other International Law Association Rules on Water Resources), ILA Report of the Berlin Conference, 21 Aug 2004, 71 I.L.A. 337; *reprinted in* **5 Weston & Carlson V.F.39: Arts. 1–3; 7–13; 16; 20–23; 26–33; 68** (Basic Document 5.56).

17.   Editors' Note. *See supra* Reading 4 (Editors' Note) in Problem 7–4 ("The Sindhu River in Punjamir and Rajatan"), at 1169.

18.   Convention on the Law of the Non-navigational Uses of International Watercourses. Concluded, 21 May 1997. Not yet in force. UN Doc. A/51/869; *reprinted in* **36 I.L.M. 700 (1997) and 5 Weston & Carlson V.F.37: Arts. 1–36** (Basic Document 5.46).

19.   Editors' Note. *See supra* Readings 7 (McCaffrey & Sinjela), 10 (Sievers), and 22 (Upadhye) in Problem 7–4 ("The Sindhu River in Punjamir and Rajatan"), at 1173, 1177, and 1187.

20.   UNEP Governing Council Decision on Cairo Guidelines and Principles for the Environmentally Sound Management of Hazardous Wastes. Adopted, 17 Jun 1987. UNEP/GC.14/17 (Annex II), UNEP/GC/DCE/14/30, UNEP ELPG No 8; *reprinted in* **5A Weston V.I.10: Guidelines 2, 4, 5, 7, 9, 12–14, 17, 19, 22, 28** (Basic Document 5.28).

21.   Experts Group on Environmental Law of the World Commission on Environment and Development, Legal Principles for Environmental Protection and Sustainable Development. Adopted, 18–20 Jun 1986. UN Doc. WCED/86/23/Add.1 (1986); *reprinted in* **5 Weston & Carlson: Arts. 1–12, 14–19, 21** (Basic Document 5.25).

22.   Basel Convention on the Control of Transboundary Movements of Hazardous Wastes and Their Disposal. Concluded, 22 Mar 1989. Entered into force, 5 May 1992. 1673 U.N.T.S 57; *reprinted in* **28 I.L.M. 657 (1989) and 5 Weston & Carlson V.I.11: Pmbl. & Arts. 1–4, 9, 10, 13, 18, 20** (Basic Document 5.30).

23.   Jane A. Dwasi, Regulation of Pesticides in Developing Countries, 32 Envtl. L. Rep. 10045, 10057 (Jan 2002).

The Basel Convention [on the Control of Transboundary Movements of Hazardous Wastes and Their Disposal **(Basic Document 5.30)**] is another international effort to protect health and the environment from harm resulting from hazardous wastes, which properly should include some pesticides. It is a global agreement ... intended to address problems and challenges posed by hazardous wastes at the international level. In the late 1980s, a tightening of environmental regulations in industrialized countries led to a dramatic rise in the cost of hazardous waste disposal. Searching for cheaper ways to get rid of the wastes, developed world industries and traders in toxic wastes began shipping hazardous wastes to developing countries and to Eastern Europe. When this activity was revealed, international outrage led to the convening of a diplomatic conference in Geneva, Switzerland, and the drafting and adoption of the Basel Convention under the auspices of UNEP.

The Basel Convention attempts to create some measure of control of international trade in hazardous wastes. It does so by obliging its members, *inter alia*: to notify the Basel Convention Secretariat of any action to prohibit the importation of hazardous wastes; to prohibit the export of hazardous wastes to parties that have prohibited the import of such wastes; to reduce the generation of hazardous wastes as much as possible; to ensure availability of adequate disposal facilities; to adopt environmentally sound management of hazardous wastes; and to consider that transboundary movement of hazardous wastes contrary to the Basel Convention is illegal and criminal [art. 4(1)–(3)].

Reports and studies indicate that hazardous wastes, whose exports to developing countries created international outrage, include banned and expired pesticides shipped to unsuspecting developing countries. Therefore, the Basel Convention would have been expected to address exports of banned, restricted, and expired pesticides to developing countries as part of hazardous wastes. The Basel Convention does include pesticides, but not pesticides *per se*, and not banned, restricted, or expired pesticides as such. What it includes in its definition of hazardous wastes in relation to pesticides would be only pesticide wastes, that is, wastes accruing in the pesticide production process.[8] Even this inclusion does not make the matter so simple because for such substances to be regarded as hazardous wastes, they must also not be intended for some use in the importing country. They must be intended or required to be disposed of.[9] Therefore, pesticides intended for use in a developing country would not be regarded under the Basel Convention as hazardous wastes, even if the export to a developing country was intended to rid manufacturers in the country of origin of banned or obsolete pesticide stocks.

The Basel Convention allows ratifying countries to apply legislation to classify or define other wastes that are not included as hazardous wastes [art. 1(1)(b)]. However, any such classifications must conform to the Basel Convention's definition of "waste" in order to be brought under its regulatory scheme. Therefore, if, for instance, [a country] considered exports of banned pesticides to its territory illegal, it would, nevertheless, not be permitted to regard such pesticides as hazardous wastes under the Basel Convention unless

---

8. "Hazardous wastes" are, first, wastes that fall under categories contained in Annex I to the Basel Convention. *See* Basel Convention, art. 1. In Annex I, wastes from the product ion, formulation, and use of biocides may be hazardous wastes.

9. "Wastes" are defined under Article 2 as substances of objects that are disposed of, are intended to be disposed of, or are required to be disposed of by the provisions of national law.

it could show that exports of such pesticides to its territory were intended for disposal.

The conclusion one would rightly draw from the Basel Convention's regulatory mechanisms is that it was not intended to deal with pesticide problems affecting developing countries.... Therefore, developing countries ... which [are] not [parties] to the Basel Convention and [do] not participate in its regulatory procedures, are not missing any benefits of measures created under the Basel Convention. Even if [they are parties] and banned or restricted pesticides were classified as hazardous wastes, the country's government would still be obliged to create effective pesticide laws within which Basel Convention procedures could be implemented.

24. Bamako Convention on the Ban of Import into Africa and the Control of Transboundary Movement and Management of Hazardous Wastes within Africa. Concluded, 30 Jan 1991. Entered in to force, 22 Apr 1998. 30 I.L.M. 773 (1991), 31 I.L.M. 164 (1992); *reprinted in* **5 Weston & Carlson V.I.14: Pmbl. & Arts. 1–6, 8, 10, 13, 20** (Basic Document 5.34).

25. Jane A. Dwasi, Regulation of Pesticides in Developing Countries, 32 Envtl. L. Rep. 10045, 10057–58 (Jan 2002).

The Bamako Convention [on the Ban of Import into Africa and the Control of Transboundary Movement and Management of Hazardous Wastes within Africa **(Basic Document 5.34)**] was created by African states as a result of their displeasure with the permissive structure of the Basel Convention.... [T]he Basel Convention had been intended to control movement of hazardous wastes to developing countries but failed to address the problem effectively....

The objective of the Bamako Convention is first and foremost to ban the importation of hazardous wastes into their territories [art. 4]. The Bamako Convention obliges African countries that are parties to it to take legal, administrative, and other measures within their areas of jurisdiction to prohibit the import of all hazardous wastes into Africa [*Id.*]. Any such imports are deemed illegal and the acts involved criminal [*Id.*] If such imports occur or if importation of hazardous wastes is carried out pursuant to consent, but the disposal of imported hazardous wastes cannot be conducted under the terms of any agreement or in an environmentally safe manner, the Bamako Convention requires that the imports be exported back to the country of origin [art. 8].

Unlike the Basel Convention, the Bamako Convention attempts to specifically regulate international trade in pesticides. It does so by banning the importation of "hazardous substances which have been banned, canceled, or refused registration by governmental regulatory action, or voluntarily withdrawn from registration in the country of manufacture for human health or environmental reasons" [art. 2(d)]. Under the Bamako Convention, such substances are considered hazardous wastes, regardless of their intended uses in the importing country. Further, the Bamako Convention contains a classification of other wastes that are considered hazardous. These include wastes from the production, formulation, and use of biocides. Wastes that are none of these but are defined as or considered to be hazardous wastes by the domestic

legislation of the party exporting, importing, or country of transit are also hazardous wastes [art. 2(b)].

The mechanisms for exercising the ban on importation of banned and unregistered pesticides include an information exchange procedure whereby Members are obliged to inform the Bamako Secretariat of any import of hazardous wastes. The Secretariat, in turn, informs the rest of the African governments in order for them to consider appropriate measures to deal with it [art. 4(1)(a) & (b)]. Parties are to ensure that those involved in the management of hazardous wastes, in this case, pesticides, take necessary steps to prevent pollution.

One of the steps suggested as a measure to prevent importation of banned and nonregistered pesticides and to manage the transboundary movement of hazardous wastes is the establishment of competent authorities in Member countries. The authorities are to act as focal points for information exchange between the Bamako Secretariat and Member countries [art. 5]. These offices must notify the Secretariat of any movement of hazardous wastes [art. 6]. Each African country that has ratified the Bamako Convention has also been required to establish a dump watch and to inform the Secretariat and Member governments of any occurrence of hazardous waste dumping [*Id.*].

The Bamako Convention ... has been lauded for taking the first bold step to regulate international trade in pesticides and other hazardous wastes.[10] It is important that the Bamako Convention recognizes that the most effective way of protecting human health and the environment from dangers posed by hazardous wastes is the reduction of their generation to a minimum in terms of quantity and hazard potential [pmbl.]. However, without going into the various areas for which the regulatory mechanisms of the Bamako Convention would not efficiently deal with the problems associated with the importation of banned, restricted, and unregistered pesticides, it is crucial [to understand that the Convention's enforcement] has been largely left to parties [to it] who agree to enforce it through their national legal systems [arts. 4.1 & 4.2]. Thus, even if [a country] had ratified the Bamako Convention, it would still be required to create effective domestic regulatory mechanisms for pesticides.

26. Stockholm Convention on Persistent Organic Pollutants. Concluded, 22 May 2001. Entered into force, 17 May 2001. UN Doc. UNEP/POPS/CONF/2; *reprinted in* **40 I.L.M. 278 (2001) and 5 Weston & Carlson V.I.14c: Pmbl. & Arts. 1–3, 6–12** (Basic Document 5.55).

27. Editor's Note. Persistent organic pollutants or "POPs" are chemical substances that persist in the environment, bioaccumulate through the food web, and pose a risk of causing adverse effects to human health and the environment. Those of greatest current concern are polychlorinated biphenyls (PCBs), dioxins, furans, aldrin, dieldrin, dichlorodiphenyltrichloroethane (DDT), endrin, chlordane, hexaclorobenzene, mirex, toxaphene, and heptachlor. There is evidence that these substances travel long distances from their

---

10. It has been rightly suggested that the Bamako Convention finds legal justification for its bold step in the precautionary principle, a principle of international law that favors preventive regulatory action for environmental protection even in the absence of conclusive scientific proof that a given substance of activity harms the environment. *See* Margo Brett Baender, *Pesticides and Precaution: The Bamako Convention as a Model for an International Convention on Pesticides Regulation*, 24 N.Y.U. J. Int'l L. & Pol'y 578 (1991).

sources of emission, including to regions where they never have been produced or used. The 2001 Stockholm Convention on Persistent Organic Pollutants **(Basic Document 5.55)**, attentive to the precautionary principle set
forth as Principle 15 of the 1992 Rio Declaration on Environment and
Development **(Basic Document 5.37)**, provides for measures and mechanisms that are hoped will reduce the emission and discharge of POPs and,
where appropriate, eliminate their production and remaining uses. Thus,
Articles 3 and 4 (in alliance with Annexes A and B) contain obligations
relating to the restriction and elimination of intentionally produced and used
POPs; Article 5 (in alliance with Annex C) contains obligations designed to
reduce or eliminate, according to the "best available techniques," unintentionally produced by-product POPs from anthropogenic sources; and Article 6
(in alliance with Annexes A, B and C) contains obligations relating to
stockpiles and wastes, with the goal being to ensure sound management of
stockpiles and wastes, and of products and articles upon becoming waste, that
consist of, contain, or are contaminated by POPs. In short, the POPs Convention provides for different approaches to different categories of POPs, including allowable exemptions relating to particular chemicals listed in the annexes
and trade between parties and non-parties. It also provides for the adoption of
transition periods in which proposed action on the POPs is to be implemented, careful management of existing stocks of POPs, elimination of POPs
where possible, and training to enforce and monitor their use. For pesticides,
governments are asked to take action to phase out their production and use of
POPs and to destroy their existing obsolete stocks.

**28.   Basel Protocol on Liability and Compensation for Damage
Resulting from Transboundary Movements of Hazardous Wastes and
Their Disposal. Concluded, 10 Dec 1999. Not yet in force. UN Doc
UNEP–CHW.1–WG–1–9–2;** *reprinted in* **5 Weston & Carlson V.J.16:
Arts. 1–6, 9, 12** (Basic Document 5.52).

29.   Editors' Note. The objective of the Protocol on Liability and
Compensation for Damage Resulting from the Transboundary Movement of
Hazardous Wastes and their Disposal **(Basic Document 5.52)** is to provide
for a comprehensive regime for liability as well as adequate and prompt
compensation for damage resulting from the transboundary movement of
hazardous wastes and other wastes, including incidents occurring because of
illegal traffic in those wastes. According to Klaus Toepfer, Executive Director
of UNEP, "the adoption of the Protocol is a major breakthrough," because
"[f]or the first time, we have a mechanism for assigning responsibility for
damage caused by accidental spills of hazardous waste during export
or import." *See* UNEP News Release: Compensation And Liability
Protocol   Adopted   By   Basel   Convention   On   Hazardous   Wastes,
at   <http://www.unep.org/Documents.Multilingual/Default.asp?DocumentID=
134&ArticleID=2086&l=en>. Fred L. Morrison and Wm. Carroll Muffett
elaborate:

> The protocol uses both strict liability and fault-based liability models.
> The person or firm who filed the notification of hazardous waste trans-
> portation is strictly liable until the material is handed over to the
> ultimate disposer [art. 4, ¶ 1]. Then the disposer is strictly liable [*Id.*].
> This strict liability, which is joint and several [art. 4, ¶ 6], is subject to
> limited exceptions [art. 4, ¶ 5; art. 9]. Domestic law can limit liability,

subject to minimum values set forth in the protocol [art. 12 and Annex B]. Fault-based liability can be based on "wrongful intentional, reckless or negligent acts or omissions" [art. 5]. If, however, fault can be shown, there is no limit on liability.[11]

Hazardous Wastes, in International, Regional and National Environmental Law 409, 427–28 (F. Morrison & R. Rüdiger eds., 2000).

After noting that litigation to establish liability under the Basel Convention is conducted in ordinary domestic courts, Morrison and Muffett go on to discuss liability for damages under the Bamako Convention on the Ban of Import into Africa and the Control of Transboundary Movement and Management of Hazardous Wastes within Africa **(Basic Document 5.34)** which, though awaiting at this writing a substantive protocol on the issue of liability and compensation called for in its Article 12, provides "a rudimentary liability scheme." Morrison and Muffett write:

> Article 4 of the Convention, which sets out the general obligations of the Parties, mandates that each party must enact national legislation imposing liability on hazardous waste generators. The Bamako approach is absolutist; requiring strict and unlimited, joint and several liability. Thus, each generator of hazardous waste whose waste, during transport, recycling or disposal causes harm to persons, private property or the environment is potentially liable for the entire cost of that harm, regardless of whether the generator acted in accordance with applicable law or with other standards of care. Because the Bamako Convention bans the import of toxic waste into Africa, this liability regime should attach only to illegal shipments and to legal intra-Africa flows of waste.

Id. at 428.

SECTION 5.   DISCUSSION NOTES/QUESTIONS

1.   As noted in John M. Johnson & George W. Ware, Pesticide Litigation Manual 1–1 (1992):

> Historians have traced the use of pesticides to the time of Homer around 1000 B.C. By 900 A.D., the Chinese were using arsenic as an insecticide in their gardens. The chemistry at their disposal was certainly more primitive, but they faced precisely the same challenge which confronts pesticide makers today: the development of substances that would kill unwanted insects, weeds, plant diseases, and other pests without harming desired plants, beneficial insects, wildlife, and, most importantly, humans.

Why has it taken so long to regulate the use of pesticides harmful to the desired natural environment? Has the international community made significant progress in this regard since the days of Homer and the ancient Chinese? Marginal progress? What more, if anything, needs to be done?

2.   In Reading 1, *supra*, the author refers to "the major accidents in Seveso, Bhopal and Basel." For a detailed discussion, see Ved P. Nanda & Bruce C. Bailey, Nature and Scope of the Problem, in Transferring Hazardous Technologies and Substances: The International Legal Challenge 3 (G. Handl & R. Lutz eds., 1989). *See also* V. Nanda & B. Bailey, *Challenges for International Environmental Law—*

---

11. The limits of liability established by Article 12 only apply to the strict liability created by Article 4, and not the fault-based liability recognized by Article 5. . . .

Seveso, Bhopal, Chernobyl, the Rhine and Beyond, 21 Law–Technology 1 (1988); Ved P. Nanda & Bruce C. Bailey, *Export of Hazardous Waste and Hazardous Technology: Challenge for International Environmental Law*, 21 Land Use & Environment Law 657 (1990).

3.   The hazards caused by a number of chemicals become evident many years after their development. The lead time before the dangers of DDT was revealed was considerable. For many years before its use was banned in the United States, DDT was a highly recommended agricultural pesticide. How should emerging international environmental law deal with such situations? Are states liable for the harms caused by activities that were thought to be safe at the time? Should they be? What are the arguments for making states retroactively liable for activities that were not known to be harmful at the time they occurred? If the environmental harm caused by such activities were considered an opportunity cost of international development, should compensation and damages be funded by a massive, general international insurance fund? If so, where would the insurance money come from? Additionally, to what extent might environmental impact assessments anticipate and foresee harm to health and the environment?

4.   What impact might modern-day terrorism play in the development of international environmental law relating to hazardous chemicals and waste? How easy or difficult would it be for a determined terrorist to obtain such substances and use them to poison the soil and water systems upon which life depends? Is existing international environmental law as it relates to hazardous chemicals and waste up to the task of protection in this regard? If not, what more needs to be done?

5.   In Ibrahim J. Wani, Poverty, Governance, The Rule of Law, and International Environmentalism: A Critique of the Basel Convention on Hazardous Wastes, 1 Kan. J. L. & Pub. Pol'y 37 (1991), the author states, at 38, that "poverty affects the priority that a government gives to environmental policy." "Until very recently," he notes, "international environmental efforts were resisted by governments in developing countries who viewed them as a form of 'ecoimperialism' and as a conspiracy against economic progress in developing countries. This suspicion resulted from a common perception in developing countries that environmental degradation is an inevitable by-product of economic development...."

These suspicions were apparently behind developing countries' opposition at the 1992 UN Conference on Environment and Development (UNCED) in Rio de Janeiro to developed country initiatives such as a then proposed forestry treaty. Given such concerns, what are the prospects for the further development of international environmental law? Do vast differences of wealth among states mean that an international environmental law that is acceptable to both developed and developing states can exist only if development efforts bring national comparative wealth closer together? Do such development efforts invariably demand that environmental considerations be given lesser priority?

6.   Developed country economies are increasingly dependent on export revenue that, in turn, is dependent upon raw materials available often in the developing countries. The ability to build and market goods for export commonly demands, however, that these raw materials be available inexpensively. Would not the evolution of an international environmental law that retards economic development among developing countries make it less likely that those countries would be able to access their raw materials for their own manufacturing industries, thus

decreasing their wealth and limiting their ability to produce goods that can compete with developed country exports? Why? Why not?

7. It is well known that, in the era of economic globalization in which we live, there are large multinational corporations (MNCs) whose gross revenues exceed the gross national products (GNPs) of dozens of countries. General Motors, for example, is a bigger economic unit than all the less developed countries of the world except China and India. Such revenues, along with a sometimes global presence, give businesses tremendous sway over the policies of countries through formal and informal contacts in the governmental policy-making establishments in their home countries as well as their host countries. Some commentators perceive MNCs as a growing international *political* force strong enough to undercut the sovereignty of even some developed countries. *See, e.g.,* Barry B. Hughes, Continuity and Change in World Politics: The Clash of Perspectives (1990); Richard J. Barnet & John Cavanagh, Global Dreams: Imperial Corporations and the New World Order (1994). Given this reality, is the international community correct to place liability for environmental harms on states that may or may not possess the real power to exercise sovereignty over what occurs as a result of corporate activity within their borders?

8. Simple and complex trading relationships among states have become a prominent feature of the modern international community. Some developing countries with export-driven economies depend, for reasons of geography and history, on another single state for a major portion of their export revenues. For example, a larger percentage of Guatemala's and Trinidad and Tobago's exports are to the United States, while an even larger percentage of Niger's exports are to France. Does this state of affairs suggest that a country's major trading partner might, for example, influence its decision to build a facility that produces toxic chemicals? Is it possible that such decisions are influenced by major aid donors? Should a more onerous duty of care to prevent environmental harm be placed on developed or more powerful countries? If so, what are the possibilities for international law to develop doctrines that transfer state responsibility and/or delineate contributory negligence? Under existing international law, to what extent, if any, would state responsibility be affected if Yoribo previously met with Bamileko and several other countries who were to be the principal consumers of PAAC's agricultural chemicals or principal purchasers of its chemical and waste disposal services and then, on the basis of their commitments to purchase the Khasa plant's products or services, decided to build the plant and facility, whereas a lack of interest might have led Yoribo not to encourage or subsidize PAAC in any way? If existing law does not allow it, to what extent should liability be transferred to these other states?

9. The United Nations Environment Programme (UNEP) is headquartered in Nairobi, Kenya. So also is its Regional Office for Africa (ROA). Covering all 53 countries of the continent, ROA's principal function is to coordinate UNEP's program of work in the region. ROA acts as the link between the various units and centers of UNEP and the countries in the region, and promotes collaboration and partnerships with organizations active in sustainable development in Africa. Through an umbrella project known as Regional Advisory Services (RAS), it provides a wide range of advisory services using either UNEP staff or consultants to advise on environmental machinery and technical requirements, review project proposals, and recommend action by governments and other organizations. It also plays host to the African Ministerial Conference on the Environment (AMCEN) which was established in 1985 as a permanent intergovernmental institution to strengthen cooperation between African governments on economic, technical and

scientific activities to halt the degradation of Africa's environment and satisfy the food and energy needs of the continent's people. For details about AMCEN, see UNEP's website at <http://www.unep.org/roa/Related_Programmes/AMCEN/index.asp>. For its constitution, see <http://www. unep.org/roa/docs/Ms_word/amcenreports/K0261748.doc>. *See also* Asian–African Handbook on Environmental Law 741(2001).

10. *Bibliographical Note.* For supplemental discussion concerning the principal themes addressed in this problem, consult the following additional specialized materials:

(a) *Books/Monographs/Reports/Symposia.* Asian–African Handbook on Environmental Law (2001); International, Regional and National Environmental Law (F. Morrison & R. Wolfrum eds., 2000); A. Bowman & A. Boyle, Environmental Damage in International and Comparative Law: Problems of Definition and Valuation (2003); G. Fowler, International Product Liability Law: A Worldwide Desk Reference Featuring Product Liability Laws & Customs in 50+ Countries (2003); Global Trends In Generation And Transboundary Movement Of Hazardous Wastes And Other Wastes: Analysis of the Data Provided by Parties to the Secretariat of the Basel Convention (2004); E. Hodgson, R. Mailman & J. Chambers, Dictionary of Toxicology (1998); International, Regional and National Environmental Law (F. Morrison & R. Wolfrum eds., 2000); A. Kellow, International Toxic Risk Management: Ideals, Interests and Implementation (1999); K. Kummer, International Management of Hazardous Wastes: The Basel Convention and Related Legal Rules (2000); L. Ringius, Radioactive waste disposal at Sea, (2000); K. Probst & T. Beierle, The Evolution of Hazardous Waste Programs: Lessons from Eight Countries (Resources for the Future) (1999); Pesticide Profiles: Toxicity, Environmental Impact, and Fate (M. Kamrin ed., 1997); P. Rao, International Environmental Law and Economics (2002); Sittig's Handbook of Toxic and Hazardous Chemicals and Carcinogens (2002); The Global Environment: Institutions, Law, and Policy (N. Vig & R. Axelrod eds., 1999).

(b) *Articles/Book Chapters.* S. Choksi, *Annual Review of Environmental and Natural Resources Law: International Law The Basel Convention on the Control of Transboundary Movements of Hazardous Wastes and Their Disposal: 1999 Protocol on Liability and Compensation,* 28 Ecology L.Q. 509 (2001); D. Fidler, *Challenges to Humanity's Health: The Contributions of International Environmental Law to National and Global Public Health,* 31 Envtl. L. Rep. 10048 (Jan 2001); K. Gregory, *The Basel Convention and The International Trade of Hazardous Waste: The Road to the Destruction of Public Health and the Environment is Paved with Good Intentions,* 10 Currents Int'l Trade L. J. 80 (2001); P. Lallas, *The Role of Process and Participation in the Development of Effective Agreements: A Study of the Global Treaty on Persistent Organic Pollutants (POPS),* 19 UCLA J. Envtl. L. & Pol'y 83 (2000/2001); J. Van Dyke, *Balancing Navigational Freedom with Environmental and Security Concerns,* Colo. J. Int'l Envtl. L. & Pol'y 19 (2003); A. Webster–Main, *Keeping Africa Out of the Global Backyard: A Comparative Study of the Basel and Bamako Conventions,*26 Environs Envtl. L. & Pol'y J. 65 (2002); N. S. Zahedi, *Implementing the Rotterdam Convention: The Challenges of Transforming Aspirational Goals into Effective Controls on Hazardous Pesticide Exports to Developing Countries,* 11 Geo. Int'l Envtl. L. Rev. 707 (Spring 1999).

Problem 7–6

A Rain Forest and the Guahibo Are Threatened
in Amazonia and Caribia

SECTION 1.   FACTS

Straddling the South American countries of Amazonia and Caribia is a rain forest, rich in biodiversity, estimated to house over fifteen percent of the Earth's remaining unknown and unspecified gene pool—a potentially valuable heritage for all humankind. Living in the rain forest, on both sides of the Amazonia–Caribia border, are a native people known as the Guahibo, who find in the rain forest support for their indigenous lifestyle and culture.

In the early 1990s, the Government of Caribia created an "Equatorial Reserve" in Caribia's part of the rain forest. It did so to ensure a sanctuary for the abundant biodiversity present in this nearly pristine forest and to safeguard the Guahibo from an onslaught of economic development that would lead to their cultural extinction. A major function of the Reserve is to forbid access by all outside groups, including missionaries, miners, hunters, and traders, who might seek to exploit the rain forest and its people.

Accomplished through a so-called debt-for-nature swap engineered by the Nature Conservancy (NC)[a] and the World Bank, the Equatorial Reserve is administered, according to the debt-for-nature agreement, by a Governing Board composed of members of the NC's local Caribian chapter, officials of the Caribian government, and members of the Guahibo tribe. Thus far the principal difficulty faced by the Board has been the prevention of encroachment into the Reserve by self-proclaimed "settlers" from the outside, especially miners, squatters, and poachers. Many of these so-called settlers have occupied, slashed, and burned parts of the "medicine valley" where many of the herbal and medicinal plants of the Guahibo are found to grow. Through strict penalties and stepped-up patrols, however, the Board has gradually reduced the violations by its own nationals to an acceptable level. The greater problem has been the encroachment of non-indigenous persons from the adjacent Guahibo reserve across the border in Amazonia.

The Amazonian Guahibo reserve was one of a number of conservation and Amerindian reservations created by the Amazonian government as a method of protecting indigenous people from the effects of a vast development

---

a. The Nature Conservancy is an international nongovernmental organization (NGO) of approximately 650,000 members worldwide that has as its objective, with forty years of experience, the purchase of land for the preservation of biological diversity by saving plants, animals, and their habitats from extinction. Its Latin American division, a principal player in trying to save Latin America's rain forests, reefs, grasslands and groves, already has helped to protect more than 20 million acres of tropical habitat in Latin America and the Caribbean.

project. The project, financed by the World Bank and called Eco–Habitación (ECOHAB), originally envisioned the widespread colonization of the northern Amazonian province of Matorral. To reduce population pressures in the eastern cities and to begin what was foreseen as a hugely profitable exploitation of Matorral, ECOHAB included an ambitious road building project and settlement plan. First, a federal highway was constructed which traversed the province along with a system of feeder roads. Next, ranching was introduced as well as "sustainable" tree farming.

Unfortunately, as has been the case elsewhere in the rain forest, neither the ranching nor the tree farming proved successful. Ranching quickly became unproductive due to the mineral leaching of rangeland, and sustainable tree farming, because of incentive mismanagement and, again, poor soils, made little headway against traditional "slash and burn" practices. To compound the problem, small quantities of gold and tin have been found in the region, leading to a surge of new immigrants. In response, the Amazonian government has proposed a second phase of ECOHAB that includes the introduction of charcoal-burning pig-iron smelters and large scale tin mining, as well as a secondary system of feeder roads to open up new land—and to these ends it again has sought financing from the World Bank.

Due to its long distance from the locus of project activities (about 1000 kilometers), the Amazonian Guahibo reserve remained relatively undisturbed during the early stages of ECOHAB. In recent years, however, a nearly lawless environment has emerged in Matorral, with the Amazonian government showing little ability or inclination to protect the reserve from encroachment. Among other developments, individual gold and tin prospectors have undertaken gold and cassiterite mining expeditions in the reserve and, in so doing, caused a considerable number of the Guahibo to move to Caribia's Equatorial Reserve in search of safer sanctuary.

Understandably, the Government of Caribia and the NC see a threat to their conservationist and protective efforts. Repeated complaints by Caribia to Amazonia have been ignored, however, and as a consequence Caribia has become increasingly strident in international circles regarding these circumstances. With approximately one-half of the Guahibo tribe residing in the contiguous Amazonian reserve, Caribia believes that the immediate problem could be contained if Amazonia would simply protect its Guahibo reserve with proper diligence under Amazonian law. However, seeing the considerable dangers that lie ahead, Caribia now desires that the vast Amazonian development projects to the south of its Guahibo reserve be stopped or, at least, sharply cut back.

To these ends, Caribia has referred its biodiversity dispute with Amazonia to arbitration under the 1992 Convention on Biological Diversity to which both countries are party and which came into force after due ratification. In its notification under Article 1 of Annex II of the Convention, Caribia alleges violation by Amazonia of Articles 3–5 and 8(j) of the Convention, stating that Amazonia's actions have threatened the conservation of biological diversity both in Caribia and in Amazonia. Both countries have signed and ratified the Convention, and both have accepted arbitration as their chosen means of dispute settlement under Article 27(3)(a) of the Convention. The President of Arbitral Tribunal, Jonathan Amarilio, has called for written memorials from each of the parties.

In addition, Caribia has filed a petition (*i.e.*, complaint) against Amazonia before the Inter–American Commission on Human Rights in respect of Amazonia's treatment of the Guahibo. Both Amazonia and Caribia are members of the Organization of American States and party to the 1969 American Convention on Human Rights. Caribia's complaint alleges multiple violations of the 1969 American Convention, which both Amazonia and Caribia have signed and ratified, as they have also, with one exception, all other potentially relevant human rights instruments.[b] The exception is 1989 ILO Convention (No. 169) Concerning Indigenous and Tribal Peoples In Independent Countries. Only Caribia has signed and ratified this convention.

Both the Biodiversity Convention's Arbitral Tribunal and the Inter–American Commission on Human Rights have announced that they will not entertain arguments relating to remedies until they have heard arguments on the alleged breaches of international law.

SECTION 2. QUESTIONS PRESENTED

1. In what way or ways, if at all, has Amazonia violated international obligations within the competence/jurisdiction of the Biodiversity Convention's Arbitral Tribunal and the Inter–American Commission on Human Rights?

2. In any event, are there any additional or alternative legal norms, procedures, and/or institutions to be recommended that might further help to prevent or discourage situations of the kind posed by this problem?

SECTION 3. ASSIGNMENTS

A. READING ASSIGNMENT

Study the Readings presented in Section 4, *infra*, and the Discussion Notes/Questions that follow. Also, to the extent possible, consult the accompanying bibliographical references.

B. RECOMMENDED WRITING ASSIGNMENT

Prepare a comprehensive, logically sequenced, and *argumentative* brief in the form of an outline of the primary and subsidiary *legal* issues you see requiring resolution by the Biodiversity Arbitral Tribunal and the ILO Commission of Inquiry. Also, from the perspective of an independent judge,

---

b. In addition to the American Convention on Human Rights and ILO Convention No.169, Amazonia and Caribia are parties to the United Nations Charter, the 1948 Convention on the Prevention and Punishment of the Crime of Genocide, the 1966 International Covenant on Economic, Social and Cultural Rights, the 1966 International Covenant on Civil and Political Rights, and the 1966 International Convention on the Elimination of All Forms of Racial Discrimination. In addition, they are signatories to the 1948 American Declaration on the Rights and Duties of Man and the 1948 Universal Declaration of Human Rights.

indicate which side ought to prevail on each issue and why. Retain a copy of your issue-outline (brief) for class discussion.

C. Recommended Oral Assignment

Assume you are legal counsel for Caribia or Amazonia (as designated by your instructor); then, relying upon the Readings (and your issue-outline if prepared), present a 15–20 minute oral argument of your government's likely positions before the Biodiversity Arbitral Tribunal and the ILO Commission of Inquiry.

D. Suggested Reflective Assignment

Consider (and recommend) alternative norms, institutions, and/or procedures that you believe might do better than existing world order arrangements to contend with situations of the kind posed by this problem. In so doing, but without insisting upon *immediate* feasibility, identify the particular transition steps that would be needed to make your alternatives a reality.

Section 4.   Readings

1. Convention on Biological Diversity. Concluded, 6 Jun 1992. Entered into force, 29 Dec 1993. 1760 U.N.T.S. 79; *reprinted in* 31 I.L.M. 818 (1992) and 5 Weston & Carlson V.H.22 (Basic Document 5.36).

2. World Resources Institute (WRI), et al., Global Biodiversity Strategy: Guidelines for Action to Save, Study, and Use Earth's Biotic Wealth Sustainably and Equitably 1–18, 27 (1992).

The Nature and Value of Biodiversity

*We cannot even estimate the number of species of organisms on
Earth to an order of magnitude, an appalling situation in terms of
knowledge and our ability to affect the human prospect positively.
There are clearly few areas of science about which so little is known,
and none of such direct relevance to human beings.*

Peter Raven, Missouri Botanical Gardens, United States

Earth's plants, animals, and microorganisms—interacting with one another and with the physical environment in ecosystems—form the foundation of sustainable development. Biotic resources from this wealth of life support human livelihoods and aspirations and make it possible to adapt to changing needs and environments. The steady erosion of the diversity of genes, species, and ecosystems taking place today will undermine progress toward a sustainable society. Indeed, the continuing loss of biodiversity is a telling measure of the imbalance between human needs and wants and nature's capacity [*see* Box 7–6.1].

The human race had 850 million members when it entered the industrial age, sharing Earth with life forms nearly as diverse as the planet has ever possessed. Today, with population nearly six times as large and resource consumption proportionately far greater, both the limits of nature and the price of overstepping them are becoming clear. A turning point is upon us. We can continue to simplify the environment to meet immediate needs, at the cost of long-term benefits, or we can conserve life's precious diversity and use it sustainably. We can deliver to the next generation (and the next) a world rich in possibilities or one impoverished of life; but social and economic development will succeed only if we do the first.

The Value of Biodiversity's Components

From both wild and domesticated components of biodiversity humanity derives all of its food and many medicines and industrial products. Economic benefits from wild species alone make up an estimated 4.5 percent of the Gross Domestic Product of the United States—worth $87 billion annually in the late 1970s. Fisheries, largely based on wild species, contributed about 100 million tons of food world-wide in 1989. Indeed, wild species are dietary mainstays in much of the world. In Ghana, three out of four people look to wildlife for most of their protein. Timber, ornamental plants, oils, gums, and many fibers also come from the wild.

The current economic value of domesticated species is even greater. Agriculture accounts for 32 percent of GDP in low-income developing countries and 12 percent in middle-income countries. Trade in agricultural products amounted to $3 trillion in 1989.

The components of biodiversity are also important to human health. Once, nearly all medicines came from plants and animals, and even today they remain vital. Traditional medicine forms the basis of primary health care for about 80 percent of people in developing countries, more than 3 billion people in all. More than 5,100 species are used in Chinese traditional medicine alone, and people in [the] northwestern [Amazon region] have tapped some 2,000 species. Traditional medicine is now encouraged by the World Health Organization, and in many countries—including industrialized countries—its use is expanding rapidly. Nearly 2,500 plant species in the Soviet Union have been used for medicinal purposes, and the demand for drug plant material has tripled in the last decade.

The Diversity of Life

Biodiversity is the totality of genes, species, and ecosystems in a region. The wealth of life on Earth today is the product of hundreds of millions of years of evolutionary history. Over the course of time, human cultures have emerged and adapted to the local environment, discovering, using, and altering local biotic resources. Many areas that now seem "natural" bear the marks of millennia of human habitation, crop cultivation, and resource harvesting. The domestication and breeding of local varieties of crops and livestock have further shaped biodiversity.

Biodiversity can be divided into three hierarchical categories—genes, species, and ecosystems—that describe quite different aspects of living systems and that scientists measure in different ways.

Genetic diversity refers to the variation of genes within species. This covers distinct populations of the same species (such as the thousands of traditional rice varieties in India) or genetic variation within a population (which is very high among Indian rhinos, for example, and very low among cheetahs). . . . Species diversity refers to the variety of species within a region. Such diversity can be measured in many ways, and scientists have not settled on a single best method. The number of species in a region—its species "richness"—is one often-used measure, but a more precise measurement, "taxonomic diversity," also considers the relationship of species to each other. For example, an island with two species of birds and one species of lizard has greater taxonomic diversity than an island with three species of birds but no lizards. Thus, even though there may be more species of beetles on earth than all other species combined, they do not account for the greater part of species diversity because they are so closely related. Similarly, many more species live on land than in the sea, but terrestrial species are more closely related to each other than ocean species are, so diversity is higher in marine ecosystems than a strict count of species would suggest.

Ecosystem diversity is harder to measure than species or genetic diversity because of communities—associations of species—and ecosystems are elusive. Nevertheless, as long as a consistent set of criteria is used to define communities and ecosystems, their number and distribution can be measured. . . .

Besides ecosystem diversity, many other expressions of biodiversity can be important. These include the relative abundance of species, the age structure of populations, the pattern of communities in a region, changes in community composition and structure over time, and even such ecological processes as predation, parasitism, and mutualism. More generally, to meet specific management or policy goals, it is often important to examine not only compositional diversity—genes, species, and ecosystems—but also diversity in ecosystem structure and function.

Human cultural diversity could also be considered part of biodiversity. Like genetic or species diversity, some attributes of human cultures (say, nomadism or shifting cultivation) represent "solutions" to the problems of survival in particular environments. And, like other aspects of biodiversity, cultural diversity helps people adapt to changing conditions. Cultural diversity is manifested by diversity in language, religious beliefs, land-management practices, art, music, social structure, crop selection, diet, and any number of other attributes of human society.

Box 7-6.1

As for modern pharmaceuticals, one-fourth of all prescriptions dispensed in the United States contain active ingredients extracted from plants, and over 3000 antibiotics—including penicillin and tetracycline—are derived from microorganisms. Cyclosporin, developed from a soil fungus, revolutionized heart and kidney transplant surgery by suppressing the immune reaction. Aspirin and many other drugs that are now synthesized were first discovered in the wild. Compounds extracted from plants, microbes, and animals were involved in developing all of the twenty best-selling drugs in the United States, drugs whose combined sales approached $6 billion in 1988.

* * *

The Value of Diversity

The sheer *variety* of life has enormous value. The variety of distinctive species, ecosystems, and habitats influence the productivity and services provided by ecosystems. As the variety of species in an ecosystem changes—a legacy of extinction or species introduction—the ecosystem's ability to absorb pollution, maintain soil fertility and micro-climates, cleanse water, and provide other invaluable services changes too. When the elephant—a voracious vegetarian—disappeared from large areas of its traditional range in Africa, the ecosystem was altered as grasslands reverted to woodlands and woodland wildlife returned. When the sea otter was all but exterminated from the Aleutian Islands by fur traders, sea urchin populations swelled and overwhelmed kelp production.

The value of variety is particularly apparent in agriculture. For generations, people have raised a wide range of crops and livestock to stabilize and enhance productivity. The wisdom of these techniques—including their contributions to watershed protection, soil fertility maintenance, and receptivity to integrated pest-management strategies—is being reaffirmed today as farmers around the world turn to alternative low-input production systems.

The genetic diversity found within individual crops is also of tremendous value. Genetic diversity provides an edge in the constant evolutionary battle between crops and livestock and the pests and diseases that prey on them. In age-old systems, several genetically distinct varieties of crops are planted together as a hedge against crop failure. The Ifugao of the Philippine island of Luzon can name more than 200 varieties of sweet potato, and Andean farmers cultivate thousands of varieties of potatoes.

Breeders and farmers also draw on the genetic diversity of crops and livestock to increase yields and to respond to changing environmental conditions. The opportunities provided by genetic engineering—which allows the transfer of genes among species—will further increase the opportunities genetic diversity provides for enhancing agricultural productivity. A wild tomato, found only in the Galapagos Islands, can grow in seawater and possesses jointless fruitstalks—a trait that has been bred into domesticated tomatoes to make them easy to harvest mechanically. A wild relative of rice collected in India provided a "resistance gene" that now protects high-yielding rice varieties in South and Southeast Asia from their nemesis, the brown plant-hopper. Plant breeding is to thank for fully half of the gains in agricultural yields in the United States from 1930 to 1980: an estimated $1 billion annually has been added to the value of US agricultural output by the widened genetic base.

Over time, the greatest value of the variety of life may be found in the opportunities it provides humanity for adapting to local and global change. The unknown potential of genes, species, and ecosystems represents a never-ending biological frontier of inestimable but certainly high value. Genetic diversity will enable breeders to tailor crops to new climatic conditions. Earth's biota—a biochemical laboratory unmatched for size and innovation—hold [sic] the still-secret cures for emerging diseases. A diverse array of genes, species, and ecosystems is a resource that can be tapped as human needs and demands change.

Because biodiversity is so closely intertwined with human needs, its conservation should rightfully be considered an element of national security. It has become increasingly apparent that national security means much more than military might. Ecological dimensions of national security cannot be ignored when countries fight over access to water or when environmental refugees strain national budgets and public infrastructure. A secure nation means not only a strong nation, but also one with a healthy and educated populace, and a healthy and productive environment as well. National security will be strongest in countries that care for their biodiversity and the services it provides.

For many, these technical definitions and economic calculations may be eclipsed by still more basic reasons for conservation. Attitudes toward biodiversity and the respect that people show for other species are strongly influenced by moral, cultural, and religious values. The reason is not surprising. Biodiversity is closely linked to cultural diversity—human cultures are shaped in part by the living environment that they in turn influence—and this linkage has profoundly helped determine cultural values. Most of the world's religions teach respect for the diversity of life and concern for its conservation. Indeed, the variety of life is the backdrop against which culture itself languishes or flourishes.

Even so, some reduction in biodiversity has been an inevitable consequence of human development, as species-rich forests and wetlands have been converted to relatively species-poor farmlands and plantations. Such conversions are themselves an aspect of the use and management of biodiversity, and there can be no doubt that they are beneficial. . . .

The many values of biodiversity and its importance for development suggest why biodiversity conservation differs from traditional nature conservation. Biodiversity conservation entails a shift from a defensive posture—protecting nature from the impacts of development—to an offensive effort seeking to meet peoples' needs from biological resources while ensuring the long-term sustainability of Earth's biotic wealth. It thus involves not only the protection of wild species but also the safeguarding of the genetic diversity of

cultivated and domesticated species and their wild relatives. This goal speaks
to modified and intensive managed ecosystems as well as natural ones, and it
is pursued in the human interest and for human benefit. In sum, biodiversity
conservation seeks to maintain the human life support system provided by
nature, and the living resources essential for development.

Losses of Biodiversity and Their Causes

*We aren't quite sure who is cutting our forests and who is going to flood
our land, but we know they live in towns, where rich people are getting
richer, and we poor people are losing what little we have.*

STATEMENT OF THE IBAN PEOPLE, SARAWAK, MALAYSIA

Biological diversity is being eroded as fast today as at any time since the
dinosaurs died out some 65 million years ago. The crucible of extinction is
believed to be in tropical forests. Around 10 million species live on earth,
according to the best estimates, and tropical forests house between 50 and 90
percent of this total. About 17 million hectares of tropical forests—an area
four times the size of Switzerland—are now being cleared annually and
scientists estimate that at these rates roughly 5 to 10 percent of tropical forest
species may face extinction within the next 30 years.... This estimate may
prove conservative, however. Rates of tropical forest loss are accelerating, and
some particularly species-rich forests are likely to be largely destroyed in our
lifetime. Some scientists believe that about 60,000 of the world's 240,000
plant species, and perhaps even higher proportions of vertebrate and insect
species, could lose their lease on life over the next three decades unless
deforestation is slowed immediately.

* * *

The dramatic losses of species and ecosystems obscure equally large and
important threats to genetic diversity. Worldwide, some 492 genetically distinct populations of tree species (including some full species) are endangered.
* * * Loss of genetic diversity could imperil agriculture. How much the genetic
base has already eroded is hard to say, but since the 1950s, the spread of
modern "Green Revolution" varieties of corn, wheat, rice, and other crops has
rapidly squeezed out native landraces. * * * Gene banks have slowed the loss
of genetic diversity, but the high costs of periodically regenerating the seeds
and the risk of mechanical failures make seed banks less than fail-safe.... In
1991, representatives of 13 national germplasm banks in Latin America
reported that between 5 and 100 percent of the maize seed collected between
1940 and 1980 is no longer viable.

The loss of genetic, species, and ecosystem diversity both stems from and
invites the loss of cultural diversity. Diverse cultures have bred and sustained
numerous varieties of crops, livestock, and habitats. By the same token, the
loss of certain crops, the replacement of traditional crops with export crops,
the extinction of species embedded in religion, mythology, or folklore, and the
degradation or conversion of homelands are cultural as well as biological
losses. Since 1900, experts say, about one Indian tribe has disappeared from
Brazil each year. Almost one half of the world's 6000 languages may die out in
the next 100 years. Of the 3000 languages expected to survive for a century,
nearly half will probably not last much longer.

Causes and Mechanisms of Biodiversity Impoverishment

The current losses of biodiversity have both direct and indirect causes. The direct mechanisms include habitat loss and fragmentation, invasion by introduced species, the over-exploitation of living resources, pollution, global climate change, and industrial agriculture and forestry. But these are not the root of the problem. * * * The roots of the biodiversity crisis are not "out there" in the forest or on the savannah, but embedded in the way we live. They lie in burgeoning human numbers, the way in which the human species has progressively broadened its ecological niche and appropriated ever more of the earth's biological productivity, the excessive and unsustainable consumption of natural resources, a continuing reduction in the number of traded products from agriculture and fisheries, economic systems that fail to set a proper value on the environment, inappropriate social structures, and weaknesses in legal and institutional systems. Just as biodiversity is an essential resource for sustainable development, finding sustainable ways to live is essential if biological diversity is to be conserved.

3.   Stockholm Declaration of the United Nations Conference on the Human Environment, adopted by the UN Conference on the Human Environment at Stockholm, 16 Jun 1972, Report of the UN Conference on the Human Environment, UN Doc. A/CONF.48/14/ Rev.1 at 3 (1973), UN Doc. A/CONF.48/14 at 2–65, and Corr. 1 (1972); *reprinted in* **11 I.L.M. 1416 (1972) and 5 Weston & Carlson V.B.3: Pmbl. & Princs. 1–3, 6, 11–13, 21–24** (Basic Document 5.14).

4.   Charter of Economic Rights and Duties of States. Adopted, 12 Dec 1974. G.A Res. 3281, 29th Sess., Supp. No. 31, at 50, UN Doc. A/9631 (1975); *reprinted in* **14 I.L.M. 251 (1975) and 4 Weston & Carlson IV.F.5: Art. 30** (Basic Document 4.9).

5.   World Charter for Nature. Adopted, 28 Oct 1982. GA Res. 37/7, UN GAOR, 37th Sess., Supp. No. 51, at 17, UN Doc. A/37/51; *reprinted in* **22 I.L.M. 455 (1983) and 5 Weston & Carlson V.B.11: Princs. 1–5, 11, 21** (Basic Document 5.21).

6.   Experts Group on Environmental Law of the World Commission on Environment and Development, Legal Principles for Environmental Protection and Sustainable Development. Adopted, 18–20 Jun 1986. UN Doc. WCED/86/23/Add.1 (1986); *reprinted in* **5 Weston & Carlson V.B.12: Arts. 1, 3, 8, 14–17** (Basic Document 5.25).

7.   Rio Declaration on Environment and Development. Adopted, 13 Jun 1992. UNCED Doc. A/CONF.151/5/Rev. 1; *reprinted in* **31 I.L.M. 874 (1992) and 5 Weston & Carlson V.B.16: Princs. 1, 3–6, 8, 9, 13, 14, 22** (Basic Document 5.37).

8.   Editors' Note. *See supra* Reading 19 (Editors' Note) in Problem 7–2 ("Hanguo Versus the Ozone Layer"), p. 1122.

9.   James P. Resor, "Debt-for-Nature Swaps: A Decade of Experience and New Directions for the Future," 48 UNASYLVA No. 1 (FAO: Issue 188, 1997), available at <http://www.fao.org/documents/show_cdr.asp?url_file=/docrep/w3247E/w3247e06.htm>.

In 1984, World Wildlife Fund [now the World Wide Fund for Nature] (WWF) initiated the debt-for-nature swap as a mechanism for enhancing conservation efforts in developing countries. The idea arose from the observation that much of the world's biological diversity is harboured in the same countries that face the greatest financial strain from foreign debt burdens. Debt-for-nature swaps leverage funds for use in local conservation efforts, based on the model of debt-equity swaps in which private sector interests buy discounted debt and exchange it for local currency investments in the indebted country. While debt-for-equity swaps did provide the initial outline for the financial mechanism, debt-for-nature swaps have a very different purpose. A debt-for-equity swap is used to generate profits for the investor. A debt-for-nature swap does not seek profit, but rather to provide additional funds for conservation activities within a country. The debt-for-nature swap differs in that there is no transfer of ownership or repatriation of capital to a foreign investor.

Debt-for-nature swaps – how they work

A debt-for-nature swap involves purchasing foreign debt, converting that debt into local currency and using the proceeds to fund conservation activities. The key to the transaction lies in the willingness of commercial banks (or governments) to sell debt at less than the full value of the original loan. This seems counterintuitive: why would any lending institution holding a promissory note for US$ 1 million, for instance, be willing to part with it for just half that amount? The answer lies in the hard economic fact that many developing countries have not been able to repay their debts in full, and may never be able to do so. As a result, commercial banks may prefer to sell debts at a discount rather than wait for an uncertain repayment in the future.

While no two debt-for-nature swaps are the same, they usually include the following steps:

1. An indebted country establishes general guidelines for a debt-for-nature programme and invites participation from conservation organizations.

2. An international conservation organization and local private and public organizations reach agreement on a conservation programme.

3. The participating conservation organizations verify that sufficient funding will exist for the debt purchase or that debt donations or partial forgiveness may be possible.

4. The partners request government approval for the swap, usually from the central bank and the Ministry of Finance, and often from the government ministry that has jurisdiction over the relevant sector where the proceeds will be used.

5. Specific terms of the swap are negotiated, including the exchange rate from foreign currency to local currency, the redemption rate and the local investment instrument. The purchase price depends on the secondary market price of the debt, which is determined by the market's view of the credit history and repayment expectations for the particular country. The amount of conservation funds generated depends on the redemption rate, which is the percentage of the face value debt that is redeemed in local currency. The redemption rate is sometimes 100 percent of the face value debt, but it is often less depending on negotiations among the parties involved. The redemption rate must exceed the purchase price of the debt by a large enough margin to make the transaction worth while.

6. The debt is acquired and is presented to the central bank of the indebted country which cancels the debt and provides funds in local currency, either in the form of cash or bonds.

7. The conservation projects are implemented over the life of the agreed programme.

Box 7-6.2

* * *

In 1987, the Government of Bolivia and Conservation International (CI) signed the first debt-for-nature swap agreement. Under that agreement, CI was able to acquire US $650,000 of Bolivian external debt at a discounted price of $100,000. In return, the Government of Bolivia undertook to provide the Beni Biosphere Reserve with maximum legal protection and to create three adjacent protected areas. It also agreed to provide $250,000 in local currency for management activities in the Beni Reserve. However, the swap raised a lot of controversy and encountered delays before implementation owing to a combination of factors: a lack of open participation by [one] organization in Bolivia; some misperceptions of the swap agreement, fueled by misleading press reports; and the newness of the debt-for-nature swap concept. . . . In the long term, however, the controversy of the Bolivian swap had the beneficial results of attracting much needed attention to conservation challenges and helping debt-for-nature swaps take root as a creative tool for financing conservation. The debt swap mechanism came to be viewed as a clever way to multiply contributions to conservation in developing countries. Donors [sic] conservation organizations liked it, since they saw a way to increase funding for badly needed conservation efforts in these countries. Many developing country governments embraced it as a tool to help manage their foreign debt situation as well as promoting selected conservation and development programmers in their countries. And, from a publicity standpoint, the idea of swapping debt for nature sold well.

* * *

One of the most important successes of debt-for-nature swaps has been their ability to influence conservation over the long term. Swaps provide a long-term source of funding which facilitates the implementation of conservation programmes with long time horizons.

For example, two separate swaps, carried out in Ecuador by Fundación Natura (an Ecuadorian NGO), WWF and The Nature Conservancy (a United States-based environmental organization), in 1987 and 1989 funded a $10 million programme. The Central Bank of Ecuador is paying out swap proceeds to Fundacióón Natura over nine years with a percentage each year being placed into an endowment fund which will exist in perpetuity. In turn, Fundación Natura is working with the Ministry of Agriculture and Livestock (responsible for National Parks) and numerous NGOs in Ecuador to carry out a variety of conservation programmes. Thus, the $10 million debt swap programme has already generated more than $10 million in local currency for conservation in Ecuador and will continue to generate funding for years to come.

However, challenges and limitations remain: organizational capacity and strategic planning on the part of conservation organizations were initially inadequate and have proved difficult to institutionalize, despite the advantages of having long-term funding in place. These challenges are further complicated when political and economic landscapes are unsteady to the point where swaps, which have substantial transaction costs and long-term payouts, are not justified. This partially explains why many countries, despite having very highly discounted debt, have not had correspondingly robust debt swap programmes. * * * Strengthening the capacity of the local conservation organizations to plan and manage funds effectively is as essential to the success of the conservation initiative as the funds are. In the early swaps, WWF and other organizations did not include sufficient investment and technical assistance to meet these organizational challenges in the original design and budgeting of the programme.

* * *

Beyond debt-for-nature swaps

Encouraged by the success of [a] 1988 debt-for-nature agreement in the Philippines and the projects financed under it, beginning in 1990 leaders of the Philippine NGO community, the Philippine Government, WWF and the United States Agency for International Development (USAID) began planning for a much larger swap to capitalize a major new institution, the Foundation for the Philippine Environment (FPE). The strategy was to capitalize FPE with an endowment fund and thus permit FPE to set its own direction and finance conservation efforts for decades to come. As a result of two large swaps—$9.8 million in 1992 and $19 million in 1993 FPE has an endowment of 640 million pesos (about US$26 million), making it the largest capitalized environmental NGO in the developing world. FPE has a Board of Trustees comprising representatives of Philippine development and conservation organizations, government representatives, the business community, academia and one international NGO (initially WWF and now the World Resources Institute). FPE is currently financing a wide variety of conservation and development projects throughout the Philippines.

As the experience in the Philippines suggests, debt swaps have been the starting point for the development of a number of new approaches for long-term financing of conservation and have also benefitted other social sectors.

* * *

Where do we go from here?

Debt-for-nature swaps have made important contributions to conservation. They have done this directly, for example in the Philippines and Ecuador where they have generated substantial funding for conservation and helped catalyse new institutions, and indirectly by providing lessons for conservation bust funds and other institutional reforms that can foster participation from diverse sets of stakeholders ranging from national monetary officials to grassroots community organizations.

However, debt swaps and conservation trusts funds have limitations, as they are largely dependent on donor grants. In the case of debt swaps, the financial multiplier enhanced donor interest in debt swaps, but several factors have eroded the potential for such multipliers and generally have decreased opportunities for debt swaps in the late 1990s and beyond. Some countries, for example the Philippines and Mexico, have undergone structural adjustment, including restructuring of their external debt, and thus the premium associated with debt conversions has decreased substantially as their own debt situation has improved.... For other countries, even when debt prices remain very low, the lack of local private conservation and development organizations will remain a limiting factor.

* * *

While there was a surge of government-to-government debt swaps in the early 1990s often with local proceeds being at least partially managed by local NGOs—these kinds of swaps also face constraints since they ultimately rely on foreign assistance budget allocations from developed countries at a time when foreign assistance and national budgets are contracting.

Given the success of debt swaps involving commercial debt and government-to-government debt, there has been much debate over the potential of conversions involving multilateral development bank (MDB) debt. This is particularly relevant for most of the highly indebted countries for whom MDB debt stock and servicing flows represent a major portion of their foreign debt. Despite a 1995 World Bank working paper arguing that MDB debt should be restructured along the lines that commercial debt and bilateral debt have been restructured, this portion of the debt pie has remained off limits. However, this offers the most significant opportunity for the next generation of debt conversions.

With debt swaps, the international community has successfully modified the debt-for-nature concept from its inception in 1984 through the mid-1990s to keep it fresh and innovative and thus an effective means for financing conservation. While debt swaps will continue to offer good opportunities on a case-by-case basis, we have reached a point of diminishing potential except perhaps until there is a major breakthrough on MDB debt. The pace and amount of debt swaps will decrease. Thus, it is necessary to look for new ways to generate more sustained funding for conservation.

The Belize PACT, which derives its funding from a $3.75 "conservation fee" paid by each of the estimated 140,000 tourists visiting Belize annually, is a step in this direction. Other possibilities for generating conservation funding from natural resource "user fees" include charging fees for timber extraction and fishing as a logical extension of the Belize PACT model, although it is to be expected that industry participants may resist initially. Several organizations, including WWF, are already pursuing this avenue to generate more funding for conservation as well as encouraging more environmentally sustainable patterns of resource use altogether.

The next challenge is to mobilize long-term financing for conservation on a commercial basis, *i.e.,* where investors can realize an economic return and still promote conservation. This could accelerate the adoption of environmentally sustainable development to replace resource liquidation practices that are common (and often preferred by financial markets) in many places. Conservationists need to engage the private sector on terms favourable for the environment—along the same lines as those followed by debt swaps over the past ten years to encourage investments that are good for conservation and the people who depend on those natural resources.

* * *

Debt-for-nature swaps have ushered in a new way of thinking about conservation and also initiated opportunities to involve institutions not previously engaged in conservation efforts. Proponents have successfully found new opportunities and tailored the mechanism to the particular national circumstances. Now there are emerging examples of harnessing similar creativity and strategic partnerships in order to tackle the greater challenge of attracting more private investment on terms that balance economic returns with conservation objectives over the long term.

10. **United Nations Charter. Concluded, 26 Jun 1945. Entered into force, 10 May 1945. 1976 Y.B.U.N. 1043;** *reprinted in* **1 Weston & Carlson I.A.1: Pmbl. & Arts. 2(7), 55, 56** (Basic Document 1.5).

11. **Universal Declaration of Human Rights. Concluded, 10 Dec 1948, GA Res. 217A, UN GAOR, 3rd Sess., Pt. I, Resolutions, at 71, UN Doc. A./810 (1948;** *reprinted in* **3 Weston & Carlson III.A.1: Arts. 1–3, 7, 17, 27, 30** (Basic Document 3.3).

12. **Convention on the Prevention and Punishment of the Crime of Genocide. Concluded, 9 Dec 1948. Entered into force, 12 Jan 1951. 78 U.N.T.S. 277;** *reprinted in* **3 Weston & Carlson III.J.1: Arts. II–IV** (Basic Document 3.2).

13. **International Convention on the Elimination of All Forms of Racial Discrimination. Concluded, 7 Mar 1966. Entered into force, 4 Jan 1969. 660 U.N.T.S. 195; reprinted in 5 I.L.M. 352 (1966) and 3 Weston & Carlson III.I.1: Pmbl. & Arts.1–3, 5** (Basic Document 3.12).

14. **International Covenant on Economic, Social and Cultural Rights. Concluded, 16 Dec 1966. Entered into force, 3 Jan 1976. 993 U.N.T.S. 3;** *reprinted in* **6 I.L.M. 360 (1967) and 3 Weston & Carlson III.A.2: Arts. 1, 2, 15, 25** (Basic Document 3.13).

15. **International Covenant on Civil and Political Rights. Concluded, 16 Dec 1966. Entered into force, 23 Mar 1976. 999 U.N.T.S. 171;** *reprinted in* **6 I.L.M. 368 (1967) and 3 Weston & Carlson III.A.3: Arts. 1, 2, 6, 27, 47,** (Basic Document 3.14).

16. **American Declaration of the Rights and Duties of Man. Adopted, 2 May 1948. O.A.S. Res. XXX, O.A.S. Off. Rec. OEA/ Ser.L/V/I.4Rev;** *reprinted in* **3 Weston & Carlson III.B.23: Pmbl. & Arts. I, II, V, VIII, IX, XI, XIII, XXII, XXIII, XXIX, XXXIII** (Basic Document 3.1).

17. **American Convention on Human Rights. Concluded, 22 Nov 1969. Entered into force, 18 Jul 1978. O.A.S. Treaty Ser. No. 36, at 1; O.A.S. Off. Rec. OAE/Ser.L./V/II.23 doc. 21 rev. 6 (1979);** *reprinted in* **9 I.L.M. 673 (1970) and 3 Weston & Carlson III.B.24: Arts. 1, 4, 16, 21** (Basic Document 3.17).

18. **ILO Convention (No. 169) Concerning Indigenous and Tribal Peoples in Independent Countries. Concluded, 27Jun 1989. Entered into force, 5 Sep 1991. 2 ILO C.R. 1436, 72 ILO Off. Bull. 59 (1989);** *reprinted in* **28 I.L.M. 1382 and 3 Weston & Carlson III.F.2: Arts. 1–8, 12–20, 24–31** (Basic Document 3.31).

19. **Draft Declaration on the Rights of Indigenous Peoples. Adopted, 26 Aug 1994. UN Doc. E/CN.4/1995/2, E/CN.4/Sub. 2/1994/56**

(28 Oct 1994); *reprinted in* 3 **Weston & Carlson III.F.4: Pmbl. & Arts. 1–4, 6–10, 12, 13, 21–23, 25–28, 30, 31, 35, 38** (Basic Document 3.43).

20. **Proposed American Declaration on the Rights of Indigenous Peoples. Approved 26 Feb 1997 by the Inter–American Commission on Human Rights at its 1333rd Session, 95th Regular Session. OEA/ Ser L/V/II.95.doc. 7, rev. 1997, at <http://scm.oas.org/Reference/en- glish/DECLARATIONS/DECL–INDIGIN–E–97.doc>: Pmbl & Arts. Iii– V, VII, XII, XIII, XVIII, XXI** (Basic Document 3.49).

21. **S. James Anaya and Robert A. Williams, "The Protection of Indigenous Peoples' Rights over Lands and Natural Resources under the Inter–American Human Rights System," 14 Harv. Hum. Rts. J. 33, 36–59 (2001).**

[*Eds.*—In this essay, the authors highlight four separate human rights cases brought before the Inter–American Commission on Human Rights in recent years, each focusing on "a central demand of the indigenous human rights movement"—*i.e.*, the protection of indigenous peoples' rights over traditional lands and natural resources. The four cases are: (1) the case of the Awas Tingni Community against the Republic of Nicaragua, filed by the Inter–American Commission before the Inter–American Court of Human Rights on 28 May 1998;[c] (2) the case of Mary and Carrie Dann against United States, Case No. 11,140, Inter–Am. Comm'n H.R. 99 (1999); (3) the case of the Maya Indigenous Communities and their Members against Belize, Case No. 12.053, Inter–Am. Comm'n H.R. 78 (2000); and (4) the case of the Carrier Sekani which, at the time of the authors' writing, was the subject of an Amended Petition and Response to the Inter–American Commission submit- ted by the Chiefs of the Member Nations of the Carrier Sekani Tribal Council against Canada (Case No. 12,279). Each of the authors was involved in representing the petitioners in these four cases at the time of the essay's writing. In addition to discussing the proposition in each case that the Inter– American human rights system recognizes and protects indigenous peoples' rights over their traditional lands and resources and, to this end, imposes corresponding international legal obligations upon its member states, they urge the state actors and other decision makers in these cases "to recognize and protect the rights of indigenous peoples in their traditional lands and resources." We begin with their summary explication of each case and thereafter turn to their principal substantive law discussion.]

II. INDIGENOUS HUMAN RIGHTS COMPLAINTS PRESENTLY BEFORE THE INTER–AMERICAN HUMAN RIGHTS SYSTEM

Of the four noted indigenous human rights cases presently working their way through the Inter–American system, by far the most significant develop- ments are occurring in the Awas Tingni Case. The case originated with a petition to the Inter–American Commission on Human Rights charging Nica- ragua with failure to take steps necessary to secure the land rights of the Mayagna (Sumo) indigenous community of Awas Tingni and of other Mayag- na and Miskito indigenous communities in Nicaragua's Atlantic Coast re-

c. *See* Caso La Communidad Mayagna (Sumo) Awas Tingni, Corte Interamericana   D.H., Caso No. 11,577, sentencia de 1 de Fe- brero de 2000.

gion.... [N]ow before the Inter–American Court of Human Rights, which ... unanimously [rejected] Nicaragua's effort to have the case dismissed on grounds of failure to exhaust domestic remedies, [the] case is the first ever heard by the Inter–American Court in which the central issue is indigenous collective rights to traditional lands and natural resources.

The case revolves around efforts by Awas Tingni and other indigenous communities of Nicaragua's Atlantic Coast to demarcate their traditional lands and to prevent logging in their territories by a Korean company under a government-granted concession. In 1998, the Inter–American Commission on Human Rights ruled favorably on the merits of the petition filed by the Awas Tingni community and recommended appropriate remedial action. The Commission's decision coincided with a judgment by the Supreme Court of Nicaragua establishing the illegality of the logging concession to the Korean company because of a procedural defect. When Nicaragua continued its refusal to demarcate Awas Tingni and other indigenous traditional lands, despite domestic constitutional and statutory provisions requiring the state to guarantee indigenous communal lands, the Inter–American Commission itself took the case to the Inter–American Court of Human Rights. In agreement with Awas Tingni, the Commission alleges that both the logging concession and the ongoing failure of Nicaragua to demarcate indigenous land constitute violations of the right to property affirmed in article 21 of the American Convention on Human Rights **[Basic Document 3.17]** and of the correlative duties of articles 1 and 2 of the Convention to guarantee the rights of the Convention.

Because the Inter–American Court possesses the power to require states that have consented to its jurisdiction (as has Nicaragua) to take remedial measures for the violation of human rights, the Awas Tingni Case will likely establish an important precedent on indigenous land rights under Inter–American and international law. The case has already attracted significant attention worldwide from indigenous, environmental, and human rights groups, as well as influential media coverage. Significantly, the World Bank has conditioned a financial aid package set for Nicaragua on the development by the government of a specific plan to demarcate the traditional lands of the Miskito and Mayagna communities. This was the first time that the World Bank had placed such a condition on an aid package.

The Inter–American Commission on Human Rights is actively involved in investigating and adjudicating petitions in three other cases involving assertions of indigenous peoples' rights to their traditional lands and resources. Among others, these cases have arisen in Belize, Canada, and the United States. Unlike Nicaragua, none of these countries is a party to the American Convention on Human Rights. However, under the Commission's Statute and Regulations, the Commission may adjudicate petitions against states that are not parties to the Convention by reference to the American Declaration on the Rights and Duties of Man **[Basic Document 3.1]**.[1] Thus, the petitions in each of these cases allege violations of the American Declaration, as well as of other sources of international human rights law.

1. *See* Statute of the Inter–American Commission on Human Rights, Art. 20; Regulations of the Inter–American Commission on Human Rights arts. 51–54. See generally Guide to International and Human Rights Practice 124 (H. Hannum ed., 3d ed. 1999).

In October 2000, the Inter–American Commission declared admissible a petition filed in 1998 by the Toledo Maya Cultural Council (TMCC) on behalf of thirty-seven indigenous Maya communities in the Toledo District of southern Belize. The petition protests government grants of logging and oil concessions to over 700,000 acres of rain forest in Maya traditional territories and the government's failure to recognize and protect Maya traditional land and resource tenure outside of small, confining reservations that were established by the British colonial government decades ago. In further action that same month, the Commission accepted a request for precautionary measures by the TMCC on behalf of the Maya. In an extraordinary measure, the Commission specifically called upon Belize to suspend all permits, licenses, and concessions for logging, oil exploration, and other natural resource development activity on lands used and occupied by the Maya communities in the Toledo District until the Commission has investigated the substantive claims raised in the case.

Significantly, the Inter–American system's recent and increased scrutiny of state action affecting indigenous peoples' rights in their traditional lands and resources reaches into all parts of the hemisphere. The Inter–American Commission has examined situations, similar to the ones concerning indigenous peoples in Belize and Nicaragua, in other countries throughout Central and South America. The international human rights community has long recognized that some of the world's worst abuses of indigenous peoples' human rights by states occur in this region. But the Commission also is currently examining two indigenous land rights cases that arise from disputes in the United States and Canada. The foreign affairs agencies of these North American countries often praise their own domestic legal and political systems as providing progressive and strong regimes of recognition and protection of indigenous rights. Nonetheless, the petitions submitted by indigenous peoples to the Inter–American Commission against the United States and Canada assert serious abuses of human rights that are anything but praiseworthy. Both cases involve the treatment of indigenous peoples' rights in their traditional lands and resources under international law, revealing that no state within the Inter–American system is above scrutiny where these rights are concerned.

In 1999, the Inter–American Commission ruled the case filed against the United States by Mary and Carrie Dann, traditional Western Shoshone ranchers, admissible and stated that the alleged infringement of Western Shoshone ancestral land rights by the United States warrants consideration. For nearly two decades the Dann sisters have asserted aboriginal title rights to Western Shoshone ancestral lands as a defense to efforts by the United States to deprive them of the use and enjoyment of those lands. The United States regards the "gradual encroachment" by non-Indians as having extinguished Western Shoshone rights to ancestral lands. This view comes despite the continuing presence of Western Shoshone people. Additionally, the United States has permitted large-scale gold mining and other environmentally damaging activity on lands still used by the Western Shoshone. Having been denied a remedy through a labyrinth of domestic legal proceedings that ended in the United States Supreme Court,[2] the Danns turned to the Inter–

2. *See* United States v. Dann, 470 U.S. 39 (1985).

American human rights system. On September 27, 1999, the Inter–American Commission, responding to the petition filed by the Dann sisters, issued its decision on admissibility, stating that the "Danns had invoked and exhausted domestic remedies of the United States" and that the petition was timely pursuant to the Commission's regulations. The Commission also concluded that, based on the facts alleged in the petition and subsequent submissions, the violations complained of are "continuing," "on going," and a *prima facie* violation of rights protected by the Inter–American system. On these bases, the Commission declared the Danns' case admissible.

Finally, in May 2000, the Inter–American Commission formally initiated consideration of a complaint filed by the Carrier Sekani Tribal Council of British Columbia, Canada, asserting violations of the Carrier Sekani indigenous peoples' aboriginal rights to land and natural resources. Submitted by the chiefs of the member First Nations of the Carrier Sekani Tribal Council, the case seeks to prevent the British Columbia provincial government from "reallocating" the timber rights in the Carrier Sekani peoples' traditional territory to large corporate logging companies. The government undertook this reallocation despite then on-going treaty negotiations to settle long-standing issues surrounding Carrier Sekani land and resource rights under a process established by the British Columbia provincial government with the backing of the Canadian federal government. The Inter–American Commission has twice requested the Canadian government to supply information relevant to the case, and convened a hearing on the case on March 2, 2000.

A great deal is at stake in these ongoing indigenous land and resource rights cases. Each concerns serious threats to the safe enjoyment of indigenous peoples' human rights, including threats to the cultural survival and physical well-being of entire indigenous communities. Furthermore, these cases test the coherence of the relationship of the American Convention and American Declaration to rules and principles of international law present in other international instruments and increasingly reflected in international practice. These cases complain of state actions that compromise the integrity of basic human rights principles.

III. PROTECTION OF INDIGENOUS PEOPLES' RIGHTS TO LAND AND NATURAL RESOURCES BY INTER–AMERICAN HUMAN RIGHTS INSTRUMENTS AND UN TREATIES

Various human rights instruments of the OAS govern the adjudication of these cases now working through the Inter–American human rights system. In the Awas Tingni case, which arises from Nicaragua, the most important instrument is the American Convention on Human Rights, since Nicaragua is a party to that multilateral treaty, as are a majority of the OAS member states. The American Convention establishes both the procedures and substantive rights that govern the adjudication of complaints by the Inter–American Commission and Inter-American Court in relation to state parties to the Convention. As already noted, the three other cases are against OAS member states that are not parties to the American Convention, and thus the principal instrument for determining the applicable substantive rights for those countries in proceedings before the Inter–American Commission is the American Declaration on the Rights and Duties of Man. The Inter–American Court considers the American Declaration to articulate general human rights obligations of OAS member states under the OAS Charter **[Basic Document 1.7]**, an organic multilateral treaty with the force of law.

Although neither the American Convention nor the American Declaration specifically mentions indigenous peoples, both include general human rights provisions that protect traditional indigenous land and resource tenure. These include provisions explicitly upholding the rights to property and to physical well being and provisions implicitly affirming the right to the integrity of culture. Thus, provisions of the American Declaration and the American Convention affirm rights of indigenous peoples to lands and natural resources on the basis of traditional patterns of use and occupancy, especially when viewed in light of other relevant human rights instruments and international developments concerning indigenous peoples.

Other human rights instruments that bear directly on an assessment of the rights and corresponding obligations of the parties include two major UN human rights treaties, the International Covenant on Civil and Political Rights **[Basic Document 3.14]** and the International Convention on the Elimination of All Forms of [Racial] Discrimination **[Basic Document 3.12]**. Each of the states involved in the cases—Canada, Belize, Nicaragua, and the United States—is a party to the Covenant on Civil and Political Rights; and each, except for Belize, is a party to the convention against discrimination. Both of these UN human rights treaties include provisions that protect indigenous peoples' rights over land and natural resources. The Inter–American Commission on Human Rights has frequently interpreted the obligations of states under the American Convention and the American Declaration by reference to obligations arising from other international instruments. The Commission has found a basis for this approach in article 29 of the American Convention, which states that "[n]o provision of this Convention shall be interpreted as ... restricting the enjoyment or exercise of any right or freedom recognized by virtue of the laws of any State Party or by virtue of another convention to which one of the said states is a party."

Interpretation of the American instruments by reference to other applicable treaties is supported by the *pro homine* principle, which favors integrating the meaning of related human rights obligations that derive from diverse sources.

A. The Right to Property

Indigenous peoples' traditional land and resource tenure is protected by Article 21 of the American Convention on Human Rights, which provides: "Everyone has the right to the use and enjoyment of his property." Similarly, article XXIII of the American Declaration on the Rights and Duties of Man affirms the right of every person "to own such private property as meets the essential needs of decent living and helps to maintain the dignity of the individual and the home." The right to property affirmed in these two instruments must be understood to attach to the property regimes that derive from indigenous peoples' own customary or traditional systems of land tenure independently of whatever property regimes derive from or are recognized by official state enactments. The Inter–American Commission on Human Rights has supported this interpretation of the right to property in [Article 18 of] its

Proposed American Declaration on the Rights of Indigenous Peoples [**Basic Document 3.49**]:

1. Indigenous peoples have the right to the legal recognition of their varied and specific forms and modalities of their control, ownership, use and enjoyment of territories and property.

2. Indigenous peoples have the right to the recognition of their property and ownership rights with respect to lands, territories and resources they have historically occupied, as well as to the use of those to which they have historically had access for their traditional activities and livelihood.

Excluding indigenous property regimes from the property protected by the American Convention and American Declaration would perpetuate the long history of discrimination against indigenous peoples. Such discriminatory application of the right to property would be in tension with the principle of non-discrimination that is part of the Inter–American human rights system's foundation.

* * *

At the outset, it should be emphasized that indigenous communities in the Americas as elsewhere will define property rights according to their own unique traditions and customs. There is no "universal," or one-size-fits-all definition of "indigenous property rights," that the Inter–American system can arbitrarily settle upon. Because each indigenous community possesses its own unique social, political, and economic history, each has adapted and adopted methods of cultural survival and development suited to the unique environment and ecosystem inhabited by that community. As a result, each indigenous community creates its own customary laws for governing its lands and resources. This process of jurisgenesis means that indigenous societies' property rights systems possess the same particularity and divergence that characterize the property rights systems of non-indigenous societies.

Generally, however, among indigenous communities a group's particular system of land tenure is recognized as embodying a property rights regime. Within the corresponding system of indigenous peoples' customary norms, traditional land tenure generally is understood as establishing the collective property of the indigenous community and derivative rights among community members. An examination of indigenous peoples' own jurisprudence, including the jurisprudence of modern indigenous judicial institutions in the United States, reveals how decision makers in indigenous communities, or tribal judges, characterize the unique systems of property rights derived from their communities' land tenure systems.

* * *

Another characteristic of indigenous property rights is that they often are not conceptualized in exclusive terms, but rather as recognized regimes of shared use and property rights between groups. Indigenous communities, for example, may migrate over time and may have overlapping land use and occupancy areas. Such patterns are simply characteristic of indigenous peoples' land tenure and resource use and do not undermine the existence or determinacy of their property rights. The International Labour Organization's

Convention No. 169 concerning Indigenous and Tribal Peoples in Independent Countries of 1989 **[Basic Document 3.31]**, expressly recognizes this principle. [Article 14(1)] requires its state parties to obey the following: "Measures shall be taken in appropriate cases to safeguard the right of the peoples concerned to use lands not exclusively occupied by them, but to which they have traditionally had access for their subsistence and traditional activities."

With their source in indigenous peoples' own customs and usages, and with characteristics that may diverge widely from property regimes that derive from state enactments, indigenous traditional and resource tenure regimes nonetheless constitute forms of property. The existence of indigenous property regimes does not depend on prior identification by the state, but rather may be discerned by objective evidence that includes indigenous peoples' own accounts of traditional land and resource tenure.

Indigenous peoples possess unique knowledge about the lands and resources that they have traditionally occupied or used, and to which they accordingly have rights under their own legal systems, as well as under domestic and international law. International and domestic legal institutions have come to recognize and respect that indigenous peoples' own knowledge can effectively establish the existence, scope, and characteristics of their traditional land tenure.... documentation is being presented to the Commission in the Maya, Dann, and Carrier Sekani cases. An increasing number of state legal systems now recognize indigenous peoples' oral history and their own documentation and mapping of their lands as evidence in legal proceedings determining land rights. In addition, expert testimony from anthropologists, geographers and other qualified scholars with relevant knowledge of indigenous peoples' customs and culture is also recognized by domestic legal systems as relevant to establishing indigenous peoples' property rights based on traditional systems of land tenure.

* * *

Thus, evidence of indigenous peoples' traditional and customary land tenure can be established by qualified expert and academic opinion, as well as by objective facts that can be discerned from the oral accounts and documentation produced by the indigenous communities concerned. Indigenous peoples' own knowledge will, in most instances, provide the most reliable proof of the existence of property rights entitled to protection under a state's legal system. Neither the international system, nor individual states should deny an indigenous groups' claimed property rights in land by excluding or ignoring evidence derived from the culture and traditions of the indigenous group or community itself.

To do so would be to perpetuate a long history of discrimination against indigenous peoples with regard to their own modalities of possession and use of lands and natural resources. In elaborating upon the requirements of the Convention on the Elimination of All Forms of Racial Discrimination **[Basic Document 3.12]**, the UN Committee on the Elimination of Discrimination (CERD) has observed:

> In many regions of the world indigenous peoples have been, and are still being, discriminated against, deprived of their human rights and fundamental freedoms ... and have lost their land and resources to

colonists, commercial companies and State enterprises. Consequently the preservation of their culture and their historical identity has been and still is jeopardized.[3]

Such patterns of discrimination against indigenous peoples cannot be allowed to persist in the modern world. Thus CERD has interpreted the convention against discrimination as requiring recognition and protection of indigenous peoples' own land and resource tenure systems, consistent with the interpretation of the right to property under the American Convention and American Declaration advanced here.

In Mabo v. Queensland (No.2) the Australian High Court exemplified the adherence to equality principles that are required to eradicate the legacies of historical discrimination affecting the enjoyment of property.[4] In that landmark case, the High Court, reversing more than a century of Australian jurisprudence and official policy, recognized "native title": that is, a right of property based on indigenous peoples' customary land tenure. In the case's leading opinion, Justice Brennan characterized as "unjust and discriminatory" the past failure of the Australian legal system to embrace and protect native title. Earlier, in Mabo v. Queensland (No. 1),[5] Justices Brennan, Toohey, and Gaudron, in a joint judgement, expressed the Court's majority view that a legislative measure targeting native title for legal extinguishment was racially discriminatory and hence invalid. Regarding the indigenous Miriam people of the Murray Islands, the justices viewed the discriminatory treatment of their claim to native title as "impairing their human rights while leaving unimpaired the human rights of those whose rights in and over the Murray Islands did not take their origins in the laws and customs of the Miriam people."

As the Australia High Court in Mabo I declared, legislation providing that the state owned all land not under formal title and ignoring indigenous peoples' historic occupancy violated Australia's Racial Discrimination Act of 1975, which implemented the United Nations Convention on the Elimination of All Forms of Racial Discrimination. The 1988 Mabo I decision thus rejected Queensland's defense that state law resolved the aboriginal challenge, opening the way for the court's 1992 landmark decision recognizing native title under Australian law.

Examined in light of the fundamental principle of non-discrimination enshrined in both the American Declaration and the American Convention, the right to property in these same instruments necessarily includes protection for those forms of property that are based on indigenous peoples' traditional patterns of land tenure. Failure to afford such protection to the property rights of indigenous peoples would accord illegitimate discriminatory treatment to their customary land tenure, in violation of the principle of equality under the law.

3. Committee on the Elimination of Racial Discrimination, General Recommendation XXIII on indigenous peoples, adopted at the Committee's 1235th meeting, 18 Aug 1997, CERD/C51/Misc. 13/Rev. (1997), ¶ 3....

4. Mabo v. Queensland [No.2] (1992), 175 C.L.R. 1 (Austl.).

5. Mabo v. Queensland [No.1] (1988), 166 C.L.R. 186 (Austl.).

B.   Rights to Physical Well–Being and Cultural Integrity

Typically for indigenous peoples, as for the indigenous communities in the cases now before the Inter–American system, land and natural resources are not mere economic commodities. The lands occupied and used by an indigenous community are crucial to its existence, continuity, and culture. The land and resource rights of indigenous peoples cannot be fully understood without an appreciation of the profound, sustaining linkages that exist between indigenous peoples and their lands. The UN Sub–Commission on the Promotion and Protection of Human Rights (formally the UN Sub–Commission on Prevention of Discrimination and Protection of Minorities) is now conducting a study on "indigenous people and their relationship to land."[6] An issue of the study observes that, through their involvement over the years at the UN, indigenous peoples have emphasized the fundamental issue of their relationship to their homelands. They have done so in the context of the urgent need for understanding by non-indigenous societies of the spiritual, social, cultural, economic and political significance to indigenous societies of their lands, territories and resources for their continued survival and vitality. Indigenous peoples have explained that, because of the profound relationship that indigenous peoples have to their lands, territories and resources, there is a need for a different conceptual framework to understand this relationship and a need for recognition of the cultural differences that exist. Indigenous peoples have urged the world community to attach positive value to this distinct relationship [as evidenced in paragraphs 10 and 18 of the report]:

> ... [A] number of elements ... are unique to indigenous peoples: (i) a profound relationship exists between indigenous peoples and their lands, territories and resources; (ii) this relationship has various social, cultural, spiritual, economic and political dimensions and responsibilities; (iii) the collective dimension of this relationship is significant; and (iv) the inter-generational aspect of such a relationship is also crucial to indigenous peoples' identity, survival and cultural viability.

Indigenous peoples' agricultural and other land use patterns provide means of subsistence, and, further, are typically linked with familial and social relations, religious practices, and the very existence of indigenous communities as discrete social and cultural phenomena. Several rights articulated in the American Convention and the American Declaration support the enjoyment of such critical aspects of indigenous peoples' cultures, in addition to the right to property discussed above. These rights include the rights to life (American Declaration, article I, American Convention, article 4), the right to preservation of health and physical integrity (American Declaration, article XI, American Convention, article 5.1), the right to religious freedom (American Declaration, article III, American Convention, article 12), the right to family and protection thereof (American Declaration, articles V–VI, American Convention, article 17), and rights to freedom of movement and residence (American Declaration, article VIII; American Convention, article 22). The Inter–American Commission on Human Rights has observed that, "[f]or

---

6. Indigenous people and their relationship to land: Second progress report on the working paper prepared by Mrs. Erica–Irene A Daes, Special Rapporteur, UN Sub–Commission on Prevention of Discrimination and Protection of Minorities, UN Doc. E/CN.4/Sub.2/1999/18 (June 1999)....

indigenous peoples, the free exercise of such rights is essential to the enjoyment and perpetuation of their culture."

The right to cultural integrity is made explicit by article 27 of the Covenant on Civil and Political Rights, which states: "In those States in which ethnic, religious or linguistic minorities exist, persons belonging to such minorities shall not be denied the right, in community with the other members of their group, to enjoy their own culture, to profess and practice their own religion, or to use their own language." Relying especially on article 27, the Inter–American Commission on Human Rights has affirmed that international law protects minority groups, including indigenous peoples, in the enjoyment of all aspects of their diverse cultures and group identities.[7] According to the Commission, the right to the integrity of, in particular, indigenous peoples' culture covers "the aspects linked to productive organization, which includes, among other things, the issue of ancestral and communal lands."[8]

In its Proposed Declaration on the Rights of Indigenous Peoples, the Commission once again articulated the obligation of states to respect the cultural integrity of indigenous peoples, expressly linking property rights and customs to the survival of indigenous cultures. Article VII of the Proposed Declaration, entitled "Right to Cultural Integrity" states:

1. Indigenous peoples have the right to their cultural integrity, and their historical and archeological heritage, which are important both for their survival as well as for the identity of their members.

2. Indigenous peoples are entitled to restitution in respect of the property of which they have been dispossessed, and where that is not possible, compensation on a basis not less favorable than the standard of international law.

3. The states shall recognize and respect indigenous ways of life, customs, traditions, forms of social, economic and political organization, institutions, practices, beliefs and values, use of dress, and languages.

The United Nations Human Rights Committee has confirmed the Commission's interpretation of the reach of the cultural integrity norm, as displayed in its General Comment on article 27 of the Covenant of Civil and Political Rights:

> [C]ulture manifests itself in many forms, including a particular way of life associated with the use of land resources, especially in the case of indigenous peoples. That right may include such traditional activities as fishing or hunting and the right to live in reserves protected by law. The enjoyment of these rights may require positive measures of protection

7. *See, e.g.* Inter–Am. C.H.R., Report on the Human Rights Situation in Ecuador, OEA/Ser.L/V./II.96, doc. 10 rev. 1 (1997) [hereinafter Report on Ecuador]; at 103–04; Inter–Amer. C.H.R., Report on the Situation of Human Rights of a Segment of the Nicaraguan Population of Miskito Origin and Resolution on the Friendly Settlement Procedure regarding the Human Rights Situation of a Segment of the Nicaraguan Population of Miskito Ori-

gin, OEA/Ser.L/V/II.62, doc. 26 (1983), OEA/Ser.L/V/II.62, doc. 26 (1984), at 76–78 (regarding the land rights of the Miskito and other indigenous communities of Nicaragua's Atlantic Coast) [hereinafter Miskito Report]; Case 7615 (Brazil), Inter–Am. C.H.R., OEA/Ser.L/V/II.66, doc. 10, rev. 1, at 24, 31 (1985) (concerning the Yanomami of Brazil).

8. Miskito Report, *supra* note 7, at 81.

and measures to ensure the effective participation of members of minority communities in decisions which affect them.[9]

Indigenous peoples' traditional land use patterns are included by the Committee as cultural elements that states must take affirmative measures to protect under article 27 regardless of whether states recognize indigenous peoples' ownership rights over lands and resources subject to traditional uses.

The Human Rights Committee found violations of article 27 in circumstances similar to those confronting the indigenous communities in the cases before the Inter–American system. In B. Ominayak, Chief of the Lubicon Lake Band of Cree v. Canada,[10] the Committee determined that Canada had violated article 27 by allowing the provincial government of Alberta to grant leases for oil and gas exploration and timber development within the ancestral territory of the Lubicon Lake Band. The Committee found that the natural resource development activity compounded historical inequities to "threaten the way of life and culture of the Lubicon Lake Band, and constitute a violation of article 27 so long as they continue."

Also significant are the Committee's pronouncements in the Länsmann cases. These two cases involved threats to reindeer herding by indigenous Sami people, through state-sanctioned rock quarrying and forestry in traditional Sami territory. In both cases, while not finding violations of the Covenant under the specific facts before it, the Committee concluded that article 27 protected Sami traditional means of livelihood in their traditional area, despite the fact that ownership to the area was in dispute.[11] Additionally, in both cases the Committee confirmed its position, articulated in an earlier case involving Sami reindeer herding, that article 27 protections extend to economic activity "where that activity is an essential element in the culture of an ethnic community."[12]

Article 27 has also been the basis of decisions by the Inter–American Commission on Human Rights in cases involving particular indigenous groups. In these decisions, the Commission has confirmed the importance and international legal obligation of protecting indigenous peoples' cultural and related property rights. In its 1985 decision concerning the Yanomami Indians of Brazil, the Commission, citing article 27, asserted that contemporary international law recognizes "the right of ethnic groups to special protection in the use of their own language, of the practice of their own religion, and in general, for all those characteristics necessary for the preservation of their cultural identity."[13] The Commission noted that the OAS and its member states list "preservation and strengthening" of the indigenous groups' cultural heritage as a "priority," and declared that Brazil's failure to protect the Yanomami from incursions by miners and others into their ancestral lands threatened the Indians' physical well being, culture, and traditions. The

9. UN Hum. Rts. Comm., General Comment No. 23 (50) (Art. 27), HRI/GEN/1/Rev.1 at 38, adopted Apr. 6, 1994 [hereinafter HRC General Comment on Art. 27], ¶ 7.

10. Communication No. 167/1984, UN Hum. Rts. Comm., A/45/40, vol. II, annex IX.A.

11. J.E. Länsmann v. Finland, Communication No. 671/1995, CCPR/C/58/D/671/1995, ¶ ¶ 2.1–2.4, 10.1–10.5 (Länsmann II).

12. Kitok v. Sweden, Communication No. 197/1985, UN Hum. Rts. Comm., doc. A/43/40, annex VII.G (1988).

13. Res. No. 12/85, Case No. 7615 Inter–Am C.H.R. 24 (1985), *in* Annual Report of the Inter–American Commission of Human Rights 1984–85, OEA/Ser.L/V/II.66, doc. 10, rev. 1 (1985).

Commission therefore recommended that the government secure the boundaries of a reserve for the Yanomami to protect their cultural heritage. Brazil responded by moving forward with the establishment of the Yanomami Reserve and by amending its constitution in 1988 to provide greater protections to Indians and their lands.

The Inter–American Commission also invoked article 27 in its consideration of the 1983 complaint filed by the indigenous peoples of Nicaragua's Atlantic Coast against the government of Nicaragua for human rights abuses committed during the early years of Nicaragua's civil war.[14] Relying specifically on the cultural rights guarantees of article 27, the Commission recommended measures to secure the indigenous communities' land rights and to develop "an adequate institutional order" that would better accommodate the distinctive cultural attributes and traditional forms of organization of the indigenous groups.[15] The Commission's recommendations were instrumental in leading the government to the negotiating table with indigenous community leaders. This negotiation process culminated in the enactment of the constitutional provisions and law that affirm indigenous peoples' land rights and establish regional governments for the indigenous communities on Nicaragua's Atlantic Coast. However, Nicaragua has not fully implemented these enactments, as illustrated by the Awas Tingni Case.

Critical to the viable continuation of indigenous peoples' cultures is the link the Human Rights Committee and Inter–American Commission have recognized between the economic and social activities of indigenous peoples and their traditional territories. Both the Human Rights Committee and the Inter–American Commission have concluded that, under international law, the states' obligation to protect indigenous peoples' right to cultural integrity necessarily includes the obligation to protect traditional lands because of the inextricable link between land and culture in this context. Thus, rights to lands and resources are property rights that are prerequisites for the physical and cultural survival of indigenous communities, and they are protected by the American Declaration, the American Convention, and other international human rights instruments, such as the Convention on the Elimination of All Forms of Racial Discrimination and the Covenant on Civil and Political Rights.

IV. INTERNATIONAL AND DOMESTIC LEGAL PRACTICE: EMERGING CUSTOMARY INTERNATIONAL LAW

The foregoing interpretations of relevant provisions of the American instruments and applicable UN human rights treaties is reinforced by an increasingly well defined and consistent pattern of international and domestic legal practice that recognizes indigenous peoples' rights to lands and natural resources. Especially significant is the international practice associated with International Labour Organization Convention (No. 169) on Indigenous and Tribal Peoples **[Basic Document 3.31]**, which has been ratified by several states in the Americas. A drafting committee that included thirty-nine states in addition to the worker and employee delegates that are part of the ILO developed the convention. It was adopted by the full conference of the ILO by an overwhelming majority of the voting delegates, including government

---

14. Miskito Report, *supra* note 7.   **15.** *Id*. at 81–82, ¶ 15.

delegates. Although none of the states involved in the cases highlighted in this Article are parties to Convention No. 169, the convention nonetheless has relevance as part of a larger body of increasingly consistent practice at the international and domestic levels. Such other international practice includes resolutions and decisions by authoritative international bodies and developments toward new declarations by the UN and OAS on the rights of indigenous peoples. At the domestic level, relevant practices include legislation, judicial decisions, and constitutional reforms that pronounce protections for indigenous land and resource rights.

Viewed comprehensively, applicable international practice incorporates and goes beyond the domain of existing treaty obligations for states within the Inter–American system. Taken together with relevant domestic legal practice, international practice gives rise to obligations of customary international law that apply more generally throughout the Inter–American system. As demonstrated by an expanding body of literature, it is evident that indigenous peoples have achieved a substantial level of international concern for their interests, and there is substantial movement toward a convergence of international opinion on the content of indigenous peoples' rights, including rights over lands and natural resources. Developments toward consensus about the content of indigenous rights simultaneously give rise to expectations that the rights will be upheld, regardless of any formal act of assent to the articulated norms. The discourse of indigenous peoples and their rights has been part of multiple international institutions and conferences in response to demands made by indigenous groups over several years backed by an extensive record of justification. The pervasive assumption has been that the articulation of norms concerning indigenous peoples is an exercise in identifying standards of conduct that are required to uphold widely shared values of human dignity. The multilateral processes that build a common understanding of the content of indigenous peoples' rights, therefore, also build expectations of behavior in conformity with those rights.

Under modern legal theory, processes that generate consensus about indigenous peoples' rights build customary international law. As a general matter, norms of customary law arise when a preponderance of states and other authoritative actors converge upon a common understanding of the norms' content and generally expect future behavior in conformity with the norms. The traditional points of reference for determining the existence and contours of customary norms include the relevant patterns of actual conduct of state actors. Today, however, actual state conduct is not the only or necessarily determinative indicia of customary norms. With the advent of modern inter-governmental institutions and enhanced communications media, states and other relevant actors increasingly engage in prescriptive dialogue. Especially in multilateral settings, explicit communication may itself bring about a convergence of understanding and expectation about rules, establishing in those rules a pull toward compliance, even in advance of a widespread corresponding pattern of physical conduct. It is thus increasingly understood that explicit communication, of the sort that is reflected in ... numerous international documents and decisions ..., builds customary rules of international law. Conforming domestic laws and related practice reinforces such customary rules of international law. Non-conforming domestic practice undermines the apparent direction of the international norm-building only to the extent the international regime holds out and eventually accepts as legitimate the non-conformity.

Although international and domestic practice varies somewhat in its recognition and protection of indigenous peoples' land and resource rights, just as state practice varies in its treatment of property rights in general, it nonetheless entails a sufficiently uniform and widespread acceptance of core principles to constitute a norm of customary international law. The relevant practice of states and international institutions establishes that, as a matter of customary international law, states must recognize and protect indigenous peoples' rights to land and natural resources in connection with traditional or ancestral use and occupancy patterns. This new and emerging customary international law, along with treaty obligations arising from outside the Inter–American system, inform an understanding of the rights that are protected by the American Convention and American Declaration.

A. International Practice

One of the most impressive achievements of the post World War II international system in protecting human rights has been the recognition of indigenous peoples as special subjects of concern. As part of this development, states and others acting through international institutions increasingly have affirmed the central importance of traditional lands and resources to the cultural survival of indigenous peoples.

The requirement that states recognize and protect indigenous peoples' rights in their traditional lands is included in the Inter–American Charter of Social Guaranties, which was adopted by the General Assembly of the Organization of American States in 1948. Article 39 of the Charter requires that states take "necessary measures ... to give protection and assistance to the Indians, safeguarding their life, liberty, and property, preventing their extermination, shielding them from oppression and exploitation, protecting them from want and furnishing them with an adequate education."[16] Further, the article recommends establishing "[i]nstitutions or services" created specifically "to safeguard [Indian] lands, legalize their ownership thereof, and prevent the invasion of such lands by outsiders."

ILO Convention No. 107 of 1957 similarly recognized indigenous peoples' rights of ownership to the lands they traditionally occupied.[17] Despite Convention No. 107's widely criticized—and now rejected—assimilationist bias in other respects, its recognition in 1957 of the right to collective land ownership by indigenous groups demonstrates the long-standing concern in international practice for protecting indigenous peoples' rights to their traditional lands.

ILO Convention No. 169 of 1989 **[Basic Document 3.31]**, a revision of Convention No. 107, is international law's most concrete manifestation of the growing recognition of indigenous peoples' rights to property in lands. Convention No. 169's land rights provisions are framed by article 13(1), which states:

16. Inter–American Charter of Social Guaranties, at Art. 39 (1948), *reprinted in* Encyclopedia of the United Nations and International Relations (E. Osmanczyk ed., 1990).

17. Convention concerning the Protection and Integration of Indigenous Populations and Other Tribal and Semi–Tribal Populations in the Independent Countries, Art. 11, 2 Jun. 1959, 107 I.L.O. 1957 [*reprinted in* 3 Weston & Carlson III.F.1].

In applying the provisions of this Part of the Convention governments shall respect the special importance for the cultures and spiritual
values of the peoples concerned of their relationship with the lands or
territories, or both as applicable, which they occupy or otherwise use, and
in particular the collective aspects of this relationship.

The Convention, which has been ratified by a significant number of American
states, speaks specifically to the property rights of indigenous peoples [in
article 14(1)]: "The rights of ownership and possession of the peoples concerned over the lands which they traditionally occupy shall be recognized."

The growing acceptance in international practice of indigenous peoples'
rights in land and natural resources is further evidenced by relevant provisions of the Proposed American Declaration on the Rights of Indigenous
Peoples, prepared by the Inter–American Commission on Human Rights in
consultation with OAS member states and representatives of indigenous
peoples. Emphasizing that such property rights originate from traditional
patterns of land tenure, the Proposed Declaration also stipulates [in article
XVIII, paras. 2 and 3(iii)]: "Nothing ... shall be construed as limiting the
right of indigenous peoples to attribute ownership within the community in
accordance with their customs, traditions, uses and traditional practices, nor
shall it affect any collective community rights over them."

The Draft United Nations Declaration on the Rights of Indigenous
Peoples **[Basic Document 3.43]**, developed by the United Nations Working
Group on Indigenous Populations and approved by UN Sub–Commission on
Prevention of Discrimination and Protection of Minorities, provides further
evidence of the increasingly widespread international recognition of and
respect for indigenous peoples' rights in lands and resources. The Draft UN
Declaration was approved by the Sub–Commission after several years of
discussions in which both states and indigenous peoples from throughout the
world took part. The Draft UN Declaration affirms [in article 26, ¶ 105]:

> Indigenous peoples have the right to own, develop, control and use
> the lands and territories, including the total environment of the lands,
> air, waters, coastal seas, sea-ice, flora and fauna and other resources
> which they have traditionally owned or otherwise occupied or used. This
> includes the right to the full recognition of their laws, traditions and
> customs, land-tenure systems and institutions for the development and
> management of resources, and the right to effective measures by States to
> prevent any interference with, alienation of or encroachment upon these
> rights.

In addition to the many documents that articulate the above principles,
examination of the active engagement of international human rights bodies
demonstrates the broad acceptance of these principles in the realm of practice
as well. The UN Human Rights Committee, the UN Committee on the
Elimination of Racial Discrimination, the relevant organs of the International
Labour Organization, and the Inter–American Commission on Human Rights
apply the prevailing understandings of indigenous peoples' land and resource
rights when they monitor human rights situations where indigenous peoples
are located and when they consider complaints brought by specific indigenous
groups.

Every major international body that has considered indigenous peoples' rights during the past decade has acknowledged the crucial importance of lands and resources to the cultural survival of indigenous peoples and communities. They also have recognized the critical need for governments to respect and protect the varied and particular forms of land tenure defined and regarded as property by indigenous peoples themselves. In addition to the international human rights institutions mentioned above, the World Bank and the European Union have pronounced and acted in favor of these rights. Indigenous peoples and their rights over land and natural resources have been discussed at a multitude of international meetings and conferences sponsored by the UN, the OAS, and other inter-governmental organizations during the last several years. In their numerous oral and written public statements at these meetings, states have concurred or acquiesced in the essential elements of the principles of indigenous peoples' land and resource rights that now find expression in several international documents.

B.   Domestic Practice

The international norms that recognize rights based on indigenous peoples' traditional landholdings and resource use are increasingly incorporated and reflected in the domestic legal practice of states throughout the American region and the world. A large number of states give formal legal recognition to indigenous peoples' communal rights in lands and natural resources based on traditional patterns of use and occupation. Throughout the Americas in particular, OAS state members have amended their constitutions or have adopted new laws to recognize and protect land and natural resource rights for indigenous peoples. In several states, judicial organs have been the architects of domestic legal doctrine recognizing such rights. Similarly, state legal systems in other parts of the world have adopted legal protections for indigenous peoples' traditional land tenure or otherwise provided them rights to land in recognition of historical tenure. . . .

Domestic legal developments are not necessarily sufficient to protect indigenous peoples in the enjoyment of their land and resource tenure. And, of course, those domestic legal advances already achieved remain far from fully implemented and translated into reality for indigenous peoples. Nonetheless, these developments signify a clear trend in the direction of the relevant international practice, and they constitute legal obligations for state officials under domestic law and give rise to expectations of conforming behavior on the part of the international community. As a result, this domestic state practice, together with relevant practice at the international level, builds customary international law. At the very least, a sufficient pattern of common practice regarding indigenous peoples' land and resource rights exists among OAS member states to constitute customary international law at the regional level.

22.   H. Elizabeth Dallam, "The Growing Voice of Indigenous Peoples: Their Use of Storytelling and Rights Discourse to Transform Multilateral Development Bank Policies," 8 Ariz. J. Int'l & Comp. L. 117, 142–48 (1991). The successes won by environmentalist groups acting in connection with pro-indigenous groups and indigenous peoples deserve enormous praise. However, pro-indigenous activists, scholars and indigenous peoples themselves have begun to question the discourse emerging out of this coalition. * * * The discourse proclaims that indigenous people know how to live in harmony with the forest and will protect it, thereby protecting the rest of the world from the damaging effects of global warming. Indeed, several of the indigenous groups themselves adopt this language. Recall Davi Kopenawa Yanomami's interview with Terence Turner. Davi stated:

> The whites have dirty spirits, the Indians, too. There are, however, places in this world that are not dirty, where nature is still clean, as *Omame* directed. The shamans know these places, they understand this cleanness, they can teach it to others.[18]

The Moxo Indians of the Chimane Forest Reserve in Amazonian Bolivia who are protesting commercial lumbering activities have stated, "We have learned to take care and maintain the ecology because we know that it guarantees our existence."[19] Thus, some indigenous groups are binding themselves to fragile ecosystems, and those indigenous groups that do not inhabit such areas cannot access the discourse or environmentalist support.

The nature of this discourse is troubling. Though the coalition between environmentalist and indigenous groups has been very successful in the past decade, it may be inadvertently closing doors for the future. Moreover, the discourse primitivizes indigenous peoples. Clad illustrates this point with the following quote from a 1981 International NGO Conference on Indigenous Peoples and the Land, held in Geneva:

> In the world of today there are two systems, two different irreconcilable "ways of life." The Indian world—collective, communal, human, respectful of nature and wise—and the western world—greedy, destructive, individualist and enemy of mother nature.[20]

The truth of these statements is questionable. As Clad asserts, "[s]uch statements not only ignore past adoption of biologically disruptive technology by aboriginal peoples, but also in a curious way buttress the fallacy of the 'noble savage,' a uniquely European concept."[21] * * * Moreover, indigenous peoples may oppose the initiatives of environmentalists. For instance, Evaristo Nugkuag of COICA [the Coordinating Body for the Indigenous Peoples' Organizations of the Amazon Basin] ... opposes debt-for-nature swaps proposed by environmentalists [on the grounds that they are "an innovative way to save 'what remains of the rich flora and fauna and natural systems of debt-burdened countries' "[22]] * * * because of the disastrous effects of a forest preservation plan that CI arranged in Bolivia. The Chimanes Indians who inhabit the Bolivian forest to be preserved offered their own conservation proposal, yet CI simply ignored it. Instead CI designated a "Permanent Production Zone" for logging of the forest. The logging practices have "wreaked havoc across the land," and "[l]ogging roads have opened up the forest to colonization, with disastrous consequences for the forest wildlife on

18. T. Turner & D. Kopenawa Yanomami, *I Fight Because I am Alive*, 15 Cultural Survival Q. 46, 62 (1991).

19. *Quoted in* K. Redford, *The Ecologically Noble Savage*, 15 Cultural Survival Q. 46, 47 (1991).

20. J. Clad, Conservation and Indigenous Peoples: A Study of Convergent Interests, 8 Cultural Survival Q. 69 (1984).

21. *Id.*

22. W. Reilly, *Debt-for-Nature Swaps: The Time Has Come*, Int'l Envtl. Aff. 135 (Spring 1990).

which the Indian depend."[23] Moreover, the Chimanes do not even have title under Brazilian law to their lands. In August, 1990, 2,000 Indians marched for one month across Bolivia in opposition to the destruction of their lands under the debt-for-nature swap. Thus, debt-for-nature swaps are a good idea in theory, yet may ignore indigenous rights to gain title to their ancestral homelands and to exercise their own development plans.

* * *

The danger in the emerging discourse that credits indigenous groups as being the best keepers of areas, such as rainforests, that are environmentally valuable, is that indigenous peoples without such lands may be excluded from the discussion. An important addition to the discourse is Nugkuag's notion that indigenous peoples should not merely be consulted about development plans but should be participants in the planning process. Moreover, indigenous peoples should explicitly bring their rights to cultural survival and self-determination ... to discussions about development plans. The right to self-determination includes the right to develop or to have control over one's resources. In particular, those indigenous groups who cannot claim to be "stewards" of their lands should enter into these conversations.

SECTION 5. DISCUSSION NOTES/QUESTIONS

1. The reasons for protecting biodiversity are utilitarian as well as ethical and cultural. The formidable strength of the utilitarian case for protecting biodiversity is demonstrated by Dr. Martin Holdgate, the former Director General of the World Conservation Union (IUCN), in his paper *Can Wildlife Pay for Itself?*, delivered at the Royal Society of Arts in London on 12 September 1992 (and wherein he defined "wildlife" to encompass both natural habitats and the wild species they support, and "pay" to mean "the direct provision of a cash return, the indirect provision of financial benefit, and the provision of social benefits more economically than engineered substitutes can do"):

> On some land, wildlife can provide all these returns as well as contribute to that intangible group of elements that we call "quality of life"—one reason why cash profit is not the only reason why people invest in this area. On much land, wildlife is the most economical form of land use—if the economic sums are done right. Undeniably, in many countries wild nature provides essentials outside the cash economy and if such products were properly valued the immense economic benefit of wildlife would become evident.

> There are many countries where forests, savannas, rivers, and coastlands are important sources of food, in the shape of meat, honey, fish, mushrooms, fruit and nuts. They are also important for fibre, fuel, medicines and building materials. Valued correctly, they are an obvious major element in the life-support system. * * * At the other end of the spectrum, direct cash benefits come from many kinds of exploitation of wildlife within formal economies. Fisheries are simply systems for cropping the wildlife of the ocean, inshore seas and fresh waters....

> As another example, 40% of the pharmaceuticals traded across the counter in North America are said to be of wild origin. The value of the substance derived from the rosy periwinkle in treating leukaemia, or of

23. D. Lewis, *Conflicts of Interests*, Geographical Mag. 18, 21 (Dec. 1990).

aconitum, in more traditional heart remedies, or of penicillin and all the other fungal-derived antibiotics, which were taken from the wild progressively once penicillin had shown its properties as a contaminant of one of Fleming's culture plates, is very obvious. The economic value of timber, latex and other materials taken from wild habitats is equally inescapable. Some years ago an estimate showed that 4.5% of North American GNP was based on the economic harvest of wild species, and that wild harvested resources contributed US $87 billion a year between 1976 and 1980.

There are also many indirect cash values. Tourism is the biggest industry—or certainly the biggest foreign exchange earner—in many developing countries. . . .

Wildlife is also immensely valuable as a source of genetic material. Crop breeders go back to the wild time and again to derive new genes that will make their strains more resistant to climate change and pests, or meet new market demands. Nature continues to diversify, and will provide such contributions without charge to humanity, so long as we maintain the ecological systems within which that diversification proceeds.

Nature also does many things for us vastly more cheaply than engineers can do. Forests on upland catchments not only stabilise the soil but regulate the run-off of water, and yield supplies. . . . In low-lying island countries like the Maldives offshore coral reefs that break the fury of the storms may make all the difference between habitability and disaster. . . .

All these benefits can be tied more or less directly to particular species or systems. Beyond—or rather on top of—them, natural ecosystems provide a free service without which we could not live. Green plants renew the oxygen we breathe, and ecosystems cycle the essential elements of carbon, nitrogen, phosphorus and sulphur. The earth would not be habitable without such processes. . . . The economy of the developed world nestles within a niche in the natural world. All societies depend on it, and without these services there would be no civilisation.

* * *

The answer to the question "can wildlife pay for itself?" is thus obviously affirmative. The real question is, however, quite different. It is: "can wildlife pay for itself within the context of our economies?" This is a much more difficult question because those economic systems are distorted in many ways. In particular, we use methods of valuation which favour the conversion of wildlife towards systems that may be less economic and less rewarding.

One reason for this incorrect valuation is the hostility to nature which is still residual in many people and communities, perhaps deriving from the struggles that our early ancestors had against their surroundings. For example, land tenure for settlers in Australia depended on the clearance of the wild vegetation that was pejoratively labelled "bush" (off which the Aboriginal inhabitants had lived sustainably for millennia). Quite recently, Brazil, the State, was subsidising the construction of roads into the forests, and granting tax concessions for forest clearance and conversion of woodland to ranchlands of far lower productivity. Even in the United Kingdom, the denuded uplands, deforested by Bronze Age or Neolithic people, are now more valued as sheep pasture than as restored forest. There is a touch of human arrogance that puts a value on manmade investment, rather than the natural systems it replaces. Only recently have economists demonstrated the economic fallacy of such an approach, and urged that we must value "natural capital" and cost its depreciation and depletion by human impact. . . .

Dr. Holdgate then raised the intriguing question: "who owns wildlife?" He wrote: "The human assumption that wildlife resources were endlessly replenished, and hence could be treated as 'open access resources' from which anyone could take what they could catch and gather might be held to imply some sort of divine ownership. Or does the sovereign state own wildlife? Or do the local communities who often live in balance with nature, so long as their populations do not grow too large, but are equally often dispossessed by urban groups with greater money and power?" How do you answer these questions?

2. The Biodiversity Convention **(Basic Document 5.36)** is a remarkably weak instrument. One of the weaknesses relates to the financial resources necessary for the protection of biological diversity. Article 20(4) states that "[t]he extent to which developing country parties will effectively implement their commitments under this Convention will depend on the effective implementation by developed country parties of their commitments under this Convention related to financial resources . . . and will take fully into account . . . that economic and social development and eradication of poverty are the first and overriding priorities of the developing country parties." In the present problem, Amazonia could argue that it cannot be held in breach of any obligations under the Convention until the developed countries provide the "new and additional financial resources to enable developing countries to meet the agreed full incremental costs to them of implementing measures which fulfill the obligations of this Convention. . . . " *Id.*, Art. 20(2).

The "Financial Mechanism" for transfer of resources is set up under Article 21 of the Convention. But even where the Financial Mechanism is in place it is possible for Amazonia to rely on Article 20(2) and argue that the alleviation of poverty, not preservation of biological diversity, should remain its first concern under the Convention. Accordingly, it may be able to press forward with the second stage of ECOHAB as a measure directed at eradicating poverty.

3. Under the facts of the present problem, neither Amazonia nor Caribia is reported to have joined the Cartagena Protocol on Biosafety to the 1992 Convention on Biological Diversity, adopted 29 January 2000 and entered into force 11 September 2003, UN Reg. No. 30619, UN Doc. NEP/CBD/ExCOP/1/3/Annex, *reprinted in* 5 Weston & Carlson V.H.26. They might well have done so. The Protocol is the first international agreement to deal specifically with the substantial concerns of both scientists and the public at large (particularly in many developing countries and in Europe) over the potential environmental and health effects of genetically modified crops. Despite the potential benefits of such technology (*e.g.*, new foods, feeds, and fibers; various crops fortified with iron or vitamins; and crops made resistant to herbicides, insecticides, extreme weather, or specific crop diseases), the issue is no small one. Today, genetically modified crops are being cultivated on about 167 million acres—with six countries accounting for 99% of this cultivation, the United States (63%), Argentina (21%), Canada (6%), Brazil (4%), China (4%), and South Africa (1%)—and significant worldwide growth is expected.

Article 4 of the Cartagena Protocol proclaims that it is intended to apply to "the transboundary movement, transit, handling and use of all living modified organisms that may have adverse effects on the conservation and sustainable use of biological diversity, taking into account risks to human health." The Protocol implements the precautionary approach contained in Principle 15 of the Rio

Declaration on Environment and Development, with the objective of "ensuring an adequate level of protection in the field of the safe transfer, handling and use of living modified organisms [LMOs] resulting from modern biotechnology that may have adverse effects on the conservation and sustainable use of biological diversity, taking also into account risks to human health, and specifically focusing on transboundary movements." (Article 1)

A major agricultural boom has been taking place in the Brazilian Amazon. Although Brazilian farmers have been planting genetically modified crops for some time, in 2003 the Brazilian government formally legalized the sale of such crops. If Amazonia had been similarly relying on genetically modified crops and had joined the Biosafety Protocol, what specific obligations would it have incurred?

4.   Nongovernmental Organizations (NGO's) and international lending institutions are playing an increasingly important role in global environmental protection. In the present problem, it was open to the Nature Conservancy (NC) or even Caribia to have adopted another route to address the problem. They could have lodged official complaints with the World Bank stating that at least the second phase of ECOHAB was required to be assessed under the Bank's Operational Directive on "environmental assessment" of October 1989, the requirements of which read in part as follows:

> The purpose of the Environmental Assessment Operational Directive (EAOD), which was issued in October 1989, is to ensure that the development options under consideration are environmentally sound and sustainable and that any environmental consequences are recognized early in the profit cycle and taken into account in project design. Environmental assessments reduce the need for project conditionality because appropriate steps can be taken in advance or incorporated into project design; the process also helps avoid costs and delays in implementation due to unanticipated environmental problems. Because assessment is the borrower's responsibility, the directive plays an important role in encouraging the development of environmental capabilities and institutions in member countries. The environmental assessment process also provides a formal mechanism to address a range of issues which have been problematic in the past. These include the requirement that the borrower should undertake an appropriate process of consultation to ensure interagency coordination and to address the concerns of affected groups and local NGOs.

> The scope, depth, and analytical techniques of an environmental assessment depend on the particular circumstances of each project. Regional and sectoral assessments, for example, can substantially reduce the work subsequently needed on specific project assessments. Regional assessments are used where a number of significant development activities with potentially cumulative impacts are planned for a reasonably localized area. They compare alternative development scenarios and recommend environmentally sustainable growth rates and land use patterns and policies. Sectoral assessments are used in designing sector investment programs. Alternative approaches that focus on a narrower range of issues may be acceptable for smaller projects with limited potential effects on the environment, and may be more effective in integrating environmental concerns into the borrower's planning process. Such approaches include integrated pest management programs, design criteria and pollution standards for small or medium-scale industrial plants, and

design criteria and construction supervision programs for small-scale rural works projects.

Since the environmental assessment is the borrower's responsibility, the ultimate success of the directive will depend on strengthening the environmental expertise within member countries. Projects with major potential impacts thus normally need to include an institutional development and training component. In addition, to help develop environmental capacity in the country, the Bank encourages the use of local expertise in the preparation of assessments and stresses the need for training courses for local specialists and consultants.

Had NC or Caribia invoked this Directive, the actions of Amazonia could have been assessed by the Bank; and if, in the present problem, ECOHAB were to be considered as having significant environmental impact according to World Bank criteria, should or would the World Bank suspend all funding or limit it for the second stage of ECOHAB?

5. In Reading 9, *supra*, James Resor, Director of Conservation Enterprises of the World Wildlife Fund–United States, explains "debt-for-nature swaps." In an omitted portion of his commentary, he elaborates on how such swaps have now expanded to embrace a number of new approaches for long-term financing, such as "debt-for-development swaps," that have benefitted social programs in addition to conservation. He then concludes: "While considerable attention initially focused on the unusual nature of the swap process, it is only a means rather than an end in itself. The ultimate success of debt-for-nature swaps depends on the viability of the programmes financed, and on the strength of the organizations and communities implementing the programmes and managing the swap proceeds." Might the ultimate success of debt-for-nature and similar swaps depend also on the extent to which they can avoid allegations of neo-imperialism on the part of the industrialized world? How might such a charge arise? Might it have to do with the way such swaps relate to the indigenous peoples who commonly are affected? Even assuming the swaps do not abuse resources or are not financially mismanaged, why should the land and resources upon which indigenous peoples have lived for generations be used to pay off debts that were not of their making?

Consider the following remarks by Robert A Williams, Jr., *Comments on Energy and the Environment: Intersecting Global Issues*, 9 Ariz. J. Int'l & Comp. L. 199, 202–203 (1992):

> The problem for human rights law and policy in addressing indigenous peoples' demands for self-determination over the territories and resources they claim—whether in the rainforest or the Arctic—is the same in many fundamental ways as it is for nation states. The question becomes: How do you create sustainable development? This perspective places indigenous peoples' claims within the same emerging context and intellectual framework used by modern human rights advocates. The emerging framework accepts the idea of a right to develop all territories under a peoples' control as a critical component of the right to self-determine. Development in this context aims at the improvement of the welfare of the entire population of a state, including its indigenous peoples.

> This right to self-determination is tempered by a recognition that environmental rights must compliment development rights. These environmental rights recognize that all human beings including indigenous peoples have the right to an environment adequate for their health and welfare, and also have the responsibility to protect that environment for the benefit of present and

future generations. Development, therefore, must occur in an environmentally sensible and sustainable context within the nation state and within boundaries of indigenous peoples' territories.

Professor Williams then goes on to express his fear:

My only fear is that indigenous peoples may lose out as non-indigenous environmentalist groups seek to link indigenous peoples' human rights to deforestation and the issue of global warming. Indigenous peoples may be denied an equal right to participate and consult in a global dialogue on the rights and responsibilities of all self-determining peoples with respect to the challenges of global warming. They may also be denied the responsibility to control their own destiny in responsible fashion. History bears witness to these denials. For the past 500 years people have hypothesized and identified what indigenous' peoples rights should be from a non-indigenous western perspective. Preventing similar denials in the future will only result if we begin listening to indigenous peoples and encouraging their contributions to a dialogue about the sources, nature and parameters of human rights for all human beings.

Professor Williams may thus be seen as somewhat at odds with Dallam's critique in Reading 22, *supra*, of the discourse which proclaims indigenous peoples to be the best guardians of fragile ecosystems. Where do you stand in this debate? Why?

6.   Regarding the rights of Aboriginal peoples in Australia, Penelope Mathew, Rosemary Hunter, and Hilary Charlesworth write, in *Law and History in Black and White*, in Thinking About Law: Perspectives on the History, Philosophy and Sociology of Law 13 (R. Hunter, R. Ingleby & R. Johnstone eds., 1995), at 33, that "[w]hile the Australian political and legal scene has been unreceptive to Aboriginal demands that white Australia recognise and make amends for its usurpation of indigenous culture, some Aboriginal groups have attempted to use the international legal arena to bring pressure on the Australian government." Why is it that indigenous peoples have begun, as further evidenced in Reading 21 (Anaya and Williams), *supra*, to resort to international law to press their claims? Is it likely that they will succeed to any substantial degree? In thinking upon this question, consider the fact that, until relatively recently, the interests of indigenous peoples were excluded from the relevant agendas of international environmental discourse for the most part, particularly noticeable when compared to the interests of the commercial world. Consider, for example, the spectacular success of the oil industry in preventing global governance in relation to energy policy in contrast to the traditional leverage of indigenous peoples when it comes to upholding their rights to sacred lands.

7.   For an account of the circumstances of the Yanomami in Venezuela that is partly responsible for the present problem, see James Brooke, *Venezuela Befriends Tribe, But What's Venezuela?*, N.Y. Times, 11 Sep 1991, at A4, col. 3.

8.   *Bibliographical Note.* For supplemental discussion concerning the principal themes addressed in this problem, consult the following additional specialized materials:

(a) *Books/Monographs/Reports/Symposia.* S. Anaya, Indigenous Peoples in International Law (2000); I. Bowles & G. Prickett, Footprints in the Jungle: Natural Resource Industries, Infrastructure, and Biodiversity Conservation (2001); J. Castellino & N. Walsh, International Law And Indigenous Peoples (2004); C. Cohen, The Human Rights of Indigenous Peoples (1998); R. Hitchcock & D. Vindig, Indigenous Peoples' Rights in Southern Africa (2005); Indigenous

Peoples, the United Nations and Human Rights (S. Pritchard ed. (1998); B. Howard, Indigenous Peoples and the State: The Struggle for Native Rights (2003); IUCN, Indigenous Peoples and Sustainability: Cases and Actions (1998); D. Ivison, P. Patton & W. Sanders, Political Theory and the Rights of Indigenous Peoples (2000); S. Jentoft, H. Minde & R. Nilse, Indigenous Peoples: Resource Management and Global Rights (2004); P. Keal, S. Smith, T. Biersteker, C. Brown, P. Cerny, J. Grieco, A.J.R. Groom, R. Higgott, G. Ikenberry, C. Kennedy–Pipe, and S. Lamy, European Conquest and the Rights of Indigenous Peoples: The Moral Backwardness of International Society (2003); A. Kiss & D. Shelton, International Environmental Law (2nd ed. 2000); R. Kuppe & R. Pots, Law & Anthropology: Indigenous Peoples, Constitutional States And Treaties Of Other Constructive Arrangements Between Indigenous Peoples And States (2005); T. McShane & M. Wells, Getting Biodiversity Projects to Work: Towards More Effective Conservation and Development (2004); P. Thornberry, Indigenous Peoples and Human Rights (2002); P. Thornberry, The Cultural Rights of Indigenous Peoples: In Search of a Glass–Ball Country (2003); L. Watters, Indigenous Peoples, The Environment And Law (2004).

(b) *Articles/Book Chapters.* S. Anaya, *International Human Rights and Indigenous Peoples: The Move Toward the Multicultural State,* 21 Ariz. J. Int'l & Comp. Law 13 (2004); F. MacKay, *Universal Rights or a Universe unto Itself? Indigenous Peoples' Human Rights and the World Bank's Draft Operational Policy 4.10 on Indigenous Peoples,* 17 Am. U. Int'l L. Rev. 527 (2002); R. Porter, *Pursuing the Path of Indigenization in the Era of Emergent International Law Governing the Rights of Indigenous Peoples,* 5 Yale H.R. & Dev. L.J. 123 (2002); A. Riley, *Indigenous Peoples and the Promise of Globalization: An Essay on Rights and Responsibilities,* 14 Kan. J.L. & Pub. Pol'y 155 (2004); R. Stavenhagen, *The Rights of Indigenous Peoples: Closing A Gap in Global Governance,* 11 Global Governance 17 (1 Jan 2005); S. Sucharitkul, *American Law in a Time of Global Interdependence: US National Reports to the XVITH International Congress of Comparative Law: Section I The Inter-temporal Character of International and Comparative Law Regarding the Rights of the Indigenous Populations of the World,* 50 A.J.C L. 3 (2002); J. Vuotto, *Awas Tingni v. Nicaragua: International Precedent for Indigenous Land Rights?,* 22 B.U. Int'l L.J. 219 (2004); S. Wiessner, *The Rights and Status of Indigenous Peoples: A Global Comparative and International Legal Analysis,* 12 Harv. Hum. Rts. J. 57 (1999); M. Wagner, *The International Legal Rights of Indigenous Peoples Affected by Natural Resource Exploitation: A Brief Case Study,* 24 Hastings Int'l & Comp. L. Rev. 491 (2001).

Part III

THE CONTRIBUTIONS OF LAW TO A PEACEFUL, JUST, EQUITABLE, AND SUSTAINABLE GLOBAL FUTURE

INTRODUCTION

The world is in unprecedented turmoil at present, making it more difficult than ever to select primary world order challenges and responses as well as depict the potential roles of law and lawyers in achieving a more humane future for the peoples of the world. The 1990s appeared to be a time of great hope about the overall prospects for enhancing global justice and building the framework for global governance. The early years of the Twenty-first Century have suffered the dark clouds cast by 11 September 2001 and the American-led response to it. Whether this encounter between a global network of violent extremists and the hegemonic United States will continue to dominate the political, legal, and moral imagination in coming years is presently both unknowable and preoccupying. Other elements of historic significance concern the relevance of the worldwide resurgence of religion as a politically potent force, and the ensuing tensions between secularism and religion; the problematic technological frontiers relating to human cloning, advanced robotics, and super-computers; and the challenges associated with a minimally regulated world economy. Of even more direct significance are issues relating to scarcities and the global maldistribution of economic benefits, including the availability of medicines and safe water. Perhaps most daunting is the increasing frequency of extreme weather causing widespread human suffering, raising questions about their relationship to global warming and the essentially unregulated emission of greenhouse gases. The 2004 South Asian tsunami and the 2005 Katrina and Rita hurricanes in the United States illustrate the magnitude of the challenge. Clarifying the complex roles of law in these settings is the main goal of this Part III.

In Part II, we emphasized the linkages between international law problem-solving and the promotion of humane world order values. These linkages were shown to be complex and often controversial, reflecting differing circumstances of development and ecology, of civilizational, ethnic, and religious orientation, of gender and class, and of historical experience and memory. In this Part III, we shift to the ways in which international law and its practitioners (including scholars, government officials, and international bureaucrats) relate to the underlying structures of world order and to the dynamics of change and struggle.

For most of the Twentieth Century, it was common for those who believed that a better world was possible and necessary to focus their attention on the sovereign state and the state system as obstacles to progress. Global reformers widely believed that the way forward involved a stronger United Nations at the expense of state sovereignty, with cumulative moves to enhance global governance, often looking ahead even to an eventual establishment of world government. Such expectations were modeled in arguably a positive way by the overall moves of the European Union toward constitutional regionalism in its five decades of existence. The spread of regional structures to other parts of the world also has given rise to a growing increase in legal arrangements of an intra-and inter-regional character.

Additionally, until the September 11 attacks on the World Trade Center and the Pentagon in 2001, it seemed quite reasonable to depict the period following upon the collapse of the Berlin War as one of globalization, acknowledging a formative role for economic forces. From an international perspective, the central issue posed was the extent to which the world economy was a self-organizing system that could operate according to the market-oriented precepts of neo-liberal capitalist logic. And it was further presumed that such a system would not only generate economic growth, the efficient use of capital, and the reduction of extreme poverty, but also would make satisfactory progress on such essential global public goods as human rights (including economic and social rights), environmental protection, and the avoidance of disruptive cycles of boom and bust. The Asian Financial Crisis, starting in 1997, raised severe doubts as to whether such a minimally regulated world economy could serve as an acceptable vehicle for the production and distribution of global public goods. These doubts gave rise to a broad-based oppositional movement, given an initial prominence by large and angry street demonstrations against the World Trade Organization (WTO) at its ministerial meetings in Seattle at the end of 1999 and later deepening and widening in various ways. Especially impressive has been the establishment of the World Social Forum whose annual meetings in the South (mainly in Porto Alegre, Brazil) have attracted hundreds of thousands of civil society activists from all parts of the world to challenge prevailing tendencies in global economic and security policy. The slogan of these meetings—"there are alternatives"—has been a way of contesting the claim that only market-driven capitalism can provide policy guidance and human benefit. These issues remain essentially unresolved and controversial, and from the perspective of international law and world order, need to be studied as matters of global economic governance, regulation for the public good, and the balance between the interests of capital and the well being of people.

But new urgencies have emerged that also require the attention of the legal profession—above all, the rethinking of the core prohibitions of the use of international force that, with due deliberation after World War II, were written into the United Nations Charter **(Basic Document 1.5)**. Various developments in recent years have cast severe doubts on the viability of the Charter approach to war and peace, as well as to global security more generally. Even before September 11, US diplomatic leadership seemed increasingly ready to rely on the use of non-defensive and essentially unilateral force to address humanitarian emergencies and the non-territorial menace of transnational terrorism. In many ways, the debate over the Kosovo interven-

tion in 1999 was formative, disclosing a willingness of the United States and its European allies, presaged by their approach to the Persian Gulf war of 1991,[a] to bypass the UN Security Council to form a "coalition of the willing" under NATO auspices and carry out a rescue operation on behalf of the Kosovar Albanians facing abusive Serb rule and the credible prospect of a new cycle of ethnic cleansing, prefigured by Serbian behavior in Bosnia.

The Security Council debate preceding the Iraq War in 2003 carried this tendency further, with a US/UK-led coalition opting for war for reasons that were unconvincing to most governments and world public opinion as expressed by unprecedented governmental and grassroots opposition, culminating on 15 February 2003 in several million persons taking part in peaceful street demonstrations in cities throughout the world. Proponents of the Iraq War had argued that the war was necessary due to threats posed by Iraqi possession of weapons of mass destruction. Not only were no such weaponry present in Iraq, but official documents now make clear that the US government in particular was guilty of "cooking" the evidence to give its allegations some credibility. As a result, it is necessary to reconsider whether the United Nations and international law can restore or even retain their relevance to the debate about the future of global security in contexts of war and peace when associated with the advocacy of humanitarian intervention, the international uses of force to combat terrorism, and recourse to war either to oppose the spread of weaponry of mass destruction or to impose regime changes on countries deemed dangerous by the US government and its partners.

These concerns are, at this writing, aggravated by the political climate in the United States. The US leadership seems increasingly captive to a radical right world view that does not fully represent the values of American society as a whole or the viewpoint of most US citizens, despite having been narrowly and controversially re-elected in 2004. This outlook is the defining feature of the George W. Bush presidency, with so many of its inner circle of advisors sporting neoconservative credentials and joining with the religious right to put the United States on the reactionary side of almost every debate about global policy and intractably opposed to any reliance on international law to resolve or mitigate world problems.[b] This turn to the right cannot be associated only with the Executive Branch. It is reflected also in Congress and in the rightward reorientation of the judiciary. True, the failures of the Bush Administration's Iraq policy and a growing dissatisfaction with the leadership of George W. Bush do give rise to some prospect of more moderate American policies in the future. At present, however, there continues to exist a central tension between the global leadership role of the United States, based on its military and economic preeminence, and the sort of world order values that are espoused in this coursebook.

a. *See* B. Weston, *Security Council Resolution 678 and Persian Gulf Decision–Making: Precarious Legitimacy*, 85 A.J.I.L. 516 (1991).

b. Thus John R. Bolton, presently US ambassador to the United Nations via a controversial recess appointment by President George W. Bush that side-stepped the advise and consent of the US Senate, stated shortly after his nomination to the post in March 2005: "It is a big mistake for us to grant any validity to international law even when it may seem in our short-term interest to do so— because, over the long term, the goal of those who think that international law really means anything are those who want to constrict the United States." *Quoted in* Samantha Power, *Comment: Boltonism*, The New Yorker, 21 Mar 2005, at 23.

At the same time, while we recognize that fundamental challenges of a new sort need to be addressed by the global security agenda, we also are mindful that, more than ever, it is important not to interpret international law on the basis of current American preoccupations or by exaggerating the significance of the United States as a global actor. There are many crucial issues of human well being other than global security that need to be addressed, and there is no acceptable reason for their neglect in deference to the American insistence that the war against terrorism crowds every other human concern to the sidelines, including racial discrimination and ethnic conflict, the oppression of women, the exploitation of children, denials of sexual freedom, the suppression of minorities, struggles for self-determination, unemployment and poverty, trafficking in arms, drugs, and people, the proliferation of refugees, involuntary migrants, and internally displaced persons, global warming, and ocean pollution—to name only a few. Other perspectives and actors are therefore important, as are different views on policy priorities.

It is vital also to revive, on a global level, the normative revolution that had such a promising start in the 1990s: efforts to provide redress of historic grievances ranging from belated compensation for Holocaust victims to protecting what few rights of indigenous peoples remain, moves to impose individual criminal accountability on political and military leaders for crimes of state, a process that gained credibility with the 1998 detention of former Chilean dictator Augusto Pinochet and moved rapidly forward thanks to a great grassroots mobilization to establish the International Criminal Court (ICC) 2002, demands for greater democratization and socially responsible practices in the operation of leading international financial institutions such as the WTO, the International Monetary Fund (IMF), and the World Bank, and international efforts to protect human rights from abusive governments, including the protection of vulnerable peoples and targeted minorities.

Part of this normative revolution was visionary in character, seeking to enhance the capacity of world order to promote democratic values and global justice. In this spirit, the commitment by civil society and many governments to make the World Court and the ICC important for the peaceful resolution of international disputes and for holding accountable leaders who commit crimes of state. Nor can the establishment of a global peoples parliament be underestimated. At stake is the imperative of converting international (i.e., interstate) law into a global law of humanity and to this end making the rule of law part of the discipline of the foreign policies of even powerful countries. The sovereignty of states has been eroding in the context of severe abuses of human rights and culture wars as manifested by a rising ethos that the International Commission on Intervention and State Sovereignty described as "the responsibility to protect"[c] and by efforts to strengthen supranational global governance in a manner that gives voice and influence to democratic forces and advocates *human* security at the expense of militarist approaches to *state* security.[d]

---

c. The Responsibility to Protect: Report of the International Commission on Intervention and State Sovereignty (Dec. 2001), *available at* <http://www.iciss.ca/report-en.asp>.

d. *But see* H. James, The End of Globalization: Lessons from the Great Depression (2001); J. R. Saul, The Collapse of Globalism: And the Reinvention of the World (2005); N. Smith, The Endgame of Globalization (2005).

In these respects, we continue, as in our past editions, to regard the great Seventeenth Century Dutch jurist, Hugo Grotius, as both inspirational and cautionary. Grotius remains inspirational because his conception of international law was a historical reaction to the barbarism of the religious warfare of his time, known as The Thirty Years War, when religious unity no longer provided normative coherence to relations among political communities in Europe. He is inspirational also because his historical moment of opportunity coincided, as indicated, with the displacement of medievalism based on localized feudal control and an overarching Christendom as a world order construct by an emergent construct that combined territorial sovereignty with an acceptance of secular governance and a farsighted realization of the positive roles that law could play in the moderation of world politics. It was this transitional reality that makes it sensible to identify a "Grotian moment" as that historical time of uncertainty and controversy when one framework of world order is being challenged by an alternative framework. In our time, the resilient framework of relations among sovereign states that has persisted since the 1648 Peace of Westphalia that ended the Thirty Years War is being challenged by several contending approaches to global governance.

It is our view that the Grotian moment we perhaps are now experiencing could move the world in one of two different directions: toward global empire or toward global democracy. In both instances, the role of law and international institutions would be globalized in a dramatic fashion sufficient to justify a re-labeling of the system as a whole. But this is an occasion to be cautious as well. A transition to global empire, even if purportedly to promote widely shared values, should not be affirmed as a step forward as it would almost certainly produce a geopolitical backlash in terms of rivalries among leading states and intensify extremist forms of violent resistance to imperial domination. As well, there is a danger in exaggerating the degree to which the state is being superseded and the extent to which civil society actors have leverage sufficient to play an emancipatory role. The state has proved to be resilient, nationalism remains a hegemonic ideology around the world, and it is not at all clear that either empire or global democracy will replace the existing statist world order in the years and decades ahead. Regionalism also is in the running, offering an attractive halfway house between statist forms of world order and an overarching structure of global governance. It may be that some sort of hybrid is the most likely world order future, combining states, regions, and globalized actors.

The vision of global democracy as the basis of world order, however, animates the many tendencies associated with global civil society at the present time. In certain respects, the guiding concept of human security as an alternative to national security constitutes a shift of emphasis from the security of the regime or state to the security of people. This shift provides a perspective for an ethical orientation to advocates of global democracy. Also involved is the possibility that the axiological fluidity of the present historical setting could produce what might be described as a "Gandhian Moment" more fundamental than the sort of shift we associate with the Grotian cluster of world order aspirations. It may be important to begin thinking seriously of a non-violent geopolitics in which wars of choice—unjustified by conditions of credible defensive necessity and lacking formal authorization by the UN Security Council—are completely abandoned out of a mixture of pragmatic and idealistic considerations. The realism of this prospect has been brilliantly depicted by Jonathan Schell in *The Unconquerable World: Power, Non-violence, and the Will of the People* (2004).

Even if the Gandhian outlook seems beyond the horizon of present plausibility, it is certainly the case that the Grotian perspective is relevant to our core undertaking in this Part III, which is to frame the basic debate about what to expect from international law. Our introductory selections suggest the fundamental disagreement about whether law can play an evolutionary role in improving the quality of planetary life, creating moral and political progress for humanity by stages, or whether certain limits on what to seek by way of law need to be preserved to avoid either utopian expectations or anti-law reactions from states that have been pushed too far by claims made under the rubric of international law. The debate is presented here by two exemplary figures: Sir Hersch Lauterpacht, unquestionably one of the greatest international jurists of the Twentieth Century, and Hedley Bull, a leading Twentieth Century political theorist of international relations with a lively awareness of the geopolitical logic giving structure to a world of sovereign states and, as well, a seriousness about the role of law and morality in producing a moderate world order as free from debilitating warfare as possible.

The three chapters that follow this stage-setting introduction and conclude this coursebook explore different dimensions of the fundamental and persisting question of situating international law within the historical circumstances of the present while at the same time keeping an eye to a better future as assessed by humane world order values. Chapter 8 ("Geopolitical Nightmares and Global Dreams") gives prominence to the renewed and newly radicalized debate about law and global security, expressing the dual reality of hope and despair. Chapter 9 ("The First Global Normative Revolution: Will it Revive?") considers the promise of a series of bold global innovations on behalf of human security that were taking shape in the 1990s and inquires whether this positive world trend has been either indefinitely derailed or merely detoured by the war/peace concerns that have risen to renewed prominence since September 11. And Chapter 10 ("Toward a Progressive Global Policy Agenda") takes seriously the social and moral agenda set forth by Kofi Annan in the *Millennium Report* delivered to the United Nations in 2000,[e] drawing attention to areas of avoidable human suffering, as well as to prospects for widening and deepening the international legal protection of human rights. This final chapter also considers the existing and emerging global governance structures that may facilitate the transition to a global rule of law and provide a growing assurance that global public goods are increasingly available on an equitable basis to the peoples of the world.

Sir Hersch Lauterpacht, "The Grotian Tradition in International Law"
23 B.Y.B.I.L. 1, 18–53 (1946)

What were the aspects of the teaching of Grotius which, notwithstanding shortcomings of method and defects of substance, lift his work above the

---

e. K. Annan, "We the Peoples": The Role of the United Nations in the 21st Century (2000), *available at* <http://www.un.org/millen-nium/sg/report/full.htm>. See an extract from this report in Chapter 10, *infra* at 1408.

plane of a mere episode, however important, in the history of international law and of its development as part of jurisprudence? ... The answer is that the principal and characteristic features of *De Jure Belli ac Pacis*[1] are identical with the fundamental and persistent problems of international law and that in nearly all of them the teaching of Grotius has become identified with the progression of international law to a true system of law in both its legal and in its ethical content. These main features of the Grotian tradition will now be considered.

1. *The Subjection of the Totality of International Relations to the Rule of Law.* In the first instance, Grotius conceives of the totality of the relations between states as governed by law. This is the central theme of the treaties and its main characteristic. There are no lacunae in that subjection of states to the rule of law. Modern international law recognized for a long time the existence of gaps which obliterated altogether the border-line between law and lawlessness in international relations. Of these gaps the admissibility of war as an absolute right of states, requiring no other legal justification, is the outstanding example. In laying down the distinction between just and unjust war Grotius rejected the claim to any such right. Neither did he concede to states the absolute faculty of action in self-preservation—a right which till recently, writers coupled with the legal power of the state to determine, with finality and to the exclusion of any outside tribunal, the justification of action in self-defence. The emphasis with which Grotius denies the absoluteness of the right to act in self-preservation is deeply impressive.... Grotius challenged the right of a state to go to war in order to ward off an anticipated attack.... It may also be noted in this connexion that he did not limit the orbit of international law to the states of Christian civilization. He recognized the binding force of treaties concluded with infidels. There was no room in his system for wars of religion—though he considered that there was a duty incumbent upon Christian states to defend one another against aggression by infidels.

2. *The Acceptance of the Law of Nature as an Independent Source of International Law.* With the affirmation of the rule of law as extending to the totality of the relations of states there is ... the view that the law thus binding upon states is not solely the product of their express will. Grotius accepted as self-evident the proposition that the sovereign–the state–is bound by the law of nations and the law of nature. The law of nations proper–*jus gentium voluntarium*–is, of course, the product of consent as manifested in the practice of states. Grotius's *jus gentium* thus conceived is not synonymous with public international law. It is distinguished from municipal law (*jus civile*), which emanates from the civil power of one state; it embraces all law– public and private, international and other–which has been sanctioned by the practice of all nations or of many nations. It is one of the component parts of international law, but not the whole of it.... Similarly, though a great deal of international law proper rests on consent, much, but not all, of it follows from the precepts of the law of nature. In a wider sense, the binding force even of that part of it that originates in consent is based on the law of nature as expressive of the social nature of man.

---

1. *See* H. Grotius, The Law of War and Peace (Kelsey ed. 1963).

It would be a mistake to judge the importance of the part played by the law of nature in *De Jure Belli ac Pacis* by reference to its use in relation to matters affecting international law proper such as treaties between states, the law of diplomatic immunities, and above all, the law of war.... The significance of the law of nature in the treatise is that it is the ever-present source for supplementing the voluntary law of nations, for judging its adequacy in the light of ethics and reason, and for making the reader aware of the fact that the will of states cannot be the exclusive or even, in the last resort, the decisive source of the law of nations.

* * *

The fact is that while within the state it is not essential to give to the ideas of a higher law—of natural law—a function superior to that of providing the inarticulate ethical premise underlying judicial decisions or, in the last resort, of the philosophical and political justification of the right of resistance, in the international society the position is radically different. There—in a society deprived of normal legislative and judicial organs—the function of natural law, whatever may be its form, must approximate more closely to that of a direct source of law. In the absence of the overriding authority of the judicial and legislative organs of the state there must assert itself—unless anarchy or stagnation are to ensue—the persuasive but potent authority of reason and principle derived from the fact of the necessary coexistence of a plurality of states. This explains the pertinacity, in the international sphere, of the idea of natural law as a legal source....

3. *The Affirmation of the Social Nature of Man as the Basis of the Law of Nature.* The place which the law of nature occupies as part of the Grotian tradition is distinguished not only by the fact of its recognition of a source of law different from and, in proper cases, superior to the will of sovereign states. What is equally significant is Grotius's conception of the quality of the law of nature which dominates his jurisprudential system. It is a law of nature largely based on and deduced from the nature of man as a being intrinsically moved by a desire for social life, endowed with an ample measure of goodness, altruism, and morality, and capable of acting on general principles and of learning from experience. He admits that man is an animal, but one different in kind from other animals. That difference consists in his impelling desire for society—not for society of any sort, but for peaceful and organized life according to the measure of his intelligence. It is a difference the essence of which is the denial of the assertion that "every animal is impelled by nature to seek only its own good." There is perhaps no political writer in whose system that conception of the nature of man is more prominent. The theme is, of course, one of the persistent problems—perhaps *the* problem—of political thought. For Machiavelli and Hobbes man is essentially selfish, anti-social, and unable to learn from experience ...; the basis of political obligation is interest pure and simple; the idea of a sense of moral duty rising supreme over desire and passion is a figment of imagination fatal alike to action and to survival. This is the typical realistic approach of contempt towards the "little breed" of man. On that line of reasoning there is no salvation for humanity but irrevocable subjection to an order of effective force which, while indifferent to the dignity of man, yet contrives to prevent his life from being

"solitary, poor, nasty, brutish, and short." The approach of Grotius and—to mention a writer as distinguished and as influential—Locke is diametrically different.

One of the salient characteristics of *De Jure Belli ac Pacis* is not only the frequency of the reliance on and appeal to the law of love, the law of charity, of Christian duty, of honour, and of goodness, and to the injunctions of divine law and the Gospel: the element of morality and the appeal to morality are, without interfering decisively with legal character of the exposition, a constant theme of the treatise. An equally persistent feature is Grotius's faith in the rational constitution of man and his capacity to see reason and to learn from experience. This aspect of *De Jure Belli ac Pacis* goes a long way towards explaining the force of the Grotian tradition in the international sphere....

4. *The Recognition of the Essential Identity of States and Individuals.* That all-pervading element of morality and rationality which is the result of Grotius's conception of law as based in the social nature and the intrinsic goodness of man is not limited to the conduct of individuals. It extends to the conduct of nations and of rulers acting on their behalf. In fact, one of the most decisive features of the teaching of Grotius is the close analogy of legal and moral rules governing the conduct of states and individuals alike.... This analogy of states and individuals has proved a beneficent weapon in the armoury of international progress. It is not the result of any anthropomorphic or organic conception of the state as being—biologically, as it were—assimilated to individuals, as being an individual person "writ large." The analogy— nay, the essential identity—of rules governing the conduct of states and of individuals is not asserted for the reason that states *are like* individuals; it is due to the fact that states *are composed of* individual human beings; it results from the fact that behind the mystical, impersonal, and therefore necessarily irresponsible personality of the metaphysical state there are the actual subjects of rights and duties, namely, individual human beings. This is the true meaning of the Grotian analogy of states and individuals. The individual is the ultimate unit of all law, international and municipal, in the double sense that the obligations of international law are ultimately addressed to him and that the development, the well-being, and the dignity of the individual human being are a matter of direct concern to international law....

* * *

... The analogy of states and individuals ... was the twin result of two distinct causes. One, which was of a transient character, was the patrimonial character of a considerable number of European states. The other, more enduring, was the realization of the true nature of rules of international law as addressing themselves to individual human beings acting on behalf of the state. The cumulative effect of these two causes was to further the scientific development of international law and to emphasize the moral content of its rules. Largely on account of the recognition of that fundamental analogy, the door was wide open for the enrichment and advancement of international law with the help of rules of private law, Roman and other, as expressive of the general principles of law recognized by civilized states. Critics of the positivist complexion have frequently raised doubts as to the propriety of that process of borrowing from private law. Even if that criticism had been justified—and it is not believed that it was—it was a lament after the event. There have been few branches of international law which have remained unaffected by the influence of private law. We have only to think of Grotius's contribution, by reference to private law, to the development of the rules of law relating to acquisition of territorial sovereignty, the principle of the freedom of the sea, and the law of state responsibility. The very notion of sovereignty, which Grotius conceived, like property, as dominion held under law, helped to deprive it of the character of absoluteness and indivisibility.... If we were to ignore or to underestimate these "illicit borrowings" we should be depriving ourselves of the possibility of understanding what is perhaps the major part of international law.... To do so would mean to jettison a substantial part of positive international law in which the rules derived by analogy have become crystallized. It would mean challenging the purpose of that significant provision of the Statute of the International Court of Justice which constitutes the general principles of international law as recognized by civilized states, one of the three principal sources of the law to be applied by the Court. To discard them as a matter of principle would mean to abandon the view, which is amply justified by experience, that upon the continued vitality of this aspect of the Grotian tradition depends the progressive approximation of international law to a system of legal rules worthy of that name.

5. *The Rejection of "Reason of State."* The recognition of the social and moral nature of man as the principal source and cause of law explains, when coupled with the persistent affirmation of the analogy of states and individuals, the fifth characteristic of the Grotian tradition, namely, his denial of the "reason of State" as a basic and decisive factor of international relations. That denial of the principle of double morality is for Grotius so obvious and so fundamental that, it would seem, he regards it as below the dignity of his work to engage in the then customary argument *ad hominem* on the subject.

A startling feature of *De Jure Belli ac Pacis* is the absence not only of any polemics, but of all reference to Machiavelli.... But although he does not mention Machiavelli by name, he takes up the issue of "reason of State" at the very beginning of the treatise. After remarking upon the usefulness of a knowledge of the law "which is concerned with the mutual relations among states or rulers of states," he points to the special necessity of studying that branch of law. For, he says, there are "in our day" persons who view it with contempt as having no reality; who consider that for a king or a state nothing is unjust which is expedient; and that the business of the state cannot be carried on without injustice. He sees an intimate connexion between the rejection of the ideas of "reason of State" and the affirmation of the legal and moral unity of mankind. He insists that if no association of men can be maintained without law, "surely also that association which binds together the human race, or binds many nations together, has need of law." This means, he says, quoting Cicero with approval, that shameful acts ought not to be committed even for the sake of one's country. It means also that the hallmark of wisdom for a ruler is to take account not only of the good of the nation committed to his care, but of the whole human race.... While denying that law is based on expediency alone, he was ready to meet the theorists of "reason of State" on the ground of their own choosing, namely, that of advantage. He records the fact that according to many the standards of justice applicable in the relations of individuals within the state do not apply to a state or the ruler of a state. The reason usually given for that assertion of the double standard of justice is, he says, that law is indispensable to individuals who, taken singly, cannot protect themselves, while great states, which dispose of everything needed for adequate protection, are in no need of law. Grotius rejects this view. Such, in his opinion, is the impact of economic interdependence or of military security that there is no state so powerful that it can dispense with the help of others.

Grotius's rejection of the ideas of *raison d'état* finds more direct expression in relation to concrete issues. It expresses itself in the denial of the right to resort to war unless in pursuance of a good legal cause; in the rigid limitation of the right of self-defence (including the right of war in order to ward off an anticipated attack); in the concession of the right–indeed, in the injunction of the duty–of passive resistance against orders and laws contrary to the law of nature and the law of God; in the concession to the subject of the right–and, again, in the injunction of the duty–to refrain from participation not only in unjust wars but also in wars the justice of which is doubtful; in his stressing of the sacredness of the principle *pacta sunt servanda*. . . .

* * *

6. *The Distinction Between Just and Unjust Wars.* In the assertion of "reason of State" and of the double standard of morality, the claim to an unrestricted right of war, though not the most conspicuous, is the most important. It is not the dagger or the poison of the hired assassin or the sharp practice of the realistic politician which expresses most truly, upon final analysis, the ideas of "*raison d'état.*" It is the infliction, without a shadow of a specific right and without a claim to any particular right, of the calamities and indignities of war and of the territorial mutilation and the very annihilation of statehood following upon defeat in war. Prior to the changes introduced by the Covenant of the League of Nations, the Pact of Paris in 1928, and the Charter of the United Nations, that central idea of "reason of State" formed part of international law. States claimed–and had–the right to resort to war not only in order to defend their legal rights but in order to destroy the legal rights of other states. In the sphere of political theory Machiavelli put the position with his usual terseness: "That war is just which is necessary." * * * But although this particular–and most important–manifestation of "reason of State" became and for centuries continued to be part of international law, it was not an unchallenged doctrine. It was opposed by the parallel and powerful current of opinion that distinguished between wars which, in law, were just and those which were not. That current of opinion is represented by yet another aspect of the Grotian tradition, namely, his denial of the absolute right of war and his consistent differentiation between just and unjust wars. Grotius did not invent that distinction. It was part of the heritage of the Middle Ages. . . .

In the elaboration of the causes of just war Grotius made no obvious advance upon the already elaborate treatment of the subject by his predecessors. The merit of his own contribution lies in the clarity and in the emphasis with which he treated the subject. For a war to be just there must exist a legal cause for it–a reason which would be recognized by a court of law as a cause for action. As he points out, war begins where judicial settlement ends. It follows that a war undertaken to enforce a claim which "is not an obligation from the point of view of strict justice" is not a just war. . . . On the other hand, the cause of just wars are limited to defence against an injury either actual or immediately threatening, to recovery of what is legally due, and to inflicting punishment. He definitely excludes wars undertaken in order to weaken a neighbour who is a potential threat to the security of the state. He says, with regard to such a war, in a passage typical of the temper of the work in its challenging rejection of *raison d'état*: "That the possibility of being attacked confers the right to attack is abhorrent to every principle of equity. Human life exists under such conditions that complete security is never guaranteed to us. For protection against uncertain fears we must rely on Divine Providence, and on a wariness free from reproach, not on force." * * * The relevant section of Book II–the shortest paragraph in the treatise consists of one sentence, significant and impressive in its brevity, referring to the causes of war: "Advantage does not confer the same right as necessity." He also denies that there is any question of a justifiable war of defence in the case of those who deserved the war waged against them.

But it was in the drawing of the practical consequences from the distinction between just and unjust wars that Grotius went beyond anything taught by his predecessors. This applies not only to the all-important question of neutrality, or to [other] matters of detail.... It applies to the more fundamental question of the duty of the subject to serve in a war which is unjust or doubtful, an aspect of his teaching which is of particular significance in view of the respect–some thought servile respect–with which Grotius treated established authority and with which he discouraged any thought of rebellion. He is emphatic that the subject when ordered to take up arms in a clearly unjust war ought to refrain from doing so. Moreover, after much careful deliberation and weighing of authorities, he considers that the obligation is the same when the justice of the war is doubtful. He admits the dangers of disobedience, but his is content to take the risk: "For when either course is uncertain that which is the lesser of two evils is free from sin; for if a war is unjust there is no disobedience in avoiding it. Moreover, disobedience in things of this kind, by its very nature, is a lesser evil than manslaughter, especially than the slaughter of many innocent men." The only concession that he is prepared to make is that in the case of a doubtful war the ruler may impose an extraordinary tax upon those refusing to carry arms. At the same time, in conformity with the view which has remained unchallenged and which is in accordance with the humanitarian character of his treatise, he lays down that the question of the justice or injustice of the war is irrelevant for the purpose of observing the rules of warfare as between the belligerents. Any other rule would add to the inherent evils of war the horrors of unrestrained licence and cruelty accentuated by what must often be an unverified *ex parte* claim to wage a just war.

International law, in the three centuries which followed *De Jure Belli ac Pacis*, rejected the distinction between just and unjust wars. War became the supreme right of sovereign states and the very hall-mark of their sovereignty. To that extent international law was deprived of a reasonable claim to be regarded as law in the accepted sense of the word. The law on the subject has now undergone a fundamental change. War has ceased to be a supreme prerogative of states ... [A]mong the imponderables which have worked in that direction, the Grotian tradition occupies a high place.

* * *

8. *The Binding Force of Promises.* The denial of the right of war, unless for a cause recognized by law, and the principle of qualified neutrality constitute the main application, with regard to the law of war, of Grotius's reflection of the ideas of reason of State. In the sphere of the law of peace, that same tendency expressed itself most conspicuously in the emphasis which he placed upon the binding force of promises and the obligation of good faith in their fulfillment.... The last exhortation, in the final chapter of the treatise, is an appeal to the sacredness of good faith. To Grotius the obligation to abide by pacts is not only the basis of municipal law and of civil society; it is of the essence of the social contract. Without it the social contract is meaningless. As such, the obligation to keep promises is the principal tenet of the law of nature. It is an obligation which binds the ruler in relation to the contract which he has entered into with his subjects; they derive a clear legal right under it. And this, he adds, "holds even between God and man." It is not surprising that to him the binding force of treaties is the basis of international law.... He lays down the modern and, in the circumstances, unexceptional rule that promises made during war or for the purpose of terminating a war are valid even if extorted by fear. The reason for this seemingly repulsive qualification is that unless this rule were adopted most wars would be incapable of termination.

This categorical affirmation of the sanctity of promises ... had a pointed meaning at a time when the Pope claimed the right to release rulers from the binding obligation of oaths and treaties, by way of interpretation of express dispensation, and when the view was widely adopted and acted upon that there is no binding force in treaties concluded not only between Christians and infidels but also those between Catholics and Protestants. But its significance goes considerably beyond that. It supplies a scientific basis ... for the "volitional" law of nations, i.e., international law based on agreement whether expressed in a treaty or implied by custom. In modern terminology, the rule *pacta sunt servanda* is the initial hypothesis of the law of nations....

9. *The Fundamental Rights and Freedoms of the Individual.* There is one perplexing aspect of the work of Grotius which appears to be alien to the spirit of his teaching as outlined so far and which calls for careful examination, namely, his attitude to the question of the freedom of the individual in his relation to constituted authority. The importance of this subject is not confined to the field of political theory. In many ways it is closely connected with international law. It has given rise to scornful and impatient reprobation of Grotius's work as a whole. What is the reason for this exception–if an exception it is–to the otherwise uniformly progressive trend of the treatise? On the face of it the record is disillusioning. Grotius justified slavery and claimed to have found support for it in the immutable canons of the law of nature. He rejected the idea of sovereignty of the people. He denied the right of resistance to oppression by the ruler. He did not see why, if an individual can voluntarily sell himself into slavery, a whole people should not be able to do so collectively. He attributed an irrevocable legal effect not only to collective voluntary submission, but also to conquest. He completed this chain of reasoning by including in his examples of unjust wars a contest waged by an oppressed people in order to regain its liberty. It is not easy to fit all this into the general pattern of the treatise. The matter becomes even more obscure when we consider the personal circumstances of its author. Here was

a refugee who escaped from the sentence of a political court set up by an arbitrary decree. Yet he deprecated resistance to oppressive rule. Here was a Dutchman, the loyal son of a people which half a century before had by force thrown off the yoke of the Spanish oppressor who, at the very moment when *De Jure Belli ac Pacis* was being written, was preparing war against the United Provinces to reimpose upon them the tyranny of alien rule. Yet Grotius considered to be unjust a war waged by an oppressed people for the sake of its freedom.

What is the explanation of these views, so foreign to the spirit of his teaching and to his personal condition? It is true that, writing as he did in a country under an absolute monarch to whom he dedicated the treatise, who bestowed a pension upon him, and from whom he might have expected the favours of remunerative appointment, he could hardly write in the vein of *Vindiciae contra Tyrannos*. It is possible that, in view of the intransigence with which the right of resistance was advocated, both in the latter tract— which appeared in 1579 but which had not by any means fallen into oblivion—and in Hotman's *Franco-Gallia*, published in 1573, he felt it incumbent upon himself to hive to the matter a special argumentative emphasis. But this in itself is an inadequate explanation. What is much more to the point is that this frowning upon rebellion and the favouring of authority were in accordance with what were considered to be the essential needs of the times. . . . At a time of general uncertainty and of loosening of traditional ties of society, national and international, order was looked upon as the paramount dictate of reason. In the period preceding the Thirty Years War the territorial sovereign state which emerged from the dissolution of the feudal system of society on the Continent of Europe had hardly taken over the functions of the feudal lord; the resulting vacuum accentuated the necessity for stability even at the expense of freedom. Considerations of this order must have weighed heavily with one in whose work the desire for peace was the dominant motive and the ever-recurring theme. This particular feature of Grotius's outlook appears clearly from his unheroic advice given to defeated peoples to yield to fate rather than to engage in a suicidal fight for liberty, for, he says, reason prefers life to freedom. Strange as it may sound, his attitude towards slavery was to a large extent determined by humanitarian considerations. Enslavement of those captured in war was an alternative preferable to the unlimited power, including the right to kill, which, in his view, the customary law of nations and, probably, the law of nature gave to the captor. His treatment of the institution of slavery is permeated throughout by a spirit of charity and mercy.

What is more important than these explanations is the fact that behind the facade of the general disapproval of the right of resistance there lay qualifications so comprehensive as to render the major proposition almost theoretical. Thus, according to Grotius, there is a right of resistance in cases in which the ruler, by virtue of an original or subsequent contract, is responsible to a free people (as was the case in Sparta); against a king who has renounced his authority or has manifestly abandoned it; who attempts to alienate his kingdom (but only so far as is necessary to prevent the transfer); who openly shows himself the enemy of the whole people–an elastic and formidable exception; who attempts to usurp that part of the sovereign power which does not belong to him; and, finally, where the people have reserved the right of resistance in certain cases. These exceptions as laid down by Grotius were relied upon as an authority for the justification of the resistance to and deposition of James II. . . .

Finally in this connexion we must bear in mind other indications of Grotius's true attitude. Thus it is significant that, notwithstanding his reluctance to sanction recourse to war, he considers as just resort to war to prevent the maltreatment by a state of its own subjects. In such cases, he says, if a ruler "should inflict upon his subjects such treatment as no one is warranted in inflicting, the exercise of the right vested in human society is not precluded." This is, on the face of it, a somewhat startling rule, for it may not be easy to see why he permits a foreign state to intervene, through war, on behalf of the oppressed while he denies to the persecuted themselves the right of resistance. Part of the answer is, perhaps, that he held such wars of intervention to be permitted only in extreme cases which coincide largely with those in which the king reveals himself as an enemy of his people and in which resistance is permitted.

However that may be, this is the first authoritative statement of the principle of humanitarian intervention–the principle that the exclusiveness of domestic jurisdictions stops where outrage upon humanity begins. The doctrine of humanitarian intervention has never become a fully acknowledged part of positive international law. But it has . . . been occasionally acted upon, and it was one of the factors which paved the way for the provisions of the Charter of the United Nations relating to fundamental human rights and freedoms. . . .

10. *The Idea of Peace.* The tenth—and not the least important—aspect of the Grotian tradition is his pacifism. He does not deny that war is a legal institution. On the contrary, he is at pains to show that war is not inconsistent with the law of nature and with many other kinds of law. There were good reasons—in addition to the recognition of a patent–fact for this initial legitimation of war. It would not be feasible . . . to introduce a measure of legal regulation into a relation not recognized by law. A corresponding method suggested itself—and was adopted—with regard to the contents of the rules of warfare. Thus Grotius's treatment of the laws of war seems to be open to the charge that, after setting out to humanize rules of war, he gives the imprimatur of law to rules of pronounced inhumanity. His answer to any such criticism would probably have been that the proper course was not to deny the character of law to practices which apparently had secured a wide degree of acceptance, but to urge a mitigation of their rigours. . . .

In general, there breathes from the pages of *De Jure Belli ac Pacis* a disapproval, amounting to hatred, of war. There is nothing in that work reminiscent of the Baconian conception of war as a healthy exercise. Grotius is clear that where the question of legal right is doubtful, a state ought to refrain from war. He proposes various methods of settling disputes, including negotiation and arbitration. He suggests that "it would be advantageous, indeed in a degree necessary, to hold certain conferences of Christian powers, where those who have no interest at stake may settle the disputes of others, and where, in fact, steps may be take to compel parties to accept peace on fair terms." He devotes a whole chapter to "warnings not to undertake war rashly, even for just causes." . . .

11. *The Tradition of Idealism and Progress.* The pacifist strain which runs through the entire work of Grotius is only one feature of the more general aspect—the last to be here considered—of the Grotian tradition, namely, what may not inappropriately be called the tradition of progress and idealism. He initiated or gave his support to progressive ideas in various fields in the sphere of international relations. He was one of the first to assist the cause of international co-operation in the suppression of crime by urging extradition of criminals as a matter of legal duty. He did more than any of the other founders of international law in developing the theory and in elucidation the practice of diplomatic immunities. He supplied the basis of the modern law of state responsibility founded on fault as distinguished from absolute liability and thus helped to displace the indiscriminating and anarchic practice of reprisals as a normal means of redressing grievances. He urged, and laid down as a rule of law, the principle of freedom of navigation on international rivers and canals. His share in the evolution of the principle of the freedom of the sea needs no elaboration. In all these matters his teaching became part of international practice, wholly or in part....

Thus in matters of economic freedom he spoke the language of uncompromising free trade expressed in terms of legal right. Men are entitled to obtain things without which life cannot comfortably be lived. And although this is an imperfect right inasmuch as the owner retains the power of disposition, no obstacles to the free acquisition of necessaries of life must be raised by "law or by conspiracy." To do that, he says, quoting Ambrose, is "to separate men from relation with their common parent, to refuse fruits freely produced for all, and to do away with the community of life." He reiterates that "all men have the right to buy such things at a fair price unless, as in time of extreme scarcity of grain, they are needed by those from whom they are sought." As if in anticipation of some modern monopolistic practices, he inquired, in this connexion, whether it is permissible for one people to make an agreement with another to sell to it exclusively products which do not grow elsewhere. He thought this permissible and not inconsistent with the law of nature provided the latter was prepared to re-sell at a fair price.

It will be noted that these various claims are not postulates of mere ideal justice. They figure in the part of the treatise which is concerned with the causes of war–one of which is "injury actually received," "an injury to that which actually belongs to us." He was clearly in advance of his time when he urged that refugees driven from their homes have the right to acquire permanent residence in another country provided they submit to the government in authority; that deserted and barren portions of national territory be given to immigrants who ask for it, and that they are entitled to take possession, subject to the sovereignty of the original people, of uncultivated land; that a state is bound to grant freedom of passage through its territory to a people which has been forced to leave its country and is seeking unoccupied lands, or desires to carry on commerce with a distant nation; that freedom of passage for the purpose of carrying on commerce extends, as a matter of right, not only to persons but also to merchandise; and that such freedom of passage includes freedom from taxation unless in return for services rendered. He urged with emphasis the right of the individual to expatriate himself from his country of origin, and he acknowledged the right of self-determination to the extent of requiring the consent of the population to the transfer of national territory. . . .

* * *

These then are the principal features of what has here been called the Grotian tradition in international law. . . . Some of these elements . . . have now become part of the positive law; others are still an aspiration. But they all explain why Grotius's work has remained an abiding force and not merely an episode, however important, in the literature of international law. . . . What Grotius did was to endow international law with unprecedented dignity and authority by making it part not only of a general system of jurisprudence but also of a universal moral code. . . . *De Jure Belli ac Pacis* is pre-eminently a treatise which must be judged not by reference to its method, but by its influence on the doctrine and on the practice of the law of nations. It satisfied the craving, in the jurist and the layman alike, for a moral content in the law. In stressing and, on the whole, maintaining the distinction between law and morality it vindicated the place of the law of nations in legal science. Last–but not least–it became identified with the idea of progress in international law.

These considerations may help to answer, to a large extent, the question whether *De Jure Belli ac Pacis* is still a proper medium of study and instruction in international law. The reply is clearly in the negative if what we have in mind is assistance in the search for a legal rule which we may assume an international court would now apply in a case before it. From this point of view most text-books and treatises are obsolete. . . .

[However, by] gaining an understanding of the Grotian tradition as a whole . . . , we may . . . obtain an insight into the persistent problems of international law in the past, in the present, and, probably for some long time to come, in the future. It is a measure of the greatness of the work of Grotius that all these questions should have found a place in his teaching and that he should have answered them in a spirit upon the acceptance of which depends the ultimate reality of the law of nations as a "law properly so called."

HEDLEY BULL, "THE GROTIAN CONCEPTION OF INTERNATIONAL SOCIETY," DIPLOMATIC INVESTIGATIONS: ESSAYS IN THE THEORY OF INTERNATIONAL RELATIONS

51–52, 64–73 (H. Butterfield & M. Wight eds., 1966)

Underlying a great deal of the theory and practice of international relations since the First World War, there is a certain conception of international society, whose imprint may be traced in the Covenant of the League of Nations, the Paris Pact, the United Nations Charter, and the Charter of the International Military Tribunal at Nuremberg. It is widely taken to contain within itself an adequate formula for orderly and just international conduct, such that the disparity between it and the actual course of events since 1919 may be ascribed to the failure of states or statesmen to behave in accordance with it, rather than to its own inherent defects. The purpose of this essay is, at the risk of losing sight of its many varieties and nuances, to state the essence of this doctrine; and to consider the adequacy of its prescriptions.

The conception of international society I have in mind may be called the Grotian conception. The reason for giving it this name does not lie in the part which the writings of Grotius have played in bringing about this twentieth century doctrine, although this has been by no means negligible; but simply in the measure of identity that exists between the one and the other. We shall have occasion to consider the difference as well as the resemblances between Grotius himself and the twentieth century neo-Grotians; but the resemblances are remarkable enough to warrant our treatment of *De Jure Belli ac Pacis* as containing the classical presentation of the same view. Two important studies, to which reference will be made, have discerned a return to Grotius in this century, and along with it a reversal of the previous trend of international legal thought, which from the seventeenth century to the early twentieth, had been away from him. The first of these studies, by Cornelius van Vollenhoven, was written in the summer of 1918 and looked forward to the resuscitation of Grotian doctrines, for which the World War seemed to have set the stage.[2] The second was published by the late Sir Hersch Lauterpacht in 1946, by which time he was able to record the penetration by these doctrines into positive international law.[e] Both these writers are concerned to contrast the position shared by Grotius and the twentieth century neo-Grotians with representative thinkers of the intervening period, Vollenhoven taking Vattel to exemplify a position contrary to that of Grotius, and Lauterpacht referring in this connection to the work of the nineteenth century international legal positivists. Vollenhoven and Lauterpacht, it should be noted, themselves embrace the broad Grotian position. It shall be our purpose, while exploring the conflict between this position and that alternative conception of international society to which Vattel and the nineteenth century positivists may be said to have contributed, to consider whether the return to Grotius does indeed constitute that advance which Vollenhoven and Lauterpacht take it to be.

The central Grotian assumption is that of the solidarity, or potential solidarity, of the states comprising international society, with respect to the enforcement of the law. This assumption is not explicitly adopted and defended by Grotius, but ... the rules which he propounds for international conduct are such as to presuppose that it is made. In the conception of international society which stands opposed to the Grotian doctrine the contrary assumption is made that states do not exhibit solidarity of this kind, but are capable of agreeing only for certain minimum purposes which fall short of that of the enforcement of the law. In the view it takes of the area of actual or potential agreement among the member states of international society it may be called pluralist where the Grotian doctrine is solidarist; and the rules it prescribes for relations among them are such as to reflect this difference.

* * *

The question at issue between the Grotians and the pluralists is not one as to what is contained in the law. It is a question as to what kind of legal rules are most appropriate to the working of the international order; a matter not of international law but of international political science. The central assumption of the Grotians, as was mentioned at the outset of our inquiry, is that there exists solidarity in international society with regard to the enforce-

2. C. van Vollenhoven, The Three Stages in the Evolution of the Law of Nations (1919)....

e. *See supra* H. Lauterpacht (p. 1270).

ment of the law. If in fact a consensus may be reached as to the nature of the distinction between just and unjust causes of war; if the international community can be brought to agree in a particular case as to which side is engaging in police action and which in crime; if the claims of the former to represent international society as a whole are in fact given credence by the active or passive support of a preponderance of states, then it may well be that it is upon Grotian principles that the international order should be shaped. But if, on the other hand, no solidarity on these matters obtains; if international society finds itself unable to agree as to the criterion of just war; if the outbreak of war typically finds international society at large, as well as the belligerents themselves, divided as to which side embodies the just cause, then our conclusion must be a different one. It may be argued of the Grotian conception in this event not merely that it is unworkable but that it is positively damaging to the international order; that by imposing upon international society a strain which it cannot bear, it has the effect of undermining those structures of the system which might otherwise be secure. And it may be said of the pluralist doctrine that so far from constituting a disguised form of *Realpolitik,* it presents a set of prescriptions more conducive to the working of the international order than those of the Grotians.

International society will be able to enforce its law only if it can mobilize superior power in its support. The existence of a system of rules favouring the victory of the just party may facilitate the imposition of the law, as the work of the police within a modern state is assisted by the legal principles we have discussed. But they will not suffice to call into being a coalition with will and force sufficient to ensure victory, where these elements are lacking. That they have been lacking in the years since the First World War, and that the provisions of the Covenant, the Paris Pact and the Charter facilitating the victory of the just party in war have not been acted upon by an international community with solidarity enough to make a reality of them, is today well enough understood.

What is less appreciated is that the Grotian doctrine may have, and perhaps has had, an influence positively detrimental to international order. For to the extent that it influences the course of events, the doctrine that war should be fought only for a just cause is injurious to the institutions with which international society had equipped itself for the limitation of war. The qualifications that the Grotian doctrine attaches to its endorsement of institutions are such as to impede their working. If one side in an armed conflict regards itself as specially privileged by the laws of war, then reciprocal observance of these laws, which is a basic condition of their efficacy, is undermined. If a state which wishes to remain neutral nevertheless discriminates in favour of one party, then unless it does so from a position of superior strength, as did the United States when it pursued a policy of "qualified neutrality" in 1940–41, it cannot expect to have the belligerent which suffers discrimination respect its wish. If the obligations of an alliance are to be qualified by the justice of the cause, this latter being something subjectively or arbitrarily determined, then an impediment exists to the conclusion or to the maintenance of alliances, which in the absence of a system of collective law enforcement may be held to be essential devices for the maintenance of security and order. If a right of intervention is proclaimed for the purpose of enforcing standards of conduct, and yet no consensus exists in the international community governing its use, then the door is open to interventions by particular states using such a right as a pretext, and the principle of territorial sovereignty is placed in jeopardy.

To show how in the twentieth century the influence of Grotian conceptions has in fact impeded the working of these institutions for the limitation of conflict would take us far afield. Three episodes may be mentioned, however, as having been especially influenced by the neo-Grotian doctrine. The first is the action of the League of Nations in imposing economic sanctions against Italy in 1935. The second is the trial and punishment of German and Japanese citizens by the International Military Tribunal of Nuremberg and that of the Far East, on charges of having begun an unjust war. The third is the war conducted in the name of the United Nations in Korea. None of these events could be regarded as having been brought about by the neo-Grotian doctrine; but each assumed the particular character it did in part because of that influence. The effects of these three episodes on the structure of international order were manifold and even contradictory; and it is possible to derive all sorts of lessons from them. But it might be argued in each case that the Grotian influence served to weaken devices for the limitation of conflict.

The view of the pluralists is not to be dismissed as a mere rationalization of state practice; it is a conception of international society founded upon the observation of the actual area of agreement between states and informed by a sense of the limitations within which in this situation rules may be usefully made rules of law. It seeks not to burden international law with a weight it cannot carry; and to have it leave room for the operation of those political forces, beyond the control of law, on which the existence of international society also depends. Thus although Oppenheim's exposition of the law allows war to be fought for any cause whatever, the political theory he presents does include a doctrine of just war; and it is partly in deference to this that he rejects the Grotian position. "The assertion that whereas all wars waged for political causes are unjust, all wars waged for international delinquencies are just, if there be no other way of getting reparation and satisfaction, is certainly incorrect in its generality. The evils of war are so great that, even when caused by an international delinquency, war cannot be justified if the delinquency was comparatively unimportant and trifling. And, on the other hand, under certain circumstances and conditions many political causes of war may correctly be called just causes. Only such individuals as lack insight into history and human nature can, for instance, defend the opinion that a war is unjust which has been caused by the desire for national unity or by the desire to maintain the balance of power which is the basis of all International Law." It may be held one of the weaknesses of the Grotian and neo-Grotian doctrines that they do not take account of the theory of the balance of power, nor face up to the question of the relationship between the prescriptions emanating from this theory and the prescriptions of international law.

Grotius is, I believe, fundamentally correct in his perception that international society cannot survive if it is to tolerate resort to war for any purpose whatever. The difference between Grotius and Oppenheim is partly explicable in terms of the fact that during the Thirty Years' War all sorts of claims were being advanced, hostile to the emergence of a society of sovereign states and a reality to its first great theoretician, that in the opening years of the twentieth century seemed remote and improbable. War to enforce the right to universal empire and war to impose a religion cannot be comprehended under the heading of "war for political causes" which Oppenheim thought international society could tolerate; and if these dangers did not seem real enough in 1905 to be worthy targets of protest, it was nevertheless still true that international society rested on the rejection of them. There is in Grotius also an awareness of a threat to international society more deadly even than these, and seeming still more remote within the confines of European international society in 1905: the war of barbarians. Grotius recognizes in addition to causes for war which are justifiable and causes which are merely persuasive (in the sense that though just causes are stated for them, these are only pretexts) a third category of causes of war which are neither justifiable nor persuasive but "wars of savages" fought without a cause of any sort. Vattel also is conscious of this possible dimension of international experience and speaks of those who begin war without pretext of any kind as "monsters unworthy of the name of men," whom nations may unite to suppress. If Oppenheim is correct in taking the divisions in international society to be too great to warrant an attempt to write a theory of just war into international law, it is also true that international society in his own time displayed on more fundamental matters a solidarity so great that it did not occur to him to call it in question.

But it is one thing to appreciate that international society presupposes abstention from war directed at certain ends and another to say that rules enjoining such abstention can usefully be made rule of law. Oppenheim's approach to the question of the place of law in international society was accompanied by an attitude of complacency about war and its use as an instrument of national policy which is rightly rejected today. But it may still be held that the method he employed, of gauging the role of law in international society in relation to the actual area of agreement between states, is superior to one which sets up the law over and against the facts. And although the solidarity exhibited by international society may increase in the future, just as it may decrease, it can still be argued that in the twentieth century the Grotian conception has proved premature.

————

THE SENSE OF THE GROTIAN CHARACTER OF INTERNATIONAL LAW, as described by Lauterpacht, was supportive of the development of a community-based dimension of international law that restricted the sovereignty of territorial states. In this regard, however, by accentuating the Grotian tradition, Lauterpacht overlooked deliberately the eighteenth and nineteenth century development of a more positivist–state-centered–conception of international law, perhaps most compellingly achieved, as Hedley Bull observes, in the work of Emmerich de Vattel, a Swiss jurist. This Vattelian tradition tended to treat the naturalist antecedents of the state system as irrelevant and to "absolutize" the state, thereby denying the existence of any kind of overarching international community on which to ground an ethos of human solidarity.

Hedley Bull's influential critique of the application of Grotian ideas is based on a more state-centric view of international society. Bull argues, in effect, that sentiments of solidarity are not sufficiently present to impose individual accountability on governmental leaders or to erect a collective security system in international life. At the same time, he is not nihilistic, recognizing the realities of international cooperation within a framework of international law that corresponds with the normal disposition of states toward moderation. In this regard, Bull trusts positivist approaches to obligation, resting on consent, as providing a more reliable set of guidelines as to the behavior of states under existing historical conditions than do more ambitious Grotian notions of solidarity.[f]

This controversy relates to the fundamental question raised by this introduction to Part III: has the historical grounding of international society moved away from a state-centric basis of world order that is limited in its capacity to impose legal constraints of any kind on the more powerful states, especially in relation to the use of force?[g] The answer could be yes, without being Grotian in Lauterpacht's sense. This is where global market forces come in. Economic globalization imposes a discipline on the shaping and sharing of power by states, but such a globalizing framework may not consistently promote world order values as presented in previous chapters or encourage a shared sense of human solidarity. As the resurgence of ethnic strife and the politics of identity suggest, globalization is consistent with such developments as political fragmentation, "failed states," ultra-nationalism, and an overall sense of world disorder. Various aspects of these new realities in international life are depicted in the next chapter, especially the tensions between the spread of universal norms (for example, in relation to civilizational values and identity politics) and the more pluralist claims of identity arising from class, gender, race, religion, and ethnic civilization.

Underlying this inquiry on international trends is the overarching question: is the time right for a Grotian move toward jurisprudential integration on behalf of a more peaceful, just, and sustainable world order? And, if so, what should be its nature? Note that states have transferred considerable sovereignty over economic policy to the World Trade Organization so as to promote the expansion of world trade and the opportunity to encourage export-led economic growth. For these goals, a common regulatory framework has been substantially achieved in the 1990s. Why is it so much more difficult to institutionalize collective action and establish common operating norms and the rule of law in other sectors of international life, such as in relation to peace and security, human rights, and environmental protection? Why have states acquiesced in the loss of sovereignty resulting from economic globalization but remain fiercely protective of sovereign rights when the matter at issue involves the social agenda or environmental protection?

f. This orientation toward world order is worked out more fully in Bull's important book, The Anarchical Society: A Study of Order in World Politics (1977).

g. For a recent argument that the United States should adhere to a unilateralist approach to foreign policy premised on military strength that is between twice and four times as much as the most powerful state, see W. Kristol & R. Kagan, *Toward a Neo-Reaganite Foreign Policy,* 75 Foreign. Aff. 18 (1996). For a skeptical view of the efficacy of international law, see J. L. Goldsmith & E.A. Posner, The Limits of International Law (2005), taking note of their conclusion, at 225, that "[i]nternational law is a real phenomenon, but international law scholars exaggerate its power and significance."

Chapter Eight

GLOBAL DREAMS AND GEOPOLITICAL NIGHTMARES

The 1990s were dominated by speculations about the shape of world order after the Cold War, and by a new realization that the world economy was being integrated in unprecedented ways. The compression of our sense of time and space together with a capacity to manage information on a global scale because of the Internet created new realities widely described under the slippery rubric of "globalization." This terminology gave a high priority to economic perspectives, the rise of global market forces and an accompanying neoliberal ideology that was weighted toward the promotion of capital efficiency and corporate profitability arguably at the expense of human well-being and even the territorial interests of citizens. Civil society activists mobilized on a transnational basis to oppose the effects of globalization, seeking a more equitable and sustainable approach to world economic policy and thereby producing an increasingly robust movement sometimes called "globalization-from-below." This project of global civil society was not one of anti-globalization as often portrayed; it was, rather, anti-neoliberal in outlook, and sought to achieve a more equitable, sustainable, and democratically regulated form of globalization.

The attacks of 11 September 2001 almost immediately superseded this economistic agenda, especially in the North and most of all in the United States. The American response to the al Qaeda challenge was conditioned to a significant degree by the presidency of George W. Bush that even before September 11 had pursued a strategic path that was unilateralist and reliant on a less constrained view of the role of force in the pursuit of claimed national interests and a presumed American role as global leader. Important treaties and promising institutional initiatives were repudiated in a defiant manner. With the sense of siege produced by September 11 and inflamed by patriotic fervor, the Bush Administration put national security at the center of its foreign policy agenda, moving to increase the military budget in dramatic ways and to augment the power of the state domestically, establishing a new cabinet level of government, the Department of Homeland Security (DHS).

There is no doubt that the magnitude and character of the September 11 attacks and the danger of future attacks generated a major challenge that could not be ignored. Nor could it be addressed fully within the framework of international law pertaining to the use of force. Adjustments in the understanding of the scope of self-defense needed to be made. Account had to be taken of an adversary that deliberately directed its violence against civilian targets, relying on suicide attackers, avoiding diplomacy, and occupying no specific territory. What was unleashed by the attacks on the World Trade Center and the Pentagon was a war without boundaries or clearly defined goals, with actors that were not states in the traditional sense. In a dark sense, al Qaeda gave further authority to the claim of the 1990s about the rise of transnational networking as a formidable strategy of economic and military power. Additionally, the United States, with its worldwide network of military bases present in more than 60 countries, its effort at achieving military control of space, and its all-oceans navies, was operating as a *global state* that made it a matter of explicit national policy to beat back any challenge to this dominance in any region of the world by, it seems, any means available.

From the perspective of international law and world order, what makes the response to September 11 so confusing is a combination of factors:

- both international law and the United Nations were premised on world order based on the interaction of territorial sovereign states, and that premise had been seriously undermined;

- the constraints on the use of international force in international law and the UN Charter **(Basic Document 1.5)** were based on a statist model of defensive necessity; so, given the apparent unworkability of deterrence or reactive postures of defense in the new context, the doctrine of self-defense had to be redefined;

- the response to September 11 combined the claim to an expanded right of self-defense, which was in some respects reasonable, with the pursuit of a project of global domination, which was destructive of international law and the war prevention roles of the United Nations as well as threatening to the sovereign rights of most states and their support of a law-governed world order.

The readings in this chapter attempt to unravel this controversy about the use of force and the global role of the United States that is casting a long shadow over the future of world order at the present time. It is possible that a more moderate leadership will emerge in the United States that pursues a responsible security policy while refraining from seeking to establish the first global empire in human history. But it is by no means assured. Nor is it clear how other major centers of state power, including China, Europe, and Russia, will respond. An interesting debate was generated by Robert Kagen's book, *Of Power and Paradise: America and Europe in the New World Order*, published in 2003 and arguing that Europe is law-oriented because it is militarily weak while the United States is power-oriented because it is militarily strong, and therefore responsible for containing aggressive forces. Kagen, a prominent neoconservative ("neocon") policy activist, advances an ultra-realist rationale for the Bush approach to American grand strategy.

What is relevant to the approach of this coursebook is the importance accorded to international law by both sides in this debate. The European outlook, generally, stresses the urgency of meeting world order challenges, to the extent possible, by reliance on law, international institutions, and diplomacy. It was this outlook that ran up against a stonewall in Washington over the question of how to deal with Iraq under Saddam Hussein. In a deep sense, the Iraq War is a continuing test of these two world order perspectives. The current difficulties encountered by the American-led occupation of Iraq bring this debate home to America in a manner that has not occurred since the Vietnam Era. So far, the traumatizing fears associated with September 11 and the absence of a draft imposing obligatory military service on young Americans, seems to explain the rather mild backlash against the failed occupation. As the war drags on and America's domestic weaknesses become more evident in the wake of Hurricane Katrina, the possibilities for change at this writing seem to be improving, but remain far from assured.

In this chapter, we begin with a letter from President George W. Bush introducing the very influential White House document titled *National Security Strategy of the United States of America* **(Basic Document 6.9)**, released in September 2002 arguing for an expanded view of national security and contending that the absence of rivalries between leading states creates an opportunity for a peaceful world that has never existed before. We add an excerpt from this presentation of American post-September 11 strategy that depicts the key claim of right relative to preemptive/preventive wars. This is followed by a succinct statement of the official American case under international law for the Iraq War written by leading officials in the Office of the Legal Advisor in the US Department of State. The implications of this approach to world order are candidly stated in a short newspaper article jointly authored by David Frum, former speech writer for President Bush, and Richard Perle, the most intellectually influential neoconservative advisor. The thesis of this article is that the United States will do what it needs to do to pursue its view of security, and that if the United Nations does not go along, then the US should withdraw. Frum and Perle have expressed their radical views of American grand strategy at greater length in *An End to Evil: How to Win the War on Terror* (2003).

More skeptical and nuanced views of the September 11 challenge, especially in the context of the Iraq War, are expressed in the remainder of the chapter. Thomas Franck considers the implications of preemption as applied to Iraq for the future of international law governing the use of force. Franck, who has endorsed realist approaches to the role of international law in the past, exhibits a critical view of the claims acted upon by the Bush Administration in its march to war.[a] Thereafter, Richard Falk explores the negative implication of the Iraq War for the future of the United Nations, arguing for the persisting vitality of the Charter framework governing the use of international force in relations among sovereign states. The chapter concludes with a short excerpt from the 2004 UN report, *A More Secure World: Our Shared Responsibility*, prepared by the Secretary–General's High-level Panel on Threats, Challenges and Change. The report argues the position that preemptive uses of force may be necessary given terrorist threats, but that their validity and legality depends upon *prior* UN Security Council authorization.

a. A more cautious and tentative view, also noteworthy, is found in J. Stromseth, *Law and*   *Force After Iraq: A Transitional Moment,* 97 A.J.I.L 628 (2003).

COVER LETTER TO NATIONAL SECURITY STRATEGY
OF THE UNITED STATES OF AMERICA
The White House, Washington, D.C., 17 September 2002

The great struggles of the twentieth century between liberty and totalitarianism ended with a decisive victory for the forces of freedom—and a single sustainable model for national success: freedom, democracy, and free enterprise. In the twenty-first century, only nations that share a commitment to protecting basic human rights and guaranteeing political and economic freedom will be able to unleash the potential of their people and assure their future prosperity. People everywhere want to be able to speak freely; choose who will govern them; worship as they please; educate their children—male and female; own property; and enjoy the benefits of their labor. These values of freedom are right and true for every person, in every society—and the duty of protecting these values against their enemies is the common calling of freedom-loving people across the globe and across the ages.

Today, the United States enjoys a position of unparalleled military strength and great economic and political influence. In keeping with our heritage and principles, we do not use our strength to press for unilateral advantage. We seek instead to create a balance of power that favors human freedom: conditions in which all nations and all societies can choose for themselves the rewards and challenges of political and economic liberty. In a world that is safe, people will be able to make their own lives better. We will defend the peace by fighting terrorists and tyrants. We will preserve the peace by building good relations among the great powers. We will extend the peace by encouraging free and open societies on every continent.

* * *

To defeat this threat we must make use of every tool in our arsenal—military power, better homeland defenses, law enforcement, intelligence, and vigorous efforts to cut off terrorist financing. The war against terrorists of global reach is a global enterprise of uncertain duration. America will help nations that need our assistance in combating terror. And America will hold to account nations that are compromised by terror, including those who harbor terrorists because the allies of terror are the enemies of civilization. The United States and countries cooperating with us must not allow the terrorists to develop new home bases. Together, we will seek to deny them sanctuary at every turn.

The gravest danger our Nation faces lies at the crossroads of radicalism and technology. Our enemies have openly declared that they are seeking weapons of mass destruction, and evidence indicates that they are doing so with determination. The United States will not allow these efforts to succeed. We will build defenses against ballistic missiles and other means of delivery. We will cooperate with other nations to deny, contain, and curtail our enemies' efforts to acquire dangerous technologies. And, as a matter of common sense and self-defense, America will act against such emerging threats before they are fully formed. We cannot defend America and our friends by hoping for the best[.] So[,] we must be prepared to defeat our enemies' plans, using the best intelligence and proceeding with deliberation. History will judge harshly those who saw this coming danger but failed to act. In the new world we have entered, the only path to peace and security is the path of action.

As we defend the peace, we will also take advantage of an historic opportunity to preserve the peace. Today, the international community has the best chance since the rise of the nation-state in the seventeenth century to build a world where great powers compete in peace instead of continually prepare for war. Today, the world's great powers find ourselves on the same side united by common dangers of terrorist violence and chaos. The United States will build on these common interests to promote global security. We are also increasingly united by common values. Russia is in the midst of a hopeful transition, reaching for its democratic future and a partner in the war on terror. Chinese leaders are discovering that economic freedom is the only source of national wealth. In time, they will find that social and political freedom is the only source of national greatness. America will encourage the advancement of democracy and economic openness in both nations, because these are the best foundations for domestic stability and international order. We will strongly resist aggression from other great powers—even as we welcome their peaceful pursuit of prosperity, trade, and cultural advancement.

Finally, the United States will use this moment of opportunity to extend the benefits of freedom across the globe. We will actively work to bring the hope of democracy, development, free markets, and free trade to every corner of the world. The events of September 11, 2001, taught us that weak states, like Afghanistan, can pose as great a danger to our national interests as strong states. Poverty does not make poor people into terrorists and murderers. Yet poverty, weak institutions, and corruption can make weak states vulnerable to terrorist networks and drug cartels within their borders.

The United States will stand beside any nation determined to build a better future by seeking the rewards of liberty for its people. Free trade and free markets have proven their ability to lift whole societies out of poverty—so the United States will work with individual nations, entire regions, and the entire global trading community to build a world that trades in freedom and therefore grows in prosperity. The United States will deliver greater development assistance through the New Millennium Challenge Account to nations that govern justly, invest in their people, and encourage economic freedom. We will also continue to lead the world in efforts to reduce the terrible toll of HIV/AIDS and other infectious diseases.

In building a balance of power that favors freedom, the United States is guided by the conviction that all nations have important responsibilities. Nations that enjoy freedom must actively fight terror. Nations that depend on international stability must help prevent the spread of weapons of mass destruction. Nations that seek international aid must govern themselves wisely, so that aid is well spent. For freedom to thrive, accountability must be expected and required.

We are also guided by the conviction that no nation can build a safer, better world alone. Alliances and multilateral institutions can multiply the strength of freedom-loving nations. The United States is committed to lasting institutions like the United Nations, the World Trade Organization, the Organization of American States, and NATO as well as other long-standing alliances. Coalitions of the willing can augment these permanent institutions. In all cases, international obligations are to be taken seriously. They are not to be undertaken symbolically to rally support for an ideal without furthering its attainment.

Freedom is the non-negotiable demand of human dignity; the birthright of every person—in every civilization. Throughout history, freedom has been threatened by war and terror; it has been challenged by the clashing wills of powerful states and the evil designs of tyrants; and it has been tested by widespread poverty and disease. Today, humanity holds in its hands the opportunity to further freedom's triumph over all these foes. The United States welcomes our responsibility to lead in this great mission.

WILLIAM H. TAFT & TODD F. BUCHWALD, "PREEMPTION, IRAQ, AND INTERNATIONAL LAW,"
97 A.J.I.L. 557, 557–63 (2003)

Preemption comes in many forms and what we think of it depends on the circumstances. One state may not strike another merely because the second might someday develop an ability and desire to attack it. Yet few would criticize a strike in the midst of an ongoing war against a second state's program to develop new types of weapons. Between these two examples lie countless fact patterns.

In the end, each use of force must find legitimacy in the facts and circumstances that the state believes have made it necessary. Each should be judged not on abstract concepts, but on the particular events that gave rise to it. While nations must not use preemption as a pretext for aggression, to be for or against preemption in the abstract is a mistake. The use of force preemptively is sometimes lawful and sometimes not.

Operation Iraqi Freedom has been criticized as unlawful because it constitutes preemption. This criticism is unfounded. Operation Iraqi Freedom was and is lawful. An otherwise lawful use of force does not become unlawful because it can be characterized as preemption. Operation Iraqi Freedom was conducted in a specific context that frames the way it should be analyzed. This context included the naked aggression by Iraq against its neighbors, its efforts to obtain weapons of mass destruction, its record of having used such weapons, Security Council action under Chapter VII of the United Nations Charter [**Basic Document 1.5**], and continuing Iraqi defiance of the Council's requirements.

On August 2, 1990, Iraq invaded Kuwait. It is easy to forget the wantonness of Iraq's invasion, which was unprovoked and carried out with particular cruelty, and the horror with which the world received news of it. That invasion rightly shaped, forever after, the way the world would look at Saddam Hussein's Iraq; and the United States, its allies and friends, and the international community as a whole came to realize that this was a menace from which the world needed special protection. In the midst of over a dozen years of an essentially ongoing conflict, conducted at different times at different levels of intensity, the Iraqi regime committed itself to comply with conditions that would have brought the story to a close. But it could never bring itself to fulfill its commitments.

Virtually immediately, the Security Council adopted UN Security Council Resolution 660, the first of many resolutions condemning Iraq's actions and demanding withdrawal from Kuwait. Additional Council actions were designed to apply further pressure and bring about Iraq's withdrawal. The Council's actions paralleled steps taken by the United States and others pursuant to the inherent right of collective self-defense recognized in Article 51 of the UN Charter. The United States moved forces to the Persian Gulf and then commenced maritime interdiction efforts in response to the Iraqi attack. But Iraq was intransigent.

Eventually, in November 1990, the Council adopted Resolution 678 [**Basic Document 2.40**], which authorized the use of "all necessary means" to uphold and implement Resolution 660 and subsequent relevant resolutions, and to restore international peace and security in the area. The resolution provided Iraq with "one final opportunity" to comply with the Council's earlier decisions and authorized the use of force "unless Iraq on or before 15 January 1991 fully implements" the Council's resolutions. It specifically invoked the authority of Chapter VII of the Charter, which permits the Security Council to respond to either a threat to, or a breach of, the peace by authorizing the use of force to maintain or restore international peace and security.

Iraq refused to comply with the resolutions by the January 15 deadline, and coalition forces commenced military operations the next day. Significantly, the Security Council did not make a further determination prior to January 15 as to whether or not Iraq had taken advantage of the "one final opportunity" it had been given two months earlier. Member states made that judgment themselves and relied on the Security Council's November decision as authority to use force.

On April 3, 1991, the Council adopted Resolution 687 [**Basic Document 2.41**]. That resolution did not return the situation to the status quo ante, the situation that might have existed if Iraq had never invaded Kuwait or if the Council had never acted. Rather, Resolution 687 declared that, upon official Iraqi acceptance of its provisions, a formal cease-fire would take effect, and it imposed several conditions on Iraq, including extensive obligations related to the regime's possession of weapons of mass destruction (WMD). As the Council itself subsequently described it, Resolution 687 provided the "conditions essential to the restoration of peace and security."

The Council's conclusion that these WMD-related conditions were essential is neither surprising in the wake of the history of aggression by the Iraqi regime against its neighbors nor irrelevant to the legal situation faced by the coalition when Operation Iraqi Freedom began in March 2003. The Iraqi regime had demonstrated a willingness to use weapons of mass destruction, including by inflicting massive deaths against civilians in large-scale chemical weapons attacks against its own Kurdish population in the late 1980s, killing thousands. On at least ten occasions, the regime's forces had attacked Iranian and Kurdish targets with combinations of mustard gas and nerve agents through the use of aerial bombs, rockets, and conventional artillery shells. There was no question that such weapons in the hands of such a regime posed dangers to the countries in the region and elsewhere, including the United States, because of the possibility both of their use by Iraq and of their transfer for use by others. After considering the nature of the threat posed by Iraq, the

Council, acting under its Chapter VII authority, established a special set of rules to protect against it.

As a legal matter, a material breach of the conditions that had been essential to the establishment of the cease-fire left the responsibility to member states to enforce those conditions, operating consistently with Resolution 678 to use all necessary means to restore international peace and security in the area. On numerous occasions in response to Iraqi violations of WMD obligations, the Council, through either a formal resolution or a statement by its president, determined that Iraq's actions constituted material breaches, understanding that such a determination authorized resort to force. Indeed, when coalition forces—American, British, and French—used force following such a presidential statement in January 1993, then Secretary–General Boutros–Ghali stated that the:

> raid was carried out in accordance with a mandate from the Security Council under resolution 678 (1991), and the motive for the raid was Iraq's violation of that resolution, which concerns the cease-fire. As Secretary–General of the United Nations, I can tell you that the action taken was in accordance with the resolutions of the Security Council and the Charter of the United Nations.[2]

It was on this basis that the United States under President Clinton concluded that the Desert Fox campaign against Iraq in December 1998, following repeated efforts by the Iraqi regime to deny access to weapons inspectors, conformed with the Council's resolutions. To be sure, that campaign did not lack critics, who raised questions about whether further Council action was required to authorize it specifically. Some said that, in the absence of a Council determination that a material breach had occurred, an individual member state or group of states could not decide that a particular set of circumstances constituted a material breach, and there was debate about whether language that the Council had used in the period leading to Desert Fox was equivalent to a determination of material breach. The US view was that whether there had been a material breach was an objective fact, and it was not necessary for the Council to so determine or state. The debate about whether a material breach had occurred and who should determine this, however, should not obscure a more important point: all agreed that a Council determination that Iraq had committed a material breach would authorize individual member states to use force to secure compliance with the Council's resolutions.

This was well understood in the negotiations leading to the adoption of Resolution 1441 on November 8, 2002 [Basic Document 2.60], and, indeed, the importance attached to the use of the phrase "material breach" was the subject of wide public discussion. The understanding of the meaning of the phrase was also reflected in the structure of Resolution 1441 itself. Thus, the preamble contained specific language recognizing the threat that Iraq's noncompliance and proliferation posed to international peace and security, recalling that Resolution 678 had authorized member states to use "all necessary means" to uphold the relevant resolutions and restore international peace and

---

2. Transcript of Press Conference by Secretary–General, Boutros Boutros–Ghali, Following Diplomatic Press Club Luncheon in Paris on 14 January, UN Doc. SG./SM/4902/Rev.1, at 1 (1993).

security, and further recalling that Resolution 687 had imposed obligations on Iraq as a necessary step for achieving the stated objective of restoring international peace and security.

After recounting and deploring Iraq's violations at some length, the resolution in operative paragraph 1 removed any doubt that Iraq's actions had constituted material breaches. Specifically, paragraph 1 stated that "Iraq has been and remains in material breach of its obligations under relevant resolutions, including resolution 687 (1991), in particular through Iraq's failure to cooperate with United Nations inspectors and the IAEA, and to complete the actions required under [the WMD and missile provisions] of resolution 687." In adopting the "material breach" language, the resolution established that Iraq's violations of its obligations had crossed the threshold that earlier practice had established for coalition forces to use force consistently with Resolution 678.

Following this decision that Iraq was in material breach, operative paragraph 2 stated the Council's decision, "while acknowledging paragraph 1 above, to afford Iraq, by this resolution, a final opportunity to comply with its disarmament obligations under relevant resolutions of the Council." The resolution then required Iraq to submit, by December 8, 2002, "a currently accurate, full, and complete declaration" that, among other things, would include information on "all aspects of its programmes to develop chemical, biological, and nuclear weapons, ballistic missiles, and other delivery systems." At the same time, the resolution established a reinforced program of weapons inspections, and demanded that Iraq cooperate "immediately, unconditionally, and actively with UNMOVIC and the IAEA."

Operative paragraph 4 stated the Council's decision that "false statements or omissions in the declarations submitted by Iraq pursuant to this resolution and failure by Iraq at any time to comply with, and cooperate fully in the implementation of, this resolution shall constitute a further material breach of Iraq's obligations." The Council in effect decided that, in view of the past behavior of Iraq, the threat it posed to others, and the fact that the opportunity it was being given to remedy its breaches was a final one, any such violations by Iraq would mean that the use of force to address this threat was consistent with Resolution 678.

No serious argument was put forward in the period following the adoption of Resolution 1441 either that the declaration submitted by Iraq was "currently accurate, full, and complete" or that Iraq had complied with and cooperated fully in the implementation of the resolution. Under Resolution 1441, the Council had already decided that any such failure to cooperate would constitute a further material breach by Iraq.

Even at this point, however, the United States returned the issue to the Council for further consideration. This course was consistent with Resolution 1441, which contemplated certain steps regarding the reporting of violations and consideration by the Council; in supporting that resolution, the United States had undertaken to "return to the Council for discussions."[3] Specifical-

---

3. UN Doc. S/PV.4644, at 3 (2002) (remarks of Ambassador Negroponte); see also Remarks on the Passage of a United Nations Security Council Resolution on Iraq, 38 Weekly Comp. Pres. Doc. 2009, 2010 (11 Nov 2002) ("The United States has agreed to discuss any material breach with the Security Council, but

ly, under operative paragraph 4, Iraqi violations that constituted "a further material breach" were to be reported to the Council for assessment under paragraphs 11 and 12. Under paragraph 11, UNMOVIC and the IAEA were directed to report immediately to the Council any interference by Iraq with inspection activities, as well as any failure by Iraq to comply with its disarmament obligations, including its obligations regarding inspections under Resolution 1441.

Under paragraph 12, the Council decided that it would convene upon receipt of a report "in order to consider the situation and the need for full compliance with all of the relevant Council resolutions in order to secure international peace and security." Paragraph 12 expressly provided for further Council consideration "upon receipt of a report in accordance with paragraphs 4 *or* 11 above."[4] It thus specifically contemplated that such a report could be provided either by UNMOVIC or the IAEA in accordance with paragraph 11 or by a member state in accordance with paragraph 4. Paragraph 4 called for violations to "be reported to the Council for assessment in accordance with paragraphs 11 and 12," without any limitation on who might submit such a report. Thus, nothing in the language of Resolution 1441 precluded a member state from submitting a report that would be the basis for the Council to convene under paragraph 12.

Violations of paragraph 4 were in fact reported to the Council, including by Secretary Colin L. Powell, whose comprehensive reports drew on human intelligence, communications intercepts, and overhead imagery regarding Iraq's ongoing efforts to pursue WMD and missile programs and conceal them from United Nations inspectors. And the Council did convene and did consider the situation, as provided by paragraph 12.

The Council held numerous formal sessions on this issue. However, nothing in Resolution 1441 required the Council to adopt any further resolution, or other form of approval, to establish the occurrence of the material breach that was the predicate for coalition forces to resort to force. The very careful wording of paragraph 12 reflected this fact clearly. Paragraph 12 contemplated that the Council would "consider" the matter, but specifically stopped short of suggesting a requirement for a further decision. As the British attorney general stated on this point, "Resolution 1441 would in terms have provided that a further decision of the Security Council to sanction force was required if that had been intended. Thus, all that resolution 1441 requires is reporting to and discussion by the Security Council of Iraq's failures, but not an express further decision to authorize force."

The language in paragraph 12 contrasts sharply with language on this point in earlier texts circulated among Council members that would have provided for the Council "to convene immediately, upon reception of a report in accordance with paragraph 8 above, in order to *decide* any measure to ensure full compliance of all its relevant resolutions" (emphasis added). The fact that this language was not included in Resolution 1441 as ultimately adopted shows that the Council decided only that it would consider the matter, but not that it would be necessary for it, or even its purpose, to make a further decision. Rather, the Council had already made the decision that

without   jeopardizing   our   freedom   ac-   4. SC Res. 1441 **[Basic Document 2.60]**,
tion.... ").   ¶ 12 (emphasis added).

violations described in paragraph 4—"false statements or omissions in the declarations submitted by Iraq pursuant to this resolution and failure by Iraq at any time to comply with, and cooperate fully in the implementation of, this resolution"—would constitute a material breach of Iraq's obligations, and thus authorize the use of force to secure Iraqi compliance with its disarmament obligations.

The similarities in this regard between Resolution 1441 and Resolution 678 are striking. Using the same terminology that it later adopted in Resolution 1441, the Council in Resolution 678 decided to allow Iraq a "final opportunity" to comply with the obligations that the Council had established in previous resolutions. The Council then authorized member states to use force "unless Iraq on or before 15 January 1991 fully implemented" those resolutions. It was clear then that coalition members were not required to return for a further Council decision that Iraq had failed to comply; nor did they do so before commencing military operations. The language of Resolution 1441 tracked the language of Resolution 678, and the resolution operated in the same way to authorize coalition forces to bring Iraq into compliance with its obligations.

What does all this tell us about Iraq and the preemptive use of force? Was Operation Iraqi Freedom an example of preemptive use of force? Viewed as the final episode in a conflict initiated more than a dozen years earlier by Iraq's invasion of Kuwait, it may not seem so. However, in the context of the Security Council's resolutions, preemption of Iraq's possession and use of weapons of mass destruction was a principal objective of the coalition forces. A central consideration, at least from the US point of view, was the risk embodied in allowing the Iraqi regime to defy the international community by pursuing weapons of mass destruction. But do US actions show a disregard for international law? The answer here is clearly no. Both the United States and the international community had a firm basis for using preemptive force in the face of the past actions by Iraq and the threat that it posed, as seen over a protracted period of time. Preemptive use of force is certainly lawful where, as here, it represents an episode in an ongoing broader conflict initiated—without question—by the opponent and where, as here, it is consistent with the resolutions of the Security Council.

DAVID FRUM & RICHARD PERLE, "UN SHOULD CHANGE— OR US SHOULD QUIT; THE WORLD BODY'S RULES PREVENT AMERICA FROM ANSWERING THREAT"

Los Angeles Times, 23 January 2004, at B13

The United Nations is the tooth fairy of American politics: Few adults believe in it, but it's generally regarded as a harmless story to amuse the children. Since 9/11, however, the UN has ceased to be harmless, and the Democratic presidential candidates' enthusiasm for it has ceased to be amusing. The United Nations has emerged at best as irrelevant to the terrorist threat that most concerns us, and at worst as an obstacle to our winning the war on terrorism. It must be reformed. And if it cannot be reformed, the United States should give serious consideration to withdrawal.

The UN has become an obstacle to our national security because it purports to set legal limits on the United States' ability to defend itself. If these limits ever made sense at all, they do not make sense now.

Yet the UN's assertion of them forces presidents and policymakers into a horrible dilemma. If we obey the UN's rules, we compromise our national security. If we defy them, we expose ourselves to accusations of hypocrisy and lawlessness.

According to the UN Charter **[Basic Document 1.5]**, nations are permitted to use military force only in two situations. Article 51 of the charter recognizes an "inherent" right to self-defense against attack. In all other cases where a nation feels threatened, it is supposed to go to the UN Security Council to seek authorization before it takes military action—even action that might forestall an attack.

The trouble is that the UN defines aggression in outdated ways. For the UN, "aggression" means invasion across national borders. Send Nazi shock troops into Poland—that's aggression. Give sanctuary to thousands of anti-American murderers, as the Taliban did in Afghanistan, that's not aggression.

In other words, if the United States had sent troops into Afghanistan to shut the camps down, we might well have been branded the aggressor. But if the US had asked the Security Council for a mandate to destroy Al Qaeda's terrorist bases, could the French, Russians and Chinese have been expected to approve? Even after 9/11, there would still have been plenty of people ready to argue that however much they deplored what Al Qaeda had done, Afghanistan—a sovereign state and United Nations member—was not an Article 51 "aggressor."

In other words, under UN rules, the US is obliged to let terrorists strike first before retaliating—and might even be prohibited from striking second. In an age when shadowy radical movements around the globe are seeking weapons that could kill hundreds of thousands of people, these rules are clearly out of date. We need new rules recognizing that harboring terrorists is just as much an act of aggression as an invasion and that those who are targeted by terrorists have an inherent right to defend themselves, preemptively if necessary.

Of course, it won't be easy to persuade the UN to adopt these changes. Many members—including some of our traditional allies—seem much more interested in constraining the United States than they are in defeating terrorism—at least terrorism that is aimed at us.

The UN member states know that the US will in the end do whatever it has to do, regardless of what the UN says. But they also know that the United States pays a price for disregarding the UN. The French in particular benefit from pushing the United States to break the UN's rules: Under French President Jacques Chirac, they are trying to fashion the European Union as a counterweight to the United States, and the image of the US as an outlaw power helps their cause.

In a little more than a decade, our world has been transformed, first by the fall of the Soviet Union and then the events of 9/11. Everything has changed—except for the UN. It remains an invention of a vanished era, designed to solve vanished problems. It must evolve or it will slide from irrelevance to oblivion. If the UN is not part of the anti-terror fight, the United States should not be part of the UN.

Thomas M. Franck, "What Happens Now? The United Nations after Iraq"

97 A.J.I.L. 607, 607–20 (2003)

I. WHO KILLED ARTICLE 2(4) AGAIN?

Thirty-three years ago I published an article in this *Journal* entitled *Who Killed Article 2(4)? or: Changing Norms Governing the Use of Force by States,* which examined the phenomenon of increasingly frequent resort to unlawful force by Britain, France, India, North Korea, the Soviet Union, and the United States. The essay concluded with this sad observation:

> The failure of the UN Charter's **[Basic Document 1.5]** normative system is tantamount to the inability of any rule, such as that set out in Article 2(4), in itself to have much control over the behavior of states. National self-interest, particularly the national self-interest of the super-Powers, has usually won out over treaty obligations. This is particularly characteristic of this age of pragmatic power politics. It is as if international law, always something of a cultural myth, has been demythologized. It seems this is not an age when men act by principles simply because that is what gentlemen ought to do. But living by power alone . . . is a nerve-wracking and costly business.[5]

The recent recourse to force in Iraq recalls this observation, which again seems all too apt. All that has changed is that we now have on offer proposed models for interstatal relations that seem even worse than the dilapidated system to which, by 1970, state misbehavior had reduced the postwar world. That once shiny new postwar system, embodied in the United Nations Charter, had been based on the assumption of states' reciprocal respect for law as their sturdy shield against the prospect of mutual assured destruction in an uncharted nuclear era. The 1970 essay regretted the loss of that vision in a miasma of so-called realpolitik.

Should international lawyers guard their faith in such circumstances? Or should we cut our coats according to the cloth? *Si non possis quod velis, velis id quod possis.* Perhaps. But, then, for one dazzling moment in the 1990s, the end of the Cold War seemed to revive faith in the Charter system, almost giving it a rebirth. Now, however, in the new millennium, after a decade's romance with something approximating law-abiding state behavior, the law-based system is once again being dismantled. In its place we are offered a model that makes global security wholly dependent on the supreme power and discretion of the United States and frees the sole superpower from all restraints of international law and the encumbrances of institutionalized multilateral diplomacy.

There is one major difference, however, between then and now. The unlawful recourses to force, during the period surveyed in the 1970 essay, were accompanied by a fig leaf of legal justification, which, at least tacitly, recognized the residual force of the requirement in Charter Article 2(4) that states "refrain in their international relations from the threat or use of force

---

5. T. Franck, *Who Killed Article 2(4)? or:*   *by States,* 64 A.J.I.L. 809, 836(1970).
Changing Norms Governing the Use of Force

against the territorial integrity or political independence of any state." Then, the aggressors habitually defended the legality of their recourse to force by asserting that their actions, taken in response to an alleged prior attack or provocation, were exercises of the right of self-defense under the terms of Charter Article 51. Now, however, in marked contrast, they have all but discarded the fig leaf. While a few government lawyers still go through the motions of asserting that the invasion of Iraq was justified by our inherent right of self-defense, or represented a collective measure authorized by the Security Council under Chapter VII of the Charter, the leaders of America no longer much bother with such legal niceties. Instead, they boldly proclaim a new policy that openly repudiates the Article 2(4) obligation. What is remarkable, this time around, is that once-obligatory efforts by the aggressor to make a serious effort to stretch law to legitimate state action have given way to a drive to repeal law altogether, replacing it with a principle derived from the Athenians at Melos: "the strong do what they can and the weak suffer what they must."[6]

In this essay I will attempt to examine whether this neo-Melian doctrine will make any difference to the way the international system works, or whether our government, by dispensing with the lawyers' shopworn casuistry, is just being realistic in exposing the yawning gap between what states always do in their ambitious pursuit of power and what they are permitted to do by the fragile normative structure.

II. THE 1970s' BOUT OF "REALISM"

Realists are supposed to take the world as they find it. By the early 1970s, the no-first-strike rule of the Charter was plainly being disobeyed by several states capable of doing as they wished, and aware that they could do so without much fear of hindrance. The question for lawyers and legal scholars was how to relate to that evident tendency. Should one help to create a new legal regime based on the conduct of those who were violating the existing order? Or should one rail against the violators, at the mortal risk of being thought cranky, "irrelevant," or even "unrealistic"?

The 1970 article was unabashedly cranky, for there was much to be cranky about, if one took the concept of law among nations seriously. The main thrust, however, was descriptive in the hope that an unvarnished understanding of the law's debasement might lead to reconsideration of longer-term costs to America of what appeared to be short-term triumphs. Such a reconsideration could only begin by understanding how the legal rhetoric then deployed by states' attorneys had ceased to be credible in disguising the illegality of their clients' scoff-law behavior. The essay sought to warn that the superpowers (and others) had severely undermined the compliance pull of the Charter's no-first-strike rule and insinuated in its place a different system, one governed by nineteenth-century principles of balance of power. Under that new normative order, each superpower would refrain from attacking the essential interests of the other, but would be freed to use

6. Thucydides, The Peloponnesian War: The Complete Writings of Thucydides 331 (Richard Crawley trans., 1934). The effort Thucydides describes, of a highly cultivated, relatively democratic Athens, destroyed in a futile effort to protect itself against every eventuality by attacking and securing the submission of all islands from which danger might emanate, is highly relevant to our times.

force at will in its own sphere of influence. States that were clients of a superpower would be freed to use force against those that were not, but would be restrained from using force against clients of the other superpower. I argued that, in the long run, such a system was no system at all and was unsustainable.

The run was longer than I had expected. For about twenty years, this bipolar arrangement more or less long characterized the world we inhabited, until the breakup of the Soviet empire, beginning in 1989. Supporting this arrangement for so long was its draconian logic: that peace could be assured by a careful balance of terror, which required the inter se equality of the Soviet Union and the United States buttressed by those two nations' supremacy over everyone else. In this context, "equality" and "supremacy" did not merely define the equation of military power among states, but also states' respective de facto normative prerogatives and precautions in the use of force. It was not exactly a system of law that would have commended itself to John Adams or Woodrow Wilson, but at about this time some regime theorists began to use the term "norms" to describe predictable patterns of behavior without ascribing any universally restraining qualities to them. There were, certainly, norms during this period. The world and its lawyers adjusted their expectations and their sights.

III.   THE OPTIMISTIC 1990s

After the Soviet side of bipolarity crumbled, the logic of the 1970s' normative balance-of-power system ceased to be convincing. Then, in the wake of our unchallenged primacy, a reasonable expectation arose that, with America's new-found muscle, a different, more enduring, and more noble stability would be achieved in international relations and, moreover, that this could be brought about by rediscovering the Charter's founding principle: that force would be used only in self-defense against an actual armed attack; or after a threat to the peace had been determined by the collective decision-making process of the Security Council acting under Chapter VII of the Charter; or, exceptionally, if the General Assembly, proceeding in accordance with the "Uniting for Peace" resolution **[Basic Document 2.14]**, had determined the existence of a "threat to the peace, breach of the peace or act of aggression."

For about a decade, the international system seemed to be moving in this direction, with Article 2(4) miraculously reborn in a post-Cold War order underwritten by a return to the law of the long-languishing Charter. This expectation was reinforced, and was facilitated by, UN-organized or-authorized military deployments in the first Gulf war, the former Yugoslavia, Somalia, and Haiti. In 1989 the United States briefly reverted to the Cold War model by invading Panama and doing so under cover of a claim to be acting in self-defense. By and large, however, the decade after the Soviet collapse seemed to presage a resurrection of Article 2(4), albeit with some flexible adaptation in practice to reflect changes of circumstance.

This ebullient period reached its high-water mark on September 12, 2001, when the Security Council unanimously passed the resolution in reaction to the attacks on the World Trade Center and the Pentagon. This resolution demonstrated not only the goodwill and collective wisdom of the Council as global decision-making forum, but also the flexibility of the Charter system in adapting old text to new exigencies. It construed the Charter-based right of self-defense to include authority to use force against nonstatal terrorist organizations, as well as "those responsible for aiding, supporting or harboring the perpetrators, organizers and sponsors of ... acts" of terrorism[7]. Two weeks later, the Council created mandatory global controls to prevent the financing of terrorism and the recruiting of terrorists, while adding procedures for monitoring and enforcing state compliance[8]. It appeared that the long dormant Charter rules regarding recourse to force not only were starting to revive—that I had reported their death prematurely—but were exhibiting an altogether unexpected capacity to grow and adapt. In a rapidly changing world, the Security Council was proving itself able to interpret and apply the rules in such a way as to make them responsive to new dangers posed by nongovernmental terrorism and terrorism-harboring states, treating these as bona fide threats to the peace against which resort to force in collective self-defense is not merely necessary but also permissible.

IV. THE RELAPSE OF 2003

The invasion of Iraq in March of 2003, and a penumbra of policy statements made concurrently by the United States, have succeeded in changing all that. Article 2(4) has died again, and, this time, perhaps for good. This is no mere happenstance. At the cutting edge of US policymaking today are persons who have never forgiven the United Nations for the General Assembly's 1975 resolution equating Zionism with racism and who, despite its subsequent repeal, see the Organization as the implacable foe of Israel and the United States. The defanging of the United Nations has remained high on their agenda and the events of September 11, 2001, have created the opportunity to achieve that once-impossible dream. Thus has Article 2(4) taken another hit; this time, however, as part of a much broader plan to disable all supranational institutions and the constraints of international law on national sovereignty. If, as now seems all too possible, this campaign succeeds within the life span of the present US administration, what sort of world order will emerge from the ruins of the Charter system?

V. DID THE IRAQ INVASION VIOLATE THE CHARTER?

Any prognosis regarding the future of world order must begin by addressing the question whether recent events have indeed had a transformative effect on the law of the international system and, if so, what that transformation portends. As in 1970, one must begin by making a clear-eyed appraisal of what has been happening. If the invasion of Iraq was nothing but an act of self-defense by the United States and its allies, or merely an exercise of police power previously authorized by the Security Council, these events would serve only to verify the continued efficacy of the Charter system. There would have been no violation of the cardinal principle of Article 2(4), as that no-first-use pledge is always subordinate to both the right of self-defense recognized by

7. SC Res. 1368 (On Threats to International Peace and Security Caused by Terrorist Acts), UN SCOR, 56th Sess., 4370th mtg., at 1, UN Doc. S/RES/1368 (2001), pmbl., ¶3, (12 Sep 2001), *reprinted in* 40 I.L.M. 1277 (2001) [and 2 Weston & Carlson II.F.28].

8. SC Res 1373 (On Threats to International Peace and Security Caused by Terrorist Acts), UN SCOR, 56th Sess., 4385th mtg., at 2–3, UN Doc S/RES/1373 (2001), ¶¶ 1, 2 (28 Sep 2001), *reprinted in* 40 I.L.M. 1278 (2001) [and 2 Weston & Carlson II.F.36].

Article 51 and the right of the Security Council, under Chapter VII, to authorize action against a threat to the peace. If, however, the invasion cannot thus be reconciled with the rules of the Charter, does the invasion of Iraq constitute a simple violation of the rules—one of many and thus of no more legal significance than a holdup of the neighborhood grocery—or should it be celebrated as a deliberate and salutary move toward UN reform? Or should these recent events be understood, more apocalyptically, as the final burial of the Charter's fundamental rules? At this point in our analysis of the systemic significance of these events, it becomes essential to focus not only on facts but also on motives for action. Needless to say, this is swampy terrain; but one must try.

The invasion of Iraq can be positioned in each of these explanatory contexts, but just barely. It can be argued that the invasion was lawful (and thus neither violative nor transformative of the Charter). It can also be argued that, while the attack on Iraq may have been technically illegal, its transformative effect on the law has been wholly benevolent. Finally, it can be argued that these events have repealed a legal regime far beyond its prime and, at last, have ushered in a new doctrine of preventive use of force that is far more responsive to the real dangers of our times.

The argument that recent events have not challenged, or have violated only *de minimis*, the Charter law pertaining to recourse to force is very difficult to sustain, although it enjoys the enthusiastic support of some American academics and the rather less enthusiastic support of State Department lawyers. Abroad, it has been advanced only by the British attorney general, supported by a prominent academic lawyer. As enunciated by Legal Adviser William Howard Taft IV of the Department of State, the argument has two prongs. The first is that the president may, "of course, always use force under international law in self-defense." The problem with that rationale is that, even if it were agreed that the right of self-defense "against an armed attack" (Charter, Art. 51) had come, through practice, to include a right of action against an imminent (as opposed to an actual) armed attack, the facts of the situation that existed in March 2003 are hard to fit within *any* plausible theory of imminence. This was a time, after all, when UN and International Atomic Energy Agency inspectors were actively engaged in situ in an apparently unrestricted search for weapons of mass destruction (WMDs) undertaken with full authorization by the Security Council. Whatever the inspectors did or did not learn about Iraqi WMDs, nothing in their reports lends any credibility to the claim of an imminent threat of armed aggression against anyone. Indeed, the memorandum of the attorney general of the United Kingdom, while supporting the right to use force, wisely omits all reference to this rationale for its exercise.[9]

The second prong of the *de minimis* argument is more sophisticated than the plea to have acted in self-defense. It avers that the attack led by Britain and the United States had already been sanctioned by the Security Council. Essential to the success of this assertion is a creative, and ultimately unsustainable, reading of three Security Council resolutions—678, 687, and 1441

---

9. Lord Goldsmith, Attorney General Clarifies Legal Basis for Use of Force Against Iraq (18 Mar 2003), *available at* <http:// www.fco.gov.uk> (statement in answer to a parliamentary question).

[Basic Documents 2.40, 2.41 & 2.60]—and of their "legislative history." According to Legal Adviser Taft, Resolution 678

> was the authorization to use force for the Gulf War in January 1991. In April of that year, the Council imposed a series of conditions on Iraq, including most importantly extensive disarmament obligations, as a condition of the ceasefire declared under UNSCR 687. Iraq has "materially breached" these disarmament obligations, and force may again be used under UNSCR 678 to compel Iraqi compliance.
>
> . . . Just last November, in resolution 1441, the Council unanimously decided that Iraq has been and remains in material breach of its obligation. 1441 then gave Iraq a "final opportunity" to comply, but stated specifically that violations of the obligations, including the obligation to cooperate fully, under 1441 would constitute a further material breach. Iraq has clearly committed such violations and, accordingly, the authority to use force to address Iraq's material breaches is clear.[10]

The British government developed this same thesis, claiming that, by Resolution 678 the Security Council had authorized "Member States to use all necessary means to restore international peace and security in the area" and that, while that authorization "was suspended but not terminated by Security Council resolution (SCR) 687 (1991)," it was "revived by SCR 1441 (2002)."[11]

This version of the meaning and intent of these three resolutions is highly problematic, and appears to have caused the resignation, on a matter of principle, of the deputy legal adviser of the British Foreign Office. Resolution 678 culminated a series of resolutions by the Security Council that condemned Iraq's invasion of Kuwait, called for the immediate withdrawal of the aggressor, imposed mandatory sanctions on Iraq until Kuwaiti sovereignty was restored, and declared the Iraqi annexation of Kuwait to be null and void. In each instance, the purpose of the resolution was solely to liberate Kuwait. Only when these measures failed to secure Iraqi withdrawal did the Council in Resolution 678, citing Chapter VII of the Charter, "authorize[] Member States co-operating with the Government of Kuwait . . . to use all necessary means to uphold and implement resolution 660 (1990) and all subsequent relevant resolutions and to restore international peace and security in the area."[12]

This sequence readily demonstrates that the restoration of Kuwaiti sovereignty was the leitmotif of Council action. That the authorization of collective measures by Resolution 678 additionally refers to the restoration of "international peace and security in the area" does not connote some expansive further mandate for contingent action against Iraq at the discretion of any individual member of the coalition of the willing. President George Bush Sr. acknowledged as much in explaining why the American military had not pursued Saddam Hussein's defeated forces to Baghdad. They were not authorized to do so.

10. W. H. Taft IV, Remarks Before National Association of Attorneys General (20 Mar 2003), *excerpted at* <http://usinfo.state.gov/dhr/Archive/2003/Oct/09–464655.html>; *see also* Sean D. Murphy, Contemporary Practice of the United States, 96 A.J.I.L. 419, 427 (2003).

11. Goldsmith, *supra* note 9.

12. SC Res. 678 **[Basic Document 2.40]**.

The resolution, however, certainly does signal that Iraq was to be subject to further post-conflict intrusive controls: those imposed by the Council in Resolution 687, as part of the cease-fire. These additional obligations are made binding by reference to Chapter VII of the Charter and they were designed, implemented, and meant to be monitored by the Security Council as a whole, not by any individual member acting at its own pleasure. Resolution 687, sometimes referred to as the "mother of all cease-fires," is not only a binding decision of the Security Council, but also an international agreement between the United Nations and Iraq, made effective only "upon official notification by Iraq to the Secretary–General and to the Security Council of its acceptance" of the provisions set out therein[13]. In legal form, then, as also in substance, this proviso manifests that it is the Security Council and the United Nations, and not individual members, who are the parties, with Iraq, to the cease-fire agreement. It is they who are entitled in law to determine whether Iraq is complying with its commitments to the Council, how long these are to remain in effect, and what is to be done in the event of their violation.

The obligations imposed by Resolution 687 are certainly onerous, and encompass everything that Iraq, thereafter, has been accused of failing to do. Baghdad had to agree to the verified destruction of its weapons of mass destruction and any industrial capacity to produce them, as well as of its medium and long-range delivery systems. Monitoring of compliance, both by a special commission to be created by the Secretary–General and by inspectors of the International Atomic Energy Agency, became mandatory. Baghdad was also required "to inform the Security Council that it will not commit or support any act of international terrorism or allow any organization directed towards commission of such acts to operate within its territory."[14] What if Iraq failed to carry out these commitments to the Council and the United Nations? Clearly, this determination was to be made by the collective security process of the Organization. To ensure such follow-up, the Council, in Resolution 687, was "to remain seized of the matter and to take such further steps as may be required for the implementation of the present resolution and to secure peace and security in the area."[15] *It* would take further steps, *not* individual member states acting without further authorization.

Neither the text nor the debates on the adoption of Resolution 687 reveal the slightest indication that the Council intended to empower any of its members, by themselves, to determine that Iraq was in material breach. Much less can the resolution be read to authorize any state to decide unilaterally to resume military action against Iraq, save in the event of an armed attack. That deduction is supported by the architecture of the Charter. For the Council to have made a prospective grant of unilateral discretion to states to deploy armed force, in the absence of an actual (or imminent) armed attack, would have been an unprecedented derogation from the strictures of Article 2(4). At the least, to be plausible, such a derogation would have had to be explicit. Moreover, such a delegation of unlimited discretion to individual states cannot be assumed because it could not have been implemented

13. SC Res. 687 [**Basic Document 2.41**].   15. *Id..*, ¶ 34.
14. *Id.*, ¶ 32.

alongside the Council's institution of an extensive system of inspections under *its* authority and control.

The UK attorney general cannot overcome these objections by an unsupported averral that a "material breach of resolution 687 revives the authority to use force under resolution 678."[16] As we have noted, the authority to use force under Resolution 678 extended exclusively to the liberation of Kuwait and to restoring peace and security in the region. In March 2003, the peace and security of the region did not require recourse to force, and the Council plainly did not think otherwise. What the Council thought is crucial. Resolution 687 would not have explicitly reserved sole discretion to the Council "to take such further steps as may be required for [its] implementation"[17] if the Council had simultaneously intended to delegate that function to the sole discretion of member states.

Thus, neither Resolution 678 nor Resolution 687 helps Washington or London make a convincing case that they acted with, rather than against, the law. Nor are their difficulties in any way alleviated by Resolution 1441. While that instrument does deplore "that the Government of Iraq has failed to comply with its commitments pursuant to resolution 687," it addresses that failure exclusively by deciding "to set up an enhanced inspection regime."[18] Anticipating further Iraqi noncompliance, the resolution makes provision for the Council to be convened immediately "in order to consider the situation and the need for full compliance ... in order to secure international peace and security," and it warns Iraq "in that context ... that it will face serious consequences as a result of its continued violations of its obligations."[19] It once again decides that the Council will "remain seized of the matter."[20] The British attorney general somehow concluded from these words that even though the Council is to convene to "consider the matter before any action is taken," no matter what the Council does or does not do, "further [military] action can be taken [by a member] without a new resolution of the Council."[21] From this he deduces that "all that resolution 1441 requires is reporting to and discussion by the Security Council of Iraq's failures, but not an express further decision to authorize force."[22] This conclusion is at best a creative interpretation. In fact, what Resolution 1441 did was to purchase unanimity for the return of the inspectors by postponing to another day, which the sponsors hoped might never be reached, the argument as to whether Resolutions 678 and 687 had authorized further enforcement at the sole discretion of one or more of the Council's members.

Perhaps to its credit, the Taft statement does not tread this tortuous path. Instead, it argues that since the Council had recognized several times that Iraq had committed a "material breach" of Resolution 687, recourse to force rested within the sole discretion of each Council member in accordance with the provision of the law of treaties on the consequences of such a "material" violation of obligations. This tack moves the argument away from a parsing of Council resolutions to the Vienna Convention on the Law of

16. Goldsmith, *supra* note 9.

17. SC Res. 687 [**Basic Document 2.41**], ¶ 34.

18. SC Res. 1441 [**Basic Document 2.60**], pmbl., ¶ 2.

19. *Id.*, ¶¶ 12, 13.

20. *Id.*, ¶ 14.

21. Goldsmith, *supra* note 9.

22. *Id.*

Treaties. But it is the United Nations, not the United States, that is the offended "party" to Resolution 687, and thus it is the Council, not the United States, that has the option under the Convention to regard the resolution as voided by Iraq's material breaches. Additionally, even if the United States were regarded as a "party" to the commitments made by Iraq in agreeing to Resolution 687, a material breach would not release Washington, as the offended party, from the obligation under the Vienna Convention "to fulfil any obligation embodied in the treaty to which it would be subject under international law independently of the [materially breached] treaty."[23] That provision, it would appear, places the United States squarely back under the obligation of Charter Article 2(4), which, in the absence of any provision in Resolution 687 to the contrary, must be regarded as an essential part of its legal context and which requires states to abstain from the use of force in the absence either of an armed attack or of prior authorization by the Security Council.

These British and US justifications do not fare well under close examination, however benevolent their intent to demonstrate compliance with the Charter. Consequently, the effect of those nations' unauthorized recourse to force against Iraq must be seen as either revising or undermining the provisions limiting the discretion of states to resort to force.

VI. A CHARTER REVISED

Well, if the Iraq invasion did not exactly conform with the law of the Charter, should it not, at least, be celebrated as a violation that has the capacity to reform the law and make it more realistic?

In international law, violators do sometimes turn out to be lawgivers. I have argued elsewhere that the Charter, as a quasi-constitutional instrument, is capable of evolving through the interpretive practice of its principal organs. That interpretive practice may sometimes be led by states with an interest in outcomes that cannot be legitimated by a narrowly originalist reading of the text. In such circumstances, violation shades into revision, sometimes to the benefit of the law and the institution charged with its implementation. The phenomenon is not unknown, also, to domestic law, though it occurs much more frequently in the international arena. The International Court has confirmed, for example, that the abstention of a permanent member of the Security Council in a vote on a substantive resolution is no longer to be taken to constitute a veto as a result of "abundant evidence" of members' practice to that effect[24]. The Court reached this conclusion despite the text of Charter Article 27(3), which requires that substantive resolutions receive "the concurring votes of the permanent members." In a similar example of the interpretive power of institutional practice, extensive UN peacekeeping operations have long been based on an evolutionary reading of the Charter's imagined "Chapter 6 1/2." Nothing in the text actually authorizes these by-and-large salubrious activities. In recent years, too, practice has seemed to legitimate such humanitarian interventions as those undertaken by regional organizations in West Africa and Kosovo, even though they had not received the

---

23. Vienna Convention on the Law of Treaties **[Basic Document 1.10]**, Art. 43.

24. Legal Consequences for States of the Continued Presence of South Africa in Namibia (South West Africa) Notwithstanding Security Council Resolution 276 (1970), Advisory Opinion, 1971 ICJ 16, 22, ¶ 22 (June 21).

requisite (Art. 53) prior authorization of the Security Council. Further evidence of this important interpretive change is afforded by the Constitutive Act of the African Union, Article 4(h) of which recognizes "the right of the Union to intervene in a Member State pursuant to a decision of the Assembly in respect of grave circumstances, namely: war crimes, genocide and crimes against humanity," when such intervention is authorized by two-thirds of the members.[25]

Even allowing that the Charter text is subject to reinterpretation in practice, it is difficult to chart the direction in which it could be said to be evolving under the impetus of the Middle Eastern events of March and April, 2003. Nevertheless, a courageous attempt to divine that direction has been made by the dean of Princeton's Woodrow Wilson School, Professor Anne–Marie Slaughter. Seeking to close the gap between Charter norms and US practice, she has proposed that the Security Council

> adopt a resolution recognizing that the following set of conditions would constitute a threat to the peace sufficient to justify the use of force: 1) possession of weapons of mass destruction or clear and convincing evidence of attempts to gain such weapons; 2) grave and systematic human rights abuses sufficient to demonstrate the absence of any internal constraints on government behavior; and 3) evidence of aggressive intent with regard to other nations.[26]

Slaughter believes that other nations would agree to such an adumbration of Charter law because they would feel "stronger and safer" in an institutional system robustly able to address the global threat of terrorism and because such a reform, based on a reinvigorated United Nations, would open up "the only forum in which other nations can make their voices heard in deliberations with the United States." The United States and everyone else needs to recognize, she concludes, that the United Nations "is the forum in which a genuine multilateral decision-making process must take place."[27]

While it is altogether admirable to seek to make the invasion of Iraq an opportunity to strengthen the UN system, this analysis, alas, takes far too optimistic a view of what the administration in Washington and the governments of most other countries have concluded from this angry episode. For the Bush administration, it has underscored the danger of subordinating the policy discretion of the world's only superpower to the perceptions and interests of institutions in which other, mostly minor and sometimes venal, governments are able to project a degree of power entirely incommensurate with reality. This view is particularly troublesome when the issue pertains to a matter, such as international terrorism, that holds far greater interest for America than for most other governments. For almost all other members of the United Nations, on the other hand, the events leading up to the invasion of Iraq demonstrated the folly of embarking upon any renegotiation of the rules pertaining to the deployment of force, however sensible, when they knew full well that Washington would ultimately apply the agreed standards unilaterally. That, to most states, was the message of Resolution 1441, which ultimately became the legal justification for the invasion of Iraq. As the

25. Constitutive Act of the African Union, July 11, 2000, Art. 4(h), *available at* <http://www.africa-union.org>.

26. A.-M. Slaughter, *Chance to Reshape the UN*, Wash. Post, 13 Apr 2003, at B7.

27. *Id.*

British attorney general put it, agreed standards are a sound basis for multilateral discussion, but not for multilateral control over action. The world's governments, their advice on Iraq spurned, now understand that the sole superpower's administration is not in the least interested in rules, old or new, if they are to be applied case by case through "a genuine multilateral decision-making process." It has no intention of subordinating its sole responsibility for protecting what it perceives to be its national security to the judgment of others.

A "genuine multilateral decision-making process" requires the willingness of each participant to accept views, perceptions, and policies it does not share, but that prevail within the institution engaging in the process. In the run-up to the Iraq invasion, it became clear that the overwhelming majority of nations—not, as some have said, just a power-jealous President Jacques Chirac of France and the feckless Chancellor Gerhard Schroder of Germany— believed either that Iraq did not have a significant number of weapons of mass destruction or, if such weapons and the necessary delivery systems existed, that they could be found by the instituted system of inspections. Very few nations accepted that credible evidence could be shown of either WMDs or an operational link between Al Qaeda and the regime in Baghdad. This was a judgment call, pure and simple, and there are indications that the majority may have been right, and the United States and Britain wrong, as to both the evidence at hand and what to do about it. But the nub of the matter is not who was right and who wrong but *who gets to decide what to do*. The UN system did not "fail" because of differences of opinion about what to do if the facts were, indeed, as asserted by Washington. Saddam Hussein had no do-or-die defenders in the Council chamber. To the extent the Council can be said to have "failed," it failed because most states had "misunderstood" the role assigned to them under the Charter and the applicable resolutions. They expected, or naively hoped, to be the jury to which evidence and arguments as to the facts would be presented and that, collegially, they would then make the final decision about what should be done; whereas the British and US governments took the view that, after the discourse ended, the decision would be up to them, alone. The problem is not one of devising new rules but of reaching agreement on who gets to apply them.

In essence, the Iraqi crisis was not primarily about what to do but, rather, who decides. There is an answer to that problem, of course, one clearly set out in Article 27 of the Charter. Through the veto, the United States, with the other four permanent members, has the right to block collective action and it takes frequent advantage of this prerogative. On the other hand, the Charter does not give the United States, or any other state, sole power to *initiate* action, except in response to an armed attack. While this deal may have seemed acceptable to America in 1945, it is apparently no longer satisfactory to the protectors of American preeminence. Nowadays, the US government does not wish to be limited in this way. Thus, the invasion of Iraq is more accurately seen as a repudiation of the central decision-making premise of the Charter system than as a genuine opening to reform, unless by reform is meant the reconstitution of the international system along the lines of an American global protectorate.

This is a sad conclusion to offer well-meaning champions of the Charter system. Unfortunately, however, this is not a time for optimistic speculation about how to make the United Nations more responsive to new challenges. Rather, reformers need first to understand that the system stands in mortal jeopardy of being destroyed altogether. If, and only if, something can be done about *that* will there be another time to talk about improving the rules.

VII. REPUDIATING THE UN SYSTEM

The US government (without, in this instance, the acquiescence of Britain) is out to disable the United Nations. Oh, yes, on its present tangent Washington will keep its membership, but primarily to block by its veto any action by others thought to be inimical to American interests. From time to time, the Bush administration may find it convenient to use the Organization to fix a famine, relocate some refugees, share some costs, even train a police force. What recent events make clear, however, is that the United States no longer considers itself subordinated in any way to the treaty rules that lie at the heart of the United Nations Charter. An anomalous situation therefore faces the Organization, which cannot expel a veto-bearing scofflaw state against its will, but which, in those circumstances, is doomed to encounter great difficulty in carrying out the wishes of its other members. Only three alternatives seem to offer themselves at present: the United States could change its policy, it could withdraw from the Organization, or the other members could withdraw to form a new system of international relations, a coalition of the *seriously* willing. None of these options are easy or probable.

Some see the present impasse as an opportunity to be rid of an international regime that is insufficiently responsive to both America's needs and the reality of our disproportionate power. The most creative of these "realist" intellectuals link the demise of the United Nations as a viable peace-and-security system to the invention of something more amenable to US interests. But *what?* According to Michael Glennon, "Ad hoc coalitions of the willing will effectively succeed it."[28] Really? Have we not already seen in the recent conflict what these ad hoc coalitions will look like: a sizable contingent from Britain, a few hundred policemen from Poland, Romania, and Bulgaria (at least until their nations are integrated into the European Union), a few soldiers from Australia and Albania, and good wishes from Israel? In practice, this prescription would require the United States to do everything alone, with Britain in tow at least until the next British elections—this in a world of rapidly intensifying animosity to almost all American projects.

To carry off such unipolarity, whatever its pros and cons, at a minimum requires a burgeoning economy and we do not have one. It also requires sociopolitical solidarity at home. To sustain such solidarity, a nation must be staunchly united. Yet, according to the eminent Republican economist Kevin Phillips, the social fabric was already badly frayed even before we began to shoulder the burden of this new global protectorate. In less than twenty years, Phillips has shown, the income gap between the richest 1 percent and the poorest 20 percent of the population has more than doubled, from a ratio of 30:1 in 1979, to one of 75:1 in 1997[29]. Thus, there looms the specter not only of vast increases in the cost of foreign undertakings, but also of a radical shift in the bearing of that burden. The nation is about to reduce spending on basic

28. M. Glennon, *Why the Security Council Failed*, Foreign Aff., May/June 2003, at 16, 34.

29. K. Phillips, *How Wealth Defines Power*, Am. Prospect, 1 May 2003, at A8, A9.

needs like education, health care, and infrastructure by $100 billion. How much solidarity can one expect from parents with children in overcrowded, crumbling classrooms in which school lunches, computer training, and after-school enrichment programs have become a dim memory? How closely tied to the common enterprise can one imagine the overtaxed middle-class home-owners and white-collar workers in America's bankrupt cities to be? Have we so soon forgotten the experience of war at home when last we pursued the logic of preeminence in Vietnam?

Solidarity is also a matter of civic pride: how we, as a people, perceive our nation; and that is at least in part conditioned by how we are perceived by others. On September 11, 2001, every nation in the world voiced its support for us, sympathy for our tragedy, and willingness to join in the war on terrorism. Now, almost every nation regards us as the world's gravest threat to peace. Even in Britain, Spain, and Italy, nations whose governments sided with us over the war in Iraq, the publics overwhelmingly oppose America's assertions of unilateral power. This opposition is not based solely on our actions in Iraq. America, in its new reality check, has concluded that it need not accommodate the values and agendas of the world regarding the environment, land mines, or an international criminal court. Having recklessly separated us from both friend and foe, the standard-bearers of triumphal unipolarity have already realized half of their fantasy: we are, now, truly alone in the world. Saddled with so much animosity, we cannot possibly count on burden sharing as we seek to implement our national interest. The self-professed realists seem blissfully unfazed by this. They will come around. "Every major country," Professor Glennon says, "faces imminent danger from terrorism, for example, and from the new surge in WMD proliferation. None will gain by permitting these threats to reach fruition."[30] In reality, however, few states regard themselves as directly threatened by terrorism in any of its present manifestations. On the contrary, they see cooperation with America, in its current mood, as an invitation to terrorist reprisal. If, up to now, they have supported American efforts to curb Al Qaeda, it is not because they regard themselves as its targets but, rather, because they have had a stake in the cooperative regime of UN collective security: the very thing Washington now seems determined to dismantle. If these states see support-ing the United States as earning them a place on the terrorist hit list, but not a place at the diplomatic table where decisions on the war against terrorism are taken, few will apply for that hollow privilege.

At the heart of the debate about the future of American foreign policy is not this or that strategy toward one or another rogue regime. It is the role of institutions and law in policymaking generally. Glennon reflects the views of many in the current US administration when he launches this bold assertion: "States are not bound by rules to which they do not agree."[31] Significantly, he deletes the Westphalian concomitant: States *are* bound by rules to which they do agree. The United States, in full compliance with its own complex constitu-tional process, accepted the regime of the UN Charter, which includes limitations on the right of unilateral recourse to force. The states that opposed an armed invasion of Iraq did so not, as Glennon conjectures, because President Chirac wanted to restrict US power but, rather, because they

---

30. Glennon, *supra* note 28, at 34.   **31.** *Id.* at 31.

shared a widespread and still-credible belief that what the Washington policy-makers had decided to do would make the problem of terrorism worse, not better. In refusing to assent to the US strategy, they were responding exactly as the Charter intended. From the perspective of the policymakers, this dissonant response was unacceptable—not primarily because it hindered the Pentagon's strategy in this instance (it did not, except for the inconvenience of precluding a simultaneous invasion through Turkey), but because it re-minded them that the United States remains treaty bound to an international regime that specifically forbids the unconstricted unilateralism Washington craves. While the usual US response to such inhibiting entanglements is to reject the treaty, the administration understands that for the United States to withdraw from the UN system would leave its machinery intact but in the hands of others, an unpalatable outcome. Thus, we now see the effort to incapacitate what Washington can neither abide nor abandon.

RICHARD FALK, "WHAT FUTURE FOR THE UN CHARTER SYSTEM OF WAR PREVENTION?"
97 A.J.I.L. 590, 590–98 (2003)
I. FRAMING AN INQUIRY

President George W. Bush historically challenged the United Nations Security Council when he uttered some memorable words in the course of his September 12, 2002, speech to the General Assembly: "Will the UN serve the purpose of its founding, or will it be irrelevant?"[32] In the aftermath of the Iraq war there are at least two answers to this question. The answer of the US government would be to suggest that the United Nations turned out to be irrelevant due to its failure to endorse recourse to war against the Iraq of Saddam Hussein. The answer of those who opposed the war is that the UN Security Council served the purpose of its founding by its refusal to endorse recourse to a war that could not be persuasively reconciled with the UN Charter [Basic Document 1.5] and international law. This difference of assessment is not just factual, whether Iraq was a threat and whether the inspection process was succeeding at a reasonable pace; it was also conceptual, even jurisprudential. The resolution of this latter debate is likely to shape the future role of the United Nations, as well as influence the attitude of the most powerful sovereign state as to the relationship between international law generally and the use of force as an instrument of foreign policy.

These underlying concerns antedate the recent preoccupation with Iraq, and were vigorously debated during the Cold War era, especially during the latter stages of the Vietnam War. But the present context of the debate regarding the interplay between sovereign discretion on matters of force and UN authority was framed in the late 1990s around the topic of humanitarian intervention, especially in relation to the Kosovo war. The burning issue in the Kosovo setting was whether "a coalition of the willing" acting under the umbrella of NATO was legally entitled to act as a residual option, given the perceived UN Security Council unwillingness to mandate a use of force despite the urgent humanitarian dangers facing the Albanian Kosovars. In

---

32. Address to the United Nations General Assembly in New York City, 38 Weekly Comp. Pres. Doc. 1529 (16 Sep 2002).

that instance, a formal mandate was sought and provided by NATO, but without what seemed to be textually required by Article 53(1) of the UN Charter, that is, lacking some expression of explicit authorization by the UN Security Council. Legal apologists for the initiative insisted that such authorization could be derived from prior UN Security Council resolutions, as well as from the willingness of the United Nations to manage the post-conflict civil reconstruction of Kosovo that amounted to a tacit assent, providing the undertaking with a retroactive certification of legality. To similar effect were arguments suggesting that the failure of the Security Council to adopt a resolution of censure introduced by those members opposed to the Kosovo war amounted to an implied acknowledgment of legality.

But the tension with the Charter rules on the use of force was so clear that these efforts at legalization seemed ineffectual, and a far preferable approach was adopted by the Independent International Commission on Kosovo, which concluded that the intervention in Kosovo was "illegal, but legitimate."[33] The troublesome elasticity of this doctrine was conditioned in two ways, first by suggesting the need for the intervening side to bear a heavy burden of persuasion as to the necessity of intervention to avoid an impending or ongoing humanitarian catastrophe. Second, there was a checklist of duties that need to be fulfilled by the intervenors to achieve legitimacy, emphasizing the protection of the civilian population, adherence to the international laws of war, and a convincing focus on humanitarian goals, as distinct from economic and strategic aims. In Kosovo the moral and political case for intervention seemed strong: a vulnerable and long abused majority population facing an imminent prospect of ethnic cleansing by Serb rulers, a scenario for effective intervention with minimal risks of unforeseen negative effects or extensive collateral damage, and the absence of significant non-humanitarian motivations on the intervening side. As such, the foundation for a principled departure under exceptional circumstances from a strict rendering of Charter rules on the use of force seemed present. The legality/legitimacy gap, however, was recognized to be unhealthy, eroding the authority of international law over time, and the Commission recommended strongly that it be closed at the earliest possible time by UN initiative. Its report urged, for example, that the permanent members of the Security Council consider agreeing not to cast adverse votes in the setting of impending humanitarian catastrophes. The adoption of such a practice would have enabled the Kosovo intervention to be approved by the Security Council even in the face of Russian and Chinese opposition, which would have been registered in the debate and by way of abstentions.

More ambitiously, the Commission proposed a three-step process designed to acknowledge within the United Nations Charter system the enforcement role of the organization in contexts of severe human rights violations. The first step consists of a framework of principles designed to limit claims of humanitarian intervention to a narrow set of circumstances, and to assure that the dynamics of implementation adhere to international humanitarian law and promote the well-being of the people being protected. The second step is to draft a resolution for adoption by the General Assembly in the form of a

---

33. Independent International Commission on Kosovo, The Kosovo Report: Conflict, International Response, Lessons Learned 185–98 (2002) (hereinafter "Kosovo Report"). [*Eds.*— Professor Falk was a member of the Commission].

Declaration on the Right and Responsibility of Humanitarian Intervention that seeks to reconcile respect for sovereign rights, the duty to implement human rights, and the responsibility to prevent humanitarian catastrophes. The third step would be to amend the Charter to incorporate these changes as they pertain to the role and responsibility of the UN Security Council, and other multilateral frameworks and coalitions that undertake humanitarian interventions. It should be noted that no progress toward closing this legitimacy/legality gap by formal or informal action within the United Nations can be anticipated at this time. There exists substantial opposition, especially among Asian countries, to any expansion of the interventionary mandate of the United Nations and other political actors in the setting of human rights. This opposition has deepened since Kosovo because of the controversial uses of force claimed by the United States in its antiterrorism campaign that have combined security and human rights arguments.

Iraq tested the UN Charter system in a way complementary to that associated with the Kosovo controversy. The Iraq test was associated with the impact of the September 11 attacks and the challenge of mega-terrorism. The initial American military response to the Al Qaeda attack and continuing threat was directed at Afghanistan, a convenient territorial target both because it seemed to be the nerve center of the terrorist organization and a country ruled by the Taliban regime that allowed Al Qaeda to operate extensive terrorist training bases within its territory, and because it lacked some crucial attributes needed for full membership in international society, including widespread diplomatic recognition. The reasonableness of waging war to supplant the Taliban regime and destroy the Al Qaeda base of operations in Afghanistan was widely accepted by the entire spectrum of countries active in world politics, although there was only the most minimal effort by the US government to demonstrate that it was acting within the UN framework. The Al Qaeda responsibility for September 11 was amply demonstrated, the prospect of future attacks seemed great and possibly imminent, and the American capability to win the war at a proportional cost seemed convincing. There was no significant international opposition to the American initiation and conduct of the Afghanistan war, and there were varying levels of support from all of America's traditional allies. International law was stretched in these novel circumstances to provide a major state with the practical option of responding with force to one important source of mega-terrorist warfare.

But when the Iraq phase of the September 11 response beyond Afghanistan began to be discussed by American leaders, most reactions around the world were highly critical, generating a worldwide peace movement dedicated to avoiding the war and a variety of efforts by governments to urge an alternative to war. The main American justification for proceeding immediately against Iraq was articulated in the form of a claimed right of preemptive warfare, abstractly explained as necessary conduct in view of the alleged interface between weaponry of mass destruction and the extremist tactics of the mega-terrorists.[34] It was argued that it was unacceptable in these circum-

---

34. Initially fully depicted in George W. Bush, *Commencement Address at the United States Military Academy in West Point, New York* (1 Jun 2002), 38 Weekly Comp. Pres. Doc. 944 (10 Jun 2002); given a more enduring and authoritative status by the emphasis in the official White House document, The National Security Strategy of the United States of America 12–16 (17 Sep 2002)[**Basic Docu-**

stances for the United States to wait to be attacked, and that preemptive warfare was essential to uphold the security of the "civilized" portion of the world. In his talk at the United Nations, Bush said, "We cannot stand by and do nothing while dangers gather."[35] It was this claim that was essentially rejected by the UN Security Council's refusal to go along with US/UK demands for a direct endorsement of recourse to war. The precise American contention was more narrowly and multiply framed in relation to the failures of Iraq to cooperate fully with the UN inspectors, the years of non-implementation of earlier Security Council resolutions imposing disarmament obligations on Iraq after the Gulf War, and, above all, by the supposedly heightened threat posed by Iraq's alleged arsenal of weapons of mass destruction.

The Iraq war was initiated, and ended militarily with rapid American battlefield victories. President Bush so declared, "In the battle of Iraq, the United States and our allies have prevailed. And now our coalition is engaged in securing and reconstructing that country."[36] The president carefully described the military operations as "a battle" rather than as "a war," subsuming the attack on Iraq within the wider, ongoing war against global terrorism, and implying that the undertaking should be seen as an element in the antiterrorism campaign launched in response to the September 11 attacks. Again, as in relation to Kosovo, the UN Security Council refrained from censuring the United States and its allies, and the United Nations seems fully willing to play whatever part is assigned to it during the current period of military occupation and political, economic, and social reconstruction, so far under exclusive US/UK control. Such acquiescence is particularly impressive given the failure of the victorious coalition in the Iraq war to find any evidence of weapons of mass destruction, or to be attacked by such weaponry despite launching a war designed to destroy the regime of Saddam Hussein. It seems reasonable to conclude that either such weaponry does not exist, or if it does exist, then deterrence was fully able to assure against a future use. That is, if such weapons were not used by Iraq to defend the survival of the regime, then it is highly unlikely that they would ever have been used in circumstances where an annihilating retaliation could be anticipated. If Iraq refrained when it had nothing to lose, why would it use such weaponry when the inevitable response would be the assured destruction of country and regime?

How should such a pattern of circumvention of Charter rules combined with the reluctance of the UN Security Council to seek censure for such violations be construed from the perspective of the future of international law? There are several overlapping modes of interpretation, each of which illuminates the issue to some extent, but none seems to provide a satisfactory account from the perspective of international law:

—The United States as the dominant state in a unipolar world order enjoys an exemption from legal accountability with respect to uses of force irreconcilable with the UN Charter system; other states, in contrast, would be

ment 6.9], *available at* <http://www.white-house. gov/nsc/nss.pdf>.

35. *Infra* note 36.

36. *Transcript of President Bush's Remarks on the End of Major Combat in Iraq,* N.Y. Times, 2 May 2003, at A16.

generally held to account unless directly protected under the United States exemption;

— The pattern of behavior confirms a skeptical trend that suggests the Charter system no longer accords, or never did accord, with the realities of world politics, and is not authoritative in relation to the behavior of states;

— The American pattern of behavior is in some tension with the Charter system, but it is a creative tension that suggests respect for the underlying values of the world community, viewing legality as a matter of degree, not either/or, and as requiring continuing adjustment to changing circumstances; as such, the claims of preemption in relation to mega-terrorism provide a reasonable doctrinal explanation for an expanded right of self-defense;

— Acknowledging the behavioral pressures of the world, the possibility exists that contested uses of force under the Charter are "illegal, yet illegitimate" either by reference to the rationale for initiating action without UN Security Council approval or on the basis of the beneficial impact of the intervention[37]. From this perspective, the failure to find weapons of mass destruction does not definitively undermine the claim that the intervention is "legitimate." It still could be judged as legitimate due to a series of effects: the emancipation of the Iraqi people from an oppressive regime, reinforced by the overwhelming evidence that the Baghdad rulers were guilty of systematic, widespread, and massive crimes against humanity, and an occupation that prepares the Iraqi people for political democracy and economic success.[38]

At this stage, it is impossible to predict how the Iraq war will impact upon the Charter system with respect to the international regulation of force. It will depend on how principal states, especially the United States, treat the issue. International law, in this crucial sense, is neither more nor less than what the powerful actors in the system, and to a lesser extent the global community of international jurists, say it is. International law in the area of the use of force cannot by itself induce consistent compliance because of sovereignty-oriented political attitudes combined with the gross disparities in power that prevent the logic of reciprocity and the benefits of mutuality from operating with respect to the security agenda of states. The "realist" school has dominated the foreign policy process of major countries throughout the existence of the modern state system, having been challenged only marginally by a Wilsonian approach that is more reliant on legalism and moralism. To the extent that restraint with respect to the use of force is advocated by realists, it is based on cost-benefit assessments, including the diplomatic virtue of prudence and the avoidance of over-extension that has been blamed throughout history for the decline of major states.

There are grounds for supposing that the approach of the Bush administration may not fit within the realist paradigm, but rather represents a militant version of Wilsonian idealism. President Bush has consistently described the war against terrorism in terms of good and evil, which works even against constraints based on calculations of self-interest and prudence. To the extent that such an orientation shapes the near future of American conduct,

37. See A.-M. Slaughter, *Good Reasons for Going Around the UN*, N.Y. Times, 18 Mar 2003, at A33.

38. See C. Krauthammer, *Iraq: A Moral reckoning*, L.A. Times, 16 May 2003, at A29; T.

Friedman, *Bored with Baghdad—Already*, N.Y. Times, 18 May 2003, § 4, at 13.

the UN Charter system will be disregarded except possibly in those circumstances where the Security Council would support an American claim to use force.

II. THE IRAQ WAR AND THE FUTURE OF THE CHARTER SYSTEM

Against the jurisprudential background depicted in the previous section, an interpretation of the Iraq precedent is necessarily tentative. It depends, in the first analysis, on whether the American battlefield victory in the Iraq war can be converted into a political victory, which will be measured in Iraq by such factors as stability, democratization, recovery of Iraqi sovereignty, and economic development. If the American occupation is viewed as successful, then the intervention is likely to be treated as "legitimate," despite being generally regarded as "illegal." Such a perception will be viewed by some as adding a needed measure of flexibility in the application of the Charter system in a world where the possible interplay of mega-terrorist tactics and weaponry of mass destruction validates recourse to anticipatory self-defense, but it will be dismissed by others as an opportunistic repudiation of legal restraints by the world's sole superpower.

There are two main conceptual explanations of this likely divergence of opinion. The first relates to issues of *factual plausibility*. The doctrine of preemption, as such, is less troublesome than its unilateral application in circumstances where the burden of persuasion as to the imminence and severity of the threat is not sustained. The diplomatic repudiation of the United States in the Security Council resulted mainly from the factual unpersuasiveness of the US arguments about the threats associated with Iraqi retention of weaponry of mass destruction and the claims of linkage between the Baghdad regime and the Al Qaeda network, and the alleged failures of deterrence and containment. There were no doubts about the brutality of Saddam Hussein's rule, but there was little support for recourse to war on such grounds. This skepticism has been heightened by the failure so far to uncover weaponry of mass destruction in the aftermath of the war, despite total access to suspicious sites and the cooperation of Iraqi scientists and weapons personnel.

The second ground of divergence relates to arguments of *retroactive justification*. Here the focus is on whether a war opposed because its side effects seemed potentially dangerous, and its advance rationale was not convincing enough to justify stretching the Charter system of restraint, could be justified after the fact. The justifications combine the quick military victory with relatively low casualty figures, as reinforced by the documentation of Saddam Hussein's criminality as an Iraqi leader. Such an argument would seem more convincing if the American-led coalition forces had been more clearly welcomed as "liberators" rather than viewed as "occupiers," and if the post-combat American presence in Iraq was less marred by violent incidents of resistance and further American casualties. It remains too early to pass judgment. If the occupation is relatively short, and is generally perceived to benefit the Iraqi people and not the American occupiers, arguments based on retroactive justification are likely to gain support, and the Iraqi precedent would be viewed not so much as destructive of the Charter system, as an extension of it based on the emerging enlargement of the role of the international community to protect societies vulnerable to abusive governments.

Of course, the issue of process is important, as well as the substantive outcome. The Iraq war represented a circumvention of the collective procedures of the Charter system with respect to uses of force in contexts not covered by the Article 51 conception of self-defense. To some extent, a favorable view of the effects of such a use of force weakens objections to unilateralism. Adopting a constructivist view of international law, much depends on the future conduct and attitudes of the United States government. Constructivism is a view of political and legal reality that places decisive emphasis on dominant mental perceptions about a given set of conditions, whether or not such perceptions are accurate as assessed from other standpoints. Will the US government in the future generally exhibit respect for the role of the Security Council or will it feel vindicated by its decision to act unilaterally in conjunction with cooperative allies, and continue to rely on such a model? If the latter interpretation shapes future American foreign policy, then the Charter system is marginalized, at least with respect to the United States.

Can the Charter system work without adherence to its procedures and restraining rules by the dominant state in the world? The constructivist answer is most clarifying. To the extent that other states continue to take the Charter system as authoritative it will certainly heavily influence international responses to challenged uses of force by states other than the United States, and will affect global attitudes toward American leadership. There will be complaints about the degree to which geopolitical realities trump international law restraints and about double standards, but these complaints have been made since the United Nations came into being, and arguably were embedded in the Charter by granting a veto to the permanent members.

The approach taken by the Security Council in its Resolution 1483 is indicative of a tension between acquiescence and opposition to the US/UK recourse to war against Iraq. The resolution divides responsibility and authority between the occupying powers and the United Nations, granting the United States/United Kingdom predominant control over the most vital concerns of security, economic and political reconstruction, and governance. At the same time, the resolution stops far short of retroactively endorsing recourse to force by the United States/United Kingdom under the factual circumstances that existed. It dodges the issue of legality/legitimacy by avoiding any formal pronouncement, while accepting as a legitimate given the realities of the outcome of the war. As a result, a high degree of ambiguity surrounds the Iraq war as precedent. Undoubtedly, this ambiguity will be reduced, and possibly eliminated, by consistent subsequent UN Security Council practice in future peace and security contexts.

III. THE CHARTER SYSTEM, MEGA–TERRORISM, AND HUMANITARIAN INTERVENTION

In the 1990s there was a definite trend toward accepting a more interventionary role for the United Nations with respect to the prevention of ethnic cleansing and genocide. The Security Council, as supported by the last three secretaries-general, reflecting a greater prominence for the international protection of human rights and less anxiety about risks of escalation than were operative during the Cold War, narrowed the degree of deference owed to the territorial supremacy of sovereign governments. As such, the domestic jurisdiction exclusion of UN intervention expressed in Article 2(7) was definitely under challenge from the widespread grassroots and governmental advocacy of humanitarian intervention in the years following the Cold War. Although the pattern of claims and practice remained contested, being resisted especially by China and other Asian countries, there was considerable support for humanitarian intervention. The UN was more insistently attacked for doing too little, as in Bosnia and Rwanda, than in doing too much.

A variant on this debate is connected with the instances of uses of force under American leadership in the post-September 11 world. In both Afghanistan and Iraq recourse to force rested on defensive claims against the new threats of mega-terrorism, but the effect in both instances was to liberate captive populations from extremely oppressive regimes, establishing patterns of governance and potential self-determination that seemed virtually impossible for the oppressed citizenry to achieve by normal modes of resistance. Even though the humanitarian *motivations* of the United States are suspect in both instances, due to a past record of collaboration with these regimes while their abusive conduct was at its worst, the effect of the interventions was emancipatory, and the declared intention of the occupation is to support human rights and democratization. Undoubtedly, such forcible liberations would not have taken place without the pressures mounted and the climate created by the September 11 attacks. Nevertheless, to the extent that mega-terrorism is associated with criminal forms of governmental authority, would it not be reasonable to construe uses of force that accomplished "regime change" as part of an enlarged doctrine of humanitarian intervention?

I think not for some obvious reasons. Recourse to war is too serious a matter to allow decisions about it to proceed on the basis of rationales that are not fully articulated and debated in advance. For this reason also, prudential considerations alone would rule out humanitarian intervention in all but the most extreme cases, and even in most of these. Who would be so crazy as to advocate humanitarian intervention on behalf of the Chechens, Tibetans, Kashmiris? Of course, there are many options open to the international community and its member states not involving the use of force that could range from expressions of disapproval to the imposition of comprehensive sanctions. The case for humanitarian intervention relying on force must be treated as a principled, and even then, a rare exception to the generalized prohibition of the Charter with respect to the use of force embodied in Article 2(4). If the Security Council does not mandate the intervention, and a coalition of the willing proceeds, the undertaking could still be substantially vindicated, as in Kosovo, if some sort of collective process was involved and the facts confirmed the imminence of a humanitarian emergency. The Kosovo Commission tackled this issue of principled humanitarian intervention, as have scholars, seeking to provide guidance that preserves the balance between the prohibition on uses of force and the moral/political imperatives to mitigate impending or ongoing humanitarian catastrophes.

But a pro-intervention argument should not be treated as acceptable in circumstances where the use of force is associated with alleged security threats posed by the menace of mega-terrorism, but the justification tendered after the fact emphasizes humanitarian intervention. In Afghanistan the security argument was sufficiently convincing as to make the humanitarian benefits of the war a political and moral bonus, but without bearing on the legal case for recourse to force, which was already convincing on the defensive grounds claimed. In Iraq, by contrast, the security and related anti-Al Qaeda arguments were unconvincing, and the claimed humanitarian benefits resulting from the war were emphasized by American officials as a way to circumvent the illegality of the American-led recourse to force. Such post hoc efforts at legalization should not be accorded much respect, especially in the context of a major war where prior efforts to obtain a mandate for the use of force were not endorsed by the Security Council even in the face of major diplomatic pressures mounted by Washington in the several months prior to the Iraq war.

IV.   A CONSTRUCTIVIST FUTURE FOR THE UN CHARTER SYSTEM

The position favored here is that the United States would be best served by adhering to the UN Charter system. This system is flexible enough to accommodate new and genuine security imperatives as well as changing values, including a shifting balance between sovereign rights and world community responsibilities. In both settings of humanitarian intervention and responses against mega-terrorism the Charter system can be *legally* vindicated *in appropriate factual circumstances*.

From this perspective recourse to war against Iraq should not have been undertaken without a *prior* mandate from the Security Council, and rather than "a failure" of the United Nations, the withholding of such a mandate represented a responsible exercise of constitutional restraint. The facts did not support the case for preemption, as there was neither *imminence* nor *necessity*. As a result, the Iraq war seemed, at best, to qualify as an instance of *preventive war*, but there are strong legal, moral, and political reasons to deny both legality and legitimacy to such a use of force. Preventive war is not an acceptable exception to the Charter system, and no effort was made by the US government to claim such a right, although the highly abstract and vague phrasing of the preemptive war doctrine in the *National Security Strategy of the United States of America* would be more accurately formulated as a "preventive war doctrine." But even within this highly dubious doctrinal setting, to be at all convincing the evidence would at least have to demonstrate a credible future Iraqi threat that could not be reliably deterred, and this was never done.

My legal constructivist position is that the United States (and the world) would benefit from a self-imposed discipline of adherence to the UN Charter system governing the use of force. Such a voluntary discipline would overcome the absence of geopolitical limits associated with countervailing power in a unipolar world. It would also work against tendencies of the United States and others to rely too much on military superiority, which encourages the formation of defensive alliances, and possibly arms races. International law is flexible enough to allow the United States, and other countries, to meet novel security needs. Beyond this, neither American values nor strategic goals should be construed to validate uses of force that cannot win support in the UN Security Council. If one considers the course of American foreign policy over the course of the last half century, adherence to the Charter system with respect to the use of force would have avoided the worst policy failures, including that of Vietnam. Deviations from the Charter system of prohibitions on the use of force can be credited with no clear successes.

It is not the Charter system that is in disarray, providing sensible grounds for declaring the project of regulating recourse to war by states a failed experiment that should now be abandoned. It is rather leading states, and above all the United States, that need to be persuaded that their interests are served and their values realized by a more diligent pursuit of a law-oriented foreign policy. The Charter system is not a legal prison that presents states with the dilemma of adherence (and defeat) and violation or disregard (and victory). Rather adherence is the best policy, if understood against a jurisprudential background that is neither slavishly legalistic nor cynically nihilistic. The law can be stretched as new necessities arise, but the stretching must to the extent possible be in accord with procedures and norms contained in the Charter system, with a factually and doctrinally persuasive explanation of why a particular instance of stretching is justified. Such positive constructivist attitudes will renew confidence in the Charter system. It is also true that constructivism can work negatively, and so if the disregard of the legal framework, public opposition, and governmental resistance present in the Iraq case is repeated in the future, then indeed the Charter system will be in a shambles before much longer.

A More Secure World: Our Shared Responsibility: Report of the [Secretary-General's] High-level Panel on Threats, Challenges and Change

UN Doc. 59/565, §§ 183–209, pp. 53–58 (2 Dec 2004)

IX. Using force: rules and guidelines

183.   The framers of the Charter of the United Nations recognized that force may be necessary for the "prevention and removal of threats to the peace, and for the suppression of acts of aggression or other breaches of the peace. Military force, legally and properly applied, is a vital component of any workable system of collective security, whether defined in the traditional narrow sense or more broadly as we would prefer. But few contemporary policy issues cause more difficulty, or involve higher stakes, than the principles concerning its use and application to individual cases.

184.   The maintenance of world peace and security depends importantly on there being a common global understanding, and acceptance, of when the application of force is both legal and legitimate. One of these elements being satisfied without the other will always weaken the international legal order—and thereby put both State and human security at greater risk.

A. The question of legality

185.   The Charter of the United Nations, in Article 2.4, expressly prohibits Member States from using or threatening force against each other, allowing only two exceptions: self-defence under Article 51, and military measures authorized by the Security Council under Chapter VII (and by extension for regional organizations under Chapter VIII) in response to "any threat to the peace, breach of the peace or act of aggression."

186.   For the first 44 years of the United Nations, Member States often violated these rules and used military force literally hundreds of times, with a paralysed Security Council passing very few Chapter VII resolutions and Article 51 only rarely providing credible cover. Since the end of the cold war,

however, the yearning for an international system governed by the rule of law has grown. There is little evident international acceptance of the idea of security being best preserved by a balance of power, or by any single—even benignly motivated—superpower.

187.   But in seeking to apply the express language of the Charter, three particularly difficult questions arise in practice: first, when a State claims the right to strike preventively, in self-defence, in response to a threat which is not imminent; secondly, when a State appears to be posing an external threat, actual or potential, to other States or people outside its borders, but there is disagreement in the Security Council as to what to do about it; and thirdly, where the threat is primarily internal, to a State's own people.

1.   Article 51 of the Charter of the United Nations and self-defence

188.   The language of this article is restrictive: "Nothing in the present Charter shall impair the inherent right of individual or collective self-defense if an armed attack occurs against a member of the United Nations, until the Security Council has taken measures to maintain international peace and security." However, a threatened State, according to long established international law, can take military action as long as the threatened attack is *imminent*, no other means would deflect it and the action is proportionate. The problem arises where the threat in question is not imminent but still claimed to be real: for example the acquisition, with allegedly hostile intent, of nuclear weaponsmaking capability.

189.   Can a State, without going to the Security Council, claim in these circumstances the right to act, in anticipatory self-defence, not just pre-emptively (against an imminent or proximate threat) but preventively (against a non-imminent or non-proximate one)? Those who say "yes" argue that the potential harm from some threats (e.g., terrorists armed with a nuclear weapon) is so great that one simply cannot risk waiting until they become imminent, and that less harm may be done (e.g., avoiding a nuclear exchange or radioactive fallout from a reactor destruction) by acting earlier.

190.   The short answer is that if there are good arguments for preventive military action, with good evidence to support them, they should be put to the Security Council, which can authorize such action if it chooses to. If it does not so choose, there will be, by definition, time to pursue other strategies, including persuasion, negotiation, deterrence and containment—and to visit again the military option.

191.   For those impatient with such a response, the answer must be that, in a world full of perceived potential threats, the risk to the global order and the norm of non-intervention on which it continues to be based is simply too great for the legality of unilateral preventive action, as distinct from collectively endorsed action, to be accepted. Allowing one to so act is to allow all.

192.   **We do not favour the rewriting or reinterpretation of Article 51.**

2.   Chapter VII of the Charter of the United Nations and external threats

193.   In the case of a State posing a threat to other States, people outside its borders or to international order more generally, the language of Chapter VII is inherently broad enough, and has been interpreted broadly enough, to

allow the Security Council to approve any coercive action at all, including military action, against a State when it deems this "necessary to maintain or restore international peace and security." That is the case whether the threat is occurring now, in the imminent future or more distant future; whether it involves the State's own actions or those of non-State actors it harbours or supports; or whether it takes the form of an act or omission, an actual or potential act of violence or simply a challenge to the Council's authority.

194.   We emphasize that the concerns we expressed about the legality of the preventive use of military force in the case of self-defence under Article 51 are not applicable in the case of collective action authorized under Chapter VII. In the world of the twenty-first century, the international community does have to be concerned about nightmare scenarios combining terrorists, weapons of mass destruction and irresponsible States, and much more besides, which may conceivably justify the use of force, not just reactively but preventively and before a latent threat becomes imminent. The question is not whether such action can be taken: it can, by the Security Council as the international community's collective security voice, at any time it deems that there is a threat to international peace and security. The Council may well need to be prepared to be much more proactive on these issues, taking more decisive action earlier, than it has been in the past.

195.   Questions of legality apart, there will be issues of prudence, or legitimacy, about whether such preventive action *should* be taken: crucial among them is whether there is credible evidence of the reality of the threat in question (taking into account both capability and specific intent) and whether the military response is the only reasonable one in the circumstances. We address these issues further below.

196.   It may be that some States will always feel that they have the obligation to their own citizens, and the capacity, to do whatever they feel they need to do, unburdened by the constraints of collective Security Council process. But however understandable that approach may have been in the cold war years, when the United Nations was manifestly not operating as an effective collective security system, the world has now changed and expectations about legal compliance are very much higher.

197.   One of the reasons why States may want to bypass the Security Council is a lack of confidence in the quality and objectivity of its decision-making. The Council's decisions have often been less than consistent, less than persuasive and less than fully responsive to very real State and human security needs. But the solution is not to reduce the Council to impotence and irrelevance: it is to work from within to reform it, including in the ways we propose in the present report.

198.   **The Security Council is fully empowered under Chapter VII of the Charter of the United Nations to address the full range of security threats with which States are concerned. The task is not to find alternatives to the Security Council as a source of authority but to make the Council work better than it has.**

3. Chapter VII of the Charter of the United Nations, internal threats and the responsibility to protect

199.   The Charter of the United Nations is not as clear as it could be when it comes to saving lives within countries in situations of mass atrocity. It "reaffirm(s) faith in fundamental human rights" but does not do much to protect them, and Article 2.7 prohibits intervention "in matters which are essentially within the jurisdiction of any State." There has been, as a result, a long-standing argument in the international community between those who insist on a "right to intervene" in man-made catastrophes and those who argue that the Security Council, for all its powers under Chapter VII to "maintain or restore international security", is prohibited from authorizing any coercive action against sovereign States for whatever happens within their borders.

200.   Under the Convention on the Prevention and Punishment of the Crime of Genocide (Genocide Convention), States have agreed that genocide, whether committed in time of peace or in time of war, is a crime under international law which they undertake to prevent and punish. Since then it has been understood that genocide anywhere is a threat to the security of all and should never be tolerated. The principle of non-intervention in internal affairs cannot be used to protect genocidal acts or other atrocities, such as large-scale violations of international humanitarian law or large-scale ethnic cleansing, which can properly be considered a threat to international security and as such provoke action by the Security Council.

201.   The successive humanitarian disasters in Somalia, Bosnia and Herzegovina, Rwanda, Kosovo and now Darfur, Sudan, have concentrated attention not on the immunities of sovereign Governments but their responsibilities, both to their own people and to the wider international community. There is a growing recognition that the issue is not the "right to intervene" of any State, but the "responsibility to protect" of *every* State when it comes to people suffering from avoidable catastrophe—mass murder and rape, ethnic cleansing by forcible expulsion and terror, and deliberate starvation and exposure to disease. And there is a growing acceptance that while sovereign Governments have the primary responsibility to protect their own citizens from such catastrophes, when they are unable or unwilling to do so that responsibility should be taken up by the wider international community— with it spanning a continuum involving prevention, response to violence, if necessary, and rebuilding shattered societies. The primary focus should be on assisting the cessation of violence through mediation and other tools and the protection of people through such measures as the dispatch of humanitarian, human rights and police missions. Force, if it needs to be used, should be deployed as a last resort.

202.   The Security Council so far has been neither very consistent nor very effective in dealing with these cases, very often acting too late, too hesitantly or not at all. But step by step, the Council and the wider international community have come to accept that, under Chapter VII and in pursuit of the emerging norm of a collective international responsibility to protect, it can always authorize military action to redress catastrophic internal wrongs if it is prepared to declare that the situation is a "threat to international peace and security", not especially difficult when breaches of international law are involved.

203.   **We endorse the emerging norm that there is a collective international responsibility to protect, exercisable by the Security Council authorizing military intervention as a last resort, in the event of genocide and other large-scale killing, ethnic cleansing or serious violations of international humanitarian law which sovereign Governments have proved powerless or unwilling to prevent.**

B.   The question of legitimacy

204.   The effectiveness of the global collective security system, as with any other legal order, depends ultimately not only on the legality of decisions but also on the common perception of their legitimacy—their being made on solid evidentiary grounds, and for the right reasons, morally as well as legally.

205.   If the Security Council is to win the respect it must have as the primary body in the collective security system, it is critical that its most important and influential decisions, those with large-scale life-and-death impact, be better made, better substantiated and better communicated. In particular, in deciding whether or not to authorize the use of force, the Council should adopt and systematically address a set of agreed guidelines, going directly not to whether force *can* legally be used but whether, as a matter of good conscience and good sense, it *should* be.

206.   The guidelines we propose will not produce agreed conclusions with pushbutton predictability. The point of adopting them is not to guarantee that the objectively best outcome will always prevail. It is rather to maximize the possibility of achieving Security Council consensus around when it is appropriate or not to use coercive action, including armed force; to maximize international support for whatever the Security Council decides; and to minimize the possibility of individual Member States bypassing the Security Council.

207.   **In considering whether to authorize or endorse the use of military force, the Security Council should always address—whatever other considerations it may take into account—at least the following five basic criteria of legitimacy:**

(a) *Seriousness of threat.* **Is the threatened harm to State or human security of a kind, and sufficiently clear and serious, to justify *prima facie* the use of military force? In the case of internal threats, does it involve genocide and other large-scale killing, ethnic cleansing or serious violations of international humanitarian law, actual or imminently apprehended?**

(b) *Proper purpose.* **Is it clear that the primary purpose of the proposed military action is to halt or avert the threat in question, whatever other purposes or motives may be involved?**

(c) *Last resort.* **Has every non-military option for meeting the threat in question been explored, with reasonable grounds for believing that other measures will not succeed?**

(d) *Proportional means.* **Are the scale, duration and intensity of the proposed military action the minimum necessary to meet the threat in question?**

(e) *Balance of consequences.* **Is there a reasonable chance of the military action being successful in meeting the threat in question, with the consequences of action not likely to be worse than the consequences of inaction?**

208. **The above guidelines for authorizing the use of force should be embodied in declaratory resolutions of the Security Council and General Assembly.**

209. We also believe it would be valuable if individual Member States, whether or not they are members of the Security Council, subscribed to them.

DISCUSSION NOTES/QUESTIONS

1. The assumption of this chapter is that the responses of international law to the debate occasioned by the Iraq War is likely to shape the future role of law and international institutions in the years ahead. Distinguish in this regard the official legal defense of the American approach to the Iraq War presented by Taft and Buchwold from the academic perspectives offered by Thomas Franck and Richard Falk. Of particular importance, are the various legal interpretations offered on the matter of *preemptive war* as claim of legal right and as world order precedent.

2. David Frum and Richard Perle, both influential figures within the neo-conconservative advisory group that has been shaping the foreign policy of the Bush Administration, argue that if the United Nations does not accept the American approach to global security, then the US should forthwith withdraw from the organization. Is this a sensible adjustment? An over-reaction? For an elaboration of these essentially nihilistic views concealed beneath a veneer of geopolitical moralism see David Frum & Richard Perle, An End to Evil: How to Win the War on Terror (2003).

3. In introducing the National Security Strategy of the United States of America (NSS 2002) **(Basic Document 6.9)**, President Bush insists that there exists an unprecedented opportunity for world peace at the present time. On what assumptions does this claim rest? What does it suggest about the shape of world order? Do you find this claim persuasive? Compare David Harvey, The New Imperialism (2003); Chalmers Johnson, The Sorrows of Empire (2004); Robert Jay Lifton, The Superpower Syndrome (2003); Clyde Prestowitz, Rogue Nation (2003); Michael Mann, The Incoherent Empire (2003); Andrew J. Bacevich, American Empire (2002); Noam Chomsky, Hegemony or Survival (2003).

4. Does the argument for preemptive/preventive war as a response to the challenge of transnational terrorism contribute a necessary adaptation to the security of the United States and the world? How is the argument framed in NSS 2002? Is this persuasive? Does it enhance the quality of world order? Could the claim be re-framed in a more constructive manner? How does the Iraq War experience shed light on the debate about this new security doctrine? Compare the framing of these issues by the UN Report, *A More Secure World* as presented in the excerpt included in this chapter.

5. If the legal claims made by the United States to engage in preemptive war against Iraq are invoked in the future by other states—for instance, India in relation to Pakistan or China in relation to Taiwan—would this settle the question of legal right? Why not?

6. The Iraq War poses fundamental issues about the nature of world order and the role of international law with respect to the use of force. Underneath this discussion is the question as to whether the attacks of September 11 require a new approach to the relationship between law and force in world politics, and specifically, about whether the UN Charter guidelines continue to be authoritative. This questioning of the prohibitions on non-defensive uses of force contained in Article 2(4) and 51 of the Charter have been under attack by international law scholars for several decades. *See*, for example, Anthony C. Arendt & Robert J. Beck, International Law and the Use of Force: Beyond the UN Charter Paradigm (1993); A. Mark Weisbrud, Use of Force: The Practice of States Since World War II (1997); and Michael Reisman, *Coercion and Self–Determination: Construing Article 2(4)*, 78 A.J.I.L 642 (1984); also the famous article by Thomas Franck, *Who Killed Article 2(4)? Or: Changing Norms Governing the Use of Force by States*, 64 A.J.I.L. 809 (1970), written 35 years ago. At the same time, this skeptical view of the narrow Charter conception of the legality of force has had many notable defenders over the years. *See generally* Louis Henkin, How Nations Behave (2d ed. 1979). Many scholars regard Oscar Schachter as providing a balanced and appropriate perspective, neither too dismissive of the restrictions nor too rigidly confining. See his *In Defense of International Rule on the Use of Force*, 53 U. Chi. L. Rev 113 (1986) and *The Right of States to Use Armed Force*, 82 Mich. L. Rev. 1620 (1984). Such a view was conceptualized, and perhaps influenced by the geopolitical realities of the Cold War, in Myres S. McDougal & Florentino P. Feliciano, Law and Minimum World Public Order (1961). Francis Boyle, World Politics and International Law (1985), among others, offers a legalist account of the constructive role played by law in regulating recourse to war with a particular stress on restraining recourse to international force, especially that of the United States. For more emphasis on the global setting that shapes the international legal order, see Richard Falk, Law in an Emerging Global Village (1998). There is an important distinction between a use of force, as in a retaliatory strike, and recourse to war, which implies a more systemic struggle between adversaries to be resolved by reliance on military capabilities and tactics. Note the solution of these problems of adapting law to the new realities of international conflict by the UN Report, *A More Secure World*, especially the idea that anticipatory self-defense may be legal under the Charter, but only if authorized by the Security Council. Is this an acceptable adjustment? Suppose the most aggressive state can bully other members of the Security Council to support its belligerent policies?

7. The Kosovo War stimulated various efforts to stretch international law governing the use of force to cope with imminent or ongoing humanitarian catastrophes in the face of a growing sensitivity to the duty of the international community to disregard sovereignty when vulnerable peoples were severely threatened. These issues were widely reviewed and debated in the 1990s, and produced two influential reports by international commissions. *See* Kosovo Report: Conflict, International Response, Lessons Learned (2000), issued by the Independent International Commission on Kosovo; also The Responsibility to Protect (2001), issued by the International Commission on Intervention and State Sovereignty. For more academic treatments of these issues, see Nicholas Wheeler, Saving Strangers: Humanitarian Intervention in International Society (2000); Humanitarian Intervention (J. Holzgrefe & R. Keohane, eds., 2003). Some efforts were made, especially journalistically, to extend this expanded role for the use of force to the quite different circumstances of the Iraq War. *See*, for instance, Anne–Marie Slaughter, *Good Reasons for Going Around the UN*, N.Y. Times, 18 Mar 2003, at A33. The most articulate and comprehensive argument for abandoning

Charter constraints on the use of force has been advanced by Michael J. Glennon, Limits of Law: Prerogatives of War: Interventionism After Kosovo (2001). *See also* W. Michael Reisman, *The Constitutional Crisis of the United Nations*, 87 A.J.I.L. 83 (1993). A similar perspective is adopted by Michael Ignatieff in lending support to an interventionist view of human rights. *See* Empire–Lite: Nation-building in Bosnia, Kosovo and Afghanistan (2003) and Human Rights as Politics and Idololatry (2001).

8. The deeper issues are structural. Did the magnitude of the attacks on September 11 create a new structure of conflict that presupposes the recasting of international law to take account of the rise of non-state actors? Does the American claim to ignore the sovereign rights of states that "harbor" terrorists validate an expanded concept of the right of self-defense? What role for international law in this new global setting? Has the impact of September 11 been either misconceived or exaggerated? Would it not be more effective to strengthen cooperative arrangements for global law enforcement as a means of restoring global security than to rely on various aspects of claims of "anticipatory self-defense?" Has not reliance on "war" proved costly in lives and resources, and ineffectual with respect to security, considering the experiences of the Afghanistan War and, especially, the Iraq War? *See supra* an excerpt from the UN Report, *A More Secure World,* at 1321.

9. Also useful for a discussion of issues raised in this chapter are the following: Rosalyn Higgins, The Development of International Law Through the Political Organs of the United Nations (1963); Myres S. McDougal & Florentino P. Feliciano, Law and World Minimum Public Order (1961); Hans Kelsen, The Law of the United Nations (1960); Inis L. Claude, Swords into Plowshares: The Problems and Progress of International Organization (4th ed. 1971); Right v. Might: International Law and the Use of Force (L. Henkin ed., 1989); Law and Force in the New International Order (L. Damrosch & D.Scheffer eds., 1991); The Future of International Law Enforcement: New Scenarios, New Law (J. Delbrück, ed., 1993); Helmut Freudenschuss, *Between Unilateralism and Collective Security: Authorizations of the Use of Force by the UN Security Council,* 5 E.J.I.L. 492 (1994); Myres S. McDougal, Harold Lasswell & Michael Reisman, *The World Constitutive Process of Authoritative Decision,* 19 J. Legal Educ. 253 (1981).

Chapter Nine

THE FIRST GLOBAL NORMATIVE REVOLUTION: MEMORIES, EXAGGERATIONS, HOPES

With the end of the Cold War, an era of preoccupying ideological conflict and political rivalry in international relations was suddenly over. The Soviet hold on Eastern Europe disintegrated, and then the Soviet Union itself collapsed. World order changed. At first, there was a sigh of relief, and from the West, exclamations of victory. Francis Fukuyama summed up this triumphalist mood of the early 1990s with his claim that "the end of history" had arrived, by which he meant that a liberal world order was now the unchallenged basis for organizing the political life of the planet, both within and among states. This outlook also encouraged the hard line in world economic policy, an all-out insistence that the only way to organize trade, development, and investment was to rely upon a market-oriented approach that accorded primacy to the efficiency of capital, a perspective that was generally labeled "globalization." The good news seemed to be that war as a regulatory mechanism for world politics was no longer necessary given this new economistic geopolitics.

But all along there were doubters. The most famous of these was Samuel P. Huntington, who startled the world with his thesis of "a clash of civilizations" and its famous sub-text of "the West against the rest."[a] In essence, Huntington anticipated new civilizational fault-lines of intense and bloody conflict, especially at the contact points between Islam and the West. Less noticed was Huntington's important claim that sovereign states might be superseded as the decisive unit of political action and human identification by the reassertion of religious and cultural identities and the framing of debate and grievances, therefore, by reference to "civilizations."

Also prominent in this period was an argument, best expressed by Robert Kaplan, to the effect that what was promised as an era of world peace is better understood in darker terms as "the coming anarchy."[b] Kaplan foresaw "failed states" in Africa and elsewhere as creating intolerable levels of chaos and destruction. He anticipated the spread of this disorder throughout the most economically disadvantaged parts of the world.

a. *See* S. Huntington, The Clash of Civilizations and the Remaking of World Order (1996).

b. *See* R. Kaplan, The Coming Anarchy: Shattering the Dreams of the Post Cold War (2000).

And there was born in 1990 the idea of a "new world order" as explained by US President George H.W. Bush in the course of mobilizing a military response to the Iraqi conquest of Kuwait. He identified the new world order with the capacity of leading states to generate an effective form of collective security under the auspices of the United Nations Security Council (UNSC). This outlook was seemingly validated by the authorization given by the UNSC to a coalition of states led by the United States to restore Kuwaiti sovereign rights by recourse to war. The 1991 Gulf War was successful in reversing the outcome of the Iraqi invasion, but it did not resolve the conflict with Iraq, and the war itself was widely criticized at the time as vesting too much discretion in the hands of one country, the United States, with respect to the means and ends of the war.[c] After the Gulf War was over the US government quietly abandoned its championship of a new world order, and reverted to its preferred status of "the sole surviving superpower," entrusted with leading the world by taking advantage of this "unipolar moment" in which its power and authority were unchallenged on the global stage.

But against this background of geopolitical maneuvers and trends were a series of other developments that seemingly led in the direction of enhancing the rule of law among states and, at the same time, diminishing the scope of their sovereign rights. In part, these developments could be understood as filling the normative (ethical, legal, religious) vacuum created by economic globalization and its rather clear neoliberal tendency to diminish the social responsibility of governments and international institutions for human suffering. This neoliberal ideological posture was subject to rising resentment around the world due to assessments made by international institutions confirming both the persistence of massive poverty on a global scale and growing disparities between rich and poor countries as well as between the rich and poor within most countries.

A growing mood of discontent that expressed itself initially in the form of an anti-globalization movement later assumed a positive stance, advocating "another globalization" based on moves toward global democracy.[d] Also noteworthy were a series of transitions in Latin America from brutal dictatorial rule to constitutional democracy. Part of the popular demand in these countries was to have some kind of accounting for past abuses of state power. The circumstances were delicate in most of these countries inasmuch as the prior oppressive leadership had voluntarily relinquished power but was unprepared to accept any procedure that might have led to criminal accountability for past wrongs. The creative compromise was to constitute "truth and reconciliation commissions," an innovative approach to achieving a symbolic repudiation of the past without causing a political crisis during the process of transition.[e] The experience was generally successful as a partial antidote to what had come to be called "a culture of impunity" with respect to crimes of state.

c. See, e.g., B. Weston, *Security Council Resolution 678 and Persian Gulf Decision–Making: Precarious Legitimacy*, 85 A.J.I.L. 516 (1991).

d. *See* D. Held, Democracy and Global Order (1995); Debating Cosmopolitics (D. Archibugi, ed., 2003).

e. For the range and effectiveness of these various commissions see P. Hayner, *Unspeakable Truths: Confronting State Terror and Atrocity* (2001).

Paralleling these developments was the establishment by the UN Security Council of separate *ad hoc* international criminal tribunals to address the criminality of behavior in the former Yugoslavia and Rwanda. In both instances, as recounted in Part I of this coursebook, flagrant international crimes had been committed, including "ethnic cleansing" in Bosnia during the mid–1990s and genocide in Rwanda during 1994.[f] The much publicized indictment and exceptionally lengthy trial of Slobodan Milosevic, the leader of Yugoslavia during the Balkan Wars, is the most notable occurrence, Milosevic having been the first head of state ever to be indicted for war crimes while still holding state power. In this same period and as likewise detailed in Part I, there took place the highly publicized British detention and extradition in response to a Spanish request of General Augusto Pinochet, the deposed dictator of Chile charged with many crimes against humanity in the course of his rule. The actual British judicial conclusion, reached by the House of Lords, sitting as the highest court, was limited to honoring the Spanish extradition request only with respect to allegations of torture for incidents that had occurred after Britain had itself legislated that torture was an international crime. But what is historically important is that a former leader of one country could be held criminally accountable in another, the biggest step in this direction since the Nuremberg Judgment **(Basic Document 7.4)** at the end of World War II, also considered in Part I.

Thus, a new momentum toward individual criminal accountability of political leaders was now evident that had major consequences for the development of a global rule of law. That it included national judicial activity in relation to crimes of state committed elsewhere was seen as an especially significant indicator that the growth of global law was more important than a rear guard action on behalf of unconditional sovereignty, a trend that gave rise also to an unprecedented interest in extending "universal jurisdiction" over serious international crimes to national courts.[g]

In such an atmosphere it is not surprising that a strong movement pushed for the establishment of a permanent international criminal court, the decision-making focus of Part I. What was especially innovative was the political process that made it happen. This process featured a close collaboration between civil society actors and dedicated, moderate governments. With surprising speed, a treaty was negotiated and sufficiently ratified to bring the International Criminal Court (ICC) into being in July 2002. Such a result was made even more impressive because this institution-building took place despite initial ambivalence and ultimately intense opposition on the part of the United States, especially at the hands of the George W. Bush presidency and a reactionary Congress. Despite this atmosphere, the ICC has the potential to become a crucial building block of humane global governance. But it could also fade unused into virtual obscurity due to subversion or neglect or both.

The 1990s achieved other significant results along the same lines. The observance of basic human rights was accorded greater attention both in the foreign policy of leading states and in the United Nations system. The UN

f. As noted *supra* in Chapter 3, at 179–81, these tribunals are continuing their activities at this writing . For valuable general inquiries, see G. Bass, Stay the Hand of Vengeance: The Politics of War Crimes Tribunals (2000); M. Minow, Between Vengeance and Forgiveness: Facing History after Genocide and Mass Violence (1998).

g. *See, e.g.,* Universal Jurisdiction S. Macedo, ed. (2004).

Conference on Human Rights and Development, held in Vienna in 1993, was notable for the establishment of the post of High Commissioner for Human Rights and for according prominence to the specific grievances of women.[h] In 1994, the Draft Declaration on the Rights of Indigenous Peoples **(Basic Document 3.43)** was circulated within the United Nations in recognition of the historic injustice done to most native peoples throughout the world. Although this document still has not been formally approved as of this writing, it represents the first time that indigenous peoples, despite their important differences, came together on matters of rights.

The erosion of state sovereignty, the migration of peoples, the resurgence of religion in various parts of the world—these and other developments gave rise to a new emphasis on the cultural and normative dimensions of world order. It also increased concerns about those who were vulnerable in such a world, by reason of migration, victimization, or exile. As well, the arousal of historical memories about past injustices contributed to the reshaping of identity by reference to cultural roots. New issues surfaced in a manner never previously considered relevant to the work of international law such as rape as a tactic of warfare or the status and rights of gays and transsexuals.[i]

The increasing salience of human rights, bolstered by media spotlighting, made an ever-stronger case for doing something about their severe violation, and indeed it was in this setting that pressures for humanitarian intervention were brought to bear with varying degrees of success.[j] In addition, due to the acceleration of history and the compression of space arising from technological innovation, especially in the area of information technologies, there arose a new attentiveness to issues of rights and justice associated with past grievance and future prospects. In the 1990s, various claims were made visible by past victims, and unprecedented symbolic, even substantive, steps were taken toward achieving a redress of historical grievances.[k]

Thus, overall, this chapter looks at some of the components of the first genuine and sustained global justice movement in human history. Also, it considers the resistance to these trends, sensitive to the derailing of this normative energy in the aftermath of September 11, especially in the context of the American grand strategy that was fashioned in response. However, as Chapter 10 argues, this derailing is not definitive; a deeper look at global prospects finds a partial revival of the encouraging moves toward global justice that occurred during the 1990s[l] The first two selections thus argue that a global justice movement that took a series of important forward steps during the 1990s, although weakened, has nonetheless endured. Elazar Barkan's introductory discussion treats comprehensively the claim that there was an upsurge of ethical initiatives in international relations in the 1990s. He is

h. *See* Vienna Declaration and Programme of Action of 25 June 1993 **(Basic Document 3.40)**.

i. For invaluable exploration of these and other emergent trends, see H. Charlesworth & C. Chinkin, The Boundaries of International Law: A Feminist Analysis (2000).

j. For helpful range of commentaries, see Globalization and Human Rights (Alison Brysk, ed., 2002).

k. For probing inquiries, see J. Thompson, Taking Responsibility for the Past: Reparations and Historical Justice (2002); The Politics of Memory: Truth, Healing & Social Justice (I. Amadiume & A. An–Na'im, eds., 2000).

l. For general commentary, see E. Barkan, The Moral Guilt of Nations (2000); Dorothy Jones, Global Justice: Defending Cosmopolitanism (1999); Janna Thompson, Justice and World Order (1992).

followed by Richard Falk who discusses this configuration of initiatives by reference to a "normative global revolution," and gives reasons for its tentative revival. The selections depict the territory, and challenge the reader to agree or dissent from the sweeping assessments being made.

In some respects, a litmus test of whether global justice and an accompanying global rule of law are truly making progress is the debate among international law specialists on the viability and desirability of "universal jurisdiction"—i.e., the degree to which national courts can and should assume legal authority to address certain designated international crimes (genocide, crimes against humanity, etc.) wherever committed and by whom. The drama of the 1990s highlighted a Belgian law that claimed such universal jurisdiction, and attracted a long list of accused parties, with such prominent potential defendants as Saddam Hussein, Henry Kissinger, Ariel Sharon, and others. A skeptical essay written from a hyper-realist perspective by Jack Goldsmith and Stephen D. Kransner begins this discussion. In contrast, a framework for the exercise of universal jurisdiction crafted by a group of scholars and jurists and published under the rubric of "The Princeton Principles on Universal Jurisdiction" is offered here as the fourth selection. This ongoing universal jurisdiction debate brings into the open the degree to which national courts will be entrusted with the admittedly delicate matter of passing judgment on the criminality of foreign state leaders for unlawful official conduct.[m] It be noted, however, that the reach of the Belgian law was greatly curtailed due to threats and other pressures brought to bear by the United States and Israel.

Chapter 9 ends with an essay by Daniele Archibugi on the globalizing of democracy, or what he labels "cosmodemocracy." Note that he is preoccupied with the democratization of international society as a whole—an idea that President Bush, judging from a speech he gave to the National Endowment for Democracy in November 2003 advocating democracy as a prerequisite for peace and stability in Iraq and the Middle East, appears nonetheless to have opposed.[n]

In sum, the overarching purpose of this chapter is to depict a crucial fork in the road, with one path entailing seemingly perpetual war as the supposed way to global security and the other promising a gradual achievement of humane global governance. This fork has been complicated by the events of September 11, and possibly the perpetual war road has already been irrevocably chosen. Mary Kaldor asks:

> Will we look back on the last decade as the "happy nineties"? Was it an interregnum between global conflicts when utopian ideas like global civil society, human rights, a global rule of law, universal jurisdiction, and global social justice seemed possible? Or was it, on another interpretation, the moment when global civil society came of age?[o]

m. For various viewpoints, most of them sympathetic to universal jurisdiction, see Macedo, *supra* note **g.**

n. *See* President Bush Discusses Freedom in Iraq and Middle East: Remarks by the President at the 20th Anniversary of the National Endowment for Democracy, United States Chamber of Commerce(Washington, DC: The White House, 9 Nov 2003), *available at* <http://www.whitehouse.gov/news/releases/2003/11/ 20031106-2.html>.

o. M. Kaldor, Global Civil Society: An Answer to War 149 (2003).

Surely, as Chou-en-Lai is reputed to have said when asked in the middle of the 20th century for his assessment of the French Revolution, "it is too early to tell."

ELAZAR BARKAN, "AMENDING HISTORICAL INJUSTICES IN INTERNATIONAL MORALITY"
The Guilt of Nations xv-xli (Barken ed., 2000)

Virginia Woolf might have said that on or about March 5, 1997, world morality—not to say, human nature—changed. The reason was unexpected: In response to accusations of profiting from Jewish suffering during World War II, Switzerland announced its intention to sell substantial amounts of its gold to create a humanitarian fund of five billion dollars. The fund is to be dispensed to Holocaust victims who lost their money in Swiss banks and, further, to amend historical injustice worldwide. The surprise is not only that Switzerland rattled the financial markets and caused a fall in the price of gold, or even that Swiss bankers appeared to deviate from their image of stability, secrecy, and respectability, but that moral issues have become so powerful in the international arena they seem to turn even tailored bankers into compassionate radicals. In the process of deciding on this plan, the traditionally conservative Swiss citizens were forced to face the distress of world suffering and to embrace a policy that shed painful light on the past of their nation. The controversy recast Swiss wartime neutrality as aiding the production of the Nazi war machine. Instead of the Swiss defending their traditional and continued national identity of neutrality, their solution seemed to place Switzerland on the verge of becoming a global moral leader.

Well, not quite. The Swiss policy can also be viewed in a more pragmatic light, as a response to new world opinion in which appearing compassionate and holding the moral high ground has become a good investment. Viewed either way, however, Switzerland had been pulled into a historical whirlwind in which the nation's very identity and self-perception as a moral people were in doubt. By advocating the creation of the new humanitarian fund, the Swiss sought to reestablish their moral image and in the process expanded the notion of guilt and restitution. . . .

The demand that nations act morally and acknowledge their own gross historical injustices is a novel phenomenon. Traditionally realpolitik, the belief that realism rather than ideology or ethics should drive politics, was the stronghold of international diplomacy. But beginning at the end of World War II, and quickening since the end of the Cold War, questions of morality and justice are receiving growing attention as political questions. As such, the need for restitution to past victims has become a major part of national politics and international diplomacy.

The transition between 1989 and 1999 in the international arena has been dramatic. It includes the horrendous wars in Africa and Yugoslavia, as well as the liberation of Eastern Europe and South Africa and the return to democracy in many Latin American countries. Even these beneficial changes from totalitarian regimes or dictatorships have been painful experiences for many countries. In several of these transitions, instead of revenge against the perpetrators, truth and reconciliation committees have tried to weigh culpability on pragmatic scales. Concurrently, as the so-called realism of the Cold

War vanished, the United Nations, NATO, and individual countries struggle to define their own places in a world that is paying increased attention to moral values. Previously the fear of the unknown, the risk of a full confrontation with the Soviet Union, and the memory of Vietnam determined the West's lack of response to human catastrophes. But the new moral frame in the nineties confuses observers/critics and participants/politicians alike. Instead of containment, the rhetoric and motivation underscored high morals. Nowhere was this confusion more pronounced than in the case of NATO's intervention in Kosovo in 1999. Was it an old-fashioned intervention by the West, imperialism under a new guise? Or was it a noble humanitarian effort to stand up to perpetrators of crimes against humanity? The lack of consistency in carrying out humanitarian policies makes a favorable judgment harder. Yet the split within Western intellectuals, who are traditionally antiwar but were predominantly supportive of NATO over Kosovo, underscored this new phenomenon.

The new international emphasis on morality has been characterized not only by accusing other countries of human rights abuses but also by self-examination. The leaders of the policies of a new internationalism—Clinton, Blair, Chirac, and Schroder—all have previously apologized and repented for gross historical crimes in their own countries and for policies that ignored human rights. These actions did not wipe the slate clean, nor, as the story told in the book makes clear, were they a total novelty or unprecedented. Yet the dramatic shift produced a new scale: Moral issues came to dominate public attention and political issues and displayed the willingness of nations to embrace their own guilt. This national self-reflexivity is the new guilt of nations.

[In 1999,] Ian Buruma highlighted some controversial aspects of the focus on identity through victimization in contemporary society. What is alarming, writes Buruma, is the extent to which so many minorities have come to define themselves above all as historical victims. Not only does it reveal ... lack of historical perspective but it also seems a very peculiar source of pride. Buruma does not negate the memory of suffering by numerous communities, but he questions when a culture, ethnic, religious, or national community bases its communal identity almost entirely on the sentimental solidarity of remembered victimhood. For that way lie historical myopia and, in extreme circumstances, even vendetta. The problem, as Buruma sees it, is that this sense of victimization impedes understanding among people; it cannot result in mutual understanding.

Victimization is a growing industry, if you will, because it enjoys public validation, says Buruma, who is obviously correct in his concern about its significance. Victimization, however, implies the existence of a perpetrator. By focusing on its effect on the victims, Buruma does not deal with the perpetrators and leaves the guilt component of the equation, and therefore its effect on the identity of the perpetrator, unexplored. It is the growth of both identities—the victim and the perpetrator, both as subjective identities—that informs this new space in international and national politics. In contrast with the potential risk and morbidity of ... autistic self-indulgent victimization, the novelty in the discourse of restitution is that it is a discussion between the perpetrators and their victims. This interaction between perpetrator and victim is a new form of political negotiation that enables the rewriting of memory and historical identity in ways that both can share. Instead of categorizing all cases according to a certain universal guideline, the discourse depends upon the specific interactions in each case. Instead of seeing the increased role of victimization as a risk, the discourse of restitution underscores the opportunities and the ambivalence embedded in this novel form of politics. The political valence of restitution is significant and particularly powerful in the post-Cold War years, but it is neither omnipotence nor panacea.

Having recognized the new phenomenon, we may ask: How does a new insight of guilt change the interaction between two nations or between a government and its minority? How does this impact on the relative power of the protagonists within a national framework and the potential resolution of historical disputes? The book describes the response to the unfolding of guilt around the globe and focuses on those cases in which perpetrators and their descendants have either formally embraced guilt or become candidates for such an admission. This is not to say that the new standard is implemented worldwide, or that it is consistent, but rather that it provides for a new threshold of morality in international politics.

What, then, is the legacy of the perpetrators? I shall try to describe the specificity of the perpetrators' bequest in the next pages, but we could say at the outset that in those cases in which the victim and the perpetrator are engaged in negotiating a resolution of historical crimes, the relative strength of the victims grows. The issue of how this new voice (or strength) is translated into concrete policies remains. Despite a new international moral frame, it is clear that the standards vary and also that there is no accepted threshold for moral action or agreement. There is, however, a mechanism of negotiation and an aspiration for justice. While the results are hardly satisfactory to either party in the short run, in addition to improving the lives of the protagonists, resolutions of long-standing international disputes have become a mark of the new international order.

Legal convention defines restitution as only one form of the possible methods to amend past injustices; there are others, such as reparations or apologies. *Restitution* strictly refers to the return of the specific actual belongings that were confiscated, seized, or stolen, such as land, art, ancestral remains, and the like. *Reparations* refers to some form of material recompense for that which cannot be returned, such as human life, a flourishing culture and economy, and identity. *Apology* refers not to the transfer of material items or resources at all but to an admission of wrongdoing, a recognition of its effects, and, in some cases, an acceptance of responsibility for those effects and an obligation to its victims. However, these are all different levels of acknowledgment that together create a mosaic of recognition by perpetrators for the need to amend past injustices. Therefore, in the current context I refer to *restitution* more comprehensively to include the entire spectrum of attempts to rectify historical injustices. *Restitution* [as used herein] refers to the integrated picture that this mosaic creates and is thus not only a legal category but also a cultural concept.

From this broader perspective, it is appropriate to ask whether or not restitution for gross historical injustices in both international and domestic conflict resolutions has become a significant trend in contemporary politics worldwide, and if so, in what way? Is it a quest to revive a perpetrating nation's moral image while reversing the effects of international injustices and national victimization of oppressed groups or merely a sideshow in a violent world? We may also ask if these trends apply at all to countries like China or Serbia?... To evaluate these questions, we should examine the role of restitution in international morality, focusing on apologies by governments for historical criminal acts and on attempts by past victims to gain access to new resources. Particularly significant is the show of any explicit intent by perpetrators to compensate their victims and descendants in order to alleviate the most immediate and enduring deprivation and suffering. On a larger scale, we should look for the role of restitution in addressing disputes over national historical identities and cultural patrimonies. It is in this sense that restitution traverses the legal boundaries between actual restitution, reparation, compensation, and even apologies for wrongdoings and acquires cultural and political significance. While restitution applies in individual disputes, and reparation is part of class action suits (such as those involving victims of Agent Orange), I limit the discussion here and throughout the book ... to cases in which the injustices have been committed against groups because of their distinct identities.

Restitution is a large part of the growing attention being paid to human rights and itself testifies to the increased attention being paid to public morality and the augmented efforts to amend past injustices. This phenomenon is most often reported in the news within the context of local or national issues, but rarely does it receive attention as a global trend. Viewed as a trend, however, it provides particular insights into national and international debates during the last generation about the extension of Enlightenment principles and human rights to peoples and groups previously excluded from such considerations and into how such extensions potentially alter the very conceptualization of those principles and rights.

A fundamental alteration focuses on the realization that victims have rights as members of groups, which has called for a reexamination of our understanding of justice. Our notion of justice is broadly founded on the Enlightenment principle that human rights accrue to individuals. Today an emerging political sense stipulates that such rights may also accrue to groups. This particular view holds that while preserving individual human rights remains crucial, this in itself is no longer sufficient because people cannot enjoy full human rights if their identity as members of a group is violated. The emerging political sense, or neo-Enlightenment morality, which, among other notions (see below), posits the need for a combination of individual and group rights, creates a modern dilemma: How can the Enlightenment principles of individual rights and justice be applied to minorities and to the traditional cultures of indigenous peoples, and what principles can be applied to resolve, or at least to negotiate, the conflicts that arise when individual rights clash with those of a group? For example, governments in general do not recognize the communal legal identity of ethnic groups. To the degree that governmental policies are aimed at a group, implementation is often directed toward the individuals who belong to it. However, by accepting a policy of restitution, governments implicitly or explicitly accept a mechanism by which group identity receives growing recognition. I shall elaborate on the global significance of this mechanism and the new ... neo-Enlightenment morality that emerges from it in the last chapter, after describing its various manifestations.

How are we to investigate the new phenomenon and new sense of civil rights informed by this new morality? I shall start by describing a number of different restitution cases within a comparative narrative framework. These stories of restitution not only will shed cultural light on questions of moral responsibilities within the public sphere, or questions of historical guilt, or individual and group rights, but will also highlight the seemingly tangible and intangible political benefits of restitution.

HISTORICAL IDENTITY AS A NEGOTIATED IDENTITY

The recognition of group rights coincided with the increased attention to the malleable role of history in forming the identity of the nation. Long ago Johann Gottfried von Herder taught us that the nation is its own history. But the current heightened prestige and attention given to the historical identity of the nation present a paradox. It arrives at a time when the tentative nature of the historical narrative has become a commonplace and when skepticism regarding a true representation of the past has reached new heights. The public encounters competing histories that paint the past of every country, as well as its national identity, in several colors. These so-called imagined communities and invented traditions have come to dominate the discussion of nationalism over the last twenty-odd years. Despite (or perhaps because of) the historical tentativeness embedded in these constructed nationalisms, the significance of the historical component of identities has only increased in contemporary culture. The classical studies by Eric Hobsbawm and Benedict Anderson, who coined these concepts, show the different aspects of national identities. While nationalists claim that the nation is primordial, historians show that it is historically specific and often recently defined. The elasticity and specific limitation of this historical construction remain debatable, but as will be evident in the pages below, when politically construed, history can under specific circumstances be instantaneous.

The impact of the paradox between well-defined, recognized, and fixed cultures, on the one hand, and a fluid postcolonial world that recognizes increasing numbers of nations, on the other, is that we have to treat historical identities as negotiated. The recognition that a national identity is intertwined with competing identities is no longer confined to radical historians. The public accepts national identities as both invented and real. Politically, however, there are constraints on what a group can legitimately imagine as its history and culture. These limitations become particularly significant when national images and other identities encroach upon one another. Consequently, competing historical narratives have to negotiate over limited space and resources.

For a group identity to become noncontroversial, or at least generally accepted, it has to be recognized not only by advocates but also by competitors. Consider the evolution of the Western perception of the Palestine Liberation Organization, which shifted from terrorist organization to representative of a national authority to a nation. Hence the discussion of identities, and consequently of restitution, centers not just on political philosophy or moral theory but also on political conditions and social movements.

As mentioned above, the novelty of the urge to amend past injustices is that it addresses history through an effort to build an interpretation of the past that both parties could share. This approach occupies a middle ground that provides both a space to negotiate identities and a mechanism to mediate between national histories. It is a discourse about nationalism and a negotiation regarding whose story and what versions of the national narratives can be legitimated, not only by supporters but also by adversaries and impartial outsiders. For instance, the Jewish Holocaust ended in 1945, but it has continued ever since to impact on the lives of its victims and certainly to shape Jewish, German, and even other identities. Slavery has ended, but its consequences continue to shape race relations. Especially when these historical injustices are viewed in relation to the ongoing social injustice of anti-Semitism or racial discrimination, the nature of the historical injustice can be subject to conflicting narratives and the impact on negotiating the conflict can be significant. Consider the controversy over the Columbian quincentenary. Were Native Americans killed by the march of history as Europeans settled America, or were they the victims of a premeditated genocide? Or were they perhaps the unfortunate victims of a biological catastrophe and structural economic and technological changes? The contending narratives shape the identity of both perpetrators and victims, as each side is invested in a particular interpretation of the historical events....

My discussion of restitution begins as primarily descriptive. I examine the opportunities that peoples create by negotiating recognition of historical injustices as part of their revised national identity in order to facilitate the closure of a conflict. The last chapter explores the implications of the comparative cases, both for international morality and as a form of negotiated justice.

A Historical Overview

To explicate restitution further as a cultural, political, and legal concept, I use it in contrast with enforced retribution—or punishment—and with the age old custom of imposed war reparations. Traditionally the winner imposed various payments on the loser. The Bible describes in some detail Abraham's demands after defeating the five kings. Three millennia later the moral entitlement of the winner had diminished very little. The Versailles Treaty (1919)[p] postulated harsh terms for the losers. In public memory the war indemnity levied upon Germany in 1919 caused, or at least heavily contributed to, World War II. The wisdom of the Versailles terms was strongly criticized along realpolitik lines and the perceived failure of the policies of vindictiveness. Having learned from experience, the Allies in 1945 did not impose reparations upon Germany. Instead the United States accepted the burden of rebuilding Europe and Japan and initiated the Marshall Plan. This introduced a novel factor into international relations: Rather than hold to a moral right to exploit enemy resources, as had been done previously, the victor underscored future reconciliation and assisted its defeated enemies to reestablish themselves. In hindsight the policy is widely celebrated.

Within this context of nonvindictiveness the modern concept of restitution was born, and it is from this point that I examine specific cases.

p. Treaty of Peace, 28 Jun 1919, 225 C.T.S.
188.

Germany, acting on vaguely comparable motivations of perceived international interests but also on its unique need to reestablish political and moral legitimacy, sought to repent for its sins under Nazism by reaching an agreement with its victims. In 1952 the Germans began to pay compensation, but instead of paying the winners, they paid those they had victimized the worst—primarily the Jews. While the Allies' Marshall Plan and their nonretributive stance toward Germany may have been imaginative politics, the innovative phenomenon in the German–Jewish agreement was that the perpetrator compensated the victims of its own volition in order to facilitate self-rehabilitation. This political arrangement benefitted both sides. In forcing an admission of war guilt at Versailles, rather than healing, the victors instigated resentment that contributed to the rise of Fascism. In contrast, Germany's voluntarily admission of responsibility for the Holocaust and consequent restitution to its victims provided a mechanism to enable Germany to move beyond its crimes and facilitate its healing.

This admission of guilt had to be done in concord with the victims. In this case the restitution agreement was formulated between West Germany and Israel, both descendant entities of the perpetrators and the victims. The idea of compensation, the rhetoric of guilt, and limited recognition-forgiveness were translated, through the legal medium of restitution, into new possibilities in international relations. The Holocaust was not undone, but as in mourning, restitution provided a mechanism for dealing with pain and recognizing loss and responsibility, while enabling life to proceed.

The agreement between Germany and the Jews turned out to be one of the most significant cornerstones of the newly formed German Federal Republic. Viewing them as a moral obligation as well as a pragmatic policy, Germany provided reparations to victims who were in no political position to enforce such payments or indeed to refuse them. The German–Jewish agreement, which included Jewish recognition of the German attempt to atone for its crimes but not forgiveness of them, became the foundation for further reconciliation between Germans and Jews, led to the rehabilitation of Germany, and contributed to the economic survival of Israel. This was the moment at which the modern notion of restitution for historical injustices was born. In the public's memory of gross historical injustices, the Holocaust is unique in the very debate about its uniqueness. It has become a yardstick for the ultimate genocide against which victims of other historical crimes measure their own suffering. The German reparations that followed the war became the gauge for future restitution claims.

A generation after Germany had begun to pay restitution to Jewish victims, other victims of World War II called for reparations. The first case was concluded when, in the late 1980s, the American government compensated Japanese Americans interned in camps during the war. The agreement was particularly successful because it quantified a historical injustice and translated it into a specific sum acceptable to both the victims as compensation and the government as an expense. The resolution quickly became a model for other groups that demanded justice. African–Americans and other victims of the slave trade were quick to cite the agreement as a precedent for their own renewed claims. Among other restitution disputes originating in World War II, the debate over art treasures looted from Germany by the Soviet Union at the end of the war is of particular interest. During the course of the war

Germany plundered, but mostly destroyed, huge amounts of European and Russian cultural treasures and sites. As the war ended, Russia turned the tables and plundered massive amounts from Germany. The Russian claim is that their twenty-seven million dead and the destruction of Russian patrimony justified Russia's plunder of art from Germany. This is at best a controversial claim. But for many Russians the museums' looted treasures became a source of national pride—the last vestige after losing the Cold War-and an integral part of Russian identity in the Duma's eyes. The swiftness with which this previously hidden and unknown loot became a national treasure bestows on the construction of invented tradition a postmodern pace. Yet Germany's relatively weak contestation of the Russian response to its claim for return of the treasures is indicative. First, it suggests a recognition that certain injustices—in this case, ... Russian looting within [the] specific context of Germany's destruction and plunder of Russia—may become ethical. Second, it suggests that in contrast with the conventional wisdom that only after a relatively long time can a national tradition be established, there may not be a minimal time or pace that is needed for inventing a national tradition. Another facet of Nazi plunder that occupied the international agenda during the mid-nineties was the role banks played, primarily in Switzerland but also in many other countries, in laundering Nazi gold and art loot. Suddenly the morality of neutrality was reexamined as an act of collaboration.

The Japanese response in the aftermath of World War II was very different from that of Germany. Following Hiroshima and Nagasaki, Japan claimed victim status and refused to acknowledge any responsibility for its war crimes. It came under a particular flood of public criticism regarding its treatment of enemy women, those who were known as the comfort women, during World War II. An initially small protest by women's organizations turned into widespread anti-Japanese sentiment in several Asian countries. But Japan did not budge. For a short period it seemed as though Japan might respond to the criticism, but this misconception quickly evaporated. A feeble official intimation that Japan was indeed responsible for the crime of enslaving women into sexual servitude during the war was never transformed into a confession of its role in the war and certainly not into a deep self-reexamination of Japanese history. Yet this was the beginning of a political debate within Japan over the war and the country's responsibility for its acts. From national commemorations to school textbooks, the debate over moral responsibility for its historical crimes is becoming more consequential within Japan than in its negotiations in the international arena.* * *

In the wake of the collapse of the Soviet system and the end of the Cold War, new sentiments of human rights spread to East Central Europe and became part of the political rhetoric. The most urgent matter governments faced was to create an infrastructure for economic prosperity. Most countries began to privatize property, but informed by the notion of rights and historical justice, they chose to combine it with some form of restitution. Thus the implementation of capitalism through privatization and restitution became not only a way to rebuild the national economy but also a way to establish a new moral national identity. Most striking in this sense was that in distinction to other parts of the world, in this region the common denominator of restitution was used to justify ethnic homogeneity. In contrast with the multicultural and multiethnic Hapsburg tradition before World War I, the new Eastern Europe opted for the monolithic nation. In every country the process of rebuilding was delayed while considerations of justice and morality conflicted with privatization. The distribution of previously state-owned property to private citizens was made more problematic by the states' need to account for the various claims of ownership. The choice each of these countries made regarding the restitution of ownership rights was a choice about its national culture. Although each country in East Central Europe chose to restitute these rights in a different way, all emphasized national homogeneity and excluded minorities. After 1989 Poland privileged the church, the Czech Republic restored private (upper-and middle-class) rights, while Romania limited initial restitution to the peasants. Each country declared its national identity, at least in part, by recognizing and sanctioning the rights of one set of victims while denying other victims theirs. This was of particular interest when Jewish and German minorities were concerned. In Eastern Europe the level of validity assigned to Jewish and German claims brings into sharp relief the relative weight of morality and pragmatic politics and of deserving and undeserving victims.

Another sphere of restitution cases resulted from the postcolonial condition. Together with the expansion of civil rights to minorities and women, there evolved a new willingness to recognize the place of indigenous peoples in the modern nation. It is here that the extension of the principle of equality to groups previously denied such treatment has, first, expanded the notion of who deserves individual human rights and, second, reformulated these rights to include group rights. During the 1960s the recognition that such rights must be extended to indigenous peoples grew in English-speaking countries, then spread to Latin America. Indigenous demands for rights translated into a call for recognizing historical injustices and amending them or, in some cases, into a call for full or semisovereignty. In their struggle for legitimacy, indigenous peoples present a major challenge to the contemporary nation-state's self-perception as a just society and a unified sovereign nation, and many of these debates are conducted within the framework of negotiating restitution. For example, legislation regarding Native American rights is influenced by the moral rhetoric of restitution and closely resembles the debate in Australia, New Zealand, and Canada. In all these countries the indigenous individual is both a minority citizen and a member of an indigenous nation. At times, especially but not limited to when indigenous groups call for full or semisovereignty, these affiliations conflict and make the nation's reexamination more difficult. During the eighties and into the mid-nineties a widespread expansion of indigenous rights occurred. Negotiating property rights—land, economic resources, and cultural property—through restitution to indigenous peoples became the norm that defines the national conversation in several contemporary pluralistic societies. As the international community pays increased attention to group and individual rights, victims of imperialism from Native Americans in the United States (and other ex-British colonies) to numerous groups in the Fourth World demand *new* rights as restitution. These rights run the gamut from exemptions from antigambling laws and casino licenses to mineral extraction, fishing treaties, and monetary compensation for traditional knowledge (copyrights). Philosophically and legally the distinction between compensation for lost development rights and reparations for repression and victimization is significant and historically has unfolded differently. Together these two types of claim have produced a new quilt of rights. While the rhetoric of restitution is gaining momentum, the practical demands face the difficulties of conflicting rights, of rival national identity claims, and of competition for resources. What is the role of restitution in negotiating the contradiction between group rights and a universal morality and in mediating the dichotomy between the rhetoric of justice and real world prosperity? Simultaneously, the notion that group suffering deserves restitution evolved in the United States between the 1950s and the 1970s as the civil rights movement and the politics of the Great Society program informed a new political morality that led to affirmative action. Although these movements were not framed in the language of restitution, they raised to public consciousness moral considerations that would inform a greater receptivity to minorities and a validation of the ethnic plurality of the nation. *E pluribus unum.* The growing legitimacy of group identity in competition with national identity became the basis of calls for domestic restitution. As survivors and descendants of past wars, colonialism, and national disputes return to demand justice, the long list of restitution claims grows, and it becomes apparent that the range of issues confronting groups of victims is similar. The cultural debate, which aims at translating these past confrontations into contemporary restitution, involves a host of specific decisions. These include questions not only about what constitutes fair reparation but also about who is entitled to it. Is blood relationship or direct lineage an essential component? Is there a statute of limitations on national injustices? These are the fundamental criteria in issues of inheritance law. In contrast, demands for compensation on the basis of shared culture, regardless of the actual blood relationship, present a new and growing challenge. One of the most widely reaching, and most morally intriguing, cases is that of the descendants of slaves....

* * *

In the United States and more recently in other countries the question of restitution for slavery has been reopened. Among the issues is the dilemma concerning the nature of the groups involved. Who are the victims, and who ought to be compensated? Descendants of slaves? All blacks? What of those of mixed race? Also, who are the perpetrators: descendants of slaveowners; all whites; the society in general? What is the relationship between the historical group that was enslaved and contemporary African Americans, between the southern slaveholders and the current US taxpayer? Have the groups been transformed in such a way that the injustices are no longer amendable? Finally, which of the wide spectrum of injustices against the slaves ought to be restituted? Even before the economic aspect is addressed, the first stage in reaching an agreement would be to retell the polarized antagonistic histories as a core of shared history to which both sides can subscribe and from which each will benefit. Similar dilemmas exist throughout the African diaspora. This attempt to resolve these competing narratives through negotiations is highly controversial, but it is a necessary stage if reparations for slavery could ever ameliorate race relations, even if it does not provide a closure to this historical injustice.

One new measure of this public morality is the growing political willingness, and at times eagerness, to admit ones ... historical guilt. As a result of admitting their guilt, the perpetrators may expect to have cleaner consciences and even direct political payoff. Either way, the apology is evidence of the public's distress in carrying the burden of guilt for inflicting suffering and possibly of its empathy with the victims. For example, Queen Elizabeth has lately found herself apologizing around the globe: to the Maoris and the Sikhs. Despite certain mockery, mostly in the conservative London press or postcolonial electronic bulletin boards, there was little downside to her apologies. In general, objections from the recipients come because they believe the apologies do not go far enough, not because they reject the notion of apologies in principle. Similar to the Maoris and the Sikhs, some among indigenous Hawaiians who received an apology from the American government on the centennial anniversary of their conquest (1993) cried hypocrisy. The Clinton administration's apology risked little yet provided most parties with a sense of accomplishment and virtue.

An apology doesn't mean the dispute is resolved, but it is in most cases a first step, part of the process of negotiation but not the satisfactory end result. Often lack of apologies, demands for apologies, and the refusal of them all are presteps in negotiations, a diplomatic dance that may last for a while, a testimony to the wish and the need of both sides to reach the negotiations stage. Consider the debate over the American government's apology for slavery. The calculus of apology involves addressing disagreements about how guilty the perpetrators were and how much and for what their descendants should repent. Despite the oft-contentious debate, the principle of apology is increasingly accepted. At the very minimum these apologies lead to a reformulated historical understanding that itself is a form of restitution and become a factor in contemporary politics and humanitarian actions.

* * *

Admitting responsibility and guilt for historical injustices is in part a result of the relative strength of the political voice the victims can mount.... But it has also become a liberal marker of national political stability and strength rather than shame. It is an attempt to recognize that nations have to come to terms with their own pasts, primarily responsibility for the others, their victims. In contrast, nondemocracies are less inclined to admit guilt because tribal ideologues and fundamentalists view the world through noncompromising lenses. Democracies are more open to it, and while clearly not all democracies are eager to amend historical injustices, they are more likely to do so than nondemocracies. But the vague standard of restitution means that the national cultural variations remain crucial.

In addition to solving a specific dispute, restitution agreements and negotiations around the globe provide possible models for other outstanding conflicts, such as peace negotiations. Bound between the conflicting principles of prosperity (utilitarianism) and morality (rights), and against the context of inequality and oppression, restitution provides a space to negotiate agreements. Neither principle exists in a pure form in restitution; rather, they inform the emerging policies around the world. The different parties that subscribe to restitution benefit from the new rhetoric by having their historical narratives and identities validated, at the cost of admitting that their histories are contaminated by injustices.

JUDGING HISTORICAL INJUSTICES

I use the concept of historical injustice here in a limited sense to refer to recognition by alleged perpetrators of their own commission of gross injustices over the last fifty years or to demands for such recognition from victims. Although history is paved with unjust, criminal, exploitative, and genocidal actions that the public has always recognized as social and political injustices, in most cases these narratives painted the injustices [as resulting from the actions] of someone else, often the enemy. Amending such injustices was not on the political agenda. In contrast, in the case of the historical injustices referred to here, perpetrators or their descendants accept, or are considering accepting, responsibility for actions that constituted gross atrocities. They do so for political and moral reasons: because they recognize that the historical injustices continue to impact on not only the well-being and identity of the victims but also on their own identity as perpetrators. It should be emphasized as well that in recognizing the most egregious historical injustices, only one layer of injustices is amended. In most cases the history of the protagonists is more complex, but other injustices, which are also part of its history, are ignored.

What constitutes such a historical injustice? Why are certain inhumanities classified as gross historical atrocities while others are merely forgotten? How does the public recognize an action or policy as a historical injustice that requires amending, as opposed to a discriminatory practice that requires change but not restitution?

Historical injustices and political and social discriminatory practices should be treated as separate and ideal types in the Weberian sense. Historical injustices are those that have ended even though their consequences continue to impact on the survivors. Discrimination is an ongoing social and political problem. The United States' approach to Native Americans may give us a good example of both. The American strategy to address *historical* injustice includes a distinct set of decisions and regulations intended as compensation and restitution for lost property. (The largest litigated case concerns the Black Hills in and around the Dakotas, and there is growing legislation that addresses the multifaceted aspects of indigenous cultural loss.) ... Separately it addresses political and social discriminatory practices and adopts a strategy that includes a set of antidiscrimination policies (welfare). Despite the dissimilar temporality and rationality, there is an overlap between historical injustices and contemporary discrimination. This is to be expected since historical injustices are numerous, but redress is limited to the victims, who continue to suffer the consequences of the original injustice but can mobilize sufficient political and moral leverage to lay blame effectively at the perpetrators' doorstep. The temporal distinctions remain significant nonetheless, especially where the current generation is unwilling to assume responsibility for past injustices. In the court of public opinion, historical events are judged out of context and in light of contemporary moral standards. The public suspends a belief in cultural pluralism and ethical relativism and, on the basis of local, provisional, and superior moral presentism as well as growing egalitarianism (more on this later), views the past as a foreign, disdained culture. It may be willing to embrace certain cultural legacies, but in true buffet style, it chooses only the very appetizing dishes. Thus in the United States the Constitution may be viewed as a sacred document, but the Founding Fathers who wrote it are denigrated as DWMs (dead white males) whose world was founded on surplus capital produced by slavery. Similarly, the public looks at wars through lenses that see only heroes and villains, winners and criminals. History spares the public the need to make subtle choices or recognize complex situations or to see that good and evil inhabit the same space. Far enough from the events and out of context, there are no instances in which suffering will not animate sympathy or in which destruction will not be denounced, often on both sides of the conflict. The parity of suffering makes everyone a potential victim in some context. The evil of Nazism clearly elicited Russian retribution that is, in hindsight, hard to justify and is the subject of current international disputes. In what way were the millions of German refugees from Central and East Europe (1945–48) victims compared with the rest of the European refugees at the time? Ought they to be recognized as victims and receive restitution, or were they unlucky perpetrators? Also, in the case of the plundered art, if both countries were to restitute what plundered treasures remained, because Germany destroyed so much, it would mean that Russia would be deprived of its own material culture while Germany would regain possession of its. Would that constitute a better or just solution? Far from the pandemonium of the war the international public is happy to take the moral high road. The presentist dilemma, of viewing history from the contemporary perspective, is whether or not such actions ought to be judged against the horror of the war or against some other global, abstract, moral standard. Is the public really in a position to legitimate retribution as justice? These questions are particularly troublesome since the delegitimation of morality as such, in public discourse. Martin Heidegger, the Frankfurt school, an array of postmodernists, and revisionist historians have been happy to lay responsibility for all injustices at the feet of technology, progress, and the Enlightenment. This clearing of any moral actors from politics presumably spares one from the need to make any moral judgment. The public, however, is not content with such an abdication of moral responsibility even if the alternative resulting standards at times conflict and are more confusing. This is also part of the new, fuzzy neo-Enlightenment morality that recognizes historical injustices despite the limitations of vague and provisional standards and resolves it through negotiation. Democracies seem to prefer limited moral standards to the total abdication of responsibility. A quilt of these local exemplars composes the spectrum of global morality. [*Eds.*—The author notes the perils of *presentism*, which he defines as the tendency to view history from a contemporary (and therefore necessarily incomplete) perspective. He continues:]

When the public judges historical events as crimes or injustices according to contemporary moral values, the judgment is often anachronistic. However, at times the criminal nature of historical actions has been indisputable; it has been clear at the time even to the perpetrators. Crimes against humanity perpetrated during World War II or in Bosnia in the 1990s fall into this category, and there is no anachronism in judging them as such. Such actions can be recognized as crimes even if they were committed by agents of a regime that was, and still may be, considered legitimate by the international community. This was the case with Nazi Germany, which led to the novelty of the Nuremberg trials. The international community views in a similar light the policies of contemporary totalitarian regimes. In other instances, changing moral and cultural canons reclassify previous actions. At times acts that were viewed as noble, even altruistic by the general public have become injustices.

Consider the legacy of archaeological efforts to excavate ancient ruins and anthropological aspirations to salvage the culture of disappearing indigenous peoples. The heroic results of those efforts by great (often) men exist in museums around the world. Over time, however, these actions have been reevaluated as appropriation and domination. Similarly, scientific efforts by physical anthropologists to study the remains of indigenous peoples have recently been reclassified as grave robbing. If the ethics of possessing certain museum collections is controversial even now, the immorality of slavery is now uncontested. When we (re)classify historical acts as injustices, we presumably determine that were we to face similar choices, we would act differently. Notwithstanding whether or not *each of us* would really act differently in a slaveowning society, the public views even historical slavery as morally wrong and may expect historical figures to have behaved accordingly. Should sentiments about this expectation increase, as a society that recognizes its own responsibility for the historical injustice of slavery we may face the dilemma of whether or not, and how, to compensate the victims. [*Eds.—* the author notes that the enterprise of archaeology, once viewed as benign or even noble, is now sometimes derided as "graverobbing" or "expropriation."]

A principled argument in favor of restitution is that no matter how long ago the injustice occurred, its legitimization only encourages other wrongdoings. The counterargument is that since there is no passage of time without changed circumstances, the perceived injustices may have been over time erased by historical changes. This is not to say that the mere passage of time lends legitimacy to the results of injustices but rather that changed circumstances do. This presentist moral predicament exists in regard to every historical injustice.

Consider, for example, the Arab–Israeli dispute in which changed conditions have reversed the moral stakes. The late-nineteenth-century Zionist national movement attempted to reverse the historical clock by returning Jews to Palestine and by eventually creating an independent Jewish state. The historical suffering by Jews was not then, and is not now, widely questioned. As a group they endured their share of injustices. After World War II there was wide international support for the establishment of Israel despite Arab opposition. Yet changing historical circumstances meant that restoring the historical right to a homeland to the Jews even in part instigated injustices against the Palestinians. Those injustices are now recognized worldwide. They were not so in 1948. There are no meta-principles by which to measure these contradictory rights or injustices. The colonial system circa 1900, which morally and politically legitimized the Zionist return, may no longer hold up. A century later the historical change recontextualized the self-identity of Palestinians and Israelis in regard to who are the victims and the perpetrators. Both Zionist and Palestinian historical narratives are being reexamined and revised according to the contemporary political situation. In this sense, present political injustices shape the historical narrative. Negotiating the resolution of the conflict includes creating the framework for the new historical narrative and national identity. The shortcomings of presentism in historical analysis are great, yet it is seductive and has political and moral power that cannot be ignored. It also enables new opportunities to resolve national conflicts.

RESTITUTION AS NEGOTIATED JUSTICE

Over the last two generations the writing of history has shifted focus from the history of perpetrators to the history of victims. Replacing the stories of elites with the histories of everyday life has necessarily illuminated the ongoing victimization of large segments of humanity along the lines of gender, class, and race discrimination. (Even though the stories themselves often underscored the agency and relative control the victims had over their own lives, the context was one of oppression.) As victorious histories of the elite and the rich are replaced by the lives of the conquered, the poor, and the victimized other, the public is confronted by history as the territory of injustice. In the democratization of historical memory, the public over time encounters its own identity, one that includes immoral acts, suffering, and oppression. Although the political system seems reluctant to take radical steps to heal contemporary injustices, it seems more willing to entertain the possibility of amending historical injustices.

Cultural property turns out to be a particularly appropriate medium for negotiating historical injustices. Cultural property embodies the group's national identity. Specific cultural objects in every society bear the mark of that society's unique identity. Demands for restitution of such objects as the Parthenon Marbles, the Benin Bronzes, and Mesoamerican treasures and of indigenous sites of cultural significance go beyond the economic value of the objects because the group's identity is invested in them. The international community increasingly recognizes these issues and attempts to formulate agreements to address cultural property as inalienable patrimony, the time limitations of historical injustices, and the place of the individual in a communal culture. UNESCO now heads efforts to codify a series of international agreements about cultural property. The significance of cultural property increases not only for reasons of national identity but also because its control carries substantial economic consequences, including the future of tourism and museums. These discussions are particularly befitting to a fuzzy moral logic, beginning from specific cases and generalizing to mediate economic interests, culture, religion, and politics within and among rival societies.

How, then, are we to look at the international order as a moral system? Admittedly a discussion of a moral international system ought to be viewed with skepticism. The public is justifiably disillusioned with the dramatic political movements or major social upheavals of the twentieth century that promised Utopian solutions only to lead to terrible wars and human disasters, which contributed to further estrangement from politics and inoculation against any belief in striking solutions. This alienation is reinforced by the inability of international organizations to put a stop to the worst human disasters. Some would go further and argue that there is no international system at all, merely anarchy. This view is too pessimistic. I think Michael Walzer is right to describe the international system as a tolerant system with a very weak regime in which some member states (nondemocratic and totalitarian) are intolerant. In extreme cases the international community uses sanctions and even force to rein in a stray (offender) government. Increasingly, however, the international system combines incremental levels of cooperation, from the most minimal general obligations to a comprehensive set of goals shared by groups of countries. At a profound level, it is a voluntary democratic system, as members determine their own willingness to commit certain resources to achieve a particular aim. The system also includes a moral standard to which countries can choose to subscribe, at times voluntarily and at times with prompting. The Nobel Peace Prize for 1997, which was awarded to the International Campaign to Ban Landmines, was a striking example of the expanded space of ethics in a new post-Cold War international politics. The organization, a coalition of about one thousand organizations in more than sixty countries, successfully applied public moral pressure to governments the world over to sign the international convention. It was praised by the Nobel Committee as an exciting new form of a broad grass roots coalition of citizens' groups that, by applying moral political pressure and working outside existing international organizations, led to world change. The convention's success is especially noteworthy, both because it seems so exceptional as a moral campaign and because it embodies a polarized view to the realpolitik of international relations. The weakness of most political campaigns with a moral edge is shaped by a public that has little appetite for activism or political responsibility, even in cases in which there is a wide commitment to achieve social justice. Instead the political agenda is formulated in a jargon of minimal governmental action. This isolationism supports a status quo informed by a market economy and a distancing from such unsavory issues as poverty and even more so from mass killings or genocides.

Moral isolationism impoverishes public culture. Thus even in the midst of prosperity public opinion does not look to the future with any great confidence or hope. The political agenda focuses instead on personal future and growing prosperity to the exclusion of other values. But few mistake this for happiness, or even moral fulfillment, in the land of uncertainty. Above all, public culture is devoid of commitment or an intellectual pledge to any course of action. Instead the political culture is predisposed to view the shortcomings and injustices embedded in every policy and therefore, absolutely abhors the idea of political commitments even in the name of a moral agenda. In *Democracy's Discontent* Michael Sandel attempts to come to terms with the malaise of contemporary public culture. Locked between postmodern nihilism, relativism, and individual liberalism, he represents the agony of public intellectuals over moral policies that are at best tentative, hesitant, and inconclusive. Contrary to conventional shibboleth, this growing alienation may be the result not of ignorance but of informed opinion. Public culture recognizes that most conflicts are too complicated to adjudicate and hence withdraws from any involvement. Which was the blameless side in the former Yugoslavia or Rwanda?

The frequent appearance that the most violent of conflicts continue unperturbed, and the notion that pariah dictators are able to ignore public opinion altogether, may make the public skeptical spectators. Nonetheless we ought to remember that even where appropriate responses were lacking, the rhetoric of war crimes and international policing did lead to international tribunals. Perhaps the limited authority of these international tribunals should be compared not only with a wishful Utopia, or even with controversial armed intervention, but with the Cold War cases of genocide in Biafra and Cambodia that went unpunished. Under no circumstances should one be less than appalled by the international response to these disasters. Yet these tribunals show the increasing desire, if not always the efficacy, of the international community to act morally.

[*Eds.*—The author notes, following Michael Walzer, that the international community operates as an imperfect moral regime with weak enforcement, in which member states have a limited freedom to be intolerant. The author goes on to contend, first, that this imperfection does not justify moral isolationism, which "impoverishes public culture." Rather, for Barkan, even the most hardened skeptic must admit that there is, at the very least, a growing international "desire" (manifested, as Barkan notes, in the increasing prevalence of tribunals, however ineffective) to "act morally."]

Morality is manifested differently in numerous other conflicts in the world; they are primarily struggles for recognition by minorities and indigenous peoples, such as the Maoris or the Hawaiian Nation, which simmer rather than explode. Power continues to play a crucial role, but morality and the appeal to world public opinion have become decisive political instruments and are manifested in negotiations of international treaties and conflicts. The abolition of apartheid in South Africa is perhaps the best recent example of the efficacy of international solidarity.

In several countries, including South Africa, Argentina, Chile, and Uruguay governments as well as nongovernmental organizations (NGOs), as they are known in the United Nations, have launched commissions of truth and reconciliation. In an effort to come to terms with the immediate authoritarian past. Those who believed that the commissions' goals were that the perpetrators admit their crimes and that the victims and their relatives simply forgive and forget were, not surprisingly, disappointed. More realistic expectations focused on improving the police and judiciary system and relieving human rights abuses. On relatively few occasions, perpetrators were prosecuted. One must not forget that the international validation (and often the finance) of these commissions conferred a prestige that in turn underscored the benefits of justice and respect for human rights as an international currency of goodwill. The impetus varied, with some countries attempting to follow the commissions with material reparations and compensations. Punishment, in contrast, has generally failed. For example, lustration and other methods have been aborted in Eastern Europe. Yet retroactive justice seriously engages a growing number of societies in their transition to democracy. In these cases, rather than aim at an absolute standard of justice or morality, the attempts are aimed at carefully negotiating justice so that it is politically feasible.

The rush to restitution since the 1980s has been informed in part by the delegitimation of armed conflict as the Cold War waned, often transferring the desire for recognition into diplomacy. Whereas, in the 1970s, radical activists within these groups resorted to violence, in the 1990s their activism has shifted to diplomacy and demands for restitution. This shift is most visible among indigenous peoples, including Native Americans, Aborigines, and Maoris.

Against this notion of increased morality, we are faced with the weak political response to human disasters and the sense of a bankrupt international system that seems to contradict the increased integration of the world economy and the necessarily high degree of cooperation. Critics view this presumed cooperation as a neocolonial system in which the rich nations are able to exploit the rest of the world (as well as the domestic poor) more efficiently. Recognizing this hegemony, we are left to ponder: What are the existing alternatives to the ills of the market economy as a global ideology? Could these be even less appealing? We find alternatives in the form of national ideologies and religious fundamentalism that reject Enlightenment values and liberalism. Notwithstanding the local popularity of these ideologies, they carry little appeal outside their own specific group. They aspire to provide a worldview and a moral guidance to their followers but are seen by outsiders as repressive totalitarian instruments. They are not candidates for adoption by outsiders, nor do they provide a mechanism to negotiate conflict resolutions. The liberal pragmatic West sees these ideologies as the cause of civil wars and other catastrophes that plague the world. While people in the West object to these ideologies, they find it hard to articulate a counterideology to which they can subscribe or even to reject these ideologies from a coherent perspective. Is Algerian fundamentalism fighting an oppressive military regime, or is it a terrorist organization? We find these questions perplexing. We embrace tradition but only in its liberal guise, as long as it is inoffensive, is open-minded, and can accommodate pluralism. Tradition, however, often sustains national tribal hate, oppression, and prejudice, which the public does not support as moral policies. The public likes nationalism for its self-definition and identity assertion but dislikes it for its racist and patriarchal manifestations. A separation of these forces, alas, is not always possible.

Short of conservative efforts to invent a cohesive past, political philosophers are very ambivalent in their attempts to point toward positive alternatives. Since the political situation is too complex and distressing, denial replaces involvement. Distancing breeds skepticism as well as guilt. Occasionally we see an ephemeral willingness to empathize with both sides of a conflict that is informed by moral presentism and in which humanitarian intervention is viewed as a noble action. The public's inability to formulate a proactive political agenda does not obliterate the distress at human catastrophes and is not for lack of caring. The closest we come as pragmatists to a positivist ideology is to reject suffering. Bosnia was horrific, yet we were equally distressed at the thought of committing resources, let alone life, to change it.

[*Eds.*—The author argues that, despite the liberal West's general inability to articulate a "coherent *riposte*" to criticisms of the widespread adoption of the market economy as political ideology, or to articulate precisely its objections to ideological and religious fundamentalist ideologies, there is nonetheless a broad and growing distress at humanitarian catastrophes, however caused. Indeed, the author notes, "[t]he closest we come as pragmatists to a positivist ideology is to reject suffering."]

THE CHALLENGE OF RESTITUTION

Against the background of a moral malaise, does restitution provide a moral opportunity? The political calculus of restitution aims to privilege a moral rhetoric, to address the needs of past victims, and to legitimate a discussion about a redistribution of resources around the globe. A strong case for restitution would underscore a moral economy that would calculate and quantify evil and would place a price on amending injustices. Such a theory of justice would obviously suffer from all the shortcomings of utilitarianism that have been exposed over the last two hundred years. After all, who could quantify genocide? Yet the moral high ground has its own disadvantages. One virtue the moral economy of restitution may present would be that it does not propose a universal solution but strives to evaluate conflicts in light of a vague standard and to be pragmatically mediated by the protagonists themselves. Would an atmosphere of restitution and apologies create motivation for the perpetrators to submit to the judgment of the victims and facilitate an economy in which distributive justice is shaped by the reciprocal contribution of the protagonists to each other's identity?

Does restitution signal a new relationship between powerful and weak nations? Does it change the relationship between the rich and the poor? In a world fraught with civil wars, ethnic cleansing, separatism, and human rights abuses, it is only too easy to reject the very notion of a moral stand. Yet victims around the world refuse this easy option. Instead they often prefer to receive even token reparations as symbolic of recognition; they are eager for the perpetrators to acknowledge the past and to provide a shared escape route for a new beginning. In this case victims and perpetrators collaborate in searching for an exit from the bonds of history. This morality may have particular cachet in our postcolonial world, in which peoples' identities include their histories and sufferings. Descendants and survivors of peoples who were conquered, colonized, dominated, decimated, or enslaved may come to recognize that a new international standard enables them to establish new relations with the descendants of the perpetrators. Each new relationship is dependent not only on moral considerations but also on political and social power relations. Beyond the moral framework, groups have to pursue their claims politically and persuade different constituencies of their just claims.

* * *

Under such new circumstances restitution may demonstrate that acting morally carries tangible and intangible political and cultural benefits. Yet we must temper our enthusiasm. It is only against the poverty of the international community's inability to prevent or mitigate human disasters that restitution provides a beacon of morality. Its attractiveness results from presenting local moral solutions in a deeply immoral and unjust world. Restitution argues for a morality that recognizes an ensemble of rights beyond individual rights, and it privileges the right of peoples to reject external impositions and decide for themselves. Does the rhetoric of restitution then open a new opportunity for victims to demand historical justice? As the language of restitution becomes central to negotiations over group rights, a door is opened to a new potential redistribution of justice. A theory of conflict resolution based on restitution may illuminate the efforts by many nations and minorities to gain partial recognition and overcome conflicting historical identities through the construction of a shared past. Contemporary international discourse underscores the growing role of guilt, mourning, and atonement in national revival and in recognizing the identity of a historically victimized group. But could restitution turn a traumatic experience into a constructive national narrative and identity? . . .

RICHARD FALK, "THE FIRST NORMATIVE GLOBAL REVOLUTION?: THE UNCERTAIN POLITICAL FUTURE OF GLOBALIZATION"

Globalizations and Civilizations 51–76 (Medhi Mozaffari, ed. 2002)

A revolutionary prospect

Jacques Barzun warns us at the outset of *From Dawn to Decadence* that "[w]e have gotten into the habit of calling too many things revolutions," and so we have. To claim, then, a "revolutionary" prospect on the horizon of international political and cultural life is to accept a heavy burden of persuasion. It is not only a matter of not contributing further to the dilution of the idea of revolution as entailing a fundamental transformation, but also of countering a historical mood of post-utopian skepticism about large jumps for the better in the human condition. The disillusionment that accompanied the failures of state socialism as reinforced by the defeat of the cultural revolution that was at the core of the turmoil of 1968, makes doubters of us all. This anti-revolutionary mood extends even to the point of admitting that seeking a promised land tends to make modest ethical gains of an incremental character unlikely, and certainly more difficult. This is due to a conservative backlash that generally achieves strict control of thought and action in the aftermath of failed revolutionary projects. This pattern of hostility to progressive social change whether domestic or international, in the main, captures the spirit of the times during the 1990s and the early 21st Century.

If revolutionary rhetoric survives at all during this period as a positive prospect, it is with reference to a set of materialist claims that market forces, integrating via computer, satellite, and optic fiber, will generate an era of abundance and health on a global scale. Cumulatively, these radical technological innovations are now, according to this view, in the process of establishing an organic form of "globalization" that will indeed diminish the role of the territorial state to the point that it is no longer satisfactory to consider world order as constituted by sovereign territorial states. Even these most extreme globalizers do not foresee the disappearance of the state, but rather its increasing virtuality, a redesigned role to facilitate world trade and investment, providing security to the extent that disruptive actors mount threats to the established order. In the background of such dramatic conceptions of the global integrative process underway is the related idea that globalization carries with it a cultural and normative code that homogenizes world society in a coherent and beneficial manner. The global media socializes people everywhere to a common consumptive life style, and, more ambitiously, promises, that in time, due to economic growth and technological innovation, poverty will disappear and material wellbeing will become attainable for everybody. Such developments may over time even lead to a system of global law and morality taking hold of the political imagination.... It is surely ironic that such a materialist vision of the future has generated such mainstream enthusiasm at this stage of world capitalism, despite its resemblance to Marxist conceptions of human and societal fulfillment.

There is the dark flip side scenario that sees the same forces of globalization moving toward self-destructive catastrophe as energy use, pollution, warming, and demographic pressure overwhelm the carrying capacity of the global ecosystem. In this understanding, the impotence of the state to stem such a globalizing juggernaut is part of our collective inability as a species to slow the human stagger toward the abyss. The plaintive and shrill calls for help associated with anti-globalization militancy, initiated in a vivid manner in late 1999 during World Trade Organization meetings at Seattle, and continued ever since, raise many questions about the viability and legitimacy of globalization. This movement from below has gained such strength that its presence at any notable gathering of globalizers from above dominates the occasion, making the encounter overshadow the substantive issues and policy changes under discussion in the official sessions. So far these demonstrations against corporate globalization have succeeded as media events but have yet to prove themselves capable of qualifying as political events that bring about change or even offer a confused public an alternative. For the first time, in the wake of the violent riots accompanying the July 2001 G–8 meetings of, heads of state, began to reevaluate, at least superficially, their approach to the management of the world economy. The leaders assembled at Genoa and their retinue of advisors seemed determined that, in view of the political turmoil generated, such meetings should no longer be held, at least within the setting of major urban centers.

There is another series of emergent innovations that have been identified as possessed of revolutionary potential, and these are associated with the frontiers of science and technology. The advent of super-intelligent machines, of really smart and versatile robots, and of human cloning and breakthroughs in biogenetics challenges our sense of the human condition and of our species' survivability in profound ways. These prospects can give rise to either the excitement of a cyberworld of abundance and longevity or a bladerunner world of sheer destructivity. I think we need as a matter of civilizational urgency to assess with great care the political, ethical, and spiritual impacts associated with this radical technology, but I do not propose to do so in this chapter.

My attempt here is to consider whether, despite the manifest despair and complacency of the age, as well as the disruptive and diversionary effects of September 11, we are not embarked upon a relatively bloodless, normative revolution of values, as well as legal procedures and institutions, which is transforming above all else our understanding of global justice. This process is also profoundly affecting our sense of political authority, accountability, and structure of relations in fundamental respects. Such a hypothesis is easy to fault, even to scorn as totally discredited by the evidence of failed and flawed efforts to pull off humanitarian interventions during the past decade or to hold leaders of states consistently accountable for crimes of state.

In a recent highly articulate repudiation of such normative projects, James Mayall writes that "[t]he revolutionary view of the future is the least plausible." Mayall wants to argue that the continuities of international society based on the co-existence and cooperation of sovereign states, although stretched in places, remains the best hope, and only realistic prospect, for sustaining even the current moderate world order that has the capacity to make modest ethical advances. This view carries forward Hedley Bull's rejection of those normative innovations that attempt, prematurely and regressively in his view, to curtail the sovereignty of states. Mayall's skepticism is explicitly grounded in the thought of David Hume about the international society of his time, with its primary insistence that we not allow our moral expectations to exceed our experience of what is attainable in the world as we know it. Of course, such Humean rhetoric is largely question-begging as the issue as to what our experience allows is a speculative matter that is constantly proving our most august pundits unable to see the handwriting on the wall. Consider, in this regard, how "experience" failed to show that East Europe would be liberated peacefully from Soviet control and domestic oppressive rule in the 1980s, that South Africa would find a way to overcome apartheid without enduring bloody civil strife, and that the standards of international human rights would emerge from their declaratory incubator to become genuine levers of influence. To the extent that experience in global affairs is demonstrative at all, it is to confirm our inability to identify the boundaries of the possible, or to give comfort to either optimistic or pessimistic turns of mind. The non-anticipation of the mega-terrorism of the sort manifested on September 11 suggests that our negative imagination is as deficient as is our sense of what is possible in a more positive sense. It also discloses the inadequacies of intelligence gathering by the state, despite billions of dollars devoted to identifying and preventing threats of a terrorist character. We should in these respects encourage receptivity to a wide range of hopeful and dangerous future scenarios, acknowledging the inadequacy of knowledge as a foundation for prediction. In effect, we need to learn to trust the imagination and the political will if we wish to be better prepared to address the future, both its promise and its menace.

It is true that revolutionary processes rarely reveal themselves in advance, and seem to unfold with such rapidity that participants are taken by surprise. Only in retrospect does a revolution disclose its efficient causes and antecedent conditions. Barzun notes "[h]ow a revolution erupts from a commonplace event—tidal wave from a ripple—is cause for endless astonishment."

Revolutionary precursors or liberal delusions?

If we look back on a century of efforts to achieve global reforms, it is possible to reach quite opposite conclusions. The Bull/Mayall view is that efforts at reform are dysfunctional to the extent that they do not respect the essential hierarchical character of an international society dominated by sovereign states of unequal size and influence. The view associated with international liberalism has been more optimistic, a confidence that small steps of an ethical and institutional character can over time produce a more peaceful and equitable world order. The view being mainly explored here is whether such reformist steps, whether implemented or not, reflect an intensifying revolutionary impulse to reconstruct world order along more normative and globalist lines that express its integrative character. The conclusion reached is that at this point such initiatives are inherently ambiguous, susceptible of interpretation along any of the three lines. The ambiguity is not likely to be removed for at least a few decades, until as the fuller impact of globalization is disclosed.

The path of such an interpretative effort leads backwards to Woodrow Wilson and the League of Nations, founded without US participation after World War I, as a tribute to Wilson's stature and popularity following in the aftermath of a senseless, cruel, and devastating experience of prolonged warfare in Europe. Was not this enactment of Wilson's vision a normative revolution of global proportions? Perhaps, if only words count. Grandiose claims were made at the time for its transformative effects, especially its project to supersede the balance-of-power diplomacy and war as the arbiter of change through the institutionalization of collective security. But was Wilson's vision ever enacted in a form, with capabilities and constitutional processes that might have had a reasonable chance of upholding its claims? Is there any evidence that Wilson himself understood or accepted the transfer of capabilities to the international level implied by his proclaimed commitment to end the war system? Did the political elites of the leading states of the world, aside from Wilson, believe that the old realist interplay of dominant sovereign states could be or should be put aside? Not much energy has to be wasted responding to such questions. A resounding "No" is all that is necessary. At the same time, there is no doubt that the League experience, as sustained by its more elaborate and successful sequel, the United Nations, provides part of the background that helps make the present argument for a normative global revolution more plausible than it would otherwise be. There has been over the course of the last century a growing institutionalization of governance at the international level, a process expressing the increasing complexity of international life, especially in economic domains, along with the search for the security and stability of transactions across the borders of sovereign states.

The same can be said about the Nuremberg and Tokyo war crimes trials held after World War II. On one level these events did put into question the idea that states were the ultimate arbiters of legality and responsibility, as well as the protective notion granting immunity from prosecution to those individuals who acted on behalf of the state. But the one-sidedness of these inquiries into criminality gave these proceedings an inevitably shaky normative status. They were vulnerable to attacks as "victors' justice" and pure hypocrisy, which could be deflected by contending that a principled framework of generalized accountability would soon follow, with codes and tribunals applicable to all members of international society. When there was no implementation of this Nuremberg Promise, cynicism seemed justified, and the experience of imposing accountability was limited to the circumstances surrounding the outcome of World War II.

As with Wilsonianism, so with the Nuremberg, a normative idea with strong potential was validated to a certain degree under special conditions, but not in a manner that would induce durable and consistent change in the behavioral practices of world order as conceived along Westphalian lines of territorial sovereignty. As such, these normative impulses, although capable of arousing extremes of enthusiasm and opposition, were not "revolutionary" in either intention or effect. The means to reach the lofty goals proclaimed were not willed into being. No suitable political project that might challenge statist world order or hegemonic patterns took shape in a credible form.

To suggest the possibility of a global normative revolution is to be aware of this background of disingenuous gestures that are made on an *ad hoc* basis without an accompanying will and social forces necessary to make structural changes. Without relevant agency and the structural changes, the rhetoric of revolution is hollow sentimentality, or a politically irrelevant utopianism. The structural changes responsive to a normative agenda, challenges several aspects of political realism embedded on a global scale in such ideas as sovereignty, statism, hegemony, marginality of law and morality, and the absence of a clear and agreed conception of *global* justice.

My position is that this normative agenda of challenge has emerged in the last decade or so, building on these earlier impulses, but now reinforced by the global setting in an unprecedented manner, making the idea of a normative revolution more politically grounded than ever before. Such grounding does not ensure its success, (hence the question mark in the title), and there are evident significant contradictory tendencies. Yet for the first time in human history a combination of social forces and practical pressures is giving the current manifestation of a project for normative revolution serious credibility, if not yet robustness. This credibility mainly arises because multidimensional forms of resistance to market-driven globalization needs to be neutralized by making the emergent order legitimate in the eyes of the peoples of the world.

It remains to ask what is meant by "normative global revolution." The idea of "normative" is associated with justice, moral values, and legal order, while that of "global" is connected with the scope of what is being proposed, but in the manner of stacked Russian dolls. Contextualizing such an outlook requires that we consider the Westphalian framework of territorial sovereignty as the established order against which the revolution is being undertaken. As such it is not a modification of a reformist sort that will enable that inherited and resilient framework to adapt yet again to altered conditions, but something that is so fundamental as to revise our perception of the core features of "the real." We will partly come to appreciate the transformative character of this process by expressing the need for and seeking out a new language of explication and appraisal that conveys the new realities in more satisfactory ways.

Barzun, quoted earlier, portrays the history of the West as a sequence of revolutions, but carried on within the boundaries of states taken as the stable elements of an established order. As expressed, "[a] revolutionary idea can succeed only if it can rally strong 'irrelevant' interests, and only the military can make it." My view explored here is that a revolutionary idea under contemporary conditions needs to rally strong support throughout global civil society, which can be conceived from a statist perspective as a domain of the internationally "irrelevant," but does not any longer depend on violence for its success.

This possibility is a result of three mutually reinforcing developments. The first of these, and the most encompassing, is the evolution of international human rights from a pious promise made in an unconvincing and nominal form back in 1950, and even earlier, to an internationally-accepted normative (and even sometimes juridical) framework for evaluating and resolving serious claims directed against inconsistent behavior in the early 21st Century. In this regard, I take seriously as the second development the empirical spread and universal endorsement accorded a democratizing ethos, although I dissent from the view that "democracy" is properly (that is, fully) delimited in minimalist and statist terms of "electoral consent" in this era of globalization and the concomitant burgeoning power of unelected corporate actors. The third development is the anti-globalization movement with its implicit indictment of the illegitimate character of the manner in which global policy is being formed and implemented, as well as with the inequities alleged to result from such processes, especially with regard to the peoples of the global South. This combination of international human rights (including distinct womens,' indigenous peoples,' and sexual identity movements), the democratic ethos, and the anti-globalization movement are what gives the normative global revolution its political shape and relevance. It is predicated upon an underlying engagement with the attainment of global justice, or, alternatively phrased, "humane global governance."

Imagining a normative global revolution: some activating conditions

The first set of normative impulses can be best understood as a continuation of World War II by the victorious coalition of states led by the United States. This meant the war crimes trials at Nuremberg and Tokyo, establishment of the United Nations, the Genocide Convention, and the Universal Declaration of Human Rights. Partly, these initiatives represented efforts to learn from the mistakes of the past, particularly they reflected the failures of the punitive approach to Germany embedded in the Versailles Treaty and the non-participation of the United States in the League of Nations. Partly, these initiatives resulted from a belated sense of shame about the failure of the liberal democracies to oppose the genocidal politics of the Nazi regime in Germany or even to proffer timely aid to the victims in their quest for places of refuge—that is, criminalizing genocide and internationalizing human rights were symbolic steps in the direction of imposing limits on sovereignty as exercised *within* territorial limits. But, in the main, these initiatives taken between 1945 and 1950 were problematic, being tainted by the victors' insistence on exempting their own behavior from legal scrutiny, failing to transfer any peacemaking capabilities to the United Nations, and through the intense adherence to notions of sovereign rights as modified by geopolitical prerogatives (most notably the veto power of the five permanent members of the UN Security Council). [The world in] 1945 was still very much of a Westphalian world, its statist logic accentuated by Soviet concerns associated with their plausible anxiety about being outmaneuvered and outvoted in any consensual procedure established at the global level. It is also the case that the main learning experience arising from the World War II experience was that idealistic approaches to international order do not succeed in providing either security or peace. The paradoxical conclusion is that the best prospects for peace result from the maintenance of deterrent strength rather than by way of demilitarizing disarmament, which tempts aggression. The so-called "lesson of Munich" was formative for Western leaders in this period, creating anxiety about placing any serious reliance on the UN as possibly diverting resources and energies from the need to rest world peace in the future on a balance-of-power logic. Neither legal nor moral norms of constraint, the logic went, but only countervailing power could induce moderation; the assumption was based on assumptions that leaders of states are generally guided by rational assessments of gains and losses associated with recourse to force and by a prudent approach to risk-taking.

The two most radical innovations in world order that were launched in this period were not widely perceived as such at the time, and perhaps for this reason were able to develop beyond most expectations of what seemed realistic. The first of these innovations was to overcome some of the weaknesses in world economic coordination that were thought to have contributed to the Great Depression of the 1930s, especially currency volatility. A complementary institutional innovation was designed to ensure that there would be ways to assist poorer countries of Asia and Africa in meeting their needs for foreign capital so to overcome their backwardness while respecting their political independence, and without appearing to be constructing new variants of economic imperialism. The IMF and World Bank, the so-called Bretton Woods institutions, as much later complemented by the World Trade Organization, designed to institutionalize periodic moves toward freer international trade and exchange rate stability, evolved into a powerful institutional triumvirate. Unlike the UN, global economic governance was seen as a capitalist enterprise, and was controlled by the Western liberal democracies from its inception. These institutional actors, along with the leading capitalist governments, provide a measure of global economic governance that has evolved over the decades in response to changing conditions, and recently functioned quite explicitly to disseminate neoliberal ideas and practices about state/society policy. This includes facilitating the adoption of market-oriented priorities of corporate globalization by countries in the South such as privatization, fiscal austerity, and the free transnational flow of capital.

The second radical innovation with enduring implications for global governance was the establishment of a regional approach to Western European recovery and reconstruction that began modestly with cooperation in relation to iron and steel production and trade among a small number of Western European countries. By the year 2001, European regionalism has matured into a quasi-confederal European Union that will launch a common currency in 2002, impressively upholds human rights of Europeans even against abuses by their own national government, contemplates a European constitution, and may in the years ahead incorporate much of Eastern Europe into an enlarged "Europe." Whether to view international financial and trade institutions and European regionalism as normative initiatives are themselves complicated and controversial matters that required extended and nuanced analysis. Certainly both initiatives have important normative implications, especially in relation to two crucial concerns: the character of global governance, the role of the state, and a concept of justice that is not limited to state/society relations. Their relevance will be assessed in the concluding section.

Undoubtedly, the great normative achievement of the cold war era involved the delegitimation of colonial rule, and the emergence of almost universal support for the right of self-determination. Of course, this achievement was rendered more difficult and remarkable because it cut against the grain of geopolitical alignments, placing the colonial powers, particularly Britain and France, as pariahs of the old order, and putting the United States in an ambivalent position. The extent of this ambivalence became evident in the setting of the Indochina Wars in which the United States supplanted

France in a sustained and futile effort to prevent indigenous nationalism from strengthening the Communist bloc.

The bipolar split of the cold war era (1945–89), combined with a realist turn in the diplomacy of major states, kept other normative developments of an inter-governmental character at a minimum: a consensus in support of the modernizing quest of the developing world and an ethos of co-existence flourished from time to time that encouraged formulating an overarching framework of shared normative ideas. The adherence of the United States to a realist understanding of global security was particularly influential, especially as the United States had traditionally challenged the European geopolitical orientation as war-prone premised on shifting alliances and the balance of power. This turn encouraged the substitution of "arms control" for "disarmament," in effect, seeking to reduce risks associated with unintended behavior without challenging the essential role of power in sustaining peace and stability within "the anarchical society" of states. This managerial diplomacy of prudence mainly focused on the distinctive problems of managing rival arsenals of nuclear weaponry, especially the dual role of this weaponry in relation to deterrence and to a resolve to forego actual use. Hence, the fascination with the acronym MAD, mutual assured destruction, but as well the crazed condition of threatening a course of action that would also lead to catastrophic self-destruction. MAD was complemented by an anti-proliferation approach to nuclear weaponry, in effect, trying to prevent additional states joining the nuclear club rather than seeking to abolish the club altogether. The prevalence of nuclearism tended to marginalize normative efforts in the security domain, especially given the implicit adoption of omnicidal prerogatives in the name of the security of state or ideological identity ("better dead than red") and the reluctance of the existing nuclear state to seek ways of reliably denuclearizing world politics.

Yet in this period, despite the ideological cleavage that affected all dimensions of global policy as coupled with the realist *zeitgeist*, there were important developments that set the stage for later developments. First of all, initiatives in civil society challenged statist approaches to both international human rights and environmental protection. Civil society actors (earlier known as NGOs), with transnational links began to promote adherence to weak, yet existent, international norms, exerting pressure especially in democratic societies for their implementation. Starting with the Iranian Revolution at the end of the 1970s, non-violent populist pressures for democratizing change were mounted under the extreme conditions of authoritarianism prevailing in Eastern Europe, as well as in relation to the racism associated with apartheid in South Africa. Secondly, militant opponents of cold war policies believed to violate fundamental norms of international law and morality began to invoke the Nuremberg idea as the basis of their refusal to support official policies. This process took place in America especially during the latter stages of the Vietnam War and later on with respect to symbolic acts of resistance by individuals seeking to prevent the deployment of nuclear weapons with first strike characteristics. In both instances, feeble or flawed inter-governmental undertakings relating to accountability that were supposed to be confined in their application to their original facts, were kept alive in a mutated form, while being generalized by civil society activists. These activists, often associated with deeply religious backgrounds, gradually came to view "democracy" through neo-natural law eyes as the spontaneous exercise of "popular sovereignty" in deference to the authority of a normative order higher than that of the secular state. Such attitudes, particularly as vindicated by varying degrees of success, helped set the stage for subsequently mounting a normative revolution of global proportions.

A final stage-setting development was the totally unexpected visionary global outlook provided by Mikhail Gorbachev during the last years of the cold war. In seeking to undertake drastic reforms internally and diplomatically, including a negotiated end to the cold war, Gorbachev revived a normative global agenda with a sweep and passion that recalled Woodrow Wilson. Unfortunately, this visionary call by Gorbachev for a more cooperative and demilitarized world order, sustained by a stronger United Nations and an increased acceptance of the rule of law, was dismissed at the time either as "propaganda" or as a feeble effort by the Kremlin to conceal the mounting evidence of Soviet decline. Unlike the efforts to deepen the commitment to human rights norms and to keep alive the Nuremberg tradition, this Gorbachev crusade led no where, despite its humane and sensible content, and has been barely acknowledged. Most regrettably, the United States, the most satisfied of superpowers, saw no need to respond to this Gorbachev approach either by way of endorsement or at least with a reform agenda of its own. Even after the collapse of the Soviet Union, Washington failed to seize the occasion to promote a system of humane global governance. Unlike the endings of major hot wars over the centuries, the end of the cold war did not induce the victorious powers to offer the peoples of the world a program of global reform that would contribute to future human well-being. The two most tangible opportunities for global reform as of the 1990s were a serious effort to achieve phased nuclear disarmament and a commitment to strengthening the capabilities and independence of the United Nations System. Despite this disappointment at the inter-governmental level, other positive developments ensued to make the hypothesis of a normative global revolution seem well worth entertaining.

The previously mentioned trends toward global economic governance and European regionalism were accelerated due to favorable geopolitical conditions for their evolution. Without cold war preoccupations, greater attention could be turned toward the coherent management of the world economy and the effective participation of Europe in a global trading and financial system that was dominated by the United States and Japan. Overall, the end of the cold war brought to the fore an economistic outlook toward the goals of global policy, particularly given the absence of serious strategic or ideological conflict. China's moves to enter the world economy and submit to the discipline of world capitalism has operated as a major factor in reorienting world order around global economic policy.

These developments taken together with a series of technological developments, especially in the broad area of information technology (IT)—the computer and Internet, as well as the rise of networking organizational schema in business operations—led to the realization that there was a sufficient disjunction between past and present to require a new descriptive vocabulary. Hence, "globalization." In some respects, the advent of globalization, especially as historically enacted according to quite contingent neoliberal precepts, represented a serious normative regression: a declining willingness to divert resources to overcome poverty and social deprivation combined with a reliance on the market and private sector to address human suffering. The point here is that the technological infrastructure that has made world integration feasible and beneficial could occur in relation to a more socially compassionate set of presiding ideas. Other "globalizations" more normatively acceptable than neoliberal globalization were possible, and yet may be negotiated to bring "peace."

This regression associated with the rise of neoliberal ideas was offset to some controversial extent by an effort to make democratic patterns of governance, by which was meant periodic multi-party elections and free markets, the foundation of legitimate state/society relations. Leaders of Western states, whether knowingly or not, became unwitting (although partial) adherents of Immanuel Kant"'s ideas about "democratic peace," and conditioned their enthusiasm for globalization by this call for democratization.

Also important was the changed role of violence in world society. There seemed to be a growing sense of obsolescence associated with major warfare as territorial gains were rarely worth the effort, and the backlash could be severe. In this sense the Gulf War of 1991 was an anomaly, and it also demonstrated the point that aggressive undertakings could generate massive responses to achieve a reversal. Of course, unsettled borders and unresolved territorial disputes still threaten future wars, but for limited ends that do not threaten international stability, with the possible and highly unlikely exceptions of wars fought by China to gain control of Taiwan or of North Korea to take over the entire Korean Peninsula or the renewed outbreak of Indo–Pakistani warfare relating to the future of Kashmir. Despite these lingering concerns, the prospect of strategic warfare is receding from the political imagination, although not smoothly as ongoing debates about missile defense systems and regimes for the prohibition of biological weaponry suggest.

As a result of this tendency, and in view of the large number of persisting forms of violent encounter, there has grown a focus on intranational violence, and on the limits of sovereign power and authority. There has emerged the awareness that international law and the UN as now constituted fit awkwardly into the new paradigm of political conflict. Both international law and the UN Charter [Basic Document 1.5] accept the idea of territorial supremacy and sovereign rights of the state, thereby rejecting any external accountability of a government or responsibility on the part of the world community to protect an abused society or ethnic minority. This tension between moral imperatives and the constitutional order generates efforts to find new normative ideas that will bridge the gap.

A further actuating circumstance is the emergence of global problems that can only be solved by the logic of collective action. The US refusal ... to back the Kyoto Protocol relating to global warming without offering a substitute measure is indicative of the vulnerability of the peoples of the world to a normative framework that is conditioned on the right of a single state to defy the collective will of the world community. The issue raised is whether collective action can be arranged either by way of a revised US assessment of its own interests or by way of procedures that take precedence over its refusal to accept a global regime of restraint. The short-term outlook is not promising, but as the evidence of harm from continued emissions of greenhouse gasses at current levels mounts, there is likely to take shape a strong political effort to insist that the United States in its behavior act as "a responsible sovereign," which might include cutting back aspects of its way of life that are globally damaging.

A further background consideration is the dual realization that armed struggles have difficulty gaining their goals, and that governments are not able to prevail over their citizenry by reliance on coercion alone. The 1980s and 1990s bore witness to a post-Gandhian rise in non-violent revolutionary challenges to established political orders and an abandonment of armed struggle strategies. The trend toward negotiated compromises was a promising, although not consistent, development. Non-violent challenges were turned back in several Asian countries, most prominently in China during 1989, and armed struggle tactics succeeded in some instances, as in inducing the NATO intervention in Kosovo that result in the expulsion of the Serb oppressive police and military forces.

My argument is simple: that a series of developments have set the stage for the unexpected surge of normativity that has taken place *globally* (and *regionally* to an uneven extent) during the last decade or so. The next section will identify the main dimensions of this normative phenomenon, to be followed by a short section assessing its sustainability.

The normative surge since 1989: a quest for global justice

Although the hypothesis being explored is that the cumulative impact of the normative initiatives underway *may* amount to a global revolution if sustained for the next decade or so. It may also fizzle, and there are also present some lively possibilities of normative global regression. The main elements of what is being presented here as the elements of the normative revolution are, by and large, not novelties, but extensions of earlier initiatives that had appeared to be stillborn with only a historical significance. That is, the *latent* normative potential of the Westphalian evolution of statism during its latest phases are the main building blocks of a possibly emergent normative global revolution. The political project associated with achieving global justice and humane global governance amounts, then, to activating these latent elements.

Accountability: justice for the perpetrators

Undoubtedly, one of the most striking developments with moral/legal/political implications, involves a multitude of efforts to hold those who act on behalf of sovereign states *internationally* accountable for their behavior, at least to the extent of severely abusive behavior. The substantive scope of "abusive" is unclear, and will undoubtedly evolve to incorporate shifting sentiments, but seems now definitely to extend to genocide, crimes against humanity, torture, rape as a military tactic, and possibly crimes against peace and severe violations of human rights. Such efforts to impose international accountability are a direct and fundamental challenge to the central Westphalian idea of territorial supremacy of the sovereign state, and the related doctrines of act of state, sovereign immunity, and superior orders. This impulse to hold leaders, and their subalterns, accountable for adherence to norms is not new, tracing its origins to medieval efforts to uphold codes of chivalry in times of war. In the last century the half-hearted insistence by the

Allies that Kaiser Wilhelm of Germany be prosecuted as a war criminal for his role in starting World War I suggested a rudimentary type of international accountability, which came to nothing.

The true precursor to the recent initiatives was, of course, the Nuremberg/Tokyo trials held after World War II. At the time, these trials seemed to promise a radical innovation in international relations, but turned out to be limited to their historical circumstances associated with the outcome of a war deemed just by its victors. Or were they? The benevolent virus of international criminal accountability had been released into the body politic, and it spread unpredictably, establishing its authority as a standard of criticism and self-judgment. This was especially the case for the United States, which was the main architect of the Nuremberg approach, and also the state most vulnerable to claims from within its own society, as well as from the broader community of liberal democracies. In fact, cold war priorities inhibited allies from complaining about US departures from the rule of law with respect to the use of international force, but it did not similarly constrain outraged citizens, especially in response to growing domestic and international opposition to the Vietnam War in the late 1960s. Notable in this regard, was the convening in Europe of a tribunal composed of well known moral authority figures to assess the criminality of American conduct in Vietnam by the British philosopher, Bertrand Russell. Also significant was Daniel Ellsberg's much publicized release of the Pentagon Papers, which he explained in public and under oath at the time as responsive to the text and teachings of the Nuremberg Judgment **[Basic Document 7.4]**

But the 1990s witnessed the inter-governmental revival of international accountability procedures, at the formal initiative of the United Nations Security Council, initially with respect to the breakup of former Yugoslavia and then shortly thereafter in relation to genocide in Rwanda. The establishment of the International Criminal Tribunal for the former Yugoslavia at The Hague in 1993 led to a renewed interest in international accountability. This interest was intensified some years later when Slobodan Milosevic was indicted in the midst of the Kosovo War, along with other high-ranking officials in Belgrade, while he was officially head of state, and again in 2001 when Milosevic was handed over for prosecution as a result of a change of government in Yugoslavia. These developments stimulated civil society and moderate governments to seek the institutionalization of international accountability through the establishment of an international criminal court. Surprisingly, this collaboration resulted in the Rome Treaty of 1998 that comes into force once it secures 60 ratifications, which seems likely within the next year or so, but without the participation of such vital states as the United States, China, Russia, and Israel[q]. There is still prevalent the idea that accountability is a selective instrument that cannot be used to judge the behavior of individuals acting on behalf of the powerful states. The silence of the West in relation to

q. The Rome Statute of the International Criminal Court (ICC) **(Basic Document 1.16)** entered into force on 1 July 2002, 60 days after the 60th instrument of ratification was deposited with the UN Secretary General. The United States, which signed the treaty in December 2000, repudiated that signature and all its attendant obligations in May 2002, and continues to insist that US forces are immune from prosecution by the ICC. For a pertinent example of this stance, see the National Security Strategy of the United States of America **(Basic Document 6.9)**. For further details concerning the ICC, see *supra* Part I of this coursebook, especially its Introduction, at 3–4, and Chapter 3, at 179–82.

Russian behavior in Chechnya is revealing of the extent to which normative principles are subordinated in favor of economistic and geopolitical goals.

Of comparable interest, and even greater salience, have been the efforts by national courts in Western Europe to claim the legal competence to punish foreign governmental officials for criminality even if committed within their own country. The landmark experience involved the criminal indictment of Augusto Pinochet for crimes committed in Chile during his period as dictatorial ruler, and his later detention in Britain for the purpose of assessing whether he could be extradited to face prosecution. This effort yielded some notable legal decisions in Britain, including a final determination by a Law Panel of the House of Lords, that Pinochet was subject to extradition, but for a very portion of the criminality charged. In the end, Pinochet was returned to Chile, being declared by the British Home Secretary as unfit to stand trial, a conclusion also reached later on slightly different grounds by Chilean courts

Subsequently, in 2001, Ariel Sharon, while Prime Minister of Israel[,] is under investigation with regard to his allegedly criminal role in connection with the massacre of Palestinian refugees at Sabra and Shatila in 1982 while he was Defense Minister. The massacre occurred at the last stage of the Lebanon War, perpetrated in West Beirut with alleged Israeli complicity by the Phalange Militia, while it was under the control of the Israel Defense Forces. The Israeli Foreign Ministry in August 2001 has reportedly prepared a map for its officials and diplomats that points out which countries have empowered their courts to prosecute for crimes against humanity and other crimes of state, and have warned of possible embarrassment to Israel.

A group of scholars and legal practitioners has formulated a set of guidelines as to the extension of universal jurisdiction to allegations of this type. There is a definite movement underway to challenge the traditional idea of sovereign immunity when it comes to crimes of state, which if it becomes established in the years ahead, will represent a major step in the struggle to bring law to bear on the behavior of governments. It will also give pause to leaders who could no longer count on immunity or asylum. It is notable that national courts function as agents of both global civil society and of an international society of states to the extent that such accountability is implemented.

It is important to ask why such a momentous set of developments has taken place in the last decade, especially given the failure during the prior half century to follow up on the Nuremberg precedent. The obvious answer relates to the absence of geopolitical inhibitions of the sort that existed during the cold war. With the fall of the Berlin Wall, it seemed to become more tenable to assert universal standards of accountability whose application would not be seen as a propaganda victory or defeat, and would not be an occasion for a heightening of superpower tensions. Also relevant was the increasing importance of international human rights, with the exemption of crimes of states [from the obligations those rights impose] thus seeming like an anomaly.

Redress of grievances: justice for the victims

Parallel [to], yet seemingly disconnected from these extraordinary moves toward international accountability, has been an unprecedented effort in an array of settings to achieve on behalf of victims some measure of redress for past grievances. It is possible to view the imposition of criminal liability on the perpetrator of abuses as also simultaneously responding to the pleas of victims and their families. Indeed, capital punishment in the United States is often defended as a form of justice for the victims, particularly since other arguments based on deterrence and prevention seem so unpersuasive. Yet it seems helpful to separate the efforts to hold perpetrators individually accountable from the efforts to obtain redress from a variety of actors associated with perpetrators (and entities such as banks and industrial firms, and even governments) in various ways.

The most salient instance of redress was associated with the efforts of Holocaust survivors and descendants to recover their share of gold that had been confiscated from them by the Nazi regime in Germany and deposited in various European banks, especially those in Switzerland. These claims, along with related claims to unclaimed bank deposits seemed suddenly to receive moral backing from important governments, including that of the United States. The Swiss Government and a consortium of its leading banks negotiated a large settlement, and "redress" became an idea whose time had definitely come. A variety of claims followed seeking recovery of earnings from slave labor, insurance proceeds, and art objects.

The experience of pursuing Holocaust claims seemed inspirational for other communities of victims. Most obviously, those in Asia/Pacific who had suffered at the hands of Japanese imperial power sought redress with a special intensity. Japan, far less than Germany, took the first step toward redress, which is an acknowledgment of wrongdoing. At present, in Japan more than 55 years after the end of World War II, school textbooks continue to whitewash the past, which itself has kept from healing the wounds of victims and those who identify most closely [with them]. Some of the Asian efforts are merely to coerce remembrance and accurate historical reconstruction through such devices as books, films, museum exhibits, and conferences detailing the Nanking Massacre of 1937. And from remembrance, the impulse to obtain redress seeks informal acknowledgments of wrongdoing, which eventually will produce a formal apology by the responsible government, and possibly some sort of offer of compensation.

The more monetary approach to redress associated with the Holocaust survivors was also emulated by Asian/Pacific survivors who have been seeking to recover damages for slave labor and other abuses endured at the hands of Japan. So-called "comfort women" abducted in various Asian occupied countries to satisfy the sexual appetites of Japanese military forces have also sought to obtain some sort of belated compensation for the abuses sustained, so far failing to find satisfaction from the Japanese judicial system. From an international law perspective, the redress process directed at Japan has encountered special difficulties arising from the waiver provision in the Japanese Peace Treaty[r] that purported to extinguish all claims of individuals on both sides of the conflict. There are important ways around this apparent barrier, but they are yet to be accepted by courts.

A form of redress that has achieved great prominence, and can be viewed also as a diluted approach to accountability, is the establishment of truth and

r. Treaty of Peace with Japan, 8 Sep 1951,
3 U.S.T. 3169, 136 U.N.T.S. 45.

reconciliation commissions to record and document past wrongs, as well as to elicit testimony and expressions of remorse by confessed wrongdoers. These commissions were established in Latin American countries in the process of making peaceful transitions from dictatorial regimes to constitutional democracies, and seemed to offer a more stable way to walk the tightrope between impunity and accountability in societies where the old order was still entrenched in the military and security forces. Ever since Nuremberg the argument has been made that one of the main functions of criminal prosecution is to build a documentary record of past wrongdoing, both to avenge the feelings of the victims and to educate the society and the world in the hope of avoiding repetition. South Africa's remarkable transition to a multi-racial democracy relied on a truth and reconciliation commission as an alternative to seeking "justice" by prosecuting those whom carried out the criminal policies of the apartheid regime. Such an attempt to make transitions to democracy successful is not without controversy, with the most severely victimized elements of the society exhibiting bitterness about letting the perpetrators of unforgivable crime get off so easily. On balance, the truth and reconciliation approach has proved to be a creative compromise, repudiating past criminality without treating those associated with the former regime so harshly as to provoke their resistance. Of course, there is no incompatibility between engaging in a truth and reconciliation process and relying on accountability procedures to deal with certain unrepentant or severe offenders.

Redress as a moral and political tactic is definitely in the mind of victim communities. Without surveying the vast array of claims, it is worth observing the issuance of apologies by leaders of dominant countries for such past abuses as colonial rule and the institution of slavery. Refusal of acknowledgement, as with respect to Armenian allegations of "genocide" by Turkey in 1915–16, has been treated by segments of international public opinion as tantamount to an endorsement of the historic abuse.

Among the most militant and persistent pursuers of redress have been indigenous peoples acting in various ways through their representatives. These initiatives have been notable for their assertiveness without any strong base of military or economic power, but through a moral and legal crusade to enjoy the protection of property and other rights, including respect for sovereignty and traditional way of life. Indigenous peoples have been able to establish a forum for networking, expressing their grievances, and positing a protective regime based on a legitimated normative order.

The logic behind the redress movement is that the victims of severe wrongdoing are entitled, even with the passage of decades or even centuries, to obtain some sort of symbolic or material form of compensation for past injustice. The relevant actors are both individual and collective, with various entities engaged as claimants and responsible party. This validation of a redress ethos reverses an earlier dominant cultural and political view that the past is a closed book as to rectification of wrongs. The new context has lent credibility to claims and contentions that were formerly dismissed as frivolous, as was the case with efforts by African–Americans to demand reparations (in the billions of dollars) for the suffering endured due to the practice and institution of slavery.

The significance of this redress ethos is difficult to assess at this stage. It does clearly form part of an increased sensitivity to issues of justice wherever and whenever, and the relevance of their resolution to a peaceful and equitable world order. Why during the 1990s? It seems evident that the end of the cold war, coupled with concerns about accountability, human rights, and democracy, led those who identified as "victims improperly acknowledged" toward adopting activist positions. In addition to this normative atmosphere, two other factors seem worth noting: the relativizing of sovereignty made states and their representatives more vulnerable to legal and moral claims than previously; and the preoccupation with the future imparted a new salience to time and history, giving to the past a present relevance.

None of these considerations is conclusive. It remains to be observed whether the redress movement is sustainable, and achieves enough tangible results to influence our understanding of the nature of global justice. What can be agreed upon is that diverse redress claims are being asserted to an unprecedented degree during this period, and that this process contributes to the impression that a normative global revolution is underway.

* * *

Conclusion

The presentation above [has] tried to make credible the case for believing that a normative global revolution is underway, but that its sustainability and outcome are highly uncertain and beset by contradictory evidence and trends, especially given the onset of the war on global terror. The goal of such a revolution is the establishment by stages of humane global governance that is responsive to the functional needs of an era of globalization. Whether the sovereign state can adapt to this revolution, or mounts a counter-revolution on behalf of a pluralist world order, is a major area of uncertainty. It would seem that rates of adaptation are uneven, with interesting collaborative opportunities evolving for states favoring normative reforms joining with civil society actors to achieve such ends as an international criminal court or a ban on anti-personnel landmines.

Another crucial uncertainty involves the direction taken by the United States, and the manner in which it chooses to discharge its global leadership, especially now that it has shifted its focus to a decidedly militarist pursuit of security. Its present anti-solidarist unilateralism and reliance on a militarist view of global security is discouraging, but it may generate counter-tendencies within the United States and elsewhere that are supportive of the normative global revolution.

In the end, the secular prospects for the normative global revolution will depend on the degree to which the anti-globalization movement converges with the struggle to promote and achieve global democracy. But even if this movement evolves in a constructive manner, its ultimate success will depend on its capacity to relate positively to the creative and visionary aspects of the religious resurgence, and not get trapped into an embrace of secular fundamentalism as a reaction to religious extremism and its mega-terrorist enactments.

"THE PRINCETON PRINCIPLES ON UNIVERSAL JURISDICTION"

Universal Jurisdiction 18–35 (Stephen Macedo ed., 2004)

The Challenge

During the last century, millions of human beings perished as a result of genocide, crimes against humanity, war crimes, and other serious crimes under international law. Perpetrators deserving of prosecution have only rarely been held accountable. To stop this cycle of violence and to promote justice, impunity for the commission of serious crimes must yield to accountability. But how can this be done, and what will be the respective roles of national courts and international tribunals?

National courts administer systems of criminal law designed to provide justice for victims and due process for accused persons. A nation's courts exercise jurisdiction over crimes committed in its territory and proceed against those crimes committed abroad by its nationals, or against its nationals, or against its national interests. When these and other connections are absent, national courts may nevertheless exercise jurisdiction under international law over crimes of such exceptional gravity that they affect the fundamental interests of the international community as a whole. This is universal jurisdiction: it is jurisdiction based solely on the nature of the crime. National courts can exercise universal jurisdiction to prosecute and punish, and thereby deter, heinous acts recognized as serious crimes under international law. When national courts exercise universal jurisdiction appropriately, in accordance with internationally recognized standards of due process, they act to vindicate not merely their own interests and values but the basic interests and values common to the international community.

Universal jurisdiction holds out the promise of greater justice, but the jurisprudence of universal jurisdiction is disparate, disjointed, and poorly understood. So long as that is so, this weapon against impunity is potentially beset by incoherence, confusion, and, at times, uneven justice.

International criminal tribunals also have a vital role to play in combating impunity as a complement to national courts. In the wake of mass atrocities and of oppressive rule, national judicial systems have often been unable or unwilling to prosecute serious crimes under international law, so international criminal tribunals have been established. Treaties entered into in the aftermath of World War II have strengthened international institutions, and have given greater clarity and force to international criminal law. A signal achievement of this long historic process occurred at a United Nations Conference in July 1998 when the Rome Statute of the International Criminal Court **[Basic Document 1.16]** was adopted. When this permanent court becomes effective, the international community will acquire an unprecedented opportunity to hold accountable some of those accused of serious crimes under international law. The jurisdiction of the International Criminal Court will, however, be available only if justice cannot be done at the national level. The primary burden of prosecuting the alleged perpetrators of these crimes will continue to reside with national legal systems.[s]

---

s. For previous discussion and details concerning the International Criminal Court, see *infra* the Introduction to Part I and Ch. 3 of this coursebook.

Enhancing the proper exercise of universal jurisdiction by national courts will help close the gap in law enforcement that has favored perpetrators of serious crimes under international law. Fashioning clearer and sounder principles to guide the exercise of universal jurisdiction by national courts should help to punish, and thereby to deter and prevent, the commission of these heinous crimes. Nevertheless, the aim of sound principles cannot be simply to facilitate the speediest exercise of criminal jurisdiction, always and everywhere, and irrespective of circumstances. Improper exercises of criminal jurisdiction, including universal jurisdiction, may be used merely to harass political opponents, or for aims extraneous to criminal justice. Moreover, the imprudent or untimely exercise of universal jurisdiction could disrupt the quest for peace and national reconciliation in nations struggling to recover from violent conflict or political oppression. Prudence and good judgment are required here, as elsewhere in politics and law.

What is needed are principles to guide, as well as to give greater coherence and legitimacy to, the exercise of universal jurisdiction. These principles should promote greater accountability for perpetrators of serious crimes under international law, in ways consistent with a prudent concern for the abuse of power and a reasonable solicitude for the quest for peace.

[*Eds.*—The document goes on to identify the formation of the "The Princeton Project on Universal Jurisdiction" and its sponsoring organizations: Princeton University's Program in Law and Public Affairs and the Woodrow Wilson School of Public and International Affairs, the International Commission of Jurists, the American Association for the International Commission of Jurists, the Urban Morgan Institute for Human Rights, and the Netherlands Institute of Human Rights. The Project convened at Princeton University in January 2001 with "an assembly of scholars and jurists from around the world, serving in their personal capacities, to develop consensus principles on universal jurisdiction." On the basis of working papers commissioned of leading scholars and discussion of them in "an ongoing process taking place in different countries and involving scholars, researchers, government experts, international organizations, and other members of international civil society," the Project participants, "united in their desire to promote greater legal accountability for those accused of committing serious crimes under international law," developed and adopted the Princeton Principles on Universal Jurisdiction, set forth as **Basic Document 6.6** in the documentary supplement to this coursebook. It is recommended that they be reviewed before continuing to the Commentary on them that follows next.]

Commentary on the Princeton Principles[1]

Why Principles? Why Now?

The Princeton Principles on Universal Jurisdiction (Principles) are a progressive restatement of international law on the subject of universal jurisdiction. Leading scholars and jurists gathered twice at Princeton University to help clarify this important area of law. The Principles contain elements of both *lex lata* (the law as it is) and *de lege ferenda* (the law as it ought to

---

1. Prepared by Steven W. Becker (J.D., DePaul University College of Law, June 2001), Sullivan Fellow, International Human Rights Law Institute. This Commentary was prepared under the direction of Professor M. Cherif Bassiouni and with the assistance of Stephen Macedo, Stephen A. Oxman, and others.

be), but they should not be understood to limit the future evolution of universal jurisdiction. The Principles are intended to help guide national legislative bodies seeking to enact implementing legislation; judges who may be required to construe universal jurisdiction in applying domestic law or in making extradition decisions; governments that must decide whether to prosecute or extradite, or otherwise to assist in promoting international criminal accountability; and all those in civil society concerned with bringing to justice perpetrators of serious international crimes.

Participants in the Princeton Project discussed several difficult threshold questions concerning universal jurisdiction. How firmly is universal jurisdiction established in international law? It is of course recognized in treaties, national legislation, judicial opinions, and the writings of scholars, but not everyone draws the same conclusions from these sources. Commentators even disagree on how to ascertain whether universal jurisdiction is well established in customary international law: for some, the acceptance by states that a practice is obligatory *(opinio juris)* is enough; for others, the consistent practice of states is required.

When it is agreed that an obligation has been created in a treaty, legal systems differ in how they incorporate international obligations into domestic law. In many legal systems, the national judiciary cannot apply universal jurisdiction in the absence of national legislation. In other systems it is possible for the judiciary to rely directly on treaties and customary international law without waiting for implementing legislation. (These and other complexities will be explored in a collection of essays being published under the auspices of the Princeton Project). Accordingly, Principle 3 encourages courts to rely on universal jurisdiction in the absence of national legislation so long as their legal systems permit them to do so. Principle 11 calls upon legislatures to enact laws enabling the exercise of universal jurisdiction. Principle 12 calls for states to provide for universal jurisdiction in future treaties and protocols to existing treaties.

Participants in the Princeton Project also carefully considered whether the time is ripe to bring greater clarity to universal jurisdiction. While it has been with us for centuries, universal jurisdiction seems only now to be corning into its own as a systematic means for promoting legal accountability. Universal jurisdiction was given great prominence by the proceedings in London involving former Chilean leader General Augusto Pinochet, and now Courts around the world are seriously considering indictments involving universal jurisdiction.

In light of current dynamics in international criminal law, some supporters of universal jurisdiction question whether now is the time to clarify the principles that should guide its exercise. Might it not be better to wait to allow for unpredictable, and perhaps surprisingly progressive, developments? Is there a danger of stunting the development of universal jurisdiction articulating guiding principles prematurely?

Everyone connected with the Princeton Project took this problem seriously. It commonly arises when codification is undertaken. Nevertheless, these concerns seem especially significant in the case of universal jurisdiction given the wide gulf between what the law of universal jurisdiction is and what advocates of greater justice would like it to be.

After considerable discussion, those who gathered in Princeton in January 2001 favored our effort to bring greater clarity and order to the use of universal jurisdiction. Our aim is to help guide those who believe that national courts have a vital role to play in combating impunity even when traditional jurisdictional connections are absent. These Principles should help clarify the legal bases for the responsible and reasoned exercise of universal jurisdiction. Insofar as universal jurisdiction is exercised, and seen to be exercised in a reasoned, lawful, and orderly manner, it will gain wider acceptance. Mindful of the need to encourage continued progress in international law, these Principles have been drafted so as to invite rather than hinder the continued development of universal jurisdiction.

The Principles are written so as to both clarify the current law of universal jurisdiction and encourage its further development. As already noted, they are addressed sometimes to the legislative, executive, or judicial branches of government, and sometimes to a combination of these.[2] The Principles are intended for a variety of actors in divergent legal systems who will properly draw on them in different ways. We acknowledge, for example, that in some legal systems, and according to some legal theories, judges are constrained in their ability to interpret existing law in light of aspirations to greater justice, or other principled aims. Nevertheless, judges on international and regional tribunals, and judges on national constitutional and supreme courts, often have greater interpretive latitude.

Our hope is that these Principles might inform and shape the practice of those judges and other officials who can act to promote greater justice and legal accountability consistent with the constraints of their offices. We also offer these Principles to help guide and inform citizens, leaders of organizations in civil society, and public officials of all sorts: all of these different actors could benefit from a clearer common understanding of what universal jurisdiction is and when and how it may reasonably be exercised.

When and How to Prosecute Based on Universality?

In defining universal jurisdiction, participants focused on the case of pure universal jurisdiction, namely, where the nature of the crime is the sole basis for subject matter jurisdiction. There has been some scholarly confusion on the role of universal jurisdiction in famous prosecutions, such as the trial in Jerusalem of Adolph Eichmann.[3] In addition, it is important to recall that simply because certain offenses are universally condemned does not mean that a state may exercise universal jurisdiction over them.

Participants in the Princeton Project debated whether states should in general be encouraged to exercise universal jurisdiction based solely on the seriousness of the alleged crime, without traditional connecting links to the

2. *See, e.g.,* Principle 3 which encourages judicial organs to rely on universal jurisdiction, Principle 11 which calls upon legislatures to enact laws enabling the exercise of universal jurisdiction, and Principle 12 which exhorts governments to include provisions for universal jurisdiction in new treaties and protocols to existing treaties.

3. *See* Attorney General of Israel v. Eichmann, 36 I.L.R. 5 (Isr. D.C., Jerusalem, 12 Dec.

1961), aff'd, 36 I.L.R. 277 (Isr. S. Ct., 29 May 1962), which is often cited as representing the exercise of universal jurisdiction by Israel, although many argue that the decision was more fundamentally predicated upon the passive personality doctrine and the protective principle under a unique Israeli statute passed by the Knesset in 1950....

victims or perpetrators of serious crimes under international law. On the one hand, the whole point of universal jurisdiction would seem to be to permit or even encourage prosecution when states find within their territory a non-citizen accused of serious crimes under international law.

In this way, universal jurisdiction maximizes accountability and minimizes impunity. The very essence of universal jurisdiction would seem, therefore, to be that national courts should prosecute alleged criminals absent any connecting factors (for example, even if the crimes were not committed against the enforcing states' citizens, or by its citizens).

There is, nevertheless, great concern that particular states will abuse universal jurisdiction to pursue politically motivated prosecutions. Mercenary governments and rogue prosecutors could seek to indict the heads of state or other senior public officials in countries with which they have political disagreements. Powerful states may try to exempt their own leaders from accountability while seeking to prosecute others, defying the basic proposition that equals should be treated equally. Members of peacekeeping forces might be harassed with unjustified prosecutions, and this might deter peacekeeping operations.

Should the Principles insist at least that the accused is physically present in the territory of the enforcing state? Should other connecting links also be required? Participants decided not to include an explicit requirement of a territorial link in Principle 1(*l*)'s definition. This was done partly to allow for further discussion, partly to avoid stifling the evolution of universal jurisdiction, and partly out of deference to pending litigation in the International Court of Justice.[4] Nevertheless, subsection (2) of Principle 1 holds that a competent and ordinary judicial body may try accused person on the basis of universal jurisdiction provided the person is present before such judicial body.

The language of Principle 1(2) does not prevent a state from initiating the criminal process, conducting an investigation, issuing an indictment, or requesting extradition, when the accused is not present.

The Principles contain a number of provisions describing the standards that legal systems and particular prosecutions would have to meet in order to exercise universal jurisdiction responsibly and legitimately. Subsections (3) and (4) of Principle 1 insist that a state may seek to extradite persons accused or convicted on the basis of universal jurisdiction provided that it has established a prima facie case of the person's guilt and provided that trials and punishments will take place in accordance with international due process norms, relevant human rights standards, and the independence and impartiality of the judiciary. Later Principles contain additional Safeguards against prosecutorial abuses: Principle 9, for example, guards against repeated prosecutions for the same crime in violation of the principle of *non bis in idem,* or the prohibition on double jeopardy[5]. Principle 10 allows states to refuse

4. See the International Court of Justice's order in the Case of Arrest Warrant of 11 April 2000 Congo v. Belg.) (8 Dec 2000) [available at http://www.icj-cji.org], in which these issues feature prominently....

5. *See* Principle 9. Note also that the drafters intended the international due process

norms in Principle 1(4) to be illustrative and not exhaustive. The right to reasonable bail (Cf. Principle 14(2)) and the right to counsel were also referred to as being included among the essential due process guarantees. *See also* Universal Declaration of Human Rights, 10 Dec 1948 [**Basic Document 3.3**], arts. 10, 11;

requests for extradition if the person sought is likely to face a death penalty sentence or to be subjected to torture or cruel or inhumane treatment or sham proceedings in violation of international due process norms. The Principles reinforce proper legal standards for courts and should help guide executive officers considering extradition requests.

Of course, effective legal processes require the active cooperation of different government agencies, including courts and prosecutors. The establishment of international networks of cooperation will be especially important to the effective development of universal jurisdiction. Therefore, Principle 4 calls upon states to comply with their international obligations to either prosecute or extradite those accused or convicted of crimes under international law, so long as these legal processes comply with international due-process norms. Universal jurisdiction can only work if different states provide each other with active judicial and prosecutorial assistance, and all participating states will need to insure that due process norms are being complied with.

All legal powers can be abused by willfully malicious individuals. The Princeton Principles do all that principles can do to guard against such abuses: they specify the considerations that conscientious international actors can and should act upon.

Which Crimes Are Covered?

The choice of which crimes to include as serious crimes under international law was discussed at length in Princeton. The ordering of the list of serious crimes was settled by historical progression rather than an attempt to rank crimes based upon their gravity.

- "Piracy" is a crime that paradigmatically is subject to prosecution by any nation based on principles of universality, and it is crucial to the origins of universal jurisdiction, so it comes first.[6]

- "Slavery" was included in part because its historical ties to piracy reach back to the Declaration of the Congress of Vienna in 1815.[7] There are but a few conventional provisions, however, authorizing the exercise of universal jurisdiction for slavery and slave-related practices.[8] The phrase slavery and slave-related practices was considered but rejected by the Princeton Assembly as being too technical in nature. However, it was agreed that the term slavery was intended to include those practices prohibited in the [1956] Supplementary Convention on the Abolition of Slavery, the Slave Trade, and Institutions and Practices Similar to Slavery **[Basic Document 3.8]**.

- "War crimes" were initially restricted to serious war crimes, namely, grave breaches of the 1949 Geneva Conventions **[Basic Document**

International Covenant on Civil and Political Rights, 19 Dec 1966 **[Basic Document 3.14]**, arts. 14, 15 [hereinafter ICCPR].

6. *See, e.g.,* Convention on the High Seas, 29 Apr 1958 **[Basic Document 5.3]**, art. 105. . . .

7. Declaration of the Congress of Vienna, 8 Feb 1815, 1 Hertslet's Commercial Treaties 9.

8. *Cf.* Convention for the Suppression of the Traffic in Persons and of the Exploitation of the Prostitution of Others, 21 Mar 1950 **[Basic Document 3.4]**, art. 11; . . . Convention Relative to the Slave Trade and Importation into Africa of Firearms, Ammunition, and Spiritous Liquors, 2 Jul 1890, art. 5, 27 Stat. 886, 17 Martens Nouveau Recueil (ser. 2) 345; Treaty for the Suppression of the African Slave Trade, 20 Dec 1841, arts. 6, 7, 10, and annex B, pt. 5, 2 Martens Nouveau Recueil (ser. 1) 392.

2.9, 2.10, 2.11, & 2.12] and Protocol I **[Basic Document 2.31]** in order to avoid the potential for numerous prosecutions based upon less serious violations. The participants, however, did not want to give the impression that some war crimes are not serious, and thus opted not to include the word "serious." The assembly agreed, though, that it would be inappropriate to invoke universal jurisdiction for the prosecution of minor transgressions of the 1949 Geneva Conventions and Protocol I .

- "Crimes against peace" were also discussed at length. While many argue that aggression constitutes the most serious international crime, others contend that defining the crime of aggression is in practice extremely difficult and divisive. In the end, crimes against peace were included, despite some disagreement, in part in order to recall the wording of Article 6(a) of the Nuremberg Charter **[Basic Document 7.4]**.

- "Crimes against humanity" were included without objection, and these crimes have now been authoritatively defined by Article 7 of the Rome Statute of the International Criminal Court **[Basic Document 1.16]**. There is not presently any conventional law that provides for the exercise of universal jurisdiction over crimes against humanity.

- "Genocide" was included without objection. Article 6 of the Genocide Convention **[Basic Document 3.2]** provides that a person accused of genocide shall be tried in a court of the State in the territory of which the act was committed. However, Article 6 does not preclude the use of universal jurisdiction by an international penal tribunal, in the event that such a tribunal is established.

- "Torture" was included without objection though some noted that there are some disagreements as to what constitutes torture. Torture is intended to include the other cruel, inhuman, or degrading treatment or punishment as defined in the Convention against Torture and Other Cruel, Inhuman, or Degrading Treatment or Punishment. **[Basic Document 3.26]**. Moreover, the Torture Convention implicitly provides for the exercise of universal jurisdiction over prohibited conduct.

Apartheid, terrorism, and drug crimes were raised as candidates for inclusion. It should be carefully noted that the list of serious crimes is explicitly illustrative, not exhaustive. Principle 2(1) leaves open the possibility that, in the future, other crimes may be deemed of such a heinous nature as to warrant the application of universal jurisdiction.

* * *

When and Against Whom Should Universal Jurisdiction Be Exercised?

Among the most difficult questions discussed in the Princeton Project was the enforcement of universal jurisdiction, and the question of when if ever to honor immunities and amnesties with respect to the commission of serious crimes under international law.

Especially difficult moral, political, and legal issues surround immunities for former or current heads of state, diplomats, and other officials (see Principle 5). Immunity from international criminal prosecution for sitting heads of state is established by customary international law, and immunity for diplomats is established by treaty. There is an extremely important distinction, however, between substantive and procedural immunity. A substantive immunity from prosecution would provide heads of state, diplomats, and other officials with exoneration from criminal responsibility for the commission of serious crimes under international law when these crimes are committed in an official capacity. Principle 5 rejects this substantive immunity ("the official position of any accused person, whether as head of state or government or as a responsible government official, shall not relieve such person of criminal responsibility nor mitigate punishment"). Nevertheless, in proceedings before national tribunals, procedural immunity remains in effect during a head of state's or other official's tenure in office, or during the period in which a diplomat is accredited to a host state. Under international law as it exists, sitting heads of state, accredited diplomats, and other officials cannot be prosecuted while in office for acts committed in their official capacities.[9]

The Princeton Principles' rejection of substantive immunity keeps faith with the Nuremberg Charter **[Basic Document 1.3]**, which proclaims: The official position of defendants, whether as Heads of State or responsible officials in Government Departments, shall not be considered as freeing them from responsibility or mitigating punishment.[10] More recently, the Statutes of the International Criminal Tribunal for the Former Yugoslavia (ICTY) **[Basic Document 2.43]** and that of the International Criminal Tribunal for Rwanda (ICTR) **[Basic Document 2.46]** removed substantive immunity for war crimes, genocide, and crimes against humanity. Principle 5 in fact tracks the language of these statutes, which, in turn, were fashioned from Article 7 of the Nuremberg Charter.

None of these statutes addresses the issue of procedural immunity. Customary international law, however, is quite clear on the subject: heads of state enjoy unqualified act of state immunity during their term of office. Similarly, diplomats accredited to a host state enjoy unqualified ex officio immunity during the performance of their official duties.[11] A head of state,

9. Lord Browne–Wilkinson provided the following reasons for his dissent from the Princeton Principles:

I am strongly in favour of universal jurisdiction over serious international crimes if, by those words, one means the exercise by an international court or by the courts of one state of jurisdiction over the nationals of another state with the prior consent of that latter state, i.e. in cases such as the ICC and Torture Convention. But the Princeton Principles propose that individual national courts should exercise such jurisdiction against nationals of a state which has not agreed to such jurisdiction. Moreover the Principles do not recognize any form of sovereign immunity: Principle 5(1). If the law were to be so established, states antipathetic to Western powers would be likely to seize both active and retired officials and military personnel of such Western powers and stage a show trial for alleged international crimes. Conversely, zealots in Western States might

launch prosecutions against, for example, Islamic extremists for their terrorist activities. It is naïve to think that, in such cases, the national state of the accused would stand by and watch the trial proceed: resort to force would be more probable. In any event the fear of such legal actions would inhibit the use of peacekeeping forces when it is otherwise desirable and also the free interchange of diplomatic personnel.

I believe that the adoption of such universal jurisdiction without preserving the existing concepts of immunity would be more likely to damage than to advance chances of international peace.

10. Nuremberg Charter **[Basic Document 1.3]**, art. 7.

11. *See* Vienna Convention on Diplomatic Relations, 18 Apr 1961 **[Basic Document 1.8]**; *see also* United States Diplomatic and Consular Staff in Tehran (U.S. v. Iran), 1980 ICJ 3 (May 24). These temporary immunities

diplomat, or other official may, therefore, be immune from prosecution while in office, but once they step down any claim of immunity becomes ineffective, and they are then subject to the possibility of prosecution.

The Principles do not purport to revoke the protections afforded by procedural immunity, but neither do they affirm procedural immunities as a matter of principle. In the future, procedural immunities for sitting heads of state, diplomats, and other officials may be called increasingly into question, a possibility prefigured by the ICTYs indictment of Slobodan Milosevic while still a sitting head of state. Whether this unprecedented action will become the source of a new regime in international law remains to be seen. Participants in the Princeton Project opted not to try and settle on principles governing procedural immunity in order to leave space for future developments.

Another possible limit on the prosecution of serious crimes under international law are statutes of limitations. Principle 6 reaffirms that statutes of limitations do not apply to crimes covered by universal jurisdiction. Conventional international law supports this position, at least as concerns war crimes and crimes against humanity.[12] Admittedly, the practice of states leaves something to be desired, here as elsewhere. Subsection (1) of Principle 13 provides that national judicial organs shall construe their own law in a manner consistent with these Principles. If a nation's law is silent as to a limitations period with respect to a certain serious crime under international law, for example genocide, a local judge could draw on this subsection and legitimately refuse to apply by analogy another statute of limitations for a crime that was codified, e.g., murder. Because the laws of many nations include limitations periods, a number of participants suggested that the Principles should exhort states to eliminate statutes of limitations for serious crimes under international law; Principle II does this.

Another significant discussion took place on the topics of amnesties and other pardons that might be granted by a state or by virtue of a treaty to individuals or categories of individuals. Some participants were very strongly against the inclusion of any principle that recognized an amnesty for serious crimes under international law. Others felt that certain types of amnesties, coupled with accountability mechanisms other than criminal prosecution, were acceptable in some cases: at least in difficult periods of political transition, as a second best alternative to criminal prosecution. Much controversy surrounds accountability mechanisms such as South Africa's Truth and Reconciliation Commission.[13] We considered trying to specify the minimum prerequisites that should have to be satisfied in order for accountability mechanisms to be deemed legitimate (including such features as individualized accountability), but in the end those assembled at Princeton decided not to try and provide general criteria. Accordingly, Principle 7 expresses only a presumption that amnesties are inconsistent with a state's obligations to

are not revoked by this subsection. Such doctrines, however, may be in the process of erosion....

12. *See* Convention on the Non–Applicability of Statutory Limitations to War Crimes and Crimes Against Humanity, 26 Nov 1968 **[Basic Document 2.22]**; European Convention on Non–Applicability of Statutory Limitations to Crimes Against Humanity and War Crimes (Inter–European), 25 Jan 1974, E.T.S. No. 82.

13. *See, e.g.,* J. Dugard, *Reconciliation and Justice: The South African Experience,* in The Future of International Human Rights (B. Weston & S. Marks eds. & contribs., 1999).

prevent impunity. Subsection (2) recognizes that if a state grants amnesties that are inconsistent with obligations to hold perpetrators of serious international crimes accountable, other states may still seek to exercise universal jurisdiction.

Who Should Prosecute?

Principle 8 seeks to specify factors that should be considered when making judgments about whether to prosecute or extradite in the face of competing national claims. The list of factors is not intended to be exhaustive. This Principle is designed to provide states with guidelines for the resolution of conflicts in situations in which the state with custody over a person accused of serious international crimes can base its jurisdiction solely on universality, and one or more other states have asserted or are in a position to exercise jurisdiction.

Originally, the drafters expressed a preference for ranking the different bases of jurisdiction so as to indicate which should receive priority in the case of a conflict. Almost without exception, the territorial principle was thought to deserve precedence. This was in part because of the longstanding conviction that a criminal defendant should be tried by his natural judge. Many participants expressed the view that societies that have been victimized by political crimes should have the opportunity to bring the perpetrators to justice, provided their judiciaries are able and willing to do so.

Although it was decided not to rank jurisdictional claims, the Principles do not deny that some traditional jurisdictional claims will often be especially weighty. For example, the exercise of territorial jurisdiction will often also satisfy several of the other factors enumerated in Principle 8, such as the convenience to the parties and witnesses, as well as the availability of evidence.

What Protections for the Accused?

If universal jurisdiction is to be a tool for promoting greater justice, the rights of the accused must be protected. Principle 9 protects accused persons against multiple prosecutions for the same crime. There was no objection among the participants as to desirability of such safeguards. Several of the participants, however, questioned whether the prohibition on double jeopardy—*non bis in idem*—was a recognized principle of international law. Under regional human rights agreements, *non bis in idem* has been interpreted to apply within a state, but not between states. It was noted, however, that the importance of the doctrine of *non bis in idem* is recognized in almost all legal systems: it qualifies as a general principle of law and, as such, could be said to apply under international law. Subsection (3) specifically grants an accused the right—and legal standing—to invoke the claim of *non bis in idem* as a defense to further criminal proceedings. This provision is designed to allow a defendant to independently raise this defense in jurisdictions that would otherwise only permit the requested state, in its discretion, to invoke the double jeopardy principle on an accused person's behalf.

Subsection (1) of Principle 10 requires that an extradition request predicated upon universality be refused if the accused is likely to face the death penalty, torture, or other cruel, degrading, or inhuman punishment or treatment. This latter phraseology should be construed in accord with its usage as described in the Torture Convention **[Basic Document 3.26]**.

There was also some discussion about whether to include a provision on trials *in absentia* in the Principles. Although generally considered anathema in common law countries, such trials are traditional in certain civil law nations, such as France, and serve a valuable function with respect to the preservation of evidence. In the end it was decided not to refer to such trials in the Principles.

Conclusion: Promoting Accountability through International Law

Several of the remaining principles have already been mentioned, and their import should be clear. Principles 11 and 12 call upon states both to adopt legislation to enable the exercise of universal jurisdiction and to include provisions for universal jurisdiction in all future treaties. The first sentence of Principle 13 was included by the drafters to memorialize their intention that nothing in the Principles should be construed as altering the existing obligations of any state under terrorism conventions.

Subsection (1) of Principle 14 calls for states to peacefully settle disputes arising out of the application of universal jurisdiction. An example of the appropriate resolution sought by this subsection is the case of *Democratic Republic of the Congo v. Belgium* [2002 ICJ 3 (Feb. 14), forthcoming],.... The case involves a dispute regarding Belgium's assertion of universal jurisdiction over the Congo's Minister of Foreign Affairs.

Universal jurisdiction is one means to achieve accountability and to deny impunity to those accused of serious international crimes. It reflects the maxim embedded in so many treaties: *aut dedere aut judicare,* the duty to extradite or prosecute. All of the participants in the Princeton Project felt it important that the Principles not be construed to limit the development of universal jurisdiction or to constrain the evolution of accountability for crimes under international law, and this conviction is made explicit in Principle 13.

National courts exercising universal jurisdiction have a vital role to play in bringing perpetrators of international crimes to justice: they form part of the web of legal instruments which can and should be deployed to combat impunity. The Princeton Principles do not purport to define the proper use of universal jurisdiction in any final way. Our hope is that these Principles can bring greater clarity and order to the exercise of universal jurisdiction, and thereby encourage its reasonable and responsible use.

JACK GOLDSMITH AND STEPHEN D. KRASNER,
"THE LIMITS OF IDEALISM"

132 Daedalus 47, 47–63 (Winter 2003)

In 1939, E. H. Carr published what was to become a modern classic on international relations, The Twenty Years Crisis, 1919–1939. Carr has usually been seen as a defender of realism and a debunker of idealism, but his thinking was much more subtle. He believed that power and interest—the bread and butter of realism—were the primary determinants of state behavior. But he also believed that peoples and their nations were motivated by normative values and aspirations, not merely by a desire to marshal power and defend material interests. Carr concluded that "Utopia and reality are thus the two facets of political science. Sound political thought and sound political life will be found only where both have their place.''

For Carr the problem of the interwar years was not international idealism itself, but rather international idealism run amuck. At the core of the international idealism he criticized was the assumption that right-minded human beings could agree on abstract normative principles to guide national behavior, and that these principles, once understood and embodied in international law, would influence nations to act with greater justice. By his account, international idealism discounted other factors, including the distribution of power and economic and political interests.

Carr famously argued that such idealism was self-defeating. Some nations, such as Germany, failed to comply with the principles of reason embodied by the League of Nations and similar institutions, and appealed instead to competing principles of law and morality to justify their self-interested and rapacious acts. Other nations, such as Britain and France, relied too heavily on the paper guarantees of international law, and not on a clear-eyed analysis of power and interest (both their own and Germany's), to secure international harmony. Carr attributed the growing international crisis in 1939 (his book was sent to the printer in July of that year) to the idealistic international institutions that were supposed to make a second world war impossible.

The kind of idealism that Carr understood to be so damaging to international peace and stability in the interwar years is again informing many aspects of international politics. Three developments in particular—the rise of universal jurisdiction, the creation of a new International Criminal Court, and recurring demands for humanitarian intervention—reflect a renewed commitment to international idealism. Supporters of these institutions and policies tend to believe that justice is best served when it is isolated from politics and power. Only by insulating international institutions and practice from the bargaining and compromise that characterize political decision-making, and from the domestic political pressure to which politicians must always be alert, can justice be fully realized. On this view, institutions and principles that minimize the influence of power better achieve justice than those in which power plays an important role; and decisions made by unaccountable actors, especially judges, are more likely to be just than decisions made by political leaders responsible to their electorates.

We believe the new international idealism suffers from four fundamental flaws:

- First, it assumes the utopian premise that a global consensus can be reached, not just on normative principles, but also on when and how they should be applied.

- Second, it minimizes considerations of power, and assumes that norms of right behavior can substitute for national capabilities and material interests.

- Third, it neglects political prudence: it offers a deontological rather than a consequentialist ethics.

- Fourth, it consistently slights the value of democratic accountability

Our claim is not that idealism in international politics is irrelevant or inherently harmful. With Carr, we believe that normative ideals can provide a hope for progress, an emotional appeal, and a ground for international action. But we also agree with Carr that ideals can be pursued effectively only if decision-makers are alert to the distribution of power ... and the consequences of their policies. The lesson Carr teaches is that when idealism is not tempered by attention to these factors, the best can become the enemy of the good, and aspiration the enemy of progress.

1

Universal jurisdiction is the power of a domestic court to try foreign citizens, including government officials, for certain egregious international crimes committed anywhere in the world. This authority is premised on the idea that human rights violations are an affront to all humanity and thus may be punished anywhere, regardless of the defendants' nationality or the place of the crime. Universal jurisdiction aims to strengthen international human rights law by marshaling politically independent domestic courts to enforce that law. The classic modern example is the Pinochet case, in which Spain attempted to extradite Pinochet from England (where he was undergoing back surgery) to stand trial in Spain for torture and related international crimes he allegedly committed in Chile. (The extradition request originally charged Pinochet with crimes against Spaniards as well, but these charges were deemed inadmissible, thus making the case one of pure "universal jurisdiction.") The House of Lords ruled that international law required England to extradite Pinochet to Spain for these crimes, but the government of Great Britain eventually sent Pinochet back to Chile after determining that he was unfit to stand trial.

The Princeton Principles of Universal Jurisdiction [**Basic Document 6.6**], a document drafted by leading scholars and jurists from around the world, are a comprehensive statement of the nature and scope of universal jurisdiction. The Principles extend universal jurisdiction to piracy, slavery, war crimes, crimes against peace, crimes against humanity, genocide, and torture. They specify that "national judicial organs may rely on universal jurisdiction even if their national legislation does not specifically provide for it." They strip all defendants—including sitting heads of state—of any official immunities. And they maintain that amnesties in particular "are generally inconsistent with the obligation of states to provide accountability for serious crimes under international law." In short, the Princeton Principles aim to replace impunity with accountability by extending universal jurisdiction as broadly as possible.

The Princeton Principles reflect conventional wisdom among idealists about the shape and direction that international law should take. The Principles will likely influence future universal jurisdiction prosecutions, because national courts interpreting international law give special deference to the views of scholars and jurists. In our view, however, the Princeton Principles are an unfortunate development that exemplifies the new idealism's failure to take seriously the contested nature of international norms, the importance of prudence, and the possibility of abuse exacerbated by the absence of democratic accountability.

International criminal law is extraordinarily vague. Virtually everyone agrees that genocide and torture and crimes against humanity are international crimes. But when we attend to the details of what acts constitute these crimes, and of when these crimes can properly be tried by courts, there is much dispute and little definitive guidance. Consider three of many examples:

- Among the most clearly defined of international crimes is torture, which the Torture Convention defines to include any act inflicted by a public official "by which severe pain or suffering, whether physical or mental, is intentionally inflicted on a person" to obtain information, punish, or intimidate.[14] Amnesty International claims that the United States violates this principle when its police use stun guns, pepper sprays, and restraint chairs, and when its prison officials use solitary confinement and related maximum security detention techniques. The United States disagrees; it believes these practices are legitimate and do not constitute torture within the meaning of the Torture Convention. There is no definitive source or judicial decision that can resolve this disagreement. Under universal jurisdiction, any national court could try these US officials if it, like Amnesty International and many other human rights groups, viewed these police practices as torture.

- A crucial issue in any universal jurisdiction prosecution is whether the defendant has an official immunity from prosecution under international law. The existence and scope of these immunities as they apply to universal jurisdiction prosecutions are contested and unsettled. The House of Lords interpreted international law to lift Pinochet's immunity as a former head of state. More recently, the International Court of Justice (ICJ) interpreted international law to hold that the Congolese foreign minister was immune from a universal jurisdiction prosecution in Belgium for alleged war crimes and crimes against humanity he committed in his country.[15] The ICJ decision technically has no precedential effect beyond the case it decided. So the scope of official immunity from a universal jurisdiction prosecution remains an open question. Under universal jurisdiction, each national court gets to determine the proper scope for itself.

- When the United States and its NATO allies bombed Yugoslavia in 1999, they violated the UN Charter's prohibition on the use of force against sovereign nations in the absence of Security Council authorization. Under the Princeton Principles, NATO officials might be subject to universal jurisdiction prosecutions for "crimes against peace." But they might not; many international lawyers believe there is a developing customary exception to the UN Charter **[Basic Document 1.5]** for certain humanitarian interventions. In addition, Amnesty International and an independent group of law professors have concluded that NATO countries committed "serious violations of the laws of war" when they purposefully destroyed civilian targets (such as a television station and electricity grids) and when they killed civilians by dropping bombs from

14. Convention Against Torture and Other Cruel, Inhuman or Degrading Treatment of Punishment **[Basic Document 3.26]**, art. 1.

15. Case Concerning the Arrest Warrant of 11 April 2000 (Democratic Republic of the Con-

go v. Belgium), 2002 ICJ 3 (Feb 14) (forthcoming).

no lower than fifteen thousand feet.[16] The prosecutor at the International Criminal Tribunal in The Hague investigated these allegations and concluded, after much internal wrangling, that they did not warrant prosecution.[17] Under a regime of universal jurisdiction, a court in any nation of the world could prosecute NATO leaders and military members and decide whether such actions constitute acceptable humanitarian intervention or criminal acts.

Because the content of international human rights law is so contested, courts exercising universal jurisdiction in good faith are likely to interpret and enforce this law in ways that affected groups will view as unconvincing, self-serving, and discriminatory. A universal jurisdiction prosecution can do more than provoke resentment among the affected groups; it can also provoke domestic unrest or international conflict. Until recently, Belgium was considering universal jurisdiction charges against both Ariel Sharon and Yassar Arafat for human rights violations each allegedly committed in the Middle East. (Such a prosecution remains a possibility. A decision by a Belgian court that Sharon or Arafat, or both, are war criminals will not likely dampen discord in the Middle East. It is much more likely to make matters worse by legitimizing views of extremists on both sides.

Proponents of universal jurisdiction claim that these leaders should be held accountable for their international crimes, no matter what the consequences. This argument presupposes a consensus on the nature of the international crimes we have just questioned. The argument also overlooks the possibility that a universal jurisdiction prosecution may cause more harm than the original crime it purports to address. Universal jurisdiction courts and prosecutors possess neither the competence nor the incentive to fully consider these harms. They are doubly unaccountable in the sense that they are relatively unaccountable to their own government (to the extent that they are politically independent), and they are completely unaccountable to the citizens of the nation whose fate they are ruling upon. It doesn't matter that they act with benevolent intent. What matters is that they may do something that harms people to whom they have no real connection and whose interests they are poorly positioned to assess. Because relevant constituencies cannot hold courts exercising universal jurisdiction accountable for the negative consequences of their rulings, the courts themselves will invariably be less disciplined and prudent than would otherwise be the case.

The inability of universal jurisdiction courts to consider the consequences of their actions in affected countries is a particular threat to amnesties, reconciliations, truth commissions, and similar programs that can successfully facilitate transitional justice. Modern international idealists tend to see these programs as a rejection of accountability. In fact, such programs often contain elements of individual accountability. More importantly, these programs are best viewed as prudential arrangements that sacrifice some benefits—such as punishment of the guilty and restoration of the respect and integrity of

16. Amnesty Report at <http://www.amnesty.org/ailib/intcam/kosovo/docs/natorep_all.doc>.

17. International Criminal Tribunal for the Former Yugoslavia, *Final Report to the Prosecutor by the Committee Established to Review the NATO Bombing Campaign Against the Federal Republic of Yugoslavia* (June 13, 2000), *available at* <http://www.un.org/icty/pressreal/nato 061300.htm>.

victims—for the sake of other values, including the minimization of human suffering, closure, a stable peace, and the like. In recent years, amnesties have been an important component in several peaceful settlements of bloody civil conflicts, including ones in Chile, Haiti, Sierra Leone, and South Africa.

As Michael Scharf correctly notes, a rejection of amnesty and an insistence on criminal prosecutions "can prolong . . . conflict, resulting in more deaths, destruction, and human suffering."[18] Consider the Truth and Reconciliation process in South Africa. Under the Princeton Principles, this process would not preclude a universal jurisdiction prosecution, in a court outside South Africa, of Apartheid-era governmental officials. This insistence on individual accountability at any cost could have terrible effects on the still-fragile South African reconciliation. And it might have precluded the reconciliation altogether (or at least made it even more rocky) had universal jurisdiction been widely practiced in the 1990s. In this way, universal jurisdiction can make political solutions to already difficult transitions to peace and democracy even more difficult.

The inability of universal jurisdiction prosecutors to weigh judiciously the consequences of their actions distinguishes them from purely domestic prosecutors, and attests to the importance of democratic accountability in the enforcement of criminal law. In a domestic prosecution, at least in the United States, the prosecutor is accountable to the community in which she serves in the sense that she is either elected (as in many states) or (as in the federal system) appointed and subject to removal by elected officials. As a result, in deciding whether and how to prosecute a crime, a domestic prosecutor will often take into account the consequences of the prosecution for community health, safety, and morale. In many instances the adverse community consequences of holding an individual accountable for a past crime can lead prosecutors to forgo prosecution, or to strike a plea deal favorable to the accused. (And of course political accountability also dampens the likelihood that this discretionary process will be abused.) Because universal jurisdiction prosecutions take place outside affected communities, universal jurisdiction courts and prosecutors lack the incentive, or the institutional capacity, to consider such tradeoffs.

The discussion thus far has proceeded on the optimistic assumption that nations will apply universal jurisdiction principles in good faith. But there is no reason to believe this will be true. It is not only the House of Lords and the Belgian courts that can prosecute under universal jurisdiction. Corrupt courts that lack political independence can as well. And many nations will have incentives to engage in politically motivated universal jurisdiction prosecutions.

The Princeton Principles rely on legal norms to preclude such prosecutions. They insist that a "state shall exercise universal jurisdiction in good faith," and add that a "state and its judicial organs shall observe international due process norms, including . . . the independence and impartiality of the judiciary." The reliance on legal norms in this context is wholly unconvincing. The Principles fail to consider why a nation with bad-faith motives to

---

18. M. Scharf, *The Amnesty Exception to the Jurisdiction of the International Criminal*   *Court*, 32 Cornell Int'l L. J. 507 (1999).

prosecute a universal jurisdiction crime would care about such due process principles—principles that, in any event, are manipulable in opportunistic ways.

To date, the costs of universal jurisdiction have not been obvious—at least in the United States and Europe—because most universal jurisdiction prosecutions have been brought by Atlantic Alliance nations against offenders in weak countries. But there is no reason to think this pattern will continue. The rate of universal jurisdiction prosecutions has increased in recent years. And, as their potential and scope become clear, as human rights groups continue to pressure nations to bring such prosecutions, and as weaker countries realize that universal jurisdiction can be a tool for creating political mischief on the international stage, especially against more powerful countries, such prosecutions will increase. Enthusiasm for universal jurisdiction might dampen in light of the ICJ's recent ruling on immunity for the Congolese foreign minister. If not, we expect that the many adverse consequences of universal jurisdiction we have discussed will become more apparent.

2

In July of 2002, international idealists realized a long-held dream: the creation of an International Criminal Court (ICC) with jurisdiction over genocide, crimes against humanity, war crimes, and, potentially, the crime of aggression.

In some respects, the ICC is an improvement over a regime of universal jurisdiction by national courts. The ICC is a centralized institution. Its treaty defines the international crimes within its jurisdiction. It also rejects universal jurisdiction, requiring instead a nexus to the territory or persons of a treaty signatory.

And yet the ICC has most of the other characteristics—and flaws—of universal jurisdiction. Its norms are still much too open-ended and contested to permit a consensus on proscribed behavior; it suppresses considerations of power; it lacks democratic accountability; and it cannot reliably balance legal benefits against possible political costs.

The ICC defines the crimes within its jurisdiction. But these definitions rely a great deal on contested international law norms, and they leave the ICC great interpretive flexibility. For example, "crimes against humanity" include "imprisonment or other severe deprivation of physical liberty in violation of fundamental rules of international law." Unfortunately, international law provides little concrete guidance about what these fundamental rules require. After listing other examples of crimes against humanity, the ICC treaty describes as a final one "other inhumane acts of a similar character intentionally causing great suffering, or serious injury to body or to physical or mental health." Such a criminal prohibition would almost certainly be void for vagueness under US law.

To take another example, the ICC includes dozens of prohibitions under the heading of "war crimes," including "willfully causing great suffering, or serious injury to body or health" of civilians, and "destroying or seizing the enemy's property unless ... imperatively demanded by the necessities of war." The scope of these prohibitions is obviously uncertain, but it is easy to imagine them being applied to NATO actions in Kosovo and [to] US actions in Afghanistan [following the events of September 11, 2001]. The ICC treaty is chock-full of many similarly vague and indeterminate criminal prohibitions.

One reason these vague norms are particularly troublesome is that the ICC prosecutor and court are unaccountable to any democratic institution or elected official. The ICC prosecutor is, to be sure, elected by a secret ballot by a majority of the signatory nations, each of which gets a single vote. But such an electoral system is problematic because, among other things, the vast majority of ICC ratifiers are weak nations that are never seriously involved in international police actions and thus have no incentive to consider the costs of zealous prosecutions. Even more importantly, the prosecutor can initiate investigations and prosecutions on his own, or at the suggestion of the UN or any signatory nation—all without review, or the threat of review, by political actors. His prosecutions are subject to legal review by the trial and appellate courts of the ICC, but these courts are similarly unaccountable to any democratic institution.

This lack of accountability means that the ICC presents many of the dangers of universal jurisdiction. Its structure is remarkably similar to the much-maligned US Independent Counsel statute[19]. By guaranteeing independence at the price of political control, it invites questionable and even politically motivated prosecutions. Legal restrictions and definitional limitations are not likely to provide real checks on the ICC's behavior, for the ICC itself is the ultimate interpreter of these norms. Experiences with the more accountable international tribunals in The Hague and Rwanda have shown that international courts will not be bound by the letter of their governing rules when justice as they conceive it requires otherwise. ICC jurisdiction can only be expected to expand.

In addition, the ICC, like a universal jurisdiction court, lacks the institutional capacity to identify and balance properly the consequences of a prosecution on potentially affected groups. The ICC treaty insists that "the most serious crimes of concern to the international community as a whole must not go unpunished and their effective prosecution must be ensured." Here again we see modern international idealism's commitment to individual accountability at the expense of national amnesties and other forms of political reconciliation. The ICC theoretically permits the prosecutor to decline to investigate when there are "substantial reasons to believe that an investigation would not serve the interests of justice." But the final call rests with the prosecutor, who there is no reason to think has the perspective, information, or incentives to make this decision wisely. (When Richard Goldstone, the Yugoslav Tribunal's first prosecutor, was asked if he "worr[ied] about the consequences to the Bosnian peace process of indicting Radovan Karadzic and Ratko Mladic," he responded that the indictment "was really done as, if you like, as an academic exercise ... Because our duty was clear.")[20]

It is true that the ICC treaty requires the court to dismiss a case if it is already under investigation in national court, "unless the State is unwilling or unable to genuinely carry out the investigation or prosecution." But the ICC has the final word on what counts as a genuine investigation based on its

---

19. 28 U.S.C. § 591 *et seq.*   **20.** G. Bass, Stay the Hand of Vengeance 6–7 (2000).

perception of whether the domestic proceedings are "inconsistent with an intent to bring the person concerned to justice," a provision that opens the possibility of double jeopardy if the prosecutor decides that a national conviction or investigation is too lenient and therefore not genuine. It is natural to expect the ICC to interpret its charter in ways that support its jurisdiction.

Perhaps the most troubling element of the ICC is its relationship to the UN Security Council. The United States argued that the ICC should prosecute only on the basis of referrals from the Security Council. The ICC drafters rejected the US proposal on the grounds that it would inject international power politics into the decision whether to prosecute, and would give each of the Big Five powers a veto over any prosecution. The drafters viewed power politics, and the opportunistic use of Security Council vetoes, as an obstacle to individual accountability under international human rights law.

The ICC in its final form does permit the Security Council to delay a prosecution for twelve-month renewable terms. But this just means that an ICC case can go forward so long as a single permanent member vetoes a resolution of delay. And even if the Security Council votes to delay an ICC initiative (as it did when it granted UN peacekeepers a twelve-month immunity from prosecution in July of 2002), many commentators believe the ICC has the power to engage in "judicial review" of the Security Council and possibly to disregard its decision.

There are at least two problems with this attempt to eliminate power politics from the enforcement of International criminal law and to subvert the recognition of national power incorporated in the UN Security Council. The first parallels a problem with universal jurisdiction: the ICC could initiate prosecutions that aggravate bloody political conflicts and prolong political instability in the affected regions. Relatedly, the possibilities for compromise that exist in a political environment guided by prudential calculation are constricted when political deliberation must compete with an independent judicial process. Many believe that the threat of prosecution by the international tribunal in The Hague made it practically impossible for NATO to reach an early deal with Milosevic, thereby lengthening the war and the suffering in the Balkans in the summer of 1999. The best strategy for stability often depends on context and contingent political factors that are not reducible to a rule of law. There is no reason to think that a politically unaccountable prosecutor and court will make such difficult, context-specific calls wisely, even assuming they had the discretion to do so.

The second problem results from what Carr would have described as a chasm between theory and practice. Proponents of the ICC believe that it may, in the words of Human Rights Watch's Kenneth Roth, "save many lives."[21] This is wishful thinking. Even if the ICC turns out not to have the disruptive effects described above, and even if it is somehow able to prosecute low-level human rights abusers, it is hard to see how the ICC can stop, or even affect, persons responsible for large-scale human rights abuses.

The main reason for this conclusion is that the ICC can only prosecute persons it can get custody over. The Milosevics, Mullah Omars, and Pol Pots of the world, however, tend to hide behind national borders, where they are

---

21. *The Court the US Doesn't Want*, The New York Review of Books (19 Nov 1998).

hard to reach. Moreover, the most notorious human rights abusers have been motivated by their own sense of mission and justice. They have seen themselves as saviors, not sinners. They have been determined to cling to power and they believe, as all leaders with a mission do, that they can reshape the world in their own image. If they have not been deterred by the threat of US military intervention, they are unlikely to worry much about an ICC that lacks any real enforcement mechanism of its own and that must depend on its members, whose decisions are uncertain, to arrest and surrender suspects.

This brings us to the US refusal to participate in the ICC. There are many reasons for the US stance, most notably the perception that the United States' disproportionate share of international policing responsibilities exposes it to a disproportionate risk of politically motivated charges being brought before the ICC.

It may seem odd that an institution that will have little effect on rogue human rights abusers could so concern the world's greatest power. But US troops, unlike rogue government officials, do not hide behind national borders. Hundreds of thousands of them are deployed around the globe, making them potentially easy to grab and bring to The Hague. (The United States is trying to counter this danger by signing bilateral agreements in which the signatories agree not to surrender nationals of the other to the ICC.)

Even if no US defendant is brought before the ICC, it can still cause mischief for the United States by being a public forum for official criticism and judgment of US military actions. For all these reasons, the ICC will more likely affect the activities of the generally human-rights-protecting but militarily active United States than rogue state actors who hide behind walls of sovereignty (or in ungoverned areas) and care little about world public opinion and international legitimacy.

Despite his opposition to the ICC treaty, President Clinton signed it in 2001, just before he left office, so that the United States could participate in ongoing negotiations. In May of 2002, however, the Bush administration officially notified the United Nations that "the United States does not intend to become a party to the treaty." In August of 2002, President Bush signed the American Servicemen's Protection Act (ASPA), a statute that enjoyed broad bipartisan support. ASPA is sometimes called the Hague Invasion Act because it authorizes the president to use all necessary means to release US officials from ICC captivity. It also bars military aid to some nations that support the ICC and it requires the president to certify that US peacekeepers will be immune from ICC prosecution.

US opposition to the ICC is important because US military and financial backing have been crucial to the operation of ad hoc international criminal tribunals. Consider how Milosevic wound up in The Hague. It was not the gravitational pull of international norms that brought him there. Rather, the United States wielded enormous diplomatic and military power to oust him from office, and then threatened to withhold some $50 million in aid to the successor regime in Yugoslavia until it turned over Milosevic to the Yugoslav tribunal.

The Milosevic episode teaches a general lesson. The ICC simply cannot, without US support, fulfill its dream of prosecuting big-time human rights abusers who hide behind national borders. This is why the ICC's alienation of the United States may actually hinder rather than enhance human rights enforcement. We have already seen this effect on peacekeeping and ad hoc international tribunals. And of course the ICC will most likely chill US military action not when central US strategic interests are at stake (as in Afghanistan), but rather in humanitarian situations (like Rwanda and perhaps Kosovo) where the strategic benefits of military action are low, and thus even a low probability of prosecution weighs more heavily. In this way, the ICC may ironically increase rather than decrease impunity for human rights atrocities.

The establishment of an ICC that is unacceptable to the world's most powerful nation (and also to other large and powerful nations, including Russia, China, Indonesia, and India) represents a folly reminiscent of the League of Nations, and portends a similar fate. The international idealists who rejected US demands for Security Council control over ICC prosecutions aimed to decouple the enforcement of international criminal law from international politics. They wanted "equal justice under law"—the equal application of international human rights law to weak and powerful nations alike. Both aims are a fantasy strongly reminiscent of the interwar idealism that Carr so effectively and presciently criticized. In demanding a full loaf of neutral justice rather than a half loaf of justice that accords with the interests of nations that can enforce it, and in creating an institution that relies on legal norms wholly removed from considerations of power, international idealists may diminish rather than enhance the protection of human rights.

3

In the last decade alone, many hundreds of thousands of people have died in the Balkans, central Africa, Afghanistan, Indonesia, Haiti, and elsewhere, some before our eyes on CNN. Humanitarian disasters, of which genocide is the most appalling, are not pretty things. No reasonable person would argue that they should simply be ignored.

The question is what to do about them. Universal jurisdiction and the ICC are institutions designed to redress and—if deterrence can be made to work—to prevent such gross human right abuses. A third practice more directly aimed at prevention or mitigation is humanitarian intervention.

Technically, humanitarian intervention in the absence of Security Council authorization violates the UN Charter. And until recently, many international idealists have viewed humanitarian intervention with suspicion on the ground that nations often use humanitarian intervention as a cover for an unjustified invasion of another country. But today many international idealists are arguing that states have a responsibility to act to prevent or rectify humanitarian catastrophes regardless of whether or not their material or security interests are at risk.

Typical of this trend is a report issued in 2001 by the International Commission on Intervention and State Sovereignty entitled *The Responsibility to Protect*.[22] The Commission was supported by a secretariat housed in Canada's Department of Foreign Affairs and International Trade and was composed of a group of international personages cochaired by Gareth Evans, a

---

22. *The Responsibility to Protect*: Report of the International Commission on Intervention   and State Sovereignty (Dec. 2001), *available at* <http://www.iciss. ca/report-en.asp>.

former foreign minister of Australia, and Mohamed Sahnoun, an Algerian diplomat and special advisor to the UN Secretary General. The report argues that each nation has an international responsibility to avoid or mitigate humanitarian disasters that could result either from conscious policy or from indifference or ineffectiveness in the face of natural calamities. This responsibility rests first with the domestic government, but if that government fails to act then other states and international organizations have a responsibility to protect.

The Commission members, echoing Secretary–General Kofi Annan's statements, aim to undermine the assertion, explicit in the UN Charter, that the principle of sovereignty precludes external intervention. Their report contends that sovereignty resides with individuals as well as states. The major purpose of government is protecting individual rights; if a government manifestly fails to protect these rights by engaging, for instance, in widespread killing or ethnic cleansing, then others have an obligation to intervene. Sovereignty and the responsibility to protect are mutually constitutive, not contradictory, principles. States that massively fail to protect individuals within their own borders are not properly exercising their sovereign authority and therefore cannot claim that external intervention is illegitimate.

No one, regardless of his understanding of international affairs, would argue that humanitarian concerns should carry no weight in decisions about intervention. The hard issue is whether nations have an obligation or responsibility to intervene for humanitarian reasons alone.

The argument that nations are obliged to intervene ignores, or, at best, minimizes, the fact that electorates in advanced industrialized democracies have been reluctant to expend blood to deal with humanitarian catastrophes that do not affect their material interests. Despite the hundreds of thousands of deaths caused by human rights abuses during the past decade, despite the millions of such deaths in the last century, humanitarian intervention has not generated any wellspring of support among domestic publics in the advanced industrialized democracies that possess the military muscle to make a difference.

Germany and Japan have been extremely reluctant to engage in overseas deployment of their military forces for any purpose, humanitarian or otherwise. No major European state has made a sustained commitment to humanitarian intervention. Indeed, no combination of European countries has the military capability to conduct a serious military intervention of any kind outside of Europe, and none appears willing to make the budgetary commitments that would make such interventions possible. European forces do have the ability to participate in peacekeeping operations, but even here the tolerance for losses can be limited. Belgium, for instance, which had several hundred troops deployed in Rwanda at the beginning of the 1994 crisis, withdrew them after ten of its soldiers were killed by Hutu militia.

The extreme caution with which American presidents have engaged in humanitarian interventions suggests that they believe that they are walking on very thin ice when they cannot convincingly tie their activities to material interests that the voting public can understand. To be sure, the Clinton administration undertook humanitarian interventions in Somalia, Haiti, Bosnia, and Kosovo. But the last two were overtly tied to the viability of NATO and American security, and even here the United States relied on high-altitude air attacks that minimized the chances for American casualties. In Somalia, Clinton extricated the United States after eighteen soldiers were killed. He did not act in Rwanda where an estimated eight hundred thousand people died—a decision that caused him no discernible political problem.

The report of the International Commission on Intervention and State Sovereignty recognizes the problematic absence of democratic support for humanitarian intervention. It suggests that

> the budgetary cost and risk to personnel involved in any military action may in fact make it politically imperative for the intervening state to be able to claim some degree of self-interest in the intervention, however altruistic its primary motive might actually be. Apart from economic or strategic interests, that self-interest could, for example, take the understandable form of a concern to avoid refugee outflows, or a haven for drug producers or terrorists, developing in one's neighbourhood.[23]

The Commission here acknowledges a gap between its own prescriptions about the moral obligation to act to mitigate humanitarian disasters, and the views held by democratic electorates in Europe, Japan, and North America—electorates whose money would be spent and whose sons and daughters could be killed.

This absence of democratic support is a fundamental problem for those who insist that nations should intervene to arrest human suffering in other nations. A basic tenet of the idealistic outlook that underlies demands for humanitarian intervention is that liberal democracy is the morally preferable form of domestic governance. In a democracy, foreign policy must have national support and be justified in terms acceptable to the voting public. But this means that political leaders cannot engage in acts of altruism abroad much beyond what constituents and/or interest groups will support. This conclusion is fatal to the interventionist project. The most we can expect is that when a nation's strategic interests dovetail with an inclination toward genuine humanitarian intervention, it will intervene—as the United States did in Bosnia, Haiti, and Kosovo.

Once again, this means that international justice will depend on the power and interest of nations, and will often result in uneven patterns of enforcement that critics deride as hypocritical. Opportunistic interventions are also what give rise to the (not unjustified) concern that many so-called humanitarian interventions are ruses for invasions motivated in large part by strategic ends. A clear eyed analysis of interventions would realize that such mixed-motive cases are probably the best we can hope for. The presence of mixed motives does not detract from the fact that some such interventions might help local populations, as the Kosovo intervention arguably did.

Arguments for the duty to intervene and prevent human suffering suffer from another problem in addition to the democratic deficit: they underplay, even if they do not ignore, questions of political prudence. Political prudence demands that foreign policy actions be judged in terms of their consequences, not their intentions.

23. *Id.* at 36.

Information affecting the cost of intervention, including the state of affairs in the target country and the price of intervention—in money spent, lives lost, and other opportunities forgone—are hard to determine. Similarly, the consequences of intervention, including the costs and likelihood of constructing a social and political order superior to that which would exist in the absence of intervention, are hard to know in advance. These factors make it all the more difficult for responsible democratic leaders to intervene, even if they were willing to ignore the absence of domestic support.

In several articles and a widely praised book, Samantha Power has been highly critical of American policy for failing to prevent or react to the genocidal policy adopted by Hutu extremists in Rwanda. She faults, among others, American Ambassador David Rawson for his failure to anticipate the scale of the killings. She quotes Rawson as follows: "Most of us thought that if a war broke out, it would be quick, that these poor people didn't have the resources, the means, to fight a sophisticated war. I couldn't have known that they would do each other in with the most economic means."[24]

Rawson was, however, far from ignorant about Rwanda. He had grown up in Burundi, the son of an American missionary. He spoke the local language. He could not, in Power's words, "have been more intimate with the region, the culture, or the peril." Yet he totally missed what was about to occur. Power argues that Rawson and others suffered from what she calls "imaginative weakness." She also claims that "US officials who did not know" or "did not fully appreciate" usually chose not to." But it would be more straightforward and obvious to say that policymakers must always make guesses about alternative states of the world with limited information and time—and absent overwhelming information to the contrary, there is no reason to reject that state of the world that is most consistent with the policy options they find most attractive.

Ex ante efforts to assess systematically the costs and benefits of any intervention are extraordinarily challenging. What is happening on the ground is rarely known with certainty. Even after the killing has begun, observers might not know whether they face a civil war or a systematic effort to murder members of a particular ethnic group. American leaders thought that bombing Serbia would provide Milosevic with the cover that he needed to withdraw from Kosovo; instead it led him to accelerate efforts at ethnic cleansing. Even ardent supporters of humanitarian intervention recognize that there must be some assessment of reasonable cost for the interveners. But it is usually difficult to know beforehand what such costs might be. How many foreign troops would have been killed if there had been a quick reaction to developments in Rwanda? How many NATO soldiers would have been lost if an aggressive, rather than cautious, air and ground campaign had been conducted against Serbia? What would the casualties be if an effective external fighting force were deployed to the Sudan? If a political leader guesses wrong, what would be the implications for his ability to secure political support from his own electorate?

Finally, and perhaps most challengingly, is the question of reconstruction. Just stopping the killing is not enough. If intervention occurs, the International Commission argues, there is an obligation to rebuild. Refugees must be

24. S. Power, A Problem from Hell 348 (2002).

allowed to return; human rights must be respected; judicial systems must be reconstructed; militaries must be demobilized.

Success requires creating institutional arrangements to which all of the relevant local actors will adhere. This is more easily done in some areas than in others. The highly developed institutional structures of Europe—the European Community, the Organization for Security and Cooperation in Europe, and NATO—offer alternatives to conventional sovereignty for the Balkans. These alternatives make it easier to maintain minority rights and prevent conflict, although even here the prospects for long-term success are uncertain. Other neighborhoods, such as ones in Africa and central Asia, are less hospitable. Building stable and tolerant societies in these areas is an enormous challenge, and there is no guarantee of success. Despite a clear security motive for intervention, widespread international support, and billions of dollars in assistance, the American-led effort to reconstruct Afghanistan might still fail. It is all the more difficult to sustain such efforts in countries where the direct security interests of powerful and rich states are not engaged.

The difficulty of assessing the costs and benefits of intervention and the absence of domestic support for purely humanitarian actions do not rule out such activities. But these considerations do suggest that it is wishful thinking to presume that the responsibility to protect will become a central norm in state decision-making. Any decision to engage in humanitarian intervention must take into account available resources, domestic support, probabilities of success, the danger of doing more harm than good, and, most importantly, the material interests of the intervener. This once again will lead, at best, to selective justice. In international politics, selective justice is the best we can hope for.

4

We have offered reasons to be pessimistic about the efficacy of three regimes—universal jurisdiction, the ICC, and (certain conceptions of) humanitarian intervention—that aim to enforce international human rights norms. Our point is not to criticize the norms themselves, but to focus attention on pathologies that may result from the inadequate institutions in which they are embedded. International institutions can damage rather than promote international ideals if they are incompatible with the interests of those states whose support is needed for their success.

Consider two successful weddings of ideals, interests, and power—the first associated with the beginning of the modern state system, and the second with its possible transformation. The treaties of Westphalia (1648) that ended the Thirty Years War are famous for embracing the principle that the prince determines the religion of his territory. But the actual terms of the treaties limited the emperor's right to regulate religious practices within the Holy Roman Empire. These restrictions, analogous to modern human rights, protected some minority religious practices, mandated the sharing of public offices in some cities with mixed populations, and most importantly, altered the domestic institutional structure of the Empire by requiring that religious questions be decided by a majority of Catholics and Protestants voting separately in the diet and courts of the Empire. These protections were largely efficacious, not because the norm of religious toleration motivated leaders (in fact no European leader believed in this norm), but rather because the Thirty Years War had shown that efforts to repress religious practices in Germany were so politically volatile that they could threaten the very existence of the Empire.

The European Union is another example. The Union has transformed the continent from one riven by war in the first half of the twentieth century to one in which war is unthinkable, at least among member states. European integration was motivated by ideals, by an aspiration among a small number of leaders to bind the states of Europe into a peaceful web of relations from which they could not extricate themselves. An important element of this integration was the creation of a human rights regime that fostered democracy and tolerance in the domestic realm. But these ideals could only be realized by grounding them in interests, economic and political, and by creating institutions that made it possible for European leaders to ensure that no nation had an incentive to defect.

The Peace of Westphalia and the European Union are institutions that successfully harnessed the power and interest of nations to enforce moral ideals. These institutions worked because each nation benefited from the institution and had an interest in complying with its terms. Unfortunately, it is not always, or even usually, possible to yoke self-interest into such a self-enforcing mechanism to promote moral ideals.

When self-enforcement fails, the alternative is a system of selective justice enforced by the powerful, one consequence of which is effective immunity for the powerful. What has not proved possible in international affairs is universal international justice based on legal norms that operate in the absence of either self-enforcement or hegemonic dominance.

This is why we believe that the norm that states ought to intervene militarily to mitigate humanitarian catastrophes will not become accepted in practice. Persons motivated to commit the abuses have nothing to gain from forgoing the abuse out of deference to international norms alone. And the leaders of democratic states—or, perhaps more to the point, American presidents—will not be able to secure the domestic political support needed to place lives at risk when their states' security interests are not directly at stake.

Universal jurisdiction and the ICC, in contrast, can matter, because they establish judicial procedures that rely on the authority and policing powers of national states for enforcement. The problem here is not that such institutional arrangements will be ineffectual. As we have suggested, these institutions can affect the costs of political action, and can have a special impact on nations like the United States that are globally active and care about public opinion and international legitimacy. The problem with these institutions is that they can do more harm than good.

The ICC and universal jurisdiction assume a consensus on human rights ideals and their applicability, and expect that compliance will follow. But no such consensus exists; non-national judicial proceedings will always be open to charges of bias, an ambiguity that Milosevic has exploited in his trial before the International Criminal Tribunal for the Former Yugoslavia (an institution that avoids many of the pitfalls of the ICC). The ICC and universal jurisdiction sever the link between norm enforcement and political accountability. One consequence of this separation is that the institutions are practically, and in some circumstances legally, discouraged from engaging in assessments of costs and benefits that are often so important for the prevention of human suffering. As a result, such institutions may worsen rather than alleviate human rights catastrophes.

DANIELE ARCHIBUGI, "COSMOPOLITAN DEMOCRACY"
Debating Cosmopolitics 3–15 (D. Archibugi ed., 2003)

If we pause to ask ourselves, at the dawn of the twenty-first century, which political institutions constitute the world's major depositories of power, we would have to reply: states. It is the same answer that any seasoned observer would have given in 1815. In the course of the last two centuries, state structures have only increased in the scale and scope of their dominion—a fact strikingly illustrated by a glance at a political map. With the exception of Antartica, the entire land-surface of the planet is now divided into the bright, bold blocks of colour that denote state's territory. If the United States is green, Canada is red; while inside borders, the colours are homogenous. The cartographical convention testifies to a certain political reality: however mixed the human experience—social, religious, ethnic— within its borders, unitary state power predominates overall. It is states that have armed forces; control police; mint currency; permit or refuse entrance to their lands; states that recognize citizen's rights and impose their duties. Since states began, there has also been a slow, complex interaction between those who hold power and those who are subject to it. In part of the world— fortunately, a growing one—the arbitrary use of government force is now subject to the checks and balances of a wider political community. The state has evolved, under the pressure of citizens, to become not only a tool of dominion but also an instrument of service. Never in the history of the human race has there been a successful structure, one which has, *de facto,* become of crucial importance to all the inhabitants of the planet. No single religion—not even all the religions put together—has ever held as much power as the world's states possess today.

Since their inception, states have had to come to terms with their own internal heterogeneity: their populations are made up of people who speak different languages, have different traditions, profess different religions and belong to different races. Some states may be more homogenous than others, but none can consider itself totally uniform. In the course of centuries, states have used a variety of means to pursue a greater degree of homogeneity: some have sought to found their own international identity on religion, others on language, blood or race; the concept of the nation-not to be found in nature-has served precisely for this purpose. States have tried to impose homogeneity on their populations through treaties and negotiations, wars and revolutions; by altering their borders, provoking exoduses or incorporating new territory. Populations have been forcibly converted to the dominant religion and vernacular languages rooted out; where this proved impossible, the diehards have been deported, repressed or even slaughtered. States have attempted to drum up support by fomenting nationalist or patriotic sentiment against a foreign menace or internal threat; they have tried to strengthen themselves internally through the creation of a unified cultural identity, drawing on the flag, national achievements, even sports teams and television programs. Other states, more enlightened, have looked for institutional devices to regulate, rather than homogenize, diversity; they have legislated for religious tolerance and, for over two hundred years, have developed forms of consensual government endorsed in constitutional charters.

States have always faced constraints, of course, both at home and abroad. International power politics imposes limitations on sovereignty: only a few states have been fully independent and not had to account for their choices to other, more powerful rivals, whether under threat of open military intervention or through lower grades of pressure. Internal adversaries have imposed a different sort of threat. Neither nature nor civil society are great respecters of a state's frontiers. Men and women love traveling and describing what they see, imitating what their neighbours do, allowing themselves to be convinced and even converted. Trade—the movement of goods and people—has flowed across state boundaries.

Only the most obtuse and despotic regimes, however, have attempted to prevent their subjects from traveling abroad and seeing what life is like elsewhere. Most states have merely sought to regulate international exchange through passports, customs authorities and financial rules. Until a short time ago, state authorization was even needed to translate books, or profess religious beliefs different from the established creed. The apparatus of norms and permits imposed by the state was a sign of its attitude towards the individual: You are mine, the state authority seemed to warn, but I benevolently allow you to travel. Going further, states have set up transnational arrangements, bilateral agreements and multilateral institutions to regulate events outside their own borders. An impressive array of sophisticated juridical constructions now exists, including international law, diplomacy and numerous intergovernmental organizations whose services states can draw upon to regulate relations among themselves.

Globalization and the state

Recently, however, the state system has been showing signs of pressure. The new fissures have not appeared overnight and there is no reason to believe that it will collapse like the Roman Empire; many critics probably exaggerate the size of the cracks. But irrespective of the depth of the present crisis, it is evident that many of the problems of the political organization of contemporary society go beyond the scope of the nation-state. Firstly, a significant number of the problems that states have to address lie outside their autonomous jurisdiction. The planet is experiencing a process of growing interdependence: the US Federal Reserve's decision to raise the interest rate may provoke a substantial rise in unemployment in Mexico; the explosion of a nuclear station in the Ukraine can trigger environmental disasters throughout Europe; the lack of prompt information about the diffusion of AIDS in Nigeria may cause epidemics throughout the world. Here, state sovereignty is not called into question by armies, missiles and armoured cars, but by elements which spontaneously escape national government control. This process has for some decades now been known as globalization. States have naturally sought to react to it, though the traditional response of creating intergovernmental institutions to manage or mediate specific systems—trade, industrial property, nuclear energy or epidemics—has met with only partial success.

Secondly, in the course of the eighties and nineties the state has been challenged by a new critique from within. I am not referring here to the classic process of revolution, whose fundamental aim is to replace one government (or form of government) with another, but to the belief of growing numbers of people that their existing state is too centralized for their needs. Political forces bent on greater local autonomy, or even secession, have gained in strength—witness the myriad smaller states that have sprung up since the dissolution of Yugoslavia, Czechoslovakia and the USSR. In Canada, Spain, Great Britain and Italy, separatist forces have consolidated their role. We have also seen the painful phenomenon of peoples left stateless, or oppressed by the alien state to which they belong. The interstate system has so far failed, for example, to provide an adequate political community for Palestinians or for Kurds.

Globalization has also brought the problem of mass migration in its wake. In Western cities whole immigrant communities with a language and culture of their own have taken root. Turks in Berlin, Chinese in Los Angeles, Arabs in Paris, Bangladeshis in London, Vietnamese in Montreal, all pose new challenges for consolidated political unity. These are minorities who do not aim at the creation of independent states but do want their cultural identity to be respected and protected. Such enclaves within existing political communities will grow in importance in the course of the next century. Will the state system be capable of meeting their needs?

Taken together, the external threats to the state from the process of globalization and the internal demands for greater autonomy give new force to the old aphorism that the state is too large for small issues, too small for bigger ones. It is here that pressures arise for a new form of world governance, more potent than anything that exists—an ideal evoked so often after the fall of the Berlin Wall. But what form should this take?

States have best met the needs of their populations where they have involved the people in running public affairs, and it must be said that one of the great successes of the state system over the last two centuries has been the quantitative extension of democracy. Despite all the uncertainties and ambiguities of the process in neophyte countries, and the persisting contradictions of low turnout and high candidacy costs in the developed nations, parliamentary democracy is increasingly emerging as a legitimate—and legitimizing—form of government. The last decade of the twentieth century will be remembered for the interminable queues of men and women in the East and South, waiting patiently outside polling stations to participate in the sacred rite of democracy—free elections—in countries where it had previously been prohibited.

Internal democracy and international system

To what extent has the new wave of democratization washed over into the international system? International political choices have never been dictated by anarchy alone. From the Congress of Vienna to the end of the Cold War, threats, wars, accords and diplomacy have regulated affairs between states; but this process has never been inspired by the principles of democracy. In place of transparency of action, there have been summits held behind closed doors; cunning diplomats and secret agents have usurped the functions of elected representatives, and judicial power has been overshadowed by intimidation or reprisal. In the final analysis, it is force—political, economic or, ultimately, military—that has regulated conflict. International institutions—the League of Nations, the UN—founded on such democratic principles as constitutional charters, transparency of action and independent judicial authority, have been hamstrung in carrying out the noble tasks that their statutes envisaged. Democracy has achieved real gains within states, but very meagre ones in the wider sphere, both in terms of relations between states and on global issues.

What explains this paradox? One argument advanced is that it is impossible to deal in a democratic fashion with undemocratic governments, and that the opportunistic conduct of democracies in foreign policy is actually caused by the existence of autocratic regimes. This thesis has been used to justify the Cold War policies of the liberal democracies: troops sent to Vietnam to check the advance of Soviet communism; apartheid in South Africa justified as a means of keeping out the "red menace"; the elected government in Chile overthrown to avoid a "second Cuba." We might, then, have expected a radical change in the foreign policy of liberal states after the fall of the Berlin Wall: this has conspicuously not been the case.

A further contention is that democracies do not fight each other. New statistical evidence has recently been adduced in support of this thesis, which proposes that if all states were democratic, the problems of war, self-determination and human rights would automatically be solved; global democracy itself would result through the simple adjustment of national systems. As an argument this is gravely flawed. Firstly, it is not clear which countries deserve the licence of "democratic," or who would be authorized to issue it in the first place. The attitudes of other states—friends or foes—will clearly be distorted by prevailing interests. To cite a few glaring examples: are we really convinced that Indonesia is more democratic than Iraq, Guatemala than Cuba, or Turkey than Serbia? If, as suggested by scholars who have tried to measure the actual levels of democracy within different countries, it emerged that in *all* these states democratic participation was either non-existent or merely formal, how do we justify the difference in attitude towards Turkey—a full member of the military community of Western democracies (NATO)—and Serbia, whom they bombed?

Secondly, the huge social and cultural variations that exist in the world inevitably entail a corresponding unevenness in political practice. The long march towards democracy has to be made by countries that walk at different speeds: the institutional system has to accept diversity. Finally, there is no historical or theoretical proof that the more democratic states really are more respectful of international legality than other powers. The United States, Great Britain and France—industrial powers who vaunt their long-established liberal-democratic traditions—do not hide the fact that they defend their own interests in the international sphere. The foreign interventions of democratic states are not always inspired by the principles of their own constitutions: the non-democratic peoples of Indochina had to conquer their independence by fighting first against the troops of democratic France and then against those of liberal-democratic America. The history of democracies is sadly scarred by aggression against communities which, if not democratically constituted, certainly had the sacrosanct right to their own independence. The history of colonialism shows that Britain, France and the United States—the last two famous for their declarations of human rights—while they may have respected these principles with increasing rigour regarding their own citizens, have not given a second thought to trampling over the rights of Indians, North Africans or Native Americans. To be democratic with your own people does not necessarily entail being democratic with others as well.

In short, something more than internal democracy is called for if we are to attempt to solve the social, political and environmental problems facing the world. What is needed is the democratization of the international community, a process joining together states with different traditions, at varying stages of development. This has been defined as the cosmopolitical democracy project.

Cosmopolitical democracy

Cosmopolitical democracy is based on the assumption that important objectives—control of the use of force, respect for human rights, self-determination—will be obtained only through the extension and development of democracy. It differs from the general approach to cosmopolitanism in that it does not merely call for global responsibility but actually attempts to apply the principles of democracy internationally. For such problems as the protection of the environment, the regulation of migration and the use of natural resources to be subjected to necessary democratic control, democracy must transcend the borders of single states and assert itself on a global level.

Many projects have envisaged a universal republic or world government founded on consensus and legality. There are real conceptual and political difficulties, however, in importing the democratic model conceived and developed at the state level on to a meta-state dimension. It is clearly not enough simply to project the process of internal development that states have undergone over the last two centuries on to a world scale. Fundamental aspects of that experience—the majority principle, the formulation of norms and the use of coercive power—will have to be reformulated, if they are to be applied globally.

Cosmopolitical democracy does not argue—as the federalist tradition does—that existing states must be dissolved to create a world state. Certain political and administrative functions can only be performed by states; but neither can the problems that states currently face be solved simply by increasing their size. The global extension of democracy thus involves both a new form of organization, which does not seek to merely reproduce the state model on a world scale, and a revision of the powers and functions of states at an international level, which will deprive them of the oligarchic power they now enjoy.

Above all, what distinguishes cosmopolitical democracy from other such projects is its attempt to create institutions which enable the voice of individuals to be heard in global affairs irrespective of their resonance at home. Democracy as a form of global governance thus needs to be realized on three different interconnected levels: within states, between states and at a world level.

Within states themselves, the aim must be to encourage the wave of popular participation that has swept the planet for the last decade, above all within countries—half the world's states that still have autocratic regimes. We should caution, however, against democratic fundamentalism; paraphrasing Robespierre, we cannot make people democratic against their will. There is a widespread attitude among some supporters of democracy (more accurately: some Western politicians) which may be summed up as: I, democratic state, teach you what you have to do—by fair means or foul. Ineffective in practice—and intolerably paternalistic—this approach is itself the very negation of democracy, which presupposes the existence of a dialogue between speakers of equal dignity. The community of democratic states may make an important contribution to the development of democracy in autocratic countries, but such support will be all the more effective if it anchors itself within civil society and works to further existing claims, in compliance with international rules.

Between states, the existing network of intergovernmental bodies—the United Nations and its various agencies—clearly needs to be strengthened. Numerous proposals have been made for the democratic reform of the UN, the General Assembly, the Security Council, the Court of International Justice and so on: all too often it has been the Western democracies that have shot them down—another example of how [loathe] the West can be to accept democratic procedures that conflict with its own interests.

Global democracy

Further problems arise on issues such as environmental protection and the defence of human rights where a democratic state contains no representatives of the communities that suffer the direct or indirect—consequences of the policies it employs. It can be argued that it is consistent with the interests of French people for a democratic French government to carry out nuclear experiments in the Pacific Ocean, if all the advantages go to France and the radioactive waste only harms people in another hemisphere[25]. No "national interest" is involved for Italy, France or Great Britain if Iraq, Iran or Turkey commit genocide against the Kurdish population; and even if these states decide to intervene outside their borders, how can it be decided whether their actions are motivated by self-interest or ethical responsibility? A parallel series of democratic institutions needs to be developed on a global level, in order to involve the world's citizens in decision making in areas such as these, irrespective of the political role they are allowed to play within their own states.

Why is international democratic practice so backward and so slow? Given the dramatic growth and efficiency of multinational enterprises and military force (think of NATO), it seems astonishing that political parties should still be confined almost exclusively to the national level[26]. The Socialist and Christian Democrat Internationals are devoid of effective power, while the Communist International, founded on the idea of the unity of the world proletariat, ceased to have an independent role long before Stalin suppressed it. Europe now has a single market, a single currency and a parliament elected

25. Government for the Environment (B. Gleeson & N. Low eds, 2000).

26. U. Beck, *Democracy beyond the Nation-State*, 45 Dissent 53, 53–55 (1999).

by universal suffrage; yet European parties operate essentially on a national basis, the most evident demonstration that political representation has remained locked inside state borders in an era in which civil and economic society has become internationalized. This is the true deficit of democracy: the existence of organized transnational interests far removed from any popular mandate. Simultaneously, new social and political subjects are appearing in international life. Movements for peace, human rights and environmental protection are playing a growing role which, while it should not be overestimated, nevertheless demands appropriate institutional channels if all the world's citizens are to participate.

What form should these institutions take? A world parliament? On the model of the European parliament is one proposal, and the Italian Peace Association has organized world assemblies, taking care to invite representatives of peoples rather than states. As far as individual duties are concerned, the statute of International Criminal Court **[Basic Document 1.16]** has now been approved; if it is effectively instituted, it will at last allow due procedure against the perpetrators of crimes against humanity. Progress is unbearably slow, but political institutions must adjust eventually to the boom! of globalization. Why shouldn't the process of democracy—which has already had to overcome a thousand obstacles within individual states—assert itself beyond national borders, when every other aspect of human life today, from economy to culture, from sport to social life, has a global dimension?

Humanitarian intervention

The model of cosmopolitical democracy summed up here has immediate policy implications. In what circumstances is the international community entitled to interfere in the domestic affairs of other states? How should it react to instances of ethnic cleansing, repression and the violation of human rights? It should be clear by now that the cosmopolitical project does not base itself upon the stubborn defence of state sovereignty. Immanuel Kant noted over two centuries ago that people had already reached such a degree of association that a violation of rights in *one* part of the world is felt everywhere'. Yet international human rights protection devices can only respond to a few of the thousands of abuses committed or consented to by governments every year; in such a situation, humanitarian intervention is too precious a concept to be decided on the hoof or, worse still, invoked to mask special interests or designs on power.

During the NATO air raids on Serbia, Tony Blair (the shrillest of the supporters of "humanitarian" war) claimed: "It's right for the international community to use military force to prevent genocide and protect human rights, even if it entails a violation of national sovereignty." Yet his argument—clearly paving the way for future military adventures in the post-Cold War era—says nothing about *which* authority may use force to violate state sovereignty, *who* such force should be used against or *which* human rights have to be protected. Studying the statements of politicians and commentators in support of military intervention to defend human rights, it becomes clear that a coherent philosophy to guide the international community (inevitably spearheaded by the liberal democracies on such occasions) simply does not exist. While the accuracy of military technology has increased so much that "smart" missiles now have a margin of error of mere meters, there is a total short-sightedness about the social objectives to be achieved by war[27]. A decade after the fall of the Berlin Wall, the seventeenth-century notion of state sovereignty is threatened by something older still: the law of the jungle.

In contrast to this, the cosmopolitical perspective on humanitarian intervention is informed by three principles: tolerance, legitimacy and effectiveness. Tolerance serves to set the violations of law within the appropriate political and anthropological framework. The history of the human race is marked by amazement at the customs of others. Europeans have been at once leaders in studying the habits of other populations, developing the whole field of anthropology, and ferocious oppressors of customs different from their own. The disease of violence and the saving antibody of toleration have cohabited here. The Spanish Conquistadors justified their genocide of the pre-Colombian peoples on the grounds of the Aztec practice of human sacrifice, during the very years in which the plazas of Spain blazed with the bonfires of oil in which heretics and witches were put to death—while the outraged cries of observers such as Bartolome de Las Casas set another standard, opposing violent repression with appeals to tolerance. Nothing could be further from the principle of global responsibility than a policy of religious or racial prejudice. Far from demonizing "otherness," cosmopolitical democracy would seek to understand the underlying reasons behind human rights conflicts and apply positive pressures to solve them.

Secondly, it is important to establish a clear gradation of methods to be used when the international community does decide to intervene within a given state. Economic or cultural sanctions (as used against the system of apartheid in South Africa) are quite a different thing to air raids. "Humanitarian intervention" at present is an umbrella term comprising an array of practices which differ widely in their juridical and political impact. Military force should only be used as an extreme measure, and then only on the basis of recognized international legitimization. By this I mean, first and foremost, the application of existing procedures, as envisaged in Chapter VII of the United Nations Charter **[Basic Document 1.5]**. These procedures are by no means perfect and may require alteration; what would be unjustifiable would be to rewrite them unilaterally, for the convenience of major states. Where these norms have proved themselves to be totally inadequate is *in* regulating intervention in cases of rights being violated inside a sovereign state—as so frequently in the last ten years. Here it is necessary for intervention to be legitimated by new, meta-state: institutions—to prevent the slogan "humanitarian intervention" being used as a cover for narrow geopolitical interests.

There is undoubtedly a contradiction here: the cosmopolitical project would delegate to structures devoid of coercive powers (international judicial bodies, institutions of the world's citizens) the job of establishing when force should be used, while asking states, who monopolize the means of military might, to acquiesce in their decisions. But if the governments that defined themselves as "enlightened" during the Gulf and Kosovo wars intend to perform their democratic mandate effectively, they should consult global civil society and international judicial authorities before flexing their muscles. Once humanitarian intervention in another state has been legitimated, a rigorous separation must be made between the responsibilities of the rulers

---

27. M. Kaldor, New and Old Wars. Organized Violence in a Global Era (1998).

and those of the ruled, especially where force is involved. It is intolerable to apply sanctions indiscriminately to all members of a community. If humanitarian interference is justified as an operation of "international policing," the principle of protecting individuals and minimizing so-called "collateral damage" must be fully espoused. A democratic order is founded on the premise that sanctions should affect only those who have violated the law.

"If a government commits any offence against a neighbouring sovereign or subject, and its own people continue to support and protect it ... they thereby become accessory and liable to punishment along with it ... In a like manner a nation must either allow itself to be liable for the damages, or give up the government altogether," wrote Adam Smith[28]. On this basis, the international community has felt authorized to repress the Iraqi and Serbian people for the actions of Saddam Hussein and Slobodan Milosevic.

In the cosmopolitical perspective, on the contrary, the citizens of an autocratic country whose government performs unlawful actions would be treated as hostages in a kidnapping: force should be precisely to guarantee the security of the citizens of the country. What is striking about the interventions in Iraq in 1991and Serbia in 1999 is the total lack of correspondence between the culprits of the crimes and the individuals who are the targets of the sanctions. Saddam Hussein and Slobodan Milosevic [were] more firmly in power than ever, while fresh waves of suffering [were] inflicted on their people. "Humanitarian intervention" may be judged effective, if it saves victims and brings presumed criminals to justice. It is this criterion of effectiveness that should be borne in mind in planning an operation.

These principles are clearly different from the ones which [inspired] the Gulf War and the "humanitarian" intervention in Kosovo. In both cases, the international alliance, guided by ... states, resorted to the use of military force long before means such as diplomacy and sanctions had been exhausted. The cosmopolitical deontology proposed here would have envisaged a very different course, basing itself on the civilians populations, the first victims of war. It would have offered a [model] of development founded on social and economic integration depriving the warmongers of mercenary arms and support. It would have asked the peoples in question to turn against dictators who spoke of ethnic cleansing or the annexing of other states. It would have risked sending in huge numbers of "blue helmets" on the ground, accompanied by numerous representatives [of] civil society and peace workers

Would this have proved effective in restoring sovereignty to Kuwait or ending the attacks on Albanians in Kosovo? It is hard to say. But one only has to see the results of interventionism based on bombing to realize that the international community's cure was much worse than the sickness. Almost a decade after the Gulf War, Saddam Hussein [was] still in power in a country crippled by dictatorship and the West's embargo. Milosevic [ruled] virtually unchallenged in Serbia while, in Kosovo, ethnic cleansing [continued], the only difference being the identity of the people on the receiving end and the direction in which the refugees [were] walking. This is not the cosmopolitical responsibility we are fighting for.

28. A. Smith, *The Law of Nations*, in Lectures on Jurisprudence 547 R. Meek, D. Raphael, & P.G. Stein eds,1978).

DISCUSSION NOTES/QUESTIONS

1. Does the idea of "a normative revolution" make sense as a way of framing a series of developments associated with global justice and global democracy? Does it exaggerate the significance of these developments? Does it overlook offsetting negative developments? Can these initiatives be revived in the world after September 11, given its preoccupations with global security? How does this supposed normative revolution relate to the labeling of the period after the cold war as the era of "globalization"?

2. Compare the approaches taken by Elazar Barkan and Richard Falk. Are their assessments compatible or in some tension? Barkan places particular emphasis on recoveries of lost assets and satisfaction of claims for restitution by Holocaust victims and their survivors. Why was such recovery deferred for more than five decades? Why did it happen in the 1990s? Was the willingness of banks and insurance companies to be more forthcoming toward Holocaust claimants part of a general climate associated with greater weight given to ethical considerations or did it primarily reflect the special leverage of the Jewish survivor community?

3. Is "universal jurisdiction" a radical idea? Why? Why not? Can such an idea be implemented given the unevenness of power and influence among sovereign states? Note that Belgium abandoned its effort under severe pressure from the United States, including even the threat by the U.S. Secretary of Defense Donald Rumsfeld that NATO might have to shift its headquarters from Brussels if Belgium persisted with this effort. Notable potential defendants such as Ariel Sharon and Henry Kissinger reportedly altered their travel plans to avoid Belgian territory. For extensive discussion of these issues see Christopher Hitchens, The Trial of Henry Kissinger (2001); Universal Jurisdiction: National Courts and the Prosecution of Serious Crimes Under International Law (S. Macedo ed., 2005); Henry A. Kissinger, *The Pitfalls of Universal Jurisdiction*, 80 Foreign Aff.86 (Jul/Aug 2001); Diane F. Orentlicher, *Settling Accounts: The Duty to Prosecute Human Rights Violations of a Prior Regime*, 100 Yale L. J. 2537 (1991); Steven R. Ratner, *Belgium's War Crimes Statute: A Postmortem*, 97 A.J.I.L 888 (2003); Marlise Simon, *Sharon Faces Belgian Trial After Term Ends*, N.Y. Times, 13 Feb 2003. On the relevance of the pursuit of Pinochet to the global justice movement see John Dinges, The Condor Years: How Pinochet and His Allies Brought Terrorism to Three Continents (2004); Peter Kornbluh, The Pinochet File: A Declassified Dossier on Atrocity and Accountability (2003).

4. How does one situate the objections to such initiatives as universal jurisdiction and the International Criminal Court (ICC) of the sort advanced *supra* by Jack Goldsmith & Stephen D. Krasner? Is their main argument one of strategic self-interest given the American role in the world or is it more grounded in a realist understanding of what is feasible given the structure of international society? In particular, is the worry about what they call "political mischief" associated with these moves toward accountability that would be aimed at embarrassing leaders in the West, and particularly, the United States. The debate between Hersch Lauterpacht and Hedley Bull at the outset of this Part III is relevant here. Do not universal jurisdiction and the ICC represent a natural evolution of the Grotian conception of contemporary international society as a time of increased integration, benefitted by a long buildup of relevant international law doctrines, principles, and rules?.

5. The issue of accountability of leaders under international criminal law illuminates any inquiry into the relationship between international law and world

order. *See* Roy S. Lee, The International Criminal Court: The Making of the Rome Statute (1999). As matters now stand, the United States opposes the International Criminal Court as an institution, yet favors *ad hoc* tribunals to prosecute alleged crimes of a similar sort, as with the leaders of former Yugoslavia, of Saddam Hussein's Iraq, and of sub-Saharan African countries. *See* The United States and the International Criminal Court: National Security and International Law (S. Sewall & C. Kaysen eds., 2000).

6.   The US Government favors unconditional sovereignty for itself and its friends, but maximal accountability, including capital punishment, for individuals associated with its enemies in the world. If law and justice require treating equals equally, how can such a position be defended? At the same time, if world order rests on the inequality of states, then such a double standard can be explained as an expression of unequal power that is evident in the treatment of other sensitive global issues. For instance, the possession of nuclear weapons is prohibited for states viewed as hostile or "evil," while retained and developed by the United States and the other nuclear weapons states. What does sovereignty mean in such a world order? Has it always been this way? Or does this two-tier structure of legal obligation reflect a rather recent convergence of geopolitics and globalization, eroding many boundaries and extending mechanisms of control without regard to sovereign rights? On the benefits and rationale for a law-ordered approach to American foreign policy, see Rule of Power or Rule of Law (N. Deller, A. Makhijani, & J. Burroughs eds., 2003); Philippe Sands, Lawless World: America and the Making and Breaking of Global Rules–From FDR's Atlantic Charter to George W. Bush's Illegal War (2005). Contrast this approach with that of Jack L. Goldsmith & Eric A. Posner, The Limits of International Law (2005)

7.   For further assessment of some of the themes in this chapter, consult the following specialized materials: George Andreopoulos, Genocide: Historical and Conceptual *Dimensions* (1994); Kader Asmal, Louise Asmal, and Ronald Suresh Roberts, Reconciliation Through Truth (1996); Jeremy Breecher & Tim Costello, Global Village or Global Pillage: Economic Reconstruction from the Bottom Up (1994); Alison Brysk, *Human Rights and Private Wrongs* ((2005); David Kennedy, The Dark Sides of Virtue: Reassessing International Humanitarianism (2004); Julie Mertus, Bait and Switch: Human Rights and US Foreign Policy (2004); Richard Minear, Victors' Justice: The Tokyo War Crimes Trial (1971); People out of Place: Globalization, Human Rights, and the Citizenship Gap (A. Brysk & G. Shafir eds., 2004); Samantha Power, A Problem from Hell: America and the Age of Genocide (2002); Steven R. Ratner & Jason S. Abrams, Accountability for Human Rights Atrocities in International Law: Beyond the Nuremberg Legacy (2d ed., 2001); Geoffrey Robertson, Crimes Against Humanity: The Struggle for Global Justice (1999); Telford Taylor, The Anatomy of the Nuremberg Trials (1992).

Chapter Ten

TOWARD A PROGRESSIVE GLOBAL
POLICY AGENDA

In introducing Part III, we dwelled on two distinct but overlapping and somewhat clashing sets of trends that seem likely to configure international law and world order for years—possibly decades—to come:

- trends that point to the transformation of our world of states into a global system wherein states remain crucial actors but in which non-territorial forms of organization and action assume increasing prominence—that is, whether the context be globalization in its various forms or the control of transnational crime and migration, at stake are proliferating demands for regulatory authority that cannot be met by international law as traditionally conceived and that therefore demand alternative as well as supplemental guidance and governance on the global and regional planes;

- trends that point to the rise of non-state actors and networks with radical programs for restructuring world order as well as to complementary revisions generated by the rise of the United States as a global state, claiming to provide for the security of the entire world while simultaneously exempting its own conduct (especially on matters relating to the use of force) from the discipline of international law—that is, the reshaping of global security is at stake, as is also the degree to which international law governing the use of force will remain a basis for guidance and subject to the authority of the United Nations.

Some of the issues raised by this dual *problematique* were addressed in Chapter 8, while Chapter 9 attempted to show the degree to which the peoples and governments of the world were acting to bring a global framework of law, ethics, and justice into being—described as a "global normative revolution." In this last Chapter 10, we carry this line of inquiry forward in two directions with the intention of providing a summary of all that has preceded as well as some sense of direction for the future.

Our dual focus emphasizes, first, what it means to be an international legal professional at this time in history, including the adoption of *a geopolitical ethos of species identity* that supplements—occasionally even overrides—existing identities associated with civilization, nation, region, religion, race, ethnicity, and gender, taking seriously the achievement of world solidarity as the greatest imperative of our time. Second, we consider promising potential moves or initiatives that might bridge the *governance gap* between the functional requirements of global and regional order and justice, on the one hand, and existing normative, institutional, and procedural realities, on the other. Without the concrete steps associated with global and regional governance, the adoption of a species identity by international lawyers will appear pious but politically irrelevant; governance initiatives devoid of species solidarity will tend mainly to recreate the injustices and grievance structures that have produced existing patterns of resentment and tension, especially among those who are or feel deprived.

In approaching these dual concerns, the style of response that lawyers bring to them is key, whether they be thinking and acting in a professional or civic leadership capacity or some combination. Three categories of analysis and assessment recommend themselves at the present critical time:

- a *system-maintaining* orientation, using existing lawmaking techniques to establish appropriate world order guidelines and implementing procedures in relation to war and peace, human rights, the world economy (including information technology), and ecological sustainability;

- a *system-reforming* orientation, extending the quality of intergovernmental cooperation as well as the activism of transnational social movements to improve the quality of world order, especially by encouraging improved regional governance structures, compulsory third-party dispute settlement, and global enforcement mechanisms;

- a *system-transforming* orientation, strengthening the global normative initiatives that began to flourish in the 1990s, providing global democratic arenas for the participation of global civil society, and ensuring that national foreign policies, of the powerful actors especially, accept the constraining discipline of international law, including the general applicability of accountability procedures to consider allegations of criminality arising from the behavior of political and military leaders at the level of the state.

These orientations to governance and security, it must be understood, are not meant to be mutually exclusive. To the contrary, they are understood to overlap to a considerable extent, as is self-evident when contemplating lasting solutions to problems of the sort studied in Part.II of this coursebook.

Also note that we do not view these system maintenance, reform, and transformation orientations as value-laden. We view them, rather, as descriptive and explanatory, capable of being either supported or rejected from whatever normative perspective one favors, including the world order values of the sort advocated throughout this coursebook. At the same time, the world order premise of these final Part III chapters is that global governance is a functional imperative that will have a transformative effect on Westphalian notions of world order; that the failure to address this imperative successfully will produce chaos unprecedented in kind and scope, including rising risks of ecological collapse; and that global governance that is not based on global democracy and global justice will give rise to oppression on a grand scale, with consequent varieties of disruptive—likely severe—resistance. We argue, therefore, that there exists a moral imperative to ensure that the constitutional character of global governance be respectful of everyone and fair to all.

This imperative, we believe, is especially important for lawyers to take seriously at every opportunity. Not that lawyers can be expected to facilitate, let alone ensure, humane global governance alone. The task is huge and multidimensional—multidisciplinary, multifaceted, multisectoral. But lawyers do bring many and diverse skills to the global policy agenda without which even modest success would be extremely problematic. In a classic essay on legal education written during World War II, Yale law professors Harold D. Lasswell and Myres S. McDougal identified many of the roles and functions that legal professionals (including international lawyers) perform—as investigators, drafters, legislators, promoters, interpreters, counsellors, advocates, negotiators, referees, judges, evaluators, planners, educators, reformers.[a] Even their enumeration is incomplete, however. As Lasswell and McDougal would be the first to argue, it is incomplete until it accounts also for the all-important identifications, expectations, and demands that invariably condition the individual and group roles and functions that lawyers perform and that consequently, as the legal profession is drawn evermore into our increasingly interdependent and interpenetrating world, give shape to international legal order, ergo world order itself.

The remainder of this closing chapter continues this discourse. In keeping with the dual concerns mentioned above, and mindful of the system-maintaining, system-reforming, and system-transforming styles of responses that lawyers are capable of bringing to them, it does so first with several selections on the professional stance toward international law and world order that we believe to be appropriate for lawyers with a commitment to enhancing the global public good, which is also itself clarified. Thereafter, the chapter offers several proposals that in our view follow from a commitment to human solidarity, a global rule of law, and a participatory approach to global democracy and world order.

Kofi A. Annan, UN Millennium Report: "We the Peoples: The Role of the UN in the 21st Century"

5–13 (2000)
available at <http://www.un.org/millennium/sg/report/full.htm>

The arrival of the new millennium is an occasion for celebration and reflection.

The world did celebrate as the clock struck midnight on New Year's Eve, in one time zone after another, from Kiribati and Fiji westward around the globe to Samoa. People of all cultures joined in—not only those for whom the millennium might be thought to have a special significance. The Great Wall of China and the Pyramids of Giza were lit as brightly as Manger Square in Bethlehem and St. Peter's Square in Rome. Tokyo, Jakarta and New Delhi joined Sydney, Moscow, Paris, New York, Rio de Janeiro and hundreds of other cities in hosting millennial festivities. Children's faces reflected the candlelight from Spitsbergen in Norway to Robben Island in South Africa. For 24 hours the human family celebrated its unity through an unprecedented display of its rich diversity.

a. *See* H. Lasswell & M. McDougal, *Legal Education and Public Policy: Professional*   *Training in the Public Interest*, 52 Yale L. J. 203 (1943).

tries and are spread unevenly within them. Second, in recent decades an imbalance has emerged between successful efforts to craft strong and well-enforced rules facilitating the expansion of global markets, while support for equally valid social objectives, be they labor standards, the environment, human rights or poverty reduction, has lagged behind.

More broadly, for many people globalization has come to mean greater vulnerability to unfamiliar and unpredictable forces that can bring on economic instability and social dislocation, sometimes at lightning speed. The Asian financial crisis of 1997–1998 was such a force—the fifth serious international monetary and financial crisis in just two decades. There is mounting anxiety that the integrity of cultures and the sovereignty of states may be at stake. Even in the most powerful countries, people wonder who is in charge, worry for their jobs and fear that their voices are drowned out in globalization's sweep.

Underlying these diverse expressions of concern is a single, powerful message: globalization must mean more than creating bigger markets. The economic sphere cannot be separated from the more complex fabric of social and political life, and sent shooting off on its own trajectory. To survive and thrive, a global economy must have a more solid foundation in shared values and institutional practices—it must advance broaden and more inclusive, social purposes.

The Challenge in 1945

This view was firmly embraced by the world's leaders who gathered in the waning days of the Second World War to rebuild a viable international order. They knew fully how an earlier era of economic globalization, in some respects as economically interdependent as ours, eroded steadily before collapsing completely under the shock of 1914. That global era rested on a political structure of imperialism, denying subject peoples and territories the right of self-rule.

Moreover, the major powers lacked adequate means for international political adjustment and peaceful change. To stabilize the European balance of power, for example, those powers resorted to carving up the African continent. In the economic sphere, the best they could do to achieve international financial stability was to hold levels of domestic economic activity hostage to shifts in their external balance of payments—contracting when in deficit, expanding when in surplus. This practice became untenable once the franchise was extended to ordinary people and governments began to respond gradually—and at first grudgingly—to people's needs for steady jobs and stable prices.

From the 20 years' crisis between the wars, however, the architects of the post–1945 world learned how utterly destructive it was for countries to turn their backs altogether on economic interdependence. Unrestrained economic nationalism and "beggar-my-neighbor" policies took root almost everywhere in the 1930s, spilling over into political revanchism, totalitarianism and militarism in some countries, isolationism in others. The League of Nations was critically wounded from the start, and in the face of those forces it stood no chance.

The Millennium Summit affords an opportunity for reflection. The General Assembly convened this gathering of Heads of State and Government to address the role of the United Nations in the twenty-first century. Both the occasion and the subject require us to step back from today's headlines and take a broader, longer-term view-of the state of the world and the challenges it poses for this Organization.

There is much to be grateful for. Most people today can expect to live longer than their parents, let alone their more remote ancestors They are better nourished, enjoy better health, are better educated, and on the whole face more favorable economic prospects. There are also many things to deplore, and to correct. The century just ended was disfigured, time and again, by ruthless conflict. Grinding poverty and striking inequality persist within and among countries even amidst unprecedented wealth. Diseases, old and new, threaten to undo painstaking progress. Nature's life-sustaining services, on which our species depends for its survival, are being seriously disrupted and degraded by our own everyday activities.

The world's people look to their leaders, when they gather at the Millennium Summit, to identify and act on the major challenges ahead.

The United Nations can succeed in helping to meet those challenges only if all of us feel a renewed sense of mission about our common endeavor. We need to remind ourselves why the United Nations exists—for what, and for whom. We also need to ask ourselves what kind of United Nations the world's leaders are prepared to support, in deeds as well as words. Clear answers are necessary to energize and focus the Organization's work in the decades ahead. It is those answers that the Millennium Summit must provide.

Of course, the United Nations exists to serve its Member States. It is the only body of its kind with universal membership and comprehensive scope, and encompassing so many areas of human endeavor. These features make it a uniquely useful forum—for sharing information, conducting negotiations, elaborating norms and voicing expectations, coordinating the behavior of states and other actors, and pursuing common plans of action. We must ensure that the United Nations performs these functions as efficiently and effectively as possible.

The United Nations is more than a mere tool, however, as its Charter makes clear; the United Nations was intended to introduce new principles into international relations, making a qualitative difference to their day-to-day conduct. The Charter's very first Article defines our purposes: resolving disputes by peaceful means, devising cooperative solutions to economic, social, cultural and humanitarian problems, and broadly encouraging behavior in conformity with the principles of justice and international law. In other words, quite apart from whatever practical tasks the United Nations is asked to perform, it has the avowed purpose of transforming relations among states, and the methods by which the worlds affairs are managed.

Nor is that all. For even though the United Nations is an organization of states, the Charter is written in the name of "we the peoples." It reaffirms the dignity and worth of the human person, respect for human rights and the equal rights of men and women and a commitment to social progress as measured by better standards of life, in freedom from want and fear alike.

Ultimately, then, the United Nations exists for and must serve the needs and hopes of people everywhere.

For its first 45 years, the United Nations lived in the grip of the cold war; prevented from fulfilling some of its core missions but discovering other critical tasks in that conflict's shadow. For 10 years now, the United Nations has been buffeted by the tumultuous changes of the new era doing good work in many instances but falling short in others. Now, the Millennium Summit offers the worlds leaders an unparalleled opportunity to reshape the United Nations well into the twenty-first century, enabling it to make a real and measurable difference to peoples lives.

I respectfully submit the present report to Member States to facilitate their preparations for the Summit and to stimulate their subsequent deliberations at the Summit. The report identifies some of the pressing challenges faced by the world's people that fall within the United Nations ambit. It proposes a number of priorities for Member States to consider; and it recommends several immediate steps that we can take at the Summit itself, to lift people's spirits and improve their lives.

All these proposals are set in the context of globalization, which is transforming the world as we enter the twenty-first century. In this new era people's actions constantly—if often unwittingly—affect the lives of others living far away. Globalization offers great opportunities, but at present its benefits are very unevenly distributed while its costs are borne by all.

Thus the central challenge we face today is to ensure that globalization becomes a positive force for all the world's people, instead of leaving billions of them behind in squalor. Inclusive globalization must be built on the great enabling force of the market but market forces alone will not achieve it. It requires a broader effort to create a shared future, based upon our common humanity in all its diversity.

That in turn requires that we think afresh about how we manage our joint activities and our shared interests, for many challenges that we confront today are beyond the reach of any state to meet on its own. At the national level we must govern better, and at the international level we must learn to govern better together. Effective states are essential for both tasks, and their capacity for both needs strengthening. We must also adapt international institutions, through which states govern together, to the realities of the new era. We must form coalitions for change, often with partners well beyond the precincts of officialdom.

No shift in the way we think or act can be more critical than this: we must put people at the center of everything we do. No calling is more noble and no responsibility greater than that of enabling men, women and children, in cities and villages around the world, to make their lives better. Only when that begins to happen will we know that globalization is indeed becoming inclusive, allowing everyone to share its opportunities.

We must do more than talk about our future; however, we must start to create it, now. Let the Millennium Summit signal the renewed commitment of Member States to their United Nations, by agreeing on our common vision.

Let the world's leaders prove their commitment by acting on it as soon as they return home.

* * *

In the early years of the United Nations, the General Assembly's timely adjournment could be predicted with precision: its absolute limit was fixed by the year's last voyage of the *Queen Mary*. That world, clearly, was a very different place from today's.

Indeed, when the United Nations was founded two-thirds of the current Members did not exist as sovereign states, their people still living under colonial rule. The planet hosted a total population of fewer than 2.5 billion, compared to 6 billion today. Trade barriers were high, trade flows minuscule and capital controls firmly in place. Most big companies operated within a single country and produced for their home market. The cost of transoceanic telephone calls was prohibitive for the average person and limited even business use to exceptional circumstances. The annual output of steel was a prized symbol of national economic prowess. The world's first computer had just been constructed; it filled a large room, bristled with 18,000 electron tubes and half a million solder joints, and had to be physically rewired for each new task. Ecology was a subject confined to the study of biology, and references to cyberspace would not have been found even in science fiction.

We know how profoundly things have changed. World exports have increased tenfold since 1950, even after adjusting for inflation, consistently growing faster than world GDP. Foreign investment has risen more rapidly, and sales by multinational firms exceed world exports by a growing margin, and transactions among corporate affiliates are a rapidly expanding segment of world trade. Foreign exchange flows have soared to more than $15 trillion daily up from $15 billion in 1973 when the regime of fixed exchange rates collapsed. A recent transnational telecommunications takeover created a firm whose market value exceeds the GDP of nearly half of all United Nations Members, though it ranks only as the worlds fourth most valuable company. Today rushed General Assembly delegates can cross the Atlantic in less than four hours and, if they so wish, conduct affairs of state on the Internet or telephone all the way.

This is the world of globalization—a new context for and a new connectivity among economic actors and activities throughout the world. Globalization has been made possible by the progressive dismantling of barriers to trade and capital mobility together with fundamental technological advances and steadily declining costs of transportation, communication and computing. Its integrative logic seems inexorable, its momentum irresistible. The benefits of integrative logic seems inexorable, its momentum irresistible. The benefits of globalization are plain to see: faster economic growth, higher living standards, accelerated innovation and diffusion of technology and management skills, new economic opportunities for individuals and countries alike.

Why, then, has globalization begun to generate a backlash, of which the events surrounding last November's World Trade Organization meeting in Seattle were but the most recent and highly visible manifestation?

Few people, groups or governments oppose globalization as such. They protest against its disparities. First, the benefits and opportunities of globalization remain highly concentrated among a relatively small number of coun-

Our predecessors, therefore, wisely chose a course of openness and cooperation. They established the United Nations, the Bretton Woods institutions, the General Agreement on Tariffs and Trade (later subsumed into the World Trade Organization) and a host of other organizations whose job it was to make the overall system work. Some supported decolonization, though the struggle for independence, which the United Nations was proud to promote, took too many years and cost too many lives. In the industrialized countries, domestic support for open markets was secured by constructing social safety nets and providing adjustment assistance to adversely affected groups and industries. We benefit from that legacy still.

Here, however, is the crux of our problem today: while the post-war multilateral system made it possible for the new globalization to emerge and flourish, globalization, in turn, has progressively rendered its designs antiquated. Simply put, our postwar institutions were built for an international world, but we now live in a global world. Responding effectively to this shift is the core institutional challenge for world leaders today. The Millennium Summit can help show the way.

The Challenge Today

How far we have moved from a strictly international world is evidenced by the changed nature of threats to peace and security faced by the world's people today. The provisions of the Charter presupposed that external aggression, an attack by one state against another, would constitute the most serious threat, but in recent decades far more people have been killed in civil wars, ethnic cleansing and acts of genocide, fueled by weapons widely available in the global arms bazaar. Technologies of mass destruction circulate in a netherworld of illicit markets, and terrorism casts shadows on stable rule. We have not yet adapted our institutions to this new reality.

Much the same is true in the economic realm. Here, the post-war institutional arrangements were premised on a world made up of separate national economies, engaged in external transactions, conducted at arms length. Globalization contradicts each of these expectations. It is hardly surprising, therefore, that the trade regime is under such stress it increasingly deals with traditionally "domestic" matters rather than border barriers. Nor are we surprised that calls for a new financial architecture are so insistent.

Globalization constrains the ability of industrialized countries to cushion the adverse domestic effects of further market opening. The developing countries had never enjoyed that privilege to begin with. As a result the public in both now feels exposed and insecure.

Globalization has also created new vulnerabilities to old threats. Criminal networks take advantage of the most advanced technologies to traffic around the world in drugs, arms, precious metals and stones—even people. Indeed, these elements of "uncivil society" are constructing global conglomerates of illicit activities.

Diseases have shaped history for millennia, spread by traders, invaders and natural carriers. But the most recent upsurge in the global transmission of pathogens, above all HIV/AIDS, has hit with a velocity and scope made possible only by open borders and unprecedented mobility.

Entirely new dimensions of globalization have emerged as well. While transborder pollution has been on the international agenda for decades, once the cumulative effects of industrialization were understood to affect global climate change, the world entered—literally, became enveloped by—a wholly new context in which conventional institutional remedies fare poorly.

The revolution in global communications has created new expectations that humanitarian suffering will be alleviated and fundamental rights vindicated. Neither governments nor international institutions have yet sorted out either the full implications of these expectations or how to meet them.

The communications revolution is being felt in other ways, too. The Internet is the fastest growing instrument of communication in the history of civilization, and it may be the most rapidly disseminating tool of any kind ever. The convergence of information technology, the Internet and e-commerce may well become as transformative as the industrial revolution. They will continue to alter the world's economic landscape and reconfigure organizational structures. They will change the way many people work and live. They already make it possible to leapfrog existing barriers to development, as entrepreneurs from Bangalore to Guadalajara and Sao Paulo will testify, and the range of such opportunities can be vastly expanded.

Perhaps most important, these technologies enable people to be connected directly who otherwise might remain divided by distance, culture and economic stratification, potentially creating, thereby, a better understanding of who we the peoples are. But none of these possibilities exists for those without access to the technology, either because the necessary infrastructure or capital is lacking, or because regulatory environments stand in the way.

And so the challenge is clear, if we are to capture the promises of globalization while managing its adverse effects, we must learn to govern better and we must learn how govern together better. The Millennium Summit, therefore, takes place at a compelling moment, not merely in symbolic but also in practical terms.

Governing Better Together

What do we mean by "governance" when applied to the international realm? What are some of its desirable attributes if our aim is to successfully manage the transition from an international to a global world?

In the minds of some, the term still conjures up images of world government, of centralized bureaucratic behemoths trampling on the rights of people and states. Nothing is less desirable. Weak states are one of the main impediments to effective governance today, at national and international levels alike. For the good of their own people and for the sake of our common aims, we must help to strengthen the capacity of those states to govern, not undermine them further. Moreover, the very notion of centralizing hierarchies is itself an anachronism in our fluid, highly dynamic and extensively networked world-an outmoded remnant of nineteenth century mindsets.

By the same token, states need to develop a deeper awareness of their dual role in our global world. In addition to the separate responsibilities each state bears towards its own society, states are, collectively the custodians of our common life on this planet—a life the citizens of all countries share.

Notwithstanding the institutional turmoil that is often associated with globalization, there exists no other entity that competes with or can substitute for the state. Successfully managing globalization, therefore, requires—first and foremost—that states act in a manner consistent with their dual role.

This implies, in turn, that decision-making structures through which governance is exercised internationally must reflect the broad realities of our times. The United Nations Security Council is an obvious case in point. Based on the distribution of power and alignments in 1945, the composition of the Council today does not fully represent either the character or the needs of our globalized world. The same holds in some major economic forums: all countries are consumers of globalization's effects, all must have a greater say in the process itself.

The unique role of the United Nations in the new global era derives from our universal membership and scope, and from the shared values embodied in our Charter. It is our job to ensure that globalization provides benefits, not just for some, but for all; that peace and security hold, not only for a few, but for the many; that opportunities exist not merely for the privileged, but for every human being everywhere. More than ever; the United Nations is needed to broker differences among states in power culture, size and interest, serving as the place where the cause of common humanity is articulated and advanced. More than ever, a robust international legal order, together with the principles and practices of multilateralism, is needed to define the ground rules of an emerging global civilization within which there will be room for the world's rich diversity to express itself fully.

Better governance means greater participation, coupled with accountability. Therefore the international public domain—including the United Nations—must be opened up further to the participation of the many actors whose contributions are essential to managing the path of globalization. Depending on the issues at hand, this may include civil society organizations, the private sector parliamentarians, local authorities, scientific associations, educational institutions and many others.

Global companies occupy a critical place in this new constellation. They, more than anyone, have created the single economic space in which we live; their decisions have implications for the economic prospects of people and even nations around the world. Their rights to operate globally have been greatly expanded by international agreements and national policies, but those rights must be accompanied by greater responsibilities—by the concept and practice of global corporate citizenship. The marks of good citizenship may vary depending upon circumstances but they will exhibit one common feature: the willingness by firms, wherever possible and appropriate, to pursue "good practices" as defined by the broader community, rather than taking advantage of the weaker regulatory systems or unequal bargaining positions of host countries.

The more integrated global context also demands a new degree of policy coherence while important gaps must be filled. The international financial architecture needs strengthening, as does the multilateral trade regime. Greater consistency must be achieved among macroeconomic, trade, aid, financial and environmental policies, so that all support our common aim of expanding the benefits of globalization. Conflict prevention, post-conflict peace-building, humanitarian assistance and development policies need to become more effectively integrated. In short, it is exceedingly difficult to successfully navigate the transition to a more global world with incomplete and incompatible policy fragments.

Formal institutional arrangements may often lack the scope, speed and informational capacity to keep up with the rapidly changing global agenda. Mobilizing the skills and other resources of diverse global actors, therefore, may increasingly involve forming loose and temporary global policy networks that cut across national, institutional and disciplinary lines. The United Nations is well situated to nurture such informal "coalitions for change" across our various areas of responsibility. Many of the networks can be virtual, overcoming, thereby, the usual constraints imposed by distance and time. The essential role that formal governance structures must continue to play is normative: defining objectives, setting standards and monitoring compliance.

For the United Nations, success in meeting the challenges of globalization ultimately comes down to meeting the needs of peoples. It is in their name that the Charter was written, realizing their aspirations remains our vision for the twenty-first century.

The peoples' concerns

But who are we, the peoples? And what are our common concerns?

Let us imagine, for a moment, that the world really is a "global village"—taking seriously the metaphor that is often invoked to depict global interdependence. Say this village has 1000 individuals, with all the characteristics of today's human race distributed in exactly the same proportions. What would it look like? What would we see as its main challenges?

Some 150 of the inhabitants live in an affluent area of the village, about 780 in poorer districts. Another 70 or so live in a neighborhood that is in transition. The average income per person is $6,000 a year and there are more middle income families than in the past. But just 200 people dispose of 86 per cent of all the wealth, while nearly half of the villagers are eking out an existence on less than $2 per day.

Men outnumber women by a small margin, but women make up a majority of those who live in poverty. Adult literacy has been increasing. Still, some 220 villagers—two thirds of them women—are illiterate. Of the 390 inhabitants under 20 years of age, three fourths live in the poorer districts, and many are looking desperately for jobs that do not exist. Fewer than 60 people own a computer and only 24 have access to the internet. More than half have never made or received a telephone call.

Life expectancy in the affluent district is nearly 78 years, in the poorer areas 64 years—and in the very poorest neighborhoods a mere 52 years. Each marks an improvement over previous generations, but why do the poorest lag so far behind? Because in their neighborhoods there is a far higher incidence of infectious diseases and malnutrition, combined with an acute lack of access to safe water, sanitation, health care adequate housing, education and work.

There is no predictable way to keep the peace in this village. Some districts are relatively safe while others are wracked by organized violence.

The village has suffered a growing number of weather-related natural disasters in recent years, including unexpected and severe storms, as well as sudden swings from floods to droughts, while the average temperature is perceptibly warmer. More and more evidence suggests that there is a connection between these two trends and that warming is related to the kind of fuel and the quantities of it, that the people and businesses are using. Carbon emissions, the major cause of warming, have quadrupled in the last 50 years. The village's water table is falling precipitously and the livelihood of one sixth of the inhabitants is threatened by soil degradation in the surrounding countryside.

Who among us would not wonder how long a village in this state can survive without taking steps to ensure that all its inhabitants can live free from hunger and safe from violence, drinking clean water, breathing clean air and knowing that their children will have real chances in life?

That is the question we have to face in our real world of 6 billion inhabitants. Indeed, questions like it were raised by the civil society participants at hearings held by the United Nations regional commissions in preparation for the Millennium Assembly in Addis Ababa, Beirut, Geneva, Tokyo and Santiago.

Similar sentiments were expressed last autumn in the largest survey of public opinion ever conducted—of 57,000 adults in 60 countries, spread across all six continents [see Box 10–1].

Strikingly, the centrality of human rights to people's expectations about the future role of the United Nations was stressed both at the hearings and in the survey. The current level of performance, especially of governments, was judged to be unsatisfactory.

The respondents in the Millennium Survey expressed equally strong views about the environment. Fully two thirds of them worldwide, said their governments had not done enough to protect the environment. In only 5 countries out of 60 was the majority satisfied with the government's efforts in this respect; people in developing countries were among the most critical.

The hearings and the survey alike gave the United Nations a mixed overall assessment. In the sampling of public opinion, governments received even lower ratings than the United Nations, in most countries a majority said their elections were free and fair, but as many as two thirds of all respondents felt that their country nevertheless, was not governed by the will of the people. Even in the world's oldest democracies many citizens expressed deep dissatisfaction.

Let there be no mistake. We have many success stories to tell and positive trends to report and I shall do both throughout this report. The United Nations global conferences in the 1990s, for example, laid a solid foundation of goals and action plans in the areas of environment and development, human rights, women, children, social development, population, human settlements and food security.

Box 10-1
Voices of the people: the world's largest ever public opinion survey
In 1999 Gallup International sponsored and conducted a Millennium Survey
of 57,000 adults in 60 countries

What matters most in life
- People everywhere valued good health and a happy family life more highly than anything else. Where economic performance was poor, they also stressed jobs.
- Where there was conflict people expressed a strong desire to live without it. Where corruption was endemic, people condemned it.

Human rights
- Respondents showed widespread dissatisfaction with the level of respect for human rights.
- In one region fewer than one in 10 citizens believed that human rights were being fully respected, while one third believed they were not observed at all.
- Discrimination by race and gender were commonly expressed concerns.

Environment
- Two thirds of all the respondents said their government had done too little to redress environmental problems in their country.
- Respondents in the developing countries were among the most critical of their government's actions in this respect.

The United Nations
- The survey showed that most people around the globe consider the protection of human rights to be the most important task for the United Nations. The younger the respondents, the greater the importance assigned to this goal.
- United Nations peacekeeping and the provision of humanitarian assistance were also stressed.
- Globally, less than half of those interviewed judged the performance of the United Nations to be satisfactory, although a majority of the young were favourably inclined.

Democracy
- In most countries the majority said their elections were free and fair.
- Despite this, two thirds of all respondents considered that their country was not governed by the will of the people. This opinion held even in some of the oldest democracies in the world.

At the national level, economic restructuring and political reforms are more widespread today than ever. The world's people are nevertheless telling us that our past achievements are not enough, given the scale of the challenges we face. We must do more, and we must do it better.

The challenges I highlight ... are not exhaustive. I [focus] on strategic priority areas where, in my view we can and must make a real difference to help people lead better lives. The challenges [cluster] into three broad categories.

Two founding aims of the United Nations whose achievement eludes us still: freedom from want, and freedom from fear. No one dreamed, when the Charter was written, that the third—leaving to successor generations an environmentally sustainable future—would emerge as one of the most daunting challenges of all.

REPORT OF THE PANEL ON UNITED NATIONS PEACE OPERATIONS[b] SUMMARY OF RECOMMENDATIONS

21 August 2000

available at <http://www.un.org/peace/reports/peace_operations/>

1. Preventive action:

(a) The Panel endorses the recommendations of the Secretary–General with respect to conflict prevention contained in the Millennium Report and in his remarks before the Security Council's second open meeting on conflict prevention in July 2000, in particular his appeal to "all who are engaged in conflict prevention and development—the United Nations, the Bretton Woods institutions, Governments and civil society organizations—[to] address these challenges in a more integrated fashion";

(b) The Panel supports the Secretary–General's more frequent use of fact-finding missions to areas of tension, and stresses Member States' obligations, under Article 2(5) of the Charter, to give "every assistance" to such activities of the United Nations.

2. Peace-building strategy:

(a) A small percentage of a mission's first-year budget should be made available to the representative or special representative of the Secretary–General leading the mission to fund quick impact projects in its area of operations, with the advice of the United Nations country team's resident coordinator;

(b) The Panel recommends a doctrinal shift in the use of civilian police, other rule of law elements and human rights experts in complex peace operations to reflect an increased focus on strengthening rule of law institutions and improving respect for human rights in post-conflict environments;

(c) The Panel recommends that the legislative bodies consider bringing demobilization and reintegration programmes into the assessed budgets of complex peace operations for the first phase of an operation in order to facilitate the rapid disassembly of fighting factions and reduce the likelihood of resumed conflict;

(d) The Panel recommends that the Executive Committee on Peace and Security (ECPS) discuss and recommend to the Secretary–General a plan to strengthen the permanent capacity of the United Nations to develop peace-building strategies and to implement programmes in support of those strategies.

b. Also known as "the Brahimi Report," after Ambassador Lakhdar Brahimi, Special Adviser to UN Secretary–General Kofi Annan and chair of the independent panel that was appointed by the Secretary–General to review UN peace operations and that issued the report after having done so.

3.   Peacekeeping doctrine and strategy:

Once deployed, United Nations peacekeepers must be able to carry out their mandates professionally and successfully and be capable of defending themselves, other mission components and the mission's mandate, with robust rules of engagement, against those who renege on their commitments to a peace accord or otherwise seek to undermine it by violence.

4.   Clear, credible and achievable mandates:

(a) The Panel recommends that, before the Security Council agrees to implement a ceasefire or peace agreement with a United Nations-led peace-keeping operation, the Council assure itself that the agreement meets threshold conditions, such as consistency with international human rights standards and practicability of specified tasks and timelines;

(b) The Security Council should leave in draft form resolutions authorizing missions with sizeable troop levels until such time as the Secretary–General has firm commitments of troops and other critical mission support elements, including peace-building elements, from Member States;

(c) Security Council resolutions should meet the requirements of peace-keeping operations when they deploy into potentially dangerous situations, especially the need for a clear chain of command and unity of effort;

(d) The Secretariat must tell the Security Council what it needs to know, not what it wants to hear, when formulating or changing mission mandates, and countries that have committed military units to an operation should have access to Secretariat briefings to the Council on matters affecting the safety and security of their personnel, especially those meetings with implications for a mission's use of force.

5.   Information and strategic analysis:

The Secretary–General should establish an entity, referred to here as the ECPS Information and Strategic Analysis Secretariat (EISAS), which would support the information and analysis needs of all members of ECPS; for management purposes, it should be administered by and report jointly to the heads of the Department of Political Affairs (DPA) and the Department of Peacekeeping Operations (DPKO).

6.   Transitional civil administration:

The Panel recommends that the Secretary–General invite a panel of international legal experts, including individuals with experience in United Nations operations that have transitional administration mandates, to evaluate the feasibility and utility of developing an interim criminal code, including any regional adaptations potentially required, for use by such operations pending the re-establishment of local rule of law and local law enforcement capacity.

7.   Determining deployment timelines:

The United Nations should define "rapid and effective deployment capacities" as the ability, from an operational perspective, to fully deploy traditional peacekeeping operations within 30 days after the adoption of a Security

Council resolution, and within 90 days in the case of complex peacekeeping operations.

8. Mission leadership:

(a) The Secretary–General should systematize the method of selecting mission leaders, beginning with the compilation of a comprehensive list of potential representatives or special representatives of the Secretary–General, force commanders, civilian police commissioners, and their deputies and other heads of substantive and administrative components, within a fair geographic and gender distribution and with input from Member States;

(b) The entire leadership of a mission should be selected and assembled at Headquarters as early as possible in order to enable their participation in key aspects of the mission planning process, for briefings on the situation in the mission area and to meet and work with their colleagues in mission leadership;

(c) The Secretariat should routinely provide the mission leadership with strategic guidance and plans for anticipating and overcoming challenges to mandate implementation, and whenever possible should formulate such guidance and plans together with the mission leadership.

9. Military personnel:

(a) Member States should be encouraged, where appropriate, to enter into partnerships with one another, within the context of the United Nations Standby Arrangements System (UNSAS), to form several coherent brigade-size forces, with necessary enabling forces, ready for effective deployment within 30 days of the adoption of a Security Council resolution establishing a traditional peacekeeping operation and within 90 days for complex peacekeeping operations;

(b) The Secretary–General should be given the authority to formally canvass Member States participating in UNSAS regarding their willingness to contribute troops to a potential operation, once it appeared likely that a ceasefire accord or agreement envisaging an implementing role for the United Nations, might be reached;

(c) The Secretariat should, as a standard practice, send a team to confirm the preparedness of each potential troop contributor to meet the provisions of the memoranda of understanding on the requisite training and equipment requirements, prior to deployment; those that do not meet the requirements must not deploy;

(d) The Panel recommends that a revolving "on-call list" of about 100 military officers be created in UNSAS to be available on seven days' notice to augment nuclei of DPKO planners with teams trained to create a mission headquarters for a new peacekeeping operation.

10. Civilian police personnel:

(a) Member States are encouraged to each establish a national pool of civilian police officers that would be ready for deployment to United Nations peace operations on short notice, within the context of the United Nations Standby Arrangements System;

(b) Member States are encouraged to enter into regional training partnerships for civilian police in the respective national pools, to promote a common level of preparedness in accordance with guidelines, standard operating procedures and performance standards to be promulgated by the United Nations;

(c) Members States are encouraged to designate a single point of contact within their governmental structures for the provision of civilian police to United Nations peace operations;

(d) The Panel recommends that a revolving on-call list of about 100 police officers and related experts be created in UNSAS to be available on seven days' notice with teams trained to create the civilian police component of a new peacekeeping operation, train incoming personnel and give the component greater coherence at an early date;

(e) The Panel recommends that parallel arrangements to recommendations (a), (b) and (c) above be established for judicial, penal, human rights and other relevant specialists, who with specialist civilian police will make up collegial "rule of law" teams.

11. Civilian specialists:

(a) The Secretariat should establish a central Internet/Intranet-based roster of pre-selected civilian candidates available to deploy to peace operations on short notice. The field missions should be granted access to and delegated authority to recruit candidates from it, in accordance with guidelines on fair geographic and gender distribution to be promulgated by the Secretariat;

(b) The Field Service category of personnel should be reformed to mirror the recurrent demands faced by all peace operations, especially at the mid-to senior-levels in the administrative and logistics areas;

(c) Conditions of service for externally recruited civilian staff should be revised to enable the United Nations to attract the most highly qualified candidates, and to then offer those who have served with distinction greater career prospects;

(d) DPKO should formulate a comprehensive staffing strategy for peace operations, outlining, among other issues, the use of United Nations Volunteers, standby arrangements for the provision of civilian personnel on 72 hours' notice to facilitate mission start-up, and the divisions of responsibility among the members of the Executive Committee on Peace and Security for implementing that strategy.

12. Rapidly deployable capacity for public information:

Additional resources should be devoted in mission budgets to public information and the associated personnel and information technology required to get an operation's message out and build effective internal communications links.

13. Logistics support and expenditure management:

(a) The Secretariat should prepare a global logistics support strategy to enable rapid and effective mission deployment within the timelines proposed and corresponding to planning assumptions established by the substantive offices of DPKO;

(b) The General Assembly should authorize and approve a one-time expenditure to maintain at least five mission start-up kits in Brindisi, which should include rapidly deployable communications equipment. These start-up kits should then be routinely replenished with funding from the assessed contributions to the operations that drew on them;

(c) The Secretary–General should be given authority to draw up to US$50 million from the Peacekeeping Reserve Fund, once it became clear that an operation was likely to be established, with the approval of the Advisory Committee on Administrative and Budgetary Questions (ACABQ) but prior to the adoption of a Security Council resolution;

(d) The Secretariat should undertake a review of the entire procurement policies and procedures (with proposals to the General Assembly for amendments to the Financial Rules and Regulations, as required), to facilitate in particular the rapid and full deployment of an operation within the proposed timelines;

(e) The Secretariat should conduct a review of the policies and procedures governing the management of financial resources in the field missions with a view to providing field missions with much greater flexibility in the management of their budgets;

(f) The Secretariat should increase the level of procurement authority delegated to the field missions (from $200,000 to as high as $1 million, depending on mission size and needs) for all goods and services that are available locally and are not covered under systems contracts or standing commercial services contracts.

14. Funding Headquarters support for peacekeeping operations:

(a) The Panel recommends a substantial increase in resources for Headquarters support of peacekeeping operations, and urges the Secretary–General to submit a proposal to the General Assembly outlining his requirements in full;

(b) Headquarters support for peacekeeping should be treated as a core activity of the United Nations, and as such the majority of its resource requirements for this purpose should be funded through the mechanism of the regular biennial programme budget of the Organization;

(c) Pending the preparation of the next regular budget submission, the Panel recommends that the Secretary–General approach the General Assembly with a request for an emergency supplemental increase to the Support Account to allow immediate recruitment of additional personnel, particularly in DPKO.

15. Integrated mission planning and support:

Integrated Mission Task Forces (IMTFs), with members seconded from throughout the United Nations system, as necessary, should be the standard vehicle for mission-specific planning and support. IMTFs should serve as the first point of contact for all such support, and IMTF leaders should have temporary line authority over seconded personnel, in accordance with agreements between DPKO, DPA and other contributing departments, programmes, funds and agencies.

16.   Other structural adjustments in DPKO:

(a) The current Military and Civilian Police Division should be restructured, moving the Civilian Police Unit out of the military reporting chain. Consideration should be given to upgrading the rank and level of the Civilian Police Adviser;

(b) The Military Adviser's Office in DPKO should be restructured to correspond more closely to the way in which the military field headquarters in United Nations peacekeeping operations are structured;

(c) A new unit should be established in DPKO and staffed with the relevant expertise for the provision of advice on criminal law issues that are critical to the effective use of civilian police in the United Nations peace operations;

(d) The Under–Secretary–General for Management should delegate authority and responsibility for peacekeeping-related budgeting and procurement functions to the Under–Secretary–General for Peacekeeping Operations for a two-year trial period;

(e) The Lessons Learned Unit should be substantially enhanced and moved into a revamped DPKO Office of Operations;

(f) Consideration should be given to increasing the number of Assistant Secretaries–General in DPKO from two to three, with one of the three designated as the "Principal Assistant Secretary–General" and functioning as the deputy to the Under–Secretary–General.

17.   Operational support for public information:

A unit for operational planning and support of public information in peace operations should be established, either within DPKO or within a new Peace and Security Information Service in the Department of Public Information (DPI) reporting directly to the Under–Secretary–General for Communication and Public Information.

18.   Peace-building support in the Department of Political Affairs:

(a) The Panel supports the Secretariat's effort to create a pilot Peace-building Unit within DPA, in cooperation with other integral United Nations elements, and suggests that regular budgetary support for this unit be revisited by the membership if the pilot programme works well. This programme should be evaluated in the context of guidance the Panel has provided in paragraph 46 above, and if considered the best available option for strengthening United Nations peace-building capacity it should be presented to the Secretary–General within the context of the Panel's recommendation contained in paragraph 47 (d) above;

(b) The Panel recommends that regular budget resources for Electoral Assistance Division programmatic expenses be substantially increased to meet the rapidly growing demand for its services, in lieu of voluntary contributions;

(c) To relieve demand on the Field Administration and Logistics Division (FALD) and the executive office of DPA, and to improve support services rendered to smaller political and peace-building field offices, the Panel recommends that procurement, logistics, staff recruitment and other support services for all such smaller, non-military field missions be provided by the United Nations Office for Project Services (UNOPS).

19. Peace operations support in the Office of the United Nations High Commissioner for Human Rights:

The Panel recommends substantially enhancing the field mission planning and preparation capacity of the Office of the United Nations High Commissioner for Human Rights, with funding partly from the regular budget and partly from peace operations mission budgets.

20. Peace operations and the information age:

(a) Headquarters peace and security departments need a responsibility centre to devise and oversee the implementation of common information technology strategy and training for peace operations, residing in EISAS. Mission counterparts to the responsibility centre should also be appointed to serve in the offices of the special representatives of the Secretary–General in complex peace operations to oversee the implementation of that strategy;

(b) EISAS, in cooperation with the Information Technology Services Division (ITSD), should implement an enhanced peace operations element on the current United Nations Intranet and link it to the missions through a Peace Operations Extranet (POE);

(c) Peace operations could benefit greatly from more extensive use of geographic information systems (GIS) technology, which quickly integrates operational information with electronic maps of the mission area, for applications as diverse as demobilization, civilian policing, voter registration, human rights monitoring and reconstruction;

(d) The IT needs of mission components with unique information technology needs, such as civilian police and human rights, should be anticipated and met more consistently in mission planning and implementation;

(e) The Panel encourages the development of web site co-management by Headquarters and the field missions, in which Headquarters would maintain oversight but individual missions would have staff authorized to produce and post web content that conforms to basic presentational standards and policy.

CARL KAYSEN AND GEORGE RATHJENS, "THE CASE FOR A VOLUNTEER UN MILITARY FORCE"
91 Daedalus 103 (Winter 2003)[c]

Since the end of the Cold War, the world has been awash in hot wars. Most have been waged within, rather than between, states. The Yearbook of the Swedish International Peace Research Institute (SIPRI) annually tabulates what it terms "major armed conflicts"—those resulting in more than one thousand battle deaths per year. Over the eleven years from 1990 to 2000 there were fifty-six such conflicts; only three were interstate (Iraq–Kuwait,

---

c. *Available also at* <http://mitpress. mit.edu/journals/pdf/daed_132_1_91_0.pdf>.

India–Pakistan, and Ethiopia–Eritrea). The average number of conflicts in any one year was about twenty-eight; the average conflict lasted two years.[1]

Typically, these civil wars have killed many more civilians than armed combatants; in addition, they have created even larger numbers of refugees. In an effort to extend humanitarian help, outsiders in recent years have attempted to intervene—in Yugoslavia, in Somalia, in Cambodia, and in Rwanda.

Unfortunately, the results have been mixed. In cases where no vital strategic interests are at stake, many nations, including the United States, have been slow to act and reluctant to expose their military personnel to the risk of casualties. Even when troops have been deployed, the duration of their deployment has often been limited by "exit strategies" and a stipulation that they will remain under national control. In order to keep outside ground troops out of harm's way, these outside forces are often, in effect, disarmed and ordered to use their weapons only in self-defense. The desire to avoid casualties in any case leads to a strong preference for employing air and naval power.

We believe that the most realistic, effective, and politically feasible alternative to this unsatisfactory state of affairs would be to create a modest standing UN military force. As we envision it, this force would be composed entirely of volunteers from member states—a sort of "UN Foreign Legion."

Such a force, numbering roughly fifteen thousand and backed up by larger forces remaining under national control, would dramatically improve the world community's rapid response capability when faced with humanitarian crises or civil unrest. Encouraging its creation would constitute an important expression of US global leadership at a critical moment in the development of multilateral institutions.

A half century ago, the establishment of the United Nations raised hopes that it might constitute an effective instrument for meeting the kinds of challenges we have just described. A Military Staff Committee, with representatives from the five permanent members of the Security Council (P–5), was organized and charged with creating a plan for a UN military force that might "take such action by air, sea, or land. . . . as may be necessary to maintain or restore international peace and security."[2] Planning began, but the committee was unable to agree on force levels or composition. As the Cold War developed, the UN effort was aborted. Since then, UN military efforts have been limited almost exclusively to peacekeeping—and then only when both the contesting parties and the P–5 members have been able to reach an agreement on UN intervention.

With the end of the Cold War, the likelihood of agreement among the P–5 has dramatically improved. Russia, for example, acquiesced in the US-led Desert Storm effort against Iraq and, more recently, in the US intervention in Afghanistan. There has been a revival of interest in increasing the UN's intervention capabilities, particularly in conflicts where enforcement may be an issue. Some proposals simply earmark selected national military units for

---

1. SIPRI Yearbook, 2001: Armaments, Disarment, and International Security, at Table 1a.1, at 54; text, at 52–55 (2001).

2. UN Charter [**Basic Document 1.5**], art. 42.

UN service; others create a standing UN force, based either on the rotating commitment of national units to a UN command, or on individuals volunteering for service (as they do for the French Foreign Legion).

In our view, the last option—an all-volunteer foreign-legion type force under UN control—would likely offer the best hope for responding effectively to humanitarian crises. To test this hypothesis, we will consider whether the availability of such a force might have made significant differences in the nature and effectiveness of some past UN interventionary efforts, specifically in four cases of intrastate conflict—those in Yugoslavia, Somalia, Cambodia, and Rwanda.

Earlier discussions have generally focused on quick reaction capability as the principal rationale for the development and maintenance of an all volunteer force under UN control. At present, however, months usually pass between the Security Council's vote and the assembly and organization of the contingents for an appropriate force. This also means that Security Council members—especially the United States because of its special role in providing logistic capacity for long-range deployments—in effect vote twice: once in the formal resolution and then, in practice, in their willingness to contribute troops, materiel, civilian personnel, and financial support.

Certainly, the ready availability of armed forces—whether volunteers or troops provided by member states—is essential to the UN's ability to act decisively. But equally vital is the ability of the UN to make a quick decision—and that, of course, is determined by the political calculations of the member nations, particularly the Security Council's P–5 members.

This brings us to the single greatest comparative advantage that a *volunteer* force would have over reliance on *national* forces earmarked for UN service (or "seconded" to it). The advantage lies in the fact that member nations would be more likely to deploy a volunteer force in actions involving a significant risk of casualties. When public sensitivity to casualties runs high—as it does in many modern democracies, including the United States—national leaders often feel compelled to follow public opinion. They then decide against intervention of any kind, or severely limit the scope of intervention, or authorize intervention only after a drawn-out debate whose duration is liable to cost lives in the affected region.

In at least two other important respects, an all volunteer force would be preferable to relying on seconded national forces. First is the issue of command and control. When nations commit their forces to UN or other multinational operations, they insist—none more so than the United States—on retaining ultimate authority over those forces, including the right to withdraw them peremptorily, or to exercise a veto over particular operations if they judge troop employment unwise or inconsistent with national interests. This problem would not arise with a volunteer UN force, except to the extent that the physical deployment of the volunteer force might depend on national forces such as logistical and air support.

A second reason to prefer a volunteer UN force is the question of capability in terms of equipment and, especially, training. The ad hoc assembly of national units is a poor basis on which to build a capable military force. Developing nations, often eager to supply troops as a way of financing their own armies, present a particular problem in this respect. Yet the UN system often must use these troops, even if the more militarily competent nations were willing to offer all the forces needed—which they rarely are.

In many situations of intervention, a long-term presence of some force will be needed to help maintain peace during a process of social and political reconstruction. The scale of the proposed UN volunteer force discussed below, however, is far too small to allow it alone to provide long-term deployments. Thus the likely need for the long-term presence of peacekeeping forces would persist.

[The case for a volunteer UN force]

In what follows, we will briefly review the history of four UN peacekeeping operations—in Yugoslavia, Somalia, Cambodia, and Rwanda—and attempt in general terms to assess the differences that a standing UN force might have made on the outcomes.[3]

The conflict in Yugoslavia, and especially in Bosnia, is probably the richest mine we have for a counterfactual analysis of the utility—and limitations—of a standing UN volunteer force. From the beginning, serious problems hampered the efforts of the international community to mitigate conflict in Yugoslavia and prevent escalation.

Germany and Austria were particularly sympathetic to Croatian and Slovenian aspirations for early independence within the boundaries they had as republics in the Yugoslav federation. Most of the rest of the world community believed, in contrast, that the maintenance of some kind of Yugoslav federation, or at least confederation, offered the best hope for peace and stability in the region. Russia, not surprisingly, was much less critical of the Serbs than were the other major powers, and the United States was much more so.

Debates persisted about whether the lead agency for international intervention should be the United Nations, the European Community/Union

---

3. The descriptions that follow are drawn from a variety of sources: (a) Susan Woodward offers a comprehensive review of the background of the conflict in Yugoslavia and operations through 1994 in Balkan Tragedy: Chaos and Dissolution after the Cold War (1996). Other particularly useful background papers are John Zametica's The Yugoslav Conflict, Adelphi Paper 270 (The International Institute for Strategic Studies, 1992), and James Steinberg's *International Involvement in the Yugoslavia Conflict*, in Enforcing Restraint: Collective Intervention in Internal Conflicts (L. Damrosch ed., 1993) [hereinafter "Damrosch"]. For . . . events in Kosovo, see SIPRI Yearbook, 2000, at 28–33; (b) The background and story of the 1991–94 intervention in Somalia can be found in T. Lyons & A. Samatar, Somalia: State Collapse, Multilateral Intervention, and Strategies for Political Reconstruction (1995); J. Clark, *Debacle in Somalia: Failure of the Collective Response*, in Damrosch, *supra*; C. Crocker, *The Lessons of Somalia*, 74 (3) Foreign Aff (May/Jun 1995); and J. Hirsch & R. Oakley, Somalia and Operation Restore Hope (US Institute of Peace, 1995); (c) For reviews of the UN intervention in Cambodia, see T. Findlay, Cambodia:

The Legacy and Lessons of UNTAC (1995); J. Shear, *The Case of Cambodia*, in Beyond Traditional Peacekeeping (D. Daniel and B. Hayes eds., 1995); S. Ratner, *The United Nations in Cambodia: A Model for Resolution of Internal Conflicts?*, in Damrosch, *supra*; W. Shawcross, Cambodia's New Deal (Carnegie Endowment for International Peace, 1994); and S. Prasso, *Cambodia: A $3 Billion Boondoggle*, Bull. Atomic Scientists (Mar/Apr 1995). *See also* UN Security Council Resolution 880, UN Doc. S/RES/880, 4 Nov 1993; (d) The conflict in Rwanda is reviewed in T. Seybolt, *Whither Humanitarian Intervention? Indications from Rwanda*, 5 (1) Breakthroughs (Spring 1996). The best overall account of events and their antecedents can be found in G. Prunier, The Rwanda Crisis: History of a Genocide (1995); e) For the East Timor conflict, see SIPRI Yearbook, 2000, at 26–28.

(EC/EU), or NATO—or even, possibly, the Western European Union (WEU) or the Organization for Security and Cooperation in Europe (OSCE). There were also differences about how to organize the international effort. Britain espoused a sharper demarcation than did the United States in force requirements and training for peacekeeping, on the one hand, and for peace enforcement on the other. Given these differences and, in the later stages of the war, differences between the government of Serbia and the local Serbs in Croatia and Bosnia, not to mention ever increasing animosities whipped to a frenzy by the nationalist leaders of the contesting factions, cease-fire and mediation efforts by the intervening powers proved fitful at best.

With memories still fresh of the Vietnam War and World War II, when Yugoslav partisans tied down some twenty German and Allied divisions for many months, outside powers were not eager to risk significant casualties in an effort to try to *enforce* a solution to the conflict. Britain and France accordingly introduced peacekeeping forces only after the Serbs and Croats had agreed to a ceasefire, by which time most of the Krajina had fallen to the Serbs.

Much later, in 1999, the fighting moved on to the Albanian-majority province of Kosovo. Serbia resisted the efforts of the Kosovo liberation movement, one part of which sought the renewal of the autonomy the province had formerly enjoyed, another part of which wanted the Kosovo Liberation Army to lead an armed campaign for independence, or possibly to join Albania in creating a Greater Albania. After negotiations between Serbia and the "Contact Group" [comprising] France, Germany, Italy, Russia, the United Kingdom, and the United States failed, NATO, without UN authorization and against the objections of Russia, initiated a bombing campaign against a variety of economic and military targets in Serbia and against Serbian military forces in Kosovo.

Nearly three months later, partly because of the bombing, partly because Serbia lost Russia's support, Serbia agreed to withdraw its large forces—about forty thousand military, paramilitary, and police—from Kosovo. The Security Council then authorized a NATO led force of some fifty thousand. After the Serbs had withdrawn and the NATO force had started its deployment, the great majority of the eight hundred thousand refugees who had fled during the Serbian repression and the bombing returned.

Had a UN volunteer force been available early on, at the very beginning of the Serbian attacks on Croatia and Bosnia, there would likely have been less sensitivity about casualties. As a result, it might have been possible to introduce the force earlier with salutary effects, particularly if it had had a mandate to engage in some enforcement actions. Such a force would have strengthened the hands of Lord Carrington, acting for the EC/EU, and of Cyrus Vance, acting for the UN, and a peaceful resolution of the conflict might have resulted. Or, had the need arisen, the UN force might have taken effective enforcement actions against Serb forces in Croatia or later in Bosnia when all sides, but particularly the Bosnian Serbs, repeatedly flouted UN injunctions proscribing attacks against "safe areas" and interference with the delivery of humanitarian relief.

The war in Somalia had its genesis in the chaotic struggle for power between clan leaders that erupted after the fall of the Siad Barre government in January of 1991. In response to looting by gangs and the prospect of famine unless order was restored, the UN became engaged early in 1992. In March of that year, it succeeded in brokering a cease-fire between the principal clan leaders in Mogadishu. It dispatched fifty unarmed peacekeepers to monitor compliance with the ceasefire and authorized the formation and deployment in April of a five-hundred troop Pakistani battalion to protect the delivery of humanitarian relief supplies.

Unfortunately, key governments, notably the United States, showed a general lack of support for the operation. Logistical and financial problems, as well as negotiations toward an agreement with Somali clan leaders for the introduction of the force, also posed difficulties. By September of 1991, when the UN force was fully deployed, the situation in Mogadishu had so degenerated that UN troops could not safeguard the delivery of food and other relief supplies. With international impunity Somali clan leaders were able to frustrate the conciliation efforts of the UN secretary-general's special representative in the field. In short, the first phase of operations in Somalia was a story of too little too late.

As the horrors of starvation and the breakdown of public order in Somalia became apparent on the nightly news, President George H. W. Bush, responding to public pressure, authorized the Marine Corps to lead a thirty-eight-thousand-troop intervention in December of 1992, with the limited objective of facilitating humanitarian relief efforts. As intended, this phase of operations lasted only a few months, but succeeded in saving many lives.

Although some US forces remained in Somalia, the UN took over the major interventionary responsibility in May of 1993 with a weaker force charged with a broader "nation-building" mandate. Unfortunately, the expanded mandate was clearly beyond UN capabilities. When eighteen Americans and a number of Pakistani troops were killed later in the year, US public opinion turned strongly against continued involvement, and President Bill Clinton announced that US forces would be withdrawn by the end of March of 1994. This third phase ended a year later, without accomplishing any of its objectives. There were further difficulties in Somalia with unity of command; national forces failed to respond to orders from field commanders because of conflicting instructions from their capitals. Such problems would not have arisen with an all-volunteer UN force.

Had a force of several thousand well trained UN volunteers been available for deployment in early 1992, the humanitarian relief mission could quite plausibly have been accomplished in less than a year without the Marine Corps intervention. Achieving the expanded objectives that the UN favored but the United States resisted, however, would have required a much larger force for a much longer period of time—and substantial commitment by the world community for nonmilitary support, also for many years. As it is, Somalia remains a failed state—a case for UN trusteeship.

The UN intervention in Cambodia grew out of the 1991 Paris Peace Agreement,[d] which was meant to end two decades of terrorism and civil war by producing a unified—and freely elected—Cambodian government. The

---

d. The Agreement, signed on 23 Oct 1991, is available at <http://www.khmerinstitute. org/docs/PPA1991.htm>.

Security Council has characterized the operation as "a major achievement of the United Nations." UN troops repatriated three hundred sixty thousand refugees and displaced persons from Thai border regions. In addition, a technically free and fair election was held with an extraordinarily high level of participation.

But, in fact, the UN's Cambodia mission must be judged a failure. Despite the high voter turnout, the UN was unable to protect opposition parties from a centrally directed government campaign of terror and intimidation. At best, 10 percent of the nation's roughly three hundred fifty thousand armed combatants were demobilized. Most significantly, the Khmer Rouge was able to sabotage the goal of national unification: although it had been a party to the Paris Peace Agreement—and a major cause of the ruthlessness of the nation's long civil war—it refused to participate in the election and to permit UN access to the parts of the country it controlled.

Might things have gone better if the UN had had an all-volunteer military force at its disposal instead of having to rely on seconded troops? Many of the sixteen thousand troops that were actually deployed were ill-equipped and ill-disciplined—problems that would not have plagued a well-trained volunteer force. Also, the force could probably have been deployed soon after the Paris accords—not eight months later, as was the case. Such earlier deployment would have made it possible to make considerably more progress in the disarmament mission. According to observers in the field, rapid deployment might also have helped to deter disorder.

Perhaps the most interesting question is whether, with a volunteer force, the UN would have been able to compel the Khmer Rouge to comply with the Paris Peace Agreement. Perhaps doing so would have been unwise, given the Khmer Rouge's military capabilities and ideological fanaticism, and given the possibility of negative reactions from China and other Southeast Asian states. Perhaps the Paris consensus might not have survived, and perhaps one or more outside parties would have resumed their support of the Khmer Rouge.

At least one moral of the story is clear: If the broader nation-building objectives of the UN intervention were to be realized—particularly in the absence of a resolution of the Khmer Rouge problem—the UN would doubt-less have had to maintain a substantial military presence in Cambodia for a number of years, as well as provide resources for the civil components of the UN mission. The Cambodian mission, then, highlights the reasons why the international community must take seriously the need not only for an enhanced volunteer UN military force, but also for a well-qualified UN "peace corps" able to help reconstruct war-ravaged societies.

From the perspective of the international community, which had recently been stung by the failure of humanitarian intervention in Somalia, the genocidal war between Hutus and Tutsis in Rwanda could not have come at a worse time or place: Africa, in April of 1994. At the time, a UN Assistance Mission (UNAMIR I) with a force of twenty-five hundred troops was already in Rwanda. Yet the immediate Security Council reaction was not to increase its strength, but to reduce it—to a mere three hundred troops. Moreover, the Security Council, ignoring the secretary-general's call for strengthening the force and increasing active intervention, limited UNAMIR I's mandate to brokering a cease-fire and assisting in relief efforts.

A month later, the UN belatedly authorized a fresh deployment of fifty-five hundred troops for UNAMIR II, again with a limited mandate. But as late as August, the UN force had not yet reached its authorized strength. After the fiasco in Somalia, there was little disposition in the world community to incur the costs of trying to stop the genocide. France was the exception; it deployed a force in Rwanda during the period of June 22 to August 22, which had some success in protecting the southwestern part of the country. (More than any other advanced industrial state, France has been willing to engage in peace enforcement operations. Relying largely on its Foreign Legion, French political leaders may not have been as sensitive as others to the risk of casualties.)

Of the cases we have considered, Rwanda provides the best example of the likely utility of a standing UN quick reaction force. Had such a force been available when the secretary-general proposed the strengthening of field capability in late April, the Security Council may well have authorized its deployment instead of voting to reduce the UNAMIR force. Assuming US logistic support—not an unreasonable assumption—the larger force could have been deployed in sufficient time to save hundreds of thousands of lives. And, considering the experience of the French, such a UN force would most likely have experienced few casualties. As it was, over a period of four and a half months, and out of a population of about eight million Rwandans, eight hundred thousand died, two million became refugees, and two million became internally displaced persons.

This review suggests that the world community could have, and in some instances likely would have, responded to each of these four crises with greater effectiveness had a well-trained and equipped all-volunteer UN force been available. Of course, the fact that interventionary forces were deployed in most of these cases for protracted periods of time—in Yugoslavia, the clock is still running—raises serious questions about the necessary size and mission of an effective UN military force.

Would a relatively small rapid deployment force be sufficient to realize UN objectives? Might a volunteer UN force be effectively supplemented by seconded national units, so that the UN force could be relieved soon enough to respond to other crises? We believe the answer to both questions is a qualified "yes."

The situations we have examined fall somewhere on the force spectrum between "classic peacekeeping" and enforcing the UN Charter's Chapter VII prohibition of aggression. Monitoring a truce line in situations where conflict has ceased and the parties have agreed to accept the intervening force usually requires a thousand troops. But stopping aggression—as the UN tried to do in Korea and Iraq—is an altogether more daunting task, requiring several hundred thousand troops.

In the intermediate situations that we have been reviewing, an intervening force will typically have a shifting variety of tasks, including:

- Preventive deployments to forestall violence between communities or states;

- Monitoring or supervising a tense situation, stalemate, cease-fire, or settlement;

- Establishing, monitoring, or supervising cantonment areas, demilitarized zones, and buffer zones between warring parties, which may involve interposition by the field force;

- Support, supervision, and implementation of a process of disarming and demobilizing the warring factions;

- Protection and support of humanitarian assistance efforts;

- Noncombatant evacuation under threat;

- Establishing protective zones;

- Protection and support of national reconstruction and reconciliation efforts, including the conduct of elections;

- Helping to restore and maintain general civil order; and

- Enforcing sanctions.

All of these tasks would have to be performed in situations where the threat of armed resistance is real and present. If it is to help achieve a political resolution of the underlying conflict, a UN military force will need to be capable of fulfilling all three of the ultimate political functions of armed force—compulsion, deterrence, and reassurance. The force must be sufficient to compel each side to stop the violence, to deter those who might resort to violence, and to reassure the general public that it need neither fight nor flee.

The most detailed and persuasive analysis of what a UN rapid reaction force should be is that of Carl Conetta and Charles Knight.[4] Examining the troop requests submitted by the commanders of the UN operations in Yugoslavia, Cambodia, Somalia, Mozambique, Haiti, and Rwanda between 1992 and 1994, Conetta and Knight concluded that meeting those requests would have required a force capable of continuous deployment of fifteen thousand troops in the field. This level of deployment would in turn have required a total force of 43,750 personnel, whose operating costs would have been about $3.5 billion per year.

We believe that the size and cost of such a force are much too large to propose to the international community. In our judgment, the size of the recommended force must fall somewhere between the smallest force that could reasonably perform the required tasks and the largest and most expensive force that member states, particularly the major powers, would allow the UN to command. We believe a force of fifteen thousand; of which eleven thousand would be deployable—half of that for long periods—meets these criteria.[e] ...

4. C. Conetta & C. Knight, Vital Force: A Proposal for the Overhaul of the UN Peace Operations System and for the Creation of a UN Legion (Commonwealth Institute, Oct 1995). Other discussions of a UN force include: (a) B. Urquhart, *For a UN Volunteer Force*," 40 (11) New York Review of Books (10 Jun 1993); (b) T. Stanley, J. Lee, & R. von Pagenhardt, To Unite Our Strength: Enhancing the United Nations Peace and Security System (1992), ch. 2; (c) Partners for Peace: Strengthening Collective Security for the 21st Century (United Nations Association of the United States, 1992), see especially ch. 3 and recommendations, at. 42; (d) Capt. E. Dennehy USCG) *et al.*, A Blue Helmet Combat Force, Policy Analysis Paper 93–101 (National Security Program, John F. Kennedy School of Government, 1993); (e) L. Haynes & T. Stanley, *To Create a United Nations Fire Brigade*, 14 Comparative Strategy 7–21 (Jan–Mar 1995); (f) Towards a Rapid Reaction Capability for the United Nations (Canadian Department of Foreign Affairs and International Trade, Sep 1995).

e. The organization and personnel of this force are shown in two tables omitted here.

A rough estimate of the annual cost of operating the force described is $1.25 billion to $1.5 billion per year. About 25 percent of this is the annual cost of equipment and facilities. These figures should be compared with UN peacekeeping expenditures of $2.5 billion in 2000. Much of the expenditure for a new voluntary force would be a substitute for, not a net addition to, current peacekeeping costs.

In addition to marshalling the force itself, the UN would need to maintain a substantial military base where the force would train and be stationed when not deployed. The base should be large enough to accommodate visits from detachments of national units from various countries for joint training with this UN force. Preparing and maintaining a base would add another substantial element of cost. But with the downsizing of military forces in many countries, facilities should be available, and at costs far lower than those of creating a new base.

Wherever the force was based, it would have to be moved to the site of its operation for any intervention. Providing it with an organic logistic capacity to make this possible would be prohibitively expensive; it would have to rely on national capabilities to provide logistic capacity. In effect, this means relying on the United States, which has provided most of the logistic support for the forces that have been seconded to the UN by member states.

* * *

The number and scale of UN interventions in recent years makes plain that the standing force we envisage could not meet all UN objectives on its own. It would require backup forces of some kind. This UN standing force might be capable of two simultaneous missions, but no more, and its operational concept should require an assessment of the success of an operation after no more than six months from initial deployment. If the intervention succeeds in damping violence and moving the conflict to the political arena, then a smaller peacekeeping force drawn from member states could replace the standing force. If not, the Security Council would be faced with the decision to either replace the standing force units with larger and perhaps more heavily armed national units or withdraw from the conflict altogether. Our plan would thus be incomplete without a provision for backup forces, included in most proposals for a rapid reaction force. These consist of national units designated for UN service in both peacekeeping and combat modes, trained and exercised to a common standard and doctrine.

For both political and operational reasons, these backup forces should be organized and deployed regionally and should consist of units designated from the national forces of cooperative states in the region. These forces would train and exercise together on a regular basis, and the UN standing force HQ would play an advisory and standard-setting role in this training process. The contributing states would benefit from the upgrading of the capabilities of their armed forces.

Meanwhile, they would have to be persuaded that doing so is politically worthwhile—that an investment in cooperative rather than competitive security is desirable.

But would the advantages of the regional forces' proximity in terms of operational ease outweigh the potential disadvantage of their having a direct interest in the conflict and its outcome? This difficult question goes to the heart of how best to balance the cooperative and competitive paths to peace and security. How one answers this question will determine, in part, how one thinks about not only the creation of regional forces, but also the very idea of a UN military force.

Schematically, appropriate coverage and operational considerations would suggest the creation of at least six such regional forces: one each for Africa, Latin America (including the Caribbean), West Asia, South Asia, East Asia, and Europe. The scale of national forces varies widely in the different regions, both in relation to each other and to the proposed UN standing force, so that the appropriate size for a regional force would also vary. Neither the UN standing force nor the national regional forces could, or should, be used to engage the national armies of states with substantial military power. The political feasibility of establishing such a regional force also varies greatly among the different regions. In both West and South Asia, for instance, major countries are in a state of ongoing hostility that would make a regional force hard to create. Perhaps the region in which such a force is most needed and might do the most immediate good is Africa; yet the possibility of creating a competent force there in the near future is not bright.

If we think of a battalion with a strength of some seven hundred fifty or one thousand as the smallest combat unit that can be effectively deployed as a constituent of a larger multinational force, then an ideal regional force might have up to twenty-five combat battalions plus independent supporting units of transport, supply, engineering, military police, medical, and sanitation troops. These would form the pool from which a force could be drawn when needed.

Withdrawing the standing force and replacing it with elements drawn from the committed backup forces would make it possible for the former to continue to serve its deterrent function in other potential conflicts. In such a replacement, the HQ element of the standing force could remain for some time to act as the memory store for the incoming forces, ensuring continuity of action.

The creation of a UN standing force would require further upgrading of the UN's Department of Peacekeeping Operations (DPKO). The capabilities and organization of the department have been substantially improved in the last several years, but much more needs to be done. Further changes should involve two levels of the UN: the Security Council and secretary-general, and the DPKO in relation to other parts of the organization. At the higher level, the Military Staff Committee or its functional equivalent must be reactivated, enlarged to include representatives from member states that are substantial contributors to ongoing field operations, and capable of functioning full-time whenever an operation is in progress. The DPKO in turn would need to add the administrative capacities required to maintain its military force, including recruitment, training, procurement, and logistics. The current UN system, whereby procurement depends on the approval of the undersecretary of the Department of Administration and Budget—an entirely separate UN department—is unworkable. The budget function must become an integral part of the DPKO's operations.

Creating the capabilities described above would in many instances make it possible for the international community to respond to crises and undertake peacemaking and enforcement operations more quickly. This could be expected to increase the likelihood of realizing several of the potential objectives of such interventions: saving lives and reducing human suffering, facilitating political settlements between contestants, and perhaps undertaking nation building activities. It would also have a broader deterrent effect, which in some cases would make diplomatic intervention alone effective in preventing armed conflict. And it would provide a strength to Security Council resolutions that is now lacking.

The advantages of early deployment should not, however, be exaggerated. In few, if any, of the above instances would the existence of such a force on its own have made much of a difference (Rwanda may be an exception). Fully capitalizing on a UN standing force's advantages will depend on various additional reforms the UN would have to undertake. Such reforms include improving staff work, quickening force deployment decision-making processes, more clearly defining mission mandates, and improving command-and-control procedures, including arrangements for civil-military coordination.

The UN cannot maintain a standing force on the basis of current financing arrangements, which are a mixture of voluntary contributions and special assessments for each operation. Instead, the support of both the standing force and traditional peacekeeping operations should be made part of the regular budget. Some larger operations—in particular, any relatively large-scale Chapter VII activities—might be best handled by special assessments. Together with the necessary strengthening of the DPKO, the creation of a standing force might result in an annual cost for peacekeeping operations (excluding large-scale Chapter VII activities) of $5–$6 billion, about twice their current level.

To put this number in some context, it is worth noting that world military expenditures in 2001 were about $835 billion. Of this, the US share was about 39 percent. The other big spenders—thirteen countries with military budgets of $10–$60 plus billion—had a 41 percent share; the share of the other 157 countries amounted to only 20 percent[5]

The creation of a volunteer UN force would require a mobilization of political will at a time when many members of the UN, including the Security Council P–5, view the organization with a mixture of skepticism and hostility. This attitude is strongest in the United States, but it is widely shared. After all, the majority of UN member states are developing countries that are among the more likely targets of outside intervention.

The most widespread objection to an all-volunteer UN force—aside from the economic costs—has been the lack of confidence in UN decision-making, and often a specific lack of confidence in UN secretaries-general. We see little basis for such concern. Developing and approving a mandate for UN operations will, for as far into the future as we can imagine, be a Security Council responsibility, with the P–5 members, at least, having veto power. Although secretaries general will presumably have executive powers, we see no need for these powers to be greater—or otherwise different than those needed for the

5. International Institute of Strategic Studies, The Military Balance 2002–3, Table 26, at. 332 *et. seq.*

management of UN operations under the present arrangement of relying on seconded forces.

In the present political mood of the United States the proposal outlined in the preceding pages may well appear to be sheer fantasy. But the underlying reality of violent intrastate conflict remains, and we cannot simply persist in looking the other way; the "CNN effect" and the activities of a host of nongovernmental organizations prevent such an option.

The US stakes in enhancing rather than undermining the capacities of the UN are of two kinds. The first is that the United States is the one power with global involvements; serious conflict anywhere is likely to involve the United States if it persists, and even more likely to involve the country if it spreads. Yet the United States has neither the capacity nor the mandate to act alone as a global policeman.

The second reason why the United States has a stake in strengthening the UN is its deep commitment to securing a liberal world order based on a global free market. The United States sees such an order as the key to achieving a minimum harmony of interests between rich and poor countries, slowly diminishing the gap between rich and poor nations through free trade and growing prosperity. Such an order cannot flourish in a world rent by widespread violent conflict.

If the United States cannot alone bear the burden of securing international order, then it must persuade others to help. The UN, backed by regional organizations—what might be called the formal international system—offers the best instrument for achieving this order, for only the formal international system has the political legitimacy to police the world.

RICHARD FALK AND ANDREW STRAUSS, "THE DEEPER CHALLENGES OF GLOBAL TERRORISM"

Debating Cosmopolitics 203–231 (D. Archibugi ed., 2003)

Answering the terrorist challenge

Audacious and gruesome terrorist attacks on the World Trade Center and the Pentagon, along with the military response, have been the defining political events of this new millennium. The most profound challenge directed at the international community, and at all of us, is to choose between two alternative visions. What we call the traditional statist response emphasizes "national security" as the cornerstone of human security. Centralization of domestic authority, secrecy, militarism, nationalism, and an emphasis on unconditional citizen loyalty, to her or his state as the primary organizing feature of international politics are all attributes of this approach.

We recommend an alternative vision, one that we call democratic transnationalism. Democratic transnationalism attempts to draw on the successes of democratic, particularly multinational democratic, orders as a model for achieving human security in the international sphere. This approach calls for the resolution of political conflict through an open transnational citizen/societal (rather than state or market) centered political process legitimized, by fairness, adherence to human rights, rule of law, and representative community participation. The promotion of security for individuals and groups through international human rights law in general, as reinforced by the incipient international criminal court with its stress on an ethos of individual legal responsibility, assessed within a reliable constitutional setting, is a crucial element of this democratic transnationalist vision, which aspires to achieve a cosmopolitan reach.

Before the events of September 11 we had argued in favour of the establishment of a distinct, global institutional voice for the peoples of the world as a beneficial next step to be taken to carry forward the transnational democratic project. We proposed the GPA, which we have variously identified as a Global Parliamentary Assembly, and interchangeably as a Global Peoples' Assembly. So far we have deliberately refrained from setting forth a detailed blueprint of our proposal, partly to encourage a wide debate about the general idea, partly to generate a sense of democratic participation in the process of establishing such a populist institution. We have expressed a tentative preference for representation on a basis that would, to the extent possible, incorporate the principle of "one person one vote." The eventual goal would be to enfranchise as voting constituents all citizens of the planet above a certain age. We have further taken the position that the GPA should not interfere in matters appropriately defined as within "the internal affairs of states," although acknowledging that the extent of such deference is bound to shift through time and often be controversial in concrete instances. The main mission of the GPA would be to play a role in democratizing the formulation and implementation of global policy. It is our conviction that such an assembly's powers should always be exercised in conformity with the Universal Declaration of Human Rights **[Basic Document 3.3]**, and other widely accepted international human rights instruments.

We believe that carrying out the transnational democratic project, including establishing the GPA, should be treated as part of the political response to the challenges posed by the sort of mega-terrorism associated with the September 11 attacks. Transnational terrorism, which consists of networks of dedicated extremists organized across many borders, of which al Qaeda is exemplary, is so constituted that its grievances, goals, recruitment tactics and membership, as well as its objects of attack, are all wholly transnational. This form of political violence is a new phenomenon. It is the frightfully dark side of an otherwise mostly promising trend toward the transnationalization of politics. This trend, a result of economic and cultural globalization, has manifested itself in a pronounced way since the street demonstrations staged against the 1999 WTO meeting in Seattle.

The state-centric structures of the international system are not adequate to address this new transnational societal activism and, in fact, the arbitrary territorial constraints on the organization of work and life have intensified various forms of frustration, which feed the rise of transnational terrorism. One cause of this frustration is that globalization in all its dimensions is bringing with it changes of great magnitude that often directly impact on the lives of individuals and regions. These changes range from growing income inequality within and between many societies to powerful assaults on cultural traditions that offend non-Western peoples. Adverse impacts of globalization on many adherents of Islam have definitely induced political extremism in recent decades even before September 11, starting with the Iranian Revolution of the late 1970s.

Even in democratic societies there is a growing sense that domestic politics is not capable of responding creatively to long range challenges of regional and global scope. It is certainly the case that the magnitude of these challenges is well beyond the capacities of even the strongest of states to shape benevolently on their own. At the same time individuals have an ever-greater incentive to influence global decision-making through their use of the technologies of globalization, especially the Internet. Information technology has given individuals an unprecedented ability to increase their leverage on public issues by making common cause with like-minded others without regard to considerations of geography or nationality.

An institutional framework such as that which would be provided by a GPA is a democratic way to begin peacefully to accommodate this new internationalization of civic politics. Individuals and groups could channel their frustrations into efforts to attempt to participate in and influence parliamentary decision waking as they have become accustomed to doing in the more democratic societies of the world. Presently, with trivial exceptions, individuals, groups and their associations are denied an official role in global political institutions where decision-making is dominated by elites who have been officially designated by states. Intergovernmental organizations, such as the United Nations [UN], the World Trade Organization [WTO] and the International Monetary Fund [IMF] are run as exclusive membership organization operated by and for states. With the possibility of direct formalized participation in the international system foreclosed, frustrated individuals and groups (especially when their governments are viewed as illegitimate or hostile) have been turning to various modes of civic resistance, both peaceful and violent. Global terrorism is at the violent end of this spectrum of transnational protest, and its apparent agenda may be mainly driven by religious, ideological and regional goals rather than by resistance directly linked to globalization. But its extremist alienation is partly, at the very least, an indirect result of globalizing impacts that may be transmuted in the political unconscious of those so afflicted into grievances associated with cultural injustices.

In addition to helping provide a non-violent and democratic channel for frustrated individuals and groups to affect meaningfully global decision-making, a GPA has the potential to provide a way of helping to resolve inter-societal and more recently civilizational conflict and polarization. Presently, the institutions around which citizen politics is formally structured are confined within distinct domestic political systems. This makes a unified human dialogue on issues of shared concern impossible and transnational remedies for perceived injustices are not available. In a globalizing world it is crucial to encourage [a] ... debate and discussion of global issues that builds consensus, acknowledges grievances, and identifies cleavages in a manner that is not dominated by the borders of sovereign territorial states, or even by innovative regional frames of reference as in Europe. As a consequence of this existing pattern of fragmentation in the political order, societies and cultures develop their own distinctive and generally self-serving distortions and myths, or perhaps, at the very least, experience exaggerated differences of perception that feed pre-existing patterns of conflict. Most persons within one society have little difficulty identifying the distorted perceptions of others, but tend to be oblivious to their own biases, an insensitivity nurtured by mainstream media especially in the midst of major crises. The oft heard American response to the September 11 attacks, "Why do they hate us so?" and the seething anger in the Muslim world that has risen to the surface in the aftermath of the attacks starkly demonstrate just how profound and tragic is "the perception gap" for societies on both sides of this now crucial civilizational and societal divide.

The establishment of a GPA provides one way to address constructively this perception gap. Like all elected assemblies, a GPA would be a forum engendering debate on the main global controversies, especially as they affect the peoples of the world. . . . Because elected delegates would be responsive to their respective constituencies, and because the media would cover proceedings, this debate would likely exert an influence far beyond the parliamentary chambers. Its echoes would be heard on editorial pages, . . . and TV, in schools and churches, and in assorted discussions at all levels of social interaction around the world. Spokespersons directly connected to aggrieved groups of citizens would have a new transnational public arena to voice their opinions and grievances, as well as to encounter opposed views. Those attacked or criticized would have ample opportunity to defend themselves and express their counter-claims. From such exchanges would come the same pull toward a less confrontational understanding between diverse groups of citizens that we find within the more successful domestic democratic systems of the world. Of course, complete agreement would never be achieved and is not even a worthy goal. Conformity of outlook is never healthy for a political community, but it is especially inappropriate in a global setting, given the unevenness of economic and cultural circumstances that exist in the world. But a GPA process could at least greatly facilitate convergent perceptions of reality, thereby making controversies about problems and solutions more likely to be productive, including a mutual appreciation and acceptance of differences in values, priorities and situations.

In addition to helping reduce the perception gap as an underlying cause of social tensions, a GPA would further promote the peaceful resolution of enduring social tensions by encouraging reliance on procedures for reaching decisions based on compromise and accommodation. Even where mutually acceptable solutions are not immediately achievable, parliamentary systems of lawmaking and communication, if functioning well, at least provide a civil forum where adversaries can peacefully debate and clarify their differences. If such institutions generate community respect and gain legitimacy, then those who do not get their way on a particular issue will be generally far more inclined to accept defeat out of a belief in the fairness of the process and with understanding that they can continue to press their case in future.

Of course, the brand of Muslim fundamentalism embraced by Osama bin Laden is illiberal and anti-democratic in the extreme. Given the existence of such extremism, it is appropriate to question the ability of liberal democratic institutions to absorb, successfully those who share the worldview of al Qaeda, or adhere to similar orientations. One of the impressive features of liberal parliamentary process, however, is its considerable ability to assimilate many of those who do reject its democratic outlook. Because [the] parliamentary process invites participation and because it has the politically powerful capacity to confer or deny the *imprimatur* of popular legitimacy upon a political position, experience at the domestic level suggests that even those

with radical political agendas will seldom decline the opportunity to participate. In the United States, for example, those on the Christian right who have
deep religious doubts about the validity of secular political institutions have
not only participated in the parliamentary process, but have done so at times
with zeal, tactical ingenuity, and considerable success despite their minority
status. In other countries, small political parties at the margins of public
opinion often exert disproportionate influence in situations where a majority
position is difficult for dominant parties to achieve. By participating in the
process they have come to accept, at least in practice, the legitimacy of these
institutions and procedures for societal decision-making.

Somewhat analogously, in the Cold War era the orthodox Soviet-inspired
critique of the American system nominally accepted by those American
Communists represented by the Communist Workers Party included a rejection of "bourgeois" rights in favor of what was then identified as "the
dictatorship of the proletariat." Yet, despite their professed rejection of
"bourgeois democracy,"their leader Gus Hall ran for President of the United
States repeatedly in an attempt to gain a tiny bit of . . . electoral legitimacy
for his position of isolation at the outermost reaches of public opinion. . . . The
relative domestic openness of the American political process helps explains
why the United States has suffered relatively little indigenous political violence in the twentieth century. During the period of heightened political
tensions in the 1960s, groups committed to violence such as the Weather
Underground, unlike al Qaeda today, could not attract popular support for
their radical rejection of the American governing process, and never became
more than a nuisance, posing only the most tangential threat to the security,
much less the stability, of the country. This lack of societal resonance soon
leads to the decay, demoralization and collapse of such extremist groups, a
dynamic of rejection that is far more effective in protecting society than law
enforcement is, even if enhanced by emergency powers as is the case . . . in
wartime conditions. To a lesser extent, the same self-destruct process seems
to have kept the right-wing militia movement from posing a major threat to
civic order, although it was indirectly responsible for inspiring the 1995
Oklahoma City bombing. This phenomenon with variations can be observed
within all of the more democratic systems of the world. The Osama bin
Ladens of the planet would be highly unlikely themselves to participate in a
global parliamentary process, but their likely ability to attract any significant
following would be substantially undermined to the extent that such an
institution existed and gave the most disadvantaged and aggrieved peoples in
the world a sense that their concerns were being meaningfully addressed.
Indeed, if such a safety valve existed, it might prevent, or at least discourage,
the emergence of the Osama syndrome, that the only way to challenge the
existing arrangement of power and influence is by engaging in totalizing
violence against its civilian infrastructure.

Civic activism: setting the stage for a GPA

We believe that the underlying preconditions for a GPA are being created
by the way that civic politics is increasingly challenging the autonomy of the
state-centric international system. In one of the most significant, if still
under-recognized, developments of the last several years, both civic voluntary
organizations and business and financial elites are engaged in creating paral-

lel structures that complement and erode the traditionally exclusive role of states as the only legitimate actors in the global political system. Individuals and groups, and their numerous transnational associations, rising up from and challenging the confines of territorial states, are promoting "globalization-from-below," and have begun to emerge into what is now recognized as being a rudimentary "global society." Business and financial elites, on their side, acting to facilitate economic globalization, have launched a variety [of] mechanisms to promote their own preferred global policy initiatives, a process that can be described as "globalization-from-above." While these new developments are rendering the territorial sovereignty paradigm partially anachronistic, they are still very far supplanting the old order, or even providing a design for a coherent democratic system of representation that operates on a truly global scale. Until the international community creates such a representative structure, the ongoing tension between the democratic ideal and the global reality will remain unresolved and will continue to be plagued by an incoherent global political structure in which the peoples of the world are not offered the sort of democratic alternative to violence that is increasingly considered the *sine qua non* of legitimate domestic . . . governance.

The organizations of global civil society

Is this coalescence of personal initiatives with an array of transnational initiatives that we identify as global civil society capable of mounting a transformative challenge to the customary role of states as the representatives of their citizens in the international system? Civil society, roughly defined as the politically organized citizenry, is mostly decentralized, broken down into non-profit organizations and voluntary associations dedicated to a wide variety of mostly liberal, humanitarian and social causes (though some decidedly illiberal and anti-liberal, of which terrorist and criminal networks are the worrisome instances). Transnationally, the largest and most prominent of these organizations bear such respected names as Amnesty International, Greenpeace, Oxfam, and the International Committee of the Red Cross. There are now more than 3,000 civil society organizations either granted consultative status by the United Nations Economic and Social Council or associated with the UN Department of Public Information.

As described by Jessica Mathews in her landmark 1997 article in Foreign Affairs,[6] global civil society gained significantly in influence during the second half, and particularly the last quarter, of the twentieth century. The early 1990s, however, was the time when civic transnationalism really came of age. If any single occasion deserves to be identified with the emergence of civil society on the global scene it would probably be the June 1992 UN Conference on the Environment and Development held in Rio de Janeiro. More than 1,500 civil society organizations were accredited to participate and 25,000 individuals from around the world took part in parallel NGO forums and activities. Civic associations and their representatives were for the first time recognized as an important and independent presence at a major world intergovernmental conference. The Rio Conference, partly responsive to this active involvement of global civil society, produced four major policy-making instruments.

---

6. J. Matthews, *Powershifts*, 76 Foreign
Aff. 50 (Jan–Feb 1997).

After Rio the pattern intensified. In the first half of the 1990s there were several other major global conferences under UN auspices at which civil society participation was an important factor. The most significant of these dealt with human rights (Vienna 1993), population (Cairo 1994), and women (Beijing 1995). The democratizing success of these global events produced a backlash among several major governments, especially the United States. The result in the short term has been the virtual abandonment of such conferences by the United Nations, supposedly for fiscal reasons, but actually because governments were afraid of losing some of their control over global policy-making. With the exception of the racism conference in Durban, South Africa, during 2001, there has been no major conference of this sort in the new millennium. It is important to evaluate this experience in the setting of the quest for global democracy. There is little doubt that these conferences in the 1990s did a great deal to establish the role and presence of civil society as a significant player in the global arena.

When the 1990s came to an end, the decade's balance sheet of accomplishments reflected for the first time in history the impact of global civil society. These transnational forces had been instrumental in promoting treaties to deal with global warming, establish an international criminal court and outlaw anti-personnel landmines. These same actors were also influential during these years in persuading the International Court of Justice [in 1996] to render an Advisory Opinion on the legality of nuclear weapons [on the Legality of the Threat or Use of Nuclear Weapons] **[Basic Document 7.10]** and in defeating an OECD attempt to gain acceptance for a multilateral investment agreement. This global populist movement at the turn of the millennium gained widespread attention through its advocacy of the cancellation of the foreign debts of the world's poorest countries. While all of these efforts to a greater or lesser extent remain works-in-progress, civil society has clearly been indispensable in achieving current levels of success.

During the formative years of the 1990s the most visible gatherings of civil society organizations took place beneath the shadow of large multilateral conferences of states. As the decade drew to a close, and with these conferences, at least in the near term, mostly foreclosed, something different began to occur. The multitude of global civil society organizations began to act on their own, admittedly in an exploratory and highly uncertain fashion, and yet independently of states and international institutions. For instance, in May 1999 at The Hague Appeal for Peace, 8,000 individuals, mostly representing civil society organizations from around the world, and given heart by the presence of such luminaries as Nobel Peace Laureates Archbishop Desmond Tutu, Jose Ramos–Horta, and Jody Williams, met to shape a strategy for the future and to agree on a common agenda. Throughout the following year there were similar though smaller meetings in Seoul, Montreal, Germany, and elsewhere.

These meetings were a prelude to the Millennium NGO Forum held at the UN in May 2000 at the initiative of UN Secretary General Kofi Annan. It was an expression of his "partnership policy" to reach out to non-state actors of both a civic and a market character. The Secretary–General invited some 1,400 individuals from international civil society to UN Headquarters in New York to present their views on global issues and to debate an organizational structure that might enable the peoples of the world to participate effectively in global decision-making. That UN Millennium Forum agreed to establish a permanently constituted assembly of civil society organizations called the Civil Society Forum that is mandated to meet at least every two to three years scheduled so as to precede the annual sessions of the UN General Assembly. While progress has been uneven, civil society has been continuing to work in the face of statist resistance and skepticism to bring this forum into fruition.

Many activists within global civil society regard this UN millennial initiative as the first step toward the establishment of a popular assembly that would meet at regular intervals, if not on a continuous basis. The emergence of such a Civil Society Forum might over time come to be recognized as an important barometer of world public opinion, and significantly, from the perspective of this chapter, could be seen as a preliminary, yet significant, step on the path to the establishment of a GPA.

The global business elite at Davos

Complicating, yet undeniably crucial to the dynamics of global democratization, are the efforts of business and finance to reshape the international order to render the global marketplace more amenable to the expansion of trade and investment. Transnational business and financial elites have so far clearly been more successful than civil society. Through their informal networks and their stature in society, financial and business elites often blend seamlessly with national and international structures of governance. State emissaries to the international system are frequently chosen directly from their ranks, and the acceptance of the neo-liberal economic ideology as tantamount to the official ideology not only of international economic institutions, but of other international organizations and most governments, has given business and banking leaders an extraordinary influence on global policy. Even in formerly exclusive arenas of state action, these private sector actors are flexing their muscles. As an indication of this expanding international influence, by bringing business and banking officials into United Nations policy-making circles for the first time, the UN Secretary–General has made "partnering" with the business community a major hallmark of his leadership. The United Nations has now established a formal business advisory council that is meant to institutionalize a permanent relationship between the business community and the UN, as well as initiated a "Global Compact" in which major multinationals sign on to a set of guidelines that commits them to uphold international standards pertaining to environment, human rights and labor practices in exchange for being given what amounts to a UN stamp of approval for their conduct.

As with civic groups, elite business participation in this emerging globalism is in the process of transforming itself into informal institutional structure that indirectly challenges the paradigm. The best example of the ability of elite business networks to extend their influence into the international system has been the World Economic Forum that has been meeting annually in Davos, Switzerland. The WEF was begun modestly three decades ago by the Swiss business visionary, Klaus Schwabr. During its early years the WEF concentrated its efforts primarily on rather humdrum management issues. In the early 1980s however, it succeeded in transforming itself into a political forum. In many ways Davos as we know it today is the legacy of earlier attempts to create transnational networks tasked with joining together international corporate and policy-making elites. Most observers agree that the most prominent of these precursors to the WEF was the highly secretive Bilderberg Conferences. Also important was David Rockefeller's Trilateral Commission (which also began in the 1970s, with an immediate display of influence on the highest levels of governmental decision-making in the industrial countries of the North before largely fading out of sight, in large part because Western governments adopted and acted upon its policy agenda). In terms of sheer concentration of super-elites from around the world, however, there has never been anything approaching the scale and salience of what has been achieved by Davos over the course of the late 1990s. Annually, 1,000 of the world's most powerful executives and another 1,000 of the world's senior policy-makers participate in a week of roundtables, discussions, lectures and presentations by world leaders.

But Davos has become much more than an assemblage of the rich and famous, although it is far less menacing and conspiratorial than its most severe critics allege, and it espouses no grandiose project that seeks to rule the world. At the same timer its advocates often make claims that stretch the reality of its considerable influence beyond the point of credibility. The WEF provides flexible arenas for discussion and recommendation that give its membership the ability to shape global policy on a continuous and effective basis. It is notable that the UN Secretary General's ideas about a partnership with business and civil society have been put forward as proposals during several high-profile appearances by Kofi Annan at Davos. In addition to encouraging the development of its own well-articulated approaches to global problems on the basis of neo-liberal precepts, the WEF conducts and disseminates its own research, which not surprisingly exhibits a consistent economistic outlook that portrays the future as market-driven. The WEF produces an annual index ranking the relative economic competitiveness of all countries in the world, which is given substantial media attention at the time of release each year.

There is no objective way to gauge the extent of influence exerted by Davos. Its own claims as a facilitator of conflict resolution are often not convincing. For example, the WEF takes credit for facilitating early meetings between the apartheid regime and the ANC, and for bringing Israeli Prime Minister Shimon Peres and PLO Chairman Yasser Arafat together in 1992, where they purportedly reached a preliminary agreement on Palestinian administration of Gaza and Jericho. The WEF is far more discreet about claiming any direct influence on global social and economic policy, being sensitive to accusations of back channel lobbying on behalf of transnational corporate interests. If the focus is placed on global economic policy then Davos together with other overlapping networks of corporate elites, such as the International Chamber of Commerce, seems to have been remarkably successful up to this time in shaping the global policy setting in directions to its liking. This success is illustrated by the expansion of international trade regimes, trends toward privatization, the maintenance of modest regulation of capital markets, the credibility accorded only to a neo-liberal interpretation of state/market relations, and the supportive collaboration of most governments, especially those in the North.

All in all the WEF has managed to position itself so as to provide a vital arena of inquiry and decision during this early stage of economic globalization. Such positioning has reduced the significance of democratic forces operating within states in relation to foreign economic policy, which in turn strengthens the argument to provide opportunities for civic participation in transnational institutional settings that will offset the impact of the multinational corporate arenas and give more voice to grassroots and populist concerns. Again, the focus on this dynamic is likely to be lost in the short-term aftermath of the September 11 attacks, which has temporarily restored the state as guardian of security to its traditional pre-eminence. Underlying globalizing trends are likely with the passage of time, however, to reassert the significance of establishing the structures of global governance in forms that take into account the goals of both market and transnational civic forces.

A GPA as the logical outcome of the process of global democratization

Putting aside the backlash against the global conference format, it seems reasonable to suggest that the international system is now exhibiting greater participation by non-state actors than ever before in its history. Without question, global civil society is unable to equal the influence, resources and power linkages of the corporate and banking communities. Nevertheless, relying on imagination and information, many of these civic networks have found ways to carve out a niche within the international order that enables effective pressures to be mounted. At the same time, there are many short-comings of such an ad hoc and improvised approach to global democracy. This transformation of the international system has been occurring in a largely uncoordinated and uneven fashion that further tends to disadvantage the concerns of the weakest and poorest. This obscures the need to connect these two types of globalizing networks (from above, from below) in a manner that is coherent, fair and efficient from the perspective of global governance.

In effect, what we have at present is a partial transplant from domestic political systems where interest group pluralism flourishes within an over-arching representative structure of parliamentary decision-making. At the global level we currently have rudimentary interest group pluralism, but it is deficient in several respects. There is a lack of accountability due to the absence of a representative structure and a low quality of functionality as a result of statist unwillingness to provide institutional capabilities for transnational political life. We believe this to be an inherently unsustainable path to a more evolved global system that is humane and comes to approximate a democratic model. What is notably missing from these intersecting forms of transnationalism is some type of unifying parliamentary body that can represent general as well as special interests.

The prevailing understanding of democracy today rejects the view that organized interest groups can validly claim to represent society as a whole. As global civil society has become more of an international presence, those opposing its agenda and activism have already begun to ask upon what basis are those within it entitled to represent the peoples of the world. Awkward questions are asked: "Who other than themselves do civil society organizations speak for?" "Who elected them?" "To whom are they accountable for their actions?" As global civil society becomes more influential, and as more ideologically diverse and antagonistic groups such as, for example, the American National Rifle Association, or for that matter Islamic fundamentalist organizations, clamour for access to global arenas of decision, this problem of representation can only become more complex and ever more hotly contested.

This illegitimacy charge can be equally leveled at the Davos improvisation, which, unlike civil society, does not even possess that degree of representativeness that comes from having within its ranks large membership organizations. Certainly those citizens who oppose mainstream globalization regard the Davos model of elite politics to be[as] extremely suspect. Such an assessment of these transnational developments suggests that the kinds of opening of the international system that have been occurring do not satisfy the demand for democratic participation. Something more is needed. Some sort of popular assembly capable of more systematically representing the diverse peoples of the world is necessary if the democratic deficit is to be meaningfully reduced. To the extent that the global undertakings are criticized for their failure to measure up to modern democratic standards, then world order seems ever more vulnerable to the charge of being more of an insiders' game than all but the most corrupt and draconian domestic political systems. Even before the events of September 11 it was evident that those whose interests were not being addressed, were unwilling to accept the legitimacy of existing global arrangements. It seems likely that given the continuation of these conditions, that the democratic deficit will grow even larger, leading to the further proliferation of various types of severe instability, which are currently causing such widespread turmoil and suffering in the world system.

The absence of a unifying parliamentary structure also means that there is currently no institutional vessel capable of bringing together the organized groupings of transnational activism that are identified with civil society and the Davos constituencies so as to facilitate dialogue, and the search for compromises and accommodations. As matters now stand, only governments have the institutional capacity to find such common ground and strike deals. As we discussed previously, there is no [formal] process for individuals and groups themselves to create a social consensus across borders or to engage formally with those acting on behalf of market forces. To the extent that solutions to global problems can be arrived at within a structure that institutionalizes interaction and allows for direct communication among competing interests, such interests will be much more likely to accept as legitimate, policy outcomes that have been fairly negotiated and agreed upon.

A GPA as a practical political project

We believe that the establishment of some sort of parliamentary assembly is necessary to begin to deal seriously with the democratic deficit. At the same time we realize that skepticism is rampant: is the creation of such a global assembly politically possible at this stage of history? For a variety of reasons, we believe that it is not Panglossian to believe it possible for the global community to take this vital step in building global democracy. After all, empirically suggesting the viability of such a project is the European Union, which has been making impressive attempts to overcome a purported regional democratic deficit. The EU already possesses a transnationally elected legislative body, the European Parliament. The European Parliament, along with the European Council and the European Commission, is one of three legislative bodies operating within the framework of the European Union. As we would expect to be the case with a globally elected assembly, the Parliament has struggled to establish credibility over time in the face of statist skepticism and media scorn. In recent years, however, the European Parliament has finally begun to gain respect, and has started to exercise significant power. Europe is, of course, far more homogeneous and economically integrated than the world at large, and the establishment of the Parliament was a part of a broader movement toward regional unity. At the same time this European evolution shows that there are no absolute political or logistical barriers to the creation and functioning of such an assembly on a transnational scale, and further, that such a development is fully compatible with the persistence of strong states and robust nationalist sentiments. In fact, on a global level, those with a pronounced interest in global governance—civil society, the corporate elite, and many governments—have an individual as well as collective stake in erecting some type of overarching democratic structure.

The role of civil society

Certain sectors of civil society in particular could likely be, and in fact are being, mobilized to lead the drive for such an assembly. This is important, because while there is the potential to find some support from corporate and political elites, it is unrealistic to expect the main initiative to come from these sectors. Most of the individuals leading business and governmental organizations tend to be institutionally conservative, as well as often too closely linked to state structures to support such a bold initiative. For these reasons, the primary energy for a global parliament will come from civil society, or nowhere.

It is rather obvious, however, that not even all civil society organizations are in favor of the creation of such an assembly. Some evidently sense that their influence would shrink in an altered world order. Nevertheless, the sentiments throughout global civil society are overwhelmingly in favor of establishing institutions and practices that will enable global democracy to flourish in the years ahead. Within this broader consensus there exists a realization that the creation of a functioning global parliament or assembly is a necessary and desirable step. The appeal of the GPA proposal to advance the agenda of global civil society seems rather obvious. At a general level, a democratically constituted assembly would be likely to address widespread societal concerns about the undemocratic nature of existing international institutions such as the World Trade Organization, the International Monetary Fund and the World Bank. It would almost certainly encourage further democratizing global reforms, as well as provide a setting for debates about the positive and negative effects of globalization. There would for the first time a widely recognized global forum in which such matters of public be concern as environmental quality, labor standards, and economic justice could be discussed from a variety of perspectives, including encounters between civil society representatives from North and South who set forth contrasting concerns embodying differing priorities. The presence of democratic structures does not, of course, guarantee that participants will consistently behave responsibly. We have learned from experience that even the most experienced and respected legislative institutions within states can act in an erratic fashion from time to time that does not reflect the real interests or values of constituents, but such is the cost incurred to sustain democratic processes as the basis of governance.

Even an initially weak and controversial global assembly could at least provide the beginnings of democratic oversight and accountability for the international system. The fact that individuals from many parts of the world would directly participate in elections would likely lead the assembly to have an impressive grassroots profile that would lend a certain populist authenticity to its pronouncements and recommendations. In all probability, at first, most governments would refuse to defer to such an assembly that operated beyond their control, but such rejectionist attitudes would be unlikely to persist very long. After all, we are living at a time when democracy has increasingly become the *sine qua non* of legitimacy around the world and the assembly would be the only institution that could validly claim to represent the peoples of global society *directly*. The comparison of its views with those of governments and market-dominated forums would likely attract media attention before long; becoming a part of public discourse would in turn influence the course of civil-political decision-making.

Besides exercising a democratic influence on the formulation of social policy, such an assembly could also be instrumental in helping to encourage compliance with international norms and standards, especially in the realm of widely supported human rights. Currently, the international system generally lacks reliable mechanisms to implement many of its laws. Civil society organizations such as Amnesty International, and even international organizations such as the International Labor Organization and the UN Human Rights Commission, attempt to address this deficiency and exert significant pressure on states by exposing failures of compliance by states, relying on a process that is often referred to as the "mobilization of shame". This pressure is premised on the importance to governments of sustaining their reputation for acting in conformity with normative standards and the reliability of established NGOs in identifying patterns of abusive behavior. In contributing to such an oversight function, a popularly elected GPA would likely soon become more visible and credible than are existing informal watchdogs that seek to expose corporate and governmental wrongdoing, and in any event, would complement such activism. A GPA would also tend to be less deferential to leading sovereign states than the more official watchdogs that function within the essentially statist framework of the United Nations System.

Perhaps most fundamentally, the mere existence and availability of the assembly would likely be helpful in promoting the peaceful resolution of international conflicts. We have already discussed how a GPA might be useful in undermining wider circles of societal support for international terrorism as a form of non-state violence. It could also in time help to reduce the likelihood of interstate violence as well. Instead of representing states, as in the United Nations and other established international organizations, delegates would directly represent various constituencies with societal roots. This means that, unlike the present system, the assembly would not be designed to reinforce artificially constructed national interests or to promote the special projects of rich and influential elites. Rather, as in multinational societies such as India or Switzerland, or in the European Parliament, most elected delegates do not consistently or mechanically vote along national lines, except possibly in instances where their national origins are directly engaged with the issue in dispute. Coalitions form in these settings on other bases, such as worldview, political orientation, class and racial solidarities, and ethical affinities. The experience of engaging in a democratic process to reach legislative compromises on the part of antagonists that are organized as opposing, but non-militarized and often shifting, coalitions may over time help establish a culture of peace. It is perhaps too optimistic to think that such a learning curve might eventually undermine reliance on the present war to sustain national and global security. It is difficult to transform the militarist mentalities associated with the pursuit of security in a world that continues to be organized around the prerogatives of sovereign national units that are heavily armed and disposed to destroy one another if the need arises. The hope is that over time the organization of international relations would come more closely to resemble decision-making within the most democratic societies of the world. Not only would an assembly tend to oppose military establishments as the foundation of global security, but it is also likely to build confidence in the perspectives of human security and in the efficacy of peaceful approaches to world order. Only when enough people begin someday to feel that non-violent structures of governance, including law enforcement, can ensure their individual and collective survival will meaningful disarmament become a genuine political option.

Any proposed institution that can credibly claim a potential for advancing causes as central to the agenda of various global civil society organizations as global democratization, labor and environmental regulation, effective global governance, peace, and human rights obviously should possess the capacity to generate broad-based support within civil society. So far, however, the nascent civil society movement that favors the establishment of such an assembly remains separate and distinct. It has not managed to gain significant levels of support, or even interest, from the issue-oriented actors that have so far been the main architects of global civil society. The present movement for an assembly consists mainly of individuals and groups who believe in holistic solutions to global problems, and seek to promote humane global governance for the world. Such proponents of a GPA are culturally influenced by a range of contemporary traditions of thought and modalities of action as varied as ecology, religion, spirituality, humanism and, most recently of all, the Internet. Each of these orientations proceeds from a premise of human solidarity and a belief in the essential unity of planet earth. Significant organizing efforts associated either with building support for the GPA or experimenting with its local enactment are under way in many different places around the world. This is an exciting development. It portends the possibility that from within civil society a truly innovative and visionary politics is beginning to take shape after centuries of dormancy. Such movement is an expression of the increasing robustness of democratic values as the foundation for all forms of political legitimacy regardless of the scale of the unit of social action being appraised. Also relevant are many types of transnational connectivity that manifest the globalizing ethos of our twenty-first-century world.

The receptivity of the business elite to a GPA

The global outlook of the corporate and financial elites represented at Davos, and elsewhere is also relevant to the prospects for furthering the cause of a GPA. The Davos network has been singularly successful in marshalling support for new international regimes that promote its interests in an open global economy. The World Trade Organization and NAFTA are two obvious examples. Certainly some within its ranks will oppose a new global parliamentary institution because a more open political system would mean a broader decision-making base, a questioning of the distribution of the benefits and burdens of economic growth, and more pressure for transnational regulation of market forces. Such developments would almost certainly be viewed with suspicion, if not hostility, by those who meet regularly at Davos to construct a world economy that is committed to the "efficient" use of capital, and dubious about any incorporation of social and normative goals into the formation of world economic policy. It would almost certainly be the case that such an assembly, if reflective of grassroots opinion around the world, would be highly critical of current modes of globalization, and hence at odds with the outcomes sought by the Davos leadership. But with transnational corporations having been, and in all likelihood continuing to be, beneficiaries of this globalization from above, those in the business world with a more enlightened sense of their long-term interest are already coming to believe that the democratic deficit must be addressed by way of stakeholder accommodations. It is perhaps relevant to recall that although hostile at first, many members of the American managerial class came under the pressure of the Great Depression and its societal unrest to realize that the New Deal was a necessary dynamic of adjustment to the claims of workers and the poor during a crisis time for capitalism. The same kind of dynamic made social democracy acceptable to the business/financial leadership of leading European countries, and helped give capitalism a more human face that enhanced its legitimacy at the level of society. In a similar vein, many of the leading figures in world business seem to find congenial the idea that some sort of democratizing improvisation along the lines we are suggesting is necessary to make globalization politically acceptable to more of the peoples of the world.

As the large street protests of the last few years in various places around the world suggested to many observers, globalization has not yet managed to achieve grassroots acceptance and societal legitimacy. Lori Wallach (the prime organizer of the Seattle anti-WTO demonstrations) said in an interview that her coalition of so many diverse groups, in addition to battling a series of distinct social issues, was held together by the "notion that the democracy deficit in the global economy is neither necessary nor acceptable."[7]

In fact, the main basis of popular support for globalization at present is not political, but economic. Globalization has either been able to deliver or to hold out the promise of delivering the economic goods to enough people to keep the anti-globalization forces from gaining sufficient ground to mount an effective challenge against it. Economic legitimacy alone is rarely able to stabilize a political system for long. Market-based economic systems have historically undergone ups and downs, particularly when they are in formation. The emerging-markets financial crisis that almost triggered a world financial meltdown in 1997 will surely not be the last crisis to emerge from the current modalities of globalization. Future economic failures are certain to generate strong and contradictory political responses. We know that standing in the wings, not only in the United States but in several other countries, are

---

7. *See FP Interview: Lori's War,* Foreign Pol'y 28 (Spring 2000) [*available at* <http://www.foreignpolicy.com/Issue119PDfs/28–55wal- lach.pdf>].

politicians, ultra-nationalists, and an array of opportunists on both the left and the right who, if given an opening, would seek to dismantle the system so as to restore territorial sovereignty, and with it, nationalism and protectionism. If the globalizing elite is seeking to find a political base that will allow it to survive economic downturns, particularly in the event that economic and social forces in powerful countries are in the future adversely affected, then it would do well to turn its attention urgently to reducing the global democratic deficit. Global terror plays a diversionary role at present, especially in the United States, but this distraction from the imperatives of global reform are not likely to persist, especially in the face of widespread economic hardship and distress.

There is a lesson to be learned from Suharto's Indonesia that offers some striking parallels to the vulnerabilities of the current global system. Indonesian citizens had come to believe in democratic practices, but the political system remained largely authoritarian, and unresponsive to the concerns of the people. As long as Indonesia was both a Cold War ally of the West and enjoyed the dramatic economic growth rates that had been sustained for nearly 30 years, American support was solid and there were enough benefits for most of the population to control political restiveness in a country with many acute ethnic and regional tensions. The great majority of the Indonesian people seemed either intimidated or willing to tolerate the country's failure to live up to the democratic ideal. But when the economy found itself in serious trouble during the last months of 1997, President Suharto had little to fall back upon internally or externally to maintain the political allegiance of the citizenry and his political edifice, which had seemed so formidable just months earlier. The Jakarta regime rapidly crumbled around him. The latent political illegitimacy of the Java-centric Indonesian government became a destabilizing factor that accompanied and intensified the economic and ethnic tribulations of the country.

The receptivity of the political elite to a GPA

Portions of the corporate elite might be persuaded that it is in their interest to support a GPA. Would not those who control state power, however, be less likely to go along with such an innovation? Surely any public institution that could reduce the global democratic deficit by claiming to speak directly for global society could eventually become an important counterweight to state and market power. The important word here is eventually. A relatively weak assembly constituted initially mainly with advisory powers would begin to address concerns about the democratic deficit while posing only a long-term threat to the citadels of state power. This being the case national leaders, whose concerns tend to be associated with short-term prerogatives, have little reason to feel significantly challenged by the establishment of such an assembly. Systemic transformation of world order that could affect successors would not to be threatening to, and might in fact appeal to those political leaders who are themselves most inclined to extend democratic ideals to all arenas of authority and decision.

Putting in place a minimally empowered, but politically saleable institutional structure that nonetheless has far-reaching transformative potential is, in fact, an approach often adopted by the most effective advocates of new global institutions. What has become the European Union, for example, began after the Second World War as the European Coal and Steel Community, a modest, skeletal framework for what would decades later evolve into an integrated European political structure that more recently poses some serious challenges to the primacy of the European state. The French Declaration of 9 May 1950 initially proposing the European Coal and Steel Community makes clear that this humble beginning was by design:

> Europe will not be made all at once, or according to a single plan, [The French Government] proposes that Franco–German production of coal and steel as a whole be placed under a common High Authority, within the framework of an organization open to the participation of the other countries of Europe. The pooling of coal and steel production should immediately provide for the setting up of common foundations for economic development as a first step in the federation of Europe, and will change the destinies of those regions which have long been devoted to the manufacture of munitions of war, of which they have been the most constant of victims.[8]

Within the European Union, by far the best model for a globally representative assembly, the European Parliament started life as an institutional vessel largely devoid of formal powers. Through time, as the sole direct representative of the European citizenry, the Parliament began to acquire an important institutional role that has given vitality to the undertaking, as well as increasingly reinforcing the European will to carry on with their bold experiment in regional governance.

One source of optimism that many national leaders can be persuaded to support this assembly project arises from the recent experience of building a coalition to push for the establishment of a permanent International Criminal Court. A large number of civil society organizations, working in collaboration with governments, have been very effective, at least so far, in building widespread cooperation among political elites around the world on behalf of a project that only a decade earlier had been dismissed as Utopian. The willingness of political leaders to support the creation of such a tribunal is quite surprising. It also lends indirect encouragement to efforts to establish a GPA because the criminal court compromises traditional sovereign prerogatives far more than would be the case initially if a global parliament comes into existence. The court has the substantive power to prosecute individuals for their failure to comply with international criminal law, which means that states have lost exclusive control over the application of penal law, which had been regarded as one of the traditional and fundamental attributes of sovereignty. Government leaders have lost their immunity to some extent in relation to international standards. By comparison a parliament with largely advisory powers would appear to be a relatively modest concession to the growing demand for a more democratic and legitimate global order, and would initially not significantly impinge upon the exercise of sovereign powers of a state. Of course, the idea of a parallel international law-making body, even if advisory, does raise the possibility in the moral and political imagination, that more centralization of authority is necessary and desirable, and this possibili-

---

8. *See*   <http://europa.eu.int/comm/dg10/ publications/brochures/docu/50ans/declen.html #declaration>.

ty, however remote, is likely to be threatening to governments administering nation-states.

Realizing the vision

While the rationale for establishing such an assembly definitely exists, this is, of course, not enough. There needs to be some liable way for this potential to be realized. We believe the formula with the best ability to take advantage of the political promise we have identified can be found in what is being called the "New Diplomacy". Unlike traditional diplomacy, which is solely conflicted among states, the New Diplomacy is based on the collaboration of civil society with whatever states are receptive, allowing for formation of flexible and innovative coalitions that shift from to issue and over time. The major success stories of global society in the 1990s were produced in this manner including the Global Warming Treaty **[Basic Document 5.48]**, the Landmines Convention **[Basic Document 2.52]** and the International Criminal Court.

This New Diplomacy (if it is to continue into this new century) is well adapted to meeting the challenge of creating a globally elected assembly. Nevertheless, the seemingly most natural way to bring a new international regime into being, a large-scale multilateral conference, does not appear well suited to this project. Despite the receptivity of some political elites, there is unlikely to be a critical mass of states in the UN General Assembly or outside its confines that would be willing to call for the convocation of such a conference. We believe that the momentum that would lead to significant state support for the assembly would undoubtedly have to be developed indirectly and gradually. Two other possible approaches seem worth considering in relation to bringing the GPA into being.

One approach that we discuss in more detail in the Summer 2000 edition of the *Stanford Journal of International Law* would be for civil society with the help of receptive states to proceed to create the assembly without resorting to a formal treaty process. Under this approach the assembly would not be formally sanctioned by the collectivity of states and hence its legitimacy would probably be contested by governments at the outset unless they chose to ignore its existence altogether. This opposition could be neutralized to some extent by widespread grassroots and media endorsement, and by the citizenry as expressed through popular elections that were taken seriously by large numbers of people and were fairly administered.

The other approach is to rely on a treaty, but to utilize what is often called the Single Negotiating Text Method as the process for coming to an agreement on the specifics of an assembly among supportive states. Pursuant to this approach after extensive consultations with sympathetic parties from civil society, business and nation-states, an organizing committee would generate the text of a treaty establishing an assembly that could serve as the basis for negotiations. Momentum could be generated as civil society organized a public relations campaign and some states were persuaded (sometimes as a result of agreed upon modifications in the draft) to accede to the treaty one at a time. As in the Ottawa Process that ultimately led to the Landmines Convention, a small core group of supportive states could lead the way. Unlike the Landmines treaty, however, which it was thought could not meaningfully come into effect before forty countries ratified it, a relatively small number of countries, say twenty, could provide the founding basis to bring such an assembly into being. Though this number is but a fraction of what would eventually be needed if the assembly wished to have some claim to global democratic legitimacy, it is worth remembering that the European Coal and Steel Community, which evolved to become the European Union, started with only six countries. After all, once the assembly was established and functioning in an impressive way the task of gaining additional state members should become easier. There would then exist a concrete organization to which states could actually be urged to join by their own citizens. As more states joined, pressure on the remaining states to allow their citizens to vote and participate would likely grow, especially if the assembly built a positive reputation in its early years. Holdout states would increasingly find themselves in the embarrassing position of being in a dwindling minority of states denying their citizens the ability to participate along with persons from foreign countries in the world's only globally elected body. It would seem increasingly perverse to proclaim democratic values at home but resist democratic practices and possibilities abroad. The exact nature of the representative parliamentary structure that should or will be created remains to be determined, and should be resolved through vigorous discussion by many different actors drawn from all corners of the world. What is clear to us, however, is that the ongoing phenomena of global democratization are part of an evolutionary social process that will persist, and intensify. While it is still too early to determine the long-term implications of the events of September 11, the future will surely find many ways to remind the peoples of the world that a commitment to global democratic governance is a matter of urgency, and that a way to move forward is through the establishment of a GPA.

Until the onset of the global terror challenge, the two dominant themes of the post-Cold War years were globalization and democracy. Proclamations are now commonplace that the world is rapidly creating an integrated global political economy and that national governments that are not freely elected lack political legitimacy. In view of this, it is paradoxical that there has not yet been a serious global debate on concrete proposals to resolve the obvious contradiction between a professed commitment to democracy at the level of the sovereign state and a manifestly undemocratic global political-economic order. Perhaps this apparent tension can be explained as a form of political inertia, and possibly by the residual sense that such democratizing proposals are still per se Utopian. Whatever the explanation, this contradiction will not be tolerated for long. Citizen groups and business and financial elites are not waiting around for governments to come up with solutions. They have taken direct and concrete action to realize their aspirations. These initiatives have created an autonomous dynamic resulting in spontaneous forms of global democratization. As this process continues in an attempt to keep pace with globalization, as it surely will, the movement for a coherent and legitimate system of global democracy will and should intensify. To political elites it will continue to become increasingly obvious that without legitimating institutions, governing the global order will be more difficult and contentious. They are likely to be plagued by the growing disinclination of citizens to accept the policy results of an ever-more encompassing system that is not based on a recognizable form of legitimate governance. To the organized networks of global civil society and business the inclination, reinforced by the practice of democratic societies, is to find direct accommodations and to work out differences. Such a process will naturally lead policy-makers to look toward familiar democratic structures to bridge present, widening cleavages. Finally, to all those who are seriously concerned about social justice, and the creation of a more peaceful global order, the democratic alternative to an inherently authoritarian global system will surely be ever more compelling.

Mario Pianta, "Democracy vs. Globalization: The Growth of Parallel Summits and Global Movements"

Debating Cosmopolitics 232–256 (D. Archibugi ed., 2003)

Political, economic, social and environmental problems of a global nature are all around us. The key decisions on such issues have been taken so far by governments (especially those of the most powerful states) and supranational institutions, as well as by a variety of large private bodies, such as financial and multinational corporations. What is the democratic foundation of such a system of global governance? Major problems of legitimacy, representativeness, accountability, participation and effectiveness are immediately evident in the present arrangements.

In this chapter, the emergence of summits as a way of assuring governance of global problems is the starting point for considering the extraordinary growth of parallel summits organized by an emerging global civil society. In the last decade, this challenge has opened the way to the growth of much broader global movements for international democracy and social and economic justice.

The growth of summits

In the last decades the urgency of global issues has led to the creation of new or the strengthening of old intergovernmental organizations, and a proliferation of international government level activities called to coordinate policy action.

The former process is associated with a *formal* transfer of power from states to supranational institutions, regulated by treaties or official agreements; as such, they are visible acts, which can be made the object of appropriate debate within countries through the usual procedures for deliberation on international issues. The creation of the World Trade Organization, the European Economic and Monetary Union, and the International Criminal Court are all examples of such developments, with widely differing degrees of popular participation in decision-making, public accountability, democratic structures and public support.

The latter process, on the other hand, leads to the emergence of *informal* supranational powers through inter-state agreements or cooperation; they still result from decisions of states—which have highly asymmetric resources, influence and force—and yet they reach well beyond the domestic sphere of state power. G8 meetings are examples of such events. Such inter-state activities tend to be much less visible and unaccountable to democratic processes, either at the domestic or at the international level.

In between these two patterns, a grey area has grown where inter-governmental organizations and powerful states have made increasingly important decisions in *informal* ways, either by stretching the official mandate of existing institutions (as in the case of the International Monetary Fund's Structural Adjustment Programmes), or by addressing, in an *ad hoc* way, emerging global problems for which no formal supranational transfer of power has yet been made (as in the case of several environmental problems).

While much of this expanding supranational decision power has remained hidden and unaccountable, largely in the hands of specialized government officials and international "technocrats", in the last two decades a model of highly visible collective action on global issues by states and inter-governmental organizations has emerged: international summits. Summits represent an important institutional innovation in the world system, combining the legitimacy of supranational organizations, the flexibility of informal meetings of states, and the high-profile exhibition of concern and action on current global problems. Summits have become more frequent and influential, with far-reaching policy consequences at the national level. In a world dominated by media and instant communication, where global problems are immediately visible everywhere, summits are often the media oriented events which "show" that the powerful of the Earth are addressing them. Moreover, they are the visible part of the growing informal decision power on supranational issues.

Summits are now a key element of the emerging governance system of an increasingly globalized world; they have a widely differing nature, but their role and activities include the tasks of *framing the issue* (as in the case of environmental or human rights issues), rule-making (as in the WTO on trade rules), providing policy guidelines for national governments (as in the IMF structural adjustment programmes) and *enforcing decisions* on individual (usually not so powerful) countries, with diplomatic pressure, embargoes or military action.

It could be argued that this is what inter-governmental cooperation has always been supposed to do. But what is new in the last decades is the extension in the range of issues addressed by summits; the greater policy impact of their decisions; their frequency which makes them part of institutionalized decision-making; the shift from bilateral to multilateral arrangements; the high media profile they have, in contrast to secretive diplomacy; in short, they are a crucial part of the shift in the balance of power from national to international decision-making. While there may be good reasons for transferring power at the supranational level in order to address increasingly global problems, this shift is not unproblematic.

The range of activities carried out by summits spans the prerogatives of political power as it has historically emerged in states. But what is missing is the democratic process developed at the state level in order to extend participation and representation of citizens and social groups, and legitimize the decisions taken. In fact, the officials attending summits are either professional diplomats or—mainly unelected—government officials.

Moreover, the rules and nature of most summits—with the partial exception of the UN—reflect a strong unbalance of power among states, with a dominance of rich Western countries, and of the United States, in many decision-making processes. While summits' decisions always follow—at least indirectly—from actions of governments, who are supposed to be accountable to their countries, most summits fail the test of democratic legitimation both when we look at the distribution of power across players involved—the governments of countries included or excluded from decisions—and when we look at the relation between decision-makers, society and citizens, and more generally those affected by the decisions taken.

The three globalizations

Global powers make decisions that have consequences for a large number of world citizens, but those making decisions have almost never been elected, cannot be replaced through democratic processes, and do not respond in any way to those who are subject to the effects of their decisions. In short, all elements of democracy are missing; no possibility of change exists through the democratic processes consolidated at the national scale. Democracy, therefore, appears to have lost substantial ground to globalization, in terms of the political and economic power exercised beyond the level of states.

But globalization is a much more complex process, and three major strategies—shaping in a fundamental way the decisions of global powers—have to be identified.

Neo-liberal globalization

Neo-liberal globalization has emerged as the dominant force of the past two decades. Moving from economic processes, from the strategies of multinational corporations and financial institutions, it has affected the decisions of governments and international institutions. As Richard Falk points out, "the characteristic policy vectors of neoliberalism involve such moves as liberalization, privatization, minimizing economic regulation, rolling back welfare, reducing expenditures on public goods, tightening fiscal discipline, favoring freer flows of capital, strict controls on organized labor, tax reductions and unrestricted currency repatriation, essentially, a politics that could be described as "predatory globalization.""[9]

Unregulated markets, dominated by multinational corporations and private financial institutions based mostly in rich countries, have been the driving force in economic growth and international integration, reducing the space for autonomous national politics in the fields of the public sphere. Neo-liberal globalization has institutionalized an overwhelming power of economic mechanisms—markets and firms—over human rights political projects, social needs and environmental priorities. It is no surprise that over the last decades political activity has lost much of its relevance and appeal; social inequalities have become dramatic; and the environmental crisis has deepened.

The political framework for neo-liberal globalization was prepared in the early 1980s by the policies of Margaret Thatcher in Britain and Ronald Reagan in the United States. In the aftermath of the collapse of the Soviet system in 1989–90, building on an unrivalled military supremacy, political power and cultural dominance, the neo-liberal project of globalization has become the new face of the hegemony of the United States.

9. R. Falk, Predatory Globalization: A Critique 2 (1999).

Globalization of rights and responsibilities

The emergence of global problems, and the necessity to confront them in a context that surpasses state dimensions, has led a second important project of globalization of rights and responsibilities. Some of the more "enlightened" states and international institutions, social organizations, and labor and environmental groups have sustained a project of universalizing human, political and social rights, along with the recognition of the responsibility that countries, governments, and people have in facing these new global problems. This project has built on common values and has defined the understanding of major global problems, having a large influence on the agenda of the UN summits on human rights, women's rights, the environment, social development, food supply, and the creation of the International Criminal Court. Among the results are new norms for international rights, declarations of principles, a new space for democratic processes, greater attention by states to the respect of rights and some innovative policies, and a broader political cooperation on a regional or global level—the case of European integration being the most significant. Civil society has asked governments and international institutions to take initiatives in this direction. In many countries, policies that supported this project were developed in parallel to economic policies of neo-liberal orientation.

However, when a conflict emerged between these two projects, neoliberal strategies have always prevailed; the project based on rights and *responsibilities,* therefore, has had a limited influence on the direction of the processes of globalization.

Globalization from below

In addressing global issues, governments, inter-governmental organizations and large firms operating in world markets are not the only actors. An increasing visibility, voice and activism has come from a large number of civil society organizations operating across national borders; they have advocated change, opposed current processes or policies, and proposed alternative solutions to global issues.

This emerging *global civil society* can be defined as the sphere of cross-border relations and collective activities outside the international reach of states and markets. This concept identifies a sphere of international relationships among heterogeneous actors who share civil values and concern for global issues, communication and meanings, advocacy actions, and self-organization experiments. From global civil society a major challenge has emerged to the strategy of neo-liberal globalization and to the failures of globalization of rights and responsibilities.

Within global civil society, the most active players are the new social movements and the network of organizations working on international themes. Their origins are in the movements of past decades on the themes of peace, human rights, solidarity, development, the environment and women's issues. Starting with these specific themes, the new movements have developed the capacity to confront problems of a global nature, to construct networks of information, to prepare common actions, to find self-organized solutions beyond national borders, interacting also in an original way with the new sites of international power.

All of this defines the emergence of an alternative project of *globalization from below* of global civil society. According to Richard Falk, who has introduced this concept, globalization from below has the potential to conceptualize widely shared world order values: minimizing violence, maximizing economic well-being, realizing social and political justice, and upholding environmental quality. Even if these values of global civil society remain far from representing a coherent alternative, they have inspired the actions of new global movements and are at the base of the resistance against the project of *neo-liberal globalization* and of the pressing for *global rights and responsibilities.*

In the last decade many cross-border campaigns and initiatives have shown how real and active global civil society can be, and have defined methods and contents of *globalization from below.* Such actions include: the campaigns for human rights, women's and children's rights; opposition to the death penalty; the peace movement; campaigns on environmental themes; the request for international labor rights; the initiatives of co-operation for development, fair trade, ethical finance and micro-credit; social self-organization; the campaigns on Third World debt, for the Tobin Tax on currency transactions, and against the international institutions—the IMF, the World Bank, the WTO. All such movements have come closer together in recent years, especially with events such as the World Social Forum of Porto Alegre in Brazil and the Assemblies of the United Nations of the People in Perugia, where their identity as global movements for international democracy and social and economic justice has become evident.

The invention of parallel summits

In order to confront the new power of summits of states and inter-governmental organizations, civil society organizations have invented parallel summits, events which could challenge the legitimacy of government summits, demand more democratic arrangements for decision-making, give visibility to the emerging global civil society, resist neo-liberal policies, and propose alternative solutions for global problems.

Parallel summits can be defined as events:

● organized by national and international civil society groups with an international participation, independent of the activities of states and firms

● in coincidence or in relation to official summits of governments and international institutions (with few major exceptions)

● addressing the same fundamental problems of official summits, with a critical perspective on government and business policies

● using the means of public information and analysis, political mobilization and protest, proposal of alternative policies

● with or without formal contacts with the official summits.

Some history

Government summits and civil society international meetings have a history as long as that of globalization itself. Charnovitz has shown that, from the late nineteenth century to the 1920s, the establishment of supranational bodies such as the League of Nations and of scores of inter-governmental organizations was accompanied by an equally strong flourishing of international non-governmental organizations and of civil society meetings. At several official summits and in the operation of the League of Nations, civil society groups were often able to articulate their proposals on a wide range of themes including peace, national liberation, economic, social and women's rights; in some cases they were even involved in official activities, opening the way to the formal recognition of NGOs in the Charter of the United Nations in 1945.

During most of the Cold War years the space for international activities of civil society was constrained and shaped by state power and policies. International mobilization of civil society had the task of putting pressure on state policies on the issues of decolonization, national self-determination, peace, human rights, development and the environment. The political movements of the 1960s and 1970s challenged the political and economic order at the national and international level with a transformative perspective still focused on state power. A major exception was the rise of the women's movement which opened the way to new forms of politics, social practices and culture based on identity politics.

In the 1980s the new social movements on peace, ecology and women took up their heritage and concentrated on specific issues which had less to do with state power and more with global challenges, often marked by the lack of adequate supranational institutions. The rapid growth of NGOs turned the advocacy of movements into practical projects and proposals of alternative policies, demanding a voice in the existing global fora.

NGOs have found a substantial opening in the UN system, in ECOSOC and other activities; however, this official recognition of civil society work at the international level has led to very modest results in terms of visibility, relevance and impact on the operation of the international system.

A new wave of state summits began in the mid–1970s spurred on by far-reaching political change—East–West detente, the completion of decolonization and a new attention to human rights and by economic developments—the end of the Bretton Woods international monetary system, the oil shocks and the emergence of the North–South divide. Existing inter-governmental organizations, starting with the UN, played a renewed and broader role, and other fora were established (the first G5 meeting was in 1975).

As global issues and supranational decision-making became increasingly important, attention and action by civil society also increased. Moving on from the traditional efforts to put pressure on national states, attention started to focus on global problems, and on the failure of states to address them in events such as summits. Symbolic actions, at first small in scale and poorly organized, were followed by a more systematic international effort by civil society organizations, resulting in explicit challenges to the legitimation and policies of summits.

In the late 1970s the first summits of non-governmental organizations working alongside the United Nations summits on the environment and human rights were organized. The first Other Economic Summit, parallel to a G7 meeting, took place in London in 1984. A protest against the International Monetary Fund meeting brought 100,000 people to West Berlin in 1988, linking the German and European traditions of the new left, the peace movement and the solidarity activism with the Third World. In 1994, seven years before the Genoa G8 summit (again, shortly after an electoral victory by right-wing leader Silvio Berlusconi), an alternative summit to the G7 held in Naples was organized by a coalition of 30 organizations, with a conference on globalization, a convention of global movements and a march with 10,000 participants. While in Seattle, Prague, Genoa, Quebec City or Barcelona the scale and attention to the protest have been much larger, the same themes and forms of action can be found with few differences in the past twenty years.

An analysis of parallel summits

The historical roots and the present diffusion of parallel summits make them an important object of analysis. A reconstruction of their development has shown the increasing importance they assume in terms of civil society activism on global issues and of demands for a more democratic world order. A specific survey was undertaken in order to investigate the nature of parallel summits, the events that occurred, their forms of organization, and their impact. A questionnaire was circulated to hundreds of civil society organizations, and dozens of newspapers, journals, NGO publications and websites were monitored in order to gather information systematically. From the findings, 89 cases of parallel summits have been selected, which are considered representative of the range of events, topics and locations, covering the period 1988–June 2002. The focus here is on the events of 2001 and of the first half of 2002, when 35 main events occurred. They will be compared with the evolution over the past 20 years presented in a previous work.

The activism of global civil society

The contemporary development of parallel summits began with the *pioneering years*, 1980–1987, when the first experiences in small events involving a limited number of NGOs were developed. The start of the recorded events was in the four years of *political transition*, 1988–1991, when seven percent of all monitored parallel summits took place and the modes of operation, organization and action were established. In the next four years of *institutional expansion*, 1992–1995, the number of parallel summits more than doubled, to 15 per cent of all meetings, including a large number of events associated with the important UN conferences of that period. Close to 20 per cent of events marked the following years of *consolidation and diffusion*, 1996–1999, when a greater variety of issues was raised and more regional meetings took place, ending with the Seattle protest against the WTO. All this accounts for 40 per cent only of all events, and the year 2000 opened the current period of *frequency and radicalization*.

In the year 2000 the same number of parallel summits were recorded as in the four previous years, while in 2001 close to a quarter of all recorded events were concentrated, and the semester of 2002 alone accounts for 15 per cent of all of global civil society. This exponential growth is the most effective indicator of the booming relevance of global civil society events.

In the period January 2001–June 2002, close to a third of the parallel summits took place in Europe, a quarter in Latin America, a sixth both in North America and Africa, and the rest in Oceania. Data for the previous period (in *Global Civil Society* 2001) covering from 1988 to June 2001, reported much higher shares for Europe and North America (53 and 23 per cent); shows the important diffusion of global civil society events in the South; and is particularly important as it suggests a shift also in the origin of participants, because the large majority of people involved tend to come from the country where the event is held or from neighboring ones.

What are the types of summit civil society sets out to challenge? Since 2001, 40 per cent of events are meetings of global movements organized independently from official summits, while this was only about 10 per cent in the past 13 years. Close to 30 per cent of parallel summits deal with regional conferences (European Union, American or Asian government meetings), and less than one third shadows UN, G8, IMF or WTO meetings. In the past this group accounted for two thirds of all parallel summits.

The key actors in the organization of parallel summits have not changed; they generally are civil society groups of the hosting country, in 80 per cent of cases also involving international networks and NGOs. In a third of the cases local groups are also active, with lesser involvement of trade unions and local authorities.

... [The] organizers of [the] parallel summits, involving varying coalitions of civil society groups, ... emerge with the following profile. In two-thirds of events—in recent months as well as in the whole period—they were active civil society organizations working on development and economic issues (trade, finance, debt and so on). Groups involved in democracy issues are active now in half of global events, as opposed to a quarter in the past. Human rights and peace organizations are present in 25–30 per cent of parallel summits, while environmental groups lose importance and are found only in one-fifth of events (almost half that in the past); a similar fall is found for the presence of trade unions. Groups active on gender, youth and other issues also appear to be less relevant than in the past.

This evidence may be associated with the two main challenges posed by parallel summits: on the one hand, resistance to neo-liberal globalization is likely to be the focus of events organized by groups active on economic, development and trade union issues; on the other hand, pressure for the globalization of rights and responsibilities may characterize those organized by human rights, environment, peace and democracy activists. The long term trends appear to be confirmed by recent developments. The growth of mobilizations around economic globalization since the late 1990s has accelerated; they dominate the present activity of global civil society. Global rights issues were the most important theme in the 1992–95 period and have since remained more or less stable in terms of overall relevance up to the present, with a modest upward dynamic after 2000. Confronting neo-liberal globalization is at present the most important issue emerging from parallel summits, but it goes hand-in-hand with demands for global rights and responsibilities.

What type of event is a parallel summit? It is always a conference, associated with street demonstrations in 80 per cent of the cases (in contrast to one-half of past parallel summits). In recent months media events and grassroots meetings have lost importance, while a broader range of fringe actions and initiatives occurred. Since January 2001, one-third of global civil society events has had more than 10,000 participants—in seven parallel summits the number of people involved was above 80,000. One fifth of cases involved between 1000 and 10,000 people, and one quarter between 200 and 500, suggesting that also global meetings with a more focused participation are on the rise. Relative to past trends, there is an increase of large demonstrations and of small events, while the smallest ones basically disappeared.

What are the objectives of the gatherings of global movements? Since 2001, in three-quarters of cases parallel summits have had three aims: networking among civil society organizations, disseminating public information and proposing alternative policies. The latter objective maintains the same relevance as in the past, while the other two aims have rapidly grown in importance. The development of stable networks of civil society organizations has emerged as a recent major priority for their action, as happened similarly to the informing of public opinion.

The two parallel needs of building up the "internal" strength, of global civil society and making more effective its external activity—based on alternative policy proposals and on the consensus of public opinion—are again confirmed. Other objectives including political confrontation and lobbying official summits, account for around 10 per cent of recent cases (while they accounted for up to one-third in the past). The relatively low priority given to lobbying official representatives may be due to the declining frequency of UN-type summits open to civil society lobbying.

Parallel summits now appear to have a substantial impact. A tentative evaluation can be provided, based on the judgment of organizers, participants or from media reports, and clearly these results have to be treated with great caution. From the evidence available, the strongest impact of parallel summits appears to be, on global civil society itself, where three-quarters of events are judged to have a medium or strong effect, and this is no different from the past. In half of the cases there is a similarly medium or strong impact on public opinion, followed by the effect of international media. While the impact of parallel summits on specific national and international policies has remained very weak, official summits have started to feel the pressure of civil society. In the last year and a half, more than 60 per cent of parallel summits have had a medium or strong impact on official conferences—stopping their activity, influencing their location or agenda—an impact twice the one estimated in the past.

Strengths and weaknesses of parallel summits did not change much after 2001. In 60 per cent of cases the wide international network of organizations is the main factor of success, followed by the strong political alliance among them; this underlines again the importance of the internal development of global movements. Mass participation is considered a success in one-third of parallel summits, while radical protest emerges as less important. The weaknesses of parallel summits are mainly due to the lack of attention of policy-makers (or to the failure to make them listen to civil society) and from the lack of "external" visibility (or to the failure to make media and public opinion listen to the message of parallel summits), both relevant in more than 50 per cent of cases. A much lower number of cases point out internal weaknesses, such as divisions among organizers (small, but on the increase), or poor participation.

With all the limitations that such data may have, there is little doubt that global civil society is coming of age. Global movements are active on all continents with a great variety of issues. Moving from protest against official summits, they have developed their own agenda, where the critique of neo-liberal globalization is joined by the proposal of alternatives and the exploration of new forms of political action. They have shown great organizational capacity in preparing global events and growing autonomy in charting their own course, independent of the pressure of the policy agenda of international institutions and from the short term considerations of national politics. Even the surge of terrorism with the attacks of September 11 2001 against the United States, and the ensuing war in Afghanistan did not slow down global activism of civil society; rather, this has led to greater attention to the issues of peace, war and violence. The millions of people around the world mobilized in the last year and a half show that global civil society has now reached a role and relevance which should not be ignored either by national politics or by supranational institutions.

The World Social Forum of Porto Alegre

For its size and importance, the second World Social Forum held in Porto Alegre, Brasil, on January 30–February 5, 2002, deserves a specific consideration. It has probably been the largest gathering of global civil society to date with 68,000 registered participants from 131 countries, representing 5,000 associations, NGOs and local authorities, 3,000 journalists and 800 members of parliament, meeting in 28 major plenaries, 100 seminars and 800 workshops. [Forty] per cent of the participants were women, 12,000 young people stayed in a city park, in a campsite named after Carlo Giuliani, the Italian youth killed by the police during the protests in July 2001. While Brasilians were by far the majority of people at the Forum, large contingencies came from Latin America (Argentina in particular) and Europe (1,000 Italians, 700 French) and smaller groups from the United States (140 delegates) and from Africa (200 participants).[10]

The Brazilian organizers had a strong institutional profile, with the systematic involvement of the President of the State of Rio Grande do Sui, of the Mayor of Porto Alegre, and of the leaders of the Workers' Party (PT) including Lula, who later won the 2002 presidential elections. The Porto Alegre experience of participatory democracy in the local budgeting process has been a key issue, receiving interest from all over the world, with hundred of local authorities planning to replicate it. The Trade Union CUT was also active, with the coalition of civil society organizations responsible for the efficient organization of the event.

Participants included activists of social movements, political organizations, women's groups, representatives of all global campaigns, as well as environmentalists, peace activists, and smaller numbers of human rights campaigners, social economy organizations, development NGOs and Trade Unions

The common analysis of global problems was the dominant theme of talks at the World Social Forum. The shared understanding of the roots of poverty, inequality, underdevelopment, hunger, environmental degradation, wars and

---

10. Correio do povo, 6 Feb 2002....

human rights violations was remarkable, with activists of all continents sharing experiences, making links and learning the relevance of new issues, in events of great impact, such as the largest plenary of the Forum featuring Noam Chomsky.

Much less attention in Porto Alegre was devoted to the diversity of strategies to address global problems and to the priorities of campaigns. Different approaches were already visible, with the obvious division between North and South perspectives, but also with an emphasis on resistance from many North Americans and Asians, and greater attention to alternative projects from Europeans and Latin Americans.

The rejection of neo-liberalism and war have emerged as the two key elements of the global movements gathered in Porto Alegre. In a document agreed [to] by hundreds of organizations (but which is not an official final document of the Forum), the "[Appeal] of Social Movements. Resistance to Neo-liberalism, War and Militarism: For Peace and Social Justice," activists define themselves as a "global movement for social justice and solidarity."[e] The first in the list of its objectives is democracy: people have the right to know about and criticize the decisions of their own governments especially with respect to dealings with international institutions.

Governments are ultimately accountable to their people. While we support the establishment of electoral and participative democracy across the world, we emphasize the need for the democratization of states and societies and the struggles against dictatorship.

Global movements in global civil society

In spite of the range and width of the global movements seen in Porto Alegre and in parallel summits all over the world, we should resist the identification of the new *global movements* with the action of *global civil society*. The latter remains the sphere of cross-border relations and collective activities outside the international reach of states and markets. It contains a variety of collective agents, operating on the basis of diverse, often conflicting projects. What identifies *global movements* is that their cross-border actions move within global civil society with a broad common project demanding

— global democracy and peace to the state system,

— global economic justice to the market system, and

— global social justice and environmental sustainability to both systems.

The commonalities among the thousands of organizations and networks animating global movements largely stop here. In order to account for the heterogeneity of actors, of the fields of interest and of the political projects within global civil society, different typologies have been proposed, distinguishing for example, on the basis of the attitude towards economic globalization:

a) *reformists* with the aim to "civilize" globalization;

b) *radical critics* with a different project for global issues;

c) *alternatives* who self-organize activities outside the mainstream of the state and market systems;

e. *Available at* <http://www.international viewpoint.org/article.php3?id_article=496>.

d) *resisters* of neo-liberal globalization.

Outside this range of perspectives typical of global movements, we can find in global civil society two other perspectives:

e) *supporters* of the current order, stressing the benefits brought by globalization;

f) *rejectionists* of global processes, favoring a return to a national dimension, often with a reactionary, nostalgic attitude.

Focusing on the strategies pursued by global movements, we can identify three major models: *resistance, lobbying*, and *production of policy alternatives*. These strategies shed new light on the vision and role of global civil society and its relationship to political and economic power.

The politics of resistance

Resisting the decisions of illegitimate and arbitrary powers in the name of higher values or broader social interests has always been the point of departure of social mobilization and political change. The demonstrations in Seattle in November–December 1999 showed the importance of the *politics of resistance* of global movements, a strategy which has culminated in the protests against the G8 summit in Genoa in July 2001 and the EU Council in Barcelona in March 2002. In between we had had dozens of large scale international demonstrations against the summits of the World Monetary Fund and the World Bank, in Washington in April 2000, Prague in September 2000, Washington again in April 2001; against the European Council meetings at Nice in December 2000 and at Gothenburg in June 2000; against the Summit of the Americas in Quebec City in April 2001; against the WTO meeting in Qatar in November 2001 when major protests were held in more than 50 cities all over the world.

The politics of resistance has been successful thanks to the convergence of four factors:

1.   The large broadening of the *social base* involved: at Seattle there was an unprecedented alliance between environmentalists and US trade unions, local groups and global campaigns; at Genoa there was the Genoa Social Forum's capacity to open up to a new generation of activists and to bring together different forces, ranging from associations to radical "social centres," from Left organizations and unions to many Catholic organizations.

2.   A *simplification of the issues* at the centre of the protest with a strong element of political opposition: at Seattle the "no" to an unjust commercial system, at Geneva the "no" to a G8 without legitimacy.

3.   The resort to a *form of radical struggle*, like civil disobedience, often successful in effectively obstructing the activities of summits.

4.   A strong *resonance in the media* and vast attention from public opinion, thanks to a long effort at public information and, above all, to the visibility of the forms of action and of the repression taking place.

The success of this strategy of global movements is indisputable, measured not only by the growth from the 60,000 demonstrators at Seattle, to the 300,000 at Genoa and Barcelona. After Seattle, the next WTO summit was organized in Qatar, the location most protected from the requests of democratization and changes in policies coming from global civil society. After Genoa,

INTERNATIONAL LAW AND WORLD ORDER

the G8 summits of the past can no longer be repeated in the same way, and the 2002 meeting has been hidden in the Canadian mountains.

These successes, nevertheless, have had a high price. Genoa was the culmination of the resistance of global movements, but also the culmination of the arbitrariness of power with the savage police repression carried out by the Italian government and the killing of Carlo Giuliani. Violence in Genoa was used by a small minority of demonstrators who threw stones, broke glass, and set vehicles and offices on fire, but violence was used in a systematic way by the police—even after the arrest of demonstrators with the aim of making peaceful protest impossible.

Since Seattle, global powers and states have tried to portray global movements as violent extremists against which repression should be exercised. After Genoa, there was the risk of a spiral of violent protest and repression. In order to avoid this, movements in Italy after Genoa, like in Sweden after Gothenburg, have had to devote a large part of their energies to prevent this spiral and defend their democratic space.

In any case, after two years of rapid expansion, the politics of resistance seems to have initiated its point of descent. Every factor of success after Genoa could transform into an element of weakness. An excessive media orientation and simplification of issues may lead to an extreme fragility of movements, with a loss of substance and credibility for their proposals for change. The spiral of violence and repression may reduce the extension of the social base involved and lose public opinion consensus. The result might be a fall in participation and a radicalization of limited sectors of the movements, without significant results on the international issues on which they started out to act.

Lobbying

At the opposite of resistance there is the lobbying model. The organizations of civil society try to influence the decisions of global powers by a systematic effort of documentation, contact with national decision-makers, and presence at international conferences. This work has led to important results in recent years, including treaties banning landmines, creating the International Criminal Court, the Kyoto protocol on the reduction of carbon emissions, and many other accords on environmental issues. Success factors of this pressure are the following:

1. The existence of *legitimate international institutions* with the mission to address particular problems of global importance; they need to be recognized by civil society and need to recognize the role civil society may in turn play in these issues. Organizations of the United Nations family are the typical examples.

2. The concentration, on the part of non-governmental organizations and associations, on very *specific requests* to well-defined decision-makers, based on practical knowledge of the relevant problems and of the most effective potential solutions.

3. A *low intensity action*, in political terms, working in direct contact with those who make decisions, seeking the broadest possible agreements on the specific themes addressed, with willingness to compromise.

4.   The use of *public opinion campaigns*, the only form of mass participation envisaged, in order to build a consensus on the general objectives, and to put pressure on policy-makers.

This path of change of the global order relies on small improvements from inside the existing institutions, and it is possible only when there is a shared horizon of political action with existing supranational powers. It offers the opportunity to effectively implement necessary changes in global rules and issues, if only minor and partial ones. The risk is to keep civil society subordinate to the decisions of governments and supranational powers, removing the resources of protest and conflict.

The experiences of the most recent global summits (Johannesburg, Qatar and Monterrey) suggest that the space for a strategy of this type is (are) increasingly limited.

The production of alternative policies

The third path of change is the capacity of global movements to produce alternative policies, autonomous from the actions of governments and traditional politics. Examples include the campaign for a Tobin Tax, and the rapid growth of Attac as a global movement demanding its introduction; the mobilization around the Jubilee 2000 campaign to cancel the debt of Southern countries; the campaigns to reform the IMF and the World Bank; the request for access to drugs by poorer countries, in particular those for the AIDS epidemic; the rejection of genetically modified organisms in Europe; the efforts on energy issues and for developing renewable energy sources; the solidarity actions, initiatives for conflict resolution and constructions of peace in the Balkans.

Ideas for alternative policies are generally present, to some extent, also in the initiatives of resistance, and in lobbying efforts. However, specific initiatives for developing alternatives have increasingly characterized the action of global movements and parallel summits since 2001, as seen above, with major international meetings such as the World Social Forum of Port Alegre held in January–February 2001, 2002 and 2003 and the four Assemblies of the People's United Nations in Perugia.

A strategy focusing on alternative policies combines in an interesting way some features of the politics of resistance and of lobbying:

1.   The alternative policies proposed by global movements target the *weak points of international institutions,* asking for radical reforms (for example of the International Monetary Fund) or for the creation of new organizations (for example to administer the Tobin Tax) able to deal with global problems. They confront well-defined international institutions, pointing out their limits and proposing ways move beyond existing arrangements; in this way such at strategy avoids the risk of subordination, typical of lobbying and the limits of a resistance without proposal.

2.   Policies of global movements combine a *broad political vision with specific demands*; moving from a concrete knowledge of the relevant fields (for example the effects of the lack of access to AIDS drugs in Africa), the appropriate proposals for solving them are advanced, changing existing power relations and institutional arrangements (*e.g.* modifying the norms on patents and on the prices of drugs set by companies).

3. The campaigns present a *high politicization* and a *high participation* because they must build a broad social base supporting their alternative project. For example, the opposition to genetically modified organisms has been transformed from an issue for biotechnology specialists to a problem for all citizens, constructing alliances among scientists, environmentalists, farmers and consumers, and raising fundamental questions to society and politics on what should be produced and consumed.

4. The construction of the *consensus of public opinion* is essential to these campaigns in order to mobilize a diversity of social forces, and to create pressure, as lobbying does, on decision-makers in national governments and supranational organisms. For example, the success of the Jubilee 2000 debt campaign is associated first with the huge involvement of the media, the churches, all sorts of civil society organizations; second to its presence in dozens of parallel summits G8, IMF–World Bank, European Council, etc.; and third to its influence on political forces and governments which has led to positive steps and legislation in several countries.

Such developments have taken place entirely *outside* the mechanisms of institutional politics, which continues to ignore the elaboration of global movements. This confirms the *autonomy* of global movements, but at the same time reveals a major weakness in this route to change: the lack of an *effective, contractual power of civil society*, of social movements, for change "from below" against existing global powers. In all sorts of fields—the requests to reform and democratize the UN, for non-military solutions to conflicts, for protection of workers and immigrants in the global economy, for the Tobin Tax, etc.—global powers have always responded in the same manner: "It is not possible." Hence the immediate popularity of the radical statement that *another world is possible*, used as a common banner by global movements.

In contrast to this stalemate, the modest ambitions of *lobbying* show that small changes are in fact feasible, and the protests of the *politics of resistance* show that global powers cannot escape radical criticism. The proposals for alternative policies coming from global movements—important as they are— risk being *innocuous* to global powers, as long as they can afford to ignore the role, ideas and influence coming from civil society.

This stalemate concerns not only global movements, but the question of global democracy itself and has important consequences for the prospects of effective governance of global problems. The ways out are three. On the one hand, states and supranational institutions have to formally recognize the role of civil society on global issues, granting rights to its organizations and movements to have a *voice* (not necessarily a *vote)* on global issues, as members, for example, of the delegations of national representatives to UN bodies, regional organizations (such as the EU) and international conferences; some very initial steps in this direction have already been taken in the case of the UN. It should be reminded that one century ago the same route was taken by the labor unions when they obtained formal recognition for the representation of workers before the government and the employers.

The second way out requires the reactivation of the mechanisms of democracy in national politics; the proposals of the movements should systematically influence the positions of national governments, and in doing so, change the balance of power in international bodies. There are many examples of success using this method: France's decision to block the negotiations for the Multilateral Agreement on Investment (MAI) at the OECD; Malaysia's decision to control the movements of capital after the Asian financial crisis; South Africa's and Brazil's decision to challenge multinational pharmaceutical companies for anti-AIDS drags; the European decisions on genetically modified organisms; even the UK decision to arrest General Pinochet. This is the concrete ground where national politics can meet civil society anew.

The third road passes through the strengthening of the global organization of civil society and movements. Stable arrangements, systematic coordination and regular meetings are important first steps, such as the ones developed after the second World Social Forum of Porto Alegre, with the Continental Social Fora and the greater, permanent role taken up by the International Council of its organizers. The search for more democratic forms of deliberation and participation of civil society also from poorer countries is a continuing challenge for the legitimacy and representativeness of global movements. The definition of a common agenda and the development of common identities, visions and policy proposals are the more difficult, but necessary steps.

The variety of strategies being pursued by social movements in confronting global powers should not be seen as a factor of division and weakness. Rather, a perspective of *globalization from below* requires a combination of capacity of resistance, radical visions, political alternatives, and instruments that introduce specific reforms. A weakness would emerge if sections of global movements confine themselves to a politics of resistance alone, seen as the way for affirming an antagonistic identity, independent of the objectives of change. Or, if other sections are co-opted and integrated into a strategy of global governance, legitimating particular international institutions.

The future of global movements is tied to their roots in society and to the capacity to affirm an alternative vision for global problems. However, much will also depend on the ability of politics to pay attention to civil society, on the response of governments, and on the effective possibilities of reform of supranational organizations.

The question of the international order, of *democracy vs. globalization*, remains too important to be left to a handful of ministers, diplomats, technocrats and military leaders. A major hope for the future has come from the global movements for democracy and justice, which have asked for (and have practiced) a more democratic order, more equal international relations, and a more just economy and society.

DECLARATION OF THE JURY OF CONSCIENCE OF THE WORLD TRIBUNAL ON IRAQ[f]

<http://www.worldtribunal.org/main/?>
Istanbul, 27 June 2005

In February 2003, weeks before an illegal war was initiated against Iraq, millions of people protested in the streets of the world. That call went

f. An "International Law Appendix" intended to validate the Jury Statement is omitted here.

unheeded. No international institution had the courage or conscience to stand up to the threat of aggression of the US and UK governments. No one could stop them. It is two years later now. Iraq has been invaded, occupied, and devastated. The attack on Iraq is an attack on justice, on liberty, on our safety, on our future, on us all. We, people of conscience, decided to stand up. We formed the World Tribunal on Iraq (WTI) to demand justice and a peaceful future. The legitimacy of the World Tribunal on Iraq is located in the collective conscience of humanity. This, the Istanbul session of the WTI, is the culmination of a series of 20 hearings held in different cities of the world focusing on the illegal invasion and occupation of Iraq. The conclusions of these sessions and/or inquiries held in Barcelona, Brussels, Copenhagen, Genoa, Hiroshima, Istanbul, Lisbon, London, Mumbai, New York, Östersund, Paris, Rome, Seoul, Stockholm, Tunis, various cities in Japan and Germany are appended to this Declaration in a separate volume.

We, the Jury of Conscience, from 10 different countries, met in Istanbul. We heard 54 testimonies from a Panel of Advocates and Witnesses who came from across the world, including from Iraq, the United States and the United Kingdom.The World Tribunal on Iraq met in Istanbul from 24–26 June 2005. The principal objective of the WTI is to tell and disseminate the truth about the Iraq War, underscoring the accountability of those responsible and underlining the significance of justice for the Iraqi people.

I. Overview of Findings

1. The invasion and occupation of Iraq was and is illegal. The reasons given by the US and UK governments for the invasion and occupation of Iraq in March 2003 have proven to be false. Much evidence supports the conclusion that a major motive for the war was to control and dominate the Middle East and its vast reserves of oil as a part of the US drive for global hegemony.

2. Blatant falsehoods about the presence of weapons of mass destruction in Iraq and a link between Al Qaeda terrorism and the Saddam Hussein régime were manufactured in order to create public support for a "preemptive" assault upon a sovereign independent nation.

3. Iraq has been under siege for years. The imposition of severe inhumane economic sanctions on 6 August 1990, the establishment of no-fly zones in the Northern and Southern parts of Iraq, and the concomitant bombing of the country were all aimed at degrading and weakening Iraq's human and material resources and capacities in order to facilitate its subsequent invasion and occupation. In this enterprise the US and British leaderships had the benefit of a complicit UN Security Council.

4. In pursuit of their agenda of empire, the Bush and Blair governments blatantly ignored the massive opposition to the war expressed by millions of people around the world. They embarked upon one of the most unjust, immoral, and cowardly wars in history.

5. Established international political-legal mechanisms have failed to prevent this attack and to hold the perpetrators accountable. The impunity that the US government and its allies enjoy has created a serious international crisis that questions the import and significance of international law, of human rights covenants and of the ability of international institutions includ-

ing the United Nations to address the crisis with any degree of authority or dignity.

6.   The US/UK occupation of Iraq of the last 27 months has led to the destruction and devastation of the Iraqi state and society. Law and order have broken down, resulting in a pervasive lack of human security. The physical infrastructure is in shambles; the health care delivery system is in poor condition; the education system has virtually ceased to function; there is massive environmental and ecological devastation; and the cultural and archeological heritage of the Iraqi people has been desecrated.

7.   The occupation has intentionally exacerbated ethnic, sectarian and religious divisions in Iraqi society, with the aim of undermining Iraq's identity and integrity as a nation. This is in keeping with the familiar imperial policy of divide and rule. Moreover, it has facilitated rising levels of violence against women, increased gender oppression and reinforced patriarchy.

8.   The imposition of the UN sanctions in 1990 caused untold suffering and thousands of deaths. The situation has worsened after the occupation. At least 100,000 civilians have been killed; 60,000 are being held in US custody in inhumane conditions, without charges; thousands have disappeared; and torture has become routine.

9.   The illegal privatization, deregulation, and liberalization of the Iraqi economy by the occupation regime has coerced the country into becoming a client economy that is controlled by the IMF and the World Bank, both of which are integral to the Washington Consensus. The occupying forces have also acquired control over Iraq's oil reserves.

10.   Any law or institution created under the aegis of occupation is devoid of both legal and moral authority. The recently concluded election, the Constituent Assembly, the current government, and the drafting committee for the Constitution are therefore all illegitimate.

11.   There is widespread opposition to the occupation. Political, social, and civil resistance through peaceful means is subjected to repression by the occupying forces. It is the occupation and its brutality that has provoked a strong armed resistance and certain acts of desperation. By the principles embodied in the UN Charter and in international law, the popular national resistance to the occupation is legitimate and justified. It deserves the support of people everywhere who care for justice and freedom.

II.   Charges

On the basis of the preceding findings and recalling the Charter of the United Nations and other legal documents indicated in the appendix, the jury has established the following charges.

A.   *Against the Governments of the US and the UK*

1.   Planning, preparing, and waging the supreme crime of a war of aggression in contravention of the United Nations Charter and the Nuremberg Principles. Evidence for this can be found in the leaked Downing Street Memo of 23rd July, 2002, in which it was revealed: "Military action was now seen as inevitable. Bush wanted to remove Saddam through military action, justified by the conjunction of terrorism and WMD. But the intelligence and

facts were being fixed around the policy." Intelligence was manufactured to willfully deceive the people of the US, the UK, and their elected representatives.

2.   Targeting the civilian population of Iraq and civilian infrastructure by intentionally directing attacks upon civilians and hospitals, medical centers, residential neighborhoods, electricity stations, and water purification facilities. The complete destruction of the city of Falluja in itself constitutes a glaring example of such crimes.

3.   Using disproportionate force and weapon systems with indiscriminate effects, such as cluster munitions, incendiary bombs, depleted uranium (DU), and chemical weapons. Detailed evidence was presented to the Tribunal by expert witnesses that leukemia had risen sharply in children under the age of five residing in those areas that had been targeted by DU weapons.

4.   Using DU munitions in spite of all the warnings presented by scientists and war veterans on their devastating long-term effects on human beings and the environment. The US Administration, claiming lack of scientifically established proof of the harmful effects of DU, decided to risk the lives of millions for several generations rather than discontinue its use on account of the potential risks. This alone displays the Administration's wanton disregard for human life. The Tribunal heard testimony concerning the current obstruction by the US Administration of the efforts of Iraqi universities to collect data and conduct research on the issue.

5.   Failing to safeguard the lives of civilians during military activities and during the occupation period thereafter. This is evidenced, for example, by "shock and awe" bombing techniques and the conduct of occupying forces at checkpoints.

6.   Actively creating conditions under which the status of Iraqi women has seriously been degraded, contrary to the repeated claims of the leaders of the coalition forces. Women's freedom of movement has severely been limited, restricting their access to the public sphere, to education, livelihood, political and social engagement. Testimony was provided that sexual violence and sex trafficking have increased since the occupation of Iraq began.

7.   Using deadly violence against peaceful protestors, including the April 2003 killing of more than a dozen peaceful protestors in Falluja.

8.   Imposing punishments without charge or trial, including collective punishment, on the people of Iraq. Repeated testimonies pointed to "snatch and grab" operations, disappearances and assassinations.

9.   Subjecting Iraqi soldiers and civilians to torture and cruel, inhuman, or degrading treatment. Degrading treatment includes subjecting Iraqi soldiers and civilians to acts of racial, ethnic, religious, and gender discrimination, as well as denying Iraqi soldiers Prisoner of War status as required by the Geneva Conventions. Abundant testimony was provided of unlawful arrests and detentions, without due process of law. Well known and egregious examples of torture and cruel and inhuman treatment occurred in Abu Ghraib prison as well as in Mosul, Camp Bucca, and Basra. The employment of mercenaries and private contractors to carry out torture has served to undermine accountability.

10.   Re-writing the laws of a country that has been illegally invaded and occupied, in violation of international covenants on the responsibilities of occupying powers, in order to amass illegal profits (through such measures as Order 39, signed by L. Paul Bremer III for the Coalition Provisional Authority, which allows foreign investors to buy and takeover Iraq's state-owned enterprises and to repatriate 100 percent of their profits and assets at any point) and to control Iraq's oil. Evidence was presented of a number of corporations that had profited from such transactions.

11.   Willfully devastating the environment, contaminating it by depleted uranium (DU) weapons, combined with the plumes from burning oil wells, as well as huge oil spills, and destroying agricultural lands. Deliberately disrupting the water and waste removal systems, in a manner verging on biological-chemical warfare. Failing to prevent the looting and dispersal of radioactive material from nuclear sites. Extensive documentation is available on air and water pollution, land degradation, and radioactive pollution.

12.   Failing to protect humanity's rich archaeological and cultural heritage in Iraq by allowing the looting of museums and established historical sites and positioning military bases in culturally and archeologically sensitive locations. This took place despite prior warnings from UNESCO and Iraqi museum officials.

13.   Obstructing the right to information, including the censoring of Iraqi media, such as newspapers (e.g., al-Hawza, al-Mashriq, and al-Mustaqila) and radio stations (Baghdad Radio), the shutting down of the Baghdad offices of Al Jazeera Television, targeting international journalists, imprisoning and killing academics, intellectuals and scientists.

14.   Redefining torture in violation of international law, to allow use of torture and illegal detentions, including holding more than 500 people at Guantánamo Bay without charging them or allowing them any access to legal protection, and using "extraordinary renditions" to send people to be tortured in other countries known to commit human rights abuses and torture prisoners.

15.   Committing a crime against peace by violating the will of the global anti-war movement. In an unprecedented display of public conscience millions of people across the world stood in opposition to the imminent attack on Iraq. The attack rendered them effectively voiceless. This amounts to a declaration by the US government and its allies to millions of people that their voices can be ignored, suppressed and silenced with complete impunity.

16.   Engaging in policies to wage permanent war on sovereign nations. Syria and Iran have already been declared as potential targets. In declaring a "global war on terror," the US government has given itself the exclusive right to use aggressive military force against any target of its choosing. Ethnic and religious hostilities are being fueled in different parts of the world. The US occupation of Iraq has further emboldened the Israeli occupation in Palestine and increased the repression of the Palestinian people. The focus on state security and the escalation of militarization has caused a serious deterioration of human security and civil rights across the world.

B.   Against the Security Council of the United Nations

   1.   Failing to protect the Iraqi people against the crime of aggression.

   2.   Imposing harsh economic sanctions on Iraq, despite knowledge that sanctions were directly contributing to the massive loss of civilian lives and harming innocent civilians.

   3.   Allowing the United States and United Kingdom to carry out illegal bombings in the no-fly zones, using false pretenses of enforcing UN resolutions, and at no point allowing discussion in the Security Council of this violation, and thereby being complicit and responsible for loss of civilian life and destruction of Iraqi infrastructure.

   4.   Allowing the United States to dominate the United Nations and hold itself above any accountability by other member nations.

   5.   Failure to stop war crimes and crimes against humanity by the United States and its coalition partners in Iraq.

   6.   Failure to hold the United States and its coalition partners accountable for violations of international law during the invasion and occupation, giving official sanction to the occupation and therefore, both by acts of commission and acts of omission becoming a collaborator in an illegal occupation.

C.   Against the Governments of the Coalition of the Willing

   Collaborating in the invasion and occupation of Iraq, thus sharing responsibility in the crimes committed.

D.   Against the Governments of Other Countries

   Allowing the use of military bases and air space, and providing other logistical support, for the invasion and occupation, and hence being complicit in the crimes committed.

E.   Against the Private Corporations which have won contracts for the reconstruction of Iraq and which have sued for and received "reparation awards" from the illegal occupation regime

   Profiting from the war with complicity in the crimes described above, of invasion and occupation.

F.   Against the Major Corporate Media

   1.   Disseminating the deliberate falsehoods spread by the governments of the US and the UK and failing to adequately investigate this misinformation, even in the face of abundant evidence to the contrary. Among the corporate media houses that bear special responsibility for promoting the lies about Iraq's weapons of mass destruction, we name the New York Times, in particular their reporter Judith Miller, whose main source was on the payroll of the CIA. We also name Fox News, CNN, NBC, CBS, ABC, the BBC and ITN. This list also includes but is not limited to, The Express, The Sun, The Observer and Washington Post.

   2.   Failing to report the atrocities being committed against Iraqi people by the occupying forces, neglecting the duty to give privilege and dignity to voices of suffering and marginalizing the global voices for peace and justice.

3. Failing to report fairly on the ongoing occupation; silencing and discrediting dissenting voices and failing to adequately report on the full national costs and consequences of the invasion and occupation of Iraq; disseminating the propaganda of the occupation regime that seeks to justify the continuation of its presence in Iraq on false grounds.

4. Inciting an ideological climate of fear, racism, xenophobia and Islamophobia, which is then used to justify and legitimize violence perpetrated by the armies of the occupying regime.

5. Disseminating an ideology that glorifies masculinity and combat, while normalizing war as a policy choice.

6. Complicity in the waging of an aggressive war and perpetuating a regime of occupation that is widely regarded as guilty of war crimes and crimes against humanity.

7. Enabling, through the validation and dissemination of disinformation, the fraudulent misappropriation of human and financial resources for an illegal war waged on false pretexts.

8. Promoting corporate-military perspectives on "security" which are counter-productive to the fundamental concerns and priorities of the global population and have seriously endangered civilian populations.

III. Recommendations

Recognizing the right of the Iraqi people to resist the illegal occupation of their country and to develop independent institutions, and affirming that the right to resist the occupation is the right to wage a struggle for self-determination, freedom, and independence as derived from the Charter of the United Nations, we the Jury of Conscience declare our solidarity with the people of Iraq.

We recommend:

1. The immediate and unconditional withdrawal of the Coalition forces from Iraq.

2. That Coalition governments make war reparations and pay compensation to Iraq for the humanitarian, economic, ecological, and cultural devastation they have caused by their illegal invasion and occupation.

3. That all laws, contracts, treaties, and institutions established under occupation, which the Iraqi people deem inimical to their interests, be considered null and void.

4. That the Guantánamo Bay prison and all other offshore US military prisons be closed immediately, that the names of the prisoners be disclosed, that they receive POW status, and receive due process.

5. That there be an exhaustive investigation of those responsible for the crime of aggression, war crimes and crimes against humanity in Iraq, beginning with George W. Bush, President of the United States of America, Tony Blair, Prime Minister of the United Kingdom, those in key decision-making positions in these countries and in the Coalition of the Willing, those in the military chain-of-command who master-minded the strategy for and carried out this criminal war, starting from the very top and going down; as well as personalities in Iraq who helped prepare this illegal invasion and supported

the occupiers. We list some of the most obvious names to be included in such investigation: prime ministers of the Coalition of the Willing, such as Junichiro Koizumi of Japan, Jose Maria Anzar of Spain, Silvio Berlusconi of Italy, José Manuel Durão Barroso and Santana Lopes of Portugal, Roh Moo Hyun of South Korea, Anders Fogh Rasmussen of Denmark; public officials such as Dick Cheney, Donald H. Rumsfeld, Paul Wolfowitz, Colin L. Powell, Condoleezza Rice, Richard Perle, Douglas Feith, Alberto Gonzales, L. Paul Bremer from the US, and Jack Straw, Geoffrey Hoon, John Reid, Adam Ingram from the UK; military commanders beginning with: Gen. Richard Myers, Gen. Tommy Franks, Gen. John P. Abizaid, Gen. Ricardo S. Sanchez, Gen. Thomas Metz, Gen. John R. Vines, Gen. George Casey from the US; Gen. Mike Jackson, Gen. John Kiszely, Air Marshal Brian Burridge, Gen. Peter Wall, Rear Admiral David Snelson, Gen. Robin Brims, Air Vice–Marshal Glenn Torpy from the UK; and chiefs of staff and commanding officers of all coalition countries with troops in Iraq and Iraqi collaborators such as Ahmed Chalabi, Iyad Allawi, Abdul Aziz Al Hakim, Gen. Abdul Qader Mohammed Jassem Mohan, among others.

6.   That a process of accountability is initiated to hold those morally and personally responsible for their participation in this illegal war, such as journalists who deliberately lied, corporate media outlets that promoted racial, ethnic and religious hatred, and CEOs of multinational corporations that profited from this war;

7.   That people throughout the world launch nonviolent actions against US and UK corporations that directly profit from this war. Examples of such corporations include Halliburton, Bechtel, The Carlyle Group, CACI Inc., Titan Corporation, Kellog, Brown and Root (subsidiary of Halliburton), DynCorp, Boeing, ExxonMobil, Texaco, British Petroleum. The following companies have sued Iraq and received "reparation awards": Toys R Us, Kentucky Fried Chicken, Shell, Nestlé, Pepsi, Phillip Morris, Sheraton, Mobil. Such actions may take the form of direct actions such as shutting down their offices, consumer boycotts, and pressure on shareholders to divest.

8.   That young people and soldiers act on conscientious objection and refuse to enlist and participate in an illegal war. Also, that countries provide conscientious objectors with political asylum.

9.   That the international campaign for dismantling all US military bases abroad be reinforced.

10.   That people around the world resist and reject any effort by any of their governments to provide material, logistical, or moral support to the occupation of Iraq.

We, the Jury of Conscience, hope that the scope and specificity of these recommendations will lay the groundwork for a world in which international institutions will be shaped and reshaped by the will of people and not by fear and self-interest, where journalists and intellectuals will not remain mute, where the will of the people of the world will be central, and human security will prevail over state security and corporate profits.

Arundhati Roy, India, Spokesperson of the Jury of Conscience

Ahmet Öztürk, Turkey

Ayşe Erzan, Turkey

Chandra Muzaffar, Malaysia

David Krieger, USA

Eve Ensler, USA

François Houtart, Belgium

Jae–Bok Kim, South Korea

Mehmet Tarhan, Turkey

Miguel Angel De Los Santos Cruz, Mexico

Murat Belge, Turkey

Rela Mazali, Israel

Salaam Al Jobourie, Iraq

Taty Almeida, Argentina

DISCUSSION NOTES/QUESTIONS

1.   What is the role of the United Nations in setting and achieving goals for the peoples of the world? Does the Secretary–General's Millennium Report express the appropriate priorities for the 21st century? If September 11 had occurred before the Report was presented to the UN General Assembly, do you think it would/should have been different in emphasis and goals? For a subsequent assessment of the Millennium goals and progress toward their realization, see the report of Secretary–General Kofi Annan, *In Larger Freedom: Towards Development, Security and Human Rights for All* (2005), *available at* <http://www.un.org/largerfreedom/>.

2.   The idea of enforcement is central to the idea of making international law relevant and effective in settings of war and peace. The Brahimi Report, *supra*, is a reaction to a range of criticisms made about the UN's performance in severe conflict settings, especially in Sub–Saharan Africa and the Balkans. Are the guidelines set forth realistic, beneficial? Too modest? Too ambitious? With the return of geopolitics and war to center stage, as it was during the Cold war, what can be expected of the United Nations? Must we look elsewhere for hopes about limiting the role of war in human affairs? To ideas associated with Gandhian perspectives of nonviolence? *See* Jonathan Schell, Unconquerable World: Power, Nonviolence, and the Will of the People (2003). *See also* Glenn D. Paige, Nonkilling Global Political Science (2002); Stuart Reis, Passion for Peace: Exercising Power Creatively (2003). Alternatively, what about civil society initiatives such as the Global Action to Prevent War? Social initiatives to reduce poverty and distress, the focus of the UN Millennium Report? All of the above? *See* Stephen Gill, Power and Resistance in the New World Order (2003); Global Backlash: Citizen Initiatives for a Just World Economy (R. Broad ed., 2002).

3.   The rise of human rights combined with media induced awareness in "real time" humanitarian catastrophe has underlined the moral imperative for international society to protect vulnerable peoples faced by terrifying ordeals. We have considered the pros and cons of humanitarian intervention in Chapter 9, but in this concluding chapter we have focused on the governance deficit. In *A UN Constabulary to Enforce the Law on Genocide and Crimes Against Humanity*, in Protection against Genocide: Mission Impossible? 105–22 (N. Riemer ed., 2000), Saul Mendlovitz and John Fousek argue that establishing a centralized enforcement capability will overcome some of the weaknesses associated with the present

ad hoc approach that failed so miserably in Rwanda in 1994 and in Bosnia during the early 1990s. Is this a feasible undertaking? Why? Why not? Are major states prepared to give the United Nations such a capability, especially if its activation is allowed to circumvent the veto power of the permanent members of the Security Council? What are some better ways of enhancing enforcement capabilities? Under present global conditions might not a regional approach be preferable? Or be at least complementary? An advantage of regionalism, especially in Africa and Asia, is to weaken the objections based on the belief that the United States and its allies are seeking to find grounds in a post-colonial era for disregarding the sovereign rights of countries in the South. Is this concern well-founded?

4. The idea of global governance that is premised on democratic values and aspires to legitimacy on the part of the peoples of the world requires new procedures and institutions for accountability, participation, policy formation, and lawmaking. In the evolution of a regional European framework, such innovative steps have been taken, although not without varieties of resistance. What about global governance? Can it build on this regional experience? On the experience of complex federal states, such as Brazil, Germany, India, and the United States? How does the global form of democratization favored by Falk and Strauss fit into this assessment? What are the arguments for and against the establishment of a global people's assembly or parliament at this time? Should this type of development be based on an inter-governmental initiative? Should it be situated within the United Nations system? How much authority? For broad philosophical perspectives, in useful chronological order, see Richard Falk, A Study of Future Worlds (1975); Stephen Toulmin, Cosmopolis: The Hidden Agenda of Modernity (1990); Andrew Linklater, The Transformation of Political Community: Ethical Foundations of the Post–Westphalia Era (1997); Cornelius F. Murphy, Jr., Theories of World Governance: A Study in the History of Ideas (1999); and Peter Singer, One World: The Ethics of Globalization (2002). On more concrete possibilities, see A Reader on Second Assembly & Parliamentary Proposals (S. Mendlovitz & R. Walker eds., 2003); Democratizing Global Governance (E. Aksu & J. Camilleri eds., 2002); From Reaction to Conflict Prevention (F. Hampson & D. Malone eds., 2002); Re-imaging Political Community (D. Archibugi, D. Held, & M. Köhler eds., 1998). And for an influential general program for the future of global democracy, see David Held, Democracy and the Global Order: From the Modern State to Cosmopolitan Governance (1995).

5. In the struggle for global democracy, the activities of global civil society are indispensable. Increasingly, the World Social Forum (WSF), meeting on an annual basis, is capturing the imagination of those around the world who yearn for a more peaceful and equitable world order. The WSF brings together activists from all parts of the world, holds its meetings (so far) in Brasil and India, and blurs the boundaries between culture and politics. It is from within global civil society also that efforts to extend the rule of law to the domain of geopolitics are most seriously attempted. In the aftermath of the Iraq War, the UN was silent, refusing to censure its most powerful member for refusing to adhere to the UN Charter's most fundamental prohibition, against waging aggressive war. It was only the dozen or so peoples' tribunals and hearings held in all parts of the world that, symbolically at least, passed judgment on the legality of the war and, as well, on the tactics used and the occupation policy pursued by the United States in Iraq. Mario Pianta, *supra*, shows how civil society organized what he calls "parallel summits" to engage in dialogue and express grievances in relation to summits organized to bring governments together under UN auspices, especially in the 1990s, on global policy issues. This dynamic interaction also provided civil society

actors with valuable access to the world media assembled for such occasions, and enabled networking to establish empowering links with likeminded individuals and groups around the world. Indeed, the phenomenon of these parallel summits, and their role as explorations in global democracy, were so threatening to the established order that leading states, both democratic and authoritarian, joined together to condemn such conferences as "spectacles" and a waste of money, thereby assuring that the UN would not be allowed to encouraged this global democratic buildup. The importance of the WSF in the early years of the 21st century partly compensates for the loss of these arenas for transnational civic action provided by conferences held under the auspices of the United Nations. *See* Alejandro Colas, International Civil Society: Social Movements in World Politics (2002); Mary Kaldor, Global Civil Society: An Answer to War (2003). Also useful is Michael Edwards, Civil Society (2004).

6.   In Democracy and the Global Order: From the Modern State to Cosmopolitan Governance (1995), David Held provides an optimistic sense of what kind of governance is needed and, in his view, follows upon the principles already agreed upon in establishing the United Nations and the European Union. Is such a liberal, optimistic vision of the future a relic of the "happy nineties" as suggested by Mary Kaldor in Global Civil Society: An Answer to War (2003)? Or is this the inevitable wave of the future arising from converging trends of complex interdependencies among societies and states, on the one hand, and the expectations of human rights and democracy, on the other? Again at issue is whether the 11 September 2001 attacks changed "everything" as some (especially American) commentators have insisted, or whether these developments have merely postponed the needed normative and functional adjustments to an ever more complex and fragile global setting that can no longer be safely and equitably regulated by relying on the primacy of states and their claims of territorial supremacy. For some useful perspectives see Amitai Etzioni, From Empire to Community: A New Approach to International Relations (2004); Richard Falk, The Declining World Order: America's Neoimperial Geopolitics (2004); Walter Russell Mead, Power, Terror, Peace, and War (2004); Anne–Marie Slaughter, A New World Order (2004).

7.   This chapter considers in some detail possible new directions to improve global governance, including an emergency peace enforcement capability within the UN to address issues of humanitarian emergencies whether of political or natural origins. The killings and mass ethnic displacements in Darfur has given renewed confirmation to the unwillingness of the UN as now constituted to deal with potential challenges of a genocidal character. The Asian tsunamis of 1998 and hurricanes Katrina and Rita in 2005 reinforce the need for such a capability in an era of extreme weather. What are reasons, if any, for not going forward with the sort of proposals developed in the Kaysen–Rathjens selection, *supra*? Financial? Utopian? A challenge to geopolitical primacy of leading states?

8.   This chapter also considers the case for a global parliament, an initiative that, like an emergency peace enforcement capability, has so far not gathered formal support within the United Nations or at the inter-governmental level. Why not? Impractical? Too expensive? Reinforces trends weakening the sovereignty of states as the sole representatives of the peoples of the world? How do you evaluate the Falk–Strauss proposal from this perspective? Are there better ways to advance the cause of global democracy? If so, what are they?

9.   The final selection in the chapter presents the outcome of the World Tribunal on Iraq (WTI), convened in Istanbul during June 2005. It was an

initiative organized exclusively by citizens joined together in a global activist network that had previously supported some sixteen earlier sessions dealing with the Iraq War held in different parts of the world. The rationale for such "tribunals" is that civil society, when states and international institutions fail to act in the face of aggressive war, has residual rights and duties to declare the law on the subject and to insist on implementation. Such a declaration is, as stated, an expression of conscience, a moral and political act, that rests upon a convincing and honest presentation of arguments and evidence relating to alleged illegality and criminality of the war and those responsible for planning and perpetrating it. What is your assessment of such an initiative? Is it invalidated because it is one-sided? Undertaken without an official imprimatur? Lacking enforcement capabilities? Or does it make a contribution to a global legal culture by taking international law seriously, exposing the violations of core principles of international law by powerful states? Offering an accurate record on the illegality of a given war and the criminality of practices relied upon? Is the basis of authority to be found in dictates of conscience? The values and norms of civil society? The formal laws and decrees of the state? For substantive guidelines, the WTI relied on the Nuremberg precedent established after World War II. For an earlier model of such an initiative, the WTI relied on the Russell Tribunal established in 1967 in the midst of the Vietnam War. On Nuremberg, see Telford Taylor, The Anatomy of the Nuremberg Trials: A personal memoir (1992). On the Russell Tribunal, see the proceedings in Against the Crime of Silence (John Duffett ed., 1968).

10.   At the beginning of this chapter, your attention was drawn to the many roles and functions that typically are assumed by lawyers, including international lawyers. It also was stressed that the identifications, expectations, and demands with which lawyers find personal and professional comfort hold out the potential for consequential influence in the furtherance of international law and the shaping of world order. What is the significance of citizenship and patriotism for the practice of law and the identity of lawyers in the present uncertain era of globalization? What is or should be the role of lawyers in relation to the world's major challenges at the present time? Are lawyers responsible for the future?

11.   Who, ultimately, is responsible for the future?

Index

References are to Pages

LAW OF THE SEA
Generally, 988 et seq., 997 et seq.
See also Ocean Resources, this index
CDEM standards, 1053, 1056
CLOS, 991
Convenience, flags of, 1071
Customary law, 1063
Exclusive economic zones (EEZ), 1007
Flag state duties
Generally, 1014
Convenience, flags of, 1071
Pollution laws, 1053, 1062
Hot pursuit, 1037
Innocent passage rights, 1065, 1070, 1093
International Convention for the Safety of Life
at Sea (SOLAS), 1053
International Maritime Organization (IMO),
1014, 1053, 1059, 1099
Marine pollution
Generally, 1051 et seq.
See also Environmental Protection, this in-
dex
Montevideo Conference, 1019
Navigation rights, 1005
Port state duties, 1014
Reprisals, 1081
Six mile limit, 1091
Three mile limit, 999, 1091
Twelve mile limits, 1006, 1091
UN convention, 991
UN involvement, 1014

LAW OF WAR
Chemical and biological weapons, 449
Chivalry, 427
Customary principles, 423
Development, 421
Geneva Conventions, this index
Hague Law, this index
Necessity, 441
Nuclear Weapons, this index
Principles, customary, 423
Proportionality, 441
Self-Defense, this index
Strategic Arms Limitation Talks, 454

LEAGUE OF NATIONS
Establishment, 38
International society, principle of, 1281

LEBANON
Sabra and Shatila massacres, 218, 581, 1365

LEGAL PERSONALITY
Generally, 796 et seq.
See also Governments, this index

LEGAL POSITIVISM
Generally, 22
Command theory, 62
Critical legal studies compared, 61
Enforceability of international law, 62

LEGALIST–MORALIST SCHOOL
Generally, 23

LESS-DEVELOPED COUNTRIES (LDC)
Generally, 940
See also Third World Perspectives, this index

LETTERS ROGATORY
Generally, 839

MAASTRICHT TREATY
Generally, 5
Human rights, 631

**MARINE MAMMAL PROTECTION ACT
(MMPA)**
Generally, 907

MARITIME ZONES
Customary international law, 123

MEDIATION
Application of international law in, 220, 233
United Nations conflict prevention, 312

MEMORANDA OF UNDERSTANDING (MOU)
Generally, 175

MERCENARIES
Generally, 359

MINES
See Landmines, this index

MINORITY RIGHTS
Generally, 558 et seq.
See also Human Rights, this index
Slavia, Candia, and Corcyra problem, 488

MONETARY POLICIES
See also Economic Well-Being, this index
Exchange rate risks, 754
Floating currency, 748, 815
International financial system, 753
Manipulation by debtor states, 783
Sundalau financial crisis problem, 747

MONISM
Domestic law applications of international law,
235

MONOPOLIES
Intellectual property laws and, 944

MONTEVIDEO CONFERENCE
Law of the seas, 1019

MONTREAL PROTOCOL
Consensus agreements, 1131
Economic incentives, 1111
Voting, 1131
Withdrawals, 1131

**MOST FAVORED NATION (MFN) TREAT-
MENT**
Generally, 762
GATT, 887

MULTINATIONAL CORPORATIONS
See also Globalization, this index
Natural resources exploitation, 1224
Subjects of international law, 367

MUNICIPAL LAW
See Domestic and International Law, this in-
dex
Definition, 17

†